online resource centre
www.oxfordtextbooks.co.uk/orc/jones_sufrin6e/

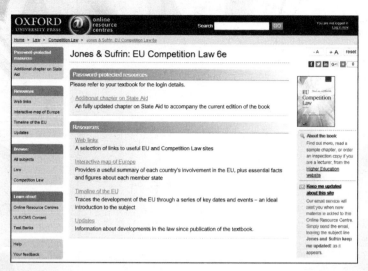

This book is accompanied by an Online Resource Centre offering additional resources and materials to support learning and to ensure that the book meets its many readers' needs.

- A **fully updated chapter on State Aid** is available online

- An **interactive map** of the European Union provides useful factual information on each country's involvement in the EU

- A **timeline** tracing the evolution of EU legal history

- **Regular updates** are an indispensable resource providing easy access to the latest changes and developments in the law

- **Annotated web links** are also offered to facilitate further study into different jurisdictions and areas of research

Please visit **www.oxfordtextbooks.co.uk/orc/jones_sufrin6e/** to find the resources. To access the additional chapter on State Aid, please enter

Username: jones_sufrin6e

Password: JS_stateaid6e

EU COMPETITION LAW

TEXT, CASES, AND MATERIALS

Sixth Edition

ALISON JONES
Solicitor, Professor of Law, King's College London

AND

BRENDA SUFRIN
Solicitor, Emeritus Professor of Law, University of Bristol

OXFORD
UNIVERSITY PRESS

OXFORD
UNIVERSITY PRESS

Great Clarendon Street, Oxford, OX2 6DP,
United Kingdom

Oxford University Press is a department of the University of Oxford.
It furthers the University's objective of excellence in research, scholarship,
and education by publishing worldwide. Oxford is a registered trade mark of
Oxford University Press in the UK and in certain other countries

Published in the United States of America by Oxford University Press
198 Madison Avenue, New York, NY 10016, United States of America

British Library Cataloguing in Publication Data
Data available

Library of Congress Control Number: 2016936831

ISBN 978–0–19–872342–4

Printed in Italy by
Grafica Veneta S.p.A.

PREFACE

Each time we have produced a new edition of this book we have commented in the Preface on the breathtaking number of developments in EU competition law that have taken place since the previous one. This edition is no exception. A host of judgments, decisions, acts, and other measures of the Court of Justice, the Commission, the EU legislature, the national courts, and national competition authorities (NCAs) of the Member States have required substantial reconsideration of, and changes to, the chapters of this book. In some cases the developments that have occurred have necessitated the significant restructuring of a chapter or even a rewriting. For example, the changes to the private enforcement landscape resulting, in particular, from the adoption of an EU Damages Directive harmonising national rules governing claims for damages in relation to violations of Articles 101 and 102, have demanded a complete rethink of Chapter 14.

Continuing uncertainty over the question of what the objectives of EU competition law are, or should be, still underpins much of the discussion of the substantive law throughout the book and renders answers to many difficult questions more elusive. Different views on this matter have divided commentators, especially in the area of Article 102. In particular, Chapter 7 considers the implications of the judgments of the General Court in *Intel* and the Court of Justice in *Post Danmark II* which deal with the question of how abusive loyalty, and other, rebates are to be identified. These judgments were eagerly awaited as many hoped that they might embrace a more 'modernised' effects-based approach to rebates. The judgments reignited the debate about the philosophical basis of EU competition law, the question of how 'abusive' conduct can, or should, be identified and whether, and if so when, presumptions of illegality should be relied upon in the context of Article 102. The judgment of the Court of Justice in the *Intel* appeal which, it is hoped, will fully address these issues, is expected to appear quite early in the life of this edition.

The debate over the objectives of EU competition law, and how they may be achieved, has also fuelled consideration of the question of how restrictions of competition within the meaning of Article 101 can be identified. A number of cases before the EU Courts, explored in Chapters 4 and 9–12, continue to raise the question of when restraints incorporated within agreements can be said to be restrictive of competition by object. A crucial new judgment examined in this edition is that of the Court of Justice in *Groupement des Cartes Bancaires*. This case provides a welcome reminder that the category of object restraints is not as broad as some expansive interpretations in earlier cases, such as *T-Mobile* and *Allianz Hungária*, suggested. Rather, it makes it clear that the category is confined to arrangements which reveal, in themselves, 'a sufficient degree of harm to competition law'. The Court of Justice judgment in *SIA 'Maxima Latvija'* reiterated that the 'by object category' is a restrictive one and confirmed that it should not extend to agreements simply because they have the potential to restrict competition.

The Commission's increasing focus on the energy, digital economy, and financial sectors has generated a number of new cases and argument as to how competition law should deal with issues arising in these sectors. How should competition law interact with regulatory rules, liberalisation programmes, and intellectual property law, and how should the existing rules evolve to deal with online practices and practices arising on multi-sided markets? Chapters 7 and 11, in particular, have to grapple with a number of these matters, including: (a) how Article 102 can control the behaviour of dominant, vertically integrated energy and telecommunications companies; (b) whether Article 102 can limit the exercise of intellectual property rights (especially the conduct of owners of standard essential patents); and (c) how Articles 101 and 102 apply to a host of distribution and other practices on online markets and platforms. Further, Chapters 4, 9, and 10 consider how Article 101 has been applied to a number of agreements occurring in the financial and insurance sectors.

It is now more than ten years since the 'modernisation' of the enforcement of Articles 101 and 102, and its effects are becoming clearer. The Commission has still not made use of its powers to make findings of inapplicability pursuant to Article 10 of Regulation 1/2003 and has never issued informal guidance on a novel question. Further, it is now relatively rare for the Commission to adopt an infringement decision outside the realm of cartels. Rather, in such cases it more frequently uses the commitments procedure provided for in Article 9 of Regulation 1/2003, taking advantage of the shorter procedure involved and the wide discretion it confers. As this system of negotiated outcomes makes appeals unlikely, and the Commission continues to pursue an aggressive enforcement policy against cartels, the majority of appeals to the EU Courts relate to cartel infringement decisions. These are principally concerned with the scope, length, and duration of cartels, procedural matters, fines, and leniency, as well as issues which span the procedural/substantive divide, such as the liability of parents for the conduct of their subsidiaries. Whether EU competition procedures, and the judicial review exercised by the General Court, are compatible with, and sufficient to satisfy, the human rights provisions of the Charter and the European Convention remains a live issue. It remains to be seen whether the expansion of the General Court, by a further 28 judges, will increase the speed of that Court's decisions.

One striking feature of the post-modernisation system seen in Chapter 11 is that the Commission has not adopted an infringement decision in relation to vertical agreements since 2005. Rather, public enforcement in this area has, until recently, been concentrated at the national level, although NCAs have not always acted consistently. The Commission is now poised to get more involved. It is particularly interested in the issue of geo-blocking and is examining barriers to cross-border online trade incorporated in distribution agreements relating to consumer goods and digital content. It thus seems likely that new EU cases will be decided in the near future.

The area of vertical restraints shows national proceedings playing an increasingly important role in the effective enforcement of EU competition law. Not only is the Commission seeking to encourage further private litigation in the national courts, but it is considering how to empower NCAs to be more effective enforcers, and to preserve their independence.

As has already been explained, these and other developments, including the adoption of a new technology transfer block exemption and accompanying Guidelines, a new De Minimis Notice, and the review of the procedural and jurisdictional provisions of the EU Merger Regulation, have once again demanded much change to the chapters in this edition. We have attempted to process these changes and to consider their wider implications for the development of EU competition law and policy fully, whilst endeavouring to keep the book manageable. Our aim with this edition is, as ever, to provide students, and others interested in competition law, with as comprehensive as possible a package of text, commentary, and materials given the confines of space. That task becomes more difficult with each edition, given not only the ever-expanding body of the law but also the ever-increasing body of literature and commentary on it. The last three years have seen a wealth of new literature, including the publication of a number of scholarly monographs, practitioner volumes, books combining law and economics, and articles in law journals. This is evidence of the continuing dynamism, excitement, and commercial importance of this area of law and its inter-disciplinary nature which sits at the interface of law and economics. As always some things we would have liked to have included have been left on the cutting-room floor but we have attempted to give readers at least a flavour of the main debates and ideas, and to provide references and further reading indicating where these may be pursued.

We would like to extend our thanks to everyone who has assisted us in the preparation of this edition, in particular, Massimiliano Kadar, Elina Stavropoulou, and Lisa Daniel, and the Centre of European Law and Dickson Poon School of Law at King's College London for its generous research funding. We also owe an enormous debt of gratitude to Emily Hoyland, Emily Spicer, Sarah Stephenson, and their colleagues at OUP, our copy-editor Joy Ruskin-Tompkins, and our proofreader, Jonathon Price, for their helpfulness and efficiency.

Our intention was to state the law as at 5 February 2016. With the cooperation and forbearance of OUP, however, we have been able to include a note at least of some later developments up until the end of March 2016. Further developments which occurred too late may be found on the Online Resource Centre that accompanies this book. The main objective of the Online Resource Centre is to set out a list of recent developments in the law, to publish the online State Aid chapter, and to provide links to helpful websites where further information can be obtained. It can be accessed at www.oxfordtextbooks.co.uk/orc/jones_sufrin6e/.

The authors would like to dedicate this edition to Gareth Jones and to Leon Paul Sufrin.

Alison Jones
Brenda Sufrin
31 March 2016

ACKNOWLEDGEMENTS

Grateful acknowledgement is made to all the authors and publishers of copyright material that appear in this book, and in particular to the following for permission to reprint material from the sources indicated:

Extracts from UK Competition Law Reports (UKCLR) and Office of Fair Trading Research Paper 2: Barriers to Entry and Exit in Competition Policy are Crown copyright material and are reproduced under Class Licence Number C01P0000148 with the permission of the Controller of HMSO and the Queen's Printer for Scotland.

Extracts from the reports of the European Court of Justice and Court of First Instance (ECR) are taken from www.curia.europa.eu. These are unauthenticated reports and are reproduced free of charge. The definitive versions are published in Reports of Cases before the Court of Justice or the Official Journal of the European Union.

Basic Books, a member of Perseus Books Group: extracts from Robert H. Bork: *The Antitrust Paradox: A Policy at War with Itself* (Basic Books, 1993), copyright © 1978 by Basic Books, LLC.

Colombia Business Law Review: William E. Kovacic, 'The Intellectual DNA of Modern U.S. Competition Law For Dominant Firm Conduct: The Chicago/Harvard Double Helix' [2007] 1(1).

Hart Publishing: extracts from G. Amato: *Antitrust and the Bounds of Power* (Hart, 1997).

Harvard Law Review Association: extracts from W. S. Comanor: 'Vertical price-fixing, vertical market restrictions, and the new antitrust policy', 98 *Harvard LR* 983 (1985), copyright © 1985 The Harvard Law Review Association.

LexisNexis: W. Allan, M. Furse, and B. Sufrin (eds.) *Butterworths Competition Law.*

Wolters Kluwer Law & Business: extracts from Common Market Law Review, Giorgio Monti, 'Article 81 EC and Public Policy', *CMLRev* (2002) 1057, 'The Scope of Collective Dominance under Article 82C', 38 *CMLRev* (2001) 131; and extracts from L. Peeperkorn, 'IP Licences and Competition Rules: Striking the Right Balance', 26 *World Competition* (2003) 527; Case IV/34.174, *Sealink/B&I Holyhead: Interim Measures* [1992] 5 CMLR 255, G. Monti, 'Restraints on Selective Distribution Agreements' (2013) *World Competition* 36(4) 489.

The Michigan Law Review Association and the author: extracts from H. Hovenkamp, 'Antitrust Policy After Chicago', 84 *Mich LR* 213 (1985), copyright © 1985 by Michigan Law Review Association.

New York University Law School: extract from Eleanor M. Fox and Lawrence A. Sullivan, 'Antitrust—Retrospective and Prospective: Where Are We Coming From? Where Are We Going?', 62 *New York University Law Review* 936 (1987).

Oxford University Press: extracts from S. D. Anderman and J. Kallaugher, *Technology Transfer and the New EU Competition Rules: Intellectual Property Licensing after Modernization* (OUP, 2006); J. Faull and A. Nikpay (eds.), *The EU Law of Competition* (3rd edn, OUP, 2014); C. Harding and J. Joshua, *Regulating Cartels in Europe* (2nd edn, OUP, 2010); and from the *Journal of European Competition Law and Practice*, B. Meyring, 'T-Mobile: Further confusion on information exchanges between competitors: Case C-8/08 *T-Mobile Netherlands and others* [2009] ECR I-4529', *JECLAP* 30 (2010).

Sweet & Maxwell Ltd: extracts from S. Bishop and M. Walker, *The Economics of EC Competition Law: Concepts, Application and Measurement* (3rd edn, Sweet & Maxwell, 2010); extracts from European Competition Law Review, A. Jones and D. Beard, 'Co-contractors, Damages and Article 81: The ECJ Finally Speaks', *ECLR* 246 (2002); extracts from European Law Review, P. Nebbia, 'Damages Actions for the Infringement of EC Competition Law: Compensation or Deterrence?', *ELRev* (2008); extracts from R. Nazzini, 'The Objective of Private Remedies in EU Competition Law', *Global Competition Litigation Review* (2011); extracts from R. J. Van den Bergh and P. D. Camesasca, *European Competition Law and Economics: A Comparative Perspective* (2nd edn, Sweet & Maxwell, 2006); and extracts from Common Market Law Reports (CMLR).

Thomson West: extracts from H. Hovenkamp, *Federal Antitrust Policy: The Law of Competition and its Practice* (4th edn, West, 2011) and H. Hovenkamp, *Federal Antitrust Policy: The Law of Competition and its Practice* (5th edn, West, 2016).

Every effort has been made to trace and contact copyright holders prior to publication but this has not been possible in every case. If notified, the publisher will undertake to rectify any errors or omissions at the earliest opportunity.

OUTLINE CONTENTS

CONTENTS

TABLE OF EUROPEAN CASES

[Page references in **bold** indicate that the item is given particular prominence in the text]

Note: Publication of the printed European Court Reports (ECR) ceased at the end of 2011. In March 2014 the European Case Law Identifier (ECLI) system was introduced. This provides a system for citing, according to a uniform format, cases in the EU Courts, and cases in the national courts of the Member States. Judgments and opinions of the EU Courts and the opinions of the Advocates General are prefaced by the letters EU, followed by either T (General Court) or C (Court of Justice), the year the opinion or decision of the Court was delivered, and an ordinal number. The CJEU has assigned an ECLI number to all EU Courts' decisions and (separately) to Advocates General's opinions from 1954. In this book we use the ECLI citation for cases from the beginning of 2012 but for previous cases we have left the ECR citation. The ECLI citation to all cases is available online on the website of the CJEU.

COMMISSION DECISIONS

NUMERICAL TABLE OF GENERAL COURT CASES

ALPHABETICAL TABLE OF GENERAL COURT CASES

OPINIONS OF THE COURT OF JUSTICE

NUMERICAL TABLE OF COURT OF JUSTICE CASES

ALPHABETICAL TABLE OF COURT OF JUSTICE CASES

EUROPEAN OMBUDSMAN

EFTA COURT

EUROPEAN COURT OF HUMAN RIGHTS

NATIONAL COURTS OF THE MEMBER STATES

DENMARK

FRANCE

GERMANY

IRELAND

TABLE OF INTERNATIONAL CASES

[Page references in **bold** indicate that the item is given particular prominence in the text]

INTERNATIONAL COURTS

PERMANENT COURT OF INTERNATIONAL JUSTICE (PCIJ)

WORLD TRADE ORGANISATION

NON-EU NATIONAL COURTS

AUSTRALIA

SINGAPORE

UNITED STATES

TABLE OF LEGISLATION

[Page references in **bold** indicate that the item is given particular prominence in the text]

EUROPEAN SECONDARY LEGISLATION

REGULATIONS

DIRECTIVES

DECISIONS (FOR COMMISSION DECISIONS IN INDIVIDUAL CASES, INCLUDING MERGER DECISIONS, SEE TABLE OF EUROPEAN CASES)

EU AND EEA NOTICES, GUIDELINES AND OTHER INFORMAL TEXTS (CHRONOLOGICAL ORDER)

RECOMMENDATIONS

NATIONAL LEGISLATION

TABLE OF EUROPEAN AND INTERNATIONAL TREATIES, CONVENTIONS, AND CHARTERS

[Page references in **bold** indicate that the item is given particular prominence in the text]

BIBLIOGRAPHY

The following are general works on EU competition law which cover the material dealt with in this book. Specialised reading is listed at the end of each chapter in the 'Further Reading' section.

ALLAN, W., FURSE, M., and SUFRIN, B. (eds.), *Butterworths Competition Law* (Butterworths, looseleaf)

AMATO, G., and EHLERMANN, C.-D., *EC Competition Law: A Critical Assessment* (Hart Publishing, 2007)

BAEL, I. VAN, and BELLIS, J.-F., *Competition Law of the European Community* (5th edn, Kluwer, 2009)

BELLAMY, G., and CHILD, G. (V. Rose and D. Bailey, eds.), *European Union Law of Competition* (7th edn, Oxford University Press, 2013 and Supplement by L. John and J. Turner, 2015)

BISHOP, S., and WALKER, M., *The Economics of EC Competition Law* (3rd edn, Sweet & Maxwell, 2010)

EZRACHI, A., *EU Competition Law: An Analytical Guide to the Leading Cases* (4th edn, Hart Publishing, 2014)

FAULL, J., and NIKPAY, A. (eds.), *The EU Law of Competition* (3rd edn, Oxford University Press, 2014)

GOYDER, J., and ALBORS-LLORENS, A., *Goyder's EC Competition Law* (5th edn, Oxford University Press, 2009)

KOKKORIS, I., *Competition Cases from the European Union* (2nd edn, Sweet & Maxwell, 2010)

KORAH, V., and LIANOS, I., *Competition Law: Text, Cases and Materials* (4th edn, Hart Publishing, 2014)

MARCO COLINO, S., *Competition Law of the EU and UK* (7th edn, Oxford University Press, 2011)

MONTI, G., *EC Competition Law* (Cambridge University Press, 2007)

MOTTA, M., *Competition Policy: Theory and Practice* (Cambridge University Press, 2004)

RODGER, B., and MACCULLOCH, A., *Competition Law and Policy in the EU and UK* (5th edn, Cavendish Publishing, 2014)

SLOT, P. J., and JOHNSTON, A., *An Introduction to Competition Law* (2nd edn, Hart Publishing, 2013)

WHISH, R., and BAILEY, D., *Competition Law* (8th edn, Oxford University Press, 2015)

BLOGS

http://chillingcompetition.com (Alfonso Lamadrid de Pablo and Pablo Ibáñez Colomo)
http://professorgeradin.blogs.com/professor_geradins_weblog/

LIST OF ABBREVIATIONS

AAC	average avoidable cost
AC	Appeal Cases
AIC	average incremental cost
AJIL	*American Journal of International Law*
All ER	All England Law Reports
Am Econ Rev	*American Economic Review*
Ant Bull	*Antitrust Bulletin*
Antitrust LJ	*Antitrust Law Journal*
ATC	average total cost
ATP	absolute territorial protection
AVC	average variable cost
Bell J Econ	*Bell Journal of Economics*
BER	Block Exemption Regulation
BEREC	Body of European Regulators for Electronic Communications
BYIL	*British Yearbook of International Law*
CAP	Common Agricultural Policy
CAT	Competition Appeal Tribunal
CBI	Confederation of British Industry
CDE	*Cahiers de Droit Européen*
CFI	Court of First Instance (renamed as General Court (GC) by the Treaty of Lisbon)
Charter	Charter of Fundamental Rights of the European Union
CISAC	International Confederation of Societies of Authors and Composers
CJ	Court of Justice
CJEU	Court of Justice of the European Union
CLI	*Competition Law Insight*
CLJ	*Cambridge Law Journal*
CLP	*Current Legal Problems*
CLPD	*Competition Law & Policy Debate*
CMA	Competition and Markets Authority (UK)
CMLR	Common Market Law Reports
CMLRev	*Common Market Law Review*
CMO	Common Organisation of Agricultural Markets
Colum LR	*Columbia Law Review*
CompAR	Competition Appeal Reports
Comp Law	*Competition Law Journal*
Cornell LR	*Cornell Law Review*
Cowp	Cowper's King's Bench Report
DG Comp	European Commission Competition Directorate-General
DGFT	Director General for Fair Trading
DOJ	Department of Justice (US)
EAGCP	European Advisory Group on Competition Policy
EBU	European Broadcasting Union
EC	European Community
ECC	European Commercial Cases
ECHR	European Convention for the Protection of Human Rights
ECJ	European Court of Justice

ECLR	*European Competition Law Review*
ECN	European Competition Network
ECR	European Court Reports
ECSC	European Coal and Steel Community
ECtHR	European Court of Human Rights
EEA	European Economic Area
EEC	European Economic Community
EFTA	European Free Trade Area
EGLR	Estates Gazette Law Reports
EHRR	European Human Rights Reports
EIPR	*European Intellectual Property Review*
ELRev	*European Law Review*
EMU	Economic and Monetary Union
EPC	European Patent Convention (1973)
ESA	EFTA Surveillance Authority
ETSI	European Telecommunications Standards Institute
EU	European Union
EuLR	European Law Reports
EUMR	European Union Merger Regulation (Reg. 139/2004)
Euratom	European Atomic Energy Community
EWCA Civ	England and Wales Court of Appeal (Civil)
EWHC	England and Wales High Court
FCO	Federal Cartel Office (Bundeskartellamt, Germany)
FIFA	International Federation of Association Football
Fordham Corp L Inst	*Fordham Corporate Law Institute*
Fordham Int'l LJ	*Fordham International Law Journal*
FRAND	fair, reasonable, and non-discriminatory
FTAIA	Foreign Trade Antitrust Improvements Act (US)
FTC	Federal Trade Commission (US)
GC	General Court (formerly the Court of First Instance)
Geo LJ	*Georgetown Law Review*
Harvard LR	*Harvard Law Review*
HHI	Herfindahl–Hirschman index
HMT	hypothetical monopolist test
HRS	Hotel Reservations Service
ICLQ	*International and Comparative Law Quarterly*
ICN	International Competition Network
ICT	information and communications technology
ILM	*International Legal Materials*
Indus & Corp Change	*Industrial and Corporate Change*
IO	industrial organisation
IOC	International Olympic Committee
IP	intellectual property
IPAC	International Competition Policy Advisory Committee
IPR	intellectual property right
IRLR	*Industrial Relations Law Reports*
JBL	*Journal of Business Law*
JECLAP	*Journal of European Competition Law and Practice*
JIEL	*Journal of International Economic Law*
JO	Journal Officiel

LIEI	*Legal Issues in European Integration/Legal Issues in Economic Integration*
LME	London Metal Exchange
LPP	legal professional privilege
LRAIC	long-run average incremental cost
MES	minimum efficient scale
MFN	most favoured nation
Mich LR	*Michigan Law Review*
MIF	multilateral interchange fee
MLP	Model Leniency Programme
MLR	*Modern Law Review*
MPV	multi-purpose vehicle
NAAT	not appreciably affect trade
NCAs	national competition authorities
New York Univ LR	*New York University Law Review*
NJECL	*New Journal of European Criminal Law*
NRA	national regulatory authority
OECD	Organisation for Economic Co-operation and Development
OFCOM	Communications Regulator (UK)
OFGEM	Office of Gas and Electricity Markets (UK)
OFT	Office of Fair Trading (UK)
OFWAT	Office of Water Services (UK)
OJ	Official Journal
OPEC	Organization of the Petroleum Exporting Countries
OTA	online travel agent
P & I	protection and indemnity
PPLR	*Public Procurement Law Review*
PPO	Public Postal Operators
PSO	public service obligation
QB	Queen's Bench
Quart J of Econ	*Quarterly Journal of Economics*
R&D	research and development
RdC	Recueil des Cours de l'Académie de droit international de La Haye
RPM	resale price maintenance
RTPA	Restrictive Trade Practices Act 1976
SEA	Single European Act 1986
SDS	selective distribution system
SEP	standard-essential patent
SGEI	service of general economic interest
SGI	service of general interest
SIEC	significant impediment to effective competition
SLC	substantial lessening of competition
SMEs	small and medium-sized enterprises
SO	statement of objections
SRMC	short-run marginal cost
SSNIP	Small but Significant Non-transitory Increase in Price
Stan LR	*Stanford Law Review*
TEU	Treaty on European Union
TFEU	Treaty on the Functioning of the European Union
TTBER	Technology Transfer Block Exemption Regulation (Reg. 772/2004) (or BER)
UKCLR	United Kingdom Competition Law Reports

UNCTAD	United Nations Conference on Trade and Development
Univ Chic LR	*University of Chicago Law Review*
Univ Mich LR	*University of Michigan Law Review*
U Pa LR	*University of Pennsylvania Law Review*
UPP	upward pricing pressure
USO	universal service obligation
WIPO	World Intellectual Property Organization
WTO	World Trade Organization
Yale LJ	*Yale Law Journal*
YEL	*Yearbook of European Law*

1

INTRODUCTION TO COMPETITION LAW

1. CENTRAL ISSUES

1. Competition law is concerned with ensuring that firms operating in the free market economy do not prevent the market from functioning optimally by acting anti-competitively.

2. The belief that competition amongst undertakings produces the best outcomes for society is based on economic theory that employs models of perfect competition and monopoly, and concepts of welfare and efficiency.

3. Competition law is concerned with preventing restrictive agreements between firms, dealing with oligopolistic markets, preventing the anti-competitive consequences of the exercise of substantial market power, and preventing mergers which lead to a concentration in market power. In the EU competition law is also concerned with State aid, whereby Member States give favourable treatment to particular undertakings.

4. There are many views about what exactly competition law should seek to achieve. It is possible for systems of competition law to simply pursue the economic objectives of welfare and efficiency. Whether competition law should do this, or should pursue other objectives, is controversial. Three main 'schools' of competition thought are known as Harvard, Chicago, and Post-Chicago. A school of political theory originating in Germany called ordoliberalism includes ideas about competition which have been influential in EU competition law.

5. Even if it is accepted that welfare and efficiency should be the sole or main goal of competition law, there are questions as to whether the welfare standard should be total/social welfare or consumer welfare, how markets work and when, and on what basis, competition authorities should intervene.

6. A system of competition law was provided for in the EC Treaty (the Treaty of Rome). Article 3(1)(g) EC provided that the activities of the EC included 'a system ensuring that competition in the internal market is not distorted'. The provision now appears in a Protocol to the Treaty on European Union (TEU) and the Treaty on the Functioning of the European Union (TFEU) which have governed the European Union since the coming into force of the Treaty of Lisbon, and the Court of Justice (CJ) has recognised that this has the same effect as Article 3(1)(g) EC. The integration of the single market is an important aspect of EU competition law.

7. Since the 1990s EU competition law has been undergoing a process of modernisation. This has led to the competition rules being applied in a more economically rigorous way. The Commission's application of the competition rules is directed to the objective of consumer welfare. The attitude of the EU Courts is more complex.

8. The development of new economy and digital markets present particular challenges for competition law.

9. EU competition law must be seen in an international context.

10. Three central concepts used in competition law are market power, market definition, and barriers to entry.

2. INTRODUCTION

'What *is* competition law?' is the first question any book on competition law must address.

The starting point is that competition law exists to protect competition in a free market economy. The terms competition *policy* and competition *law* are often used synonymously but competition law can be described as the means by which competition policy is implemented in respect of firms operating in the marketplace.

A free market economy is an economic system in which the allocation of resources is determined by supply and demand in free markets and is not directed by government regulation. This contrasts with an economy run by central government planning, such as that which existed in Soviet Russia. States which adopt a market economy do so because they consider it to be the form of economic organisation which brings the greatest benefits to society. The basis of a free market is competition between firms. Competition law seeks to protect that competition by controlling the exercise of market power, either by single firms or by firms acting together, which leads to higher prices, less choice, and lower quality and less innovation in products and services.

The foundation of free market theory is usually located in the work of Adam Smith in the eighteenth century.[1] He thought that governments should remove artificial obstacles to the operation of free markets, such as price controls, and allow competition to flourish. Individuals pursuing their own self-interest competing in the marketplace would be led by the 'invisible hand' to achieve the general good:

> Every individual necessarily labours to render the annual revenue of the society as great as he can. He generally neither intends to promote the public interest, nor knows how much he is promoting it . . . He intends only his own gain, and he is in this, as in many other cases, led by an invisible hand to promote an end which was no part of his intention. Nor is it always the worse for society that it was no part of his intention. By pursuing his own interest he frequently promotes that of the society more effectually than when he really intends to promote it. I have never known much good done by those who affected to trade for the public good.[2]

From this developed the concept of the market as an efficient and self-regulating mechanism with which governments should not interfere. Faith in the market was shaken to its core by the Great Depression of the 1930s, but it recovered to become by the latter part of the twentieth century the great organising principle of western economies, exported around the world, particularly after the fall of the Communist regimes of the Soviet Union and eastern Europe which was celebrated as the triumph of free market capitalism over central planning. The high priests of the free market are those belonging to the 'Chicago School' of economics, which has had a profound influence on the development of competition law and is discussed later.[3]

The adoption of a free market economy does not mean that all areas are left to unbridled competition. Adam Smith himself believed that governments should provide for certain public institutions which individuals would have no interest in undertaking as they would not yield profit. Furthermore, sectors such as health services or the provision of utilities may be subject to governmental intervention or government controls even though it is possible to operate them for profit. States have varying views about how far the free market should be tempered or supplemented by a social component.[4]

It may seem ironic that competition laws interfere with the freedom of firms to compete as they wish in order to promote competition. However, similar paradoxes face democratic governments in

---

[1] See Adam Smith, *The Wealth of Nations* (1776, reprinted Penguin, 1999).

[2] Ibid., Book IV.

[3] See Section 4.B.i, p. 14 ff.

[4] For the argument that competition does not always benefit society and that in certain scenarios competition yields sub-optimal results, see M. E. Stucke, 'Is Competition Always Good?' (2013) 1(1) *J of Antitrust Enforcement* 162.

other spheres, such as the question of how far the liberties of individuals should be constrained in order to uphold liberty itself.

Competition rules are necessary to deal with market imperfections and failures. In particular, left alone to determine their own conduct, firms are likely to combine or collude in a way which is profitable to them but which works to the detriment of society as a whole. Adam Smith himself described the tendency of those operating within the same trade to conspire to fix prices,[5] in what we now call cartels. On markets where only a few firms operate without any one of them dominating (called an oligopoly) they may be able to behave as monopolists by acting together without conspiring. Either way the firms can together exercise market power. Further, competition between firms may produce a 'winner' which dominates the market, or 'natural' monopolies may exist on a market. These firms can then exercise market power. Positions of market power may also be created if firms are allowed to merge freely with one another. Competition laws therefore need to be framed:

(a) to prevent restrictive agreements between firms which have anti-competitive consequences;

(b) to deal with oligopolistic markets;

(c) to deal with the prejudicial consequences of market power enjoyed by dominant firms; and

(d) to prevent mergers which lead to a concentration in market power.

In respect of terminology it should be noted that in general parlance competition law is often called by its American name, 'antitrust law'. However, the European Commission (the EU competition authority) uses the term 'antitrust' to denote the areas of competition law other than merger control and State aid. The reader will find, nevertheless, that many of the sources quoted in this book use 'antitrust' in its more general meaning.

State aid rules concern aids given by Member States to particular firms which distort competition. State aid is not dealt with in the printed edition of this book but is the subject of a separate chapter available online.[6]

3. THE ECONOMICS OF COMPETITION LAW

In this section we set out some basic concepts of microeconomics and welfare economics (the branch of economics which deals with efficiency) and seek to show why competition is thought to achieve efficiency and produce the greatest benefits to society in the form of welfare.[7]

A. BASIC CONCEPTS OF WELFARE ECONOMICS

(i) Demand Curves and Consumer and Producer Surplus

Consumers are all different. They place different values on things, have different preferences and different incomes, and will consequently be willing to pay different prices for a particular product. The maximum amount a consumer is willing to pay for a product is his reservation price.

Although suppliers might like to charge each consumer his individual reservation price, in practice this is not usually feasible.[8] The supplier must therefore consider the relationship between the

---

[5] *The Wealth of Nations*, n. 1.

[6] See the Online Resource Centre for the State aid chapter.

[7] See D. Geradin, A. Layne-Farrar, and N. Petit, *EU Competition Law and Economics* (Oxford University Press, 2012), 2.10–2.34; J. Faull and A. Nikpay (eds.), *The EU Law of Competition* (3rd edn, Oxford University Press, 2014) (Faull and Nikpay), Chap. 1, 1.21–1.119. Many of the team who write Faull and Nikpay are past or present European Commission officials.

[8] Although it is becoming more possible where customers buy or book online and the supplier has mined data they have previously provided online and so can make targeted offers.

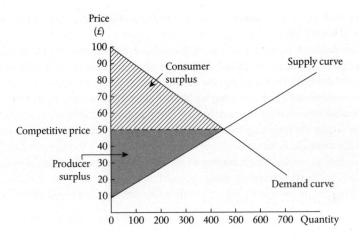

Figure 1.1 Demand curve and consumer and producer surplus

consumer's willingness to pay and the quantity which will be bought on the market as a whole. If only buyers with very high reservation prices are supplied, the quantity produced will be smaller than if buyers with lower reservation prices are supplied. Conversely, if greater quantities are produced the price will have to fall to incorporate buyers with lower reservation prices. The relationship between price and supply is represented by the market demand curve. The demand curve normally slopes downwards from left to right.

Assuming that the market price is £50 we can see that some consumers will be paying £50 for a product for which they would have paid more. This results in what is known as *consumer surplus* and is shown by the hatched area in Fig. 1.1. It is the difference between the buyers' reservation price and the market price.[9]

The supply curve shows the marginal cost of production. In Fig. 1.1 we see that the producer is selling the output for more than it costs to produce. This results in what is known as *producer surplus* and is shown by the shaded area in Fig. 1.1.

(ii) Elasticity of Demand (Own Price Elasticity)

The amount by which the quantity demanded increases as price reduces (and vice versa) will depend on the market in question and the elasticity of demand for the product.

Price elasticity of demand measures the sensitivity of the quantity demanded to the price. Demand is said to be *inelastic* if an increase in price leads to an insignificant fall in demand. Conversely, demand is *elastic* if an increase in price leads to a significant fall in demand.

Technically, price elasticity of demand is the percentage change in the quantity of a product demanded divided by the corresponding percentage change in its price. The result will be a negative figure as the fall in demand will be expressed as a negative figure from the starting point. If demand for widgets[10] falls by 2 per cent as a result of a 1 per cent price increase, the change in demand will be expressed as −2 per cent. The demand elasticity is then −2 divided by 1 (the price increase), which is −2.[11] Typically, elasticity falls as one moves down the demand curve, so that at higher

---

[9] The concept of consumer surplus was first described by Alfred Marshall, *Principles of Economics* (8th edn, Macmillan, 1920).

[10] A widget is traditionally a mythical product with no specific characteristics used in competition law examples. Despite the recent use of 'widget' to describe particular products it still retains its characterless role as the Everyman of competition law discourse.

[11] This figure is often expressed without the minus (as it is always negative). The bigger the negative number, the 'higher' the elasticity, e.g. elasticity of −5 is higher than elasticity of −1.

prices demand is more elastic. Economic theory puts the dividing line between elastic and inelastic demand at −1. Demand is elastic at a figure below, or more negative, than −1. It is inelastic between −1 and 0. In markets where demand is inelastic shortages will lead to higher prices. So a bad harvest may be better for food producers than a good one. This was true, for example, when a frost disaster struck the Brazil coffee harvest in 1995.[12]

The position of an individual firm on the market will be different from that of producers on the market as a whole. Even if the demand for petrol is inelastic, the price for any individual brand will be elastic. If Esso puts up the price of its petrol but Shell does not, drivers will seek Shell garages. If, however, all the sellers of petrol increase the price the quantity demanded may not change significantly, at least in the short run.[13]

(iii) Cross-elasticity of Demand

As already explained, elasticity of demand measures the relationship between the price of the product and the demand for it. In contrast, *cross price elasticity of demand* measures how much the demand for one product (A) increases when the price of *another* (B) goes up. It is measured by the percentage change in the quantity demanded of product A divided by the percentage increase in the price of B. Cross-elasticity of demand is crucial to market definition.[14]

Cross price elasticity is positive if the price increase in B leads to an increase in demand for A, and this suggests that A and B are substitute products. The Brazil coffee shortage, although leading to an increase in the price of coffee, did not cause consumers to stop purchasing coffee and to purchase tea instead. This indicated that consumers did not consider tea was a substitute for coffee. An important point to note when considering two products is that there may be cross price elasticity in one direction and not in the other. Although coffee drinkers may not purchase tea when the price of coffee increases, this does not mean that tea drinkers would not purchase coffee if there was a similar price rise in tea. If products are complements of each other, rather than substitutes, the cross price elasticity figure will be negative rather than positive. If the price of petrol goes up the demand for big-engine gas-guzzling cars may go down.

(iv) Profit Maximisation

An assumption is made for the purposes of welfare economics that firms act rationally and in a way which maximises profits.[15] Whether firms do always behave in this way is doubtful.[16] It will be seen

---

[12] D. Begg, G. Vernasca, S. Fischer, and R. Dornbusch, *Economics* (10th edn, McGraw-Hill, 2011), 76–77.

[13] The demand for petrol is not totally inelastic, although elasticity is low. Arguments about governments taking action on the environment by discouraging driving through higher petrol taxes are predicated on the assumption of some elasticity in the demand for petrol. In the long run consumers may change their travelling habits, lifestyle, and/or buy more fuel-efficient or electric cars.

[14] See Section 15.B, p. 56 ff.

[15] Known as 'rational choice theory' which assumes that individuals always make prudent and logical decisions which are of the greatest benefit to them. Profits represent the difference between the total cost of producing goods or providing a service and the revenue earned by selling them.

[16] Behavioural economics has cast doubt on rational choice theory; see H. A. Simon, 'Theories of Decision-making in Economic and Behavioral Sciences' (1959) 49 *Am Econ Rev* 253; R. Van den Bergh, 'Behavioural Antitrust: Not Ready for the Main Stage' (2013) 9(1) *J of Competition Law and Economics* 203; S. Bhattacharya and R. Van den Bergh, 'The Contribution of Management Studies to Understanding Firm Behaviour and Competition Law' (2014) 37 *World Competition* 517. Furthermore, the seminal work of A. A. Berle and G. C. Means, *The Modern Corporation and Private Property* (revised edn 1968, Harcourt Brace and World, 1932) explored the consequences of the separation of ownership from control in all but the smallest companies. In the layers of complex organisation which make up modern businesses, decisions may be made by managers and executives facing uncertain future events and a large number of variables. Their expectations may be misplaced, they may be averse to risk-taking, and they may be most concerned with corporate or individual survival or the growth of the company rather than its profitability. See also J. E. Parkinson, *Corporate Power and Responsibility* (Oxford University Press, 1993), particularly Chaps. 2–4.

later that, in particular where a firm has a monopoly, the managers may prefer a 'quiet life' to profit maximisation. Nevertheless, welfare economics is predicated on this basis.

(v) Economies of Scale and Scope

Economies of scale occur when the average cost of producing a commodity falls as more is produced. If a widget factory produces only one widget that one widget must bear the whole cost of establishing and running the factory. If it produces 100,000 widgets, however, the costs are spread over 100,000 widgets. Some costs (variable costs) may increase with production (energy and labour for example, although they may not increase proportionately to the number of extra units). However, some costs may not increase at all: for example, the driver of a lorry delivering widgets will be paid the same whether the lorry is full or half empty.

Economies of scale result where efficiency in production is achieved as output is increased. There inevitably comes a point, however, when the average cost ceases to fall and economies of scale can no longer be reaped. That point is called the minimum efficient scale (MES). The MES is of great significance in competition law since it has important repercussions for market structure. Where the MES is very large in relation to the market, i.e. a producer has to supply a large quantity of products on the market before the MES is reached, only a few firms, possibly only one, will be able to operate efficiently on the market. A 'natural monopoly' occurs where it is less costly for just one firm to serve the market than for the market to be divided between more players. On a competitive market, however, the MES is low in comparison to overall demand so that numerous firms can operate efficiently on the market.

Economies of scope occur where it is cheaper to produce two different products jointly than each separately. This may result from factors such as shared assembly lines or shared personnel which enable the firm to make costs savings by producing a range of goods rather than the individual products on their own. Economies of scope may mean that a multi-product firm has lower unit costs than a single-product firm.

B. PERFECT COMPETITION AND EFFICIENCY

(i) Perfect Competition

The theory of perfect competition presents a model of a market in which efficiency is maximised and cannot, therefore, be improved by the application of competition rules.

A perfectly competitive market is one in which there is a large number of buyers and sellers (firms with very small market shares can operate at minimal costs since the MES is small in comparison to the size of the market); the product is homogeneous; all the buyers and sellers have perfect information;[17] there are no barriers to entry or exit so that sellers can come on to, and leave, the market freely;[18] there are no transaction costs (buyers and sellers do not incur costs or fees to participate in the market); and there are no externalities (firms do not impose uncompensated costs on others but rather, each bears the full cost of its production process). The result is that each seller is insignificant in relation to the market as a whole and has no influence on the product's price. Consequently, sellers are price-takers, not price-makers.

In a perfectly competitive market the price does not exceed marginal cost. The marginal cost to a firm is the cost of producing one extra unit of the product. So if it costs £100 to produce ten widgets but £105 to produce 11, the marginal cost is £5. On such a market the firm will always be able to add to profit where the marginal cost of producing a unit is less than the price. The producer will therefore increase production until the price obtained per unit equals marginal cost. If the price is below marginal cost the firm will have to respond by reducing output. In other words, in a perfectly

---

[17] Buyers and sellers know of every change in price or demand and so respond immediately to such changes.

[18] For a discussion of barriers to entry, see Section 15.C, p. 79 ff.

competitive market a firm's marginal revenue (the rise in what the firm earns by one extra unit of output) equals marginal cost.[19]

Where the price charged for a product is at marginal cost the firm makes only a 'normal' profit, that is a rate of profit that is just sufficient to keep the firm in the industry. All the factors of production used to make the product must be taken into account when computing the cost, including the capital. The firm has to make enough of a return on the capital employed in the business to make it worthwhile staying on the market. When economists talk of zero profits they mean that there is no profit above the 'normal' level, which is assessed in relation to the 'opportunity cost'. Opportunity costs are the value of what has to be given up to do something else. The capital employed in the business must therefore reap a profit to compensate the business for the profit which would come from a different outlay.

The relationship between marginal and average cost is important. The average cost is the costs of the firm evened out over all the units produced.[20] When the marginal cost of the next unit exceeds the average cost of the existing units, producing the next unit raises average costs. In that case the firm can decrease costs by reducing supply. If, on the other hand, the marginal cost of the next unit is less than the average cost of the existing units, an extra unit reduces average costs. In that case the firm can decrease costs by increasing supply. So the producer will produce at the point at which the average cost curve and the marginal cost curve intersect.

(ii) Allocative Efficiency

The fact that on a perfectly competitive market the market price equals the marginal cost is said to lead to *allocative efficiency*.

Allocative efficiency results from the fact that goods are produced in the quantities valued by society. The supplier will expand production to the point where market price and marginal cost coincide. The supplier will not make more but neither, if it is acting rationally to maximise profits, will it make less. Everyone who is willing and able to purchase the product at its cost of production will be able to do so. The result is a market which is in equilibrium. Allocative efficiency is a state in which none of the players, sellers or buyers, could be made better off without someone being made worse off. It is sometimes known as Pareto optimal after the Italian economist, Vilfredo Pareto (1848–1923), who first developed the theory.

(iii) Productive Efficiency

Similarly, *productive* (or technical) efficiency results from perfectly competitive markets. Goods are produced at the lowest possible cost. Every firm must produce at minimum cost or lose its custom to others, make losses, and eventually be obliged to leave the market. Given the perfect information in the market any cost-cutting techniques will be copied by the other firms and the market price will be lowered generally. There is therefore downward pressure on costs and cost reductions are passed on to customers because of the competitive pressure from other suppliers.

(iv) Dynamic Efficiency

Dynamic efficiency is a third type of efficiency. Allocative and productive efficiency describe static situations, but dynamic efficiency is concerned with how well a market delivers innovation and

---

[19] The reason for this is that although the *industry's* demand curve is downward sloping, the demand curve for *each individual firm* is horizontal, which means that however much it sells it will get the market price. For further explanation of this, see D. W. Carlton and J. M. Perloff, *Modern Industrial Organization* (4th edn, Pearson Addison Wesley, 2005), Chap. 3.

[20] See further, Chap. 7 for a discussion of costs in relation to pricing abuses.

technological progress. The relation of dynamic efficiency to the concept of perfectly competitive markets is complex and it can be argued that innovation may be better delivered by monopolistic rather than competitive markets and that the ability to achieve market power is an important spur to innovation.[21] Many economists argue that dynamic efficiency is the most important kind of efficiency for increasing the 'welfare' which is discussed later.

C. MONOPOLY

At the opposite end of the spectrum to perfect competition lies monopoly. A monopoly is a market where there is only one seller. This may be because there are barriers which prevent other firms from entering the market or because there is a natural monopoly.

Theory predicts that as the firm is not constrained by any competitors it will price as high as possible. The monopoly price will be above the competitive market price. However, the price that the monopolist charges is still affected by demand and is constrained to some extent by products from outside the market. As the price rises some customers will not purchase the product but will use their resources to purchase something else instead. The firm usually faces a downward-sloping demand curve, so the higher the price it charges the lower the demand for its product.

If a monopolist sells just one unit it may receive a very high price for that unit but that price is unlikely to cover its costs. The monopolist will therefore wish to sell more units but in order to do so it must lower the price in order to attract customers with lower reservation prices. Unless the monopolist can *price discriminate* between customers, the monopolist must lower the price on all units, not just the extra ones. The producer's marginal revenue is the extra amount the monopolist obtains from selling the extra unit, but because it involves lowering the price across the board the marginal revenue is less than the selling price. This means that the monopolist will sell units only up to the point at which the marginal revenue equals the marginal cost. A monopolist's marginal revenue is below the market price. This in turn means that the quantity supplied of the product will be less than that which would be supplied on a competitive market. Thus prices are higher than those resulting on a competitive market and output is restricted. This is illustrated in Fig. 1.2.

Figure 1.2 shows that, in the absence of price discrimination, the marginal revenue curve is always under the demand curve.[22] Because price is above the competitive price the monopolist makes abnormal profits but some consumers who would have paid the competitive (marginal cost) price are deprived of the product. Some of the consumer surplus identified in Fig. 1.1 is therefore transferred to the producer as monopoly profit but some is lost altogether. The horizontally hatched triangle in Fig. 1.2 shows this *deadweight loss of monopoly*, the loss of consumer surplus which is not turned into profit for the producer.

According to this theory, therefore, the main distinction between perfect competition and pure monopoly is that the monopolist's price exceeds marginal cost, while the competitor's price equals marginal cost. This monopoly pricing leads to a transfer of wealth from consumer to producer (the vertically hatched area in Fig. 1.2). It is for this reason that firms operating on a competitive market may wish to emulate the effect of monopoly by colluding, for example, to set their prices at above the competitive level and by reducing output.

From an efficiency point of view the transfer of wealth to the monopolist may be immaterial. The behaviour does not, however, simply lead to a redistribution of income but also results in the misallocation in resources and a deadweight loss. It is this loss to efficiency as a whole that is of greatest concern.

---

[21] See Section 3.G, p. 12.

[22] If the monopolist is able to practise perfect price discrimination, i.e. charge each customer his reservation price, the marginal revenue curve and the demand curve are the same.

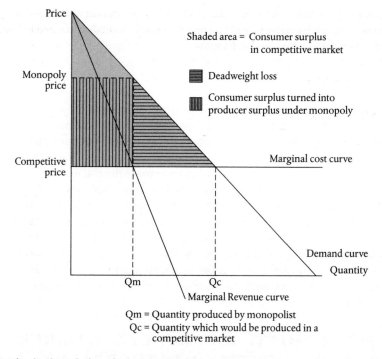

Qm = Quantity produced by monopolist
Qc = Quantity which would be produced in a
    competitive market

Figure 1.2 The deadweight loss due to monopoly

This seeming technicality, so trivial at first glance, is the basis of the economist's most general condemnation of monopoly: it leads to an allocation of resources that is inefficient in the sense of failing to satisfy consumer wants as completely as possible.[23]

In this respect, therefore, the objection to monopoly is not the popular concern—that the monopolist is able to charge excessively for its product—but that monopoly is inefficient.[24] Consumers who would have bought the product at the competitive price will spend their money on other things and welfare is not maximised as allocative inefficiency occurs. However, it is also possible to consider that the redistribution of benefits to producers from consumers who buy at above the competitive price is itself a form of inefficiency—distributive inefficiency.[25]

Another important objection to monopoly is that a monopolist will not have the same pressure as firms operating on a competitive market to reduce its costs. This was identified by Leibenstein as, and has become known as, 'X-inefficiency'. It describes internal inefficiencies and rising costs due, for example, to high salaries, excessive perks, overmanning, and the lack of need to minimise the cost of production.[26] A monopolist may also waste resources, for example defending its monopoly position, maintaining excess capacity, and indulging in excessive product differentiation.[27] These

[23] F. M. Scherer and D. Ross, *Industrial Market Structure and Economic Performance* (3rd edn, Houghton Mifflin, 1990), 23.

[24] Economists have often sought to quantify the deadweight loss. The starting point was Harberger's article in 1954 in which he calculated the loss in the US as less than 0.1% of national income: see A. C. Harberger, 'Monopoly and Resource Allocation' (1954) 44 *Am Econ Rev* 77–87. In a mass of further studies this has been found to be a great underestimate (for the literature on this, see Scherer and Ross, n. 23, 661–667). Cowling and Mueller calculated it as 7%: see K. Cowling and D. C. Mueller, 'The Social Costs of Monopoly Power' (1978) 88 *Economic Journal* 724–748, although Scherer and Ross, n. 23, describe these results as 'exaggerated'. In this, as in much else in economics, there are wide differences in views.

[25] Geradin, Layne-Farrar, and Petit, n. 7, 2.29.

[26] H. Leibenstein, 'Allocative efficiency vs. "X-efficiency" ' (1966) 56 *Am Econ Rev* 392–415.

[27] See, e.g., R. Posner, 'The Social Costs of Monopoly and Regulation' (1975) J *of Political Economy* 83.

inefficiencies will be reflected in higher prices. Moreover, a monopolist not subject to competitive pressures may have little incentive to innovate and to improve its production methods although, as already noted, the opposite may be true on some markets.

D. OLIGOPOLY

Oligopoly is a market structure lying between perfect competition and monopoly on the spectrum. On an oligopolistic market there are only a few leading firms, so the market is 'concentrated'. Given their small number they know each other's identity and recognise that they are affected by the output and pricing decisions of the others. This mutual awareness may lead to tacit (that is, understood or implied without being stated) collusion between them. It may also lead them to collude expressly. However, some oligopolistic markets are characterised by fierce competition. Thus in some markets the price appears to be set above the competitive level and to approximate monopoly pricing, but in others it is not. A wealth of economic literature has been produced setting out economic models of oligopoly to explain why this occurs. Oligopolistic markets are problematic for those responsible for drafting and applying the competition rules. The mainstream explanations of oligopolistic behaviour and the way in which EU competition law attempts to deal with oligopolistic markets are described in Chapter 9. Many markets are oligopolistic and present a major problem for competition authorities.

E. PERFECT COMPETITION, MONOPOLY, MARKET POWER, AND COMPETITION IN THE REAL WORLD

Monopolies and oligopolies do exist. Monopolies may be created and maintained by State regulation (utilities and transport markets, for example) and/or may be natural. Pure monopoly is relatively rare outside these circumstances but some markets, although not 100 per cent monopolised, may be dominated by one firm which holds a very large share of the market. Other markets may be oligopolistic, dominated by two, three, or four sellers. Even though there may be a fringe of smaller sellers on this type of market, they may present the same concerns for competition law as those arising on a monopolistic market.[28]

The analysis of perfectly competitive markets presents a number of problems. The main problem is that in the real world perfectly competitive markets hardly ever exist.[29] Rather, the model of perfect competition is just that—a model. It is a useful starting point because it demonstrates the concepts of productive and allocative efficiency. In reality, however, markets do not possess all the characteristics of perfect competition. It is very unlikely that an infinite number of firms will be operating at identical costs levels, that producers will not benefit from economies of scale, and that sellers and buyers have perfect information across an atomistic market. Important caveats must thus be attached to the theory that the perfectly competitive market is superior. In particular, in most markets economies of scale make the attainment of perfect competition impossible and in some monopolies are 'natural' because of the MES. Further, it is not actually clear that profit maximisation is the policy which firms always pursue.

The reality is that most markets lie somewhere between perfect competition and monopoly, in a state of 'imperfect' or 'monopolistic' competition where firms make differentiated or heterogeneous products[30] which consumers regard as imperfect substitutes, so that each firm has some degree of

---

[28] For a more detailed discussion see, Chaps. 5–7 and 9.

[29] Carlton and Perloff, n. 19, 84, suggest that the buying and selling of shares on the New York Stock Exchange comes close to satisfying the assumptions for perfect competition. And see von Hayek's views on information, Section 4.H, p. 24.

[30] Or products which consumers think of as differentiated. The differentiation and heterogeneity may mainly be in their minds, perhaps as the result of clever branding or advertising.

market power in that if it raises its prices it will not lose all its customers. The model of perfect competition is nonetheless still useful as a benchmark against which to measure the competitiveness of real markets. The difference between the perfectly competitive and monopolistic (or oligopolistic) market focuses attention on the crucial question: whether the firm or firms have sufficient market power to raise prices above the competitive level and keep them there.

F. THE CONCEPT OF WELFARE: TOTAL (SOCIAL) WELFARE, CONSUMER WELFARE, AND EFFICIENCY TRADE-OFFS

Welfare is the measure of how well a market is performing. A perfectly competitive market maximises welfare because it leads to efficiency. However, there are different concepts of welfare: total (otherwise called *social*) welfare and consumer welfare.

We have already seen that producer surplus is the profit a producer makes by selling goods above the cost of production. Consumer surplus is the difference between what consumers would be prepared to pay for goods and what they do pay. *Total welfare* is the sum of these two surpluses. The objection to monopoly, it will be recalled, is that it does not just transfer some consumer surplus to producers but that some surplus (the deadweight) is totally lost to the market. That is a loss to total welfare.

Consumer welfare can for present purposes be equated with consumer surplus (the aggregate measure of the surplus of all consumers).[31] If competition policy is concerned with consumer welfare rather than total welfare it will be concerned with the transfer of surplus from producers to consumers.[32] However, total welfare may be maximised by such a transfer. In other words, prohibiting conduct and transactions which reduce consumer welfare may not allow efficiency gains which maximise total welfare.[33] Efficiency and consumer welfare may pull in different directions. In contrast, a competition policy which chooses to pursue total welfare as an objective is concerned only with the loss of efficiency represented by the deadweight 'triangle' and is not concerned about the redistributive effects of efficiency gains.[34] This is sometimes called 'the constant dollar' (or constant euro) philosophy, as no value judgment is made as to who, producer or consumer, has the dollar. In this respect it should be noted that producers may have shareholders who include institutions such as pension funds and life assurance firms whose members and policyholders benefit from the company profits. Employees too may benefit from increased profits. It is not necessarily justifiable to privilege the buyer (the consumer) above the seller (the producer) as if the welfare of one is inherently more precious than that of the other.[35] Furthermore, as we shall see, the term 'consumers' in EU competition law includes customers on intermediate markets,[36] so where the customers are not final consumers but intermediate buyers a consumer welfare standard favours the buying *firm* over the selling one.

Moreover, although theory accords prime position to allocative efficiency, improving overall efficiency may require a trade-off between different types of efficiencies, which may have an effect on the relationship between producer and consumer surplus. This is discussed in the following extract, which explains what is meant by a *potential Pareto* (or *Kaldor Hicks*) *improvement*. Whereas a *Pareto improvement* is an action by which nobody loses and at least one person benefits, *a potential Pareto*

---

[31] See M. Motta, *Competition Policy* (Cambridge University Press, 2004), 18.

[32] See R. J. Van den Bergh and P. D. Camesasca, *European Competition Law and Economics: A Comparative Perspective* (2nd edn, Sweet & Maxwell, 2006), 37. As noted in Section 4.B.i, p. 17 the influential American commentator Robert Bork used the terminology 'consumer welfare' differently.

[33] See P. Akman, *The Concept of Abuse in EU Competition Law* (Hart Publishing, 2012), 37–44.

[34] Compensating redistribution can be achieved by other policies, such as taxation, if thought desirable.

[35] Akman, n. 33, 39; J. Farrell and M. L. Katz, 'The Economics of Welfare Standards in Antitrust' (2006) 2(2) *Competition Policy International* 3.

[36] See Section 8.B.v, p. 39.

improvement is a concept which deals with a situation where different efficiency goals are not consistent with each other, by providing that where there are both winners and losers the winners must win more than the losers lose.

> ## R. J. Van den Bergh and P. D. Camesasca, *European Competition Law and Economics: A Comparative Perspective* (2nd edn, Sweet & Maxwell, 2006), 29–30
>
> In some cases, allocative efficiency may conflict with other efficiency goals: productive efficiency and dynamic efficiency . . . Productive or technical efficiency implies that output is maximised by using the most effective combination of inputs; hence internal slack (also called X-inefficiency) is absent. The goal of productive efficiency implies that more efficient firms, which produce at lower costs, should not be prevented from taking business away from less efficient ones. Obviously, the achievement of productive efficiency is not a Pareto improvement since the less efficient firms are made worse off. Dynamic efficiency is achieved through the invention, development and diffusion of new products and production processes that increase social welfare. Whereas productive efficiency and allocative efficiency are static notions, progressiveness or dynamic efficiency refers to the rate of technological progress. Again, there will be losers in the dynamic competitive struggle, so that Pareto improvements cannot be reached. To enable policy decisions when the different efficiency goals are not consistent with each other, welfare economics offers the alternative criterion of Kaldor-Hicks efficiency.
>
> A Kaldor-Hicks improvement allows changes in which there are both winners and losers, but requires that the gainers gain more than the losers lose. This condition being satisfied, the winners could compensate the losers . . . and still have a surplus left for themselves . . . A Kaldor-Hicks improvement is also referred to as a potential Pareto improvement, since actual compensation would again satisfy the Pareto criterion. The central value judgment underlying Kaldor-Hicks efficiency is that an exchange of money has a neutral impact on aggregate well-being, which may not be the case when the incomes of gainers and losers differ. By using the Kaldor-Hicks criterion total welfare is maximised. This welfare notion may allow clearing mergers that enable the merging firms to achieve important scale economies and thus improve productive efficiency, but at the same time enable previously independent firms to collude and raise prices above competitive levels. In terms of total welfare, it is irrelevant that producers rather than consumers capture the surplus produced by achieving efficiencies, as the monopoly overcharge paid by purchasers to stockholders is treated as a transfer from one member of a society to another and so is ignored in the balance.

The question of trade-off between efficiencies and the relationship between efficiency and consumer welfare poses difficult problems for EU competition law. These issues are discussed further in the following chapters of this book.

G. DYNAMIC COMPETITION

The trade-off between different types of efficiencies already mentioned is particularly acute when dynamic efficiencies are concerned:

> . . . an improvement in terms of dynamic efficiency does not satisfy the Pareto criterion, since this will harm less innovative firms which will lose customers to their technically superior competitors. However, such improvements may satisfy the Kaldor-Hicks criterion since benefits both to pioneering firms and consumers may outweigh losses to non-innovative firms.[37]

---

[37] Begg, Vernasca, Fischer, and Dornbusch, n. 12, 31. And see the litigation culminating in Case C-501/06 P, *GlaxoSmithKline Services Unlimited v Commission* [2009] ECR I-9291, discussed in Chap. 4, where it was argued that increased prices to consumers were outweighed by dynamic efficiencies resulting from the undertaking concerned having more profit to plough back into the research and development of pharmaceuticals.

It is often claimed that monopolies have fewer incentives to innovate than firms in competitive markets but it is also argued that substantial market power is an incentive to innovate. The Austrian economist Joseph Schumpeter took issue with the idea that competition is a better spur to innovation than monopoly. He considered that a monopolist may be more willing to bear the risks and costs of invention and technical development.[38] Schumpeter's argument is that competition in innovation is more important than price competition because it is a more effective means of obtaining an advantage over one's competitors. This is known as 'Schumpterian rivalry', where firms compete in a constant race to bring new products on to the market in 'gales of creative destruction', competition is dynamic, and positions of market power are short term as further innovation hands the advantage to another player. This involves accepting that short-term positions of substantial market power may arise but that this is not necessarily inimical to consumer welfare.[39] Nevertheless, recent research has shown that monopolies and tight oligopolies are less conducive to innovation than less concentrated markets.[40] Concepts of dynamic efficiency and dynamic competition are particularly important in respect of the 'new economy' of high technology markets.[41]

4. SCHOOLS OF COMPETITION ANALYSIS AND THEORIES AND CONCEPTS RELEVANT TO COMPETITION LAW

A. THE STRUCTURE → CONDUCT → PERFORMANCE PARADIGM AND THE HARVARD SCHOOL

The S→C→P paradigm holds that the structure of the market determines the firm's conduct and that conduct determines market performance (for example profitability, efficiency, technical progress, and growth). The model thus seeks to establish that certain industry structures lead to certain types of conduct which then lead to certain kinds of economic performance. In particular, highly concentrated industries cause conduct which leads to poor economic performance, especially reduced output and monopoly prices.

This theory stems mainly from work done at Harvard University, initially in the 1930s, particularly by E. S. Mason,[42] and then by J. S. Bain in the 1950s.[43] The theory was developed through empirical studies of American industries rather than from theoretical models. The conclusion that market structure dictated performance led to a belief that competition law should be concerned with *structural* remedies rather than *behavioural* remedies. The focus of attention was, therefore, on concentrated industries. Bain considered that most industries were more concentrated than was necessary (economies of scale were not substantial in most industries); that barriers to entry were widespread and very high and so new firms were prevented from entering markets; and that the monopoly pricing associated with oligopolies began to occur at relatively low levels of concentration.

---

[38] J. A. Schumpeter, *Capitalism, Socialism and Democracy* (Harper, 1942).

[39] See D. Hildebrand, 'The European School in EC Competition Law' (2002) 25 *World Competition* 3.

[40] P. Aghion, N. Bloom, R. Blundell, R. Griffith, and P. Howitt, 'Competition and Innovation: An Inverted-U Relationship' (2005) 120 *Quart J of Econ* 701, cited by the then Director General of DG Comp, Alexander Italianer, 'Level Playing-field and Innovation in Technology Markets', Conference on Antitrust in Technology, Palo Alto, 28 January 2013, <http://www.ec.europa.eu/competition/speeches/text/sp2013_01_en.pdf>.

[41] See Section 12 and e.g. Case T-201/04, *Microsoft v Commission* [2007] ECR II-3601, discussed in Chap. 7.

[42] See E. S. Mason, *Economic Concentration and the Monopoly Problem* (Harvard University Press, 1957).

[43] See J. S. Bain, *Barriers to New Competition* (Harvard University Press, 1956) and *Industrial Organization* (2nd edn, Wiley, 1968).

These influential conclusions coincided with a general trend of US Congressional policies which sought to protect small businesses and which were suspicious of business expansion. This led in the 1960s to an interventionist antitrust enforcement policy in the US.[44] Criticism of the Bainian analysis, led by the Chicago School, centred particularly on the fact that the conclusions drawn from the empirical studies were flawed,[45] that they wrongly found barriers to entry to be pervasive, and wrongly found economies of scale to be rare. Consequently, the policy of condemning so many business practices as anti-competitive was misconceived. Despite the rise of the Chicago School, the S→C→P paradigm remains a basic tool of competition analysis. Although mainstream economics no longer holds that structure *dictates* performance, it accepts that structure is important to the ability of firms to behave anti-competitively. As Hovenkamp says:

The S-C-P left certain marks that seem all but indelible—for example, the greatly increased attention to market definition, barriers to entry, and proof of market power that even the most convinced members of the Chicago School acknowledge to be important. Antitrust without structural analysis has become impossible, thanks largely to the S-C-P writers. To be sure, they may have gone too far in emphasizing structure over conduct, but that is a question of balance, not of basic legitimacy. Not even S-C-P's most vehement critics would roll the clock back completely.[46]

B. THE CHICAGO SCHOOL, POST-CHICAGO, AND NEO-CHICAGO

(i) The Chicago School

'Chicago' antitrust theory does not exist in a vacuum. Rather, it is part of what is known as Chicago economics, a school of neoclassical, libertarian, free-market economics called after the university where many of its originators and adherents did (and still do) their work.[47] Put very simply, Chicago economics holds that people are rational and that markets work and are self-correcting. Chicago thinking has had a lasting influence on the economic policies of governments throughout the world.

The foundations of Chicago competition analysis are rigorously theoretical. Even while the S→C→P paradigm was becoming established as the dominant ideology of the day, Chicago scholars were decrying it and developing an alternative model based on neoclassical price theory. Although the S→C→P model has never been entirely eclipsed, Chicago School economics produced a 'revolution' in competition thinking in the US and then around the world.[48] Although it has been strongly criticised in its turn, its influence on competition law is profound.

---

[44] E.g., *Brown Shoe Co v United States*, 370 US 294, 82 S.Ct 1502 (1962); *FTC v Consolidated Foods Corp*, 380 US 592, 85 S.Ct 1220 (1965); *FTC v Procter & Gamble Co*, 386 US 568, 87 S.Ct 1224 (1967); *United States v Arnold, Schwinn & Co*, 388 US 365, 87 S.Ct 1856 (1967).

[45] Inter alia, in that they used accounting rates of return to calculate profits although they are unreliable indicators of monopoly profits; that they used cross-sectional data rather than data on a particular industry; that they were not a proper test unless based on long-run rather than short-run performance; and that the researchers did not always consider that the structural variables were not exogenous, i.e. that the concentration was itself determined by the economic conditions of the industry. There is modern work with the S→C→P model (notably by John Sutton) which takes account in particular of this last, very serious concern: see further Carlton and Perloff, n. 19, 246–274.

[46] H. Hovenkamp, *Federal Antitrust Policy: The Law of Competition and its Practice* (4th edn, West, 2011), 45.

[47] The description here relates to the Chicago School from the 1960s. The macroeconomist Milton Friedman, who opposed Keynesianism and developed monetarism during the 1960s, worked at Chicago from 1944 to 1977. Other leading Chicagoans include George Stigler, Robert Lucas, and Eugene Fama.

[48] See generally R. Posner, 'The Chicago School of Antitrust Analysis' (1979) 127 *U Pa LR* 92. The main proponents of its antitrust ideas, besides Posner, include George Stigler, Harold Demsetz (although he worked after 1971 at the University of California), Yale Brozen, and Robert Bork.

The fundamental Chicago view[49] is that the pursuit of efficiency, by which is meant allocative efficiency[50] as defined by the market, should be the sole goal of competition law. Chicago does not espouse sentimentality for small businesses or the corner store but places trust in the market, which it holds to be robust when it comes to competition. The identity of the winners or losers is irrelevant so long as efficiency is achieved. Indeed, since the writers consider that few barriers to entry exist, that industries frequently benefit from economies of scale, and that businesses are profit-maximisers, the Chicago School places much belief in the ability of the market to correct and achieve efficiency itself without interference from governments or competition laws.

Hovenkamp sets out the basic tenets of the Chicago School in the following extract from an article written in 1985. Although critical of some of the views, Hovenkamp nonetheless describes himself as a 'fellow traveler' (sic).

H. Hovenkamp, 'Antitrust Policy After Chicago' [1985] 84 *Univ Mich LR* 213, 226–229

. . . the following discussion summarizes a few of the model's basic assumptions and principles that have been particularly important in Chicago School antitrust scholarship.

(1) Economic efficiency, the pursuit of which should be the exclusive goal of the antitrust laws, consists of two relevant parts: allocative efficiency and productive efficiency . . . Occasionally practices that increase a firm's productive efficiency reduce the market's allocative efficiency. For example, construction of a large plant and acquisition of large market share may increase a firm's productive efficiency by enabling it to achieve economies of scale; however, these actions may simultaneously reduce allocative efficiency by facilitating monopoly pricing. A properly defined antitrust policy will attempt to maximize net efficiency gains . . .

(2) Most markets are competitive, even if they contain a relatively small number of sellers. Furthermore, product differentiation tends to undermine competition far less than was formerly presumed. As a result, neither high market concentration nor product differentiation are the anti-competitive problems earlier oligopoly theorists believed them to be . . .

(3) Monopoly, when it exists, tends to be self-correcting; that is, the monopolist's higher profits generally attract new entry into the monopolist's market, with the result that the monopolist's position is quickly eroded. About the best that the judicial process can do is hasten the correction process . . .

(4) 'Natural' barriers to entry are more imagined than real. As a general rule investment will flow into any market where the rate of return is high. The one significant exception consists of barriers to entry that are not natural—that is, barriers that are created by government itself. In most markets the government would be best off if it left entry and exit unregulated . . .

(5) Economies of scale are far more pervasive than economists once believed, largely because earlier economists looked only at intra-plant or production economics, and neglected economies of distribution. As a result, many more industries than were formerly thought may operate most economically only at fairly high concentration levels . . .

(6) Business firms are profit-maximizers. That is, their managers generally make decisions that they anticipate will make the firm more profitable than any alternative decision would. The model would not be undermined, however, if it should turn out that many firms are not profit maximizers, but are motivated

---

[49] We can only describe here the views of Chicago School scholars generally. There are considerable divergences of view among them, see further e.g. D. Crane, 'Chicago, Post-Chicago and Neo-Chicago' (2009) 76 *Univ Chic LR* 191.

[50] Chicago theory holds that the market itself punishes those who are productively inefficient. As the conditions for Pareto-efficiency can rarely be fulfilled, Chicago usually uses 'potential' Pareto-efficiency as the guide, which means a policy whereby the total gains of all those who gain should be greater than the total losses of all those who lose, see Section 3.F, p. 11 ff.

by some alternative goal, such as revenue maximization, sales maximization, or 'satisficing.' . . .[51] The integrity of the market efficiency model requires only that a few firms be profit-maximizers. In that case, the profits and market shares of these firms will grow at the expense of other firms in the market . . .

(7) Antitrust enforcement should be designed in such a way as to penalize conduct precisely to the point that it is inefficient, but to tolerate or encourage it when it is efficient . . . During the Warren Court era,[52] antitrust enforcement was excessive, and often penalized efficient conduct . . .

(8) The decision to make the neoclassical market efficiency model the exclusive guide for antitrust policy is nonpolitical.

A clear statement of the view that 'efficiency is all' is set out in Robert Bork's celebrated polemic, *The Antitrust Paradox*.[53]

R. H. Bork, *The Antitrust Paradox: A Policy at War with Itself* (Basic Books, 1978, reprinted with a new Introduction and Epilogue, 1993), 90–91

Antitrust is about the effects of business behavior on consumers. An understanding of the relationship of that behavior to consumer well-being can be gained only through basic economic theory. The economic models involved are essential to all antitrust analysis, but they are simple and require no previous acquaintance with economics to be comprehended. Indeed, since we can hardly expect legislators, judges, and lawyers to be sophisticated economists as well, it is only the fact that the simple ideas of economics are powerful and entirely adequate to this field that makes it conceivable for the law to frame and implement useful policy.

Consumer welfare is greatest when society's economic resources are allocated so that consumers are able to satisfy their wants as fully as technological constraints permit. Consumer welfare, in this sense, is merely another term for the wealth of the nation. Antitrust thus has a built-in preference for material prosperity, but it has nothing to say about the ways prosperity is distributed or used. Those are matters for other laws. Consumer welfare, as the term is used in antitrust, has no sumptuary or ethical component, but permits consumers to define by their expression of wants in the marketplace what things they regard as wealth. Antitrust litigation is not a process for deciding who should be rich or poor, nor can it decide how much wealth should be expended to reduce pollution or undertake to mitigate the anguish of the cross-country skier at the desecration wrought by snowmobiles. It can only increase collective wealth by requiring that many lawful products, whether skis or snowmobiles, be produced and sold under conditions most favorable to consumers.

The role of the antitrust laws, then, lies at that stage of the economic process in which production and distribution of goods and services are organized in accordance with the scale of values that consumers choose by their relative willingness to purchase. The law's mission is to preserve, improve, and reinforce the powerful economic mechanisms that compel businesses to respond to consumers. 'From a social point of view,' as Frank H. Knight puts it, 'this process may be viewed under two aspects, (a) the assignment or allocation of the available productive forces and materials among the various lines of industry,

---

[51] 'Satisficing' is when management adopts certain goals for profits, sales, etc. and tries to meet, but not necessarily exceed, them. The goals may not be set high in the first place, so that management will not seem a failure if it does not achieve them, and it is unwilling to be in a position where the shareholders demand ever higher goals in the future. See Simon, n. 16.

[52] Earl Warren was Chief Justice of the Supreme Court from 1953 until 1968.

[53] Robert Bork (1927–2012) was President Reagan's nominee for the Supreme Court in 1987 but he was rejected by the Senate.

and (b) the effective *co-ordination* of the various means of production in each industry into such groupings as will produce the greatest result.' . . .

These two factors may conveniently be called *allocative efficiency* and *productive efficiency* . . . These two types of efficiency make up the overall efficiency that determines the level of our society's wealth, or consumer welfare. The whole task of antitrust can be summed up as the effort to improve allocative efficiency without impairing productive efficiency so greatly as to produce either no gain or a net loss in consumer welfare. That task must be guided by basic economic analysis, otherwise the law acts blindly upon forces it does not understand and produces results it does not intend.

It should be noted from the second paragraph of this extract that Bork equates 'consumer welfare' with the 'wealth of the nation'. Thus his conception of 'consumer welfare' is what is usually called 'total' or 'social' welfare.[54] The confusion arising from this use of the term 'consumer welfare' has been called the 'Chicago trap' and should be borne in mind when reading Chicago School sources.[55] Bork pursued his conception of consumer welfare in the extract from the Epilogue to his book when it was reprinted in 1993. Critics had argued that efficiency could not be the sole pursuit of competition law without becoming inconsistent with other government policies, such as those pursuing distributive goals. Bork made a riposte to this.

R. H. Bork, *The Antitrust Paradox: A Policy at War with Itself* (Basic Books, 1978, reprinted with a new Introduction and Epilogue, 1993), 426–429

Of the two, the issue of the goals of antitrust seems to have fared somewhat better than the law's capacity to deal with economics. Fifteen years ago, the question of what goals antitrust serves, and hence what factors a judge may properly consider in deciding an antitrust case, had not been addressed in any systemic fashion. The answers given by courts and commentators were hardly more than slogans of a more or less appealing variety, depending on your taste for populist rhetoric. Though the preservation of competition was often cited as the aim of the law, there seemed no agreed definition of what, for the purposes of antitrust, competition is.

'Competition,' the courts assured us, meant the preservation or comfort of small businesses, the advancement of first amendment values, the preservation of political democracy, the preservation of local ownership, and so on ad infinitum. Judges could and did choose among the items they had invented and placed in this grab bag in order to legislate freely. Cornucopias have their attractions but, when it comes to finding and applying a policy to guide adjudication, horns of plenty make anything resembling a rule of law impossible.

The argument of this book, of course, is that competition must be understood as the maximization of consumer welfare or, if you prefer, economic efficiency. That requires economic reasoning because courts must balance, when they conflict, possible losses of efficiency in the allocation of resources with possible gains in the productive use of those resources. In a word, the goal is maximum economic efficiency to make us as wealthy as possible. The distribution of that wealth or the accomplishment of noneconomic goals are the proper subjects of other laws and not within the competence of judges deciding antitrust cases.

By and large, with some ambiguity at times, the more recent cases have adopted a consumer welfare model. Aside from some explicit statements to that effect, the best evidence for the proposition is that

---

[54] See Section 3.F, p. 11.

[55] See K. Cseres, *Competition Law and Consumer Protection* (Kluwer Law International, 2005), 331–332; P. Akman, 'Consumer versus "Customer": The Devil in the Detail' (2010) 37 *J of Law and Society* 315.

courts now customarily speak the language of economics rather than pop sociology and political philoso-phy. If the conversion from a multi-goal jurisprudence is not complete, it is nevertheless very substantial. Explicit opposition to the consumer welfare thesis comes less from judges than from the academics. The objections are generally of two kinds: denial that an exclusive consumer welfare focus is to be found in the various antitrust statutes; and insistence that such a policy is not desirable.

. . . A different line of attack comes from those who observe, quite correctly, that people value things other than consumer welfare, and, therefore, quite incorrectly, that antitrust ought not be confined to advancing that goal. As non sequiturs go, that one is world class. There may be someone identified with the Chicago School who thinks all human activity can be analyzed in terms of economics and efficiency, but that is not true of most Chicagoans and certainly constitutes no part of my argument. No one body of law can protect everything that people value. If antitrust could, we would need no other statutes. If we trace the implications of the proposition, it results in judges deciding cases as if the Sherman Act said: 'A restraint of trade shall consist of any contract, combination, or conspiracy that fails to produce, in the eyes of the court, the optimum mix of consumer welfare and other good things that Americans want.' That is inevitably the result of bringing into judicial consideration an open-ended list of attractive-sounding goals to be weighed against consumer welfare.

Nor is there any force to the argument that the consumer welfare cannot be the exclusive mission of antitrust since that mission will be rendered less effective unless all other government policies pursue the same goal. Of course, antitrust will be less effective in promoting consumer welfare if government simultaneously subsidizes small business. A tariff policy designed to keep American companies viable will be less effective if government allows foreign competitors to set up manufacturing operations in the United States. That fact does not state a reason for a judge to alter the way he construes the tariff laws or other laws that apply to foreign companies' operations here. Many statutory policies conflict to some degree with other statutory policies. Whether or not they should do so, and to what degree, is a subject for legislation rather than adjudication.

In any event, no matter what policy goals or combination of goals one attributes to antitrust, the effec-tiveness of the law in forwarding those policies will be diminished by other public policies. That fact tells us nothing about how judges should go about deciding cases under the antitrust statutes.

The following extract is from the 2001 second edition of Posner's seminal book first published in 1976. The author is takes issue with the 'populist' view that would seek to use competition laws to promote goals other than efficiency and addresses the issue of using competition law to promote the interests of small business.

R. A. Posner, *Antitrust Law* (2nd edn, University of Chicago Press, 2001), 25

Antitrust enforcement is not only an ineffectual, but a perverse, instrument for trying to promote the interests of small business as a whole. Antitrust objectives and the objectives of small business people are incompatible at a very fundamental level. The best overall antitrust policy from a small-business standpoint is no antitrust policy. By driving a wedge between the prices and the costs of the larger firms in the market (a market cannot be effectively cartelized unless the large firms in it participate in the cartel), monopoly enables the smaller firms to survive even if their costs are higher than those of the large firms. The only kind of antitrust policy that would benefit small business would be one that sought to prevent large firms from underpricing less efficient small firms by sharing their lower costs with consumers in the form of lower prices. Apart from raising in acute form the question whether society should promote small business at the expense of the consumer, such a policy would be unworkable because it would require comprehensive and continuing supervision of the prices of large firms. There are no effective shortcuts.

For example, if mergers between large firms are forbidden because of concern that they will enable the firms resulting from such mergers to take advantage of economies of scale and thereby underprice smaller firms operating at a less efficient scale, one or more of the larger firms will simply expand until the efficient scale of operation is reached.

Perhaps the most contentious of all Chicago School claims is that the pursuit of efficiency as the sole goal of competition law is non-political. The essential argument is that since competition policy is dictated only by microeconomics it is ideology-free. The adoption of such a policy is, however, in itself ideological. Chicago proclaims itself as neutral because it believes only in market forces. The idea that this is an apolitical stance is challenged by Fox and Sullivan in an 1987 article. In particular, the authors stress that the law should not only be about economics. Rather, economics should be used as a tool to support the system which is aimed at supporting consumers and a dynamic system of competition law.

E. M. Fox and L. A. Sullivan, 'Antitrust—Retrospective and Prospective: Where Are We Coming From? Where Are We Going?' (1987) 62 *New York Univ LR* 936, 956–959

Economists have both praised and criticized mainstream antitrust law. Many economists, especially those with Chicago leanings, think that because antitrust is about markets, as is microeconomics, antitrust law should be economics. They react as though the law is out of kilter whenever it diverges from their particular economic insight; and they so react regardless of whether the law diverges because empirical processes have not validated factual assumptions, or because the law has identified social goals other than or in addition to allocative efficiency. Law is not economics. Nor were the antitrust laws adopted to squeeze the greatest possible efficiency out of business. Nonetheless, we would not want an antitrust system that hurts consumers rather than helps them. Most people agree that economics is a tool that can help keep the system on course to help consumers and to facilitate dynamic competition. Economic analysts have provided important insights into why business acts the way it does, and what the probable effect of a practice will be on the marketplace. Despite the consensus that economics can play a supporting role, the Chicago School, in the name of law and economics, has waged ideological warfare, assaulting antitrust itself. Commitment and belief fuel the debate on both sides. While others seem aware that the debate is about values, Chicagoans seem not to be. They often claim the imperative of science for their policy prescriptions. But on points of basic difference between Chicagoans on the one hand and realists or traditionalists on the other, the Chicago assertions are not provable. They are not matters of fact. They cannot be derived from economics. The basic difference between Chicagoans and traditionalists is a difference of vision about what kind of society we are and should strive to be . . .

. . . The Chicago beliefs are compatible with only the most minimal law. In antitrust, the most minimal law, given the existence of the statutes, is law that proscribes only clear cartel agreements and mergers that would create a monopoly in a market that included all perceptible potential competition. Let us review the characteristics that underlie this minimalist approach to antitrust.

First, the Chicago School claims that it has the right prescription for efficiency. This is unprovable; some would say highly suspect, and others would say wrong. Economic experts have intense debates as to what scheme is likely to produce a more efficient or a more dynamic, inventive economy. Economics does not provide a conclusive answer. Within a wide range, the answer is indeterminate . . .

Second, the Chicago School always opts for norms that presuppose that markets are robust and that firms, imbued with perfect knowledge and risk neutrality, move their resources quickly and easily to the most profitable opportunity. Data about how people actually behave belie these assumptions . . . Yet Chicagoans continue to press for legal rules that accept these assumptions as true . . . It is this mind-set that led Judge Posner to dissent in a recent case in which a prisoner was blinded in jail and sued prison authorities for neglect . . . A majority of the appellate court thought that appointment of counsel was improperly denied to the prisoner, but Judge Posner disagreed . . . Assuming the existence of a market for lawyers that would function like a Chicago model market, Judge Posner argued that if the prisoner's case was any good, a lawyer would have taken it on contingency. The fact that no lawyer did 'proved' that the prisoner's case lacked merit . . .[56]

Third, the Chicago School defines competition in terms of efficiency; defines efficiency as the absence of inefficiency; defines inefficiency in terms of artificial output restraint; . . . and thus concludes that any activity that does not demonstrably limit output is efficient and therefore pro-competitive. Thus, it 'proves' that almost all business activity is efficient—a neat trick.

Fox and Sullivan thus question the bases of many of the views on which the Chicago concept of efficiency is hung and hence challenge its faith in the ability of the market to correct itself. Criticisms have also been made of the Chicagoans' belief that barriers to entry are rare outside government regulation,[57] that potential competition polices the market as well as existing competitors because, in the absence of barriers to entry, monopolists will be challenged by new entrants if they reap monopoly profits, and that most markets are competitive. The Chicago model is criticised for being 'static' and concentrating too much on long-term effects rather than on short-term effects and of competition as a process. Above all, it is argued that the neoclassical market efficiency model of Chicago is too simple to account for or predict business behaviour in the real world. However, note should be taken of the warning by the American scholar in the extract in Section 4.B.iv that one should be wary of oversimplistic depictions of the Chicago School as some kind of extremist ideology. Whatever criticisms can be and have been made of the Chicago School, it undeniably changed competition law thinking profoundly. It placed rigorous economic analysis at the centre of competition law. After Chicago it is impossible to accept the S→C→P paradigm without qualification, or not to think of efficiency as a central concern. It shed new light on many matters.

(ii) Post-Chicago

'Post-Chicago School' scholars recognise that economics may give indications of what questions to ask, but does not always yield definitive answers, and certainly not answers which are necessarily value-free. Post-Chicago (or 'new industrial economics') stresses the effect that the strategic conduct of firms can have in different market situations. Post-Chicago makes heavy use of game theory (see Section 4.C) to examine how firms may indulge in strategic entry deterrence. So, for example, the Chicago belief that predatory pricing is rarely rational conduct[58] is replaced in Post-Chicago analysis by considering that in some circumstances it can be adopted as a rational strategy to prevent new competitors entering the market,[59] and the Chicago 'single monopoly profit theorem' has been countered with new thinking about leverage.[60] In short, Post-Chicago competition scholarship admits of more complexities than either the Harvard or Chicago approaches and 'helps observers understand why conduct thought benign in light of Chicago School teaching might in fact lessen competition'.[61] It also attempts to deal with the importance of dynamic competition.[62] However,

---

[56] The case concerned was *Merritt v Faulkner*, 697 F.2d 761 (7th Cir. 1983).

[57] See the discussion of barriers to entry in Section 15.C, p. 79 ff.

[58] Chicago scholars differ about this: Bork said 'never' rational, but others are less absolutist.

[59] See Chap. 7.

[60] Important in the debate about practices such as 'tying' by dominant undertakings, see Chap. 7.

[61] E. Gellhorn, W. Kovacic, and S. Calkins, *Antitrust Law and Economics* (5th edn, West, 2004), 97; see further A. Cucinotta, R. Pardolesi, and R. Van den Bergh, *Post-Chicago Developments in Antitrust Law* (Edward Elgar, 2002).

[62] See Section 3.G, p. 12.

Post-Chicago analysis is heavily theoretical and makes greater demands on competition authorities and decision-makers because of the very wealth of models and theories that may fall to be considered, and it is has been criticised for offering little by way of empirical verification and therefore of being of limited practical utility.[63]

(iii) Neo-Chicago

'Neo-Chicago' is a recently coined term to describe those who are faithful to the core tenets of the Chicago School but take on board the criticisms made of it and present an intellectually reinvigorated Chicago.[64]

(iv) Conclusion

There is a continuing debate about the ideas of Chicago. A book edited by Pitofsky[65] in 2008 elicited a fierce defence from those who consider that Pitofsky (as distinct from some of the contributors to that volume) perpetuated the misrepresentation of Chicago as an extremist conservative ideology. Many scholars take the view that labels of 'Chicago', 'Post-Chicago', and so on are not helpful and should be abandoned other than in a historical context. There is much to be said for this. The distinction between Harvard, Chicago, and Post-Chicago could always be drawn too starkly. A leading American scholar and member (and former Chairman) of the FTC has counselled caution against seeing the history of US antitrust in rigid Harvard/Chicago/Post-Chicago terms and considers that doing so distorts the understanding not only of the evolution of US antitrust but also of its relationship with EU antitrust policy. Rather, many scholars and judges have held more nuanced views and cannot be as neatly pigeon-holed as some descriptions of their work have suggested.

William E. Kovacic, 'The Intellectual DNA of Modern U.S. Competition Law For Dominant Firm Conduct: The Chicago/ Harvard Double Helix' [2007] 1(1) *Columbia Business LR* 8–10

More recent developments in trans-Atlantic competition policy have accentuated my doubts about the conventional Chicago/Post-Chicago framework. In reading the work of foreign scholars . . . and participating in international conferences I have become convinced that the Chicago/Post-Chicago School framework seriously distorts discussions about U.S. abuse of dominance policy and its relationship to EU competition policy. The tendency is to explain U.S. experience in terms of a Chicago/Post-Chicago dialectic and the subsequent preoccupation with branding ideas with Chicago or Post-Chicago labels prevents Americans and Europeans from understanding why the U.S. system developed as it did and from seeing more accurately why their systems differ . . .

. . . The first problem is the implication that Chicago and Post-Chicago perspectives have little in common. The frequently-voiced suggestion that the Chicago School and the Post-Chicago School are antonyms overlooks important connections between the two bodies of thought. Many Post-Chicago School scholars build upon theoretical or empirical propositions advanced by Chicago School

---

[63] See Crane, n. 49; B. H. Kobayashi and T. J. Muris, 'Chicago, Post-Chicago, and Beyond: Time to Let Go of the 20th Century' (2012) 78 *Antitrust LJ* 147; cf. D. Rubenfield, 'On the Foundations of Antitrust Law and Economics' in R. Pitofsky (ed.), *How Chicago Overshot the Mark: The Effect of Conservative Economic Analysis on US Antitrust* (Oxford University Press, 2008), 51, 55, who considers that 'This new post-Chicago School perspective should be given substantial credit for its influence on courts and the competition authorities' (i.e. of the US).

[64] D. S. Evans and A. Jorge Padilla, 'Designing Antitrust Rules for Assessing Unilateral Practices: A Neo-Chicago Approach' (2005) 72 *Univ Chic LR* 7; Crane, n. 49.

[65] Pitofsky, n. 63.

exponents . . . Some Chicago scholars appear to acknowledge the value of Post-Chicago ideas, at least so far as finding similarities between the modern Post-Chicago scholarship and early Chicago School views on antitrust policy . . . The tendency to focus on differences between these schools obscures how developments in competition policy, both in theory and practice, often are incremental and cumulative, with significant borrowings across bodies of thought that sometimes, or often, are depicted as being distinct and self-contained . . .

. . . A second problem with explaining modern U.S. antitrust experience as a Chicago School/Post-Chicago School contest is the suggestion that each school is monolithic and single-minded. Neither body of literature features such a uniformity of preferences . . .

. . . A third problem with framing the modern policy debate in terms of a Chicago School/Post-Chicago School dialectic is that it incorrectly attributes antitrust perspectives to a single source when they instead stemmed from more diverse intellectual influences. The perceived origins of ideas can affect views about whether the ideas are legitimate. One way to discredit an idea is to depict its brand and the originators of the brand as violating norms of reasonable thought. In modern discourse about competition policy, commentators sometimes depict Chicago School advocates as extremists, close-minded fanatics, or mere 'ideologues' . . . If one agrees that Chicago School views are unduly extreme, it is a short step to conclude that a competition policy system assumed to be guided chiefly by Chicago School views is itself extremist, unsoundly ideological, and unworthy of emulation.

From the point of view of EU competition law, what is important is not the labels and the politics, but the ideas, theories, and insights which this rich period of (mainly) American discourse has yielded and which inform so many of the debates which rage over the application of the EU rules, as discussed in the subsequent chapters of this book.

C. GAME THEORY

Game theory is central to much modern industrial organisation theory and stems from work done in the 1940s by von Neumann and Morgenstern.[66] It models strategic interactions between firms—their conflict and cooperation—as 'games' in which each firm plans its own strategy, for example with regard to pricing or output, in the light of assumptions about the strategy which will be adopted by its competitors. Game theory is in particular an important tool in analysing the conduct of oligopolies and is discussed further in that context in Chapter 9. It is important in Post-Chicago analysis, as already explained.[67]

D. CONTESTABLE MARKETS THEORY

Contestable markets theory[68] places the main emphasis on freedom of entry to, and exit from, a market. It attaches importance not to the structure of the market but to its contestability. So long as 'hit-and-run' entry by competitors is possible the behaviour of firms operating on the market will be constrained and they will perform efficiently and price competitively. The minimum conditions for a contestable market are instantaneous entry and costless exit and, crucially, the inability of the incumbent to respond to entry by another competitor by lowering its prices. This last point is vital because otherwise the incumbent firm can keep its prices at monopoly level and only lower them

[66] J. von Neumann and O. Morgenstern, *The Theory of Games and Economic Behaviour* (Princeton University Press, 1944).

[67] In Section 4.B.ii.

[68] W. J. Baumol, J. Panzar, and R. Willig, *Contestable Markets and the Theory of Industry Structure* (Harcourt Brace Jovanovich, 1982); W. J. Baumol, 'Contestable Markets: An Uprising in the Theory of Industry Structure' (1982) 72 *Am Econ Rev* 1.

when it needs to respond to competition. In reality, again, the conditions for perfect contestability are rarely found.[69] However, the term 'contestable market', meaning one with low barriers to entry and exit where the threat of entry does significantly constrain the incumbent, is used more loosely and is often found in competition law discourse.[70] The Commission looked at the contestability of the market and therefore approved a merger despite a highly concentrated market and high market shares in its *Syniverse/MACH* decision.[71]

E. RAISING RIVALS' COSTS

Raising rivals' costs describes strategic behaviour of a firm which is designed to raise the costs of its rivals relative to its own.[72] It normally requires some degree of market power (or, for some strategies, political power or influence). It includes interfering with the production or selling methods of rivals, lobbying for or supporting government regulation which has a differential impact on the rivals' costs, raising the price of inputs, tying, raising switching costs (so that customers find it difficult or expensive to change to the rival's goods or services), and indulging in rapid product innovation in primary markets.[73] Some behaviour which raises rivals' costs may also increase welfare and whether competition law should sanction or allow it often depends on the particular circumstance of the case. In the following chapters of this book we will come across many examples of behaviour which can raise rivals' costs.

F. TRANSACTION COST ECONOMICS

Transaction cost economics is based on the theory first developed by Ronald Coase in *The Nature of the Firm*.[74] Transaction costs are the costs a firm incurs by trading with other parties. Coase's argument was that a firm can choose to organise its activities by doing things itself (so internalising the costs) or by using other parties to do them (i.e. using the market). A firm may have a choice between producing the inputs necessary for production itself or obtaining them from other parties. Similarly it may have a choice between doing its own distribution or using independent distributors. The first of these options in each case involves vertical integration while the second involves agreements with others. Which is chosen will depend on its comparative efficiency. The insight from transaction cost economics for competition law is that competition law should not be designed so as to force firms to take less efficient options for doctrinaire reasons of promoting more competitive markets.

Transaction cost research has identified efficiency reasons for which firms use various forms of internal organization and has underscored the importance of contractual techniques in curbing opportunistic behavior that, if left unchecked, undermines business arrangements that increase efficiency. By showing that the main purpose of many forms of economic organization—for example, joint ventures, vertical integration, and restrictive distribution contracts—often is to reduce costs, transaction costs scholars have spurred a reevaluation of antitrust doctrines that have treated such arrangements with hostility.[75]

---

[69] Sunk costs, for example, will be a hindering factor, see Section 15.C.iii.a, p. 82.

[70] S. Bishop and M. Walker, *The Economics of EC Competition Law* (3rd edn, Sweet & Maxwell, 2010), 3.35.

[71] M.6690, *Syniverse/MACH* [2014] OJ C60/7, 29 May 2013; see G. Goeteyn and S. Ashall, 'Away From Market Shares? The Increasing Importance of Contestability in EU Competition Law Case' (2015) 6 *JECLAP* 197.

[72] T. G. Krattenmaker and S. C. Salop, 'Anti-competitive Exclusion: Raising Rivals' Costs to Achieve Power Over Price' (1986) 96 *Yale LJ* 209.

[73] See Carlton and Perloff, n. 19, 371–379.

[74] (1937) 4 *Economica* 38. See also the work of Oliver Williamson, particularly 'Transaction Cost Economics' in R. Schmalensee and R. D. Willig (eds.), *Handbook of Industrial Organization, Vol. 1* (North-Holland, 1989), 135.

[75] Gellhorn, Kovacic, and Calkins, n. 61, 101. See also Van den Bergh and Camesasca, n. 32, 94–98; P. L. Joskow, 'The Role of Transaction Cost Economics in Antitrust and Public Utility Regulatory Policies' (1991) 7 *J of Law, Economics & Organization* 53.

Transaction cost economics was taken on board by the Post-Chicago School, but in contrast to other ideas which Post-Chicago adopts, such as the anti-competitive effects of strategic behaviour, transaction cost economics points to a *less* expansive application of competition rules.

G. WORKABLE COMPETITION

The theory of 'workable competition' was developed in the 1940s.[76] It was associated with the Harvard School and held that as perfect competition was usually impossible to attain, competition policy should aim to produce the best competitive arrangement practically attainable. This too presented difficulties. The criteria by which workability can be assessed may be divided into structure, conduct, and performance criteria but it may be hard to assess whether or not they have been satisfied in any particular industry; and if some are satisfied and some not, it may be hard to decide whether workability has been attained without making subjective value judgments.[77] Workable competition, in short, does not provide a very workable basis for developing a sound competition policy. The Court of Justice (CJ) referred to workable competition in 1976 in *Metro I*, equating it with 'the degree of competition necessary to ensure the observance of the basic requirements and the attainment of the objectives of the EEC Treaty'.[78]

H. THE AUSTRIAN SCHOOL

The Austrian School embraces a theory of dynamic competition which goes beyond that advanced by Schumpeter.[79] As with Chicago, the Austrian School's conception of competition policy is just one facet of a wider school of economic theory,[80] one of whose leading figures was von Hayek.[81] Von Hayek's conception of competition was that it is a 'discovery process'. He considered that the market is only discovered through the rivalry of firms competing for consumers' custom, as information about what consumers want only becomes known as they respond to firms' efforts to do better than their competitors. This is in contrast to the theory of a perfectly competitive market, which posits that both consumers and competitors have perfect information. The logical conclusion of von Hayek's view is that competition laws should not interfere with rivalrous competitive behaviour at all, not even by prohibiting cartels, because such intervention distorts the discovery process.[82]

I. EFFECTIVE COMPETITION

The concept of *effective competition* is important in EU competition law. A dominant position is defined for the purposes of Article 102 TFEU[83] as involving an undertaking's power to 'prevent effective competition being maintained on the relevant market'[84] and under the EU Merger Regulation (the EUMR) the grounds for the prohibition of a merger are that it would 'significantly impede

---

[76] J. M. Clark, 'Towards a Concept of Workable Competition' (1940) 30 *Am Econ Rev* 241–256; see also S. Sosnick, 'A Critique of Concepts of Workable Competition' (1958) 72 *Quart J of Econ* 380–423.

[77] See further Scherer and Ross, n. 23, 52–55; Van den Bergh and Camesasca, n. 32, 70–73.

[78] Case 26/76, *Metro v Commission (Metro I)* [1977] ECR 1875, para. 20.

[79] See Section 3.G, p. 12.

[80] Originating with Carl Menger, Professor of Economics at the University of Vienna, 1873–1903.

[81] Von Hayek's most famous work is *The Road to Serfdom* (Routledge, 1944).

[82] See further F. von Hayek, *Law, Legislation and Liberty* (reprinted Routledge, 2013); Van den Bergh and Camesasca, n. 32, 88.

[83] One of the two main EU competition law articles, previously Art. 82 (and before 1999, Art. 86). See Chaps. 5–7.

[84] Case 27/76, *United Brands v Commission* [1978] ECR 207, para. 65; Case 85/76, *Hoffmann-La Roche & Co AG v Commission* [1979] ECR 461, para. 38.

effective competition'.[85] In *Continental Can* the Court said that the competition provisions, Articles 101 and 102, both seek to achieve the same aim, '*viz.* the maintenance of effective competition'.[86] The General Court (GC) said in *GlaxoSmithKline* that 'the competition referred to in Article 3(1)(g) EC[87] and Article [101 TFEU] is taken to mean effective competition, that is to say, the degree of competition necessary to ensure the attainment of the objectives of the Treaty'.[88] Bishop and Walker explain that 'effective competition' should be outcome-based.

S. Bishop and M. Walker, *The Economics of EC Competition Law* (3rd edn, Sweet & Maxwell, 2010), 20–21

2-008 . . . The economic goal of EC competition law is the protection and promotion of effective competition. But this is a goal only because of the benefits that it delivers to European consumers. What matters therefore are the outcomes for consumers that competition in a particular market delivers—not the particular form that the competition process takes. Whether a market is characterized by effective competition or not therefore depends on the outcomes it produces.

This raises the question of what outcomes are produced by effective competition and how can they be distinguished from those produced by less than effective competition. The practical application of competition law ought to be interested less in outcomes that are desirable in some theoretical, abstract sense and more in outcomes that are feasible for regulatory intervention to achieve . . . To draw this distinction requires consideration of the various economic models of competition and the implications each type of model has for consumer welfare.

Effective competition is therefore the means to an end, not the end itself.

5. ORDOLIBERALISM

Ordoliberalism is a school of thought[89] which originated in Germany in the 1930s and was nurtured at the University of Freiburg during the Nazi era.[90] It became a key element of post-war thinking in Germany and provided the theoretical foundations for the German social market economy. It has

---

[85] Council Reg. 139/2004 [2004] OJ L124/1, Art. 2(3), previously Council Reg. 4064/89 [1990] OJ L257/13, see Chap. 15.

[86] Case 6/72, *Europemballage Corp and Continental Can Co Inc v Commission* [1973] ECR 215, para. 225.

[87] For the fate of Art. 3(1)(g) under the Treaty of Lisbon see Section 8.A, p. 32 ff.

[88] Case T-168/01, *GlaxoSmithKline Services Unlimited v Commission* [2006] ECR II-2969, para. 109. The Treaty referred to here was the EC Treaty. For the objectives of the EC Treaty, see Section 8.A, p. 31 ff.

[89] Or perhaps more accurately a 'family of ideas', see M. Marquis, 'Introduction, Summary, Remarks' in C.-D. Ehlermann and M. Marquis (eds.), *European Competition Law Annual 2007: A Reformed Approach to Article 82* (Hart Publishing, 2008), xxxi.

[90] The leading ordoliberal theorists were the economist Walter Eucken (see W. Eucken, 'Die Wettbewerbsordnung und ihre Verwirklichung' (1949) 2 ORDO—*Jahrbuch für die Ordnung der Wirtschaft und Gesellschaft* 1–99, reprinted and translated in (2006) 2(2) *Competition Policy International* 219 (C. Ahlborn and C. Grave), and the lawyers Franz Böhm and Hans Grossmann-Doerth. See further D. Gerber, 'Constitutionalizing the Economy: German Neoliberalism, Competition Law and the "New Europe"' (1994) 42 *Am J of Comparative Law* 25; V. Vanberg, 'The Freiburg School: Walter Eucken and Ordoliberalism', Freiburg Discussion Papers on Constitutional Economics, No. 04/11 (2004), <www.eonstor.eu/dspace/bitstream/10419/4343/1/04_llbw.pdf>; C. Ahlborn and C. Grave, 'Walter Eucken and Ordoliberalism: An Introduction from a Consumer Welfare Perspective' (2006) 2(2) *Competition Policy International* 197; G. Schnyder and M. Siems, 'The Ordoliberal Variety of Neoliberalism' in S. J. Konzelmann and M. Fovargue-Davies (eds.), *Banking Systems in the Crisis: The Faces of Liberal Capitalism* (Routledge, 2013), 250; available at <http://ssrn.com/abstract=2142529>.

been developed over the years by succeeding generations of adherents.[91] Ordoliberalism advocates an 'economic constitution' whereby competition and economic freedom are embedded into the law so that there is neither unconstrained private power nor discretionary government intervention in the economy.[92] For ordoliberals, a competitive market is 'a system of decentralized economic planning based on individual economic freedom legally protected by the system of private law of property and contract' and it is the role of competition law 'to protect competition *as a system* within which individuals are free to make their choices on the market'.[93] Ordoliberalism therefore conceives 'the competitive process as a process resulting from the exercise of individual economic liberties'[94] and competition laws as the 'rules of the game'.

The constituent elements of ordoliberalism have been summarised as follows:

- Competition results from individual freedom of producers to choose what they want to offer and of consumers to choose what they want to buy.

- Competition is understood as a dynamic system (process) of interaction between choice-making individuals who by making their choices reveal their preferences and produce the kind of information that other individuals need to make their choices.

- It is the fundamental role of the system of private law to provide individuals with legal rights the unrestricted use of which forms the basis of competitive rivalry among producers and of consumers' freedom of choice among alternative sources of supply.

- It is the task of the state to provide laws against restraints of such competitive rivalry and to enforce them as rules of the game with which market participants have to comply.[95]

6. POSSIBLE GOALS OF COMPETITION LAW

A. GENERAL

There are profound disagreements about the goals which competition laws should seek to achieve. We briefly set out here some of the candidates.[96] Some of these goals are irreconcilable with each other, but others overlap or may coexist. The fundamental division is between (a) the pursuit of solely economic goals, in the form of economic efficiency and welfare (the 'welfarist' approach) and (b) a wider range of policy objectives. It should be noted, however, that the term 'ordoliberal' is sometimes tossed around to denote any approach in EU law which is not welfarist whereas, as we have seen in Section 5, the principles of ordoliberalism are more precise.

B. ECONOMIC EFFICIENCY AND WELFARE

The welfarist approach to competition law holds that its aim is to maximise welfare by promoting efficient markets, as explained in Section 2. This is an economic aim and its focus is on the *outcome* in welfare

---

[91] It is therefore erroneous to represent it by reference only to its initial form: see P. Behrens, 'The Ordoliberal Concept of "Abuse" of a Dominant Position and its Impact on Article 102 TFEU', <http://ssrn.com/abstract=2658045>, who criticises D. Gerber, *Law and Competition in Twentieth Century Europe* (Oxford University Press, 1998), for doing this.

[92] W. Möschel, 'Competition Policy from an Ordo Point of View' in A. Peacock and H. Willgerodt (eds.), *German Neo-liberals and the Social Market Economics* (Macmillan, 1989), 142.

[93] Behrens, n. 91, 11.

[94] H. Schweitzer, 'The History, Interpretation and Underlying Principles of Section 2 Sherman Act and Article 82 EC' at <http://cadmus.eui.eu/bitstream/handle/1814/7626/LAW-2007-32.pdf>, p. 41.

[95] Behrens, n. 91, 12.

[96] See further, e.g., G. Monti, *EC Competition Law* (Cambridge University Press, 2007), Chap. 2; K. Coates, *Competition Law and Regulation of Technology Markets* (Oxford University Press, 2011), Chap. 2; R. Nazzini, *The Foundations of European Union Competition Law: The Objectives and Principles of Article 102* (Oxford University Press, 2011), Chap. 2; Geradin, Layne-Farrar, and Petit, n. 7, 1.61–1.69; D. Zimmer (ed.), *The Goals of Competition Law* (Edward Elgar, 2012).

terms. The welfarist approach largely originated in the 'Chicago School' as discussed in Section 4.B. Whether the welfare standard should be consumer welfare or total (social) welfare is a subsidiary question, but the generally prevailing view is that it should be consumer welfare. A commentator explains why competition authorities (including the European Commission) usually prefer consumer welfare:

> ### R. Nazzini, *The Foundations of European Union Competition Law: The Objectives and Principles of Article 102* (Oxford University Press, 2011), 44–45
>
> First, consumer welfare, as a test, is easier to apply than social welfare. It is more straightforward to argue—although not necessarily to prove—that as a result of the exclusion of a competitor or of an agreement between firms prices will be higher, than to explain why the aggregate producer and consumer surplus will be lower. . . .
>
> Secondly, consumer welfare is a politically acceptable way of arguing for an economic approach to competition law. The very mention of the word 'consumer' evokes ideas of fairness, redistribution, and protection of the many and vulnerable, making this rhetoric attractive to politicians, policy-makers, and competition officials. On the other hand, the consumer welfare objective may be applied so that, in many circumstances, it leads to precisely the same consequences as a social welfare objective . . . Consumer welfare can be used as a populist slogan to sell, to the public, an economic approach to competition law.
>
> Thirdly, consumer welfare is a politically acceptable way to disguise a non-interventionist agenda. It would be more difficult politically to argue that a tying practice by a dominant undertaking should be allowed because it does not make any difference to the sum of industry profits and consumer surplus than to argue that it should be allowed because an integrated product is good for consumers.

C. ECONOMIC FREEDOM AND THE PROCESS OF COMPETITION

Competition law aimed at securing economic freedom is concerned not with direct effects on consumers but with the maintenance of a system which protects individual economic freedom of action and allows all citizens to participate in the market. The law therefore protects market participants from the undue economic power of others. The focus is on *structure and process* rather than outcomes. The 'economic freedom' theory is associated with ordoliberalism, as discussed in Section 5. Advocating the protection of the process of competition as the goal of competition is not solely the preserve of ordoliberals.[97] The difference is that ordoliberals wish to protect the process as a way of protecting the right of individuals to participate in the market.

D. PROTECTING COMPETITORS

It is often claimed that the goal of economic freedom leads to competition laws whose aim is to protect competitors for their own sake. However, competition laws can aim at dispersing economic power and favouring small businesses without being influenced by ordoliberalism as such. That was true of US antitrust law in the 1960s, for example. Competition laws which protect competitors may, for instance, protect small firms from the dominant firm's (efficient) low pricing, or force a dominant firm to give access to its resources to a smaller firm in order to allow the latter to compete with it. In some circumstances it may be necessary to protect particular competitors in order to prevent a welfare loss.

---

[97] See the discussion in N. Dunne, *Competition Law and Economic Regulation* (Cambridge University Press, 2015), 28–30 and the critique of the competitive process approach in N. Petit, '*Intel*, Leveraging Rebates and the Goals of Article 102', <http//:ssrn.com/abstract=2567628>, 24–28.

However, there is a difference between, on the one hand, protecting competitors and the competitive process as a means of achieving economic welfare and, on the other hand, protecting particular competitors for their own sake or maintaining a particular market structure as a matter of principle.

A policy which protects competitors for their own sake may accord with popular sentiment which is distrustful of 'large' firms. It can be described as 'populist',[98] and may enable a government to nurture small businesses, and to promote a society in which citizens are encouraged to be their own boss, run their own business, and behave in an entrepreneurial manner. The dispersal of market power may prevent the redistribution of wealth from consumers to firms with market power but the protection of small and inefficient businesses may also take wealth from consumers and lead to a loss in economic welfare.

E. FAIRNESS

fair ₤ v. ₰N4lang

'Fairness' is sometimes put forward as an objective of competition laws. 'Fairness' is a nebulous concept in this context. Aiming for fairness can mean, or can lead to, the protection of smaller competitors, as discussed in Section D, but being 'fair' to competitors in this way may protect inefficiency and so lead to the 'unfairness' of consumers paying higher prices than necessary. Competition laws concerned with fairness therefore need to be clear about whom fairness protects. One possible application of fairness is to ensure that equally efficient competitors are not excluded from the market by the anti-competitive practices of dominant firms. Competition law may have specific provisions about fairness, as EU law does[99] but the main protection for customers afforded by competition law is through the protection of *free* competition. There is disagreement about the extent to which ordoliberalism is concerned with fairness as an objective of competition law.[100] 'Fair competition' is mentioned in the Preamble to the TFEU, as explained in Section 8.

Competition laws concerned with fairness should be distinguished from laws against unfair trading practices such as deceptive, fraudulent, or unethical behaviour. The latter are best dealt with by *Consumer* specific legislation, including consumer protection legislation outlawing conduct such as misleading *protector* advertising and aggressive marketing techniques.[101]

F. PUBLIC POLICY AND SOCIO-POLITICAL FACTORS

Competition law may be used to service other policies, such as social, employment, industrial, environmental, and/or regional policy (for example, by prohibiting mergers which will cause job losses, or allowing restrictive agreements which will preserve declining industries for a little longer or produce environmental benefits). The pursuit of such policies may be inconsistent with the pursuit of efficiency. In some countries socio-political objectives are set out in the competition legislation. For example, South Africa's competition law has six purposes, one of which is 'to promote the greater spread of ownership, in particular to increase the ownership stakes of historically disadvantaged persons';[102] China's competition law is stated to be enacted for the purpose, inter alia, of 'promoting the healthy development of the socialist market economy'.[103]

---

[98] See R. A. Posner, *Antitrust Law* (2nd edn, University of Chicago Press, 2001), 25, and Section 4.B.i.

[99] See Section 8.B.ii, p. 35.

[100] See Behrens, n. 91; cf. Akman, n. 33, 151.

[101] See the EU Dir. on Unfair Commercial Practices, 2005/29/EC [2005] OJ L149/22. However the *AstraZeneca* case, Case C-457/10 P, *AstraZeneca AB and AstraZeneca plc v Commission* EU:C:2012:770, which concerned misrepresentations made to public authorities, was dealt with under the EU competition rules, see Chap. 7, Section 14.

[102] Competition Act no. 89 of 1998, s. 2(f).

[103] Anti-Monopoly Law, Art. 1; see M. Furse, *Antitrust Law in China, Korea, and Vietnam* (Oxford University Press, 2009), Chap. 2-1.

G. THE EU DIMENSION OF THE SINGLE MARKET

The objectives of EU competition law have a special dimension in the imperative of the integration of the single market. This is discussed in Section 8.B.iii.

7. US ANTITRUST LAW

It is impossible to discuss EU competition law without some reference to US law because of the influence which American legal scholars, practitioners, and economists have had on competition law thinking.[104]

The US was one of the first jurisdictions to adopt a proper 'modern' system of competition law.[105] The US Congress passed the Sherman Act in 1890.[106] It is still in force. Section 1 states:

Every contract, combination in the form of trust or otherwise, or conspiracy, in restraint of trade or commerce among the several States, or with foreign nations, is hereby declared to be illegal. Every person who shall make any contract or engage in any combination or conspiracy hereby declared to be illegal shall be deemed guilty of a felony . . .[107]

Section 2 states:

Every person who shall monopolize, or attempt to monopolize, or combine or conspire with any other person or persons, to monopolize any part of the trade or commerce among several States, or with foreign nations, shall be deemed guilty of a felony . . .

None of the expressions used in the Sherman Act, such as 'in restraint of trade' or 'monopolize' were defined.

The most popular explanation for the passing of the Sherman Act is that it was to combat the power of the 'trusts'. It had become common for the owners of stocks held in competing companies to transfer the stocks to trustees who then controlled the activities of those competitors and consequently lessened competition between them (this is why it has become known as 'antitrust' law). The activities of the railroad companies gave rise to particular concern. It is also claimed, however, that the Sherman Act was more of a protectionist measure passed in response to pressure by farmers, small businesses, or those desiring to stop the transfer of wealth from consumers to big business.[108] Chicago scholars[109] have argued that it was passed to preserve economic efficiency, but since the theories of allocative efficiency, dead-weight loss, and Pareto-efficiency had not then been

---

[104] A good example is the influential article written by Barry Hawk castigating the European approach to vertical restraints, which at the time fundamentally differed from that in the US: B. Hawk, 'System Failure: Vertical Restraints and EC Competition Law' (1995) 32 *CMLRev* 973, see Chap. 11, Section 3.A.

[105] Canada was the first (Act for the Prevention and Suppression of Combinations Formed in Restraint of Trade, 1889). For a historical survey of rules in respect of monopolies and cartels, see N. Green, 'From Rome to Rome: The Evolution of Competition Law into a Twenty-first Century Religion' [2010] *Comp Law* 7; the UK courts developed a doctrine of restraint of trade at common law, but this never developed into a system of competition law: see *Chitty On Contracts* (32nd edn, Sweet & Maxwell, 2015), Chap. 16.

[106] 'An Act to protect trade and commerce against unlawful restraints and monopolies', 15 USC, 2 July 1890. It was supplemented by later statutes, the Clayton Act (1914), the Federal Trade Commission Act (1914), the Robinson-Patman Act (1936), the Celler-Kefauver Act (1950), and the Hart-Scott-Rodino Antitrust Improvements Act 1976.

[107] See further Chap. 4, Section 2.D.

[108] See E. T. Sullivan (ed.), *The Political Economy of the Sherman Act* (Oxford University Press, 1991) for a collection of essays written between 1959 and 1989 on the Sherman Act, published to mark the centenary of the Act. The articles display the wide divergence of views between some of the most eminent names in antitrust thinking, as well as historians and Department of Justice officials.

[109] For the Chicago School, see Section 4.B. For Robert Bork's Chicago view of the intention of Congress, see R. H. Bork, *The Antitrust Paradox* (Basic Books, 1978, reprinted with a new Introduction and Epilogue, 1993), Chap. 2.

formulated it cannot have been conceived in exactly this way.[110] The argument about the conception of US antitrust is not merely about history, but is important when considering what the objective of that law is now and in the 'struggle for the soul of antitrust'. It may seem to the neutral observer that in passing the Sherman Act Congress made a law without a discernible policy behind it and that the policy only emerged later. However, according to Richard Posner, a leading exponent of the Chicago School, the motives of the legislators of 1890 are irrelevant.[111]

US law developed in a series of judicial decisions in the half-century following the Sherman Act in a rather ad hoc manner and reflected the experiences of the American economy as it went through an industrial revolution, the Depression (when antitrust enforcement was relaxed),[112] and the New Deal.[113] In the 1940s and 1950s the 'workable competition' hypothesis[114] was influential.[115] In the 1950s the S→C→P paradigm[116] led to a belief that markets were fragile and to an antitrust policy which intervened to protect small businesses against large firms.[117] Chicago School thinking[118] had a profound impact on the development of antitrust enforcement in the US from the 1970s onwards. In the US the ascendancy of Chicago during the 1970s and 1980s led to a change of direction in the application of antitrust law.[119]

The Bush administrations (2000–2008) took a non-interventionist stance towards the conduct of big business, particularly in respect of merger control and the application of s. 2 of the Sherman Act. This culminated in the 2008 report of the Department of Justice (DOJ) setting out a policy of restrained enforcement of s. 2.[120] In 2009 the Obama administration repudiated this policy and withdrew the report.[121]

There are four particular features of US antitrust law which distinguish it from EU law.[122] These need to be borne in mind when looking at US cases or reading American commentators. First, the US competition authorities, the DOJ Antitrust Division and the FTC, enforce the antitrust laws by bringing actions before the ordinary federal courts: they are primarily prosecutors rather than decision-makers (although the FTC does have administrative adjudication powers and both agencies shape the application of the law by issuing guidelines, making speeches, negotiating settlements, and so on).

---

[110] Marshall's *Principles of Economics*, n. 9, was first published in 1890 and Pareto published his theory in 1909. For a good account of the history of the US legislation, see Gellhorn, Kovacic, and Calkins, n. 61, 22–36.

[111] Posner, n. 98, 24–26.

[112] It has been claimed that this prolonged the Depression, see J. D. Harkrider, 'Lessons from the Great Depression' (2009) 23 *Antitrust* 6.

[113] The New Deal was a federal policy begun under President Roosevelt in 1933 to aid those thrown out of employment in the Depression. Collusion between competitors was first encouraged and then prosecuted.

[114] See Section 4.G, p. 24.

[115] See the Report of the Attorney General's National Committee to Study the Antitrust Laws (1955).

[116] See Section 4.A, p. 13.

[117] A policy which Posner describes as 'populist' because he sees it as based on 'a hostility towards wealth and power and a suspicion of capitalism but a suspicion that falls short of an endorsement of socialism': Posner, n. 98, 24. 'Populism' is a term that has been attached to various political movements in different countries (e.g., late nineteenth-century Russia) but in general means the preferences of 'ordinary people'. It is characterised by the defence of the little man against powerful organisations, such as governments, large firms, and trade unions.

[118] See Section 4.B.

[119] See generally Pitofsky, n. 63; Crane, n. 49 (a review of the Pitofsky book). For a highly critical view of the influence of Chicago on US antitrust policy, see C. E. Mueller, 'Antitrust Economics and the "The Flying Dutchman": How Economists Ruined Antitrust in Reagan's 1980s' (2008) 32 *Antitrust Law and Economics Rev* 1.

[120] *Competition and Monopoly: Single-Firm Conduct Under Section 2 of the Sherman Act*, United States Department of Justice (2008). The Federal Trade Commission (FTC) did not endorse the report and three of the four Commissioners disassociated themselves from its conclusions, see FTC Press Release, 8 September 2008.

[121] See the speech by the Assistant Attorney General of the DOJ Antitrust Division, Christine A. Varney, 'Vigorous Antitrust Enforcement In This Challenging Era', 11 May 2009, available on the DOJ website, <http://www.justice.gov/atr/public/speeches/245711.htm>.

[122] There are more than four differences of course (e.g., s. 1 of the Sherman Act is structured differently from the EU counterpart, Art. 101 TFEU) but the four mentioned here are particularly crucial.

The DOJ may bring criminal as well as civil proceedings for violations of the Sherman Act. The state governments (through their attorneys general) may also prosecute federal antitrust infringements and the states have their own state antitrust laws. This is in contrast to the position in the EU where the competition authority, the Commission, enforces the rules by taking decisions binding on the firms concerned, acting as both prosecutor and judge.[123] Secondly, in the US the antitrust laws are the subject of a large amount of private litigation (including collective and 'treble damages' actions) again before the ordinary federal courts, whereas in Europe private litigation has hitherto been secondary to public enforcement.[124] The result of these two factors is that US law has been developed on a case-by-case basis by the courts, while in the EU it has been primarily developed by an administrative authority with the EU Courts acting only to review the legality of the authority's actions or to interpret the law on references from national courts. Thirdly, s. 2 of the Sherman Act forbids 'monopolization' and attempts to 'monopolize'. It is thus crucially different from the corresponding provision in EU law, Article 102, which forbids the 'abuse of a dominant position'. So in the US anti-competitive conduct by which market power is *acquired* is an offence, whereas Article 102 can be applied only against the conduct of firms which are already in a dominant position. Finally, US law does not have the EU imperative of the integration of the single market.

8. EU COMPETITION LAW

A. THE OBJECTIVES OF THE EU AND THE ROLE OF THE COMPETITION RULES

An examination of the *raison d'être* of the EU is beyond the scope of a book on competition law. However, it is useful to look briefly at the aims and objectives of the EU in order to understand the context within which the competition rules are set.[125]

The fourth Preamble to the Treaty of Rome, which established the EEC (later the EC),[126] included the recognition that:

the removal of existing obstacles calls for concerted action in order to guarantee steady expansion, balanced trade and fair competition.

The objectives of the (E)EC were set out in Article 2 of the Treaty of Rome, which in its final form stated:[127]

The Community shall have as its task, by establishing a common market and an economic and monetary union and by implementing the common policies or activities referred to in Articles 3 and 4, to promote throughout the Community a harmonious, balanced and sustained development of economic activities, a high level of employment and of social protection, equality between men and women, sustainable and non-inflationary growth, a high degree of competitiveness and convergence of economic performance, a high level of protection and improvement of the quality of the environment, the raising of the standard of living and quality of life, and economic and social cohesion and solidarity among Member States.

The Community therefore had a number of wide-ranging and aspirational goals which it sought to achieve through economic integration. The creation of the common market was not an end

---

[123] See Chaps. 2 and 13.

[124] The 'modernisation' of EU law in 1 May 2004 was aimed, inter alia, at encouraging greater private enforcement. The Damages Dir., 2014/104/EU [2014] OJ L349/1, was adopted to facilitate and encourage private enforcement, see Chap. 14.

[125] For a historical analysis of the foundational phase of EU competition law, see K. K. Patel and H. Schweitzer (eds.), *The Historical Foundations of EU Competition Law* (Oxford University Press, 2013).

[126] See Chap. 2.

[127] Following the coming into force of the Treaty of Amsterdam on 1 May 1999.

in itself, but one of the means of achieving the promotion of the matters listed in Article 2. The 'common market' means an area where direct and indirect barriers to trade between Member States are removed and a common import and export policy adopted towards the outside world as far as commercial transactions are concerned. The single market is the 'internal' aspect of the common market. The economic integration of the Member States was taken further by progress towards Economic and Monetary Union (EMU).[128]

Article 3 of the Treaty of Rome set out a broad range of the 'activities' of the Community necessary for the purposes set out in Article 2. This included a highly significant provision, Article 3(1)(g), (originally Article 3(f))[129] which stated that the activities should include:

a system ensuring that competition in the internal market is not distorted.

Article 3(1)(g) was of great importance because it embedded the principle of undistorted competition in the fundamental provisions of the Treaty. The Court saw it as the foundation for the specific competition rules and referred to it in interpreting those rules, most famously in the seminal *Continental Can* case.[130]

The Treaty of Lisbon subsumed the EC into the EU and amended both the TEU and the EC Treaty, now renamed the Treaty on the Functioning of the European Union (TFEU), as from 1 December 2009.[131] The fourth Preamble is repeated in the TFEU. The objectives of the EU are now set out in Article 3(1) TEU:

The Union's aim is to promote peace, its values and the well-being of its peoples.

The reference to 'values' relates to Article 2 TEU which states:

The Union is founded on the values of respect for human dignity, freedom, democracy, equality, the rule of law and respect for human rights, including the rights of persons belonging to minorities. These values are common to the Member States in a society in which pluralism, non-discrimination, tolerance, justice, solidarity and equality between women and men prevail.

Article 3(3) states:

The Union shall establish an internal market. It shall work for the sustainable development of Europe based on balanced economic growth and price stability, a highly competitive social market economy, aiming at full employment and social progress, and a high level of protection and improvement of the quality of the environment. It shall promote scientific and technological advance …

'Internal market' is defined in Article 26 TFEU[132] which states:

The internal market shall comprise an area without internal frontiers in which the free movement of goods, persons, services and capital is ensured in accordance with the provisions of these Treaties.[133]

Neither the TEU nor the TFEU replicates Article 3(1)(g). As can be seen from Article 3(3), the provision in the TEU on the establishment of the internal market contains nothing about competition.

---

[128] The third and final stage of EMU entailed the creation of the Eurozone.

[129] And then Art. 3(g). The renumbering was brought about by the Treaties of Maastricht (the TEU) and Amsterdam in 1993 and 1999 respectively. In this book the provision is referred to as 'Art. 3(1)(g)' throughout, unless otherwise indicated. Until the 1993 amendments it read: '*the institution of* a system ensuring that competition in the common market is not distorted' (emphasis added).

[130] Case 6/72, *Continental Can* [1973] ECR 215, discussed further in Chaps. 5 and 7. See also Case C-68/94, *French Republic v Commission* [1998] ECR I-1375.

[131] The specific competition provisions (Arts. 101–106) remain unchanged by Lisbon, other than minor amendments such as replacing 'common market' with 'internal market' and an addition to one of the procedural articles, Art. 105 (ex Art. 85 EC), see Chap. 2.

[132] Previously Art. 14(2) of the Treaty of Rome (ex Art. 7a). The concept of the 'internal market' was first formally enshrined in the Treaty by the Single European Act 1986 (SEA).

[133] 'These Treaties' refers to the TFEU and the Treaty on European Union (TEU).

There is therefore no Treaty provision referring to undistorted competition.[134] Instead the principle appears in one of the Protocols annexed to and forming 'an integral part'[135] of the Treaties. Protocol No. 27 on the Internal Market and Competition states that the High Contracting Parties,

Considering that the internal market as set out in Article 3 of the Treaty on European Union includes a system ensuring that competition is not distorted, Have agreed that: To this end, the Union shall, if necessary, take action under the provisions of the Treaties, including under Article 352 of the Treaty on the Functioning of the European Union.

Moreover, Article 3(1)(b) TFEU states that one of the areas in which the Union has exclusive competence is:

The establishing of the competition rules necessary for the functioning of the internal market.

The consensus among competition lawyers was that the cumulative effect of these provisions was to leave the position in respect of 'undistorted competition' unchanged. When the Lisbon Treaty was agreed the Commission issued a press release declaring that it would carry on enforcing competition policy as before.[136] That the position is indeed unchanged was confirmed by the CJ in its preliminary ruling in *TeliaSonera*, concerning the interpretation of one of the competition articles, Article 102.[137]

Case C-52/09, *Konkurrensverket v TeliaSonera Sverige AB* [2011] ECR I-527

Court of Justice

20. In order to answer those questions, it must be observed at the outset that Article 3(3) TEU states that the European Union is to establish an internal market, which, in accordance with Protocol No 27 on the internal market and competition, annexed to the Treaty of Lisbon (OJ 2010 C 83, p. 309), is to include a system ensuring that competition is not distorted.

21. Article 102 TFEU is one of the competition rules referred to in Article 3(1)(b) TFEU which are necessary for the functioning of that internal market.

22. The function of those rules is precisely to prevent competition from being distorted to the detriment of the public interest, individual undertakings and consumers, thereby ensuring the well-being of the European Union (see, to that effect, Case C-94/00 *Roquette Frères* . . . paragraph 42).

Furthermore, in its Opinion finding that the draft agreement on the accession of the EU to the ECHR was incompatible with the TEU and Protocol 8, the CJ placed competition policy among the fundamental provisions to which the pursuit of the EU's objectives were entrusted:

---

[134] The removal of the reference to free and undistorted competition from the body of the Treaties is attributed to the insistence of President Sarkozy of France. The provision disappeared on the night of 21 June 2007 during the final last-minute negotiations on the Treaty of Lisbon. President Sarkozy was reported as saying at the time, 'Competition as an ideology, as a dogma: what has it done for Europe?', *Financial Times*, 26 June 2007, p. 12.

[135] Art. 51 TEU.

[136] MEMO 07/250, 23 June 2007. For the Commission, the competition community, and some Member States, the inclusion of free and undistorted competition among the Union's fundamental provisions was taken for granted. It was not foreseen that it would be a sticking point in the Treaty negotiations. The episode was a salutary reminder that for some Member States the concept of competition as a central organising principle of European integration was still open to question.

[137] For the substantive issues in this case, see Chap. 7.

The pursuit of the EU's objectives, as set out in Article 3 TEU, is entrusted to a series of fundamental provisions, such as those providing for the free movement of goods, services, capital and persons, citizenship of the Union, the area of freedom, security and justice, and competition policy. Those provisions, which are part of the framework of a system that is specific to the EU, are structured in such a way as to contribute—each within its specific field and with its own particular characteristics—to the implementation of the process of integration that is the *raison d'être* of the EU itself.[138]

In describing the major developments in competition policy and enforcement over the previous 40 years the Commission said in its 2010 report that there had been a constant process of adaptation in order to contribute to the major objectives of the EU:

Building the Single Market, making it deliver for consumers and achieving a competitive social market economy.[139]

B. THE OBJECTIVES OF EU COMPETITION LAW

(i) General

It is clear from Protocol 27, as from Article 3(1)(g) before it, that the function of EU competition law is to ensure that competition in the internal market is not distorted, in order to achieve the objectives of the EU. The policy which should be pursued in fulfilment of that function is another matter. We have already noted that in *Continental Can* in 1974 the Court said that the competition provisions, Articles 101 and 102, both seek to achieve the aim of the maintenance of effective competition,[140] and that the EUMR uses the criterion of 'effective competition' by which to judge the compatibility of mergers with the single market.[141] That still leaves open what goals should be pursued to achieve effective competition. We have already seen that there are various objectives which competition laws can pursue and which of these EU competition law should pursue is still a matter of debate after more than 50 years.[142] It is not a merely theoretical concern but one of great practical importance as it may affect how the competition rules are interpreted and how they are applied in individual cases. It is a particular issue in respect of Article 102, which deals with abuses of market power, as discussed in Chapter 7.[143]

(ii) The Competition Provisions

The substantive antitrust provisions, Articles 101, 102, and 106,[144] do not expressly articulate any particular policy. However, they do contain concepts which are significant in discerning the objectives of

---

[138] *Opinion 2/13* EU:C:2014:2454, para. 172.

[139] Commission Report on Competition Policy 2010, COM(2011)328 final, 10.6.2011, para. 1.

[140] Case 6/72, *Continental Can* [1973] ECR 215, para. 25.

[141] Council Reg. 139/2004 [2004] OJ L24/1, n. 85, Art. 2(3).

[142] See generally, e.g., C.-D. Ehlermann and L. Laudati (eds.), *European Competition Law Annual 1997: Objectives of Competition Policy* (Hart Publishing, 1998); L. Parret, 'The Objectives of EU Competition Law and Policy' (2010) 6 *European Competition Journal* 339; Nazzini, n. 96; Akman, n. 33; P. Akman, 'The Role of "Freedom" in EU Competition Law' (2014) 34 *Legal Studies* 183; Geradin, Layne-Farrar, and Petit, n. 7, 1.61–1.80. For the history of the EU competition rules see Gerber, n. 90; Gerber, n. 91; A. Weitbrecht, 'From Freiburg to Chicago and Beyond—The First 50 Years of European Competition Law' [2008] *ECLR* 81; Patel and Schweitzer, n. 125.

[143] See, for example, the opposing arguments which erupted in the wake of the GC's judgment in Case T-286/09, *Intel v Commission* EU:T:2014:547: W. Wils, 'The Judgment of the EU General Court in *Intel* and the So-called "More Economic Approach" to Abuse of Dominance' (2014) 37 *World Competition* 405; C. Ahlborn and D. Piccinin, 'The *Intel* Judgment and Consumer Welfare—A Response to Wouter Wils', 2015/1 *CLPD* 60; Petit, n. 97; L. Peeperkorn, 'Conditional Pricing: Why the General Court is wrong in *Intel* and what the Court of Justice can do to rebalance the assessment of rebates' [2015] 1 *Concurrences* 43–63.

[144] Art. 106 deals with the application of the rules to public undertakings and those granted special rights, see Chap. 8.

the rules. There is the reference to 'fair competition' in the fourth Preamble.[145] There are also references to fairness and to consumers in the exemption provision in Article 101(3) (a 'fair share' of benefit to consumers), the prohibition of the exploitation of customers (which includes consumers[146]) by unfair prices and unfair trading conditions in Article 102(a) as regards dominant firms, and a prohibition on limiting production, markets, or technical development to the prejudice of consumers in Article 102(b). As regards consumers, they must therefore be relevant to all abuses covered by Article 102,[147] and to Article 101 as a whole, given that Articles 101 and 102 serve the same end.[148] This is not the same as saying that the aim of the provisions is consumer welfare in the technical sense.

(iii) The Single Market

As we have seen, competition policy was included in the list of Community activities set out in Article 3 of the Treaty of Rome from the inception of the Community in 1958. It was embedded in the Treaty as part of a set of wide policy instruments oriented towards the objective of European economic integration. Competition policy was thought necessary to underpin the internal market aspect of the common market because there was no point in dismantling, by means of the free movement provisions, State measures which divided the Community territorially and compartmentalised the market if private undertakings could erect and maintain barriers to trade between Member States by carving up markets between them and indulging in anti-competitive practices. Economic integration was therefore promoted both by free movement and by competition.[149]

The role of competition law as an instrument of single market integration is crucial to an understanding of EU competition law. It differentiates EU law from any other system of competition law, whether in the Member States, the US, or elsewhere. This is seen most strikingly in respect of the law on vertical restraints.[150] Both the EU Courts and the Commission have repeatedly stressed the fundamental nature of the competition rules in achieving the single market.[151]

---

[145] See Section 8.A, pp. 31–32.

[146] For the customer/consumer terminology, see Section 8.B.v.a.

[147] The abuses specifically listed in Art. 102 are not an exhaustive list of the specific ways in which Art. 102 can be infringed, see Chap. 7.

[148] Case 6/72, *Continental Can* [1973] ECR 215, para. 25.

[149] See J. Baquero Cruz, *Between Competition and Free Movement: The Economic Constitutional Law of the European Community* (Hart Publishing, 2002). In general it is true to say that the free movement provisions apply to State measures and the competition provisions to those of private actors. However, this statement masks a number of complexities. First, in some cases the free movement provisions can bind private parties, in particular where 'collective' private action is concerned in the area of free movement of persons and services, such as Case 36/74, *Walrave & Koch v Association Union Cycliste Internationale* [1974] ECR 1405 and Case 415/93, *Union Royal Belge des Sociétés de Football Association ASBL & others v Jean-Marc Bosman* [1995] ECR I-4921 (both cases concerned the rules of sporting organisations). Secondly, some situations raise both free movement and competition issues, e.g. *Bosman* (on the right of professional football players to move between clubs when out of contract) and Cases 403 and 429/08, *Football Association Premier League v QC Leisure and Karen Murphy v Media Protection Services Ltd* [2011] ECR I-9083 (on the selling of TV rights to the Premier League); see also Case C-309/99, *Wouters v Algemene Raad van de Nederlandse Orde van Advocaten* [2002] ECR I-1577, on the rules of the Dutch Bar, discussed in Chap. 3. Thirdly, it is possible to impugn some State measures on competition grounds and the application of the competition rules to State action has become a significant aspect of competition law in the EU, as discussed in Chap. 8.

[150] From Cases 56 and 58/64, *Etablissements Consten SA & Grundig-Verkaufs-GmbH v Commission* [1966] ECR 299 onwards; see Chap. 11.

[151] See Case C-126/97, *Eco Swiss China Time Ltd v Benetton International NV* [1999] ECR I-3055, para. 36; Case C-453/99, *Courage Ltd v Crehan* [2001] ECR I-6297, para. 20; Case T-168/01, *GlaxoSmithKline Services* [2006] ECR II-2969, para. 11 ('indispensable for the achievement of the missions entrusted to the Community'); Commission Guidelines on the application of Article 81(3) of the Treaty [2004] OJ C101/97, para. 13; Commission Guidelines on vertical restraints [2010] OJ C130/1, para. 7. For the development of the convergence of competition and market integration, see C. D. Ehlermann, 'The Contribution of EC Competition Policy to the Single Market' (1992) 29 *CMLRev* 257; K. Mortelmans, 'Towards Convergence of the Rules on Free Movement and Competition' (2001) 38 *CMLRev* 613; R. O'Loughlin, 'EC Competition Rules and Free Movement Rules: An Examination of the Parallels and their furtherance by the ECJ *Wouters* Decision' [2003] *ECLR* 62; Baquero Cruz, n. 149.

The continuing importance of the single market goal to competition law is seen in recent case law. In *GlaxoSmithKline* the CJ confirmed that agreements limiting parallel imports have the object of restricting competition contrary to Article 101(1),[152] referring to 'the Treaty's objective of achieving the integration of national markets through the establishment of a single market'.[153] In *Sot. Lélos* the CJ held a dominant undertaking's refusal to supply in order to prevent parallel trade between Member States is prima facie an abuse under Article 102 for that reason alone (although capable of objective justification);[154] *Pierre Fabre* was driven by the wish to stop contractual provisions (*in casu* selling over the internet) from preventing inter-Member State trade;[155] and the finding in *Football Association Premier League* that the arrangements for selling Premier League TV rights contravened Article 101 as well as the free movement of services provisions was because they resulted in the artificial partitioning of the single market.[156] Further, in the Guidance on Article 102 enforcement priorities[157] the Commission says that in addition to exclusionary abuses (the subject of the Guidance) it may intervene in relation to 'certain behaviour that undermines the efforts to achieve an integrated internal market'. In the *Swedish Connectors* case the Commission's reason for intervening in the anti-congestion arrangements of the Swedish electricity transmission operator was that they segmented the internal market.[158] In September 2015 Commissioner Vestager stressed the importance of the Commission's e-commerce inquiry[159] in revealing and removing barriers to the single market and contributing to the EU's Digital Single Market strategy.[160]

(iv) The Development of the Law

There has been a great deal of argument about the influence of ordoliberalism on the drafting of the EEC competition provisions in 1956–1957.[161] Certainly, the main debate during the drafting was between the French and German delegations, but their positions appear to have been more nuanced and complex than has sometimes been supposed.[162] It has been persuasively concluded that:

---

[152] Case C-501/06 P, *GlaxoSmithKline* [2009] ECR I-9291, paras. 59–62, disapproving on this point the judgment of the GC, see Chap. 4.

[153] Ibid., para. 61.

[154] Cases C-468–478/06, *Sot. Lélos kai Sia EE and others v GlaxoSmithKline AEVE Farmakeftikon Proionton* [2008] ECR I-7139, see Chap. 7.

[155] Case C-439/09, *Pierre Fabre Dermo-Cosmétique SAS v Président de l'Autorité de la Concurrence* [2011] ECR I-9419.

[156] Case C-403/08, *Football Association Premier League* [2011] ECR I-9083; see the comments of the Commissioner on this in the speech 'Competition—What's in it for Consumers?', European Competition and Consumer Day, Poznan, 24 November 2011, SPEECH/11/803.

[157] Guidance on the Commission's Enforcement Priorities in Applying Article 82 of the EC Treaty to Abusive Exclusionary Conduct by Dominant Undertakings [2009] OJ C45/2 (the Guidance Paper), para. 7 (discussed in Chaps. 5–7).

[158] COMP/39.351, *Swedish Interconnectors* [2010] OJ C142/28 (settled with a commitments decision, see Chap. 7, Section 17, p. 574).

[159] IP/15/4921, see Chap. 11, Section 3.C.iii.

[160] <http://ec.europa.eu/priorities/digital-single-market/index_en.htm>, see Section 12.

[161] See Gerber, n. 91; P. Akman, 'Searching for the Long-Lost Soul of Article 82EC' (2009) 29 *OJLS* 267; Akman, n. 33; Behrens, n. 91; H. Schweitzer, 'The History, Interpretation and Underlying Principles of Section 2 Sherman Act and Article 82 EC' in Ehlermann and Marquis, n. 89, 119.

[162] Particularly in respect of what is now Art. 102. The French legislation on agreements between undertakings strongly influenced the wording of what is now Art. 101, see L. F. Pace and K. Seidel, 'The Drafting and Role of Regulation 17: A Hard-Fought Compromise' in Patel and Schweitzer, n. 125, 54, 59. There was also an American influence. The ECSC competition provisions, which were the pattern for the later EEC ones, were based on a draft prepared at the behest of Jean Monnet by the Harvard antitrust lawyer Robert Bowie, who was an adviser to John McCloy, the US High Commissioner for Germany and a close ally of Monnet, [1959–62] OJ Spec. Ed. 87. See Chap. 2. The EU competition rules also apply to the EEA.

The EC Treaty was indeed a collective work, moulded by various influences, all of which are reflected in the various provisions referring to competition policy. In other words, the Treaty's commitment to 'undistorted competition' enshrines a multi-faceted concept.[163]

There was an important German influence in the competition Directorate General (then DG IV) at the beginning because of the powerful presence of German officials[164] and the drafting of Regulation 17, the provision which implemented the competition rules, was greatly influenced by the external experts, who were all German.[165] Although those concerned were not necessarily ordoliberals, ordoliberalism provided the intellectual and theoretical framework for the development of EU competition law but, as we saw in Section 6, ordoliberalism is not a static body of ideas and it has itself developed and changed over the relevant period.

In *Continental Can*, the first judgment on Article 102, the Court said:

Article [102] is not only aimed at practices which may cause damage to consumers directly, but also at those which are detrimental to them through their impact on an effective competition structure such as is mentioned in Article [3(1)(g)] ...[166]

This looks to the protection of consumers, but not just at immediate direct effects on them. It looks also at the protection of the market structure because of possible long-term effects on consumers. As Articles 101 and 102 have the same aim this applies to both provisions. As we see in the cases discussed throughout this book, the rules have often been applied in a very interventionist way, to protect competitors rather than competition, to favour small or medium-sized enterprises, and to keep markets open. Although not couched expressly in 'freedom' terms much of the decisional practice and many judgments, particularly on Article 102, reflect ordoliberal principles. A previous Director-General of Competition acknowledged:

The case-law of the European courts and also the decisional practice of the Commission were initially influenced by ordoliberal thought which has its origin in the so-called Freiburg School ... The protection of individual economic freedom—as a value in itself—was regarded as the primary objective of competition policy.[167]

(v) 'Modernisation', the 'More Economic Approach', and the Consumer Welfare Standard

a. 'Modernisation' and the Commission

'Modernisation' is often used to describe the major reform in the enforcement of EU competition law which took place in 2004 when Regulation 1/2003 came into force.[168] However, it should be understood as a wider and deeper phenomenon. During the 1990s the Commission began a move towards a realignment of competition law in line with the economic thinking on efficiency and welfare previously discussed.[169] Furthermore, the Commission adopted an 'effects' approach to applying the consumer welfare standard. 'Modernisation' therefore encompasses the gradual revolution

---

[163] Geradin, Layne-Farrar, and Petit, n. 7, 1.70.

[164] E.g. Hans von der Groeben from the German Economics Ministry, who was one of the authors of the Spaak Report (the report by an intergovernmental committee of the six Member States of the ECSC which formed the basis for what became the EEC and Euratom) was the chairman of the group who drafted the competition articles during the Treaty negotiations. He became the first Commissioner for Competition, 1958–1967. E.-J. Mestmäcker, an ordoliberal (see his paper 'Wettbewerbsfreiheit und Wohlfahrt' (Freedom of Competition and Welfare), Max Planck Law Research Paper No. 12/2, 2012, available at <http://ssrn.com/abstract=1983193>) was special adviser to DGIV, 1960–1970.

[165] Pace and Seidel, n. 162, 72.

[166] Case 6/72, *Continental Can* [1973] ECR 215, para. 12.

[167] P. Lowe, 'Consumer Welfare and Efficiency—New Guiding Principles of Competition Policy?', 13th International Competition and 14th European Competition Day, Munich, 27 March 2007, <http://ec.europa.eu/competition/speeches/index_2007.html>.

[168] Council Reg. 1/2003 [2003] OJ L1/1 and the accompanying secondary legislation and Notices.

[169] See Section 3, p. 3 ff.

in the interpretation and application of the substantive law which has taken place both before 2004[170] and afterwards. This is often called the 'more economic' approach. The effect of modernisation in this sense on the application of the competition provisions, Articles 101 and 102, and the EUMR[171] is seen throughout this book.

As modernisation progressed the instruments and pronouncements emanating from the Commission proclaimed its conversion to the efficiency and consumer welfare standard.[172] In a highly significant speech in July 2001 Commissioner Monti said:

. . . the goal of competition policy, in all its aspects, is to protect consumer welfare by maintaining a high degree of competition in the common market. Competition should lead to lower prices, a wider choice of goods, and technological innovation, all in the interest of the consumer.[173]

The policy continued under successive Competition Commissioners. Commissioner Kroes said in 2005:

Consumer welfare is now well established as the standard the Commission applies when assessing mergers and infringements of the Treaty rules on cartels and monopolies. Our aim is simple: to protect competition in the market as a means of enhancing consumer welfare and ensuring an efficient allocation of resources. An effects-based approach, grounded in solid economics, ensures that citizens enjoy the benefits of a competitive, dynamic market economy.[174]

Commissioner Almunia reaffirmed this in 2011:

Consumer welfare is not just a catchy phrase. It is the cornerstone, the guiding principle of EU competition policy.[175]

The 2004 Guidelines on Article 101(3) state that:

[t]he objective of Article [101] is to protect competition on the market as a means of enhancing consumer welfare and of ensuring an efficient allocation of resources.[176]

---

[170] This could first be discerned in the approach to the assessment of mergers under the regime which came into operation in 1990 (Council Reg. 4064/89 [1990] OJ L257/13, see Chap. 15). See also the Notice on the definition of the relevant market [1997] OJ C372/51; the Green Paper on vertical restraints, COM (96) 721 final, paving the way for the reform of the Commission's much-criticised policy towards vertical restraints in 1999 (Commission Reg. 2790/99 [1999] OJ L336/21 and the Guidelines on vertical restraints [2000] OJ C291/1 (since amended), see Chap. 11); the 1999 White Paper on the modernisation of enforcement and procedure (Commission White Paper on modernisation of the rules implementing Articles 81 and 82 of the EC Treaty [1999] OJ C132/1); Guidelines and block exemptions on horizontal cooperation agreements in 2000 (Guidelines on the applicability of Article 81 of the EC Treaty to horizontal cooperation agreements [2001] OJ C3/2; Commission Reg. 2658/2000 on specialisation agreements [2000] OJ L304/3; Commission Reg. 2659/2000 on categories of research and development agreements [2000] OJ L304/7 (since amended)).

[171] Now Council Reg. 139/2004 [2004] OJ L24/1.

[172] Particularly after the appointment of an economist, Mario Monti, as Commissioner responsible for competition in 1999, see e.g M. Monti, 'European Competition Policy for the 21st Century', SPEECH/00/389, 20 October 2000, <http://www.ec.europa.eu./competition/speeches/> and in [2000] *Fordham Corp L Inst*, Chap. 15. In 1998 Jacobs AG reminded the CJ that 'the primary purpose of Art. [102] is to prevent distortion of competition—and in particular to safeguard the interests of consumers—rather than to protect the position of particular competitors', Case C-7/97, *Oscar Bronner GmbH & Co KG v Mediaprint* [1998] ECR I-7791, para. 58 of his Opinion, see Chap. 7.

[173] M. Monti, 'The Future for Competition Policy in the European Union', Merchant Taylor's Hall, London, 9 July 2001, SPEECH/01/340, <http://www.ec.europa.eu/competition/speeches/>. The fact that he said that the protection of consumer welfare was *the* goal rather than *a* goal was acclaimed by the then Deputy Assistant Attorney General of the US DOJ Antitrust Division who said that '[w]e in the United States applaud Commissioner Monti's bold leadership in embracing the consumer welfare model of competition policy', William J. Kolasky, 'North Atlantic Competition Policy: Converging Towards What?', Address given at the BIICL 2nd Annual International and Comparative Law Conference, London, 17 May 2002, available on the DOJ website, <http://www.usdoj.gov/atr/public/speeches/speech_kolasky.htm>.

[174] 'Delivering Better Markets and Better Choices', European Consumer and Competition Day, London, 15 September 2005, SPEECH/05/512, <http://ec.europa.eu/competition/speeches/>.

[175] 'Competition—what's in it for consumers?', Poznan, 24 November 2011, SPEECH/1/2003803, <http://ec.europa.eu/competition/speeches/>.

[176] Guidelines on the application of Article 81(3) [now Article 101(3)] of the Treaty [2004] OJ C101/97, para. 13 (the Article 101(3) Guidelines).

Subsequent Guidelines and similar documents proclaim a similar stance.[177] The 2009 Guidance Paper on the Commission's enforcement priorities in applying Article 102 (the Guidance Paper) states that the Commission will focus on those types of conduct that are most harmful to consumers.[178] The whole rhetoric of the Commission in its press releases, speeches by officials, policy documents, reports, and all other publications is to stress that its activities are for the benefit of European *consumers*.

The adoption of the consumer welfare standard means that the Commission seeks to apply the competition rules (by preventing restrictive agreements, anti-competitive conduct by dominant firms, and mergers which would significantly impede effective competition) to deliver lower prices, greater output, greater choice, higher quality, and more innovation in products and services. Adopting the standard also means that the Commission has rejected not only broader objectives such as economic freedom[179] and the protection of competitors but also the total/social welfare standard. In other words, the Commission *is* concerned with distributive effects.[180] The reasons that lead competition authorities to prefer the consumer welfare to the total welfare standard are explained in the extract from Nazzini set out in Section 6.B.[181] Bishop and Walker (who also make the point that competition authorities must be careful to see consumer welfare in a dynamic rather than static context) say as follows apropos of EU law.[182]

> ## S. Bishop and M. Walker, *The Economics of EC Competition Law* (3rd edn, Sweet & Maxwell, 2010), 31–32
>
> 2-019... The economic goal of EC competition law appears to be concerned with improving allocative efficiency in ways that do not impair productive efficiency so greatly as to produce no increase (or even net reduction) in total consumer welfare. Given that competition law enforcement should not, in general, be concerned with detailed micro-regulation of industries, this is a reasonable policy objective. Direct regulation of a firm's efficiency is likely to be fraught with difficulty and, given the informational constraints under which regulators usually work, is likely to be prone to substantial errors.
>
> So the conclusion . . . is that the welfare standard for EC competition law is consumer welfare, not social welfare, but that in most cases the distinction is not important because maximising consumer welfare and maximising social welfare require the same outcomes. However, there are times when it does matter (for instance, in some mergers), and on these occasions the focus is on consumer welfare.

The application of the consumer welfare standard in EU law can be confused by the meaning given to the word 'consumers'. The word appears in both Article 101(3) and in Article 102(b).[183] Consumers also feature in the EUMR, which refers to ' the interests of the intermediate and ultimate

---

[177] Such as Guidelines on the assessment of horizontal mergers [2004] OJ C31/03, para. 8; Guidelines on the assessment of non-horizontal mergers [2008] OJ C265/7, para. 10; Guidelines on vertical restraints [2010] OJ C130/1, para. 7; Guidelines on technology transfer agreements [2014] OJ L89/3, para. 5.

[178] The Guidance Paper, n. 157, para. 5.

[179] See generally L. Lovdahl Gormesen, 'The Conflict between Economic Freedom and Consumer Welfare in the Modernisation of Article 82' (2007) 3 *European Competition Journal* 329.

[180] There is support for this in the wording of Art. 101(3) which demands that a 'fair share' of the efficiency gains resulting from anti-competitive agreements must be passed on to consumers, see Chap. 4.

[181] P. 27.

[182] See also, in respect of Bishop and Walker's point about the difference between total and consumer welfare often being insignificant, E. Fox, 'Is Efficiency All That Counts'? in Pitofsky, n. 65, 77, 78.

[183] See Section 8.B.ii, p. 35.

consumers'.[184] The normal (and popular) conception of a 'consumer' is a private end-user and the current Commission rhetoric emphasises the benefits that the enforcement of the competition rules has for individual citizens. However, 'consumers' has long been interpreted in EU competition law as encompassing all indirect and direct users and not just private end-users, i.e. it includes intermediate customers as well, as can be seen from the EUMR.[185] The problems with this are that the interests of intermediate customers and end-users may well not coincide, and intermediate customers may be competitors of the supplier in downstream markets. This can cause complications,[186] particularly in Article 102 cases.

The decisions that the Commission has taken since modernisation, however, can often be criticised from a consumer welfare perspective. This is particularly true of Article 102 decisions, such as *Microsoft*,[187] *Tomra*,[188] and *Telefónica*[189] discussed in Chapter 7.

The 'consumer welfare approach' to EU competition law is frequently called the 'more economic approach'. Commentators have rightly pointed out, however, that this phrase embraces different matters.[190] The least controversial, which receives support from nearly all sides, is the rigorous use of economic methods in establishing facts and other essential factors. The most controversial is the reorientation to the consumer welfare goal.

H. Schweitzer and K. K. Patel, 'EU Competition Law in Historical Context: Continuity and Change' in Patel and Schweitzer (eds.), *The Historical Foundations of EU Competition Law* (Oxford University Press, 2013), 207, 220

In its most far-reaching version, the 'more economic approach' is a proposition to redefine the goals of EU competition law. A different aspect of the 'more economic approach' is the suggestion to make greater use of economic theories and methods to establish the relevant facts of the case and provide evidence for the appropriateness of a given market definition or anti-competitive effect of a given type for unilateral conduct…Finally, the 'more economic approach' in a 'light' form can be understood to suggest a review of the test for anti-competitive conduct in light of recent insights of economic theory with a view to determining whether the EU competition [sic] can be interpreted in a more concise and unerring manner.

---

b. The Consumer Welfare Standard and the Case Law of the Court

The adoption by the Commission of the consumer welfare standard has not been wholeheartedly embraced by the EU Courts.

---

[184] In appraising a merger the Commission shall take into account, inter alia, 'the interests of the intermediate and ultimate consumers, and the development of technical and economic progress provided that it is to consumers' advantage and does not form an obstacle to competition', EUMR, Art. 2(1)(b). Exactly the same provision appeared in the original Merger Reg., 4064/89 [1990] OJ L257/13. Note also that recital 29 of the EUMR refers to a merger's potential efficiencies counteracting the effects on competition and 'in particular the potential harm to consumers' (there was no similar recital in 4064/89).

[185] See as well as the EUMR, the Article 101(3) Guidelines, n. 176, para. 84 (direct or indirect users . . . including producers that use the products as an input . . . In other words . . . customers of the parties to the agreement and subsequent purchasers); Guidance Paper on Article 102, para. 19, n. 2. For a discussion of the concept of 'consumer' in EU competition law generally, see A. Jones and A. Albors-Llorens, 'The Images of the "Consumer" in EU Competition Law' (2016), <http://papers.ssrn.com/sol3/papers.cfm?abstract_id=2750922>.

[186] See P. Akman, '"Consumer" versus "Customer": the Devil in the Detail' (2010) 37 J of Law and Society 315.

[187] COMP/37.792, [2007] OJ L32/23.

[188] COMP/38.113, *Prokent/Tomra* [2008] OJ C219/11.

[189] COMP/38.784, [2008] OJ C83/6.

[190] Ahlborn and Piccinin, n. 143, 61.

It will be recalled that in *Continental Can* the CJ said that the competition provisions were aimed at practices which were detrimental to consumers through their impact on an effective competition structure as well as those causing damage to them directly.[191] The EU Courts have repeated this on many subsequent occasions, including the recent cases of in *TeliaSonera*[192] and *Post Danmark I*.[193] In 2000 the CJ said in *Hoechst* that the function of the competition rules:

. . . is, as follows from the fourth preamble to the Treaty, Article 3[(1)(g)] and Articles [101] and [102], to prevent competition being distorted to the detriment of the public interest, individual undertakings and consumers.[194]

In 2006 the GC gave two judgments on Article 101 in which it identified the 'well-being' or 'welfare' of the final consumer as the objective. The first was *Österreichische Postsparkasse* in which it said that the ultimate purpose of the rules 'is to increase the well-being of consumers'.[195] The second was *GlaxoSmithKline* where the GC said, in a clear endorsement of the consumer welfare standard:

However, as the objective of the Community competition rules is to prevent undertakings, by restricting competition between themselves or with third parties, from reducing the welfare of the final consumer of the products in question . . .[196]

In *GlaxoSmithKline* this was crucial to one of the findings in the case, as it prevented an agreement from falling within the prohibition of anti-competitive agreements in Article 101(1) by reason of its object alone. Although the object of the agreement was to restrict parallel trade the GC held that could not, on the facts of the case, be equated with the object of reducing the welfare of the final consumer.[197]

In the appeal in *GlaxoSmithKline* the CJ firmly disapproved of the GC's statement on the object of agreements and parallel trade:

. . . it must be borne in mind that the Court has held that, like other competition rules laid down in the Treaty, Article [101] aims to protect not only the interests of competitors or of consumers, but also the structure of the market and, in so doing, competition as such. Consequently, for a finding that an agreement has an anti-competitive object, it is not necessary that final consumers be deprived of the advantages of effective competition in terms of supply or price (see, by analogy, *T-Mobile Netherlands and Others*, cited above, paragraphs 38 and 39).[198]

The *T-Mobile* case referred to by the CJ is to a preliminary reference ruling it gave after the GC's *GlaxoSmithKline* judgment in which it said that the competition rules were designed to protect 'not only the interests of individual competitors or consumers but also to protect the structure of the market and thus competition as such'.[199] This appears to assume that the aim is the protection of competitors as well as consumers (without any indication that the interests of the two groups might conflict) and stress that they also protect the market structure and 'competition as such'.

---

[191] Case 6/72, *Continental Can* [1973] ECR 215, para. 26.

[192] Case C-52/09, *Konkurrensverket v TeliaSonera Sverige AB* [2011] ECR I-527, para. 24.

[193] Case C-209/10, *Post Danmark A/S v Konkurrencerådet (Post Danmark I)* EU:C:2012:172, para. 20.

[194] Cases 46/87 and 227/88, *Hoechst v EC Commission* [1989] ECR 2859, para. 25. This was repeated in Case C-94/00 *Roquette Frères* [2002] ECR I-9011, para. 42.

[195] Cases T-213 and 214/01, *Österreichische Postsparkasse AG v Commission* and *Bank für Arbeit und Wirtschaft AG v Commission* [2006] ECR II-1601, para. 115.

[196] Case T-168/01, *GlaxoSmithKline Services* [2006] ECR II-2969, para. 118.

[197] See further Chap. 4.

[198] Case C-501/06 P, *GlaxoSmithKline Services* [2009] ECR I-9291, para. 63, repeated in Case C-68/12, *Protimonopolný úrad Slovenskej republiky v Slovenská sporiteľňa as* EU:C:2013:71, para. 18.

[199] Case C-8/08, *T-Mobile Netherlands BV v Raad van bestuur van de Nederlandse Mededingingsautoriteit* [2009] ECR I-4529, para. 38. See also Kokott AG in her Opinion in Case C-95/04 P, *British Airways v Commission* [2007] ECR I-2331, para. 86, which described Art. 102 as not being 'only or primarily designed to protect the immediate interests of individual competitors or consumers but to protect the structure of the market and thus competition as such (as an institution) . . .'

Being concerned with restraints on the abuse of market power Article 102 cases frequently raise questions about the protection of particular competitors and the structure of competition, particularly as Article 102 has been mainly concerned with practices that exclude competitors. As will be seen from the discussion in Chapter 7, the approach of the EU Courts has been inconsistent. Looking at the jurisprudence of the EU Courts in the last ten years, since the Commission's official endorsement of the consumer welfare standard, we see a confused picture with no straightforward trajectory. The *British Airways* judgment was clearly concerned with the protection of a competitor, and the CJ held that demonstrating prejudice to consumers was unnecessary. *Microsoft* was mainly concerned with the alteration of the balance of competition in favour of Microsoft and with disadvantage to competitors. In *TeliaSonera*[200] the CJ said[201] that the function of the rules is 'to prevent competition from being distorted to the detriment of the public interest, individual undertakings and consumers, thereby ensuring the well-being of the European Union'. The phrase 'well-being of the Union' is a clear reference to the aims of the EU set out in Article 3(1) TEU ('well-being of its peoples').[202] However, in *TeliaSonera* and *Deutsche Telekom*[203] the CJ approved the application of the as efficient competitor (AEC) test,[204] which is used to apply the consumer welfare standard, to margin squeeze pricing,[205] although in *Deutsche Telekom* it held that the conduct was an abuse even though avoiding the conduct would entail increasing its prices to consumers in the short term.[206] At the time of writing the high-water mark of the consumer welfare approach in Article 102 cases is *Post Danmark I*[207] in which the CJ (re)asserted the principle that Article 102 does not protect inefficient competitors from exclusion from the market and applied the AEC test to selective low pricing. However, in *Intel*[208] the GC was mainly concerned with competitors' freedom of access to the market and it denied that the AEC test was relevant to exclusive rebates. *Post Danmark II*[209] was a mixture with the CJ inter alia, referring to consumer welfare but also holding that the AEC was not always applicable and that there was no *de minimis* threshold to establish a breach of Article 102.

There is no doubt that recent judgments do have more regard for the interests of consumers than earlier ones. The language of the EU Courts has shifted. In general, however, although the Courts are concerned with consumers they have not adopted the consumer welfare standard as such. It is therefore not possible to say at present that consumer welfare is the objective of EU competition law.

9. PUBLIC POLICY CONSIDERATIONS AND EU COMPETITION LAW

The question of the objectives of EU competition law raises the issue of how far, if at all, what one can call 'non-competition' factors, such as employment, the environment, or social policy, can or should be taken into account in the application of the competition law.[210] This is not an argument about

---

[200] Case C-52/09, *Konkurrensverket v TeliaSonera Sverige AB* [2011] ECR I-527.

[201] As seen in the extract in Section 8.A, p. 33.

[202] See Section 8.B.

[203] Case C-280/08 P, *Deutsche Telekom v Commission* [2010] ECR I-9555.

[204] See Chap 7.7.D.

[205] See also Case T-336/07, *Telefónica and Telefónica de España v Commission* EU:T:2012:172, upheld in Case C-295/12 P, *Telefónica SA v Commission* EU:C:2014:2062, where the point was not appealed.

[206] Case C-280/08 P, *Deutsche Telekomm* [2010] ECR I-9555, para. 181. The CJ considered that in the longer term competitive pressure would lead to a reduction in prices (para. 182).

[207] Case C-209/10, *Post Danmark A/S v Konkurrencerådet (Post Danmark I)* EU:C:2012:172.

[208] Case T-286/09, *Intel v Commission* EU:T:2014:547, on appeal Case C-413/14 P, judgment pending.

[209] Case C-23/14, *Post Danmark A/S v Konkurrencerådet (Post Danmark II)* EU:C:2015:651.

[210] See G. Monti, 'Article 81 EC and Public Policy' (2002) 30 CMLRev 1057; A. C. Witt, 'Public Policy Goals under EU Competition Law' (2012) 8 *European Competition Journal* 443.

whether there should be social, regional, employment, environmental, or other policies but a matter of whether, and to what extent, these may be or should be pursued as part of a *competition* policy.

The adoption by the Commission of the consumer welfare standard makes it particularly difficult to take other considerations into account. As we have seen, the whole philosophy of the 'modernised' approach to competition policy is that it should be concerned only with welfare and efficiency. Moreover, the 2004 reforms, which decentralised the enforcement of EU competition law to the national competition authorities of the Member States[211] and gave encouragement to the private enforcement of the competition rules in the national courts, made the exclusion of other considerations expedient. It is one thing for the Commission to balance competition against other EU policies, but quite another for national courts and authorities to do so.[212]

EU competition policy does not stand alone in splendid isolation. As explained in Section 8.A, it was stated in the EC Treaty to be one of a number of activities undertaken to achieve the objectives of the Treaty, and its role has not changed under the Treaty of Lisbon. Article 7 TFEU provides generally for consistency between all EU policies and activities:

The Union shall ensure consistency between its policies and activities, taking all of its objectives into account and in accordance with the principle of conferral of powers.

Articles 8–13 TFEU set out specific matters that must be taken into account (the 'policy-linking' or 'flanking' clauses).[213] The effect of these provisions on competition law is a matter of debate. For example, Odudu argues that they are not relevant to enforcement in any particular competition case[214] whereas Townley argues that they can provide a legal base for non-efficiency considerations in individual cases.[215] Hitherto the EU Courts have not addressed the legal effect of the policy-linking clauses.

There are in practice two ways in which non-welfare or efficiency issues and other EU policies can be taken into account.[216] A matter may be excluded from the scope of competition law altogether,[217] or the matter may be covered by the competition rules but other considerations may be taken into account in their application in what has been described as a compromise or 'balancing' exercise.[218]

---

[211] Council Reg. 1/2003 [2003] OJ L1/1; Commission Notice on cooperation within the network of competition authorities [2004] OJ C101/43.

[212] In the Commission White Paper on modernisation of the rules implementing Articles 81 and 82 of the EC Treaty [1999] OJ C132/1, the Commission first proposed decentralisation and turned its face against using Art. 101(3) to take into account public policy: see Chap. 4. Member States do pursue objectives which do not fit with the efficiency approach. In 2006 Member State governments interfered with merger transactions in the energy sector in order to protect national companies from 'foreign' takeovers, thus incurring the wrath of the Commission which considered the actions contrary to the EUMR. The Commission took infringement proceedings under Art. 258 TFEU against Spain in respect of the conditions the Spanish energy regulator had imposed on the takeover of the Spanish energy company Endesa by the German company E.ON, Case C-196/07, *Spain v Commission* [2008] ECR I-41 (summary, the full judgment is available only in Spanish and French): see Press Release IP/06/1426.

[213] Similar, though less extensive, clauses also appeared in the EC Treaty. In the TFEU they are equality between men and women, known as 'gender mainstreaming' (Art. 8); high level of employment, social protection, the fight against social exclusion, and a high level of education, training, and protection of human health (Art. 9); combating gender, racial or ethnic origin, religion or belief, disability, age, or sexual orientation discrimination (Art. 10); environmental protection, in particular promoting sustainable development (Art. 11); consumer protection (Art. 12); and (as regards inter alia the internal market) animal welfare (Art. 13). There are also provisions in respect of agriculture, fisheries, transport, research and technological development, and space.

[214] Relying on the minimum price for tobacco products case, Case C-221/08, *Commission v Ireland* [2010] ECR I-1669, in which what is now Art. 168(1) TFEU was argued, and on the apparent lack of direct effect: O. Odudu, 'The Wider Concerns of Competition Law' (2010) 30 *OJLS* 599, 606–607.

[215] C. Townley, *Article 81 EC and Public Policy* (Hart Publishing, 2009), 50–54. See also Monti, n. 96, 90–91.

[216] See generally O. Odudu, *The Boundaries of EC Competition Law* (Oxford University Press, 2006), Chap. 7; Townley, n. 215.

[217] Some matters are excluded from the competition rules by the Treaties themselves: e.g. national security connected with the production or trade in arms (Art. 346 TFEU; for the application of this in the context of mergers, see Chap. 15). For the position of undertakings entrusted with services of general economic interest, see Art. 106(2) TFEU, discussed in Chap. 8.

[218] See Townley, n. 215, Chap. 2.

Examples of the former are the CJ's exclusion of collective bargaining agreements between employer and employees on the ground that such arrangements fall within the ambit of social policy,[219] and cases finding that an entity is not an 'undertaking' and its agreements or conduct therefore not subject to the competition rules.[220]

The EUMR contains specific provisions on the ability of Member States to take account of certain public policy considerations in respect of mergers to which the Regulation applies.[221] In respect of antitrust, the issue has arisen mainly in respect of Article 101 and is therefore discussed in Chapter 4.

10. INDUSTRIAL POLICY

There is a particular question of the relationship of competition law to the EU's industrial policy.[222] 'Industrial policy' can be defined in many ways, but at its widest it includes all State acts and policies which relate to industry. It can encompass such policies as employment, protecting domestic industry from foreign competition, regional development, encouraging 'national champions', and fostering particular sectors. Industrial policy may also be 'horizontal' and aimed at 'competitiveness' across the whole economy.[223] The EU's industrial policy provision is now Article 173 TFEU.[224] It adopts a competitiveness strategy:

The Union and the Member States shall ensure that the conditions necessary for the competitiveness of the Union's industry exist.[225]

This entails speeding up the adjustment of industry to structural changes; encouraging an environment favourable to initiative and to the development of small and medium-sized undertakings (SMEs); encouraging an environment favourable to cooperation between undertakings; and fostering better exploitation of the industrial potential of policies of innovation, research, and technological development.[226] However, nothing in Article 173 can provide a basis for Union measures which, inter alia, 'could lead to a distortion of the competition'.[227]

In 2004 the Commission issued a Communication, *A pro-active competition policy for a competitive Europe*,[228] which set competition at the heart of industrial policy rather than in opposition to it. The Commission said that '[T]he goal of a pro-active competition policy is to support the competitive process in the internal market and to induce firms to engage in competitive and dynamically efficiency-enhancing behaviour'. This was in the context of the Lisbon Strategy[229] whereby the EU

---

[219] Case C-67/96, *Albany International BV v Stichting Bedrijfspensioenfonds Textielindustrie* [1999] ECR I-6025: see Chap. 3.

[220] E.g., Case C-205/03 P, *Federación Nacional de Empresas de Instrumentación Científica, Médica, Técnica y Dental (FENIN) v Commission* [2006] ECR I-6295 (CJ, aff'g Case T-319/99, *FENIN v Commission* [2003] ECR II-357); Cases C-264, 306, 354, and 355/01, *AOK Bundesverband and others v Ichtyol-Gesellschaft Cordes and others* [2004] ECR I-2493: see further Chaps. 3 and 8.

[221] Council Reg. 139/2004 [2004] OJ L124/1, Art. 21(4); see Chap. 15.

[222] See W. Sauter, *Competition Law and Industrial Policy in the EU* (Oxford University Press, 1997); N. Petit and N. Neyrinck, 'Industrial Policy and Competition Enforcement: Is there, Could There and Should There Be a Nexus?', Global Competition Law Centre Conference 2012, <http://papers.ssrn.com/sol3/papers.cfm?abstract_id=2225903>.

[223] See Petit and Neyrinck, n. 222, for an account of the different forms of industrial policies.

[224] Previously Art. 157 EC.

[225] Art. 173(1) TFEU.

[226] Art. 173(1).

[227] Art. 173(3).

[228] COM(2004)293 final.

[229] Originally declared at the Lisbon European Council in March 2000 and relaunched in February 2005 in the Communication of the Commission to the Spring European Council, *Working together for growth and jobs: A new start for the Lisbon Strategy*, COM(2005)24, 2 February 2005.

set itself the strategic goal of becoming the most competitive and dynamic knowledge-based economy in the world by 2010, capable of sustainable economic growth and more and better jobs and greater social cohesion.

The Lisbon Agenda was replaced for the current decade with the 'EU 2020' strategy, which required 'well functioning markets where competition and consumer access stimulate growth and innovation' in order to gear the single market to serve the goals of EU 2020.[230] In the 2011 Competition Report the Commission said:

Competition enforcement and advocacy also serve other wider longer-term objectives such as enhancing consumer welfare, supporting the EU's growth, jobs and competitiveness in line with the Europe 2020 Strategy for smart, sustainable and inclusive growth.[231]

The two areas of competition policy most likely to be relevant to industrial policy are merger control and State aid.[232] However, an analysis of possible industrial policy influence on Commission merger decisions has not shown industrial policy considerations to systematically override competition-related ones.[233]

On the new Commission's assumption of office in 2014 President Junker's Mission Letter to the Competition Commissioner exhorted her to focus, inter alia, on:

Mobilising competition policy tools and market expertise so that they contribute, as appropriate, to our jobs and growth agenda, including in areas such as the digital single market, energy policy, financial services, industrial policy and the fight against tax evasion. In this context, it will be important to keep developing an economic as well as a legal approach to the assessment of competition issues and to further develop market monitoring in support of the broader activities of the Commission.[234]

The Commissioner has said that competition enforcement is 'a political endeavour in the EU' in that it plays a role in the process of European integration and helps the Commission reach its overall goals. Nevertheless 'decision-making in individual competition cases cannot be bent to political priorities' and competition enforcement 'follows its own principles and rules—and they are cast in stone'.[235]

11. THE APPLICATION OF COMPETITION LAW

A. FORM, EFFECTS, AND THEORIES OF HARM

The EU competition provisions are drafted in broad terms. Article 101 TFEU covers the prohibition of restrictive agreements, Article 102 TFEU deals with abuses of market power ('dominant position'), and the EUMR is intended to preclude mergers which would significantly impede effective competition. The Commission and the EU Courts have been subjected to much criticism over the

---

[230] Commission Working Document, 'Consultation on the Future "EU 2020" Strategy', COM(2009)647 final, 9–10.

[231] Commission Report on Competition Policy 2011, 9. See also Commissioner Almunia, 'Industrial policy and Competition policy: Quo vadis Europa?', 10 February 2012, SPEECH/12/83, <http://europa.eu/rapid/press-release_SPEECH-12-83_en.pdf>.

[232] See the Online Resource Centre for the State aid chapter. Commissioner Vestager has stated that it is her role to support the Commission's energy policy by ensuring that subsidies do not distort the market, see <http://ec.europa.eu/commission/2014-2019/vestager/announcements/values-competition-policy_en>, 13 October 2015.

[233] Petit and Neyrinck, n. 222, 25–29. The Commissioner commented on the prohibited merger between Deutsche Börse and NYSE Euronext (M.6166, IP/12/94, 1 February 2012) that the price of creating a European champion would have been harm to customers (SPEECH/12/131, 28 February 2012). There is evidence, however, that the Commission has used its merger regulation powers to open up the market in network industries, see Petit and Neyrinck, 28.

[234] <http//:ec.europa.eu/commission/sites/cwt/files/commissioner_mission_letters/vestager_en.pdf>. Some of these matters, particularly tax evasion, relate to State aid rather than to antitrust and mergers. For the Digital Single Market strategy, see Section 12, p. 50.

[235] Speech, 'The Values of Competition Law', <http://ec.europa.eu/commission/2014-2019/vestager/announcements/values-competition-policy_en>, 13 October 2015.

years for failing to take a sufficiently economically rigorous approach to the application of the provisions and for instead adopting a 'form-based' approach. This means prohibiting certain agreements or conduct as a matter of course because they are presumed to be anti-competitive, without examining their actual or likely effects in the particular case. The process of 'modernisation' has included a move towards the application of a proper 'effects-based' approach and the Commission has displayed a greater determination to use rigorous economic analysis in its decision-making. This is one meaning of the 'more economic approach' as discussed in Section 8.[236] It will be seen in Chapter 4 that in respect of Article 101 it was the EU Courts which took the lead in moving away from a form-based approach to a more effects-based analysis.[237] The effects-based approach is taken in the Article 101(3) Guidelines which the Commission issued in 2004 to accompany Regulation 1/2003[238] and in all the Guidelines it has published since in respect of the application of Article 101 to particular types of agreement.[239] The Commission's determination to follow a 'more economic' approach was epitomised by the creation of the post of Chief Competition Economist in 2003 in the wake of a number of merger cases in which the GC annulled prohibition decisions of the Commission for inadequate economic reasoning.[240] The situation over an effects-based approach to Article 102 is still confused and a matter of dispute. The Commission Guidance on Article 102 enforcement priorities[241] adopted an effects-based approach, but the EU Courts have continued to eschew this in respect of some of the most heavily contested areas of Article 102, in particular exclusionary rebates. This is discussed in Chapter 7.

The application of competition rules prohibiting agreements, conduct, or mergers should ideally require the party alleging that the competition rules have been infringed to spell out a convincing *theory of harm*. In the following extract two economists set out the characteristics of a well-developed theory of harm.

H. Zenger and M. Walker, 'Theories of Harm in European Competition Law: A Progress Report' in J. Bourgeois and D. Waelbrock (eds.), *Ten Years of Effects-based Approach in EU Competition Law* (Bruylant, 2012), 185 and available at <http://ssrn.com/abstract=2009296>

The requirement to present a theory of harm imposes a logically consistent approach to the assessment of anti-competitive behaviour. If the theory of harm is made explicit by competition authorities, then this makes it much harder for internally inconsistent or speculative competition concerns to survive the process of assessment.

A well-developed theory of harm has the following characteristics:

- it should articulate how competition, and, ultimately, consumers will be harmed relative to an appropriately defined counter-factual;

---

[236] P. 40.

[237] Case C-234/89, *Delimitis v Henninger Bräu AG* [1991] ECR I-935 was of particular significance in this regard.

[238] See n. 176.

[239] Guidelines on the assessment of horizontal mergers [2004] OJ C31/03; Guidelines on the assessment of non-horizontal mergers [2008] OJ C265/7; Guidelines on vertical restraints [2010] OJ C130/1; Guidelines on horizontal co-operation agreements [2011] OJ C11/1; Guidelines on technology transfer agreements [2014] OJ L89/3.

[240] Case T-342/99, *Airtours plc v Commission* [2002] ECR II-2585; Case T-310/01, *Schneider Electric SA v Commission* [2002] ECR II-4071; Case T-5/02, *Tetra Laval BV v Commission* [2002] ECR II-4381, aff'd Case C-12/03 P, *Commission v Tetra Laval* [2005] ECR I-987.

[241] The Guidance Paper, n. 157.

- it should be internally logically consistent;
- it should be consistent with the incentives that the various parties face; and
- it should be consistent with (or at least not inconsistent with) the available empirical evidence.

Two important points should be noted in respect of the effects-based approach. First, adopting a consumer welfare objective and following an effects-based approach are not synonymous, although they are both part of 'modernisation' and are often both described as 'more economic'. It is possible to apply a consumer welfare standard while using form-based rules.[242] Secondly, there is a need for legal certainty in the application of competition law. It is not acceptable to have a system of competition law in which it is impossible for firms to tell in advance whether their agreements or arrangements comply with it, so an effects-based approach should contain the elements which make such judgments possible.

B. OVER- AND UNDER-ENFORCEMENT: TYPE 1 AND TYPE 2 ERRORS

One reason for using effects-based analysis is to achieve an optimal level of enforcement of the competition rules. Ideally EU law should avoid both over- and under-enforcement. Over-enforcement means prohibiting agreements, conduct, or mergers where there is no actual or likely anti-competitive harm. These are called Type 1 errors, or 'false positives'.[243] Under-enforcement means failing to prohibit such things where there is anti-competitive harm. These are called Type 2 errors, or 'false negatives'. Over-enforcement of competition rules may be as harmful as under-enforcement. Indeed, the generally prevailing view is that it is *more* harmful because preventing things which are in reality not anti-competitive chills pro-competitive activity and stunts innovation. Whether a competition law system is equally, or more, worried about Type 1 or Type 2 errors affects the entire way in which the law is applied.

C. THE USE OF ECONOMIC ANALYSIS

Both the consumer welfare standard and the effects-based approach involve extensive use of economic analysis[244] and undertakings involved in competition issues make heavy use of economists.[245] Economic analysis, however, does not necessarily tell the competition authority what the outcome of any given agreement or conduct will be. Economics employs assumptions, economists may come to different conclusions on any given matter, and economics does not provide the answer to every question. The economic view that monopoly is inefficient and that the exercise of market power leads to prices above the competitive level is only the starting point to the application of the law in any particular case. Furthermore, even if there is agreement that competition law should achieve consumer welfare, there can be disagreement about how allocative, productive, and dynamic efficiencies should be weighed against one another, what are the welfare implications of certain practices, or whether the protection of competitors in the short term is necessary to protect competition, and thus consumer welfare, in the longer term. We see these debates played out in

---

[242] And 'fairness' or 'economic freedom' objectives could be pursued through an effects-based approach, although that might be more difficult, see further Ahlborn and Piccinin, n. 143, 61.

[243] The way the terminology 'Type 1' and 'Type 2' errors is used is not standardised. Some commentators use the labels the other way round. However, this book uses Type 1 errors to describe false positives and Type 2 to describe under-enforcement.

[244] See D. Neven, 'Competition Economics and Antitrust in Europe' (2006) 21(48) *Oxford Review of Economic Policy* 742.

[245] For a highly critical view of this, see Wils, n. 143.

the cases discussed throughout this book. Merger control, for example, discussed in Chapter 15, involves predicting the future effects of transactions that have not yet taken place.

It was seen in Section 4 that there are fashions in economic theory and schools of antitrust analysis, and that today's orthodoxy may be overtaken by new ideas. Nevertheless, given that competition policy is concerned with economic structures, conduct, and effects, it must be correct that its application should be as economically sound as possible. Faull and Nikpay explain the advantages and limitations of economic analysis in competition cases.[246]

J. Faull and A. Nikpay (eds.), *The EU Law of Competition* (3rd edn, Oxford University Press, 2014), 3–4

1.02 The growing acceptance and importance of economics in competition policy raises questions regarding the usefulness of economics, both for devising competition rules and for deciding on competition cases. A word of caution is appropriate in this respect. Economic thinking and economic models have proved not to be perfect guides. . . .

1.03 Economic theories and models are built on and around assumptions. This approach has the benefit of making explicit the various elements relied upon in arriving at a particular conclusion or insight. At the same time, these assumptions by definition do not cover (all) real world situations. In addition, when the assumptions are changed the outcomes of the models may look very different. It is for these reasons that the application of economic theories may not always be able to give a clear and definitive answer, for example as to what will happen in a market when companies merge, or when companies try to collude or engage in specific types of conduct.

1.04 The best that the application of economic principles can do in general is to provide a coherent framework of analysis, to provide relevant lines of reasoning, to identify the main issues to be checked in the context of certain theories of competitive harm, and possibly to exclude certain outcomes. The application of empirical methods may further help to test the relevance of theories of harm. In this way, economics helps to tell the most plausible story. In individual cases, it will be necessary first to find the concepts and the model that best fit the actual market conditions of the case and then to proceed with the analysis of the actual or possible competition consequences. Economic insights can also be useful in the formulation of policy rules, indicating under what conditions anti-competitive outcomes are very unlikely, very likely, or rather likely, and helping to devise safe harbours.

---

12. THE NEW ECONOMY

The 'new economy' is a term which covers markets characterised by rapid innovation and technological change, such as electronic communications, software, computer hardware, search engines, internet-based businesses, social media, biotechnology, and aerospace. The features of these markets variously include the creation, exploitation of, and reliance on intellectual property rights; the need for complementary products, services, or platforms to work together; and a high degree of technical complexity and technological sophistication. In some of these markets 'network effects' or 'network externalities' are crucially important. Direct network effects means that the product becomes more valuable the more users it has (as with telephones and social media platforms); indirect network effects means that increases in the usage of one product increases the value of complementary ones (such as software and operating systems). New economy industries pose particular

---

[246] See also J. Briones, 'A Balance of the Impact of Economic Analysis on the EU Competition Policy' (2009) 32 *World Competition* 27; S. Bishop, 'Snake-oil with Mathematics is Still Snake-oil: Why Recent Trends in the Application of So-called "Sophisticated" Economics is Hindering Good Competition Enforcement' (2013) 9 *European Competition Journal* 67.

challenges for competition law. For example, competition between undertakings is not normally so much on price as on innovation (they may display 'Schumpterian rivalry');[247] the usual ways of defining markets may not work well, particularly if they involve multi-sided platforms;[248] and competition may not be *in* markets but *for* markets (markets may 'tip' towards one firm whose products become the standard).[249]

The new economy includes many two- (or multi-)sided markets (for convenience here described as 'multi-sided'). Multi-sided markets are markets in which firms have to compete simultaneously for more than one group of customers.[250] These markets are often described as 'platforms' although the exact definition of what constitutes a 'platform' is a matter of dispute.[251] Examples include games machine manufacturers who need customers to buy the consoles and game developers to write games for them, newspapers and other media which need to attract both advertisers and readers/viewers, and estate agents who need both buyers and sellers. For a multi-sided market to work there must be users or customers on both sides. A price rise to one side may lose sales to both groups and, indeed, it may be necessary to subsidise one side in order to attract the other. One side may even not be charged at all (estate agents may levy fees only on the successful seller, and newspapers may be given away free). There has been a recent explosion in online multi-sided platforms in the new economy, such as search engines, comparison shopping services, social media networks, payment systems, video-sharing, and online marketplaces. Platforms can be *transaction* or *non-transaction* markets.[252] In a transaction market the platform brings together users from each side and enables them to enter into transactions with each other. Examples are eBay, Airbnb, and payment cards. In a non-transaction market the two sides do not transact with each other. An example is social media sites, where the platform facility is provided free of charge to users on one side who interact between themselves but there is no (direct) transaction between the users and the advertisers on the other side who make use of their data.

There has long been discussion about the application of competition law to the new economy[253] but the recent rapid and exponential expansion in digital markets has given the matter more urgency. One argument is that as competition law must preserve the incentives for firms to innovate, the application of the rules to these markets should be modified to fully accommodate the dynamic competition there. It is even suggested that there is no need for antitrust intervention in high-tech markets because the pace of technological innovation, and low barriers to

---

[247] See Section 3.G, p. 12.

[248] For market definition and multi-sided platforms, see Section 15.B.

[249] Microsoft and its Windows operating system is the obvious instance. In the early 1980s the battle between the Betamax and VHS video formats was won by VHS to the total extinction of Betamax.

[250] There is an enormous literature on the theory of multi-sided markets. See, e.g., B. Caillaud and B. Julien, 'Chicken and Egg: Competition Among Intermediation Service Providers' (2003) 34(2) *RAND J of Economics* 309; J.-C. Rochet and J. Tirole, 'Platform Competition in Two-Sided Markets (2003) 1 *J of the European Economic Association* 990; D. S. Evans, 'The Antitrust Economics of Multi-sided Platform Markets' (2003) 20 *Yale J on Regulation* 325; J.-C. Rochet and J. Tirole, 'Two-sided Markets: A Progress Report (2006) 37(3) *RAND J of Economics* 645; M. Armstrong, 'Competition in Two-sided Markets' (2006) 37(3) *RAND J of Economics* 668; A. Lamadrid de Pablo, 'The Double Duality of Two-sided Markets' [2015] *Comp Law* 5; D. Auer and N. Petit, 'Two-sided Markets and the Challenge of Turning Economic Theory into Antitrust Policy', <http://ssrn.com/abstract=2552337>.

[251] See, for example, the problem of definition in the Commission's Consultation questionnaire, n. 267.

[252] L. Filistrucchi, D. Geradin, E. van Damme, and P. Affeldt, 'Market Definition in Two-sided Markets: Theory and Practice' (2014) 10(2) *J of Competition Law and Economics* 293.

[253] See, e.g., J. Temple Lang, 'European Community Antitrust Law—Innovation Markets and High Technology Industries' [1996] *Fordham Corp L Inst* 519; C. Veljanovski, 'EC Antitrust in the New Economy: Is the European Commission's View of the Network Economy Right?' [2001] *ECLR* 115; C. Ahlborn, D. S. Evans, and A. J. Padilla, 'Competition Policy in the New Economy: Is European Competition Law up to the Challenge?' [2001] *ECLR* 156; M. Monti, 'Defining the Boundaries, Competition Policy in High Tech Sectors', Speech at UBS Warburg Conference, Barcelona, 11 September 2001; D. S. Evans and R. Schmalensee, 'Some Economic Aspects of Antitrust Analysis in Dynamically Competitive Industries', NBER Working Paper 8268, May 2001; R. Lind and P. Muysert, 'Innovation and Competition Policy: Challenges for the New Millennium' [2003] *ECLR* 87.

entry, make it impossible to maintain entrenched positions of market power.[254] The Commission does not agree with this[255] and does not refrain from enforcing competition law in new economy markets.[256] Indeed, at the time of writing the Commission has instituted proceedings against Google in a controversial application of Article 102 to 'net neutrality'.[257] Conversely, it has been suggested that 'ordinary' competition law may be unable to deal adequately with the challenges of the digital economy and that new instruments, or a 'law of the platform', may be needed. The European Commission launched its Digital Single Market Strategy (DSMS) in May 2015[258] which raised a number of concerns about the growing influence of online platforms. Pursuant to this governments of the Member States have examined the issues.[259] Some European politicians and others, concerned with what they perceive as the inordinate power of companies such as Google and Amazon, have argued that online platforms should not be left to the ordinary competition rules but should be subject to a specific regime of regulation. In September 2015 the Commission launched a public consultation, further to the DSMS, on 'the regulatory environment for platforms, online intermediaries, data and cloud computing and the collaborative economy'.[260] The Commission also launched an inquiry into the e-commerce sector,[261] within the framework of the DSMS, under the powers in Article 17 of Regulation 1/2003[262] in order to examine the problems raised by new forms of digital distribution and online selling.[263]

There are particular concerns about 'big data', which means the structured, unstructured, and semi-structured data which is produced in great volume and variety and at great velocity by every transaction, interaction, and social media exchange online, and through mobile devices, sensors, and so on, and which has the potential to be 'mined'.[264] As the Competition Commissioner remarked, 'These incredibly powerful tools, like search engines and social media, are available for free. In many cases, that's because we as consumers have a new currency that we can use to pay for them—our data.'[265] Big data issues, particularly the protection of privacy, are major features of the DSMS, but the Commission's view is that privacy problems are not a matter for competition law. Competition law should rather concern itself with big data as an asset.[266]

It is submitted that it would not be desirable to subject certain areas of the digital economy to some 'special' regime of competition law, not least because of the difficulties of delineating what

---

[254] See Chap. 6, Section 6.E.

[255] Alexander Italianer, 'Level Playing-field and Innovation in Technology Markets', Conference on Antitrust in Technology, Palo Alto, 28 January 2013, <http://www.ec.europa.eu/competition/speeches/text/sp2013_01_en.pdf>.

[256] See, e.g., Case C-202/07 P, *France Télécom v Commission* [2009] ECR I-2369; Case T-201/04, *Microsoft* [2007] ECR II-3601; COMP/40.099, *Google (Android)*, IP/15/4780, MEMO/15/4782.

[257] COMP/39.740, *Google*, IP/15/4780, MEMO/15/4781, discussed in Chap. 7, Section 14.D.

[258] <http://ec.europa.eu/priorities/digital-single-market/index_en.htm; IP/15/4919>.

[259] In the UK the issue was dealt with by the House of Lords Select Sub-Committee on the EU Internal Market, <http://www.parliament.uk/business/committees/committees-a-z/lords-select/eu-internal-market-subcommittee/inquiries/parliament-2015/online-platforms/>.

[260] <https://ec.europa.eu/digital-agenda/en/news/public-consultation-regulatory-environment-platforms-online-intermediaries-data-and-cloud>.

[261] IP/15/4919.

[262] See Chap. 9, Section 4.C.ii.

[263] See Chap. 11. The Commission announced its preliminary findings from the inquiry on 18 March 2016, IP/16/922. These confirmed the Commission's suspicions of the prevalence of geo-blocking, i.e. preventing consumers from purchasing goods and accessing digital content online across the EU.

[264] The EU is in the process of adopting a new General Data Protection Reg.

[265] Margrethe Vestager, 'Competition in a Big Data World', Speech, 18 January 2016, <http://ec.europa.eu/commission/2014-2019/vestager/announcements/competition-big-data-world_en>.

[266] Ibid. See also Director-General Laitenberger, 'The Digital Single Market, Consumers and EU Competition Policy, Speech, 21 September 2015, <http://ec.europa.eu/competition/speeches/text/sp2016_01_en.pdf>; D. Sokol and R. Comerford, 'Does Antitrust Have a Role to Play in Regulating Big Data?', <http://ssrn.com/abstract=2723693>.

kind of 'platform' such a regime would cover[267] and of making meaningful economic or legal distinctions between one form of transaction and another.[268] There is no evidence yet that 'ordinary' competition law, itself a fluid and ever-developing area of law, cannot cope with the new phenomena. As for regulation, we see in Section 13, that regulation should be used only where competition law is unable to deal with market failures and such inability in respect of digital markets has yet to be demonstrated.

13. EU COMPETITION LAW AND REGULATION

Since the last quarter of the twentieth century many State-owned, and often vertically integrated, monopolies throughout Europe have been wholly or partly privatised.[269] Sectors previously monopolised by State enterprises legally protected from competition have been opened up, a process known as liberalisation. The EU has pursued a far-reaching programme of liberalisation and harmonisation in respect of the transport, postal services, energy, and telecommunications (electronic communications) markets.[270] However liberalisation can lead, at least in the short term, to private monopolies replacing public ones. There are particular problems in sectors where the provision of services depends on the use of network infrastructures (such as railway lines or telephone lines) which cannot feasibly be duplicated and where control of the network may create a 'bottleneck' monopoly which hinders downstream competitors. Moreover, some services—such as the supply of water, sewage, and basic postal services—may need to be the subject of a public service obligation such as 'universal service' (USO). As the market does not provide satisfactory outcomes to these problems (i.e. there is 'market failure'), the liberalised sectors are often subject to 'regulation'. Regulation 'consists of public interventions which affect the operation of markets through command and control'.[271] This typically involves setting up a regulatory body which implements controls on prices and quality, fixes terms of contracts, mandates and polices access by downstream competitors, and oversees the obligations of the undertaking such as the USO.[272] There are at present no EU-wide regulators as such[273] although EU law may provide for a regulatory regime in Member States through regulations and directives. The relevant EU sector legislation may require the establishment

---

[267] The Commission's list of examples of platforms in its consultation questionnaire has been criticised as including undertaking such as Netflix which appear to be straightforward distributors rather than a platform.

[268] For a good review of the arguments, see <http://chillingcompetition.com/2015/11/24/> (Alfonso Lamadrid de Pablo); K. Coates, 'An Emerging Competition Law for a New Economy? Introductory Remarks for the Chillin Competition Panel', <http://twentyfirstcentury competition.com>, 21 January 2016; J. Verhaert, 'The Challenges involved with the Application of Article 102 TFEU to the New Economy: A Case Study of Google' [2014] *ECLR* 265; M. Kadar, 'European Competition Law in the Digital Era', <http://ssrn/com/abract=2703062>. On 4 April 2016 the governments of ten Member States (Bulgaria, the Czech Republic, Denmark, Estonia, Latvia, Lithuania, Luxembourg, Poland, Sweden, and the UK) sent a joint letter to the Commission urging it to desist from new ex ante regulation of online platforms.

[269] Private rather than public ownership is a major plank of the neoliberal ideology which drives globalised capitalism.

[270] It has been pursued through directives adopted under the special procedure laid down in Art. 106(3) TFEU and through Council harmonisation directives under Art. 114 TFEU (ex Art. 95 EC).

[271] T. Prosser, *Law and the Regulators* (Oxford University Press, 1997), 4. See generally, Dunne, n. 97.

[272] Prosser, n. 271, 5–6. Obviously this is a generality. The functions of the regulators differ between sectors and different States organise regulation differently. The regulators in the UK include OFWAT (water), OFGEM (energy), the Rail Regulator, and, pursuant to the Communications Act 2003, OFCOM.

[273] Though note that the expression 'regulator' is often used loosely to mean 'competition authority'. As far as EU-wide sector regulators are concerned, the Commission proposed an EU-wide authority for electronic communications during negotiations on the reform of the electronic communications legislation. The Member States did not accept this. Instead a new body, the Body of European Regulators for Electronic Communications (BEREC) consisting of the heads of the 27 Member States' NCAs, was created, Reg. 1211/2009 [2009] OJ L239/1.

of an independent national regulatory authority (NRA) and specify in detail the powers and duties it must possess. Under the 2009 electronic telecommunications reform package[274] the Commission may become closely involved in regulatory remedies chosen by the NRAs.

Although it has been persuasively argued that competition law is 'conceptually very similar' to some types of regulation, namely the type of regulation that encourages or promotes competitive markets, rather than that which pursues public policy objectives (some regulation pursues both),[275] there are differences between regulation and competition law.[276]

First, regulation normally acts *ex ante* (in advance) whereas competition law (other than merger control) normally acts *ex post* (reacting to conduct which is taking place or has taken place).[277] Where prices are concerned, for example, a regulator sets out in advance what the undertaking may charge while a competition authority will step in only if and when it appears that an undertaking's pricing infringes the competition rules. On the other hand, the desire of undertakings to comply with competition laws means that in practice competition law does have considerable *ex ante* effect.[278]

Secondly, regulatory agencies often possess more extensive and detailed information about the whole industry and the wider issues affecting the market than do competition authorities. The latter concentrate on the specific conduct in issue.

Thirdly, competition authorities generally try to avoid behavioural remedies whereas sector regulators provide detailed rules on matters such as prices and conditions which require close monitoring. Regulation is more *dirigiste* than competition law.

Fourthly, the position of a regulator may be affected by its closeness to the market players and to the government (despite liberalisation many States retain a financial stake in former State-owned monopolies).

Fifthly, regulation may be a transitory phase which is replaced by competition law in the long term.

The last point is important. Sector regulation should be put in place only where competition law is unable to deal with market failures. The European Commission may ultimately veto the decision of an NRA to subject a particular market to *ex ante* regulation if it thinks it unnecessary. The Commission favours the replacement of regulation with competition law whenever possible.[279] In the 2009 Electronic Communications Directive the Commission looked forward to a time when the sector is no longer subject to *ex ante* regulation:

The aim is progressively to reduce *ex-ante* sector specific rules as competition in the markets develops and, ultimately, for electronic communications to be governed by competition law only. Considering that

---

[274] See Dir. 2009/140/EC [2009] OJ L337/3 on a common regulatory framework for electronic communications, and Dir. 2009/136 [2009] OJ L137/11, which amend the electronics communications directives of 2002 (21/2002, 22/2002, 58/2002).

[275] Coates, n. 96, 2.03–2.04.

[276] P.-A. Buigues and R. Klotz, 'Margin Squeeze in Regulated Industries: The CFI Judgment in the *Deutsche Telekom* Case' (2008) *GCP* (July (1)) 1, 17; J. C. Laguna de Paz, 'Regulation and Competition Law' [2012] *ECLR* 77; R. O'Donoghue and A. J. Padilla, *The Law and Economics of Article 102* (3rd edn, Hart Publishing, 2013), 45–47; N. Dunne, 'Between Competition Law and Regulation: Hybridised Approaches to Market Control' (2014) 2 *J of Antitrust Enforcement* 225.

[277] Monopoly control is generally *ex post*, and so, in the current regime under Reg. 1/2003, is the control of anti-competitive agreements (although there is the possibility of interim measures or injunctions). Merger control is *ex ante* (the EU merger regime requires prior notification of mergers with a 'Community dimension', see Chap. 15). R. O'Donoghue and A. J. Padilla, *The Law and Economics of Article 102* (2nd edn, Hart Publishing, 2013), 44–47.

[278] Coates, n. 96, 2.2.17–2.2.19.

[279] For example, see Commission Recommendation on relevant product and service markets within the electronic communications sector susceptible to *ex ante* regulation in accordance with Directive 2002/21/EC on a common regulatory framework for electronic communications networks and services [2007] OJ L344/65, which sets out three cumulative criteria to be applied in determining whether a market is one in which *ex ante* regulation may be warranted.

the markets for electronic communications have shown strong competitive dynamics in recent years, it is essential that *ex-ante* regulatory obligations only be imposed where there is no effective and sustainable competition.[280]

Competition laws can apply to regulated sectors concurrently with regulatory regimes.[281] Member States vary as to whether NRAs may apply competition rules as well as regulatory rules.[282] The relationship between sector-specific regulation and EU competition law was clarified in *Deutsche Telekom*[283] and *Telefónica*[284] in which the EU Courts held that an undertaking could infringe Article 102 by applying a pricing policy which constituted an abusive 'margin squeeze' even though the prices had been approved by the national telecommunications regulator, as the competition rules supplemented by *ex post* review the legislative framework adopted by the Union legislator for *ex ante* regulation of the telecommunications market.[285] The CJ and GC held that regulatory approval does not remove an undertaking's liability for infringing the competition rules unless the restrictive effects of its conduct are caused wholly by the national law and the undertaking has no room for manoeuvre.[286] The Commission cannot be bound by a decision taken by a national body[287] which, although bound to respect the Treaty provisions, operates under national law which might have different sectoral objectives to Union law.[288] The position is different in the US where the Supreme Court has declined to apply ordinary competition law (s. 2 of the Sherman Act) to conduct in the regulated telecommunications sector on the grounds that it is the regulatory regime which is designed to deter and remedy anti-competitive harm.[289] The Supreme Court does not want to impose upon undertakings intervention from two different sources. However, the US has a federal sector regulation regime[290] so the dynamics of the relationship with federal antitrust law are different from those of the relationship between EU competition law and national regulation in the Member States.

In the EU the pharmaceutical sector is also subject to regulation but not in the way, and for the reasons, previously discussed. Regulation of the pharmaceutical sector arises from the operation of the national healthcare systems in the Member States and the resulting interest of the Member States in controlling, directly or indirectly, the price of pharmaceuticals. The differing national regimes of price controls lead to wide variations in prices between Member States.[291] The degree of price regulation in this sector is a major factor in competition cases concerning parallel trade in

---

[280] Dir. 2009/140/EC, n. 274, recital 5.

[281] See G. Monti, 'Managing the Intersection of Utilities Regulation and EC Competition Law' (2008) 4 *Competition Law Review* 121.

[282] In the UK the sector regulators have concurrent powers to apply the Competition Act 1998 and the Enterprise Act 2002 in their sectors. See generally *Butterworths Competition Law* (Butterworths, looseleaf), Div. IX.

[283] Case C-280/08 P, *Deutsche Telekom* [2010] ECR I-9555. See D. Geradin and R. O'Donoghue, 'The Concurrent Application of Competition Law and Regulation: The Case of Margin Squeeze Abuses in the Telecommunications Sector' (2005) 1 J *of Competition Law and Economics* 355, GCLC Working Paper 04/05, 51–65.

[284] Case T-336/07, *Telefónica* EU:T:2012:172, aff'd Case C-295/12 P, *Telefónica* EU:C:2014:2062; Case T-398/07, *Spain v European Commission* EU:T:2012:173. See also COMP/39.525, *Telekomunikacja Polska* 22 June 2011; Case T-486/11, *Orange Polska SA v Commission* EU:T:2015:1002; D. Kamiński, A. Rogozińska, and B. Sasinowska, '*Telekomunikacja Polska* Decision: Competition Law Enforcement in Regulated Markets' (2011) 3 *Competition Policy Newsletter* 3.

[285] Case C-280/08 P, *Deutsche Telekom* [2010] ECR I-9555, para. 92. See further Chap. 7.

[286] Ibid., paras. 80–89.

[287] Ibid., para. 90.

[288] Case T-271/03, *Deutsche Telekom* [2008] ECR II-477, para. 113.

[289] *Verizon Communications Inc v Trinko LLP*, 540 US 398, 124 S.Ct 872 (2004), see Chap. 7.

[290] See Hovenkamp, n. 46, Chap. 19.

[291] There are also EU harmonisation measures in the pharmaceutical sector, see particularly Dir. 2001/83/EC on the Community code relating to medicinal products for human use [2001] OJ L211/67 and Council Dir. 89/105 on transparency of measures regulating the prices of medicinal products for human use and their inclusion in the scope of national health insurance systems [1989] OJ L40/8.

pharmaceuticals.[292] The Commission conducted a sector inquiry into the pharmaceutical sector which reported in 2009.[293]

As seen in Section 12 there is currently a debate in the EU about the desirability of subjecting online platforms to a regulatory regime amid fears in some quarters that competition law cannot adequately deal with perceived market failures in those markets.

14. COMPETITION LAW AND THE INTERNATIONAL CONTEXT

The effects of anti-competitive practices and the exercise of market power can be felt in States far away from that in which the undertaking concerned is located. Many undertakings in today's globalised economy are truly 'multinational' in the sense that they have a presence throughout the world. One of the most important issues in competition law is the international application and enforcement of competition laws and there are increasing developments in international cooperation in competition matters. States throughout the world, including many developing countries, have put in place systems of competition law. The international aspects of competition law arise throughout this book, but are discussed as a whole in Chapter 16.

15. MARKET POWER, MARKET DEFINITION, AND BARRIERS TO ENTRY

A. MARKET POWER

Economists usually define market power as the ability to price above short-run marginal cost and, in the long run, above average total cost.[294] Therefore firms that, individually or collectively, are able to restrict output, increase prices above the competitive level, and earn monopoly profits are said to have market power. Concomitantly, they can influence the variety or quality of goods or services, innovation, and the other parameters of competition.[295] Most firms have some market power in the short term,[296] but it is 'substantial' market power which endures for a significant period of time that matters.[297] In this section we introduce the concepts of market definition and barriers to entry which are central to the assessment of market power in EU competition law and to the discussion throughout this book.

In 1981 a seminal paper by William Landes and Richard Posner triggered a continuing debate about the assessment of market power and the point at which the degree of market power warrants antitrust proceedings.[298] Landes and Posner advocated the use of the Lerner index to assess market power.[299] This expresses the concept of market power 'as the setting of price in excess of marginal

---

[292] Cases C-468–478/06, *Sot. Lélos* [2008] ECR I-7139; Case C-501/06, *GlaxoSmithKline* [2009] ECR I-9291.

[293] See Chap. 9, Section 4.C.

[294] See Carlton and Perloff, n. 19, 642; Bishop and Walker, n. 70, 3-002; Faull and Nikpay, n. 7, 1.22. For market power in EU competition law generally, see L. Ortiz Blanco, *Market Power in EU Antitrust Law* (Hart Publishing, 2012).

[295] Guidance Paper, see n. 202, para. 11.

[296] For instance, customers and competitors will need time to react to the price increase.

[297] There are other concepts of market power, such as the power to exclude competitors, which are also relevant to competition law; Monti, n. 96, 124–127; Bishop and Walker, n. 70, 3-041; and see Chap. 6.

[298] W. M. Landes and R. A. Posner, 'Market Power in Antitrust Cases' (1981) 94 *Harvard LR* 937. See the discussion in J. Vickers, 'Market Power in Competition Cases' (2006) 2 *European Competition Journal* 3.

[299] A. P. Lerner, 'The Concept of Monopoly and the Measurement of Monopoly Power' (1934) *Review of Economic Studies* 157.

cost by measuring the proportional deviation of price at the firm's profit-maximizing output from the firm's marginal costs at that output'.[300]

There are two ways of measuring a firm's market power, 'direct' and 'indirect'. The 'direct' method involves estimating the market power by using econometric methods, particularly the residual demand curve (the demand curve facing a single firm).[301] This requires data which is often not available and even if it is the estimation of market power in this way may prove problematic, but it has considerable support amongst economists.[302]

The 'indirect' method involves a structural approach. First, the 'relevant market' is defined and, secondly, the power on that market of the undertaking under review is assessed using market share and 'barriers to entry' analysis. Barriers to entry are vital to the determination of market power by this method since it is these which enable a firm already in the market to earn monopoly profits without attracting other firms to enter that market. The 'indirect' method is the one most commonly used by competition authorities throughout the world.[303] It is used by the European Commission[304] and has the imprimatur of the CJ.[305]

Under the 'indirect' method, therefore, the determination of the relevant market (or 'antitrust market', the concept of the relevant market is unique to competition law[306]) is of crucial importance. This raises the important question of how a market is identified and defined.[307]

The size of a firm's market share, both in absolute terms and relative to those of its competitors, is the usual starting point for assessing market power.[308] It is not normally sufficient on its own for, as already noted, a more detailed analysis of the economic features of the market, such as barriers to entry, will also be required in order to determine the competitive constraints to which the firm is subject. However, in some areas of EU competition law market share stands proxy

---

[300] Van den Bergh and Camesasca, n. 32, 110, give the simplest formulation as $L = (P − MC)/P$. See also Vickers, n. 298, 4–6.

[301] Called 'residual' as it is demand not met by other firms in the market: see Carlton and Perloff, n. 19, 66–69.

[302] For the arguments, see Motta, n. 31, 116–117; Vickers, n. 298, 7. See also J. B. Baker and T. F. Bresnahan, 'Estimating the Residual Demand Curve Facing a Single Firm' (1988) 6 *International J of Industrial Organization* 283; Monti, n. 96, 290, 150–153; J. A. Keyte and N. R. Stoll, 'Markets? We Don't Need No Stinking Markets! The FTC and Market Definition' (2004) 49 *Ant Bull* 593; S. Bhattacharya and R. Van den Bergh, n. 16, 533–535; L. Kaplow, 'Why (Ever) Define Markets?' (2010) 124 *Harvard LR* 437 (in which the author argues that 'the market definition process is incoherent as a matter of basic economic principle and hence should be abandoned entirely') and see the discussion of this article in *Antitrust Bulletin* Special Issue: Louis Kaplow, 'Why (Ever) Define Markets?' (2012) 57(4) *Ant Bull.*

[303] However, the revised US Horizontal Merger Guidelines published by the DOJ and FTC in 2010 (<http://www/justice.gov/atr/file/810276/download>) introduced Upward Pricing Pressure as an alternative to market definition in the assessment of mergers of firms producing differentiated products (Section 6.1). The Upward Pricing Pressure concept was developed in the work of Farrell and Shapiro (see the updated version, J. Farrell and C. Shapiro, 'Antitrust Evaluation of Horizontal Mergers: An Economic Alternative to Market Definition' Working Paper, 5 February 2010, <http://faculty.haas.berkeley.edu/shapiro/alternative.pdf>). It uses the value of diverted sales to measure the extent of the competitive constraint on a merging firm's product that is eliminated by the merger; see, e.g., OECD Policy Roundtable on market definition, DAF/COMP(2012)19, <http://www.oecd.org/daf/competition/Marketdefinition2012.pdf>, 5.1; G. das Varma, 'Will Use of the Upward Pressure Test Lead to an Increase in the Level of Merger Enforcement?' (2009) 24(1) *Antitrust* 27; J. J. Simons and M. B. Coate, 'Upward Pressure on Price Analysis: Issues and Implications for Merger Policy' (2010) 6 *European Competition Journal* 377; M. B. Coate and J. H. Fischer, 'Is Market Definition Still Needed After All These Years' (2014) 2(2) *J of Antitrust Enforcement* 422.

[304] Commissioner Almunia said that 'snazzier analytical tools' do not make the intermediate step of market definitions unnecessary, but that these tools are complementary. He gave the example of the *Unilever/Sara Lee* merger as a case in which market definition and various economic methods were all used. SPEECH 11/561, 8 September 2011.

[305] Case 6/72, *Continental Can* [1973] ECR 215, para. 32 and subsequent case law: see Section 15.B.ii, p. 57 and Chap. 6.

[306] 'Antitrust market' includes markets in merger cases, although the Commission now uses 'antitrust' to denote areas of competition law other than mergers.

[307] On market definition generally, see the OECD Roundtable document, DAF/COMP(2012), n. 303, 19. See also, in respect of Art. 102 TFEU, the discussion in Chap. 6.

[308] See the Guidance Paper, n. 157, para. 13 and Chap. 6.

for market power. The current thinking of the Commission, in line with mainstream economic theory, is that many agreements between undertakings are not anti-competitive unless a degree of market power is present, although that degree may be less than that required to put an undertaking into a 'dominant position' for the purpose of Article 102. Block exemption regulations, which exempt categories of agreements from the prohibition in Article 101(1) TFEU, are therefore drafted to apply only to situations in which the undertakings' market shares are below certain thresholds.[309] This approximation of market share with market power is simplistic but considered the most practicable way of enabling the block exemptions to be applied. The use of market share as the sole determinant is likely to overestimate rather than underestimate the market power of the undertakings concerned.[310]

B. MARKET DEFINITION AND EU COMPETITION LAW

(i) The Importance of Market Definition

It is only by defining the relevant market that a firm's market power can be assessed by the 'indirect' method. The purpose of defining the relevant market is to identify which products are such close substitutes for one another that they exert competitive pressure on the behaviour of the suppliers of those products. Suppose, for example, you are suspicious that Y, the only producer of yellow widgets, is exercising market power and engaging in monopoly pricing. A preliminary question which must be asked is whether or not the product has substitutes to which customers could easily turn. If it does, then if Y raises prices it will lose customers. If customers can buy blue widgets, which are perfect substitutes, from other firms a rise in the price of yellow widgets will lead customers to buy (cheaper) blue ones instead. Saying that Y has a 'monopoly' over the sale of yellow widgets is meaningless in economic terms. Similarly, suppose Y is the sole manufacturer of all colours of widgets. Y will still not be able to raise prices without losing customers if blodgets, which are made by other firms which can expand output, are perfect substitutes for widgets. The problem of market definition is that it is often difficult to decide which products or services are in the same market. It is obvious, for example, that steel beams and chewing-gum are not in the same market, but what about coffee and tea, vodka and whisky, bananas and apples, Eurostar and cross-Channel ferries?

It is important to remember that market definition is not an end in itself. Rather, it is 'a tool for aiding the competitive assessment by identifying those substitute products or services which provide an effective constraint on the competitive behaviour of the products or services being offered in the market by the parties under investigation'.[311] So the guiding principle is that a relevant market is 'something worth monopolising'.[312]

We now consider how the relevant market has been defined for the purposes of EU competition law. We also outline the way in which the EU institutions go about, or should go about, actually determining what the relevant market is in any given case.[313]

---

[309] So below the threshold there is a 'safe harbour'. See, e.g., Commission Reg. 330/2010 [2010] OJ L102/1 on vertical restraints, Chap. 11; Commission Reg. 1217/2010 [2010] OJ L335/36 on research and development agreements, and Commission Reg. 1218/2010 [2010] OJ L335/43 on specialisation agreements, Chap. 10; Commission Reg. 316/2014 on technology transfer agreements [2014] OJ L93/17, Chap. 12.

[310] For the reasons why this is so, see Section 15.C.i, p. 79.

[311] Bishop and Walker, n. 70, 4-002.

[312] Ibid., 4-005.

[313] See further Faull and Nikpay, n. 7, 1.134–1.189; O'Donoghue and Padilla, n. 276, Chap. 3.

(ii) The Definition of the Relevant Market

The definition of the relevant market is necessary in EU competition law in respect of the following:

- the application Article 101 TFEU, where the determination of the market is ordinarily necessary before it can be determined whether or not an agreement has as its appreciable effect the prevention, restriction, or distortion of competition;[314]

- the determination of whether or not an agreement *appreciably* restricts inter-Member State trade;[315]

- the determination of whether or not an agreement substantially eliminates competition in the internal market for the purposes of Article 101(3);

- the determination of whether a block exemption is applicable or not, because of the market share thresholds in current block exemptions;[316]

- establishing a breach of Article 102 TFEU prohibiting the abuse of a dominant position[317] as the application of the Article requires the existence of a dominant position in a given market 'which presupposes that such a market has already been defined';[318]

- the application of the EUMR, as the test is whether a merger would significantly impede effective competition, in particular by creating or strengthening a dominant position.[319]

However, market definition plays a different role in Article 101 cases from that in Article 102 (and merger) cases.[320] In Article 101 cases concerning horizontal price-fixing cartels, for example, it may be unnecessary for the Commission to define the market precisely as the Commission is entitled to use as the relevant market the group of products over which the undertakings have colluded.[321] In the *Lombard Club* case, which concerned a horizontal cartel, the GC held that it was justified for the Commission to use a broad market definition including many banking products that might in other contexts have belonged to separate markets, provided that an effect on competition in that market could be shown.[322]

The EU Courts define the relevant market in terms of substitutability ('interchangeability'). The CJ has adopted a definition of a relevant market which describes the market as consisting of products[323] which are interchangeable with each other but not (or only to a limited extent) interchangeable with those outside it. This interchangeability may be with other products (widgets as substitutes for blodgets) or with the same products from elsewhere (widgets from France as

---

[314] Cases T-374, 375, 384, and 388/94, *European Night Services v Commission* [1998] ECR II-3141, paras. 93–95 and 105; Case T-62/98, *Volkswagen AG v Commission* [2002] ECR II-2707, para. 230. However, note the position re cartels, discussed at n. 321.

[315] See Case C-439/11 P, *Ziegler SA v Commission* EU:C:2013:513.

[316] See n. 309 and accompanying text.

[317] Case 6/72, *Continental Can* [1973] ECR 215, para. 32. On the other hand, if the conduct complained of would not amount to an abuse even if the undertaking concerned *was* in a dominant position, it may not be necessary to define the market.

[318] Case T-62/98, *Volkswagen* [2002] ECR II-2707, para. 230; Case T-111/08, *MasterCard Inc and Others v Commission* EU:T:2012:260, para. 171.

[319] EUMR, Art. 2(2) and (3). See further Chap. 15.

[320] Case T-62/98, *Volkswagen* [2002] ECR II-2707, para. 230; Cases T-259–264 and 271/02, *Raiffeisen Zentralbank Österreich and Others v Commission* (the *Lombard Club* case) [2006] ECR II-5169 (aff'd on appeal, Cases C-125, 113, 135, and 137/07 P, *Erste Group Bank AG v Commission* [2009] ECR I-8681, paras. 62–63); see also Case T-61/99, *Adriatica di Navigazione v Commission* [2003] ECR II-5349.

[321] See, e.g., Cases T-71, 74, 87, and 93/03, *Tokai Carbon Co Ltd v Commission* [2005] ECR II-10, para. 90; COMP/39.181, *Candle Waxes Cartel* [2009] OJ C295/17, para. 263 (the point was not raised in the appeals).

[322] Cases T-259–264 and 271/02, *The Lombard Club case* [2006] ECR II-5169.

[323] Or services. The words 'products' and 'product market' encompass both products and services, as appropriate.

substitutes for widgets from the UK). The relevant market therefore has both a product aspect (the product market) and a geographical aspect (the geographic market). The CJ has said of the *relevant product market*:

…the definition of the relevant market is of essential significance, for the possibilities of competition can only be judged in relation to those characteristics of the products in question by virtue of which those products are particularly apt to satisfy an inelastic need and are only to a limited extent interchangeable with other products.[324]

This approach to product market definition uses a 'functional interchangeability' yardstick based on the 'qualitative' criteria of characteristics, price, and intended use. In some cases this approach has led to controversial decisions delineating very narrow markets. In *United Brands*, for example, the CJ upheld the finding that the market for bananas was separate from the market for other fruit.[325] The Commission and the EU Courts have (at least in the past) been criticised for focusing too much attention on characteristics, price, and use. If too much attention is placed on factors which in reality tell us little about a relevant market then decisions are of course likely to be arbitrary. In particular, if the market is not determined scientifically, reference to factors such as product characteristics, intended use, and consumer preference may mean that too much subjectivity is introduced into the determination. In many circumstances this may result in the adoption of too narrow a market definition. In some cases, moreover, characteristics and intended use are not particularly useful to the determination of the relevant market. They will not shed light when trying to determine, for example, whether or not sparkling mineral water is in the same market as still mineral water, tap water, orange juice, or tonic water. All of these products have similar characteristics and uses.[326] Likewise, the fact that two products serving the same function have significantly different prices (as is the case, for example, with many consumer products such as watches, pens, perfumes, handbags) does not necessarily put them into different markets. Consumers commonly make a trade-off between price and (actual or perceived) quality and the existence of different versions may constrain the pricing decisions of the producers.

In *United Brands* the CJ gave the following definition of the *relevant geographic market*:

The opportunities for competition under Article [102 TFEU] must be considered having regard to the particular features of the product in question and with reference to a clearly defined geographic area in which it is marketed and where the conditions of competition are sufficiently homogeneous for the effect of the economic power of the undertaking concerned to be able to be evaluated. . . . The conditions for the application of Article [102] to an undertaking in a dominant position presuppose the clear delimitation of the substantial part of the Common Market in which it may be able to engage in abuses which hinder effective competition and this is an area where the objective conditions of competition applying to the product in question must be the same for all traders.[327]

In some cases there may also be a temporal aspect, although this is usually considered as a feature of the product and therefore part of the delineation of the product market.

The definition of the relevant market involves 'complex economic assessments' by the Commission. For the question of the intensity of judicial review by the GC of such assessments, see Chapter 13.

[324] Case 6/72, *Continental Can* [1973] ECR 215, para. 32; see similarly Case 85/76, *Hoffmann-La Roche* [1979] ECR 461, para. 28 and Case 322/81, *Nederlandsche Banden-Industrie Michelin v Commission (Michelin 1)* [1983] ECR 3461, para. 37.

[325] See Chap. 6.

[326] See the merger case M.190, *Nestlé/Perrier* [1992] OJ L356/1, discussed in Chap. 15.

[327] Case 27/76, *United Brands* [1978] ECR 207, paras. 11 and 44.

(iii) The Commission Notice on the Definition of the Relevant Market for the Purposes of EU Competition Law

a. The Publication of the Notice

In 1997 the Commission published a Notice on the definition of the relevant market for the purposes of Community competition law (the Market Definition Notice) to 'provide guidance as to how the Commission applies the concept of relevant product and geographic market in its ongoing enforcement of [Union] competition law' (para. 1).[328] The Commission had previously been criticised for taking an approach to market definition in Article 101 and Article 102 cases which was insufficiently economically rigorous and the Notice provides a 'modernised' framework for determining the relevant market on economic principles. It reflected the new practice the Commission had developed in the area of merger control after the EUMR came into force in 1990.[329] The Notice is still current.

The Commission states that market definition is a tool to identify and define the boundaries of competition between firms and that it serves to establish the framework within which the Commission applies competition policy (para. 2). By publishing the Notice the Commission sought to increase transparency in respect of the procedures it follows and the evidence upon which it relies in reaching decisions on market definition, and thus assist undertakings in their decision-making.[330] As in respect of other Notices, by adopting and publishing its rules of conduct the Commission has imposed a limit on the exercise of its discretion and must not depart from them on pain of being penalised for breach of fundamental principles of law such as equal treatment or protection of legitimate expectations.[331]

The Commission's approach set out in the Notice is outlined in this chapter since it describes the economic analysis which should be used to define the relevant market in all competition cases. It should be noted, however, that the process described in the Notice is at odds with some earlier Commission decisions and case law, such as the treatment of 'unique suitability'.[332]

The case law and the relevant Commission decisions in specific contexts are described in subsequent chapters.

b. The Definition of the Relevant Market in the Notice

The definition of the relevant market adopted by the Commission in the Notice is based on that of the CJ, as already set out.

Commission Notice on the Definition of the Relevant Market for the Purposes of Community Competition Law [1997] OJ C372/5

7. . . . A relevant product market comprises all those products and/or services which are regarded as interchangeable or substitutable by the consumer, by reason of the products' characteristics, their prices and their intended use.

---

[328] [1997] OJ C372/5.

[329] See Chaps. 6 and 15.

[330] Market Definition Notice, paras. 4 and 5. The GC confirmed this role of the Notice in Case T-446/05, *Amann & Söhne GmbH & Co KG v Commission* [2010] ECR II-1255, paras. 137–139.

[331] Case T-446/05, *Amann & Söhne* [2010] ECR II-1255, para. 137, following Cases C-189, 202, 208, and 213/02 P, *Dansk Rørindustri A/S and Others v Commission* [2005] ECR I-5425, paras. 209–211, see Chap. 2, Section 5, p. 108.

[332] The treatment of 'unique suitability' in para. 43 of the Notice differs from that in Case 27/76, *United Brands v Commission* [1978] ECR 207, discussed in Section 15.B.vii.b, p. 71 and Chap. 6.

8. . . . The relevant geographic market comprises the area in which the undertakings concerned are involved in the supply and demand of products or services, in which the conditions of competition are sufficiently homogeneous and which can be distinguished from neighbouring areas because the conditions of competition are appreciably different in those areas.

Paragraph 7 was cited by the GC in *CEAHR*.[333] The problem, of course, is to identify what products are considered substitutes by consumers.

(iv) Demand and Supply Substitution

We have seen that the relevant market depends on the determination of which products in which areas are substitutes for one another. If a product has perfect substitutes the sole producer of such a product has no market power, because if that supplier tries to exploit his monopoly by raising the price his customers will turn to the substitutes. There are two aspects to substitutability. *Demand substitution* is concerned with the ability of users of the product to switch to substitute products. *Supply substitution* is concerned with the ability of producers of similar products to switch to producing the relevant product. *Potential competition* is also important. The behaviour of an undertaking on a market will be constrained if potential competitors are easily able to enter the market. Potential competition is, however, ordinarily taken into account not at the stage of market definition but further on in the competitive assessment when an undertaking's position on the already defined market is considered.[334]

When defining the relevant market both demand and supply substitutability have to be considered.[335] The Notice indicates however that the Commission mainly focuses on demand-side substitution.

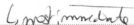

Commission Notice on the Definition of the Relevant Market for the Purposes of Community Competition Law [1997] OJ C372/5

13. . . . From an economic point of view, for the definition of the relevant market, demand substitution constitutes the most immediate and effective disciplinary force on the suppliers of a given product, in particular in relation to their pricing decisions. A firm or a group of firms cannot have a significant impact on the prevailing conditions of sale, such as prices, if its customers are in a position to switch easily to available substitute products or to suppliers located elsewhere. Basically, the exercise of market definition consists in identifying the effective alternative sources of supply for the customers of the undertakings involved, in terms both of products/services and of geographic location of suppliers.

14. The competitive constraints arising from supply side substitutability other than those described in paragraphs 20 to 23 and from potential competition are in general less immediate and in any case require an analysis of additional factors. As a result such constraints are taken into account at the assessment stage of competition analysis.

Paragraph 13 was approved by the GC in *easyJet*.[336]

---

[333] Case T-427/08, *Confédération européenne des associations d'horlogers-réparateurs (CEAHR) v Commission* [2010] ECR II-5865, para. 68.

[334] See Chap. 6.

[335] The Commission lost the *Continental Can* case (Case 6/72, [1973] ECR 215) on the issue of demand substitution, see Chap. 6.

[336] Case T-177/04, *easyJet v Commission* [2006] ECR II-1931, para. 99.

(v) Demand Substitution

a. Measuring Demand Substitution

Demand substitution identifies which products a consumer considers to be substitutes for another. Unless products are totally homogeneous there will be no perfect substitutes. However, most products do have imperfect substitutes. Whether or not products are substitutes for one another is dependent on a number of factors, particularly customer preference, whether customers can switch immediately or need time to adapt, whether there is similarity in quality or price, and whether the substitutes are available. The matter may be complicated if some customers can switch to substitutes but others cannot or if a product has several uses and there are substitutes for some of those uses but not for others. As already explained, products may be substitutes in one direction and not in the other (asymmetrical substitution). For example, in *Microsoft*[337] the Commission found that while a streaming media player was a substitute for a media player which delivered less functionality, substitution the other way round was not readily available as less powerful media players did not satisfy consumer demand for features such as streaming or video playback. In *AstraZeneca* purchasers had only gradually switched from one product to another but it could not be concluded from this that the first product exercised a significant competitive constraint over the other.[338]

b. The SSNIP Test

Interchangeability is gauged by measuring 'cross-elasticity of demand', as described earlier.[339] The primary method favoured by the Commission for measuring this, set out in the Notice, is the hypothetical monopolist test (HMT), put into effect by using the SSNIP test. This is a 'quantitative' test that reflects the more economically rigorous approach adopted by the Commission to market definition.

SSNIP stands for a Small but Significant Non-transitory Increase in Price.[340] The test[341] has been adopted by competition authorities around the world.[342] It reflects contemporary economic analysis. The test is as follows: a small (5–10 per cent) rise in the price of widgets is assumed. It is then asked whether this price increase would cause widget customers to purchase blodgets, or to purchase widgets from another area, to such an extent that the price rise is unprofitable (customers who are able and willing to switch are called 'marginal' customers). If the answer is yes, then blodgets and/or widgets from the other area form part of the same market. The test is then repeated for that bigger bundle of products until the point is reached when the price rise would be profitable.

Commission Notice on the Definition of the Relevant Market for the Purposes of Community Competition Law [1997] OJ C372/5

15. The assessment of demand substitution entails a determination of the range of products which are viewed as substitutes by the consumer. One way of making this determination can be viewed as a speculative experiment, postulating a hypothetical small, lasting change in relative prices and evaluating the likely

---

[337] COMP/37.792, [2007] OJ L32/23, para. 415, on appeal Case T-201/04, *Microsoft* [2007] ECR II-3601; see also Case T-340/03, *France Télécom SA v Commission* [2007] ECR II-107, paras. 88–90.

[338] Case T-321/05, *AstraZeneca v Commission* [2010] ECR II-2805, paras. 89–107. See Chap. 6, Section 5.B.i.j, p. 307.

[339] See Section 3.A.iii, p. 5.

[340] Note that where buying (procurement) markets are concerned, the test may involve a postulated *reduction* in price, as in the merger case, Case T-151/05, *Nederlandse Vakbond Varkenshouders (NVV) v Commission* [2009] ECR II-1219 where in defining the geographic market the question arose as to whether a reduction in the prices paid for pigs by slaughterhouses in some areas would lead to pig farmers exporting their pigs to slaughterhouses in other areas.

[341] Van den Bergh and Camesasca, n. 32, 131, say that, 'The so-called SSNIP test is not a test in itself but a conceptual framework, within which several quantitative tests can be employed to address the market delineation question'.

[342] It was pioneered by the US Department of Justice in 1982. See now the US 2010 Horizontal Merger Guidelines, section 4, <http://www.justice.gov/atr/horizontal-merger-guidelines-08192010>.

reactions of customers to that increase. The exercise of market definition focuses on prices for operational and practical purposes, and more precisely on demand substitution arising from small, permanent changes in relative prices. This concept can provide clear indications as to the evidence that is relevant in defining markets.

16. Conceptually, this approach means that, starting from the type of products that the undertakings involved sell and the area in which they sell them, additional products and areas will be included in, or excluded from, the market definition depending on whether competition from these other products and areas affect or restrain sufficiently the pricing of the parties' products in the short term.

17. The question to be answered is whether the parties' customers would switch to readily available substitutes or to suppliers located elsewhere in response to a hypothetical small (in the range 5 to 10 per cent) but permanent relative price increase in the products and areas being considered. If substitution were enough to make the price increase unprofitable because of the resulting loss of sales, additional substitutes and areas are included in the relevant market. This would be done until the set of products and geographical areas is such that small, permanent increases in relative prices would be profitable. The equivalent analysis is applicable in cases concerning the concentration of buying power, where the starting point would then be the supplier and the price test serves to identify the alternative distribution channels or outlets for the supplier's products. In the application of these principles, careful account should be taken of certain particular situations as described within paragraphs 56 and 58.

18. A practical example of this test can be provided by its application to a merger of, for instance, soft-drink bottlers. An issue to examine in such a case would be to decide whether different flavours of soft drinks belong to the same market. In practice, the question to address would be whether consumers of flavour A would switch to other flavours when confronted with a permanent price increase of 5 to 10 per cent for flavour A. If a sufficient number of consumers would switch to, say, flavour B, to such an extent that the price increase for flavour A would not be profitable owing to the resulting loss of sales, then the market would compromise at least flavours A and B. The process would have to be extended in addition to other available flavours until a set of products is identified for which a price rise would not induce a sufficient substitution in demand.

19. Generally, and in particular for the analysis of merger cases, the price to take into account will be the prevailing market price. This may not be the case where the prevailing price has been determined in the absence of sufficient competition. In particular for the investigation of abuses of dominant positions, the fact that the prevailing price might already have been substantially increased will be taken into account.[343]

An economist explains the significance and advantages of the Commission's use of the SSNIP test when defining markets as follows:[344]

The success of the SSNIP is no accident. The question that it asks goes to the core of why we care about market definition in the first place. We can only answer the question of whether, for instance, a 70 per cent share of a 'market' is likely to give a company market power if that 'market' is an economically meaningful market. The key question is whether substitution to other products or other geographic regions is a substantial, or only a trivial, limitation on the conduct of the parties offering those products. We want to include within the market everything that offers substitution to the products at issue for significant numbers of consumers and to exclude from the market all those things that are not realistic substitutes. The SSNIP test is a convenient way of doing this.

The EU Courts have approved the use of the SSNIP test, for example in *AstraZeneca*.[345]

---

[343] This is a reference to the 'cellophane fallacy'. See the discussion in Section 15.B.v.d, p. 65.

[344] W. Bishop, 'Editorial: The Modernisation of DGIV' [1997] *ECLR* 481.

[345] Case T-321/05, *AstraZeneca v Commission* [2010] ECR II-2805, paras. 86–7 where the GC said, '[i]n order to evaluate the merits of the applicants' arguments, both in principle and in the specific circumstances of this case, it

The practical problem, however, is actually applying the SSNIP test. How are customers' reactions to the hypothetical price rise to be gauged? The Commission attempts to answer this question in paragraphs 25–52 of the Notice. It stresses that it has an open approach to empirical evidence and recognises that the types of evidence which will be relevant and influential will depend on the industry, product, or services in question. The Commission can ordinarily establish the potential market from preliminary information available or submitted by firms involved. Frequently, the matter may boil down to a question as simple as 'Is product A in the same market as product B?' Where this is so, the case may be determined without a precise definition of the market being necessary. Where greater precision in market definition is necessary, the Commission may contact the main customers and companies in the industry, professional associations, and companies in upstream markets to ascertain their views. It may address written requests for information to the market players (including asking their views on reactions to hypothetical price increases and on market boundaries), enter into discussions with them, and even carry out visits to or inspections of the premises of the parties and/or their customers and competitors. Where consumers are concerned it is recognised that asking hypothetical questions may lead to biased results and that interviewees may behave in practice differently from how they answer survey questions.[346] Research on consumer behaviour has led economists to favour 'conjoint analysis' whereby the 'trade-offs' which consumers make when confronted with different products (between, e.g., price and quality, reliability and trendiness) can be built into the analysis.[347]

The Commission will consider quantitative tests devised by economists for the purpose of delineating markets.[348] These include elasticity estimates, tests based on similarity of price movements over time (price correlation analysis),[349] causality calculations,[350] regression analysis, and price convergence analysis. In particular, it will consider evidence of recent substitution in the past available as a result of actual events or shocks in the market ('shock analysis'), including the entry of other competitors into the market or the introduction of new products.[351] Indeed, the Commission indicates that 'this sort of information will normally be fundamental for market definition'.[352] Evidence of the consequences of past launches of new products on the sales of existing products is also described as useful.

---

is necessary to place them in the theoretical framework adopted by the Commission in the Notice on market definition for the purposes of determining competitive constraints' and went on to refer to paras. 15–19 of the Notice. On appeal, Case C-457/10 P, *AstraZeneca*, the market definition point was not taken. See also Case T-151/05, *NVV v Commission* [2009] ECR II-1219.

[346] See M. Hughes and N. Beale, 'Customer Surveys in UK Merger Cases—The Art and Science of Asking the Right People the Right Questions' [2005] *ECLR* 297; CC2com1/OFT 1230, 'Good practice and design in the design and presentation of consumer survey evidence in merger inquiries' (2011), <https://www.gov.uk/government/publications/mergers-consumer-survey-evidence-design-and-presentation>.

[347] See B. Dunbow, 'Understanding Consumers: The Value of Stated Preferences in Antitrust Proceedings' [2003] *ECLR* 141; D. Hildebrand, *The Role of Economic Analysis in the EC Competition Rules* (Kluwer Law International, 2002), 329–331; D. Hildebrand, 'The European School in EC Competition Law' (2002) 25 *World Competition* 3; D. Hildebrand, 'Using Conjoint Analysis for Market Definition: Application of Modern Market Research Tools to Implement the Hypothetical Monopolist Test' (2006) 29 *World Competition* 315.

[348] Market Definition Notice, para. 39.

[349] See G. J. Stigler and R. A. Sherwin, 'The Extent of the Market' (1985) 28 *J of Law and Economics* 555.

[350] Causality tests try to determine if there is causation from one series of prices to another, or if they mutually determine each other. The most widely accepted testing procedure recently has been 'Granger causality', a method set out in C. Granger, 'Investigating Causal Relations by Econometric Models and Cross-spectral Methods' (1969) 37 *Econometrica* 424, see Van den Bergh and Camesasca, n. 32, 137.

[351] As well as things like natural disasters, strikes, sudden exchange rate changes, regulatory intervention, and the introduction of new technology.

[352] Para. 38. Economics is not an experimental science. The consequences of something happening which really affects the products available on the market (e.g., a shortage arising from a natural disaster) are therefore particularly significant.

The wide range of tests that can be employed in the attempt to define markets were discussed in a 1999 report prepared by an economics consultancy for the UK competition authority, the OFT.[353] The report demonstrated that there are problems of some kind with all the tests (although these are being continually refined and improved). For example:

Generally, tests based on price trends alone should be treated with caution, as they do not allow an assessment of whether prices could be profitably raised by market participants. However, the paucity of the data available often prevents the analyst from estimating more appropriate demand models, so that antitrust markets are defined on the basis of price tests alone.[354]

Bishop and Walker accept that price correlation analysis has several weaknesses[355] but consider that nevertheless it can provide useful information to aid market definition. One of its attractions is that it has 'relatively low information requirements and ease of use'[356] which is particularly important when, as in merger investigations, competition authorities are working to very tight deadlines.[357] There is general agreement that price correlation, Granger causality, and cointegration[358] tests may identify economic markets but do not necessarily establish antitrust markets, i.e. do not answer the question 'Is this market worth monopolising?'[359] The HMT can also be implemented through critical loss analysis.[360] This seeks to identify the smallest percentage of sales which, if lost, would make a SSNIP unprofitable, i.e. 'the critical loss is the point where the two opposing effects of a price increase offset each other so that the net effect in profits is nil'.[361] Critical loss analysis has drawbacks and in particular is unsuitable in two-sided markets.[362]

However, although quantitative techniques are not 'magic bullets' they can, when used correctly and rigorously, be helpful tools.[363] Faull and Nikpay conclude that the value of the SSNIP test is in directing the attention to asking the right questions:

In our view, the complexity of the SSNIP test should not, however, be overemphasized. The most important aspect of SSNIP is its conceptual side, not its quantitative side . . . Even when no detailed data are available, it is useful to think of the market definition question in terms of SSNIP. By asking a question

---

[353] OFT 266, 'Quantitative techniques in competition analysis', Research Paper 17, prepared by LECG Ltd.

[354] Ibid., para. 2.25.

[355] Price correlation analysis is based on the idea that if two products are in the same market their prices will move in the same way over time. Similarity, however, may result from products in different markets being subject to the same changes in external forces (common shocks), such as the increase in the price of a raw material needed for both. This could result in a spurious correlation: see Motta, n. 31, 108.

[356] Bishop and Walker, n. 70, 10.02.

[357] See Chap. 15 for the time periods applicable under the EUMR. Price correlation analysis was used, inter alia, in the leading merger cases of *Nestlé/Perrier* [1992] OJ L356/1, *Guinness/Grand Metropolitan* [1998] OJ L288/24, *Lonrho/Gencor* [1997] OJ L11/30, M.4439, *Ryanair/Aer Lingus* [2008] 4 CMLR 667, *BMG/Sony* [2005] OJ L65/30. Merger simulation, which attempts to directly calculate how much prices are likely to rise post-merger, may also be used in merger cases, as it was in *Volvo/Scania* [2001] OJ L143/74.

[358] Cointegration analysis looks at the relationship between economic data series, such as price series, and examines whether it is stable over the long term.

[359] OFT 266, n. 353, para. 8.7; Bishop and Walker, n. 70, 10-73; H. Wills, 'Market Definition: How Stationarity Tests Can Improve Accuracy' [2002] ECLR 4.

[360] See Van den Bergh and Camesasca, n. 32, 137–140; Faull and Nikpay, n. 7, 1.289–1.294; Geradin, Layne-Farrar, and Petit, n. 7, 4.35–4.36; OECD Roundtable on market definition, n. 303, 3.2.3; D. P. O'Brien and A. L. Wickelgreen, 'A Critical Analysis of Critical Loss Analysis' (2003) 70 *Antitrust LJ* 161; B. Harris and C. Veljanovski, 'Critical Loss Analysis: Its Growing Use in Competition Law' [2003] *ECLR* 213; I. Kokkoris, 'Critical Loss Analysis: Critically Ill?' [2005] *ECLR* 518; Ø. Daljord, 'An Exact Arithmetic SSNIP Test for Asymmetric Products' (2009) 5(3) *J of Competition Law and Economics* 563; K. Hüschelrath, 'Critical Loss Analysis in Market Definition and Merger Control' (2009) 3 *European Competition Journal* 757; A. Ten Kate and G. Niels, 'The Concept of Critical Loss for a Group of Differentiated Products' (2010) 6(2) *J of Competition Law and Economics* 321.

[361] O'Donoghue and Padilla, n. 276, 110.

[362] Geradin, Layne-Farrar, and Petit, n. 7, 4.36. For two-sided markets, see Section 15.B.vii.i, p. 74.

[363] OFT 266, n. 353, para. 18.12.

which is directly linked to the purpose of antitrust analysis (is the exercise of market power an issue for this collection of products?), it brings a certain structure and consistency to the market definition exercise. The SSNIP concept provides for a framework within which to consider the question of economic substitution.[364]

c. Switching Costs

Paragraph 42 of the Notice discusses 'switching costs'. Two prima facie demand substitutes will not be considered to belong to one market if there are obstacles which will prevent or hinder customers from changing.

42. *Barriers and costs associated with switching demand to potential substitutes.*

   There are a number of barriers and costs that might prevent the Commission from considering two prima facie demand substitutes as belonging to one single product market. It is not possible to provide an exhaustive list of all the possible barriers to substitution and of switching costs. These barriers or obstacles might have a wide range of origins, and in its decisions, the Commission has been confronted with regulatory barriers or other forms of State intervention, constraints arising in downstream markets, need to incur specific capital investment or loss in current output in order to switch to alternative inputs, the location of customers, specific investment in production process, learning and human capital investment, retooling costs of other investments, uncertainty about quality and reputation of unknown suppliers, and others.

Switching costs are therefore the price which consumers pay for changing to another product. They are not necessarily financial but cover inconvenience and hassle as well. Switching costs may act as barriers to entry[365] and may be created or increased by incumbent firms as an exclusionary tactic.

d. The Cellophane Fallacy

A major problem with the SSNIP test is known as the 'cellophane fallacy'. Paragraph 19 of the Notice recognises the difficulties presented by the cellophane fallacy (although it does not refer to it as such). The fallacy arises from the fact that the SSNIP test cannot identify whether the current price is already a monopoly price resulting from the exercise of market power. It is named after the subject matter of a US case in which the Supreme Court erroneously accepted Du Pont's argument that cellophane was not a separate relevant market but competed directly and closely with other flexible packaging materials such as aluminium foil, polythene, and wax paper.[366]

   The difficulty is that a profit-maximising firm will price as high as it can. If X is the sole supplier of widgets it will normally set the price of widgets at a level where other products constrain it. If the marginal cost of a widget is £5 but blodgets, which perform the same function as widgets, are sold at their marginal cost of £10, X will sell widgets at just under £10. That way X still makes a supranormal profit and does not lose out to the blodget manufacturers. At the price of £10 blodgets and widgets are substitutes, and X can argue, as Du Pont did in *Cellophane*, that since it cannot raise the price without losing sales it must be operating on a competitive market. Yet X is already making a monopoly profit. It may have no substitutes at its competitive price of £5 but will at £10. In the *Cellophane* case the Supreme Court found that the market was that for all flexible wrapping materials as other materials competed with cellophane at its current price. It did not ask, however, whether or not cross-elasticity between cellophane and other materials was only high *because Du Pont was already exercising market power*. The Notice recognises this difficulty and states that using the prevailing market price as the base figure from which to hypothesise the 5–10 per cent price rise of the SSNIP

---

[364] Faull and Nikpay, n. 7, 1.151 (L.Peeperkorn and V. Verouden).

[365] See Section 15.C.iii, p. 81 ff.

[366] *United States v El du Pont de Nemours & Co*, 351 US 377 (1956).

test may be inappropriate where that price has been determined in the absence of competition. This means that great care will have to be exercised if using the SSNIP test to determine whether or not an incumbent on a market has a 'dominant position' for the purposes of Article 102. Recognition of the cellophane fallacy prevented the Commission using the SSNIP test in the Article 101 case *MasterCard*.[367]

In contrast, in merger cases it has only to be decided whether or not the merger will create or increase market power. The SSNIP test is thus much more reliable since the prevailing market price is the appropriate starting point from which to assess the effects of the merger.

The cellophane fallacy is a great problem because in very many markets prices do reflect some degree of market power and the failings of the SSNIP test in dealing with these is a serious limitation on its utility in non-merger cases. Furthermore, it is not just an issue where prices are already set above the competitive level, but also where the prevailing price is too low.[368] Although the Notice recognises the problem it makes no suggestions for dealing with it. Geradin, Layne-Farrar, and Petit suggest how the problem should be approached.

> ## D. Geradin, A. Layne-Farrar, and N. Petit, *EU Competition Law and Economics* (Oxford University Press, 2012), 185–186
>
> 4.46 To guard against the cellophane fallacy, one could estimate the competitive price before conducting a hypothetical monopolist test with a SSNIP or a critical loss test. In practice, however, if determining the competitive price were easy, we would not need to conduct any other tests. We could simply compare the actual price the undertaking was charging in the marketplace with the competitive one to assess that undertaking's market power—we would not need any HMT or critical loss estimation. Alternatively, one could ignore the HMT test and instead rely on qualitative evidence to determine the relevant market. The point of the HMT and critical loss tests, however, is to provide meaningful structure to the assessment of markets, to ensure that physically similar products are included in the same market only when consumers view them as substitutes, and to identify those seemingly dissimilar products that should be included in a market because consumers substitute among them. It is difficult to impossible to achieve those goals through qualitative analysis alone. As a result, the Commission's Discussion Paper observes that '[t]he SSNIP test at prevailing prices remains useful in the sense that it is indicative of substitution patterns at those prices'.[369]
>
> The best approach, then, is to conduct a SSNIP or critical loss test, but compare the results against other measures to ensure that the market has not been defined too broadly and thus falsely indicated a lack of market power. One way to do [that] is to consider multiple tests with qualitative checks, where consistent results among all of the evidence would offer the most reliable market definition.

e. Characteristics and Intended Use

Despite the limitations of analysing the characteristics and intended use of a product when defining the market, the Notice indicates that such an analysis may be useful as a preliminary step when considering the possible substitutes.

---

[367] COMP/34.579, *MasterCard* 19 December 2007, on appeal Case T-111/08, *MasterCard Inc v Commission* EU:T:2012:260 and Case C-382/12 P, *MasterCard Inc v Commission* EU:C:2014:2201.

[368] See P. Crocioni, 'The Hypothetical Monopolist Test: What It Can and Cannot Tell You' [2002] *ECLR* 355.

[369] This is a reference to the Commission Staff Discussion Paper on the application of Article 82 to exclusionary abuses, Brussels, 9 December 2005, para. 15, see Chap. 5.

Commission Notice on the Definition of the Relevant Market for the Purposes of Community Competition Law [1997] OJ C372/5

36. An analysis of the product characteristics and its intended use allows the Commission, as a first step, to limit the field of investigation of possible substitutes. However, product characteristics and intended use are insufficient to show whether two products are demand substitutes. Functional interchangeability or similarity in characteristics may not, in themselves, provide sufficient criteria, because the responsiveness of customers to relative price changes may be determined by other considerations as well. For example, there may be different competitive constraints in the original equipment market for car components and in spare parts, thereby leading to a separate delineation of two relevant markets. Conversely, differences in product characteristics are not in themselves sufficient to exclude demand substitutability, since this will depend to a large extent on how customers value different characteristics.

However, as has already been noted, in the past an analysis of the characteristics and use of the product were the usual criteria for identifying substitutability and it was above all the experience of the Commission after 1990 in defining markets for the purpose of merger control which led it to favour the more economic SSNIP test. The case law of the EU Courts and the decisions of the Commission discussed in this book are replete with considerations of characteristics and use in market definition.[370] It is the examination of the characteristics of the product which have given rise to the greatest problems, as in the *United Brands* case, where the CJ famously had to decide whether bananas were in a separate market from fruit.[371] In some cases, however, a consideration of the use of the product can be crucial because it can then be determined that it has no substitutes. Since the publication of the Notice the Commission itself has continued to use characteristics and use where appropriate, in particular where there is insufficient data to apply the SSNIP test, as is often the case.[372] In its *Michelin II* decision of 2001,[373] the Commission held, without mentioning the SSNIP test, that the market for new replacement tyres for lorries and buses was separate to that for retreads. It took into account the 'analysis of their specific characteristics and their uses by final consumers'[374] based on surveys of those consumers (the haulier firms). In the Article 102 decisions, *Microsoft*,[375] *Wanadoo*,[376] and *Clearstream*,[377] the Commission relied heavily on qualitative analysis, although in *Wanadoo* it also referred to the SSNIP test.[378] In short, the examination of characteristics and use is often not in

---

[370] See particularly Chap. 6.

[371] Case 2/76, *United Brands v Commission* [1978] ECR 207.

[372] See, for example, *Van den Bergh Foods Ltd* [1998] OJ L246/1, particularly paras. 130–138, where the Commission held that impulse ice cream (bought as individual portions in shops for immediate consumption) and take-home ice cream (multi-packs of single items designed for storage and consumption at home) were in different markets (it also distinguished catering ice cream, sold in bulk to catering establishments, from impulse and take-home ice cream, and it distinguished between the markets for industrial (produced for wide-scale distribution) and 'artisan' (produced, distributed, and consumed locally on a small scale) ice cream. The decision was upheld in Case T-65/98, *Van den Bergh Foods Ltd v Commission* [2003] ECR II-4653, where the GC said that the 'distinction on the basis of the consumer's intended purpose in purchasing the ice cream in turn determines the differences in characteristics and price between impulse and take-home products' (para. 132).

[373] [2002] OJ L58/25, upheld Case T-203/01, *Michelin v Commission (Michelin II)* [2003] ECR II-4071: see further Chap. 6.

[374] Case T-203/01, *Michelin II* [2003] ECR II-4071, para. 116 (see n. 373).

[375] COMP/37.792, *Microsoft* [2007] OJ L32/23.

[376] COMP/38.233, 16 July 2003, upheld Case T-340/03, *France Télécom* [2007] ECR II-107.

[377] COMP/38.096, 2 June 2004, upheld Case T-301/04, *Clearstream Banking v Commission* [2009] ECR II-3155.

[378] See further Chap. 6.

practice confined to the 'first step' as suggested in paragraph 36 of the Notice, particularly in view of the very real difficulties caused by the cellophane fallacy in so many non-merger cases.

f. Price

The price of products may affect whether or not they are in the same market. Price may be a reflection of a product's characteristics. This is so with products which are available in cheap utility and in luxury versions, such as pens, watches, cosmetics, and perfume, where the price difference relates to characteristics which do not necessarily affect use and function. In such cases the utility and luxury versions may be in separate product markets. For example, in *CEAHR* the GC accepted the Commission's distinction between cheap watches and luxury/prestige watches costing 60 to 160 times as much.[379] However, cheap and luxury products may also be part of a continuous chain of substitution in which a rise in the price of the cheapest model may lead consumers to switch to the next cheapest, and so on.[380] The switching may be one way, however, so that there are two markets, one for lower quality and higher quality versions, and one for higher quality alone.[381] An example of a case where price put products into different markets is *Microsoft* where the Commission held that higher level operating systems and basic workgroup server systems were in different markets because it would be 'extremely cost inefficient' for a customer to buy a (more expensive) higher level system just to fulfil basic workgroup functions.[382]

(vi) Supply Substitution

In *Continental Can*[383] the CJ held that the market must be defined by reference both to supply-side and demand-side substitutability. If a manufacturer of one product can readily switch production to another product then both products may be in the same market.[384] The difficulty is to distinguish supply-side substitutability from potential competition. The Notice concludes that it is a matter of timescale. If a producer of one product can switch production to another in the short term, without significant cost or risk, then those two products will be found to be in the same market. If a producer can enter the market but only in the longer term and after incurring some cost, then that producer is not relevant at the stage of market definition. It will be important, however, when assessing market power: if the producer can enter the market then it is a potential competitor and its existence will have a constraining effect on those operating on the market. Supply substitution is likely to be possible only where producers make products which, while not substitutes for one another from the consumer's perspective are, nonetheless, similar. An example, given by the Commission in its Notice, is markets for paper.[385]

---

[379] Case T-427/08, *CEAHR* [2010] ECR II-586, paras. 73–74. The phrase 'luxury/prestige' was the Commission's interpretation of the description 'watches worth repairing' contained in the complaint whose rejection was the subject of the case.

[380] For chains of substitution, see Section 15.B.vii.a, p. 70.

[381] COMP/38.233, *Wanadoo*; and see O'Donoghue and Padilla, n. 276, 132–133.

[382] COMP/37.792, *Microsoft* [2007] OJ L32/23, para. 376.

[383] Case 6/72, *Continental Can* [1973] ECR 215.

[384] The SSNIP test can be applied to supply-side substitution by postulating whether the price increase would be rendered unprofitable by other suppliers moving to produce the product; see G. Niels, 'The SSNIP Test: Some Common Misconceptions' (2004) *Comp Law* 267; Bellamy and Child (V. Rose and D. Bailey (eds.)), *European Union Law of Competition* (7th edn, Oxford University Press, 2013), 4.053.

[385] In M.166, *Torras/Sarrio* (1992) the Commission relied upon supply-side substitution in considering a merger in the paper sector. See also M.458, *Electrolux/AEG* (all models and sizes of washing machines found to be in the same market, ditto for dishwashers, fridges, microwaves, and so on); Case T-65/96, *Kish Glass and Co Ltd v Commission* [2000] ECR II-1885 (different thicknesses of glass in the same market).

Commission Notice on the Definition of the Relevant Market for the Purposes of Community Competition Law [1997] OJ C372/5

20. Supply-side substitutability may also be taken into account when defining markets in those situations in which its effects are equivalent to those of demand substitution in terms of effectiveness and immediacy. This means that suppliers are able to switch production to the relevant products and market them in the short term. . . . without incurring significant additional costs or risks in response to small and permanent changes in relative prices. When these conditions are met, the additional production that is put on the market will have a disciplinary effect on the competitive behaviour of the companies involved. Such an impact in terms of effectiveness and immediacy is equivalent to the demand substitution effect.

21. These situations typically arise when companies market a wide range of qualities or grades of one product; even if, for a given final customer or group of consumers, the different qualities are not substitutable, the different qualities will be grouped into one product market, provided that most of the suppliers are able to offer and sell the various qualities immediately and without the significant increases in costs described above. In such cases, the relevant product market will encompass all products that are substitutable in demand and supply, and the current sales of those products will be aggregated so as to give the total value or volume of the market. The same reasoning may lead to group different geographic areas.

22. A practical example of the approach to supply-side substitutability when defining product markets is to be found in the case of paper. Paper is usually supplied in a range of different qualities, from standard writing paper to high quality papers to be used, for instance, to publish art books. From a demand point of view, different qualities of paper cannot be used for any given use, i.e., an art book or a high quality publication cannot be based on lower quality papers. However, paper plants are prepared to manufacture the different qualities, and production can be adjusted with negligible costs and in a short time-frame. In the absence of particular difficulties in distribution, paper manufacturers are able therefore, to compete for orders of the various qualities, in particular if orders are placed with sufficient lead time to allow for modification of production plans. Under such circumstances, the Commission would not define a separate market for each quality of paper and its respective use. The various qualities of paper are included in the relevant market, and their sales added up to estimate total market value and volume.

23. When supply-side substitutability would entail the need to adjust significantly existing tangible and intangible assets, additional investments, strategic decisions or time delays, it will not be considered at the stage of market definition. Examples where supply-side substitution did not induce the Commission to enlarge the market are offered in the area of consumer products, in particular for branded beverages. Although bottling plants may in principle bottle different beverages, there are costs and lead times involved (in terms of advertising, product testing and distribution) before the products can actually be sold. In these cases, the effects of supply-side substitutability and other forms of potential competition would then be examined at a later stage.

The GC referred to paragraphs 20–23 in *Amann & Söhne*, to determine 'in the light of those considerations, whether the Commission correctly applied the criterion of supply-side substitutability'.[386] That case concerned industrial thread. The Commission concluded that there were two markets from the point of view of the supply side, automotive (for use in the motor industry) and non-automotive (for use in clothing, embroidery, footwear, etc.). Automotive thread is manufactured to higher specifications, to comply with ISO standards, although it can be used in the non-automotive sector also. The Commission found that non-automotive thread producers would have no interest in incurring the higher costs associated with automotive thread production solely on the ground that it might sell that thread to motor industry customers. The GC confirmed that the Commission

---

[386] Case T-446/05, *Amann & Söhne* [2010] ECR II-1255, para. 73.

had committed no manifest error in finding that there was no supply substitution here and that the automotive and non-automotive markets were distinct.[387]

Whether supply-side issues are taken into account at the market definition stage can be of utmost importance in cases where the only issue is market share and there is no 'later stage' as referred to at the end of paragraph 23 of the Notice. As already explained, a feature of recent block exemption regulations is that they apply only to agreements where the parties have market shares below a particular threshold.[388] Supply-side substitution taken into account at the market definition stage may widen the market and enable the parties concerned to take advantage of the block exemption, although they would have too large a share of a narrower market. Furthermore, in cases where the question is whether an undertaking is in a dominant position, too little emphasis on supply-side substitutability may lead to over-narrow definitions of the market, a matter which is not necessarily remedied by taking into account potential competition at the next stage of the assessment of market power. In particular, in effect a presumption of dominance for the purposes of Article 102 is triggered at a market share of 50 per cent so the dynamics of the assessment may be skewed by omitting supply-side substitutability.[389]

(vii) Particular Issues in Market Definition

a. Chains of Substitution

Demand-side substitutability can be complicated by the existence of a 'chain of substitution', where B is a substitute for A and C is a substitute for B, etc. This can occur in geographic as well as product markets.[390] For example, two shops may compete for the customers who live between them, but for customers who live the far side of either of them the substitute may be different:

Shop A ← customer 1 → **Shop B** ← customer 2 → **Shop C** ← customer 3 → **Shop D**

In this example, shops A and B are substitutes for customer 1, shops B and C are substitutes for customer 2, and shops C and D are substitutes for customer 3. Shops A and D, A and C, B and D are not direct substitutes for any customer. How then are the boundaries of the geographic market to be drawn? In product markets chains of substitution can arise from products with multiple uses or from versions of products sold at different prices as noted earlier. The Commission's Notice discusses the chain of substitution problem in paragraphs 57 and 58, and at the end of paragraph 57 concludes that the real question is how far the existence of substitutes has a constraining influence on an undertaking's pricing policy. So a chain of substitution can place a series of products into a single market if a SSNIP in respect of products in one part of the chain would be unprofitable because customers would switch to products elsewhere in the chain.

57. In certain cases, the existence of chains of substitution might lead to the definition of a relevant market where products or areas at the extreme of the market are not directly substitutable. An example might be provided by the geographic dimension of a product with significant transport costs. In such cases, deliveries from a given plant are limited to a certain area around each plant by the impact of transport costs. In principle, such an area could constitute the relevant geographic market. However, if the distribution of plants is such that there are considerable overlaps between the areas around different plants, it is possible that the pricing of those products will be constrained by a chain substitution effect, and lead to the definition of a broader geographic market. The same reasoning may apply if product B is a demand substitute for products A and C. Even if products A and C are not direct demand substitutes, they might be found to be in the same relevant product market since their respective pricing might be constrained by substitution to B.

---

[387] Ibid., paras. 74–88.

[388] See p. 56 and the instruments listed in n. 309. The Notice on agreements of minor importance [2014] OJ C291/1, see Chap. 3, also uses market share thresholds.

[389] For a more detailed discussion, see Chap. 6.

[390] For geographic market definition, see further Section 15.B.viii, p. 75.

58. From a practical perspective, the concept of chains of substitution has to be corroborated by actual evidence, for instance related to price inter-dependence at the extremes of the chains of substitution, in order to lead to an extension of the relevant market in an individual case. Price levels at the extremes of the chains would have to be of the same magnitude as well.[391]

Chains of substitution are discussed further in Chapter 6.

b. Distinct Groups of Customers and Price Discrimination

Customers as a whole have different preferences and priorities but exercises in market definition have to recognise that some customers may be able to turn to a substitute in response to a price rise while for others it is impossible. A person who cannot drive, for example, cannot respond to an increase in rail fares by driving him- or herself in a car, and customers may be 'locked in' because of previous choices they have made. The most (in)famous case of this problem in EU law is *United Brands*[392] in which the CJ confirmed the Commission's finding that there was a market for bananas separate from that for other fruit partly on the grounds that for some consumers (the very young, the old, and the sick) bananas were a uniquely suitable fruit (they can be mashed up for babies, are easily digestible, are easy to handle, and can be eaten by people with no teeth). This reasoning, however, is incorrect. The fact that bananas satisfy a unique need of a particular class of customers does not mean that bananas constitute a separate market if the average customer is not so limited in their choice of fruit and can respond to a price rise in bananas by buying other fruit. Although it may be possible at point of sale to discriminate *in favour* of certain customers (such as students or old-age pensioners) on production of identification, it is generally not possible to discriminate in the same way *against* individuals, for example pensioners, and to charge them a higher price. If it is impossible to discriminate against the 'infra-marginal' customers who cannot switch—the young, old, and sick—by charging them a higher price, then the behaviour of marginal customers (who are able to switch) must be taken into account. It is the marginal customers who affect a supplier's pricing decisions and whose behaviour is, consequently, crucial in the determination of the market. One group of customers which has a particular need for the product is difficult to exploit unless it can somehow be kept separate from other customers and the other customers can be prevented from making sales on to the special class (arbitrage) or the profits from the special class outweigh the loss of the marginal customers.

In the Notice the Commission recognises (despite *United Brands*) that a distinct group of customers will be relevant to market definition only where they constitute a separate market and price discrimination between the different groups of customers is possible:

43. The extent of the product market might be narrowed in the presence of distinct groups of customers. A distinct group of customers for the relevant product may constitute a narrower, distinct market when such a group could be subject to price discrimination. This will usually be the case when two conditions are met: (a) it is possible to identify clearly which group an individual customer belongs to at the moment of selling the relevant products to him, and (b) trade among customers or arbitrage by third parties should not be feasible.

United Brands is examined in Chapter 6.

c. The Structure of Supply and Demand

The structure of supply and demand may be important in determining the relevant market and may cause identical products to fall into different markets because the dynamics of the transactions

---

[391] Bellamy and Child, n. 384, 4.063, point out that the last sentence of para. 58 only applies to chains in geographic markets.

[392] Case 27/76, *United Brands* [1978] ECR 207.

concerning them differ. The structure of supply and demand may also create 'sub-markets'. This is seen further in Chapter 6.

d. One Market or Two?

Special problems of market definition arise where products are connected with one another but are not substitutes. Demand substitutability does not help with the issue of determining whether certain products are one whole product (or 'system') or whether they are separate. One aspect of this is the matter of 'aftermarkets'. In other situations the products may be supplied at the same time, or may be part of a range sold together. What, for instance, about size 38 and size 42 shoes (they are not substitutes for one another, so does that mean there are separate product markets for each size of shoe?).[393] Is a pair of shoes one product or two (a right and left shoe are not substitutes for one another)? What about the shoes and the laces (again, they are not substitutes for one another)? The division of products into separate markets can be crucial in cases concerning allegations of 'tying' or 'bundling' which may constitute an abuse of a dominant position contrary to Article 102.[394] In *Microsoft* the GC held that the criterion for assessing the distinctiveness of products in Article 102 cases is consumer demand.[395]

e. Aftermarkets

An 'aftermarket' is a market comprising complementary ('secondary') products or services that are purchased after another ('primary') product to which they relate. Many durable goods, such as cars, need compatible spare parts and some need a constant supply of 'consumables' (vacuum cleaners and bags, photocopiers and toner cartridges, and so on). Furthermore, durables may need servicing and repair. The customer may be 'locked in'—the owner of a Ford Focus needs spare parts which fit a Ford Focus, not those which fit a Honda Civic. The Notice, paragraph 56, says that this is an area 'where the application of the principles above has to be undertaken with care'. It recognises that 'constraints on substitution imposed by conditions in the connected markets' must be taken into account. Although the normal approach to market definition may result in an aftermarket consisting of one brand of spare parts where compatibility with a primary product is important, that may not be, in certain situations, a 'relevant product market' for the purpose of the competition rules. Paragraph 56 of the Notice says:

a different market definition may result if significant substitution between secondary products is possible or if the characteristics of the primary products make quick and direct consumer responses to relative price increases of the secondary products feasible.

This recognises that if customers can see the costs they will incur in the aftermarket when buying the primary product (i.e. they can estimate the 'whole-life' cost of the primary and secondary products together) the decision as to which brand of primary product to purchase may be influenced by those costs. In such a case the primary and secondary products comprise one single unified 'system' market and the competition is between the 'systems'.

In *CEAHR* the GC confirmed this approach to market definition in respect of aftermarkets and cited paragraph 56[396] although it annulled the Commission decision in issue, inter alia because of the incorrect application of the approach.[397] The Commission had rejected a complaint from

---

[393] See the definition of the tyre market in Case 322/81, NV *Nederlandsche Banden-Industrie Michelin v Commission* (*Michelin I*) [1983] ECR 3461, discussed in Chap. 6.

[394] See further Chap. 7.

[395] Case T-201/04, *Microsoft* [2007] ECR II-3601, para. 917.

[396] Case T-427/08, *CEAHR* [2010] ECR II-586, para. 70.

[397] The decision, COMP/39.097, 10 July 2008, was also annulled because of the Commission's inadequate explanation of why there was insufficient Community interest to pursue the investigation: see further Chap. 13. On the annulment of the decision rejecting the complaint the Commission opened proceedings against the watch manufacturers, COMP/39.097, *Independent Watches Repairers*, IP/11/952, but ultimately rejected the complaint again, 29 July 2014.

independent watch repairers about the alleged collusive behaviour of luxury/prestige watch manufacturers in refusing to supply them with spare parts. The Commission found that there were no separate markets in spare parts for, and the repair and maintenance of, luxury/prestige watches (those costing between €1,500 and €4,000 new). Rather, they were part of the highly competitive primary product market. The GC found that the Commission had not satisfactorily established whether the different brands of spare parts were substitutes for one another or that consumers could or would reasonably switch to another primary product in order to avoid a price increase for spare parts. In respect of the latter:

The factors raised by the Commission merely indicate a purely theoretical possibility of switching to another primary product, which is not a sufficient demonstration for the purposes of the definition of the relevant market. That definition is based on the concept that effective competition exists, which presupposes that a sufficient number of consumers would actually switch to another primary product in the event of a moderate price increase for spare parts in order to make such an increase unprofitable.[398]

Further, the Commission argued that purchasers of the primary product (the watch) were influenced by price increases in the repair and maintenance market when making their original choice between the luxury brands, thus making this a 'systems' market. The GC held that the Commission had not shown this to be so, and indeed had said itself that the cost of repairs was minor and insignificant compared to the price of the watch.[399]

f. Markets for Raw Materials and 'Inputs'

A raw material may constitute a separate product market even though the derivative product made from it forms part of a wide product market which has a number of substitutes. This was established in *Commercial Solvents*.[400] There may also be a market consisting of a resource or facility which an undertaking does not market to third parties but uses solely for its own production purposes. The EU Courts have held that this 'input' may constitute a potential or hypothetical market separate from that for the product or service in which it is used.[401] The point is important in cases of refusal to supply under Article 102 where the existence of two markets, rather than one, is crucial.[402]

g. Markets Created by State Regulation

A relevant market may be affected by State regulation. Legislation may, for example, define a statutory market. Such regulation may mean that no substitutes are permitted for a particular product or service. In *General Motors*[403] and *British Leyland*[404] national regulations required conformity or type-approval certificates from importers of motor vehicles and provided that they could only be issued by the vehicle manufacturer. In both cases the CJ held that the provision of the certificates was a separate market and not part of the motor car market.

h. Markets in the New Economy

The high technology markets of the new economy are characterised by dynamic competition, where the threat to existing products comes from new products.[405] The implicit assumption underlying the SSNIP test, however, is that the products compete on price. Concentrating on hypothetical

---

[398] Case T-427/08, *CEAHR* [2010] ECR II-586, para. 102.

[399] Para. 22 of the Commission decision.

[400] Cases 6 and 7/73, *Istituto Chemioterapico Italiano Spa & Commercial Solvents v Commission* [1974] ECR 223.

[401] Case C-418/01, *IMS Health GmbH & Co OHG v NDC Health GmbH & Co KG* [2004] ECR I-5039, paras. 43–45; Case T-201/04, *Microsoft* [2007] ECR II-3601, para. 335; Case T-301/04, *Clearstream* [2009] ECR II-3155, paras. 65–66.

[402] See Chap. 7.

[403] Case 26/75, *General Motors v Commission* [1975] ECR 1367.

[404] Case 226/84, *British Leyland v Commission* [1986] ECR 3263.

[405] See Section 12, p. 48.

price rises instead of the competitive constraints stemming from product innovation may lead in dynamically competitive industries to the identification of over-narrow markets.

Application of the SSNIP test in an industry where competition is performance-based (almost always true when product innovation is present) rather than purely price-related is likely to create a downward bias in the definition of the size of the relevant product market, and a corresponding upward bias in the assessment of market power.[406]

It has therefore been argued that the importance of market definition should be downplayed in new economy markets and that overreliance on market shares should be avoided.[407] Market definition in the new economy is a particular problem in merger cases, where the merging parties may be hoping to produce innovative products which do not yet exist. The concept of an 'innovation market' may be useful here. An innovation market consists of the research and development (R&D) directed to a particular new or improved product or process and its close substitutes. Bishop and Walker consider that: (a) where possible it is probably better to define standard product markets than more speculative innovation markets; (b) there are competition issues that are best analysed using the innovation market concept; but (c) where the issue is best analysed using innovation markets, market shares should be interpreted with great care.[408]

Many markets in the new economy are multi-sided. Multi-sided markets are discussed in the next paragraph.

i. Multi-Sided Markets

As already explained, a multi-sided market is one where the firms have to compete simultaneously for more than one group of customers and it may be necessary to subsidise customers on one side or even provide the product or service for free.[409] There is a problem of how to apply market definition tests in multi-sided markets: if the SSNIP test or critical loss analysis is applied to one side of the market in the usual way it may lead to incorrect, particularly over-narrow, definitions.[410] The enormous importance of online platforms in modern life has attracted much attention to the issue of how markets should be defined in respect of them, in order to avoid both Type 1 and Type 2 errors.[411] Although there is general agreement amongst economists that the SSIP test should be adjusted in multi-sided markets there is little agreement about exactly how that should be done. Complicating factors include differences between transaction and non-transaction markets[412] and whether one side receives the services for free. Four particular questions have been identified: (a) should a single SSNIP test be applied to both sides of the market, or a separate test be applied to each side; (b) how should the 10 per cent price increase be allocated among different groups of users; (c) how to deal with the fact that a price increase can affect both sides of a platform; and (d) from what baseline should the 10 per cent be calculated.[413]

---

[406] D. Teece and M. Coleman, 'The Meaning of Monopoly: Antitrust Analysis in High-technology Industries' [1998] *Ant Bull* 801, 827–828.

[407] Overreliance on market shares is criticised in relation to all markets, as discussed in Chap. 6, but in the new economy context it is considered particularly damaging.

[408] Bishop and Walker, n. 70, 4-44. The Commission uses the concept 'innovation and new products markets' in the Horizontal Cooperation Guidelines [2010] OJ C11/1, para. 119.

[409] Section 12, p. 48.

[410] See D. S. Evans and M. D. Noel, 'Defining Antitrust Markets When Firms Operate Two-sided Platforms' (2005) 3 *Colum Business LR* 557.

[411] See, e.g., Lamadrid de Pablo, n. 250; Filistrucchi, Geradin, van Damme, and Affeldt, n. 252; F. Thépot, 'Market Power in Online Search and Social Networking: A Matter of Two-sided Markets' (2013) 36 *World Competition* 195.

[412] See Section 12, p. 49.

[413] Auer and Petit, n. 250, 26–30.

In *MasterCard MIF*,[414] which concerned MasterCard's multilateral interchange fees for cross-border payment card transactions, the two sides were an upstream market where the different card schemes competed in persuading financial institutions to join their schemes and where they provided services to those institutions, and a downstream market where the financial institutions competed for acquiring services, i.e. contracting with merchants (such as retailers) so that they would accept payments by card. The Commission recognised the two-sided nature of the market and the indirect network effects, and held that the relevant market was the downstream one for acquiring payment cards.[415]

j. Markets in the Pharmaceutical Sector

The Commission defines markets in the pharmaceutical sector by reference to the third level of the WHO/EphMRA Anatomical Therapeutical Chemical (ATC) classification which groups medicines in terms of therapeutic indications, i.e. intended use. Where appropriate in the circumstances of the case, however, an analysis may be carried out at another level, such as four (mode of action) or five (individual active substances).[416] The GC in *AstraZeneca* approved the Commission's approach.[417] *AstraZeneca* also established that pharmaceutical markets can be narrowly delineated by reference to the *means* by which the treatment is effected, rather than to the condition being treated.[418] Furthermore *AstraZeneca* shows that the general principles of market definition apply in the pharmaceutical sector and that they are not excluded by regulation in the sector or by reimbursement of the cost of medicine by national health systems.

k. Markets on the Buying Side (Procurement Markets)

The previous discussion is predicated on markets defined on the supply side. However, it is also possible to define markets on the demand side, that is, in terms of what is being bought. This is illustrated in the *British Airways* case, discussed in Chapters 6 and 7.[419] A number of merger cases have involved procurement markets, for example *NewsCorp/Telepiù*[420] and *NVV v Commission*.[421] The SSNIP test is applied by postulating a 5–10 per cent *reduction* in price in buying markets.

(viii) The Geographic Market

The CJ in *United Brands* stressed the importance of defining the market from a geographic perspective.[422] Because market definition is determined by reference to substitutability it is possible that even firms producing identical products will not operate in the same market if they operate within mutually exclusive geographic areas. However where, for example, a customer in England

---

[414] COMP/34.579, *MasterCard* 19 December 2007.

[415] Ibid., para. 316 (the market definition point was not raised on appeal, Case T-111/08, *MasterCard Inc v Commission* EU:T:2012:260, aff'd Case C-382/12 P, *MasterCard Inc v Commission* EU:C:2014:2201). See also COMP/37.860, *Morgan Stanley/Visa International and Visa Europe* 3 October 2007, appeal dismissed Case T-461/07, *Visa Europe v Commission* [2011] ECR II-1729 and COMP/38.606, *Groupement des Cartes Bancaires* 17 October 2007, upheld Case T-491/07, *Groupement des Cartes Bancaires v Commission* EU:T:2012:633, overturned on appeal on another point, Case C-67/13 P, *Groupement des Cartes Bancaires v Commission* EU:C:2014:2022.

[416] COMP/37.507/F3, *AstraZeneca*, 15 June 2005, para. 3.

[417] Case T-321/05, *AstraZeneca v Commission* [2010] ECR II-2805; aff'd Case C-457/10 P, *AstraZeneca* EU:C:2012:770. See J. Westin, 'Defining Relevant Market in the Pharmaceutical Sector in the Light of the *Losec* Case—Just How Different is the Pharmaceutical Market?' [2011] *ECLR* 57.

[418] See further Chap. 6.

[419] Case C-95/04 P, *British Airways* [2007] ECR I-2331.

[420] M.2876, [2004] OJ L110/73 (broadcasting rights).

[421] Case T-151/05, *Nederlandse Vakbond Varkenshoudes (NVV) v Commission* [2009] ECR II-1219, the appeal from M.3605, *Sovion/HMG* (purchase of pigs by slaughterhouses).

[422] Case 27/76, *United Brands* [1978] ECR 207.

may be able to substitute French widgets for English ones, the English producer will not have market power if the small but significant price rise causes his customers to purchase French widgets instead. Whether or not the geographic market in a particular product is global, regional, national, or local depends on a number of factors, including the cost of transport, the nature of the product, and legal regulation (including intellectual property rights). If transport costs are high relative to the value of the product, as in the case of paving slabs or concrete tiles, a geographic market may be small, perhaps even local. There may be chains of substitution in geographic markets, as explained earlier.[423]

In paragraph 8 of the Notice the Commission describes the geographic market as comprising an area 'in which the conditions of competition are sufficiently homogeneous', faithfully following the CJ's definition in *United Brands*,[424] although the rest of the Notice does not stress this aspect. Rather the Commission appears to recognise that the behaviour of undertakings may be constrained by imports from areas where the conditions of competition are *not* the same. In *Deutsche Bahn*[425] the GC held that 'the definition of the geographical market does not require the objective conditions of competition between traders to be perfectly homogenous. It is sufficient if they are "similar" or "sufficiently homogeneous" and accordingly, only areas in which the objective conditions of competition are "heterogeneous" may not be considered to constitute a uniform market.'

The Commission adopts the SSNIP test for determining the geographic as well as the product market. It indicates the type of evidence it considers to be relevant to the determination of the geographic market. Techniques such as critical loss analysis may be used here as well.

Commission Notice on the Definition of the Relevant Market for the Purposes of Community Competition Law [1997] OJ C372/5

28. The Commission's approach to geographic market definition might be summarized as follows: it will take a preliminary view of the scope of the geographic market on the basis of broad indications as to the distribution of market shares between the parties and their competitors, as well as a preliminary analysis of pricing and price differences at national and Community or EEA level. This initial view is used basically as a working hypothesis to focus the Commission's enquiries for the purposes of arriving at a precise geographic market definition.

29. The reasons behind any particular configuration of prices and market shares need to be explored. Companies might enjoy high market shares in their domestic markets just because of the weight of the past, and conversely, a homogeneous presence of companies throughout the EEA might be consistent with national or regional geographic markets. The initial working hypothesis will therefore be checked against an analysis of demand characteristics (importance of national or local preferences, current patterns of purchases of customers, product differentiation/brands, other) in order to establish whether companies in different areas do indeed constitute a real alternative source of supply for consumers. The theoretical experiment is again based on substitution arising from changes in relative prices, and the question to answer is again whether the customers of the parties would switch their orders to companies located elsewhere in the short term and at a negligible cost.

30. If necessary, a further check on supply factors will be carried out to ensure that those companies located in differing areas do not face impediments in developing their sales on competitive terms

---

[423] See Section 15.B.vii.a, p. 70.

[424] Case 2/76, *United Brands* [1978] ECR 207, para. 11.

[425] Case T-229/94, *Deutsche Bahn AG v Commission* [1997] ECR II-1689, para. 92; see also Case T-51/89, *Tetra Pak Rausing SA v Commission (Tetra Pak I)* [1990] ECR II-309, paras. 91 and 92.

throughout the whole geographic market. This analysis will include an examination of requirements for a local presence in order to sell in that area the conditions of access to distribution channels, costs associated with setting up a distribution network, and the presence or absence of regulatory barriers arising from public procurement, price regulations, quotas and tariffs limiting trade or production, technical standards, monopolies, freedom of establishment, requirements for administrative authorizations, packaging regulations, etc. In short, the Commission will identify possible obstacles and barriers isolating companies located in a given area from the competitive pressure of companies located outside that area, so as to determine the precise degree of market interpenetration at national, European or global level.

. . .

44. The type of evidence the Commission considers relevant to reach a conclusion as to the geographic market can be categorized as follows:

45. *Past evidence of diversion of orders to other areas.* In certain cases, evidence on changes in prices between different areas and consequent reactions by customers might be available. Generally, the same quantitative tests used for product market definition might as well be used in geographic market definition, bearing in mind that international comparisons of prices might be more complex due to a number of factors such as exchange rate movements, taxation and product differentiation.

46. *Basic demand characteristics.* The nature of demand for the relevant product may in itself determine the scope of the geographical market. Factors such as national preferences or preferences for national brands, language, culture and life style, and the need for a local presence have a strong potential to limit the geographic scope of competition.

47. *Views of customers and competitors.* Where appropriate, the Commission will contact the main customers and competitors of the parties in its enquiries, to gather their views on the boundaries of the geographic market as well as most of the factual information it requires to reach a conclusion on the scope of the market when they are sufficiently backed by factual evidence.

48. *Current geographic pattern of purchases.* An examination of the customers' current geographic pattern of purchases provides useful evidence as to the possible scope of the geographic market. When customers purchase from companies located anywhere in the Community or the EEA on similar terms, or they procure their supplies through effective tendering procedures in which companies from anywhere in the Community or the EEA submit bids, usually the geographic market will be considered to be Community-wide.

49. *Trade flows/pattern of shipments.* When the number of customers is so large that it is not possible to obtain through them a clear picture of geographic purchasing patterns, information on trade flows might be used alternatively, provided that the trade statistics are available with a sufficient degree of detail for the relevant products. Trade flows, and above all, the rationale behind trade flows provide useful insights and information for the purpose of establishing the scope of the geographic market but are not in themselves conclusive.

50. *Barriers and switching costs associated to divert orders to companies located in other areas.* The absence of trans-border purchases or trade flows, for instance, does not necessarily mean that the market is at most national in scope. Still, barriers isolating the national market have to be identified before it is concluded that the relevant geographic market in such a case is national. Perhaps the clearest obstacle for a customer to divert its orders to other areas is the impact of transport costs and transport restrictions arising from legislation or from the nature of the relevant products. The impact of transport costs will usually limit the scope of the geographic market for bulky, low-value products, bearing in mind that a transport disadvantage might also be compensated by a comparative advantage in other costs (labour costs or raw materials). Access to distribution in a given area, regulatory barriers still existing in certain sectors, quotas and custom tariffs might also constitute barriers isolating a geographic area from the competitive pressure of companies located outside that area. Significant switching costs in procuring supplies from companies located in other countries constitute additional sources of such barriers.

51. On the basis of the evidence gathered, the Commission will then define a geographic market that could range from a local dimension to a global one, and there are examples of both local and global markets in past decisions of the Commission.

52. The paragraphs above describe the different factors which might be relevant to define markets. This does not imply that in each individual case it will be necessary to obtain evidence and assess each of these factors. Often in practice the evidence provided by a subset of these factors will be sufficient to reach a conclusion, as shown in the past decisional practice of the Commission.

In *Amman & Söhne* the Commission defined a supply-side EEA-wide geographic market for automotive thread as motor manufacturers commonly have factories located in several different countries and in order to reduce costs need a uniform thread which can be used in all of them. The relevant market in industrial thread for other sectors, where these features were not present, was regional only (Benelux and the Nordic countries).[426]

The Commission says the methodology set out in the Notice 'might lead to different results depending on the nature of the competition issue being examined'. In particular:

the scope of the geographic market might be different when analysing a concentration, where the analysis is essentially prospective, from an analysis of past behaviour. The different time horizon considered in each case might lead to the result that different geographic markets are defined for the same products depending on whether the Commission is examining a change in the structure of supply, such as a concentration or a cooperative joint venture, or examining issues relating to certain past behaviour.[427]

It will be seen in later chapters that the EU's approach to the geographic market has been criticised in the past for failing to give sufficient attention to substitutability between different geographic areas. As in the case of the product market, the geographic market has often been drawn narrowly. Commissioner Almunia addressed some of these criticisms when he said:

defining the markets affected by a merger which involves companies and competitors with operations in several regions of the world can be a very complex exercise. However, we try to respond to the challenge by constantly adjusting our market definitions to changing market realities. In telecommunication equipment and enterprise software applications, for instance, our definitions have become EU-wide if not worldwide. Also, in the pharmaceutical sector, some ingredients are now usually considered to be sold on a worldwide basis.

And then, there is another point to make. I do not believe that globalisation makes all markets automatically worldwide—that depends on the prevailing competitive conditions. For example, the scope of the markets for electricity distribution or for consumer goods does not change simply because some suppliers—utilities and retailers—extend their operations into more countries. Customers in these countries may still be faced with very different prices and choices. In sum, when it comes to the geographic scope of markets, we apply a simple maxim: we take the markets as we find them.[428]

(ix) The Temporal Market

The Market Definition Notice does not refer to a separate temporal dimension of the market, i.e. the time over which the market operates. Many markets do not have a temporal aspect and where

---

[426] Case T-446/05 P, *Amann & Söhne* [2010] ECR II-1255, paras. 78–80.

[427] Market Definition Notice, para. 12.

[428] Joaquín Almunia, 'Policy Objectives in Merger Control', SPEECH/11/561, Fordham, New York, 8 September 2011.

they do it may be an inherent part of the definition of the product market and analysed as such. The temporal dimension may be particularly relevant when considering transport markets.[429]

C. BARRIERS TO ENTRY AND EXPANSION

(i) The Role of Barriers to Entry

A firm with a 100 per cent share of a market may not, in economic terms, have a monopoly. Market shares tell us nothing about why the firm has such a high market share or about potential competition. It tells us only about the current state of competition. A firm will not be able to charge monopoly prices if other firms can freely enter the market and compete with it. Excessive prices indicate to others that entry to the market is profitable. Whether or not a firm really does have a monopolist's power over price is, therefore, dependent on how vulnerable it is to new entrants. Such vulnerability to new entrants is dependent upon 'barriers to entry'. A firm can exercise market power for a significant time only if barriers to entry exist. As Bork states:[430] '[t]he concept of barriers to entry is crucial to antitrust debate . . . The ubiquity and potency of the concept are undeniable.'

It is difficult to give any definition of 'barriers to entry' without taking sides in a long-standing debate. To put it as neutrally as possible, however, a barrier to entry is something which prevents or hinders the emergence of potential competition which would otherwise constrain the incumbent undertaking. A barrier to expansion is something which prevents or hinders an existing competitor from expanding output. The term 'barriers to entry' is used in the present discussion to include both barriers to entry and barriers to expansion, unless the context otherwise requires. However, it should be noted that barriers to entry may be high although barriers to expansion are low.[431] The height of barriers to entry, as well as their existence, must always be taken into account.

(ii) The Definition of a Barrier to Entry

The seminal work on barriers to entry was that of J. S. Bain who belonged to the Harvard School.[432] Bain described barriers to entry as:

the extent to which, in the long run, established firms can elevate their selling prices above the minimal average costs of production and distribution . . . without inducing potential entrants to enter the industry.[433]

This defines barriers to entry in an effects-based way. In contrast, Stigler, a leading exponent of the Chicago School,[434] adopted a narrower definition, focusing on the differences in demand and cost conditions suffered by incumbent firms and potential entrants respectively. He defined a barrier to entry as:

a cost of producing (at some or every rate of output) which must be borne by a firm which seeks to enter the industry but is not borne by firms already in the industry.[435]

---

[429] In Cases T-374, 375, 384, and 388/94, *European Night Services* [1998] ECR II-3141, where the GC annulled an Art. 101 Commission decision on a joint venture, the Commission raised during the appeal the matter of confining the business transport market to early morning and late evening rather than all round the clock.

[430] Bork, n. 103, 310–311.

[431] See Geradin, Layne-Farrar, and Petit, n. 7, 4.69; e.g. entry may require large capital investment while expansion of existing plant does not.

[432] See Section 4.A, p. 13.

[433] J. S. Bain, *Industrial Organization* (2nd edn, John Wiley, 1968), 242. See also J. S. Bain, 'Economies of Scale, Concentration, and the Condition of Entry in Twenty Manufacturing Industries' (1954) 44 *Am Econ Rev* 15, and *Barriers to New Competition*, n. 43.

[434] See Section 4.B, p. 14.

[435] G. J. Stigler, *The Organization of Industry* (Irwin, 1968), 67; see also W. Baumol and R. Willig, 'Fixed Costs, Sunk Costs, Entry Barriers and Sustainability of Monopoly' (1981) 95 *Quart J of Econ* 405, 408, and C. von Weizsäcker, 'A Welfare Analysis of Barriers to Entry' (1980) 11 *Bell J Econ* 399, 400. D. Carlton, 'Why Barriers to Entry are Barriers

Gilbert's definition follows Bain but emphasises 'first-mover advantages' (the advantages the firm derives simply from being on the market before its potential competitors) rather than absolute costs advantages:

a barrier to entry is a rent that is derived from incumbency. It is the additional profit that a firm can earn as a sole consequence of being established in an industry.[436]

The essential debate remains whether the definition of Bain or of Stigler and the Chicago School is the more appropriate. The Bain approach results in many things being identified as barriers. Conversely, the definition adopted by Stigler means that very few things constitute barriers to entry.[437] For example, Bain's approach, unlike Stigler's, accepts that market conduct may operate as a barrier to entry because the definition is effects-based.[438] Further, Bain's definition admits that economies of scale may operate as a barrier to entry, since they deter new entrants and so allow prices to remain above minimum unit cost. Stigler's definition does not, however, accept that economies of scale operate as a barrier since both incumbents and new competitors have to face them at the time they enter the market.[439] There is therefore a lack of the asymmetry which the Stigler definition demands.

It is the Bain approach which today has the greatest influence in industrial economics and which is ordinarily used in competition law decisions in both the EU and the US.[440] Herbert Hovenkamp explains why this is so.

H. Hovenkamp, *Federal Antitrust Policy: The Law of Competition and its Practice* (4th edn, West, 2011), 39–40

The difference between the two definitions of entry barriers can be quite substantial. For example, under the Bainian definition economies of scale is a qualifying barrier to entry. If scale economies are significant, then incumbent firms with established markets may have a large advantage over any new entrant, who will enter the market at a low rate of output. As a result, scale economies can permit incumbent firms to earn monopoly returns up to a certain point without encouraging new entry.

By contrast, scale economies are not a qualifying entry barrier under the Stiglerian definition. Both incumbent firms and new entrants had to deal with them at the time of entry; so scale economies are not a cost that applies only to new entrants.

The Stiglerian conception of entry barriers is based on a powerful analytic point: entry barrier analysis should distinguish desirable from undesirable entry. If prospective entrants face precisely the same costs that incumbents faced but still find entry unprofitable, then this market has probably already attained the

to Understanding' (2004) 94(2) *Am Econ Rev* 466, 468, says that 'Although Stigler's definition of "barrier" as a differential cost is concise and unambiguous, it does raise the question of why it should be called a "barrier". Why not call it "differential cost advantage?" This may seem overly pedantic, but introduction of unnatural use of language can lead to confusion. Consider, for example, an industry where the government restricts the numbers of firms to 100. It issues 100 licences to operate that are then sold in an open market. The entry restriction is likely to be inefficient, but as long as all firms have access to the (artificially) scarce license at the market-clearing price, there is no entry barrier according to Stigler's definition. All firms earn a normal rate of return. Yet there is a restriction to entry. It seems to mangle the English language to refuse to call this entry restriction a "barrier to entry".'

[436] R. Gilbert, 'Mobility Barriers and the Value of Incumbency' in R. Schmalensee and R. Willig (eds.), *Handbook of Industrial Organization*, Vol. 1 (North-Holland, 1989), 478. For absolute costs advantages, see Section 15.C.iii, p. 82.

[437] All Stiglerian entry barriers are Bainian entry barriers as well, but not vice versa.

[438] R. P. McAfee, H. M. Mialon, and M. A. Williams, 'What is a Barrier to Entry?' (2004) 94(2) *Am Econ Rev* 461, 462 comment that 'Bain's definition is flawed in that it builds the consequences of the definition into the definition itself'.

[439] McAfee, Mialon, and Williams, n. 438, say that the present tense 'is' in Stigler's definition is confusing as '[l]iterally, the definition implies that a cost that only entrants (not incumbents) have to bear today is an entry barrier, even if incumbents had to bear it in the past (when they entered the market)'.

[440] See the US *Horizontal Merger Guidelines* 2010 (<http://www/justice.gov/atr/file/810276/download>).

appropriate number of players, even though monopoly profits are being earned. For example, suppose that minimum efficient scale (MES) in a market requires a 30% market share. Such a market has room for only three MES firms—and a three-firm market is quite likely to perform oligopolistically or else be conducive to collusion. The Stiglerian approach to entry barriers would say that, although monopoly profits are being earned in the industry, entry barriers should not be counted as high because entry by a fourth firm is not socially desirable. Additional entry would force at least one firm to be of suboptimal size, and eventually one of the four would probably exit the market. . . . The socially desirable solution to the problem of oligopoly performance in this market is not to force entry of a fourth, inefficiently small firm; but rather to look for alternative measures that make collusion more difficult.

Nevertheless, antitrust analysis has mainly used the Bainian rather than the Stiglerian definition of entry barriers. The Bainian definition is written into the 2010 Horizontal Merger Guidelines promulgated by the Justice Department's Antitrust Division and the Federal Trade Commission (FTC) . . . In all antitrust decisions except for a few in the FTC, tribunals have relied on the Bainian definition . . .

Although the Stiglerian approach to entry barriers offers a useful insight into the relationship between market structure and socially desirable entry, there are nevertheless good reasons for antitrust policy to prefer the Bainian approach. In particular, the Bainian definition is free of the value judgment of what constitutes socially desirable entry. This is important because the existence of entry barriers is not itself an antitrust violation. The antitrust policy maker does not use entry barrier analysis in order to consider whether further entry into a market is socially desirable; the market itself will take care of that question. Rather, the question is whether a particular practice is plausibly anti-competitive. This distinction is critically important because we know so little about the minimum efficient scale of operation in any given market.

The various definitions of barriers to entry are summed up in the OECD's Roundtable report of 2005.[441]

The proper identification of barriers to entry is vital to the determination of market power. If factors are too readily identified as entry barriers a firm may be wrongly found to have market power and its conduct may then be constrained by competition laws. Similarly a merger between two firms may be prohibited even though it does not lead to the firms acquiring market power. This may mean that the competitive process is actually harmed by competition law since it interferes with and impedes the behaviour of firms operating on a competitive market. On the other hand, if the possibility of entry barriers is too easily dismissed, undertakings which do have market power may escape the prohibitions of competition law and mergers which create or strengthen market power might be allowed.

(iii) Types of Barrier to Entry

We have seen[442] that Post-Chicago and modern industrial organisation theory stresses the strategic conduct of undertakings. It looks to the effect which conduct has on structure, rather than vice versa, and considers that whether a new entrant will enter a market will depend, at least in part, on the conditions of competition it will face post-entry. Thus predatory behaviour by the incumbent firm may constitute a barrier to entry. The theory also emphasises the importance that 'sunk costs' may have on a firm's decision to enter a market. Sunk costs are costs which cannot be recovered on exiting a market.[443]

---

[441] OECD Policy Roundtable on barriers to entry, DAF/COMP(2005)42, available at <http://www.oecd.org/daf/competition/abuse/36344429.pdf>, 2.2.

[442] At Section 4.B.ii, p. 20.

[443] See R. Schmalensee, 'Sunk Costs and Antitrust Barriers to Entry' (2004) 94(2) Am Econ Rev 471.

The list of barriers to entry considered in Sections a–c follows that in the OECD report.[444] The OECD divides barriers to entry into two types, structural and strategic, but notes that '[s]ome arguably spill over from one category to the other, and none of them should be viewed in isolation because they can interact with and magnify each other'.[445] The report considers sunk costs separately, because they 'permeate the whole discussion'.

a. Sunk Costs

Sunk costs[446] can generally affect entry in two ways. First, because the money has already gone an incumbent undertaking can rationally ignore sunk costs when making pricing decisions so it may deter some entrants that are equally, and maybe even more, efficient. Secondly, sunk costs make entry more risky as if entry turns out to be a failure the sunk costs will be irrecoverable. Examples of sunk costs are:[447]

- start-up phase losses;
- investments in human capital such as recruiting and training costs;
- investments in highly specialised equipment or buildings with limited resale value;
- advertising and promotion costs;
- R&D that does not yield results with alternative uses;
- expenses of complying with government regulations.

b. Structural Barriers

Structural barriers[448] arise from the basic conditions in the industry and are normally factors out of the incumbents' direct control or originate from their general efforts to compete and not from specific entry-deterring strategies. They include:

- *Absolute costs advantages,*[449] which are advantages which the incumbent enjoys but which are not available to entrants, such as exclusive access to necessary resources or technology.[450]
- *Economies of scale and scope.*[451] In the absence of sunk costs economies of scale and scope do not deter or prevent entry.
- *High capital costs.* The OECD says that 'high' has two meanings: absolute and relative.[452] Whether high capital costs constitute a barrier to entry is a matter of debate. Bain considered that capital requirements could give rise to barriers to entry because of the amount a new entrant would need to enter the market at an efficient scale.[453] However, in Bork's view:

---

[444] See also the 'slightly adapted version' of the list in Geradin, Layne-Farrar, and Petit, n. 7, 2.104–2.124. See also OFT Research Paper 2, 'Barriers to Entry and Exit in Competition Policy'; OFT 1282, 'Barriers to Entry, Expansion and Exit in Retail Banking' (2010).

[445] OECD Roundtable, n. 441, section 3.

[446] Ibid., section 3.1.

[447] Ibid., section 3.1.

[448] Ibid., section 3.2.

[449] Ibid., section 3.2.1.

[450] They have been described as arising 'if some factor of production is denied to the potential entrant and, but for this omitted factor, the latter firm would be as efficient as the incumbent firm', Van den Bergh and Camesasca, n. 32, 142, referring to R. J. Gilbert, 'Mobility Barriers and the Value of Incumbency' in R. Schmalensee and R. D. Willig (eds.), *The Handbook of Industrial Organization, Vol. I* (North-Holland, 1989). Cost advantages may not endure in high technology markets with a rapid rate of innovation, and in those markets the timescale of change will be important.

[451] OECD Roundtable, n. 441, sections 3.2.2 and 3.2.3. For economies of scale and scope see Section 3.A.v, p. 6.

[452] OECD Roundtable, n. 441, section 3.2.4.

[453] Bain, n. 43, where he reported on a survey of 20 US industries. Capital requirements are therefore linked to economies of scale.

Capital requirements exist and certainly inhibit entry—just as talent requirements for playing professional football exist and inhibit entry. Neither barrier is in any sense artificial or the proper subject of special concern for antitrust policy.[454]

The Commission explained in the Discussion Paper on Article 102 that:[455]

in some cases [financial strength] may be one of the factors that contribute to a finding of a dominant position, in particular in those cases where (i) finance is relevant to the competitive process in the industry under review; (ii) there are significant asymmetries between competitors in terms of their internal financing capabilities; and (iii) particular features of the industry make it difficult for firms to attract external funds[456]

The OECD says that it is probably most useful to think about how capital costs affect a potential entrant's decision.[457]

- *Reputational effects* whereby the incumbent has a strong reputation for reliability or quality. The effects will be greater where customers will incur significant risk, inconvenience, or expense in trying new products.[458]

- *Network effects.*[459] Network effects are discussed earlier.[460] They have been described as 'among the determinants of the conditions of entry in many industries, and they can create a truly formidable entry obstacle, sufficient to permit prices to persist above competitive level[s] for a substantial period of time without attracting entry'.[461]

- *Legal and regulatory barriers*[462] include all kinds of rules, restrictions, and conditions imposed by governments on entry on to or operation within a market. They include intellectual property rights (IPRs). The Chicago School views them as the most substantial barriers to entry. If legal and regulatory barriers are manipulated by incumbents they can be seen as strategic barriers too.[463]

- *Barriers to exit.*[464] The costs of exiting a market may deter undertakings from entering it in the first place. High costs of exit (including sunk costs) make entry riskier. The OECD report points out that high barriers to exit may make incumbents respond more aggressively to entrants, thus creating more barriers to entry.

- *First-mover advantages*[465] are the advantages that the incumbent derives from being the first in the market and which mean that subsequent entrants cannot compete on equal terms. First-mover advantages include some of the barriers to entry already mentioned, such as network effects, reputation, and IPRs.

---

[454] Bork, n. 109, 320.

[455] Commission Staff Discussion Paper, n. 369, para. 40.

[456] Ibid.

[457] OECD Roundtable, n. 441, section 3.2.4, citing Schmalensee's 'pragmatic approach' in R. Schmalensee, 'Horizontal Merger Policy: Problems and Changes' (1987) 1 *Economic Perspectives* 4, that if business people think the cost of capital is a barrier to entry, then that will affect their decisions about entry and become a *de facto* barrier.

[458] OECD Roundtable, n. 441, section 3.2.5.

[459] Ibid., section 3.2.6.

[460] See Section 12, p. 48.

[461] G. J. Werden, 'Network Effects and Conditions of Entry: Lessons from the Microsoft Case' (2001) 69 *ALJ* 8 (discussing the US case).

[462] OECD Roundtable, n. 441, section 3.2.7.

[463] See, e.g., Case C-457/10 P, *AstraZeneca* EU:C:2012:770, discussed in Chap. 7.

[464] OECD Roundtable, n. 441, section 3.2.8.

[465] Ibid., section 3.2.9.

- *Vertical integration* means that an undertaking operates at more than one stage of the production and distribution chain.[466] It may be difficult for an entrant to enter at only one stage and the vertical integration may endow the incumbent with advantages that can be replicated only by a similarly integrated entrant. It can be argued, however, that when vertical integration takes place barriers to entry are only added up and are not multiplied. Vertical integration may therefore accompany monopoly but is not an indicator of it.[467] Vertically integrated firms may discriminate in favour of their own downstream operations, which becomes a strategic barrier, as in the cases on margin squeeze discussed in Chapter 7.[468]

c. Strategic Behaviour by Incumbents

Strategies which deter entry may be intentionally created or enhanced for that purpose.[469] Sometimes the strategies are used to pre-empt entry and sometimes they are used in retaliation against entry that has already occurred. Threats are an effective deterrent if (and only if) they are credible. Some of the practices below are discussed in Chapter 7 as they constitute conduct which can amount to an abuse of a dominant position for the purposes of Article 102 insofar as they 'foreclose' the market, i.e. have exclusionary effects.

- *Predatory pricing*[470] is where an incumbent prices below cost to deter entrants or drive out competitors. See further Chapter 7.

- *Limit pricing* is where the incumbent does not price below cost but deliberately fails to maximise short-term profit, so that it leaves too little residual demand for entry to be profitable. It normally works only if there are economies of scale or scope, because it depends on the entrant being unable to operate efficiently at the available level of demand.[471] The potential entrants also need to believe that the incumbent will maintain that level of output whether or not the new entry occurs.

- *Intentional over-investment in capacity and sunk costs.*[472] An incumbent undertaking may over-invest in sunk assets so that it operates with significant spare capacity. The threat of this spare capacity being used may deter a potential entrant, as the incumbent may be able to manufacture large quantities of the product using that spare capacity at a very low unit cost.

- *Fidelity (loyalty) and bundled rebates*[473] comprise pricing practices whereby undertakings give discounts and rebates to customers in exchange for the customers' loyalty in not buying elsewhere or for buying certain amounts. See further Chapter 7.

- *Product differentiation and advertising.*[474] There is an extensive economics literature about the extent to which advertising, reputation, and goodwill may operate as barriers to entry. There can be economies of scale in advertising and advertising expenditures will usually be sunk costs.[475]

---

[466] Ibid., section 3.2.10.

[467] See C. Baden Fuller, 'Art. 86 EEC: Economic Analysis of the Existence of a Dominant Position' (1979) 4 *ELRev* 423, 440 and the economic literature cited there; D. Harbord and T. Hoehn, 'Barriers to Entry and Exit in European Competition Policy' (1994) 14 *International Review of Law and Economics* 411, 419; V. Korah, 'Concept of a Dominant Position Within The Meaning of Art. 86' (1980) 17 *CMLRev* 395, 408.

[468] Chap. 7, Section 9, p. 407 ff.

[469] OECD Roundtable, n. 441, section 3.3.

[470] Ibid., section 3.3.1.

[471] Ibid., section 3.3.2.

[472] Ibid., section 3.3.3, which cites A. M. Spence, 'Entry, Capacity, Investment and Oligopolistic Pricing' (1977) 8 *Bell J Econ* 53 and A. Dixit, 'The Role of Investment in Entry Deterrence' (1980) 90 *Economic Journal* 9 on the theory of this strategy.

[473] OECD Roundtable, n. 441, section 3.3.4.

[474] Ibid., section 3.3.5.

[475] Although a brand image built up by advertising might be deployable in a separate market, e.g. the name Virgin is applied to many different products and services. The Commission described advertising and promotion as sunk costs in the merger decision *Nestlé/Perrier* [1992] OJ L356/1, para. 97.

Bain considered advertising a barrier to entry.[476] Advertising builds up goodwill and reputation, and the first brand in the market may enjoy a classic first-mover advantage which will operate as a barrier to entry to later entrants.[477] Stigler's view, however, was that advertising is not a barrier to entry: it reduces consumer search costs and is pro-competitive.[478] Advertising and brand reputation may contribute to rendering the undertaking's product a 'must-stock' item, which can in turn make the undertaking an 'unavoidable trading partner'. There is also a significant literature on brand proliferation and product differentiation as barriers to entry.[479] Van den Bergh and Camesasca explain that the insights of modern industrial organisation theory show that advertising and product differentiation can reduce consumer welfare in some circumstances.

R. J. Van den Bergh and P. D. Camesasca, *European Competition Law and Economics: A Comparative Perspective* (2nd edn, Sweet & Maxwell, 2006), 145–146

Recent work in modern industrial organisation has further contributed to our understanding of product differentiation and advertising as entry barriers. It now appears that a cautious approach is warranted. Product differentiation and advertising can, under certain conditions, reduce consumer welfare. Advertising may be used either to increase the objective knowledge of products or to create consumers' preferences for a particular brand, thereby making the demand for those products less elastic and market entry by newcomers more difficult. However, to qualify as an entry barrier and not just as an entry impediment, the effects of advertising must last sufficiently long to enable incumbent firms to earn super-normal profits persistently. On the latter point the relevant empirical evidence is mixed: some researchers found that the effects of advertising lasted for several years, whereas others found that advertising effects are gone within a year . . . Modern industrial organisation stresses the importance of sunk costs in assessing whether advertising may function as a barrier to entry. Sunk costs are central to the calculations of potential entrants: advertising costs to build consumer loyalty are normally sunk costs unless an exiting firm could either sell its brand name or use it somewhere else without a loss. The higher advertising and promotion expenditures that cannot be recovered on exiting a particular market, the more entry will be deterred. . . . Recent literature in industrial organisation on product differentiation also includes the view that it may be used as an instrument to obstruct market entry. To deter entrants looking for unfulfilled product design or brand image niches, established sellers might seek to crowd product space with enough brands (brand proliferation) so that no room for profitable new entry remains. . . .

The Commission Staff Discussion Paper said:[480]

it may be difficult to enter an industry where experience or reputation is necessary to compete effectively, both of which may be difficult to obtain as an entrant. Factors such as consumer loyalty to a particular brand, the closeness of relationships between suppliers and customers, the importance of promotion or advertising,

---

[476] Bain, n. 43. See also M. Spence, 'Notes on Advertising, Economies of Scale and Entry Barriers' (1980) 95 *Quart J of Econ* 493; J. Sutton, *Sunk Costs and Market Structure: Price Competition, Advertising, and the Evolution of Concentration* (MIT Press, 1991).

[477] See R. Schmalensee, 'Entry Deterrence in the Ready-to-eat Breakfast Cereal Industry' (1978) 9 *Bell J Econ* 305.

[478] G. Stigler, 'The Economics of Information' (1961) 69 *J of Political Economy* 213; see Van den Bergh and Camesasca, n. 32, 144–145.

[479] See Bain, n. 43; R. Schmalensee, 'Product Differentiation Advantages of Pioneering Brands' (1981) 72 *Am Econ Rev* 349. Bain considered product differentiation a barrier to entry but the Chicago School does not.

[480] Commission Staff Discussion Paper, n. 369, para. 40.

or other reputation advantages will be taken into account. Advertising and other investments in reputation are often sunk costs which cannot be recovered in the case of exit and which therefore make entry more risky.

- *Tying.*[481] Tying and bundling, whereby a dominant undertaking makes the purchase of one product conditional on the purchase of another, or 'bundles' them together, are discussed in Chapter 7.

- *Exclusive dealing arrangements*[482] are vertical arrangements whereby customers contract with an incumbent undertaking to purchase all their requirements of the relevant product from that undertaking. They raise similar issues to fidelity rebates, which may have the same effect. They are discussed in Chapter 7. The OECD report notes that an incumbent undertaking operating on a market where it is necessary to use distributors may sign exclusive contracts with enough of the available distributors (rather than directly with the customers) to mean that new entrants would need in effect to vertically integrate, a requirement that would render entry riskier and therefore less likely.

- *Patent hoarding.*[483] Although IPRs can be structural barriers (both as legal and regulatory barriers and as first-mover advantages) the way in which they are used by their holders can also be strategic barriers. The OECD mentions the practice of 'patent hoarding' whereby an undertaking acquires numerous patents that block the feasible methods of competing and thereby builds a 'fortress' around its market position. These may be patents that the undertaking has no intention of exploiting commercially, but are simply deterrents to entry.[484]

Although not specifically listed in the OECD Roundtable document, switching costs, discussed earlier in respect of their possible effect on market definition, can also constitute barriers to entry. Switching costs are structural barriers but can also be exploited by undertakings and so form strategic barriers. Furthermore, opportunity costs can act as barriers. Opportunity costs, the value of what has to be given up to do something else,[485] can be classed as an absolute cost advantage for the incumbent.

The Commission sets out the forms that barriers to entry can take in the 2004 Horizontal Merger Guidelines, which are discussed in Chapter 15.[486] In the Guidelines the Commission takes a broad view of barriers to entry, considering that they can comprise legal or technical advantages or may exist because of the established position of the incumbent firms on the market. The Commission also deals with barriers to entry in the Guidance Paper, as discussed in Chapter 6 where the decisional practice of the Commission and the case law in respect of Article 102 are considered.

16. CONCLUSIONS

1. Competition law upholds the workings of the free market economy by policing the conduct of firms as they compete in the market. Whether anti-competitive harm should be judged by the effects on competitors, on the structure of competition, on consumers, on society in some broader sense, or by some combination of these, is a matter of long-standing debate.

2. There is currently a consensus in mainstream economics that competition law systems should be designed to maximise 'welfare' although there are differences of opinion as to whether this should

---

[481] OECD Roundtable, n. 441, section 3.3.6.

[482] Ibid., section 3.3.7.

[483] Ibid., section 3.3.8. The practice is also addressed in in the OECD Roundtable report *Intellectual Property Rights*, DAF(2004)24, <http://www.oecd.org/daf/competition/abuse/34306055.pdf>.

[484] The abuse of IPRs is discussed in Chaps. 7 and 12.

[485] See Section 3.A.iii.

[486] [2004] OJ C31/5. See also the Article 101(3) Guidelines, n. 176, paras. 114–115.

be 'total welfare' or 'consumer welfare'. In the past (at least) EU competition law has sought to achieve a more diffuse range of objectives. The debate about the aims of EU competition law is affected by the fact that competition is but one of a range of policies pursued by the EU and that EU competition policy serves as a tool of the single market. At present the view of the European Commission, the EU competition authority, is that competition law should be directed to consumer welfare. The EU Courts currently tend to express the objectives of EU competition law in wider terms.

3. The belief that competition produces the best outcomes for society is based on neoclassical economic theory. This teaches that in competitive markets prices are kept down, and other benefits, such as quality, choice, and innovation, flow to consumers, whereas in markets which are monopolised output is reduced, prices rise, and consumers are deprived of choice, quality, and innovation. Competition is said to produce 'efficiency'. The matter is complicated by the fact that there are different aspects to efficiency and, in particular, the need to take account of dynamic efficiencies may make the application of competition law in any specific situation a complex exercise. Even where there is agreement about the ultimate objectives of competition law there is much debate about how to achieve efficiency and maximise consumer welfare and in any particular case there may be room for argument about the analysis of the market, the effects of the transaction or conduct under review, and the desirability of intervention.

4. A central concept of competition law is 'market power'. Market power is usually defined as the ability to profitably raise prices above the competitive level for a significant period of time.

5. Market definition and barriers to entry are both employed in assessing market power. There are difficulties involved in defining markets and identifying (and even defining) a barrier to entry. The imprecise nature of these concepts should be borne in mind in all cases where the application of competition rules is being considered. If markets are wrongly defined and barriers to entry imagined the application of the competition rules can take a wrong turn and prohibit conduct which might otherwise achieve economic efficiency and maximise welfare.

17. FURTHER READING

A. BOOKS

AKMAN, P., *The Concept of Abuse in EU Competition Law* (Hart Publishing, 2012), Chap. 1

AMATO, G., *Antitrust and the Bounds of Power* (Hart Publishing, 1997)

BAIN, J. S., *Barriers to New Competition* (Harvard University Press, 1956)

BAIN, J. S., *Industrial Organization* (2nd edn, John Wiley, 1968)

BAQUERO CRUZ, J., *Between Competition and Free Movement* (Hart Publishing, 2002)

BEGG, D., VERNASCA, G., FISCHER, S., and DORNBUSCH, R., *Economics* (10th edn, McGraw-Hill, 2011)

BELLAMY and CHILD (V. Rose and D. Bailey, eds.), *European Union Law of Competition* (7th edn, Oxford University Press, 2013 and Supplement by L. John and J. Turner, 2015), Chap. 4

BISHOP, S., and WALKER, M., *The Economics of EC Competition Law: Concepts, Application and Measurement* (3rd edn, Sweet & Maxwell, 2010)

BORK, R. H., *The Antitrust Paradox: A Policy at War with Itself* (Basic Books, 1978, reprinted with a new Introduction and Epilogue, 1993)

CARLTON, D. W., and PERLOFF, J. M., *Modern Industrial Organization* (4th edn, Pearson Addison Wesley, 2005)

CASSIDY, J., *How Markets Fail: The Logic of Economic Calamities* (Allen Lane, 2009)

COATES, K., *EC Competition Law in Technology Markets* (Oxford University Press, 2010), Chap. 2

CSERES, K., *Competition Law and Consumer Protection* (Kluwer Law International, 2005), 331–332

CUCINOTTA, A., PARDOLESI R., and VAN DEN BERGH, R., *Post-Chicago Developments in Antitrust Law* (Edward Elgar, 2002)

DUNNE, N., *Competition Law and Economic Regulation* (Cambridge University Press, 2015)

ELHAUGE, E., and GERADIN, D., *Global Competition Law and Economics* (2nd edn, Hart Publishing, 2011), Chap. 1

FATUR, A., *EU Competition Law and the Information and Communication Technology Network Industries* (Hart Publishing, 2012)

FAULL, J., and NIKPAY, A. (eds.), *The EU Law of Competition* (3rd edn, Oxford University Press, 2014), Chap. 1

GAL, M. S., *Competition Policy for Small Market Economies* (Harvard University Press, 2003)

GELLHORN, E., KOVACIC, W. E., and CALKINS, S., *Antitrust Law and Economics* (5th edn, West, 2004)

GERADIN, D., LAYNE-FARRAR, A., and PETIT, N., *EU Competition Law and Economics* (Oxford University Press, 2012)

GERADIN, D., ZENGER, H., and STEPHAN, A., *EU Cartel Law and Economics* (Oxford University Press, 2016)

GERBER, D., *Law and Competition in Twentieth Century Europe: Protecting Prometheus* (Oxford University Press, 1998)

HILDEBRAND, D., *The Role of Economics Analysis in the EC Competition Rules* (Kluwer Law International, 2002)

HOVENKAMP, H., *The Antitrust Enterprise, Principle and Execution* (Harvard University Press, 2005)

HOVENKAMP, H., *Federal Antitrust Policy: The Law of Competition and its Practice* (4th edn, West, 2011)

HYLTON, K. N., *Antitrust Law and Economics* (Edward Elgar, 2010)

JACQUEMIN, A. P., and DE JONG, H. W., *European Industrial Organisation* (Macmillan, 1997)

LIANOS, I., and SOKOL, D., *The Global Limits of Competition Law* (Stanford University Press, 2012)

MATEUS, A. M., and MOIREIRA, T., *Competition Law and Economics* (Edward Elgar, 2010)

MERCURO, N., and MEDEMA, S. G., *Economics and the Law: From Posner to Post-Modernism* (Princeton University Press, 1999)

MOTTA, M., *Competition Policy* (Cambridge University Press, 2004)

NAZZINI, R., *The Foundations of European Union Competition Law: The Objectives and Principles of Article 102* (Oxford University Press, 2011), Chap. 2

NIELS, G., JENKINS, H., and KAVANAGH, J., *Economics for Competition Lawyers* (2nd edn, Oxford University Press, 2016)

ODUDU, O., *The Boundaries of EC Competition Law* (Oxford University Press, 2006), Chap. 2

ORTIZ BLANCO, L., *Market Power in EU Antitrust Law* (Hart Publishing, 2012)

PATEL, K. K., and SCHWEITZER, H., *The Historical Foundations of EU Competition Law* (Oxford University Press, 2013)

PITOFSKY, R. (ed.), *How Chicago Overshot the Mark: The Effect of Conservative Economic Analysis on US Antitrust* (Oxford University Press, 2008)

POSNER, R. A., *Antitrust Law* (2nd edn, University of Chicago Press, 2001)

POSNER, R. A., *A Failure of Capitalism* (Harvard University Press, 2009)

POSNER, R. A., *The Crisis of Capitalist Democracy* (Harvard University Press, 2010)

SAUTER, W., *Competition Law and Industrial Policy in the EU* (Oxford University Press, 1997)

SCHERER, F. M., and ROSS, D., *Industrial Market Structure and Economic Performance* (3rd edn, Houghton Mifflin, 1990), Chaps. 1, 2, and 4

SCHWEITZER, H. and PATEL, K.K. (eds.), *The Historical Foundations of EU Competition Law* (Oxford University Press, 2013)

STIGLER, G. J., *The Organization of Industry* (Irwin, 1968)

STIGLITZ, J., *Freefall: Free Markets and the Sinking of the Global Economy* (Penguin, 2010)

TOWNLEY, C., *Article 81 EC and Public Policy* (Hart Publishing, 2009)

VAN DEN BERGH, R. J., and CAMESASCA, P. D., *European Competition Law and Economics: A Comparative Perspective* (2nd edn, Sweet & Maxwell, 2006)

VIVES, X. (ed.), *Competition Policy in the EU: Fifty Years on from the Treaty of Rome* (Oxford University Press, 2009)

ZIMMER, D. (ed.), *The Goals of Competition Law* (Edward Elgar, 2012)

B. CHAPTERS IN BOOKS

MÖSCHEL, W., 'Competition Policy from an Ordo Point of View' in A. Peacock and H. Willgerodt (eds.), *German Neo-liberals and the Social Market Economics* (Macmillan, 1989), 142

SCHNYDER, G., and SIEMS, M., 'The Ordoliberal Variety of Neoliberalism' in S. J. Konzelmann and M. Fovargue-Davies (eds.), *Banking Systems in the Crisis: The Faces of Liberal Capitalism* (Routledge, 2013) 250; available at <http://ssrn.com/abstract=2142529>

SCHWEITZER, H., 'The History, Interpretation and Underlying Principles of Section 2 Sherman Act and Article 82 EC' in C.-D. Ehlermann and M. Marquis (eds.), *European Competition Law Annual 2007: A Reformed Approach to Article 82*, 119

SCHWEITZER, H., and PATEL, K. K., 'EU Competition Law in Historical Context: Continuity and Change' in Patel and Schweitzer (eds.), *The Historical Foundations of EU Competition Law* (Oxford University Press, 2013), 207

ZENGER, H., and WALKER, M., 'Theories of Harm in European Competition Law: A Progress Report', available at <http://ssrn.com/abstract=2009296> and in J. Bourgeois and D. Waelbrock (eds.), *Ten Years of Effects-based Approach in EU Competition Law* (Bruylant, 2012), 185

C. ARTICLES

AKMAN, P., 'Searching for the Long-lost Soul of Article 82' (2009) 29 *OJLS* 267

AKMAN, P., '"Consumer" versus "Customer": The Devil in the Detail' (2010) 37 *J of Law and Society* 315

AKMAN, P., 'The Role of Freedom in EU Competition Law' (2014) 34(2) *Legal Studies* 183

ANDRIYCHUK, O., 'The Dialectics of Competition Law: Sketching the Ordo-Austrian Approach to Antitrust' (2012) 35 *World Competition* 355

ANTITRUST BULLETIN SPECIAL ISSUE: Louis Kaplow, 'Why (Ever) Define Markets?' (2012) 57(4) *Ant Bull*

ASHALL, S., 'Away From Market Shares? The Increasing Importance of Contestability in EU Competition Law Case' (2015) 6 *JECLAP* 197

AUER, D., and PETIT, N., 'Two-sided Markets and the Challenge of Turning Economic Theory into Antitrust Policy', <http://ssrn.com/abstract=2552337>

BAIN, J. S., 'Economies of Scale, Concentration, and the Condition of Entry in Twenty Manufacturing Industries' (1954) 44 *Am Econ Rev* 15

BEHRENS, P., 'The Ordoliberal Concept of "Abuse" of a Dominant Position and its Impact on Article 102 TFEU', <http://ssrn.com/abstract=2658045>

BISHOP, S., 'Snake-oil with Mathematics is Still Snake-oil: Why Recent Trends in the Application of So-called "Sophisticated" Economics is Hindering Good Competition Enforcement' (2013) 9 *European Competition Journal* 67

BRIONES, J., 'A Balance of the Impact of Economic Analysis on the EU Competition Policy' (2009) 32 *World Competition* 27

CAILLAUD, B., and JULIEN, B., 'Chicken and Egg: Competition Among Intermediation Service Providers' (2003) 34(2) *RAND J of Economics* 309

CARLTON, D. W., and KEATING, B., 'Rethinking Antitrust in the Presence of Transaction Costs: Coasian Implications' (2015) 46 *Rev of Industrial Organization* 307, <http://ssrn.com/abstract=2561783>

COATE, M. B., and FISCHER, J. H., 'Is Market Definition Still Needed After All These Years' (2014) 2(2) *J of Antitrust Enforcement* 422

CRANE, D., 'Chicago, Post-Chicago and Neo-Chicago' (2009) 76 *Univ Chic LR* 1911

CROCIONI, P., 'The Hypothetical Monopolist Test: What it Can and Cannot Tell You' [2002] *ECLR* 355

DUNBOW, B., 'Understanding Consumers: The Value of Stated Preferences in Antitrust Proceedings' [2003] *ECLR* 141

DUNNE, N., 'Between Competition Law and Regulation: Hybridised Approaches to Market Control' (2014) 2 *J of Antitrust Enforcement* 225

EASTERBROOK, F. H., 'The Limits of Antitrust' (1984) 63(6) *Texas LR* 1

FARRELL, J., and KATZ, M. L., 'The Economics of Welfare Standards in Antitrust' (2006) 2(2) *Competition Policy International* 3

FILISTRUCCHI, L., GERADIN, D., VAN DAMME, E., and AFFELDT, P., 'Market Definition in Two-sided Markets: Theory and Practice' (2014) 10(2) *J of Competition Law and Economics* 293

FOX, E. M., 'The New American Competition Policy: From Antitrust to Pro-efficiency?' [1981] *ECLR* 439

FOX, E. M., 'The Modernisation of Antitrust: A New Equilibrium' (1981) 66 *Cornell LR* 1140

FOX, E. M., 'Consumer Beware Chicago' (1984–1985) 84 *Mich LR* 1714

FOX, E. M., 'What is Harm to Competition? Exclusionary Practices and Anti-competitive Effect' (2002) 70 *ALJ* 371

FOX, E. M., and SULLIVAN, L. A., 'Antitrust—Retrospective and Prospective: Where Are We Coming From? Where Are We Going?' (1987) 62 *New York Univ LR* 936

GERBER, D., 'Constitutionalizing the Economy: German Neo-liberalism, Competition Law and the "New Europe"' (1994) 42 *Am J of Comparative Law* 25

GREEN, N., 'From Rome to Rome: The Evolution of Competition Law into a Twenty-first Century Religion' [2010] *Comp Law* 25

HARBORD, D., and HOEHN, T., 'Barriers to Entry and Exit in European Competition Policy' (1994) 14 *International Review of Law and Economics* 41

HILDEBRAND, D., 'The European School in EC Competition Law' (2002) 25 *World Competition* 3

HOVENKAMP, H., 'Antitrust after Chicago' (1984–1985) 84 *Mich LR* 213

HÜSCHELRATH, K., 'Critical Loss Analysis in Market Definition and Merger Control' (2009) 3 *European Competition Journal* 757

HÜSCHELRATH, K., 'The Costs and Benefits of Antitrust Enforcement: Identification and Measurement' (2012) 35 *World Competition* 121

JONES, A., and ALBORS-LLORENS, A., 'The Images of the "Consumer" in EU Competition Law' (2016), <http://papers.ssrn.com/sol3/papers.cfm?abstract_id=2750922>

KAPLOW, L., 'Why (Ever) Define Markets?' (2010) 124 *Harvard LR* 437

KOVACIC, W., 'The Intellectual DNA of Modern U.S. Competition Law For Dominant Firm Conduct: The Chicago/Harvard Double Helix' (2007) 1 *Colum Business LR* 1

LAMADRID DE PABLO, A., 'The Double Duality of Two-sided Markets' [2015] Comp Law 5

LANDES, W. M., and POSNER, R. A., 'Market Power in Antitrust Cases' (1981) 94 Harvard LR 937

LEIBENSTEIN, H., 'Allocative Efficiency vs. "X-efficiency"' (1966) 56 Am Econ Rev 392

LOVDAHL GORMESEN, L., 'The Conflict between Economic Freedom and Consumer Welfare in the Modernisation of Article 82' (2007) 3 European Competition Journal 329

LOWE, P., 'The Design of Competition Policy Institutions for the 21st Century—The Experience of the European Commission and DG Competition' (2008) 3 Competition Policy Newsletter 1

MANNE, G. A., and WRIGHT, J. D., 'Innovation and the Limits of Antitrust' (2010) 1 J of Competition Law and Economics, Special Issue, 'The Limits of Antitrust Revisited'

MARSDEN, P., and WHELAN, P., 'Consumer Detriment and its Application in EC and UK Competition Law' [2006] ECLR 569

MUELLER, C. E., 'Antitrust Economics and the "The Flying Dutchman": How Economists Ruined Antitrust in Reagan's 1980s' (2008) 34(2) Antitrust Law and Economics Review 1

PARRET, L., 'The Objectives of EU Competition Law and Policy' (2010) 6 European Competition Journal 339

PETIT, N., and NEYRINCK, N., 'Industrial Policy and Competition Enforcement: Is There, Could There

and Should There Be a Nexus?', available at <http://ssrn.com/abstract=2225903>

POSNER, R. A., 'The Social Costs of Monopoly and Regulation' [1975] J of Political Economy 83

POSNER, R. A., 'The Chicago School of Antitrust Analysis' (1979) 127 U Pa LR 925

ROCHET, J.-C., and TIROLE, J., 'Two-sided Markets: A Progress Report' (2006) 35(3) RAND J of Economics 645

STUCKE, M. E., 'Is Competition Always Good?' (2013) 1(1) J of Antitrust Enforcement 162

THÉPOT, F., 'Market Power in Online Search and Social Networking: A Matter of Two-sided Markets' (2013) 36 World Competition 195

TOWNLEY, C., 'Which Goals Count in Article 101 TFEU?: Public Policy and its Discontents' [2011] ECLR 441

VANBERG, V., 'The Freiburg School: Walter Eucken and Ordoliberalism', Freiburg Discussion Papers on Constitutional Economics, No 04/11 (2004), <www.eonstor.eu/dspace/bitstream/10419/4343/1/04_llbw.pdf>

VELJANOVSKI, C., 'Markets without Substitutes: Substitution versus Constraints as the Key to Market Definition' [2010] ECLR 122

WEITBRECHT, A., 'From Freiburg to Chicago and Beyond—The First 50 Years of European Competition Law' [2008] ECLR 81

WITT, A. C., 'Public Policy Goals under EU Competition Law' (2012) 8 European Competition Journal 443

2

THE COMPETITION LAW AND INSTITUTIONS OF THE EUROPEAN UNION

1. CENTRAL ISSUES

1. The entity now called the European Union (EU), originally the European Economic Community (EEC), was created by the Treaty of Rome in 1957. The EEC later became the European Community (EC), the major 'pillar' of the European Union. On 1 December 2009 the Treaty of Lisbon came into force and the EU replaced and succeeded the EC. The EC has ceased to exist.

2. The Treaties governing the EU are the Treaty on European Union (TEU), the Treaty on the Functioning of the European Union (TFEU), and the Charter of Fundamental Rights of the European Union (the Charter). Until 1 December 2009 the competition rules were contained in the Treaty of Rome, and competition law was EC law rather than EU law. It is now EU law. The competition rules are contained in the TFEU.

3. The Council has played a relatively minor role in the development of competition law. In 1962 Council Regulation 17 gave wide powers to enforce and apply the competition rules to the Commission. Regulation 17 was replaced by Regulation 1/2003, which took effect on 1 May 2004.

4. The Commission is divided into Directorates-General. One of these, the Directorate-General for Competition (DG Comp) is responsible for competition policy. One Commissioner has responsibility for the competition portfolio.

5. The national competition authorities (NCAs) of the Member States and the national courts share with the Commission the responsibility for the application and enforcement of the EU competition rules.

6. The Court of Justice of the European Union (CJEU) comprises the Court of Justice (CJ) and the General Court (GC), previously the Court of First Instance (CFI). These are together referred to in this book as the 'EU Courts'. They play an important part in developing the competition rules, through hearing appeals from Commission decisions and (at present only as regards the CJ) by hearing preliminary references from the national courts of the Member States.

7. The general principles of EU law and fundamental human rights (now largely embodied in the Charter) apply, and are particularly important in competition law, which entails the imposition of penalties and sanctions upon legal persons.

8. Two main provisions, Articles 101 and 102 TFEU, set out the antitrust rules. Merger control is provided for in Regulation 139/2004, the European Merger Regulation (EUMR). These are amplified by rafts of delegated legislation, Notices and other instruments, Commission decisions in individual cases, and by the case law of the EU Courts.

9. The EU and three other States form the European Economic Area (EEA) and in effect the EU competition rules apply throughout the EEA, and not just to the EU.

10. The 'modernisation' of EU competition law, of which the linchpin is Regulation 1/2003, took EU competition law into a new era.

2. INTRODUCTION

In this chapter we describe the EU institutions concerned with competition law. We then set out the competition provisions and briefly explain the way in which those rules are applied and enforced. Public and private enforcement of the competition rules are discussed more fully in Chapters 13 and 14. As the printed edition of this book does not deal with the State aid rules this chapter discusses the legal provisions and the powers of the institutions in respect only to antitrust and mergers, and the words 'competition law' should be understood in this sense unless the context otherwise requires.[1]

On 1 May 2004 a fundamental change took place in the way that EU competition law is applied and enforced as regards Articles 101 and 102. Council Regulation 17,[2] the first regulation implementing what are now Articles 101 and 102, which had governed enforcement since 1962, was replaced by Council Regulation 1/2003.[3] Regulation 1/2003 is the main legislative plank in the process of the 'modernisation' of EU competition law enforcement. Other reforms and developments both before and after 1 May 2004 are also part of the modernisation programme.[4]

3. INTRODUCTION TO THE EUROPEAN UNION

A. THE EUROPEAN UNION AND THE EUROPEAN COMMUNITY

The EU has its foundation in the EEC. After the Second World War three European Communities were created: the European Coal and Steel Community (ECSC), 1951, created by the Treaty of Paris; the European Atomic Energy Community (Euratom), 1957; and the EEC, created by the Treaty of Rome, 1957. The ECSC Treaty was concluded for 25 years and expired on 23 July 2002.[5] Euratom is under the control of the EU but is a legally distinct entity.[6]

The Treaty of Rome governing the EEC was amended several times, including by the Treaty of Amsterdam in 1999 which effected a renumbering of the Articles of the Treaty. The most significant amendments were made by the Treaty on European Union (TEU)[7] which entered into force on 1 November 1993. The TEU created a new entity, the European Union (EU), which marked a new stage in the process of European integration. Inter alia it expanded the ambit of the EEC to include more powers, particularly in the fields of economic and monetary union and citizenship, and renamed it the European Community (EC).[8]

The Treaty of Lisbon came into force on 1 December 2009. It amended both the TEU and the EC Treaty. The EC was subsumed into the EU which replaced and succeeded it[9] so that the 'European Community' ceased to exist. Since 1 December 2009, therefore, it is EU competition law rather than

---

[1] See the Online Resource Centre for the State aid chapter.

[2] [1959–62] OJ Spec. Ed. 87.

[3] [2003] OJ L1/1.

[4] See Chap. 1, Section 8.B.v, p. 37 ff.

[5] For the effect of this on the competition rules applicable to the coal and steel sectors, see Section 4.A.iii.a.

[6] See further <http://ec.europa.eu//euratom/index.html>.

[7] Known as 'Maastricht' after the Dutch town where it was signed. At the time the number of Member States had risen, through successive waves of accessions, to 12.

[8] The EU comprised three 'pillars': (a) the existing three Communities; (b) cooperation in the Common Foreign and Security Policy; and (c) cooperation in Justice and Home Affairs.

[9] Art. 1 TEU, as amended by the Treaty of Lisbon.

EC competition law. The amended EC Treaty was renamed the Treaty on the Functioning of the Union (TFEU).[10] The TEU and the TFEU, which have the 'same legal value',[11] are together referred to in this book as 'the Treaties'. The Charter of Fundamental Rights, which had been 'solemnly proclaimed' in 2000,[12] was rendered legally binding by the amendments to Article 6 TEU made by the Treaty of Lisbon. Article 6 states that it has the 'same legal value' as the TEU and TFEU.[13]

As at 5 February 2016, the EU comprises 28 Member States, ten of which entered in 2004.[14] The 2004 enlargement was one of the reasons for the 'decentralisation' of enforcement in Regulation 1/2003.

B. THE EU TREATIES

The TEU establishes the EU, states its values and objectives, sets out the respective competences of the EU and the Member States, and provides for the EU institutions and for the Common Defence and Security policy. The TFEU contains more detailed provisions and the rules of substantive law. The competition rules, including the State aid rules, are set out in Articles 101–109 TFEU. The aims and objectives of the EC Treaty, and now the TEU and the TFEU, have provided the context for the application of the competition rules. In particular, the single market objective influences the way in which the competition rules are interpreted and applied.

C. THE NON-JUDICIAL EU INSTITUTIONS

(i) Introduction

The Treaties establish the EU's autonomous institutions and the rules governing them. They confer legislative, executive, and judicial powers upon the institutions to enable the achievement of the EU's tasks. The main institutions of the EU are the European Parliament, the Council, the Commission, the Court of Justice of the European Union, the European Central Bank, and the Court of Auditors.[15] In this section we consider the roles of the Council and the Commission in respect of EU competition law, and note also the Advisory Committees provided for by Regulation 1/2003 and Regulation 139/2004, and the Ombudsman.[16] The EU Courts are considered in Section 5.

(ii) The Council

The Council, which is comprised of representatives of each Member State, takes the final step in the passing of primary EU legislation,[17] concludes agreements with foreign countries, and plays a key role in the EU budget. In the sphere of EU competition law it does not, however, play a role on

---

[10] For the full consolidated texts of the TEU, as amended, and the TFEU, see [2008] OJ C115/1.

[11] Art. 1 TEU.

[12] By the Council, Parliament, and Commission. It was politically approved by the Member States at the Nice European Council summit in December 2000: [2000] OJ C364/1.

[13] See also Declaration 1 to the Treaties. The UK, Poland, and the Czech Republic have a partial opt-out from the Charter, Protocol 30 to the Treaties.

[14] The original Member States were Belgium, France, Germany, Italy, Luxembourg, and the Netherlands; Denmark, Ireland, and the UK acceded in 1973; Greece in 1981; Spain and Portugal in 1986; Austria, Finland, and Sweden in 1995; Cyprus, the Czech Republic, Estonia, Hungary, Latvia, Lithuania, Malta, Poland, Slovakia, and Slovenia in 2004; Bulgaria and Romania in 2007; and Croatia in 2013.

[15] Note also the advisory bodies, the Economic and Social Committee and the Committee of the Regions: Art. 300 TFEU.

[16] The role of the European Parliament in the legislative process in the sphere of competition policy is generally limited to a consultative role. Nonetheless, it can be influential.

[17] Often in concert with the European Parliament: see the legislative procedures now set out in Arts 295 and 296 TFEU.

a day-to-day basis. Nonetheless, it has been responsible for the adoption of a number of important legislative acts in respect of competition law. In particular, by Regulation 17 and Regulation 1/2003, the Council conferred power on the Commission to enforce the competition rules.[18] It has also given the Commission power to adopt regulations exempting groups of agreements from the application of the competition rules (block exemptions),[19] and it adopted the European Merger Regulation (EUMR), conferring power on the Commission to rule on the compatibility with the internal market of mergers above certain turnover thresholds.[20]

The delegation to the Commission of the routine enforcement of the competition rules has meant that the development and enforcement of competition law has not generally been subject to the delays and compromises that have been encountered in other areas of EU activity. Where the Council plays a significant role, progress is dependent on the political will of the Member States, reflecting their differing views and interests. Notably, the original Merger Regulation[21] took 16 years to reach the statute book.

(iii) The Commission and DG Comp

The Commission is the key enforcer of the competition rules.[22] It has power, for example, to take decisions finding an infringement of the EU competition rules and fining those responsible. EU competition law is primarily applied through a 'public' enforcement system rather than through private litigation[23] and for over 50 years the Commission has both enforced the competition rules and played the central role in developing the law.

One of the Commissioners has responsibility for competition. Currently it is Margrethe Vestager, the Danish Commissioner.[24] Administratively the European Commission is divided into separate Directorates-General. The Competition Directorate-General, known as DG Comp, deals with competition.[25] It is headed by a Director-General,[26] has three Deputy Directors-General,[27] and a Chief Competition Economist, and is divided into Directorates. One of the Directorates is dedicated to the investigation and prosecution of cartels in all sectors.

Although one Commissioner is responsible for the competition portfolio, formal decisions taken by the Commission must be adopted by the College of Commissioners as a whole,[28] subject to some delegation of investigatory and procedural matters. The significance of DG Comp being part of the Commission as a whole and not a stand-alone body was explained by the then Director-General in the following passage.[29]

---

[18] And, in Council Reg. 1/2003, on the NCAs of the Member States.

[19] See Chap. 4.

[20] Reg. 139/2004 [2004] OJ L24/1, replacing Reg. 4064/89 [1989] OJ L395/1.

[21] The legal basis for the merger regulation is Art. 103 TFEU (ex Art. 83 EC), which requires a qualified majority, and Art. 352 TFEU (ex Art. 308 EC), which requires unanimous approval in the Council and the consent of Parliament.

[22] The Commission is 'required to ensure the application of the principles' laid down in the competition Articles, Case T-99/04, *AC-Treuhand AG v Commission* [2008] ECR II-1501, para. 163; Cases C-189, 202, 208, and 213/02 P, *Dansk Rørindustri A/S and others v Commission* [2005] ECR I-5425, para. 170; Cases 100–103/80, *Musique Diffusion Française SA v Commission (Pioneer)* [1983] ECR 11025, para. 105.

[23] Although the latter is now actively encouraged; see Chap. 14.

[24] The previous four were Joaquín Almunia (2010–2014), Neelie Kroes (2004–2010), Mario Monti (1999–2004), and Karel Van Miert (1993–1999).

[25] Before 1999 the Directorate-General dealing with competition was known as DG IV.

[26] As at 5 February 2016, Johannes Laitenberger.

[27] One responsible for each of Antitrust, Mergers, and State Aid.

[28] Decisions may be passed by a simple majority: Art. 219 TFEU. The Legal Service of the Commission also plays an important role in competition matters.

[29] But see Chap. 13 for criticism of the fact that Commission decisions are taken by a (political) body (the College of Commissioners) which has had no part in the proceedings.

P. Lowe, 'The Design of Competition Policy Institutions for the 21st Century—The Experience of the European Commission and DG Competition' (2008) 3 *Competition Policy Newsletter* 1, 6

The European Commission finds itself in a substantially different position to a national authority. In the first place, its institutional independence should not be in question. As reflected in the EU treaties, its independence from national and political interests is fundamental to its mission of promoting the 'common interest' of the European Union as a whole.

Secondly, the Commission has delegated fully its powers to investigate a case, and manage the due process, to DG Competition. The Commissioner for Competition is in addition empowered to take decisions on cases and problems which raise no significant policy issue. These arrangements offer a solid guarantee of the integrity and impartiality of investigations and their conclusions, while reserving all key decisions on cases and policy for the college of Commissioners as a whole.

Thirdly, a competition authority certainly needs to be independent and impartial. But it should not be isolated or uninformed. It needs to be fully aware of the market and the regulatory environment around competition law enforcement. And it needs to be in a position to influence legislators and regulators, particularly when competition problems can be better addressed by new or amended regulation. This only underlines the advantage of EU competition policy of having the work of the Competition Commissioner and DG Competition fully embedded within the Commission. Finally, it is worth underlining again that the Commission as an institution, and not just DG Competition, retains the role of Europe's competition authority.

Particularly since 2008, when DG Comp became concerned with the application of the State aid rules during the financial crisis, it has worked in close cooperation with the Directorates-General for Financial Markets and for Economic and Monetary Affairs.

The office of Chief Competition Economist was created in 2003, mainly in response to a series of judgments annulling Commission merger decisions[30] which convinced the Commission that its decisions should be subjected to a more rigorous internal regime of economic oversight. The role of the Chief Competition Economist and his team is to give independent guidance on methodological issues of economics and econometrics in the application of the competition rules; to contribute to individual competition cases, in particular those involving complex economic issues and quantitative analysis; to contribute to the development of general policy instruments; and to assist with cases before the EU Courts.[31] He or she is responsible for coordinating the activities of the Economic Advisory Group on Competition Policy (EAGCP)[32] and acts as a focus for economics debates within DG Comp.

Details of DG Comp, its Directorates, and staff can be found on its website.[33] The informative website is critical to those practising or studying EU competition law. For example, relevant legislation,

---

[30] Case T-342/99, *Airtours plc v Commission* [2002] ECR II-2585; Case T-310/01, *Schneider Electric SA v Commission* [2002] ECR II-4071; Case T-5/02, *Tetra Laval BV v Commission* [2002] ECR II-4381, *aff'd* by the CJ, Case C-12/03 P, *Commission v Tetra Laval* [2005] ECR I-987. See further Chap. 15.

[31] <http://ec.europa.eu/dgs/competition/economist/role_en.htm>. See further L.-H. Röller and P. A. Buigues, 'The Office of the Chief Competition Economist at the European Commission', <http://ec.europa.eu/dgs/competition/economist/officechiefecon_ec.pdf>; the Chief Competition Economist has successively been Professor Lars-Hendrik Röller, Professor Damian Neven, Professor Kai-Uwe Kühn, and (since 2013) Professor Massimo Motta.

[32] EAGCP is a group of academic industrial organisation economists whose members represent different fields of research and academic research centres in Europe. Members are nominated by the Commissioner on the proposal of the Chief Economist. EAGCP's role is to support DG Comp's economic reasoning in competition policy analysis. The Commissioner or the Director-General may also ask EAGCP members on an ad hoc basis to provide economic advice on particular issues (see, e.g., EAGCP's July 2005 opinion on the reform of Art. 102, discussed in Chaps. 5 and 6).

[33] <http://ec.europa.eu/competition/index_en.html>.

Commission decisions, daily news, weekly updates, press releases, speeches, articles, proposals, and Commission publications such as the Competition Policy Brief,[34] the Competition Merger Brief, and annual reports can be found on the website. The site also provides links to the sites of the Member States' NCAs, the European Competition Network (ECN), the International Competition Network (ICN), and other international organisations concerned with competition policy, such as the Organisation for Economic Co-operation and Development (OECD), the World Trade Organization (WTO), and the United Nations Conference on Trade and Development (UNCTAD).

Under the regime brought into effect on 1 May 2004 by Council Regulation 1/2003[35] to modernise the enforcement of the rules, the NCAs and national courts of the Member States share the enforcement of the competition rules with the Commission. The ECN was created by the Commission and NCAs to achieve, amongst other things, a harmonious and consistent application of the competition rules.

(iv) The Advisory Committee on Restrictive Practices and Dominant Positions and the Advisory Committee on Concentrations

Regulation 1/2003 provides for an Advisory Committee on Restrictive Practices and Dominant Positions.[36] It is 'the forum where experts from the various [national] competition authorities[37] discuss individual cases and general issues of Community competition law'.[38] The role and powers of the Advisory Committee were strengthened by Regulation 1/2003. A similar Advisory Committee on Concentrations has functions under the EU Merger Regulation.[39]

(v) The European Ombudsman

Article 228 TFEU provides for a European Ombudsman, elected by the European Parliament, who is empowered to deal with complaints in respect of maladministration by EU institutions (other than the CJEU acting in a judicial capacity). This includes complaints against the Commission in its enforcement of the competition rules.[40]

D. EU LEGISLATIVE AND OTHER ACTS

EU acts adopted by the autonomous EU institutions (the Council, the Commission, and the European Parliament), such as regulations, directives, decisions, recommendations, and opinions, flesh out the basic principles set out in the Treaties.[41] Most general legislative acts, intended to apply in all of the Member States, are adopted by regulation or directive.

It has already been seen that a number of regulations have been adopted by the Council to ensure that the objectives of the European competition rules are carried out. In the field of competition the

---

[34] Replacing the former *Competition Policy Newsletter*.

[35] [2003] OJ L1/1: see Chap. 13.

[36] Art. 14.

[37] Those of the Member States.

[38] Commission Notice on cooperation within the Network of Competition Authorities [2004] OJ C101/43, para. 58.

[39] Reg. 139/2004, Art. 19.

[40] The first decision on such a complaint was issued on 30 September 2008, case 1881/2006/JF; see Chap. 13.

[41] Art. 288 TFEU defines the main characteristics of each of these measures. Other *sui generis* acts adopted by one of the EU institutions may also be capable of producing legal effects: Case 22/70, *Commission v Council (ERTA)* [1971] ECR 263. Under the TFEU there is a distinction between 'legislative' and 'non-legislative' acts: see Arts. 289–290.

Commission has adopted a number of regulations under powers delegated to it by the Council and applies the competition rules to undertakings by means of decisions.[42] Decisions contain a statement of reasons (grounds) and an operative part which is formulated in Articles. The grounds and the operative part must be consistent with one another.[43]

E. THE EU COURTS

The Court of Justice of the European Union (CJEU) comprises the Court of Justice (CJ) and the General Court (GC).[44] They are together referred to in this book as 'the EU Courts'.[45] Provision is also made for specialist courts. The GC, previously called the Court of First Instance (CFI),[46] was established in 1989.

In the context of EU competition law the EU Courts hear two main types of action. First, there are actions brought directly before the EU Courts. Article 263 TFEU provides for the review of the legality of acts adopted by the EU institutions. This includes challenging the legality of the Commission's competition decisions and of a number of other administrative acts of the Commission in the competition field which are capable of affecting the interests of individuals. Challenges are normally made in the first instance to the GC.[47] In addition, Article 261 TFEU gives the EU Courts 'unlimited jurisdiction' to review fines or periodic penalties imposed by the Commission, Article 265 TFEU provides an action for failure to act, and Article 340 TFEU provides for damages for non-contractual liability.

Competition cases form a significant part of the GC's work and the GC has developed considerable competition law expertise. Nevertheless, the intensity (or lack of it) with which the GC reviews Commission competition decisions is a major issue in the enforcement of EU competition law which has human rights implications.[48] Appeals on points of law can be made from the GC to the CJ.[49] The CJ takes a limited view of its role in such appeals[50] and it is often necessary to look at the GC judgment rather than that of the CJ to find a full analysis of the issues.

Secondly, the national courts apply Articles 101 and 102, which are directly applicable. Article 267 TFEU provides a procedure whereby a national court or tribunal may (and in some circumstances must) request the CJ to give a preliminary ruling on a question on the interpretation or validity of EU law where a decision on the question is necessary to enable that court or tribunal to give judgment.[51] At present these references are still made directly to the CJ and are not dealt with by

---

[42] The Commission also has powers under Art. 106(3) TFEU, which deals with public undertakings and those to whom Member States grant special or exclusive rights, to adopt directives (addressed to Member States) without the participation of the Council: see Chap. 8.

[43] In Cases T-9/11 etc., *Air Canada v Commission* EU:T:2015:994 the Commission decision in the *Air Freight* cartel decision, 9 November 2010, was annulled for inconsistency between the two parts; see Chap. 13, Section 8.A.v.c, p. 997.

[44] The CJEU 'shall ensure that in the interpretation and application of the Treaties the law is observed': Art. 17 TEU. For the EU Courts generally, see A. Arnull, *The European Union and its Court of Justice* (2nd edn, Oxford University Press, 2006).

[45] In 2003 provision was made for specialist courts to be attached to the GC and this is now contained in Art. 257 TFEU. No specialist court has yet been established except for the Civil Service Tribunal (2005) which is to be merged with the GC (see IP/496/15 and IP 497/15).

[46] The name was changed by the Treaty of Lisbon.

[47] For the derogations see Art. 256(1) TFEU and the Protocol on the Statute of the CJEU, Art. 51. See further Chap. 13 and Cases C-68 and 30/95, *France v Commission* [1998] ECR I-1375.

[48] See Chap. 13.

[49] Protocol on the Statute of the Court of Justice, Art. 51.

[50] See Chap. 13.

[51] Final courts must refer. For a full discussion, see P. Craig and G. de Búrca, *EU Law: Text, Cases, and Materials* (6th edn, Oxford University Press, 2015), Chap. 13.

the GC.[52] The CJ refuses to give a ruling on a reference from a body that does not constitute a 'court or tribunal' within the criteria laid down in the case law.[53] On these grounds it refused to rule on a reference from the Greek competition authority on an important point concerning the application of Article 102 but accepted a reference on the same issue from a Greek court.[54] The CJ does give rulings on points of EU law which are crucial to the interpretation of domestic law in the case before the referring court. This is important in competition law where most Member States have domestic laws which deliberately mirror the EU rules and are interpreted in line with them. Leading rulings in EU competition law have been given in such cases.[55]

The EU Courts' volume of work can cause severe delays for litigants despite the existence of an expedited procedure.[56] In a number of appeals from Commission decisions[57] the CJ has held the duration of proceedings before the GC to be excessive. There have been frequent calls for the creation of a specialist competition court to remedy the delay problem, but despite the provision for the setting up of specialist courts in Article 257 TFEU this has not been done. Instead, in December 2015 the Council reformed the GC by providing that the number of judges should be increased in stages until they number 56 (instead of 28) by September 2019 to enable the GC to deliver judgments within a reasonable time.[58]

The issue of whether the judicial architecture should be reformed to encompass a specialist competition court also arises in the context of the debate about whether the current arrangements for judicial review of Commission proceedings is adequate and in particular whether it satisfies the requirements of the ECHR.[59]

F. GENERAL PRINCIPLES OF EU LAW AND FUNDAMENTAL (HUMAN) RIGHTS

We have seen in Section 3.A. that the EU has its own Charter of Fundamental Rights which is of 'equal value' to the TEU and TFEU. Prior to the Charter the EU Courts had already developed a body of law known as the general principles of law and fundamental (or 'human') rights, based on national laws of Member States and international treaties to which the Member States are signatories, particularly the European Convention on Human Rights (ECHR). The Charter can 'perhaps best be described as a creative distillation of the rights contained in the various European and international agreements and national constitutions on which the ECJ had for some years already drawn'.[60]

---

[52] Art. 256 TFEU provides that the GC shall have jurisdiction to give preliminary rulings 'in specific areas laid down by the Statute'. The Statute of the Court does not yet lay down any such areas and all preliminary rulings continue to go to the CJ.

[53] See in particular Case C-54/96, *Dorsch Consult* [1997] ECR I-4961; Cases C-110–147/98, *Gabalfrisa and Others* [2000] ECR I-1577; Case C-195/98, *Österreichischer Gewerkschaftsbund* [2000] ECR I-10497; Case C-516/99, *Schmid* [2002] ECR I-4573; Case C-103/97, *Köllensperger and Atzwanger* [1999] ECR I-551.

[54] Case C-53/03, *Synetairismos Farmakopoion Aitolias & Akarnanias (Syfait) v GlaxoSmithKline* [2005] ECR I-4609 (reference refused); Cases C-468–478/06, *Sot. Lélos kai Sia and others EE v GlaxoSmithKline AEVE Farmakeftikon Proionton* [2008] ECR I-7139 (preliminary ruling given).

[55] E.g. the refusal to supply case, Case C-7/97, *Oscar Bronner GmbH & Co KG v Mediaprint* [1998] ECR I-7791.

[56] Rules of Procedure of the General Court [2015] OJ L105/1, Art. 151. For the problems of the GC, see D. Hadrousĕk and M. Smolek, 'Solving the European Union's General Court' (2015) 40 *ELRev* 188.

[57] E.g. Case C-580/12, *Guardian Industries and Guardian Europe v European Commission* EU:C:2014:2363 (almost four years, seven months); Case C-467/13, *ICF v European Commission* EU:C:2014:2274 (almost five years).

[58] Council Reg. 2015/2422 [2015] OJ L341/14, amending Protocol No. 3 on the Statute of the CJEU. The increase is effected in part by merging the Civil Service Tribunal with the GC as from September 2016.

[59] See Chap. 13.

[60] P. Craig and G. de Búrca, *EU Law: Text, Cases, and Materials* (6th edn, Oxford University Press, 2015), 396. The CJ cited the Charter for the first time in Case C-540/03, *European Parliament v Council* [2006] ECR I-5769, para. 38. It has been applied in a number of competition cases, such as Case C-407/08 P, *Knauf Gips v Commission* [2010] ECR I-6375; Case C-272/09 P, *KME Germany AG v Commission* [2011] ECR I-13125; and Case C-17/10, *Toshiba v Úřad pro ochranu hospodářské soutěže* EU:C:2012:72.

There are three overlapping sources of fundamental rights in EU law. Article 6(1) TEU provides for the recognition of the rights, freedoms, and principles set out in the Charter and Article 6(3) TEU provides for fundamental rights derived from (a) the ECHR and (b) the constitutional traditions common to the Member States to constitute general principles of EU law. Many of the Charter's provisions directly correspond to those in the ECHR. Article 6(2) TEU provides that the EU will accede to the ECHR, but until that happens the EU is not formally bound by the ECHR.[61] Nevertheless, Article 6(3) ensures that the special significance of the ECHR for the EU continues, and Article 52(3) of the Charter provides for its provisions to be interpreted in accordance with the ECHR:

In so far as this Charter contains rights which correspond to rights guaranteed by the Convention for the Protection of Human Rights and Fundamental Freedoms, the meaning and scope of those rights shall be the same as those laid down by the said Convention. This provision shall not prevent Union law providing more extensive protection.

Subsidiarity, the principle whereby the Union does not take action unless it is more effective than action taken at national, regional, or local level is also a general principle of EU law and is now enshrined in Article 5 TEU. It applies only to areas not within the exclusive competence of the Union and, by Article 3(1)(b) TFEU, 'the establishing of the competition rules necessary for the functioning of the internal market' *is* an area of exclusive Union competence. The institutional arrangements in Regulation 1/2003 set up to effect the modernisation of competition law, inter alia by decentralising enforcement to Member States, were specifically expressed to be in accordance with the principle of subsidiarity.[62] It should be noted that the EU competition rules apply only to agreements and practices when they *affect trade between Member States* or to mergers that have an *EU [previously Community] dimension*[63] (matters that do not have such effect or dimension are of national concern only as they do not concern the functioning of the internal market) and the GC said in *GlaxoSmithKline* that the limitation of Article 101(1) to agreements which may affect inter-Member State trade gives 'concrete form' to the principle of subsidiarity.[64]

Fundamental rights are of great importance in respect of the enforcement of EU law, and are dealt with in that context in Chapter 13.

4. THE COMPETITION PROVISIONS

A. GENERAL

(i) Article 3(1)(g) of the EC Treaty

The omission of an equivalent provision in the body of the TEU or TFEU to Article 3(1)(g) of the EC Treaty is discussed in Chapter 1.[65] It is explained there that the relegation of the words 'a system ensuring that competition is not distorted' to a Protocol is of no significance.[66] When examining the way in which the EU Courts have hitherto interpreted the competition provisions it is impossible to ignore Article 3(1)(g). Article 3(1)(g) was crucial to the judgment in *Continental Can*, the seminal

---

[61] Case C-501/11 P, *Schindler v European Commission* EU:C:2013:522, para. 32. A draft accession agreement between the EU and the Council of Europe was agreed at the beginning of April 2013 but was held by the CJ to be incompatible with EU law, Opinion C-2/13, EU:C:2014:2454: the relationship between the ECHR and EU law is described in paras. 37–45. See also P. Gragl, *The Accession of the European Union to the ECHR* (Hart Publishing, 2013).

[62] Council Reg. 1/2003 [2003] OJ L1/1, recital 34.

[63] As at 5 February 2016 the relevant wording of the Merger Reg. had not been changed to reflect the demise of the EC. However, in this book the terminology 'EU dimension' or 'Union dimension' is used.

[64] Case T-168/01, *GlaxoSmithKline Services Unlimited* [2006] ECR II-2969, para. 201.

[65] See Chap. 1, Section 8.B.

[66] Case C-52/09, *Konkurrensverket v TeliaSonera Sverige AB* [2011] ECR I-527, paras. 20–22.

competition case in 1973 on what is now Article 102 TFEU.[67] The words of Article 3(1)(g), now in Protocol 27, must therefore always be borne in mind when looking at the provisions which set out the competition rules in greater detail.

(ii) The Main Treaty Provisions and the Merger Regulation

The main competition rules are contained in Chapter 1 of Title VII of the TFEU. Section 1 (Articles 101–106) deals with rules applying to undertakings.[68] Section 2 (Articles 107–109) deals with State aid. Merger control has never been expressly contained in any Treaty provision. It is provided for in Council Regulation 139/2004.[69]

(iii) Particular Sectors

The basic position is that the competition rules cover all areas of the economy. However, the following should be noted about the position of certain sectors.

a. Coal and Steel

Coal and steel passed into the scope of the EC Treaty and thence into that of the TEU and TFEU upon the expiry of the European Coal and Steel Community Treaty on 23 July 2002.[70] In the appeal from the *Reinforcing Bars Cartel* decision[71] the GC annulled a decision in respect of a breach of Article 65(1) ECSC which the Commission had purported to adopt after the expiry of the Treaty. The GC confirmed that upon the expiry of the Treaty the coal and steel sectors had passed within the *lex generalis* of the EC Treaty but held that this did not give the Commission competence to take a decision under provisions that had expired.[72]

b. Atomic Energy

The Euratom Treaty of 1957 established the European Atomic Energy Community in respect of the non-military use of nuclear energy. Article 305(2) EC provided that the EC competition provisions applied to nuclear energy insofar as they did not derogate from the Euratom Treaty. That article was repealed by the Treaty of Lisbon. The sector is therefore subject to no special provisions. The Commission took a number of decisions on horizontal cooperation agreements in the industry despite Article 305(2).

c. Agriculture

The common agricultural policy (CAP)[73] was reformed in 2013 and set out in four Council regulations.[74] One of these, Regulation 1308/2013 (the 'Common Market Organisation (CMO)

---

[67] Case 6/72, *Europemballage Corp and Continental Can Co Inc v Commission* [1973] ECR 215, para. 23. See Chaps. 5 and 7. See also Case C-68/94, *French Republic v Commission* [1998] ECR I-1375.

[68] Broadly, any entity engaged in commercial activities: see Chap. 3.

[69] [2004] OJ L24/1, replacing Council Reg. 4064/89 [1989] OJ L395/1, as amended by Council Reg. 1310/97 [1997] OJ L180/1.

[70] The Commission issued a Communication in June 2002 explaining how the EC rules would in future apply to coal and steel: [2002] OJ C152/5. It stated that it did not intend to initiate proceedings under the EC rules in respect of agreements it had previously authorised under the ECSC regime unless 'owing to substantial factual or legal developments' they were clearly not eligible for exemption under the EC Treaty: [2002] OJ C152/5, paras. 28–29.

[71] COMP/37.956, 17 December 2002, on appeal Cases T-27/03 etc., *SP SpA v Commission* [2007] ECR II-4331. The Commission readopted the *Concrete Reinforcing Bars* decision under Reg. 1/2003, COMP/37.956, 30 September 2009. On appeal, Cases T-472/09 etc., *SP v Commission* EU:T:2014:1040 the GC upheld that base of jurisdiction although the decision was partially annulled on other grounds.

[72] See also Case C-201/09 P, *Arcelor Mittal v Commission* [2011] ECR I-2239.

[73] Art. 39 TFEU.

[74] Reg. 1305/2013 [2013] OJ L347/487, Reg. 1306/2013 [2013] OJ L347/549, Reg. 1307/2013 [2013] OJ L347/608, and Reg. 1308/2013 [2013] OJ L347/671; there is also a transitional Regulation, Council Reg. 1310/2013 [2013] OJ L347/865.

Regulation'), contains the competition rules applicable to agriculture. Article 206 thereof states that the standard competition rules apply to agricultural products, save for some specific derogations set out in the Regulation, some of which existed in the pre-2013 regime. The continuing ones allow: agreements which do not exclude competition, impair CAP objectives, or entail the charging of identical prices;[75] the withdrawal of products from the market by producer organisations in the fruit and vegetable sector;[76] and certain activities of inter-branch organisations.[77] The new derogations concern: the joint sale or commercialisation of their products by the producers of olive oil, beef, veal, and arable crops through producer organisations;[78] and the temporary waiver of Article 101 in respect of measures carried out by producers in order to address severe market imbalances (only possible after a Commission decision).[79] The Commission has adopted Guidelines concerning the implementation of the new rules regarding joint sales by producers of olive oil, beef and veal, and arable crops.[80]

In respect of fisheries and aquaculture products the competition rules are set out in a separate Regulation, Regulation 1379/2013.[81] As with agriculture products, the standard competition rules apply subject to some derogations.

d. Transport

The transport sector, once characterised by national legal monopolies in respect of rail and air transport, has since 2000 gradually been liberalised and brought within the general competition regime.[82] In the rail sector, freight was fully liberalised from 1 January 2007 and international passenger services as from 1 January 2010.[83] Council Regulation 487/2009[84] provides for block exemptions in the air transport sector but currently there are no such exemptions in force. The maritime transport sector was previously subject to a specially generous regime but this has been significantly amended and curtailed.[85] In respect of inland transport there remains a limited block exemption for technical agreements and agreements of groups of small and medium-sized undertakings (SMEs).[86]

e. Other Sectors Subject to Liberalisation

The EU embarked on programmes of liberalisation and/or harmonisation of the energy, telecommunications, broadcasting, and financial services sectors with the aim of opening them up to greater competition. The issue of the relationship between competition law and the specific regulatory

---

[75] Reg. 1308/2013, Art. 209.

[76] Reg. 1308/2013, Art. 23.

[77] Reg. 1308/2013, Art. 210. This is subject to a number of conditions.

[78] Reg. 1308/2013, Arts. 169–171. This is subject to a number of conditions.

[79] Reg. 1308/1213, Art. 222.

[80] [2015] OJ C431/1, MEMO/15/6188, IP/15/6187.

[81] [2013] OJ L354/1, Art. 40.

[82] The EU provisions on transport generally are set out in Arts. 90–100 TFEU. The exclusion of certain maritime transport services from Reg. 1/2003 by Art. 32 was removed by Council Reg. 1419/2006 [2006] OJ L269/1. Until Reg. 411/2004 [2004] OJ L68/1 the competition rules did not apply to aviation between the EU and third countries. Reg. 1/2003 now applies to the enforcement of the competition rules in the transport sector. See L. Ortiz Blanco and B. Van Houtte (eds.), *EU Competition Law and Regulation in the Transport Sector* (2nd edn, Oxford University Press, 2016).

[83] Dir. 2007/58/EC [2007] OJ L315/44. See IP/09/2001.

[84] [2009] OJ L148/1.

[85] Council Reg. 246/2009 [2009] OJ L79/1 gives the Commission power to adopt block exemptions in respect of international liner consortia. Pursuant to this the Commission adopted Reg. 906/2009 [2009] OJ L256/31, extended by Reg. 697/14 [2014] OJ L184/3 to 2020. The Commission issued Guidelines on the application of Art. 101 to maritime transport services in 2008 [2008] OJ C245/2. These expired on 26 September 2013 and the Commission did not renew them. Parties must now rely on the general law, including the Horizontal Cooperation Guidelines [2011] OJ C11/1.

[86] Council Reg. 169/2009 [2009] L61/1, a codified version of Council Reg. 1017/68 [1968] OJ L175/1.

regimes which apply to these sectors was discussed in Chapter 1.[87] There has been little sympathy for the claims that these sectors should receive favourable treatment and should be protected from the competitive process and there has been a plethora of recent competition decisions concerning them.[88] The Commission is also much concerned with the application of the competition rules to professional services.[89]

f. Sport

Sport is not immune from the EU competition rules.[90] This was made clear by the CJ in *Meca-Medina*.[91]

Early cases on EU law and sport concerned the application of the free movement provisions to sporting rules. The CJ established that the practice of sport was subject to Community law insofar as it constituted an economic activity.[92] Competition law is therefore applied to the commercial aspects of sport[93] which have huge economic impact in the EU.[94] The Commission has been particularly concerned with the joint sale and acquisition of media rights to sporting events[95] and with ticketing arrangements (including exclusivity deals concerning the sponsors' credit cards).[96] Furthermore, cases on the commercial aspects of sport have reached the CJ from national courts.[97]

---

[87] See Chap. 1, Section 13.

[88] See Chap. 7. The Commission undertook a sector inquiry under Reg. 1/2003, Art. 17 in respect of the energy sector, see Chap. 9. Art. 102 is rigorously applied to the energy sector in order to make liberalisation effective. See P. Cameron, *Competition in Energy Markets* (2nd edn, Oxford University Press, 2007). For 'universal service' obligations, see further Chap. 8.

[89] The Commission has produced two reports: *Report on Competition in Professional Services*, COM/2004/0083 final, February 2004; and *Professional Services—Scope for More Reform*, COM/2005/0405 final, in September 2005. As a follow-up to these reports the European Parliament passed a resolution in December 2006 supporting the Commission's moves to rid the professional services sector of overly restrictive regulation (which is often put in place, or maintained, by the actions of Member States). For a discussion of the regulation of the legal profession in the Netherlands, see the discussion of Case C-309/99, *Wouters v Algemene Raad van de Nederlandse Orde van Advocaten* [2002] ECR I-1577 in Chap. 4. See further I. E. Wendt, *EU Competition Law and Liberal Professions: An Uneasy Relationship?* (Martinus Nijhoff, 2012).

[90] See generally Annex 1 to the Staff Working Document accompanying the Commission White Paper on Sport of July 2007, 'The EU and Sport: Background and Context', SEC(2007)935, accompanying the White Paper, COM(2007) 391 final; P. Kienapfel and A. Stein, 'The Application of Articles 81 and 82 EC in the Sports Sector (2007) 3 *Competition Policy Newsletter* 6; E. Szyszcak, 'Competition and Sport' (2007) 32 *ELRev* 95; S. Van den Bogaert and A. Vermeersch, 'Sport and the EC Treaty: A Tale of Uneasy Bedfellows?' (2006) 31 *ELRev* 821; S. Weatherill, '"Fair Play Please": Recent Developments in the Application of EC Law to Sport' (2003) 40 *CMLRev* 51; O. Budzinski and S. Szymanski, 'Are Restrictions of Competition by Sports Associations Horizontal or Vertical in Nature? (2015) 11 J of Competition Law and Economics 409.

[91] Case C-519/04, *Meca-Medina and Majcen v Commission* [2006] ECR I-6991. The CJ set aside the judgment of the GC (Case T-313/02, [2004] ECR II-3291) which had granted sporting rules a more extensive 'safe harbour' from the competition provisions (although the outcome for the appellants had been the same).

[92] Case 36/74, *Walrave and Koch v Association Union Cycliste Internationale* [1974] ECR 1405; see also Case 13/76, *Donà v Mantero* [1976] ECR 1333. Subsequently, the free movement rules were applied to the transfer system in professional football in Case C-415/93, *URBSFA v Bosman* [1995] ECR I-4921.

[93] See section 3 of Annex 1 to the Commission Staff Working Document, n. 90.

[94] The Commission's website (last accessed 5 February 2016) states that in 2004 it amounted to €407 billion, representing 3.7% of EU GDP and employing 15 million people (5.4% of the labour force), <http://ec.eu/competition/sectors/sports/overview_en.html>.

[95] COMP/37.398, *Joint selling of the commercial rights of the UEFA Champions League* [2003] OJ L291/25; COMP/37.214, *Deutsche Bundesliga* [2005] OJ L134/46; COMP/38.173, *FA Premier League* 22 March 2006; and Annex 1 to the Commission Staff Working Document, n. 90, section 3. The saga of litigation over the rules of the European Broadcasting Union (EBU) was largely to do with the television rights to sporting events: Cases T-528, 542, 543, and 546/93, *Métropole Télévision SA v Commission* [1996] ECR II-649; Case T-206/99, *Métropole Télévision SA v Commission* [2001] ECR II-1057; Cases T-185, 216, 299, and 300/00, *Métropole Télévision SA (M6) v Commission* [2002] ECR II-3805. For the sale of media rights, see also T. Toft, 'Developments in European Law', Speech to the Sports and Law Congress, Berlin, 28 April 2006, <http://ec.europa.eu/competition/speeches/text/sp2006_003_en.pdf>.

[96] COMP/33.384 and COMP/33.378, *FIFA World Cup 1990* [1992] OJ L326/31; COMP/36.888, *1998 Football World Cup* [2000] OJ L5/55; COMP/39.177, *Which?/DFB, Mastercard and FIFA*, IP/05/519.

[97] Such as Cases C-403 and 429/08, *Football Association Premier League v QC Leisure* and *Karen Murphy v Media Protection Services Ltd* [2011] ECR I-9083 (broadcasting of FAPL matches in the UK using unauthorised non-UK decoder): the cases also concerned the free movement of services.

Bodies regulating sports may be an association of undertakings for the purposes of Article 101 or be in a dominant[98] or collectively dominant[99] position for the purposes of Article 102.

Meca-Medina[100] concerned the Olympic swimming doping rules of the IOC. The CJ held that the competition rules do not apply to matters which are of a 'purely sporting interest and, as such, have nothing to do with economic activity'[101] but recognised 'the difficulty of severing the economic aspects from the sporting aspects of a sport'.[102] It said:

> . . . it is apparent that the mere fact that a rule is purely sporting in nature does not have the effect of remov-ing from the scope of the Treaty the person engaging in the activity governed by that rule or the body which has laid it down.
>
> If the sporting activity in question falls within the scope of the Treaty, the conditions for engaging in it are subject to all the obligations which result from the various provisions of the Treaty . . .[103]

In *Meca-Medina* the Court accepted that sports regulatory bodies may have rules which are necessary for regulating sporting activity even if they limit competition, because such a limitation is 'inher-ent in the organisation and proper conduct of competitive sport and its very purpose is to ensure healthy rivalry between athletes'.[104] Nevertheless, EU law must be the judge of whether the rules are compatible with the competition rules in that they must comply with the principle of proportional-ity and not apply excessive penalties. The outcome of the application of these principles in *Meca-Medina* was that the Court found the Commission to be justified in considering that the IOC doping rules were legitimate and that the penalties imposed (exclusion from the sport for two years) were compatible with the competition rules.

The Commission does not intervene in what it considers to be pure sporting issues, and coop-erates with sporting bodies in trying to reach a consensus on regulatory and organisational mat-ters with economic implications.[105] In 2012 Commissioner Almunia and the President of UEFA, Michel Platini, issued a joint statement on UEFA's Financial Fair Play policy (clubs' football-related income should at least match football-related expenditure), which was presented primarily as a State aid issue.[106] The Commission's acceptance of this policy has since been challenged in litigation in various Member States but an Article 267 reference to the CJ by a Belgian court was dismissed on

---

[98] See, e.g., Case C-49/07, *Motosykletistiki Omospondia Ellados NPID (MOTOE) v Elliniko Dimosio* [2008] ECR I-4863 (Greek Motorcycling Federation), discussed in Chap. 8.

[99] See Case T-193/02, *Laurent Piau v Commission* [2005] ECR II-209 (FIFA).

[100] Case C-519/04, *Meca-Medina* [2006] ECR I-6991. The case was brought by two long-distance swimmers from Spain and Slovenia against the Commission for rejecting their complaint that the IOC's action in barring them from the sport for two years for failing a drugs test infringed the competition rules.

[101] Ibid., para. 25.

[102] Ibid., para. 26.

[103] Ibid., paras. 27–28.

[104] Ibid., para. 45.

[105] See COMP/39.732, *BRV/FIA, FIM and others* 4 August 2011 (Commission rejected a complaint re FIA regu-lations on Formula 1 engine specifications, citing *Meca-Medina*); COMP/36.583, *FGTB/FIFA/Ligue Football/SETCA/ URBSFA* 28 May 2002 (Commission investigated FIFA's international player transfer rules and FIFA adopted rules acceptable to the Commission); COMP/35.163, *FIA*, COMP/36.638, *FIA/FOA*, and COMP/36.776, *GTR/FIA* [2001] OJ C169/5, IP/01/1523 (Commission closed its investigations into various aspects of FIA's regulations and practices after the parties, in order to prevent conflicts of interest, agreed to limit the FIA's regulatory role and to remove certain restrictions on the parties' commercial activities); COMP/36.851, *UEFA* [1999] OJ C363/2 (Commission rejected a complaint against UEFA's 'home and away' rule—each club must play its home matches at its own ground—on the grounds that it was a purely sporting rule and as such outside the competition rules, IP/99/965); COMP/37.362, *UEFA* (Commission closed its investigation into the UEFA rule precluding more than one club be-longing to the same owner from taking part in the same competition on the grounds that the rule was justified by the need to guarantee the integrity of football competitions, IP/02/942).

[106] IP/12/264. The Commission's argument was that when their finances are not soundly managed, and football clubs therefore experience financial difficulties, there is a particular risk that public authorities may be tempted to grant State aid.

procedural grounds.[107] The GC has supported the Commission's disinclination to become involved in policing sports disputes. In *Laurent Piau* it upheld the Commission's rejection of a complaint about UEFA's rules on licensing football agents.[108] In 2012 it dismissed three appeals against Commission rejections of complaints, one of which concerned the sanctions imposed on Juventus in the Italian match-rigging scandal.[109] The Commission has a section of its website devoted to competition law and sport, which also covers the application of the State aid rules which are relevant, for example, where public authorities give support to sports infrastructure and/or financial benefits to undertakings concerned with sport.[110]

g. Security Connected with Military Equipment

Article 346(1)(b)[111] provides that the Treaty provisions shall not preclude any Member State from taking 'such measures as it considers necessary for the protection of the essential interests of its security which are connected with the production of or trade in arms, munitions and war material; such measures shall not adversely affect the conditions of competition in the internal market regarding products which are not intended for specifically military purposes'. This provision has, for example, been used by Member States to retain jurisdiction over mergers with a military significance.[112] A list of the products covered by Article 346(1)(b) is contained in a Council decision of 1958.[113] The provision has to be interpreted strictly and it is for the Member State seeking to rely on it to prove that it is necessary to have recourse to it in order to protect its essential security interests.[114]

B. THE SUBSTANTIVE COMPETITION PROVISIONS OF THE TFEU

The substantive competition provisions of the TFEU are summarised here.[115] The provisions are dealt with more fully in later chapters.

---

[107] Case C-299/15, *Striani and others* EU:C:2015:519. The reference was defective. Striani's complaint to the Commission had been rejected, COMP/40.105, 12 December 2014. Striani alleged, inter alia, that FFP contravenes the competition rules and also EU rules on free movement of capital, workers, and services, and human rights. One argument of many European football clubs against FFP is that it protects the status quo. See S. Bastianon, 'A New Era After Bosman or Just a Washout' (2015) 11(1) *Competition Law Review* 11. UEFA itself recognised that the policy was particularly problematic following the sale in February 2015 of the television rights to FAPL matches to Sky and BT for three years from 2016–2017 for over £5 billion.

[108] Case T-193/02, *Laurent Piau v Commission* [2005] ECR II-209.

[109] Case T-273/09, *Associazione 'Giùlemanidallajuve' v Commission* EU:T:2012:129; the decision was case COMP/39.464, *Supporters Juventus Turin—FIGC-CONI-UEFA-FIFA*; the scandal involved certain Italian teams influencing referee appointments. Juventus were, inter alia, relegated to Serie B (along with Lazio and Fiorentina), forfeited two Serie A titles, and were excluded from the 2006–2007 Champions League. The other two cases were Case T-508/09, *Cañas v Commission* EU:T:2012:152, upheld Case C-269/12 P, *Cañas v Commission* EU:C:2013:415 (anti-doping sanctions in tennis) and Case T-341/10, *F91 Diddeleng* EU:T:2012:183 (rules of the Luxembourg FA).

[110] For example, in 2013 the Commission opened an investigation into State aid allegedly given by Spain to Real Madrid in connection with property transactions, SA 33754, [2013] OJ C69/08.

[111] Ex Art. 296(1)(b) EC.

[112] See Chap. 15. For Art. 326 generally, see P. Koutrakos, *Trade, Foreign Policy and Defence in EU Constitutional Law* (Hart Publishing, 2001).

[113] Council decision 255/58, <http://register.consilium.europa.eu/doc/srv?l=EN&f=ST%2014538%202008%20REV%204>.

[114] Case C-284/05, *Commission v Finland* [2009] ECR I-11705, paras. 46–49.

[115] In these Articles the Treaty of Lisbon replaced the words 'common market' in the EC Treaty with 'internal market'. This makes no substantive difference.

(i) Article 101 TFEU (ex Article 81 EC, ex Article 85 EC)

Article 101 is set out in three parts: Article 101(1) prohibits agreements, decisions of associations of undertakings, and concerted practices which have as their object or effect the prevention, restriction, or distortion of competition and which may affect trade between Member States. Article 101(2) states that such agreements are void. Article 101(3) provides that Article 101(1) may be 'declared inapplicable' in respect of agreements, decisions, or concerted practices or of categories of such agreements which are on balance beneficial as they satisfy the criteria set out in that provision. The provisions governing the analysis of an agreement are split, therefore, between Article 101(1) and Article 101(3). This 'bifurcation' of Article 101 has caused great difficulties.[116]

The wording in Article 101(3) that Article 101(1) 'may ... be declared inapplicable' to certain agreements left open, deliberately perhaps, the question of how and by whom this declaration was to be made. The Council in 1962 conferred exclusive power on the Commission to exempt agreements from the prohibition of Article 101(1),[117] and later enabled it to adopt 'block exemption' regulations exempting categories of agreements from the prohibition. The system of individual notification and exemption was abolished by the Council in Regulation 1/2003[118] and from 1 May 2004 Article 101(3) has had direct effect and is applied directly by the Commission, national courts, and NCAs as an exception to the Article 101(1) prohibition.

(ii) Article 102 TFEU (ex Article 82 EC, ex Article 86 EC)

Article 102 prohibits an undertaking which holds a dominant position in the internal market, or a substantial part of it, from abusing that position insofar as it may affect inter-Member State trade. It contains no express provision for exception or exemption.

(iii) Articles 106 and 37 TFEU (ex Articles 86 and 31 EC, ex Articles 90 and 31 EC)

Article 106 deals with the application of the competition rules (and other rules of the Treaties) to public undertakings and those given special or exclusive rights by Member States. It contains a limited exemption (Article 106(2)) from the Treaty rules for such undertakings. That limitation has, however, been construed narrowly.

Article 37 is situated in the part of the TFEU concerned with the free movement of goods. It requires Member States which have State monopolies of a commercial character to eliminate discrimination between nationals of Member States regarding the conditions under which goods are procured and marketed.

C. THE PROCEDURAL PROVISIONS

(i) Article 103 TFEU (ex Article 87 EC)

Article 103 confers a general power on the Council to adopt secondary legislation to give effect to the principles laid down in Articles 101 and 102. It provides:

1. The appropriate regulations or directives to give effect to the principles set out in Articles 101 and 102 shall be laid down by the Council on a proposal from the Commission and after consulting the European Parliament.

---

[116] See Chap. 4.

[117] Reg. 17 [1959–62] OJ Spec. Ed. 87, Art. 9.

[118] [2003] OJ L1/1.

2. The regulations or directives referred to in paragraph 1 shall be designed, in particular:

   (a) to ensure compliance with the prohibitions laid down in Article 101(1) and in Article 102 by making provision for fines and periodic penalty payments;

   (b) to lay down detailed rules for the application of Article 101(3), taking into account the need to ensure effective supervision on the one hand, and to simplify administration to the greatest possible extent on the other;

   (c) to define, if need be, in the various branches of the economy, the scope of the provisions of Articles 101 and 102;

   (d) to define the respective functions of the Commission and of the Court of Justice of the European Union in applying the provisions laid down in this paragraph;

   (e) to determine the relationship between national laws and the provisions contained in this Section or adopted pursuant to this Article.

a. Implementing Legislation

The Council has adopted regulations pursuant to Article 103 implementing Articles 101 and 102. The most important of these regulations is Regulation 1/2003, which replaced Regulation 17 of 1962 on 1 May 2004. Regulation 1/2003 confers power to enforce the competition rules on the Commission and on the NCAs of the Member States.

b. Block Exemptions

The Council has adopted regulations delegating power to the Commission to adopt regulations granting block exemptions, by which Article 101(1) is declared to be inapplicable to specified types of agreements.[119] The Commission has issued a number of block exemptions under these delegated powers. Some of these are general (such as those on vertical restraints[120] and horizontal cooperation agreements[121]) and some relate only to particular sectors (for example, motor vehicle distribution,[122] insurance,[123] and maritime transport[124]).

c. Other Regulations and Measures Adopted by the Commission

The Commission has also adopted secondary legislation which implements Council Regulation 1/2003. For example, Regulation 773/2004[125] governs proceedings by the Commission, covering matters such as the Commission's powers while carrying out investigations under Regulation 1/2003, the handling of complaints[126] by the Commission, and the hearings that Regulation 1/2003 requires the Commission to carry out. Directives are not often used in the area of competition policy[127] but, unusually, the *Commission* has power under Article 106 to issue directives in order to ensure the application of that Article.

---

[119] See Chap. 4.

[120] Commission Reg. 330/2010 [2010] OJ L1021.

[121] Commission Reg. 1217/2010 on research and development agreements [2010] OJ L335/36; Commission Reg. 1218/2010 on specialisation agreements [2010] OJ L335/43.

[122] Commission Reg. 461/2010 [2010] OJ L129/52.

[123] See Commission Reg. 267/2010 [2010] OJ L83/1, made pursuant to Council Reg. 1534/91 [1991] OJ L143/1 empowering the Commission to adopt block exemptions for certain types of agreements in the insurance sector. It expires on 31 March 2017.

[124] Commission Reg. 906/2009 [2009] OJ L256/31, adopted pursuant to Council Reg. 246/2009.

[125] [2004] OJ L123/18.

[126] Complaints to the Commission that undertakings have infringed the competition rules. See Chap. 13, Section 12.

[127] But note Dir. 2014/104/EU [2014] OJ L349/1 on certain rules governing actions for damages under national law for infringements of the competition rules of the Member States and of the European Union (the Damages Dir.), discussed in Chap. 14.

(ii) Article 104 TFEU (ex Article 84 EC, ex Article 88 EC)

Article 104 confers power on 'authorities in Member States' to apply the competition rules prior to the Council's adoption of implementing rules.[128] Article 104 was designed as a transitional provision but it remained significant in conferring power on the NCAs to act whenever EU implementing legislation did not apply.[129] All sectors of the economy are now subject to Regulation 1/2003 and Article 104 is therefore without practical purpose.

(iii) Article 105 TFEU (ex Article 89 EC)

Article 105 imposes a general duty on the Commission to ensure compliance with the competition rules:

1. Without prejudice to Article 104, the Commission shall ensure the application of the principles laid down in Articles 101 and 102. On application by a Member State or on its own initiative, and in co-operation with the competent authorities in the Member States, who shall give it their assistance, the Commission shall investigate cases of suspected infringement of these principles. If it finds that there has been an infringement, it shall propose appropriate measures to bring it to an end.

2. If the infringement is not brought to an end, the Commission shall record such infringement of the principles in a reasoned decision. The Commission may publish its decision and authorise Member States to take the measures, the conditions and details of which it shall determine, needed to remedy the situation.

3. The Commission may adopt regulations relating to the categories of agreement in respect of which the Council has adopted a regulation or a directive pursuant to Article 103(2)(b).

Article 105 originally included the words 'as soon as it takes up its duties' between the words 'shall' and 'ensure' in the first line. This suggested that it was merely a transitional provision enabling the Commission to enforce Articles 101 and 102 prior to the adoption of implementing legislation.[130] The change of wording (effected by the Treaty of Amsterdam) recognises that it is not a temporary measure, but confers on the Commission a permanent residual power to intervene.

Article 105(3) was added by the Treaty of Lisbon. It gives the Commission a general power to adopt regulations governing categories of agreements, i.e. block exemptions,[131] although it is dependent on a prior Council regulation. Previously the Commission could only do this following specific ad hoc Council regulations.

D. THE EUROPEAN MERGER REGULATION (EUMR)

The current Merger Regulation, 139/2004, was adopted by the Council pursuant to Article 103 and Article 352 TFEU (ex Article 308 EC). It replaced, with effect from 1 May 2004, the original Merger Regulation, Regulation 4064/89.[132] The EUMR applies to concentrations with a 'Community [now EU] dimension'.[133]

---

[128] See Cases 209–213/84, *Ministère Public v Lucas Asjes (Nouvelles Frontières)* [1986] ECR 1425.

[129] An example of this prior to 1 May 2004 was international flights between Community and non-Community airports. The UK adopted regulations, the EC Competition Law (Arts 88 and 89) Enforcement Regulations 1996 (SI 1996/2199), to enable the competition authorities to act in such cases and asserted jurisdiction over the proposed alliance between British Airways and American Airlines on this basis.

[130] The Commission asserted jurisdiction under Art. 105 over a proposed alliance between British Airways and American Airlines at the time when air transport between a Community airport and a non-Member State was not covered by the relevant legislation (see n. 129): Commission Notice concerning the Alliance Agreement between British Airways and American Airlines [1996] OJ C288/4.

[131] For block exemptions generally, see Chap. 4.

[132] [1989] OJ L395/1, as amended by Council Reg. 1310/97 [1997] OJ L180/1. Art. 352, the residual legislative power, was used as one of the bases for both Reg. 4064/89 and Reg. 139/2004 as it was thought that, on its own, Art. 103 was an inadequate basis for legislation to control mergers: see Chap. 15.

[133] For the terminology see n. 63.

E. OTHER RELEVANT TREATY PROVISIONS

Other provisions of the TFEU may interact with the competition provisions. For example, the provisions relating to the free movement of goods, Articles 34–36, and relating to the free movement of services, Articles 56–62. There is a significant interface between the free movement rules and the competition provisions. The free movement rules are also of particular importance when dealing with intellectual property rights. Articles 114 and 115 permit the EU institutions to adopt measures to achieve the approximation of national rules which affect the establishment and functioning of an internal market.

5. COMMUNICATIONS AND NOTICES

The Commission issues Communications and Notices (some of which are called 'Guidelines') which play a significant role in EU competition law. They are important statements of how the Commission deals with certain matters and are essential to an understanding of how the competition rules are applied in practice. Some Notices state the Commission's view of the substantive law and explain the approach the Commission takes to particular kinds of agreements, practices, or mergers[134] and some set out the principles by which the Commission exercises its powers and administrative discretion.[135] A number of Notices were issued to accompany Regulation 1/2003 and its flanking legislation in order to flesh out the details of the new enforcement system.[136] The Notices are crucial to an overall picture of the competition rules and in practice they influence the way in which firms conduct business. The Notices do not have legislative force and are sometimes referred to as 'soft law'.[137] However, the CJ has held that they may form rules of practice from which the Commission cannot depart in an individual case without giving reasons that are compatible with the principles of equal treatment and legitimate expectation.[138] We see throughout this book instances in which cases before the EU Courts are fought on the issue of whether the Commission did or did not properly follow or apply one or more of its Notices.[139] Particular issues arise in respect of the Notice which the Commission issued in December 2009 on its enforcement priorities in the application of

---

[134] Such as the Guidelines on vertical restraints [2010] OJ C130/1; Guidelines on horizontal cooperation agreements [2011] OJ C11/1; Guidelines on the assessment of horizontal mergers [2004] OJ C31/5.

[135] Such as the Guidelines on the method of setting fines imposed pursuant to Article 23(2)(a) of Regulation No. 1/2003 [2006] OJ C210/5 (the Fining Guidelines) and Commission Notice on Immunity from Fines and Reduction of Fines in Cartel Cases [2006] OJ C298/17 (the Leniency Notice).

[136] Notice on cooperation within the network of competition authorities [2004] OJ C101/43; Notice on cooperation between the Commission and the courts of the EU Member States [2004] OJ C101/54; Notice on the handling of complaints by the Commission [2004] OJ C101/65; Notice on informal guidance relating to novel questions [2004] OJ C101/78; Notice on the effect on trade concept in Article 81 and Article 82 [2004] OJ C101/81; Guidelines on the application of Article 81(3) [now Article 101(3)] of the Treaty [2004] OJ C101/97 (the Article 101(3) Guidelines).

[137] L. Senden, *Soft Law in European Community Law* (Hart Publishing, 2004); S. Lefevre, 'Interpretative Communications and the Implementation of Community Law at National Level' (2004) 29 *ELRev* 808; H. A. Cosma and R. Whish, 'Soft Law in the Field of EU Competition Policy' (2003) 14 *European Business LR* 25; N. Petit and M. Rato, 'From Hard to Soft Enforcement of EC Competition Law—A Bestiary of "Sunshine" Enforcement Instruments', <http://ssrn.com/abstract=1270109>. The European Parliament was extremely critical in 2007 of the widespread use of 'soft law', see European Parliament Resolution of 4 September 2007 on institutional and legal implications of the use of 'soft law' instruments (2007/2028(INI)).

[138] Cases C-189, 202, 208, and 213/02 P, *Dansk Rørindustri A/S and Others v Commission* [2005] ECR I-5425, paras. 209–213; Case C-397/03 P, *Archer Daniels Midland Co v Commission* [2006] ECR I-4429; Case C-226/11, *Expedia Inc v Autorité de la Concurrence* EU:C:2012:795, para. 28; Case T-446/05 P, *Amann & Söhne GmbH & Co KG v Commission* [2010] ECR II-1255, paras. 137–139; Case C-439/11 P, *Ziegler SA v Commission* EU:C:2013:513, para. 60; H. C. H. Hofman, 'Negotiated and Non-negotiated Administrative Rule-making: The Example of EC Competition Policy' (2006) 43 *CMLRev* 153; Senden, n. 137.

[139] Particularly in respect of the Fining Guidelines (currently [2006] OJ C210/2) and the Leniency Notice (currently [2006] OJ C298/17), and see Chap. 13.

Article 102 to exclusionary abuses.[140] This is dealt with in Chapters 5–7. The Notices are not binding on the courts or NCAs of the Member States.[141]

6. THE COMPETITION RULES AND THE EUROPEAN ECONOMIC AREA

The agreement establishing the EEA came into force on 1 January 1994. The EEA creates a free trade area between the EU and the European Free Trade Area (EFTA) countries with the exception of Switzerland.[142] The competition rules in the EEA are modelled on those in the EC Treaty (now the TFEU). References to trade between the contracting parties, however, replace references to trade between Member States. The agreement effectively extends to the territory of the relevant EFTA States the EU competition rules and all the rules governing the internal market, including intellectual property.

Article 53 EEA is modelled on Article 101 TFEU, Article 54 EEA is modelled on Article 2, Article 59 EEA is modelled on Article 106, and Article 57 EEA effectively applies the rules set out in the EUMR to the EEA.

The EFTA Surveillance Authority (ESA) is entrusted, together with the Commission, with the enforcement of the EEA competition rules. The EEA Agreement sets out when the ESA or the Commission has jurisdiction over a particular case. Essentially the ESA has jurisdiction where:

(a) only trade between the EFTA States is affected; or

(b) trade between one or more EFTA States and the EU is affected and the turnover of the undertakings concerned in the EFTA States is one-third or more of the total turnover of those undertakings in the EEA as a whole.[143] Where, however, trade in the EU is affected to an appreciable extent the Commission and not the ESA has jurisdiction.[144] The Commission has jurisdiction in all other cases.

The EEA Agreement also established an EFTA Court. This court has jurisdiction in competition matters to deal with appeals from the ESA, infringement actions brought by the ESA against EFTA States, and the settlement of disputes between two or more EFTA States.[145]

7. MODERNISATION

As already explained, on 1 May 2004 Council Regulation 1/2003[146] brought in a new era in EU competition law. Regulation 1/2003 is a decentralising measure whereby a greater role than previously is given to the NCAs and national courts of the Member States to share with the Commission the enforcement and application of the competition rules.

---

[140] Guidance on Commission's Enforcement Priorities in Applying Article 82 of the EC Treaty to Abusive Exclusionary Conduct by Dominant Undertakings [2009] OJ C45/2.

[141] Case C-360/09, *Pfleiderer AG v Bundeskartellamt* [2011] ECR I-5161; Case C-226/11, *Expedia Inc v Autorité de la Concurrence* EU:C:2012:795; Case C-23/14, *Post Danmark A/S v Konkurrencerådet (Post Danmark II)* EU:C:2015:651, para. 52.

[142] Switzerland did not join the EEA after membership was rejected in a referendum. As Austria, Finland, and Sweden joined the EU on 1 January 1995, the only States which are in the EEA and not also in the EU are Liechtenstein, Iceland, and Norway. Switzerland has special arrangements with the EU.

[143] EEA Agreement, Art. 56(1)(a) and (b).

[144] Ibid., Art. 56(1)(c) and (3).

[145] Ibid., Art. 108(2).

[146] [2003] OJ L1/1.

Regulation 1/2003 did not, in itself, change the substantive law but, as will be seen throughout this book, the mechanisms for enforcement and application have impacted on the development of the substantive law and an appreciation of how the law is, and has been, enforced is necessary to a proper understanding of it. Many of the cases discussed in this book were decided under the previous enforcement system. That system is described, where the context requires, when the present system is examined. In Chapter 4 we look at the linchpin of the reforms, the rendering of Article 101(3) directly applicable.

Regulation 1/2003 effected the voluntary surrender by the European Commission of some of its monopoly powers. It contains measures of decentralisation to the NCAs and to national courts and created the European Competition Network (ECN), comprising the Commission and the NCAs. Nevertheless, it must be stressed that despite the changes brought into effect by Regulation 1/2003 the Commission remains at the heart of the system, at the centre of the development and application of EU competition law and policy, as it has been since 1962.[147]

8. CONCLUSIONS

1. The EU competition rules are primarily contained in Chapter 1 of Title VII of the TFEU.

2. The two main competition Articles are Article 101 TFEU which applies to agreements between undertakings and Article 102 which applies to the conduct of undertakings in a 'dominant position'.

3. Articles 101 and 102 are supplemented by Article 106 (public undertakings and undertakings with special or exclusive rights) and by Articles concerned with powers and procedures (Articles 103, 104, and 105).

4. The competition Articles were held by the ECJ to be a specific working out of Article 3(1)(g) EC which is in effect now Protocol 27 to the TEU and TFEU.

5. The control of mergers is governed by Council Regulation 139/2004 (the EUMR).

6. The EU competition rules are primarily enforced by administrative bodies by way of 'public' enforcement.

7. The European Commission enforces the EU competition rules through DG Comp, the Competition Directorate-General. However, the modernisation embodied in Regulation 1/2003 decentralised enforcement to the NCAs of the Member States which form, together with the Commission, the European Competition Network (ECN).

8. The competition rules are directly applicable and can be enforced in national courts.

9. The enforcement and application of the competition rules must be seen in the context of the EU legal order as whole.

9. FURTHER READING

A. BOOKS

ARNULL, A., *The European Union and its Court of Justice* (2nd edn, Oxford University Press, 2006)

BELLAMY and CHILD (V. Rose and D. Bailey, eds.), *European Union Law of Competition* (7th edn, Oxford University Press, 2013, and Supplement (L. John and J. Turner, eds.) 2015), 1.001–1.081

CHALMERS, D., DAVIES, G., and MONTI, G., *European Union Law* (3rd edn, Cambridge University Press, 2014), Chaps. 1–4

CRAIG, P., and DE BÚRCA, G., *EU Law: Text, Cases, and Materials* (6th edn, Oxford University Press, 2015), Chaps. 1, 2, 4, 11

---

[147] Indeed, it has been argued that the Commission in fact executed a 'strategic coup', by marginalising national laws and in effect centralising rather than decentralising control of the application of the competition rules: see S. Wilkes, 'Agency Escape: Decentralization or Dominance of the European Commission in the Modernisation of Competition Policy' (2005) 18 *Governance* 431.

DASHWOOD, A., DOUGAN, M., RODGER, B., SPAVENTA, E., and WYATT, D., *Wyatt and Dashwood's European Union Law* (6th edn, Hart Publishing, 2011), Chaps. 1–3

GOYDER, J., and ALBORS-LLORENS, A., *Goyder's EC Competition Law* (5th edn, Oxford University Press, 2009), Chaps. 2–5

GRAGL, P., *The Accession of the European Union to the ECHR* (Hart Publishing, 2013)

HARTLEY, T. C., *The Foundations of European Community Law* (8th edn, Oxford University Press, 2014)

SENDEN, L., *Soft Law in European Community Law* (Hart Publishing, 2004)

DE VRIES, S., BERNITZ, U., and WEATHERILL, S., (eds.), *The Protection of Fundamental Rights in the EU after Lisbon* (Hart Publishing, 2013)

DE VRIES, S., BERNITZ., U., and WEATHERILL, S. (eds.), *The EU Charter of Fundamental Rights as a Binding Instrument* (Hart Publishing, 2015)

WARD, I., *A Critical Introduction to European Law* (3rd edn, Cambridge University Press, 2009)

B. ARTICLES

COSMA, H. A., and WHISH, R., 'Soft Law in the Field of EU Competition Policy' (2003) 14 *European Business Law Review* 25

HADROUSĔK, D., and SMOLEK, M., 'Solving the European Union's General Court' (2015) 40 *ELRev* 188

LEFEVRE, S., 'Interpretative Communications and the Implementation of Community Law at National Level' (2004) 29 *ELRev* 808

SYRPIS, P., 'The Treaty of Lisbon: Much Ado . . . But About What?' (2008) 37 *Industrial Law Journal* 219

3

ARTICLE 101 TFEU: THE ELEMENTS

1. CENTRAL ISSUES

1. Chapters 3 and 4 set out and introduce the core elements of Article 101. The way in which this provision applies to specific types of business agreements (e.g. cartels, horizontal cooperation agreements, distribution agreements, and intellectual property licensing agreements) is discussed in greater detail in later chapters, especially Chapters 9–12.

2. Article 101(1) prohibits agreements, and other joint conduct or collusion, between two or more independent undertakings which have as their object or effect the prevention, restriction, or distortion of competition and which affect trade between Member States.

3. The CJ held that Article 101(1) applies only if the agreement appreciably affects competition and trade.

4. Article 101(3) provides that the Article 101(1) prohibition may be declared inapplicable to agreements which fulfil its four criteria, broadly where beneficial aspects of the agreement outweigh its restrictive effects.

5. This Chapter focuses on the following issues:

   (a) *who* Article 101 applies to, i.e. which entities constitute an 'undertaking' and are consequently bound to comply with the competition rules;

   (b) what constitutes *joint* conduct caught by Article 101(1) (an agreement or concerted practice between undertakings or a decision by an association of undertakings) and how this is distinguished from unilateral conduct falling outside of its scope;[1] and

   (c) when an agreement appreciably *affects trade* between Member States and so falls within the jurisdictional scope of Article 101(1).

6. Chapter 4 focuses on the question of *which* agreements are prohibited by Article 101. In particular:

   (a) when an agreement appreciably 'restricts' competition (by object or effect) for the purposes of Article 101(1); and

   (b) when the beneficial aspects of the agreement enable it to satisfy the conditions of Article 101(3) and 'trump' the restrictive effects identified under Article 101(1).

2. INTRODUCTION

Article 101 precludes certain restrictive agreements, or other collusion, between independent market operators, whether 'horizontal' (between parties operating at the same level of the economy, often actual or potential competitors) or 'vertical' (between parties operating at different levels, for example an agreement between a manufacturer and its distributor). In this chapter the scheme of Article 101 and some of the key elements of Article 101(1) are considered. Chapter 4 focuses on the relationship between Article 101(1) and Article 101(3) and the substantive question of which agreements restrict competition and/or meet the Article 101(3) criteria.

---

[1] This issue is further examined in Chap. 9.

How the provisions of Article 101 are interpreted and applied depends, of course, upon the policy objectives being pursued in its enforcement. It has been seen in Chapter 1 that the answer to the question 'what are the goals of Article 101?' is not entirely straightforward. Although the view set out by the Commission in its guidelines in recent years, including the Guidelines on the application of Article 81(3) [now Article 101(3)] (the 'Article 101(3) Guidelines'), is that:[2]

[t]he objective of Article [101] is to protect competition on the market as a means of enhancing consumer welfare and of ensuring an efficient allocation of resources. Competition and market integration serve these ends since the creation and preservation of an open single market promotes an efficient allocation of resources throughout the Community for the benefit of consumers;[3]

court judgments also stress the importance of the single market imperative and the structure of competition. Indeed, in *GlaxoSmithKline Services Unlimited v Commission* the CJ held that the competition rules are designed 'to achieve the Treaty's objective of achieving the integration of national markets through the establishment of a single market',[4] and aim 'to protect not only the interests of competitors or of consumers, but also the structure of the market and, in so doing, competition as such'.[5] Further, the question of whether it is possible to isolate competition policy under Article 101 from other Treaty goals and objectives is controversial. In this and other chapters it will be seen that 'non-competition' factors have sometimes been influential in the context of the interpretation of Article 101.

3. THE TEXT OF ARTICLE 101

Article 101 provides:

1. The following shall be prohibited as incompatible with the common market: all agreements between undertakings, decisions by associations of undertakings and concerted practices which may affect trade between Member States and which have as their object or effect the prevention, restriction or distortion of competition within the common market, and in particular those which:

   (a) directly or indirectly fix purchase or selling prices or any other trading conditions;

   (b) limit or control production, markets, technical development, or investment;

   (c) share markets or sources of supply;

   (d) apply dissimilar conditions to equivalent transactions with other trading parties, thereby placing them at a competitive disadvantage;

   (e) make the conclusion of contracts subject to acceptance by the other parties of supplementary obligations which, by their nature or according to commercial usage, have no connection with the subject of such contracts.

2. Any agreements or decisions prohibited pursuant to this Article shall be automatically void.

3. The provisions of paragraph 1 may, however, be declared inapplicable in the cases of:

   — any agreement or category of agreements between undertakings;

   — any decision or category of decisions by associations of undertakings;

---

[2] [2004] OJ C101/97, para. 13.

[3] See Guidelines on the application of Article 81(3) [now Article 101(3)] of the Treaty (the Article 101(3) Guidelines) [2004] OJ C101/97, para. 13.

[4] Cases C-501, 513, 515, and 519/06 P, [2009] ECR I-9291, para. 61.

[5] Ibid., para. 63. See also Case C-8/08, *T-Mobile Netherlands BV v Raad van Bestuur van de Nederlandse Mededingingsautoriteit* [2009] ECR I-4529, para. 38.

   — any concerted practice or category of concerted practices,

      which contributes to improving the production or distribution of goods or to promoting technical or economic progress, while allowing consumers a fair share of the resulting benefit, and which does not:

(a) impose on the undertakings concerned restrictions which are not indispensable to the attainment of these objectives;

(b) afford such undertakings the possibility of eliminating competition in respect of a substantial part of the products in question.

4. THE SCHEME OF ARTICLE 101

A. THE THREE PARAGRAPHS

It can be seen from the text that Article 101 is in three parts.

(i) The Prohibition

For the prohibition in Article 101(1) to apply the following must be established:

(a) collusion or joint conduct—an agreement or concerted practice between two or more undertakings or a decision by an association of undertakings;

(b) collusion which appreciably[6] restricts competition—that is, which has as its object or effect the prevention, restriction, or distortion of competition. An illustrative, but not exhaustive, list of examples of such preventions, restrictions, or distortions is set out; and

(c) an appreciable effect on trade between Member States.

(ii) Nullity

Although Article 101(2) states that an agreement, decision, or concerted practice prohibited by Article 101(1) is automatically void, the CJ has held that the nullity affects *only* the clauses in the agreement prohibited by the provision (see further Section 6).[7]

(iii) Legal Exception—Declaration of Inapplicability

The Article 101(1) prohibition may be declared inapplicable to an agreement, etc.,[8] which fulfils the four criteria (two positive and two negative) set out in Article 101(3). Between 1962 and 2004, agreements could benefit from Article 101(3) only if they were specifically 'exempted' from the Article 101(1) prohibition by virtue of either an *individual exemption* granted by the Commission following notification of the agreement to it, or a *block exemption*, granted by EU regulation to certain categories of agreement. The Commission had *sole* power under Regulation 17 of 1962 to declare Article 101(1) inapplicable to individual agreements pursuant to Article 101(3).[9] From 1 May 2004, however, it has not been possible to gain an individual exemption for an agreement from the Commission (although block exemptions remain) and the Commission's exclusive competence to

---

[6] Art. 101 itself does not provide that the effect on competition and trade must be an appreciable one, the appreciability requirement has been added by the CJ, see Section 5.D and E.

[7] Case 56/65, *Société Technique Minière (STM) v Maschinenbau Ulm GmbH* [1966] ECR 235. See Section 6 and Chap. 14.

[8] Unless the context otherwise requires, or the discussion is specifically about one or other category of collusion, the word 'agreement' is used as shorthand to cover agreements, decisions, and concerted practices.

[9] Reg. 17 [1959–62] OJ Spec. Ed. 87, Art. 9(1), see Chaps. 2, 4, and 13.

apply Article 101(3) has been removed. Regulation 1/2003[10] makes it clear that the Commission, the national competition authorities (NCAs), and national courts may apply Article 101(3) individually to agreements whenever an agreement's compatibility with the provision is questioned.

B. THE CONSEQUENCES OF INFRINGEMENT

Severe consequences may result for parties to an agreement which contravenes Article 101(1) but which does not meet the four criteria set out in Article 101(3). Not only is Article 101 enforced publicly by the Commission and NCAs (which may investigate a violation of the rules and impose fines or other sanctions on undertakings (and/or, in some Member States, executives or employees working within them[11]) found to be in breach), but private litigants may bring tortious or other proceedings against an infringing undertaking before a national court (and this is increasingly becoming a reality in the EU). Public and private enforcement are considered in detail in Chapters 13 and 14 respectively.

C. BURDEN AND STANDARD OF PROOF

The burden is on the Commission, or other person, alleging an infringement of Article 101(1) to prove the same. Once this is established, the burden shifts on to the undertakings claiming the benefit of Article 101(3) to establish that the agreement meets its criteria.[12]

The standard of proof depends upon the forum of the proceedings.[13] Antitrust proceedings brought by the Commission are characterised as administrative. Nonetheless, because they may culminate in non-negligible stigma for the legal or natural persons involved and the imposition of punitive fines, which are treated as *de facto* criminal charges for the purposes of Article 6(1) of the European Convention on Human Rights (ECHR), this has important consequences for the procedures carried out by the Commission and the standard of review of its decisions that must be conducted by the EU Courts. In particular, the CJ has confirmed that 'the presumption of innocence resulting in particular from Article 6(2) of the ECHR . . . applies to the procedures relating to infringements of the competition rules applicable to undertakings that may result in the imposition of fines or periodic penalties payments'[14] and that the Commission must establish 'sufficiently precise and coherent proof'[15] of an infringement—the Commission must provide 'a firm, precise and consistent body of evidence' to justify its view.[16] Consequently, 'any doubt of the Court must benefit the undertaking' to which an infringement decision is addressed.[17] 'The Court cannot therefore conclude that the Commission has established the existence of the infringement at issue to the requisite legal standard if it still entertains doubts on that point, in particular in proceedings for the annulment of a decision imposing a fine.'[18]

[10] [2003] OJ L1/1, see Chap. 13.

[11] In the UK, for example, in addition to corporate fines, sanctions against *individuals* are available (imprisonment, fines, and/or disqualification from acting as a director) in certain circumstances, see Enterprise Act 2002, Part 6, s. 204 and Chap. 9.

[12] See Reg. 1/2003, Art. 2. Cases C-204, 205, 211, 213, 217, and 219/00 P, *Aalborg Portland A/S v Commission (Cement)* [2004] ECR I-123, para. 78 and Chap. 13.

[13] Case C-74/14, *'Eturas' UAB v Lietuvos Respublikos konkurencijos taryba* EU:C:2016:42, see n. 296 and text.

[14] Case C-199/92 P, *Hüls AG v Commission* [1999] ECR I-4287, paras. 149–150.

[15] Cases 29 and 30/83, *Compagnie Royale Asturienne des Mines SA and Rheinzink GmbH v Commission* [1984] ECR 1679. The standard of proof in civil litigation will be a matter for the national courts of the relevant Member State, see Chap. 14.

[16] Cases C-89, 104, 114, 116, 117, and 125–129/85, *Ahlström Osakeyhtiö and Others v Commission (Woodpulp)* [1993] ECR I-1307, para. 127.

[17] Case T-442/08, *International Confederation of Societies of Authors and Composers (CISAC) v Commission* EU:T:2013:188, para. 91.

[18] Case T-348/08, *Aragonesas Industrias y Energía, SAU v Commission* [2011] ECR II-7583, paras. 92–93.

5. THE INTERPRETATION AND APPLICATION OF ARTICLE 101(1)

A. 'UNDERTAKING' AND 'ASSOCIATIONS OF UNDERTAKINGS'

(i) Every Entity Engaged in an Economic Activity: The Constituent Elements of an Undertaking

Article 101 applies to agreements and concerted practices between *undertakings* and decisions by *associations of undertakings*. Undertaking has the same meaning for the purposes of both Article 101 and Article 102[19] so the concept determines 'the categories of actors to which the competition rules apply'.[20] The term 'undertaking' is not defined in the Treaty but it is settled in the case law that it 'encompasses every entity engaged in an economic activity, regardless of the legal status of the entity and the way in which it is financed'.[21] Entities engaged in economic activity must respect the principles of competition, whilst entities performing tasks in the public interest fall outside the scope of the rules.[22] The critical question, therefore, is what constitutes 'economic activity'. The fine distinctions that have been drawn in the cases have turned on the *functions* performed by the particular bodies involved in the case. The cases seem to establish, however, that the characteristic features of an 'economic activity' is (a) the offering of goods or services on the market,[23] (b) where that activity 'could, at least in principle, be carried on by a private undertaking in order to make profits'.[24] If these requirements are satisfied it is irrelevant that the body is not in fact profit-making[25] or that it is not set up for an economic purpose.[26]

(ii) The Legal Status or Form or the Entity is Immaterial

Because the notion of an undertaking focuses on the nature of the activity carried out by the entity concerned (a functional approach is adopted),[27] the legal personality of the entity is not decisive. The

---

[19] See Cases T-68, 77, and 78/89, *Società Italiana Vetro SpA v Commission* [1992] ECR II-1403, para. 358. Many of the cases discussed in this chapter concern Art. 102, not Art. 101.

[20] Case C-67/96, *Albany International BV (Albany) v Stichting Bedrijfspensioenfonds Textielindustrie* [1999] ECR I-5751, Jacobs AG, para. 206.

[21] Case C-41/90, *Höfner and Elser v Macrotron GmbH* [1991] ECR I-1979, para. 21. See also, e.g., Cases C-159 and 160/91, *Poucet and Pistre v Assurances Générales de France* [1993] ECR I-637, para. 17; Case 364/92, *SAT Fluggesellschaft mbH v Eurocontrol* [1994] ECR I-43, para. 18; Cases C-180–184/98, *Pavlov v Stichting Pensioenfonds Medische Specialisten* [2000] ECR I-6451, para. 74; and Case C-138/11, *Compass-Datenbank GmbH v Republik Österreich* EU:C:2012:449, para. 35.

[22] For the view that the Treaty contains a public/private divide and that the different treatment of these entities is 'justified by a presumption underlying the rules of the private sphere that its occupants are self-interested and the presumption underlying rules of the public sphere that its occupants operate in pursuit of the public interest', see O. Odudu, *The Boundaries of EC Competition Law: The Scope of Article 81* (Oxford University Press, 2006), 45–56.

[23] See, e.g., Case C-475/99, *Firma Ambulanz Glöckner v Landkreis Südwestpfalz* [2001] ECR I-8089, para. 19, Case C-35/96 *Commission v Italy* [1998] ECR I-3851, para. 36, and Case C-205/03 P, *FENIN v Commission* [2006] ECR I-6295, para. 25.

[24] Case C-67/96, *Albany* [1999] ECR I-5751, Jacobs AG, para. 311. Cases C-180–184/98, *Pavlov* [2000] ECR I-6451, para. 201. See Odudu, n. 22, 26–45 (the three positive requirements of economic activity are that the entity must: 'offer goods or services to the market; bear the economic or financial risk of the enterprise; and have the potential to make profit from the activity').

[25] Cases 96–102, 104, 105, 108, and 110/82, *NV IAZ International Belgium SA v Commission* [1983] ECR 3369; Case C-67/96, *Albany* [1999] ECR I-5751. In the UK the OFT investigated price-fixing by private schools, many of which are non-profit-making charitable organisations, see *Independent Schools*, 20 November 2006.

[26] Case 155/73, *Italy v Sacchi* [1974] ECR 409. See also COMP/33.384 and COMP/33.378, *The Distribution of Package Tours During the 1990 World Cup* [1992] OJ L326/31, see n. 39 and text.

[27] Focusing on the activity carried out rather than the nature of the actor that performed it, see O. Odudu, 'The Meaning of Undertaking within Article 101' (2005) 7 *Cambridge Yearbook of European Legal Studies* 209 citing

notion may encompass natural persons, legal persons, and/or State and public bodies (even if they supply public services or if the entity is subject to a public service obligation). As well as companies and partnerships, therefore, individuals,[28] trade associations,[29] agricultural cooperatives,[30] P & I clubs,[31] collecting societies,[32] and professional bodies[33] have been found to be undertakings for the purposes of the rules. The fact that the business occupation of a body is viewed as a liberal profession is not inconsistent with the fact that it may be an undertaking or an association of undertakings engaged in an economic activity.[34] In *Wouters v Algemene Raad van de Nederlandse Orde van Advocaten*,[35] for example, the CJ made it clear that members of the Bar which offered, for a fee, services in the form of legal assistance carried out an economic activity and so were undertakings for the purposes of the rules. Neither the complex and technical nature of the services provided nor the fact that the profession was regulated altered this conclusion.[36] Similarly, in *Ordem dos Técnicos Oficiais de Contas v Autoridade da Concorrência*,[37] the CJ confirmed that chartered accountants, who offer accounting services for remuneration and assume the financial risks related to the exercise of those activities, carry on economic activity and are therefore undertakings.

Although in some circumstances it may be inappropriate to apply the competition rules to functions carried out by sporting bodies,[38] the concept of an undertaking does catch bodies carrying out activities having a connection with sport when they constitute economic activities.[39] In a case concerning the 1990 World Cup, for example, the Commission held that the international football federation (FIFA), the Italian FA (FIGC), and the local organising committee, which carried out economic activities, were all undertakings within the meaning of Article 101(1).[40] Further, in *Motosykletistiki Omospondia Ellados NPID (MOTOE) v Ellinkio Dimosio*,[41] the CJ held that a legal (non-profit-making) entity which organised motorcycling events and entered into sponsorship, advertising, and insurance contracts designed to exploit those events commercially was an undertaking even though it was also vested with public powers (authorising the organisation of motorcycling events) which were not of an economic nature.

A. Deringer, *The Competition Law of the European Economic Community: A Commentary on the EEC Rules of Competition (Articles 85 to 90) Including the Implementing Regulations and Directives* (Commerce Clearing House, 1968), 5.

[28] COMP/29.559, *RAI/UNITEL* [1978] OJ L157/39, COMP/28.996, *Reuter/BASF* [1976] OJ L254/40, COMP/38.279, *French Beef* [2003] OJ L209/12, aff'd (but fines reduced) in Cases T-217 and 245/03, *FNSEA v Commission* [2004] ECR II-271, Cases C-101 and 110/07, *Coop de France bétail et viande v Commission, FNSEA v Commission* [2008] ECR I-10193, but not, it seems, employees, see nn. 91–93 and text. See also Case 42/84, *Remia BV and others v Commission* [1985] ECR 2545; COMP/29.290, *Vaessen BV/Moris* [1979] OJ L19/32.

[29] Case 96/82, *NV IAZ International Belgium v Commission* [1983] ECR 3369.

[30] See Case C-250/92, *Gøttrup-Klim e.a. Grovvareforeninger and Others v Dansk Landbrugs Grovvareselskab AmbA* [1994] ECR I-5641.

[31] Protection and Indemnity clubs, COMP/30.373, *P & I Clubs* [1985] OJ L376/2.

[32] Which engage in the commercial provision of services, see e.g. Case 127/73, *Belgische Radio en Televisie v SV SABAM* [1974] ECR 313.

[33] See generally M. Monti, 'Competition in Professional Services: New Light and New Challenges', Speech to the German Federal Bar Association (Bundesanwaltskammer), 21 March 2003.

[34] COMP/33.407, *AICIA v CNSD* [1993] OJ L203/27, para. 40.

[35] Case C-309/99, [2002] ECR I-1577.

[36] Case C-309/99, *Wouters* [2002] ECR I-1577, paras. 46–49, 64.

[37] Case C-1/12, EU:C:2013:127.

[38] For the discussion of when rules inherent in sport are subject to Art. 101, see Chap. 2.

[39] COMP/33.384 and COMP/33.378, *The Distribution of Package Tours During the 1990 World Cup* [1992] OJ L326/31, especially paras. 44–60. See also Case C-519/04 P, *Meca-Medina v Commission* [2006] ECR I-6991, and Case C-49/07, *Motosykletistiki Omospondia Ellados NPID (MOTOE) v Elliniko Dimosio* [2008] ECR I-4863.

[40] *The Distribution of Package Tours*, ibid. French organisers of the 1998 World Cup were also found to have infringed Art. 102 by discriminating on grounds of nationality: COMP/36.888, *1998 World Cup Finals* [2000] OJ L5/55.

[41] Case C-49/07, *MOTOE* [2008] ECR I-4863.

(iii) Public Bodies and Bodies Performing Public Functions Which Are Not Economic

a. Distinction Between Economic Activities and Activities Which Must Necessarily be Carried out by the State or Which Fulfil a Social Function

It has been seen that public bodies may constitute an undertaking.[42] Indeed, an entity may be an undertaking even where it does not have an independent legal personality but forms part of a State's general administration.[43] The case law does however draw an important distinction between entities engaged in 'economic' activities (undertakings, subject to the competition law rules), and those which act 'in the exercise of official authority' or in connection with the exercise of 'public powers' (immune from the application of the rules whether a public or private entity insofar as any activity conducted cannot be separated from the exercise of public powers).[44]

Nonetheless it is often not easy to determine whether the entity is offering goods or services on the market which could be carried out by a private firm to make a profit[45] or whether it is performing public tasks. In *Höfner and Elser v Macrotron*, the CJ focused on the responsibilities of the relevant entity, holding that employment procurement activities were economic in nature since they had not always been, and are not necessarily, carried out by public entities.

Case C-41/90, *Höfner and Elser v Macrotron* [1991] ECR I-1979

Under German law on the promotion of employment (the AFG) the Bundesanstalt für Arbeit (Federal Office for Employment, the Bundesanstalt), a public agency, had a monopoly in employment recruitment. Nevertheless the Bundesanstalt tolerated private agencies dealing with the recruitment of business executives. This case concerned a dispute which arose in the German courts between a private recruitment agency and a company for which it had provided recruitment services in breach of the Bundesanstalt's exclusive right. The private agency sought to recover fees payable under the terms of the recruitment contract. The German courts took the view that the claim should fail on the grounds that the contract had been concluded in breach of German law and was void. The Oberlandesgericht München referred a number of questions to the CJ under Article 267 TFEU, including whether the Bundesanstalt had committed an abuse of a dominant position.[46] This necessitated consideration of whether the Bundesanstalt was an undertaking for the purposes of the competition rules.

Court of Justice

21. It must be observed, in the context of competition law, first that the concept of an undertaking encompasses every entity engaged in an economic activity, regardless of the legal status of the entity and the way in which it is financed and, secondly, that employment procurement is an economic activity.

---

[42] See also Chap. 8.

[43] 90/456/EEC, *Spanish International Express Courier Services* [1990] OJ L233/19; COMP/26.870, *Aluminium Products* [1985] OJ L92/1. See also Case 42/83, *Commission v Italy* [1985] ECR 873, paras. 16–20 and Case C-138/11, *Compass-Datenbank GmbH v Republik Österreich* EU:C:2012:449, para. 35.

[44] But see, e.g., Case C-67/96, *Albany* [1999] ECR I-5751, Case C-309/99, *Wouters v Algemene Raad van de Nederlandse Orde van Advocaten* [2002] ECR I-577, and Art. 106(2) (which provides that undertakings entrusted with the operation of services of general economic interest or having the character of a revenue-producing monopoly are subject to the competition rules only insofar as the application of the rules does not obstruct the performance of the tasks assigned to them). Art. 106(2), like all derogations from the main Treaty objectives, is construed narrowly, see Chap. 8. A finding that an entity is not an undertaking obviates the need for reliance on Art. 106(2).

[45] Cases C-264, 306, 354, and 355/01, *AOK Bundesverband v Ichthyol-Gesellschaft Cordes, Hermani & Co* [2004] ECR I-2493, Jacobs AG, para. 27 ('If there were no possibility of a private undertaking carrying on a given activity, there would be no purpose in applying the competition rules to it').

[46] This aspect of the case is discussed in Chaps. 7 and 8.

22. The fact that employment procurement activities are normally entrusted to public agencies cannot affect the economic nature of such activities. Employment procurement has not always been, and is not necessarily, carried out by public entities. That finding applies in particular to executive recruitment.

23. It follows that an entity such as a public employment agency engaged in the business of employment procurement may be classified as an undertaking for the purpose of applying the Community competition rules.

24. It must be pointed out that a public employment agency which is entrusted, under the legislation of a Member State, with the operation of services of general economic interest, such as those envisaged in Article 3 of the AFG, remains subject to the competition rules pursuant to Article [106(2)] unless and to the extent to which it is shown that their application is incompatible with the discharge of its duties: see Case 155/73, *Sacchi* . . .

In contrast, the CJ has held that the rules do not apply to the exercise of sovereign powers of the State, tasks performed in the public interest, or administrative functions. In *Bodson*,[47] the competition rules were not applicable because the local authority was carrying out an administrative duty, granting concessions for funeral services. The CJ stressed that Article 101 would not apply to communes acting in their capacity as public authorities and entrusted with the 'operation of a public service'.[48] Further, in *SAT Fluggesellschaft mbH v Eurocontrol*,[49] the CJ indicated that Eurocontrol (European Organisation for the Safety of Air Navigation), which performed tasks which were in the public interest (maintaining and improving air navigation safety), was not an undertaking even though it collected route charges (which were set not by it but by the Contracting States). The supervision of airspace was a duty typically reserved to public authorities. In a later case also involving Eurocontrol,[50] the CJ confirmed that Eurocontrol would not act as an undertaking even when conducting economic activities if those activities were connected with, and inseparable from, the exercise of its public powers.[51]

In *Diego Calì*,[52] the CJ referred to *Eurocontrol* when dealing with a case concerning anti-pollution surveillance and intervention entrusted by the national port authority at Genoa to a *private* limited company, SEPG. A port user, Diego Calì, challenged charges levied on it by SEPG in respect of services provided, on the grounds that SEPG had abused its dominant position contrary to Article 102. The CJ found that SEPG was not an undertaking since it carried out services relating to the protection of the environment which were not of an economic nature but which were essential functions of the State. The purpose of the activity was to guarantee safety and to protect the port environment and to ensure public assets were properly protected in the interest of the State and citizens.[53]

22. The anti-pollution surveillance for which SEPG was responsible in the oil port of Genoa is a task in the public interest which forms part of the essential functions of the State as regards protection of the environment in maritime areas.

23. Such surveillance is connected by its nature, its aim and the rules to which it is subject with the exercise of powers relating to the protection of the environment which are typically those of a public authority. It is not of an economic nature justifying the application of the Treaty rules on competition . . .

---

[47] Case 30/87, *Corinne Bodson v SA Pompes funèbres des régions libérées* [1988] ECR 2479.

[48] Ibid., para. 18.

[49] Case C-364/92, [1994] ECR I-43.

[50] Case C-113/07, *SELEX Sistemi Integrati SpA (SELEX Sistemi) v Commission* [2009] ECR I-2207.

[51] See also nn. 85–89 and text.

[52] Case C-343/95, *Diego Calì e Figli Srl v SEPG* [1997] ECR I-1547.

[53] Ibid., Cosmas AG, paras. 44–46.

24. The levying of a charge by SEPG for preventive anti-pollution surveillance is an integral part of its surveillance activity in the maritime area of the port and cannot affect the legal status of that activity (Case C-364/92 *SAT Fluggesellschaft v Eurocontrol* . . . paragraph 28). Moreover, as stated in paragraph 8 of this judgment, the tariffs applied by SEPG have been approved by the public authorities.

The outcome of *Eurocontrol*, and *Diego Calì*, thus turned upon the CJ's assessment that these tasks, in contrast to those carried out in *Höfner and Elser*, could only be performed by or on behalf of a public body.[54] They make it clear that the fact that a product or a service supplied by a public entity is provided in return for remuneration is not sufficient for the activity to be classified as an economic one, especially if it is not independently set by the entity. Similarly, in *Compass-Datenbank GmbH v Republik Österreich*,[55] the CJ held that a public authority which stored data 'in relation to undertakings, on the basis of a statutory obligation on those undertakings to disclose the data and power of enforcement related thereto' exercised 'public powers'[56] even though it charged those who wished to search that data and/or provided print-outs for it:[57]

42. With regard to the fact that the making available to interested persons of the data in such a database is remunerated, it should be noted that . . . to the extent that the fees or payments due for the making available to the public of such information are not laid down directly or indirectly by the entity concerned but are provided for by law, the charging of such remuneration can be regarded as inseparable from that making available of data. Thus, the charging by the Republik Österreich of fees or payments due for the making available to the public of that information cannot change the legal classification of that activity, meaning that it does not constitute an economic activity.

In a line of cases concerning pension funds and social security schemes (for example, relating to healthcare or accident insurance), the CJ has drawn a distinction between: (a) entities which, fulfilling an exclusively social function, (i) carry out an activity which is based on the principle of solidarity ('the redistribution of income between those who are better off and those who, in view of their resources . . . would be deprived'[58] or 'the inherently uncommercial act of involuntary subsidization of one social group by another'[59]) or involves an element of cross-subsidy (for example, because benefits paid or the scope of coverage are not proportionate to contributions, contributions are not proportionate to risk, benefits may be payable even though contributions due have not been paid) and (ii) is subject to State supervision as to how the scheme functions (which are not undertakings);[60] and (b) entities which operate in the same way as, or in competition with, ordinary commercial enterprises in the same sector (which are undertakings even if the scheme has a social objective). For example, in *Poucet et Pistre*,[61] it was held that a French body running a compulsory social security

---

[54] Odudu states that it is not feasible to profit from the provision of public goods and services and that '[b]oth *Eurocontrol* and *Diego Calì* show recognition that effective provision of a public good is impossible absent the coercive power of the state'. He identifies the two characteristics of public goods that make profit impossible: they are non-rivalrous in consumption (once produced, an infinite number of consumers can enjoy them without increased production cost or diminished enjoyment by others); and the benefits are non-excludable (it is not possible to prevent people from enjoying the benefits once the good is produced), Odudu, n. 22, 42–45.

[55] Case C-138/11, EU:C:2012:449.

[56] Ibid., para. 40.

[57] The fact that the public entity relied on intellectual property rights to protect the data also did not mean that it necessarily acted as an undertaking, Case C-138/11, EU:C:2012:449, paras. 47–50.

[58] Cases C-159–160/91, *Poucet et Pistre v Assurances Générales de France* [1993] ECR I-637, para. 10.

[59] Case C-70/95, *Sodemare SA v Regione Lombardia* [1997] ECR I-3395, Fennelly AG, para. 29. In his book, Odudu considers that a number of elements possessed by redistributive activity can be identified: (a) compulsion; (b) control over cost; (c) control over price; and (d) absence of link between cost and price, see Odudu, n. 22, 39–42.

[60] See Case C-350/07, *Kattner Stahlbau GmbH v Maschinenbau- und Metall- Berufsgenossenschaft* [2009] ECR I-1513 (a body to which firms in an industry must be affiliated in respect of insurance against accidents at work and occupational diseases is not an undertaking, but fulfils a social function, where such a body operates within the framework of a scheme which applies the principle of solidarity and is subject to State supervision).

[61] Cases C-159–160/91, *Poucet et Pistre* [1993] ECR I-637.

scheme was not an undertaking. In this case, benefits received under the scheme administered were not proportionate to contributions and contributions made were proportionate to income (there was an element of cross-subsidy).

18. Sickness funds, and the organizations involved in the management of the public social security system, fulfil an exclusively social function. That activity is based on the principle of national solidarity and is entirely non-profit-making. The benefits paid are statutory benefits bearing no relation to the amount of contributions.

19. Accordingly, that activity is not an economic activity and, therefore, the organizations to which it is entrusted are not undertakings within the meaning of Articles [101] and [102].

Further, in *Cisal v INAIL*,[62] the CJ found that an institution providing compulsory insurance against accidents at work and occupational diseases applied the principle of solidarity and did not carry out an economic activity for the purposes of competition law;[63] and in *AOK Bundesverband*,[64] the CJ held that sickness funds fulfilled 'an exclusively social function, which is founded on the principle of national solidarity and is entirely non-profit making'.[65] In particular, the funds were obliged to offer benefits to members which were not dependent upon the amount of contributions, and an equalisation of costs and risks was operated between the funds. This conclusion was not affected by the fact that latitude was available to the funds when setting their contribution rate and that some competition with one another did exist.[66] Further, the Court held that the fund associations' practice of fixing maximum purchasing amounts was linked to their social functions and did not, therefore, constitute an activity of an economic nature.[67]

EU law does not therefore detract from the powers of the Member States to organise their social security systems,[68] but the fact that such a system has a social aim is not in itself sufficient to preclude the activity in question from being classified as economic activity; it has been seen that the scheme must both apply 'the principle of solidarity' and be 'subject to supervision by the State'.[69] Thus, in contrast:

- in *Fédération Française des Sociétés d'Assurance*,[70] a non-profit-making body operating a pension scheme was found to be an undertaking—the entity operated in the same way as other insurance companies, the rules were like those of private schemes, and there was no mutuality or cross-subsidy between the beneficiaries;

---

[62] Case C-218/00, *Cisal di Battistello Venanzio & Co v Istituto nazionale per l'assicurazione contro gli infortuni sul lavoro (INAIL)* [2002] ECR I-691.

[63] Contributions were not systematically set at a rate proportionate to the risk of insurance, the amount of benefits paid were not necessarily proportionate to earnings, there was no direct link between the contributions paid and the benefits granted, and the amount of benefits and contributions were, in the last resort, fixed by the State. Compulsory affiliation of the scheme was essential to its financial balance and for the application of the principle of solidarity, ibid., paras. 31–46, Jacobs AG, paras. 71–82. See also Case C-350/07, *Kattner Stahlbau GmbH v Maschinenbau- und Metall-Berufsgenossenschaft* [2009] ECR I-1513.

[64] Cases C-264, 306, 354, and 355/01, *AOK Bundesverband v Ichthyol-Gesellschaft Cordes, Hermani & Co* [2004] ECR I-2493. The CJ rejected the view of its Advocate General that the funds were undertakings and that their 'purchasing cartel' was subject to the competition rules unless exempt by virtue of Art. 106(2), see Chap. 8.

[65] Ibid., para. 51.

[66] Contrast Jacobs AG in his Opinion in Cases C-264, 306, 354, and 355/01, *AOK Bundesverband v Ichthyol-Gesellschaft Cordes, Hermani & Co* [2004] ECR I-2493, para. 42.

[67] See also discussion of Case C-205/03 P, *FENIN v Commission* [2006] ECR I-6295, n. 74 and text.

[68] Case C-218/00, *Cisal di Battistello Venanzio & Co v Istituto nazionale per l'assicurazione contro gli infortuni sul lavoro (INAIL)* [2002] ECR I-691, para. 31 (relying in particular on Case C-158/96, *Kohll* [1998] ECR I-1931, para. 17).

[69] Case C-350/07, *Kattner Stahlbau* [2009] ECR I-1513, paras. 42–43. See also Case C-437/09, *AG2R Prévoyance v Beaudout Père et Fils SARL* [2011] ECR I-973, paras. 53–65.

[70] Case C-244/94, *Fédération Française des Sociétés d'Assurance and Others v Ministère de l'Agriculture et de la Pêche* [1995] ECR I-4013.

- in *Albany International BV v Stichting Bedrijfspensioenfonds Textielindustrie*[71] a supplementary pension fund (affiliation to which was compulsory in the textile industry) was found to be an undertaking even though affiliation to the scheme was compulsory, the supplementary pension scheme was designed to top up an extremely limited statutory pension, the sectoral pension fund was non-profit-making, and the pension fund was obliged to accept all workers without a medical examination.[72] The CJ accepted that the social objectives which the pension fund was required to pursue might make the service it provided less competitive than those offered by other insurance companies. These factors did not, however, detract from the fact that the activities it engaged in were economic ones. The pension fund determined the amount of contributions made and benefits received (the latter were dependent upon the results of the investments made by it) and it could, in certain circumstances, grant exemption from affiliation to the fund. The social objectives were relevant, however, to the CJ's finding that the public authority could nonetheless confer on a pension fund the exclusive right to manage a supplementary pension scheme in a given sector.[73]

b. Purchasing of Goods and Services by an Entity Not Engaged in Economic Activity

In *Federación Nacional de Empresas de Instrumentación Científica, Médica, Técnica y Dental (FENIN) v Commission*,[74] it had to be considered when 'purchasing' of goods and services by a public entity that discharges social functions might constitute economic activity. In this case, an association of the undertakings which marketed medical goods and equipment to bodies forming part of the Spanish Health Service (SNS) complained to the Commission that SNS organisations were guilty of an abuse of a dominant position, in particular because they systematically took an average of 300 days to pay their debts. The Commission rejected the complaint on the ground that the organisations in question were not undertakings when they participated in the management of the national health service. Consequently, they were not acting as undertakings when they purchased medical goods and supplies. The GC affirmed; bodies forming part of the SNS did not act as an undertaking when *purchasing* medical goods and equipment for the purpose of using them for activities of a purely social nature (to provide free health services to SNS members).[75] The Court stressed that it was the *supply* function (the offering of goods and services on a market) of the entity that was important when determining whether economic activity was carried out and not the purchasing function.[76] In providing health services, SNS operated according to the principle of solidarity. It was funded from social security contributions and other State funding and it provided services free of charge to its members on the basis of universal cover. If the activity for which the entity purchased goods was not an economic one, it made no difference that the entity might wield very considerable economic power, even giving rise to a monopsony.[77] The GC did not consider whether the fact that SNS did charge some patients (not covered by SNS) for care would alter the conclusion on the undertaking question. Although this point was raised on appeal it had not been put to the Commission and so was held not to be relevant for the purposes of reviewing the legality of the Commission's decision.[78]

---

[71] Case C-67/96, [1999] ECR I-5751. The case concerned a dispute between the fund and Albany, a textile business, which wished to be exempted from the affiliation.

[72] Ibid., paras. 77–87. See also Cases C-180–184, *Pavlov* [2000] ECR I-6451.

[73] See discussion of the case in Chap. 8.

[74] Case C-205/03 P, *FENIN v Commission* [2006] ECR I-6295, Case T-319/99, [2003] ECR II-351.

[75] See also Cases C-264, 306, 354, and 355/01, *AOK Bundesverband v Ichthyol-Gesellschaft Cordes, Hermani & Co* [2004] ECR I-2493.

[76] Case T-319/99, [2003] ECR II-351, para. 36.

[77] Ibid., para. 37. Contrast the view of Jacobs AG in Case C-218/00, *Cisal di Battistello Venanzio & Co v Istituto nazionale per l'assicurazione contro gli infortuni sul lavoro (INAIL)* [2002] ECR I-691, para. 71.

[78] Ibid., paras. 40–43.

On appeal, the CJ,[79] in a very short judgment, upheld the decision of the GC and rejected FENIN's argument that the GC had adopted too narrow a definition of economic activity since it had failed to consider whether purchasing activity is in itself an economic activity which may be dissociated from the service subsequently provided or because the subsequent activity—the provision of medical treatment—was itself an economic activity. Again, the CJ stressed that the characteristic feature of an economic activity consists in offering of goods and services on a given market.

Case C-205/03, *Federación Nacional de Empresas de Instrumentación Científica, Médica, Técnica y Dental (FENIN) v Commission* [2006] ECR I-6295

Court of Justice

23. In support of the first part of its plea, FENIN argues that the [GC] adopted a definition of economic activity which is too narrow, holding that that activity necessarily consists of the offer of goods or services on a given market and excluding all purchasing activity from that definition. FENIN submits that the approach of the [GC] would enable many bodies to avoid the competition rules of the Treaty, even though competition is affected by the conduct of such bodies.

24. The Commission submits that it is precisely the act of placing goods or services on a given market which characterises the concept of economic activity and not purchasing activity as such. Accordingly, there is no need to dissociate the purchase from the use to which the purchased goods are put.

Findings of the Court

25. The [GC] rightly held, in paragraph 35 of the judgment under appeal, that in Community competition law the definition of an 'undertaking' covers any entity engaged in an economic activity, regardless of the legal status of that entity and the way in which it is financed (Case C-41/90 *Höfner and Elser* . . . , paragraph 21, and Joined Cases C-264/01, C-306/01, C-354/01, and C-355/01 *AOK-Bundesverband* . . . , paragraph 46). In accordance with the case-law of the Court of Justice, the [GC] also stated, in paragraph 36 of the judgment under appeal, that it is the activity consisting in offering goods and services on a given market that is the characteristic feature of an economic activity (Case C-35/96 *Commission v Italy* . . . , paragraph 36).

26. The [GC] rightly deduced, in paragraph 36 of the judgment under appeal, that there is no need to dissociate the activity of purchasing goods from the subsequent use to which they are put in order to determine the nature of that purchasing activity, and that the nature of the purchasing activity must be determined according to whether or not the subsequent use of the purchased goods amounts to an economic activity.

27. It follows that the first part of the single plea raised by FENIN in support of its appeal, that the purchasing activity of the SNS management bodies constitutes an economic activity in itself, dissociable from the service subsequently provided and which, as such, should have been examined separately by the [GC], must be dismissed as unfounded.

The judgment in *FENIN* thus makes it clear that *purchasing* for consumption is not economic activity; it will only do so if the goods and services acquired are subsequently used as an input for an economic activity, the offering of goods and services on a market. This means that public bodies (even if wielding substantial purchasing power) will escape the reach of competition law unless the goods or services are bought for an economic activity. Although the view could be taken that economic

---

[79] Case C-205/03 P, *FENIN v Commission* [2006] ECR I-6295.

activity should depend equally on buyers and sellers so that there is no reason why the concept of an undertaking should apply only to one side of the equation,[80] the Court was perhaps mindful of the 'dangerous territory' it enters in this area and felt it needed to find a balance between the protection of undistorted competition 'and respect for the power of the Member States'.[81] The decision reached in this case will inevitably lead to difficult questions of when purchasing in a particular case is sufficiently closely linked to the provision of goods or services by the purchaser to constitute economic activity[82] and how purchasing should be treated when only some or a small proportion of the goods acquired are used in connection with an economic activity.

(iv) The Notion of an Undertaking is a Relative Concept

As the notion of undertaking focuses on the nature of the activity carried out by the entity concerned, it is clear that it is 'a relative concept in the sense that a given entity might be regarded as an undertaking for one part of its activities while the rest fall outside the competition rules'.[83] Thus 'the fact that, for the exercise of part of its activities, an entity is vested with public powers does not, in itself, prevent it from being classified as an undertaking . . . in respect of the remainder of its economic activities'.[84]

In *SELEX Sistemi Integrati SpA (SELEX Sistemi) v Commission*,[85] for example, the Commission argued that Eurocontrol was not an undertaking, relying on a previous finding of the CJ that:

[t]aken as a whole, Eurocontrol's activities, by their nature, their aim and the rules to which they are subject, are connected with the exercise of powers relating to the control and supervision of air space which are typically those of a public authority (air space management and development of air safety).[86]

Although, on appeal, the EU Courts stressed the need to review each of Eurocontrol's individual activities,[87] the CJ held that Eurocontrol would only be subject to competition law insofar as it engaged in economic activities which are not connected with the exercise of public powers.[88] As Eurocontrol's activity of assisting the national administrations was connected with (and inseparable from) the exercise of public powers the organisation was not, in carrying out that activity, acting as an undertaking.[89] In contrast, in MOTOE,[90] the CJ held that a legal (non-profit-making) person which organised motorcycling events and entered into sponsorship, advertising, and insurance contracts designed to exploit those events commercially, *was* an undertaking even though it was also vested

---

[80] Contrast the (prior) conclusion reached by the UK's Competition Appeal Tribunal in *Bettercare Group Ltd v DGFT* [2002] CAT 7 (the conclusion by a public entity of commercial contracts with private sector bodies was an economic activity and that it made no difference whether it acted as purchaser, rather than the supplier, of the services in question (especially where the purchaser was in a position to generate the effects which the competition rules seek to prevent) and see, e.g., J. Skilbeck, 'The EC Judgment in *AOK*: Can a Major Public Sector Purchaser Control the Prices It Pays or Is It Subject to Competition Law?' (2004) 44 PPLR NA95–97 and J. Skilbeck, 'Just When is a Public Body an "Undertaking": *FENIN* and *Bettercare* Compared' (2003) 4 PPLR NA75–77 (although this approach to public procurement might bring short-term savings it may ultimately cause the disappearance of innovative and competitive suppliers) and L. Montana and J. Jellis, 'The Concept of Undertakings in EC Competition Law and its Application to Public Bodies: Can You Buy Your Way into Article 82?' [2003] *Comp Law* 110 (arguably this means that suppliers will be made to make sacrifices in the name of the principle of solidarity) and Chap. 8.

[81] Case C-205/03 P, *FENIN v Commission* [2006] ECR I-6295, Maduro AG, para. 26.

[82] See, e.g., Cases C-180–4/98, *Pavlov* [2000] ECR I-6451.

[83] Case C-475/99, *Firma Ambulanz Glöckner v Landkreis Südwestpfalz* [2001] ECR I-8089, Jacobs AG, para. 72.

[84] Case C-49/07, *MOTOE* [2008] ECR I-4863, para. 25.

[85] Case T-155/04, [2006] ECR II-4797, Case C-113/07 P, [2009] ECR I-2207.

[86] Case C-364/92, *SAT Fluggesellschaft mbH v Eurocontrol* [1994] ECR I-43, para. 30.

[87] Case T-155/04, *SELEX Sistemi* [2006] ECR II-4797, paras. 50–94.

[88] Case C-113/07 P, *SELEX Sistemi* [2009] ECR I-2207 (the GC had erred in law in finding that it did constitute an undertaking).

[89] Ibid.

[90] Case C-49/07, *MOTOE* [2008] ECR I-4863.

with public powers (authorising the organisation of motorcycling events) and carried out activities which were not of an economic nature.

(v) Employees and Trade Unions

Although individuals may act as independent economic actors and constitute an undertaking, it seems that employees in an employment relationship and which do not bear the financial risks of the business, but perform work for and under the direction of their employers, do not 'in themselves constitute "undertakings" within the meaning of Community competition law'.[91]

In *Albany*, Advocate General Jacobs[92] clearly set out his view that the competition rules were not structured to be applicable to employees who did not perform the 'functions' of undertakings. Rather, he considered work and labour to be distinct from the provision of goods or services. Consequently, trade unions would not be characterised as undertakings (or associations of undertakings) insofar as they act as agents for their members (employees).[93]

(vi) Single Economic Units

a. The undertaking as a Single Economic Unit—Natural Persons, Legal Persons, Principal–Agent and Parent–Subsidiary Relationships

It has long been held that the term undertaking[94] is not necessarily synonymous with natural or legal personality[95] but denotes 'an economic unit ... even if in law that economic unit consists of several persons, natural or legal'.[96] The concept is thus aimed at economic units 'which consist of a unitary organization of personal, tangible and intangible elements which pursues a specific economic aim on a long-term basis and can contribute to the commission of an infringement'.[97] Consequently, an undertaking may be comprised of simply a natural person (a single individual), a legal person, or a group of persons (made up of natural or legal persons such as two or more companies within a corporate group), for example:

- an individual sole trader (natural persons);[98]
- a legal person, such as a company and partnership,[99] made up of a collection of individual persons. In this context, the cases do not look behind the legal personality; individuals working

---

[91] Case C-22/98, *Criminal Proceedings Against Becu* [1999] ECR I-5665, para. 26 and see further nn. 100 and 261 and text (rather the employees form part of the undertaking within which they work). Whether or not agreements relating to self-employed workers fall outside Art. 101 depends on whether the worker 'acts under the direction of his employer as regards, in particular, his freedom to choose the time, place and content of his work ... does not share in the employer's commercial risks ... and ... forms an integral part of that employer's undertaking', Case C-413/13, *FNV v Netherlands* EU:C:2014:2411.

[92] See also his Opinion in Cases C-180–184/98, *Pavlov* [2000] ECR I-6451. The CJ in Case C-67/96, *Albany* [1999] ECR I-5751 did not rule specifically on whether or not, or when, employees or trade unions qualify as undertakings for the purposes of the competition rules, as it held that collective agreements concluded between trade unions and employers relating to conditions of employment and working conditions fell outside Art. 101(1) altogether, see n. 222 and text.

[93] If the employee does not constitute an undertaking, the trade union could not constitute an association of undertakings.

[94] See further W. Wils, 'The Undertaking as Subject of E.C. Competition Law and the Imputation of Infringements to Natural or Legal Persons' (2000) 25 *ELRev* 99 and A. Jones, 'The Boundaries of an Undertaking in EU Competition Law' (2012) 8 *European Competition Journal* 301.

[95] COMP/35.691, *Pre-insulated Pipe Cartel* [1999] OJ L24/1, para. 154 ('The subject of the competition rules in the Treaty is the "undertaking", a concept not necessarily identical with the notion of corporate legal personality in national commercial company or fiscal law').

[96] Case 170/83, *Hydrotherm Gerätebau GmbH v Compact de Dott Ing Mario Adredi & CSAS* [1984] ECR 2999, para. 11; Case C-97/08 P, *Akzo Nobel v Commission* [2009] ECR I-8237, para. 55.

[97] Case T-11/89, *Shell International Chemical Co v Commission* [1992] ECR II-757, para. 311.

[98] See Case C-309/99, *Wouters v Algemene Raad van de Nederlandse Orde van Advocaten* [2002] ECR I-1577.

[99] See, e.g., Case 258/78, *Nungesser v Commission* [1982] ECR 2015 and *Breeders' rights: roses* [1985] OJ L369/9. See also sporting bodies, n. 39 and text, trade associations (Case 96/82, *NV IAZ International Belgium v Commission* [1983]

within the legal person, and not accepting individual risk, are treated as constituent elements of it. Thus in *Becu*, for example, the CJ held that dock workers, performing work for and under the direction of their employers, were to be viewed as being incorporated into the undertaking concerned and forming part of the 'economic unit';[100]

- principal and agent. The close economic links which exist in many agency relationships have led the CJ to recognise that an independently owned agent may lose its character as an independent trader and operate as an auxiliary organ 'forming an integral part of the principal's undertaking'[101] in certain circumstances; in particular where the agent does not take on any (or only a negligible portion of) financial and commercial risk linked to sales of goods to third parties on behalf of the principal (see further Chapter 11);[102]

- parent and subsidiary. Such entities will constitute an economic unit if the subsidiary 'enjoys no economic independence'[103] or if the entities 'form an economic unit within which the subsidiary has no real freedom to determine its course of action on the market'[104] but carries out the instructions issued by the parent company controlling it. The formal separation of those entities resulting from distinct legal identity is not therefore decisive. The relevant question is not whether two given companies are separate legal persons but, rather, whether they behave together as a single unit on the market (see further Section c below).[105]

b. Consequences of the Single Economic Unit Doctrine

The economic unit doctrine has a number of important consequences. First, it affects the substantive reach of Article 101: agreements and concerted practices between the parent and subsidiary (or other entities) forming part of the same economic unit, and concerned merely with the internal allocation of tasks between them, fall outside Article 101 (as they are part of the same undertaking, such arrangements are intra-undertaking rather than arrangements between independent undertakings).[106] In *Viho*,[107] for example, the CJ confirmed that the Commission had been correct to reject a complaint that Parker's distribution agreements concluded with its 100 per cent owned subsidiaries infringed Article 101. Parker controlled the sales, advertising, and marketing policy of its subsidiaries which had no real autonomy to determine their course of action. Consequently, agreements

---

ECR 3369), and agricultural cooperatives (Case C-250/92, *Gøttrup-Klim e.a. Grovvareforeninger and Others v Dansk Landbrugs Grovvareselskab AmbA* [1994] ECR I-5641).

[100] Case C-22/98, *Criminal Proceedings Against Becu* [1999] ECR I-5665, para. 26. See also Case C-413/13, *FNV v Netherlands* EU:C:2014:2411 (and n. 91) and the view of Jacobs AG in Case 67/96, *Albany* [1996] ECR I-5457, n. 92 and text. There is thus a difficult line to be drawn between legal entities, economic units, and cartels. Firms such as companies and partnerships inevitably eliminate competition, and result in price-fixing and market-sharing competition, between individuals within them. Characterisation of a partnership as an undertaking renders such arrangements per se legal under Art. 101. In contrast an agreement between independent competing undertakings to fix prices and share markets is almost invariably illegal under Art. 101, see e.g., R. H. Bork, *The Antitrust Paradox: A Policy at War with Itself* (Basic Books, 1978, reprinted with a new Introduction and Epilogue, 1993), 264–265 and H. Hovenkamp and C. R. Leslie, 'The Firm as Cartel Manager' (2011) 64(3) *Vanderbilt LR* 813, 818 ('[t]he lines between firms, cartels and joint ventures are notoriously indistinct').

[101] Case C-266/93, *Bundeskartellamt v Volkswagen and VAG Leasing GmbH* [1995] ECR I-3477, paras. 18–19. Contrast Cases 56 and 58/64, *Consten and Grundig* [1966] ECR 299, 340, n. 219 and text.

[102] Case C-279/06, *CEPSA* [2008] ECR I-6681, para. 36.

[103] Case 22/71, *Béguelin Import Co v SAGL Import Export* [1971] ECR 949, para. 8.

[104] Case 15/74, *Centrafarm BV and Adriaan De Peijper v Sterling Drug Inc* [1974] ECR 1183, para. 41.

[105] Case T-325/01, *DaimlerChrysler AG v Commission* [2005] ECR II-3319, para. 85.

[106] Case 15/74, *Centrafarm BV and Adriaan De Peijper v Sterling Drug Inc* [1974] ECR 1183, para. 41. See also Case 170/83, *Hydrotherm Gerätebau GmbH v Compact de Dott. Ing. Mario Adreoli* [1984] ECR 2999, para. 41 (the Commission had submitted that Art. 101 was not applicable to agreements where their sole object was the allocation of tasks within the same economic unit but that it would apply to agreements having a wider scope, see also Trabucchi AG) and Case 30/87, *Bodson v Pompes Funèbres* [1988] ECR 2479, para. 19.

[107] Case C-73/95 P, *Viho Europe BV v Commission* [1996] ECR I-5457.

and arrangements between these companies were not caught by Article 101(1): the activity constituted internal allocation of functions of a single enterprise and not the collusive action required to trigger Article 101.[108]

Case C-73/95 P, *Viho Europe BV v Commission* [1996] ECR I-5457

This case concerned a complaint made by a Dutch company, Viho, which marketed office equipment on a wholesale basis which had been unable to obtain Parker Pen Ltd products (writing utensils) on conditions equivalent to those granted to Parker's subsidiaries and independent distributors. It complained to the Commission that Parker's distribution system (which prohibited exports between Member States, divided the common market into national markets, and maintained artificially high prices on those national markets) was in breach of Article 101(1). Parker sold its products through 100 per cent owned subsidiary companies in Germany, Belgium, France, Spain, and the Netherlands. Sales and marketing of the products through the subsidiaries were controlled by an area team of three directors.

The Commission rejected the complaint finding that as Parker's subsidiary companies were wholly dependent on it, and enjoyed no real autonomy, the distribution system did not go beyond the normal allocation of tasks within a group of undertakings. The EU Courts[109] confirmed that the Commission had correctly classified the Parker Group as one economic unit.

Court of Justice

13. The appellant claims that the fact that the conduct in question occurs within a group of companies does not preclude the application of Article [101(1)], since the division of responsibilities between the companies in the Parker group aims to maintain and partition national markets by means of absolute territorial protection. The evaluation of such conduct, which has harmful effects on competition, should not therefore depend on whether it takes place within a group or between Parker and its independent distributors. The appellant points out that such territorial protection prevents third parties such as itself from obtaining supplies freely within the Community from the subsidiary which offers the best commercial terms, so as to be able to pass such benefits on to the customer.

14. Consequently, the appellant considers that Article [101(1)], interpreted in the light of Articles 2 and [3(1)(c) and (g)] ... must apply, since the referral policy in question goes far beyond a mere internal allocation of tasks within the Parker group.

15. It should be noted, first of all, that it is established that Parker holds 100 per cent of the shares of its subsidiaries in Germany, Belgium, Spain, France and the Netherlands and that the sales and marketing activities of its subsidiaries are directed by an area team appointed by the parent company and which controls, in particular, sales targets, gross margins, sales costs, cash flow and stocks. The area team also lays down the range of products to be sold, monitors advertising and issues directives concerning prices and discounts.

16. Parker and its subsidiaries thus form a single economic unit within which the subsidiaries do not enjoy real autonomy in determining their course of action in the market, but carry out the instructions issued to them by the parent company controlling them (Case 48/69, *ICI v E.C. Commission* ...; Case 15/74, *Centrafarm v Sterling Drug* ...; Case 16/74, *Centrafarm v Winthrop* ...; Case 30/87, *Bodson v Pompes Funèbres* ...; and Case 66/86, *Ahmed Saeed Flugreisen and Others v Zentrale zur Bekämpfung unlauteren Wettbewerbs* ...).

---

[108] The US Supreme Court in *Copperweld Corp v Independence Tube Corp*, 467 US 36 (1984) has held that since a parent and a wholly owned subsidiary have a complete unity of interest and because a parent can assert full control at any moment if a subsidiary fails to act in a parent's interest, the parent and subsidiary have a unity of purpose or common design that belies the existence of an agreement for antitrust purposes.

[109] Case T-102/92, [1995] ECR II-17 (holding that Art. 101(1) referred only to relations between economic entities which were capable of competing with one another. It did not cover agreements or concerted practices between entities belonging to the same group if they formed an economic unit).

17. In those circumstances, the fact that Parker's policy of referral, which consists essentially in dividing various national markets between its subsidiaries, might produce effects outside the ambit of the Parker group which are capable of affecting the competitive position of third parties cannot make Article [101(1)] applicable . . . . On the other hand, such unilateral conduct could fall under Article [102] if the conditions for its application, as laid down in that article[,] were fulfilled.

18. The [GC] was therefore fully entitled to base its decision solely on the existence of a single economic unit in order to rule out the application of Article [101(1)] to the Parker group.

This case establishes that unilateral behaviour of an undertaking and its internal allocation of duties, even if within a group of connected companies, falls outside the scope of Article 101. In contrast, the complaints lodged by Viho about the arrangements between Parker and its *independent distributors*, i.e. firms which were not connected to Parker by any type of ownership or control, culminated with a Commission decision finding that the distribution arrangements were in breach of Article 101(1) and with the parties being fined.[110] In *Hydrotherm Gerätebau GmbH v Compact del Dott Ing Mario Andreoli & C Sas*,[111] the CJ also confirmed that a natural person, a limited partnership, and another firm constituted (and so counted as) a single economic unit when they were all controlled by the same natural person.[112]

Although the rationale underpinning this line of judgments has not been made explicit, in *Hydrotherm* the CJ stated that where entities form part of the same economic unit, competition between the parties is impossible.[113] The Court thus seems to consider that the arrangements between such entities resemble the internal workings of the firm and that the unity of purpose that they pursue renders meaningless the application of Article 101 to agreements between them (there is no competition to be protected[114]). If the subsidiary's strategy is determined by the parent, the parent and subsidiary will pursue a common course irrespective of the existence of any agreement between them: 'the unified conduct on the market of the parent company and its subsidiaries takes precedence over the formal separation between those companies as a result of their separate legal personalities'.[115]

Secondly, and more controversially, the doctrine has been relied on as a mechanism for attributing liability and responsibility for an infringement of the competition law rules committed by a subsidiary to its parent company ('attribution of liability' cases).[116] Where an undertaking or economic

---

[110] See the appeals to the GC in Case T-66/92, *Herlitz AG v Commission* [1994] ECR II-531, and Case T-77/92, *Parker Pen Ltd v Commission* [1994] ECR II-549.

[111] Case 170/83, [1984] ECR 2999.

[112] The economic unit concept was relevant in this case to the question of whether a block exemption applied (see now, for example, the technology transfer block exemption which applies only to 'bilateral' agreements discussed in Chap. 12). The terminology used in this case is confusing in that the judgment also refers to the partnership and the firm as undertakings and so concludes that the block exemption regulation can be applied 'even if several legally independent undertakings participate in the agreement as one contracting party provided that those undertakings constitute an economic unit for the purposes of the agreement', para. 12. This suggests that the undertaking as an economic unit can be comprised of a number of undertakings, which are natural or legal persons, see also Case 15/74, *Centrafarm BV and Adriaan De Peijper v Sterling Drug Inc* [1974] ECR 1183, para. 32 and Case T-102/92, *Viho Europe BV v Commission* [1995] ECR II-117, paras. 47–53.

[113] Case 170/83, [1984] ECR 2999, para. 11, but see also Case T-102/92, [1995] ECR II-17.

[114] For an interesting account of the cases dealing with this issue and the principles underpinning them, see Lenz AG in Case C-73/95 P, *Viho Europe BV v Commission* [1996] ECR I-5457, paras. 31–73, especially para. 67.

[115] Case T-102/92, *Viho Europe BV v Commission* [1995] ECR II-117, para. 50. See also Case T-9/99, *HFB Holdings v Commission* [2002] ECR II-1487, paras. 54–68 and Case C-97/08 P, *Akzo Nobel v Commission* [2009] ECR I-8237, para. 55.

[116] Some have complained that such a use of the concept of an undertaking is unconvincing, illogical, and breaches fundamental principles, in particular the principle of personal responsibility, the presumption of innocence, and of limited liability, see, e.g., J. Joshua, Y. Botteman, and L. Atlee, '"You Can't Beat the Percentage"—The

entity infringes competition rules, 'it falls, according to the principle of personal responsibility, to that entity to answer for that infringement'.[117] As decisions cannot be addressed to an undertaking, they must be addressed, and liability imputed, to a legal person (or persons) on whom fines may be imposed. The economic unit doctrine has been interpreted to allow a fine to be imposed not only on the legal entity which has actually infringed the competition rules but its parent.[118] As the 'parent company and its subsidiary form a single economic unit and therefore a single undertaking' a decision imposing fines can be addressed 'to the parent company, without having to establish the personal involvement of the latter in the infringement'.[119] Fines can be imposed on the 'guilty' party(ies); responsibility for an offence attaches to those bearing personal responsibility.[120] Indeed, the Commission's policy in cartel cases is now, wherever possible, to hold parent companies (and top group holding companies[121]) jointly and severally liable with their (infringing) subsidiaries (Chapter 13 discusses fining policy more fully[122]). This policy sends out a strong message and maximises the total level of fines both by augmenting the maximum cap on the level of fines which can be imposed (which is 10 per cent of the turnover of the undertaking as a whole[123]) and by enhancing the risk of an uplift in the fine for recidivism or deterrence.[124] A competition authority may also be particularly keen to attribute responsibility to a parent company where, for example, the subsidiary is unable to pay any fine imposed or where it wishes to impose liability on a parent company which operated the agreement, and concocted the breach, outside the EU.[125]

Thirdly, the single economic unit doctrine has also been relied upon in private litigation. For example, claimants before the English courts have sought to anchor an action for damages in the UK by bringing it against a member of the economic unit domiciled in the UK (a UK subsidiary) where another member of that unit (for example, a non-UK parent) has committed the violation of the competition law rules.[126]

Parental Liability Presumption in EU Cartel Enforcement' in *Global Competition Review—The European Antitrust Review* 2012, 3, S. Thomas, 'Guilty of a Fault that One has not Committed: The Limits of the Group-Based Sanction Policy Carried out by the Commission and the European Courts in EU-Antitrust Law' (2012) 3 *JECLAP* 11, K. Hofstetter and M. Ludescher, 'Fines against Parent Companies in EU Antitrust Law: Setting Incentives for "Best Practice Compliance"' (2010) 33 *World Competition* 55, and M. Bronckers and A. Vallery, 'No Longer Presumed Guilty? The Impact of Fundamental Rights on Certain Dogmas of EU Competition Law' (2011) 34 *World Competition* 535.

[117] Case C-97/08 P, *Akzo Nobel v Commission* [2009] ECR I-8237, para. 56.

[118] See Case 48/69, *Imperial Chemical Industries v Commission (Dyestuffs)* [1972] ECR 619, paras. 11 and 131–140. This is the case even if the parent is a non-operational holding company not involved in economic activity, see e.g., Case C-440/11 P, *Commission v Stichting Administratiekantoor Portielje and Gosselin Group NV* EU:C:2013:514.

[119] Case C-97/08 P, *Akzo Nobel v Commission* [2009] ECR I-8237, paras. 58–59.

[120] Case T-146/09, *Parker ITR Srl and Parker-Hannifin Corp v Commission* EU:T:2013:258 (appeal before the CJ, Case C-434/13 P *Commission v Parker Hannifin Manufacturing and Parker-Hannifin* EU:C:2014:2456), paras. 85–86.

[121] '[T]he existence of intermediary companies between the subsidiary and the parent company does not affect the possibility of applying the presumption that the parent company in fact exercises decisive influence over the subsidiary', Case T-343/06, *Shell Petroleum v Commission* EU:T:2012:478, para. 52. See also Case C-90/09 P, *General Química SA v Commission* [2011] ECR I-1, paras. 88–89.

[122] Cases C-231–233/11, *Commission v Siemens AG Österreich* EU:C:2014:256 (the Commission only determines joint and serveral liability from an external perspective, and does not have power to determine the shares to be paid by the legal persons that make up that undertaking from the perspective of their internal relationship).

[123] See Reg. 1/2003 [2003] OJ L1/1, Art. 23(2) and Chap. 13.

[124] To maximise the deterrent effect of fines, the Commission's 'invariable policy today is to hold a group parent automatically responsible for cartel infringements committed down the line by its wholly owned subsidiaries', Joshua et al., n. 116, 3–4.

[125] Cases 48, 49, and 51–57/69, *ICI v Commission (Dyestuffs)* [1972] ECR 619, paras. 125–146 (by use of its power to control its subsidiaries established in the EU, the applicant had been able to ensure that its decisions were implemented on that market). In this way the single economic entity doctrine avoids the need for the extraterritorial application of EU competition law and enables the competition rules to be applied to companies outside the jurisdiction without recourse to the more controversial 'implementation' or 'effects' doctrines, see Chap. 16.

[126] See, in particular, *Provimi v Aventis* [2003] EWHC 961 (Comm), *Cooper Tire & Rubber v Shell Chemicals* [2009] EWHC 2609 (Comm), [2010] EWCA Civ 864 (appeal dismissed), and *Toshiba Carrier UK Ltd v KME Yorkshire Ltd* [2012] EWCA Civ 1190.

Finally, some EU secondary legislation and Commission Notices also utilise the same idea. For example, most of the block exemptions[127] and the Commission's Notice on agreements of minor importance[128] apply only to firms which do not exceed specified market shares. These provisions require that, when calculating market shares, the shares of all entities closely 'connected' (as defined therein) to the entity that actually entered into the agreement must be taken into account.[129] Similarly, the activities of the whole group must be considered when determining whether or not the parties to the agreement are competing undertakings.[130] Although the definition of connected entities in these provisions is designed to provide legal certainty, some of the language used within them is confusing, as it suggests an approach to the concept of undertaking which is not evidently consistent with the notion of an undertaking as defined by the EU Courts.[131]

The question of whether the concept of an undertaking does, or should, have the same meaning in each of the diverse scenarios described above, in particular in substantive reach and in attribution of liability cases, is explored in the section below.

c. The Boundaries of the Economic Unit: Parent and Subsidiary

Given the significant consequences that flow from the acceptance of the single economic unit doctrine, a critical issue is exactly how broadly the concept of an economic unit extends and, in particular, exactly when a subsidiary has sufficient independence to prevent the doctrine from applying. Although there is relatively little case law which deals with the question of when an agreement falls outside the ambit of Article 101 on this basis (and so when the concept of an undertaking affects the substantive reach of Article 101), there are a greater number of 'attribution of liability' cases which shed light on the question. These cases clarify that the parent and subsidiary[132] will constitute a single economic unit where the parent is able to, *and does actually*, exercise decisive influence over the policy and direct the conduct of its subsidiary, so that the subsidiary does not enjoy real autonomy or independence in determining its course of action in the market.[133] Liability can be imputed to a parent in this way even where the parent is a 'financial investor'.[134] Critically, the cases establish:

(a) that where a parent holds a 100 per cent shareholding in a subsidiary, or a de minimis amount less than 100 per cent,[135] a rebuttable presumption that the parent does in fact exercise decisive influence over the commercial policy and conduct of its subsidiary applies. This was clearly established in *Akzo Nobel*.[136]

---

[127] See Chap. 4.

[128] Commission Notice on agreements of minor importance which do not appreciably restrict competition under Article 101(1) [2014] OJ C291/1.

[129] See, e.g., ibid., para. 16.

[130] See, e.g., Chap. 10.

[131] See Jones, n. 94.

[132] Also that the acts of an agent can be imputed to a principal where the two companies act as a single entity on the market (where the agent must be treated as an auxiliary body forming an integral part of the principal's business who must carry out the principal's instructions and, like a commercial employee, forms an economic unit within that undertaking), see COMP/39.406, *Marine Hoses* 28 January 2009, para. 330 and Case T-66/99, *Minoan Lines v Commission* [2003] ECR II-5515, paras. 121–129 and Chap. 11.

[133] Case 48/69, *Imperial Chemical Industries v Commission (Dyestuffs)* [1972] ECR 619, paras. 125–146.

[134] See, e.g., COMP/39.610, *Power Cables* 2 April 2014 and Case T-395/09, *Gigaset AG (formerly Arques Industries AG) v Commission* EU:T:2014:23.

[135] See, e.g., Case T-299/08, *Elf Aquitaine v Commission* [2011] ECR II-2149 (aff'd Case C-404/11 P, EU:C:2012:56) and Case C-508/11, *Eni SpA v Commission* EU:C:2013:289.

[136] Case C-97/08 P, *Akzo Nobel NV v Commission* [2009] ECR I-8237, para. 60. See also Case C-286/98 P, *Stora Kopparbergs Bergslags AB v Commission* [2000] ECR I-9925, para. 29 and Cases C-201 and 216/09 P, *ArcelorMittal Luxembourg SA v Commission* [2011] ECR I-2239.

Case C-97/08 P, *Akzo Nobel NV and Others v Commission* [2009] ECR I-8237

Court of Justice

58. It is clear from settled case-law that the conduct of a subsidiary may be imputed to the parent company in particular where, although having a separate legal personality, that subsidiary does not decide independently upon its own conduct on the market, but carries out, in all material respects, the instructions given to it by the parent company (see, to that effect, *Imperial Chemical Industries v Commission*, paragraphs 132 and 133; *Geigy v Commission*, paragraph 44; Case 6/72 *Europemballage and Continental Can v Commission* . . ., paragraph 15; and *Stora*, paragraph 26), having regard in particular to the economic, organisational and legal links between those two legal entities (see, by analogy, *Dansk Rørindustri and Others v Commission*, paragraph 117, and *ETI and Others*, paragraph 49).

59. That is the case because, in such a situation, the parent company and its subsidiary form a single economic unit and therefore form a single undertaking . . . Thus, the fact that a parent company and its subsidiary constitute a single undertaking within the meaning of Article [101] enables the Commission to address a decision imposing fines to the parent company, without having to establish the personal involvement of the latter in the infringement.

60. In the specific case where a parent company has a 100% shareholding in a subsidiary which has infringed the Community competition rules, first, the parent company can exercise a decisive influence over the conduct of the subsidiary (see, to that effect, *Imperial Chemical Industries v Commission*, paragraphs 136 and 137) and, second, there is a rebuttable presumption that the parent company does in fact exercise a decisive influence over the conduct of its subsidiary (see, to that effect, *AEG-Telefunken v Commission*, paragraph 50, and *Stora*, paragraph 29).

61. In those circumstances, it is sufficient for the Commission to prove that the subsidiary is wholly owned by the parent company in order to presume that the parent exercises a decisive influence over the commercial policy of the subsidiary. The Commission will be able to regard the parent company as jointly and severally liable for the payment of the fine imposed on its subsidiary, unless the parent company, which has the burden of rebutting that presumption, adduces sufficient evidence to show that its subsidiary acts independently on the market (see, to that effect, *Stora*, paragraph 29).

In such cases joint and several liability for the parent firm follows unless it adduces sufficient evidence to show that the subsidiary acted independently. A hotly contested issue is exactly when the presumption can be rebutted in practice;[137]

(b) the ability to, and actual, exercise of decisive influence can be ascertained in other situations 'on the basis of a body of factual evidence, including, in particular, any management power exercised by the parent company or companies over their subsidiary'. In such cases 'account must be taken of all the relevant factors relating to the economic, organisational and legal links which tie the subsidiary to its parent company and, therefore, of economic reality' and 'the exercise of decisive influence may be inferred from a body of consistent evidence, even if some of that evidence, taken in isolation, is insufficient to establish the existence of such influence . . .'.[138] For example, decisive influence may be found where: the parent holds a majority interest in a subsidiary[139] or a minority

---

[137] See Joshua et al., n. 116, 3 and R. Burnley, 'Group Liability for Antitrust Infringements: Responsibility and Accountability' (2010) 33 *World Competition* 595. The Commission is obliged to consider the rebuttal evidence and if it fails to do so its decision will be overturned, see e.g. Case T-185/06, *L'Air liquide SA v Commission* [2011] ECR II-2809, Case T-517/09, *Alstom v Commission* EU:T:2014:999 and Case C-446/11 P, *Commission v Edison SpA* EU:C:2013:798.

[138] Cases C-293 and 294/13 P, *Fresh Del Monte Produce Inc v Commission* EU:C:2015:416, paras. 76–77.

[139] Case T-141/89, *Tréfileurope Sales SARL v Commission* [1995] ECR II-791. See also Cases 6 and 7/73, *Istituto Chemioterapico Italiano SpA and Commercial Solvents Corp v Commission* [1974] ECR 223 (parent and subsidiary in which the parent held a 51% shareholding were to be treated as an economic unit).

interest which is allied to rights greater than those normally granted to minority shareholders;[140] or a parent has negative control[141] over its subsidiary, at least where two or more parents have negative control over a joint venture (JV)[142] and so cooperate to determine the JV's commercial policy—that is, in situations where the parents have the power to exercise, and have actually exercised, *joint control* over a JV. In *Dow*,[143] for example, both the CJ and the GC upheld the Commission's finding that Dow (and the other parent EI Du Pont) was jointly and severally liable for the infringement of its JV and formed part of the same economic unit with it.

Relying amongst other things[144] on the fact that the Commission had found that they had acquired joint control of the JV when appraising it on its creation under the EU Merger Regulation (EUMR),[145] the EU Courts accepted that the parents had been found to have the power to jointly control their JV and further that, in the light of all the economic, legal, and organisational links, control had actually been exercised. It was not therefore accepted that the parents could not be liable as they merely exercised joint negative control over the JV and only had a right of veto over its commercial strategy (and did not have the power to exercise decisive influence over its day-to-day management). The GC stated:

The 'negative' nature of the joint control is not sufficient to preclude the exercise of decisive influence over [JV]. Even if parent companies are not able to impose decisions on their joint venture, they are able to prevent their joint venture from taking certain decisions and thereby exercise decisive influence over its business strategy … The 'negative' nature of the control that the applicant held over [JV] did not therefore prevent it from exercising over [JV] sufficient decisive influence to enable the Commission to impute to it the unlawful conduct of that joint venture.[146]

In *Fresh Del Monte Produce Inc v Commission*[147] the CJ also held that the exercise of joint control, by two parents, of their subsidiary did not preclude a finding of the existence of an economic unit comprising one of those parent companies and the subsidiary, and in some cases the GC has even gone so far as to hold that where two companies are placed in a position analogous to that in which a single company owns the entire share capital of its subsidiary, it is possible to apply the *presumption* that a parent company in fact exercises decisive influence over its subsidiary. In *Avebe*, for example, it held that a JV, on the one hand, and its parents, on the other 'do form an economic unit . . . in the context of which the unlawful conduct of the subsidiary may be imputed to the parent companies, who become liable by virtue of the fact that they in reality control its marketing policy'.[148] Further in *Shell*

---

[140] Case T-132/07, *Fuji Electric System Co Ltd v Commission* [2011] ECR II-4091, para. 183.

[141] The EUMR also applies to changes in the quality of control.

[142] The term JV can be used to describe a wide spectrum of commercial arrangements between firms. In competition law, it is frequently used to describe an entity which (a) constitutes a separate business entity, and (b) is jointly controlled by at least two parents.

[143] Case T-77/08, *The Dow Chemical Co v Commission* EU:T:2012:47, Case C-179/12 P, *The Dow Chemical Co v Commission* EU:C:2013:605. See also COMP/39.639, *Optical Disk Drive* 21 October 2015 (where the Commission confirmed that parents and their JV, Philips, Lite-On and Philips & Lite-On Digital Solutions, could, as a single economic entity, obtain immunity from fines for being the first to reveal the existence of the cartel, see further Chap. 13).

[144] E.g., the facts that each had the right to participate on a Members' Committee which approved certain matters pertaining to the strategic direction of the JV, that they had both withdrawn from the chloroprene rubber market and participated on it only through their JV. Net profits or losses of the JV were allocated in equal proportions to the two parents.

[145] M.663, 21 February 1996. The EU Courts held however that the fact that the Commission had found that the JV was an autonomous full-function JV for the purposes of the EUMR (see further Chap. 15) did not mean that it was autonomous in the sense that it was free from the exercise of decisive influence by its parent on its commercial conduct and policies. The operational autonomy required of full-function JVs under the EUMR thus does not 'mean that the joint venture enjoys autonomy as regards the adoption of its strategic decisions (and that it is not therefore under the decisive influence exercised by its parent companies for the purposes of the application of Article [101])', Case T-77/08, *The Dow Chemical Co v Commission* EU:T:2012:47, para. 93, aff'd Case C-179/12 P EU:C:2013:605, para. 65.

[146] Case T-77/08, ibid., para. 92.

[147] Cases C-293 and 294/13 P, EU:C:2015:416, paras. 76–100.

[148] Case T-314/01, *Avebe v Commission* [2006] ECR II-3085, para. 141.

Petroleum NV v Commission[149] the Court endorsed the Commission's view that the situation (notwithstanding the coexistence of two legal parent entities) was analogous to that in which a single parent company controls fully its subsidiary, so entitling the Commission to rely on the *Akzo* presumption. In this case the parents jointly appointed the members of the board of directors of the subsidiaires, had equal representation in two supervisory committees, and a body coordinated the operational activity and governed all the group companies.

What is not entirely clear, however, is whether the concept of an undertaking developed in the attribution of liability line of cases is identical to that developed in the substantive reach cases. If the notions are the same, the consequences are far-reaching and the doctrine potentially excludes a relatively wide spectrum of behaviour from Article 101(1), in particular, agreements between:

- persons bound together by a contractual relationship which results in one person working for and under the direction of another and so being integrated within that other (for example, an employment or agency contract) or one person controlling the behaviour of another;[150]

- a parent and a subsidiary, where the latter has no freedom to determine its course of action or economic independence as the parent has sufficient rights to exercise, and does actually exercise, positive control over its behaviour;

- (possibly) a parent and a subsidiary, where the former has sufficient rights to veto strategic decisions of the latter, and actually exercises such negative control over its behaviour;

- subsidiaries/sister companies[151] which are controlled (within the meaning set out earlier) by the same parent; and

- a JV and its parent(s) or between parents which have the power to, and do actually, exercise jointly control and decisive influence over the JV's behaviour.

Because of the functional approach taken to the concept of an undertaking, however, it would seem that even if such a broad exclusion from Article 101 potentially applies, it would relate only to conduct which concerns the internal working of, or the internal allocation of responsibilities within, the economic unit.[152] In the context of a JV, for example, this would suggest that only conduct inherent to the working and operation of the JV would fall outside Article 101.[153] Although, therefore, the conduct of the JV, when acting within its scope, would be regarded as the conduct of a single entity, Article 101 could 'apply to agreements between the parents outside the scope of the joint venture'.[154] The question of whether the entities are acting as a single undertaking would thus appear likely to turn on the complex question of whether the conduct limits competition among the parents and the JV outside its core operations/the scope of the JV.

---

[149] Case T-343/06, EU:T:2012:478, Case C-585/12 P, EU:C:2013:236 (appeal withdrawn).

[150] See also, e.g., Commission Consolidated Jurisdictional Notice under Council Regulation (EC) No. 139/2004 on the control of concentrations between undertakings [2008] OJ C95/1, para. 20, the Commission's decision in COMP/39.188, *Bananas* 15 October 2008 where the Commission found that the combination of a partnership, capital links, and a distribution agreement was sufficient to give Del Monte the possibility to exercise decisive influence on the way Weichert ran its business and that Del Monte did exercise such influence, paras. 383–385, *aff'd* Case T-587/08, *Del Monte* EU:T:2013:129 and Cases C-293 and 294/13 P, EU:C:2015:416.

[151] Commission Guidelines on the applicability of Article 101 of the Treaty on the Functioning of the European Union to horizontal co-operation agreements [2011] OJ C11/1, para. 11 (Horizontal Cooperation Guidelines) ('the same is true for sister companies, that is to say companies over which decisive influence is exercised by the same parent company. They are consequently not considered to be competitors even if they are both active on the same relevant product and geographic markets').

[152] But see Case C-73/95 P, *Viho Europe BV v Commission* [1996] ECR I-5457, paras. 14–18 and Wils, n. 94, 107.

[153] This of course leaves a difficult line to be drawn between conduct relating to the working of the economic unit (exempted from Art. 101) and that which goes beyond it (falling within Art. 101). Unilateral conduct could be caught by Art. 102, however.

[154] Draft Horizontal Cooperation Guidelines, SEC(2011) 528/2, para. 11, 'and with regard to the agreement between the parents to create the joint venture' (this part of the paragraph was not repeated in the final version of the Guidelines, however).

d. The Boundaries of an Economic Unit: A Single Concept?

Support can be found for the view that the concept of an undertaking is the same in the substantive reach and attribution of liability line of cases. Not only do the cases all hinge on the interpretation of the term 'undertaking', without any explicit suggestion that the concept should be considered differently in differing scenarios, but: (a) in *Flat Glass*[155] the GC clarified that the term 'undertaking' has the same meaning in Article 102 as the one given to it in the context of Article 101; and (b) in *Hydrotherm*[156] the CJ held that 'in competition law, the term "undertaking" must be understood as designating an economic unit . . .'. Further, in both *Dyestuffs*[157] and *Viho*,[158] the CJ held that the consequence of the economic doctrine was both that Article 101(1) was inapplicable to arrangements between entities within the economic unit (intra-undertaking agreements) and that the actions of the subsidiary could be attributed to the parent company[159] and in some cases there has been cross-referral between the lines of cases.[160] It could also be argued that a single concept would provide the greatest coherence to the system.

Nonetheless, caution should be exercised before concluding that a single approach, rather than a context-specific approach, will be adopted to the concept of an economic unit/undertaking in the future. For example, the CJ's judgment in *Dow* lends some support for the view that the cases demand different approaches to be adopted in the separate contexts in which the concept is used; in this case it specifically confined its comments about the single economic unit and undertaking concept to circumstances in which imputation of liability was at issue. At paragraph 58 it stated:

> Where two parent companies each have a 50% shareholding in the joint venture which committed an infringement of the rules of competition law, *it is only for the purposes of establishing liability for participation in the infringement of that law* and only in so far as the Commission has demonstrated, on the basis of factual evidence, that both parent companies did in fact exercise decisive influence over the joint venture, that those three entities can be considered to form a single economic unit and therefore form a single undertaking for the purposes of Article [101 TFEU]. (*emphasis added*)

Other factors also arguably militate in favour of a context-specific approach to the concept of an undertaking being adopted.[161] For example, the attribution of liability cases have considerably expanded the concept of an undertaking without specific reference to the underlying objectives of the doctrine or to its consequences for the reach and scope of Article 101. The underpinning objectives in the two lines of cases might suggest different interpretations of the concept in the

---

[155] Cases T-68 and 77–78/89, *Società Italiano Vetro SpA v Commission* [1992] ECR II-1403, paras. 357–358.

[156] Case 170/83, *Hydrotherm Gerätebau GmbH v Compact de Dott Ing Mario Adredi & CSAS* [1984] ECR 2999, para. 11. See also Horizontal Cooperation Guidelines, para. 11, n. 151.

[157] Case 48/69, *Imperial Chemical Industries v Commission (Dyestuffs)* [1972] ECR 619, paras. 132–136.

[158] Case C-73/95 P, *Viho Europe BV v Commission* [1996] ECR I-5457, para. 16. In Case T-102/92, *Viho Europe BV v Commission* [1995] ECR II-117 the GC relied on cases concerning parental liability in its judgment upholding the Commission's conclusion that agreements between Parker Pen and its subsidiaries fell outside Art. 101(1). Indeed it concluded that the Commission had been correct in finding that because the subsidiaries' conduct could be *imputed* to the parent the integrated distribution system fell outside Art. 101.

[159] See also Kokott AG in Case C-440/11 P, *Commission v Stichting Administratiekantoor Portielje and Gosselin Group NV* EU:C:2012:763, para. 31 and Bot AG in Cases C-201 and 216/09 P, *ArcelorMittal Luxembourg SA v Commission* EU:C:2010:634, para. 178.

[160] See, e.g., Case T-112/05, *Akzo Nobel v Commission* [2007] ECR II-5049, paras. 63–64, aff'd Case C-97/08 P, *Akzo Nobel v Commission* [2009] ECR I-8237, paras. 72–78, and Case T-132/07, *Fuji Electric System Co Ltd v Commission* [2011] ECR II-4091, para. 180.

[161] In, for example, Singapore, the Competition Commission held that two entities may not form a single economic entity in one context (for instance, where the issues is whether agreements between the entities should be excluded from its prohibition of anti-competitive agreements) even though they may do so in another context (for instance, where the issue is whether to hold one of the companies liable for the other's competition infringement or whether to treat them as a single economic entity for the purposes of analysing the competitive effects of a merger), see CCS 400/003/06, *Qantas-Orangestar Cooperation Agreement*, 5 March 2007, para. 31. But see also the later cases of CCS 700/002/11, *Ball Bearing Manufacturers International Cartel*, 27 May 2014 and CCS 700/003/11, *Freight Forwarders Price Fixing Agreement*, 11 December 2014.

diverse contexts. In attribution of liability cases, the issue is when it is appropriate to ignore the legal personality of the entity that committed the infringement and to impose liability on a parent for an infringement it did not itself commit—when can the parent be said to have 'personal responsibility' for the violation?—but in substantive reach cases the policy is to take outside the scope of Article 101 only arrangements which resemble the internal workings of a firm and/or arrangements between entities which are in any event bound to pursue a common policy on a market. Indeed, in *Del Monte* the GC held that when determining whether the conduct of one firm (Weichert) could be imputed to another (Del Monte), the applicant's reference to *Suiker Unie* and *BMW* were irrelevant

since those judgments concern legal issues and have factual backgrounds that differ from those of the present case. *Suiker Unie and Others v Commission* concerns the applicability of Article [101] to agreements concluded between trade representatives and principals. *BMW Belgium and Others v Commission* concerns direct responsibility in the light of a fine which the Commission imposed on car dealers for having agreed on an export prohibition. In neither of those decisions was the Court required to examine and determine the question whether the conditions for the imputation to one undertaking of an infringement committed by another were satisfied.[162]

In addition, although the expansive interpretation given to the concept of an undertaking in attribution of liability cases is in itself controversial (and has been argued to infringe principles of personal responsibility, limited liability, and the presumption of innocence[163]), it seems that there must at least be some doubt over the question of whether, in particular, negative control over a subsidiary or JV is/ should be sufficient to ensure that a parent and that subsidiary/JV pursue a common course of conduct so that the conduct escapes scrutiny under Article 101. Indeed, application of the concept in such a way as to exclude such conduct from the scope of Article 101 might raise concerns that the conduct of an entity controlled by a group of competitors, and used as a vehicle for cooperation between them, could be put beyond the scope of Article 101. Such an interpretation would also seem to conflict with decisions adopted by the Commission in cases which specifically dealt with the application of Article 101 to arrangements between parent and joint venture, see for example, *IJsselcentrale*,[164] *Gosmé/ Martell-DMP*,[165] and with jurisprudence dealing with 'associations of undertakings' which have generally interpreted this concept broadly to encompass entities used as an institutionalised mechanism for coordinating the members/shareholders' conduct (see Section 5.A.vii.a).

e. The Boundaries of the Economic Unit on a Dynamic Basis

Because an undertaking constitutes an economic unit which can be made up of several legal persons, its constitution may change over time, especially following a corporate reorganisation or a sale of the responsible entity to another or its absorption into another entity. This is of particular relevance in cases where the Commission wishes to impose a fine on responsible persons within the economic unit. '[R]eorganisations, disposals of undertakings and other changes can lead to the situation in which at the time a cartel offence is penalised the person who conducts an undertaking which participated in the cartel is not the person who conducted the undertaking at the time of the infringement.'[166]

The general rule flowing from the principle of personal responsibility[167] is that liability should attach to the original operator managing the undertaking in question at the time the infringement

---

[162] Case T-587/08, *Del Monte* EU:T:2013:129, para. 151. In the appeal the CJ discussed imputation of liability without referring to the other line of cases, Cases C-293 and 294/13 P, EU:C:2015:416.

[163] See articles cited in n. 116.

[164] COMP/32.732, [1991] OJ L28/3.

[165] COMP/32.186, [1991] OJ L185/21. Each parent held 50% of the capital and half the supervisory board had to be drawn from each parent's shareholders.

[166] Case C-280/06, *ETI and Others* [2007] ECR I-10893, Kokott AG, para. 73.

[167] Ibid. ('what is decisive for the attribution of cartel offences is the principle of personal responsibility, which is founded in the rule of law and the principle of fault … Personal responsibility means that in principle a cartel offence is to be attributed to the natural or legal person who operates the undertaking who participates in the cartel').

was committed; responsibility is personal in nature and cannot be avoided by transferring relevant business activities to another.[168] An infringing undertaking (which is still in existence) must therefore ordinarily answer itself for its unlawful activity and remains, subject to the limitation rules, liable for its past infringements even if it sells the subsidiary or assets that were the vehicle of the infringement.[169] Conversely, subsequent purchasers or transferees are not normally held responsible for prior breaches but only in respect of continuous, repeat, or new infringements by the entity committed after the date of transfer.[170] In exceptional circumstances, however, in order to ensure that liability for an infringement is not avoided and the application of penalties thwarted through means of organisational change (for example, where the transferor ceases to exist, and has been absorbed within the new operator, or is left as an empty shell), liability may be transferred to a new operator which, in economic terms, can be regarded as the successor of the original operation or 'if he continues the undertaking which participated in the cartel'[171] (the 'economic continuity' test is satisfied). In *Parker-Hanifin v Commission*[172] the CJ explained:

40. The Court has noted that, when an entity that has committed an infringement of the competition rules is subject to a legal or organisational change, this change does not necessarily create a new undertaking free of liability for the conduct of its predecessor that infringed the competition rules, when, from an economic point of view, the two entities are identical. If undertakings could escape penalties by simply changing their identity through restructurings, sales or other legal or organisational changes, the objective of suppressing conduct that infringes the competition rules and preventing its reoccurrence by means of deterrent penalties would be jeopardised (judgment in *ETI and Other*, …, paragraphs 41 and 42 …).

41. The Court has thus held that where two entities constitute one economic entity, the fact that the entity that committed the infringement still exists does not as such preclude imposing a penalty on the entity to which its economic activities were transferred. In particular, applying penalties in this way is permissible where those entities have been under the control of the same person and have therefore, given the close economic and organisational links between them, carried out, in all material respects, the same commercial instructions (judgments in *ETI and Others*, …, paragraphs 48 and 49 …, and *Versalis v Commission*, …, paragraph 52).

Liability under the economic continuity principle may thus be transferred to a new operator where, for example:

(a) the legal entity responsible for running the entity has ceased to exist in law and is absorbed into the business of a new owner.[173] The change in the legal form and/or name does not create a new undertaking free of liability for the conduct of its predecessor when from 'an economic point of view, the two are identical'.[174] The Commission may identify the 'combination of

---

[168] Case C-49/92 P, *Commission v Anic Partecipazioni* [1999] ECR I-4125.

[169] COMP/37.027, *Zinc Phosphate* [2003] OJ L153/1, para. 238.

[170] Assuming that, in the case of a transfer of a legal entity, the parental liability conditions are satisfied. If not, the acquiring entity cannot be held liable—only the acquired, infringing entity will attract liability.

[171] Case T-335/94, *Limburgse Vinyl Maatschappijand v Commission* [1999] ECR II-931, para. 76.

[172] Case C-434/13, *Commission v Parker Hannifin Manufacturing Srl and Parker-Hannifin Corp* EU:C:2014:2456.

[173] See, e.g., Cases T-259–264 and 271/02, *Raiffeissen Zentralbank Osterreich v Commission* [2006] ECR II-5169, Case T-349/08, *Uralita v Commission* [2011] ECR II-373, and Case T-194/06, *SNIA v Commission* [2011] ECR II-3119, *aff'd* Case C-448/11 P, EU:C:201:801. But contrast Case C-49/92, *Commission v Anic Partecipazioni* [1999] ECR I-4125, para. 145 (where the legal person responsible for running the undertaking had not ceased to exist in law) and Case T-9/99 *HFB and Others v Commission* [2002] ECR II-1487, para. 104.

[174] Cases 29 and 30/83, *CRAM and Rheinzink v Commission* [1984] ECR 1679, para. 9. Case C-280/06 *ETI and Others* [2007] ECR I-10893, Kokott AG ('having regard to economic continuity ensures that legal persons cannot escape their responsibility under antitrust law merely by changing their legal form or their name. The same must be true for example in respect of a merger in which the original operator of the undertaking which participated in the cartel surrenders its legal personality to another legal person which is its successor in law', para. 78).

physical and human elements which contributed to the commission of the infringement' and then impose liability on the legal person which has become responsible for their operation;[175] or

(b) the legal person that committed the infringement still exists but no longer carries on an economic activity in the relevant market and there are close structural links between the original and new operators which are under the control of the same person.[176] In such circumstances the existence of the structural links between the original and new operators justifies the imposition of liability on both (the new operator being jointly and severally liable for the fine).[177] In *ETI*, for example, the CJ held that responsibility for past antitrust infringements committed by AAMS, an organ of the State, on the cigarette market, could be attributed to its successor company, ETI. AAMS's tobacco business (manufacture and sales) had been transferred in 1999 by the Italian Government to ETI which, at that time, was also owned by the Italian Ministry of Economy and Finance. In 2003, ETI was privatised and acquired by British American Tobacco. The CJ held that liability could be imposed on ETI in respect of infringements committed by AAMS if it, and AAMS, constituted one economic entity—if they answered to, and were owned and subject to control by, the same public entity. Applying penalties in this way 'is permissible where those entities have been subject to control by the same person within the group and have therefore given the close economic and organisational links between them carried out, in all material respects, the same commercial instructions'.[178]

Although in *Hoescht* the GC held that the principle of personal liability cannot 'be called into question by the principle of economic continuity in cases where...an undertaking involved in the cartel has transferred a part of its business to an independent third party and there is no structural link between the initial operator and the new operator (see, to that effect, Opinion of Advocate General Kokott in *ETI and Others*, paragraph 82)',[179] in *Parker-Hanifin* the CJ clarified that where an infringing business had been transferred into a new subsidiary, simply for the purpose of transferring that business to a third party, the economic continuity principle may apply. '[F]or the purpose of establishing the existence of economic continuity, the relevant date for assessing whether the transfer of activities is within a group or between independent undertakings must be that of the transfer itself'; the economic links need therefore to exist only *at the time of* the acquisition and two distinct transactions, an internal transaction and a subsequent transfer to a third party, cannot be treated as one.

In *ETI* Advocate General Kokott indicated that although the criterion of economic continuity is not intended to substitute for the principle of personal responsibility, new circumstances of 'economic continuity' might be recognisable where the effective enforcement of competition law requires a derogation from the principle of personal responsibility in order to ensure that an offence is punished effectively according to fault; for example, where organisational changes are made 'abusively' in an attempt to circumvent liability to pay a fine.[180]

---

[175] Case T-6/89, *Enichem v Commission* [1991] ECR II-1623, 237.

[176] Cases C-204/00 P etc, *Aalborg Portland and Others v Commission* [2004] ECR I-123, para. 359, and Case C-280/06, *ETI and Others* [2007] ECR I-10893, paras. 41 and 48.

[177] Case T-40506, *ArcelorMittal v Commission* [2009] ECR II-789, paras. 112–117.

[178] Case C-280/06, *ETI and Others* [2007] ECR I-10893, para. 49.

[179] Case T-161/05, *Hoescht v Commission* [2009] ECR II-3555, para. 61.

[180] Case C-280/06, *ETI and Others* [2007] ECR I-10893, Kokott AG, para. 82.

(vii) Associations of Undertakings

a. Institutionalised Forms of Cooperation

Article 101(1) applies not only to agreements and concerted practices between undertakings, but to decisions by associations of undertakings. In *Wouters*[181] Advocate General Léger stated that the concept

seeks to prevent undertakings from being able to evade the rules on competition on account simply of the form in which they coordinate their conduct on the market. To ensure that this principle is effective, Article [101(1)] covers not only direct methods of coordinating conduct between undertakings (agreements and concerted practices) but also institutionalised forms of cooperation, that is to say, situations in which economic operators act through a collective structure or a common body.[182]

An association of undertakings 'consists of undertakings of the same general type and makes itself responsible for representing and defending their common interests vis-à-vis other economic operators, government bodies and the public in general'.[183] Thus it has been found to apply to: trade associations (which may provide a forum for competitors in a particular industry to get together and to discuss matters which may be to their mutual interest and a perfect vehicle through which undertakings in a specific industry coordinate action), agricultural cooperatives,[184] an association of collecting societies,[185] a body set up by statute and with public functions if it represents the trading interests of the members (even if there are some members appointed by the government or another public authority),[186] and professional associations (even if governed by a public law statute).[187] It has also been found that *Visa*[188] and *MasterCard*[189] are associations of undertakings. Such a categorisation means that their recommendations, rules, and other unilateral acts designed to coordinate the behaviour of members may constitute decisions which are brought within Article 101 without separate proof of a concerted practice or agreement between the individual members of the association.

b. The Relationship between Associations of Undertakings and Undertakings

A particular feature of Article 101, which applies to agreements between undertakings and the decisions of associations of undertakings, is that an entity has sometimes been found to be acting both jointly with its parents/members (as an association of undertakings) and unilaterally as a single undertaking at the same time. In *Laurent Piau*,[190] for example, the GC held that although a sporting association constituted an association of undertakings it also constituted an undertaking insofar

---

[181] Case C-309/99, [2002] ECR I-1577.

[182] Ibid., Léger AG, para. 62.

[183] Ibid., para. 61.

[184] Case C-250/92, *Gøttrup-Klim e.a. Grovvareforeninger and Others v Dansk Landbrugs Grovvareselskab AmbA* [1994] ECR I-5641.

[185] See COMP/38.698, *CISAC Agreement* 16 July 2008, partially annulled on appeal, Case T-442/08, *International Confederation of Societies of Authors and Composers (CISAC) v Commission* EU:T:2013:188, see Chap. 9.

[186] Case 123/83, *BNIC v Clair* [1985] ECR 391.

[187] See Case C-35/96, *Commission v Italy* [1998] ECR I-3851, paras. 36–38 (dealing with a professional association of custom agents); Cases C-180–184/98, *Pavlov* [2000] ECR I-6451, paras. 73–77; and Case C-309/99, *Wouters* [2002] ECR I-577, para. 65.

[188] E.g. COMP/29.373, *Visa International* [2002] OJ L318/17.

[189] See COMP/34.579, *Europay (Eurocard-MasterCard)* 19 December 2007. In this case the Commission rejected MasterCard's argument that its public listing on the New York Stock Exchange had changed the organisation's governance so fundamentally that any decision of its board no longer qualified as a decision of an association (an institutionalised form of coordination of the banks' conduct) but rather constituted a 'unilateral' act by which each member bank bilaterally agrees to abide, *aff'd* Case T-111/08, *MasterCard Inc v Commission* EU:T:2012:260, paras. 241–260 and Case C-382/12 P, EU:C:2014:2201, paras. 62–77 (the banks still participated in the decision-making process and shared a commonality of interest with MasterCard).

[190] Case T-193/02, *Piau v Commission* [2005] ECR II-209, para. 69.

as it engaged in economic activity in a market itself. This reasoning is not entirely easy, however. If the association is viewed as an undertaking and a single economic actor, the parents/members are viewed as part of that economic unit and not as separate undertakings. But if the parents are not undertakings, the sporting association cannot be an association of undertakings.

A further question arising is whether an association of undertakings which carries out non-economic activity should be subject to the competition rules. It would seem that such non-economic activity should not be caught as, in essence, the conduct of the association is treated as the joint conduct of its members/shareholders (whose actions are not caught unless they are economic in nature).[191] Indeed, in *Wouters*,[192] the CJ suggests that a functional approach should be adopted to the concept of an association of undertakings in the same way as it applies to the concept of an undertaking. In that case it was argued that the Bar of the Netherlands, a body governed by public law, should not constitute an association of undertakings when exercising regulatory powers in order to perform a task of public interest. The CJ held that the 'rules of competition do not apply to activity which, by its nature, its aim and the rules to which it is subject does not belong to the sphere of economic activity . . . or which is connected with the exercise of the powers of a public authority . . .'.[193] It held, however, that in adopting the regulatory rules the association was neither fulfilling a social function based on the principle of solidarity nor exercising powers which are typically those of a public authority. Rather, it was acting as the regulatory body of a profession, the practice of which constitutes an economic activity. It thus concluded that the Bar of the Netherlands must be regarded as an association of undertakings within the meaning of Article 101(1) when adopting a regulation such as one which prohibited certain multidisciplinary partnerships. 'Such a regulation constitutes the expression of the intention of the delegates of the members of a profession that they should act in a particular manner in carrying on their economic activity.'[194]

Similarly, in *Ordem dos Técnicos Oficiais de Contas (OTOC) v Autoridade da Concorrência*,[195] the CJ held that a professional association of chartered accountants was to be regarded as an association of undertakings when it adopted a regulation providing that certain compulsory training to be undertaken by chartered accountants could be provided only by OTOC. Even though OTOC was regulated by public law and required to adopt binding rules putting in place a system of compulsory training for its members and to ensure a quality service, it could not be regarded, when adopting the rules, as exercising powers which are typically those of a public authority and the rules at issue could not be regarded as not belonging to the sphere of economic activity (they had a direct impact on the market for compulsory training for chartered accountants[196]). The CJ also held that it was immaterial that OTOC did not seek to make a profit: 'that does not prevent an entity which carries out

---

[191] But for the view that '[i]f the functional definition of undertaking given in *Höfner* captures all economic activity then associations of undertakings must be addressed when engaged in non-economic activity, otherwise the association would be an undertaking in its own right and "associations of undertakings" otiose', see Odudu, n. 22, 52–53. See also Cases 209–215 and 218/78, *Van Landewyck and Others v Commission* [1980] ECR 3125, paras. 87–88; Cases 96–102, 104, 105, 108, and 110/82, *NV IAZ International Belgium SA v Commission* [1983] ECR 3369, paras. 19–20; and Cases T-25, 26, 30–32, 34–39, 42–46, 48, 50–71, 87, 88, 103, and 104/95, *Cimenteries CBR v Commission* [2000] ECR II-491, para. 1320.

[192] Case C-309/99, [2002] ECR I-1577.

[193] Ibid., para. 57.

[194] Ibid., para. 64. The Court found this view to be supported by the facts that: the governing body of the Bar was composed exclusively of members of the Bar elected solely by members of the profession; when adopting regulatory measures the Bar was not required to be guided by reference to specified public-interest criteria (it was authorised to act where to do so would be in the interest of the proper practice of the profession); and the regulation influenced the conduct of the members of the Bar on the market in legal services (which indicated it did not fall outside the sphere of economic activity).

[195] Case C-1/12, EU:C:2013:127.

[196] It did not matter therefore that the rules would not affect competition on the market on which the members of the professional association practise their profession as it could do so on the market on which the professional association itself has an economic activity, Case C-1/12, EU:C:2013:127, para. 45.

operations on the market from being considered an undertaking, where the corresponding offer of services exists in competition with that of other operators which do seek to make a profit'.[197]

B. THE MEANING OF 'AGREEMENT', 'DECISION', AND 'CONCERTED PRACTICE'

(i) Introduction

Article 101(1) prohibits joint not individual conduct. The reference to 'agreements between undertakings, decisions by associations of undertakings and concerted practices' requires some element of 'collusion' between independent undertakings. Although the terms 'agreement', 'decision', and 'concerted practice' are distinguishable from each other by their intensity and the forms in which they manifest themselves, they overlap and nothing turns legally on whether the conduct results from one or the other (the precise characterisation of the cooperation does not alter the legal analysis to be conducted).[198] Each must be understood in the light of the concept inherent in the competition rules that each economic operator must determine independently the policy which it intends to adopt. Collectively they draw a critical dividing line between collusive practices (caught by Article 101)[199] and independent behaviour (falling outside of its scope).

In effect, while that provision distinguishes between 'concerted practices', 'agreements between undertakings' and 'decisions by associations of undertakings', the aim is to have the prohibitions of that article catch different forms of coordination and collusion between undertakings (see Case C-49/92 P, *Commission v Anic Partecipazioni . . .*, paragraph 112). Accordingly . . . a precise characterisation of the nature of the cooperation at issue in the main proceedings is not liable to alter the legal analysis to be carried out under Article [101].[200]

In cases involving complex infringements it may not, therefore, be necessary to characterise an infringement either as, for example, an agreement on the one hand or a concerted practice on the other. The conduct may present elements of both. A difficulty explored below, however, is to ascertain and define the minimum degree or loosest form of interaction necessary between undertakings for it to be shown that they have colluded.

In many Article 101 cases the existence of an agreement is not in doubt. There may be doubt, however, as to the precise terms of the agreement and/or as to whether the terms can be said to restrict competition. In other cases, frequently where it is suspected that a serious violation of the competition rules has been committed (for example, horizontal or vertical price-fixing), evidence that independent undertakings agreed or concerted to fix prices will, effectively, prove a violation of Article 101(1).[201] If detected, severe consequences may follow for those involved in the infringement (see Section 4.B and Chapters 13 and 14). In such cases, the parties who have been 'colluding' are likely to do so in an amorphous way and/or to try and conceal the existence of the practice rather than attempt to try to defend its legitimacy. The challenge for the competition authorities in such cases therefore is to uncover such covert operations and, where evidence is skimpy, to determine whether or not the behaviour on the market results from collusion, which is prohibited under Article 101, or independent behaviour, which is not. Proof of collusion may be founded upon either

---

[197] Ibid., para. 57.

[198] Case C-238/05, *Asnef-Equifax, Servicios de Información sobre Solvencia y Crédito, SL v Asociación de Usuarios de Servicios Bancarios (Ausbanc)* [2006] ECR I-11125.

[199] Case C-49/92 P, *Commission v Anic* [1999] ECR I-4125, paras. 112 and 131.

[200] Case C-238/05, *Asnef-Equifax, Servicios de Información sobre Solvencia y Crédito, SL v Asociación de Usuarios de Servicios Bancarios (Ausbanc)* [2006] ECR I-11125.

[201] As the agreement has as its 'object' the restriction of competition, its anti-competitive 'effect' does not need to be demonstrated, see Chap. 4.

direct evidence, which may be difficult to uncover[202] in cases involving serious violations of the rules, or indirect or circumstantial evidence from which such conduct may be inferred.

(ii) Agreement

a. A Concurrence of Wills

The term 'agreement' has been given a liberal construction. In *Bayer AG v Commission*,[203] the GC set out what has now become the classic definition of the concept, holding that proof of an agreement must be founded upon 'the existence of the subjective element that characterizes the very concept of the agreement, that is to say a concurrence of wills between economic operators on the implementation of a policy, the pursuit of an objective, or the adoption of a given line of conduct on the market'.[204] It is 'clear from the case-law that in order for there to be an agreement . . . it is sufficient that the undertakings in question should have expressed their joint intention to conduct themselves on the market in a specific way'.[205]

So long as there is a concurrence of wills, constituting the faithful expression of the parties' intention,[206] its form is unimportant; whether or not the conduct amounts to a contract under national law, whether or not it is intended to be legally binding, whether or not sanctions are provided for a breach, and whether it is in writing or oral.[207] It covers 'gentlemen's agreements',[208] standard conditions of sale,[209] trade association rules (which are treated as an agreement between the members to abide by the rules),[210] and agreements entered into to settle disputes, such as trade mark delimitation agreements.[211] An agreement exists once the parties agree on 'good neighbour rules' or 'establish practice and ethics' or 'certain rules of the game which it is in the interests of all of us to follow'.[212] Further, an agreement which has been terminated may be caught by Article 101(1) in respect of the period after termination if the effects of the agreement continue to be felt.[213] Agreements may be caught even if they are encouraged or approved by national law[214] or entered into after consultation with the national authorities.[215] It is no defence that an undertaking was bullied into concluding the

---

[202] I.e. smoking-gun evidence which does not require inferences to establish the agreement or other collusion alleged. Written or parol evidence may be used. The Commission has broad investigative powers which may help it uncover direct evidence and the Commission's leniency programme is designed to encourage participants to come forward with direct evidence, see Chaps. 9 and 13.

[203] Case T-41/96, [2000] ECR II-3383, *aff'd* on appeal Cases C-2 and 3/01 P, [2004] ECR I-23.

[204] Ibid.

[205] Case T-41/96, *Bayer AG v Commission* [2000] ECR II-3383, para. 67, *aff'd* on appeal Cases C-2 and 3/01 P, [2004] ECR I-23, relying on, e.g., Case 41/69, *ACF Chemiefarma NV v Commission* [1970] ECR 661, para. 112. See also Case C-49/92, *Commission v Anic Partecipazioni* [1999] ECR I-4125, paras. 79 and 122.

[206] Case T-41/96, *Bayer AG v Commission* [2000] ECR II-3383, para. 69, *aff'd* on appeal Cases C-2 and 3/01 P, [2004] ECR I-23. See also Case T-62/98, *Volkswagen AG v Commission* [2000] ECR II-2707, *aff'd* Case C-338/00 P, *Volkswagen AG v Commission* [2003] ECR I-9189.

[207] See, e.g., Case 28/77, *Tepea BV v Commission* [1978] ECR 1391.

[208] Case 41/69, *ACF Chemiefarma NV v Commission* [1970] ECR 661 (an export cartel was extended within the EU through a gentlemen's agreement. So long as the parties had declared themselves willing to abide by the gentlemen's agreement that was sufficient).

[209] Case C-277/87, *Sandoz prodotti farmaceutici SpA v Commission* [1990] ECR I-45.

[210] COMP/30.804, *Nuovo Cegam* [1984] OJ L99/29.

[211] See Chap. 12.

[212] Cases 209–215 and 218/78, *Van Landewyck v Commission* [1980] ECR 3125, paras. 85 and 86.

[213] Case T-7/89, *SA Hercules Chemicals NV v Commission* [1991] ECR II-1711, see n. 224 and text.

[214] See Cases 43 and 63/82, *VBVB & VBBB v Commission* [1984] ECR 19; COMP/26.870, *Aluminium Imports from Eastern Europe* [1985] OJ L92/1; COMP/29.525 and COMP/30.000, *AROW/BNIC* [1982] OJ L379/1.

[215] Cases 240–242, 261, and 262/82, *SSI v Commission* [1985] ECR 3831. For the position where the State *requires* or encourages undertakings to enter into anti-competitive agreements, see Section 5.F and Chap. 8.

agreement,[216] or that an undertaking had cheated or never intended to implement or to adhere to the terms of the agreement.

undertakings concerned, by taking part without publicly distancing themselves, gave the other participants the impression that they subscribed to what was discussed and would act in conformity with it. The notion of 'agreement' is objective in nature. The actual motives (and hidden intentions) which underlay the behaviour adopted are irrelevant.[217]

b. Agreements between Undertakings Operating at Different Levels of the Economy or in Separate Markets

Article 101(1) applies to agreements concluded between two or more undertakings (bilateral or multilateral agreements). It has been seen that it is not applicable where agreements are concluded between companies forming part of a single economic entity, such as a parent and subsidiary/distributor or a principal and its agent.[218] In the course of argument in *Consten and Grundig v Commission*[219] it was suggested that, in a similar way, Article 101(1) should not be applied to agreements concluded between undertakings operating at different levels of the economy. If a producer could restrict the actions of its commercial representative without triggering the operation of Article 101(1) it should also be able to restrict the action of independent distributors. Article 101 should not be concerned with agreements concluded between entities which were not competitors and which were not on an equal footing. Rather, any such conduct considered to be restrictive of competition should be dealt with under Article 102. The CJ rejected these arguments, holding that Article 101(1) could apply to vertical arrangements. The wording of the provision did not suggest that a distinction between horizontal and vertical agreements should be drawn. The agreement had not been concluded between a manufacturer and an entity integrated within it but had been concluded between independent undertakings. Further, the fact that the agreement was not concluded between competitors was immaterial. Article 101 applied to all agreements between undertakings which had the potential to distort competition within the common market.

Cases 56 and 58/64, *Etablissements Consten SA and Grundig-Verkaufs-GmbH v Commission* [1966] ECR 299, 339–340

In 1957 Grundig, a German manufacturer of radios, tape recorders, dictaphones, and televisions, appointed Consten as its exclusive agent for France. Consten agreed, amongst other things, not to handle any competing products, to order a minimum quantity of Grundig products, to stock accessories and spare parts, and to provide after-sales services. In return, Grundig agreed not to deliver the product for sale in France and imposed export and re-export restrictions on all distributors in other Member States. The Grundig trade mark, Gint, was registered in France in Consten's name. Under the agreements Consten, therefore, had absolute territorial protection. No one else was entitled to sell Grundig products in France either actively or passively. In fact, UNEF, a Parisian company, started importing and selling Grundig products at more favourable prices in France. Consten commenced proceedings in the French courts contending that UNEF had failed to respect its contract with Grundig, that it was indulging in unfair competition, and that it was infringing Consten's trade mark rights. It also brought proceedings against

---

[216] Case T-25/95, *Cimenteries CBR SA v Commission* [2000] ECR II-491, para. 2557.

[217] See, e.g., COMP/36.700, *Industrial and Medical Gases* [2003] OJ L84/1 (the Commission rejected the arguments of undertakings alleged to be members of a cartel, Air Liquide and Westfalen, that they had not actially taken part in the agreements or ever intended to implement them), *aff'd* on appeal Case T-304/02, *Hoek Loos NV v Commission* [2006] ECR II-1887.

[218] See also Chap. 11.

[219] Cases 56 and 58/64, *Consten and Grundig* [1966] ECR 299.

Leissner in Strasbourg which had obtained Grundig products for resale in France. UNEF complained to the Commission and, in 1963, the agreement was notified to the Commission for examination. The French court adjourned its proceedings to await the Commission's decision.

The Commission concluded that the agreements did infringe Article 101(1) and could not be individually exempted under Article 101(3). Consten and Grundig appealed to the Court of Justice. One of their pleas was that Article 101(1) applied only to 'horizontal' and not 'vertical' agreements. This argument was supported by the Italian Government.

Court of Justice

The complaints concerning the applicability of Article [101(1)] to sole distributorship contracts

The applicants submit that the prohibition in Article [101(1)] applies only to so-called horizontal agreements. The Italian Government submits furthermore that sole distributorship contracts do not constitute 'agreements between undertakings' within the meaning of that provision, since the parties are not on a footing of equality. With regard to these contracts, freedom of competition may only be protected by virtue of Article [102].

Neither the wording of Article [101] nor that of Article [102] gives any ground for holding that distinct areas of application are to be assigned to each of the two Articles according to the level in the economy at which the contracting parties operate. Article [101] refers in a general way to all agreements which distort competition within the Common Market and does not lay down any distinction between those agreements based on whether they are made between competitors operating at the same level in the economic process or between non-competing persons operating at different levels. In principle, no distinction can be made where the Treaty does not make any distinction.

Furthermore, the possible application of Article [101] to a sole distributorship contract cannot be excluded merely because the grantor and the concessionnaire are not competitors inter se and not on a footing of equality. Competition may be distorted within the meaning of Article [101(1)] not only by agreements which limit it as between the parties, but also by agreements which prevent or restrict the competition which might take place between one of them and third parties. For this purpose, it is irrelevant whether the parties to the agreement are or are not on a footing of equality as regards their position and function in the economy. This applies all the more, since, by such an agreement, the parties might seek, by preventing or limiting the competition of third parties in respect of the products, to create or guarantee for their benefit an unjustified advantage at the expense of the consumer or user, contrary to the general aims of Article [101].

It is thus possible that, without involving an abuse of a dominant position, an agreement between economic operators at different levels may affect trade between Member States and at the same time have as its object or effect the prevention, restriction or distortion of competition, thus falling under the prohibition of Article [101(1)].

In addition, it is pointless to compare on the one hand the situation, to which Article [101] applies, of a producer bound by a sole distributorship agreement to the distributor of his products with on the other hand that of a producer who includes within his undertaking the distribution of his own products by some means, for example, by commercial representatives, to which Article [101] does not apply. These situations are distinct in law and, moreover, need to be assessed differently, since two marketing organizations, one of which is [i]ntegrated into the manufacturer's undertaking whilst the other is not, may not necessarily have the same efficiency. The wording of Article [101] causes the prohibition to apply, provided that the other conditions are met, to an agreement between several undertakings. Thus it does not apply where a sole undertaking integrates its own distribution network into its business organization. It does not thereby follow, however, that the contractual situation based on an agreement between a manufacturing and a distributing undertaking is rendered legally acceptable by a simple process of economic analogy—which is in any case incomplete and in contradiction with the said Article. Furthermore, although in the first case the Treaty intended in Article [101] to leave untouched the internal organization of an undertaking and to render it liable to be called in question, by means of Article [102], only in cases where it reaches such a degree of seriousness as to amount to an abuse of a dominant position, the same reservation could not apply when the impediments to competition result from agreement between two different undertakings which then as a general rule simply require to be prohibited.

Finally, an agreement between producer and distributor which might tend to restore the national divisions in trade between Member States might be such as to frustrate the most fundamental objectives of the Community. The Treaty, whose preamble and content aim at abolishing the barriers between States, and which in several provisions gives evidence of a stern attitude with regard to their reappearance, could not allow undertakings to reconstruct such barriers. Article [101(1)] is designed to pursue this aim, even in the case of agreements between undertakings placed at different levels in the economic process.

The submissions set out above are consequently unfounded.

In *AC-Treuhand AG v Commission*[220] the CJ also made it clear that Article 101(1) catches agreements between undertakings, even where the purpose of the agreement is to restrict competition on a market on which one of the undertakings is not active. Accordingly, the CJ confirmed that a consultancy firm may infringe Article 101(1) where it actively contributes to the implementation and continuation of a cartel among producers operating on a market (for example, through organising meetings, collecting and supplying data, and moderating disputes between cartel members), even if it does not itself operate on the cartelised market. It thus rejected AC-Treuhand's argument that Article 101(1) is directed only at the parties who agree to alter their conduct on the market and confirmed that it may also apply to intermediaries assisting or facilitating the functioning of a cartel.[221] The CJ reiterated that the main objective of Article 101(1) is to ensure that competition remains undistorted so it had to be possible to put a stop to the active contribution of an undertaking to a restriction of competition even where that contribution did not relate to an economic activity forming part of the relevant market on which the restriction came about (or was intended to come about).

c. Collective Bargaining Agreements

Article 101(1) *does not* apply to collective agreements between workers and employers intended to improve working conditions which belong to the realm of social policy. In *Albany*[222] the CJ held that agreements concluded by representatives of employers and workers in a sector would not be caught by Article 101(1) insofar as those agreements related to the improvement of conditions of work and employment. Not only was it an objective of the Treaty to ensure that competition in the common market was not distorted, but one of the Treaty's objectives was to achieve a high level of employment and social protection. The latter objective would be thwarted if Article 101(1) applied to agreements adopted by management and labour to improve conditions of work and employment. Consequently, such agreements fell outside the scope of Article 101(1) of the Treaty altogether.

---

[220] Case C-194/14 P, EU:C:2015:717, paras. 26–47 (but contrast Wahl AG in his Opinion in this case, EU:C:2015:350), *aff'g* Case T-27/10, *AC-Treuhand AG v Commission* EU:T:2014:59. See also Case T-99/04, *AC-Treuhand AG v Commission* [2008] ECR II-1501.

[221] In February 2015, the Commission also imposed a fine of €14.96 million on ICAP a broker that had facilitated several cartels in the sector of Yen interest rate derivatives, COMP/39.861, IP/15/1404.

[222] Case C-67/96, [1999] ECR I-5751, see especially paras. 46–64. See also Cases C-115–117/97, *Brentjens' Handelsonderneming BV v Stichting Bedrijfspensioenfonds voor de Handel in Bouwmaterialen* [1999] ECR I-6025, para. 57, Cases C-180–184/98, *Pavlov* [2000] ECR I-6451, para. 67, and Case C-437/09, *AG2R Prévoyance v Beaudout Père et Fils SARL* [2011] ECR I-973, paras. 28–36. See also nn. 91–93 and text.

d. Participation in Meetings—Acceptance of an Offer to Collude

A participant in a meeting at which an anti-competitive agreement is concluded will be taken to have participated in that agreement, unless it can establish that it did not have any anti-competitive intention when it attended the meeting, and that the other participants were aware of this.[223] It appears, therefore, that the participant tacitly accepts an offer to collude by not publicly distancing itself from the agreement.[224] It is no defence that the participant did not put the initiatives into effect. Evidence of prices or other behaviour not reflecting those discussed at the meeting are not, therefore, sufficient to prove that it had not participated in the scheme.[225] The CJ set this position out clearly in *Cement*.[226]

Cases C-204, 205, 211, 213, 217, and 219/00 P, *Aalborg Portland AS v Commission* [2004] ECR I-123

Court of Justice

81. According to settled case-law, it is sufficient for the Commission to show that the undertaking concerned participated in meetings at which anti-competitive agreements were concluded, without manifestly opposing them, to prove to the requisite standard that the undertaking participated in the cartel. Where participation in such meetings has been established, it is for that undertaking to put forward evidence to establish that its participation in those meetings was without any anti-competitive intention by demonstrating that it had indicated to its competitors that it was participating in those meetings in a spirit that was different from theirs (see Case C-199/92 P, *Hüls v Commission* . . ., paragraph 155, and Case C-49/92 P, *Commission v Anic* . . ., paragraph 96).

82. The reason underlying that principle of law is that, having participated in the meeting without publicly distancing itself from what was discussed, the undertaking has given the other participants to believe that it subscribed to what was decided there and would comply with it.

83. The principles established in the case-law cited at paragraph 81 of this judgment also apply to participation in the implementation of a single agreement. In order to establish that an undertaking has participated in such an agreement, the Commission must show that the undertaking intended to contribute by its own conduct to the common objectives pursued by all the participants and that it was aware of the actual conduct planned or put into effect by other undertakings in pursuit of the same objectives or that it could reasonably have foreseen it and that it was prepared to take the risk (*Commission v Anic*, paragraph 87).

84. In that regard, a party which tacitly approves of an unlawful initiative, without publicly distancing itself from its content or reporting it to the administrative authorities, effectively encourages the continuation of the infringement and compromises its discovery. That complicity constitutes a passive mode

---

[223] See, e.g., Case C-510/06 P, *Archer Daniels Midland Co v Commission* [2009] ECR I-1843, paras. 119–120 and Case T-3/89, *Atochem v Commission* [1991] ECR II-867, paras. 53–54.

[224] An undertaking may also try to show that an agreement has come to an end by showing that it publicly distanced itself from the cartel. If it cannot do so, the Commission may rightly assume that a cartel extended beyond the date of the last cartel meeting, see e.g., Case T-23/10, *Arkema France v Commission* EU:T:2014:62 and Case T-519/09, *Toshiba Corp v Commission* EU:T:2014:263 (on appeal before the Court of Justice Case C-373/14 P).

[225] Case T-3/89, *Atochem v Commission* [1991] ECR II-867, para. 100 and Case T-53/03, *British Plasterboard v Commission* [2008] ECR II-1333, para. 85 ('[W]here an undertaking participates, even without taking an active part, in meetings between undertakings with an anti-competitive object and does not publicly distance itself from what occurred at those meetings, thus giving the impression to the other participants that it subscribes to the results of the meetings and will act in conformity with them, it may be considered as established that it participates in the cartel resulting from those meetings').

[226] Cases C-204, 205, 211, 213, 217, and 219/00 P, *Aalborg Portland AS v Commission* [2004] ECR I-123. See also n. 220 and text.

of participation in the infringement which is therefore capable of rendering the undertaking liable in the context of a single agreement.

85. Nor is the fact that an undertaking does not act on the outcome of a meeting having an anti-competitive purpose such as to relieve it of responsibility for the fact of its participation in a cartel, unless it has publicly distanced itself from what was agreed in the meeting (see Case C-291/98 P, *Sarrió v Commission* . . ., paragraph 50).

86. Neither is the fact that an undertaking has not taken part in all aspects of an anti-competitive scheme or that it played only a minor role in the aspects in which it did participate material to the establishment of the existence of an infringement on its part. Those factors must be taken into consideration only when the gravity of the infringement is assessed and if and when it comes to determining the fine (see, to that effect, *Commission v Anic*, paragraph 90).

e. Vertical Agreements and Unilateral Conduct

It is clear that the word 'agreement' catches terms and conditions even if imposed by one party on another. If the terms are accepted the fact that one of the parties was unwilling to accept them does not prevent the agreement from being formed (although fines may be reserved for the principal beneficiaries of the activity involved).[227] In *BMW*,[228] an agreement was found to have been concluded which incorporated export bans imposed on reluctant BMW dealers.

A further related question is the extent to which the term agreement can encompass what, at first sight at least, appears to be a purely unilateral policy or unilateral conduct pursued by one of the parties to an agreement. The question of when behaviour is truly unilateral (where the aims can be achieved without the participation of another) and when unilateral behaviour is merely *apparent* (receiving explicit or tacit acquiescence by another) is an important and difficult one which has provoked considerable litigation. The former, even if restrictive of competition or hindering parallel imports, falls outside Article 101.

Take, for example, a vertical agreement between a supplier and a dealer. Such agreements are unlikely to incorporate provisions in the EU imposing resale price maintenance or incorporating an export ban as these generally constitute clear violations of Article 101(1).[229] What would be the position, therefore, if on its face an agreement appears to comply with Article 101 but the supplier subsequently unilaterally announces that it will not deal with dealers that do not adhere to minimum recommended prices or who sell outside their allotted territory *or* if it is understood that if dealers do not adhere to minimum recommended prices and/or if they sell outside their allotted territory, they will not be supplied? Can an agreement to adhere to minimum resale prices or an export ban between the supplier and dealers be established and/or can a dealer that continues to accept supply be said to have 'tacitly' acquiesced in the supplier's policy and to have agreed to adhere to the anti-competitive terms? Does it make any difference whether or not the dealers do in fact adhere to the terms or whether they price cut or make sales outside their territory and/or whether the policy manifests itself before or after the agreement was concluded?

The Commission has been prepared to find the existence of an agreement based on seemingly unilateral conduct. For example, in *AEG*, AEG-Telefunken (a developer and manufacturer of consumer electronic products) notified its selective distribution system to the Commission;[230] the Commission

---

[227] The Commission may decline to impose a fine on a party that has acted unwillingly, against its own economic interest, or under duress, see, e.g., COMP/35.733, *Volkswagen* [1998] OJ L124/60, on appeal Case T-62/98, *Volkswagen AG v Commission* [2000] ECR II-2707, the appeal to the CJ was dismissed, Case C-338/00 P, *Volkswagen AG v Commission* [2003] ECR I-9189. See Chap. 13 for a discussion of the Commission's fining policy.

[228] Case 32/78, *BMW v Commission* [1979] ECR 2435.

[229] Such agreements are generally assumed to restrict competition (Art. 101(1)) and not to meet the conditions of Art. 101(3), see further Chaps. 4 and 11.

[230] A selective distribution system is one where the supplier limits the number or, more usually, the type of outlets that sell its products. They are discussed in greater detail in Chap. 11.

indicated that it did not infringe Article 101(1). Subsequently, however, the Commission received numerous complaints alleging that AEG had refused to supply certain resellers which would not adhere to a policy of charging minimum prices (and so in effect the agreement incorporated a resale price maintenance provision).[231] AEG argued that the acts complained of were not part of its agreement with resellers, but were decisions that it had taken unilaterally. Both the Commission and the Court rejected this argument. The CJ held that a refusal to approve distributors who satisfied the qualitative criteria necessary to become a member of the selective distribution system would be unlawful. This behaviour

on the part of the manufacturer does not constitute, on the part of the undertaking, unilateral conduct which, as AEG claims, would be exempt from the prohibition contained in Article [101(1)]. On the contrary, it forms part of the contractual relations between the undertaking and resellers. Indeed, in the case of the admission of a distributor, approval is based on the acceptance, tacit or express, by the contracting parties of the policy pursued by AEG which requires *inter alia* the exclusion from the network of all distributors who are qualified for admission but are not prepared to adhere to that policy.[232]

The Court thus found that the resellers' admission to the network was dependent upon their acceptance, express or tacit, of AEG's policy.

A similar approach has been adopted in other cases, many involving export bans imposed on distributors. In *Ford*,[233] the Commission concluded that Ford's decision to cease supply of right-hand-drive cars to German dealers formed an integral part of the agreements with the dealers. The CJ upheld its finding that admission to the Ford AG dealer network implied acceptance by the contracting parties of the policy pursued by Ford with regard to the models delivered to the German market. In *Sandoz*,[234] the CJ also affirmed the Commission's view that Sandoz's policy of sending invoices to customers with the words 'export prohibited' upon them did not constitute unilateral conduct, but, on the contrary, formed part of the general framework of commercial relations which the undertaking maintained with its customers. The Court stressed the uniform and systematic repetition of this practice noting that customers

were sent the same standard invoice after each individual order . . . The repeated orders of the products and the successive payments without protest by the customer of the prices indicated on the invoice bearing the words 'export prohibited', constituted a tacit acquiescence on the part of the latter in the clauses stipulated in the invoice.[235]

In each of these cases the apparently unilateral conduct was read into the agreement even though, in the export ban cases at least, it did not operate to the dealer's advantage.[236] In both *Bayer AG v Commission*[237] and *Volkswagen v Commission*,[238] however, the GC annulled Commission decisions which had found that unilateral conduct formed part of an agreement.[239] Indeed, in *Bayer AG v Commission*,[240] the EU Courts made it clear that the Commission had pushed the concept of an

---

[231] See Chaps. 4 and 11.

[232] Case 107/82, *AEG-Telefunken v Commission* [1983] ECR 3151, para. 38.

[233] Cases 228 and 229/82, *Ford Werke AG and Ford of Europe Inc v Commission* [1984] ECR 1129. See also Case C-279/87, *Tipp-Ex GmbH v Commission* [1990] ECR I-261.

[234] Case C-277/87, *Sandoz prodotti farmaceutici SpA v Commission* [1990] ECR I-45.

[235] Ibid., paras. 7–12.

[236] See, e.g., H. H. Lidgard, 'Unilateral Refusal to Supply: An Agreement in Disguise?' [1997] *ECLR* 354.

[237] Case T-41/96, *Bayer AG v Commission* [2000] ECR II-3383, *aff'd* Cases C-2 and 3/01 P, [2004] ECR I-23.

[238] Case T-208/01, [2003] ECR II-5141, *aff'd* Case C-74/04 P, [2006] ECR I-6585.

[239] See also Case T-368/00, *General Motors Nederland BV and Opel Nederland BV v Commission* [2003] ECR II-4491 (annulling a finding of the Commission that Opel and dealers in the Netherlands had agreed to a policy of preventing exports), *aff'd* Case C-551/03 P, *General Motors BV v Commission* [2006] ECR I-3173 and Case T-67/01, *JCB Service v Commission* [2004] ECR II-49, *aff'd* Case C-167/04, *JCB Service v Commission* [2006] ECR I-8935 (annulling a finding of an agreement to fix retail prices and discounts).

[240] Case T-41/96, [2000] ECR II-3383, and Cases C-2 and 3/01 P, [2004] ECR I-23.

agreement too far and stressed that a finding of an agreement will not be upheld in the absence of evidence of a concurrence of wills between the undertakings. In this case the Commission[241] had imposed a fine of €3 million on Bayer AG for taking action to prevent parallel imports in the pharmaceutical market. Bayer reduced the volumes of the drug supplied to its French and Spanish distributors. As these dealers had obligations to supply their home markets' requirements, this curbed their ability to engage in parallel trade and sales of the drug Adalat into the UK. The Commission found that the export ban was an integral element in the continuous commercial relations between Bayer and its wholesalers (which were aware of Bayer's policy and continued to place and renew orders for the product).

On appeal the GC[242] considered that the Commission erred when deciding that the wholesalers' continuation of commercial relations with Bayer amounted to their acquiescence in its restrictive supply policy. In fact, their actual conduct was contrary to that policy—a concurrence of wills between Bayer and the wholesalers, designed to prevent or limit exports of Adalat, had not been established. The GC drew a distinction between cases in which a genuinely unilateral measure had been adopted (without express or implied participation of another) and those in which the unilateral character of the measure was merely apparent, receiving at least the tacit acquiescence of the dealers.[243] It also held that the Commission could not rely on case law precedents, in which a concurrence of wills had been found, to call into question the Court's conclusion that neither agreement nor acquiescence in Bayer's policy had been established. In distinguishing AEG and Ford the GC stressed that the practices of the manufacturers in those cases, refusing to approve distributors who satisfied the qualitative criteria, were not unilateral but part of the contractual relations between the manufacturers and resellers since admission to the selective distribution networks in those cases was based on the acceptance, tacit or express, by the contracting parties, of the policy pursued by the supplier.[244]

Case T-41/96, *Bayer AG v Commission* [2000] ECR II-3383

General Court

B. The concept of an agreement within the meaning of Article [101(1)]

66. The case-law shows that, where a decision on the part of a manufacturer constitutes unilateral conduct of the undertaking, that decision escapes the prohibition in Article [101(1)] (Case 107/82 *AEG v Commission* . . . , paragraph 38; Joined Cases 25/84 and 26/84 *Ford and Ford Europe v Commission* . . . , paragraph 21; Case T-43/92 *Dunlop Slazenger v Commission* . . . , paragraph 56).

67. It is also clear from the case-law that in order for there to be an agreement within the meaning of Article [101(1)] it is sufficient that the undertakings in question should have expressed their joint intention to conduct themselves on the market in a specific way (Case 41/69 *ACF Chemiefarma v Commission* . . . , paragraph 112; Joined Cases 209/78 to 215/78 and 218/78 *Van Landewyck and Others v Commission* . . . , paragraph 86; Case T-7/89 *Hercules Chemicals v Commission* . . . , paragraph 256).

68. As regards the form in which that common intention is expressed, it is sufficient for a stipulation to be the expression of the parties' intention to behave on the market in accordance with its terms (see,

---

[241] COMP/34.279, [1996] OJ L201/1. See also discussion of Cases C-501, 513, 515, and 519/06 P, *GlaxoSmithKline Services v Commission* [2009] ECR I-9291, Chap. 4, and Case C-468–478/06, *Sot. Lélos kai Sia EE v GlaxoSmithKline AEVE* [2008] ECR I-7139, Chap. 7.

[242] Case T-41/96, [2000] ECR II-3383, *aff'd* Cases C-2 and 3/01 P, [2004] ECR I-23.

[243] Case T-41/96, ibid., paras. 66–71.

[244] See further Case 107/82, *AEG-Telefunken AG v Commission* [1983] ECR 3151, paras. 38 and 66–185 (in a selective distribution system admission to the network may be based on acceptance by the distributors of the policy pursued by the producers, para. 170).

in particular, *ACF Chemiefarma*, paragraph 112, and *Van Landewyck*, paragraph 86), without its having to constitute a valid and binding contract under national law (*Sandoz*, paragraph 13).

69. It follows that the concept of an agreement within the meaning of Article [101(1)], as interpreted by the case-law, centres around the existence of a concurrence of wills between at least two parties, the form in which it is manifested being unimportant so long as it constitutes the faithful expression of the parties' intention.

70. In certain circumstances, measures adopted or imposed in an apparently unilateral manner by a manufacturer in the context of his continuing relations with his distributors have been regarded as constituting an agreement within the meaning of Article [101(1)] (Joined Cases 32/78, 36/78 to 82/78 *BMW Belgium and Others v Commission* . . ., paragraphs 28 to 30; *AEG*, paragraph 38; *Ford and Ford Europe*, paragraph 21; . . . *Metro II* . . ., paragraphs 72 and 73; *Sandoz*, paragraphs 7 to 12; Case C-70/93 *BMW v ALD* . . ., paragraphs 16 and 17).

71. That case-law shows that a distinction should be drawn between cases in which an undertaking has adopted a genuinely unilateral measure, and thus without the express or implied participation of another undertaking, and those in which the unilateral character of the measure is merely apparent. Whilst the former do not fall within Article [101(1)], the latter must be regarded as revealing an agreement between undertakings and may therefore fall within the scope of that article. That is the case, in particular, with practices and measures in restraint of competition which, though apparently adopted unilaterally by the manufacturer in the context of its contractual relations with its dealers, nevertheless receive at least the tacit acquiescence of those dealers.

72. It is also clear from that case-law that the Commission cannot hold that apparently unilateral conduct on the part of a manufacturer, adopted in the context of the contractual relations which he maintains with his dealers, in reality forms the basis of an agreement between undertakings within the meaning of Article [101(1)] if it does not establish the existence of an acquiescence by the other partners, express or implied, in the attitude adopted by the manufacturer (*BMW Belgium*, paragraphs 28 to 30; *AEG*, paragraph 38; *Ford and Ford Europe*, paragraph 21; *Metro II*, paragraphs 72 and 73; *Sandoz*, paragraphs 7 to 12; *BMW v ALD*, paragraphs 16 and 17).

In addition, the GC held that the Commission had *not* shown that Bayer had sought to obtain agreement or acquiescence from its wholesalers to adhere to its policy or that the wholesalers had acquiesced, explicitly or implicitly, in the policy. Rather the evidence demonstrated that they had sought to circumvent the policy.[245] It was not 'open to the Commission to achieve a result, such as the harmonization of prices in the medicinal products markets, by enlarging or straining the scope' of the Treaty rules.[246]

The GC's judgment was upheld by the CJ. The CJ started by stating that its judgment was confined to the question of whether there was an agreement within the meaning of Article 101. 'It should be made clear, therefore, that neither the possible application of other aspects of Article [101], nor Article [102] . . ., nor any other possible definitions of the relevant market are at issue in these proceedings.'[247] The CJ did not therefore deny that Article 102 proceedings might have been possible, if a position of dominance had been established.[248] Like the GC, the CJ stressed that it was not open for the Commission automatically to assume that the expression of a unilateral policy by one of the parties established an agreement. Such a broad approach would confuse Article 101 with Article 102. It also considered that the GC had been correct to find that the Commission could not rely on the case law precedents to call into question the analysis leading the GC to conclude that,

---

[245] Case T-41/96, *Bayer AG v Commission* [2000] ECR II-3383, paras. 151–157.

[246] Case T-41/96, [2000] ECR II-3383, para. 179.

[247] Cases C-2 and 3/01 P, [2004] ECR I-23, para. 42.

[248] See discussion of refusal to deal in Chap. 7.

in this case, acquiescence by the wholesalers in Bayer's policy was not established. It thus distinguished cases such as *AEG* and *Ford* on the basis that admission to the network in those cases was based on adherence to the manufacturer's policy.

Cases C-2 and 3/01 P, *Bundesverband der Arzneimittel-Importeure EV and Commission v Bayer AG* [2004] ECR I-23

Court of Justice

102. For an agreement within the meaning of Article [101(1)] to be capable of being regarded as having been concluded by tacit acceptance, it is necessary that the manifestation of the wish of one of the contracting parties to achieve an anti-competitive goal constitute an invitation to the other party, whether express or implied, to fulfil that goal jointly, and that applies all the more where, as in this case, such an agreement is not at first sight in the interests of the other party, namely the wholesalers.

103. Therefore, the [GC] was right to examine whether Bayer's conduct supported the conclusion that the latter had required of the wholesalers, as a condition of their future contractual relations, that they should comply with its new commercial policy.

. . .

141. . . . [I]t is important to note that this case raises the question of the existence of an agreement prohibited by Article [101(1)]. The mere concomitant existence of an agreement which is in itself neutral and a measure restricting competition that has been imposed unilaterally does not amount to an agreement prohibited by that provision. Thus, the mere fact that a measure adopted by a manufacturer, which has the object or effect of restricting competition, falls within the context of continuous business relations between the manufacturer and its wholesalers is not sufficient for a finding that such an agreement exists.

142. The case of *Sandoz* concerned an export ban imposed by a manufacturer in the context of continuous business relations with wholesalers. The Court of Justice held that there was an agreement prohibited by Article [101(1)]. However, as the [GC] points out in paragraphs 161 and 162 of the judgment under appeal, that conclusion was based upon the existence of an export ban imposed by the manufacturer which had been tacitly accepted by the wholesalers. In that regard, at paragraph 11 of the *Sandoz* judgment, the Court of Justice held that [t]he repeated orders of the products and the successive payments without protest by the customer of the prices indicated on the invoices, bearing the words export prohibited, constituted a tacit acquiescence on the part of the latter in the clauses stipulated in the invoice and the type of commercial relations underlying the business relations between Sandoz PF and its clientele. The existence of a prohibited agreement in that case therefore rested not on the simple fact that the wholesalers continued to obtain supplies from a manufacturer which had shown its intention to prevent exports, but on the fact that an export ban had been imposed by the manufacturer and tacitly accepted by the wholesalers. Therefore, the appellants cannot usefully rely on the *Sandoz* judgment in support of their plea that the [GC] erred in law by requiring acquiescence of the wholesalers in the measures imposed by the manufacturer.

143. Nor can the appellants rely on *AEG*, *Ford* and *BMW Belgium*, arguing that business relations in the wholesale trade in pharmaceutical products are comparable to a selective distribution system such as that which was at issue in those cases. As has been stated in paragraph 141 of this judgment, the relevant question is that of the existence of an agreement within the meaning of Article [101(1)].

144. As has been stated in paragraph 106 of this judgment, in the *AEG* and *Ford* judgments the need to demonstrate the existence of an agreement within the meaning of Article [101(1)] was not at issue. The existence of an agreement capable of infringing that provision having already been established, the question raised was whether the measures adopted by the manufacturer formed part of that agreement and therefore had to be taken into account when examining the compatibility of that agreement with Article [101(1)]. In that regard, the [GC] rightly pointed out that, in those judgments, the Court of Justice

had held that, at the time of a distributor's admission, its authorisation was based on its adherence to the policy pursued by the manufacturer . . .

145. A similar analysis must be drawn from the judgment in *BMW Belgium*, in which the question was whether Article [101(1)] of the [EC] Treaty must be interpreted as [prohibiting] a motor vehicle manufacturer which sells its vehicles through a selective distribution system from agreeing with its authorised dealers that they are not to supply vehicles to independent leasing companies where, without granting an option to purchase, those companies make them available to lessees residing or having their seat outside the contract territory of the authorised dealer in question, or from calling on such dealers to act in such a way (paragraph 14).

In *Volkswagen v Commission*,[249] the GC also annulled a Commission decision[250] in which the Commission had found that VW had set the selling price of the VW Passat in Germany in an agreement with its dealers;[251] unilateral calls by the manufacturer, intended to influence the dealer,[252] did not provide sufficient evidence of an agreement between them. 'In doing so, the Commission is seeking to impose a new legal approach which not only enlarges the meaning of agreement, but also changes the rules on the burden of proof in its favour.'[253] The EU Courts also rejected the Commission's argument that acquiescence in the supplier's policy could be inferred simply from the dealer being part of a selective distribution network and that signature of an agreement which complies with competition law implied tacit acceptance of *future* unlawful variations of the agreement.[254] Rather, acquiescence and the existence of an agreement had to be established.[255] A request by a manufacturer did not relieve the Commission of its obligation to prove that there was a concurrence of wills on the part of the parties to the dealership agreement (established either from the clauses of the dealership agreement or from the conduct of the parties, in particular from tacit acquiescence by the dealers in the manufacturer's request).[256]

The EU Courts in both *Bayer* and *Volkswagen* thus admonished the Commission for too easily finding an agreement where none existed. It is now apparent that simply continuing to participate in a selective distribution system or accepting supplies under the terms of a distribution agreement will be insufficient to establish liability. A dealer that signs up to a distribution agreement or selective distribution network in no way binds itself to accept future variations in the way the agreement is operated. Where, however, the dealer knows of the supplier's policy at the time it enters contractual relations, it may then be concluded that the contract was dependent upon the dealer accepting that policy.

In the absence of any direct documentary evidence of a written agreement incorporating the allegedly unilateral policy, the Commission (or other person trying to prove a violation) will have

---

[249] Case T-208/01, [2003] ECR II-5141, *aff'd* Case C-74/04 P, [2006] ECR I-6585.

[250] COMP/36.693, [2001] OJ L262/14 (imposing a fine of €30.96 million on Volkswagen).

[251] Case T-208/01 [2003] ECR II-5141, paras. 30–35, *aff'd* Case C-74/04 P, [2006] ECR I-6585.

[252] By definition the calls were intended to influence the dealer in the performance of the contract, Case T-208/01, ibid., paras. 30–57.

[253] Ibid., para. 19, *aff'd* on appeal Case C-74/04, [2006] ECR I-6585, para. 38. See also, e.g., Case T-67/01, *JCB Service v Commission* [2004] ECR II-49 (the GC annulled a Commission finding that a supplier's policy of drawing up lists of recommended retail prices amounted to resale price maintenance, see especially paras. 121–133. This finding of the GC was not challenged before the CJ Case C-167/04, *JCB Service v Commission* [2006] ECR I-8935).

[254] The Commission's case amounted to a claim that a dealer who signed a dealership which complies with competition law is deemed to have accepted in advance a later unlawful variation of the contract.

[255] In contrast in COMP/35.733, *Volkswagen* [1998] OJ L124/60 (*aff'd* Case T-62/98, *Volkswagen AG v Commission* [2000] ECR II-2707, Case C-338/00 P, *Volkswagen AG v Commission* [2003] ECR I-9189), acquiescence in or acceptance of the policy had been established. See further Chap. 11.

[256] In this case the Commission had not attempted to show that the dealers had tacitly acquiesced in the manufacturer's request but had argued that the concurrence was part of the dealership agreement.

to establish to the requisite legal standard that there is a concurrence of wills sufficient to trigger Article 101(1). In *Activision Blizzard Germany GmbH v Commission*,[257] the CJ expressly clarified that the standard of proof required for the purposes of establishing an anti-competitive agreement is the same whether in the framework of a vertical or a horizontal relationship.[258] Although an important difference is that in the framework of a vertical relationship between a manufacturer and a distribution a certain measure of contact between the parties is lawful, in each case it is still necessary to ask whether an agreement can be inferred from all the evidence having regard to all the relevant factors, and the economic and legal context specific to the case.[259] The cases demonstrate, nonetheless, that great care will need to be exercised by firms in this area and that this requirement does not provide a mechanism for parties to avoid the application of Article 101 by operating an agreement informally—if it can be established that an invitation to pursue the policy has been accepted, at least tacitly, or acquiesced in by the other party to the contract, the actions may be found to have spilled over into an agreement.

f. Hub and Spoke Arrangements

Anti-competitive agreements (or concerted practices) may have both horizontal and vertical elements. For example, collusion between retailers as to the price at which they will sell a particular product could be achieved, directly, or indirectly, through the intermediary of a supplier. In such a case it could be critical to determine both whether a vertical price-fixing agreement exists (between the supplier and the relevant retailers) and/or whether there is in fact an agreement or a concerted practice between the supplier and retailers to fix the retail prices of the product (see Section 5.B.iii.d, pp. 160–161). In the latter scenario, the violation has a horizontal element and so may become an even more serious infringement of the competition rules.[260]

g. Agreements Concluded by Employees

An agreement (or concerted practice) can arise from the actions of employees acting within the scope of their employment. EU law holds that the undertaking will be liable even if the employees were not authorised or instructed to act in that way by senior management—personal conduct on the part of, or the assent of, a representative authorised under the undertaking's constitution is not required. In *Protimonopolný úrad Slovenskej republiky v Slovenská sporiteľňa as*, the CJ thus clarified that:

> it is not necessary for there to have been action by, or even knowledge on the part of, the partners or principal managers of the undertaking concerned; action by a person who is authorised to act on behalf of the undertaking suffices.[261]

This is particularly relevant in situations where employees have entered into secret collusive conspiracies to rig markets. Undertakings should have in place, and should enforce, a compliance programme to prevent breaches of the competition rules.[262] Although EU law does not provide sanctions (disqualification, fines, and/or imprisonment) for the individual employees, such sanctions are available in some EU Member States.

h. Recommendations by Bodies Constituted under Statutory Powers

Several cases have raised the question of whether there is an 'agreement' where undertakings are represented on a body constituted under statutory powers to make recommendations in respect

---

[257] Case C-260/09 P, [2011] ECR I-419.

[258] Ibid., para. 71.

[259] Ibid., para. 72.

[260] See, e.g., discussion of Case 1022/1/1/03, *JJB Sports plc v Office of Fair Trading* [2004] CAT 17, *aff'd* [2006] EWCA Civ 1318 at n. 304 and text.

[261] Case C-68/12, EU:C:2013:71, para. 25.

[262] See further Chap. 13.

of a certain industry, etc. The CJ has held that there is not an agreement even when the trade representatives are in the majority on the committee, provided that the public authorities have not delegated their power of decision and that the matters to be fixed (e.g., tariffs) are fixed with due regard for public-interest criteria.[263]

(iii) Concerted Practices

a. Description of a Concerted Practice

It has been seen that Article 101(1) is aimed at explicit collusion whatever form it takes, whether through a formal agreement or a more informal arrangement. The term concerted practice[264] aims to forestall the possibility of undertakings evading the application of Article 101 by colluding in a manner falling short of an agreement. Classic descriptions of a concerted practice were set out by the CJ in *ICI v Commission (Dyestuffs)*[265] and *Suiker Unie*.[266] In *Dyestuffs*, it held that the purpose of the term was to preclude:

co-ordination between undertakings which, without having reached the stage where an agreement, properly so called, has been concluded, knowingly substitutes practical co-operation between them for the risks of competition.[267]

In *Suiker Unie*, it confirmed that the concept in no way required 'the working out of an actual plan'.[268] Further, it is clear that although the concept 'does not deprive economic operators of a right to adapt intelligently to the existing and anticipated conduct of their competitors',[269] it does:

preclude any direct or indirect contact between such operators, the object or effect whereof is either to influence the conduct on the market of an actual or potential competitor or to disclose to such a competitor the course of conduct which they themselves have decided to adopt or contemplate adopting on the market.[270]

Although the concept does not require an actual plan or a 'meeting of the minds',[271] it does seem to require *reciprocal* cooperation or a joint intention to conduct themselves in a specific way, disclosed through direct or indirect contact, designed to influence the conduct of an actual or potential competitor or to reveal to them the course of conduct that will or may be adopted on the market. Where therefore firms engage in conduct designed to remove strategic uncertainty about each other's future conduct on the market, they are not acting independently and so their conduct is subject to Article 101:

[T]he criteria of coordination and cooperation necessary for determining the existence of concerted practice are understood in the light of the notion inherent in the Treaty provisions on competition, according to which an economic operator must determine independently the policy which he intends to adopt on the common market (judgment in *T-Mobile Netherlands and Others*, C-8/08 ..., paragraph 32).[272]

---

[263] See, e.g., Case C-96/94, *Centro Servizi Spediporto Srl v Spedizioni Marittima del Golfo Srl* [1995] ECR I-2883; Case C-38/97, *Autotrasporti Librandi Snc di Librandi F. & C. v Cuttica spedizioni servizi internationali Srl* [1998] ECR I-5955, and Chap. 8. See also the discussion of decisions by association of undertakings above, especially nn. 35 and 192 and text.

[264] The definition of concerted practice is explored further in Chap. 9.

[265] Cases 48, 49, and 51–57/69, *ICI v Commission* [1972] ECR 619.

[266] Cases 40–48, 50, 54–56, 111, and 113–114/73, *Re the European Sugar Cartel; Coöperatieve Vereniging 'Suiker Unie' UA v Commission* [1975] ECR 1663.

[267] Cases 48, 49, and 51–57/69, *ICI v Commission* [1972] ECR 619, paras. 64 and 65.

[268] Cases 40–48, 50, 54–56, 111, and 113–114/73, *Suiker Unie* [1975] ECR 1663, para. 173.

[269] Case C-89/85, *Woodpulp* [1993] ECR I-1307, para. 71.

[270] Cases 40–48, 50, 54–56, 111, and 113–114/73, *Suiker Unie* [1975] ECR 1663, para. 174.

[271] Case T-587/08, *Del Monte* EU:T:2013:129 ('the intervener's complaint that the contested decision does not mention a meeting of minds between it and Dole or the existence of a common course of conduct is irrelevant, since the conduct in question falls within the specific legal classification of a concerted practice and not of an anti-competitive agreement'), the appeal to the CJ on substantive grounds was dismissed, Cases C-293 and 294/13 P, EU:C:2015:416.

[272] Case C-286/13 P, *Dole Food and Dole Fresh Fruit Europe v Commission* EU:C:2015:184, para. 199.

b. The Need for the Concertation to be Implemented on the Market

One important difference between the concept of an agreement and the concept of a concerted practice is that the latter term implies a requirement that the concertation should be practised or implemented on the market. This matter arose in the appeals from the Commission's decision in *Polypropylene*[273] where one of the issues to be decided was if it mattered whether the parties' conduct was characterised as an agreement or a concerted practice. One of the arguments raised by some of the parties was that although an agreement would be caught by Article 101(1) even if it was not implemented, as intended, on the market, direct or indirect conduct which has not been implemented on a market did not amount to a concerted *practice*. An agreement, however informal and whether or not successful or acted upon, is a consensual act. In contrast, the word 'practice', in the concept of concerted practice, implied proof not only of concertation but *also of the fact that* steps have been taken to give effect to the concertation. There would, therefore, be no actual concerted *practice* if the parties only *plotted* to coordinate their behaviour but did not carry out that plot by conduct on the market. The arguments supporting this view and academic writings on this issue are fully reviewed in the Opinion of Advocate General Vesterdorf designated by the President of the GC.[274]

The CJ accepted that the concept of a concerted practice does require both concertation between the undertakings *and* 'subsequent conduct on the market, and a relationship of cause and effect between the two'.[275] However, it held that once evidence had been adduced of concertation it is presumed that undertakings taking part in the concerted action and remaining active on the market—especially where the concertation takes place on a regular basis—take account of the information exchanged with competitors in determining their conduct on the market. It is therefore for the undertaking to establish that concertation had not been followed by conduct on the market.

Case C-199/92 P, *Hüls AG v Commission (Polypropylene)* [1999] ECR I-4287

Court of Justice

158. The Court of Justice has consistently held that a concerted practice refers to a form of co-ordination between undertakings which, without having been taken to a stage where an agreement properly so-called has been concluded, knowingly substitutes for the risks of competition practical co-operation between . . .

159. The criteria of co-ordination and co-operation must be understood in the light of the concept inherent in the provisions of the Treaty relating to competition, according to which each economic operator must determine independently the policy which he intends to adopt on the market . . .

160. According to that case law, although that requirement of independence does not deprive economic operators of the right to adapt themselves intelligently to the existing and anticipated conduct of their competitors, it does however strictly preclude any direct or indirect contact between such operators, the object or effect whereof is either to influence the conduct on the market of an actual or potential

---

[273] COMP/31.149, *Polypropylene* [1986] OJ L230/1, appeals substantially dismissed by both the GC and the CJ: see, e.g., Case C-51/92 P, *SA Hercules Chemicals NV v Commission* [1999] ECR I-4235, and Case C-199/92 P, *Hüls AG v Commission* [1999] ECR I-4287.

[274] See Case T-7/89, [1991] ECR II-1711, 1923–1946. The AG was appointed following the order of the CJ referring this and other cases to the GC soon after its establishment. The AG considered that failed attempts to concert would not be caught by Art. 101(1). The GC did not specifically address this point, since it took the view that having participated in and having obtained information from meetings with competitors an undertaking would be bound to take it into account, directly or indirectly, when determining its conduct on the market: see, e.g., Case T-7/89, *SA Hercules Chemicals NV v Commission* [1991] ECR II-1711, para. 260.

[275] Case C-199/92 P, *Hüls AG v Commission* [1999] ECR I-4287, para. 161. See also Case C-8/08, *T-Mobile Netherlands and Others* EU:C:2009:343, paras. 38 and 39 and Case C-286/13 P, *Dole* EU:C:2015:184, paras. 125–126. But see Case C-74/14, *'Eturas' UAB v Lietuvos Respublikos konkurencijos taryba* EU:C:2016:42, especially n. 298 and text.

competitor or to disclose to such a competitor the course of conduct which they themselves have decided to adopt or contemplate adopting on the market, where the object or effect of such contact is to create conditions of competition which do not correspond to the normal conditions of the market in question, regard being had to the nature of the products or services offered, the size and number of the undertakings and the volume of the said market . . .

161. It follows, first, that the concept of a concerted practice, as it results from the actual terms of Article [101(1)], implies, besides undertakings' concerting with each other, subsequent conduct on the market, and a relationship of cause and effect between the two.

162. However, subject to proof to the contrary, which the economic operators concerned must adduce, the presumption must be that the undertakings taking part in the concerted action and remaining active on the market take account of the information exchanged with their competitors for the purposes of determining their conduct on that market. That is all the more true where the undertakings concert together on a regular basis over a long period, as was the case here, according to the findings of the [GC].

163. Secondly, contrary to Hüls's argument, a concerted practice as defined above is caught by Article [101(1)], even in the absence of anti-competitive effects on the market.

164. First, it follows from the actual text of that provision that, as in the case of agreements between undertakings and decisions by associations of undertakings, concerted practices are prohibited, regardless of their effect, when they have an anti-competitive object.

165. Next, although the very concept of a concerted practice presupposes conduct by the participating undertakings on the market, it does not necessarily mean that that conduct should produce the specific effect of restricting, preventing or distorting competition.

166. Lastly, that interpretation is not incompatible with the restrictive nature of the prohibition laid down in Article [101(1)] . . . since, far from extending its scope, it corresponds to the literal meaning of the terms used in that provision.

167. Consequently, contrary to Hüls's argument, the [GC] was not in breach of the rules applying to the burden of proof when it considered that, since the Commission had established to the requisite legal standard that Hüls had taken part in polypropylene producers' concerting together for the purpose of restricting competition, it did not have to adduce evidence that their concerting together had manifested itself in conduct on the market or that it had had effects restrictive of competition; on the contrary, it was for Hüls to prove that that did not have any influence whatsoever on its own conduct on the market.

It can be seen from this extract that the Court emphasised both that: (a) the question whether or not the parties had engaged in a concerted practice was distinct from the question whether or not that concertation had restricted competition;[276] and (b) although a concerted practice requires concertation *and also* subsequent conduct, there is a presumption that concertation has been followed by conduct and has been taken into account where the undertakings concerned remained active on the market. This is true whether the undertakings concert together on a regular basis over a long period or whether the concerted practice stems from a single meeting.[277] This presumption of a causal connection stems from Article 101 and so forms an integral part of EU law.[278] As it is very hard to envisage circumstances in which an undertaking can establish that its conduct was *not* influenced by information acquired through concerting with others, the most important question appears to be whether or not there was collusion.

---

[276] Where it is found that the object of the concerted practice is to restrict competition, a restriction of competition is also assumed, see Chap. 4.

[277] Case C-8/08, *T-Mobile Netherlands BV v Raad van bestuur van de Nederlandse Mededingingsautoriteit* [2009] ECR I-4529.

[278] Ibid., para. 52. See also A. Gerbandy, Case Comment (2010) 47 *CMLRev* 1199.

The importance of the concept of a concerted practice does not thus result so much from the distinction between it and an agreement as from the distinction between forms of collusion falling under Article [101(1)] and mere parallel behaviour with no element of concertation.[279]

The following are examples of the type of conduct which might be used to establish that the parties involved have engaged in a 'concerted practice'.

c. Direct Contact—Frequent or Isolated Exchanges, or Disclosure, of Information

Even if undertakings do not agree to fix prices or share markets, etc., the sharing or exchange of sensitive information may constitute a mechanism for substituting practical cooperation between them for the risks of competition, for example reciprocal exchanges of strategic information (even if only on a single occasion).[280] In *Suiker Unie*,[281] for example, documents established that the parties had contacted each other and that they pursued the aim of removing in advance any uncertainty about the future conduct of their competitors. This conduct facilitated the coordination of their commercial behaviour.

In *PVC*,[282] the Commission considered that the term concerted practice was particularly apt to cover the involvement of some undertakings, for example Shell. Shell, whilst not a full member of the cartel, had cooperated with it. It was thus able to adapt its own market behaviour in the light of this contact. Similarly, in *Belgian Brewers*[283] the Commission took the view that, in respect of one of the cartels it found to be operating on the Belgian market—the private label cartel—it could not establish an agreement from available evidence, but that a concerted practice was proven. Meetings between the brewers had clearly served to influence the market behaviour of the competitors and to report on market behaviour to competitors.

At the meetings not only was information exchanged but prices and customers were discussed. From statements . . . it is clear that the aim of the meetings was, firstly, to prevent a price war and adopt a position on prices and, secondly, to share out customers by not making (real) offers to the customers of other brewers.[284]

Further, in *T-Mobile Netherlands BV v Raad van bestuur van de Nederlandse Mededingingsautoriteit*,[285] the CJ confirmed that a concerted practice could result not only from meetings which occurred on a regular basis over a long period but from an isolated exchange of information. In this case competing mobile telephone network operators had met only on a single occasion and discussed the reduction of certain standard dealer remunerations for postpaid subscriptions (packages whereby customers pay a fixed subscription charge and are invoiced subsequently for the number of minutes called). The CJ stressed that Article 101 precluded contact between firms which might influence the conduct on the market of competitors or disclose to them its decisions or intentions concerning its own conduct on the market.[286] The number, frequency, and form of meetings between competitors required to concert, however, depended on both the subject matter of the concerted action and the particular market conditions. The CJ also confirmed that the presumption that a concerted practice would influence the conduct of the undertakings participating in the practice where they remain active on that market was an integral part of EU law which had to be applied by a national court.

---

[279] COMP/31.149, *Polypropylene* [1986] OJ L230/1, para. 87.

[280] Case C-8/08, *T-Mobile* [2009] ECR I-4529, paras. 54–62.

[281] Cases 40–48, 50, 54–56, 111, and 113–114/73, *Suiker Unie* [1975] ECR 1663.

[282] COMP/31.865, [1994] OJ L239/14.

[283] COMP/37.614, [2003] OJ L200/1.

[284] Ibid., para. 254.

[285] Case C-8/08, [2009] ECR I-4529.

[286] Ibid., paras. 32–35.

> **Case C-8/08, *T-Mobile Netherlands BV v Raad van bestuur van de Nederlandse Mededingingsautoriteit* [2009] ECR I-4529**
>
> ### Court of Justice
>
> 59. Depending on the structure of the market, the possibility cannot be ruled out that a meeting on a single occasion between competitors . . . may, in principle, constitute a sufficient basis for the participating undertakings to concert their market conduct and thus successfully substitute practical cooperation between them for competition and the risks that that entails . . .
>
> 60. . . . [T]he number, frequency, and form of meetings between competitors needed to concert their market conduct depend on both the subject-matter of that concerted action and the particular market conditions. If the undertakings concerned establish a cartel with a complex system of concerted actions in relation to a multiplicity of aspects of their market conduct, regular meetings over a long period may be necessary. If, on the other hand . . . the objective of the exercise is only to concert action on a selective basis in relation to a one-off alteration in market conduct with reference simply to one parameter of competition, a single meeting between competitors may constitute a sufficient basis on which to implement the anti-competitive object which the participating undertakings aim to achieve.
>
> 61. In those circumstances, what matters is not so much the number of meetings held between the participating undertakings as whether the meeting or meetings which took place afforded them the opportunity to take account of the information exchanged with their competitors in order to determine their conduct on the market in question and knowingly substitute practical cooperation between them for the risks of competition. Where it can be established that such undertakings successfully concerted with one another and remained active on the market, they may justifiably be called upon to adduce evidence that that concerted action did not have any effect on their conduct on the market in question.

In *Bananas,*[287] the Commission also found that three banana importers, Chiquita, Dole, and Weichert, which had engaged in direct bilateral pre-pricing communications (prior to setting their weekly quotation prices), had taken part in a concerted practice to coordinate quotation prices for bananas. They repeatedly communicated over a two-year period in relation to price-setting factors (factors relevant for setting of quotation prices) before quotation prices were set. As the communications were about future pricing policies the participants could not fail to take the information into account when determining the policy which they intended to pursue on the market. Further, the Commission held that the bilateral exchange of quotation prices after they had been set provided a monitoring mechanism for the pre-pricing communications. It thus considered that it had demonstrated cooperation (that the parties had knowingly adopted or adhered to collusive devices which facilitated the coordination of their commercial behaviour) and subsequent conduct on the market sufficient to establish the existence of a concerted practice.

The Commission's decision was upheld on appeal and the CJ reiterated that the requirement of independence precludes direct or indirect conduct between operators designed to disclose to actual or potential competitors decisions or intentions concerning their own conduct on the market. Consequently, 'the exchange of information between competitors is liable to be incompatible with the competition rules if it reduces or removes the degree of uncertainty as to the operation of the market in question, with the result that competition between undertakings is restricted ...'.[288]

The concept of a concerted practice may also encompass a disclosure of strategic information by one undertaking to a competitor (whether by, for example, mail, email, phone call, or orally at a

---

[287] COMP/39.188, 15 October 2008, *aff'd* Cases T-587/08, *Del Monte* EU:T:2013:129 and T-588/08 P, *Dole* EU:T:2013:130 and Cases C-293 and 294/13 P, *Del Monte* EU:C:2015:416 and Case C-286/13 P, *Dole* EU:C:2015:184. Weichert's appeal, Case T-2/09, was dismissed as it was lodged out of time, *aff'd* Case C-73/10 P.

[288] Case C-286/13 P, *Dole* EU:C:2015:184, para. 121.

meeting) where the recipient requests the information or accepts it.[289] A recipient of such strategic information will be presumed to have accepted the information tendered to it in this way, and to have altered its conduct accordingly, unless it publicly distances itself from, and clearly states that it does not wish to receive, it:

mere attendance at a meeting where a company discloses its pricing plans to competitors is likely to be caught by Article 101, even in the absence of an explicit agreement to raise prices. When a company receives strategic information from a competitor (be it in a meeting, by mail or electronically), it will be presumed to have accepted the information and adapted its market conduct accordingly unless it responds with a clear statement that it does not wish to receive such data.[290]

In *Polypropylene*,[291] for example, although the Commission had concluded that an agreement existed between the undertakings, the GC[292] confirmed that the Commission had been correct to classify the meetings in the alternative as a concerted practice. The clear purpose of the competing undertakings participating in meetings, during which information was exchanged about, for example, prices and sales volumes, was to disclose to each other the course of conduct which each of the producers itself contemplated adopting on the market.[293] Participants clearly had the aim of eliminating any uncertainty about the future conduct of their competitors. They were bound to take into account the course of conduct upon which other participants had decided.

Even if, therefore, parties have not actually agreed to exchange price information its simple exchange may be prohibited where the behaviour of the undertakings eliminates 'the risks of competition and the hazards of competitors' spontaneous reactions . . .'.[294] The exchange of sensitive information exacerbates the problems of, and increases transparency on, oligopolistic markets where there is already limited opportunity for competition.[295]

In *'Eturas' UAB v Lietuvos Respublikos konkurencijos taryba*,[296] the CJ set out detailed guidance as to how the existence of a concerted practice can be proved in the context of an online travel system, and how an alleged conspirator can publicly distance itself from concertation instigated through an electronic communication. In this case the question arose as to whether travel agents, which participated in the online system, engaged in a concerted practice when the administrator sent messages, via a personal electronic mailbox, to members relating to the capping of the level of online discounts which the travel agents should grant to customers. Some of travel agents alleged that as they had not opened and read the message they could not be presumed to have been aware of the message and so could not have engaged in a concerted practice. The competition authority, in contrast, alleged that, in the absence of any opposition on the part of the agents, they could be presumed to have participated in the concerted practice.

On a reference to it from the Lithuanian Supreme Administrative Court, the CJ held, stressing the obligation of economic operators to determine their policy on the market independently, that

---

[289] See, e.g., Cases T-25/95 etc., *Cimenteries CBR SA v Commission* [2000] ECR II-491, Cases T-202/98 etc., *Tate & Lyle, Napier Brown and British Sugar* [2001] ECR II-2035, *aff'd* Case C-359/01 P, *British Sugar* [2004] ECR I-4933.

[290] Horizontal Cooperation Guidelines, para. 62, relying on Cases T-202/98 etc., *Tate & Lyle* [2001] ECR II-2035, *aff'd* Case C-359/01 P, para. 54, Case C-199/92, *Hüls v Commission* [1999] ECR I-4287, para. 162 and Case C-49/92 P, *Anic v Commission* [1999] ECR I-4125, para. 121.

[291] COMP/31.149, *Polypropylene* [1986] OJ L230/1.

[292] The judgments of the CJ focused mainly on procedural arguments, but see, e.g., Case C-199/92 P, *Hüls AG v Commission* [1999] ECR I-4287.

[293] E.g., Case T-7/89, *SA Hercules Chemicals NV v Commission* [1992] ECR II-1711, para. 259, see Case C-199/92 P, *Hüls v Commission* [1999] ECR I-4287, para. 155; Case C-49/92 P, *Commission v Anic* [1999] ECR I-4125, para. 96; Case C-291/98 P, *Sarrió SA v Commission* [2000] ECR I-9991, para. 50.

[294] Cases 48, 49, and 51–57/69, *ICI v Commission (Dyestuffs)* [1972] ECR 619, para. 119. But such conduct may be hard to distinguish from a unilateral decision, for example to send a price list to the press for publication or to make a price announcements in advance, see discussion in Chap. 9.

[295] See Chap. 9.

[296] Case C-74/14, EU:C:2016:42.

although passive modes of participation in an infringement (such as presence at meetings at which anti-competitive agreements were concluded without that undertaking opposing them) were indicative of collusion, the question of whether a dispatch of a message constituted sufficient evidence to establish that its addressees were aware, or ought to have been aware, was a question which had to be determined in the national proceedings following an assessment of evidence.[297] Although the concerted practice could be established, not only from direct evidence but through indicia (provided that they were objective and consistent), the presumption of innocence precludes the referring court from inferring that the travel agencies concerned ought to have been aware of the content of that message simply from the mere dispatch of the message at issue in the main proceedings; it could be inferred, however, from the dispatch of the message together with other objective and consistent indicia, so long as the travel agencies had the ability to rebut it (for example, by proving that they did not receive that message, that they did not look at the section in question or did not look at it until some time had passed since that dispatch). An agency could also rebut a presumption that it had concerted by showing that it had publicly distanced itself from the concertation, reporting it to authorities or establishing that it had systematically not adhered to the cap.[298]

Case C-74/14, 'Eturas' UAB v Lietuvos Respublikos konkurencijos taryba EU:C:2016:42

43. Secondly, it must be pointed out that the case at issue in the main proceedings, as presented by the referring court, is characterised by the fact that the administrator of the information system at issue sent a message concerning a common anticompetitive action to the travel agencies participating in that system, a message which could only be consulted in the 'Notices' section of the information system in question and to which those agencies did not expressly respond. Following the dispatch of that message, a technical restriction was implemented which limited the discounts that could be applied to bookings made via that system to 3%. Although that restriction did not prevent the travel agencies concerned from granting discounts greater than 3% to their customers, it nevertheless required them to take additional technical steps in order to do so.

44. Those circumstances are capable of justifying a finding of a concertation between the travel agencies which were aware of the content of the message at issue in the main proceedings, which could be regarded as having tacitly assented to a common anticompetitive practice, provided that the two other elements constituting a concerted practice, noted in paragraph 42 above, are also present. Depending on the referring court's assessment of the evidence, a travel agency may be presumed to have participated in that concertation if it was aware of the content of that message.

45. However, if it cannot be established that a travel agency was aware of that message, its participation in a concertation cannot be inferred from the mere existence of a technical restriction implemented in the system at issue in the main proceedings, unless it is established on the basis of other objective and consistent indicia that it tacitly assented to an anticompetitive action.

46. In the third place, it must be pointed out that a travel agency may rebut the presumption that it participated in a concerted practice by proving that it publically distanced itself from that practice or reported it to the administrative authorities. In addition, according to the case-law of the Court, in a case such as that at issue in the main proceedings, which does not concern an anticompetitive meeting, public distancing or reporting to the administrative authorities are not the only means of rebutting the presumption that a company has participated in an infringement; other evidence may also be adduced with a view

---

[297] Ibid., paras. 26–38.

[298] Ibid., paras. 39–49. The latter statement, that the presumption of a causal connection between the concertation and the market conduct of the undertakings participating in the practice, could be rebutted by evidence of a systematic application of a discount exceeding the cap in question is not easy to reconcile with prior case law, see especially nn. 275–279 and text.

to rebutting that presumption (see, to that effect, judgment in *Total Marketing Services* v *Commission*..., paragraphs 23 and 24).

47. As regards the examination of whether the travel agencies concerned publicly distanced themselves from the concertation at issue in the main proceedings, it must be noted that, in particular circumstances such as those at issue in the main proceedings, it cannot be required that the declaration by a travel agency of its intention to distance itself be made to all of the competitors which were the addressees of the message at issue in the main proceedings, since that agency is not in fact in a position to know who those addressees are.

48. In that situation, the referring court may accept that a clear and express objection sent to the administrator of the E-TURAS system is capable of rebutting that presumption.

49. As regards the possibility of rebutting the presumption of participation in a concerted practice by means other than public distancing or reporting it to the administrative authorities, it must be held that, in circumstances such as those at issue in the main proceedings, the presumption of a causal connection between the concertation and the market conduct of the undertakings participating in the practice, referred to in paragraph 33 of the present judgment, could be rebutted by evidence of a systematic application of a discount exceeding the cap in question.

d. Indirect Contact/Sharing of Information and Hub and Spoke Arrangements

More difficult to categorise are situations where undertakings do not directly pass information to each other but disclose information which is nonetheless received by competitors, for example because the information was published publicly by an undertaking (perhaps on a website or to investors[299]) or because the information was received and published or transferred by an intermediary (such as a newspaper or trade journal, an independent consultant, a trade association, or a mutual customer or supplier). In such situations it is necessary to assess carefully on the facts whether or not the undertakings have acted independently, adapting their conduct to that of their competitors, or whether they have engaged in indirect contact designed to influence the conduct of their competitors.

While it is correct to say that this requirement of independence does not deprive economic operators of the right to adapt themselves intelligently to the existing or anticipated conduct of their competitors, it does, none the less, strictly preclude any direct or indirect contact between such operators by which an undertaking may influence the conduct on the market of its actual or potential competitors or disclose to them its decisions or intentions concerning its own conduct on the market where the object or effect of such contact is to create conditions of competition which do not correspond to the normal conditions of the market in question, regard being had to the nature of the products or services offered, the size and number of the undertakings involved and the volume of that market ...[300]

In *Wood Pulp*,[301] for example, the CJ found that no collusion had been established where undertakings had announced their price increases in advance and the information had been rapidly transferred between both buyers and sellers by means of publication in the trade press.

Exchanges of information between competitors (A and C) may also take place through the intermediary of a common customer or supplier (B). For example B might act as a 'hub' collating and distributing competitively sensitive information relating to its retailers (A and C, the 'spokes'). Information exchanged in this way may be of a type which reduces the uncertainty over the pricing

---

[299] E.g., earnings calls with industry analysts are often monitored by competitors.

[300] Case C-8/08, *T-Mobile* [2009] ECR I-4529, para. 33.

[301] Cases C-89, 104, 114, 116–117, and 125–129/85, *Re Wood Pulp Cartel: Ahlström Osakeyhtiö v Commission (Wood Pulp II)* [1993] ECR I-1307, see further Chap. 11.

intentions or output of rival retailers; for example, it may reveal future pricing intentions. The question of exactly when a vertical information exchange (a frequent and often necessary practice in many supplier/customer relationships) may also support the existence of a concerted practice involving competitors at the upstream or downstream level is controversial.[302] Although an agreement or concerted practice can be presumed where a competitor discloses strategic information directly to another competitor and the latter accepts it (and does not publicly distance itself from it), such a presumption should, arguably, not be made simply because A passed strategic information (for example about its intended retail pricing) to B, who then passed the information to C, as there may have been valid business justification for A sharing this information with B.

There is no EU case which explicitly deals with this issue (although in *e-books*[303] the Commission accepted commitments before terminating proceedings in which it was investigating whether five principal publishers had engaged, with Apple, in a concerted practice to raise the retail prices of electronic books). Nonetheless it has been considered in some Member States, including the courts of England & Wales. In *JJB Sports plc v Office of Fair Trading*,[304] for example, the appellant sought to challenge the OFT's finding that it unlawfully participated in various price-fixing arrangements through participating in indirect exchanges of price information with competing retailers through the intermediary of Umbro. The Court of Appeal considered that a concerted practice may be established where retailer A intended that the information be passed on by B and that retailer C knew that the information had been provided by A to B and used that information in setting its prices and that the Competition Appeal Tribunal 'may have gone too far if it intended [its] suggestion to extend to cases in which A did not, in fact, foresee that B would make use of the pricing information to influence market conditions or in which C did not, in fact, appreciate that the information was being passed to him with A's concurrence'.[305] Where a horizontal conspiracy is found, the intermediary may also be found liable and to have facilitated the operation of the cartel.[306]

e. Parallel Behaviour

Market data may show that undertakings have acted in parallel (for example, that competing undertakings increased prices at the same moment, offered the same discounts and/or terms and conditions to customers, etc.). In the context of Article 101 a crucial question is whether such parallel behaviour results from independent or concerted action; it prohibits collusion but not 'mere parallel behaviour with no element of concertation'.[307] The question of whether parallel behaviour can constitute a concerted practice or furnish proof of a concerted practice, and the CJ's important judgment in *Ahlström Osakeyhtiö v Commission (Wood Pulp)*[308] on this issue, is examined in Chapter 9. Chapter 9 also explores further the circumstances in which exchanges of information (direct or indirect) between undertakings may constitute an infringement of the rules.

---

[302] See e.g., P. J. G. Van Cayseele, 'Hub-and-spoke Collusion: Some Nagging Questions Raised by Economists' (2014) 5 *JECLAP* 164 and also, Commission's Guidelines on Vertical Restraints [2010] OJ C130/01, para. 211; Horizontal Cooperation Guidelines, para. 55.

[303] COMP/39.847 (the proceedings were terminated when, in December 2012 and July 2013, the companies offered a number of commitments, which addressed the Commission's concerns, see further Chap. 11).

[304] Case 1022/1/1/03, [2004] CAT 17 (Judgment on Liability). See also, fines imposed on 18 companies (distributors and manufacturers) by the Belgian Competition Authority for hub and spoke arrangements in personal care and hygiene products, 22 June 2015 and discussion of national cases in Van Cayseele, n. 302.

[305] *Argos Ltd and Littlewoods Ltd v OFT, JJB Sports plc v OFT* [2006] EWCA Civ 1318, para. 91 (the higher substantive test was satisfied on the facts).

[306] See n. 221 and accompanying text.

[307] COMP/31.149, *Polypropylene* [1986] OJ L230/1, para. 87.

[308] Case C-89/85, *Woodpulp* [1993] ECR I-1307.

f. Concerted Practice and Vertical Arrangements

A concerted practice may be operated horizontally between colluding competitors but also vertically between a manufacturer and its distributors. In *Pioneer*,[309] for example, the Commission found that Pioneer and its European exclusive distributors had engaged in concerted practices to prevent the parallel import of Pioneer products from the UK and Germany into France.

(iv) Decisions by Associations of Undertakings

a. Medium for a Cartel

Trade and other associations perform a plethora of legitimate functions which promote the competitiveness of the industry as a whole. However, membership of an association, particularly a trade association, may also tempt the undertakings meeting within its auspices to collude together and to coordinate their action. Indeed, studies have shown that where players wish to coordinate their action on a market, coordination through a trade association or some other vehicle may be critical when there are a relatively large number of players on the market.

Trade associations can play a particularly important role when [a] cartel involves a large number of firms. Hay and Delley (1974) found that trade associations were involved in more than 80 per cent of the cartels they studied that had more than 15 members, and in 100 per cent of cartels with more than 25 members. Levenstein and Suslow (2006) found that 29 per cent of the cartels in their sample involved trade associations. In 2003 the Commission found Treuhand AG, a Swiss consultancy, guilty of cartel behaviour because it facilitated a cartel even though it did not itself produce or sell the relevant product. The actual cartel was for organic peroxides and included Akzo Group, Atofina SA and Peroxid Chemic GmbH. The Commission found that AC-Treuhand had actively organised the cartel and provided support to it, such as organising meetings, providing and sharing information and storing contracts.[310]

In *Re Belgian Roofing Felt Cartel*,[311] for example, an agreement was discovered between members of Belasco (Société Coopérative des Asphalteurs Belges) which was intended to ensure control of the Belgian roofing market. The parties had agreed, amongst other things, to adopt a common price list and minimum selling prices for roofing felt, to set quotas for sales on the Belgian market, and to advertise jointly their 'Belasco' products. The agreement was implemented by resolutions passed at the general meeting of Belasco. Belasco actively participated in the operations in a number of ways: in particular, it employed an accountant who monitored compliance with quotas at the end of each year so that penalties could be levied on members which had exceeded their quotas. Further, Belasco financed the joint advertising of the 'Belasco' trade mark which fostered users' impression of a homogeneous product. Members were not, therefore, able to compete by differentiating their products.

It may be that in many situations the conduct adopted by the members of an association may be characterised as an agreement or a concerted practice. However, the prohibition of decisions may facilitate the proof and prohibition of collusive devices operated through associations. The concept has been interpreted broadly to catch conduct designed to coordinate the conduct of the members contrary to Article 101(1),[312] whether engaged in through resolutions of the association, recommendations, the operation of certification schemes, or through the association's constitution itself.

---

[309] COMP/29.595, [1980] OJ L60/1, aff'd Cases 100–103/80, *SA Musique Diffusion française SA v Commission* [1983] ECR 1825, especially paras. 75–76. See also Case 86/82, *Hasselblad (GB) Ltd v Commission* [1984] ECR 883, paras. 24–29 and Case T-43/92, *Dunlop Slazenger International Ltd v Commission* [1994] ECR-II 441 and, in the UK, Case 1022/1/1/03, *JJB Sports plc v Office of Fair Trading* [2004] CAT 17, paras. 150–163, 637–670, aff'd [2006] EWCA Civ 1318.

[310] S. Bishop and M. Walker, *The Economics of EC Competition Law: Concepts, Application and Measurement* (3rd edn, Sweet & Maxwell, 2010), para. 5.016, see also n. 220 and text and Chap. 9.

[311] Case 246/86, *Re Roofing Felt Cartel: S.C. Belasco v Commission* [1989] ECR 2117.

[312] Case 96/82, *NV IAZ International Belgium v Commission* [1983] ECR 3369.

b. Trade Association Recommendations

A recommendation by an association to its members, which has no binding effect, will constitute a decision, if in reality it is intended to determine, or is likely to have the effect of determining, the members' conduct. In *IAZ*,[313] a recommendation made by an association of water-supply undertakings that its members should not connect 'unauthorised' appliances (without a conformity label supplied by another Belgian trade association) to the mains systems was held to be a binding decision capable of restricting competition within the meaning of Article 101(1). The practice discriminated against non-Belgian producers of the appliances. Similarly, in *FENEX*,[314] the Commission held that the recommendation of tariffs by a Dutch association to its member forwarding companies constituted a decision by an association of undertakings within the meaning of Article 101(1). Although the tariffs merely took the form of recommendations, the procedure for drawing up and circulating the tariffs was a habitual activity of the association and was accompanied by circulars drafted in more mandatory terms. The Commission concluded that the circulation of the tariffs had to be interpreted as a faithful reflection of the association's resolve to coordinate the conduct of its members on the relevant market.

c. Medium for Exchange of Information

More subtly, the association may simply collect and disseminate sensitive information and facilitate its exchange between competitors. Were the association to be used, for example, as a vehicle for exchanging information on the prices that the members intended to charge for their products, etc., the parties are likely to be found to be operating a concerted practice.[315]

d. Certification Schemes

Certification schemes operated by members of an association may, in reality, be designed to exclude non-members from business opportunities or to preclude foreign undertakings from penetrating the domestic market of the association's members.[316] The word 'decision', in addition to catching acts of the association which are binding on its members, may also catch these types of more informal methods of coordinating members' actions. In *Stichting Certificatie Kraanverhuurbedrijf and the Federatie van Nederlandse Kraanbedrijven v Commission*,[317] the Commission fined both FNK and SCK after an examination of agreements that they had notified.[318] Not only were the rules of FNK providing for the charging of 'reasonable' rates by its members caught by Article 101(1), but SCK's rules on the certification of the crane-hire trade were also caught. The prohibition on the certificate holders from hiring cranes from non-affiliated firms without valid certification plates (and not affiliated to SCK) restricted competition between affiliated firms and substantially restricted access to the market by other firms.

e. The Trade Association's Constitution

The constitution and rules of a trade association may themselves qualify as a decision (and an agreement) within Article 101(1).[319]

---

[313] COMP/29.995, *Anseau* [1982] OJ L167/39, on appeal Case 96/82, ibid.

[314] COMP/34.983, [1996] OJ L181/28.

[315] See Cases 40–48, 50, 54–56, 111, and 113–114/73, *Suiker Unie* [1975] ECR 1663. See also COMP/31.370 and COMP/31.446, *UK Agricultural Tractor Exchange* [1992] OJ L68/19, upheld on appeal, Case T-34/92, *Fiatagri and Ford New Holland v Commission* [1994] ECR II-905, and Case T-35/92, *John Deere Ltd v Commission* [1994] ECR II-957, on appeal to the CJ Case C-7/95 P, *John Deere Ltd v Commission* [1998] ECR I-3111, see Chap. 9.

[316] As in *Anseau*, n. 313. See also Case 8/72, *Vereeniging van Cementhandelaren v Commission* [1972] ECR 977.

[317] COMP/34.179, *Stichting Certificatie Kraanverhuurbedrijf and Federatie van Nederlandse Kraanbedrijven* [1995] OJ L312/79; on appeal Cases T-213/95 and T-18/96, *Stichting Certificatie Kraanverhuurbedrijf and Federatie van Nederlandse Kraanbedrijven v Commission* [1997] ECR II-1739.

[318] After a preliminary examination of the agreements ([1994] OJ L117/30), the Commission suspended the parties' immunity from fines that arose on the notification of an agreement to the Commission (Reg. 17 [1959–62] OJ Spec. Ed. 87, Art. 15(6)).

[319] COMP/27.958, *National Sulphuric Acid* [1980] OJ L260/24.

f. Governmental Intervention

The fact that a governmental body has either approved of or even imposed an obligation on an association to adopt a scale of compulsory tariffs for the association's members does not alter any resolution's (or other decision's) status as a decision of an association of undertakings.[320]

(v) Complex Arrangements and Single Continuous Infringements

A cartel operated through an agreement or concerted practice can consist of a whole complex set of arrangements affecting a number of products and spread out over a number of different countries and over a lengthy period of time. Where a cartel operates, for example, on a global basis it may also involve a number of sub-agreements affecting different products/services, operated in different countries and some firms may leave and others may join during its tenure. In such cases it is necessary to determine the scope of the cartel (in terms of product and geographical reach) as well as the time period over which it operated and its members—for example, whether the arrangements are sufficiently linked that it can be said that there is one single and continuous cartel or whether there are a number of smaller cartels.

The concept of a single continuing infringement is '[d]esigned to capture the dynamic of one and the same cartel under Article [101]'[321] operated over a period of time (as opposed to multiple separate cartel agreements). The Commission summarised the nature of the concept in the *Shrimp* case:

378. . . . The notion of a single infringement covers precisely a situation in which several undertakings participated in an infringement in which continuous conduct in pursuit of a single economic aim was intended to distort competition and where individual infringements were linked to one another by the same object (elements as a whole sharing the same aim) and the same subjects (same undertakings who are aware that they are participating towards the same object). The existence of synergies and the complementarity between the different lines of conduct are objective indicia of the existence of such an overall plan.

In such circumstances 'it would be artificial to split up such continuous conduct, characterised by a single purpose, by treating it as consisting of several separate infringements, when what was involved was a single infringement which progressively would manifest itself in both agreements and concerted practices'.[322] Where a single and continuous cartel infringement can be established responsibility for the infringement as a whole can be attributed not only to those undertakings that participate in the whole infringement but also[323] to an undertaking who 'participated directly only in one or some of the constituent elements of that cartel, if it is shown that it knew, or must have known, that the collusion in which it participated was part of an overall plan and that the overall plan included all the constituent elements of the cartel'.[324] A finding that old conduct forms part of

---

[320] COMP/33.407, *AICIA v CNSD* [1993] OJ L203/27, paras. 42–44.

[321] J. Joshua, 'Single Continuous Infringement of Article 81 EC: Has the Commission Stretched the Concept Beyond the Limit of its Logic?' (2009) 5 *European Competition Journal* 451, 451 ('[d]eriving its rationale from the temporal dimension of the common law conspiracy as "an agreement with a continuance in time", the continuing infringement concept was also intended, by focusing on bad conduct as much as on the element of consensus, to capture and translate to an EC context the "offensiveness" implicit in criminal conspiracy', 452). See also D. Bailey, 'Single, Overall Agreement in EU Competition Law' (2010) 47 *CMLRev* 473.

[322] COMP/39.579, *Consumer Detergents*, 13 April 2011 [2011] OJ C193/14, paras. 36–37.

[323] But see Case T-68/09, *Soliver NV v Commission* EU:T:2014:867 (where the GC found that the Commission had failed to establish that Soliver, a fringe player, should be held responsible for the wider cartel agreement participated in by the three larger car glass producers. The Commission had not established that Soliver was aware, or should have been aware, of the cartel as a whole and that the contacts it had with its competitors were implementations of a wider cartel).

[324] Case 39.633, *Shrimps*, 27 November 2013, para. 380, citing Cases T-147/89 etc., *Buchmann v Commission* [1995] ECR II-1057; Case T-9/99 *HFB and Others v Commission* [2002] ECR II-1487, para. 231; Cases T-101/05 etc., *BASF and UCB v Commission* [2007] ECR II-4949, para. 160.

an agreement which has endured over a long period may also avoid the applicability of the five-year limitation period.[325]

Harding and Joshua note the huge significance of the concept, some of its salient features, the difficulties in definition, and that, because of the consequences that follow, the finding of a wider single continuous cartel is usually (but not always) in the interest of the Commission.

C. Harding and J. Joshua, *Regulating Cartels in Europe* (2nd edn, Oxford University Press, 2010), 175–177

Aggregation into a single infringement may well increase the size of the market and extent of trade affected, increase the number of participants, and perhaps extend the duration, all of which would add to the gravity of the infringement and justify higher fines. For the participants, there may be exposure to additional legal risks, notably prosecution in other jurisdictions, the transfer of the liability of core players to minor actors, and increased exposure to consequent civil liability claims. Time bars may be removed in relation to earlier activities, now joined to more recent cartel operations. The only possible consolation for cartel participants would be the capping of penalties in terms of the maximum which might be imposed for a single infringement . . .

On the other hand, the consequences of disaggregation or decortications into multiple separate cartels are various. On the whole it is likely to increase prosecution effort and costs, it may multiply the involvement of different enforcement agencies, and complicate the legal process, especially the management of leniency applications . . . There is likely to be a larger number of smaller fines, which may or may not in aggregate match the larger single fine resulting from the single infringement. On the other hand, there may be a prosecutorial advantage in disaggregation, if this allows large corporate structures to be broken down, so that different companies within the same group may be dealt with in relation to separate cartels according to their different involvement in the same market.

Such considerations confirm the significance of the criteria for cartel definition and deciding whether there may be a single or multiple cartels. In . . . reviewing the activities of alleged cartel participants, the [GC] has used a vocabulary of 'complementary' action as descriptive of single infringement and cartel: the acts must be 'closely linked', an 'integrated set of arrangements', 'interwoven and uninterrupted', or be bound together by a 'sufficient definite and decisive causal link'. Evidence of such complementarity would include, in the Court's view, the period of application, the objective, and the content, including the methods used. More specifically, the Commission in its decisions on cartels has identified a number of 'objective elements' as indicia of a single infringement: common objective; similarity of products or services; similarity of behaviour in different geographical areas, commonality of membership, modus operandi, personnel, and the nature of meetings. But the factual complexities of and variations as between actual cases may render the organization of such criteria for purposes of overall assessment a difficult matter. As Joshua has commented:

. . . rarely does the Commission explain how the components are interlinked or what degree of knowledge is required. No doubt the Commission often reaches the 'right' solution intuitively. The danger is that if the exercise becomes a mere recitation, it fuels accusation that the result is 'political'. It also does not help that, to the extent the Commission has developed and articulated any principled test, its application on the ground is not entirely consistent . . . if the distinction between a single and many conspiracies is clear enough conceptually, its empirical application is beset with difficulty.

Part of the problem is the organizational complexity of some cartels, which may have core and minor memberships, national or regional subsets, and an overarching or 'global' coordination, all of which may

---

[325] But see Cases T-101/05 etc., ibid., where the Commission's finding of a single continuous agreement was not upheld (and the decision found to be time-barred). See also, e.g., Case T-655/11, *FSL Holdings v Commission* EU:T:2015:383 and Case T-104/13, *Toshiba v Commission* EU:T:2015:610. Occasionally, fines may be maximised by finding not a single cartel but a series of cartels over a number of different markets, see n. 333 and text and Chap. 13.

be matters of evidential difficulty. Some cartels may resemble 'hub and spoke' conspiracies, with which there may be little awareness on the spoke of the main or core conspiracy at the hub. It may be necessary for regulators and courts to master a complex factual scenario in order to define the limits of a cartel and thus the extent of liability.

It may be argued that a convincing and reliable test may be based on elements of interdependence and knowledge. 'Interdependence' describes well the idea of a chain of activities which all contribute in a necessary and decisive way to the goals of the cartel organization—the resulting network of activity of linked but crucial actions defines the infrastructure and scope of the cartel. But it is also necessary for this interdependent activity to be performed with knowledge of its purpose and significance, an awareness which characterizes the action and also supplies a justifiable mental element as a basis for liability. Thus in the *Treuhand* case, the consultancy firm was aware that its servicing of the cartel's activities was a necessary part of the success of those activities. On the other hand, in the *Choline Chloride Cartel* . . . [t]he earlier involvement of the American and Canadian companies was not necessary or decisive for the later operation of the cartel in Europe. A *knowing interdependence* may therefore be put forward as a test of cartel scope and perpetrator liability, separating 'core' involvement from acts of ancillary, unknowing, and uninformed support for minor actors who are thus outside the cartel and not liable in a significant way for the cartel's activity.

Cartel identification and definition is thus an issue of some complexity, but one that must be mastered, since the existence and identify of the cartel must first be proven for the offence or infringement to be properly prosecuted. A crucial problem would seem to be that of sorting the peripheral accessory players and their activities from the essential participation.

The concept of a single continuous infringement was first used in *Polypropylene*,[326] a case concerning a long-lasting cartel in the petrochemical industry. Fifteen firms were held by the Commission to have infringed the competition rules by participating in a framework agreement to fix prices and sales volumes. The Commission considered that the cartel, which was based on an overall framework agreement or a common and detailed plan manifested in a series of more detailed sub-agreements worked out from time to time, constituted a single continuing agreement for the purpose of Article 101(1). Some firms claimed they were not liable as they had not participated in all aspects of the arrangements. The GC held that the Commission was justified in treating the entire course of the collusion as one single agreement. For there to be an 'agreement' for the purposes of Article 101(1) it was sufficient for the undertakings to have 'expressed their joint intention to conduct themselves on the market in a specific way'.[327] In this case the undertakings had, throughout the whole course of the arrangements, pursued the single economic aim of distorting the polypropylene market.

Since then the Commission has frequently relied on the concept which has facilitated the application of Article 101 to cartels 'which are "not born fully grown" but develop organically as the members conceive ever more sophisticated ways to achieve their objectives while reducing the risk of detection'.[328]

---

[326] COMP/31.149, *Polypropylene* [1986] OJ L230/1; on appeal Cases T-1/89, *Rhône-Poulenc v Commission* [1991] ECR II-867; T-2/89, *Petrofina SA v Commission* [1991] ECR II-1087; T-3/89 *Atochem v Commission* [1991] ECR II-1177; T-6/89, *Enichem Anic SpA v Commission* [1991] ECR II-1623; T-7/89, *SA Hercules Chemicals NV v Commission* [1991] ECR II-1711, etc. The appeals by the companies to the CJ were broadly dismissed: see Case C-51/92 P, *Hercules Chemicals NC v Commission* [1999] ECR I-4235; Case C-199/92 P, *Hüls AG v Commission* [1999] ECR I-4287; Case C-200/92 P, *ICI v Commission* [1999] ECR I-4399, etc., although the appeal by the Commission against the partial annulment of its decision against Enichem was mainly successful, Case C-49/92 P, *Commission v Anic Partecipazioni* [1999] ECR I-4125.

[327] See especially Case T-1/89, *Rhône-Poulenc v Commission* [1991] ECR II-867, para. 120, relying on Case 41/69, *ACF Chemiefarma NV v Commission* [1970] ECR 661, para. 112.

[328] Joshua, n. 321, 459.

In *Bananas*,[329] for example, the GC and CJ affirmed a Commission decision finding that three competitors which had engaged in bilateral price communications with each other (between Dole and Chiquita, Dole and Weichert, where Chiquita knew or, at least foresaw, that Dole communicated with Weichert) were party to a single and continuous infringement having as its object the restriction of competition and holding Chiquita and Dole responsible for the entire single and continuous infringement (while Weichert was held responsible only for the part of the infringement relating to the collusive agreements with Dole).

The CJ clarified that where the infringement results from a series of acts or from continuous conduct forming part of an overall plan, with the same object of distorting competition, the Commission is entitled to attribute liability on the basis of participation in the infringement as a whole, even if it is established that the undertaking concerned directly participated in only one of some of the constituent elements of the infringement. This will be the case, for example, where the undertaking concerned intended to contribute by its own conduct to the common objectives pursued by all the participants and was aware of the actual conduct planned or put into effect by the other undertakings in pursuit of the same objectives or that it could reasonably have foreseen it and that it was prepared to take the risk.

Cases C-293 and 294/13 P, *Fresh Del Monte Produce Inc v Commission* EU:C:2015:416

156. According to settled case-law, an infringement of Article [101(1)] can result not only from an isolated act, but also from a series of acts or from continuous conduct, even if one or more aspects of that series of acts or continuous conduct could also, in themselves and taken in isolation, constitute an infringement of that provision. Accordingly, if the different actions form part of an 'overall plan' because their identical object distorts competition within the common market, the Commission is entitled to impute responsibility for those actions on the basis of participation in the infringement considered as a whole (judgment in *Commission v Verhuizingen Coppens* ..., paragraph 41 ...).

157. An undertaking which has participated in such a single and complex infringement, by its own conduct, which meets the definition of an agreement or concerted practice having an anti-competitive object within the meaning of Article [101(1)] and was intended to help bring about the infringement as a whole, may also be responsible for the conduct of other undertakings in the context of the same infringement throughout the period of its participation in the infringement. That is the position where it is shown that the undertaking intended, through its own conduct, to contribute to the common objectives pursued by all the participants and that it was aware of the offending conduct planned or put into effect by other undertakings in pursuit of the same objectives or that it could reasonably have foreseen it and was prepared to take the risk (judgment in *Commission v Verhuizingen Coppens*..., paragraph 42...).

158. An undertaking may thus have participated directly in all the forms of anti-competitive conduct comprising the single and continuous infringement, in which case the Commission is entitled to attribute liability to it in relation to that conduct as a whole and, therefore, in relation to the infringement as a whole. Equally, the undertaking may have participated directly in only some of the forms of anti-competitive conduct comprising the single and continuous infringement, but have been aware of all the other unlawful conduct planned or put into effect by the other participants in the cartel in pursuit of the same objectives, or could reasonably have foreseen that conduct and have been prepared to take the risk. In such cases, the Commission is also entitled to attribute liability to that undertaking in relation to all the forms

---

[329] COMP/39.188, 15 October 2008, aff'd Cases T-587/08, *Fresh Del Monte Produce v Commission* EU:T:2013:129 and T-588/08 P, *Dole Food and Dole Germany v Commission* EU:T:2013:130 and Cases C-293 and 294/13 P, *Fresh Del Monte v Commission* EU:C:2015:416 and Case C-286/13 P, *Dole Food Company Inc v Commission* EU:C:2015:184. Contrast Case T-655/11, *FSL Holdings v Commission* EU:T:2015:383.

of anti-competitive conduct comprising such an infringement and, accordingly, in relation to the infringement as a whole (judgment in *Commission v Verhuizingen Coppens...*, paragraph 43).

159. On the other hand, if an undertaking has directly taken part in one or more of the forms of anti-competitive conduct comprising a single and continuous infringement, but it has not been shown that that undertaking intended, through its own conduct, to contribute to all the common objectives pursued by the other participants in the cartel and that it was aware of all the other offending conduct planned or put into effect by those other participants in pursuit of the same objectives, or that it could reasonably have foreseen all that conduct and was prepared to take the risk, the Commission is entitled to attribute to that undertaking liability only for the conduct in which it had participated directly and for the conduct planned or put into effect by the other participants, in pursuit of the same objectives as those pursued by the undertaking itself, where it has been shown that the undertaking was aware of that conduct or was able reasonably to foresee it and prepared to take the risk (judgment in *Commission v Verhuizingen Coppens* ..., paragraph 44).

In *Trelleborg Industrie v Commission*,[330] an appeal from the Commission's *Marine Hoses* decision, the GC also set out the salient features of a single and continuous infringement and to distinguish these from single, repeated infringements. The GC explained that as in cartel cases the existence of an infringement frequently had to be pieced together from fragmentary evidence (see further Chapter 9), coincidences and indicia might be relied on to provide information not only about the mere existence of anti-competitive practices or agreements, but also about their duration or the period of application. Thus the Commission might be entitled to support a finding of continuous infringement by relying on evidence that actions formed part of an overall plan—for example, establishing the identical nature of the objectives of the practices at issue, the identical nature of the undertakings which participated in the infringement, the identical nature of the detailed rules for its implementation, the fact that the natural persons involved on behalf of the undertakings and/or the geographical scope of the practices are identical—even if evidence of the infringement has not been produced in relation to all specific periods.[331]

Cases T-147 and 148/09 *Trelleborg Industrie v Commission* EU:T:2013:259

General Court

– The existence of a continuous infringement

57. It should be borne in mind that, in most cases, the existence of an anti-competitive practice or agreement must be inferred from a number of coincidences and indicia which, taken together, may, in the absence of another plausible explanation, constitute evidence of an infringement of the competition rules. Such coincidences and indicia, when evaluated overall, may provide information not just about the mere existence of anti-competitive practices or agreements, but also about the duration of continuous anti-competitive practices or the period of application of anti-competitive agreements (see, to that effect, *Aalborg Portland and Others v Commission*, paragraph 52 above, paragraph 57, and Case C-105/04 P *Nederlandse Federatieve Vereniging voor de Groothandel op Elektrotechnisch Gebied* v *Commission* . . ., paragraphs 94 to 96 . . .).

58. Furthermore, such an infringement may be the consequence not only of an isolated act but also of a series of acts or indeed of continuous conduct. That interpretation cannot be challenged on the

---

[330] Cases T-147 and 148/09, EU:T:2013:259.

[331] Ibid., paras. 50–71.

ground that one or more elements of that series of acts or of that continuous conduct might also constitute in themselves, and taken in isolation, an infringement of the competition rules. Where the various actions form part of an 'overall plan', owing to their identical object, which distorts competition within the common market, the Commission is entitled to impute liability for those actions according to participation in the infringement considered as a whole (see *Aalborg Portland and Others v Commission*, . . . paragraph 258 and *Nederlandse Federatieve Vereniging voor de Groothandel op Elektrotechnisch Gebied v Commission*, . . . paragraph 110).

59. As regards the lack of evidence that there was an agreement during certain specific periods or, at least, the lack of evidence of its implementation by an undertaking during a given period, it should be recalled that the fact that evidence of the infringement has not been produced in relation to certain specific periods does not preclude the infringement from being regarded as established during a longer overall period than those periods, provided that such a finding is supported by objective and consistent indicia. In the context of an infringement extending over a number of years, the fact that a cartel is shown to have applied during different periods, which may be separated by longer or shorter periods, has no effect on the existence of the cartel, provided that the various actions which form part of the infringement pursue a single purpose and fall within the framework of a single and continuous infringement (*Nederlandse Federatieve Vereniging voor de Groothandel op Elektrotechnisch Gebied v Commission*, . . . paragraphs 97 and 98; see also, to that effect, *Aalborg Portland and Others v Commission*, . . . paragraph 260).

60. In that regard, several criteria have been identified by the case-law as relevant for assessing whether there is a single infringement, namely the identical nature of the objectives of the practices at issue (Case T-21/99 *Dansk Rørindustri v Commission* . . . paragraph 67; see also, to that effect, Case C-113/04 P *Technische Unie v Commission* . . . paragraphs 170 and 171; and Case T-43/02 *Jungbunzlauer v Commission* . . . paragraph 312), the identical nature of the goods or services concerned (see, to that effect, judgment of 15 June 2005 in Joined Cases T-71/03, T-74/03, T-87/03 and T-91/03 *Tokai Carbon and Others v Commission*, . . . paragraphs 118, 119 and 124, and *Jungbunzlauer v Commission*, paragraph 312), the identical nature of the undertakings which participated in the infringement (*Jungbunzlauer v Commission*, paragraph 312), and the identical nature of the detailed rules for its implementation (*Dansk Rørindustri v Commission*, paragraph 68). Furthermore, whether the natural persons involved on behalf of the undertakings are identical and whether the geographical scope of the practices at issue is identical are also factors which may be taken into consideration for the purposes of that examination.

61. The case-law therefore permits the Commission to assume that the infringement—or the participation of an undertaking in the infringement—has not been interrupted, even if it has no evidence of the infringement in relation to certain specific periods, provided that the various actions which form part of the infringement pursue a single purpose and are capable of falling within the framework of a single and continuous infringement; such a finding must be supported by objective and consistent indicia showing that an overall plan exists.

62. If those conditions are satisfied, the concept of continuous infringement . . . allows the Commission to impose a fine in respect of the whole of the period of infringement taken into consideration and establishes the date on which the limitation period begins to run, namely the date on which the continuous infringement ceased.

63. However, the undertakings accused of collusion may attempt to rebut that presumption by submitting indicia and evidence proving that, on the contrary, the infringement—or their participation in it—did not continue during those same periods.

Nonetheless, a finding of a single and continuous infringement must be made sufficiently clearly and precisely. In *Airfreight*,[332] for example, the GC annulled fines imposed by the Commission on 13 companies it found to have participated in the airfreight cartel. The GC held that although the Commission had described a single and continuous agreement in its statement of reasons, that

---

[332] Cases T-9/11 etc., *Air Canada v Commission* EU:T:2015:994.

finding was not clearly reflected in the operative part of the decision. Contradictions and inconsistencies in the decision infringed rights of defence and precluded review by the Court.

In *Treuhand*,[333] the applicant, in contrast to the cases described above, challenged the Commission's decision finding two parallel but similar cartels (and imposing two separate fines)—the applicant contended that they formed one single infringement and so there had been an infringement of Regulation 1/2003 (Article 23(2)) as the fines imposed on it related to the same infringement but together exceeded 10 per cent of its total turnover (the maximum fine permitted under the Regulation). The GC upheld the finding of the Commission. Recalling that the notion of a single infringement covers a situation in which undertakings participate in continuous, complementary conduct in pursuit of a single economic aim linked by the same object and the same subjects, it was necessary to take into account circumstances capable of establishing, or of casting doubt on, that link, such as the period of implementation the content and the objectives of the various acts. On the facts, it found that the GC and Commission had been correct to find that there was not a single continuous infringement and the members of the two cartels did not have a common project nor a common objective: the parties of the two cartels were not all the same; the products did not form part of the same market and were not complementary; the cartels did not have the same duration; and indeed some of the undertakings in one cartel were buyers in the other cartel market.

C. OBJECT OR EFFECT OF THE PREVENTION, RESTRICTION, OR DISTORTION OF COMPETITION

Agreements and other collusive practices are not prohibited unless they have as their object or the effect the prevention, restriction, or distortion of competition. The way in which this phrase is interpreted determines the types of agreements which are prohibited and the scope of application of Article 101(1). Further, the way in which Article 101(1) is interpreted has a crucial impact on the role played by and the interpretation of Article 101(3)—as the latter excepts from the Article 101(1) prohibition agreements which satisfy its conditions. The relationship and interaction of these two paragraphs and the question of what issues should be considered under each Article has caused enormous controversy and is fully explored in Chapter 4.

D. AN APPRECIABLE EFFECT ON COMPETITION AND TRADE

The CJ has held that 'in order to come within the prohibition imposed by Article [101], the agreement must affect trade between Member States and the free play of competition to an appreciable extent'.[334] The concept of appreciability was accepted by the CJ in *Völk v Vervaecke*.

Case 5/69, *Völk v Vervaecke* [1969] ECR 295, 302

The case concerned an exclusive distribution agreement concluded between Mr Völk, the owner of a company, Erd & Co, which manufactured washing machines, and Vervaecke, a Belgian company which distributed household electrical appliances. Under the agreement, Vervaecke had the exclusive right to sell Völk's products in Belgium and Luxembourg. According to the Commission, Erd & Co had only 0.08 per cent of the market for the production of washing machines EU-wide, 0.2 per cent of the market

---

[333] Case T-27/10, *AC-Treuhand v Commission* EU:T:2014:59, *aff'd* Case C-194/14 P, EU:C:2015:717.

[334] Case 22/71, *Béguelin Import Co v SAGL Import Export* [1971] ECR 949, para. 16 (even though the text of Art. 101(1) does not require it).

in Germany, and 0.6 per cent of the market in Belgium and Luxembourg. Following a dispute which raised the validity of the agreement before the German courts, the Oberlandesgericht in Munich made an Article 234 reference to the EU Courts. In particular, it asked the CJ whether, in considering if an agreement fell within Article 101(1), regard had to be had to the proportion of the market that the grantor had.

Court of Justice

If an agreement is to be capable of affecting trade between Member States it must be possible to foresee with a sufficient degree of probability on the basis of a set of objective factors of law or of fact that the agreement in question may have an influence, direct or indirect, actual or potential, on the pattern of trade between Member States in such a way that it might hinder the attainment of the objectives of a single market between States. Moreover the prohibition in Article [101(1)] is applicable only if the agreement in question also has as its object or effect the prevention, restriction or distortion of competition within the common market. Those conditions must be understood by reference to the actual circumstances of the agreement. Consequently an agreement falls outside the prohibition in Article [101] when it has only an insignificant effect on the markets, taking into account the weak position which the persons concerned have on the market of the product in question. Thus an exclusive dealing agreement, even with absolute territorial protection, may, having regard to the weak position of the persons concerned on the market in the products in question in the area covered by the absolute protection, escape the prohibition laid down in Article [101(1)].

This case clarifies that EU law is not concerned with agreements concluded between parties that hold a weak position on the market and which have an insignificant effect on intra-Community trade and/or on competition. The insignificant position held by the undertakings means the agreement does not threaten the EU objectives.[335] Because the concept of appreciability is of huge practical importance to undertakings, particularly small and medium-sized ones, the Commission has, over the years, issued a series of Notices indicating when, in its view, an agreement is likely to fall outside Article 101 on this ground. The Commission's interpretation of appreciability is now fleshed out in two separate Notices—one dealing with the effect on trade concept and one dealing with agreements of minor importance which do not appreciably restrict competition. The former Notice is dealt with in the section below, whilst the latter is dealt with in Chapter 4.

E. AN APPRECIABLE EFFECT ON TRADE BETWEEN MEMBER STATES

(i) Jurisdictional Limit

The concept of an effect on trade between Member States sets out a jurisdictional limit to the prohibition laid down in Article 101 (it is also a requirement that any abuse of a dominant position should affect trade for the purposes of Article 102). The criterion confines the scope of the application of Articles 101 and 102 to agreements having a minimum level of cross-border effects within the EU, hence the practices must *appreciably* affect trade between Member States.[336] It has been interpreted broadly, although it is accepted that the EU has no jurisdiction over conduct whose effect is confined to one Member State.[337] The meaning of an effect on trade has been clarified in the case law. The

---

[335] Rather, it is more appropriate that they should be examined, if at all, within the framework of national competition legislation.

[336] Guidelines on the effect on trade concept contained in Arts 81 and 82 of the Treaty (Guidelines on the effect on trade concept) [2004] OJ C101/81, para. 13.

[337] Case 22/78, *Hugin v Commission* [1979] ECR 1869.

Commission has also prepared a Notice on the concept of effect on trade between Member States[338] which seeks to set out the principles developed by the Court and to spell out when agreements and conduct may 'appreciably' affect trade between Member States. It aims 'to set out the methodology for the application of the effect on trade concept and to provide guidance on its application in frequently occurring situations'.[339] In paragraphs 58–109 of the Guidelines it applies the general principles set out in the cases to common types of agreements and abuses, for example: different types of agreements and abuse covering or implemented in several Member States; agreements and abuses covering a single or only part of a Member State; agreements and abuses involving imports and exports with undertakings located in third countries; and agreements and practices involving undertakings located in third countries. The Guidelines are, of course, without prejudice to the interpretation given to the concept by the EU Courts.[340]

(ii) The Tests

The Commission's Notice stresses, relying on case law of the Court,[341] that '[t]he concept of "trade" is not limited to traditional exchanges of goods and services across borders. It is a wider concept, covering all cross-border economic activity, including establishment. This interpretation is consistent with the fundamental objective of the Treaty to promote free movement of goods, services, persons and capital.'[342] An agreement will be found to 'affect trade' if it interferes with the pattern of trade between Member States.[343] There must be an impact on the flow of goods and services or other relevant economic activities involving at least two Member States. An agreement or practice may also be found to affect trade if it is liable to interfere with the structure of competition in the common market, for example where it eliminates or threatens to eliminate competitors operating within the Union. This latter structural test is more commonly used in the context of Article 102 than Article 101.[344]

(iii) Pattern of Trade Test

In *Société Technique Minière v Maschinenbau Ulm*,[345] the CJ set out a broad interpretation of the requirement that an agreement should affect trade so that it is easily satisfied. All that is necessary is that 'it must be possible to foresee with a sufficient degree of probability on the basis of a set of objective factors of law or of fact that the agreement in question may have an influence, direct or indirect, actual or potential, on the pattern of trade between Member States . . .'.[346]

The test requires the following to be shown:

(a) a sufficient degree of probability on the basis of a set of objective factors of law of fact;[347]

(b) an influence on the pattern of trade between Member States;[348]

(c) a direct or indirect, actual or potential influence on the pattern of trade.[349]

---

[338] [2004] OJ C101/81.

[339] Guidelines on the effect on trade concept, para. 3.

[340] Ibid., para. 5.

[341] See, e.g., Case 172/80, *Züchner v Bayerische Vereinsbank AG* [1981] ECR 2021, para. 18, and Case C-309/99, *Wouters v Algemene Raad van de Nederlandse Orde van Advocaten* [2002] ECR I-1577, Case C-41/90, *Höfner and Elser v Macrotron* [1991] ECR I-1979.

[342] Guidelines on the effect on trade concept, para. 19.

[343] Case 56/65, *STM* [1966] ECR 235.

[344] See Case 6–7/73, *Istituto Chemioterapico Italiano SpA and Commercial Solvents Corp v Commission* [1974] ECR 223, especially para. 5, and Chap. 5.

[345] Case 56/65, [1966] ECR 235.

[346] Ibid., 249, and Case 5/69, *Völk v Vervaecke* [1969] ECR 295, 302.

[347] Guidelines on the effect on trade concept, paras. 25–32.

[348] Ibid., paras. 33–35.

[349] Ibid., paras. 36–43.

An agreement will, therefore, be caught even if it is not established that the agreement will affect the pattern of trade if it can be shown that it is *capable* of having such an effect,[350] for example if it is anticipated that it will affect the pattern of trade in the future. As it is only a jurisdictional criterion it is not necessary to establish that it actually has cross-border effects. Relevant factors to the determination will be: the nature of the agreement and practice; the nature of the products; and the position and importance of the undertakings involved.

The fact that the influence on trade need only be direct, indirect, actual, or potential means that a broad range of agreements will be caught including, for example: agreements affecting goods or services that are not traded, but which are used in the supply of a final product, which is traded;[351] and agreements which do not actually affect trade but which, taking account of foreseeable market developments, may affect trade in the future. In *AEG v Commission*,[352] the CJ held that the fact that there was little inter-State trade did not mean that Article 101(1) was inapplicable if it could reasonably be expected that the patterns of trade in the future might change. The Commission states, however, that the inclusion of indirect and potential effects in the analysis of effects on trade between Member States does not mean that the analysis can be based on remote, hypothetical, or speculative effects.

For instance, an agreement that raises the prices of a product which is not tradable reduces the disposable income of consumers. As consumers have less money to spend they may purchase fewer products imported from other Member States. However, the link between such income effects and trade between Member States is generally in itself too remote to establish [EU] law jurisdiction.[353]

(iv) An Increase in Trade

In *Consten and Grundig*,[354] the parties argued before the CJ that their distribution agreement did not produce an effect on trade within the meaning of Article 101(1) since it increased trade between Member States (in the absence of the agreement, Grundig products might not have been sold in France at all). This argument was partially supported by a textual analysis of the Treaty since, in at least one language (Italian), the text suggested that the effect on trade should be a harmful or prejudicial one. The CJ[355] rejected this argument, ruling that 'the fact that an agreement encourages an increase, even a large one, in the volume of trade between states is not sufficient to exclude the possibility that the agreement may "affect" such trade . . .'.[356] Rather, it examined the contract, which precluded anyone other than Consten from importing Grundig products into France, and prohibited Consten from re-exporting the products into other Member States, concluding that it 'indisputably affects trade between Member States'. Instead of attempting to adopt a literal interpretation of the provision the CJ adopted an interpretation which respected the aims and spirit of the Treaty. It was important that agreements such as the exclusive distribution agreement at issue in that case should be capable of being scrutinised under the provisions. The aim of the Treaty was not to increase trade as an end in itself, but to create a system of undistorted competition. The CJ concluded that Article 101 applied to any agreement which might threaten the freedom of trade between Member States in a manner which might harm the attainment of the single market. The term pattern of trade is neutral, it is not a condition that trade is restricted or reduced.

---

[350] Ibid., para. 26.

[351] Case 123/83, *BNIC v Clair* [1985] ECR 391, para. 29.

[352] Case 107/82, [1983] ECR 3151, para. 60; see also *AEI/Reyrolle Parsons re Vacuum Interrupters* [1977] OJ L48/32.

[353] Guidelines on the effect on trade concept, para. 43.

[354] Cases 56 and 58/64, *Consten and Grundig* [1966] ECR 299.

[355] The argument was, however, supported by Roemer AG. He took the view that the effect on trade would have to be an unfavourable one before the prohibition applied.

[356] Cases 56 and 58/64, *Consten and Grundig* [1966] ECR 299, 341.

(v) Partitioning of the Internal Market

Many vertical IP licensing agreements are capable of an effect on trade between Member States because of their tendency to incorporate territorial restrictions and their ability to partition the common market. In *Consten and Grundig* the CJ found that the nature of the territorial restrictions was to affect trade.[357] Similarly, other agreements concerning imports or exports, containing provisions sharing markets between a manufacturer and its distributor or between distributors *inter se*, are capable of affecting trade between Member States.[358]

Even an agreement covering third countries and undertakings located in third countries may appreciably affect trade between Member States where it is capable of affecting cross-border economic activity inside the Union, for example an agreement preventing a distributor appointed for a territory outside the EU from making sales outside its contractual territory (and, consequently, into the EU). If, in the absence of the agreement, resale to the EU would be both possible and likely, it may be capable of affecting patterns of trade inside the EU.[359] Whether or not an agreement with an undertaking outside the EU will affect trade will depend on factors such as the object of the agreement (whether the object of the agreement is to restrict competition within the EU), the prices for the contractual products charged in the EU and those charged outside the EU, the level of customs duties, and transport costs. Further, the product volumes exported compared to the total market for those products in the territory of the common market must not be insignificant.[360]

It is also possible that an agreement may have an effect on trade even if it does not appear to do so at first sight. The impact on inter-State trade may be revealed on a closer examination of the agreement. In *Delimitis v Henninger Bräu*,[361] for example, a beer-supply agreement between a German brewer and a German café proprietor imposed an obligation on the latter to purchase beer only from the brewer. In derogation from this obligation, however, it included an access clause permitting the café proprietor to purchase competing beer from suppliers in other Member States. The CJ ruled that the national court would have to examine the agreement in greater detail. It was critical to determine whether or not this 'access' clause was hypothetical or real. The contract obliged the café proprietor to purchase a specific quantity of the brewer's beer each year. It had to be determined, therefore, whether or not this clause stipulating the minimum quantity of the brewer's beer to be purchased in reality left the café proprietor with a real opportunity to purchase beer from brewers in other Member States. If it did not, the agreement would produce an effect on inter-State trade, despite the access clause. On the other hand, if the agreement left a real possibility for foreign brewers to supply the outlet, the agreement was not in principle capable of affecting trade between Member States.

(vi) Agreements Operating in One Member State

It tends to be assumed that an agreement between parties situated in different Member States affects trade between Member States.[362] It can be seen from *Delimitis* that an agreement which operates in only one Member State is also quite capable of affecting trade between Member States.

Similarly, national cartels, especially those dominating the whole or a large part of a market, tend to reinforce compartmentalisation and make it more difficult for undertakings from other Member States to penetrate the market.[363] The CJ has consistently held that the fact that a cartel relates only

---

[357] See n. 354 and text.

[358] Case 161/84, *Pronuptia de Paris GmbH v Pronuptia de Paris Irmgard Schillgallis* [1986] ECR 353, para. 27.

[359] Case C-306/96, *Javico International and Javico AF v Yves Saint Laurent Parfums SA* [1998] ECR I-1983, paras. 15–29.

[360] Ibid.

[361] Case C-234/89, [1991] ECR I-935.

[362] See, e.g., Guidelines on the effect on trade concept, paras. 61–72.

[363] Case 8/72, *Vereeniging van Cementhandelaren v Commission* [1972] ECR 977. But see Cases C-215 and 216/96, *Bagnasco v Banca Popolare di Novara (BPN) and Cassa di Risparmio di Genova e Imperia SpA (Carige)* [1999] ECR I-135, paras. 38–53, n. 368 and text.

to the marketing of products in a single Member State is not sufficient to exclude the possibility that trade between Member States might be affected.[364] Indeed, the cartel is likely to be successful only if the members can defend themselves against foreign competition. If they do not, and the product covered by the agreement is tradable, the cartel is likely to be undermined by competition from undertakings in other Member States. The agreement in *Belasco*,[365] for example, specifically provided for protective and defensive measures to be taken against foreign undertakings. Where the relevant product or service affected by the cartel is easily transmissible across borders it is likely that an effect on trade will be found. A Dutch cartel agreement which operated in order to restrict competition in the market for mobile cranes was held to have an effect on intra-Union trade. Since the cranes could travel at speeds of between 63 and 78 k.p.h., the agreement was likely to affect German and Belgian firms operating near the Dutch border.[366] The Commission reached a similar conclusion in *Luxembourg Brewers*[367] in respect of a cartel designed to insulate the Luxembourg market against imports of beer from other Member States.

In *Carlo Bagnasco v BPN*[368] and *Dutch Banks*,[369] the CJ and Commission respectively concluded that purely national banking agreements were not capable of affecting trade between Member States. *Bagnasco*, for example, concerned retail banking services (guarantees for current account credit facilities) and the CJ considered that trade was not capable of being appreciably affected because the potential for trade in the products was very limited. The market was not particularly susceptible to imports and retail banking services were not an important factor affecting the choice made by undertakings from other Member States when determining whether or not to establish themselves in another Member State. Although somewhat out of line with other case law and decisions setting out extensive EU jurisdiction, the cases may be explicable by virtue of a reluctance at the time to apply EU law to cases which essentially have a national impact and so can be dealt with at a national level. Since 2004, however, such cases may be appraised by the appropriate NCA under Article 101 (if an effect on trade is found) as well as domestic law.[370]

(vii) Restrictions on Competition and Restrictions on Trade

It is clear that so long as the agreement as a whole affects trade between Member States it is immaterial that the clause (or clauses) which restricts competition does not itself affect trade.[371]

(viii) Agreements which Appreciably Affect Trade between Member States

The Commission's Notice dealing with the effect on trade concept also deals with the quantitative element of the criterion, the question of when an agreement will *appreciably* affect trade between Member States.[372] It states that EU law limits jurisdiction to agreements and practices capable of having effects on trade of a certain magnitude. In particular, appreciability can be appraised by reference to the position and importance of the undertakings on the relevant market. The Commission

---

[364] Case C-246/86, *S.C. Belasco v Commission* [1989] ECR 2117, para. 33.

[365] Ibid., paras. 35–38.

[366] COMP/34.179, *Stichting Certificatie Kraanverhuurbedrijf and Federatie van Nederlandse Kraanbedrijven* [1995] OJ L312/79.

[367] COMP/37.800, [2002] OJ L253/21, paras. 77–81.

[368] Case C-215/96, [1999] ECR I-135. See also Guidelines on the effect on trade concept, para. 60.

[369] COMP/31.499, [1991] OJ L271/28.

[370] But see discussion of Reg. 1/2003, Art. 3 in Chap. 13.

[371] See Case 193/83, *Windsurfing International Inc v Commission* [1986] ECR 611.

[372] Commission Guidelines on the effect on trade concept, paras. 44–57.

considers that appreciability can be measured both in absolute terms (turnover) and in relative terms, comparing the position of the relevant undertakings with others on the market (market share).[373] In paragraphs 50–57, the Commission seeks to quantify appreciability, stressing however that the assessment depends on the circumstances of each individual case. It does, however, indicate when trade is normally not capable of being appreciably affected. It sets out a negative rebuttable presumption, defining the absence of an appreciable effect on trade between Member States (the NAAT-rule). In contrast to its Notice on agreements of minor importance, the Commission states that the rule applies to *all* agreements irrespective of the restrictions contained within them (i.e. it applies even to agreements containing object (or hardcore) restraints, see further Chapter 4).[374] Agreements which do not fall within its negative definition of appreciability do not, however, necessarily appreciably affect trade.

At paragraph 52 the Commission states its view that 'in principle agreements are not capable of appreciably affecting trade between Member States when the following *cumulative* conditions are met' (emphasis added):[375]

(a) The aggregate market share of the parties on any relevant market within the Community affected by the agreement does not exceed 5 per cent,[376] and

(b) In the case of horizontal agreements, the aggregate annual Community turnover of the undertakings concerned in the products covered by the agreement does not exceed 40 million Euro.[377] In case of agreements concerning joint buying of products the relevant turnover shall be the parties' combined purchases of the products covered by the agreement.

In the case of vertical agreements, the aggregate annual Community turnover of the supplier in the products covered by the agreement does not exceed 40 million Euro. In the case of licence agreements the relevant turnover shall be the aggregate turnover of the licensees in the products incorporating the licensed technology and the licensor's own turnover in such products. In cases involving agreements concluded between a buyer and several suppliers the relevant turnover shall be the buyer's combined purchase of the products covered by the agreement.

Paragraph 52 also provides marginal relief for those that outgrow the Notice in two successive calendar years. In cases where the presumption applies the Commission will not normally institute proceedings. Further, where undertakings assumed in good faith that an agreement is covered by the negative presumption, the Commission will not impose fines.[378]

In contrast, paragraph 53 states that for agreements that, by their very nature, are capable of affecting trade between Member States, such as agreements concerning imports and exports or covering several Member States, there is a *rebuttable positive presumption* that the effects on trade are appreciable when the turnover of the parties exceeds €40 million. It may also often be presumed that effects are appreciable where the 5 per cent threshold is exceeded. These rebuttable presumptions will obviously be of central importance when these issues are litigated before national courts.

---

[373] Ibid., para. 46.

[374] Ibid., para. 50.

[375] The NAAT-rule does not apply in emerging markets. In such cases appreciability may have to be assessed on the basis of the position of the parties on related product markets or their strength in technologies relating to the agreement.

[376] See Case C-439/11 P, *Ziegler SA v Commission* EU:C:2013:513.

[377] The turnover threshold is calculated on the basis of total EU sales excluding tax during the last financial year by the undertakings concerned. Sales between entities that form part of the same undertaking are excluded, Commission Guidelines on the effect on trade concept, para. 54.

[378] Commission Guidelines on the effect on trade concept, para. 50.

(ix) The Relationship Between EU and National Law

The breadth of the effect on trade criterion determines the scope of Article 3 of Regulation 1/2003 which determines the relationship between Articles 101 and 102 and national law. The effect on trade criterion can therefore have a substantive outcome. Essentially, Article 3 provides that whenever an NCA or national court applies national competition laws to an agreement or practice that affects trade between Member States, it must also apply Articles 101 and 102. The application of national competition law may not, however, lead to the prohibition of agreements which affect trade between Member States but which do not restrict competition within the meaning of Article 101(1), or which fulfil the conditions of Article 101(3) or which are covered by an EU block exemption. Further, a national authority cannot authorise an agreement prohibited by EU law. The relationship between EU and national law is dealt with more fully in Chapter 13.

F. AGREEMENTS REQUIRED BY NATIONAL LEGISLATION OR ENCOURAGED BY NATIONAL GOVERNMENTS

National law or national regulatory regimes may affect competition in a market. Case law makes it clear that Article 101 is not applicable to the anti-competitive activities of a firm if the restrictive effects on competition originate solely from the implementation of national law, for example where national law requires an agreement or creates a framework eliminating any possible competitive conduct.[379] In such a case the anti-competitive effect results not from the autonomous conduct of the firms but from the national law and not the agreement.[380] Article 101 is concerned with the conduct of undertakings and not with laws or regulations of Member States.[381]

Where, however, national law leaves room for competition, firms must comply with the competition rules. This position is clearly spelt out by the GC in its judgment in *Atlantic Container Line*.

Cases T-191 and 212–214/98, *Atlantic Container Line v Commission* [2003] ECR II-3275, para. 1130

General Court

1130. According to the case-law, Articles [101] and [102] apply only to anti-competitive conduct in which undertakings engage on their own initiative. If anti-competitive conduct is required of undertakings by national law or if the latter creates a legal framework eliminating any possibility of competitive conduct on their part, Articles [101] and [102] do not apply. In such a situation, the restriction of competition is not attributable, as is implied by those provisions, to the autonomous conduct of the undertakings. Articles [101] and [102] may apply, by contrast, if it is found that the national legislation does not preclude undertakings

---

[379] Where a Member State takes measures which lead to an infringement of the antitrust rules by a firm, the Commission may be able to issue an infringement decision against that State, see Chap. 8.

[380] See, e.g., Cases C-94 and 202/04, *Cipolla v Fazari* [2006] ECR I-11421 (a Member State may violate its EU obligations 'where a Member State requires or encourages the adoption of agreements; contrary to Article [101] or reinforces their effects, or where it divests its own rules of the character of legislation by delegating to private economic operators responsibility for taking decisions affecting the economic sphere', para. 47). But contrast Case C-466/05, *Criminal Proceedings against Doulamis* [1998] ECR I-1377, paras. 19–22 (legislation prohibiting dental care providers from advertising does not infringe EU law where there is no evidence that it encourages, reinforces, or codifies concerted practices or decisions by undertakings or delegates responsibility to private operators). A national authority is duty-bound to disapply national legislation which violates EU law, see Case C-198/01, *Consorzio Industrie Fiammiferi (CIF) v Autorità Garante della Concorrenza e del Mercato* [2003] ECR I-8055 discussed in Chap. 13.

[381] See Cases C-94 and 202/04, ibid but see n. 379.

from engaging in autonomous conduct which prevents, restricts or distorts competition (Joined Cases C-359/95 P and C-379/95 P *Commission and France v Ladbroke Racing* . . ., paragraph 33; . . . in Case C-198/01 *Consorzia Industrie Fiammiferi*, paragraphs 52 to 55, and Case C-207/01 *Altair Chimica*, paragraphs 30, 35 and 36; Case T-111/96 *ITT Promédia v Commission* . . ., paragraph 96; *Irish Sugar* . . ., paragraph 130; Case T-513/93 *Consiglio Nazionale degli Spedizionieri Doganali v Commission* . . ., paragraphs 58 and 59; and Case T-154/98 *Asia Motor France and Others v Commission* . . ., paragraphs 78 to 91). Consequently, if a national law merely allows, encourages or makes it easier for undertakings to engage in autonomous anti-competitive conduct, those undertakings remain subject to the Treaty competition rules (see *inter alia* Joined Cases 89/85, 104/85, 114/85, 116/85, 117/85 and 125/85 to 129/85 *Ahlström v Commission* . . ., paragraph 20, and *Consorzia Industrie Fiammiferi*, cited above, paragraph 56).

Agreements between undertakings may therefore be caught even if they are encouraged or approved by national law or entered into after consultation with the national authorities.[382] Indeed, in both *Competition Authority v Beef Industry Development Society Ltd (BIDS)*[383] and *Coop de France bétail et viande v Commission*[384] undertakings were found to have violated Article 101 even though national governments had some knowledge of, or involvement with, the relevant agreements concluded.[385]

G. COMMISSION NOTICES

The Commission has issued a number of Notices/Guidelines which provide useful guidance on the interpretation of Article 101.[386] Although they are not rules of law which the Commission (or a court) is always bound to observe, they nevertheless form rules of practice from which the Commission itself may not depart without giving reasons that are compatible with the principle of equal treatment.[387] The following are of particular significance:[388]

- Commission Notice concerning its assessment of certain subcontracting agreements;[389]
- Guidelines on the application of Article 101 to Vertical Restraints;[390]
- Guidelines on the application of Article 101 to horizontal cooperation agreements;[391]
- Guidelines on the application of Article 101 to technology transfer agreements;[392]
- Commission Notice on restrictions directly related and necessary to the concentration;[393]

---

[382] See further Chap. 1.

[383] Case C-209/07, [2008] ECR I-8637.

[384] Cases C-101 and 110/07 P, [2008] ECR I-10193.

[385] Indeed, governments, or their agencies, may put forward or encourage firms to conclude voluntary agreements to achieve important health, environmental, or other policy objectives, or be sympathetic to, and encourage, arrangements put together by entities operating in an industry in crisis. Such action may undermine compliance with competition law by sending mixed signals to businesses as to what is permitted and what is prohibited. Competition agencies thus increasingly engage in advocacy with government departments providing advice on the effects of, and alternatives to, restrictions of competition in any aspect of the law or a proposed change in the law.

[386] These are discussed further in subsequent chapters, especially Chaps. 4 and 9–12.

[387] See Chap. 2, Section 5.

[388] See also, e.g., Notice on the application of the competition rules to the postal sector [1998] OJ C39/2.

[389] [1979] OJ C1/2, see Chap. 11.

[390] [2010] OJ C130/10.

[391] [2011] OJ C11/01.

[392] [2014] OJ C 89/03, see Chap. 12.

[393] [2005] OJ C 56/24. Although this Notice applies to merger cases, it provides guidance on the question of when contractual restraints fall outside Art. 101(1) on the grounds that they are 'ancillary' to a pro-competitive merger or agreement, see Chaps. 4 and 15.

- Commission Notice on agreements which do not appreciably restrict competition under Article 101(1) of the Treaty on the Functioning of the European Union (De Minimis Notice);[394]
- Guidelines on the application of Article 81(3) of the Treaty [now Article 101(3)].[395]

H. EXTRATERRITORIALITY

The question of when and in what circumstances the competition rules may be applied to the acts (which appreciably effect trade between Member States) of overseas undertakings (which are not established in the EU) is controversial and politically sensitive and is explored in Chapter 16.

6. ARTICLE 101(2)

It has been seen that despite the clear wording of Article 101(2), the nullity provided for in that provision applies only to individual *clauses* in the agreement affected by the Article 101(1) prohibition. In *Société Technique Minière v Maschinenbau Ulm GmbH*,[396] the CJ held that the agreement as a whole is void only where those clauses are not severable from the remaining terms of the agreement;[397] the question of severability is matter of national, not EU, law.[398] Each national court will, therefore, have to apply its own national rules on severance to determine the impact of Article 101(2) on the arrangements before it.[399]

The nullity affected by Article 101(2) is automatic and is not dependent upon any prior decision to that effect.[400] The English Court of Appeal has taken the view, however, that the nullity imposed by Article 101(2) is not absolute. Rather, it has only the same temporaneous or transient effect as the prohibition in Article 101(1) (an agreement will cease to be void if the agreement itself ceases to restrict competition or to affect trade within the meaning of Article 101(1)).[401]

7. EXCLUSIONS

In the UK, the Competition Act 1998 (CA 1998) provides that the Chapter I prohibition (modelled on Article 101(1)) does not apply to agreements 'excluded' by, or as a result of, other provisions of the Act.[402] Thus transactions that constitute mergers under the Enterprise Act 2002 merger regime or concentrations with an EU dimension under the EU Merger Regulation are excluded as are, for example: agreements subject to competition scrutiny under special enactments; agreements required to comply with planning obligations or a legal requirement; certain agreements made by an undertaking entrusted with the operation of services of general economic interest or of a revenue-producing monopoly; and certain agreements relating to agricultural products.[403]

---

[394] [2014] OJ C 291/01.

[395] [2004] OJ C101/97, discussed in Chap. 4.

[396] Case 56/65, [1966] ECR 234, 250.

[397] It thus interpreted Art. 101(2) with reference only to its purpose in EU law and to ensure compliance with the Treaty.

[398] See also Case 319/82, *Société de Vente de Ciments et Bétons de l'Est v Kerpen & Kerpen GmbH & Co KG* [1983] ECR 4173, para. 11. See Chap. 14.

[399] See further, Chap. 14 and, e.g., C. Cauffman, 'The Impact of Voidness for Infringements of Article 101 TFEU on Related Contracts' (2012) 8 *European Competition Journal* 95.

[400] See Reg. 1/2003, Art. 1.

[401] *Passmore v Morland plc* [1999] 3 All ER 1005, see further Chap. 14.

[402] See especially Competition Act 1998, s. 50 of and Schs. 1–4 to the Act.

[403] Ibid., Schs. 2 and 3.

Although Article 101 does not itself refer to any express exclusions, in practice a number of agreements are excluded from its scope in a similar way. For example, the scheme of the EU Merger Regulation is such that, with certain limited exceptions, merger transactions that constitute a 'concentration' are assessed either under any applicable national competition legislation, or, where the transaction has an EU dimension, under the provisions of the Merger Regulation itself. The idea is that concentrations, which include certain joint venture agreements, should not generally be appraised under Article 101.[404] In addition, derogations apply in relation to certain agricultural agreements[405] and Article 346(1)(b) TFEU provides that nothing in the Treaty shall preclude the application by Member States of measures 'it considers necessary for the protection of the essential interests of its security which are connected with the production of or trade in arms, munitions, and war material'. Further, it has been mentioned that Article 106(2) TFEU provides that the competition rules do not apply to some activities of public bodies or bodies entrusted with public services. It has also been seen that in interpreting the elements of Article 101(1), the CJ has excluded from its ambit agreements belonging to the realm of social policy, agreements concluded by firms carrying out tasks of a public or social nature, agreements between entities which form part of the same undertaking or economic unit, agreements required by national legislation, and matters which are of a purely sporting interest and, as such, have nothing to do with economic activity.

8. CONCLUSIONS

Agreements that infringe Article 101(1) and which do not meet the conditions of Article 101(3) are prohibited. Severe consequences potentially flow for those that violate Article 101. It is therefore of utmost importance for a firm to know whether any agreement it concludes may violate Article 101(1).

The discussion in this chapter has established that the following agreements (or conduct) will fall outside Article 101(1) and escape the prohibition altogether:

1. Agreements which are not concluded by two or more entities engaged in economic activity;
2. Agreements between entities which are part of the same economic unit, for example certain parent and subsidiary or principal and agent relationships;
3. Collective agreements between employers and workers;
4. Unilateral conduct not explicitly or tacitly accepted by another or by another party to a contract;
5. Agreements which constitute a 'concentration' within the meaning of the Merger Regulation;
6. Agreements which relate to the production of, or trade in, certain agricultural products;
7. Agreements which do not appreciably affect trade between Member States (although such agreements may be subject to national competition law);
8. Agreements which are necessary for the performance of a task of general economic interest entrusted to them by a Member State (see Article 106(2));
9. Agreements required by national law; and
10. Agreements which are truly extraterritorial.

In Chapter 4 it is seen that agreements between undertakings which appreciably affect trade also fall outside Article 101(1) if they do not appreciably restrict competition or are excepted, or exempted, from the prohibition under Article 101(3).

---

[404] For discussion of the complicated question of which transactions fall to be assessed within the procedure of the Merger Reg., Council Reg. 139/2004 [2004] OJ L24/1, and not under Art. 101, see Chaps. 10 and 15.

[405] See Reg. 1184/2006 [2006] OJ L214/7 and Reg. 1308/2013 [2013] OJ L347/671 and J. Blockx and J. Vandenberghe, 'Balancing Commercial Relations Along the Food Supply Chain: The Agricultural Exemption from EU Competition Law after Regulation 1308/2013' (2014) 10 *European Competition Journal* 387.

9. FURTHER READING

A. BOOKS

HARDING, C., and JOSHUA, J., *Regulating Cartels in Europe* (2nd edn, Oxford University Press, 2010)

ODUDU, O., *The Boundaries of EC Competition Law: The Scope of Article 81* (Oxford University Press, 2006)

B. ARTICLES

ALBORS-LLORENS, A., 'Horizontal Agreements and Concerted Practices in EC Competition Law: Unlawful and Legitimate Contacts between Competitors' (2006) 51 *Ant Bull* 837

BAILEY, D., 'Single, Overall Agreement in EU Competition Law' (2010) 47 *CMLRev* 473

CAUFFMAN, C., 'The Impact of Voidness for Infringements of Article 101 TFEU on Related Contracts' (2012) 8 *European Competition Journal* 95

JONES, A., 'The Boundaries of an Undertaking in EU Competition Law' (2012) 8 *European Competition Journal* 301

JOSHUA, J., 'Single Continuous Infringement of Article 81 EC: Has the Commission Stretched the Concept Beyond the Limit of its Logic?' (2009) 5 *European Competition Journal* 451

JOSHUA, J., BOTTEMAN, Y., and ATLEE, L., '"You Can't Beat the Percentage"—The Parental Liability Presumption in EU Cartel Enforcement' in *Global Competition Review—The European Antitrust Review 2012*, 3

THOMAS, S., 'Guilty of a Fault that One has not Committed. The Limits of the Group-based Sanction Policy Carried out by the Commission and the European Courts in EU-Antitrust Law' (2012) 3 *JECLAP* 11

WESSELY, T., 'Polyproplyene Appeal Cases' (2001) 38 *CMLRev* 739

WILS, W., 'The Undertaking as Subject of EC Competition Law and the Imputation of Infringements to Natural or Legal Persons' (2000) 25 *ELRev* 99

4

THE RELATIONSHIP BETWEEN ARTICLE 101(1) AND ARTICLE 101(3) TFEU

1. CENTRAL ISSUES

1. It is seen in Chapter 3 that, essentially, the scheme of Article 101 is that: Article 101(1) prohibits agreements between undertakings which appreciably affect trade between Member States and which have as their object or effect an appreciable restriction of competition; whilst Article 101(3) provides that the prohibition may be declared inapplicable to any agreement which satisfies its four conditions.

2. In this chapter the relationship between Article 101(1) and Article 101(3) is explored. Broadly, it focuses on the substantive question of *which* agreements contravene the objectives of Article 101 and so should be prohibited; that is, which agreements have as their object or effect the appreciable restriction of competition and, if so, when do such agreements satisfy the conditions of Article 101(3).

3. In conducting substantive assessment issues of primary importance include: (a) how is analysis to be divided between Article 101(1) and Article 101(3); and (b) how is it determined whether an agreement restricts competition by object (where a restriction of competition is assumed without a need to establish a restrictive effect)? These two matters have a significant impact on the burden of proof. The burden of proving a breach of Article 101(1) rests on the person alleging the same, whilst the burden of establishing that the Article 101(3) criteria are satisfied rests on those undertakings claiming its benefit.

4. The Commission states that it takes an economic approach to Article 101 based on a consumer welfare objective; Article 101(1) is about identifying the anti-competitive object or effect of an agreement (agreements which adversely affect competition by restricting inter-brand or intra-brand competition) whilst Article 101(3) allows the balancing of offsetting efficiencies against these restrictive effects. However, not all of the case law of the EU Courts is easy to reconcile with this approach. Rather, it indicates that, in certain circumstances at least, broader objectives may be relevant under both Article 101(1) and Article 101(3).

2. INTRODUCTION AND BACKGROUND

A. ARTICLE 101(1) AND ARTICLE 101(3)

This chapter examines the question of which agreements, etc. falling within the scope of Article 101 (which appreciably affect trade between Member States), contravene the objectives of Article 101 and are prohibited by it. Substantive analysis under Article 101 is conducted in two parts. First, an agreement has to be scrutinised to determine whether it infringes Article 101(1), i.e. whether it appreciably restricts[1] competition (by object or effect). If it does not, that is the end of the story. If it does, it must, secondly, be determined whether or not the agreement meets the criteria set out in Article 101(3). Article 101(1) may be declared inapplicable to any agreement which provides specified benefits (broadly, it improves the production or distribution of goods or services or promotes technical or economic progress), allows consumers a fair share of the benefit, does not contain any indispensable restrictions, and does not eliminate competition in a substantial part of the products in question.

This section starts by examining possible ways of reconciling the two parts of Article 101 and how they have been balanced over time. Section 3 then examines more closely how agreements are analysed under Article 101(1), whilst Section 4 considers the analysis required under Article 101(3). The chapter concludes that the jurisprudence in this sphere is not all easy to reconcile and some rationalisation of the case law is required.

B. POSSIBLE WAYS OF RECONCILING ARTICLE 101(1) AND ARTICLE 101(3)

The bifurcated structure of Article 101 has, to some extent, complicated its interpretation and led to uncertainty as to the correct role for, and analysis required by, each part. Key questions arising are what objectives influence the interpretation of Article 101 and what factors are taken into account at each stage, i.e.: (a) what constitutes a restriction of competition for the purposes of Article 101(1); and (b) in what circumstances should such restrictions be 'trumped' by Article 101(3) benefits? Finding the right balance between the application of Article 101(1) and Article 101(3) has proved to be extremely difficult.

The wording of Article 101(1) and Article 101(3) itself does not define their relationship. A number of different approaches may be adopted, or advocated, as to how they should be reconciled. For example:

(1) One way of reconciling the two parts is to adopt a literal or broad interpretation of Article 101(1), bringing many agreements within its net, and conducting a more detailed analysis of the anti-competitive, pro-competitive, and other aspects of the agreement within the more structured framework of Article 101(3). In this scenario the requirement that the agreement restricts competition serves a jurisdictional function (bringing within its ambit all potentially problematic agreements). The rigorous substantive assessment is then completed under Article 101(3).

(2) A second approach is to conduct a more detailed analysis when determining whether an agreement restricts competition (Article 101(1)) and to thereby confine the role of Article 101(3). An assessment of an assumed (in object cases), actual, or likely (in effect cases) adverse impact on consumer welfare is made when determining whether it restricts competition. Article 101(3) then plays a more limited role, excepting agreements assumed to restrict competition *and*, perhaps, allowing other demonstrable public policy benefits (such as benefits to environment, health, industry, culture, or employment) to be balanced against identified anti-competitive effects.

(3) A third approach is to divide the substantive appraisal more evenly between the two parts. There are a number of ways in which this division could be effected, but one method could be to use Article 101(1) to identify presumed, actual, or likely anti-competitive effects and Article 101(3) to enable the parties to establish that the agreement achieves offsetting efficiencies or pro-competitive effects (the analysis as a whole would thus determine whether the agreement adversely impacts on consumer welfare). For example, Article 101(1) could become concerned with allocative efficiency (and, essentially, deadweight loss resulting from contrived restrictions of output) whilst Article 101(3) could become a productive and dynamic efficiency inquiry, available to allow the parties

---

[1] The words 'prevention, restriction, or distortion' are intended to cover any interference with competition, and are synonymous, so the term 'restriction' will generally be used as shorthand in this text to cover all three.

to demonstrate that the restraints in the agreement are necessary to achieve efficiencies which will be passed on to consumers and compensate them for the resulting allocative inefficiencies.[2] An important issue would be whether public policy factors should also be relevant to the assessment and, if so, whether they are relevant at the Article 101(1) or Article 101(3) stage of the analysis (or both).

The discussion in Sections C–F establishes that the Commission initially adopted an approach close to (1) but that many commentators urged it to take an approach closer to (2) (which it was argued would be in line with the jurisprudence of the EU Courts). Further, that although neither the EU Courts' nor the Commission's current approach equates *exactly* to any of those outlined the modern approach most closely resembles (3).

C. THE INTERPRETATION OF 'OBJECT OR EFFECT IS THE PREVENTION, RESTRICTION, OR DISTORTION OF COMPETITION'—THE EARLY APPROACH

Following the setting up of the notification and exemption system by Regulation 17, the Commission was able to play an extremely influential role in the interpretation of Article 101. One of the most strident criticisms made of the Commission's application of the competition rules until the 1990s was its failure to adopt a sufficiently realistic economic interpretation of Article 101(1), in particular, when determining whether or not an agreement restricts competition. In short, it was complained that the Commission found many agreements were caught within the widely cast net of Article 101(1) but subsequently completed its analysis, by authorising (or exempting) many agreements, using Article 101(3)[3] (the analysis thus resembled approach (1) set out in Section 2.B).

This approach seems to have been motivated both by ideology and practicalities. Arguably, the Commission utilised Article 101, in accordance with the ordoliberal philosophy, to limit restrictions on conduct (restraints on economic freedom), to promote rivalry between undertakings operating on a market,[4] as well as to prevent interferences with the single market project.[5] Further, a broad jurisdictional interpretation of Article 101(1) cemented the Commission's central role in the moulding and shaping of EU competition policy since it had the exclusive right to apply Article 101(3) through the system of 'notification and exemption'.[6]

This approach raised both conceptual and practical difficulties. First, businesses found it hard to understand why their agreement was characterised as restrictive of competition, simply because it imposed restrictions on the conduct of one of the parties. Secondly, until 1 May 2004 when Regulation 1/2003 came into force, negative procedural consequences resulted from this approach. Parties fearful that their agreement might infringe Article 101(1) had either to notify their agreement to the Commission (which had the exclusive right to grant individual exemptions but had limited resources to grant such exemptions in practice)[7] or draft it to fall within a block exemption

---

[2] See, e.g., O. Odudu, *The Boundaries of EC Competition Law: The Scope of Article 81* (Oxford University Press, 2006), Chaps. 5–7.

[3] See, e.g., COMP/23.013, *Goodyear Italiana-Euram* [1975] OJ L38/10, COMP/171, 856, 172, 117, 28.173, *Campari* [1978] OJ L70/69, para. 7, part IIA, COMP/27.442, *Vacuum Interrupters* [1977] OJ L48/32, COMP/27.093, *De Laval-Stork* [1977] OJ L215/11, para. 6, and COMP/28.796, *Beecham/Parke, Davis* [1979] OJ L70/11.

[4] See J. Faull and A. Nikpay (eds.), *The EU Law of Competition* (3rd edn, Oxford University Press, 2014), 3.160–3.166.

[5] See Chap. 1 and, e.g., Faull and Nikpay, ibid.

[6] See Reg. 17 [1959–1962] OJ Spec. Ed. 87, Arts. 9(1) and 4. This enabled it to influence the form and way in which agreements were operated through its application of Art. 101(3). In contrast, had it adopted a narrower, more effects-based approach to Art. 101(1), greater enforcement of agreements would have been delegated to the national level and the uniform interpretation of the competition rules might have been compromised.

[7] Reg. 17 [1959–1962] OJ Spec. Ed. 87, Art. 9(1). Notification was a time- and cost-consuming exercise and the Commission could not grant more than a few individual exemptions each year (see, e.g., Case T-67/01, *JCB Service v Commission* [2004] ECR II-49 (*aff'd* Case C-167/04, [2006] ECR I-8935) concerning an agreement notified to the Commission in 1973 but not dealt with until 2000.

(discussed in Section 4.E below). The Commission's monopoly over Article 101(3) effectively also made it impossible for national courts and National Competition Authorities (NCAs) to participate fully in the enforcement process.

The Commission was subjected to significant criticism for this approach[8] and it was argued that a more sophisticated approach to Article 101(1) was required because:

- the legal rules followed by the Commission under Article 101(1) were overbroad (wrongly favouring the freedom of individual traders over consumer welfare) and did not provide sufficiently transparent, precise, and operable criteria to determine which agreements restricted competition and for businesses to apply;[9]

- the approach adopted led to the condemnation under Article 101(1) of innocuous agreements which did not in fact restrict competition through anti-competitive effects.[10] Because of the unlikelihood of gaining an exemption, pro-competitive agreements were being deterred and Type 1 errors may have occurred;

- if a consideration of anti- and pro-competitive effects was conducted under Article 101(1), many of the procedural problems experienced in consequence of the notification and exemption system would fall away; and critically

- the advocated approach was necessitated by the case law of the EU Courts which had not interpreted the concept of a restriction of competition under Article 101(1) so broadly as the Commission. Although it has been clear since the CJ's judgment in *Établissements Consten SàRL and Grundig-Verkaufs-GmbH v Commission*[11] that there is no need to take account of the effects of an agreement if its *object* is to restrict competition, it was maintained that in other, 'effect', cases, a series of judgments commencing with *Société Technique Minière v Maschinenbau Ulm GmbH (STM)*[12] (and including cases such as *Nungesser v Commission*,[13] *Erauw-Jacquéry Sprl v La Hesbignonne Société Coopérative*,[14] *Remia BV and NV Verenigde Bedrijven Nutricia v Commission*,[15] *Pronuptia de Paris GmbH v Pronuptia de Paris Irmgard Schillgallis*,[16] *Brasserie de Haecht (No. 1)*,[17] *Gøttrup-Klim Grovvareforeninger and Others v Dansk Landbrugs Grovvareselskab AmbA*,[18] and *Delimitis v Henninger Bräu*)[19] required the drawing up of a competition balance sheet and a weighing of anti- and pro-competitive effects under Article 101(1).[20]

---

[8] See, e.g., R. Joliet, *The Rule of Reason in Antitrust Law* (Nijhoff, 1967); I. Forrester and C. Norall, 'The Laïcization of Community Law: Self-help and the Rule of Reason: How Competition is and could be Applied' (1984) 21 *CMLRev* 11; V. Korah, 'EEC Competition Policy—Legal Form or Economic Efficiency?' (1986) 39 *CLP* 85; B. E. Hawk, 'System Failure: Vertical Restraints and EC Competition Law' (1995) 32 *CMLRev* 973; J. S. Venit, '*Pronuptia*: Ancillary Restraints or Unholy Alliances' (1986) 11 *ELRev* 213; R. Whish and B. Sufrin, 'Article 85 and the Rule of Reason' (1987) 7 *YEL* 1. See also, A. Jones, 'Analysis of Agreements under US and EC Antitrust Law—Convergence or Divergence?' (2006) 51 *Ant Bull* 691.

[9] See, e.g., Hawk, ibid.

[10] Since many of the agreements prohibited created or increased competition they should not have required authorisation under Art. 101(3), see, e.g., Roemer AG in his Opinion in Cases 56 and 58/64, *Établissements Consten S.à.R.L and Grundig-Verkaufs-GmbH v Commission* [1966] ECR 299.

[11] Ibid.

[12] Case 56/65, [1966] ECR 235.

[13] Case 258/78, [1982] ECR 2015.

[14] Case 27/87, [1988] ECR 1919.

[15] Case 42/84, [1985] ECR 2545.

[16] Case 161/84, [1986] ECR 353.

[17] Case 23/67, [1967] ECR 407.

[18] Case C-250/92, [1994] ECR I-5641.

[19] Case C-234/89, [1991] ECR I-935.

[20] See Section 3.

D. SECTION 1 OF THE SHERMAN ACT

During the debate, reference was frequently made to the need for greater economic analysis, similar perhaps to 'rule of reason' analysis conducted in the US. Section 1 of the Sherman Act 1890 (the US equivalent of Article 101) provides that '[e]very contract, combination in the form of a trust or otherwise, or conspiracy, in restraint of trade or commerce among the several States, or with foreign nations, is declared to be illegal . . .' but contains no legal exception to the prohibition.

Since the main objective of a contract is to restrain the conduct of the parties to it, the US Supreme Court soon recognised that a literal interpretation of the section might result in many (or all) agreements being held to be illegal.[21] 'Every agreement concerning trade, every regulation of trade, restrains. To bind, to restrain, is of their very essence.'[22] The US courts thus construed the section to mean that contracts must not restrain trade unreasonably.[23] Eventually, and following the emergence of a consensus that the paramount goal of the Sherman Act is consumer welfare and efficiency, this has become an inquiry into the competitive significance of the restraint.[24] In determining whether or not an agreement does restrain competition unreasonably the courts traditionally adopted two separate approaches—per se and rule of reason analysis.[25]

Some agreements, such as 'cartel' arrangements among competitors to fix price, restrict output, share markets, or rig bids,[26] are automatically held to restrain competition unreasonably; they are considered to be so likely to be anti-competitive that the court will not waste time or resources requiring that anti-competitive effects must be proved and/or hearing justifications for the agreement, they are illegal per se. This bright-line rule focuses *solely* on whether the conduct took place, not on its effect.

There are certain agreements or practices which because of their pernicious effect on competition and lack of any redeeming virtue are conclusively presumed to be unreasonable and therefore illegal without elaborate inquiries as to the precise harm they have caused or the business excuse for their use.[27]

By the 1960s a relatively large number of restraints had been categorised as illegal per se. For the sake of business certainty and litigation efficiency the courts were prepared to tolerate the invalidation of some agreements that might not have been proved to be unreasonable following a fuller analysis.[28] Towards the end of the 1970s, however, the Supreme Court began, as it embraced a consumer welfare objective, to retreat from this position. Indeed, since 1977 the presumptive and prevailing standard has been the 'rule of reason'.[29] Under this analysis, agreements are not assumed to restrain trade unreasonably but are assessed in their legal and economic context to determine:

whether the restraint imposed is such as merely regulates and perhaps thereby promotes competition or whether it is such as may suppress or even destroy competition. To determine that question the court must ordinarily consider the facts peculiar to the business to which the restraint is applied; its condition before and after the restraint was imposed; the nature of the restraint and its effect, actual or probable.[30]

---

[21] But see the approach adopted in *United States v Trans-Missouri Freight Ass'n*, 166 US 290 (1897).

[22] *Chicago Board of Trade v United States*, 246 US 231, 238 (1918), per Brandeis J.

[23] *Standard Oil Co of New Jersey v United States*, 221 US 1 (1911); *United States v American Tobacco Co*, 221 US 106 (1911).

[24] *National Society of Professional Engineers v United States*, 435 US 679 (1978).

[25] As the law has developed, however, the boundary between the two categories has become increasingly blurred so that 'there is often no bright line separating per se from Rule of Reason analysis', *NCAA v Board of Regents of Univ of Okla*, 468 US 85, 104 (1984). This has led some courts to conclude that there has been a move, away from fixed categories, to a continuum, *Polygram Holding, Inc v Federal Trade Commission*, 416 F.3d 29, 35 (DC Cir. 2005) and Jones, n. 8.

[26] *United States v Socony-Vaccuum Oil Co*, 310 US 150 (1940).

[27] *Northern Pac R Co v United States*, 356 US 1, 5 (1958).

[28] *Arizona v Maricopa County Medical Society*, 457 US 332, 344 (1982).

[29] *Continental TV, Inc v GTE Slyvania Inc*, 433 US 36 (1977).

[30] *Chicago Board of Trade v United States*, 246 US 231, 238 (1918), per Brandeis J.

In short, the anti- and pro-competitive aspects of the agreement are weighed before an agreement is condemned as illegal.[31]

Not all commentators agreed that EU case law supported an approach identical or similar to the US rule of reason under Article 101(1).[32] Nonetheless, the core message was simple—a more economic approach in tune with the objectives underlying Article 101 was required, especially under Article 101(1).

E. MODERNISATION

(i) Substantive Analysis and Procedural Steps

Eventually, the Commission recognised that the status quo was no longer tenable: the notification system was failing and some change was obligatory. Not only did it set about reformulating its interpretation of Article 101, reviewing and rethinking its analysis over a number of years,[33] but it resolved the procedural problems arising by proposing that its monopoly over Article 101(3) should be revoked. On 1 May 2004, Council Regulation 1/2003 abolished the Commission's exclusive right to rule on the compatibility of an agreement with Article 101(3), rendering Article 101(3) directly applicable as a legal exception to Article 101(1)[34] by the Commission, the NCAs, and the national courts.[35]

The Commission's current framework for analysis of agreements is set out in its Guidelines on the application of Article 81(3) [now Article 101(3)] of the Treaty (the Article 101(3) Guidelines),[36] which is elucidated further in specific Guidelines dealing with horizontal cooperation, vertical agreements, and technology transfer agreements, respectively.[37] These Guidelines state that consumer welfare should be the benchmark against which agreements are tested under Article 101 and that substantive appraisal should be conducted at both the Article 101(1) and 101(3) stages:

- Article 101(1) is about identifying agreements with a restrictive object or effect; whilst

- Article 101(3) is about identifying pro-competitive effects and balancing those against the anti-competitive effects identified under Article 101(1).

The Commission does not therefore believe that a 'rule of reason' style analysis, balancing anti- and pro-competitive should be conducted at the Article 101(1) stage. Rather, its view is that Article 101(1) is simply about identifying restrictions on inter- or intra-brand competition and it is Article 101(3), not Article 101(1), which provides the appropriate forum for weighing the

---

[31] The rule of reason analysis has proved hard to apply in practice and there is limited guidance from the Supreme Court on this issue. The circuit courts have adopted their own methods and have developed approaches, tailoring the extent of the inquiry to the suspect conduct in each case, see, e.g., *Polygram Holding, Inc v FTC*, 416 F.3d 29, 33–34 (DC Cir. 2005).

[32] See, e.g., Whish and Sufrin, n. 8.

[33] It reviewed and overhauled the working of Art. 101 between 1996 and 2004. See further Chaps. 9–12.

[34] Reg. 1/2003, Art. 1 provides that agreements which are caught by Art. 101(1) and which do not satisfy the conditions of Art. 101(3) are prohibited, no prior decision to that effect being required. Further that agreements which are caught by Art. 101(1), but which satisfy the conditions of Art. 101(3), are not prohibited, no prior decision to that effect being required.

[35] Reg. 1/2003, Arts. 7–10, 5, and 3. The Commission is seeking to encourage greater 'private' enforcement of EU competition law, see Chap. 14.

[36] See Guidelines on the application of Article 81(3) [now Article 101(3)] of the Treaty (the Article 101(3) Guidelines) [2004] OJ C101/97.

[37] See Commission Guidelines on the applicability of Article 101 of the Treaty on the Functioning of the European Union to horizontal co-operation agreements [2011] OJ C11/1 (Horizontal Cooperation Guidelines), Guidelines on Vertical Restraints [2010] OJ C130/1, Guidelines on the application of Article 101 of the Treaty on the Functioning of the European Union to technology transfer agreements [2014] OJ C89/3 and Chaps. 9–12.

restrictive effects identified at this stage against the economic benefits and efficiencies created by the agreement.[38] Otherwise, Article 101(3) would be rendered virtually redundant.

Although it will be seen that the EU cases on this issue are difficult to reconcile, some judgments of the GC, including *Métropole Télévision (M6) v Commission*,[39] support the view of the Commission that Article 101(3) provides the main forum for weighing anti- and pro-competitive aspects of an agreement.

M6 concerned an appeal from a Commission decision holding that the creation of the joint venture, Télévision par Satellite (TPS), did not infringe Article 101(1) but that certain clauses in the notified agreements infringed Article 101(1) and could be exempted under Article 101(3) *only* for a period of three years. Amongst other things, the applicants argued that the Commission had been wrong to exempt the clauses. Rather, the reasoning adopted by the Commission indicated that these clauses *favoured* competition and did not restrict it. Had the Commission, therefore, correctly applied Article 101(1) using the rule of reason, weighing the pro- and anti-competitive effects of the agreement, the Commission should have found that the agreement did not restrict competition.[40]

The GC did not accept this argument, observing that, contrary to the applicants' assertions, the existence of such a rule had not been confirmed by the EU Courts. Echoing the view of the Commission, that such an interpretation would be difficult to reconcile with the rules prescribed by Article 101, it stated that Article 101(3) provided the correct forum for weighing the pro- and anti-competitive aspects of the agreement. The Court recognised that some EU cases, such as STM,[41] favoured a 'more flexible' interpretation of the Article 101(1) prohibition,[42] but held that they did not establish the existence of a rule of reason. Rather, such a rule had not been confirmed by the Courts and the cases simply formed part of a broader trend in the case law according to which it is not necessary to hold, wholly abstractly, that any agreement restricting the freedom of action of one or more of the parties is necessarily caught by Article 101(1).[43]

Case T-112/99, *Métropole Télévision (M6) v Commission* [2001] ECR II-2459

General Court

72. According to the applicants, as a consequence of the existence of a rule of reason in [EU] competition law, when Article [101(1)] is applied it is necessary to weigh the pro and anti-competitive effects of an agreement in order to determine whether it is caught by the prohibition laid down in that article. It should, however, be observed, first of all, that contrary to the applicants' assertions the existence

---

[38] See White Paper on the Modernisation of the Rules Implementing Articles 85 and 86 of the EC Treaty [now Articles 101 and 102 TFEU] [1999] OJ C132/1, paras. 56–57. See also G. Monti, 'Article 81 EC and Public Policy' (2002) 39(5) CMLRev 1057, 1061.

[39] Case T-112/99, *Métropole Télévision SA (M6) v Commission* [2001] ECR II-2459. See also Case T-65/98, *Van den Bergh Foods* [2003] ECR II-4653, aff'd Case C-552/03 P, *Unilever Bestfoods v Commission* [2006] ECR I-9091, Case T-328/03, *O2 (Germany) GmbH & Co OHG v Commission* [2006] ECR II-1231.

[40] Case T-112/99, M6 [2001] ECR II-2459, para. 69.

[41] Case 56/65, [1966] ECR 235, 249. See also Case 258/78, *Nungesser and Eisele v Commission* [1982] ECR 2015; Case 161/84, *Pronuptia de Paris GmbH v Pronuptia de Paris Irmgard Schillgallis* [1986] ECR 353; Cases T-374, 375, 384, and 388/94, *European Night Services v Commission* [1998] ECR II-3141; and Case C-250/92, *Gøttrup-Klim Grovvareforening and Others v Dansk Landbrugs Grovvareselskab AmbA* [1994] ECR I-5641, paras. 31–35.

[42] Case T-112/99, M6 [2001] ECR II-2459, para. 75.

[43] For the argument (rejected) that Art. 101(1) could not apply as the agreement did *not* restrain the freedom of action of one of the parties to the agreement, see Case T-99/04, *AC-Treuhand AG v Commission* [2008] ECR II-1501, paras. 124–128 ('it is not therefore to be ruled out that an undertaking may participate in the implementation of such a restriction even if it does not restrict its own freedom of action on the market on which it is primarily active', para. 127).

of such a rule has not, as such, been confirmed by the [EU] courts. Quite to the contrary, in various judgments the Court of Justice and the [GC] have been at pains to indicate that the existence of a rule of reason in [EU] competition law is doubtful (see Case C-235/92 P *Montecatini v Commission* . . . paragraph 133 (. . . even if the rule of reason did have a place in the context of Article [101(1)]of the Treaty), and Case T-14/89 *Montedipe v Commission* . . . paragraph 265, and in Case T-148/89 *Tréfilunion v Commission* . . . paragraph 109).

73. Next, it must be observed that an interpretation of Article [101(1)], in the form suggested by the applicants, is difficult to reconcile with the rules prescribed by that provision.

74. Article [101] expressly provides, in its third paragraph, for the possibility of exempting agreements that restrict competition where they satisfy a number of conditions, in particular where they are indispensable to the attainment of certain objectives and do not afford undertakings the possibility of eliminating competition in respect of a substantial part of the products in question. It is only in the precise framework of that provision that the pro and anti-competitive aspects of a restriction may be weighed (see, to that effect, Case 161/84 *Pronuptia* . . . paragraph 24, and Case T-17/93 *Matra Hachette v Commission* . . . paragraph 48, and *European Night Services and Others v Commission* . . . paragraph 136). Article [101(3)] would lose much of its effectiveness if such an examination had to be carried out already under Article [101(1)].

75. It is true that in a number of judgments the Court of Justice and the [GC] have favoured a more flexible interpretation of the prohibition laid down in Article [101(1)] (see, in particular, *Société technique minière* and *Oude Luttikhuis and Others* . . . *Nungesser and Eisele v Commission* and *Coditel and Others* . . . *Pro nuptia* . . . and *European Night Services and Others v Commission* . . . as well as the judgment in Case C-250/92 *DLG* . . . paragraphs 31 to 35).

76. Those judgments cannot, however, be interpreted as establishing the existence of a rule of reason in [EU] competition law. They are, rather, part of a broader trend in the case-law according to which it is not necessary to hold, wholly abstractly and without drawing any distinction, that any agreement restricting the freedom of action of one or more of the parties is necessarily caught by the prohibition laid down in Article [101(1)]. In assessing the applicability of Article [101(1)] to an agreement, account should be taken of the actual conditions in which it functions, in particular the economic context in which the undertakings operate, the products or services covered by the agreement and the actual structure of the market concerned (see, in particular, *European Night Services and Others v Commission* . . . paragraph 136, *Oude Luttikhuis* . . . paragraph 10, and *VGB and Others v Commission* . . . paragraph 140, as well as the judgment in Case C-234/89 *Delimitis* . . . paragraph 31).

77. That interpretation, while observing the substantive scheme of Article [101] and, in particular, preserving the effectiveness of Article [101(3)], makes it possible to prevent the prohibition in Article [101(1)] from extending wholly abstractly and without distinction to all agreements whose effect is to restrict the freedom of action of one or more of the parties. It must, however, be emphasised that such an approach does not mean that it is necessary to weigh the pro and anti-competitive effects of an agreement when determining whether the prohibition laid down in Article [101(1)] applies.

In M6 the GC appears, therefore, to reject both the first two of the possible approaches set out in Section 2.B and to favour the third (one which divides the substantive appraisal between Article 101(1) and 101(3)).[44] It indicates that the Article 101 appraisal should be divided into five parts: (1) the Commission (or other person seeking to demonstrate the same) must establish that the agreement restricts competition (identify the anti-competitive aspects)—whether by object or effect; when this burden is discharged the parties (or the undertakings seeking the benefit of Article 101(3)) must establish that (2) the agreement achieves pro-competitive benefits (identified in Article 101(3));

---

[44] But see, e.g., Monti, n. 38.

(3) consumers attain a fair share of those benefits; (4) the agreement is indispensable to the attainment of the benefits; and (5) there is no possibility of an elimination of competition.[45]

This supposition leads to two further questions. Was the GC correct to interpret previous case law this way? If so, exactly how is the envisaged division in analysis made in practice: in particular, what constitutes a restriction of competition for the purpose of Article 101(1) and what 'pro-competitive' 'aspects of a restriction' can be weighed against them under Article 101(3)? In seeking to answer these questions the discussion in Sections 3 and 4 indicates that, unfortunately, the position does not seem to be quite as clear as the GC in M6 suggests.

(ii) Categories of Analysis: Clear Rules or More Complex Standards?

Even if it is correct that the goal of Article 101 is to identify agreements that harm consumer welfare and that the analysis should be divided between Article 101(1) and Article 101(3) in the way that the Commission suggests, it still leaves the conundrum of how to achieve that objective within the Article 101 framework. How can rules or standards to identify such conduct be constructed which will be both sufficiently:

(a) clear—so as to enable firms to comply with them and courts or other decision-makers to administer them; and

(b) accurate—identifying and prohibiting conduct which harms the objectives of the Article whilst permitting those that may promote competition?

Although at first sight it might appear necessary to ensure accuracy that actual or likely anti-competitive effects should be identified under Article 101(1) and balanced against any pro-competitive benefits in each individual case, such an approach is likely to impose too high a burden on firms (especially small ones), competition agencies (and other claimants), and courts, creating a risk both that pro-competitive agreements will be deterred and too little enforcement/condemnation of harmful agreements will occur. A trade-off thus needs to be made between more complex standards, requiring detailed factual and economic analysis, which are more difficult and costly to apply, and simpler bright-line rules, which may be less accurate but which are easier and less costly to apply (they require less sophisticated analysis and less emphasis on expert economic evidence) and which provide greater clarity and legal certainty (and a patent deterrent to the practice at issue). It may also be necessary to consider whether an approach which may sometimes condemn legitimate business practices (false positives or 'Type 1' errors) and so potentially chill pro-competitive conduct is a lesser or greater evil than one which may sometimes allow anti-competitive practices to escape antitrust prohibitions (false negatives or 'Type 2' errors).[46] In seeking to balance accuracy (based on widely accepted economic principles), administrability, consistency, objectivity, and transparency,[47] most competition law systems accept that some sorting of agreements into categories is required and so:

- apply rules against agreements which are very likely to cause anti-competitive effects and unlikely to have offsetting benefits (such agreements may be prohibited per se (as in the US) or *presumed* to be incompatible with the competition law rules);

- apply rules in favour of agreements which are very unlikely to cause anti-competitive effects—in some systems, such agreements may benefit from a safe harbour or a presumption of compatibility with the rules; and

---

[45] These steps have similarities to the four steps taken in US rule of reason analysis, see Jones, n. 8.

[46] See Chap. 1.

[47] See, e.g., OECD Policy Roundtables: Resale Price Maintenance (2008), available at <http://www.oecd.org/daf/competition/43835526.pdf>.

- conduct more detailed and complex analysis in relation to agreements whose effects are more ambiguous—which require closer individual scrutiny of anti-competitive and pro-competitive effects.

The question of how any such categories are to be drawn, how flexibly they are applied, and which agreements fall within each category is generally controversial. In the EU four main categories of antitrust analysis are used in the assessment of agreements (see further Fig. 4.1 below):

(a) agreements found to have as their object the restriction of competition are assumed to restrict competition appreciably. Although such agreements are, theoretically, justifiable under Article 101(3), in practice it often proves hard or impossible to do so. The Commission's view is that they are presumed *not* to satisfy the conditions of Article 101(3) (consequently, the safe harbour of a block exemption (see point (c)) will not apply);

(b) agreements between undertaking which have a weak position on the market fall outside the scope of Article 101(1) where they do not have a significant or appreciable effect on competition;

(c) agreements between undertakings which satisfy conditions set out in an EU block exemption are assumed to satisfy the conditions of Article 101(3) and to be compatible with Article 101. The block exemptions operate as a safe harbour for agreements which can only be withdrawn prospectively;

(d) other agreements are analysed individually to determine whether they have as their effect the restriction of competition and, if so, whether the agreement satisfies the four conditions of Article 101(3).

The question of which agreements fall within each of the categories, and so how broadly each category applies, is explored in the remainder of this chapter and subsequently in Chapter 9–12.

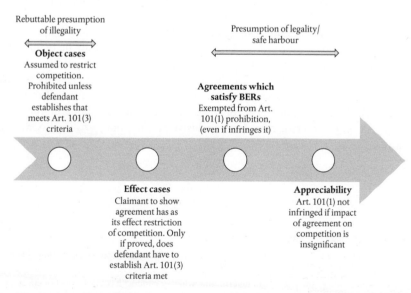

Figure 4.1 Categories of antitrust analysis under Article 101

3. ARTICLE 101(1), AGREEMENTS WHICH HAVE AS THEIR OBJECT OR EFFECT THE PREVENTION, RESTRICTION, OR DISTORTION OF COMPETITION

A. OBJECT OR EFFECT

In *STM*[48] the CJ clarified that the words 'object or effect' in Article 101(1) are not cumulative, but are alternative conditions.

Finally, for the agreement at issue to be caught by the prohibition contained in Article [101(1)] it must have as its 'object or effect the prevention, restriction or distortion of competition …'.

The fact that these are not cumulative but alternative requirements, indicated by the conjunction 'or', leads first to the need to consider the precise purpose of the agreement, in the economic context in which it is to be applied. This interference with competition referred to in Article [101(1)] must result from all or some of the clauses of the agreement itself. Where, however, an analysis of the said clauses does not reveal the effect on competition to be sufficiently deleterious, the consequences of the agreement should then be considered and for it to be caught by the prohibition it is then necessary to find that those factors are present which show that competition has in fact been prevented or restricted or distorted to an appreciable extent.[49]

An agreement, decision, or concerted practice[50] is thus caught if *either* its object *or* its effect is the restriction of competition.[51] Where it is shown that the 'precise purpose' of an agreement is to restrict competition, a restriction of competition is assumed and a violation of Article 101 is proved unless it can be demonstrated that the agreement satisfies the Article 101(3) criteria. In contrast, where the object of the agreement is not found to restrict competition, the burden of proving that this is its *effect* is on the person alleging the breach. Only where this is established does the burden shift on to the parties to defend it under Article 101(3).

A vital question is, therefore, how can agreements which restrict competition by object be identified? The discussion below indicates that although it can generally be predicted with a reasonable degree of certainty that some types of agreement will be found to have as their object restriction of competition, the exact boundary and extent of the category is extremely controversial. In particular, a contested issue is whether the interpretation of restriction by object adopted in the EU is drawn in accordance with the objectives underpinning the rules and so as to yield minimal error costs (over-inclusive presumptions of illegality may lead to false positives).[52]

---

[48] Case 56/65, *STM* [1966] ECR 235, 249.

[49] Ibid. See also, e.g., Case C-209/07, *Competition Authority v Beef Industry Development Society Ltd and Barry Brothers (Carrigmore) Meals Ltd (BIDS)* [2008] ECR I-8637, para. 15.

[50] The criteria laid down for the purpose of determining whether conduct has as its object or effect the restriction of competition are applicable irrespective of whether the case entails an agreement, a decision, or a concerted practice, see Case C-8/08, *T-Mobile* [2009] ECR I-4529.

[51] Case 56/65, *STM* [1966] ECR 235, 249. See also Case C-234/89, *Delimitis v Henninger Bräu* [1991] ECR I-935, para. 13 and Cases T-374, 375, 384, and 388/94, *European Night Services v Commission* [1998] ECR II-3141, para. 136.

[52] See Case C-67/13 P, *Groupement des Cartes Bancaires (CB) v Commission* EU:C:2014:2204, Wahl AG.

B. AGREEMENTS THAT RESTRICT COMPETITION BY OBJECT: RESTRAINTS WHICH REVEAL A SUFFICIENTLY DELETERIOUS IMPACT ON COMPETITION

(i) Identifying the Category of Object Restraints

In *STM*[53] the CJ indicated that agreements are restrictive of competition by object where an analysis of the purpose of the agreement, taking account of its clauses and the economic context in which it operates, reveals a sufficiently deleterious impact on competition;[54] the category is designed to encompass coordination which 'reveals in itself a sufficient degree of harm to competition law'.[55] 'The distinction between "infringements by object" and "infringements by effect"' thus 'arises from the fact that certain forms of collusion between undertakings can be regarded, by their very nature, as being injurious to the proper functioning of normal competition'.[56] A bright-line rule is applied; 'object' restraints are assumed to have a 'pernicious' effect on competition (and to be so unlikely to produce efficiencies), so that costs do not need to be incurred in demonstrating restrictive effects.[57]

Case law consistently reiterates that to identify agreements incorporating object restrictions, 'regard must be had inter alia to the content of its provisions, the objectives it seeks to ascertain and the economic and legal context of which it forms part'.[58] It is the case law of the EU Courts, therefore (rather than the Treaty itself[59]), which sheds light on the question of which clauses are likely to be problematic and how much analysis of the clauses in the context in which they are operated is required.[60]

When assessing the objective or purpose of the agreement, closer regard in the cases is 'paid to the wording of its provision and to the objectives which it is intended to attain'[61] than to the subjective intention of the parties.[62] Indeed, although the parties' intention to restrict competition or violate Article 101(1) can be taken into account it is not a necessary condition to a finding of

[53] Case 56/65, *STM* [1966] ECR 235, 249.

[54] See generally, e.g., A. Jones, 'Left Behind by Modernisation? Restrictions by Object under Article 101(1)' (2010) 6 *European Competition Journal* 649; M. Mahtani, 'Thinking Outside the Object Box: An EU and UK Perspective' (2012) 8 *European Competition Journal* 1; D. Bailey, 'Restrictions of Competition by Object under Article 101 TFEU' (2012) 49 *CMLRev* 559; P. Ibáñez Colomo, 'Market Failure, Transaction Costs and Article 101(1) TFEU Case-law' (2012) 5 *ELRev* 541, L. Peeperkorn, 'Defining "By Object" Restrictions' [2015] 3 *Concurrences* 40; and P. Ibáñez Colomo, 'Copyright Licensing and the EU Digital Single Market Strategy' in R. D. Blair and D. D. Sokol (eds.), *Handbook of Antitrust, Intellectual Property and High Technology* (Cambridge University Press, 2016).

[55] Case C-67/13P, *CB* EU:C:2014:2204, para. 57.

[56] Case C-209/07, *BIDS* [2008] ECR I-8637, para. 17.

[57] See Case C-8/08, *T-Mobile* [2009] ECR I-4529, Kokott AG, para. 43. Although the idea has similarities to the rule of per se illegality adopted in the US, any alleged economic justifications or pro-competitive aspects of the agreement may, in theory, be weighed against the restrictive elements at the Art. 101(3) stage.

[58] Case C-501/06 P, *GlaxoSmithKline Services Unlimited (GSK) v Commission* [2009] ECR I-9291, para. 58.

[59] Although in Case C-8/08, *T-Mobile* [2009] ECR I-4529, para. 37 the CJ held that 'it is apparent from Article [101(1)(a)] that concerted practices may have an anti-competitive object if they "directly or indirectly fix purchase or selling prices or any other trading conditions"' it has never been suggested that tying or price discrimination (listed in Art. 101(c) and (d)) should be restrictive by object, see e.g. Bailey, n. 54. See also discussion of *Wouters* in n. 178 and text. The Commission has published a Staff Working Document setting out guidance as to what constitutes a restriction of competition 'by object' (see MEMO/14/440, 25 June 2014, Commission's Staff Working Document, Guidance on restrictions of competition 'by object' for the purposes of defining which agreements may benefit from the *De Minimis* Notice, SWD(2014) 198 final). The Guidance accompanied the publication of the Commission's new Notice on agreements of minor importance, the benefit of which does not extend to agreements containing restrictions by object, see n. 132 and text.

[60] Object categorisation is not affected by the fact that an undertaking adversely affected and complaining about the agreement is operating illegally on the relevant market: Case C-68/12, *Protimonopolný úrad Slovenskej republiky v Slovenská sporiteľňa as* EU:C:2013:71, paras. 14–21.

[61] Case C-209/07, *BIDS* [2008] ECR I-8637, para. 21.

[62] Although intention can be taken into account: Case C-8/08, *T-Mobile* [2009] ECR I-4529, para. 27.

a restrictive purpose.[63] Conversely, the fact that the parties did not intend to restrict competition and infringe Article 101 will not necessarily deprive an agreement of an anti-competitive object. Intention and the object of the agreement is thus generally determined objectively, and the parties' subjective intent cannot be relied upon to exculpate otherwise anti-competitive behaviour. In *Competition Authority v Beef Industry Development Society Ltd (BIDS)*,[64] for example, the CJ rejected the parties' argument that by acting to reduce capacity on the Irish beef market they had not acted with an anti-competitive purpose or an intention to injure competition and the welfare of consumers, but with the intention of rationalising the beef industry and so making it more competitive by reducing, but not eliminating, production overcapacity.

[T]o determine whether an agreement comes within the prohibition laid down in Article [101(1)], close regard must be paid to the wording of its provisions and to the objectives which it is intended to attain. In that regard, even supposing it to be established that the parties to an agreement acted without any subjective intention of restricting competition, but with the object of remedying the effects of a crisis in their sector, such considerations are irrelevant for the purposes of applying that provision.[65]

(ii) Content—The Clauses in the Agreement

When identifying the content of the agreement it may be necessary to consider not only its express terms but the behaviour of the parties as '[t]he way in which an agreement is actually implemented may reveal a restriction of competition by object even where the formal agreement does not contain an express provision to that effect'.[66]

Jurisprudence has, over the years, clarified that agreements containing certain clauses are liable, in principle, to be found to pursue a restrictive objective. In particular, arrangements between competitors:

(a) to fix prices, limit output, share markets (see *European Night Services v Commission*[67] and *Toshiba Corporation v Commission*[68]) or rig bids;

(b) to reduce capacity (see *BIDS*[69]);

(c) designed, directly or indirectly, to fix purchase or selling prices through exchanges of information (see *T-Mobile Netherlands BV v Raad van bestuur van de Nederlandse Mededingingsautoriteit*);[70] and/or

(d) to boycott a competitor (collective exclusive dealing).[71]

---

[63] An intent to restrict competition may be relevant to a determination that the agreement is restrictive by object, see e.g., Case T-368/00, *General Motors Nederland and Opel Nederland* [2003] ECR II-4491.

[64] Case C-209/07, *BIDS* [2008] ECR I-8637.

[65] Ibid., para. 21.

[66] Article 101(3) Guidelines, para. 22. See also discussion of agreements and unilateral conduct in Chap. 3, Section 5.B.ii.e.

[67] Cases T-374, 375, 384, and 388/94, [1998] ECR II-3141, para. 136 and see further Chap. 9.

[68] Case C-373/14 P, EU:C:2016:26 (rejecting the argument raised that, as the parties to the alleged market-sharing agreement operated in different geographic markets, they were not actual or potential competitors so the agreement was not restrictive of competition by object, see n. 109 and text).

[69] Case C-209/07, [2008] ECR I-8637.

[70] Case C-8/08, [2009] ECR I-4529, paras. 36–43.

[71] See COMP/33.884, *Nederlandse Federatieve Vereniging voor de Groothandel op Elektrotechnisch Gebied and Technische Unie* [2000] OJ L39/1 (collective exclusive dealing arrangements by association intended to prevent supplies to undertakings not belonging to that associations), aff'd Cases T-5 and 6/00, *Nederlandse Federatieve Vereniging voor de Groothandel op Elektrotechnisch Gebied v Commission* [2003] ECR II-5761 and Case C-105/04 P, [2006] ECR I-8725), Case C-68/12, *Protimonopolný* EU:C:2013:71 and Staff Working Document, n. 59, 2.5. In the US, the courts distinguish between 'classic' collective boycott cases which are likely to result in predominantly anti-competitive effects, for example, where firms with market power boycott suppliers or customers in order to discourage them from doing

An assumption that these types of *'naked'* cartel activity (agreements which seek to constrain competition between the parties without producing any objective countervailing benefits[72]) restrict competition seems justifiable. There is growing international acceptance that such activity poses a serious threat to economies and consumers.[73] Parties to cartels deliberately set out to interfere with fundamental parameters of competition, to contradict the principles of the free market economy, and to act instead to protect the prosperity of the participants as a whole. Indeed, in *Groupement des Cartes Bancaires (CB) v Commission*,[74] the CJ recognised that since horizontal price-fixing by cartels, 'may be considered so likely to have negative effects, in particular on the price, quantity or quality of the goods and services, that it may be considered redundant, for the purposes of applying Article [101(1)], to prove that they have actual effects on the market …'.[75]

The extent to which the object category should be utilised more broadly than this, however, is contentious (especially given the difficulty of justifying restrictions of object under Article 101(3)). One controversy in the EU is that it has consistently been held that certain vertical restraints constitute, in principle, restrictions by object even though they are not made between competitors, but between providers of complementary goods and services, and generally provide scope for efficiencies. The category of object restrictions has thus been held to include agreements between non-competitors (for example, suppliers and distributors):[76]

(a) involving vertical price-fixing (resale price maintenance);[77]

(b) conferring absolute territorial protection (ATP) on a distributor or otherwise aimed at partitioning national markets according to national borders or limiting parallel trade;[78] and

(c) certain selective distribution agreements.[79]

These cases are explored in greater detail in Chapter 11. However, a few comments are made about the cases governing ATP here. Ever since *Consten and Grundig*[80] in 1966, it has been held that distribution agreements which provide a distributor with an exclusive sales territory and protection from sales by others within the territory (creating ATP) have as their object the restriction of competition. It will be remembered that this case concerned an exclusive distribution agreement

---

business with competitors (illegal per se) and others which are appraised under the rule of reason, see, e.g., *FTC v Indiana Federation of Dentists*, 476 US 447 (1986).

[72] M. Monti, 'Fighting Cartels Why and How? Why Should We Be Concerned With Cartels and Collusive Behaviour?', Third Nordic Competition Policy Conference, Stockholm, 11–12 September 2000. See also L. Peeperkorn, 'Conditional Pricing: Why the General Court is Wrong in *Intel* and What the Court of Justice Can Do to Rebalance the Assessment of Rebates' [2015] 1 *Concurrences* 43–63 ('Even if a cartel is formed, by mistake, by a group of producers who collectively are too small to control the market—and who will thus fail to produce an appreciable negative effect on the market as any price rise they initiate will be met by customers going to the non-participating competitors resulting in serious loss of market share for the cartel participants—not allowing such a cartel does not risk destroying any efficiencies').

[73] See Chap. 9.

[74] Case C-67/13 P, EU:C:2014:2204.

[75] Ibid., para 51.

[76] Restrictions in intellectual property licensing agreements (between non-competitors) on the determination of prices for the licensed products or providing ATP for the licensee, also ordinarily have as their *object* the restriction of competition within the meaning of Art. 101(1), see Chap. 12 and, e.g., Case 258/78, *Nungesser v Commission* [1982] ECR 2015 and Cases C-403 and 429/08, *Football Association Premier League Ltd and Others v QC Leisure and Others and Karen Murphy v Media Protection Services Ltd (Murphy)* EU:C:2011:631 (contrast Case 27/87, *Erauw-Jacquéry Sprl v La Hesbignonne Société Coopérative* [1988] ECR 1919; Case 62/79, *Coditel v Ciné Vog Films (Coditel I)* [1980] ECR 881).

[77] See e.g., Case 26/76, *Metro-SB-Grossmärkte GmbH v Commission (Metro I)* [1977] ECR 1875 and Chap. 11.

[78] See especially Cases 56 and 58/64, *Consten and Grundig* [1966] ECR 299.

[79] Case C-439/09, *Pierre Fabre v Président de l'Autorité de la concurrence* EU:C:2011:277, see nn. 99 and 122 and text and Chap. 11.

[80] Cases 56 and 58/64, [1966] ECR 299. It has been reiterated in a series of cases since then, see e.g. Case C-501/06 P, *GSK* [2009] ECR I-9291, para. 61, Case T-360/09, *E.ON Ruhrgas AG v Commission* EU:T:2012:332, and Cases C-403 and 429/08, *Murphy* EU:C:2011:631. See also, e.g., Case 86/82, *Hasselblad v Commission* [1984] ECR 883, para. 46.

concluded between Grundig, a German manufacturer of electronic products, and Consten. The agreement obliged Consten not to handle competing products, to order a minimum quantity of Grundig products, to stock accessories and spare parts, to provide after-sales services, and not to sell Grundig products outside France. In return, Grundig agreed not to deliver the product for sale in France itself and to prohibit all other distributors from seeking sales, actively or passively, within France. To reinforce the territorial protection Grundig assigned to Consten the rights to the Grundig trade mark GINT, in France. The provisions in the agreement were therefore intended to confer ATP upon Consten and to prevent all parallel trade in Grundig products. The Commission held that the agreement was designed to restrict competition. The exclusive contract and ancillary arrangements (in particular, in relation to the trade mark) had the object of relieving Consten of the competition of other undertakings insofar as it involved the import or wholesale trade in Grundig products in France. Further, an exemption was refused.

The parties appealed to the CJ, challenging the Commission's decision on several grounds. In particular, they vigorously denied that the arrangements restricted competition and complained that the Commission had erred in its application of Article 101(1) since it had failed to base itself on the 'rule of reason'. It had been wrong simply to conclude that the object of its agreement was to restrict competition without considering its effect. Broadly, their argument hinged on the fact that the provisions had been essential to enable Grundig to penetrate the French market. The Commission had wrongly considered the transaction with hindsight, *ex post*, when matters had turned out well. If, however, it had taken account of the market at the time that the agreement was entered into, *ex ante*, when matters looked risky and uncertain, it would have been apparent that the distributor would not have proceeded without the territorial protection. The exclusivity was crucial to encourage the distributor to take on an uncertain new venture and invest resources in promoting the new product on the French market. Such a distributor would have to persuade French consumers to purchase Grundig products instead of other competing brands of electrical products available and established on the French market and other distributors would have to be prevented from taking a 'free ride'[81] on Consten's promotional and investment efforts. They would have been able to import the products more cheaply from Germany[82] (this was, in fact, exactly what UNEF, a Parisian company, and Leissner in Strasbourg had done).

The parties thus argued that despite the fact that the agreement resulted in the existence of only one distributor of Grundig products in France (there was a restriction on *intra-brand competition*), the agreement led to an increase in competition for electrical products in France (there was an increase in *inter-brand competition*). French consumers wishing to purchase such products now also had the option to purchase Grundig products in addition to those of the other manufacturers on the market. Consequently, the Commission had been wrong to focus solely on the restriction in intra-brand competition and to make an assumption of anti-competitive effects. It should instead have considered the effects of the disputed contract upon competition between Grundig and its competitors' products.

The notion that the Commission's decision should have been marked with greater market analysis was supported by Advocate-General Roemer[83] who agreed that Article 101(1) should not have been applied on the basis of purely theoretical considerations to a situation which might, upon closer inspection, reveal no appreciable adverse effects on competition. Article 101(1) required a consideration of the effects of the agreement on the market. This could not be established without looking at the market *in concreto* and without taking account of competition between similar products. In a case like this one, where the agreement had already been implemented, the Commission should have made a comparison between two market situations: that after making the agreement and that which would have arisen had there been no agreement. If Grundig would not have found

---

[81] For a more detailed discussion of the free-rider arguments, see Chap. 11.

[82] The German distributors would not have to engage in such high levels of promotion and investment.

[83] Cases 56 and 58/64, *Consten and Grundig* [1966] ECR 299.

an outlet for its products in the absence of supplying a sole concessionaire, the exclusive distribution agreement clearly promoted competition. It would have been necessary for Grundig to gain access to or penetrate the new market. In the view of the Advocate General, therefore, Article 101(1) should not be applied if, in the absence of the agreement appointing a single distributor exclusively in France, Grundig would not have found an outlet for its products.

In this case the CJ did not agree with its Advocate-General but upheld the Commission's decision.[84] It held that the agreement giving Consten a monopoly over the sale of Grundig products in France (ATP) had as its *object* the restriction of competition so that an assessment of its *effect* was unnecessary.

Cases 56 and 58/64, *Établissements Consten SàRL and Grundig-Verkaufs-GmbH v Commission* [1966] ECR 299, 342–343

Court of Justice

The complaints concerning the criterion of restriction on competition

The applicants and the German Government maintain that since the Commission restricted its examination solely to Grundig products the decision was based upon a false concept of competition and of the rules on prohibition contained in Article [101(1)], since this concept applies particularly to competition between similar products of different makes; the Commission, before declaring Article [101(1)] to be applicable, should, by basing itself upon the 'rule of reason', have considered the economic effects of the disputed contract upon competition between the different makes. There is a presumption that vertical sole distributorship agreements are not harmful to competition and in the present case there is nothing to invalidate that presumption. On the contrary, the contract in question has increased the competition between similar products of different makes. The principle of freedom of competition concerns the various stages and manifestations of competition. Although competition between producers is generally more noticeable than that between distributors of products of the same make, it does not thereby follow that an agreement tending to restrict the latter kind of competition should escape the prohibition of Article [101(1)] merely because it might increase the former.

Besides, for the purpose of applying Article [101(1)], there is no need to take account of the concrete effects of an agreement once it appears that it has as its object the prevention, restriction or distortion of competition.

Therefore the absence in the contested decision of any analysis of the effects of the agreement on competition between similar products of different makes does not, of itself, constitute a defect in the decision.

It thus remains to consider whether the contested decision was right in founding the prohibition of the disputed agreement under Article [101(1)] on the restriction on competition created by the agreement in the sphere of the distribution of Grundig products alone. The infringement which was found to exist by the contested decision results from the absolute territorial protection created [by] the said contract in favour of Consten on the basis of French law. The applicants thus wished to eliminate any possibility of competition at the wholesale level in Grundig products in the territory specified in the contra[c]t essentially by two methods.

First, Grundig undertook not to deliver even indirectly to third parties products intended for the area covered by the contract. The restrictive nature of that undertaking is obvious if it is considered in the light of the prohibition on exporting which was imposed not only on Consten but also on all the other sole concessionnaires of Grundig, as well as the German wholesalers.

---

[84] Ibid.

Secondly, the registration in France by Consten of the GINT trade mark, which Grundig affixes to all its products, is intended to increase the protection inherent in the disputed agreement, against the risk of parallel imports into France of Grundig products, by adding the protection deriving from the law on industrial property rights. Thus no third party could import Grundig products from other Member States of the [Union] for resale in France without running serious risks.

The defendant properly took into account the whole distribution system thus set up by Grundig. In order to arrive at a true representation of the contractual position the contract must be placed in the economic and legal context in the light of which it was concluded by the parties. Such a procedure is not to be regarded as an unwarrantable interference in legal transactions or circumstances which were not the subject of the proceedings before the Commission.

The situation as ascertained above results in the isolation of the French market and makes it possible to charge for the products in question prices which are sheltered from all effective competition. In addition, the more producers succeed in their efforts to render their own makes of product individually distinct in the eyes of the consumer, the more the effectiveness of competition between producers tend[s] to diminish. Because of the considerable impact of distribution costs on the aggregate cost price, it seems important that competition between dealers should also be stimulated. The efforts of the dealer are stimulated by competition between distributors of products of the same make. Since the agreement thus aims at isolating the French market for Grundig products and maintaining artificially, for products of a very well-known brand, separate national markets within the [EU], it is therefore such as to distort competition in the Common Market.

It was therefore proper for the contested decision to hold that the agreement constitutes an infringement of Article [101(1)]. No further considerations, whether of economic data (price differences between France and Germany, representative character of the type of appliance considered, level of overheads borne by Consten) or of the corrections of the criteria upon which the Commission relied in its comparisons between the situations of the French and German markets, and no possible favourable effects of the agreement in other respects, can in any way lead, in the face of abovementioned restrictions, to a different solution under Article [101(1)].

In its judgment the CJ, although recognising the importance of competition between producers (inter-brand competition), held that agreements which restricted competition between distributors (intra-brand competition) could also restrict competition for the purposes of Article 101(1). It was important that competition between dealers should be stimulated, and intra-brand as well as inter-brand competition maintained. In particular, restrictions on intra-brand competition might facilitate brand differentiation and diminish competition between producers. The agreement in question eliminated any possibility of competition between distributors of Grundig products and led to the isolation of the French market and so distorted competition and infringed Article 101(1). The Commission had not, therefore, erred by failing to consider the effects of the agreement for the purposes of Article 101(1).

There seems little doubt that the Court's judgment in *Consten and Grundig* was influenced not only by its view as to the pernicious effects of the agreement's provisions from a competition perspective, but also by the effects of the agreement from the single market perspective.[85] Whatever the economic justifications for the agreement the affront to the single market goal in this case was too severe.[86] Arguably, it was this factor that played a central part in the categorisation of the agreement. The object of the agreement was to grant *ATP* and to eliminate competition at a wholesale level in Grundig products in the territory. The French market had been isolated and the French distributor sheltered from all effective (intra-brand) competition. The Court sent out a clear

---

[85] See also, e.g., Case T-360/09, *E.ON Ruhrgas* EU:T:2012:332.

[86] See Chap. 1.

message: agreements which divide up the internal market and preclude all cross-border trade in the contract product will not be tolerated.

G. Amato, *Antitrust and the Bounds of Power* (Hart Publishing, 1997), 48–49

In the leading case in this area, *Consten and Grundig*, of 1966 . . . the Commission challenged the exclusive agreement for France that Grundig had given to Consten and had strengthened by barring its wholesale distributors in Germany and other countries from selling to France, where the price of Grundig products was kept higher than elsewhere, net of French tax. The parties maintained, first before the Commission itself and then before the Court of Justice, that Article [101] referred primarily to inter-brand competition, and that as far as intra-brand restrictions went, one had to presume efficiency in promoting inter-brand competition failing proof of the contrary. This argument copied word-for-word approaches of the Chicago School, which in fact at the time the American courts themselves had rejected, in the name of protection (dropped later in the *Sylvania* case) for the right of each distributor or retailer to exercise freedom of trade without restraint. Our court did not accept the arguments either, but for very different reasons. It accepted that inter-brand competition was the most relevant for the purposes of prohibition under Article [101], but added that this did not *a priori* exempt intra-brand restrictions, with the consequence—inconceivable today (and perhaps in earlier times too) for an American court—that the fact that the Commission was not concerned to ascertain the size of inter-brand competition was irrelevant. On this basis, the absolute territorial protection by which the exclusivity for France was guaranteed was illegitimate. It is indeed true, said the Court, that imports have an effect on the supply planning that Consten may engage in and on the organization of services it may offer customers. But a margin of risk is inherent in commercial activity, and in any case 'the more manufacturers isolate themselves from each other in consumers' eyes, the more competition among them is reduced. Moreover, competition among wholesale distributors of products of one and the same brand enlivens the downstream market of sales to final consumers'.

As we can see, these are very important assertions of principle that bring the decision close to the American ones of the 1960s. But there are two important differences, one explicit and the other implicit. The explicit one is that the need for intra-brand competition is based on protection not of an individual right (freedom of trade) but of a general and objective principle (competitiveness of the market in all its segments). The implicit one is that such a pervasive and rigorous principle is asserted to the extent that it serves to protect another principle, a higher one in 1966, that of market integration. For the territory protected by Consten's rigid exclusivity coincided with that of the French State, and both the Commission and the Court saw this protection as persistence of the segmentation of economic activities along national frontiers, violating the 'Grundnorm' of the whole [EU] system.

In Chapter 11 it will be seen that the question whether this strict stance taken towards vertical territorial (and price) restraints was, or remains, appropriate has been much debated. In the US, in particular, the category of agreements considered illegal per se has, to prevent false positives and to allow antitrust scrutiny of more ambivalent agreements, changed over time (and, in fact, dramatically in the last 30 years), reflecting changes in ideology and economic thinking.[87] Some have hoped that the EU Courts might also reconsider the boundaries of the 'object' category of restraints (or the Commission may reconsider object categorisation) where necessary to reflect economic and other developments or new experience collected in relation to restraints.[88] The EU Courts, however,

---

[87] See, e.g., A. Jones, 'Completion of the Revolution in Antitrust Doctrine on Restricted Distribution: *Leegin* and its Implications for EC Competition Law' (2008) 53 *Ant Bull* 903, 918–920.

[88] See, e.g., Peeperkorn, n. 54.

generally strive for consistency in their case law,[89] and, have not to date shown an inclination to deviate from the starting point that vertical price and territorial restrictions are in principle restrictive of competition.

(iii) The Importance of Context in Identifying the Purpose or Objective of the Agreement

It is important to remember that the category of object restraints is not as simple as constituting a definitive and clear list.[90] Rather it has been seen that the purpose/objective of the agreement, taking account of its content and the context in which it is operated, is central to the issue. The list of restraints set out above consequently provides an illustration of agreements/restraints whose purpose is (in most contexts) likely to be sufficiently deleterious. The objective and the context of the agreement could, however, require the category of object restricts to be:

- expanded beyond these listed clauses—to include other 'new' restraints whose anti-competitive nature becomes obvious once its objective, and/or context, is taken into account (see Section iv below); or

- narrowed—to exclude agreements containing the listed restraints where it is clear from the purpose pursued and/or the context in which it operates that an assumption of anti-competitive effects is not warranted (see Section v below).

(iv) The Objective of the Agreement and the Context in Which it Operates: Expanding the List of Object Restraints

The cases establish that the list of restraints is not closed. Consequently, an important question which is frequently arising (and considered in subsequent chapters) is whether, and if so when, 'new types' of conduct which have not been classified as restrictive by object in past case law of the EU Courts may be so treated (for example, multilateral interchange fees (MIFs),[91] most favoured nation clauses,[92] patent settlement agreements,[93] or no-poach agreements—agreements between competitors not to solicit or hire each other's employees[94]). What exactly is required to demonstrate that the clauses and context of the agreement are sufficient to establish an anti-competitive objective?

There has been acute concern that some rulings of the CJ have adopted too broad an interpretation of a restriction by object, suggesting that the category can be expanded to a somewhat unclear extent. In *T-Mobile*,[95] for example, although the CJ had to consider a case in which the practice at issue indirectly facilitated the fixing of prices between competing mobile operators in the Netherlands, the CJ made some expansive statements, particularly in paragraphs 31 and 43 of its judgment, about the concept of an object restraint.

31. With regard to the assessment as to whether a concerted practice, such as that at issue in the main proceedings, pursues an anti-competitive object, it should be noted, first, as pointed out by the Advocate

---

[89] Case 4/73, *Nold v Commission* [1974] ECR 491. See also A. Arnull, 'Owning Up to Fallibility: Precedent and the Court of Justice' (1993) 30 *CMLRev* 247.

[90] See Case C-209/07, *BIDS* [2008] ECR I-8637, Trstenjack AG and articles cited in n. 54.

[91] See n. 175 and text and Chap. 9.

[92] See Chap. 11.

[93] See Chap. 12.

[94] Or perhaps to agree salaries, see e.g., G. Gürkaynak, A. Güner and C. Özkanli, 'Competition Law Issues in the Human Resources Field' (2013) 4 *JECLAP* 201 and in the US, *United States v Adobe Systems* 17 March 2011 (consent decree enjoining the defendant technology companies from colluding to refrain from soliciting, cold-calling, recruiting, or otherwise competing for employees of the other).

[95] Case C-8/08, [2009] ECR I-4529.

General at point 46 of her Opinion, that in order for a concerted practice to be regarded as having an anti-competitive object, it is sufficient that it has the potential to have a negative impact on competition. In other words, the concerted practice must simply be capable in an individual case, having regard to the specific legal and economic context, of resulting in the prevention, restriction or distortion of competition within the common market. Whether and to what extent, in fact, such anti-competitive effects result can only be of relevance for determining the amount of any fine and assessing any claim for damages.

…

43. In the light of all the foregoing considerations, the answer to the first question must be that a concerted practice pursues an anti-competitive object for the purpose of Article [101(1)] where, according to its content and objectives and having regard to its legal and economic context, it is capable in an individual case of resulting in the prevention, restriction or distortion of competition within the common market. It is not necessary for there to be actual prevention, restriction or distortion of competition or a direct link between the concerted practice and consumer prices. An exchange of information between competitors is tainted with an anti-competitive object if the exchange is capable of removing uncertainties concerning the intended conduct of the participating undertakings.

Although both broad and narrow constructions of this judgment have been argued to be possible,[96] in *Allianz Hungária Biztosító Zrt, Generali-Providencia Biztosító Zrt v Gazdasági Versenyhivatal*[97] the CJ, when asked to consider the question of whether a number of bilateral agreements concluded between insurance companies and car repairers (or a Car Repairers' Association) were restrictive of competition by object,[98] stated that:[99]

agreements would … amount to a restriction of competition by object in the event that the referring court found that it is likely that, having regard to the economic context, competition on that market would be eliminated or seriously weakened following the conclusion of those agreements. In order to determine the likelihood of such a result, that court should in particular take into consideration the structure of that market, the existence of alternative distribution channels and their respective importance and the market power of the companies concerned.

Indeed, the Court stressed that vertical agreements could have significant restrictive potential and, in particular, that they would be treated as restrictive by object where they implement or affirm a horizontal agreement which is restrictive by object.

These judgments bolstered the impression that the object category was 'inexorably getting larger';[100] a view which was fuelled by the Commission's publication, in June 2014, of a Staff Working Document on 'restrictions of competition "by object"'[101] adopting a liberal approach to the issue—this guidance was, however, revised in 2015 and some of the broader statements made in the original document were taken out of it. Two principal concerns arise about this standpoint. First, the broad approach manifest appears to be out of tune with the objectives underpinning the

---

[96] See Bailey, n. 54, 589 (the broad being that the test of capability sets the threshold for finding infringements by object very low and the narrow being that the CJ simply made it clear that a finding of an anti-competitive object does not depend upon an assessment of its actual impact on competition and that, in the circumstances of the case, the restriction was obvious).

[97] Case C-32/11, EU:C:2013:160.

[98] These agreements did not contain any of the restraints identified as severe or obvious ones in previous case law. The concern about the restrictions in this case arose, however, because of the market power of the insurers involved and the concentrated structure of the market.

[99] Case C-32/11, *Allianz Hungária Biztosító Zrt, Generali-Providencia Biztosító Zrt v Gazdasági Versenyhivatal* EU:C:2013:160, para. 48. In Case C-439/09, *Pierre Fabre* EU:C:2011:277 the CJ also cast doubt on the traditional view that selective distribution agreements require some form of analysis of the restrictive effects of the agreement, stating that they necessarily affect competition and 'are to be considered, in the absence of objective justification, as "restrictions by object"', see further n. 121 and text and Chap. 11.

[100] R. Whish and D. Bailey, *Competition Law* (8th edn, Oxford University Press, 2015), 125.

[101] SWD(2014) 198 final.

rules and is liable to extend the category of object restraints well beyond agreements containing 'obvious' restrictions of competition. Secondly, the suggestion that an abbreviated analysis of market structure and market power is required inappropriately blurs the analysis required in object and effects cases respectively. Indeed, the proposition that any agreement which, following such an abbreviated market analysis, can be shown to have the potential to have a negative impact on competition is restrictive by object could, at its broadest construction, do away with the need for effects analysis completely. The claimant's obligation under Article 101(1) to demonstrate restrictive effects may then too easily be sidestepped and the burden shifted to the parties to defend their agreement under Article 101(3).

A judgment which has, consequently, been welcomed is that of the CJ in *CB*[102] which sets out an important reminder that, as recognised in *STM*, the category of object restrictions should be interpreted *restrictively* and reserved exclusively for agreements which inherently reveal a sufficient degree of harm to competition—it is only then that the Commission (or other claimant) should be exempted from demonstrating actual anti-competitive effects. Importantly, the CJ clarified that if there is a need to conduct a detailed market analysis to assess the impact of the agreement, it should not constitute an object restriction; the category is consequently inappropriate for cases involving complex measures or where experience[103] with the restraint is limited.

On the facts of the *CB* case, the CJ held that the GC had erred in affirming a Commission decision finding that a number of measures designed to achieve interoperability within a system for payment and withdrawal by bank cards were restrictive of competition by object. It criticised the GC for:

- ruling that the concept of restriction of competition by 'object' was not to be interpreted 'restrictively';

- not explaining why the measures were by their very nature harmful to the proper functioning of normal competition rather than just being capable of restricting competition (on the contrary, the CJ considered that as the GC had conducted an assessment of the potential effects of the measures, it has thereby make it clear that they did not reveal a sufficient degree of harm to competition); and

- taking insufficient account of the fact that restraints had been incorporated to ensure the success of the system, in particular through combating free-riding and balancing issuing/acquisition activities.

In so doing the Court distinguished *BIDS*,[104] a case in which the arrangements were intended to change appreciably the structure of the market through the withdrawal of competitors, from *CB* on the grounds that the purpose of the arrangement in *CB* was not to reduce overcapacity but to achieve a given ratio between the issuing and acquisition activities of the member of the grouping in order to develop the CB system. The CJ referred the matter back to the GC to determine whether the Commission had established that the agreement had as its effect the restriction of competition.

---

[102] Case C-67/13 P, EU:C:2014:2204.

[103] The importance of experience was also stressed by the CJ in Case C-286/13 P, *Dole Food Co Inc and Dole Fresh Fruit Europe v Commission (Dole)* EU:C:2015:184, para. 115 ('certain collusive behaviour, such as that leading to horizontal price-fixing by cartels, may be considered so likely to have negative effects, in particular on the price, quantity or quality of the goods and services, that it may be considered redundant, for the purposes of applying [Article 101(1) TFEU], to prove that they have actual effects on the market. Experience shows that such behaviour leads to falls in production and price increases, resulting in poor allocation of resources to the detriment, in particular, of consumers (judgment in Case C-67/13 P, *CB v Commission* ..., paragraph 51)'). See also Wathelet AG in his Opinion in Case C-373/14, *Toshiba Corp v Commission* EU:C:2015:427.

[104] Case C-209/07, *BIDS* [2008] ECR I-8637.

Case C-67/13 P, *Groupement des Cartes Bancaires (CB) v Commission* EU:C:2014:2204

– Examination of whether there is a restriction of competition by 'object' within the meaning of Article [101(1)]

48. It must be recalled that, to come within the prohibition laid down in Article [101(1)], an agreement, a decision by an association of undertakings or a concerted practice must have 'as [its] object or effect' the prevention, restriction or distortion of competition in the internal market.

49. In that regard, it is apparent from the Court's case-law that certain types of coordination between undertakings reveal a sufficient degree of harm to competition that it may be found that there is no need to examine their effects (see, to that effect, judgment in *LTM*, 56/65 ..., paragraphs 359 and 360; judgment in *BIDS*, paragraph 15, and judgment in *Allianz Hungária Biztosító and Others*, C-32/11..., paragraph 34...).

50. That case-law arises from the fact that certain types of coordination between undertakings can be regarded, by their very nature, as being harmful to the proper functioning of normal competition (see, to that effect, in particular, judgment in *Allianz Hungária Biztosító and Others*...paragraph 35...).

51. Consequently, it is established that certain collusive behaviour, such as that leading to horizontal price-fixing by cartels, may be considered so likely to have negative effects, in particular on the price, quantity or quality of the goods and services, that it may be considered redundant, for the purposes of applying Article [101(1)], to prove that they have actual effects on the market (see, to that effect, in particular, judgment in *Clair*, 123/83,..., paragraph 22). Experience shows that such behaviour leads to falls in production and price increases, resulting in poor allocation of resources to the detriment, in particular, of consumers.

52. Where the analysis of a type of coordination between undertakings does not reveal a sufficient degree of harm to competition, the effects of the coordination should, on the other hand, be considered and, for it to be caught by the prohibition, it is necessary to find that factors are present which show that competition has in fact been prevented, restricted or distorted to an appreciable extent (judgment in *Allianz Hungária Biztosító* ..., paragraph ...).

53. According to the case-law of the Court, in order to determine whether an agreement between undertakings or a decision by an association of undertakings reveals a sufficient degree of harm to competition that it may be considered a restriction of competition 'by object' within the meaning of Article [101(1)], regard must be had to the content of its provisions, its objectives and the economic and legal context of which it forms a part. When determining that context, it is also necessary to take into consideration the nature of the goods or services affected, as well as the real conditions of the functioning and structure of the market or markets in question (see, to that effect, judgment in *Allianz Hungária Biztosító and Others*..., paragraph 36...).

54. In addition, although the parties' intention is not a necessary factor in determining whether an agreement between undertakings is restrictive, there is nothing prohibiting the competition authorities, the national courts or the Courts of the European Union from taking that factor into account (see judgment in *Allianz Hungária Biztosító and Others*..., paragraph 37...).

55. In the present case, it must be noted that, when the General Court defined in the judgment under appeal the relevant legal criteria to be taken into account in order to ascertain whether there was, in the present case, a restriction of competition by 'object' within the meaning of Article [101(1)], it reasoned as follows, in paragraphs 124 and 125 of that judgment:

'124. According to the case-law, the types of agreement covered by Article 81(1)(a) to (e) EC do not constitute an exhaustive list of prohibited collusion and, accordingly, the concept of infringement by object should not be given a strict interpretation (see, to that effect, [judgment in *BIDS*], paragraphs 22 and 23).

125. In order to assess the anti-competitive nature of an agreement or a decision by an association of undertakings, regard must be had *inter alia* to the content of its provisions, its objectives and

the economic and legal context of which it forms a part. In that regard, it is sufficient that the agreement or the decision of an association of undertakings has the potential to have a negative impact on competition. In other words, the agreement or decision must simply be capable in the particular case, having regard to the specific legal and economic context, of preventing, restricting or distorting competition within the common market. It is not necessary for there to be actual prevention, restriction or distortion of competition or a direct link between [that agreement or decision] and consumer prices. In addition, although the parties' intention is not a necessary factor in determining whether an agreement is restrictive, there is nothing prohibiting the Commission or the Community judicature from taking it into account (see, to that effect, [judgment in *T-Mobile*...], paragraphs 31, 39 and 43, and [judgment in *GlaxoSmithKline*...] paragraph 58...).'

56. It must be held that, in so reasoning, the General Court in part failed to have regard to the case-law of the Court of Justice and, therefore, erred in law with regard to the definition of the relevant legal criteria in order to assess whether there was a restriction of competition by 'object' within the meaning of Article [101(1)].

57. First, in paragraph 125 of the judgment under appeal, when the General Court defined the concept of the restriction of competition 'by object' within the meaning of that provision, it did not refer to the settled case-law of the Court of Justice mentioned in paragraphs 49 to 52 of the present judgment, thereby failing to have regard to the fact that the essential legal criterion for ascertaining whether coordination between undertakings involves such a restriction of competition 'by object' is the finding that such coordination reveals in itself a sufficient degree of harm to competition.

58. Secondly, in the light of that case-law, the General Court erred in finding, in paragraph 124 of the judgment under appeal, and then in paragraph 146 of that judgment, that the concept of restriction of competition by 'object' must not be interpreted 'restrictively'. The concept of restriction of competition 'by object' can be applied only to certain types of coordination between undertakings which reveal a sufficient degree of harm to competition that it may be found that there is no need to examine their effects, otherwise the Commission would be exempted from the obligation to prove the actual effects on the market of agreements which are in no way established to be, by their very nature, harmful to the proper functioning of normal competition. The fact that the types of agreements covered by Article [101(1)] do not constitute an exhaustive list of prohibited collusion is, in that regard, irrelevant.

59. It is, however, necessary to examine whether those errors of law were capable of vitiating the General Court's analysis as regards the characterisation of the measures at issue in the light of Article [101(1)].

...

65. Although it is apparent from the judgment under appeal that the General Court took the view that the restrictive object of the measures at issue could be inferred from their wording alone, the fact remains that it did not at any point explain, in the context of its review of the lawfulness of the decision at issue, in what respect that wording could be considered to reveal the existence of a restriction of competition 'by object' within the meaning of Article [101(1)].

...

69. However, although the General Court thereby set out the reasons why the measures at issue, in view of their formulas, are capable of restricting competition and, consequently, of falling within the scope of the prohibition laid down in Article [101(1)], it in no way explained—contrary to the requirements of the case-law referred to in paragraphs 49 and 50 above—in what respect that restriction of competition reveals a sufficient degree of harm in order to be characterised as a restriction 'by object' within the meaning of that provision, there being no analysis of that point in the judgment under appeal.

70. Although, as the General Court correctly found in paragraphs 76 and 140 to 144 of the judgment under appeal, the fact that the measures at issue pursue the legitimate objective of combatting free-riding does not preclude their being regarded as having an object restrictive of competition, the fact remains that that restrictive object must be established.

71. It follows that the General Court, in its characterisation of the measures at issue, not only vitiated the judgment under appeal by defective reasoning, but also misinterpreted and misapplied Article [101(1)].

72. It is indeed clear, in particular, from paragraphs 204 and 247 of the judgment under appeal, that the General Court rejected on several occasions the appellant's claim that it was apparent from formulas prescribed for the measures at issue that the latter sought to develop the acquisition activities of the members in order to achieve an optimal rate of balance between issuing and acquisition activities. On the other hand, it is not disputed—as is apparent, in particular, from paragraphs 198, 199, 245, 247 and 327 of the judgment under appeal—that those formulas encouraged the members of the Grouping, in order to avoid the payment of fees introduced by those measures, not to exceed a certain volume of CB card issuing that enabled them to achieve a given ratio between the issuing and acquisition activities of the Grouping.

73. After stating, in paragraph 83 of the judgment under appeal, that the Grouping is active on the 'payment systems market', the General Court found, in paragraph 102 of that judgment, in its assessment of the facts—which is not subject to appeal and is not challenged in these proceedings—that, in the present case, in a card payment system that is by nature two-sided, such as that of the Grouping, the issuing and acquisition activities are 'essential' to one another and to the operation of that system: first, traders would not agree to join the CB card payment system if the number of cardholders was insufficient and, secondly, consumers would not wish to hold a card if it could not be used with a sufficient number of traders.

74. Having therefore found, in paragraph 104 of the judgment under appeal, that there were 'interactions' between the issuing and acquisition activities of a payment system and that those activities produced 'indirect network effects', since the extent of merchants' acceptance of cards and the number of cards in circulation each affects the other, the General Court could not, without erring in law, conclude that the measures at issue had as their object the restriction of competition within the meaning of Article [101(1)].

75. Having acknowledged that the formulas for those measures sought to establish a certain ratio between the issuing and acquisition activities of the members of the Grouping, the General Court was entitled at the most to infer from this that those measures had as their object the imposition of a financial contribution on the members of the Grouping which benefit from the efforts of other members for the purposes of developing the acquisition activities of the system. Such an object cannot be regarded as being, by its very nature, harmful to the proper functioning of normal competition, the General Court itself moreover having found, in particular in paragraphs 76 and 77 of the judgment under appeal, that combatting free-riding in the CB system was a legitimate objective.

76. In that regard, as the Advocate General observed at point 149 of his Opinion, the General Court wrongly held, in paragraph 105 of the judgment under appeal, that the analysis of the requirements of balance between issuing and acquisition activities within the payment system could not be carried out in the context of Article [101(1)] on the ground that the relevant market was not that of payment systems in France but the market, situated downstream for the issue of payment cards in that Member State.

77. In so doing, the General Court confused the issue of the definition of the relevant market and that of the context which must be taken into account in order to ascertain whether the content of an agreement or a decision by an association of undertakings reveals the existence of a restriction of competition 'by object' within the meaning of Article [101(1)].

78. In order to assess whether coordination between undertakings is by nature harmful to the proper functioning of normal competition, it is necessary, in accordance with the case-law referred to in paragraph 53 above, to take into consideration all relevant aspects—having regard, in particular, to the nature of the services at issue, as well as the real conditions of the functioning and structure of the markets—of the economic or legal context in which that coordination takes place, it being immaterial whether or not such an aspect relates to the relevant market.

79. That must be the case, in particular, when that aspect is the taking into account of interactions between the relevant market and a different related market (see, by analogy, judgment in *Delimitis*,…, paragraphs 17 to 23, and judgment in *Allianz Hungária Biztosító and Others*…, paragraph 42) and, all the more so, when, as in the present case, there are interactions between the two facets of a two-sided system.

80. Admittedly, it cannot be ruled out that the measures at issue, as the General Court found in paragraphs 198, 227 and 234 of the judgment under appeal, hinder competition from new entrants—in

the light of the difficulty which those measures create for the expansion of their acquisition activity—and even lead to their exclusion from the system, on the basis, as BPCE argued at the hearing, of the level of fees charged pursuant to those measures.

81. However, as the Advocate General observed in point 131 of his Opinion, such a finding falls within the examination of the effects of those measures on competition and not of their object.

82. It must therefore be found that, while purporting to examine, in paragraphs 161 to 193 of the judgment under appeal, the 'options' left open to the members of the Grouping by the measures at issue—at the end of which it concluded, in paragraph 194 of that judgment, that 'in practice MERFA left two options open to the banks subject to it: payment of a fee or limiting the issue of CB cards'—the General Court in fact assessed the potential effects of those measures, analysing the difficulties for the banks of developing acquisition activity on the basis of market data, statements made by certain banks and documents seized during the inspections, and thereby indicating itself that the measures at issue cannot be considered 'by their very nature' harmful to the proper functioning of normal competition.

83. In that regard, the General Court erred, in paragraphs 197 and 198 of the judgment under appeal, in finding that the measures at issue could be regarded as being analogous to those examined by the Court of Justice in the *BIDS* judgment, in which the Court of Justice held that the arrangements referred to ('the BIDS arrangements'), concluded between the ten principal beef and veal processors in Ireland, members of BIDS ..., had as their object the restriction of competition within the meaning of Article [101(1)].

84. By providing for a reduction of the order of 25% in processing capacity, the BIDS arrangements were intended, essentially, as their own wording makes clear, to enable several undertakings to implement a common policy which had as its object the encouragement of some of them to withdraw from the market and the reduction, as a consequence, of the overcapacity which affects their profitability by preventing them from achieving economies of scale. The object of the BIDS arrangements was therefore to change, appreciably, the structure of the market through a mechanism intended to encourage the withdrawal of competitors in order, first, to increase the degree of concentration in the sector concerned by reducing significantly the number of undertakings supplying processing services and, secondly, to eliminate almost 75% of excess production capacity (*BIDS* judgment, paragraphs 31 to 33).

85. In the judgment under appeal, the General Court made no such finding, nor indeed was it argued before it that the measures at issue, like the BIDS arrangements, were intended to change appreciably the structure of the market concerned through a mechanism intended to encourage the withdrawal of competitors and, accordingly, that those measures revealed a degree of harm such as that of the BIDS arrangements.

86. Although the General Court found, in paragraph 198 of the judgment under appeal, that the measures at issue encouraged the members of the Grouping not to exceed a certain volume of CB card issuing, the objective of such encouragement was, according to its own findings in paragraphs 245, 247 and 327 of that judgment, not to reduce possible overcapacity on the market for the issue of payment cards in France, but to achieve a given ratio between the issuing and acquisition activities of the members of the Grouping in order to develop the CB system further.

87. It follows that the General Court could not, without erring in law, characterise the measures at issue as restrictions of competition 'by object' within the meaning of Article [101(1)].

...

92. In the light of all the foregoing, it must be found that, in holding that the measures at issue had as their object a restriction of competition within the meaning of Article [101(1)], the General Court erred in law and failed to observe the standard of review required under the case-law.

In *SIA 'Maxima Latvija' v Konkurences padome*[105] the CJ reiterated this approach, stressing the restrictive nature of the 'by object category' and that it should only be expanded outside the established

---

[105] Case C-345/14, EU:C:2015:784.

category of restraints where the agreement 'reveals in itself a sufficient degree of harm to competition for it to be considered that it is not appropriate to assess its effects'.[106] The CJ thus held that as a commercial lease incorporating a clause giving the tenant the right to oppose the lease of commercial premises in the shopping centre to other tenants was not 'among the agreements which it is accepted may be considered, by their very nature, to be harmful to the proper functioning of competition',[107] the agreement had to be assessed in the economic and legal context in which it occurred to determine its effects.

22. Even if the clause at issue in the main proceedings could potentially have the effect of restricting the access of Maxima Latvija's competitors to some shopping centres in which that company operates a large shop or hypermarket, such a fact, if established, does not imply clearly that the agreements containing that clause prevent, restrict or distort, by the very nature of the latter, competition on the relevant market, namely the local market for the retail food trade.

23. Taking account of the economic context in which agreements, such as those at issue in the main proceedings are to be applied, the analysis of the content of those agreements would not, in the light of the information provided by the referring court, show, clearly, a degree of harm with regard to competition sufficient for those agreements to be considered to constitute a restriction of competition 'by object' within the meaning of Article 101(1) TFEU.

(v) The Objective of the Agreement and the Context in Which it Operates: Narrowing the List of Object Restraints

In a number of cases it has also been argued that an agreement containing severe restraints identified as restrictive by object in past case law (and set out in Section ii above) should *not* be characterised as restrictive by object as, examined in context, it is clear that its precise purpose is not to restrict competition but to achieve a pro-competitive or other legitimate objective (see also discussion of ancillary restraints below).

In *BIDS*, the CJ rejected the parties' plea that they had simply acted to deal with an industry crisis on the grounds that this 'type of arrangement conflicts patently with the concept inherent in the [TFEU] provisions relating to competition, according to which each economic operator must determine independently the policy which it intends to adopt on the common market'.[108] Further, in *Toshiba Corp v Commission*[109] the CJ rejected the argument that a market-sharing agreement should not have been found to be restrictive of competition by object by the Commission and GC, as they had failed adequately to analyse the economic and legal context, in particular by failing to ascertain whether entry by Japanese producers into the EEA market was an economically viable strategy for them. The Court stressed that the analysis of the context of which the practice forms part must 'be limited to what is strictly necessary in order to establish the existence of a restriction of competition by object'.[110] Further that as the GC had examined, and ruled out, Toshiba's argument that it could not restrict competition because the Japanese and EEA producers were not competitors, the GC had carried out correct sufficient analysis of the context.

31. . . . It is in that context that the General Court found, first, in paragraph 230 of the judgment under appeal, that, since Article 101 TFEU also concerns potential competition, the Gentlemen's Agreement was capable

---

[106] Ibid., para. 20.

[107] Ibid., para. 21.

[108] Ibid., para. 34. An agreement could restrict competition by object even if that was not its sole aim: 'Indeed, an agreement may be regarded as having a restrictive object even if it does not have the restriction of competition as its sole aim but also pursues other legitimate objectives . . . It is only in connection with Article [101(3)] that matters such as those relied upon by BIDS may, if appropriate, be taken into consideration for the purposes of obtaining an exemption from the prohibition laid down in Article [101(1)]', para. 21.

[109] Case C-373/14 P, EU:C:2016:26.

[110] Ibid., para. 29.

of restricting competition, unless insurmountable barriers to entry to the European market existed that ruled out any potential competition from Japanese producers.

32. Secondly, in paragraphs 232 and 233 of the judgment under appeal, the General Court held that those barriers could not be classified as insurmountable, which was shown by the fact that Hitachi had accepted projects coming from customers situated in Europe.

33. The General Court also held, in paragraph 231 of the judgment under appeal, that the Gentlemen's Agreement represented a 'strong indication that a competitive relationship existed' between the two categories of producers, which, as the Advocate General observes in point 100 of his Opinion, constitutes an element of the relevant economic and legal context.

34. The analysis which the General Court thus carried out is in accordance with the criteria set out in paragraphs 24 to 29 of this judgment in order to establish an infringement of Article 101(1) TFEU as a restriction by object, without a more detailed analysis of the relevant economic and legal context being necessary.

Nonetheless, in some judgments the CJ has accepted that inherently restrictive arrangements may be necessary to achieve a legitimate public policy objective or regulatory aim, for example 'the proper practice of the legal profession'[111] or the organisation and proper conduct of competitive sport[112] (see further discussion of ancillary restraints below).

What has been less clear, however, is whether severe restraints incorporated within a cooperative arrangement between the parties, and which are argued to be 'ancillary' to that productive activity, are to be characterised as restrictive by object. This question has been crucial in some situations where the Commission's (or others') characterisation of certain agreements as restrictive of competition by object has been hotly contested, for example in cases involving the setting of MIFs[113] as an integral part of the operation of a payment system, see further Chapter 9 and discussion of *MasterCard* below.

One view is that, as such agreements do not obviously reveal a sufficiently deleterious and obvious risk to competition or restrictive purpose, they should not be assumed to restrict competition and should be condemned only if found to restrict competition in fact. Such an approach would have parallels to that adopted by the US courts, which applies an 'ancillary restraints' doctrine to distinguish per se restraints from restraints which have to be analysed under the rule of reason ('characterisation'). In *Broadcast Music, Inc ('BMI') v Columbia Broadcasting System Inc*,[114] in particular, the US Supreme Court drew a sharp distinction between:

- practices between competitors which facially appear to be one that would always or almost always tend to restrict competition and decrease output—such as naked price-fixing and market-sharing agreements with no purpose except stifling competition which are illegal per se; and

- practices designed to increase economic efficiency and render markets more, rather than less, competitive—such as agreements where price-fixing and market division are 'ancillary' to cooperative productive activity engaged in by the agreeing parties, which must be analysed under the rule of reason.

In this case the Court thus warned that 'easy labels do not always supply ready answers' and held that the blanket copyright licence at issue in that case, concluded by BMI and ASCAP, although literally constituting 'price fixing', should not automatically be condemned as illegal per se. Rather

---

[111] Case C-309/99, *Wouters v Algemene Raad van de Nederlandse Orde van Advocaten* [2002] ECR I-1577, at paras. 106–110, see n. 178 and text.

[112] Case C-519/04 P, *Meca-Medina v Commission* [2006] ECR I-6991, paras. 45–47, see n. 194 and text.

[113] In Chap. 9 it will be seen that even though these arrangements involve horizontal price restraints, no ruling of the EU Courts has upheld this view.

[114] *Broadcast Music, Inc v Columbia Broadcasting System, Inc*, 441 US 1 (1979). See also *NCAA v Board of Regents of the University of Oklahoma*, 468 US 85 (1984).

it should be analysed under the rule of reason as it had the potential to achieve efficiencies by eliminating the costs of individual negotiation.[115]

A counter-argument could be that as such agreements contain clauses which are inherently suspicious, they should be assumed to restrict competition—to restrict competition by object; efficiency justifications for the agreement can be raised at the Article 101(3) stage. It has been seen, however, that despite the theoretical existence of Article 101(3) in object cases, in practice it is difficult to justify such agreements under Article 101(3) and to know when arguments so presented will be accepted (a perception of per se illegality has been created for most object cases). Further, it is difficult to see how holding that such agreements are restrictive of competition by object would meet the objectives underpinning Article 101; rather it would seem to create a risk of infringement for technical reasons and wrongly condemning pro-competitive agreements and false positives. Indeed, although such agreements may have the potential to restrict competition it is hard to see that they reveal a sufficiently deleterious and obvious risk to competition, as required by the CJ in *STM* and *CB*.

The CJ's ruling in *CB* (discussed above) in particular lends support for the view that such restrictions should not be found to restrict competition by object. The CJ stressed the narrow nature of the object category, confining it to agreements revealing a sufficient degree of harm to competition, Secondly, it distinguished cases, such as *CB*, where the purpose of the arrangement is to achieve a pro-competitive commercial objective (for example, where complex pricing rules are used in two-sided markets), from other cases where naked horizontal price or output restraints are specifically intended to eliminate competitors and competition from the market. The Court indicated that in the former circumstances, a detailed analysis or a careful study of the evidence is required to determine whether it has as its effect the restriction of competition. Indeed, the Commission seems to endorse such an approach in its Horizontal Cooperation Guidelines and By Object Guidance and it ensures that Article 101 analysis is in line with merger analysis.[116]

Similarly, although the EU Courts have held that certain vertical restraints are, in principle, restrictive of competition by object, it has been accepted that an assumption of anti-competitive effects should not be applied where other circumstances, falling within the economic and legal context of the agreement, justify a finding that such an agreement is not liable to impair competition.[117] Indeed: in *Coditel II*, the CJ held that an exclusive territorial licence conferring ATP on a broadcaster was not as such restrictive of competition;[118] in *Murphy*,[119] the CJ ruled that a broadcasting licensing agreement containing territorial limitations aimed at partitioning national markets, would not have to be regarded as restrictive by object where other circumstances falling within its economic and legal context justified the finding that such an agreement is not liable to impair competition; in the Guidelines on Vertical Restraints, the Commission states that severe vertical restraints (such as bans on selling outside a specified sales territory) will fall outside Article 101(1) altogether for two years where a manufacturer needs to encourage substantial investments by a distributor in order

---

[115] Under this approach, the initial inquiry as to whether the restraint is ancillary is distinct from the substantive rule of reason analysis conducted; the fact that it is ancillary to legitimate joint activity is not therefore enough to establish as a matter of law that the agreement does not unreasonably restrain trade and so falls outside s. 1 of the Sherman Act, rather this is a separate issue to be considered.

[116] See Horizontal Cooperation Guidelines, paras. 128, 160–161, and 205–206, discussed in Chap. 10, Commission Staff Working Document, n. 59, pp. 5–6, C. E. Mosso, 'The Contribution of Merger Control to the Definition of Harm to Competition', GCLC Conference, Brussels, February 2016 (object restrictions have no equivalent in merger analysis rather each merger is analysed to determine its likely impact of the merger on the main market parameters of competition) and Chap. 10.

[117] For the view that the objective necessity test will be deemed to be fulfilled in the case of ATP where, in particular, the agreement (a) does not exceed the scope of an intellectual property right that (b) is not exhausted, see Ibáñez Colomo, 'Copyright Licensing and the EU Digital Single Market Strategy', n. 54.

[118] Case 262/81, *Coditel v Ciné Vog Films (Coditel II)* [1982] ECR 3381. See also Case 27/87, *Erauw-Jacquéry v La Hesbignonne* [1988] ECR 1919 (and Chap. 12).

[119] Cases C-403/08 and C-429/08, *Murphy* EU:C:2011:631.

to start developing a market—for example, where the distributor needs to invest in launching and establishing a new brand on the market.[120] and in *Pierre Fabre v Président de l'Autorité de la concurrence*,[121] the CJ held that although selective distribution agreements restriction competition 'by object', they will fall outside Article 101(1) where objectively justified.[122] On the facts of that case, however, the CJ held that a ban on internet selling, which was 'liable to restrict competition', did not constitute a proportionate measure to achieve a legitimate aim. These issues are considered further in Chapters 11 and 12.

(vi) Is an Assumption that an Agreement Restricts Competition Warranted Where, Taking Account of the Market Structure and Market Power of the Parties, a Restriction of Competition is in Fact Unlikely?

It has been seen that in *Cartes Bancaires* the CJ held that if an analysis of effects is required, an assumption of a restriction of competition is not appropriate. By the same token, it is not possible for the parties to an agreement to escape the assumption of a restriction of competition applied in 'object' cases by showing that the agreement does not, or is not likely to, have an actual restrictive effect[123] (whether on prices or other parameters of competition),[124] for example because the market shares of the parties are low or because of other specific features of the market.[125] Indeed, the case law indicates that an analysis of the effects of an agreement has no place in object cases so once an agreement has been characterised as restrictive of competition by object, the actual effect of the agreement need not be considered—the agreement is simply assumed to restrict competition. This seems to be the core reason why the CJ, in *GlaxoSmithKline Services Unlimited (GSK) v Commission*,[126] overturned the ruling of the GC.[127]

GSK concerned the general sales conditions for the supply of certain pharmaceuticals products to Spanish wholesalers which GSK had notified (under the old notification and exemption system) to the Commission, seeking confirmation that the agreement did not infringe Article 101. The arrangements incorporated (in clause 4) a dual pricing system which resulted in Spanish wholesalers being charged a higher price for drugs resold in other Member States than for those resold in Spain. GSK admitted that the purpose of this provision was to restrict parallel trade, but argued that parallel trade benefited only the intermediaries (the parallel importers and exporters). In contrast, the restriction on parallel trade benefited final consumers as it provided GSK with additional resources for investment in the research and development (R&D) of new medicines. The Commission rejected these arguments, concluding both that (a) the general sales conditions infringed Article 101(1)—they had as their object and effect the restriction of competition; and (b) they did not merit an exemption as GSK had not proved its case under Article 101(3).

[120] Guidelines on Vertical Restraints, para. 61.

[121] Case C-439/09, EU:C:2011:277.

[122] On the facts of that case, however, the Court of Justice held that a ban on internet selling, which was 'liable to restrict competition', did not constitute a proportionate measure to achieve a legitimate aim.

[123] Case C-286/13 P, *Dole* EU:C:2015:184, paras. 111–135.

[124] 'Accordingly, . . . there is no need to consider the effects of a concerted practice where its anti-competitive object is established', Case C-8/08, *T-Mobile* [2009] ECR I-4529, para. 31.

[125] See Article 101(3) Guidelines, para. 22.

[126] Case C-501/06 P, [2009] ECR I-9291 and Case T-168/01, [2006] ECR II-2969.

[127] See also Cases C-101 and 110/07 P, *Coop de France bétail et viande v Commission* [2008] ECR I-10193 (the CJ held that the GC had taken the (adverse) economic context into account when making its determination that the purpose of the agreement fixing minimum purchasing prices and suspending imports of beef into France was to restrict competition; 'since the [GC] concluded that it was established that the object of the Agreement . . . was anticompetitive, it correctly ruled . . . that the Commission was not bound to research the actual effects on competition of the measure', para. 88).

The GC ruled that the Commission had been right to find that the agreement infringed Article 101(1) but annulled the decision insofar as it had rejected GSK's exemption application.[128] With regard to the violation of Article 101(1), however, the GC held that the Commission had been wrong to characterise the agreement as restrictive by object. Although it held that it was true that an agreement intended to prevent parallel trade unfavourably had, in principle, to be regarded as having its object the restriction of competition, the Court stated that Article 101(1) also required an abridged analysis designed to determine whether the agreement restricted competition, to the detriment of final consumers. The GC concluded that, in this case, the specific characteristics of the pharmaceutical sector, which led to prices of medicine being largely shielded from the free play of supply and demand by regulation, meant that *no* assumption could be made that parallel trade would reduce prices and increase the welfare of final consumers. Despite the special circumstances that existed in *GSK*, the conclusion drawn by the GC seemed potentially to open the possibility for parties to argue that an agreement should not be presumed to restrict competition because of the particular facts of the case and so to bring effects analysis into object cases.[129]

The Commission appealed this aspect of the GC's judgment and the CJ upheld the Commission's view that the agreement was indeed restrictive by object. The Court stressed that in principle agreements aimed at prohibiting or limiting parallel trade have as their object the prevention of competition and that that principle applies in the pharmaceutical sector. Further, that an agreement tending to restore national divisions in trade between Member States might be such as to frustrate the Treaty's single market objective and that it was not necessary for an agreement to be considered to have as its object the restriction of competition, that it be presumed to deprive final consumers of the advantages of effective competition in terms of price.

Case C-501/06 P, *GlaxoSmithKline Services v Commission* [2009] ECR I-9291

Court of Justice

58. According to settled case-law, in order to assess the anti-competitive nature of an agreement, regard must be had inter alia to the content of its provisions, the objectives it seeks to attain and the economic and legal context of which it forms a part. . . . In addition, although the parties' intention is not a necessary factor in determining whether an agreement is restrictive, there is nothing prohibiting the Commission or the Community judicature from taking that aspect into account (see, to that effect, *IAZ International Belgium and Others v Commission*, . . . , paragraphs 23 to 25).

59. With respect to parallel trade, the Court has already held that, in principle, agreements aimed at prohibiting or limiting parallel trade have as their object the prevention of competition (see, to that effect, Case 19/77 *Miller International Schallplaten v Commission* . . . , paragraphs 7 and 18, and Joined Cases 32/78, 36/78 to 82/78 *BMW Belgium and Others v Commission* . . . , paragraphs 20 to 28 and 31).

60. As observed by the Advocate General in point 155 of her Opinion, that principle, according to which an agreement aimed at limiting parallel trade is a 'restriction of competition by object', applies to the pharmaceuticals sector.

61. The Court has, moreover, held in that regard, in relation to the application of Article [101] and in a case involving the pharmaceuticals sector, that an agreement between producer and distributor which

---

[128] The GC held that the Commission had not adequately refuted GSK's evidence of efficiencies, see further Section 4.

[129] Indeed, it has been seen that in *Consten and Grundig*, the parties argued passionately that their agreement conferring ATP on Consten had been essential to its operation. Roemer AG supported their view, but the CJ held that since the *object of* the agreement was to restrict competition a consideration of the effects was not necessary, Cases 56 and 58/64, *Consten and Grundig* [1966] ECR 299, 342–343.

might tend to restore the national divisions in trade between Member States might be such as to frustrate the Treaty's objective of achieving the integration of national markets through the establishment of a single market. Thus on a number of occasions the Court has held agreements aimed at partitioning national markets according to national borders or making the interpenetration of national markets more difficult, in particular those aimed at preventing or restricting parallel exports, to be agreements whose object is to restrict competition within the meaning of that article of the Treaty (Joined Cases C-468/06 to C-478/06 *Sot. Lélos kai Sia and Others* . . . , paragraph 65 and case-law cited).

62. With respect to the [GC]'s statement that, while it is accepted that an agreement intended to limit parallel trade must in principle be considered to have as its object the restriction of competition, that applies in so far as it may be presumed to deprive final consumers of the advantages of effective competition in terms of supply or price, the Court notes that neither the wording of Article [101(1)] nor the case-law lend support to such a position.

63. First of all, there is nothing in that provision to indicate that only those agreements which deprive consumers of certain advantages may have an anti-competitive object. Secondly, it must be borne in mind that the Court has held that, like other competition rules laid down in the Treaty, Article [101] aims to protect not only the interests of competitors or of consumers, but also the structure of the market and, in so doing, competition as such. Consequently, for a finding that an agreement has an anti-competitive object, it is not necessary that final consumers be deprived of the advantages of effective competition in terms of supply or price (see, by analogy, *T-Mobile* . . . , paragraphs 38 and 39).

64. It follows that, by requiring proof that the agreement entails disadvantages for final consumers as a prerequisite for a finding of anti-competitive object and by not finding that that agreement had such an object, the [GC] committed an error of law.

65. However, where the grounds of a judgment of the [GC] are contrary to Community law, that judgment need not be set aside if the operative part of the judgment appears to be well founded on other legal grounds (see, to that effect, Case C-30/91 P *Lestelle v Commission* . . . , paragraph 28, and Case C-294/95 P *Ojha v Commission* . . . , paragraph 52).

66. That is the case here. It suffices to note that in point 2 of the operative part of the judgment under appeal, the [GC] confirmed Article 1 of the contested decision, by which the Commission had found that the agreement infringed Article [101(1)]. Accordingly, it is not necessary to set aside point 2 of the operative part of the judgment under appeal.

67. In the light of all the aforegoing considerations, GSK's appeal must be dismissed as unfounded in so far as it seeks to establish that the agreement was compatible with Article [101(1)].

(vii) Object Cases, Appreciability, Market Definition, and Market Power

In the preceding discussion it has been seen that restrictions of competition by object are assumed to constitute a threat to the attainment of the Treaty's objectives, irrespective of their actual effects. The person alleging the infringement is not, therefore, generally required to demonstrate the relevant market, the existence of market power, or actual or likely harm to competition. In Chapter 3, however, it was seen that the CJ has made it clear that 'in order to come within the prohibition imposed by Article [101(1)], the agreement must affect trade between Member States and the free play of competition to an appreciable extent';[130] EU law is not concerned with agreements which have an 'insignificant effect on the market, taking into account the weak position which the persons concerned have on the market of the product in question' (Völk).[131] Further, that the Commission has issued a series of Notices indicating when, in its view, an agreement is likely to be considered to be

---

[130] Case 22/71, *Béguelin Import Co v GL Import-Export SA* [1971] ECR 949.

[131] Case 5/69, *Völk v Vervaecke* [1969] ECR 295, 302.

of minor importance and enabling undertakings to judge for themselves whether their agreements fall outside the Article 101(1) prohibition by virtue of their minor importance.

In Chapter 3 the Notice on the Effect on Trade Concept was examined which sets out guidance as to when an agreement (even one containing an object restraint) is unlikely to affect trade between Member States appreciably. A separate Notice governs agreements of minor importance which do not appreciably restrict competition. Although the current Notice on agreements of minor importance (De Minimis Notice), published in 2014[132] utilises market share thresholds to quantify what is *not* likely to constitute an appreciable restriction, paragraph 13 of the Notice provides that the thresholds (and Notice) do *not* apply to agreements which have as their object the restriction of competition (this was the reason why the Commission published an accompanying Staff Working Document setting out guidance on what it considers to constitute a restriction by object):

Notice on agreements of minor importance which do not appreciably restrict competition under Article 101(1) of the Treaty on the Functioning of the European Union (De Minimis Notice) [2014] OJ C291/01

2. The Court of Justice has also clarified that an agreement which may affect trade between Member States and which has as its object the prevention, restriction or distortion of competition within the internal market constitutes, by its nature and independently of any concrete effects that it may have, an appreciable restriction of competition. This Notice therefore does not cover agreements which have as their object the prevention, restriction or distortion of competition within the internal market.

...

13. In view of the clarification of the Court of Justice referred to in point 2, this Notice does not cover agreements which have as their object the prevention, restriction or distortion of competition within the internal market. The Commission will thus not apply the safe harbour created by the market share thresholds set out in points 8, 9, 10 and 11 to such agreements. For instance, as regards agreements between competitors, the Commission will not apply the principles set out in this Notice to, in particular, agreements containing restrictions which, directly or indirectly, have as their object: a) the fixing of prices when selling products to third parties; b) the limitation of output or sales; or c) the allocation of markets or customers. Likewise, the Commission will not apply the safe harbour created by those market share thresholds to agreements containing any of the restrictions that are listed as hardcore restrictions in any current or future Commission block exemption regulation, which are considered by the Commission to generally constitute restrictions by object.

The judgment referred to in this extract is *Expedia Inc v Authorité de la Concurrence*.[133] Although the CJ's judgment in *Völk* established that even object restraints may fall outside Article 101(1) on de minimis grounds (in that case it will be remembered the agreement conferred ATP on the distributor but the parties had an exceptionally small market shares of less than 1 per cent), the CJ ruled in *Expedia* that an agreement which is restrictive of competition by object is so injurious to competition that it always constitutes an appreciable restriction of competition (paragraph 37). Many, including the Commission, consequently take the view that this judgment overrules the ruling in *Völk*. Indeed, the Commission stated in a press release that the judgment in *Expedia* 'has established that a

[132] Notice on agreements of minor importance which do not appreciably restrict competition under Article 101(1) of the Treaty on the Functioning of the European Union (De Minimis Notice) [2014] OJ C291/01. The previous notice was set out in [2001] OJ C368/13.

[133] Case C-226/11, EU:C:2012:795.

restriction with an anticompetitive object constitutes, by its very nature, an appreciable restriction of competition'.[134]

Although the Commission's view is now reflected in the 2014 De Minimis Notice, it should be noted that if the CJ did intend to overrule *Völk* in *Expedia*, it did not do so as clearly as it could have. In particular, prior to paragraph 37, it relies on *Völk* both as authority for the settled position that an agreement falls outside Article 101(1) if it has only an insignificant effect on the market and also as a case in which it was found 'that an exclusive dealing agreement, even with absolute territorial protection, has only an insignificant effect on the market . . . taking into account the weak position which the persons concerned have in that market'.[135] Further, it concludes that an NCA can only apply Article 101(1) to an agreement, stated by the national court to be restrictive by object, 'provided that that agreement constitutes an appreciable restriction of competition'.[136]

Case C-226/11, *Expedia Inc v Authorité de la Concurrence* EU:C:2012:795

In this case the French competition authority had found that a joint venture created by SNCF and Expedia for the reservation and sale of train tickets over the internet infringed Article 101 and French law and imposed financial penalties on both SNCF and Expedia. The parties alleged on appeal that as their market shares fell below 10 per cent, the agreement should have fallen outside the competition rules on de minimis grounds. The Cour de Cassation concluded that the agreement at issue had an anti-competitive object but stayed proceeding to refer to the CJ the question of whether the national finding would be precluded if the parties' market shares did not reach the thresholds specified by the Commission in the De Minimis Notice.

Court of Justice

The question referred for a preliminary ruling

14. By its question, the referring court seeks to know, essentially, whether Article 101(1) TFEU and Article 3(2) of Regulation No 1/2003 must be interpreted as precluding a national competition authority from applying Article 101(1) TFEU to an agreement between undertakings that may affect trade between Member States, but that does not reach the thresholds specified by the Commission in its *de minimis* notice.

15. It should be noted that Article 101(1) TFEU prohibits as incompatible with the internal market all agreements between undertakings, decisions by associations of undertakings and concerted practices which may affect trade between Member States and which have as their object or effect the prevention, restriction or distortion of competition within the internal market.

16. It is settled case-law that an agreement of undertakings falls outside the prohibition in that provision, however, if it has only an insignificant effect on the market (. . . *Völk* v *Vervaecke* . . ., paragraph 7; . . . P *John Deere* v *Commission* . . . , paragraph 77; . . . *Bagnasco* . . . , paragraph 34; and . . . *Asnef-Equifax* . . . , paragraph 50).

17. Accordingly, if it is to fall within the scope of the prohibition under Article 101(1) TFEU, an agreement of undertakings must have the object or effect of perceptibly restricting competition within the common market and be capable of affecting trade between Member States (. . . *BMW* . . . , paragraph 18; . . . *Javico* [1998] . . . , paragraph 12; and . . . *Pedro IV Servicios* . . . , paragraph 68).

---

[134] IP/13/685.

[135] Case C-226/11, *Expedia* EU:C:2012:795, para. 22.

[136] Ibid., para. 38.

18. With regard to the role of Member State authorities in the enforcement of Union competition law, the first sentence of Article 3(1) of Regulation No 1/2003 establishes a close link between the prohibition of the agreements set out in Article 101 TFEU and the corresponding provisions of national competition law. Where the national competition authority applies provisions of national law prohibiting cartels to an agreement of undertakings which is capable of affecting trade between Member States within the meaning of Article 101 TFEU, the first sentence of Article 3(1) requires Article 101 TFEU also to be applied to it in parallel (. . . *Toshiba Corporation* . . . , paragraph 77).

19. Under Article 3(2) of Regulation No 1/2003, the application of national competition law may not lead to the prohibition of such agreements if they do not restrict competition within the meaning of Article 101(1) TFEU.

20. It follows that the competition authorities of the Member States can apply the provisions of national law prohibiting cartels to an agreement of undertakings which is capable of affecting trade between Member States within the meaning of Article 101 TFEU only where that agreement perceptibly restricts competition within the common market.

21. The Court has held that the existence of such a restriction must be assessed by reference to the actual circumstances of such an agreement (Case 1/71 *Cadillon* . . . , paragraph 8). Regard must be had, inter alia, to the content of its provisions, the objectives it seeks to attain and the economic and legal context of which it forms a part (. . . *GlaxoSmithKline Services* . . ., paragraph 58). It is also appropriate to take into consideration the nature of the goods or services affected, as well as the real conditions of the functioning and the structure of the market or markets in question (see, to that effect, *Asnef-Equifax* . . ., paragraph 49).

22. In its examination, the Court found, inter alia, that an exclusive dealing agreement, even with absolute territorial protection, has only an insignificant effect on the market in question, taking into account the weak position which the persons concerned have in that market, (*Völk*, paragraph 7, and *Cadillon*, paragraph 9). In other cases, however, it did not base its decision on the position of the persons concerned in the market in question. Accordingly, in paragraph 35 of *Bagnasco and Others*, it found that an agreement between the members of a banking association which excludes the right, with regard to the opening of current-account credit facilities, to adopt a fixed interest rate cannot have an appreciable restrictive effect on competition, since any variation of the interest rate depends on objective factors, such as changes occurring in the money market.

23. It is apparent from paragraphs 1 and 2 of the *de minimis* notice that the Commission intends to quantify therein, with the help of market share thresholds, what is not an appreciable restriction of competition within the meaning of Article 101 TFEU and the case-law cited in paragraphs 16 and 17 of the present judgment.

24. With regard to the wording of the *de minimis* notice, its non-binding nature, for both the competition authorities and the courts of the Member States, is emphasised in the third sentence of paragraph 4 thereof.

. . .

28. It is apparent from [paragraph 4], first, that the purpose of that notice is to make transparent the manner in which the Commission, acting as the competition authority of the European Union, will itself apply Article 101 TFEU. Consequently, by the *de minimis* notice, the Commission imposes a limit on the exercise of its discretion and must not depart from the content of that notice without being in breach of the general principles of law, in particular the principles of equal treatment and the protection of legitimate expectations (see, to that effect, . . . *Dansk Rørindustri and Others* v *Commission* . . . , paragraph 211). Furthermore, it intends to give guidance to the courts and authorities of the Member States in their application of that article.

29. Consequently, and as the Court has already had occasion to point out, a Commission notice, such as the *de minimis* notice, is not binding in relation to the Member States (see, to that effect, . . . *Pfleiderer* . . . , paragraph 21).

. . .

31. Consequently, in order to determine whether or not a restriction of competition is appreciable, the competition authority of a Member State may take into account the thresholds established in paragraph 7 of the *de minimis* notice but is not required to do so. Such thresholds are no more than factors among others that may enable that authority to determine whether or not a restriction is appreciable by reference to the actual circumstances of the agreement.

32. Contrary to what Expedia argued during the hearing, the proceedings brought and penalties imposed by the competition authority of a Member State, on undertakings that enter into an agreement that has not reached the thresholds defined in the *de minimis* notice, cannot infringe, as such, the principles of legitimate expectations and legal certainty, having regard to the wording of paragraph 4 of that notice.

33. Furthermore, as the Advocate General pointed out in point 33 of her Opinion, the principle of the lawfulness of penalties does not require the *de minimis* notice to be regarded as a legal measure binding on the national authorities. Cartels are already prohibited by the primary law of the European Union, that is, by Article 101(1) TFEU.

34. In so far as Expedia, the French Government and the Commission have, in their written observations or during the hearing, questioned the finding made by the national court that it is not disputed that the agreement at issue in the main proceedings had an anti-competitive object, it should be remembered that, in proceedings under Article 267 TFEU, which is based on a clear separation of functions between the national courts and the Court of Justice, any assessment of the facts in the main proceedings is a matter for the national court (. . . *Winner Wetten* . . . , paragraph 49 . . .).

35. Moreover, it should be noted that, according to settled case-law, for the purpose of applying Article 101(1) TFEU, there is no need to take account of the concrete effects of an agreement once it appears that it has as its object the prevention, restriction or distortion of competition (see, to that effect, . . . *Consten and Grundig v Commission* . . . ; . . . *KME Germany and Others v Commission* . . . paragraph 65; and . . . *KME Germany and Others* v *Commission* . . . , paragraph 75).

36. In that regard, the Court has emphasised that the distinction between 'infringements by object' and 'infringements by effect' arises from the fact that certain forms of collusion between undertakings can be regarded, by their very nature, as being injurious to the proper functioning of normal competition (. . . *('BIDS')* . . . , paragraph 17, and . . . *T-Mobile* . . . , paragraph 29).

37. It must therefore be held that an agreement that may affect trade between Member States and that has an anti-competitive object constitutes, by its nature and independently of any concrete effect that it may have, an appreciable restriction on competition.

38. In light of the above, the answer to the question referred is that Article 101(1) TFEU and Article 3(2) of Regulation No 1/2003 must be interpreted as not precluding a national competition authority from applying Article 101(1) TFEU to an agreement between undertakings that may affect trade between Member States, but that does not reach the thresholds specified by the Commission in its *de minimis* notice, provided that that agreement constitutes an appreciable restriction of competition within the meaning of that provision.

In spite of the ambiguity, the case is being interpreted as deciding the point that in object cases an appreciable restriction of competition is assumed; the market consequently does not need to be defined for this purpose. In *Ziegler SA v Commission*,[137] however, the EU Courts had to deal with the argument that the Commission had failed to define the relevant market for the purposes of determining whether the agreement had an appreciable effect on trade.[138] The CJ held that the Commission did have to define the market if it chose to apply its Notice on the effect on trade concept. Nonetheless it rejected Ziegler's argument on the facts as the GC had found that the Commission had provided a sufficiently detailed description of the relevant sector, including supply, demand, and scope, to allow

---

[137] Case C-439/11 P, EU:C:2013:513.

[138] See Chap. 3, Section 5.E, pp. 171–177.

the Court to verify the Commission's basic assertions that the combined market share far exceeded the 5 per cent threshold set out in that Notice.[139]

(viii) Restrictions by Object and 'Hardcore' Restraints

The previous discussion sets out the types of contractual provisions that have caused a finding that an agreement has as its object the restriction of competition. These object restraints broadly correspond with a list of 'hardcore' restraints, identified by the Commission in its Notices, Guidelines, and block exemptions, as agreements presumed to infringe Article 101(1) and presumed *not* to satisfy the Article 101(3) criteria (for which reason the block exemption regulations do not apply).[140] Indeed, in the section above, it was seen that the Commission equates 'hardcore' with object restrictions in paragraph 13 of its De Minimis Notice.

Caution needs to be adopted to this approach, however. First, as a matter of law, it is not for the Commission to expand and codify the category of object restraints in this way; rather it has been seen that an agreement only restricts competition by object if its precise purpose can be said to restrict competition (there is no such thing as a definitive list of object restraints).[141] Secondly, the Commission has sought to create the impression that object and hardcore restrictions are most unlikely to satisfy the conditions of Article 101(3)—so bringing EU law on object restraints more closely in line with the US per se rule, where a conclusive presumption of unreasonableness is applied. It is seen in Section 4 below, however, that all agreements are capable of satisfying the conditions of Article 101(3) even those incorporating object restraints. If the Commission were more willing to accept this, the controversy surrounding object categorisation might be somewhat assuaged.

C. AGREEMENTS THAT DO NOT RESTRICT COMPETITION BY OBJECT: ANALYSING THEIR EFFECTS

(i) General

Where the object of an agreement cannot be said to restrict competition, an analysis of its *effect* becomes crucial.

Where…an analysis of the said clauses does not reveal the effect on competition to be sufficiently deleterious, the consequence of the agreement should then be considered and for it to be caught by the prohibition it is then necessary to find that those factors are present that show that competition has in fact been prevented or restricted or distorted to an appreciable extent. The competition in question must be understood within the actual context in which it would occur in the absence of the agreement in dispute.[142]

It has been seen that the Commission's view is that consumer welfare should be the benchmark against which agreements are tested and that: Article 101(1) is about identifying restrictions on inter- or intra-brand competition; whilst Article 101(3), not Article 101(1), provides the forum for weighing the restrictive effects identified at this stage against the economic benefits and efficiencies created by the agreement.[143]

---

[139] Case C-439/11 P, EU:C:2013:513, paras. 57–89.

[140] Article 101(3) Guidelines, para. 23. See also, e.g., COMP/39.579, *Consumer Detergents* [2011] OJ C193/14, 13 April 2011, paras. 53–54.

[141] See Case C-439/09, *Pierre Fabre* EU:C:2011:277 and Mazák AG in his Opinion in this case, EU:C:2010:718, para. 29 (the fact that the Commission has categorised it as a hardcore restraint does not necessarily mean that it has the object or effect of restricting competition).

[142] Case 56/65, *STM* [1966] ECR 234, 249.

[143] See White Paper on the Modernisation of the Rules Implementing Articles 85 and 86 of the EC Treaty [now Articles 101 and 102 TFEU] [1999] OJ C132/1, paras. 56–57.

(ii) Appraisal of an Agreement in its Legal and Economic Context

The CJ in both *STM*[144] and *Brasserie de Haecht v Wilkin (No. 1)*[145] stressed the need to examine an agreement which did not have as its object the restriction of competition in its market context to determine its effect. In *STM*, the CJ dealt with an exclusive distribution agreement which, in contrast to that concerned in *Consten and Grundig*, did not confer ATP (or a complete monopoly over the right to distribute in France) on the distributor. The contractual arrangements did admit the possibility of parallel imports from distributors in other Member States. In this case the CJ did not hold that the object of the agreement was to restrict competition. Rather, accepting similar arguments to those raised by the parties (but rejected by the Court) in *Consten and Grundig*, it indicated that an exclusive distribution agreement would not restrict competition if the appointment of an exclusive distributor was necessary in order to enable a manufacturer to penetrate a new market.[146] Before it could be determined whether the agreement restricted competition, the agreement should be examined in the light of the competition which would occur if the agreement in question were not or had not been made. In this case it seemed that the economic justifications for the agreement might outweigh the territorial restrictions inherent in the agreement.

> ### Case 56/65, *Société Technique Minière v Maschinenbau Ulm GmbH* [1966] ECR 234, 249–250
>
> The parties entered into an agreement by which a French company was given exclusive rights to distribute in France the equipment (levelling machines) of a German manufacturer. The French company was free to re-export the equipment outside France. The parties fell out, and in litigation in the French courts the French company claimed that the agreement was void under Article 101(2) because it infringed Article 101(1). The Cour d'Appel Paris asked the Court of Justice on a preliminary reference how it should assess the compatibility of this type of agreement with Article 101(1).
>
> ### Court of Justice
>
> #### The effects of the agreement on competition
>
> . . . The competition in question must be understood within the actual context in which it would occur in the absence of the agreement in dispute. In particular it may be doubted whether there is an interference with competition if the said agreement seems really necessary for the penetration of a new area by an undertaking. Therefore, in order to decide whether an agreement containing a clause 'granting an exclusive right of sale' is to be considered as prohibited by reason of its object or of its effect, it is appropriate to take into account in particular the nature and quantity, limited or otherwise, of the products covered by the agreement, the position and importance of the grantor and the concessionnaire on the market for the products concerned, the isolated nature of the disputed agreement or, alternatively, its position in series of agreements, the severity of the clauses intended to protect the exclusive dealership or, alternatively, the opportunities allowed for other commercial competitors in the same products by way of parallel re-exportation and importation.

Brasserie de Haecht concerned the compatibility of a beer-supply agreement, containing a beer tie, with Article 101(1). In many Member States brewers conclude agreements with outlets such as

---

[144] Case 56/65, *STM* [1966] ECR 235, 249–250.

[145] Case 23/67, [1967] ECR 407.

[146] In line with *STM* the CJ has also held that where exclusivity provisions do not give a licensee of intellectual property (IP) rights ATP, restrictions in a licensing agreement may fall outside Art. 101(1) if necessary to protect the investment of the licensee, see Chap. 12.

public houses, which, in return for certain benefits from the brewer, oblige the outlet to purchase beer (and perhaps other drinks) exclusively from the brewer (or another named supplier). The CJ held that in considering whether there was a restriction of competition, it was necessary to take account of the whole market context in which the beer-supply agreement operated, including the simultaneous existence of similar contracts.

The CJ built upon the foundations of *Brasserie de Haecht* in *Delimitis v Henninger Bräu*.[147] It held that the object of a commitment to purchase beer and other drinks exclusively from named suppliers was not to restrict competition. On the contrary, the Court specifically referred to the benefits which flowed from such an agreement, for example the guarantee for a supplier of an outlet for its product; the assurance that the retailer would concentrate its sales efforts on the distribution of the contract goods; the ability of the retailer to gain access to the market on favourable terms; and the guarantee for the retailer of supply of products. Since the object of the agreement was not to restrict competition, the agreement would only be prohibited by Article 101(1) if this was its effect. In determining the effect, it is first necessary to define the relevant market. It must then be ascertained whether there is a concrete possibility for new competitors to penetrate the market or existing competitors to expand taking account of the number and size of producers operating on the market, the existence of networks of agreements, the saturation of the market, and brand loyalty, etc. If analysis shows that there is no denial of access to the market, an agreement cannot be found to restrict competition. Conversely, if access is inhibited it must then be assessed whether the agreement in question (which is taken to mean the agreements of that particular producer or brewer) contributes appreciably to that situation.

Case C-234/89, *Delimitis v Henninger Bräu* [1991] ECR I-935

Delimitis and a brewer concluded an agreement in which the brewer let a public house to Delimitis. In return, Delimitis undertook to obtain beer and soft drinks from the brewer or its subsidiaries. On the termination of the agreement a dispute arose as to the agreement's compatibility with Article 101. On a preliminary reference the Court of Justice set out guidelines in order to enable the national court to assess the compatibility of the agreement with Article 101. The extract below deals with Article 101(1).

Court of Justice

The compatibility of beer supply agreements with Article [101(1)]

10. Under the terms of beer supply agreements, the supplier generally affords the reseller certain economic and financial benefits, such as the grant of loans on favourable terms, the letting of premises for the operation of a public house and the provision of technical installations, furniture and other equipment necessary for its operation. In consideration for those benefits, the reseller normally undertakes, for a predetermined period, to obtain supplies of the products covered by the contract only from the supplier. That exclusive purchasing obligation is generally backed by a prohibition on selling competing products in the public house let by the supplier.

11. Such contracts entail for the supplier the advantage of guaranteed outlets, since, as a result of his exclusive purchasing obligation and the prohibition on competition, the reseller concentrates his sales efforts on the distribution of the contract goods. The supply agreements, moreover, lead to co-operation with the reseller, allowing the supplier to plan his sales over the duration of the agreement and to organize production and distribution effectively.

12. Beer supply agreements also have advantages for the reseller, inasmuch as they enable him to gain access under favourable conditions and with the guarantee of supplies to the beer distribution market.

---

[147] Case C-234/89, [1991] ECR I-935. See V. Korah, 'The Judgment in *Delimitis*: A Milestone Towards a Realistic Assessment of the Effects of an Agreement or a Damp Squib?' [1992] *EIPR* 167.

The reseller's and supplier's shared interest in promoting sales of the contract goods likewise secures for the reseller the benefit of the supplier's assistance in guaranteeing product quality and customer service.

13. If such agreements do not have the object of restricting competition within the meaning of Article [101(1)], it is nevertheless necessary to ascertain whether they have the effect of preventing, restricting or distorting competition.

14. In its judgment in Case 23/67 *Brasserie De Haecht v Wilkin* . . . , the Court held that the effects of such an agreement had to be assessed in the context in which they occur and where they might combine with others to have a cumulative effect on competition. It also follows from that judgment that the cumulative effect of several similar agreements constitutes one factor amongst others in ascertaining whether, by way of a possible alteration of competition, trade between Member States is capable of being affected.

15. Consequently, in the present case it is necessary to analyse the effects of a beer supply agreement, taken together with other contracts of the same type, on the opportunities of national competitors or those from other Member States, to gain access to the market for beer consumption or to increase their market share and, accordingly, the effects on the range of products offered to consumers.

16. In making that analysis, the relevant market must first be determined. The relevant market is primarily defined on the basis of the nature of the economic activity in question, in this case the sale of beer. Beer is sold through both retail channels and premises for the sale and consumption of drinks. From the consumer's point of view, the latter sector, comprising in particular public houses and restaurants, may be distinguished from the retail sector on the grounds that the sale of beer in public houses does not solely consist of the purchase of a product but is also linked with the provision of services, and that beer consumption in public houses is not essentially dependent on economic considerations. The specific nature of the public house trade is borne out by the fact that the breweries organize specific distribution systems for this sector which require special installations, and that the prices charged in that sector are generally higher than retail prices.

17. It follows that in the present case the reference market is that for the distribution of beer in premises for the sale and consumption of drinks. That finding is not affected by the fact that there is a certain overlap between the two distribution networks, namely inasmuch as retail sales allow new competitors to make their brands known and to use their reputation in order to gain access to the market constituted by premises for the sale and consumption of drinks.

18. Secondly, the relevant market is delimited from a geographical point of view. It should be noted that most beer supply agreements are still entered into at a national level. It follows that, in applying the [EU] competition rules, account is to be taken of the national market for beer distribution in premises for the sale and consumption of drinks.

19. In order to assess whether the existence of several beer supply agreements impedes access to the market as so defined, it is further necessary to examine the nature and extent of those agreements in their totality, comprising all similar contracts tying a large number of points of sale to several national producers (judgment in Case 43/69 *Bilger v Jehle* . . .). The effect of those networks of contracts on access to the market depends specifically on the number of outlets thus tied to national producers in relation to the number of public houses which are not so tied, the duration of the commitments entered into, the quantities of beer to which those commitments relate, and on the proportion between those quantities and the quantities sold by free distributors.

20. The existence of a bundle of similar contracts, even if it has a considerable effect on the opportunities for gaining access to the market, is not, however, sufficient in itself to support a finding that the relevant market is inaccessible, inasmuch as it is only one factor, amongst others, pertaining to the economic and legal context in which an agreement must be appraised (Case 23/67 *Brasserie De Haecht*, cited above). The other factors to be taken into account are, in the first instance, those also relating to opportunities for access.

21. In that connection it is necessary to examine whether there are real concrete possibilities for a new competitor to penetrate the bundle of contracts by acquiring a brewery already established on the market together with its network of sales outlets, or to circumvent the bundle of contracts by opening new public

houses. For that purpose it is necessary to have regard to the legal rules and agreements on the acquisition of companies and the establishment of outlets, and to the minimum number of outlets necessary for the economic operation of a distribution system. The presence of beer wholesalers not tied to producers who are active on the market is also a factor capable of facilitating a new producer's access to that market since he can make use of those wholesalers' sales networks to distribute his own beer.

22. Secondly, account must be taken of the conditions under which competitive forces operate on the relevant market. In that connection it is necessary to know not only the number and the size of producers present on the market, but also the degree of saturation of that market and customer fidelity to existing brands, for it is generally more difficult to penetrate a saturated market in which customers are loyal to a small number of large producers than a market in full expansion in which a large number of small producers are operating without any strong brand names. The trend in beer sales in the retail trade provides useful information on the development of demand and thus an indication of the degree of saturation of the beer market as a whole. The analysis of that trend is, moreover, of interest in evaluating brand loyalty. A steady increase in sales of beer under new brand names may confer on the owners of those brand names a reputation which they may turn to account in gaining access to the public-house market.

23. If an examination of all similar contracts entered into on the relevant market and the other factors relevant to the economic and legal context in which the contract must be examined shows that those agreements do not have the cumulative effect of denying access to that market to new national and foreign competitors, the individual agreements comprising the bundle of agreements cannot be held to restrict competition within the meaning of Article [101(1)]. They do not, therefore, fall under the prohibition laid down in that provision.

24. If, on the other hand, such examination reveals that it is difficult to gain access to the relevant market, it is necessary to assess the extent to which the agreements entered into by the brewery in question contribute to the cumulative effect produced in that respect by the totality of the similar contracts found on that market. Under the [EU] rules on competition, responsibility for such an effect of closing off the market must be attributed to the breweries which make an appreciable contribution thereto. Beer supply agreements entered into by breweries whose contribution to the cumulative effect is insignificant do not therefore fall under the prohibition under Article [101(1)].

25. In order to assess the extent of the contribution of the beer supply agreements entered into by a brewery to the cumulative sealing-off effect mentioned above, the market position of the contracting parties must be taken into consideration. That position is not determined solely by the market share held by the brewery and any group, to which it may belong, but also by the number of outlets tied to it or to its group, in relation to the total number of premises for the sale and consumption of drinks found in the relevant market.

26. The contribution of the individual contracts entered into by a brewery to the sealing-off of that market also depends on their duration. If the duration is manifestly excessive in relation to the average duration of beer supply agreements generally entered into on the relevant market, the individual contract falls under the prohibition under Article [101(1)]. A brewery with a relatively small market share which ties its sales outlets for many years may make a significant contribution to a sealing-off of the market as a brewery in a relatively strong market position which regularly releases sales outlets at shorter intervals.

27. The reply to be given to the first three questions is therefore that a beer supply agreement is prohibited by Article [101(1)], if two cumulative conditions are met. The first is that, having regard to the economic and legal context of the agreement at issue, it is difficult for competitors who could enter the market or increase their market share to gain access to the national market for the distribution of beer in premises for the sales and consumption of drinks. The fact that, in that market, the agreement in issue is one of a number of similar agreements having a cumulative effect on competition constitutes only one factor amongst others in assessing whether access to that market is indeed difficult. The second condition is that the agreement in question must make a significant contribution to the sealing-off effect brought about by the totality of those agreements in their economic and legal context. The extent of the contribution made by the individual agreement depends on the position of the contracting parties in the relevant market and on the duration of the agreement.

The analysis required by the CJ in this case highlights the importance of looking at the contractual restraint, not abstractly as a restraint, but in the context in which it operates before its effect can be determined. Irrespective of the fact that the judgment in *Delimitis* dealt only with beer-supply agreements it affirmed the general need for an economic approach when determining the compatibility of an agreement with Article 101(1) and an assessment of the impact of the agreement on inter-brand competition. Indeed, in *SIA 'Maxima Latvija' v Konkurences padome*,[148] the CJ held that the same approach should be applied to assess the compatibility of a commercial lease incorporating a clause giving the tenant the right to oppose the lease of commercial premises in the shopping centre to other tenants with Article 101(1). As such an agreement was not restrictive of competition by object,[149] it has to be considered whether, assessed in the economic and legal context in which it occurred, it had as its effect the restriction of competition. This required an analysis of (a) factors which determined access to the relevant market (and assessing whether there were real concrete possibilities for a new competitor to establish itself),[150] and (b) the conditions under which competitive forces operate on the relevant market, including the number and size of operators present on the market, the degree of concentration and customer fidelity to existing brands, and consumer habits.[151]

It is only if, after a thorough analysis of the economic and legal context in which the agreements at issue in the main proceedings occur and the specificities of the relevant market, it is found that access to that market is made difficult by all the similar agreements found on the market, that it will then be necessary to analyse to what extent they contribute to any closing-off of that market, on the basis that only agreements which make an appreciable contribution to that closing-off are prohibited … To assess the extent of the contribution of each of the agreements at issue in the main proceedings to the cumulative closing-off effect, the position of the contracting parties on the market in question and the duration of the agreements must be taken into consideration.[152]

In *European Night Services*[153] the GC also stressed the need for an effects-based approach to Article 101(1) in the context of horizontal agreements. In many cases parties operating at the same level of the economy may conclude an agreement which does not have the sole purpose of coordinating the parties' market conduct. For example, parties may create a joint venture[154] to pool their resources, perhaps to facilitate or speed up new entry into a market, to share financial risks, to achieve cost savings, or even to enable entry into a new market (each undertaking individually may not have the necessary skills or technology to make entry feasible). Such agreements may cause concern competition concerns,[155] but in *European Night Services v Commission* the GC emphasised that where such an agreement does not contain obvious restrictions of competition, the actual conditions in which an agreement functions must be taken into account when considering whether or not it has the effect of restricting competition. In particular, account has to be taken of 'the economic context in which the undertakings operate, the products or services covered by the agreement and the actual structure of the market concerned'.[156] The importance of examining the conditions of competition, including existing and *potential* competition, was stressed. This was necessary:

---

[148] Case C-345/14, EU:C:2015:784.

[149] See n. 105 and text.

[150] Case C-345/14, EU:C:2015:784, para. 27.

[151] Ibid., para. 28.

[152] Ibid., para. 29.

[153] Cases T-374, 375, and 388/94, [1998] ECR II-3141.

[154] In some circumstances, the establishment of a joint venture amounts to a concentration for the purposes of the EU Merger Reg., Council Reg. 139/2004 [2004] OJ L24/1, discussed further in Chaps. 10 and 15.

[155] See Chap. 10.

[156] Cases T-374, 375, and 388/94, [1998] ECR II-3141, para. 136.

in order to ascertain whether, in the light of the structure of the market and the economic and legal context within which it functions, there are real concrete possibilities for the undertakings concerned to compete among themselves or for a new competitor to penetrate the relevant market and compete with the undertakings already established.[157]

Similarly, in *O2 (Germany) GmbH & Co OHG v Commission*[158] the GC held that the general method of analysis under Article 101(1) required an examination of the economic and legal context in which the agreement was concluded. In making the assessment, competition had to be understood in the context in which it would occur in the absence of the agreement in dispute.

71. The examination required in the light of Article [101(1)] consists essentially in taking account of the impact of the agreement on existing and potential competition (see, to that effect, Case C-234/89, *Delimitis* . . .) and the competition situation in the absence of the agreement (*Société minière et technique* . . .), those two factors being intrinsically linked.

72. The examination of competition in the absence of an agreement appears to be particularly necessary as regards markets undergoing liberalization or emerging markets . . . where effective competition may be problematic owing, for example, to the presence of a dominant operator, the concentrated nature of the market structure or the existence of significant barriers to entry—factors referred to, in the present case, in the Decision.[159]

(iii) The Analytical Framework Set out by the Commission in its Guidelines

In its Article 101(3) Guidelines, the Commission sets out its interpretation of the relationship between Article 101(1) and Article 101(3). It commences by stressing that in Article 101(1) 'effects' cases, there is no presumption of anti-competitive effects, rather, the likely impact of the agreement on inter- or intra-brand competition must be determined. Two counterfactuals may thus need to be used:

- one to determine whether the agreement restricts inter-brand competition—whether the agreement restricts actual or potential competition that would have existed without the agreement;[160] and

- one to determine whether it restricts intra-brand competition (whether the agreement restricts actual or potential competition that would have existed in the absence of the contractual restraints).

This requires proof that the agreement either (a) affects 'actual or potential competition to such an extent that on the relevant market negative effects on prices, output, innovation or the variety or quality of goods and services can be expected with a reasonable degree of probability'[161] or (b) restricts a supplier's distributors from competing with each other, since potential competition that could have existed between the distributors absent the restraint is restricted.

---

[157] Ibid. For joint ventures generally, see Chap. 10.

[158] Case T-328/03, [2006] ECR II-1231. See, e.g., M. Marquis, 'O2 *(Germany) v Commission* and the Exotic Mysteries of Article [101(1)]' (2007) 32 *ELRev* 29.

[159] Case T-328/03, [2006] ECR II-1231, paras. 71–72. In this case the GC found that the Commission had not carried out an economic analysis of the effect of the agreement on the competitive situation.

[160] The need to consider the impact of the agreement as against the counterfactual—the position which would have existed in the absence of the agreement—has been stressed in a number of cases, see, e.g., Case 56/65, *STM* [1966] ECR 235.

[161] Article 101(3) Guidelines, para. 24. This could be because the agreement restricts actual or potential competition between the parties or between any one of the parties and third parties that could have existed absent the agreement, Article 101(3) Guidelines, paras. 25–26.

If, following these principles, it is concluded that the transaction is not restrictive of competition, the Commission states that restraints 'ancillary' to the main non-restrictive transaction also fall outside Article 101(1).[162]

The Commission relies on cases such as *Delimitis, European Night Services*, and *O2* to support its view that a restriction of competition may be established by proof that anti-competitive effects are the expected consequence of a restriction (i.e. a reduction in output or an increase in price).[163] This does not necessarily mean that 'an assessment of the positive and negative effects of the agreement from the point of view of competition must be carried out at the stage of Article [101(1)]'.[164] Rather, potential anti-competitive effects are determined through an examination of whether the parties individually or jointly have or obtain some degree of market power and, if so, whether the agreement contributes to the creation, maintenance, or strengthening of that market power or allows the parties to exploit it.[165] Where the parties have no such market power, the agreement cannot have anti-competitive effects, and, therefore, cannot be said to restrict competition. The scarcity of the case law and economically reasoned Commission decisions in this area, however, make it difficult to draw conclusions as to the *degree* of market power required to establish anti-competitive effects. The Article 101(3) Guidelines state only that the requisite degree is 'less than the degree of market power required for a finding of dominance under Article [102]'.[166] This, combined with the moderately low market share thresholds, of 20–30 per cent, that are set out in the block exemptions,[167] which *exempt* agreements from the Article 101(1) prohibition, may cause firms to be concerned that market power issues will arise under Article 101(1) where relatively low market share thresholds are exceeded (10–20 per cent for agreements between competitors and 15–30 per cent for agreements between non-competitors).

The Commission also relies on cases such as *STM* as authority for the proposition that territorial or customer *intra-brand* restraints are caught by Article 101(1) unless 'objectively necessary' for the existence of an agreement of that type or nature.

The question is not whether the parties in their particular situation would not have accepted to conclude a less restrictive agreement, but whether given the nature of the agreement and the characteristics of the market a less restrictive agreement would not have been concluded by undertakings in a similar setting. For instance, territorial restraints in an agreement between a supplier and a distributor may for a certain period of time fall outside Article 101(1), if the restraints are objectively necessary in order for the distributor to penetrate a new market.[168]

This sweeping approach potentially brings many vertical and IP licensing agreements within the ambit of Article 101 whether or not the parties have market power and/or the ability to affect prices or output on the market, for example by foreclosing access to supply or distribution channels to competitors. It is not at all clear that such a broad approach is dictated by *STM*, which clearly seems to require an assessment of the competitive situation in the absence of the agreement in dispute *and* a determination of the strength of the parties' position on the market prior to an assessment of the compatibility of an agreement with Article 101(1).

---

[162] Article 101(3) Guidelines, paras. 28–31.

[163] Ibid., 18 and 24 and Case T-328/03, *O2 (Germany) GmbH & Co OHG v Commission* [2006] ECR II-1231, para. 68.

[164] Case T-328/03, *O2 (Germany) GmbH & Co OHG v Commission* [2006] ECR II-1231, paras. 69–71.

[165] Article 101(3) Guidelines, paras. 17–27.

[166] Ibid., para. 26.

[167] See Section 4.E.

[168] Article 101(3) Guidelines, para. 18(2) and Chap. 11.

(iv) Ancillary Restraints or Restraints Objectively Necessary to a Transaction Which Does Not Have as Its Purpose the Restriction of Competition

The Commission relies in its Guidelines on a line of cases for the view that restraints which are ancillary to the implementation of a non-restrictive agreement do not restrict competition within the meaning of Article 101(1):

a. *Remia and Nutricia*

In *Remia and Nutricia*[169] the CJ recognised that a non-compete clause on the sale of a business was likely to be an essential part of an agreement to sell a business. Viewed *ex post*, a non-compete clause may appear to restrict competition between the parties. However, when assessed *ex ante* it may become clear that competition is not restricted. No undertaking would be willing to purchase the business without an assurance from the vendor that it will not remain in business in such a way that it would still be able to exploit the goodwill and the customers of the business sold. Nonetheless, the Court held that the non-compete clause must be limited to what is necessary to make the transaction viable. If it is broader than required for the sale, for example if it precludes the vendor from setting up any business within a wide geographic area for an indefinite period of time, it will restrict competition within the meaning of Article 101(1).[170]

17. It should be stated at the outset that the Commission has rightly submitted ... that the fact that non-competition clauses are included in an agreement for the sale of an undertaking is not of itself sufficient to remove such clauses from the scope of Article [101(1)].

18. In order to determine whether or not such clauses come within the prohibition in Article [101(1)], it is necessary to examine what would be the state of competition if those clauses did not exist.

19. If that were the case, and should the vendor and the purchaser remain competitors after the transfer, it is clear that the agreement for the transfer of the undertaking could not be given effect. The vendor, with his particularly detailed knowledge of the transferred undertaking, would still be in a position to win back his former customers immediately after the transfer and thereby drive the undertaking out of business. Against that background non-competition clauses incorporated in an agreement for the transfer of an undertaking in principle have the merit of ensuring that the transfer has the effect intended. By virtue of that very fact they contribute to the promotion of competition because they lead to an increase in the number of undertakings in the market in question.

20. Nevertheless, in order to have that beneficial effect on competition, such clauses must be necessary to the transfer of the undertaking concerned and their duration and scope must be strictly limited to that purpose. The Commission was therefore right in holding that where those conditions are satisfied such clauses are free of the prohibition laid down in Article [101(1)].

b. *Pronuptia*

In *Pronuptia de Paris GmbH v Pronuptia de Paris Irmgard Schillgallis*[171] the CJ set out guidelines for a national court ruling on the compatibility of a distribution franchising agreement with Article 101(1). It held that restrictions essential to the successful operation of a distribution franchise agreement, which provided a means for an undertaking to derive financial benefit from its expertise without investing its own capital and a means for traders who do not have expertise to benefit from the franchisor's experience and reputation, would not restrict competition. In particular, the franchisor should be able to communicate know-how without running the risk that it would be used

---

[169] Case 42/84, [1985] ECR 2545. Merger transactions are now ordinarily appraised under the EU Merger Reg. rather than Art. 101, see Chap. 15.

[170] Ibid., paras. 17–36.

[171] Case 161/84, [1986] ECR 353.

to benefit competitors and to take measures necessary to maintain the identity and reputation of the network.[172] The Court thus considered that restrictions within the agreement would fall outside Article 101(1) if objectively necessary to the successful operation of the franchising transaction. The Court considered, however, that 'far from being necessary for the protection of the know-how provided or the maintenance of the network's identity and reputation, certain provisions restrict competition between the members of the network. That is true of provisions which share markets between the franchisor and franchisees or between franchisees or prevent franchisees from engaging in price competition with each other.'[173]

c. Gøttrup-Klim

In *Gøttrup-Klim Grovvareforening and Others v Dansk Landbrugs Grovvareselskab AmbA*[174] the CJ was asked by a Danish court whether a clause in the statutes of Dansk Landbrugs Grovvareselskab AmbA (a Danish cooperative association distributing farm supplies (DLG)) restricted competition within the meaning of Article 101(1). The object of DLG was to provide its members with farm supplies (such as fertiliser) at the lowest possible prices and to offer its members other services, particularly in the area of finance. In 1988 the statutes of DLG were changed because of increasing competition from the claimants in this case. Essentially, the disputed clause precluded some of DLG's members from holding membership of, or any other kind of participation in, associations, societies, or other forms of cooperative organisation in competition with DLG, with regard to the purchase and sale of fertilisers and plant-protection products. The statutes provided that members which infringed this rule would be excluded from DLG (and some members were in fact excluded). DLG had notified the amendment to the Commission for negative clearance or exemption, but at the time of the proceedings before the CJ, it had still not received an answer to the letter of notification. In the proceedings before the CJ the Commission stated in reply to a question from the Court that the amendment to the statutes did not infringe the Article 101(1) prohibition.

DLG contended that the aim of the clause was not to restrict competition. On the contrary it (a) enabled the members to stand up to a few very large multinational producers of fertilisers and plant-protection products in order to obtain lower purchase prices for Danish farmers, and (b) prevented competitors' representatives from taking part in the association's management bodies (shareholders' committee and board of directors) in which business secrets were discussed. The Danish authorities did not take the view that the statutes as amended infringed Danish competition law. Nonetheless, the claimants challenged the compatibility of the provision with Article 101 and sought compensation and damages in respect of the loss sustained from their exclusion from DLG. The Danish court referred the matter to the CJ using the procedure set out in Article 267 TFEU. In particular it asked whether a provision in the statutes of a commercial cooperative society excluding members that participated in a cooperative organisation which competed with it was contrary to Article 101(1). The CJ replied that it would not, so long as the provision was restricted to what was necessary to ensure that the cooperative functioned properly and maintained its contractual power in relation to producers.

In *MasterCard*[175] the EU Courts also had to deal with arguments relating to ancillary restraints.

---

[172] Ibid., paras. 16–17, see also Chap. 10.

[173] Ibid., para. 23.

[174] Case C-250/92, *Gøttrup-Klim* [1994] ECR I-5641.

[175] Case T-111/08, *MasterCard, Inc v Commission* EU:T:2012:260, Case C-382/12 P, *MasterCard and Others v Commission* EU:C:2014:2201. See also, e.g., Case T-360/09, *E.ON Ruhrgas* EU:T:2012:332 (finding that a side letter providing for market sharing is not ancillary to an agreement for the construction and operation of a gas pipe line), paras. 60–82 and Case T-112/99, *M6* [2001] ECR II-2459, paras. 103–117 (the GC rejected the parties' argument that two clauses—an exclusivity clause granting TPS the exclusive right to broadcast general-interest channels and a clause essentially granting TPS the right of first refusal with regard to special-interest channels produced by the parties— were 'ancillary' to the operation of the non-restrictive joint venture; it found that the clauses were not objectively necessary for the operation of the joint venture and, even if they were, the Commission had not committed a manifest error in concluding that the restrictions were not proportionate to, or exceeded what was necessary for, the creation of the joint venture).

d. MasterCard

The CJ in *MasterCard, Inc v Commission*[176] summarised the core of the Commission's decision in *MasterCard*:

11. By the decision at issue, the Commission found that the appellants had infringed Article [101 TFEU] and Article 53 of the Agreement on the European Economic Area. That decision includes the considerations set out below:

  – Interchange fees concern the relationship between issuing and acquiring banks on settlement of card transactions and correspond to a sum deducted in favour of the issuing bank. These fees must be distinguished from the costs charged to merchants by the acquiring bank (merchant service charges; 'MSC'). The decision at issue relates only to the MIF, and not to the interchange fees agreed bilaterally between issuing and acquiring banks or the interchange fees set collectively at national level.

  – It is necessary to distinguish between three different product markets in the sphere of open bank card systems: first of all, the 'inter-systems market', in which the various card systems compete; then the 'issuing market', in which the issuing banks compete for the business of the cardholders; and, lastly, the 'acquiring market', in which the acquiring banks compete for the merchants' business. The relevant market for the purposes of the decision at issue is made up of the national acquiring markets in the Member States of the EEA.

  – The appellants' decisions in relation to the setting of the MIF constitute decisions by an association of undertakings within the meaning of Article [101(1) TFEU], notwithstanding the changes in MasterCard's structure and governance arising from the IPO.

  – The MIF have the effect of inflating the base of the MSC, while the latter could be lower if there were no MIF and if there were a prohibition of unilateral pricing *a posteriori* of transactions by the issuing banks, that is to say, a rule prohibiting issuing and acquiring banks from defining the amount of the interchange fees after a purchase has been made by one of the issuing bank's cardholders from one of the acquiring bank's merchants and the transaction has been submitted for payment ('prohibition of *ex post* pricing'). The MIF therefore lead to a restriction of price competition between acquiring banks to the detriment of merchants and their customers.

  – MIF cannot be regarded as 'ancillary restrictions' in so far as they are not objectively necessary for the operation of an open payment card scheme. The scheme could function simply on the basis of the remuneration of issuing banks by cardholders, of acquiring banks by merchants, and of the owner of the scheme by the fees paid by the issuing and acquiring banks. Unlike restrictions which are necessary for implementing a main operation, restrictions which are merely desirable for the commercial success of that operation, or which offer greater efficiency, can be examined only within the framework of Article [101(3)] EC.

  – With regard to the impact of the requirement, in the context of the MasterCard system, that all Maestro or MasterCard cards should be accepted irrespective of the issuing bank (the 'Honour All Cards Rule'), the elimination of the MIF would not mean that the issuing banks could freely and unilaterally set interchange fees, since that risk could be avoided by a rule having effects less restrictive of competition, such as the prohibition of *ex post* pricing.

  – As regards Article [101(3)], the economic arguments put forward by the appellants in relation to the role of the MIF in the balancing of the MasterCard system and its maximisation are inadequate for the purposes of establishing that the MIF generate objective advantages. The appellants notably did not produce evidence to show that any objective advantages counterbalanced the disadvantages of the MIF for merchants and their customers.

MasterCard sought annulment of the decision; one argument was that the setting of the MIF in the payment system operated by MasterCard did not produce restrictive effects and/or was objectively necessary to the operation of the payment card system (without it the acquiring banks would be at the mercy of the issuing banks so the main operation would be difficult or even impossible to implement in its absence). On appeal, the CJ held that the GC had been correct to uphold the Commission's findings that MIFs were not objectively necessary, and so were not ancillary restrictions. In determining if a restriction is objectively necessary, it held that the correct test was whether MasterCard could function without a MIF—whether the operation would be impossible to carry

---

[176] Case C-382/12 P, EU:C:2014:2201.

out in the absence of the restriction in question—and not whether or not the absence of the restriction would have adverse consequences on MasterCard's business. The CJ confirmed that in testing the counterfactual in an ancillary restraints analysis, the Commission can rely on the existence of realistic alternatives that are less restrictive of competition; it is not limited to postulating simply the absence of the restriction, but may also consider other possible developments that may realistically occur. In so ruling the CJ explored the meaning of an ancillary restriction and how the concept relates to the rule of reason debate and the analysis required under Article 101(3).

Case C-382/12 P, *MasterCard, Inc v Commission* EU:C:2014:2201

Court of Justice

89. It is apparent from the case-law of the Court of Justice that if a given operation or activity is not covered by the prohibition rule laid down in Article [101(1)], owing to its neutrality or positive effect in terms of competition, a restriction of the commercial autonomy of one or more of the participants in that operation or activity is not covered by that prohibition rule either if that restriction is objectively necessary to the implementation of that operation or that activity and proportionate to the objectives of one or the other (see to that effect, in particular, judgments in *Remia and Others* v *Commission,…* paragraphs 19 and 20; *Pronuptia de Paris,…* paragraphs 15 to 17; *DLG,…* paragraph 35, and *Oude Luttikhuis and Others,…* paragraphs 12 to 15).

90. Where it is not possible to dissociate such a restriction from the main operation or activity without jeopardising its existence and aims, it is necessary to examine the compatibility of that restriction with Article [101] in conjunction with the compatibility of the main operation or activity to which it is ancillary, even though, taken in isolation, such a restriction may appear on the face of it to be covered by the prohibition rule in Article [101(1)].

91. Where it is a matter of determining whether an anti-competitive restriction can escape the prohibition laid down in Article [101(1)] because it is ancillary to a main operation that is not anti-competitive in nature, it is necessary to inquire whether that operation would be impossible to carry out in the absence of the restriction in question. Contrary to what the appellants claim, the fact that that operation is simply more difficult to implement or even less profitable without the restriction concerned cannot be deemed to give that restriction the 'objective necessity' required in order for it to be classified as ancillary. Such an interpretation would effectively extend that concept to restrictions which are not strictly indispensable to the implementation of the main operation. Such an outcome would undermine the effectiveness of the prohibition laid down in Article [101(1)].

92. However, that interpretation does not mean that there has been an amalgamation of, on the one hand, the conditions laid down by the case-law for the classification—for the purposes of the application of Article [101(1)]—of a restriction as ancillary, and, on the other hand, the criterion of the indispensability required under Article [101(3)] in order for a prohibited restriction to be exempted.

93. In that regard, suffice it to note that those two provisions have different objectives and that the latter criterion relates to the issue whether coordination between undertakings that is liable to have an appreciable adverse impact on the parameters of competition, such as the price, the quantity and quality of the goods or services, which is therefore covered by the prohibition rule laid down in Article [101(1)], can none the less, in the context of Article [101(3)], be considered indispensable to the improvement of production or distribution or to the promotion of technical or economic progress, while allowing consumers a fair share of the resulting benefits. By contrast, as is apparent from paragraphs 89 and 90 of the present judgment, the objective necessity test referred to in those paragraphs concerns the question whether, in the absence of a given restriction of commercial autonomy, a main operation or activity which is not caught by the prohibition laid down in Article [101(1)] and to which that restriction is secondary, is likely not to be implemented or not to proceed.

94. In ruling, in paragraph 89 of the judgment under appeal, that '[o]nly those restrictions which are necessary in order for the main operation to be able to function in any event may be regarded as falling within

the scope of the theory of ancillary restrictions', and in concluding, in paragraph 90 of the judgment under appeal, that 'the fact that the absence of the MIF may have adverse consequences for the functioning of the MasterCard system does not, in itself, mean that the MIF must be regarded as being objectively necessary, if it is apparent from an examination of the MasterCard system in its economic and legal context that it is still capable of functioning without it', the General Court did not, therefore, err in law.

95. In those circumstances, the first part of the first plea in the main appeal must be rejected.

. . .

106. . . . [A]s is apparent from paragraphs 96 and 97 of the present judgment, the appellants are critical of the fact that the General Court relied on the premiss of a prohibition of *ex post* pricing—a scenario which, in their view, would not occur, in the absence of MIF, without a regulatory intervention, and which in any event would not differ from that resulting from the existence of the MIF—in order to conclude in paragraph 96 of the judgment under appeal that '[t]he fact that there are default transaction settlement procedures less restrictive of competition than the MIF precludes the latter from being regarded as objectively necessary for the operation of the MasterCard system'.

107. It must be noted in that regard that, as is apparent from paragraphs 89 and 90 of the present judgment, in the context of the assessment, for the purposes of the application of Article [101(1)], of the ancillary nature of a given restriction of commercial autonomy in relation to a main operation or activity, it is necessary to consider not only whether that restriction is necessary for the implementation of the main operation or activity, but also whether that restriction is proportionate to the underlying objectives of that operation or activity.

108. It should be pointed out that, irrespective of the context or aim in relation to which a counterfactual hypothesis is used, it is important that that hypothesis is appropriate to the issue it is supposed to clarify and that the assumption on which it is based is not unrealistic.

109. Accordingly, in order to contest the ancillary nature of a restriction, as referred to in paragraphs 89 and 90 of the present judgment, the Commission may rely on the existence of realistic alternatives that are less restrictive of competition than the restriction at issue.

110. In that regard, as is apparent from paragraph 97 of the present judgment, the appellants also submit, in essence, that the General Court wrongly failed to penalise the Commission for not having tried, in the decision at issue, to understand how competition would function in the absence both of the MIF and of the prohibition of *ex post* pricing, a prohibition which the appellants would not have chosen to adopt without a regulatory intervention.

111. However, the alternatives on which the Commission may rely in the context of the assessment of the objective necessity of a restriction are not limited to the situation that would arise in the absence of the restriction in question but may also extend to other counterfactual hypotheses based, inter alia, on realistic situations that might arise in the absence of that restriction. The General Court was therefore correct in concluding, in paragraph 99 of the judgment under appeal, that the counterfactual hypothesis put forward by the Commission could be taken into account in the examination of the objective necessity of the MIF in so far as it was realistic and enabled the MasterCard system to be economically viable.

The doctrine of ancillary restraints is not without difficulties. First, as *MasterCard* illustrates, it is by no means easy to identify whether or not a particular restraint is 'ancillary', or necessary and proportionate, to the operation of the particular agreement or what the counterfactual is. Secondly, its relationship to ordinary effects analysis is somewhat unclear. Some of the jurisprudence indicates that it is only if a main transaction does not restrict competition, that individual restraints in the agreement ancillary to it, i.e. directly related and necessary to its implementation and proportionate to the main non-restrictive distribution or joint venture agreement, will be held to be compatible with Article 101(1).[177] In *MasterCard*, however, the appeals related to the questions of (a) whether

---

[177] Article 101(3) Guidelines, paras. 28–29.

the restraints were objectively necessary to the aims of the agreement and, *if not*, (b) whether restrictive effects had been identified.

(v) Restraints Inherent in the Pursuit of a Legitimate (Public Policy?) Objective: *Wouters* and *Meca-Medina*

In *Wouters v Algemene Raad van de Nederlandse Orde van Advocaten*,[178] the CJ considered the compatibility with Article 101(1) of rules[179] adopted in the Netherlands which prohibited members of the Bar practising in full partnership with accountants. It held that although the rules had an adverse effect on competition and limited production and technical development within the meaning of Article 101(1)(b) (partnerships of lawyers and accountants would, for example, be able to offer a wider range of services and result in economies of scale), account had to be taken of the objectives of the restrictions and the overall context in which they were adopted; not every agreement that restricted the freedom of action of the parties necessarily fell within the prohibition of Article 101(1).

Case C-309/99, *Wouters v Algemene Raad van de Nederlandse Orde van Advocaten* [2002] ECR I-1577

Court of Justice

73. By its second question the national court seeks, essentially, to ascertain whether a regulation such as the 1993 Regulation which, in order to guarantee the independence and loyalty to the client of members of the Bar who provide legal assistance in conjunction with members of other liberal professions, adopts universally binding rules governing the formation of multi-disciplinary partnerships, has the object or effect of restricting competition within the common market and is likely to affect trade between Member States.

. . .

86. It appears to the Court that the national legislation in issue in the main proceedings has an adverse effect on competition and may affect trade between Member States.

87. As regards the adverse effect on competition, the areas of expertise of members of the Bar and of accountants may be complementary. Since legal services, especially in business law, more and more frequently require recourse to an accountant, a multi-disciplinary partnership of members of the Bar and accountants would make it possible to offer a wider range of services, and indeed to propose new ones. Clients would thus be able to turn to a single structure for a large part of the services necessary for the organisation, management and operation of their business (the 'one-stop shop' advantage).

88. Furthermore, a multi-disciplinary partnership of members of the Bar and accountants would be capable of satisfying the needs created by the increasing interpenetration of national markets and the consequent necessity for continuous adaptation to national and international legislation.

89. Nor, finally, is it inconceivable that the economies of scale resulting from such multi-disciplinary partnerships might have positive effects on the cost of services.

90. A prohibition of multi-disciplinary partnerships of members of the Bar and accountants, such as that laid down in the 1993 Regulation, is therefore liable to limit production and technical development within the meaning of Article [101(1)(b)].

. . .

---

[178] Case C-309/99, [2002] ECR I-1577.

[179] The Bar was created by legislation which imposed an obligation on it to ensure the proper practice of the profession and power to adopt measures to contribute to that end.

97. However, not every agreement between undertakings or every decision of an association of undertakings which restricts the freedom of action of the parties or of one of them necessarily falls within the prohibition laid down in Article [101(1)]. For the purposes of application of that provision to a particular case, account must first of all be taken of the overall context in which the decision of the association of undertakings was taken or produces its effects. More particularly, account must be taken of its objectives, which are here connected with the need to make rules relating to organisation, qualifications, professional ethics, supervision and liability, in order to ensure that the ultimate consumers of legal services and the sound administration of justice are provided with the necessary guarantees in relation to integrity and experience (see, to that effect, Case C-3/95 *Reisebüro Broede . . .* paragraph 38). It has then to be considered whether the consequential effects restrictive of competition are inherent in the pursuit of those objectives.

98. Account must be taken of the legal framework applicable in the Netherlands, on the one hand, to members of the Bar and to the Bar of the Netherlands, which comprises all the registered members of the Bar in that Member State, and on the other hand, to accountants.

99. As regards members of the Bar, it has consistently been held that, in the absence of specific Community rules in the field, each Member State is in principle free to regulate the exercise of the legal profession in its territory (Case 107/83 *Klopp . . .* paragraph 17, and *Reisebüro*, paragraph 37). For that reason, the rules applicable to that profession may differ greatly from one Member State to another.

100. The current approach of the Netherlands, where Article 28 of the Advocatenwet entrusts the Bar of the Netherlands with responsibility for adopting regulations designed to ensure the proper practice of the profession, is that the essential rules adopted for that purpose are, in particular, the duty to act for clients in complete independence and in their sole interest, the duty, mentioned above, to avoid all risk of conflict of interest and the duty to observe strict professional secrecy.

101. Those obligations of professional conduct have not inconsiderable implications for the structure of the market in legal services, and more particularly for the possibilities for the practice of law jointly with other liberal professions which are active on that market.

102. Thus, they require of members of the Bar that they should be in a situation of independence *vis-à-vis* the public authorities, other operators and third parties, by whom they must never be influenced. They must furnish, in that respect, guarantees that all steps taken in a case are taken in the sole interest of the client.

103. By contrast, the profession of accountant is not subject, in general, and more particularly, in the Netherlands, to comparable requirements of professional conduct.

104. As the Advocate General has rightly pointed out in paragraphs 185 and 186 of his Opinion, there may be a degree of incompatibility between the 'advisory' activities carried out by a member of the Bar and the 'supervisory' activities carried out by an accountant. The written observations submitted by the respondent in the main proceedings show that accountants in the Netherlands perform a task of certification of accounts. They undertake an objective examination and audit of their clients' accounts, so as to be able to impart to interested third parties their personal opinion concerning the reliability of those accounts. It follows that in the Member State concerned accountants are not bound by a rule of professional secrecy comparable to that of members of the Bar, unlike the position under German law, for example.

105. The aim of the 1993 Regulation is therefore to ensure that, in the Member State concerned, the rules of professional conduct for members of the Bar are complied with, having regard to the prevailing perceptions of the profession in that State. The Bar of the Netherlands was entitled to consider that members of the Bar might no longer be in a position to advise and represent their clients independently and in the observance of strict professional secrecy if they belonged to an organisation which is also responsible for producing an account of the financial results of the transactions in respect of which their services were called upon and for certifying those accounts.

106. Moreover, the concurrent pursuit of the activities of statutory auditor and of adviser, in particular legal adviser, also raises questions within the accountancy profession itself, as may be seen from the Commission Green Paper 96/C/321/01 'The role, the position and the liability of the statutory auditor within the European Union' (OJ 1996 C 321, p. 1; see, in particular, paragraphs 4.12 to 4.14).

107. A regulation such as the 1993 Regulation could therefore reasonably be considered to be neces-sary in order to ensure the proper practice of the legal profession, as it is organised in the Member State concerned.

108. Furthermore, the fact that different rules may be applicable in another Member State does not mean that the rules in force in the former State are incompatible with [EU] law (see, to that effect, Case C-108/96 *Mac Quen and Others* . . . paragraph 33). Even if multi-disciplinary partnerships of lawyers and accountants are allowed in some Member States, the Bar of the Netherlands is entitled to consider that the objectives pursued by the 1993 Regulation cannot, having regard in particular to the legal regimes by which members of the Bar and accountants are respectively governed in the Netherlands, be attained by less restrictive means (see, to that effect, with regard to a law reserving judicial debt-recovery activity to lawyers, *Reisebüro*, paragraph 41).

109. In light of those considerations, it does not appear that the effects restrictive of competition such as those resulting for members of the Bar practising in the Netherlands from a regulation such as the 1993 Regulation go beyond what is necessary in order to ensure the proper practice of the legal profession (see, to that effect, Case C-250/92 *DLG* . . . paragraph 35).

110. Having regard to all the foregoing considerations, the answer to be given to the second question must be that a national regulation such as the 1993 Regulation adopted by a body such as the Bar of the Netherlands does not infringe Article [101(1)], since that body could reasonably have considered that that regulation, despite the effects restrictive of competition that are inherent in it, is necessary for the proper practice of the legal profession, as organised in the Member State concerned.

The reasoning in this case is not easy. Despite appearing to find that the conduct had 'an adverse effect on competition' (in terms of services that could be offered and economies of scope) and was liable to limit production and technical development, the CJ indicated that the regulation at issue did not infringe Article 101(1) (by object or effect)[180] 'since the association could reasonably have considered that, despite its inherent restrictive effect on competition, it was necessary for the proper practice of the legal profession as organized in the Member States concerned'.[181] The objective of the rules was to ensure that the ultimate consumers of legal services and the sound administration of justice were provided with the necessary guarantees in relation to integrity and experience. For example, members of the Bar might not be in a position to advise and represent clients independ-ently if they belonged to an organisation which was also responsible for producing an account for the financial results of the transactions in respect of which their services were called upon and for certifying those accounts. As the agreement did not infringe Article 101(1), it did not have to be determined whether the rules of ethics could have been exempted through the application of Article 101(3).[182] In so ruling the CJ did not, as it had done with respect to collective bargaining agreements in *Albany*,[183] consider that reasonable rules relating to the regulation of the provision

---

[180] The CJ had after all made it clear that the rules might have negative effects on prices, innovation, and/or the variety or quality of goods and services that could be expected.

[181] Case C-309/99, [2002] ECR I-1577, at paras. 106–110. Contrast Léger AG in his Opinion in this case (the rule of reason in EU competition law was strictly confined to a 'purely competitive balance-sheet of the effects of the agreement' and social concerns, and considerations connected with the pursuit of the public interest, were relevant only to the Art. 101(3) appraisal, paras. 104–105).

[182] Or, perhaps through Art. 106(2) on the grounds that the rules were necessary to the task entrusted by statute to the Dutch Bar Council. The CJ considered, however, that it was precluded from applying Art. 106(2) as the Bar Council was not an entrusted undertaking or group of undertakings within the meaning of Art. 106, Case C-309/99, [2002] ECR I-1577, paras. 111–116. Contrast, e.g., Léger AG, paras. 114 and 201. Art. 106 is discussed in Chap. 8.

[183] Case C-67/96, *Albany International BV v Stichting Bedrijfspensioenfonds Textielindustrie* [1999] ECR I-5751, dis-cussed in Chap. 3.

of professional services should fall outside Article 101(1) altogether. Rather, it appeared to weigh the anti-competitive effects of the agreement against benefits which were *not* economic efficiency benefits.

The approach taken in *Wouters* is not easy to reconcile with all of the jurisprudence, for example *BIDS* or the GC's (later) judgment in *Laurent Piau*.[184] In the latter case the GC held, distinguishing *Wouter*, that the actual principle of a licence, required by FIFA (a private body which was not acting according to power delegated by a public authority) as a condition for carrying on the occupation of players' agent, constituted a 'barrier to access to that economic activity and therefore necessarily affects competition' which could be accepted 'only in so far as the conditions set out in Article [101(3)] are satisfied'.[185] Further, if the approach in *M6* and the Commission's analytical framework is correct, it might have been expected that the CJ in *Wouters* would (in line with the approach taken in *Piau* and *BIDS*) have found that the agreement restricted competition (in terms of the services that could be offered and economies of scope)[186] and held that the justifications raised by the parties could then only have been appraised when determining whether the rules of ethics could be excepted through the application of Article 101(3). The CJ did not, however, take this course. Had it done so, the referring national court, which did not, at this time, have jurisdiction to rule on the compatibility of the agreement with Article 101(3), would have been compelled to rule that the regulations, or at least the restrictive rules within them, were void. This has led some to argue that, because the CJ considered that the Bar Association had not been unreasonable in considering that the restrictive rules were warranted by reference to the objective pursued, it conflated and operated Article 101(1) and Article 101(3) as if they were a single provision in order to avoid this consequence.[187] Even if, however, this explains *why* the Court might have decided to adopt this course of action, the case still stands for authority that some balancing of the restriction(s) identified against *other* legitimate objectives can take place under Article 101(1).

The question of how widely this 'Wouters' exception applies has been much debated—for example, it has been argued that it applies where restraints are ancillary to a regulatory aim, such as ensuring legal integrity and experience ('reasonable' regulatory rules fall outside Article 101(1)).[188] Another argument is that the CJ transposed free movement-style analysis to the competition sphere in this case, allowing the association of undertakings, which in this case was acting within a mandate from a public sector body, to pursue, in a non-discriminatory and proportionate way, an objective in the public interest (in this case the proper exercise of a profession) which could not be achieved by other less restrictive measures (so allowing the Court to take account of non-competition factors relating to domestic interests).[189]

---

[184] Case T-193/02, *Laurent Piau v Commission* [2005] ECR II-209 (appeal dismissed by Order of the CJ, Case C-171/05 P, [2006] ECR I-37).

[185] Ibid., para. 101. The regulations, or at least the restrictive rules within them, would thus have been void as they had not been notified to the Commission for exemption, see Reg. 17, [1959–1962] OJ Spec. Ed. 87, Art. 4.

[186] The CJ had after all made it clear that the rules might have negative effects on prices, innovation, and/or the variety or quality of goods and services that could be expected.

[187] See J. Goyder and A. Albors-Llorens, *Goyder's EC Competition Law* (5th edn, Oxford University Press, 2009), 115–116. For the view that *Wouters* is explicable by the fact that the rule was promulgated not by an undertaking but by an association of undertakings, see Odudu, n. 2, 53.

[188] Whish and Bailey, n. 100, 138–142.

[189] See also M. Monti, *EC Competition Law* (Cambridge University Press, 2007), 110–113. For the view that the rule in *Wouters* was to deal with market failures—information asymmetries that are typically present in professional service—see Ibáñez Colomo, 'Market Failure, Transaction Costs and Article 101(1) TFEU Case-law', n. 54, 550.

G. Monti, 'Article 81 EC and Public Policy' (2002) 30 *CMLRev* 1057, 1087–1088

This is a remarkable *ratio decidendi* for the Court intertwines principles of competition law and free movement . . . In simple terms, the line of reasoning followed is this: we know from *Cassis de Dijon* that an indistinctly applicable domestic rule which is an obstacle to the free movement of goods does not fall under the prohibition in Article [34] if it is necessary to satisfy a mandatory requirement relating to, for example, fairness of commercial transactions or the defence of the consumer. The same approach has been applied in relation to other freedoms. In *Wouters*, the Court relies on this line of case-law, specifically referring to *Reisbüro Vroede*, a case in relation to the regulation of the legal profession in the context of Article [56] (freedom to provide services) where it held that a non-discriminatory rule of German law which infringed Article [56] might be justified in the public interest. The Court then holds that the principle created by this case-law (labelled by many commentators a 'rule of reason') applies *mutatis mutandis* to Article [101]. Having transposed a rule from the free movement case-law into the competition case-law, the Court was free to say that the prohibition in Article [101] could not apply. This reasoning incorporates the rule of reason deployed in the free movement area as a mechanism for justifying an agreement otherwise unlawful under Article [101(1)]. It is ironic that while the Court (most explicitly in *Métropole*) has regularly refused to adopt an *American-style* rule of reason in Article [101] (whereby the legality of an agreement would depend upon whether, on balance it increased consumer welfare) it has in *Wouters* given strong indications that what I shall call the *European-style rule of reason*, developed in the free movement field, can apply to competition cases so that an anti-competitive agreement necessary to preserve a domestic mandatory requirement of public policy is allowed to escape the application of Article [101]. Thus *Wouters* is another in a line of cases that exemplifies what Mortelmans[190] labelled a 'convergence' in the application of the rules on free movement and competition. The purpose of convergence in this case is to allow the Court to take into account non-competition factors which relate to *domestic* interests.

If this interpretation is correct then *Wouters* may require a distinction to be drawn between public policy considerations which remove practices from the scope of Article 101(1) altogether (reasons of general interest may justify the non-application of Article 101 to certain restrictions of competition when they are necessary) and economic justifications which are treated differently[191] (in free movement law it is established that purely economic justifications, or financial concerns,[192] cannot constitute a legitimate public policy objective and be relied on to substantiate a restriction on free movement).

This latter interpretation seems compatible with other cases in which the *Wouters* exception has been invoked (albeit unsuccessfully)[193] and both: (a) *Meca-Medina*,[194] where the Court held that

---

[190] K. Mortelmans, 'Towards Convergence in the Application of the Rules on Free Movement and on Competition' (2001) 38 *CMLRev* 613.

[191] See e.g., E. Rousseva and M. Marquis, 'Hell Freezes Over: A Climate Change for Assessing Exclusionary Conduct under Article 102 TFEU' (2013) 4 *JECLAP* 32, 49.

[192] The CJ rejected the argument raised in *BIDS* that the parties need to ride an economic storm or crisis and so the purpose of the agreement was not to restrict competition.

[193] See, e.g., Case C-1/12, *Ordem dos Técnicos Oficiais de Contas (OTOC) v Autoridade da Concorrência* EU:C:2013:127 (the CJ held that rules adopted by a professional association of chartered accountants providing that certain compulsory training to be undertaken by chartered accountants could be provided only by OTOC was not necessary to achieve a legitimate objective (in that case to guarantee the quality of the services offered by chartered accountants). The rules eliminated all competition rather than putting in place criteria to ensure training bodies equal access to the market), Case T-90/11, *Ordre national des pharmaciens v Commission* EU:T:2014:1049 (the GC upheld the Commission's decision fining three French pharmacists' trade bodies for various decisions: (a) setting minimum prices for certain medical analyses through restrictions on rebates and (b) restricting the development of laboratory groups which competed with pharmacists, and rejecting justifications for the conduct based on *Wouters*), Cases C-184/13 etc., *API v Ministero delle Infrastrutture e dei Trasporti* EU:C:2014:2147 and Case 136/12, *Consiglio nazionale dei geologi v AGCM* EU:C:2013:489.

[194] Case C-519/04 P, *Meca-Medina v Commission* [2006] ECR I-6991. See also ongoing investigation into the sporting rules of the International Skating Union, COMP/40.208.

restraints on freedom of action resulting from anti-doping rules do not constitute a restriction of competition[195] if inherent in, and justified by, a legitimate objective in that case the organisation and proper conduct of competitive sport;[196] and (b) the Commission's statement in its Guidelines on Vertical Restraints that severe restraints in vertical agreements

> may be objectively necessary in exceptional cases for an agreement of a particular type or nature and therefore fall outside Article 101(1). For example, a hardcore restriction may be objectively necessary to ensure that a public ban on selling dangerous substances to certain customers for reasons of safety or health is respected.[197]

Nonetheless, the analysis conducted in *Wouters* undoubtedly has conceptual similarities to, and parallels with, other cases in which the courts have accepted that restraints which are objectively necessary to the operation of a pro-competitive commercial transaction may fall outside Article 101(1).

(vi) Appreciability

Where an agreement does not contain object or 'hardcore' restraints, the Commission's De Minimis Notice provides that the agreement is not likely to restrict competition appreciably if the aggregate market share held by the parties to the agreement does not exceed certain thresholds—10 per cent (for competitors) or 15 per cent (for non-competitors). Where it is difficult to classify the agreement, the 10 per cent threshold applies and where competition in a market is restricted by the cumulative effect of agreements entered into by different suppliers and distributors, the threshold is reduced to 5 per cent.[198]

When calculating market shares, the market shares of 'connected undertakings' are included. The Notice also contains provisions governing the situation where undertakings meet the thresholds, but subsequently outgrow them.

> ## Notice on agreements of minor importance which do not appreciably restrict competition under Article 101(1) of the Treaty on the Functioning of the European Union (De Minimis Notice) [2014] OJ C291/01
>
> ### I.
>
> 3. In this Notice the Commission indicates, with the help of market share thresholds, the circumstances in which it considers that agreements which may have as their effect the prevention, restriction or distortion of competition within the internal market do not constitute an appreciable restriction of competition under Article 101 of the Treaty. This negative definition of appreciability does not imply that agreements between undertakings which exceed the thresholds set out in this Notice constitute an appreciable

---

[195] '[T]he penal nature of the anti-doping rules . . . are capable of producing adverse effects on competition because they could, if penalties were ultimately to prove unjustified, result in an athlete's unwarranted exclusion from sporting events', ibid., para. 47.

[196] Case C-519/04 P, *Meca-Medina* [2006] ECR I-6991, paras. 45–47. The CJ set aside the judgment of the GC which had held that the sporting rules had nothing to do with economic activity and so fell outside the scope of Art. 101, Case T-313/02, [2004] ECR II-3291.

[197] [2010] OJ C130/1, para. 60.

[198] Access to a market is unlikely to be foreclosed by the cumulative effect of parallel networks of agreements, however, where they cover less than 30% of the market. This provision is particularly important in the context of distribution agreements, for example beer-supply agreements, which operate in a similar way to other agreements on the market. Beer-supply agreements will not restrict competition at all however if they do not significantly contribute to a cumulative effect caused by the network on the market, see Case 234/89, *Delimitis* [1991] ECR I-935, paras. 24–26, discussed n. 147 and text.

restriction of competition. Such agreements may still have only a negligible effect on competition and may therefore not be prohibited by Article 101(1) of the Treaty.

4. Agreements may also fall outside Article 101(1) of the Treaty because they are not capable of appreciably affecting trade between Member States. This Notice does not indicate what constitutes an appreciable effect on trade between Member States. Guidance to that effect is to be found in the Commission's Notice on effect on trade, in which the Commission quantifies, with the help of the combination of a 5 % market share threshold and a EUR 40 million turnover threshold, which agreements are in principle not capable of appreciably affecting trade between Member States. Such agreements normally fall outside Article 101(1) of the Treaty even if they have as their object the prevention, restriction or distortion of competition.

5. In cases covered by this Notice, the Commission will not institute proceedings either upon a complaint or on its own initiative. In addition, where the Commission has instituted proceedings but undertakings can demonstrate that they have assumed in good faith that the market shares mentioned in points 8, 9, 10 and 11 were not exceeded, the Commission will not impose fines. Although not binding on them, this Notice is also intended to give guidance to the courts and competition authorities of the Member States in their application of Article 101 of the Treaty.

6. The principles set out in this Notice also apply to decisions by associations of undertakings and to concerted practices.

7. This Notice is without prejudice to any interpretation of Article 101 of the Treaty which may be given by the Court of Justice of the European Union.

II.

8. The Commission holds the view that agreements between undertakings which may affect trade between Member States and which may have as their effect the prevention, restriction or distortion of competition within the internal market, do not appreciably restrict competition within the meaning of Article 101(1) of the Treaty:

(a) if the aggregate market share held by the parties to the agreement does not exceed 10 % on any of the relevant markets affected by the agreement, where the agreement is made between undertakings which are actual or potential competitors on any of those markets (agreements between competitors); or

(b) if the market share held by each of the parties to the agreement does not exceed 15 % on any of the relevant markets affected by the agreement, where the agreement is made between undertakings which are not actual or potential competitors on any of those markets (agreements between non-competitors).

9. In cases where it is difficult to classify the agreement as either an agreement between competitors or an agreement between non-competitors the 10 % threshold is applicable.

10. Where, in a relevant market, competition is restricted by the cumulative effect of agreements for the sale of goods or services entered into by different suppliers or distributors (cumulative foreclosure effect of parallel networks of agreements having similar effects on the market), the market share thresholds set out in point 8 and 9 are reduced to 5 %, both for agreements between competitors and for agreements between non-competitors. Individual suppliers or distributors with a market share not exceeding 5 %, are in general not considered to contribute significantly to a cumulative foreclosure effect. A cumulative foreclosure effect is unlikely to exist if less than 30 % of the relevant market is covered by parallel (networks of) agreements having similar effects.

11. The Commission also holds the view that agreements do not appreciably restrict competition if the market shares of the parties to the agreement do not exceed the thresholds of respectively 10 %, 15 % and 5 % set out in points 8, 9 and 10 during two successive calendar years by more than 2 percentage points.

12. In order to calculate the market share, it is necessary to determine the relevant market. This consists of the relevant product market and the relevant geographic market. When defining the relevant market, reference should be had to the Notice on the definition of the relevant market. The market shares are to be calculated on the basis of sales value data or, where appropriate, purchase value data. If value data are not available, estimates based on other reliable market information, including volume data, may be used.

...

14. The safe harbour created by the market share thresholds set out in points 8, 9, 10 and 11 is particularly relevant for categories of agreements not covered by any Commission block exemption regulation. The safe harbour is also relevant for agreements covered by a Commission block exemption regulation to the extent that those agreements contain a so-called excluded restriction, that is a restriction not listed as a hardcore restriction but nonetheless not covered by the Commission block exemption regulation.

15. For the purpose of this Notice, the terms 'undertaking', 'party to the agreement', 'distributor' and 'supplier' include their respective connected undertakings.

16. For the purpose of the Notice 'connected undertakings' are:

(a) undertakings in which a party to the agreement, directly or indirectly:

    i. has the power to exercise more than half the voting rights, or

    ii. has the power to appoint more than half the members of the supervisory board, board of management or bodies legally representing the undertaking, or

    iii. has the right to manage the undertaking's affairs;

(b) undertakings which directly or indirectly have, over a party to the agreement, the rights or powers listed in (a);

(c) undertakings in which an undertaking referred to in (b) has, directly or indirectly, the rights or powers listed in (a);

(d) undertakings in which a party to the agreement together with one or more of the undertakings referred to in (a), (b) or (c), or in which two or more of the latter undertakings, jointly have the rights or powers listed in (a);

(e) undertakings in which the rights or the powers listed in (a) are jointly held by:

    i. parties to the agreement or their respective connected undertakings referred to in (a) to (d), or

    ii. one or more of the parties to the agreement or one or more of their connected undertakings referred to in (a) to (d) and one or more third parties.

17. For the purposes of point (e) in point 16, the market share held by these jointly held undertakings is apportioned equally to each undertaking having the rights or the powers listed in point (a) in point 16.

D. CONCLUSIONS ON THE APPROACH REQUIRED UNDER ARTICLE 101(1)

The sections above highlight the crucial distinction that Article 101 draws between agreements which restrict competition by object or effect. Object restraints are, on account of their injurious nature, assumed to produce anti-competitive effects and to restrict competition appreciably within the meaning of Article 101(1). This assumption cannot be rebutted by proving that anti-competitive effects did not in fact result from the agreement (the parties may, however, seek to justify such an agreement by establishing that it meets the conditions of Article 101(3)). Although some commentators have regretted the fact that the Court has adopted this formalistic interpretation of a provision drafted in terms of economic concepts,[199] the wording of Article 101(1) makes it clear that such a

---

[199] Korah, n. 8, 92–93 ('[t]o see whether an agreement restricts competition, it is not enough to examine its provisions. One needs to know about the market and the commercial reasons for inserting restrictive provisions').

distinction is warranted and, pragmatically, *so long as* the category is realistically thought through and confined, the finding that some contracts or contractual provisions have as their object the restriction of competition is sensible as it eradicates the need to prove, at cost, the adverse consequences of provisions which are in practice likely to lead to inefficiency and are unlikely to have any redeeming justification. The controversial issue is thus which agreements fall within the object category.

The jurisprudence of the EU Courts makes it clear that the content, objective, and context of an agreement are all crucial factors in determining whether it has a restrictive object within the meaning of Article 101(1); purpose is generally determined objectively so the subjective intent of the parties is not a necessary or sufficient condition to establish a restriction by object (it may, however, be taken into consideration). Further, the cases hold that an established category or list of clauses can be predicted to be likely to be found, in principle, to have a restrictive purpose. Although this list has not been narrowed or reconsidered over time (on the contrary, competition agencies and claimants have sought to apply the category more expansively), the cases do make it clear that there is not such a thing as a definitive list of object restraints. Indeed, in *CB* the CJ reiterated that the category of object restraints is a narrow one and confined to agreements containing sufficiently deleterious and obvious restraints which in themselves reveal a sufficient degree of harm to competition. Consequently, a restraint can only be found to be restrictive of competition by object if it can be shown why, taking account of the objectives and context of the agreement, the measure reveals a sufficient degree of harm to competition. If the measures do not reveal a sufficiently deleterious aim in the context which they operated, in particular because they seem ancillary to a legitimate objective pursued by the parties, the agreement cannot be said to be restrictive of competition by object. A quick look at context is thus important for determining whether an object characterisation is appropriate; if, however, a detailed investigation of the legal and economic context is required to determine the impact of the agreement on competition, a fuller examination of the effects of the agreement is required.

Many of the recent cases of the EU Courts have focused on the question of whether particular agreements can be said to be restrictive by object and there has been relatively little attention paid to the difficult but vital question of how it is determined when other agreements restrict competition. Nonetheless, a line of cases makes it clear that where the object of the agreement cannot be said to restrict competition, it is necessary to conduct a detailed analysis of the effects of the agreement in the context in which operates taking account of the position that would have occurred in the absence of the agreement. In such cases restrictive effect may be demonstrated by establishing that the agreement affects actual or potential competition to such an extent that on the relevant market negative effects on prices, output, innovation, or the variety or quality of goods and services can be expected; it will allow the parties to create, maintain, strengthen, or exploit market power (see, for example, *Delimitis, European Night Services, M6*, and *O2*).

Some cases also hold that restraints which are objectively necessary to a pro-competitive agreement (for example, certain restraints on intra-brand competition are necessary to allow the supplier to penetrate a new market) or other legitimate objective fall outside Article 101(1). Thus proportionate restraints *objectively necessary* to the implementation of a main non-restrictive operation (which would be impossible to implement without the restriction) do not infringe Article 101(1).[200] These cases are often referred to as 'ancillary' restraints cases.

---

[200] But see the view of Léger AG in Case C-309/99, *Wouters v Algemene Raad van de Nederlandse Orde van Advocaten* [2002] ECR I-1577, para. 103 ('Confronted with certain classes of agreement . . . [the CJ] has drawn up a competition balance-sheet and, where the balance is positive, has held that the clauses necessary to perform the agreement fell outside the prohibition laid down by Article [101(1)]'). See also Case 1035/1/1/04, *The Racecourse Association (the 'RCA') v OFT* [2005] CAT 29, where the UK's Competition Appeal Tribunal (CAT) confessed to having 'some difficulty in reconciling' the approach in *Gøttrup-Klim* and *Wouters* with that in *M6*. It considered that the analysis required under Art. 101(1) by the CJ in *Gøttrup-Klim* and *Wouters* was a rather more flexible exercise than the GC had been willing to appreciate in *M6*.

On a close analysis of cases arising under Article 101(1), the so-called ancillary restraints doctrine seems to two perform functions. First, the concept seems to play an important role in characterisation: if a restraint (even a severe one) seems objectively necessary to the pursuit of a legitimate objective (efficiency-enhancing or public policy), it will not be found to be restrictive of competition by object; its precise purpose cannot be said to restrict competition, see, for example, *CB*, *Pierre Fabre*, and *Wouters* discussed above. Secondly, it operates to remove an agreement from Article 101(1) entirely if it is established that the restraints at issue are necessary and proportionate to the achievement of a legitimate objective; the agreement will not then be found to restrict competition in fact (here the Courts have conducted an analysis which is arguably reminiscent of the European-style rule of reason analysis conducted in internal market case law, suggesting that some weighing of the anti-competitive aspects of the agreement against its legitimate objective is required).

Where the doctrine plays a 'characterisation' role, a finding that the restraints are not ancillary will result in the agreement being found to infringe Article 101(1)—as its object is then found to restrict competition (see, for example, *Pierre Fabre* and *Murphy*). Where, however, it is relied upon in the context of agreements which do not have as their object the restriction of competition, it operates as just one mechanism for considering whether the agreement restricts competition in fact (has as its effect the restriction of competition). The agreement will not restrict competition and will fall outside Article 101(1) altogether if it is objectively necessary to the pursuit of a legitimate objective. When the doctrine is used in this latter context, however, a finding that the restrictions are not objectively necessary does not necessarily mean that the agreement infringes Article 101(1); rather in some cases it has been held that a more detailed analysis must be conducted to determine if the agreement (including all the restraints at issue) has as its effect the restriction of competition (see, for example, *MasterCard* discussed above).

It is submitted that the use of the ancillary restraints idea as a mechanism for characterisation seems logical. The second use of the doctrine, however, is more problematic to the scheme of Article 101 envisaged by the Commission and the GC in M6. Indeed its use in this way seems undoubtedly to require some consideration of the benefits pursued by the agreement and the indispensability of the restraints within it to its operation.

4. ARTICLE 101(3)

A. APPLICATION OF ARTICLE 101(3)

Although a number of block exemptions exempt certain categories of agreement from Article 101(3) (see Section E), it has not been possible, since 2004, to notify an agreement to the Commission seeking an 'individual' exemption decision from the Commission. Article 101(3) can, however, be applied in individual cases in a variety of different ways. For example, the Commission (and NCAs and national courts) has to consider the application of Article 101(3) in proceedings where it is raised by persons seeking to rely on it. It might also have to apply Article 101(3) when adopting commitment or non-infringements decisions or when providing 'informal guidance'.[201] Nonetheless, since 'modernisation' there have been very few cases dealing with the application of Article 101(3) in individual cases (most cases brought by the Commission/NCAs relate to object infringements and provide little scope for Article 101(3) arguments to be raised and no non-infringement decisions[202] have been adopted). Consequently, there is little post-modernisation jurisprudence providing clarification of how these important criteria are interpreted. The Commission's Article 101(3) and other

---

[201] See Reg. 1/2003 [2003] OJ L1/1, Arts. 9 and 10, Commission notice on informal guidance relating to novel questions concerning Articles 81 and 82 of the EC Treaty [now Articles 101 and 102 TFEU] that arise in individual cases (guidance letters) [2004] OJ C101/78, and Chap. 13.

[202] The Commission has not adopted a non-infringement decision and NCAs are not entitled to adopt such a decision, see Chap. 13.

Guidelines provide some guidance to business, shedding light on the Commission's thinking as to how the criteria apply.

B. BURDEN AND STANDARD OF PROOF

Agreements meeting the conditions of block exemption are assumed to meet the Article 101(3) criteria (and the benefit of a block exemption can only be withdrawn prospectively). In an individual case, however, those claiming the benefit of Article 101(3) have the burden[203] of establishing, by means of convincing argument and evidence, that *all* four[204] Article 101(3) criteria are satisfied:[205] (1) that the agreement achieves benefits; (2) that a fair share of those benefits are passed on to consumers; (3) that the agreement does not contain any indispensable restraints; and (4) that it does not eliminate competition in respect of a substantial part of the products in question. The exception rule applies only for as long as the four conditions are met.[206]

Once undertakings have submitted evidence to support an argument that Article 101(3) is satisfied, it is for the fact-finder to examine whether, on the balance of probabilities,[207] the agreement in question does meet these criteria. In the Commission's analytical framework it narrowed the role of Article 101(1) to the identification of negative effects on competition and, correspondingly, sought to limit the role of Article 101(3)[208] to the determination of whether efficiencies achieved by the agreement outweigh negative effects, so that the agreement is on balance pro-competitive.

Agreements that restrict competition may at the same time have pro-competitive effects by way of efficiency gains. Efficiencies may create additional value by lowering the cost of producing an output, improving the quality of the product or creating a new product. When the pro-competitive effects of an agreement outweigh its anti-competitive effects the agreement is on balance pro-competitive and compatible with the objectives of the [EU] competition rules. The net effect of such agreements is to promote the very essence of the competitive process, namely to win customers by offering better products or better prices than those offered by rivals. This analytical framework is reflected in Article [101(1)] and Article [101(3)]. The latter provision expressly acknowledges that restrictive agreements may generate objective economic benefits so as to outweigh the negative effects of the restriction of competition.[209]

It is frequently argued that the Commission has, post-modernisation and in the Article 101(3) Guidelines, imposed an excessively high burden of proof on those seeking to establish that the conditions of Article 101(3) are met.[210] Challenging the Commission's approach is not easy, however, as it now rarely rules on the compatibility of an agreement with Article 101(3) and when reviewing a Commission decision, the GC assesses only whether the evidence the Commission relies on 'is factually accurate, reliable and consistent' and also whether 'it contains all the information which must be taken into account for the purpose of assessing a complex situation and whether it is capable of substantiating the conclusions drawn from it'[211] (see further Chapter 13). In *MasterCard*, for example,

[203] Reg. 1/2003, Art. 2.

[204] The requirements are cumulative, see Case T-528/93, *Métropole Télévision SA v Commission* [1996] ECR II-649, para. 93 and Case C-68/12, *Protimonopolný* EU:C:2013:71, paras. 31–34.

[205] Case T-168/01, *GSK* [2006] ECR II-296, para. 235.

[206] It ceases to apply when that is no longer the case, Article 101(3) Guidelines, para. 44. Under the old notification system an exemption was granted to an agreement for a specified period of time.

[207] See Case C-501/06 P, *GSK* [2009] ECR I-9291, paras. 93–95 where the CJ makes it clear that parties need to demonstrate that it is more likely than not that the agreement satisfies the Art. 101(3) conditions.

[208] The Article 101(3) Guidelines increased the bar for those seeking to justify their agreement under Art. 101(3), in terms of the level and sophistication of evidence required. The Horizontal, Vertical, and Technology Transfer Guidelines provide more specific guidance on how the Commission considers the Art. 101(3) criteria apply to those agreements, see Chaps. 10, 11, and 12.

[209] Article 101(3) Guidelines, para. 33.

[210] See, e.g., Case T-111/08, *MasterCard Inc v Commission* EU:T:2012:260, para. 194.

[211] Ibid., para. 202.

the GC rejected the parties' arguments relating to Article 101(3), holding that the Commission had examined the arguments and evidence put forward by the parties and had properly been able to conclude that the Article 101(3) conditions were not fulfilled.[212] The GC's judgment was affirmed on appeal.[213]

C. ANY AGREEMENT MAY IN PRINCIPLE BENEFIT FROM ARTICLE 101(3)

Although the Commission considers that there is a presumption that an agreement containing hardcore, or object, restraints is unlikely to fulfil the Article 101(3) criteria, it is clear that any fact-finder in a case must examine whether or not it does. Any agreement may in principle benefit from it (including agreements containing object restraints). Indeed, in *GSK*,[214] the GC[215] held that the Commission (the fact-finder in that case as the parties had notified the agreement to it under the old notification system set up by Regulation 17) had not adequately discharged its burden of examining the Article 101(3) arguments put forward by the parties in respect of an agreement designed to prevent parallel trade in its pharmaceutical products, and refuting them by means of substantiated evidence.[216]

Case T-168/01, *GlaxoSmithKline Services Unlimited v Commission* [2006] ECR II-2969

General Court

233. Any agreement which restricts competition, whether by its effects or by its object, may in principle benefit from an exemption (*Consten and Grundig v Commission* . . . 342, 343 and 347, and Case T-17/93 *Matra Hachette v Commission* . . . paragraph 85), as the Commission, moreover, observed at recital 153 to the Decision and at the hearing.

234. The application of that provision is subject to certain conditions, satisfaction of which is both necessary and sufficient (*Remia and Others v Commission* . . . paragraph 38, and *Matra Hachette v Commission* . . . paragraph 104). First, the agreement concerned must contribute to improving the production or distribution of the goods in question, or to promoting technical or economic progress; second, consumers must be allowed a fair share of the resulting benefit; third, it must not impose on the participating undertakings any restrictions which are not indispensable; and, fourth, it must not afford them the possibility of eliminating competition in respect of a substantial part of the products in question.

235. Consequently, a person who relies on Article [101(3)] must demonstrate that those conditions are satisfied, by means of convincing arguments and evidence (Joined Cases 43/82 and 63/82 *VBVB and VBBB v Commission* . . . paragraph 52, and *Aalborg Portland and Others v Commission* . . . paragraph 78).

236. The Commission, for its part, must adequately examine those arguments and that evidence (*Consten and Grundig v Commission* . . . 347), that is to say, it must determine whether they demonstrate that the conditions for the application of Article [101(3)] are satisfied. In certain cases, those arguments and that evidence may be of such a kind as to require the Commission to provide an explanation or

---

[212] Ibid., paras. 194–237.

[213] Case C-382/12 P. *MasterCard and Others v Commission* EU:C:2014:2201.

[214] Case T-168/01, [2006] ECR II-2969, paras. 247–252, this aspect of the judgment was *aff'd* Cases C-501 and 513, 515, and 519/06 P. See also Case T-17/93, *Matra Hachette v Commission* [1994] ECR II-595, para. 85.

[215] The CJ upheld the GC's ruling with regard to Art. 101(3), Case C-501/06 P, [2009] ECR I-9291.

[216] In some respects the GC held that the Commission had sought to reject the arguments on the basis of evidence which was, to say the least, fragmentary and of limited relevance or value.

justification, failing which it is permissible to conclude that the burden of proof borne by the person who relies on Article [101(3)] has been discharged (*Aalborg Portland and Others v Commission*, paragraph 55 above, paragraph 79). As the Commission agrees in its written submissions, in such a case it must refute those arguments and that evidence.

It will be seen in later chapters, however, that given the Commission's presumption against hard-core restraints (and its view that the more severe the restriction the less likely it is to satisfy the Article 101(3) conditions[217]) and the dearth of guidance on when agreements containing such restraints might satisfy the Article 101(3) criteria, undertakings are reluctant in practice to incorporate such restraints within their agreements.

D. THE ARTICLE 101(3) CRITERIA

(i) Criterion 1: The Agreement Must Lead to an Improvement in the Production or Distribution of Goods or the Promotion of Technical or Economic Progress

a. Article 101(3) Benefits

Criterion 1 requires that the agreement: (1) lead to an improvement in the production of goods or services;[218] (2) lead to an improvement in the distribution of goods or services; (3) promote technical progress; and/or (4) promote economic progress. The benefits referred to are not subjective ones that result to the parties to the agreement (for example, from the exercise of market power) and must be derived from empirical data and facts not just economic theory. The CJ has stressed that the improvement must 'show appreciable objective advantages of such a character as to compensate for the disadvantages which they cause in the field of competition'[219] and that improvement within the meaning of Article 101(3) 'cannot be identified with all the advantages which the parties obtain from the agreement in their production or distribution activities';[220] consequently it will not apply if the parties are 'primary beneficiaries' of the benefits flowing from the arrangement.

b. Efficiency Gains

This first limb permits the parties to establish that, despite the fact that the agreement restricts competition, efficiency gains, cost efficiencies,[221] and qualitative efficiencies, creating value in the form of new or improved products (dynamic efficiencies),[222] will result from the economic activity that forms the object of the agreement (there must be a causal link between the agreement and the claimed efficiencies).[223] The Commission's Article 101(3) Guidelines state that parties must substantiate efficiency claims by showing the nature of the claimed efficiencies, the link between the agreement and the efficiencies, the likelihood and magnitude of each claimed efficiency, and how and when each claimed efficiency would be achieved.[224]

---

[217] Article 101(3) Guidelines, para. 46. See further in particular discussion of indispensability, n. 276 and text.

[218] Although Art. 101(3) does not make specific reference to services, services are covered by analogy: see, e.g., COMP/30.373, *P & I Clubs* [1985] OJ L376/2 and Article 101(3) Guidelines, para. 48.

[219] Cases 56 and 58/64, *Consten and Grundig* [1966] ECR 299, 348.

[220] Case C-382/12 P, *MasterCard Inc v Commission* EU:C:2014:2201, para. 234.

[221] Article 101(3) Guidelines, paras. 64–68.

[222] Ibid., paras. 69–72.

[223] Ibid., para. 45.

[224] Ibid., paras. 51 and 52–59. Examples of different types of efficiencies are given at paras. 59–72.

Parties may, therefore, establish that the agreement will improve production or distribution or promote technical or economic progress, for example through cost reduction (such as those originating from: development of new production technologies and methods; synergies resulting from an integration of existing assets; economies of scale or scope; or better production planning)[225] and/or through improvement in the quality and choice of goods and services.[226]

A number of joint venture agreements have succeeded on the grounds that new or better products will be produced and that the cooperation permitted the parties to do so more quickly or cheaply and/or through the sharing of risk or cost, through the pooling of technical expertise and/or by making the venture financially viable.[227] In *Ford/Volkswagen*,[228] for example, the Commission held that the parties' creation of a joint venture company to develop and produce a multi-purpose vehicle (MPV) in Portugal would improve the production of goods and promote technical development. It would rationalise product development and manufacturing and establish a new and modern manufacturing plant which would be using the latest production technology. In addition, the parties' pooling of technical knowledge would be converted into a significantly improved and innovative MPV. In the context of vertical and intellectual property licensing agreements the Commission has taken account of the fact that the agreement will improve production and distribution of products through, for example, permitting an increase in production capacity, conferring incentives to promote a product, and conferring incentives to concentrate sales efforts, and/or through reduction in transaction costs.[229]

In *GSK*[230] Glaxo argued that the territorial restraints in the distribution agreements were necessary to stimulate and support costly and risky global R&D in a market where inter-brand competition was driven by innovation not price and where in many Member States the prices were controlled by public authorities. The agreement would thus encourage competition upstream by encouraging innovation and, on the market itself, by optimising the distribution of medicines. In particular, it was stressed that the strong competitive pressure to innovate would ensure that any additional profits made would be ploughed into investment in R&D. The GC considered that the Commission had been wrong to reject the evidence raised, which appeared 'relevant, reliable and credible' and, to some extent, to be corroborated by Commission documents.[231]

c. Non-competition Factors

A controversial issue is whether the first head of Article 101(3) permits the parties to rely on broader public policy benefits achieved by the agreement.[232] In its White Paper on modernisation the

---

[225] Ibid., paras. 64–68.

[226] The enhancing potential of the agreement may not therefore be cost reduction but quality improvement resulting from technical and technological advance. R&D, technology licensing, and joint production, and distribution agreements may all be capable of realising these qualitative efficiencies, ibid., paras. 69–72.

[227] See, e.g., COMP/28.796, *Beecham/Parke, Davis* [1979] OJ L70/11 (R&D agreement would promote 'technical progress' by creating a product for the prevention or treatment of an impairment for which there was no known marketed compound and where the pooling of research capacities was a major factor in providing a reasonable likelihood of success); COMP/27.093, *De Laval-Stork* [1977] OJ L215/11 (R&D agreement would enable the parties to penetrate a market more easily and quickly, reach optimal size, work at greater capacity, and share the latest technical advances) and Chap. 10.

[228] COMP/33.814, [1993] OJ L20/14.

[229] See, e.g., COMP/23.013, *Goodyear Italiana-Euram* [1975] OJ L38/10; COMP/171, 856, 172, 117, and 28.173, *Campari* [1978] OJ L70/69.

[230] Case T-168/01, [2006] ECR II-2969.

[231] Ibid., paras. 233–307. On appeal, Cases C-501, 513, 515, 519/06 P, [2009] ECR I-9291, the CJ ruled that the GC had not erred in law in finding that the Commission had erroneously failed to take into account certain facts highlighted by GSK in its request for exemption, including the specific structural features of the pharmaceuticals sector.

[232] This question was of importance in the modernisation debate. An acceptance that Art. 101(3) permitted a balancing of public and private interests and/or of conflicting EU policies might have militated against the proposals; it might have been considered unwise to delegate this task to a multiplicity of bodies, including national courts.

Commission stated that Article 101(3) is intended 'to provide a legal framework for the economic assessment of restrictive practices and not to allow the application of the competition rules to be set aside because of political considerations'.[233] In its Article 101(3) Guidelines, the discussion of the first condition of Article 101(3) is headed 'Efficiency gains' and *only* efficiency gains are discussed within it. Although it states that '[g]oals pursued by other Treaty provisions can be taken into account to the extent that they can be subsumed under the four conditions of Article [101(3)]'[234] its reliance on the ruling of the GC in *Matra Hachette* suggests that it considers that these factors may only be taken into account 'supererogatorily' on condition that they can be subsumed under the four conditions of Article 101(3).[235]

Case T-17/93, *Matra Hachette v Commission* [1994] ECR II-595

General Court

139. As regards the argument based on the reference to 'exceptional circumstances', the Court observes that, although the Commission refers to them, in particular in paragraphs 23 and 28, and in paragraph 36, in which the Decision concludes its examination of the condition under review and considers the project's impact on public infrastructures and on employment, and its impact on European integration, the latter paragraph ends with the following sentence: 'This would not be enough to make an exemption possible unless the conditions of Article [101(3)] were fulfilled, but it is an element which the Commission has taken into account'. The Court considers that it is clear from the latter sentence that the 'exceptional circumstances' thus referred to in the Decision were taken into consideration by the Commission only supererogatorily. In other words, it is sufficiently established that, if those circumstances had not been referred to, the operative part of the decision adopted would have been exactly the same as that of the contested Decision. It follows that the applicant's argument that, on the contrary, the individual exemption decision granted for the project in question was adopted only on the basis of the 'exceptional circumstances' surrounding the project must be rejected.

The Commission thus seems to take the view that past practice 'has never shown that the competition rules were "set aside" for political considerations . . . rather public policy considerations have been used to supplement the economic benefits which the agreement generates'.[236]

A narrow view, that only improvements in economic efficiency can be taken into account under Article 101(3), is certainly the one which sits best with the Commission's view of Article 101's objectives and how Article 101(1) and (3) now interact. It requires, however, a strained interpretation of past judgments and decisional practice. It has been seen that the CJ has, when construing the competition provisions, adopted a teleological interpretation[237] so that it is conceivable that, despite its actual wording, the criteria set out in Article 101(3) might be interpreted broadly against the

---

[233] [1999] OJ C132/1, para. 56. See, e.g., C.-D. Ehlermann in C.-D. Ehlermann and L. Laudati (eds.), *European Competition Law Annual 1997: Objectives of Competition Policy* (Hart Publishing, 1998), 480; R. Wesseling, 'The Commission White Paper on Modernisation of EC Antitrust Law: Unspoken Consequences and Incomplete Treatment of Alternative Options' [1999] *ECLR* 420; Monti, n. 38.

[234] Article 101(3) Guidelines, para. 42. The following words incorporated in the draft guidelines were not repeated in the final version of the document: 'It is not, on the other hand, the role of Article [101] and the authorities enforcing this Treaty provision to allow undertakings to restrict competition in pursuit of general interest aims.'

[235] See Faull and Nikpay, n. 4, 3.458–3.459.

[236] Monti, n. 38, 1090–1091. If the Commission is attempting to go further than this, however, and is seeking to deny even the more limited role of socio-political factors under Art. 101(3), then the view is difficult, if not impossible, to square with previous decisional practice and case law.

[237] See, e.g., Case 6/72, *Europemballage Corp and Continental Can Co, Inc v Commission* [1973] ECR 215 (discussed in Chap. 5); Cases C-68/94 and 30/95, *France v Commission* [1998] ECR I-1375 (discussed in Chaps. 9 and 15).

backdrop of the wider EU aims and objectives.[238] Indeed, pursuit of a sole consumer welfare objective may produce results inconsistent with other EU policies; the TFEU specifically provides in some places that the formulation and implementation of *all* EU policies and actions should take account of certain 'policy-linking' clauses, such as environmental protection, employment, culture, health, consumer protection, industrial policy, and/or the elimination of regional disparities. Indeed, some authority can be found to support the relevance of all these goals in the Article 101(3) context.[239]

In *Metro I*,[240] the CJ took the view that the fact that an agreement might lead to stability in the labour market was a matter which could be taken into account within the first criterion of Article 101(3). The agreement in question constituted 'a stabilizing factor with regard to the provision of employment which, since it improves the general conditions of production, especially when market conditions are unfavourable, comes within the framework of the objective to which reference may be had pursuant to Article [101(3)]'.[241] Further, in *Métropole Télévision SA v Commission*[242] the GC stated that 'the Commission is entitled to base itself on considerations connected with the pursuit of the public interest in order to grant exemption under Article [101(3)]'.[243] Both of these judgments related to the position pre-modernisation when the Commission had a monopoly over the application of Article 101(3). In 2011, however, in *Premier League Ltd v QC Leisure* and *Murphy v Media Protection Services Ltd*[244] the CJ referred to the applicant's argument that the agreement was justifiable under Article 101(3) on the grounds that the restraints were necessary to ensure that the intellectual property rights holder was appropriately remunerated and to encourage the public to attend football stadiums. It rejected the arguments on the facts, holding that the exclusive broadcast licensing agreement restricted competition by object and did not meet the conditions of Article 101(3), but did not specifically state whether such arguments were cognisable under Article 101(3) at all.

This attitude is also reflected in a number of the Commission's older decisions (although these may not reflect current Commission thinking). In *Ford/Volkswagen*,[245] for example, the Commission noted, in exempting the agreement, that the joint venture would lead to the creation of a number of jobs and substantial foreign investment in one of the poorest regions of the EU.[246]

36. In the assessment of this case, the Commission also takes note of the fact that the project constitutes the largest ever single foreign investment in Portugal. It is estimated to lead, *inter alia*, to the creation of about 5 000 jobs and indirectly create up to another 10 000 jobs, as well as attracting other investment in the supply industry. It therefore contributes to the promotion of the harmonious development of the [EU] and the reduction of regional disparities which is one of the basic aims of the Treaty. It also furthers European market integration by linking Portugal more closely to the [EU] through one of its important industries. This would not be enough to make an exemption possible unless the conditions of Article [101(3)] were fulfilled, but it is an element which the Commission has taken into account.

---

[238] Art. 101(3) could therefore be construed to permit authorisation of agreements which provide benefits, e.g., from a regional, social, environmental, cultural, and/or industrial perspective, see Monti, n. 38.

[239] See Chap. 1 (and discussion of Arts. 8–13 TFEU), C. Townley, *Article 101 and Public Policy* (Hart Publishing, 2009), and Odudu, n. 2, 161.

[240] Case 26/76, *Metro-SB-Grossmärkte GmbH v Commission (Metro I)* [1977] ECR 1875.

[241] Ibid., para. 43.

[242] Cases T-528, 542, 543, and 546/93, [1996] ECR II-649. See also Case T-193/02, *Laurent Piau v Commission* [2005] ECR II-209 (appeal dismissed by Order of the CJ, Case C-171/05 P, [2006] ECR I-37), para. 103 (a licence system for players' agents required by FIFA resulted in a qualitative selection, appropriate for the attainment of the objective of raising professional standards for the occupation of players' agents rather than a quantitative restriction on access to that occupation).

[243] Cases T-528, 542, 543, and 546/93, [1996] ECR II-649, para. 118.

[244] Cases C-403 and 429/08, EU:C:2011:43.

[245] COMP/33.814, [1993] OJ L20/14.

[246] The Commission found that the agreement would promote harmonious development, reduce regional disparities, and contribute to the integration of the European market, COMP/33.814, [1993] OJ L20/14, paras. 23, 28, and 36.

Although the Commission emphasised that these broader factors would not have caused the agreement to merit an exemption had the other conditions of Article 101(3) not been fulfilled,[247] these factors do appear to have been relevant to its final decision. Further, in an appeal from this decision the Commission argued that it was possible, when determining whether the agreement contributed to technical and economic progress, to take into account factors such as the maintenance of employment.[248] Arguably, this decision is difficult to justify on pure efficiency grounds and it symbolises the infiltrations of other policy objectives into EU competition law.[249]

In a series of decisions in the 1980s, the Commission also exempted agreements concluded between competitors designed to ensure an orderly reduction of capacity between the undertakings which were operating in an industry in crisis (crisis cartels). Although it might be argued that such agreements produce demonstrable efficiencies (such as the removal of inefficient capacity from the industry and increasing capacity utilisation rate, see also Chapter 9) in some of the cases the Commission also stressed the social benefits resulting from the agreements. In *Synthetic Fibres*,[250] for example, the Commission, in authorising an agreement between competitors to reduce capacity, accepted that the decision to embark on an orderly reduction in output satisfied the first criterion of Article 101(3).[251]

In a free market economy it ought to be principally a matter for the individual undertaking to judge the point at which overcapacity becomes economically unsustainable and to take the necessary steps to reduce it . . . In the present case, however, market forces by themselves had failed to achieve the capacity reductions necessary to re-establish and maintain in the longer term an effective competitive structure within the common market. The producers concerned therefore agreed to organise for a limited period and collectively, the needed structural adjustment.

The Commission thus recognised that, ordinarily, individual undertakings should make their own decision about reduction in capacity. However, in this case market forces had not achieved the reductions necessary. The agreement would enable the establishment and maintenance in the long term of effective competitive structures and would improve technical efficiency by enabling the undertakings to specialise. The eventual result would be to raise profitability and restore competitiveness.

[The] coordination of plant closures will also make it easier to cushion the social effects of the restructuring by making suitable arrangements for the retraining and redeployment of workers made redundant. It can be concluded then that the agreement contributes to improving production and promoting technical and economic progress.[252]

Similarly, in *Stichting Baksteen*[253] the Commission, when exempting an agreement for the restructuring of the Dutch brick industry, took account of the fact that the agreement allowed the restructuring to be carried out in acceptable social conditions and in a way which would lead to the redeployment of employees. The Commission held that the social advantages resulting to employees would promote economic progress for the purposes of Article 101(3).[254] In Chapter 9 it will be seen that the Commission did not take such a benevolent approach during the recent financial and economic crisis and has referred to these cases as examples of arrangements which achieved efficiency gains by removing inefficient capacity from the market.

---

[247] Ibid., para. 36.

[248] Case T-17/93, *Matra Hachette v Commission* [1994] ECR II-595, para. 96.

[249] See G. Amato, *Antitrust and the Bounds of Power: The Dilemma of Liberal Democracy in the History of the Market* (Hart Publishing, 1997), 58–63, and Chap. 10.

[250] COMP/30.810, [1984] OJ L207/17.

[251] Ibid., paras. 30–31.

[252] Ibid., paras. 37–38.

[253] COMP/34.456, [1994] OJ L131/15.

[254] Ibid., paras. 27–28.

In *Exxon/Shell*[255] the Commission held that a reduction in pollution would lead to a technological improvement for the purposes of Article 101(3). Further, in *European Council of Manufacturers of Domestic Appliances (CECED)*[256] it exempted an agreement concluded between 95 per cent of the producers and importers of washing machines operating on the EU market that restricted their freedom to manufacture or import the least energy-efficient washing machines. The agreement was found to restrict competition within the meaning of Article 101(1). The agreement, by restricting the parties' autonomy to produce or import less environmentally friendly machines,[257] had the object of controlling one important product characteristic on which there was competition, thereby restricting competition between the parties and reducing consumer choice. Nonetheless the Commission considered that the agreement met the criteria set out in Article 101(3). It would reduce the potential energy consumption of new machines and consequently lessen pollution, create more technically efficient machines, and focus future R&D on furthering energy efficiency.[258] It also seems that the production of a product which increases safety for a consumer may constitute a technical improvement.[259]

(ii) Criterion 2: Allowing Consumers a Fair Share of the Resulting Benefit

Although the second criterion of Article 101(3) requires that it must be established that the agreement allows consumers a fair share of the benefit, the Article 101(3) Guidelines indicate that this condition should be considered only after it has been determined that the restrictions incorporated in the agreement are indispensable (see Criterion 3). This is because the requirement that consumers receive a fair share of the benefits 'implies a balancing of pro-competitive and anti-competitive effects. This balancing exercise should not include restrictions that in any event are unnecessary to achieve the efficiencies.'[260] The Article 101(3) Guidelines states that the agreement allows consumers a fair share of the benefit, by showing that there is a pass-on of the cost and quality efficiencies to consumers.[261] This accords with the Commission's view that the objective of Article 101 is consumer not total welfare.[262]

a. Consumer

Consumer is interpreted broadly to include not only final consumers (end-users) but also intermediate consumers, including wholesalers and retailers, that purchase products in the course of their trade or business.[263] Consumers can be undertakings or private individuals. It is clear that not all

---

[255] COMP/33.640, [1994] OJ L144/20.

[256] COMP/36.718, [2000] OJ L187/47. See also COMP/39.579, *Consumer Detergents* [2011] OJ C193/14, paras. 53–54, COMP/34.950, *Eco-Emballages* [2001] OJ L233/37 (negative clearance), and COMP/34.493, *DSD* [2001] OJ L319/1 (exemption) and Chap. 10.

[257] It did not directly restrict output as the agreement was only to cease to produce the least energy efficient machines. Limited effects on output might arise only indirectly, through reduced demand.

[258] The Commission considered that the other elements of Art. 101(3) were also satisfied, see Chap. 9. See IP/00/148 ('When I took office as Commissioner responsible for Competition, I stressed before the European Parliament that environmental concerns are in no way contradictory with competition policy. This decision clearly illustrates this principle, enshrined in the Treaty, provided that restrictions of competition are proportionate and necessary to achieving the environmental objectives aimed at, to the benefit of current and future generations' (then) Commissioner Monti).

[259] COMP/29.146, *BMW Belgium NV and Belgian BMW Dealers* [1978] OJ L46/33. See also COMP/34.493, *DSD* [2001] OJ L319/1.

[260] Faull and Nikpay, n. 4, 3.489.

[261] Article 101(3) Guidelines, paras. 83–104.

[262] See Chap. 1.

[263] COMP/21.353, *Kabel und Metallwerke Neumeyer AG and Etablissements Luchaire SA Agreement* [1975] OJ L222/34.

individual consumers need to derive a benefit from the agreement for Article 101(3) to apply. Rather it is the overall effect on consumers in the relevant markets that must be favourable. '[I]t is the beneficial nature of the effect on all consumers in the relevant markets that must be taken into consideration, not the effect on each member of that category of consumers.'[264]

Two further issues arising in relation to the consumer benefit requirement are (a) whether the benefits must result to the same consumers in the same market as those suffering anti-competitive effects; and (b) whether it is possible to take account of the fact that future consumers will benefit when current consumers will be hurt by the arrangement. Although the Article 101(3) Guidelines state that the benefits must be felt by consumers in the same market as that in which the anti-competitive effects take place,[265] in *MasterCard*[266] the CJ held that it is necessary to take into account the objective advantages flowing from the measure not only on the market in which the restriction has been established but also, in particular where there is an undisputed interaction between the two markets, in other markets (in the case of a two-sided system, other groups of consumers associated with that system). The CJ held that some advantage must, however, flow to the market where the restrictive measures are felt, if the consumers on the affected markets are not substantially the same. As in that case no advantages were found to flow from the MIF to the merchants (affected by the restriction), it was not necessary to examine the advantages flowing to cardholders since these could not by themselves be of such a character to compensate for the disadvantages resulting from those fees.[267]

A broad reading of the cases might also suggest that all consumer benefits (whether current or future) should be taken into account, so long as some benefit to consumers affected by the restriction can be established. Such an interpretation would also be compatible with the approach adopted under Article 102 where both the short-term and longer-term effects of a strategy may be relevant to the assessment. Clearly, however, even if future benefits to future consumers are relevant, it may be extremely difficult for the parties to provide convincing evidence that such benefits will result to consumers.[268]

b. Fair Share

The Commission describes the concept of fair share in its Article 101(3) Guidelines.

85. The concept of 'fair share' implies that the pass-on of benefits must at least compensate consumers for any actual or likely negative impact caused to them by the restriction of competition found under Article [101(1)]. In line with the overall objective of Article [101] to prevent anti-competitive agreements, the net effect of the agreement must at least be neutral from the point of view of those consumers directly or likely affected by the agreement. If such consumers are worse off following the agreement, the second condition of Article [101(3)] is not fulfilled. The positive effects of an agreement must be balanced against and compensate for its negative effects on consumers. When that is the case consumers are not harmed by the agreement. Moreover, society as a whole benefits because the efficiencies lead either to fewer resources being used to produce the output consumed or to the production of more valuable products and thus to a more efficient allocation of resources.

---

[264] Case C-238/05, *Asnef-Equifax v Asociación de Usuarios de Servicios Bancarios (Ausbanc)* [2006] ECR I-11125, para. 70.

[265] Unless 'the group of consumers affected by the restriction and benefiting from the efficiency gains [on a different market] are substantially the same', Article 101(3) Guidelines, para. 43.

[266] Case C-382/12 P, EU:C:2014:2201.

[267] Ibid., paras. 242–243. See also Case T-86/95, *Compagnie Générale Maritime v Commission* [2002] ECR II-1011, para. 343 and, e.g., C. Townley, 'The Relevant Market: An Acceptable Limit to Competition Analysis?' [2011] ECLR 490.

[268] See C. Townley, 'Inter-generational Impacts in Competition Law: Remembering Those Not Yet Born' [2011] ECLR 580.

The Guidelines also explain that it is *not* necessary that consumers receive a share of each and every efficiency gain identified under the first condition, nor that the pass-on must occur immediately or within a specified period of time.[269] Further, that the pass-on will have to be greater, the greater the restriction of competition.[270]

Where consumers are forced to pay a higher price without attaining other benefits from the agreement, this criterion will not be satisfied. Some agreements have been refused an exemption on the ground that consumers will not receive a fair share of the benefit. For example, in *VBBB and VBVB*[271] the Commission held that the consumers would not benefit from the parties' agreement to fix the retail prices of books. On the contrary, consumers would be forced to pay a higher price and would be deprived of the opportunity to pay lower prices. The Commission has also refused exemption to agreements that are clearly designed to restrict competition and force consumers to pay a higher price for products in the absence of other compensating benefits. In *SPO and others v Commission*,[272] for example, the GC heard an appeal against the Commission's refusal of an exemption to a Dutch building association. The purpose of the agreement in question was to protect the members from ruinous competition. The Court upheld the Commission's decision, stating that 'by taking action to counteract what they regard as ruinous competition, the applicants necessarily restrict competition and therefore deprive consumers of its benefits'.[273] In contrast, however, to the decision it took in *SPO* the Commission in *Synthetic Fibres*[274] concluded that consumers would benefit from an agreement between competitors on a market to reduce capacity. Although prices might rise initially, there was sufficient competition on the market and considerable countervailing purchasing power to limit these increases. Further, the agreement would result in a healthier, more competitive industry in the long run.[275]

(iii) Criterion 3: Indispensable Restrictions

An agreement which satisfies the first two positive criteria set out in Article 101(3) must only contain restrictions which are indispensable to the achievement of the benefits shown to result from the agreement. Such restrictions may be indispensable only for a period of time.

It has been seen that the Commission seeks to distinguish this inquiry from that made under the doctrine of ancillary restraints by asking whether the restrictive agreement and restrictions make it possible to perform the activity in question more efficiently, i.e. 'if its absence would eliminate or significantly reduce the efficiencies that follow from the agreement or make it significantly less likely that they will materialize'.[276] In *MasterCard* the CJ also stressed the separate nature of the ancillary restraints and indispensability requirements and their different objectives. The indispensability criterion 'relates to the issue whether coordination between undertakings

---

[269] Article 101(3) Guidelines, paras. 86–89.

[270] Ibid., paras. 90–91.

[271] COMP/428, *VBBB and VBVB* [1982] OJ L54/36, *aff'd* in Cases C-43 and 63/82, *VBVB and VBBB v Commission* [1984] ECR 19.

[272] Case T-29/92, [1995] ECR II-289.

[273] Ibid., para. 294.

[274] COMP/30.810, [1984] OJ L207/17.

[275] Ibid., paras. 39–41.

[276] Article 101(3) Guidelines, para. 79 (and not whether the restraint is necessary to the implementation of the agreement). But see Case C-1/12, *OTOC* EU:C:2013:127, where the CJ relies on the same factors to state both that the agreement went beyond what was necessary to achieve a legitimate objective (and so did not fall outside Art. 101(1)) and that the restrictions could not be regarded as essential for the purposes of Art. 101(3). In COMP/36.253, *P&O Stena Line* [1999] OJ L163/61 the Commission granted an exemption to a joint venture which combined the parties' services on a particular ferry route. It accepted the argument that less restrictive alternatives, such as joint scheduling, or pooling, would not enable the parties to achieve the benefits, such as cost savings and increased frequency in service, of their joint venture. The Commission expended much effort in its exemption decisions in ensuring that agreements were not more restrictive than they needed to be to achieve their accepted benefits.

that is liable to have an appreciable adverse impact on the parameters of competition...can none the less, in the context of Article [101(3)], be considered indispensable to the improvement of production or distribution or to the promotion of technical or economic progress, while allowing consumers a fair share of the resulting benefits. By contrast...the objective necessity test...concerns the question whether, in the absence of a given restriction of commercial autonomy, a main operation or activity which is not caught by the prohibition laid down in Article [101(1)] and to which that restriction is secondary, is likely not to be implemented or not to proceed.'[277] On the facts the CJ held that the GC had not erred in rejecting both the argument that the MIF was objectively necessary for the operation of the MasterCard system and that the MIF had contributed to increasing the output of the system.[278]

The Commission states that this condition, an application of the EU principle of proportionality,[279] implies a twofold test.

Guidelines on the application of Article 81(3) [now Article 101(3)] of the Treaty (the Article 101(3) Guidelines) [2004] OJ C101/97

73. According to the third condition of Article [101(3)] the restrictive agreement must not impose restrictions, which are not indispensable to the attainment of the efficiencies created by the agreement in question. This condition implies a two-fold test. First, the restrictive agreement as such must be reasonably necessary in order to achieve the efficiencies. Secondly, the individual restrictions of competition that flow from the agreement must also be reasonably necessary for the attainment of the efficiencies.

74. In the context of the third condition of Article [101(3)] the decisive factor is whether or not the restrictive agreement and individual restrictions make it possible to perform the activity in question more efficiently than would have been the case in the absence of the agreement or the restriction concerned. The question is not whether in the absence of the restriction the agreement would not have been concluded, but whether more efficiencies are produced with the agreement or restriction than in the absence of the agreement.[280]

Restrictions will not therefore be indispensable if the efficiencies specific to the agreement can be achieved by other practicable and less restrictive means, or if individual restrictions are not reasonably necessary to produce the efficiencies. In *Protimonopolný úrad Slovenskej republiky v Slovenská sporiteľňa as*,[281] for example, the CJ rejected an argument that an anti-competitive agreement was required to eliminate undertakings operating illegally on the market. The CJ stressed that even if some efficiency could be demonstrated by the parties from forcing those undertakings to comply with national law (for example, from protecting the conditions for healthy competition and so seeking to promote economic progress on the market), less restrictive measures could have been adopted. In

---

[277] Case C-382/12 P, *MasterCard and Others v Commission* EU:C:2014:2201, para. 93.

[278] Ibid., paras. 232–234.

[279] The principle of proportionality essentially requires that an action (whether of the EU or of a State or, in this case, parties to an agreement) should not go beyond what is necessary to achieve the objectives of the Treaty, see discussion of principle in, e.g., P. Craig and G. de Búrca, *EU Law: Text, Cases, and Materials* (6th edn, Oxford University Press, 2015), 551–558.

[280] See Article 101(3) Guidelines, para. 18.

[281] Case C-68/12, EU:C:2013:71.

particular, rather than taking steps to eliminate the undertaking themselves, the parties could have lodged a complaint with competent authorities.

The Commission takes the view that provisions which are 'restrictive by object' or hardcore restraints are not generally indispensable.[282] The list of 'hardcore' restraints in the block exemptions thus provide useful guidance on the types of provisions that the Commission considers are dispensable and not essential to achieving the benefits produced by a particular type of agreement.

J. Faull and A. Nikpay (eds.), *The EU Law of Competition* (3rd edn, Oxford University Press, 2014)

3.494 …Once it is found that the agreement in question is necessary in order to produce the efficiencies the indispensability of each restriction of competition flowing from the agreement must be assessed. A restriction is indispensable if its absence would eliminate or significantly reduce the efficiencies achieved by the agreement or make it significantly less likely that they will materialize. The assessment of alternative solutions must take into account the actual and potential improvement in competition by the elimination of a particular restriction or the application of a less restrictive alternative. The third condition of Article 101(3) thus incorporates a sliding scale. The more restrictive the restraint, the stricter the test under the third condition. Restrictions that are identified as hardcore restrictions in Commission block exemption regulations or guidelines and notices are unlikely to be considered indispensable.

It is reiterated, however, that *every* agreement is potentially capable of exemption. In later chapters of this book, it will be seen that the Commission has since the publication of these Guidelines been prepared to concede that even hardcore restraints may sometimes satisfy the Article 101(3) criteria (see especially Chapter 11) and examples will be given of some such exceptional cases.[283]

(iv) Criterion 4: The Agreement Must Not Afford the Parties the Possibility of Eliminating Competition

The last requirement is that the agreement as a whole must not lead to the elimination of competition. This criterion appears to reflect the view that short-term efficiency gains must not be outweighed by longer-term losses stemming from the elimination of competition.

The Commission states in the Article 101(3) Guidelines that '[u]ltimately the protection of rivalry and the competitive process is given priority over potentially pro-competitive efficiency gains which could result from restrictive agreements'.[284] Further, it sets out its view that rivalry between undertakings on the market should be preserved since rivalry is the essential driver of economic efficiency, including dynamic efficiency.

When competition is eliminated the competitive process is brought to an end and short-term efficiency gains are outweighed by longer-term losses stemming *inter alia* from expenditures incurred by the incumbent to maintain its position (rent seeking), misallocation of resources, reduced innovation and higher prices.[285]

---

[282] See, e.g., Article 101(3) Guidelines, para. 46 (these types of restraints are unlikely to satisfy the first two conditions of Art. 101(3) since they neither create objective economic benefits nor benefit consumers).

[283] See, e.g., Chaps. 9 and 11.

[284] Article 101(3) Guidelines, para. 105.

[285] Ibid.

This criterion thus requires an analysis of the competitive restraints imposed on the parties, the degree of competition existing prior to the agreement, and the impact of the agreement on competition. Sources of competition, through actual and potential competitors, must be analysed along with the impact of the agreement on these competitive constraints.

The Commission considers, in its assessment, the market shares of the parties, the incentives for actual competitors to compete, the impact of the agreement on the various parameters of competition, the actual market conduct of the parties (where the agreement has been implemented), past competitive interaction, the closeness of competition previously existing between the competitors, and the scope of potential competition.

When assessing barriers to entry the Commission stresses that it takes into account the real possibility for new entry into the market.[286] At paragraph 116 of the Guidelines the Commission sets out some hypothetical examples of how this fourth condition is applied.

The Guidelines also explore the relationship between this requirement (and Article 101(3) more generally) with Article 102.[287] The following principles are set out:

(a) the application of Article 101(3) does not prevent the application of Article 102;

(b) conduct which is abusive should not be permitted under Article 101(3).[288] Article 101(3) could however be used to authorise an agreement concluded by a dominant undertaking which does not constitute an abuse of a dominant position;[289]

(c) not all agreements infringing Article 101 constitute an abuse of a dominant position.

E. BLOCK EXEMPTIONS

(i) General

A number of EU regulations[290] grant exemption to categories of agreements that satisfy their conditions. They are adopted for a specified period of time and kept under review during that period. In *Pierre Fabre*,[291] the CJ held, when interpreting the block exemption applicable to vertical agreements, that as undertakings have the option of asserting that Article 101(3) applies on an individual basis to their agreement, it is not necessary to give a broad interpretation of the block exemption provisions.

(ii) Current Block Exemptions

Some block exemptions pertain to specific sectors. Others, however, apply more generally to vertical, horizontal, and technology transfer agreements respectively. The latter block exemptions are discussed in further detail in Chapters 10–12. Table 4.1 sets out the block exemptions currently in force.

---

[286] Ibid., para. 115 and see Chap. 1.

[287] Ibid., para. 106.

[288] Ibid. In COMP/34.395 and COMP/35.436, *Van den Bergh Foods* [1998] OJ L264/1, upheld on appeal Case T-65/98, *Van den Bergh Foods* [2003] ECR II-4653, *aff'd* Case C-552/03 P, *Unilever Bestfoods v Commission* [2006] ECR I-9091, the Commission declined to grant an exemption to conduct found to contravene Art. 102. The finding of dominance influenced the Commission's decision that the agreement would substantially eliminate competition within the meaning of Art. 101(3), see paras. 242–246.

[289] Article 101(3) Guidelines, para. 106.

[290] Although some have been adopted by the Council a majority have been adopted by the Commission following authorisation from the Council.

[291] Case C-439/09, EU:C:2011:277.

Table 4.1 Block exemptions currently in force

Regulation	Categories of agreements covered	Enabling legislation (Council Regulation)[292] (where relevant)
Commission Regulation 316/2014[293]	Technology transfer agreements	Regulation 19/65[294] (amended by Council Regulation 1215/99 and 1216/2000)[295]
Commission Regulation 330/2010[296]	Vertical agreements	
Commission Regulation 461/2010[297]	Vertical agreements and concerted practices in the motor vehicle sector	
Commission Regulation 1218/2010[298]	Specialisation agreements	Regulation 2821/71[299]
Commission Regulation 1217/2010[300]	R&D agreements	
Commission Regulation 267/2010[301]	Agreements in the insurance sector	Council Regulation 1534/91[302]
Commission Regulation 906/2009[303]	Liner shipping consortia	Council Regulation 246/2009[304]
Council Regulation 169/2009[305]	Rail, road, and inland waterway sectors	

(iii) Direct Applicability

Agreements falling within the ambit of one of the block exemptions are automatically exempt from the Article 101(1) prohibition and the national courts are, and always have been, free to apply the terms of the block exemption should the validity of the agreement be raised before such a court. Article 288 TFEU specifically provides that regulations are directly applicable.

If an agreement does not fall precisely within the scope of a block exemption the national court may not extend it to cover the agreement.[306] The general rule is that if the conditions of the block exemption are not met the regulation ceases to apply in its entirety. However, in the block exemption applying to vertical and technology transfer agreements, for example, the regulations distinguish between provisions which, if inserted, mean that the block exemption does not apply and

---

[292] Although Council Reg. 487/2009 [2009] OJ L148/1 authorises the granting of block exemptions in the air transport sector, none have been adopted.

[293] [2014] OJ L93/17.

[294] [1965–1966] OJ Spec. Ed. 35.

[295] [1999] OJ L148/1 and [1999] OJ L148/5.

[296] [2010] OJ L102/1.

[297] [2010] OJ L129/52.

[298] [2010] OJ L335/43.

[299] [1971] OJ Spec. Ed. 1032.

[300] [2010] OJ L335/36.

[301] [2010] OJ L83/1. On 17 March 2016 the Commission published a report on the functioning of this block exemption, which expires at the end of March 2017. Broadly, it is considering whether an industry-specific block exemption is still required or appropriate.

[302] [1991] OJ L143/1.

[303] [2009] OJ L256/31 (amended and extended by Reg. 697/2014 [2014] OJ L184/3).

[304] [2009] OJ L79/1.

[305] [2009] OJ L61/1.

[306] See also n. 291 and text.

provisions which are not covered by the block exemption but which do not prevent the remaining provisions of the agreement benefiting from the regulation.

Where the conditions of a block exemption are not met (for example, the market share thresholds are exceeded or the agreement incorporates 'hardcore' restraints identified within it), the national court will, of course, be bound to determine whether or not the agreement infringes Article 101(1) and, where it does, whether it individually meets the Article 101(3) criteria.[307]

(iv) Market Share Thresholds

The new block exemptions, adopted since 1999, have generally sought to reflect the economic objective underpinning the competition law rules so operate by providing a rule of thumb that agreements concluded by undertakings which meet specified market share thresholds (and so are unlikely to have significant market power) are unlikely to raise competition problems. Most block exemptions thus now contain market share thresholds. For example, Regulation 330/2010, relating to vertical agreements, applies only where the relevant undertakings' market shares are below 30 per cent, Regulation 316/2014, the technology transfer block exemption, applies only where the parties' market shares do not exceed 20 or 30 per cent of the market (depending upon whether the parties are competitors or non-competitors), and the R&D and specialisation block exemptions apply only provided the parties do not exceed market share thresholds of 25 and 20 per cent respectively.[308]

(v) 'Hardcore' Restraints

Most block exemptions also contain a list of hardcore restraints which, if included within the agreement, preclude the application of the block exemption. This reflects the Commission's view that agreements containing hardcore restraints are presumed to violate Article 101 (in most cases they will be restrictive of competition by object and are unlikely to satisfy the Article 101(3) conditions) and so cannot benefit from a block exemption.

(vi) Withdrawal of Block Exemptions

Regulation 1/2003 provides that the Commission may withdraw the benefit of any Commission block exemption when 'it finds that in any particular case an agreement, decision or concerted practice to which the exemption Regulation applies has certain effects which are incompatible with Article [101(3)]'.[309] Withdrawal was threatened on several occasions under some of the old regulations[310] and actually occurred in *Langnese-Iglo*.[311] The CJ made clear, however, that the benefit of the block exemption (in that case Regulation 1984/83 applying to exclusive purchasing agreements) could not be withheld in advance from *future* agreements.[312] Some block exemptions, however, now specifically provide for the Commission to withdraw their benefit to specified categories of agreements (rather than individual agreements) by regulation.[313]

Regulation 1/2003 also provides NCAs with power to withdraw the benefit of any Commission block exemption where the agreement, to which the regulation applies, has 'effects which are

---

[307] It has been seen, however, that an agreement which contains clauses specifically prohibited by a regulation is unlikely to satisfy Art. 101(3).

[308] Above those market shares, however, the restraints may pose competition problems on account of the market power so an individual assessment is required, see especially Chaps. 10–12.

[309] Reg. 1/2003 [2003] OJ L1/1, Art. 29(1).

[310] See, e.g., *Tetra Pak/BTG* [1988] OJ L272/27.

[311] COMP/34.072, *Langnese-Iglo* [1993] OJ L183/19.

[312] Case C-279/95 P, *Langnese-Iglo v Commission* [1998] ECR I-5609, paras. 207–209.

[313] See, e.g., Chap. 11.

incompatible with Article [101(1)] in the territory of a Member State, or in a part thereof, which has all the characteristics of a distinct geographic market'.[314]

(vii) Safe Harbours

The block exemptions are designed to provide legal certainty for undertakings. Undertakings know that agreements satisfying their conditions are valid and compatible with Article 101. Clearly, the introduction of market share thresholds detracts somewhat from this objective,[315] although their incorporation goes hand in hand with the desire that they reflect the economic goals underpinning Article 101. Further, the relatively low market share thresholds set out for those wishing to benefit from the safe harbour do not fit neatly within the analytical framework constructed by the Commission in its Article 101(3) Guidelines. The block exemptions were initially adopted as an essential response to the broad interpretation given to Article 101(1). Exemption under Article 101(3) was vital to the validity of many agreements. Although it is understood that the Commission now intends the block exemptions to operate as safe harbours and considers that agreements which do not satisfy these requirements do not necessarily infringe Article 101(1),[316] it is arguable that agreements satisfying their conditions will, in most cases, be unlikely to affect actual or potential competition to such an extent that a negative effect on prices, output, innovation, or the variety or quality of goods and services can be expected on the market (and so arguably do not infringe Article 101(1)). The existence of the block exemptions, although providing welcome legal certainty, therefore concentrates attention on Article 101(3) and may confuse the question of what analysis is required under Article 101(1).

F. UNILATERAL ACTION AND ARTICLE 101(3)

It was seen in Chapter 3 that in certain circumstances seemingly unilateral conduct of one party to a contract might actually form part of the contractual arrangements between it and a co-contractor, for example where it has been explicitly or tacitly accepted by the latter. In many cases the Commission has relied on such behaviour to find a breach of Article 101(1). Similarly, in *Ford Werke AG v Commission*[317] the Commission relied both on the terms of the agreement and on the way in which it was operated by Ford when it issued a decision refusing Ford an exemption for its selective distribution system. The CJ held that the Commission was entitled, when considering the terms of the agreement, to take account not only of the written terms of the agreement but also the way the agreement was operated. In this case Ford had essentially refused to supply right-hand-drive cars to its German dealers in order to protect the higher prices which the distributors charged in the UK. That apparently unilateral decision was, in this case, found to form part of the contractual arrangements since admission to the network involved implicit acceptance by the dealers of the terms imposed by Ford.

5. CONCLUSIONS

1. The challenge for a system of competition law is to design a set of transparent and predictable rules which can be used to determine as accurately as possible, and at a tolerable cost, which agreements so harm competition that they should be prohibited and deterred. It has been seen in this chapter that this challenge has been rendered particularly difficult in the EU both by the lack of clarity over Article 101's objectives and its bifurcated structure.

---

[314] Reg. 1/2003 [2003] OJ L1/1, Art. 29(2). See, e.g., Chap. 11.

[315] See especially Chap. 12.

[316] See the Verticals Guidelines, para. 120.

[317] Cases 228 and 229/82, [1984] ECR 1129.

2. The Commission has moved away from its broad, jurisdictional approach to Article 101(1) which created an expansive role for Article 101(3) and (at the time) a pressing need for block exemptions. It now seeks to adopt a more realistic approach to Article 101(1) and Article 101(3) based on a consumer welfare objective.

3. In modernising its approach to Article 101, the Commission has not accepted that Article 101(1) provides the correct forum for weighing pro- and anti-competitive effects on the basis that this approach would result in Article 101(3) being 'cast aside'. Rather, the Commission considers that Article 101(1) is about identifying restrictive effects on competition (it is for the Commission, or other person trying to prove the same, to demonstrate the restriction except where restrictions of competition are assumed (object cases)), whilst Article 101(3) provides the forum, for the person seeking to rely on it, to prove that counteracting efficiencies resulting from the agreement outweigh the effect of those restrictions.[318]

4. The difficulty with this structure is that it requires a strained view of some of the jurisprudence. A number of judgments of the CJ support the view that the weighing of pro- and anti-competitive effects should be conducted within the framework of Article 101(1) (restrictions of competition necessary and proportionate to a legitimate objective fall outside Article 101(1)). Further, precedent indicates that public policy objectives may, in certain circumstances, be taken into account. These cases suggest a rather different picture of the analysis to be conducted under Article 101, indicating a narrower interpretation of Article 101(1) and less emphasis on Article 101(3). Further, they suggest that both Article 101(1) and Article 101(3) may still have a role to play in the pursuit of public policy objectives.

6. FURTHER READING

A. BOOKS

AMATO, G., *Antitrust and the Bounds of Power* (Hart Publishing, 1997), Chap. 4

ODUDU, O., *The Boundaries of EC Competition Law: The Scope of Article 81* (Oxford University Press, 2006)

TOWNLEY, C., *Article 81 EC and Public Policy* (Hart Publishing, 2009)

B. CHAPTERS IN BOOKS

IBÁÑEZ COLOMO, P., 'Copyright Licensing and the EU Digital Single Market Strategy' in R. D. Blair and D. D. Sokol (eds.), *Handbook of Antitrust, Intellectual Property and High Technology* (Cambridge University Press, 2016)

C. ARTICLES

BAILEY, D., 'Restrictions of Competition by Object under Article 101 TFEU' (2012) 49 *CMLRev* 559

HAWK, B. E., 'System Failure: Vertical Restraints and EC Competition Law' (1995) 32 *CMLRev* 973

IBÁÑEZ COLOMO, P., 'Market Failure, Transaction Costs and Article 101(1) TFEU Case-law' (2012) 37 *ELRev* 541

JONES, A., 'Analysis of Agreements under US and EC Antitrust Law—Convergence or Divergence?' (2006) 51 *Ant Bull* 691

JONES, A., 'Left Behind by Modernisation? Restrictions by Object under Article 101(1)' (2010) 6 *European Competition Journal* 649

KORAH, V., 'EEC Competition Policy—Legal Form or Economic Efficiency' (1986) 39 *CLP* 85

MONTI, G., 'Article 81 and Public Policy' (2002) 39 *CMLRev* 1057

SUFRIN, B., 'The Evolution of Article 81(3) of the EC Treaty' (2006) 51 *Ant Bull* 915

WHISH, R., and SUFRIN, B., 'Article 85 and the Rule of Reason' [1987] *YEL* 1

---

[318] The weighing is conducted therefore within the framework of Art. 101(3) rather than under Art. 101(1).

5

INTRODUCTION TO ARTICLE 102 TFEU

1. CENTRAL ISSUES

1. Article 102 TFEU (previously Article 82 EC) deals with the unilateral conduct of undertakings in a 'dominant position'.

2. Article 102 prohibits one or more undertakings which hold a dominant position in the internal market or a substantial part of it abusing that position insofar as it may affect inter-Member State trade. For an infringement of Article 102 to be established, therefore, five cumulative elements must be established.

3. 'Undertaking' has the same meaning as it does in respect of Article 101. 'One or more undertakings' means that independent undertakings may together hold a 'collective' dominant position. The meaning of an effect on inter-Member State trade is set out in the Commission Guidelines on the effect on trade concept, which explain the case law.

4. The elements of 'dominant position' and 'abuse' are particularly difficult both to define and to establish. The holding of a 'dominant position' is not prohibited, only the 'abuse' of the dominant position. Article 102 does not apply to conduct whereby non-dominant firms achieve dominance.

5. The way in which the Commission and the EU Courts have interpreted Article 102 has been extremely controversial. Article 102 has mainly been applied to 'exclusionary abuses', i.e. to conduct which impedes effective competition by excluding (foreclosing) competitors. It has often been applied in a formalistic way, focusing on the form of the conduct and drawing presumptions from that, rather than analysing the actual effects on the market. Further, it has often been applied in order to protect competitors rather than to protect the competitive process for the benefit of consumers.

6. The Commission wishes to 'modernise' the approach to Article 102. It wishes to realign Article 102 to take an effects-based approach directed to the objective of consumer welfare. In 2003 the Commission embarked upon a review of the application of Article 102 to exclusionary abuses. The review resulted first in a DG Comp Staff Discussion Paper in 2005 and culminated in the official publication in February 2009 of Commission Guidance on its enforcement priorities in applying Article 102 to abusive exclusionary conduct (the Guidance Paper).

7. The Guidance Paper states that it is not intended to constitute a statement of the law. Instead, it sets out the principles which will guide the Commission in deciding when to intervene. The Commission is concerned about conduct that has an adverse impact on consumers. It takes a consumer welfare approach.

8. The EU Courts have been slow to depart from the established case law. Recent judgments of the EU Courts have taken an approach different from that of the Commission in the Guidance Paper and the Court of Justice has stated that the Guidance Paper merely sets out the Commission's administrative practice in the choice of cases it will pursue as a matter of priority.

2. INTRODUCTION

Article 102 is designed to deal with monopoly and substantial market power. It focuses not on agreements *between* undertakings (as Article 101 does) but on the unilateral behaviour of undertakings which hold a 'dominant position'.[1] It constrains the behaviour of undertakings which are not sufficiently restrained by other competitors operating on the market by prohibiting the 'abuse' of a dominant position. Article 102 applies only to the conduct of undertakings which are already dominant and not to any anti-competitive conduct by which an undertaking *achieves* dominance, or to unilateral conduct by a non-dominant firm which causes harm to consumers despite that lack of dominance.[2]

Article 102 prohibits an undertaking with a dominant position from exploiting that position, for example by charging unfair prices or by limiting production to the prejudice of consumers. In addition, it is clear from the case law that the provision also covers anti-competitive conduct by which a dominant undertaking excludes actual or potential competitors from the market.[3] Article 102 therefore applies to so-called 'exclusionary' conduct as well as to conduct that exploits consumers directly.

The application of Article 102 by the Commission and the EU Courts has often been highly controversial. This is principally due to the following:

- questionable findings that an undertaking is dominant for the purposes of the Article;

- an emphasis on the *form* that the behaviour of the dominant undertaking takes, rather than on its *effects*;

- an absence of coherent and consistent principles or a clear analytical or intellectual framework of analysis in the approach to Article 102.[4] This has stemmed partly from a failure to identify the policy objectives being pursued in the enforcement of the prohibition. The application of Article 102 raises very starkly the question of whether the law should protect competitors for their own sake or whether it should focus on consumers. In the application of Article 102 and the debate surrounding it we see played out the arguments about the purposes of competition law which we noted in Chapter 1;

- the effect that the imperative of single market integration has played.

3. THE TEXT OF ARTICLE 102

Article 102 provides:[5]

Any abuse by one or more undertakings of a dominant position within the internal market or in a substantial part of it shall be prohibited as incompatible with the internal market insofar as it may affect trade between Member States. Such abuse may, in particular, consist in:

(a) directly or indirectly imposing unfair purchase or selling prices or other unfair trading conditions;

(b) limiting production, markets or technical development to the prejudice of consumers;

---

[1] It does, however, as explained in Section 7 and in Chap. 7, include conduct which involves entering into agreements with other parties.

[2] For comments on this 'enforcement gap' see L.-H. Roeller, 'Exploitative Abuses', in C.-D. Ehlermann and M. Marquis (eds.), *European Competition Law Annual 2007: A Reformed Approach to Article 82* (Hart Publishing, 2008); I. Kokkoris, 'Are We Underenforcing Article 102 TFEU' in F. Etro and I. Kokkoris (eds.), *Competition Law and the Enforcement of Article 102* (Oxford University Press, 2010), Chap. 9. The lack of application of Art. 102 to the unilateral behaviour of non-dominant firms was remarked upon by the Commission in its press release on the initial findings of the e-commerce inquiry, IP/16/922.

[3] See Case 6/72, *Europemballage Corp and Continental Can Co Inc v Commission* [1973] ECR 215 and Chap. 7 *passim*.

[4] See, e.g., J. Temple Lang and R. O'Donoghue, 'Defining Legitimate Competition: How to Clarify Pricing Abuses under Article 82EC' (2002) 26 *Fordham Int'l LJ* 83, 84.

[5] The wording of Art. 102 TFEU is unchanged from that of Art. 82 EC other than the substitution of 'internal market' for 'common market'.

(c) applying dissimilar conditions to equivalent transactions with other trading parties, thereby placing them at a competitive disadvantage;

(d) making the conclusion of contracts subject to acceptance by the other parties of supplementary obligations which, by their nature or according to commercial usage, have no connection with the subject of such contracts.

The burden of proving an infringement of Article 102 rests on the party or authority alleging the infringement.[6] The question of the burden of proof where 'objective justification' is pleaded is discussed in Chapter 7.[7]

4. THE SCHEME OF ARTICLE 102

A. THE PROHIBITION

Article 102 prohibits undertakings from committing an abuse of a dominant position held within the internal market or a substantial part of it where that abuse may have an effect on trade between Member States. Although sub-paragraphs (a)–(d) set out examples of abuses, they do not provide an exhaustive list of specific types of prohibited conduct.[8]

The provision does not set out a separate procedure for declaring an undertaking to be dominant and so subject to Article 102. An undertaking is dominant simply when it satisfies the criteria for dominance and its conduct then becomes potentially subject to the prohibition.

Article 102 contains no express exception provision equivalent to that in Article 101(3).[9] It is, however, open to a dominant undertaking to plead that its conduct is 'objectively justified'.[10] Further, although it must be established that the dominant position is held 'in a substantial part of the internal market' and there must be an *appreciable* effect on inter-Member State trade, there is no de minimis threshold equivalent to that adopted by the CJ in respect of restrictions of competition under Article 101(1).[11]

It can be seen from the text of Article 102 that five elements must be established before the prohibition applies. They are:

(a) one or more undertakings;

(b) a dominant position;

(c) the dominant position must be held within the internal market or a substantial part of it;

(d) an abuse; and

(e) an effect on inter-State trade.

It is often extremely difficult to determine whether or not these criteria have been satisfied, in particular whether an undertaking holds a 'dominant position' and/or whether it has committed an

---

[6] Reg. 1/2003, Art. 2.

[7] Chap. 7, Section 5.E, p. 374.

[8] See Case 6/72, *Continental Can* [1973] ECR 215; Case C-333/94 P, *Tetra Pak International SA v Commission* [1996] ECR I-5951 (*Tetra Pak II*), para. 37; Case C-95/04 P, *British Airways v Commission* [2007] ECR I-2331, para. 57; Case T-201/04, *Microsoft v Commission* [2007] ECR II-3601, para. 860; Case C-280/08 P, *Deutsche Telekom v Commission* [2010] ECR I-9555, para. 173.

[9] Although it was possible to apply for a negative clearance under Reg. 17, Art. 2 (JO 204/62 (1959–1962) OJ Spec. Ed. 87). It is possible under Reg. 1/2003, Art. 10 for the Commission to make a finding of inapplicability (although this has never yet been done): see Chap. 13.

[10] See Chap. 7, Section 5.

[11] Case C-23/14, *Post Danmark A/S v Konkurrencerådet (Post Danmark II)* EU:C:2015:651, paras. 72–74. For the appreciability of the effect on inter-Member State trade see Section 5.E. See Chap. 3 for de minimis in respect of Art. 101.

'abuse' of that dominant position. The problems in the application of Article 102 have mainly concerned those two elements.

The question whether an undertaking is dominant requires, according to the case law of the CJ, the definition of the market on which the undertaking is alleged to be dominant.[12] The undertaking's position on the market must then be assessed. It is crucial that these definitions and assessments are made properly. It is not an offence to hold a dominant position as Article 102 does not prohibit the holding of a dominant position but only an abuse of it.[13] However, some behaviour which may be competitive, or at least neutral, from a competition perspective when engaged in by an undertaking on a competitive market may be prohibited when engaged in by a dominant undertaking. An incorrect finding of dominance may consequently lead to a ruling that an undertaking's pro-competitive behaviour is abusive conduct prohibited by Article 102 (a Type 1 'false positive' error). Furthermore, it was seen in Chapter 3 that a firm which unilaterally acts anti-competitively by imposing export bans[14] or resale prices[15] is not prohibited from doing so by Article 101(1), which applies only to agreements. If the undertaking concerned is not dominant the conduct falls outside Article 102 as well and is therefore legal. Dominant and non-dominant firms are in crucially different positions. In addition, if the concept of an abuse is found to encompass an unjustifiably wide spectrum of behaviour, Article 102 may come perilously close to forbidding the dominance itself.

The question of what amounts to an 'abuse' is a vexed one. It requires a determination of what conduct can and what conduct cannot legitimately be carried out by a dominant undertaking. This, of course, depends partly upon the purposes of the whole provision. As already stated, it has often been unclear what objectives were being pursued in the enforcement of Article 102.

This chapter, after setting out the consequences of infringing Article 102, considers the five elements of Article 102 in turn and deals with general issues concerning their scope, interpretation, and application. Chapters 6 and 7 respectively consider in greater detail (a) how it is ascertained whether an undertaking holds a dominant position and (b) what conduct constitutes an abuse of a dominant position. It is important to realise, however, that the different elements of Article 102 cannot always be considered separately from one another. In particular, the questions whether an undertaking is in a dominant position and whether it has committed an abuse may be interrelated and intertwined.[16] As we shall see, it has even been argued that there should be no need to establish a preliminary and separate assessment of dominance, but that the analysis of dominance and abuse should be integrated.[17]

B. THE ENFORCEMENT OF ARTICLE 102

(i) Infringement Decisions, Fines, and Other Remedies

The Commission may investigate undertakings it believes may have committed a breach of Article 102. Where the Commission finds that a violation of Article 102 has been committed, it can issue a decision ordering the undertaking to put an end to the abuse (by taking positive or negative

---

[12] Case 6/72, *Continental Can* [1973] ECR 215. For the argument that market power may be able to be measured directly, rather than by going through the 'indirect method' via market definition, see Chap. 1, Section 15.A, p. 55 and Chap. 6.

[13] This point was reiterated by the CJ in Case C-209/10, *Post Danmark A/S v Konkurrencerådet (Post Danmark I)* EU:C:2012:172, paras. 21–22.

[14] Cases C-2 and 3/01 P, *Bundesverband der Arzneimittel-Importeure EV and Commission v Bayer AG* [2004] ECR I-23, 5141.

[15] Case C-74/04 P, *Commission v Volkswagen AG* [2006] ECR I-6585.

[16] See T. Eilmansberger, 'Dominance—The Lost Child? How the Effects-based Rules Could and Should Change Dominance Analysis' (2006) 2 *European Law Journal* 15.

[17] Report by EAGCP, July 2005, see Chap. 6, Section 3.C, p. 289.

measures) and can, where certain conditions are met, impose structural remedies.[18] Further, it can impose fines on the undertaking of up to 10 per cent of its turnover in the preceding year of business. The Commission has imposed substantial fines on undertakings found to have committed a breach of Article 102. In *Intel*[19] the Commission imposed a fine of over €1 billion on a single undertaking.

The difficulties involved in determining whether or not an infringement of Article 102 has been committed and the controversy surrounding many of the Commission's decisions taken under Article 102 have rendered the Commission's willingness to impose heavy fines in respect of breaches of the Article extremely contentious. Moreover, as shown by *Microsoft*, behavioural remedies such as ordering an undertaking to supply or to cease tying products together, may be more significant for the undertaking than a large fine.[20]

(ii) Complaints

The great majority of Article 102 cases arise from complaints.[21] Both the Commission and the national competition authorities (NCAs) inaugurate cases after receiving complaints, and the latter may ultimately come before the CJ in an Article 267 reference. The complaints are usually made by competitors, not customers,[22] and Article 102 is increasingly deployed as a weapon in the commercial struggle between the players on the market. This has become particularly noticeable in the high technology sector, with the Commission opening investigations, for example, after complaints from Microsoft about Google,[23] and Apple and Microsoft about Motorola.[24]

(iii) Commitments Decisions

Under Regulation 1/2003, Article 9, the Commission can take 'commitments decisions'[25] whereby it accepts binding commitments from undertakings under investigation rather than proceeding to a final prohibition decision under Article 7. Under the Regulation 17 regime the Commission brought several Article 102 proceedings to a close by accepting commitments from the parties, but it could not make these binding.[26] Since 2004 the Commission has made enthusiastic use of Article 9 commitments decisions including in energy markets where Article 102 has been applied in pursuance of liberalisation. The termination of cases by commitment decisions has serious implications for the development of the law on Article 102, as the nature of the procedure means that it is never established whether according to the Commission the impugned conduct *did* amount to an infringement of Article 102 and the matter never goes before the EU Courts. This exacerbates the uncertainty surrounding the question of what conduct can constitute an abuse, particularly given the contentious nature of the subject matter of some of the cases settled in this way, and it dilutes the control of the Commission by the EU Courts. Nevertheless most Commission Article 102 proceedings do now terminate in commitments rather than infringement decisions, and one can appreciate the attractions to both the Commission and the parties of handling the matter in this way.

---

[18] Reg. 1/2003, Art. 7. See Chap. 13. The power to impose remedies of a structural nature, i.e. to order divestment and break-up companies was introduced by Reg. 1/2003 and did not appear in Reg. 17.

[19] Case COMP/37.990, *Intel*, upheld Case T-286/09, *Intel* EU:T:2014:547, see Chap. 7.

[20] Case T-201/04, *Microsoft* [2007] ECR II-3601.

[21] For complaints to the Commission, see Chap. 12. In some Member States actions may involve national sector regulators.

[22] Because they relate to 'exclusionary' rather than 'exploitative' abuse, see Chap. 7.

[23] COMP/39.740, *Google*, IP/15/4780, MEMO/15/4781.

[24] COMP/39.986, *Motorola*, IP/12/345.

[25] See Chap. 13, Section 7.E.iii.

[26] E.g., *Digital Undertaking*, Commission Press Release IP/97/868.

(iv) Enforcement by the NCAs

Regulation 1/2003 requires Member States to empower their designated competition authorities to apply Article 102 (and Article 101).[27] Article 5 provides that the NCAs shall have powers to take infringement, commitments, and fining decisions and take interim measures. The Regulation itself does not give them the power to impose structural remedies.[28] The CJ held in *Tele2 Polska* that NCAs do not have power to make a finding that there has been no infringement of Article 102. Only the Commission can do that.[29]

(v) Judicial Review in Article 102 Cases

The issue of the standard and intensity of the judicial review of the Commission's decisions in competition cases is discussed in Chapter 13.[30] However, a few preliminary points should be made here about Article 102 cases. Article 102 cases tend to be highly fact-specific. Many of the Commission's decisions are controversial, to say the least, and the extent to which they are reviewed by the GC is therefore of great concern. The EU Courts decline to substitute their own assessment of 'complex economic matters' for that of the Commission, but since 2011 the CJ has ceased talking of the GC looking for 'manifest errors of assessment'[31] and instead referred to the GC conducting an 'in-depth review'.[32] The Article 102 appeal *Telefónica* was one of the judgments in 2014 in which the CJ discussed the standard of judicial review.[33] Even when concerned only with 'manifest errors of assessment' however, the GC has in some cases conducted a highly detailed review.[34]

There is an appeal from the GC to the CJ on a point of law only. There is a narrow line between points of fact and points of law. At times the CJ's classification of a plea as 'inadmissible' because it considers it a point of fact and not law has been highly frustrating.[35] It is worth noting that it is very rare for the Commission to lose Article 102 cases on the substance. It has a success rate which has been described as 'staggering'.[36]

(vi) Private Actions in National Courts and Article 267 References

Article 102, like Article 101, is directly effective.[37] It is possible, therefore, that an entity injured by a breach of Article 102 may bring proceedings before a national court seeking an injunction or damages in respect of loss resulting from the breach.[38]

---

[27] Reg. 1/2003, Art. 35.

[28] See Chap. 13. National law may give the NCA such powers.

[29] Case C-375/09, *Prezes Urzędu Ochrony Konkurencji i Konsumentów v Tele2 Polska sp. z o.o., now Netia SA* [2011] ECR I-3055.

[30] Chap. 13, Section 8.A.vii. And see in respect of merger decisions, Chap. 15.

[31] See the GC's approach in Case T-201/04, *Microsoft* [2007] ECR II-3601, paras. 87–89.

[32] The reason for this is the compatibility of the EU's enforcement system with human rights requirements.

[33] Case C-295/12 P, *Telefónica SA v Commission* EU:C:2014:2062.

[34] For example, Case T-321/05, *AstraZeneca v Commission* [2010] ECR II-2805.

[35] For example, in Case C-95/04 P, *British Airways v Commission* [2007] ECR I-2331.

[36] R. O'Donoghue and A. J. Padilla, *The Law and Economics of Article 102* (2nd edn, Hart Publishing, 2013), 86, quoting, inter alia, research by the former Chief Competition Economist which showed the Commission's success rate in defending challenges to its decisions as 98%. See D. Neven, 'Competition Economics and Antitrust in Europe' (2006) 21(48) *Economic Policy* 742; and C. Ahlborn and D. S. Evans, 'The *Microsoft* Judgment and its Implications for Competition Policy Towards Dominant Firms in Europe' (2008–2009) 75 *Antitrust LJ* 887.

[37] See Case 127/73, *Belgische Radio en Télévisie and Société belge des auteurs, compositeurs et editeurs v SV SABAM and NV Fonior* [1974] ECR 313. The equivalent Article of the ECSC Treaty, Art. 66(7), did not have direct effect because it conferred sole jurisdiction on the Commission; see Case C-128/92, *H. J. Banks & Co Ltd v British Coal Corp* [1994] ECR I-1209, paras. 18–19.

[38] See Chap. 14.

Further, a party to a contract concluded with a dominant undertaking may claim that clauses within it are prohibited by Article 102 and consequently void or unenforceable.[39] That party may also bring proceedings to recover benefits conferred under a prohibited provision.

National courts before which Article 102 is raised may make references to the CJ for preliminary rulings under Article 267, as explained in Chapter 2. Many leading cases on Article 102 have come before the CJ in this way.[40] The use of commitments decisions by the Commission, and the consequent paucity of appeals from Commission infringement decisions to the EU Courts, make the Article 267 route even more significant for the development of the law.

5. THE INTERPRETATION AND APPLICATION OF ARTICLE 102

A. THE MEANING OF ONE OR MORE UNDERTAKINGS

(i) General

'Undertaking' is interpreted in the same way for the purpose of Article 102 as for Article 101. It has been construed broadly and 'encompasses every entity engaged in an economic activity'.[41] If an entity is not engaged in an economic activity, the fact that the members who comprise it do carry out such activity will not render the entity itself an 'undertaking' for the purposes of Article 102. In *Wouters*[42] the CJ thus held that the Dutch Bar was not itself an undertaking in respect of Article 102 although the individual members of the Bar *were* undertakings for the purposes of Article 101. Two points of particular importance arise when considering the meaning of the term 'undertaking' within the context of Article 102. First, since State regulation is a frequent source of an entity's market power, it is crucial to know to what extent public bodies or bodies with a special connection with the State will be characterised as undertakings and so potentially subject to Article 102. Secondly, it must be considered what is meant by 'one or more undertakings' in Article 102. So far, in this chapter reference has been made to individual undertakings. It is clearly envisaged, however, that Article 102 should apply to the conduct of more than one undertaking. Is Article 102 confined to the conduct of undertakings which are part of the same single economic entity (in which a united policy may be pursued) or does Article 102 go further and prohibit the conduct of one or more *independent* undertakings?

(ii) Public Bodies and Bodies Performing Public Functions

The term 'undertaking' applies to any entity engaged in commercial activities whether or not it is a State entity, even if it has no identity separate from that of the State.[43] Further, it is clear from Article 4(3) TEU and Article 106(1) TFEU that the State itself cannot confer immunity upon undertakings from the application of the rules. The fact that an undertaking's market power has been

---

[39] For the effect of this see, e.g., *English Welsh and Scottish Railway Ltd v E.ON UK plc* [2007] EWHC 599 (Comm).

[40] Such as Case 311/84, *Centre Belge d'Etudes du Marché-Télémarketing v Compagnie Luxembourgeoise de Télédiffusion SA et Information Publicité Benelux SA* [1985] ECR 3261; Case C-7/97, *Oscar Bronner GmbH & Co KG v Mediaprint* [1998] ECR I-7791; Case C-418/01, *IMS Health GmbH & Co OHG v NDC Health GmbH & Co KG* [2004] ECR I-5039; Cases C-468–478/06, *Sot. Lélos kai Sia and others EE v GlaxoSmithKline AEVE Farmakeftikon Proionton* [2008] ECR I-7139.

[41] See Chap. 3, Section 5, p. 116.

[42] Case C-309/99, *Wouters v Algemene Raad van de Nederlandse Orde van Advocaten* [2002] ECR I-1577, para. 112.

[43] See Chap. 3 and Chap. 8. For two important CJ judgments concerning the status of undertakings exercising some public powers, see Case C-113/07, *SELEX Systemi Integrati SpA v Commission* [2009] ECR I-2207 and Case C-49/07, *Motosykletistiki Omospondia Ellados NPID (MOTOE) v Ellinkio Dimosi* [2008] ECR I-4863.

created by State action is no defence to an action based on Article 102 unless the narrow exception set out in Article 106(2) TFEU applies. This provision states that '[u]ndertakings entrusted with the operation of services of general economic interest or having the character of a revenue-producing monopoly' are subject to the competition rules unless those rules 'obstruct the performance, in law or in fact, of the particular tasks assigned to them'. This topic is discussed in Chapter 8.

(iii) One or More Undertakings—Collective Dominance

a. The Development of the Collective Dominance Concept

Initially it was believed that the term 'one or more undertakings' referred only to bodies which were part of the same economic entity, i.e. that the purpose of the term was to ensure that the conduct of all bodies within the corporate group was taken into account when assessing whether or not a breach of Article 102 had occurred. Thus circumstances such as those which arose in *Continental Can* and *Commercial Solvents* would be caught. In *Continental Can*[44] a US company held an 85.8 per cent share in a German company (SLW). It formed a wholly owned Belgian subsidiary through which it acquired a Dutch company which was a competitor of SLW. The Commission held that the American parent had, through SLW, a dominant position in a substantial part of the common market and that an abuse of the dominant position was committed when it used its Belgian subsidiary to take over the Dutch company.[45] Similarly, in *Commercial Solvents*[46] a US parent and its 51 per cent owned Italian subsidiary were involved in a refusal to supply a third party in Italy with a raw material produced by the parent. The subsidiary followed the policy laid down by the parent and both were held to have abused a dominant position. The view that Article 102 might be confined to situations where bodies formed part of the same economic unit or the same corporate group found support from a statement of the CJ in *Hoffmann La-Roche*.[47]

Such an interpretation would, however, have meant that the term 'undertaking' in Article 102 has a different meaning from that which it has in Article 101. In Chapter 3 it was explained that the term 'undertaking' applies to all bodies which form part of the same economic entity. Bodies within the same corporate group are treated as a single undertaking if the bodies 'form an economic unit within which the subsidiary has no real freedom to determine its course of action on the market, and if the agreements or practices are concerned merely with the internal allocation of tasks as between the undertakings'.[48] If interpreted in the same way, Article 102 would apply to the behaviour of all bodies which form an economic unit even if the Article had referred only to an abuse by *an* undertaking of a dominant position. So what interpretation should be given to the phrase 'one or more undertakings'?

It has now been established that 'one or more undertakings' can refer to legally independent undertakings which together hold a 'collective dominant position' on the market. Article 102 therefore applies both to dominant positions held by single firms and to those held collectively. However, the issue of what exactly constitutes a collective (or 'joint') dominant position and how it is established has had a long and tortuous evolution, and involves not only Article 102 but also the EU Merger Regulation (EUMR).[49]

---

[44] Case 6/72, *Continental Can* [1973] ECR 215.

[45] *Continental Can Co Inc* [1972] OJ L7/25. The CJ annulled the Commission's decision on the ground of an erroneous definition of the market (see Chap. 6) but the point about the aggregation of the activities of the group was not doubted.

[46] Cases 6 and 7/73, *Istituto Chemioterapico Italiano SpA and Commercial Solvents Corp v Commission* [1974] ECR 223.

[47] Case 85/76, *Hoffmann-La Roche & Co AG v Commission* [1979] ECR 461, para. 39.

[48] Case 15/74, *Centrafarm BV and Adriaan De Peijper v Sterling Drug Inc* [1974] ECR 1147, para. 41, repeated in Case 30/87, *Bodson v Pompes funèbres des régions libérées SA* [1988] ECR 2479, para. 19.

[49] See Chap. 15. For collective dominance generally see G. Monti, 'The Scope of Collective Dominance Under Article 82 EC' (2001) 38 *CMLRev* 131.

b. Situations Giving Rise to Collective Dominance

The concept of collective dominance initially arose in respect of undertakings which were linked by licences or agreements. However, in the first case in which the concept was accepted, *Flat Glass*,[50] the GC spoke of entities 'united by such economic links that . . . together they hold a dominant position vis-à-vis the other operators on the same market'.[51] This opened the door to the possibility that a collective dominant position could be held by legally independent undertakings which operate on an oligopolistic market. Oligopolies present great problems for competition laws. We see in Chapter 3 that Article 101 applies to agreements and concerted practices between undertakings. However, as explained in Chapter 9, undertakings on oligopolistic markets may act in parallel without expressly colluding. Rather, recognising their 'interdependence' they 'tacitly' collude. Such tacit collusion (or 'tacit coordination') is not caught by Article 101. Therefore, if 'economic links' include the interdependence of undertakings on an oligopolistic market the application of Article 102 might be a way of dealing with the 'oligopoly problem'.

There is also an issue of oligopolies in respect of the regulation of mergers. The concept of a 'dominant position' appears not only in Article 102 but also in the EUMR.[52] It was important to know whether the concept in the EUMR covered collective as well as single firm dominance. If it did the EUMR could be applied to the creation and strengthening of a collective dominant position and thus could prevent anti-competitive oligopolistic market structures being created in the first place, or strengthened.[53]

Following the *Flat Glass* judgment there was a stream of cases and decisions both on Article 102 and on the EUMR. The EU Courts have cited their merger judgments in Article 102 cases and vice versa, so the development of collective dominance in the context of Article 102 cannot be separated from its development under the EUMR. The case law must be read as a whole. It establishes in effect that collective dominance is of two types.

- What has been called 'non-oligopolistic'[54] or 'expressly or pure collusive' ('traditional')[55] collective dominance where there are contractual, commercial, or structural links between the parties or direct or indirect contact. The parties may be operating on an oligopolistic market but their collusion is express rather than tacit.

- 'Oligopolistic' collective dominance which arises on tightly oligopolistic markets where the undertakings can coordinate their behaviour without express collusion and have the incentive to do so. This is the form of collective dominance that is relevant to the application of both Article 102 and the EUMR.

The EU Courts have sometimes advanced the law on oligopolistic collective dominance in cases which concerned non-oligopolistic collective dominance.[56]

---

[50] Cases T-68, 77, and 78/89, *Società Italiano Vetro SpA v Commission* [1992] ECR II-1403 (the *Italian Flat Glass Cartel* appeal), paras. 357–358; Cases C-395 and 396/96 P, *Compagnie Maritime Belge Transports SA v Commission* [2000] ECR I-1365; Cases T-191 and 212–214/98, *Atlantic Container Line & Others v Commission* [2003] ECR II-3275, para. 595.

[51] Cases T-68, 77, and 78/89, *Società Italiano Vetro* [1992] ECR II-1403, para. 358.

[52] Council Reg. 139/2004 [2004] OJ L124/1, on the control of concentrations between undertakings, Art. 2(2) and (3), previously Council Reg. 4064/89 [1989] OJ L395/1.

[53] The Commission's stretching of the collective dominance concept to deal with the situation where a merger has anti-competitive effects without creating or strengthening a single dominant position was the subject of Case T-342/99, *Airtours plc v Commission* [2002] ECR II-2585. The importance of dominance in respect of the EUMR was lessened by the changes made in Art. 2(2) and (3) by Reg. 139/ 2004, see further Chaps. 9 and 15.

[54] See R. Nazzini, *The Foundations of European Union Competition Law: The Objectives and Principles of Article 102* (Oxford University Press, 2011), Chap. 11; J. Faull and A. Nikpay (eds.), *The EU Law of Competition* (3rd edn, Oxford University Press, 2014), 4.220–4.240.

[55] See L. Ortiz Blanco, *Market Power in EU Antitrust Law* (Hart Publishing, 2012), Chap. 10.

[56] See particularly Cases C-395 and 396/96 P, *Compagnie Maritime Belge Transports* [2000] ECR I-1365 and Case T-193/02, *Laurent Piau v Commission* [2005] ECR II-209.

c. Oligopolistic Collective Dominance

Given the importance of the concept of collective dominance in respect of tacit collusion between oligopolists and of mergers, the case law is fully discussed in Chapters 9 and 15. We set out here, however, some points about non-oligopolistic collective dominance.

d. Non-oligopolistic Collective Dominance

In *Flat Glass* the Commission found that three Italian flat glass producers had all infringed Article 101(1) by concluding agreements to, inter alia, fix prices and sales quotas, and had infringed Article 102 by abusing their collective dominant position (although the Commission did not adduce any evidence to establish the latter infringement apart from that relied on to establish the breach of Article 101).[57] On appeal the GC quashed the Commission's decision that there had been an infringement of Article 102 on the grounds that it was not sufficient simply to recycle the facts constituting an infringement of Article 101 in order to deduce that the behaviour constituted an abuse of a collective dominant position. Nevertheless, the GC expressed the view, as already explained, that Article 102 *could* apply to independent undertakings and that Article 102 was not confined to one or more undertakings within the same corporate group.

In a series of decisions it applied the concept of collective dominance to undertakings bound together by contractual links. In *French-West African Shipowners' Committees*,[58] *CEWAL*,[59] and *Trans-Atlantic Conference Agreement (TACA)*,[60] the Commission used collective dominance in relation to shipowners which were members of liner conferences, and which had concluded agreements regulating the operation of trade on shipping routes. In *French-West African Shipowners' Committees* the Commission imposed fines on shipowners that had participated in cargo-sharing systems on international routes. The Committees monitored the quota systems and imposed penalties on those that exceeded the quotas without approval. The Commission found that the agreements infringed Article 101(1)[61] and could not be exempted under Article 101(3).[62] In addition, the Commission considered that the shipowners had infringed Article 102 because, as a result of the conference, they had presented themselves as a united front to shippers and, consequently, the position of the shipowners on the market for cargo between France and the African States had to be assessed collectively. Since the Committees had been set up by a group of shipowners covering virtually the entire market, the agreement resulted in the creation of a collective dominant position to their advantage. Their practices, which endeavoured to eliminate effective competition for non-Committee shipping lines, constituted an abuse of the dominant position within the meaning of Article 102(b) by limiting the supply of liner services available to shippers.[63]

Similarly, in both *CEWAL*[64] and *TACA*,[65] the Commission found that members of a liner conference were collectively dominant on certain international shipping routes from Northern Europe.

---

[57] *Flat Glass* [1989] OJ L33/44.

[58] [1992] OJ L134/1.

[59] [1993] OJ L34/20. The finding of collective dominance was upheld on appeal: Cases T-24/93 etc., *Compagnie Maritime Belge Transports SA v Commission* [1996] ECR II-1201 and Cases C-395 and 396/96 P, *Compagnie Maritime Belge* [2000] ECR I-1365.

[60] *Transatlantic Conference Agreement* [1999] OJ L95/1, on appeal, Case T-191/98, *Atlantic Container Line* [2003] ECR II-3275.

[61] The object and effect of the agreements was to share markets amongst the members and to limit the supply of transport services available, contrary to Art. 101(1)(c) and (b) respectively.

[62] Further, and because the objective of the agreements was not to fix common rates of the participants, it did not fall within the terms of the block exemption then in force dealing with 'liner conferences', Reg. 4056/86.

[63] Both the practice of imposing penalties on shipowners which had exceeded their quotas and the application of conditions protecting their own interests against those of newcomers wishing to serve the routes infringed Art. 102.

[64] [1993] OJ L34/20.

[65] [1999] OJ L95/1 finding that the TACA members held a collective dominant position on the relevant market and abused that collective dominant position between 1994 and 1996, first, by entering into an agreement to place restrictions on the availability and content of service contracts and, secondly, by altering the competitive structure

In these cases the agreements enabled the undertakings to present a 'united front' to shippers. Although it does not seem that it was strictly necessary to use Article 102, since Article 101 was applicable (Article 102 would only have been vital had the agreement been block exempted under Article 3 of Regulation 4056/86), the cases fitted neatly within the GC's formulation in *Flat Glass*. The parties were undoubtedly united by 'economic links'. The GC in the *TACA* appeal held that these links (a tariff, enforcement provisions and penalties, a secretariat, and annual business plans of the TACA) were 'capable of justifying a collective assessment of the position on the relevant market of the members of that conference for the purposes of the application of Article [102] of the Treaty, in so far as those links are such as to allow them to adopt together, as a single entity which presents itself as such on the market vis-à-vis users and competitors, the same line of conduct on that market'.[66] In *Irish Sugar*[67] the Commission found Irish Sugar and one of its distributors to be collectively dominant. In this case the producer and the distributor were linked *vertically* by agreements and other factors (such as close management relationships) which created a clear parallelism of interest, such as a significant equity holding which Irish Sugar held in the distributor. The links between the companies were very strong, and only just failed to satisfy the criteria for being a single economic entity.[68]

In *Almelo* where the undertakings were all regional electricity distributors in the Netherlands the CJ said that a dominant position involved the undertakings being 'linked in such a way that they adopt the same conduct on the market'.[69] In this case the undertakings adopted uniform supply conditions drawn up by their trade association. The most significant statement of what constitutes a collective dominant position for the purposes of Article 102 was in *Compagnie Maritime Belge*,[70] the appeal from the *CEWAL* decision. There the CJ said that a collective dominant position could be held by undertakings which 'present themselves or act together on a particular market as a collective entity'.[71] That must be established by examining the economic links or factors which give rise to a connection between them.[72] It must then be decided whether that collective entity holds a dominant position.[73] As already explained, the undertakings involved in the CEWAL liner conference were linked by express agreements, but nevertheless the CJ said that the existence of an agreement or other links in law were not indispensable to a finding of collective dominance.[74] Because of the importance of this judgment in developing the application of collective dominance to the tacit collusion of oligopolists the judgment is discussed in Chapter 9.

In the appeal from the *TACA* decision the GC stated that it was not a requirement for establishing the existence of a dominant position that the elimination of effective competition (which the

---

of the market so as to reinforce the TACA's dominant position. The finding of collective dominance was upheld on appeal but the finding of abuse and fines were annulled, see Cases T-191 and 214–216/98, *Atlantic Container Line* [2003] ECR II-3275 but see the Commission's revised decision [2003] OJ L26/53.

[66] Cases T-191 and 214–216/98, *Atlantic Container Line* [2003] ECR II-3275, para. 602.

[67] [1997] OJ L25/1. The GC upheld the finding of collective dominance: Case T-228/97, *Irish Sugar plc v Commission* [1999] ECR II-2969.

[68] See Chap. 3, Section 5.A.vi, p. 125. 'The various terms used in the contested decision to describe the applicant's position on the market before February 1990 are the result of the special nature of its links with SDL before that date. The Commission claims to have established the existence of infringements of Article [102] of the Treaty from 1985 to February 1990 committed by the applicant alone, by SDL alone, or by both together. Having accepted the applicant's argument that it did not control the management of SDL, despite holding 51% of [SDL's] capital, the Commission decided that even if it was not possible to regard the applicant and SDL as a single economic entity, they had, together at least, held a dominant position on the market in question', Case T-228/97, *Irish Sugar plc v Commission* [1999] ECR II-2969, para. 28.

[69] Case C-393/92, *Almelo v NV Energiebedrijf Ijsselmij* [1994] ECR I-1477, para. 42, see also Case C-140/94, *DIP v Comune di Bassano del Grappa* [1995] ECR I-3257, para. 27.

[70] Cases C-395 and 396/96 P, *Compagnie Maritime Belge* [2000] ECR I-1365.

[71] Ibid., para. 36.

[72] Ibid., para. 41.

[73] Ibid., para. 39.

[74] Ibid., para. 45.

GC had stipulated in the merger case *Airtours*)[75] must result in the elimination of *all* competition between the undertakings concerned.[76]

Sports organisations may hold a collective dominant position. In *Laurent Piau* the GC said that it was 'unrealistic' to claim that FIFA could not be in a collective dominant position in respect of the market for football players' agents' services. It was irrelevant that FIFA was not itself an economic operator buying agents' services as it was the emanation of the national associations and the clubs, which did.[77]

There are also difficult cases where allegations of a collective dominant position arising from national legislation or regulation have been made. These have been rejected by the CJ, mainly on the grounds that the measures did not result in the undertakings concerned ceasing to compete with one another.[78]

B. A DOMINANT POSITION

The definition of a dominant position is set out in the case law of the CJ. The meaning of 'dominant position' and the way in which it is decided whether any particular undertaking holds such a position are considered in detail in Chapter 6. One important point should be noted here, however. Although many undertakings found to infringe Article 102 are large multinational firms, dominance relates to an undertaking's market power on a particular market and not to the size of the market or the size of the firm. Markets can be defined very narrowly[79] (Boosey & Hawkes were found to be dominant in the market for brass instruments for British-style brass bands)[80] and small firms can be dominant. If they commit an abuse of that position it may well not have an appreciable effect on inter-Member State trade and so could be subject only to national competition provisions. Even if the other elements of Article 102 *are* satisfied the Commission, currently concentrating on the Microsofts, Intels, Samsungs, and Googles of this world, is unlikely to bring proceedings. NCAs, however, also apply Article 102 and furthermore Article 102 can be enforced in private litigation.

C. A DOMINANT POSITION WITHIN A SUBSTANTIAL PART OF THE INTERNAL MARKET

(i) Purpose of the Requirement

The dominant position of the undertaking must be held within the internal market or within a substantial part of it. The purpose of this requirement is to exclude from the Article's scope purely localised monopoly situations in which there is no Union interest. Together with the necessity that the abuse of a dominant position has an effect on trade between Member States, the requirement determines the limit of the EU's jurisdiction.

(ii) Meaning of a Substantial Part of the Internal Market

A 'substantial part' does not simply mean substantial in geographic terms. It is not a matter of counting hectares. In *Suiker Unie* the CJ stated that:

---

[75] Case T-342/99, *Airtours plc v Commission* [2002] ECR II-2585, para. 63.

[76] Cases T-191 and 212–214/98, *Atlantic Container Line* [2003] ECR II-3275, para. 130.

[77] Case T-193/02, *Laurent Piau* [2005] ECR II-209, paras. 112–116. This was a case, like *Atlantic Container Line*, where, although dealing with a situation where there were express agreements between the parties concerned, the GC made important statements which relate to tacit collusion and oligopolistic collective dominance.

[78] See Case C-96/94, *Centro Servizi Spediporto v Spedizioni Marritima del Golfo* [1995] ECR I-2883, Case C-140/94, *DIP v Comune di Bassano del Grappa* [1995] ECR I-3257, and Case C-70/95, *Sodemare v Regione Lombardia* [1997] ECR I-3395.

[79] For the principles of market definition, see Chap. 1, Section 15.B, p. 56 ff.

[80] *BBI/Boosey & Hawkes* [1987] OJ L286/36.

[f]or the purpose of determining whether a specific territory is large enough to amount to a 'substantial part of the common market' within the meaning of Article [102 TFEU] the pattern and volume of the production and consumption of the said product as well as the habits and economic opportunities of vendors and purchasers must be considered.[81]

(iii) Relevance of Volume of Production

In *Suiker Unie* the CJ compared the volume of sugar production in Belgium, Luxembourg, and southern Germany to that of Community production overall. It held that each of those markets was a substantial part of the common market. The CJ has never specified whether there is a particular percentage of the EU market which could automatically be said to satisfy the 'substantial' criterion. However, Advocate General Warner, in his Opinion in the *ABG Oil* case, considered that the Dutch petrol market, which was approximately 4.6 per cent of the overall Community (as it then was) market, was substantial. He stated that:

[t]here is . . . in my opinion, in this kind of field, a danger in focusing attention exclusively on percentages. The opposite of 'substantial' is 'negligible', and what may seem negligible when looked at in the terms of a percentage may seem otherwise when looked at in absolute terms. The population of Luxembourg is, I believe, about 0.23 per cent of the population of the whole Community. I would however shrink from saying that one who had a monopoly, or near monopoly, of the Luxembourg market for a particular product was exempt from the application of Article [102].[82]

(iv) A Member State is Likely to be a Substantial Part of the Internal Market

In a number of cases individual Member States have been held to be a 'substantial part'[83] of the internal market, as have parts of Member States.[84] As the EU is enlarged the concept of what is a 'substantial part' of it may alter, with previously substantial parts becoming more insignificant so that older cases on this point may no longer be a reliable guide. It is difficult to imagine, however, that a single Member State would be held not to constitute a substantial part of the internal market even in an EU of more than 28 Member States. It would be politically insensitive. As the process of European integration proceeds, however, the delineation of geographic markets may become broader and it may become rarer for a position of dominance to be found to exist in a single Member State other than in the case of statutory monopoly.

(v) Transport Cases

What constitutes a 'substantial part' of the internal market may depend on the nature of the market in issue. For example, there have been a number of transport cases in which very small areas have

---

[81] Cases 40–48, 50, 54–56, 111, 113, and 114/73, *Coöperatieve Vereniging 'Suiker Unie' UA v Commission* [1975] ECR 1663, para. 371.

[82] Case 77/77, *Benzine en Petroleum Handelsmaatschappij BV v Commission* [1978] ECR 1513, 1537. The CJ held that the undertaking's conduct could not constitute an abuse and did not address the dominance issue.

[83] The UK was held to be a substantial part of the common market in Case 226/84, *British Leyland plc v Commission* [1986] ECR 3263, as was Belgium in Case 127/73, *Belgische Radio en Televisie and Société belge des auteurs, compositeurs et editeurs v SV SABAM and NV Fonior* [1974] ECR 313 and Case 26/75, *General Motors Continental NV v Commission* [1975] ECR 1367.

[84] E.g., the south-east of England in Case 22/78, *Hugin Kassaregister AB and Hugin Cash Registers Ltd v Commission* [1979] ECR 1869. A number of local markets in a Member State may be aggregated together to form a 'substantial part', as in Case C–323/93, *Société Civile Agricole du Centre d'Insémination de la Crespelle v Coopérative d'Elevage et d'Insémination Artificielle du Département de la Mayenne* [1994] ECR I-5077, where there was a series of local statutory monopolies in bovine insemination services which together covered the whole of France. See also Case 30/87, *Bodson v Pompes Funèbres des Régions Libérées* [1988] ECR 2479.

been found to be substantial. In both *Sealink/B&I Holyhead: Interim Measures*[85] and *Sea Containers Ltd/ Stena Sealink Ports*[86] Holyhead Harbour in Wales was held to be a substantial part of the common market. In the former case the Commission stated:

40. . . . The port of Holyhead constitutes a substantial part of the Common Market because it is a port providing one of the main links between two member-States; more especially, it provides the direct link between Great Britain and the capital city of Ireland. It should also be noted that this is, at least for passengers and cars, the most popular ferry route between Ireland and Great Britain.

In *Port of Roscoff*[87] the Commission emphasised the importance that might be played by the catchment area served by the port. In *Merci Convenzionali* the CJ looked to the volume of traffic handled by the port of Genoa. After stressing its importance in relation to the overall volume of imports and exports by sea to and from Italy, the Court held that the market 'may be regarded as constituting a substantial part of the common market'.[88] The Commission has also found the activities at the port of Rødby[89] and various airports to involve substantial parts of the internal market.[90]

The transport cases suggest, therefore, that, once it has been established that the routes or traffic concerned are significant in anything other than a purely domestic context, the 'substantial part' criterion will be satisfied.[91] Indeed, the full application of Article 102 to maritime and air transport would be impossible in the absence of such an interpretation.

D. ABUSE

As with 'dominant position' the meaning of 'abuse' is to be found in the case law of the CJ. The definition of abuse, and the issue of what conduct can amount to an abuse, is the subject of Chapter 7. However, a preliminary point to note is that a distinction is commonly made between 'exploitative' and 'exclusionary' abuses. An *exploitative* abuse is conduct whereby the dominant undertaking takes advantage of its market power to exploit its customers. An *exclusionary* abuse is conduct which impedes effective competition by excluding (foreclosing) competitors.[92] The application of Article 102 has been mainly concerned with exclusionary abuses. The Commission Guidance Paper on enforcement priorities, discussed in Section 6.C, is concerned only with exclusionary abuses.

E. AN EFFECT ON TRADE BETWEEN MEMBER STATES

(i) General

Article 102 applies only if the abuse of a dominant position *appreciably* affects trade between Member States. As in the context of Article 101, this requirement marks the jurisdictional divide between EU and national law. The concept of an effect on trade is interpreted in the same way under

---

[85] [1992] 5 CMLR 255, Commission's *XXIInd Annual Report on Competition Policy* (1992), point 219.

[86] [1994] OJ L15/8.

[87] Reported as *Irish Continental Group v CCI Morlaix* [1995] 5 CMLR 177, para. 58.

[88] Case C-179/90, *Merci Convenzionali Porto di Genova SpA v Siderurgica Gabrielli SpA* [1991] ECR I-5889, para. 15; see also Case C-266/96, *Corsica Ferries France SA v Gruppo Antichi Ormeggiatori del Porto di Genova Coop arl* [1998] ECR I-3949, para. 38.

[89] *Port of Rødby* [1994] OJ L55/52.

[90] E.g., *FAG-Flughafen Frankfurt/Main AG* [1998] OJ L72/30; *Alpha Flight Services/Aéroports de Paris* [1998] OJ L230/10; *Portuguese Airports* [1999] OJ L69/31, on appeal Case C-163/99, *Portugal v Commission* [2001] ECR I-2613; *Ilmailulaitos/Luftfartsverket* [1999] OJ L69/24; *Spanish Airports* [2000] OJ L208/36.

[91] See Case 66/86, *Ahmed Saeed Flugreisen and Silver Line Reisebüro GmbH v Zentrale zur Bekämpfung unlauteren Wettbewerbs eV* [1989] ECR 803; *British Midland v Aer Lingus* [1992] OJ L96/34, 596.

[92] This is a basic distinction. The complications over the categorisation of abuses are discussed in Chap. 7.

the two Articles.[93] Thus an agreement or conduct will affect trade if it interferes with the pattern of trade between Member States or if it interferes with the effective competitive structure in the internal market (even if there is no alteration to the flow of goods or services between Member States). The latter test was first adopted by the Court in *Commercial Solvents*.[94] The approach is particularly germane to Article 102 cases in which abusive conduct might result in a competitor leaving the market, which was indeed the position in *Commercial Solvents*, but the GC in *Intel* said it applied not only to eliminating a competitor but also to weakening one.[95] In *Commercial Solvents* Zoja, an Italian pharmaceutical company, claimed it was being driven out of the market for a certain type of anti-TB drug by the conduct of the dominant supplier of the necessary raw material. At the time (the early 1970s) there was an insignificant incidence of TB in the EEC and Zoja was principally manufacturing for export to the developing world. The CJ said that whether or not there was trade between Member States in the drugs was immaterial:

33. The Community authorities must therefore consider all the consequences of the conduct complained of for the competitive structure in the Common Market without distinguishing between production intended for sale within the market and that intended for export. When an undertaking in a dominant position with[in] the Common Market abuses its position in such a way that a competitor in the Common Market is likely to be eliminated, it does not matter whether the conduct relates to the latter's exports or its trade within the Common Market, once it has been established that this elimination will have repercussions on the competitive structure within the Common Market.[96]

In judging the effect on trade it is necessary to look at the conduct as a whole, and not at individual transactions in isolation.[97]

Hugin,[98] however, showed that not all alteration in the competitive structure affects trade. The case concerned the supply of cash register spare parts by a Swedish undertaking to a servicing and repair firm in south-east England at a time prior to Sweden joining the EU. The servicing firm's activities were confined to the London area and there was no inter-State trade in the spare parts. The CJ quashed the Commission's decision on the ground that there was no effect on trade between Member States. The alteration in the competitive structure if the firm went out of business would not be felt outside one part of the UK. The CJ stated:

17. . . . The interpretation and application of the condition relating to effects on trade between Member States contained in Articles [101 and 102 TFEU] must be based on the purpose of that condition which is to define, in the context of the law governing competition, the boundary between the areas respectively covered by Community law and the law of the Member States. Thus Community law covers any agreement or any practice which is capable of constituting a threat to freedom of trade between Member States in a manner which might harm the attainment of the objectives of a single market between the Member States, in particular by partitioning the national markets or by affecting the structure of competition within the common market. On the other hand conduct the effects of which are confined to the territory of a single Member State is governed by the national legal order.

This case established, therefore, that before trade between Member States will be affected, the alteration in the effective competitive structure has to have some repercussion beyond the borders of a single Member State.

---

[93] See Chap. 3.

[94] Cases 6 and 7/73, *Commercial Solvents* [1974] ECR 223.

[95] Case T-286/09, *Intel v Commission* EU:T:2014:547, para. 275. The competitor concerned was Intel's 'sole significant competitor at the worldwide level' and was being foreclosed from 'the most important sales channels'.

[96] Cases 6 and 7/73, *Commercial Solvents* [1974] ECR 223, para. 33. This paragraph does not say '*effective* competitive structure' but the phrase appears elsewhere in the judgment (e.g. para. 32) and in subsequent cases, see Case 22/79, *Greenwich Film Production v SACEM* [1979] ECR 3275, para. 11 and Case T-286/09, *Intel* EU:T:2014:547, para. 275.

[97] Case T-286/09, *Intel* EU:T:2014:547, para. 269.

[98] Case 22/78, *Hugin Kassaregister AB and Hugin Cash Registers Ltd v Commission* [1979] ECR 1869.

The meaning of an appreciable effect on inter-Member State trade for the purposes of Article 102 is now spelt out in the Commission Guidelines on the effect on trade concept which it adopted as part of the modernisation programme. The Guidelines explain how Article 102 applies where the dominant undertaking is pursuing several practices in an overall strategy not all of which have an effect on inter-Member State trade.

Commission Guidelines on the Effect of Trade Concept Contained in Articles 81 and 82 of the Treaty [2004] OJ C101/81

17. In the case of Article [102] it is the abuse that must affect trade between Member States. This does not imply, however, that each element of the behaviour must be assessed in isolation. Conduct that forms part of an overall strategy pursued by the dominant undertaking must be assessed in terms of its overall impact. Where a dominant undertaking adopts various practices in pursuit of the same aim, for instance practices that aim at eliminating or foreclosing competitors, in order for Article [102] to be applicable to all the practices forming part of this overall strategy, it is sufficient that at least one of these practices is capable of affecting trade between Member States.

The Guidelines then deal with four situations: abuse of a dominant position covering several Member States; abuse of a dominant position covering a single Member State; abuse of a dominant position covering only part of a Member State; and abuses involving trade with third countries or practices involving undertakings in third countries. The principles set out in the Notice are basically a summing-up of the case law.

(ii) Abuse of a Dominant Position Covering Several Member States

Not surprisingly, the Commission takes the view that both exclusionary and exploitative abuses in which a dominant undertaking engages in more than one Member State are normally by their very nature capable of affecting trade between Member States.[99]

(iii) Abuse of a Dominant Position Covering a Single Member State

Where an undertaking has a dominant position which covers the whole of a Member State the Guidelines distinguish between exclusionary and exploitative abuses. Where exclusionary abuses are concerned, trade between Member States is normally capable of being affected because the abuse will generally make it more difficult for competitors from other Member States to penetrate the market.[100] There are a number of cases that illustrate this.[101] An example is *Greek Lignite and Electricity Markets*[102] in which a State-owned electricity company in Greece had a near-monopoly of the exploitation rights of an important raw material. The Commission held that this situation discouraged potential entrants on to the market from exercising their right of establishment in Greece.[103] Also,

---

[99] Guidelines on the effect on trade concept, paras. 73–76.

[100] Ibid., para. 93.

[101] E.g. Case 322/81, NV *Nederlandsche Banden-Industrie Michelin v Commission* (Michelin I) [1983] ECR 3461; Case T-65/89, *BPB Industries and British Gypsum* [1993] ECR II-389.

[102] COMP/38.700, *Greek Lignite and Electricity Markets* 5 March 2008, finally upheld Case C-554/12 P, *Commission v DEI* EU:C:2014:2085.

[103] COMP/38.700, *Greek Lignite and Electricity Markets*, para. 244.

exclusionary abuses may affect the competitive structure in a Member State in a way that affects inter-Member State trade. The Guidelines explain:

94. Exclusionary abuses that affect the competitive market structure inside a Member State, for instance by eliminating or threatening to eliminate a competitor, may also be capable of affecting trade between Member States. Where the undertaking that risks being eliminated only operates in a single Member State, the abuse will normally not affect trade between Member States. However, trade between Member States is capable of being affected where the targeted undertaking exports to or imports from other Member States . . . and where it also operates in other Member States. . . . An effect on trade may arise from the dissuasive impact of the abuse on other competitors. If through repeated conduct the dominant undertaking has acquired a reputation for adopting exclusionary practices towards competitors that attempt to engage in direct competition, competitors from other Member States are likely to compete less aggressively, in which case trade may be affected, even if the victim in the case at hand is not from another Member State.

In the case of exploitative abuses, such as price discrimination and excessive pricing, if only domestic customers are affected there will normally be no inter-Member State trade effect. But the Guidelines explain how, nevertheless, there may be:

95. However, it may do so if the buyers are engaged in export activities and are disadvantaged by the discriminatory pricing or if this practice is used to prevent imports . . . Practices consisting of offering lower prices to customers that are the most likely to import products from other Member States may make it more difficult for competitors from other Member States to enter the market. In such cases trade between Member States is capable of being affected.

The Guidelines further explain that once the undertaking's *dominant position* covers a whole Member State it will normally not matter whether the *abuse* affects only some of the territory or only some customers.[104]

(iv) Abuse of a Dominant Position Covering only Part of a Member State

If a dominant position is held in only part of a Member State it will, of course, be a matter of whether that part is a 'substantial part of the internal market'. If so, then it is again a matter of deciding whether access by competitors from other Member States is made more difficult by the abuse. If it is, inter-Member State trade must normally be considered as being appreciably affected.[105] It should be remembered that a part of a Member State comprising only a port or airport is capable of being a substantial part of the internal market.[106]

(v) Abuses Involving Trade with Third Countries

Abuses involving trade outside the EU will be caught by Article 102 if they are implemented in the EU.[107] If the conduct relates to imports or exports to and from the EU there may be an effect on cross-border activity. Imports into one Member State may affect the conditions of competition there, and this may have a knock-on effect in others.[108] Where the object is to restrict competition inside the EU the requisite effect on inter-Member State trade is more readily established than when it is predominantly to restrict competition outside it.[109] A more detailed analysis is necessary where

---

[104] Guidelines on the effect on trade concept, para. 96.

[105] Ibid., para. 90.

[106] Ibid., para. 91, and see Section 5.C.v, p. 269.

[107] See Chap. 16.

[108] Guidelines on the effect on trade concept, para. 101.

[109] Ibid., para. 103.

the practice is not aimed at competition inside the EU, to identify exactly how, if at all, patterns of trade between Member States will be affected.[110] Thus, the conduct of liner conferences operating on routes between European ports and third countries was held to affect inter-Member State trade in that it obstructed the activities of competitors operating from ports in other Member States, limited the choice of services available to shippers in various Member States, and disturbed normal trade patterns in the common market.[111]

(vi) Regulation 1/2003, Article 3

The question of whether an effect on inter-Member State trade exists acquired an added significance after 1 May 2004. Regulation 1/2003, Article 3 provides that where an NCA applies national law to an abuse prohibited by Article 102 it *must* also apply Article 102. This means that if there is an effect on inter-Member State trade the NCA cannot deal with conduct which meets the other criteria of Article 102 by applying national law alone, although Article 3(2) does allow stricter national laws to be applied to conduct which affects inter-Member State trade and Article 3(3) permits national provisions which predominantly pursue an aim different from Article 102.[112] The judgment in *Tele2 Polska*[113] to the effect that NCAs may not make findings that there has been no infringement of Article 102 reinforced the significance of the inter-Member State trade condition.

6. THE REVIEW OF ARTICLE 102

A. THE INAUGURATION OF THE REVIEW

In 2003 DG Comp initiated a major internal review of its policy on Article 102. It had already reviewed its approach to Article 101 and to mergers[114] and considered it time to look at Article 102. In particular this was desirable in the light of the reform whereby under Regulation 1/2003 the NCAs have 'parallel competence' with the Commission to apply Article 102. The Commission considered that 'a policy which is clear on the substantive interpretation of the Article is essential to make the system work' and that a 'credible policy on abusive conduct must be compatible with mainstream economics'.[115] However, where the modernised 'more economics-based' approach to Article 101 was concerned the Court had been in the vanguard, and the Commission was walking through an open door.[116] This was not so with regard to Article 102.[117]

During the review the Chief Economist of DG Comp commissioned a report from EAGCP, the Economic Advisory Group on Competition Policy, which was published in July 2005 (the EAGCP report).[118]

---

[110] Ibid., paras. 106–109.

[111] E.g. *CEWAL* [1993] OJ L34/20, where a liner conference operating between the North Sea ports and the coast of West Africa was held to have infringed Art. 102. The inter-Member State trade point was not appealed.

[112] See further Chap. 13, Section 10.

[113] See n. 29.

[114] Culminating in the new EUMR, Council Reg. 139/2004 [2004] OJ L24/1.

[115] Speech by the then Director-General of DG Comp, Philip Lowe, at Fordham Corporate Law Institute 30th Annual Conference on International Antitrust Law and Policy, 23 October 2003 [2003] *Fordham Corp L Inst* 163.

[116] See Chap. 4.

[117] As shown by two GC judgments in 2003, Case T-203/01, *Manufacture Française des Pneumatiques Michelin v Commission (Michelin II)* [2003] ECR II- 4071 and Case T-219/99, *British Airways v Commission* [2003] ECR II-5917, discussed in Chap. 7.

[118] For EAGCP, see Chap. 2. The EAGCP report is available at <http://ec.europa.eu/dgs/competition/economist/eagcp_july_21_05.pdf>.

B. THE STAFF DISCUSSION PAPER

The review resulted in the publication in December 2005 of a DG Comp Staff Discussion Paper on the application of the Article to exclusionary abuses (the Discussion Paper).[119]

The Discussion Paper dealt only with the application of Article 102 to *exclusionary* abuses (defined as behaviour by a dominant undertaking which is likely to have a foreclosure effect on the market)[120] which are the main focus of Article 102 enforcement.[121] The thrust of the Discussion Paper was to reorientate the application of Article 102 in exclusionary abuse cases to an 'effects-based' analysis and to the consumer welfare standard. It stated that the objective of Article 102 with regard to exclusionary abuses was 'the protection of competition on the market as a means of enhancing consumer welfare and of ensuring an efficient allocation of resources'.[122]

The Discussion Paper was put out for public consultation and stimulated wide-ranging debate.[123] Broadly speaking the direction of the Discussion Paper was welcomed but there was much disagreement about the specific proposals and concern as to how far undertakings would be faced with even less legal certainty about the behaviour prohibited to dominant undertakings.[124] The outcome of the consultation was widely expected to be the publication of guidelines similar to the guidelines on Article 101(3).[125] However, there was a major problem as to how any guidelines embodying a reform in the law could be reconciled with the case law unless the EU Courts themselves changed their approach.

C. THE GUIDANCE PAPER

(i) The Road to the Guidance Paper

Two months after the publication of the Discussion Paper, Advocate General Kokott referred to the relationship between any new approach by the Commission to Article 102 and the case law of the Court in her Opinion in the *British Airways* appeal:

> . . . even if its administrative practice were to change, the Commission would still have to act within the framework prescribed for it by Article [102] as interpreted by the Court of Justice.[126]

The subsequent judgment of the CJ in the case in March 2007 took a highly conservative and formalistic approach to Article 102, showing little regard for consumers. Its treatment of rebates was at odds with the effects-based and consumer welfare analysis suggested by the Commission in the Discussion Paper.[127] The controversial GC judgment in *Microsoft* in September 2007 likewise concentrated on competitors and market structure rather than consumers.[128]

---

[119] Brussels, December 2005, <http://ec.europa.eu//competition/antitrust/art82/discpaper2005.pdf>.

[120] Discussion Paper, para. 1.

[121] See Section 5.D, and Chap. 7. The Discussion Paper dealt specifically with only the main types of exclusionary abuses.

[122] Discussion Paper, para. 4.

[123] The Commission received more than 100 submissions in response which are still available on the Commission's website: <http://ec.europa.eu/competition/antitrust/art82/contributions.html>. The Commission held a public hearing on the topic in June 2006, which is also available on the website, <http://ec.europa.eu/competition/antitrust/art82/hearing.html>.

[124] '. . . the upswing is good but the downswing and the follow-through needs a lot of work' as the Director General said in Brussels, 14 June 2006, summing up the responses to the Discussion Paper.

[125] The Discussion Paper itself described its contents as 'possible principles for the Commission's application of Article 82' (para. 1) and was written in a similar format to the Article 101(3) Guidelines. The Director General said at the public hearing that the Commission was looking to take a decision about issuing draft Guidelines by the end of 2006.

[126] Case C-95/04 P, *British Airways* [2007] ECR I-2331, Kokott AG, para. 28. The AG made the same point in a post-Guidance Paper case, Case C-109/10 P, *Solvay SA v European Commission* [2011] ECR I-10329, para. 21 of her Opinion.

[127] Cf. Discussion Paper, paras. 134–176. The case is discussed in Chap. 7.

[128] Case T-201/04, *Microsoft* [2007] ECR II-3601; see also Case T-271/03, *Deutsche Telekom v Commission* [2008] ECR II-477 and the CJ judgment in Cases C-468–478/06, *Sot. Lélos* [2008] ECR I-7139 which, although an Art. 102 case

As one commentator remarked:

Cynics might point out that the European courts' interpretation of Article [102] has been guided to a large extent by the Commission's historic approach, which was formalistic in nature. Subsequently, the Commission's creative leeway is restricted by its own historic analysis which was approved by the European courts. Having been embedded in the European case law, this structured analysis cannot easily be changed.[129]

Indeed, the *British Airways* and *Deutsche Telekom* judgments were appeals from Commission decisions in 1999 and 2001 respectively in which the decisions were upheld. In *Microsoft*, however, the Commission had conducted an effects analysis and examined the consumer welfare aspects.[130]

Faced with the attitude of the EU Courts and the difficulty of drafting guidelines in an area so rife with disagreements even among those who advocated effects-based analysis and the consumer welfare objective, the Commission finally adopted in February 2009 not 'guidelines' but 'Guidance' on the Commission's *enforcement priorities* in applying Article 102 to abusive exclusionary conduct by dominant undertakings (the Guidance Paper).[131]

(ii) The Content of the Guidance Paper

The Guidance Paper specifically states that it is not intended to be a statement of the law and that it is without prejudice to the interpretation of Article 102 by the EU Courts.[132] Rather, it sets out the *enforcement priorities* that will guide the Commission's action in applying Article 102 to exclusionary conduct by dominant undertakings.[133] The Commission therefore sets out what kinds of conduct it considers egregious enough to warrant expending its resources on intervention. It focuses on 'those types of conduct that are most harmful to consumers'.[134] It makes it clear that it is not concerned with protecting competitors but with protecting an effective competitive process because of the benefits that will deliver to consumers.

Guidance on the Commission's Enforcement Priorities in Applying Article 82 of the EC Treaty to Abusive Exclusionary Conduct by Dominant Undertakings [2009] OJ C45/2

5. In applying Article [102] to exclusionary conduct by dominant undertakings, the Commission will focus on those types of conduct that are most harmful to consumers. Consumers benefit from competition

---

on refusal to supply, was outside the range of abusive conduct covered by the Discussion Paper. The only radical development in this period in the jurisprudence was the GC's judgment on the 'object' issue in the application of Art. 101 in Case T-168/01, *GlaxoSmithKline* [2006] ECR II-2969 against which, rather ironically in this context, the Commission appealed. The judgment was disapproved on this point by the CJ in Cases C-501, 513, 515, and 519/06 P, *GlaxoSmithKline Services Unlimited v Commission* [2009] ECR I-9291.

[129] A. Ezrachi, 'The Commission's Guidance on Article 82EC and the Effects Based Approach—Legal and Practical Challenges' in A. Ezrachi (ed.), *Article 82EC: Reflections on its Recent Evolution* (Hart Publishing, 2009), 51, 56. Or, as Hamlet put it, 'hoist with one's own petard'.

[130] COMP/37.792, *Microsoft* 24 March 2004, see Chap. 7.

[131] Guidance on the Commission's Enforcement Priorities in Applying Article 82 of the EC Treaty to Abusive Exclusionary Conduct by Dominant Undertakings [2009] OJ C45/2. The Guidance Paper was originally published on the Commission website in December 2008 but after minor amendments the final version appeared in the Official Journal on 9 February 2009. See generally P. Akman, 'The European Commission's Guidance on Article 102 TFEU: From *Inferno* to *Paradiso*?' (2010) 73 *MLR* 605; D. Geradin, 'Is the Guidance Paper on the Commission's Enforcement Priorities in Applying Article 102 TFEU to Abusive Exclusionary Conduct Useful?', available at <http://ssrn.com/abstract=1569502>.

[132] Guidance Paper, para. 3.

[133] Ibid., para. 2.

[134] Ibid., para. 5.

through lower prices, better quality and a wider choice of new or improved goods and services. The Commission, therefore, will direct its enforcement to ensuring that markets function properly and that consumers benefit from the efficiency and productivity which result from effective competition between undertakings.

6. The emphasis of the Commission's enforcement activity in relation to exclusionary conduct is on safeguarding the competitive process in the internal market and ensuring that undertakings which hold a dominant position do not exclude their competitors by other means than competing on the merits of the products or services they provide. In doing so the Commission is mindful that what really matters is protecting an effective competitive process and not simply protecting competitors. This may well mean that competitors who deliver less to consumers in terms of price, choice, quality and innovation will leave the market.

The Commission says of the Guidance Paper on its website:

The Communication provides comprehensive guidance to the business community and competition law enforcers at national level on how the Commission uses an economic and effects-based approach to establish its enforcement priorities under Article 102 in relation to exclusionary conduct.[135]

The Guidance Paper does not deal with exploitative abuses,[136] discrimination,[137] or abuses by undertakings in a collective dominant position. It contains an introductory section setting out the purpose of the Guidance;[138] an explanation of its general approach to exclusionary conduct, including a short section on market power and dominance and a general section on price-based exclusionary conduct;[139] and then a part applying that approach to specific forms of exclusionary conduct.[140] These are exclusive dealing, including conditional rebates; tying and bundling; predation; and some exclusionary refusals to supply, under which the Commission includes margin squeezes[141] but expressly does not cover, for example, refusals to supply to prevent parallel trade.[142] It does not, of course, cover 'new' types of abusive conduct with which the Commission has become concerned since publication of the Guidance Paper, such as standard essential patents[143] and (lack of) net neutrality.[144]

Throughout the Guidance Paper the Commission sets out a general rule as to what will 'normally' be its approach but then leaves some 'wriggle room' by adding a proviso to cover other situations where it may wish to take enforcement action because of the particular circumstances of the case. It has thus retained a wide degree of administrative discretion. This has been criticised as still leaving undertakings without sufficient legal certainty although the Guidance Paper says that its publication will 'help undertakings better assess whether certain behaviour is likely to result in intervention by the Commission'.[145]

---

[135] <http://ec.europa.eu/competition/antitrust/art82/index.html>. See also MEMO/08/761.

[136] Guidance Paper, para. 7.

[137] In the sense discussed in Chap. 7, Section 15.

[138] Guidance Paper, paras. 1–8.

[139] Ibid., paras. 9–31.

[140] Ibid., paras. 32–90.

[141] But see now Case C-280/08 P, *Deutsche Telekom* [2010] ECR I-9555.

[142] Guidance Paper, para. 77. This means that it does not deal with the situation in Cases C-468–478/06, *Sot. Lélos* [2008] ECR I-7139.

[143] See Chap. 7, Section 14.C.ii.

[144] See Chap. 7, Section 14.D. The Commission appears to treat this in COMP/39.740, *Google*, IP/15/4780, MEMO/15/4781, as a type of discrimination.

[145] Guidance Paper, para. 2.

The Commission's decision to issue a document on its enforcement priorities rather than fully fledged Guidelines met with a mixed response. It was said that:

In a world where the European Courts cling to old case law like castaways to a wreckage, guidelines for the Commission's enforcement priorities may be the best that can be achieved at present. The inability of the European Courts to provide intellectual leadership regarding the modernisation of these rules is all the more surprising as they have been at the forefront of modernisation in the areas of restrictive agreements and EC merger control.[146]

The detailed provisions of the Guidance Paper are discussed further in Chapters 6 and 7.

(iii) The Effect of the Guidance Paper

No Guidelines or Guidance can change the existing case law of the EU Courts.[147] The Guidance *could*, however, influence the way that the EU Courts approach the interpretation of Article 102 in future.

After the publication of the Guidance Paper the EU Courts had to deal with appeals from Commission decisions taken before its publication, or taken pursuant to proceedings initiated before its publication. In *Tomra*[148] and *Intel*[149] the EU Courts held that the Guidance Paper was irrelevant to such cases and applied the existing case law, eschewing an effects-based approach and focusing on competitors rather than consumers.[150] *Intel* concerned loyalty rebates, the treatment of which is one of the most contentious issues in Article 102 jurisprudence.[151] The GC held, following *Hoffmann-La Roche* but contrary to the new effects-based approach to rebates in the Guidance Paper, that it was unnecessary to show the potential to restrict competition. The GC also held that it was not necessary to apply the as efficient competitor (AEC) test (which the Guidance Paper adopts as the standard in price-based abuses and the CJ had employed in recent pricing cases) because loyalty rebates do not concern pricing but exclusivity.

In the Article 267 reference *TeliaSonera*, Advocate General Mazák described the Guidance Paper as 'a useful point of reference'[152] and considered margin squeeze as a type of refusal to supply, in line with the Commission in the Guidance Paper. The CJ however held, contrary to the Guidance Paper but without referring to it, that margin squeeze is a separate abuse from refusal to supply.[153]

The final blow fell in *Post Danmark II*, an Article 267 reference which also concerned rebates. The CJ accepted the *Hoffmann-La Roche* approach to loyalty rebates without demur and described the AEC test as 'one tool among many'. Faced with arguments about the AEC, and its centrality in the Guidance Paper, the Court stated:

…that document merely sets out the Commission's approach as to the choice of cases that it intends to pursue as a matter of priority; accordingly, the administrative practice followed by the Commission is not binding on national competition authorities and courts.[154]

---

[146] Linklaters Press Release, 2 December 2008.

[147] See L. Lovdahl Gormesen, 'Why the European Commission's Enforcement Priorities on Article 82 Should Be Withdrawn' [2010] *ECLR* 45 who argues that for this reason the Commission should withdraw the Guidance Paper.

[148] Case C-549/10 P, *Tomra Systems v Commission* EU:C:2012:221. Case C-280/08 P, *Deutsche Telekom* [2010] ECR I-9555 was another judgment where the CJ affirmed the upholding by the GC of a controversial pre-Guidance Paper decision, Case T-271/03, *Deutsche Telekom v Commission* [2008] ECR II-477.

[149] Case T-286/09, *Intel* EU:T:2014:547, on appeal Case C-413/14 P, judgment pending.

[150] The cases are discussed in Chap. 7, Section 11.

[151] See Chap. 7, Section 11.E.

[152] Case C-52/09, *Konkurrensverket v TeliaSonera Sverige AB* [2011] ECR I-527, n. 21 of the Opinion.

[153] Case C-52/09, *TeliaSonera* [2011] ECR I-527, paras. 55–56, followed in Case T-336/07, *Telefónica and Telefónica de España v Commission* EU:T:2012:172, aff'd Case C-295/12 P, *Telefónica SA* EU:C:2014:2062. See the discussion of the cases in Chap. 7, Section 9, p. 409 ff.

[154] Case C-23/14, *Post Danmark II* EU:C:2015:651, para. 52.

However, one should not conclude from this that the EU Courts are not influenced by the Guidance Paper. Some judgments since its publication show a tendency to recognise the principles in the Guidance Paper. Of particular significance in this regard is the ruling in *Post Danmark I*,[155] which applied the AEC standard and the incremental cost standard in predatory pricing,[156] formulated an efficiencies defence in line with paragraph 30 of the Guidance Paper, inserted a reference to consumers in the definition of an abuse in *Hoffmann-La Roche*,[157] and generally took a robust and economics-based attitude to the application of Article 102. Although the EU Courts have not adopted the consumer welfare standard as the sole objective of Article 102 the post-Guidance Paper judgments do pay more attention to the effects on consumers as shown in the cases discussed in Chapter 7. *Post Danmark II*, although dismissing the Guidance Paper as 'administrative practice' did take a less rigid approach to certain types of rebate than had been taken in previous cases.[158]

Undertakings will obviously look at the Guidance Paper for enlightenment as to what conduct the Commission considers an infringement of Article 102 worth pursuing because of its impact on consumers. However, the degree to which the Guidance Paper is riddled with caveats and exceptions will make it difficult for an undertaking to mount a challenge to action by the Commission on the ground that it has breached legitimate expectations.[159] Furthermore, *Treuhand*[160] has made it clear that legitimate expectations cannot hinder the Commission's duty to enforce the competition rules. As one commentator said:

> The announcement that Commission intervention against certain practices will be an enforcement priority cannot be taken as an indication of the lawfulness of other behaviour that breaches art.[102] according to settled case law. A dominant company cannot invoke a right to equal treatment to complain that the Commission did not keep its promise to focus its resources on pursuing somebody else's exclusionary abuses.
>
> The Guidance does not assure companies that their infringing conduct will go unpunished if it does not fall under the new enforcement priorities. Therefore, it cannot give rise to legitimate expectations.[161]

Article 102 is directly applicable and may be enforced in national courts, and more private enforcement of the competition rules is being actively encouraged.[162] The national courts are bound by the case law and must look to that rather than to Notices from the Commission as the CJ made clear in *Post Danmark II*. NCAs (and national regulators as in the *Post Danmark* cases) must also follow the case law and should they not do so would be liable to be overturned by their national courts applying the case law. NCAs may, however, be influenced by the Commission in the cases that they prioritise for enforcement (they may find the Guidance Paper inspiring although not binding) and some NCAs already apply an effects-based analysis to cases under both Article 102 and their domestic equivalents.[163]

As for the Commission itself, it can simply refrain from bringing cases where there is no consumer harm according to its consumer welfare/effects approach. Such inactivity could be challenged by a

---

[155] Case C-209/10, *Post Danmark I* EU:C:2012:172; see E. Rousseva and M. Marquis, 'Hell Freezes Over: A Climate Change for Assessing Exclusionary Conduct under Article 102 TFEU' (2012) 4 *JECLAP* 32.

[156] Although this had in effect been done in Case C-62/86 *AKZO Chemie BV v Commission* [1991] ECR I-3359.

[157] Case C-209/10, *Post Danmark I* EU:C:2012:172, para. 24; see Chap. 7, Section 3.D.i, p. 356.

[158] Case C-23/14, *Post Danmark II* EU:C:2015:651, paras 28–50, see Chap. 7, Section 11.F.iii, p. 464.

[159] Moreover, the legal status of the Guidance is unclear, see further O'Donoghue and Padilla, n. 36, 74. See Chap. 2 for the status of 'Guidelines', described by the CJ in Cases C-189, 202, 208, and 213/02 P, *Dansk Rørindustri A/S and others v Commission* [2005] ECR I-5425, para. 209 as rules of practice rather than rules of law.

[160] Case T-99/04, *AC-Treuhand AG v Commission* [2008] ECR II-1501, para. 163.

[161] M. Kellerbauer, 'The Commission's New Enforcement Priorities in Applying Article 82EC to Dominant Companies' Exclusionary Conduct: A Shift Towards a More Economic Approach?' [2010] *ECLR* 175, 185 (the author is a member of the Commission Legal Service but was writing in a personal capacity).

[162] See Chap. 14.

[163] Discussion between representatives of NCAs at the GCR Conference on Dominance and Unilateral Conduct, Brussels, 9 February 2010.

disgruntled complainant but the GC established in the leading *Automec* case that the Commission is entitled to set its own priorities.[164] The Commission is bound by the case law but it may well be able to subtly move matters along because of the dynamics of the 'appeal' process to the GC which takes the form of a judicial review.[165] The consumer welfare/effects approach to Article 102 espoused by the Commission will generally result in fewer findings of abuse than a more formalistic/protection of competitors one. It is difficult to envisage how a decision finding an abuse after an analysis of anti-competitive foreclosure and effects on consumers could be successfully appealed by an undertaking because a stricter standard would not have found an abuse. A major hindrance to the development of the case law is the Commission's current preference for settling Article 102 cases by commitments decisions, which never go to the EU Courts. That makes Article 267 preliminary references ever more crucial to the development of the law, and in those cases the CJ is not limited to considering only 'errors of law' in the GC's judicial review. Notably, *TeliaSonera* and the *Post Danmark* cases were all Article 267 rulings (all in appeals from national regulators).

In conclusion, the path to modernising what has been called 'the last of the steam-powered trains'[166] is not straightforward. Ultimately, the Commission needs the EU Courts on board if the steam-powered train is to be transformed into the TGV. However, there is no doubt that the Guidance Paper has affected the whole discourse on Article 102 and that it is impossible to discuss Article 102 without taking it on board.

7. THE RELATIONSHIP BETWEEN ARTICLE 102 AND ARTICLE 101

Articles 101 and 102 are not mutually exclusive and they serve the same aim.[167] In *Hoffmann-La Roche*[168] the CJ confirmed that both Articles 101 and 102 may apply to the same contractual arrangements. When dealing with an exclusive requirements contract concluded by a dominant undertaking the Commission was, therefore, at liberty to proceed under either Article 101 or Article 102. The CJ held that:

the question might be asked whether the conduct in question does not fall within Article [101] and possibly within its paragraph (3) thereof. However, the fact that agreements of this kind might fall within Article [101] and in particular within paragraph (3) thereof does not preclude the application of Article [102], since this latter article is expressly aimed in fact at situations which clearly originate in contractual relations so that in such cases the Commission is entitled, taking into account the nature of the reciprocal undertakings entered into and to the competitive position of the various contracting parties on the market or markets in which they operate to proceed on the basis of Article [101] or Article [102].[169]

The fact that Article 101 and Article 102 can be applied to the same agreements or practices is a powerful argument for aligning the approach to the two provisions.[170] An agreement entered into

---

[164] Case T-24/90, *Automec Srl v Commission (Automec II)* [1992] ECR II-2223. However, the discretion of the Commission is not unlimited: see Case T-427/08, *Confédération européenne des associations d'horlogers-réparateurs (CEAHR) v Commission* [2010] ECR II-5865, Chap. 13, Section 12.F, p. x, for a case in which the GC annulled the Commission's decision not to pursue a complaint because the Commission had not adequately assessed the matter; see W. Wils, 'Discretion and Prioritisation in Public Antitrust Enforcement' (2011) 34 *World Competition* 353.

[165] See Chap. 13, Section 8.A.i, p. 992 ff.

[166] B. Sher, 'The Last of the Steam-powered Trains: Modernising Article 82' [2004] *ECLR* 243.

[167] Case 6/72, *Continental Can* [1973] ECR 215, para. 25.

[168] Case 85/76, *Hoffmann-La Roche* [1979] ECR 461. See also Cases C-395 and 396/96 P, *Compagnie Maritime Belge* [2000] ECR I-1365, para. 33.

[169] Case 85/76, *Hoffmann-La Roche* [1979] ECR 461, para. 116.

[170] See, e.g., *Van den Bergh (Irish Ice Cream)* [1998] OJ L246/1, and the subsequent appeals, and exclusive dealing generally, Chap. 7, Section 10. In COMP/39.612, *Périndopril (Servier)* 9 July 2014, IP14/799, on appeal Case T-691/14,

by a dominant undertaking may infringe Article 102 even though it complies with Article 101. This includes an agreement which benefits from a block exemption and is therefore exempt from Article 101 by virtue of Article 101(3). In *Tetra Pak I*[171] the Commission found[172] that Tetra Pak had committed an abuse of a dominant position when it acquired an undertaking which held an exclusive patent licence. The patent licence fell under a block exemption. The GC confirmed that an undertaking could commit an abuse of a dominant position by operating an agreement which was exempted under a block exemption even if the benefit of the block exemption had not been withdrawn. Otherwise an exemption under Article 101(3) would also operate as an exemption from Article 102.[173]

Where the individual application of Article 101(3) by NCAs or national courts is concerned the Notice on the application of Article 101(3) states that the concept of the elimination of competition in respect of a substantial part of the products in question, which precludes the exemption of an agreement from the Article 101(1) prohibition, is an 'autonomous Community law concept specific to Article 101(3)'[174] which is narrower than 'dominance' under Article 102.[175] The Notice makes it clear that Article 101(3) cannot be applied to permit an agreement that constitutes an *abuse* of a dominant position.[176] Not all restrictive agreements entered into by dominant firms will, however, constitute an abuse. The Notice gives the example of a dominant firm's participation in a non-full-function joint venture.

It has been argued that it would be preferable if only Article 101 were applied to the vertical arrangements of dominant undertakings, leaving Article 102 to deal with abusive unilateral conduct that cannot be caught by Article 101.[177] One complication which arises with the applicability of both Articles to the same conduct is the difference in the position as regards the burden of proof[178] and the fact that (at least hitherto) arrangements such as exclusive dealing have been subject to less rigorous economic analysis under Article 102 than under Article 101.[179]

The relationship between Article 101 and Article 102 is also relevant in the context of undertakings found to be 'collectively dominant' for the purposes of Article 102.[180] Both Article 101 and Article 102 may apply to the conduct of such undertakings. It is possible that the agreement between the parties will infringe Article 101 and that the behaviour conducted in consequence of the agreement will amount to an abuse of a collective dominant position. Moreover, the collective dominant position may arise from agreements between the parties.

Servier SAS v Commission, judgment pending, the Commission applied both Art. 101 and Art. 102 to agreements and transactions of a dominant firm which implemented a strategy of excluding competitors and delaying the introduction of generic medicines.

[171] Case T-51/89, *Tetra Pak Rausing v Commission (Tetra Pak I)* [1990] ECR II-309.

[172] [1988] OJ L272/27.

[173] Such a situation is unlikely to occur now, as the current trend is for block exemptions to contain market share thresholds above which the block exemption is not applicable, see Chap. 4.

[174] [2004] OJ C101/97, para. 106.

[175] See Case T-395/94, *Atlantic Container Line* [2002] ECR II-875, para. 330.

[176] Notice on the application of Article 101(3), para. 106.

[177] See E. Rousseva, 'Modernising by Eradicating: How the Commission's New Approach to Article 81 EC Dispenses with the Need to Apply Article 82 to Vertical Restraints' (2005) 42 *CMLRev* 587; E. Rousseva, *Rethinking Exclusionary Abuses in EU Competition Law* (Hart Publishing, 2010), 460–473.

[178] See also I. Lianos, 'Categorical Thinking in Competition Law and the "Effects-based Approach" in Article 82' in A. Ezrachi (ed.), *Article 82EC: Reflections on its Recent Evolution* (Hart Publishing, 2009), 19, 26–30.

[179] See O'Donoghue and Padilla, n. 36, 35–36; Chap. 7, Section 10; Lianos, n. 178, 19, 26–30; Case C-552/03 P, *Unilever Bestfoods (Ireland) Ltd v Commission (Van Den Bergh)* [2006] ECR I-9091.

[180] See Section 5.A.iii, p. 264.

8. CONCLUSIONS

1. Article 102 is a powerful regulatory tool. However, its application has suffered from a lack of a proper theoretical framework and from confused policy goals. Protecting competitors for their own sake can lead to consumer detriment by penalising efficient pro-competitive conduct. Even protecting competitors in order to protect the competitive process has often been done without sufficient analysis of the real impact on consumers. It is argued that there is a danger of too many 'false positive' errors, i.e. over-enforcement which chills competition and harms consumers.

2. The Commission wished to published Guidelines similar to those published in respect to Article 101 and to mergers. It hoped to set out its concept of an abuse in a way orientated to a consumer welfare objective and using effects-based analysis. Instead it had to limit itself to 'Guidance' as to its 'enforcement priorities'. It is difficult not to read the Guidance as an explanation of what the Commission considers constitutes an abuse, but the document itself states that it is not a statement of the law, and the CJ has described it as merely setting out the administrative practice of the Commission.

3. The approach taken by the Guidance Paper has had a mixed reception in the EU Courts. Some cases decided since its publication have taken a completely different approach but there are some issues on which the EU Courts and the Commission agree. However at the moment there is, overall, a dissonance between the Commission's adherence to consumer welfare and EU Courts' continued adherence to the established case law.

9. FURTHER READING

A. BOOKS

AKMAN, P., *The Concept of Abuse in EU Competition Law* (Hart Publishing, 2012), Chap. 2

EHLERMANN, C.-D., and MARQUIS, M. (eds.), *European Competition Law Annual 2007: A Reformed Approach to Article 82* (Hart Publishing, 2008)

FAULL, J., and NIKPAY, A. (eds.), *The EU Law of Competition* (3rd edn, Oxford University Press, 2014), Chap. 4

JOLIET, R., *Monopolization and Abuse of Dominant Position* (Nijhoff, 1970)

NAZZINI, R., *The Foundations of European Union Competition Law: The Objectives and Principles of Article 102* (Oxford University Press, 2011), Chaps. 4 and 11

O'DONOGHUE, R., and PADILLA, A. J., *The Law and Economics of Article 102* (2nd edn, Hart Publishing, 2013), Chaps. 1 and 2

ORTIZ BLANCO, L., *Market Power in EU Antitrust Law* (Hart Publishing, 2012), Chap. 10

PACE, L. F. (ed.), *European Competition Law: The Impact of the Commission's Guidance on Article 102* (Edward Elgar, 2011)

ROUSSEVA, E., *Rethinking Exclusionary Abuses in EU Competition Law* (Hart Publishing, 2010), Chap. 1

B. CHAPTERS IN BOOKS

LIANOS, I., 'Categorical Thinking in Competition Law and the Effects-based Approach in Article 82' in A. Ezrachi (ed.), *Article 82EC: Reflections on its Recent Evolution* (Hart Publishing, 2009), 19

MESTMÄCKER, E.-J., 'The Development of German and European Competition Law with Special Reference to the EU Commission's Article 82 Guidelines of 2008' in L. F. Pace (ed.), *European Competition Law: The Impact of the Commission's Guidance on Article 102* (Edward Elgar, 2011), 43

C. ARTICLES

AKMAN, P., 'The European Commission's Guidance on Article 102 TFEU: From *Inferno* to *Paradiso*' (2010) 73 *MLR* 605

ALLAN, B., 'Article 102: A Commentary on DG Competition's Discussion Paper' [2006] *Competition Policy International* 43

GERADIN, D., 'Is the Guidance Paper on the Commission's Enforcement Priorities in Applying Article 102 TFEU to Abusive Exclusionary Conduct Useful?', available at <http://ssrn.com/abstract=1569502>

KELLERBAUER, M., 'The Commission's New Enforcement Priorities in Applying Article 82 EC to Dominant Companies' Exclusionary Conduct: A Shift Towards a More Economic Approach?' [2010] *ECLR* 175

KROES, N., 'Tackling Exclusionary Practices to Avoid Exploitation of Market Power: Some Preliminary Thoughts on the Policy Review of Article 82' [2005] *Fordham Corp L Inst* 381

LOVDAHL GORMESEN, L., 'Why the European Commission's Enforcement Priorities on Article 82 Should Be Withdrawn' [2010] *ECLR* 45

MONTI, G., 'The Scope of Collective Dominance Under Article 82 EC' (2001) 38 *CMLRev* 131

NAZZINI, R., 'The Wood Began to Move: An Essay on Consumer Welfare, Evidence and Burden of Proof in Article 82 EC Cases' (2006) 31 *ELRev* 518

PETIT, N., 'From Formalism to Effects—The Commission's Communication on Enforcement Priorities in Applying Article 82 EC' (2009) 32 *World Competition* 485

SHER, B., 'The Last of the Steam-powered Trains: Modernising Article 82' [2004] *ECLR* 243

6

ARTICLE 102 TFEU: DOMINANT POSITION

1. CENTRAL ISSUES

1. Article 102 can only apply to undertakings which, singly or collectively, are in a dominant position. A 'dominant position' was defined by the Court of Justice in *Hoffmann-La Roche* and *United Brands* in terms of an undertaking's independence and ability to prevent effective competition. This is normally equated with substantial market power (SMP), which is the ability to profitably raise prices above the competitive level for a significant period of time.

2. Dominance can be measured 'directly' or 'indirectly'. EU law measures it 'indirectly' for the purposes of Article 102 by defining the market and then assessing the undertaking's degree of market power on that market.

3. Historically, the market has been defined in Article 102 cases by employing qualitative factors such as characteristics and intended use. The Commission now advocates the use of quantitative techniques such as the small but significant non-transitory increase in price (SSNIP) test.

4. Once the market is defined, the case law places heavy reliance on market shares in order to assess the degree of market power.

5. The case law establishes that once an undertaking has 50 per cent of the market there is a presumption that it is dominant.

6. Barriers to entry (and expansion) are also taken into account and the lower the market share, the greater the importance that is attached to them. A wide range of barriers to entry and other factors indicating dominance have been taken into account in the cases.

7. The cases do not establish a figure below which an undertaking cannot be found dominant.

8. In the Guidance Paper on the Commission's enforcement priorities in applying Article 102 to exclusionary abuses the Commission states that market shares are a 'useful first indication' of the market structure and the relative importance of the undertakings active on it. The Commission maintains the position that undertakings with market shares below 40 per cent could be considered dominant. The Guidance Paper does not establish a 'safe harbour'.

9. The usual way of assessing dominance is problematic in some new economy markets.

2. INTRODUCTION

As explained in Chapter 5, Article 102 only applies to undertakings in a dominant position. Whether or not an undertaking holds a 'dominant position' is therefore of central importance to Article 102.[1] Clearly the term is not intended only to refer to a complete monopolist (the sole undertaking on a relevant market). It is intended also to encompass undertakings which have a certain degree of

---

[1] The concept of a 'dominant position' is also a term employed in the EU Merger Reg. (the EUMR), Council Reg. 139/2004 [2004] OJ L24/1, see Chap. 15.

market power.[2] The difficulty is to determine what degree of market power is necessary before Article 102 applies.

Perfect competition is rarely encountered outside textbooks; almost all firms have some market power, though most have very little. Accordingly, the relevant question in antitrust cases is not whether market power is present, but whether it is important.[3]

The initial problem in respect of Article 102 is to identify with sufficient clarity the point at which an undertaking becomes, and can know it becomes, dominant and so potentially subject to the prohibition. This will be at some point on the spectrum of market power. As we saw in Chapter 1, economists usually describe *substantial* market power (SMP) as the ability of a firm to raise prices above the competitive level without attracting new entrants and losing sales to competitors so rapidly that the price increase is unprofitable and must be rescinded.[4] Another way of looking at SMP is to relate it to the power to exclude competitors, but there are problems with this.[5] In US law, monopoly power for the purposes of s. 2 of the Sherman Act has been defined as 'the power to control prices or to exclude competition'.[6] In the following sections we consider how 'dominant position' has been defined and conceptualised by the EU Courts and the Commission.

3. THE DEFINITION OF A DOMINANT POSITION

A. THE DEFINITION OF A DOMINANT POSITION IN THE CASE LAW

The CJ has defined dominance in terms of an undertaking's 'economic strength' and its ability to act independently on the market.

In *United Brands* the CJ said that an undertaking would hold a dominant position where it could prevent effective competition being maintained by virtue of its ability to behave independently of the usual competitive constraints facing an entity operating on a market.[7]

Case 27/76, *United Brands v Commission* [1978] ECR 207

Court of Justice

65. The dominant position referred to in this Article relates to a position of economic strength enjoyed by an undertaking which enables it to prevent effective competition being maintained on the relevant market by giving it the power to behave to an appreciable extent independently of its competitors, customers and ultimately of its consumers.

---

[2] Although the words 'monopoly' and 'monopolist' are sometimes used as a shorthand to cover both situations.

[3] R. Schmalensee, 'Another Look at Market Power' (1981–1982) 95 *Harvard LR* 1789, 1790.

[4] See W. Landes and R. Posner, 'Market Power in Antitrust Cases' (1980–1981) 94 *Harvard LR* 937, and Chap. 1.

[5] S. Bishop and M. Walker, *The Economics of EC Competition Law* (3rd edn, Sweet & Maxwell, 2010), 3-041; D. Geradin, A. Layne-Farrar, and N. Petit, *EU Competition Law and Economics* (Oxford University Press, 2012), 4.57; R. Nazzini, *The Foundations of European Union Competition Law: The Objectives and Principles of Article 102* (Oxford University Press, 2011), 335–342.

[6] See *Standard Oil Co of New Jersey v United States*, 221 US 1 (1911); *United States v E I du Pont de Nemours & Co*, 351 US 377 (1956); *United States v Grinnell Corp*, 384 US 563 (1966).

[7] See also *Continental Can Co Inc* [1972] JO L7/25, para. 3, where the Commission described dominance in terms of independence and power over price. On appeal, Case 6/72, *Europemballage Corp and Continental Can Co Inc v Commission* [1973] ECR 215, the CJ did not expressly comment on the Commission's formulation of dominance, but it was approved by Roemer AG at [1973] ECR 215, 257 and implicitly by the Court.

66. In general a dominant position derives from a combination of several factors which, taken separately, are not necessarily determinative.

In *Hoffmann-La Roche* in 1979 the CJ elaborated on this definition. It emphasised that a position of dominance did not preclude some competition and particularly focused on the ability of the undertaking to influence the conditions of competition occurring on the market.

Case 85/76, *Hoffmann-La Roche & Co AG v Commission* [1979] ECR 461, paras. 38–39

Court of Justice

38. The dominant position thus referred to relates to a position of economic strength enjoyed by an undertaking which enables it to prevent effective competition being maintained on the relevant market by affording it the power to behave to an appreciable extent independently of its competitors, its customers and ultimately of its consumers.

39. Such a position does not preclude some competition, which it does where there is a monopoly or quasi-monopoly, but enables the undertaking which profits by it, if not to determine, at least to have an appreciable influence on the conditions under which that competition will develop, and in any case to act largely in disregard of it so long as such conduct does not operate to its detriment.

The definition of dominance in *United Brands* and *Hoffmann-La Roche* has become settled case law.[8]

The definition presupposes a dominant supplier. However, it is clear that the dominant position may be on the buying, rather than the selling, side. In that case the issue will be one of the independence of the undertaking from its suppliers. *British Airways v Commission*, for example, concerned the position of BA as a dominant buyer of air travel agency services.[9]

The formulation of dominance in *Hoffmann-La Roche* is problematic. The CJ test uses a concept of 'independence' which is more nebulous than power over price and, particularly as the independence has to exist only 'to an appreciable extent' and is compatible with continuing competition on the market, it brings inherent uncertainty to the operation of Article 102. Commentators have questioned whether the reference both to the ability of the undertaking to impede effective competition—which implies the power to exclude competitors—and to behave independently are two separate elements.[10] It is observed, however, that in subsequent case law the EU Courts 'have never drawn any distinction between them'.[11]

[8] See recently Case C-52/09, *Konkurrensverket v TeliaSonera Sverige AB* [2011] ECR I-527, para. 23, Case C-457/10 P, *AstraZeneca AB and AstraZeneca plc v Commission* EU:C:2012:770, para. 175. See also the merger case, Case T-210/01, *General Electric v Commission* [2005] ECR II-5575, para. 117, where the GC expressed it thus: 'However, even the existence of lively competition on a particular market does not rule out the possibility that there is a dominant position on that market, since the predominant feature of such a position is the ability of the undertaking concerned to act without having to take account of this competition in its market strategy and without for that reason suffering detrimental effects from such behaviour (*Hoffmann-La Roche v Commission*, paragraph 70, and Case 27/76 *United Brands v Commission*...). Thus, the fact that there may be competition on the market is indeed among the relevant factors for the purposes of ascertaining whether a dominant position exists, but it is not in itself a decisive factor in that regard.'

[9] Case C-95/04 P, *British Airways v Commission* [2007] ECR I-2331. See also, e.g., *Re Eurofima* [1973] CMLR D217; Case 298/83, *CICCE v Commission* [1985] ECR 1105.

[10] T. Eilmansberger, 'Dominance—The Lost Child? How the Effects-based Rules Could and Should Change Dominance Analysis' (2006) 2 *European Law Journal* Special Issue 15, 16.

[11] Geradin, Layne-Farrar, and Petit, n. 5, 4.51.

The 'act independently' criterion has been criticised as inherently flawed in that it does not satisfactorily distinguish between dominant and non-dominant firms. No successful firm, it is said,[12] can act to an appreciable extent independently of its of its consumers (unless it is a monopolist operating in a market protected by insurmountable barriers to entry and facing completely inelastic demand[13]). It really amounts to a matter of appreciable independence from competitors, and that comes back to a matter of the ability to sustain an above competitive level price rise. Moreover, the 'independence' referred to in *Hoffmann-La Roche*, it is argued, is not the ability to set price independently of demand but the ability to behave, to an appreciable extent, unconstrained by competitive pressure and demand discipline.[14] The GC equated 'independence' with the ability to maintain high prices in *AstraZeneca*:

Next, it must in any event be pointed out that a finding of market power, that is to say the ability of an undertaking to behave to an appreciable extent independently of its competitors, its customers and, ultimately, consumers, in the sense that it is in particular able to maintain prices at a higher level while retaining a much higher market share than those of its competitors . . .[15]

The 'position of economic strength' enabling the undertaking 'to prevent effective competition' element in *Hoffmann-La Roche* implies a power to exclude. The problem here is the chicken-and-egg conundrum as exclusionary behaviour is one form of the abuse of a dominant position forbidden by Article 102.[16] Faull and Nikpay conclude that this element merely requires that the ability to harm competition must derive from the position of economic strength which is the hallmark of dominance, namely SMP.[17]

B. DOMINANT POSITION IN THE GUIDANCE PAPER

In the Guidance Paper the Commission has a short section on 'market power'.[18] It starts with the *United Brands/Hoffmann-La Roche* definition. It relates 'independence' to the degree of competitive constraint upon an undertaking: dominance entails insufficiently effective competitive constraints so that the undertaking has SMP over a period of time. An undertaking that can sustain price rises above the competitive level can generally be regarded as dominant.

It will be noted that by paragraph 11 the Commission has equated dominance with power over price.

> ### Guidance on the Commission's Enforcement Priorities in Applying Article 82 of the EC Treaty to Abusive Exclusionary Conduct by Dominant Undertakings [2009] OJ C45/2
>
> 9. The assessment of whether an undertaking is in a dominant position and of the degree of market power it holds is a first step in the application of Article [102]. According to the case-law, holding a

---

[12] See, e.g., J. P. Azevedo and M. Walker, 'Dominance: Meaning and Measurement' [2002] *ECLR* 363, 364. The authors suggest that a better test would be 'the ability to restrict output substantially in the market-place'.

[13] R. O'Donoghue and A. J. Padilla, *The Law and Economics of Article 102* (2nd edn, Hart Publishing, 2013), 142.

[14] J. Faull and A. Nikpay (eds.), *The EU Law of Competition* (3rd edn, Oxford University Press, 2014), 4.125.

[15] Case T-321/05, *AstraZeneca v Commission* [2010] ECR II-2805, para. 267. On appeal the CJ affirmed the passage which includes para. 267 without commenting on it directly, Case C-457/10 P, *AstraZeneca* EU:C:2012:770, paras. 177–181.

[16] See further Geradin, Layne-Farrar, and Petit, n. 5, 4.57.

[17] Faull and Nikpay, n. 14, 4.126. See also Faull and Nikpay's reconciliation of the Guidance Paper's approach to dominance with the *Hoffmann-La Roche* definition in Section 3.B.

[18] Guidance on the Commission's Enforcement Priorities in Applying Article 82 of the EC Treaty to Abusive Exclusionary Conduct by Dominant Undertakings [2009] OJ C45/2 (the Guidance Paper), paras. 9–15.

dominant position confers a special responsibility on the undertaking concerned, the scope of which must be considered in the light of the specific circumstances of each case…

10. Dominance has been defined under Community law as a position of economic strength enjoyed by an undertaking, which enables it to prevent effective competition being maintained on a relevant market, by affording it the power to behave to an appreciable extent independently of its competitors, its customers and ultimately of consumers…This notion of independence is related to the degree of competitive constraint exerted on the undertaking in question. Dominance entails that these competitive constraints are not sufficiently effective and hence that the undertaking in question enjoys substantial market power over a period of time. This means that the undertaking's decisions are largely insensitive to the actions and reactions of competitors, customers and, ultimately, consumers. The Commission may consider that effective competitive constraints are absent even if some actual or potential competition remains…In general, a dominant position derives from a combination of several factors which, taken separately, are not necessarily determinative…

11. The Commission considers that an undertaking which is capable of profitably increasing prices above the competitive level for a significant period of time does not face sufficiently effective competitive constraints and can thus generally be regarded as dominant…In this Communication, the expression 'increase prices' includes the power to maintain prices above the competitive level and is used as short-hand for the various ways in which the parameters of competition—such as prices, output, innovation, the variety or quality of goods or services—can be influenced to the advantage of the dominant undertaking and to the detriment of consumers…

In paragraph 11 the Commission makes the important point that the power to maintain supra-competitive prices is not the only hallmark of SMP. It also includes the power to maintain the depression of output or innovation, or the production of poor quality and/or choice of goods or services,[19] so 'increase prices' is employed as an umbrella term.

Faull and Nikpay explain that the Guidance Paper is consistent with the case law.[20]

J. Faull and A. Nikpay (eds.), *The EU Law of Competition* (3rd edn, Oxford University Press, 2014), 4.133–4.134

4.133 The question then is whether dominance requires more than the possession of substantial and durable market power. The case law appears to place emphasis on the dominant undertaking's ability to harm competition rather than on its ability to raise price substantially above the competitive level for a significant period of time…It could be argued that there is a tension between a structural definition of dominance as substantial and durable market power, adopted by the Commission in its guidance, and a behavioural definition of dominance as ability to harm competition, adopted by the EU Courts.

4.134 This tension may be more apparent than real and can be reconciled. The ability of a dominant undertaking to harm competition presupposes substantial and durable market power. If a firm is subject to effective competitive pressure and, therefore, has no substantial market power it is unlikely to be able to harm competition within the meaning of Article 102 because competitors and customers will generally be able to neutralize any potentially anti-competitive behaviour of the firm in question. The application of a prohibition of abusive unilateral conduct to such firms would give rise to a high risk of error that would

---

[19] See Azevedo and Walker, n. 12.

[20] See similarly L. Ortiz Blanco, *Market Power in EU Antitrust Law* (Hart Publishing, 2012), 47: 'in effect, the traditional definition of a dominant position, based on the concept of independence, and the more modern one, which requires the capacity to maintain supra-competitive prices, basically refer to the same thing. In a market economy that focuses on profit, independence can only lead to price increases, and, at the same time, improvements in the results or the positions of the companies', and Geradin, Layne-Farrar, and Petit, n. 5, 4.52.

not be counterbalanced by the magnitude and likelihood of the harm that they can inflict on the economy. It can be concluded therefore, that the definition of dominance in the case law and that in the Guidance on Article 102 are coextensive and both equally consistent with the text and purpose of Article 102.

C. EFFECTS-BASED ANALYSIS AND THE CONCEPT OF DOMINANCE

We explained in Chapter 5 how the reform, or 'modernisation', of Article 102 centres on the widely accepted idea that an effects-based analysis of Article 102 concerned only with consumer welfare should be adopted. It can be argued from this that if a rigorous economic approach is taken to determining whether the conduct of an undertaking harms consumers the preliminary question of whether an undertaking is in a dominant position need not be separately answered.[21] This approach was urged by a report prepared for the Commission, during the internal review which led to the Discussion Paper,[22] by the Economic Advisory Group on Competition Policy (EAGCP).[23] This was not a suggestion of 'abuse, *ergo* dominance' but a plea for an *integrated* examination of the issues as a whole.[24]

Report by the EAGCP, 'An Economic Approach to Article 102', Brussels, 14–15 July 2005, available at <http://ec.europa.eu/dgs/competition/economist/eagcp_july_21_05.pdf>

In proposing to reduce the role of separate assessments of dominance and to integrate the substantive assessment of dominance with the procedure for establishing competitive harm itself, we depart from the tradition of case law concerning Art. [102], but *not*, we believe, from the legal norm itself. Art. [102] is concerned not just with dominance as such, but with abuses of dominance. The case law tradition of having separate assessments of dominance and of abusiveness of behaviour simplifies procedures, but this simplification involves a loss of precision in the implementation of the legal norm. The structural indicators which traditionally serve as proxies for 'dominance' provide an appropriate measure of power in some markets, but not in others. In a market in which these indicators do not properly measure the firm's ability to impose abusive behaviour on others, the competition authority's intervention under traditional modes of procedure is likely to be inappropriate, too harsh in some cases and too lenient in others. Given that the Treaty itself does not provide a separate definition of dominance, let alone call for any of the traditionally used indicators as such, it seems more appropriate to have the implementation of the Treaty itself focus on the abuses and to treat the assessment of dominance in this context.

Lawyers are likely to have more trouble than economists with the inconvenient fact that ever since *Continental Can* in 1974[25] the EU Courts have said that, in applying Article 102, first dominance must be established and then the conduct under review judged abusive or not. However, commentators also disagreed with EAGCP's suggestion for other reasons, particularly arguing that it *is* possible for anti-competitive effects to be caused by the conduct of non-dominant undertakings,[26] that a

---

[21] See *Eastman Kodak Co v Image Technical Services Inc*, 504 US 451, 112 S.Ct 2072 (1992) for this approach in the US.

[22] DG Comp Staff Discussion Paper on the application of Article 82 of the Treaty to exclusionary abuses, Brussels, December 2005, see Chap. 5.6.B, p. 275.

[23] For EAGCP, see Chap. 2, Section 3.C.iii, p. 95.

[24] J. Vickers, 'Market Power in Competition Cases' (2006) 2 *European Competition Journal* Special Issue 3, 11.

[25] See Case 6/72, *Continental Can* [1973] ECR 215.

[26] See, e.g., G. Monti, 'The Concept of Dominance in Article 82' (2006) 2 *European Competition Journal* 31, 45–46, discussing in particular predatory pricing; I. Kokkoris, *A Gap in the Enforcement of Article 82* (BIICL, 2009).

dominance 'screen' is desirable for administrative reasons to avoid Type 1 'false positive errors', and that a requirement of a preliminary finding of dominance provides a 'safe harbour', freeing the vast majority of undertakings from the need to worry about accusations of abuse.[27]

4. ESTABLISHING DOMINANCE

We now consider how the existence of a 'dominant position' is actually established, that is, how it is decided whether or not a particular undertaking is dominant.

In *Continental Can* the CJ stressed that dominance exists only in relation to a particular market and not in the abstract. It held that 'the definition of the relevant market is of essential significance'[28] to the determination of whether or not an undertaking is dominant. Commission decisions applying Article 102 will be quashed if the market is not properly defined.[29] In accordance with this judgment the practice of the Commission in ascertaining dominance is to follow a two-stage procedure by first identifying the relevant market and, secondly, examining the undertaking's position on that market and analysing the competitive constraints which the undertaking faces.[30] It does this by looking at the market share of the undertaking concerned and at 'other factors indicating dominance' including barriers to entry and expansion.

The two-stage procedure can be problematic. Not only are markets notoriously difficult to define,[31] but the process of market definition may be hard to separate from what is supposed to be the second step, assessing the undertaking's power on that market. It can be difficult to determine which factors should be taken into account when defining markets and which factors should be taken into account when considering the undertaking's position on the market. For example, it may not be easy to decide whether account should be taken of the presence of a producer which can switch its production to making a particular product when defining the market (supply-side substitutability) or when assessing the competitive constraints that the allegedly dominant undertaking faces on a particular market (potential competition). In addition, the question whether a particular undertaking is dominant can be hard to disentangle from the question whether or not it has committed an abuse of its dominant position.[32]

The Commission has often been criticised for finding that an undertaking occupies a 'dominant position' where, in reality, it has little market power. In particular it has been criticised for defining markets too narrowly,[33] for being too ready to find that an undertaking is dominant on a particular market by relying heavily on market shares, for finding dominance to exist at comparatively low market shares, and/or for not taking a sufficiently rigorous view of what amounts to a barrier to entry. This approach, coupled with the wide interpretation given to the term 'abuse',[34] means that

---

[27] Vickers, n. 24, 11–12; G. J. Werden, 'Competition Policy on Exclusionary Conduct: Towards an Effects-based Analysis' (2006) 2 *European Competition Journal* 53, 55–57; Faull and Nikpay, n. 14, 4.137–4.138.

[28] Case 6/72, *Continental Can* [1973] ECR 215, para. 32. See also Case C-7/97, *Oscar Bronner GmbH & Co KG v Mediaprint* [1998] ECR I-7791, para. 32; Case C-52/07, *Kanal 5 Ltd and TV 4 AB* [2008] ECR I-9275, para. 19.

[29] In *Continental Can* itself the CJ quashed the Commission's decision on account of its failure to define adequately the market from the supply side.

[30] However, in COMP/37.990, *Intel*, upheld Case T-286/09, *Intel v Commission* EU:T:2014:547, on appeal Case C-413/14 P, judgment pending, the Commission left open the question of whether there was one relevant market, CPUs for all computers, or three separate markets (CPUs for respectively desktops, laptops, and servers). It made no difference to the finding of dominance either way.

[31] See Chap. 1, Section 15.B, p. 56 ff.

[32] In some cases it has been indicated that the undertaking must be dominant, since if it was not it could not possibly have engaged in the conduct concerned: see Section 6.C.v.k, p. 342.

[33] In Art. 102 cases where the Commission is investigating what it suspects to be a breach of Art. 102 it may begin its case with a predisposition to a finding of dominance. This may encourage a narrow market definition. In merger cases the Commission may be more objective in its definition of the market.

[34] See Chap. 7.

the Commission has played a notably interventionist role in the market through the application of Article 102. If a more stringent approach was taken to identifying abusive conduct, findings of dominance would be less significant.

5. MARKET DEFINITION IN ARTICLE 102 CASES

A. GENERAL

Chapter 1 explained that the purpose of defining the relevant market is to identify those products and services that are such close substitutes for the product or service under consideration that they operate as a competitive constraint on the behaviour of the suppliers of the latter. In this chapter we focus on market definition in Article 102 cases, always remembering that market definition is not an end in itself. Rather, it is a preliminary step and a tool necessary to answer the real question: does this firm occupy a dominant position for the purposes of Article 102?

The market must be defined anew, and a fresh analysis of the conditions of competition made, each time Article 102 is applied. The Commission cannot rely on findings of dominance in previous cases.[35]

In most Article 102 cases the undertaking concerned will argue that the market is a wide one (for example, all fruit, rather than just bananas). The broader the market, the less likely the finding of dominance.[36] The assessment of the relevant market is therefore crucial. If it is defined too narrowly, an undertaking's position will be exaggerated and a finding of dominance made more likely. Furthermore, there may be a question as to whether a 'market' exists at all.[37]

It was seen in Chapter 1 that in the Market Definition Notice the Commission identifies three main competitive constraints to which firms are subject: demand substitutability, supply substitutability, and potential competition.[38] Demand and, to a more limited extent, supply substitutability are relevant to the determination of the market. Potential competition is relevant when considering the allegedly dominant undertaking's position on the relevant market once defined although, as we saw in Chapter 1, potential competitors may in certain narrow circumstances be considered supply substitutes.[39]

B. THE PRODUCT MARKET

(i) Demand Substitution

a. Substitutability

As we saw in Chapter 1, the Market Definition Notice prefers quantitative methods for measuring substitutability rather than qualitative methods which look at characteristics, price, and intended use. In particular it adopts the SSNIP test which essentially asks whether a small (5–10 per cent) but non-transitory increase in price of one product (product A) will cause purchasers to purchase

---

[35] Cases T-125/97 etc., *Coca-Cola v Commission* [2000] ECR II-1733, para. 82.

[36] Occasionally the undertaking argues for a narrow definition: e.g., in Case C-62/86, *AKZO Chemie BV v Commission* [1991] ECR I-3359, the undertaking argued for a narrow market definition as in the narrow niche market it was relatively weak, but in the wider market as a whole it had a large market share, see Section 5.B.i.e, p. 301.

[37] See the discussion on 'input' markets in Section 5.B.i.i, p. 306 and Case T-219/99, *British Airways plc v Commission* [2003] ECR II-5917, *aff'd* Case C-95/04 P, *British Airways* [2007] ECR I-2331.

[38] Commission Notice on the definition of the relevant market for the purposes of Community competition law [1997] OJ C372/5, para. 13.

[39] Chap. 1, Section 15.B.vi, p. 68.

sufficient of another product instead (product B) to make the price increase unsustainable.[40] However, the use of the SSNIP test in Article 102 cases is complicated by the 'cellophane fallacy'.[41]

The problems of identification using characteristics, price, and intended use are illustrated here by two leading Article 102 cases, *United Brands* and *Michelin I*.[42] These are followed by a case in the new economy, *Wanadoo (France Télécom)* which employed both a qualitative assessment of characteristics and use and also the SSNIP test.

b. The *United Brands* Case

In *United Brands* the CJ had to consider why people eat bananas and whether or not consumers treat bananas as reasonably interchangeable with other kinds of fresh fruit.[43] It decided that there was only a small degree of substitutability between bananas and other fruit, partly because of the unique appearance, taste, softness, seedlessness, and easy handling nature of the banana. The judgment does not make it clear why these distinctive characteristics should impact on the determination of the product market.

Case 27/76, *United Brands v Commission* [1978] ECR 207

United Brands (UBC) was a US company, with a European subsidiary, which produced bananas. The Commission found that United Brands had abused its dominant position on the banana market in a number of different ways, in particular by engaging in excessive and discriminatory pricing and refusal to supply. One argument raised in the appeal was that the Commission had been wrong to find that there was a separate market for bananas because bananas formed part of a wider fresh fruit market in that they were reasonably interchangeable with other kinds of fresh fruit such as apples, oranges, grapes, peaches, and strawberries. The Commission contended that bananas were a separate market because of their unique physical, functional, and economic characteristics and because Food and Agriculture Organization studies had demonstrated only low cross-elasticity between bananas and other fruit.

Court of Justice

12. As far as the product market is concerned it is first of all necessary to ascertain whether, as the applicant maintains, bananas are an integral part of the fresh fruit market, because they are reasonably interchangeable by consumers with other kinds of fresh fruit such as apples, oranges, grapes, peaches, strawberries, etc. or whether the relevant market consists solely of the banana and is a market sufficiently homogeneous and distinct from the market of other fresh fruit.

13. The applicant submits in support of its argument that bananas compete with other fresh fruit in the same shops, on the same shelves, at prices which can be compared, satisfying the same needs: consumption as a dessert or between meals.

14. The statistics produced show that consumer expenditure on the purchase of bananas is at its lowest between June and December when there is a plentiful supply of domestic fresh fruit on the market.

15. Studies carried out by the Food and Agriculture Organization (FAO) (especially in 1975) confirm that banana prices are relatively weak during the summer months and that the price of apples for example has a statistically appreciable impact on the consumption of bananas in the Federal Republic of Germany.

---

[40] See Chap. 1, Section 15.B.v.b, p. 61.

[41] See Chap. 1, Section 15.B.v.d, p. 65.

[42] Case 27/76, *United Brands v Commission* [1978] ECR 207; Case 322/81, *NV Nederlandsche Banden-Industrie Michelin v Commission (Michelin I)* [1983] ECR 3461.

[43] Mayras AG confidently declared: 'As far as eating habits are concerned there is no doubt that a mother who gives her young child a fruit yoghurt will not give him a banana as well...' [1978] ECR 207, 312.

16. Again according to these studies some easing of prices is noticeable at the end of the year during the 'orange season'.

17. The seasonal peak periods when there is a plentiful supply of other fresh fruit exert an influence not only on the prices but also on the volume of sales of bananas and consequently on the volume of imports thereof.

18. The applicant concludes from these findings that bananas and other fresh fruit form only one market and that UBC's operations should have been examined in this context for the purpose of any application of Article [102 TFEU].

19. The Commission maintains that there is a demand for bananas which is distinct from the demand for other fresh fruit especially as the banana is a very important part of the diet of certain sections of the community.

20. The specific qualities of the banana influence customer preference and induce him not to readily accept other fruits as a substitute.

21. The Commission draws the conclusion from the studies quoted by the applicant that the influence of the prices and availability of other types of fruit on the prices and availability of bananas on the relevant market is very ineffective and that these effects are too brief and too spasmodic for such other fruit to be regarded as forming part of the same market as bananas or as a substitute therefor.

22. For the banana to be regarded as forming a market which is sufficiently differentiated from other fruit markets it must be possible for it to be singled out by such special features distinguishing it from other fruits that it is only to a limited extent interchangeable with them and is only exposed to their competition in a way that is hardly perceptible.

23. The ripening of bananas takes place the whole year round without any season having to be taken into account.

24. Throughout the year production exceeds demand and can satisfy it at any time.

25. Owing to this particular feature the banana is a privileged fruit and its production and marketing can be adapted to the seasonal fluctuations of other fresh fruit which are known and can be computed.

26. There is no unavoidable seasonal substitution since the consumer can obtain this fruit all the year round.

27. Since the banana is a fruit which is always available in sufficient quantities the question whether it can be replaced by other fruits must be determined over the whole of the year for the purpose of ascertaining the degree of competition between it and other fresh fruit.

28. The studies of the banana market on the Court's file show that on the latter market there is no significant long term cross-elasticity any more than—as has been mentioned—there is any seasonal substitutability in general between the banana and all the seasonal fruits, as this only exists between the banana and two fruits (peaches and table grapes) in one of the countries (West Germany) of the relevant geographic market.

29. As far as concerns the two fruits available throughout the year (oranges and apples) the first are not interchangeable and in the case of the second there is only a relative degree of substitutability.

30. This small degree of substitutability is accounted for by the specific features of the banana and all the factors which influence consumer choice.

31. The banana has certain characteristics, appearance, taste, softness, seedlessness, easy handling, a constant level of production which enable it to satisfy the constant needs of an important section of the population consisting of the very young, the old and the sick.

32. As far as prices are concerned two FAO studies show that the banana is only affected by the prices—falling prices—of other fruits (and only of peaches and table grapes) during the summer months and mainly in July and then by an amount not exceeding 20 per cent.

33. Although it cannot be denied that during these months and some weeks at the end of the year this product is exposed to competition from other fruits, the flexible way in which the volume of imports and

their marketing on the relevant geographic market is adjusted means that the conditions of competition are extremely limited and that its price adapts without any serious difficulties to this situation where supplies of fruit are plentiful.

34. It follows from all these considerations that a very large number of consumers having a constant need for bananas are not noticeably or even appreciably enticed away from the consumption of this product by the arrival of other fresh fruit on the market and that even the personal peak periods only affect it for a limited period of time and to a very limited extent from the point of view of substitutability.

35. Consequently, the banana market is a market which is sufficiently distinct from the other fresh fruit markets.

It will be noted from this extract that the CJ was concerned with the question of whether the banana could be 'singled out by such special features distinguishing it from other fruits that it is only to a limited extent interchangeable with them and is only exposed to their competition in a way that is hardly perceptible' (paragraph 22). The 'special features' identified were first that the banana was a 'privileged fruit' (paragraph 25) in that it was not seasonal and, secondly, that it had 'certain characteristics' making it suitable for the very young, the old, and the sick (paragraph 31). These characteristics, apart from constant availability, were appearance, taste, softness, seedlessness, and easy handling. This is a strange list. Softness, seedlessness, and easy handling may make bananas suitable for the young, old, and sick but it is difficult to see why their appearance does and it is never explained what is so special about their taste. Moreover, as we saw in Chapter 1,[44] it is wrong to conclude from the dependence of one group of customers that a product forms a separate market unless it is possible to price discriminate at the point of sale and to prevent arbitrage. This is now recognised in the Notice.[45] It may be that if the question arose again bananas would still be held to constitute a separate market, but it is most unlikely that this would be on the basis of their 'special suitability' for certain customers.[46] Rather, evidence would be sought from technology such as supermarket scanners, which would enable own-price and cross-price elasticities to be measured.[47]

c. The *Michelin* Case

In *Michelin I* the Commission found that Michelin had abused a dominant position on the market for new replacement tyres for lorries, buses, and similar vehicles.[48] Michelin claimed, inter alia, that the Commission's definition of the market was narrow and arbitrary and that Michelin did not hold a dominant position on the wider tyre market.[49] The CJ had to determine whether or not the Commission had correctly defined the market. In considering this question a number of facts had to be taken into account: that lorries and buses need larger tyres than cars and vans; that there are different sizes of lorry and bus tyres; that tyre manufacturers supply their tyres separately to new lorry and bus manufacturers *and* to dealers who fit tyres on lorries and buses as replacements; and that tyre dealers also fit retreaded or remoulded tyres to vehicles whose owners do not want new replacement tyres. Which, if any, of these tyres were substitutes for each other so that they formed part of the same product market?

---

[44] See Chap. 1, Section 15.B.vii.b, p. 71.

[45] Para. 43.

[46] Moreover, changes in market conditions would affect the conclusion: many more fruits, for example, are now available in Europe all year round, and kitchen technology is such that few fruits cannot be pulped (although blenders were in fact readily available in the mid-1970s!).

[47] See O'Donoghue and Padilla, n. 13, 98.

[48] [1981] OJ L353/33.

[49] Michelin also challenged the definition of the geographic market as being the Netherlands. See Section 5.C, p. 312.

Case 322/81, *Nederlandsche Banden-Industrie Michelin v Commission* [1983] ECR 3461

Court of Justice

(aa) The market in replacement tyres for heavy vehicles

37. As the Court has repeatedly emphasized, most recently in its judgment of 11 December 1980 in Case 31/90 *NV L'Oreal and SA L'Oreal* v. *PVBA De Nieuwe AMCK*...for the purposes of investigating the possibly dominant position of an undertaking on a given market, the possibilities of competition must be judged in the context of the market comprising the totality of the products which, with respect to their characteristics, are particularly suitable for satisfying constant needs and are only to a limited extent inter-changeable with other products. However, it must be noted that the determination of the relevant market is useful in assessing whether the undertaking concerned is in a position to prevent effective competition from being maintained and behave to an appreciable extent independently of its competitors and customers and consumers. For this purpose, therefore, an examination limited to the objective characteristics only of the relevant products cannot be sufficient: the competitive conditions and the structure of supply and demand on the market must also be taken into consideration.

38. Moreover, it was for that reason that the Commission and Michelin NV agreed that new, original-equipment tyres should not be taken into consideration in the assessment of market shares. Owing to the particular structure of demand for such tyres characterized by direct orders from car manufacturers, competition in this sphere is in fact governed by completely different factors and rules.

39. As far as replacement tyres are concerned, the first point which must be made is that at the user level there is no interchangeability between car and van tyres on the one hand and heavy-vehicle tyres on the other. Car and van tyres therefore have no influence at all on competition on the market in heavy-vehicle tyres.

40. Furthermore, the structure of demand for each of those groups of products is different. Most buyers of heavy-vehicle tyres are trade users, particularly haulage undertakings, for whom, as the Commission explained, the purchase of replacement tyres represents an item of considerable expenditure and who constantly ask their tyre dealers for advice and long-term specialized services adapted to their specific needs. On the other hand, for the average buyer of car or van tyres the purchase of tyres is an occasional event and even if the buyer operates a business he does not expect such specialized advice and service adapted to specific needs. Hence the sale of heavy-vehicle tyres requires a particularly specialized distribution network which is not the case with the distribution of car and van tyres.

...

42. The Commission rightly examined the structure of the market and demand primarily at the level of dealers to whom Michelin NV applied the practice in question. Michelin NV has itself stated, although in another context, that it was compelled to change its discount system to take account of the tendency towards specialization amongst its dealers, some of whom, such as garage owners, no longer sold tyres for heavy vehicles and vans. This confirms the differences existing in the structure of demand between differ-ent groups of dealers. Nor has Michelin NV disputed that the distinction drawn between tyres for heavy vehicles, vans and cars is also applied by all its competitors, especially as regards discount terms, even if in the case of certain types of tyre the distinctions drawn by different manufacturers may vary in detail.

43. Nevertheless, it cannot be deduced from the fact that the conduct to which exception is taken in this case affects dealers that Michelin NV's position ought to be assessed on the basis of the propor-tion of Michelin heavy-vehicle tyres in the dealers' total turnover. Since it is a question of investigating whether Michelin NV holds a dominant position in the case of certain products, it is unimportant that the dealers also deal in other products if there is no competition between those products and the products in question.

44. On the other hand, in deciding whether a dominant position exists, neither the absence of elasticity of supply between different types and dimensions of tyres for heavy vehicles, which is due to differences

in the conditions of production, nor the absence of interchangeability and elasticity of demand between those types and dimensions of tyre from the point of view of the specific needs of the user allow a number of smaller markets, reflecting those types and dimensions, to be distinguished, as Michelin NV suggests. Those differences between different types and dimensions of tyre are not vitally important for dealers, who must meet demand from customers for the whole range of heavy-vehicle tyres. Furthermore, in the absence of any specialization on the part of the undertakings concerned, such differences in the type and dimensions of a product are not a crucial factor in the assessment of an undertaking's market position because in view of their similarity and the manner in which they complement one another at the technical level, the conditions of competition on the market are the same for all the types and dimensions of the product.

45. In establishing that Michelin NV has a dominant position the Commission was therefore right to assess its market share with reference to replacement tyres for lorries, buses and similar vehicles and to exclude consideration of car and van tyres.

(bb) The taking into consideration of competition from retreads

...

48. ...[I]t must first be recalled that although the existence of a competitive relationship between two products does not presuppose complete interchangeability for a specific purpose, it is not a pre-condition for a finding that a dominant position exists in the case of a given product that there should be a complete absence of competition from other partially interchangeable products as long as such competition does not affect the undertaking's ability to influence appreciably the conditions in which that competition may be exerted or at any rate to conduct itself to a large extent without having to take account of that competition and without suffering any adverse effects as a result of its attitude.

49. It is clear from the facts, as established from the parties' statements and those made by the witnesses examined at the hearing during the administrative procedure, that it cannot be denied that new tyres and retreads are interchangeable to some degree but only to a limited extent and not for all purposes. Although Michelin NV has produced calculations to show that the price and quality of retreads are comparable to those of new tyres and that a number of users do in fact consider the two groups of products interchangeable for their purposes; it has nevertheless admitted that in terms of safety and reliability a retread's value may be less than that of new tyre and, what is more, the Commission has shown that a number of users have certain reservations, which may or may not be justified, regarding the use of a retread, particularly on a vehicle's front axle.

50. In order to assess the effect of this limited competition from retreads on Michelin NV's market position it must be borne in mind that at least some retreads are not put on sale but are produced to order for the user as some transport undertakings attach importance to having their own tyre carcasses retreaded in order to be sure of not receiving damaged carcasses. It must be acknowledged that there has been no agreement between the parties as regards the percentage of tyres retreaded in this way as a form of service; the Commission has estimated it at 80 per cent to 95 per cent of retreads whereas Michelin NV maintains that it is only 15 to 20 per cent and that in most cases the order is placed in the name of the dealer and not that of the user. Despite that disagreement between the parties it may [be] said that a proportion of retreads reaching the consumer stage are not in competition with new tyres because they involve a service provided directly by the retreading firms to the users.

51. Furthermore, in assessing the size of Michelin NV's market share in relation to its competitors' it must not be overlooked that the market in renovated tyres is a secondary market which depends on supply and prices on the market in new tyres since every retread is made from a tyre which was originally a new tyre and there is a limit to the number of occasions on which a tyre may be retreaded. Consequently a considerable proportion of demand will inevitably always be satisfied by new tyres. In such circumstances the possession by an undertaking of a dominant position in new tyres gives it a privileged position as regards competition from retreading undertakings and this enables it to conduct itself with greater independence on the market than would be possible for a retreading undertaking.

52. It is clear from the considerations set out above that the partial competition to which manufacturers of new tyres are exposed from retreading undertakings is not sufficient to deprive a manufacturer of new tyres of the economic power which he possesses by virtue of his dominant position on the market in new tyres. In assessing Michelin NV's position in relation to the strength and number of its competitors the Commission was therefore right to take into consideration a market share [of] 57 to 65 per cent on the market in new replacement tyres for heavy vehicles. Compared with the market shares of Michelin NV's main competitors amounting to 4 to 8 per cent, that market share constitutes a valid indication of Michelin NV's preponderant strength in relation to its competitors, even when allowance is made for some competition from retreads.

The CJ thus upheld the Commission's decision.[50] It will be noted that in paragraph 48 the CJ considered that in the context of finding a dominant position it is not necessary that products be completely interchangeable—partial interchangeability is enough. The issue is whether the other product exerts a competitive restraint.[51]

The definition of the replacement tyre market was revisited 20 years later in a second Commission decision finding that Michelin's discount and rebate system was an abuse of its dominant position.[52] The Commission concluded that new replacement tyres for trucks and buses in France and retreaded tyres for trucks and buses in France were two separate markets and that Michelin had a dominant position on both of them.[53] The Commission's reasons for separating new tyres and retreads were essentially the same as they had been in 1981:[54] the supply and demand for the two types of tyre were different; retreaders were skilled *service* providers who did not necessarily have any links to tyre dealers, whereas new tyres were supplied to dealers; the retread market was a secondary 'after-sales' market, in which new tyres were the raw material and the purpose was to prolong the life of the tyre to avoid purchasing another new one; and, finally, there was still a safety issue in that many final (haulier) customers perceived retreads as less safe ('the situation that prevailed in 1981 has thus not changed significantly').[55] The Commission did not employ the SSNIP test in *Michelin II*.

d. The *France Télécom* Case

In *Wanadoo*[56] the Commission defined the relevant market as the French market for high-speed internet access for residential customers (the products with which the infringement of predatory pricing was concerned were internet access services based on ADSL technology).[57] The Commission examined the differences in performance between high- and low-speed internet access and concluded that the differences were clearly perceived by consumers, and that an analysis of price differences between them showed that consumers were prepared to pay a premium for the extra performance and convenience of high speed.[58] On appeal, France Télécom pleaded, inter alia, that the Commission should have considered the market as comprising both high-speed and low-speed access.[59]

---

[50] [1981] OJ L353/33.

[51] See also Case T-301/04, *Clearstream Banking v Commission* [2009] ECR II-3155, para. 64.

[52] COMP/36.041, *Michelin* [2001] OJ L143/1 (*Michelin II*).

[53] On appeal, Case T-203/01, *Manufacture Française des Pneumatiques Michelin v Commission* (*Michelin II*) [2003] ECR II-4071, neither the market definition nor the finding of dominance were challenged.

[54] *Michelin II* decision, paras. 109–118, despite the heavy criticism of the market definition in *Michelin I*, see e.g., V. Korah, 'The *Michelin* Decision of the Commission' (1982) 7 *ELRev* 130.

[55] *Michelin II* decision, para. 116.

[56] COMP/38.233, 16 July 2003.

[57] Asynchronous Digital Subscriber Line. It allows broadband services to be provided over the traditional telephone copper wire.

[58] COMP/38.233, para. 187.

[59] France Télécom had succeeded to the rights of Wanadoo (WIN) following a merger. On appeal to the CJ, Case C-202/07 P, *France Télécom SA v Commission* [2009] ECR I-2369 the market definition was not challenged.

Case T-340/03, *France Télécom SA v Commission* [2007] ECR II-107

General Court

78. According to settled case-law (Case 322/81 *Michelin* v *Commission* … paragraph 37; Case T-65/96 *Kish Glass* v *Commission*…paragraph 62; and Case T-219/99 *British Airways* v *Commission*…paragraph 91), for the purposes of investigating the possibly dominant position of an undertaking on a given product market, the possibilities of competition must be judged in the context of the market comprising the totality of the products or services which, with respect to their characteristics, are particularly suitable for satisfying constant needs and are only to a limited extent interchangeable with other products or services. Moreover, since the determination of the relevant market is useful in assessing whether the undertaking concerned is in a position to prevent effective competition from being maintained and to behave to an appreciable extent independently of its competitors and, in this case, of its service providers, an examination to that end cannot be limited solely to the objective characteristics of the relevant services, but the competitive conditions and the structure of supply and demand on the market must also be taken into consideration.

79. If a product could be used for different purposes and if these different uses are in accordance with economic needs, which are themselves also different, there are good grounds for accepting that this product may, according to the circumstances, belong to separate markets which may present specific features which differ from the standpoint both of the structure and of the conditions of competition. However, this finding does not justify the conclusion that such a product, together with all the other products which can replace it as far as concerns the various uses to which it may be put and with which it may compete, forms one single market.

80. The concept of the relevant market in fact implies that there can be effective competition between the products which form part of it and this presupposes that there is a sufficient degree of interchangeability between all the products forming part of the same market in so far as a specific use of such products is concerned (Case 85/76 *Hoffmann-La Roche* v *Commission*…paragraph 28).

81. It is also apparent from the Commission Notice on the definition of the relevant market for the purposes of Community competition law…that '[a] relevant product market comprises all those products and/or services which are regarded as interchangeable or substitutable by the consumer, by reason of the products' characteristics, their prices and their intended use'.

82. It must be stated that there is not a mere difference in comfort or quality between high- and low-speed access. It is clear from the evidence provided by the Commission (recital 175 of the decision), which was not contradicted by WIN, that some applications available with high-speed access are simply not feasible with low-speed access, including, for example, the downloading of very voluminous video files or interactive network games. WIN also confirmed, in its reply of 4 March 2002 to the first statement of objections, that there are 'audiovisual/multimedia activities … more specific to ADSL'. In addition, the study undertaken by the Centre de recherche pour l'étude et l'observation des conditions de vie (Research Centre for the Study and Monitoring of Living Standards) (Crédoc) on behalf of WIN which it presented in an annex to its application also describes new uses developed on the internet by the extense service and which are specific to high-speed access, that is, playing network games, listening to radio online, watching a video online and shopping online. According to that study, moreover, the subscriber with high-speed access goes online far more often and, on average, for considerably longer than the low-speed access user.

83. As regards the differences in technical features and performances, it is clear from the Commission's contentions (recitals 181 to 187 of the decision), which have not been denied by the applicant, that an important technical feature of high-speed internet access is the specific nature of the modems used. A high-speed internet access modem cannot be used for low-speed internet access and vice versa (recital 181 of the decision). In addition, in the case of high-speed access, the connection is always on and the telephone line always available for making calls.

84. In addition, in the case of the French market, it should be pointed out that, for the period investigated, the offers of high-speed access involved download speeds in the region of 512 kbits/s (recital 185 of the decision). The offers of traditional low-speed access (limited to 56 kbits/s) and of ISDN (integrated services digital network) (64 or 128 kbits/s) only allowed speeds of 4 to 10 times less. The ADSL offers with download speeds of 128 kbits/s, which, according to the applicant, bear witness to the continuity between low-speed and high-speed, only became available at the end of the period covered by the decision. In addition, even in the case of an offer of 128 kbits/s, the difference between low-speed and high-speed access is considerable. The difference in performance was therefore considerable during the period investigated.

85. In addition to the differences in use, features and performances, there is a significant price differential between low-speed and high-speed access (recitals 188 to 192 of the decision).

86. As regards the degree of substitutability, it is appropriate to recall, in addition to the case-law cited in paragraph 78 above, the criteria laid down by the Commission in its Notice on the definition of the relevant market for the purposes of Community competition law (see paragraph 81 above).

87. According to that notice, the assessment of demand substitution entails a determination of the range of products which are viewed as substitutes by the consumer. One way of making this determination can be viewed as a speculative experiment, postulating a hypothetical small but lasting change in relative prices and evaluating the likely reactions of customers to that increase. In paragraph 17 of the notice, the Commission states '[t]he question to be answered is whether the parties' customers would switch to readily available substitutes … in response to a hypothetical small (in the range 5 to 10%) but permanent relative price increase in the products and areas being considered'.

88. In recital 193 of the decision, the Commission admits that low-speed and high-speed access indeed present some degree of substitutability. It adds in recital 194, however, that the operation of such substitutability is extremely asymmetrical, the migrations of customers from offers of high-speed to low-speed access being negligible compared with the migrations in the other direction. However, according to the Commission, if the products were perfectly substitutable from the point of view of demand, the rates of migration should be identical or at least comparable.

89. It should be pointed out, in this respect, that, first of all, it is clear from the information gathered by WIN and reproduced in Table 7 of the decision that the migration rates of high-speed subscribers to integral low-speed offers were very low during the period covered, in spite of the difference in price between those services, which should have prompted numerous internet users to turn to low-speed access. This large discrepancy in the rates of migration between low-speed and high-speed access and between high-speed and low-speed access does not lend credence to the argument that those services are interchangeable in the eyes of consumers. In the application, WIN also failed to adduce any evidence to cast doubt on that analysis.

90. Secondly, it transpires that, according to a survey carried out on behalf of the Commission and presented by WIN in an annex to its application, 80% of subscribers would maintain their subscription in response to a price increase in the range 5 to 10%. According to paragraph 17 of the Notice on the definition of the relevant market for the purposes of Community competition law (see paragraph 87 above), this high percentage of subscribers who would not abandon high-speed access in response to a price increase of 5 to 10% provides a strong indication of the absence of demand-side substitution.

91. Consequently, on the basis of all the foregoing, it should be held that the Commission was right to find that a sufficient degree of substitutability between high-speed and low-speed access did not exist and to define the market in question as that of high-speed internet access for residential customers.

It will be noted that the GC cited the case law of the CJ on identifying substitute products by reference to characteristics and use. However, it also referred to the Market Definition Notice and to the SSNIP test (paragraph 87) and to a survey showing that 80 per cent of subscribers to the high-speed service would be impervious to a 5–10 per cent price increase. The GC concluded that this 'provides a strong indication' of the absence of demand-side substitution.[60]

e. Chains of Substitution and Products with Multiple Applications

Hoffmann-La Roche demonstrates the chain of substitution problem discussed in Chapter 1.[61] Hoffmann-La Roche (HLR) challenged the Commission's finding that it had committed a number of abuses of dominant positions held on several separate vitamin markets. Two of the vitamins concerned, C and E, had two distinct uses. In each case the vitamin had a bio-nutritive use for which there were no substitutes, and an antioxidant use. Both vitamins C and E and other products could be used for the antioxidant use. HLR claimed that the two vitamins were in the same market for antioxidants together with these other products. The CJ, concentrating on the bio-nutritive use, upheld the Commission's finding that the vitamins each constituted a separate market. The reasoning was not, however, entirely satisfactory. In particular, the judgment can be criticised for the Court's failure to take account of the two distinct uses. If HLR could not profitably increase the price to customers in the bio-nutritive market without also losing customers in the antioxidant market, then arguably they should have been found to form part of the same market.

Case 85/76, *Hoffmann-La Roche & Co AG v Commission* [1979] ECR 461

Court of Justice

28. If a product could be used for different purposes and if these different uses are in accordance with economic needs, which are themselves also different, there are good grounds for accepting that this product may, according to the circumstances, belong to separate markets which may present specific features which differ from the standpoint both of the structure and of the conditions of competition. However this finding does not justify the conclusion that such a product together with all the other products which can replace it as far as concerns the various uses to which it may be put and with which it may compete, forms one single market. The concept of the relevant market in fact implies that there can be effective competition between the products which form part of it and this presupposes that there is a sufficient degree of interchangeability between all the products forming part of the same market in so far as a specific use of such products is concerned. There was no such interchangeability, at any rate during the period under consideration, between all the vitamins of each of the groups C and E and all the products which, according to the circumstances, may be substituted for one or other of these groups of vitamins for technological uses which are themselves extremely varied.

29. On the other hand there may be some doubt whether, for the purpose of delimiting the respective markets of the C and E groups of vitamins, it is necessary to include all the vitamins of each of these groups in a market corresponding to that group, or whether, on the contrary, each of these groups must be placed in a separate market, one comprising vitamins for bio-nutritive use and the other vitamins for technological purposes.

30. However, in order to calculate the market shares of Roche and its competitors correctly this question did not have to be answered because, as the Commission has rightly pointed out, if it had been necessary to draw this distinction, it would have to be drawn for Roche's competitors as well as for Roche itself, and—in the absence of any indication to the contrary by the applicant—in similar proportions with the result that the market shares in percentages would remain unchanged. Finally Roche, in answer to a question put to it by the Court, has stated that all the vitamins of each group, irrespective of the ultimate

---

[60] It may not have needed SSNIP tests to convince the Court that low-speed internet access is no substitute for high-speed.

[61] Chap. 1, Section 15.B.vii.a, p. 70.

intended use of the product, were subject to the same price system so that they could not be split up into specific markets. It follows from the foregoing that the Commission has correctly delimited the relevant markets in its contested decision.

In one sense the narrow definition in *Hoffmann-La Roche* is of no concern if it is remembered that market definition is not an end in itself, but a step towards assessing market power. What matters is the recognition that markets are not impermeable and may be subject to competitive pressures from *outside* the market.[62] The problem, however, is that a narrow market definition may be more likely to result in a finding of dominance because of the importance accorded to market share in making that finding, as discussed in Section 6. The Market Definition Notice, paragraph 57,[63] recognises that where chains of substitution are present practical problems may arise in determining both the geographic and the product market. It will be recalled that the Commission's conclusion is that the crucial question is the extent to which the existence of substitutes constrains an undertaking's pricing policy.[64]

AKZO[65] shows how the particular circumstances of the case can influence the definition of the market where there are chains of substitution. AKZO produced organic peroxides, which had multiple uses. They were used in polymer manufacture, where in some fields of application they had limited substitutes but the main organic peroxide, benzoyl peroxide, could also be used as a bleaching agent in flour-milling in the UK and Ireland. AKZO argued that the relevant market should be considered as that for flour additives (where its market share was low). The Commission found that the relevant market was the organic peroxides market as a whole. AKZO's share of the whole peroxides market was 50 per cent. The CJ upheld the Commission's definition of the market because AKZO's conduct—lowering its prices in the flour-milling sector in order to protect its position in the polymer sector—as well as its internal documentation, showed that the undertaking itself treated the market as a single one.

In the extract from *France Télécom*[66] it can be seen at paragraph 79 that the GC explained that a product used for separate purposes may belong to separate markets and that this does not mean that the product, along with all its replacements for the different uses, can be placed in one single market.

f. The Structure of Supply and Demand

The importance of the structure of supply and demand in market definition was first stated in *Michelin I*, paragraph 37.[67]

The *Michelin* cases show that the structure of supply and demand may cause identical products to fall into different markets. It is seen in the extract that the CJ upheld the Commission finding that identical new heavy-vehicle tyres and retreads formed two separate product markets and that the market for the supply of heavy-vehicle tyres to vehicle manufacturers as original equipment was distinct from the market for the supply to dealers to be fitted as replacements. In both cases the EU Courts stressed the difference in the dynamics of the transactions.[68] Conversely, different types of heavy-vehicle tyres, although not substitutes for each other, were in the same market. This was

---

[62] See, e.g., C. W. Baden Fuller, 'Article 86: Economic Analysis of the Existence of a Dominant Position' (1979) 4 *ELRev* 423; and V. Korah, 'Concept of a Dominant Position within the Meaning of Art 86' (1980) 17 *CMLRev* 395.

[63] See Chapter 1, Section 15.B.vii.a, p. 70.

[64] As it has demonstrated in a number of merger cases, such as M.1806, *AstraZeneca/Novartis*.

[65] Case C-62/86, *AKZO* [1991] ECR I-3359.

[66] Section 5.B.i.d, p. 298.

[67] See Section 5.B.i.c, p. 295.

[68] See also Case C-333/94 P, *Tetra Pak International SA v Commission (Tetra Pak II)* [1996] ECR I-5951, para. 13.

because dealers had to stock all tyres and the conditions of competition were the same for all types and dimensions.

Similarly, in *Van den Bergh Foods* the Commission emphasised the structure of supply and demand in finding that the markets for single wrapped individual ice cream and individual portions of soft ice cream were distinct. Although the consumer might perceive the two types of ice cream to be reasonably interchangeable, the competitive conditions under which they were offered to the retail trade were different and distinct. Soft ice cream had, for example, to be processed by the retailer and so required the installation of special processing and dispensing machines; it was not self-service and was not normally branded. Similarly, single wrapped ice cream was distinct from multiple packs of ice cream sold in supermarkets.

> The consumer's point of view is . . . not in every instance the sole criterion in the determination of a product market; nor is an examination limited only to the objective characteristics of the products in question sufficient. The competitive conditions and the structure of supply and demand on the market must also be taken into consideration.[69]

The importance of the structure of supply and demand was stressed in *France Télécom*[70] and in *Clearstream* where primary clearing and settlement services to intermediaries in respect of securities issued under German law was held to be a relevant market.[71]

g. One Product or Market or Two

The question of whether a product is to be considered a single whole or as a number of separate products[72] is illustrated by *Microsoft*.[73] There the Commission took action against Microsoft for infringing Article 102 by 'tying' in that it supplied its Windows desktop operating system with the Windows Media Player ready installed. As the issue of whether products are distinct is inextricably bound up with that of the abuse of tying, it is discussed in Chapter 7.

h. Primary and Secondary Markets (Aftermarkets)

Microsoft concerned complementary products. An 'aftermarket' is a particular instance of complementary products. As explained in Chapter 1, an aftermarket is a product or service which is complementary to, and follows on from, another, such as spare parts,[74] consumables, or maintenance services. Competition issues can arise when the supplier of the original (primary) product or equipment also supplies the product or service in the secondary market, the aftermarket (in some markets the producer makes more money from the sale of consumables than from the original product). There are two possible scenarios.

First, the supplier may not be the only source of products or services in the aftermarket as the primary product may be compatible with different brands.[75] In this situation the supplier may try to ensure that its customers obtain the aftermarket goods or services from itself rather the competitors. Where the supplier is in a dominant position on the market for the primary product the steps it takes to this end may constitute the abuse of 'tying' or 'bundling'. This was so in *Hilti*[76] and

---

[69] [1998] OJ L246/1, para. 133. The decision was upheld on appeal, Case T-65/98, *Van den Bergh Foods Ltd v Commission* [2003] ECR II-4653, aff'd Case C-552/03 P, *Unilever Bestfoods (Ireland) Ltd v Commission* [2006] ECR I-9091, where the definition of the market was not challenged.

[70] Case T-340/03, *France Télécom* [2007] ECR II-107, para. 78.

[71] Case T-301/04, *Clearstream Banking* [2009] ECR II-3155, para. 65.

[72] See Chap. 1, Section 15.B.vii.d, p. 72.

[73] COMP/37.792, 24 March 2004, upheld Case T-201/04, *Microsoft v Commission* [2007] ECR II-3601.

[74] A replacement for an integral part of the original product, produced by the supplier of that product and/or by independent manufacturers. Motor vehicle tyres have never been considered 'spare parts' in this sense.

[75] This means that the primary product producer does not have intellectual property rights (IPRs) which prevent competitors making compatible spare parts or consumables. For refusal to license as an abuse, see Chap. 7.

[76] Case T-30/89, *Hilti AG v Commission* [1991] ECR II-439.

Tetra Pak II.[77] The dominant manufacturer of the primary product may therefore seek to present itself as supplying an indivisible 'system' consisting of the durable primary product and, for example, an ongoing supply of the consumable and a maintenance and repair service. If there is found to be only one product, consisting of the 'system', then tying or bundling is not an issue.

Secondly, the supplier may be the only source of products or services in the aftermarket which are compatible with the primary product. The one brand of spare parts, complements, etc. has no substitutes. In this scenario there are two further possibilities:

- the supplier is dominant on the market for the primary product; or
- the supplier is not dominant on the market for the primary product.

In the first case on spare parts and aftermarkets, *Hugin*,[78] the undertaking was not dominant on the primary market. The Commission defined the market narrowly, finding that the spare parts were a separate market from the original equipment supplied. The justification for this approach is that the original equipment and its spare parts or consumables are not substitutes for one another. The result is that where only the supplier's brand in the aftermarket is compatible with the primary product an undertaking with a small share of the original equipment market may be found to be dominant in the aftermarket and find its behaviour constrained by Article 102. This was what happened in *Hugin* itself.

Hugin was a Swedish producer of cash registers and their spare parts. It had approximately 12 per cent of the Community cash register market. After-sales, maintenance, and repair services of Hugin machines were conducted by local subsidiaries, agents, and distributors in, inter alia, all the Member States. Hugin decided no longer to supply machines or their spare parts to Liptons, a small firm in south-east England which sold, leased, repaired, serviced, and reconditioned cash registers, including Hugin machines. Without the spare parts Liptons could not continue servicing and repairing Hugin machines. The Commission held that the relevant product market consisted of Hugin spare parts required by the independent undertakings which maintained and repaired Hugin cash registers and since Hugin was the sole supplier of those spare parts it was dominant on that market (and had abused its dominance by refusing to continue to supply). The CJ upheld the finding on the relevant market and dominance.[79]

The finding that the market was defined not as the market for spare parts needed by the owners of Hugin machines, but by general repairers and servicers of the machines, is problematic.[80] For example, if the focus of the case was the independent repairer, an analysis was needed of the feasibility of their shifting their business to dealing with other brands of machine. Moreover, the interests of the ultimate consumer—the owners of Hugin machines— were not considered. Nevertheless, the principle established in *Hugin*, that one brand of spare parts can constitute a separate product market for the purposes of Article 102, has been applied in a number of cases, including the motor industry cases, *Volvo*[81] and *Renault*.[82] There it was held that spare parts for cars constitute a separate market from the cars themselves.

The *Hugin* principle was applied to consumables in *Hilti*. Hilti was dominant in the market for nail guns for the construction industry. The guns were used together with cartridge strips and nails. Nails compatible with Hilti guns were made not only by Hilti but by a number of independent firms,

---

[77] *Tetra Pak II*, discussed in text at n. 86.

[78] [1978] OJ L22/23, on appeal Case 22/78, *Hugin Kassaregister AB and Hugin Cash Registers Ltd v Commission* [1979] ECR 1869.

[79] The CJ quashed the Commission finding of abuse on the grounds that it had not been established that there was an effect on inter-Member State trade, see Section 5.E.i.

[80] Baden Fuller, n. 62, 423.

[81] Case 238/87, *AB Volvo v Erik Veng* [1988] ECR 6211.

[82] Case 53/87, *CICCRA v Renault* [1988] ECR 6039.

who complained that Hilti was indulging in practices designed to ensure that purchasers of the guns bought only Hilti's own nails. The Commission held that these practices constituted an abuse.[83] Hilti argued that the consumables were useless without the nail guns and that the guns and consumables formed a 'powder-actuated fastening system' which was in competition with, and in the same market as, other forms of construction fastening systems. Since the nail guns, cartridges, and nails were not distinct but formed one indivisible product, its conduct in 'tying' the sales together could not constitute an abuse. These arguments were rejected the GC.[84]

Case T-30/89, *Hilti AG v Commission* [1991] ECR II-439

General Court

66. The Court takes the view that nail guns, cartridge strips and nails constitute three specific markets. Since cartridge strips and nails are specifically manufactured, and purchased by users, for a single brand of gun, it must be concluded that there are separate markets for Hilti-compatible cartridge strips and nails, as the Commission found in its decision (paragraph 55).

67. With particular regard to the nails whose use in Hilti tools is an essential element of the dispute, it is common ground that since the 1960s there have been independent producers, including the interveners, making nails intended for use in nail guns. Some of those producers are specialized and produce only nails, and indeed some make only nails specifically designed for Hilti tools. That fact in itself is sound evidence that there is a specific market for Hilti-compatible nails.

68. Hilti's contention that guns, cartridge strips and nails should be regarded as forming an indivisible whole, 'a powder-actuated fastening system' is in practice tantamount to permitting producers of nail guns to exclude the use of consumables other than their own branded products in their tools. However, in the absence of general and binding statements or rules, any independent producer is quite free, as far as Community competition law is concerned, to manufacture consumables intended for use in equipment manufactured by others, unless in doing so it infringes a patent or some other industrial or intellectual property right. Even on the assumption that, as the applicant has argued, components of different makes cannot be interchanged without the system characteristics being influenced, the solution should lie in the adoption of appropriate laws and regulations, not in unilateral measures taken by nail gun producers which have the effect of preventing independent producers from pursuing the bulk of their business.

In paragraph 68 the GC states that independent producers are free, as far as competition law is concerned, to manufacture consumables. This statement is revealing of the policy behind the narrow market definition adopted in some of the cases. It is not, as the wording suggests, that competition law *allows* independents to manufacture but that Article 102 may preclude the producer of the original equipment foreclosing others from the market.[85]

In *Tetra Pak II*[86] the Commission refused to accept that Tetra Pak supplied 'systems' and held rather that it operated on four separate product markets. The following extract is from the judgment of the GC, which was confirmed by the CJ.

---

[83] *Eurofix-Bauco v Hilti* [1988] OJ L65/19.

[84] Aff'd Case C-53/92 P, *Hilti AG v Commission* [1994] ECR I-667.

[85] See Chap. 7.

[86] *Elopak Italia/Tetra Pak* [1991] OJ L72/1, upheld Case T-83/91, *Tetra Pak International SA v Commission* [1994] ECR II-755, aff'd Case C-333/94 P, *Tetra Pak II* [1996] ECR I-5951.

Case T-83/91, *Tetra Pak Rausing v Commission* [1994] ECR II-755

Tetra Pak produced aseptic cartons for packaging ultra-heat treated milk and the machines for process-ing the milk and filling the cartons. It also produced non-aseptic cartons for pasteurized (non-aseptic) milk and the machines for pasteurizing the milk and filling those cartons. The Courts confirmed the Commission's finding that there were four product markets concerned: aseptic packaging machines, asep-tic cartons, non-aseptic machines, and non-aseptic cartons.

General Court

82. First, and contrary to the arguments of the applicant, consideration of commercial usage does not support the conclusion that the machinery for packaging a product is indivisible from the cartons. For a considerable time there have been independent manufacturers who specialize in the manufacture of non-aseptic cartons designed for use in machines manufactured by other concerns and who do not manu-facture machinery themselves. It is apparent in particular from the Decision … and not disputed by the applicant, that, until 1987, Elopak, which was set up in 1957, manufactured only cartons and accessory equipment, for example handling equipment. Moreover, also according to the Decision … and not con-tested by the applicant, approximately 12 per cent of the non-aseptic carton sector was shared in 1985 between three companies manufacturing their own cartons, generally under licence and acting, for ma-chinery, only as distributors. In those circumstances, tied sales of machinery and cartons cannot be con-sidered to be in accordance with commercial usage, given that such sales were not the general rule of the non-aseptic sector and that there were only two manufacturers in the aseptic sector, Tetra Pak and PKL.

83. Furthermore, the applicant's argument as to the requirements for the protection of public health and its interests and those of its customers cannot be accepted. It is not for the manufacturers of com-plete systems to decide that, in order to satisfy requirements in the public interest, consumable products such as cartons constitute, with the machines with which they are intended to be used, an inseparable integrated system. According to settled case-law, in the absence of general and binding standards or rules, any independent producer is quite free, as far as Community competition law is concerned, to manufac-ture consumables intended for use in equipment manufactured by others, unless in doing so it infringes a competitor's intellectual property right: see Case T-30/89, *Hilti v. EC Commission* … and Case C-53/92P, *Hilti v. EC Commission* …

84. In those circumstances, whatever the complexity in this case of aseptic filling processes, the pro-tection of public health may be guaranteed by other means, in particular by notifying machine users of the technical specifications with which cartons must comply in order to be compatible with those machines, without infringing manufacturers' intellectual property rights. Moreover, even on the assumption, shared by the applicant, that machinery and cartons from various sources cannot be used together without the characteristics of the system being affected thereby, the remedy must lie in appropriate legislation or regulations, and not in rules adopted unilaterally by manufacturers, which would amount to prohibiting independent manufacturers from conducting the essential part of their business.

85. It follows that the applicant's argument that the markets in machinery for packaging a product and those in packaging cartons are inseparable cannot be accepted.

In *Info-Lab/Ricoh*,[87] however, the Commission held there was no separate market for empty toner cartridges compatible with a specific (Ricoh) photocopy machine. No producer or dealer produced or sold empty toner cartridges. There was no consumer demand for such a product. Rather, car-tridge and powder were always sold together as a single product.

As explained in Chapter 1 it may be that the interaction between the primary market and the aftermarket is such that the primary and secondary products form one single 'system' market and

---

[87] Case IV/36.431, rejection of a complaint by decision: see (1999) 1 *Competition Policy Newsletter* 35.

the competition is between the 'systems' as a whole. Whether this is so mainly depends on the likely reactions of customers to moderate price increases in the aftermarket, so that a separate aftermarket consisting of the secondary products or services of one brand of primary product will be a relevant market only if (a) switching to other brands of secondary products is not possible and (b) there are high switching costs in the market for the primary product.[88] In the *Pelikan/Kyocera* decision[89] the Commission held that Kyocera was not dominant in the aftermarket for its own brand of printer cartridges because customers made purchasing decisions based on whole-life costs and commonly used the 'total cost per page' criterion when choosing a printer. Printers are a product where the long-term costs in the aftermarket significantly exceed those for the primary product.[90] The Commission did not expressly state that this was a 'systems' market, but did find that the intense competition on the primary market so restrained Kyocera's behaviour on the aftermarket that it could not be dominant on the latter. This, in effect, amounted to the same thing.[91] The Commission applied the principles in *Pelikan/Kyocera* to another printers-and-cartridges case, *EFIM*, in which it rejected a complaint alleging that the conduct of four manufacturers of inkjet printers illegally excluded competitors from the aftermarket. It held that purchasers of printers were well informed about the prices for consumables and that such was the balance between the capital cost of the printer and the total cost of consumables over the printer's lifetime that consumers had a strong incentive to switch printer brand were the price of consumables for that brand to rise. The primary market was intensely competitive and therefore, 'even if' each of the various markets for cartridges constituted separate relevant markets, the manufacturers were not dominant on their respective aftermarkets.[92]

The Commission found a different situation on the mainframe computer market in its *IBM Maintenance Services* Commitments Decision where it held that the conditions as to the lack of ability of customers to switch to other brands of secondary products, and the presence of high switching costs in the primary product market, were fulfilled. There was therefore a separate aftermarket on which IBM was dominant.[93]

i. Markets for Raw Materials and Inputs

In *Commercial Solvents* it was held that a raw material, aminobutanol, used to produce ethambutol, an anti-TB drug, constituted a product market of its own.[94] Zoja manufactured ethambutol from aminobutanol which had been manufactured by Commercial Solvents. Other, non-ethambutol-based, anti-TB drugs were on the market. The CJ held that the relevant market was not the market for the derivatives (the drugs) but the market for the raw material. There may have been substitute drugs which could be used to combat TB but a manufacturer of ethambutol, such as Zoja, could not operate without aminobutanol.[95]

---

[88] See Case T-427/08, *CEAHR v Commission* [2010] ECR II-5865; F. Domanico and M. Angeli, 'An Analysis of the IBM Commitment Decision concerning the aftermarket for IBM mainframe computers' (2012) 1 *Competition Policy Newsletter*.

[89] *Pelikan/Kyocera*, see Commission's *XXVth Report on Competition Policy* (1995), pp. 41–42.

[90] Apparently, volume for volume, ink in toner cartridges is more expensive than the finest champagne.

[91] See also *Info-Lab/Ricoh*, Case IV/36.431.

[92] COMP/39.391, *EFIM*, rejection decision 20 May 2009; upheld Case T-296/09, *European Federation of Ink and Ink Cartridge Manufacturers (EFIM) v Commission* [2011] ECR II-425, aff'd Case C-59/12 P, *EFIM v Commission* EU:C:2013:575.

[93] COMP/39.692, *IBM Maintenance Services*, 13 December 2011. The aftermarket consisted of inputs needed to provide maintenance services for IBM mainframes which could not be sourced outside IBM, and for maintenance services for the mainframes.

[94] Cases 6 and 7/73, *Istituto Chemioterapico Italiano SpA and Commercial Solvents Corp v Commission (Commercial Solvents)* [1974] ECR 223.

[95] Other possible ways of producing ethambutol, using thiophenol or butatone, were dismissed by the CJ as they were uncertain and experimental and had not been used on an industrial scale.

The concept developed in *Commercial Solvents*, that a raw material (or any 'input') can be distinguished from the derivative produced with, or from, it has proved of great importance in the Article 102 jurisprudence. The raw material in *Commercial Solvents* was an input into a production process and had been previously sold by Commercial Solvents to Zoja. The question has arisen, however, as to whether there can be a market in an 'input' which the producer of the 'input' does not offer for sale but uses only for its own purposes. In *Magill*[96] the CJ upheld the Commission's definition of a market in 'television listings' although the broadcasting companies did not sell them for publication. In *Bronner*[97] the CJ accepted that there could be a market in schemes for the home delivery of newspapers even though the undertaking concerned had developed its scheme solely to distribute its own newspapers and did not 'sell' it independently. In *IMS*[98] the CJ said that there could be a 'potential' or 'hypothetical' market in inputs which a dominant undertaking decided not to market independently. In that case the 'input' was a system for representing pharmaceutical sales data over which the undertaking claimed copyright. The undertaking used it to produce the sales reports it sold to pharmaceutical companies. There was no suggestion that the undertaking had ever contemplated 'selling' (licensing) the scheme to others. Nevertheless, the CJ found that there could be a 'market' for it. All that is needed is that two stages of production can be identified. In *Microsoft* the 'input' was the IPRs over its Windows technology.[99] The point can be of great importance in cases (such as *Magill*, *Bronner*, *IMS*, and *Microsoft*) where the alleged abuse is a refusal to supply, because there can be such an abuse only where two markets are involved and the undertaking is dominant in the upstream market.[100]

j. Markets in the Pharmaceutical Sector

The general principles of market definition in the pharmaceutical sector are explained in Chapter 1. They are illustrated by *AstraZeneca*.[101] There the Commission defined the relevant market as consisting of proton pump inhibitors (PPIs) used for the treatment of acid-related gastrointestinal conditions. PPIs act by operating directly on the proton pump (PP) which pumps acid into the stomach. From the early 1990s it was accepted by the scientific community that PPIs are superior to the previous treatment by antihistamines (H2 blockers) which block only one of the stimulants of the PP (the histamine receptors in the parietal cells). From then on sales of PPIs gradually increased at the expense of sales of H2 blockers. In *AstraZeneca* the issue was whether H2 blockers and other ulcer medicines exert such competitive pressure on PPIs that they should be considered part of the same market. They treat the same condition but with different therapeutic effects (although only PPIs are effective in respect of some of the most serious conditions). The Commission concluded that the market should be defined as that for PPIs. The fact that the replacement of H2 blockers by PPIs as the treatment of choice was only gradual was caused not by competitive constraints from the former but by the conservative caution of prescribing doctors. Doctors and patients were not sensitive to relative price changes. The GC, affirmed by the CJ, therefore held that the Commission was entitled to take the view that, in principle, the gradual nature of the increase in sales of a new product substituting for an existing product cannot in itself suffice to conclude that the existing product exercises a significant competitive constraint over the new one.[102] The GC pointed out that the issue in the case

[96] Cases C-241–242/91 P, *RTE & ITP v Commission (Magill)* [1995] ECR I-743.

[97] Case C-7/97, *Oscar Bronner* [1998] ECR I-7791.

[98] Case C-418/01, *IMS Health GmbH & Co OHG v NDC Health GmbH & Co KG* [2004] ECR I-503, paras. 43–44.

[99] Case T-201/04, *Microsoft* [2007] ECR II-3601, para. 335.

[100] See Chap. 7, Section 13.

[101] COMP/37.507, 15 June 2005, upheld Case T-321/05, *AstraZeneca v Commission* [2010] ECR II-2805, *aff'd* Case C-457/10 P, *AstraZeneca* EU:C:2012:770.

[102] Case T-321/05, *AstraZeneca* [2010] ECR II-2805, para. 90.

was concerned only with whether PPIs were subject to competitive constraints, and not with any competitive constraints that PPIs might have exercised over other products.[103]

k. Markets on the Buying Side (Procurement Markets)

It is possible for a buyer to be in a dominant position. The complications of market definition in such situations are illustrated by a case which concerned BA's system of rewards to travel agents for selling BA tickets. BA is a supplier of services—air travel. However, like any other supplier it must also *purchase* goods and services as inputs into its business. The issue in the case was BA's relationship with travel agents. The Commission held that the travel agents supplied a service to BA by selling tickets for BA flights.[104] That service, 'air travel agency services' in the UK, was a relevant market. The Commission found that BA was the dominant buyer in this market and that it had abused its dominance. It concentrated not on BA as a provider of air transport services to persons wanting to fly, but on BA as a buyer of services from numerous travel agents. BA argued that the market identified by the Commission did not really exist and that even if it did it was not the relevant market to consider here. It claimed that the Commission should have looked instead at its position on the air transport market. The GC upheld the Commission's definition of the market.[105]

Case T-219/99, *British Airways plc v Commission* [2003] ECR II-5917

General Court

89. The Commission took the view in the contested decision that the product market to be taken into consideration, for the purposes of establishing the dominant position of BA, is comprised by the services which airlines purchase from travel agents for the purposes of marketing and distributing their airline tickets (recital 72). In the Commission's view, that practice by airlines has the effect of creating a market for air travel agency services distinct from the air transport markets.

90. The Commission has also taken the view that the relevant geographic market in this case was the territory of the United Kingdom, given the national dimension of travel agents' business.

91. According to settled case-law (Case 322/81 *Michelin* v. *Commission*...paragraph 37; Case T-65/96 *Kish Glass* v. *Commission*...paragraph 62, confirmed on appeal by order of the Court of Justice in Case C-241/00 P *Kish Glass* v. *Commission*...), for the purposes of investigating the possibly dominant position of an undertaking on a given product market, the possibilities of competition must be judged in the context of the market comprising the totality of the products or services which, with respect to their characteristics, are particularly suitable for satisfying constant needs and are only to a limited extent interchangeable with other products or services. Moreover, since the determination of the relevant market is useful in assessing whether the undertaking concerned is in a position to prevent effective competition from being maintained and behave to an appreciable extent independently of its competitors and, in this case, its service providers, an examination to that end cannot be limited to the objective characteristics only of the relevant services, but the competitive conditions and the structure of supply and demand on the market must also be taken into consideration.

92. It is clear from BA's pleadings that it itself acknowledges the existence of an independent market for air travel agency services, since it states in paragraph 11.34 of its application that travel agents themselves

---

[103] Ibid., para. 97.

[104] COMP/34.780, *Virgin/BA* [2000] OJ L30/1.

[105] And also the finding of a dominant position, see Section 6.B.vi, p. 325, and the Commission's controversial finding of abuse: see Chap. 7. The GC's judgment was affirmed Case C-95/04 P, *British Airways* [2007] ECR I-2331, where the market definition point was not appealed.

operate in a competitive market, competing with each other to provide the best possible service to their customers.

93. In that regard, although travel agents act on behalf of the airlines, which assume all the risks and advantages connected with the transport service itself and which conclude contracts for transport directly with travellers, they nevertheless constitute independent intermediaries carrying on an independent business of providing services (see, to that effect, the judgment in *VVR*...[106] at paragraph 20).

94. As the Commission states in recital 31 of the contested decision, that specific business of travel agents consists, on the one hand, in advising potential travellers, reserving and issuing airline tickets, (and) collecting the price of the transport and remitting it to the airlines, and, on the other hand, in providing those airlines with advertising and commercial promotion services.

95. In that regard, BA itself states that travel agents are and will remain, in the short term at least, a vital distribution channel for airlines, allowing them efficiently to sell seats on the flights they offer, and that there is a mutual dependence between travel agents and airlines which are not in themselves in a position to market their air transport services effectively.

96. As BA has also stated, travel agents offer a wider range of air routes, departure times and arrival times than any airline could. Travel agents filter information concerning various flights for the benefit of travellers faced with the proliferation of different air transport fare structures, which arise from the real-time pricing systems operated by airlines.

97. BA has further recognised that the role which travel agents play in the distribution of airline tickets explains why airlines seek to offer them advantages so that they sell seats on their flights. The irreplaceable nature of the services which travel agents provide to airlines is thus borne out by all the payments which the airlines make to them.

98. Finally, BA has itself emphasised that major travel agents individually negotiate agreements for the distribution of air tickets and that they are thus in a position to set the airlines in competition.

99. That specific nature of the services provided to airlines by travel agents, without any serious possibility of the airlines substituting themselves for the agents in order to carry out the same services themselves, is corroborated by the fact that, at the time of the events of which complaint is made, 85 per cent of air tickets sold in the territory of the United Kingdom were sold through the intermediary of travel agents.

100. The Court therefore considers that the services of air travel agencies represent an economic activity for which, at the time of the contested decision, airlines could not substitute another form of distribution of their tickets, and that they therefore constitute a market for services distinct from the air transport market.

101. With regard to the fact that the restrictions on competition which the Commission imputes to BA's performance reward schemes arise from the position which BA holds in its capacity not as supplier but as purchaser of air travel agency services, this is irrelevant having regard to the definition of the market in question. Article [102] applies both to undertakings whose possible dominant position is established, as in this case, in relation to their suppliers and to those which are capable of being in the same position in relation to their customers.

102. BA itself acknowledged at the hearing, moreover, that it is possible both for a seller and for a purchaser to hold a dominant position within the meaning of Article [102].

103. BA cannot therefore validly argue that, in order to define the product market in question, with a view to assessing the effects on competition of the financial advantages which it allows to travel agents established in the United Kingdom, it is necessary to determine whether a single supplier of air transportation services on a particular route can profitably increase its prices.

---

[106] This is a reference to Case 311/87, *VZW Vereniging van Vlaamse Reisbureaus v VZW Sociale Dienst van de Plaatselijke en Gewestelijke Overheidsdiensten* [1987] ECR 3801, which concerned price-fixing amongst Belgian travel agents.

104. Such a parameter, which might be relevant in relation to each airline, is not of such a kind as to enable measurement of BA's economic strength in its capacity not as provider of air transport services but as purchaser of travel agency services, on all routes to and from United Kingdom airports, either in relation to all other airlines regarded in the same capacity as purchasers of air travel agency services or in relation to travel agents established in the United Kingdom.

105. BA's objections to the relevance of the product market adopted by the Commission, based on the possible marginalisation of the distribution of airline tickets through the intermediary of travel agents, on the exclusive specialisation of airlines by geographical destinations, and on the independent behaviour of an airline in a monopoly situation on certain routes, therefore have no bearing.

106. Those arguments are based on situations which are either hypothetical or foreign to the conditions of competition operating in the product market in question constituted by air travel agency services, both between the agents providing those services and between the airlines using them.

107. The Commission did not therefore make any error of assessment in defining the relevant product market as that for services provided by travel agents in favour of airlines, for the purposes of establishing whether BA holds a dominant position on that market in its capacity as bidder for those services.

l. Markets in the New Economy and Multi-sided Markets

We discuss the problems of market definition in the new economy, where network effects are commonly found, and of two- (or multi-)sided platforms, in Chapter 1.[107] The Commission has embarked upon an action against Google, alleging it has infringed Article 102 in respect of the operation of its vertical search engine. The definition of the market can be expected to be a major feature of any decision in that case.[108]

(ii) Supply Substitution

In *Continental Can* the CJ held that the market must be defined from the supply side as well as the demand side. In that case the Commission found three separate markets consisting of different types of metal containers for food packaging. The Court found that the Commission had not explained why these products were in separate markets and were not all part of a larger light metal container market. In particular, it had not set out why competitors could not enter the identified markets by a simple adaptation of their production facilities.

Case 6/72, *Europemballage Corp and Continental Can Co Inc v Commission* [1973] ECR 215

Court of Justice

32. For the appraisal of SLW's dominant position and the consequences of the disputed merger, the definition of the relevant market is of essential significance, for the possibilities of competition can only be judged in relation to those characteristics of the products in question by virtue of which those products are particularly apt to satisfy an inelastic need and are only to a limited extent interchangeable with other products.

33. In this context recitals Nos 5 to 7 of the second part of the decision deal in turn with a 'market for light containers for canned meat products', a 'market for light containers for canned seafood', and a

---

[107] Chapter 1, Section 15.B.vii.h and i, p. 73 ff.

[108] COMP/39.740, *Google*, IP/15/4780, MEMO/15/4781 (SO).

'market for metal closures for the food packing industry, other than crown corks', all allegedly dominated by SLW and in which the disputed merger threatens to eliminate competition. The decision does not, however, give any details of how these three markets differ from each other, and must therefore be considered separately. Similarly, nothing is said about how these three markets differ from the general market for light metal containers, namely the market for metal containers for fruit and vegetables, condensed milk, olive oil, fruit juices and chemico-technical products. In order to be regarded as constituting a distinct market, the products in question must be individualized, not only by the mere fact that they are used for packing certain products, but by particular characteristics of production which make them specifically suitable for this purpose. Consequently, a dominant position on the market for light metal containers for meat and fish cannot be decisive, as long as it has not been proved that competitors from other sectors of the market for light metal containers are not in a position to enter this market, by a simple adaptation, with sufficient strength to create a serious counterweight.

The CJ also held that the Commission should not have dismissed the possibility of the customers themselves commencing manufacture of their own cans.[109]

Subsequent to *Continental Can* it is common for supply-side substitution to be considered. For example, in *Michelin*[110] the CJ held that there was no elasticity of supply between tyres for heavy vehicles and car tyres 'owing to significant differences in production techniques and in the plant and tools needed for their manufacture. The fact that time and considerable investment are required in order to modify production plant for the manufacture of light-vehicle tyres instead of heavy-vehicle tyres or vice versa means that there is no discernible relationship between the two categories of tyre enabling production to be adapted to demand on the market.' Similarly, in *Tetra Pak I*[111] the Commission dismissed the feasibility of supply-side substitution. Manufacturers of other types of milk-packaging machinery were not readily able to switch to producing aseptic packaging machinery and cartons. In *Clearstream* the GC said the Commission was correct in finding that no other institution could provide in the near future the full clearing and settlement services for securities issued under German law, given that the undertaking concerned was the final depository for 90 per cent of all existing German securities.[112]

The difficulty is to distinguish supply-side substitution from potential competition, which is considered at the stage of assessing market power on the defined market.[113] In Chapter 1 it was seen that the Commission considers in the Market Definition Notice, paragraphs 20–23, that supply substitution is relevant to market definition only when a supplier is able to switch production in the short term without incurring significant additional costs or risks. Only where the impact is effective and immediate is it equivalent to the demand substitution effect. The GC said in *Atlantic Container Line*:

Although potential competition and supply-side substitution are conceptually different issues ... those issues overlap in part, as the distinction lies primarily in whether the restriction of competition is immediate or not.[114]

---

[109] Case 6/72, *Continental Can* [1973] ECR 215, para. 36.

[110] Case 322/81, *Michelin I* [1983] ECR 3461, para. 41. The issue of supply substitutability was not addressed in the decision, [1981] OJ L353/33.

[111] *TetraPak (BTG Licence)* [1988] OJ L272/27, paras. 36–38, upheld Case T-51/89, *Tetra Pak Rausing SA v Commission (Tetra Pak I)* [1990] ECR II-309 where the market definition was not challenged.

[112] Case T-301/04, *Clearstream* [2009] ECR II-3155, paras. 58–63.

[113] The approach in the US is to take no account of supply-side substitutability at the market definition stage but to consider other undertakings switching production only at the next stage.

[114] Cases T-191 and 212–214/98, *Atlantic Container Line v Commission* [2003] ECR II-3275, para. 834.

Although it could be argued that it does not matter *when* the possibility of other producers switching is considered so long as it *is* considered, the reliance EU law places on market shares makes the proper definition of the market crucial.

C. THE GEOGRAPHIC MARKET

We saw in Chapter 1 that the relevant market has a geographic as well as a product dimension and that the Market Definition Notice explains at length how the geographic market is determined.[115]

It is clear from the case law that legal regulation may create national markets, as in the type-approval certificate cases.[116] In some cases an undertaking has a statutory monopoly. In *AKZO*[117] the geographic market was defined by the fact that the UK and Ireland were the only Member States which permitted the use of bleaching agents in flour. Narrow geographic markets may be created through factors such as EU regulation (as was the case with sugar),[118] high transport costs, language, marketing infrastructures, consumer preference,[119] or national or local regulations.[120] In cases involving the transport sector narrow geographic markets have been defined (in these cases the geographic and product markets may in effect be the same). The Commission has, for example, defined as separate markets the air route between Dublin and Heathrow,[121] the air route between Brussels and Luton,[122] and in *Sealink/B&I Holyhead: Interim Measures* the ferry route between Holyhead and Dun Laoghaire.[123] In the latter decision the Commission distinguished the 'northern', 'southern', and 'central' corridor routes between Great Britain and Ireland. Further, within the 'central corridor' it distinguished the Liverpool and Holyhead routes, concluding that 'potential competition from Liverpool does not constrain the market power of Sealink at Holyhead'.

One of the most notorious cases on the geographic market is *Michelin I* where the CJ upheld the Commission's finding that there was a separate market for heavy-vehicle new replacement tyres in the Netherlands.

Case 322/81, *Nederlandsche Banden-Industrie Michelin v Commission* [1983] ECR 3461

Court of Justice

23. The applicant's first submission under this head challenges the Commission's finding that the substantial part of the common market on which it holds a dominant position is the Netherlands. Michelin NV maintains that this geographical definition of the market is too narrow. It is contradicted by the fact that the Commission itself based its decision on factors concerning the Michelin group as a whole such as its

---

[115] See Chap. 1, Section 15.B.viii, p. 75 ff.

[116] Case 26/75, *General Motors v EC Commission* [1975] ECR 1367; Case 226/84, *British Leyland v Commission* [1986] ECR 3263.

[117] Case C-62/86, *AKZO* [1991] ECR I-3359.

[118] See *Napier Brown-British Sugar* [1988] OJ L284/41; *Irish Sugar* [1997] OJ L258/1.

[119] In the merger case *Nestlé/Perrier* [1992] OJ L356/1 (see Chap. 15), for example, the Commission found that the relevant geographic market for mineral water was limited to France. Irrespective of European integration, French consumers obstinately continued to choose local products.

[120] As in *DSD*, Case C-385/07 P, *Der Grüne Punkt—Duales System Deutschland GmbH v Commission* [2009] ECR I-6155, which concerned the German recycling regime. In Case 27/76, *United Brands* [1978] ECR 207 the geographic market in the EEC was held not to include France, the UK, or Italy because of their special import regimes for bananas, stemming in the case of the first two from their former colonial ties.

[121] *British Midland v Aer Lingus* [1992] OJ L96/34.

[122] *London European-Sabena* [1988] OJ L317/47.

[123] IV/34.174, 11 June 1992.

technological lead and financial strength which, in the applicant's view, relate to a much wider market or even the world market. The activities of Michelin NV's main competitors are world-wide too.

24. The Commission maintains that this objection concerns less the definition of the market than the criteria used to establish the existence of a dominant position. Since tyre manufacturers have on the whole chosen to sell their products on the various national markets through the intermediary of national subsidiaries, the competition faced by Michelin NV is on the Netherlands market.

25. The point to be made in this regard is that the Commission addressed its decision not to the Michelin group as a whole but only to its Netherlands subsidiary whose activities are concentrated on the Netherlands market. It has not been disputed that Michelin NV's main competitors also carry on their activities in the Netherlands through Netherlands subsidiaries of their respective groups.

26. The Commission's allegation concerns Michelin NV's conduct towards tyre dealers and more particularly its discount policy. In this regard the commercial policy of the various subsidiaries of the groups competing at the European or even the world level is generally adapted to the specific conditions existing on each market. In practice dealers established in the Netherlands obtain their supplies only from suppliers operating in the Netherlands. The Commission was therefore right to take the view that the competition facing Michelin NV is mainly on the Netherlands market and that it is at that level that the objective conditions of competition are alike for traders.

27. This finding is not related to the question whether in such circumstances factors relating to the position of the Michelin group and its competitors as a whole and to a much wider market may enter into consideration in the adoption of a decision as to whether a dominant position exists on the relevant product market.

28. Hence the relevant substantial part of the common market in this case is the Netherlands and it is at the level of the Netherlands market that Michelin NV's position must be assessed.

The question whether or not customers could easily have bought Michelin or other tyres outside the Netherlands was not asked. Rather, the geographic market appears to have been confined to the area in which the Commission found that the abuse had been committed.[124]

In some cases the EU Courts have been more sceptical about narrowly drawn markets. In *Alsatel v Novasam*,[125] for example, it did not accept that the evidence established that a particular region of France, rather than the country as a whole, was the geographic market for telephonic installations. In *BPB*,[126] however, a national market was found despite the existence of pressure from imports from elsewhere. The market was defined as being just the UK and Ireland.

In *Michelin II*[127] the Commission was careful to devote considerable attention to the delineation of the geographic market. Taking into account the CJ's judgment of 1983 the company argued that the new replacement tyre market was no longer national but had become international in the intervening years. The Commission refuted this. It said that what mattered was 'to assess the real capacity of dealers to obtain supplies from outside their national territory and the similarities or differences in the supply structure'.[128] Michelin argued that 'the structure of competition on the replacement tyre market is worldwide: the main players . . . compete on a world scale'.[129] The Commission denied that this situation implied that there were not national markets:

123. The argument that the largest international tyre producers compete in numerous countries and across the European Union in no way means that it can be supposed that the relevant geographic market is the

---

[124] Bishop and Walker, n. 5, para. 4.70. See also the criticism in V. Korah, 'The Michelin Decision of the Commission' (1982) 7 *ELRev* 130.

[125] Case 247/86 [1988] ECR 5987.

[126] *BPB Industries* [1989] OJ L10/50, upheld Case T-65/89, *BPB Industries and British Gypsum Ltd v Commission* [1993] ECR II-389, *aff'd* Case C-310/93 P, *BPB Industries plc and British Gypsum Ltd v Commission* [1995] ECR I-865.

[127] *Michelin* [2001] OJ L143/1.

[128] Ibid., para. 124.

[129] Ibid., para. 121.

world market. This situation is perfectly compatible with the existence of conditions of competition that are appreciably different in each of the relevant countries. This was already the situation in the tyre industry at the time, when the Court of Justice found that the Dutch new replacement tyre market was a national market.

The Commission took into account the fact that the large manufacturers still organised their distribution and sales along national lines;[130] that there were considerable differences in the large manufacturers' market shares from country to country which 'are hardly compatible with the theory of a European market characterised by homogeneous competition';[131] and that there were appreciable price differences from country to country.[132] It also rejected the argument that the hauliers could easily purchase their tyres from abroad if they wished: among the reasons for this was the structure of the road haulage industry in France which was composed in the main of small firms[133] which meant, inter alia, that they were unlikely to have the resources to surmount the linguistic obstacles to intra-Community trade.[134] As far as the retread market was concerned the Commission held that since the retread market was a market for the provision of *services* rather than goods 'it is a national market and therefore at most of national dimension'. Moreover there were differences in the structure of demand within the Community which helped to set the French market apart, including the fact that in France the predominant method of retreading was 'mould-cure' and custom retreading, rather than 'precure' treading.[135]

In *British Airways* geographic market definition arose in a case involving the dominance of a buyer, not a supplier. As we have seen, the GC upheld the Commission's definition of the product market as being air travel agency services. The geographic market was defined as the UK.[136]

Case T-219/99, *British Airways plc v Commission* [2003] ECR II-5917

General Court

108. As for the geographic market to be taken into consideration, consistent case-law shows that it may be defined as the territory in which all traders operate in the same or sufficiently homogeneous conditions of competition in so far as concerns specifically the relevant products or services, without it being necessary for those conditions to be perfectly homogeneous (Case T-83/91 *Tetra Pak* v. *Commission*...paragraph 91, confirmed on appeal by judgment in Case C-333/94 P *Tetra Pak* v. *Commission* (*Tetra Pak II*)...).

109. It can hardly be denied that, in the overwhelming majority of cases, travellers reserve airline tickets in their country of residence. Although BA has argued that not all tickets sold by travel agents in the United Kingdom are necessarily sold to residents of that country, it has acknowledged that transactions taking place outside the United Kingdom could not be quantified.

110. Moreover, as the Commission has stated in recital 83 of the contested decision, without challenge from BA, IATA's rules on the order of using the coupons in airline tickets prevent tickets sold outside the territory of the United Kingdom from being used for flights departing from United Kingdom airports.

---

[130] Ibid., paras. 125–131.

[131] Ibid., para. 133.

[132] Ibid., paras. 134–141.

[133] 'Micro-enterprises' in EU-speak, see *Michelin* [2001] OJ L143/1, para. 144.

[134] Ibid., para. 144.

[135] Ibid., para. 157. Mould-cure involves industrial retreading plants and, unlike the precure method, usually requires an intermediary between the retreader and the haulier.

[136] Under IATA rules tickets bought outside the UK could not be used to depart from non-UK airports.

111. Since the distribution of airline tickets takes place at national level, it follows that airlines normally purchase the services for distributing those tickets on a national basis, as is shown by the agreements signed to that end by BA with travel agents established in the United Kingdom.

112. Nor has any doubt been cast on the fact that airlines structure their commercial services at the national level, that travel agents' handling of air tickets is carried out in the context of IATA's national plans for bank settlement and, in this case, through the Billing and Settlement Plan for the United Kingdom (BSPUK).

113. Nor has BA challenged the Commission's statement that BA applies its performance reward schemes to travel agents established in the United Kingdom in a uniform manner over the whole of the territory of that Member State.

114. Nor has BA denied that the disputed financial incentives apply only to sales of BA tickets carried out in the United Kingdom, even if those incentives form part of agreements concluded with travel agents whose activities extend to more than one Member State.

115. Contrary to what BA maintains, the fact that BA concludes global agreements with certain travel agents is not capable of establishing that the latter increasingly deal with airlines on the international level. As is shown in recital 20 of the contested decision, which BA has not challenged, those global agreements were signed with only three travel agents and only for the winter season 1992/1993. Moreover, those agreements were merely added to local agreements made in the countries concerned.

116. It does not therefore appear that the Commission erred in defining the relevant geographic market as the United Kingdom market, for the purposes of demonstrating that BA held a dominant position on that market in its capacity as the purchaser of air travel agency services provided by agents established in the United Kingdom.

117. The plea alleging incorrect definition of the relevant product and geographic market cannot therefore be accepted.

Again the difficulty involved in defining the geographic market, as when defining product markets, can be tempered if competition from outside the market is taken into account when assessing market power. If that is done, over-narrow market definitions and the rather artificial distinction between market definition and market power assessment are not so misleading. However, the size, financial strength, and degree of diversification of competitors at world level does not necessarily deprive an undertaking of dominance in the relevant geographical market.

D. THE TEMPORAL MARKET

The temporal dimension of the market is often ignored and the Market Definition Notice does not refer to it. Many markets do not have a temporal dimension.[137] It can, however, be relevant when considering transport markets, for example.[138] In such markets the temporal dimension may in fact be an inherent part of the definition of the product market.

In *United Brands*[139] there was evidence that the demand for bananas fluctuated from season to season depending on the availability of other fruits. This suggested that there were different seasonal markets and that in the summer at least bananas were part of a wider fruit market. The Commission disregarded this evidence and defined a single year-round market consisting only of bananas. The CJ

---

[137] Case 322/81, *Michelin I* [1983] ECR 3461, para. 59.

[138] See Cases T-374–375, 384, and 388/94, *European Night Services v Commission* [1998] ECR II-3141, Chap. 1, Section 15.B.ix, p. 78.

[139] Case 27/76, *United Brands* [1978] ECR 207.

did not pursue the issue. In *ABG Oil*[140] the Commission looked at the oil market just in the period of the OPEC crisis in the 1970s.

E. THE *TETRA PAK II* CASE

Tetra Pak II[141] is set out here as a good illustration of the complexities of market definition and of the application of the principles of demand substitution. The aftermarket aspect of the case has already been discussed.[142] The following extract deals with the issue of the interchangeability of different forms of packaging. The GC judgment was affirmed by the CJ.

Case T-83/91, *Tetra Pak Rausing v Commission* [1994] ECR II-755

Tetra Pak produced aseptic cartons for packaging ultra-heat treated milk and the machines for processing the milk and filling the cartons. It also produced non-aseptic cartons for pasteurised (non-aseptic) milk and the machines for pasteurising the milk and filling those cartons. The GC confirmed the Commission's finding that there were four product markets concerned: aseptic packaging machines, aseptic cartons, non-aseptic machines, and non-aseptic cartons.

General Court

64. In this case, the 'interchangeability' of aseptic packaging systems with non-aseptic systems and of systems using cartons with those using other materials must be assessed in the light of all the competitive conditions on the general market in systems for packaging liquid food products. Accordingly, in the specific context of this case, the applicant's approach of dividing that general market into differentiated sub-markets depending on whether the packaging systems are used for packaging milk, dairy products other than milk or non-dairy products by virtue of the specific characteristics of the packaging of those different categories of products, in which the possibility exists that various kinds of substitutable equipment may be used, would lead to a compartmentalization of the market which would not reflect economic reality. There is a comparable structure of supply and demand for both aseptic and non-aseptic machinery and cartons, however they are used, since all belong to one sector, the packaging of liquid food products. Whether they are used for packaging milk or other products, aseptic and non-aseptic machinery and cartons not only share the same characteristics of production but also satisfy identical economic needs. In addition, a not insignificant proportion of Tetra's Pak's customers operate in both the milk sector and the fruit juice sector, as the applicant has admitted. In all those respects, therefore, this case is distinguishable from the situation contemplated in Case 85/76, *Hoffmann-La Roche* v. *EC Commission*…relied on by the applicant, in which the Court of Justice had first considered the possibility of finding that there were two separate markets for one product which, unlike in this case, was used in two ways in wholly distinct sectors, one 'bio-nutritive' and the other 'technological'…Furthermore, as both parties have submitted, Tetra Pak machinery and cartons of the same type were uniformly priced whether they were intended for packaging milk or other products, which confirms that they belong to a single product market. There is accordingly no need, contrary to the applicant's arguments, to find that there are differentiated sub-markets for packaging systems of the same type depending on whether they are used for packaging a particular category of products.

65. Accordingly, in order to ascertain whether the four markets defined in the Decision were indeed separate markets during the period in question, it is necessary—as the Commission submits—to determine

---

[140] [1977] OJ L117/1 (the decision was annulled on appeal on the abuse issue: Case 77/77, *Benzine Petroleum Handelsmaatschappij BV v Commission* [1978] ECR 1513, see Chap. 7).

[141] *Elopak Italia/Tetra Pak* [1992] OJ L72/1, upheld by the GC, and by the CJ, Case C-333/94 P, *Tetra Pak II* [1996] ECR I-5951. See V. Korah, 'The Paucity of Economic Analysis in the EEC Decisions on Competition—*Tetra Pak II*' [1993] *CLP* 148.

[142] See Section 5.B.i.h, p. 304 ff.

in particular which products were sufficiently interchangeable with aseptic and non-aseptic machinery and cartons in the predominant milk sector. To the extent that the carton-packaging systems were used primarily for packaging milk, a dominant position in that sector was sufficient evidence, if relevant, of a dominant position on the market as a whole. Any such dominant position could not be called in question by the existence of substitutable equipment, alleged by the applicant, in the non-milk product packaging sector, since such equipment accounted for only a very small proportion of all products packaged in cartons during the period covered by the Decision. The predominance of the milk-packaging sector is clearly demonstrated by data given in the Decision (recital 6) and not disputed by the applicant...Those figures indicate that, notwithstanding a decrease, the majority of Tetra Pak aseptic cartons were used for packaging milk during the period in question. As for non-aseptic cartons, 100 per cent were used for packaging milk until 1980 and 99 per cent thereafter, according to the same source. For all those reasons, the Commission was entitled to take the view that it was not necessary to carry out a separate analysis of the non-milk-packaging sector.

66. In the milk-packaging sector, the Commission correctly based itself, in this case, on the test of sufficient substitutability of the different systems for packaging liquid foods, as laid down by the Court of Justice: see in particular Case 6/72, *Europemballage and Continental Can* v. *EC Commission* ... and Case 85/76 *Hoffmann La Roche* v. *EC Commission*...It is also in accordance with case-law (see Joined Cases 6 & 7/73, *Commercial Solvents* v. *EC Commission)* that the Commission applied the test of sufficient substitutability of products at the stage of the packaging systems themselves, which constitute the market in intermediate products on which Tetra Pak's position must be assessed, and not at the stage of the finished products, in this case the packaged liquid food products.

67. In order to assess the interchangeability for packers of the packaging systems, the Commission necessarily had to take account of the repercussions of the final consumers' demand on the packers' intermediate demand. It found that the packers could influence consumer habits in the choice of types of product packaging only by promotion and publicity in a long and costly process, extending over several years, as Tetra Pak had expressly acknowledged in its reply to the statement of objections. In those circumstances, the various types of packaging could not be considered to be sufficiently interchangeable for packers, whatever their bargaining power, referred to by the applicant.

68. It is therefore exclusively to assess the effect of final demand on the packers' intermediate demand that the Commission referred to the lack of perfect substitutability, which concerned only the packaged products and not the packaging systems. In particular, the Commission correctly considered that, because of the small proportion of the retail price of milk accounted for by the cost of its packaging, 'small but significant changes in the relative price of the different packages would not be sufficient to trigger off shifts between the different types of milk with which they are associated because the substitution of different milks is less than perfect' (decision in *Tetra Pak I*...). The applicant's complaints that the Commission based itself on the model of perfect competition and defined the relevant markets solely by reference to consumer demand must accordingly be rejected.

69. The [General Court] therefore holds first that the Commission was entitled to find that during the period in question there was not sufficient interchangeability between machinery for aseptic packaging in cartons and machinery for non-aseptic packaging whatever the material used. At the level of demand, aseptic systems are distinguished by their inherent characteristics, satisfying specific consumer needs and preferences in relation to the duration and quality of conservation and to taste. Moreover, to move from packaging UHT milk to packaging fresh milk requires the setting up of a distribution system which ensures that the milk is continuously kept in a refrigerated environment. Furthermore, at the level of supply, the manufacture of machinery for the aseptic packaging of UHT milk in cartons requires complex technology, which only Tetra Pak and its competitor PKL have succeeded in developing and making operational during the period considered in the Decision. Manufacturers of non-aseptic machinery using cartons, operating on the market closest to the market in the aseptic machinery in question, were therefore not in a position to enter the latter market by modifying their machinery in certain respects for the market in aseptic machinery.

70. As for aseptic cartons, they also constituted a market distinct from that in non-aseptic packaging. At the level of the packers' intermediate demand, aseptic cartons were not sufficiently interchangeable with non-aseptic packages, including cartons, for the same reasons as those already set out in the preceding paragraph in relation to machinery. At the level of supply, the documents before the Court indicate that notwithstanding the absence of insurmountable technical problems, manufacturers of non-aseptic cartons were not in a position in the circumstances in question to adapt to the manufacture of aseptic cartons. The fact that on that market there was only one competitor of Tetra Pak, namely PKL, with only 10 per cent of the market in aseptic cartons during the period in question, demonstrates that the conditions of competition were such that in practice there was no possibility for manufacturers of non-aseptic cartons to enter the market in aseptic cartons, in particular given the lack of aseptic filling machines.

71. Secondly, the Court holds that, during the period in question, aseptic machinery and cartons were not sufficiently interchangeable with aseptic packaging systems using other materials. According to the data provided in the documents before the Court, which are not disputed by the applicant, no such substitutable equipment existed, with the exception of the arrival on the market towards the end of the relevant period of systems for aseptic packaging in plastic bottles, returnable glass bottles and pouches in France, Germany and Spain respectively. However, each of those new products was introduced in only one country and, what is more, accounted for only a marginal share of the UHT-milk-packaging market. According to information provided by the applicant, that share has been only 5 per cent of the market in France since 1987. In the Community as a whole, in 1976, all UHT milk was packaged in cartons. The observations submitted by the applicant in response to the statement of objections indicate that in 1987 approximately 97.7 per cent of UHT milk was packaged in cartons. At the end of the period in question, that is 1991, cartons still accounted for 97 per cent of the UHT-milk-packaging market, the remaining 3 per cent being held by plastic containers, as the applicant indicated in answer to a written question from the Court. The marginal share of the market thus held by aseptic containers made out of other materials demonstrates that those containers cannot be considered, even during the last years of the period covered by the Decision, as products which are sufficiently interchangeable with aseptic systems using cartons (see *Commercial Solvents* v. *EC Commission*...).

72. Thirdly, the Court finds that non-aseptic machinery and cartons constituted markets which were distinct from those in non-aseptic packaging systems using materials other than cartons. It has already been shown...that, because of the marginal proportion of the price of milk attributable to packaging costs, packers would have been led to consider that containers—in this case cartons, glass or plastic bottles and non-aseptic pouches—were easily interchangeable only if there had been an almost perfect substitutability of final consumer demand. In the light of their very different physical characteristics and the system of doorstep delivery of pasteurized milk in glass bottles in the UK, that form of packaging was not interchangeable for consumers with packaging in cartons. Moreover, the fact that environmental factors led some consumers to prefer certain types of packaging, such as returnable glass bottles, did not promote the substitutability of those containers with cartons. Consumers who were aware of those factors did not consider those containers to be interchangeable with cartons. The same applies to consumers who, conversely, were attracted to a certain convenience in using products packaged in cartons. As for plastic bottles and plastic pouches, they were on the market only in countries where consumers accepted that type of packaging, in particular, according to information in the Decision which is not disputed by the applicant, Germany or France. Furthermore, according to the same source, that packaging was used for only approximately one-third of pasteurised milk in France and 20 per cent in Germany. It follows that those products were not in practice sufficiently interchangeable with non-aseptic cartons throughout the Community during the period covered by the Decision.

73. Analysis of the markets in the milk-packaging sector thus shows that the four markets concerned, defined in the Decision, were indeed separate markets.

74. Moreover and in any event, the Court finds that an examination of the substitutability of the various packaging systems in the fruit-juice sector, fruit juices being the largest category of liquid foods other than milk, shows that in that sector also there was no sufficient interchangeability either between aseptic and non-aseptic systems or between systems using cartons and systems using other materials.

75. The market in the carton packaging of fruit juices was held mainly by aseptic systems during the period in question. In 1987, 91 per cent of cartons used for packaging fruit juice were aseptic. That proportion remained stable until 1991, when 93 per cent of all cartons were aseptic according to Tetra Pak's reply to a written question from the Court. The marginal share held by non-aseptic cartons for packaging fruit juice, which continued for several years as has been shown, demonstrates that in practice they were barely interchangeable with aseptic cartons.

76. Nor were aseptic machinery and cartons sufficiently interchangeable with equipment using other materials for packaging fruit juice. The tables provided by Tetra Pak in answer to a written question from the Court show that during the period in question the two major rival types of packaging in the fruit-juice sector were glass bottles and cartons. In particular, the tables indicate that in 1976 in the Community more than 76 per cent of fruit-juice (by volume) was packaged in glass bottles, 9 per cent in cartons and 6 per cent in plastic bottles. The share held by cartons reached approximately 50 per cent of the market in 1987 and 46 per cent in 1991. The share held by glass bottles increased from 30 to 39 per cent between those dates and the share held by plastic bottles remained negligible, decreasing from approximately 13 per cent to 11 per cent.

77. Taking into account their very different characteristics, concerning both price and presentation, weight and the way in which they are stored, cartons and glass bottles could not be considered to be sufficiently interchangeable. In relation particularly to comparative prices, both parties' answers to a written question from the Court show that the total cost to the packer of packaging fruit juice in non-returnable glass bottles is significantly higher by approximately 75 per cent than that of packaging in aseptic cartons.

78. It follows from all the above considerations that the Commission has established to the requisite legal standard that the markets in aseptic machinery and cartons and those in non-aseptic machinery and cartons were insulated from the general market in systems for packaging liquid foods.

6. ASSESSING MARKET POWER

A. GENERAL

Once the market has been defined the power which the undertaking has on that market must be assessed in order to determine whether the undertaking is 'dominant'.[143]

It is possible, although rare in the absence of a statutory monopoly, for an undertaking to have 100 per cent of a market.[144] As seen in Chapter 1, however, even an undertaking with a 100 per cent market share does not necessarily possess substantial market power. Market shares do not indicate why the undertaking has 100 per cent of the market or tell us about potential competition. They do not explain, for example, whether the undertaking has a high market share because it produces the best products most efficiently, or because the minimum efficient scale of production means that it is a 'natural' monopoly. Nor do they indicate whether or not the undertaking is vulnerable to market entry. The vulnerability of an undertaking to market entry will be dependent upon whether or not there are 'barriers to entry' to the market. This is why barriers to entry, discussed in Chapter 1, is such a central concept.

We saw in Chapter 1 that there is an ongoing debate about what constitutes a barrier to entry or expansion (hereafter, unless the context otherwise requires 'barriers to entry') and even about how

---

[143] See Landes and Posner, n. 4; Schmalensee, n. 3.

[144] See Chap. 1. *GVL* [1981] OJ L370/49 is an example of a monopoly which was not in that category (a collecting society in Germany). And see the discussion of dominance in high technology markets in the new economy, Section 6.E, p. 344 ff.

the term should be defined. It should also be noted that there is an argument that the disciplining effect of potential, as distinct from existing, competitors can be exaggerated.[145]

EU law on barriers to entry does not follow Stigler.[146] In the past at least, a very wide variety of factors have been found to be barriers to entry or, in the terminology often used by the EU Courts, 'other factors indicating dominance'.[147] Account is also taken of evidence of the actual competition on the market, for example how undertakings have been affected (or not) in periods of economic downturn.[148]

Sections 6.B–6.E set out the approach of the EU Courts and the Commission to date when determining whether or not an undertaking is dominant on a particular market. It will be seen that reliance is placed first on the market shares of the undertakings concerned and then on barriers to entry and other factors indicating dominance. Throughout these sections it will be seen that one criticism of the case law and decisions taken under Article 102 has been their tendency to place too great an emphasis on market shares and the failure, at least in the past, to display rigorous economic analysis when dealing with barriers to entry. On the contrary, barriers to entry have often been seen as pervasive. When combined with the tendency to define markets narrowly, the importance attached to market shares and the broad approach to barriers to entry mean that an undertaking's market power may be considerably exaggerated. Undertakings which do not in reality have market power may, therefore, be precluded or deterred from engaging in conduct which is pro-competitive or at least neutral from a competition perspective (Type 1 errors). Competition law may then have the perverse effect of inhibiting the competitive process on the market.

Hitherto the Commission has not issued a general Notice on market power analogous to that on market definition.[149] However, the matter is considered in the Guidance Paper, paragraphs 9–18. In paragraph 12 the Commission says that the assessment of dominance will take into account the competitive structure of the market and in particular:

- the market position of the dominant undertaking and its competitors (i.e. current market shares);
- constraints imposed by credible threats of expansion or entry (barriers to expansion or entry); and
- countervailing buyer power.

The Commission is now committed to taking an economically rigorous approach to the assessment of dominance.[150]

B. MARKET SHARES

(i) General

Market share relates to the first indent in paragraph 12 of the Guidance Paper. Market shares indicate the *present* state of the market.

---

[145] See E. M. Fox and L. A. Sullivan, 'Antitrust—Retrospective and Prospective: Where Are We Coming From? Where Are We Going?' (1987) 62 *New York Univ LR* 936, 975: 'Potential competition is not an existing alternative source of supply; it does not satisfy buyers' desires for choice or the opportunity for buyers to play one seller against another; and it is normally an inconsequential source of pressure to innovate.'

[146] G. J. Stigler, *The Organization of Industry* (Irwin, 1968), discussed in Chap. 1, Section 15.C.ii, p. 79.

[147] 'Other' meaning factors other than market share. The Commission now uses the term 'barriers to entry': see, e.g., Commission Guidelines on the assessment of horizontal mergers under the Council Regulation on the control of concentrations between undertakings [2004] OJ C31/5 and the Guidance Paper.

[148] See O'Donoghue and Padilla, n. 13, 171–173.

[149] Although it has issued Guidelines on market analysis and the assessment of significant market power under the regulatory framework for electronic communications and services [2002] OJ C165/6. See also the Guidelines on horizontal mergers and on non-horizontal mergers, discussed in Chap. 15.

[150] See Faull and Nikpay, n. 14, 4.122–4.217.

If an undertaking has a statutory monopoly over a relevant market, that is the end of the matter. It is in a dominant position. In the absence of statutory monopoly it has been settled case law since *Hoffmann-La Roche*[151] that the starting point for the assessment of dominance is market share.

The EU Courts have placed great reliance on market shares although, as already explained, economic theory holds that in the absence of barriers to entry high market shares are not themselves indicative of dominance. Critics of this reliance point, inter alia, to the fact that it depends on the uncertain art of market definition and that market definition is an 'in or out' (zero-one fallacy) game, whereas in reality products are often imperfect substitutes for one another and undertakings may be constrained by the existence of products which are outside the defined market. One suggestion is that it may be possible to devise a 'weighted market share' approach 'to take account of the fact that substitutability is a matter of degree in market power assessment'. This would involve taking into account imperfect substitutes when calculating the market share of a product but with a lesser weight than if it were a more perfect substitute.[152] Another problem with reliance on market share is that market share analysis is 'static' and not suited for application to dynamically competitive markets such as those in the new economy.[153]

(ii) The Calculation of Market Shares

The calculation of market shares is dealt with in the Market Definition Notice, which explains that in some industries sales figures may not be the most appropriate basis for the calculation.

Commission Notice on the Definition of the Relevant Market for the Purposes of Community Competition Law [1997] OJ C372/5

53. The definition of the relevant market in both its product and geographic dimensions allows the identification of the suppliers and the customers/consumers active on that market. On that basis, a total market size and market shares for each supplier can be calculated on the basis of their sales of the relevant products in the relevant area. In practice, the total market size and market shares are often available from market sources, i.e., companies' estimates, studies commissioned from industry consultants and/or trade associations. When this is not the case, or when available estimates are not reliable, the Commission will usually ask each supplier in the relevant market to provide its own sales in order to calculate total market size and market shares.

54. If sales are usually the reference to calculate market shares, there are nevertheless other indications that, depending on the specific products or industry in question, can offer useful information such as, in particular, capacity, the number of players in bidding markets, units of fleet in aerospace, or the reserves held in the case of sectors such as mining.

55. As a rule of thumb, both volume sales and value sales provide useful information. In cases of differentiated products, sales in value and their associated market share will usually be considered to better reflect the relative position and strength of each supplier …

Pursuant to this approach market share has, for example, been calculated using the number of subscribers signed up to a high-speed internet service;[154] the number of units shipped;[155] the units sold

---

[151] Case 85/76, *Hoffmann-La Roche & Co AG v Commission* [1979] ECR 461.

[152] Vickers, n. 24, 8–10.

[153] See Section 6.E, p. 344.

[154] COMP/38.233, *Wanadoo* 16 July 2003.

[155] Case T-201/04, *Microsoft* [2007] ECR II-3601, paras. 555–585 and 1038.

and the shares of the installed base (i.e. the number of the relevant machines installed in a given market at a particular point in time);[156] and by the number of retail telecommunications lines and by revenues.[157]

(iii) High Market Shares

The higher the market share the more likely a finding of dominance. In *Hoffmann-La Roche*[158] the CJ, although recognising that the significance of market shares may vary from market to market, and acknowledging the relevance of other factors, held that 'very large shares' held over 'some time' are in themselves indicative of dominance unless there are 'exceptional circumstances'.[159]

Case 85/76, *Hoffmann-La Roche & Co AG v Commission* [1979] ECR 461

39.... The existence of a dominant position may derive from several factors which, taken separately, are not necessarily determinative but among these factors a highly important one is the existence of very large market shares.

40. A substantial market share as evidence of the existence of a dominant position is not a constant factor and its importance varies from market to market according to the structure of these markets, especially as far as production, supply and demand are concerned...

41. Furthermore although the importance of the market shares may vary from one market to another the view may legitimately be taken that very large shares are in themselves, and save in exceptional circumstances, evidence of the existence of a dominant position. An undertaking which has a very large market share and holds it for some time, by means of the volume of production and the scale of the supply which it stands for—without those having much smaller market shares being able to meet rapidly the demand from those who would like to break away from the undertaking which has the largest market share—is by virtue of that share in a position of strength which makes it an unavoidable trading partner and which, already because of this secures for it, at the very least during relatively long periods, that freedom of action which is the special feature of a dominant position.

In *AKZO* the CJ explained what was meant by a 'very high market share' within the meaning of the test set out in *Hoffmann-La Roche*. It interpreted it as 50 per cent of the market:

With regard to market shares the Court has held that very large shares are in themselves, and save in exceptional circumstances, evidence of the existence of a dominant position: Case 85/76 *Hoffmann-La Roche* v. *EC Commission*. That is the situation where there is a market share of 50 per cent such as that found to exist in this case.[160]

The CJ confirmed this in *AstraZeneca*.[161]

---

[156] COMP/38.113, *Prokent/Tomra* 29 March 2006, para. 59. The Commission said that this favoured Tomra, the undertaking under investigation, as a calculation on sales *value* would have given Tomra a greater market share (the point was not taken on appeal, Case T-155/06, *Tomra Systems v Commission* [2010] ECR II-4361).

[157] COMP/39.525, *Telekomunikacja Polska* 22 June 2011, upheld Case T-486/11, *Orange Polska SA v Commission* EU:T:2015:1002 where the market definition was not challenged.

[158] Case 85/76, *Hoffmann-La Roche* [1979] ECR 461, para. 41.

[159] See also, e.g., Case C-457/10 P, *AstraZeneca* EU:C:2012:770, para. 176.

[160] Case C-62/86, *AKZO* [1991] ECR I-3359, para. 60.

[161] Case C-457/10 P, *AstraZeneca* EU:C:2012:770, para. 176.

The outcome of *Hoffmann-La Roche* and *AKZO* is generally interpreted as in effect providing a presumption of dominance at 50 per cent of the market, although Faull and Nikpay argue that it is not a legal presumption but rather a permissible inference on the facts of individual cases.[162] If it is a presumption it is a rebuttable one and weaker at 50 per cent than above 70 per cent. Even when dealing with firms with very high market shares the EU Courts refer to evidence of other indications of dominance which show that the 'exceptional circumstances' referred to in *Hoffmann-La Roche* are not present. In *AKZO* itself the CJ said that the Commission had 'rightly pointed out that other factors confirmed AKZO's predominance in the market'.[163] In *Hilti*[164] and *Tetra Pak II*[165] the GC held, citing *Hoffmann-La Roche*, that market shares respectively of 70–80 per cent and 90 per cent were in themselves evidence of a dominant position but noted that barriers to entry were high.[166] In *AstraZeneca*, where the market shares in some Member States were in the 80–90 per cent region the GC said approvingly that the Commission 'did not base its examination exclusively on AZ's market share, but took care to conduct an in-depth analysis of competitive conditions by taking into account various factors …'.[167] It is the Commission's practice to take great care to examine whether 'exceptional circumstances' are present when dealing with undertakings with extremely high market shares. This was so in *Microsoft*, for example, where it examined barriers to entry (in particular network effects) even though Microsoft had a market share of over 90 per cent,[168] and in *Intel* where there were market shares of over 70 and 80 per cent in the various relevant markets.[169]

There is also a question of what holding a very large market share 'for some time' in *Hoffmann-La Roche* means. In *AstraZeneca* the CJ rendered this as 'a long period'.[170] Bellamy and Child suggest that a high and stable market share for 'a period of five years would probably afford sufficient evidence while any period of less than three years, especially in a dynamic market, might be considered too short for a high market share to be an indicator of dominance'.[171]

(iv) Relative Market Shares

Market shares must be looked at in relative as well as absolute terms, as recognised in paragraph 13 of the Guidance Paper. This means that when considering the market shares of the undertaking under scrutiny it is also necessary to consider the market shares of its competitors. The CJ said in *Hoffmann-La Roche* that 'the relationship between the market shares of the undertaking concerned and of its competitors, especially those of the next largest' was a relevant factor.[172] The market power of an undertaking with a market share of 51 per cent will be considerably different depending on whether, for example, it simply has one competitor with a 49 per cent share of the

---

[162] Faull and Nikpay, n. 14, 4.158–4.160.

[163] Case C-62/86, *AKZO* [1991] ECR I-3359, para. 61.

[164] Case T-30/89, *Hilti* [1991] ECR II-439, paras. 91–94, *aff'd* Case C-53/92 P, *Hilti AG* [1994] ECR I-667.

[165] Case T-83/91, *Tetra Pak* [1994] ECR II-755, paras. 109–110, *aff'd* Case C-333/94 P, *Tetra Pak II* [1996] ECR I-5951.

[166] See also Case T-395/94, *Atlantic Container Line* [2002] ECR II-875, para. 328, and Case T-228/97, *Irish Sugar plc v Commission* [1999] ECR II-2969, paras. 71–104.

[167] Case T-321/05, *AstraZeneca* [2010] ECR II-2805, para. 244.

[168] COMP/37.792, *Microsoft* 24 March 2004, paras. 448–464 and 515–540.

[169] COMP/37.990, *Intel* 13 May 2009, paras. 853–912.

[170] Case C-457/10 P, *AstraZeneca* EU:C:2012:770, para. 176.

[171] Bellamy and Child (V. Rose and D. Bailey, eds.), *European Union Law of Competition* (7th edn, Oxford University Press, 2013), 10.026. In 'bidding markets' where contracts are awarded by a competitive tendering process and the 'winner takes all', market shares are not necessarily a useful indicator of dominance, see Bellamy and Child, 10.027, and Geradin, Layne-Farrar, and Petit, n. 5, 4.63, although see the merger case, Case T-210/01, *General Electric v Commission* [2005] ECR II-5575, paras. 148 ff where the GC agreed with the Commission that it was an indicator of market strength for an undertaking to maintain or increase its market share over a number of years on a bidding market.

[172] Case 85/76, *Hoffmann-La Roche* [1979] ECR 461, para. 48.

market, three competitors which have 16, 16, and 17 per cent of the market respectively, or 49 competitors each with 1 per cent of the market. The differentials in market share are extremely significant. A market where there are two undertakings, A with 51 per cent and B with 49 per cent, is an oligopoly. It is not dominated by A, although there may be a position of collective dominance with B.[173]

In *United Brands*[174] UBC was held to be dominant although its market share was only 45 per cent. That was however almost twice as large as the share of its nearest competitor. In *Michelin I*[175] Michelin was found dominant with a market share of 57–65 per cent where the remainder was fragmented, the competitors each having only 4–8 per cent. In *Michelin II* there was some uncertainty about Michelin's exact market share in France but it was taken as being over 50 per cent and thus over five times greater than that of its nearest competitor,[176] and in *British Airways*[177] BA's share was seven times greater. In *AstraZeneca* the CJ agreed with the GC that the 'generally very large' market shares of AstraZeneca (AZ) indicated that its market power was 'out of all comparison to those of the other market players'.[178] Once an undertaking has a market share as large as 70 per cent it is bound to have at least twice the share of its nearest competitor.[179] In these circumstances it will be very difficult indeed for the undertaking to preclude a finding of dominance. There is no case where an undertaking with such a high market share has not been held dominant. It will therefore be appreciated why narrow market definitions may be fatal for undertakings and how important it is to make a realistic determination of the market.

(v) Market Share and the Commission Guidance Paper

In the Guidance Paper the Commission says that market shares provide it with a *useful first indication* of market structure[180] and downplays the reliance on market share.

Guidance on the Commission's Enforcement Priorities in Applying Article 82 of the EC Treaty to Abusive Exclusionary Conduct by Dominant Undertakings [2009] OJ C45/2

13. Market shares provide a useful first indication for the Commission of the market structure and of the relative importance of the various undertakings active on the market…However, the Commission will interpret market shares in the light of the relevant market conditions, and in particular of the dynamics of the market and of the extent to which products are differentiated. The trend or development of market shares over time may also be taken into account in volatile or bidding markets.

…

15. Experience suggests that the higher the market share and the longer the period of time over which it is held, the more likely it is that it constitutes an important preliminary indication of the existence of a dominant position and, in certain circumstances, of possible serious effects of abusive conduct, justifying

---

[173] For collective dominance in respect of Art. 102 see Chap. 5, Section 5.A.iii, p. 264 ff.

[174] Case 27/76, *United Brands* [1978] ECR 207.

[175] Case 322/81, *Michelin I* [1983] ECR 3461.

[176] *Michelin* [2001] OJ L143/1.

[177] Case T-219/99, *British Airways* [2003] ECR II-5917.

[178] Case C-457/10 P, *AstraZeneca* EU:C:2012:770, para. 177, *aff'g* para. 253 of Case T-321/05, *AstraZeneca* [2010] ECR II-2805. AZ's market shares in different Member States are set out in paras. 246–252 of the GC judgment.

[179] See also COMP/38.113, *Prokent Tomra* 29 March 2006, paras. 84–85, upheld Case T-155/06, *Tomra* [2010] ECR II-4361, *aff'd* Case C-549/10 P, *Tomra Systems ASA v Commission* EU:C:2012:221.

[180] The same phrase appears in the Horizontal Merger Guidelines [2004] OJ C31/3, para. 14.

an intervention by the Commission under Article [102].[181] However, as a general rule, the Commission will not come to a final conclusion as to whether or not a case should be pursued without examining all the factors which may be sufficient to constrain the behaviour of the undertaking.

It will be noted that in the last sentence the Commission does not completely preclude reaching a finding of dominance without looking at 'all the factors'. Nevertheless, as already mentioned, in recent cases the Commission has examined all the factors very carefully, and there is no case where it has reached a conclusion on market share alone. The Guidance Paper is notable for making no reference to the significance of 50 per cent of the market, let alone to presumptions at that level.

(vi) Low Market Shares and Dominance

It is important to know the minimum market share at which an undertaking is likely to be found to be dominant. The crucial range is 40–50 per cent for above that the market share is 'very high' and below that dominance is unlikely though possible. The lower the market share of the undertaking the greater the significance which attaches to the other factors indicating dominance. The lowest share at which an undertaking has been found dominant for the purposes of Article 102 is 39.7 per cent in *British Airways*. The market definition aspect of *British Airways* has been dealt with already.[182] As is apparent from the following extract from the GC judgment, there were a number of special circumstances which led the GC to uphold the Commission's finding that BA was dominant with such a low market share.

BA argued, inter alia, that the Commission should not have found it dominant as a buyer without taking into account the intense competition it faced as a supplier of air transport services; that the Commission had not explained how its dominance as a buyer of air travel agency services arose from its successful position in air transport; that its market share did not establish a position of dominance; that its market share was falling; that it was not an 'obligatory business partner' of the travel agents; and finally, that if it *were* dominant it would not have had to spend substantial sums on improving its services. The following extract omits the table referred to in paragraph 211.

Case T-219/99, *British Airways v Commission* [2003] ECR II-5917

General Court

197. For the purposes of establishing whether BA holds a dominant position on the United Kingdom market for air travel agency services, there is no need to assess its economic strength on that market by reference to the competition between airlines providing services on each of the routes served by BA and its competitors to and from United Kingdom airports.

198.…[T]hose various United Kingdom markets in air transport services are distinct from air travel agency services, including the distribution of air tickets in particular.

…

209. The Court still needs to examine whether the reasoning followed by the Commission in order to establish BA's dominant position, on the basis of the evidence which it thus lawfully used, might not be vitiated by errors of assessment.

---

[181] The Commission has a footnote here referring to the relationship between degrees of dominance and the finding of abuse. See further Chap. 7, Section 3.D.iv, p. 358.

[182] See Section 5.B.i.k, p. 308.

210. In that respect, account must be taken of the highly significant indicator which is the fact that the undertaking in question holds large shares of the market and of the ratio between the market share held by the undertaking concerned and that of its nearest rivals (*Hoffmann-La Roche*...at paragraphs 39 and 48), particularly since the nearest rivals hold only marginal market shares (see, to that effect, Case 27/76 *United Brands* v. *Commission*...paragraph 111).

211. As is shown by the table reproduced below [not shown], which is taken from recital 41 of the contested decision and the factual accuracy which BA has not been able to disprove...not only is BA's market share in the total of air ticket sales handled by BSPUK[183] to be regarded as large, but it invariably constitutes a multiple of the market shares of each of its five main competitors on the United Kingdom market for air travel agency services. . . .

212. The economic strength which BA derives from its market share is further reinforced by the world rank it occupies in terms of international scheduled passenger-kilometres flown, the extent of the range of its transport services and its hub network.

213. According to BA's own statements, its network operations allow it, in comparison with its five competitors, to offer a wider choice of routes and more frequent flights.

214. It is further shown by recital 38 of the contested decision, not challenged by BA, that, in 1995, it operated 92 of the 151 international routes from Heathrow Airport and 43 of the 92 routes in service at Gatwick, that is to say several times the number of routes served by each of its three or four nearest rivals (operating) from those two airports.

215. As a whole, the services operated by BA on routes to and from United Kingdom airports have the cumulative effect of generating the purchase by travellers of a preponderant number of BA air tickets through travel agents established in the United Kingdom, and, correspondingly, at least as many transactions between BA and those agents for the purposes of supplying air travel agency services, particularly in the distribution of BA air tickets.

216. It necessarily follows that those agents substantially depend on the income they receive from BA in consideration for their air travel agency services.

217. BA is therefore wrong to deny that it is an obligatory business partner of travel agents established in the United Kingdom and to maintain that those agents have no actual need to sell BA tickets. BA's arguments are not capable of calling into question the finding, in recital 93 of the contested decision, that BA enjoys a particularly powerful position in relation to its nearest rivals and the largest travel agents.

218. The facts of this case therefore show that BA was in a position, unilaterally by circular of 17 November 1997, to impose a reduction as from 1 January 1998 of its rates of commission in force up to that date and to extend its new performance reward scheme to all travel agents established in the United Kingdom.

219. In those circumstances, neither the possibly modest size of the share of BA ticket sales in the business of some of the main agencies, which has moreover merely been alleged, nor the alleged fluctuations of BA's share in the total figure of air ticket sales by travel agents established in the United Kingdom can call into question the Commission's finding that BA holds a dominant position on the United Kingdom market for air travel agency services.

220. Nor are the great dependence of United Kingdom travel agents upon BA and BA's corresponding freedom of manoeuvre in relation to other companies using the services of air travel agencies capable of being called into question by the fact that those agents do not normally hold stocks of air tickets.

221. Such a purely logistical circumstance is not of such a kind as to affect the dominant position which BA derives from its preponderant weight on the United Kingdom market for air travel agency services.

222. The argument that, as an undertaking in a dominant position, BA would have no interest in spending considerable sums improving its services so as to compete more effectively with its rivals is irrelevant in that it concerns the United Kingdom air transport markets and not the United Kingdom market for air travel agency services which the Commission took to establish the dominant position of BA.

---

[183] The Billing and Settlement Plan for the United Kingdom.

223. Finally, for the same reason, neither the decline in the percentage of BA air ticket sales nor the advance in market share of certain rival companies is sufficiently large to call into question the existence of BA's dominant position on the United Kingdom market for air travel agency services.

224. In this case, the reduction in BA's market share cannot, in itself, constitute proof that there is no dominant position. The position which BA still occupies on the United Kingdom market for air travel agency services remains very largely preponderant. As the table in paragraph 211 above shows, a substantial gap remained, during the whole of the period of the infringement found by the Commission, between, on the one hand, BA's market share and, on the other, both the market share of its closest rival and the cumulative shares of its five main competitors on the United Kingdom market for air travel agency services.

225. The Commission was therefore right to hold that BA held a dominant position on the United Kingdom market for air travel agency services.

It should also be noted that in *Gøttrup Klim* the CJ did not dismiss the possibility of an undertaking with 36 and 32 per cent of two relevant markets being in a dominant position:

While an undertaking which holds market shares of that size may, depending on the strength and number of its competitors, be considered to be in a dominant position, those market shares cannot on their own constitute conclusive evidence of the existence of a dominant position.[184]

As with the presumption of dominance at 50 per cent of the market, the fact that it is possible to have a dominant position, and thus be subject to Article 102, at a market share even lower than 40 per cent is a striking feature of EU competition law. It is frequently argued[185] that there should be a 'safe harbour' in respect of Article 102, similar to that provided by the block exemptions in respect of Article 101, whereby a finding of dominance would be ruled out at, say, below a 40 per cent market share. Such a 'dominance screen' could possibly allow some firms with market power to escape Article 102 but would, it is argued, generate legal certainty for undertakings and avoid Type 1 errors (generally considered to be more damaging in respect of unilateral behaviour than Type 2 errors). The Commission, which had never ruled out the possibility of finding dominance at a market share of 20–40 per cent,[186] sets out a *qualified* safe harbour in the Guidance Paper.

Guidance on the Commission's Enforcement Priorities in Applying Article 82 of the EC Treaty to Abusive Exclusionary Conduct by Dominant Undertakings [2009] OJ C45/2

14. The Commission considers that low market shares are generally a good proxy for the absence of substantial market power. The Commission's experience suggests that dominance is not likely if the undertaking's market share is below 40 % in the relevant market. However, there may be specific cases below that threshold where competitors are not in a position to constrain effectively the conduct of a dominant undertaking, for example where they face serious capacity limitations. Such cases may also deserve attention on the part of the Commission.

---

[184] Case C-250/92, *Gøttrup Klim v KLG* [1994] ECR I-5641.

[185] See the comments received on the Commission Staff Discussion Paper, <http://ec.europa.eu/competition/antitrust/art82/contributions.html>. The Discussion Paper, para. 31, did not merely fail to rule out dominance below 40%, it expressly said that undertakings with market share below 25% were merely 'not likely' to enjoy a dominant position.

[186] See Commission's *Xth Report on Competition Policy* (1981), point 150. The EUMR, Reg. 139/2004, recital 32, states a presumption that a concentration will not be liable to impede effective competition where the merging undertakings' aggregate market share is less than 25%. The Guidelines on the assessment of significant market

The Guidance Paper is therefore a disappointment to those who argue for a real safe harbour. Dominance below 40 per cent is 'not likely' but the Commission reserves its position over certain 'specific cases'. In this, paragraph 14 is like many other places in the Guidance Paper where the Commission sets out a general position and then qualifies it.

(vii) Market Shares in the Case of Collective Dominance

Most of the existing Article 102 cases finding a collective dominant position concern situations involving undertakings with combined market shares above 90 per cent in a 'quasi-monopoly'.[187] However, in *Atlantic Container Line*[188] a liner conference with market shares of 60–70 per cent on various markets was held to be in a collective dominant position and the GC rejected the argument that a market share in excess of 50 per cent could not suffice to found a presumption of a collective dominant position. In cases of 'oligopolistic' collective dominance, where the undertakings can co-ordinate their behaviour without express collusion or structural links,[189] the situation may well be different because the significance of high market shares is not the same.[190]

C. OTHER FACTORS INDICATING DOMINANCE AND BARRIERS TO ENTRY

(i) General

A wide range of matters have been held by the EU Courts and the Commission to constitute 'other factors indicating dominance'. In *United Brands* and *Hoffmann-La Roche* the CJ held that a dominant position derives from a combination of several factors which, taken separately, are not necessarily determinative.[191] It should be noted, however, that carrying out a full economic analysis before a finding of dominance is made would preclude any one factor (including market share) being determinative, so the inclusion of the word 'necessary' in this famous sentence is unfortunate. The 'other factors indicating dominance' comprise both matters to do with the undertaking itself and barriers to entry and expansion.

(ii) Indications from the Undertaking

a. The Undertaking's Own Assessment of its Position

The EU Courts and the Commission have sometimes relied on an undertaking's own internal documentation as indicating its dominance. Such evidence was referred to in *BBI/Boosey & Hawkes* ('"automatic first choice" of all the top brass bands')[192] and *AKZO* ('AKZO regards itself as the world leader in the peroxides market').[193] In *Prokent/Tomra* several company documents found during the Commission's dawn raid referred to its dominant position.[194] The opinions of managers, however,

---

power under the regulatory framework for electronic communications [2002] OJ C165/15, para. 75, say that undertakings with market shares of no more than 25% are not likely to enjoy a single dominant position on the market concerned.

[187] Case T-228/97, *Irish Sugar plc v Commission* [1999] ECR II-2969, aff'd, Case C-497/99 P, *Irish Sugar plc v Commission* [2001] ECR I-5333; Cases C-395 and 396/96 P, *Compagnie Maritime Belge Transports SA v Commission* [2000] ECR I-1365, discussed in Chap. 9. Case T-193/02, *Laurent Piau v Commission* [2005] ECR II-209 concerned the position of FIFA.

[188] Cases T-191/98, 212–214/98, *Atlantic Container Line* [2003] ECR II-3275, paras. 931–935.

[189] See Chap. 5, Section 5.A.iii, p. 264.

[190] Monti, n. 26, 136–138; Ortiz Blanco, n. 20, 168–172. For oligopolistic collective dominance see Chap. 9.

[191] Case 27/76, *United Brands* [1978] ECR 207, para. 66; Case 85/76, *Hoffmann-La Roche* [1979] ECR 461, para. 39.

[192] *BBI/Boosey & Hawkes* [1987] OJ L286/36, para. 18.

[193] Case C-62/86, *AKZO* [1991] ECR I-3359, para. 61.

[194] COMP/38.113, *Prokent/Tomra* 29 March 2006.

are not incontrovertible evidence of their truth. Managers may try to 'talk up' the undertaking's position to convince themselves, others, or both.[195]

b. Profits

Since a monopolist can reap the benefits of its market power by earning monopoly profits, it is possible that profit margins could be used as a means of identifying market power. It has been argued, however, that no significant relationship between profit margins and market power exists.[196] Moreover it may be difficult to determine whether or not an undertaking is in fact earning monopoly profits. Perhaps for this reason profitability assessment has not been much used in EU cases as a tool to assist in the assessment of dominance, although in *Microsoft* the Commission was impressed by the fact that Microsoft was operating on a profit margin of approximately 81 per cent.[197] EU cases have demonstrated that a lack of profits is not necessarily a contra-indication of dominance. In *United Brands*[198] and *Michelin I*[199] the CJ held that an undertaking's economic strength is not measured by profitability alone.[200] On the contrary, losses, at least if temporary, may demonstrate the economic strength of the undertaking which has the ability to absorb them.

c. Performance Indicators and Price Levels

An undertaking's economic performance can be an indicator of dominance. In *Hoffmann-La Roche*[201] the CJ took spare manufacturing capacity into account as a factor indicating dominance, although it did not distinguish between idle and excess capacity. Capacity is idle when its use would not be profitable because the market price is less than the cost of its use. It is found on both competitive and non-competitive markets. Excess capacity means that the undertaking is producing less output than the optimal output the plant is designed to produce, so that it could increase its output without its unit costs increasing.[202]

The ability of an undertaking to obtain premium prices was relevant in *United Brands*[203] and in *BBI/Boosey & Hawkes*.[204] In *AstraZeneca* it was relevant that AZ was able to maintain its prices at a higher level than those of its competitors while retaining a much higher share. This was a consequence of the way in which public health systems operate in covering the cost of medicines and the resulting insensitivity of prescribing doctors and patients.[205]

d. Overall Size and Strength and Range of Products (Portfolio Power)

In its decision in *Hoffmann-La Roche* the Commission took into account the undertaking's position as the world's largest vitamin producer and leading pharmaceuticals producer and the wide range

---

[195] The same problem of taking account of internal documentation arises when it is used to show that an abuse has been committed: see Chap. 7.

[196] See R. H. Bork and J. G. Sidak, 'The Misuse of Profit Margins to Infer Market Power' (2013) 9 *Journal of Competition Law and Economics* 511 (published after Judge Bork's death).

[197] As a percentage of revenues in the year ending 30 June 2003, COMP/37.792, *Microsoft* 24 March 2004, para. 464.

[198] Case 27/76, *United Brands* [1978] ECR 207, paras. 126–128.

[199] Case 322/81, *Michelin I* [1983] ECR 3461, para. 59.

[200] See also COMP/39.985, *Motorola—Enforcement of GPRS Standard Essential Patents* 29 April 2014, para. 251, where the Commission cited *Michelin I* in dismissing Motorola's argument about its unprofitability/losses.

[201] Case 85/76, *Hoffmann-La Roche* [1979] ECR 461, para. 48.

[202] Excess capacity can be used against potential competitors as a form of strategic entry deterrence.

[203] Case 27/76, *United Brands* [1978] ECR 207, para. 91.

[204] *BBI/Boosey & Hawkes* [1987] OJ L286/36, para. 18.

[205] Case T-321/05, *AstraZeneca* [2010] ECR II-2805, paras. 256–268, *aff'd* Case C-457/10 P, *AstraZeneca* EU:C:2012:770, paras. 178–180.

of vitamins it manufactured.[206] The CJ rejected the assertion that these factors were indicators of dominance, saying:

45. The fact that Roche produces a far wider range of vitamins than its competitors must similarly be rejected as being immaterial. The Commission regards this as a factor establishing a dominant position and asserts that 'since the requirements of many users extend to several groups of vitamins, Roche is able to employ a sales and pricing strategy which is far less dependent than that of the other manufacturers on the conditions of competition in each market.'

46. However, the Commission has itself found that each group of vitamins constitutes a specific market and is not, or at least not to any significant extent, interchangeable with any other group or with any other products (Recital 20 to the decision) so that the vitamins belonging to the various groups are as between themselves products just as different as the vitamins compared with other products of the pharmaceutical and food sector. Moreover, it is not disputed that Roche's competitors, in particular those in the chemical industry, market besides the vitamins which they manufacture themselves, other products which purchasers of vitamins also want, so that the fact that Roche is in a position to offer several groups of vitamins does not in itself give it any advantage over its competitors, who can offer, in addition to a less or much less wide range of vitamins, other products which are also required by the purchasers of these vitamins.

47. Similar considerations lead also to the rejection as a relevant factor of the circumstance that Roche is the world's largest vitamin manufacturer, that its turnover exceeds that of all the other manufacturers and that it is at the head of the largest pharmaceuticals group in the world. In the view of the Commission these three considerations together are a factor showing that there is a dominant position, because 'it follows that the applicant occupies a preponderant position not only within the Common Market but also on the world market; it therefore enjoys very considerable freedom of action, since its position enables it to adapt itself easily to the developments of the different regional markets. An undertaking operating throughout the markets of the world and having a market share which leaves all its competitors far behind it does not have to concern itself unduly about any competitors within the Common Market.' Such reasoning based on the benefits reaped from economics of scale and on the possibility of adopting a strategy which varies according to different regional markets is not conclusive, seeing that it is accepted that each group of vitamins constitutes a group of separate products which require their own particular plant and form a separate market, in that the volume of the overall production of products which are different as between themselves does not give Roche a competitive advantage over its competitors, especially over those in the chemical industry, who manufacture on a world scale other products as well as vitamins and have in principle the same opportunities to set off one market against the other as are offered by a large overall production of products which differ from each other as much as the various groups of vitamins do.[207]

Although size is not therefore per se an indicator of dominance on a particular market, it has been found relevant in some situations. In *Michelin* the CJ took into account the advantages Michelin NV derived from belonging to a group of undertakings which operated throughout Europe and the world.[208] In *Soda Ash–Solvay*[209] the Commission considered Solvay's manufacturing strength with plant in six other Member States to be part of the 'relevant economic evidence' to be taken into account in assessing dominance. The geographical spread of an undertaking's operations has also been held to be an advantage where it makes it less vulnerable to natural disasters[210] and/or other fluctuations.[211] In *AstraZeneca* the GC approved the Commission's taking into account as 'relevant indicia' (although not as in themselves sufficient to warrant a finding of dominance) the fact that AZ's resources and performances outclassed those of its competitors, inter alia, as regards its general financial solidity, R&D resources, and marketing resources. AZ's turnover, unlike its competitors',

---

[206] Case IV/29.020, *Vitamins* [1976] OJ L223/27 at recitals 5, 6, and 21.

[207] Case 85/76, *Hoffmann-La Roche* [1979] ECR 461, paras. 45–47.

[208] Although without specifying what these were: Case 322/81, *Michelin I* [1983] ECR 3461, para. 55.

[209] [2003] OJ L10/10, para. 138.

[210] As with the banana plantations in Case 27/76, *United Brands* [1978] ECR 207, para. 75.

[211] See *Elopak Italia/Tetra Pak* [1991] OJ L72/1, para. 101.

was derived almost exclusively from the sale of pharmaceutical products and these superior resources were devoted to its pharmaceutical business.[212]

It can be seen from the previous discussion that in *Hoffmann-La Roche* the CJ overturned the Commission's finding that the wide range of vitamins produced by the undertaking was an indication of dominance because each vitamin was a separate market. It is otherwise if the undertaking benefits from the diversity of products. In *Tetra Pak II*[213] the Commission held that the diversity 'allows it, if necessary, to make financial sacrifices on one or other of its products without affecting the overall profitability of its operations'. This is a polite way of saying that a 'deep pocket' can facilitate practices such as predatory pricing.[214]

(iii) Barriers to Entry and Expansion

The second indent in paragraph 12 of the Guidance Paper refers to the constraints imposed on an undertaking by credible threats of future entry or expansion. Barriers to entry and expansion are important because where they exist competitors cannot enter or expand on the market and erode the incumbent's existing market share. The Commission explains the importance of potential expansion by existing competitors or potential entry by new ones in paragraph 16 of the Guidance Paper. It considers that such entry or expansion is only a curb on the putatively dominant undertaking if it is 'likely, timely and significant': these concepts are explained in that paragraph. Small-scale or niche entry is not enough, for example. In paragraph 17 the Commission sets out a number of forms that barriers to entry or expansion can take. In the last sentence the Commission says that persistent high market shares may indicate the existence of barriers to entry and expansion.

Guidance on the Commission's Enforcement Priorities in Applying Article 82 of the EC Treaty to Abusive Exclusionary Conduct by Dominant Undertakings [2009] OJ C45/2

16. Competition is a dynamic process and an assessment of the competitive constraints on an undertaking cannot be based solely on the existing market situation. The potential impact of expansion by actual competitors or entry by potential competitors, including the threat of such expansion or entry, is also relevant. An undertaking can be deterred from increasing prices if expansion or entry is likely, timely and sufficient. For the Commission to consider expansion or entry likely it must be sufficiently profitable for the competitor or entrant, taking into account factors such as the barriers to expansion or entry, the likely reactions of the allegedly dominant undertaking and other competitors, and the risks and costs of failure. For expansion or entry to be considered timely, it must be sufficiently swift to deter or defeat the exercise of substantial market power. For expansion or entry to be considered sufficient, it cannot be simply small-scale entry, for example into some market niche, but must be of such a magnitude as to be able to deter any attempt to increase prices by the putatively dominant undertaking in the relevant market.

17. Barriers to expansion or entry can take various forms. They may be legal barriers, such as tariffs or quotas, or they may take the form of advantages specifically enjoyed by the dominant undertaking, such as economies of scale and scope, privileged access to essential inputs or natural resources, important technologies...or an established distribution and sales network...They may also include costs and other impediments, for instance resulting from network effects, faced by customers in switching to a new

---

[212] Case T-321/05, *AstraZeneca* [2010] ECR II-2805, paras. 284–286; the CJ dismissed the appeal against this finding as inadmissible as the cross-appellant did not indicate how it was vitiated by legal error, Case C-457/10 P, *AstraZeneca* EU:C:2012:770, para. 185.

[213] *Elopak Italia/Tetra Pak* [1991] OJ L72/1, para. 101.

[214] One of the abuses which was found in Case C-333/94 P, *Tetra Pak II* [1996] ECR I-5951: see Chap. 7.

supplier. The dominant undertaking's own conduct may also create barriers to entry, for example where it has made significant investments which entrants or competitors would have to match...or where it has concluded long-term contracts with its customers that have appreciable foreclosing effects. Persistently high market shares may be indicative of the existence of barriers to entry and expansion.

The way in which dominance is derived from a combination of factors in addition to market share is illustrated by some of the leading cases on Article 102.

(iv) Some Leading Cases on Barriers to Entry

a. *United Brands*

Case 27/76, *United Brands v Commission* [1978] ECR 207

The issues in *United Brands* were first whether bananas were a separate relevant market from other fruit (see Section 5.B in the discussion on market definition) and if so whether, secondly, United Brands was dominant on it.

Court of Justice

67. In order to find out whether UBC is an undertaking in a dominant position on the relevant market it is necessary first of all to examine its structure and then the situation on the said market as far as competition is concerned.

68. In doing so it may be advisable to take account if need be of the facts put forward as acts amounting to abuses without necessarily having to acknowledge that they are abuses.

...The structure of UBC

69. It is advisable to examine in turn UBC's resources for and methods of producing, packaging, transporting, selling and displaying its product.

70. UBC is an undertaking vertically integrated to a high degree.

71. This integration is evident at each of the stages from the plantation to the loading on wagons or lorries in the ports of delivery and after those stages, as far as ripening and sale prices are concerned, UBC even extends its control to ripener/distributors and wholesalers by setting up a complete network of agents.

72. At the production stage UBC owns large plantations in Central and South America.

73. In so far as UBC's own production does not meet its requirements it can obtain supplies without any difficulty from independent planters since it is an established fact that unless circumstances are exceptional there is a production surplus.

74. Furthermore several independent producers have links with UBC through contracts for the growing of bananas which have caused them to grow the varieties of bananas which UBC has advised them to adopt.

75. The effects of natural disasters which could jeopardize supplies are greatly reduced by the fact that the plantations are spread over a wide geographic area and by the selection of varieties not very susceptible to diseases.

76. This situation was born out by the way in which UBC was able to react to the consequences of hurricane 'Fifi' in 1974.

77. At the production stage UBC therefore knows that it can comply with all the requests which it receives.

78. At the stage of packaging and presentation on its premises UBC has at its disposal factories, manpower, plant and material which enable it to handle the goods independently.

79. The bananas are carried from the place of production to the port of shipment by its own means of transport including railways.

80. At the carriage by sea stage it has been acknowledged that UBC is the only undertaking of its kind which is capable of carrying two thirds of its exports by means of its own banana fleet.

81. Thus UBC knows that it is able to transport regularly, without running the risk of its own ships not being used and whatever the market situation may be, two thirds of its average volume of sales and is alone able to ensure that three regular consignments reach Europe each week, and all this guarantees it commercial stability and well being.

82. In the field of technical knowledge and as a result of continual research UBC keeps on improving the productivity and yield of its plantations by improving the draining system, making good soil deficiencies and combating effectively plant disease.

83. It has perfected new ripening methods in which its technicians instruct the distributor/ripeners of the Chiquita banana.

84. That is another factor to be borne in mind when considering UBC's position since competing firms cannot develop research at a comparable level and are in this respect at a disadvantage compared with the applicant.

85. It is acknowledged that at the stage where the goods are given the final finish and undergo quality control UBC not only controls the distributor/ripeners which are direct customers but also those who work for the account of its important customers such as the Scipio group.

86. Even if the object of the clause prohibiting the sale of green bananas was only strict quality control, it in fact gives UBC absolute control of all trade in its goods so long as they are marketable wholesale, that is to say before the ripening process begins which makes an immediate sale unavoidable.

87. This general quality control of a homogeneous product makes the advertising of the brand name effective.

88. Since 1967 UBC has based its general policy in the relevant market on the quality of its Chiquita brand banana.

89. There is no doubt that this policy gives UBC control over the transformation of the product into bananas for consumption even though most of this product no longer belongs to it.

90. This policy has been based on a thorough reorganization of the arrangements for production, packaging, carriage, ripening (new plant with ventilation and a cooling system) and sale (a network of agents).

91. UBC has made this product distinctive by large-scale repeated advertising and promotion campaigns which have induced the consumer to show a preference for it in spite of the difference between the price of labelled and unlabelled bananas (in the region of 30 to 40 per cent) and also of Chiquita bananas and those which have been labelled with another brand name (in the region of 7 to 10 per cent).

92. It was the first to take full advantage of the opportunities presented by labelling in the tropics for the purpose of large-scale advertising and this, to use UBC's own words, has 'revolutionized the commercial exploitation of the banana' (Annex II to the application, p. 10).

93. It has thus attained a privileged position by making Chiquita the premier banana brand name on the relevant market with the result that the distributor cannot afford not to offer it to the consumer.

94. At the selling stage this distinguishing factor—justified by the unchanging quality of the banana bearing this label—ensures that it has regular customers and consolidates its economic strength.

95. The effect of its sales networks only covering a limited number of customers, large groups or distributor/ripeners, is a simplification of its supply policy and economies of scale.

96. Since UBC's supply policy consists—in spite of the production surplus—in only meeting the requests for Chiquita bananas parsimoniously and sometimes incompletely UBC is in a position of strength at the selling stage.

...

121. UBC's economic strength has thus enabled it to adopt a flexible overall strategy directed against new competitors establishing themselves on the whole of the relevant market.

122. The particular barriers to competitors entering the market are the exceptionally large capital investments required for the creation and running of banana plantations, the need to increase sources of supply in order to avoid the effects of fruit diseases and bad weather (hurricanes, floods), the introduction of an essential system of logistics which the distribution of a very perishable product makes necessary, economies of scale from which newcomers to the market cannot derive any immediate benefit and the actual cost of entry made up, *inter alia*, of all the general expenses incurred in penetrating the market such as the setting up of an adequate commercial network, the mounting of very large-scale advertising campaigns, all those financial risks, the costs of which are irrecoverable if the attempt fails.

123. Thus, although, as UBC has pointed out, it is true that competitors are able to use the same methods of production and distribution as the applicant, they come up against almost insuperable practical and financial obstacles.

124. This is another factor peculiar to a dominant position.

125. However UBC takes into account the losses which its banana division made from 1971 to 1976—whereas during this period its competitors made profits—for the purpose of inferring that, since dominance is in essence the power to fix prices, making losses is inconsistent with the existence of a dominant position.

126. An undertaking's economic strength is not measured by its profitability; a reduced profit margin or even losses for a time are not incompatible with a dominant position, just as large profits may be compatible with a situation where there is effective competition.

127. The fact that UBC's profitability is for a time moderate or non-existent must be considered in the light of the whole of its operations.

128. The finding that, whatever losses UBC may make, the customers continue to buy more goods from UBC which is the dearest vendor, is more significant and this fact is a particular feature of the dominant position and its verification is determinative in this case.

129. The cumulative effect of all the advantages enjoyed by UBC thus ensures that is has a dominant position on the relevant market.

b. *Hoffmann-La Roche*

Case 85/76, *Hoffmann-La Roche & Co AG v Commission* [1979] ECR 461

The case concerned Hoffmann-La Roche's practices on various vitamin markets.

Court of Justice

48. ... [T]he relationship between the market shares of the undertaking concerned and of its competitors, especially those of the next largest, the technological lead of an undertaking over its competitors, the existence of a highly developed sales network and the absence of potential competition are relevant factors, the first because it enables the competitive strength of the undertaking in question to be assessed, the second and third because they represent in themselves technical and commercial advantages and

the fourth because it is the consequence of the existence of obstacles preventing new competitors from having access to the market. As far as the existence or non-existence of potential competition is concerned it must, however, be observed that, although it is true—and this applies to all the groups of vitamins in question—that because of the amount of capital investment required the capacity of the factories is determined according to the anticipated growth over a long period so that access to the market by new producers is not easy, account must also be taken of the fact that the existence of considerable unused manufacturing capacity creates potential competition between established manufacturers. Nevertheless Roche is in this respect in a privileged position because, as it admits itself, its own manufacturing capacity was, during the period covered by the contested decision, in itself sufficient to meet world demand without this surplus manufacturing capacity placing it in a difficult economic or financial situation.

49. It is in the light of the preceding considerations that Roche's shares of each of the relevant markets, complemented by those factors which in conjunction with the market shares make it possible to show that there may be a dominant position, must be evaluated. Finally, it will also be necessary to consider whether Roche's submissions relating to the implication of its conduct on the market, mainly as far as concerns prices, are of such a kind as to alter the findings to which the examination of the market shares and the other factors taken into account might lead.

c. *Michelin*

Case 322/81, *Nederlandsche Banden-Industrie Michelin v Commission* [1983] ECR 3461

As discussed in Section 5.B. in relation to market definition, this case concerned Michelin's position on the tyre market. The Commission's definition of the market as being that for new replacement lorry and bus tyres was upheld. The alleged abuse concerned the terms Michelin offered its dealers. This part of the judgment deals with the assessment of dominance.

Court of Justice

53. The applicant challenges next the relevance of the other criteria and evidence used by the Commission to prove that a dominant position exists. It claims that it is not the only undertaking to have commercial representatives, that the numbers employed by its main competitors are even larger in relative terms and that its wide range of products is not a competitive advantage because the different types of tyre are not interchangeable and it does not require dealers to purchase its whole range of tyres.

54. It also claims that the Commission took no account of a number of evidential factors which were incompatible with the existence of a dominant position. For instance, dealers' net margins on Michelin tyres and competing tyres are comparable and the cost per mile of Michelin tyres is the most favourable for users. Since 1979 Michelin NV has made a loss. As its production capacity is insufficient, its competitors, which are also financially stronger and more diversified than the Michelin group, can at any moment replace the quantities which it supplies. Lastly, because users of heavy-vehicle tyres are experienced trade buyers they have the ability to act as a counterpoise to the tyre manufacturers.

55. In reply to those arguments it should first be observed that in order to assess the relative economic strength of Michelin NV and its competitors on the Netherlands market the advantages which those undertakings may derive from belonging to groups of undertakings operating throughout Europe or even the world must be taken into consideration. Amongst those advantages, the lead which the Michelin group has over its competitors in the matters of investment and research and the special extent of its range of products, to which the Commission referred in its decision, have not been denied. In fact in the case of certain types of tyres the Michelin group is the only supplier on the market to offer them in its range.

56. That situation ensures that on the Netherlands market a large number of users of heavy-vehicle tyres have a strong preference for Michelin tyres. As the purchase of tyres represents a considerable investment for a transport undertaking and since much time is required in order to ascertain in practice the cost-effectiveness of a type or brand of tyre, Michelin NV therefore enjoys a position which renders it largely immune to competition. As a result, a dealer established in the Netherlands normally cannot afford not to sell Michelin tyres.

57. It is not possible to uphold the objections made against those arguments by Michelin NV, supported on this point by the French Government, that Michelin NV is thus penalized for the quality of its products and services. A finding that an undertaking has a dominant position is not in itself a recrimination but simply means that, irrespective of the reasons for which it has such a dominant position, the undertaking concerned has a special responsibility not to allow its conduct to impair genuine undistorted competition on the common market.

58. Due weight must also be attached to the importance of Michelin NV's network of commercial representatives, which gives it direct access to tyre users at all times. Michelin NV has not disputed the fact that in absolute terms its network is considerably larger than those of its competitors or challenged the description, in the decision at issue, of the services performed by its network whose efficiency and quality of service are unquestioned. The direct access to users and the standard of service which the network can give them enables Michelin NV to maintain and strengthen its position on the market and to protect itself more effectively against competition.

59. As regards the additional criteria and evidence to which Michelin NV refers in order to disprove the existence of a dominant position, it must be observed that temporary unprofitability or even losses are not inconsistent with the existence of a dominant position. By the same token, the fact that the prices charged by Michelin NV do not constitute an abuse and are not even particularly high does not justify the conclusion that a dominant position does not exist. Finally, neither the size, financial strength and degree of diversification of Michelin NV's competitors at the world level nor the counterpoise arising from the fact that buyers of heavy-vehicle tyres are experienced trade users are such as to deprive Michelin NV of its privileged position on the Netherlands market.

60. It must therefore be concluded that the other criteria and evidence relevant in this case in determining whether a dominant position exists confirm that Michelin NV has such a position.

61. Michelin NV's submissions disputing that it has a dominant position on a substantial part of the common market are therefore unfounded.

d. Eurofix-Bauco v Hilti

For the market definition aspects of this case[215] see the discussion of market definition in Section 5.[216] The case concerned the consumables (nails and cartridges) for Hilti's nail guns.

Eurofix-Bauco v Hilti [1988] OJ L65/19

Commission

69. In addition to the strength derived from its market share and the relative weakness of its competitors, Hilti has other advantages that help reinforce and maintain its position in the nail gun market:

— its biggest selling nail gun, the DX 450, has certain novel technically advantageous features which are still protected by patents,

— Hilti has an extremely strong research and development position and is one of the leading companies worldwide not only in nail guns but also other fastening technologies,

---

[215] Upheld, Case T-30/89, *Hilti AG* [1991] ECR II-439 and Case C-53/92 P, *Hilti* [1994] ECR I-667.

[216] Section 5.B.i.h, p. 302.

— Hilti has a strong and well-organised distribution system—in the EEC it has subsidiaries and independent dealers integrated into its selling network who deal mostly direct with customers, and

— the market for nail guns is relatively mature, which may discourage new entrants since sales or market shares can only be obtained at the expense of existing competitors in the market for replacements.

70. The foregoing considerations lead to the conclusion that Hilti holds a dominant position in the EEC for nail guns, as well as the markets for Hilti-compatible nails and cartridge strips. These are the relevant markets for the purposes of this Decision. It should be stressed that, in this particular case, the relevant markets for Hilti compatible nails and cartridge strips are important because of Hilti's large share of sales of nail guns. Because of this large share, independent manufacturers of nails and cartridge strips must manufacture nails and/or cartridge strips which can be used in Hilti tools if they are to produce for more than a small segment of the market thus achieving the economies of scale necessary to be both competitive and profitable.

71. Hilti's market power and dominance stem principally from its large share of the sales of nail guns coupled with the patent protection for its cartridge strips. The economic position it enjoys is such that it enables it to prevent effective competition being maintained on the relevant markets for Hilti-compatible nails and cartridge strips. In fact Hilti's commercial behaviour, which has been described above and is analysed below, is witness to its ability to act independently of, and without due regard to, either competitors or customers on the relevant markets in question. In addition, Hilti's pricing policy also described above reflects its ability to determine, or at least to have an appreciable influence on the conditions under which competition will develop. This behaviour and its economic consequences would not normally be seen where a company was facing real competitive pressure. Therefore the Commission considers that Hilti holds a dominant position in the two separate relevant markets for Hilti-compatible nails and cartridge strips.

(v) Summary of Barriers to Entry for the Purposes of Article 102

This section summarises the main barriers to entry which have been held to indicate dominance in Article 102 cases. They are also summed up in paragraph 17 of the Guidance Paper.[217] This section should be read in the light of the section on barriers to entry in Chapter 1.[218]

a. Economies of Scale and Scope and Sunk Costs

In *United Brands* (paragraph 122) the CJ recognised that economies of scale can operate as a barrier to entry. It also referred to sunk costs when it spoke of 'costs which are irrecoverable if the attempt fails'.[219] Whether or not competitors can enter a market on a small scale depends on the characteristics of the market. In *Intel*, the Commission found that in respect of the x86CPU market there were (a) significant sunk costs in R&D, (b) significant sunk costs in plant production, and (c) resulting significant economies of scale which meant that the minimum efficient scale was high relative to overall market demand, so that there were significant barriers to entry. Furthermore, once entry had taken place expanding output would have required additional sunk investment into new property, plant, and equipment and several years' lead time.[220] The Commission explained the link between economies of scale, sunk investments, and high fixed costs:

In general, a high share of fixed costs is indicative of significant barriers to entry and expansion. These barriers to entry give rise to market power, which in turn enables a firm to set prices above marginal costs. In the presence of fixed costs, pricing above marginal cost is necessary for a firm to generate profits and thus

---

[217] See Section 6.C.iii, p. 331.

[218] Chap.1, Section 15.C.

[219] Case 27/76, *United Brands* [1978] ECR 207, para. 122.

[220] COMP/37.990, *Intel* 13 May 2009, para. 866, upheld Case T-286/09, *Intel v Commission* EU:T:2014:547.

remain viable. As long as barriers to entry remain moderate, new entrants could be expected to compete away any supra-competitive profits, leading to more or less comparable levels of net profits across companies (after accounting for risk). The higher the proportion of fixed costs in a given industry, the more concentrated it is likely to be, because higher mark-ups are necessary for firms to remain profitable.[221]

In *Telefónica* the Commission also noted the significant sunk costs for new operators and the fact that the incumbent benefited from economies of scale and scope whereas new operators would have to secure a sufficient number of customers while facing higher unit costs.[222]

b. Access to Key Inputs or Facilities

New entrants may be unable to enter the market because of lack of access to key inputs. This can cover items such as airport slots or things which are covered by IPRs or mean there is no access to raw materials. In *BPB*[223] a new entrant to the market would have needed access to the raw material, gypsum. There was no access to this in the UK without opening new mines. The only alternative was thus to import it. This would incur cost and risk and therefore relates to access to financial resources as discussed in Section 6.C.v.c. Where key inputs are unavailable to new entrants, refusals to supply can amount to strategic entry-deterring behaviour by the incumbent undertaking and may in certain circumstances amount to an abuse of a dominant position: see *Commercial Solvents* and the case law on refusal to supply and the essential facilities doctrine discussed in Chapter 7. Access to facilities is a particular problem in network industries, where it may be dealt with by sector regulation.

c. Access to Financial Resources and the Need for Investment

In *United Brands*[224] and *Hoffmann-La Roche*[225] the CJ considered that the need for large-scale capital investment constituted a barrier to entry. In *Continental Can*[226] the Commission also appeared to consider that the undertaking's access to international capital markets was an indicator of its dominance.

d. Legal and Regulatory Barriers and Intellectual Property Rights

State or regulatory measures which subject a market to licensing requirements, or grant to a particular undertaking a statutory monopoly, an exclusive concession (such as in the provision of undertaking services in *Bodson v Pompes Funèbres*[227]), or exclusive access to finite resources (such as radio frequencies in *Decca Navigator*[228] or airport slots in *British Midland–Aer Lingus*[229]) are obvious barriers to entry. Most legal and regulatory barriers to entry can be classified as absolute costs advantages.[230] They are structural factors which are characteristics inherent in the relevant market and they may impact differently on new entrants than on incumbents.[231] The EU Courts and the Commission have

---

[221] COMP/37.990, *Intel* 13 May 2009, para. 878.

[222] COMP/38.784, *Wanadoo España v Telefónica* 4 July 2007, paras. 224–226, upheld Case T-336/07, *Telefónica and Telefónica de España v Commission* EU:T:2012:172, para. 154, *aff'd* Case C-295/12 P, *Telefónica SA v Commission* EU:C:2014:2062.

[223] *BPB Industries* [1989] OJ L10/50, para. 120.

[224] Case 27/76, *United Brands* [1978] ECR 207, para. 122.

[225] Case 85/76, *Hoffmann-La Roche* [1979] ECR 461, para. 49.

[226] *Continental Can Co Inc* [1972] JO L7/25, para. 13.

[227] Case 30/87, *Bodson v Pompes Funèbres des Régions Libérées* [1988] ECR 2479.

[228] [1989] OJ L43/7.

[229] [1992] OJ L96/34.

[230] See D. Harbord and T. Hoehn, 'Barriers to Entry and Exit in European Competition Policy' (1994) 14 *International Review of Law and Economics* 411.

[231] Faull and Nikpay, n. 14, 4.189.

frequently held such measures to be factors indicating dominance and many cases on Article 102 concern statutory monopolists.[232]

Although not legal regulation as such, it was found in *AstraZeneca*[233] that the organisation and dynamics of the health and social security systems in the Member States made it more difficult for competitors to gain market share. This gave AZ first-mover advantages.

IPRs are a particular type of legal right granted by national (or European) law. The CJ has consistently held that the mere possession of IPRs does not necessarily confer a dominant position.[234] The legal monopoly may not equate to an economic monopoly if the relevant market is wider than the protected product. The issue is how far the possession of the IPRs enables the holder to prevent effective competition. The fact that access to a market is protected by IPRs may therefore be relevant as a barrier to entry.[235] IPRs can be classified as absolute cost advantages and also first-mover advantages. IPRs were found to be barriers to entry in *Hugin*,[236] *Eurofix-Bauco v Hilti*,[237] and *Tetra Pak II*.[238] In *Intel* the Commission remarked on the 'significant intellectual property-related barriers that any new entrant would have to overcome'[239] and the strength of the patent protection enjoyed by AZ, and its rigorous enforcement of its rights, were major factors contributing to the finding of dominance in *AstraZeneca*.[240] Cases on refusal to license copyrights have arisen because without access to the copyright-protected material the competitor is unable to enter the market.[241] The Commission is also concerned with standard-essential patents (SEPs), where an undertaking has a patent which is necessary to the technical standard adopted by an industry for a particular product or process.[242] Ownership of a SEP should not be considered as necessarily conferring dominance. That should depend on factors such as whether compliance with the standard is necessary to enter the market and whether competition from other technologies is possible.[243] In its first decision on SEPs,[244] the Commission found that it was indispensable for manufacturers of mobile devices to comply with the GPRS standard which was owned by Motorola. The first (and hitherto only) case to reach the EU Courts on SEPs, *Huawei*, was an Article 267 reference which asked only about abuse, not dominance.[245]

---

[232] E.g. Case 311/84, *Centre Belge d'Etudes du Marché-Télémarketing v Compagnie Luxembourgeoise de Télédiffusion SA and Information Publicité Benelux SA* [1985] ECR 3261; Cases C-241–242/91 P, *Magill* [1995] ECR I-743; Case 226/84, *British Leyland* [1986] ECR 3263; IV/34.174 *Sealink/B&I Holyhead: Interim Measures* 11 June 1992, and other transport cases; Case C-23/14, *Post Danmark A/S v Konkurrencerådet (Post Danmark II)* EU:C:2015:651.

[233] Case C-457/10 P, *AstraZeneca* EU:C:2012:770.

[234] Case 24/67, *Parke Davis v Probel* [1968] ECR 55; Cases C-241–242/91 P, *Magill* [1995] ECR I-743.

[235] The issue here is with patents, copyrights, and designs: it is unlikely that the holding of a trade mark alone would confer dominance although the ownership of a popular brand name may constitute a barrier to entry.

[236] Case 22/78, *Hugin* [1979] ECR 1869, where the CJ seemed to accept the argument that the spare parts were protected by the UK's Design Copyright Act 1968.

[237] [1988] OJ L65/19.

[238] Case C-333/94 P, *Tetra Pak II* [1996] ECR I-5951.

[239] COMP/37.990, *Intel* 13 May 2009, para. 858.

[240] Case T-321/05, *AstraZeneca* [2010] ECR II-2805, paras. 270–275, *aff'd* Case C-457/10 P, *AstraZeneca* EU:C:2012:770, paras. 186–188.

[241] Case C-418/01, *IMS Health* [2004] ECR I-503; Cases C-241–242/91 P, *Magill* [1995] ECR I-743 (although unlike the GC (Cases T-69/70 and 76/89, *RTE, ITP, BBC v Commission* [1991] ECR II-485) the CJ treated the lack of the *information* as being the barrier to entry and interpreted the undertakings' behaviour as a refusal to supply the *information* rather than a refusal to license: see Chap. 7).

[242] For SEPs, see further Chap. 7, Section 14.C.ii, p. 547.

[243] See further the discussion in O'Donoghue and Padilla, n. 13, 703–704.

[244] COMP/39.985, *Motorola—Enforcement of GPRS Standard Essential Patents* 29 April 2014, MEMO/14/322. Motorola's GPRS patents were previously an issue in the merger case M.6381, *Google/Motorola* 13 February 2012.

[245] Case C-170/13, *Huawei Technologies v ZTE* EU:C:2015:477.

e. Superior Technology

The superior technology of an undertaking has been found to be a factor indicating dominance. This can be seen from the extracts set out from *United Brands, Hoffmann-La Roche, Michelin, Eurofix-Bauco v Hilti,* and *Tetra Pak* in Section 6.C.iv. It is, however, questionable from an economic point of view to hold that an undertaking's technological superiority operates as a barrier to entry per se. It is true that expenditure on technological development can be a sunk cost of entry but it is also true that a new entrant on to the market may not have to spend the same resources on R&D as the incumbent on the market: there is no need to reinvent the wheel.[246] Superior technology could not operate as a barrier to entry according to Stigler[247] since it does not represent a cost to the new entrant which was not borne by the incumbent.

f. Established Distribution and Sales Networks

The overall efficacy of the undertaking's commercial arrangements has been held to contribute to its dominant position in several cases. This is particularly marked in *United Brands* (paragraphs 75–95 of the judgment), which was also a case of vertical integration, in *Michelin* (paragraph 58), and in *Eurofix-Bauco* (paragraph 69) where the CJ and the Commission took into account the effectiveness of the undertakings' distribution networks. These judgments may be criticised for failing to explain sufficiently *why* a new entrant could not replicate these arrangements. Otherwise, the authorities appear simply to be penalising the undertaking in respect of its efficiency.[248] In the Discussion Paper the Commission listed 'a highly developed distribution and sales network' as barriers to entry and expansion and simply stated that 'the allegedly dominant undertaking may have its own dense outlet network, established distribution logistics or wide geographical coverage that would be difficult for rivals to replicate'.[249] In the Guidance Paper, paragraph 17, they are simply listed without comment, with a reference to *Hoffmann-La Roche*.

g. Vertical Integration

Vertical integration has been considered a barrier to entry. This can appear to condemn an undertaking in respect of its efficiency. Further, it can be argued that when vertical integration takes place the barriers to entry are only added up and are not multiplied. Vertical integration may therefore accompany monopoly but is not an indicator of it.[250] Nonetheless in *United Brands* vertical integration was an important factor in the finding of dominance. Clearly, in the context of the growing and marketing of highly perishable bananas, this vertical integration played an important part in UBC's ability to get its bananas across the world as quickly as possible. It is quite another thing, however, to hold that this vertical integration constituted a barrier to entry. There was no explanation in the case of why, or even if, the vertical integration was to be regarded as a barrier to entry.[251] However, in a number of telecommunication cases it has been found that the benefits to a vertically integrated undertaking of operating on both upstream and downstream markets gave it a competitive advantage over competitors operating at only one level of the market.[252] The discrimination of a vertically

---

[246] See V. Korah, 'Concept of a Dominant Position Within The Meaning of Art. 86' (1980) 17 *CMLRev* 395, 408, and 410; Harbord and Hoehn, n. 230, 411, 419; Baden Fuller, n. 62, 423, 437.

[247] See Chap. 1, Section 15.C.ii.

[248] Despite the CJ's protestations in, inter alia, *Michelin* (para. 57) that finding an undertaking has a dominant position is not a reproach, the consequences are such that it is invariably to the undertaking's disadvantage.

[249] Discussion Paper, para. 40.

[250] See Baden Fuller, n. 62, 423, 440 and the economic literature cited there; Harbord and Hoehn, n. 230, 411, 419; Korah, n. 62, 395, 408.

[251] See also *Soda Ash–Solvay* [2003] OJ L10/10, where the Commission gave Solvay's production of the raw material (salt) as a factor indicating its dominance.

[252] See Case T-340/03, *France Télécom* [2007] ECR II-107; COMP/38.784, *Wanadoo España v Telefónica* 4 July 2007; COMP/39.525, *Telekomunikacja Polska* 22 June 2011, upheld Case T-486/11, *Orange Polska v Commission* EU:T:2015:1002.

integrated undertaking in favour of its own downstream operations may constitute a strategic barrier to entry and amount to an abuse.[253]

h. Advertising, Reputation, Product Differentiation

In *United Brands* the CJ considered that advertising and promotion had enhanced UBC's large market share, because it had 'induced the customer to show a preference for' branded Chiquita bananas despite a large price differential with unlabelled and differently labelled bananas.[254] United Brands had 'thus attained a privileged position by making Chiquita the premier banana brand name'.[255] The Court did not appear to contemplate the possibility that consumers might have been swayed by the quality of the product rather than by advertising. It concluded that among the barriers faced by new competitors would be 'the mounting of very large-scale advertising campaigns'.[256] Similarly, in the merger case of *Nestlé/Perrier*[257] the Commission considered it relevant to the existence of a dominant position that any new entrant to the market would face formidable advertising and promotion requirements. The Commission considered the difficulty of access to distribution outlets in a brand-crowded market and referred to the problem of shelf-space in retail stores. In *BBI/Boosey & Hawkes*[258] (instruments for British-style brass bands) the Commission relied on the goodwill and reputation enjoyed by Boosey & Hawkes, listing among 'other factors which tend . . . to support a preliminary finding of dominance' the 'strong buyer preference for B&H instruments' and 'its close identification with the brass band movement'. In *Intel* the Commission found that Intel's extensive advertising campaigns and product differentiation constituted barriers.[259]

i. Opportunity Costs

Opportunity costs are the value of something which must be given up in order to achieve or acquire something else and can be classified as an absolute cost advantage for the incumbent undertaking. In *British Midland–Aer Lingus*[260] the Commission considered as a barrier to entry to the Heathrow–Dublin air route the opportunity costs involved in an airline having to divert its Heathrow airport slots, currently employed for other (profitable) routes, to service the less profitable Irish destination.

j. Switching Costs

Switching costs are costs which a customer would have to bear were it to move its custom to a competitor. They can include having to invest in new infrastructure, staff training or procedures, or having to sacrifice advantages obtained from the existing supplier (such as frequent flyer programmes).[261] Network effects may make it unattractive to change supplier.[262] The costs to the customers in switching supplier were taken into account in, inter alia, *Tetra Pak I*,[263] *IMS/NDC*,[264] and *Microsoft*.[265] Switching costs arising from, for example, the loss of rebates or the privileges attached

---

[253] As in the margin squeeze cases, and in *Google*, see Chap. 7, Sections 9 and 14.D respectively.

[254] Case 27/76, *United Brands* [1978] ECR 207, para. 91.

[255] Ibid., para. 93.

[256] Ibid., para. 122.

[257] [1992] OJ L356/1, at recital 97. See Chap. 15.

[258] *BBI/Boosey & Hawkes* [1987] OJ L286/36, para. 18.

[259] COMP/37.990, *Intel* 13 May 2009, paras. 867–870. Between 1997 and 2007 Intel spent 14–17% of its annual turnover on advertising and marketing the relevant product, CPUs.

[260] *British Midland–Aer Lingus* [1992] OJ L96/34.

[261] See R. J. Van den Bergh and P. D. Camesasca, *European Competition Law and Economics: A Comparative Perspective* (2nd edn, Sweet & Maxwell, 2006), 146.

[262] Network effects are particularly significant in new economy industries, see Section 6.E.

[263] [1988] OJ L272/37.

[264] *NDC Health/IMS: Interim Measures* [2002] OJ L59/18.

[265] COMP/37.792, *Microsoft* 24 March 2004.

to long-term or exclusive supply contracts may be strategic behaviour on the part of a dominant firm which constitutes an abuse. Switching costs are first-mover advantages.

k. Conduct

An undertaking's ability to act in a certain way may indicate that it is dominant and moreover its conduct may constitute a barrier to entry.

In *United Brands* the Commission considered that the undertaking's geographical price discrimination and export bans were evidence of its dominance and the CJ said that its economic strength had 'enabled it to adopt a flexible overall strategy directed against new competitors'.[266] In *Eurofix-Bauco* the Commission said that the undertaking's behaviour was 'witness to its ability to act independently of, and without due regard to, either competitors or customers . . . This behaviour and its economic consequences would not normally be seen where a company was facing real competitive pressure.'[267]

This reasoning causes some concern on account of its circularity: the conduct leads to finding dominance which leads to finding the conduct is an abuse because the undertaking is dominant. It is justified, however, in some circumstances so long as caution is exercised. First, some conduct *is* impossible without market power. Secondly, some conduct may operate as a strategic entry barrier.[268] If the conditions of post-entry competition are an important factor in undertakings' decisions about entering markets, predatory behaviour may deter entry, and practices such as exclusive dealing, tying, and refusals to supply may foreclose markets to new entrants.[269] Modern industrial organisation theory, by emphasising the analysis of strategic competition, makes the incumbent undertakings' conduct a major consideration in assessing dominance. Giving a prime place to conduct in the assessment of market power is one reason why the issue of ascertaining whether an undertaking is dominant, and the issue of deciding whether it has abused that position, cannot be neatly separated. The Guidance Paper states that the fact that the undertaking has made significant investments which entrants or competitors would have to match can constitute a barrier (citing in a footnote *United Brands* for this).[270]

l. An Unavoidable Trading Partner

In *Hoffmann-La Roche* the CJ described the undertaking as being in a position vis-à-vis its customers where it was an 'unavoidable trading' partner.[271] The railway operators were described as being in a position of 'economic dependence' on the supplier of rail services in *Deutsche Bahn*.[272] In *British Airways* the GC confirmed the Commission's finding that BA was an 'obligatory business partner' for travel agents.[273] In view of BA's leading position on the UK air transport market it was imperative that travel agents could offer their customers BA tickets. In these situations there is no countervailing buyer (or, in the BA situation, supplier) power to dilute the power of the undertaking in question. An undertaking can therefore be an unavoidable trading partner not because there is no other source of the undertaking's product or service but because it has become a 'must-stock' product, perhaps as the result of advertising, marketing, and/or product differentiation, as was found to be

---

[266] Case 27/76, *United Brands* [1978] ECR 207, para. 121.

[267] [1988] OJ L65/19 at recital 71. See similarly *ECS/AKZO* [1985] OJ L374/1 at recital 56, upheld in Case C-62/86, *AKZO* [1991] ECR I-3359, para. 61.

[268] See Chap. 1.

[269] For a discussion of these practices as abuses see Chap. 7.

[270] Guidance Paper, para. 17.

[271] Case 85/76, *Hoffmann-La Roche* [1979] ECR 461, para. 41, reproduced in Section 6.B.iii, p. 322.

[272] Case T-229/94, *Deutsche Bahn v Commission* [1997] ECR II-1689, para. 57.

[273] Case T-219/99, *British Airways* [2003] ECR II-5917, para. 217, upholding *Virgin/BA* [2000] OJ L30/1, para. 92.

the case in *Intel*.[274] Such a situation can both indicate that the undertaking is dominant and act as a barrier to entry.[275]

D. COUNTERVAILING BUYER POWER

Countervailing buyer power is mentioned in the third indent of paragraph 12 of the Guidance Paper. As the essence of dominance is defined as the independence of an undertaking from, inter alia, its customers,[276] it follows that an undertaking constrained by a powerful buyer may not be in a dominant position.[277] However, it is not enough that powerful buyers extract favourable terms from the supplier *for themselves*: in order to counter a finding of dominance. They must be able to protect *the market itself* by defeating any price increase through paving the way for new entry or leading existing competitors to expand production. This is possible, for example, where the buying side is highly concentrated.[278] It is possible that powerful buyers able to get a good deal for themselves could constitute a market for market definition purposes separate from that of other customers.[279] The Guidance Paper says of countervailing buyer power:

18. Competitive constraints may be exerted not only by actual or potential competitors but also by customers. Even an undertaking with a high market share may not be able to act to an appreciable extent independently of customers with sufficient bargaining strength. . . . Such countervailing buying power may result from the customers' size or their commercial significance for the dominant undertaking, and their ability to switch quickly to competing suppliers, to promote new entry or to vertically integrate, and to credibly threaten to do so. If countervailing power is of a sufficient magnitude, it may deter or defeat an attempt by the undertaking to profitably increase prices. Buyer power may not, however, be considered a sufficiently effective constraint if it only ensures that a particular or limited segment of customers is shielded from the market power of the dominant undertaking.

In *Prokent/Tomra*[280] a supplier of reverse vending machines with over 70 per cent of the relevant markets argued that it was constrained by the power of its customers, the supermarkets, and other retail outlets. The Commission said that the concentration on the demand side was much lower than that on the supply side.

COMP/38.113, *Prokent Tomra* 29 March 2006

89. The existence of buyer power on the demand side requires that there are either credible alternative suppliers to which the customers could turn, or that customers are able to sponsor new entrants. However, in the absence of established competitors which achieve significant and stable market shares,

---

[274] COMP/37.990, *Intel* 13 May 2009.

[275] See also Case C-23/14, *Post Danmark II* EU:C:2015:651, where the referring court had found that the undertaking's statutory monopoly in respect of certain types of post made it an 'unavoidable trading partner' in respect of another segment of the postal market.

[276] Case 85/76, *Hoffmann-La Roche* [1979] ECR 461, para. 38.

[277] See Case T-228/97, *Irish Sugar* [1999] ECR II-2969, paras. 97–104 where such a situation was considered (although held not to apply on the facts).

[278] As, e.g., in the merger cases, M/1225, *Enso/Stora*; M.495, *Behringwerke/Armour Pharmaceutical*. In *Irish Sugar* [1997] OJ L258/1, paras. 97–98, however, the GC held that where a supplier controls over 90% of a market, the presence of one or more large customers is not capable of affecting the dominant position of the supplier where there are a number of customers who are not equally strong and whose demand cannot be aggregated.

[279] Discussion Paper, para. 42; the Notice on the definition of the relevant market, para. 43, acknowledges that the ability of an undertaking to price discriminate may put customers in different markets. For the technique of market definition where there is market power on the demand side, see I. Kokkoris, 'Buyer Power Assessment in Competition Law: A Boon or a Menace?' (2006) 29 *World Competition* 139.

[280] On appeal, Case T-155/06, *Tomra* [2010] ECR II-4361, the dominance point was not argued.

there cannot be a credible threat of even the largest customers moving all or a very large proportion of their requirements away from Tomra, by way of a bidding process or otherwise. Procurement of reverse vending equipment is not part of the core activities of retail groups. The circumstances of the case do not suggest that they are likely to act in a strategic manner in order to subsidise and actively build up competing suppliers to which large parts of the demand could be diverted. There is no evidence for any such behaviour of sponsoring new entry in the period under investigation. Moreover, such behaviour would have been prone to free riding, as building up a competitor would have resulted in a public good. Therefore, there was no substantial countervailing buyer power which would have been able to challenge Tomra's dominance in any of the markets concerned.

Even a monopoly buyer (monopsonist) may be unable to constrain the behaviour of a dominant firm to a significant extent. This is notably so in respect of pharmaceutical companies and national health services.[281] In *AstraZeneca* the argument that AZ was constrained by the public authorities which paid for the drugs was dismissed after an analysis of the way in which AZ's first-mover advantages enabled it to maintain both high prices and high market share.[282]

In *Motorola* the Commission distinguished countervailing buyer power from *bargaining power*. The SEP case against Motorola was initiated by a complaint from Apple, a would-be licensee, and Motorola claimed there was therefore countervailing buyer power. The Commission dismissed this, saying that 'Motorola's interpretation of countervailing buyer power would mean that it would be impossible to establish the existence of a dominant position in cases where the conduct is directed against a purchaser that is economically strong on a market for a product the dominant undertaking needs access to for its own activities'.[283] It is possible for both seller and buyer to hold a dominant position within the meaning of Article 102.[284]

E. DOMINANT POSITIONS IN THE NEW ECONOMY

As we saw in Chapter 1,[285] much competition in the new economy is on innovation rather than on price. Markets may be difficult to define, especially in respect of multi-sided platforms, network effects are important, and markets may 'tip' towards one product. In some markets there are very low barriers to entry (shown by the number of multinational businesses begun by young entrepreneurs in college bedrooms and the like) but in others they are high, because of network effects for example. Assessing dominance in high technology industries therefore presents particular difficulties.[286]

It is often argued that dominant positions in the new economy tend to be temporary and fragile, for ever under threat from innovating competitors. Even where their way is blocked by IPRs, new enterprises may be incentivised to innovate 'round' the barrier to entry rather than through it. In

---

[281] In the UK case *Genzyme*, where there was only one drug efficacious in treating a rare disease, the Competition Appeal Tribunal (CAT) described the monopoly buyer, the NHS, as being in a 'relatively weak' bargaining position, *Genzyme Ltd v OFT* [2004] CAT 4, [2004] CompAR 358, para. 250. There was no alternative to Genzyme's Cerezyme for treating Gaucher's Disease patients, and without it they would die.

[282] COMP/37.507, *Generics/AstraZeneca* 15 June 2005, upheld Case T-321/05, *AstraZeneca* [2010] ECR II-2805, paras. 256–268, *aff'd* Case C-457/10 P, *AstraZeneca* EU:C:2012:770, paras. 178–180. In the UK, for example, the answer to the monopoly pricing of a pharmaceutical company would be for the relevant authority, the National Institute for Health and Care Excellence (NICE) to refuse to license it for use in the NHS on financial grounds in the first place. This is sometimes done in respect of, e.g., new cancer drugs whose only effect would be to prolong life expectancy. However, the drug in issue in *AstraZeneca*, Losec (Omneprazole), is a very widely prescribed first-line treatment for gastro-intestinal disorders.

[283] COMP/39.985, *Motorola—Enforcement of GPRS Standard Essential Patents* 29 April 2014, para. 246.

[284] Ibid., citing Case T-219/99, *British Airways* [2003] ECR II-5917, para. 102.

[285] In Chap. 1, Section 12, p. 48.

[286] See e.g. D. Teece and M. Coleman, 'The Meaning of Monopoly: Antitrust Analysis in High–technology Industries' [1998] *Ant Bull* 801, 853–857; R. Hartman, D. Teece, W. Mitchell, and T. Jorde, 'Assessing Market Power in Regimes of Rapid Technological Change' (1993) 2 *Indus & Corp Change* 317.

the next extract the authors argue that large market shares are not a good basis from which to find dominance in new economy industries.

C. Ahlborn, D. Evans, and A. Padilla, 'Competition Policy in the New Economy: Is Competition Law Up to the Challenge?' [2001] *ECLR* 156, 162

...[I]n new economy industries, the incumbent typically has a large market share since competition is often a matter of 'winner-takes-most'. Their large market share, however, is under permanent threat from innovating competitors and they are only able to retain their position if they continue to innovate...

Equating high market shares with dominance in the case of these 'fragile monopolists' of the new economy is potentially very damaging to innovation and competition, as E.C. competition law imposes a 'special responsibility' to the market upon dominant firms...Apart from the fact that this special responsibility often prohibits welfare-enhancing action where it has a negative effect on rivals' profits, in the new economy it prevents companies with high market shares (which nevertheless are under competitive threat and do not have the power to act independently of competitors and customers) to compete vigorously on an equal footing with their rivals.

A better test of market power is contestability. If the market is contestable, as new economy markets often are...a firm with a high market share does not enjoy a position of dominance because potential entry imposes an effective competitive constraint on its conduct; i.e., it cannot act independently of its (potential) competitors.

Some economists consider that the implications of network effects can be exaggerated.[287] Although in some markets consumers may be better served by one network, in others there is room for several networks and the important question is whether they connect to each other. There are multiple mobile telephone networks, for example, but consumers are unlikely to subscribe to one which did not connect to others.[288] Moreover, it is not necessarily true that once a network has 'won' it cannot be dislodged. If a new product offers clearly superior benefits consumers may be prepared to bear the switching costs, and there are always *new* consumers coming on stream.

It may be that the ephemeral nature of market power in new economy markets can also be exaggerated. One commentator argues that the enormous market shares of some companies may drop, but their share remains very high (e.g. Microsoft) and that the relative size of a market may change by the introduction of new products, but if customers remain who want the 'old' product then the dominant firm may remain dominant but over a smaller market (e.g. IBM and mainframe computers).[289] The market power may be more enduring than it seems.

There is a general consensus, nevertheless, that competition authorities need to be sensitive to the special characteristics of new economy markets and refrain from moving against apparent dominant positions which may be transitory.[290] In *France Télécom*[291] the undertaking claimed

---

[287] See, e.g., C. Veljanovski, 'Antitrust in the New Economy: Is the European Commission's View of the Network Economy Right?' [2001] *ECLR* 115.

[288] There is also a distinction between 'single-homing' (the customer can have access only to one network/ platform/facility) and 'multi-homing' (e.g., the internet user is connected to a number of networks or able to use a number of search engines).

[289] See K. Coates, 'An Emerging Competition Law for a New Economy? Introductory Remarks for the Chillin Competition Panel', <http://twentyfirstcentury competition.com>.

[290] Teece and Coleman, n. 286, 801; C. Ahlborn, D. S. Evans, and A. J. Padilla, 'Competition Policy in the New Economy: Is European Competition Law up to the Challenge?' [2001] *ECLR* 156; R. Lind and P. Muysert, 'Innovation and Competition Policy: Challenges for the New Millennium' [2003] *ECLR* 87.

[291] Case T-340/03, *France Télécom* [2007] ECR II-107, *aff'd* Case C-202/07 P, *France Télécom* [2009] ECR I-2369.

that market shares were not a reliable indicator in the context of an emerging market. The GC said that the fact that this was a fast-growing market could not preclude application of the competition rules[292] but it did examine the claimant's contention that the market should be looked at from a dynamic perspective by assessing potential as well as actual competition, and found that the Commission had taken proper account of this.[293] In *Microsoft* the Commission examined the network effects carefully and concluded that the barriers to entry were such that the dominant position was far from transitory:

In industries exhibiting strong network effects, consumer demand depends critically on expectations about future purchases. If consumers expect a firm with a strong reputation in the current (product) generation to succeed in the next generation, this will tend to be self-fulfilling as the consumers direct their purchases to the product that they believe will yield the greatest network gains.[294]

The decision in the *Google* case will, it is hoped, shed further light on the finding of dominance in digital markets.[295]

7. CONCLUSIONS

1. The definition in the case law of what constitutes a 'dominant position' is now usually interpreted as substantial market power which enables the undertaking concerned to profitably raise prices above the competitive level over a significant period of time.

2. The way that dominance is assessed for the purposes of Article 102 puts great emphasis on market shares. However, market definition is an inexact science which places products either in a market or outside it, whereas in reality there are degrees of substitution. Further, market shares are a static measurement that does not reflect dynamic developments in the market and potential competition.

3. The situation is exacerbated by the broad approach taken to barriers to entry and expansion.

4. The danger is that undertakings may be found to be in a dominant position when in reality they do not have significant market power.

5. Dominance has been found in EU law at market shares of 40 per cent. Moreover, the EU Courts and the Commission have not ruled out finding dominance below that point. There are good arguments for a dominance 'screen' or 'safe harbour' whereby undertakings with shares of the market below a certain point would have the legal certainty of knowing they were not subject to Article 102.

6. The danger with Article 102 is generally considered to be its over-, rather than under-, inclusiveness (i.e. the danger is of Type 1 'false positive' errors).

7. Particular care needs to be taken over findings of dominance in new economy markets whose dynamics mean that competition is often centred on innovation rather than price.

---

[292] Case T-340/03, *France Télécom* [2007] ECR II-107, para. 10.

[293] Ibid., paras. 110–113.

[294] COMP/37.792, *Microsoft*, para. 438, upheld Case T-201/04, *Microsoft* [2007] ECR II-3601. The Commission also noted (para. 520) that the easier it is to find technicians to service the product (*in casu* Microsoft work group server operating systems) the more customers will buy it, and the more customers buy it, the more technicians will learn to service it, thus making it even more popular with customers, and so on.

[295] COMP/39.740, *Google*, IP/15/4780, MEMO/15/4781 (SO). For the abuse issues, see Chap. 7, Section 14.D, p. 553. The statement of objections was sent in April 2015 (the decision in *Microsoft* came three and a half years after the first SO). In the meantime, see I. Lianos and E. Motchenkova, 'Market Dominance and Search Quality in the Search Engine Market' (2013) 9 *J of Competition Law and Economics* 419.

8. FURTHER READING

A. BOOKS

BAIN, J. S., *Barriers to New Competition* (Harvard University Press, 1956)

SUTTON, J., *Sunk Costs and Market Structure: Price Competition, Advertising, and the Evolution of Concentration* (MIT Press, 1991)

VAN DEN BERGH, R. J., and CAMESASCA, P. D., *European Competition Law and Economics: A Comparative Perspective* (2nd edn, Sweet & Maxwell, 2006), Chap. 4

B. ARTICLES

AHLBORN, C., EVANS, D. S., and PADILLA, A. J., 'Competition Policy in the New Economy: Is European Competition Law up to the Challenge?' [2001] *ECLR* 156

AZEVEDO, J. P., and WALKER, M., 'Dominance: Meaning and Measurement' [2002] *ECLR* 363

BADEN FULLER, C. W., 'Article 86 EEC: Economic Analysis of the Existence of a Dominant Position' (1979) 4 *ELRev* 423

BISHOP, W., 'Editorial: The Modernisation of DGIV' [1997] *ECLR* 481

BISHOP, W., and CAFFARRA, C., 'Editorial, Dynamic Competition and Aftermarkets' [1998] *ECLR* 265

BORK, R. H., and SIDAK, J. G., 'The Misuse of Profit Margins to Infer Market Power' (2013) 9 *J of Competition Law and Economics* 511

EILMANSBERGER, T., 'Dominance—The Lost Child? How the Effects-Based Rules Could and Should Change Dominance Analysis' (2006) 2 *European Law Journal* Special Issue 15

FJELL, K., and SØRGARD, L., 'How to Test for Abuse of Dominance?' (2006) 2 *European Law Journal* 69

FOX, E. M., and SULLIVAN, L. A., 'Antitrust—Retrospective and Prospective: Where Are We Coming From? Where Are We Going?' (1987) 62 *New York Univ LR* 936

HARBORD, D., and HOEHN, T., 'Barriers to Entry and Exit in European Competition Policy' (1994) 14 *International Review of Law and Economics* 411

HARTMAN, R., TEECE, D., MITCHELL, W., and JORDE, T., 'Assessing Market Power in Regimes of Rapid Technological Change' (1993) 2 *Indus & Corp Change* 317

KAPLOW, L., 'Market Definition, Market Power' (2015) 43 *International J of Industrial Organization* 148

KOKKORIS, I., 'Buyer Power Assessment in Competition Law: A Boon or A Menace?' (2006) 29 *World Competition* 139

KOKKORIS, I., *A Gap in the Enforcement of Article 82* (BIICL, 2009)

KORAH, V., 'Concept of a Dominant Position within the Meaning of Article 86' (1980) 17 *CMLRev* 395

KORAH, V., 'The *Michelin* Decision of the Commission' (1982) 7 *ELRev* 13

KORAH, V., 'The Paucity of Economic Analysis in the EEC Decisions on Competition—*Tetra Pak II*' [1993] *CLP* 148

LANDES, D., and POSNER, R. A., 'Market Power in Antitrust Cases' (1981) 94 *Harvard LR* 937

LIANOS, I., and MOTCHENKOVA, E., 'Market Dominance and Search Quality in the Search Engine Market' (2013) 9 *J of Competition Law and Economics* 419

LIND, R., and MUYSERT, P., 'Innovation and Competition Policy: Challenges for the New Millennium' [2003] *ECLR* 87

MONTI, G., 'The Concept of Dominance in Article 82' (2006) 2 *European Competition Journal* 31

MÖSCHEL, W., 'Market Definition with Branded Goods and Private Label Products' [2014] *ECLR* 29

MULDOOM, D., 'The *Kodak* Case: Power in Aftermarkets' [1996] *ECLR* 473

MURPHY, F., and LIBERATORE, F., 'Abuse of Regulatory Procedures—The *Astra-Zeneca* Case' [2009] *ECLR* 223

SCHMALENSEE, R., 'Entry Deterrence in the Ready-to-eat Breakfast Cereal Industry' (1978) 9 *Bell J Econ* 305

SCHMALENSEE, R., 'Product Differentiation Advantages of Pioneering Brands' (1981) 72 *Am Econ Rev* 349

SCHMALENSEE, R., 'Another Look at Market Power' (1981–1982) 95 *Harvard LR* 1789

SCHMALENSEE, R., 'Ease of Entry: Has the Concept Been Applied too Readily?' (1987) 56 *Antitrust LJ* 41

SHAPIRO, C., 'Aftermarkets and Consumer Welfare: Making Sense of *Kodak*' (1995) 63 *Antitrust LJ* 483

SPENCE, M., 'Notes on Advertising, Economies of Scale and Entry Barriers' (1980) 95 *Quart J of Econ* 493

TEECE, D., and COLEMAN, M., 'The Meaning of Monopoly: Antitrust Analysis in High-technology Industries' [1998] *Ant Bull* 801

TEMPLE LANG, J., 'Monopolisation and the Definition of "Abuse" of a Dominant Position under Article 86 EEC Treaty' (1979) 16 *CMLRev* 345

VELJANOVSKI, C., 'Antitrust in the New Economy: Is the European Commission's View of the Network Economy Right?' [2001] *ECLR* 115

VICKERS, J., 'Market Power in Competition Cases' (2006) 2 *European Competition Journal* Special Issue 3

WERDEN, G. J., 'Competition Policy on Exclusionary Conduct: Towards an Effects-based Analysis' (2006) 2 *European Competition Journal* 53

WESTIN, J., 'Defining Relevant Market in the Pharmaceutical Sector in the Light of the Losec Case—Just How Different is the Pharmaceutical Market?' [2011] *ECLR* 57

7

ARTICLE 102 TFEU: CONDUCT WHICH CAN BE AN ABUSE

1. CENTRAL ISSUES

1. The definition of (exclusionary) abuse was laid down by the Court of Justice (CJ) in *Hoffmann-La Roche* in 1979. This leads to a difficult distinction between 'competition on the merits' and conduct which is an abuse.

2. The main concern of the Commission in applying Article 102 has been with what are called 'exclusionary' rather than 'exploitative' abuses.

3. The EU Courts have held that dominant undertakings have a 'special responsibility' to the competitive process. That principle has had a major effect on the type of conduct which has been held to be abusive.

4. The Guidance on the Commission's Enforcement Priorities in Applying Article 82 (2009) deals only with exclusionary abuses and covers in detail only the main exclusionary abuses: predatory pricing, exclusive dealing (single branding), discounts and rebates, tying, and refusal to supply.

5. The Guidance Paper adopts a concept of *anti-competitive foreclosure* to identify those cases which are an enforcement priority for the Commission. This has two elements, exclusion of competitors and harm to consumers.

6. The Guidance Paper adopts the 'as efficient competitor' (AEC) test in respect of pricing abuses. The CJ has adopted the AEC test in respect of predatory pricing and margin squeeze but considers it only one tool amongst others in respect of rebates.

7. The EU predatory pricing rules centre on the AEC test. The Guidance Paper adopts a 'sacrifice' test for predatory pricing.

8. The conduct of dominant undertakings may infringe Article 102 even where it has been approved by national sector regulators. This has been shown in cases on 'margin squeeze' in the telecommunications sector.

9. The application of Article 102 to exclusive dealing and rebates has treated some of these practices as virtually per se abuses ('by object' abuses) and others as requiring only a capability of restricting competition. The Guidance Paper considers their likely or actual effects rather than their form. However, there is still a question of how the effects are to be measured, and how far presumptions should be used to assess them.

10. The *Microsoft* case involved a 'technological tie' whereby two elements are integrated into the product sold to the consumer.

11. The idea that it can be an abuse for a dominant undertaking to refuse to supply another party is contrary to fundamental notions of freedom of contract. There is also a danger that it may be harmful to consumer welfare as it may discourage innovation and investment. Nevertheless, the case law establishes that in certain situations it can be an abuse for a dominant undertaking to refuse to supply. These mainly concern competitors on downstream markets. There is a special problem over vertically integrated undertakings and the licensing of intellectual property rights (IPRs).

12. The Commission has paid less attention to exploitative abuses. One exploitative abuse is the charging of unfair prices. There is great difficulty in assessing whether a price is excessive. It is a question of assessing whether the price is excessive in relation to the 'economic value' of the product or service in issue.

13. Article 102(c) specifically prohibits discrimination which puts the other trading parties at a competitive disadvantage. In general, price discrimination may be welfare-enhancing or otherwise depending on the circumstances of the case.

14. Refusals to supply may be abusive simply on the grounds that they prevent or hinder parallel trade between Member States.

2. INTRODUCTION

In this chapter we consider the meaning of 'abuse' in Article 102 and examine the types of conduct which may constitute an abuse.[1] This must be seen in the context of the objectives of EU competition law in general and of Article 102 in particular, as discussed in Chapter 1 and Chapter 5.

In Chapter 5 we explained that in 2003 the Commission embarked upon a review of Article 102 aimed at 'modernising' its application which culminated in the Guidance Paper on enforcement priorities in respect of exclusionary abuses.[2] The reason for this was the belief that Article 102 should be applied with a consumer welfare objective rather than to protect competition and particular competitors for their own sakes. Further, the Commission wished to take an effects-based, rather than a form-based, approach to the application of Article 102. The practice of judging the conduct of dominant firms by its form, considering some conduct abusive by object, and looking at effects on competitors rather than consumers will be seen from the cases and decisions discussed in this chapter. The extent to which this approach has changed, or not changed, over the years will be observed.

3. THE MEANING OF ABUSE

A. GENERAL

Article 102 does not forbid the holding of a dominant position but only the abuse thereof.[3] The meaning of 'abuse' is of vital importance. Although the term is not defined, Article 102 sets out what abuse 'may, in particular, consist in':

(a) directly or indirectly imposing unfair purchase or selling prices or other unfair trading conditions;

(b) limiting production, markets or technical development to the prejudice of consumers;

(c) applying dissimilar conditions to equivalent transactions with other trading parties, thereby placing them at a competitive disadvantage;

(d) making the conclusion of contracts subject to acceptance by the other parties of supplementary obligations which, by their nature or according to commercial usage, have no connection with the subject of such contracts.

---

[1] See generally, Bellamy and Child (V. Rose and D. Bailey, eds.), *European Union Law of Competition* (7th edn, Oxford University Press, 2013 and Supplement by L. John and J. Turner, 2015), Chap. 10; J. Faull and A. Nikpay (eds.), *The EU Law of Competition* (3rd edn, Oxford University Press, 2014), Chap. 4; R. O'Donoghue and A. J. Padilla, *The Law and Economics of Article 102* (2nd edn, Hart Publishing, 2013).

[2] Guidance on the Commission's Enforcement Priorities in Applying Article 82 of the EC Treaty to Abusive Exclusionary Conduct by Dominant Undertakings [2009] OJ C45/2 (the Guidance Paper).

[3] Reiterated in Case C-209/10, *Post Danmark A/S v Konkurrencerådet (Post Danmark I)* EU:C:2012:172, para. 21; see also Case C-23/14, *Post Danmark A/S v Konkurrencerådet (Post Danmark II)* EU:C:2015:651, para. 67. In Case C-52/09, *Konkurrensverket v TeliaSonera Sverige AB (TeliaSonera)* [2011] ECR I-527, para. 24, the CJ said, 'Whilst Article 102 TFEU does not prohibit an undertaking from acquiring, *on its own merits*, [emphasis added] the dominant position in a market', which could suggest that where the dominant position has been acquired otherwise, such as by the past conferment of a legal monopoly, special considerations might apply, and see E. Rousseva and M. Marquis, 'Hell Freezes Over: A Climate Change for Assessing Exclusionary Conduct under Article 102 TFEU' (2013) 4 *JECLAP* 32.

Unlike Article 101 there is no reference to 'object or effect the restriction of competition' which could help to clarify why particular conduct might be an abuse. Article 102 does not indicate what 'theory of harm' it embodies.

B. TYPES OF ABUSE COVERED BY ARTICLE 102 TFEU

(i) Categories of Abuse

The two most important categories of abuse are 'exploitative' and 'exclusionary'.[4]

Exploitative abuses are conduct whereby the dominant undertaking takes advantage of its market power to exploit its trading partners (customers or suppliers).

Exclusionary abuses are conduct whereby the dominant undertaking prevents or hinders competition on the market. The CJ understood 'exclusionary abuse' in *Post Danmark I* to refer to 'practices that cause consumers harm through their impact on competition'.[5]

In addition, *discrimination* abuses, where the dominant undertaking applies discriminatory prices or conditions to its customers or suppliers, thereby placing some of them at a 'competitive disadvantage', are expressly covered by Article 102(c). There appears to be a type of abuse which comprises conduct which divides the *single market*[6] and it has been suggested that there is a type of abuse which can be described as a *reprisal* abuse, which comprises conduct specifically aimed at disciplining or punishing another undertaking. Reprisal abuses are normally a form of exclusionary abuse.[7]

It appears that a new form of abuse may be becoming identifiable, that of harming innovation without necessarily excluding competitors.[8] This is discernible in *Microsoft*[9] and in aspects of the ongoing *Google* investigation.[10]

It must be emphasised that these categories of abuse—exploitative, exclusionary, discrimination, single market—are not mutually exclusive. The same conduct may be exploitative *and* may make it more difficult for a competitor to gain access to the market, or may be both exclusionary and discriminatory. For example, discriminatory prices offered to customers (prohibited by Article 102(c)) may also exclude competitors by charging lower prices to customers who might otherwise purchase from the competitor.[11] Limiting production and tying can also simultaneously exploit customers and exclude competitors. Similarly, conduct aimed at dividing the single market may be also exclusionary in that it excludes a competitor distributor from the territory the dominant undertaking is trying to protect[12] or exploitative in that the object is to charge consumers higher prices.[13]

---

[4] See J. Temple Lang, 'Monopolisation and the Definition of "Abuse" of a Dominant Position under Article 86 EEC Treaty' (1979) 16 *CMLRev* 345.

[5] Case C-209/10, *Post Danmark I* EU:C:2012:172, para. 20.

[6] See Cases C-468–478/06, *Sot. Lélos kai Sia and others EE v GlaxoSmithKline AEVE Farmakeftikon Proionton* [2008] ECR I-7139, discussed in Section 17.

[7] See J. Temple Lang, 'Monopolisation and the Definition of "Abuse" of a Dominant Position under Article 86 EEC Treaty' (1979) 16 *CMLRev* 345, 363–364 and J. Temple Lang, 'Reprisals and Overreaction by Dominant Companies as an Anti-competitive Abuse under Article 82(b)' [2008] *ECLR* 11. The best example of a 'reprisal' abuse is the termination of supply in Case 27/76, *United Brands v Commission* [1978] ECR 207, discussed in Section 13.E, p. 532, which was also exclusionary.

[8] See P. Ibáñez Colomo, 'Restrictions on Innovation in EU Competition Law' (2016) 41 *ELRev* forthcoming, <http://ssrn.com/abstract=2699395>.

[9] Case T-201/04, *Microsoft v EC Commission* [2007] ECR II-3601, see Chap. 7, Section 13.

[10] COMP/39.740, *Google*, IP/15/4780, MEMO/15/4781.

[11] See Case C-95/04 P, *British Airways v Commission* [2007] ECR I-2331, where this was held to be so.

[12] As in Cases C-468–478/06, *Sot. Lélos* [2008] ECR I-7139.

[13] Case 226/84, *British Leyland v Commission* [1986] ECR 3323.

C. ARTICLE 102 COVERS EXPLOITATIVE AND EXCLUSIONARY ABUSES

(i) The *Continental Can* Case

Article 102 clearly covers exploitative abuses and abusive discrimination as these are expressly provided for in Article 102(a), which prohibits the imposition of unfair prices or trading conditions, and Article 102(c). It was not clear in the early days of the EEC whether 'abuse'[14] went beyond this and also covered conduct which had structural effects on competition by excluding or disadvantaging other competitors, i.e. exclusionary abuses.[15] The argument was exemplified by the debate between René Joliet, later a judge at the CJ, and E.-J. Mestmäcker who was then special adviser to DGIV. Joliet argued that the prohibition of conduct because of its structural effects would be tantamount to the prohibition of the dominant position itself, which was not the purpose of Article 102. Rather, its purpose was to control the abusive exploitation of existing power (which he accepted would involve regulatory intervention).[16] Mestmäcker, an ordoliberal,[17] argued that an abuse could also consist of conduct restricting the competition remaining on the dominated market by preventing or hindering current or potential competition.[18]

The Commission considered that Article 102 *could* be applied to prohibit conduct affecting the structure of the market.[19] In 1972 (before the Commission had a tailor-made system of merger control[20]) it issued its decision in *Continental Can*, finding that an undertaking which had merged with another had committed an abuse of a dominant position.[21] In the appeal the CJ confirmed this broad view of abuse.[22] In the following extract from *Continental Can* the references to what are now Articles 101 and 102 TFEU have been left as references to Articles 85 and 86 of the EEC Treaty as they were then, because the extract deals with those Articles in the context of their relationship with Articles 2 and 3(f) (later Article 3(1)(g)).

Case 6/72, *Europemballage Corp and Continental Can Co Inc v Commission* [1973] ECR 215

Continental Can Co Inc, a US company, manufactured metal packaging. It acquired an 85.8 per cent share in a German metal can manufacturer, SLW. Through SLW it formed a wholly owned subsidiary under Belgian law, Europemballage, through which it acquired TDV, another can manufacturer. The Commission adopted a decision holding that this was contrary to Article 86 (now Article 102 TFEU) on the grounds that through SLW Continental Can held a dominant position in a substantial part of the common market

---

[14] '. . . d'exploiter de façon abusive' in French; '*mibbräuchliche Ausnutzung*' in German.

[15] See the debate about the origins of Art. 102 in, e.g., P. Behrens, 'The Ordoliberal Concept of "Abuse" of a Dominant Position and its Impact on Article 102 TFEU', <http://ssrn.com/abstract=2658045>; H. Schweitzer, 'The History, Interpretation and Underlying Principles of Section 2 Sherman Act and Article 82 EC' in C.-D. Ehlermann and M. Marquis (eds.), *European Competition Law Annual 2007: A Reformed Approach to Article 82* (Hart Publishing, 2008), 119; P. Akman, 'Searching for the Long-lost Soul of Article 82EC' (2009) 29 *OJLS* 267; P. Akman, *The Concept of Abuse in EU Competition Law* (Hart Publishing, 2012).

[16] See R. Joliet, *Monopolization and Abuse of Dominant Position* (Nijhoff, 1970).

[17] See recently E.-J. Mestmäcker, 'Wettbewerbsfreiheit und Wohlfahrt' (Freedom of Competition and Welfare), Max Planck Law Research Paper No. 12/2 (2012), available at <http://ssrn.com/abstract=1983193>.

[18] For ordoliberalism, see Chap. 1, Section 5, p. 25.

[19] *Le Problème de la Concentration dans le Marché Commun*, Etudes CEE, Série Concurrence No. 3, 1966, particularly paras. 25–27.

[20] The first merger Reg. was adopted in 1989, see Chap. 15.

[21] *Continental Can Co Inc* [1972] OJ L7/25.

[22] Case 6/72, *Europemballage Corp and Continental Can Co Inc v Commission* [1973] ECR 215.

in the markets for light packaging for preserved meat, fish, and crustacea and for metal caps for glass jars, and that by Europemballage's purchase of a majority shareholding in TDV Continental Can had abused this dominant position by practically eliminating competition in the relevant market.

On appeal the CJ annulled the decision on the grounds that the Commission had wrongly defined the relevant market because it had failed properly to take into account supply-side substitutability.[23] Nevertheless, and contrary to the Opinion of Advocate General Roemer, the Court held that where there *was* a dominant position it was possible for a merger to amount to an abuse within what was then Article 86 EEC.

Court of Justice

20. Article 86 (1) of the Treaty says 'Any abuse by one or more undertakings of a dominant position within the common market or in a substantial part of it shall be prohibited as incompatible with the common market in so far as it may affect trade between Member States'. The question is whether the word 'abuse' in Article 86 refers only to practices of undertakings which may directly affect the market and are detrimental to production or sales, to purchasers or consumers, or whether this word refers also to changes in the structure of an undertaking, which lead to competition being seriously disturbed in a substantial part of the Common Market.

21. The distinction between measures which concern the structure of the undertaking and practices which affect the market cannot be decisive, for any structural measure may influence market conditions, if it increases the size and the economic power of the undertaking.

22. In order to answer this question, one has to go back to the spirit, general scheme and wording of Article 86, as well as to the system and objectives of the Treaty. These problems thus cannot be solved by comparing this Article with certain provisions of the ECSC Treaty.

23. Article 86 is part of the chapter devoted to the common rules on the Community's policy in the field of competition. This policy is based on Article 3 (f) of the Treaty according to which the Community's activity shall include the institution of a system ensuring that competition in the Common Market is not distorted. The applicants' argument that this provision merely contains a general programme devoid of legal effect, ignores the fact that Article 3 considers the pursuit of the objectives which it lays down to be indispensable for the achievement of the Community's tasks. As regards in particular the aim mentioned in 3(f), the Treaty in several provisions contains more detailed regulations for the interpretation of which this aim is decisive.

24. But if Article 3(f) provides for the institution of a system ensuring that competition in the Common Market is not distorted, then it requires a fortiori that competition must not be eliminated. This requirement is so essential that without it numerous provisions of the Treaty would be pointless. Moreover, it corresponds to the precept of Article 2 of the Treaty according to which one of the tasks of the Community is 'to promote throughout the Community a harmonious development of economic activities'. Thus the restraints on competition which the Treaty allows under certain conditions because of the need to harmonize the various objectives of the Treaty, are limited by the requirements of Articles 2 and 3. Going beyond this limit involves the risk that the weakening of competition would conflict with the aims of the Common Market.

25. With a view to safeguarding the principles and attaining the objectives set out in Articles 2 and 3 of the Treaty, Articles 85 to 90 have laid down general rules applicable to undertakings. Article 85 concerns agreements between undertakings, decisions of associations of undertakings and concerted practices, while Article 86 concerns unilateral activity of one or more undertakings. Articles 85 and 86 seek to achieve the same aim on different levels, *viz.* the maintenance of effective competition within the Common Market. The restraint of competition which is prohibited if it is the result of behaviour falling under Article 85, cannot become permissible by the fact that such behaviour succeeds under the influence

---

[23] See Chap. 6, Section 5.B.ii, p. 310.

of a dominant undertaking and results in the merger of the undertakings concerned. In the absence of explicit provisions one cannot assume that the Treaty, which prohibits in Article 85 certain decisions of ordinary associations of undertakings restricting competition without eliminating it, permits in Article 86 that undertakings, after merging into an organic unity, should reach such a dominant position that any serious chance of competition is practically rendered impossible. Such a diverse legal treatment would make a breach in the entire competition law which could jeopardize the proper functioning of the Common Market. If, in order to avoid the prohibitions in Article 85, it sufficed to establish such close connections between the undertakings that they escaped the prohibition of Article 85 without coming within the scope of that of Article 86, then, in contradiction to the basic principles of the Common Market, the partitioning of a substantial part of this market would be allowed. The endeavour of the authors of the Treaty to maintain in the market real or potential competition even in cases in which restraints on competition are permitted, was explicitly laid down in Article 85(3)(b) of the Treaty. Article 86 does not contain the same explicit provisions, but this can be explained by the fact that the system fixed there for dominant positions, unlike Article 85(3), does not recognize any exemption from the prohibition. With such a system the obligation to observe the basic objectives of the Treaty, in particular that of Article 3 (f), results from the obligatory force of these objectives. In any case Articles 85 and 86 cannot be interpreted in such a way that they contradict each other, because they serve to achieve the same aim.

26. It is in the light of these considerations that the condition imposed by Article 86 is to be interpreted whereby in order to come within the prohibition a dominant position must have been abused. The provision states a certain number of abusive practices which it prohibits. The list merely gives examples, not an exhaustive enumeration of the sort of abuses of a dominant position prohibited by the Treaty. As may further be seen from letters (c) and (d) of Article 86 (2), the provision is not only aimed at practices which may cause damage to consumers directly, but also at those which are detrimental to them through their impact on an effective competition structure, such as is mentioned in Article 3(f) of the Treaty. Abuse may therefore occur if an undertaking in a dominant position strengthens such position in such a way that the degree of dominance reached substantially fetters competition, i.e., that only undertakings remain in the market whose behaviour depends on the dominant one.

27. Such being the meaning and the scope of Article 86, of the EEC Treaty the question of the link of causality raised by the applicants which in their opinion has to exist between the dominant position and its abuse, is of no consequence, for the strengthening of the position of an undertaking may be an abuse and prohibited under Article 86 of the Treaty, regardless of the means and procedure by which it is achieved, if it has the effects mentioned above.

Continental Can is the foundational judgment on Article 102. First, it clarified that Article 102 does not set out an exhaustive list of prohibited conduct. This important principle has been repeated and applied many times.[24] However, it is argued that it is 'very difficult to think of unilateral conduct that falls outside these four clauses of Article 102 TFEU and which should be subject to competition law' but that if there *was* the principle of legal certainty would prevent Article 102 being applied to it.[25] Rather, it is a matter of there being no limit to the specific forms of conduct which fall within the provisions. Article 102(a) is wide enough to encompass all exploitative behaviour, Article 102(b) can cover all exclusionary abuses,[26] Article 102(c) contains a wide discrimination principle, and Article 102(d) catches all tying and bundling.

---

[24] E.g., Case C-333/94 P, *Tetra Pak International SA v Commission (Tetra Pak II)* [1996] ECR I-5951, para. 37; Cases C-395 and 396/96 P, *Compagnie Maritime Belge Transports SA v Commission* [2000] ECR I-1365, para. 112; Case C-95/04 P, *British Airways* [2007] ECR I-2331, paras. 57–58; Case T-201/04, *Microsoft* [2007] ECR II-3601, paras. 860–861 (Art. 102 must be interpreted as a whole); Case C-280/08, *Deutsche Telekom v Commission* [2010] ECR I-9555, para. 173.

[25] O'Donoghue and Padilla, n .1, 256–258.

[26] See J. Temple Lang, 'How Can the Problems of Exclusionary Abuses under Article 102 TFEU Be Resolved?' (2012) 37 *ELRev* 136.

Secondly, the CJ established that the object of Article 102 is not just to protect consumers directly from the exploitation of market power, but also to protect them from conduct which through its impact on the structure of competition is detrimental to them indirectly. Therefore Article 102 applies to exclusionary, as well as to exploitative, abuses. Paragraph 26 of *Continental Can* is one of the important passages in EU competition law.

Thirdly, a merger could be prohibited irrespective of the fact that the dominant undertaking had not exploited, or otherwise used, its market power in concluding the transaction. Thus conduct by a dominant undertaking may constitute an abuse even without use of market power.

Fourthly, the *way* in which the CJ interpreted Article 102 was significant. In determining the scope of the provision the Court looked to the basic objectives of the Community and construed Article 102 as a specific application of Article 3(f).[27] This 'teleological' reasoning was an early indication of how the competition rules would be interpreted.[28]

(ii) The Application of Article 102 since *Continental Can*

Since *Continental Can* the story of Article 102 has predominantly been one of action against exclusionary abuses. There have been few cases in which an undertaking's exploitation of its dominant position has been prohibited.[29] This is partly because a dominant undertaking's ability to exploit its customers for a significant period of time indicates that there is something wrong with the market. For example, the ability to reap supra-competitive profits by charging excessive prices should in theory act as a spur to attract new competitors on to the market. In some markets in which this cannot happen, such as those with high barriers to entry because of network effects or high minimum efficient scale, the solution may be to impose price controls through sector regulation. In situations other than this the Commission, like other competition authorities, prefers to take action against anti-competitive practices which are preventing entry and causing the market failure, rather than tackle the high prices directly. Tackling high prices directly is an unattractive option for competition authorities. First, there are problems in identifying what is an excessive price and, secondly, there is the matter of the remedy. Competition authorities do not like acting as price regulators. However, the Commission has made it clear that there is no question of Article 102 being applied *only* to exclusionary abuses: 'Article 102 can properly be applied, where appropriate, to situations in which a dominant undertaking's behaviour directly prejudices the interests of consumers, notwithstanding the absence of any effect on the structure of competition.'[30] Moreover, as the imposition of 'unfair' prices and conditions is expressly listed as an abuse in Article 102(a) the Commission could not pursue a policy of never prosecuting in such cases and it will take action where the circumstances warrant it.[31] As a Commission official put it: 'the [EEC] Founding Fathers' faith in competition as a process of rivalry between competitors was not strong enough to tolerate customer/consumer exploitation in the short run'.[32]

The prohibition of exclusionary behaviour may benefit consumers by protecting the competitive structure. Indeed, the view that consumer welfare is the objective of competition law holds that consumer benefit is the *only* reason for this prohibition. However, such a prohibition also *directly* benefits competitors. It prevents their exclusion from the market. The prohibition of exclusionary behaviour

---

[27] Later Art. 3(1)(g), now Protocol 27, see Chap. 1, Section 8.A, p. 31 ff.

[28] E.g. Cases 6 and 7/73, *Istituto Chemioterapico Italiano SpA and Commercial Solvents Corp v Commission* [1974] ECR 223, para. 32.

[29] See Section 16.

[30] *1998 World Cup* [2000] OJ L5/55, para. 100.

[31] See the (then) Competition Commissioner, Mario Monti in C.-D. Ehlermann and I. Atanasiu (eds.), *European Competition Law Annual 2003: What is an Abuse of a Dominant Position?* (Hart Publishing, 2006), 3, 6–7; Director-General of DG Comp, Philip Lowe in [2003] *Fordham Corp L Inst* 163, 169–170. The cases on excessive pricing are discussed in Section 16.A, p. 566.

[32] L. Gyselen, 'Rebates: Competition on the Merits or Exclusionary Practice?' in Ehlermann and Atanasiu, n. 31, 287, 290. This contrasts with the US Sherman Act, s. 2, which is not applied to exploitative conduct.

may, therefore, allow competition authorities to go beyond the objective of protecting competition as a way of benefiting consumers. We see cases in this chapter where Article 102 has been applied to protect particular *competitors* rather than *competition* and where it is questionable whether preventing the exclusion of the competitors did, in fact, benefit consumers.[33]

D. THE BROAD NATURE OF THE CONCEPT OF ABUSE

(i) The Definition of 'Abuse'

In *Hoffmann La-Roche* (repeated with minor linguistic differences in *Michelin I*[34]) the CJ gave a definition of the concept of an (exclusionary) abuse which has been the foundation of the jurisprudence ever since.[35]

Case 85/76, *Hoffmann-La Roche & Co AG v Commission* [1979] ECR 461

Court of Justice

91. For the purpose of rejecting the finding that there has been an abuse of a dominant position the interpretation suggested by the applicant that an abuse implies that the use of the economic power bestowed by a dominant position is the means whereby the abuse has been brought about cannot be accepted. The concept of abuse is an objective concept relating to the behaviour of an undertaking in a dominant position which is such as to influence the structure of a market where, as a result of the very presence of the undertaking in question, the degree of competition is weakened and which, through recourse to methods different from those which condition normal competition in products or services on the basis of the transactions of commercial operators, has the effect of hindering the maintenance of the degree of competition still existing in the market or the growth of that competition.

In *Post Danmark I* in 2012 the CJ (Grand Chamber) added an express consumer detriment element, prefacing this with 'applies in particular':

In that regard, it is also to be borne in mind that Article [102] applies, in particular, to the conduct of a dominant undertaking that, through recourse to methods different from those governing normal competition on the basis of the performance of commercial operators, has the effect, to the detriment of consumers, of hindering the maintenance of the degree of competition existing in the market or the growth of that competition (see, to that effect, *AKZO* v Commission, paragraph 69; *France Télécom* v Commission, paragraphs 104 and 105; and Case C-280/08 P *Deutsche Telekom* v Commission..., paragraphs 174, 176 and 180 and case-law cited).[36]

However, subsequent cases have returned to the original *Hoffmann–La Roche* formulation.[37]

---

[33] See, e.g., Cases 6 and 7/73, *Commercial Solvents* [1974] ECR 223; Case 22/78, *Hugin Kassaregister AB and Hugin Cash Registers Ltd v Commission* [1979] ECR 1869; Case T-201/04, *Microsoft* [2007] ECR II-3601. In Case C-280/08 P, *Deutsche Telekom* [2010] ECR I-9555, the application of Art. 102 was to the short-term *detriment* to consumers in the form of higher prices.

[34] Case 322/81, *NV Nederlandsche Banden-Industrie Michelin v Commission (Michelin I)* [1983] ECR 3461, para. 70.

[35] See, e.g., Case C-62/86, *AKZO Chemie BV v Commission* [1991] ECR I-3359, para. 69; Case C-202/07 P, *France Télécom v Commission* [2009] ECR I-2369, para. 104; Case C-280/08 P, *Deutsche Telekom* [2010] ECR I-9555, para. 174; Case C-52/09, *TeliaSonera* [2011] ECR I-527, para. 27.

[36] C-209/10, *Post Danmark I* EU:C:2012:172, para. 24.

[37] Case C-549/10 P, *Tomra Systems ASA v European Commission* EU:C:2012:221, para. 17; Case C-457/10 P, *AstraZeneca v Commission* EU:C:2012:770, para. 74.

In *Hoffmann-La Roche* the CJ related abuse to the weakening of the structure of competition, in a passage which has been important in more recent cases:[38]

> ## Case 85/76, *Hoffmann-La Roche & Co AG v Commission* [1979] ECR 461
>
> ### Court of Justice
>
> 123. . . . Since the course of conduct under consideration is that of an undertaking occupying a dominant position on a market where for this reason the structure of competition has already been weakened, within the field of application of Article [102] any further weakening of the structure of competition may constitute an abuse of a dominant position.

(ii) The Market Power Does Not Need to be Used for an Abuse to be Committed

As already noted, *Continental Can* established that the dominant undertaking does not need to be *using* its dominance to commit the abuse.[39] However, it is the fact that the undertaking is dominant that renders its behaviour abusive. The dominance means that the behaviour has effects which the behaviour of a non-dominant undertaking would not have. Since a dominant undertaking may be prohibited from some conduct even though it is not actually using its market power, some strategies possible for, and permitted to, non-dominant firms will be prohibited. It may abuse its position by engaging in conduct which is acceptable when carried out by its competitors and irrespective of any intention to commit an abuse.[40]

(iii) The Special Responsibility of Dominant Undertakings

The EU Courts have consistently stressed that although the finding that an undertaking is in a dominant position is not a reproach, dominant firms have a 'special responsibility' towards the competitive process. This idea was first expressed by the CJ in *Michelin I*:

> A finding that an undertaking has a dominant position is not in itself a recrimination but simply means that, irrespective of the reasons for which it has such a dominant position, the undertaking concerned has a special responsibility not to allow its conduct to impair genuine undistorted competition on the common market.[41]

The special responsibility arises irrespective of the reasons for which the undertaking has a dominant position but in *Post Danmark I* the CJ accorded particular importance to the origin of the dominant position in a legal monopoly:

> According to equally settled case-law, a dominant undertaking has a special responsibility not to allow its behaviour to impair genuine, undistorted competition on the internal market (Case C-202/07 P *France Telecom*

---

[38] E.g. Case C-23/14, *Post Danmark II* EU:C:2015:651, para. 72.

[39] Case 6/72, *Continental Can* [1973] ECR 215, particularly paras. 26–27.

[40] Case T-111/96, *ITT Promedia v Commission* [1998] ECR II-2937, para. 139, and see the case law in the rest of this chapter.

[41] Case 322/81, *Michelin I* [1983] ECR 3461, para. 57. See also, e.g., Case T-228/97, *Irish Sugar plc v Commission* [1999] ECR II-2969, para. 112; Case T-201/04, *Microsoft* [2007] ECR II-3601, para. 229; Case C-202/07 P, *France Télécom* [2009] ECR I-2369, para. 105; Case C-52/09, *TeliaSonera* [2011] ECR I-527, para. 24; Case C-457/10 P, *AstraZeneca* EU:C:2012:770, para. 134. See further K. McMahon, 'A Reformed Approach to Article 82 and the Special Responsibility Not to Distort Competition' in A. Ezrachi (ed.), *Article 82 EC: Reflections on Its Recent Evolution* (Hart Publishing, 2009), 121.

v *Commission* . . . paragraph 105 and case-law cited). When the existence of a dominant position has its origins in a former legal monopoly, that fact has to be taken into account.[42]

This is highly significant in respect of dominant undertakings in liberalised markets where the incumbents are still reaping the advantages of their previous legal monopoly.[43]

The principle that dominant firms have a 'special responsibility' towards the competitive process is a key element in the application of Article 102.[44] It imposes what is in effect a positive, or affirmative, duty on the dominant undertaking to act in certain ways. The consequences of the imposition of special responsibility will be seen in the discussion throughout this chapter.

(iv) Super-dominance

A line of case law has suggested that the dominant undertaking's special responsibility increases with its degree of dominance. The idea first appeared in *Tetra Pak II*[45] where the CJ approved the GC's statement that '[t]he actual scope of the special responsibility imposed on an undertaking in a dominant position must therefore be considered in the light of the specific circumstances of the case'.[46] The 'special circumstances' there included the undertaking's 'quasi-monopoly'.[47] In *Compagnie Maritime Belge* Advocate General Fennelly spoke of the 'super-dominance' of monopolists and quasi-monopolists and of the 'particularly onerous special responsibility' upon undertakings enjoying 'a position of dominance approaching a monopoly'.[48] While not expressly endorsing this the CJ did state that the scope of the special responsibility was affected by the circumstances of the case and the competition existing on the market. It indicated that an undertaking with a very large market share and only one competitor would be more likely to be found to have abused its dominant position than a dominant undertaking with a lesser degree of market power.[49] In *Deutsche Post AG: Interception of Cross-Border Mail* the Commission said that the 'actual scope of the dominant firm's special responsibility must be considered in relation to the degree of dominance held by the firm and to the special characteristics of the market which may affect the competitive situation'. The GC made much of the undertaking's 'quasi-monopoly' in *Microsoft*.[50]

The concept of super-dominance has long been criticised as lacking economic or legal foundation.[51] In *TeliaSonera* the referring court asked, inter alia, whether the degree of market dominance held by the undertaking was relevant to establishing whether the impugned pricing practice was abusive. Advocate General Mazák recommended that the answer was 'no', saying that Article 102 'makes no reference to a "super-dominant" position'.[52] The CJ agreed.

---

[42] Case C-209/10, *Post Danmark I* EU:C:2012:172, para. 23.

[43] See Case T-486/11, *Orange Polska SA v Commission* EU:T:2015:1002, paras. 177–178 where, citing *Post Danmark I*, the GC took the former legal monopoly into account when setting the fine. See further Rousseva and Marquis, n. 3, 32; and see the exceptions the Commission makes to its position on refusal to supply in the Guidance Paper, para. 82, in Section 13.F, p. 536.

[44] In Case C-457/10 P, *AstraZeneca* EU:C:2012:770, paras. 134 and 149 it was used to condemn as an abuse the failure to maintain in force a regulatory authorisation, see Section 14.C.i.b, p. 545.

[45] Case C-333/94 P, *Tetra Pak II* [1996] ECR I-5951, para. 24.

[46] Case T-83/91, *Tetra Pak International SA v Commission* [1994] ECR II-755, para. 115.

[47] Ibid., para. 31.

[48] Cases C-395 and 396/96 P, *Compagnie Maritime Belge Transports SA v Commission* [2000] ECR I-1365, Fennelly AG, para. 137. This is the source of the term 'super-dominance'.

[49] Ibid., paras. 112–119.

[50] Case T-201/04, *Microsoft* [2007] ECR II-3601, e.g., at paras. 435 and 775.

[51] See L. Ortiz Blanco, *Market Power in EU Antitrust Law* (Hart Publishing, 2012), 49–50 and the literature there cited.

[52] Case C-52/09, *TeliaSonera* [2011] ECR I-527, para. 41 of the Opinion.

Case C-52/09, *Konkurrensverket v TeliaSonera Sverige AB* [2011] ECR I-527

Court of Justice

79. As stated in paragraph 23 of this judgment, the dominant position referred to in Article 102 TFEU relates to a position of economic strength enjoyed by an undertaking which enables it to prevent effective competition being maintained on the relevant market by affording it the power to behave to an appreciable extent independently of its competitors, its customers and ultimately of consumers.

80. Accordingly, that provision, as stated by the Advocate General in point 41 of his Opinion, does not envisage any variation in form or degree in the concept of a dominant position. Where an undertaking has an economic strength such as that required by Article 102 TFEU to establish that it holds a dominant position in a particular market, its conduct must be assessed in the light of that provision.

81. Of course, that does not mean that an undertaking's strength is not relevant to the assessment of the lawfulness of the conduct in the market of such an undertaking in the light of Article 102 TFEU. The Court itself has based its analyses on the fact that an undertaking enjoyed a position of super-dominance or a quasi-monopoly (see, to that effect, Case C-333/94 P *Tetra Pak* v *Commission* . . . paragraph 31, and *Compagnie maritime belge transports and Others* v *Commission*, paragraph 119). Nonetheless the degree of market strength is, as a general rule, significant in relation to the extent of the effects of the conduct of the undertaking concerned rather than in relation to the question of whether the abuse as such exists.

82. It follows that the application of a pricing practice resulting in margin squeeze by an undertaking may constitute an abuse of a dominant position where that undertaking has such a position, and, as a general rule, the degree of dominance in the market concerned is not relevant in that regard.

The CJ confirmed paragraphs 80 and 81 in *Tomra*.[53]

The CJ thus considers that as a general rule the degree of market power held by a dominant undertaking is irrelevant to whether its conduct constitutes an abuse. Rather, it is relevant only to the *extent of the effects* of the conduct. It may therefore affect the lawfulness of the conduct insofar as effects play a part in Article 102 analysis. As usual, the CJ enters the caveat 'as a general rule'. One cannot therefore say that super-dominance as a determinant of what conduct can constitute an abuse is completely dead. Moreover, the CJ said in *Post Danmark*, apropos the special responsibility, that the fact that the existence of a dominant position has its origins in a legal monopoly has to be taken into account.[54] It may be, therefore, that previous legal monopoly is in some cases substituting for 'super-dominance' as a relevant factor.

(v) Abuse is an Objective Concept

In *Hoffmann-La Roche*[55] the CJ said that the notion of an abuse is an 'objective concept'. This reinforces the fact that it is not essential to a finding of an abuse that the dominant undertaking has used its dominant position.[56] Further, it means that the characterisation of a dominant undertaking's conduct as abusive does not imply fault and does not depend on the undertaking's subjective intent to exclude competitors or weaken competition. For example, in *Clearstream* the GC stated that the undertaking's argument that it had not pursued an anti-competitive objective was irrelevant to the legal characterisation of the facts.[57] In *Michelin II* the GC stated that establishing the anti-competitive

---

[53] Case C-549/10 P, *Tomra Systems ASA v Commission* EU:C:2012:221, para. 39.

[54] Case C-209/10, *Post Danmark I* EU:C:2012:172, para. 23.

[55] Case 85/76, *Hoffmann-La Roche* [1979] ECR 461, para. 91.

[56] See Kirschner AG in Case T-51/89, *Tetra Pak Rausing SA v Commission (Tetra Pak I)* [1990] ECR II-309, para. 64.

[57] Case T-301/04, *Clearstream Banking v Commission* [2009] ECR II-3155, paras. 142–144, citing Case T-65/89, *BPB Industries Plc and British Gypsum Ltd v Commission* [1993] ECR II-389, para. 70.

object and the anti-competitive effect are the same thing for the purposes of Article 102 and that if it is shown that the object pursued by the conduct of an undertaking in a dominant position is to limit competition, that conduct will also be liable to have such an effect.[58]

However, the presence of an anti-competitive objective may 'reinforce' the conclusion that there is an abuse of a dominant position even though it is not a condition for such a finding.[59] Anti-competitive intent is one of the factors which may be taken into account in establishing abuse, but an intent to compete on the merits does not save conduct from being abusive, as the CJ stated in *Tomra*.

Case C-549/10 P, *Tomra Systems ASA v European Commission* EU:C:2012:221

Court of Justice

16. By their first ground of appeal, the appellants seek, in essence, to establish that the General Court was wrong to endorse an alleged finding by the Commission of anti-competitive intent on the part of the Tomra group, in particular by failing to take into account internal documents proving that the Tomra group was intent on competing on the merits.

17. In order to assess whether this ground of appeal is well founded, it must be recalled that the concept of abuse of a dominant position prohibited by Article 102 TFEU is an objective concept relating to the conduct of a dominant undertaking which, on a market where the degree of competition is already weakened precisely because of the presence of the undertaking concerned, through recourse to methods different from those governing normal competition in products or services on the basis of the transactions of commercial operators, has the effect of hindering the maintenance of the degree of competition still existing in the market or the growth of that competition (see Case C-52/09 *TeliaSonera* . . . paragraph 27 and case-law cited).

18. None the less, the Commission, as part of its examination of the conduct of a dominant undertaking and for the purposes of identifying any abuse of a dominant position, is obliged to consider all of the relevant facts surrounding that conduct (see, to that effect, C-95/04 P *British Airways* v *Commission* . . . paragraph 67).

19. It must be observed in that regard that where the Commission undertakes an assessment of the conduct of an undertaking in a dominant position, that assessment being an essential prerequisite of a finding that there is an abuse of such a position, the Commission is necessarily required to assess the business strategy pursued by that undertaking. For that purpose, it is clearly legitimate for the Commission to refer to subjective factors, namely the motives underlying the business strategy in question.

20. Accordingly, the existence of any anti-competitive intent constitutes only one of a number of facts which may be taken into account in order to determine that a dominant position has been abused.

21. However, the Commission is under no obligation to establish the existence of such intent on the part of the dominant undertaking in order to render Article [102] applicable.

22. In that regard, the General Court correctly stated, in paragraph 36 of the judgment under appeal, that it was perfectly legitimate for the contested decision to concentrate primarily on Tomra's anti-competitive conduct, since it was precisely that conduct which it was the Commission's task to establish. The existence of an intention to compete on the merits, even if it were established, could not prove the absence of abuse.

---

[58] Case T-203/01, *Manufacture Française des Pneumatiques Michelin v Commission (Michelin II)* [2003] ECR II-4071, para. 241, echoing what the GC had said in Case T-228/97, *Irish Sugar* [1999] ECR II-2969, para. 170, albeit not so clearly.

[59] Case T-301/04, *Clearstream* [2009] ECR II-3155, para. 142; Case T-321/05, *AstraZeneca v Commission* [2010] ECR II-2805, para. 359.

As seen later in this chapter there are some types of conduct where the undertaking's intent is of particular relevance in establishing an abuse, for example predatory pricing,[60] and 'vexatious litigation'.[61]

It appears that conduct may be abusive even if the dominant undertaking obtains no advantage, either financial or competitive, for itself. The discriminatory distribution of tickets by the French body which organised the 1998 World Cup was condemned as abusive although it was accepted that the body had not gained any commercial or other advantage from its actions.[62]

E. EXCLUSIONARY ABUSES: DISTINGUISHING ILLEGITIMATE FROM LEGITIMATE CONDUCT

(i) The Problem of Applying the *Hoffmann-La Roche* Definition

The principle that a dominant undertaking has a special responsibility to the competitive process and that any conduct which strengthens the dominant position or further weakens the competitive structure may be an abuse potentially brings within the prohibition an indefinite spectrum of conduct. The parameters of that spectrum are the subject of judgments by the EU Courts, decisions of the Commission, and an enormous body of literature. The difficulty is that anything done by a dominant undertaking may improve its market position in comparison to those of its competitors. New and attractive products, better quality, better service, good advertising, and low prices may all attract custom from the competitors. Should improving market share as a result of the dominant undertaking's increased efficiency and unbeatable products be forbidden? Obviously such a finding would be absurd.

The key to distinguishing between illegitimate and legitimate conduct lies in the judgments in *Hoffmann-La Roche* and *Michelin I*.[63] In these cases the CJ spoke respectively of 'recourse to methods different from those which condition normal competition in products or services on the basis of the transactions of commercial operators' and 'recourse to methods different from those governing normal competition in products or services based on traders' performance'.[64] The Court thus distinguished between anti-competitive behaviour and 'competition on the basis of performance'. A dominant undertaking providing a superior product at a low price which reflects its costs is competing on performance. Its conduct is not prohibited even though its competitors, producing inferior products at less attractive prices, lose customers. This is the natural operation of the market. In contrast, a dominant undertaking which almost gives away its products, below cost, in order to attract customers from its competitors and drive them out of business, is acting anti-competitively. The term most often used (in English) to denote what *Hoffmann-La Roche* refers to 'as normal competition in products or services on the basis of the transactions of commercial operators' is 'competition on the merits'.[65] The enduring difficulty with Article 102 is where and how the line is drawn between anti-competitive conduct and competition on the merits. Prohibiting conduct that is in

---

[60] See Case C-62/86, *AKZO* [1991] ECR I-3359.

[61] Case T-111/96, *ITT Promedia* [1998] ECR II-2937.

[62] *1998 World Cup* [2000] OJ L5/55, para. 102; cf. Case T-155/04, *SELEX Sistemi Integrati SpA v Commission* [2006] ECR II-4797, para. 108 (where, however, the context was the issue of whether an entity (Eurocontrol) was carrying out an economic activity).

[63] See Section 3.D.i, p. 356.

[64] The phraseology in English of *Hoffmann-La Roche* and *Michelin* is ungainly and unhelpful. For an explanation of the source of the original German in *Hoffmann-La Roche* and its translation see J. Kallaugher and B. Sher, 'Rebates Revisited: Anti-competitive Effects and Exclusionary Abuse Under Article 82' [2004] *ECLR* 263.

[65] E.g. Case C-202/07 P, *France Télécom* [2009] ECR I-2369, para. 106; Case C-549/10 P, *Tomra* EU:C:2012:221, para. 42; Case C-209/10, *Post Danmark* I EU:C:2012:172, para. 22; Case 457/10 P, *AstraZeneca* EU:C:2012:770, paras. 93 and 134; Guidance Paper, paras. 1 and 6.

fact pro-competitive (making Type 1 errors) may be detrimental to consumers and to social welfare, stifling innovation and hindering dynamic competition. Moreover, companies need to be able to pursue business strategies in the knowledge that they are behaving legally, in other words there needs to be a sufficient degree of legal certainty in the interpretation and application of Article 102. In the discussion in this chapter of the types of conduct which may constitute an abuse we see over and over again the conflict between applying Article 102 in a way which is economically literate and rational and formulating workable rules in the light of which undertakings can plan commercial strategies.

Temple Lang and O'Donoghue, writing in 2002, deplored the lack of clarification about what kind of conduct constitutes an abuse.

J. Temple Lang and R. O'Donoghue, 'Defining Legitimate Competition: How to Clarify Pricing Abuses under Article 82EC' (2002) 26 *Fordham Int'l LJ* 83, 83–84

Although a now universally-accepted distinction is drawn in the European Community ('Community') competition law between exploitative and exclusionary (or anti-competitive) abuses . . . very little effort has been made to clarify the general principles about the kinds of behavior that are contrary to Article [102] . . . which prohibits abuse of a dominant position. The case law and practice has arisen pragmatically, and largely in response to complaints to the European Commission and appeals to the Community Courts against Commission decisions adopted on the basis of such complaints. With the exception of specialized Notices and guidance in the telecommunications and postal sectors, the Commission has not attempted to develop any kind of general or comprehensive statement on abusive behavior. There have been several consequences of this unplanned growth. First, the Commission and the Community Courts have dealt with individual cases that were said to raise questions of abuse by reference to the facts of the individual case, seemingly without having any clear general analytical or intellectual framework for doing so. Second, a number of basic questions have not been answered or even discussed, because due to the accidents of litigation or otherwise, they did not arise in any of the cases that have been decided. Finally, the influence that economic thinking has had on the Community rules on distribution, horizontal agreements, and mergers has not been felt, to the same extent or at all, in the interpretation and application of Article [102].

The Commission's initiative to 'modernise' the application of Article 102 to exclusionary abuses, described in Chapter 5, was an attempt to inject intellectual coherence and interpret the vague and unscientific language of the EU Courts in terms of economic principle.

(ii) The Implications of Competition on the Merits: It is Not the Role of Article 102 to Keep Less Efficient Competitors on the Market

Modernisation put the interests of consumers at the centre of the application of Article 102. Ironically, almost all exclusionary abuse cases arise not from action by customers or consumers (who may be very happy with the predatory (low) prices, low prices arising from a margin squeeze, or bundled products) but from complaints or legal action by competitors. However, competition on the merits may hurt competitors. The CJ made an important statement in *Post Danmark*, making it clear that it is not the function of Article 102 to protect less efficient competitors and that excluding competitors is not necessarily detrimental to competition.

> ### Case C-209/10, *Post Danmark A/S v Konkurrencerådet*, EU:C:2012:172
>
> #### Court of Justice
>
> 21. It is settled case-law that a finding that an undertaking has such a dominant position is not in itself a ground of criticism of the undertaking concerned (Case 322/81 *Nederlandsche Banden-Industrie-Michelin v Commission* . . . paragraph 57, and Joined Cases C-395/96 P and C-396/96 P *Compagnie maritime belge transports and Others* v *Commission* . . . paragraph 37). It is in no way the purpose of Article [102] to prevent an undertaking from acquiring, on its own merits, the dominant position on a market (see, inter alia, *TeliaSonera Sverige*, paragraph 24). Nor does that provision seek to ensure that competitors less efficient than the undertaking with the dominant position should remain on the market.
>
> 22. Thus, not every exclusionary effect is necessarily detrimental to competition (see, by analogy, *TeliaSonera Sverige*, paragraph 43). Competition on the merits may, by definition, lead to the departure from the market or the marginalisation of competitors that are less efficient and so less attractive to consumers from the point of view of, among other things, price, choice, quality or innovation.[66]

(iii) Tests for Determining what is 'Competition on the Merits'

While it may be comparatively easy to identify conduct at the extremes of the spectrum as being competition on the merits or an exclusionary abuse,[67] the concept does not provide a tool for objectively drawing a line between 'good' and 'bad' conduct in the middle. In *Microsoft*,[68] for example, the GC confined the 'merits' of a product, on which competition should be based, to its 'intrinsic merits' separate from the way that it was distributed or to the way it worked with other products (*in casu*, interoperability).

There are a number of economic tests which can aid identification of competition on the merits. Each of these has its drawbacks but nevertheless they can be useful as analytical tools.[69] The best known tests are:

- The 'as efficient competitor' or 'equally efficient competitor' test (AEC test). The test is used to apply the consumer welfare standard.[70] The 'as efficient competitor' is a 'hypothetical competitor having the same costs as the dominant company'.[71] The idea behind this test is that conduct should be unlawful only if it is capable of excluding such a competitor, because only some kind of anti-competitive conduct can exclude equally efficient rivals. It has drawbacks in allowing the exclusion of less efficient new competitors which could in time have become as efficient. Furthermore, conduct caught by the AEC test might nevertheless enhance consumer welfare

---

[66] See also the then Commissioner Neelie Kroes on the review of Art. 102 in 2005, 'I like aggressive competition—including by dominant companies—and I don't care if it may hurt competitors—as long as it ultimately benefits consumers. That is because the main and ultimate objective of Article 102 is to protect consumers, and this does, of course, require the protection of an undistorted competitive process on the market', 'Preliminary Thoughts on Policy Review of Article 102', Fordham Corporate Law Institute, SPEECH/05/537, 23 September 2005.

[67] See the Guidance Paper, para. 22, for the Commission's examples of what are termed 'naked restrictions', and Case T-286/09, *Intel v Commission* EU:T:2014:547, paras. 203–320, on appeal Case C-413/14 P, judgment pending.

[68] Case T-201/04, *Microsoft* [2007] ECR II-3601, para. 1046.

[69] See, e.g., OECD Policy Brief (2006), 'What is Competition on the Merits?', available at <http://78.41.128.130/dataoecd/10/27/37082099.pdf>; J. Vickers, 'Abuse of Market Power' (2005) 115 *Economic Journal* F244; K. Fjell and L. Sørgard, 'How to Test for Abuse of Dominance?' (2006) 2 *European Law Journal* 69; O'Donoghue and Padilla, n. 1, 227–237.

[70] Chap. 1, Section 3.F, and see C. Ahlborn and D. Piccinin, 'The *Intel* Judgment and Consumer Welfare—A Response to Wouter Wils' [2015] 1 *CLPD* 60, 64–65.

[71] OECD Policy Brief (2006), 4.

(the test may not have the necessary correlation to consumer welfare), and it is not useful in situations where the efficiency of competitors is not an issue.[72] The CJ has endorsed the AEC test in respect of predatory[73] and selective low[74] pricing and margin squeeze.[75] It has rejected its use in loyalty rebate cases.[76] In *Post Danmark II* it described the test as 'one tool amongst others'.[77] The Guidance Paper adopts the AEC test as the standard by which pricing policies are normally assessed but allows for exceptions.[78]

- The 'profit sacrifice' test. This examines the dominant undertaking's conduct to see if it involves sacrificing profits in circumstances where it would only be rational to do so if the undertaking was thereby able to exclude competitors. The obvious example is predatory pricing (pricing below cost to drive competitors from the market). It does not, however, capture other types of anti-competitive exclusionary conduct and can catch welfare-enhancing conduct such as investing in research and development (R&D) (which if successful might result in an innovation so successful that competitors are eliminated).[79] The Guidance Paper adopts a profit sacrifice test as the usual test for predatory pricing.[80]

- The 'no economic sense' test. This is similar to the profit sacrifice test, but more inclusive as it does not depend on the one element of sacrificing profits. It states that conduct should be considered abusive only if it makes no economic sense except for its tendency to lessen or exclude competition. The test has been used by the US Department of Justice (DOJ) when arguing cases under s. 2 of the Sherman Act.[81] Like the other tests it has its proponents and detractors.[82] The Guidance Paper, paragraph 22, adopts what is in effect a no economic sense test when it says that where conduct can only raise obstacles to competition and create no efficiencies anti-competitive effect may be inferred.

- The consumer welfare balancing test. The various versions of this test involve balancing the positive and negative effects of the conduct on consumer welfare. As the OECD says, '[t]hey all have a degree of intuitive appeal because they attempt to use consumer welfare effects themselves, rather than indirect factors such as profit sacrifice, as the gauge of dominant firm conduct'.[83] O'Donoghue and Padilla conclude:

Although proponents of the consumer harm test have made its operational features as useful as possible, complex and precarious balancing acts are still likely to be necessary in marginal cases where

---

[72] E.g., Case C-457/10 P, *AstraZeneca* EU:C:2012:770, where the undertaking was held to have misused the patent system to exclude competitors.

[73] Case C-62/86, *AKZO* [1991] ECR I-3359.

[74] Case C-209/10, *Post Danmark I* EU:C:2012:172.

[75] Case C-280/08 P, *Deutsche Telekom* [2010] ECR I-9555; Case C-52/09, *TeliaSonera* [2011] ECR I-527.

[76] Case C-549/10 P, *Tomra* EU:C:2012:221. See also the GC in Case T-286/09, *Intel v Commission* EU:T:2014:547, on appeal Case C-413/14 P, judgment pending.

[77] Case C-23/14, *Post Danmark II* EU:C:2015:651, para. 61.

[78] Guidance Paper, paras. 23 and 24, see Section 7.D, p. 383 ff.

[79] See S. Salop, 'Exclusionary Conduct, Effect on Consumers, and the Flawed Profit-Sacrifice Standard' (2005–2006) 73 *Antitrust LJ* 311; E. Elhauge, 'Defining Better Monopolisation Standards' (2003–2004) 56 *Stan LR* 253, 271 ('Sacrificing profits is neither sufficient nor necessary to show that conduct that excludes rivals is undesirable, nor does it even correlate well with the desirability of such conduct').

[80] Guidance Paper, paras. 64–65.

[81] E.g., in its briefs in *Microsoft*, available at <http://www.doj.gov/atr/cases/f7200/7230.htm>; *United States v AMR Corp*, 335 F.3d 1109 (10th Cir. 2005) (*American Airlines*); *United States v Dentsply International Inc*, 399 F.3d 181 (3d Cir. 2005).

[82] The criticisms are summed up in O'Donoghue and Padilla, n. 1, 230; cf. G. J. Werden, 'Competition Policy on Exclusionary Conduct: Towards an Effects-based Analysis' (2006) 2 *European Competition Journal* 53, who suggests that the 'no economic sense' test should generally be applied (note that, although writing in a personal capacity, Werden was at the time Senior Economic Counsel at the US DOJ).

[83] OECD Policy Brief (2006), 5.

the cost of error is likely to be high. Moreover, if issues of proportionality come into play, economics contributes very little by way of predictability and the outcomes will represent matters of policy rather than precision.[84]

- The 'own efficiency' test.[85] This asks whether the monopolist has improved its own efficiency by the conduct under review, or whether it has impaired a competitor's efficiency (regardless of whether it has impaired its own efficiency). The former would be permitted and the latter would be prohibited. This test seems to be most suitable where the alleged exclusionary conduct is of the 'refusal to deal' kind,[86] and it still requires a determination of whether the conduct is efficient or not.

F. FORM- AND EFFECTS-BASED ANALYSIS

One of the most criticised aspects of the application of Article 102 has been the use of 'form' rather than 'effects' based analysis.[87] This means that conduct is condemned as an exclusionary abuse because it takes a certain form, rather than because of its effects in the particular case. Where conduct is condemned as an abuse because of its form it is often called a 'per se' abuse. However, given that there is always the possibility (however unlikely in practice and notwithstanding the more absolutist language in some older cases) of the conduct being objectively justified,[88] it is more accurately described as presumptively abusive or *virtually* or *akin to* per se abusive (and the words 'per se abuse' should be understood in that way). Recently these types of abuses have often been called 'by object' abuses, reflecting the Article 101 terminology. This is appropriate because, as we saw in Chapter 4, all restrictions by object under Article 101 are in theory eligible for exemption under Article 101(3). Moreover, the description of Article 101 'object' restrictions in *Cartes Bancaires* in 2014 as those that 'may be considered so likely to have negative effects...that it may be considered redundant,...to prove that they have actual effects on the market...'[89] also describes conduct which is condemned as abusive because it is presumed to have anti-competitive effects. One argument for having such a category of abuses is that it provides 'a clear and easy to apply general prohibition rule' which lays the burden of showing any possible objective justification upon the dominant undertaking which 'has the best access to all relevant information, and has a stronger risk-bearing capacity than its smaller competitors'.[90]

In view of the confusion of calling abuses 'per se' when they are open to objective justification this chapter uses the term 'by object' abuses where possible.

We see the issue of 'by object' versus 'by effects' abuses played out in many of the cases discussed in this chapter. We also see that in some cases the argument is whether the conduct should merely be *capable* of anti-competitive effects rather than produce *actual* or *likely* effects before being found abusive. Furthermore, even if competitors are shown to be (potentially) excluded by the conduct, should it be assumed that consumers are thereby harmed as a result? This goes back to the question of why exclusionary abuses are prohibited. If the competition rules only protect competition as a means of protecting consumers, then exclusion which does not harm consumers should be permitted.[91]

---

[84] O'Donoghue and Padilla, n. 1, 237.

[85] Put forward in a leading article in 2003, see E. Elhauge, 'Defining Better Monopolisation Standards' (2003–2004) 56 *Stan LR* 253.

[86] See Section 13, p. 496 ff.

[87] For form- and effects-based analysis generally, see Chap. 1, Section 11.B.

[88] For objective justification, see Section 5.

[89] Case C-67/13 P, *Groupement des Cartes Bancaires* EU:C:2014:2204, para. 51.

[90] W. Wils, 'The Judgment of the EU General Court in *Intel* and the So-called "More Economic Approach" to Abuse of Dominance' (2014) 4 *World Competition* 405, writing with reference to the rules on loyalty rebates.

[91] For a full discussion of the effects issue, see Akman, *The Concept of Abuse in EU Competition Law*, n. 15, 130–143.

G. APPRECIABILITY

There is no appreciability threshold or de minimis doctrine in respect of abusive conduct under Article 102. This was confirmed by the CJ in *Post Danmark II*.[92]

Case C-23/14, *Post Danmark A/S v Konkurrencerådet (Post Danmark II)* EU:C:2015:651

Court of Justice

72. In addition, since the structure of competition on the market has already been weakened by the presence of the dominant undertaking, any further weakening of the structure of competition may constitute an abuse of a dominant position (judgment in *Hoffmann-La Roche* v *Commission*, 85/76,..., paragraph 123).

73. It follows that fixing an appreciability (*de minimis*) threshold for the purposes of determining whether there is an abuse of a dominant position is not justified. That anti-competitive practice is, by its very nature, liable to give rise to not insignificant restrictions of competition, or even of eliminating competition on the market on which the undertaking concerned operates.

74. It follows from the foregoing considerations that Article [102] must be interpreted as meaning that, in order to fall within the scope of that article, the anti-competitive effect of a rebate scheme operated by a dominant undertaking must be probable, there being no need to show that it is of a serious or appreciable nature.

It will be noted that the Court based the lack of an appreciability threshold on paragraph 123 of *Hoffmann-La Roche*, which said that *any* further weakening of the competitive structure of a market on which there is a dominant firm may constitute an abuse. The Court concluded from this that an anti-competitive practice by the dominant undertaking is *by its very nature* liable to give rise to restrictions which are significant. The GC in *Intel* had already found that there is no appreciability criterion under Article 102, stating that this had been rejected by the CJ in paragraph 123 of *Hoffmann-La Roche*.[93]

Although there cannot be an appreciability threshold under Article 102 predicated on market share as in the Commission's de minimis Notice applicable to Article 101,[94] the dismissal of any concept of appreciability in respect of abusive conduct is striking. However, it is likely to be of importance mainly as regards conduct which is abusive by object, as vividly demonstrated in *Intel*.[95] Where conduct is judged by its effects taking into account 'all the circumstances', as in *Post Danmark II* itself, where the effects must be 'probable' the issue of appreciability may be subsumed into the general analysis. Moreover, the Commission and national competition authorities (NCAs) could be expected to desist from enforcement action in any case where there were no significant anti-competitive effects, although private litigants in national courts might not.

---

[92] Case C-23/14, *Post Danmark II* EU:C:2015:651. This was implicit in the earlier case, Case C-549/10 P, *Tomra* EU:C:2012:221, see Section 11.F.ii.d.

[93] Case T-286/09, *Intel* EU:T:2014:547, para. 116, on appeal Case C-413/14 P, judgment pending, see Section 11.E.iii.

[94] Notice on agreements of minor importance [2014] OJ C57/1, see Chap. 3.

[95] Such as exclusive purchasing, loyalty (exclusivity rebates), and tying.

4. THE COMMISSION'S APPROACH TO EXCLUSIONARY ABUSES IN THE GUIDANCE PAPER: THE 'ANTI-COMPETITIVE FORECLOSURE' CONCEPT

The publication of the Commission's Guidance Paper is discussed in Chapter 5.[96] In the Guidance Paper the Commission adopts the concept of 'anti-competitive foreclosure' as the normal standard for intervention.[97] It is important to note that this is not just 'foreclosure' but '*anti-competitive* foreclosure'. This is explained in paragraph 19 as a situation where the exclusion of competitors is likely to result in the dominant undertaking being in a position where it can profitably increase prices to the detriment of consumers.[98] In paragraph 20 the Commission explains how it will generally assess this. Anti-competitive foreclosure therefore comprises two elements:

- foreclosure (the hindrance, exclusion, or elimination of actual or potential competitors); and
- consumer harm.

Guidance on the Commission's Enforcement Priorities in Applying Article 82 of the EC Treaty to Abusive Exclusionary Conduct by Dominant Undertakings [2009] OJ C45/2

19. The aim of the Commission's enforcement activity in relation to exclusionary conduct is to ensure that dominant undertakings do not impair effective competition by foreclosing their competitors in an anti-competitive way, thus having an adverse impact on consumer welfare, whether in the form of higher price levels than would have otherwise prevailed or in some other form such as limiting quality or reducing consumer choice. In this document the term 'anti-competitive foreclosure' is used to describe a situation where effective access of actual or potential competitors to supplies or markets is hampered or eliminated as a result of the conduct of the dominant undertaking whereby the dominant undertaking is likely to be in a position to profitably increase prices . . . to the detriment of consumers. The identification of likely consumer harm can rely on qualitative and, where possible and appropriate, quantitative evidence. The Commission will address such anti-competitive foreclosure either at the intermediate level or at the level of final consumers, or at both levels.[99]

20. The Commission will normally intervene under Article [102] where, on the basis of cogent and convincing evidence, the allegedly abusive conduct is likely to lead to anti-competitive foreclosure. The Commission considers the following factors to be generally relevant to such an assessment:

- the position of the dominant undertaking: in general, the stronger the dominant position, the higher the likelihood that conduct protecting that position leads to anti-competitive foreclosure,

- the conditions on the relevant market: this includes the conditions of entry and expansion, such as the existence of economies of scale and/or scope and network effects. Economies of scale mean that

---

[96] See Chap. 5, Section 6.C, p. 275.

[97] For general commentary on the Guidance Paper, see N. Petit, 'From Formalism to Effects? The Commission's Communication on Enforcement Priorities in Applying Article 82' (2009) 32 *World Competition* 485; P. Akman, 'The European Commission's Guidance on Article 102 TFEU: From *Inferno* to *Paradiso*?' (2010) 73 *MLR* 605; L. Lovdahl Gormesen, 'Why the European Commission's Enforcement Priorities on Article 82 Should Be Withdrawn' [2010] *ECLR* 45; L. F. Pace (ed.), *European Competition Law: The Impact of the Commission's Guidance on Article 102* (Edward Elgar, 2011).

[98] 'Increase prices' is used as shorthand for the other parameters of competition as well: influencing output, innovation, variety, and quality, Guidance Paper, para. 11, see Chap. 6, Section 3.B.

[99] For the footnote at this point of the Guidance, see text accompanying n. 101.

competitors are less likely to enter or stay in the market if the dominant undertaking forecloses a significant part of the relevant market. Similarly, the conduct may allow the dominant undertaking to 'tip' a market characterised by network effects in its favour or to further entrench its position on such a market. Likewise, if entry barriers in the upstream and/or downstream market are significant, this means that it may be costly for competitors to overcome possible foreclosure through vertical integration,

- the position of the dominant undertaking's competitors: this includes the importance of competitors for the maintenance of effective competition. A specific competitor may play a significant competitive role even if it only holds a small market share compared to other competitors. It may, for example, be the closest competitor to the dominant undertaking, be a particularly innovative competitor, or have the reputation of systematically cutting prices. In its assessment, the Commission may also consider in appropriate cases, on the basis of information available, whether there are realistic, effective and timely counterstrategies that competitors would be likely to deploy,

- the position of the customers or input suppliers: this may include consideration of the possible selectivity of the conduct in question. The dominant undertaking may apply the practice only to selected customers or input suppliers who may be of particular importance for the entry or expansion of competitors, thereby enhancing the likelihood of anti-competitive foreclosure . . . In the case of customers, they may, for example, be the ones most likely to respond to offers from alternative suppliers, they may represent a particular means of distributing the product that would be suitable for a new entrant, they may be situated in a geographic area well suited to new entry or they may be likely to influence the behaviour of other customers. In the case of input suppliers, those with whom the dominant undertaking has concluded exclusive supply arrangements may be the ones most likely to respond to requests by customers who are competitors of the dominant undertaking in a downstream market, or may produce a grade of the product—or produce at a location—particularly suitable for a new entrant. Any strategies at the disposal of the customers or input suppliers which could help to counter the conduct of the dominant undertaking will also be considered,

- the extent of the allegedly abusive conduct: in general, the higher the percentage of total sales in the relevant market affected by the conduct, the longer its duration, and the more regularly it has been applied, the greater is the likely foreclosure effect,

- possible evidence of actual foreclosure: if the conduct has been in place for a sufficient period of time, the market performance of the dominant undertaking and its competitors may provide direct evidence of anti-competitive foreclosure. For reasons attributable to the allegedly abusive conduct, the market share of the dominant undertaking may have risen or a decline in market share may have been slowed. For similar reasons, actual competitors may have been marginalised or may have exited, or potential competitors may have tried to enter and failed,

- direct evidence of any exclusionary strategy: this includes internal documents which contain direct evidence of a strategy to exclude competitors, such as a detailed plan to engage in certain conduct in order to exclude a competitor, to prevent entry or to pre-empt the emergence of a market, or evidence of concrete threats of exclusionary action. Such direct evidence may be helpful in interpreting the dominant undertaking's conduct.

21. When pursuing a case the Commission will develop the analysis of the general factors mentioned in paragraph 20, together with the more specific factors described in the sections dealing with certain types of exclusionary conduct, and any other factors which it may consider to be appropriate. This assessment will usually be made by comparing the actual or likely future situation in the relevant market (with the dominant undertaking's conduct in place) with an appropriate counterfactual, such as the simple absence of the conduct in question or with another realistic alternative scenario, having regard to established business practices.

Many of the factors listed in paragraph 20 of the Guidance concern the structure of the market and are factors the Commission customarily takes into account in both antitrust and merger analysis. These relate to the 'foreclosure' part of the test. The Commission will also take any other appropriate factors into account, including those that are conduct-specific. Paragraph 21 also states that the Commission will base its assessment on an appropriate 'counterfactual' (meaning a 'but for' analysis in which it tries to determine what would be the situation in the absence of the impugned conduct). The assessment of consumer harm is mainly contained in the last sentence of paragraph 19. The Guidance Paper is open to the criticism that although 'anti-competitive foreclosure' has consumer harm as one of its elements the treatment of many of the specific abuses in the Guidance Paper assumes such harm readily.[100]

Paragraph 19 has an important footnote[101] which says that '"consumers" encompasses all direct and indirect users, including intermediate producers'. That is the established interpretation of 'consumer' in EU competition law.[102] However here the footnote also states that 'where intermediate users are actual or potential competitors of the dominant undertaking, the assessment focuses on the effects of the conduct on users further downstream'. This is significant in respect of abuses (such as refusals to supply and margin squeezes) where the intermediate customers are downstream competitors of the dominant undertaking. In such situations emphasis on the effects on those competitor-customers may distort the analysis of the effects on the final consumers.

Paragraph 22 turns away from an effects-based analysis and says that there may be conduct which is so egregious that its anti-competitive effect can be inferred. This can be seen as an application of the 'no economic sense' test.

22. There may be circumstances where it is not necessary for the Commission to carry out a detailed assessment before concluding that the conduct in question is likely to result in consumer harm. If it appears that the conduct can only raise obstacles to competition and that it creates no efficiencies, its anti-competitive effect may be inferred. This could be the case, for instance, if the dominant undertaking prevents its customers from testing the products of competitors or provides financial incentives to its customers on condition that they do not test such products, or pays a distributor or a customer to delay the introduction of a competitor's product.

An example of these abuses is the 'naked restrictions' in *Intel*[103] where the undertaking paid customers to delay or restrict the marketing of rivals' products. However, the inclusion of testing restrictions in paragraph 22 has been criticised.[104]

5. OBJECTIVE JUSTIFICATION, EFFICIENCY, AND OTHER DEFENCES

A. GENERAL

Although Article 102 does not contain an exemption provision similar to Article 101(3), the EU Courts have developed the concept of 'objective justification' by which otherwise abusive conduct may escape infringing Article 102. The main debate has been about to what extent, if any, efficiencies can provide objective justification.

The defence of objective justification means that there are no 'per se' abuses under Article 102. Conduct which is often described as per se abusive, because it is presumptively abusive or abusive

---

[100] See, e.g., P. Marsden, 'Some Outstanding Issues from the European Commission's Guidance on Article 102 TFEU: Not-so-faint Echoes of Ordoliberalism' in F. Etro and I. Kokkoris (eds.), *Competition Law and the Enforcement of Article 102* (Oxford University Press, 2010), Chap. 3.

[101] See n. 99.

[102] See Chap. 1, Section 8.B.v.a, p. 40.

[103] Case T-286/09, *Intel* EU:T:2014:547, paras. 198–220, see Section 14.F, p. 558.

[104] O'Donoghue and Padilla, n. 1, 449–450.

'by object'[105] is open to the possibility of justification. That possibility may be more theoretical than real, because the chances of the defence succeeding are extremely unlikely, but it exists. The difficulties of proving objective justification mean, however, that once an abuse is prima facie abusive it is will almost inevitably infringe Article 102.

In this section we look first at the *Post Danmark I* ruling; secondly, at objective necessity; thirdly, at efficiencies; fourthly, at the question of the burden of proof; and fifthly at the problems with the objective justification defence. We then consider the 'protecting its own commercial interests' defence which may be conceptualised as a type of objective justification, and at the 'meeting competition' defence.

B. OBJECTIVE JUSTIFICATION IN *POST DANMARK I*

In *Post Danmark I* in 2012 the CJ stated that conduct with anti-competitive effects may be justified and set out the conditions that a successful efficiencies defence must fulfil.[106]

Case C-209/10, *Post Danmark A/S v Konkurrencerådet* EU:C:2012:172

The facts of the case, an Article 267 reference, are given later in this chapter.[107] The CJ ruled on the application of Article 102 to certain types of pricing and then said that it was for the referring court to decide whether there were anti-competitive effects. Even if there were, however, it was open to the dominant undertaking to provide justification for its conduct.

Court of Justice

40. If the court making the reference, after carrying out that assessment, should nevertheless make a finding of anti-competitive effects due to Post Danmark's actions, it should be recalled that it is open to a dominant undertaking to provide justification for behaviour that is liable to be caught by the prohibition under Article [102] (see, to this effect, Case 27/76 *United Brands and United Brands Continentaal* v *Commission* . . . paragraph 184; Joined Cases C-241/91 P and C-242/91 P *RTE and ITP* v *Commission* . . . paragraphs 54 and 55; and *TeliaSonera Sverige*, paragraphs 31 and 75).

41. In particular, such an undertaking may demonstrate, for that purpose, either that its conduct is objectively necessary (see, to that effect, Case 311/84 *CBEM* . . . paragraph 27), or that the exclusionary effect produced may be counterbalanced, outweighed even, by advantages in terms of efficiency that also benefit consumers (Case C-95/04 P *British Airways* v *Commission* . . . paragraph 86, and *TeliaSonera Sverige*, paragraph 76).

42. In that last regard, it is for the dominant undertaking to show that the efficiency gains likely to result from the conduct under consideration counteract any likely negative effects on competition and consumer welfare in the affected markets, that those gains have been, or are likely to be, brought about as a result of that conduct, that such conduct is necessary for the achievement of those gains in efficiency and that it does not eliminate effective competition, by removing all or most existing sources of actual or potential competition.

---

[105] See Section 3.F, p. 365.

[106] Whether *Post Danmark I* means that 'objective necessity' is a synonym for 'objective justification' and that 'efficiency' is a separate defence, is a moot point. Rousseva and Marquis, n. 3, 32 consider that they are separate. In COMP/39.525, *Telekomunikacja Polska* 22 June 2011, paras. 873–874, upheld Case T-486/11, *Orange Polska* EU:T:2015:1002, the Commission referred to a dominant undertaking providing an objective justification *or* demonstrating that its conduct produces efficiencies.

[107] Section 8.D, p. 391.

> 43. In the present case, it is enough to state, with regard to the considerations set out at paragraph 11 above, that the mere fact that a criterion explicitly based on gains in efficiency was not one of the factors appearing in the schedules of prices charged by Post Danmark cannot justify a refusal to take into account, where necessary, such gains in efficiency, provided that their actual existence and their extent have been established in accordance with the requirements set out in paragraph 42 above.

In paragraphs 41 and 42 the CJ identifies two particular grounds of justification (a) objective necessity and (b) efficiencies. By prefacing this with 'in particular' the CJ does not rule out there being other grounds of justification. The reference in paragraph 40 of the judgment to *United Brands*[108] where the undertaking pleaded that it was merely protecting its own commercial interests suggests that the CJ considers that this is another type of justification rather than a separate defence. In *AstraZeneca*, however, the CJ referred to 'the absence . . . of the defence of legitimate interests . . . *or in the absence of objective justification*' (emphasis added).[109]

C. OBJECTIVE NECESSITY

Post Danmark I did not elaborate on the meaning of 'objective necessity'. In *Télémarketing (CBEM)*,[110] cited in paragraph 41, the Court said that an abuse would be committed where the dominant undertaking engaged in certain conduct 'without any objective necessity'[111] and referred to the possibility of the refusal to supply in that case being justified by technical or commercial requirements relating to the nature of television, the service at issue.[112] Conduct necessary to protect legitimate public-interest objectives could in principle be objectively justified[113] and this could include the health and safety of consumers. However, in both *Hilti*[114] and *Tetra Pak II*[115] claims that tie-ins were justified in order to ensure public safety were rejected on the grounds that safety is ensured by public authorities enforcing safety regulations and not by private undertakings indulging in exclusionary practices.[116] In *AstraZeneca* the CJ said that the imposition of pharmacovigilance obligations on a dominant undertaking could constitute objective justification for deregistering a marketing authorisation, although it was not proved to be so in that case.[117] In *FAG-Flughafen-Frankfurt/Main*[118] the undertaking argued that the refusal to allow independent ramp-handling and self-handling services at an airport was objectively justified by space and capacity restraints and the Commission only rejected this after carefully considering technical reports.[119]

---

[108] Case 27/76, *United Brands* [1978] ECR 207.

[109] Case C-457/10 P, *AstraZeneca* EU:C:2012:770, para. 134.

[110] Case 311/84, *Centre Belge d'Etudes du Marché-Télémarketing v Compagnie Luxembourgeoise de Télédiffusion SA and Information Publicité Benelux SA (Centre Belge, CBEM, or Télémarketing)* [1985] ECR 3261.

[111] Ibid., para. 27.

[112] Ibid., para. 26.

[113] See P. Lowe, 'DG Competition's Review of the Policy on Abuse of Dominance' [2004] *Fordham Corp L Inst* 163 (the author was then Director-General of DG Comp).

[114] Case T-30/89, *Hilti AG v Commission* [1991] ECR II-1439, para. 118.

[115] Case C-333/94 P, *Tetra Pak II* [1996] ECR I-5951.

[116] R. Nazzini, *The Foundations of European Union Competition Law: The Objectives and Principles of Article 102* (Oxford University Press, 2011), 317–320, describes this as a 'social welfare' defence.

[117] Case C-457/10 P, *AstraZeneca* EU:C:2012:770, para. 135. The argument was raised for the first time before the GC.

[118] [1998] L72/30.

[119] But note the commitments decision COMP/39.315, *ENI* 29 September 2010, where capacity constraints did not prevent the view of the Commission that there was an abuse.

In the Guidance Paper the Commission relates 'objectively necessary' to 'factors external to the undertaking'. The only examples it gives are health and safety reasons, and it repeats what was said in *Hilti* and *Tetra Pak II*.[120]

Guidance on the Commission's Enforcement Priorities in Applying Article 82 of the EC Treaty to Abusive Exclusionary Conduct by Dominant Undertakings [2009] OJ C45/2

29. The question of whether conduct is objectively necessary and proportionate must be determined on the basis of factors external to the dominant undertaking. Exclusionary conduct may, for example, be considered objectively necessary for health or safety reasons related to the nature of the product in question. However, proof of whether conduct of this kind is objectively necessary must take into account that it is normally the task of public authorities to set and enforce public health and safety standards. It is not the task of a dominant undertaking to take steps on its own initiative to exclude products which it regards, rightly or wrongly, as dangerous or inferior to its own product . . .

The limitation to 'external factors' is seen in the Commission's decisional practice. As well as being necessary the conduct, as stated in paragraph 29, must be 'proportionate'. In *Telekomunikacja Polska*[121] the Commission referred to 'allegedly abusive conduct that is actually necessary on the basis of factors external to the dominant undertaking and is proportionate'. The plea of the Romanian Power Exchange in *OPCOM/Romanian Power Exchange* that its discriminatory treatment of power exchanges from Member States other than Romania was justified by the need to avoid an unlawful cash flow mismatch in VAT payments, was dismissed by the Commission on the grounds that creating this barrier to entry was neither proportionate nor necessary.[122] Faull and Nikpay point out that the objective necessity defence 'does not require any balancing between the negative effects on competition of the conduct and its benefits . . . as long as the conduct is necessary to the achievement of the objective and proportionate to it, an objective necessity defence is made out'.[123] There is as yet no case in which an abuse has been justified as objectively necessary.

D. EFFICIENCIES

In setting out the conditions for an 'efficiency defence' the CJ in *Post Danmark I* referred to its judgment in *British Airways* (repeated in *TeliaSonera*[124]) where it accepted that the dominant undertaking's conduct could be justified by efficiencies (earlier cases did not refer to efficiencies as such):

It has to be determined whether the exclusionary effect arising from such a system, which is disadvantageous for competition, may be counterbalanced, or outweighed, by advantages in terms of efficiency which also benefit the consumer. If the exclusionary effect of that system bears no relation to advantages for the market and consumers, or if it goes beyond what is necessary in order to attain those advantages, that system must be regarded as an abuse.[125]

---

[120] See Section 5.C, p. 371.

[121] COMP/39.525, *Telekomunikacja Polska* 22 June 2011, para. 874, upheld Case T-486/11, *Orange Polska* EU:T:2015:1002.

[122] [2014] OJ C 314/7, IP/14/214, STATEMENT/14/48. The Commission noted that no other European power exchange faced with a similar situation took such measures.

[123] Faull and Nikpay, n. 1, 4.291.

[124] Case C-52/09, *TeliaSonera* [2011] ECR I-527, para. 76.

[125] Case C-95/04, *British Airways* [2007] ECR I-2331, para. 69.

Despite the Court's reference to *British Airways* and *TeliaSonera* the efficiency defence set out in paragraph 42 of *Post Danmark I* is stricter. The dominant undertaking must show:

- the likely efficiency gains counteract any likely negative effects on competition and consumer welfare;

- the gains have been, or are likely to be, brought about as a result of the conduct;

- the conduct is necessary for the achievement of the efficiency gains; and

- the conduct does not eliminate effective competition, by removing all or most existing sources of actual or potential competition.

In effect paragraphs 41–42 of *Post Danmark I*, which were repeated in *Post Danmark II*,[126] adopted the efficiency test set out in paragraph 30 of the Guidance Paper. Paragraph 30 is similar to the efficiencies section in the Horizontal Merger Guidelines.[127]

Guidance on the Commission's Enforcement Priorities in Applying Article 82 of the EC Treaty to Abusive Exclusionary Conduct by Dominant Undertakings [2009] OJ C45/2

30. The Commission considers that a dominant undertaking may also justify conduct leading to foreclosure of competitors on the ground of efficiencies that are sufficient to guarantee that no net harm to consumers is likely to arise. In this context, the dominant undertaking will generally be expected to demonstrate, with a sufficient degree of probability, and on the basis of verifiable evidence, that the following cumulative conditions are fulfilled:[128]

- the efficiencies have been, or are likely to be, realised as a result of the conduct. They may, for example, include technical improvements in the quality of goods, or a reduction in the cost of production or distribution,

- the conduct is indispensable to the realisation of those efficiencies: there must be no less anticompetitive alternatives to the conduct that are capable of producing the same efficiencies,

- the likely efficiencies brought about by the conduct outweigh any likely negative effects on competition and consumer welfare in the affected markets,

- the conduct does not eliminate effective competition, by removing all or most existing sources of actual or potential competition. Rivalry between undertakings is an essential driver of economic efficiency, including dynamic efficiencies in the form of innovation. In its absence the dominant undertaking will lack adequate incentives to continue to create and pass on efficiency gains. Where there is no residual competition and no foreseeable threat of entry, the protection of rivalry and the competitive process outweighs possible efficiency gains. In the Commission's view, exclusionary conduct which maintains, creates or strengthens a market position approaching that of a monopoly can normally not be justified on the grounds that it also creates efficiency gains.

31. It is incumbent upon the dominant undertaking to provide all the evidence necessary to demonstrate that the conduct concerned is objectively justified. It then falls to the Commission to make the ultimate assessment of whether the conduct concerned is not objectively necessary and, based on a weighing-up of any apparent anti-competitive effects against any advanced and substantiated efficiencies, is likely to result in consumer harm.

---

[126] Case C-23/14, *Post Danmark II* EU:C:2015:651, paras. 48–49.

[127] Horizontal Merger Guidelines [2004] OJ C31/5, paras. 76–88, see Chap. 15. Note in particular the requirement of 'merger specificity' in the Guidelines.

[128] The Commission's footnote here refers to the Article 101(3) Guidelines.

There is as yet no recorded case or decision where the efficiency defence has succeeded. In *Microsoft*, six months after *British Airways*, the GC rejected Microsoft's arguments that its conduct was objectively justified.[129] In a number of preliminary reference rulings the CJ has referred to the possibility of the exclusionary effects of the conduct being counterbalanced or outweighed by advantages in terms of efficiency, but this has been left to the national court.[130]

E. THE BURDEN OF PROOF

In *Microsoft* the GC considered the burden of proof in claims of objective justification. Paragraph 31 of the Guidance Paper reflects these parts of *Microsoft*.

Case T-201/04, *Microsoft v Commission* [2007] ECR II-3601

688 [and 1114].[131] The Court notes, as a preliminary point, that although the burden of proof of the existence of the circumstances that constitute an infringement of Article [102] is borne by the Commission, it is for the dominant undertaking concerned, and not for the Commission, before the end of the administrative procedure, to raise any plea of objective justification and to support it with arguments and evidence. It then falls to the Commission, where it proposes to make a finding of an abuse of a dominant position, to show that the arguments and evidence relied on by the undertaking cannot prevail and, accordingly, that the justification put forward cannot be accepted.

It appears from this, and from paragraph 42 of *Post Danmark*, that the evidential burden in respect of objective justification is on the dominant undertaking, in that once an abuse has been prima facie established it is up to the undertaking to adduce evidence and arguments that its conduct was justified. However, as the Commission, or other party alleging the infringement, bears the ultimate burden of proof under Article 2 of Regulation 1/2003, it is for that party to show that the conduct was not objectively justified in the light of the evidence put forward.[132]

F. THE DIFFICULTIES OF THE EFFICIENCY DEFENCE

There is yet to be any Article 102 case in which the conduct has been saved from infringing Article 102 because of efficiencies. Efficiency claims are usually dismissed with little discussion, as is shown in the cases discussed throughout this chapter. The problems with the defence include the following.[133]

---

[129] Case T-201/04, *Microsoft v Commission* [2007] ECR II-3601, paras. 666–712 and 1090–1167. See the discussion of *Microsoft* in Section 12.E.iii and Section 13.D.

[130] See Case C-52/09, *TeliaSonera* [2011] ECR I-527, para. 76; Case C-23/14, *Post Danmark II* EU:C:2015:651, paras. 48–49; see also Case C-52/07, *Kanal 5 Ltd v Föreningen Svenska Tonsättares Internationella Musikbyrå (STIM) upa* [2008] ECR I-9275, para. 47, where the CJ said that objective justification could arise from the task and method of financing public service undertakings.

[131] *Microsoft* covered two separate abuses. The identical passage appears in both halves of the judgment. The passage was repeated in Case T-301/04, *Clearstream* [2009] ECR II-3155, para. 185.

[132] See also R. Nazzini, 'The Wood Began to Move: An Essay on Consumer Welfare, Evidence and Burden of Proof in Article 102 EC Cases' (2006) 31 *ELRev* 518, 535: 'The analysis of the jurisprudence on objective justification demonstrates that this concept is not technically a defence. Rather it is used to explain the shifting of the evidential burden to the dominant undertaking once a prima facie case of abuse has been established', and further, Nazzini, n. 116, 289–294. See also Jacobs AG in his Opinion in Case C-53/03, *Synetairismos Farmakopoion Aitolias & Akarnanias (Syfait) v GlaxoSmithKline* [2005] ECR I-4609, para. 72.

[133] O'Donoghue and Padilla, n. 1, 287 note that it has been suggested that the Commission only pursues cases in which there are no offsetting efficiencies to the anti-competitive harm, but comment that this is difficult to reconcile with the Commission rejecting so few complaints on efficiency grounds.

First, the requirements of the defence are stringent. For example, the dominant undertaking has to ensure no net harm to competition and consumer welfare, but that balancing exercise is notoriously difficult and the undertaking needs to make the assessment before it implements its commercial policy.

Secondly, the requirements are subject to a high standard of proof. The Guidance Paper demands that the satisfaction of the conditions is demonstrated 'with a sufficient degree of probability, and on the basis of verifiable [i.e. quantifiable] evidence'. In *Post Danmark I* the CJ talked of taking efficiency gains into account where 'their actual existence and their extent have been established…'.[134] This standard of proof is in sharp contrast to the case law which allows the abusive conduct itself to be found by object, capability, or 'likely' anti-competitive effects.[135]

Thirdly, the fourth condition in *Post Danmark I*, i.e. that the conduct 'does not eliminate effective competition, by removing all or most existing sources of actual or potential competition' is inherently problematic when applied to the exclusionary conduct of a dominant undertaking. For example, in refusal to supply cases the refusal would not be a prima facie abuse in the first place without the (likely) elimination of effective competition in the downstream market.[136] It has been suggested that the requirement of 'effective' competition needs, therefore, to be read as 'existing' competition.[137] The danger is that the 'elimination of competition' condition means that consumers are deprived of the benefits of efficiencies because of the degree of dominance of the supplier.

Fourthly, the formulation of the efficiency defence appears to be narrow, and focused on the specific transaction. In *Michelin II*, for example, the GC dismissed claims about economies of scale[138] and in *British Airways* it dismissed arguments about high fixed costs.[139]

Post Danmark and the Guidance Paper in effect import Article 101(3) into Article 102. However, there are cogent reasons for arguing that a provision designed as an exemption for negotiated agreements between independent undertakings which restrict competition is not suitable for application *ex post* to the unilateral actions of dominant undertakings where the theory of harm is far more difficult.[140] It is not a matter of the desirability of taking efficiencies into account before finding an infringement of Article 102 but rather of at what stage of the analysis they should be taken into account and the conditions that they need to fulfil.

G. PROTECTING THE UNDERTAKING'S OWN COMMERCIAL INTERESTS

'Protection of the undertaking's own commercial interests' as a defence was first accepted in *United Brands* where the undertaking cut off supplies to a distributor to discipline it for participating in a rival's promotion. A 'commercial interest' has been described as 'an interest consistent

---

[134] Case C-209/10, *Post Danmark I* EU:C:2012:172, para. 43.

[135] See Sections 8–17 of this chapter. For a discussion of which standard applies to which abuse.

[136] See, e.g., Case C-7/97, *Oscar Bronner GmbH & Co KG v Mediaprint* [1998] ECR I-7791; Case C-418/01, *IMS Health GmbH & Co OHG v NDC Health GmbH & Co KG* [2004] ECR I-5039; Case T-201/04, *Microsoft* [2007] ECR II-3601.

[137] Faull and Nikpay, n. 1, 4.296.

[138] Case T-203/01, *Michelin II* [2003] ECR II-4071, para. 108.

[139] Case T-219/99, *British Airways v Commission* [2003] ECR II-5917, paras. 284–285. In the appeal, Case C-95/04 P, *British Airways* [2007] ECR I-2331, the CJ refused to review the matter on grounds of jurisdiction, see Section 11.F.c, p. 455.

[140] See further Akman, *The Concept of Abuse in EU Competition Law*, n. 15, 280–284; Nazzini, n. 116, 304–309; D. Walbroeck, 'The Assessment of Efficiencies under Article 102 TFEU and the Commission's Guidance Paper' in Etro and Kokkoris, n. 100, 115.

with the rational profit-maximizing behaviour of a non-dominant undertaking'.[141] The CJ said in *United Brands*:

189. Although it is true, as the applicant points out, that the fact that an undertaking is in a dominant position cannot disentitle it from protecting its own commercial interests if they are attacked, and that such an undertaking must be conceded the right to take such reasonable steps as it deems appropriate to protect its said interests, such behaviour cannot be countenanced if its actual purpose is to strengthen this dominant position and abuse it.

190. Even if the possibility of a counter-attack is acceptable that attack must still be proportionate to the threat taking into account the economic strength of the undertakings confronting each other.[142]

The CJ thus established the principle that Article 102 does not prevent an undertaking from protecting its own commercial interests when they are attacked. However, the principle does not apply if the undertaking's 'actual purpose is to strengthen this dominant position and abuse it', i.e. if the undertaking has an anti-competitive intent. Furthermore, the undertaking's response must be 'reasonable' and 'proportionate'.

The EU Courts and the Commission have relied on *United Brands* many times when considering a claim that the undertaking was merely protecting its own commercial interests.[143] The question of what is 'reasonable and proportional' arose in *BBI/Boosey & Hawkes*, another case in which a dominant undertaking cut off an existing customer.[144] In this case it seems to have been the undertaking's *immediate* withdrawal of supplies which was unacceptable. It was not proportional to the threat it faced. In *Tetra Pak I* Advocate General Kirschner said of proportionality:

Applied to the conduct of an undertaking in a dominant position, that principle has the following meaning: the undertaking in a dominant position may act in a profit-oriented way, strive through its efforts to improve its market position and pursue its legitimate interests. But in so doing it may employ only such methods as are necessary to pursue those legitimate aims. In particular it may not act in a way which, foreseeably, will limit competition more than is necessary.[145]

The protecting legitimate commercial interests defence has particularly been raised in cases of refusal to supply.[146] It played an important part in *Sot. Lélos*.[147] The pharmaceutical company's arguments were in effect an efficiency defence, but the CJ's judgment treated the matter as protection of its legitimate commercial interests.[148] The CJ said that the competition rules are incapable of being interpreted in such a way that in order to defend its own commercial interests the undertaking has no choice but to leave a particular market altogether.[149] There is little doubt that conduct protecting the dominant undertaking's interests would be justified if it consisted of legitimate business practices such as cutting off supplies to a bad debtor.[150]

---

[141] Nazzini, n. 116, 300.

[142] Case 27/76, *United Brands v Commission* [1978] ECR 207.

[143] See, e.g., Case T-65/89, *BPB Industries and British Gypsum* [1993] ECR II-389, para. 69; Cases T-24–26 and 28/93, *Compagnie Maritime Belge Transports v Commission* [1996] ECR II-1201, para. 107; Case T-228/97, *Irish Sugar* [1999] ECR II-2969, para. 112; Cases T-191 and 212–214/98, *Atlantic Container Line v Commission* [2003] ECR II-3275, paras. 1113–1114 (the GC said that according to the case law objective justification applied only to practices reasonably taken to protect the undertaking's commercial interests); Case T-203/01, *Michelin II* [2003] ECR II-4071, para. 55; Cases C-468–478/06, *Sot. Lélos* [2008] ECR I-7139, para. 39; Case T-301/04, *Clearstream* [2009] ECR II-3155, para. 132.

[144] *BBI/Boosey & Hawkes: Interim Measures* [1987] OJ L282/36, para. 19. The customer entered into competition with the supplier.

[145] Case T-51/89, *Tetra Pak Rausing SA v Commission* [1990] ECR II-309, para. 68 of the Opinion.

[146] As in Case 27/76, *United Brands* [1978] ECR 207 and *BBI/Boosey & Hawkes* [1987] OJ L282/36.

[147] Cases C-468–478/06, *Sot. Lélos* [2008] ECR I-7139.

[148] See Section 17, p. 575 ff.

[149] Cases C-468–478/06, *Sot. Lélos* [2008] ECR I-7139, para. 68.

[150] See *BBI/Boosey & Hawkes* [1987] OJ L282/36.

H. THE 'MEETING COMPETITION' DEFENCE

The 'meeting competition defence' is the plea that the dominant undertaking is merely reacting to competition in a proportionate and reasonable way. It is an aspect of the 'protecting legitimate commercial interests' defence,[151] and most relevant to pricing or margin squeeze cases where the dominant undertaking's prices are alleged to be predatory[152] and/or exclusionary of equally efficient competitors.[153] The 'meeting competition' defence cannot save predatory pricing from constituting an abuse: in *France Télécom*,[154] the CJ confirmed that there is no absolute right for a dominant undertaking to align its prices with those of its competitors.

6. DOMINANCE AND ABUSE ON DIFFERENT MARKETS

The dominant position may be held on a different market from that where the effects of the abuse are felt.

The earliest cases involved dominant undertakings which abused their position on one market in order to gain advantages on a downstream, or ancillary, market and/or to reserve to themselves an activity on that market. The prevention of such 'leverage' has been a major theme in the application of Article 102, as the rest of this chapter reveals. In the leading case of *Commercial Solvents*[155] the dominant undertaking was held to have abused its position on a raw material market when it refused to supply it to a producer of a derivative drug because the dominant undertaking wished to enter the market in the derivative drug itself.

In *Centre Belge*[156] Luxembourg television stopped accepting telesales advertisements on its television station unless the sales agent phone number used was that of its own subsidiary. This could be seen both as a refusal to supply and as contractual tying. Either way the statutory monopolist's purpose was to exclude other undertakings from competing with its own subsidiary on the ancillary market. The CJ considered the conduct an abuse:[157]

an abuse within the meaning of Article [102] is committed where, without any objective necessity, an undertaking holding a dominant position on a particular market reserves to itself or to an undertaking belonging to the same group an ancillary activity which might be carried out by another undertaking as part of its activities on a neighbouring but separate market, with the possibility of eliminating all competition from such undertaking.

Tying, where the firm dominant in one market uses its position to encourage or force customers also to buy from it products which fall into other markets, is a clear instance of a situation where the dominant position on one market is used to affect competition on another second market. The

---

[151] See COMP/38.784, *Wanadoo España v Telefónica* 4 July 2007 (*Telefónica*), para. 638.

[152] See Section 8.E, p. 394.

[153] As in margin squeeze cases, see COMP/38.784, *Wanadoo España v Telefónica* 4 July 2007, para. 639.

[154] Case C-202/07 P, *France Télécom* [2009] ECR I-2369, paras. 47–48, aff'g Case T-340/03, *France Télécom SA v Commission* [2007] ECR II-107. And see the unsuccessful 'meeting competition' plea in the selective pricing cases, Cases C-395 and 396/96 P, *Compagnie Maritime Belge* [2000] ECR I-1365, and Case T-228/97, *Irish Sugar* [1999] ECR II-2969.

[155] Cases 6 and 7/73, *Commercial Solvents* [1974] ECR 223.

[156] Case 311/84, *Centre Belge* [1985] ECR 3261. See also Case C-260/89, *Elliniki Radiophonia Tileorasi (ERT) v DEP* [1991] ECR I-2925, paras. 37–38 where the CJ held that it was contrary to Art. 102 for a television monopoly to pursue a discriminatory broadcasting policy which favoured its own programmes (the case also raised Art. 106 issues which are discussed in Chap. 8).

[157] Case 311/84, *Centre Belge* [1985] ECR 3261, para. 27.

markets concerned do not necessarily have to be up- or downstream, or ancillary to one another.[158] As we see in Section 12, tying may sometimes be 'defensive' in that it is aimed not at preventing competition on the second market but at protecting the dominant position on the first.[159] In *BPB Industries*[160] too, the undertaking tried to protect its dominant position on one market by conduct on another. In that case British Gypsum, which was dominant in the *plasterboard* market, promised priority delivery of *plaster* to plasterboard customers who stayed loyal to it and did not buy plasterboard from importers. This was held to be an abuse.[161]

In *British Airways*[162] the impugned conduct was the way in which BA paid commission to travel agents selling its tickets, which was said to put pressure on the agents to push BA tickets. The Commission did not try to prove that BA was dominant on any air route. Instead, it defined a market consisting of UK air travel agency services in which BA was dominant (as a *buyer*)[163] and held that it had abused this dominant position in order to gain anti-competitive advantages in the air transport market. To this extent *British Airways* is an application of the original principle in *Commercial Solvents*. However, the reality was rather different. The case stemmed from the intense rivalry in air transport. The Commission found an abuse on one (arguably rather artificial) market, assessing BA as dominant (with an unprecendently low market share), and identifying the effects of the abuse on another market where the powerful position of the undertaking was in effect the source of the dominance on the first market. The GC upheld the Commission.[164]

In *Tetra Pak II* an undertaking was held to have infringed Article 102 by predatory (i.e. below cost) pricing where it was dominant on one market and the predatory pricing took place on another. The dominant undertaking was not directly using its dominance to commit the abuse but the dominance facilitated cross-subsidisation. Unlike *BPB Industries* the dominant undertaking was not trying to protect its dominant position. The case involved two carton markets: aseptic and non-aseptic. They were separate, distinct markets.[165] Neither was ancillary to the other nor upstream or downstream of the other. The Commission held that Tetra Pak was dominant on the aseptic market but made no finding of dominance with regard to the non-aseptic market. It held, however, that Tetra Pak had abused its dominant position on the aseptic market by its conduct on the non-aseptic market which was designed to obtain a competitive advantage on the latter. The Commission's decision was upheld.

Case C-333/94 P, *Tetra Pak International SA v Commission* [1996] ECR I-5951

Court of Justice

27. It is true that application of Article [102] presupposes a link between the dominant position and the alleged abusive conduct, which is normally not present where conduct on a market distinct from the dominated market produces effects on that distinct market. In the case of distinct, but associated, markets, as in the present case, application of Article [102] to conduct found on the associated, non-dominated, market and having effects on that associated market can only be justified by special circumstances.

---

[158] For tying generally, see Section 12, p. 473 ff. See, e.g., *De Poste-La Poste* [2002] OJ L61/32 where the statutory monopolist in the basic letter service tried to exclude competition on the business-to-business market.

[159] See Section 12.C, p. 476.

[160] Case T-65/89, *BPB Industries and British Gypsum* [1993] ECR II-389.

[161] See also *De Poste-La Poste* [2002] OJ L61/32.

[162] *Virgin/British Airways* [2000] OJ L30/1.

[163] See Chap. 6.

[164] Case T-219/99, *British Airways v Commission* [2003] ECR II-5917. BA did not appeal the point to the CJ, in Case C-95/04 P, *British Airways* [2007] ECR I-2331.

[165] For market definition in the case, see Chap. 6, Section 5.E.

28. In that regard, the [General Court] first considered, at paragraph 118 of its judgment, that it was relevant that Tetra Pak held 78 per cent of the overall market in packaging in both aseptic and non-aseptic cartons, that is to say seven times more than its closest competitor. At paragraph 119, it stressed Tetra Pak's leading position in the non-aseptic sector. Then, in paragraph 121, it found that Tetra Pak's position on the aseptic markets, of which it held nearly a 90 per cent share, was quasi-monopolistic. It noted that that position also made Tetra Pak a favoured supplier of non-aseptic systems. Finally, at paragraph 122, it concluded that, in the circumstances of the case, application of Article [102] was justified by the situation on the different markets and the close associative links between them.

29. The relevance of the associative links which the [General Court] thus took into account cannot be denied. The fact that the various materials involved are used for packaging the same basic liquid products shows that Tetra Pak's customers in one sector are also potential customers in the other. That possibility is borne out by statistics showing that in 1987 approximately 35 per cent of Tetra Pak's customers bought both aseptic and non-aseptic systems. It is also relevant to note that Tetra Pak and its most important competitor, PKL, were present on all four markets. Given its almost complete domination of the aseptic markets, Tetra Pak could also count on a favoured status on the non-aseptic markets. Thanks to its position on the former markets, it could concentrate its efforts on the latter by acting independently of the other economic operators.

30. The circumstances thus described, taken together and not separately, justified the [General Court], without any need to show that the undertaking was dominant on the non-aseptic markets, in finding that Tetra Pak enjoyed freedom of conduct compared with the other economic operators on those markets.

31. Accordingly, the [General Court] was right to accept the application of Article [102] of the Treaty in this case, given that the quasi-monopoly enjoyed by Tetra Pak on the aseptic markets and its leading position on the distinct, though closely associated, non-aseptic markets placed it in a situation comparable to that of holding a dominant position on the markets in question as a whole.

The reference to *AKZO* in paragraph 25 is strange since ultimately only one relevant market was held to exist in that case, so the dominant position and the abuse were actually on the same market.[166] *Tetra Pak II* extended the previous law because the abuse was committed on a non-dominated market, unrelated vertically to the dominated one, in order to gain an advantage in the former. The Court stated in paragraph 27 that Article 102 can be applied to conduct by a dominant undertaking on a distinct, non-dominated market only where it is justified by 'special circumstances'. The special circumstances in this case were the 'close associative links' between the two markets, the quasi-monopolistic position (a 90 per cent market share) held by Tetra Pak on the dominated market, and its leading position on the non-dominated market. Both types of carton were used for packaging the same basic liquid, and many customers bought on both markets. Its powerful position on the dominated market meant that Tetra Pak could concentrate its efforts on the associated market where it enjoyed a greater freedom of action than its competitors. It was thus in a position *comparable to that of holding a dominant position on the two markets as a whole* (paragraph 31). *Tetra Pak II* does not mean that dominance on one market can always be abused by conduct on another distinct market, but rather that it is a possibility where particular circumstances mean that the undertaking's dominance gives it significant advantages on the second market. In *TeliaSonera*, the CJ stressed that Article 102 gives no explicit guidance about requirements as to where on the product markets the abuse took place. So 'while Article 102 TFEU presupposes a link between the dominant position and the alleged abusive conduct, which is normally not present where conduct on a market distinct from the dominated market produces effects on that distinct market, the application of Article 102 TFEU

---

[166] Case C-62/86, *AKZO* [1991] ECR I-3359. Organic peroxides had various uses but the Court accepted that it was all one market: see Chap. 6.

to conduct found on the associated, non-dominated, market and having effects on that associated market can nonetheless be justified by special circumstances . . .'.[167]

7. GENERAL ISSUES IN RESPECT OF ABUSES CONCERNING PRICES

A. EXPLOITATIVE AND EXCLUSIONARY PRICING POLICIES

Many cases and decisions on Article 102 concern the pricing policies of dominant firms. One of the most serious consequences of a firm being found to be in a dominant position is that its pricing policies may be condemned as abusive. Although some pricing practices, such as excessive pricing, are impossible or at least unlikely in the absence of market power, others, such as discriminatory pricing in the form of discount and rebate schemes, can be practised by any firm, and in non-dominated markets may be applauded as lively competition. Competition on price is the most basic form of competition but where dominant firms are concerned the Court has constantly reiterated that not all competition by means of price can be regarded as legitimate.[168]

For convenience this chapter deals with pricing abuses under various headings and the sections on exclusionary price-based abuses, with the exception of margin squeeze, follow the categorisation used in the Commission Guidance Paper.[169] However, it must be appreciated that many of these abuses are interrelated and that pricing policies may be characterised under more than one head and may arise in combination. Exploitative pricing abuses are discussed in Section 16.

B. PRICE DISCRIMINATION

(i) What is Price Discrimination?

Price discrimination[170] occurs where the same commodity is sold at different prices to different customers despite identical costs, i.e. the sales have different ratios of price to marginal cost. It also covers sales at the same price despite different costs. Price discrimination covers a wide range of practices. As seen below predatory pricing and rebate policies, for example, may involve price discrimination.

Price discrimination is 'persistent' when a supplier maintains a policy of obtaining a higher rate of return from some customers than from others. The ability to practise persistent price discrimination is a characteristic of market power. In a competitive market the customers who are charged the higher price are able to take their custom elsewhere. Persistent discrimination against some customers shows that it is difficult or impossible for them to change suppliers. Price discrimination occurs in competitive markets too but it tends to be sporadic, i.e. it changes frequently and customers may be in a favoured group today and a disfavoured one tomorrow.

---

[167] Case C-52/09, *TeliaSonera* [2011] ECR I-527, paras. 84–86. The markets in *TeliaSonera* were vertically related.

[168] See, e.g., Case C-62/86, *AKZO* [1991] ECR I-3359, para. 70; Case C-209/10, *Post Danmark I* EU:C:2012:172, para. 25.

[169] The Guidance Paper, unlike the CJ more recently (Case C-52/09, *TeliaSonera* [2011] ECR I-527), deals with margin squeeze as a type of refusal to supply, see Section 9.D, p. 426.

[170] See F. M. Scherer and D. Ross, *Industrial Market Structure and Economic Performance* (3rd edn, Houghton & Mifflin, 1990), Chap. 13; L. Phlips, *The Economics of Price Discrimination* (Cambridge University Press, 1983); H. Varian, 'Price Discrimination' in R. Schmalensee and R. Willig (eds.), *Handbook of Industrial Organisation*, Vol. 1 (North-Holland, 1989), Chap. 10; D. Geradin, A. Layne-Farrar, and N. Petit, *EU Competition Law and Economics* (Oxford University Press, 2012), 4.452–4.452; O'Donoghue and Padilla, n. 1, 781–789.

All customers have a 'reservation price', the maximum price they will pay for the product.[171] In *perfect (first-degree) discrimination* the supplier charges each customer his reservation price. This is often impossible and the supplier can only practise *imperfect (second degree)* discrimination whereby he identifies different groups of customers with similar reservation prices and charges each group accordingly. He can do this by offering different 'deals' in the form of goods or services in different packages and letting customers 'self-select' by choosing which they want. In *third-degree discrimination* the supplier identifies different groups of customers by some easily observable or ascertainable characteristic, such as old-age pensioners or students.[172] Information technology makes price discrimination easier in some markets because suppliers may have detailed data on individual buyers because of the data gathered from the use of loyalty cards and similar schemes, and the footprint consumers leave online.

Price discrimination works only if arbitrage is not feasible. Arbitrage is where the customers trade amongst themselves so that the customers charged the lowest prices sell on to those charged more. There is no incentive to do this if the difference in prices charged is insufficient to recompense the selling customer for the costs involved. Arbitrage is often impossible. In *United Brands*,[173] for example, it was difficult to transport bananas, a highly delicate and perishable product, between Member States. Price discrimination is easier in respect of services consumed on the spot than in respect of goods because of the lack of opportunities for arbitrage.[174]

The general consensus among economists is that price discrimination is welfare-enhancing if it increases output.[175] Price discrimination may be pro-competitive in industries with high fixed (or sunk) costs and low marginal costs if an undertaking can charge above marginal cost to customers willing to pay in order to recover some fixed costs, while charging lower, marginal cost prices, to others.[176] This may in particular be a feature of high technology markets in the new economy. However, it is also possible for price discrimination to be anti-competitive and produce adverse effects on efficiency. It depends on the facts of the case. The problem for competition law is to develop the tools for distinguishing the situations in which price discrimination is welfare-enhancing from those in which it is not. In *Post Danmark I* the CJ clarified that the fact that the practice of a dominant undertaking may be described as 'price discrimination' cannot of itself suggest that an exclusionary abuse exists.[177]

(ii) Primary Line and Secondary Line Injury

Price discrimination may involve primary line or secondary line injury. Primary line injury prejudices the supplier's competitors. Price discrimination can cause primary line injury by having exclusionary (foreclosure) effects on competitors. For example, in *Irish Sugar*[178] and *Compagnie Maritime Belge*[179] the dominant undertakings were held to have pursued selective (and therefore discriminatory) low pricing policies in order to exclude their competitors. Secondary line injury is where the impact is on the undertaking's trading partners. If a supplier sells a product to X more cheaply than

---

[171] See Chap. 1.

[172] M. Motta, *Competition Policy* (Cambridge University Press, 2004), 492.

[173] Case 27/76, *United Brands v Commission* [1978] ECR 207.

[174] D. Begg, G. Vernasca, S. Fischer, and R. Dornbusch, *Economics* (10th edn, McGraw-Hill, 2011), 190.

[175] There is a large literature on the economics of price discrimination, but see in particular R. Schmalensee, 'Output and Welfare Implications of Third Degree Price Discrimination' (1981) 71 *Am Econ Rev* 242; H. R. Varian, 'Price Discrimination and Social Welfare' (1985) 75 *Am Econ Rev* 870.

[176] See D. Ridyard, 'Exclusionary Pricing and Price Discrimination Abuses under Article 102—An Economic Analysis' [2002] *ECLR* 286, 287–278; J. Temple Lang and R. O'Donoghue, 'Defining Legitimate Competition: How to Clarify Pricing Abuses under Article 102EC' (2002) 26 *Fordham Int'l LJ* 83, 89–90.

[177] Case C-209/10, *Post Danmark I* EU:C:2012:172, para. 30; see further Sections 8.D and 8.I, pp. 391 and 402.

[178] Case T-228/97, *Irish Sugar plc* [1999] ECR II-2969.

[179] Cases C-395 and 396/96 P, *Compagnie Maritime Belge* [2000] ECR I-1365.

to Y, and X and Y are competing manufacturers who need the product as an input, then X's costs will be lower than Y's. The supplier *may* have distorted competition between them as a result. However, in some cases the supplier may compete with the customer on the downstream market.

Primary and secondary line injury may arise from the same scenario. In *British Airways*[180] the differential rebates given to travel agents for selling BA tickets were held to have both an excluding effect on BA's competitor airlines (primary line), and to cause distortions to competition between the agents (secondary line).

Primary line injury through exclusionary price discrimination is a major issue in EU competition law. Secondary line injury through discriminatory pricing is expressly listed as an abuse in Article 102(c)[181] although in several cases discussed in this chapter the Commission has also used Article 102(c) in respect of primary line discrimination.[182]

C. COSTS LEVELS

When looking at pricing abuses, it is necessary to understand costs terminology.[183]

1. *Total cost* The total costs of production.

2. *Average Total Cost (ATC)* The total costs involved in the production of one unit of output (i.e. total cost divided by the number of units produced).

3. *Total costs are of two kinds*:

   (a) Fixed costs. Those which do not change with output over a given time period.

   (b) Variable costs. Those which do change with output.

4. *Average Variable Cost (AVC)* The variable costs involved in the production of one unit (i.e. the variable costs added up and divided by the number of units produced).

5. *Marginal Cost* The increase in total costs of a firm caused by increasing its output by one extra unit.

6. *Short-run Marginal Cost (SRMC)* The marginal cost based on a firm's existing plant and equipment, not on that which would be the most efficient.

7. *Avoidable Costs* The costs that will not be incurred if an undertaking ceases a particular operation. They are variable costs plus any fixed costs that are incurred during the period under examination (they cannot include sunk costs because sunk costs have already been spent and cannot be recovered).

8. *Average Avoidable Cost (AAC)* The average of the costs that could have been avoided if the undertaking had not produced a discrete amount of extra output.[184]

9. *(Long-run) Average Incremental Cost ((LR)AIC)* The average of all the (variable and fixed) costs that an undertaking incurs to produce a particular product.[185] The standard is useful in industries where there are large fixed costs but low, or even negligible, variable costs (because the main cost is the provision of a network for example, as is the case with telecommunications). LRAIC includes product-specific fixed costs made before the period under examination and is useful in the case of multi-product undertakings where there are fixed costs common to a number of different activities carried on by an undertaking resulting in economies of scope. LRAIC does

---

180 Case C-95/04 P, *British Airways* [2007] ECR I-2331.

181 See Section 15.B, p. 559.

182 See Geradin, Layne-Farrar, and Petit, n. 170, 4.999–5.004.

183 See also Chap. 1.

184 The definition of average avoidable cost given in the Guidance Paper, para. 26, n. 2.

185 The definition of LRAIC given in the Guidance Paper, para. 26, n. 2.

not include true common costs.[186] The Guidance Paper says that LRAIC and ATC are good proxies for one another and are the same in respect of a single product undertaking.[187] It also explains that in the case of multiple products, any costs that could have been avoided by not producing a particular product or range are not considered to be common costs.[188]

10. *Stand-alone Costs* The costs which are involved in producing a product without taking into account that some of those costs are shared with the production of other products (i.e. that there are common costs).

The following should be noted:

- average variable cost is always lower than average total cost;.
- long run means a period of time long enough for all the factors of production to be costlessly varied (i.e. the period needed for complete adjustment);
- short run means a period of time so short that the factors of production cannot be costlessly varied (i.e. a period too short for complete adjustment).

D. THE GENERAL APPROACH IN THE GUIDANCE PAPER TO PRICE-BASED EXCLUSIONARY CONDUCT: THE 'AS EFFICIENT COMPETITOR' STANDARD

Paragraphs 23–27 of the Guidance Paper set out the general principles the Commission applies when deciding whether to intervene in respect of a dominant undertaking's pricing conduct. It will act with a view to preventing anti-competitive foreclosure and will *normally* intervene where the conduct has been, or is capable of, hampering competition from 'as efficient' competitors. The Commission thus adopts the AEC test. However, the Commission lodges a proviso (paragraph 24) saying that 'in certain circumstances' competitive constraints may be exerted by *less* efficient competitors which should be taken into account when assessing foreclosure. The example given is of a competitor which, in the absence of abusive conduct, might benefit from demand-led advantages such as network and learning effects which could enhance its efficiency.[189] The proviso is an example of the Commission's strategy throughout the Guidance Paper of setting out the normal rule but expressly reserving some freedom to depart from it in certain circumstances. Here it means that the Commission can take account of dynamic efficiencies. However, as a result undertakings can never be sure that their case will not be one where the Commission is concerned with the exclusion of less efficient competitors.[190] The Commission will assess whether a competitor is 'as efficient' by examining the costs and sales price data of the dominant undertaking itself, but if this information is unavailable the Commission is prepared to use that of the competitor. The problem here is that the use of the competitor's data alone cannot tell the Commission whether the competitor is 'as efficient'.[191]

---

[186] See however Case C-209/10, *Post Danmark I* EU:C:2012:172, where the national competition authority (NCA) had included some common costs in its calculation of LRAIC.

[187] See Guidance Paper, para. 26, n. 2.

[188] Ibid., para. 26, n. 2.

[189] Ibid., para. 24.

[190] Less efficient competitors can provide consumers with choice that some may value. See Case T-201/04, *Microsoft* [2007] ECR II-3601, para. 652; N. Petit, 'From Formalism to Effects? The Commission's Communication on Enforcement Priorities in Applying Article 82' (2009) 32 *World Competition* 485, 491.

[191] A practitioner made the point that given the Commission's extensive powers of investigation and of sanctioning non-cooperation (see Chap. 13) it may merely be issuing a warning to dominant undertakings to produce the data it requires: L. Kjølbe, 'Rebates Under Article 82EC: Navigating Uncertain Waters' [2010] *ECLR* 66, 74.

Guidance on the Commission's Enforcement Priorities in Applying Article 82 of the EC Treaty to Abusive Exclusionary Conduct by Dominant Undertakings [2009] OJ C45/2

C. Price-based Exclusionary Conduct

23. The considerations in paragraphs 23 to 27 apply to price-based exclusionary conduct. Vigorous price competition is generally beneficial to consumers. With a view to preventing anti-competitive foreclosure, the Commission will normally only intervene where the conduct concerned has already been or is capable of hampering competition from competitors which are considered to be as efficient as the dominant undertaking . . .

24. However, the Commission recognises that in certain circumstances a less efficient competitor may also exert a constraint which should be taken into account when considering whether particular price-based conduct leads to anti-competitive foreclosure. The Commission will take a dynamic view of that constraint, given that in the absence of an abusive practice such a competitor may benefit from demand-related advantages, such as network and learning effects, which will tend to enhance its efficiency.

25. In order to determine whether even a hypothetical competitor as efficient as the dominant undertaking would be likely to be foreclosed by the conduct in question, the Commission will examine economic data relating to cost and sales prices, and in particular whether the dominant undertaking is engaging in below-cost pricing. This will require that sufficiently reliable data be available. Where available, the Commission will use information on the costs of the dominant undertaking itself. If reliable information on those costs is not available, the Commission may decide to use the cost data of competitors or other comparable reliable data.

26. The cost benchmarks that the Commission is likely to use are average avoidable cost (AAC) and long-run average incremental cost (LRAIC) . . . Failure to cover AAC indicates that the dominant undertaking is sacrificing profits in the short term and that an equally efficient competitor cannot serve the targeted customers without incurring a loss. LRAIC is usually above AAC because, in contrast to AAC (which only includes fixed costs if incurred during the period under examination), LRAIC includes product specific fixed costs made before the period in which allegedly abusive conduct took place. Failure to cover LRAIC indicates that the dominant undertaking is not recovering all the (attributable) fixed costs of producing the good or service in question and that an equally efficient competitor could be foreclosed from the market . . .

27. If the data clearly suggest that an equally efficient competitor can compete effectively with the pricing conduct of the dominant undertaking, the Commission will, in principle, infer that the dominant undertaking's pricing conduct is not likely to have an adverse impact on effective competition, and thus on consumers, and will therefore be unlikely to intervene. If, on the contrary, the data suggest that the price charged by the dominant undertaking has the potential to foreclose equally efficient competitors, then the Commission will integrate this in the general assessment of anti-competitive foreclosure (see Section B [of the Guidance] above), taking into account other relevant quantitative and/or qualitative evidence.

The Commission therefore favours using AAC and LRAIC as its benchmarks. As it points out in a footnote, in most cases AAC and AVC are the same, as are LRAIC and ATC in the case of single-product undertakings.

E. THE GENERAL APPROACH OF THE EU COURTS TO PRICING ABUSES

The CJ in effect applied the AEC principle in the 1991 predatory pricing case of *AKZO* where it established that whether or not low prices amounted to an abuse depended on their relationship to the dominant undertaking's own costs.[192] Since then it has firmly established the AEC test as

---

[192] Case C-62/86, *AKZO* [1991] ECR I-3359.

the standard to be used in predatory pricing, selective pricing, and margin squeeze cases.[193] The EU Courts do not apply the AEC test to loyalty rebates[194] and in respect of standardised retroactive rebates the CJ described the AEC test in *Post Danmark II*[195] as 'one tool amongst many' whose application would depend on the circumstances. The current approach of the Courts therefore differs from the principles set out in respect of rebates in the Guidance Paper.[196]

In *Michelin I* the CJ said that in deciding whether the undertaking's discount system was abusive it was necessary to consider all the circumstances and decide whether the practice tended to remove or restrict the buyer's freedom to choose his sources of supply, to bar competitors from access to the market, to apply dissimilar conditions to equivalent transactions with other trading parties, or to strengthen the dominant position by distorting competition. This principle now invariably appears in all judgments on pricing abuses.[197]

8. PREDATORY PRICING

A. GENERAL

Predatory pricing is the practice whereby an undertaking prices its product so low that competitors cannot live with the price and are driven from the market.[198] Once the competitors are excluded from the market the undertaking hopes to increase prices to monopoly levels and recoup its losses. It is anti-competitive because, although it means low prices in the short term, its effects are to strengthen the power of the dominant undertaking to the prejudice of consumers. Predatory pricing can exclude firms which are *equally as efficient* as the predator.[199]

The intractable problem for competition authorities is to identify where robust price competition ends and predatory pricing begins: '[p]redatory pricing is one of the most daunting subjects confronting nations with competition policies'.[200] False positives (Type 1 errors) and false negatives (Type 2 errors) are both prejudicial to consumer welfare, but many commentators argue that in particularly in respect of predatory pricing the avoidance of Type 1 errors should be the priority.

Opinions differ as to how often predatory pricing occurs. The strategy of the predator is to sacrifice profit-maximisation in the short term in order to reap monopoly profits in the long term. It has been argued that it is hardly ever a rational business strategy and very rare. This view was famously

---

[193] Case C-209/10, *Post Danmark I* EU:C:2012:172; Case C-280/08 P, *Deutsche Telekom* [2010] ECR I-9555; Case C-52/09, *TeliaSonera* [2011] ECR I-527.

[194] Case C-549/10 P, *Tomra* EU:C:2012:221; Case T-286/09, *Intel v Commission* EU:T:2014:547, on appeal Case C-413/14 P, judgment pending, see Section 11.

[195] Case C-23/14, *Post Danmark II* EU:C:2015:651.

[196] Case T-203/01, *Michelin II* [2003] ECR II-4071; Case C-95/04 P, *British Airways* [2007] ECR I-2331; Case C-549/10 P, *Tomra* EU:C:2012:221; see Section 11.

[197] Case C-280/08 P, *Deutsche Telekom* [2010] ECR I-9555, para. 175; Case 52/09, *TeliaSonera* [2011] ECR I-527, para. 28; Case C-209/10, *Post Danmark I* EU:C:2012:172, para. 26; Case C-549/10 P, *Tomra* EU:C:2012:221, para. 71 (which omits the 'applying dissimilar conditions' phrase); Case T-336/07, *Telefónica and Telefónica de España v Commission* EU:T:2012:172, para. 175, aff'd Case C-295/12 P, *Telefónica SA v Commission* EU:C:2014:2062; Case C-23/14, *Post Danmark II* EU:C:2015:651, para. 29. In some cases 'thereby placing them at a competitive disadvantage' is added to the phrase about applying dissimilar conditions.

[198] See generally P. L. Joskow and A. K. Klevorick, 'A Framework for Analyzing Predatory Pricing Policy' (1979) 89 *Yale LJ* 213; S. Bishop and M. Walker, *The Economics of EC Competition Law* (3rd edn, Sweet & Maxwell, 2010), 6.084–6.112; O'Donoghue and Padilla, n. 1, Chap. 6. Conduct, other than low pricing, designed to drive competitors out of the market can also be described as 'predatory'.

[199] Although some economists argue that the efficiency of the entrant is irrelevant: what matters is whether there is room for another player in a non-cooperative Nash equilibrium (a market where all the participants are pursuing their best possible strategy given the strategies of all the others, see Chap. 9); see, e.g., L. Phlips, *Competition Policy: A Game-Theoretic Perspective* (Cambridge University Press, 1995), 233.

[200] E. Fox, 'Price Predation—US and EEC: Economics and Values' [1989] *Fordham Corp L Inst* 687, 687.

adopted by Bork: '[i]t seems unwise . . . to construct rules about a phenomenon that probably does not exist or which, should it exist in very rare cases, the courts would have grave difficulty in distinguishing from competitive price behavior'.[201] The mainstream view now is that predatory pricing can occur in certain factual circumstances.

The rationality of predatory pricing generally is conditioned upon the existence of barriers to entry. Otherwise, after one competitor is knocked out by low prices others will enter when the incumbent raises them again. The incumbent will never be able to enjoy the fruits of its predation. However, it is important to appreciate that predatory pricing may itself *constitute* a barrier to entry. Industrial organisation theory suggests that the conditions of post-entry competition are a major factor in decisions about market entry and that the presence of a known predator on the market is a disincentive to entry. In this way predatory pricing not only drives out existing competitors, but also repels potential competition. It may be easier to deter potential competitors through predatory pricing than to expel existing ones, as incumbents may have incurred sunk costs and have an incentive to remain on the market. Further, it is unlikely that all the actors on the market have perfect information. It is also argued that a predatory price may give the potential entrant erroneous signals about price levels in the market, which will deter entry as it will not appear worthwhile.

Predatory pricing is often considered feasible only where firms operate multi-market because if the firm operates in only one market it is more rational for it to absorb the new entrant (by merger or take-over, insofar as that is permitted by the competition authorities), or to accommodate it, rather than incur greater losses by undercutting. Losses suffered by the predator are suffered *today*, and may be heavy: the profits above the competitive level are *tomorrow* if and when the predation strategy works, and are inherently uncertain. There is also the problem that in exiting the entrant may dispose of its assets to other competitors still on the market. Where a firm is multi-market, however, it may be able to offset the losses on one market from the profits on another. Moreover, a firm which establishes a reputation for aggressive reaction to competition in one market may deter entrants into others, so predation in one market may protect several others. The firm may be multi-market in a geographical rather than a product sense, so that a reputation for predation in one geographic market may deter entrants elsewhere.[202] It has also been argued that predation can be a rational strategy only for a firm that has a very high market share.[203]

The current consensus can be summed up as saying that predatory pricing can be a rational strategy where the conditions are right. In particular, it may be rational in new economy markets.[204] The Commission and the EU Courts consider that it can and does occur and that it infringes Article 102 when it does. The problem is to identify it. Most predatory pricing theory centres around costs levels. The basic concept is that a dominant firm prices below cost. However a firm's costs, and the relationship between its costs and prices, may be difficult to compute. Particular problems arise where a firm uses the same production capacity to make different products.

[201] R. Bork, *The Antitrust Paradox* (Basic Books, 1978, reprinted with new Introduction and Epilogue, Free Press, Macmillan, 1993), 154. This conclusion was based, inter alia, on a study in the US by J. McGee, 'Predatory Price Cutting; The Standard Oil (New Jersey) Case' (1958) 1 *J of Law and Economics* 137, described by R. T. Rapp, 'Predatory Pricing and Entry Deterring Strategies: The Economics of *AKZO*' [1986] *ECLR* 233, n. 1 as 'a work combining exceptionally bad economics and equally bad history' and its influence on US courts as showing 'that bad economic history can have a long, happy life'. For the influence on US courts see *Matsushita Elec Indust Co Ltd v Zenith Radio Corp*, 475 US 574 (1986), where the Supreme Court, having quoted Bork, McGee, and others said, 'for this reason, there is a consensus among commentators that predatory pricing schemes are rarely tried, and even more rarely successful', before rejecting claims of predatory pricing by a cartel.

[202] But see R. Selten, 'The Chain Store Paradox' (1978) 9 *Theory and Decision* 127–159 for a model of how predation in a series of geographic markets would be impossible.

[203] Rapp, n. 201, 234; see also H. Hovenkamp, *Federal Antitrust Policy* (4th edn, West, 2011), 381–382.

[204] Bork's thesis was formulated before the explosion of the new economy.

B. THE AREEDA–TURNER TEST

In a seminal *Harvard Law Review* article Areeda and Turner put forward a test for identifying predatory pricing.[205] Under this test a price lower than reasonably anticipated short-run marginal cost (SRMC) is predatory, whilst a price equal to or higher than reasonably anticipated SRMC is not predatory.[206]

SRMC is, however, almost impossible to compute in practice, as it is a question of looking back to determine what the firm's marginal cost was during a past period of time. The Areeda–Turner test therefore uses average variable cost (AVC) as a surrogate for SRMC. The test is stated as follows:

- a price at or above reasonably anticipated AVC should be conclusively presumed lawful;
- a price below reasonably anticipated AVC should be conclusively presumed unlawful.

Despite criticisms of the shortcomings in the Areeda–Turner test it has been highly influential in antitrust thinking and some version of it is commonly used in US antitrust cases.[207] It formed the basis for the argument in the *AKZO* case.

C. THE TEST LAID DOWN IN *AKZO*

(i) The *AKZO* Case

The Commission first considered predatory pricing in *AKZO*.[208]

ECS was a small UK firm which produced benzoyl peroxide, a catalyst used in plastics production and also (in the UK and Ireland) as a bleaching agent in flour-milling. ECS concentrated on the flour sector, where its major customer was Allied Mills. AKZO, a multinational chemicals company, produced benzoyl peroxide but concentrated on the plastics sector. The Commission found that when ECS expanded its operations in the plastics sector (capturing one of AKZO's largest customers) AKZO retaliated by threatening to attack ECS's business in the UK flour sector by reducing prices. It then supplied benzoyl peroxide to the UK flour sector at low prices, offering large discounts to ECS's best customers. The Commission adopted a decision holding that AKZO had abused a dominant position contrary to Article 102.[209]

The Commission found that AKZO was dominant in the organic peroxides market as a whole[210] and had infringed Article 102 by pursuing a course of predation against ECS designed to drive it from the plastics sector. It fined AKZO ECU 10 million and ordered it to terminate the infringement. It required AKZO to refrain from offering or applying prices which would result in customers in respect of whose business it was competing with ECS paying prices dissimilar to those applied to comparable customers. The Commission decision finding predation focused on AKZO's threats[211] and its eliminatory intent. The decision did not adopt the Areeda–Turner rule or lay down specific

---

[205] P. Areeda and D. Turner, 'Predatory Pricing and Related Practices Under Section 2 of the Sherman Act' (1975) 88 *Harvard LR* 697.

[206] 'Reasonably anticipated' means that a firm's conduct is not judged *ex post facto*. The marginal cost is judged by what seemed reasonable at the time. If the SRMC turned out to be higher than anticipated the firm should not be condemned for predatory pricing.

[207] See J. Brodley and D. Hay, 'Predatory Pricing: Competing Economic Theories and the Evolution of Legal Standards' (1981) 66 *Cornell LR* 738; J. Hurwitz and W. Kovacic, 'Judicial Analysis of Predation: The Emerging Trends' (1982) 35 *Vanderbilt LR* 63; E. Elhauge and D. Geradin, *Global Competition Law and Economics* (2nd edn, Hart Publishing, 2011), 353–368; Hovenkamp, n. 203, 372–379.

[208] *ECS/AKZO* [1985] OJ L374/1; upheld Case C-62/86, *AKZO* [1991] ECR I-3359.

[209] [1985] OJ L374/1. ECS had originally obtained an interim injunction in the High Court in London to prevent AKZO from implementing its threats, and those proceedings were terminated by agreement.

[210] See Chap. 6 for the market definition aspects of the case.

[211] It uncovered the evidence of these to support ECS's contentions when it conducted a dawn raid (see Chap. 13) on AKZO's premises.

rules about the point at which low prices become predatory, and abusive. It suggested that even prices above ATC could be predatory.[212]

On appeal AKZO argued that since it had not reduced its prices below AVC, under the Areeda–Turner test its prices were not predatory. The CJ confirmed the Commission's definition of the market and the finding of dominance. It did accept AKZO's arguments that some costs which the Commission had classified as variable were, in this case, fixed. The CJ confirmed that AKZO had been guilty of predatory pricing,[213] but set out a more structured, costs-based test for identifying it.

Case C-62/86, *AKZO Chemie BV v Commission* [1991] ECR I-3359

Court of Justice

66. AKZO disputes the relevance of the criterion of lawfulness adopted by the Commission, which it regards as nebulous or at least inapplicable. It maintains that the Commission should have adopted an objective criterion based on its costs.

67. In that respect, it states that the question of the lawfulness of a particular level of prices cannot be separated from the specific market situation in which the prices were fixed. There is no abuse if the dominant undertaking endeavours to obtain [an] optimum selling-price and a positive coverage margin. A price is optimum if the undertaking may reasonably expect that the offer of another price or the absence of a price would produce a less favourable operating profit in the short term. Furthermore, coverage margin is positive if the value of the order exceeds the sum of the variable costs.

68. According to AKZO, a criterion based on an endeavour to obtain an optimal price in the short term cannot be rejected on the grounds that it would jeopardise the viability of the undertaking in the long term. It is only after a certain time that the undertaking in . . . question could take measures to eliminate the losses or withdraw from a loss-making branch of business. In the meantime the undertaking would have to accept 'optimum orders' in order to reduce its deficit and to ensure continuity of operation.

69. It should be observed that, as the Court held in Case 85/76, *Hoffmann-La Roche* v. *E.C. Commission* . . . paragraph 91, the concept of abuse is an objective concept relating to the behaviour of an undertaking in a dominant position which is such as to influence the structure of a market where, as a result of the very presence of the undertaking in question, the degree of competition is weakened and through recourse to methods which, different from those which condition normal competition in products or services on the basis of the transactions of commercial operations, has the effect of hindering the maintenance of the degree of competition still existing in the market or the growth of that competition.

70. It follows that Article [102] prohibits a dominant undertaking from eliminating a competitor and thereby strengthening its position by using methods other than those which come within the scope of competition on the basis of quality. From that point of view, however, not all competition by means of price can be regarded as legitimate.

71. Prices below average variable costs (that is to say, those which vary depending on the quantities produced) by means of which a dominant undertaking seeks to eliminate a competitor must be regarded as abusive. A dominant undertaking has no interest in applying such prices except that of eliminating competitors so as to enable it subsequently to raise its prices by taking advantage of its monopolistic position, since each sale generates a loss, namely the total amount of the fixed costs (that is to say, those which remain constant regardless of the quantities produced) and, at least, part of the variable costs relating to the unit produced.

72. Moreover, prices below average total costs, that is to say, fixed costs plus variable costs, but above average variable costs, must be regarded as abusive if they are determined as part of a plan for eliminating

---

[212] *ECS/AKZO* [1985] OJ L374/1, para. 79.

[213] It annulled the Commission's decision in respect of offers made to one particular customer and reduced the fine to ECU 7.5 million.

a competitor. Such prices can drive from the market undertakings which are perhaps as efficient as the dominant undertakings but which, because of their smaller financial resources, are incapable of withstanding the competition waged against them.

73. These are the criteria that must be applied to the situation in the present case.

74. Since the criterion of legitimacy to be adopted is a criterion based on the costs and strategy of the dominant undertaking itself, AKZO's allegation concerning the inadequacy of the Commission's investigation with regard to the cost structure and the pricing policy of its competitors must be rejected at the outset.

The *AKZO* test states that prices below AVC 'must be regarded as abusive' because there is no profit-maximising reason for them. The only explanation for them is that they are intended to eliminate competitors. This sets out a strong presumption that pricing below AVC is abusive. It presumes eliminatory intent. The Court went on to hold that above AVC but below ATC prices can also be abusive if they are part of a plan to eliminate competitors (thus differing from the Areeda–Turner test, under which there is no predation where prices are above AVC). There is no presumption as to the undertaking's intention, so the onus is on the Commission, or other party alleging abuse. Eliminatory intent was found in *AKZO* from the direct threats and from the price cuts.

The CJ did not expressly deal with the situation where prices are at or above ATC. Nor did it say anything *expressly* about the dominant undertaking's possibility of recouping its losses, although it can be argued that it is implicit in paragraph 71.[214]

The test in *AKZO* is therefore:

- prices below AVC are presumed to be predatory;
- prices above AVC but below ATC (the 'grey' area) are not *presumed* predatory but are predatory if they are proved to be part of a plan to eliminate a competitor.

The *AKZO* test was reaffirmed in *Tetra Pak II*[215] and *France Télécom*.[216] It was further developed in *Post Danmark I*.[217]

(ii) The Criteria Laid Down in *AKZO*

a. Problems with Costs-based Tests

Costs-based criteria for predatory pricing are inherently problematic. The problems include:

- AVC is an unsatisfactory substitute for SRMC, because the AVC cost curve tends to be U-shaped and gives the undertaking a lot of room for manoeuvre. Marginal cost rises and falls more dramatically than AVC because AVC averages out the cost of one additional unit over the entire output being produced. The assumption that SRMC and AVC are equivalent holds good only in the long run.[218]
- It is difficult to draw a rigid demarcation line between fixed and variable categories. Classification is dependent upon the industry and the time period in issue. The longer the time period, the more costs become variable. In *AKZO* the parties submitted to the Court very different calculations of AKZO's costs. The Court stated that 'an item of cost is not fixed or

---

[214] Fennelly AG argued this in his Opinion in Cases C-395 and 396/96 P, *Compagnie Maritime Belge* [2000] ECR I-1365.

[215] Case C-333/94 P, *Tetra Pak II* [1996] ECR I-5951.

[216] Case C-202/07 P, *France Télécom* [2009] ECR I-2369.

[217] Case C-209/10, *Post Danmark I* EU:C:2012:172.

[218] Bishop and Walker, n. 198, 6.097.

variable by nature' and overruled the Commission's classification of the labour costs as variable rather than fixed as in this case there was no direct correlation between labour costs and quantities produced.[219] In *Wanadoo Interactive*[220] the Commission classified the advertising of the undertaking's residential broadband services as a variable rather than a fixed cost, which the undertaking disputed.[221] Areeda and Turner recognised the problem of classification and proposed that certain costs should always be considered fixed (interest on debt, depreciation, taxes which do not vary with output).[222]

- They are unsatisfactory in markets in which AVC (or SRMC) is minimal (such as digital markets in the new economy).[223]

In *AKZO* the CJ gave no guidance as to the allocation of costs in multi-product/service firms. This was, however, addressed by the Commission in *Deutsche Post* where it applied the (LR)AIC standard when dealing with a statutory monopolist (DPAG) which was also active on a competitive market.[224] In *Post Danmark I*,[225] the CJ dealt with the application of AIC to a multi-service undertaking, which also involved a universal service obligation (USO).

b. Rational Reasons for Below AVC Pricing

There can be rational, non-predatory reasons for pricing under AVC: for example, the launch of new lines, obsolete stock clearance, and using continuous production facilities. It may be better for an undertaking to sell temporarily at a loss and make some return rather than none at all. As paragraph 71 of *AKZO* only sets out a presumption, circumstances such as these could be recognised and the presumption rebutted. Multi-sided markets[226] present a particular problem, as undertakings may choose to price by charging only one side of the market or charging very low prices on one side. Such a charging strategy may be perfectly rational, and not anti-competitive:[227] the Guidance Paper recognises that in multi-sided markets it may be necessary to look at revenues and costs of both sides at the same time.[228]

c. Ascertaining Intention between AVC and ATC

Under the *AKZO* test the intention of the undertaking is the crucial factor when prices are in the 'grey' area between AVC and ATC. The test accepts that pricing at that level can be a rational, non-predatory strategy in certain circumstances because the undertaking will be covering the variable costs and at least some part of the fixed costs on every unit sold. However, all undertakings might be

---

[219] *ECS/AKZO* [1985] OJ L374/1, para. 95.

[220] COMP/38.233, 16 July 2003.

[221] The GC dismissed the appeal on this point in Case T-340/03, *France Télécom SA v Commission* [2007] ECR II-107 on procedural grounds, and likewise the plea that the Commission had calculated its recovery of costs incorrectly.

[222] P. Areeda and D. Turner, *Antitrust Law* (Little Brown, 1978), para. 715c.

[223] But cf. E. Elhauge, 'Why Above-cost Price Cuts to Drive Out Entrants Are Not Predatory—And the Implications for Defining Costs and Market Power' (2003) 112 *Yale LJ* 681, 710–711 ('The fact that marginal or variable costs are uniformly low in an industry thus raises no difficulty if one is careful to consider all (and only) costs that are variable during the period of alleged predation. Different problems might be raised, however, if the equally efficient rival has a different ratio of fixed to variable costs than the alleged predator, or if the alleged predatory price is timed after the predator has incurred a fixed or sunk cost that the rival must decide whether to incur in the future').

[224] *Deutsche Post* [2001] OJ L125/27. The Commission examined the cost of providing the mail-order parcels service (which was open to competition) and deducted from it the costs shared with the services in respect of which DPAG had a USO. The incremental cost was the additional cost which DPAG incurred solely as a result of the mail-order service. The Commission disregarded the common fixed costs shared with the universal service, apparently because of the extra costs arising from the USO, see Temple Lang and O'Donoghue, n. 176, 156.

[225] See Section 8.D, p. 391.

[226] See Chap. 1, Section 12, p. 48.

[227] See Geradin, Layne-Farrar, and Petit, n. 170, 4.527.

[228] Guidance Paper, para. 26, n. 3. For the issue of low prices in the digital economy see Section 8.H, p. 401.

said to intend to eliminate their competitors by the very fact that they are participating in the struggle for custom in the marketplace. The Court therefore means intending to eliminate competitors by competition which is not on the merits, and therefore not, in the words of *Hoffmann-La Roche*, 'normal' competition, but the distinction between 'normal' price competition and predatory pricing is the very thing this test is trying to identify. 'Determined as part of a plan' seems to denote some degree of systematic and deliberate strategy and the EU Courts treat 'plan' to eliminate and 'intent' to eliminate as synonymous.[229]

A finding of intention to eliminate must be established 'on the basis of sound and consistent evidence'[230] which may be 'direct' or 'indirect'.[231] Documentary evidence from the allegedly predating undertaking is 'direct evidence' of an intention to predate. In *AKZO* eliminatory intention was derived partly from company documentation. However, words may be open to different interpretations and what seemed like an exhortationary address to the troops in the sales department at the time may read like threats of ruthless predatory intent months or years afterwards.[232] *AKZO* itself may have made proving intent more difficult as undertakings are now advised to be more careful in what they record. Nevertheless, in *Wanadoo* (*France Télécom*) the Commission relied, inter alia, upon internal documents to show that the undertaking (WIN) had dropped its price for residential high-speed broadband access in order to 'pre-empt' the developing market. WIN disputed the scope and significance of the documents, alleging that some were merely informal or impromptu. The GC pointed out that some of the incriminating words and phrases came from management-level staff and were expressed in the context of formal presentations for the taking of a decision or of a very detailed framework letter[233] and did not consider the phrase 'our pre-emption of the ASDL market is imperative' could be read as anything other than a strategy to 'pre-empt'.[234] WIN claimed on appeal that this amounted to the GC finding a plan of predation on 'subjective' instead of 'objective' factors. The CJ rejected this, holding that the GC had deduced a 'strategy to pre-empt' from 'objective factors such as that of the undertaking's internal documents'.[235] It has been said that despite the GC's suggestions in *France Télécom* about the sufficiency of direct evidence such as internal documents, in practice the Commission always relies on 'indirect' corroborative evidence as well.[236] The type of indirect evidence used is illustrated by *Tetra Pak II* where factors such as the duration and scale of the losses, and the tactics of specially importing the products into Italy in order to sell them at a loss there, were taken into account in identifying a predatory strategy.

The Commission indicates the evidence it will consider in identifying a predatory strategy in paragraphs 20, 65, and 66 of the Guidance Paper.[237]

D. THE *POST DANMARK I* CASE

Post Danmark I[238] is significant for the way it developed *AKZO* in respect both of the costs benchmarks which can be used and of the position where prices are between ATC and AVC but no intent to eliminate competitors has been shown. The case was a preliminary reference in respect of the pricing

---

[229] Case T-83/91, *Tetra Pak International SA v Commission (Tetra Pak II)* [1994] ECR II-755, para. 151; Case T-340/03, *France Télécom* [2007] ECR II-107, para. 197.

[230] Case T-83/91, *Tetra Pak II* [1994] ECR II-755, para. 151.

[231] For a discussion of the required evidence generally see Geradin, Layne-Farrar, and Petit, n. 170, 4.272–4.278.

[232] See, e.g., *Napier Brown/British Sugar* [1988] OJ L284/41 where an internal memo which said '[i]f we are to succeed in seeing off the Whitworths threat, we MUST attack on all fronts. It is time to get nasty!' did not go down well with the Commission.

[233] Case T-340/03, *France Télécom* [2007] ECR II-107, para. 202.

[234] Ibid., para. 206.

[235] Para. 98.

[236] Rousseva and Marquis, n. 3, 32, and available at <http://ssrn.com/abstract=2171693>.

[237] See Section 8.G, p. 399.

[238] Case C-209/10, *Post Danmark I* EU:C:2012:172.

practices of Post Danmark (PD) on the liberalised unaddressed mail market in Denmark. PD had a statutory monopoly and USO in respect of normal addressed mail under a certain weight. For this purpose it had a network covering the whole national territory, which it also used for its unaddressed mail business. A competitor on the latter market claimed that PD was enticing away its three biggest customers through selective price reductions. The Konkurrencerådet (Danish competition authority)[239] could not establish that PD had intentionally sought to eliminate competition. Examining its costs by reference to the concept of average incremental cost (AIC) in order to take account of the shared infrastructure, the Konkurrencerådet found that in two cases (Spar and SuperBest) PD's prices were above ATC and in one (the Coop) they were below ATC but above AIC. As it found no intention to eliminate, the Konkurrencerådet, following the *AKZO* criteria, held that PD had not abused its dominant position by predatory pricing. However, it found that PD had abused it by practising a policy of selective price reductions which amounted to price discrimination, in that it had pursued a pricing policy for the competitor's former customers which was different from its policy for its pre-existing customers, without being able to justify the difference on cost-related grounds.

The referring court defined 'incremental costs' in the case as those 'destined to disappear in the short and medium term (three to five years), if PD were to give up its business activity of distributing unaddressed mail' and the ATC as 'average incremental costs to which were added a portion, determined by estimation, of Post Danmark's common costs connected to activities other than those covered by the universal service obligation'.[240] As there were common costs arising from the use of the network infrastructure for both the USO obligations and the unaddressed mail, the costs of the USO could be reduced over three to five years if PD were to give up the unaddressed mail business. The Konkurrencerådet therefore included in its estimation of the average incremental costs (AIC) not only the fixed and variable costs attributable solely to distributing unaddressed mail but also a certain proportion of the common costs.[241] The CJ commented on this method of assessment that 'in the specific circumstances of the case . . . such a method of attribution would seem to seek to identify the great bulk of the costs attributable to the activity of unaddressed mail' (the CJ was not asked in the reference about the *correctness* of the assessment methodology).[242] As we have already seen[243] incremental cost normally includes only the fixed and variable costs incurred in providing the particular product or service, and none of the common costs.

On the abuse issue the CJ said that price discrimination cannot of itself suggest that there is an exclusionary abuse; that the prices above ATC could not be considered to have anti-competitive effects; and that selective low prices may not be considered to amount to an exclusionary abuse merely because the price is lower than ATC but higher than AIC.

Case C-209/10, *Post Danmark A/S v Konkurrencerådet*, EU:C:2012:172

Court of Justice

35. . . . [I]t was found, among other things, that the price offered to the Coop group did not enable Post Danmark to cover the average total costs attributed to the activity of unaddressed mail distribution taken as a whole, but did enable it to cover the average incremental costs pertaining to that activity, as estimated by the Danish competition authorities.

---

[239] Confirmed by the appeals tribunal, Konkurrenceankenævnet.

[240] Case C-209/10, *Post Danmark I* EU:C:2012:172, para. 31.

[241] Seventy-five per cent of the attributable common costs of logistical capacity and 25% of non-attributable common costs, *Post Danmark I*, ibid., paras. 32–33.

[242] Ibid., para. 34. Mengozzi AG was firmly in favour of using AIC rather than AVC, Opinion, paras. 33–37.

[243] See Section 7.C, p. 382.

36. Moreover, it is common ground that, in the present case, the prices offered to the Spar and SuperBest groups were assessed as being at a higher level than those average total costs, as estimated by those authorities. In those circumstances, it cannot be considered that such prices have anti-competitive effects.

37. As regards the prices charged the Coop group, a pricing policy such as that in issue in the main proceedings cannot be considered to amount to an exclusionary abuse simply because the price charged to a single customer by a dominant undertaking is lower than the average total costs attributed to the activity concerned, but higher than the average incremental costs pertaining to the latter, as respectively estimated in the case in the main proceedings.

38. Indeed, to the extent that a dominant undertaking sets its prices at a level covering the great bulk of the costs attributable to the supply of the goods or services in question, it will, as a general rule, be possible for a competitor as efficient as that undertaking to compete with those prices without suffering losses that are unsustainable in the long term.

39. It is for the court making the reference to assess the relevant circumstances of the case in the main proceedings in the light of the finding made in the previous paragraph. In any event, it is worth noting that it appears from the documents before the Court that Forbruger-Kontakt managed to maintain its distribution network despite losing the volume of mail related to the three customers involved and managed, in 2007, to win back the Coop group's custom and, since then, that of the Spar group.

40. If the court making the reference, after carrying out that assessment, should nevertheless make a finding of anti-competitive effects due to Post Danmark's actions, it should be recalled that it is open to a dominant undertaking to provide justification for behaviour that is liable to be caught by the prohibition under Article [102] (see, to this effect, Case 27/76 *United Brands and United Brands Continentaal* v *Commission* . . . paragraph 184; Joined Cases C-241/91 P and C-242/91 P *RTE and ITP* v *Commission* . . . paragraphs 54 and 55; and *TeliaSonera Sverige*, paragraphs 31 and 75).

. . .

45. . . . On those grounds, the Court (Grand Chamber) hereby rules:

Article [102] must be interpreted as meaning that a policy by which a dominant undertaking charges low prices to certain major customers of a competitor may not be considered to amount to an exclusionary abuse merely because the price that undertaking charges one of those customers is lower than the average total costs attributed to the activity concerned, but higher than the average incremental costs pertaining to that activity, as estimated in the procedure giving rise to the case in the main proceedings. In order to assess the existence of anti-competitive effects in circumstances such as those of that case, it is necessary to consider whether that pricing policy, without objective justification, produces an actual or likely exclusionary effect, to the detriment of competition and, thereby, of consumers' interests.

The CJ noted that the Konkurrencerådet had recourse to incremental costs rather than the variable costs concept used in the *AKZO* case law[244] but accepted for the purposes of the ruling the Konkurrencerådet's use of the ATC and AIC benchmarks, whatever the peculiarities of their calculation (adding only the non-USO common costs to ATC and adding some common costs to AIC). As AIC is lower than ATC but always higher than AVC some of the prices in the case fell within the 'grey' area identified in *AKZO* between ATC and AVC where intent to eliminate is necessary for an abuse. PD's intention to eliminate had not been proved, so applying *AKZO* without further ado would have rendered these prices not abusive. However, the CJ still left it open to the national court to find that the pricing was abusive *if it made a finding of anti-competitive effects*.[245] The CJ clearly thought this would be unlikely because if, as here, the dominant undertaking is setting its prices at a

---

[244] Case C-209/10, *Post Danmark I* EU:C:2012:172, para. 31.
[245] Ibid., para. 40.

level covering the bulk of its attributable costs, *as a general rule* an equally efficient competitor would be able to compete without suffering long-term unsustainable losses,[246] and in this case the competitor had actually remained on the market and won back some of the customers.[247] Although in paragraph 37 the CJ specifically talked about below ATC prices charged to a *single customer*, paragraph 38, to which paragraphs 39 and 40 refer ('it is for the court making the reference to assesses the relevant circumstances . . . in the light of the finding made in the previous paragraph') makes a general point about the ability of equally efficient competitors to compete, i.e. it applied the AEC test. It is clear from paragraph 37 that mere selectivity alone does not make a below ATC price abusive.

It is reasonable to conclude from this that the CJ has added to the *AKZO* test in providing for anti-competitive effects as an alternative to intent where prices are between ATC and AIC. The question then arises whether effects could also be an alternative where prices are between AIC and AVC.[248] It is illogical that effects should be relevant when prices are above AIC but not when they are below it, but it has been argued that given the 'indirect' evidence admissible to show intent, an intent-based test and an effects-based test may actually converge.[249]

E. THE 'MEETING COMPETITION' DEFENCE AND PREDATORY PRICING

In *France Télécom* the dominant undertaking, WIN, claimed that in pricing below cost it was only meeting competition and that it had an absolute right to 'align' its prices with its competitors. The CJ upheld the GC[250] in saying that it did not.

Case C-202/07 P, *France Télécom v Commission* [2009] ECR I-2369

Court of Justice

43. Accordingly, in paragraph 176 of the judgment under appeal, the [General Court] noted, first, that recital 315 of the contested decision contests WIN's right to align its prices on those charged by its competitors only in so far as the exercise of that option 'would result in its not recovering the costs of the service in question'.

44. Next, the Court explained, in paragraphs 178 to 182 of the judgment under appeal, the reasons why such a right to align could be based neither on Commission Decision 83/462/EEC of 29 July 1983 relating to a proceeding under Article [102] (IV/30.698—ECS/AKZO: interim measures) . . . nor the judgment in *AKZO v Commission*, upon which the appellant relies.

45. Lastly, the Court determined whether limiting WIN's right to align its prices on those of its competitors, inasmuch as it 'would result in its not recovering the costs of the service in question', was compatible with Community law.

46. To that end, the Court refers in paragraphs 185 and 186 of the judgment under appeal to the Community case-law according to which Article [102] imposes specific obligations on undertakings in a dominant position. In particular, the Court recalled that, although the fact that an undertaking is in a

---

[246] Ibid., para. 38.

[247] On 13 February 2013 the Danish Supreme Court, applying this ruling, overturned the Konkurrencerådet's decision.

[248] See the discussion in Faull and Nikpay, n. 1, 4.342.

[249] Rousseva and Marquis, n. 3. For general comments on *Post Danmark I*, see S. Barazza, '*Post Danmark*: The CJEU Calls for an Effect-based Assessment of Pricing Policies' (2012) 3 *JECLAP* 466; R. Subiotto and D. Little, 'The Application of Article 102 TFEU by the European Commission and the European Courts' (2012) 3 *JECLAP* 175.

[250] Case T-340/03, *France Télécom* [2007] ECR II-107.

dominant position cannot deprive it of the right to protect its own commercial interests if they are at-tacked and such an undertaking must be allowed the right to take such reasonable steps as it deems ap-propriate to protect those interests, it is not possible, however, to countenance such behaviour if its actual purpose is to strengthen that dominant position and abuse it.

47. It was on the basis of that case-law that the [General Court] thus found, in paragraph 187 of the judgment under appeal, that WIN cannot rely on any absolute right to align its prices on those of its com-petitors in order to justify its conduct where that conduct constitutes an abuse of its dominant position.

48. Nor can the appellant object that the Court merely made such a finding without ascertaining whether, in the present case, WIN's conduct was abusive. The Court specifically rejected, inter alia in paragraphs 195 to 218 and 224 to 230 of the judgment under appeal, all the appellant's arguments seek-ing to question whether that abusive conduct existed, as found in the contested decision.

It should be noted that the CJ said that a dominant undertaking does not have an *absolute* right to align. The problem in pleading a meeting competition defence in predatory pricing cases is that the *AKZO* test is formulated in intent terms. If the undertaking is pricing below cost and the intent is presumed (below AVC), or has been proved (in the 'grey area') then that is the end of the matter. The 'right to align' has been taken away by the fact of the undertaking's dominance, which imposes on it 'specific obligations' (paragraph 46) which, as the GC said, deprives it 'of the right to adopt a course of conduct or take measures which are not in themselves abuses and which would even be unobjec-tionable if adopted or taken by non-dominant undertakings'.[251] The GC rejected the plea that below-cost pricing could be justified by the efficiencies to be garnered through economies of scale.[252]

F. RECOUPMENT

(i) The Issue of the Possibility of Recoupment

The concept of predatory pricing rests on the assumption that the predator sacrifices short-term profits for future gains. It hinges on the possibility that the predator can recoup its losses, i.e. that short-term loss is more than compensated for in the long term when, after the competitor's exit, the undertaking can raise prices to monopoly level. If there are no barriers to entry to the market the undertaking will not be able to recoup if it continually has to price low in order to fight off new competitors (although predation may constitute a barrier to entry). The economics literature em-phasises that the ability to recoup is central to recognising predatory pricing as a rational strategy in certain conditions. It is another matter, however, to say that it should be *necessary* for the party alleging predation to show that recoupment is possible or likely[253] before predatory pricing can be found.

In the US the courts do not find predatory pricing unless the plaintiff demonstrates that the alleged predator had a dangerous probability of recouping its investment in below-cost prices.[254] It means in effect that even if the plaintiff can show below-cost prices[255] and an anti-competitive intent, there will be no antitrust violation.[256] The result of this, especially when wedded to the sceptical judicial

---

[251] Ibid., para. 186.

[252] Ibid., para. 217.

[253] Depending on the standard of proof which is applied.

[254] This stems from the 1993 Supreme Court ruling in *Brooke Group Ltd v Brown & Williamson Tobacco Corp*, 509 US 209, 113 S.Ct 2578 (1993).

[255] They were below AVC in *Brooke Group*.

[256] *Brooke Group* was an action brought under the Robinson–Patman Act, 15 USC §13(a) on price discrimination but the analysis applies equally to s. 2 of the Sherman Act. See J. B. Baker, 'Predatory Pricing after *Brooke Group*: An Economic Perspective' (1994) 62 *Antitrust LJ* 585.

attitude to predatory pricing shown in the *Matsushita* case,[257] is that it is very hard for predatory pricing actions to succeed in the US courts.[258] The US position reflects the view that consumer welfare is the objective of s. 2 of the Sherman Act. Without proof of actual or likely consumer harm there is no violation.

There are good arguments against making feasibility of recoupment part of the legal test. For example, there are problems wherever the burden of proof is placed, predicting recoupment is difficult, and the 'recoupment' gained by the firm may, for example, consist of deterring entrants in other markets, which is impossible to measure.[259]

(ii) The EU Case Law

EU law differs from US law. In *AKZO* the CJ did not expressly consider whether recoupment made predation a plausible strategy, but it is argued that it is implicit in paragraph 71.[260] The question of whether a possibility or likelihood of recoupment is part of the test for predatory pricing was expressly raised in *Tetra Pak II* and answered in the negative—at least in the circumstances of that case, where the principles laid down in *AKZO* were confirmed and developed.[261] Tetra Pak's share of the dominated market (aseptic cartons) was over 90 per cent although the impugned pricing conduct took place on the unrelated non-dominated market.

Tetra Pak was found to have engaged in predatory pricing in the non-aseptic carton market. This included selling at below AVC in Italy. The CJ held that the Commission did not have to prove that Tetra Pak could recoup.

Case C-333/94 P, *Tetra Pak International SA v Commission* [1996] ECR I-5951

Court of Justice

39. In its fourth plea, Tetra Pak submits that the [General Court] erred in law when, at paragraph 150 of the judgment under appeal, it characterised Tetra Pak's prices in the non-aseptic sector as predatory without accepting that it was necessary for that purpose to establish that it had a reasonable prospect of recouping the losses so incurred.

40. Tetra Pak considers that the possibility of recouping the losses incurred as a result of predatory sales is a constitutive element in the notion of predatory pricing. That is clear, it claims, from paragraph 71 of the *AKZO* judgment. Since, however, both the Commission and the [General Court] accept that sales below cost took place only on the non-aseptic markets, on which Tetra Pak was not found to hold a dominant position, it had no realistic chance of recouping its losses later.

41. In *AKZO* this Court did indeed sanction the existence of two different methods of analysis for determining whether an undertaking has practised predatory pricing. First, prices below average variable costs must always be considered abusive. In such a case, there is no conceivable economic purpose other than the elimination of a competitor, since each item produced and sold entails a loss for the undertaking.

---

[257] *Matsushita Elec Indust Co Ltd v Zenith Radio Corp*, 475 US 574 (1986), see n. 201.

[258] It is not difficult for a properly advised defendant to raise sufficient doubts as to the possibility of recoupment. How courts can judge the possibility of recoupment is discussed in C. Scott Hemphill, 'The Role of Recoupment in Predatory Pricing Analyses' (2001) 53 *Stan LR* 1581.

[259] See Temple Lang and O'Donoghue, n. 176, 144–145.

[260] See Fennelly AG in para. 136 of his Opinion in Cases C-395 and 396/96 P, *Compagnie Maritime Belge* [2000] ECR I-1365.

[261] Case C-333/94 P, *Tetra Pak II* [1996] ECR I-5951.

Secondly, prices below average total costs but above average variable costs are only to be considered abusive if an intention to eliminate can be shown.

42. At paragraph 150 of the judgment under appeal, the [General Court] carried out the same examination as did this Court in *AKZO*. For sales of non-aseptic cartons in Italy between 1976 and 1981, it found that prices were considerably lower than average variable costs. Proof of intention to eliminate competitors was therefore not necessary. In 1982, prices for those cartons lay between average variable costs and average total costs. For that reason, in paragraph 151 of its judgment, the [General Court] was at pains to establish—and the appellant has not criticized it in that regard—that Tetra Pak intended to eliminate a competitor.

43. The [General Court] was also right, at paragraphs 189 to 191 of the judgment under appeal, to apply exactly the same reasoning to sales of non-aseptic machines in the United Kingdom between 1981 and 1984.

44. Furthermore, it would not be appropriate, in the circumstances of the present case, to require in addition proof that Tetra Pak had a realistic chance of recouping its losses. It must be possible to penalize predatory pricing whenever there is a risk that competitors will be eliminated. The [General Court] found, at paragraphs 151 and 191 of its judgment, that there was such a risk in this case. The aim pursued, which is to maintain undistorted competition, rules out waiting until such a strategy leads to the actual elimination of competitors.

In paragraph 44 the CJ stressed that the important factor in the determination of predation is the risk that competitors will be eliminated. This could be shorthand for saying that once that happened Tetra Pak would be able to raise prices. Economic theory, however, suggests that the possibility of recoupment can only be judged after a thorough analysis of the structure of the market and other factors. The CJ did not say in paragraph 44 that it would *never* be necessary to show the feasibility of recoupment, but only that it would not be appropriate *in the circumstances of the present case*. Those circumstances included the fact that Tetra Pak had a quasi-monopoly and that the alleged predation was on a market distinct from the dominated one (so that Tetra Pak could cross-subsidise). Further, there was clear evidence from the data uncovered by the Commission that Tetra Pak was pursuing a deliberate strategy of eliminating competitors.

In *Compagnie Maritime Belge* Advocate General Fennelly considered that the possibility of recoupment should be an essential part of the test for predatory pricing[262] but the CJ did not address the point. However in *France Télécom* the GC held that proof of recoupment was not a precondition to a finding of predatory pricing.[263] On appeal Advocate General Mazák considered that in the light of paragraph 44 of *Tetra Pak II* (no need '*in the circumstances of the present case*') proof of the possibility of recoupment should be required as without that possibility 'consumers and their interests should, in principle not be harmed'.[264] However, the CJ upheld the GC in the most trenchant terms. It recited the *AKZO* and *Tetra Pak II* case law and said that EU law does not require proof of the possibility of recoupment. Such proof might, nevertheless, be a relevant factor in excluding economic justification for below AVC pricing or assist in establishing an eliminatory plan (paragraph 111). The CJ also considered in paragraph 107 that the abuse arises from the objective of elimination of competitors which will harm the competitive process —there is no mention of effects on consumers.

---

[262] Para. 136 of his Opinion in *Compagnie Maritime Belge* [2000] ECR I-1365.

[263] Case T-340/03, *France Télécom* [2007] ECR II-107. Both above and below AVC pricing were involved.

[264] Case C-202/07 P, *France Télécom* [2009] ECR I-2369, paras. 73–74 of the Opinion.

Case C-202/07 P, *France Télécom SA v Commission* [2009] ECR I-2369

Court of Justice

103. In considering the merits of the first part of this ground of appeal, it is necessary to note at the outset that, according to settled case-law, Article [102] is an application of the general objective of European Community action laid down by Article 3(1)(g) EC, namely, the institution of a system ensuring that competition in the common market is not distorted. Thus, the dominant position referred to in Article [102] relates to a position of economic strength enjoyed by an undertaking which enables it to prevent effective competition being maintained on the relevant market by affording it the power to behave to an appreciable extent independently of its competitors, its customers and ultimately of the consumers (Case 85/76 *Hoffmann-La Roche v Commission* . . . paragraph 38).

104. In that context, in prohibiting the abuse of a dominant market position in so far as trade between Member States is capable of being affected, Article [102] refers to conduct which is such as to influence the structure of a market where the degree of competition is already weakened and which, through recourse to methods different from those governing normal competition in products or services on the basis of the transactions of commercial operators, has the effect of hindering the maintenance of the degree of competition still existing in the market or the growth of that competition (*Hoffman[n]-La Roche v Commission*, paragraph 91; Case 322/81 *Nederlandsche Banden-Industrie-Michelin v Commission* . . . paragraph 70; *AKZO v Commission*, paragraph 69; and Case C-95/04 P *British Airways v Commission* . . . paragraph 66).

105. Therefore, since Article [102] refers not only to practices which may cause damage to consumers directly, but also to those which are detrimental to them through their impact on an effective competition structure (Case 6/72 *Europemballage and Continental Can v Commission* . . . paragraph 26), an undertaking which holds a dominant position has a special responsibility not to allow its behaviour to impair genuine undistorted competition on the common market (*Nederlandsche Banden-Industrie-Michelin v Commission*, paragraph 57).

106. As the Court has already stated, it follows that Article [102] prohibits a dominant undertaking from eliminating a competitor and thereby strengthening its position by using methods other than those which come within the scope of competition on the basis of quality. From that point of view, not all competition by means of price can be regarded as legitimate (*AKZO v Commission*, paragraph 70).

107. In particular, it must be found that an undertaking abuses its dominant position where, in a market the competition structure of which is already weakened by reason precisely of the presence of that undertaking, it operates a pricing policy the sole economic objective of which is to eliminate its competitors with a view, subsequently, to profiting from the reduction of the degree of competition still existing in the market.

108. In order to assess the lawfulness of the pricing policy applied by a dominant undertaking, the Court, in paragraph 74 of *AKZO v Commission*, relied on pricing criteria based on the costs incurred by the dominant undertaking and on its strategy.

109. Thus, the Court of Justice has held, first, that prices below average variable costs must be considered prima facie abusive inasmuch as, in applying such prices, an undertaking in a dominant position is presumed to pursue no other economic objective save that of eliminating its competitors. Secondly, prices below average total costs but above average variable costs are to be considered abusive only where they are fixed in the context of a plan having the purpose of eliminating a competitor (see *AKZO v Commission*, paragraphs 70 and 71, and *Tetra Pak v Commission*, paragraph 41).

110. Accordingly, contrary to what the appellant claims, it does not follow from the case-law of the Court that proof of the possibility of recoupment of losses suffered by the application, by an undertaking in a dominant position, of prices lower than a certain level of costs constitutes a necessary precondition to establishing that such a pricing policy is abusive. In particular, the Court has taken the opportunity to

dispense with such proof in circumstances where the eliminatory intent of the undertaking at issue could be presumed in view of that undertaking's application of prices lower than average variable costs (see, to that effect, *Tetra Pak v Commission*, paragraph 44).

111. That interpretation does not, of course, preclude the Commission from finding such a possibility of recoupment of losses to be a relevant factor in assessing whether or not the practice concerned is abusive, in that it may, for example where prices lower than average variable costs are applied, assist in excluding economic justifications other than the elimination of a competitor, or, where prices below average total costs but above average variable costs are applied, assist in establishing that a plan to eliminate a competitor exists.

112. Moreover, the lack of any possibility of recoupment of losses is not sufficient to prevent the undertaking concerned reinforcing its dominant position, in particular, following the withdrawal from the market of one or a number of its competitors, so that the degree of competition existing on the market, already weakened precisely because of the presence of the undertaking concerned, is further reduced and customers suffer loss as a result of the limitation of the choices available to them.

113. The [General Court] was right therefore to hold, in paragraph 228 of the judgment under appeal, that demonstrating that it is possible to recoup losses is not a necessary precondition for a finding of predatory pricing.

G. PREDATORY PRICING IN THE GUIDANCE PAPER AND THE SACRIFICE PRINCIPLE

The Guidance Paper states that the Commission will decide whether to intervene in a possible predatory pricing case (pursuant to the general AEC) on the basis of whether the undertaking deliberately incurs losses or foregoes profits in the short term ('sacrifice') so as to foreclose actual or potential competitors with a view to maintaining or strengthening market power thereby causing consumer harm. The Guidance Paper reflects the *AKZO* test but the Commission will use AAC and LRAIC rather than AVC and ATC in assessing the 'sacrifice'.[265] Pricing below AAC is clear evidence of sacrifice. LRAIC and ATC are the same in single-product undertakings but LRAIC may be lower in the case of multi-product undertakings. Subsequent to the Guidance Paper the CJ accepted the use of LRAIC in *Post Danmark I*, as already discussed. The Commission does not rule out justification by efficiencies but considers that the conditions in the Guidance Paper[266] are unlikely to be satisfied in cases of predatory pricing.[267]

The Guidance Paper does not mention the word 'recoupment'. The Commission, indicating when it will intervene, nevertheless says that consumers are most likely to be harmed if the dominant undertaking can reasonably expect an increase in market power after its conduct has ended.[268] An increase in market power, however, does not necessarily denote an ability to recoup, which will depend on the specific circumstances.[269] The Commission will intervene not only if prices can be increased again, but also if the conduct could prevent or delay a lowering of prices.

[265] The Commission had already used the LRAIC standard in the *Deutsche Post AG* decision in 2001 ([2001] OJ L125/27). See also the Notice on the Application of the Competition Rules to Access Agreements in the Telecommunications Sector [1998] OJ C265/2, paras. 114 and 115.

[266] Guidance Paper, para. 30, see Section 5.D, p. 373.

[267] Ibid., para. 74.

[268] Ibid., para 70.

[269] See E. Rousseva, *Rethinking Exclusionary Abuses in EU Competition Law* (Hart Publishing, 2010), 408.

Guidance on the Commission's Enforcement Priorities in Applying Article 82 of the EC Treaty to Abusive Exclusionary Conduct by Dominant Undertakings [2009] OJ C45/2

63. In line with its enforcement priorities, the Commission will generally intervene where there is evidence showing that a dominant undertaking engages in predatory conduct by deliberately incurring losses or foregoing profits in the short term (referred to hereafter as 'sacrifice'), so as to foreclose or be likely to foreclose one or more of its actual or potential competitors with a view to strengthening or maintaining its market power, thereby causing consumer harm . . .

(a) Sacrifice

64. Conduct will be viewed by the Commission as entailing a sacrifice if, by charging a lower price for all or a particular part of its output over the relevant time period, or by expanding its output over the relevant time period, the dominant undertaking incurred or is incurring losses that could have been avoided. The Commission will take AAC as the appropriate starting point for assessing whether the dominant undertaking incurred or is incurring avoidable losses. If a dominant undertaking charges a price below AAC for all or part of its output, it is not recovering the costs that could have been avoided by not producing that output: it is incurring a loss that could have been avoided [40]. Pricing below AAC will thus in most cases be viewed by the Commission as a clear indication of sacrifice . . .

65. However, the concept of sacrifice does not only include pricing below AAC . . . In order to show a predatory strategy, the Commission may also investigate whether the allegedly predatory conduct led in the short term to net revenues lower than could have been expected from a reasonable alternative conduct, that is to say, whether the dominant undertaking incurred a loss that it could have avoided . . . The Commission will not compare the actual conduct with hypothetical or theoretical alternatives that might have been more profitable. Only economically rational and practicable alternatives will be considered which, taking into account the market conditions and business realities facing the dominant undertaking, can realistically be expected to be more profitable.

66. In some cases it will be possible to rely upon direct evidence consisting of documents from the dominant undertaking which clearly show a predatory strategy . . . such as a detailed plan to sacrifice in order to exclude a competitor, to prevent entry or to pre-empt the emergence of a market, or evidence of concrete threats of predatory action . . .

(b) Anti-competitive foreclosure

67. If sufficient reliable data are available, the Commission will apply the equally efficient competitor analysis, described in paragraphs 25 to 27, to determine whether the conduct is capable of harming consumers. Normally only pricing below LRAIC is capable of foreclosing as efficient competitors from the market.

68. In addition to the factors already mentioned in paragraph 20, the Commission will generally investigate whether and how the suspected conduct reduces the likelihood that competitors will compete. For instance, if the dominant undertaking is better informed about cost or other market conditions, or can distort market signals about profitability, it may engage in predatory conduct so as to influence the expectations of potential entrants and thereby deter entry. If the conduct and its likely effects are felt on multiple markets and/or in successive periods of possible entry, the dominant undertaking may be shown to be seeking a reputation for predatory conduct. If the targeted competitor is dependent on external financing, substantial price decreases or other predatory conduct by the dominant undertaking could adversely affect the competitor's performance so that its access to further financing may be seriously undermined.

69. The Commission does not consider that it is necessary to show that competitors have exited the market in order to show that there has been anti-competitive foreclosure. The possibility cannot be excluded that the dominant undertaking may prefer to prevent the competitor from competing vigorously

and have it follow the dominant undertaking's pricing, rather than eliminate it from the market altogether. Such disciplining avoids the risk inherent in eliminating competitors, in particular the risk that the assets of the competitor are sold at a low price and stay in the market, creating a new low cost entrant.

70. Generally speaking, consumers are likely to be harmed if the dominant undertaking can reasonably expect its market power after the predatory conduct comes to an end to be greater than it would have been had the undertaking not engaged in that conduct in the first place, that is to say, if the undertaking is likely to be in a position to benefit from the sacrifice.

71. This does not mean that the Commission will only intervene if the dominant undertaking would be likely to be able to increase its prices above the level persisting in the market before the conduct. It is sufficient, for instance, that the conduct would be likely to prevent or delay a decline in prices that would otherwise have occurred. Identifying consumer harm is not a mechanical calculation of profits and losses, and proof of overall profits is not required. Likely consumer harm may be demonstrated by assessing the likely foreclosure effect of the conduct, combined with consideration of other factors, such as entry barriers . . . In this context, the Commission will also consider possibilities of re-entry.

72. It may be easier for the dominant undertaking to engage in predatory conduct if it selectively targets specific customers with low prices, as this will limit the losses incurred by the dominant undertaking. 73. It is less likely that the dominant undertaking engages in predatory conduct if the conduct concerns a low price applied generally for a long period of time.

(c) Efficiencies

74. In general it is considered unlikely that predatory conduct will create efficiencies. However, provided that the conditions set out in Section III D are fulfilled, the Commission will consider claims by a dominant undertaking that the low pricing enables it to achieve economies of scale or efficiencies related to expanding the market.

In a footnote to paragraph 63 of the Guidance Paper the Commission specifically says that it may pursue predatory practices by dominant undertakings on secondary markets on which they are not yet dominant. This may particularly be so where a dominant undertaking on a market protected by a legal monopoly uses its profits there to cross-subsidise its activities in another market. Cross-subsidisation has never been held to be an abuse *in itself*. It is the below-cost prices on the subsidised market, or other abusive practices, which may infringe Article 102.[270]

H. PREDATORY PRICING IN NEW AND DIGITAL ECONOMY MARKETS

We have noted previously the particular characteristics of markets in the new economy.[271] One of these is the 'tipping' effect, whereby the competitor who wins takes most (or all) of the market because its product or service becomes the standard. Predatory pricing may therefore be a highly rational strategy in such markets: low pricing may achieve the critical mass of customers which results in the undertaking winning the competition 'for' the market. Further, high technology markets commonly have very high fixed costs and very low variable costs which may confuse predatory pricing tests based on average variable cost.

France Télécom, discussed in Sections 8.E and 8.F, concerned a new economy market, WIN's ADSL services.[272] WIN was a 72 per cent owned subsidiary of France Télécom which at the relevant

---

[270] See *Deutsche Post* [2001] OJ L125/27; Case C-333/94 P, *Tetra Pak II* [1996] ECR I-5951.

[271] See Chap. 1, Section 12, p. 48 and Chap. 6.

[272] COMP/38.233, *Wanadoo Interactive*, 16 July 2003. See R. Klotz and J. Fehrenbach (2003) 3 *Competition Policy Newsletter* 10.

time had almost 100 per cent of the wholesale ADSL services for internet service providers. The Commission found that in one period WIN's prices were below AVC and thereafter they were above AVC but still below ATC.[273] It also found that the undertaking deliberately pursued a pricing policy which made losses but 'was designed to take the lion's share of a booming market at the expense of other competitors'.[274] Indeed, one competitor went out of business. WIN claimed that its conduct was perfectly rational, in that its pricing attracted new customers who would be profitable in less than five years. It claimed this was a rational way of developing a new market and reaching profitability in the medium term. The Commission, however, saw this reasoning as demonstrating that the pricing *was* predatory, '[i]ndeed, the recoupment of initial losses over a certain period of time is in the most common settings the very objective of a predatory pricing behaviour . . . Admitting WIN's reasoning in this respect would have led to the conclusion that by essence predatory pricing can simply not exist.'[275] The Commission also rejected the argument that it was inappropriate for it to intervene in a market at a nascent stage.[276] The Commission's refusal to take a 'hands off' approach while the ADSL market developed was upheld on appeal.[277] The Commission is currently pursuing a predatory pricing case against Qualcomm, alleging that it sold its UTMS baseband chipsets below cost with the aim of forcing a main rival out of the market.[278]

Nevertheless, it is doubtful that normal predatory pricing rules can be applied to some markets in the new economy without Type 1 errors. We have already noted the problems of multi-sided markets.[279] As Rato and Petit say of the ICT sector 'the fact that no price is charged to consumers does not mean that no price is charged at all, or that none of the dominant firm's costs are recouped'. Often customers can use the basic service for free and then are charged when they move on to premium services with added features.[280] In the digital economy providers may supply their services for free and make money from their customers in other ways, particularly by the commodification of their personal data. The Commission, which had been looking at the possibility of an investigation of Google for predatory pricing in distributing its Android system for free, did not pursue this when it opened proceedings against Google in respect of Android in April 2015. It confined itself to tying and bundling and similar charges in connection with the installation on Android of Google apps.[281]

I. SELECTIVE ABOVE-COST PRICING

Predatory pricing may involve not just low prices across the board but selectively targeting the low prices on certain customers. The Guidance Paper recognises this practice in paragraph 72. There are cases, however, in which prices which were *not* below costs, and did not involve the dominant

---

[273] The Commission calculated the costs in a way which it claimed was highly favourable to Wanadoo, e.g. treating customer acquisition costs as capital expenditures. This lowered Wanadoo's AVC (and therefore the significant cost level for the *AKZO* test).

[274] And see Klotz and Fehrenbach, n. 272, 11.

[275] Ibid., 12.

[276] See Chap. 1, Section 12, p. 48. The Commission fined WIN €10.35 million and later placed WIN's accounts under review until the end of 2006, to ensure month by month that its prices were not anti-competitive. The situation in *France Télécom* was in effect a type of margin squeeze (see Section 9) but because of the relationship between WIN and France Télécom at the relevant time it was not analysed as such but dealt with as predatory pricing.

[277] Case T-340/03, *France Télécom* [2007] ECR II-107 and Case C-202/07 P, *France Télécom* [2009] ECR I-2369.

[278] IP/15/6271.

[279] In Chap. 1, Section 12, p. 48.

[280] M. Rato and N. Petit, 'Abuse of Dominance in Technology-enabled Markets: Established Standards Reconsidered?' (2013) 9 *European Competition Journal* 1, 50–51.

[281] IP/15/4780; MEMO/15/4782; IP/16/1492; MEMO/16/1484.

undertakings making losses (although they may have made reduced profits), have also been held to infringe Article 102. If predatory pricing is defined as below-cost pricing to eliminate competitors, such selective low pricing cannot be properly described as such. The cases where selective above-cost prices have been held to be abusive— *Hilti*,[282] *Compagnie Maritime Belge*,[283] and *Irish Sugar*[284]— all had special features, and in the later case of *Post Danmark I*[285] the CJ clarified that prices above average incremental cost are presumed to be legal.

In *Hilti* the dominant undertaking offered lower, but above-cost, prices to competitors' customers as part of a tying strategy.[286] In *Compagnie Maritime Belge* the Commission found that undertakings in a collective dominant position had engaged in predatory conduct through selective low pricing targeted at a competitor's customers.[287] The undertakings were parties to a liner conference[288] (CEWAL) which faced competition from an independent shipping line (G & C). Among the practices it adopted to counter this threat was the use of 'fighting ships', specially designated CEWAL vessels whose sailing dates were close to those of G & C ships and on which CEWAL dropped its rates to match those of G & C. The Commission found this an abuse of CEWAL's collective dominant position[289] without an analysis of CEWAL's costs. The prices caused the members of CEWAL some revenue losses, but did not appear to have been below their total costs. The shipping lines appealed, inter alia, on the grounds that as their prices were not predatory within the *AKZO* test they were not an abuse.

The GC upheld the Commission, focusing on CEWAL's intent to eliminate G & C and the possible effect of its actions[290] and rejected the argument that CEWAL was merely trying to *meet* rather than *beat* the competition, saying that its response to G & C was not reasonable and proportionate.[291] Advocate General Fennelly saw this as a case of a 'super-dominant' entity setting out to exclude a competitor. In such a situation targeted, selective price cuts designed to eliminate would be an abuse regardless of the relationship of the prices to costs.[292]

The CJ held that the prices charged were abusive,[293] but its judgment was couched in narrower terms than the wide sweep of the Advocate General's Opinion. It concentrated on the specifics of the case.

---

[282] Case C-53/92P, *Hilti AG v Commission* [1994] ECR I-667.

[283] Cases C-395 and 396/96 P, *Compagnie Maritime Belge* [2000] ECR I-1365.

[284] Case T-228/97, *Irish Sugar* [1999] ECR II-2969.

[285] Case C-209/10, *Post Danmark I* EU:C:2012:172.

[286] See further Section 12.

[287] *CEWAL* [1993] OJ L34/20.

[288] A 'liner conference' is a group of two or more vessel-operators providing international liner services for carrying cargo on a particular route or routes within specified geographical limits, which has an agreement or arrangement within the framework of which they operate under uniform or common freight rates and other agreed conditions. At the time Council Reg. 4056/86, [1986] OJ L378/4, provided a (generous) block exemption for liner conferences which, inter alia, allowed horizontal price-fixing between the members of the conference. Art. 8 of Reg. 4056/86 provided that an abuse of a dominant position within Art. 102 was prohibited and that the Commission had power to withdraw the benefit of the exemption if the exemption brought about effects incompatible with Art. 102. This provision was referred to by the GC in Cases T-68/89 etc., *Società Italiana Vetro SpA v Commission* [1992] ECR II-1403, para. 359, as support for interpreting Art. 102 as applying to collective dominance. Reg. 4056/86 was repealed by Council Reg. 1419/2006 [2006] OJ L269/1.

[289] For the collective dominance aspects of the case, see Chap. 5.

[290] Cases T-24–26 and 28/93, *Compagnie Maritime Belge Transports v Commission* [1996] ECR II-1201.

[291] Case T-24/93, *Compagnie Maritime Belge* [1996] ECR II-1201, para. 148.

[292] Cases C-395 and 396/96 P, *Compagnie Maritime Belge* [2000] ECR I-1365, Fennelly AG, para. 137.

[293] The fines on the shipping lines were, however, annulled for procedural reasons as the Commission had not stated in its statement of objections that it intended to impose fines on the individual members. They were re-imposed, *Compagnie Maritime Belge* [2005] OJ L171/28, appeal dismissed Case T-276/04, *Compagnie Maritime Belge* [2008] ECR II-1277.

Cases C-395 and 396/96 P, *Compagnie Maritime Belge and Others v Commission* [2000] ECR-1365

Court of Justice

111. The third ground of appeal concerns the question whether the alleged abuse, as defined in the contested decision and the defence, can properly be so characterised.

112. It is settled case-law that the list of abusive practices contained in Article [102] of the Treaty is not an exhaustive enumeration of the abuses of a dominant position prohibited by the Treaty (Case 6/72 *Europemballage and Continental Can* v. *Commission* . . . paragraph 26).

113. It is, moreover, established that, in certain circumstances, abuse may occur if an undertaking in a dominant position strengthens that position in such a way that the degree of dominance reached substantially fetters competition (*Europemballage and Continental Can*, paragraph 26).

114. Furthermore, the actual scope of the special responsibility imposed on a dominant undertaking must be considered in the light of the specific circumstances of each case which show that competition has been weakened (Case C-333/94 P *Tetra Pak* v. *Commission* . . ., paragraph 24).

115. The maritime transport market is a very specialised sector. It is because of the specificity of that market that the Council established, in Regulation No. 4056/86, a set of competition rules different from that which applies to other economic sectors. The authorisation granted for an unlimited period to liner conferences to co-operate in fixing rates for maritime transport is exceptional in light of the relevant regulations and competition policy.

116. It is clear from the eighth recital in the preamble to Regulation No. 4056/86 that the authorisation to fix rates was granted to liner conferences because of their stabilising effect and their contribution to providing adequate efficient scheduled maritime transport services. The result may be that, where a single liner conference has a dominant position on a particular market, the user of those services would have little interest in resorting to an independent competitor, unless the competitor were able to offer prices lower than those of the liner conference.

117. It follows that, where a liner conference in a dominant position selectively cuts its prices in order deliberately to match those of a competitor, it derives a dual benefit. First, it eliminates the principal, and possibly the only, means of competition open to the competing undertaking. Second, it can continue to require its users to pay higher prices for the services which are not threatened by that competition.

118. It is not necessary, in the present case, to rule generally on the circumstances in which a liner conference may legitimately, on a case by case basis, adopt lower prices than those of its advertised tariff in order to compete with a competitor who quotes lower prices, or to decide on the exact scope of the expression 'uniform or common freight rates' in Article 1(3)(b) of Regulation No. 4056/86.

119. It is sufficient to recall that the conduct at issue here is that of a conference having a share of over 90 per cent of the market in question and only one competitor. The appellants have, moreover, never seriously disputed, and indeed admitted at the hearing, that the purpose of the conduct complained of was to eliminate G & C from the market.

120. The [GC] did not, therefore, err in law, in holding that the Commission's objections to the effect that the practice known as 'fighting ships', as applied against G & C, constituted an abuse of a dominant position were justified. It should also be noted that there is no question at all in this case of there having been a new definition of an abusive practice.

121. The grounds of appeal concerning fighting ships must therefore be rejected as inadmissible or unfounded.

The CJ stated that the 'special responsibility' of dominant undertakings has to be considered in the light of the circumstances in each case (paragraph 114), and confined its remarks thereafter to the facts of the case and stressed the specialised nature of the maritime transport sector (paragraph 115).[294] It considered that a competitor to a liner conference in a dominant position would have to offer *lower* prices than the conference (paragraph 116). In that context selective price-cutting deliberately made in order to meet the prices of the only competitor was an abuse. The CJ declined to say (paragraph 118) when a liner conference *could* legitimately drop its prices from its advertised tariff in order to compete with a competitor. The general question of when above-cost price competition designed to eliminate a new competitor is illegitimate, remained unanswered. However, in paragraph 119 the CJ noted that the conference had over 90 per cent of the market, and its comments about liner conferences in paragraphs 116–117, read with the reference to *Tetra Pak II*, suggested that undertakings in a monopolistic or quasi–monopolistic position have a particularly heavy responsibility towards the competitive process.[295]

In *Irish Sugar*,[296] Irish Sugar was the sole producer of sugar beet in Ireland and Northern Ireland. It reacted to increasing imports from other Member States by a variety of practices,[297] inter alia dropping its prices to customers identified as most vulnerable to the imports, although the reductions do not seem to have taken prices below total cost. As in *CEWAL* the Commission held that the conduct was abusive because of the intent to exclude competition (shown by company documents) and the selective, targeted nature of the price cuts. The appeal to the GC, on the grounds that it was only defending its position as it was entitled to do, was rejected.

Case T-228/97, *Irish Sugar plc v Commission* [1999] ECR II-2969

General Court

111. The case law shows that an 'abuse' is an objective concept referring to the behaviour of an undertaking in a dominant position which is such as to influence the structure of a market where, as a result of the very presence of the undertaking in question, the degree of competition is already weakened and which, through recourse to methods different from those governing normal competition in products or services on the basis of the transactions of commercial operators, has the effect of hindering the maintenance of the degree of competition still existing in the market or the growth of that competition (*Hoffmann-La Roche*, paragraph 91 . . .). It follows that Article [102] of the Treaty prohibits a dominant undertaking from eliminating a competitor and thereby reinforcing its position by having recourse to means other than those within the scope of competition on the merits. From that point of view, not all competition on price can be regarded as legitimate (*AKZO*, paragraph 70 . . .). The prohibition laid down in Article [102] is also justified by the consideration that harm should not be caused to consumers (*Continental Can*, paragraph 26; *Suiker Unie*, paragraphs 526 and 527 . . .).

112. Therefore, whilst the finding that a dominant position exists does not in itself imply any reproach to the undertaking concerned, it has a special responsibility, irrespective of the causes of that position, not to allow its conduct to impair genuine undistorted competition on the Common Market (*Michelin* paragraph 57 . . .). Similarly, whilst the fact that an undertaking is in a dominant position cannot deprive it of its entitlement to protect its own commercial interests when they are attacked, and whilst such an undertaking must be allowed the right to take such reasonable steps as it deems appropriate to protect those interests, such behaviour cannot be allowed if its purpose is to strengthen that dominant position and thereby abuse it (*United Brands*, paragraph 189; *BPB Industries*, paragraph 69; Case 83/91 *Tetra Pak II*, paragraph 147; Case T-24/93 *CMB*, paragraph 107 . . .).

. . .

---

[294] And thus the liner conference had already been given a lot of leeway, see n. 288.

[295] Nazzini sees the CJ in *Compagnie Maritime Belge* as applying a dynamic AEC efficient competitor test: Nazzini, n. 116, 242–243.

[296] [1997] OJ L258/1.

[297] Such as target rebates, export rebates, and product swaps.

189. Thus, even if the existence of a dominant position does not deprive an undertaking placed in that position of the right to protect its own commercial interests when they are threatened (see paragraph 112 above), the protection of the commercial position of an undertaking in a dominant position with the characteristics of that of the applicant at the time in question must, at the very least, in order to be lawful, be based on criteria of economic efficiency and consistent with the interests of consumers. In this case, the applicant has not shown that those conditions were fulfilled.

Again, this case concerned an undertaking with a very high market share. In paragraph 189 the GC refers to an undertaking 'with the characteristics of that of the applicant at the time in question' and relates the abuse to that. According to this judgment the ability of such undertakings to react to encroachments on their market position is limited, as they have to act in a way 'based on criteria of economic efficiency' and consistent with consumers' interests.

Compagnie Maritime Belge and *Irish Sugar* had a number of features in common:

- the infringing undertakings were in collective dominant positions;
- the collectively dominant undertakings had a market position which gave them a position of 'super-dominance' or quasi-monopoly (although the implications of 'super-dominance' must now be read in the light of the CJ's remarks in *TeliaSonera*[298]);
- an exclusionary intent was clearly identified;
- in both cases the undertakings were engaged in a range of exclusionary practices and there were cumulative effects from a number of abuses.

In addition, *Compagnie Maritime Belge* concerned a liner conference in the maritime transport sector created by horizontal agreements, and as such already benefited from favourable treatment by the competition rules.

A US commentator, engaging in a debate as to whether above-cost price cuts can be predatory because they can exclude new entrants who would, in time, become as efficient as the incumbent dominant undertaking,[299] concludes that above-cost price cuts should never be held predatory, but that care should be taken in measuring costs.

E. Elhauge, 'Why Above-Cost Price Cuts to Drive Out Entrants are not Predatory—And the Implications for Defining Costs and Market Power' (2003) 112 *Yale LJ* 681, 682–687

Even when incumbents do have market power, restrictions on their ability to adopt reactive above-cost price cuts are unlikely to achieve the objective of encouraging and protecting entry because less efficient entrants cannot survive in the long run, and entrants who are (or will predictably become) more efficient need no encouragement or protection. Further, such restrictions will have harmful effects by raising prices and lowering productive efficiency during any period of price restriction, inflicting wasteful transition and entry costs, as well as distorting innovation and price flexibility in response to changing market conditions. And the restrictions will discourage the creation of more efficient incumbents and entrants, which is ultimately far more important.

---

[298] Case C-52/09, *TeliaSonera* [2011] ECR I-527, paras. 78–82, see Section 3.D.iv, p. 359.

[299] See also A. Edlin, 'Stopping Above-cost Predatory Pricing' (2002) 111 *Yale LJ* 952; Geradin, Layne-Farrar, and Petit, n. 170, 4.284–4.291; Rousseva and Marquis, n. 3.

> This analysis reaffirms the wisdom of the position that antitrust law should not recognize any claim of above-cost predatory pricing. It also helps specify just what should count as costs. Costs should be defined in whatever way assures that an incumbent pricing at cost could not deter or drive out an equally efficient entrant. This test should be met by a cost measure that includes all costs that are varied by the allegedly predatory increase in output, since short-term threats or pricing strategies that exceed short-term costs should not be able to deter long-term investments or entry. Alternatively, if short-term pricing could deter such long-term decisions, this test would be met by a cost measure that reflected the magnitude of predator costs for the sorts of costs that are variable to the rival during the period of entry or investment decisions influenced by the short-term existence or threat of such pricing.

The case of *Post Danmark* has already been discussed.[300] We have seen that in the judgment the CJ ruled that discriminatory pricing was not of itself abusive, and that selective low prices cannot be considered to amount to an exclusionary abuse merely because the price is lower than ATC but higher than AIC. However, PD had offered prices which were above its own ATC to two customers. The CJ said in respect of this:

In those circumstances, it cannot be considered that such prices have anti-competitive effects.[301]

This is a highly significant statement. In the judgment the CJ mentioned *Compagnie Maritime Belge* only in support of the principle of the special responsibility of dominant undertakings, and did not mention *Irish Sugar* at all. However, Advocate General Mengozzi discussed both cases, and concluded that they were only 'marginally relevant' to *Post Danmark* for three reasons: first, in those cases there was documentary evidence of intention to exclude; secondly, they concerned undertakings in near monopoly positions; and, thirdly, the pricing was one of a series of other practices which constituted abuses.[302] Given the words '[i]n those circumstances' it cannot be concluded, therefore, that above-ATC pricing could *never* be an abuse, although normally it will not be so as it will not exclude equally efficient competitors.

The Guidance Paper does not rule out intervention in cases of above-cost selective pricing.[303] It does not specifically deal with the issue, although it says in paragraph 72 that it is easier to engage in predatory conduct if the dominant undertaking selectively targets specific customers. However, paragraph 63 defines 'sacrifice' to include '*foregoing profits*' as well as incurring losses and in paragraph 24 the Commission contemplates intervening to protect less efficient competitors in some situations. Article 102 might therefore still be enforced against such pricing in exceptional circumstances.

9. MARGIN SQUEEZE

A. GENERAL

Margin squeeze occurs where a vertically integrated undertaking which is dominant on the upstream market for an input sets its prices at such a level that its competitors on the downstream

---

[300] Case C-209/10, *Post Danmark I* EU:C:2012:172, see Section 8.D, p. 391.

[301] Case C-209/10, *Post Danmark I* EU:C:2012:172, para. 37.

[302] Ibid., Mengozzi AG, paras. 91–94.

[303] The Discussion Paper, DG Comp Staff Discussion Paper on the application of Article 82 of the Treaty to exclusionary abuses, Brussels, December 2005, see Chap. 5, Section 6.B, treated the idea of above-ATC selective pricing as an abuse with circumspection (para. 127). It would be an abuse only in exceptional situations. An example was where 'companies in a collective dominant situation apply a clear strategy to collectively exclude or discipline a competitor by selectively undercutting the competitor and thereby putting pressure on its margins, while collectively sharing the loss of revenues' (para. 128), i.e. the situation in *Compagnie Maritime Belge* itself.

market cannot compete with it for the supply of products or services to customers.[304] The dominant undertaking can apply a margin squeeze by setting a high price for the input, charging low prices on the downstream market, or by a combination of the two. Margin squeeze can occur in both regulated and non-regulated sectors but it has proved a particular issue in the EU following the liberalisation of the telecommunications sector which is intended to bring about competition in retail services. Despite liberalisation the previous State-owned monopoly often retains control of the network infrastructure whilst also being in competition on the downstream retail market.

The first Commission decision on margin squeeze was an interim measure under the ECSC Treaty. In *National Carbonizing* the Commission stated that an 'enterprise in a dominant position may have an obligation to arrange its prices so as to allow a *reasonably efficient* manufacturer of the derivatives a margin sufficient to enable it to survive in the long term' (emphasis added).[305] The second decision was *Napier Brown/British Sugar*[306] where the Commission found that British Sugar (BS) had abused its dominant position in the industrial sugar market by maintaining a price for its own retail sugar which did not reflect its repackaging and selling costs. Napier Brown (NB), which was dependent on BS for supplies of industrial sugar, could not therefore viably compete on the retail market. The Commission said that if BS maintained its reduced margin NB, or any company *equally efficient* in repackaging as BS but without a self-produced source of industrial sugar, would have to leave the market.[307] The GC recognised the concept of price or margin squeezing in *Industrie des poudres sphériques*:

178. . . . Price squeezing may be said to take place when an undertaking which is in a dominant position on the market for an unprocessed product and itself uses part of its production for the manufacture of a more processed product, while at the same time selling off surplus unprocessed product on the market, sets the price at which it sells the unprocessed product at such a level that those who purchase it do not have a sufficient profit margin on the processing to remain competitive on the market for the processed product.[308]

The Commission referred to margin squeeze in its 1998 Telecommunications Notice.[309]

The current EU law on margin squeeze is set out in a series of cases in the telecommunications sector, *Deutsche Telekom*,[310] *TeliaSonera*,[311] and *Telefónica*.[312]

---

[304] See, e.g., R. Downing and A. Jones, 'Margin Squeezes in Telecommunications Markets' in S. Anderman and A. Ezrachi (eds.), *Intellectual Property and Competition Law: New Frontiers* (Oxford University Press, 2011); N. Dunne, 'Margin Squeeze: From Broken Regulation to Legal Uncertainty' (2011) 70 *CLJ* 34; N. Dunne, 'Margin Squeeze: Theory, Practice, Policy', Parts I and II [2012] *ECLR* 29 and 61; D. W. Carlton, 'Should "Price Squeeze" be a Recognized Form of Anti-competitive Conduct?' (2008) 4 *J of Competition Law and Economics* 271; J. G. Sidak, 'Abolishing the Price Squeeze as a Theory of Antitrust Liability' (2008) 4 *J of Competition Law and Economics* 279; A. M. Panner, 'Are Price Squeezes Anti-competitive?' (2009) 1 *Global Competition Policy*; H. Hovenkamp and E. Hovenkamp, 'The Viability of Antitrust Price Squeeze Claims', available at <http://ssrn.com/abstract=1156974>; O'Donoghue and Padilla, n. 1, Chap. 7; Bishop and Walker, n. 198, 6.119–6.139; G. Faella and R. Pardolesi, 'Squeezing Price Squeeze under EC Antitrust Law' (2010) 6 *European Competition Journal* 255; Geradin, Layne-Farrar, and Petit, n. 170, 4.340–4.370; Faull and Nikpay, n. 1, 4.638–4.693.

[305] *National Coal Board, National Smokeless Fuels Ltd and the National Carbonizing Company Ltd*, 79/185/ECSC [1976] OJ L35/6 at 7.

[306] [1988] OJ L284/41.

[307] *Napier Brown* [1988] OJ L284/41, para. 66.

[308] Case T-5/97, *Industrie des poudres sphériques SA v Commission* [2000] ECR II-3755; the GC upheld the Commission's rejection of the downstream competitor's complaint about the dominant undertaking's pricing.

[309] Notice on the Application of the Competition Rules to Access Agreements in the Telecommunications Sector [1998] OJ C265/12, paras. 117–119.

[310] Case C-280/08 P, *Deutsche Telekom* [2010] ECR I-955.

[311] Case C-52/09, *TeliaSonera* [2011] ECR I-527; Case note, W. Wurmnest (2012) 49 *CMLRev* 721.

[312] Case C-295/12 P, *Telefónica SA v Commission* EU:C:2014:2062.

B. THE CASE LAW

(i) *Deutsche Telekom*

In *Deutsche Telekom*[313] the Commission found that Deutsche Telekom (DT) had effected a margin squeeze by charging its competitors on the retail market in Germany a higher price for access to the 'local loop',[314] to which it was obliged to offer access under German law pursuant to the EU telecommunications regime,[315] than it was charging its own retail end-user customers. Therefore the competitors could not offer retail prices which were competitive with DT's unless they could find additional efficiency gains elsewhere. The Commission found that even when DT raised its own retail prices (from 2002) the margin between the wholesale access price and its retail prices was insufficient to cover its own downstream costs. DT's prices had been approved by the German telecommunications regulator (RegTP) and the Commission refused to take into account the fact that losses on the access charges were still subsidised by higher telephone charges as Germany had not yet implemented the relevant directive.[316]

The Commission held that there was a margin squeeze where:[317]

. . . the difference between the retail prices charged by a dominant undertaking and the wholesale prices it charges its competitors for comparable services is negative, or insufficient to cover the product-specific costs to the dominant operator of providing its own retail services on the downstream market.

Although the Commission did in fact proceed to analyse the likely exclusionary effects of DT's prices, it stated that once a margin squeeze was shown it was not necessary to assess the effects on competition, as by proving the existence of a margin squeeze the Commission had done enough to establish the existence of an abuse.[318]

The GC dismissed DT's arguments that it could not have infringed Article 102 as its prices had been approved by RegTP[319] and that DT had been left insufficient scope by the regulator to adjust its retail prices to avoid the margin squeeze (the GC proceeded on the basis that the wholesale access price was fixed and that DT did not have scope to adjust it).[320] The GC said the Commission was correct in identifying the abuse as consisting of the unfair 'spread' between the wholesale and resale prices[321] and that the wholesale and retail prices did not have to be abusive taken individually in themselves. The GC thus considered a margin squeeze as a separate abuse, independent from predatory pricing. The GC also upheld the Commission's finding that the AEC test was the correct one in that the relevant costs benchmark for calculating the spread was DT's own costs and not those of the competing undertakings.[322] This was required on grounds of legal certainty as a dominant undertaking cannot

---

[313] COMP/37.451, 37.578, and 37.579, *Deutsche Telekom AG* [2003] OJ L263/9. The decision was adopted before the inauguration of the review of Art. 102.

[314] The local loop is the physical circuit connecting the network termination point at a subscriber's premises to the main distribution frame or equivalent facility in the fixed public telephone network: Case T-271/03, *Deutsche Telekom* [2008] ECR II-477, para. 3.

[315] Decision No. 223a of the Federal Ministry of Post and Telecommunications of 28 May 1997, pursuant to the EU legislative regime for the telecommunications sector (since amended).

[316] Dir. 90/388/EEC [1990] OJ L192/10, which required Member States to rebalance historic charging structures. In *Deutsche Telekom* the Commission used what was in effect AAC as the cost measure. The GC accepted that the calculation was a matter of complex economic assessment (Case T-271/03, *Deutsche Telekom* [2008] ECR II-477, para. 185) and that the Commission had not made a manifest error.

[317] [2003] OJ L263/9, para. 107.

[318] Ibid., paras. 179–180.

[319] Case T-271/03, *Deutsche Telekom* [2008] ECR II-477, paras. 106–120. For the distinction between regulation and competition law see further Chap. 1, Section 13, p. 51.

[320] Ibid., paras. 121–151.

[321] Ibid., para. 167. The GC dismissed the plea that the Commission had wrongly calculated DT's prices, paras. 195–212.

[322] Ibid., paras. 194 and 237.

be expected to make commercial decisions on the basis of the costs of a competitor about which it cannot have proper information, and also on the basis of the principle of 'equality of opportunity'. The GC did not, however, agree with the Commission that proof of a margin squeeze was alone sufficient to establish an abuse. Rather, the Commission had to demonstrate anti-competitive effects related to the barriers to entry that the pricing practices *could have created* for the growth of competition.[323] The small market shares gained by the competitors could be evidence of the anti-competitive effects of DT's pricing despite the worse development of competition in the telecommunications markets in other Member States.[324] The CJ upheld the GC's judgment.

Case C-280/08 P, *Deutsche Telekom v Commission* [2010] ECR I-955

Court of Justice

80. According to the case-law of the Court of Justice, it is only if anti-competitive conduct is required of undertakings by national legislation, or if the latter creates a legal framework which itself eliminates any possibility of competitive activity on their part, that Articles [101] and [102] [do] not apply. In such a situation, the restriction of competition is not attributable, as those provisions implicitly require, to the autonomous conduct of the undertakings. Articles [101] and [102] may apply, however, if it is found that the national legislation leaves open the possibility of competition which may be prevented, restricted or distorted by the autonomous conduct of undertakings (Joined Cases C-359/95 P and C-379/95 P *Commission and France* v *Ladbroke Racing* . . . paragraphs 33 and 34 and the case-law cited).

81. The possibility of excluding anti-competitive conduct from the scope of Articles [101] and [102] on the ground that it has been required of the undertakings in question by existing national legislation or that the legislation has precluded all scope for any competitive conduct on their part has thus been accepted only to a limited extent by the Court of Justice (see Case 41/83 *Italy* v *Commission* . . . paragraph 19; Joined Cases 240/82 to 242/82, 261/82, 262/82, 268/82 and 269/82 *Stichting Sigarettenindustrie and Others* v *Commission* . . . paragraphs 27 to 29; and Case C-198/01 *CIF* . . . paragraph 67).

82. Thus, the Court has held that if a national law merely encourages or makes it easier for undertakings to engage in autonomous anti-competitive conduct, those undertakings remain subject to Articles [101] and [102] (Joined Cases 40/73 to 48/73, 50/73, 54/73 to 56/73, 111/73, 113/73 and 114/73 *Suiker Unie and Others* v *Commission* . . . paragraphs 36 to 73, and *CIF*, paragraph 56).

83. According to the case-law of the Court, dominant undertakings have a special responsibility not to allow their conduct to impair genuine undistorted competition on the common market (Case 322/81 *Nederlandsche Banden-Industrie-Michelin* v *Commission* . . . paragraph 57).

84. It follows from this that the mere fact that the appellant was encouraged by the intervention of a national regulatory authority such as RegTP to maintain the pricing practices which led to the margin squeeze of competitors who are at least as efficient as the appellant cannot, as such, in any way absolve the appellant from responsibility under Article [102] (see, to that effect, Case 123/83 *Clair* . . . paragraphs 21 to 23).

85. Since, notwithstanding such interventions, the appellant had scope to adjust its retail prices for end-user access services, the General Court was entitled to find, on that ground alone, that the margin squeeze at issue was attributable to the appellant.

86. In the present case, it must be noted that the appellant does not deny the existence of such scope in the arguments put forward in the first part of the first ground of appeal. In particular, the appellant does not challenge the General Court's findings in paragraphs 97 to 105 and 121 to 151 of the judgment under

---

[323] Ibid., para. 235.
[324] Ibid., paras. 242–243.

appeal that, in essence, the appellant was able to make applications to RegTP for authorisation to adjust its retail prices for end-user access services, specifically retail prices for narrowband access services for the period between 1 January 1998 and 31 December 2001, and retail prices for broadband access services for the period from 1 January 2002.

87. Instead, in its various complaints and arguments the appellant merely underlines the encouragement provided by RegTP's intervention, and states, in particular, that RegTP itself considered and approved the margin squeeze at issue in the light both of national and European Union telecommunications law and of Article [102] and, moreover, that the Bundesgerichtshof held in a judgment of 10 February 2004 that the appellant cannot take the place of RegTP in assessing whether a pricing practice is contrary to Article [102].

88. For the reasons set out in paragraphs 80 to 85 of the present judgment, such arguments cannot, however, in any way alter the fact that that pricing practice is attributable to the appellant, since it is common ground that the appellant had scope to adjust its retail prices for end-user access services, and, therefore, such arguments are ineffective as a means of challenging the General Court's findings on that point.

89. In particular, the appellant cannot complain that the General Court did not consider whether there was 'fault' on its part by failing to use the scope which it had to apply to RegTP for authorisation to adjust its retail prices for end-user access services. The existence or otherwise of any 'fault' in such conduct cannot alter the finding that the appellant had scope to adopt that conduct, and can be taken into account only in determining whether that conduct was an infringement and at the stage of setting the level of the fines.

90. Moreover, as the General Court held in paragraph 120 of the judgment under appeal, the Commission cannot, in any event, be bound by a decision taken by a national body pursuant to Article [102] EC (see, to that effect, Case C-344/98 *Masterfoods and HB* . . . paragraph 48). In the present case, the appellant does not, indeed, deny that RegTP's decisions are not binding on the Commission.

. . .

124. As regards, in the first place, the complaints as to whether the General Court's findings are well founded, it must be borne in mind, in relation to the question whether the infringements were committed intentionally or negligently and are, therefore, liable to be punished by a fine in accordance with the first subparagraph of Article 15(2) of Regulation No 17, that it follows from the case-law of the Court that that condition is satisfied where the undertaking concerned cannot be unaware of the anti-competitive nature of its conduct, whether or not it is aware that it is infringing the competition rules of the Treaty (see Joined Cases 96/82 to 102/82, 104/82, 105/82, 108/82 and 110/82 *IAZ International Belgium and Others* v *Commission* . . . paragraph 45, and *Nederlandsche Banden-Industrie-Michelin* v *Commission*, paragraph 107).

125. In the present case, the General Court took the view in paragraphs 296 and 297 of the judgment under appeal that that condition was satisfied, since the appellant could not have been unaware that, notwithstanding the authorisation decisions of RegTP, it had genuine scope to set its retail prices for end-user access services and, moreover, the margin squeeze entailed serious restrictions on competition, particularly in view of its monopoly on the wholesale market in local loop access services and its virtual monopoly on the retail market in end-user access services.

126. It must be held that such reasoning, which is based on findings of fact which, in the absence of any allegation of distortion, are for the General Court alone to assess, is not vitiated by any error of law.

127. In so far as the appellant complains that the General Court did not take RegTP's decisions or the lack of any precedent in the European Union into account, it is sufficient to note that such arguments are merely intended to show that the appellant was unaware that the conduct complained of in the decision at issue was unlawful in the light of Article [102]. Such arguments must, therefore, in accordance with the case-law cited in paragraph 124 of the present judgment, be rejected as unfounded.

. . .

169. . . . [I]n order to consider whether the present complaint is well founded, the Court must consider whether the General Court was right, in particular in paragraphs 166 and 168 of the judgment under

appeal, to find that, even if the appellant does not have scope to adjust its wholesale prices for local loop access services, its pricing practices can nevertheless be categorised as an abuse within the meaning of Article [102] where, irrespective of whether those wholesale prices and the retail prices for end-user access services are, in themselves, abusive, the spread between them is unfair, namely, according to that judgment, where that spread is either negative or insufficient to cover the appellant's product-specific costs of providing its own services, so that a competitor who is as efficient as the appellant is prevented from entering into competition with the appellant for the provision of end-user access services.

170. In that regard, it has consistently been held that Article [102] is an application of the general objective of European Community action, namely the institution of a system ensuring that competition in the common market is not distorted. Thus, the dominant position referred to in Article [102] relates to a position of economic strength enjoyed by an undertaking which enables it to prevent effective competition being maintained on the relevant market by affording it the power to behave to an appreciable extent independently of its competitors, its customers and ultimately of consumers (see Case 85/76 *Hoffmann-La Roche* v *Commission* . . . paragraph 38, and Case C-202/07 P *France Télécom* v *Commission* . . . paragraph 103).

171. In the present case, it must be borne in mind that, as is apparent from paragraphs 50 to 52 of the present judgment, the appellant does not deny that it enjoys a dominant position on all the relevant service markets, namely both on the wholesale market in local loop access services and on the retail market in end-user access services.

172. As regards the abusive nature of the appellant's pricing practices, it must be noted that subparagraph (a) of the second paragraph of Article [102] expressly prohibits a dominant undertaking from directly or indirectly imposing unfair prices.

173. Furthermore, the list of abusive practices contained in Article [102] is not exhaustive, so that the practices there mentioned are merely examples of abuses of a dominant position. The list of abusive practices contained in that provision does not exhaust the methods of abusing a dominant position prohibited by the Treaty (see *British Airways* v *Commission*, paragraph 57 and the case-law cited).

174. In that regard, it must be borne in mind that, in prohibiting the abuse of a dominant position in so far as trade between Member States is capable of being affected, Article [102] refers to the conduct of a dominant undertaking which, on a market where the degree of competition is already weakened precisely because of the presence of the undertaking concerned, through recourse to methods different from those governing normal competition in products or services on the basis of the transactions of commercial operators, has the effect of hindering the maintenance of the degree of competition still existing in the market or the growth of that competition (see, to that effect, *Hoffman[n]-La Roche* v *Commission*, paragraph 91; *Nederlandsche Banden-Industrie-Michelin* v *Commission*, paragraph 70; Case C-62/86 *AKZO* v *Commission* . . . paragraph 69; *British Airways* v *Commission*, paragraph 66; and *France Télécom* v *Commission*, paragraph 104).

175. It is apparent from the case-law of the Court that, in order to determine whether the undertaking in a dominant position has abused such a position by its pricing practices, it is necessary to consider all the circumstances and to investigate whether the practice tends to remove or restrict the buyer's freedom to choose his sources of supply, to bar competitors from access to the market, to apply dissimilar conditions to equivalent transactions with other trading parties, thereby placing them at a competitive disadvantage, or to strengthen the dominant position by distorting competition (see, to that effect, *Nederlandsche Banden-Industrie-Michelin* v *Commission*, paragraph 73, and *British Airways* v *Commission*, paragraph 67).

176. Since Article [102] thus refers not only to practices which may cause damage to consumers directly, but also to those which are detrimental to them through their impact on competition, a dominant undertaking, as has already been observed in paragraph 83 of the present judgment, has a special responsibility not to allow its conduct to impair genuine undistorted competition on the common market (see, to that effect, *France Télécom* v *Commission*, paragraph 105 and the case-law cited).

177. It follows from this that Article [102] prohibits a dominant undertaking from, inter alia, adopting pricing practices which have an exclusionary effect on its equally efficient actual or potential competitors,

that is to say practices which are capable of making market entry very difficult or impossible for such competitors, and of making it more difficult or impossible for its co-contractors to choose between various sources of supply or commercial partners, thereby strengthening its dominant position by using methods other than those which come within the scope of competition on the merits. From that point of view, therefore, not all competition by means of price can be regarded as legitimate (see, to that effect, *Nederlandsche Banden-Industrie-Michelin* v *Commission*, paragraph 73; *AKZO* v *Commission*, paragraph 70; and *British Airways* v *Commission*, paragraph 68).

178. In the present case, it must be noted that the appellant does not deny that, even on the assumption that it does not have the scope to adjust its wholesale prices for local loop access services, the spread between those prices and its retail prices for end-user access services is capable of having an exclusionary effect on its equally efficient actual or potential competitors, since their access to the relevant service markets is, at the very least, made more difficult as a result of the margin squeeze which such a spread can entail for them.

179. At the hearing the appellant submitted, however, that the test applied in the judgment under appeal for the purpose of establishing an abuse within the meaning of Article [102] required it, in the circumstances of the case, to increase its retail prices for end-user access services to the detriment of its own end-users, given the national regulatory authorities' regulation of its wholesale prices for local loop access services.

180. It is true, as paragraphs 175 to 177 of the present judgment have already shown, that Article [102] aims, in particular, to protect consumers by means of undistorted competition (see Joined Cases C-468/06 to C-478/06 *Sot. Lélos kai Sia and Others* . . . paragraph 68).

181. However, the mere fact that the appellant would have to increase its retail prices for end-user access services in order to avoid the margin squeeze of its competitors who are as efficient as the appellant cannot in any way, in itself, render irrelevant the test which the General Court applied in the present case for the purpose of establishing an abuse under Article [102].

182. By further reducing the degree of competition existing on a market—the end-user access services market—already weakened precisely because of the presence of the appellant, thereby strengthening its dominant position on that market, the margin squeeze also has the effect that consumers suffer detriment as a result of the limitation of the choices available to them and, therefore, of the prospect of a longer-term reduction of retail prices as a result of competition exerted by competitors who are at least as efficient in that market (see, to that effect, *France Télécom* v *Commission*, paragraph 112).

183. In those circumstances, in so far as the appellant has scope to reduce or end such a margin squeeze, as observed in paragraphs 77 to 86 of the present judgment, by increasing its retail prices for end-user access services, the General Court correctly held in paragraphs 166 to 168 of the judgment under appeal that that margin squeeze is capable, in itself, of constituting an abuse within the meaning of Article [102] in view of the exclusionary effect that it can create for competitors who are at least as efficient as the appellant. The General Court was not, therefore, obliged to establish, additionally, that the wholesale prices for local loop access services or retail prices for end-user access services were in themselves abusive on account of their excessive or predatory nature, as the case may be.

. . .

195. As a preliminary point, it must be noted that, contrary to Vodafone's contention, the present complaint is admissible even though it partly reiterates the arguments put forward at first instance, since, in accordance with the case-law cited in paragraph 25 of the present judgment, the complaint is that, by resorting to the as-efficient-competitor test notwithstanding the fact that the appellant is not subject to the same legal and material conditions as its competitors, the General Court applied an incorrect legal test to the application of Article [102] to the pricing practices at issue and, therefore, committed an error of law on that point.

196. As to whether that complaint is well founded, as is apparent from paragraph 186 of the judgment under appeal and from paragraphs 4 and 12 of the present judgment, the as-efficient-competitor test used

by the General Court in the judgment under appeal consists in considering whether the pricing practices of a dominant undertaking could drive an equally efficient economic operator from the market, relying solely on the dominant undertaking's charges and costs, instead of on the particular situation of its actual or potential competitors.

197. In the present case, as is apparent from paragraph 169 of the present judgment, the appellant's costs were taken into account by the General Court in order to establish the abusive nature of the appellant's pricing practices where the spread between its wholesale prices for local loop access services and its retail prices for end-user access services was positive. In such circumstances, the General Court considered that the Commission was entitled to regard those pricing practices as unfair within the meaning of Article [102], where that spread was insufficient to cover the appellant's product-specific costs of providing its own services.

198. In that regard, it must be borne in mind that the Court has already held that, in order to assess whether the pricing practices of a dominant undertaking are likely to eliminate a competitor contrary to Article [102], it is necessary to adopt a test based on the costs and the strategy of the dominant undertaking itself (see *AKZO* v *Commission*, paragraph 74, and *France Télécom* v *Commission*, paragraph 108).

199. The Court pointed out, inter alia, in that regard that a dominant undertaking cannot drive from the market undertakings which are perhaps as efficient as the dominant undertaking but which, because of their smaller financial resources, are incapable of withstanding the competition waged against them (see *AKZO* v *Commission*, paragraph 72).

200. In the present case, since, as is apparent from paragraphs 178 and 183 of the present judgment, the abusive nature of the pricing practices at issue in the judgment under appeal stems in the same way from their exclusionary effect on the appellant's competitors, the General Court did not err in law when it held, in paragraph 193 of the judgment under appeal, that the Commission had been correct to analyse the abusive nature of the appellant's pricing practices solely on the basis of the appellant's charges and costs.

201. As the General Court found, in essence, in paragraphs 187 and 194 of the judgment under appeal, since such a test can establish whether the appellant would itself have been able to offer its retail services to end-users otherwise than at a loss if it had first been obliged to pay its own wholesale prices for local loop access services, it was suitable for determining whether the appellant's pricing practices had an exclusionary effect on competitors by squeezing their margins.

202. Such an approach is particularly justified because, as the General Court indicated, in essence, in paragraph 192 of the judgment under appeal, it is also consistent with the general principle of legal certainty in so far as the account taken of the costs of the dominant undertaking allows that undertaking, in the light of its special responsibility under Article [102], to assess the lawfulness of its own conduct. While a dominant undertaking knows what its own costs and charges are, it does not, as a general rule, know what its competitors' costs and charges are.

203. Those findings are not affected by what the appellant claims are the less onerous legal and material conditions to which its competitors are subject in the provision of their telecommunications services to end-users. Even if that assertion were proved, it would not alter either the fact that a dominant undertaking, such as the appellant, cannot adopt pricing practices which are capable of driving equally efficient competitors from the relevant market, or the fact that such an undertaking must, in view of its special responsibility under Article [102], be in a position itself to determine whether its pricing practices are compatible with that provision.

204. The appellant's complaint concerning the misapplication of the as-efficient-competitor test must, therefore, be rejected.

. . .

251. It should be borne in mind that, in accordance with the case-law cited in paragraph 174 of the present judgment, by prohibiting the abuse of a dominant position in so far as trade between Member States is capable of being affected, Article [102] refers to the conduct of a dominant undertaking which,

through recourse to methods different from those governing normal competition in products or services on the basis of the transactions of commercial operators, has the effect of hindering the maintenance of the degree of competition still existing in the market or the growth of that competition.

252. The General Court therefore held in paragraph 235 of the judgment under appeal, without any error of law, that the anti-competitive effect which the Commission is required to demonstrate, as regards pricing practices of a dominant undertaking resulting in a margin squeeze of its equally efficient competitors, relates to the possible barriers which the appellant's pricing practices could have created for the growth of products on the retail market in end-user access services and, therefore, on the degree of competition in that market.

253. As is already apparent from paragraphs 177 and 178 of the present judgment, a pricing practice such as that at issue in the judgment under appeal that is adopted by a dominant undertaking such as the appellant constitutes an abuse within the meaning of Article [102] if it has an exclusionary effect on competitors who are at least as efficient as the dominant undertaking itself by squeezing their margins and is capable of making market entry more difficult or impossible for those competitors, and thus of strengthening its dominant position on that market to the detriment of consumers' interests.

254. Admittedly, where a dominant undertaking actually implements a pricing practice resulting in a margin squeeze of its equally efficient competitors, with the purpose of driving them from the relevant market, the fact that the desired result is not ultimately achieved does not alter its categorisation as abuse within the meaning of Article [102]. However, in the absence of any effect on the competitive situation of competitors, a pricing practice such as that at issue cannot be classified as exclusionary if it does not make their market penetration any more difficult.

255. In the present case, since, as has already been noted in paragraph 231 of the present judgment, the wholesale local loop access services provided by the appellant are indispensable to its competitors' effective penetration of the retail markets for the provision of services to end-users, the General Court was entitled to hold in paragraph 237 of the judgment under appeal, as paragraphs 233 to 236 of the present judgment have already shown, that a margin squeeze resulting from the spread between wholesale prices for local loop access services and retail prices for end-user access services, in principle, hinders the growth of competition in the retail markets in services to end-users, since a competitor who is as efficient as the appellant cannot carry on his business in the retail market for end-user access services without incurring losses.

256. The appellant has not challenged that finding. For the reasons already set out in paragraphs 233 to 236 of the present judgment, the complaint concerning the failure to take into account revenues from any provision of other telecommunications services to end-users must be rejected as unfounded. The argument relating to paragraph 238 of the judgment under appeal concerning the possibility of cross-subsidisation must be rejected as ineffective for the reasons stated in paragraphs 238 to 241 of the present judgment.

257. In addition, in paragraph 239 of the judgment under appeal, the General Court found—as, in the absence of an allegation of distortion, it is for the General Court alone to do—that 'the small market shares acquired by . . . competitors in the retail . . . market [in end-user access services] since the market was liberalised by the entry into force of the TKG on 1 August 1996 are evidence of the restrictions which the applicant's pricing practices have imposed on the growth of competition in those markets'. In that regard, contrary to what is claimed by the appellant, it is clear from the expression 'have imposed' that the General Court did find a causal connection between the appellant's pricing practices and the small market shares acquired by competitors. The appellant's complaint on that point is, therefore, unfounded.

258. Furthermore, the General Court concluded in paragraph 244 of its judgment, which also remained unchallenged in the present appeal, that the appellant had not produced any evidence to rebut the findings in the decision at issue that its pricing practices actually restricted competition in the retail market in end-user access services.

259. In those circumstances, it must be concluded that the General Court was correct to hold that the Commission had established that the particular pricing practices of the appellant gave rise to actual exclusionary effects on competitors who were at least as efficient as the appellant itself.

The Court of Justice in *Deutsche Telekom* thus established the following main points:

- the approval by a national sector regulator of a dominant undertaking's prices does not mean that those prices cannot constitute an abuse under Article 102 as it is not possible for the actions of a national sector regulator to immunise a dominant undertaking's conduct from the application of the EU competition rules; a dominant undertaking escapes liability for infringement of the competition rules only if the anti-competitive conduct is required of it by national legislation or if the national framework eliminates any possibility of competitive activity—mere encouragement is not enough;[325]

- margin squeeze is a stand-alone abuse, independent of excessive pricing of the input or predatory pricing downstream; the essence of a margin squeeze is the unfairness of the spread between the wholesale and retail prices;[326]

- the test for identifying a margin squeeze abuse is the AEC test, i.e. whether the dominant undertaking's downstream operation could trade profitably if it was subject to the same pricing regime as the downstream competitors;[327]

- in order for a margin squeeze to constitute an abuse there must be anti-competitive effects in the form of exclusionary effects on as efficient competitors; it is a question of whether the pricing is *capable* of making market entry more difficult or impossible, and thus of strengthening the dominant position to the detriment of consumers' interests;[328]

- DT should have avoided the margin squeeze even if it meant raising its prices to consumers on the downstream market.[329]

(ii) *TeliaSonera*

In *TeliaSonera*, an Article 267 reference, the CJ clarified and elaborated upon the principles it set out in *Deutsche Telekom*. TeliaSonera was in an analogous position to Deutsche Telekom—a vertically integrated former State monopolist which retained ownership, inter alia, of the local loop. TeliaSonera offered access to the local loop to operators supplying broadband to end-users. It also offered broadband connection services via the local loop directly to end-users. It had no statutory obligation to grant access on the wholesale market to the downstream competitors in the retail market,[330] which distinguished the case from the situation in *Deutsche Telekom*. Moreover, it appears that there were a number of alternative technologies available to provide users with broadband services.[331] Nevertheless, the Konkurrensverket (the Swedish competition authority) alleged that TeliaSonera had abused its dominant position by applying a margin squeeze in that the spread between its wholesale and retail prices was not sufficient to cover the costs which TeliaSonera itself had to incur in order to supply its services to end-users.

---

[325] Case C-280/08 *Deutsche Telekom* [2010] ECR I-9555, paras. 80–90.

[326] Ibid., paras. 157, 159, and 183.

[327] Ibid., paras. 198–203.

[328] Ibid., paras. 252–255.

[329] Ibid., para. 181.

[330] The access subject to the dispute was not covered by the obligations laid down in Reg. 2887/2000 [2000] OJ L336/4 on unbundled access to the local loop.

[331] Case C-52/09, *TeliaSonera* [2011] ECR I-527, Mazák AG, para. 20; this was why the referring court specifically asked the CJ (Question 7 of the reference) whether the input had to be indispensable for there to be an abuse.

Case C-52/09, *Konkurrensverket v TeliaSonera Sverige AB* [2011] ECR I-527

Court of Justice

25. As regards the abusive nature of pricing practices such as those in the main proceedings, it must be noted that subparagraph (a) of the second paragraph of Article 102 TFEU expressly prohibits a dominant undertaking from directly or indirectly imposing unfair prices.

26. Furthermore, the list of abusive practices contained in Article 102 TFEU is not exhaustive, so that the list of abusive practices contained in that provision does not exhaust the methods of abusing a dominant position prohibited by EU law (*Deutsche Telekom* v *Commission*, paragraph 173 and case-law cited).

. . .

28. In order to determine whether the dominant undertaking has abused its position by the pricing practices it applies, it is necessary to consider all the circumstances and to investigate whether the practice tends to remove or restrict the buyer's freedom to choose his sources of supply, to bar competitors from access to the market, to apply dissimilar conditions to equivalent transactions with other trading parties, or to strengthen the dominant position by distorting competition (*Deutsche Telekom* v *Commission*, paragraph 175 and case-law cited).

29. Those are the principles in the light of which the referring court must examine the pricing practice at issue in the main proceedings in order to establish whether it constitutes an abuse of any dominant position that may be held by TeliaSonera.

30. In particular, after ascertaining whether the other conditions for the applicability of Article 102 TFEU are satisfied in the present case—including whether TeliaSonera holds a dominant position and whether trade between Member States was affected by its conduct—it is for the referring court to examine, in essence, whether the pricing practice introduced by TeliaSonera is unfair in so far as it squeezes the margins of its competitors on the retail market for broadband connection services to end users.

31. A margin squeeze, in view of the exclusionary effect which it may create for competitors who are at least as efficient as the dominant undertaking, in the absence of any objective justification, is in itself capable of constituting an abuse within the meaning of Article 102 TFEU (see, to that effect, *Deutsche Telekom* v *Commission*, paragraph 183).

32. In the present case, there would be such a margin squeeze if, inter alia, the spread between the wholesale prices for ADSL input services and the retail prices for broadband connection services to end users were either negative or insufficient to cover the specific costs of the ADSL input services which TeliaSonera has to incur in order to supply its own retail services to end users, so that that spread does not allow a competitor which is as efficient as that undertaking to compete for the supply of those services to end users.

33. In such circumstances, although the competitors may be as efficient as the dominant undertaking, they may be able to operate on the retail market only at a loss or at artificially reduced levels of profitability.

34. It must moreover be made clear that since the unfairness, within the meaning of Article 102 TFEU, of such a pricing practice is linked to the very existence of the margin squeeze and not to its precise spread, it is in no way necessary to establish that the wholesale prices for ADSL input services to operators or the retail prices for broadband connection services to end users are in themselves abusive on account of their excessive or predatory nature, as the case may be (*Deutsche Telekom* v *Commission*, paragraphs 167 and 183).

35. In addition, as maintained by TeliaSonera, before the spread between the prices of those services can be regarded as squeezing the margins of competitors of the dominant undertaking, account must be taken not only of the prices of services supplied to competitors which are comparable to the services

which TeliaSonera itself must obtain to have entry to the retail market, but also of the prices of comparable services supplied to end users on the retail market by TeliaSonera and its competitors. Similarly, a comparison must be made between the prices actually applied by TeliaSonera and its competitors over the same period of time.

. . .

The prices to be taken into account

38. The Stockholms tingsrätt seeks to ascertain, first, whether, for that purpose, account should be taken not only of the retail prices applied by the dominant undertaking for services to end users, but also those applied by competitors for those services.

39. It must be recalled, in that regard, that the Court has already made clear that Article 102 TFEU prohibits a dominant undertaking from, inter alia, adopting pricing practices which have an exclusionary effect on its equally efficient actual or potential competitors (see, to that effect, *Deutsche Telekom* v *Commission*, paragraph 177 and case-law cited).

40. Where an undertaking introduces a pricing policy intended to drive from the market competitors who are perhaps as efficient as that dominant undertaking but who, because of their smaller financial resources, are incapable of withstanding the competition waged against them, that undertaking is, accordingly, abusing its dominant position (see, to that effect, *Deutsche Telekom* v *Commission*, paragraph 199).

41. In order to assess the lawfulness of the pricing policy applied by a dominant undertaking, reference should be made, as a general rule, to pricing criteria based on the costs incurred by the dominant undertaking itself and on its strategy (see, to that effect, Case C-62/86 *AKZO* v *Commission* . . . paragraph 74, and *France Télécom* v *Commission*, paragraph 108).

42. In particular, as regards a pricing practice which causes margin squeeze, the use of such analytical criteria can establish whether that undertaking would have been sufficiently efficient to offer its retail services to end users otherwise than at a loss if it had first been obliged to pay its own wholesale prices for the intermediary services (see, to that effect, *Deutsche Telekom* v *Commission*, paragraph 201).

43. If that undertaking would have been unable to offer its retail services otherwise than at a loss, that would mean that competitors who might be excluded by the application of the pricing practice in question could not be considered to be less efficient than the dominant undertaking and, consequently, that the risk of their exclusion was due to distorted competition. Such competition would not be based solely on the respective merits of the undertakings concerned.

44. Furthermore, the validity of such an approach is reinforced by the fact that it conforms to the general principle of legal certainty, since taking into account the costs and prices of the dominant undertaking enables that undertaking to assess the lawfulness of its own conduct, which is consistent with its special responsibility under Article 102 TFEU, as stated in paragraph 24 of this judgment. While a dominant undertaking knows its own costs and prices, it does not as a general rule know those of its competitors (*Deutsche Telekom* v *Commission*, paragraph 202).

45. That said, it cannot be ruled out that the costs and prices of competitors may be relevant to the examination of the pricing practice at issue in the main proceedings. That might in particular be the case where the cost structure of the dominant undertaking is not precisely identifiable for objective reasons, or where the service supplied to competitors consists in the mere use of an infrastructure the production cost of which has already been written off, so that access to such an infrastructure no longer represents a cost for the dominant undertaking which is economically comparable to the cost which its competitors have to incur to have access to it, or again where the particular market conditions of competition dictate it, by reason, for example, of the fact that the level of the dominant undertaking's costs is specifically attributable to the competitively advantageous situation in which its dominant position places it.

46. It must therefore be concluded that, when assessing whether a pricing practice which causes a margin squeeze is abusive, account should as a general rule be taken primarily of the prices and costs of the undertaking concerned on the retail services market. Only where it is not possible, in particular

circumstances, to refer to those prices and costs should those of its competitors on the same market be examined.

The absence of any regulatory obligation to supply

47. It is apparent from the order for reference that, contrary to the case which gave rise to *Deutsche Telekom* v *Commission*, TeliaSonera, as stated in paragraph 6 of this judgment, was not under any regulatory obligation to supply ADSL input services to operators.

. . .

53. The special responsibility which a dominant undertaking has not to allow its conduct to impair genuine undistorted competition in the internal market concerns specifically the conduct, by commission or omission, which that undertaking decides on its own initiative to adopt (see, to that effect, the order in Case C-552/03 P *Unilever Bestfoods* v *Commission* . . . paragraph 137).

54. TeliaSonera maintains, in that regard, that, in order specifically to protect the economic initiative of dominant undertakings, they should remain free to fix their terms of trade, unless those terms are so disadvantageous for those entering into contracts with them that those terms may be regarded, in the light of the relevant criteria set out in Case C-7/97 *Bronner* . . . as entailing a refusal to supply.

55. Such an interpretation is based on a misunderstanding of that judgment. In particular, it cannot be inferred from paragraphs 48 and 49 of that judgment that the conditions to be met in order to establish that a refusal to supply is abusive must necessarily also apply when assessing the abusive nature of conduct which consists in supplying services or selling goods on conditions which are disadvantageous or on which there might be no purchaser.

56. Such conduct may, in itself, constitute an independent form of abuse distinct from that of refusal to supply.

57. Moreover, it must be observed that since the Court was, in the said paragraphs of *Bronner*, called upon, in essence, only to interpret Article [102] with regard to the conditions under which a refusal to supply may be abusive, the Court did not make any ruling on whether the fact that an undertaking refuses access to its home-delivery scheme to the publisher of a rival newspaper where the latter does not at the same time entrust to it the carrying out of other services, such as sales in kiosks or printing, constitutes some other form of abuse of a dominant position, such as tied sales.

58. Moreover, if *Bronner* were to be interpreted otherwise, in the way advocated by TeliaSonera, that would, as submitted by the European Commission, amount to a requirement that before any conduct of a dominant undertaking in relation to its terms of trade could be regarded as abusive the conditions to be met to establish that there was a refusal to supply would in every case have to be satisfied, and that would unduly reduce the effectiveness of Article 102 TFEU.

59. It follows that the absence of any regulatory obligation to supply the ADSL input services on the wholesale market has no effect on the question of whether the pricing practice at issue in the main proceedings is abusive.

Whether an anti-competitive effect is required and whether the product offered by the undertaking must be indispensable

60. The referring court seeks to ascertain, thirdly, whether the abusive nature of the pricing practice in question depends on whether there actually is an anti-competitive effect and, if so, how that effect can be determined. Moreover, it seeks to ascertain whether the product offered by TeliaSonera on the wholesale market must be indispensable for entry onto the retail market.

61. It must be observed in that regard that, bearing in mind the concept of abuse of a dominant position explained in paragraph 27 of this judgment, the Court has ruled out the possibility that the very existence of a pricing practice of a dominant undertaking which leads to the margin squeeze of its equally efficient competitors can constitute an abuse within the meaning of Article 102 TFEU without it being

necessary to demonstrate an anti-competitive effect (see, to that effect, *Deutsche Telekom* v *Commission*, paragraphs 250 and 251).

62. The case-law has furthermore made clear that the anti-competitive effect must relate to the possible barriers which such a pricing practice may create to the growth on the retail market of the services offered to end users and, therefore, on the degree of competition in that market (*Deutsche Telekom* v *Commission*, paragraph 252).

63. Accordingly, the practice in question, adopted by a dominant undertaking, constitutes an abuse within the meaning of Article 102 TFEU, where, given its effect of excluding competitors who are at least as efficient as itself by squeezing their margins, it is capable of making more difficult, or impossible, the entry of those competitors onto the market concerned (see, to that effect, *Deutsche Telekom* v *Commission*, paragraph 253).

64. It follows that, in order to establish whether such a practice is abusive, that practice must have an anti-competitive effect on the market, but the effect does not necessarily have to be concrete, and it is sufficient to demonstrate that there is an anti-competitive effect which may potentially exclude competitors who are at least as efficient as the dominant undertaking.

65. Where a dominant undertaking actually implements a pricing practice resulting in a margin squeeze on its equally efficient competitors, with the purpose of driving them from the relevant market, the fact that the desired result, namely the exclusion of those competitors, is not ultimately achieved does not alter its categorisation as abuse within the meaning of Article 102 TFEU.

66. However, in the absence of any effect on the competitive situation of competitors, a pricing practice such as that at issue in the main proceedings cannot be classified as an exclusionary practice where the penetration of those competitors in the market concerned is not made any more difficult by that practice (see, to that effect, *Deutsche Telekom* v *Commission*, paragraph 254).

67. In the present case, it is for the referring court to examine whether the effect of TeliaSonera's pricing practice was likely to hinder the ability of competitors at least as efficient as itself to trade on the retail market for broadband connection services to end users.

68. In that examination that court must take into consideration all the specific circumstances of the case.

69. In particular, the first matter to be analysed must be the functional relationship of the wholesale products to the retail products. Accordingly, when assessing the effects of the margin squeeze, the question whether the wholesale product is indispensable may be relevant.

70. Where access to the supply of the wholesale product is indispensable for the sale of the retail product, competitors who are at least as efficient as the undertaking which dominates the wholesale market and who are unable to operate on the retail market other than at a loss or, in any event, with reduced profitability suffer a competitive disadvantage on that market which is such as to prevent or restrict their access to it or the growth of their activities on it (see, to that effect, *Deutsche Telekom* v *Commission*, paragraph 234).

71. In such circumstances, the at least potentially anti-competitive effect of a margin squeeze is probable.

72. However, taking into account the dominant position of the undertaking concerned in the wholesale market, the possibility cannot be ruled out that, by reason simply of the fact that the wholesale product is not indispensable for the supply of the retail product, a pricing practice which causes margin squeeze may not be able to produce any anti-competitive effect, even potentially. Accordingly, it is again for the referring court to satisfy itself that, even where the wholesale product is not indispensable, the practice may be capable of having anti-competitive effects on the markets concerned.

73. Secondly, it is necessary to determine the level of margin squeeze of competitors at least as efficient as the dominant undertaking. If the margin is negative, in other words if, in the present case, the wholesale price for the ADSL input services is higher than the retail price for services to end users, an effect which is at least potentially exclusionary is probable, taking into account the fact that, in such a

situation, the competitors of the dominant undertaking, even if they are as efficient, or even more efficient, compared with it, would be compelled to sell at a loss.

74. If, on the other hand, such a margin remains positive, it must then be demonstrated that the application of that pricing practice was, by reason, for example, of reduced profitability, likely to have the consequence that it would be at least more difficult for the operators concerned to trade on the market concerned.

75. That said, it must be borne in mind that an undertaking remains at liberty to demonstrate that its pricing practice, albeit producing an exclusionary effect, is economically justified (see, to that effect, Case C-95/04 P *British Airways* v *Commission* . . . paragraph 69, and *France Télécom* v *Commission*, paragraph 111).

76. The assessment of the economic justification for a pricing practice established by an undertaking in a dominant position which is capable of producing an exclusionary effect is to be made on the basis of all the circumstances of the case (see, to that effect, *Nederlandsche Banden-Industrie-Michelin* v *Commission*, paragraph 73). In that regard, it has to be determined whether the exclusionary effect arising from such a practice, which is disadvantageous for competition, may be counterbalanced, or outweighed, by advantages in terms of efficiency which also benefit the consumer. If the exclusionary effect of that practice bears no relation to advantages for the market and consumers, or if it goes beyond what is necessary in order to attain those advantages, that practice must be regarded as an abuse (*British Airways* v *Commission*, paragraph 86).

77. It must then be concluded that, in order to establish that a pricing practice resulting in margin squeeze is abusive, it is necessary to demonstrate that, taking into account, in particular, the fact that the wholesale product is indispensable, that practice produces, at least potentially, an anti-competitive effect on the retail market which is not in any way economically justified.

. . .

The relevance of the fact that the supply concerned is to a new customer

94. The point must be made that the abusiveness of a pricing practice such as that at issue in the main proceedings must be assessed not only with regard to the possibility that the effect of that practice may be that equally efficient operators who are already active in the relevant market may be driven from it, but also by taking into account any barriers which the practice is capable of creating in the way of operators who are potentially equally efficient and who are not yet present on the market (see, to that effect, *Deutsche Telekom* v *Commission*, paragraph 178).

95. Consequently, whether the pricing practice at issue is liable to drive out from the market concerned existing clients of the dominant undertaking or rather new clients of that undertaking is not, as a general rule, relevant to the assessment of whether the practice is abusive.

The opportunity to recoup losses

. . .

98. However, a margin squeeze is the result of the spread between the prices for wholesale services and those for retail services and not of the level of those prices as such. In particular, that squeeze may be the result not only of an abnormally low price in the retail market, but also of an abnormally high price in the wholesale market.

99. Consequently, an undertaking which engages in a pricing practice which results in a margin squeeze on its competitors does not necessarily suffer losses.

100. In any event, even if the dominant undertaking suffers losses in order to squeeze the margins of its competitors, there can be no requirement that, in order to establish the existence of an abuse, evidence must be produced of the capacity to recoup any such losses.

101. The possibility that competitors may be driven from the market does not depend on either the fact that the dominant undertaking suffers losses or the fact that that undertaking may be capable of recouping

its losses, but depends solely on the spread between the prices applied by the dominant undertaking on the markets concerned, the result of which may be that it is not the dominant undertaking itself which suffer losses but its competitors.

102. Lastly, in the event that the dominant undertaking were nonetheless to apply a price on the retail market which was so low that sales would engender losses, beyond the fact that such conduct is likely to constitute an autonomous form of abuse, namely the application of predatory prices, the Court has in any event already rejected the argument that, even in such a case, proof of the possibility of recoupment of losses suffered by the application, by an undertaking in a dominant position, of prices lower than a certain level of costs constitutes a necessary precondition to establishing that such a pricing policy is abusive (see, to that effect, *France Télécom* v *Commission*, paragraph 110).

103. It follows that whether the dominant undertaking is able to recoup any losses suffered as a result of applying the pricing practice at issue has no relevance to the matter of establishing whether that pricing practice is abusive.

In *TeliaSonera* the CJ therefore confirmed and developed its judgment in *Deutsche Telekom* to establish:

- a margin squeeze may constitute an abuse if the spread between the wholesale and retail prices is either negative or insufficient to cover the costs which the dominant undertaking has to incur to supply its own retail services to end-users;[332]

- the unfairness of the pricing practice relates to the very existence of the margin squeeze and not to the excessive or predatory nature of the wholesale or retail prices (following *Deutsche Telekom*, paragraphs 167 and 183);[333]

- the question is whether there are exclusionary effects on as efficient competitors; in ascertaining this the relevant costs and prices are normally those of the undertaking itself (following *Deutsche Telekom*, paragraph 202).[334] *TeliaSonera* added the proviso that in some circumstances the prices and costs of the competitors on the retail market should be used instead;[335]

- margin squeeze is an independent form of abuse distinct from that of refusal to supply. In the absence of any regulatory duty to supply there may be a margin squeeze abuse even if there is no duty to supply according to the *Bronner* criteria.[336] There may be a margin squeeze even if the wholesale product is not indispensable to the supply of the retail product (indispensability is one of the criteria for a duty to supply according to *Bronner*);[337]

- although it is necessary to demonstrate anti-competitive effects, as the CJ held in *Deutsche Telekom* (paragraphs 250 and 251), those effects need not be concrete but need only potentially exclude competitors;[338] where the input is indispensable at least potentially anti-competitive effects are probable;[339] where it is not indispensable, pricing which causes a margin squeeze may still be capable of having anti-competitive effects;[340]

[332] Case C-52/09, *TeliaSonera* [2011] ECR I-527, paras. 32–33.

[333] Ibid., para. 34.

[334] Ibid., para. 44.

[335] Ibid., paras. 45–46.

[336] Ibid., paras. 54–59. For the criteria in Case C-7/97, *Oscar Bronner GmbH & Co KG v Mediaprint* [1998] ECR I-7791 see the discussion of refusal to supply as an abuse, in Section 13.B, p. 497 ff.

[337] Case C-52/09, *TeliaSonera* [2011] ECR I-527, para. 72.

[338] Ibid., para. 65.

[339] Ibid., para. 71.

[340] Ibid., para. 72.

- an effect which is at least potentially exclusive is probable where the pricing is negative, i.e. the input price is higher than the dominant undertaking's retail price to end-users but there may be anti-competitive effects even where it remains positive;[341]
- it is normally irrelevant whether the affected competitors on the downstream market are existing or new customers of the dominant undertaking;[342]
- as in the case of predatory pricing, the ability to recoup is irrelevant;[343]
- a margin squeeze can be objectively justified on the basis of efficiencies.[344]

Furthermore, the CJ also held that the degree of dominance held by TeliaSonera on the upstream wholesale market was irrelevant;[345] the finding of a margin squeeze abuse does not depend on the undertaking dominant on the upstream market also being dominant on the downstream retail market;[346] and 'the fact that the markets concerned are growing rapidly and involve new technology, requiring high levels of investment, is not, as a general rule, relevant to establishing whether the pricing practice at issue constitutes an abuse'.[347]

(iii) *Telefónica*

The Commission adopted a decision in 2007 imposing a fine of nearly €152 million on Telefónica for abusing a dominant positions for wholesale ADSL broadband in Spain at both national and regional level between 2001 and 2006.[348] Before the liberalisation of the telecommunications markets in Spain in 1998 Telefónica had a statutory monopoly over the retail provision of landline telecommunications services and it continued to be the only Spanish telecommunications operator with a nationwide fixed telephone network. It used that network both to provide wholesale broadband services to other telecommunications operators to enable them to supply retail broadband services to end-users and to provide its own retail broadband services directly to end-users. The decision is notable for the Commission's careful analysis of Telefónica's costs and of the possible prejudicial effects on consumers, including the finding that retail broadband prices were too high.[349] The Commission found that Telefónica had imposed unfair prices in the form of a margin squeeze between its wholesale and retail prices in that the margin between its wholesale and retail prices was insufficient to cover the costs that an operator equally as efficient as Telefónica would have to incur. It assessed this on the basis of Telefónica's downstream costs, using LRAIC as the appropriate standard.

Under Spanish law Telefónica was under a regulatory duty to supply the wholesale product to the downstream competitors. There were price controls at the wholesale level but the Commission found that these were maximum prices and that Telefónica had scope to reduce them itself or to apply to the regulator to reduce them. The retail prices were not controlled during the relevant period and Telefónica was free to increase them.[350] Telefónica claimed that margin squeeze was a type of constructive refusal to supply and that the Commission could not deduce from the *regulatory* duty to supply that there was a duty to supply under Article 102, as that would depend on the

---

[341] Ibid., paras. 73–74.

[342] Ibid., paras. 92–95.

[343] Ibid., paras. 96–103.

[344] Ibid., paras. 31 and 75–76.

[345] Ibid., paras. 78–82; see the discussion of 'super-dominance', see Section 3.D.iv, p. 358.

[346] Ibid., paras. 83–89.

[347] Ibid., para. 104.

[348] COMP/38.784, *Wanadoo España v Telefónica* 4 July 2007.

[349] Ibid., in particular Section E and paras. 543–544.

[350] Ibid., paras. 665–675.

fulfilment of the *Bronner* criteria,[351] which it submitted were not satisfied here.[352] The Commission, without stating that it agreed that margin squeeze was a type of refusal to supply,[353] did say that this case was fundamentally different from the situation in *Bronner* in two particular ways which meant that the legal test laid down by the CJ in *Bronner* was not applicable. First, the dominant undertaking had a regulatory duty to supply which resulted from the balancing by the public authorities of the incentives of Telefónica and its competitors to invest and innovate. Secondly, Telefónica's *ex ante* incentives to invest were not at stake because the infrastructure had been built up before the advent of broadband and at a time when Telefónica benefited from special or exclusive rights.[354] These two circumstances, which have been called the 'Telefónica exceptions',[355] were later repeated in the section on refusal to supply in the Guidance Paper.[356]

Before the GC delivered judgment in the appeal[357] the CJ had pronounced on margin squeeze in *Deutsche Telekom* and *TeliaSonera*. The GC followed those judgments. It therefore held that in order to establish that a margin squeeze constituted an abuse there was no need to show excessive or predatory prices as the abuse lay in the spread; that the applicable test is AEC, normally based on the dominant undertaking's own costs but in exceptional circumstances using those of the competitors;[358] and that the applicability of the competition provisions was not excluded by *ex ante* regulatory approval. On the refusal to supply issue the GC did not consider the 'Telefónica exceptions' as, following *TeliaSonera*, it held that margin squeeze is a distinct type of abuse from refusal to supply and that the indispensability criterion in *Bronner* is relevant only to an assessment of the *effects* of the margin squeeze.

The CJ dismissed large parts of the appeal on the grounds that they were inadmissible as being challenges to findings of fact.[359] However, in upholding the GC the CJ did make a number of important points, confirming its stance in *Deutsche Telekom* and *TeliaSonera*.

Case C-295/12 P, *Telefónica and Telefónica de España v Commission* EU:C:2014:2062

Court of Justice

117. The appellants maintain, in their first complaint, that the General Court erred in its failure to take account of the non-essential nature of inputs in its examination of the effect of their conduct on the retail market, thus failing to have due regard for the principles established by the Court in *TeliaSonera Sverige*....

---

[351] Case C-7/97, [1998] ECR I-7791, see Section 13.B.vi, p. 504.

[352] COMP/38.784, *Wanadoo España v Telefónica* 4 July 2007, paras. 299–301.

[353] A view which it did, nevertheless, set out 18 months later in the Guidance Paper, para. 80.

[354] COMP/38.784, *Wanadoo España v Telefónica* 4 July 2007, paras. 303–304.

[355] D. Geradin, 'Refusal to Supply and Margin Squeeze: A Discussion of Why the *"Telefonica* Exceptions" are Wrong', TILEC Discussion Paper No. 2011-009, available at <http://papers.ssrn.com/sol3/papers.cfm?abstract_id=1762687>.

[356] Guidance Paper, para. 82, see Section 13.F, p. 534.

[357] Case T-336/07, *Telefónica and Telefónica de España v Commission* EU:T:2012:172; Spain brought a parallel appeal against the decision, Case T-398/07, *Spain v Commission* EU:T:2012:173.

[358] The GC held that the Commission had not manifestly erred in its calculation of Telefónica's costs. The Commission examined whether the dominant undertaking's downstream arm could operate profitably on the basis of the charges applied by its upstream arm using LRAIC as the cost measure (COMP/38.784, *Wanadoo España v Telefónica* 4 July 2007, paras. 310 and 397) and by two methods of analysing profitability, the period-by-period method and the discounted cash flow method (paras. 310–542). The former measured Telefónica's profitability year by year and the latter allowed for below-cost pricing in the initial period. Both led to the conclusion that the downstream arm could not cover its costs. The GC subjected the Commission decision to detailed scrutiny but concluded that there was no manifest error of assessment with the choice of methodology or the details of the calculations (paras. 198–265). See also Nazzini, n. 116, 230–232.

[359] Or were pleas not raised before the GC.

118. That complaint must be rejected as unfounded as it is based on a misinterpretation of paragraph 69 of the judgment in *TeliaSonera Sverige* ..., in which the Court simply stated that, when assessing the effects of the margin squeeze, the question whether the wholesale product is indispensable may be relevant, with the result that the General Court was not obliged to take account of it.

...

124. ...[I]n order to establish that a practice such as margin squeeze is abusive, that practice must have an anti-competitive effect on the market, although the effect does not necessarily have to be concrete, it being sufficient to demonstrate that there is a potential anti-competitive effect which may exclude competitors who are at least as efficient as the dominant undertaking (see *TeliaSonera Sverige* ..., paragraph 64)...

...

128. In the first place, the appellants maintain that the General Court endorsed a misinterpretation of the case-law established in *Bronner* ...by taking the view that the Commission had the power to regulate ex post the price conditions to which the use of non-essential infrastructure is subject. That argument is unfounded, since it amounts to a claim that Article 102 TFEU is applicable in the present context only if the requirements established in *Bronner* ...are satisfied. It should be recalled in that regard that Article 102 TFEU is of general application and cannot be restricted, inter alia, as the General Court was correct to point out at paragraph 293 of the judgment under appeal, by the existence of a regulatory framework adopted by the EU legislature for ex ante regulation of the telecommunications markets.

...

133. ...[T]he fact that an undertaking's conduct complies with a regulatory framework does not mean that such conduct complies with Article 102 TFEU.

...

135. ...[T]he Commission's implementation of Article 102 TFEU is not subject to any prior consideration of action taken by national authorities.

C. CASES AND DECISIONS OUTSIDE THE TELECOMMUNICATIONS SECTOR

The earlier cases and decisions of *National Carbonising*, *Napier Brown*, and *Industrie des poudres sphériques* have been noted.[360] In 2007 the Commission initiated proceedings against the German energy undertaking, RWE, in respect of the gas transmission market.[361] The Commission came to the preliminary view that RWE, which controlled the gas transmission network in North Rhine-Westphalia, had intentionally set its transmission tariffs at an artificially high level in order to squeeze the margins of its competitors on the downstream gas supply markets.[362] It had done this by maintaining elevated network tariffs and an asymmetric cost structure. The Commission also considered that other conduct of RWE amounted to a refusal to supply. RWE offered commitments to divest itself of its transmission network which the Commission accepted and made binding by a commitments decision under Article 9 of Regulation 1/2003.[363]

---

[360] See Section 9.A, p. 408.

[361] MEMO/07/186.

[362] COMP/39.402, RWE—*Gas Foreclosure* Commitments Decision 18 March 2009, [2009] OJ C133/10, IP/09/410.

[363] For the conclusion of Art. 102 proceedings by adopting commitments decisions, see Chap. 13, Section 7.E.iii, p. 945.

D. MARGIN SQUEEZE IN THE GUIDANCE PAPER

In the Guidance Paper on Article 102, the Commission considers margin squeezes as a type of constructive refusal to supply (paragraphs 75–90). It explains why:

80. Finally, instead of refusing to supply, a dominant undertaking may charge a price for the product on the upstream market which, compared to the price it charges on the downstream market . . . does not allow even an equally efficient competitor to trade profitably in the downstream market on a lasting basis (a so-called 'margin squeeze'). In margin squeeze cases the benchmark which the Commission will generally rely on to determine the costs of an equally efficient competitor are the LRAIC of the downstream division of the integrated dominant undertaking . . .[364]

Although a margin squeeze could amount to a constructive refusal to supply where the *Bronner* criteria are met, *TeliaSonera* and *Telefónica* have now established that margin squeeze is not dependent on the indispensability of the input or the other *Bronner* criteria. The Guidance Paper sets out some special circumstances where the Commission considers the normal criteria on refusal to supply do not apply.[365] These correspond to the 'Telefónica exceptions' already mentioned,[366] and are dealt with in Section 13 on refusal to supply.

E. US LAW ON MARGIN SQUEEZE

The law stated by the EU Courts in *Deutsche Telekom*, *TeliaSonera*, and *Telefónica* differs significantly from US law. The Supreme Court held in *linkLine*[367] that prices which 'squeeze' the margin for as efficient competitors downstream are not an antitrust offence contrary to s. 2 of the Sherman Act unless there is an antitrust duty to deal on the upstream wholesale market[368] or the downstream retail price is predatory according to the normal principles on predatory pricing (as laid down in *Brooke Group*).[369] The Supreme Court rejected the idea later accepted by the CJ that the 'spread' itself can be illegal. It can only be a matter of refusal to supply or predatory pricing ('excessive' pricing is not in practice an issue for s. 2[370] and the US test concentrates solely on the downstream price). Moreover, in *Verizon v Trinko* the Supreme Court had already declined to apply s. 2 to a refusal to supply in the telecommunications sector where the regulatory authority had jurisdiction over questions of access.[371]

F. COMMENT

The conclusion on refusal to supply, which was contrary to the Opinion of the Advocate General in *TeliaSonera*,[372] is difficult to rationalise. Logic suggests that if one has no duty to supply one can have

---

[364] The Guidance Paper states, in nn. 8 and 9 to para. 80, that it includes in this situation a scenario where an integrated supplier of a system of complementary products refuses to sell one of the products on an unbundled basis to a competitor that produces the other complementary product. It also states that it might in some cases use the LRAIC of the downstream competitor as the benchmark when the dominant undertaking's costs cannot be allocated clearly between up- and downstream operations.

[365] Guidance Paper, para. 82.

[366] In Section 9.B.iii, p. 424.

[367] *Pacific Bell Telephone Co v linkLine Communications Inc*, 129 S.Ct. 1109 (2009); see F. Enrique González Díaz and J. Padilla, 'The *linkLine* Judgment—A European Perspective' (2009) 1 *Global Competition Policy*.

[368] Which, following *Verizon Communications Inc v Trinko LLP*, 540 US 398, 124 S.Ct 872 (2004) is highly unlikely; see Section 13.G, p. 537.

[369] *Brooke Group Ltd v Brown & Williamson Tobacco Corp*, 509 US 209 (1993).

[370] The Sherman Act s. 2 is not applied to situations of excessive pricing.

[371] *Verizon Communications Inc v Trinko*, 540 US 398, 124 S.Ct 872 (2004).

[372] Case C-52/09, *TeliaSonera* [2011] ECR I-527, Mazák AG, paras. 21–23.

no duty to supply at a particular price. However, EU law has reached the position that an undertaking which does not infringe Article 102 by refusing to supply (because the conditions laid down in the case law for a duty to supply are not fulfilled)[373] can nevertheless infringe if it *does* supply at a price deemed to give rise to an abusive margin squeeze. A vertically integrated dominant undertaking which has no regulatory duty to supply may therefore decide not to supply at all, which may be more anti-competitive and have detrimental welfare implications. The CJ's rationale for this seemingly bizarre state of affairs is that were the established refusal to supply conditions required to be fulfilled before a dominant undertaking's terms of trade could be abusive, it 'would unduly reduce the effectiveness of Article 102'.[374] The CJ does not clearly explain why this is so. However, although the divorce of margin squeeze from refusal to supply means that the indispensability of the input to the downstream competitor is not a necessary condition for the pricing to constitute an abuse, it may be relevant to the issue of whether there are anti-competitive effects as indispensability renders at least potential anti-competitive effects 'probable'.[375] In other words the CJ's concern is with anti-competitive effects, not the indispensability of the input. The judgments in *TeliaSonera* and *Telefónica* in respect of the independence of margin squeeze from refusal to supply differ both from US law and from the position of the Commission in the Guidance Paper.[376] It has been suggested that the CJ's stance stems from a failure to distinguish between horizontal and vertical foreclosure.

R. Nazzini, *The Foundations of European Union Competition Law: The Objectives and Principles of Article 102* (Oxford University Press, 2011), 274–275

The Court might have been induced in error because margin squeeze consists in the modulation of upstream and downstream prices. The refusal to supply test must, therefore, necessarily be complemented by the as efficient competitor test. This does not mean, however, that margin squeeze is a form of customer foreclosure analogous to predation, rebates, or exclusivity. But, regrettably, an analogy with non-vertical foreclosure is what the Court probably had in mind when it said that it would be absurd to hold that all abuses relating to the dominant undertaking's prices or trading terms presuppose a duty to deal. Thus the Court failed to distinguish horizontal foreclosure practices in which the dominant undertaking only deals with customers and vertical foreclosure practices in which the issue is whether and, if so, on what terms, the dominant undertaking must deal with its competitors so as to allow them to compete effectively. It is only in relation to vertical foreclosure that Article 102 requires the conditions for a duty to deal to be established as a safeguard against over-deterrence of market-wide investments.

The fact that in EU law it is the unfair 'spread' which identifies a margin squeeze abuse means that both upstream and downstream prices are taken into account, whereas if the issue is whether prices downstream are predatory only the one market is relevant. Although the dismissal of the predatory pricing standard can be criticised as protecting competitors and risking consumer welfare[377] the conceptualisation of a margin squeeze as a stand-alone abuse independent of predatory (and excessive) pricing has the advantage of being better able to reflect the realities of the situation

---

[373] See Case C-7/97, *Bronner* [1998] ECR I-7791.

[374] Case C-52/09, *TeliaSonera* [2011] ECR I-527, para. 58, followed by the GC in T-336/07, *Telefónica* EU:T:2012:172, para. 181.

[375] Case C-52/09, *TeliaSonera* [2011] ECR I-527, paras. 69–72.

[376] As already noted, the Commission in the *Deutsche Telekom* decision took the view that the *Bronner* refusal to supply conditions did not apply because the situation fell within what it considers exceptions to those conditions, not because it expressly rejected the classification of a margin squeeze as a refusal to supply.

[377] See J. G. Sidak, 'Abolishing the Price Squeeze as a Theory of Antitrust Liability' (2008) 4 J of Competition Law and Economics 279.

and behaviour of a vertically integrated undertaking, in particular internal transfer pricing, cross-subsidies, and the leveraging of market power.[378]

In *Deutsche Telekom*, *TeliaSonera*, and *Telefónica* the CJ endorsed the AEC test as applicable to margin squeeze cases. This aligns margin squeeze with predatory pricing. The AEC test, by using the dominant undertaking's own costs as the benchmark, should ensure that the competition rules are applied only to prevent the anti-competitive foreclosure of those whose exclusion from the market would be detrimental to welfare. The test also has the advantage spelt out in the cases of complying with the principle of legal certainty and enabling the dominant undertaking to assess the lawfulness or otherwise of its own conduct. Moreover, in *Deutsche Telekom* the CJ (followed by the GC in *Telefónica*) approved the GC's finding that the AEC test chimed with principle of 'equality of opportunity' between economic operators, referring to the CJ having consistently held that this was necessary to guarantee a system of undistorted competition.[379] This is an interesting importation from the case law on Article 106, which the CJ has since confirmed.[380] However, the CJ left the door open to the use of the downstream competitors' own costs (the 'reasonably efficient competitor' test) in *TeliaSonera* (paragraph 45) holding that the costs and prices of competitors could be relevant in certain circumstances. The CJ summed these up as situations where 'it not possible' to use those of the dominant undertaking.[381] This reasonably efficient competitor test deprives dominant undertakings of the legal certainty the CJ thinks important and makes life more difficult for dominant undertakings. The application of the AEC test can be extremely problematic as is seen in the arguments about the methodology used to calculate the margin squeeze in *Deutsche Telekom* and *Telefónica*: in particular the very fact of the vertical integration and the complications of regulated prices make carrying out the test difficult. It is important that opportunity costs are taken into account.[382]

The EU Courts have made it clear that it cannot be assumed that a margin squeeze will always cause harm to consumers. Rather, it is necessary to consider the likely anti-competitive effects of the pricing in either the upstream or downstream markets, and the impact of any ruling on innovation upstream. However, it is not necessary to show concrete effects as it is sufficient to demonstrate an anti-competitive effect which may potentially exclude competitors.[383] There is therefore a need to demonstrate a coherent theory of harm relating to entry barriers to the retail market and thus to the degree of competition on that market.[384] It is notable, however, that in *Telefónica* the GC upheld the Commission's reliance on 'probable' anti-competitive effects despite the fact that the decision was taken six years after the start of the abuse. The Commission was not required to show that the effects had materialised.[385] The CJ accepted in *Deutsche Telekom* (where the upstream prices were regulated) that it may be that the only way a dominant undertaking can avoid the margin squeeze

---

[378] See further Faella and Pardolesi, n. 304, 256–259; J. Meisel, 'The Law and Economics of Margin Squeezes in the US versus the EU' (2012) 8 *European Competition Journal* 383, 397–398.

[379] Case C-280/08 P, *Deutsche Telekom* [2010] ECR I-9555, para. 230, followed by the GC in T-336/07, *Telefónica* EU:T:2012:172, para. 204.

[380] Case C-553/12 P, *Commission v Dimosia Epicheirisi Ilektrismou AE (DEI) (Greek Lignite)* EU:C:2014:2083, see Chap. 8, Section 5.B.xiii, p. 617.

[381] Only the first example in para. 45, the non-identification of the dominant undertaking's own costs, can strictly be described as 'not possible'. The other examples are situations where the CJ does not consider it *acceptable* to use those costs and presumably it is in this sense that 'possible' must be construed.

[382] See further S. C. Salop, 'Refusals to Deal and Price Squeezes by an Unregulated Vertically Integrated Monopolist' (2010) 76 *Antitrust LJ* 709; Meisel, n. 378, 396–397; L. Colley and S. Burnside, 'Margin Squeeze Abuse' (2006) 2 *European Competition Journal*, Special Issue, 185, 193–195.

[383] Case C-52/09, *TeliaSonera* [2011] ECR I-527, para. 64.

[384] W. Wurmnest, Case note on *TeliaSonera* (2012) 49 *CMLRev* 721.

[385] The GC expressly rejected the argument that the higher degree of probability of 'in all likelihood' required under the EUMR in Case T-5/02, *Tetra Laval BV v Commission* [2002] ECR II-4381, para. 153, *aff'd* on appeal Case C-12/03 P, *Commission v Tetra Laval* [2005] ECR I-987, concerning assessment of a conglomerate merger, should apply here.

is to increase its retail prices to consumers. This seems a regrettable outcome to the application of the competition rules, and can only be justified by the longer-term benefits to consumers in the future which can be expected to arise through the maintenance of competition. Today's consumers have to make sacrifices for tomorrow's. However, it should be recalled that at the beginning of the *TeliaSonera* judgment the CJ stated the function of the competition rules as being 'to prevent competition from being distorted to the detriment of the public interest, individual undertakings and consumers, thereby ensuring the well-being of the European Union'[386] and this denotes a longer-term view than the immediate short-term interests of consumers.[387]

The margin squeeze cases provide the fullest treatment yet of the relationship between regulation and Article 102 and the resulting situation for dominant undertakings is not a happy one.[388] The main reasons for finding that *ex ante* sector regulation does not preclude the application of the competition rules to the same conduct—that EU competition law cannot be prevented from applying by decisions of national regulators and that regulation and competition law may pursue different objectives[389]—are perfectly understandable, but the result leaves dominant undertakings in a difficult position and produces unsatisfactory outcomes. The undertakings are subject to two separate sets of rules and can infringe Article 102 even though they have done everything required of them by the sector regulator.[390] Moreover, the situation in which a vertically integrated dominant undertaking finds itself may have been largely created by the regulator. In *Deutsche Telekom* the wholesale price was taken as having been fixed by the regulator and so in respect of an abuse which was founded on the spread between two prices, the dominant undertaking had no power over one of them. DT was held to have 'scope' for remedying the margin squeeze because the 'State compulsion' defence was attenuated to the narrowest of circumstances and it therefore infringed Article 102 by failing to take the initiative and request an alteration to the second (retail) price. In *TeliaSonera* the CJ said that a dominant undertaking may infringe by omission as well as commission,[391] and DT was liable for having failed to apply to the regulator to change the retail price in favour of its competitors. In effect the dominant undertaking in this situation is put under a duty to help its competitor by taking positive action in a situation in which regulation has failed to achieve the best competitive outcome. There has been not just a market failure but a regulatory failure. It is doubtful, however, whether competition authorities should attempt to remedy defects in regulation by application of the competition rules or use competition law to achieve what are regulatory rather than competition objectives.[392] In both *Deutsche Telekom* and *Telefónica* the argument that the Commission should have brought proceedings against the Member State under Article 258 for failure to properly implement the telecommunications Directives, instead of against the undertakings under Article 102, was dismissed.[393]

---

[386] Case C-52/09, *TeliaSonera* [2011] ECR I-527, para. 22.

[387] See the discussion in Chap. 1, Section 8.B.

[388] See in particular D. Geradin and R. O'Donoghue, 'The Concurrent Application of Competition Law and Regulation: The Case of Margin Squeeze Abuses in the Telecommunications Sector' (2005) *J of Competition Law and Economics* 355, GCLC Working Paper 04/05; N. Dunne, 'Margin Squeeze: Theory, Practice, Policy', Part II [2012] *ECLR* 61.

[389] See Chap. 1, Section 13.

[390] The GC dismissed claims that the principle of legitimate expectation had been breached, Case T-271/03, *Deutsche Telekom* [2008] ECR II-477, paras. 267–269; the CJ held the appeal against this was inadmissible, Case C-280/08, [2010] ECR I-9555, paras. 105–110.

[391] Case C-52/09, *TeliaSonera* [2011] ECR I-527, para. 53.

[392] Geradin and O'Donoghue, n. 388, sections IV and V; Dunne, 'Margin Squeeze: Theory, Practice, Policy', n. 304, 63–66.

[393] Case T-271/03, *Deutsche Telekom* [2008] ECR II-477, paras. 46–47; T-336/07, *Telefónica* EU:T:2012:172, para. 307; and see Dunne, 'Margin Squeeze: Theory, Practice, Policy', n. 304, 66.

G. SUMMARY

The EU Courts have established that margin squeeze is a stand-alone abuse, independent from predatory and excessive pricing, and based on the unfair spread between the vertically integrated dominant undertaking's wholesale and retail prices. The test is normally the AEC, i.e. whether the undertaking could survive on the downstream market if it were subject to the pricing policy it imposed on its downstream competitors. However, in some situations the competitors' own costs will be used as the benchmark instead. A number of factors are normally irrelevant to the existence of an abuse: the degree of dominance of the vertically integrated undertaking on the upstream market; whether it is dominant on the downstream market; whether the market involves new technology; whether the vertically integrated undertaking can recoup losses; and whether the downstream competitors are new or existing customers. Margin squeeze is a separate form of abuse from refusal to supply and it is not necessary that the input is indispensable. A margin squeeze will infringe Article 102 only if it has anti-competitive effects, but the effect need not be concrete and it is enough that competitors are potentially excluded. Anti-competitive effects are considered 'probable' if the input is indispensable or the margin is negative. A dominant undertaking's prices may infringe Article 102 even if they have been approved by a sector regulator and the undertaking will escape liability only if it had no room for manoeuvre whatsoever. A margin squeeze that produces exclusionary effects may nevertheless be objectively justified.

The conceptualisation of margin squeeze as a separate abuse from excessive and predatory pricing more readily captures the anti-competitive effects of vertical integration. However, the application of Article 102 to situations approved by regulators raises many difficulties and the separation of margin squeeze from refusal to supply, freeing it from the requirement of indispensability of the input (contrary to the view of the Commission in the Guidance Paper) is problematic. Dominant undertakings in the EU are left widely exposed to margin squeeze claims and this may impact prejudicially on their incentives to invest and innovate.

10. EXCLUSIVITY OBLIGATIONS AND EXCLUSIVE DEALING

A. GENERAL

The main issue in respect of the application of Article 102 to exclusivity obligations concerns exclusive purchasing agreements (also called requirements contracts and single branding). These are arrangements by which a customer is obliged to obtain all or most of its requirements for the relevant product from one supplier.[394] The term 'exclusive dealing' is often used interchangeably with 'exclusive purchasing' but in the Guidance Paper[395] the Commission employs 'exclusive dealing' to encompass both exclusive purchasing and conditional rebates (discussed in Section 11) because they may have similar same effects.[396] For the sake of clarity, therefore, this chapter uses 'exclusive purchasing' to describe single branding/requirements contracts.

Article 102 can apply to *de facto*, as well as contractual, exclusivity. *De facto* exclusivity occurs where there is no stipulation of exclusivity but the arrangements are such that exclusivity results. *Van Den Bergh*,[397] the paradigm case of this,[398] concerned the practice whereby ice cream manufacturers

---

[394] See P. Lugard, 'Eternal Sunshine on a Spotless Policy? Exclusive Dealing under Article 82 EC' (2006) 2 *European Competition Journal* 163.

[395] Guidance Paper, paras. 32–46.

[396] Ibid., para. 32.

[397] [1998] OJ L246/1, upheld Case T-65/98, *Van den Bergh Foods Ltd v Commission* [2003] ECR II-4653; *aff'd* Case C-552/03 P, *Unilever Bestfoods (Ireland) Ltd v Commission* [2006] ECR I-9091.

[398] As recognised in the Guidance Paper, para. 33.

provide retail outlets with freezers but prohibit any other supplier's brand being stored there.[399] This is considered to create a strategic barrier to entry and to reduce the intensity of competition be-tween incumbent firms, because in practice it is impractical for a retailer to accommodate a second freezer and he has no incentive to do so.[400] In *Van den Bergh* HB entered into distribution agreements with retailers in Ireland under which freezer cabinets were made available to them (either loaned with no direct charge or leased for an uncollected nominal sum with the maintenance and repair done by HB) exclusively for the storage and display of HB's impulse ice cream at the point of sale. The Commission found that these arrangements infringed Article 102 as well as Article 101.

B. EXCLUSIVE PURCHASING

In *Hoffmann-La Roche* the CJ spoke in terms which suggest that exclusive purchasing is abusive 'by object' when entered into by dominant suppliers (i.e. abusive insofar as it is not objectively justified, although the objective justification possibility was not expressly spelt out in the judgment):

An undertaking which is in a dominant position on the market and ties purchasers—even if it does so at their request—by an obligation or promise on their part to obtain all or most of their requirements exclusively from the said undertaking abuses its dominant position within the meaning of Article [102] . . .[401]

The objection to exclusive purchasing commitments involving dominant suppliers is that they are exclusionary and foreclose competitors from the market. The argument against holding them abusive by object is that they should be judged by their effects in the specific context of the case. Moreover, what should matter is whether they harm *consumers*.

In *Hoffmann-La Roche* the Court referred to an exclusive purchasing obligation covering 'all or most' of the customer's requirements.[402] Guidance as to what this means can be derived from the Verticals Regulation where a non-compete obligation is defined as including an obligation on a buyer to purchase 80 per cent of its requirements from one source.[403] In *Intel*[404] the GC suggested that exclusivity arrangements covering 80 per cent of a customer's requirements in one (comparatively small) segment of its demand amounted to 'most' of its requirements.[405]

The abusive nature of exclusive purchasing is not removed by the presence of an 'English clause' whereby the customer is allowed to switch suppliers without penalty if the dominant undertak-ing cannot or will not match more favourable terms offered by another supplier.[406] In *Hoffmann-La Roche*[407] the dominant firm argued that the English clause denuded the loyalty rebate provision[408] of its anti-competitive nature. The Court held that, on the contrary, the clause exacerbated the abuse by enabling Hoffmann-La Roche to learn of its competitors' offers.[409] Moreover, English clauses 'increase the likelihood that a competitor lowering prices will not gain market share but will prompt

---

[399] The issue relates to 'impulse ice cream', i.e. ice cream sold in individually wrapped portions for immediate consumption, not ice cream bought in multi-packs from supermarkets.

[400] The practice was also considered in the UK under the Fair Trade Act 1973 by the Mergers and Monopolies Commission (MMC) in its report, *Ice Cream: A Report on the Supply in the UK of Ice Cream for Immediate Consumption*, Cm. 2524 (TSO, 1994), and by the Competition Commission in its report, *The Supply of Impulse Ice Cream* Cm. 4510 (TSO, 2000).

[401] Case 85/76, *Hoffmann-La Roche* [1979] ECR 461, para. 89.

[402] See also *Soda-Ash–ICI* [2003] OJ L10/33, para. 142.

[403] Reg. 330/2010 [2010] OJ L102/1, Art. 1(b); for the Verticals Reg., see Chap. 11.

[404] Case T-286/09, *Intel* EU:T:2014:547.

[405] On this point, see further Section 11.E.iii.

[406] See also the discussion of 'most favoured nation' (MFN) clauses in Chap. 11, Section 2.B.iv, p. 755.

[407] Case 85/76, *Hoffmann-La Roche* [1979] ECR 461.

[408] See Section 11.E.

[409] Case 85/76, *Hoffmann-La Roche*, paras. 107–108. The Commission objected to an English clause in *IRI/Nielsen*, *XXXVIth Report on Competition Policy* (1996), part 64.

the incumbent supplier to match the lower price'.[410] The Verticals Guidelines say that even where there is no express exclusive purchasing arrangement English clauses can 'be expected to have the same effect as a single branding obligation'.[411]

In *Van den Bergh*[412] a more effects approach was taken to the application of Article 102 to exclusive purchasing. The Commission found that HB held a dominant position in the Irish impulse ice cream market (its market share was 75 per cent) and that its inducement of the retailers to accept the distribution arrangements infringed Article 102.[413] The Commission held that the agreements also infringed Article 101,[414] dismissing HB's argument, in respect to both Articles, that the application of the competition rules to the exclusivity provisions in the freezer agreements would be tantamount to interference with its property rights, contrary to Article 345 TFEU.[415] The GC upheld the decision, but not before considering the effects of the agreements on the market very carefully, applying the principle in *Delimitis* in respect of Article 101.[416] When it came to Article 102 the GC did not simply view the inducements to enter the arrangements as abusive by object but held that they breached Article 102 because of their effects in preventing competitors gaining access to the market,[417] thus taking a similar approach to that it had taken in respect of Article 101. The GC considered it significant that 40 per cent of the retail outlets were foreclosed by HB's freezer policy. The CJ upheld the judgment without expressly considering the Article 102 test.[418] However, subsequent cases such as *Solvay*[419] and *ICI*,[420] in which only Article 102 was in issue, have continued to take a more absolute view of exclusivity, citing and following *Hoffmann-La Roche*.

In *BPB Industries* the incentives to exclusivity were not only loyalty rebates[421] but also priority deliveries at times of shortage. The Commission's condemnation of this as an abuse was upheld by the GC on the basis of *Hoffmann-La Roche*.[422]

Exclusive purchasing agreements have been the subject of several commitments decisions under Article 9(1) of Regulation 1/2003.[423] These include cases resulting from the Commission's push to liberalise the European energy market[424] in which the Commission adopted commitments decisions whereby vertically integrated suppliers agreed to abandon long-term exclusive supply agreements: see *Distrigaz*[425] and *EDF—Long Term Electricity Contracts in France*.[426] The Commission is also

---

[410] Faull and Nikpay, n. 1, 4.404.

[411] Verticals Guidelines [2010] OJ C130/10, para. 129; see also the discussion on MFN clauses, Chap. 11.

[412] See n. 397.

[413] See I. Lianos, 'Categorical Thinking in Competition Law and the Effects-based Approach in Article 82' in Ezrachi, n. 41, 19, 24–25, who makes the often overlooked point that what was condemned under Art. 102 was the inducement of retailers who had not yet concluded the agreements, rather than the agreements themselves.

[414] See Chap. 11 Section 4.B.ii, p. 787.

[415] Then Art. 295 EC.

[416] Case C-234/89, *Stergios Delimitis v Henninger Bräu* [1991] ECR I-9350, see Chap. 4.

[417] Para. 160 of the GC judgment: Case T-65/98, *Van den Bergh Foods Ltd v EC Commission* [2003] ECR II-4653.

[418] The CJ (n. 397) briefly dismissed the appeal by Order, finding the grounds of appeal inadmissible or unfounded.

[419] Cases T-57 and 58/01, *Solvay v Commission* [2009] ECR II-4621, para. 365 (judgment overruled on the procedural pleas, Case C-109/10 P, *Solvay SA v European Commission* [2011] ECR I-10329 where the substantive arguments were not considered).

[420] Case T-66/01, *ICI v Commission* [2009] ECR II-2631, para. 315.

[421] See Section 11.E, p. 437 ff.

[422] *BPB Industries* [1989] OJ L10/50, paras. 141–147, upheld Case T-65/89, *BPB* [1993] ECR II-389, para. 68.

[423] For commitments decisions, see Chap. 13, Section 7.E.iii.

[424] A number of Art. 102 proceedings were opened in the wake of the energy sector inquiry.

[425] COMP/337.966, 11 October 2007, Pre-liberalisation, Distrigaz was the only gas supplier on the wholesale Belgian gas market. Two problems identified by the Commission were the duration of the contracts and the volume of gas tied. The commitments decision limits the ability of Distrigaz to enter into long-term supply contracts and an average of 70% of the market is to be open to competitors each year.

[426] COMP/39.386, 17 March 2010, IP/10/290. The Commission was concerned that EDF's supply contracts could prevent other electricity suppliers entering and expanding on the French electricity market. EDF will now ensure that every year a significant number of customers are free to contract with other suppliers.

pursuing exclusive purchasing in the technology sector—in December 2015 it sent a statement of objections (SO) to Qualcomm alleging it had paid significant amounts to a tablet and smartphone manufacturer in return for them using Qualcomm's chipsets exclusively.[427]

C. EXCLUSIVE DISTRIBUTION

There are few cases on exclusive distribution arrangements entered into by dominant undertakings, but limiting the customers' avenues of supply and foreclosing competitors can constitute an abuse.[428] In *DeBeers/Alrosa*[429] the Commission was concerned with an agreement between De Beers, the world's leading diamond mining company,[430] and Alrosa, a Russian company which was the world's second largest diamond producer, accounting for over 98 per cent of Russian diamond production. The agreement provided, in effect, that Alrosa would distribute almost all its diamonds sold outside the former USSR through De Beers. The Commission considered that the agreement would lead to *de facto* distribution exclusivity for De Beers and viewed it as the outcome of a long relationship between De Beers and Alrosa aimed at jointly regulating the volume, assortment, and prices of rough diamonds on the world market. De Beers gave commitments to phase out its purchases from Alrosa, and ultimately to cease purchasing them altogether.[431]

D. EXCLUSIVE PURCHASING IN THE GUIDANCE PAPER

The Guidance Paper deals with exclusive purchasing along with rebates in a section on 'exclusive dealing'. The Commission, applying its general effects-based approach, sets out the factors it considers relevant in determining whether to intervene in exclusivity arrangements. It makes the point that it is not concerned just with the effect on the customer who is party to the agreement. After all, the particular customer may be perfectly happy with the deal he has negotiated with the dominant supplier and the *quid pro quo* for his agreement to purchase exclusively. Rather, the Commission is concerned with customers overall and with the final consumers. It will be particularly concerned where consumers as a whole will not benefit, which is likely to be the case where the dominant firm has exclusive contracts with many customers so that competing undertakings are prevented from entering or expanding.[432] In paragraph 36 the Commission explains that it will treat as an enforcement priority those cases where anti-competitive foreclosure is likely as the dominant undertaking is an 'unavoidable trading partner' because, for example, its brand is a 'must stock item' or the competitors are unable for reasons of capacity constraints to satisfy the entire demand of each individual customer. The Commission considers that if competitors can compete on equal terms for each individual customer's entire demand, exclusive purchasing obligations are generally unlikely to hamper effective competition unless the switching of supplier by customers is rendered difficult due to the duration of the exclusive purchasing obligation, and that in general, the longer the duration of the obligation, the greater the likely foreclosure effect.[433] However, it says that if the dominant

---

[427] IP/15/6271.

[428] See *Hachette*, Commission's *VIIIth Report on Competition* (1978), paras. 115–115; *Visa International*, Commission's *XXVIth Report on Competition* (1996), para. 63; and Faull and Nikpay, n. 1, 4.406.

[429] COMP/38.381, 22 February 2006.

[430] Its market share was omitted from the decision, but for much of the 20th century it controlled over 80% of the world supply of rough diamonds.

[431] The GC, Case T-170/06, *Alrosa v Commission* [2007] ECR II-2601, annulled the decision on the grounds that the remedy infringed the principles of proportionality and freedom of contract but the judgment was set aside by the CJ, Case C-441/07 P, *Commission v Alrosa* [2010] ECR I-5949; see further Chap. 13, Section 7.E.iii.

[432] Guidance Paper, para. 34.

[433] Ibid., para. 36.

undertaking is an unavoidable trading partner for all or most customers, even an exclusive purchasing obligation of short duration can lead to anti-competitive foreclosure.[434]

The Guidance Paper accepts that exclusive purchasing contracts could be justified by efficiencies: the Commission will consider evidence of advantages to particular customers if the exclusive dealing is necessary for the dominant undertaking to make relationship-specific investments in order to supply them.[435]

11. DISCOUNTS AND REBATES

A. GENERAL

Granting discounts and rebates is a common commercial practice and a major way in which suppliers compete on price but the case law on Article 102 establishes that where undertakings are dominant their discounting and rebating policies are severely constrained.

The concern of the Commission and the EU Courts over rebates has centred on the exclusionary primary line injury they may cause.[436] The application of Article 102 to discounts and rebates is one of the most contentious areas of EU competition law.[437] In brief, the criticisms are that the law has distinguished between different types of discounts and rebates in a way that makes no economic sense; that it has assumed that an exclusionary effect on competitors means consumer harm; and that it has taken no account of the reasons why undertakings adopt certain discounting and rebating practices and the fact that these might be pro-competitive. In particular there is much controversy about EU law condemning certain types of rebates as a 'by object' abuse or as 'capable' of excluding competitors without sufficient analysis of the effects on the market.

The Guidance Paper set out a new approach to rebates, which adopted the as efficient competitor (AEC) test to determine whether a rebate could lead to anti-competitive foreclosure.[438] This has not been followed in the subsequent case law.[439]

---

[434] Ibid., para. 36. Marsden, n. 100, Chap. 3, 62–63 criticises the Commission for appearing inherently suspicious of the customer's desire for the dominant undertaking's product, which simply reflects past consumer demand and future expectations of that demand. The Commission thus casts 'normal business operations' in a 'pejorative light'. He concludes that 'a policy document that supposedly prioritizes abuses that most harms consumers should actually set out and apply some test for consumer harm, rather than assume that such harm is likely when retailers and their largest suppliers agree exclusive deals'.

[435] Guidance Paper, para. 46.

[436] Thus they fall within Art. 102(b) in 'limiting production, markets or technical development to the prejudice of consumers', see Temple Lang and O'Donoghue, n. 176, 83; J. Temple Lang, 'How Can the Problems of Exclusionary Abuses under Article 102 TFEU be Resolved?' (2012) 37 ELRev 136. However, Art. 102(c) which should be applied to discrimination affecting downstream markets, has been expressly relied upon in some cases of primary line injury; see Geradin, Layne-Farrar, and Petit, n. 170, 4.499–4.505, and Section 15, p. 559 ff, where Art. 102(c) is discussed.

[437] See, e.g., Temple Lang and O'Donoghue, n. 176; J. Kallaugher and B. Sher, 'Rebates Revisited: Anti-competitive Effects and Exclusionary Abuse under Article 82' [2004] ECLR 263; C. Ahlborn and D. Bailey, 'Discounts, Rebates and Selective Pricing by Dominant Firms: A Trans-Atlantic Comparison' (2006) 2 European Competition Journal 101; D. Spector, 'Loyalty Rebates: An Assessment of Competition Concerns and a Proposed Structured Rule of Reason' (2005) 1 Competition Policy International 89; Geradin, Layne-Farrar, and Petit, n. 170, 4.159–4.219; J. Temple Lang, 'How Can the Problems of Exclusionary Abuses under Article 102 TFEU be Resolved?' (2012) 37 ELRev 136; H. Zenger, 'Loyalty Rebates and the Competitive Process' (2012) 8 J of Competition Law and Economics 717, who says at 763 that there 'is no benefit in continuing to adhere to a delusive and antiquated theory of anticompetitive rebates that had no counterpart in economic reality even at the time when it was written down'; P. Ibáñez Colomo, 'Post Danmark II, or the Quest for Administrability and Coherence in Article 102 TFEU' LSE, Law, Society and Economy Working Papers 15/2015, <http://ssrn.com/abstract=2636407>.

[438] Guidance Paper, paras. 37–46; see Section 11.G, p. 471.

[439] The situation is complicated by the Commission's position in defending its decisions before the EU Courts.

B. TERMINOLOGY OF DISCOUNTS AND REBATES

Before turning to the decisions and case law it is useful to understand the terminology of discounts and/or rebates.[440] Technically a discount is a deduction from a price list and a rebate is refund granted retrospectively, but the terms are often used synonymously, particularly in the earlier case law. In this chapter the term 'rebate' is used to encompass both discounts and rebates, unless the context otherwise requires.

- *Quantity* rebates are reductions given to a purchaser who buys a certain objective amount (such as ten widgets for the price of nine).

- *'Loyalty'* or *'fidelity'* or *'exclusivity'* rebates are rebates given in return for exclusivity, whereby the supplier gives a rebate to a customer who purchases all (or nearly all)[441] of its requirements for the product from that supplier.

- *Target* rebates are rebates given to customers who buy more than a target (threshold) amount in a certain period (the reference period). The target may be set according to the customer's perceived capacity to absorb the goods, and is often set according to its previous purchases, i.e. the customer is required to buy a certain amount in excess of its purchases in the past. Target rebates can be retroactive (rolled back) or incremental, and standardised or individualised.

- *Rolled-back* (retroactive) rebates are those awarded on *all* purchases once the customer reaches a set threshold. If the threshold is 100 widgets, once the customer reaches that threshold it gets a rebate on the first 100 as well as the 101st onwards.

- *Incremental* rebates are those awarded only on purchases *above* the threshold.

- *Standardised* rebates are schemes where all customers get the same rebates on the same conditions.

- *Individualised* rebates are where customers are set different thresholds and/or different rebates.

- *'Loyalty-inducing'* or *'fidelity-building'* rebates are not a separate category of rebates but a concept developed in EU law to describe rebates which, while not strictly loyalty rebates given in return for exclusivity as such, are perceived as having analogous effects. The term is often used in respect of target rebate schemes.

- *Aggregated* (or *multi-product* or *bundled*) rebates are schemes whereby discounts are given on aggregated purchases of products belonging to different product markets. If the dominant supplier of widgets also supplies blodgets, and offers a discount scheme whereby purchases of blodgets (for which the customer is not dependent on the supplier) are aggregated with those of widgets for discount purposes, the customer will have an incentive to buy the blodgets from the dominant widget supplier.[442] This can have the effects of a tie.[443]

- *Selective* or *'targeted'* rebates (not to be confused with the target rebates described previously) are rebates offered only to certain customers or classes of customers who the supplier identifies to be likely to switch to or from a competitor. Whether selective, targeted low prices can be an abuse has already been discussed.[444]

- The *non-contestable* and *contestable portions of demand* is terminology introduced in the Guidance Paper. The *non-contestable portion of demand* is the amount which the customer would purchase

---

[440] See D. Ridyard, 'Exclusionary Pricing and Price Discrimination Abuses Under Article 102—An Economic Analysis' [2002] *ECLR* 286; Bishop and Walker, n. 198, 6.037–6.062.

[441] This is generally taken as meaning more than 80%, by analogy with the non-compete obligation definition in the Verticals Reg., Commission Reg. 330/2010 [2010] OJ L102/1, Art. 1(1)(d), and see Section 10.B, p. 431.

[442] See Case 85/76, *Hoffmann-La Roche* [1979] ECR 461 and *Elopak Italia/Tetra Pak* [1991] OJ L72/1.

[443] And is treated as such in the Guidance Paper, paras. 59–61.

[444] See Section 8.I, p. 402 ff.

from the dominant undertaking in any event. The *contestable portion of demand* is the amount for which the customer may prefer, and be able to find, substitutes.

C. CATEGORIES OF REBATES IN EU LAW

In *Intel* the GC distinguished three kinds of rebates in EU law.[445] *Intel* is on appeal to the CJ[446] but the GC's categorisation, elaborated upon in the light of the subsequent CJ judgment in *Post Danmark II*,[447] is used in this chapter as an organisational tool.

(i) Quantity Rebates

Quantity rebates are rebates linked solely to the quantity of purchases made from the dominant undertaking. *Michelin II*[448] established that a quantity discount scheme which is 'loyalty-inducing' will be treated as a target rebate scheme (which falls within *Intel's* third category) rather than as a simple quantity rebate. It is now clear from *Post Danmark II* that a standardised retroactive rebate given on the basis of the aggregate orders placed by the customer over a given period, rather than one granted in respect of each individual order, will also not qualify as a 'simple quantity rebate scheme' for the purposes of applying Article 102.[449] Quantity rebates are fixed objectively and applicable to all possible purchasers and therefore rebates linked to an estimate of each customer's presumed capacity of absorption are loyalty rebates.[450] Furthermore, a simple quantity discount must be non-discriminatory, not just on paper but in fact.[451]

(ii) Exclusivity Rebates

'Exclusivity rebates' is the term used by the GC in *Intel* for what have hitherto been called in the decisions and cases 'loyalty' or 'fidelity' rebates. They are conditional on the customer obtaining all or most of its requirements for the product from the dominant undertaking.[452] 'All or most' of the customer's requirements appears from *Intel* to include all or most of its requirements in one particular segment of its demand. In that case, in order to obtain the rebate one customer was required to purchase 95 per cent of its requirements for the central processing units (x86 CPUs) in one market segment (corporate desktop computers) from Intel, but that represented only 28 per cent of the customer's total requirements for x86 CPUs across all its computers.[453] This dilutes the meaning of 'exclusivity'. Furthermore, the exclusivity condition need not be contained in a formal obligation. In *Intel* there were no written contracts or other communications produced which evidenced the exclusivity. The GC held that this was irrelevant, as 'it is sufficient that the undertaking in a dominant position indicates in a credible manner to its customer that the grant of a financial advantage depends on exclusive or quasi-exclusive supply'.[454]

---

[445] Case T-286/09, *Intel* EU:T:2014:547, paras. 74–78.

[446] Case C-413/14 P, *Intel v Commission*, judgment pending.

[447] Case C-23/14, *Post Danmark II* EU:C:2015:651.

[448] Case T-203/01, *Michelin II* [2003] ECR II-4071.

[449] Case C-23/14, *Post Danmark II* EU:C:2015:651, para. 28.

[450] See the Commission decision *Deutsche Post* [2001] OJ L125/27, para. 33; see also Case T–228/97, *Irish Sugar plc* [1999] ECR II-2969, paras. 213 and 218.

[451] Case C-163/99, *Portugal v Commission* [2001] ECR I-2613 (*Portuguese Airports*), where the 'quantity discount' was so constructed that in practice it favoured Portuguese over non-Portuguese airlines. See Section 15.C.

[452] See the discussion of exclusive purchasing in Section 10.B, p. 430.

[453] Case T-286/09, *Intel* EU:T:2014:547, para. 129.

[454] Ibid., para. 106.

(iii) 'Rebates Falling Within The Third Category'

'Rebates falling within the third category' is how the GC in *Intel* described rebates which are neither quantity rebates on the one hand nor directly linked to a condition of exclusivity or quasi-exclusivity on the other. They may however have exclusionary effects because they are 'fidelity-building'.[455] The cases on this type of rebate have mainly involved target rebate schemes[456] but *Post Danmark II* appears to include within this category quantity rebates which relate to aggregate rather than to individual orders.

D. QUANTITY REBATES

The CJ confirmed in *Post Danmark II* that it is settled case law that quantity discounts linked solely to the volume of purchases from the manufacturer concerned are not, in principle, liable to infringe Article 102.[457] The case law referred to stems from *Hoffmann-La Roche* which, as we see below, drew a sharp distinction between quantity rebates and loyalty rebates.[458] Quantity rebates are presumptively lawful because they are 'deemed to reflect gains in efficiency and economies of scale made by the undertaking in a dominant position'.[459] A quantity rebate would not be presumptively legal if the price charged was predatory according to the normal predatory pricing principles.[460]

E. EXCLUSIVITY (LOYALTY/FIDELITY) REBATES

(i) The Nature of Exclusivity Rebates

As we have seen, provisions whereby a customer contractually commits itself to buying all its requirements of a product from a dominant supplier are a 'by object' abuse. However, a supplier may offer a customer a rebate if it buys all its requirements for the product from that supplier, or a rebate system may be set up so that it rewards customers who *do* buy exclusively. Such rebates may have the same effect as an exclusive purchasing agreement. In the *European Sugar Cartel* case[461] the CJ, for the first time, distinguished between true quantity rebates and loyalty rebates:

> . . . the rebate at issue is not to be treated as a quantity rebate exclusively linked with the volume of purchases from the producer concerned but has rightly been classified by the Commission as a loyalty rebate designed, through the grant of a financial advantage, to prevent customers obtaining their supplies from competing producers.[462]

Ever since the seminal 1979 judgment in *Hoffmann-La Roche*, in which the CJ treated exclusivity rebates as 'by object' abuses, debate has raged about the proper treatment of such rebates, which many economists and other commentators argue may have pro- rather than anti-competitive effects. The pro-competitive effects include more efficient recovery of fixed costs, providing better incentives to retailers, reducing double marginalisation, and resolving 'hold-up' problems. Anti-competitive effects arise mainly from the possibility of leverage, although it is argued that this happens only when certain assumptions apply.[463]

---

[455] Ibid., para. 78.

[456] Case 322/81, *Michelin I* [1983] ECR 3461; Case T-203/01, *Michelin II* [2003] ECR II-4071; Case C-95/04 P, *British Airways* [2007] ECR I-2331.

[457] Case C-23/14, *Post Danmark II* EU:C:2015:651, para. 27.

[458] Case 85/76, *Hoffmann-La Roche* [1979] ECR 461, para. 90.

[459] Case T-286/09, *Intel* EU:T:2014:547, para. 75, on appeal Case C-413/14 P, judgment pending; see also Case T-203/01, *Michelin II* [2003] ECR II-4071, para. 58.

[460] For predatory pricing see Case C-62/86, *AKZO* [1991] ECR I-3359, and Section 8.

[461] Case 40/73, *Suiker Unie v Commission* [1975] ECR 1663.

[462] Ibid., para. 513.

[463] See the discussion in O'Donoghue and Padilla, n. 1, 464–471.

(ii) The *Hoffmann-La Roche* Case and Subsequent Case Law

a. *Hoffmann-La Roche*: The Abusive Nature of Loyalty Rebates

In the seminal case of *Hoffmann-La Roche* the CJ laid down the basis for the treatment of exclusivity rebates which remains the foundation of the law.

Case 85/76, *Hoffmann-La Roche v Commission* [1979] ECR 461

Hoffmann-La Roche (HLR) supplied a number of vitamins. The Commission held that it was in a dominant position[464] and had abused its position by giving loyalty rebates to 22 large customers. HLR appealed. The Court dealt with three arguments on the question of the loyalty rebates: whether such rebates are an abuse, what was the nature of the rebates in this case, and whether they were saved from infringing Article 102 by the presence in the contracts of an 'English clause'.

Court of Justice

89. An undertaking which is in a dominant position on the market and ties purchasers—even if it does so at their request—by an obligation or promise on their part to obtain all or most of their requirements exclusively from the said undertaking abuses its dominant position within the meaning of Article [102], whether the obligation in question is stipulated without further qualification or whether it is undertaken in consideration of the grant of a rebate. The same applies if the said undertaking, without tying the purchasers by a formal obligation, applies, either under the terms of agreements concluded with these purchasers or unilaterally, a system of fidelity rebates, that is to say discounts conditional on the customer's obtaining all or most of its requirements—whether the quantity of its purchases be large or small—from the undertaking in a dominant position.

90. Obligations of this kind to obtain supplies exclusively from a particular undertaking, whether or not they are in consideration of rebates or of the granting of fidelity rebates intended to give the purchaser an incentive to obtain his supplies exclusively from the undertaking in a dominant position, are incompatible with the objective of undistorted competition within the Common Market, because—unless there are exceptional circumstances which may make an agreement between undertakings in the context of Article [101] and in particular of paragraph (3) of that Article, permissible—they are not based on an economic transaction which justifies this burden or benefit but are designed to deprive the purchaser of or restrict his possible choice of sources of supply and to deny other producers access to the market. The fidelity rebate, unlike quantity rebates exclusively linked with the volume of purchases from the producer concerned, is designed through the grant of a financial advantage to prevent customers from obtaining their supplies from competing producers. Furthermore, the effect of fidelity rebates is to apply dissimilar conditions to equivalent transactions with other trading parties in that two purchasers pay a different price for the same quantity of the same product depending on whether they obtain their supplies exclusively from the undertaking in a dominant position or have several sources of supply. Finally, these practices by an undertaking in a dominant position and especially on an expanding market tend to consolidate this position by means of a form of competition which is not based on the transactions effected and is therefore distorted.

In this famous passage the CJ says that dominant firms cannot enter into exclusive purchasing agreements and cannot operate rebate schemes which have the same effect as exclusive purchasing agreements: in other words, they are 'by object' abuses. The illegality does not depend on assessing the effects of the rebate on the market in the particular case, as it is assumed that if a dominant firm

---

[464] For the dominance aspects of this case see Chap. 6.

rewards customers for not buying elsewhere it is bound to have an exclusionary foreclosure effect on competitors. The Court also held that the abuse was exacerbated rather than remedied by the presence of an English clause.[465] It will be noted that in *Hoffmann-La Roche* there was no mention of the effect of the assumed exclusion of competitors on consumers.

Subsequent to *Hoffmann-La Roche* the EU Courts have dealt with exclusivity payments in a number of cases. In *BPB Industries and British Gypsum* the undertaking inaugurated a system of payments for promotional and advertising expenses to customers (builders' merchants) in Great Britain who bought exclusively from it,[466] and in Northern Ireland it offered rebates to those buying exclusively from BG and not dealing with the importers.[467] Both schemes were condemned as abuses on the grounds that a dominant undertaking may not give rebates or other advantages conditional upon exclusivity.[468] In the *Soda Ash* cases the Commission condemned a pricing structure based on 'top slice' rebates, whereby customers got the basic tonnage, which would have been bought from the dominant undertaking anyway (the 'non-contestable' share in recent terminology), at the normal price, but were offered substantial discounts on extra amounts above that. These were held to be exclusionary loyalty rebates.[469]

In *Tomra*, a case mainly concerned with retroactive target rebates[470] the CJ restated the law laid down in *Hoffmann-La Roche*:

In the event that an undertaking in a dominant position makes use of a system of rebates, the Court has ruled that that undertaking abuses that position where, without tying the purchasers by a formal obligation, it applies, either under the terms of agreements concluded with these purchasers or unilaterally, a system of loyalty rebates, that is to say, discounts conditional on the customer's obtaining—whether the quantity of its purchases is large or small—all or most of its requirements from the undertaking in a dominant position (see Case 85/76 *Hoffman[n]-La Roche* . . . . , paragraph 89, and Case 322/81 *Nederlandsche Banden-Industrie-Michelin v Commission* . . . , paragraph 71.[471]

The reference to *Michelin I* was to the CJ's judgment in 1983[472] where it quoted *Hoffmann-La Roche* on exclusivity rebates in the course of a case on target rebates. Since then there had been nearly 30 years of relentless criticism of the EU Courts' position on loyalty rebates. *Tomra* was therefore an acute disappointment to those who believe that loyalty rebates should be judged by an effects-based test showing actual foreclosure and not condemned per se.

---

[465] Case 85/76, *Hoffmann-La Roche* [1979] ECR 461, paras. 107–108. For 'English clauses' see Section 10.B, p. 431.

[466] According to the Commission's decision these were devised after the managing director asked the marketing director how the company could 'reward the loyalty of merchants who remained exclusively with us', *BPB Industries plc* [1989] OJ L10/50, para. 58.

[467] The company also put in place a system of priority deliveries for loyal customers.

[468] Case T-65/89, *BPB Industries* [1993] ECR II-389, aff'd on appeal Case C-310/93 P, *BPB Industries PLC and British Gypsum Ltd v Commission* [1995] ECR I-865.

[469] *Soda Ash–ICI* and *Soda Ash–Solvay* [1991] OJ L152/40 and 152/21, annulled for procedural reasons, Cases T-30/91 etc., *Solvay v Commission* [1995] ECR II-1775, aff'd Cases C-286–288/96 P, *Commission v Solvay* [2000] ECR I-2391; replaced by *Soda Ash–Solvay* [2003] OJ L10/10 and *Soda Ash–ICI* [2003] OJ L10/33, upheld in respect of *Solvay*, Cases T-57 and 58/01, *Solvay v Commission* [2009] ECR II-4621, annulled for procedural reasons Case C-109/10 P, *Solvay SA v Commission* [2011] ECR I-10329 (but note Kokott AG rejecting criticism of the *Hoffmann-La Roche* position) upheld in respect of ICI, Case T-66/01, *ICI v Commission* [2009] ECR II-2631. The Commission also held the rebates to be discriminatory contrary to Art. 102(c) in that the basic tonnage was set at a different figure for each customer, so giving them different costs, see Section 15.

[470] See Section 11.F.ii.d, p. 460. The rebates condemned as loyalty rebates were rebates found by the Commission to be tailored precisely to each customer's estimated requirements.

[471] Case C-549/10 P, *Tomra* EU:C:2012:221, para. 70. The suggestion that para. 71 of the judgment could be read as the CJ softening its stance towards exclusivity rebates (see the 5th edition of this book, p. 460) was put forward in argument in *Intel* but rejected by the GC (Case T-286/09, *Intel v Commission* EU:T:2014:547, para. 97).

[472] Case 322/81, *Michelin I* [1983] ECR 3461.

(iii) The *Intel* Case

In *Intel*[473] the Commission imposed a fine of €1.06 billion on Intel for a number of practices found to infringe Article 102. These included giving rebates (wholly or partially hidden) on its x86 CPUs to computer manufacturers (OEMs) such as Dell and HP which were conditional on the OEMs purchasing 80–100 per cent of their requirements from Intel.[474] The Commission took the view that its Guidance Paper was not applicable to existing proceedings[475] and set out its understanding of the existing case law stemming from *Hoffmann-La Roche* as requiring no evidence of actual foreclosure.[476] Nevertheless, in line with the approach to rebates set out in the Guidance Paper[477] the Commission did apply the AEC test in order to demonstrate that Intel's conditional rebates *were* 'capable of causing or likely to cause anti-competitive foreclosure (which is likely to result in consumer harm)'[478] even though the case law did not require it to do so. Intel denied that it had ever imposed exclusivity obligations.[479]

The decision was subjected to considerable criticism, inter alia on the grounds that the theory of harm the Commission put forward in respect of the effect of the rebates on the OEM's purchasing strategy was highly speculative, that the analysis of the evidence was flawed, and that the analysis of 'harm to competition and consumers' in paragraphs 1597–1616 was entirely theoretical.[480] The outcome of the appeal to the GC was eagerly awaited. That judgment, in 2014, provided a longer and more detailed consideration of exclusivity rebates than anything in the previous case law. In it the GC confirmed that exclusivity rebates which enable the undertaking to leverage the non-contestable portion of demand are 'by object' abuses and infringe Article 102, subject only to the possibility of objective justification. It also made a number of other controversial points. The judgment unleashed a storm of comment, most of it highly critical.[481] The case is on appeal to the CJ.[482]

---

[473] COMP/37.990, *Intel*, decision of 13 May 2009.

[474] In Dell's case, for example, the rebate was conditional on 100% exclusivity. In HP's case it was 95%: when AMD offered HP one million CPUs *free* it took only 160,000 of them in order to stay within Intel's limit (COMP/37.990, *Intel*, decision of 13 May 2009, paras. 956–957).

[475] Such as these were. The decision was adopted shortly after the publication of the Guidance Paper but the dawn raids had occurred in 2005.

[476] COMP/37.990, *Intel*, decision of 13 May 2009, paras. 920–923. It also cited Case T-201/04, *Microsoft* [2007] ECR II-3601, as showing that the EU Courts do not look at the actual impact of the alleged anti-competitive conduct on the market.

[477] See Section 11.G, p. 471.

[478] COMP/37.990, *Intel*, decision of 13 May 2009, para. 925.

[479] Case T-286/09, *Intel* EU:T:2014:547, para. 106.

[480] D. Geradin, 'The Decision of the Commission of 13 May 2009 in the *Intel* Case: Where is the Foreclosure and Consumer Harm?' (2009) 2 *JECLAP* 9.

[481] See, e.g., N. Petit, '*Intel*, Leveraging Rebates and the Goals of Article 102 TFEU', <http://ssrn.com/abstract=2567628>; L. Peeperkorn, 'Conditional Pricing: Why the General Court is Wrong in *Intel* and What the Court of Justice Can Do to Rebalance the Assessment of Rebates' [2015] 1 *Concurrences* 43; P. Ibáñez Colomo, '*Intel* and Article 102 TFEU Case Law: Making Sense of a Perpetual Controversy', LSE, Law, Society and Economy Working Papers 29/201; J. Venit, 'Case T-286/09, *Intel v Commission*—The Judgment of the General Court: All Steps Backward and No Steps Forward' (2014) 10 *European Competition Journal* 203; W. Wils, 'The Judgment of the EU General Court in *Intel* and the So-called "More Economic Approach" to Abuse of Dominance' (2014) 37 *World Competition* 405 (which approves the judgment); P. Rey and J. Venit, 'An Effects-based Approach to Article 102: A Response to Wouter Wils' (2015) 38 *World Competition* 3; R. Whish, '*Intel v Commission*: Keep Calm and Carry On!' (2015) 6 *JECLAP* 1; P. Nihoul, 'The Ruling of the General Court in *Intel*: Towards the End of an Effects-based Approach in European Competition Law?' (2014) 5 *JECLAP* 521; D. Geradin, 'Loyalty Rebates after *Intel*: Time for the European Court of Justice to Overrule *Hoffmann-La Roche*' (2015) 11 *J of Competition Law and Economics* 579; and the symposium in the first issue of *Competition Law and Policy Debate* [2015] 1 *CLPD* especially B. Allan, 'Loyalty and Fidelity Rebates: A Sense of Déjà Vu Again' [2015] 1 *CLPD* 50; C. Ahlborn and D. Piccinin, 'The *Intel* Judgment and Consumer Welfare—A Response to Wouter Wils' [2015] 1 *CLPD* 60; and M. Dolmans and T. Graf, 'Dealing with *Intel* Intelligently Delineating the Scope and Limits of the Court's Ruling' [2015] 1 *CLPD* 76.

[482] Case C-413/14 P, *Intel v Commission*, judgment pending.

In the judgment the GC said that what it called 'exclusivity rebates' are by their very nature capable of foreclosing competitors (at least insofar as rebates which leverage the dominant undertaking's economic power from the non-contestable to the contestable share of the customer's demand are concerned). It characterised exclusivity rebates as a matter of exclusivity, not pricing.[483] A financial advantage granted for the purpose of inducing a customer to obtain all or most of its requirements from the undertaking in a dominant position means that that customer has an incentive not to obtain, in respect of the part of its requirements concerned by the exclusivity condition, supplies from competitors of the undertaking in a dominant position.[484] A foreclosure effect occurs not only where access to the market by competitors is made impossible but also where it is made more difficult, and a financial incentive which induces exclusivity is by its very nature capable of making access more difficult.[485] The GC justified its approach by recourse to the principle of the special responsibility of dominant undertakings[486] and by stating that a supplier in a strong dominant position, as Intel was, is to a large extent an 'unavoidable trading partner',[487] which enables it to use its economic power on the non-contestable share of the demand as leverage to secure the contestable share also.[488] This means that the approach to exclusivity conditions taken on competitive markets[489] does not apply to a market where competition is already restricted because of the dominant position.[490]

Case T-286/09, *Intel v Commission* EU:T:2014:547

General Court

84. It follows that, according to the case-law, it is only in the case of rebates falling within the third category that it is necessary to assess all the circumstances, and not in the case of exclusivity rebates falling within the second category.

85. That approach can be justified by the fact that exclusivity rebates granted by an undertaking in a dominant position are by their very nature capable of restricting competition.

86. The capability of tying customers to the undertaking in a dominant position is inherent in exclusivity rebates. The grant by an undertaking in a dominant position of a rebate in consideration of a customer's obtaining all or most of its requirements implies that the undertaking in a dominant position grants a financial advantage designed to prevent customers from obtaining their supplies from competing producers. It is therefore not necessary to examine the circumstances of the case in order to determine whether that rebate is designed to prevent customers from obtaining their supplies from competitors.

87. It should moreover be noted that exclusivity rebates granted by an undertaking in a dominant position are by their very nature capable of foreclosing competitors. A financial advantage granted for the purpose of inducing a customer to obtain all or most of its requirements from the undertaking in a dominant position means that that customer has an incentive not to obtain, in respect of the part of its requirements concerned by the exclusivity condition, supplies from competitors of the undertaking in a dominant position.

---

[483] Case T-286/09, *Intel* EU:T:2014:547, para. 99.

[484] Ibid., para. 87.

[485] Ibid., para. 88.

[486] Ibid., para. 90.

[487] Ibid., paras. 91–92.

[488] Ibid., para. 93.

[489] Exemplified by Case C-234/89, *Delimitis v Henninger Bräu AG* [1991] ECR I-935.

[490] Case T-286/09, *Intel* EU:T:2014:547, para. 89.

88. In that context, it should be observed that a foreclosure effect occurs not only where access to the market is made impossible for competitors, but also where that access is made more difficult (see, to that effect, *Michelin I*, paragraph 74 above, paragraph 85; Case C-52/09 *TeliaSonera Sverige*…, paragraph 63, and *Michelin II*, paragraph 75 above, paragraph 244). A financial incentive granted by an undertaking in a dominant position in order to induce a customer not to obtain, in respect of the part of its requirements concerned by the exclusivity condition, supplies from its competitors is by its very nature capable of making access to the market more difficult for those competitors.

89. Although exclusivity conditions may, in principle, have beneficial effects for competition, so that in a normal situation on a competitive market, it is necessary to assess their effects on the market in their specific context (see, to that effect, Case C-234/89 *Delimitis*…, paragraphs 14 to 27), those considerations cannot be accepted in the case of a market where, precisely because of the dominant position of one of the economic operators, competition is already restricted (see, to that effect, Case C-310/93 P *BPB Industries and British Gypsum* v *Commission*, paragraph 11, and the Opinion of Advocate General Léger in that case, points 42 to 45).

90. That approach is justified by the special responsibility that an undertaking in a dominant position has not to allow its conduct to impair genuine undistorted competition in the common market and by the fact that, where an economic operator holds a strong position in the market, exclusive supply conditions in respect of a substantial proportion of purchases by a customer constitute an unacceptable obstacle to access to the market (see, to that effect, Case T-65/89 *BPB Industries and British Gypsum* v *Commission*…, paragraphs 65 to 68). In that case, the exclusivity of supply causes additional interference with the structure of competition on the market. Thus, the concept of abuse in principle includes any obligation to obtain supplies exclusively from an undertaking in a dominant position which benefits that undertaking (see, to that effect, *Hoffmann-La Roche*, paragraph 71 above, paragraphs 120, 121 and 123, Case C-310/93 P *BPB Industries and British Gypsum*, paragraph 89 above, paragraph 11, and the Opinion of Advocate General Léger in that case, paragraph 89 above, points 46 and 47).

91. Furthermore, it must also be stated that it is inherent in a strong dominant position, such as that occupied by the applicant, that, for a substantial part of the demand, there are no proper substitutes for the product supplied by the dominant undertaking. The supplier in a dominant position is thus, to a large extent, an unavoidable trading partner (see, to that effect, *Hoffmann-La Roche*, paragraph 71 above, paragraph 41; Case C-95/04 P *British Airways*, paragraph 74 above, paragraph 75; and Case T-155/06 *Tomra*, paragraph 72 above, paragraph 269). In the present case, the applicant does not contest the findings made in the contested decision that its position on the market during the period of the infringement found in this case was that of an unavoidable trading partner.

92. It follows from the position of unavoidable trading partner that customers will in any event obtain part of their requirements from the undertaking in a dominant position ('the non-contestable share'). The competitor of an undertaking in a dominant position is not therefore in a position to compete for the full supply of a customer, but only for the portion of the demand exceeding the non-contestable share ('the contestable share'). The contestable share is thus the portion of a customer's requirements which can realistically be switched to a competitor of the undertaking in a dominant position in any given period, as the Commission states at recital 1009 of the contested decision. The grant of exclusivity rebates by an undertaking in a dominant position makes it more difficult for a competitor to supply its own goods to customers of that dominant undertaking. If a customer of the undertaking in a dominant position obtains supplies from a competitor by failing to comply with the exclusivity or quasi-exclusivity condition, it risks losing not only the rebates for the units that it switched to that competitor, but the entire exclusivity rebate.

93. In order to submit an attractive offer, it is not therefore sufficient for the competitor of an undertaking in a dominant position to offer attractive conditions for the units that that competitor can itself supply to the customer; it must also offer that customer compensation for the loss of the exclusivity rebate. In order to submit an attractive offer, the competitor must therefore apportion the rebate that the undertaking in a dominant position grants in respect of all or almost all of the customer's requirements, including the non-contestable share, to the contestable share alone. Thus, the grant of an exclusivity rebate by an

unavoidable trading partner makes it structurally more difficult for a competitor to submit an offer at an attractive price and thus gain access to the market. The grant of exclusivity rebates enables the undertaking in a dominant position to use its economic power on the non-contestable share of the demand of the customer as leverage to secure also the contestable share, thus making access to the market more difficult for a competitor.

94. Lastly, it should be noted that it is open to the dominant undertaking to justify the use of an exclusivity rebate system, in particular by showing that its conduct is objectively necessary or that the potential foreclosure effect that it brings about may be counterbalanced, outweighed even, by advantages in terms of efficiency that also benefit consumers (see, to that effect, *Hoffmann-La Roche*, paragraph 71 above, paragraph 90; Case C-95/04 P *British Airways*, paragraph 74 above, paragraphs 85 and 86; and Case C-209/10 *Post Danmark...*, paragraphs 40 and 41 and the case-law cited). However, in the case in point, the applicant has put forward no argument in that regard.

...

98. Second, the applicant relies on Case C-280/08 P *Deutsche Telekom* v *Commission...*, paragraph 175, *TeliaSonera*, paragraph 88 above, paragraph 28, and *Post Danmark*, paragraph 94 above, paragraph 26. In those judgments, the Court of Justice held that, 'in order to determine whether the undertaking in a dominant position has abused such a position by its pricing practices, it is necessary to consider all the circumstances...'.

99. However, the scope of that case-law is limited to pricing practices and does not affect the legal characterisation of exclusivity rebates. Case C-280/08 P *Deutsche Telekom*, paragraph 98 above, and *TeliaSonera*, paragraph 88 above, concerned margin squeeze practices and *Post Danmark*, paragraph 94 above, concerned low price practices, so that those three cases concerned pricing practices. However, the present case does not relate to a pricing practice. As regards the rebates granted to the various OEMs, the complaint made against the applicant in the contested decision is not based on the exact amount of the rebates and thus on the prices charged by the applicant, but on the fact that the grant of those rebates was conditional on exclusive or quasi-exclusive supply. Different treatment of exclusivity rebates and pricing practices is justified by the fact that, unlike an exclusive supply incentive, the level of a price cannot be regarded as unlawful in itself.

The judgment held that the following were all irrelevant to the finding of abuse:

a. The AEC Test

The GC considered that there was no requirement to use the AEC test[491] in the case of exclusivity rebates where the non-contestable share is being leveraged.[492] The AEC test is applicable where it is impossible to assess whether a price is abusive without comparing it to other prices and costs as a price cannot be unlawful in itself.[493] Exclusivity rebates, however, are a matter of exclusivity, not pricing. The GC referred to *Tomra* where the CJ did not consider it necessary to show that an as efficient competitor would have to charge 'negative' prices in order to compete with a target rebate scheme.[494] The GC also said that the AEC test was concerned only with showing the *impossibility* of an as efficient competitor being able to access the market and not whether access was *more difficult*.[495]

---

[491] Which asks whether equally efficient competitors could compete with the dominant undertaking's prices without incurring a loss.

[492] Case T-286/09, *Intel* EU:T:2014:547, paras. 140–166, particularly para. 150.

[493] Ibid., para. 152.

[494] See Section 11.F.ii.d, p. 460.

[495] Case T-286/09, *Intel* EU:T:2014:547, para. 150.

b. Evidence of Actual or Potential Foreclosure Effects

It is not necessary to finding (leveraging type) exclusivity rebates an abuse that at least potential foreclosure is established.[496] The abuse stems from the fact that the rebates are by their very nature capable of restricting competition. In this regard the GC distinguished exclusivity rebates both from 'rebates falling within the third category'[497] and from pricing practices such as margin squeeze and low prices. As in respect of its approach to the AEC test, the GC based the latter distinction on the legal characterisation of exclusivity rebates as being concerned with exclusivity rather than with pricing.[498] Even where the abuse is historic the Commission is not required to prove actual foreclosure effects, direct damage to consumers, or a causal link between such damage and the practices in issue.[499]

c. The Amount of the Rebate

It is irrelevant that the amount of the rebate is small. It is not the level of the rebates which is the issue, but the exclusivity for which they are given, 'the rebate must only be capable of inducing the customer to purchase exclusively, irrespective of whether the competing supplier could have compensated the customer for the loss of the rebate if that customer switched supplier'.[500]

d. The Short Duration of the Supply Contracts and the Right to Terminate at Short Notice

The short duration of supply contracts, and the right to terminate at short notice (even a period of 30 days) does not affect the abusive nature of the contracts, which stems from the fact that any financial incentive to purchase exclusively from a dominant undertaking constitutes an additional interference with the structure of competition.[501]

e. The (Small) Portion of the Market Concerned in the Relevant Conduct: There is No 'Appreciable Effect' or 'De Minimis' Criterion in Respect of Article 102

In *Intel* the part of the x86 CPU market covered by the rebates was between 0.3 and 2 per cent. The small size of the part of the market concerned was not a relevant consideration.[502] The GC said that the CJ had already rejected the application of an 'appreciable effect' criterion or a de minimis threshold in the application of Article 102 in *Hoffmann-La Roche*.[503] For the issue of appreciability in Article 102 generally, see Section 3.G.

f. The Rebates Being Granted in Response to Customer's Requests and Buying Power

The fact that rebates are given in response to customer buying power does not justify making them subject to an exclusive supply condition. The GC said that the customers' buying power did not alter the fact that the dominant undertaking was an unavoidable trading partner.[504]

---

[496] Ibid., paras. 95–100.

[497] See Section 11.F.

[498] Case T-286/09, *Intel* EU:T:2014:547, para. 99.

[499] Ibid., paras. 102–105.

[500] Ibid., para. 108.

[501] Ibid., para. 114.

[502] Ibid., paras. 114–124.

[503] Ibid., para. 116. Subsequent to *Intel*, the CJ held in Case C-23/14, *Post Danmark II* EU:C:2015:651, para. 73 that fixing an appreciability threshold in respect of Art. 102 was not justified.

[504] Case T-286/09, *Intel* EU:T:2014:547, paras. 138–140.

g. The Rebates Cover Only an Insignificant Proportion of the Customer's Total Requirement and Apply Only to a Certain Segment of the Customer's Demand

As we have already seen[505] a rebate amounting to 28 per cent of the customer's total demand was held to be 'exclusive' because it amounted to 95 per cent of its demand in one segment of demand. The GC justified this by reference to the CJ's *Tomra* judgment[506] in which it said that competitors of the dominant undertaking must be able to compete on the merits for the entire market and not just for a part of it.

It is striking that the GC chose so trenchantly to endorse the object/per se approach to what it called exclusivity rebates and to reject the move towards more effects-based analysis as seen in recent CJ judgments such as *TeliaSonera*[507] and *Post Danmark I*.[508] The strictness of the standard applied by the GC is compounded by the findings as to the irrelevance of the small amount of the rebate and the short duration, and the extension of 'exclusivity' to one segment of the customer's demand. Furthermore, the finding that there is no appreciability threshold in respect of Article 102 means that, as effects do not have to be shown, the provision may be applied to exclusive rebates which have in reality very little impact on the market.

The GC was careful to point out in *Intel* that it is open to a dominant undertaking to objectively justify its exclusivity rebates, but that Intel had not put forward any arguments in that regard.[509] However, there are as yet no Article 102 cases where a prima facie abuse has been saved by being objectively justified, and that possibility seems more theoretical than realistic and practical.[510]

It will be interesting, to say the very least, to see what the CJ does in the *Intel* appeal.[511]

(iv) *Post Danmark II*

Post Danmark II,[512] discussed in the following section, was not a case on exclusivity rebates. Nevertheless, in the course of its ruling the CJ said apropos of them:

> It is also settled case law that a loyalty rebate, which by offering customers financial advantages tends to prevent them from obtaining all or most of their requirement from competing manufacturers, amounts to an abuse within the meaning of [Article 102] (see judgments in *Nederlandsche Banden-Industrie-Michelin v Commission*, 322/81,..., paragraph 71, and *Tomra Systems and Others v Commission*, C-549/10 P,..., paragraph 70).[513]

F. 'REBATES FALLING WITHIN THE THIRD CATEGORY'

(i) Types of Third Category Rebates

Third category rebates are described in *Intel* by reference to what they are *not*. They are rebates which are not simple quantity rebates but are not directly linked to an exclusivity condition. Nevertheless they may, according to the cases, have a 'loyalty-inducing' or 'fidelity-building' effect

---

[505] Section 11.C.ii.

[506] Case C-549/10 P, *Tomra* EU:C:2012:221, para. 42, see Section 11.F, ii.d, p. 461.

[507] Case C-52/09, *TeliaSonera* [2011] ECR I-527.

[508] Case C-209/10, *Post Danmark I* EU:C:2012:172.

[509] Intel had argued, rather, than it had not stipulated exclusivity.

[510] For objective justification, see Section 5, p. 369.

[511] Case C-413/14 P, judgment pending.

[512] Case C-23/14, *Post Danmark II* EU:C:2015:651.

[513] Ibid., para. 27.

(the terms are synonymous).[514] This concept was first used by the EU Courts in *Michelin II*[515] and has been employed in cases on what are called 'target rebates' (see the terminology in Section 11.B) which are described in *Intel* as 'rebate systems depending on the attainment of individual sales objectives which do not constitute exclusivity rebates, since those systems do not contain any obligation to obtain all or a given proportion of supplies from the dominant undertaking'.[516] The GC in *Intel* did not suggest what rebate systems other than target rebates are included in its third category but the standardised retroactive rebates in *Post Danmark II* were described by the CJ as neither simple quantity rebates nor loyalty rebates.[517] That suggests that they, too, fall within the 'third category'. It is important to note that the CJ in *Post Danmark II* did not use the contentious 'fidelity-building/loyalty-inducing' terminology, although it did refer to the 'suction effect', another target rebate case concept,[518] and it referred in its reasoning to its target rebate judgments.[519] Therefore in this chapter we discuss the rebates in issue in *Post Danmark II* as being another type of rebate in the 'third category'.

(ii) Target Rebates

Target rebate schemes, while not expressly rewarding exclusivity as such, may strongly encourage the customer to stay with the supplier. This is why the EU Courts use the much-criticised description 'loyalty-inducing' or 'fidelity-building'. These rebates are seen in the Article 102 cases as enmeshing the customer into deals with the dominant supplier which competitors cannot match, thereby having an exclusionary effect and foreclosing the market. There is particular concern with the so-called 'suction effect' (the 'effect at the margin') in rolled-back rebates, whereby the nearer the customer gets to the target the more difficult it is for a competitor to entice it away, as by switching even a small portion of its demand from the dominant undertaking the customer would lose all the retroactive rebate.[520]

The fundamental question about target rebates is whether they infringe Article 102 only if they are shown to have anti-competitive effects on the market. Current emphasis on economic analysis and on consumer harm as the test for whether the behaviour of the dominant firm amounts to an abuse suggests two things: first, that the actual or likely exclusionary effects in a particular case should be assessed, rather than presumed and, secondly, that it should not be presumed that the exclusion of *competitors* harms *consumers*. However, as we see below, this is not how the case law has hitherto treated target rebates.

a. *Michelin I*: The Abusive Nature of Target Rebates

The first case on target rebates was *Michelin I* in 1983. The rebates were held to be an abuse. The CJ described the rebates (paragraph 73) as removing or restricting the buyer's 'freedom to choose his sources of supply' in line with paragraph 90 of *Hoffmann-La Roche* in relation to loyalty rebates.

---

[514] Case T-286/09, *Intel* EU:T:2014:547, para. 78.

[515] Case T-203/01, *Michelin II* [2003] ECR II-4071.

[516] Case T-286/09, *Intel* EU:T:2014:547, para. 78.

[517] Case C-23/14, *Post Danmark II* EU:C:2015:651, para. 28.

[518] See Section 11.F.ii.

[519] Case 322/81, *Michelin I* [1983] ECR 3461, Case C-95/04 P, *British Airways* [2007] ECR I-2331, and Case C-549/10 P, *Tomra* EU:C:2012:221.

[520] See Case C-95/04 P, *British Airways* [2007] ECR I-2331, para. 74; *Tomra* EU:C:2012:221, paras. 78–79; Guidance Paper, para. 40.

Case 322/81, *Nederlandsche Banden-Industrie Michelin v Commission* [1983] ECR 3461

Michelin supplied heavy-vehicle new replacement tyres to tyre dealers who sold both Michelin tyres and competing brands. It ran a fixed invoice discount and a cash discount for early payment, which were the same for all dealers. These were not found to infringe Article 102. Michelin also offered a discount linked to an annual sales target which was personal to each dealer. A proportion of this variable discount was paid in advance, initially every month and then every four months as an advance on the annual sum. The full sum became payable only if the dealer attained a pre-determined sales target. The target was fixed for each dealer by a Michelin sales representative at the beginning of each year. The discount was basically geared to turnover and to the proportion of Michelin tyres sold and the aim was to ensure that the dealer sold more Michelin tyres than he had in the year before although if times were hard it might be sufficient to equal the previous year. Towards the end of each sales year Michelin's sales representative would urge the dealer to place an order big enough to obtain the full discount. The Commission held that the scheme infringed Article 102. This finding was upheld by the Court of Justice.

Court of Justice

70. As regards the application of Article [102] to a system of discounts conditional upon the attainment of sales targets, such as described above, it must be stated first of all that in prohibiting any abuse of a dominant position on the market in so far as it may affect trade between Member States Article [102] covers practices which are likely to affect the structure of a market where, as a direct result of the presence of the undertaking in question, competition has already been weakened and which, through recourse to methods different from those governing normal competition in products or services based on traders performance, have the effect of hindering the maintenance or development of the level of competition still existing on the market.

71. In the case more particularly of the grant by an undertaking in a dominant position of discounts to its customers the court has held in its judgments of 16 December 1975 in Joined Cases 40 to 48, 50, 54, to 56, 111, 113 and 114/73 *Cooperatieve Vereniging 'Suiker Unie' UA and others* v. *Commission* . . . and . . . in Case 85/76 *Hoffmann-La Roche* v. *Commission* . . . that in contrast to a quantity discount, which is linked solely to the volume of purchases from the manufacturer concerned, a loyalty rebate, which by offering customers financial advantages tends to prevent them from obtaining their supplies from competing manufacturers, amounts to an abuse within the meaning of Article [102].

72. As regards the system at issue in this case, which is characterized by the use of sales targets, it must be observed that this system does not amount to a mere quantity discount linked solely to the volume of goods purchased since the progressive scale of the previous year's turnover indicates only the limits within which the system applies. Michelin NV has moreover itself pointed out that the majority of dealers who bought more than 3 000 tyres a year were in any case in the group receiving the highest rebates. On the other hand the system in question did not require dealers to enter into any exclusive dealing agreements or to obtain a specific proportion of their supplies from Michelin NV, and that this point distinguishes it from loyalty rebates of the type which the court had to consider in its judgment of 13 February 1979 in *Hoffmann-La Roche*.

73. In deciding whether Michelin NV abused its dominant position in applying its discount system it is therefore necessary to consider all the circumstances, particularly the criteria and rules for the grant of the discount, and to investigate whether, in providing an advantage not based on any economic service justifying it, the discount tends to remove or restrict the buyer's freedom to choose his sources of supply, to bar competitors from access to the market, to apply dissimilar conditions to equivalent transactions with other trading parties or to strengthen the dominant position by distorting competition.

74. It is in the light of those considerations that the submissions put forward by the applicant in answer to the two objections raised in the contested decision to the discounted system in general, namely that

Michelin NV bound tyre dealers in the Netherlands to itself and that it applied to them dissimilar conditions in respect of equivalent transactions, must be examined.

. . .

81. The discount system in question was based on an annual reference period. However, any system under which discounts are granted according to the quantities sold during a relatively long reference period has the inherent effect, at the end of that period, of increasing pressure on the buyer to reach the purchase figure needed to obtain the discount or to avoid suffering the expected loss for the entire period. In this case the variations in the rate of discount over a year as a result of one last order, even a small one, affected the dealer's margin of profit on the whole year's sales of Michelin heavy-vehicle tyres. In such circumstances, even quite slight variations might put dealers under appreciable pressure.

82. That effect was accentuated still further by the wide divergence between Michelin NV's market share and those of its main competitors. If a competitor wished to offer a dealer a competitive inducement for placing an order, especially at the end of the year, it had to take into account the absolute value of Michelin NV's annual target discount and fix its own discount at a percentage which, when related to the dealer's lesser quantity of purchases from that competitor, was very high. Despite the apparently low percentage of Michelin NV's discount, it was therefore very difficult for its competitors to offset the benefits or losses resulting for dealers from attaining or failing to attain Michelin NV's targets, as the case might be.

83. Furthermore, the lack of transparency of Michelin NV's entire discount system, whose rules moreover changed on several occasions during the relevant period, together with the fact that neither the scale of discounts nor the sales targets or discounts relating to them were communicated in writing to dealers meant that they were left in uncertainty and on the whole could not predict with any confidence the effect of attaining their targets or failing to do so.

84. All those factors were instrumental in creating for dealers a situation in which they were under considerable pressure, especially towards the end of a year, to attain Michelin NV's sales targets if they did not wish to run the risk of losses which its competitors could not easily make good by means of the discounts which they themselves were able to offer. Its network of commercial representatives enabled Michelin NV to remind dealers of this situation at any time so as to induce them to place orders with it.

85. Such a situation is calculated to prevent dealers from being able to select freely at any time in the light of the market situation the most favourable of the offers made by the various competitors and to change supplier without suffering any appreciable economic disadvantage. It thus limits the dealers' choice of supplier and makes access to the market more difficult for competitors. Neither the wish to sell more nor the wish to spread production more evenly can justify such a restriction of the customer's freedom of choice and independence. The position of dependence in which dealers find themselves and which is created by the discount system in question, is not therefore based on any countervailing advantage which may be economically justified.

86. It must therefore be concluded that by binding dealers in the Netherlands to itself by means of the discount system described above Michelin NV committed an abuse, within the meaning of Article [102], of its dominant position in the market for new replacement tyres for heavy vehicles. The submission put forward by the applicant to refute that finding in the contested decision must therefore be rejected.

In paragraph 73 the CJ said that it is necessary to consider 'all the circumstances' in judging whether the discount *tends to* remove the buyers' freedom to choose or bar competitors from the market. The circumstances it considered were the features and rules of the scheme, rather than any demonstrable effects on the market. The particular objections to the scheme were that it required the customer to purchase more than in the preceding period; it set a different target for each customer based on exceeding the previous purchases (i.e. it was individualised); it had a long reference period (a year); it was retroactive; it was not transparent so that dealers were left in a state of uncertainty; and the design and operation of the scheme put heavy pressure on the dealers.[521] On this basis it could be argued that a more transparent scheme, with a short reference period and variations which exerted less pressure at the end of the period, would be less likely to infringe Article 102. However, in *Irish Sugar* the GC upheld a decision[522] unequivocally condemning rebate schemes which are conditional on the customer buying more than in a previous period:

the Commission has not committed an error of assessment in taking the view that a rebate granted by an undertaking in a dominant position by reference to an increase in purchases made over a certain period, without that rebate being capable of being regarded as a normal quantity discount (point 153), as the applicant does not deny, constitutes an abuse of that dominant position, since such a practice can only be intended to tie the customers to which it is granted and place competitors in an unfavourable competitive position.[523]

Target rebates are seen as loyalty-inducing in that they put pressure on the customer to stay with the supplier in order to ensure that the rebate at the end of the reference period is obtained. Nevertheless, in *Coca-Cola*[524] the Commission settled proceedings against Coca-Cola by accepting individually set targets of less than three months because the Commission considered that the scheme did not substantially impede the customers from switching suppliers.[525]

b. *Michelin II*

In *Michelin II*[526] Michelin operated a wide range of pricing schemes in respect of the supply of replacement tyres for heavy vehicles in France. The schemes were complex. The forms of discounts, rebates, and payments in respect of which Michelin appealed from the prohibition decision[527] were primarily quantity rebates based on standardised volume targets (*rappels quantitatifs*); a 'service bonus' scheme; and arrangements known as the 'Michelin Friends Club'.

The quantity rebates were given according to a grid. Rebates were a percentage of the tyre dealers' annual turnover and increased with the volumes purchased during the reference period (a year) but the target volumes were not based on estimates of each dealer's purchase requirements. The grid had a large number of 'steps'. When a dealer went up a step by hitting a particular target the extra discount was 'rolled back'. *Michelin II* was the first time that the Commission had made a decision on a *standardised* target scheme. The Commission held that it infringed Article 102.

The Commission also objected to the 'service bonus' whereby the dealer earned 'points' for compliance with various commitments entered into with Michelin. The operation of the scheme left considerable discretion to Michelin. The Commission said the service bonus scheme was unfair, loyalty-inducing, and (in some parts) equivalent to tied sales.

The 'Michelin Friends Club' was an arrangement by which, in return for additional payments, larger dealers could enter into a closer relationship with Michelin thus maintaining the dealer's 'température Michelin'. The Commission found the Club terms to be abusive as they were loyalty-inducing and left the dealers completely dependent on Michelin.[528]

---

[521] See in particular para. 81.

[522] *Irish Sugar* [1997] OJ L258/1.

[523] Case T-228/97, *Irish Sugar plc* [1999] ECR II-2969, para. 213; *aff'd* on appeal, Case C-497/99 P, *Irish Sugar plc v Commission* [2001] ECR I-5333. The Commission decision (para. 150) found that the lack of transparency in Irish Sugar's rebate scheme was in itself an abuse.

[524] Commission, *XIXth Report on Competition Policy* (1989), para. 50.

[525] The Commission's clearance in 1997 of the *Coca-Cola/Amalgamated Beverages* merger [1997] OJ L218/15 was on the basis that Coca-Cola undertook to adopt the 1989 undertakings (para. 212 of the decision).

[526] Case T-203/01, *Michelin II* [2003] ECR II-4071.

[527] [2002] OJ L143/1.

[528] 'Certainly the members of the Club all shared the feeling that there could be no turning back . . . The commitment they had all entered into could fairly be described as a lifetime one', Case T-203/01 P, *Michelin II* [2003] ECR II-4071, para. 326.

On appeal the GC upheld the Commission's decision in its entirety.[529] Paragraphs 54 and 55 of the judgment rehearsed again the definition of abuse from *Hoffmann-La Roche*, and the special responsibility of dominant undertakings laid down in *Michelin I*. It then continued as set out in the following extract. The judgment was the first time the EU Courts employed the concept of 'loyalty-inducing', which the Commission had used in its decision. As in *Michelin I*, the exclusionary effect was linked to the removal or restriction of the buyer's freedom to choose sources of supply (paragraph 60).

Case T-203/01, *Manufacture Française Des Pneumatiques Michelin v Commission* [2003] ECR II-4071

General Court

56. With more particular regard to the granting of rebates by an undertaking in a dominant position, it is apparent from a consistent line of decisions that a loyalty rebate, which is granted in return for an undertaking by the customer to obtain his stock exclusively or almost exclusively from an undertaking in a dominant position, is contrary to Article [102]. Such a rebate is designed through the grant of financial advantage, to prevent customers from obtaining their supplies from competing producers (Joined Cases 40/73 to 48/73, 50/73, 54/73 to 56/73, 111/73, 113/73 and 114/73 *Suiker Unie and Others* v. *Commission* . . . paragraph 518; *Hoffmann-La Roche* v. *Commission* . . . paragraphs 89 and 90; *Michelin* v. *Commission* . . . paragraph 71; and Case T-65/89 *BPB Industries and British Gypsum* v. *Commission* . . . paragraph 120).

57. More generally, as the applicant submits, a rebate system which has a foreclosure effect on the market will be regarded as contrary to Article [102] if it is applied by an undertaking in a dominant position. For that reason, the Court has held that a rebate which depended on a purchasing target being achieved also infringed Article [102] (*Michelin* v. *Commission* . . .).

58. Quantity rebate systems linked solely to the volume of purchases made from an undertaking occupying a dominant position are generally considered not to have the foreclosure effect prohibited by Article [102] (see *Michelin* v. *Commission* . . . paragraph 71, and Case C-163/99 *Portugal* v. *Commission* . . . paragraph 50). If increasing the quantity supplied results in lower costs for the supplier, the latter is entitled to pass on that reduction to the customer in the form of a more favourable tariff (Opinion of Advocate General Mischo in *Portugal* v. *Commission* . . . at point 106). Quantity rebates are therefore deemed to reflect gains in efficiency and economies of scale made by the undertaking in a dominant position.

59. It follows that a rebate system in which the rate of the discount increases according to the volume purchased will not infringe Article [102] unless the criteria and rules for granting the rebate reveal that the system is not based on an economically justified countervailing advantage but tends, following the example of a loyalty and target rebate, to prevent customers from obtaining their supplies from competitors (see *Hoffmann-La Roche* v. *Commission*, cited at paragraph 54 above, paragraph 90; *Michelin* v. *Commission* . . . paragraph 85; *Irish Sugar* v. *Commission* . . . paragraph 114; and *Portugal* v. *Commission* . . . paragraph 52).

60. In determining whether a quantity rebate system is abusive, it will therefore be necessary to consider all the circumstances, particularly the criteria and rules governing the grant of the rebate, and to investigate whether, in providing an advantage not based on any economic service justifying it, the rebates tend to remove or restrict the buyer's freedom to choose his sources of supply, to bar competitors from access to the market, to apply dissimilar conditions to equivalent transactions with other trading parties or to strengthen the dominant position by distorting competition (see *Hoffmann-La Roche* v. *Commission* . . . paragraph 90; *Michelin* v. *Commission* . . . paragraph 73; and *Irish Sugar* v. *Commission* . . . paragraph 114).

. . .

---

[529] Despite finding that the Commission was wrong to suggest that the CJ in *Michelin I* had expressly held that a reference period could not exceed three months, *Michelin II*, para. 85, referring to para. 216 of the decision.

62. . . . [T]he Court points out that the mere fact of characterising a discount system as quantity rebates does not mean that the grant of such discounts is compatible with Article [102]. It is necessary to consider all the circumstances, particularly the criteria and rules governing the grant of the discounts, and to investigate whether, in providing an advantage not based on any economic service justifying it, the quantity rebates tend to remove or restrict the buyer's freedom to choose his sources of supply, to bar competitors from access to the market, to apply dissimilar conditions to equivalent transactions with other trading parties or to strengthen the dominant position by distorting competition (see the case-law cited at paragraph 60 above).

. . .

64. It is apparent from the contested decision that the Commission considers that the quantity rebate system applied by the applicant constitutes an infringement of Article [102] because it is unfair, it is loyalty-inducing and it has a partitioning effect . . .

65. However, it may be inferred generally from the case-law that any loyalty-inducing rebate system applied by an undertaking in a dominant position has foreclosure effects prohibited by Article [102] (see paragraphs 56 to 60 above), irrespective of whether or not the rebate system is discriminatory. In *Michelin v. Commission* . . . the Court, when considering the lawfulness of Commission Decision 81/969/ EEC of 7 October 1981 . . . (. . . *Bandengroothandel Frieschebrug BV/NV Nederlandsche Banden-Industrie Michelin*) . . ., the NBIM Decision), did not uphold the Commission's claim that the rebate system applied by Michelin was discriminatory but nevertheless held that it infringed Article [102] because it placed dealers in a position of dependence in relation to Michelin.

66. This Court considers that it is necessary, first, to consider whether the Commission had good reason to conclude, in the contested decision, that the quantity rebate system was loyalty-inducing or, in other words, that it sought to tie dealers to the applicant and to prevent them from obtaining supplies from the applicant's competitors. As the Commission acknowledges in its defence, moreover, the alleged unfairness of the system was closely linked to its loyalty-inducing effect. Furthermore, it must be held that a loyalty-inducing rebate system is, by its very nature, also partitioning, since it is designed to prevent the customer from obtaining supplies from other manufacturers.

. . .

95. It follows from all of the foregoing that a quantity rebate system in which there is a significant variation in the discount rates between the lower and higher steps, which has a reference period of one year and in which the discount is fixed on the basis of total turnover achieved during the reference period, has the characteristics of a loyalty-inducing discount system.

96. Admittedly, as the applicant points out, the aim of any competition on price and any discount system is to encourage the customer to purchase more from the same supplier.

97. However, an undertaking in a dominant position has a special responsibility not to allow its conduct to impair genuine undistorted competition on the common market (*Michelin v. Commission* . . . paragraph 57). Not all competition on price can be regarded as legitimate (*AKZO v. Commission* . . . paragraph 70, and *Irish Sugar v. Commission* . . . paragraph 111). An undertaking in a dominant position cannot have recourse to means other than those within the scope of competition on the merits (*Irish Sugar v. Commission* . . . paragraph 111).

98. In those circumstances, it is necessary to consider whether, in spite of appearances, the quantity rebate system applied by the applicant is based on a countervailing advantage which may be economically justified (see, in that regard, *Michelin v. Commission* . . . paragraph 73; *Irish Sugar v. Commission* paragraph 114; and *Portugal v. Commission* . . . paragraph 52) or, in other words, if it rewards an economy of scale made by the applicant because of orders for large quantities. If increasing the quantity supplied results in lower costs for the supplier, the latter is entitled to pass on that reduction to the customer in the form of a more favourable tariff (Opinion of Advocate General Mischo in *Portugal v. Commission* . . . point 106).

. . .

100. It must be borne in mind that, according to settled case-law, discounts granted by an undertaking in a dominant position must be based on a countervailing advantage which may be economically justified (*Michelin* v. *Commission* . . . paragraph 85; *Irish Sugar* v. *Commission* . . . paragraph 114; and *Portugal* v. *Commission* . . . paragraph 52). A quantity rebate system is therefore compatible with Article [102] if the advantage conferred on dealers is justified by the volume of business they bring or by any economies of scale they allow the supplier to make (*Portugal* v. *Commission*, paragraph 52).

. . .

107. It is then necessary to examine whether the applicant has established that the quantity rebate system, which presents the characteristics of a loyalty-inducing rebate system, was based on objective economic reasons (see, in that regard, *Irish Sugar* v. *Commission* . . . paragraph 188, and *Portugal* v. *Commission* . . . paragraph 56).

108. It must be stated that the applicant provides no specific information in that regard. It merely states that orders for large amounts involve economies and that the customer is entitled to have those economies passed on to him in the price that he pays (point 57 of the application). It also refers to its reply to the statement of objections and to the transcript of the hearing (reply, point 91). Far from establishing that the quantity rebates were based on actual cost savings (Opinion of Advocate General Mischo in *Portugal* v. *Commission* . . . point 118), the applicant merely states generally that the quantity rebates were justified by economies of scale in the areas of production costs and distribution (transcript of the hearing, p. 62).

109. However, such a line of argument is too general and is insufficient to provide economic reasons to explain specifically the discount rates chosen for the various steps in the rebate system in question (see, in that regard, *Portugal* v. *Commission* . . . paragraph 56).

110. It follows from all of the foregoing that the Commission was entitled to conclude, in the contested decision, that the quantity rebate system at issue was designed to tie truck tyre dealers in France to the applicant by granting advantages which were not based on any economic justification. Because it was loyalty-inducing, the quantity rebate system tended to prevent dealers from being able to select freely at any time, in the light of the market situation, the most advantageous of the offers made by various competitors and to change supplier without suffering any appreciable economic disadvantage. The rebate system thus limited the dealers' choice of supplier and made access to the market more difficult for competitors, while the position of dependence in which the dealers found themselves, and which was created by the discount system in question, was not therefore based on any countervailing advantage which might be economically justified (see *Michelin* v. *Commission* . . . paragraph 85).

111. The applicant cannot find support in the transparent nature of the quantity rebate system. A loyalty-inducing rebate system is contrary to Article [102], whether it is transparent or not. Furthermore, the quantity rebates formed part of a complex system of discounts, some of which on the applicant's own admission constituted an abuse . . . The simultaneous application of various discount systems—namely, the quantity rebates, the service bonus, the progress bonus, and the bonuses linked to the PRO Agreement and the Michelin Friends Club—which were not obtained on invoice, made it impossible for the dealer to calculate the exact purchase price of Michelin tyres at the time of purchase. That situation inevitably put dealers in a position of uncertainty and dependence on the applicant.

. . .

113. It follows from the foregoing that the Commission was correct to find that the quantity rebate system applied by the applicant infringed Article [102], *inter alia*, because it was loyalty-inducing.

. . .

140. The granting of a discount by an undertaking in a dominant position to a dealer must be based on an objective economic justification (*Irish Sugar* v. *Commission* . . . paragraph 218). It cannot depend on a subjective assessment by the undertaking in a dominant position of the extent to which the dealer has met his commitments and is thus entitled to a discount. As the Commission points out in the contested decision (recital 251), such an assessment of the extent to which the dealer has met his commitments enables the undertaking in a dominant position to put strong pressure on the dealer . . . and allow[s] it, if necessary, to use the arrangement in a discriminatory manner.

141. It follows that a discount system which is applied by an undertaking in a dominant position and which leaves that undertaking a considerable margin of discretion as to whether the dealer may obtain the discount must be considered unfair and constitutes an abuse by an undertaking of its dominant position on the market within the meaning of Article [102] (see, in that regard, *Hoffmann-La Roche* v. *Commission* . . . paragraph 105). Because of the subjective assessment of the criteria giving entitlement to the service bonus, dealers were left in uncertainty and on the whole could not predict with any confidence the rate of discount which they would receive by way of service bonus (see, in that regard, *Michelin* v. *Commission* . . . paragraph 83).

. . .

237. The Court points out that Article [102] prohibits, in so far as it may affect trade between Member States, any abuse of a dominant position within the common market or in a substantial part thereof. Unlike Article [101(1)], Article [102] contains no reference to the anti-competitive aim or anti-competitive effect of the practice referred to. However, in the light of the context of Article [101], conduct will be regarded as abusive only if it restricts competition.

238. In support of its argument, the applicant refers to the consistent line of decisions which show that an abuse is an objective concept referring to the behaviour of an undertaking in a dominant position which is such as to influence the structure of a market where, as a result of the very presence of the undertaking in question, the degree of competition is already weakened and which, through recourse to methods different from those governing normal competition in products or services on the basis of the transactions of commercial operators, has the *effect* of hindering the maintenance of the degree of competition still existing in the market or the growth of that competition (*Hoffmann-La Roche* v. *Commission* . . . paragraph 91; *Michelin* v. *Commission* . . . paragraph 70; *AKZO* v. *Commission* . . . paragraph 69; and *Irish Sugar* v. *Commission* . . . paragraph 111; emphasis added).

239. The effect referred to in the case-law cited in the preceding paragraph does not necessarily relate to the actual effect of the abusive conduct complained of. For the purposes of establishing an infringement of Article [102], it is sufficient to show that the abusive conduct of the undertaking in a dominant position tends to restrict competition or, in other words, that the conduct is capable of having that effect.

240. Thus, in *Michelin* v *Commission* (cited at paragraph 54 above), the Court of Justice, after referring to the principle reproduced at paragraph 238 above, stated that it is necessary to consider all the circumstances, particularly the criteria and rules for the grant of the discount, and to investigate whether, in providing an advantage not based on any economic service justifying it, the discount tends to remove or restrict the buyer's freedom to choose his sources of supply, to bar competitors from access to the market, to apply dissimilar conditions to equivalent transactions with other trading parties or to strengthen the dominant position by distorting competition (paragraph 73). It concluded that Michelin had infringed Article [102], since its discount system [was] calculated to prevent dealers from being able to select freely at any time in the light of the market situation the most favourable of the offers made by the various competitors and to change supplier without suffering any appreciable economic disadvantage (paragraph 85).

241. It follows that, for the purposes of applying Article [102], establishing the anti-competitive object and the anti-competitive effect are one and the same thing (see, in that regard, *Irish Sugar* v *Commission*, cited at paragraph 54 above, paragraph 170). If it is shown that the object pursued by the conduct of an undertaking in a dominant position is to limit competition, that conduct will also be liable to have such an effect.

The judgment firmly linked the legality of quantity rebates to efficiencies. At paragraph 58 the GC stated that quantity rebates are 'deemed' to lower suppliers' costs, and in paragraph 59 that quantity rebates are not an abuse unless the system is not based on an economically justified countervailing advantage. Michelin, however, did not establish what exactly were the costs savings (paragraphs 108–109) and the Commission was entitled to find it loyalty-inducing (paragraph 110) and therefore not prima facie lawful.

According to the GC, in respect to loyalty-inducing rebates the 'effect' of hindering the maintenance of the degree of competition still existing on the market, referred to in the definition of the abuse concept in *Hoffmann-La Roche* and *Michelin I*,[530] need not relate to an *actual* effect (*Michelin II*, paragraph 239). It is sufficient to show that the conduct *tends* to restrict competition, i.e. that the conduct is *capable* of having that effect. Moreover, anti-competitive object and anti-competitive effect are the same thing for the purposes of Article 102 (paragraph 241).

Michelin II was not appealed to the CJ.

c. British Airways

In *Virgin/British Airways*[531] the Commission found British Airways (BA) to be in a dominant position as a buyer in the market for air travel agency services and fined it €6.8 million for offering travel agents commission schemes which included extra payments in return for meeting or exceeding their previous year's sales of BA tickets. The commission was retroactive. This meant that 'when a travel agent is close to one of the thresholds for an increase in commission rate selling relatively few extra BA tickets can have a large effect on his commission income. Conversely a competitor of BA who wishes to give a travel agent an incentive to divert some sales from BA to the competing airline will have to pay a much higher rate of commission than BA on all of the tickets sold by it to overcome this effect'.[532] The Commission held that the schemes were exclusionary. It said that the fact that BA's competitors had nevertheless been able to gain market share from BA could not indicate that the schemes had had no effect as 'it can only be assumed that competitors would have had more success in the absence of these abusive commission schemes'.[533] The decision also condemned the schemes for being discriminatory, contrary to Article 102(c), in that the different levels of commission the travel agents received distorted competition between them.[534]

The GC upheld the decision.[535] In the part of the judgment concerning the exclusionary effect on competitors the GC followed *Michelin II* very closely.[536] The GC agreed with the Commission that concrete effects on the market did not have to be proved and that it was sufficient to demonstrate that the conduct *tends* to restrict competition, i.e. that it is *capable* of having such an effect.[537] The GC was satisfied that the BA scheme had this capability, in particular because of its 'very noticeable effect at the margin'[538] and the inability of the competitors to make competitive counter-offers to the agents.[539] The GC agreed with the Commission that the fact that the market shares of some of BA's competitors had actually increased during the relevant period did not disprove the exclusionary effect of the commission payments.[540] Furthermore, it stated that Article 102 is aimed at the protection of the competitive structure and so dismissed the argument that there was no proof of consumer harm.[541] However, the GC was prepared to accept that the rebates could be objectively justified if it could be determined that the schemes were based on 'economically justified

---

[530] At paras. 91 and 70 respectively. See Section 3.D.i, p. 356.

[531] COMP/34.780, [2000] OJ L30/1. The decision, which resulted from a complaint from rival airline Virgin about the incentives which British Airways (BA) gave travel agents to push its tickets to their customers, predated the *Michelin II* decision but the GC judgment in the *British Airways* appeal was delivered after the *Michelin II* judgment.

[532] COMP/34.780, *Virgin/BA* [2000] OJ L30/1, para. 29.

[533] Ibid., para. 107.

[534] Ibid., paras. 108–111, see further Section 15.B.

[535] Case T-219/99, *British Airways* [2003] ECR II-5917.

[536] In particular, paras. 241–247 are almost identical to paras. 54–59 of *Michelin II*.

[537] Case T-219/99, *British Airways* [2003] ECR II-5917, para. 293.

[538] Ibid., para. 272.

[539] Ibid., para. 276.

[540] Ibid., para. 298. The GC cited its own judgment in Cases T-24–26 and 28/93, *Compagnie Maritime Belge Transports and Others v Commission* [1996] ECR II-1201, para. 149 for this approach.

[541] Case T-219/99, *British Airways* [2003] ECR II-5917, para. 311.

considerations'.[542] In this case it found that they were not, dismissing arguments about the relevance of the high fixed costs in the air transport industry.[543]

BA appealed. In the intervening three years there had been an ever more intensive debate about the correct approach to rebates, and a general consensus had emerged that the law needed to be realigned towards a concern with effects on consumers rather than with presumptions about tendencies and capabilities.[544] Furthermore, the Commission had set out an innovative way of assessing the exclusionary effects of rebates in the 2005 Staff Discussion Paper.[545] Nevertheless, the *British Airways* judgment was upheld by the CJ.

Case C-95/04 P, *British Airways v Commission* [2007] ECR I-2331

BA's first plea was that Article 102(b) required limiting production, markets, or technical development *to the prejudice of consumers* and that the GC should therefore have verified whether BA had actually limited the markets of rival airlines and whether a prejudice to consumers had resulted.

Court of Justice

57. Concerning, first, the plea that the [General Court] wrongly failed to base its argument on the criteria in subparagraph (b) of the second paragraph of Article [102] in assessing whether the bonus schemes at issue were abusive, the list of abusive practices contained in Article [102] is not exhaustive, so that the practices there mentioned are merely examples of abuses of a dominant position (see, to that effect, Case C-333/94 P *Tetra Pak* v *Commission* . . . paragraph 37). According to consistent case-law, the list of abusive practices contained in that provision does not exhaust the methods of abusing a dominant position prohibited by the EC Treaty (Case 6/72 *Europemballage and Continental Can* v *Commission* . . . paragraph 26; Joined Cases C-395/96 P and C-396/96 P *Compagnie maritime belge transports a.o.* v *Commission* . . . paragraph 112).

58. It follows that discounts and bonuses granted by undertakings in a dominant position may be contrary to Article [102] even where they do not correspond to any of the examples mentioned in the second paragraph of that article. Thus, in determining that fidelity discounts had an exclusionary effect, the Court based its argument in *Hoffmann-La Roche* and *Michelin* on Article [102] . . . in its entirety, and not just on subparagraph (b) of its second paragraph. Moreover, in its judgment in Joined Cases 40/73 to 48/73, 50/73, 54/73 to 56/73, 111/73, 113/73 and 114/73 *Suiker Unie and Others* v *Commission* . . . paragraph 523, concerning fidelity rebates, the Court expressly referred to subparagraph (c) of the second paragraph of Article [102], according to which practices constituting abuse of a dominant position may consist, for example, in applying dissimilar conditions to equivalent transactions with other trading parties, thereby placing them at a competitive disadvantage.

59. The plea that the [General Court] erred in law by not basing its argument on the criteria in subparagraph (b) of the second paragraph of Article [102] is therefore unfounded.

---

[542] Ibid., para. 271.

[543] Ibid., paras. 284–285.

[544] For the arguments for a new approach to rebates see, e.g., B. Sher, 'Price Discounts and *Michelin II*; What Goes Around, Comes Around' [2002] *ECLR* 482; Temple Lang and O'Donoghue, n. 176, 83; J. Kallaugher and B. Sher, 'Rebates Revisited: Anti-competitive Effects and Exclusionary Abuse under Article 102' [2004] *ECLR* 263; D. Spector, 'Loyalty Rebates: An Assessment of Competition Concerns and a Proposed Structured Rule of Reason' (2005) 1 *Competition Policy International* 89; C. Ahlborn and D. Bailey, 'Discounts, Rebates and Selective Pricing by Dominant Firms' (2006) 2 *European Competition Journal* 101. For a defence of the more traditional position, see Gyselen, n. 32, 287. See also J. Temple Lang, 'How Can the Problems of Exclusionary Abuses under Article 102 TFEU be Resolved?' (2012) 37 *ELRev* 136.

[545] DG Comp Discussion Paper on the application of Article 82 of the Treaty to exclusionary abuses, paras. 151–176, see Chap. 5, Section 6.B.

60. Nor does it appear that the Court's assessment of the exclusionary effect of the bonus schemes in question was based on a misapplication of the case-law of the Court of Justice.

61. In the *Hoffmann-La Roche* and *Michelin* judgments, the Court of Justice found that certain discounts granted by two undertakings in a dominant position were abusive in character.

62. The first of those two judgments concerned discounts granted to undertakings whose business was the production or sale of vitamins, and the grant of which was, for most of the time, expressly linked to the condition that the co-contractor obtained its supplies over a given period entirely or mainly from Hoffmann-La Roche. The Court found such a discount system an abuse of a dominant position and stated that the granting of fidelity discounts in order to give the buyer an incentive to obtain its supplies exclusively from the undertaking in a dominant position was incompatible with the objective of undistorted competition within the common market (*Hoffmann-La Roche*, paragraph 90).

63. In *Michelin*, unlike in *Hoffmann-La Roche*, Michelin's co-contractors were not obliged to obtain their supplies wholly or partially from Michelin. However, the variable annual discounts granted by that undertaking were linked to objectives in the sense that, in order to benefit from them, its co-contractors had to attain individualised sales results. In that case, the Court found a series of factors which led it to regard the discount system in question as an abuse of a dominant position. In particular, the system was based on a relatively long reference period, namely a year, its functioning was non-transparent for co-contractors, and the differences in market share between Michelin and its main competitors were significant (see, to that effect, *Michelin*, paragraphs 81 to 83).

64. Contrary to BA's argument, it cannot be inferred from those two judgments that bonuses and discounts granted by undertakings in a dominant position are abusive only in the circumstances there described. As the Advocate General has stated in point 41 of her Opinion, the decisive factor is rather the underlying factors which have guided the previous case-law of the Court of Justice and which can also be transposed to a case such as the present.

65. In that respect, *Michelin* is particularly relevant to the present case, since it concerns a discount system depending on the attainment of individual sales objectives which constituted neither discounts for quantity, linked exclusively to the volume of purchases, nor fidelity discounts within the meaning of the judgment in *Hoffmann-La Roche*, since the system established by Michelin did not contain any obligation on the part of resellers to obtain all or a given proportion of its supplies from the dominant undertaking.

66. Concerning the application of Article [102] to a system of discounts dependent on sales objectives, paragraph 70 of the *Michelin* judgment shows that, in prohibiting the abuse of a dominant market position in so far as trade between Member States is capable of being affected, that article refers to conduct which is such as to influence the structure of a market where, as a result of the very presence of the undertaking in question, the degree of competition is already weakened and which, through recourse to methods different from those governing normal competition in products or services on the basis of the transactions of commercial operators, has the effect of hindering the maintenance of the degree of competition still existing in the market or the growth of that competition.

67. In order to determine whether the undertaking in a dominant position has abused such a position by applying a system of discounts such as that described in paragraph 65 of this judgment, the Court has held that it is necessary to consider all the circumstances, particularly the criteria and rules governing the grant of the discount, and to investigate whether, in providing an advantage not based on any economic service justifying it, the discount tends to remove or restrict the buyer's freedom to choose his sources of supply, to bar competitors from access to the market, to apply dissimilar conditions to equivalent transactions with other trading parties or to strengthen the dominant position by distorting competition (*Michelin*, paragraph 73).

68. It follows that in determining whether, on the part of an undertaking in a dominant position, a system of discounts or bonuses which constitute neither quantity discounts or bonuses nor fidelity discounts or bonuses within the meaning of the judgment in *Hoffmann-La Roche* constitutes an abuse, it first has to be determined whether those discounts or bonuses can produce an exclusionary effect, that is to say whether they are capable, first, of making market entry very difficult or impossible for competitors

of the undertaking in a dominant position and, secondly, of making it more difficult or impossible for its co-contractors to choose between various sources of supply or commercial partners.

69. It then needs to be examined whether there is an objective economic justification for the discounts and bonuses granted. In accordance with the analysis carried out by the [General Court] in paragraphs 279 to 291 of the judgment under appeal, an undertaking is at liberty to demonstrate that its bonus system producing an exclusionary effect is economically justified.

70. With regard to the first aspect, the case-law gives indications as to the cases in which discount or bonus schemes of an undertaking in a dominant position are not merely the expression of a particularly favourable offer on the market, but give rise to an exclusionary effect.

71. First, an exclusionary effect may arise from goal-related discounts or bonuses, that is to say those the granting of which is linked to the attainment of sales objectives defined individually (*Michelin*, paragraphs 70 to 86).

72. It is clear from the findings of the [General Court] in paragraphs 10 and 15 to 17 of the judgment under appeal that the bonus schemes at issue were drawn up by reference to individual sales objectives, since the rate of the bonuses depended on the evolution of the turnover arising from BA ticket sales by each travel agent during a given period.

73. It is also apparent from the case-law that the commitment of co-contractors towards the undertaking in a dominant position and the pressure exerted upon them may be particularly strong where a discount or bonus does not relate solely to the growth in turnover in relation to purchases or sales of products of that undertaking made by those co-contractors during the period under consideration, but extends also to the whole of the turnover relating to those purchases or sales. In that way, relatively modest variations—whether upwards or downwards—in the turnover figures relating to the products of the dominant undertaking have disproportionate effects on co-contractors (see, to that effect, *Michelin*, paragraph 81).

74. The [General Court] found that the bonus schemes at issue gave rise to a similar situation. Attainment of the sales progression objectives gave rise to an increase in the commission paid on all BA tickets sold by the travel agent concerned, and not just on those sold after those objectives had been attained (paragraph 23 of the judgment under appeal). It could therefore be of decisive importance for the commission income of a travel agent as a whole whether or not he sold a few extra BA tickets after achieving a certain turnover (paragraphs 29 and 30 of the grounds for the Commission's decision, reproduced in paragraph 23 of the judgment under appeal). The [General Court], which describes that characteristic and its consequences in paragraphs 272 and 273 of the judgment under appeal, states that the progressive nature of the increased commission rates had a 'very noticeable effect at the margin' and emphasises the radical effects which a small reduction in sales of BA tickets could have on the rates of performance-related bonus.

75. Finally, the Court took the view that the pressure exerted on resellers by an undertaking in a dominant position which granted bonuses with those characteristics is further strengthened where that undertaking holds a very much larger market share than its competitors (see, to that effect, *Michelin*, paragraph 82). It held that, in those circumstances, it is particularly difficult for competitors of that undertaking to outbid it in the face of discounts or bonuses based on overall sales volume. By reason of its significantly higher market share, the undertaking in a dominant position generally constitutes an unavoidable business partner in the market. Most often, discounts or bonuses granted by such an undertaking on the basis of overall turnover largely take precedence in absolute terms, even over more generous offers of its competitors. In order to attract the co-contractors of the undertaking in a dominant position, or to receive a sufficient volume of orders from them, those competitors would have to offer them significantly higher rates of discount or bonus.

76. In the present case, the [General Court] held in paragraph 277 of the judgment under appeal that BA's market share was significantly higher than that of its five main competitors in the United Kingdom. It concluded, in paragraph 278 of that judgment, that the rival airlines were not in a position to grant travel agents the same advantages as BA, since they were not capable of attaining in the United Kingdom a level

of revenue capable of constituting a sufficiently broad financial base to allow them effectively to establish a reward scheme similar to BA's (paragraph 278 of the judgment under appeal).

77. Therefore, the [General Court] was right to examine, in paragraphs 270 to 278 of the judgment under appeal, whether the bonus schemes at issue had a fidelity-building effect capable of producing an exclusionary effect.

At this point the CJ refused to review the GC's finding that the bonus scheme was capable of an exclusionary effect, in particular because of the strong effect at the margin and the competitors' inability to make competitive counter-offers, because it would not review the GC's findings of fact. It continued by examining the GC's assessment of the objective justification for the scheme.

84. Discounts or bonuses granted to its co-contractors by an undertaking in a dominant position are not necessarily an abuse and therefore prohibited by Article [102]. According to consistent case-law, only discounts or bonuses which are not based on any economic counterpart to justify them must be regarded as an abuse (see, to that effect, *Hoffmann-La Roche*, paragraph 90, and *Michelin*, paragraph 73).

85. As has been held in paragraph 69 of this judgment, the [General Court] was right, after holding that the bonus schemes at issue produced an exclusionary effect, to examine whether those schemes had an objective economic justification.

86. Assessment of the economic justification for a system of discounts or bonuses established by an undertaking in a dominant position is to be made on the basis of the whole of the circumstances of the case (see, to that effect, *Michelin*, paragraph 73). It has to be determined whether the exclusionary effect arising from such a system, which is disadvantageous for competition, may be counterbalanced, or outweighed, by advantages in terms of efficiency which also benefit the consumer. If the exclusionary effect of that system bears no relation to advantages for the market and consumers, or if it goes beyond what is necessary in order to attain those advantages, that system must be regarded as an abuse.

87. In this case, correctly basing its examination upon the criteria thus inferred from the case-law, the [General Court] examined whether there was an economic justification for the bonus schemes at issue. In paragraphs 284 and 285 of the judgment under appeal, it adopted a position in relation to the arguments submitted by BA, which concerned, in particular, the high level of fixed costs in air transport and the importance of aircraft occupancy rates. On the basis of its assessment of the circumstances of the case, the [General Court] came to the conclusion that those systems were not based on any objective economic justification.

Again, the CJ refused to review the GC's findings of fact on this issue, but just stated that the GC had not committed an error of *law*. Unfortunately this meant that BA's arguments about the fixed costs were again not reviewed.

90. The [General Court] did not therefore make any error of law in holding that the bonus schemes at issue had a fidelity-building effect, that they therefore produced an exclusionary effect, and that they were not justified from an economic standpoint.

...

96. Concerning BA's argument that the [General Court] did not examine the probable effects of the bonus schemes at issue, it is sufficient to note that, in paragraphs 272 and 273 of the judgment under appeal, the [General Court] explained the mechanism of those schemes.

97. Having emphasised the very noticeable effect at the margin, linked to the progressive nature of the increased commission rates, it described the exponential effect on those rates of an increase in the number of BA tickets sold during successive periods, and, conversely, the disproportionate reduction in those rates in the event of even a slight decrease in sales of BA tickets in comparison with the previous period.

98. On that basis, the [General Court] was able to conclude, without committing any error of law, that the bonus schemes at issue had a fidelity-building effect. It follows that BA's plea accusing the Court of not examining the probable effects of those schemes is unfounded.

99. Moreover, in paragraph 99 of its appeal, BA acknowledges that, in its judgment, the [General Court] rightly held that travel agents were given an incentive to increase their sales of BA tickets. In addition, in paragraph 113 of its appeal, it states that, if the [General Court] had examined the actual or probable impact of the bonus schemes at issue on competition between travel agents, it would have concluded that that impact was negligible.

100. It follows that BA is not seriously denying that those schemes had a fidelity-building effect on travel agents and thus tended to affect the situation of competitor airlines.

101. Concerning BA's allegations of evidence showing that no exclusionary effect arose from the bonus schemes at issue, of which evidence the [General Court] is alleged to have taken insufficient account, it is sufficient to note that this part of the second plea is inadmissible on an appeal for the reasons already set out in paragraph 78 of this judgment.

Again, the CJ rejected as inadmissible the plea that the GC had taken insufficient account of BA's evidence of the lack of exclusionary effects. It did deal with BA's plea that the GC should have examined whether BA's conduct involved a prejudice to consumers.

105. It should be noted first that, as explained in paragraphs 57 and 58 of this judgment, discounts or bonuses granted by an undertaking in a dominant position may be contrary to Article [102] even where they do not correspond to any of the examples mentioned in the second paragraph of that article.

106. Moreover, as the Court has already held in paragraph 26 of its judgment in *Europemballage and Continental Can*, Article [102] is aimed not only at practices which may cause prejudice to consumers directly, but also at those which are detrimental to them through their impact on an effective competition structure, such as is mentioned in Article 3(1)(g) EC.

107. The [General Court] was therefore entitled, without committing any error of law, not to examine whether BA's conduct had caused prejudice to consumers within the meaning of subparagraph (b) of the second paragraph of Article [102], but to examine, in paragraphs 294 and 295 of the judgment under appeal, whether the bonus schemes at issue had a restrictive effect on competition and to conclude that the existence of such an effect had been demonstrated by the Commission in the contested decision.

In this judgment the CJ confirmed that a system whereby the rebate is conditional on purchasing mainly or exclusively from the dominant undertaking is abusive, on the basis of *Hoffmann-La Roche* (paragraph 62); and that other types of discount or rebate such as that in *Michelin I* (paragraph 65) must be judged in the light of the circumstances, but in particular in the light of two criteria (paragraph 67). These are:

(a) whether the discounts or bonuses are *capable* of producing an exclusionary effect (see also paragraph 77) in that they make market entry very difficult or impossible for competitors and make it more difficult or impossible for the other party to choose other sources of supply (paragraph 68); and

(b) whether there is objective economic justification for the system (paragraph 69).

In assessing the *capability* of a scheme to cause exclusion (paragraph 73) the CJ stressed the effect of a 'roll-back' retroactive provision. It referred to the 'very noticeable effect at the margin' which the roll-back feature of the BA schemes produced. It did not require that concrete, or even actual or likely, effects should be shown. It said that the GC had explained the mechanism of the schemes, their effect at the margin, and so on (paragraph 97), and so had been able to conclude that they did have a 'fidelity-building effect'. The GC's actual assessment of whether the schemes were exclusionary was not reviewed, because of lack of jurisdiction.

The CJ's second criterion recognises that loyalty-inducing rebates could be objectively justified. Paragraph 86 describes this in terms of countervailing efficiencies which produce benefits for consumers.

The CJ rejected the plea that the GC should have examined whether the schemes infringed Article 102(b) which refers to 'prejudice to consumers' on the grounds that the list of abuses in Article 102 is not exhaustive (paragraphs 57 and 58), the decisive factor being rather the (unspecified and unexplained) 'underlying factors' which have guided the previous case law (paragraph 64),[546] and that in order to show a detrimental effect on consumers it is only necessary to conclude that there is a restrictive effect on *competition* (paragraphs 106 and 107). In paragraphs 106 and 107 the CJ rejected an effects-based approach to Article 102 and ignored any consideration of economic notions of consumer welfare or proof of consumer harm.[547] This case was a major reason for the Commission abandoning any idea of 'Guidelines' on Article 102 embodying a 'modernised' approach to Article 102 and settling instead for Guidance on 'enforcement priorities'.

d. *Tomra*

In *Tomra*[548] the Commission applied Article 102 to the exclusive dealing and rebate schemes of Tomra, a firm holding market shares of more than 80 per cent in various national markets in the supply of reverse vending machines (RVM).[549] Tomra's agreements with its supermarket customers featured exclusivity clauses, individualised quantity commitments, and retroactive rebate schemes the thresholds of which usually corresponded to the total or almost total machine requirements of its customers. The decision set out the law on rebates according to the case law of the EU Courts as already described but then went on to examine the likely and actual effects along the lines suggested in the Staff Discussion Paper.[550] In particular the Commission found that the nature of the market was such that customers would at first buy only a small number of machines from a new competitor and that these would have to be supplied at very low, or even negative, prices in order to match the effect of Tomra's rebates.[551] Tomra did not advance any arguments claiming that its exclusivity arrangements were objectively justified.[552]

Before Tomra's appeal to the GC was heard the Guidance Paper was published. Tomra argued, inter alia, along the lines of the Guidance Paper[553] (a) that in order to prove that the market was foreclosed the Commission should have determined the minimum viability threshold necessary to operate on the market and then have determined whether the part of the demand tied by

---

[546] For criticism of this statement, see Temple Lang and O'Donoghue, n. 544.

[547] For a critical analysis of the law on rebates after the CJ's *British Airways* judgment, see Rousseva, n. 269, 173–218.

[548] COMP/38.113, *Prokent/Tomra* 29 March 2006. Tomra was fined €24 million. See F. Maier-Rigaud and D. Vaigauskaite, 'Prokent/Tomra, a Textbook Case? Abuse of Dominance under Perfect Information' (2006) 2 EC *Competition Policy Newsletter*, 19.

[549] Used by supermarkets to collect empty drink containers from consumers and return the deposit to them.

[550] See Chap. 5, Section 6.B. The decision (in 2006) was adopted during the Commission's review of Art. 102, three months after the publication of the Staff Discussion Paper which contained an extensive section on assessing the foreclosure effects of rebate schemes.

[551] COMP/38.113, *Prokent/Tomra* 29 March 2006, paras. 165–166.

[552] Nor in respect of the loyalty rebates, see the GC judgment, Case T-155/06, *Tomra* [2010] ECR II-4361, para. 224.

[553] See Section 11.G, p. 471.

Tomra's practices was sufficiently large to have exclusionary effects on competitors and (b) that the Commission should have examined whether Tomra's prices were below its costs. The GC dismissed the appeal and the case went to the CJ.

The appeal to the CJ was the first case it had heard on rebates since *British Airways* five years before and the first since the Guidance Paper. Commentators saw *Tomra* as the opportunity for the CJ to reshape the law and take it in a 'modern' direction, moving away from form-based rules and presumptions and towards effects-based analysis, in particular adopting the kind of approach set out in the Guidance Paper. In the event the CJ trenchantly upheld the GC.

Case C-549/10 P, *Tomra Systems ASA v European Commission* EU:C:2012:221

Court of Justice

40. It is true that, as is stated in paragraph 239 of the judgment under appeal, the Commission did not establish a precise threshold beyond which the practices of the Tomra group would be capable of excluding its competitors from the market in question.

41. However, in paragraph 240 of the judgment under appeal, the General Court properly approved the Commission's reasoning that, by foreclosing a significant part of the market, the Tomra group had restricted entry to one or a few competitors and thus limited the intensity of competition on the market as a whole.

42. In fact, and as stated by the General Court in paragraph 241 of the judgment under appeal, the foreclosure by a dominant undertaking of a substantial part of the market cannot be justified by showing that the contestable part of the market is still sufficient to accommodate a limited number of competitors. First, the customers on the foreclosed part of the market should have the opportunity to benefit from whatever degree of competition is possible on the market and competitors should be able to compete on the merits for the entire market and not just for a part of it. Second, it is not the role of the dominant undertaking to dictate how many viable competitors will be allowed to compete for the remaining contestable portion of demand.

43. Further, the General Court stated, in paragraph 242 of the judgment under appeal, that only an analysis of the circumstances of the case, such as the analysis carried out by the Commission in the contested decision, may make it possible to establish whether the practices of an undertaking in a dominant position are capable of excluding competition. It would, however, be artificial to establish without prior analysis the portion of the tied market beyond which the practices of a dominant undertaking may have an exclusionary effect on competitors.

44. The General Court accordingly determined, following that analysis of the circumstances of this case, in paragraph 243 of the judgment under appeal, that a considerable proportion (two fifths) of total demand during the period and in the countries under consideration was foreclosed to competition.

45. That conclusion of the General Court cannot be regarded as containing any error of law.

46. As regards the appellants' argument that the Commission should have applied the 'minimum viable scale' test, suffice it to observe that, first, the General Court was correct to hold that the determination of a precise threshold of foreclosure of the market beyond which the practices at issue had to be regarded as abusive was not required for the purposes of applying Article 102 TFEU and, secondly, in the light of the findings made in paragraph 243 of the judgment under appeal, it was, in any event, in the present case, proved to the requisite legal standard that the market had been closed to competition by the practices at issue.

. . .

68. The General Court was correct to observe, in paragraph 289 of the judgment under appeal, that, for the purposes of proving an abuse of a dominant position within the meaning of Article 102 TFEU, it

is sufficient to show that the abusive conduct of the undertaking in a dominant position tends to restrict competition or that the conduct is capable of having that effect.

69. As regards rebates granted by a dominant undertaking to its customers, the Court has stated that those may infringe Article 102 TFEU, even where they do not correspond to any of the examples mentioned in the second paragraph of that Article 102 (see, to that effect, *British Airways* v *Commission*, paragraph 58 and case-law cited).

70. In the event that an undertaking in a dominant position makes use of a system of rebates, the Court has ruled that that undertaking abuses that position where, without tying the purchasers by a formal obligation, it applies, either under the terms of agreements concluded with these purchasers or unilaterally, a system of loyalty rebates, that is to say, discounts conditional on the customer's obtaining—whether the quantity of its purchases is large or small—all or most of its requirements from the undertaking in a dominant position (see Case 85/76 *Hoffman[n]-La Roche* . . . paragraph 89, and Case 322/81 *Nederlandsche Banden-Industrie-Michelin* v *Commission* . . . paragraph 71).

71. In that regard, it is necessary to consider all the circumstances, particularly the criteria and rules governing the grant of the rebate, and to investigate whether, in providing an advantage not based on any economic service justifying it, the rebates tend to remove or restrict the buyer's freedom to choose his sources of supply, to bar competitors from access to the market, or to strengthen the dominant position by distorting competition (see *Nederlandsche Banden-Industrie-Michelin* v *Commission*, paragraph 73).

72. As regards the present case, it is clear from paragraph 213 of the judgment under appeal that a rebate system must be regarded as infringing Article 102 TFEU if it tends to prevent customers of the dominant undertaking from obtaining their supplies from competing producers.

73. Contrary to what is claimed by the appellants, the invoicing of 'negative prices', in other words prices below cost prices, to customers is not a prerequisite of a finding that a retroactive rebates scheme operated by a dominant undertaking is abusive.

74. As the General Court was fully entitled to observe, in paragraph 258 of the judgment under appeal, the third part of the second and fourth pleas in law submitted at first instance was based on an incorrect premiss. The fact that the retroactive rebate schemes oblige competitors to ask negative prices from Tomra's customers benefiting from rebates cannot be regarded as one of the fundamental bases of the contested decision in showing that the retroactive rebate schemes are capable of having anti-competitive effects. Further, the General Court correctly stated, in paragraph 259 of the judgment under appeal, that a whole series of other considerations relating to the retroactive rebates operated by Tomra underpinned the contested decision as regards its conclusion that those types of practices were capable of excluding competitors in breach of Article 102 TFEU.

75. In that regard, the General Court observed, more particularly, that, according to the contested decision, in the first place, the incentive to obtain supplies exclusively or almost exclusively from Tomra was particularly strong when thresholds, such as those applied by Tomra, were combined with a system whereby the achievement of the bonus threshold or, as the case may be, a more advantageous threshold benefited all the purchases made by the customer during the reference period and not exclusively the purchasing volume exceeding the threshold concerned (paragraph 260 of the judgment under appeal). Secondly, the rebate schemes were individual to each customer and the thresholds were established on the basis of the customer's estimated requirements and/or past purchasing volumes and represented a strong incentive for buying all or almost all the equipment needed from Tomra and artificially raised the costs of switching to a different supplier, even for a small number of units (paragraphs 261 and 262 of the judgment under appeal). Third, the retroactive rebates often applied to some of the largest customers of the Tomra group with the aim of ensuring their loyalty (paragraph 263 of the judgment under appeal). Lastly, Tomra failed to show that their conduct was objectively justified or that it generated significant efficiency gains which outweighed the anti-competitive effects on consumers (paragraph 264 of the judgment under appeal).

76. Accordingly, it is apparent from all the reasoning set out in paragraphs 260 to 264 of the judgment under appeal, referred to above, that the General Court came to the conclusion that the third part of the

second and fourth pleas in law submitted at first instance was based on an incorrect premiss as regards the evidential value, in respect of whether the rebates scheme at issue was anti-competitive, of the specific characteristics of that scheme, irrespective of the precise level of prices charged.

77. The General Court took its reasoning further by stating, in paragraph 266 of the judgment under appeal, that the Commission, in the contested decision, first, did not state that the rebate schemes automatically resulted in negative prices and, second, did not maintain that showing that is a prerequisite to finding those rebate schemes to be abusive.

78. The General Court added, in that regard, in paragraph 267 of the judgment under appeal, that the exclusionary mechanism represented by retroactive rebates does not require the dominant undertaking to sacrifice profits, since the cost of the rebate is spread across a large number of units. If retroactive rebates are given, the average price obtained by the dominant undertaking may well be far above costs and ensure a high average profit margin. However, retroactive rebate schemes ensure that, from the point of view of the customer, the effective price for the last units is very low because of the 'suction effect'. The General Court therefore rejected as ineffective the claims made by Tomra that there were errors of fact in the analysis within the contested decision of the level of prices charged by them.

79. The General Court was therefore justified in ruling, in essence, in paragraphs 269 to 271 of the judgment under appeal, that the loyalty mechanism was inherent in the supplier's ability to drive out its competitors by means of the suction to itself of the contestable part of demand. When such a trading instrument exists, it is therefore unnecessary to undertake an [analysis] of the actual effects of the rebates on competition given that, for the purposes of establishing an infringement of Article 102 TFEU, it is sufficient to demonstrate that the conduct at issue is capable of having an effect on competition, as recalled in paragraph 68 of this judgment.

80. That being the case, the alleged absence, in the judgment under appeal, of an examination of the arguments raised by the applicants at first instance, on the need to compare the prices charged by them with their costs, which underlies both the complaint of a procedural irregularity and that of an error of law, cannot mean that the judgment under appeal is vitiated by an error of law. The Commission established the existence of an abuse of a dominant position by relying on the other considerations set out in paragraphs 260 to 264 of the judgment under appeal, and the General Court correctly found that that analysis was adequate and sufficient to establish the existence of that abuse. Accordingly, neither the Commission nor the General Court was obliged to examine the question of whether the prices charged by the Tomra group were or were not lower than their long-run average incremental costs, and accordingly this ground of appeal must fail in the context of the present appeal.

81. The appellants' arguments that the Commission's Guidance (see paragraph 52 of this judgment) provides for a comparative analysis of prices and costs cannot invalidate that conclusion. As the Advocate General observes in point 37 of his Opinion, the Guidance, published in 2009, has no relevance to the legal assessment of a decision, such as the contested decision, which was adopted in 2006.

The most notable aspects of the judgment are as follows.

- First, the question of how much of the market must be foreclosed before the target rebates can be an abuse. Although the GC had satisfied itself that in this case 40 per cent of the market was foreclosed and the CJ affirmed the judgment on this basis, in paragraph 42 the CJ set out the principle that 'competitors should be able to compete on the merits for the entire market and not just for a part of it'. That 'suggests that if a dominant firm grants loyalty rebates to customers whose combined purchases amount to 10 per cent of the market (hence, leaving the other 90 per cent up for grabs by new entrants), that firm would nevertheless have committed an abuse . . .'[554]

---

[554] Geradin, Layne-Farrar, and Petit, n. 170, 4.217. The appreciability issue was also addressed by the CJ in *Post Danmark II*, see Section 11.F.iii, p. 464.

- Secondly, the CJ rejected the argument that a costs-based test (i.e. AEC) must be applied to rebates and said that it did not matter whether or not the dominant undertaking was sacrificing profits or charging negative prices (paragraphs 73–78).[555] Rather, the CJ stressed the 'suction effect' (paragraph 78).

- Thirdly, the considerations which were taken into account in concluding that the target rebates were capable of excluding competitors (paragraph 75) are likely to be present in the majority of such schemes, i.e. the rebates were retroactive (rolled-back); they were individualised and based on the customer's estimated requirements; the thresholds corresponded to the customer's total requirements or a large proportion thereof; and they were offered to the largest customers.

- Fourthly, the CJ was content that the rebates are 'capable' of excluding competition. It did not require the demonstration of actual or likely effects. There is no theory of harm in respect of effects on consumers. This is a good example of the assumption that the foreclosure of competitors harms consumers without demonstrating why that is so.[556]

The comments in paragraph 81 of the judgment about the effect of the Guidance Paper are considered in Chapter 5, Section 6.C.iii.

(iii) Retroactive Standardised Rebates in *Post Danmark II*

The second *Post Danmark* case was a further preliminary reference from a Danish court concerned with proceedings between the Danish competition authority (Konkurrencerådet) and Post Danmark (PD). The position of PD is described in Section 8.D where the first *Post Danmark* case is discussed.[557] Briefly, PD had a statutory monopoly over a large part (amounting in the relevant period to 70 per cent) of the bulk mail distribution market in Denmark. PD operated a volume rebate scheme which applied to all of a customer's bulk mail, whether covered by the statutory monopoly or not. At the beginning of each year PD entered into agreements with its customers setting out the estimated quantities of mailings for the year. The rebates were given on the basis of those estimates and varied on a scale from 6 per cent to 16 per cent.[558] At the end of the year there was an adjustment up or down if the mail sent was higher or lower than the estimate. It was a standardised scheme, so all customers were entitled to receive the same rebates, but it was retroactive as the rebate was given on the aggregate quantities over the one-year reference period. The Konkurrencerådet found that PD had a 95 per cent share of the bulk mail market as a whole and that it had abused its dominant position by operating a rebate scheme that had an anti-competitive exclusionary effect on the market.

The Commercial Court asked a number of questions in its reference.[559] The CJ interpreted these as asking in essence:

First, for clarification of 'the criteria that are to be applied in order to determine whether a rebate scheme, such as that at issue in the main proceedings, is liable to have an exclusionary effect on the market contrary to Article [102]' and also 'what relevance is to be attached, in the context of that assessment, to the fact that the rebate scheme is applicable to the majority of customers on the market';[560] those questions are answered in paragraphs 22–50 of the judgment.

Secondly, 'the relevance to be attached to the as-efficient-competitor test in assessing a rebate scheme under Article [102]';[561] answered in paragraphs 52–62.

---

[555] See further the consideration of whether a costs-based test is necessary in *Post Danmark II*.

[556] See further Marsden, n. 100, 64–66.

[557] Case C-209/10, *Post Danmark I* EU:C:2012:172, see p. 391.

[558] Sixteen per cent applied where the customer sent over two million items a year or items worth over DKK 20 million.

[559] Case C-23/14, *Post Danmark II* EU:C:2015:651, para. 20.

[560] Ibid., para. 21.

[561] Ibid., para. 51.

Thirdly, 'whether Article [102] must be interpreted as meaning that, in order to fall within the scope of that article, the anti-competitive effect of a rebate scheme, such as that at issue in the main proceedings, must be, on the one hand, probable and, on the other, serious or appreciable'; answered in paragraphs 63–74.

Case C-23/14, *Post Danmark A/S v Konkurrencerådet* EU:C:2015:651 (*Post Danmark II*)

Court of Justice

28. So far as the rebate scheme at issue in the main proceedings is concerned, it must be observed that that scheme cannot be regarded as a simple quantity rebate linked solely to the volume of purchases, since the rebates at issue are not granted in respect of each individual order, thus corresponding to the cost savings made by the supplier, but on the basis of the aggregate orders placed over a given period. Moreover, it was not coupled with an obligation for, or promise by, purchasers to obtain all or a given proportion of their supplies from Post Danmark, a point which served to distinguish it from loyalty rebates within the meaning of the case-law referred to in paragraph 27 above.

29. In those circumstances, in order to determine whether the undertaking in a dominant position has abused that position by applying a rebate scheme such as that at issue in the main proceedings, the Court has repeatedly held that it is necessary to consider all the circumstances, particularly the criteria and rules governing the grant of the rebate, and to investigate whether, in providing an advantage not based on any economic service justifying it, the rebate tends to remove or restrict the buyer's freedom to choose his sources of supply, to bar competitors from access to the market, to apply dissimilar conditions to equivalent transactions with other trading parties or to strengthen the dominant position by distorting competition (judgments in *British Airways* v *Commission*, C-95/04 P..., paragraph 67, and *Tomra Systems and Others* v *Commission*, C-549/10 P..., paragraph 71).

30. Having regard to the particularities of the present case, it is also necessary to take into account, in examining all the relevant circumstances, the extent of Post Danmark's dominant position and the particular conditions of competition prevailing on the relevant market.

31. In that regard, it first has to be determined whether those rebates can produce an exclusionary effect, that is to say whether they are capable, first, of making market entry very difficult or impossible for competitors of the undertaking in a dominant position and, secondly, of making it more difficult or impossible for the co-contractors of that undertaking to choose between various sources of supply or commercial partners. It then has to be examined whether there is an objective economic justification for the discounts granted (judgment in *British Airways* v *Commission*, C-95/04 P..., paragraphs 68 and 69).

32. As regards, in the first place, the criteria and rules governing the grant of the rebates, it must be recalled that the rebates at issue in the main proceedings were 'retroactive', in the sense that, if the threshold initially set at the beginning of the year in respect of the quantities of mail was exceeded, the rebate rate applied at the end of the year applied to all mailings presented over the reference period and not only to mailings exceeding the threshold initially estimated. On the other hand, a customer whose volume of mailings proved to be lower than the quantity estimated had to reimburse Post Danmark.

33. It is apparent from the case-law that the contractual obligations of co-contractors of the undertaking in a dominant position and the pressure exerted upon them may be particularly strong where a discount does not relate solely to the growth in purchases of products of that undertaking made by those co-contractors during the period under consideration, but extends also to those purchases in aggregate. In that way, relatively modest variations in sales of the products of the dominant undertaking have disproportionate effects on co-contractors (see, to that effect, judgment in *British Airways* v *Commission*, C-95/04 P...paragraph 73).

34. In addition, it must be pointed out that the rebate scheme at issue in the main proceedings was based on a reference period of one year. However, any system under which discounts are granted

according to the quantities sold during a relatively long reference period has the inherent effect, at the end of that period, of increasing the pressure on the buyer to reach the purchase figure needed to obtain the discount or to avoid suffering the expected loss for the entire period (judgment in *Nederlandsche Banden-Industrie-Michelin* v *Commission*, 322/81,..., paragraph 81).

35. Consequently, as the Advocate General stated in points 37 and 38 of her Opinion, such a rebate scheme is capable of making it easier for the dominant undertaking to tie its own customers to itself and attract the customers of its competitors, and thus to secure the suction to itself of the part of demand subject to competition on the relevant market. That suction effect is further enhanced by the fact that, in the case in the main proceedings, the rebates applied without distinction both to the contestable part of demand and to the non-contestable part of demand, that is to say, in the latter case, to addressed advertising mail weighing less than 50 grams covered by Post Danmark's statutory monopoly.

36. In the case in the main proceedings, according to the file placed before the Court, for 25 of Post Danmark's largest customers, representing approximately one-half of the volume of transactions on the relevant market during the period at issue, approximately two-thirds of mail sent in the form of direct advertising mail not covered by the monopoly could not be transferred from Post Danmark to Bring Citymail without an adverse impact on the scale of the rebates. If that were established, a matter which it is for the referring court to ascertain, the incentive to obtain all or a substantial proportion of their supplies from Post Danmark would be particularly strong, reducing significantly customers' freedom of choice as to their sources of supply.

37. Moreover, as regards the standardisation of the rebate scale, whereby all customers were entitled to receive the same rebate on the basis of their aggregate purchases over the reference period, such a characteristic admittedly supports the conclusion that, in principle, the rebate scheme implemented by Post Danmark did not result in the application of dissimilar conditions to equivalent transactions with other trading parties, within the meaning of Article [102(c)].

38. However, the mere fact that a rebate scheme is not discriminatory does not preclude its being regarded as capable of producing an exclusionary effect on the market, contrary to Article [102]. Indeed, in the judgment in *Nederlandsche Banden-Industrie-Michelin* v *Commission* (322/81,..., paragraphs 86 and 91), the Court, having rejected the Commission's complaint that the discount system applied by Michelin was discriminatory, nevertheless held that it infringed Article [102] since it made dealers dependent upon Michelin.

39. As regards, in the second place, the extent of Post Danmark's dominant position and the particular conditions of competition prevailing on the bulk mail market, the order for reference states that Post Danmark held 95% of that market, access to which was protected by high barriers and which market was characterised by the existence of significant economies of scale. Post Danmark also enjoyed structural advantages conferred, inter alia, by the statutory monopoly on the distribution of letters weighing up to 50 grams that concerned 70% of all bulk mail. In addition, Post Danmark enjoyed unique geographical coverage encompassing all of Denmark.

40. An undertaking which has a very large market share is by virtue of that share in a position of strength which makes it an unavoidable trading partner and which secures for it freedom of action (judgment in *Hoffmann-La Roche* v *Commission*, 85/76,..., paragraph 41). In those circumstances, it is particularly difficult for competitors of that undertaking to outbid it in the face of discounts based on overall sales volume. By reason of its significantly higher market share, the undertaking in a dominant position generally constitutes an unavoidable business partner in the market (see judgment in *British Airways* v *Commission*, C-95/04 P,..., paragraph 75).

41. That fact, together with the factors mentioned in paragraph 39 above which contribute to clarifying the competitive situation on the relevant market, supports the conclusion that competition on that market was already very limited.

42. In those circumstances, it must be held that a rebate scheme operated by an undertaking, such as the scheme at issue in the main proceedings, which, without tying customers to that undertaking by a formal obligation, nevertheless tends to make it more difficult for those customers to obtain supplies from

competing undertakings, produces an anti-competitive exclusionary effect (see, to that effect, judgment in *Tomra Systems and Others* v *Commission*, C-549/10 P,..., paragraph 72).

43. In addition, the referring court also wishes to know what relevance is to be attached, in the context of assessing the rebate scheme implemented by Post Danmark, to the fact that that scheme applies to the majority of customers on the market.

44. The fact that the rebates applied by Post Danmark concern a large proportion of customers on the market does not, in itself, constitute evidence of abusive conduct by that undertaking.

45. Indeed, in a case that concerned, inter alia, the assessment of the loyalty rebates applied by a dominant undertaking, the Court held that there was no need to ascertain the number of contracts which contained the clause at issue and the number which did not (judgment in *Suiker Unie and Others* v *Commission*, 40/73 to 48/73, 50/73, 54/73 to 56/73, 111/73, 113/73 and 114/73,..., paragraph 511).

46. However, the fact that a rebate scheme, such as that at issue in the main proceedings, covers the majority of customers on the market may constitute a useful indication as to the extent of that practice and its impact on the market, which may bear out the likelihood of an anti-competitive exclusionary effect.

47. Lastly, should the referring court find that there are anti-competitive effects attributable to Post Danmark, it should be recalled that it is nevertheless open to a dominant undertaking to provide justification for behaviour liable to be caught by the prohibition set out in Article [102].

48. In particular, a dominant undertaking may demonstrate that the exclusionary effect arising from its conduct may be counterbalanced, or outweighed, by advantages in terms of efficiency which also benefit the consumer (see judgments in *British Airways* v *Commission*, C-95/04 P,..., paragraph 86, and *TeliaSonera Sverige*, C-52/09,..., paragraph 76).

49. In that last regard, it is for the dominant undertaking to show that the efficiency gains likely to result from the conduct under consideration counteract any likely negative effects on competition and consumer welfare in the affected markets, that those gains have been, or are likely to be, brought about as a result of that conduct, that such conduct is necessary for the achievement of those gains in efficiency and that it does not eliminate effective competition, by removing all or most existing sources of actual or potential competition (judgment in *Post Danmark*, C-209/10,..., paragraph 42).

50. In the light of the foregoing considerations, the answer to the first and second subparagraphs of Question 1, and the first subparagraph of Question 3, is that in order to determine whether a rebate scheme, such as that at issue in the main proceedings, implemented by a dominant undertaking is capable of having an exclusionary effect on the market contrary to Article [102], it is necessary to examine all the circumstances of the case, in particular, the criteria and rules governing the grant of the rebates, the extent of the dominant position of the undertaking concerned and the particular conditions of competition prevailing on the relevant market. The fact that the rebate scheme covers the majority of customers on the market may constitute a useful indication as to the extent of that practice and its impact on the market, which may bear out the likelihood of an anti-competitive exclusionary effect.

...

51. By the third and fourth subparagraphs of Question 1, the referring court asks, in essence, the Court to clarify the relevance to be attached to the as-efficient-competitor test in assessing a rebate scheme under Article [102].

52. Given that the referring court has mentioned, in the fourth subparagraph of Question 1, the communication from the Commission entitled 'Guidance on the Commission's enforcement priorities in applying Article [102] to abusive exclusionary conduct by dominant undertakings', it must be observed, as a preliminary point, that that document merely sets out the Commission's approach as to the choice of cases that it intends to pursue as a matter of priority; accordingly, the administrative practice followed by the Commission is not binding on national competition authorities and courts.

53. The application of the as-efficient-competitor test consists in examining whether the pricing practices of a dominant undertaking could drive an equally efficient competitor from the market.

54. That test is based on a comparison of the prices charged by a dominant undertaking and certain costs incurred by that undertakings as well as its strategy (see judgment in *Post Danmark*, C-209/10,..., paragraph 28).

55. The as-efficient-competitor test has been specifically applied by the Court to low-pricing practices in the form of selective prices or predatory prices (see, in respect of selective prices, judgment in *Post Danmark*, C-209/10,..., paragraphs 28 to 35, and in respect of predatory prices, judgments in *AKZO* v *Commission*, C-62/86,..., paragraphs 70 to 73, and *France Télécom* v *Commission*, C-202/07 P.,..., paragraphs 107 and 108), and margin squeeze (judgment in *TeliaSonera Sverige*, C-52/09,..., paragraphs 40 to 46).

56. As regards the comparison of prices and costs in the context of applying Article [102] to a rebate scheme, the Court has held that the invoicing of 'negative prices', that is to say, prices below cost prices, to customers is not a prerequisite of a finding that a retroactive rebate scheme operated by a dominant undertaking is abusive (judgment in *Tomra Systems and Others* v *Commission*, C-549/10 P.,..., paragraph 73). In that same case, the Court specified that the absence of a comparison of prices charged with costs did not constitute an error of law (judgment in *Tomra Systems and Others* v *Commission*, C-549/10 P.,..., paragraph 80).

57. It follows that, as the Advocate General stated in points 61 and 63 of her Opinion, it is not possible to infer from Article [102] or the case-law of the Court that there is a legal obligation requiring a finding to the effect that a rebate scheme operated by a dominant undertaking is abusive to be based always on the as-efficient-competitor test.

58. Nevertheless, that conclusion ought not to have the effect of excluding, on principle, recourse to the as-efficient-competitor test in cases involving a rebate scheme for the purposes of examining its compatibility with Article [102].

59. On the other hand, in a situation such as that in the main proceedings, characterised by the holding by the dominant undertaking of a very large market share and by structural advantages conferred, inter alia, by that undertaking's statutory monopoly, which applied to 70% of mail on the relevant market, applying the as-efficient-competitor test is of no relevance inasmuch as the structure of the market makes the emergence of an as-efficient competitor practically impossible.

60. Furthermore, in a market such as that at issue in the main proceedings, access to which is protected by high barriers, the presence of a less efficient competitor might contribute to intensifying the competitive pressure on that market and, therefore, to exerting a constraint on the conduct of the dominant undertaking.

61. The as-efficient-competitor test must thus be regarded as one tool amongst others for the purposes of assessing whether there is an abuse of a dominant position in the context of a rebate scheme.

62. Consequently, the answer to the third and fourth subparagraphs of Question 1 is that the application of the as-efficient-competitor test does not constitute a necessary condition for a finding to the effect that a rebate scheme is abusive under Article [102]. In a situation such as that in the main proceedings, applying the as-efficient-competitor test is of no relevance.

...

63. By Question 2 and the second subparagraph of Question 3, which should be answered together, the referring court asks, in essence, whether Article [102] must be interpreted as meaning that, in order to fall within the scope of that article, the anti-competitive effect of a rebate scheme, such as that at issue in the main proceedings, must be, on the one hand, probable and, on the other, serious or appreciable.

64. As regards, in the first place, the likelihood of an anti-competitive effect, it is apparent from the case-law cited in paragraph 29 above that, in order to determine whether a dominant undertaking has abused its position by operating a rebate scheme, it is necessary, inter alia, to examine whether that rebate tends to remove or restrict the buyer's freedom to choose his sources of supply, to bar competitors from access to the market, to apply dissimilar conditions to equivalent transactions with other trading parties or to strengthen the dominant position by distorting competition.

65. In that regard, and as the Advocate General stated in point 80 of her Opinion, the anti-competitive effect of a particular practice must not be of purely hypothetical.

66. The Court has also held that, in order to establish whether such a practice is abusive, that practice must have an anti-competitive effect on the market, but the effect does not necessarily have to be concrete, and it is sufficient to demonstrate that there is an anti-competitive effect which may potentially exclude competitors who are at least as efficient as the dominant undertaking (judgment in *TeliaSonera Sverige*, C-52/09,…, paragraph 64).

67. It follows that only dominant undertakings whose conduct is likely to have an anti-competitive effect on the market fall within the scope of Article [102].

68. In that regard, the assessment of whether a rebate scheme is capable of restricting competition must be carried out in the light of all relevant circumstances, including the rules and criteria governing the grant of the rebates, the number of customers concerned and the characteristics of the market on which the dominant undertaking operates.

69. Such an assessment seeks to determine whether the conduct of the dominant undertaking produces an actual or likely exclusionary effect, to the detriment of competition and, thereby, of consumers' interests (judgment in *Post Danmark*, C-209/10,…paragraph 44).

70. As regards, in the second place, the serious or appreciable nature of an anti-competitive effect, although it is true that a finding that an undertaking has a dominant position is not in itself a ground of criticism of the undertaking concerned (judgment in *Post Danmark*, C-209/10,…, paragraph 21), the conduct of such an undertaking may give rise to an abuse of its dominant position because the structure of competition on the market has already been weakened (see, to that effect, judgments in *Hoffmann-La Roche* v *Commission*, 85/76,…, paragraph 123, and *France Télécom* v *Commission*, C-202/07 P,…, paragraph 107).

71. Consequently, the Court has repeatedly held that a dominant undertaking has a special responsibility not to allow its behaviour to impair genuine, undistorted competition on the internal market (see judgment in *Post Danmark*, C-209/10,…, paragraph 23 and the case-law cited).

72. In addition, since the structure of competition on the market has already been weakened by the presence of the dominant undertaking, any further weakening of the structure of competition may constitute an abuse of a dominant position (judgment in *Hoffmann-La Roche* v *Commission*, 85/76,…, paragraph 123).

73. It follows that fixing an appreciability (*de minimis*) threshold for the purposes of determining whether there is an abuse of a dominant position is not justified. That anti-competitive practice is, by its very nature, liable to give rise to not insignificant restrictions of competition, or even of eliminating competition on the market on which the undertaking concerned operates.

74. It follows from the foregoing considerations that Article [102] must be interpreted as meaning that, in order to fall within the scope of that article, the anti-competitive effect of a rebate scheme operated by a dominant undertaking must be probable, there being no need to show that it is of a serious or appreciable nature.

This ruling is of great interest and significance. It has clarified some issues although others remain unclear. The CJ relied heavily on its previous case law but also went beyond it on some matters. The most important aspects of the ruling are as follows (all emphasis is added).

- Loyalty rebates are abusive (paragraph 27, already set out in Section 11.E.iv). The CJ thus confirmed that there is a category of 'by object' abuses under Article 102.

- Simple quantity rebates are not in principle liable to infringe Article 102, but retroactive rebates given on aggregate orders are not to be classed as simple quantity rebates (paragraph 28). The category of rebates which are presumptively lawful is very narrow.

- The rebates in this case were neither simple quantity rebates nor loyalty rebates (paragraph 28). Therefore it was necessary (paragraph 29) to consider 'all the circumstances' to determine whether the rebate *tended* to do what is listed there.[562] Paragraph 29 reproduces paragraph 67 of *British Airways* (which itself quoted *Michelin I*). In paragraph 31 the Court repeated paragraph 68 of *British Airways* when it says that it first has to be determined whether the rebates *can* produce an exclusionary effect, i.e. whether they are *capable* of making market entry difficult or impossible and of making it difficult or impossible for co-contractors to choose sources of supply.

- However, in paragraph 46 the Court referred to indications which 'may bear out the *likelihood of an anti-competitive exclusionary effect*' and in paragraph 47 talked of the possibility of objective justification 'should the referring court find that there are anti-competitive effects'. Moreover, in paragraphs 63–74 the Court talked of assessing whether there are actual or likely (although not concrete, see paragraph 66) exclusionary effects which are '*probable*' (paragraph 73). In the latter part of the judgment the Court referred to its rulings in *TeliaSonera* and *Post Danmark I* both of which, as we have seen earlier in this chapter, took an effects-based approach to Article 102. Above all, in paragraph 67 the Court said that only dominant undertakings 'whose conduct is likely to have an anti-competitive effect on the market' fall within Article 102. It appears, however, that the Court considers that an assessment of whether rebates are *capable* of restricting competition (paragraph 68) seeks thereby to determine whether the conduct produces *actual or likely exclusionary effects* to the detriment of competition and thus of *consumers'* interests (paragraph 69).

- The 'criteria and rules particularly the criteria and rules governing the grant of the rebate' which had to be examined included the retroactivity of the rebates and the 'relatively long reference period' of one year (paragraphs 32–34), which created a strong suction effect, particularly as the rebates applied both to mail covered by the monopoly and that not covered (paragraphs 35–36).[563]

- The circumstances to be examined also included the extent of the dominant position and the particular conditions of competition on the market (paragraph 30). As regards the dominant position it was relevant that PD had 95 per cent of the market and enjoyed structural advantages, inter alia from the statutory monopoly and significant economies of scale. The CJ considered that the 'very large market share' made it an 'unavoidable trading partner' (paragraph 40). The fact that the rebate scheme covered the majority of the customers on the market was not of itself evidence of an abuse, but could indicate the extent of the practice and its impact (paragraph 46).

- There is no requirement to apply the AEC test in every case. It is merely 'one tool amongst others' (paragraph 61). Its use is not excluded in principle but it is not relevant in a case like *Post Danmark II* where there were high barriers to entry, structural advantages, a statutory monopoly, and a very high market share (paragraphs 58–60). Notably, one of reasons given for excluding its application in this case was that the emergence of an as efficient competitor was 'practically impossible' (paragraph 59) and furthermore the Court considered that in a market such as this a *less* efficient competitor might exert a competitive restraint (paragraph 60). However, *Post Danmark II* means that passing the AEC test does not necessarily rule out an abuse. Failing the AEC test, if one were applied, is likely to be more significant.

---

[562] I.e. remove or restrict the buyer's freedom to choose his sources of supply, bar competitors from access to the market, apply dissimilar conditions to equivalent transactions with other trading parties, or strengthen the dominant position by distorting competition.

[563] The CJ here used the 'non-contestable' and 'contestable' terminology used by the Commission in the Guidance Paper, paras. 37–45.

- There is no appreciability/de minimis threshold under Article 102.[564] The anti-competitive effect must be 'probable' but need not be 'serious' or 'appreciable'. The normal meaning of 'probable' is 'more likely than not' or 'expected to happen'.[565] The word 'serious' appears to be synonymous with 'appreciable' and relate to the impact of the anti-competitive effect rather than to its nature.

The question is whether the effects-based approach taken to standardised retroactive rebates in *Post Danmark II* should also apply to target rebates. The latter are also, according to the case law, neither quantity rebates nor loyalty rebates and the CJ in *Post Danmark II* quoted extensively from its target rebate case law in the first part of the ruling. Only when the matter of actual or likely effects were in issue did the Court turn instead to its *TeliaSonera* and *Post Danmark I* judgments. This is understandable, in that '*Post Danmark I* hinted at the emergence of a set of principles common to all price-based exclusionary conduct'.[566] Unlike the GC in *Intel* the CJ in *Post Danmark II* did not suggest that the rebates with which it was concerned were not about prices but exclusivity. Admittedly, individualised target rebates may be more conducive to anti-competitive foreclosure effects than the type of standardised rebates in *Post Danmark II*, but that should be reflected in the outcome of the examination of 'all the circumstances', rather than in the test which is applied.

G. REBATES IN THE GUIDANCE PAPER

The section of Guidance Paper on rebates presented an different approach to that hitherto taken in the case law. It is the most radical part of the Guidance Paper and sets out a new methodology for determining whether rebates are abusive.[567] The Guidance Paper broadly follows the Commission's proposals in the Staff Discussion Paper,[568] but is less complex.[569]

Paragraphs 37–45 of the Guidance Paper deal with what the Commission calls 'conditional rebates', defined as 'rebates granted to customers to reward them for a particular form of purchasing behaviour'. The Commission accepts that such rebates may stimulate demand and benefit consumers. However, they can also have foreclosure effects.[570]

The section on rebates must be read in conjunction with the general section on price-based exclusionary conduct, paragraphs 23–27.[571] The Commission is therefore concerned with the anti-competitive foreclosure of as efficient competitors. However, the Commission notes that conditional rebates can have such foreclosure effects without necessarily entailing a sacrifice for the dominant undertaking.[572] The question the Commission asks is what price a competitor would need to offer to compensate customers for the loss of the conditional rebate if the customer switched part of its demand away from the dominant undertaking.

The concepts used in the assessments are 'contestable' and 'non-contestable' portions of a customer's demand[573] and the 'relevant range'. A portion of demand may be 'non-contestable' because, for example, the dominant undertaking supplies a 'must-stock' product (to which consumers have brand loyalty) or because the competitors have capacity constraints and could not satisfy all the customer's demand. The Commission's concern is that the dominant undertaking may grant

---

[564] See Section 3.G, p 366.

[565] In Case T-201/04, *Microsoft* [2007] ECR II-3601, paras. 560–563 (see Section 13.D) the GC refused to indulge in making distinctions between 'likely to' and 'high probability'.

[566] Ibáñez Colomo, n. 437, 13.

[567] See Faull and Nikpay, n. 1, 4.429–4.467, for a full discussion of the Guidance Paper treatment of rebates.

[568] Discussion Paper, paras. 151–169. For the Discussion Paper generally, see Chap. 5, Section 6.B.

[569] See Marsden, n. 100, 64–66.

[570] Guidance Paper, para. 37.

[571] See Section 7.D.

[572] Guidance Paper, para. 37. The assessment of conditional rebates is therefore different from that for predation which, according to paras. 64–66, always entails a sacrifice, para. 37, n. 3.

[573] For the terminology, see Section 11.B.

conditional rebates in order to use the non-contestable portion as leverage to decrease the price for the contestable portion.[574] The market may be significantly foreclosed if retroactive rebates make it less attractive for customers to switch small amounts of contestable demand. Therefore the Commission will try to estimate the price which a competitor would have to offer to compensate for the loss of the rebate if the customer were to switch part of its demand (the 'relevant range'). The effective price the competitor has to match is the normal list price less the rebate lost by switching.[575] The Commission, using a method similar to the tests for predatory pricing, will apply costs levels to assess whether an as efficient competitor could compete profitably notwithstanding the rebate. If the effective price remains above the dominant undertaking's LRAIC the rebate is not 'normally' capable of anti-competitive foreclosure.[576] If it is below AAC 'as a general rule' it is capable of foreclosing as efficient competitors whereas if it is between LRAIC and AAC the Commission 'will investigate whether other factors point to the conclusion that entry or expansion even by equally efficient competitors is likely to be affected'.[577] One important factor is whether the rebate is retroactive or incremental.[578] The Commission will consider efficiencies in respect of exclusive dealing in line with the principles laid out in the section of the Guidance Paper on objective necessities and efficiencies.[579] The Commission considers that transaction-related costs advantages (which are passed on to consumers) are more likely with standardised volume targets than with individualised ones.[580]

The Guidance Paper presents considerable practical difficulties, particularly in respect of the 'contestable share',[581] making it difficult for undertakings to assess with confidence whether their business strategies are lawful.

J. Faull and A. Nikpay (eds.), *The EU Law of Competition* (3rd edn, Oxford University Press, 2014), 437 (Manuel de la Mano, Renato Nazzini, and Hans Zenger)

4.465. First, it is undoubtedly correct that the AECT poses certain challenges in terms of practical administrability, since it is a far more complex pricing test than the standard predation test. The primary difficulty it entails is the determination of the contestable share of demand, an exercise that often leaves room for subjective judgment.

4.466. Secondly, this uncertainty is amplified from the perspective of firms which try to devise their pricing schemes so as to comply with the competition rules. After all, what turns to be viewed as contestable by a competition authority *ex post* may differ substantially from the firm's own best judgment *ex ante*, when it competed for incremental sales.

4.467. As a result, it has been argued that DT firms may be reluctant to use loyalty rebates to compete fiercely for expanded output, out of a concern that any margin of error would ultimately be used against them in an investigation. However, there is little or no evidence that such reluctance is widespread and, in any event, effective steps can be taken by firms to minimize the risk of violating the Article 102 Enforcement Priorities Guidance standard.[582]

---

[574] Guidance Paper, para. 39.

[575] Ibid., paras. 41–42.

[576] Ibid., para. 43. For LRAIC (long-run average incremental cost), see Section 7.C, p. 382.

[577] Guidance Paper, para. 44.

[578] Ibid., para. 45.

[579] Ibid., para. 46, referring to paras. 28–31.

[580] Ibid., para. 46.

[581] L. Kjølbe, 'Rebates Under Article 82EC: Navigating Uncertain Waters' [2010] *ECLR* 66.

[582] The authors suggest that firms that grant retroactive rebates can use multiple thresholds to minimise compliance risks, and refer to H. Zenger, 'Devising Loyalty Rebates that Comply with the As-efficient-competitor Test' [2013] 3 *Concurrences* 16.

Apparently the Commission decided to close an investigation into various rebating practices in *Velux*, having applied the Guidance Paper methodology and concluding that there were no anti-competitive foreclosure effects.[583] As already noted, in *Intel* the Commission followed the Guidance Paper and applied the AEC test.

The EU Courts have considered the effect of the Guidance Paper section on rebates in three cases. In *Tomra* the CJ dismissed its relevance to a decision adopted in 2006[584] and in *Intel* the GC dismissed its relevance to a post-Guidance Paper decision where the statement of objections had been sent in 2007.[585] As we have seen, in the Article 267 reference *Post Danmark II*, the CJ said that a matter of the administrative practice of the Commission was not binding on NCAs and national courts.[586] The EU Courts have yet to deal with an appeal from a decision in a case where the investigation began after the publication of the Guidance Paper. The question of the effect of the Guidance Paper generally is discussed in Chapter 5.[587] However, as we have seen, in recent cases the Courts have adopted some of the terminology of the Guidance Paper rebates section, particularly 'non-contestable' and 'contestable' portions of demand, and have concentrated on the possibility of leverage, as the Guidance Paper does.

H. CONCLUSIONS

The situation with rebates, pending the outcome of the *Intel* appeal to the CJ, is as follows. Quantity rebates are presumptively lawful. However, that category is drawn very narrowly and comprises only 'simple' rebates, applicable to all customers without discrimination, linked solely to objective amounts granted in respect of each individual order. Loyalty or 'exclusivity' rebates are in the 'by object' category of abuses and are unlawful unless objectively justified, which is unlikely. This treatment of loyalty rebates is despite the cogent arguments as to their possible pro-competitive effects. Retroactive standardised rebates are considered in the light of (a) the nature and operation of the scheme and (b) the extent of the dominant position and the conditions of competition on the market and are subject to an 'actual or likely effects' test. Target rebates are considered 'loyalty-inducing' and have so far been subject to a 'capable' of exclusionary effects test. However, it is arguable that after *Post Danmark II* they could now be subject to an 'actual or likely effects' test, like retroactive standardised rebates. The Commission is unlikely to bring proceedings against rebate schemes which do not meet its criteria as an enforcement priority under the Guidance Paper, but NCAs and national courts can continue to follow the case law without any regard to the principles set out in the exclusive dealing and rebates section of the Guidance Paper.

12. TYING AND BUNDLING

A. GENERAL

Tying and bundling are closely connected practices. For convenience they are dealt with together in this section. They encompass practices whereby an undertaking supplies a product (the tying product)[588] on condition that the customer also obtains something else (the tied product) from the supplier, or the undertaking only supplies the two things together or ensures that the two things only work properly together and do not work at all or as well with competitors' products.

---

[583] See S. Albaek and A. Claici, 'The *Velux* Case—An In-depth Look at Rebates and More' (2009) 2 *Competition Policy Newsletter* 44.

[584] Case C-549/10 P, *Tomra* EU:C:2012:221, para. 81.

[585] Case T-286/09, *Intel* EU:T:2014:547, paras. 154–156.

[586] Case C-23/14, *Post Danmark II* EU:C:2015:651, para. 52.

[587] Chap. 5, Section 6.B.

[588] Or service. Throughout this section 'product' includes 'service' unless otherwise stated.

Tying and bundling can be practised by non-dominant undertakings but in this chapter we are concerned with the possibility that it can constitute an abuse under Article 102 when pursued by an undertaking in a dominant position.

The concepts of tying and bundling for the purposes of Article 102 are described in the Guidance Paper.[589]

48. 'Tying' usually refers to situations where customers that purchase one product (the tying product) are required also to purchase another product from the dominant undertaking (the tied product). Tying can take place on a technical or contractual basis . . . 'Bundling' usually refers to the way products are offered and priced by the dominant undertaking. In the case of pure bundling the products are only sold jointly in fixed proportions. In the case of mixed bundling, often referred to as a multi-product rebate, the products are also made available separately, but the sum of the prices when sold separately is higher than the bundled price.

Contractual tying 'occurs when the customer who purchases the tying product undertakes also to purchase the tied product (and not the alternatives offered by competitors)'.[590] Suppose X makes both widgets and blodgets. X is the monopoly supplier of widgets but the blodget market is competitive. Customers for widgets need to buy blodgets as well. If X refuses to supply widgets unless the customers buy its blodgets rather than those of its competitors that is a contractual tie. Contractual tying can also be effected through offering non-financial inducements, such as refusing to honour guarantees on the tying product if the tied product is not bought[591] or offering priority delivery to customers who take both products.[592]

Technical tying occurs 'when the tying product is designed in such a way that it only works properly with the tied product (and not with the alternatives offered by competitors)'[593] or where the two products are physically integrated so that they are only sold together. The latter type of technical tying is a form of *pure bundling*, and sometimes called *technical bundling*. *Microsoft*[594] was a case of this type.

Pure bundling means that the products are only sold together, in fixed proportions, as stated in paragraph 48 of the Guidance Paper. The elements of a package are not supplied separately. For example, where services are tied to products the supplier may quote a price for the product which includes the service (such as repair and maintenance). A customer who does not want the service will normally still have to pay the full price (or be offered only a reduction which does not reflect the true cost of the service element). Pure bundling includes, as already mentioned, technical tying as in *Microsoft*.

Mixed bundling is also known as a multi-product rebate or economic tying. Instead of providing that the customer must obtain the tied product from itself in order to be supplied with the tying product, or technically tying them together, the supplier offers a financially advantageous deal if the customer buys both. For example, if the normal unit price for widgets is £10 and the competitive unit price for blodgets is £5 the dominant widget supplier may offer both together for £13.

As the Commission explains in the Guidance Paper,[595] for Article 102 potentially to apply the undertaking needs to be dominant in the tying product market but not necessarily in the tied product market. In bundling cases it needs to be dominant in one of the bundled markets. In the case of aftermarkets the undertaking needs to be dominant in the tying and/or the tied market.

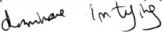

---

[589] See also the Horizontal Merger Guidelines [2008] OJ C265/6, paras. 96–97; see also Case T-210/01, *General Electric v Commission* [2005] ECR II-5575, para. 406.

[590] Guidance Paper, para. 48, n. 2.

[591] See *Eurofix-Bauco v Hilti* [1988] OJ L65/19, para. 44.

[592] See Case T-65/89, *BPB Industries* [1993] ECR II-389.

[593] Guidance Paper, para. 48, n. 2.

[594] Case T-201/04, *Microsoft* [2007] ECR II-3601.

[595] Guidance Paper, para. 50, n. 3.

B. THE COMMERCIAL RATIONALE FOR TYING AND BUNDLING

Tying and bundling may make good commercial and economic sense for reasons which are not necessarily anti-competitive. They can be used as methods for obtaining royalties or fees for the use of a process or product, i.e. as a metering device.[596] They can enable a supplier to 'spread the risk' when trying to penetrate a new market. They can also allow the supplier to achieve economies of scale which are then reflected in the price reduction offered to customers, or to offer a 'bundle' which is more attractive (and of greater value) to consumers than the sum of its separate parts. They can therefore have beneficial effects on consumer welfare. Suppliers may also tie products or services together in order to ensure their optimal performance and maintain the supplier's reputation, or to ensure safety, although the EU Courts have not proved receptive to the latter justification.[597]

C. THE ECONOMIC ARGUMENTS OVER TYING AND BUNDLING

The basic objection to tying and bundling by dominant undertakings is that it enables 'monopoly leveraging' of market power—the projection of dominance from one market to another. In other words, the dominant undertaking uses its position on the market where it is dominant to foreclose competition on another market and acquire substantial market power there too ('offensive leveraging'). The fear is that the dominant supplier can extract two monopoly prices, one from the tying and one from the tied product. This may lead to competition laws proscribing the practice as per se illegal.[598] The Chicago School argues that the extraction of two profits is not possible and advanced the 'single monopoly profit theorem' which was a powerful riposte to the per se illegality position. An explanation of this is set out in the judgment of Judge Easterbrook in a US case.[599]

> ### Schor v Abbott Laboratories, 457 F.3d 608 (7th Cir. 2006)
>
> The basic point is that a firm that monopolizes some essential component of a treatment (or product or service) can extract the whole monopoly profit by charging a suitable price for the component alone. If the monopolist gets control of another component as well and tries to jack up the price of that item, the effect is the same as setting an excessive price for the monopolized component. The monopolist can take its profit just once; an effort to do more makes it worse off and is self-deterring . . .
>
> The monopolist's profit-maximizing strategy is not to take over the market in related products . . . But to promote competition among the other producers. The less the complements cost, the more the monopolist can charge for its own product . . .
>
> We appreciate the potential reply that it is impossible to say that a given practice 'never' could injure consumers. A creative economist could imagine unusual combinations of costs, elasticities, and barriers to entry that would cause injury in the rate situation . . . But just as rules of per se illegality condemn

---

[596] E.g. *Vaassen/Moris* [1979] OJ L19/32, where the patentee of a device for filling *saucissons de Boulogne* supplied it royalty-free but on the condition that customers bought their sausage skins from him. This was an easy way of monitoring, and charging for, the use of the device (but found to be contrary to Art. 101(1)).

[597] See the *Hilti* and *Tetra Pak II* cases (in Section 12.E.i), p. 477.

[598] The US modified its previous absolute per se illegality rule in *Jefferson Parish Hospital District No. 2 v Hyde*, 466 US 2 (1984).

[599] See the discussion in J. Vickers, 'Some Economics of Abuse of Dominance' in X. Vives (ed.), *Competition Policy in the EU: Fifty Years on from the Treaty of Rome* (Oxford University Press, 2009), 71, 79. R. A. Posner, *Antitrust Law* (2nd edn, University of Chicago Press, 2001), 197–209 also sets out the Chicago position.

practice[s] that almost always injure consumers, so antitrust law applies rules of per se legality to practices that almost never injure consumers.

Lower prices almost always benefit consumers. Subjecting all low prices to litigation, and the inevitable risk of error in a search for the rate instances in which consumers could be made worse off in the long run by low prices today, would make it more risky for firms to reduce prices, and they would be less inclined to do so—to consumers' considerable detriment. That's why in Matsushita and Brooke Group the Supreme Court held that low prices are lawful, even if the seller has considerable market power, unless rivals have been driven out of the market and recoupment is either ongoing or imminent. It is why any firm's unilateral conduct is almost always deemed lawful unless it creates a dangerous probability of success in monopolizing . . .

Just so with arguments that low prices are designed to 'leverage' a firm from one monopoly to another. As long as rivals continue to sell, and no second monopoly is in prospect, the search for the rare situation in which that second monopoly just might allow the firm to gain a profit by injuring consumers is not worth the candle. The search itself (and the risk of error in the judicial process) has much more chance of condemning a beneficial practice than of catching a detrimental one. A price high enough to avoid condemnation under predatory-pricing rules cannot be condemned under a 'monopoly leveraging' theory that is just a predatory pricing variant without the intellectual discipline of that doctrine.

Post-Chicagoans, however, have argued that it is possible for tying to serve as a mechanism for leveraging market power because the single monopoly profit theorem depends on certain assumptions. One of these is that the two products are used in fixed proportions, another is that the market for the tied good has a competitive, constant, returns-to-scale structure. The economics of tying and bundling[600] have generated a large and lively literature.[601] Ultimately this shows that these practices may have both pro- and anti-competitive effects. Everything will depend on the facts of each case.

Leveraging can also be 'defensive'. The theory of defensive leveraging concentrates on the prolongation of power in the tying market. In this model the dominant undertaking eliminates competitors on the tied market in order to prevent entry on to the tying market, or make it more difficult, by depriving the entrant of access to the consumable. It may also be that the dominant undertaking wishes to exclude the competitor in the tied market where there is a possibility that the tied product may in time become a substitute for the tying product.[602]

[600] For the economics, see Bishop and Walker, n. 198, 6-063–6-083; Motta, n. 172, 7.3; R. J. Van den Bergh and P. D. Camesasca, *European Competition Law and Economics: A Comparative Perspective* (2nd edn, Sweet & Maxwell, 2006), 265–270; O'Donoghue and Padilla, n. 1, 599–609; Rousseva, n. 269, 239–245; Elhauge and Geradin, n. 207, 562–571.

[601] The seminal article setting out the arguments against the Chicago position is M. Whinston, 'Tying, Foreclosure and Exclusion' (1990) 80 *Am Econ Rev* 837; see also J. Choi and C. Stefanadis, 'Tying, Investment and Dynamic Leverage Theory' (2001) 32 *RAND J of Economics* 52; K.-U. Kuhn, R. Stillman, and C. Caffarra, 'Economic Theories of Bundling and their Policy Implications in Abuse Cases' (2005) 1 *European Competition Journal* 85; D. Crane and J. Wright, 'Can Bundled Discounting Increase Consumer Prices Without Excluding Rivals?' (2009) 5 *Competition Policy International* 209; D. S. Evans and M. Salinger, 'Why Do Firms Bundle and Tie? Evidence from Competitive Markets and Implications for Tying Law' (2005) 22 *Yale J on Regulation* 37; B. Nabeluff, 'Exclusionary Bundling' (2005) 50 *Ant Bull* 321. An article published in 2009, E. Elhauge, 'Tying, Bundled Discounts, and the Death of the Single Monopoly Profit Theory' (2009) 123 *Harvard LR* 399 attracted much debate, see particularly P. Seabright, 'The Undead? A Comment on Professor Elhauge's Paper' (2009) 5 *Competition Policy International* 243; H. First, 'No Single Monopoly Profit, No Single Policy Prescription?' (2009) 5 *Competition Policy International* 199; and Elhauge's response, E. Elhauge, 'The Failed Resurrection of the Single Monopoly Profit Theory', Harvard Discussion Paper No. 664 (2010) 6 *Competition Policy International* 155.

[602] D. Carlton and M. Waldman, 'The Strategic Use of Tying to Preserve and Create Market Power in Evolving Industries' (2002) 33 *RAND J of Economics* 194; see generally P. Këllezi, 'Rhetoric or Reform: Does the Law of Tying and Bundling Reflect the Economic Theory' in Ezrachi, n. 41, 148, 152 ff.

D. TYING AND BUNDLING AND ARTICLE 102

The Guidance Paper says:

49. Tying and bundling are common practices intended to provide customers with better products or offerings in more cost effective ways. However, an undertaking which is dominant in one product market (or more) of a tie or bundle (referred to as the tying market) can harm consumers through tying or bundling by foreclosing the market for the other products that are part of the tie or bundle (referred to as the tied market) and, indirectly, the tying market.

EU competition law is concerned with tying because of the leverage problem, which may result in the foreclosure of competitors from the market.[603] Tying can do this because the supplier is dominant in the market for the *tying* product, so the customer has difficulty going elsewhere for it and therefore cannot or does not shop around for the *tied* product; mixed bundling can have a foreclosure effect because it offers a price the competitors on the tied market cannot match. Mixed bundling is a type of pricing policy. Contractual tying can be seen as a refusal to supply as well as a tie,[604] although as we will see, the competition rules on tying and refusal to supply differ.[605]

Article 102(d) specifically lists tying as a type of abuse:

making the conclusion of contracts subject to acceptance by the other parties of supplementary obligations which, by their nature or according to commercial usage, have no connection with the subject of such contracts.

However, the case law shows that tying and bundling may infringe Article 102 even if it does not fit within that provision.

E. THE CASE LAW

(i) Contractual Tying

Hilti and *Tetra Pak II* concerned consumables in an aftermarket tied to a primary product. In both cases the Commission found an abuse after very little analysis of the market and the appeals to the EU Courts concentrated on the issues of market definition[606] and objective justification.

Eurofix-Bauco/Hilti [1988] OJ L65/19

Hilti was dominant in the supply of nail guns for the construction industry which were protected by patents. The cartridge strips were also protected by Hilti's patents. The nails fired out of the cartridge strips were not, however, so protected and there were small, independent manufacturers of Hilti-compatible nails. Hilti followed a number of practices to ensure that customers for its cartridges also bought its nails and did not buy nails from the independent suppliers: (a) making the sale of patented cartridge strips conditional upon taking a corresponding complement of nails; (b) reducing discounts on cartridges where the customer did not order nails as well; (c) inducing its distributors not to supply certain customers so that the independent nail producers could not get hold of Hilti cartridges; (d) refusing supplies of cartridges to long-standing customers who might resell to independent nail producers; (e) frustrating or delaying

---

[603] In the *cause célèbre* merger case *GE/Honeywell*, Case T-210/01, *General Electric v Commission* [2005] ECR II-5575 the fear (inter alia) that the merged entity might bundle its products in the future and thereby exclude competitors caused the Commission, unlike the US authorities, to prohibit the transaction, see Chap. 15.

[604] See, e.g., Case 311/84, *Centre Belge* [1985] ECR 3261; *Napier Brown/British Sugar* [1988] OJ L284/41 (delivered pricing).

[605] See Section 13 for refusal to supply and see Rousseva, n. 269, 228–230.

[606] See Chap. 6, Section 5.B.i.h, p. 302.

applications for licences of right of the cartridge strip technology; and (f) refusing to honour guarantees on nail guns if non-Hilti nails had been used with them.

The Commission held that the nail guns, cartridges, and nails each constituted a separate relevant product market and that Hilti was dominant in the EEC in all of them. It held that Hilti had infringed Article 102 by the practices above which were designed to tie the nails to the cartridges and thus to prevent or limit the entry of independent producers of Hilti-compatible consumables into the markets. Hilti claimed that the practices were objectively justified in that safety required that Hilti guns were only used with Hilti consumables and it claimed that the nails produced by the independents were sub-standard. The Commission rejected Hilti's claim of objective justification on safety and quality grounds.

Commission

74. Hilti has abused its dominant position in the EEC in the relevant market for nail guns and most importantly the markets for Hilti-compatible cartridge strips and nails. It has done this principally through its attempts to prevent or limit the entry of independent producers of Hilti-compatible consumables into these markets. Hilti's attempts to block or limit such entry went beyond the means legitimately available to a dominant company. The different aspects of Hilti's commercial behaviour were designed to this effect and were aimed at preventing Hilti-compatible cartridge strips from being freely available. Without such availability of Hilti-compatible cartridge strips, for which in the EEC Hilti until recently enjoyed protection afforded by patents, independent producers of Hilti-compatible nails have been severely restricted in their penetration of the market. Furthermore, customers have been obliged to rely on Hilti for both cartridges and nails for their Hilti nail guns. By limiting the effective competition from new entrants Hilti has been able to preserve its dominant position. The ability to carry out its illegal policies stems from its power on the markets for Hilti-compatible cartridge strips and nail guns (where its market position is strongest and the barriers to entry are highest) and aims at reinforcing its dominance on the Hilti-compatible nail market (where it is potentially more vulnerable to new competition) . . . Most of the abuses took place in or were centred on the UK which constitutes a substantial part of the common market. However, at least one of these abuses had direct effects in another Member State and in addition the strategy of Hilti was aimed indirectly at the whole EEC in its attempt both to stop new entrants into the market (who might start exporting) and to prevent otherwise profitable arbitrage.

75. Making the sale of patented cartridge strips conditional upon taking a corresponding complement of nails constitutes an abuse of a dominant position, as do reduced discounts and other discriminatory policies described above on cartridge-only orders. These policies leave the consumer with no choice over the source of his nails and as such abusively exploit him. In addition, these policies all have the object or effect of excluding independent nail makers who may threaten the dominant position Hilti holds. The tying and reduction of discounts were not isolated incidents but a generally applied policy.

The GC upheld the decision, dismissing pleas about the products forming a 'system' and refusing to accept that Hilti's conduct was justified by safety concerns.[607] The judgment was affirmed by the CJ.[608]

The facts of *Tetra Pak II* have already been given.[609] One of the abuses was tying the supply of non-aseptic packaging machines to the supply of cartons which the machines filled. Customers had to obtain the cartons only from Tetra Pak itself[610] and were obliged to obtain all maintenance and repair services and the supplies of spare parts from Tetra Pak. Tetra Pak claimed that the machines and the cartons formed 'integrated distribution systems' and that in any event the tie was justified

---

[607] Case T-30/89, *Hilti* [1991] ECR II-1439.

[608] Case C-53/92 P, *Hilti* [1994] ECR I-667.

[609] Case C-333/94 P, *Tetra Pak II* [1996] ECR I-5951. See Section 6, p. 377, Section 8.F, p. 395.

[610] Or from a company it designated. As there were no independent distributors the Commission pointed out that this clause was superfluous.

for technical reasons, considerations of public liability and health, and by the need to protect its reputation. The Commission rejected these arguments and said that the system of tied sales, 'which again limits outlets and makes contracts subject to acceptance of conditions (the purchase of cartons) which have no connection with their purpose (the sale of machines), constitutes a serious infringement of Article [102]'.[611] The GC upheld this, referring to the tied-sales clause intending to 'strengthen Tetra Pak's dominant position by reinforcing its customers' economic dependence on it'.[612]

On appeal to the CJ Tetra Pak claimed in particular that Article 102(d) prohibited tying only where the supplementary obligations imposed had by their nature, or according to commercial usage, no connection with the subject of the contract. The CJ upheld the finding of the GC that there was no natural link in this case. It also held, however, that as the examples in Article 102 are not exhaustive, a tie may constitute an abuse even if there is a natural link or the tied sale is in accordance with commercial usage.

Case C-333/94 P, *Tetra Pak International SA v Commission* [1996] ECR I-5951

Court of Justice

34. In its third plea, Tetra Pak submits that the [General Court] erred in law in holding that the tied sales of cartons and filling machines were contrary to Article [102] in circumstances where there was a natural link between the two and tied sales were in accordance with commercial usage.

35. Tetra Pak interprets Article [102 (d)] as prohibiting only the practice of making the conclusion of contracts dependent on acceptance of additional services which, by nature or according to commercial usage, have no link with the subject-matter of the contracts.

36. It must be noted, first, that the [General Court] explicitly rejected the argument put forward by Tetra Pak to show the existence of a natural link between the machines and the cartons. In paragraph 82 of the judgment under appeal, it found: 'consideration of commercial usage does not support the conclusion that the machinery for packaging a product is indivisible from the cartons. For a considerable time there have been independent manufacturers who specialise in the manufacture of non-aseptic cartons designed for use in machines manufactured by other concerns and who do not manufacture machinery themselves'. That assessment, itself based on commercial usage, rules out the existence of the natural link claimed by Tetra Pak by stating that other manufacturers can produce cartons for use in Tetra Pak's machines. With regard to aseptic cartons, the [General Court] found, at paragraph 83 of its judgment, that 'any independent producer is quite free, as far as Community competition law is concerned, to manufacture consumables intended for use in equipment manufactured by others, unless in doing so it infringes a competitor's intellectual property right'. It also noted, at paragraph 138, rejecting the argument based on the alleged natural link, that it was not for Tetra Pak to impose certain measures on its own initiative on the basis of technical considerations or considerations relating to product liability, protection of public health and protection of its reputation. Those factors, taken as a whole, show that the [General Court] considered that Tetra Pak was not alone in being able to manufacture cartons for use in its machines.

37. It must, moreover, be stressed that the list of abusive practices set out in the second paragraph of Article [102] is not exhaustive. Consequently, even where tied sales of two products are in accordance with commercial usage or there is a natural link between the two products in question, such sales may still constitute abuse within the meaning of Article [102] unless they are objectively justified. The reasoning of the [General Court] in paragraph 137 of its judgment is not therefore in any way defective.

---

[611] *Elopak Italia/Tetra Pak* [1991] OJ L72/1, para. 117.
[612] Case T-83/91, *Tetra Pak* [1994] ECR II-755, para. 140.

It is clear from *Tetra Pak II* that, once it is shown that the products or services tied together are distinct, a dominant undertaking cannot rely on the words about nature and commercial usage in Article 102(d). 'Commercial usage' may merely have been established by the dominant undertaking itself[613] and the Court stressed the non-exhaustive character of the particular examples listed in the Article, thereby emasculating the conditions in that sub-paragraph. *Hilti* and *Tetra Pak II* were both driven by concerns about the structure of the market, not about the extraction of monopoly profits or the direct protection of consumers. In *Tetra Pak II* the monopoly profit could have been extracted from the tying product (the machines), had Tetra Pak wished.[614]

(ii) Mixed Bundling

Two of the cases and settlements concerning mixed bundling involved Coca-Cola. In *Coca-Cola Italia Undertaking* (1989)[615] the Commission's SO alleged that Coca-Cola's practice of offering discounts to retailers based on a package of cola and non-cola was an abuse. Coca-Cola agreed not to make discounts on cola conditional on the retailers buying non-cola, and the case was settled on that basis. In *Coca-Cola Undertaking* (2005)[616] Coca-Cola agreed, inter alia, to no longer offer a rebate to its customers if the customer agreed to buy other products together with its best-selling products or to reserve shelf space for the entire group of products.

In the aftermarket case, *Digital Undertaking*,[617] Digital, a computer supplier, offered a package of hardware maintenance services and software support services for its systems. The primary product market of computer systems was competitive but the Commission alleged that by offering customers the package in the aftermarket Digital abused its dominant position on the software support market for Digital systems as it made it uneconomic for customers to buy the hardware maintenance from a third party. Competitors in the hardware maintenance market were therefore excluded from servicing Digital systems. The Commission settled the proceedings when Digital undertook, inter alia, to offer hardware maintenance services on a stand-alone basis and to price its package in a way which fell below the list prices of the individual component services only insofar as the reduction reflected the passing on to customers of costs savings or other benefits stemming from the efficient packaging together of the different elements.

(iii) Technical Bundling and the *Microsoft* Case

In 1984 the Commission came to a settlement with IBM[618] after it had alleged that IBM had infringed Article 102 by, inter alia, tying various computer products together.[619]

---

[613] See V. Korah, 'The Paucity of Economic Analysis in the EEC Decisions on Competition: *Tetra Pak II*' [1993] *CLP* 150; see also Case T-201/04, *Microsoft* [2007] ECR II-3601, para. 940.

[614] See Korah, ibid.

[615] Commission's *XIXth Report on Competition Policy* (1989), para. 50.

[616] [2005] OJ L253/21.

[617] Commission Press Release IP/97/868. Cf. the *Pelikan/Kyocera* case, *XXVth Report on Competition Policy* (1995), part 87: see Chap. 6. See also D. Maldoom, 'The *Kodak* Case: Power in Aftermarkets' [1996] *ECLR* 473; M. Dolmans and V. Pickering, 'The 1997 Digital Undertaking' [1998] *ECLR* 108; P. Andrews, 'Aftermarket Power in the Computer Services Market: The Digital Undertaking' [1998] *ECLR* 176.

[618] See Commission, *XIVth Report on Competition Policy* (1984) paras. 94–95.

[619] This involved not offering central processing units (CPUs) without a capacity of main memory included in the price (memory bundling); and not offering CPUs without the basic software included in the price (software bundling). IBM did not admit it had a dominant position or that it had committed an abuse but nevertheless undertook to offer its CPUs in the EEC either without main memory or with only such capacity as was strictly required for testing. IBM was also alleged to have committed an abuse by failing to disclose interface information, see Section 13.D, p. 521, and by discriminating between users of IBM software, i.e. refusing to supply certain software installation services to users of non-IBM CPUs. In 2010 the Commission examined complaints (from rival software suppliers) that IBM had tied its mainframe hardware with its operating system. The Commission closed the proceedings on 20 September 2011 and the complaints were withdrawn.

In *Microsoft*[620] the Commission returned to the issue of tying in software markets. The Commission adopted a decision finding that Microsoft had abused its dominant position on the client PC operating systems market, where Microsoft's Windows system had over 90 per cent of the market, by supplying Windows to the computer manufacturers (OEMs) with its Windows Media Player (WMP) pre-installed. The Commission's conclusions were based on the finding that the Windows operating system and the WMP were two distinct products and that by bundling them together Microsoft was leveraging its monopoly power on to the media player market where it faced more competition. The Commission held that for tying to infringe Article 102 four elements must be present (see paragraph 794 in the extract from the Commission's decision): two separate products; dominance in the tying market; the customers are given no choice to obtain the tying product alone; and the tying forecloses competition. The Commission held all four conditions were present in this case. In this extract the Commission explains the detrimental effects of Microsoft's practices.

Microsoft, Commission Decision COMP/37.792, 24 March 2004

Commission

(794) Tying prohibited under [Article 102] of the Treaty requires the presence of the following elements: (i) the tying and tied goods are two separate products; (ii) the undertaking concerned is dominant in the tying product market; (iii) the undertaking concerned does not give customers a choice to obtain the tying product without the tied product; and (iv) tying forecloses competition.

. . .

(979) Through tying WMP with Windows, Microsoft uses Windows as a distribution channel to anti-competitively ensure for itself a significant competition advantage in the media player market. Competitors, due to Microsoft's tying, are *a priori* at a disadvantage irrespective of whether their products are potentially more attractive on the merits.

(980) Microsoft thus interferes with the normal competitive process which would benefit users in terms of quicker cycles of innovation due to unfettered competition on the merits. Tying of WMP increases the content and applications barrier to entry which protects Windows and it will facilitate the erection of such a barrier for WMP. A position of market strength achieved in a market characterised by network effects—such as the media player market—is sustainable, as once the network effects work in favour of a company which has gained a decisive momentum, they will amount to entry barriers for potential competitors . . .

(981) This shields Microsoft from effective competition from potentially more efficient media player vendors which could challenge its position. Microsoft thus reduces the talent and capital invested in innovation of media players, not least its own . . . and anti-competitively raises barriers to market entry. Microsoft's conduct affects a market which could be a hotbed for new and exciting products springing forth in a climate of undistorted competition.

(982) Moreover, tying of WMP allows Microsoft to anti-competitively expand its position in adjacent media-related software markets and weaken effective competition to the eventual detriment of consumers.

It is notable that the Commission took a more 'effects-based' approach in *Microsoft* than it had done in the past, in *Hilti* and *Tetra Pak II*. It did not assume foreclosure of competitors. Instead it said:[621]

There are indeed circumstances relating to the tying of WMP which warrant a closer examination of the effects that tying has on competition in this case. While in classical tying cases, the Commission and the Courts considered the foreclosure effect for competing vendors to be demonstrated by the bundling of a

---

[620] COMP/37.792, 24 March 2004. The case also concerned a refusal to supply, discussed in Section 13.D, p. 521.

[621] COMP/37.792, *Microsoft* 24 March 2004, para. 841.

separate product with the dominant product, in the case at issue, users can and do to a certain extent obtain third party media players through the internet, sometimes for free. There are therefore indeed good reasons not to assume without further analysis that tying WMP constitutes conduct which by its very nature is liable to foreclosure competition.

It carefully set out the effects of Microsoft's tying practice. First, installing WMP on Windows provided a more efficient distribution system than was available to the competitors and led to the 'ubiquity' of WMP.[622] That meant, secondly, that content providers and software developers increasingly used the WMP format to the detriment of the main competitors and their technologies.[623] That led, thirdly, to network effects which in the end would result in the market 'tipping' to WMP: it is not necessary for a competition authority to wait until the tipping has actually occurred, by which time meaningful intervention would be too late.[624]

Microsoft was fined €497,196,304.[625] More seriously for Microsoft the Commission ordered it to offer the OEMs a version of Windows without the WMP. The OEMs must be able to choose between Windows alone and a 'package' of Windows plus the WMP. If they choose the former they can install a rival media player. Consumers therefore have a choice of media player when they buy their PC. Microsoft is not allowed to offer any technological, commercial, or contractual term or inducement to make the bundled version the more attractive, and the unbundled version of Windows must work as well as the bundled version.

The Commission's decision raised a number of difficult and controversial issues. Among these was how far even dominant suppliers should be free to develop new versions of their products with 'built in' features. Microsoft appealed to the GC.[626]

Meanwhile, in the US the competition authorities charged Microsoft with an illegal tie by bundling its own Internet Explorer browser (IE) with its Windows operating system, but the case was dropped.[627] The DOJ was highly critical of the EU *Microsoft* decision:

Imposing antitrust liability on the basis of product enhancements and imposing 'code removal' remedies may produce unintended consequences. Sound antitrust policy must avoid chilling innovation and competition even by 'dominant' companies. A contrary approach risks protecting competitors, not competition, in ways that may ultimately harm innovation and the consumers that benefit from it. It is significant that the U.S. district court considered and rejected a similar remedy in the U.S. litigation.

While the imposition of a civil fine is a customary and accepted aspect of EC antitrust enforcement, it is unfortunate that the largest antitrust fine ever levied will now be imposed in a case of unilateral competitive conduct, the most ambiguous and controversial area of antitrust enforcement. For this fine to surpass even the fines levied against members of the most notorious price fixing cartels may send an unfortunate message about the appropriate hierarchy of enforcement priorities.[628]

---

[622] Ibid., paras. 843–878.

[623] Ibid., paras. 879–944.

[624] Ibid., para. 946.

[625] The fine included that for the other abuse investigated, refusal to supply interface information. This was not a case where the Commission refrained from imposing a fine because of the novelty of the case: it said that as regards the tying/bundling abuse it was not applying a new rule but that *Hilti* and *Tetra Pak II* should have been sufficient guidance to Microsoft in making it clear that its conduct infringed Art. 102: 'the software industry is not exempted from the application of competition law' (ibid., para. 1057).

[626] Case T-201/04, *Microsoft* [2007] ECR II-3601; there was no further appeal to the CJ.

[627] The District Court held that they were two products and that the browser/operating system package constituted a per se illegal tie-in (87 F. Supp.2d 30 (DDC 2000)), but the Court of Appeals sent it back to be tried under a rule of reason analysis (253 F.3d 34 (DCC 2001)). The Court of Appeals was concerned that the bundling of the system and browser served consumer welfare, in that consumers welcome being able to buy a computer with a browser ready installed, rather than having to shop around for one. The US DOJ then withdrew the tying claim, so it was not retried (the States which were also plaintiffs withdrew their claims likewise).

[628] Assistant Attorney General for Antitrust, R. Hewitt Pate, Issues Statement on the EC's Decision in its Microsoft Investigation, 24 March 2004, <http://www.justice.gov/archive/atr/public/press_releases/2004/202976.htm>.

In the *Microsoft* appeal the GC, having stated at the outset the limited nature of its judicial function where complex economic and technical appraisals were concerned,[629] stuck closely to its brief of establishing that the Commission had provided adequate reasoning based on factually accurate, reliable, and consistent evidence capable of substantiating its conclusions. It confirmed (in paragraph 859) that the four factors set out in the Commission's decision,[630] i.e. two products, dominance in the tying market, no choice, and foreclosure, were correct.

The Commission's conclusions were based on the premiss that there were two products, desktop operating systems and media players. Microsoft therefore claimed, first, that it did not supply two distinct products but one integrated one and that therefore it could not commit the abuse of tying or bundling. It argued that it was relevant to ask whether there was consumer demand for the tying product (Windows) without the tied product (WMP). The GC upheld the Commission's decision that there were two products.

Case T-201/04, *Microsoft v Commission* [2007] ECR II-3601

General Court

917. First of all, it must be observed that, as the Commission correctly states at recital 803 to the contested decision, the distinctness of products for the purpose of an analysis under Article [102] has to be assessed by reference to customer demand. Furthermore, Microsoft clearly shares that opinion . . .

918. The Commission was also correct to state, at the same recital, that in the absence of independent demand for the allegedly tied product, there can be no question of separate products and no abusive tying.

919. Microsoft's argument that the Commission thus applied the wrong test and that it ought in reality to have ascertained whether what was alleged to be the tying product was regularly offered without the tied product or whether customers 'want[ed] Windows without media functionality' cannot be accepted.

920. In the first place, the Commission's argument finds support in the case-law (see, to that effect, Case C-333/94 P *Tetra Pak II* . . . paragraph 36; Case T-30/89 *Hilti* . . . paragraph 67; and Case T-83/91 *Tetra Pak II* . . . paragraph 82).

921. In the second place, as the Commission correctly observes in its pleadings, Microsoft's argument, based on the concept that there is no demand for a Windows client PC operating system without a streaming media player, amounts to contending that complementary products cannot constitute separate products for the purposes of Article [102], which is contrary to the Community case-law on bundling. To take Hilti, for example, it may be assumed that there was no demand for a nail gun magazine without nails, since a magazine without nails is useless. However, that did not prevent the Community Courts from concluding that those two products belonged to separate markets.

922. In the case of complementary products, such as client PC operating systems and application software, it is quite possible that customers will wish to obtain the products together, but from different sources. For example, the fact that most client PC users want their client PC operating system to come with word-processing software does not transform those separate products into a single product for the purposes of Article [102].

923. Microsoft's argument ignores the particular intermediary role played by OEMs, who combine hardware and software from different sources in order to offer a ready-to-use PC to the end user. As the Commission very correctly observes at recital 809 to the contested decision, if OEMs and consumers were able to obtain Windows without Windows Media Player, that would not mean that they would choose to obtain Windows without a streaming media player. OEMs follow consumer demand for a preinstalled media player on the operating system and offer a software package including a streaming media

---

[629] Case T-201/04, *Microsoft* [2007] ECR II-3601, paras. 85–89, but see now Chap. 13, Section 8.A.vii, p. 1000.
[630] COMP/37.792, *Microsoft* 24 March 2004, para. 794.

player that works with Windows, the difference being that that player would not necessarily be Windows Media Player.

924. In the third place, and in any event, Microsoft's argument cannot succeed because, as the Commission observes at recital 807 to the contested decision, there exists a demand for client PC operating systems without streaming media players, for example by companies afraid that their staff might use them for non-work-related purposes. That fact is not disputed by Microsoft.

925. Next, the Court finds that a series of factors based on the nature and technical features of the products concerned, the facts observed on the market, the history of the development of the products concerned and also Microsoft's commercial practice demonstrate the existence of separate consumer demand for streaming media players.

926. In the first place, it must be borne in mind that the Windows client PC operating system is system software while Windows Media Player is application software. As the Commission explains at recital 37 to the contested decision, ' "[s]ystem software" controls the hardware of the computer, to which it sends instructions on behalf of "applications" fulfilling a specific user need, such as word processing', and '[o]perating systems are system software products that control the basic functions of a computer and enable the user to make use of such a computer and run application software on it'. More generally, it is clear from the description of those products at recitals 324 to 342 and 402 to 425 to the contested decision that client PC operating systems and streaming media players clearly differ in terms of functionalities.

927. In the second place, there are distributors who develop and supply streaming media players on an autonomous basis, independently of client PC operating systems. Thus, Apple supplies its QuickTime player separately from its client PC operating systems. A further particularly convincing example is that of RealNetworks, Microsoft's main competitor on the streaming media players market, which neither develops nor sells client PC operating systems. It must be pointed out, in that regard, that according to the case-law the fact that there are on the market independent companies specialising in the manufacture and sale of the tied product constitutes serious evidence of the existence of a separate market for that product (see, to that effect, Case C-333/94 P *Tetra Pak II* . . . paragraph 36; Case T-30/89 *Hilti* . . . paragraph 67; and Case T-83/91 *Tetra Pak II* . . . paragraph 82).

928. Likewise, in the third place, Microsoft, as it confirmed in answer to a written question put by the Court, develops and markets versions of Windows Media Player which are designed to work with its competitors' client PC operating systems, namely Apple's Mac OS X and Sun's Solaris. Similarly, RealNetworks' RealPlayer works with, inter alia, the Windows, Mac OS X, Solaris and some UNIX operating systems.

929. In the fourth place, Windows Media Player can be downloaded, independently of the Windows client PC operating system, from Microsoft's Internet site. Likewise, Microsoft releases upgrades of Windows Media Player, independently of releases or upgrades of its Windows client PC operating system.

930. In the fifth place, Microsoft engages in promotions specifically dedicated to Windows Media Player (see recital 810 to the contested decision).

931. In the sixth place, as the Commission pertinently observes at recital 813 to the contested decision, Microsoft offers SDK licences which differ according to whether they relate to the Windows client PC operating system or to Windows Media technologies. There is thus a specific SDK licence for Windows Media Player.

932. Last, and in the seventh place, in spite of the bundling applied by Microsoft, a not insignificant number of customers continue to acquire media players from Microsoft's competitors, separately from their client PC operating system, which shows that they regard the two products as separate.

933. The foregoing facts demonstrate to the requisite legal standard that the Commission was correct to conclude that client PC operating systems and streaming media players constituted two separate products for the purposes of Article [102].

934. That conclusion is not undermined by Microsoft's other arguments.

935. In the first place, as regards Microsoft's argument that the integration of Windows Media Player in the Windows operating system from May 1999 constitutes a normal and necessary step in the evolution of that system and is in keeping with the constant improvement of its media functionality, it is sufficient to observe that the fact that tying takes the form of the technical integration of one product in another does not have the consequence that, for the purpose of assessing its impact on the market, that integration cannot be qualified as the bundling of two separate products.

936. As Microsoft itself acknowledged in answer to a question put to it by the Court at the hearing, its decision to supply WMP 6 as a functionality integrated in the Windows operating system from May 1999 was not the consequence of a technical constraint. At that time there was nothing to prevent Microsoft from distributing WMP 6 in the same way as it had distributed its previous player, NetShow, which since June 1998 had been included on the Windows 98 installation CD: and none of the four Windows 98 default installations provided for the installation of NetShow, which had to be installed by users if they wished to use it.

937. Furthermore, Microsoft's argument that the integration of Windows Media Player in the Windows operating system was dictated by technical reasons is scarcely credible in the light of the content of certain of its own internal communications. Thus, it follows from Mr Bay's email of 3 January 1999 to Mr Gates (see paragraph 911 above) that the integration of Windows Media Player in Windows was primarily designed to make Windows Media Player more competitive with RealPlayer by presenting it as a constituent part of Windows and not as application software that might be compared with RealPlayer.

938. In the second place, Microsoft cannot claim that the Commission fails to show that media functionality is not linked, by nature or according to commercial usage, to client PC operating systems.

939. First, it follows from the considerations set out at paragraphs 925 to 932 above that client PC operating systems and streaming media players do not, by their nature, constitute indissociable products. While it is true that there is a link between a client PC operating system such as Windows and application software such as Windows Media Player, in the sense that both products are on the same computer from the user's perspective and that a media player will only work when an operating system is present, that does not mean that the two products are not dissociable in economic and commercial terms for the purpose of competition rules.

940. Second, as the Commission rightly observes, it is difficult to speak of commercial usage in an industry that is 95% controlled by Microsoft.

941. Third, Microsoft cannot rely on the fact that vendors of competing client PC operating systems also bundle those systems with a streaming media player. On the one hand, Microsoft has not adduced any evidence that such bundling was already carried out by its competitors at the time when the abusive bundling commenced. On the other hand, moreover, it is clear that the commercial conduct of those competitors, far from invalidating the Commission's argument, corroborates it. As may be seen from recitals 822 and 823 to the contested decision and as the Commission observes in its pleadings, some vendors of non-Microsoft operating systems who supply their operating systems with a media player make the installation of the media player optional, or allow it to be uninstalled, or offer a selection of different media players.

942. Fourth, and in any event, it is settled case-law that even when the tying of two products is consistent with commercial usage or when there is a natural link between the two products in question, it may none the less constitute abuse within the meaning of Article [102], unless it is objectively justified (Case C-333/94 P *Tetra Pak II* . . . paragraph 37).

943. Finally, in the third place, the argument which Microsoft put forward at the hearing, that the unbundled version of Windows which it placed on the market pursuant to the remedy had met with no success, must also be rejected. As already stated at paragraph 260 above, the lawfulness of a Community measure must be assessed on the basis of the matters of fact and of law existing at the time when the measure was adopted. Furthermore, any doubts as to the effectiveness of the remedy ordered by the Commission do not in themselves prove that its finding as to the existence of two separate products is wrong.

944. The Court concludes from all of the foregoing considerations that the Commission was correct to find that client PC operating systems and streaming media players constituted separate products.

The test for determining whether products are distinct for the purposes of Article 102 is thus 'consumer demand' (paragraphs 917–918). One relevant issue was not whether consumers wanted Windows without media functionality but whether they necessarily wanted them from the same source (paragraphs 921–922); a second was the important role of the OEMs (paragraph 923); and a third was that some operating systems users (e.g. kill-joy employers) did not want built-in media players (paragraph 924). The GC also looked at features of the market and at aspects of Microsoft's commercial practice. It noted that operating systems and streaming media players have different functionality (paragraph 926); distributors supply media players separately from any supply of a PC client operating system (paragraph 927); Microsoft distributed versions of the WMP designed to work with its competitors' operating systems (paragraph 928); WMP could be downloaded independently from Microsoft's internet site (paragraph 929); Microsoft engaged in WMP-specific promotion (paragraph 930); Microsoft applied different licensing arrangements to Windows and to WMP (paragraph 931); and some consumers obtained media players from the competitors, separately from their PC operating system (paragraph 932).

Secondly, Microsoft argued that the situation did not fall within Article 102(d) and that the Commission had added a foreclosure element not expressly provided for in Article 102(d).[631] The GC confirmed that the second paragraph of Article 102 is not exhaustive and that the Commission's 'four factors' could be deduced from the very concept of bundling and from the case law.

Case T-201/04, *Microsoft v Commission* [2007] ECR II-3601

General Court

850. The Court finds that Microsoft's arguments are purely semantic and cannot be accepted.

851. It is appropriate to recall the way in which the Commission structures its argument relating to bundling in the contested decision.

852. At recital 794 to the contested decision, the Commission states that tying prohibited under Article [102] requires the presence of the four factors set out at paragraph 842 above.

853. Next, it examines Microsoft's conduct in the light of those four factors (recitals 799 to 954 to the contested decision).

854. So, the Commission first observes that Microsoft has a dominant position on the client PC operating systems market (recital 799 to the contested decision). The Court notes that Microsoft does not dispute that fact.

855. Second, the Commission says that streaming media players and client PC operating systems are two separate products (recitals 800 to 825 to the contested decision).

856. Third, the Commission states that Microsoft does not give customers the choice of obtaining Windows without Windows Media Player (recitals 826 to 834 to the contested decision).

857. Fourth, the Commission claims that the tying of Windows Media Player forecloses competition in the media players market (recitals 835 to 954 to the contested decision). It observes, in particular, that in classical tying cases both it and the Community Courts 'considered the foreclosure effect for competing vendors to be demonstrated by the bundling of a separate product with the dominant product' (recital 841 to the contested decision). The Commission states, however, that in the present case there are good reasons not to assume without further analysis that tying Windows Media Player constitutes conduct which by its very nature is liable to foreclose competition (ibid.). The Commission considers, in essence, that 'tying [Windows Media Player] with the dominant Windows makes [Windows Media Player] the platform of choice for complementary content and applications which in turn [creates a risk of] foreclosing competition in the market for media players' (recital 842 to the contested decision). Furthermore, '[t]his has

---

[631] Case T-201/04, *Microsoft* [2007] ECR II-3601, paras. 845–847.

spillover effects on competition in related products such as media encoding and management software (often server-side), but also in client PC operating systems for which media players compatible with quality content are an important application' (ibid.).

858. Last, the Commission examines the basis on which Microsoft relies in its attempt to demonstrate that the abusive conduct imputed to it is objectively justified (recitals 955 to 970 to the contested decision).

859. The Court considers that the Commission's analysis of the constituent elements of bundling is correct and that it is consistent both with Article [102] and with the case-law. The Commission was correct to rely on the factors set out at recital 794 to the contested decision and on the fact that the tying was without objective justification in deciding whether Microsoft's conduct constituted abusive tying. Those factors can be deduced both from the very concept of bundling and from the case-law (see, in particular, Case T-30/89 *Hilti v Commission* . . . upheld in Case C-53/92 P *Hilti v Commission* . . . (both cases being referred to below as 'Hilti') and judgments of the [General Court] and the Court of Justice in *Tetra Pak II*, paragraph 293 above).

860. It must be borne in mind that the list of abusive practices set out in the second paragraph of Article [102] is not exhaustive and that the practices mentioned there are merely examples of abuse of a dominant position (see, to that effect, Case C-333/94 P *Tetra Pak II*, paragraph 293 above, paragraph 37). It is settled case-law that the list of practices contained in that provision is not an exhaustive enumeration of the abuses of a dominant position prohibited by the EC Treaty (Case 6/72 *Europemballage and Continental Can v Commission* . . . paragraph 26, and *Compagnie maritime belge transports and Others v Commission*, paragraph 229 above, paragraph 112).

861. It follows that bundling by an undertaking in a dominant position may also infringe Article [102] where it does not correspond to the example given in Article [102(d)]. Accordingly, in order to establish the existence of abusive bundling, the Commission was correct to rely in the contested decision on Article [102] in its entirety and not exclusively on Article [102 (d)].

862. In any event, the Court holds that the constituent elements of abusive tying identified by the Commission at recital 794 to the contested decision coincide effectively with the conditions laid down in Article[102 (d)].

863. The Court thus rejects Microsoft's argument that in the present case the Commission applied conditions which differ, from two perspectives, from those laid down in Article [102(d)].

864. In the first place, when the Commission states that it is necessary to examine whether the dominant undertaking 'does not give customers a choice to obtain the tying product without the tied product', it is merely expressing in different words the concept that bundling assumes that consumers are compelled, directly or indirectly, to accept 'supplementary obligations', such as those referred to in Article [102(d)].

865. In the present case, as the Court will explain in greater detail at paragraphs 962 and 965 below, that coercion is mainly applied first of all to OEMs, who then pass it on to the end user. The end user is directly exposed to that coercion in the less frequent situation in which, rather than deal through an OEM, he acquires a Windows client PC operating system directly from a retailer.

866. In the second place, it cannot be claimed that the Commission introduced a new condition relating to the foreclosure of competitors from the market in order to establish the existence of abusive bundling within the meaning of Article [102(d)].

867. In that regard, the Court observes that, while it is true that neither that provision nor, more generally, Article [102] as a whole contains any reference to the anti-competitive effect of bundling, the fact remains that, in principle, conduct will be regarded as abusive only if it is capable of restricting competition (see, to that effect, Case T-203/01 *Michelin v Commission* . . . ('Michelin II'), paragraph 237).

868. Furthermore, as will be made explicit at paragraphs 1031 to 1058 below, the applicant cannot claim that the Commission relied on a new and highly speculative theory to reach the conclusion that a foreclosure effect exists in the present case. As indicated at recital 841 to the contested decision, the Commission considered that, in light of the specific circumstances of the present case, it could not merely assume, as it normally does in cases of abusive tying, that the tying of a specific product and a dominant

product has by its nature a foreclosure effect. The Commission therefore examined more closely the actual effects which the bundling had already had on the streaming media player market and also the way in which that market was likely to evolve.

869. In light of the foregoing, the Court considers that the question of the bundling must be assessed by reference to the four conditions set out at recital 794 to the contested decision (see paragraph 842 above) and to the condition relating to the absence of objective justification.

870. The second condition set out at recital 794 to the contested decision must be considered to be met, because it is common ground that Microsoft has a dominant position on the market for what is alleged to be the tying product, namely client PC operating systems. The arguments which Microsoft puts forward in relation to the first three parts of the first plea (see paragraph 839 above) will be examined in conjunction with the four other conditions which must be satisfied to substantiate the finding of abusive tying. In carrying out that examination, the Court will proceed as follows. First, it will examine the condition relating to the existence of two separate products in the light of the arguments advanced by Microsoft on the second and third parts of the plea. Second, it will examine the condition to the effect that the conclusion of contracts is made subject to supplementary obligations, in the light of the arguments which Microsoft puts forward in support of the third part of the plea. Third, the Court will analyse the condition relating to the restriction of competition on the market in the light of the submissions made by Microsoft in connection with the first part of the plea. Fourth, it will examine the objective justifications on which the applicant relies, taking into account the arguments which it puts forward in connection with the second part of the plea.

Thirdly, Microsoft said that there was no restriction of *actual* (rather than *hypothetical*) customer choice. It argued that there was no 'coercion' or supplementary obligation involved. Consumers did not pay more for the WMP functionality of Windows. They did not have to use it. They could install and use third party media players. The GC held all of this irrelevant. It was not necessarily true that the WMP was free just because there was no separate charge for it and, anyway, it was not required that consumers had to pay a certain price for the tied product.[632] Nor did Article 102(d), as could be seen from *Hilti*, demand that the consumers had to use the tied product.[633] Although both OEMs and consumers *could* install and/or use other media players, they had little incentive to do so.[634] This last point was vital for the issue of foreclosure.

Fourthly, Microsoft claimed that the Commission had failed to prove that the integration of WMP with Windows involved foreclosure of competition. It argued that the Commission, recognising that it was not dealing with a 'classical tying case', had applied a 'highly speculative theory, relying on a prospective analysis of the possible reactions of third parties, in order to reach the conclusion that the tying at issue was likely to foreclose competition'.[635] The GC rejected this too.

Case T-201/04, *Microsoft v Commission* [2007] ECR II-3601

General Court

1046. Thus, the release of the bundled version of Windows and Windows Media Player as the only version of the Windows operating system capable of being pre-installed by OEMs on new client PCs had the direct and immediate consequence of depriving OEMs of the possibility previously open to

---

[632] Ibid., paras. 968–969.

[633] Ibid., para. 970.

[634] Ibid., para. 971.

[635] Ibid., para. 1032.

them of assembling the products which they deemed most attractive for consumers and, more particularly, of preventing them from choosing one of Windows Media Player's competitors as the only
media player. On this last point, it must be borne in mind that at the time RealPlayer had a significant
commercial advantage as market leader. As Microsoft itself acknowledges, it was only in 1999 that it
succeeded in developing a streaming media player that performed well enough, given that its previous
player, NetShow, 'was unpopular with customers because it did not work very well' (recital 819 to the
contested decision). It must also be borne in mind that between August 1995 and July 1998 it was
RealNetworks' products—first RealAudio Player, then RealPlayer—that were distributed with Windows.
There is therefore good reason to conclude that if Microsoft had not adopted the impugned conduct
competition between RealPlayer and Windows Media Player would have been decided on the basis of
the intrinsic merits of the two products.

. . .

1052. As the Commission asserts at recital 870 to the contested decision, while downloading is in
itself a technically inexpensive way of distributing media players, vendors must deploy major resources
to 'overcome end-users' inertia and persuade them to ignore the pre-installation of [Windows Media
Player]'.

1053. Second, Microsoft has put forward no argument capable of calling in question the Commission's
finding that the other methods of distributing streaming media players mentioned in the contested decision, namely bundling the media player with other software or Internet access services, and retail sale,
are only a 'second-best solution and [do] not rival the efficiency and effectiveness of distributing software
pre-installed on [Windows] PCs' (recitals 872 to 876 to the contested decision).

1054. It follows from the foregoing that in the analysis set out at recitals 843 to 878 to the contested decision, which is the first stage of its reasoning, the Commission demonstrated to the
requisite legal standard that the bundling of Windows and Windows Media Player from May 1999
inevitably had significant consequences for the structure of competition. That practice allowed
Microsoft to obtain an unparalleled advantage with respect to the distribution of its product and to
ensure the ubiquity of Windows Media Player on client PCs throughout the world, thus providing
a disincentive for users to make use of third-party media players and for OEMs to pre-install such
players on client PCs.

1055. Admittedly, as Microsoft contends, a number of OEMs continue to add third-party media players
to the packages which they offer to their customers. It is also common ground that the number of media
players and the extent of the use of multiple players are continually increasing. However, those factors do
not invalidate the Commission's conclusion that the impugned conduct was likely to weaken competition
within the meaning of the case-law. Since May 1999 vendors of third-party media players have no longer
been able to compete through OEMs to have their own products placed instead of Windows Media Player
as the only media player on the client PCs assembled and sold by OEMs.

1056. It should further be noted that the merits of the findings made above are borne out by data
examined by the Commission in the third stage of its reasoning. More particularly, as will be explained
at paragraphs 1080 to 1084 below, the data mentioned at recitals 905 to 926 to the contested decision
show a clear tendency in favour of using Windows Media Player to the detriment of competing media
players.

1057. It follows from information communicated by Microsoft itself during the administrative
procedure and referred to at recitals 948 to 951 to the contested decision that the significant growth
in the use of Windows Media Player has not come about because that player is of better quality
than competing players or because those media players, and particularly RealPlayer, have certain
defects.

1058. In the light of all the foregoing considerations, the Court concludes that the Commission's findings in the first stage of its reasoning are in themselves sufficient to establish that the fourth constituent

element of abusive bundling is present in this case. Those findings are not based on any new or speculative theory, but on the nature of the impugned conduct, on the conditions of the market and on the essential features of the relevant products. They are based on accurate, reliable and consistent evidence which Microsoft, by merely contending that it is pure conjecture, has not succeeded in showing to be incorrect.

1059. It follows from the foregoing that it is not necessary to examine the arguments which Microsoft puts forward against the findings made by the Commission in the other two stages of its reasoning. None the less, the Court considers that it should examine them briefly.

1060. In the second stage of its reasoning, the Commission seeks to establish that the ubiquity of Windows Media Player as a result of its bundling with Windows is capable of having an appreciable impact on content providers and software designers.

1061. The Commission's theory is based on the fact that the market for streaming media players is characterised by significant indirect network effects or, to use the expression employed by Mr Gates, on the existence of a 'positive feedback loop' (recital 882 to the contested decision). That expression describes the phenomenon where, the greater the number of users of a given software platform, the more there will be invested in developing products compatible with that platform, which, in turn reinforces the popularity of that platform with users.

1062. The Court considers that the Commission was correct to find that such a phenomenon existed in the present case and to find that it was on the basis of the percentages of installation and use of media players that content providers and software developers chose the technology for which they would develop their own products (recital 879 to the contested decision). The Commission correctly stated, first, that those operators tended primarily to use Windows Media Player as that allowed them to reach the very large majority of client PC users in the world and, second, that the transmission of content and applications compatible with a given media player was in itself a significant competitive factor, since it increased the popularity of that media player, and, in turn, favoured the use of the underlying media technology, including codecs, formats (including DRM) and server software (recitals 880 and 881 to the contested decision).

. . .

1078. In the third stage of its reasoning, the Commission examines the evolution of the market in light of market surveys carried out by Media Metrix, Synovate and Nielsen/NetRatings and concludes that the data in those surveys 'consistently point to a trend in favour of usage of [Windows Media Player] and Windows Media formats to the detriment of the main competing media players (and media player technologies)' (recital 944 to the contested decision).

1079. The Court finds that the conclusion referred to in the preceding paragraph is correct.

. . .

1088. It follows from the foregoing considerations that the final conclusion which the Commission sets out at recitals 978 to 984 to the contested decision concerning the anti-competitive effects of the bundling is well founded. The Commission is correct to make the following findings:

- Microsoft uses Windows as a distribution channel to ensure for itself a significant competitive advantage on the media players market (recital 979 to the contested decision);
- because of the bundling, Microsoft's competitors are a priori at a disadvantage even if their products are inherently better than Windows Media Player (ibid.);
- Microsoft interferes with the normal competitive process which would benefit users by ensuring quicker cycles of innovation as a consequence of unfettered competition on the merits (recital 980 to the contested decision);
- the bundling increases the content and applications barriers to entry, which protect Windows, and facilitates the erection of such barriers for Windows Media Player (ibid.);
- Microsoft shields itself from effective competition from vendors of potentially more efficient media players who could challenge its position, and thus reduces the talent and capital invested in innovation of media players (recital 981 to the contested decision);

- by means of the bundling, Microsoft may expand its position in adjacent media-related software markets and weaken effective competition, to the detriment of consumers (recital 982 to the contested decision);
- by means of the bundling, Microsoft sends signals which deter innovation in any technologies in which it might conceivably take an interest and which it might tie with Windows in the future (recital 983 to the contested decision).

1089. The Commission therefore had ground to state, at recital 984 to the contested decision, that there was a reasonable likelihood that tying Windows and Windows Media Player would lead to a lessening of competition so that the maintenance of an effective competition structure would not be ensured in the foreseeable future. It must be made clear that the Commission did not state that the tying would lead to the elimination of all competition on the market for streaming media players. Microsoft's argument that, several years after the beginning of the abuse at issue, a number of third-party media players are still present on the market therefore does not invalidate the Commission's argument.

1090. It follows from all of the foregoing considerations that Microsoft has put forward no argument capable of vitiating the merits of the findings made by the Commission in the contested decision concerning the condition relating to the foreclosure of competition. The Court must therefore conclude that the Commission has demonstrated to the requisite legal standard that the condition was satisfied in the present case.

The section on foreclosure is the most interesting part of the judgment.[636] The GC concerned itself with the threat to the structure of competition. In paragraph 1034 it talked of 'appreciably altering the balance of competition in favour of Microsoft', and in paragraph 1054 it deduced from the *first stage of the Commission's reasoning*, i.e. just its findings as to the ubiquity of WMP, that the Commission had demonstrated to the requisite legal standard that the bundling 'inevitably had significant consequences for the structure of competition'.[637] It was assumed that this advantage led to foreclosure.[638] The GC thought it unnecessary to examine the further stages of the Commission's reasoning, i.e. the impact on the software developers and the evolution of the market,[639] although it did so for the sake of completeness. The emphasis of the judgment is on the market structure, on the fact that the ubiquity of WMP gave it an advantage unrelated to its 'intrinsic merits'[640] (which means its qualities rather than its advantages in distribution).[641]

Microsoft argued that its behaviour was objectively justified.[642] It defended its 'business model' as having benefits for software developers, OEMs, and consumers. The GC answered that some of the benefits could be achieved without integration and the fact that software developers and site creators were convenienced by knowing that WMP was present on nearly all client PCs in the world was

---

[636] For comment on this see, e.g., C. Ahlborn and D. S. Evans, 'The *Microsoft* Judgment and its Implications for Competition Policy Towards Dominant Firms in Europe' (2008–2009) 75 *Antitrust LJ* 887; Rousseva, n. 269, 252–255; L. Lovdahl Gormsen, 'Why the European Commission's Enforcement Priorities on Article 82 EC Should be Withdrawn' [2010] *ECLR* 45, 48; D. Howarth and K. McMahon, '"Windows has Performed an Illegal Operation": The Court of First Instance's Judgment in *Microsoft v Commission*' [2008] *ECLR* 117.

[637] The point at para. 1055 where the GC in effect speculates that an increase in the use of the competitors' products might have been greater in the absence of the impugned conduct recalls the finding about the rise in Virgin's market share in *British Airways*: see Section 11.F.c, p. 454 ff.

[638] Case T-201/04, *Microsoft* [2007] ECR II-3601, para. 1058.

[639] Ibid., para. 1059.

[640] Ibid., para. 1046.

[641] Ahlborn and Evans, n. 636, 887.

[642] At this point in the judgment the GC clarified where the burden of proof lies when objective justification is raised. See Section 5.E, p. 374.

exactly why the integration led to foreclosure.[643] The GC dismissed the claim that the removal of WMP from Windows would lead to a degradation of the latter.[644] Above all the GC stressed that the Commission had not ordered Microsoft to cease supplying Windows with WMP, but only to also supply Windows without it.

The Commission's remedy in *Microsoft*, the supply of an alternative 'naked' version of Windows without WMP installed, was not a success. OEMs had no interest in such a product.[645] It would have been different had the Commission ordered Microsoft *not* to supply Windows with WMP.

In 2009 the Commission sent an SO to Microsoft saying that Microsoft might have infringed Article 102 by tying its Internet Explorer (IE) browser to Windows in that Windows was only supplied with IE ready installed.[646] The matter was concluded with a commitments decision whereby Microsoft undertook to provide users of Windows PCs who have IE set as a default web browser with a browser 'Choice Screen' and to allow OEMs to choose which browser to install.[647] The 'Choice Screen' was made operational on 1 March 2010. The commitments decision meant that the Commission did not have to produce a fully reasoned decision and the possibility of the technical tying issue being re-examined in the GC did not arise. However, on 6 March 2013 the Commission fined Microsoft €561 million for failing to comply with its commitments.[648]

(iv) The *Google/Android* Investigation

In April 2015 the Commission opened proceedings against Google in respect of its Android mobile operating system.[649] The Commission is concerned with allegations concerning the tying or bundling of certain Google applications and services with the Android system 'to the detriment of consumers and developers of innovative services and products'.[650] Android is an open-source system which is distributed for free and the allegations relate to the installing by OEMs of Google's core apps and the Google Mobile Services suite.[651]

---

[643] Case T-201/04, *Microsoft* [2007] ECR II-3601, para. 1151.

[644] Ibid., paras. 1164–1166.

[645] The GC said that the lawfulness of the Commission decision had to be judged at the time of its adoption. The fact that the remedy had not worked was irrelevant and could not be taken into account by the GC looking at the separate product issue with hindsight (para. 943). According to Ahlborn and Evans, n. 636 (who acted for or on behalf of Microsoft), between the date of the naked Windows being made available and the date of the oral hearing in the case no OEM in the world chose to install it. Retailers bought 11,787 copies of the naked Windows XP, less than 0.005% of those sold in Europe.

[646] MEMO/09/15. The tying of Windows and IE was the subject of the DOJ proceedings in the US discussed in the text at n. 627, p. 482.

[647] IP/09/1941, [2010] OJ C36/7. In a speech on 21 October 2009 in Brussels, 'Competition and Consumers in the 21st Century', SPEECH/09/486, available at <http://europa.eu/rapid/press-release_SPEECH-09-486_en.htm>, Neelie Kroes said, 'In IT we have stopped dominant companies abusing their position to restrict consumer choice. No matter how big those infringers are—we have consistently said that no company is above the law. Our message to these companies is: You can't run away or spend your way around Europe's rules. Speaking of this—promising news on Microsoft, don't you think? In the New Year we hope that hundreds of millions of consumers in Europe will get a choice of which web browser to use on their computers.'

[648] IP/13/2013. The Commission found that Microsoft failed to roll out the browser choice screen with its Windows 7 Service Pack 1 from May 2011 to July 2012, so that 15 million Windows users in the EU did not see the choice screen during that period.

[649] COMP/40.009, *Google (Android)*, IP/15/4780.

[650] MEMO/15/4782; IP/16/1492; MEMO/16/1484. See further <http://chillingcompetition.com/2013/09/05/some-thoughts-on-the-new-anti-google-android-complaint-post-13/>; <http://chillingcompetition.com/2013/09/09/some-thoughts-on-the-new-anti-google-android-complaint-post-33-bundling-allegations/>; and <http://chillingcompetition.com/2013/09/16/android-google-and-bundling-some-follow-up-thoughts/>.

[651] The initial problem is whether Google is dominant in respect of Android.

F. TYING AND BUNDLING IN THE GUIDANCE PAPER

(i) General

We have seen that in *Microsoft* the GC agreed with the Commission that tying prohibited under Article 102 requires the presence of the following elements:

- the tying and the tied goods are two separate products;
- the undertaking concerned is dominant in the tying product market;
- the undertaking concerned does not give customers a choice to obtain the tying product without the tied product; and
- the tying forecloses competition.

The Commission deals with tying and bundling in paragraphs 47–74 of the Guidance Paper. It does 'not approach tying practices from a presumption of harm'.[652] It will normally take action under Article 102 where an undertaking is dominant in the tying market and: (a) the tying and tied products are distinct products; and (b) the tying practice is likely to lead to anti-competitive foreclosure.[653] The Guidance Paper says nothing about the lack of choice/coercion condition. The matter of dominance is discussed in Chapter 6.

(ii) The Tying and the Tied Goods are Two Separate Products

Both the case law and the Guidance Paper recognise that there must be distinct products involved. The problem is that almost any product can be broken down into smaller parts:

A coat can be sold without its buttons, a desk without its drawers . . . The market would come to a standstill, however, if the antitrust laws gave every customer a legal right to atomize his purchases as much as he chose.[654]

In some cases the separation is clear. This was so in *Centre Belge*,[655] for example, where the television company tied the use of its own sales agents to the sale of its advertising slots and in *Napier Brown/British Sugar*[656] where the undertaking adopted a delivered pricing policy which, by only providing the product and the delivery together, excluded competition on the separate although ancillary transport market. However, it is more difficult when there is a possibility that the undertaking is supplying a 'system' consisting of several components, as in *Hilti* and *Tetra Pak II*.[657] The issue is even more difficult where IT markets are concerned.

The test for whether there are distinct products is 'consumer demand'—is there actual or potential consumer demand for the products separately? However, there may be demand for only one of them on a stand-alone basis. In *Microsoft* the GC approved the Commission's statement that there can be no abusive tying in the absence of independent demand for the allegedly *tied* product.[658] It rejected the relevance of Microsoft's arguments that there was no demand for the tying product separately. Nevertheless, the inconvenient fact in *Microsoft* was that there was no longer any such

---

[652] Faull and Nikpay, n. 1, 4.529.

[653] Guidance Paper, para. 50.

[654] Hovenkamp, n. 203, 436–437.

[655] Case 311/84, *Centre Belge* [1985] ECR 3261. The CJ treated this as a refusal to supply scenario: see Section 13.

[656] [1988] OJ L284/41.

[657] See also Case T-427/08, *Confédération européenne des associations d'horlogers-réparateurs v Commission (CEAHR)* [2010] ECR II-5865, see Chap. 1, Section 15.B.vii.e, p. 72.

[658] Case T-201/04, *Microsoft* [2007] ECR II-3601, para. 918.

demand and so it proved once the remedy was implemented. Once consumers had tasted operating systems with media functionality a 'naked' system was unwanted and the OEMs saw no point in purchasing it. Arguably the lack of demand for a naked version of Windows should have led to the adoption of a different separate product test in the first place.

The Guidance Paper states:

51. Whether the products will be considered by the Commission to be distinct depends on customer demand. Two products are distinct if, in the absence of tying or bundling, a substantial number of customers would purchase or would have purchased the tying product without also buying the tied product from the same supplier, thereby allowing stand-alone production for both the tying and the tied product [citing paragraphs 917, 921, and 922 of *Microsoft*]. Evidence that two products are distinct could include direct evidence that, when given a choice, customers purchase the tying and the tied products separately from different sources of supply, or indirect evidence, such as the presence on the market of undertakings specialised in the manufacture or sale of the tied product without the tying product [citing paragraph 67 of *Hilti*] or of each of the products bundled by the dominant undertaking, or evidence indicating that undertakings with little market power, particularly in competitive markets, tend not to tie or not to bundle such products.

It is clear from the second sentence that the test is whether, without the tie, a substantial number of customers would purchase the tied product *from the same supplier*. That is not the same as asking whether there would be a demand for the tying product *if the tied product did not exist*. In *Hilti* and *Tetra Pak II* the answer to that would be 'no' because the machinery was useless without the consumables.[659]

The Guidance Paper does not specifically mention the 'commercial usage' test in Article 102(d) which the CJ dismissed as not decisive in *Tetra Pak II*[660] and which is unhelpful where the dominant undertaking has a quasi-monopoly. Nevertheless, the last sentence of paragraph 51 contemplates using evidence of the practices of undertakings with little market power in competitive markets, if relevant.

Consumer demand can change, sometimes very quickly, and nowhere more so than in the new economy.[661] New products are brought on to the market but may become commonly integrated into others, or products may be introduced which in time are broken down and the elements sold separately. Where new products are concerned, the 'commercial usage' test is again unhelpful. If the purpose of the rules on tying is the welfare of consumers then the inquiry about distinct products is just part of the overall assessment of whether 'the efficiencies of tying outweighs the inherent reduction in choice for the consumer'.[662] Although there are usually consumers whose wants are different from those of the majority the consumer welfare test has to ensure that *most* consumers are better off and that consumer gains exceed consumer losses.

(iii) Lack of Customer Choice/Coercion

The lack of customer choice referred to as an element of the abuse in *Microsoft*[663] is sometimes described as 'coercion'. The complications of using 'coercion' and 'lack of choice' as conditions for identifying abusive tying and bundling are graphically demonstrated by *Microsoft* because although a customer may in some cases have to buy the tied product in order to obtain the tying product in a case such as *Microsoft*, the customer is given the tied product with no price increase, does not have to

---

[659] The GC relied on *Hilti* and *Tetra Pak II* in paras. 920–921 of the *Microsoft* judgment. See Ahlborn and Evans, n. 636.

[660] Case C-333/94 P, *Tetra Pak II* [1996] ECR I-5951, para. 37.

[661] The Court has to consider the position at the date of the adoption of the decision, Case T-201/04, *Microsoft* [2007] ECR II-3601COMP/37.792, para. 943.

[662] See the comments of Linklaters on the Discussion Paper, <http://ec.europa.eu/competition/antitrust/art82/127.pdf>, 17.

[663] See, e.g., Case T-201/04, *Microsoft* [2007] ECR II-3601, paras. 865 and 963.

use it, and can use competitors' products instead. The Guidance Paper does not mention this criterion, as it does not regard 'coercion' as a separate element of the assessment of tying.[664]

(iv) Anti-competitive Foreclosure

The Guidance Paper adopts an effects-based approach to tying. This specific section of the Guidance Paper, like the others, must be read in the light of the overall principle that the Commission's enforcement activity is focused on foreclosure which is 'anti-competitive' in that it operates to the detriment of consumers, so it is the effects on consumers which is the issue. The factors for identifying anti-competitive foreclosure set out in paragraphs 53–58 have to be read in conjunction with those in paragraph 20.[665]

The Commission will take into account whether the dominant undertaking's strategy is a lasting one, for example through technical tying;[666] whether the undertaking is dominant in respect of more than one product in the bundle;[667] and whether there are insufficient customers who buy the tied product alone to sustain competitors, in which case those customers may face higher prices.[668] The Commission is also concerned with inputs to a production process where a dominant undertaking may use tying to prevent customers avoiding a rise in the price of the tying product:[669]

56. If the tying and the tied product can be used in variable proportions as inputs to a production process, customers may react to an increase in price for the tying product by increasing their demand for the tied product while decreasing their demand for the tying product. By tying the two products the dominant undertaking may seek to avoid this substitution and as a result be able to raise its prices.

The Commission also highlights the situation where the tying product market is regulated so that, constrained in its pricing freedom in the tying market, the undertaking may use tying to raise prices in the tied market instead.[670]

The Guidance Paper recognises both 'offensive and 'defensive' leverage[671] and one of the factors the Commission will consider is the effect of tying in reducing the number of alternative tied product suppliers to the prejudice of those trying to enter the tying market alone.[672]

(v) Multi-product Rebates (Mixed Bundling)

The Guidance Paper deals specifically with multi-product rebates.[673] The Commission's approach to multi-product rebates is similar to its approach to rebates generally.[674] It would prefer to examine whether the incremental revenue covers the incremental costs for each product in the discounted bundle but, since that is not usually possible, the Commission will normally use the incremental price as a proxy. It will normally intervene only if the price of each product in the dominant undertaking's bundle falls below LRAIC. This is the application of the AEC test to what is in essence

---

[664] See Faull and Nikpay, n. 1, 4.488–4.491.

[665] See Section 4, p. 367.

[666] Guidance Paper, para. 53.

[667] Ibid., para. 54.

[668] Ibid., para. 55.

[669] Ibid., para. 56.

[670] Ibid., para. 57.

[671] Ibid., para. 52. For offensive and defensive leverage see Section 12.C, p. 476.

[672] Ibid., para. 58.

[673] Ibid., paras. 59–61.

[674] See Section 11.G, p. 471.

a pricing issue. Where both the dominant undertaking and its competitors are selling identical bundles[675] the Commission will examine whether the price of the *bundle* is predatory.[676]

(vi) Efficiencies

If the conditions laid down in paragraph 30 of the Guidance Paper for the 'efficiency defence' are fulfilled the Commission will consider efficiency claims.[677] It will look at claims of savings in production or distribution, reduced transaction costs for customers and suppliers, and enabling pass-on of efficiencies stemming from the supplier producing or purchasing large quantities of the tied product. Notably, it will also examine the possibility that combining two products into a single new one might 'enhance the ability to bring such a product to the market to the benefit of consumers'.

13. REFUSAL TO SUPPLY

A. GENERAL

It is possible for a dominant undertaking to infringe Article 102 by refusing to supply its products or services or grant access to its facilities. This includes 'constructive' refusals, where the offer is such that the supplier knows it is unacceptable, or the terms are unreasonable or supply is unduly delayed.[678] Unilateral refusals to supply by non-dominant firms are not caught by the competition rules, as seen in *Bayer*.[679] This is an example of conduct being prohibited only because of the dominant position.

Dominant undertakings do not have an absolute duty to supply all those who request them to do so. However, in certain situations a refusal to supply is an abuse. EU law has been mainly concerned with vertically integrated undertakings dominant in an upstream market refusing to supply competitors in the downstream market. This is the only refusal to supply scenario that is dealt with in the Guidance Paper. In this section, parts B to D deal with the 'upstream/downstream' cases, and part E with the others. Refusal to supply as a way of hindering parallel trade is dealt with in Section 17.

Holding refusal to supply to be an abuse is contrary to deep-seated principles of freedom of contract and property which hold that one should be free to deal with whom one chooses and dispose of one's property as one chooses.[680] It also threatens the dominant undertaking's incentives to invest and innovate, which is harmful to dynamic efficiency and welfare. There are particular concerns in respect of intellectual property rights (IPRs). The EU position on when and why in the name of competition a duty to supply should be imposed has been developed in a stream of decisions and judgments beginning with *Commercial Solvents*[681] in 1973.

---

[675] Or could do so in a timely way without being deterred by possible additional costs.

[676] Guidance Paper, para. 61.

[677] Ibid., para. 62.

[678] E.g., in *Napier Brown/British Sugar* [1988] OJ L284/41 the downstream competitor asked for industrial sugar, but British Sugar was prepared to offer only 'special grain' sugar and at so high a price that the competitor could not use it; see also IV/34.174, *Sealink/B&I Holyhead: Interim Measures* 11 June 1992; *Deutsche Post AG: Interception of cross-border mail* [2001] OJ L331/40; Case T-301/04, *Clearstream* [2009] ECR II-3155; COMP/39.525, *Telekomunikacja Polska* 22 June 2011, upheld Case T-486/11, *Orange Polska* EU:T:2015:1002; COMP/39.692, *IBM Maintenance Services* Commitments Decision 13 December 2011.

[679] Cases C-2 and 3/01 P, *Bundesverband der Arzneimittel-Importeure EV and the Commission v Bayer AG (Bayer)* [2004] ECR I-23.

[680] See Jacobs AG in Case C-7/97, *Bronner* [1998] ECR I-7791.

[681] Cases 6 and 7/73, *Commercial Solvents* [1974] ECR 223.

Conduct which can be classified under some other heading of abuse, such as tying, can also be seen as a refusal to supply. In *Centre Belge*[682] the condition that advertisers could buy advertising time on television only if they used the television company's own telesales agency was both a refusal to supply and a tie, as was the delivered pricing policy in *Napier Brown/British Sugar*.[683] The difficulty with this is that the law has developed different principles in respect of tying and refusal to supply.[684] In the Guidance Paper the Commission states that it will deal with refusals to supply customers who do not agree to tying arrangements in accordance with the principles on tying and bundling.[685]

Refusal to supply as an abuse raises the question of the appropriate remedy. Article 3 of Regulation 17 provided that where the Commission finds an infringement of Article 102 'it may by decision require the undertakings . . . concerned to bring such infringement to an end'. In *Commercial Solvents* the CJ established that the Commission could order an undertaking positively to do certain acts or to provide certain advantages which had been wrongfully withheld, including making specific orders about what exactly the dominant undertaking should supply to whom. This continues to be the position under Article 7 of Regulation 1/2003.[686] Some proceedings in the energy sector have been resolved by the dominant undertaking agreeing to divest itself of assets.[687]

B. THE EXCLUSION OF COMPETITORS FROM DOWNSTREAM MARKETS

(i) The *Commercial Solvents* case

Commercial Solvents was the first case in which a refusal to supply was held to be capable of infringing Article 102.

Cases 6 and 7/73, *Istituto Chemioterapico Italiano SpA and Commercial Solvents Corp v Commission* [1974] ECR 223

Commercial Solvents (CSC) supplied aminobutanol, a raw material from which a derivative, ethambutol, could be produced. CSC's Italian subsidiary, Istituto, resold aminobutanol in Italy to Zoja, an Italian pharmaceutical company which made ethambutol-based anti-TB drugs from it. In 1970 Zoja cancelled its orders for aminobutanol from Istituto as independent distributors were supplying it cheaper. When this proved unsatisfactory Zoja placed new orders with Istituto. However, CSC had decided no longer to supply aminobutanol to the EEC but only an upgraded product, dextroaminobutanol, which Istituto would convert into ethambutol itself, manufacturing its own ethambutol-based drugs. Zoja was therefore refused supplies. Zoja could not obtain supplies on the world market as all its searches led back to CSC. Zoja complained to the Commission which held that CSC was dominant in the market for aminobutanol and had abused its position by refusing to supply it to Zoja, a refusal which would lead to the elimination of

---

[682] Case 311/84, *Centre Belge* [1985] ECR 3261.

[683] *Napier Brown/British Sugar* [1988] OJ L284/41.

[684] As can be seen by comparing the discussion in Section 12 with that in this section. In J.-Y. Art and G. S. McCurdy, 'The European Commission's Media Player Remedy in its *Microsoft* Decision: Compulsory Code Removal Despite the Absence of Tying or Foreclosure' [2004] *ECLR* 694, Microsoft's lawyers argued that the WMP part of *Microsoft* should have been judged under refusal to supply rather than tying principles.

[685] Guidance Paper, para. 77.

[686] [2003] OJ L1/1.

[687] COMP/39.402, *RWE—Gas Foreclosure* Commitments Decision 18 March 2009, see Section 13.B.vi, p. 508.

one of the principal manufacturers of ethambutol in the common market. CSC appealed to the CJ, which upheld the finding of dominance on the raw material market[688] and the finding of abuse.[689]

Court of Justice

24. It appears from the documents and from the hearing that the suppliers of raw material are limited, as regards the EEC, to Istituto, which, as stated in the claim by CSC, started in 1968 to develop its own specialities based on ethambutol, and in November 1969 obtained the approval of the Italian government necessary for the manufacture and in 1970 started manufacturing its own specialities. When Zoja sought to obtain further supplies of aminobutanol, it received a negative reply. CSC had decided to limit, if not completely to cease, the supply of nitropropane and aminobutanol to certain parties in order to facilitate its own access to the market for the derivatives.

25. However, an undertaking being in a dominant position as regards the production of raw material and therefore able to control the supply to manufacturers of derivatives, cannot, just because it decides to start manufacturing these derivatives (in competition with its former customers) act in such a way as to eliminate their competition which in the case in question, would amount to eliminating one of the principal manufacturers of ethambutol in the Common Market. Since such conduct is contrary to the objectives expressed in Article [3(1)(g)] of the Treaty and set out in greater detail in Articles [101 and 102], it follows that an undertaking which has a dominant position in the market in raw materials and which, with the object of reserving such raw materials for manufacturing its own derivatives, refuses to supply a customer, which is itself a manufacturer of these derivatives, and therefore risks eliminating all competition on the part of this customer, is abusing its dominant position within the meaning of Article [102]. In this context it does not matter that the undertaking ceased to supply in the spring of 1970 because of the cancellation of the purchases by Zoja, because it appears from the applicants' own statement that, when the supplies provided for in the contract had been completed, the sale of aminobutanol would have stopped in any case.

26. It is also unnecessary to examine, as the applicants have asked, whether Zoja had an urgent need for aminobutanol in 1970 and 1971 or whether this company still had large quantities of this product which would enable it to reorganize its production in good time, since that question is not relevant to the consideration of the conduct of the applicants.

27. Finally CSC states that its production of nitropropane and aminobutanol ought to be considered in the context of nitration of paraffin, of which nitropropane is only one of the derivatives, and that similarly aminobutanol is only one of the derivatives of nitropropane. Therefore the possibilities of producing the two products in question are not unlimited but depend in part on the possible sales outlets of the other derivatives.

28. However the applicants do not seriously dispute the statement in the Decision in question to the effect that 'in view of the production capacity of the CSC plant it can be confirmed that CSC can satisfy Zoja's needs, since Zoja represents a very small percentage (approximately 5–6 per cent) of CSC's global production of nitropropane'. It must be concluded that the Commission was justified in considering that such statements could not be taken into account.

29. These submissions must therefore be rejected.

According to paragraph 25 of the judgment, the factors leading to the finding of abuse were:

- CSC was using its dominant position on the raw material market to affect competition on the derivatives market;

---

[688] See Chap. 6.

[689] It also upheld the finding of an effect on inter-Member State trade on the basis that the elimination of Zoja as a competitor would affect the competitive structure of the common market: see Chap. 5.E, p. 271.

- CSC was refusing to supply an existing customer[690] because it wanted to compete with it downstream; and

- the refusal risked eliminating the customer from the downstream market.

CSC had, in effect, decided to integrate vertically. The CJ did not consider whether this strategy might produce efficiencies, and there was no discussion in the judgment about the possible benefits to the end-user, the consumer.

The *Commercial Solvents* principle was applied to a deliberate move to remove a competitor from a downstream market in *Napier Brown/British Sugar*,[691] where the dominant supplier of industrial sugar, which itself produced the derivative retail sugar, refused to supply industrial sugar to a competitor on the downstream market who was an existing customer. *Commercial Solvents* involved the supply of physical products to existing customers but in *Centre Belge* the CJ applied the *Commercial Solvents* principle to *new* customers deprived of the provision of a *service*.[692]

(ii) The Supply of Spare Parts, and Aftermarkets

An early application of the *Commercial Solvents* principle involved the supply of spare parts. The CJ established in *Hugin*[693] that an undertaking which refuses to supply spare parts and services for its product may infringe Article 102 even though it is dominant only in the market for its own spare parts and not the primary product market.[694] In *Hugin* the undertaking stopped supplying the customer which repaired and serviced its machines, because it wanted to carry out those operations itself. Like Commercial Solvents, it wanted to integrate vertically. The Commission held the refusal to continue supplying was an abuse because it would lead to an existing customer being unable to carry out a particular line of business. As in *Commercial Solvents* the Commission did not consider questions of efficiencies or the advantages of the vertical integration to consumers (the owners of the machines). The CJ annulled the decision because it found no effect on inter-Member State trade but did not suggest that Hugin's conduct was not an abuse.

The CJ dealt obliquely with refusal to supply spare parts in two Article 267 references concerning the licensing of IPRs covering car parts, *Renault*[695] and *Volvo*.[696] In both cases the undertakings were trying to protect their own dealers. In *Renault* the Court held that a refusal by the car manufacturer to license did not necessarily constitute an abuse, but would do so if it gave rise to 'certain abusive conduct . . . such as the arbitrary refusal to deliver spare parts to independent repairers'.[697] The Commission cited *Volvo* in its 2012 commitments decision *IBM Maintenance Services*.[698] There maintenance services for IBM mainframe computers were offered both by IBM itself and by third parties (TPMs). The Commission was concerned with aspects of IBM's dealings with TPMs in respect of the supply of spare parts and other resources which TPMs needed. These included restricted

---

[690] It was not material that Zoja had previously cancelled its purchases from Istituto (see para. 25, last sentence).

[691] *Napier Brown/British Sugar* [1988] OJ L284/41.

[692] Case 311/84, *Centre Belge* [1985] ECR 3261, paras. 25–27.

[693] Case 22/78, *Hugin* [1979] ECR 1869.

[694] The CJ annulled the decision because it found no effect on inter-Member State trade, but it confirmed the finding of dominance. As discussed in Chap. 6, however, the spare parts of a particular brand do not always constitute a separate relevant market. In Case T-427/08, *Confédération européenne des associations d'horlogers-réparateurs (CEAHR) v Commission* [2010] ECR II-5865 (see Chap. 1, Section 15.B.vii.e) the Commission's rejection of a complaint from independent watch repairers about the refusal of luxury watch manufacturers to continue to supply them with spare parts was annulled, partly on the grounds that the Commission had wrongly defined the market.

[695] Case 53/87, *CICCRA v Renault* [1988] ECR 6039.

[696] Case 238/87, *AB Volvo v Erik Veng* [1988] ECR 6211.

[697] Case 53/87, *CICCRA* [1988] ECR 6039, para. 16.

[698] COMP/39.692, *IBM Maintenance Services* 13 December 2011.

access to spare parts, unreasonable terms for the supply of some parts, unreasonably delayed access, and withheld information. The Commission considered the cumulative effect might amount to a constructive refusal to supply that could raise concerns under Article 102(b) as the conduct had the potential to lead to the exclusion of the few existing rival firms that competed with IBM on the downstream market which might limit markets to the prejudice of consumers. IBM gave commitments as to its future practices and contractual conditions.[699]

(iii) The 'Essential Facilities' Concept

The *Commercial Solvents* principle and its subsequent application has given rise to the issue of the concept of 'essential facilities' in EU law.

The definition of an 'essential facility' is fraught with difficulty. The basic proposition is that competitors downstream need access to something owned or controlled by a vertically integrated dominant undertaking in order to provide products or services to customers. It is sometimes referred to as a 'bottleneck monopoly'. A refusal to grant access to an essential facility may be a breach of the special responsibility that the holder of the facility has as a dominant undertaking.

The 'essential facilities' concept originated in US law, where it has proved to be highly contentious.[700] When the Commission used the expression in 1992 it was therefore employing terminology which was familiar to competition lawyers and the subject of much debate in the US context. The CJ itself has never used the expression 'essential facility'.[701] Indeed, it has carefully avoided doing so and has preferred the term 'indispensable'. However, much of the discourse on refusal to supply has been couched in terms of essential facilities or, as one scholar has called it, 'the epithet that dares not speak its name'.[702] It is therefore a convenient expression to use so long as one does not accord it legal significance. When we speak of 'essential facilities' in this chapter we are therefore referring to resources which are indispensable or, as the Commission puts it in the Guidance Paper, 'objectively necessary' for competitors.[703]

Refusal to supply 'essential facilities' has arisen widely in relation to access to physical infrastructures (where the term 'essential facilities' is most suitable) and networks, particularly in liberalised sectors of the economy where facilities indispensable to the operations of competitors downstream are still held by the incumbent. It is the imposition of a 'duty to deal' outside those situations which is the most problematic.

(iv) The Commission Decisions on 'Essential Facilities' in EU Law

The Commission did not use the expression 'essential facility' until *B&I/Sealink* in 1992[704] but it is possible, particularly with hindsight, to see the essential facilities rationale in the earlier cases, even *Commercial Solvents* itself.[705] This is also true of the Commission decision *London-European Sabena*[706]

---

[699] See F. Domanico and M. Angeli, 'An Analysis of the IBM Commitment Decision Concerning the Aftermarket for IBM Mainframe Computers' (2012) 1 *Competition Policy Newsletter*.

[700] The present position in US law is described in Section 13.G, p. 537.

[701] Although the GC has, see Cases T-374–375, 384, and 388/94, *European Night Services v Commission* [1998] ECR II-3141, para. 191 and Case T-52/00, *Coe Clerici Logistics SpA v Commission* [2003] ECR II-2123, para. 62. And see, e.g., Jacobs AG in Case C-7/97, *Bronner* [1998] ECR I-7791, Opinion, paras. 33 and 45–53.

[702] S. Anderman, 'The Epithet That Dares Not Speak Its Name: The Essential Facilities Concept in Article 82 EC and IPRs After the *Microsoft* Case' in Ezrachi, n. 41, 87.

[703] Guidance Paper, para. 83.

[704] IV/34.174, *Sealink/B&I Holyhead: Interim Measures* 11 June 1992.

[705] See J. Temple Lang, 'Defining Legitimate Competition: Companies' Duties to Supply Competitors and Access to Essential Facilities' (1994) 18 *Fordham Int'l LJ* 437 and the Commission's citation of cases in *Sealink/B&I*.

[706] [1988] OJ L317/47. The airline Sabena, which was dominant in Belgium in the computer reservation services market, refused to give a rival airline access to the system. The Commission found that the refusal, which was to pressurise the rival either to withdraw from the London–Brussels route or to raise prices, and to punish it for not using Sabena's ground-handling services, was an abuse.

and *British-Midland/Aer Lingus*[707] which both concerned the airline industry and are best seen in the context of the Commission's drive to liberalise the European air transport sector using the competition rules.

IV/34.174, *Sealink/B&I Holyhead: Interim Measures* 11 June 1992

Sealink Harbours was the owner and operator of the port at Holyhead, in Wales, and as such was held by the Commission to be in a dominant position on the market on the British side for port facilities for ferry services on the 'central corridor' route between Wales and Ireland (Holyhead to Dublin and Dun Laoghaire). It ran ferries on that route. B&I ran ferries from the port on the same route. B&I used a particular berth and the limitations of the harbour were such that whenever Sealink's ferries passed the berth the drawing away of water and turbulence meant that B&I had to cease all loading and unloading activity. B&I complained that Sealink intended to introduce a new timetable which would cause greater disruption to B&I's schedules in this way. The Commission adopted a decision providing for interim measures, ordering Sealink to return to its previous timetable. The matter never went to a final decision as the dispute was settled.

Commission

41. A dominant undertaking which both owns or controls and itself uses an essential facility, i.e., a facility or infrastructure without access to which competitors cannot provide services to their customers, and which refuses its competitors access to that facility or grants access to competitors only on terms less favourable than those which it gives its own services, thereby placing the competitors at a competitive disadvantage, infringes Article [102], if the other conditions of that Article are met . . .[708] A company in a dominant position may not discriminate in favour of its own activities in a related market (Case C-260/89 *Elliniki Radiophonia*, paragraphs 37–38) . . . The owner of an essential facility which uses its power in one market in order to strengthen its position in another related market, in particular, by granting its competitor access to that related market on less favourable terms than those of its own services, infringes Article [102] where a competitive disadvantage is imposed upon its competitor without objective justification.

. . .

42. The owner of the essential facility, which also uses the essential facility, may not impose a competitive disadvantage on its competitor, also a user of the essential facility, by altering its own schedule to the detriment of the competitor's service, where, as in this case, the construction or the features of the facility are such that it is not possible to alter one competitor's service in the way chosen without harming the other's. Specifically, where, as in this case, the competitor is already subject to a certain level of disruption from the dominant undertaking's activities, there is a duty to the dominant undertaking not to take any action which will result in further disruption. That is so even if the latter's actions make, or are primarily intended to make its operations more efficient. Subject to any objective elements outside its control, such an undertaking is under a duty not to impose a competitive disadvantage upon its competitor in the use of the shared facility without objective justification, as seemed to be accepted by SHL in 1989.

[707] [1992] OJ L96/34. This did not involve an upstream/downstream market situation. Aer Lingus refused to interline the tickets of another airline (British Midland) when the latter began competing on the London (Heathrow)–Dublin air-route. The Commission held that the refusal was an abuse. It condemned refusals to interline where they have significant effects on competition (and are not objectively justified). See the Commission's *XXIInd Report on Competition Policy* (1992), point 218. Aer Lingus was dominant only because of the narrowly defined market (Heathrow–Dublin air route) and no more than a minnow in the wider European airline market.

[708] The Commission here cited Cases 6 and 7/73, *Commercial Solvents* [1974] ECR 223; Case 311/84, *Centre Belge* [1985] ECR 3261; Case 53/87, *CICCRA* [1988] ECR 6039; Case 238/87, *AB Volvo v Erik Veng* [1988] ECR 6211; Case C-260/89, *Elliniki Radiophonia Tileorasi (ERT) v DEP* [1991] ECR I-2925; Cases T-69–70/89, *RTE, ITP, BBC v Commission (Magill)* [1991] ECR II-485 (the CJ judgment had not yet been given); Case C-18/88, *LRTT v GB-INNO-BM SA* [1991] ECR I-5941; and the Commission decisions *National Carbonising* [1976] OJ L35/6; *London-European/Sabena* [1988] OJ L317/47; *British Midland/Aer Lingus* [1992] OJ L96/34.

In the first sentence of paragraph 41 the Commission laid down the basic principle that an owner of an 'essential facility' may have to provide non-discriminatory access to a competitor. The Commission developed the theme in further decisions concerning ports. In *Sea Containers Ltd/ Stena*[709] Stena Sealink (previously Sealink, the port authority and ferry operator involved in *Sealink/ B&I Holyhead*) refused to give the requested access to a company wanting to operate a new fast ferry service on the Wales–Ireland central corridor route by lightweight catamaran. The Commission, repeating the *B&I* decision, held this was an abuse. The *Sea Containers/Stena* decision made it clear that the duty to supply essential facilities set out in *Sealink/B&I* applies to new as well as to existing customers. This was also shown in another decision taken on the same day, *Port of Rødby*, in which the Commission held that Denmark had infringed Article 106(1) in conjunction with Article 102.[710]

The Commission decision in *European Night Services*[711] was taken under Article 101. It raised similar issues to the Article 102 cases although the Commission did not actually use the expression 'essential facilities'. Railway undertakings in the UK, France, Germany, and the Netherlands formed a joint venture to provide overnight passenger rail services between the UK and the Continent via the Channel Tunnel. The Commission granted an exemption conditional on the parent companies providing locomotives, train crews, and train paths to any other undertaking wishing to compete in the running of a similar service, on the same terms as they gave to the joint venture. The GC annulled the decision, inter alia,[712] in respect of the condition as regards the locomotives and train crews. It held that the Commission had not properly analysed why the requirement to supply was appropriate and had not supplied adequate reasoning for imposing this condition. The GC expressly referred to 'essential facilities'. It stressed that a facility can be essential only if there are no substitutes. Mere advantage to the competitor is not enough. This judgment showed a disinclination to apply the essential facilities concept too widely, a disinclination which was vindicated by the CJ's *Bronner* judgment[713] two months later.

(v) Problems with 'Essential Facilities'

In *B&I/Sealink* 'essential facilities' were defined as 'a facility or infrastructure without access to which competitors cannot provide services to their customers'. This definition provides only a starting point. 'Essential facilities' should be narrowly confined since a finding that an undertaking's resources or assets fall within that category may result in the undertaking being forced to share them with its competitors. This represents a severe interference with an undertaking's rights which can only be justified where there would otherwise be a serious effect on competition irremediable by less intrusive measures.

There has to be some way of identifying assets to which access by competitors is truly 'essential' or 'indispensable' rather than merely desirable. Even when these are identified there may be practical problems about access or sharing. Some facilities (ports for example) have limited physical capacity, and the question arises *which* competitors should be given access. There is also the matter of the terms on which access is given. If the parties are left to settle their own terms the owner of

---

[709] IV/34.689, *Sea Containers Ltd/Stena Sealink* [1994] OJ L15/8.

[710] *Port of Rødby (Euro-port) v Denmark* [1994] OJ L55/5. The publicly owned port authority operated the only ferry to Puttgarden in Germany jointly with German national railways. The Danish Government refused to grant other ferry companies either access to the port or permission to build another terminal in the immediate vicinity. The Commission held that the double refusal had the effect of eliminating a potential competitor and infringed Art. 102. For Art. 106, which deals with the application of the competition rules to public undertakings, see Chap. 8. See also COMP/35.388, *Morlaix (Port of Roscoff)* [1995] 5 CMLR 177.

[711] [1994] OJ L259/20.

[712] Cases T-374–375, 384, and 388/94, *European Night Services* [1998] ECR II-3141. Other aspects of this case are dealt with in Chap. 4. The requirement that train paths should be provided was quashed because it was based on false premises to do with the relevant transport directive (91/440 [1991] OJ L237/25).

[713] Case C-7/97, *Bronner* [1998] ECR I-7791.

the facility may be able to impose a price which is prohibitively high.[714] If the terms are to be set by an authority such as the Commission, however, the authority ends up acting as a price regulator.[715]

Outside the area of access to facilities in liberalised sectors where existing facilities, such as networks, were built with public money the concept of refusal to supply as an abuse needs to be treated with great caution.[716] An overenthusiastic approach may result in undertakings having to share with competitors assets which they have developed over many years at great expense. Robbing firms of the fruits of their endeavours may be injurious to the public interest and consumer welfare as it removes incentives to innovation.

The following extract is the conclusion from Areeda's critical survey of the essential facilities doctrine in US law. He considers that it should be treated with the greatest circumspection, in particular because of the dangerous disincentive to innovation. Obviously, his remarks relate to the doctrine in US law at the time of writing, but the first two sentences of paragraph 6 were cited with approval by the US Supreme Court in *Verizon v Trinko*.[717]

P. Areeda, 'Essential Facilities: An Epithet in Need of Limiting Principles' (1990) 58 *Antitrust LJ*, 841, 852–853

I conclude by offering six principles that should limit application of the essential facilities concept.

(1) There is no general duty to share. Compulsory access, if it exists at all, is and should be very exceptional . . .

(2) A single firm's facility, as distinct from that of a combination, is 'essential' only when it is both critical to the plaintiff's competitive vitality and the plaintiff is essential for competition in the marketplace. 'Critical to the plaintiff's competitive vitality' means that the plaintiff cannot compete effectively without it and that duplication or practical alternatives are not available.

(3) No one should be forced to deal unless doing so is likely substantially to improve competition in the marketplace by reducing price or by increasing output or innovation. Such an improvement is unlikely (a) when it would chill desirable activity; (b) [when] the plaintiff is not an actual or potential competitor; (c) when the plaintiff merely substitutes itself for the monopolist or shares the monopolist's gains; or (d) when the monopolist already has the usual privilege of charging the monopoly price for its resources . . .

(4) Even when all these conditions are satisfied, denial of access is never per se unlawful; legitimate business purpose always saves the defendant. What constitutes legitimacy is a question of law for the courts. Although the defendant bears the burden of coming forward with a legitimate business purpose, the plaintiff bears the burden of persuading the tribunal that any such claim is unjustified.

(5) The defendant's intention is seldom illuminating, because every firm that denies its facilities to rivals does so to limit competition with itself and increase its profits. Any instruction on intention must ask whether the defendant had an intention to exclude by *improper* means. To get ahead in the marketplace is not, itself the kind of intention that contaminates conduct . . .

(6) No court should impose a duty to deal that it cannot explain or adequately and reasonably supervise. The problem should be deemed [irremediable] by antitrust law when compulsory access requires the court to assume the day-to-day controls characteristic of a regulatory agency. Remedies may be practical

---

[714] See Case C-242/95, *GT–Link A/S v De Danske Statsbaner (DSB)* [1997] ECR I-4449, where the CJ held that excessive duties levied by a public undertaking on a ferry company in breach of Art. 106, in conjunction with Art. 102, had to be repaid.

[715] For the difficulty in settling the terms of supply, see Case T-167/08, *Microsoft* EU:T:2012:323.

[716] But for the problems of identifying assets acquired with public money, and of treating them differently, see Section 13.F, p. 536.

[717] 540 US 398, 124 S.Ct. 872 (2004).

(a) when admission to a consortium is at stake, especially at the outset, (b) when divestiture is otherwise appropriate and effective, or (c) when, as in *Otter Tail*, a regulatory agency already exists to control the terms of dealing. However, the availability of a remedy is not reason to grant one. Compulsory sharing should remain exceptional.

(vi) The *Bronner* Case

Bronner was an Article 267 reference[718] in which the CJ set out the limited circumstances in which access to a facility will be ordered. Both the Advocate General and the CJ referred to the CJ's 1995 judgment in *Magill*,[719] which concerned IPRs. Refusals to supply which involve IPRs raise particular problems, and the IPRs cases are all dealt with together in Section 13.C. However, in order to understand the *Magill* reference points in *Bronner*, an outline of the case is given here.

Magill concerned an Irish publisher who wanted to publish a composite television listings magazine. However, the broadcasters whose programmes could be received in Ireland at the time refused permission to publish their schedules, which were protected by copyright under Irish and UK law. The CJ found that in exceptional circumstances a refusal to supply material protected by an IPR could be an abuse. The exceptional circumstances in *Magill* were that there was no substitute for a weekly television guide; the refusal to supply was preventing the appearance of a new product for which there was consumer demand; there was no justification for the refusal; and the refusal enabled the television companies to reserve the downstream market to themselves by denying access to the indispensable raw material.

Bronner was notable for the Opinion of Advocate General Jacobs urging the necessity of confining the essential facilities concept within strict limits. He reminded the Court that the primary purpose of Article 102 is to protect consumers, not competitors.

Case C-7/97, *Oscar Bronner GmbH & Co KG v Mediaprint* [1998] ECR I-7791

Bronner published a newspaper, *Der Standard*, which had approximately 3.6 per cent of the daily newspaper market in Austria in terms of circulation and 6 per cent in terms of advertising revenue. Mediaprint published two daily newspapers in Austria, which together had a combined market share of 46.8 per cent of circulation and 42 per cent of advertising revenues. For the distribution of its newspapers Mediaprint had established a nationwide home-delivery scheme. Bronner wanted Mediaprint to include *Der Standard* in its delivery scheme but Mediaprint refused. Mediaprint did include another newspaper it did not publish in its scheme but it did the whole of the printing and distribution in respect of that paper. Bronner sought an order from the Austrian courts requiring Mediaprint to cease abusing its alleged dominant position on the home-delivery market and requiring it to include *Der Standard* in its home-delivery service in return for reasonable remuneration. It claimed that other methods of sale, such as postal delivery, were less advantageous than home-delivery and that given the small circulation of *Der Standard* it would be entirely unprofitable for it to organise its own home-delivery service. The Austrian court referred to the CJ two questions as to whether the conduct in issue amounted to an abuse of a dominant position.

Advocate General Jacobs

56. First, it is apparent that the right to choose one's trading partners and freely to dispose of one's property are generally recognized principles in the laws of the Member States, in some cases with constitutional status. Incursions on those rights require careful justification.

---

[718] There was no appreciable effect on inter-Member State trade and therefore the case actually involved a question of Austrian law, which mirrors Art. 102. The reference was admissible, paras. 12–22 of the judgment.

[719] Cases C-241–242/91 P, *RTE & ITP v Commission* [1995] ECR I-743, known as '*Magill*'.

57. Secondly, the justification in terms of competition policy for interfering with a dominant undertaking's freedom to contract often requires a careful balancing of conflicting considerations. In the long term it is generally pro-competitive and in the interest of consumers to allow a company to retain for its own use facilities which it has developed for the purpose of its business. For example, if access to a production, purchasing or distribution facility were allowed too easily there would be no incentive for a competitor to develop competing facilities. Thus while competition was increased in the short term it would be reduced in the long term. Moreover, the incentive for a dominant undertaking to invest in efficient facilities would be reduced if its competitors were, upon request, able to share the benefits. Thus the mere fact that by retaining a facility for its own use a dominant undertaking retains an advantage over a competitor cannot justify requiring access to it.

58. Thirdly, in assessing this issue it is important not to lose sight of the fact that the primary purpose of Article [102] is to prevent distortion of competition—and in particular to safeguard the interests of consumers—rather than to protect the position of particular competitors. It may therefore, for example, be unsatisfactory, in a case in which a competitor demands access to a raw material in order to be able to compete with the dominant undertaking on a downstream market in a final product, to focus solely on the latter's market power on the upstream market and conclude that its conduct in reserving to itself the downstream market is automatically an abuse. Such conduct will not have an adverse impact on consumers unless the dominant undertaking's final product is sufficiently insulated from competition to give it market power.

Court of Justice

38. Although in *Commercial Solvents* v. *Commission* and *CBEM*, cited above, the Court of Justice held the refusal by an undertaking holding a dominant position in a given market to supply an undertaking with which it was in competition in a neighbouring market with raw materials (*Commercial Solvents* v. *Commission*, paragraph 25) and services (*CBEM*, paragraph 26) respectively, which were indispensable to carrying on the rival's business, to constitute an abuse, it should be noted, first, that the Court did so to the extent that the conduct in question was likely to eliminate all competition on the part of that undertaking.

39. Secondly, in *Magill*, at paragraphs 49 and 50, the Court held that refusal by the owner of an intellectual property right to grant a licence, even if it is the act of an undertaking holding a dominant position, cannot in itself constitute abuse of a dominant position, but that the exercise of an exclusive right by the proprietor may, in exceptional circumstances, involve an abuse.

40. In *Magill*, the Court found such exceptional circumstances in the fact that the refusal in question concerned a product (information on the weekly schedules of certain television channels) the supply of which was indispensable for carrying on the business in question (the publishing of a general television guide), in that, without that information, the person wishing to produce such a guide would find it impossible to publish it and offer it for sale (paragraph 53), the fact that such refusal prevented the appearance of a new product for which there was a potential consumer demand (paragraph 54), the fact that it was not justified by objective considerations (paragraph 55), and that it was likely to exclude all competition in the secondary market of television guides (paragraph 56).

41. Therefore, even if that case-law on the exercise of an intellectual property right were applicable to the exercise of any property right whatever, it would still be necessary, for the *Magill* judgment to be effectively relied upon in order to plead the existence of an abuse within the meaning of Article [102] in a situation such as that which forms the subject-matter of the first question, not only that the refusal of the service comprised in home delivery be likely to eliminate all competition in the daily newspaper market on the part of the person requesting the service and that such refusal be incapable of being objectively justified, but also that the service in itself be indispensable to carrying on that person's business, inasmuch as there is no actual or potential substitute in existence for that home-delivery scheme.

42. That is certainly not the case even if, as in the case which is the subject of the main proceedings, there is only one nationwide home-delivery scheme in the territory of a Member State and, moreover, the

owner of that scheme holds a dominant position in the market for services constituted by that scheme or of which it forms part.

43. In the first place, it is undisputed that other methods of distributing daily newspapers, such as by post and through sale in shops and at kiosks, even though they may be less advantageous for the distribution of certain newspapers, exist and are used by the publishers of those daily newspapers.

44. Moreover, it does not appear that there are any technical, legal or even economic obstacles capable of making it impossible, or even unreasonably difficult, for any other publisher of daily newspapers to establish, alone or in co-operation with other publishers, its own nationwide home-delivery scheme and use it to distribute its own daily newspapers.

45. It should be emphasised in that respect that, in order to demonstrate that the creation of such a system is not a realistic potential alternative and that access to the existing system is therefore indispensable, it is not enough to argue that it is not economically viable by reason of the small circulation of the daily newspaper or newspapers to be distributed.

46. For such access to be capable of being regarded as indispensable, it would be necessary at the very least to establish, as the Advocate General has pointed out at point 68 of his Opinion, that it is not economically viable to create a second home-delivery scheme for the distribution of daily newspapers with a circulation comparable to that of the daily newspapers distributed by the existing scheme.

47. In the light of the foregoing considerations, the answer to the first question must be that the refusal by a press undertaking which holds a very large share of the daily newspaper market in a Member State and operates the only nationwide newspaper home-delivery scheme in that Member State to allow the publisher of a rival newspaper, which by reason of its small circulation is unable either alone or in co-operation with other publishers to set up and operate its own home-delivery scheme in economically reasonable conditions, to have access to that scheme for appropriate remuneration does not constitute abuse of a dominant position within the meaning of Article [102].

In this ruling the CJ avoided using the term 'essential facilities', despite its use by the Advocate General, and preferred 'indispensable'. It referred back again to *Commercial Solvents*. In paragraph 41 the CJ listed four factors which would have to be present before the refusal could be an abuse:

- first, the refusal would have to be likely to eliminate all competition in the downstream market *from the person requesting access*;
- secondly, the refusal must be incapable of objective justification;
- thirdly, the access must be indispensable to carrying on the other person's business; and
- fourthly, there must be no actual or potential substitute for it.

These criteria were patently not fulfilled in *Bronner*.

In *Bronner* the CJ took a restrictive view of the obligation to grant access to facilities. It stressed that the refusal must be likely to *eliminate* all competition from the undertaking requesting access, not merely make it harder for it to compete. Access must also be *indispensable,* not desirable or convenient, and there must be no actual or potential substitute for the requested facility. Moreover, in paragraphs 45–46 the CJ held that in the case before it access could have been indispensable only if it was not economically viable to create a home-delivery system for a newspaper *with a comparable circulation to the dominant firm's*. It was not enough to show it was not viable for a small-circulation paper. *Bronner* left many questions unanswered. It did not address the problems about pricing, for example, or how the facility owner should deal with competing claims for access, or the role of competition authorities in essential facilities scenarios. The judgment sidestepped the question whether the case law on IPRs (i.e. *Magill*), is applicable to other property rights. It did, however, make it quite clear that an obligation to grant access to a facility will arise only in exceptional circumstances and that the key issues are *indispensability* and *non-substitutability*. *Bronner*, of course, was an easy case for the CJ. It concerned a facility built up by a private undertaking with its own resources and a situation in which the other undertaking was operating satisfactorily on the downstream market without access to it. If the CJ had considered that it was a situation suitable for the application of the essential facilities doctrine then all dominant firms owning or controlling a facility someone else might have found useful were at risk, and incentives to innovation would have been seriously undermined. However, it was made apparent that facilities are not lightly to be considered 'indispensable' or access lightly required. The essential facilities doctrine was 'reined in' by the CJ[720] which showed it was alive to the harm to competition which can arise from an over-broad application of a duty to deal.

In some decisions since *Bronner* the Commission appears to have relaxed the requirement about the elimination of competition. In *Telekomunikacja Polska*, where the Commission found that the dominant telecommunications incumbent (TP) had proposed unreasonable conditions for whole-sale access and delayed negotiations over access to its network the Commission said:

> The establishment of likely effects of a refusal to supply does not mean that rivals were actually forced to exit the market. It is sufficient that rivals are disadvantaged and consequently compete less aggressively.[721]

The Commission considered that it was of crucial importance to the competitors to obtain a minimum critical network size. TP's delaying tactics had prevented the competitors from reaching the critical customer size rapidly and so prevented them from climbing the 'investment ladder' earlier.[722] In *ENI*, the Commission's preliminary view was that the *Bronner* test was satisfied if the refusal was 'likely to lead either to the elimination or the prevention of the development of effective competition on the downstream market resulting in consumer harm'.[723] The 'effective competition' standard echoes the *Microsoft* judgment.[724]

In *TeliaSonera*, the margin squeeze case, it will be recalled that the CJ said that the *Bronner* conditions do not necessarily apply when assessing the abusive nature of conduct which consists in supplying services or selling goods on conditions which are disadvantageous or on which there might be no purchaser.[725] The Commission cited this in its *IBM Mainframe Services* commitments decision.[726] In its *Telefónica* margin squeeze decision[727] the Commission considered that the *Bronner* conditions did not have to be satisfied in the circumstances of the case which fundamentally differed from those in *Bronner*.[728] The point was not discussed on appeal because the GC, following *TeliaSonera*, considered margin squeeze to be an abuse independent of refusal to supply[729] but the 'Telefónica exceptions', as they have been called[730] appear in the Guidance Paper and are therefore discussed in that context.[731]

---

[720] As the Commission recognised in IV/36.431, *Info-Lab*, see (1999) 1 *Competition Policy Newsletter* 35 where Ricoh, a photocopier manufacturer, refused to supply a toner producer with empty cartridges compatible with Ricoh machines. The Commission held that Ricoh did not have a dominant position on a relevant market but that, even if it had, in the light of *Bronner* such forced cooperation could be envisaged only under exceptional circumstances which did not pertain there.

[721] COMP/39.525, 22 June 2011, para. 815, upheld Case T-486/11, *Orange Polska* EU:T:2015:1002, where the point was not raised.

[722] COMP/39.525, *Telekomunikacja Polska* 22 June 2011, para. 818, see D. Kamiński, A. Rogozińska, and B. Sasinowska, 'Telekomunikacja Polska Decision: Competition Law Enforcement in Regulated Markets' (2011) 3 *Competition Policy Newsletter* 3; see also Case T-301/04, *Clearstream* [2009] ECR II-3155.

[723] COMP/39.315, ENI Commitments Decision 29 September 2010, para. 40.

[724] See Section 13.D, p. 521 ff.

[725] Case C-52/09, *TeliaSonera* [2011] ECR I-527, para. 55; see Section 9.B.ii, p. 417 ff.

[726] COMP/39.692, *IBM Maintenance Services* Commitments Decision 13 December 2011, para. 37.

[727] COMP/38.784, *Wanadoo España v Telefónica* 4 July 2007.

[728] As explained in Section 9.B.iii, p. 424 ff.

[729] Case T-336/07, *Telefónica* EU:T:2012:172, aff'd Case C-295/12 P, *Telefónica* EU:C:2014:2062.

[730] D. Geradin, 'Refusal to Supply and Margin Squeeze: A Discussion of Why the "Telefonica Exceptions" are Wrong', TILEC Discussion Paper No. 2011-009, available at <http://papers.ssrn.com/sol3/papers.cfm?abstract_id=1762687>.

[731] In Section 13.F.

The markets most ripe for the application of the essential facilities doctrine in the EU are those concerning transport and utility infrastructures originally developed with public money. Where competition is being brought on to markets which have previously been statutory monopolies, duplication of facilities such as networks may not be feasible. Liberalisation therefore cannot be fully realised unless the new competitors are given access to the incumbent's established facilities. Incumbents, however, have strong incentives to delay such access and discriminate against downstream competitors.[732] The Commission decisions discussed in this section demonstrate how the essential facilities concept can be used to open up transport markets, for example.[733] It can be applied both through, and alongside, sector-specific regulation. The Commission has also been active in using Article 102 in the energy sector. In *RWE* the Commission was concerned that RWE was restricting its downstream competitors' access to its gas transmission network. It adopted a commitments decision whereby RWE undertook to divest itself of part of its network.[734] In *ENI* one of the Commission's objections was the dominant gas company's strategic under-investment which limited the access of competitors.[735] According to the commitments decision ENI had embarked on a strategy of deliberately avoiding capacity expansions in order to limit third party access.[736] The Commission considered that the mere fact that current capacities are fully used does not suffice to exclude an abuse, and that a 'dominant essential facility holder' is under an obligation to take all possible measures to remove the capacity constraints and organise its business to maximise the capacity available.[737] Like RWE, ENI undertook to divest itself of some of its assets and businesses. *ENI* raises the question of the existence of a 'duty to invest' as well as a 'duty to supply', at least in the case of incumbents in liberalised sectors and it will be recalled that the CJ in *Post Danmark* said in respect of the special responsibility of dominant undertakings that the origin of the dominant position in a former legal monopoly was a fact to be taken into account. Unfortunately where cases are terminated by commitments decisions the principles therein do not come before the EU Courts.

The Commission has dealt specifically with access agreements in the telecommunications sector.[738]

(vii) Refusal to Supply in the Financial Industry

The Commission intervened in the financial services sector when it issued a Notice on cross-border credit transfers, because it considered that access to payment systems is vital if banks are to compete on relevant markets.[739] It took its first decision on a refusal to supply in the financial sector in

---

[732] See the discussion in O'Donoghue and Padilla, n. 1, 807–809.

[733] And see also *GVG/FS* [2004] OJ L11/17 where the Italian State-owned railway company (FS) abused its dominant position on the Italian passenger rail market by refusing to enter into an international grouping with a German railway company. FS gave undertakings to grant access.

[734] COMP/39.402 *RWE—Gas Foreclosure* Commitments Decision 18 March 2009 (for commitments decisions, see Chap. 13); the Competition Commissioner's press release said this, along with the other remedies, would result in more customer choice and that she was satisfied 'that RWE will no longer be able to use the control of its network to favour its own gas supply affiliate over its competitors', IP/09/410. See also, e.g., COMP/39.316 *Gaz de France* Commitments Decision 3 December 2009 and COMP/39.389 *German Electricity Wholesale Markets and German Electricity Balancing Markets (E.ON)* Commitments Decision 26 November 2008, [2009] OJ C36/8. In March 2015 the Commission sent a statement of objections to Bulgarian Energy Holdings alleging that it may have infringed Art. 102 by hindering competitors' access to key gas infrastructures in Bulgaria, COMP/39.849 *BEH Gas* IP/15/4651.

[735] COMP/39.315, *ENI* Market Test Notice 5 March 2010 [2010] OJ C55/13.

[736] COMP/39.315, *ENI* Commitments Decision 29 September 2010, paras. 57–60.

[737] Ibid., paras. 57–60, n. 43, citing IV/34.689, *Sea Containers Ltd/Stena Sealink* [1994] OJ L15/8 and *Port of Rødby* [1994] OJ L55/5.

[738] Commission Notice on access agreements in the telecommunications sector [1998] OJ C265/2.

[739] Commission Notice on the application of the competition rules to cross-border credit transfers [1995] OJ C251/3; see also *SWIFT*, XXVIIth Report on Competition Policy (1997), 143.

Clearstream.[740] Clearstream (CBF) was the Central Securities Depository (CSD) for securities issued under German law and kept in collective safe custody. It was the only such recognised depository in Germany. The Commission found it was in a dominant position in the market for the provision of primary clearing and settlement services for securities issued according to German law to CSDs in other Member States and to international CSDs (ICSDs). It held that CBF and its parent had infringed Article 102 in denying Euroclear Bank (EB) clearing and settlement services for two years (and, for a period, in charging it discriminatory prices which were higher than those charged to other security depositories outside Germany). ED was a direct competitor of CBF's sister company, CBL. Although the infringement had ceased the Commission adopted the decision (without imposing a fine) 'to make it clear that the competition rules are being applied in the financial industry'.[741] The Commission said that CBF's behaviour qualified as a refusal to supply contrary to Article 102 because it was an unavoidable trading partner, new entry into its activity being unrealistic for the foreseeable future; EB could not duplicate the requested services; and CBF's behaviour had the effect of impairing EB's ability to provide efficient cross-border clearing and settlement services to clients. The Commission referred to EB's 'legitimate expectation' that it would be supplied with services within a reasonable period of time. The Commission stated that anti-competitive practices committed by market players in the area of cross-border clearing and settlement 'are a major source of inefficiencies that harm consumers'.[742] The GC upheld the Commission decision. The judgment contains several references to the *Microsoft* judgment.[743]

Case T-301/04, *Clearstream Banking v Commission* [2009] ECR II-3155

General Court

140. According to settled case-law, the concept of abuse is an objective concept relating to the behaviour of an undertaking in a dominant position which is such as to influence the structure of a market where, as a result of the very presence of the undertaking in question, the degree of competition is weakened and which, through recourse to methods different from those which condition normal competition in products or services on the basis of the transactions of commercial operators, has the effect of hindering the maintenance of the degree of competition still existing on the market or the growth of that competition (*Hoffmann-La Roche v Commission*, paragraph 49 above, paragraph 91; see also Case T-203/01 *Michelin v Commission*, paragraph 132 above, paragraph 54, and the case-law cited).

141. Accordingly, the conduct of an undertaking in a dominant position may be regarded as an abuse within the meaning of Article [102] even in the absence of any fault (Case T-65/89 *BPB Industries and British Gypsum v Commission* . . . paragraph 70).

142. Consequently, the applicants' argument that they did not pursue an anti-competitive objective is irrelevant to the legal characterisation of the facts. In that context, proving that it was the applicants' objective to postpone the grant of access in order to prevent a customer and competitor of the Clearstream group from providing its services effectively may reinforce the conclusion that there is an abuse of a dominant position but is not a condition for such a finding.

143. It should also be noted that, in the present case, access was refused to EB which was, at the same time, a customer of CBF on the German market for securities in collective custody, but also

---

[740] COMP/38.096, *Clearstream Banking AG and Clearstream International SA* 2 June 2004; IP/04/705 and MEMO/04/705.

[741] IP/04/705.

[742] MEMO/04/705.

[743] Case T-201/04, *Microsoft* [2007] ECR II-3601, see Section 13.D, p. 521 ff.

a direct competitor of CBL—a sister company of CBF and the only other ICSD in the European Union—on the downstream market for clearing and settlement of cross-border securities transactions. While the contested decision does not establish that the applicants intended to cause EB a competitive disadvantage, it assesses on the other hand the reasoning for and consequences of that refusal to provide services in the context of EB's position and that of the entire Clearstream group on the relevant market. Thus, the Commission puts forward various indicia to suggest that the applicants' intention was to exclude EB from the provision of their services and, therefore, to hinder competition in the provision of cross-border secondary clearing and settlement services (recitals 234 and 300 of the contested decision). However, given that the abuse of a dominant position is an objective concept, it is not necessary to rule on that point.

144. The effect referred to in the case-law cited in paragraph 140 above does not necessarily relate to the actual effect of the abusive conduct complained of. For the purposes of establishing an infringement of Article [102], it is sufficient to show that the abusive conduct of the undertaking in a dominant position tends to restrict competition or, in other words, that the conduct is capable of having that effect (Case T-203/01 *Michelin v Commission*, paragraph 132 above, paragraph 239).

145. It must therefore be examined whether the Commission has proved in the present case that the applicants' conduct tended to restrict competition on the market in secondary clearing and settlement services.

146. As explained in relation to the examination of the first plea in law, the contested decision shows that the Commission carried out a full analysis of the market in services. On that basis, the Commission was entitled to conclude that CBF held a de facto monopoly and was therefore an indispensable trading partner in the provision of primary clearing and settlement services on the market in question. In addition, it found that the barriers to entry on that market, in terms of regulations, technical requirements, interest by market participants, cost of entry, cost for consumers and likelihood of being able to provide competitive products, were so significant that the possibility of new market entries exercising a competitive constraint on CBF in the foreseeable future could be excluded (recitals 205 to 215 of the contested decision).

147. In that regard, it follows from the case-law of the Court of Justice that, in order to find the existence of an abuse within the meaning of Article [102], the refusal of the service in question must be likely to eliminate all competition on the market on the part of the person requesting the service, such refusal must not be capable of being objectively justified, and the service must in itself be indispensable to carrying on that person's business (Case C-7/97 *Bronner* . . . paragraph 41). According to settled case-law, a product or service is considered necessary or essential if there is no real or potential substitute (see Joined Cases T-374/94, T-375/94, T-384/94 and T-388/94 *European Night Services and Others v Commission* . . . paragraph 208, and the case-law cited).

148. With regard to the condition of elimination of all competition, it is not necessary, in order to establish an infringement of Article [102], to demonstrate that all competition on the market would be eliminated, but what matters is that the refusal at issue is liable to, or is likely to, eliminate all effective competition on the market. It is for the Commission to establish such a risk of the elimination of all effective competition (*Microsoft v Commission*, paragraph 47 above, paragraphs 563 and 564).

In paragraph 144 the GC says that in establishing an abuse it is sufficient to show that the conduct 'tends to' or 'is capable of' restricting competition. Although the Court also cited the *Bronner* 'likely elimination of all competition on the market on the part of the person requesting the service' test (paragraph 147) and the *Microsoft* 'elimination of all effective competition' test (paragraph 148) it was content with the Commission's conclusion that the refusal had merely 'hindered' EB:

[T]he applicants' refusal to provide it with primary clearing and settlement services for registered shares hindered EB's capacity to provide comprehensive, pan-European and innovative services. That harmed innovation and competition in the provision of cross-border secondary clearing and settlement services and ultimately the consumers within the single market.[744]

It has been suggested that this standard can be explained by the fact that the case concerned the emergence of a pan-European settlement and clearing market and that it is therefore of limited precedential value.[745]

C. REFUSAL TO SUPPLY AND INTELLECTUAL PROPERTY RIGHTS

(i) General

Refusal to supply in respect of intellectual property rights (IPRs) is one aspect of the problematic interface between competition law and intellectual property law.[746] Neither the EU Courts nor the Commission has applied the phrase 'essential facilities' to IPRs but the leading case on IPRs, *Magill*,[747] featured significantly in *Bronner*[748] and, in turn, *Bronner* was relied upon in the intellectual property case *IMS*.[749] The arguments on this matter centre around the fact that the law has already put in place a regime to deal with intellectual property; that compulsory licensing of IPRs is a dangerous disincentive to innovation; and that the law to date has not properly explained why some situations are so 'exceptional' that the normal rights of an IPR owner to exclude others should be eroded.

Obviously, the existence of IPRs will prevent undertakings competing on certain markets. Although the EU Courts have held that the ownership of IPRs does not necessarily mean that an undertaking holds a dominant position,[750] some rights can nonetheless constitute a barrier to entry under any conception of that term.[751] An undertaking cannot usually produce or use something protected by IPRs without the consent of the rights holder. IPRs owners frequently license their rights to others and Chapter 12 deals with the application of Article 101 to such agreements. Article 102 may be relevant, however, when the rights holder is in a dominant position and refuses to give licences to those wanting them.

(ii) The *Car Parts* Cases

The matter first came before the CJ in two Article 267 references, *Volvo* and *Renault*.[752] In essence the CJ was asked whether it is an abuse for a car manufacturer to refuse to license the design rights on its car parts to third parties wishing to manufacture and sell such parts[753] The CJ held that a refusal to license was not normally an abuse, but might become so in certain circumstances.

---

[744] Case T-301/04, *Clearstream* [2009] ECR II-3155, para. 149.

[745] Nazzini, n. 116, 268–269.

[746] See also the issue of standard-essential patents, discussed in Section 14.C.ii of this chapter, and Chap. 12 on the licensing of IPRs.

[747] Cases C-241–242/91 P, *Magill* [1995] ECR I-743.

[748] Case C-7/97, *Bronner* [1998] ECR I-7791.

[749] Case C-418/01, *IMS Health GmbH & Co OHG v NDC Health GmbH & Co KG* [2004] ECR I-5039.

[750] See Chap. 6, Section 6.C.v.d, p. 338.

[751] See Chap. 1, Section 15.C.

[752] Case 238/87, *AB Volvo v Erik Veng* [1988] ECR 6211 and Case 53/87, *CICCRA and Maxicar v Renault* [1988] ECR 6039, decided on the same day.

[753] The cases arose after the CJ had confirmed in Case 22/78, *Hugin* [1979] ECR 1869 that an undertaking may be dominant on the market for its own spare parts even if the primary product market is competitive.

Case 238/87, *AB Volvo v Erik Veng* [1988] ECR 6211

Court of Justice

8. It must also be emphasized that the right of the proprietor of a protected design to prevent third parties from manufacturing and selling or importing, without its consent, products incorporating the design constitutes the very subject-matter of his exclusive right. It follows that an obligation imposed upon the proprietor of a protected design to grant to third parties, even in return for a reasonable royalty, a licence for the supply of products incorporating the design would lead to the proprietor thereof being deprived of the substance of his exclusive right, and that a refusal to grant such a licence cannot in itself constitute an abuse of a dominant position.

9.[754] It must however be noted that the exercise of an exclusive right by the proprietor of a registered design in respect of car body panels may be prohibited by Article [102] if it involves, on the part of an undertaking holding a dominant position, certain abusive conduct such as the arbitrary refusal to supply spare parts to independent repairers, the fixing of prices for spare parts at an unfair level or a decision no longer to produce spare parts for a particular model even though many cars of that model are still in circulation, provided that such conduct is liable to affect trade between Member States.

The references in the judgments to the 'very subject-matter of the exclusive right' and the 'exercise of an exclusive right' are to concepts which the Court had already developed to deal with the tension between IPRs and Community law, mainly in the area of the free movement of goods and services. The outcome of their application in *Volvo* and *Renault* was that the CJ held that a refusal to grant licences would be an abuse only if it involved or gave rise to 'certain abusive conduct'. In effect the car makers were given a choice: either they could license third parties, or they could retain their monopoly and ensure, inter alia, that they did not arbitrarily refuse to supply independent repairers, did not charge unfairly, and continued to supply parts for old models. One way of looking at this is to see an order to license as a *remedy* for other abuses.[755] The examples of abusive conduct given are not unproblematic, however, including the issue of what is an 'unfair' price.[756] The refusal to supply spare parts to independent repairers was classed as an abuse even though it involved the supply of products to new, rather than existing, customers, albeit within a very particular context.[757]

(iii) The *Magill* Case

Magill[758] concerned copyright in 'television listings' (television programme schedules). Under UK and Irish law copyright protected not only literary works which resulted from creative or intellectual endeavour but also compilations of information resulting from 'skill, judgment and labour' or the 'sweat of the brow', including listings of programmes to be broadcast.[759] Such compilations were

---

[754] Para. 9, with only insignificant changes in wording, was repeated in Case 53/87, *Renault* [1988] ECR 6039, para. 16.

[755] See the discussion in J. Temple Lang, 'Anti-competitive Non-Pricing Abuses under European and National Antitrust Law' [2003] *Fordham Corp L Inst* 235, 292–301.

[756] See Section 16.A, p. 566. And see generally V. Korah, 'No Duty to License Independent Repairers to Made Spare Parts: The *Renault*, *Volvo* and *Bayer* and *Hennecke* Cases' [1988] *EIPR* 381. The extent to which a car manufacturer has power to charge excessively in the aftermarket for spare parts without affecting sales in the competitive foremarket is questionable, see Chap. 6, Section 5.B.i.h, p. 302 ff.

[757] EU competition law has special provisions covering motor vehicle distribution, see Chap. 11.

[758] Cases C-241–242/91 P, *Magill* [1995] ECR I-743, on appeal from Cases T-69–70/89, 76/89, *RTE, ITP, BBC (Magill) v Commission* [1991] ECR II-485, on appeal from *Magill TV Guide* [1989] OJ L78/43.

[759] At the time of the *Magill* decision the relevant UK law was the Copyright Act 1956 which, according to *Independent Television Publications v Time Out* [1984] FSR 64, protected programme listings. The Broadcasting Act 1990, s. 176 specifically provides that persons broadcasting television and radio programmes in the UK have to

not protected by intellectual property laws in the other Member States of the EU, where copyright covered only the fruits of creative or intellectual effort. The EU Courts have said on several occasions that where intellectual property laws are not harmonised EU law recognises the *existence* of rights granted by the Member States.

In 1985 RTE had a statutory monopoly over television broadcasting in Ireland and the BBC and IBA had a statutory duopoly in the UK (including Northern Ireland). Most viewers in Ireland and Northern Ireland could receive the channels of all three broadcasters. RTE and the BBC owned the copyright in the programme listings for their respective channels and ITP owned the copyright in the listings of the IBA franchised channels. RTE, the BBC, and ITP each published a weekly TV guide containing only their own individual weekly programme listings. They also gave listings information to the press to be published according to strictly enforced licensing conditions. An Irish publisher, Magill, started to publish a comprehensive weekly TV guide giving details of all programmes available to viewers in the Irish Republic and Northern Ireland, but the television companies obtained injunctions against it in national legal proceedings. Magill complained to the Commission that the television companies, by refusing to give out reliable advance listings information and protecting their listings by enforcing their copyright, were infringing Article 102.

The EU Courts and the Commission appear to have been influenced by the fact that the UK and Ireland were alone among the Member States in affording copyright protection to TV listings, and that composite TV guides could therefore be published in the other Member States, where they were popular and common.[760] The case became perceived as a battle between the protection of national IPRs and competition law, for if the TV companies' refusal to deal with Magill *was* an abuse the only remedy was, in effect, to order them to give the publisher a licence of their copyrights.

The Commission found that the television companies had infringed Article 102.[761] It held that each was dominant in the market for its weekly listings and that their policies in restricting the availability of the information were driven by a desire to protect their own individual weekly guides in the downstream market. The GC upheld the Commission. The GC related the position under Article 102 to the case law on IPRs in the context of the free movement of goods and services.[762] RTE and ITP appealed. The CJ confirmed the finding of abuse but its judgment was strikingly different to that of the GC. It concentrated on the specific scenario in issue and eschewed extended discussion about the nature of IPRs and their relationship to the competition rules.[763] Rather, it treated the matter as a straightforward refusal to supply and applied the principles laid down in previous Article 102 case law.

Cases C-241–242/91 P, *RTE & ITP v Commission* [1995] ECR I-743 (*Magill*)

Court of Justice

(a) Existence of a dominant position

46. So far as dominant position is concerned, it is to be remembered at the outset that mere ownership of an intellectual property right cannot confer such a position.

---

make information about the programme schedules available to any person in the UK who wants to publish it: the actual dispute in *Magill* therefore became a dead issue as regards the UK during the course of the case, which explains why the BBC was not party to the appeal to the CJ.

[760] See particularly the Commission's submissions to the GC, [1991] ECR II-485, summarised in paras. 43–59 of the judgment, culminating in the Commission's statement in para. 59 that 'copyright should not subsist in compilations of banal information'.

[761] *Magill TV Guide* [1989] OJ L78/43.

[762] There were three separate judgments, but the crucial paras. are the same in all three.

[763] See particularly para. 58 of the judgment. The CJ did not follow Gulmann AG, who recommended in his Opinion setting aside the GC judgment, primarily to uphold the inviolability of IPRs.

47. However, the basic information as to the channel, day, time and title of programmes is the necessary result of programming by television stations, which are thus the only source of such information for an undertaking, like Magill, which wishes to publish it together with commentaries or pictures. By force of circumstance, RTE and ITP, as the agent of ITV, enjoy, along with the BBC, a *de facto* monopoly over the information used to compile listings for the television programmes received in most households in Ireland and 30–40 per cent. of households in Northern Ireland. The appellants are thus in a position to prevent effective competition on the market in weekly television magazines. The [General Court] was therefore right in confirming the Commission's assessment that the appellants occupied a dominant position (*Michelin, paragraph 30*)

(b) Existence of an abuse

48. With regard to the issue of abuse, the arguments of the appellants and IPO wrongly presuppose that where the conduct of an undertaking in a dominant position consists of the exercise of a right classified by national law as 'copyright', such conduct can never be reviewed in relation to Article [102].

49. Admittedly, in the absence of Community standardization or harmonization of laws, determination of the conditions and procedures for granting protection of an intellectual property right is a matter for national rules. Further, the exclusive right of reproduction forms part of the author's rights, so that refusal to grant a licence, even if it is the act of an undertaking holding a dominant position, cannot in itself constitute abuse of a dominant position (*Volvo* v. *Veng*, paragraphs 7 and 8).

50. However, it is also clear from that judgment (paragraph 9) that the exercise of an exclusive right by the proprietor may, in exceptional circumstances, involve abusive conduct.

51. In the present case, the conduct objected to is the appellants' reliance on copyright conferred by national legislation so as to prevent Magill—or any other undertaking having the same intention—from publishing on a weekly basis information (channel, day, time and title of programmes) together with commentaries and pictures obtained independently of the appellants.

52. Among the circumstances taken into account by the [General Court] in concluding that such conduct was abusive was, first, the fact that there was, according to the findings of the [General Court], no actual or potential substitute for a weekly television guide offering information on the programmes for the week ahead. On this point, the [General Court] confirmed the Commission's finding that the complete lists of programmes for a 24-hour period—and for a 48-hour period at weekends and before public holidays— published in certain daily and Sunday newspapers, and the television sections of certain magazines covering, in addition, 'highlights' of the week's programmes, were only to a limited extent substitutable for advance information to viewers on all the week's programmes. Only weekly television guides containing comprehensive listings for the week ahead would enable users to decide in advance which programmes they wished to follow and arrange their leisure activities for the week accordingly. The [General Court] also established that there was a specific, constant and regular potential demand on the part of consumers (see the *RTE* judgment, paragraph 62, and the *ITP* judgment, paragraph 48).

53. Thus the appellants—who were, by force of circumstance, the only sources of the basic information on programme scheduling which is the indispensable raw material for compiling a weekly television guide—gave viewers wishing to obtain information on the choice of programmes for the week ahead no choice but to buy the weekly guides for each station and draw from each of them the information they needed to make comparisons.

54. The appellants' refusal to provide basic information by relying on national copyright provisions thus prevented the appearance of a new product, a comprehensive weekly guide to television programmes, which the appellants did not offer and for which there was a potential consumer demand. Such refusal constitutes an abuse under heading (b) of the second paragraph of Article [102].

55. Second, there was no justification for such refusal either in the activity of television broadcasting or in that of publishing television magazines (*RTE* judgment, paragraph 73, and *ITP* judgment, paragraph 58).

56. Third, and finally, as the [General Court] also held, the appellants, by their conduct, reserved to themselves the secondary market of weekly television guides by excluding competition on that market

(*Commercial Solvents*, paragraph 25) since they denied access to the basic information which is the raw material indispensable for the compilation of such a guide.

57. In the light of all those circumstances, the [General Court] did not err in law in holding that the appellants' conduct was an abuse of a dominant position within the meaning of Article [102].

58. It follows that the plea in law alleging misapplication by the [General Court] of the concept of abuse of a dominant position must be dismissed as unfounded. It is therefore unnecessary to examine the reasoning of the contested judgments in so far as it is based on Article [36 TFEU].

It can be seen that in this judgment the CJ said (paragraph 48) that while it is not true that the exercise of IPRs can *never* be reviewed under Article 102, a refusal to grant a licence to reproduce cannot *in itself* constitute an abuse of a dominant position (paragraph 49). It cited *Volvo* as establishing that a refusal might constitute an abuse *in exceptional circumstances*. In this case the exceptional circumstances were:

- there was no substitute for a composite weekly television guide, for which there was a specific, constant, and regular potential demand on the part of consumers;
- the appellants' refusal to supply prevented the appearance of a new product for which there was a potential consumer demand[764] (an abuse under Article 102(b), in 'limiting production, markets or technical development to the prejudice of consumers');
- there was no justification for such refusal;
- the appellants were reserving to themselves the secondary market of weekly television guides by excluding all competition on the market.

The following points should also be noted:

- The CJ based its finding of dominance on the fact that the TV companies had a *de facto* monopoly over the listings, i.e. they were responsible for producing the TV schedules and were the only source of advance information about them (paragraph 47). The Commission (paragraph 22) based the finding of dominance on both the *de facto* monopoly and the legal monopoly stemming from the copyright. The GC based it on the legal monopoly (paragraph 63 of the *RTE* judgment). The CJ did not even mention the existence of the IPRs in its discussion of dominance in paragraph 47.
- The CJ (paragraphs 53 and 56) described the undertakings' conduct in terms of refusal to supply a raw material. It did not use essential facilities terminology. It referred back to *Commercial Solvents* (paragraph 56), seeing the present case as an example of the established abuse of a dominant undertaking trying to exclude competition on a downstream market.
- Unlike the car makers in *Volvo* and *Renault* the television companies were not given a choice of how they could avoid committing an abuse. Although the judgment did not mention compulsory licensing there was only one way in which the abuse could be remedied.[765]
- The judgment established the norm that refusal to license is *not* generally an abuse. The judgment was less of an assault on IPRs than it was on the exploitation of compilations of information gained as a by-product of an undertaking's main business. It is possible to see *Magill* as a limitation of the power wielded by statutory monopolists. The power of the television companies in respect of the TV guides arose as a result of their privileged position on a broadcasting market with few channels.

[764] The AG on the other hand (paras. 93–102 of the Opinion) thought that the fact that the product Magill wanted to produce was new and would compete with the right holders' own products was a reason to find that the refusal to supply was *not* abusive.

[765] The existence of the Copyright Tribunal in the UK meant that the Commission itself did not have to become involved in price-setting.

It was unclear whether the 'list' of exceptional circumstances in *Magill* was cumulative or not. In particular it was unclear whether the hindrance of a new product was a necessary, or a separate and sufficient, ground for holding the refusal to supply the IPR to be abusive. If the television companies had already produced their own composite guides by cross-licensing each other, the composite guide of a third party would not have been a new product, but the undertakings would still have reserved for themselves a special position on the secondary market. In *Tiercé Ladbroke*,[766] which concerned Ladbroke's complaint that the French *sociétés de courses* and their associated companies refused to supply broadcasts of French horse races to Ladbroke's betting shops in Belgium, the GC said that the refusal to supply could constitute an abuse only if *either* the product or service was essential to the activity in question *or* the introduction of a new product demanded by consumers was being prevented.[767] The GC thus suggested that a refusal to supply which precluded the introduction of a new product might constitute an abuse for that reason alone, even if the access demanded was not 'essential'. In other words, the GC read the 'exceptional circumstances' in *Magill* as severable, not cumulative.[768] In the *IMS* case, however, the CJ considered the circumstances as cumulative.

(iv) The *IMS* Case

a. The Facts of *IMS*

The *IMS* case concerned the '1860 brick structure', a system for representing regional pharmaceutical sales data in Germany. It consisted of a grid superimposed on the map of Germany, breaking down the country into small geographical 'bricks' based on factors including postcodes, administrative and political boundaries, and the location of doctors and pharmacies.[769] IMS collected pharmaceutical sales information from wholesalers, formatted it in accordance with the brick structure so enabling it to be analysed in various ways, and provided sales reports to its customers, the pharmaceutical companies. The brick structure had been developed over many years, in collaboration by IMS with the pharmaceutical industry[770] and the Commission found that it had become the *de facto* industry standard. IMS's competitors[771] attempted to develop similar brick structures but IMS claimed that these infringed its copyright and obtained interim injunctions in the German courts to restrain their use. The competitors complained to the Commission that IMS's refusal to license the brick structure meant that it was impossible for them to provide pharmaceutical data services to customers as they could not present data in a way acceptable to the customers without infringing IMS's copyright and there was no prospect of the customers changing to a radically different structure. The Commission found that the brick structure was indispensable to carrying on business in the relevant market; there was no actual or potential substitute for it; there was no objective justification for IMS's refusal to license; and that there were 'exceptional circumstances' in the *Magill* sense. It ordered interim measures[772] which were suspended pending the appeal.[773]

---

[766] Case T-504/93, *Tiercé Ladbroke SA v Commission* [1997] ECR-II 923. Ladbrokes was appealing to the GC against the Commission's rejection of its complaint.

[767] Ibid., para. 131.

[768] The GC dismissed Ladbroke's appeal. The *sociétés de courses* did not operate betting shops in Belgium, so the downstream market issue did not arise. Showing films of the races was not essential to providing services in betting shops, and the *sociétés de courses* were not discriminating (contrary to Art. 102(c)) as they did not license anybody in the relevant market (Belgium).

[769] There were around 21,500 pharmacies and 287,000 doctors in Germany (*IMS/NDC* [2002] OJ L59/18, para. 14). German privacy laws prevent the production of data which can identify sales in individual pharmacies.

[770] There was considerable dispute about the extent of this collaboration.

[771] One of the competitors, PII, was founded by a former director of IMS, and later taken over by NDC.

[772] COMP/38.044, *NDC Health/IMS: Interim Measures* [2002] OJ L59/18. IMS was to give a licence on request and on a non-discriminatory basis to all undertakings currently on the German regional sales data services market.

[773] Case T-184/01 R, *IMS Health v Commission* [2001] ECR II-3193, para. 125, aff'd Case C-481/01 P(R), *IMS Health v Commission* [2002] ECR I-3401.

In the meantime, litigation between IMS and NDC was ongoing in Germany and a preliminary reference was made to the CJ asking about the interpretation of Article 102 in the context of IMS's refusal to license. Before the ruling was given, however, a German court gave judgment on the issue of IMS's claim to copyright in the brick structure, holding that the brick structure was protected by copyright but that this did not prevent other parties from developing a similar structure. Moreover, NDC began to compete more successfully with IMS. The Commission therefore withdrew the interim measures.[774] The CJ however proceeded to give its ruling on the preliminary reference.

b. The CJ Ruling

The ruling of the CJ, which largely followed the Opinion of Advocate General Tizzano, set out the conditions in which a refusal to supply a copyright is an abuse, and left the German court to decide whether the conditions were satisfied in the situation before it.

Case C-418/01, *IMS Health GmbH & Co OHG v NDC Health GmbH & Co KG* [2004] ECR I-5039

The Landgericht Frankfurt am Main asked three questions:

- first, whether it was an abuse not to grant a licence in a situation where the competitor was seeking access to the same geographical and product market and the customers would only accept a product based on material protected by the copyright;
- secondly, was the participation of the customers in developing the copyright material relevant;
- thirdly, were the costs which the customers would occur in switching to a product protected by a different data bank relevant.

The Court held that the second and third questions both concerned factors which had to be taken into consideration in determining whether the protected structure was indispensable for the relevant marketing studies. The following extract is the part of the judgment dealing with the first question.

Court of Justice

34. According to settled case-law, the exclusive right of reproduction forms part of the owner's rights, so that refusal to grant a licence, even if it is the act of an undertaking holding a dominant position, cannot in itself constitute abuse of a dominant position (judgment in Case 238/87 *Volvo* . . . paragraph 8, and *Magill*, paragraph 49).

35. Nevertheless, as is clear from that case-law, exercise of an exclusive right by the owner may, in exceptional circumstances, involve abusive conduct (*Volvo*, paragraph 9, and *Magill*, paragraph 50).

36. The Court held that such exceptional circumstances were present in the case giving rise to the judgment in *Magill*, in which the conduct complained of by the television channels in a dominant position involved invoking the copyright conferred by national legislation on the weekly listings of their programmes in order to prevent another undertaking from publishing information on those programmes together with commentaries, on a weekly basis.

37. According to the summary of the *Magill* judgment made by the Court at paragraph 40 of the judgment in *Bronner*, the exceptional circumstances were constituted by the fact that the refusal in question concerned a product (information on the weekly schedules of certain television channels), the supply of which was indispensable for carrying on the business in question, (the publishing of a general television guide), in that, without that information, the person wishing to produce such a guide would find it impossible to publish it and offer it for sale (paragraph 53), the fact that such refusal prevented the emergence of a new product for which there was a potential consumer demand (paragraph 54), the fact that it was

---

[774] Commission Decision 2003/741/EC, [2003] OJ L268/69; IP/03/1159.

not justified by objective considerations (paragraph 55), and was likely to exclude all competition in the secondary market (paragraph 56).

38. It is clear from that case-law that, in order for the refusal by an undertaking which owns a copyright to give access to a product or service indispensable for carrying on a particular business to be treated as abusive, it is sufficient that three cumulative conditions be satisfied, namely, that that refusal is preventing the emergence of a new product for which there is a potential consumers demand, that it is unjustified and such as to exclude any competition on a secondary market.

39. In light of the order for reference and the observations submitted to the Court, which reveal a major dispute as regards the interpretation of the third condition, it is appropriate to consider that question first.

The third condition, relating to the likelihood of excluding all competition on a secondary market

40. In that regard, it is appropriate to recall the approach followed by the Court in the *Bronner* judgment, in which it was asked whether the fact that a press undertaking with a very large share of the daily newspaper market in a Member State which operates the only nationwide newspaper home-delivery scheme in that Member State refuses paid access to that scheme by the publisher of a rival newspaper, which by reason of its small circulation is unable either alone or in cooperation with other publishers to set up and operate its own home-delivery scheme under economically reasonable conditions, constitutes the abuse of a dominant position.

41. The Court, first of all, invited the national court to determine whether the home delivery schemes constituted a separate market (*Bronner*, paragraph 34), on which, in light of the circumstances of the case, the press undertaking held a de facto monopoly position and, thus, a dominant position (paragraph 35). It then invited the national court to determine whether the refusal by the owner of the only nationwide home-delivery scheme in a Member State, which used that scheme to distribute its own daily newspapers, to allow the publisher of a rival daily newspaper access to it deprived that competitor of a means of distribution judged essential for the sale of its newspaper (paragraph 37).

42. Therefore, the Court held that it was relevant, in order to assess whether the refusal to grant access to a product or a service indispensable for carrying on a particular business activity was an abuse, to distinguish an upstream market, constituted by the product or service, in that case the market for home delivery of daily newspapers, and a (secondary) downstream market, on which the product or service in question is used for the production of another product or the supply of another service, in that case the market for daily newspapers themselves.

43. The fact that the delivery service was not marketed separately was not regarded as precluding, from the outset, the possibility of identifying a separate market.

44. It appears, therefore, as the Advocate General set out in points 56 to 59 of his Opinion, that, for the purposes of the application of the earlier case-law, it is sufficient that a potential market or even hypothetical market can be identified. Such is the case where the products or services are indispensable in order to carry on a particular business and where there is an actual demand for them on the part of undertakings which seek to carry on the business for which they are indispensable.

45. Accordingly, it is determinative that two different stages of production may be identified and that they are interconnected, the upstream product is indispensable in as much as for supply of the downstream product.

46. Transposed to the facts of the case in the main proceedings, that approach prompts consideration as to whether the 1860 brick structure constitutes, upstream, an indispensable factor in the downstream supply of German regional sales data for pharmaceutical products.

47. It is for the national court to establish whether that is in fact the position, and, if so be the case, to examine whether the refusal by IMS to grant a licence to use the structure at issue is capable of excluding all competition on the market for the supply of German regional sales data on pharmaceutical products.

The first condition, relating to the emergence of a new product

48. As the Advocate General stated in point 62 of his Opinion, that condition relates to the consideration that, in the balancing of the interest in protection of copyright and the economic freedom of its owner, against the interest in protection of free competition the latter can prevail only where refusal to grant a licence prevents the development of the secondary market to the detriment of consumers.

49. Therefore, the refusal by an undertaking in a dominant position to allow access to a product protected by copyright, where that product is indispensable for operating on a secondary market, may be regarded as abusive only where the undertaking which requested the licence does not intend to limit itself essentially to duplicating the goods or services already offered on the secondary market by the owner of the copyright, but intends to produce new goods or services not offered by the owner of the right and for which there is a potential consumer demand.

50. It is for the national court to determine whether such is the case in the dispute in the main proceedings.

The second condition, relating to whether the refusal was unjustified

51. As to that condition, on whose interpretation no specific observations have been made, it is for the national court to examine, if appropriate, in light of the facts before it, whether the refusal of the request for a licence is justified by objective considerations.

52. Accordingly, the answer to the first question must be that the refusal by an undertaking which holds a dominant position and is the owner of an intellectual property right over a brick structure which is indispensable for the presentation of data on regional sales of pharmaceutical products in a Member State, to grant a licence to use that structure to another undertaking which also wishes to supply such data in the same Member State, constitutes an abuse of a dominant position within the meaning of Article [102] where the following conditions are fulfilled:

— the undertaking which requested the licence intends to offer, on the market for the supply of the data in question, new products or services not offered by the copyright owner and for which there is a potential consumer demand;

— the refusal is not justified by objective considerations;

— the refusal is such as to reserve to the copyright owner the market for the supply of data on sales of pharmaceutical products in the Member State concerned by eliminating all competition on that market.

In this ruling the CJ laid down (paragraphs 38 and 52) that three *cumulative* conditions made the refusal to license a copyright an abuse:

• first, a 'new product' was involved;

• secondly, access to the protected material was 'indispensable' so that the refusal would exclude *any/all* (paragraphs 38 and 52) competition on a secondary market (not, as in *Bronner*, all competition from the person requesting access);

• thirdly, the refusal was unjustified.

One view of the judgment is that the CJ came down firmly on the 'side' of the IPR holder, in that there is a presumption against the licence (see paragraph 48). The CJ repeated that a refusal to grant a licence cannot in itself constitute an abuse (paragraph 34). It allowed for the possibility of compulsory licences but only in 'exceptional circumstances' (paragraph 35). It incorporated into the exceptional circumstances the requirement of 'indispensability' in the *Bronner* sense, which sets the bar at a high level, and it demanded that the party requiring the licence intends to offer new goods and services for which there is a potential consumer demand. On the other hand, the 'indispensable' and 'new product' requirements are such that everything will turn on the application of these conditions to the facts of the case. In *IMS* the CJ referred everything back to the national court without giving any indication as to whether the requirements were in fact satisfied in the case. In *IMS* there was room for argument about whether NDC was providing a 'new product'.[775] The Commission stated in its Decision that the sales reports of the firms 'differ markedly'.[776] It came down to a matter of whether this would fulfil the condition of not 'essentially duplicating' the right holder's product. The key to this is the interests of consumers. In paragraph 48 the Court said that the only situation in which free competition can override the rights of the copyright holder is where the refusal prevents the development of the secondary market to the detriment of consumers (in other words limiting production to the detriment of consumers as provided for in Article 102(b)). The licence is not ordered to protect the competitor but to protect consumers.

The CJ did require that the development of a secondary market be affected. As the Commission had done it spelt two markets out of the situation in *IMS*. The Court said (paragraph 44) that it is enough if a 'potential or even hypothetical' market can be identified upstream. It only required that 'two different stages of production' can be identified.[777] The question here is how hypothetical can the market for the input be. The upstream market in *IMS* was a very artificial one: IMS only developed the brick structure in order to produce its own sales reports. It was different in *Magill* where the television listings existed as a by-product of the broadcasting activities and would have existed whether or not the broadcasters had published their own magazines. As one commentator said (critically) of the Commission decision in *IMS*, it was enough 'even if the input is a competitive advantage of a kind which has never previously been marketed or licensed by any company, and which it would not be economically rational to license to a direct competitor'.[778] There are few production processes that cannot be divided as in *IMS* if one thinks hard enough and anything protected by an IPR can on this basis form an upstream market. One can compare *IMS* on this point with the judgment of the US Supreme Court in *Verizon v Trinko*,[779] set out in Section 13.G, where the fact that 'the services allegedly withheld are not otherwise marketed or available to the public' and existed 'only deep in the bowels of Verizon' was a factor in holding the refusal to deal lawful.[780]

The *IMS* ruling gave little flavour of the underlying factual situation. It is necessary to read the Commission decision to fully appreciate that *IMS*, like *Magill*, involved a 'weak' copyright. Indeed, the Commission seemed to consider that IMS had more or less hijacked the industry standard.[781] If *IMS* could be taken as turning on the particular facts of how the brick structure had been developed and the copyright acquired, it could be viewed as a response to a quirk of national law. Some commentators considered that the cases should be viewed in this light—as exceptional responses to unsatisfactory copyright laws—and argued that there was no reason to suppose that the same approach would be taken to strong patent rights, for example.[782] However, *Magill and IMS* were relied upon by the GC in the *Microsoft* case, where any IPRs concerned were certainly not the product of quirks of copyright laws. As far as the indispensability requirement is concerned it should be

---

[775] Unlike *Bronner*, where the CJ made it clear that that the conditions laid down there were not satisfied.

[776] According to the customers the coverage of parts of Germany was more complete and they provided more detail on types of information, [2002] OJ L59/18, para. 15.

[777] It can be argued that by saying that it was a matter of whether two *stages of production* can be identified the Court was abandoning the requirement of two *markets*: it is enough that there are two *products*. See J. Venit, 'The IP/Antitrust Interface After *IMS Health*' in Ehlermann and Atanasiu, n. 31, 609, 625.

[778] J. Temple Lang, 'Anti-competitive Non-Pricing Abuses under European and National Antitrust Law' [2003] *Fordham Corp L Inst* 235, 307.

[779] 540 US 398, 124 S.Ct 872 (2004).

[780] Moreover *IMS* did not involve leveraging. IMS was not leveraging its dominance from the upstream to the downstream market: see Venit, n. 777.

[781] And see F. Fine, 'NDC/IMS: A Logical Application of the Essential Facilities Doctrine' [2002] *ECLR* 457; F. Fine, 'NDC/IMS: In Response to Professor Korah' (2002) 70 *Antitrust LJ* 247.

[782] See, e.g., M. Delrahim, 'Forcing Firms to Share the Sandbox: Compulsory Licensing of Intellectual Property Rights and Antitrust', BIICL Conference, 10 May 2004, available at <http://www.usdoj.gov/atr/public/speeches/203627.htm> (Delrahim was at the time US Deputy Assistant Attorney General, DOJ Antitrust Division).

noted that the Commission withdrew its interim decision in August 2003 because the situation had changed, in that NDC had succeeded in concluding contracts with some larger pharmaceutical companies and there was no longer a threat that it might be eliminated from the market. The Commission stated that its decision was without prejudice to whether the improvement in NDC's position had been caused by the German judgment on the copyright. If it was not caused by this it throws doubt on how indispensable the 1860 brick structure was in the first place.

D. REFUSAL TO SUPPLY AND INTEROPERABILITY— THE *MICROSOFT* CASE

A particular kind of refusal to supply arises in the IT sector in respect of 'interface information'. Providers of software need to be able to make products which operate with other systems and programs. This is known as 'interoperability'. For this they require interface information, i.e. information about the systems and programs of other producers with which their products need to be compatible and usable. This information may be protected by IPRs (copyright). It may be obtainable by decompilation (reverse engineering) but this can be impossible or not practically or economically feasible.[783] Where there is a dominant undertaking on a software market it may be essential to the competitive viability of other providers that their products are compatible with those of that undertaking.

The Commission first addressed this issue in 1984 when it dealt with a number of IBM's practices.[784] It alleged that IBM had abused its dominant position by failing to supply other manufacturers with interface information needed to make competitive products work with IBM's System/370. A settlement was reached by which IBM, while not admitting the existence of a dominant position or any abuse thereof, undertook to disclose sufficient interface information to enable competitors in the EEC to attach hardware and software products of their own design to System/370.[785]

The *Microsoft* investigation began in 1998 after Sun Microsystems lodged a complaint. Microsoft had over 90 per cent of the PC operating systems market. The Commission described this as approaching a near monopoly and Microsoft as being in an 'overwhelmingly dominant position'.[786] Sun complained of Microsoft's refusal to disclose to those who provided server operating systems sufficient interface information to enable them to create 'workgroup server operating systems' (WGOS) that would operate satisfactorily with Microsoft's Windows desktop and server operating systems. Microsoft had previously supplied full interoperability information to server producers but cut it back after entering that market itself. Five years and three statements of objections after the investigation began the Commission held that Microsoft held a dominant position on both the client PC operating systems market and the WGOS market and that it had committed an abuse by refusing to supply the interface information. Microsoft was fined €497,196,304[787] and ordered to make the relevant information available to undertakings on the WGOS market within 120 days and ensure that the information was kept updated on an ongoing basis and in a timely manner.[788]

In the decision the Commission examined whether the *Bronner* and *Magill*[789] criteria were fulfilled, although it noted that it was 'of interest' that this was a case (unlike *Bronner* and *Magill*) of

---

[783] For the arguments about the possibilities of reverse engineering in *Microsoft*, see text at n. 791.

[784] For the tying aspects, see Section 12.E.iii, p. 480.

[785] See Commission, *XIVth Report on Competition Policy* (1984) parts 94–95.

[786] COMP/37.792, *Microsoft* 24 March 2004, para. 435.

[787] The fine was also in respect of the tying abuse, see Section 12.E.iii, p. 480.

[788] To be enforced by the appointment of a 'monitoring trustee' to ensure that the disclosures are complete and accurate. For this issue see Chap. 13, Section 7.E.ii.b, p. 944. The dispute between the Commission and Microsoft as to whether Microsoft was complying with the obligation to supply the information on fair and reasonable terms led to the imposition of a periodic penalty payment, Case T-167/08, *Microsoft v Commission* EU:T:2012:323.

[789] The decision was adopted a month before the CJ's *IMS* ruling.

the disruption of previous levels of supply.[790] It held that the criteria were fulfilled. In doing so the Commission followed the 'effects-based' approach to the application of Article 102 which it set out the following year in the Discussion Paper. It examined the facts closely, identified effects on consumers, and considered the issues of incentives to innovation.

The Commission found that the information was indispensable by adopting a two-stage approach. First, it considered what degree of interoperability with Windows non-Microsoft WGOS required in order for the competitors to be able to remain viably on the market and, secondly, it appraised whether the information that Microsoft refused to disclose was indispensable to attaining that. On the basis of customer surveys the Commission found that although the competitors' systems had features and functionalities which customers preferred to those of Microsoft's this was trumped by the attraction of full interoperability with Windows. It concluded that the competitors' systems had to be able to interoperate with Windows on an equal footing with Microsoft's own systems if they were to compete viably with them and that this was not possible without the information Microsoft refused to disclose. There were no substitutes for disclosure by Microsoft. Microsoft argued, inter alia, that reverse engineering was a means of its competitors accessing the information but the Commission held that reverse engineering required 'considerable efforts with uncertain chances of success'[791] and that the viability of products produced by reverse engineering depended on Microsoft not breaking the compatibility (for instance by upgrading the operating system): '[r]everse engineering is therefore an unstable basis for a business model'.[792] The Commission held, with regard to the criteria of the elimination of competition, that the refusal to supply put Microsoft's competitors 'at a strong competitive disadvantage . . . to an extent where there is a risk of elimination of competition'.[793] This would impact on technical development to the prejudice of consumers contrary to Article 102(b)[794] because the competitors would, at best, be confined to niche existences and there would be little scope for innovation,[795] while Microsoft's incentives to innovate would be diminished by the disappearance of its competitors.[796] The Commission rejected Microsoft's plea that the refusal to supply was justified by the fact that the information was protected by IPRs and that forced disclosure would lessen its incentives to innovate. Even if there was such a disincentive the Commission held that 'the possible negative impact of an order to supply on Microsoft's incentives to innovate is outweighed by its positive impact on the level on innovation of the whole industry (including Microsoft)'.[797]

The *Microsoft* decision stretched the *Magill* criteria. For example, the Commission held not that the refusal prevented the appearance of a specific new product but rather that 'technical development' would be limited. The Commission therefore hedged its bets. In case the Microsoft situation did not satisfy the principles laid down in the previous cases it argued that there was no 'exhaustive checklist' of exceptional circumstances and that it could have regard to other circumstances, i.e. that a refusal to supply should be examined on a case-by-case basis so that refusal that did not fit exactly within the *Bronner* or *Magill* criteria could still be an abuse.[798]

---

[790] I.e. like *Commercial Solvents* and *Centre Belge*: COMP/37.792, *Microsoft* 24 March 2004, para. 556.

[791] COMP/37.792, *Microsoft* 24 March 2004, para. 685.

[792] Ibid., para. 686.

[793] Ibid., para. 589.

[794] Ibid., paras. 693–701.

[795] Ibid., para. 700.

[796] Ibid., para. 725.

[797] Ibid., para. 783.

[798] Ibid., para. 555. In the Discussion Paper of 2005 the Commission reinforced this argument by placing interoperability in a separate category of refusal to supply. It said that 'it may not be appropriate to apply to such refusals to supply information the same high standards for intervention as those described in the previous subsections' (which set out the principles derived from the previous cases, by that time including *IMS*): Discussion Paper, paras. 271–272.

Before the GC the Commission argued that it was entitled to take account of all the particular circumstances surrounding the refusal and identified three particular characteristics in this case: (a) the information related to interoperability, 'a matter to which the Community legislature attaches particular importance'; (b) Microsoft was using its 'extraordinary power' on one market to eliminate competition on an adjacent market; and (c) the case involved the disruption of previous levels of supply.[799] The GC examined first whether the Commission was justified in finding that the highest standard—the *Magill/IMS* exceptional circumstances test—was satisfied and, having decided that it was, upheld the Commission decision without expressly considering the position had it not been.[800] However, the GC had to give an expansive interpretation of the criteria in the case law in order to do this and it might have been preferable had it seized the opportunity to consider the other relevant special circumstances put forward by the Commission.[801]

The GC applied the 'manifest error of assessment' standard of review. The GC said that the 'review of complex economic appraisals made by the Commission is necessarily limited to checking whether the relevant rules on procedure and on stating reasons have been complied with, whether the facts have been accurately stated and whether there has been any manifest error of assessment or a misuse of powers . . .'.[802] The 'manifest error' standard is particularly significant in *Microsoft* where the Commission was making predictions about the elimination of competition and the effects on innovation rather than judging past events.[803]

In respect of the *Magill/IMS* criteria the GC reiterated what was said in *IMS*, i.e. that in order for a refusal to supply to be abusive on the grounds that it denies access to an indispensable product or service two markets must be involved but the upstream market may merely be 'hypothetical'.[804] It examined the Commission decision in the light of the four conditions established in the case law—indispensability; elimination of competition; new product; no objective justification—and upheld it.

Case T-201/04, *Microsoft v Commission* [2007] ECR II-3601

General Court

332. It also follows from that case-law that the following circumstances, in particular, must be considered to be exceptional:

- in the first place, the refusal relates to a product or service indispensable to the exercise of a particular activity on a neighbouring market;

- in the second place, the refusal is of such a kind as to exclude any effective competition on that neighbouring market;

- in the third place, the refusal prevents the appearance of a new product for which there is potential consumer demand.

333. Once it is established that such circumstances are present, the refusal by the holder of a dominant position to grant a licence may infringe Article [102] unless the refusal is objectively justified.

334. The Court notes that the circumstance that the refusal prevents the appearance of a new product for which there is potential consumer demand is found only in the case-law on the exercise of an intellectual property right.

---

[799] COMP/37.792, *Microsoft* 24 March 2004, paras. 316–317.

[800] Ibid., para. 712.

[801] See P. Larouche, 'The European *Microsoft* Case at the Crossroads of Competition Policy and Innovation: Comment on Ahlborn and Evans' (2008–2009) 75 *Antitrust LJ* 933, 959.

[802] Case T-210/04, *Microsoft* [2007] ECR II-3601, para. 87.

[803] For the recent cases on the standard of review, see Chap. 13, Section 8.A.vii, p. 1000.

[804] Case C-418/01, *IMS* [2004] ECR I-5039, paras. 43–44.

335. Finally, it is appropriate to add that, in order that a refusal to give access to a product or service indispensable to the exercise of a particular activity may be considered abusive, it is necessary to distinguish two markets, namely, a market constituted by that product or service and on which the undertaking refusing to supply holds a dominant position and a neighbouring market on which the product or service is used in the manufacture of another product or for the supply of another service. The fact that the indispensable product or service is not marketed separately does not exclude from the outset the possibility of identifying a separate market (see, to that effect, *IMS Health* . . . paragraph 43). Thus, the Court of Justice held, at paragraph 44 of *IMS Health* . . . that it was sufficient that a potential market or even a hypothetical market could be identified and that such was the case where the products or services were indispensable to the conduct of a particular business activity and where there was an actual demand for them on the part of undertakings which sought to carry on that business. The Court of Justice concluded at the following paragraph of the judgment that it was decisive that two different stages of production were identified and that they were interconnected in that the upstream product was indispensable for supply of the downstream product.

336. In the light of the foregoing factors, the Court considers that it is appropriate, first of all, to decide whether the circumstances identified in *Magill* and *IMS Health* . . . as described at paragraphs 332 and 333 above, are also present in this case. Only if it finds that one or more of those circumstances are absent will the Court proceed to assess the particular circumstances invoked by the Commission . . .

On the indispensability condition the GC confirmed the Commission's approach to finding indispensability through the twofold test described, and its conclusion was that the test was satisfied.[805] On the other conditions it concluded as follows.

Case T-201/04, *Microsoft v Commission* [2007] ECR II-3601

General Court

Elimination of competition

– The applicable criterion

560. In the contested decision, the Commission considered whether the refusal at issue gave rise to a 'risk' of the elimination of competition on the work group server operating systems market (recitals 585, 589, 610, 622, 626, 631, 636, 653, 691, 692, 712, 725, 781, 992 and 1070 to the contested decision). Microsoft contends that that criterion is not sufficiently strict, since according to the case-law on the exercise of an intellectual property right the Commission must demonstrate that the refusal to license an intellectual property right to a third party is 'likely to eliminate all competition', or, in other words, that there is a 'high probability' that the conduct in question will have such a result.

561. The Court finds that Microsoft's complaint is purely one of terminology and is wholly irrelevant. The expressions 'risk of elimination of competition' and 'likely to eliminate competition' are used without distinction by the Community judicature to reflect the same idea, namely that Article [102] does not apply only from the time when there is no more, or practically no more, competition on the market. If the Commission were required to wait until competitors were eliminated from the market, or until their elimination was sufficiently imminent, before being able to take action under Article [102], that would clearly run counter to the objective of that provision, which is to maintain undistorted competition in the common market and, in particular, to safeguard the competition that still exists on the relevant market.

562. In this case, the Commission had all the more reason to apply Article [102] before the elimination of competition on the work group server operating systems market had become a reality because that

---

[805] Case T-210/04, *Microsoft* [2007] ECR II-3601, paras. 369–436.

market is characterised by significant network effects and because the elimination of competition would therefore be difficult to reverse (see recitals 515 to 522 and 533 to the contested decision).

563. Nor is it necessary to demonstrate that all competition on the market would be eliminated. What matters, for the purpose of establishing an infringement of Article [102], is that the refusal at issue is liable to, or is likely to, eliminate all effective competition on the market. It must be made clear that the fact that the competitors of the dominant undertaking retain a marginal presence in certain niches on the market cannot suffice to substantiate the existence of such competition.

564. Last, it must be borne in mind that it is for the Commission to establish that the refusal to supply gives rise to a risk of the elimination of all effective competition. As already stated at paragraph 482 above, the Commission must base its assessment on accurate, reliable and coherent evidence which comprises all the relevant data that must be taken into consideration in order to assess a complex situation and which are capable of substantiating the conclusions drawn from them.

... The new product

643. It must be emphasised that the fact that the applicant's conduct prevents the appearance of a new product on the market falls to be considered under Article [102(b)] ... which prohibits abusive practices which consist in 'limiting production, markets or technical developments to the ... prejudice of consumers'.

644. Thus, at paragraph 54 of *Magill* ... the Court of Justice held that the refusal by the broadcasting companies concerned had to be characterised as abusive within the meaning of that provision because it prevented the appearance of a new product which the broadcasting companies did not offer and for which there was a potential consumer demand.

645. It is apparent from the decision at issue in that case that the Commission had, more specifically, considered that by their refusal, the broadcasting companies limited production or markets to the prejudice of consumers (see the first paragraph of recital 23 to Commission Decision 89/205/EEC ... *Magill TV Guide/ITP, BBC and RTE* ...). The Commission had found that that refusal prevented publishers from producing and publishing a weekly television guide for consumers in Ireland and Northern Ireland, a type of guide not then available on that geographic market. Although each of the broadcasting companies concerned published a weekly television guide, each guide was devoted to that particular broadcaster's own programmes. In finding an abuse of a dominant position by those broadcasting companies, the Commission had emphasised the harm which the absence of a general weekly television guide on the market in Ireland and in Northern Ireland caused to consumers, who, if they wished to know what programmes were being offered in the coming week, had no alternative to buying the weekly guides of each channel and themselves extracting the relevant information in order to make comparisons.

646. In *IMS Health* ... the Court of Justice, when assessing the circumstance relating to the appearance of a new product, also placed that circumstance in the context of the damage to the interests of consumers. Thus, at paragraph 48 of that judgment, the Court emphasised, with reference to the Opinion of Advocate General Tizzano in that case ... that that circumstance related to the consideration that, in the balancing of the interest in protection of the intellectual property right and the economic freedom of its owner against the interest in protection of free competition, the latter can prevail only where refusal to grant a licence prevents the development of the secondary market, to the detriment of consumers.

647. The circumstance relating to the appearance of a new product, as envisaged in *Magill* and *IMS Health* ... cannot be the only parameter which determines whether a refusal to license an intellectual property right is capable of causing prejudice to consumers within the meaning of Article [102(b)] ... As that provision states, such prejudice may arise where there is a limitation not only of production or markets, but also of technical development.

648. It was on that last hypothesis that the Commission based its finding in the contested decision. Thus, the Commission considered that Microsoft's refusal to supply the relevant information limited technical development to the prejudice of consumers within the meaning of Article [102(b)] ... (recitals 693 to 701 and 782 to the contested decision) and it rejected Microsoft's assertion that it had not been demonstrated that its refusal caused prejudice to consumers (recitals 702 to 708 to the contested decision).

649. The Court finds that the Commission's findings at the recitals referred to in the preceding paragraph are not manifestly incorrect.

650. Thus, in the first place, the Commission was correct to observe, at recital 694 to the contested decision, that '[owing] to the lack of interoperability that competing work group server operating system products can achieve with the Windows domain architecture, an increasing number of consumers are locked into a homogeneous Windows solution at the level of work group server operating systems'.

651. It must be borne in mind that it has already been stated at paragraphs 371 to 422 above that Microsoft's refusal prevented its competitors from developing work group server operating systems capable of attaining a sufficient degree of interoperability with the Windows domain architecture, with the consequence that consumers' purchasing decisions in respect of work group server operating systems were channelled towards Microsoft's products . . .

652. The limitation thus placed on consumer choice is all the more damaging to consumers because, as already observed at paragraphs 407 to 412 above, they consider that non-Microsoft work group server operating systems are better than Windows work group server operating systems with respect to a series of features to which they attach great importance, such as 'reliability/availability of the . . . system' and 'security included with the server operating system'.

653. In the second place, the Commission was correct to consider that the artificial advantage in terms of interoperability that Microsoft retained by its refusal discouraged its competitors from developing and marketing work group server operating systems with innovative features, to the prejudice, notably, of consumers (see, to that effect, recital 694 to the contested decision). That refusal has the consequence that those competitors are placed at a disadvantage by comparison with Microsoft so far as the merits of their products are concerned, particularly with regard to parameters such as security, reliability, ease of use or operating performance speed (recital 699 to the contested decision).

654. The Commission's finding that '[i]f Microsoft's competitors had access to the interoperability information that Microsoft refuses to supply, they could use the disclosures to make the advanced features of their own products available in the framework of the web of interoperability relationships that underpin the Windows domain architecture' (recital 695 to the contested decision) is corroborated by the conduct which those competitors had adopted in the past, when they had access to certain information concerning Microsoft's products . . .

655. The Commission was careful to emphasise, in that context, that there was 'ample scope for differentiation and innovation beyond the design of interface specifications' (recital 698 to the contested decision). In other words, the same specification can be implemented in numerous different and innovative ways by software designers.

656. Thus, the contested decision rests on the concept that, once the obstacle represented for Microsoft's competitors by the insufficient degree of interoperability with the Windows domain architecture has been removed, those competitors will be able to offer work group server operating systems which, far from merely reproducing the Windows systems already on the market, will be distinguished from those systems with respect to parameters which consumers consider important (see, to that effect, recital 699 to the contested decision).

. . .

658. Nor would Microsoft's competitors have any interest in merely reproducing Windows work group server operating systems. Once they are able to use the information communicated to them to develop systems that are sufficiently interoperable with the Windows domain architecture, they will have no other choice, if they wish to take advantage of a competitive advantage over Microsoft and maintain a profitable presence on the market, than to differentiate their products from Microsoft's products with respect to certain parameters and certain features. It must be borne in mind that, as the Commission explains at recitals 719 to 721 to the contested decision, the implementation of specifications is a difficult task which requires significant investment in money and time

659. Last, Microsoft's argument that it will have less incentive to develop a given technology if it is required to make that technology available to its competitors (see paragraph 627 above) is of no relevance

to the examination of the circumstance relating to the new product, where the issue to be decided is the impact of the refusal to supply on the incentive for Microsoft's competitors to innovate and not on Microsoft's incentives to innovate. That is an issue which will be decided when the Court examines the circumstance relating to the absence of objective justification.

660. In the third place, the Commission is also correct to reject as unfounded Microsoft's assertion during the administrative procedure that it was not demonstrated that its refusal caused prejudice to consumers (recitals 702 to 708 to the contested decision).

661. First of all, as has already been observed at paragraphs 407 to 412 above . . . contrary to Microsoft's contention, consumers consider non-Microsoft work group server operating systems to be better than Windows work group server operating systems on a number of features to which they attach great importance.

662. Next, Microsoft cannot rely on the fact that consumers never claimed at any time during the administrative procedure that they had been forced to adopt a Windows work group server operating system as a consequence of its refusal to disclose interoperability information to its competitors. In that connection, it is sufficient to point out that Microsoft does not dispute the Commission's findings at recitals 705 and 706 to the contested decision. Thus, at recital 705 to the contested decision, the Commission observes that it is developers of complementary software required to interoperate with Microsoft's systems who 'depend on the interface information' and that '[c]ustomers will not always exactly know what is disclosed by Microsoft to other work group operating system vendors and what is not'. At recital 706 to the contested decision, the Commission states '[w]hen confronted with a "choice" between putting up with interoperability problems that render their business processes cumbersome, inefficient and costly, and embracing a homogeneous Windows solution for their work group network, customers will tend to opt for the latter proposition' and that '[o]nce they have standardised on Windows, they are unlikely to report interoperability problems between their client PCs and the work group servers'.

663. Furthermore, Microsoft's own statements concerning the disclosures made under the United States settlement show that those disclosures had the consequence of offering greater choice to consumers (see recital 703 to the contested decision).

664. Last, it must be borne in mind that it is settled case-law that Article [102] . . . covers not only practices which may prejudice consumers directly but also those which indirectly prejudice them by impairing an effective competitive structure (Case 85/76 *Hoffmann-La Roche v Commission* . . . paragraph 125, and *Irish Sugar v Commission* . . . paragraph 232). In this case, Microsoft impaired the effective competitive structure on the work group server operating systems market by acquiring a significant market share on that market.

665. The Court concludes from all of the foregoing considerations that the Commission's finding to the effect that Microsoft's refusal limits technical development to the prejudice of consumers within the meaning of Article [102(b)] . . . is not manifestly incorrect. The Court therefore finds that the circumstance relating to the appearance of a new product is present in this case.

. . . The absence of objective justification

688. The Court notes, as a preliminary point, that although the burden of proof of the existence of the circumstances that constitute an infringement of Article [102] . . . is borne by the Commission, it is for the dominant undertaking concerned, and not for the Commission, before the end of the administrative procedure, to raise any plea of objective justification and to support it with arguments and evidence. It then falls to the Commission, where it proposes to make a finding of an abuse of a dominant position, to show that the arguments and evidence relied on by the undertaking cannot prevail and, accordingly, that the justification put forward cannot be accepted.

689. In the present case, as the Commission found at recital 709 to the contested decision and as Microsoft expressly confirmed in the application, Microsoft relied as justification for its conduct solely on the fact that the technology concerned was covered by intellectual property rights. It made clear that if it were required to grant third parties access to that technology, that 'would . . . eliminate future incentives to invest in the creation of more intellectual property' (recital 709 to the contested decision). In the reply,

the applicant also relied on that fact that the technology was secret and valuable and that it contained important innovations.

690. The Court considers that, even on the assumption that it is correct, the fact that the communication protocols covered by the contested decision, or the specifications for those protocols, are covered by intellectual property rights cannot constitute objective justification within the meaning of *Magill* and *IMS Health* . . . Microsoft's argument is inconsistent with the raison d'être of the exception which that case-law thus recognises in favour of free competition, since if the mere fact of holding intellectual property rights could in itself constitute objective justification for the refusal to grant a licence, the exception established by the case-law could never apply. In other words, a refusal to license an intellectual property right could never be considered to constitute an infringement of Article [102] even though in *Magill* and *IMS Health* . . . above, the Court of Justice specifically stated the contrary.

691. It must be borne in mind that, as stated at paragraphs 321, 323, 327 and 330 above, the Community judicature considers that the fact that the holder of an intellectual property right can exploit that right solely for his own benefit constitutes the very substance of his exclusive right. Accordingly, a simple refusal, even on the part of an undertaking in a dominant position, to grant a licence to a third party cannot in itself constitute an abuse of a dominant position within the meaning of Article [102] . . . It is only when it is accompanied by exceptional circumstances such as those hitherto envisaged in the case-law that such a refusal can be characterised as abusive and that, accordingly, it is permissible, in the public interest in maintaining effective competition on the market, to encroach upon the exclusive right of the holder of the intellectual property right by requiring him to grant licences to third parties seeking to enter or remain on that market. It must be borne in mind that it has been established above that such exceptional circumstances were present in this case.

692. The argument which Microsoft puts forward in the reply, namely that the technology concerned is secret and of great value to the licensees and contains important innovations, cannot succeed either.

693. First, the fact that the technology concerned is secret is the consequence of a unilateral business decision on Microsoft's part. Furthermore, Microsoft cannot rely on the argument that the interoperability information is secret as a ground for not being required to disclose it unless the exceptional circumstances identified by the Court of Justice in *Magill* and *IMS Health*, above, are present, and at the same time justify its refusal by what it alleges to be the secret nature of the information. Last, there is no reason why secret technology should enjoy a higher level of protection than, for example, technology which has necessarily been disclosed to the public by its inventor in a patent-application procedure.

694. Second, from the moment at which it is established that—as in this case—the interoperability information is indispensable, that information is necessarily of great value to the competitors who wish to have access to it.

695. Third, it is inherent in the fact that the undertaking concerned holds an intellectual property right that the subject-matter of that right is innovative or original. There can be no patent without an invention and no copyright without an original work.

696. The Court further observes that in the contested decision the Commission did not simply reject Microsoft's assertion that the fact that the technology concerned was covered by intellectual property rights justified its refusal to disclose the relevant information. The Commission also examined the applicant's argument that if it were required to give third parties access to that technology there would be a negative impact on its incentives to innovate (recitals 709 and 712 to the contested decision).

697. The Court finds that, as the Commission correctly submits, Microsoft, which bore the initial burden of proof (see paragraph 688 above), did not sufficiently establish that if it were required to disclose the interoperability information that would have a significant negative impact on its incentives to innovate.

698. Microsoft merely put forward vague, general and theoretical arguments on that point. Thus, as the Commission observes at recital 709 to the contested decision, in its response of 17 October 2003 to the third statement of objections Microsoft merely stated that '[d]isclosure would . . . eliminate future incentives to invest in the creation of more intellectual property', without specifying the technologies or products to which it thus referred.

699. In certain passages in the response referred to in the preceding paragraph, Microsoft envisages a negative impact on its incentives to innovate by reference to its operating systems in general, namely both those for client PCs and those for servers.

700. In that regard, it is sufficient to note that, at recitals 713 to 729 to the contested decision, the Commission quite correctly refuted Microsoft's arguments relating to the fear that its products would be cloned. It must be borne in mind, in particular, that the remedy prescribed in Article 5 of the contested decision does not, and is not designed to, allow Microsoft's competitors to copy its products (see paragraphs 198 to 206, 240 to 242 and 656 to 658 above).

701. It follows that it has not been demonstrated that the disclosure of the information to which that remedy relates will significantly reduce—still less eliminate—Microsoft's incentives to innovate.

702. In that context, the Court observes that, as the Commission correctly finds at recitals 730 to 734 to the contested decision, it is normal practice for operators in the industry to disclose to third parties the information which will facilitate interoperability with their products and Microsoft itself had followed that practice until it was sufficiently established on the work group server operating systems market. Such disclosure allows the operators concerned to make their own products more attractive and therefore more valuable. In fact, none of the parties has claimed in the present case that such disclosure had had any negative impact on those operators' incentives to innovate.

. . .

704. Last, the Court finds that Microsoft's assertion that in the contested decision the Commission applied a new evaluation test when rejecting the objective justification which Microsoft had submitted is based on a misreading of that decision.

705. That assertion is based on a single sentence in recital 783 to the contested decision, which is in a part of that decision containing the findings of the Commission's analysis, at recitals 560 to 778, of the refusal at issue.

706. That sentence reads as follows:

'[A] detailed examination of the scope of the disclosure at stake leads to the conclusion that, on balance, the possible negative impact of an order to supply on Microsoft's incentives to innovate is outweighed by its positive impact on the level of innovation of the whole industry (including Microsoft)'.

707. However, that sentence must be read in conjunction with the one coming immediately afterwards in the same recital, which states that '. . . the need to protect Microsoft's incentives to innovate cannot constitute an objective justification that would offset the exceptional circumstances identified'.

708. It must also be compared with recital 712 to the contested decision, where the Commission sets out the following considerations:

'It has been established above . . . that Microsoft's refusal to supply [creates a risk of elimination of] competition in the relevant market for work group server operating systems, that this is due to the fact that the refused input is indispensable to carry on business in that market and that Microsoft's refusal has a negative impact on technical development to the prejudice of consumers. In view of these exceptional circumstances, Microsoft's refusal cannot be objectively justified merely by the fact that it constitutes a refusal to license intellectual property. It is therefore necessary to assess whether Microsoft's arguments regarding its incentives to innovate outweigh these exceptional circumstances.'

709. In other words, in accordance with the principles laid down in the case-law . . . the Commission, after establishing that the exceptional circumstances identified by the Court of Justice in *Magill* and *IMS Health* . . . were present in this case, then proceeded to consider whether the justification put forward by Microsoft, on the basis of the alleged impact on its incentives to innovate, might prevail over those exceptional circumstances, including the circumstance that the refusal at issue limited technical development to the prejudice of consumers within the meaning of Article [102(b)] . . .

710. The Commission came to a negative conclusion but not by balancing the negative impact which the imposition of a requirement to supply the information at issue might have on Microsoft's incentives to innovate against the positive impact of that obligation on innovation in the industry as a whole, but

after refuting Microsoft's arguments relating to the fear that its products might be cloned (recitals 713 to 729 to the contested decision), establishing that the disclosure of interoperability was widespread in the industry concerned (recitals 730 to 735 to the contested decision) and showing that IBM's commitment to the Commission in 1984 was not substantially different from what Microsoft was ordered to do in the contested decision (recitals 736 to 742 to the contested decision) and that its approach was consistent with Directive 91/250 (recitals 743 to 763 to the contested decision).

711. It follows from all of the foregoing considerations that Microsoft has not demonstrated the existence of any objective justification for its refusal to disclose the interoperability at issue.

712. As the exceptional circumstances identified by the Court of Justice in *Magill* and *IMS Health* . . . were also present in this case, the first part of the plea must be rejected as wholly unfounded.

As seen from the preceding extracts of the judgment, the GC upheld the Commission decision on the basis that the *Magill/IMS* exceptional circumstances were present. In doing so the GC gave an elastic interpretation to those exceptional circumstances. It should also be noted that the GC did not confine its statements to copyrights.

- *Indispensability*. The GC upheld the Commission's finding that it was indispensable for the competitors' systems to work as seamlessly with Windows as Microsoft's own products[806] even though a fringe of competitors unable to do so were operating on the market. The interface information might have been greatly more convenient for the competitors, but they *were* functioning without it. Indispensability in *Microsoft* did not mean exclusion from the market.[807]

- *Elimination of competition*. First, the GC interpreted this requirement as meaning the elimination of *effective* competition on the downstream market (paragraph 563). The continued existence of fringe competitors in niche markets was irrelevant. Secondly, the GC was content that the Commission should demonstrate merely a 'risk' of the elimination of effective competition and accepted that the Commission did not have to wait for the elimination of competition before it could act. It dismissed as semantics all Microsoft's arguments about a difference between 'risk', 'likely to', and 'high probability' (paragraphs 560–561) despite the oft-quoted plea of a Microsoft lawyer at the hearing that there is a world of difference between a risk of getting bird flu and the likelihood of getting it.[808] Unlike *Magill*, where the refusal to supply entirely excluded the potential entrant from the market, the competitors in *Microsoft* were on the market but might leave it, or become marginalised, at some future time. This all involved speculation as to how the (constantly evolving, high technology) market would develop in the future. As has been pointed out, this is akin to the kind of prediction that is undertaken in merger cases, where the EU Courts have held the Commission to a rigorous standard of proof.[809] In *Microsoft*, however, the GC was happy that the Commission had established a 'risk' based on accurate, reliable, and coherent evidence.[810] Furthermore, it has been pointed out that in Article 102 cases which may take years to reach the GC (over three in *Microsoft*) any 'risk' foreseen by the Commission at the time of the decision may or may not have materialised to a greater or lesser

---

[806] The Commission explained further at the hearing that this included a non-Windows WGOS being able to 'talk' to a Microsoft WGOS just as if it were itself a Microsoft WGOS: Case T-210/04, *Microsoft* [2007] ECR II-3601, para. 237.

[807] See D. Ridyard, 'Compulsory Access under EC Competition Law—A New Doctrine of "Convenient Facilities" and the Case for Price Regulation' [2004] *ECLR* 670.

[808] Said on Day Three of the *Microsoft* hearing, 26 April 2009, Ahlborn and Evans, n. 636, 927; D. Beard, '*Microsoft*: What Sort of Landmark?' (2008) 4 *Competition Policy International* 39.

[809] See Beard, ibid., 42–43; for mergers, see Chap. 15.

[810] Case T-210/04, *Microsoft* [2007] ECR II-3601, paras. 564, 620.

extent. The problem is then how far the Court could employ the benefit of hindsight, given the limitations of judicial review.[811]

- A *'new product'*. The GC said that the Commission had not made a manifest error in failing to identify a specific new product for which there was actual or potential consumer demand whose emergence was prevented by the refusal to supply. It was enough that the refusal limited 'technical developments to the prejudice of consumers' within Article 102(b). Having noted that in *IMS* itself the CJ was concerned about refusals which prevented the development of the secondary market to the detriment of consumers,[812] the GC said that the appearance of a 'new product' was not the only relevant parameter (paragraphs 646–647). It noted that Article 102(b) applies to the limitation of technical development as well as production and markets. Accordingly the Commission was correct in considering that the test included (as yet unspecified and unknown) products emerging from innovation by the competitors which would not occur if the competitors left the market and/or were unable to develop products fully compatible with Windows. The lack of interoperability meant that consumers were increasingly locked in to Windows WGOS (paragraph 650). The GC also agreed with the Commission's view that the competitors would not have any interest in just 'cloning' Microsoft's products but had every reason to develop differentiated products (paragraph 658). However, it has been argued that mere cloning could be profitable for competitors if they could compete with Microsoft on price.[813] Notably (paragraph 659), Microsoft's argument that it would have less incentive to develop new technology if it were required to divulge it to competitors was held by the GC to be irrelevant to the 'new product' condition which was concerned only with the *competitors'* incentives to innovate (Microsoft's incentives were considered an objective justification issue). The GC thus endorsed the Commission's view that a refusal to supply may be abusive not because it excludes competitors but because it is likely to hinder future innovation.

In dealing with Microsoft's plea of objective justification the GC provided clarification of how the defence actually works (paragraph 688). The case itself, however, demonstrates how difficult it is to separate out objective justification from the initial finding of abuse (see paragraph 659). The GC rejected Microsoft's plea that the fact that the information was covered by IPRs justified its refusal to disclose, on the grounds that it would lead to the conclusion that a refusal to license could never be an abuse. It also rejected Microsoft's pleas that disclosure would have a negative impact on its incentives to innovate, dismissing them as 'vague and theoretical arguments' which did not specify the technologies or products concerned (paragraph 698). The judgment suggests, therefore, that the defence might succeed if a greater level of detail were given. However, in paragraph 696 the GC puts the burden of proof on the dominant undertaking to demonstrate that its incentives would be harmed by compulsory licensing and, especially where (as here) the evolution of high technology markets is involved, it is questionable whether it would ever be possible to discharge that burden. The GC's judgment on this point should also be contrasted to its willingness to accept, without similar specificity, the claims about 'technical development' being limited and assuming that the refusal to deal will lead to consumer harm. One curious point on objective justification is the GC's treatment of the Commission's statement that the positive impact on the industry as a whole outweighed the negative impact on Microsoft's incentives.[814] Microsoft argued before the GC that this introduced a whole new test into the application of Article 102,[815] and the GC's attempt to try to

---

[811] See further on this, Beard, n. 808, 47.

[812] Case C-418/01, *IMS* [2004] ECR I-5039, para. 48.

[813] D. Howarth and K. McMahon, '"Windows has performed an Illegal Operation": The Court of First Instance's Judgment in *Microsoft v Commission*' [2008] *ECLR* 117, 124.

[814] COMP/37.792, *Microsoft* 24 March 2004, para. 783.

[815] Case T-210/04, *Microsoft* [2007] ECR II-3601, paras. 669–670.

explain away what the Commission was saying is unconvincing (paragraphs 705–710).[816] From the efficiencies point of view it can be argued that the Commission was correct[817] although it is also said that balancing tests are 'an inherently unreliable and unpredictable method to address mandatory access cases'.[818]

As with the tying part of the judgment,[819] *Microsoft* is significant not only in respect of the substantive law on refusal to supply and IPRs but also in the context of the 'modernisation' of Article 102 and the Commission's review. First, the GC concentrated on looking at the position of the competitors and stressed the fall in their market share and the rise in Microsoft's (for example, paragraph 428). Secondly, it emphasised the disadvantage to the competitors and deduced consumer prejudice from that. Thirdly, as already noted, the GC in paragraph 664 repeated that Article 102 is concerned with the impairment of the competitive structure, but said that Microsoft had done that by acquiring a significant market share and did not explain how it led to consumer detriment in this case.

The GC has also been criticised for failing to engage sufficiently with the implications of networks effects. One American commentator has suggested that the GC, instead of straining to apply the existing rules, could instead have asked the 'important questions', i.e. (a) are consumers and the market seriously disadvantaged by denial of full access to interoperability information and if 'yes', (b) would the respondent and the market be seriously disadvantaged by a duty to grant access?[820]

E. REFUSAL TO SUPPLY IN SITUATIONS NOT INVOLVING UPSTREAM/DOWNSTREAM MARKETS

Refusals to supply where the issue is not one of vertical foreclosure of competitors in downstream markets are not covered in the refusal to supply section of the Guidance Paper and have mainly concerned the supply of products for distribution or resale and a dominant firm protecting its commercial interests.

In *United Brands* the Commission held that UBC had abused its dominant position on the banana market by refusing to continue supplying its Chiquita bananas to its Danish ripener/distributor, Oelsen, in response to Oelsen taking part in an advertising and promotion campaign for Standard Fruit's 'Dole' bananas. Oelsen was not under an exclusive purchasing obligation but UBC argued that Oelsen had sold fewer and fewer Chiquitas in comparison to Doles, and had taken less trouble in ripening them. Without gainsaying UBC's allegations, the CJ upheld the Commission's finding that the refusal to supply infringed Article 102.

---

[816] I.e. that if the sentence was read in conjunction with other passages of the decision it was clear that the Commission was considering whether the alleged impact on Microsoft's innovation incentives might prevail over the presence of the exceptional circumstances laid down in *Magill* and *IMS*.

[817] C. Ritter, 'Refusal to Deal and Essential Facilities: Does Intellectual Property Require Special Deference Compared to Tangible Property?' (2005) 3 *World Competition* 281, 298.

[818] D. Geradin, 'Limiting the Scope of Article 82 EC: What Can the EU Learn from the Supreme Court's Judgment in *Trinko*, in the Wake of *Microsoft*, *IMS* and *Deutsche Telekom*?' (2004) 41 *CMLRev* 1526, 1542.

[819] See Section 12.E.iii, p. 480 ff.

[820] E. Fox, '*Microsoft* (EC) and Duty to Deal: Exceptionality and the Transatlantic Divide' (2008) 4 *Competition Policy International* 25, 29. The Commission initiated a further investigation in January 2008 for refusing 'to disclose interoperability information across a broad range of products, including information related to its Office suite, a number of its server products, and also in relation to the so called.NET Framework': MEMO/08/19. In July 2009, the Commission announced that Microsoft had 'made proposals in relation to disclosures of interoperability information that would improve interoperability' between third party products and several Microsoft products: MEMO/09/352.

Case 27/76, *United Brands v Commission* [1978] ECR 207

Court of Justice

182. . . . [I]t is advisable to assert positively from the outset that an undertaking in a dominant position for the purpose of marketing a product—which cashes in on the reputation of a brand name known to and valued by the consumers—cannot stop supplying a long standing customer who abides by regular commercial practice, if the orders placed by that customer are in no way out of the ordinary.

183. Such conduct is inconsistent with the objectives laid down in Article [3(1)(g)] of the Treaty, which are set out in detail in Article [102], especially in paragraphs (b) and (c), since the refusal to sell would limit markets to the prejudice of consumers and would amount to discrimination which might in the end eliminate a trading party from the relevant market.

. . .

189. Although it is true, as the applicant points out, that the fact that an undertaking is in a dominant position cannot disentitle it from protecting its own commercial interests if they are attacked, and that such an undertaking must be conceded the right to take such reasonable steps as it deems appropriate to protect its said interests, such behaviour cannot be countenanced if its actual purpose is to strengthen this dominant position and abuse it.

190. Even if the possibility of a counter-attack is acceptable that attack must still be proportionate to the threat taking into account the economic strength of the undertakings confronting each other.

191. The sanction consisting of a refusal to supply by an undertaking in a dominant position was in excess of what might, if such a situation were to arise, reasonably be contemplated as a sanction for conduct similar to that for which UBC blamed Oelsen.

192. In fact UBC could not be unaware of that fact that by acting in this way it would discourage its other ripener/distributors from supporting the advertising of other brand names and that the deterrent effect of the sanction imposed upon one of them would make its position of strength on the relevant market that much more effective.

193. Such a course of conduct amounts therefore to a serious interference with the independence of small and medium sized firms in their commercial relations with the undertaking in a dominant position and this independence implies the right to give preference to competitors' goods.

194. In this case the adoption of such a course of conduct is designed to have a serious adverse effect on competition on the relevant banana market by only allowing firms dependant upon the dominant undertaking to stay in business.

195. The applicant's argument that in its view the 40 per cent fall in the price of bananas on the Danish market shows that competition has not been affected by the refusal to supply Oelsen cannot be upheld.

196. In fact this fall in prices was only due to the very lively competition—called at the time the 'banana war'—in which the two transnational companies UBC and Castle and Cooke engaged.

Whilst affirming that dominant undertakings are justified in acting to prevent attacks on their commercial interests,[821] the CJ nevertheless judged UBC's response to be disproportionate despite recognising that UBC was in the midst of a 'banana war'.[822] It is not clear, given Oelsen's conduct, what the CJ meant when it stated, in paragraph 182, that a dominant undertaking could not stop supplying a regular customer who 'abides by regular commercial practice'[823] but that statement was relied

[821] For the protection of commercial interests as a defence, see Section 5.G.

[822] In para. 196. As discussed in Chap. 6, UBC was found dominant with 45% of a narrowly drawn market (bananas rather than fruit) despite evidence of what the Court itself called 'very lively competition'.

[823] It has been argued that 'the Court of Justice inferred an anti-competitive motive on United Brands' part, without, as far as one can see, a scintilla of evidence, and then condemned United Brands for having had this improper

upon by the CJ in its 2008 judgment *Sot. Lélos* on a refusal to supply to prevent parallel trade.[824] The Guidance Paper says that exclusive dealing principles will be applied to the punishment of customers situation.[825]

In *Boosey & Hawkes*[826] B&H, which the Commission held to be dominant in the British-style brass band instrument market, refused to have further dealings with two firms, one a distributor of its instruments and the other a repairer, who formed a company to manufacture and market competing instruments. The Commission took interim measures, ordering B&H to recommence supplies. Again, the Commission recognised the right of dominant undertakings to protect their interests when attacked but refused to accept that B&H's conduct was justified and proportionate. The Commission saw a dominant undertaking trying to exclude others from the market and seemed only reluctantly to admit that in the circumstances 'even a dominant producer is entitled to review its commercial relations'.

BP v Commission[827] was a rare case of the Commission losing an Article 102 case on the substance. The CJ held there was no duty to supply where during the 1973 OPEC oil boycott an oil supplier dealt with the shortage by supplying its regular, long-term rather than occasional customers. The Commission had found that the refusal to deal with occasional customers on the basis of what they ordered in a previous period was an abuse.[828] However, the CJ held that the supply strategy was reasonable in the circumstances and that the refusal to supply ABG was justified.

Refusal to supply on grounds of nationality infringes Article 102.[829]

F. REFUSAL TO SUPPLY IN THE GUIDANCE PAPER

The Guidance Paper deals with refusals to supply in paragraphs 75–90. It is limited to the situation in which a vertically integrated dominant undertaking competes downstream with a buyer it refuses to supply (see paragraph 77). No other refusal to supply scenarios are dealt with.

The refusal to supply section states the basic principle of freedom to contract with whom one chooses before setting out the reasons for taking great care before competition law intervenes.

75. When setting its enforcement priorities, the Commission starts from the position that, generally speaking, any undertaking, whether dominant or not, should have the right to choose its trading partners and to dispose freely of its property. The Commission therefore considers that intervention on competition law grounds requires careful consideration where the application of Article [102] would lead to the imposition of an obligation to supply on the dominant undertaking . . . The existence of such an obligation—even for a fair remuneration—may undermine undertakings' incentives to invest and innovate and, thereby, possibly harm consumers. The knowledge that they may have a duty to supply against their will may lead dominant undertakings—or undertakings who anticipate that they may become dominant—not to invest, or to invest less, in the activity in question. Also, competitors may be tempted to free ride on investments made by the dominant undertaking instead of investing themselves. Neither of these consequences would, in the long run, be in the interest of consumers.

---

motive', resulting in the CJ effectively precluding dominant undertakings 'from refusing to supply customers who either directly or indirectly wage an assault on their businesses': P. Jebsen and R. Stevens, 'Assumptions, Goals, and Dominant Undertakings: The Regulation of Competition Under Art. 86 of the European Union' (1996) 64 *Antitrust LJ* 443, 510–511.

[824] Cases C-468–478/06, *Sot. Lélos* [2008] ECR I-7139, see Section 17, p. 576.

[825] Guidance Paper, para. 77.

[826] *BBI/Boosey & Hawkes* [1987] OJ L286/36. There were other alleged abuses by B&H, such as engaging in vexatious litigation (see Section 14.B, p. 540).

[827] Case 77/77, *BP v Commission* [1978] ECR 1513.

[828] *ABG Oil* [1977] OJ L117/1. The Court upheld the Commission's finding that for the duration of the crisis each supplier was in a dominant position in respect of its former customers.

[829] See, e.g., Case 7/82, *GVL v Commission* [1983] ECR 483 where the German collecting society refused to offer its services to artists established outside Germany unless they were of German nationality.

The Guidance Paper makes no distinction between refusal to license IPRs and other refusals. It says that the concept of refusal to supply includes 'a broad range of practices' such as refusing to supply products to existing or new customers, refusal to license IPRs, including for purposes of interface information, or refusal to grant access to an essential facility or network.[830] It covers 'constructive refusals' such as undue delay, degradation of supply, or imposing unreasonable conditions.[831] The Guidance Paper also considers margin squeeze as a type of refusal to supply[832] but this has been overtaken by the judgment of the CJ in *TeliaSonera*, which held that margin squeeze was a distinct abuse from refusal to supply.[833]

The Guidance Paper sets out a test (paragraph 81) for when the Commission will consider it a priority to intervene. It comprises three cumulative conditions:

(a) the refusal relates to a product or service that is objectively necessary to be able to compete on a downstream market;

(b) the refusal is likely to lead to the elimination of effective competition in the downstream market;

(c) the refusal is likely to lead to consumer harm.

On condition (a), the objective necessity of the input (the term the Commission uses instead of 'essential facility' or 'indispensable') the Commission relies on *Microsoft* for saying that this does not mean that without it no competitor could enter or survive on the downstream market.[834] The test is whether an alternative source of supply is capable of allowing competitors to exert a competitive constraint.

On condition (b) the Commission states that if the objective necessity of the input is shown the refusal to supply is generally liable to eliminate, immediately or over time, effective competition in the downstream market.[835] The requirement for the elimination of *effective competition* comes from *Microsoft* and the Commission has preferred this to the standard in the non-IPR cases, *Commercial Solvents* and *Bronner*, which, as we have seen, requires the elimination of competition from the person requesting access.[836]

On condition (c), the impact on consumer harm, the Commission says it will normally pursue the case if the likely negative effects of the refusal outweigh over time the negative effects of ordering supply. It then continues:[837]

The Commission considers that consumer harm may, for instance, arise where the competitors that the dominant undertaking forecloses are, as a result of the refusal, prevented from bringing innovative goods or services to market and/or where follow-on innovation is likely to be stifled . . . This may be particularly the case if the undertaking which requests supply does not intend to limit itself essentially to duplicating the

---

[830] Guidance Paper, para. 78.

[831] Ibid., para. 79.

[832] Ibid., para. 80.

[833] Case C-52/09, *TeliaSonera* [2011] ECR I-527, see Section 9.B.ii, p. 416.

[834] Guidance Paper, para. 83.

[835] Ibid., para. 85. Nazzini, n. 116, 267 takes issue with this, saying that proof of the effect of the refusal on downstream competition is a free-standing element of the test, and pointing out that the Commission itself in para. 85 sets out a number of factors which affect the likelihood of effective competition being eliminated. These include a high market share in the downstream market, the extent to which the dominant undertaking is comparatively capacity constrained downstream, the substitutability between the dominant undertaking's output and that of its downstream competitors, and the proportion of downstream competitors that are affected by the refusal. Marsden, n. 100, 68 considers that the list of factors in para. 85 shows the Commission's concern with dominance per se rather than with the conduct.

[836] Nazzini, n. 116, 267, argues that elimination of all competition and elimination of competition from the person requiring access amount in reality to the same thing as indispensability is an objective concept so a refusal capable of excluding one competitor must be capable of excluding all.

[837] Guidance Paper, para. 87.

goods or services already offered by the dominant undertaking on the downstream market, but intends to produce new or improved goods or services for which there is a potential consumer demand or is likely to contribute to technical development . . .

The reference to innovation is not confined to IPR situations. Rather than distinguish between IPR and non-IPR cases on the basis that IPR refusals require prevention of a new product/technical development, therefore, the Commission has applied the need for 'consumer harm' to all cases. The concern with the stifling of innovation reflects the *Microsoft* judgment.

The Commission says it will apply the paragraph 81 criteria to both new and existing customers. However, the termination of existing supply is more likely to be found abusive. This is because:

For example, if the dominant undertaking had previously been supplying the requesting undertaking, and the latter had made relationship-specific investments in order to use the subsequently refused input, the Commission may be more likely to regard the input in question as indispensable. Similarly, the fact that the owner of the essential input in the past has found it in its interest to supply is an indication that supplying the input does not imply any risk that the owner receives inadequate compensation for the original investment. It would therefore be up to the dominant company to demonstrate why circumstances have actually changed in such a way that the continuation of its existing supply relationship would put in danger its adequate compensation.[838]

The three conditions laid down in paragraph 81 for enforcement priority are subject to a proviso (paragraph 82). In certain situations, such as (a) where sector regulation has already provided for supply obligations or (b) the upstream position of the dominant undertaking has been developed through state protection or state financing, the Commission's normal wariness about the intervention having negative effects on investment and innovation incentives is eased. In such cases the Commission will not be concerned if the three paragraph 81 conditions are not fulfilled and will revert to its general enforcement standard set out in the Guidance Paper, i.e. likely anti-competitive foreclosure.

82. In certain specific cases, it may be clear that imposing an obligation to supply is manifestly not capable of having negative effects on the input owner's and/or other operators' incentives to invest and innovate upstream, whether ex ante or ex post. The Commission considers that this is particularly likely to be the case where regulation compatible with Community law already imposes an obligation to supply on the dominant undertaking and it is clear, from the considerations underlying such regulation, that the necessary balancing of incentives has already been made by the public authority when imposing such an obligation to supply. This could also be the case where the upstream market position of the dominant undertaking has been developed under the protection of special or exclusive rights or has been financed by state resources. In such specific cases there is no reason for the Commission to deviate from its general enforcement standard of showing likely anti-competitive foreclosure, without considering whether the three circumstances referred to in paragraph 81 are present.

The exceptional situations in this paragraph are the 'Telefónica exceptions' which appeared in the Commission's margin squeeze decision *Wanadoo España v Telefónica*, discussed earlier.[839] They have both been criticised[840] by those who argue in respect of the first that regulation pursues broader objectives than competition law and that national regulators may impose an obligation to supply in circumstances where the Commission is not entitled to impose one; and in respect of the second that 'it is difficult to apply in practice and is likely to lead to unpredictable and erroneous results'[841]

---

[838] Ibid., para. 84. There is no case law cited in support of this paragraph.

[839] COMP/38.784, *Wanadoo España v Telefónica* 4 July 2007, see Section 9.B.iii, p. 423.

[840] See D. Geradin, 'Refusal to Supply and Margin Squeeze: A Discussion of Why the "*Telefonica* Exceptions" are Wrong', TILEC Discussion Paper No. 2011-009, available at <http://papers.ssrn.com/sol3/papers.cfm?abstract_id=1762687>; Geradin, Layne-Farrar, and Petit, n. 170, 4.351–4.354, 4.366–4.367; Faella and Pardolesi, n. 304, 271–273.

[841] Geradin, Layne-Farrar, and Petit, n. 170, 4.354.

because how far the dominant undertaking's position has been developed in that way may not be clear-cut and in particular which parts of the assets were paid for pre- rather than post-liberalisation may be difficult to determine.[842] One answer to this is that the Commission 'still needs to prove an elimination of effective competition and consumer harm and these [exceptions] simply provide a (rebuttable) presumption that the indispensability condition is met'.[843]

The Guidance Paper states that the Commission will consider efficiencies claims. Paragraph 89 reflects the kinds of arguments that were raised in *Microsoft*:

The Commission will consider claims by the dominant undertaking that a refusal to supply is necessary to allow the dominant undertaking to realise an adequate return on the investments required to develop its input business, thus generating incentives to continue to invest in the future, taking the risk of failed projects into account. The Commission will also consider claims by the dominant undertaking that its own innovation will be negatively affected by the obligation to supply, or by the structural changes in the market conditions that imposing such an obligation will bring about, including the development of follow-on innovation by competitors.

Citing *Microsoft* the Guidance Paper says that it is for the dominant undertaking to demonstrate the negative impact of an obligation to supply on its own level of innovation.[844]

G. REFUSAL TO SUPPLY AND THE 'ESSENTIAL FACILITIES' DOCTRINE IN US LAW

We noted earlier that the essential facilities doctrine originated in US law. Section 2 of the Sherman Act prohibits the acquisition or maintenance of monopoly power. In *United States v Colgate & Co*[845] the Supreme Court said that in the absence of any purpose to create or maintain a monopoly a private trader may freely 'exercise his own independent discretion as to parties with whom he may deal' and the US courts have consequently been generally reluctant to condemn refusals to deal. However, they have held that such refusals do come within s. 2, by way of exception to the *Colgate* principle, in certain limited circumstances, and some courts have applied an 'essential facilities' doctrine.[846] There is some question as to whether the doctrine is really part of the recognised exceptions to the *Colgate* principle, or whether it is a separate principle.[847] In any event, many American commentators are highly critical of the doctrine. We have already seen that Areeda expressed caution about it[848] and Hovenkamp says the 'so-called essential facilities doctrine is one of the most troublesome, incoherent and unmanageable bases for Sherman section 2 liability. The antitrust world would almost certainly be a better place if it were jettisoned, with a little fine tuning of the general doctrine of the monopolist's refusal to deal to fill in the resulting gaps.'[849]

---

[842] See also Mazák AG in Case C-52/09, *TeliaSonera* [2011] ECR I-527, para. 27 of the Opinion. The Commission is also criticised for ignoring the dominant undertaking's future incentives to invest, D. Geradin, 'Refusal to Supply and Margin Squeeze: A Discussion of Why the "*Telefonica* Exceptions" are Wrong', TILEC Discussion Paper No. 2011-009, available at <http://papers.ssrn.com/sol3/papers.cfm?abstract_id=1762687>.

[843] Faull and Nikpay, n. 1, 4.690.

[844] Guidance Paper, para. 90, citing para. 659 of *Microsoft*.

[845] 250 US 300, 39 S.Ct 465 (1919).

[846] The leading cases are discussed by the Supreme Court in *Verizon v Trinko*, 540 US 398, 124 S.Ct. 872 (2004); see also Elhauge and Geradin, n. 207, 425–449.

[847] See L. Hancher, 'Case note on *Oscar Bronner*' (1999) 36 *CMLRev* 1289.

[848] P. Areeda, 'Essential Facilities: An Epithet in Need of Limiting Principles' (1990) 58 *Antitrust LJ* 841, extracted in Section 13.B.v, p. 503.

[849] Hovenkamp, n. 203, 336, and Chap. 7 generally. Jacobs AG, reviewing the US position in Case C-7/97, *Bronner* [1998] ECR I-7791, para. 46 of his Opinion, pointed out that s. 2 of the Sherman Act and Art. 102 protect competition in different ways. The Sherman Act prohibits the acquisition or maintenance of monopoly power, whereas Art. 102 regulates the actions of companies in dominant positions. See further H. Schweitzer, 'The History, Interpretation and Underlying Principles of Section 2 Sherman Act and Article 82 EC' in Ehlermann and Marquis, n. 15, 119.

In 2004 a case concerning a refusal to supply where the essential facilities doctrine was raised finally came before the Supreme Court. The case concerned the telecommunications sector, which is regulated under federal law. The Supreme Court dismissed the claim that there was a refusal to deal under s. 2 and was less than enthusiastic about the essential facilities doctrine. The extracts from the case rehearse again (albeit in the context of the US provisions) the dangers of forcing undertakings to share with or supply competitors and should be compared with the similar arguments of Advocate General Jacobs in *Bronner*.

Verizon Communications Inc v Trinko LLP, 540 US 398, 124 S.Ct 872 (2004)

Customers who received local telephone services from competing local exchange carriers (LEC) brought an action against the incumbent LEC alleging that it had breached its duty to share under the Telecommunications Act 1996 and that its failure to share violated s. 2 of the Sherman Act. The Supreme Court held that the duties under the 1996 Act could not be enforced through a s. 2 claim, but the Act did not affect any liability which the LEC had under general antitrust law. It therefore examined the customers' claims under antitrust law. The Court held (paragraph 6) that even if the essential facilities doctrine existed it served no purpose here as the question of access was taken care of by the 1996 Act.

Supreme Court of the United States (Justice Scalia delivered the opinion of the Court)

III

[2] . . . The mere possession of monopoly power, and the concomitant charging of monopoly prices, is not only not unlawful; it is an important element of the free-market system. The opportunity to charge monopoly prices—at least for a short period—is what attracts 'business acumen' in the first place; it induces risk taking that produces innovation and economic growth. To safeguard the incentive to innovate, the possession of monopoly power will not be found unlawful unless it is accompanied by an element of anti-competitive *conduct*.

[3] Firms may acquire monopoly power by establishing an infrastructure that renders them uniquely suited to serve their customers. Compelling such firms to share the source of their advantage is in some tension with the underlying purpose of antitrust law, since it may lessen the incentive for the monopolist, the rival, or both to invest in those economically beneficial facilities. Enforced sharing also requires antitrust courts to act as central planners, identifying the proper price, quantity, and other terms of dealing—a role for which they are ill-suited. Moreover, compelling negotiation between competitors may facilitate the supreme evil of antitrust: collusion. Thus, as a general matter, the Sherman Act 'does not restrict the long recognized right of [a] trader or manufacturer engaged in an entirely private business, freely to exercise his own independent discretion as to parties with whom he will deal.' *United States* v. *Colgate & Co*, 250 U.S. 300, 307 . . . (1919).

[4] However, '[t]he high value that we have placed on the right to refuse to deal with other firms does not mean that the right is unqualified.' *Aspen Skiing Co* v. *Aspen Highlands Skiing Corp*, 472 U.S. 585, 601 . . . (1985). Under certain circumstances, a refusal to cooperate with rivals can constitute anti-competitive conduct and violate § 2. We have been very cautious in recognizing such exceptions, because of the uncertain virtue of forced sharing and the difficulty of identifying and remedying anti-competitive conduct by a single firm. The question before us today is whether the allegations of respondent's complaint fit within existing exceptions or provide a basis, under traditional antitrust principles, for recognizing a new one.

Justice Scalia then reviewed the case law and continued:

[6] We conclude that Verizon's alleged insufficient assistance in the provision of service to rivals is not a recognized antitrust claim under this Court's existing refusal-to-deal precedents. This conclusion would be unchanged even if we considered to be established law the 'essential facilities' doctrine crafted by some lower courts, under which the Court of Appeals concluded respondent's allegations might state a claim. See generally Areeda, Essential Facilities: An Epithet in Need of Limiting Principles, 58 Antitrust L.J. 841 (1989). We have never recognized such a doctrine, see *Aspen Skiing Co*, 472 U.S., at 611, n. 44, 105 S.Ct. 2847; *AT & T Corp v. Iowa Utilities Bd.*, 525 U.S., at 428, 119 . . . (opinion of BREYER, J.), and we find no need either to recognize it or to repudiate it here. It suffices for present purposes to note that the indispensable requirement for invoking the doctrine is the unavailability of access to the 'essential facilities'; where access exists, the doctrine serves no purpose. Thus, it is said that 'essential facility claims should . . . be denied where a state or federal agency has effective power to compel sharing and to regulate its scope and terms.' P. Areeda & H. Hovenkamp, Antitrust Law, p. 150, 773e (2003 Supp.). Respondent believes that the existence of sharing duties under the 1996 Act supports its case. We think the opposite: The 1996 Act's extensive provision for access makes it unnecessary to impose a judicial doctrine of forced access. To the extent respondent's 'essential facilities' argument is distinct from its general § 2 argument, we reject it.

IV

[7] Finally, we do not believe that traditional antitrust principles justify adding the present case to the few existing exceptions from the proposition that there is no duty to aid competitors. Antitrust analysis must always be attuned to the particular structure and circumstances of the industry at issue. Part of that attention to economic context is an awareness of the significance of regulation . . .

Against the slight benefits of antitrust intervention here, we must weigh a realistic assessment of its costs. Under the best of circumstances, applying the requirements of § 2 'can be difficult' because 'the means of illicit exclusion, like the means of legitimate competition, are myriad.' *United States v. Microsoft Corp*, 253 F.3d 34, 58 (C.A.D.C.2001) . . . Mistaken inferences and the resulting false condemnations 'are especially costly, because they chill the very conduct the antitrust laws are designed to protect.' *Matsushita Elec. Industrial Co v. Zenith Radio Corp*, 475 U.S. 574, 594 . . . (1986). The cost of false positives counsels against an undue expansion of § 2 liability . . .

Even if the problem of false positives did not exist, conduct consisting of anti-competitive violations of § 251 may be, as we have concluded with respect to above-cost predatory pricing schemes, 'beyond the practical ability of a judicial tribunal to control.' *Brooke Group Ltd v. Brown & Williamson Tobacco Corp*, 509 U.S. 209, 223 . . . (1993). Effective remediation of violations of regulatory sharing requirements will ordinarily require continuing supervision of a highly detailed decree. We think that Professor Areeda got it exactly right: 'No court should impose a duty to deal that it cannot explain or adequately and reasonably supervise. The problem should be deemed irremedia[ble] by antitrust law when compulsory access requires the court to assume the day-to-day controls characteristic of a regulatory agency.' Areeda, 58 Antitrust L.J., at 853. In this case, respondent has requested an equitable decree to '[p]reliminarily and permanently enjoi[n] [Verizon] from providing access to the local loop market . . . to [rivals] on terms and conditions that are not as favorable' as those that Verizon enjoys. App. 49–50. An antitrust court is unlikely to be an effective day-to-day enforcer of these detailed sharing obligations.

In paragraph 6 Justice Scalia points out that the Supreme Court has never recognised the essential facilities doctrine, which has been 'crafted by some lower courts'. Given that it could not apply in this case he states that there is 'no need either to recognize or repudiate it here'. However, the tenor of the judgment is unsympathetic towards it. Earlier he is careful to confine the Court's existing refusal to deal precedents to their own facts. Even taking into account the CJ's conservative approach in *Bronner*, refusals to deal and essential facilities are an area of divergence between US and EU law. Some commentators argue strongly that the EU should take the same robust approach to demands for access to the facilities of others as the Supreme Court has taken.[850] The divergence on refusal to supply demonstrates the difference between US law's concern with incentives to innovate—and the assumption in the case of refusal to supply that a requirement to deal will chill incentives—and the requirement in EU law that it is for the dominant undertaking to demonstrate negative impact on innovation.[851] Also, it should be remembered when reading *Trinko* that the relationship between sector regulation and competition law is different in the EU and the US. In the US regulation law is federal, whereas in the EU there are only national regimes.[852]

14. OTHER EXCLUSIONARY PRACTICES

A. GENERAL

Any exclusionary conduct by a dominant undertaking may be capable of constituting an exclusionary abuse. Miscellaneous exclusionary conduct which has come before the EU Courts or Commission includes alleging to third parties that a competitor is a bad debtor;[853] buying up a competitor's machines;[854] monopolising the specialist advertising media;[855] putting pressure on a shipping line to stop carrying the competitor's product by threatening to withdraw the dominant undertaking's own custom;[856] 'inducing' a competitor shipping line to join a liner conference;[857] and a liner conference pressurising the Zairean Government to observe the exclusive dealing provisions in their agreements and exclude rival carriers.[858]

In this section we discuss some specific exclusionary practices which have been held to infringe Article 102, some of which are of particular importance in the ICT sector.

B. PURSUIT OF LEGAL PROCEEDINGS, VEXATIOUS LITIGATION, AND ENFORCING LEGAL RIGHTS

It may be an abuse for a dominant undertaking to pursue legal proceedings against a competitor. This was suggested by *BBI/Boosey & Hawkes*[859] but the Commission did not pursue the point, concentrating rather on the refusal to supply aspect.[860] In *ITT Promedia*[861] Belgacom, the dominant supplier of voice telephony services in Belgium was engaged in a dispute with Promedia about the

---

[850] See in particular D. Geradin, 'Limiting the Scope of Article 82 EC: What Can the EU Learn from the Supreme Court's Judgment in *Trinko*, in the Wake of *Microsoft, IMS* and *Deutsche Telekom*?' (2004) 41 *CMLRev* 1526.

[851] See further Marsden, n. 100, 68–72.

[852] See the margin squeeze case, Case C-280/08 P, *Deutsche Telekom* [2010] ECR I-9555 for the interaction between EU competition rules and national sector regulators.

[853] *BBI/Boosey & Hawkes* [1987] OJ L282/36.

[854] *Elopak Italia/Tetra Pak* [1991] OJ L72/1, para. 165.

[855] Ibid.

[856] *Irish Sugar* [1997] OJ L258/1, paras. 120–122, on appeal Case T–228/97, *Irish Sugar* [1999] ECR II-2969.

[857] *Transatlantic Conference Agreement (TACA)* [1999] OJ L95/1. On appeal, Cases T-191 and 212–214/98, *Atlantic Container* [2003] ECR II-3275 the GC held that the Commission had not proved that the alleged 'inducement' had occurred so overturned the decision on that ground.

[858] Cases C-395 and 396/96 P, *Compagnie Maritime Belge* [2000] ECR I-1365, paras. 80–88.

[859] *BBI/Boosey & Hawkes* [1987] OJ L282/36.

[860] See Section 13.E, p. 534.

[861] Case T-111/96, *ITT Promedia NV v Commission* [1998] ECR II-2937.

publication of telephone directories. Promedia complained to the Commission that Belgacom was abusing its dominant position by conducting national litigation against it. The Commission rejected the complaint on the grounds that the conduct of litigation by a dominant firm could be abusive only if two cumulative criteria, not present here, were met: (a) that the action could not reasonably be considered as an attempt to establish its rights and could therefore serve only to harass the opposite party; and (b) it was conceived in the framework of a plan whose goal was to eliminate competition. Promedia appealed, alleging that the Commission had applied the criteria incorrectly. The GC recognised the fundamental right, since enshrined in Article 47 of the Charter, of access to the courts. It expressly said that it was not necessary for it to rule on the correctness of the criteria[862] and confined itself to holding that they had been properly applied. The implication of the GC judgment, however, was that the criteria themselves are correct. This was confirmed by the GC in *Protégé International*.[863] The following extract from *ITT* deals with the first criterion.

Case T-111/96, *ITT Promedia v EC Commission* [1998] ECR II-2937

General Court

60. . . . [A]s the Commission has rightly emphasised, the ability to assert one's rights through the courts and the judicial control which that entails, constitute the expression of a general principle of law which underlies the constitutional traditions common to the Member States and which is also laid down in Articles 6 and 13 of the European Convention for the Protection of Human Rights and Fundamental Freedoms of 4 November 1950 (see Case 222/84, *Johnson* v. *Chief Constable of the Royal Ulster Constabulary* . . .). As access to the Court is a fundamental right and a general principle ensuring the rule of law, it is only in wholly exceptional circumstances that the fact that legal proceedings are brought is capable of constituting an abuse of a dominant position within the meaning of Article [102].

61. Second, since the two cumulative criteria constitute an exception to the general principle of access to the courts, which ensures the rule of law, they must be construed and applied strictly, in the manner which does not defeat the application of the general rule (see, *inter alia*, Case T-105/95, *WWF UK* v. *E.C. Commission* . . .).

. . .

72. According to the first of the two cumulative criteria set out by the Commission in the contested decision, legal proceedings can be characterised as an abuse, within the meaning of Article [102], only if they cannot reasonably be considered to be an attempt to assert the rights of the undertaking concerned and can therefore only serve to harass the opposing party. It is therefore the situation existing when the action in question is brought which must be taken into account in order to determine whether that criterion is satisfied.

73. Furthermore, when applying that criterion, it is not a question of determining whether the rights which the undertaking concerned was asserting when it brought its action actually existed or whether that action was well founded, but rather of determining whether such an action was intended to assert what that undertaking could, at that moment, reasonably consider to be its rights. According to the second part of that criterion, as worded, it is satisfied solely when the action did not have that aim, that being the sole case in which it may be assumed that such action could only serve to harass the opposing party.

The *ITT* test asks not whether the rights claimed by the dominant undertaking exist, but whether the undertaking may reasonably consider that they do. The GC judgment therefore confirms that

---

[862] Ibid., para. 57.

[863] Case T-119/09, *Protégé International Ltd v Commission* EU:T:2012:421.

litigation *can* be an abuse, but only in limited circumstances where it is, in effect, vexatious or 'sham'. Moreover, the GC held that Belgacom was entitled to rely on its rights under national law unless and until it was ruled that the national law had been invalidated.[864]

In *AstraZeneca* the Commission considered the question of whether a patent holder's defence to an action for a declaration of invalidity could be an abuse. The Commission differentiated between *defending* an action and *initiating* an action, but as it viewed the costs and delays at issue as having arisen from AZ's misrepresentations to the patent authorities rather than from its defence of legal proceedings, the question was not pursued.[865]

The issue of bringing an injunction to protect IPRs arises in respect of standard-essential patents and is discussed in Section 14.C.ii.[866]

The GC also held in *ITT v Promedia* that a dominant undertaking which sought performance of a contract would commit an abuse only if the claim went beyond what it could reasonably expect from the contract.[867] However, the CJ held that it was an abuse for the dominant liner conference in *Compagnie Maritime Belge*[868] to insist on the Zairean authorities keeping strictly to the terms of the exclusive contract they had signed. This meant that Zaire could not continue giving a small amount of trade to a new competitor.

C. THE MISUSE OF INTELLECTUAL PROPERTY RIGHTS OR OTHER REGULATORY PROCEDURES

(i) The *AstraZeneca* Case

The CJ confirmed in *AstraZeneca*[869] that it can be an abuse for a dominant undertaking to make misrepresentations to regulatory authorities or to take steps with regard to regulatory procedures in order to exclude competitors.

The Commission fined AstraZeneca (AZ) €60 million[870] for (a) misrepresenting certain dates to national patent offices and national courts in order to obtain extra patent protection for Losec[871] in the form of supplementary protection certificates (SPCs) to which it would otherwise not have been entitled; and (b) misusing marketing authorisation procedures by switching Losec from capsule to tablet form in order to hinder generic versions of the drugs coming on to the market, and to hinder parallel imports. By deregistering the capsule marketing authorisation AZ prevented generic drug manufacturers from making use of simplified marketing authorisation procedures which were open to generic producers only if the authorisation for the original product was still in force. The Commission found that depriving the generic manufacturers of the ability to use the faster and simpler procedure delayed the entry on to the market of the generic product.

The decision was taken at a time when the Commission was increasingly concerned with delays in generic medicines coming on to the market and with delays in the development of new medicines to compete with those already available.[872]

---

[864] Case T-111/96, *ITT Promedia* [1998] ECR II-2937, paras. 93–95.

[865] COMP/.37.507, *Generics/AstraZeneca* 15 June 2005, paras. 736–739.

[866] P. 547.

[867] Case T-111/96, *ITT Promedia* [1998] ECR II-2937, para. 129.

[868] Cases C-395 and 396/96 P, *Compagnie Maritime Belge* [2000] ECR I-1365, paras. 72–88.

[869] Case C-457/10 P, *AstraZeneca v Commission* EU:C:2012:770.

[870] COMP/ 37.507, *Generics/AstraZeneca*, 15 June 2005.

[871] An anti-ulcer medicine which is the main oral proton pump inhibitor. For the market definition and dominance aspects of the case, see Chap. 6, Section 5.B.i.j, p. 307 and Section C.

[872] See the Commission inquiry into the pharmaceutical sector, 8 July 2009, and IP/09/1098.

a. Misrepresentations to National Patent Offices and National Courts

The GC[873] upheld the Commission's finding that the presentation of the relevant dates which AZ made to the national patent offices and courts amounted to the giving of misleading information.[874] The GC cited the case law establishing that an abuse of a dominant position does not necessarily have to involve the dominant undertaking using its economic power in order to engage in the infringing conduct. It said that giving public authorities misleading information making possible the grant of an exclusive right to which the undertaking was not entitled constituted a practice falling outside the scope of competition on the merits which may be particularly restrictive of competition. In this case the public authorities had a limited discretion to verify the information provided to them which was a relevant factor in assessing whether the misrepresentations were liable to raise regulatory obstacles to competition. The GC referred to the special responsibility of a dominant undertaking which required it, in this situation, at least to inform the public authorities of any error it had made so that the matter could be rectified. As far as intention is concerned, the GC said that although abuse is an objective concept and so does not require deliberation and bad faith, nevertheless intention can constitute a relevant factor to be taken into account to support the conclusion that an undertaking has abused its dominant position.

The GC held that it was irrelevant whether or not the public authorities to whom misrepresentations were made were actually misled or not, and whether the exclusive rights obtained were afterwards revoked, as the abusive nature of the behaviour could not depend on the contingencies of third parties' reactions. Nor was it relevant whether or not the exclusive right obtained had actually been enforced as the mere possession of an IPR normally keeps competitors away. To make the application of Article 102 dependent on whether or not the dominant undertaking had exercised its right in legal proceedings would render it conditional on the competitors having contravened public regulations.

The GC held that finding that the unlawful acquisition of an exclusive right constituted an abuse did not depend on it having the effect of eliminating all competition. It rejected the argument that for the misrepresentations to constitute an abuse there must have been a direct effect on competition. It was only necessary that they were *capable* of restricting competition. The ability of the practice to restrict competition could be *indirect* provided that it could be shown that it was *actually liable* to do so. The existence of specific remedies within the patent system did not mean that in this situation proof of anti-competitive effect was required. On appeal the CJ affirmed the judgment of the GC.

Case C-457/10 P, *AstraZeneca AB and AstraZeneca plc v Commission* EU:C:2012:770

Court of Justice

[The third ground of appeal, that the GC had taken a legally flawed approach to competition on the merits.]

98. Regarded in the light of the facts found by the General Court, which the appellants have expressly stated that they are not calling into question, the third ground of appeal raised by them is tantamount to an argument that where an undertaking in a dominant position considers that it can, in accordance with a legally defensible interpretation, lay claim to a right, it may use any means to obtain that right, and even have recourse to highly misleading representations with the aim of leading public authorities into error. Such an approach is manifestly not consistent with competition on the merits and the specific responsibility on such an undertaking not to prejudice, by its conduct, effective and undistorted competition within the European Union.

---

[873] Case T-321/05, *AstraZeneca v Commission* [2010] ECR II-2805.

[874] It did, however, hold that the abuse started later than the Commission had found.

99. Lastly, contrary to what the EFPIA submits, the General Court did not hold that undertakings in a dominant position had to be infallible in their dealings with regulatory authorities and that each objectively wrong representation made by such an undertaking constituted an abuse of that position, even where the error was made unintentionally and immediately rectified. It is sufficient to note in this connection that, first, that example is radically different from AZ's conduct in the present case, and that, secondly, the General Court pointed out, at paragraphs 357 and 361 of the judgment under appeal, that the assessment of whether representations made to public authorities for the purposes of improperly obtaining exclusive rights are misleading must be made *in concreto* and may vary according to the specific circumstances of each case. It thus cannot be inferred from that judgment that any patent application made by such an undertaking which is rejected on the ground that it does not satisfy the patentability criteria automatically gives rise to liability under Article [102].

[The fourth ground of appeal, that the GC erred in holding that the mere fact of applying for an SPC was sufficient to constitute an abuse.]

. . .

105. As is apparent, inter alia, from paragraph 357 of the judgment under appeal, the General Court examined in the present case whether, in the light of the context in which the practice in question had been implemented, that practice was such as to lead the public authorities wrongly to create regulatory obstacles to competition, for example by the unlawful grant of exclusive rights to the dominant undertaking. It held in this connection that the limited discretion of public authorities or the absence of any obligation on their part to verify the accuracy or veracity of the information provided could be relevant factors to be taken into consideration for the purposes of determining whether the practice in question was liable to raise regulatory obstacles to competition.

106. Contrary to what the appellants submit, that examination by the General Court is not in any way based on the assumption that the practice in question constitutes an 'abuse in itself', regardless of its anti-competitive effect. On the contrary, the General Court expressly pointed out, at paragraph 377 of the judgment under appeal, that representations designed to obtain exclusive rights unlawfully constitute an abuse only if it is established that, in view of the objective context in which they are made, those representations are actually liable to lead the public authorities to grant the exclusive right applied for.

. . .

111. So far as concerns the fact that the misleading representations did not enable AZ to obtain SPCs in Denmark and that in Ireland and the United Kingdom the SPCs were ultimately issued on the basis of the correct date, it must be stated that the General Court did not err in law in holding, at paragraphs 602 to 604 of the judgment under appeal, that that fact does not mean that AZ's conduct in those countries was not abusive, since it is established that those representations were very likely to result in the issue of unlawful SPCs. In addition, as the Commission has pointed out, in so far as the impugned conduct forms part of an overall strategy seeking to unlawfully exclude manufacturers of generic products from the market by means of obtaining SPCs in breach of the regulatory framework which established them, the existence of an abuse is not affected by the fact that that strategy did not succeed in some countries.

112. Lastly, as regards the circumstances which, according to the appellants, must be present in order to be able to find that the misleading representations were such as to restrict competition, it is sufficient to note that in actual fact they amount to a requirement that current and certain anti-competitive effects be shown. However, it follows from the Court's case-law that, although the practice of an undertaking in a dominant position cannot be characterised as abusive in the absence of any anti-competitive effect on the market, such an effect does not necessarily have to be concrete, and it is sufficient to demonstrate that there is a potential anti-competitive effect (see, to that effect, *TeliaSonera Sverige*, paragraph 64).

b. Withdrawal of the Marketing Authorisations

In respect of the misuse of marketing authorisation procedures the GC distinguished the situation from what it described as the 'essential facilities' cases, referring to *Bronner* and *Microsoft*. It observed that as a result of the EU scheme for marketing authorisations for generic products[875] AZ could not prevent national authorities from using the relevant data when giving authorisations under the abridged procedure. So this was not a 'refusal to supply' scenario.[876] The GC rejected the argument that, as the undertaking was entitled under the relevant rules to request the withdrawal of its marketing authorisations for Losec capsules, the deregistration could not constitute an abuse because 'the illegality of abusive conduct under [Article 102] is unrelated to its compliance or non-compliance with other legal rules'.[877] The GC held that in cases of conduct by which regulatory procedures are used without any basis in competition on the merits, evidence that the conduct is *capable* of restricting competition is sufficient to classify it as an abuse of a dominant position.[878]

In this case the Commission had established that the deregistration was not based on the legitimate protection of an investment that was part of competition on the merits.[879] The Court said that although a dominant undertaking is under no obligation to protect the interests of its competitors that does not make practices implemented solely to exclude competitors compatible with Article 102: the desire of a dominant undertaking to protect its own commercial interests does not justify recourse to practices falling outside the scope of competition on the merits.[880] Therefore, in the absence of objective justification a dominant undertaking 'cannot use regulatory procedures solely in such a way as to prevent or make more difficult the entry of competitors on the market'.[881] The GC did, however, annul the decision to the extent that it found that the deregistration was capable of restricting parallel imports in Denmark and Norway on the grounds that the Commission had not established this. The CJ affirmed the judgment of the GC.

Case C-457/10 P, *AstraZeneca AB and AstraZeneca plc v Commission* EU:C:2012:770

[The fifth ground of appeal, that the GC had misinterpreted the concept of 'competition on the merits'.]

129. As a preliminary point it must be stated that, as the General Court observed at paragraph 804 of the judgment under appeal, the preparation by an undertaking, even in a dominant position, of a strategy whose object it is to minimise the erosion of its sales and to enable it to deal with competition from generic products is legitimate and is part of the normal competitive process, provided that the conduct envisaged does not depart from practices coming within the scope of competition on the merits, which is such as to benefit consumers.

130. However, contrary to what the appellants submit, conduct like that impugned in the context of the second abuse—consisting in the deregistration, without objective justification and after the expiry of the exclusive right to make use of the results of the pharmacological and toxicological tests and clinical trials granted by Directive 65/65, of the MAs for Losec capsules in Denmark, Sweden and Norway, by which AZ intended, as the General Court held at paragraph 814 of the judgment under appeal, to hinder the introduction of generic products and parallel imports—does not come within the scope of competition on the merits.

131. In this connection, it must in particular be stated that, as the General Court observed at paragraph 675 of that judgment, after the expiry of the period of exclusivity referred to above, conduct designed, inter alia, to prevent manufacturers of generic products from making use of their right to benefit from

---

[875] Established by Dir. 65/65 [1965–1966] OJ Special Edition 24, as amended.

[876] Case T-321/05, *AstraZeneca* [2010] ECR II-2805, paras. 678–684.

[877] Ibid., para. 677.

[878] Ibid., para. 824.

[879] Ibid., paras. 675, 812.

[880] Ibid., para. 816.

[881] Ibid., para. 817.

those results was not based in any way on the legitimate protection of an investment which came within the scope of competition on the merits, precisely because, under Directive 65/65, AZ no longer had the exclusive right to make use of those results.

132. Furthermore, the General Court was correct to hold, at paragraph 677 of that judgment, that the fact, relied on by the appellants, that under Directive 65/65 AZ was entitled to request the withdrawal of its MAs for Losec capsules in no way causes that conduct to escape the prohibition laid down in Article 82 EC. As that court pointed out, the illegality of abusive conduct under Article 82 EC is unrelated to its compliance or non-compliance with other legal rules and, in the majority of cases, abuses of dominant positions consist of behaviour which is otherwise lawful under branches of law other than competition law.

133. Moreover, as the Advocate General observes in point 78 of his Opinion, the primary purpose of Directive 65/65 is to safeguard public health while eliminating disparities between certain national provisions which hinder trade in medicinal products within the Union, and it therefore does not, as claimed by the appellants, pursue the same objectives as Article 82 EC in such a way that the application of the latter is no longer required for the purposes of ensuring effective and undistorted competition within the internal market.

134. It is important to point out, in this context, that an undertaking which holds a dominant position has a special responsibility in that latter regard (see Case C-202/07 P *France Télécom* v *Commission* [2009] ECR I-2369, paragraph 105) and that, as the General Court held at paragraphs 672 and 817 of the judgment under appeal, it cannot therefore use regulatory procedures in such a way as to prevent or make more difficult the entry of competitors on the market, in the absence of grounds relating to the defence of the legitimate interests of an undertaking engaged in competition on the merits or in the absence of objective justification.

. . .

[The sixth ground of appeal, that the GC erred in law in considering that the impugned conduct tended to restrict competition.]

148. . . . The situation which characterises the second abuse is not in any way comparable to a compulsory licence or to the situation which gave rise to the judgment in *IMS Health*, relied upon by the appellants, which concerned the refusal by an undertaking in a dominant position, which was the owner of an intellectual property right in a 'brick structure', to grant its competitors a licence for the use of that structure.

149. In fact, the possibility provided for in Directive 65/65 of deregistering a MA is not equivalent to a property right. Consequently, the fact that, in the light of its special responsibility, an undertaking in a dominant position cannot make use of such a possibility in such a way as to prevent or render more difficult the entry of competitors on the market, unless it can, as an undertaking engaged in competition on the merits, rely on grounds relating to the defence of its legitimate interests or on objective justifications, does not constitute either an 'effective expropriation' of such a right or an obligation to grant a licence, but a straightforward restriction of the options available under European Union law.

150. The fact that the exercise of such options by an undertaking in a dominant position is limited or made subject to conditions in order to ensure that competition already weakened by the presence of that undertaking is not subsequently undermined is in no way an exceptional case and does not justify a derogation from Article [102], unlike a situation in which the unfettered exercise of an exclusive right awarded for the realisation of an investment or creation is limited.

. . .

153. The General Court therefore did not commit any error of law in rejecting, at paragraphs 678 to 684 of the judgment under appeal, the appellants' argument that the compatibility with Article [102] of the conduct impugned in the context of the second abuse should be assessed in accordance with the criteria applied, inter alia, in *IMS Health*, or in holding, at paragraphs 824 and 826 of the judgment under appeal, that, for the purposes of characterising that conduct as an abuse of a dominant position, it is sufficient to demonstrate that it is such as to restrict competition and, in particular, to constitute an impediment to generic products entering the market and to parallel imports.

154. The General Court was also fully entitled, in ascertaining whether the Commission had actually proved this in respect of generic products, to hold, at paragraphs 829 to 835 of the judgment under appeal, that the fact that the regulatory framework offers alternative means, which are longer and more costly, to obtain a MA did not prevent the conduct of an undertaking in a dominant position from being abusive where that conduct, considered objectively, has the sole purpose of rendering the abridged procedure provided for by the legislator in point 8(a)(iii) of the third paragraph of Article 4 of Directive 65/65 unavailable and therefore of excluding the producers of generic products from the market for as long as possible and of increasing the costs incurred by them in overcoming barriers to entry to the market, thereby delaying the significant competitive pressure exerted by those products.

In this highly significant judgment the CJ concurred with the GC in widening the reach of Article 102. A dominant undertaking may commit an abuse even if it is exercising legal rights. The marketing authorisation part of the judgment places severe limitations on the strategies adopted by dominant pharmaceutical companies for managing the life-cycle of their products and extracting the maximum return from their investments in innovation. Despite accepting that a dominant undertaking has no duty to protect its competitors the EU Courts in effect imposed an obligation on AZ to maintain in force its marketing authorisations in order to assist its competitors to enter the market. This was on the basis of the 'special responsibility' and a particular interpretation of 'competition on the merits'. Moreover, the requirement was only that there was sufficient evidence of the conduct's capability of anti-competitive effects rather than of actual or likely effects. AZ's intentions were accorded more importance than such effects and there was no emphasis on consumers.

AstraZeneca must be seen in the context of the Commission's policy on generic drugs and the position of 'blockbuster' medicines,[882] and it is highly fact-specific. It left pharmaceutical companies, at least, in a difficult and uncertain position in respect of what positive obligations can be imposed upon them and the extent of their freedom to pursue their own commercial interests.[883] O'Donoghue and Padilla suggest five principles they might follow. First, assess the impact of the conduct on generic competition; secondly, consider whether the new replacement is advantageous relative to the replaced product; thirdly, if it is, are there legitimate reasons why they do not offer both new and old products; fourthly, ask whether the same decision would have been taken in the absence of generic competition; and, fifthly, think about internal evidence suggesting a subjective intention to reduce generic competition.[884]

(ii) Standard-essential Patents and Patent Ambushes

Standard-setting agreements are those whereby undertakings in a particular industry or market define, usually through a standard-setting organisation (SSO), technical or quality requirements with which current or future products, production processes, services, or methods may comply.[885] Patents which are essential to the technology incorporated in such standards are known as standard-essential patents (SEPs).[886] Negotiations before the standard is adopted usually cover the use of SEPs and the owners of such patents are normally required to commit themselves to licensing their rights

---

[882] See, e.g., the Competition Commissioner's Press Release at the time of the decision, IP/05/737.

[883] For a consideration of the issues, see F. Murphy and F. Liberatore, 'Abuse of Regulatory Procedures—the *Astra-Zeneca Case*' [2009] *ECLR* 223, 289, and 314 (in three parts, written before the GC judgment).

[884] O'Donoghue and Padilla, n. 1, 669–670.

[885] See Chap. 10.

[886] See D. Geradin and M. Rato, 'Can Standard-setting Lead to Exploitative Abuse? A Dissonant View of Patent Hold-up, Royalty-stacking and the Meaning of FRAND' (2007) 3 *European Competition Journal* 146; P. Chappatte, 'FRAND Commitments—The Case for Antitrust Intervention' (2009) 5 *European Competition Journal* 320; D. Geradin, 'Ten Years of DG Competition Effort to Provide Guidance on the Application of Competition Rules to the Licensing

to third parties on FRAND terms (fair, reasonable, and non-discriminatory).[887] The owner of an SEP may be in a dominant position but this is not necessarily so. There are an increasing number of disputes concerning SEPs, particularly in the ICT sector.

A 'patent ambush' is where a party to a standard-setting agreement conceals that it has patents and patent technology relevant to the technology incorporated in the standard, and then attempts to enforce its rights. Where an undertaking is in a dominant position on the relevant market a patent ambush can be an exclusionary abuse in that the undertaking concerned may gain control over the standard, thereby excluding potentially competing technologies and raising barriers to entry.[888] In *Rambus*[889] the Commission was concerned with the conduct of an undertaking it considered had engaged in a 'patent ambush' in respect of the DRAM standard.[890] Because Rambus was not in a dominant position during the standard-setting procedure, the Commission dealt with the matter as one of excessive pricing for the royalties it claimed for the use of the patents and adopted a commitments decision whereby Rambus agreed to cap the royalties.[891]

Even in the absence of a patent ambush there can be disputes about the licensing of SEP-encumbered patents. In the mobile communications sector in particular the SSOs have not developed robust dispute resolution mechanisms capable of dealing with the contentious issues arising between the leading players in the sector[892] and in the 'smartphone wars' the likes of Google, Apple, Samsung, and Microsoft are litigating across the globe. In a number of actions before EU national courts SEP holders have sued for patent infringement and the Commission initiated proceedings against two SEP holders on the basis that bringing an action for an injunction amounts to an abuse of a dominant position. In *Motorola*[893] the Commission took a prohibition decision (without imposing a fine) against Motorola for bringing an action in Germany for an injunction against Apple for alleged infringement of the Electronic Telecommunications Standards Institute (ETSI) General Packet Radio Service (GPRS) SEPs. Motorola had committed to licensing them on FRAND terms and Apple was a willing licensee, prepared to take a licence on terms to be set by the German court. Moreover, Motorola had sought to prevent Apple challenging the validity it its patents. Therefore, said the Commission, the injunction action was an abuse. Such an action would not, however, be abusive if the SEP holder was only taking reasonable steps to protect its own interests, for example where the potential licensee was financially distressed, the potential licensee's assets were in a jurisdiction that does not adequately provide for the enforcement of damages, or the potential licensee was unwilling to take a licence on FRAND terms.[894] The Commission's action against Samsung alleged that Samsung had infringed Article 102 by seeking injunctions in actions in various Member States to

---

of Standard-essential Patents: Where Do We Stand?', available at <http://ssrn.com/abstract=2204359>; M. Rato and N. Petit, 'Abuse of Dominance in Technology-enabled Markets: Established Standards Reconsidered?' (2013) 9 *European Competition Journal* 1, 58–64; N. Petit, 'Injunctions for FRAND-pledged SEPs: The Quest for an Appropriate Test of Abuse under Article 102 TFEU' (2013) 9 *European Competition Journal* 677; A. Jones, 'Standard-essential Patents: FRAND Commitments, Injunctions and the Smartphone Wars' (2014) 10 *European Competition Journal* 1.

[887] See Guidelines on horizontal co-operation agreements [2011] OJ C11/1, paras. 283–287. In the US, they are called RAND terms (the 'fair' is dropped).

[888] See Commission MEMO/09/544, issued at the time of the *Rambus* Commitments Decision.

[889] COMP/38.636, Commitments Decision 9 December 2009 [2010] OJ C30/17; IP/09/1867; MEMO/09/544.

[890] Dynamic Random Access Memory chips. They are used to temporarily store data, particularly on PCs. At the time of the decision DRAMs compliant with the standard (the JEDEC standard) had approximately 95% of the (world) market and were used in nearly all PCs, see IP/09/1867.

[891] See Section 16.A.i, p. 571; and O'Donoghue and Padilla, n. 1, 715–725.

[892] Jones, n. 886, 8. The issues which arise include: how valid patents can be identified; how infringement can be tested in relation to a portfolio of SEPs; the enforcement of SEPs following their transfer to a third party; the assessment of FRAND royalties; and what happens when negotiations over these issues break down.

[893] COMP/39.985, *Motorola—Enforcement of GPRS Standard Essential Patents* [2014] OJ C344/6; MEMO/14/322; IP/14/490.

[894] Ibid., para. 23.

enforce its patents which were necessary to comply with the ETSI 3G UMTS[895] standard and which Samsung had agreed to license on FRAND terms. The case was settled by a commitments decision in which Samsung undertook not to seek, for five years, an injunction in the EEA against potential licensees complying with the conditions set out in the decision.[896]

Broadly speaking, the Commission's approach in *Motorola* and *Samsung* favours the potential licensee, in that seeking an injunction is an abuse unless special conditions apply (the potential licensee's financial situation, etc.). In Germany, however, where a significant amount of the relevant litigation has taken place, the courts tend to be more favourable to the patent holder.[897] In the *Orange-Book-Standard* case[898] the Bundesgerichtshof held that a company would abuse its dominant position by seeking an injunction only in special circumstances.

The concept that a SEP holder abuses a dominant position by bringing an injunction for a prohibitory injunction (or for the recall of products) against an alleged infringer/potential licensee runs into two major problems. The first is the familiar difficulties over the interface between IPRs and competition law.[899] The second is that classifying bringing legal proceedings as an abuse risks breaching the fundamental right of access to the courts, enshrined in Article 47 of the Charter, and the protection of intellectual property guaranteed by Article 17(2) of the Charter. We have seen in Section 13.B that according to *ITT Promedia* litigation can be an abuse only in 'wholly exceptional circumstances'.[900]

The issue finally came before the CJ in *Huawei Technologies*,[901] a preliminary reference from the Landgericht Düsseldorf, which was seised of a dispute between two Chinese ICT companies in which a SEP holder was alleging infringement of its patent. The German court was fully aware of the difference between the Commission's approach and the *Orange-Book-Standard*. It asked the CJ a series of detailed question which the CJ summed up asking, essentially:

… in what circumstances the bringing of an action for infringement, by an undertaking in a dominant position and holding an SEP, which has given an undertaking to the standardisation body to grant licences to third parties on FRAND terms, seeking an injunction prohibiting the infringement of that SEP or seeking the recall of products for the manufacture of which the SEP has been used, is to be regarded as constituting an abuse contrary to Article 102 TFEU.[902]

The CJ began by rehearsing the *Hoffmann-La Roche* definition of abuse[903] and stating that it was 'settled case law' that the exercise of an exclusive right linked to an IPR by the proprietor may, in exceptional circumstances, involve abusive conduct for the purposes of Article 102.[904] It cited *Volvo*, *Magill*, and *RTE* for this proposition but made it clear that the circumstances in the present case had to be distinguished from those in the refusal to supply cases.[905] It then proceeded to identify the exceptional circumstances in the SEP situation which could lead to the exercise of an exclusive

---

[895] Universal Mobile Telecommunications System.

[896] COMP/39.939, *Samsung—Enforcement of ETSI Standard Essential Patents* 29 April 2014 [2014] OJ C 30/8, IP/14/490, MEMO/14/322.

[897] This is partly because of the bifurcated nature of the court process in respect of patent cases, in that patent infringement cases come before specialist patent chambers of the Higher District Courts whereas challenges to the validity of patents are heard by the Federal Patent Court.

[898] BGH, 6 May 2009, KZR 39/06, GRUR 2009, 694.

[899] As in the refusal to supply cases involving two markets: *Magill*, *IMS*, and *Microsoft*, see Section 13 C. and D.

[900] Case T-111/96, *ITT Promedia* [1998] ECR II-2937, para. 60; Case T-119/09, *Protégé International Ltd v Commission* EU:T:2012:421.

[901] Case C-170/13, *Huawei Technologies v ZTE* EU:C:2015:477; see N. Banasevic, 'Editorial: The Implications of the Court of Justice's *Huawei/ZTE* Judgment' (2015) 6 *JECLAP* 463.

[902] *Huawei*, para. 44.

[903] Ibid., para. 45.

[904] Ibid., para. 47.

[905] Ibid., para. 48.

right linked to an IPR—in the form of bringing an action—being abusive, but it did not mention *ITT*. The circumstances are (a) the fact that the patent at issue is essential to a standard established by a standardisation body[906] and (b) that the patent at issue obtained SEP status only in return for the proprietor's irrevocable undertaking, given to the standardisation body in question, that it is prepared to grant licences on FRAND terms.[907] Given that these circumstances create legitimate expectations on the part of third parties, Article 102 may in principle provide a defence against actions by the SEP holder.[908] The CJ recognised that the holder cannot in principle be deprived of the right to bring an action to enforce its exclusive rights but stated that in order to do so without infringing Article 102 'specific requirements' must be met.[909] These are that: (a) prior to bringing proceedings the holder must alert the alleged infringer to the alleged infringement;[910] (b) after the alleged infringer has expressed willingness to take a licence on FRAND terms, the holder must present it with a specific written offer for a licence on FRAND terms;[911] and (c) the alleged infringer must not have accepted the offer or promptly and in writing submitted a counter-offer.[912] Where no agreement is reached after the counter-offer the parties 'may by common agreement' have the amount of the royalty independently determined.[913] Furthermore, the alleged infringer 'cannot be criticised' for challenging the validity of the relevant patents[914] (presumably meaning that the alleged infringer may challenge without penalty). These conditions apply only to proceedings 'liable to prevent products complying with the standard in question manufactured by competitors from appearing or remaining on the market' and so do not apply to actions for the rendering of accounts or damages in respect of an alleged infringer's past acts of use of the SEP.[915]

Case C-170/13, *Huawei Technologies v ZTE* EU:C:2015:477

Court of Justice

49. It is characterised, first, as the referring court has observed, by the fact that the patent at issue is essential to a standard established by a standardisation body, rendering its use indispensable to all competitors which envisage manufacturing products that comply with the standard to which it is linked.

50. That feature distinguishes SEPs from patents that are not essential to a standard and which normally allow third parties to manufacture competing products without recourse to the patent concerned and without compromising the essential functions of the product in question.

51. Secondly, the case in the main proceedings may be distinguished by the fact, as is apparent from paragraphs 15 to 17 and 22 of the present judgment, that the patent at issue obtained SEP status only in return for the proprietor's irrevocable undertaking, given to the standardisation body in question, that it is prepared to grant licences on FRAND terms.

52. Although the proprietor of the essential patent at issue has the right to bring an action for a prohibitory injunction or for the recall of products, the fact that that patent has obtained SEP status means that its

---

[906] Ibid., paras. 49–50.
[907] Ibid., para. 51.
[908] Ibid., paras. 53–54.
[909] Ibid., paras. 59–60.
[910] Ibid., paras. 60–61.
[911] Ibid., paras. 63–64.
[912] Ibid., paras. 65–67.
[913] Ibid., para. 68.
[914] Ibid., para. 69.
[915] Ibid., paras. 52–53 and 72–73. This was the CJ's response to a specific question (Question 5) put by the Landgericht.

proprietor can prevent products manufactured by competitors from appearing or remaining on the market and, thereby, reserve to itself the manufacture of the products in question.

53. In those circumstances, and having regard to the fact that an undertaking to grant licences on FRAND terms creates legitimate expectations on the part of third parties that the proprietor of the SEP will in fact grant licences on such terms, a refusal by the proprietor of the SEP to grant a licence on those terms may, in principle, constitute an abuse within the meaning of Article 102 TFEU.

54. It follows that, having regard to the legitimate expectations created, the abusive nature of such a refusal may, in principle, be raised in defence to actions for a prohibitory injunction or for the recall of products. However, under Article 102 TFEU, the proprietor of the patent is obliged only to grant a licence on FRAND terms. In the case in the main proceedings, the parties are not in agreement as to what is required by FRAND terms in the circumstances of that case.

55. In such a situation, in order to prevent an action for a prohibitory injunction or for the recall of products from being regarded as abusive, the proprietor of an SEP must comply with conditions which seek to ensure a fair balance between the interests concerned.

56. In this connection, due account must be taken of the specific legal and factual circumstances in the case (see, to that effect, judgment in *Post Danmark*, C-209/10, EU:C:2012:172, paragraph 26 and the case-law cited).

57. Thus, the need to enforce intellectual-property rights, covered by, inter alia, Directive 2004/48, which—in accordance with Article 17(2) of the Charter—provides for a range of legal remedies aimed at ensuring a high level of protection for intellectual-property rights in the internal market, and the right to effective judicial protection guaranteed by Article 47 of the Charter, comprising various elements, including the right of access to a tribunal, must be taken into consideration (see, to that effect, judgment in *Otis and Others*, C-199/11, EU:C:2012:684, paragraph 48).

58. This need for a high level of protection for intellectual-property rights means that, in principle, the proprietor may not be deprived of the right to have recourse to legal proceedings to ensure effective enforcement of his exclusive rights, and that, in principle, the user of those rights, if he is not the proprietor, is required to obtain a licence prior to any use.

59. Thus, although the irrevocable undertaking to grant licences on FRAND terms given to the standardisation body by the proprietor of an SEP cannot negate the substance of the rights guaranteed to that proprietor by Article 17(2) and Article 47 of the Charter, it does, none the less, justify the imposition on that proprietor of an obligation to comply with specific requirements when bringing actions against alleged infringers for a prohibitory injunction or for the recall of products.

60. Accordingly, the proprietor of an SEP which considers that that SEP is the subject of an infringement cannot, without infringing Article 102 TFEU, bring an action for a prohibitory injunction or for the recall of products against the alleged infringer without notice or prior consultation with the alleged infringer, even if the SEP has already been used by the alleged infringer.

61. Prior to such proceedings, it is thus for the proprietor of the SEP in question, first, to alert the alleged infringer of the infringement complained about by designating that SEP and specifying the way in which it has been infringed.

62. As the Advocate General has observed in point 81 of his Opinion, in view of the large number of SEPs composing a standard such as that at issue in the main proceedings, it is not certain that the infringer of one of those SEPs will necessarily be aware that it is using the teaching of an SEP that is both valid and essential to a standard.

63. Secondly, after the alleged infringer has expressed its willingness to conclude a licensing agreement on FRAND terms, it is for the proprietor of the SEP to present to that alleged infringer a specific, written offer for a licence on FRAND terms, in accordance with the undertaking given to the standardisation body, specifying, in particular, the amount of the royalty and the way in which that royalty is to be calculated.

64. As the Advocate General has observed in point 86 of his Opinion, where the proprietor of an SEP has given an undertaking to the standardisation body to grant licences on FRAND terms, it can be

expected that it will make such an offer. Furthermore, in the absence of a public standard licensing agreement, and where licensing agreements already concluded with other competitors are not made public, the proprietor of the SEP is better placed to check whether its offer complies with the condition of non-discrimination than is the alleged infringer.

65. By contrast, it is for the alleged infringer diligently to respond to that offer, in accordance with recognised commercial practices in the field and in good faith, a point which must be established on the basis of objective factors and which implies, in particular, that there are no delaying tactics.

66. Should the alleged infringer not accept the offer made to it, it may rely on the abusive nature of an action for a prohibitory injunction or for the recall of products only if it has submitted to the proprietor of the SEP in question, promptly and in writing, a specific counter-offer that corresponds to FRAND terms.

67. Furthermore, where the alleged infringer is using the teachings of the SEP before a licensing agreement has been concluded, it is for that alleged infringer, from the point at which its counter-offer is rejected, to provide appropriate security, in accordance with recognised commercial practices in the field, for example by providing a bank guarantee or by placing the amounts necessary on deposit. The calculation of that security must include, inter alia, the number of the past acts of use of the SEP, and the alleged infringer must be able to render an account in respect of those acts of use.

68. In addition, where no agreement is reached on the details of the FRAND terms following the counter-offer by the alleged infringer, the parties may, by common agreement, request that the amount of the royalty be determined by an independent third party, by decision without delay.

69. Lastly, having regard, first, to the fact that a standardisation body such as that which developed the standard at issue in the main proceedings does not check whether patents are valid or essential to the standard in which they are included during the standardisation procedure, and, secondly, to the right to effective judicial protection guaranteed by Article 47 of the Charter, an alleged infringer cannot be criticised either for challenging, in parallel to the negotiations relating to the grant of licences, the validity of those patents and/or the essential nature of those patents to the standard in which they are included and/or their actual use, or for reserving the right to do so in the future.

70. It is for the referring court to determine whether the abovementioned criteria are satisfied in the present case, in so far as they are relevant, in the circumstances, for the purpose of resolving the dispute in the main proceedings.

71. It follows from all the foregoing considerations that the answer to Questions 1 to 4, and to Question 5 in so far as that question concerns legal proceedings brought with a view to obtaining the recall of products, is that Article 102 TFEU must be interpreted as meaning that the proprietor of an SEP, which has given an irrevocable undertaking to a standardisation body to grant a licence to third parties on FRAND terms, does not abuse its dominant position, within the meaning of Article 102 TFEU, by bringing an action for infringement seeking an injunction prohibiting the infringement of its patent or seeking the recall of products for the manufacture of which that patent has been used, as long as:

- prior to bringing that action, the proprietor has, first, alerted the alleged infringer of the infringement complained about by designating that patent and specifying the way in which it has been infringed, and, secondly, after the alleged infringer has expressed its willingness to conclude a licensing agreement on FRAND terms, presented to that infringer a specific, written offer for a licence on such terms, specifying, in particular, the royalty and the way in which it is to be calculated, and
- where the alleged infringer continues to use the patent in question, the alleged infringer has not diligently responded to that offer, in accordance with recognised commercial practices in the field and in good faith, this being a matter which must be established on the basis of objective factors and which implies, in particular, that there are no delaying tactics.

The judgment gives no indication of what constitutes FRAND terms, beyond the reference to 'conditions which seek to ensure a fair balance between the interests concerned'. It is also unclear as to what is the position where the parties do not reach an agreement following the counter-offer (paragraph 68). The judgment says that they 'may' by common agreement request a third party determination, but not that they 'must', and not what happens if such common agreement is not forthcoming. Furthermore, as the judgment focuses on the impact in the market for the products implementing the standard, and on the legitimate expectations created by giving FRAND commitments, it is not completely clear that its reasoning would apply to an injunction action by a patent assertion entity[916] and/or to an undertaking to which the original SEP owner had sold the patent.

D. SEARCH ENGINE PRACTICES

(i) General

The *Google* case[917] concerns the application of Article 102 to search engine practices. The case is discussed as a whole in this section although it raises issues such as findings of dominance, discrimination, essential facilities, and unfair practices which arise elsewhere in this chapter and in Chapter 6. It also raises the issue of whether hindering innovation, even in the absence of the exclusion of competitors, can be an abuse in itself. In the US Google has simultaneously been the subject of an FTC investigation.

Google provides general web search services. It also operates specialised 'vertical' search services, which are search engines focusing on specific product or service areas, such as Google Shopping and Google Flights. In November 2010 the Commission opened an investigation into alleged anti-competitive practices by Google after receipt of complaints from 17 undertakings.[918] The Commission found that Google had a 90 per cent share of the market for general web search services (horizontal searches) in the EEA and had a strong position in the market for online search advertising. The Commission had four concerns:[919]

(a) the favourable treatment, within Google's web search results, of links to Google's own specialised web search services as compared to links to competing specialised web search services, i.e. services allowing users to search for specific categories of information such as restaurants, hotels, or products (known as 'comparison shopping services' or the Vertical Search Abuse);

(b) the use by Google without consent of original content from third party web sites in its own specialised web search services (known as 'content scraping');

(c) agreements that oblige third party web sites ('publishers') to obtain all or most of their online search advertisements from Google ('exclusivity arrangements' or 'AdSense'); and

(d) contractual restrictions on the transferability of online search advertising campaigns to rival search advertising platforms and the management of such campaigns across Google's Adwords and rival search advertising platforms ('transferability restrictions' or 'AdWords').

After protracted negotiations[920] Google proposed commitments, which were market tested[921] and met with such criticism, particularly in respect of the comparison shopping services,[922] that the

---

[916] An entity whose business is primarily to purchase and manage patents rather than produce products itself (also known as a non-practising entity).

[917] COMP/39.740.

[918] Including Microsoft and Oracle, IP/10/162.

[919] IP/13/371; see also MEMO/13/383.

[920] See, e.g., Statement of Vice-President Almunia on the Google Antitrust Investigation, SPEECH/12/372, 21 May 2012.

[921] IP/13/371, MEMO/13/383, 25 April 2013, see Chap. 13, Section 7.E.iii.c, p. 952.

[922] There were claims that the commitments could benefit rather than disadvantage Google in ensuring that its own specialist services are prominently labelled as such, which, given the strength of the Google brand, could make them more attractive to searchers. A spokesman for one of the complainants, Foundem, was quoted in the *Daily Telegraph* on 26 April 2013 as saying that any settlement should stop Google abusing its monopoly, not require it to change the way it does so.

Commission finally abandoned the commitments procedure[923] in respect of comparison shopping in April 2015 and issued a statement of objections (SO) instead.[924] It continued to 'actively investigate' the other three concerns.[925]

(ii) The Comparison Shopping Charge (the Vertical Search Abuse)

The alleged vertical search abuse concerns the favourable treatment, within Google's web search results, of links to Google's own specialised web search services as compared to links to competing specialised web search services, so-called 'search bias'. To remedy these the Commission proposed accepting Google's commitments that for five years it would:

- label promoted links to its own specialised search services so that users can distinguish them from natural web search results,

- clearly separate these promoted links from other web search results by clear graphical features (such as a frame), and

- display links to three rival specialised search services close to its own services, in a place that is clearly visible to users.[926]

The improved commitments which the Commission initially considered accepting in February 2014 included more detailed provisions on the rival specialised search services.[927]

From the opening of the investigation it was never clear on what basis Google was alleged to have infringed Article 102 in respect of vertical searches. There has been much discussion about whether it could or should be characterised as a refusal to supply or essential facilities case where Google would be required to actively assist its competitors. Either way, many commentators have taken issue with competition authorities trying to ensure 'net neutrality', arguing that interference in the search engine market will be costly to consumers, impede innovation, and discourage welfare-enhancing developments in dynamic markets.[928] The Memo and Press Release issued by the Commission when it sent the SO appears to conceptualise the abuse as some form of discrimination,[929] but without any reference to refusal to supply (the extract below retains the Commission's bold font). As is apparent from the second and eighth paragraphs of the Memo below, the Commission also considers that 'stifling innovation' and lowering rivals' incentives to innovate infringes Article 102 even though there is no suggestion of excluding those rivals.[930] The Commission has not indicated how it has assessed Google's dominant position, although this is a multi-sided platform (which makes both the assessment of dominance and the application of Article 102 more difficult).[931]

---

[923] After Google had offered two improved sets of commitments, IP/14/116, MEMO/14/87.

[924] IP/15/4780, MEMO/15/4781.

[925] MEMO/15/4781.

[926] IP/13/371. These commitment proposals followed a settlement between Google and the FTC in the US in respect of Google's search-related practices, see FTC Press Release, 3 January 2013, available at <http://ftc.gov/opa/2013/01/google.shtm> and <https://www.ftc.gov/system/files/documents/public_statements/295971/130103googlesearchstmtofcomm.pdf>. In the press release following the FTC settlement the FTC said that it had concluded that 'the introduction of Universal Search, as well as additional changes made to Google's search algorithms—even those that may have had the effect of harming individual competitors—could plausibly be justified as innovations that improved Google's product and the experience of users'.

[927] MEMO/14/87.

[928] G. A. Manne and J. D. Wright, 'If Search Neutrality is the Answer, What's the Question?', available at <http://papers.ssrn.com/sol3/papers.cfm?abstract_id=1807951>; D. Crane, 'Search Neutrality as an Antitrust Principle', available at <http://papers.ssrn.com/sol3/papers.cfm?abstract_id=1961742>; G. Manne and J. Wright, 'Google and the Limits of Antitrust: The Case Against the Case Against Google' (2011) 34 Harvard J of Law and Public Policy 171.

[929] See the discussion of exclusionary discrimination in P. Ibáñez Colomo, 'Exclusionary Discrimination under Article 102 TFEU' (2014) 51 CMLRev 141.

[930] See further Ibáñez Colomo, n. 8.

[931] For multi-sided markets, see A. Lamadrid de Pablo, 'The Double Duality of Two-sided Markets' [2015] Comp Law 5 and Chap. 1, Section 15.B.vii.i, p. 74.

Commission Memo/15/4781 of 15 April 2015

The Commission's preliminary conclusions in the Statement of Objections

The Statement of Objections alleges that Google treats and has treated more favourably, in its general search results pages, Google's own comparison shopping service 'Google Shopping' and its predecessor service 'Google Product Search' compared to rival comparison shopping services.

Google's conduct may therefore artificially divert traffic from rival comparison shopping services and hinder their ability to compete, to the detriment of consumers, as well as stifling innovation.

More specifically, the preliminary conclusions are:

- Google systematically **positions and prominently displays** its comparison shopping service in its general search results pages, **irrespective of its merits**. This conduct started in 2008.
- Google does not apply to its own comparison shopping service the **system of penalties**, which it applies to other comparison shopping services on the basis of defined parameters, and which can lead to the lowering of the rank in which they appear in Google's general search results pages.
- Froogle, Google's first comparison shopping service, did not benefit from any favourable treatment, and performed poorly.
- As a result of Google's **systematic favouring of its subsequent comparison shopping services** 'Google Product Search' and 'Google Shopping', both experienced **higher rates of growth**, to the detriment of rival comparison shopping services.
- Google's conduct has a **negative impact on consumers and innovation**. It means that users do not necessarily see the most relevant comparison shopping results in response to their queries, and that incentives to innovate from rivals are lowered as they know that however good their product, they will not benefit from the same prominence as Google's product.

The Statement of Objections takes the preliminary view that in order to remedy the conduct, Google should **treat its own comparison shopping service and those of rivals in the same way**. This would not interfere with either the algorithms Google applies or how it designs its search results pages.

It would, however, mean that when Google shows comparison shopping services in response to a user's query, the most relevant service or services would be selected to appear in Google's search results pages.

It will be noted that the Commission's objections are that Google has 'artificially diverted' traffic from the competitors' sites towards its own sites. Its own comparison shopping services have experienced 'higher rates of growth' to the detriment of competitors. Google's conduct has negatively impacted consumers and innovation. However, the Commission does not mention anti-competitive foreclosure or exclusion. It takes the preliminary view that Google should exercise search neutrality.

Google submitted its reply to the SO at the end of August 2015. Its General Counsel explained its defence.[932]

Kent Walker, 27 August 2015, <http://googlepolicyeurope. blogspot.co.uk>

The SO says that Google's displays of paid ads from merchants (and, previously, of specialized groups of organic search results) 'diverted' traffic away from shopping services. But the SO doesn't back up that

---

[932] See also an article commissioned by Google in connection with the US case, R. Bork and J. G. Sidak, 'What Does the Chicago School Teach About Internet Search and the Antitrust Treatment of Google?' (2011) 8 *J of Competition Law and Economics* 663.

claim, doesn't counter the significant benefits to consumers and advertisers, and doesn't provide a clear legal theory to connect its claims with its proposed remedy.

Our response provides evidence and data to show why the SO's concerns are unfounded. We use traffic analysis to rebut claims that our ad displays and specialized organic results harmed competition by preventing shopping aggregators from reaching consumers. Economic data spanning more than a decade, an array of documents, and statements from complainants all confirm that product search is robustly competitive. And we show why the SO is incorrect in failing to consider the impact of major shopping services like Amazon and eBay, who are the largest players in this space. The universe of shopping services has seen an enormous increase in traffic from Google, diverse new players, new investments, and expanding consumer choice. Google delivered more than 20 billion free clicks to aggregators over the last decade in the countries covered by the SO, with free traffic increasing by 227% (and total traffic increasing even more).

Moreover, the ways people search for, compare, and buy products are rapidly evolving. Users on desktop and mobile devices often want to go straight to trusted merchants who have established an online presence. These kinds of developments reflect a dynamic and competitive industry, where companies are continuing to evolve their business models and online and offline markets are converging.

But our central point is our consistent commitment to quality—the relevance and usefulness of our search results and the ads we display. In providing results for people interested in shopping, we knew we needed to go beyond the old-fashioned '10 blue links' model to keep up with our competitors and better serve our users and advertisers. We developed new ways to organize and rank product information and to present it to users in useful formats in search and ads. In 2012, as part of that effort, in addition to our traditional ads, we introduced the Google Shopping Unit as a new ad format …

(iii) The Alleged Content Scraping Abuse

Google's content scraping practices involve using the original content of other sites in its own specialised search results. Copyrighted materials can be protected but the other sites cannot stop Google 'crawling' through their websites without blocking them from the Google search results. In effect the other sites are complaining that they do not like the terms upon which Google does business with them. Doubts have been raised as to how far this is a competition concern.[933] The Competition Commissioner suggested that the concern is about reducing competitors' incentives to invest,[934] which again raises the issue of whether the possible hindrance of innovation is an abuse in itself. Nevertheless, Google offered commitments that it would:

- offer all websites the option to opt out from the use of all their content in Google's specialised search services, while ensuring that any opt-out does not unduly affect the ranking of those websites in Google's general web search results;

- offer all specialised search web sites that focus on product search or local search the option to mark certain categories of information in such a way that such information is not indexed or used by Google;

- provide newspaper publishers with a mechanism allowing them to control on a web-page-per-web-page basis the display of their content in Google News.[935]

---

[933] See, e.g., R. Nazzini, 'Google and the (Ever-stretching) Boundaries of Article 102 TFEU' (2015) 6 JECLAP 301, 310–311; <http://chillingcompetition.com>, 14 February 2013 and 13 June 2013.

[934] Statement of Vice-President Almunia on the Google Antitrust Investigation, SPEECH 12/372, 21 May 2012.

[935] IP/13/371, MEMO/13/383.

(iv) The Alleged Exclusivity (AdSense) Abuse

The Commission is claiming that Google is entering into exclusive purchasing arrangements in that advertisers must obtain all or most of their online search advertisements from Google as a condition of advertising there at all.[936] In the 2013 commitments Google offered to:

no longer include in its agreements with publishers any written or unwritten obligations that would require them to source online search advertisements exclusively from Google.[937]

(v) The Alleged Transferability Restrictions or 'AdWords' Abuse

The Commission's concern is with the 'portability' of online advertising campaigns and, again, raises exclusive purchasing issues. In the 2013 commitments Google offered to:

no longer impose obligations that would prevent advertisers from managing search advertising campaigns across competing advertising platforms.

It has been noted[938] that the Commission appears to want the 'seamless' transfer of advertising campaigns[939] and that it is unclear how high the switching costs involved in a transfer which is not 'seamless' have to be before the situation becomes one of *de facto* exclusivity.

E. THE ACQUISITION OF INTELLECTUAL PROPERTY RIGHTS AND/OR COMPETING TECHNOLOGIES

It was seen in Chapter 5 that in *Tetra Pak*[940] the acquisition by a dominant undertaking of an exclusive patent licence was held to be an abuse even though the licence agreement did not infringe Article 101 as it fell within the block exemption regulation.[941] The GC said that although the acquisition of an exclusive licence by a dominant undertaking is not an abuse per se, it may be an abuse, and was on the facts of this case. The principle in *Tetra Pak I* is a striking example of the onerous nature of the 'special responsibility' towards the competitive process imposed on dominant firms. In *Périndopril (Servier)* the Commission held that it was an abuse for a dominant pharmaceutical company to shut out a competing technology, inter alia by buying out a number of competitors which had developed competing medicines.[942]

F. NAKED RESTRICTIONS

'Naked restrictions' is a term used by the Commission in *Intel* to describe payments to customers to delay, restrict, or cancel the marketing of competing products.[943] The Commission said that the scope of these restrictions was more specific than that of the conditional rebates in that case, being of shorter duration and focused on a specific product/line of products but that the two

---

[936] For the application of Art. 102 to such arrangements generally, see Section 10.

[937] IP/13/371, MEMO/13/383.

[938] Nazzini, n. 933, 311–312.

[939] Statement of Vice-President Almunia on the Google Antitrust Investigation, SPEECH/12/372, 21 May 2012.

[940] Case T-51/89, *Tetra Pak Rausing v Commission (Tetra Pak I)* [1990] ECR II-309.

[941] Reg. 2349/84 [1984] OJ L219/15 on patent licensing agreements (replaced by Reg. 240/96 [1996] OJ L31/2 on Technology Transfer Agreements and subsequently by Reg. 772/2004 [2004] OJ L123/11 (see Chap. 12)).

[942] COMP/39.612, *Périndopril (Servier)* 9 July 2014, IP14/799, on appeal Case T-691/14, *Servier SAS v Commission*, judgment pending. The Commission also found the patent settlement and 'pay-for-delay' agreements to be in breach of Art. 101, see Chap. 12, Section 5.B.iii.

[943] COMP/37.990, *Intel* 13 May 2009. The Commission's treatment of these practices was foreshadowed by para. 22 of the Guidance Paper.

types of conduct complemented each other and formed part of a single foreclosure strategy.[944] The Commission likened the payments, which it said had an anti-competitive object, to the conduct of the dominant undertaking in *Irish Sugar* in persuading certain wholesalers and retailers to swap the products they had bought from a competitor for the undertaking's own.[945] The Commission's treatment of these practices was foreshadowed by paragraph 22 of the Guidance Paper, in which it referred to practices in respect of which anti-competitive effect can be inferred without carrying out a detailed assessment.[946] The GC upheld the Commission. It rejected the plea that the use of the concept 'naked restriction' denoted a novel type of abuse.

Case T-286/09, *Intel v Commission* EU:T:2014:547

General Court

211....[T]he Commission did not rely exclusively on the anti-competitive object of the three naked restrictions. In addition to referring to *Irish Sugar*, paragraph 199 above, it relied on additional circumstances confirming the capability of the naked restrictions to restrict competition, even though reference to such circumstances is not essential in order to characterise them as abusive under Article [102].

212. In the first place, the Commission demonstrated to the requisite legal standard that the payments which were subject to the conditions...were a factor which had been taken into account by [the customers] in their decisions to delay, cancel or in some other way restrict the marketing of their computers equipped with AMD CPUs. That confirms the capability of those payments to restrict competition. In that context, it should be noted that characterisation of a naked restriction as abusive depends solely on the capability to restrict competition, and that characterisation does not therefore require proof of an actual effect on the market or of a causal link (see, as regards exclusivity rebates, paragraphs 103 and 104 above).

...

219. Third, it is necessary to reject the applicant's argument that the use of the concept of 'naked restriction' constitutes a novel type of abuse. It must be stated that the legal characterisation of an abusive practice does not depend on the name given to it, but on the substantive criteria used in that regard. Thus, the mere use of the concept of 'naked restriction' does not provide a sufficient basis on which to conclude that the substantive criteria applied are new. As regards the substantive criteria applied in the present case, it is clear from the wording of point (b) of the second subparagraph of Article [102] that limiting markets constitutes an abuse. Moreover, it is not novel in competition law that a practice which clearly does not come within competition on the merits is regarded as unlawful (see, to that effect, *Hoffmann-La Roche*, paragraph 71 above, paragraph 91, and *AKZO* v *Commission*..., paragraph 70).

220. Lastly, even if the characterisation as abusive of the practices at issue were indeed 'novel', that would not call in question the Commission's power to prohibit them. Even in the area of the calculation of fines, the General Court has already held that the fact that conduct with the same features has not been examined in past decisions does not exonerate an undertaking (see, to that effect, *Michelin I*, paragraph 74 above, paragraph 107, and *AstraZeneca*, paragraph 64 above, paragraph 901).

G. VERTICAL AND HORIZONTAL INTEGRATION

It is not an infringement of Article 102 for a dominant undertaking to integrate vertically, but actions taken in pursuit of a policy of vertical integration may infringe. Many cases finding a refusal to

---

[944] Ibid., para. 1642.

[945] Case T-228/97, *Irish Sugar* [1999] ECR II-2969. The 'persuasion' was found to involve financial threats.

[946] See Section 4, p. 369.

supply[947] or tying[948] to infringe Article 102 involved actions taken by a dominant undertaking which would enable it to integrate vertically.

In *Continental Can*[949] it was established that Article 102 could apply to mergers whereby an undertaking strengthened its dominant position. Since the EU Merger Regulation regime has been in force, however, the general rule is that the Regulation alone applies to mergers falling within its scope.[950]

15. DISCRIMINATION

A. GENERAL

Many of the exclusionary practices discussed in this chapter, such predatory pricing, margin squeezes, rebates, tying, and refusals to supply, involve discrimination in some form. However, there is a question as to what extent, if at all, discrimination can be abusive outside those specific situations. It will be remembered that in *Post Danmark I* the CJ said that price discrimination is not of itself suggestive of an exclusionary abuse.[951] In particular there is a question as to whether a dominant firm can infringe Article 102 simply by discriminating in favour of its own downstream operations (sometimes known as 'self-preferencing'). This is the issue at the heart of the *Google* case,[952] discussed in Section 14.E.

The Commission expressly excluded discrimination from the ambit of the Guidance Paper. There have been some cases in which discrimination in favour of the dominant undertaking's downstream operations have been held to infringe Article 102(c), as discussed later in this section, but these have all been in particular circumstances. A more general duty not to discriminate, i.e. a concept of 'exclusionary discrimination', would push at what hitherto have been the boundaries of Article 102 and ought to be based on a convincing theory of harm. Such a theory is not readily discernible from the Commission's Memo in *Google*[953] but should, if the Commission is venturing down that route, be set out in any final decision in that case. However, the idea that there is a general duty on vertically integrated dominant undertakings not to discriminate against competitors in downstream markets is a controversial one[954] as such discrimination, which is very common, may be pro-competitive and may reflect competition on the merits.

B. ARTICLE 102(C) TFEU

Article 102(c) expressly prohibits a specific form of discrimination. It states that an abuse may, in particular, consist in:

applying dissimilar conditions to equivalent transactions with other trading parties, thereby placing them at a competitive disadvantage.

Article 102(c) therefore deals with secondary line injury, i.e. between the customers of the dominant undertaking. 'Dissimilar conditions' includes dissimilar prices.

---

[947] Such as Cases 6 and 7/73, *Commercial Solvents* [1974] ECR 223 and Case 22/78, *Hugin* [1979] ECR 1869.

[948] E.g., the *Digital Undertaking*, IP/97/868.

[949] Case 6/72, *Continental Can* [1973] ECR 215; see Section 3.C.i.

[950] Council Reg. 139/2004 [2004] OJ L24/1, see Chap. 15.

[951] Case C-209/10 P, *Post Danmark I* EU:C:2012:172, para. 30.

[952] COMP/39.740.

[953] See the discussion in Section 14.E.

[954] See the discussion in P. Ibáñez Colomo, 'Exclusionary Discrimination under Article 102 TFEU' (2014) 51 *CMLRev* 141.

There are a number of problems in the application of Article 102(c). First, 'equivalent transactions' refers to the fact that discrimination involves different prices or conditions for transactions entailing the same costs.[955] However, identifying equivalence is difficult as the elements which make up a transaction are complex, but the EU Courts and the Commission have often assumed that transactions are equivalent without a sufficient analysis.[956] Secondly, an infringement of Article 102(c) has sometimes been found without identifying any competitive disadvantage. Thirdly, financial disadvantage has been too easily equated with competitive disadvantage.

In some cases, particularly older ones, Article 102(c) has been applied to situations of primary line injury where dissimilar prices or conditions were offered to different customers, in order to prejudice the supplier's competitors, without a proper analysis of whether the conditions in Article 102(c) were satisfied. This can be traced back to *Hoffmann-La Roche* itself[957] and was a feature of *Michelin I*[958] and *Irish Sugar*.[959] In *British Airways*,[960] *Clearstream*,[961] and *Solvay*[962] conduct which was held to be exclusionary was also condemned as price discrimination contrary to Article 102(c). The use of Article 102(c) in exclusionary situations has been widely criticised,[963] one problem being that the standard of proof for 'competitive disadvantage' in Article 102(c) is far lower than that pertaining to exclusionary abuses generally.

C. ARTICLE 102(C) AND NON-VERTICALLY INTEGRATED UNDERTAKINGS

A non-vertically integrated undertaking will normally have an interest in discriminating between its customers only if it can thereby take account of factors such as their different elasticities of demand (in which case the question of whether the transactions are 'equivalent' arises) or possibly if it is preparing to enter the downstream market. However, there are some cases in which a non-vertically integrated dominant undertaking has discriminated in favour of certain customers on nationality, or similar, grounds.

In the first *Corsica Ferries* case[964] the port operator in Genoa charged different prices for pilotage services depending on whether the vessels were sailing between two domestic (Italian) ports[965] or were on an international route. In *Aéroports de Paris*[966] the airport authority at Orly and Charles de Gaulle in Paris charged different levels of fees to companies it licensed to provide

---

[955] For price discrimination generally, see Section 7.B.

[956] E.g., railway traffic via German ports and via Belgian and Dutch ones (Case T-229/94, *Deutsche Bahn AG v Commission* [1997] ECR II-1689), and transactions with exclusive and non-exclusive customers (in the loyalty rebate cases).

[957] Case 85/76, *Hoffmann-La Roche & Co AG v Commission* [1979] ECR 461, para. 90, which does not actually mention Art. 102(c) but says that 'the effect of fidelity rebates is to apply dissimilar conditions to equivalent transactions with other trading parties . . .'. The Commission had characterised the rebates as contrary to Art. 102(c).

[958] Case 322/81, *Michelin I* [1983] ECR 3461, where, nevertheless, the CJ annulled the Commission's finding of discrimination contrary to Art. 102(c) on the facts (paras. 90–91).

[959] Case T–228/97, *Irish Sugar* [1999] ECR II-2969, aff'd Case C-497/99 P, *Irish Sugar* [2001] ECR I-5333. See also Case T-65/89, *BPB Industries* [1993] ECR II-389, aff'd Case C-310/93 P, *BPB Industries* [1995] ECR I-865.

[960] Case C-95/04, *British Airways* [2007] ECR I-2331.

[961] Case T-301/04, *Clearstream* [2009] ECR II-3155. In *Clearstream* the customer competed with the dominant undertaking's sister company.

[962] Cases T-57 and 58/01, *Solvay* [2009] ECR II-4621; the Commission decision was annulled for procedural reasons, Case C-109/10 P, *Solvay* [2011] ECR II-10329, without the substance of the Art. 102 issues being discussed.

[963] See, e.g., Temple Lang and O'Donoghue, n. 176; Rousseva, n. 269, 215–217; Nazzini, n. 116, 249–250; Geradin, Layne-Farrar, and Petit, n. 170, 4.475–4.505; Rousseva and Marquis, n. 3, 32.

[964] Case C-18/93, *Corsica Ferries Italia Srl v Corporazione dei Piloti del Porto di Genova* [1994] ECR I–1783.

[965] Maritime cabotage.

[966] Case T-128/98, *Aéroports de Paris v Commission* [2000] ECR II–3929, aff'd Case C-82/01, [2002] ECR I-9297.

ground-handling services. In none of these cases was there found to be any objective justification for the differentials.[967] In *Portuguese Airports*[968] the airport authority applied a seemingly uniform system of quantity discounts which was so constructed that it gave larger discounts to Portuguese airlines than to others. This was found to infringe Article 102(c) and the CJ took the opportunity to discuss the application of Article 102(c) to quantity discounts. The airport operator, inter alia, gave discounts on landing fees to airlines depending on the number of planes they landed. There were a number of discount bands and the highest rate of discount could be earned only by airlines with a very large number of landings. The only airlines to qualify for this high rate were the two Portuguese carriers, TAP and Portugalia. The CJ said that while it was inherent in any quantity discount system that the largest buyers obtained the highest reductions, nevertheless it could be discriminatory if the system included thresholds that only a few very large users could reach and which gave them disproportionate rewards.[969] The relevant passage from *Portuguese Airports* was cited in *Solvay* where the CJ applied Article 102(c) to 'quantity' rebates in an exclusionary situation.[970] In *1998 World Cup* organisers of the Football World Cup in France infringed Article 102 by setting up a ticket distribution system which indirectly discriminated against non-French residents/nationals[971] and in *OPCOM/ Romanian Power Exchange*[972] OPCOM, the Romanian power exchange, discriminated against electricity traders established in EU countries other than Romania by requiring them to obtain a Romanian VAT registration even though they had a VAT registration in their own country.

In *British Airways* the airline paid differing amounts of Commission to travel agents depending on whether they had increased their BA ticket sales. The application of Article 102(c) was part of an action against BA for an exclusionary abuse against a competitor.[973] It is notable that in *Post Danmark II* the CJ said that in principle the retroactive standardised rebate scheme did not result in the application of dissimilar conditions contrary to Article 102(c).[974]

D. VERTICALLY INTEGRATED UNDERTAKINGS

Where a vertically integrated dominant undertaking price discriminates between its own downstream operation and its downstream competitors it may be committing an exclusionary abuse such as a margin squeeze which is a matter of Article 102(b). The relatively few cases in which Article 102(c) has been applied mainly concern transport infrastructures, liberalised industries, and/or statutory authorities. The paucity of cases may reflect the fact that Article 102(c) was designed to deal with 'pure' secondary discrimination between third party customers. It is difficult to see transactions with an undertaking's associated company as 'equivalent' to a transaction with a third party. The cases where Article 102(c) has been used include *Deutsche Post: Interception of Cross-Border Mail*,[975] where the German postal authority was held to have discriminated without objective justification between different types of mail coming into Germany;[976] *Deutsche Bahn*[977] where a

[967] See also *Brussels National Airport (Zaventem)* [1995] OJ L216/8; *Ilmailulaitos/Luftsfartverket (Finnish Airports)* [1999] OJ L69/24; *Spanish Airports* [2000] OJ L208/36.

[968] Case C-163/99, *Portugal v Commission* [2001] ECR I-2613.

[969] Ibid., paras. 50–53.

[970] Cases T-57 and 58/01, *Solvay* [2009] ECR II-4621, para. 396.

[971] *1998 World Cup* [2000] OJ L5/55.

[972] COMP/39.984, 5 March 2014.

[973] See Section 11.F.ii.c, p. 454.

[974] Case C-23/14, *Post Danmark II* EU:C:2015:651, para. 37.

[975] [2002] OJ L331/40.

[976] Statutory monopolists entrusted with a 'service of general economic interest' have a limited exemption from the competition rules under Art. 106(2) of the Treaty. This is discussed in Chap. 8.

[977] *HOV SVZ/MCN* [1994] OJ L104/34, on appeal Case T-229/94, *Deutsche Bahn AG v Commission* [1997] ECR II–1689, aff'd Case C-436/97, *Deutsche Bahn AG v Commission* [1999] ECR I-2387.

national rail operator applied different prices in respect of railway traffic via German ports and traffic via Belgian and Dutch ones; and *GT Link*[978] where the State port authority discriminated in favour of its own ferry services.[979] In *Clearstream*, the facts of which are given earlier,[980] the undertaking had a role conferred by regulation,[981] and had charged higher prices to a competitor of its sister company.

Google is a vertically integrated undertaking operating in a network industry but there are no indications from the Commission so far that it will apply Article 102(c) in the current proceedings[982] rather than a more general concept of discrimination.

E. GEOGRAPHICAL PRICE DISCRIMINATION

Article 102(c) has been applied to geographical price discrimination. Such discrimination involves charging different prices for the same products or services in different geographical territories. Artificial price differences across the EU should be eliminated or reduced by arbitrage and parallel trade (and indeed the price differences should encourage parallel trade) but this may be impeded by other factors. In both leading cases on geographical price discrimination, *United Brands*[983] and *Tetra Pak II*,[984] Article 102(c) was applied and the dominant undertaking was found to have taken measures to prevent parallel trade.

Case 27/76, *United Brands v Commission* [1978] ECR 207

United Brands shipped its bananas across the Atlantic and unloaded them at Rotterdam and Bremerhaven. At those ports it sold them to its approved ripener/distributors from various Member States at different prices. The prices reflected the different prices in the retail markets in the Member States. The contractual conditions under which the bananas were sold contained a prohibition on the distributors reselling the bananas while they were still green (the 'green banana clause'). The Commission concluded that this clause was simply a tactic to reinforce the price differences because once the bananas had started to turn yellow they were so perishable that it was not possible to export them to other Member States. The Commission also found that United Brands' practice of supplying the distributors with less than they ordered made them sell locally instead of in other markets. The Commission held that these practices infringed Article 102. United Brands appealed, inter alia on this issue.

Court of Justice

. . .

227. Although the responsibility for establishing the single banana market does not lie with the applicant, it can only endeavour to take 'what the market can bear' provided that it complies with the rules for the regulation and co-ordination of the market laid down by the Treaty.

228. Once it can be grasped that differences in transport costs, taxation, customs duties, the wages of the labour force, the conditions of marketing, the differences in the parity of currencies, the density of competition may eventually culminate in different retail selling price levels according to the Member

---

[978] Case C-242/95, *GT-Link A/S v DE Danske Statsbaner* [1997] ECR I-4449.

[979] See also *German Electricity Balancing Markets (E.ON)* Commitments Decision [2009] OJ C36/8, where the Commission considered that E.ON's discrimination in favour of its own production affiliate led it to discriminate between domestic balancing energy and imported balancing energy, contrary to Art. 12 TFEU.

[980] Case T-301/04, *Clearstream Banking* [2009] ECR II-3155, see Section 13.B.vii, p. 509.

[981] It was the Central Securities Depository for securities issued under German law.

[982] COMP/39.740, see Section 14.D.

[983] Case 27/76, *United Brands v Commission* [1978] ECR 207.

[984] Case C-333/94 P, *Tetra Pak II* [1996] ECR I-5951.

States, then it follows those differences are factors which UBC only has to take into account to a limited extent since it sells a product which is always the same and at the same place to ripener/distributors who—alone—bear the risks of the consumer's market.

229. The interplay of supply and demand should, owing to its nature, only be applied to each stage where it is really manifest.

230. The mechanisms of the market are adversely affected if the price is calculated by leaving out one stage of the market and taking into account the law of supply and demand as between the vendor and the ultimate consumer and not as between the vendor (UBC) and the purchaser (the ripener/distributor).

231. Thus, by reason of its dominant position UBC, fed with information by its local representatives, was in fact able to impose its selling price on the intermediate purchaser. This price and also the 'weekly quota allocated' is only fixed and notified to the customer four days before the vessel carrying the bananas berths.

232. These discriminatory prices, which varied according to the circumstances of the Member States, were just so many obstacles to the free movement of goods and their effect was intensified by the clause forbidding the resale of bananas while still green and by reducing the deliveries of the quantities ordered.

233. A rigid partitioning of national markets was thus created at price levels, which were artificially different, placing certain distributor/ripeners at a competitive disadvantage, since compared with what it should have been competition had thereby been distorted.

234. Consequently the policy of differing prices enabling UBC to apply dissimilar conditions to equivalent transactions with other trading parties, thereby placing them at a competitive disadvantage, was an abuse of a dominant position.

The unconvincing reasoning in this part of the *United Brands* judgment has been savagely criticised.[985] For example, treating the law of supply and demand as normative or prescriptive ('to be applied', paragraph 229) rather than descriptive; allowing an undertaking to take into account different retail conditions and taking what the market can bear only if it bears the risks of the consumer market, thus giving undertakings an incentive to vertically integrate; describing the discriminatory prices as 'just so many obstacles to the free movement of goods' (paragraph 232) whereas differential pricing would normally stimulate parallel trade;[986] and favouring profits going to distributors rather than producers. The real objection to the price discrimination in *United Brands* was of course that it offended against the concept of the single market.

In *Tetra Pak II* the Commission found wide disparities in the prices that Tetra Pak charged for its milk packaging machinery and cartons in different Member States despite the fact that the geographical market was Community-wide. It held these prices differences to be due to artificial partitioning of the market and not to objective market conditions.[987] The decision was upheld by the GC, which found that 'those disparities in price could not be attributed to objective market conditions'.[988]

In *Irish Sugar*[989] the dominant undertaking operated a system of 'sugar export rebates', granted on sales of industrial sugar to companies exporting to other Member States. The Commission found that this practice discriminated against customers of industrial sugar supplying the domestic Irish

---

[985] W. Bishop, 'Price Discrimination under Article 86: Political Economy in the European Court' (1981) 44 *MLR* 282; L. Zanon, 'Price Discrimination under Article 102 of the EEC Treaty: A Comment on the *UBC* Case' (1982) 31 *ICLQ* 36; M. Siragusa, 'The Application of Article 86 to the Pricing Policy of Dominant Companies: Discriminatory and Unfair Prices' (1979) 16 *CMLRev* 179.

[986] The problem in *United Brands* was rather the buttressing 'green banana' clause which did not intensify the effect of the differing prices but neutralised it.

[987] E.g., customers for the machines could purchase cartons only from Tetra Pak itself or a company designated by it, and so customers in high-price countries were not free to purchase from third parties in lower-price areas.

[988] Case T-83/91, *Tetra Pak Rausing v Commission* [1994] ECR II-755, para. 170. See also Case T-168/01, *GlaxoSmithKline Services Unlimited v Commission* [2006] ECR II-2969, para. 177.

[989] [1997] OJ L258/1, [1997] 5 CMLR 666.

market. The GC upheld the Commission's finding that this was an abuse, holding that market mechanisms were distorted by pricing according to the location of the customers' buyers.

Whether or not geographical price discrimination is an abuse in the absence of measures taken by the dominant undertaking to partition the market is unclear. In *Tetra Pak II* the GC reiterated that setting different prices could be justified by local conditions. In *United Brands*, however, local conditions did not justify variations in retail prices. This suggests that once the Member States are held to be in the same geographic market and costs are the same, objective justification for price discrimination between them will be hard to prove. However, in the absence of buttressing measures (such as the 'green banana clause') the ability to maintain different prices in different geographical areas suggests that there are different geographic markets, and so Article 102(c) should not apply.[990] Where there are buttressing measures these are likely to be abusive themselves.

F. COMPETITIVE DISADVANTAGE AND ARTICLE 102(C)

The abuse set out in Article 102(c) is the application of dissimilar conditions to equivalent transactions with other trading parties 'thereby placing them at a competitive disadvantage'. In respect of the export rebates in *Irish Sugar*, the GC did not accept that the non-export customers suffered no competitive disadvantage.[991] However, in *United Brands* the CJ applied Article 102(c) even though the ripener/distributors from different Member States were not in competition with one another (partly because of the measures United Brands had taken to prevent parallel trade, such as the 'green banana clause') and greengrocers in Ireland certainly did not compete with those in Germany. Likewise, in *Corsica Ferries I* the CJ applied Article 102(c) regardless of the fact that the domestic and international shipping lines were not competing with each other.[992] In *Deutsche Post: Interception of Cross-Border Mail*, the Commission answered the argument that customers were not put at a competitive disadvantage by having to pay more than others for their cross-border mail: the Commission pointed out that the list in Article 102 is not exhaustive:

In any event, the Court of Justice has stated that the list of abuses mentioned in Article [102] itself is not exhaustive and thus only serves as examples of possible ways for a dominant firm to abuse its market power . . . Article [102] may be applied even in the absence of a direct effect on competition between undertakings on any given market. This provision may . . . also be applied in situations where a dominant undertaking's behaviour causes damage directly to consumers . . . The senders of the disputed mailings are consumers of postal services. Due to the behaviour of DPAG, these consumers are affected negatively by having to pay prices for these services which are higher than those charged to other senders and by having their mailings delayed significantly. Likewise, the German addressees are to be regarded as consumers who are affected in a negative manner by the behaviour of DPAG. Having their incoming mail delayed may prevent the addressees from benefiting from commercial offers made by the senders.[993]

The Commission here was saying that directly damaging consumers may infringe Article 102, although of course consumers will usually not be 'in competition' with one another. Since Deutsche Post was a statutory monopolist the consumers had no alternative supplier: nor indeed did the shipping lines in *Corsica Ferries*. Moreover, both *Deutsche Post* and *Corsica Ferries* involved discrimination in the context of inter-Member State transactions, while *United Brands*, as we have seen, involved compartmentalising the common market. In such situations one can expect that EU law will disapprove of discriminatory behaviour, but it is difficult to reconcile this with the wording of Article 102(c).

---

[990] See further Geradin, Layne-Farrar, and Petit, n. 170, 4.525–4.541.

[991] Case T-228/97, *Irish Sugar plc* [1999] ECR II-2969, paras. 140–149.

[992] Case C-18/93, *Corsica Ferries Italia Srl v Corporazione dei Piloti del Porto di Genova* [1994] ECR I-1783. The CJ did not mention the issue at all: the AG did, but stated that it did not matter, Van Gerven AG, para. 34.

[993] [2002] OJ L331/40, para. 133.

In *British Airways* the target bonus/commission scheme operated by British Airways, the facts of which are given in Section 11.F.iii.c,[994] was found by the Commission to infringe Article 102 because of its capability to exclude competitors.[995] It was also held to specifically infringe Article 102(c) because it discriminated between the travel agents in giving different rewards to different agents for selling the same number of tickets. This was upheld by the GC[996] and the CJ.

Case C-95/04 P, *British Airways v Commission* [2007] ECR I-2331

Court of Justice

143. The specific prohibition of discrimination in subparagraph (c) of the second paragraph of Article [102] forms part of the system for ensuring, in accordance with Article 3(1)(g) EC, that competition is not distorted in the internal market. The commercial behaviour of the undertaking in a dominant position may not distort competition on an upstream or a downstream market, in other words between suppliers or customers of that undertaking. Co-contractors of that undertaking must not be favoured or disfavoured in the area of the competition which they practise amongst themselves.

144. Therefore, in order for the conditions for applying subparagraph (c) of the second paragraph of Article [102] to be met, there must be a finding not only that the behaviour of an undertaking in a dominant market position is discriminatory, but also that it tends to distort that competitive relationship, in other words to hinder the competitive position of some of the business partners of that undertaking in relation to the others (see, to that effect, *Suiker Unie*, paragraphs 523 and 524).

145. In that respect, there is nothing to prevent discrimination between business partners who are in a relationship of competition from being regarded as being abusive as soon as the behaviour of the undertaking in a dominant position tends, having regard to the whole of the circumstances of the case, to lead to a distortion of competition between those business partners. In such a situation, it cannot be required in addition that proof be adduced of an actual quantifiable deterioration in the competitive position of the business partners taken individually.

146. In paragraphs 237 and 238 of the judgment under appeal, the [General Court] found that travel agents in the United Kingdom compete intensely with each other, and that that ability to compete depended on two factors, namely 'their ability to provide seats on flights suited to travellers' wishes, at a reasonable cost' and, secondly, their individual financial resources.

147. Moreover, in the part of the judgment under appeal relating to the examination of the fidelity-building effect of the bonus schemes at issue, the [General Court] found that the latter could lead to exponential changes in the revenue of travel agents.

148. Given that factual situation, the [General Court] could, in the context of its examination of the bonus schemes at issue having regard to subparagraph (c) of the second paragraph of Article [102], move directly, without any detailed intermediate stage, to the conclusion that the possibilities for those agents to compete with each other had been affected by the discriminatory conditions for remuneration implemented by BA.

149. The [General Court] cannot therefore be accused of an error of law in not verifying, or in verifying only briefly, whether and to what extent those conditions had affected the competitive position of BA's commercial partners. The [General Court] was therefore entitled to take the view that the bonus schemes at issue gave rise to a discriminatory effect for the purposes of subparagraph (c) of the second paragraph of Article [102]. The second part of the fifth plea is therefore unfounded.

---

[994] P. 455.

[995] *Virgin/British Airways* [2000] OJ L30/1.

[996] Case T-219/99, *British Airways v Commission* [2003] ECR II-5917.

Paragraph 144 therefore restates the requirement that for discrimination to be an abuse under Article 102(c) there must be competitive disadvantage. However, the Court assumed that the different financial arrangements the agents had with BA because of the different rebates they received automatically meant that some were at a competitive disadvantage compared to others. Paragraphs 144 and 145 only require that the behaviour of the dominant undertaking 'tends' to distort competition and expressly do not require proof of an actual quantifiable deterioration in the individual's competitive position. The standard of proof, therefore, is low, as was also demonstrated in *Clearstream*.[997]

In *Kanal*[998] the CJ was asked in effect whether the fact that a copyright management organisation calculates the royalties paid with respect to remuneration due for the television broadcast of musical works protected by copyright differently according to whether the broadcasting companies are commercial or public constituted an abuse of a dominant position. The CJ said that it could, if it put the companies at a competitive disadvantage. However, the practice was capable of being objectively justified because of the task and method by which public services were financed. The matter was referred back to the national court.

16. EXPLOITATIVE ABUSES

A. UNFAIRLY HIGH OR LOW PRICING

(i) Unfairly High Prices

a. General

Article 102(a) provides that an abuse may consist in directly or indirectly imposing 'unfair purchase or selling prices or other unfair trading conditions'.[999] We have discussed unfairly *low* prices on the selling side in the sections on predatory pricing and other exclusionary pricing abuses. Here we look at unfairly *high* prices. Excessive pricing is the most obvious way in which a monopolist can exploit its position. We saw in Chapter 1 that monopoly prices are likely to be higher than those in competitive markets and excessive prices match the popular conception of the evils of monopoly. However, it is argued that the free market economy needs the lure of monopoly pricing: '[t]he opportunity to charge monopoly prices—at least for a short period—is what attracts "business acumen" in the first place; it induces risk taking that produces innovation and economic growth'.[1000] Excessive prices may therefore be pro- rather than anti-competitive because high prices and profits may act as a signal to attract new competitors on to the market.[1001] Where high barriers to entry prevent this the spectre of competition authorities acting as price regulators arises. Price regulation, however, is the antithesis of the free market and competition authorities are rarely equipped to act as price

---

[997] Case T-301/04, *Clearstream* [2009] ECR II-3155. For a scathing criticism of the lack of attention paid the 'competitive disadvantage' requirement by the EU Courts, see Faull and Nikpay, n. 1, 4.921–4.926.

[998] Case C-52/07, *Kanal 5 Ltd v Föreningen Svenska Tonsättares Internationella Musikbyrå (STIM) upa* [2008] ECR I-9275.

[999] See generally A. Svetlicinii and M. Botta, 'Article 102 TFEU as a Tool for Market Regulation' (2012) 8 *European Law Journal* 473; T. Ackermann, 'Excessive Pricing and the Goals of Competition Law' and J. P. Terhechte, 'Excessive Pricing and the Goals of Competition Law: An Enforcement Perspective—Comment on Ackermann' in D. Zimmer (ed.), *The Goals of Competition Law* (Edward Elgar, 2012), Chaps. 18 and 19 respectively; M. Furse, 'Excessive Prices, Unfair Prices and Economic Value' (2008) 4 *European Competition Journal* 59; Geradin, Layne-Farrar, and Petit, n. 170, 4.475–4.542.

[1000] *Verizon Communications Ltd v Trinko* 540 US 398, 124 S.Ct 872, para. 2 (Scalia J).

[1001] But against this view, see A. Ezrachi and D. Gilo, 'Are Excessive Prices Really Self-correcting?' (2009) 5 *J of Competition Law and Economics* 249 who argue that high prices alone are not sufficient reason to persuade a new entrant to compete with the incumbent.

regulators. They should not be called upon to arbitrate how profits ought to be shared out amongst the players on the market where there is no issue of anti-competitive exclusion (the error into which the CJ fell in *United Brands* over the matter of geographic price discrimination[1002]).

The Commission has not much concerned itself with high prices,[1003] agreeing with the view that in many circumstances interference with high prices and profits per se is a disincentive to innovation and investment and considering it preferable to solve problems of unfair pricing by taking action against exclusionary conduct whereby dominant firms seek to preserve their dominance.[1004] A former Director-General of DG Comp said of high prices:

High prices certainly harm consumers in the short run. But is that a sufficient case for intervention by a competition authority? What if high prices would in the medium term attract entry and spur competition? If there are no high or insurmountable barriers to entry, it might well be that high prices are actually likely to be, on balance and with a longer term perspective, good for consumers. There is much more for consumers to gain through increased competition than a mere decrease in prices: competition brings more choice, scope for differentiation in quality, innovation, etc.[1005]

Price regulation is better restricted to situations of natural or legal monopoly, where it can be applied within a system of *ex ante* sector regulation. Outside that regulatory context, exploitative high prices which do not have exclusionary potential are better dealt with by contract or consumer protection laws rather than competition law. There are, however, cases on the application of Article 102 to high prices in situations not involving exclusion, and we look at these in this section.

b. Ascertaining What Constitutes an Unfairly High Price: The Concept of 'Economic Value'

The main problem in applying Article 102(a) is to identify what constitutes an unfair price. In *General Motors*[1006] the CJ introduced the concept of 'economic value' to which the price charged should relate. There a car manufacturer was charging a high price for the production of documentation without which car owners could not bring their cars into Belgium. The documentation was obviously cheap to produce, but the 'value' to the customers was great since without the certificate the car could not be imported. On the facts the Court accepted that no abuse had been committed[1007] and so the meaning of 'economic value' or excessive prices was not pursued.

In the leading case of *United Brands* the Commission condemned UBC for charging excessive prices for Chiquita bananas in Germany, Denmark, and Benelux. It compared the prices with those for unbranded bananas, competitors' bananas, and with the price of Chiquitas in Ireland, and it said that the prices were 'excessive in relation to the economic value of the product supplied'.

The CJ annulled the decision in respect of unfair prices, because the Commission had failed to do its homework properly. It had not presented sufficient evidence and had not analysed UBC's costs. However, the CJ accepted that 'excessive' prices can constitute an abuse and that charging a price which has no relation to the product's 'economic value' would be excessive (paragraph 250).

[1002] Where the CJ preferred the distributors over the producers, see Section 15.E, p. 562.

[1003] Although note the special sector of telecommunications, e.g. the investigation into prices in mobile telephone services in the EC (Press Releases IP/98/141, IP 98/707, IP (98) 1036). The Commission found 14 cases of discrimination and high prices but closed its files when prices were reduced or there was action by the domestic regulator.

[1004] See Commission, *XXIVth Report on Competition Policy* (1994), point. 207.

[1005] P. Lowe, 'Consumer Welfare and Efficiency—New Guiding Principles of Competition Policy?', 13th International Conference on Competition and 14th European Competition Day, 27 March 2007.

[1006] Case 26/75, *General Motors v Commission* [1975] ECR 1367.

[1007] Because the high price had been a temporary blip while national procedures were changed.

Case 27/76, *United Brands v Commission* [1978] ECR 207

Court of Justice

248. The imposition by an undertaking in a dominant position directly or indirectly of unfair purchase or selling prices is an abuse to which exception can be taken under Article [102].

249. It is advisable therefore to ascertain whether the dominant undertaking has made use of the opportunities arising out of its dominant position in such a way as to reap trading benefits which it would not have reaped if there had been normal and sufficiently effective competition.

250. In this case charging a price which is excessive because it has no reasonable relation to the economic value of the product supplied would be such an abuse.

251. This excess could, *inter alia*, be determined objectively if it were possible for it to be calculated by making a comparison between the selling price of the product in question and its cost of production, which would disclose the amount of the profit margin; however the Commission has not done this since it has not analysed UBC's costs structure.

252. The questions therefore to be determined are whether the difference between the costs actually incurred and the price actually charged is excessive, and, if the answer to this question is in the affirmative, whether a price has been imposed which is either unfair in itself or when compared to competing products.

253. Other ways may be devised—and economic theorists have not failed to think up several—of selecting the rules for determining whether the price of a product is unfair.

254. While appreciating the considerable and at times very great difficulties in working out production costs which may sometimes include a discretionary apportionment of indirect costs and general expenditure and which may vary significantly according to the size of the undertaking, its object, the complex nature of its set up, its territorial area of operations, whether it manufactures one or several products, the number of its subsidiaries and their relationship with each other, the production costs of the banana do not seem to present any insuperable problems.

. . .

258. The Commission bases its view that prices are excessive on an analysis of the differences—in its view excessive—between the prices charged in the different Member States and on the policy of discriminatory prices which has been considered above.

. . .

260. Having found that the prices charged to ripeners of the other Member States were considerably higher, sometimes by as much as 100 per cent, than the prices charged to customers in Ireland it concluded that UBC was making a very substantial profit.

. . .

264. However unreliable the particulars supplied by UBC may be . . . the fact remains that it is for the Commission to prove that the applicant charged unfair prices.

265. UBC's retraction, which the Commission has not effectively refuted, establishes beyond doubt that the basis for the calculation adopted by the latter to prove the UBC's prices are excessive is open to criticism and on this particular point there is doubt which must benefit the applicant, especially as for nearly 20 years banana prices, in real terms, have not risen on the relevant market.

266. Although it is also true that the price of Chiquita bananas and those of its principal competitors is different, that difference is about 7 per cent, a percentage which has not been challenged and which cannot automatically be regarded as excessive and consequently unfair.

267. In these circumstances it appears that the Commission has not adduced adequate legal proof of the facts and evaluations which formed the foundation of its finding that UBC had infringed Article [102] of the Treaty by directly and indirectly imposing unfair selling prices for bananas.

What is the economic value of a banana other than what a customer is prepared to pay for it? The Court considered the excess might be determined by comparing the selling and production costs (the 'cost+ standard'), which would disclose the profit margin (paragraph 251), but it did not suggest the level at which the profit would become excessive. In paragraph 252 the Court said that finding the price is 'excessive' by these means is not the end of the matter: it must then be determined whether the excessive price is *unfair*. So the Court in effect set out a two-stage test:

(a) is the price excessive; *and if it is*

(b) is the price either unfair in itself or when compared to competing products?

This means that a finding that prices are high in relation to the costs of production is not a sufficient condition for an infringement of Article 102. The CJ clarified in *Scippacercola and Terezakis*[1008] that whether the price is 'unfair in itself' or 'when compared to competing products' are alternatives.

In 2004 the Commission adopted the *Scandlines* decision,[1009] rejecting complaints of excessive pricing, in which it systematically analysed the *United Brands* judgment. Two ferry operators complained about the port fees charged by the port authority at Helsingborg, Sweden, in respect of the services provided to ferry operators active on the Helsingborg–Elsinore route between Sweden and Denmark. The Commission adopted the two-stage methodology set out in paragraph 252 of *United Brands* and confirmed that the two stages are cumulative, not alternative. The Commission rejected the contention that examining whether a price was excessive was just a question of 'cost+', i.e. of determining the supplier's costs, adding a profit margin, and considering any price above this excessive. Rather, the economic value had to be determined with regard to the particular circumstances of the case and taking into account non-cost-related factors, particularly demand-side aspects of the product or service concerned. The demand side was relevant because 'customers are notably willing to pay more for something specific attached to the product/service that they consider valuable. This specific feature does not necessarily imply higher production costs for the provider. However it is valuable for the customer and also for the provider, and thereby increases the economic value of the product/service.'[1010]

In deciding whether the price was excessive in *British Leyland*[1011] the CJ looked at the large increases in price over time. Like *General Motors* the case concerned type approval certificates. The manufacturer had demanded exponentially higher prices for these as a way of discouraging individuals from importing cars into the UK from Member States where they were cheaper. The price was condemned as 'excessive and discriminatory' but viewed by the CJ as a part of a policy of maintaining price differentials and compartmentalising the common market rather than as a simple garnering of monopoly profits.

In a number of cases the comparison has been made with products in other geographic areas. In *United Brands* the CJ dismissed the comparison with Ireland for lack of proper analysis, not because it

---

[1008] Case C-159/08 P, *Scippacercola and Terezakis v Commission* [2009] ECR I-46, para. 47, confirming the rejection of a complaint of excessive prices at Athens Airport.

[1009] COMP/36.568, *Scandlines Sverige v Port of Helsingborg* 23 July 2004 and COMP/36.570, *Sundbesserne v Port of Helsingborg* 23 July 2004 (*Scandlines*).

[1010] *Scandlines*, para. 227. See the comment on this decision in (2004) 3 *EC Competition Policy Newsletter* 40 (M. Lamalle, L. Lindström-Rossi, and A. C. Teixara). The complainants withdrew their appeal to the GC against the decision. The *Scandlines* approach was followed in the UK case *Attheraces Ltd v The British Horseracing Board Ltd* [2005] EWHC 3015 (Ch), on appeal [2007] EWCA Civ 38, which was a perfect example of the problem of ascertaining 'economic value'. The supply of 'pre-race data' amassed by the British horse-racing authorities pursuant to running horse racing was valuable to ATR which operated online and television gambling sites and channels. The Court of Appeal said the object of Art. 102 was the protection of consumers and that if ATR succeeded in obtaining the pre-race data at a lower price there was no suggestion that it would have charged the customers less. Any 'unfairness' to ATR was not a concern of competition law: 'Despite its elaborate legal and economic arguments and the high levels of moral indignation, the case is about who is going to get their hands on ATR's revenues from overseas bookmakers' (para. 214). The case was cited by Mazák AG in Case C-52/09, *TeliaSonera* [2011] ECR I-527, para. 30 of his Opinion.

[1011] Case 226/84, *British Leyland v Commission* [1986] ECR 3263.

rejected the comparison as a technique. In *Bodson v Pompes Funèbres des Régions Libérées*,[1012] which concerned funeral services in areas of France where there were monopoly concessions granted by local authorities, the CJ talked of whether the price was 'fair' in comparison with prices in areas where there were no such concessions. In *Ministère Public v Tournier*[1013] it said in the context of a complaint about the high charges imposed by the French copyright collecting society, SACEM, that:

38. When an undertaking holding a dominant position imposes scales of fees for its services which are appreciably higher than those charged in other member-States and where a comparison of the fee levels has been made on a consistent basis, that difference must be regarded as indicative of an abuse of a dominant position. In such a case it is for the undertaking in question to justify the difference by reference to objective dissimilarities between the situation in the member-State concerned and the situation prevailing in all the other member-States.

In *Deutsche Grammophon*[1014] the CJ said that the fact that the price of the product in one Member State was different from that when re-imported from another did not necessarily constitute an abuse, but it would be a determining factor if the difference was very marked and unjustified by any objective criteria.

Comparing the price of products across different Member States is difficult, however, because of the different factors which might be affecting those prices, as demonstrated by *United Brands* itself.[1015] The same is true of comparisons with competing products, where direct comparators may be hard to find. Cases where there were comparators available include *General Motors*, where the type approval certificate prices were considerably higher than other manufacturers, and *United Brands* where the Commission was overturned for simply finding the higher price of Chiquita bananas as excessive without further analysis. In *Deutsche Post: Interception of Cross-Border Mail*[1016] the Commission said that when judging whether a price is excessive in a market which is open to competition, the normal test is to compare the prices of the dominant operator with those charged by competitors. However, DPAG had a statutory monopoly which encompassed, inter alia, the forwarding and delivery of cross-border mail in Germany. It (wrongfully) classified certain categories of incoming mail from the UK as unauthorised remail[1017] and levied a charge which the British Post Office had to pay before the mail was released for delivery. Given the undertaking's monopoly the normal comparison with competitors was impossible, and in the absence of 'reliable cost accounting' the Commission compared the cross-border tariff with the domestic tariff and held the former to be excessive as it had 'no sufficient or reasonable relationship to real costs or to the real value of the service provided'.[1018]

In cases concerning excessive prices in respect of products covered by IPRs the issue of a comparison with non-IPR-protected products has arisen. In *Parke, Davis*[1019] the CJ said that the higher price of a patented compared with a non-patented product did not necessarily mean that an abuse had been committed. In *Renault*,[1020] however, it suggested that a car manufacturer which refused to license its

---

[1012] Case 30/87, [1988] ECR 2479, para. 31.

[1013] Case 395/87, [1989] ECR 2521, para. 38. See also Case C-351/12, *OSA—Ochranný svaz autorský pro práva k dílům hudebním o.s. v Léčebné lázně Mariánské Lázně a.s.* EU:C:2014:110, para. 87.

[1014] Case 78/70, *Deutsche Grammophon v Metro* [1971] ECR 487.

[1015] See also Case C-159/08 P, *Scippacercola* [2009] ECR I-46, where the complainants' attempts to compare the prices at Athens airports with those at airports in other Member States did not convince the Commission.

[1016] [2002] OJ L331/40. The case raised issues in respect of competition rules and undertakings granted monopoly rights by the State, and the application of Art. 106(2): see Chap. 8.

[1017] DPAG's policy towards remailing was also the subject of a preliminary reference to the CJ, Cases C-147–148/97, *Deutsche Post AG v Gesellschaft für Zahlungssysteme mbH (GZS) and Citicorp Kartenservice GmbH* [2000] ECR I-825 (*Deutsche Post*), discussed in Chap. 8.

[1018] *Deutsche Post* [2001] OJ L125/27, paras. 159–167.

[1019] Case 24/67, *Parke, Davis & Co v Probel* [1968] ECR 55.

[1020] Case 53/87, *Renault* [1988] ECR 6039, para. 16, see Section 13.C.ii, p. 511.

IPRs in respect of its spare parts to other manufacturers might commit an abuse if it charged 'unfair prices' for its own parts. The idea that IPR owners are not entitled to extract the maximum return from their monopoly position raises serious questions about the value of such rights. If cost-price comparisons are used to detect excessive pricing the undertaking's past research costs, including research costs which do not result in commercially exploitable products, need to be considered. This is particularly true in high technology markets in the new economy. Large resources may be devoted to the development of new products by a number of competitors and the undertaking which 'wins' the market may reap huge rewards (for a time at least). The incentive of that level of profit is, it is argued, necessary to persuade undertakings to incur R&D costs which may never be recovered.[1021]

Other cases in which the question of excessive prices has arisen include *Duales System Deutschland* in which DSD charged a fee for all the packaging bearing its 'Green Dot' logo even where customers showed that they did not use DSD's system for taking back and recovering packaging. The CJ upheld the GC's finding that this amounted to an abuse under Article 102(a) on the basis of 'economic value'.[1022] The Commission had said that an infringement of Article 102(a) exists where the price charged for a service is 'clearly disproportionate to the cost of supplying it'.[1023] In *Kanal*[1024] the CJ said that calculating royalties for broadcast music on the basis of the revenue of companies broadcasting those works and the amount of music broadcast was in principle reasonable and would not constitute an abuse unless there was some more accurate method available for identifying the music with the audience which did not involve a disproportionate increase in costs. In the commitments decision *Standard & Poor's*[1025] the Commission was able to use an international standard, the ISO costs-recovery principle,[1026] as its benchmark in coming to the view that the charges of the ratings agency, S&P, for distributing US International Securities Identification Numbers (ISINs) were unfairly high.

In *Rambus*,[1027] the undertaking undertook to cap (worldwide) for five years the royalty rates it charged for licences of its DRAM chips in the context of the Commission's concerns about a possible patent ambush.[1028] This was a case of unfair prices in the context of an exclusionary abuse. There is great difficulty in applying the principles laid down in *United Brands* to royalty rates charged by holders of SEPs.[1029]

(ii) Low Prices on the Buying Side

Although there is little case law on it, it is possible that unfairly low purchase prices may constitute an abuse where the dominant position is on the buying side. *CICCE v Commission*[1030] concerned a

---

[1021] This is particularly true also of the pharmaceutical industry, and the cost of R&D played a major part in e.g. Cases C-468–478/06, *Sot. Lélos* [2008] ECR I-7139 and Case C-501/06 P, *GlaxoSmithKline Services Unlimited v Commission* [2009] ECR I-9291.

[1022] Case T-289/01, *Der Grüne Punkt–Duales System Deutschland GmbH v Commission* [2007] ECR II-1691, aff'd Case C-385/07 P, *Der Grüne Punkt Duales System Deutschland GmbH v Commission* [2009] ECR I-6155. The case concerned Germany's highly developed system for making users responsible for disposing of packaging.

[1023] *DSD* [2001] OJ L166/1, para. 111. See also Case C-351/12, *OSA* EU:C:2014:110, para. 88.

[1024] Case C-52/07, *Kanal* [2008] ECR I-9275, see Section 15.F.

[1025] COMP/39.592, Commitments decision 15 November 2011; IP/11/1354, paras. 26–30 of the decision. S&P undertook not to impose any licensing charges on 'indirect' users and to charge 'direct' users no more than the amounts set out in the decision, which were set by reference to S&P's costs data.

[1026] ISO standard 6166 was developed at international level as a public service to the financial services industry.

[1027] COMP/38.636; Commitments decision 9 December 2009, Summary [2010] OJ C30/17; IP/09/1867; MEMO/09/544.

[1028] See Section 14.C.ii, p. 548.

[1029] See the discussion of SEPs in Section 14.C.ii, and for the issue of 'fair and reasonable' (FRAND) terms in respect of SEPs, see Chap. 10, Section 8.A. Another case, *Qualcomm*, in which the Commission had received complaints about the royalties being charged for an SEP, ended with the Commission closing its formal proceedings without taking commitments: MEMO/09/516.

[1030] Case 298/83, *CICCE v Commission* [1985] ECR 1105, upholding the Commission.

complaint about the allegedly low prices paid as licence fees for the showing of films on French television. The Commission dismissed the complaint on the ground that the complainant had produced insufficient evidence but did not deny that low prices could constitute an abuse.

B. IMPOSING UNFAIR TRADING CONDITIONS AND ENTERING INTO RESTRICTIVE AGREEMENTS

Article 102(a) expressly condemns unfair conditions, and Article 102(c) condemns discriminatory conditions. In a number of cases conditions imposed by dominant undertakings on their customers have been condemned as abuses because they were unfair, and some of these have been dealt with under other heads of abuse. In many cases the unfair or discriminatory trading conditions are imposed in pursuit of a policy to exclude competitors. For example, the Commission's 1994 investigation into Microsoft's licensing practices concerned Microsoft's standard agreements for licensing its software to PC manufacturers, which discouraged the latter from using competitors' products. Microsoft used: (a) 'per processor' 'per system' licences which required payment of royalties on every computer made by a PC manufacturer either containing a particular processor type or belonging to a particular model series, whether or not the computer was shipped with Microsoft software pre-installed; (b) 'minimum commitment' clauses which required licensees to pay for a minimum number of copies of a product regardless of actual use; and (c) had excessively long licence agreements. The Commission reached a settlement with Microsoft.[1031] Microsoft undertook not to enter licence contracts of more than one year's duration, not to impose minimum commitments, and not to use per processor clauses.[1032]

In *Tetra Pak II*[1033] the terms on which the dominant undertaking dealt with its customers (in pursuance of a marketing policy which aimed to restrict supply and compartmentalise national markets) were found to be unfairly onerous. They included placing limitations on the purchasers' use of the machines, binding purchasers to Tetra Pak's repair and maintenance services, and reserving to Tetra Pak the right to make surprise inspections. The rental payments were so high in comparison to sale prices that the supplier had to be taken to have relinquished its property rights to the hirer. Lease terms which exceeded the technological (though not the physical) life of the machine were abusive. Further, clauses imposing penalties for breach of any of the terms of the agreements at Tetra Pak's discretion also infringed Article 102, as these were aimed at ensuring compliance with the terms of the agreements which were in themselves abuses.

The terms on which DSD did business in respect of its 'Green Dot' logo in Germany were considered unfair in *Duales System Deutschland* as DSD charged licence fees in circumstances where the trade mark was not actually being used. This was an infringement of Article 102(a) as '[u]nfair commercial terms exist where an undertaking in a dominant position fails to comply with the principle of proportionality'.[1034] The CJ rejected DSD's argument that the Commission's decision had amounted to an obligation to grant a licence to use the logo.[1035]

In *AAMS v Commission*[1036] the terms of the distribution agreements which the dominant wholesale distributor of cigarettes in Italy imposed on foreign producers were held to be unfair. They were also

---

[1031] *Microsoft*, IP/94/653 of 17 July 1994. The US FTC also reached a settlement with Microsoft.

[1032] Per system clauses would be allowed if the licensees were given flexibility not to buy Microsoft products and not to have to pay for what they did not buy. See also Case C-310/93 P, *BPB Industries* [1995] ECR I-865, n. 959, where the company had applied dissimilar conditions to equivalent transactions on one market in order to strengthen its dominance on the other. Another example of customers (allegedly) suffering unfair conditions in pursuit of an exclusionary policy was the conditions imposed by IBM in COMP/39.692, *IBM Maintenance Services* Commitments Decision 13 December 2011.

[1033] Case C-333/94 P, *Tetra Pak II* [1996] ECR I-5951.

[1034] [2001] OJ 1166/1, para. 112, *aff'd* on appeal, see also Section 16.A.i.b, p. 571 on the excessive pricing finding.

[1035] Case C-385/07 P, *Der Grüne Punkt–Duales System Deutschland* [2009] ECR I-6155.

[1036] Case T-139/98, *Amministrazione Autonoma dei Monopoli di Stato (AAMS) v Commission* [2001] ECR II-3413.

objectionable in that they limited the foreign producers' access to the Italian market, contrary to the imperative of the single market.[1037]

In a number of cases concerning performing rights societies the Commission has found the society to have committed abuses by virtue of the terms on which the society did business. For example, in *GEMA*[1038] the society wished to prevent members leaving it for direct relationships with undertakings such as record companies. Its rules took the rights to works even after the member's resignation, provided for long periods of withdrawal, and made payments to the social fund payable only to members of 20 years' standing. GEMA also discriminated on grounds of nationality.[1039]

A dominant undertaking entering into restrictive agreements may be caught by both Article 101 and Article 102. In *Ahmed Saeed*[1040] the CJ, in the context of an agreement fixing air tariffs, said that what appeared to be an agreement could really be the imposition on the other party of the dominant undertaking's will, the agreement simply constituting 'the formal measure setting the seal on an economic reality characterised by the fact that an undertaking in a dominant position has succeeded in having the tariffs in question applied by other undertakings'.

In *FENIN*[1041] a group of suppliers to the bodies which run the Spanish national health service (SNS) complained to the Commission that SNS was abusing its position as a dominant buyer by persistently paying its debts late (an average of 300 days). The suppliers said that the bodies took advantage of the fact that the suppliers could exert no commercial pressure on them. The SNS organisations were held not to be 'undertakings' for the purpose of Article 102[1042] and therefore the question of whether a practice such as late payment could constitute an abuse was not addressed.

The dearth of cases and decisions on the imposition of unfair trading conditions can be explained by the prevalence of other legislative regimes, such as consumer protection and unfair competition and general contract and tort laws. Some of these rules have been enacted at EU level.[1043]

C. INEFFICIENCY AND LIMITING PRODUCTION

The Article 102(b) prohibition of 'limiting production, markets, or technical development to the prejudice of consumers' has been applied to dominant undertakings operating inefficiently and unable to meet demand, particularly public undertakings with statutory monopolies where Article 102 has applied in conjunction with Article 106.[1044] In *Port of Genoa*[1045] the Court held that an undertaking with the exclusive right to organise dock work at Genoa, which refused to use modern technology and thus raised costs and caused delays, was in breach of Article 102. In *Höfner v Macrotron* the Court held that a State employment agency which was unable to meet the demand for its services would infringe Article 102.[1046] This type of abuse can, however, also be committed by private undertakings.

[1037] See Section 17, p. 574.

[1038] [1971] OJ L134/15.

[1039] Contrary to Art. 18 TFEU; see also Case 7/82, *GVL v Commission* [1983] ECR 483. See also *1998 Football World Cup* [2000] OJ L5/55.

[1040] Case 66/86, *Ahmed Saeed Flugreisen and Silver Line Reiseburo GmbH v Zentrale zur Bëkämpfung Unlauteren Wettwerbs eV* [1989] ECR 803.

[1041] Case C-205/03 P, *Federación Española de Empresas de Tecnología Sanitaria (FENIN) v Commission* [2006] ECR I-6295.

[1042] See the discussion of the concept of an undertaking for the purposes of Arts. 101 and 102 in Chap. 3, Section 5.A.iii.b.

[1043] Such as Council Dir. 93/13/EEC [1993] OJ L95/29 on unfair contract terms.

[1044] See further Chap. 8. The issue often arises in cases in which the special or exclusive rights given to the undertaking are being challenged by a would-be entrant.

[1045] Case C-179/90, *Merci Convenzionali Porto di Genova v Siderurigica Gabrielle* [1991] ECR I-5889.

[1046] Case C-41/90, *Höfner v Macrotron* [1991] ECR I-1979; see also Case C-55/96, *Job Centre Co-op arl* [1997] ECR I-7119; *Dutch Express Delivery Services* [1994] OJ L10/47; Case C-475/99; *Ambulanz Glöckner v Landkreis Südwestpfalz* [2001] ECR I-8089; Case T-556/08, *Slovenská Pošta* EU:C:2015:189.

In *P & I Clubs*,[1047] which concerned associations providing marine insurance, the Commission stated that it would intervene in situations only where there is 'clear and uncontroversial evidence that a very substantial share of the demand is being deprived of a service that it manifestly needs'.[1048] In the E.ON electricity case, where the Commission accepted commitments, one of the charges was that E.ON had limited its production of electricity in order to raise prices in the wholesale market.[1049]

17. CONDUCT HINDERING INTER-MEMBER STATE TRADE

Practices dividing markets or hindering trade between Member States in the EU may be abusive as contrary to single market integration.[1050] The excessive prices charged for the type approval certificates in *British Leyland*[1051] were held to be an abuse because they both hindered parallel imports and exploited consumers. In *United Brands*[1052] the 'green banana clause' UBC imposed on its ripener/distributors, prohibiting them from reselling the bananas while they were still green, was treated by the CJ and the Commission as tantamount to an export ban (bananas once yellow were so perishable that exporting them was not feasible) which reinforced UBC's policy of geographical price discrimination.[1053] UBC claimed throughout that the necessary measure of quality control had never been understood, applied, or enforced as an export ban, but it was nevertheless held to infringe Article 102. The unfair distribution terms imposed by the dominant undertaking in *AAMS*[1054] hindered the trade in cigarettes between Member States. In *Swedish Interconnectors*[1055] the Commission objected to the steps taken by the Swedish electricity network operator to reduce congestion in the Swedish grid by, in effect, limiting export to neighbouring countries. The operator gave commitments which bound it to remedy the problem by other means, which would not result in segmenting the internal market.[1056] Another commitments decision in respect of the energy sector was *Bulgarian Energy Holding* where the Commission was concerned that clauses in BEH's wholesale energy contracts contained territorial restrictions amounting to export bans.[1057]

The issue of whether a refusal to supply in order to restrict parallel imports between Member States is an abuse on that ground alone arose in the context of the pharmaceutical sector.[1058] Greek pharmaceutical wholesalers were in dispute with GlaxoSmithKline who they claimed refused to

---

[1047] [1999] OJ L125/12.

[1048] *P & I Clubs* [1999] OJ L125/12, para. 128. The undertakings, in a collective dominant position, offered only a single insurance product. They amended their arrangements so there was no longer any question of an infringement of Art. 102.

[1049] COMP/39.388, *German Electricity Balancing Markets (E.ON)* Commitments Decision [2009] OJ C36/8.

[1050] See, e.g., Case 40/73, *Suiker Unie v EC Commission* [1975] ECR 1663; *Eurofix-Bauco* [1988] OJ L65/19; Case C-333/94 P, *Tetra Pak II* [1996] ECR I-5951; Case T-65/89, *BPB Industries Plc and British Gypsum Ltd v Commission* [1993] ECR II-389; Case T-228/97, *Irish Sugar plc v Commission* [1999] ECR II-2969.

[1051] Case 226/84, *British Leyland v EC Commission* [1986] ECR 3263.

[1052] Case 27/76, *United Brands* [1978] ECR 207.

[1053] See Section 15.E, p. 562.

[1054] Case T-139/98, *Amministrazione Autonoma dei Monopoli di Stato (AAMS) v Commission* [2001] ECR II-3413.

[1055] COMP/39.351, *Swedish Interconnectors* [2010] OJ C142/28; see M. Sadowska and B. Willems, 'Market Integration and Economic Efficiency at Conflict? Commitments in the *Swedish Interconnectors* Case' (2013) 36 *World Competition* 99.

[1056] By dividing the Swedish transmission market into bidding zones and building a new transmission line.

[1057] COMP/39.767, *Bulgarian Energy Holdings* 10 December 2015, IP/15/6289. The commitments involved a far-reaching industry restructuring, see Chap. 13, Sections 7.E.ii and 7.E.iii.

[1058] Outside the pharmaceutical sector see *Polaroid/SSI* where Polaroid allegedly refused to supply a customer with the quantities ordered because of concerns that it intended to export some of the products. Polaroid agreed to supply the full amount and the Commission closed its file: see *XIIIth Report on Competition Policy* (1983), point 157.

fulfil all their orders in respect of certain pharmaceuticals in order to prevent them exporting to other Member States in which prices were higher. The efforts of pharmaceutical companies to prevent such parallel trade had resulted in Article 101 proceedings, as seen in Chapters 3 and 4.[1059] The first case to reach the CJ on the application of Article 102 was *Syfait*,[1060] an Article 267 reference from the Greek Competition Commission. Advocate General Jacobs considered that in the context of the European pharmaceutical sector it was not necessarily an abuse to refuse to supply to prevent parallel trade.[1061] He recognised special circumstances pertaining to trade in pharmaceuticals. First, the price differentials between Member States were due to pervasive and diverse State intervention; secondly, Community and Member State regulation imposed obligations on pharmaceutical undertakings and wholesalers to ensure adequate stocks; thirdly, parallel trade could have potentially negative consequences on R&D incentives; and, fourthly, end consumers could not be assumed to benefit from parallel trade, given that the Member States' public authorities are the main purchasers and that parallel trade does not necessarily result in any price competition discernible to the end consumers. In the circumstances, therefore, a refusal to supply that aimed thereby to limit parallel trade was capable of objective justification and thus of not constituting an abuse. The Advocate General was careful to say that his conclusion was 'highly specific' to the peculiarities of the European pharmaceutical market.[1062] The CJ refused to give judgment on the grounds that the reference was inadmissible because the Greek Competition Commission is not a 'court or tribunal of a Member State' within Article 267 from which the CJ can accept a reference. The Advocate General's Opinion, however, showed both a reluctance to widen the ambit of refusal to supply abuses simply on single market grounds, and a sympathetic stance towards the pharmaceutical industry.

The same matter involving the same parties came before the CJ again on a reference from a Greek court in *Sot. Lélos* (often known as *Glaxo Greece*).[1063] In the meantime the GC had delivered the Article 101 judgment, *GlaxoSmithKline* (or *Glaxo Spain*) in which Advocate General Jacob's arguments in *Syfait* were largely accepted.[1064]

In *Sot. Lélos* the CJ reframed the questions it was asked as:

- whether there is an abuse of a dominant position contrary to Article 102 if a pharmaceuticals company occupying such a position on the national market for certain medicinal products refuses to meet orders sent to it by wholesalers on account of the fact that those wholesalers are involved in parallel exports of those products to other Member States (paragraph 28); and

- the relevance of a series of factors such as the degree of regulation to which the pharmaceuticals sector is subject in Member States, the impact of parallel trade on the pharmaceuticals companies' revenues, and the question whether parallel trade is capable of generating financial benefits for the ultimate consumers of the medicinal products (paragraph 29).

The CJ ruled that 'there can be no escape' from Article 102 for the practices of an undertaking in a dominant position which are aimed at avoiding all parallel exports between Member States

---

[1059] See Cases C-2 and 3/01 P, *Bayer* [2004] ECR I-23, discussed in Chap. 3 (where it was held that there was no breach of Art. 101(1) as the refusal was a unilateral act and did not constitute an agreement: it was not claimed that Bayer was dominant) and Case C-501/06 P, *GlaxoSmithKline* [2009] ECR I-9291.

[1060] Case C-53/03, *Synetairismos Farmakopoion Aitolias & Akarnanias (Syfait) v GlaxoSmithKline plc and GlaxoSmithKline AEVE* [2005] ECR I-4609.

[1061] Ibid., Opinion, paras. 77–104.

[1062] Ibid., Opinion, paras. 101–102.

[1063] See R. O'Donoghue and L. Macnab, 'Dominant Firms' Duties to Deal with Pharmaceutical Parallel Traders Following *Glaxo Greece*' (2009) 5 *Competition Policy International* 153; S. Kingston, 'Casenote on *Sot. Lélos*' (2009) 46 *CMLRev* 683.

[1064] The GC said that an agreement restricting parallel trade in the pharmaceutical sector was not restrictive by object because it could not be assumed that it reduced consumer welfare, Case T-168/01, *GlaxoSmithKlineServices* [2006] ECR II-2969, see Chap. 4. A year after the *Sot. Lélos* ruling the CJ overruled the GC on that point, Case C-501/06 P, *GlaxoSmithKline Services* [2009] ECR I-9291.

(paragraph 66). The peculiarities of the EU pharmaceutical sector did not alter this. However, the CJ was prepared to accept that the practices could be objectively justified by the undertaking's need to protect its own commercial interests and so it could refuse to meet orders which are out of the ordinary.

This means that there is a different rule for refusals to supply to prevent parallel trade than for others. As the Commission recognises in the Guidance Paper, EU law normally starts from the position that 'any undertaking, whether dominant or not, should have the right to choose its trading partners'.[1065] That is why the 'exceptional circumstances' in the case law already discussed,[1066] which impose a duty to supply in derogation from this principle, are so important. In respect of parallel trade refusals, however, the position is that they are prima facie abusive, and can escape Article 102 only by objective justification.

Cases C-468–478/06, *Sot. Lélos kai Sia EE v GlaxoSmithKline AEVE Farmakeftikon Proionton* [2008] ECR I-7139

Court of Justice

The existence of a refusal to supply liable to eliminate competition

34. The established case-law of the Court shows that the refusal by an undertaking occupying a dominant position on the market of a given product to meet the orders of an existing customer constitutes abuse of that dominant position under Article [102] where, without any objective justification, that conduct is liable to eliminate a trading party as a competitor (see, to that effect, Joined Cases 6/73 and 7/73 *Istituto Chemioterapico Italiano and Commercial Solvents v Commission* . . . paragraph 25, and Case 27/76 *United Brands and United Brands Continentaal v Commission* . . . paragraph 183).

35. With regard to a refusal by an undertaking to deliver its products in one Member State to wholesalers which export those products to other Member States, such an effect on competition may exist not only if the refusal impedes the activities of those wholesalers in that first Member State, but equally if it leads to the elimination of effective competition from them in the distribution of the products on the markets of the other Member States.

36. In this case it is common ground between the parties in the main proceedings that, by refusing to meet the Greek wholesalers' orders, GSK AEVE aims to limit parallel exports by those wholesalers to the markets of other Member States in which the selling prices of the medicinal products in dispute are higher.

37. In respect of sectors other than that of pharmaceutical products, the Court has held that a practice by which an undertaking in a dominant position aims to restrict parallel trade in the products that it puts on the market constitutes abuse of that dominant position, particularly when such a practice has the effect of curbing parallel imports by neutralising the more favourable level of prices which may apply in other sales areas in the Community (see, to that effect, Case 26/75 *General Motors Continental v Commission* . . . paragraph 12) or when it aims to create barriers to re-importations which come into competition with the distribution network of that undertaking (Case 226/84 *British Leyland v Commission*, paragraph 24). Indeed, parallel imports enjoy a certain amount of protection in Community law because they encourage trade and help reinforce competition (Case C-373/90 *X* [1992] ECR I-131, paragraph 12).

. . .

39. In order to determine whether the refusal by a pharmaceuticals company to supply medicinal products to such wholesalers indeed falls within the prohibition laid down in Article [102], in particular at point (b) of the second paragraph of that article, it must be examined whether, as GSK AEVE maintains, there are

---

[1065] Guidance Paper, para. 75.

[1066] See Sections 13.B, 13.C, and 13.D.

objective considerations based on which such a practice cannot be regarded as an abuse of the dominant position occupied by that undertaking (see, to that effect, *United Brands and United Brands Continentaal v Commission*, paragraph 184, and Case C-95/04 P *British Airways v Commission* . . . paragraph 69).

The abusive nature of the refusal to supply

. . .

49. It should be recalled that in paragraph 182 of its judgment in United Brands and *United Brands Continentaal v Commission* the Court held that an undertaking in a dominant position for the purpose of marketing a product—which cashes in on the reputation of a brand name known to and valued by consumers—cannot stop supplying a long-standing customer who abides by regular commercial practice, if the orders placed by that customer are in no way out of the ordinary. In paragraph 183 of the same judgment, the Court held that such conduct is inconsistent with the objectives laid down in [Article 3(1)(g) EC], which are set out in detail in Article [102], particularly in points (b) and (c) of the second paragraph of that article, since the refusal to sell would limit the markets to the prejudice of consumers and would amount to discrimination which might in the end eliminate a trading party from the relevant market.

50. In paragraph 189 of the judgment in *United Brands and United Brands Continentaal v Commission*, the Court stated that, although the fact that an undertaking is in a dominant position cannot deprive it of its right to protect its own commercial interests if they are attacked, and that such an undertaking must be conceded the right to take such reasonable steps as it deems appropriate to protect those interests, such behaviour cannot be accepted if its purpose is specifically to strengthen that dominant position and abuse it.

51. It must be examined in this context whether, as GSK AEVE claims, particular circumstances are present in the pharmaceuticals sector, by reason of which the refusal by an undertaking in a dominant position to supply clients in a given Member State who engage in parallel exports to other Member States where prices for medicines are higher does not, generally speaking, constitute an abuse.

The consequences of parallel trade for the ultimate consumers

52. The first thing to consider is GSK AEVE's argument that parallel trade in any event brings only few financial benefits to the ultimate consumers.

53. In that connection, it should be noted that parallel exports of medicinal products from a Member State where the prices are low to other Member States in which the prices are higher open up in principle an alternative source of supply to buyers of the medicinal products in those latter States, which necessarily brings some benefits to the final consumer of those products.

54. It is true, as GSK AEVE has pointed out, that, for medicines subject to parallel exports, the existence of price differences between the exporting and the importing Member States does not necessarily imply that the final consumer in the importing Member State will benefit from a price corresponding to the one prevailing in the exporting Member State, inasmuch as the wholesalers carrying out the exports will themselves make a profit from that parallel trade.

55. Nevertheless, the attraction of the other source of supply which arises from parallel trade in the importing Member State lies precisely in the fact that that trade is capable of offering the same products on the market of that Member State at lower prices than those applied on the same market by the pharmaceuticals companies.

56. As a result, even in the Member States where the prices of medicines are subject to State regulation, parallel trade is liable to exert pressure on prices and, consequently, to create financial benefits not only for the social health insurance funds, but equally for the patients concerned, for whom the proportion of the price of medicines for which they are responsible will be lower. At the same time, as the Commission notes, parallel trade in medicines from one Member State to another is likely to increase the choice available to entities in the latter Member State which obtain supplies of medicines by means of a public procurement procedure, in which the parallel importers can offer medicines at lower prices.

57. Accordingly, without it being necessary for the Court to rule on the question whether it is for an undertaking in a dominant position to assess whether its conduct vis-à-vis a trading party constitutes abuse in the light of the degree to which that party's activities offer advantages to the final consumers, it is clear that, in the circumstances of the main proceedings, such an undertaking cannot base its arguments on the premise that the parallel exports which it seeks to limit are of only minimal benefit to the final consumers.

The impact of State price and supply regulation in the pharmaceutical sector

. . .

64. On the other hand, it should be recalled that, where a medicine is protected by a patent which confers a temporary monopoly on its holder, the price competition which may exist between a producer and its distributors, or between parallel traders and national distributors, is, until the expiry of that patent, the only form of competition which can be envisaged.

65. In relation to the application of Article [101] the Court has held that an agreement between producer and distributor which might tend to restore the national divisions in trade between Member States might be such as to frustrate the objective of the Treaty to achieve the integration of national markets through the establishment of a single market. Thus on a number of occasions the Court has held agreements aimed at partitioning national markets according to national borders or making the interpenetration of national markets more difficult, in particular those aimed at preventing or restricting parallel exports, to be agreements whose object is to restrict competition within the meaning of that Treaty article (see, for example, Joined Cases 96/82 to 102/82, 104/82, 105/82, 108/82 and 110/82 *IAZ International Belgium and Others v Commission* . . . paragraphs 23 to 27; Case C-306/96 *Javico* . . . paragraphs 13 and 14; and Case C-551/03 P *General Motors v Commission* . . . paragraphs 67 to 69).

66. In the light of the abovementioned Treaty objective as well as that of ensuring that competition in the internal market is not distorted, there can be no escape from the prohibition laid down in Article [102] for the practices of an undertaking in a dominant position which are aimed at avoiding all parallel exports from a Member State to other Member States, practices which, by partitioning the national markets, neutralise the benefits of effective competition in terms of the supply and the prices that those exports would obtain for final consumers in the other Member States.

67. Although the degree of price regulation in the pharmaceuticals sector cannot therefore preclude the Community rules on competition from applying, the fact none the less remains that, when assessing, in the case of Member States with a system of price regulation, whether the refusal of a pharmaceuticals company to supply medicines to wholesalers involved in parallel exports constitutes abuse, it cannot be ignored that such State intervention is one of the factors liable to create opportunities for parallel trade.

68. Furthermore, in the light of the Treaty objectives to protect consumers by means of undistorted competition and the integration of national markets, the Community rules on competition are also incapable of being interpreted in such a way that, in order to defend its own commercial interests, the only choice left for a pharmaceuticals company in a dominant position is not to place its medicines on the market at all in a Member State where the prices of those products are set at a relatively low level.

69. It follows that, even if the degree of regulation regarding the price of medicines cannot prevent any refusal by a pharmaceuticals company in a dominant position to meet orders sent to it by wholesalers involved in parallel exports from constituting an abuse, such a company must nevertheless be in a position to take steps that are reasonable and in proportion to the need to protect its own commercial interests.

70. In that respect, and without it being necessary to examine the argument raised by GSK AEVE that it is necessary for pharmaceuticals companies to limit parallel exports in order to avoid the risk of a reduction in their investments in the research and development of medicines, it is sufficient to state that, in order to appraise whether the refusal by a pharmaceuticals company to supply wholesalers involved in parallel exports constitutes a reasonable and proportionate measure in relation to the threat that those exports represent to its legitimate commercial interests, it must be ascertained whether the orders of the

wholesalers are out of the ordinary (see, to that effect, *United Brands and United Brands Continentaal v Commission*, paragraph 182).

71. Thus, although a pharmaceuticals company in a dominant position, in a Member State where prices are relatively low, cannot be allowed to cease to honour the ordinary orders of an existing customer for the sole reason that that customer, in addition to supplying the market in that Member State, exports part of the quantities ordered to other Member States with higher prices, it is none the less permissible for that company to counter in a reasonable and proportionate way the threat to its own commercial interests potentially posed by the activities of an undertaking which wishes to be supplied in the first Member State with significant quantities of products that are essentially destined for parallel export.

72. In the present cases, the orders for reference show that, in the disputes which gave rise to those orders, the appellants in the main proceedings have demanded not that GSK AEVE should fulfil the orders sent to it in their entirety, but that it should deliver them quantities of medicines corresponding to the monthly average sold during the first 10 months of 2000. In 6 of the 11 actions in the main proceedings, the appellants asked for those quantities to be increased by a certain percentage, which was fixed by some of them at 20%.

73. In those circumstances, it is for the referring court to ascertain whether the abovementioned orders are ordinary in the light of both the previous business relations between the pharmaceuticals company holding a dominant position and the wholesalers concerned and the size of the orders in relation to the requirements of the market in the Member State concerned (see, to that effect, *United Brands and United Brands Continentaal v Commission*, paragraph 182, and Case 77/77 *Benzine en Petroleum Handelsmaatschappij and Others v Commission*, paragraphs 30 to 32).

74. Those considerations equally deal with the argument raised by GSK AEVE, namely the impact of State regulation on the supply of medicinal products, and more particularly the argument that undertakings that engage in parallel exports are not subject to the same obligations regarding distribution and warehousing as the pharmaceuticals companies and are therefore liable to disrupt the planning of production and distribution of medicines.

75. It is true that in Greece, as is apparent from paragraph 8 of this judgment, national legislation places pharmaceuticals wholesalers under an obligation to supply the needs of a defined geographical area with a range of pharmaceutical products. It is equally true that, in cases where parallel trade would effectively lead to a shortage of medicines on a given national market, it would not be for the undertakings holding a dominant position but for the national authorities to resolve the situation, by taking appropriate and proportionate steps that were consistent with national legislation as well as with the obligations flowing from Article 81 of Directive 2001/83.

76. However, a producer of pharmaceutical products must be in a position to protect its own commercial interests if it is confronted with orders that are out of the ordinary in terms of quantity. Such could be the case, in a given Member State, if certain wholesalers order from that producer medicines in quantities which are out of all proportion to those previously sold by the same wholesalers to meet the needs of the market in that Member State.

77. In view of the foregoing, the answer to the questions referred should be that Article [102] must be interpreted as meaning that an undertaking occupying a dominant position on the relevant market for medicinal products which, in order to put a stop to parallel exports carried out by certain wholesalers from one Member State to other Member States, refuses to meet ordinary orders from those wholesalers is abusing its dominant position. It is for the national court to ascertain whether the orders are ordinary in the light of both the size of those orders in relation to the requirements of the market in the first Member State and the previous business relations between that undertaking and the wholesalers concerned.

The CJ (paragraphs 52–57) considered that final consumers and social security systems did derive some benefit from parallel trade and that an undertaking in GSK's position could not argue from the basis that the benefit to final consumers was only minimal (paragraph 57). It considered the effect of price controls by Member States but stressed that for patented pharmaceuticals it is only parallel trade which can provide any competition (paragraph 64). Although the features of the pharmaceutical sector did not remove it from the normal competition rules against restrictions on parallel trade the Court did, however, recognise the effect of national intervention on the opportunities for parallel trade (paragraph 67). It accepted that the undertaking had a right to protect its own commercial interests and said (paragraph 68) that the competition rules could not be interpreted in such a way that it left an undertaking in Glaxo's position with no way to do this but to leave the market (which here would have meant ceasing to supply in Greece). The CJ therefore made the very important concession that although Glaxo could not, without infringing Article 102, cease honouring the 'ordinary orders of an existing customer' it *could* refuse orders which were 'out of the ordinary'. It was left to the national court to draw the difficult line between 'ordinary' and 'out of the ordinary' orders.[1067] The method for this assessment is to examine the orders in the light of the previous business relations between the distributor and the supplier and the size of the order in relation to the market requirements in the Member State concerned to see if they are 'out of all proportion' (paragraphs 73 and 76).

The ruling is notable for the way in which it treated Glaxo's arguments about the need to limit parallel trade in order to maintain profits for investment in R&D (also the argument in *GlaxoSmithKline*). In its formulation of the questions referred to it (paragraph 29) the CJ referred to 'the pharmaceutical companies revenues' and in paragraph 70 it simply treated their protection as a 'legitimate commercial interests' matter. It did not engage in any discussion about justifying the hindrance of parallel trade on 'efficiency' grounds and indeed specifically stated that it is unnecessary to examine the R&D question.

The judgment only dealt with the position of existing customers, because that was the subject matter of the case. This does not mean that there is not also a duty to supply new customers, particularly given the prima facie nature of the abuse. Obviously different criteria for assessing the reasonable and proportionate nature of the refusal to protect legitimate commercial interests would need to be devised since there would be no 'ordinary' orders for comparison. The size of the market in the Member State would still be germane however.

18. ABUSE AND COLLECTIVE DOMINANCE

It was explained in Chapter 5 that a 'dominant position' may be held by a single undertaking or by one or more independent undertakings which hold a collective dominant position. This concept and its application are explored in Chapter 9, in the context of cartels and oligopolies and the question of what can amount to the abuse of a collective dominance position is discussed there.[1068] In some of the cases discussed in this chapter, the dominant position being abused was a collective one.[1069] It should be noted here, however, that in *Irish Sugar* the GC said that it was not necessary for the collective dominant position to be *abused* collectively. It is possible therefore that an undertaking may individually commit an abuse of a dominant position held collectively with other undertakings, at least insofar as the abuse is committed to protect the collective dominant position.[1070]

[1067] This concept of 'ordinary' orders is found in *United Brands* which the CJ cites. *United Brands* was, however, a totally different scenario, a reprisal against customers dealing with a competitor, see Section 13.E, p. 532.

[1068] See Chap. 9, Section 4.B.ii, p. 706.

[1069] See, e.g., Case C-395 and 396/96 P, *Compagnie Maritime Belge* [2000] ECR I-1365; Case T-193/02, *Laurent Piau* [2005] ECR II-209.

[1070] Case T-228/97, *Irish Sugar* [1999] ECR II-2969, para. 66.

19. CONCLUSIONS

1. The matter of what conduct on the part of a dominant undertaking can constitute an infringement of Article 102 should be put on a sound and consistent economic footing. Conduct should be judged by its effects on the market, not on its form. However, theoretically sound, effects-based rules that are too complex or impractical are not a good basis on which to build a sound competition policy. Undertakings need legal certainty and they should be able to adopt commercial policies in the knowledge that their conduct is legal.

2. An abuse of a dominant position should only be found on the basis of a clearly articulated theory of harm.

3. The Guidance Paper is a welcome move which helps to clarify when certain types of conduct merit intervention by the Commission. According to the EU Courts the Guidance Paper is, however, only an administrative document setting out enforcement priorities, which does not bind either them, national courts, or NCAs. The EU Courts have not hesitated to diverge from their approach to topics such as loyalty rebates, margin squeeze, and the AEC test.

4. The EU Courts have not adopted the Commission's welfarist approach to Article 102. They continue to hold that Article 102 is concerned with the impact of conduct on an effective competitive structure. However, the language of the Courts reflects more concern with effects on consumers than it has in the past. The judgments are not always consistent, but *TeliaSonera* and *Post Danmark I*, in particular, show a more 'modern' approach.

5. The increasing use of commitments decisions is unfortunate for the development of the law. Commitments negotiated between undertakings and the Commission do not result in a finding that (perhaps novel) conduct does indeed constitute an abuse and the questions at issue do not come before the EU Courts. The development of the jurisprudence on Article 102 is becoming more dependent on cases in national courts which reach the CJ under the preliminary reference procedure, but in such cases the Court is not called upon to apply the law to the facts.

6. There is a growing trend for undertakings in the digital economy to use Article 102 as a major weapon in their commercial battles, particularly since Article 102 is applied in a more interventionist way than s. 2 of the US Sherman Act. This is shown by the cases arising from the 'smartphone wars' and the *Google* investigation.

20. FURTHER READING

A. BOOKS

AKMAN, P., *The Concept of Abuse in EU Competition Law* (Hart Publishing, 2012)

BELLAMY and CHILD (V. Rose and D. Bailey, eds.), *European Union Law of Competition* (7th edn, Oxford University Press, 2013 and Supplement by L. John and J. Turner, 2015), Chap. 9, 9.049–9.064, Chap. 10, 10.053–10.152

BISHOP, S., and WALKER, M., *The Economics of EC Competition Law: Concepts, Application and Measurement* (3rd edn, Sweet & Maxwell, 2010), Chap. 6

BORK, R., *The Antitrust Paradox* (Basic Books, 1978, reprinted with a new Introduction and Epilogue, 1993), Chap. 7

EHLERMANN, C.-D., and ATANASIU, I. (eds.), *European Competition Law Annual 2003: What is Abuse of a Dominant Position?* (Hart Publishing, 2006)

EHLERMANN, C.-D., and ATANASIU, I. (eds.), *European Competition Law Annual 2005: The Interaction Between Competition Law and Intellectual Property Law* (Hart Publishing, 2007)

EHLERMANN, C.-D., and MARQUIS, M., *European Competition Law Annual 2007: A Reformed Approach to Article 82 EC* (Hart Publishing, 2008)

ETRO, F., and KOKKORIS, I. (eds.), *Competition Law and the Enforcement of Article 102* (Oxford University Press, 2010)

EZRACHI, A. (ed.), *Article 82 EC: Reflections on its Recent Evolution* (Hart Publishing, 2009)

GERADIN, D., LAYNE-FARRAR, A., and PETIT, N., *EU Competition Law and Economics* (Oxford University Press, 2012), 4.131–4.542

HOVENKAMP, H., *Federal Antitrust Policy* (4th edn, West, 2011), Chaps. 6, 7, 8, and 10

JOLIET R., *Monopolization and Abuse of Dominant Position* (Nijhoff, 1970)

LANGER, J., *Tying and Bundling as a Leveraging Concern Under EC Competition Law* (Kluwer Law International, 2008)

LOVDHAL GORMSEN, L., *A Principled Approach to Abuse of Dominance in European Competition Law* (Cambridge University Press, 2010)

MOTTA, M., *Competition Policy* (Cambridge University Press, 2004), Chaps. 2 and 7

NAZZINI, R., *The Foundations of European Union Competition Law: The Objectives and Principles of Article 102* (Oxford University Press, 2011)

O'DONOGHUE, R., and PADILLA, A. J., *The Law and Economics of Article 102* (2nd edn, Hart Publishing, 2013), Chaps. 5–16

PACE, L. F. (ed.), *European Competition Law: The Impact of the Commission's Guidance on Article 102* (Edward Elgar, 2011)

PETROVIC, U., *Competition Law and Standard-Essential Patents: A Transatlantic Perspective* (Kluwer Law International, 2014)

PHLIPS, L., *The Economics of Price Discrimination* (Cambridge University Press, 1983)

POSNER, R. A., *Antitrust Law* (2nd edn, University of Chicago Press, 2001), Chaps. 7 and 8

ROUSSEVA, E., *Rethinking Exclusionary Abuses in EU Competition Law* (Hart Publishing, 2010)

SCHERER, F. M., and ROSS, D., *Industrial Market Structure and Economic Performance* (3rd edn, Houghton Mifflin, 1990), Chaps. 13 and 16

SCHMIDT, H., *Competition Law, Innovation and Antitrust* (Edward Elgar, 2009)

VAN DEN BERGH, R. J., and CAMESASCA, P. D., *European Competition Law and Economics: A Comparative Perspective* (2nd edn, Sweet & Maxwell, 2006), Chap. 7

B. CHAPTERS IN BOOKS

ACKERMANN, T., 'Excessive Pricing and the Goals of Competition Law' in D. Zimmer (ed.), *The Goals of Competition Law* (Edward Elgar, 2012), Chap. 18

DOWNING, R., and JONES, A., 'Margin Squeezes in Telecommunications Markets' in S. Anderman and A. Ezrachi (eds.), *Intellectual Property and Competition Law: New Frontiers* (Oxford University Press, 2011)

FOX, E., 'Abuse of Dominance and Monopolisation: How to Protect Competition Without Protecting Competitors' in C.-D. Ehlermann and I. Atanasiu (eds.), *European Competition Law Annual 2003: What is Abuse of a Dominant Position?* (Hart Publishing, 2006), 69

HATZOPOULOS, V., 'The EC Essential Facilities Doctrine' in G. Amato and C.-D. Ehlermann (eds.), *EC Competition Law: A Critical Assessment* (Hart Publishing, 2007), 333

HOWARTH, D., 'Unfair and Predatory Pricing under Article 82 EC: From Cost-price Comparisons to the Search for Strategic Standards' in G. Amato and C.-D. Ehlermann (eds.), *EC Competition Law: A Critical Assessment* (Hart Publishing, 2007), 249

JONES, A., 'Refusal to Deal—EC and US Law Compared' in P. Marsden (ed.), *Handbook of Research in Trans-Atlantic Antitrust* (Edward Elgar, 2006), Chap. 8, 236–286

LANGER, J., 'A Four-step Test to Assess the Exclusionary Effects of Bundling under Article 82 EC' in G. Amato and C.-D. Ehlermann (eds.),

EC Competition Law: A Critical Assessment (Hart Publishing, 2007), 297

MARSDEN, P., 'Some Outstanding Issues from the European Commission's Guidance on Article 102 TFEU: Not-So-Faint Echoes of Ordoliberalism' in F. Etro and I. Kokkoris (eds.), *Competition Law and the Enforcement of Article 102* (Oxford University Press, 2010), Chap. 3

ROELLER, L.-H., 'Exploitative Abuses' in C.-D. Ehlermann and M. Marquis (eds.), *European Competition Law Annual 2007: A Reformed Approach to Article 82* (Hart Publishing, 2008)

ROUSSEVA, E., 'Objective Justification and Article 82 EC in the Era of Modernisation' in G. Amato and C.-D. Ehlermann (eds.), *EC Competition Law: A Critical Assessment* (Hart Publishing, 2007), 377

TERHECHTE, J. P., 'Excessive Pricing and the Goals of Competition Law: An Enforcement Perspective—Comment on Ackermann' in D. Zimmer (ed.), *The Goals of Competition Law* (Edward Elgar, 2012), Chap. 19

VICKERS, J., 'How Does the Prohibition of Abuse of Dominance Fit with the Rest of Competition Policy?' in C.-D. Ehlermann and I. Atanasiu (eds.), *European Competition Law Annual 2003: What is Abuse of a Dominant Position?* (Hart Publishing, 2006), 147

VICKERS, J., 'Some Economics of Abuse of Dominance' in X. Vives (ed.), *Competition Policy in the EU: Fifty Years on from the Treaty of Rome* (Oxford University Press, 2009), 71

C. ARTICLES

AHLBORN, C., and BAILEY, D., 'Discounts, Rebates and Selective Pricing by Dominant Firms: A Trans-Atlantic Comparison' (2006) 2 *European Competition Journal* 101

AHLBORN, C., and EVANS, D. S., 'The *Microsoft* Judgment and its Implications for Competition Policy Towards Dominant Firms in Europe' (2008–2009) 75 *Antitrust LJ* 887

AHLBORN, C. and PICCININ, D., 'The *Intel* Judgment and Consumer Welfare—A Response to Wouter Wils' [2015] 1 *CLPD* 60

AHLBORN, C., EVANS, D. S., and PADILLA, J., 'The Logic and Limits of Exceptional Circumstances Test in *Magill* and *IMS Health*' (2005) *Fordham Int'l LJ* 1062

AKMAN, P., '"Consumer Welfare" and Article 82: Practice and Rhetoric' (2009) 32 *World Competition* 71

AKMAN, P., 'Searching for the Long-lost Soul of Article 82EC' (2009) 29 *OJLS* 267

ALLAN, B., 'Article 102: A Commentary on DG Competition's Discussion Paper' (2006) 2 *Competition Policy International* 43

ALLAN, B., 'Loyalty and Fidelity Rebates: A Sense of Déjà Vu Again' [2015] 1 *CLPD* 50

ANDREANGELI, A., 'Interoperability as an "Essential Facility" in the *Microsoft* Case—Encouraging Competition or Stifling Innovation' (2009) 34 *ELRev* 584

ANDREWS, P., 'Aftermarket Power in the Computer Services Market: The Digital Undertaking' [1998] *ECLR* 176

AREEDA, P., 'Essential Facilities: An Epithet in Need of Limiting Principles' (1990) 58 *Antitrust LJ* 841

AREEDA, P., and TURNER, D., 'Predatory Pricing and Related Practices under Section 2 of the Sherman Act' (1975) 88 *Harvard LR* 697

BARAZZA, S., '*Post Danmark*: The CJEU Calls for an Effect-based Assessment of Pricing Policies' (2012) 3 *JECLAP* 466

BEARD, D., '*Microsoft*: What Sort of Landmark?' (2008) 4 *Competition Policy International* 33

BISHOP, W., 'Price Discrimination under Article 86: Political Economy in the European Court' (1981) 66 *MLR* 282

BORK., R., and SIDAK, J. G., 'What Does the Chicago School Teach About Internet Search and the Antitrust Treatment of Google?' (2011) 8 *J of Competition Law and Economics* 663

BORLINI, L., 'Methodological Issues of the "More Economic Approach" to Unilateral Exclusionary Conduct' (2009) 5 *European Competition Journal* 409

BRODLEY, J., and HAY, D., 'Predatory Pricing: Competing Economic Theories and the Evolution of Legal Standards' (1981) 66 *Cornell LR* 738

BUNDESKARTELLAMT, 'Competition Law Forum Debate on Reform of Article 102: A "Dialectic" on Competing Approaches' (2006) 2 *European Competition Journal* 211

CAPOBIANCO, A., 'The Essential Facility Doctrine: Similarities and Differences between the American and European Approaches' (2001) 26 *ELRev* 548

CARLTON, D., 'Should "Price Squeeze" be a Recognized Form of Anticompetitive Conduct?' (2008) 4 *J of Competition Law and Economics* 271

CARLTON, D., and WALDMAN, W., 'The Strategic Use of Tying to Preserve and Create Market Power in Evolving Industries' (2002) 33 *RAND J of Economics* 194

CHOI, J., and STEFANADIS, C., 'Tying, Investment and Dynamic Leverage Theory' (2001) 32 *RAND J of Economics* 52

COLE, M., 'Ordoliberalism and its Influence on EU Tying Law' [2015] *ECLR* 255

COLLEY, L., and BURNSIDE, S., 'Margin Squeeze Abuse' (2006) 2 *European Competition Journal* 185

CRANE, D., and WRIGHT, J., 'Can Bundled Discounting Increase Consumer Prices Without Excluding Rivals?' (2009) 5 *Competition Policy International* 209

DOHERTY, B., 'Just What Are Essential Facilities?' (2001) 38 *CMLRev* 397

DOLMANS, M., and GRAF, T., 'Dealing with *Intel* Intelligently: Delineating the Scope and Limits of the Court's Ruling' [2015] 1 *CLPD* 76

DUNNE, N., 'Margin Squeeze: From Broken Regulation to Legal Uncertainty' (2011) 70 *CLJ* 34

DUNNE, N., 'Margin Squeeze: Theory, Practice, Policy', Parts I and II [2012] *ECLR* 29 and 61

EDELMAN, B., 'Does Google Leverage Market Power Through Tying and Bundling?' (2015) 11 *J of Competition Law and Economics* 365

EILMANSBERGER, T., 'How to Distinguish Good from Bad Competition under Article 102 EC: In Search of Clearer and More Coherent Standards for Anti-competitive Abuses' (2005) 42 *CMLRev* 129

ELHAUGE, E., 'Defining Better Monopolisation Standards' (2003–2004) 56 *Stan LR* 253

ELHAUGE, E., 'Tying, Bundled Discounts, and the Death of the Single Monopoly Profit Theory' (2009) 123 *Harvard LR* 399

EVANS, D. S., and SALINGER, M., 'Why Do Firms Bundle and Tie? Evidence from Competitive Markets and Implications for Tying Law' (2005) 22 *Yale J on Regulation* 37

EZRACHI, A., and GILO, D., 'Are Excessive Prices Really Self-correcting?' (2009) 5 *J of Competition Law and Economics* 249

FAELLA, G., and PARDOLESI, R., 'Squeezing Price Squeeze under EC Antitrust Law' (2010) 6 *European Competition Journal* 255

FINE, F., 'NDC/IMS: A Logical Application of the Essential Facilities Doctrine' [2002] *ECLR* 457

FINE, F., 'NDC/IMS: In Response to Professor Korah' (2002) 70 *Antitrust LJ* 247

FIRST, H., 'No Single Monopoly Profit, No Single Policy Prescription?' (2009) 5 *Competition Policy International* 199

FJELL, K., and SØRGARD, L., 'How to Test for Abuse of Dominance?' (2006) 2 *European Competition Journal* 69

FOX, E., 'Price Predation—US and EEC: Economics and Values' [1989] *Fordham Corp L Inst* 687

FOX, E., 'What is Harm to Competition? Exclusionary Practices and Anti-competitive Effect' (2002) 70 *Antitrust LJ* 371

FOX, E., 'We Protect Competition, You Protect Competitors' (2003) 26 *World Competition* 149

FURSE, M., 'Excessive Prices, Unfair Prices and Economic Value' (2008) 4 *European Competition Journal* 59

GERADIN, D., 'Limiting the Scope of Article 82 EC: What Can the EU Learn from the Supreme Court's Judgment in *Trinko*, in the Wake of *Microsoft*, *IMS* and *Deutsche Telekom*?' (2004) 41 *CMLRev* 1526

GERADIN, D., 'The Decision of the Commission of 13 May 2009 in the *Intel* Case: Where is the Foreclosure and Consumer Harm?' (2009) 2 *JECLAP* 9

GERADIN, D., 'Is the Guidance Paper on the Commission's Enforcement Priorities in Applying Article 102 TFEU to Abusive Exclusionary Conduct Useful?' (2010), <http://ssrn.com/abstract=1569502>

GERADIN, D., 'Refusal to Supply and Margin Squeeze: A Discussion of Why the "Telefonica Exceptions" are Wrong', TILEC Discussion Paper No. 2011-009, <http://ssrn.com/abstract=1750226>

GERADIN, D., 'Ten Years of DG Competition Effort to Provide Guidance on the Application of Competition Rules to the Licensing of Standard-Essential Patents: Where Do We Stand?' (2013), <http://ssrn.com/abstract=2204359>

GERADIN, D., and O'DONOGHUE, R., 'The Concurrent Application of Competition Law and Regulation: The Case of Margin Squeeze Abuses in the Telecommunications Sector' (2005) 1 *J of Competition Law and Economics* 355

GERADIN, D., and RATO, M., 'Can Standard-setting Lead to Exploitative Abuse? A Dissonant View of Patent Hold-up, Royalty-stacking and the Meaning of FRAND' (2007) 3 *European Competition Journal* 146

GOHARI, R. S., 'Margin Squeeze in the Telecommunications Sector: A More Economics-based Approach' (2012) 2 *World Competition* 205

HANCHER, P., 'Case Note on *Oscar Bronner*' (1999) 36 *CMLRev* 1289

HOPPNER, T., 'Competition Law in Intellectual Property Litigation: The Case for a Compulsory Licence Defence under Article 102 TFEU' (2011) 7 *European Competition Journal* 297

HOWARTH, D., and MCMAHON, K., '"Windows has performed an Illegal Operation": The Court of First Instance's Judgment in *Microsoft v Commission*' [2008] *ECLR* 117

IBÁÑEZ COLOMO, P., 'Exclusionary Discrimination under Article 102 TFEU' (2014) 51 *CMLRev* 141

IBÁÑEZ COLOMO, P., '*Intel* and Article 102 TFEU Case Law: Making Sense of a Perpetual Controversy', LSE, Law, Society and Economy Working Papers 29/2014

IBÁÑEZ COLOMO, P., '*Post Danmark II*, or the Quest for Administrability and Coherence in Article 102 TFEU', LSE, Law, Society and Economy Working Papers 15/2015, <http://ssrn.com/abstract=2636407>

INCARDONA, R., 'Modernization of Article 82 EC and Refusal to Supply' (2006) 2 *European Competition Journal* 337

JEBSEN, P., and STEVENS, R., 'Assumptions, Goals and Dominant Undertakings: The Regulation of Competition Under Article 86 of the European Union' (1996) 64 *Antitrust LJ* 443

JONES, A., 'Distinguishing Predatory Prices from Competitive Ones' [1995] *EIPR* 252

JONES, A., 'Standard-essential Patents: FRAND Commitments, Injunctions and the Smartphone Wars' (2014) 10 *European Competition Journal* 1

KALLAUGHER, J., and SHER, B., 'Rebates Revisited: Anti-competitive Effects and Exclusionary Abuse Under Article 82' [2004] *ECLR* 263

KATE, A., and NIELS, G., 'On the Rationality of Predatory Pricing: The Debate between Chicago and Post-Chicago' (2002) 47 *Ant Bull* 1

KELLERBAUER, M., 'The Commission's New Enforcement Priorities in Applying Article 82EC to Dominant Companies' Exclusionary Conduct: A Shift Towards a More Economic Approach?' [2010] *ECLR* 175

KINGSTON, S., 'Casenote on *Sot. Lélos* (2009) 46 *CMLRev* 683

KJØLBE, L., 'Rebates Under Article 82 EC: Navigating Uncertain Waters' [2010] *ECLR* 66

KJØLBE, L., 'Article 82 EC as Remedy to Patent System Imperfections: Fighting Fire with Fire?' (2009) 32 *World Competition* 163

KLEIN, B., and SHEPARD WILEY, J., 'Competitive Price Discrimination as an Antitrust Justification for IP Refusals to Deal' (2003) 70 *Antitrust LJ* 599

KORAH, V., 'The Paucity of Economic Analysis in the EEC Decisions on Competition: *Tetra Pak II*' (1993) 46 *CLP* 150

KORAH, V., 'The Interface between Intellectual Property and Antitrust: the European Experience' (2002) 69 *Antitrust LJ* 801

KROES, N., 'Tackling Exclusionary Practices to Avoid Exploitation of Market Power: Some Preliminary Thoughts on the Policy Review of Article 82' [2005] *Fordham Corp L Inst* 381

KUHN, K.-U., STILLMAN, R., and CAFFARRA, C., 'Economic Theories of Bundling and their Policy Implications in Abuse Cases' (2005) 1 *European Competition Journal* 85

LAROUCHE, P., 'The European *Microsoft* Case at the Crossroads of Competition Policy and Innovation: Comment on Ahlborn and Evans' (2008) 75 *Antitrust LJ* 933

LIANOS, I., 'Competition Law and Intellectual Property Rights: Is the Property Rights Approach Right?' (2005–2006) 8 *Cambridge Yearbook of European Legal Studies* 153

LOVDAHL GORMESEN, L., 'The Conflict between Economic Freedom and Consumer Welfare in the Modernisation of Article 82' (2007) 3 *European Competition Journal* 329

LOVDAHL GORMESEN, L., 'Why the European Commission's Enforcement Priorities on Article 82 Should Be Withdrawn' [2010] *ECLR* 45

LUGARD, P., 'Eternal Sunshine on a Spotless Policy? Exclusive Dealing under Article 82 EC' (2006) 2 *European Competition Journal* 163

MCGEE, J., 'Predatory Price Cutting: The Standard Oil (New Jersey) Case' (1958) 1 *J of Law and Economics* 137

MAIER-RIGAUD, F., 'Article 82 Rebates: Four Common Fallacies' (2006) 2 *European Competition Journal* 85

MANNE, G., and WRIGHT, J., '*Google* and the Limits of Antitrust: The Case Against the Case Against Google' (2011) 34 *Harvard J of Law & Public Policy* 171

MATEUS, A., 'Predatory Pricing: A Proposed Structured Rule of Reason' (2011) 7 *European Competition Law* 243

MEISEL, J., 'The Law and Economics of Margin Squeezes in the US versus the EU' (2012) 8 *European Competition Journal* 383

MOORE, D. W., and WRIGHT, J. D., 'Conditional Discounts and the Law of Exclusive Dealing' (2015) 22 *George Mason LR* 1205

MOURA DE SILVA, M., 'Predatory Pricing and the Recoupment Test: Do Not Go Gentle Into That Good Night' [2009] *ECLR* 61

MÜLLER, U., and RODENHAUSEN, A., 'The Rise and Fall of the Essential Facilities Doctrine' [2008] *ECLR* 310

MURPHY, F., and LIBERATORE, F., 'Abuse of Regulatory Procedures—The *Astra-Zeneca* Case' [2009] *ECLR* 289 and 314

NABELUFF, B., 'Exclusionary Bundling' (2005) 50 *Ant Bull* 321

NAZZINI, R., 'The Wood Began to Move: An Essay on Consumer Welfare, Evidence and Burden of Proof in Article 82 EC Cases' (2006) 31 *ELRev* 518

NAZZINI, R., '*Google* and the (Ever-stretching) Boundaries of Article 102 TFEU' (2015) 6 *JECLAP* 301

NIHOUL, P., 'The Ruling of the General Court in *Intel*: Towards the End of an Effects-based Approach in European Competition Law?' (2014) 5 *JECLAP* 521

O'DONOGHUE, R., and MACNAB, L., 'Dominant Firms' Duties to Deal with Pharmaceutical Parallel Traders Following *Glaxo Greece*' (2009) 5 *Competition Policy International* 153

PANNER, A. M., 'Are Price Squeezes Anticompetitive?' (2009) April (1) *Global Competition Policy*

PEEPERKORN, L., 'Conditional Pricing: Why the General Court is Wrong in *Intel* and What the Court of Justice Can Do to Rebalance the Assessment of Rebates' [2015] 1 *Concurrences* 43

PEEPERKORN, L., and ROUSSEVA, E., 'Article 102 TFEU: Exclusive Dealing and Rebates' (2011) 2 *JECLAP* 36

PETIT, N., 'Injunctions for FRAND-pledged SEPs: The Quest for an Appropriate Test of Abuse under Article 102 TFEU' (2013) 9 *European Competition Journal* 677

PETIT, N., '*Intel*, Leveraging Rebates and the Goals of Article 102 TFEU' (2015), <http://ssrn.com/abstract=2567628>

PETIT, N., 'Theories of Self-preferencing under Article 102 TFEU: A Reply to Bo Vesterdorf' (2015), <http//:ssrn.com/abstract=2592253>

PITOFSKY, R., PATTERSON, D., and HOOKS, J., 'The Essential Facilities Doctrine under US Antitrust Law' (2002) 70 *Antitrust LJ* 443

RAPP, R. T., 'Predatory Pricing and Entry Deterring Strategies: The Economics of *AKZO*' [1986] *ECLR* 233

RATO, M., and PETIT, N., 'Abuse of Dominance in Technology-enabled Markets: Established Standards Reconsidered?' (2013) 9 *European Competition Journal* 1

REY, P., and VENIT, J., 'An Effects-based Approach to Article 102: A Response to Wouter Wils' (2015) 38 *World Competition* 3

RIDYARD, D., 'Essential Facilities and the Obligation to Supply Competitors' [1996] *ECLR* 438

RIDYARD, D., 'Exclusionary Pricing and Price Discrimination Abuses under Article 102—An Economic Analysis' [2002] *ECLR* 286

RIDYARD, D., 'Compulsory Access under EC Competition Law—A New Doctrine of "Convenient Facilities" and the Case for Price Regulation' [2004] *ECLR* 670

RIDYARD, D., 'The Commission's Article 82 Guidelines: some Reflections on the Economic Issues' [2009] *ECLR* 230

RITTER, C., 'Refusal to Deal and Essential Facilities: Does Intellectual Property Require Special Deference compared to Tangible Property?' (2005) 3 *World Competition* 281

Rousseva, E., 'Modernizing by Eradicating: How the Commission's New Approach to Article 81 EC Dispenses with the Need to Apply Article 82 EC to Vertical Restraints' (2005) 42 *CMLRev* 587

Rousseva, E., and Marquis, M., 'Hell Freezes Over: A Climate Change for Assessing Exclusionary Conduct under Article 102 TFEU' (2012) 4 *JECLAP* 32

Schmalensee, R., 'Output and Welfare Implications of Third Degree Price Discrimination' (1981) 71 *Am Econ Rev* 242

Scott Hemphill, C., 'The Role of Recoupment in Predatory Pricing Analyses' (2001) 53 *Stan LR* 1581

Seabright, P., 'The Undead? A Comment on Professor Elhauge's Paper' (2009) 5 *Competition Policy International* 243

Sher, B., 'Price Discounts and *Michelin II*: What Goes Around, Comes Around' [2002] *ECLR* 482

Sher, B., 'The Last of the Steam-powered Trains: Modernising Article 82' [2004] *ECLR* 243

Sidak, J. G, 'Abolishing the Price Squeeze as a Theory of Antitrust Liability' (2008) 4 *J of Competition Law and Economics* 279

Sidak, J. G, and Teece, D. J., 'Dynamic Competition in Antitrust Law' (2009) 5 *J of Competition Law and Economics* 581

Spector, D., 'Loyalty Rebates: An Assessment of Competition Concerns and a Proposed Structured Rule of Reason' (2005) 1 *Competition Policy International* 89

Spector, D., 'From Harm to Competitors to Harm to Competition: One More Effort, Please!' (2006) 2 *European Competition Journal* 145

Subiotto, R., and Little, D., 'The Application of Article 102 TFEU by the European Commission and the European Courts' (2012) 3 *JECLAP* 175

Svetlicinii, A., and Botta, M., 'Article 102 TFEU as a Tool for Market Regulation' (2012) 8 *European Law Journal* 473

Temple Lang, J., 'Defining Legitimate Competition: Companies' Duties to Supply Competitors and Access to Essential Facilities' (1994) 18 *Fordham Int'l LJ* 437

Temple Lang, J., 'The Principle of Essential Facilities in European Community Competition Law—The Position since *Bronner*' (2000) 1 *J of Network Industries* 375

Temple Lang, J., 'Anti-competitive Non-pricing Abuses under European and National Antitrust Law' [2003] *Fordham Corp L Inst* 235

Temple Lang, J., 'Reprisals and Overreaction by Dominant Companies as an Anti-competitive Abuse under Article 82(b)' [2008] *ECLR* 11

Temple Lang, J., 'How Can the Problems of Exclusionary Abuses under Article 102 TFEU be Resolved?' (2012) 37 *ELRev* 136

Temple Lang, J., and O'Donoghue, R., 'Defining Legitimate Competition: How to Clarify Pricing Abuses under Article 102 EC' (2002) 26 *Fordham Int'l LJ* 83

Venit, J., 'Case T-286/09, *Intel v Commission*—The Judgment of the General Court: All Steps Backward and No Steps Forward' (2014) 10 *European Competition Journal* 203

Verhaert, J., 'The Challenges Involved with the Application of Article 102 TFEU to the New Economy: A Case Study of *Google*' [2014] *ECLR* 265

Vesterdorf, B., 'Theories of Self-preferencing and Duty to Deal—Two Sides of the Same Coin?' [2015] 1 *CLPD* 4

Vickers, J., 'Abuse of Market Power' (2005) 115 *Economic Journal* F244

Werden, G., 'Competition Policy on Exclusionary Analysis: Towards an Effects-based Analysis?' (2006) 2 *European Competition Journal* 53

Whinston, M., 'Tying, Foreclosure and Exclusion' (1990) 80 *Am Econ Rev* 837

Whish, R., '*Intel v Commission*: Keep Calm and Carry On!' (2015) 6 *JECLAP* 1

Wils, W., 'The Judgment of the EU General Court in *Intel* and the So-called "More Economic Approach" to Abuse of Dominance' (2014) 37 *World Competition* 405

Zenger, H., 'Loyalty Rebates and the Competitive Process' (2012) 8 *J of Competition Law and Economics* 717

8

COMPETITION, THE STATE, AND PUBLIC UNDERTAKINGS: ARTICLE 106 TFEU

1. CENTRAL ISSUES

1. Article 4(3) TEU contains the principle of Union loyalty. Member States are required to take any appropriate measures to ensure fulfilment of their Union obligations, facilitate the achievement of the Union's tasks, and refrain from any measure that could jeopardise the attainment of the Union's objectives.

2. Article 106 TFEU addresses the application of the competition rules (and other rules of the Treaties) to State measures in respect of public undertakings and to undertakings granted special or exclusive rights, and to undertakings entrusted with services of general economic interest (SGEIs).

3. Article 106(1) is a prohibition addressed to Member States. Its object is to prevent Member States from depriving Treaty rules of their effectiveness by the measures they adopt in respect of public undertakings and those to which they grant special or exclusive rights.

4. The cases show that Article 106(1) is infringed if, in merely exercising the special or exclusive rights, the undertaking cannot avoid abusing its dominant position or if it is thereby led to abuse its dominant position. Some cases, however, have suggested that the very granting of special or exclusive rights is contrary to Article 106(1).

5. SGEIs may be economic or non-economic. Non-economic services are not subject to the competition rules. Economic services are subject to the competition rules. However, Article 106(2) provides a derogation from, inter alia, the competition rules for undertakings entrusted with SGEIs if otherwise they would be obstructed in the performance of their tasks.

6. It may be a crucial factor in the application of Article 106(2) that the undertaking has 'universal service' obligations (USO). Further, it may be important to shield an undertaking from competition so that it can cross-subsidise from profitable sectors to uneconomic ones and competitors cannot come in and 'cherry pick' the profitable parts of the operation.

7. Article 106(3) provides the Commission with special supervisory and policing powers to ensure the application of the Article. It can adopt directives as well as issue decisions.

8. Article 14 TFEU specifically deals with SGEIs. They are also the subject of an article in the Charter of Fundamental Rights and services of general interest are dealt with in a Protocol attached to the TEU and TFEU.

2. INTRODUCTION

In this chapter we discuss how competition law applies to the actions of the State when it intervenes in the market. We look at two matters: first, the obligation on Member States, derived from Article 4(3) TEU, not to adopt or maintain in force measures which could deprive the competition provisions of their effectiveness; and, secondly, the provisions of Article 106 which deal with undertakings to which a Member State has granted special or exclusive rights, and with undertakings entrusted with services of general economic interest (SGEIs). State aid (Articles 107–109) is outside the scope of the printed edition of this book[1] but it is mentioned where it interacts with the issues discussed in this chapter, particularly in respect of SGEIs.

The State plays some part in the marketplace, directly or indirectly, in all the Member States, although the means and extent of this vary. The means and extent have also changed over time since the inception of the EEC. In 1957 there was still a fashion for nationalisation. Since then there has been a move in Europe away from public ownership, and indeed a revolution in the way that public services are delivered.[2] There has been increasing 'marketisation', whereby Member States have turned to the market to provide services to the public, and the distinction between public and private providers has been partly eroded. This is due not only to shifts in ideology but also to technological and economic advances which mean that the arguments for publicly owned monopolies in sectors such as telecommunications and electricity-generation have been transformed.[3] The EU has pursued a programme of liberalisation whereby sectors in which there were formerly State-owned monopolies have been opened up to competition and competition law is employed alongside the liberalising measures to make this effective. Liberalisation, which has been described as inspired as much by the desire to increase the integration of the market as by increasing competition (national monopolies tend to maintain the compartmentalisation of the internal market),[4] has been accompanied by the imposition of public service obligations (PSOs) such as universal service (USO) on undertakings operating on the liberalised market and by the strengthening of consumer and user rights.[5]

The original version of the Treaty of Rome was neutral as between public and private ownership. Article 295 EC[6] stated that the Treaty in no way prejudiced the rules in Member States governing the system of property ownership. That Article, now Article 345 TFEU, is unchanged but it is arguable that the insertion by the TEU (Maastricht) of what is now Article 119 TFEU,[7] represented a shift in policy which favours private over public ownership. Article 119 says that the activities of the Member States and the Union shall be conducted 'in accordance with the principle of an open market economy with free competition'.

The answer to the question as to which, if any, areas of activity the normal principles of competition law should not apply, belongs in the political rather than the legal realm. However, the original Treaty of Rome contained nothing about the limits to competition law and the provision of public

---

[1] See the Online Resource Centre for the State aid chapter. For the interface between State aid and Art. 106, see Section 9.

[2] For an analysis of the development of the law in this area, see L. Hancher, 'Community, State and Market' in P. Craig and G. de Búrca (eds.), *The Evolution of EU Law* (Oxford University Press, 1999), 721 and E. Szyszczak, *The Regulation of the State in Competitive Markets in the EU* (Hart Publishing, 2007). And see generally J. Faull and A. Nikpay (eds.), *The EU Law of Competition* (3rd edn, Oxford University Press, 2014), Chap. 6 (J. L. Buendia Sierra); J. L. Buendia Sierra, *Exclusive Rights and State Monopolies in EC Law* (Oxford University Press, 1999); T. Prosser, *The Limits of Competition Law* (Oxford University Press, 2005).

[3] See G. Amato, *Antitrust and the Bounds of Power: The Dilemma of Liberal Democracy in the History of the Market* (Hart Publishing, 1997), 88–89; E. Szyszczak, 'Public Service Provision in Competitive Markets' (2001) 20 *YEL* 35.

[4] See Hancher, n. 2, 722.

[5] See the Commission's comments on this in the 2007 Communication, para. 2.2 (cited in n. 14).

[6] Ex Art. 222.

[7] Ex Art. 4 EC.

services, save for a provision about State aid in the inland transport sector in respect of 'certain obligations inherent in the concept of a public service' being permitted,[8] and a derogation in what is now Article 106(2)[9] pertaining to 'services of general economic interest' (SGEIs). The 'services of general economic interest' concept was not defined and appeared nowhere else in the Treaty or in secondary legislation. Before 1990[10] the application of competition law to State-owned, State-controlled, or State-privileged undertakings was not a significant issue. It has become so because of technological, ideological, social, and economic changes, the increasing sophistication and reach of EU competition law, and the more aggressive enforcement of the law.

The debate about the relationship between competition law and public services resulted in the introduction into the Treaty of Rome by the Treaty of Amsterdam of what is now (with some modification) Article 14 TFEU,[11] and the inclusion in the Charter of Fundamental Rights of the European Union of Article 36, both of which proclaim the value and importance of 'services of general economic interest'.[12] Protocol No. 26 on 'services of general interest' is attached to the TEU and the TFEU by the Treaty of Lisbon.[13] The Commission has complemented these provisions with a series of Communications on services of general interest,[14] the latest being 'A Quality Framework for Services of General Interest in Europe' in December 2011 (the 2011 Communication).[15]

There are two ways in which the application of EU competition law to public services can be limited. First, the activity can be found not to be 'economic', and therefore not subject to Articles 101 and 102 in the first place. Secondly, it can be found to be economic but allowed to take advantage of a derogation from the rules (in particular, the derogation provided in Article 106(2)).

Whether or not an activity is economic determines whether or not an entity is an 'undertaking' subject to the competition rules, as discussed in Chapter 3.[16] It will be recalled that 'undertaking' is a concept of EU law and that it is immaterial how the entity is regarded in national law. The fundamental question is whether it carries out commercial activities and not whether it is governed by public law or is non-profit-making.[17] It was also seen in Chapter 3 that bodies which exercise public powers which can be seen as part of the prerogatives of the State, such as air traffic control in *Eurocontrol*[18] and the anti-pollution surveillance in *Diego Cali*,[19] are not engaging in activities of an

---

[8] Art. 73 EC, ex Art. 77. The Article was at issue in Case C-280/00, *Altmark Trans GmbH, Regierungspräsidium Magdeburg v Nahverkehrsgesellschaft Altmark GmbH* [2003] ECR I-7747 on whether compensation for services of general economic interest is a State aid: see Section 9, p. 646.

[9] Ex Art. 86(2) EC, ex Art. 90(2).

[10] The early 1990s saw the four major Art. 267 rulings, Case C-41/90, *Höfner v Macrotron* [1991] ECR I-1979; Case C-179/90, *Merci Convenzionali v Porto di Genova* [1991] ECR I-5889; Case C-260/89, *Elliniki Radiophonia Tileorasi (ERT) v DEP* [1991] ECR I-2925; and Case C-18/88, *RTT v GB-Inno-BM SA* [1991] ECR I-5973; and the telecommunications cases between the Commission and Member States, Case C-202/88, *France v Commission* [1991] ECR I-1223 (the *Telecommunications Equipment* case) and Cases C-271, 281, and 289/90, *Spain, Belgium & Italy v Commission* [1992] ECR I-5833 (the *Telecommunications Services* case).

[11] Ex Art. 16 EC, ex Art.7d EC. For the Article and the way in was modified see Section 6.A.i, p. 623.

[12] See Section 6.A.i, p. 623 ff.

[13] See Section 6.A.i, p. 623 ff.

[14] Communication on Services of General Interest in Europe [1996] OJ C281/03; Communication on Services of General Interest [2001] OJ C17/4; Communication on 'Services of General Interest, including Social Services of General Interest: a New European Commitment' accompanying the Communication on 'A Single Market for 21st Century Europe', COM(2007) 725 final. The 2007 Communication followed the Commission's Green and White Papers of 2003 and 2004, COM(2003) 270 final and COM(2004) 374, 12 May 2004 respectively.

[15] Communication from the Commission to the European Parliament, the Council, the European Economic and Social Committee and the Committee of the Regions, COM(2011) 900 final. It was accompanied by a Commission Staff Working Document SEC(2010) 1545 final, since supplemented by another, SWD(2013) 53/final/2.

[16] Chap. 3.5.A.iii, p. 116.

[17] See Case C-41/90, *Höfner v Macrotron* [1991] ECR I-1979.

[18] Case C-364/92, *SAT Fluggesellschaft v Eurocontrol* [1994] ECR I-43, and Case C-113/07, *SELEX Systemi Integrati SpA v Commission*, [2009] ECR I-2207.

[19] Case C-343/95, *Diego Cali v SEPG* [1997] ECR I-1547.

economic nature.[20] Where it has been necessary to determine the status of various types of social security and health insurance funds the EU Courts have used the concept of 'solidarity' to distinguish economic from non-economic activities.[21]

3. ARTICLE 4(3) TEU

Article 4(3) TEU contains the principle of Union loyalty which previously appeared in Article 10 EC.[22] It requires Member States to take any appropriate measures to ensure fulfilment of their obligations under the Treaties or resulting from acts of the institutions; to facilitate the achievement of the Union's tasks; and to refrain from measures which could jeopardise the attainment of the Union's objectives. The CJ held in *Inno v ATAB* that pursuant to this Member States are under a duty not to adopt or maintain in force measures which could deprive the competition provisions of their effectiveness.

Case 13/77, *NV GB-Inno-BM SA v ATAB* [1977] ECR 2115

The CJ was asked by the Belgian Court of Cassation about the compatibility with Community law of Belgian rules prohibiting the sale of tobacco at less than the price fixed by the manufacturers or importers.

Court of Justice

28. First, the single market system which the Treaty seeks to create excludes any national system of regulation hindering directly or indirectly, actually or potentially, trade within the Community.

29. Secondly, the general objective set out in Article [3(1)(g) EC] is made specific in several Treaty provisions concerning the rules on competition, including Article [102], which states that any abuse by one of more undertakings of a dominant position shall be prohibited as incompatible with the Common Market in so far as it may affect trade between Member States.

30. [Article 4(3) TEU] provides that Member States shall abstain from any measure which could jeopardize the attainment of the objectives of the Treaty.

31. Accordingly, while it is true that Article [102] is directed at undertakings, nonetheless it is also true that the Treaty imposes a duty on Member States not to adopt or maintain in force any measure which could deprive that provision of its effectiveness.

32. Thus Article [106] provides that, in the case of public undertakings and undertakings to which Member States grant special or exclusive rights, Member States shall neither enact nor maintain in force any measure contrary, *inter alia*, to the rules provided for in Articles [101 to 109 TFEU].

33. Likewise, Member States may not enact measures enabling private undertakings to escape from the constraints imposed by Articles [101 to 109 TFEU].

34. At all events, Article [102] prohibits any abuse by one or more undertakings of a dominant position, even if such abuse is encouraged by a national legislative provision.

---

[20] Case C-138/11, *Compass-Datenbank GmbH* EU:C:2012:449, para. 36.

[21] See Cases C-159–160/91, *Poucet and Pistre v Assurances Générales de France* [1993] ECR I-637 and the other cases discussed in Chap. 3, Section 5.A.iii.a, p. 118. See N. Boeger, 'Solidarity and EC Competition Law' (2007) 32 *ELRev* 319; A. Winterstein, 'Nailing the Jellyfish: Social Security and Competition Law' [1999] *ECLR* 324.

[22] Previously Art. 5.

> 35. In any case, a national measure which has the effect of facilitating the abuse of a dominant position capable of affecting trade between Member States will generally be incompatible with Articles [34] and [35], which prohibits quantitative restrictions on imports and exports and all measures having equivalent effect.

The effect of Article 4(3) together with Articles 101 and 102 is that a Member State may not require or favour the adoption of agreements, decisions, or concerted practices contrary to Article 101, or conduct contrary to Article 102, or reinforce their effects, and may not deprive its own legislation of its official character by delegating responsibility for taking decisions affecting the economic sphere to private traders.[23]

We saw in Chapter 3 that Article 101 is not applicable to the anti-competitive activities of a firm if the restrictive effects on competition originate solely from the implementation of national law. Undertakings may therefore plead a 'State compulsion' defence and seek to show that their behaviour was not autonomous but dictated by national provisions. The EU Courts have made it clear that such a plea will succeed only if the undertaking had no room for manoeuvre at all.[24] The same situation pertains to Article 102, as illustrated in the margin squeeze cases discussed in Chapter 7.[25]

We also saw in Chapter 3 that there is no agreement between undertakings where the undertakings sit on statutory boards which simply make recommendations.[26] The position on this was illustrated by the *Anonima Petroli* ruling, in which an Italian court asked about the compatibility with Article 4(3) TEU, in conjunction with Article 101,[27] of Italian legislation which provided that the price of haulage services could not be lower than minimum operating costs and ultimately left the fixing of those costs to a body (the Osservatorio) composed of representatives of the State, haulage associations, and customer associations. The CJ looked first at three issues: (a) whether an agreement, decision, or concerted practice between private economic operators existed, or whether the tariffs had the character of legislation; (b) whether the public authorities had delegated their powers to private operators; and (c) whether there was an effect on inter-Member State trade (this point is omitted from the extracts from the judgment below). Interestingly the CJ then considered, (d), whether the restrictions were limited to what was necessary to ensure the implementation of legitimate objectives, i.e. it applied the justification test in *Wouters*,[28] discussed in Chapter 4.

---

[23] Case 267/86, *Van Eycke v ASPA NV* [1988] ECR 4769, para. 16; Cases C-140–142/94, *DIP and Others v Commune di Bassano del Grappa and Commune di Chioggia* [1995] ECR I-3257, para. 15; Case C-266/96, *Corsica Ferries France SA v Gruppo Antichi Ormeggiatori del Porto di Genova* [1998] ECR I-3949, paras. 35, 36, and 49; Cases C-67/96, 115–117/97 and 219/97, *Albany International BV v Stichting Bedrijfspensioenfonds Textielindustrie* [1999] ECR I-5751, para. 65; Case C-202/04, *Cipolla and ors* [2006] ECR I-11421, para. 758; Case C-437/09, *AG2R Prévoyance v Beaudout* [2011] ECR I-973, paras. 24 and 37. It was made clear in Case C-2/91, *Meng* [1993] ECR I-5797, para. 14, Case C-185/91, *Reiff* [1993] ECR I-5847, para. 14, and Case C-245/91, *Ohra* [1993] ECR I-5851 that Art. 4(3) applies in respect of competition only in combination with Art. 101 or Art. 102. The fate of Art. 3(1)(g) EC, referred to in para. 29 of *INNO v ATAB*, under the Treaty of Lisbon (see Chap. 1, Section 8.B.i) appears to have made no difference to the principle established in that case, see Case C-327/12, *Ministero dello Sviluppo Economico v SOA Nazionale Costruttori—Organismo di Attestazione* EU:C:2013:827, para. 37; Case C-184/13, *API-Anonima Petroli Italiana SpA v Ministero delle Infrastrutture e dei Trasporti* EU:C:2014:2147.

[24] See Cases C-359 and 379/95 P, *Commission and France v Ladbroke Racing* [1996] ECR I-6265 and the cases referred to in Chap. 3, Section 5.F.

[25] Case C-280/08 P, *Deutsche Telekom v Commission* [2010] ECR I-9555, paras. 80–85.

[26] Chap. 3, Section 5.B.ii.h, p. 152; see, e.g., Case C-96/94, *Centro Servizi Spediporto Srl v Spedizioni Marittima del Golfo Srl* [1995] ECR I-2883.

[27] And with Arts. 49 and 56 on the free movement of services, and Art. 96 on transport.

[28] Case C-309/99, *Wouters v Algemene Raad van de Nederlandse Orde van Advocaten* [2002] ECR I-1577.

Cases C-184–187, 194, 195, and 208/13, *API-Anonima Petroli Italiana SpA v Ministero delle Infrastrutture e dei Trasporti* EU:C:2014:2147

Court of Justice

28. It should be noted, as is apparent from the Court's settled case-law, that, although it is true that Article 101 TFEU is concerned solely with the conduct of undertakings and not with laws or regulations emanating from Member States, that article, read in conjunction with Article 4(3) TEU, which lays down a duty of cooperation between the European Union and the Member States, none the less requires the latter not to introduce or maintain in force measures, even of a legislative or regulatory nature, which may render ineffective the competition rules applicable to undertakings (see judgments in *Cipolla and Others*, C-94/04 and C-202/04, EU:C:2006:758, paragraph 46, and *Sbarigia*, C-393/08, EU:C:2010:388, paragraph 31).

29. Article 101 TFEU, read in conjunction with Article 4(3) TEU, is infringed where a Member State requires or encourages the adoption of agreements, decisions or concerted practices contrary to Article 101 TFEU or reinforces their effects, or where it divests its own rules of the character of legislation by delegating to private economic operators responsibility for taking decisions affecting the economic sphere (see judgments in *Centro Servizi Spediporto*, C-96/94, EU:C:1995:308, paragraph 21; *Arduino*, C-35/99, EU:C:2002:97, paragraph 35; and *Cipolla and Others*, EU:C:2006:758, paragraph 47).

. . .

32. As regards, in the first place, whether it is possible to conclude on the basis of the legislation at issue in the main proceedings that an agreement, decision or concerted practice exists between private economic operators, it should be noted that the committee which established, in the cases in the main proceedings, the minimum operating costs, namely the Osservatorio, is composed principally of representatives of professional associations of carriers and customers. At the material time in the main proceedings, of the 10 members of the Osservatorio chosen by the President of the Consulta, 8 represented the views of associations of carriers and customers, the decree appointing those members stating moreover that they were appointed 'as representatives' of the association or the undertaking to which they belong.

33. Moreover, decisions of the Osservatorio are approved by a majority of its members, without a State representative having a right of veto or a casting vote which might make it possible to rebalance power between the public authorities and the private sector, unlike the situation at issue in the judgments in *Reiff* (C-185/91, EU:C:1993:886, paragraph 22); *Delta Schiffahrts- und Speditionsgesellschaft* (C-153/93, EU:C:1994:240, paragraph 21); *Centro Servizi Spediporto* (EU:C:1995:308, paragraph 27); and *Librandi* (EU:C:1998:454, paragraph 35).

34. A tariff established by a professional organisation such as the Osservatorio may none the less have the character of legislation, inter alia, where the members of that organisation are experts who are independent of the economic operators concerned and they are required, under the law, to set tariffs taking into account not only the interests of the undertakings or associations of undertakings in the sector which has appointed them but also the public interest and the interests of undertakings in other sectors or users of the services in question (see, to that effect, judgments in *Reiff*, EU:C:1993:886, paragraphs 17 to 19 and 24; *Delta Schiffahrts- und Speditionsgesellschaft*, EU:C:1994:240, paragraphs 16 to 18 and 23; *DIP and Others*, C-140/94 to C-142/94, EU:C:1995:330, paragraphs 18 and 19; *Commission* v *Italy*, C-35/96, EU:C:1998:303, paragraph 44; and *Arduino*, EU:C:2002:97, paragraph 37).

35. However, according to the information in the order for reference, the national legislation establishing the Consulta and the Osservatorio does not indicate the guiding principles which those bodies must observe and does not contain any provision such as to prevent the representatives of the professional organisations from acting in the exclusive interest of the profession.

. . .

38. In those circumstances, the national legislation at issue in the main proceedings does not contain either procedural arrangements or substantive requirements capable of ensuring, that, when establishing minimum operating costs, the Osservatorio conducts itself like an arm of the State working in the public interest.

39. As regards, in the second place, whether the public authorities delegated their powers, in terms of setting tariffs, to private operators, the Court observes that Article 83a(1),(2) and (4a) of amended Decree-Law No 112/2008 merely provides that the Osservatorio 'shall fix' the various types of costs referred to by the national legislation at issue in the main proceedings. It is apparent from the case-file submitted to the Court of Justice that the public authorities do not exercise any review over the assessments of the Osservatorio regarding the criteria for fixing minimum operating costs or the rate set.

40. Similarly, it is not apparent that other bodies or public associations are consulted before those costs are set by decree and brought into force.

41. It follows from the foregoing considerations that, in the light of the composition and the method of operation of the Osservatorio, on the one hand, and of the absence both of any public-interest criteria laid down by law in a manner sufficiently precise to ensure that carriers' and customers' representatives in fact operate in compliance with the general public interest that the law seeks to achieve and of actual review and of the power to adopt decisions in the last resort by the State, on the other, the Osservatorio must be regarded as an association of undertakings within the meaning of Article 101 TFEU when it adopts decisions fixing minimum operating costs for road transport such as those at issue in the main proceedings.

...

46. Lastly, it should however be noted that the legislation at issue in the main proceedings making mandatory a decision of an association of undertakings which has the object or effect of restricting competition or restricting the freedom of action of the parties or of one of them does not necessarily fall within the prohibition laid down in Article 101(1) TFEU, read in conjunction with Article 4(3) TEU.

47. For the purposes of application of that provision to a particular case, account must first of all be taken of the overall context in which a decision of the association of undertakings was taken or produces its effects and, more specifically, of its objectives. It has then to be considered whether the consequential effects restrictive of competition are inherent in the pursuit of those objectives (see judgments in *Wouters and Others*, C-309/99, EU:C:2002:98, paragraph 97, and *Consiglio nazionale dei geologi and Autorità garante della concorrenza e del mercato*, C-136/12, EU:C:2013:489, paragraph 53).

48. In that context, it is important to verify whether the restrictions thus imposed by the rules at issue in the main proceedings are limited to what is necessary to ensure the implementation of legitimate objectives (see, to that effect, judgments in *Meca-Medina and Majcen* v *Commission*, C-519/04 P, EU:C:2006:492, paragraph 47, and *Consiglio nazionale dei geologi and Autorità garante della concorrenza e del mercato*, EU:C:2013:489, paragraph 54).

49. However, without there being any need to consider whether the case-law cited in paragraphs 47 and 48 of this judgment is applicable to national legislation prescribing a horizontal price agreement, it is sufficient to note that the legislation at issue in the main proceedings cannot, in any event, be justified by a legitimate objective.

50. According to Article 83a(4) of amended Decree-Law No 112/2008, the fixing of minimum operating costs is intended to protect, in particular, road safety.

51. Although it cannot be ruled out that the protection of road safety may constitute a legitimate objective, the fixing of minimum operating costs does not appear appropriate, either directly or indirectly, for ensuring that that objective is attained.

52. In that regard, the Court would point out that the legislation at issue in the main proceedings merely refers, in a general manner, to the protection of road safety, without establishing any link whatsoever between the minimum operating costs and the improvement of road safety.

4. ARTICLE 106

The application of EU rules to public undertakings and those granted special or exclusive rights is dealt with in Article 106.[29]

Article 106 states:

1. In the case of public undertakings and undertakings to which Member States grant special or exclusive rights, Member States shall neither enact nor maintain in force any measure contrary to the rules contained in the Treaties, in particular to those rules provided for in Article 18 and Articles 101 to 109.

2. Undertakings entrusted with the operation of services of general economic interest or having the character of a revenue-producing monopoly shall be subject to the rules contained in the Treaties, in particular to the rules on competition, in so far as the application of such rules does not obstruct the performance, in law or in fact, of the particular tasks assigned to them. The development of trade must not be affected to such an extent as would be contrary to the interests of the Union.

3. The Commission shall ensure the application of the provisions of this Article and shall, where necessary, address appropriate directives or decisions to Member States.

A. THE OBJECTIVES OF ARTICLE 106

As will be appreciated from its wording, Article 106 is applied in conjunction with another Article, since its function is to limit the ways in which State measures protecting certain undertakings hinder the operation of the Treaties. Article 106 does not deal only with competition, despite its position in the competition chapter of the TFEU. It deals rather with the application of *all* the rules in the Treaties ('the Treaty rules'), although it mentions in particular the competition rules (Articles 101–109 TFEU) and the prohibition on discrimination on the grounds of nationality (Article 18 TFEU). Article 106 does, however, have particular relevance to the competition provisions and especially Article 102, because public undertakings and undertakings granted special or exclusive rights frequently hold a dominant position.[30]

Article 106 is a specific manifestation of the duty of Union loyalty contained in Article 4(3) TEU.

B. THE FORMAT OF ARTICLE 106

Article 106 contains three interrelated provisions.

(i) Article 106(1): Prohibition Addressed to Member States

The prohibition in Article 106(1) is addressed to Member States, not to undertakings. It prohibits Member States from enacting or maintaining in force any measures in relation to public undertakings and undertakings to which they have granted special or exclusive rights which are contrary to the Treaty rules. It is designed to prevent Member States from depriving the Treaty rules of their effectiveness through the measures they adopt in respect of public undertakings or through measures which enable private undertakings to escape the constraints of the competition provisions. The CJ confirmed in the *Greek Lignite* case, *DEI*, that the provision is applicable to public undertakings on the one hand and to undertakings granted special or exclusive rights on the other. It is not necessary to show that the public undertaking has been granted special or exclusive rights.[31]

---

[29] Ex Art. 86, ex Art. 90.

[30] But not inevitably: the usual criteria of dominance apply, and the exclusive right has to be over a relevant market: see Case 30/87, *Bodson v Pompes Funèbres des Régions Libérées* [1988] ECR 2479, paras. 26–29.

[31] Case C-553/12 P, *Commission v Dimosia Epicheirisi Ilektrismou AE (DEI)* EU:C:2014:2083, paras. 56–58.

(ii) Article 106(2): Provision Addressed to Undertakings Providing for Limited Immunity from the Treaty Rules

Article 106(2) is addressed to the undertakings themselves. It gives a limited derogation from the Treaty rules to 'undertakings entrusted with the operation of services of general economic interest or having the character of a revenue producing monopoly' insofar as that is necessary for the carrying out of their tasks. Despite being addressed to undertakings, Article 106(2) can be invoked by Member States in relation to exclusive rights they have granted.

(iii) Article 106(3): Policing and Legislative Powers of the Commission

Article 106(3) provides that the Commission may address decisions to Member States to ensure the observance of Article 106. This is an expedited enforcement mechanism which does not have to comply with the procedures of the general enforcement provision, Article 258 TFEU, which provides for infraction proceedings brought by the Commission against Member States.

It also gives the Commission power to issue directives to Member States to ensure the application of the Article. The power does not have to be exercised within the detailed procedural framework ordinarily applicable to the adoption of directives, which involves other Union institutions and is set down in Articles 289–297 TFEU.

5. ARTICLE 106(1)

A. DEFINITIONS

When considering Article 106(1) it is first necessary to determine the meaning of the concepts it employs, in particular the terms 'public undertakings', 'granted special or exclusive rights', and 'measures'.

(i) 'Public Undertakings'

Determining the meaning of 'public undertakings' is a two-step procedure. First, one must ask whether a particular body is an 'undertaking' and secondly, if it is, whether it is a 'public' undertaking.

The answer to the first question, what constitutes an undertaking, has already been considered in the context of Articles 101 and 102[32] and recalled in Section 2.[33] The second question is whether an undertaking is a 'public' undertaking. Again, this is a Union concept[34] because Article 106(1) would be deprived of its effect if Member States were free to choose their own conception of 'public undertaking'. State participation in the ownership or running of undertakings comes in an almost indefinite range of guises and the Union concept must embrace them all.

The concept of a 'public undertaking' is defined Article 2(b) of the Transparency Directive:[35]

'public undertakings' means any undertaking over which the public authorities may exercise directly or indirectly a dominant influence by virtue of their ownership of it, their financial participation therein or the rules

---

[32] Chap. 3.5.A and Chap. 5.5.A.

[33] See p. 589.

[34] See Cases 188–190/88, *Transparency Directive* [1982] ECR 2545, Reischl AG, para. 9.

[35] Now Commission Directive 2006/111/EC on the transparency of financial relations between Member States and public undertakings as well as on financial transparency within certain undertakings [2006] OJ L318/17 (codifying Commission Dir. 80/723 [1980] OJ L195/35 and its subsequent modifications).

which govern it. A dominant influence on the part of the public authorities shall be presumed when these authorities, directly or indirectly in relation to an undertaking:

(i) hold the major part of the undertaking's subscribed capital: or

(ii) control the majority of votes attaching to shares issued by the undertakings; or

(iii) can appoint more than half of the members of the undertaking's administrative, managerial or supervisory body.

The key to the concept is therefore control by the State. This can be through ownership or through some contractual, financial, or structural connection between the State and the undertaking. In *Greek Lignite*, for example, the Commission held that the former legal electricity monopoly company in Greece was a public undertaking as 51 per cent of the voting stock was held by the State.[36]

(ii) Undertakings Granted Special or Exclusive Rights

Special or exclusive rights may be granted in the whole of a national territory or in only part of it.[37] Difficulties have arisen over the definition of 'special and exclusive rights'. Two categories are involved here: 'special' and 'exclusive' are not synonymous. Entities with such rights may or may not be public undertakings.

Exclusive rights are the most easily identified. They exist where a monopoly has been granted by the State to one entity to engage in a particular economic activity on an exclusive basis. They have been held to have been conferred, for example, upon broadcasting monopolies,[38] and upon undertakings granted the sole right to operate employment recruitment services,[39] the sole right to operate on a particular air route,[40] the sole right to supply unloading services at a port,[41] the sole right to provide bovine insemination services,[42] the exclusive right to receive and manage the contributions made under a compulsory social insurance scheme,[43] and the exclusive right to manage copyright relating to a certain category of works.[44] The rights granted to the television duopoly in the Greek television case, *ERT*,[45] were designated as 'special or exclusive'. Rather strangely, however, the CJ described the three firms who were entitled to collect waste for recycling in Copenhagen, as holding 'exclusive' rights.[46] It is important to note that the grant of intellectual property rights does not entail the granting of exclusive rights for the purposes of Article 106(1) because it involves laws which lay down criteria which any undertaking is free to satisfy: there is no question of a closed class.[47]

---

[36] COMP/38.700, *Greek Lignite and Electricity Markets* 5 March 2008, para. 5, the point was not taken on appeal. The State's holding could never fall below 51%.

[37] E.g., Case 30/87, *Bodson* [1988] ECR 2479 (funeral services in particular French communes); Case C-179/90, *Merci Convenzionali* [1991] ECR I-5889 (unloading services in the port of Genoa); Case C-323/93, *Société Civile Agricole du Centre d'Insémination de la Crespelle v Coopérative d'Elevage et d'Insémination Artificielle du Département de la Mayenne (Crespelle)* [1994] ECR I-5077 (exclusive rights to provide bovine insemination services in defined areas of France).

[38] Case 155/73, *Sacchi* [1974] ECR 409.

[39] Case C-41/90, *Höfner v Macrotron* [1991] ECR I-1979.

[40] Case 66/86, *Ahmed Saeed Flugreisen and Silver Line Reiseburo GmbH v Zentrale zur Bëkampfung Unlauteren Wettwerbs eV* [1989] ECR 803; *Sterling Airways/SAS Denmark*, Commission's *Xth Report on Competition Policy* (1980), paras. 136–138.

[41] Case C-179/90, *Merci Convenzionali* [1991] ECR I-5889.

[42] Case C-323/93, *Crespelle* [1994] ECR I-5077.

[43] Case C-437/09, *AG2R Prévoyance v Beaudout* [2011] ECR I-973.

[44] Case C-351/12, *OSA—Ochranný svaz autorský pro práva k dílům hudebním o.s. v Léčebné lázně Mariánské Lázně a.s.* EU:C:2014:110, para. 82.

[45] Case C-260/89, *ERT* [1991] ECR I-2925.

[46] Case C-209/98, *Entreprenørforeningens Affalds (FFAD), acting for Sydhavnens Sten and Grus ApS v Københavns Kommune (Sydhavnens)* [2000] ECR I-3743.

[47] See also Case C-327/12, *Ministero dello Sviluppo Economico v SOA Nazionale Costruttori—Organismo di Attestazione* EU:C:2013:827, where anybody who satisfied the relevant conditions could become a certification body.

What amounts to 'special rights' has been defined by the CJ as a result of a series of challenges brought by Member States to directives issued by the Commission under Article 106(3) in pursuance of its objective to liberalise the telecommunications market. This liberalisation inevitably meant ensuring the removal of the protection hitherto given by Member States to national telecommunications operators.

France v Commission, the *Telecommunications Equipment* case,[48] concerned the challenge by France to Directive 88/301 on competition in the markets in telecommunications terminal equipment.[49] According to Article 2, Member States which had granted special or exclusive rights to undertakings for the importation, marketing, connection, bringing into service of telecommunications terminal equipment, and/or maintenance of such equipment were to ensure that those rights were withdrawn. The CJ held that Article 2 was void insofar as it concerned the withdrawal of *special* rights because:

45. . . . neither the provisions of the directive nor the preamble thereto specify the type of rights which are actually involved and in what respect the existence of such rights is contrary to the various provisions of the Treaty.

46. It follows that the Commission has failed to justify the obligation to withdraw special rights regarding the importation, marketing, connection, bringing into service and/or maintenance of telecommunications terminal equipment.

The *Telecommunications Services*[50] case concerned a similar challenge by Spain, Belgium, and Italy to Directive 90/388 on competition in the markets for telecommunications services.[51] Again the CJ annulled the provisions concerning the requirement to withdraw all special rights. In this directive the Commission had defined 'special or exclusive rights' in Article 1 as being 'rights granted by a Member State or a public authority to one or more private or public bodies through any legal, regulatory or administrative instrument reserving them the right to provide a service or undertake an activity'. The CJ held that this was inadequate as it did not make it possible 'to determine the type of special rights with which the directive is concerned or in what respect the existence of those rights is contrary to the various provisions of the Treaty'.[52]

As a result of these cases, the Commission set out an extended definition of the meaning of 'special rights' in the field of telecommunications in the Preamble to Directive 94/46.[53] A special right is:

granted by a Member State to a limited number of undertakings through any legislative, regulatory or administrative instruments which, within a given geographical area, limits to two or more, otherwise than according to objective, proportional and non-discriminatory criteria, the number of undertakings which are authorised to provide any such service, or designates, otherwise than according to such criteria, several competing undertakings, as those which are authorised to provide any such service, or confers on any undertaking or undertakings otherwise than according to such criteria, legal or regulatory advantages which substantially affect the ability of any other undertaking to provide that same telecommunications service in the same geographical area under substantially equivalent conditions.

This definition can be taken as generally applicable.[54] It identifies as 'special rights' those which are given by the State to a limited number of undertakings chosen in a subjective and discretionary manner.[55] In *Ambulanz Glöckner* the CJ referred to a special or exclusive right existing where 'protection is conferred by a legislative measure on a limited number of undertakings which may

---

[48] Case C-202/88, [1991] ECR I-1223.

[49] [1988] OJ L131/73.

[50] Cases C-271, 281, and 289/90, [1992] ECR I-5833.

[51] [1990] OJ L192/10.

[52] [1992] ECR I-5833, para. 31.

[53] Now Dir. 2002/77/EC [2002] OJ L249/21, Art. 1(6).

[54] There is a similar definition in Dir. 2006/111/EC, n. 35, Art. 2(g).

[55] See also the Commission's statement at the hearing in the *Telecommunications Services* case, Cases C-271, 281, and 289/90, [1992] ECR I-5833, quoted by Jacobs AG, para. 50.

substantially affect the ability of other undertakings to exercise the economic activity in question in the same geographical area under substantially equivalent conditions'.[56]

In *Inno v ATAB* the CJ doubted whether special or exclusive rights could result from allowing manufacturers and importers of a particular product to impose resale price maintenance.[57] In *Banchero*[58] it held that Italian laws on the distribution of tobacco did not entail special or exclusive rights as, although they governed access to the market, all undertakings were treated in the same way. Further, in *GEMA*[59] the Commission held that an authors' rights society did not enjoy special or exclusive rights even though legislation required authors to exercise their rights through such a society, because there was no limit on the number of rights societies which could exist.[60] As with exclusive rights, special rights involve the creation of some sort of limited, closed class. In *UEFA*[61] the GC dismissed the claim that the designation by the UK of the European Football Championship final stages as of major importance to society[62] meant that those broadcasters (the BBC and ITV) who were prepared to take non-exclusive broadcasts were thereby given special or exclusive rights within Article 106(1). It was open to all broadcasters to acquire the rights and the only reason that the pay-TV companies were uninterested in doing so was that their business model required exclusivity.

(iii) 'Measures'

The word 'measures' also appears in Article 4 TEU which obliges Member States to fulfil their Treaty obligations and not to jeopardise the objectives of the Treaties, and in Article 34 TFEU which prohibits, inter alia, measures having an equivalent effect to quantitative restrictions on imports between Member States.[63] 'Measures' must emanate from a branch of the public administration acting as a public authority. It does not include the actions of private undertakings, rather than the State actions which allow or authorise them, so that anti-competitive conduct engaged in by undertakings on their own initiative must be dealt with by Articles 101 and 102.[64] It is possible, however, that an exclusive or special right could be granted by a public authority through a private law contract which had a regulatory effect.[65]

B. MEASURES WHICH ARE FORBIDDEN BY ARTICLE 106(1)

(i) Introduction

There is some uncertainty about what measures violate Article 106(1). In some cases there is clearly a violation of Article 106(1) in that some aspect of the State's arrangements inherently infringes a Treaty rule in itself. A good example, which does not involve the competition rules, is

---

[56] Case C-475/99, *Ambulanz Glöckner v Landkreis Südwestpfalz* [2001] ECR I-8089, para. 24; see also Case C-351/12, *OSA* EU:C:2014:110, para. 82.

[57] Case 13/77, [1977] ECR 2115: the point did not actually have to be answered because of the reply given to an earlier question.

[58] Case C-387/93, *Banchero* [1995] ECR I-4663.

[59] [1971] OJ L134/15.

[60] See also Case C-327/12, *Ministero dello Sviluppo Economico v SOA Nazionale Costruttori—Organismo di Attestazione* EU:C:2013:827 where any undertaking that satisfied certain conditions could become an attestation organisation.

[61] Case T-55/08, *UEFA v Commission* [2011] ECR II-271, aff'd Cases C-201, 204, and 205/11 P, *UEFA and FIFA v Commission* EU:C:2013:519.

[62] Pursuant to Dir. 89/552/EEC [1989] OJ L298/23 as amended.

[63] See Dir. 70/50 [1970] OJ Spec. Ed. 17 on the abolition of measures which have an effect equivalent to quantitative restrictions on imports and are not covered by other provisions, which defined measures as 'laws, regulations, administrative provisions, administrative practices, and all instruments issued from a public authority, including recommendations'.

[64] Case C-202/88, *France v Commission* [1991] ECR I-1223, para. 55.

[65] See Faull and Nikpay, n. 2, 6.34.

Merci Convenzionali,[66] where Italian laws reserved the loading and unloading of ships at an Italian port to certain dock-work companies whose worker-members had to be of Italian nationality. This infringed what is now Article 45 TFEU[67] on the free movement of workers, which specifically applies the prohibition of nationality discrimination in situations governed by Union law.[68] In other cases the measures taken by the Member State *result in* violations of the Treaties. The problem is that where the measures result in violations of the competition rules there are suggestions in some cases that the very fact of granting monopoly rights may itself be a violation. If this is so, the neutrality as to the organisation of economic activities within the Member States discussed at the beginning of the chapter is seriously eroded and the right of Member States to make certain economic choices is limited.

It has been clear since the *Telecommunications Equipment* case in 1991 that Member States do not have unassailable rights to create legal monopolies under any conditions they choose.

Case C-202/88, *France v Commission* [1991] ECR I-1223

France challenged the Telecommunications Terminal Equipment Directive, 88/301, *inter alia*, on the grounds that the Commission had no competence to adopt it on the basis of Article 106(3). France claimed that Article 106 did not allow the Commission to interfere with the granting of special or exclusive rights by Member States because Article 106(1) presupposed the existence of special or exclusive rights so the granting of such rights could not itself constitute a 'measure' within the Article.

Court of Justice

21. . . . [I]t must be held in the first place that the supervisory power conferred on the Commission includes the possibility of specifying, pursuant to Article [106(3)], obligations arising under the Treaty. The extent of that power therefore depends on the scope of the rules with which compliance is to be ensured.

22. Next, it should be noted that even though that article presupposes the existence of undertakings which have certain special or exclusive rights, it does not follow that all the special or exclusive rights are necessarily compatible with the Treaty. That depends on different rules, to which Article [106(1)] refers.

. . .

51. It should be observed that a system of undistorted competition, as laid down in the Treaty, can be guaranteed only if equality of opportunity is secured as between the various economic operators. To entrust an undertaking which markets terminal equipment with the task of drawing up the specifications for such equipment, monitoring their application and granting type-approval in respect thereof is tantamount to conferring upon it the power to determine at will which terminal equipment may be connected to the public network, and thereby placing that undertaking at an obvious advantage over its competitors.

52 Consequently, the Commission was justified in seeking to entrust responsibility for drawing up technical specifications, monitoring their application and granting type-approval to a body independent of public or private undertakings offering competing goods and/or services in the telecommunications sector.

In this judgment the CJ introduced the concept of 'equality of opportunity', which has played an important role in subsequent cases. This could not be guaranteed if the undertaking given the task of controlling specifications and issuing type approval certificates in respect of telecommunications

---

[66] Case C-179/90, *Merci Convenzionali* [1991] ECR I-5889.

[67] Then Art. 48 EC.

[68] Then Art. 7 EC, now Art. 18 TFEU; Case C-179/90, *Merci Convenzionali* [1991] ECR I-5889, paras. 10–13.

equipment also marketed that equipment itself, in competition with the other suppliers it was overseeing.

As Edward and Hoskins[69] say:

It follows from *France* v. *Commission* that Member States have not retained complete sovereignty in relation to the creation of legal monopolies. Rather, the creation of such monopolies must be balanced with the principle of free competition.

It is therefore a question of examining the cases to determine how that balance is struck. The principles are not easy to discern. There has to be some link between the State measures and the abuse. However, the cases are inconsistent and difficult to categorise. We therefore look first at the main cases chronologically to see how the law has developed and then see what, if any, conclusions can be drawn from them.

(ii) *Höfner v Macrotron*

Case C-41/90, *Höfner v Macrotron* [1991] ECR I-1979

The reference arose from an action in a German court between a company and the recruitment consultants it had employed to find it a sales director. In a dispute about fees the company claimed that the contract between the parties was void as it infringed the German law on the promotion of employment, the Arbeitsförderungsgesetz (the AFG). The AFG conferred on the Bundesanstalt, the Federal Office for Employment, the exclusive right to put prospective employees and employers in contact with one another. Nevertheless, to some extent the Bundesanstalt tolerated the existence and activities of independent recruitment consultants and it appeared that the Bundesanstalt was unable, on its own, to meet the demand for executive recruitment. The questions referred by the Oberlandesgericht raised the issue of whether there was an abuse of a dominant position involved and whether Article 106(1) was infringed by the exclusive rights. The Court first held that the Bundesanstalt was an undertaking for the purposes of Articles 102 and 106.[70] It then considered the possible infringements.

Court of Justice

24. It must be pointed out that a public employment agency which is entrusted, under the legislation of a Member State, with the operation of services of general economic interest, such as those envisaged in Article 3 of the AFG, remains subject to the competition rules pursuant to Article [106(2)] unless and to the extent to which it is shown that their application is incompatible with the discharge of its duties (see judgment in Case 155/73 *Sacchi* . . .).

25. As regards the manner in which a public employment agency enjoying an exclusive right of employment procurement conducts itself in relation to executive recruitment undertaken by private recruitment consultancy companies, it must be stated that the application of Article [102] cannot obstruct the performance of the particular task assigned to that agency in so far as the latter is manifestly not in a position to satisfy demand in that area of the market and in fact allows its exclusive rights to be encroached on by those companies.

26. Whilst it is true that Article [102] concerns undertakings and may be applied within the limits laid down by Article [106(2)] to public undertakings or undertakings vested with exclusive rights, or specific rights, the fact nevertheless remains that the Treaty requires the Member States not to take or maintain in force measures which could destroy the effectiveness of that provision (see judgment in Case 13/77

---

[69] D. Edward and M. Hoskins, 'Art. 90: Deregulation and EC Law. Reflections Arising from the XVI FIDE Conference' (1995) 32 *CMLRev* 157, 160.

[70] See Chap. 3, Section 5.A.iii, p.118.

GB-Inno-BM . . . paragraphs 31 and 32). Article [106(1)] in fact provides that the Member States are not to enact or maintain in force, in the case of public undertakings and the undertakings to which they grant special or exclusive rights, any measure contrary to the rules contained in the Treaty, in particular those provided for in Articles [101] to [109].

27. Consequently, any measure adopted by a Member State which maintains in force a statutory provision that creates a situation in which a public employment agency cannot avoid infringing Article [102] is incompatible with the rules of the Treaty.

28. It must be remembered, first, that an undertaking vested with a legal monopoly may be regarded as occupying a dominant position within the meaning of Article [102] of the Treaty (see judgment in Case 311/84 *CBEM*, [1985] ECR 3261) and that the territory of a Member State, to which that monopoly extends, may constitute a substantial part of the common market (judgment in Case C 322/81 *Michelin* . . . paragraph 28).

29. Secondly, the simple fact of creating a dominant position of that kind by granting an exclusive right within the meaning of Article [106(1)] is not as such incompatible with Article [102] (see Case 311/84 *CBEM*, above, paragraph 17). A Member State is in breach of the prohibition contained in those two provisions only if the undertaking in question, merely by exercising the exclusive right granted to it, cannot avoid abusing its dominant position.

30. Pursuant to Article [102(b)], such an abuse may in particular consist in limiting the provision of a service, to the prejudice of those seeking to avail themselves of it.

31. A Member State creates a situation in which the provision of a service is limited when the undertaking to which it grants an exclusive right extending to executive recruitment activities is manifestly not in a position to satisfy the demand prevailing on the market for activities of that kind and when the effective pursuit of such activities by private companies is rendered impossible by the maintenance in force of a statutory provision under which such activities are prohibited and non-observance of that prohibition renders the contracts concerned void.

32. It must be observed, thirdly, that the responsibility imposed on a Member State by virtue of Articles [102 and [106(1)] is engaged only if the abusive conduct on the part of the agency concerned is liable to affect trade between Member States. That does not mean that the abusive conduct in question must actually have affected such trade. It is sufficient to establish that the conduct is capable of having such an effect (see Case 322/81 *Michelin*, above, paragraph 104).

33. A potential effect of that kind on trade between Member States arises in particular where executive recruitment by private companies may extend to the nationals or to the territory of other Member States.

34. In view of the foregoing considerations, it must be stated in reply to the fourth question that a public employment agency engaged in employment procurement activities is subject to the prohibition contained in Article [102], so long as the application of that provision does not obstruct the performance of the particular task assigned to it. A Member State which has conferred an exclusive right to carry on that activity upon the public employment agency is in breach of Article [106(1)] where it creates a situation in which that agency cannot avoid infringing Article [102]. That is the case, in particular, where the following conditions are satisfied:

- the exclusive right extends to executive recruitment activities;
- the public employment agency is manifestly incapable of satisfying demand prevailing on the market for such activities;
- the actual pursuit of those activities by private recruitment consultants is rendered impossible by the maintenance in force of a statutory provision under which such activities are prohibited and non-observance of that prohibition renders the contracts concerned void;
- the activities in question may extend to the nationals or to the territory of other Member States.

In *Höfner v Macrotron* the CJ said (at paragraph 29) that the fact of creating a dominant position by granting exclusive rights is not as such incompatible with the Treaties. However, a Member State will infringe if the undertaking in question, *merely by exercising the exclusive right granted to it, cannot avoid* abusing its dominant position. In this case the criterion was fulfilled as German law had given the undertaking a monopoly over executive recruitment services, the demand for which it was incapable of satisfying. Such limitation of the service offered to customers constituted an abuse under Article 102(b), and so the Member State had created a situation in which the agency could not avoid infringing the Article.[71] This was reiterated in *Job Centre* where Italian law gave public place-ment offices a monopoly to act as employment intermediaries. Again, the statutory monopolist was unlikely to be able to satisfy the demand on the employment market for recruitment services. The Member State had therefore created a situation in which the provision of a service was limited, contrary to Article 102(b).[72]

(iii) ERT v DEP

In its ruling in *ERT*, given eight weeks after that in *Höfner v Macrotron*, the Court did not talk of the abuse being unavoidable but of the exclusive rights being liable to create a situation where the undertaking is *led to infringe* Article 102.

Case C-260/89, *Elliniki Radiophonia Tileorassi Anonimi Etaira (ERT) v Dimotiki Etairia Pliroforissis (DEP)* [1991] ECR I-2925

The Thessaloniki Regional Court referred to the CJ under Article 267 various questions concerning the position of the Greek radio and television undertaking (ERT) to which the Greek Government had granted exclusive rights in regard to the original broadcasting and retransmitting of programmes in Greece. Greek law prohibited any person from engaging in activities for which ERT had an exclusive right without ERT's authorisation. The Mayor of Thessaloniki and a municipal company, DEP, set up a televi-sion station and began to broadcast television programmes. ERT sought an injunction and the seizure of the new station's technical equipment.

Court of Justice

10. In Case C-155/73 *Sacchi* . . . paragraph 14, the Court held that nothing in the Treaty prevents Member States, for considerations of a non-economic nature relating to the public interest, from removing radio and television broadcasts from the field of competition by conferring on one or more establishments an exclusive right to carry them out.

11. Nevertheless, it follows from Article [106(1) and (2)] that the manner in which the monopoly is or-ganized or exercised may infringe the rules of the Treaty, in particular those relating to the free movement of goods, the freedom to provide services and the rules on competition.

12. The reply to the national court must therefore be that Community law does not prevent the grant-ing of a television monopoly for considerations of a non-economic nature relating to the public interest. However, the manner in which such a monopoly is organized and exercised must not infringe the provi-sions of the Treaty on the free movement of goods and services or the rules on competition.

. . .

27. As a preliminary point, it should be observed that Article [3(1)(g)] of the Treaty states only one objective for the Community which is given specific expression in several provisions of the Treaty relating to the rules on competition, including in particular Articles [101], [102] and [106].

---

[71] See para. 27 of the judgment.

[72] Case C-55/96, *Job Centre Coop arl* [1997] ECR I-7119. The Commission came to a similar conclusion in *Spanish Courier Services* [1990] OJ L233/19 (courier services reserved to Post Office which could not offer complete services). For inefficiency and the limitation of production and services as an abuse, see Chap. 7.

28. The independent conduct of an undertaking must be considered with regard to the provisions of the Treaty applicable to undertakings, such as, in particular, Articles [101], [102] and [106(2)].

29. As regards Article [101], it is sufficient to observe that it applies, according to its own terms, to agreements 'between undertakings'. There is nothing in the judgment making the reference to suggest the existence of any agreement between undertakings. There is therefore no need to interpret that provision.

30. Article [102] declares that any abuse of a dominant position within the common market or in any substantial part of it is prohibited as incompatible with the common market in so far as it may affect trade between Member States.

31. In that respect it should be borne in mind that an undertaking which has a statutory monopoly may be regarded as having a dominant position within the meaning of Article [102] (see the judgment in Case C-311/84 *CBEM* v. *CLT and IBP* . . . paragraph 16) and that the territory of a Member State over which the monopoly extends may constitute a substantial part of the common market (see the judgment in Case C-322/81 *Michelin* v. *Commission* . . . paragraph 28).

32. Although Article [102] does not prohibit monopolies as such, it nevertheless prohibits their abuse. For that purpose Article [102] lists a number of abusive practices by way of example.

33. In that regard it should be observed that, according to Article [106(2)], undertakings entrusted with the operation of services of general economic interest are subject to the rules on competition so long as it is not shown that the application of those rules is incompatible with the performance of their particular task (see in particular, the judgment in *Sacchi*, cited above, paragraph 15).

34. Accordingly it is for the national court to determine whether the practices of such an undertaking are compatible with Article [102] and to verify whether those practices, if they are contrary to that provision, may be justified by the needs of the particular task with which the undertaking may have been entrusted.

35. As regards State measures, and more specifically the grant of exclusive rights, it should be pointed out that while Articles [101] and [102] are directed exclusively to undertakings, the Treaty none the less requires the Member States not to adopt or maintain in force any measure which could deprive those provisions of their effectiveness (see the judgment in Case C-13/77 *Inno* v. *ATAB* . . . paragraphs 31 and 32).

36. Article [106(1)] thus provides that, in the case of undertakings to which Member States grant special or exclusive rights, Member States are neither to enact nor to maintain in force any measure contrary to the rules contained in the Treaty.

37. In that respect it should be observed that Article [106(1)] prohibits the granting of an exclusive right to retransmit television broadcasts to an undertaking which has an exclusive right to transmit broadcasts, where those rights are liable to create a situation in which that undertaking is led to infringe Article [102] by virtue of a discriminatory broadcasting policy which favours its own programmes.

38. The reply to the national court must therefore be that Article [106(1)] prohibits the granting of an exclusive right to transmit and an exclusive right to retransmit television broadcasts to a single undertaking, where those rights are liable to create a situation in which that undertaking is led to infringe Article [102] by virtue of a discriminatory broadcasting policy which favours its own programmes, unless the application of Article [102] obstructs the performance of the particular tasks entrusted to it.

In this case the CJ said that the Treaty did not prevent the granting of a monopoly (*in casu* a television monopoly) but stressed, as it had in *Inno v ATAB*,[73] that Member States are prohibited from adopting measures which deprive the competition rules of their effectiveness. This means that the manner in which the monopoly is organised may infringe the competition rules (paragraph 11). The Court therefore concluded that the rules did prohibit the granting of an exclusive right to retransmit TV

---

[73] Case 13/77, *NV GB-Inno-BM* [1977] ECR 2115.

broadcasts to an undertaking which has exclusive rights to transmit broadcasts where those rights *are liable to create a situation in which that undertaking is led* to infringe Article 102 by virtue of a discriminatory broadcasting policy which favours its own programmes (paragraphs 37 and 38). In *ERT* the cumulation of rights in the hands of the monopolist did not result in an unavoidable infringement of Article 102 but did result in a situation where the monopolist was perceived as being led to infringe because it would inevitably discriminate in favour of retransmitting its own programmes rather than those of anyone else. There was no evidence that ERT had done this. The Court was concerned with the possibility of an abuse.

(iv) *Merci Convenzionali*

In the next case, *Merci Convenzionali*, six months later, the Court talked of the exclusive rights *inducing* an abuse.

Case C-179/90, *Merci Convenzionali Porto di Genova v Siderurgica Gabrielli SpA* [1991] ECR I-5889

By Italian law Merci had the exclusive right to organise the loading, unloading, and other handling of goods within the Port of Genoa through a dock-work company. There was a delay in unloading Siderurgica's ship, caused in particular by the dock-work company's workers being on strike. The exclusive rights meant that the vessel's crew were not able to do the work themselves. Siderurgica demanded compensation for the damage it suffered due to the delay and the reimbursement of the charges it had paid to Merci, which it claimed were unfair given the service it had received, or rather, not received. The Tribunale di Genoa made an Article 267 reference, asking, inter alia, whether Article 106(1) in conjunction with Article 102 precluded the Italian rules. The CJ confirmed in paragraph 14 that an undertaking with a statutory monopoly over a substantial part of the common market could be regarded as having a dominant position within Article 102.

Court of Justice

16. It should next be stated that the simple fact of creating a dominant position by granting exclusive rights within the meaning of Article [106(1)] is not as such incompatible with Article [102].

17. However, the Court has had occasion to state, in this respect, that a Member State is in breach of the prohibitions contained in those two provisions if the undertaking in question, merely by exercising the exclusive rights granted to it, cannot avoid abusing its dominant position (see the judgment in Case C-41/90 *Höfner*, cited above, paragraph 29) or when such rights are liable to create a situation in which that undertaking is induced to commit such abuses (see the judgment in Case C-260/89 *ERT*, cited above, paragraph 37).

18. According to subparagraphs (a), (b) and (c) of the second paragraph of Article [102], such abuse may in particular consist in imposing on the persons requiring the services in question unfair purchase prices or other unfair trading conditions, in limiting technical development, to the prejudice of consumers, or in the application of dissimilar conditions to equivalent transactions with other trading parties.

19. In that respect it appears from the circumstances described by the national court and discussed before the Court of Justice that the undertakings enjoying exclusive rights in accordance with the procedures laid down by the national rules in question are, as a result, induced either to demand payment for services which have not been requested, to charge disproportionate prices, to refuse to have recourse to modern technology, which involves an increase in the cost of the operations and a prolongation of the time required for their performance, or to grant price reductions to certain consumers and at the same time to offset such reductions by an increase in the charges to other consumers.

20. In these circumstances it must be held that a Member State creates a situation contrary to Article [102] where it adopts rules of such a kind as those at issue before the national court, which are capable of affecting trade between Member States as in the case of the main proceedings, regard being had to the factors mentioned in paragraph 15 of this judgment relating to the importance of traffic in the Port of Genoa.

In this judgment the CJ cited *ERT* for the proposition that a Member State infringes Article 102 where it grants rights which are liable to *induce* the undertaking to commit abuses (paragraphs 17 and 19). The abuses were unfair payment demands and prices (Article 102(a)), inefficiency (Article 102(b)), and discrimination between customers (Article 102(c)). So we reach the position that although, as the Court said in *Merci* (paragraph 16), the simple fact of creating a dominant position by granting exclusive rights is not incompatible with Article 106(1), the granting of rights which induce or lead to the undertakings committing abuses *is* incompatible.[74]

(v) *RTT v GB-Inno-BM*

The *GB-Inno-BM* ruling, three days after *Merci*, involved the cumulation of rights in the hands of one undertaking. This was similar to *ERT*.

Case C-18/88, *RTT v GB-Inno-BM SA* [1991] ECR I-5973

Under Belgian law RRT held a monopoly over the establishment and operation of the public telephone system. The law also provided that only equipment supplied by RTT or approved by it could be connected to its network. GB-Inno sold in its shops telephones which had not been approved by RTT. RTT brought proceedings in the Commercial Court for an order that GB-Inno should not sell telephones without informing the purchasers that they were not approved. The Commercial Court asked the Court, inter alia, whether a Member State was precluded from granting to the company operating the public telephone network the power to lay down the standards for telephone equipment and to check that economic operators meet those standards when it is competing with those operators on the market for terminals.

Court of Justice

15. Under Belgian law, the RTT holds a monopoly for the establishment and operation of the public telecommunications network. Moreover, only equipment supplied by the RTT or approved by it can be connected to the network. The RTT thus has the power to grant or withhold authorization to connect telephone equipment to the network, the power to lay down the technical standards to be met by that equipment, and the power to check whether the equipment not produced by it is in conformity with the specifications that it has laid down.

16. At the present stage of development of the Community, that monopoly, which is intended to make a public telephone network available to users, constitutes a service of general economic interest within the meaning of Article [106(2)].

17. The Court has consistently held that an undertaking vested with a legal monopoly may be regarded as occupying a dominant position within the meaning of Article [102] and that the territory of a Member State to which that monopoly extends may constitute a substantial part of the common market (judgments in Case C-41/90 *Höfner* . . . paragraph 28, and in Case C-260/89 *ERT* . . . paragraph 31).

---

[74] See also Case C-18/93, *Corsica Ferries Italia Srl v Corpo dei Piloti del Porto di Genova* [1994] ECR I-1783.

18. The Court has also held that an abuse within the meaning of Article [102] is committed where, without any objective necessity, an undertaking holding a dominant position on a particular market reserves to itself an ancillary activity which might be carried out by another undertaking as part of its activities on a neighbouring but separate market, with the possibility of eliminating all competition from such undertaking (judgment in Case 311/84 *CBEM* . . .).

19. Therefore the fact that an undertaking holding a monopoly in the market for the establishment and operation of the network, without any objective necessity, reserves to itself a neighbouring but separate market, in this case the market for the importation, marketing, connection, commissioning and maintenance of equipment for connection to the said network, thereby eliminating all competition from other undertakings, constitutes an infringement of Article [102].

20. However, Article [102] applies only to anti-competitive conduct engaged in by undertakings on their own initiative (see judgment in Case C-202/88 *France* v. *Commission* 'Telecommunications terminals' . . .), not to measures adopted by States. As regards measures adopted by States, it is Article [106(1)] that applies. Under that provision, Member States must not, by laws, regulations or administrative measures, put public undertakings and undertakings to which they grant special or exclusive rights in a position which the said undertakings could not themselves attain by their own conduct without infringing Article [102].

21. Accordingly, where the extension of the dominant position of a public undertaking or undertaking to which the State has granted special or exclusive rights results from a State measure, such a measure constitutes an infringement of Article [106] in conjunction with Article [102].

22. The exclusion or the restriction of competition on the market in telephone equipment cannot be regarded as justified by a task of a public service of general economic interest within the meaning of Article [106(2)]. The production and sale of terminals, and in particular of telephones, is an activity that should be open to any undertaking. In order to ensure that the equipment meets the essential requirements of, in particular, the safety of users, the safety of those operating the network and the protection of public telecommunications networks against damage of any kind, it is sufficient to lay down specifications which the said equipment must meet and to establish a procedure for type-approval to check whether those specifications are met.

23. According to the RTT, there could be a finding of an infringement of Article [106(1)] only if the Member State had favoured an abuse that the RTT itself had in fact committed, for example by applying the provisions on type-approval in a discriminatory manner. It emphasizes, however, that the order for reference does not state that any abuse has actually taken place, and that the mere possibility of discriminatory application of those provisions by reason of the fact that the RTT is designated as the authority for granting approval and is competing with the undertakings that apply for approval cannot in itself amount to an abuse within the meaning of Article [102].

24. That argument cannot be accepted. It is sufficient to point out in this regard that it is the extension of the monopoly in the establishment and operation of the telephone network to the market in telephone equipment, without any objective justification, which is prohibited as such by Article [102], or by Article [106(1)] in conjunction with Article [102], where that extension results from a measure adopted by a State. As competition may not be eliminated in that manner, it may not be distorted either.

25. A system of undistorted competition, as laid down in the Treaty, can be guaranteed only if equality of opportunity is secured as between the various economic operators. To entrust an undertaking which markets terminal equipment with the task of drawing up the specifications for such equipment, monitoring their application and granting type-approval in respect thereof is tantamount to conferring upon it the power to determine at will which terminal equipment may be connected to the public network, and thereby placing that undertaking at an obvious advantage over its competitors (judgment in Case C-202/88, paragraph 51).

26. In those circumstances, the maintenance of effective competition and the guaranteeing of transparency require that the drawing up of technical specifications, the monitoring of their application, and the granting of type-approval must be carried out by a body which is independent of public or private

undertakings offering competing goods or services in the telecommunications sector (judgment in Case C-202/88, paragraph 52).

27. Moreover, the provisions of the national regulations at issue in the main action may influence the imports of telephone equipment from other Member States, and hence may affect trade between Member States within the meaning of Article [102].

28. Accordingly, it must first be stated, in reply to the national court's questions, that Articles [3(1)(g) EC], [106] and [102] preclude a Member State from granting to the undertaking which operates the public telecommunications network the power to lay down standards for telephone equipment and to check that economic operators meet those standards when it is itself competing with those operators on the market for that equipment.

It will be noticed here that there was no allegation that RTT had actually behaved improperly in its authorisation of equipment. The objection was that the State measures in effect extended the monopoly position from one market to another, by giving the undertaking the authorisation power over its competitors, a situation which if brought about by the conduct of an undertaking rather than by State measures would have constituted an abuse, as the Court pointed out at paragraphs 18–20.[75] In paragraph 25 the Court also referred to the principle of 'equality of opportunity' between economic operators which appeared in *France v Commission*.[76] The rights conferred on the undertakings in both *ERT* and *GB-Inno-BM SA* were also contrary to Article 106(1) since they created a conflict of interest in bundling together regulatory functions and commercial activities. This was also so in *Silvano Raso*[77] where an Italian law gave the exclusive right to supply temporary labour to other dock-work companies operating in a port to an undertaking which was also authorised to carry out dock-work itself. Again the CJ said that the company would have a conflict of interest:[78]

29. That is because merely exercising its monopoly will enable it to distort in its favour the equal conditions of competition between the various operators on the market in dock-work services (Case C-260/89, *ERT v. DRP* . . . and Case C-18/88, *GB-Inno-BM SA*).

30. The result is that the company in question is led to abuse its monopoly by imposing on its competitors in the dock-work market unduly high costs for the supply of labour or by supplying them with labour less suited to the work to be done.

(vi) *Corbeau*

In *Corbeau*, the CJ appeared to suggest that the very granting of special or exclusive rights, even where the elements in the cases previously discussed are not present, might be contrary to Article 106(1).

Case C-320/91, *Corbeau* [1993] ECR I-2533

Belgian law conferred a monopoly on the Belgian Post Office, the Régie des Postes, in respect of the collection, transporting, and delivery of various forms of correspondence. Criminal sanctions were imposed for infringing the monopoly. Corbeau set up his own postal service in the Liège area, whereby

---

[75] See Case 311/84, *Centre Belge d'Etudes du Marché-Télémarketing v Compagnie Luxembourgeoise de Télédiffusion SA and Information Publicité Benelux SA* [1985] ECR 3261 (quoted in para. 18 of the *GB-Inno-BM* judgment) and the cases discussed in Chap. 7.

[76] See Section 5.B.i, p. 599.

[77] Case C-163/96, *Silvano Raso* [1998] ECR I-533.

[78] Ibid., para. 28.

personal collection would be made from the sender's premises and delivery made before noon next day in the same area, although deliveries outside the area were made by putting the items in the ordinary post. Corbeau was prosecuted for infringing the Post Office's monopoly. The Liège court referred questions to the Court concerning the compatibility of the post office monopoly with Articles 101, 102, and 106, whether the monopoly should be modified to comply with Article 106(1), the application of Article 106(2), and whether the post office was in a dominant position. (The part of the judgment concerning Article 106(2) is reproduced in Section 6.E.iii.)

Court of Justice

7. With regard to the facts in the main proceedings, the questions referred to the Court must be understood as meaning that the national court is substantially concerned with the question whether Article [106] must be interpreted as meaning that it is contrary to that Article for the legislation of a Member State which confers on a body such as the Régie des Postes the exclusive right to collect, carry and distribute mail to prohibit an economic operator established in that State from offering, under threat of criminal penalties, certain specific services on that market.

8. To reply to that question, as thus reformulated, it should first be pointed out that a body such as the Régie des Postes, which has been granted exclusive rights as regards the collection, carriage and distribution of mail, must be regarded as an undertaking to which the Member State concerned has granted exclusive rights within the meaning of Article [106(1)].

9. Next it should be recalled that the Court has consistently held that an undertaking having a statutory monopoly over a substantial part of the Common Market may be regarded as having a dominant position within the meaning of Article [102] (see the judgments in Case C-179/90 *Merci Convenzionali Porto di Genova* . . . paragraph 14 and in Case C-18/88 *RTT v. GB-Inno-BM* . . . paragraph 17).

10. However, Article [102] applies only to anti-competitive conduct engaged in by undertakings on their own initiative, not to measures adopted by States (see the *RTT v. GB-Inno-BM* judgment, cited above, paragraph 20).

11. The Court has had occasion to state in this respect that although the mere fact that a Member State has created a dominant position by the grant of exclusive rights is not as such incompatible with Article [102], the Treaty none the less requires the Member States not to adopt or maintain in force any measure which might deprive those provisions of their effectiveness (see the judgment in Case C-260/89 *ERT* . . . paragraph 35).

12. Thus Article [106(1)] provides that in the case of public undertakings to which Member States grant special or exclusive rights, they are neither to enact nor to maintain in force any measure contrary to the rules contained in the Treaty with regard to competition.

13. That provision must be read in conjunction with Article [106(2)] which provides that undertakings entrusted with the operation of services of general economic interest are to be subject to the rules on competition in so far as the application of such rules does not obstruct the performance, in law or in fact, of the particular tasks assigned to them.

14. That latter provision thus permits the Member States to confer on undertakings to which they entrust the operation of services of general economic interest, exclusive rights which may hinder the application of the rules of the Treaty on competition in so far as restrictions on competition, or even the exclusion of all competition, by other economic operators are necessary to ensure the performance of the particular tasks assigned to the undertakings possessed of the exclusive rights.

There was no suggestion in *Corbeau* that the Régie des Postes had acted abusively. The challenge raised by Corbeau's defence to the criminal charges was to the monopoly itself.[79] The CJ answered this in paragraphs 7–12 of the judgment. In paragraph 11 it said that the mere grant of exclusive

---

[79] Since *Corbeau* the postal sector has been liberalised.

rights was not in itself incompatible with the Treaty but also that Member States are not to adopt or maintain measures which may deprive the competition provisions of their effectiveness. It then quoted Article 106(1) and turned immediately to Article 106(2). It never clearly identified which, if any, features of the Belgian legislation were contrary to Article 106(1) and Article 102.[80] This case did not concern an undertaking accused of acting abusively, the extension of the monopoly into a neighbouring market, a conflict of interest, or the bundling of regulatory functions with entrepreneurial activities. It did however, as Hancher notes,[81] appear to suggest that, in order to ensure the *effet utile* or effectiveness of Articles 106(1) and 102 and despite the Court's statement to the contrary at paragraph 11, the very existence of national rules conferring a dominant position on an undertaking is unacceptable unless the rights at issue can be justified under Article 106(2) (see paragraphs 13 and 14). In effect, it reversed the burden of proof: exclusive rights are not prima facie legal, but prima facie illegal unless they are objectively justified or fulfil the Article 106(2) criteria.[82]

(vii) *La Crespelle*

The CJ did not pursue the line it took in *Corbeau* in the next case, *La Crespelle*,[83] where it again held that a Member State contravenes the Treaty only if, in merely exercising the exclusive right granted to it, the undertaking cannot avoid abusing its dominant position: it is not possible automatically to impute the abuse to the existence of the right. In this case, where the exclusive right concerned bovine insemination centres, there was nothing in the grant of exclusive rights which made the alleged abuse—excessive pricing—unavoidable. The same approach can be seen in *Corsica Ferries*,[84] where the CJ held that the grant of the exclusive right to offer compulsory piloting services in a port was not in itself an infringement of Article 106(1) but the approval of the discriminatory tariffs, which were contrary to Article 102(c), *was* an infringement. Similarly, in *Banchero* the CJ held that Article 106(1) was infringed only where the undertaking cannot avoid abusing its dominant position.[85]

(viii) *Albany*

Albany concerned the Dutch regime of compulsory affiliation to sectoral pension funds.[86]

Case C-67/96, *Albany International BV v Stichting Bedrijfspensioenfonds Textielindustrie* [1999] ECR I-5751

Under Dutch law pension provision included a system whereby, at the request of the representatives of employers and employees in a particular sector of the economy, affiliation to a sectoral pension fund was made compulsory for all undertakings in that sector. This was to provide a pension supplementary to the basic State pension. Various undertakings brought proceedings in the Dutch courts challenging the compulsory affiliation regime on the grounds that they provided equivalent supplementary pension

---

[80] As Jacobs AG pointed out in his Opinion in Cases C-67/96, 115–117/97, and 219/97, *Albany International BV v Stichting Bedrijfspensioenfonds Textielindustrie* [1999] ECR I-5751, para. 417.

[81] See L. Hancher, 'Casenote on *Corbeau*' (1994) 31 *CMLRev* 105, 111.

[82] See Faull and Nikpay, n. 2, 6.81, which says that in effect this brings the approach to Arts. 106(1) and 102 in line with the approach to the free movement of goods.

[83] Case C-323/93, *La Crespelle* [1994] ECR I-5077.

[84] Case C-18/93, *Corsica Ferries Italia Srl v Corpo dei Piloti del Porto di Genova* [1994] ECR I-1783.

[85] Case C-387/93, *Banchero* [1995] ECR I-4663.

[86] See L. Gyselen, 'Case Note on *Albany, Brentjens'* and *Drijvende Bokken*' (2000) 37 *CMLRev* 425.

schemes themselves. The Dutch courts referred to the CJ the question, inter alia, whether the exclusive rights conferred on the sectoral pension funds infringed the Treaty.[87]

Court of Justice

90. It must be observed at the outset that the decision of the public authorities to make affiliation to a sectoral pension fund compulsory, as in this case, necessarily implies granting to that fund an exclusive right to collect and administer the contributions paid with a view to accruing pension rights. Such a fund must therefore be regarded as an undertaking to which exclusive rights have been granted by the public authorities, of the kind referred to in Article [106(1)].

91. Next, it should be noted that according to settled case-law an undertaking which has a legal monopoly in a substantial part of the common market may be regarded as occupying a dominant position within the meaning of Article [102] (see Case C-179/90 *Merci Convenzional Porto di Genova* . . . paragraph 14, and Case C-18/88 *GB-Inno-BM* . . . paragraph 17).

92. A sectoral pension fund of the kind at issue in the main proceedings, which has an exclusive right to manage a supplementary pension scheme in an industrial sector in a Member State and, therefore, in a substantial part of the common market, may therefore be regarded as occupying a dominant position within the meaning of Article [102].

93. It must not be forgotten, however, that merely creating a dominant position by granting exclusive rights within the meaning of Article [106(1)] is not in itself incompatible with Article [102]. A Member State is in breach of the prohibitions contained in those two provisions only if the undertaking in question, merely by exercising the exclusive rights granted to it, is led to abuse its dominant position or when such rights are liable to create a situation in which that undertaking is led to commit such abuses (*Höfner and Elser*, cited above, paragraph 29; Case C-260/89 *ERT* . . . paragraph 37; *Merci Convenzionali Porto di Genova*, cited above, paragraphs 16 and 17; Case C-323/93 *Centre d'Insémination de la Crespelle* . . . paragraph 18; and Case C-163/96 *Raso and Others* . . . paragraph 27).

94. Albany contends in that connection that the system of compulsory affiliation to the supplementary pension scheme managed by the Fund is contrary to the combined provisions of Articles [102 and 106]. The pension benefits available from the Fund do not, or no longer, match the needs of the undertakings. The benefits are too low, are not linked to wages and, consequently, are generally inadequate. Employers have therefore to make other pension arrangements. The system of compulsory affiliation deprives those employers of any opportunity of arranging for comprehensive pension cover from an insurance company. Pension arrangements spread over a number of insurers would increase administrative costs and reduce efficiency.

95. It should be remembered that, in *Höfner and Elser*, cited above, paragraph 34, the Court held that a Member State which conferred on a public employment agency an exclusive right of recruitment was in breach of Article [106(1)] where it created a situation in which that office could not avoid infringing Article [102], in particular because it was manifestly incapable of satisfying the demand prevailing on the market for such activities.

96. In the present case, it is important to note that the supplementary pension scheme offered by the Fund is based on the present norm in the Netherlands, namely that every worker who has paid contributions to that scheme for the maximum period of affiliation receives a pension, including the State pension under the AOW, equal to 70 per cent of his final salary.

97. Doubtless, some undertakings in the sector might wish to provide their workers with a pension scheme superior to the one offered by the Fund. However, the fact that such undertakings are unable

---

[87] See also Cases C-115–117/97, *Brentjens' Handelsonderneming BV v Stichting Bedrijfspensioenfonds voor de Handel in Bouwmaterialen* [1999] ECR I-6025 and Case C-219/97, *Maatschappij Drijvende Bokken BV v Stichting Pensioenfonds voor de Vervoer-en Havenbedrijven* [1999] ECR I-6121, which raised the same issue. The cases also raised questions about the application of the competition rules to collective agreements between employers and employees. For these aspects, see Chap. 3.

> to entrust the management of such a pension scheme to a single insurer and the resulting restriction of competition derive directly from the exclusive right conferred on the sectoral pension fund.
>
> 98. It is therefore necessary to consider whether, as contended by the Fund, the Netherlands Government and the Commission, the exclusive right of the sectoral pension fund to manage supplementary pensions in a given sector and the resultant restriction of competition may be justified under Article [106(2)] as a measure necessary for the performance of a particular social task of general interest with which that fund has been charged.

The CJ then proceeded to consider whether the exclusive right and the restriction of competition could indeed be justified under Article 106(2). This part of the judgment is reproduced in Section 6.E.[88]

It can be seen from this previous extract that the CJ said once again that the granting of exclusive rights is not contrary to the Treaty unless merely by exercising the right the undertaking is led to commit an abuse (paragraph 93) or unless an abuse is unavoidable (paragraph 95). However, the Court did not proceed to consider whether the undertaking here *was* put in such a position, but instead turned to see whether the justification under Article 106(2) applied.[89] This can be contrasted with *Dusseldorp* where the CJ actually found the provision to be contrary to Article 106(1) in conjunction with Article 102 before turning to consider the application of Article 106(2).[90] It is notable that in *Albany* the CJ, unlike Advocate General Jacobs in his Opinion (paragraphs 441–468), was not concerned that the pension funds with the exclusive rights were also the authority able to grant exemptions from compulsory participation in the pension schemes.

(ix) *Deutsche Post*

In *Deutsche Post* the undertaking concerned was a State monopoly with the exclusive right to collect, carry, and deliver certain categories of mail in Germany, and which carried out the obligations flowing from the Universal Postal Convention (UPC).

Cases C-147–148/97, *Deutsche Post AG v Gesellschaft für Zahlungssysteme mbH (GZS) and Citicorp Kartenservice GmbH* [2000] ECR I-825

Under the Universal Postal Convention 1989 the Contracting States are obliged to forward and deliver international mail addressed to persons resident in their country which is passed to them by the postal services of other contracting parties. The Convention provides for the receiving state to charge a fixed fee for the costs of delivering the mail (terminal dues). The Convention also provides, inter alia, that where senders resident in country A cause mail addressed to addressees in country A to be posted in bulk in country B, country A is entitled to either charge its full internal rate for the items or to return them to their origin (Article 25). Various credit-card companies based in Germany electronically transmitted

---

[88] See Section 6.E.iii, p. 638.

[89] See L. Gyselen, 'Case Note on *Albany, Brentjens'* and *Drijvende Bokken*' (2000) 37 *CMLRev* 425. In Case C-209/98, *Sydhavnens* [2000] ECR-3743 the CJ decided the exclusive right did *not* infringe Art. 106(1) but still proceeded to examine the application of Art. 106(2).

[90] Case C-203/96, *Chemische Afvalstoffen Dusseldorp BV v Minister van Volkshuisvesting, Ruimtelijke Ordening en Milieubeheer* [1998] ECR I-4075. The CJ held that a Dutch prohibition on a company exporting its waste oil filters for treatment in Germany amounted, in practice, to imposing an obligation on it to deliver the filters to the Dutch undertaking which held the exclusive right to incinerate dangerous waste. For the Art. 106(2) aspects of the case, see Section 6.E.iii, p. 636.

the data for their customers' bills to processing centres outside Germany which prepared the German customers' bills and posted them back to Germany. In one case this resulted in the bills being posted in Denmark, where the rate for international mail is lower than the internal rate in Germany. Deutsche Post was merely paid the terminal dues. It demanded the full internal rate. The credit companies refused to pay. In the course of the subsequent litigation the German courts referred to the Court questions about whether it was contrary to Article 106 and Article 102 (and Article 56, on the freedom to provide services) for Deutsche Post to exercise its rights under Article 25 of the Convention to charge the internal postage rate.

Court of Justice

37. . . . [I]t should first be noted that a body such as Deutsche Post, which has been granted exclusive rights as regards the collection, carriage and delivery of mail, must be regarded as an undertaking to which the Member State concerned has granted exclusive rights within the meaning of Article [106(1)] (Case C-320/91 *Corbeau* . . . paragraph 8).

38. Also, it is settled case-law that an undertaking having a statutory monopoly over a substantial part of the common market may be regarded as holding a dominant position within the meaning of Article [102] (see Case C-179/90 *Merci Convenzionali Porto di Genova* v. *Siderurgica Gabrielli* . . . paragraph 14, Case C-18/88 *RTT* v. *GB-Inno-BM* . . . paragraph 17, and *Corbeau*, cited above, paragraph 9).

39. The Court has had occasion to state in this respect that although the mere fact that a Member State has created a dominant position by the grant of exclusive rights is not as such incompatible with Article [102], the Treaty none the less requires the Member States not to adopt or maintain in force any measure which might deprive that provision of its effectiveness (see Case C-260/89 *ERT* . . . paragraph 35, and *Corbeau*, cited above, paragraph 11).

40. Article [106(1)] thus provides that in the case of undertakings to which Member States grant special or exclusive rights, they are neither to enact nor to maintain in force any measure contrary, in particular, to the rules contained in the Treaty with regard to competition (see *Corbeau*, paragraph 12).

41. That provision must be read in conjunction with Article [106(2)] which provides that undertakings entrusted with the operation of services of general economic interest are to be subject to the rules contained in the Treaty in so far as the application of such rules does not obstruct the performance, in law or in fact, of the particular tasks assigned to them.

42. A final point to note is that the UPC proceeds on the basis of a market in letter-post where the postal services of the various Contracting States of the Universal Postal Union are not in competition.

43. In that context, the UPC is designed to establish rules ensuring that international items of mail addressed to residents of a Contracting State and passed on by the fundamental principles of the UPC, set out in Article 1 thereof, is the obligation of the postal administration of the Contracting State to which international mail is sent to forward and deliver it to addressees resident in its territory using the most rapid means of its letter post. In that regard, the States which have adopted the Convention of the Universal Postal Union constitute a single postal territory, in which the freedom of transit of reciprocal international mail is in principle guaranteed.

44. For the postal services of the Member States, performance of the obligations flowing from the UPC is thus in itself a service of general economic interest within the meaning of Article [106(2)].

45. In the present case, German legislation assigns the operation of that service to Deutsche Post.

46. As has been noted in paragraph 5 of this judgment, postal services initially delivered international mail without being paid for that task. However, when it became apparent that the flows of postal traffic between two Contracting States frequently did not balance out, so that the postal services of the various Contracting States had to process quantities of international mail which differed greatly, specific provisions were laid down in that regard, one of which is Article 25 of the UPC.

47. Under Article 25(3) of the UPC, the postal services of the Contracting States may in particular, in the cases referred to in Article 25(1) and (2), charge postage on items of mail at their internal rates.

48. The grant to a body such as Deutsche Post of the right to treat international items of mail as internal post in such cases creates a situation where that body may be led, to the detriment of users of postal services, to abuse its dominant position resulting from the exclusive right granted to it to forward and deliver those items to the relevant addressees.

49. It is accordingly necessary to examine the extent to which exercise of such a right is necessary to enable a body of that kind to perform its task of general interest pursuant to the obligations flowing from the UPC and, in particular, to operate under economically acceptable conditions.

50. If a body such as Deutsche Post were obliged to forward and deliver to addressees resident in Germany mail posted in large quantities by senders resident in Germany using postal services of other Member States, without any provision allowing it to be financially compensated for all the costs occasioned by that obligation, the performance, in economically balanced conditions, of that task of general interest would be jeopardised.

51. The postal services of a Member State cannot simultaneously bear the costs entailed in the performance of the service of general economic interest of forwarding and delivering international items of mail, which is their responsibility by virtue of the UPC, and the loss of income resulting from the fact that bulk mailings are no longer posted with the postal services of the Member State in which the addressees are resident but with those of other Member States.

52. In such a case, it must be regarded as justified, for the purposes of the performance, in economically balanced conditions, of the task of general interest entrusted to Deutsche Post by the UPC, to treat cross-border mail as internal mail and, consequently, to charge internal postage.

. . .

54. Article [106(2)] therefore justifies, in the absence of an agreement between the postal services of the Member States concerned fixing terminal dues in relation to the actual costs of processing and delivering incoming trans-border mail, the grant by a Member State to its postal services of the statutory right to charge internal postage on items of mail where senders resident in that State post items, or cause them to be posted, in large quantities with the postal services of another Member State in order to send them to the first Member State.

. . .

56. On the other hand, in so far as part of the forwarding and delivery costs is offset by terminal dues paid by the postal services of other Member States, it is not necessary, in order for a body such as Deutsche Post to fulfil the obligations flowing from the UPC, that postage be charged at the full internal rate on items posted in large quantities with those services.

57. It is to be remembered that a body such as Deutsche Post which has a statutory monopoly over a substantial part of the common market may be regarded as holding a dominant position within the meaning of Article [102].

58. Thus, the exercise by such a body of the right to demand the full amount of the internal postage, where the costs relating to the forwarding and delivery of mail posted in large quantities with the postal services of a Member State other than the State in which both the senders and the addressees of that mail are resident are not offset by the terminal dues paid by those services, may be regarded as an abuse of a dominant position within the meaning of Article [102].

59. In order to prevent a body such as Deutsche Post from exercising its right, provided for by Article 25(3) of the UPC, to return items of mail to origin, the senders of those items have no choice but to pay the full amount of the internal postage.

60. As the Court has stated in relation to a refusal to sell on the part of an undertaking holding a dominant position within the meaning of Article [102], such action would be inconsistent with the objective laid down by Article [3(1)(g)] of the EC Treaty] . . . as explained in Article [102], in particular in subparagraphs (b) and (c) of its second paragraph (Case 27/76 *United Brands* v. *Commission* . . . paragraph 183).

In this judgment the CJ said that Deutsche Post had been granted exclusive rights within the meaning of Article 106(1), and that Article 106(1) had to be read in conjunction with Article 106(2). In saying this (paragraphs 40–41), the Court repeated the wording in paragraphs 12–13 of the *Corbeau* judgment. The performance of the obligations of the UPC was a service of general economic interest within the meaning of Article 106(2) (paragraph 44). The Court held that granting Deutsche Post the right under the UPC to treat international mail as internal mail *did* create a situation where 'it may be led, to the detriment of users of postal services, to abuse its dominant position' (paragraph 48). It therefore said it must examine whether the exercise of the right was necessary to perform its task of general interest 'under economically acceptable conditions' (paragraph 49). It concluded that it *was* necessary, because of the financial loss Deutsche Post would otherwise incur.[91] However, it would be an abuse of a dominant position if Deutsche Post were to charge the full internal postage without offsetting the terminal dues against the money demanded from the senders.

(x) *Ambulanz Glöckner*

A similar approach to *Deutsche Post* was taken in *Ambulanz Glöckner*.

Case C-475/99, *Ambulanz Glöckner v Landkreis Südwestpfalz* [2001] ECR I-8089

The provision of the public ambulance service in Germany was governed by legislation referred to in the judgment below as the 'RettDG 1991'. This distinguished between 'emergency transport' and 'patient transport' (non-emergency). Emergency transport in the *Land* of Rheinland-Pfalz was entrusted to two medical aid organizations which also ran a non-emergency service. Ambulanz Glöckner had previously also provided a non-emergency service. However, when it applied to the relevant public authority for a renewal of its permit, the two medical aid organizations objected, claiming that competition on the non-emergency market would affect their ability to provide the emergency service. As a result the public authority refused Ambulanz Glöckner a permit.

Court of Justice

39. It must be borne in mind that the mere creation of a dominant position through the grant of special or exclusive rights within the meaning of Article [106(1)] is not in itself incompatible with Article [102]. A Member State will be in breach of the prohibitions laid down by those two provisions only if the undertaking in question, merely by exercising the special or exclusive rights conferred upon it, is led to abuse its dominant position or where such rights are liable to create a situation in which that undertaking is led to commit such abuses (see *Pavlov*, cited above, paragraph 127).

40. It is settled case-law that an abuse within the meaning of Article [102] is committed where, without any objective necessity, an undertaking holding a dominant position on a particular market reserves to itself an ancillary activity which could be carried out by another undertaking as part of its activities on a neighbouring but separate market, with the possibility of eliminating all competition from that undertaking (judgment in Case C-18/88 *GB-Inno-BM* . . . paragraph 18). Where the extension of the dominant position of an undertaking to which the State has granted special or exclusive rights results from a State measure, such a measure constitutes an infringement of Article [106] in conjunction with Article [102] (*GB-Inno-BM*, paragraph 21, and Case C-203/96 *Dusseldorp and Others* . . . paragraph 61).

41. In the present case, the argument put forward by Ambulanz Glöckner is indeed that it is excluded from the market for patient transport as a result of the application of Paragraph 18(3) of the RettDG 1991,

---

[91] See Section 6.E.iii, p. 640.

which, in its submission, enables the medical aid organisations, acting in concertation with the public authorities, to restrict access to that market.

42. The Commission also contends that the extension of the dominant position on the urgent transport market to the related, but separate, market for patient transport is due to the changes made in the federal legislation governing the latter type of transport, then in the legislation of the Land of Rheinland-Pfalz and, in particular, to the adoption of Paragraph 18(3) of the RettDG 1991. Such a restriction of competition, it contends, constitutes a breach of Article [106] in conjunction with Article [102] thereof.

43. As far as those arguments are concerned, it must be concluded that, in enacting Paragraph 18(3) of the RettDG 1991, the application of which involves prior consultation of the medical aid organisations in respect of any application for authorisation to provide non-emergency patient transport services submitted by an independent operator, the legislature of the Land of Rheinland-Pfalz gave an advantage to those organisations, which already had an exclusive right on the urgent transport market, by also allowing them to provide such services exclusively. The application of Paragraph 18(3) of the RettDG 1991 therefore has the effect of limiting markets . . . to the prejudice of consumers within the meaning of Article [102(b)], by reserving to those medical aid organisations an ancillary transport activity which could be carried on by independent operators.

The objections of the CJ were, once again, that the State measure resulted in the undertaking extending its dominant position on to another market (the urgent transport market and the patient transport market were held to be related but separate) which could have been provided by an independent operator. The CJ went on to consider whether Article 106(2) applied.[92]

(xi) *Connect Austria*

In *Connect Austria*[93] the Austrian regulatory agency charged an applicant for a new standard digital mobile telecommunications licence fees that were greatly in excess of those it charged the incumbent public undertaking. This was likely to lead to the public undertaking extending or strengthening its dominant position, and the distorted competition 'would therefore result from a State measure which creates a situation where equality of opportunity for the various economic operators concerned cannot be ensured',[94] thus infringing Article 106(1) in conjunction with Article 102. The extension of the dominant position appeared to come from the State measure itself, not from any conduct by the undertaking. In paragraph 84 the CJ said (without citing any previous case law):

If inequality of opportunity between economic operators, and therefore distorted competition, results from a State measure, such a measure constitutes an infringement of Article [106(1)] in conjunction with Article [102].

(xii) *MOTOE*

In *MOTOE* the reference concerned administrative powers given to a sports body which also competed in the market with those it authorised.[95]

---

[92] For this aspect, see Section 6.E.iii, p. 641.

[93] Case C-462/99, *Connect Austria Gesellschaft für Telekommunikation GmbH v Telekom-Control-Kommission* [2003] ECR I-5147.

[94] Ibid., para. 87.

[95] See A. Veermersch, 'Casenote on Case C-49/07' (2009) 46 *CMLRev* 1327.

Case C-49/07, *Motosykletistiki Omospondia Ellados NPID (MOTOE) v Ellinkio Dimosi* [2008] ECR I-4863

Greek legislation (Road Traffic Code, Article 49) requires authorisation from the Minister for Public Order for motorcycling competitions on public or private roads and spaces. The Code provides that authorisation can only be given following the consent of ELPA (Automobile and Touring Club of Greece), the official Greek representative of FIM (International Motorcycling Federation). ELPA, a non-profit-making association, organised motorcycling events in Greece and entered into sponsorship, advertising, and insurance contracts in that connection. MOTOE, another non-profit-making association, also organised motor-cycling events in Greece. ELPA failed to give its consent to various events MOTOE wanted to hold. MOTOE sued for damages. On an Article 267 reference one of the questions asked by the Greek court concerned the authorisation power granted to ELPA in the situation where it also competed on the market with those it authorised.

Court of Justice

48. As regards, third, the question whether Articles [102 and 106(1)] preclude a national rule, such as Article 49 of the Greek Road Traffic Code, which confers on a legal person like ELPA, which can itself take on the organisation of motorcycling events and their commercial exploitation, the power to give consent to applications for authorisation to organise those events, without that power being made subject to restrictions, obligations and review, it should be recalled that the mere creation or reinforcement of a dominant position through the grant of special or exclusive rights within the meaning of Article [106(1)] is not in itself incompatible with Article [102].

49. On the other hand, a Member State will be in breach of the prohibitions laid down by those two provisions if the undertaking in question, merely by exercising the special or exclusive rights conferred upon it, is led to abuse its dominant position or where such rights are liable to create a situation in which that undertaking is led to commit such abuses (*Höfner and Elser*, cited above, paragraph 29; *ERT*, cited above, paragraph 37; Case C-179/90 *Merci convenzionali porto di Genova* . . . paragraphs 16 and 17; and Case C-323/93 *Centre d'insémination de la Crespelle* . . . paragraph 18). In this respect, it is not necessary that any abuse should actually occur (see, to that effect, Case C-55/96 *Job Centre* . . . paragraph 36).

50. In any event, Articles [102 and 106(1)] are infringed where a measure imputable to a Member State, and in particular a measure by which a Member State confers special or exclusive rights within the meaning of Article [106(1)], gives rise to a risk of an abuse of a dominant position (see, to that effect, *ERT*, cited above, paragraph 37; *Merci convenzionali porto di Genova*, cited above, paragraph 17; and Case C-380/05 *Centro Europa 7* . . . paragraph 60).

51. A system of undistorted competition, such as that provided for by the Treaty, can be guaranteed only if equality of opportunity is secured as between the various economic operators. To entrust a legal person such as ELPA, which itself organises and commercially exploits motorcycling events, the task of giving the competent administration its consent to applications for authorisation to organise such events, is tantamount *de facto* to conferring upon it the power to designate the persons authorised to organise those events and to set the conditions in which those events are organised, thereby placing that entity at an obvious advantage over its competitors (see, by analogy, Case C-202/88 *France* v *Commission* . . . paragraph 51, and Case C-18/88 *GB Inno BM*. . . paragraph 25). Such a right may therefore lead the undertaking which possesses it to deny other operators access to the relevant market. That situation of unequal conditions of competition is also highlighted by the fact, confirmed at the hearing before the Court, that, when ELPA organises or participates in the organisation of motorcycling events, it is not required to obtain any consent in order that the competent administration grant it the required authorisation.

52. Furthermore, such a rule, which gives a legal person such as ELPA the power to give consent to applications for authorisation to organise motorcycling events without that power being made subject by that rule to restrictions, obligations and review, could lead the legal person entrusted with giving that consent to distort competition by favouring events which it organises or those in whose organisation it participates.

53. In the light of the foregoing, the answer to the questions referred must be that a legal person whose activities consist not only in taking part in administrative decisions authorising the organisation of motor-cycling events, but also in organising such events itself and in entering, in that connection, into sponsorship, advertising and insurance contracts, falls within the scope of Articles [102 and 106]. Those articles preclude a national rule which confers on a legal person, which organises motorcycling events and enters, in that connection, into sponsorship, advertising and insurance contracts, the power to give consent to applications for authorisation to organise such competitions, without that power being made subject to restrictions, obligations and review.

One of the reasons the CJ gave in *MOTOE* for finding that the national rule infringed Article 106(1) was that it created inequality of opportunity (paragraph 51), a concept already seen in *France v Commission*, *GB-Inno-BM*, and *Connect Austria*. It also, as in *GB-Inno-BM*, created a conflict of interest in giving ELPA regulatory powers over commercial activities events in which it competed with others. The CJ said again that Article 106(1) and Article 102 preclude a national rule which, inter alia, is liable to create a situation in which the undertaking is led to commit an abuse, and that it is not necessary that any abuse actually occurs (paragraph 49).

(xiii) *DEI*

The issues of equality of opportunity and the strengthening or extension of a dominant position over another market were explored in the *Greek Lignite* case. Lignite is coal ore from which electricity can be produced. It is the cheapest combustible for producing electricity in Greece, where the extensive lignite deposits are State-owned. The Greek Government gave PCC, the former monopoly generator of electricity in Greece prior to liberalisation (and now a limited liability company in which the State had a controlling shareholding), rights to explore and exploit approximately half of the lignite deposits. No exploitation rights over the remaining deposits were granted to anyone. The Commission concluded that these arrangements infringed Article 106(1) in conjunction with Article 102[96] in that by granting and maintaining quasi-monopolistic lignite exploration rights in favour of PCC Greece had created inequality of opportunity between economic operators on the wholesale electricity market and thus distorted competition, thereby reinforcing the PCC's dominant position on that market.[97] *Greek Lignite* was an unusual case post-2000 in that it originated in an Article 106(3) infringement decision. The real problem of the Commission in *Greek Lignite* was that it considered the situation in the Greek electricity market after liberalisation to be unsatisfactory. Unable to attack directly the Greek Government's failure to grant exploitation licences for the remaining deposits to PCC's competitors, it turned to the 'equality of opportunity' concept but did not identify what abuse PCC was being led to commit.

On appeal the GC annulled the decision.[98] It held that it was not enough to establish that a State measure simply distorted competition by creating inequality of opportunity. Rather, a breach of Article 106(1) in combination with Article 102 required an abuse to be identified. The GC distinguished the case from other cases discussed in this chapter because it considered that in those the way in which the undertaking was led, or would or could be led, to abuse its rights was identified. In this case the Commission had held it was an infringement just to maintain PCC in a dominant position. However, the mere exercise of its licence could not amount to the undertaking extending its dominant position. On appeal by the Commission the CJ set aside the GC's judgment. It agreed with the decision. In the extract below the Court deals first with the issue of inequality of opportunity

---

[96] COMP/38.700, *Greek Lignite* 5 March 2008.

[97] Ibid., paras. 190 and 238.

[98] Case T-169/08, *Dimosia Epicheirisi Ilektrismou AE (DEI) v Commission* EU:T:2012:448.

and then with the issue of the extension of the dominant position. The undertaking had argued that the theory of the extension of the dominant position was governed by four conditions, which were not fulfilled here (paragraph 61 of the judgment) in that: (a) the State measure had not awarded DEI special or exclusive rights over a neighbouring and separate market; (b) DEI had no power to determine the activity of its competitors or impose costs upon them; (c) the Commission had not examined the impact on the interests of consumers; and (d) the Commission had defined lignite as an essential facility but had failed to show that it was in this case.

Case C-553/12 P, *Commission v Dimosia Epicheirisi Ilektrismou AE (DEI)* EU:C:2014:2083

39. It should be recalled that, pursuant to Article [106(1)], Member States are not to enact or maintain in force, in the case of public undertakings and the undertakings to which they grant special or exclusive rights, any measure contrary to the rules contained in the EC Treaty, in particular those provided for in Article [102].

40. In so far as it may affect trade between Member States, the abuse of a dominant position within the common market or in a substantial part thereof is prohibited by Article [102].

41. It should be noted that, according to the case-law, a Member State is in breach of the prohibitions laid down by Article [106(1)] in conjunction with Article [102] if it adopts any law, regulation or adminis-trative provision that creates a situation in which a public undertaking or an undertaking on which it has conferred special or exclusive rights, merely by exercising the preferential rights conferred upon it, is led to abuse its dominant position or when those rights are liable to create a situation in which that undertak-ing is led to commit such abuses (see, to that effect, the judgments in *Connect Austria*,…, paragraph 80, and *MOTOE*,…, paragraph 49 and the case-law cited). In that respect, it is not necessary that any abuse should actually occur (judgments in *GB-Inno-BM*,…, paragraphs 23 to 25; *Raso and Others*,…, paragraph 31; and *MOTOE*,…, paragraph 49).

42. Thus, a Member State will be in breach of those provisions where a measure imputable to a Member State gives rise to a risk of an abuse of a dominant position (see the judgment in *MOTOE*,…, paragraph 50 and the case-law cited).

43. It is clear from the Court's case-law that a system of undistorted competition, such as that provided for by the Treaty, can be guaranteed only if equality of opportunity is secured as between the various economic operators (see the judgments in *GB-Inno-BM*,…, paragraph 25; *MOTOE*,…, paragraph 51; and *Connect Austria*,…, paragraph 83 and case-law cited).

44. It follows that if inequality of opportunity between economic operators, and thus distorted compe-tition, is the result of a State measure, such a measure constitutes an infringement of Article [106(1)] read together with Article [102] (see the judgment in *Connect Austria*,…, paragraph 84).

45. The Court has moreover had occasion to state in that regard that, although the mere fact that a Member State has created a dominant position by the grant of exclusive rights is not as such incompat-ible with Article [102], the EC Treaty none the less requires the Member States not to adopt or maintain in force any measure which might deprive that provision of its effectiveness (judgments in *ERT*, C-260/89,…, paragraph 35; *Corbeau*, C-320/91,…, paragraph 11; and *Deutsche Post*, C-147/97 and C-148/97,…, paragraph 39).

46. It follows from the matters addressed in paragraphs 41 to 45 above that, as the Advocate General states in point 55 of his Opinion, infringement of Article [106(1)] in conjunction with Article [102] may be established irrespective of whether any abuse actually exists. All that is necessary is for the Commission to identify a potential or actual anti-competitive consequence liable to result from the State measure at issue. Such an infringement may thus be established where the State measures at issue affect the structure of the market by creating unequal conditions of competition between companies, by allowing the public undertaking or the undertaking which was granted special or exclusive rights to maintain (for example by

hindering new entrants to the market), strengthen or extend its dominant position over another market, thereby restricting competition, without it being necessary to prove the existence of actual abuse.

47. In those circumstances, it follows that, contrary to the General Court's analysis in paragraphs 105 and 118 of the judgment under appeal, it is sufficient to show that that potential or actual anti-competitive consequence is liable to result from the State measure at issue; it is not necessary to identify an abuse other than that which results from the situation brought about by the State measure at issue. It also follows that the General Court erred in law in holding that the Commission, by finding that DEI, a former monopolistic undertaking, continued to maintain a dominant position on the wholesale electricity market by virtue of the advantage conferred upon it by its privileged access to lignite and that that situation created inequality of opportunity on that market between the applicant and other undertakings, had neither identified nor established to a sufficient legal standard the abuse to which, within the meaning of Article [102], the State measure in question had led or could have led DEI.

...

65. In addition, the Court must disregard the claimed 'conditions of application' of the theory of the extension of a dominant position, which are summarised in paragraph 61 above and which, according to DEI, follow from the case-law of the Court.

66. It is settled case-law that practices by an undertaking in a dominant position which tend to extend that position to a neighbouring but separate market by distorting competition amount to abuse of a dominant position within the meaning of Article [102] (see, to that effect, the judgment in *Connect Austria*,…, paragraphs 81 and [102]and case-law cited).

67. Similarly, the Court has previously stated that the extension of a dominant position, without any objective justification, is prohibited 'as such' by Article [106(1)] in conjunction with Article [102], where that extension results from a State measure. As competition may not be eliminated in that manner, it may not be distorted either (see, to that effect, the judgments in *Spain and Others* v *Commission*, C-271/90, C-281/90 and C-289/90,…, paragraph 36, and *GB-Inno-BM*,…, paragraphs 21, 23 and 24).

68. It is therefore not necessary, as claimed by DEI, for the Commission to show, in every case, that the undertaking concerned enjoys a monopoly or that the State measure at issue awards it exclusive or special rights over a neighbouring and separate market, or that it has any regulatory powers. Having regard to the case-law referred to in paragraphs 41 to 44 above, the claim that there is an obligation on the Commission to show the impact of the infringement of the combined provisions of Articles [106(1)] and [102] on the interests of consumers must also be rejected; Article [102] may moreover cover practices which are harmful as a result of their impact on an effective competition structure (see, to that effect, the judgment in *Europemballage and Continental Can* v *Commission*, 6/72,…, paragraph 26). Finally, DEI's argument that the Commission defined lignite as an essential facility is based on a false premiss, as the Commission only referred to DEI's situation of 'quasi-monopoly' on the electricity wholesale market.

This judgment is highly significant. It establishes (citing paragraph 84 of *Connect Austria*) that inequality of opportunity 'and thus distorted competition' resulting from State measures constitutes an infringement of Article 106(1) in conjunction with Article 102 without any abuse occurring or existing. There needs simply to be identified 'a potential or actual anti-competitive consequence liable to result from the State measure'. An infringement can therefore be established where the measures affect the structure of the market by allowing the undertaking concerned to maintain, strengthen, or extend its dominant position over another market, without any necessity to identify any abuse other than that situation. Where the dominant position is extended as a result of the State measure, without any objective justification, it is prohibited 'as such'. Furthermore, there is no need to show an impact on the interests of consumers—the CJ referred back to *Continental Can*[99] in holding that Article 102 covers practices which are harmful to an effective competition structure.

---

[99] Case 6/72, *Europemballage Corp and Continental Can Co Inc v Commission* [1973] ECR 215, see Chap. 7.

(xiv) *Slovenská Pošta*

In *Slovakian Hybrid Mail Services* the delivery of hybrid mail[100] in Slovakia had been open to competition but by legislation in 2008 it was in effect 're-monopolised' and reserved to Slovenská Pošta, an undertaking wholly owned by the Slovak State. The service offered by Slovenská Pošta did not include many of the added features which the private operators had been offering and which customers valued.[101] The Commission held, on the basis of *Höfner v Macrotron*, that granting an exclusive right to an undertaking manifestly unable to satisfy the demand infringed Article 106 in conjunction with Article 102.[102] It was also a case of extending the public undertaking's monopoly—here from ordinary mail to hybrid mail. The decision was upheld by the GC.[103]

C. SUMMARY OF THE SITUATIONS WHICH INFRINGE ARTICLE 106(1) IN CONJUNCTION WITH ARTICLE 102

As we have seen in the previous section, the cases variously establish that a Member State infringes Article 106(1) in conjunction with Article 102 if it creates a situation in which a public undertaking or one on which it has conferred special or exclusive rights cannot avoid committing an abuse, or is led to, or induced to, commit an abuse. This can be summed up as saying that a Member State infringes the provisions 'where a measure imputable to a Member State gives rise to a risk of an abuse of a dominant position'.[104] Measures may also infringe simply because they create inequality of opportunity and thus distorted competition. It is not possible to neatly categorise the case law and, even if it were, the categories would not be closed. However, looking at the case law one can identify the following.

(i) Inability to Meet Demand

It is clear from *Höfner v Macroton*[105] that Article 106(1) is infringed where a statutory monopoly is set up in such a way that it is incapable of meeting the demand in the reserved sector. This was also the case in *Job Centre Coop arl*,[106] *AG2R Prévoyance*,[107] and *Slovenská Pošta*.[108] *Merci Convenzionali* showed that Article 106(1) is infringed where the monopolist is enabled to behave inefficiently, exploit customers, and not modernise.[109] In *Ambulanz Glöckner* the Advocate General discussed the possible causes for inefficiency or inability to meet demand. He considered that a Member State is only liable under Article 106(1) if the fault is in the system it has set up, and not where the only reason that an organisation is 'manifestly not able to satisfy demand' is inefficient management.[110] The CJ did not address this point in its judgment. Besides *Slovenská Pošta* there are a number of other cases of this type in the

---

[100] Where the content is transferred electronically from the sender to the postal service operator who prints it out, puts it in envelopes, and sorts and delivers it.

[101] Such as tracking services and seven days a week delivery.

[102] COMP/39.562, 7 October 2008.

[103] Case T-556/08, *Slovenská Pošta* EU:C:2015:189; see also Case C-437/09, *AG2R Prévoyance v Beaudout* [2011] ECR I-973.

[104] Case 553/12 P, *DEI* EU:C:2014:2083, para. 42.

[105] See Section 5.B.ii, p. 600.

[106] Case C-55/96, [1997] ECR I-7119.

[107] Case C-437/09, [2011] ECR I-973.

[108] Case T-556/08, *Slovenská Pošta* EU:C:2015:189.

[109] See Section 5.B.iv, p. 604.

[110] Case C-475/99, *Ambulanz Glöckner* [2001] ECR I-8089, Jacobs AG, para. 148.

postal[111] and telecommunications[112] sectors which were the subject of Article 106(3) decisions.[113] The abuses at issue under this head are violations of Article 102(b), 'limiting production, markets or technical development to the prejudice of consumers'.

(ii) The Cumulation of Rights Conferred on an Undertaking Create a Conflict of Interest

Cumulation of rights was an issue in *France v Commission*, *GB-Inno-BM*,[114] *ERT*,[115] *Raso*,[116] and *MOTOE*[117] where some type of 'regulatory' function given to the monopoly would enable it to disadvantage competitors in a downstream market.

The CJ did not appear to find the dual role of the pension funds in *Albany* (as both managers of the scheme and the authority with power to grant exemptions whereby companies could be allowed to insure with other undertakings) to constitute a conflict of interest. The Court held the situation justified because '[e]xercise of that power of exemption involves an evaluation of complex data relating to the pension schemes involved and the financial equilibrium of the fund, which necessarily implies a wide margin of appreciation'.[118] In that case, however, the Court concentrated on the application of Article 106(2) rather than Article 106(1) and, as we have seen,[119] passed rather quickly over the issue of Article 106(1) altogether. It is therefore unclear whether there was no infringement of Article 106(1) or whether the Court was applying Article 106(2) at this point.

(iii) The Extension of the Dominant Position

According to the CJ in *DEI* the extension of a dominant position, without any justification, is prohibited 'as such'.[120] As well as *DEI*, cases where Article 106(1) has been infringed by measures enabling an undertaking to extend its monopoly into neighbouring markets include *GB-Inno-BM SA* which can be classified under this head as well as head (ii) (cumulation of rights), as can *ERT*. The telecommunications case *France v Commission*[121] was also a matter of extension of rights as was *Connect Austria*.[122] In *Ambulanz Glöckner* the CJ said that the fact that the medical aid organisations providing emergency transport were consulted by the authorities about the permit applications of other undertakings wishing to operate in the non-emergency market gave the aid organisations an advantage in the latter. The 'essential facilities' case, *Port of Rødby*,[123] concerned an infringement of Article 106(1) as the port authority was able to refuse access to the port it controlled, thus eliminating competition from a competitor ferry company.

---

[111] See *Dutch Express Delivery Services* [1994] OJ L10/47; *Spanish Express Courier Services* [1990] OJ L233/19.

[112] See *Italian GSM* [1995] OJ L280/49; *Spanish GSM* [1997] OJ L79/19.

[113] See Section 8.B, p. 644.

[114] Case C-18/88, *GB-Inno-BM SA* [1991] ECR I-5973, see Section 5.B.v, p. 605.

[115] Case C-260/89, *ERT* [1991] ECR I-2925, Section 5.B.iii, p. 602.

[116] Case C-163/96, *Raso* [1998] ECR I-533, see Section 5.B.v, p. 607.

[117] Case C-49/07, *MOTOE* [2008] ECR I-4863, see Section 5.B.xii, p. 615.

[118] Case C-67/96, *Albany* [1999] ECR I-5751, para. 119. Jacobs AG was not so sanguine and considered that Art. 106(1) was infringed, see paras. 441–468.

[119] Section 5.B.viii, p. 609.

[120] Case C-553/12 P, *DEI* EU:C:2014:2083, see Section 5.B.xiii, p. 617.

[121] Case C-202/88, *France v Commission* [1991] ECR I-1223, Section 5.B.i, p. 599.

[122] Case C-462/99, *Connect Austria* [2003] ECR I-5147.

[123] [1994] OJ L55/52, see Chap. 7.

(iv) Inequality of Opportunity and Distortion of Competition

Inequality of opportunity was an issue in a number of cases such as *France v Commission*, *GB-Inno-BM*, *Connect Austria*, and *MOTOE*. The CJ has established in *DEI*[124] that a measure which creates inequality of opportunity and distorts competition thereby infringes Article 106(1) in conjunction with Article 102 without any need to identify any abuse. Rather, what needs to be shown is a potential or actual anti-competitive consequence.

(v) Pricing Abuses

Undertakings with exclusive rights may be enabled to commit pricing abuses. Indeed, price discrimination has featured in a number of cases concerning the conduct of undertakings given control over transport infrastructures.[125] *GT-Link*, where the port authority was guilty of price discrimination in waiving harbour duties in respect of its own ferry services and those of its partners but charging them to its competitors on the ferry market, is also a case where there was a cumulation of rights and where the undertaking was extending its monopoly into a downstream market.[126] In *OSA* the CJ held that excessive prices charged by a collecting society could be an abuse.[127]

(vi) Refusal to Supply

There may be refusal to supply in cases involving 'essential facilities', as in *Port of Rødby*. The refusal to deliver incoming cross-border mail in *Deutsche Post*[128] unless extra payments were made was treated as a refusal to supply.

(vii) 'Automatic' Abuse

In *Corbeau*[129] the Court found an infringement without seeking to identify any abuse. It appeared to consider that a monopoly which was too wide infringed Article 106(1) for that reason alone and did not identify any abuse. Buendia Sierra calls it the 'automatic abuse doctrine'.[130] No other case is such a clear example of this, though Buendia Sierra detects the same approach in *Deutsche Post* and *Dusseldorp*. In all these cases the Court was considering Article 106(1) en route to discussing the application of Article 106(2). In *Albany*,[131] the nature of the abuse was not clear, and the CJ concentrated on the application of Article 106(2). The Court did not however seem to be suggesting that the monopoly was too wide.

---

[124] Case C-553/12 P, *DEI* EU:C:2014:2083.

[125] See, e.g., Case C-266/96, *Corsica Ferries France* [1998] ECR I-3949 (discussed in Section 6.E.iii, p. 636); Case C-163/99, *Portugal v Commission* [2002] ECR I-2613 (concerning the landing fees at Portuguese airports, and discussed in Chap. 7); *Spanish Airports* [2000] OJ L208/36.

[126] Case C-242/95, *GT-Link A/S v Danske Staatsbaner (DSB)* [1997] ECR I-4449. In this case the Court in effect imposed on undertakings in this position an obligation to maintain a transparent accounting system demonstrating that they did not favour their own operations. Otherwise they would not be able to avoid a finding of abuse.

[127] Case C-351/12, *OSA* EU:C:2014:110.

[128] Cases C-147–148/97, *Deutsche Post* [2000] ECR I-825. See Section 5.B.ix, p. 611 and Section 6.E.iii, p. 640.

[129] Case C-320/91, *Corbeau* [1993] ECR I-2533, Section 5.B.vi, p. 607.

[130] Buendia Sierra in Faull and Nikpay, n. 2, 6.77.

[131] Case C-67/96, *Albany* [1999] ECR I-5751, Section 5.B.viii, p. 609.

6. ARTICLE 106(2)

A. THE INSTITUTIONAL SETTING OF SERVICES OF GENERAL ECONOMIC INTEREST

(i) Article 14 TFEU and Protocol 26

In the period leading up to the Intergovernmental Conference of 1996 the Commission suggested that a new paragraph should be inserted into Article 3 of the EC Treaty, adding 'a contribution to the promotion of services of general interest' to the activities of the Community. Instead, the Treaty of Amsterdam which came into force in 1999 added a new 'Principle', latterly Article 16, to the EC Treaty. Article 16, expanded by the Treaty of Lisbon, is now Article 14 TFEU.

a. Article 14 TFEU

Without prejudice to Article 4 of the Treaty on European Union or to Articles 93,[132] 106 and 107[133] of this Treaty, and given the place occupied by services of general economic interest in the shared values of the Union as well as their role in promoting social and territorial cohesion, the Union and the Member States, each within their respective powers and within the scope of application of the Treaties, shall take care that such services operate on the basis of principles and conditions, particularly economic and financial conditions, which enable them to fulfil their missions. The European Parliament and the Council, acting by means of regulations in accordance with the ordinary legislative procedure, shall establish these principles and set these conditions without prejudice to the competence of Member States, in compliance with the Treaties, to provide, to commission and to fund such services.

The two additions which did not appear in Article 16 EC are the phrase 'particularly economic and financial conditions' towards the end of the first sentence, and the whole second sentence which gives the EU power to legislate to establish the principles and conditions under which SGEIs operate.

Article 14 needs to be read in the context of the post-Lisbon Treaties as a whole. The 'shared values of the Union' is an important feature of the TEU. According to Article 2 the Union is founded on values common to the Member States, which are 'respect for human dignity, freedom, democracy, equality, the rule of law and respect for human rights, including the rights of persons belonging to minorities'. Article 3 TEU states that the Union is working for the sustainable development of Europe based on a highly competitive *social market* economy.

b. Protocol (No. 26) on Services of General Interest

A Protocol on *services of general interest* (rather than just SGEIs) was attached to the TEU and TFEU by the Treaty of Lisbon.

Article 1
The shared values of the Union in respect of services of general economic interest within the meaning of Article 14 of the Treaty on the Functioning of the European Union include in particular:

- the essential role and the wide discretion of national, regional and local authorities in providing, commissioning and organising services of general economic interest as closely as possible to the needs of the users;

- the diversity between various services of general economic interest and the differences in the needs and preferences of users that may result from different geographical, social or cultural situations;

---

[132] Art. 93 TFEU (ex Art. 73 EC) is a specific provision dealing with State aid in the transport sector.
[133] Art. 107 TFEU is the general provision on State aid.

– a high level of quality, safety and affordability, equal treatment and the promotion of universal access and of user rights.

Article 2

The provisions of the Treaties do not affect in any way the competence of Member States to provide, commission and organise non-economic services of general interest.

The Protocol therefore contains two Articles, one expanding on the meaning of Article 14 TFEU, and one which states that the Treaties do not in any way affect the competence of Member States in respect to non-economic services of *general interest*.

(ii) Article 36 of the Charter of Fundamental Rights

Article 36 of the Charter of Fundamental Rights of the European Union is entitled 'Access to Services of General Economic Interest'. It states:

The Union recognises and respects access to services of general economic interest as provided for in national laws and practices, in accordance with the Treaties, in order to promote the social and territorial cohesion of the Union.

This provision is about *access to* SGEIs rather than to their content or establishment because the Charter is about *rights*. It appears in Chapter IV of the Charter, 'Solidarity', and elevates access to SGEIs to the status of a fundamental right.

(iii) Commission Communications on Services of General Economic Interest and Services of General Interest

The Commission has issued a number of Communications and other documents on SGEIs and services of general interest.[134] These attempt to grapple with the problem of what services are, and are not, subject to the internal market and competition rules. The December 2011 Communication 'A Quality Framework for Services of General Interest in Europe'[135] (the Quality Framework) was adopted at the same time as a package of measures on SGEIs and State aid[136] to deal, inter alia, with the issues in the *Altmark* case,[137] and on SGEIs and public procurement.

B. THE CONCEPTS AND TERMINOLOGY OF 'SERVICES OF GENERAL ECONOMIC INTEREST' AND 'SERVICES OF GENERAL INTEREST'

The phrase '*services of general economic interest*' (SGEIs) has appeared in what is now Article 106(2) TFEU, since the inception of the EEC. It has appeared in what is now Article 14 TFEU since 1999, as already explained. It now appears in Protocol 26 and Article 36 of the Charter as well. Article 106(2) gives a limited derogation from (inter alia) the competition rules to undertakings entrusted with such services, in certain circumstances. What amounts to an SGEI is the subject of a considerable

---

[134] See Section 2, p. 589.

[135] COM(2011) 900 final.

[136] A Decision ([2012] OJ L7/3), two Communications ([2012] OJ C8/4 and [2012] OJ C8/15) and a de minimis Reg. (Reg. 360/12 [2012] OJ L114/8). See also the Staff Working Document on the application of the State aid rules to SGEIs and social services of general interest, mainly concerning State aid, procurement, social services and transport SWD(2013) 53/final/2, <http://ec.europa.eu/competition/state_aid/overview/new_guide_eu_rules_procurement_en.pdf>.

[137] Case C-280/00, *Altmark Trans GmbH, Regierungspräsidium Magdeburg v Nahverkehrsgesellschaft Altmark GmbH* [2003] ECR I-7747.

body of case law. The phrase is an unhappy one because of the placing of the word 'economic'. It is the service to which the word 'economic' really applies, rather than the 'interest'. It also overlaps with the concept of a service of *general interest*. The words *service of general interest* appear only in Protocol 26.

In the 2011 Communication the Commission admits that 'the debate on services of general interest suffers from a lack of clarity on terminology. The concepts are used interchangeably and inaccurately.' The Commission therefore sets out what it understands by the various concepts,[138] which it describes as 'dynamic and evolving'. It says that in doing this it is bound by EU primary law and by the case law of the Court (which is discussed in the following sections of this chapter).

Service of general interest (SGI): SGI are services that public authorities of the Member States classify as being of general interest and, therefore, subject to specific public service obligations (PSO). The term covers both economic activities (see the definition of SGEI below) and non-economic services. The latter are not subject to specific EU legislation and are not covered by the internal market and competition rules of the Treaty. Some aspects of how these services are organised may be subject to other general Treaty rules, such as the principle of non-discrimination.

Service of general economic interest (SGEI): SGEI are economic activities which deliver outcomes in the overall public good that would not be supplied (or would be supplied under different conditions in terms of quality, safety, affordability, equal treatment or universal access) by the market without public intervention. The PSO is imposed on the provider by way of an entrustment and on the basis of a general interest criterion which ensures that the service is provided under conditions allowing it to fulfil its mission.

Social services of general interest (SSGI): these include social security schemes covering the main risks of life and a range of other essential services provided directly to the person that play a preventive and socially cohesive/inclusive role . . . While some social services (such as statutory social security schemes) are not considered by the European Court as being economic activities, the jurisprudence of the Court makes clear that the social nature of a service is not sufficient in itself to classify it as non-economic . . . The term social service of general interest consequently covers both economic and non-economic activities.

Universal service obligation (USO): USO are a type of PSO which sets the requirements designed to ensure that certain services are made available to all consumers and users in a Member State, regardless of their geographical location, at a specified quality and, taking account of specific national circumstances, at an affordable price. The definition of specific USO are set at European level as an essential component of market liberalization of service sectors, such as electronic communications, post and transport.

Public service: Public service is used in article 93 TFEU in the field of transport. However, outside this area, the term is sometimes used in an ambiguous way: it can relate to the fact that a service is offered to the general public and/or in the public interest, or it can be used for the activity of entities in public ownership. To avoid ambiguity, this Communication does not use the term but follows the terminology 'service of general interest' and 'service of general economic interest'.

The Commission therefore makes it clear that SGEIs are a subset of services of general interest (SGIs). SGIs comprise:

- non-economic (i.e. non-market) services, to which the competition and internal market rules[139] do not apply in the first place. They are services of general interest but not services of general economic interest;

- services of general *economic* interest (i.e. market services) which are subject to the competition rules and the internal market rules since their activities are *economic* in nature.

Whether a service falls into the category of 'economic' or 'non-economic' services depends on the application of the concept of an 'economic activity'. Services provided as part of the prerogatives of the State are non-economic.[140] It is 'economic' services, SGEIs, which are the subject of Article 106(2).

---

[138] Previously explained in the 2007 Communication, see n. 14.

[139] Other EU rules, such as the principle of non-discrimination may, however, apply.

[140] Such as the police and the justice system.

C. THE PURPOSE OF ARTICLE 106(2)

Article 106(2) provides a limited derogation from the Treaty rules in order to deal with the activities of undertakings entrusted by the State with certain tasks. It provides that the Treaty rules shall apply to two sorts of undertaking—revenue-producing monopolies and those entrusted with SGEIs—only insofar as that does not obstruct the performance of their tasks. It is subject to the proviso that the exception should not affect trade to an extent contrary to the interests of the Union. Unlike Article 106(1), Article 106(2) is addressed to undertakings themselves and not to Member States, although Member States may rely on Article 106(2)[141] and, as we have seen, the two provisions may be applied together. As with Article 106(1), the competition rules are singled out for special mention and Article 106(2) is particularly important in relation to the application of Article 102.

Article 106(2) does not state what value is to be accorded to SGEIs and in particular does not say that 'universal service' (USO) should be protected or promoted.[142] In the past the provision tended to be construed narrowly (like other derogations in the Treaty), an interpretation which preserved the widest possible application of the competition rules.[143] However, from the case of *Corbeau* in 1993[144] onwards the Court has been more willing to accept that providers of public services may need to be protected from the full rigours of competition and has become more flexible in the way in which the criteria in Article 106(2) are applied. As Article 106(2) is a derogation from the normal rules it is for those claiming its benefit to show that its terms are satisfied.[145]

D. UNDERTAKINGS HAVING THE CHARACTER OF A REVENUE-PRODUCING MONOPOLY

This is a reference to undertakings which exploit their exclusive rights to raise revenue for the State. They may constitute commercial monopolies and so be subject to the rules laid down in Article 37 TFEU. Article 37 applies to 'any body through which a Member State, in law or in fact, either directly or indirectly supervises, determines or appreciably influences imports or exports between Member States'. Article 37 appears among the free movement provisions, but the CJ has said that it aims to eliminate distortions in competition in the internal market as well as discrimination against the products and trade of other Member States.[146]

E. UNDERTAKINGS ENTRUSTED WITH THE OPERATION OF SERVICES OF GENERAL ECONOMIC INTEREST

(i) 'Undertakings Entrusted With . . .'

'Undertaking' has the meaning previously discussed.[147] The legal status of the undertaking in national law is immaterial. It can be a public or private undertaking, but the important thing is that the State has assigned it certain tasks by a positive act conferring on it certain functions or by granting

---

[141] See, e.g., Case C-203/96, *Dusseldorp* [1998] ECR I-4075.

[142] See M. Ross, 'Art. 16 EC and Services of General Interest: From Derogation to Obligation?' (2000) 25 *ELRev* 22, 24; see further Case T-289/03, *BUPA v Commission* [2008] ECR II-18, and Section 6.E.ii, p. 630.

[143] See Case 127/73, *BRT v SABAM* [1974] ECR 313.

[144] Case C-320/91, [1993] ECR I-2533.

[145] Case C-157/94, *Commission v Netherlands* [1997] ECR I-5699, para. 58; Case T-556/08, *Slovenská Pošta* EU:C:2015:189, para 358.

[146] For a discussion of Art. 37 see Bellamy and Child (V. Rose and D. Bailey, eds.), *European Union Law of Competition* (7th edn, Oxford University Press, 2013), 11.036–11.045.

[147] See Chaps. 3 and 5.

it a concession. Merely tolerating, approving, or endorsing its activities is insufficient. So, according to the Commission, the Member States' approval of the Eurocheque system did not mean that Article 106(2) applied to the banks concerned.[148] The CJ held that an authors' rights society was not within the provision merely because it was subject to obligations imposed on all monopolies by national law[149] but the Commission has left open the question of whether a rights society might be 'entrusted' if the Member State's legislation described the functions and status of the society in an appropriate way.[150] The CJ held that the collecting society in *OSA* was not within Article 106(2). Although it was given exclusive rights to manage certain copyrights the State had not assigned any tasks to it and it managed private interests (albeit intellectual property rights which were protected by law).[151] In *Dusseldorp* the Advocate General said that an undertaking is 'entrusted' with a service where 'certain obligations are imposed on it by the State in the general economic interest'.[152]

In *BUPA* the Irish Government introduced a risk equalisation scheme in respect of private medical insurance (PMI) following the liberalisation of the sector. Under the scheme, insurers with a risk profile below the average were liable to pay a levy and those with a profile above the average were entitled to receive payments. The result of this was in effect to transfer funds from the private insurer, BUPA, to other operators. BUPA claimed that this amounted to illegal State aid. The question arose as to whether or not the PMI scheme adopted by Ireland had an SGEI mission. The question was relevant as compensation paid for the supply of SGEIs may not, in certain conditions, constitute State aid.[153] In an appeal from the decision holding that the scheme did not constitute State aid on these grounds, BUPA claimed that the insurers had not been 'entrusted' with an SGEI mission as required by Article 106(2).

Case T-289/03, *BUPA v Commission* [2008] ECR II-18

General Court

178. . . . [A]s the case-law shows, the provision of the service in question must, by definition, assume a general or public interest. Thus, SGEIs are distinguished in particular from services in the private interest, even though that interest may be more or less collective or be recognised by the State as legitimate or beneficial (see, to that effect, *Züchner*, paragraph 97 above, paragraph 7, and *GVL v Commission*, paragraph 98 above, paragraphs 31 and 32). In addition, as the applicants claim, the general or public interest on which the Member State relies must not be reduced to the need to subject the market concerned to certain rules or the commercial activity of the operators concerned to authorisation by the State. The mere fact that the national legislature, acting in the general interest in the broad sense, imposes certain rules of authorisation, of functioning or of control on all the operators in a particular sector does not in principle mean that there is an SGEI mission (see, to that effect, *GVL v Commission*, paragraph 98 above, paragraph 32, and *GB-Inno-BM*, paragraph 98 above, paragraph 22).

179. On the other hand, the recognition of an SGEI mission does not necessarily presume that the operator entrusted with that mission will be given an exclusive or special right to carry it out. It follows from a reading of paragraph 1 together with paragraph 2 of Article [106 TFEU] that a distinction must be drawn between a special or exclusive right conferred on an operator and the SGEI mission which, where appropriate, is attached to that right (see, in that regard, *Merci Convenzionali Porto di Genova*, paragraph 97

---

[148] *Uniform Eurocheques* [1985] OJ L35/43.

[149] *GEMA* [1971] OJ L134/15.

[150] COMP/38.698, *CISAC Agreement*, on appeal decisions partially annulled on other grounds, Cases T-442/08 etc., *CISAC v Commission* EU:T:2013:188.

[151] Case C-351/12, *OSA* EU:C:2014:110, para. 81.

[152] Case C-203/96, *Dusseldorp* [1998] ECR I-4075, Jacobs AG, para. 103.

[153] Case C-280/00, *Altmark* [2003] ECR I-7747, see Section 9, p. 646.

above, paragraphs 9 and 27; *Almelo*, paragraph 97 above, paragraphs 46 to 50; and *Albany*, paragraph 101 above, paragraphs 98 and 104 to 111). The grant of a special or exclusive right to an operator is merely the instrument, possibly justified, which allows that operator to perform an SGEI mission. Therefore . . . the Commission's finding at recital 47 to the contested decision, which refers to paragraphs 14 and 15 of the communication on services of general interest, that the attribution of an SGEI mission may also consist in an obligation imposed on a large number of, or indeed on all, the operators active on the same market, is not vitiated by an error (see, with respect to an SGEI mission entrusted in the context of a non-exclusive concession governed by public law, *Almelo*, paragraph 97 above, paragraph 47).

180. Consequently, the applicants' argument that the existence of an SGEI mission is precluded because all PMI insurers are subject to certain obligations cannot succeed.

181. In the second place, it must be borne in mind that, in essence . . . the wording of Article [106(2)], as such, require[s] that the operator in question be entrusted with an SGEI mission by an act of a public authority and that the act clearly define the SGEI obligations in question (see, to that effect, *Züchner*, paragraph 97 above, paragraph 7; Case 66/86 *Ahmed Saeed Flugreisen* . . . paragraph 55; *GT-Link*, paragraph 97 above, paragraph 51; *Altmark*, paragraph 89; and *Olsen v Commission*, paragraph 166 above, paragraph 186).

182. In the present case, contrary to the theory put forward by the applicants, the relevant Irish legislation does not involve any regulation or authorisation whatsoever relating to the activity of PMI insurers, but must be characterised as an act of a public authority creating and defining a specific mission consisting in the provision of PMI services in compliance with the PMI obligations . . . Furthermore, with the stated object of serving the general interest by allowing what is at present approximately half of the Irish population to benefit from alternative cover for certain health care, in particular hospital care, the above mentioned PMI obligations restrict the commercial freedom of the PMI insurers to an extent going considerably beyond ordinary conditions of authorisation to exercise an activity in a specific sector (see paragraph 191 et seq. below).

183. . . . Furthermore, since the system chosen by Ireland does not provide for the grant of exclusive or special rights, but for the achievement of the mission by all operators active on the Irish PMI market, which is a choice open to the Member State (see paragraph 179 above), it follows that, contrary to what the applicants appear to claim, there can be no requirement that each of the operators subject to the PMI obligations be separately entrusted with that mission by an individual act or mandate.

184. Accordingly, the complaint that the activity of the PMI insurers is governed by 'normal' regulatory obligations and that there is no act of a public authority creating and entrusting an SGEI mission must be rejected.

In this case, therefore, the GC drew a distinction between a State imposing general regulatory rules on a sector and entrusting undertakings with an SGEI mission. It did not matter that the SGEI was entrusted to a number of undertakings and not to just one. Being entrusted with an SGEI did not necessarily mean that an undertaking had to be granted a special or exclusive right. It was therefore not required that each undertaking concerned had to be individually entrusted with the SGEI rather than just being subject to the scheme laid down by the State.

(ii) Operation of Services of General Economic Interest

The word 'services' is construed to cover the widest spectrum of activities and is not limited to the meaning of the term as used in the free movement provisions. 'Services of general economic interest' denotes activities that need to be carried out in the public interest. As the Advocate General said in *Dusseldorp*:[154]

---

[154] Case C-203/96, *Dusseldorp* [1998] ECR I-4075, Jacobs AG, para. 105.

The reason for the assignment of particular tasks to undertakings is often that the tasks need to be undertaken in the public interest but might not be undertaken, usually for economic reasons, if the service were to be left to the private sector.

In the *Telecommunications Equipment* case the CJ explained that Article 106(2) reconciles the interests of Member States and the Union:[155]

In allowing derogations to be made from the general rules of the Treaty in certain circumstances, that provision seeks to reconcile the Member States' interest in using certain undertakings, in particular in the public sector, as an instrument of economic or fiscal policy with the Community's interest in ensuring compliance with the rules on competition and the preservation of the unity of the common market.

Further, this passage refers to undertakings which are used as instruments of economic or fiscal policy. In *Albany International* the CJ applied the same principle to social policy.[156]

In *BUPA*, as seen in the next extract (paragraph 172), the GC stated that an SGEI has to satisfy certain minimum criteria derived from the case law. These are, in addition to the act of entrusting, that the mission has to be 'universal' and 'compulsory'. Within those criteria the Member States have a wide discretion.

The most obvious candidates for recognition as SGEIs on this basis are the utilities, as the Commission stated in its *XXth Report on Competition Policy*.[157] However, the concept of SGEIs has been expanded significantly beyond this. The EU Courts or the Commission have accepted as SGEIs, inter alia, the administration of major waterways;[158] the operation of non-economically viable air routes;[159] the operation of the electricity supply network;[160] the distribution of water;[161] the operation of the basic, as distinct from extra 'added-value', postal service;[162] the operation of public telecommunications networks;[163] television services;[164] employment recruitment;[165] mooring services in ports;[166] the treatment of waste;[167] regional development;[168] sectoral supplementary pension funds;[169] the performance of obligations flowing from the Universal Postal Convention;[170] the provision of emergency ambulance services;[171] and the provision of private medical insurance.[172] The Commission held that in principle the provision of banking services to people who have difficulty

---

[155] Case C-202/88, *France v Commission* [1991] ECR I-1223, para. 12; see also Case C-157/94, *Commission v Netherlands (Re Electricity Imports)* [1997] ECR I-5699, para. 39.

[156] Case C-67/96, *Albany* [1999] ECR I-5751, paras. 103–105.

[157] (1990), Introduction, 12.

[158] Case 10/71, *Ministère Public of Luxembourg v Muller* [1971] ECR 723.

[159] Case 66/86, *Ahmed Saeed* [1989] ECR 803.

[160] Case C-393/92, *Gemeente Almelo* [1994] ECR I-1477; in Case C-157/94, *Commission v Netherlands (Re Electricity Imports)* [1997] ECR I-5699 the Commission did not contest that the monopoly electricity distributor in the Netherlands provided a service of general economic interest.

[161] *Navewa-Anseau* [1982] OJ L167/48.

[162] *Dutch Courier Services* [1990] OJ L10/47, [1990] 4 CMLR 947; *Spanish Courier Services* [1990] OJ L233/19, [1991] 4 CMLR 560; Case C-320/91, *Corbeau* [1993] ECR I-2533.

[163] Case 41/83, *Italy v Commission* [1985] ECR 873.

[164] Case 155/73, *Sacchi* [1974] ECR 430.

[165] Case 41/90, *Höfner* [1991] ECR I-1979.

[166] Case C-266/96, *Corsica Ferries France SA v Gruppo Antichi Ormeggiatori del Porto di Genova* [1998] ECR I-3949.

[167] Case C-209/98, *Sydhavnens* [2000] ECR I-3743.

[168] Case T-260/94, *Air Inter v Commission* [1997] ECR II-997, para. 40, see Section 6.E.iii, p. 640.

[169] Case C-67/96, *Albany* [1999] ECR-5751.

[170] Joined Cases C-147–148/97, *Deutsche Post* [2000] ECR I-825.

[171] Case C-475/99, *Ambulanz Glöckner* [2001] ECR I-8089. Jacobs AG considered that non-emergency ambulance services were also services of general economic interest, see para. 175.

[172] Case T-289/03, *BUPA* [2008] ECR II-18; see M. G. Ross, 'A Healthy Approach to Services of General Economic Interest? The *BUPA* Judgment of the Court of First Instance' (2009) 34 *ELRev* 127.

in accessing basic banking services could be an SGEI (although it was not in the case concerned).[173] The CJ did not, however, accept that commercial port operations are SGEIs[174] and it has sometimes left open the status of the services provided, and said that even if they were of general economic interest the other criteria in Article 106(2) were not fulfilled.[175]

Extracts from the judgments in the leading cases on what amounts to an SGEI service of general economic interest are set out in Section 6.E.iii as they usually deal also with the question of whether non-compliance with the Treaty rules is essential to the fulfilment of the entrusted tasks. However, the following extract from *BUPA*, the facts of which have already been given, deals with the width of the Member States' discretion to define SGEIs and with what is meant by 'universal service'.

Case T-289/03, *BUPA v Commission* [2008] ECR II-18

General Court

166. As regards competence to determine the nature and scope of an SGEI mission within the meaning of the Treaty, and also the degree of control that the Community institutions must exercise in that context, it follows from paragraph 22 of the Communication on SGEIs . . . [2000] and from the case-law of the [General Court] that Member States have a wide discretion to define what they regard as SGEIs and that the definition of such services by a Member State can be questioned by the Commission only in the event of manifest error (see Case T-17/02 *Fred Olsen v Commission* . . . paragraph 216 and the case-law there cited).

167. That prerogative of the Member State concerning the definition of SGEIs is confirmed by the absence of any competence specially attributed to the Commission and by the absence of a precise and complete definition of the concept of SGEI in Community law. The determination of the nature and scope of an SGEI mission in specific spheres of action which either do not fall within the powers of the Community, within the meaning of the first paragraph of Article [5 TEU], or are based on only limited or shared Community competence, within the meaning of the second paragraph of that article,[176] remains, in principle, within the competence of the Member States. As the defendant and Ireland maintain, the health sector falls almost exclusively within the competence of the Member States. In that sector, the Community can engage, under Article [168 TFEU] and [5 TEU], only in action which is not legally binding, while fully respecting the responsibilities of the Member States for the organisation and provision of health services and medical care. It follows that the determination of SGEI obligations in this context also falls primarily within the competence of the Member States. That division of powers is also reflected, generally, in Article [14 TFEU], which provides that, given the place occupied by SGEIs in the shared values of the Union as well as their role in promoting social and territorial cohesion, the Community and the Member States, each within their respective powers and within the scope of application of the Treaty, are to take care that such services operate on the basis of principles and conditions which enable them to fulfil their missions.

168. In that regard, the applicants cannot validly rely on Case 41/83 *Italy v Commission*, paragraph 100 above (paragraph 30), to demonstrate the need for full and unrestricted control by the Community institutions of the existence of an SGEI mission in the health sector . . .

---

[173] *La Banque Postale, les Caisses d'Épargne et de Prévoyance and the Crédit Mutuel, for the distribution of the Livret A and Livret Bleu*, 10 May 2007.

[174] Case C-179/90, *Merci Convenzionali* [1991] ECR I-5889; Case C-242/95, *GT-Link v De Danske Statsbaner (DSB)* [1997] ECR I-4449.

[175] E.g., Case C-203/96, *Dusseldorp* [1998] ECR I-4075.

[176] Art. 5 TEU replaced Art. 5 EC to which this judgment actually refers. Both Articles deal with the competence of respectively the EU and the EC. Art. 5 TEU is more detailed and specific but does not alter the principle upon which the GC relied here.

169. Consequently, the control which the Community institutions are authorised to exercise over the use of the discretion of the Member State in determining SGEIs is limited to ascertaining whether there is a manifest error of assessment. In the contested decision (recital 44), the Commission did in fact exercise that control by considering whether Ireland's assessment of the presence of an SGEI mission and of the characterisation of the PMI obligations as SGEI obligations was vitiated by a manifest error.

170. Accordingly, the complaint that the Commission unlawfully delegated to the Irish authorities the definition of the SGEIs in question and that it failed to exercise full and unrestricted control of the assessment made by those authorities with respect to a strict and objective definition of the SGEIs in Community law cannot be upheld.

iii) The existence of an SGEI mission in the present case

. . .

172. . . . . In that regard, the Court notes at the outset that even though the Member State has a wide discretion when determining what it regards as an SGEI, that does not mean that it is not required, when it relies on the existence of and the need to protect an SGEI mission, to ensure that that mission satisfies certain minimum criteria common to every SGEI mission within the meaning of the EC Treaty, as explained in the case-law, and to demonstrate that those criteria are indeed satisfied in the particular case. These are, notably, the presence of an act of the public authority entrusting the operators in question with an SGEI mission and the universal and compulsory nature of that mission. Conversely, the lack of proof by the Member State that those criteria are satisfied, or failure on its part to observe them, may constitute a manifest error of assessment, in which case the Commission is required to make a finding to that effect, failing which the Commission itself makes a manifest error. Furthermore, it follows from the case-law on Article [106(2)] that the Member State must indicate the reasons why it considers that the service in question, because of its specific nature, deserves to be characterised as an SGEI and to be distinguished from other economic activities (see, to that effect, *Merci Convenzionali Porto di Genova*, paragraph 97 above, paragraph 27, and *Enirisorse*, paragraph 131 above, paragraphs 33 and 34). In the absence of such reasons, even a marginal review by the Community institutions . . . with respect to the existence of a manifest error by the Member State in the context of its discretion would not be possible.

173. It is in the light of those considerations that the Court will examine the complaints whereby the applicants seek to demonstrate that in this case the Commission was wrong to accept the existence of an SGEI mission.

. . .

4) The universal and compulsory nature of the services coming within the SGEI mission

185. The applicants submit that the fact that the PMI services are not universal and compulsory by nature supports their conclusion that there is no SGEI mission in this case.

General observations

186. As regards the universal nature of the PMI services, it must be noted at the outset that, contrary to the theory put forward by the applicants, it does not follow from Community law that, in order to be capable of being characterised as an SGEI, the service in question must constitute a universal service in the strict sense, such as the public social security scheme. In effect, the concept of universal service, within the meaning of Community law, does not mean that the service in question must respond to a need common to the whole population or be supplied throughout a territory (see, in that regard, *Ahmed Saeed Flugreisen*, paragraph 181 above, paragraph 55; *Corsica Ferries France*, paragraph 97 above, paragraph 45; and *Olsen v Commission*, paragraph 166 above, paragraph 186 et seq.). As stated at recital 47 to the contested decision, with reference to paragraph 14 of the communication on SGEIs, although those characteristics correspond to the classical type of SGEI, and the one most widely encountered in Member States, that does not preclude the existence of other, equally lawful, types of SGEIs which the Member States may validly choose to create in the exercise of their discretion.

187. Accordingly, the fact that the SGEI obligations in question have only a limited territorial or material application or that the services concerned are enjoyed by only a relatively limited group of users does not necessarily call in question the universal nature of an SGEI mission within the meaning of Community law. It follows that the applicants' restrictive understanding of the universal nature of an SGEI, based on certain Commission reports or documents, the content of which, moreover, is not legally binding, is not compatible with the scope of the discretion which Member States have when defining an SGEI mission. Consequently, that argument must be rejected as unfounded.

188. As regards the argument that the PMI services represent only optional, indeed 'luxury', financial services, intended to provide complementary or supplementary cover by reference to the compulsory universal services provided for by the public health insurance system, the Court observes that the compulsory nature of the service in question is an essential condition of the existence of an SGEI mission within the meaning of Community law. That compulsory nature must be understood as meaning that the operators entrusted with the SGEI mission by an act of a public authority are, in principle, required to offer the service in question on the market in compliance with the SGEI obligations which govern the supply of that service. From the point of view of the operator entrusted with an SGEI mission, that compulsory nature—which in itself is contrary to business freedom and the principle of free competition—may consist, inter alia, particularly in the case of the grant of an exclusive or special right, in an obligation to exercise a certain commercial activity independently of the costs associated with that activity (see also, to that effect, paragraph 14 of the communication on SGEIs). In such a case, that obligation constitutes the counterpart of the protection of the SGEI mission and of the associated market position by the act which entrusted the mission. In the absence of an exclusive or special right, the compulsory nature of an SGEI mission may lie in the obligation borne by the operator in question, and provided for by an act of a public authority, to offer certain services to every citizen requesting them (see also, to that effect, paragraph 15 of the communication on SGEIs).

189. Contrary to the applicants' opinion, however, the binding nature of the SGEI mission does not presuppose that the public authorities impose on the operator concerned an obligation to provide a service having a clearly predetermined content . . . In effect, the compulsory nature of the SGEI mission does not preclude a certain latitude being left to the operator on the market, including in relation to the content and pricing of the services which it proposes to provide. In those circumstances, a minimum of freedom of action on the part of operators and, accordingly, of competition on the quality and content of the services in question is ensured, which is apt to limit, in the community interest, the scope of the restriction of competition which generally results from the attribution of an SGEI mission, without any effect on the objectives of that mission.

190. It follows that, in the absence of an exclusive or special right, it is sufficient, in order to conclude that a service is compulsory, that the operator entrusted with a particular mission is under an obligation to provide that service to any user requesting it. In other words, the compulsory nature of the service and, accordingly, the existence of an SGEI mission are established if the service-provider is obliged to contract, on consistent conditions, without being able to reject the other contracting party. That element makes it possible to distinguish a service forming part of an SGEI mission from any other service provided on the market and, accordingly, from any other activity carried out in complete freedom (see, to that effect, *GT-Link*, paragraph 97 above, paragraph 53, and *Merci Convenzionali Porto di Genova*, paragraph 97 above, paragraph 27).

The GC therefore held that Ireland's PMI scheme did have an SGEI mission. This was despite it not being 'a universal service in the strict sense' of responding to a need common to the entire population or being supplied throughout a territory. It did not matter that there was a limited territorial or material application or that the services concerned were enjoyed by only a relatively limited group of users (paragraph 187). The important thing was the compulsory nature of the service and the fact that the service provider was obliged to contract, on consistent conditions, and could not refuse the other contracting party (paragraph 190). It is these features which define an SGEI.

(iii) Obstruct the Performance of the Particular Tasks Assigned to Them

Even if an activity is accepted as an SGEI it still has to be shown that compliance with the Treaty rules would 'obstruct the performance' of the particular tasks assigned to the undertaking.

Until 1993 the CJ took a very strict view of the 'obstruct the performance' test. Thus, in *Höfner v Macrotron* the CJ accepted that the Bundesanstalt had been entrusted with SGEIs but said that such an undertaking remained subject to the competition rules 'unless and to the extent to which it is shown that their application is *incompatible* with the discharge of its duties'[177] (emphasis added); in *Merci Convenzionali*[178] it said that even if SGEIs had been involved it would not have been necessary for the undertaking to infringe the Treaty rules; in *British Telecom*[179] it said that Italy had failed to establish that compliance by BT with the competition rules would obstruct it in carrying out its tasks; and in *GB-Inno-BM SA*[180] it did not accept that the undertaking entrusted with the public telephone network also needed power to lay down the standards for telephone equipment and to check rival equipment suppliers' compliance with them.[181]

The CJ changed its approach in *Corbeau*,[182] and recognised that Article 106(2) contains what is in effect a proportionality requirement. The facts of *Corbeau* have already been given. It will be recalled that the CJ considered both Article 106(1) and Article 106(2) and seemed to say that Member States may grant special or exclusive rights only insofar as they entrust undertakings with SGEIs and the criteria in Article 106(2) are fulfilled.[183] The Court went on to consider the application of Article 106(2).

Case C-320/91, *Corbeau* [1993] ECR I-2533

Court of Justice

15. As regards the services at issue in the main proceedings, it cannot be disputed that the Régie des Postes is entrusted with a service of general economic interest consisting in the obligation to collect, carry and distribute mail on behalf of all users throughout the territory of the Member State concerned, at uniform tariffs and on similar quality conditions, irrespective of the specific situations or the degree of economic profitability of each individual operation.

16. The question which falls to be considered is therefore the extent to which a restriction on competition or even the exclusion of all competition from other economic operators is necessary in order to allow the holder of the exclusive right to perform its task of general interest and in particular to have the benefit of economically acceptable conditions.

17. The starting point of such an examination must be the premise that the obligation on the part of the undertaking entrusted with that task to perform its services in conditions of economic equilibrium presupposes that it will be possible to offset less profitable sectors against the profitable sectors and hence justifies a restriction of competition from individual undertakings where the economically profitable sectors are concerned.

18. Indeed, to authorize individual undertakings to compete with the holder of the exclusive rights in the sectors of their choice corresponding to those rights would make it possible for them to concentrate on the economically profitable operations and to offer more advantageous tariffs than those adopted by

---

[177] Case C-41/90, *Höfner v Macrotron* [1991] ECR I-1979, para. 24.

[178] Case C-179/90, *Merci Convenzionali* [1991] ECR I-5009.

[179] Case 41/83, *Italy v Commission* [1985] ECR 873.

[180] Case C-18/88, *RTT v GB-Inno-BM SA* [1991] ECR I-5973.

[181] See also Case 66/86, *Ahmed Saeed* [1989] ECR 803; Commission Decision, *Dutch Courier Services* [1990] OJ L10/47.

[182] Case C-320/91, *Corbeau* [1993] ECR I-2533.

[183] Ibid., para. 14.

the holders of the exclusive rights since, unlike the latter, they are not bound for economic reasons to offset losses in the unprofitable sectors against profits in the more profitable sectors.

19. However, the exclusion of competition is not justified as regards specific services dissociable from the service of general interest which meet special needs of economic operators and which call for certain additional services not offered by the traditional postal service, such as collection from the senders' address, greater speed or reliability of distribution or the possibility of changing the destination in the course of transit, in so far as such specific services, by their nature and the conditions in which they are offered, such as the geographical area in which they are provided, do not compromise the economic equilibrium of the service of general economic interest performed by the holder of the exclusive right.

20. It is for the national court to consider whether the services at issue in the dispute before it meet those criteria.

21. The answer to the questions referred to the Court by the Tribunal Correctionnel de Liège should therefore be that it is contrary to Article [106] for legislation of a Member State which confers on a body such as the Régie des Postes the exclusive right to collect, carry and distribute mail, to prohibit, under threat of criminal penalties, an economic operator established in that State from offering certain specific services dissociable from the service of general interest which meet the special needs of economic operators and call for certain additional services not offered by the traditional postal service, in so far as those services do not compromise the economic equilibrium of the service of general economic interest performed by the holder of the exclusive right. It is for the national court to consider whether the services in question in the main proceedings meet those criteria.

In this judgment the Court accepted that the operation of a basic postal system providing a universal service is an SGEI and that the normal principles of competition law will not apply to the extent necessary to preserve it through cross-subsidy. The undertaking must have 'economically acceptable conditions' (paragraph 16) and be able to perform its task in 'conditions of economic equilibrium' (paragraph 17). If competitors are allowed to come in and 'cherry-pick' or 'cream-skim' the most profitable parts of the system the holder of the exclusive right required to operate the universal service cannot operate under economically acceptable conditions. The Court said, however, in paragraph 19 that this does not justify the exclusion of competition from additional services, separable from the basic public service, if these could be offered by other undertakings without compromising the economic viability of the latter. *Corbeau* is a paradoxical case: it is the high-water mark of hostility by the Court to the very existence of statutory monopoly in the context of Article 106(1) but the dawn of a much more flexible and generous (to incumbents) interpretation of Article 106(2).

The CJ elaborated on the *Corbeau* ruling in *Commission v Netherlands*. It said again that the entrusted undertaking must be allowed 'economically acceptable conditions'. It also said that the undertaking does not have to prove that there is no other way but the impugned measure whereby it could carry out its task.[184]

Case 157/94, *Commission v Netherlands (Re Electricity Imports)* [1997] ECR I-5699

Court of Justice

52. . . . [I]t is not necessary, in order for the conditions for the application of Article [106(2)] to be fulfilled, that the financial balance or economic viability of the undertaking entrusted with the operation of a service of general economic interest should be threatened. It is sufficient that, in the absence of the rights at

---

[184] Cf. Darmon AG in Case C-393/92, *Almelo* [1994] ECR I-1477, on this point.

issue, it would not be possible for the undertaking to perform the particular tasks entrusted to it, defined by reference to the obligations and constraints to which it is subject.

53. Moreover, it follows from the *Corbeau* judgment . . . that the conditions for the application of Article [106(2)] are fulfilled in particular if maintenance of those rights is necessary to enable the holder of them to perform the tasks of general economic interest assigned to it under economically acceptable conditions.

. . .

58. Whilst it is true that it is incumbent upon a Member State which invokes Article [106(2)] to demonstrate that the conditions laid down by that provision are met, that burden of proof cannot be so extensive as to require the Member State, when setting out in detail the reasons for which, in the event of elimination of the contested measures, the performance, under economically acceptable conditions, of the tasks of general economic interest which it has entrusted to an undertaking would, in its view, be jeopardized, to go even further and prove, positively, that no other conceivable measure, which by definition would be hypothetical, could enable those tasks to be performed under the same conditions.

In *Corbeau* the Court did not consider whether the universal service provision could be achieved by a less extreme measure than granting a monopoly. Universal service and cross-subsidisation are not inseparable: it is possible for the State to subsidise the universal service, for example. It will be noted that it was left (*Corbeau*, paragraph 21) to the national court actually to determine whether or not the additional services *were* severable and able to be operated by other undertakings without prejudicing the economic equilibrium of the traditional postal service. This left the national court with a difficult task involving extensive economic analysis. It had to decide the extent of the cross-subsidisation, and how far this was necessary to maintain the 'economic equilibrium'.[185] Cross-subsidisation is a problematic issue, particularly in respect of network monopolies.

Issues similar to those in *Corbeau* arose in *Almelo* where the Court dealt with a preliminary reference from a Dutch court seised of litigation between regional and local electricity distributors concerning, inter alia, the legality of an exclusive purchasing clause.

Case C-393/92, *Gemeente Almelo and Others v Energiebedrijf Ijsselmij NV* [1994] ECR I-1477

Court of Justice

46. Article [106(2)] provides that undertakings entrusted with the operation of services of general economic interest may be exempted from the application of the competition rules contained in the Treaty in so far as it is necessary to impose restrictions on competition, or even to exclude all competition, from other economic operators in order to ensure the performance of the particular tasks assigned to them (see the judgment in Case C-320/91 *Corbeau* . . . paragraph 14).

47. As regards the question whether an undertaking such as IJM has been entrusted with the operation of services of general interest, it should be borne in mind that it has been given the task, through the grant of a non-exclusive concession governed by public law, of ensuring the supply of electricity in part of the national territory.

48. Such an undertaking must ensure that throughout the territory in respect of which the concession is granted, all consumers, whether local distributors or end-users, receive uninterrupted supplies of

[185] See L. Hancher, 'Casenote on *Corbeau*' (1994) 31 *CMLRev* 105, 119–120. For the issue of the direct effect of Art.106, see Section 7, p. 643.

electricity in sufficient quantities to meet demand at any given time, at uniform tariff rates and on terms which may not vary save in accordance with objective criteria applicable to all customers.

49. Restrictions on competition from other economic operators must be allowed so far as they are necessary in order to enable the undertaking entrusted with such a task of general interest to perform it. In that regard, it is necessary to take into consideration the economic conditions in which the undertaking operates, in particular the costs which it has to bear and the legislation, particularly concerning the environment, to which it is subject.

50. It is for the national court to consider whether an exclusive purchasing clause prohibiting local distributors from importing electricity is necessary in order to enable the regional distributor to perform its task of general interest.

Here again, the CJ accepted that the undertaking provided a service of general economic interest and that Article 106(2) allows the restrictions of competition necessary for the performance of its universal service obligations (although it was for the national court to make the decision whether the actual restriction at issue in the case was necessary for that purpose). Ross comments that *Almelo*, reinforcing *Corbeau*, was a movement towards recognising the value of public service independently of its economic viability because 'it clearly indicated that the availability of the derogation was to be measured by a balancing exercise based upon competing priorities rather than inhibiting that choice by insisting upon narrow economic tests to be satisfied before the normal market rules can be disapplied'.[186]

In *Dusseldorp*,[187] however, where the Court was dealing with an undertaking with a monopoly over certain waste incineration, it was less flexible and reverted to a previous, more stringent approach. It said that even if the task could constitute a task of general economic interest it was for the Dutch Government to show to the satisfaction of the national court that the objective could not be equally achieved by other means, and that Article 106(2) could apply only if it was shown that without the contested measure the undertaking could not carry out its entrusted task.[188]

In some cases, unlike *Corbeau* and *Almelo*, the Court has not left the decision to the national court but has actually decided that the conditions in Article 106(2) were satisfied. This can be seen in *Corsica Ferries France*, *Albany*, and *Deutsche Post*.

Case C-266/96, *Corsica Ferries France SA v Gruppo Antichi Ormeggiatori del Porto di Genova Coop and Others* [1998] ECR I-3949

Under Italian law ships from other Member States were required to use the services of local mooring companies who held exclusive concessions in each port. Corsica Ferries claimed that the Genoa and La Spezia mooring groups were abusing their dominant positions by preventing shipping companies using their own staff to carry out mooring operations, in the excessive nature of the price of the service which bore no relation to the actual cost of the service provided, and in fixing tariffs that varied from port to port for equivalent services. The Italian court asked, inter alia, whether the Treaty prohibited national measures which put the mooring companies in the position to act in this way.

---

[186] M. Ross, 'Art. 16 EC and Services of General Interest: From Derogation to Obligation' (2000) 25 *ELRev* 22, 25.

[187] Case C-203/96, *Dusseldorp* [1998] ECR I-4075.

[188] Ibid., para. 67.

Court of Justice

36. The national court asks whether there is an abuse, on the part of the Genoa and La Spezia mooring groups, of their dominant position on a substantial part of the Common Market by virtue of the exclusive rights conferred upon them by the Italian public authorities.

37. There are three aspects of the abuse alleged in this case. It is said to reside in the grant of exclusive rights to local mooring groups, preventing shipping companies from using their own staff to carry out mooring operations, in the excessive nature of the price of the service, which bears no relation to the actual cost of the service provided, and in the fixing of tariffs that vary from port to port for equivalent services.

38. As regards the definition of the market in question, it appears from the order for reference that it consists in the performance on behalf of third persons of mooring services relating to container freight in the ports of Genoa and La Spezia. Having regard, *inter alia*, to the volume of traffic in those ports and their importance in intra-Community trade, those markets may be regarded as constituting a substantial part of the Common Market (Case C-179/90, *Merci Convenzionali Porto di Genova* . . . and Case C-163/96, *Raso and Others* . . .

39. As far as the existence of exclusive rights is concerned, it is settled law that an undertaking having a statutory monopoly in a substantial part of the Common Market may be regarded as having a dominant position within the meaning of Article [102] of the Treaty (Case C-41/90, *Höfner and Elser* v. *Macrotron* . . . Case C-260/89, *ERT* v. *DEP* . . . *Merci Convenzionali Porto di Genova* . . . and *Raso and Others* . . .

40. Next, it should be pointed out that although merely creating a dominant position by granting exclusive rights within the meaning of Article [106 (1)] is not in itself incompatible with Article [102], a Member State is in breach of the prohibitions contained in those two provisions if the undertaking in question, merely by exercising the exclusive rights granted to it, is led to abuse its dominant position or if such rights are liable to create a situation in which that undertaking is led to commit such abuses (Case C-41/90, *Höfner and Elser* v. *Macrotron* . . . Case C-260/89, *ERT* v. *DEP* . . . *Merci Convenzionali Porto di Genova* . . . Case C-323/93, *Centre d'Insemination de la Crespelle* . . . *Raso and others* . . .).

41. It follows that a Member State may, without infringing Article [102], grant exclusive rights for the supply of mooring services in its ports to local mooring groups provided those groups do not abuse their dominant position or are not led necessarily to commit such an abuse.

42. In order to rebut the existence of such abuse, the Genoa and La Spezia mooring groups rely on Article [106(2)], which provides that undertakings entrusted with the operation of services of general economic interest are to be subject to the competition rules contained in the Treaty only in so far as their application does not obstruct the performance, in law or in fact, of the particular tasks assigned to them. Article [106(2)] further provides that, in order for it to apply, the development of trade must not be affected to such an extent as would be contrary to the interests of the Community.

43. They maintain that the tariffs applied are indispensable if a universal mooring service is to be maintained. On the one hand, the tariffs include a component corresponding to the additional cost of providing a universal mooring service. On the other hand, the difference in the tariffs from one port to another, which, according to the file, result from account being taken, when the tariffs are calculated, of corrective factors reflecting the influence of local circumstances—which would tend to indicate that the services provided are not equivalent—are justified by the characteristics of the service and the need to ensure universal coverage.

44. It must therefore be considered whether the derogation from the rules of the Treaty provided for in Article [106(2)] may fall to be applied. To that end, it must be determined whether the mooring service can be regarded as a service of general economic interest within the meaning of that provision and, if so, first, whether performance of the particular tasks assigned to it can be achieved only through services for which the charge is higher than their actual cost and for which the tariff varies from one port to another, and secondly, whether the development of trade is not affected to such an extent as would be contrary to the interests of the Community (see, to that effect, Case C-157/94, *E.C. Commission* v. *Netherlands* . . .).

45. It is evident from the file on the case in the main proceedings that mooring operations are of general economic interest, such interest having special characteristics, in relation to those of other economic activities, which is capable of bringing them within the scope of Article [106(2)] Mooring groups are obliged to provide at any time and to any user a universal mooring service, for reasons of safety in port waters. At all events, Italy could properly have considered that it was necessary, on grounds of public security, to confer on local groups of operators the exclusive right to provide a universal mooring service.

46. In those circumstances it is not incompatible with Articles [102] and [106(1)] to include in the price of the service a component designed to cover the cost of maintaining the universal mooring service, inasmuch as it corresponds to the supplementary cost occasioned by the special characteristics of that service, and to lay down for that service different tariffs on the basis of the particular characteristics of each port.

47. Consequently, since the mooring groups have in fact been entrusted by the Member State with managing a service of general economic interest within the meaning of Article [106(2)], and the other conditions for applying the derogation from application of the Treaty rules which is laid down in that provision are satisfied, legislation such as that at issue does not constitute an infringement of Article [102], read in conjunction with Article [106(1)].

As in *Corbeau*, the CJ considered that the exclusive rights could escape the prohibition in Article 106(1) if they satisfied Article 106(2). However, the Court did not leave this determination to the national court, but said that the mooring operations were SGEIs provided on a universal basis and that it was, in the circumstances, not incompatible with the Treaty to include supplementary costs related to the running of that service and to charge varying tariffs (paragraph 46). Therefore there was no infringement of Article 106(1). There is no explanation of how the Court reached its conclusions in paragraph 46, or of how the supplementary costs arose or what cross-subsidisation was taking place.

The CJ also made a clear decision on the application of Article 106(2) in *Albany*. It will be remembered from the earlier discussion of Article 106(1)[189] that the case concerned the Dutch regime of compulsory affiliation to sectoral pension schemes. The Court considered whether the derogation in Article 106(2) applied, and held that it did because the scheme involved a service of general economic interest which had to operate under 'economically acceptable conditions'.

Case C-67/96, *Albany International BV v Stichting Bedrijfspensioenfonds Textielindustrie* [1999] ECR I-5751

Court of Justice

102. It is important to bear in mind first of all that, under Article [106(2)], undertakings entrusted with the operation of services of general economic interest are subject to the rules on competition in so far as the application of such rules does not obstruct the performance, in law or in fact, of the particular tasks assigned to them.

103. In allowing, in certain circumstances, derogations from the general rules of the Treaty, Article [106(2)] seeks to reconcile the Member States' interest in using certain undertakings, in particular in the public sector, as an instrument of economic or fiscal policy with the Community's interest in ensuring compliance with the rules on competition and preservation of the unity of the common market (Case C-202/88 *France* v. *Commission* . . . paragraph 12, and Case C-157/94 *Commission* v. *Netherlands* . . . paragraph 39).

---

[189] See Section 5.B.viii, p. 609.

104. In view of the interest of the Member States thus defined they cannot be precluded, when determining what services of general economic interest they entrust to certain undertakings, from taking account of objectives pertaining to their national policy or from endeavouring to attain them by means of obligations and constraints which they impose on such undertakings (*Commission v Netherlands*, cited above, paragraph 40).

105. The supplementary pension scheme at issue in the main proceedings fulfils an essential social function within the Netherlands pensions system by reason of the limited amount of the statutory pension, which is calculated on the basis of the minimum statutory wage.

106. Moreover, the importance of the social function attributed to supplementary pensions has recently been recognised by the Community legislature's adoption of Council Directive 98/49/EC of 29 June 1998 on safeguarding the supplementary pension rights of employed and self-employed persons moving within the Community (OJ 1998 L209, p. 46).

107. Next, it is not necessary, in order for the conditions for the application of Article [106(2)] to be fulfilled, that the financial balance or economic viability of the undertaking entrusted with the operation of a service of general economic interest should be threatened. It is sufficient that, in the absence of the rights at issue, it would not be possible for the undertaking to perform the particular tasks entrusted to it, defined by reference to the obligations and constraints to which it is subject (*Commission v. Netherlands*, cited above, paragraph 52) or that maintenance of those rights is necessary to enable the holder of them to perform tasks of general economic interest which have been assigned to it under economically acceptable conditions (Case C-320/91 *Corbeau* . . . paragraphs 14 to 16, and *Commission v. Netherlands*, cited above, paragraph 53).

108. If the exclusive right of the fund to manage the supplementary pension scheme for all workers in a given sector were removed, undertakings with young employees in good health engaged in non-dangerous activities would seek more advantageous insurance terms from private insurers. The progressive departure of 'good' risks would leave the sectoral pension fund with responsibility for an increasing share of 'bad' risks, thereby increasing the cost of pensions for workers, particularly those in small and medium-sized undertakings with older employees engaged in dangerous activities, to which the fund could no longer offer pensions at an acceptable cost.

109. Such a situation would arise particularly in a case where, as in the main proceedings, the supplementary pension scheme managed exclusively by the Fund displays a high level of solidarity resulting, in particular, from the fact that contributions do not reflect the risk, from the obligation to accept all workers without a prior medical examination, the continuing accrual of pension rights despite exemption from the payment of contributions in the event of incapacity for work, the discharge by the Fund of arrears of contributions due from an employer in the event of insolvency and the indexing of the amount of pensions in order to maintain their value.

110. Such constraints, which render the service provided by the Fund less competitive than a comparable service provided by insurance companies, go towards justifying the exclusive right of the Fund to manage the supplementary pension scheme.

111. It follows that the removal of the exclusive right conferred on the Fund might make it impossible for it to perform the tasks of general economic interest entrusted to it under economically acceptable conditions and threaten its financial equilibrium.

. . .

123. The answer to the third question must therefore be that Articles [102] and [106] do not preclude the public authorities from conferring on a pension fund the exclusive right to manage a supplementary pension scheme in a given sector.

It is important to note that, again, the Court (paragraph 107) did not demand that the economic viability of the entrusted undertaking should be threatened without the exclusive right. Article 106(2) can apply where it is necessary to provide economically acceptable conditions. Here again this meant preventing 'cherry-picking': without the exclusive rights other insurers would be able to offer a better deal to companies with predominantly young, healthy workforces. Paragraph 107 was repeated by the CJ in *AG2R Prévoyance*.[190]

The cross-subsidy argument did not succeed, however, in *Air Inter* where the proportionality requirement was not satisfied. There the Commission challenged the granting of exclusive rights on two internal French air routes to Air Inter. The undertaking claimed that domestic air transport in France was based on cross-subsidy between profitable and unprofitable routes, but the Commission and the GC were not convinced.

Case T-260/94, *Air Inter v Commission* [1997] ECR II-997

General Court

138. The application of those articles could, however, be excluded only in as much as they 'obstructed' performance of the tasks entrusted to the applicant. Since that condition must be interpreted strictly, it was not sufficient for such performance to be simply hindered or made more difficult. Furthermore, it was for the applicant to establish any obstruction of its task (see, to that effect, Case 155/73, *Sacchi* . . .).

139. In that regard, the applicant merely asserts that the organization of domestic air transport was based on a system of cross-subsidy between profitable routes and unprofitable routes and that the exclusivity which had been granted to it on the Orly–Marseille and Orly–Toulouse routes was justified by its obligation to operate the unprofitable routes regularly and at tariffs that were not prohibitive, in order to contribute to regional development. It does not put a figure on the probable loss of revenue if other air carriers are allowed to compete with it on the two routes in question. Nor has it shown that that loss of income will be so great that it will be forced to abandon certain routes forming part of its network.

140. In any event, the domestic air network system combined with the internal cross-subsidy system to which the applicant refers in support of its case did not constitute an aim in themselves, but were the means chosen by the French public authorities for developing the French regions. The applicant has not argued and still less established that, following the entry into force of Regulation 2408/92, there was no appropriate alternative system capable of ensuring that regional development and in particular of ensuring that loss-making routes continue to be financed (see also the order of the President of the Court in Case C-174/94 R, *France* v. *E.C. Commission* . . .).

141. Consequently, the applicant has not shown that the contested decision would obstruct the performance in law or in fact of the particular task assigned to it. It follows that the plea of infringement of Article [106(2)] cannot be accepted either.

In *Deutsche Post*,[191] the facts of which are given in a previous section,[192] the CJ had to consider a statutory monopolist's exercise of a right (charging for international mail as though it were internal mail) stemming from an international convention. It held that the German Post Office was justified in doing this. Fulfilling the obligations under the UPC was a service of general economic interest and the Court simply stated without further explanation that levying the charges in issue was necessary to the performance of the task in economically balanced conditions. Otherwise the task would be jeopardised.[193] It has been argued that this was very favourable treatment of Deutsche Post and that the need for cross-subsidisation should have been more closely examined.[194]

---

[190] Case C-437/09, *AG2R Prévoyance v Beaudout* [2011] ECR I-973, para. 76.

[191] Cases C-147–148/97, *Deutsche Post* [2000] ECR I-825.

[192] Section 5.B.ix, p. 611.

[193] Cases C-147–148/97, *Deutsche Post* [2000] ECR I-825, para. 50.

[194] See A. Bartosch, 'Casenote on Cases C-147–148/97, *Deutsche Post AG v Gesellschaft für Zahlungssysteme mbH (GZS) and Citicorp Kartenservice GmbH*' (2001) 38 CMLRev 195, 207–208: 'If it were permitted to split up the whole

In *Ambulanz Glöckner*, however, the CJ again took an approach to the cross-subsidisation issue which greatly favoured the incumbent. It identified the emergency ambulance service as being a service of general economic interest subject to universal service but held the extension of provider's exclusive rights to the non-emergency market was justified so that it could subsidise the emergency from the non-emergency service.

Case C-475/99, *Ambulanz Glöckner v Landkreis Südwestpfalz* [2001] ECR I-8089

Court of Justice

55. With regard to those arguments, the medical aid organisations are incontestably entrusted with a task of general economic interest, consisting in the obligation to provide a permanent standby service of transporting sick or injured persons in emergencies throughout the territory concerned, at uniform rates and on similar quality conditions, without regard to the particular situations or to the degree of economic profitability of each individual operation.

56. However, Article [106(2)], read in conjunction with paragraph (1) of that provision, allows Member States to confer, on undertakings to which they entrust the operation of services of general economic interest, exclusive rights which may hinder the application of the rules of the Treaty on competition in so far as restrictions on competition, or even the exclusion of all competition, by other economic operators are necessary to ensure the performance of the particular tasks assigned to the undertakings holding the exclusive rights (Case C-320/91 *Corbeau* . . . paragraph 14).

57. The question to be determined, therefore, is whether the restriction of competition is necessary to enable the holder of an exclusive right to perform its task of general interest in economically acceptable conditions. The Court has held that the starting point in making that determination must be the premise that the obligation, on the part of the undertaking entrusted with such a task, to perform its services in conditions of economic equilibrium presupposes that it will be possible to offset less profitable sectors against the profitable sectors and hence justifies a restriction of competition from individual undertakings in economically profitable sectors (*Corbeau*, paragraphs 16 and 17).

58. In the case before the national court, for the reasons advanced by the Landkreis, the ASB, the Vertreter des öffentlichen Interesses, Mainz, and the Austrian Government, which are set forth in paragraph 53 above and which are for the national court to assess, it appears that the system put in place by the RettDG 1991 is such as to enable the medical aid organisations to perform their task in economically acceptable conditions. In particular, the evidence placed before the Court shows that the revenue from non-emergency transport helps to cover the costs of providing the emergency transport service.

59. It is true that, in paragraph 19 of *Corbeau*, the Court held that the exclusion of competition is not justified in certain cases involving specific services, severable from the service of general interest in question, if those services do not compromise the economic equilibrium of the service of general economic interest performed by the holder of the exclusive rights.

60. However, that is not the case with the two services now under consideration, for two reasons in particular. First, unlike the situation in *Corbeau*, the two types of service in question, traditionally assumed by the medical aid organisations, are so closely linked that it is difficult to sever the non-emergency transport services from the task of general economic interest constituted by the provision of the public ambulance service, with which they also have characteristics in common.

of the universal service into its different elements for the purposes of applying Article [106(2)], it would become possible for the entrusted undertaking to compete effectively with regard to those elements that can be operated profitably and to ask for a derogation from the application of the Treaty's competition rules wherever this is not feasible. Article [106(2)] could therefore be relied on for each individual operation within the universal service that can be shown to operate at a loss'.

61. Second, the extension of the medical aid organisations' exclusive rights to the non-emergency transport sector does indeed enable them to discharge their general-interest task of providing emergency transport in conditions of economic equilibrium. The possibility which would be open to private operators to concentrate, in the non-emergency sector, on more profitable journeys could affect the degree of economic viability of the service provided by the medical aid organisations and, consequently, jeopardise the quality and reliability of that service.

62. However, as the Advocate General explains in point 188 of his Opinion, it is only if it were established that the medical aid organisations entrusted with the operation of the public ambulance service were manifestly unable to satisfy demand for emergency ambulance services and for patient transport at all times that the justification for extending their exclusive rights, based on the task of general interest, could not be accepted.

63. In this regard, Ambulanz Glöckner contends that Paragraph 18(3) of the RettDG 1991 does indeed promote the creation of a situation in which the medical aid organisations are not always able to satisfy all demand for patient transport services at acceptable prices (see, by analogy, Case C-41/90 *Höfner and Elser* . . . paragraph 31, and Case C-55/96 *Job Centre* . . . paragraph 35). On the other hand, the Landkreis and the ASB maintain that the public ambulance service is incontestably able to satisfy both demand for emergency transport and that for patient transport, even without private undertakings.

64. It is for [the] national court to determine whether the medical aid organisations which occupy a dominant position on the markets in question are in fact able to satisfy demand and to fulfil not only their statutory obligation to provide the public emergency ambulance services in all situations and 24 hours a day but also to offer efficient patient transport services.

65. Consequently, a provision such as Paragraph 18(3) of the RettDG 1991 is justified under Article [106(2)] provided that it does not bar the grant of an authorisation to independent operators where it is established that the medical aid organisations entrusted with the operation of the public ambulance service are manifestly unable to satisfy demand in the area of emergency transport and patient transport services.

In *Slovakian Hybrid Mail Services*[195] the Commission stated that the presumption in the Postal Directive[196] of prima facie justification under Article 106(2) for services covered by the 'reserved area' as defined in that directive did not apply in that case because the hybrid service had previously been liberalised without endangering the public service. Therefore, extending the monopoly to cover hybrid mail again needed specific justification. Under the Postal Directive it is only possible to subsidise the universal service through extending or maintaining the reserved areas. It was not possible to finance any other type of service.[197] The decision was upheld by the GC.[198]

In *OTOC*[199] there was no cross-subsidisation issue. The case concerned the rules for the training of chartered accountants in Portugal. The CJ doubted, on the documents before it, whether 'compulsory training of chartered accountants is of general economic interest exhibiting special characteristics as compared with that of other economic activities' but even if it was the CJ was doubtful that the restrictions on competition were necessary to the performance of OTOC's tasks and therefore the application of the competition rules would not obstruct it.[200]

[195] COMP/39.562, 7 October 2008.

[196] Dir. 97/67 [1998] OJ L15/14 as amended.

[197] COMP/39.562, *Slovakian Hybrid Mail* 7 October 2008, paras. 165–167. For the sectoral regime in the postal sector, see Bellamy and Child, n. 146, 12.135–12.147.

[198] Case T-556/08, *Slovenská Pošta v Commission* EU:C:2015:189, see particularly paras. 354–424.

[199] Case C-1/12, *Ordem dos Técnicos Oficiais de Contas (OTOC) v Autoridade da Concorrência* EU:C:2013:81.

[200] Ibid., paras 104–107. OTOC is the Portuguese Order of Chartered Accountants, empowered by statute to plan, organise, and provide compulsory training schemes for members. OTOC adopted a regulation the effect of which was to impose stricter conditions on independent providers than on its own training operation.

F. NO EFFECT ON TRADE CONTRARY TO THE INTERESTS OF THE UNION

Article 106(2) contains the proviso that 'the development of trade must not be affected to such an extent as would be contrary to the interests of the Union'. This is similar to the proviso in Article 36 TFEU that the derogation from the free movement provisions should not be 'a means of arbitrary discrimination or a disguised restriction on trade between Member States', but unlike that proviso the tailpiece to Article 106(2) has not so far been of importance. It was pleaded by the Commission in the electricity cases[201] but the CJ held that the Commission had provided no explanation to demonstrate such an effect on trade. The proviso must denote something different from the phrase 'affect trade between Member States' in Articles 101 and 102 because without such an effect on trade those Articles cannot apply at all. It may, however, simply be a further proportionality requirement. In *De Post-La Poste* the Commission held that the undertaking with a statutory monopoly over the general letter mail in Belgium had infringed Article 102 by operating a tying policy in order to exclude competitors from the neighbouring business-to-business (B2B) market. The undertaking did not rely on Article 106(2) in its defence, but the Commission went out of its way to say that, if it had, the sealing off of a national market would have impeded trade to an extent contrary to the Community interest.[202]

7. THE DIRECT EFFECT OF ARTICLE 106(1) AND (2)

A. ARTICLE 106(1)

As Article 106(1) prohibits Member States from enacting or maintaining measures contrary to rules contained in the Treaties it applies, as we have seen, only in conjunction with some other rule. Whether or not individuals may invoke Article 106(1) before a national court, i.e. whether Article 106(1) is directly effective, therefore depends on whether the rule infringed by the Member State is itself directly effective. In *Höfner v Macrotron*, for example, the litigant was able to claim in the German court that the German laws breached Article 106(1) because they led to an infringement of Article 102, which is directly effective. The litigant was therefore able to rely on the Articles in conjunction with one another.

B. ARTICLE 106(2)

There are four questions raised by Article 106(2): is the undertaking 'entrusted' with a task; is that task a 'service of general economic interest'; would the task be obstructed by complying with the Treaty rules; and would a derogation from the Treaty rules have an effect on trade contrary to the interests of the Union?

As far as the first two questions are concerned, the Court confirmed long ago that Article 106(2) is directly effective in that a national court may decide whether or not an undertaking has been entrusted with a service of general economic interest.[203]

As for the third question, whether the task would be obstructed, for a long time it appeared from the judgment in *Muller*[204] that the national courts were not competent to answer it and that only the

---

[201] Case 157/94, *Commission v Netherlands (Re Electricity Imports)* [1997] ECR I-5699, paras. 66–72; Case C-159/94, *Commission v France (Re Electricity and Gas Imports)* [1997] ECR I-5815, paras. 109–116.

[202] COMP/37.859, [2002] OJ L61/32, paras. 80–81.

[203] Case 127/73, *BRT v SABAM* [1974] ECR 313.

[204] Case 10/71, *Ministère Public of Luxembourg v Muller* [1971] ECR 723; see also Case 155/73, *Sacchi* [1974] ECR 409; Case 172/82, *Syndicat National des Fabricants Raffineurs d'Huile de Graissage v Inter Huiles* [1983] ECR 555.

Community institutions could decide the point in favour of the undertaking. However, the CJ expressly said at paragraph 34 of the *ERT* judgment[205] that it is for the national court to verify whether the application of the competition rules would obstruct the undertaking's task. The CJ also left this determination to the national court in, for example, *Corbeau* and *Almelo*.

The fourth question is more problematic as it requires an assessment of whether the *interests of the Union* would be adversely affected. At first sight the issue seems more suited to a decision by the Commission than to a judgment by a national court. However, it may be that this is not an additional requirement at all, but part of the overall proportionality requirement to which the first sentence is subject.[206] If this is so Article 106(2) as a whole has direct effect. On the other hand, it can also be argued that only the first sentence of Article 106(2) has direct effect and that the Commission alone has competence to declare that the interest of the Union is being infringed. There is as yet no ruling of the EU Courts on the point.

8. ARTICLE 106(3)

A. THE AMBIT OF THE PROVISION

Article 106(3) provides that the Commission shall ensure the application of the Article[207] and gives it the supervisory and policing powers with which to do this. These powers are in addition to the general powers conferred upon the Commission elsewhere in the Treaties. Under Article 106(3) the Commission can adopt two types of measure, decisions addressed to Member States (not to the undertakings themselves, in respect of whom the Commission must use its powers under Regulation 1/2003) and directives. The Commission may use these powers either to deal with some existing infringement of the Treaty rules or to take steps to prevent future infringements. The adoption of directives to deal with the latter has proved particularly contentious.

B. DECISIONS

The power to issue decisions addressed to Member States provides the Commission with an enforcement mechanism in respect of infringements of the Treaty in addition to the general power in Article 258 TFEU.[208] However, the Commission still has to comply with the general principles of Union law, such as giving reasons and allowing the addressee to be heard, and failure to do so means that the decision can be quashed.[209] In *max.mobil*[210] the GC held that the Commission was under an obligation to examine complaints based on Article 106 diligently and objectively. However, the CJ overruled the GC and held that the Commission's refusal to act under Article 106(3) is not susceptible to judicial review.[211] The Commission has adopted Article 106(3) decisions in a number of the cases discussed in this chapter and in Chapter 7, such as *Spanish Courier Services*,[212] *ANA*,[213] and the

---

[205] Case C-260/89, *ERT* [1991] ECR I-2925; see Section 5.B.iii, p. 602; see also Case 66/86, *Ahmed Saeed* [1989] ECR 803, paras. 55–57.

[206] See Buendia Sierra in Faull and Nikpay, n. 2, 6.214.

[207] This is a specific manifestation of the Commission's general duty of enforcement and supervision under Art. 17 TEU.

[208] Cases C-48 and 66/90, *Netherlands and Koninklijke PTT Netherland v Commission* [1992] ECR I-565.

[209] Ibid.

[210] Case T-54/99, *max.mobil* [2002] ECR II-313.

[211] Case C-141/02 P, *max.mobil* [2005] ECR I-1283.

[212] [1990] OJ L233/19.

[213] [1999] OJ L69/31, confirmed on appeal, Case C-163/99, *Portugal v Commission* [2001] ECR I-2613, concerning discriminatory landing charges at Portuguese airports, discussed in Chap. 7.

essential facilities case, *Port of Rødby*,[214] but it has adopted less since 2000.[215] Most of the cases dealt with in this chapter were Article 267 references. Following the *Altmark* judgment the Commission issued a decision, now replaced with another, on State aid and public service compensation.[216]

C. DIRECTIVES

The reason that the adoption of directives under Article 106(3) can prove contentious is that the Commission can thereby legislate alone, without going through any of the usual legislative procedures laid down in Articles 289–297. Although in practice it normally consults Parliament and the Member States the latter do not have any opportunity to vote against the measures in the Council and the Commission can act where there is no political consensus. This became an issue with regard to liberalisation where there is a thin line to be drawn between harmonisation under Articles 114 and 115 TFEU and what is 'appropriate' under Article 106(3). Directives adopted under Article 106(3) have been challenged by Member States claiming that the wrong legal base was used for their adoption. The Commission used its Article 106(3) powers for the first time in adopting the Transparency Directive[217] which was challenged by France, Italy, and the UK. The CJ confirmed that the Commission was entitled to proceed under Article 106(3) in adopting the Directive, a preventive measure which was aimed at creating greater transparency in the financial relationship between Member States and public undertakings, as it was necessary to its duty of surveillance under the Article.[218]

The Commission used Article 106(3) as the legal basis for two directives in the telecommunications sector, on telecommunications equipment[219] and telecommunications services,[220] both of which were challenged by Member States. In the *Telecommunications Equipment* case the CJ held that Article 106(3) does not give the Commission a general legislative power, but a specific one to deal with State measures concerning legal monopolies.

Case C-202/88, *France v Commission (Telecommunications Equipment)* [1991] ECR I-1223

Court of Justice

23. As regards the allegation that the Commission has encroached on the powers conferred on the Council by Articles [103 and 114 TFEU], those provisions have to be compared with Article [106], taking into account their respective subject-matter and purpose.

24. Article [114] is concerned with the adoption of measures for the approximation of the provisions laid down by law, regulation or administrative action in Member States which have as their object the establishment and functioning of the internal market. Article [103] is concerned with the adoption of any appropriate regulations or directives to give effect to the principles set out in Articles [101] and [102], that is to say the competition rules applicable to all undertakings. As for Article [106], it is concerned with measures adopted by the Member States in relation to undertakings with which they have specific links referred to in the provisions of that article. It is only with regard to such measures that Article [106]

---

[214] [1994] 5 CMLR 457, discussed in Chap. 7.

[215] See J. L. Buendia Sierra, 'Applying Article 106.1 TFEU by the European Commission and the EU Courts' in P. Lowe, G. Monti, and M. Marquis (eds.), *European Competition Law Annual 2013* (Hart Publishing, 2016).

[216] See Section 9, p. 646.

[217] Dir. 80/723/EEC [1980] OJ L195/35, now Dir. 2006/111/EC [2006] OJ L318/17, see n. 35.

[218] Cases 188–190/80, *France, Italy and the UK v Commission* [1982] ECR 2545.

[219] Dir. 88/301/EEC [1988] OJ L131/73.

[220] Dir. 90/388 [1990] OJ L192/10.

imposes on the Commission a duty of supervision which may, where necessary, be exercised through the adoption of directives and decisions addressed to the Member States.

25. It must therefore be held that the subject-matter of the power conferred on the Commission by Article [106(3)] is different from, and more specific than, that of the powers conferred on the Council by either Article [114] or Article [103].

26. It should also be noted that, as the Court held in Joined Cases 188 to 190/80 (*France, Italy and United Kingdom v. Commission* . . . paragraph 14), the possibility that rules containing provisions which impinge upon the specific sphere of Article [106] might be laid down by the Council by virtue of its general power under other articles of the Treaty does not preclude the exercise of the power which Article [106] confers on the Commission.

27. The plea in law alleging lack of powers on the part of the Commission must therefore be rejected.

In this case, although the CJ upheld the Commission's power to legislate over telecommunications equipment it did annul Article 7 of the Directive, which required Member States to ensure the telecommunications monopolies did not enter into certain types of long-term contracts. The Court said that 'anti-competitive conduct engaged in by undertakings on their own initiative' could be dealt with only by individual decisions adopted under Articles 101 and 102 and that Article 106(3) was not an appropriate basis. Likewise in the *Telecommunications Services* case[221] the CJ upheld the Commission's right to use Article 106(3) for measures which were necessary for its surveillance function.[222]

The Member States look jealously at the Commission's use of its Article 106(3) powers and the Commission strives to distinguish its surveillance and supervisory powers from other measures. The Open Network Provision Directive,[223] to which the Services Directive was an accompaniment, was adopted under Article 114 because it was a harmonisation measure, dealing with the conditions for access to, and use of, public networks and services.

The Constitutional Treaty of 2004, which never came into force,[224] would have amended Article 106(3) to read:

The Commission shall ensure the application of this Article and shall, where necessary, adopt appropriate European regulations or decisions.

This would, in effect, have enacted the case law discussed earlier and clarified the limited extent of the Commission's powers. In the event the Treaty of Lisbon left Article 106(3) unchanged.

9. SERVICES OF GENERAL ECONOMIC INTEREST AND STATE AID

The printed edition of this book does not cover State aid, which is instead available on the Online Resource Centre, but it should be noted here that there is a major issue over the financing of SGEIs and State aid. In particular the question is whether, or in what circumstances, compensation for SGEIs is to be considered a State aid under Article 107. A series of cases[225] culminated in the ruling

---

[221] Cases C-271, 281, and 289/90, *Spain, Belgium and Italy v Commission* [1992] ECR I-5833.

[222] Although Art. 8 was annulled on the same grounds as Art. 7 of the Equipment Dir., Dir. 88/301/EEC [1988] OJ L131/73 and the provisions on special rights were annulled for inadequacy of reasons.

[223] Council Dir. 90/387/EEC [1990] OJ L192/1.

[224] It was rejected by referenda in France and the Netherlands.

[225] Case 240/83, *ADBHU* [1985] ECR 531; Case T-106/95, *Fédération Française des Sociétés d'assurances (FFSA)* [1997] ECR II-229; Case C-53/00, *Ferring* [2001] ECR I-9067.

in *Altmark*,[226] where the CJ established that compensation that does not exceed what is necessary to cover the minimum possible costs incurred in the discharge of public service obligations is not a State aid.[227] Following the judgment the Commission adopted a decision, 2005/842 now replaced by 2012/21, specifying that certain types of compensation paid by Member States to undertakings dealing with SGEIs are compatible with Article 106(2) and exempt from the State aid notification obligation under Article 108.[228]

10. CONCLUSION ON SERVICES OF GENERAL ECONOMIC INTEREST

The significance of SGEIs in the Union is summed up in the following passage.

E. Szyszczak, *The Regulation of the State in Competitive Markets in the EU* (Hart Publishing, 2007), 215–216

The creation of a European idea of services of general economic interest has largely been as a result of negative integration processes. In particular the use of Article [106(1)] to attack public monopolies through the national courts and the use of Article [106(2)] to defend services of general interest from the full rigour of the competition and free market rules. Within this process the European Courts have created ideas of how services of general economic interest should be regulated and how they should perform in competitive markets. The EC Commission, through soft law processes, has built up a concept of a European idea of services of general economic interest, attempting a balance between national and EU competence. Legislative intervention has been through the use of concepts such as public service obligations in the liberalisation processes, and more recently in finding ways in which the state may fund services of general economic interest that are compatible with the new attitudes towards state aid in the EU.

Thus we have only a partial concept of services of general economic interest at the EU level, complemented by national models. However, the litigation and debate over the role of services of general economic interest form part of a wider debate over the future economic and social constitution of Europe and the political battle over competing visions of the European Social Model . . .

11. CONCLUSIONS

1. Since 1990 the question of the relationship between competition law and public services has gone from being a side issue to a matter of central concern. This has been due in part to the programme of liberalisation which has introduced competition into sectors previously subject to statutory monopolies. It has given Article 106 increased significance.

2. The case law on Article 106(1) is inconsistent. It may be infringed in conjunction with Article 102 where the State measure will in some way lead to the undertaking concerned committing an abuse but it may also be infringed because it extends the dominant position to another market. Where the measure creates inequality of opportunity there is no need to show anything more than an actual or potential anti-competitive consequence. There are cases where the very granting of the exclusive

---

[226] Case C-280/00, *Altmark* [2003] ECR I-7747.

[227] See S. Santamato and N. Pesaresi, 'Compensation for Services of General Economic Interest: Some Thoughts on the *Altmark* Ruling' (2004) 1 *Competition Policy Newsletter* 1.

[228] [2012] OJ L7/3 (adopted under Art. 106(3)).

right seems to infringe because of its width. Some cases are unclear because the Court has proceeded to the application of Article 106(2) without a proper conclusion on Article 106(1).

3. EU policy on the role of SGEIs has developed to the point where they are seen as a core unifying factor in the enlarged Union. Since 1994 the EU Courts have taken a more liberal attitude to Article 106(2) alongside their more hardline approach to Article 106(1).

4. The case law on Article 106 reflects the tensions that exist within the EU and between Member States on the different choices that can be made in respect of the delivery of public services and to what extent they can be fully marketised.

12. FURTHER READING

A. BOOKS

BELLAMY and CHILD (V. Rose and D. Bailey, eds.), *European Union Law of Competition* (7th edn, Oxford University Press, 2013 and Supplement by L. John and J. Turner, 2015), Chap. 11

BUENDIA SIERRA, J. L., *Exclusive Rights and State Monopolies in EC Law* (Oxford University Press, 2000)

CREMONA, M. (ed.), *Market Integration and Public Service in the EU* (Oxford University Press, 2011)

FAULL, J., and NIKPAY, A., *The EU Law of Competition* (3rd edn, Oxford University Press, 2014), Chap. 6 (J. L. Buendia Sierra)

HANCHER, L., and SAUTER, W., *EU Competition and Internal Market Law in the Healthcare Sector* (Oxford University Press, 2012)

PROSSER, T., *The Limits of Competition Law* (Oxford University Press, 2005)

SAUTER, W., *Public Services in EU Law* (Cambridge University Press, 2014)

SZYSZCZAK, E., *The Regulation of the State in Competitive Markets in the European Union* (Hart Publishing, 2007)

B. CHAPTERS IN BOOKS

BARNARD, C., 'EU Citizenship and the Principle of Solidarity' in M. Dougan and E. Spaventa (eds.), *Social Welfare and the Law* (Hart Publishing, 2005)

FLYNN, L., 'Competition Policy and Public Services in EC Law after the Maastricht and Amsterdam Treaties' in D. O'Keefe and P. Twomey (eds.), *Legal Issues of the Amsterdam Treaty* (Hart Publishing, 1999)

GARCIA, E. M., 'Public Service, Public Services, Public Functions, and Guarantees of the Rights of Citizens: Unchanging Needs in a Changed Context' in M. Freedland and S. Sciarra (eds.), *Public Services and Citizenship in European Law* (Clarendon Press, 1998)

HANCHER, L., 'Community, State and Market' in P. Craig and G. de Búrca (eds.), *The Evolution of EU Law* (Oxford University Press, 1999)

SAUTER, W., 'Universal Service Obligations and the Emergence of Citizens' Rights in European Telecommunications Liberalisation' in M. Freedland and S. Sciarra (eds.), *Public Services and Citizenship in European Law* (Clarendon Press, 1998)

SZYSZCZAK, E., 'Public Service and the Limits to Competition Law' in C. Graham and F. Smith (eds.), *Competition, Regulation and the New Economy* (Hart Publishing, 2004)

VAN MIERT, K., 'Liberalization of the Economy of the European Union: The Game is Not (Yet) Over' in D. Geradin (ed.), *The Liberalization of State Monopolies in the European Union and Beyond* (Kluwer, 2000)

C. ARTICLES

BARTOSCH, A., 'Casenote on Cases C-147–8/97, *Deutsche Post AG v Gesellschaft für Zahlungssysteme mbH (GZS) and Citicorp Kartenservice GmbH*' (2001) 38 *CMLRev* 195

BOEGER, N., '"New" Social Democracy before the Court of Justice' (2005–2006) 8 *Cambridge Yearbook of European Legal Studies* Chap. 5

BOEGER, N., 'Solidarity and EC Competition Law' (2007) 32 *ELRev* 319

EDWARD, D., and HOSKINS, M., 'Article 90: Deregulation and EC Law. Reflections Arising from the XVI FIDE Conference' (1995) 32 *CMLRev* 157

GYSELEN, L., 'Case Note on *Albany, Brentjens*' and *Drijvende Bokken*' (2000) 37 *CMLRev* 425

HANCHER, L., 'Casenote on *Corbeau*' (1994) 31 *CMLRev* 105

HANCHER, L., and BUENDIA SIERRA, J. L., 'Cross-subsidization and EC Law' (1998) 35 *CMLRev* 901

ROSS, M. G., 'Article 16 EC and Services of General Interest: From Derogation to Obligation?' (2000) 25 *ELRev* 22

ROSS, M. G., 'Promoting Solidarity: From Public Services to a European Model of Competition?' (2007) 44 *CMLRev* 1057

ROSS, M. G., 'A Healthy Approach to Services of General Economic Interest? The *BUPA* Judgment of the Court of First Instance' (2009) 34 *ELRev* 127

SANTAMATO, A., and PESARESI, N., 'Compensation for Services of General Economic Interest: Some Thoughts on the Altmark Ruling' (2004) 1 *Competition Policy Newsletter* 1

SAUTER, W., 'Casenote on Case T-289/03, *BUPA v Commission*' (2009) 46 *CMLRev* 269

SLOT, P. J., 'Applying the Competition Rules in the Healthcare Sector' [2003] *ECLR* 580

SZYSZCZAK, E., 'Public Service Provision in Competitive Markets' (2001) 20 *YEL* 35

TESAURO, G. 'The Community's Internal Market in the Light of the Recent Case-law of the Court of Justice' (1995) 15 *YEL* 1

VAN DE GRONDEN, J. W., 'Purchasing Care: Economic Activity or Service of General Economic Interest?' [2004] *ECLR* 87

VEERMERSCH, A., 'Casenote on Case C-49/07, *Motosykletistiki Omospondia Ellados NPID v Ellinkio Dimosi*' (2009) 46 *CMLRev* 1327

9

CARTELS AND OLIGOPOLY

1. CENTRAL ISSUES

1. This chapter deals with explicit and tacit collusion. Collusion is most likely to occur on oligopolistic markets, that is markets on which there are only a few suppliers.

2. Firms may explicitly collude by concluding naked agreements to fix prices, restrict output, share markets, or rig bids ('hardcore' cartels).

3. Hardcore cartel activity leads to higher prices, deadweight loss, and reduced incentives for firms to keep costs low and to innovate. They 'diminish social welfare, create allocative inefficiency and transfer wealth from consumers to the participants in the cartel'.

4. Since the 1990s, the Commission has increasingly focused its resources on detecting cartels and fining undertakings involved. The number of cartel decisions adopted each year and the fines imposed have increased dramatically since 2000. In some Member States, as in the US, cartel activity constitutes a criminal offence.

5. Another problem for consumer welfare is tacit collusion. Economic theory predicts that, on some oligopolistic markets, the players will recognise that the profitability of what they do is dependent on the behaviour of other firms operating on the market, and that they are all better off if they charge higher prices and earn greater profits. They are thus able to coordinate their behaviour in a similar way to those operating a cartel, without explicitly colluding or agreeing to do so. Such coordination is known as tacit collusion or tacit coordination.

6. A significant problem for competition law is how to deal with tacit collusion. Although the EU Merger Regulation can be used *ex ante* to prevent mergers likely to create conditions conducive to tacit collusion (see Chapter 15), this chapter focuses on whether, and if so when, Article 101 or Article 102 can be used *ex post* to condemn the behaviour of firms engaged in tacit collusion or behaviour that may be facilitating or strengthening tacit collusion on a market.

2. INTRODUCTION

A. CARTELS AND OLIGOPOLY

This chapter examines explicit collusion and tacit collusion (or tacit coordination). Both explicit and tacit collusion may result in a reduction of social welfare, mainly through the raising of prices and the restriction of output. These practices may also damage variety and innovation on a market.

Explicit collusion occurs where undertakings collude, collectively, to exploit their joint economic power and to improve their profitability by raising prices, restricting output, sharing markets, or rigging bids. Tacit collusion occurs where undertakings operating on some oligopolistic markets, set their prices 'as if' there had been some explicit collusion between them. Oligopolists may recognise their interdependence and, without direct communication, align their conduct and charge supra-competitive prices as a rational response to market circumstances. Market conditions may, therefore, dictate that without any explicit cooperation between the undertakings, they align their behaviour in a manner which maximises the profits of the players involved.

This chapter considers how EU competition law applies to undertakings operating cartels or other agreements which may be akin to cartel conduct and to undertakings that tacitly coordinate their behaviour on an oligopolistic market. It commences by examining what exactly cartel conduct is, the incentives for, and practical difficulties involved in, collusion, and the difference between explicit and tacit collusion. Section 3 then focuses on how cartels, other agreements akin to cartels, or agreements which may be used to bolster cartels or facilitate explicit or tacit collusion on a market are treated under Article 101. Section 4 then considers the problem of tacit collusion and whether, in particular, Articles 101 and 102 operate as effective mechanisms for dealing with it. The Chapter also considers other options that EU competition law might offer to deal with tacit collusion, either *ex ante* or *ex post*.

B. EXPLICIT AND TACIT COLLUSION

(i) Cartels and Explicit Collusion

a. Introduction

In a Recommendation of the OECD Council Concerning Effective Action Against Hard Core Cartels, a 'hardcore' cartel was defined as:

an anti-competitive agreement, anti-competitive concerted practice, or anti-competitive arrangement by competitors to fix prices, make rigged bids (collusive tenders), establish output restrictions or quotas, or share or divide markets by allocating customers, suppliers, territories or lines of commerce.[1]

Of all agreements, cartels most contradict the principles of the free market economy as the operators specifically attempt to eliminate or limit the free play of competition. Further, they differ from other agreements considered in this book,[2] in that they are 'naked'. 'They seek to restrict competition without producing any objective countervailing benefits.'[3] They lead to higher prices (transferring wealth from consumers to the cartel), deadweight loss (allocative inefficiency), and, ordinarily, productive inefficiency and dynamic harm resulting from reduced incentives to innovate and to strive for efficiency; they thus 'diminish social welfare'.[4] The costs of forming and enforcing the cartel are also welfare-reducing:[5]

Cartels harm consumers and have pernicious effects on economic efficiency. A successful cartel raises price above the competitive level and reduces output. Consumers (which include businesses and governments) choose either not to pay the higher price for some or all of the cartelised product that they desire thus forgoing the product, or they pay the cartel price and thereby unknowingly transfer wealth to the cartel operators. Further, a cartel shelters its members from full exposure to market forces, reducing pressures on them to control costs and to innovate. All of these effects harm efficiency in a market economy.[6]

---

[1] OECD Publication C(98)35/FINAL, May 1998, available on the OECD's website, <http://www.oecd.org>. The ICN Cartel Working Group has also prepared Reports on Cartel Settlements (2008) and Cooperation between Competition Agencies in Cartel Investigations (2006).

[2] See especially Chaps. 10–12.

[3] M. Monti, 'Fighting Cartels Why and How? Why Should We Be Concerned with Cartels and Collusive Behaviour?', 3rd Nordic Competition Policy Conference, Stockholm, 11–12 September 2000. As they are intrinsically detrimental to the competitive process and are not reasonably related to the lawful realisation of cost-reducing or output-enhancing efficiencies they cannot be held lawful under competition law.

[4] Commission, *XXXIInd Report on Competition Policy* (2002), part 26.

[5] R. Van den Bergh and P. Camesasca, *European Competition Law and Economics: A Comparative Perspective* (2nd edn, Sweet & Maxwell, 2006), 5.2.1.2.

[6] *Fighting Hard Core Cartels: Recent Progress and Challenges Ahead* (OECD, 2003), and 'Hard Core Cartels—Harm and Effective Sanctions' (OECD Policy Brief, May 2002), both available at <http://www.oecd.org>.

The formation and successful operation of a cartel is easier for firms operating in an oligopolistic market, where each firm's profits are strongly dependent upon the course of action chosen by its competitors.

b. Oligopolistic Interdependence, the Prisoners' Dilemma, and Theory of Games

'[V]irtually anything can happen'[7] on oligopolistic markets (where only a few players operate on a market). Although economic pricing theories seeking to explain oligopolistic behaviour are numerous[8] and some oligopolistic markets gravitate towards price warfare, on others firms recognise that the price and output decisions they take are affected by the choices made by their rivals—i.e. that they are interdependent—and succeed in maintaining prices well above production costs for years.[9]

Because firms in an oligopolistic market recognise that their profits are dependent on the strategies of others on the market, pricing decisions resemble a game or contest between them. In the 1940s the pioneering work of von Neumann and Morgenstern[10] laid the foundation for the development of a new branch of economics, 'game theory', which deals with the strategic interaction of firms and which is now highly developed. Game theory is a helpful tool used to explain and predict the behaviour of firms on an oligopolistic market.

The basic model applied to illustrate decision-making on such a market is the 'prisoners' dilemma'. It demonstrates how both cooperative and non-cooperative outcomes may result on an oligopolistic market. It explains the incentives that exist for firms operating on a market to agree to coordinate their behaviour and to charge prices which are higher than those which would occur on a competitive market. It also exemplifies, through the Nash non-cooperative equilibrium, the practical difficulties involved in operating such an agreement and consequently helps to predict which market conditions are likely to result in price levels above the competitive price. The Nash non-cooperative equilibrium arises 'when, given the behaviour of all other firms in the market, no firm wishes to change its behaviour (i.e. each firm maximises profit, given the behaviour of all the other firms)'.[11] In the extract, Bishop and Walker explain insights from game theory and how it is relevant to the study of oligopoly.

S. Bishop and M. Walker, *The Economics of EC Competition Law: Concepts, Application and Measurement* (3rd edn, Sweet & Maxwell, 2010), 2.020–2.022

Oligopoly Models

2.020 Neither the paradigm of perfect competition nor that of monopoly provide adequate descriptions of competition in most industries. While the models of perfect competition and monopoly provide a good basis for understanding the basic economic principles, particularly in illustrating the detrimental welfare consequences of monopoly, neither model provides a solid framework on which to base policy prescriptions. These models ignore the interaction between firms and how this interaction may affect the outcomes of the competitive process. In the model of perfect competition, each firm is so small that it can put as much or as little for sale on the market without affecting the market price. For this reason, a firm in a competitive market has no reason to worry about what other firms will do when it makes its own plans.

---

[7] F. M. Sherer and D. Ross, *Industrial Market Structure and Economic Performance* (3rd edn, Houghton Mifflin, 1990), 199.

[8] See, e.g., Cournot's and Bertrand's oligopoly pricing model, discussed in e.g., S. Bishop and M. Walker, *The Economics of EC Competition Law: Concepts, Application and Measurement* (3rd edn, Sweet & Maxwell, 2010), 2.23–2.28.

[9] Sherer and Ross, n. 7, 199.

[10] J. von Neumann and O. Morgenstern, *The Theory of Games and Economic Behaviour* (Princeton University Press, 1944). See, e.g., J. Tirole, *The Theory of Industrial Organization* (MIT Press, 1988) and Chap. 1.

[11] Bishop and Walker, n. 8, 2.020.

For example, a farmer selling his product in an international market does not consider whether his output will affect the market price but instead takes the market price as a given that he cannot affect. At the other extreme, the monopolist can directly set the market price as it has no rivals to worry about.

But in most markets, firms do need to take into account the commercial decisions of rivals when formulating their own commercial strategy. In most markets, firms recognise that changes in their own plans—*e.g.* prices, planned production and additions to capacity—may affect the decisions of other firms in the industry and will take this into account when making commercial decisions. When addressing what constitutes effective competition, these interactions between firms must be taken into account. This requires one to examine more realistic models of competition: models of oligopolistic behaviour. It is the outcomes produced by these models which should underpin our understanding of effective competition.

With advances in game theory, economic models of competition have become much more sophisticated and have started to take explicit account of the interactions between competing firms. Until the 1970s, the examination of oligopoly received little attention, reflecting the lack of analytical tools available in this area. But since that time, a new branch of economics—non-co-operative game theory—has grown up which addresses directly the strategic interactions between firms. Non-co-operative game theory sees competition between firms as each firm trying to do the best it can subject to the actions of its competitors. A key concept in this analysis is that of the Nash non-co-operative equilibrium. An equilibrium is a Nash non-co-operative equilibrium when, given the behaviour of all other firms in the market, no firm wishes to change its behaviour (*i.e.* each firm maximises profit given the behaviour of all the other firms).

2.021 The concept of a non-co-operative Nash equilibrium can be illustrated by reference to the following game, commonly known as the Prisoners' Dilemma. There are two firms, A and B, who must each decide whether to charge a high price or to charge a low price. There are therefore four possible outcomes: they could both charge high prices, both charge low prices, or one or other could charge a low price whilst the other charges a high price. The numbers in each box in Figure 2.4 denote the profits resulting from the outcome of the decisions of the two firms. The first number in each box shows the profits firm A makes whilst the second number shows the profits firm B makes. For example, if both firms choose a low price, each firm makes profits of 4 (see bottom right quadrant).

| | | **FIRM B** | |
		High	Low
FIRM A	**High**	10,10	0,30
	Low	30,0	4,4

Figure 2.4 Illustrating a Nash Equilibrium

2.022 Considering the various outcomes, both firms would prefer an outcome in which both charged a high price to that in which they both charged a low price. In this case, both firms would earn profits of 10 (top left quadrant). But if firm A chooses a high price, what is the best action that firm B can take? With firm A choosing a high price, if firm B also chooses a high price it earns profits of 10 (top left). But if firm B chooses a low price, it earns profits of 30 as a result of undercutting firm A (top right). Hence, given that firm A chooses a high price, firm B's best strategy is to charge a low price.

But if firm B charges a low price, what is the best course of action for firm A? With firm B charging a low price, if firm A charges a high price, it earns zero profits (top right) but if it charges a low price, firm A earns profits of 4 (bottom right quadrant). Hence, firm A will charge a low price if firm B charges a low price. This outcome (the shaded area) represents a Nash equilibrium: the best firm A can do if firm B charges a low price is also to choose a low price and vice versa. In this example, it is also the only Nash equilibrium. In each of the other three quadrants, at least one of the firms wishes to change its behaviour given the behaviour of the other firm. So in the top left quadrant both firms wish to change their behaviour, in the bottom left Firm B wants to change and in the top right Firm A wants to change.

This simple model shows that while both firms prefer a situation in which both firms charge a high price, the incentive to charge a low price while the rival firm charges a high price results in both firms charging a low price.

The model demonstrates that firms operating on a market realise that the profitability of what they do is dependent on the behaviour of other firms operating on the market. If firms compete vigorously with one another and charge low prices their overall profits will be considerably less than if they increase prices and increase profits. They are all better off if they coordinate their behaviour and charge higher prices—there is therefore a strong *incentive* to collude explicitly on such markets. As Adam Smith noted in *The Wealth of Nations*:

people of the same trade seldom meet together, even for merriment and diversion, but the conversation ends in a conspiracy against the public, or in some contrivance to raise prices.

A player on the market nevertheless knows that if its competitor charges a high price, it will be better off if it charges a low price (and cheats on any cartel agreement). Further, that if its competitor charges a low price it must also do so. The Nash equilibrium for a one-shot game is, therefore, for the two firms to lower prices: it is better for both firms to charge a low price, whatever decision the other takes. Where, however, the game is repeated, it may be possible through recurring market interaction for collusion at the high price to be sustained.

c. Alignment, Detection, and Punishment of Deviation: Markets Prone to Explicit Collusion

The prisoners' dilemma illustrates that achieving and sustaining a cartel or collusive strategy is not easy. Its success is dependent upon the parties being able to interact over a period of time and to:

(a) align their behaviour (the competitors must reach an understanding on prices, output, or another factor of competition);

(b) monitor the market so that deviations from the collusive strategy can quickly be detected (it is the fear of retaliation and punishment that makes the collusion sustainable); and

(c) punish those that cheat on the cartel agreement.

It is also important that any alignment of behaviour and increase in price is not counteracted by buyer power or new entry into the market. Clearly it will be easier to align behaviour where the players explicitly collude to do so and on some markets rather than others: for example, alignment is more feasible where there are fewer players on the market; the players are of similar sizes; their products are very similar (there is little non-price competition for the product); and their cost structures are similar (there will then be less disagreement as to the collusive price to be charged).

Further, the cartel members will need to be able to monitor the market and detect cheating on the collusive arrangement, and to find a mechanism for punishing those that do so that cheating becomes unprofitable. Cheating on a cartel is obviously easier the less transparent the markets, the greater the number of firms, where products are differentiated, and where demand is unpredictable. The incentive to deviate from the collusive strategy is also affected by the 'punishment' that can be levied on a firm that cheats. Punishment usually takes the form of a promise of loss of profits once the collusion is uncovered: i.e. the other firms lower price and expand output so that prices revert to the non-collusive or competitive price. The operation of internal enforcement mechanisms is inevitably time-consuming and expensive and on some markets may be impossible. These difficulties become more acute the larger the number of participants and the greater the differentiation in their products. The more elaborate the monitoring and enforcement devices, the more vulnerable the cartel is to detection by competition authorities. This indicates that markets with the following characteristics are more likely to support the successful operation of a cartel.

Fewer Firms and Higher Market Concentration

The fewer the number of operators on the market, or controlling the market, the simpler it is to co-ordinate actions, the cheaper the costs of collusion, the easier it is to detect cheating, and the easier it is to keep the arrangement secret. Further, the larger the market share that each undertaking has the greater the potential profits to be earned from successful collusion (the bigger the share that each will receive of the collusive pie). The greater the anticipated rewards the more likely they are to outweigh the risks of detection.

Barriers to Entry

Barriers to entry are important to the successful operation of a cartel. In the absence of barriers, an increase in price will attract new competitors into the market.

Homogeneous Goods

It will be much easier for firms to collude where products are homogeneous/similar and where the main dimension of competition is price competition (competition is not multidimensional); the possibility for non-price competition through product differentiation and cost of collusion is reduced, and the likelihood of successful collusion increased. Many of the Commission's decisions prohibiting the operation of a cartel have been taken against undertakings whose products offer little scope for differentiation, for example steel tubes, vitamins, sugar, cement, cartonboard, pvc, soda ash, polypropylene.[12]

Firms with Similar Cost Structures or Operating Efficiencies and Market Shares

The more similar the cost structures, the easier it is for the firms to cooperate on prices to be charged. Otherwise, for example, lower-cost firms are likely to want lower prices than other cartel members.

Market Transparency

The more transparent the market, the easier it will be for firms to monitor what their competitors are doing and to detect cheating on, or deviation from, any cartel arrangement.

Mechanisms for Coordination

To be successful cartels may need considerable coordination—to allow alignment of behaviour and to ensure the stability of the cartel. Cartel members thus often, in addition to price-fixing, agree to share markets and/or to adhere to quotas (restriction of output is ordinarily essential to sustain a price rise). The allocation of markets, customers, and quotas may be easier to implement and police than price increases.[13] Other agreements between firms may also facilitate collusion between them, for example by rendering the market more transparent through agreements to exchange information or vertical agreements containing provisions such as meeting competition clauses or resale price maintenance.[14]

---

[12] See, e.g., COMP/31.371, *BELASCO* [1986] OJ L232/15, *aff'd* on appeal Case 246/86, *Re Roofing Felt Cartel: BELASCO v Commission* [1989] ECR 2117, where cartel members took steps, e.g. through standardisation and joint advertising, to foster an impression in consumers that their products were homogeneous.

[13] See, e.g., discussion of the global lysine cartel uncovered in the US, S. Hammond, 'Caught in the Act: Inside an International Cartel', Speech at OECD Competition Committee Working Party No. 3 Public Prosecutors Program, Paris, 18 October 2005 and *BELASCO* ibid. (where the trade association of which the parties to the cartel were members employed an accountant which fined undertakings who exceeded the quota allocated to them under the terms of the cartel agreement).

[14] How provisions requiring buyers to sell at minimum resale prices and other provisions, e.g. meeting competition clauses (a clause providing that a seller will meet any lower price offered to the buyer by a competing seller) and/or most favoured nation clauses (requiring a supplier to offer any price reduction offered to one buyer to all buyers), might facilitate collusion is discussed further in Chap. 11.

Dispersed Buyers with No Controlling Purchasing Power

Where buyers are numerous and dispersed it is almost impossible to advertise price-cuts or reductions and, consequently, to cheat on the cartel without it being brought to the attention of the other members. Further, it will be easier to operate a cartel where individual buyers do not have controlling purchasing power.

Demand Patterns

Cyclical changes in demand may lead to the breakdown of a cartel. In these circumstances undertakings may find it difficult to determine whether the decline in demand for their products is due to a reduction in demand as a whole or to another member cheating on the cartel. This uncertainty may cause the members to deviate from the terms of the cartel. Further, where large orders are put in for a product occasionally (rather than on a regular basis) there may be a greater temptation for cheating since the gains from cheating in each case will obviously be greater.

Depressed Conditions or Low Innovation Rate

Firms operating in industries in recession or suffering from declining demand may be tempted to adopt price-fixing or other collusive agreements to maintain profits.

In a speech, the (then) Competition Commissioner Mario Monti referred to these types of factors as those likely to lead to collusive arrangements between market operators. He stated his belief, however, that cartel agreements might also operate outside industries with these traditional characteristics, and a number of the cartels unearthed bear this statement out.

M. Monti, 'Fighting Cartels Why and How? Why Should We Be Concerned with Cartels and Collusive Behaviour?', 3rd Nordic Competition Policy Conference, Stockholm, 11–12 September 2000

As we all know, cartels do not occur with the same frequency in all sectors. Indeed, some sectors have been particularly prone to cartelisation. These sectors are generally characterised by a relatively high degree of concentration, significant barriers to entry, homogeneous products, similar cost structures and mature technologies. In such stable sectors it is easier to reach consensus on the collusive outcome and to maintain it. The steel, cement and chemical industries can be mentioned as examples of sectors that fit this description and in which the Commission has in the past uncovered cartels.

However, our experience shows that cartel behaviour is not limited to such traditional industries. Recent investigations concerning the banking sector and the liberal professions demonstrate that we should certainly not lose sight of other sectors. In the case of the liberal professions collusion has generally involved the fixing of tariffs. In these sectors it is often quite difficult to assess with precision the level of quality. Price competition is therefore quite an important aspect of competition. It is also interesting to note that in these cases the cartels have virtually always been operated by a trade association. The involvement of an association is necessary due to the large number of operators. One study has found that trade associations were involved in most of the cases that involved more than 10 undertakings. Moreover, in the case of the liberal professions the rules of the association can be a very effective weapon in maintaining discipline.

d. The Desire to Combat and Eliminate Cartels

Because of their harmful effects to consumer welfare and efficiency, cartels have provoked strong and hostile reactions from competition enforcement authorities. They have been described as 'the supreme evil of antitrust',[15] the most 'egregious' violation of competition law,[16] and as 'cancers on the open market economy'.[17]

Although it is arguable that in the long run most cartels will break down without the intervention of any competition authority, the Commission (like other competition agencies) has uncovered a number of cartels that have been operated successfully over long periods of time.[18] In the meantime loss to society as a whole is suffered. Indeed, in 2000 the OECD, in *Hard Core Cartels*, urging an OECD anti-cartel programme,[19] estimated that cartels cost society billions and thwart the gains sought to be achieved through global market liberalisation.[20] 'The average increase from price fixing is estimated to amount to 10% of the selling price and the corresponding reduction of output to be as high as 20%. In some recent big cases prices have been increased by the cartel participants 30% (graphite electrodes) and 50% (citric acid).'[21] At the EU level, cartels also thwart attempts to liberalise and integrate European markets.

It is essential to ensure that the removal of State measures that have shielded companies from competition is not replaced by collusion, having the same effect. Companies that have been used to the absence of effective competition, may have a particularly strong incentive to collude rather than to compete. Indeed, liberalisation of markets and removal of other regulatory obstacles to effective competition increases competition and thereby the payoffs from successful collusion. The higher the degree of competition in a market, the greater the incentive to form a cartel and the greater the harm to the economy and consumers.[22]

It is thus widely accepted that cartels should be deterred[23] and there is now 'a global trend toward enhanced sanctions combined with common enforcement techniques'.[24] Many competition authorities agree that one of the, if not the, most important objective of the competition rules is to detect, punish, prevent, and eliminate the operation of 'hardcore' cartels and work together through formal and informal bilateral and multilateral arrangements to combat such cartels.[25] They are prepared to coordinate searches and investigations across jurisdictions, and are increasingly allocating their scarce resources towards the detection and elimination of cartels.

---

[15] *Verizon Communications v Law Offices of Curtis V. Trinko*, 540 US 398, 408 (2004).

[16] 'Recommendation of the Council Concerning Effective action Against Hard Core Cartels', OECD Publication C(98)35/FINAL, of May 1998, available on the OECD's website, <http://www.oecd.org>.

[17] Monti, n. 3.

[18] See, e.g., COMP/33.133-A, *Soda Ash* [1991] OJ L152/1 (thought to have been in operation since the 19th century), annulled on procedural grounds Case T-30/91, *Solvay SA v Commission* [1995] ECR II-1775 (see Chap. 13) but readopted COMP/33.133-C, [2003] OJ L10/1, see Case T-57/01, *Solvay v Commission* [2009] ECR II-4621, COMP/30.907, *Peroxygen Products* [1985] OJ L35/1, and COMP/37.857, *Organic Peroxides* [2005] OJ L110/44 (the cartel was found to have lasted 20 years), *aff'd* Case T-120/04, *Peróxidos Orgánicos SA v Commission* [2006] ECR II-4441. In the US a series of cases were taken between 1988 and 1997 against bid-rigging on school milk markets. In some cases, it was thought that the bid-rigging had occurred since the late 1960s, see, e.g., Department of Justice Press Release, 25 April 1997, 'Minnesota, Iowa Dairies agreed to plead guilty and will each pay $1 million for participating in milk price fixing conspiracy'.

[19] The findings of this programme were published in OECD, *Fighting Hard Core Cartels*, n. 6.

[20] OECD estimated, for example, that the Graphite electrodes cartel affected $6 billion in commerce worldwide and that the harm of such cartel was up to 65% of this sum, in *Fighting Hard Core Cartels*, n. 6, 97. See also OFT 386, 'The development of targets for consumer savings arising from competition policy', Economic Discussion Paper 4, June 2002.

[21] Monti, n. 3.

[22] Ibid.

[23] See, e.g., R. H. Bork, *The Antitrust Paradox* (Basic Books, 1978, reprinted with a new Introduction and Epilogue, 1993), 67.

[24] See, e.g., G. C. Shaffer and N. H. Nesbitt, 'Criminalizing Cartels: A Global Trend?', University of Minnesota Law School Legal Studies Research Paper Series, Research Paper No. 11–26 (2011), 3.

[25] An International Anti-cartel Enforcement Workshop has been held each year since 1999 for cartel investigators and prosecutors. International cooperation is discussed in Chap. 16.

In the US, Richard Posner comments that '[t]he elimination of the formal cartel from . . . industries is an impressive, and remains the major, achievement of American antitrust law'.[26] Hardcore cartel activity is prosecuted criminally in the US and, since the mid-1990s, the Department of Justice (DOJ) has concentrated its enforcement resources on international cartels that victimise American consumers and businesses. Huge fines are now imposed on corporations and executives, and executives are sent to prison for long periods. Individual jail sentences are believed by many to be the most effective deterrent to cartel activity.[27] Further, firms in breach may be liable to treble damages to persons injured by the violation and may exceed any fine imposed.[28]

If the Commission once felt inhibited about acting against national champions and industrial giants engaged in the operation of cartels, this can no longer be said to be the case. It is determined to take vigorous action against cartels, believing that their effect is to deprive consumers of the benefits of undistorted competition. The fight against cartels has, since the end of the 1990s, been one of the principal concerns of the Commission[29] and it deploys all the resources necessary to take effective action against them despite the major effort in terms of manpower and lengthy procedure that their identification and combating involves.[30] This policy did not soften during the 2008 financial and economic crisis in order to allow firms to weather the crisis and to prevent ruinous competition between them.

If we create the impression that it is OK to 'turn a blind eye' to cartels or for an executive to fail to ask questions about suspicious behaviour, then we create only more trouble—not only in competition, but across all our markets. This sort of misbehaviour is infectious. They breed the sorts of complacent cultures that have generated our current financial and economic situation.[31]

The hardening attitude of the Commission towards cartels in the last 20 years has been reflected by a number of factors, for example:

- the creation of an entire cartel directorate (Directorate F) within DG Comp to focus on cartel activity;
- increasing numbers of cartel decisions have been adopted since 2000;[32]
- increasing fines are imposed on cartel members (see Tables 9.1 and 9.2 and Chapter 13).[33]

---

[26] R. A. Posner, *Antitrust Law* (University of Chicago Press, 1976), 39.

[27] See, e.g., speech of S. D. Hammond, 'The Evolution of Criminal Antitrust Enforcement Over the Last Two Decades', 25 February 2010.

[28] See Chap. 14.

[29] See Monti, n. 3.

[30] See, e.g., Commission, *XXIIIrd Report on Competition Policy* (1993), part 209.

[31] N. Kroes, 'Private and public enforcement of EU competition law—5 years on', Brussels, 12 March 2009.

[32] See cartel statistics, available on DG Comp's website at: <http://ec.europa.eu/competition/cartels/statistics/statistics.pdf>. This was facilitated by the abolition of the notification and authorisation system in 2004, enabling the Commission to refocus its activities and to divert resources from scrutinising (mainly innocuous) notified agreements to uncovering the most serious infringements of competition law.

[33] <http://ec.europa.eu/competition/cartels/statistics/statistics.pdf>. The spike in the level of fines has partly resulted from the Commission's revision, in 2006, of its Fining Guidelines with the specific objective of providing more effective sanctions and deterrents for cartels and multiplying the level of fines in cases of infringements of long duration and recidivism. The change in policy has led to a growing number of complaints that the administrative procedure is 'quasi-criminal' in nature and so is incompatible with due process principles set out in the European Convention for the Protection of Human Rights and Fundamental Freedoms 1950 and that the fines may be leading to hardship for struggling companies and their shareholders and employees as well as consumers as fines are indirectly channelled back to them through higher prices. Even though fines are high, however, some argue that they are still not sufficiently high to achieve deterrence and that criminal sanctions for individuals involved are necessary, alternatively or additionally, to 'focus the mind of potential cartelists', see nn. 35–36 and text. Fining policy is discussed in detail in Chap. 13.

Table 9.1 Level of Fines 1990 to January 2016 (Adjusted for Court Judgments)

Year	Amount in Euros
1990–1994	344,282,550
1995–1999	270,963,500
2000–2004	3,157,348,710
2005–2009	7,926,161,498
2010–2014	7,831,270,579
2015–2016	502,320,000
Total	20,032,346,837

Table 9.2 Highest Fines Imposed for Individual Cartels (Adjusted for Court Judgments) (to January 2016)*

Commission Decision	Total Fines (in €)
TV and Computer Monitor Tubes	1,409,588,000 (including 705.296 million for Philips)
Car Glass	1,185,500,000 (including 715 million for Saint Gobain)
Euro Interest Rate Derivatives (EIRD)	1,042,749,000 (including 465.861 million for Deutsche Bank AG)
Automotive Bearings	953,306,000 (including 370.481 million for Schaeffler)
Elevators and Escalators	832,422,250
Vitamins	790,515,000 (including €462 million for Hoffmann-La Roche)
Yen Interest Rate Derivatives (YIRD)	684,679,000
Gas Insulated Switchgear	675 445 000 (including 396.562 million for Siemens)
Gas	640,000,000 (including 320 million for both E.ON and GDF Suez)
LCD	631,925,000

* See <http://ec.europa.eu/competition/cartels/cases/cases.html> and <http://ec.europa.eu/competition/cartels/statistics/statistics.pdf>.

Although these fines are imposed on undertakings following the Commission's administrative procedure,[34] a number of the Member States have criminalised cartel activity, or certain types of it,[35] and the view that *individuals* responsible for violation of cartel rules should be punished is gaining traction.[36] In the UK, for example, criminal sanctions exist for individuals and it is possible for directors of companies in breach of the competition rules to be disqualified from acting as directors for a period of up to 15 years where they contributed to a breach or knew, or should have known, of the

---

[34] Reg. 1/2003 [2003] OJ L1/1, Art. 23(5) (which 'shall not be of a criminal law nature').

[35] Some form of criminal regime exists in more than 30 jurisdictions including, e.g., Canada, US, Japan, France, Austria, Norway, South Korea, Iceland, Slovakia, Slovenia, Ireland, Romania, Denmark, Germany, UK, Estonia, Hungary, Czech Republic, South Africa, Mexico, and Australia. The more States that have criminal regimes the harder it will be for an individual to avoid extradition.

[36] See, e.g., C. Beaton-Wells and A. Ezrachi (eds.), *Criminalising Cartels: Critical Studies of an International Regulatory Movement* (Hart Publishing, 2011), but see, e.g., A. Jones and R. Williams, 'The UK Response to the Global Effort Against Cartels: Is Criminalization Really the Solution? (2014) 2 *J of Antitrust Enforcement* 1. The EU legislature could, possibly, require Member States to impose criminal penalties for European cartel offences. For a discussion of this issue see, e.g., W. Wils, 'Does the Effective Enforcement of Articles 81 and 82 Require Not Only Fines on Undertakings but also Individual Penalties, in Particular Imprisonment?' in C.-D. Ehlermann (ed.), *European Competition Law Annual 2001: Effective Private Enforcement of EC Antitrust Law* (Hart Publishing, 2002); P. H. Roshowicz, 'The Appropriateness of Criminal Sanctions in the Enforcement of Competition Law' [2004] *ECLR* 12 and G. J Werden and M. J. Simon, 'Why Price Fixers Should Go to Prison' (1987) 32 *Ant Bull* 917.

breach.[37] In *Generali*,[38] the CJ also ruled that an undertaking may be excluded by public authorities from tendering for public contracts where it has committed an infringement of competition law, for which it was fined, even if the procurement procedure is not covered by the EU Procurement Directive. Other factors that reflect the hardening attitude towards cartels include:

- the introduction in 1996 and refinement (in 2002 and 2006) of a successful leniency programme encouraging parties to blow the whistle and to confess to their participation in an illegal cartel;[39]

- the Commission's introduction of a procedure for the settlement of cartel cases (in return for a 10 per cent discount on fines).[40] The purpose of the procedure is to speed up investigations, to reduce the number of infringement decisions appealed to the GC, and so to free up Commission resources enabling it to handle more cartel cases;

- increased international cooperation focused on the elimination of international hardcore cartel activity; and

- the Commission's initiative to encourage greater private enforcement of the competition rules, see further Chapter 14.

(ii) Tacit Collusion, Coordinated Effects on an Oligopolistic Market

In Chapter 1 it was seen that in the 1930s and 1940s an ascendant view was that the structure of a market affected outcome on that market and that concentrated markets delivered poorer outcomes for consumers and higher profitability for firms. Many of the assumptions of the 'structuralists' have, however, been challenged. Indeed, game theory, for example, indicates that although in some oligopolistic markets players may coordinate their behaviour, coordination will not always occur.[41] Although, therefore, undertakings operating on a market on which there are only a few players *may* align their conduct and charge supra-competitive prices as a rational response to market circumstances, this is by no means an inevitable outcome.

The prisoners' dilemma[42] provides a framework for understanding when an oligopolistic market may be conducive to collusion and when it may not. Indeed, the game illustrates that, even without explicit collusion between the parties, *tacit* collusion may occur. A and B know, even without conferring, that if they both choose a high price they will, collectively, maximise their profits (by raising their prices and restricting their output). Further, that although in a one-shot game, A and B may reduce prices and achieve a result that is disadvantageous for both parties, where the game is played continually, they may reconsider their situation independently and realise that they are both much better off if they decide to charge a high price. Oligopolists thus have heightened awareness of other firms' presence on the market and recognise their interdependence; tacit collusion occurs where firms simply understand that if they compete less vigorously they will be able to earn higher profits and that, conversely, cutting prices will simply lead to their rivals following suit. Because economists consider the outcome or effects to be similar to explicit collusion, they generally describe this behaviour as tacit collusion. Lawyers in contrast may feel uncomfortable with this terminology as it is not neutral and suggests the existence of a joint conduct (targeted by Article 101) between

re profit
oligopoly

---

[37] Enterprise Act 2002.

[38] Case C-470/13, EU:C:2014:2469.

[39] The leniency rules are discussed in Chap. 13.

[40] See <http://ec.europa.eu/comm/competition/cartels/legislation/settlements.html> and IP/08/1056 and the UK settlement of the investigation of price-fixing by independent schools, available at <http://www.oft.gov.uk/news-and-updates/press/2006/88–06#.UelH275wbiw>. This issue is discussed further in Chap. 13.

[41] G. Stigler, 'A Theory of Oligopoly' (1964) 72 *J of Political Economy* 44.

[42] Discussed at n. 11 and text.

the parties.[43] Nonetheless, in this chapter the terms tacit collusion and tacit coordination are used interchangeably.

To be conducive to such tacit collusion, the market must possess features which make it feasible or likely. Thus, it is necessary for the firms to have the incentive to avoid competing, to realise their mutual interdependence, to be able successfully to engage in a common form of behaviour, i.e. to align their conduct (this is of course more difficult to achieve without explicit collusion), to monitor what their competitors are doing on the market, and to realise that if they deviate from the common behaviour they will be punished or disciplined (with low prices and low profits). These markets are likely to have similar characteristics to those which facilitate explicit collusion. For example, the market is likely to be transparent and characterised by high concentration, barriers to entry, homogenous products, firms with similar cost and demand structures, and a common high valuation of future profits, some mechanism for alignment (through either signalling[44] or a focal point[45]), and a mechanism for punishing those deviating from parallelism (perhaps through costly price wars or expansion of output). In contrast, coordination is liable to be difficult to sustain on markets characterised by differentiated products, volatile demand or demand booms, the existence of large and sophisticated buyers, and ease of entry or cost asymmetries.[46]

C. COMPETITION LAW AND COLLUSION (EXPLICIT AND TACIT)

Explicit collusion in fixing prices, restricting output, and/or sharing markets through an agreement, decision, or concerted practice falls within the scope of, and is prohibited by, Article 101(1). The difficulty with *tacit* collusion is that although the impact of such coordination on the market is the same as, or at least similar to, where it is explicit (and consumer welfare is harmed), the parties have not in fact *agreed* or otherwise explicitly cooperated with each other to coordinate their behaviour. How then should the competition rules deal with tacit collusion?

In the EU, the European Commission has utilised the merger rules to try and prevent mergers between firms, which are likely to *create* a market situation in which coordinated effects (tacit collusion between the parties) or unilateral effects on an oligopolistic market are likely, or more likely (see Chapter 15).[47] But what can be done about markets which are already concentrated and on which tacit collusion is, or may be, occurring? Can action be taken *ex post* as opposed to *ex ante*? As the tacit collusion stems from the *structure* of the market, should the Commission adopt a structural solution and try to deconcentrate the market, perhaps by ordering the firms operating on the market to sell off parts of their business?[48] In the US in the 1960s, there was serious support for the view that unreasonable market power should be condemned and that there should be power to dissolve firms found to possess it.[49] Indeed, in 1968 a White House Task Force on Antitrust Policy proposed legislation that would permit

---

[43] See, e.g., R. Whish and D. Bailey, *Competition Law* (8th edn, Oxford University Press, 2015), 597–598.

[44] By signalling, e.g. making price announcements in advance, firms may be able to indicate what their future pricing policy will be. It will be a question of degree whether or not this type of conduct can be characterised as concerted behaviour contrary to Art. 101(1), see nn. 267–270 and text.

[45] A practice of recommending prices can operate as a focal point and facilitate alignment of behaviour, see Chap. 11. So too can historical price leadership.

[46] See, e.g., Van den Bergh and Camesasca, n. 5, 5.2.3.

[47] It has the power to prevent mergers that will significantly impede effective competition by leading to coordinated and unilateral (or non-coordinated) effects, see Chap. 15.

[48] Such an outcome is, since 1 May 2004, now theoretically possible but only so long as a breach of Art. 101 or Art. 102 is established, see Reg. 1/2003, Art. 7 and the discussion in Chap. 13. See discussion of UK's market investigation powers, n. 322 and text.

[49] See, e.g., C. Kaysen and D. Turner, *Antitrust Policy* (Harvard University Press, 1959), 110–119 and 266–272 and criticisms of these 'startling' conclusions set out in Bork, n. 23), 176.

deconcentration of markets where four or fewer firms had a combined market share of 70 per cent or more *unless* the defendant could establish that such a step would reduce efficiency.[50] Support for this kind of legislation was, however, abandoned following 'post-1970s scepticism about ambitious governmental interventions in the economy'.[51]

Alternatively, should tacit collusion be viewed as a problem stemming from the anti-competitive *behaviour* of the oligopolists?[52] Since the effects of tacit collusion are similar to cases in which there is explicit collusion and the firms' decisions could be seen as not having been taken truly unilaterally (but rather taking into account the anticipated reaction of their competitors), could parallel behaviour or conscious parallelism, without any proof of actual collusion between the undertakings, be prohibited as an illegal concerted practice under Article 101 or as an abuse of a collective dominant position under Article 102? In the US, Richard Posner was a proponent of the view that the concepts of contract, combination, or conspiracy in s. 1 of the Sherman Act 1890 were capable of reaching, and an appropriate mechanism for dealing with, tacit collusion.[53] This view has not, however, been accepted by the US Supreme Court[54] or the CJ.

Sections 3 and 4 consider the extent to which Article 101 or Article 102 may be applied as an effective tool against tacit collusion on a market. They also consider the extent to which those Articles can be used to prevent *other* behaviour of oligopolistic firms operating on the market, for example practices which might lead to or encourage tacit collusion by rendering the market more transparent or discouraging or prohibiting deviation from a collusive strategy.

3. CARTELS, INFORMATION EXCHANGES, AND RESTRICTIONS ON NON-PRICE TRADING CONDITIONS, ADVERTISING, AND PROMOTION

A. 'HARDCORE' CARTELS

(i) Price-fixing Agreements, Output Restrictions, Restrictions Limiting or Controlling Production, and Market-sharing Agreements

Article 101(1)(a)–(c) specifically provides that agreements etc. which 'directly or indirectly fix purchase or selling prices or any other trading conditions', 'limit or control production, markets, technical development, or investment' or 'share markets or sources of supply' constitute examples of conduct which may be prohibited by the Article. Indeed, these provisions encapsulate classic 'hardcore cartel' activity, operated by fixing prices and/or by imposing quotas on the members and/or by

---

[50] The White House Task Force Report on Antitrust Policy (the Neal Report), 1968 recommended adoption of this Concentrated Industries Act (it was endorsed by 11 of its 13 members) but the views set out in this Report reflected the beliefs of the Harvard School which subsequently were challenged and criticised, particularly by members of the Chicago School, see e.g. H. Hovenkamp, 'The Neal Report and the Crisis in Antitrust', University of Iowa Legal Studies Research Paper, No. 09-09, March 2009.

[51] Posner, n. 26 (deconcentration would confer few benefits and even if it were effective its social costs would exceed its social benefits) and Hovenkamp ibid.

[52] Other approaches might be regulatory or investigatory ones, see e.g. Whish and Bailey, n. 43, 567 and discussion of market investigations later in this chapter.

[53] See R. Posner, 'Oligopoly and the Antitrust Laws: A Suggested Approach' (1969) 21 *Stan LR* 1562 (but see now Posner, n. 26). Contrast, e.g., D. F. Turner, 'The Definition of Agreement under the Sherman Act: Conscious Parallelism and Refusals to Deal' [1962] 75 *Harvard LR* 655.

[54] See, in particular, *Theatre Enterprises v Paramount Film Distributing Corp*, 346 US 537 (1954).

sharing markets between them. In some situations, cartel members may also limit price competition and share the market between them by engaging in collusive tendering.

In *Dyestuffs*,[55] the CJ stressed the importance of price competition between competitors:

The function of price competition is to keep prices down to the lowest possible level . . . Although every producer is free to change his prices, taking into account in so doing the present or foreseeable conduct of his competitors, nevertheless it is contrary to the rules on competition contained in the Treaty for a producer to co-operate with his competitors, in any way whatsoever, in order to determine a co-ordinated course of action relating to a price increase and to ensure its success by prior elimination of all uncertainty as to each other's conduct regarding the essential elements of that action, such as the amount, subject-matter, date and place of the increases.[56]

Article 101 thus targets all agreements which may directly or indirectly facilitate level pricing whether by suppliers or retailers including, for example, agreements: fixing or prohibiting discounts, rebates,[57] or other financial concessions;[58] to consult on price lists;[59] to give warning of price increases to provide reassurance that a price war will not break out;[60] to pursue a collaborative strategy of higher pricing;[61] to exchange price information and price lists;[62] and/or the discussion and implementation of target prices.

[I]f a system of imposed selling prices is clearly in conflict with that provision [Article 101], the system of [target prices] is equally so. It cannot in fact be supposed that the clauses of the agreement concerning the determination of target prices are meaningless. In fact the fixing of a price, even one which merely constitutes a target, affects competition because it enables all the participants to predict with a reasonable degree of certainty what the pricing policy pursued by their competitors will be.[63]

Similarly, a restriction of output automatically creates an imbalance between supply and demand and causes an increase in market prices[64] and market-sharing agreements provide each cartelist with exclusivity in a particular geographical area, or over a particular customer group, which it is free to exploit. Indeed, from the perspective of the Commission, geographical market-sharing agreements are viewed particularly seriously as, in addition to restricting competition, they thwart the objective of integrating the single market by dividing up the EU.

Market sharing agreements are particularly restrictive of competition and contrary to the achievement of a single market. Agreements or concerted practices for the purpose of market-sharing are generally based on

---

[55] Cases 48, 49, and 51–57/69, *ICI v Commission (Dyestuffs)* [1972] ECR 619.

[56] Ibid, paras. 115 and 118.

[57] Case 311/85, *ASBL Vereniging van Vlaamse Reisbureaus v ASBL Sociale Dienst van de Plaatselijke en Gewestelijke Overheidsdiensten* [1987] ECR 3801. See also COMP/37.766, *Dutch Beer* [2008] OJ C122/1.

[58] E.g., COMP/400, *IFTRA Rules on Glass Containers* [1974] OJ L160/1.

[59] COMP/30.064, *Cast Iron Steel Rolls* [1983] OJ L137/1.

[60] See COMP/37.152, *Plasterboard* [2005] OJ L166/8, see Case T-50/03, *Saint-Gobain Gyproc Belgium NV v Commission* [2008] ECR II-114.

[61] COMP/33.708–33.711, *British Sugar plc, Tate & Lyle plc, Napier Brown & Co Ltd, James Budgett Sugars Ltd (British Sugar)* [1999] OJ L76/1, substantially upheld by the GC, Case T-202/98, *Tate & Lyle v Commission* [2001] ECR II-2035, on appeal Case C-359/01 P, [2004] ECR I-4933.

[62] Cases T-25/95 etc., *Cimenteries CBR SA v Commission* [2000] ECR II-491, para. 1531 (at least where it underpins another anti-competitive agreement), broadly aff'd Cases C-204/00 P etc., *Aalborg Portland A/S v Commission* [2004] ECR I-123. See also COMP/400, *IFTRA Rules on Glass Containers* [1974] OJ L160/1 ('It is contrary to the provisions of Article [101(1)] . . . for a producer to communicate to his competitors the essential elements of his price policy such as price lists, the discounts and terms of trade he applies, the rates and date of any change to them and the special exceptions he grants to specific customers') and discussion of information exchange, Section 3.B.

[63] Case C-8/72, *Vereeniging van Cementhandelaren v Commission* [1972] ECR 977, para. 21.

[64] Organization of the Petroleum Exporting Countries (OPEC), for example, is designed to coordinate and unify petroleum prices of Member Countries and to stabilise oil prices. In 1973 voluntarily restriction of outputs and adherence to quotas, led to the world price of oil quadrupling within a year. The increase in wealth to the participants was so enormous that, initially at least, there was little temptation to cheat on the arrangement.

the principle of mutual respect of the national markets of each Member State for the benefit of producers resident there. The direct object and result of their implementation is to eliminate the exchange of goods between the Member States concerned. The protection of their home market allows producers to pursue a commercial policy—particularly a pricing policy—in that market which is insulated from the competition of other parties to the agreement in other Member States, and which can sometimes only be maintained because they have no fear of competition from that direction.[65]

In Chapter 4 it was seen that these types of 'naked' cartel activity have as their *object* the restriction of competition and are assumed to restrict competition.[66] This is so even if: the agreement has proved difficult to apply in practice (and may not, therefore, have had the effect of restricting competition);[67] a participant always intended to ignore the terms of the agreement and that it did, in fact, cheat on the cartel (when cheating the undertaking inevitably relies on the existence of the agreement or concerted practice and will not gain unless the others adhere to its terms);[68] price control is in place;[69] the subjective motive of the parties to any such agreement may have been to deal with an industry crisis or overcapacity;[70] and/or the parties had acted with the knowledge, or with support from, a national government.[71]

a. Examples of Price-fixing Agreements

Since the end of the 1990s the Commission has adopted numerous cartel decisions. Many of these have involved some element of price-fixing or price coordination, either alone or together with other anti-competitive practices such as customer allocation. For example, the Commission has condemned price coordination by French federations in the beef sector and by undertakings selling: aluminium fluoride; sodium chlorate; synthetic rubber; calcium carbide; magnesium-based reagents; concrete reinforcing bars; stainless steel, synthetic rubber, bleaching chemicals, acrylic glass, road bitumen, copper fittings, methylglucamine; Dutch industrial gases; zinc phosphates; carbonless paper; vitamin products; graphite electrodes; lysine; plasterboard; airfreight; LCD panels; washing powder; bananas; glass for cathode ray tubes; refrigeration compressors; mounting for windows and window doors; freight forwarders; water management products; and TV and computer monitor tubes, automotive wire harnesses, shrimps, flexible polyurethane foam, car and truck bearings, steel abrasives, canned mushrooms, envelopes, parking heaters, and retail food packaging.[72]

In many of the cases, the price-fixing was supplemented by other restrictive operations such as measures designed: to limit imports;[73] to allocate sales quotas;[74] to share markets;[75] to share

---

[65] Commission's *Ist Report on Competition Policy* (1971), para. 2.

[66] Cases T-374, 375, 384, and 388/94, *European Night Services v Commission* [1998] ECR II-3141, Case C-67/13 P, *Groupement des Cartes Bancaires v Commission* EU:C:2014:2204.

[67] COMP/34.503, *Ferry Operators* [1997] OJ L26/23.

[68] See COMP/31.371, *BELASCO* [1986] OJ L232/15, *aff'd* on appeal, Case 246/86, *Re Roofing Felt Cartel: BELASCO v Commission* [1989] ECR 2117.

[69] See COMP/37.614/F3, *Belgian Brewers* [2003] OJ L200/1, para. 247, *aff'd* Case T-38/02, *Groupe Danone v Commission* [2005] ECR II-4407 (small reduction in fine) *aff'd* Case C-3/06 P, *Groupe Danone v Commission* [2007] ECR I-1331.

[70] See, e.g., Case C-209/07, *Competition Authority v Beef Industry Development Society Ltd and Barry Brothers (Carrigmore) Meals Ltd (BIDS)* [2008] ECR I-8637 and Cases C-101 and 110/07 P *Coop de France bétail et viande v Commission* [2008] ECR I-10193.

[71] Ibid. and see n. 167 and text.

[72] See <http://ec.europa.eu/competition/cartels/cases/cases.html>.

[73] COMP/38.279, *French Beef* [2003] OJ L209/12, *aff'd* (but fines reduced) in Cases T-217 and 245/03, *FNCBV v Commission* [2004] ECR II-239, Cases C-101 and 110/07, *Coop de France Bétail, FNSEA and others v Commission* [2008] ECR I-10193.

[74] COMP/37.027, *Zinc Phosphate* [2003] OJ L153/1.

[75] See, e.g., COMP/36.490, *Graphite Electrodes* [2002] OJ L100/1, on appeal Cases T-236/01, *Tokai Carbon v Commission* [2004] ECR II-1181 (some of the fines reduced on appeal), Cases C-301 and 308/04 P, *SGL v Commission* [2006] ECR I-5915 (fine increased on SGL).

customers;[76] and/or to fix other trading conditions (such as transport costs).[77] In *Cartonboard*,[78] for example, the Commission fined 19 producers of cartonboard for, over a long period of time, planning and implementing uniform and regular price increases within the Union, planning and coordinating price initiatives in advance, freezing market shares, controlling output, and organising the exchange of confidential information.

A number of these cartels have been global ones. For example, the Commission's decision in *Vitamins*[79] followed criminal proceedings in the US.[80] The parties had agreed target and minimum prices, quotas (agreeing to maintain the status quo in respect of market shares), and provided for compensation payments to be paid in case quotas were exceeded. Elaborate provisions for monitoring and enforcing the agreements were also established and a formal structure and management was involved in the operation of the agreements, including most senior levels of management.

Article 101(1) applies to price-fixing agreements relating not only to goods but also to services and in all economic sectors, including the financial sector. Indeed, in *Fine Art Auction Houses*[81] the Commission found that Christie's and Sotheby's had fixed commission fees and other trading conditions between 1993 and 2000, cartels have been uncovered in the transport sector (for example, aviation and ferry services),[82] and an increasing number of investigations have focused on the financial sector. In 1992, in *Eurocheque: Helsinki Agreement*[83] the Commission imposed heavy fines on French banks and Eurocheque for operating a scheme under which the same commission was charged for both Eurocheque transactions and the use of Carte Bleu; the scheme eliminated the positive features of the Eurocheque system (that it was free to the payee) and competition between Eurocheques and Carte Bleu. Further, it imposed fines on banks in *German Banks*[84] and *Austrian Banks* ('Lombard Club').[85] In the latter case, the Commission found that the Austrian banks had concluded agreements about interest rates and charges/fees and by meeting regularly had coordinated their conduct with respect to every essential factor of competition. In a series of cases the Commission has also imposed fines on undertakings involved in cases relating to the manipulation of financial benchmarks such as London Interbank Offered Rate (LIBOR) and the Euro Interbank Offered Rate (EURIBOR) (including Swiss Franc, Euro, and Yen interest rate derivatives).[86]

---

[76] See Case C-172/14, *ING Pensii v Consiliul Concurentnei* EU:C:2015:484, COMP/39.234, *Synthetic Rubber* [2007] OJ L182/31, Cases T-44 and 45/07 *Kaučuk v Commission* [2011] ECR II-4629.

[77] COMP/36.700, *Dutch Industrial Gases* [2003] OJ L84/1, *aff'd* Case T-303/02, *Westfalen Gassen Nederland v Commission* [2006] ECR II-4567 and Case T-304/02, *Hoek Loos NV v Commission* [2006] ECR II-1887.

[78] COMP/33.833, [1994] OJ L243/1, in a series of appeals, see e.g. Case T-334/94, *Sarrió SA v Commission* [1998] ECR II-1439, the GC broadly upheld the fines imposed but the CJ reduced three fines, referred two cases back to the GC for reassessment, and dismissed the remainder of the appeals: see, e.g., Case C-286/98 P, *Stora Kopparbergs Bergslags AB v Commission* [2000] ECR I-9925.

[79] COMP/37.512, [2003] OJ L6/1, see Cases T-15 and 26/02, [2006] ECR II-497 (reducing some of the fines) and Table 9.2.

[80] The defendants also agreed to pay US customers more than $1 billion in damages, see 'Status Report: An Overview of Recent Developments in the Antitrust Division's Criminal Enforcement Program', DOJ Antitrust Division, 25 February 2004. High fines were also imposed on companies such as SGL Carbon and Archer Daniels Midland for their participation in the graphite electrode and lysine cartels respectively.

[81] COMP/37.784, [2002] OJ L200/92 (a significant fine was imposed on Sotheby's, although Christie's escaped a fine in consequence of its cooperation with the Commission).

[82] See, e.g., COMP/39.258, *Airfreight* [2014] OJ C371/57 (but fines annulled in Cases T-9/11 etc., *Air Canada v Commission* EU:T:2015:994) and COMP/37.444, *SAS/Maersk Air* [2001] OJ L265/15.

[83] COMP/30.717, [1992] OJ L95/50, partially annulled and fines reduced on appeal, see Case T-39/92, *Groupement des Cartes Bancaires v Commission* [1994] ECR II-49. But see COMP/30.717, *Uniform Eurocheques* [1985] OJ L35/43 and n. 147 and text.

[84] COMP/37.919, [2003] OJ L15/1, annulled Case T-44/02, *Dresdner Bank v Commission* [2006] ECR II-356.

[85] COMP/36.571, [2004] OJ L56/1, *aff'd* (but fine reduced on Österreichische Postsparkasse AG) see Cases T-259–264 and 271/02, *Raiffeisen Zentralbank Österreich v Commission* [2006] ECR II-5169, Case C-125/07 *Raiffeisen Zentralbank Österreich v Commission* [2009] ECR I-8681.

[86] The Commission e.g. imposed fines of €1.71 billion on 4 December 2013 in cartels in the Euro and Yen interest rate derivatives (EIRD and YIRD) markets, a fine of €14.9 million on 4 February 2015 on ICAP for participation in and facilitating several cartels in the YIRD sector, and in October 2014 fines of €61.6 million and €32.3 million

The Commission has also been concerned that high levels of regulation (including State or self-regulation) within the sphere of professional services in Europe serve to restrict competition. Although it accepts that some carefully targeted regulation may be necessary in the liberal professions to deal with specific issues arising, such as asymmetry of information between customers and service providers, externalities, and to ensure adequate and sufficient supply of these services, it has been concerned that anti-competitive practices, such as the fixing of prices or recommended prices,[87] is widespread.[88] It has therefore adopted two reports on the subject, a 'Report on Competition in Professional Services'[89] and 'Professional Services—Scope for More Reform'[90] which have examined the question of whether the regulatory regimes existing for lawyers, notaries, accountants, architects, engineers, and pharmacies can be adapted or modernised to spur economic growth and value to consumers. In the first report the Commission states that 'within an otherwise competitive market, price regulation is unlikely to ensure prices that are lower than competitive levels'.[91] Further, that price recommendations 'like fixed prices, may have a significant negative effect on competition. First, recommended prices may facilitate the coordination of prices between service providers. Secondly, they can mislead consumers about reasonable price levels.'[92]

Although the Commission called for restrictions to be reviewed and, where not objectively justified, removed or replaced by less restrictive rules[93] and for national competition authorities (NCAs) to deal with remaining restraints (since in most cases the professional rules have their origin and effect in a single Member State), the Commission has been prepared to take infringement procedures itself. In particular, it takes the view that rules relating to price are likely to constitute automatic violations of Article 101(1), even if in practice an increase in price may be very difficult to sustain in this sphere.[94] In *Belgian Architects*,[95] the Commission fined the Belgian Architects' Association in respect of its operation of a recommended minimum fee scale, laying down fees as a percentage of the value of work realised. The practice had as its object the restriction of competition since it sought to coordinate the pricing behaviour of architects which was unnecessary for the proper practice of the profession. Rather, the architects should have been free to charge a fee commensurate with their skills, efficiency, costs, and reputation.[96]

---

on banks involved in cartels influencing Swiss Franc LIBOR and Swiss Franc interest derivatives. For a discussion of the competition and other investigations that have occurred around the globe, see Pieter J. F. Huizing, 'Parallel Enforcement of Rate Rigging: Lessons to be Learned from LIBOR' (2015) 3 *J of Antitrust Enforcement* 173.

[87] Communication from the Commission, Report on Competition in Professional Services, COM(2004) 83 final, 9 February 2004, available at: <http://eur-lex.europa.eu/legal-content/EN/TXT/?uri=celex:52004DC0083>, Table 2 indicating that recommended prices existed in Austria, Belgium, Denmark, Greece, Ireland, Luxembourg, Portugal, and Spain.

[88] Ibid., para. 1 (occupations requiring special training in the liberal arts or sciences, for example lawyers, notaries, accountants, architects, engineers, and pharmacists).

[89] 'Report on Competition in Professional Services', n. 87. Table 1 indicates that professions with fixed, minimum, or maximum prices exist in Austria, Belgium, France, Germany, Greece, Italy, Luxembourg, the Netherlands, and Spain.

[90] 'Professional Services—Scope for More Reform. Follow-up on Competition in Professional Services', SEC(2005) 1064.

[91] Ibid., para. 32.

[92] Ibid., para. 37.

[93] Ibid., para. 90.

[94] 'Since the number of practitioners in these markets is high, cartel discipline is difficult to maintain and cheating very attractive. The non-sustainability of price cartels under such circumstances is also confirmed by empirical evidence . . . Current European competition law, however allows the relevant economic evidence to be pushed aside if the objective to fix prices or control output can be proven, and the (lack of) economic impact on the market will only be taken into account when determining the ultimate fine.' Van den Bergh and Camesasca, n. 5, 5.3.1.1. For an examination of developments in Ireland, see C. Boate and K. MacGuill, 'Regulating Competition in Professional Services—A Balancing Act' (2013) 9 *European Competition Journal* 105.

[95] COMP/38.549, [2005] OJ L004/10.

[96] For the view that specific problems may result from trying to introduce competition in markets for professional services in the ordinary way, Camesasca, n. 5, Box 5.3.

b. Examples of Output Restrictions and Restrictions Limiting or Controlling Production

A number of the cases dealing with price-fixing have also involved sales quotas. In many cases the implementation of quotas is easier to operate than adherence to a pricing policy: no undertaking can benefit from price-cutting if it is obliged to adhere to sales restrictions, and the adherence to quotas may be easier to monitor. Further, a decision to adhere to quotas may facilitate collusion where participants with different cost structures cannot agree on the prices to be charged for their products.[97]

The *Quinine Cartel*[98] was the first case in which the Commission fined undertakings for the operation of a cartel which raised prices by means of a limitation on production. In particular, certain French companies had agreed not to manufacture synthetic quinidine. The parties contended that, in any event, the companies did not have either the expertise or the resources to manufacture quinidine. The Court dismissed those arguments:

> The fact relied upon that, when the gentlemen's agreement was concluded, the French undertakings were not in a position to manufacture synthetic quinidine does not render lawful such a restriction which entirely precluded them from taking up this activity.[99]

In *Polypropylene*[100] the EU Courts upheld the Commission's finding that the object of meetings to fix target prices and sale volume targets was anti-competitive and in *Zinc Producer Group*[101] the Commission held that an agreement to fix prices, to adhere to production quotas, and to refrain from the building of new production capacity without the consent of the Group, infringed Article 101(1). Market share quotas were also found to constitute the central plank of the *Zinc Phosphate* cartel.[102] In this case the parties calculated initial market shares and sales quotas were allocated at the European level on this basis. A monitoring system was set up and pressure brought to bear on those that did not comply. The parties also agreed on 'bottom' prices, and on some occasions, the allocation of customers. The cartel in this case appeared to have been concluded in response to a prior period of low prices, aggressive price-cutting, and targeting of mutual customers.

A practice in the professions which can cause significant reductions in competition in the spectrum of services offered is the use of business structure regulations. It will be remembered that in *Wouters v Algemene Raad van de Nederlandse Orde van Advocaten*[103] the CJ held that a professional rule that prevented lawyers from working in partnership with accountants, despite constituting a restriction on production and technical development within the meaning of Article 101(1)(b), did not restrict competition. Rather, it accepted that restrictions were required to ensure the proper practice of the profession as organised in a Member State, and which did not go beyond what was necessary to ensure the proper practice of the legal profession, did not infringe Article 101(1). In the Commission's report on competition in professional services, however, the Commission set out its view that such restrictions 'may have a negative economic impact',[104] particularly where collaboration is prevented

---

[97] See discussion of OPEC, n. 64.

[98] COMP/26.623, *Quinine Cartel* [1969] OJ L192/5.

[99] Case 41/69, *ACF Chemiefarma NV v Commission* [1970] ECR 661. See also COMP/31.371, *BELASCO* [1986] OJ L232/15, on appeal, Case 246/86, *Re Roofing Felt Cartel: BELASCO v Commission* [1989] ECR 2117 (where an accountant monitored compliance with quotas and imposed penalties upon those that had exceeded them).

[100] COMP/31.149, *Polypropylene* [1986] OJ 1230/1, appeals substantially dismissed by both the GC and the CJ: see, e.g., Case C-51/92 P, *SA Hercules NV v Commission* [1999] ECR I-4235 and Case C-199/92 P, *Hüls AG v Commission (Polypropylene)* [1999] ECR I-4287. See also, e.g., COMP/33.833, *Cartonboard* [1994] OJ L243/1.

[101] COMP/30.350, [1984] OJ L220/27. See also, e.g., COMP/36.545, *Amino Acid* [2001] OJ L152/24, appeal dismissed in part, Case T-224/00, *Archer Daniels Midlands Co and Archer Daniels Ingredients Ltd v Commission* [2003] ECR II-2597, aff'd Case C-397/03 P, *Archer Daniels Midlands Co and Archer Daniels Ingredients Ltd v Commission* [2006] ECR I-4429.

[102] COMP/37.027, [2003] OJ L153/1, see especially paras. 65–72.

[103] Case C-309/99, [2002] ECR I-1577 (discussed in Chap. 4).

[104] Communication from the Commission, Report on Competition in Professional Services, n. 87, para. 60.

between members of the same profession or between professions where there is no overriding need to protect independence or ethical standards.

Communication from the Commission, 'Report on Competition in Professional Services', COM(2004) 83 final (Brussels, 9 February 2004)

4.5 Business structure regulations

59. A number of professions are subject to sector-specific regulations on business structure. These regulations can restrict the ownership structure of professional services companies, the scope for collaboration with other professions and, in some cases, the opening of branches, franchises or chains.

60. Business structure regulations may have a negative economic impact if they inhibit providers from developing new services or cost-efficient business models. For example, these regulations might inhibit lawyers and accountants from providing integrated legal and accountancy advice for tax issues or prevent the development of one-stop shops for professional services in rural areas. Certain ownership regulations such as prohibition of incorporation can also reduce access to capital in professional services markets, hindering new entry and expansion.

61. On the other hand, it is argued that business structure and ownership regulation may be necessary to ensure practitioner's personal responsibility and liability towards clients and avoid conflicts of interest. It has also been suggested that these regulations may be necessary to ensure practitioners' independence. If professional service companies were controlled or influenced by non-professionals, this might compromise practitioners' judgement or respect for professional value.

62. In the Commission's view business structure regulations appear to be least justifiable in cases where they restrict the scope for collaboration between members of the same profession. Collaboration between members of the same profession would appear less likely to reduce the profession's independence or ethical standards

63. Business structure regulations appear likewise to be less justifiable in professions where there is no overriding need to protect practitioners' independence. The architectural and engineering professions, for example, function effectively without these regulations in most Member States. It therefore appears unlikely that business structure regulations are essential to protect consumers of these services.

64. Business structure regulations appear to be more justifiable in markets where there is a strong need to protect practitioners' independence or personal liability. There might however be alternative mechanisms for protecting independence and ethical standards which are less restrictive of competition. In some markets, stringent ownership restrictions might therefore be replaced or partially replaced by less restrictive rules.

c. Examples of Market Sharing

The Commission and Court have acted against all forms of geographical market-sharing: whether through agreements to refrain from exporting from home markets; agreements to make sales only through the home manufacturer; agreements to limit sales to home markets; or agreements between EU and non-EU undertakings to protect the EU market from low-priced imports.[105] For example, in *Cement*[106] the Commission found that EU cement producers had operated a systematic and

---

[105] See, e.g., COMP/35.860, *Seamless Steel Tubes* [2003] OJ L140/1, on appeal Case T-44/00, *Mannesmannröhren-Werke AG v Commission* [2004] ECR II-2223 (fine reduced), Cases C-403/04 etc., *Sumitomo Metal Industries Ltd v Commission* [2007] ECR I-729.

[106] COMP/33.126 and COMP/33.322, [1994] OJ L343/1, *aff'd* Cases T-25/95 etc., *Cimenteries CBR SA v Commission* [2000] ECR II-491, broadly *aff'd* Cases C-204/00 P etc., *Aalborg Portland v Commission* [2004] ECR I-123.

well-policed policy of, amongst other things, dividing markets on the basis of the 'home market principle' (refraining from exporting to other Member States). The parties made concerted efforts to stem cross-frontier flows and to reduce trade between Member States and a number of bilateral and multilateral agreements (relating to, for example, the exchange of sensitive price information) backed up the main agreement.

In *Peroxygen Products*[107] the Commission also fined producers of hydrogen peroxide a total of €9 million for operating agreements which included a 'home market' rule (and which had excluded virtually all trade between Member States (prices varied enormously between States) and in *Soda Ash*[108] the Commission imposed fines (of approximately €7 million) on ICI and Solvay, the two largest producers of synthetic soda ash in the Union, for the operation of an agreement under which ICI was exclusively to supply the UK and Ireland and Solvay was exclusively to supply continental Europe. Although the formal written agreement had been abandoned in 1972 (on the UK's accession to the EU) the Commission found that the agreement/concerted practice in fact continued unaltered.

In *SAS/Maersk*[109] the Commission imposed fines of €52.5 million for market-sharing in the air transport sector; broadly the parties agreed to withdraw from each other's routes and to share out domestic routes. In this case, the parties had notified a cooperation agreement to the Commission. The Commission became suspicious, however, that the agreements were more far-reaching than the notified agreements made out and uncovered the market-sharing agreement following investigations conducted at the parties' premises. In *Gas*,[110] the Commission imposed very significant fines[111] on E.ON AG and GDF Suez SA (two of the largest players in the EU gas industry) for an agreement (in place since 1975) not to sell gas, transported through a jointly built and owned MEGAL pipeline, into each other's home markets. The market-sharing arrangement was maintained after the EU gas market was liberalised in 2000 and, by helping the parties to maintain their strong positions in the German and French gas markets respectively, had thwarted the liberalisation process. Through adopting this decision the Commission sought to send a strong message to energy incumbents that it would not tolerate anti-competitive behaviour which deprived customers of choice. On appeal, the GC confirmed that an agreement between actual or potential competitors not to penetrate each other's home market was restrictive by object and upheld the Commission's decision.[112]

Market-sharing, through customer allocation, is also prohibited. In *Methylglucamine*,[113] for example, the parties sought to maintain the status quo of 50 per cent market share for both companies by trying to prevent switching by their respective customers from one to the other supplier and agreeing not to compete for each other's customers. Further, in *Luxembourg Brewers*,[114] four Luxembourg brewers agreed (in signed writing)[115] not to supply beer, for an unlimited duration, to any customer tied to another by an exclusive purchasing commitment or beer tie.[116]

---

[107] COMP/30.907, [1985] OJ L35/1.

[108] COMP/33.133, [1991] OJ L152/1, annulled on procedural grounds Case T-30/91, *Solvay SA v Commission* [1995] ECR II-1775 (see Chap. 13) but readopted COMP/33.133, [2003] OJ L10/1, see Case T-57/01, *Solvay v Commission* [2009] ECR II-4621.

[109] COMP/37.444, [2001] OJ L265/15, *aff'd* Case T-241/01, *Scandinavian Airlines System AB v Commission* [2005] ECR II-2917. But see discussion of the OneWorld, Skyteam, and Star airline alliances in Ch. 10, pp. 725–728.

[110] COMP/39.401, *Gas* [2009] OJ C248/5.

[111] See Table 9.2.

[112] Case T-360/09, *E.ON Ruhrgas AG v Commission* EU:C:2011:389 (it annulled the Commission's finding insofar as it had not done so and consequently reduced the level of the fines).

[113] COMP/37.978, [2004] OJ L38/18. See also, e.g., COMP/39.234, *Synthetic Rubber* [2007] OJ L182/31, Cases T-44 and 45/07, *Kaučuk v Commission* [2011] ECR II-4629.

[114] COMP/37.800, [2002] OJ L253/21, *aff'd* Case T-49/02, *Brasserie nationale SA v Commission* [2005] ECR II-3033.

[115] Interbrew disclosed details of the arrangement following an investigation into its practices on the Belgian beer market, see n. 117 and text.

[116] See discussion of single branding agreements in Chaps. 4 and 11.

When taking on a new customer, each would consult one another to check that a beer tie did not bind the customer to another. The parties also had measures in place that impeded trade from other Member States, and which were designed to keep foreign brewers out of the market. The Commission held that this agreement had as its object the restriction of competition. Similarly *Belgian Brewers*[117] Interbrew and Danone shared out their distribution channels and pursued a policy of non-aggression.

(ii) Collusive Tendering or Bid-rigging

Collusive tendering occurs where undertakings collaborate on responses to invitations to tender for the supply of goods and services. The practice can take different forms (for example, bid rotation, bid suppression, market allocation, or cover pricing) and is liable to limit price competition between the parties by allowing the tenderers to share markets between themselves. Instead of competing to submit the lowest possible tender at the tightest possible margin, the parties may agree on the lowest offer to be submitted or agree amongst themselves who should and should not bid and who should be the most successful bidder.[118] The practice will automatically infringe Article 101(1).

> In a system of tendering, competition is of the essence. If the tenders submitted by those taking part are not the result of individual economic calculation, but of knowledge of the tenders by other participants or of concertation with them competition is prevented, or at least distorted and restricted.[119]

Evidence suggests that bid-rigging, at least in some countries, may be rather widespread, in particular in government procurement cases, and that they may lead to greater price increases than ordinary price-fixing. The extract from OFT 368, a UK discussion paper, makes this point.

OFT 386, 'The Development of Targets for Consumer Savings Arising from Competition Policy', Economic Discussion Paper 4, June 2002, Chap. 5, paras. 5.3–5.8

Evidence from US bid rigging cases

5.3 Froeb, Koyak and Werden (1993) noted that in the five years to 1993, 70 per cent of the cartel cases investigated by the US Department of Justice (DoJ) involved bid rigging rather than price fixing, bid rigging in government procurement being typical. Perhaps for this reason, much of the empirical literature on the effect of cartels concentrates on bid rigging. While there are exceptions, in general, the evidence suggests that cartels lead to prices well in excess of 10 per cent, and sometimes in excess of 20 per cent, of competitive levels.

---

[117] COMP/37.614, [2003] OJ L200/1, para. 247, *aff'd* Case T-38/02, *Groupe Danone v Commission* [2005] ECR II-4407 (small reduction in fine) and Case C-3/06 P [2007] ECR I-1331. 'After the Commission, on its own initiative, uncovered a cartel on the Belgian beer market, InBev provided information under the auspices of the Commission's leniency policy that it was also involved in cartels in other European countries. This led to surprise inspections on brewers in France, Luxembourg, Italy, and the Netherlands. These investigations led to decisions condemning cartels in Belgium (see IP/01/1739 upheld by the [GC] and CJ, see CJE/07/13), France (see IP/04/1153, not appealed) and Luxembourg (see IP/01/1740, upheld by the CFI). The Italian investigation was closed without charges being brought' (IP/07/509). The Dutch cartel decision was adopted on 18 April 2007.

[118] It must be distinguished from joint bidding made openly and with knowledge of the party seeking the tenders/work.

[119] COMP/26.918, *Re The European Sugar Cartel* [1973] OJ L140/17, para. 42.

School milk markets

5.4 Some recent papers refer to bid rigging cartels in school milk markets. These markets lend themselves to collusion for several reasons set out in Porter and Zona (1999):

- Price competition is the only dimension of competition,
- Demand is inelastic and stable,
- Firms face similar costs of production,
- Building a new plant would be unattractive solely on the basis of higher margins made on school milk contracts, and this reduces the scope for new entry,
- Markets tend to be concentrated and localised (transport costs reduce the scope of supply side substitution) which facilitates market sharing,
- The 'game' is repeated year by year and multi-market contact is enhanced by disaggregated contracts staggered throughout the year,
- Although tendering is by sealed bid auctions, immediately after contracts are won, bids and bidders are made public so cheating can be observed,
- Competitors can obtain each other's list prices for sales of milk to retail customers which may facilitate signalling, and
- Parties often meet through trade associations or by being customers of each other.

. . .

Bid rigging cases in Europe

5.8 The European Commission imposed record fines for bid rigging in the Pre-Insulated Pipe cartel. The Commission does not provide a formal analysis of how much higher prices were during the periods when the conspiracy had effect. However, there is a suggestion that the cartel inflated prices in Denmark by 15–20 per cent or more, whilst information from one of the cartel meetings suggests that prices in most other markets were inflated by about the same amount. Given the US evidence of bid rigging against the public sector, price rises of 15–20 per cent would certainly seem plausible.

The Commission has now unearthed a number of such cases.[120] In *Pre-Insulated Pipe Cartel*[121] it imposed fines in excess of €92 million on ten undertakings it had found to be engaged in market-sharing, price-fixing, and bid-rigging in the market for pipes used for district heating systems (contracts for the supply of pipes were almost all awarded on the basis of competitive tendering procedures). The parties had also tried to squeeze out of the market the only competitor that had refused to participate in the cartel and had deliberately flouted the EU Public Procurement Rules. Further, in *Lifts and Escalators*[122] the Commission imposed fines of €992 million on four firms for operating a number of bid-rigging cartels for the installation and maintenance of lifts and escalators in Belgium, Germany, Luxembourg, and the Netherlands. The Commission was particularly outraged by this cartel since it affected a vast market for the sale, installation, maintenance, and modernisation of lifts and escalators (including in the buildings of the Commission itself and the courts in Luxembourg!)

---

[120] In a number of jurisdictions, including, e.g., Germany, bid-rigging is a specific criminal offence and forms of bid-rigging have been tackled by a number of NCAs.

[121] COMP/35.691, *Pre-Insulated Pipe* [1999] OJ L24/1; decision substantially upheld on appeal (although some fines reduced) see, e.g., Cases T-9/99 etc., *HFB Holdings v Commission* [2002] ECR II-1487, *aff'd* Cases C-189/02 P etc., *Dansk Rørindustri A/S* [2005] ECR I-5425. See also COMP/31.572 and COMP/32.571, *Building and Construction Industry in the Netherlands* [1992] OJ L92/1, *aff'd* Case T-29/92, *SPO v Commission* [1995] ECR II-289, COMP/39.406, *Marine Hoses* [2009] OJ C168/6, see on appeal, e.g., Case T-146/09, *Parker-Hannifin* EU:T:2013:258, Case C-434/13, *Commission v Parker Hannifin Manufacturing Srl and Parker-Hannifin Corp* EU:C:2014:2456, COMP/38.899, *Gas Insulated Switchgear* [2008] OJ C5/7, on appeal see, e.g., Cases C-231–233/11 P, *Commission v Siemens* EU:C:2014:256.

[122] COMP/38.823, [2007] OJ C75/19, Cases T-138/07 etc., *Schindler Holding v Commission* [2011] ECR II-4819.

and the cartel would have long-term effects because of the maintenance contracts which lasted decades. In *International Removals Services*[123] the Commission reiterated the serious nature of bid-rigging when it condemned a cartel in which participants had agreed on prices, allocated removal contracts between themselves by way of bid-rigging in the form of bogus 'cover quotes', and benefited from a system of financial compensation called 'commissions'.

(iii) Bolstering Provisions

Provisions designed to reinforce or bolster the operation of a hardcore cartel, such as: measures designed to block imports;[124] refusals to supply or boycott customers who purchase from sellers outside the cartel; boycotts of competitors refusing to participate in the cartel arrangements;[125] collective exclusive dealing;[126] or information-sharing arrangements (see further Section 3.B below)[127] are also likely to infringe Article 101(1).

(iv) Characterisation—Is It a Cartel?

In Chapter 4 it was stressed that although agreements to fix prices, limit output, share markets, or rig bids ordinarily restrict competition by object and rarely satisfy the conditions of Article 101(3): (a) there is no such thing as a fixed list of object restraints—rather in making such an assessment account must be taken not only of the content of the agreement but of its precise purpose in the context in which it is operates; and (b) all agreements, even those containing object restraints may be capable of satisfying the conditions of Article 101(3). Although naked cartel activity, including price-fixing agreements, generally falls into 'the category of manifest infringements under Article [101(1)] which it is always impossible to exempt under Article [101(3)] because of the total lack of benefit to the consumer'[128] this begs the question of what exactly cartel activity is. In some situations the Commission has sought to stretch the boundaries of the object category to encompass more complex interactions which go beyond arrangements simply relating to the fixing of price, restricting of output, or sharing of markets (see further, for example, the discussion of information exchange and restrictions on advertising below).

Conversely, parties have sometimes sought to argue that their agreements incorporating price, production, and/or output restraints are not purely designed to restrict price or output etc. but are necessary, or ancillary, to some successful collaboration or efficiency-enhancing integration between them that benefits consumer welfare.[129] In such cases crucial questions are: does the agreement restrict competition (in particular does it have as its 'object' or 'effect' the restriction of competition and/or are the restraints objectively necessary to a pro-competitive arrangement);[130] and, if so, does it satisfy the conditions of Article 101(3) (the Commission's view is that object restraints rarely meet the Article 101(3) criteria)? Of importance to the first question, of course, is the CJ's judgment

---

[123] COMP/38.543, [2009] OJ C188/52.

[124] See, e.g., COMP/31.204, *Meldoc* [1986] OJ L348/50, COMP/37.800, *Luxembourg Brewers* [2002] OJ L253/21, *aff'd* Case T-49/02, *Brasserie nationale SA v Commission* [2005] ECR II-3033.

[125] COMP/35.691, *Pre-Insulated Pipe* [1999] OJ L24/1; decision substantially upheld on appeal (although some fines reduced) Cases T-9/99 etc., *HFB Holdings v Commission* [2002] ECR II-1487, *aff'd* Case C-189/02 P, *Dansk Rørindustri A/S* [2005] ECR I-5425. See also COMP/31.572 and COMP/32.571, *Building and Construction Industry in the Netherlands* [1992] OJ L92/1, *aff'd* Case T-29/92, *SPO v Commission* [1995] ECR II-289.

[126] See, e.g., COMP/33.884, *Nederlandse Federative Vereniging voor de Groothandel op Elektrotechnisch Gebied and Technische Unie (FEG and TU)* [2000] OJ L39/1.

[127] Cases T-25/95 etc., *Cimenteries CBR SA v Commission* [2000] ECR II-491, para. 1531, broadly *aff'd* Cases C-204/00 P etc., *Aalborg Portland A/S v Commission* [2004] ECR I-123, COMP/400, *IFTRA Rules on Glass Containers* [1974] OJ L160/1.

[128] Commission's *Xth Report on Competition Policy* (1980), 115.

[129] See Chap. 10.

[130] See Chap. 4 and also Chap. 11.

in *Groupement des Cartes Bancaires*.[131] In this case it will be remembered that the CJ stressed that object classification should be used sparingly and only for coordination that 'reveals in itself a sufficient degree of harm to competition'. Further, that it found that the GC had erred when assessing whether the Commission has been correct to find that a number of measures (including pricing measures) designed to achieve interoperability of systems for payment and withdrawal by bank cards issued by Carte Bancaire members were restrictive of competition by object.

a. Price-fixing

The controversy of how multilateral interchange fees (MIFs) set in card payment schemes should be analysed under Article 101(1) and (3) neatly demonstrates the difficulties that arise in this area. Although the Commission in the past indicated that arrangements incorporating MIFs infringed Article 101(1) only if they had a restrictive effect, it has retreated from this approach in subsequent cases (see, for example, *Visa*[132]). Further although in *Visa International-Multilateral Interchange Fee*[133] it decided that the agreement met the Article 101(3) criteria,[134] in *MasterCard*[135] it declined to do so— finding that no objective advantages under Article 101(3) had been demonstrated. Subsequently, the Commission has opened further proceedings against MasterCard[136] and Visa Europe[137] and a number of NCAs have brought similar actions.[138]

The EU Courts have not yet had to rule on the question of whether such arrangements are, or are not, restrictive of competition by object (this matter did not have to be decided in the *MasterCard* appeal as the decision at issue was not based on the existence of an infringement by object, but on the effects of the MIF[139]), but in *MasterCard* they upheld the Commission's finding that the arrangements restricted competition in fact[140] and did not meet the Article 101(3) criteria.[141] In particular, in relation to Article 101(3), the GC stated that even if it could be inferred from the evidence that the MIF contributed to increasing the output of the MasterCard system, that was not sufficient to establish that the first condition of Article 101(3) was satisfied; the primary beneficiaries of such an increase were the MasterCard payment organisation and participating banks. Case law specified that the improvement demanded in Article 101(3) could not be identified with all the advantages which the parties obtain from the agreement in their production or distribution activities.

---

[131] Case C-67/13P, *Groupement des Cartes Bancaires v Commission* EU:C:2014:2204.

[132] In *Visa* the Commission took the preliminary view that the MIFs had as their object (as well as their effect) the appreciable restriction of competition as they inflated the base on which acquirers set the merchant service charges and were not objectively necessary (the case was resolved by a commitments decision, however). Although the Commission originally reiterated this approach in its Staff Working Document providing guidance on restrictions of competition by object, relying on its preliminary conclusion in *Visa* for a statement that joint setting by banks of so-called MIFs in the payment card market is to be considered as price-fixing which is restrictive by object, this statement does not appear in the revised version, Commission's Staff Working Document, Guidance on restrictions of competition 'by object' for the purposes of defining which agreements may benefit from the *De Minimis* Notice, SWD(2014) 198 final.

[133] COMP/29.373, [2002] OJ L318/17.

[134] See also discussion of the case in Chap. 4.

[135] COMP/34.579, [2009] OJ C264/8.

[136] COMP/40.049, IP/13/314 (the Commission sent a statement of objections on 9 July 2015).

[137] See COMP/39.398, IP/10/1684 (the Commission set out its preliminary view that the MIF set by Visa restricted competition between banks without benefiting consumers by contributing to technical and economic progress. The proceedings in relation to both Visa immediate debit card transactions and credit cards, have been resolved by commitments under Reg. 1/2003, Art. 9, decisions of 8 December 2010 and 26 February 2014.

[138] A number of complaints have been lodged before, or investigations launched and/or concluded by, NCAs including France, Germany, and Hungary (where fines of €1.75 million were imposed on both Visa and MasterCard), Italy, Poland, and the UK.

[139] Case C-382/12 P, EU:C:2014:2201, para. 186.

[140] See discussion of the case in Chap. 4.

[141] Case C-382/12 P, EU:C:2014:2201 and Case T-111/08, EU:T:2012:260.

The improvements had to display appreciable objective advantages so as to compensate for the disadvantages which they cause in the field of competition.

The question of how payment card fees should be dealt with under competition law has therefore been controversial and different approaches have been advocated and adopted at the EU and national level. In 2015, the EU legislature sought to deal with some of the problems arising by adopting a Regulation capping interchange fees for payments using consumer debit and credit cards (the caps came into force on 9 December 2015).[142] As this Regulation does not deal with all the potential competition law issues arising, however, the Commission has not terminated existing proceedings in this area.[143]

A number of other cases have also involved price-fixing with 'unusual characteristics'. In *Reims II*[144] the Commission held that the fixing of terminal dues,[145] payable by post offices for the delivery of letters in other Member States, would lead to an improvement in efficiency[146] and eliminate cross-subsidy and in *Uniform Eurocheques*[147] the Commission exempted, for a limited period, an agreement which fixed commissions for the cashing of Eurocheques. The Commission found that the agreement (a) improved payment methods and (b) benefited users (all currencies were available and interest-free credit was available whilst the cheques were being cleared). The restrictions were essential in the circumstances and did not lead to an elimination of competition.

b. Joint Selling and Collective Licensing

On a number of occasions, the Commission has considered whether joint distribution, joint selling, or collective licensing arrangements infringe Article 101. It is ordinarily hostile to joint selling or sales joint ventures as they restrict competition between the parents on the supply side and limit purchaser's choice: they effectively operate as horizontal price-fixing agreements.[148] Particularly when dealing with copyright, or other neighbouring rights, however, the Commission has sometime been persuaded that joint selling or licensing may be beneficial and meet the criteria of Article 101(3).[149]

In *UIP*,[150] for example, the Commission granted an exemption to agreements creating United International Pictures BV (UIP) a joint film distribution company established by Paramount Pictures Corp, Universal Studios Inc, and Metro-Goldwyn Mayer Inc. UIP distributed and licensed on an exclusive basis feature motion pictures, short subjects, and trailers produced by the parties for showing in cinemas. Following modifications to the agreement, in particular by limiting the effect of the exclusivity provisions by allowing UIP only a right of first refusal to the parent companies' films,[151] the Commission was prepared to accept that the Article 101(3) requirements

---

[142] Regulation 2015/751 of 29 April 2015 on interchange fees for card-based payment transactions [2015] OJ L123/1, see, e.g., A. De Matteis and S. Giordano, 'Payment Cards and Permitted Multilateral Interchange Fees (MIFs): Will the European Commission Harm Consumers and the European Payment Industry?' (2015) 6 *JECLAP* 85.

[143] See n. 136 and text.

[144] COMP/36.748, [1999] OJ L275/17 and COMP/38.170, [2004] OJ L56/76.

[145] The remuneration that public postal operators (PPO) pay each other for the delivery of incoming cross-border mail. The receiving PPO is remunerated by the sending PPO for the delivery of the latter's mail.

[146] The agreement would lead to a correlation between the terminal dues paid and cost and improve the quality of service for cross-border mail.

[147] COMP/30.717, [1985] OJ L35/43. But see COMP/30.717-A, *Eurocheque: Helsinki Agreement* [1992] OJ L95/50, partially annulled and fines reduced on appeal, see Case T-39/92, *Groupement des Cartes Bancaires v Commission* [1994] ECR II-49.

[148] But see Commission's Guidelines on joint selling of olive oil, beef and veal and arable crops, 27 November 2015 (providing guidance to farmers clarifying how they can, under certain conditions, cooperate to jointly sell these products without infringing Art. 101).

[149] See also the decision of the US Supreme Court, *Broadcast Music Inc v Columbia Broadcasting System Inc*, 441 US 1 (1979).

[150] COMP/30.566, [1989] OJ L226/35.

[151] This meant that the parent company concerned had first to offer its product for distribution in the EU to UIP, but if UIP elected not to distribute a picture, the parent company could impose its distribution on UIP or distribute the film independently, either itself or through a third party.

were met. The cooperation produced economic benefits for the production and distribution of motion pictures and for consumers, which could not be achieved in the absence of the joint venture and which outweighed its disadvantages. In particular, the creation of UIP made possible a more effective and rationalised distribution of the parents' products, avoiding duplication of distribution organisations, and creating an economically viable distribution network in a deteriorating market where high financial risks were present. When the parties applied for an extension of the exemption the Commission required further amendments to the agreements before issuing a comfort letter.[152]

In *IFPI*[153] the International Federation of the Phonic Industry notified a reciprocal agreement in the name of national collecting societies of music record companies. The main objective of the agreement was to facilitate the grant of a multi-territorial licence[154] which broadcasters could exploit *globally*, and not just nationally, by simulcasting sound recordings on to the global digital network of the internet. It thus enabled the creation of a new type of licence, ensured effective administration and protection of producers' rights in the face of global internet exploitation, and provided broadcasters with an alternative to obtaining a licence from the local society in every country in which their internet transmissions could be accessed. Although the agreement did involve some prices restrictions between the parties, the Commission concluded that the restrictions were indispensable to the agreement, would lead to substantial economic benefits, and would improve the distribution of music, which would benefit consumers.

Broadcasting rights to sports matches or competitions are also frequently sold collectively on behalf of clubs or participants by sports associations. The agreements often involve exclusivity, leading to a concern that they will distort competition between broadcasters, encourage media concentration, and stifle the development of new products and services such as internet sports services and new generation mobile phones.[155] The Commission has consequently taken a keen interest in such cases. For example, in *Joint selling of the commercial rights of the UEFA Champions League*[156] it, following revision of their terms, exempted regulations concerning the joint selling of the commercial rights to the UEFA Champions League on behalf of the clubs participating in the league (see further Chapter 10).

c. Buying Prices

Price-fixing amongst buyers can have quite different effects to price-fixing by sellers. Whilst the latter may obviously be liable to maximise sellers' profits and to extract higher prices from purchasers, the former may be designed to achieve lower prices for members which may then be passed on to their customers (see further discussion of joint purchasing agreements in Chapter 10).[157] Nonetheless, horizontal agreements restricting the parties' freedom to negotiate buying prices might produce anti-competitive effects (particularly through increasing buyer power and/or facilitating collusion downstream) and so be prohibited by Article 101. For example, agreement by cartel members on the purchase price of a key raw material may facilitate the operation of the cartel at the downstream

---

[152] IP/99/681.

[153] COMP/38.014, [2003] OJ 107/46.

[154] Ordinarily, collecting societies have the right to grant licences for exploitation of sound recordings in their territory only.

[155] The Commission is concerned that exclusivity agreements do not lead to other broadcasters being excluded from the market altogether. Thus a long duration of exclusivity may be prohibited if there is a risk that a broadcaster might prevent its competitors gaining access.

[156] COMP/37.398, [2003] OJ L291/25.

[157] See Research Paper prepared by RBB for the OFT on cooperation by purchasers, 'The Competitive Effects of Buyer Groups', January 2007 and T. Björkroth, 'Joint Purchasing Agreements in the Food Supply Chain: Who's in the Sheep's Clothing?' (2013) 9 *European Competition Journal* 175 and *Covisint* discussed n. 221 and text.

level.[158] Indeed, in both the Spanish and Italian raw tobacco cases,[159] the Commission imposed fines on companies active in raw tobacco processing for colluding on the prices paid to (as well as the quantities bought from) tobacco growers and in its Guidelines on the assessment of horizontal co-operation agreements[160] the Commission states:

205. Joint purchasing arrangements restrict competition by object if they do not truly concern joint purchasing, but serve as a tool to engage in a disguised cartel, that is to say, otherwise prohibited price fixing, output limitation or market allocation.

206. Agreements which involve the fixing of purchase prices can have the object of restricting competition within the meaning of Article 101(1). However, this does not apply where the parties to a joint purchasing arrangement agree on the purchasing prices the joint purchasing arrangement may pay to its suppliers for the products subject to the supply contract. In that case an assessment is required as to whether the agreement is likely to give rise to restrictive effects on competition within the meaning of Article 101(1). In both scenarios the agreement on purchase prices will not be assessed separately, but in the light of the overall effects of the purchasing agreement on the market.

d. Output and Production Limitations

The Commission has been prepared to accept that agreements which limit output or production may not infringe Article 101. As with joint purchasing, where such restrictions are ancillary to a beneficial R&D, production, or specialisation agreement (and truly concern R&D, production or specialisation and do not serve simply as a tool to engage in a disguised cartel), the terms in such agreements are not liable to be found to be restrictive of competition by object and may satisfy the terms of Article 101(3) where restrictive effects are identified.[161]

In the past at least, it is also seen in Chapter 4 that the Commission has been sympathetic to parties that notified 'crisis cartels' (for example, restructuring agreements) for exemption.[162] In these cases it permitted undertakings operating in industries suffering severe difficulties to conclude co-operation agreements providing, for example, for an orderly reduction in overcapacity where the economic effect of the improved rationalisation outweighs the disadvantages of the reduced competition in the short term. However, it would not allow the restructuring to be achieved by unacceptable means such as price-fixing or market-sharing. Further, it would regard the restrictions as indispensable only if the agreement was concerned solely with the reduction of capacity and was limited from the outset to a period necessary for its setting up and implementation.[163]

These decisions are old ones, however, and at the start of the most recent financial and economic crisis the Commission indicated that it would not be willing to tolerate crisis cartels, at least where it could be expected that market forces would be able to remedy structural overcapacity.[164] In particular, (then) Competition Commissioner Neelie Kroes, indicated that not only would the Commission not turn a blind eye to cartels, but it would be vigilant for them, recognising that anti-competitive

---

[158] See, e.g., COMP/30.350, *Zinc Producer Group* [1984] OJ L220/7. It may also harm welfare by causing the input suppliers to reduce output.

[159] COMP/38.238, *Spanish Raw Tobacco* [2004] OJ L102/14, Cases T-37/05 etc., *World Wide Tobacco España v Commission* [2011] ECR II-41, COMP/38.281, *Italian Raw Tobacco* [2005] OJ L353/45, Cases T-11–12/06, *Romana Tabacchi v Commission* [2011] ECR II-6681. See also the current investigation in COMP/40.018, *Car Battery Recycling*, IP/15/5254.

[160] [2011] OJ C11/1.

[161] See Chap. 10.

[162] One of the Commission's objectives was to ensure the elimination of overcapacity in an industry and to enable the industry to recover its profitability, Commission, *XXIst Report on Competition Policy* (1991), 207 ff.

[163] See, e.g., in COMP/31.055, *ENI/Montedison* [1987] OJ L5/13, for 15 years there was an agreement between two large petrochemical groups for rationalisation of their production capacities and transfer of certain businesses, leading to a *de facto* specialisation by each party.

[164] But see B. Wardhaugh, 'Crisis Cartels: Non-economic Values, the Public Interest and Institutional Considerations' (2014) 10 *European Competition Journal* 311.

collaboration is a hugely tempting mechanism for firms to employ to shield themselves from ruin-ous competition in a climate of rising competition for a shrinking demand:

> If I may quickly mention the issue of so-called 'crisis-cartels' . . . There may be many temptations in 2009 to cut corners, but encouraging cartelists and others would be guaranteeing disaster. It would drag down recov-ery, increase consumer harm and create more cartel and cartel cases into the future. No-one wins—today's softness is tomorrow's nightmare.[165]

This hard-line stance has, however, raised some concern, especially in cases where, for example, governments may have endorsed or encouraged industry-wide measures to permit the weathering of an industry storm or even pressured industry members to adopt voluntary measures to achieve broader public policy objectives. This type of disquiet was perhaps experienced by the Irish courts, which had to adjudicate on the compatibility of a crisis cartel in the *BIDS* case (made with the knowl-edge of the Irish Government) with Article 101(3). In Chapter 4 it is seen that the CJ in *BIDS* held, fol-lowing a reference to it from the Irish Supreme Court, that because an agreement to reduce capacity had as its object the restriction of competition, the fact that the parties did not intend to harm con-sumers but to benefit them through rationalisation of the industry was not relevant under Article 101(1). The objective pursued might, however, be relevant under Article 101(3). When the matter re-turned to the Irish Supreme Court, the only matter remaining to be resolved, therefore, was whether or not the arrangements could benefit from Article 101(3). The Irish Supreme Court[166] felt that this issue should be remitted to the Irish High Court for decision, but nonetheless expressed a view on some general legal points that would be relevant to the assessment. In particular, it stressed that the case was far removed from a cartel scheme hatched in a smoke-filled room,[167] indicated (having regard to the Commission's previous decisions in *Synthetic Fibres* and *Dutch Bricks (Stichting Baksteen)*) that the agreement was likely to realise substantial efficiencies (even if the value of those efficiencies could not be demonstrated), and pointed out that no consumers had complained and that power-ful buyers (such as Tesco) were unlikely to tolerate the passing on of any price increases. The court noted further that restraints designed to prevent players who had been paid to leave the industry from re-entering and acquiring capacity seemed indispensable to the success of the arrangements.

When the matter reverted to the Irish High Court the Commission intervened in the case to submit observations to the court on the application of Article 101(3). The opinion indicates that the Commission considers that it will only be in relatively rare circumstances that parties to an agreement involving a reduction in capacity will be able to demonstrate efficiencies, that the restric-tive agreement is indispensable to achieve those efficiencies (and that they cannot be achieved by market forces), and that any benefits would be passed on to consumers.[168] Before the High Court had an opportunity to reach its decision on the application of Article 101(3), however, BIDS withdrew its claim for exemption and agreed to pay a substantial proportion of the competition authority's costs. The authority has now published a guidance note on agreements to reduce capacity which is based on its experience in the *BIDS* case.[169]

In another case the Commission granted an exemption to an agreement which restricted the type of goods that the parties to the agreement could produce or import. In *European Council of Manufacturers of Domestic Appliances*[170] the Commission exempted an agreement concluded between 95 per cent of the producers and importers of washing machines operating on the EU market that restricted their

---

[165] Speech by N. Kroes, 'Tackling cartels—a never-ending task', 8 October 2009.

[166] *Competition Authority v Beef Industry Development Society Ltd* [2009] IESC 72.

[167] Not only had the agreement been concluded with the knowledge of the Irish Government but it had been no-tified to the Irish competition authority. The latter felt it was anti-competitive, however, and for this reason brought proceedings before the Irish courts to have the agreement struck down.

[168] Available at <http://ec.europa.eu/competition/court/antitrust_amicus_curiae.html>.

[169] Notice on Agreements to Reduce Capacity, 16 June 2011, available at <http://www.tca.ie/images/uploaded/documents/N-11–001%20Notice%20on%20Agreements%20to%20Reduce%20Capacity.pdf>.

[170] COMP/36.718, [2000] OJ L187/47.

freedom to manufacture or import the least energy-efficient washing machines. The agreement was found to restrict competition within the meaning of Article 101(1).[171] Nonetheless the Commission considered that the agreement met the criteria set out in Article 101(3) since it would reduce the potential energy consumption of new machines and consequently lessen pollution, create more technically efficient machines, and focus future R&D on furthering energy efficiency. Such economic and technical progress would benefit society and consumers. The Commission considered that the restrictions were indispensable to the agreement, which would not substantially eliminate competition.

e. Collusive Tendering

It is also rather unlikely that bid-rigging would meet the Article 101(3) criteria.[172] In *FIEC/CEETB*,[173] however, the Commission indicated that it would take a favourable view of an agreement designed to standardise and reduce the cost of the tendering process between building contractors and sub-contractors but which would not in any way limit either the firms who could tender or the prices at which they could tender (see further Chapter 10).

B. INFORMATION-SHARING AGREEMENTS

(i) Exchange of Information between Competitors

The dissemination and exchange of information between competitors and the creation of a transparent market may be harmless or even highly beneficial to the competitive structure of the market, especially where it forms part of a horizontal cooperation agreement, for example a standardisation or a R&D agreement[174] or the information is also disclosed to consumers.[175] In particular, the transparency created in a market by information exchanges can produce significant efficiencies and benefits to both suppliers and customers. 'Many sectors of our economies now depend upon ready access to detailed information.'[176] For example, information exchange may allow suppliers to adapt their businesses and perform better, to improve commercial strategies, to improve effective allocation of resources, to increase internal efficiency (for example, by benchmarking their processes and performance against other industry performance), to promote innovation, to understand market trends and demand, and/or to improve product positioning. From a consumer's perspective it may increase transparency, reduce search costs, and help them choose the most suitable products or services. Trade associations thus frequently collect industry data on prices, outputs, capacity, and investment and circulate information to their members which may make it easier for undertakings to plan their own business strategies. Further, the theory of perfect competition rests upon the assumption that there is perfect freedom of information. A market characterised by many buyers and sellers should, therefore, positively benefit from such transparency. Where information is available

---

[171] See Chap. 4, IP/01/1659 (where the Commission indicated its intention to take a similar approach to environmental agreements for water heaters and dishwashers) and contrast, e.g., COMP/39.579, *Consumer Detergents* [2011] OJ C193/14.

[172] See, e.g., COMP/30.064, *Cast Iron and Steel Rolls* [1983] OJ L317/1.

[173] COMP/31.014, [1988] OJ C52/2.

[174] See Chap. 10.

[175] See Commission's Guidelines on the applicability of Article 101 of the Treaty on the Functioning of the European Union to horizontal co-operation agreements [2011] OJ C11/1 (Horizontal Cooperation Guidelines), especially paras. 57–58 and 64–71 and, e.g., M. Bennett and P. Collins, 'The Law and Economics of Information Sharing: The Good, the Bad and the Ugly' (2010) 6 *European Competition Journal* 311, K. U. Kühn and X. Vives, 'Information exchanges among firms and their impact on competition' (Office for Official Publications of the European Community, Luxembourg, 1995), OECD Roundtable on Information Exchange, DAF/COMP(2010)37, and V. Robertson, 'A Counterfactual on Information Sharing: The Commission's Horizontal Guidelines 2011 Applied to the Leading Cases' (2013) 36 *World Competition* 459.

[176] Bennett and Collins, ibid., 311.

generally, consumers with complete knowledge of what is on offer may fully utilise their power of choice.

Information exchanges may, however, also present the opportunity for competitors to coordinate their behaviour and to achieve and maintain a collusive equilibrium over time. They may be used to bolster or facilitate the operation of a cartel. Where the information is exchanged deliberately to support price-fixing or other hardcore cartel activity the Commission or other enforcing authority will obviously take a dim view.[177] In *Methylglucamine*,[178] for example, cartel meetings (where price increases and customer allocation were agreed) normally started with an exchange of information and views on the worldwide demand for the product, referring to the volumes sold to the respective main clients during the previous year. In this case, however, the Commission concluded that this practice had not materialised into a full systematic exchange of sales data.[179]

As information exchanges ancillary to a cartel or a horizontal cooperation agreement are assessed in the broader context of, and in combination with, the cartel or cooperation arrangements in which they are operated, this section focuses on how 'stand-alone' information exchanges (which are not dependent on a cartel or another arrangement between the parties) are analysed under the EU competition law rules. Stand-alone agreements, involving the exchange of strategic information, '[b]y artificially increasing transparency in the market, . . . can facilitate coordination (that is to say, alignment) of companies' competitive behaviour and result in restrictive effects on competition'.[180] Indeed, at worst, an information exchange may be a mechanism designed purely for coordinating behaviour. Further, even if not designed to do so it may have the effect of facilitating collusion. For example, information exchanged about firms' past, current, or future behaviour may provide a focal point facilitating competitors' coordination of price or output levels on a market and facilitate identification of deviations from it. It may also allow firms operating on a market to determine quickly whether competitors are deviating from a coordinated strategy (it may contribute to the internal stability of the coordinated strategy) or whether new entrants may be threatening a collusive strategy (it may contribute to the external stability of the coordinated strategy). Information-sharing arrangements may also present opportunities to foreclose competitors from a market, for example where the information exchange provides the recipients with a significant competitive advantage over rivals in the relevant market or in a downstream market.[181] A stand-alone information exchange may therefore in *itself* be sufficient to establish a violation of Article 101(1).[182]

(ii) Assessing the Competitive Effects of an Information-sharing Arrangement under Article 101(1) and Article 101(3)

a. Characterisation

Although a category of information exchange may be equated with cartel activity and considered to be restrictive by object, the majority of information agreements are assessed individually in their market context to determine their actual or likely effects on competition. Apart from the de minimis principle, no safe harbour applies for the latter arrangements and there are relatively few bright lines or clear rules for business to adhere to in this area.

---

[177] See, e.g., COMP/31.572 and COMP/32.571, *Building and Construction Industry in the Netherlands* [1992] OJ L92/1, aff'd Case T-29/92, *SPO v Commission* [1995] ECR II-289.

[178] COMP/37.978, [2004] OJ L38/18.

[179] Ibid., paras. 76–82.

[180] Horizontal Cooperation Guidelines, para. 65.

[181] Ibid., paras. 69–71.

[182] See, e.g., Case T-141/94, *Thyssen Stahl v Commission* [1999] ECR II-347, paras. 379–392.

b. Object Restrictions

In Chapter 4 it was seen that although in *T-Mobile Netherlands BV v Raad van bestuur van de Nederlandse Mededingingsautoriteit*[183] the CJ clarified that a private[184] information exchange designed to remove uncertainties concerning the intended conduct of the participating firms and facilitating, directly or indirectly, the fixing of selling prices falls within the category of restraints which are restrictive by object,[185] the CJ went further in its ruling than perhaps was required for the case. It stated that 'an exchange of information which is capable of removing uncertainty between participants as regard the timing, extent and details of the modifications to be adopted by the undertakings concerned must be regarded as pursuing an anti-competitive object' and that 'in order for a concerted practice to be regarded as having an anti-competitive object, it is sufficient that it has the potential to have a negative impact on competition . . .'.[186]

Some of the difficulties with the approach of the CJ in *T-Mobile* are explored in the extract below.

B. Meyring, 'T-Mobile: Further Confusion on Information Exchanges Between Competitors' (2010) 1 *JECLAP* 30

Analysis

It has often been highlighted that the [*T-Mobile*] ruling makes clear that one single meeting between competitors can be enough for a serious violation of Article [101] and can trigger the presumption that participants have considered what was discussed at this meeting when they determine their market conduct. The judgment is also important in that it highlights that [Article 101] goes beyond protecting final consumers and also aims to protect competitors as well as a competitive market structure as such. Finally, the judgment contains interesting and controversial language on the assessment of information exchanges. This is the focus of this paper. At the outset, the Court summarises its approach to the distinction between violations by object and violations by effect. It points out that both concepts are alternatives and that, contrary to the national court's view, there is no need to analyse the effects of a specific practice once it is established that its object was to restrict competition.

The role of the economic context in the assessment remains, however, unclear. On the one hand, the Court holds that the conduct must be *capable* of restricting competition in its '*specific legal and economic context*', even in the framework of a restriction by object. In other words, this seems to indicate that conduct that might aim at a restriction of competition but cannot achieve this purpose because of a specific economic or regulatory context cannot be treated as a violation by object. This is in line with the statement according to which '*the intention of the parties is not an essential factor*'. On the other hand, the Court reemphasises that it is irrelevant '*whether and to what extent*' anti-competitive effects in fact materialise.

Even though this seems to be what point 31 says ('*it is sufficient*'), it would be wrong to conclude that any potential to have a negative impact is sufficient to establish that a practice is a restriction by object. First, this would do away with restrictions by effect altogether because practices that are not even capable of having anti-competitive effects will not produce such effects in any event—and all other restrictions would be restrictions by object. Second, the concept of a violation by object is a narrow one. As the Court

---

[183] Case C-8/08, [2009] ECR I-4529, paras. 36–43.

[184] For the view that public information exchanges relating to future (or current) prices are less likely to produce anti-competitive effects than private exchanges, see Bennett and Collins, n. 175, 334 and discussion of public announcements, nn. 267– 270 and text.

[185] The same principles apply to the exchange of price information between distributors, see COMP/25.757, *Hasselblad* [1982] OJ L161/18, on appeal Case 86/82, *Hasselblad v Commission* [1984] ECR 883: where a market is not oligopolistic, the Commission has been prepared to accept that even the exchange of individual and confidential information concerning costs, sales volumes, and market shares may not infringe Art. 101: COMP/33.815, 35.842, *Eudim* [1996] OJ C111/8.

[186] Case C-8/08, *T-Mobile* [2009] ECR I-4529, para. 31.

notes in point 29, restrictions by object are only the severest forms of collusion that '*can be regarded, by their very nature, as being injurious to the proper functioning of normal competition*'. These practices are hardcore cartels and it is indeed common sense that these are prohibited, whether or not they actually turn out to be effective in the individual case. In its Guidelines on the application of Article [101(3)], the Commission speaks of restrictions that '*have such a high potential of negative effects on competition that it is unnecessary . . . to demonstrate any actual effects on the market*' (point 21).

Practices outside this category may or may not affect competition, depending on their economic context. They merit and require a careful analysis as to their effects on competition. It would be inappropriate to circumvent this requirement by simply classifying them as restrictions by object.

The Court argues that '*an exchange of information which is capable of removing uncertainties between participants as regards the timing, extent and details of the modifications to be adopted by the undertaking concerned must be regarded as pursuing an anticompetitive object*' (point 41). This is a bold statement and it is worth recalling that, in the case at hand, the parties had discussed contemplated modifications of their standard remuneration for dealers. This discussion related to a strategic choice that would be implemented in the future. Moreover, the request for a preliminary ruling suggests that the future levels of remuneration were not unilaterally set and then exchanged but were '*discussed*', which implies that the aim of the conversations was to determine the right level. Advocate General Kokott sets out in her opinion that the discussions indeed resulted in a coordination of market conduct (at point 36). It is not surprising that the Court classifies such a discussion as a restriction by object. However, it seems very odd in this context to elaborate, as the Court does, on information exchanges. Where two competitors discuss, on the basis of their market knowledge and strategic planning, how their competing products should best be priced, we would hardly speak of an information exchange but rather of a price fixing cartel. And it seems obvious to treat such a discussion as a violation by object. The legal assessment of the information exchange in this framework would be irrelevant, and would only obscure the real issue. The fact that the discussion covered other conditions should not make any difference to this part of the analysis.

The phrase '*information exchange*' appears in none of the three preliminary questions, and the legal analysis of information exchanges as such seems to be irrelevant for the case that the national Court has to decide. By focusing on the exchange of confidential information, the [CJ] produced statements that are confusing and far too broad. The question in this case was not when information exchanges are legal but where precisely is the line in the sand that separates violations by object from practices that turn on the analysis of their effect. The Court has missed an opportunity to provide more clarity as to the crucial question when precisely a practice is a restriction by object. It has also failed to acknowledge, like Advocate General Kokott at point 37 of her opinion, that not every exchange of information between competitors has an anticompetitive object.

E. Practical significance

The judgment leads to further confusion in the competition law analysis of information exchanges. Whereas the Court's *John Deere* judgment had used a checklist approach to analyse the effects of an information exchange between competitors, the Maritime Transport Guidelines and the cases on AC Nielsen in Finland, Norway, and Sweden have moved to a more economic approach to effects. The [CJ's] judgment in *T-Mobile Netherlands* should not be misinterpreted as advocating a simplistic *per se* approach to such cases. Rather, it makes clear that an information exchange that is ancillary to a cartel must be treated together with the cartel and as a *per se* violation. The Court could have stated this more clearly.

The question of when an information exchange should be characterised as restrictive by object arose again in *Bananas*.[187] In this case the Commission fined three banana importers for engaging in

---

[187] Case COMP/39.188, *Bananas*, 15 October 2008, *aff'd* Cases T-587/08, *Fresh Del Monte Produce v Commission* EU:T:2013:129 and T-588/08 P, *Dole Food and Dole Germany v Commission* EU:T:2013:130 and Cases C-293 and 294/13 P, *Fresh Del Monte v Commission* EU:C:2015:416 and Case C-286/13 P, *Dole Food Co Inc v Commission* EU:C:2015:184.

a concerted practice concerning the fixing, development, and evolution of prices. It found that the parties' regular pattern of communications relating to price-setting factors (such as the sales situation, supply and demand conditions liable to affect price levels for the coming weeks, and price trends and/or indications of quotation prices for the coming week) restricted competition by object; they were ultimately aimed at reducing or eliminating uncertainty as to the future pricing behaviour of the parties (the setting of quotation prices) and to maximise the price that they could individually and/or collectively obtain.[188] On appeal the argument was rejected that, as the pre-pricing communications were not able to remove uncertainty as to the setting of actual prices, they could not be considered to be restrictive by object. In particular, the CJ upheld the Commission's finding that the conduct could be regarded, by its very nature, to be harmful to the proper functioning of competition, reiterating (as in *T-Mobile*) that economic operators must determine their policy independently on the market and that conduct was liable to be incompatible with the competition law rules if it reduced or removed the degree of uncertainty as to the operation of the market in question.[189]

Case C-286/13 P, *Dole Food Co Inc v Commission* EU:C:2015:184

122. In particular, an exchange of information which is capable of removing uncertainty between participants as regards the timing, extent and details of the modifications to be adopted by the undertakings concerned in their conduct on the market must be regarded as pursuing an anticompetitive object (see, to that effect, judgment in *T-Mobile*..., paragraph 41).

123. Moreover, a concerted practice may have an anticompetitive object even though there is no direct connection between that practice and consumer prices. Indeed, it is not possible on the basis of the wording of Article [101(1)] to conclude that only concerted practices which have a direct effect on the prices paid by end users are prohibited (see, to that effect, judgment in *T-Mobile*..., paragraph 36).

124. On the contrary, it is apparent from Article [101(1)(a)] that concerted practices may have an anticompetitive object if they 'directly or indirectly fix purchase or selling prices or any other trading conditions' (judgment in *T-Mobile*..., paragraph 37).

125. In any event, Article [101], like the other competition rules of the Treaty, is designed to protect not only the immediate interests of individual competitors or consumers but also to protect the structure of the market and thus competition as such. Therefore, in order to find that a concerted practice has an anticompetitive object, there does not need to be a direct link between that practice and consumer prices (judgment in *T-Mobile*..., paragraphs 38 and 39).

...

129. As observed by the Advocate General at points 115 and 116 of her Opinion, it is apparent from the extremely detailed findings of the General Court, first, that bilateral pre-pricing communications were exchanged between the Dole companies and other undertakings in the banana sector and, as part of those communications, the undertakings discussed their own quotation prices and certain price trends. Moreover, the Dole companies do not contest that finding.

130. Second, the General Court found, at paragraph 574 of the judgment under appeal, that quotation prices were relevant to the market concerned, since, on the one hand, market signals, market trends or indications as to the intended development of banana prices could be inferred from those quotation prices, which were important for the banana trade and the prices obtained and, on the other, in some transactions the actual prices were directly linked to the quotation prices.

131. Third, at paragraph 580 of the judgment under appeal, the General Court found that the Dole employees involved in the pre-pricing communications participated in the internal pricing meetings.

---

[188] Ibid.

[189] Case C-286/13 P, *Dole* EU:C:2015:184, paras. 119–121.

132. Furthermore, those findings of the General Court are to a large extent based on statements made by Dole Food and the Dole companies have not alleged any form of distortion in that regard.

133. Accordingly, the General Court was entitled to take the view, without erring in law, that the conditions for the application of the presumption referred to at paragraph 127 above were fulfilled in the present case, with the result that the Dole companies' claims that that court infringed the principle governing the burden of proof and the presumption of innocence are unfounded.

134. It also follows that the General Court was entitled to take the view, as it did at paragraphs 553 and 585 of the judgment under appeal, without erring in law, that it was permissible for the Commission to conclude that, as they made it possible to reduce uncertainty for each of the participants as to the foreseeable conduct of competitors, the pre-pricing communications had the object of creating conditions of competition that do not correspond to the normal conditions on the market and therefore gave rise to a concerted practice having as its object the restriction of competition within the meaning of Article [101].

Although, as in *T-Mobile*, the statements in this case seem potentially to extend the category of object restraints to an overly broad and somewhat uncertain group of information-exchange agreements, it must be remembered both that: (a) (as in *T-Mobile*) the statements were made in the context of a case in which the conduct at issue was found to be designed to facilitate the fixing of selling prices; and (b) in *CB* the CJ stressed that the category of object restrictions is a narrow one, reserved exclusively for agreements which inherently reveal a sufficient degree of harm to competition. An approach closely in tune with economic effects might suggest that only a relatively narrow category of information-sharing agreements should potentially be considered to be restrictive by object—in particular, the private sharing of disaggregated, confidential information relevant, or relating, to future pricing or output intentions between competitors.[190] In its Horizontal Cooperation Guidelines, the Commission provides only one example of an information exchange that restricts competition by object, that is information exchanges 'on companies' individualised intentions concerning future conduct regarding prices or quantities'.[191] The Commission states that such exchanges are likely to allow competitors to arrive at a common higher price level and are less likely to be made for pro-competitive reasons than exchanges of actual data. Further, that 'private exchanges between competitors on their individualised intentions regarding future prices or quantities would normally be considered and fined as cartels because they generally have the object of fixing prices or quantities'.[192]

c. Analysing Other Information Exchanges

Where an agreement is not found to have as its object the restriction of competition, it will need to be assessed individually in its market context to determine its actual or likely effect. 'For an information exchange to have restrictive effects on competition within the meaning of Article 101(1), it must be likely to have an appreciable adverse impact on one (or several) of the parameters of competition such as price, output, product quality, product variety or innovation.'[193] A particular concern is that information exchanges can facilitate interdependent behaviour by creating the conditions

---

[190] See, e.g., Bennett and Collins, n. 175, 329–331 and Swedish Competition Authority, *The Pros and Cons of Information Sharing* (2006) and B. Meyring, 'T-Mobile: Further Confusion on Information Exchanges Between Competitors' (2010) 1 JECLAP 31.

[191] Horizontal Cooperation Guidelines, para. 73. It does, however, also state that in assessing whether any specific exchange is restrictive by object, the Commission will pay particular attention to the legal and economic context in which the information exchange takes place and whether by its very nature the exchange may possibly lead to a restriction of competition.

[192] Ibid., paras. 72–74.

[193] Ibid., para. 75.

for it—by increasing transparency, reducing complexity, buffering instability, or compensating for asymmetry.[194] The CJ in *Asnef-Equifax, Servicios de Información sobre Solvencia y Crédito, SL v Asociación de Usuarios de Servicios Bancarios (Ausbanc)* stated:[195]

the appraisal of the effects of agreements or practices . . . entails the need to take into consideration the actual context to which they belong, in particular the economic and legal context in which the undertakings concerned operate, the nature of the goods or services affected, as well as the real conditions of the functioning and the structure of the market or markets in question . . .

Accordingly . . . the compatibility of an information exchange system . . . with the [EU] competition rules cannot be assessed in the abstract. It depends on the economic conditions on the relevant markets and on the specific characteristics of the system concerned, such as, in particular, its purpose and the conditions of access to it and participation in it, as well as the type of information exchanged—be that, for example, public or confidential, aggregated or detailed, historical or current—the periodicity of such information and its importance for the fixing of prices, volumes or conditions of service.

Two factors are, therefore, particularly relevant in the marking of the assessment: (a) the specific characteristics of the system—its purpose, conditions of access and participation, and the type of information exchanged; and (b) the nature and economic conditions of the relevant market.

(a) When determining the likely effect of the information exchange on competition it is necessary to assess a number of factors including the type of information exchanged and the nature of the data, in the context of the facts of the case and the market in which the information exchange is operated.[196] Statistical information which enables undertakings to assess the level of demand and output in the market or the costs of its competitors may be beneficial and is not of itself objectionable.[197] Similarly, exchange of technical or other information that does not restrict the parties' freedom to determine their market behaviour independently should not be objectionable. However, exchange of strategic data (that reduces strategic uncertainty in the market), such as information relating to prices, individual output or sales figures,[198] capacity increases,[199] costs,[200] demand, investment plans,[201] new technology and research projects, or other business secrets, is liable to decrease the parties' incentive to compete and increase opportunities for coordinated activity. It has been seen that the exchange of particularly sensitive, confidential data may be sufficient to establish a restriction by object. In *Cobelpa/VNP*,[202] for example, the Commission held that although there was nothing wrong in a trade association exchanging information on industry output and sales, in this case, where the information exchanged identified the output and sales of individual undertakings, the practice was prohibited. By exchanging information about matters normally regarded as confidential (especially where the information was not available to consumers) the parties were replacing practical cooperation for the normal risks of competition. It made no difference that the information could have been obtained from elsewhere.

The nature of the data (whether it is individualised or aggregated) and its age is also important. The exchange of aggregated industry-wide data (which does not identify the performance of individual competitors), even if it relates to output or price, is less likely to enable firms to coordinate their behaviour or to detect deviations from a coordinated strategy. Similarly, if the information

---

[194] Ibid., para. 77.

[195] Case C-238/05, [2006] ECR I-11125, para. 54.

[196] Horizontal Cooperation Guidelines, paras. 86–94.

[197] Case T-334/94, *Sarrió SA v Commission* [1998] ECR II-1439.

[198] See COMP/31.370 and 31.466, *UK Agricultural Tractor Registration Exchange* [1992] OJ L68/19.

[199] See, e.g., COMP/243, 244, 245, *Re Cimbell* [1972] OJ L303/24.

[200] See, e.g., COMP/400, *IFTRA Glass Containers* [1974] OJ L160/1; COMP/27.000, *IFTRA Aluminium* [1975] OJ L228/3.

[201] See, e.g., COMP/30.350, *Zinc Producer Group* [1984] OJ L220/27.

[202] COMP/312 and 366, [1977] OJ L242/10.

exchanged is 'historic'[203] rather than current it is unlikely to facilitate the coordination of conduct on a market in the future.[204] In contrast, exchanges are more likely to facilitate 'a common understanding on the market and punishment strategies by allowing the coordinating companies to single out a deviator or entrant'[205] when the data exchanged is individualised and/or when it relates to future or current conduct. Other factors, such as the frequency of the exchange, whether the information exchanged is in the public domain,[206] and whether the information exchange is public or private,[207] may also to be relevant to the assessment. 'The fact that information is exchanged in public may decrease the likelihood of a collusive outcome on the market to the extent that non-coordinating companies, potential competitors, as well as customers may be able to constrain potential restrictive effect on competition.'[208] The purpose of the exchange and conditions of access may also be important to the assessment.

(b) In assessing information agreements close attention also needs to be paid to the structure of the market. The tendency for firms to fall in line with the behaviour of their competitors is particularly strong in oligopolistic markets. The improved knowledge of market conditions aimed at by information agreements strengthens the connection between the undertakings, in that they are enabled to react very efficiently to one another's actions, and thus lessens the intensity of competition.[209] Information exchanges are therefore more likely to be problematic on oligopolistic markets which are conducive to interdependent coordinated behaviour, in particular, markets with a few players which are sufficiently transparent, concentrated, complex, stable, and symmetric: 'In those types of markets companies can reach a common understanding on the terms of coordination and successfully monitor and punish deviations.'[210]

In *UK Agricultural Tractor Registration Exchange*,[211] eight UK manufacturers and importers of agricultural tractors operated an information-exchange agreement that identified the volume of retail sales and market shares of each of the manufacturers individually. The Commission condemned the exchange taking account of the fact that:

(i)   the market was highly concentrated (the eight manufacturers/importers had approximately 87–88 per cent of the relevant market);

(ii) there were high barriers to entry into the market;

---

[203] There may be no objection under Art. 101(1) if information as to the production or sales of particular undertakings is made publicly available under the auspices of a trade association provided the information is sufficiently historical that it no longer has any real impact on future behaviour, COMP/31.370 and COMP/31.466, *UK Agricultural Tractor Registration Exchange* [1992] OJ L68/19.

[204] 'Aggregated information at the industry level is unlikely to be useful for coordination. It is difficult to come to a focal point or monitor and understanding when firms cannot see from the information how their individual competitors are performing. Likewise, information which is significantly historic in nature is unlikely to be useful for present or future coordination . . . Of course, what qualifies as "historic" will depend upon the nature of the market and the competitive interaction within the sector', Bennett and Collins, n. 175, 331.

[205] Horizontal Cooperation Guidelines, para. 89.

[206] Art. 101(1) may be infringed even if the information could have been obtained from other, less convenient, sources, see, e.g., Case C-238/05, *Asnef-Equifax v Asociación Usuarios de Servicios Bancarios (Ausbanc)* [2006] ECR I-11125, para. 58.

[207] Any 'market transparency' attained may be offset by the fact that the information remains private to the undertakings concerned, see, e.g., COMP/31.370 and 31.466, *UK Agricultural Tractor Registration Exchange* [1992] OJ L68/19.

[208] Horizontal Cooperation Guidelines, para. 94. The public information exchanges will, of course, be caught by Art. 101(1) only if it can be established that the parties have engaged in an agreement to exchange the information or concerted to do so.

[209] Commission's *VIIth Report on Competition Policy* (1977), part 7(2).

[210] Horizontal Cooperation Guidelines, para. 77.

[211] COMP/31.370 and 31.466, [1992] OJ L68/19, Case T-34/92, *Fiatagri & Ford New Holland v Commission* [1994] ECR II-905 and Case T-35/92, *John Deere Ltd v Commission* [1994] ECR II-957; Case C-7/95 P, *John Deere Ltd v Commission* [1998] ECR I-3111.

(iii) there were insignificant extra-Union imports;

(iv) the information exchanged was detailed and identified the exact retail sales and shares of the undertakings which were generally trade secrets between competitors; and

(v) the members met regularly.

First, the Commission held that the exchange of information prevented hidden competition by creating transparency on a market which was already highly concentrated and largely shielded from outside competition. Where demand was stable, a forecast of a competitor's future actions could be largely determined on the basis of past transactions. The forecast would be more effective the more accurate and recent the information was. The exchange of information could, however, truly be categorised as historic from a certain period of time (for example, if it was more than one year old).[212] Although the Commission recognised that there were benefits of transparency in a competitive market, in this case the concentration of the market was not low and the market transparency was not in any way directed towards the benefit of consumers. The information in this case enabled each participant accurately to establish its rivals' market position and to see immediately if a rival increased its market share (for example, by price reductions or other marketing incentives). It limited price competition since competitors would be able to react quickly to changes in market positions (this would, of course, mean that there was little incentive for a potential initiator to take steps to improve its position). Information would thus limit the possibility of surprise or secrecy if a rival received information disclosing sensitive information about its competitors. It would then be able to react quickly and eliminate any possible advantage to be gained by the initiator.

Secondly, the information would also be likely to increase barriers to entry since participants would know immediately of new market entrants and would be able to react accordingly.

The Commission's analysis was upheld by the EU Courts. In *John Deere Ltd v Commission*,[213] the GC accepted that a truly competitive market would benefit from transparency but that exchanges of precise information at short intervals on a highly concentrated market would be likely to impair competition existing between the traders.

Case T-35/92, *John Deere Ltd v Commission* [1994] ECR II-957

General Court

51. The Court observes that, as the applicant points out, the Decision is the first in which the Commission has prohibited an information exchange system concerning sufficiently homogeneous products which does not directly concern the prices of those products, but which does not underpin any other anti-competitive arrangement either. As the applicants correctly argue, on a truly competitive market transparency between traders is in principle likely to lead to the intensification of competition between suppliers, since in such a situation, the fact that a trader takes into account information made available to him in order to adjust his conduct on the market is not likely, having regard to the atomized nature of the supply, to reduce or remove for the other traders any uncertainty about the foreseeable nature of its competitors' conduct. On the other hand, the Court considers that, as the Commission argues this time, general use, as between main suppliers and, contrary to the applicant's contention, to their sole benefit and consequently to the exclusion of the other suppliers and of consumers, of exchanges of precise information at short intervals, identifying registered vehicles and the place of their registration is, on a highly concentrated oligopolistic market such as the market in question and on which competition is as a result already greatly

---

[212] See also COMP/34.936, *CEPI/Cartonboard* [1996] OJ C310/3.

[213] Case T-35/92, [1994] ECR II-957, aff'd Case C-7/95 P, *John Deere Ltd v Commission* [1998] ECR I-3111. See also COMP/36.096, *Wirtschaftsvereinigung Stahl* [1998] OJ L1/10, although the Commission's decision condemned information-sharing in a concentrated market with high barriers to entry was annulled by the GC, essentially on the grounds that the Commission's decision was marred by errors of fact, Case T-16/98, [2000] ECR II-1217.

reduced and exchange of information facilitated, likely to impair substantially the competition which exists between traders (see paragraph 81). In such circumstances, the sharing, on a regular and frequent basis, of information concerning the operation of the market has the effect of periodically revealing to all the competitors the market positions and strategies of the various individual competitors.

52. Furthermore, provision of the information in question to all suppliers presupposes an agreement, or at any rate a tacit agreement, between the traders to define the boundaries of dealer sales territories by reference to the United Kingdom postcode system, as well as an institutional framework enabling information to be exchanged between the traders through the trade association to which they belong and, secondly, having regard to the frequency of such information and its systematic nature, it also enables a given trader to forecast more precisely the conduct of its competitors, so reducing or removing the degree of uncertainty about the operation of the market which would have existed in the absence of such an exchange of information. Furthermore, the Commission correctly contends, at points 44 to 48 of the Decision, that whatever decision is adopted by a trader wishing to penetrate the United Kingdom agricultural tractor market, and whether or not it becomes a member of the agreement, that agreement is necessarily disadvantageous for it. Either the trader concerned does not become a member of the information exchange agreement and, unlike its competitors, then forgoes the information exchanged and the market knowledge which it provides; or it becomes a member of the agreement and its business strategy is then immediately revealed to all its competitors by means of the information which they receive.

53. It follows that the pleas that the information exchange agreement at issue is not of such a nature as to infringe the [EU] competition rules must be dismissed.

. . .

81. Secondly, with regard to the type of information exchanged, the Court considers that, contrary to the applicant's contention, the information concerned, which relates in particular to sales made in the territory of each of the dealerships in the distribution network, is in the nature of business secrets. Indeed, this is admitted by the members of the agreement themselves, who strictly defined the conditions under which the information received could be disseminated to third parties, especially to members of their distribution network. The Court also observes that, as stated above (in paragraph 51), having regard to its frequency and systematic nature the exchange of information in question makes the conduct of a given trader's competitors all the more foreseeable for it in view of the characteristics of the relevant market as analyzed above, since it reduces, or even removes, the degree of uncertainty regarding the operation of the market, which would have existed in the absence of such an exchange of information, and in this regard the applicant cannot profitably rely on the fact that the information exchanged does not concern prices or relate to past sales. Accordingly, the first part of the plea, to the effect that there is no restriction of competition as a result of alleged 'prevention of hidden competition', must be dismissed.

In *Eudim*,[214] in contrast, the Commission held that information sharing in a market that was competitive on both the purchasing and selling side did not infringe Article 101(1).

In *Asnef-Equifax, Servicios de Información sobre Solvencia y Crédito, SL v Asociación de Usuarios de Servicios Bancarios (Ausbanc)*[215] Ausbanc challenged the exchange of information between financial institutions on the solvency of customers and borrower default. Following an Article 267 reference to it the CJ set out guidance for the referring court to determine the compatibility of the provisions for exchange with Article 101(1). With regard to the question of whether the agreement had as its effect the restriction of competition, the CJ stressed the importance of considering whether supply on the market was highly concentrated, whether information identified competitors individually, and whether access to the information was available in a non-discriminatory manner to all operators.

---

[214] COMP/33.815 and 35.842, [1996] OJ C111/8.
[215] Case C-238/05, [2006] ECR I-11125. Contrast, Case C-172/14, *ING Pensii v Consiliul Concuretnei* EU:C:2015:484.

Case C-238/05, *Asnef-Equifax, Servicios de Información sobre Solvencia y Crédito, SL v Asociación de Usuarios de Servicios Bancarios (Ausbanc)* [2006] ECR I-11125

55. As indicated at paragraph 47 of this judgment, registers such as the one at issue in the main proceedings, by reducing the rate of borrower default, are in principle capable of improving the functioning of the supply of credit. As the Advocate General observed, in substance, at point 54 of his Opinion, if, owing to a lack of information on the risk of borrower default, financial institutions are unable to distinguish those borrowers who are more likely to default, the risk thereby borne by such institutions will necessarily be increased and they will tend to factor it in when calculating the cost of credit for all borrowers, including those less likely to default, who will then have to bear a higher cost than they would if the institutions were in a position to evaluate the probability of repayment more precisely. In principle, registers such as that mentioned above are capable of reducing such a tendency.

56. Furthermore, by reducing the significance of the information held by financial institutions regarding their own customers, such registers appear, in principle, to be capable of increasing the mobility of consumers of credit. In addition, those registers are apt to make it easier for new competitors to enter the market.

57. None the less, whether or not there is in the main proceedings a restriction of competition within the meaning of Article [101(1) TFEU] depends on the economic and legal context in which the register exists, and in particular on the economic conditions of the market as well as the particular characteristics of the register.

58. In that regard, first of all, if supply on a market is highly concentrated, the exchange of certain information may, according in particular to the type of information exchanged, be liable to enable undertakings to be aware of the market position and commercial strategy of their competitors, thus distorting rivalry on the market and increasing the probability of collusion, or even facilitating it. On the other hand, if supply is fragmented, the dissemination and exchange of information between competitors may be neutral, or even positive, for the competitive nature of the market (see, to that effect, *Thyssen Stahl v Commission*, paragraphs 84 and 86). In the present case, it is common ground, as may be seen from paragraph 10 of this judgment, that the referring court premi[s]ed its reference for a preliminary ruling on the existence of 'a fragmented market', which it is for that court to verify.

59. Secondly, in order that registers such as that at issue in the main proceedings are not capable of revealing the market position or the commercial strategy of competitors, it is important that the identity of lenders is not revealed, directly or indirectly. In the present case, it is apparent from the decision for referral that the Tribunal de Defensa de la Competencia imposed on Asnef-Equifax, which accepted it, a condition that the information relating to lenders contained in the register not be disclosed.

60. Thirdly, it is also important that such registers be accessible in a non-discriminatory manner, in law and in fact, to all operators active in the relevant sphere. If such accessibility were not guaranteed, some of those operators would be placed at a disadvantage, since they would have less information for the purpose of risk assessment, which would also not facilitate the entry of new operators on to the market.

61. It follows that, provided that the relevant market or markets are not highly concentrated, that the system does not permit lenders to be identified and that the conditions of access and use by financial institutions are not discriminatory, an information exchange system such as the register is not, in principle, liable to have the effect of restricting competition within the meaning of Article [101(1) TFEU].

62. While in those conditions such systems are capable of reducing uncertainty as to the risk that applicants for credit will default, they are not, however, liable to reduce uncertainty as to the risks of competition. Thus, each operator could be expected to act independently and autonomously when adopting a given course of conduct, regard being had to the risks presented by applicants. Contrary to Ausbanc's contention, it cannot be inferred solely from the existence of such a credit information

> exchange that it might lead to collective anti-competitive conduct, such as a boycott of certain potential borrowers.
>
> 63. Furthermore, since, as the Advocate General observed, in substance, at point 56 of his Opinion, any possible issues relating to the sensitivity of personal data are not, as such, a matter for competition law, they may be resolved on the basis of the relevant provisions governing data protection. In the main proceedings, it is apparent from the documents before the Court that, under the rules applicable to the register, affected consumers may, in accordance with the Spanish legislation, check the information concerning them and, where necessary, have it corrected, or indeed deleted.

The CJ in *Asnef-Equifax* also recognised that the referring court might need to carry out an Article 101(3) assessment in order to resolve the dispute at issue.[216] For example, the court might be required to determine whether objective economic advantages, such as helping to prevent over-indebtedness for consumers of credit and leading to a greater overall availability of credit, might be such as to offset the disadvantages of any restriction of competition identified. The CJ stressed that in making the Article 101(3) determination, it was not necessary that all consumers should benefit from the system. Rather, it was not inconceivable that some applicants for credit would be faced with increased interest rates or refused credit. This circumstance was not in itself sufficient to prevent the condition that consumers be allowed a fair share of the benefit from being satisfied since 'it is the beneficial nature of the effect on all consumers in the relevant markets that must be taken into consideration, not the effect on each member of that category of consumers'.[217] Indeed, the exchange in this situation might be capable of leading to a greater overall availability of credit, including for applicants for whom interest rates might be excessive if lenders did not have appropriate knowledge of their personal system.

d. Business-to-Business (B2B) Exchanges

B2B e-marketplaces, which allow industrial buyers and sellers to transact business online over the internet, have become common.[218] Although such marketplaces may create huge efficiency gains in purchasing and supply chain management there has also been a concern that such markets would create an ideal climate for collusion, due to increased communication and transparency in the market,[219] exchange of confidential information, and foreclosure. The Commission, however, recognises the clear advantages that may result from such marketplaces and has sought to develop a coherent approach to their assessment and has in many cases accepted that such agreements do not infringe Article 101(1) at all.[220] In *Covisint*,[221] for example, the Commission sent a comfort letter clearing the creation of the Covisint Automotive Internet Marketplace (the agreement did not infringe Article 101(1)). Six car manufacturers notified to the Commission a joint venture to serve the procurement needs of major car makers and suppliers and to reduce costs and improve efficiency in the supply chain. The Commission noted in its press release that in general B2B marketplaces should have pro-competitive effects by creating more transparency, integrating markets, and creating marketing efficiencies by reducing search and information costs and improving inventory

---

[216] But see, e.g., COMP/30.525, *International Energy Program* [1983] OJ L376/30.

[217] Case C-238/05, *Asnef-Equifax v Asociación Usuarios de Servicios Bancarios (Ausbanc)* [2006] ECR I-11125, para. 70.

[218] J. Lüking, 'B2B e-Marketplaces and EU Competition Law: Where Do We Stand?' (2001) 3 *Competition Policy Newsletter* 14. See also S. Stroux, 'B2B e-Market-places: The Emerging Competition Law Issues' (2001) 24 *World Competition* 125 and D. Lancefield, 'The Regulatory Hurdles Ahead in B2B' [2001] *ECLR* 9.

[219] OFT 308, 'E-Commerce and Its Implications for Competition Policy', para. 6.54.

[220] See, e.g., M. Monti, 'European Competition Policy for the 21st Century' [2000] *Fordham Corp L Inst*, Chap. 15 and 'Competition in the New Economy', 10th International Conference on Competition of the Bundeskartellamt, Berlin, 21 May 2001.

[221] COMP/38.064, IP/01/1155 (a negative clearance comfort letter).

management, leading ultimately to lower prices for the end consumer. In this case the Commission was satisfied that potential competition concerns had been eliminated:

Covisint is open to all firms in the industry on a non-discriminatory basis, is based on open standards, allows both shareholders and other users to participate in other B-2-B exchanges, does not allow joint purchasing between car manufacturers or for automotive-specific products, and provides for adequate data protection, including firewalls and security rules.

It has also sent negative clearance comfort letters in relation to B2B electronic marketplaces set up in other sectors.[222] In an article by a Commission official in the *Competition Policy Newsletter* several guidelines are set out for companies considering setting up e-marketplaces.[223]

C. RESTRICTIONS ON NON-PRICE TRADING CONDITIONS, ADVERTISING, AND PROMOTION

(i) General

Agreements relating to non-price trading conditions or relating to advertising or promotion may restrict important methods of competition between undertakings operating on the market and so chill competition between them. Such restraints may be tantamount to price-fixing or other hardcore cartel activity (for example, an agreement not to grant credit to buyers), may be used to complement and facilitate the operation of a hardcore cartel agreement or may have the effect of facilitating tacit collusion between firms.

(ii) Restrictions on Non-price Trading Conditions

a. Introduction

Because non-price competition may also be an important part of competition between undertakings, Article 101(1)(a) prohibits not only collusive practices directly or indirectly fixing price but also those fixing 'any other trading conditions'. Restraints on such trading conditions may constitute or bolster hardcore cartel activities. In *Fine Art Auction Houses*,[224] for example, Christie's and Sotheby's fixed not only the commissions that they charged but other conditions as well, such as payment conditions, guarantees, and advances. In some cases, however, it may be advantageous for undertakings to have access to suitably drafted terms and conditions and/or to adopt common quality or technical standards. In such cases, it is possible that the agreements will not infringe Article 101(1) at all or that they will meet the criteria of Article 101(3).[225]

b. Uniform Terms and Conditions

The use of printed forms setting out standard terms and conditions to be applied by undertakings will not necessarily infringe Article 101(1). However, where the terms and conditions relate to 'important secondary aspects of competition',[226] that is, to any aspect of a supplier's offer which has economic value in the eyes of the customer, they may infringe Article 101(1).

---

[222] See *Eutilia/Endorsial*, IP/01/1775; *Eurex*, IP/02/4; *Inreon*, IP/02/761; *Centradia*, IP 02/943; *Water Portal*, IP/02/956; and J. Lüking, 'B2B e-Marketplaces and EC Competition Law: Where Do We Stand?' (2001) 3 *Competition Policy Newsletter* 14.

[223] Lüking, ibid.

[224] COMP/37.784, [2002] OJ L200/92.

[225] COMP/32.265, *Concordato Incendio* [1990] OJ L15/27.

[226] COMP/30.174, *Vimpoltu* [1983] OJ L200/44.

In *Fabricants de Papiers Peints de Belgique*,[227] the Commission found that general conditions of sale concluded by Belgian manufacturers of wallpaper, which related to terms of delivery, returns policy, lengths of rolls, etc. infringed Article 101(1) and did not satisfy the conditions of Article 101(3).

c. Customer Services

Prohibitions on parties to an agreement offering customers special services such as the loan of products or special delivery arrangements are likely to cause an infringement of Article 101(1).[228]

d. Product Quality

The adoption of a common quality label (establishing that products meet a minimum quality standard) will not necessarily infringe Article 101(1). However, a provision restricting suppliers from producing products of a different, inferior standard (and limiting the quality of products supplied) is likely to do so.[229]

e. Technical Development

Similarly, the adoption of a label identifying products that achieve a certain common technical standard will not infringe Article 101(1) where the quality mark is freely available and the parties are free to market products of a different or inferior standard.[230] There may, however, be an infringement of Article 101(1) where the agreement limits technical development[231] or is used to hinder imports, as in *IAZ*.[232]

In *IAZ* a Belgian trade association agreed with Belgian manufacturers and sole importers for washing machines and dishwashers that only appliances with a 'conformity' label could be connected to the mains. To receive a conformity label the appliances had to comply with technical standards laid down by Belgian law. In fact, the label was available only to Belgian manufacturers or sole importers of products. Thus parallel imports of the appliances were made impossible in practice.

(iii) Restrictions on Advertising and Promotion

The advertising and promotion of a product may be an extremely important aspect of competition between undertakings. It may be a vital means of distinguishing the products, in the eyes of the consumer, from those of competitors and may draw attention to the different characteristics, prices, and qualities of the relevant products. It can also provide an important mechanism for entering a new market.

Restrictions on the ability of parties to an agreement to advertise are likely to be seen as a restriction on their competitive freedom and competition.[233] The Commission has shown particular concern about restrictions on advertising in the liberal professions.

---

[227] COMP/426, [1974] OJ L237/3.

[228] See, e.g., COMP/324, *VCH* [1972] OJ L13/34.

[229] COMP/32.202, *Belgian Association of Pharmacists* [1990] OJ L18/33. But see also *European Council of Manufacturers of Domestic Appliances* [2000] OJ L187/47, Chap. 4 and Case C-309/99, *Wouters v Algemene Raad van de Nederlandse Orde van Advocaten* [2002] ECR I-1577.

[230] Notice on Cooperation Agreements [1968] JO C75/3, para. II(8).

[231] See, e.g., COMP/29.151, *Video Cassette Recorders* [1978] OJ L47/42.

[232] COMP/29.995, *Anseau* [1982] OJ L167/39; on appeal Case 96/82, *IAZ International Belgium NV v Commission* [1983] ECR 3369.

[233] See, e.g., COMP/39.579, *Consumer Detergents* [2011] OJ C193/14 (the Commission treated restrictions on promotional activity as a form of price collusion in the context of the case).

Communication from the Commission, 'Report on Competition in Professional Services', COM(2004) 83 final (Brussels, 9 February 2004)

42. A large number of the EU professions are subject to sector-specific advertising regulation . . . in some cases advertising as such is prohibited. In others, specific media or advertising methods such as radio advertising, televisions advertising or 'cold calling' or specific types of advertising content are proscribed. In certain cases, there is a lack of clarity in existing advertising regulations which, in itself, may deter professions from employing certain advertising methods.

43. According to economic theory, advertising may facilitate competition by informing consumers about different products and allowing them to make better informed purchasing decisions. Advertising restrictions may thus reduce competition by increasing the costs of gaining information about different products, making it more difficult for consumers to search for the quality and price that best meets their needs. It is also widely recognised that advertising, and in particular comparative advertising, can be a crucial competitive tool for new firms entering the market and for existing firms to launch new products.

44. The proponents of advertising restrictions emphasise the asymmetry of information between practitioners and consumers of professional services. According to this argument, consumers find it difficult to assess information about professional services and therefore need particular protection from misleading or manipulative claims.

45. There is, however, an increasing body of empirical evidence which highlights the potentially negative effects of some advertising restrictions. This research suggests that restrictions may under certain circumstances increase the fees for professional services without having a positive effect on the quality of those services. The implication of these findings is that advertising restrictions as such do not, necessarily, provide an appropriate response to asymmetry of information in professional services. Conversely, truthful and objective advertising may actually help consumers to overcome the asymmetry and to make more informed purchasing decisions.

In general, where parties agree jointly to advertise industry products or products of a common brand, there is no infringement of Article 101(1) so long as the parties are also free to advertise individually. However, different rules may apply in an oligopolistic market where product differentiation and advertising may play a more vital role.

In *Milchförderungsfonds*,[234] the German dairy industry established a milk promotion fund. The fund was financed by a voluntary levy on milk delivered to dairies. The purpose of the fund was to promote the export of milk products. Brand-advertising campaigns and subsidised sales were conducted abroad. The Commission considered that the campaign distorted competition within the meaning of Article 101(1) and artificially strengthened the position of German exporters abroad. Although generic advertising, which did not commend the products solely on the ground of their national origin and did not disparage foreign products, would have benefited all exporters, brand-oriented advertising appreciably reduced the possibility of sales for competing brands. Individual manufacturers benefited from the campaign without having to suffer a corresponding cost which otherwise would have been reflected in the sales price.

In *BELASCO*,[235] Belgian manufacturers jointly advertised and promoted their products, which were sold under a common trade mark, through the association, BELASCO. The Commission considered that the purpose of the standardisation of the products and the joint advertising was to reinforce the other provisions of the agreement which provided for a common price list and sales

---

[234] COMP/28.930, [1985] OJ L35/35.
[235] COMP/31.371, *BELASCO* [1986] OJ L232/15.

quotas. The fostering of an impression in consumers that their products were homogeneous limited the scope of competition by means of product differentiation.

The Commission has, on occasion, accepted that it may be advantageous for undertakings to rationalise and coordinate their advertising efforts, particularly in the context of trade fairs.[236]

D. PROVING A BREACH

(i) Agreement, Concerted Practice, or Decision Required: Distinguishing Joint from Unilateral Conduct

It has been seen that naked cartel activity is liable to be found to restrict competition by object, not to satisfy the conditions of Article 101(3), and to result in significant fines (or other penalties) being imposed on those involved. This means that such activity tends to be hidden and/or that firms seek to find more amorphous mechanisms for coordinating their conduct on the market (for example, through signalling how they will behave in the future to their competitors). The challenge for competition authorities, or other claimants, in cases where a cartel is suspected, is therefore to establish that the undertakings involved have engaged in collusive activity prohibited by Article 101(1)[237]— through an agreement or concerted practice between undertakings or a decision by an association of undertakings. In Chapter 3 it was seen that although these concepts are interpreted broadly to catch:

- formal and informal agreements;

- recommendations and certain other conduct of trade associations and associations of undertakings; and[238]

- coordination between undertakings which, without having reached the stage where an agreement, properly so called, has been concluded, knowingly substitutes practical cooperation between them for the risks of competition.[239] In particular, cooperation between undertakings which have not made an actual plan as to how they will behave on the market but who are not determining their conduct *independently*. For example, where competitors share data/information either directly (for example, through reciprocal exchanges of strategic information[240] or a disclosure of strategic information by one undertaking to a competitor where the recipient requests the information or accepts it)[241] or indirectly (for example, 'through a common agency (for example, a trade association) or a third party such as a market research organisation or through the companies' suppliers or retailers');[242]

---

[236] See, e.g., COMP/28.775, *UNIDI* [1984] OJ L322/10.

[237] The fact that the parties have cheated on the cartel agreement during its course cannot be used to demonstrate that there is no agreement or concerted practice because the parties were not committed to the scheme. On the contrary, cheating may be part and parcel of ordinary cartel activity which may be characterised by sporadic price wars or outbreaks of conflict, see, e.g., COMP/35.691, *Pre-Insulated Pipes* [1999] OJ L24/1, para. 132.

[238] In a number of cartels uncovered by the Commission, a significant role has been played by a trade association, a fiduciary company, or other intermediary, see Chap. 3. Where this is the case the intermediary may be held responsible for the breach and fined, see, e.g., Case 246/86, *Re Roofing Felt Cartel: BELASCO v Commission* [1989] ECR 2117 and COMP/37.857, *Organic Peroxides* [2005] OJ L110/44, *aff'd* Case T-120/04, *Peróxidos Orgánicos SA v Commission* [2006] ECR II-4441, Case C-194/14 P, *AC-Treuhand AG v Commission* EU:C:2015:717 and Case T-99/04, *AC-Treuhand AG v Commission* [2008] ECR II-1501 and Chap. 4.

[239] Cases 48, 49, and 51–57/69, *ICI v Commission* [1972] ECR 619, paras. 64 and 65.

[240] See Case C-8/08, *T-Mobile* [2009] ECR I-4529 (see Chap. 3), paras. 54–62 and Case COMP/39.188, *Bananas*, n. 187.

[241] See Chap. 3.

[242] Horizontal Cooperation Guidelines, para. 55.

the challenge is to define the exact boundary between joint conduct caught by Article 101(1) and unilateral conduct falling outside it and to demonstrate (through direct or circumstantial evidence) that collusion has taken place.

(ii) Parallel Conduct, Explicit and Tacit Collusion

a. The Problem

An important question that has arisen is whether the concepts of agreement, decision, and concerted practice are broad enough to catch parallel conduct arising from tacit collusion on a market, where firms determine their strategy by taking account of the likely response of their competitors; in particular, whether tacit collusion constitutes a mechanism for substituting practical cooperation between undertakings (caught by Article 101(1)) or independent behaviour (outside its scope).[243] Although the judgment of the CJ in *Dyestuffs*[244] arguably left the position open, in *Re Wood Pulp Cartel: Ahlström Oy v Commission (Wood Pulp)*[245] the CJ made it clear that parallel conduct or tacit collusion is not in itself prohibited by Article 101(1). Further, that although parallel behaviour may furnish circumstantial proof of explicit collusion it will not do so if the behaviour can be explained by the conditions of competition on the market, for example that the conditions have led to tacit collusion of the undertaking's behaviour (there is a plausible explanation for the conduct other than collusion).

b. The *Dyestuffs* Case

In *Dyestuffs*,[246] three general and uniform increases in the prices of dyestuffs had taken place within the EU over a period of years. The Commission concluded that the increases had occurred as a result of a concerted practice operating between ten producers (and in fact it had discovered significant evidence of actual direct/indirect contact between the parties).[247] The CJ upheld the decision finding that the behaviour constituted a concerted practice. In so doing, the Court relied upon the facts that: price increases had been announced in advance (the announcements eliminating all uncertainty between them as regards their future conduct and the risk inherent in any independent change in conduct); the announcements rendered the market transparent as regards the rates of increase; and given the number of producers on the market, it did not consider that it was possible to say that the market was an oligopolistic one. It was not plausible, therefore, that the parallel conduct could have been brought into effect within a period of two to three days without prior concertation. The Court concluded that, taking into account the nature of the market in the products in question, the conduct of the undertakings was designed to replace both the risks of competition and the hazards of competitors' spontaneous reactions with cooperation.

There were suggestions and concern after the Court's judgment that its interpretation of the term 'concerted practice' would be used broadly to catch rational, and purely parallel, market behaviour.[248] In particular, the Court characterised behaviour as apparently innocuous as making price announcements in advance as an impermissible means of indirect communication.[249] Arguably,

---

[243] In addition, if tacit collusion cannot be *equated* with a concerted practice, whether parallel conduct by firms operating on an oligopolistic market can ever be used as circumstantial evidence to justify a finding that an agreement or concerted practice existed between the undertakings.

[244] Case 48/69, *ICI v Commission* [1972] ECR 619.

[245] Cases C-89, 104, 114, 116–117, and 125–129/85, [1993] ECR I-1307.

[246] Case 48/69, *ICI v Commission* [1972] ECR 619.

[247] COMP/26.267, *Re Cartel in Aniline Dyes* [1969] OJ L195/11.

[248] See, e.g., V. Korah, 'Concerted Practices' (1973) 36 *MLR* 260; R. Joliet, 'La notion de pratique concertée et l'arrêt I.C.I. dans une perspective comparative' [1974] *CDE* 251.

[249] See Section 4.A.iii, 698–700.

however, these concerns were overstated given that the Commission had, in this case, discovered significant evidence of actual direct/indirect contact between the parties[250] and the CJ specifically stated that 'parallel behaviour may not by itself be identified with a concerted practice' although it could provide 'strong evidence of such a practice if it leads to conditions of competition which do not correspond to the normal conditions of the market, having regard to the nature of the products, the size and number of the undertakings, and the volume of the said market'.[251] The CJ thus stressed that a producer was 'free to charge his prices, taking into account in so doing the present or foreseeable conduct of his competitors'. In contrast, he was precluded from cooperating 'with his competitors, in any way whatsoever, in order to determine a coordinated course of action relating to a price increase to ensure its success by prior elimination of all uncertainty as to each other's conduct'.[252] Consequently,

the judgment was not so much worrying because of its definition of a concerted practice but more because it so easily assumed, without a detailed study of the market characteristics and without evidence of concertation, that parties had cooperated. Although the Court recognised the need to consider the specific features of the market in weighing the evidence, . . . it only did so superficially.[253]

c. *Suiker Unie* and *Züchner*

In both *Suiker Unie*[254] and *Züchner*[255] the CJ stressed that Article 101(1) did not prevent an undertaking from adapting its behaviour intelligently to the existing or anticipated conduct of competitors. In accordance with these judgments the Commission, in *Zinc Producer Group*,[256] accepted the legitimacy of parallel/oligopolistic behaviour. It held that:

parallel pricing behaviour in an oligopoly producing homogeneous goods [would] not in itself be sufficient evidence of a concerted practice.[257]

Thus, parallel action explicable in terms of barometric price leadership (that is to say, linked to a change in the market conditions, for example an increase in the price of the main raw material) would not be sufficient evidence of a concerted practice.

d. *Wood Pulp*

The CJ in *Wood Pulp*[258] delivered the clearest judgment on the relationship between conscious parallelism (or tacit collusion) and concerted practices. The Commission found that 43 pulp producers operating on the bleached sulphate wood pulp market had breached Article 101(1).[259] In particular, it found that concertation between many of the Finnish, US, and Canadian undertakings with regard to both announced and transaction prices in the pulp market had led to prices which were both artificially high and rigid. The Commission considered that the parallel behaviour was not

---

[250] The Commission found proof of concertation from the similarity of the content of the orders sent by the producers to their subsidiaries or representatives on the various markets, to make the increases (sometime sent on the same day (at the same hour), and couched in similar terms). It also discovered records of meetings of the producers in Basel and London.

[251] Cases 48, 49, and 51–57/69, [1972] ECR 619, para. 66.

[252] Ibid., para. 118.

[253] G. van Gerven and E. N. Varona, 'The *Wood Pulp* Case and the Future of Concerted Practices' (1994) 31 *CMLRev* 575, 590.

[254] Cases 40/73 etc., *Re the European Sugar Cartel: Coöperatieve Vereniging 'Suiker Unie' UA v Commission* [1975] ECR 1663.

[255] Case 172/80, *Züchner v Bayerische Vereinsbank* [1981] ECR 2021.

[256] COMP/30.350, [1984] OJ L220/27.

[257] Ibid., paras. 75–76.

[258] Cases C-89, 104, 114, 116–117, and 125–129/85, [1993] ECR I-1307.

[259] COMP/29.725, [1985] OJ L85/1.

explicable as rational behaviour.[260] It could not be explained as independently chosen parallel conduct in a narrow oligopolistic market (the market was characterised by a large number of producers, customers, and products; the market was not inherently transparent, but was only so as a result of the producers' deliberately chosen strategy of making price announcements in advance and there was no clear price leader, etc.).

The Court annulled much of the Commission's decision and many of the fines on substantive grounds. It considered two separate points: first whether or not the price announcements were in themselves prohibited by Article 101(1) and, secondly, whether they provided evidence of a concerted practice and concertation in advance prices.

The Court reiterated its previous holdings that parallel conduct could not be used to establish the existence of a concerted practice unless, taking account of the nature of the products, the size and the number of undertakings, and the volume of the market in question, it could not be explained otherwise than by concertation. Parallel behaviour would furnish proof of concertation only where it constituted the only plausible explanation for such conduct. Every producer was free to react intelligently to market forces and to alter its course of action, taking into account in so doing the present or foreseeable conduct of its competitors.

The Court was not prepared to reject, as the Commission had done, the protestations that the undertakings' behaviour was a consequence, not of a concerted practice, but of non-collusive interdependence or conscious parallelism. It commissioned two independent reports from economic experts to analyse the wood pulp market and the evidence involved. The reports were extremely damaging to the Commission's case. On the facts and relying on experts' reports, the Court found that the system of quarterly price announcements did not, of itself, amount to an infringement of Article 101(1)[261] and that this system and the parallelism of announced prices were not evidence of concertation. Further, it could not be said that the system of advance price announcements and parallel behaviour was not explicable otherwise than by concertation. The Commission had failed sufficiently to appreciate that the wood pulp market had oligopolistic tendencies, being characterised by oligopolies and oligopsonies (on the buying side) in particular pulp types. Also the market was inherently transparent. Paper manufacturers were in constant touch with a number of pulp suppliers and exchanged price information amongst themselves and the transparency was reinforced both by a number of common agents that operated throughout the market and an active trade press.

The system of advanced announced prices was, therefore, explicable as a rational response to the fact that the pulp market was a long-term one and met a legitimate business concern of customers.

Cases C-89, 104, 114, 116–117, and 125–129/85, *Re Wood Pulp Cartel: Ahlström Oy v Commission* [1993] ECR I-1307

Court of Justice

70. Since the Commission has no documents which directly establish the existence of concertation between the producers concerned, it is necessary to ascertain whether the system of quarterly price announcements, the simultaneity or near-simultaneity of the price announcements and the parallelism of price announcements as found during the period from 1975 to 1985 constitute a firm, precise and consistent body of evidence of prior concertation.

71. In determining the probative value of those different factors, it must be noted that parallel conduct cannot be regarded as furnishing proof of concertation unless concertation constitutes the only plausible explanation for such conduct. It is necessary to bear in mind that, although Article [101] . . . prohibits

---

[260] Although the Commission relied on some documentary evidence to supplement its finding, this was excluded by the Court.

[261] Cases C-89, 104, 114, 116–117, and 125–129/85, [1993] ECR I-1307.

any form of collusion which distorts competition, it does not deprive economic operators of the right to adapt themselves intelligently to the existing and anticipated conduct of their competitors (see *Suiker Unie*, . . . paragraph 174).

72. Accordingly, it is necessary in this case to ascertain whether the parallel conduct alleged by the Commission cannot, taking account of the nature of the products, the size and the number of the undertakings and the volume of the market in question, be explained otherwise than by concertation.

. . .

126. Following that analysis, it must be stated that, in this case, concertation is not the only plausible explanation for the parallel conduct. To begin with, the system of price announcements may be regarded as constituting a rational response to the fact that the pulp market constituted a long-term market and to the need felt by both buyers and sellers to limit commercial risks. Further, the similarity in the dates of price announcements may be regarded as a direct result of the high degree of market transparency, which does not have to be described as artificial. Finally, the parallelism of prices and the price trends may be satisfactorily explained by the oligopolistic tendencies of the market and by the specific circumstances prevailing in certain periods. Accordingly, the parallel conduct established by the Commission does not constitute evidence of concertation.

127. In the absence of a firm, precise and consistent body of evidence, it must be held that concertation regarding announced prices has not been established by the Commission. Article 1(1) of the contested decision must therefore be annulled.

e. Conclusions on Article 101 and Parallel Behaviour

It is clear that purely parallel behaviour on a market is not prohibited by Article 101. Rather, the concept of a concerted practice appears to demand *reciprocal* cooperation, through direct or indirect contact, designed to influence the conduct of an actual or potential competitor or to disclose to them the course of conduct that will or may be adopted on the market.[262]

Where direct evidence of reciprocal cooperation is not available, parallel behaviour may, however, furnish circumstantial proof of an agreement or concerted practice if it is not the kind of behaviour which would be anticipated on the market involved (whether the parallel conduct alleged by the Commission cannot, taking into account the nature of the products, the size and number of the undertakings, and the volume of the market in question, be explained otherwise than by concertation) and if there is no other plausible explanation for the conduct. In *Wood Pulp* the CJ's judgment describes the market characteristics in meticulous detail. In particular, it seems clear that the number of undertakings on the market, the homogeneity of the product, and the transparency of the market will be relevant to the analysis. The market structure may, therefore, provide a plausible explanation for the behaviour. It can be seen from *Wood Pulp* itself that explanations may well be available outside a tight oligopoly situation.

It is unclear whether, on the proof of parallel behaviour, the evidential burden shifts onto the accused to establish that there *is* a plausible explanation for the conduct. In *Wood Pulp*, the Advocate General appeared to consider that '[t]he burden of proof cannot be shifted simply by a finding of parallel conduct. Unless the Court can be satisfied by a set of presumptions having a solid basis, concertation is not established.'[263] If in accordance with the presumption of innocence that applies in Article 101 cases, the onus does not shift it seems impossible to imagine how the Commission (or any other) could establish that there is no other plausible explanation for

---

[262] See also Chap. 3 and, e.g., A. Albors-Lorens, 'Horizontal Agreements and Concerted Practices in EC Competition Law: Unlawful and Legitimate Contacts between Competitors' [2006] 51 *Ant Bull* 837 and A. Jones, '*Wood Pulp*: Concerted Practice and/or Conscious Parallelism' [1993] *ECLR* 273, 275–276.

[263] [1993] ECR I-1307, Darmon AG, para. 195. This conclusion seems to be necessitated by the presumption of innocence that applies in competition law cases, see further Chap. 13.

the parallel conduct. It would thus seem inadvisable to rely solely on economic evidence to establish the existence of a cartel. Rather, other evidence is required to corroborate a case. Indeed, in *Cartonboard*[264] the Commission stated:

> Had they been challenged, the producers could as a result of this elaborate scheme of deception have attributed the series of uniform, regular and industry-wide price increases in the cartonboard sector to the phenomenon of 'oligopoly behaviour'. They could argue that it made sense for all the producers to decide of their own volition to copy an increase initiated by one or other of the market leaders as soon as it became publicly known; unlawful collusion as such would not necessarily be indicated. Customers might well suspect and even accuse them of operating a cartel; and given the relatively large number of producers, economic theory would be stretched to its limits and beyond, but unless direct proof of collusion were forthcoming— and they went to some lengths to ensure it was not—the producers must have had hopes of defeating any investigation into their pricing conduct by the competition authorities by invoking the defence of oligopolistic interdependence.[265]

It is clear, however, that where plausible explanations are raised each of those must be ruled out by the Commission. In *CISAC*,[266] for example, the GC annulled a Commission decision finding a concerted practice as it had neither proven its existence by factors other than parallel conduct nor provided sufficient evidence to render implausible explanations of the undertakings for their parallel conduct.

(iii) Unilateral Price Announcements in Advance and Price Signalling

Like reciprocal exchanges of price information, price announcements in advance on a market may signal to other players on the market what a firm's future price policy will be and may facilitate alignment of their behaviour and tacit collusion on an oligopolistic market. An important question therefore is whether price announcements in advance constitute indirect contact with a competitor sufficient to establish a concerted practice to fix prices? In *Dyestuffs*,[267] the CJ considered that advance price communications provided, in the circumstances, proof of a concerted practice. It held that the announcements rendered the market artificially transparent and eliminated all uncertainty between the operators as regards the rates of increase, future conduct, and the risks inherent in an independent change of conduct. The Court commented:

> . . . the undertakings taking the initiative . . . announced their intentions of making an increase some time in advance, which allowed the undertakings to observe each other's reactions on the different markets, and to adapt themselves accordingly. By means of these advance announcements the various undertakings eliminated all uncertainty between them as to their future conduct and, in doing so, also eliminated a large part of the risk usually inherent in any independent change of conduct on one or several markets. This was all the more the case since these announcements, which led to the fixing of general and equal increases in prices for the markets in dyestuffs, rendered the market transparent as regard the percentage rates of increase. Therefore, by the way in which they acted, the undertakings in question temporarily eliminated with respect to prices some of the preconditions for competition on the market which stood in the way of the achievement of parallel uniformity of conduct.[268]

---

[264] COMP/33.833, Cartonboard [1994] OJ L243/1. In 2015 the Commission closed an investigation into parallel pricing on cement and cement related markets, COMP/39.520, Cement (proceedings initiated 6 December 2010). In a series of judgments, however, see e.g., Case C-247/14, *HeidelbergCement AG v Commission* EU:C:2016:149 the CJ annulled a Commission decision requesting information, broadly on the grounds that the Commission had not specified the purpose of the request and the alleged infringement precisely enough, see Chap. 13.

[265] Ibid., para. 73.

[266] Case T-442/08, *International Confederation of Societies of Authors and Composers (CISAC) v Commission* EU:T:2013:188.

[267] Cases 48, 49, and 51–57/69, *ICI v Commission (Dyestuffs)* [1972] ECR 619.

[268] Ibid., paras. 100–103.

This case must, however, be assessed in the light of its own particular facts and, now, the judgment of the CJ in *Wood Pulp*.[269] In the latter case the Commission found concertation in respect of both announced and actual transaction prices. The CJ, however, held that price announcements in advance did not, in themselves, constitute an infringement of Article 101(1).

64. In this case, the communications arise from the price announcements made to users. They constitute in themselves market behaviour which does not lessen each undertaking's uncertainty as to the future attitude of its competitors. At the same time when each undertaking engages in such behaviour, it cannot be sure of the future conduct of the others.

65. Accordingly, the system of quarterly price announcements on the pulp market is not to be regarded as constituting in itself an infringement of Article [101](1).

Further, the Court held that it had not been established that the system amounted to a means of indirect communication between the competitors. The announcements served the need of customers desiring the information to plan the cost of their paper products. This provided a plausible or alternative explanation for the parallel behaviour.

G. van Gerven and E. N. Varona, 'The *Wood Pulp* Case and the Future of Concerted Practices' (1994) 31 *CMLRev* 575, 595

It is clear that in deciding whether price signalling is illegal, one should not overlook the circumstances. In the *Wood Pulp* case, it was established that (i) there was a clear lawful business justification for advance price communications, since the price of wood pulp constituted a major proportion of the cost of paper and it was the paper producers themselves which had requested prior announcement; (ii) the announcements were made to customers. If, given the high transparency of the market, firms become aware of the prospective pricing of their competitors, so be it. If a rival adapts its pricing to the information it has obtained, it merely 'adapts intelligently to existing or anticipated conduct of its competitors' as allowed by the *Dyestuffs* and *Suiker Unie* judgments.

Firstly, as Advocate Darmon pointed out in his opinion, if price signalling does not correspond to a legitimate business justification, such advance announcements may very well be considered as an illegal exchange of information. In the end, as so often in antitrust law, the decisive question in practice may be whether there is a valid business reason for the particular market conduct. In the *Wood pulp* judgment, the Court had no difficulty finding such a valid business reason for the price announcements and, therefore, it was easy and correct to conclude that the system of price announcements did not give rise to a concerted practice. However, price signalling, if not warranted by any legitimate explanation and clearly not in the individual (non-collusive) self-interest of the individual companies may constitute sufficient evidence of concertation.

Secondly, in *Wood Pulp*, it appeared that the trade press was also very rapidly informed of the advance price announcements but the Court went out of its way to state that most of the wood pulp producers did not send as a matter of course their announced prices to the trade press and that if, sporadically, this was done, such communications were made at the request of the press. Thus the Court implicitly rejected the Commission's claim that wood pulp producers had deliberately made the market transparent or increased transparency by talking to the press.

The Commission will inevitably be sensitive to attempts by oligopolists to make the market artificially more transparent than it otherwise would be. Indeed, the Commission is currently investigating whether public announcements and price signalling in the *Container Line Shipping*[270] market

---

[269] Cases C-89, 104, 114, 116–117, and 125–129/85, *Wood Pulp* [1993] ECR I-1307.

[270] COMP/39.850, Press Release 22 November 2013. See also COMP/39.520, *Cement* (proceedings closed 14 August 2015), on appeal Cases C-247, 248, 267, and 268/14 P, *Heidelberg Cement* (discussed in Chap. 13). Other NCAs have also been concerned about this type of conduct, see, e.g., the draft price announcement order published

may be sufficient to establish a concerted practice between the operators there. Although the Commission is market testing commitments offered by the 15 container liner shipping companies which are designed to address its concern (including commitments to change the way they make price announcements and not to make them more than 31 days before their entry into force),[271] when opening proceedings in the Commission expressed concern about:

regular public announcements of price increase intentions through press releases on their websites and in the specialised trade press. These announcements are made several times a year and contain the amount of increase and the date of implementation, which is generally similar for all announcing companies. The announcements are usually made by the companies successively a few weeks before the announced implementation date.

The Commission has concerns that this practice may allow the companies to signal future price intentions to each other and may harm competition and customers by raising prices on the market for container liner shipping transport services on routes to and from Europe. The Commission will now investigate whether this behaviour amounts to a concerted practice in breach of Article 101…

(iv) Uncovering Collusion

Even though the terms agreement, decision, and concerted practice have been interpreted broadly parties are likely to operate any offending cartel arrangements covertly in order to make detection difficult. A competition authority's task of proving the existence of the cartel is consequently an onerous one.

M. Monti, 'Fighting Cartels Why and How? Why Should We Be Concerned with Cartels and Collusive Behaviour?', 3rd Nordic Competition Policy Conference, Stockholm, 11–12 September 2000

Fighting cartels is not an easy business to be in. Companies operating cartels are of course very much aware of the illegality of their conduct under the antitrust laws. For that reason, cartels are typically operated in secrecy and considerable efforts are devoted by the participants to avoiding detection by the authorities. Meetings are held in exotic places around the globe. Incriminating documents are destroyed or stored outside the premises of the companies. Practices are arranged so as to simulate normal market behaviour and so on.

In order to be successful a competition authority must be able to play a number of different cards. In particular, a successful fight against cartels presupposes an effective leniency programme, effective enforcement powers and sanctions, and close cooperation amongst competition authorities.

Because of the difficulty confronting the Commission in proving the existence of a breach, Regulation 1/2003 confers broad powers of investigation on the Commission to aid it in the task of gathering the evidence it requires to establish a breach (see further Chapter 13). Despite the existence of these powers, difficulties remain in uncovering covertly operated cartels. Many competition authorities now encourage undertakings to cooperate with them prior to or during cartel investigations and to destabilise the nervous and unstable existence of cartels through the operation of

following the UK Competition and Markets Authority into aggregates, cement, and ready-mixed concrete, <https://www.gov.uk/cma-cases/aggregates-cement-and-ready-mix-concrete-market-investigation> and n. 322 and text.

[271] COMP/39.850, *Container Line Shipping*, Press Release 16 February 2016.

'leniency' regimes.[272] Leniency regimes have become a key part of policy in the fight against cartels. Authorities operating such schemes believe that the public interest in terminating and eradicating cartels outweighs the public interest in punishing those involved in the operation of cartels.[273]

The leniency regime in the US, for example, seems to have been particularly successful for three reasons:[274] (a) it makes a genuinely good offer—complete immunity from a big penalty (fines and/or imprisonment) for the first to come forward; (b) it generates and exploits a nervousness that other cartel members may well be tempted by the same offer and win the race to obtain it; and (c) 'the ploy is reinforced by the general knowledge that only the first whistle-blower gets the big prize. It is thus reminiscent of the classical "Prisoner's Dilemma"—whether to play ball now, and quickly, or risk losing altogether. The strategy thus promotes within the cartel the sense of a higher risk, first, that somebody will blow the whistle and, secondly and consequently, of the other members being convicted. This serves to outweigh the previous benefits of solidarity, that is, of big profit from the offence plus a low risk of detection and conviction.'[275]

The Commission has operated a leniency regime since 1996, amending and improving it in 2002 and 2006.[276] Central to both the 2002 and 2006 Notices is the provision that total immunity is available but only to the *first* undertaking to submit evidence to the Commission (subject to other conditions also being satisfied). This provides a strong incentive for a cartel member to blow the whistle prior to its co-collaborators and destabilises the game of collusion set up by the members.[277] The leniency regime is generally perceived to have operated extremely successfully and firms have cooperated with the Commission in a high proportion of the cases occurring since 1996.[278]

Although total immunity from fines has now been granted in a number of cases, the Commission, like most competition authorities, aims to ensure that its policy is not dependent upon the leniency programme—the Commission has made it clear that it will search for and find out about cartels whether or not one of the members blows the whistle.[279] Nonetheless, the existence of the leniency regime has had an effect on the nature of cartel decisions and appeals: in many cases the dispute now revolves around the nature and duration of the infringement, which firms should be given what credit for cooperation under the relevant Leniency Notice, and other factors (such as the principle of equal treatment) which affect the level of the fine. The leniency regime is dealt with fully in Chapter 13 but two other important points are stressed here. First, the Notice cannot give whistle-blowers immunity from the civil law consequences of their participation in an illegal agreement. The Commission has however sought to ensure that the possibility of private enforcement does not deter leniency applicants and so undermine public enforcement (see further Chapter 14). Secondly,

---

[272] See, e.g., C. Harding and J. Joshua, *Regulating Cartels in Europe* (2nd edn, Oxford University Press, 2010), Chap. 8, C. Beaton-Wells and C. Tan, *Anti-Cartel Enforcement in a Contemporary Age: Leniency Religion* (Hart Publishing, 2015), and L. M. Marx and C. Mezzetti, 'Effects of Antitrust Leniency on Concealment Efforts by Colluding Firms' (2014) 2 *J of Antitrust Enforcement* 305.

[273] See 'Report on Leniency Programs to Fight Hard Core Cartels' (OECD, 2001), and the 'Anti-Cartel Enforcement Manual' of the ICN's Cartel Working Group, April 2006, available at <http://www.internationalcompetitionnetwork.org/working-groups/current/cartel/manual.aspx>. See also the ECN Model Leniency Programme explained in Chaps. 13 and 14.

[274] Harding and Joshua, n. 272, 235.

[275] Ibid.

[276] Commission Notice on immunity from fines and reduction of fines in cartel cases [2006] OJ C298/17, see also 1996 and 2002 Notices, [1996] OJ C207/4 and [2002] OJ C45/3.

[277] Reductions in fines are also available to those who are not eligible for total immunity but who nevertheless provide the Commission with evidence that represents significant added value. Essentially, greater reductions are offered to those that provide evidence first, see Chap. 13.

[278] But see, e.g., A. Stephan, 'An Empirical Assessment of the European Leniency Notice' (2009) 5 *J of Competition Law and Economics* 537.

[279] 'Companies that engage in cartels will be found out, whether or not one of their members blows the whistle. And when such cartels are found out, the punishment will be severe because the Commission will not tolerate companies cheating consumers and business customers by fixing prices and depriving them of the benefits of the Single Market.' N. Kroes, 'Flat Glass Cartel and Non-Horizontal Mergers', 28 November 2007.

a leniency application to the Commission does not constitute an application to any other competition authority within the European Competition Network (ECN) or elsewhere across the globe. An undertaking applying for leniency will, therefore, need to consider simultaneous applications in all States where leniency programmes are operated and where a breach of the rules may have been committed.

4. OLIGOPOLY

A. THE OLIGOPOLY PROBLEM AND ARTICLE 101

This section considers how if at all Article 101 or Article 102 can deal with the problem of tacit collusion that may arise on some oligopolistic markets. In this chapter it has been seen that although Article 101 does not reach tacit collusion, competition agencies are vigilant for cartel activity on oligopolistic markets which are prone to collusion. Further, that agreements, such as information-sharing agreements, which may increase transparency or otherwise facilitate collusion on oligopolistic markets, may be prohibited by Article 101. In Chapters 10 and 11 it will also be seen that cooperation and vertical agreements may be scrutinised particularly closely where there is a risk that they may facilitate collusion between undertakings (especially on oligopolistic markets). Another question which arises, however, is whether Article 102 may control the behaviour of firms operating on an oligopolistic market.

B. OLIGOPOLY AND ARTICLE 102

(i) 'One or More Undertakings'—Collective Dominance

It was seen in Chapter 5 that in *Flat Glass*[280] the GC confirmed that Article 102 applies to 'collective' dominant positions held by one or more *economically independent* undertakings, as well as to those held by single undertakings.

Cases T-68, 77, and 78/89, *Società Italiana Vetro SpA v Commission (Flat Glass)* [1992] ECR II-1403

General Court

357. The Court notes that the very words of the first paragraph of Article [102] provide that 'one or more undertakings' may abuse a dominant position. It has consistently been held, as indeed all the parties acknowledge, that the concept of agreement or concerted practice between undertakings does not cover agreements or concerted practices among undertakings belonging to the same group if the undertakings form an economic unit . . . It follows that when Article [101] refers to agreements or concerted practices between 'undertakings', it is referring to relations between two or more economic entities which are capable of competing with one another.

358. The Court considers that there is no legal or economic reason to suppose that the term 'undertaking' in Article [102] has a different meaning from the one given to it in the context of Article [101]. There is nothing in principle, to prevent two or more independent economic entities from being, on a specific market, united by such economic links that, by virtue of that fact, together they hold a dominant position vis-à-vis the other operators on the same market. This could be the case, for example, where two or more independent undertakings jointly have, through agreements or licences, a technological lead affording

---

[280] Cases T-68 and 77–78/89, *Società Italiana Vetro SpA v Commission* [1992] ECR II-1403, paras. 357–358.

them the power to behave to an appreciable extent independently of their competitors, their custom-ers and ultimately of their consumers (judgment of the Court in *Hoffmann-La Roche* . . . ., paragraphs 38 and 48).

359. The Court finds support for that interpretation in the wording of Article 8 of Council Regulation 4065/86 . . . laying down detailed rules for the application of Articles [101] and [102] to maritime trans-port. Article 8(2) provides that the conduct of a liner conference benefiting from an exemption from a prohibition laid down by Article [101(1)] may have effects which are incompatible with Article [102]. A request by a conference to be exempted from the prohibition laid down by Article [101(1)] necessarily presupposes an agreement between two or more independent economic undertakings.

It was also seen that although the examples given by the Court in this case of when such economic links would exist (for example, where two or more independent undertakings jointly have, through agreements or licences, a technological lead) caused speculation that Article 102 might apply only to 'non-oligopolistic' collective dominance,[281] the broad statements made in paragraph 358, and subsequent case law, confirm that 'oligopolistic' collective dominance (where the links are derived from the economic interdependence between the undertakings on an oligopolistic market or the structure of the market dictates that undertakings operating upon it may tacitly collude) is also covered by Article 102. Although therefore the early decisions of the Commission subsequent to *Flat Glass* concerned cases of non-oligopolistic collective dominance (where the undertakings were linked by express agreements),[282] the concept of collective dominance has been developed more broadly in a line of judgments given both in the context of Article 102 and the EU Merger Regulation (EUMR).[283] In particular: in *Almelo*,[284] the CJ clarified that 'in order for such a collective dominant position to exist, the undertakings in the group must be linked in such a way that they adopt the same conduct on the market';[285] in *Gencor*[286] the GC confirmed (in the context of the EUMR) that a 'relationship of interdependence existing between the parties to a tight oligopoly' which would make alignment of conduct likely, constituted a sufficient economic link on which to hinge a finding of collective dominance; and in *Airtours*[287] (again in the context of the EUMR) the GC built on *Gencor* stating that a collective dominant position would exist where each member of a dominant oligopoly would 'consider it possible, economically rational, and hence preferable, to adopt on a lasting basis a common policy on the market with the aim of selling at above competitive prices, without having

[281] This latter narrower view of the concept was supported by the Court's reliance on Art. 8(2) of Council Reg. 4056/86 [1986] OJ L378/1. which provided that Art. 102 could be applied to agreements between undertakings even though they have been exempted under the Regulation. If this position had been correct it is hard to see how much the concept of an abuse of a collective dominant position could usefully have added.

[282] COMP/32.450, *French-West African Shipowners' Committees* [1992] OJ L134/1, COMP/32.448 and COMP/32.450, *CEWAL* [1993] OJ L34/20, COMP/35.134, *Trans-Atlantic Conference Agreement (TACA)* [1999] OJ L95/1, COMP/34.621 and COMP/35.059/F-3, *Irish Sugar* [1997] OJ L258/1.

[283] The EUMR developments are also discussed in greater detail in Chap. 15.

[284] Case C-393/92, *Almelo v NV Energiebedrijf Ijsselmij* [1994] ECR I-1477.

[285] Ibid., paras. 42–43 ('It is for the national court to consider whether there exist between the regional electricity distributors in the Netherlands links which are sufficiently strong for there to be a collective dominant position in a substantial part of the common market'), see also, e.g., Case C-96/94, *Centro Servizi Spediporto Srl v Spedizioni Marittima de Golfo Srl* [1995] ECR I-2883, Case C-70/95, *Sodemare SA v Regione Lombardia* [1997] ECR I-3395, and Cases T-24/93 etc., *Compagnie Maritime Belge Transports SA v Commission* [1996] ECR II-1201.

[286] Case T-102/96, *Gencor Ltd v Commission* [1999] ECR II-753.

[287] Case T-342/99, *Airtours v Commission* [2002] ECR II-2585. See also Case T-464/04, *Independent Music Publishers and Labels Association (Impala) v Commission* [2006] ECR II-2289. Although in the appeal from the GC's judgment in *Impala*, Case C-413/06 P, *Bertelsmann and Sony Corp v Commission* [2008] ECR I-4951, the CJ expressed the test in a slightly different way, the criteria it set out for establishing collective dominance are similar to and compatible with those set out by the GC.

to enter into an agreement or resort to a concerted practice within the meaning of Article 101 . . .'. It considered that a finding of collective dominance could be established if:

first, each firm knew how other members were behaving (they could monitor the market to see if they were adopting the common policy);

secondly, tacit co-ordination was sustainable over time, (i.e., there was not an incentive to depart from the common policy on the market); and

thirdly, the foreseeable reactions of competitors (actual and potential) and customers would not jeopardize the results expected from the common policy.

Over time it has become clear that the concept of collective dominance is interpreted in the same way for the purposes of both the EUMR and Article 102. Indeed, the judgments under the EUMR frequently rely on case law developed under Article 102 and vice versa.[288] Crucially in *CEWAL*, known on appeal as *Compagnie Maritime Belge*, and *TACA*, the CJ and the GC respectively relied on the CJ's EUMR ruling in *France v Commission* when defining collective dominance in the context of Article 102. The *Compagnie Maritime Belge* judgment devotes a number of paragraphs to the meaning and means of establishing the existence of collective dominance.

Cases C-395 and 396/96 P, *Compagnie Maritime Belge Transports SA v Commission* [2000] ECR I-1365

Court of Justice

35. In terms of Article [102], a dominant position may be held by several 'undertakings'. The Court of Justice has held, on many occasions, that the concept of 'undertaking' in the chapter of the Treaty devoted to the rules on competition presupposes the economic independence of the entity concerned (see, in particular, Case 22/71 *Béguelin Import v G.L. Import Export* . . .

36. It follows that the expression 'one or more undertakings', in Article [102] implies that a dominant position may be held by two or more economic entities legally independent of each other, provided that from an economic point of view they present themselves or act together on a particular market as a collective entity. That is how the expression 'collective dominant position', as used in the remainder of this judgment, should be understood.

37. However, a finding that an undertaking has a dominant position is not in itself a ground of criticism but simply means that, irrespective of the reasons for which it has such a dominant position, the undertaking concerned has a special responsibility not to allow its conduct to impair genuine undistorted competition on the common market (see *Michelin*, paragraph 57).

38. The same applies as regards undertakings which hold a collective dominant position. A finding that two or more undertakings hold a collective dominant position must, in principle, proceed upon an economic assessment of the position on the relevant market of the undertakings concerned, prior to any examination of the question whether those undertakings have abused their position on the market.

39. So, for the purposes of analysis under Article [102], it is necessary to consider whether the undertakings concerned together constitute a collective entity *vis-à-vis* their competitors, their trading partners and consumers on a particular market. It is only where that question is answered in the affirmative that it is appropriate to consider whether that collective entity actually holds a dominant position and whether its conduct constitutes abuse.

40. In the contested judgment, the [GC] was careful to examine separately those three elements, namely the collective position, the dominant position and the abuse of such a position.

---

[288] See, e.g., Case T-102/96, *Gencor Ltd v Commission* [1999] ECR II-753, para. 273 and COMP/34.621 and COMP/35.059/F-3, *Irish Sugar* [1997] OJ L258/1, aff'd Case T-228/97, *Irish Sugar plc v Commission* [1999] ECR II-2969, para. 46.

41. In order to establish the existence of a collective entity as defined above, it is necessary to examine the economic links or factors which give rise to a connection between the undertakings concerned (see, *inter alia*, Case C-393/92 *Almelo* [1994] ECR I-1477, paragraph 43, and Joined Cases C-68/94 and C-30/95 *France and Others v Commission* . . . paragraph 221).

42. In particular, it must be ascertained whether economic links exist between the undertakings concerned which enable them to act together independently of their competitors, their customers and consumers (see *Michelin*).

43. The mere fact that two or more undertakings are linked by an agreement, a decision of associations of undertakings or a concerted practice within the meaning of Article [101(1)] of the Treaty does not, of itself, constitute a sufficient basis for such a finding.

44. On the other hand, an agreement, decision or concerted practice (whether or not covered by an exemption under Article [101(3)]) may undoubtedly, where it is implemented, result in the undertakings concerned being so linked as to their conduct on a particular market that they present themselves on that market as a collective entity *vis-à-vis* their competitors, their trading partners and consumers.

45. The existence of a collective dominant position may therefore flow from the nature and terms of an agreement, from the way in which it is implemented and, consequently, from the links or factors which give rise to a connection between undertakings which result from it. Nevertheless, the existence of an agreement or of other links in law is not indispensable to a finding of a collective dominant position; such a finding may be based on other connecting factors and would depend on an economic assessment and, in particular, on an assessment of the structure of the market in question.

In this judgment the CJ thus reiterates that a dominant position within the meaning of Article 102 can be held by two or more undertakings provided that they *present themselves or act together on a particular market as a collective entity*. It then states that the proof of the existence of a collective dominant position involves a two-stage process: it is necessary first to establish the existence of a collective entity and then, where the position is established, to prove that the collective entity holds a dominant position. In establishing the existence of a collective entity, the Court held that the 'economic links or factors which give rise to a connection between the undertakings concerned' could, but would not necessarily, be established by an agreement, decision, or concerted practice within the meaning of Article 101 concluded by the undertakings (the *CEWAL* agreement[289] did in fact provide such requisite links). The Court stresses, however, in paragraph 45 that 'the existence of an agreement or of other links in law is not indispensable to a finding of a collective dominant position; such a finding may be based on other connecting factors and would depend on an economic assessment and, in particular, on an assessment of the structure of the market in question'. This indicates that, as the GC held in both *Gencor* and *Airtours*, undertakings which are able to engage in a parallel manner on a market by tacitly coordinating their behaviour may be found collectively to hold a dominant position on a market. This approach is supported by the GC judgments in *Atlantic Container Lines AB (TACA)*[290] and *Laurent Piau*.[291] In the *TACA* case there were again contractual links in place between the parties,[292] but the GC gave support to a broad view of the links required to establish a finding of

---

[289] COMP/32.448 and COMP/32.450, *CEWAL* [1993] OJ L34/20.

[290] Cases T-191 and 214–216/98, *Atlantic Container Line AB v Commission* [2003] ECR II-3275, para. 602.

[291] Case T-193/02, *Laurent Piau v Commission* [2005] ECR II-209.

[292] See Chap 5.

collective dominance by relying on both EUMR and Article 102 cases.[293] More clearly, the GC in *Laurent Piau*[294] stated, relying on *Airtours*,[295] that:

[t]hree cumulative conditions must be met for a finding of collective dominance: first, each member of the dominant oligopoly must have the ability to know how the other members are behaving in order to monitor whether or not they are adopting the common policy; second, the situation of tacit coordination must be sustainable over time, that is to say, there must be an incentive not to depart from the common policy on the market; thirdly, the foreseeable reaction of current and future competitors, as well as of consumers, must not jeopardise the results expected from the common policy.

In conclusion, it now seems clear from the case law that:

(a) the concept of a collective dominant position is defined in the same way for the purposes of both the EUMR and Article 102 (although an important difference between the provisions is, of course, that in Article 102 cases a collective dominant position must exist as a threshold matter (it prohibits only abuses of a dominant or collective dominant position not abuses that may lead to the creation of a collective dominant position), whilst in merger cases the Commission may act to prevent mergers which lead to coordinated effects through the creation of a collective dominant position or to the strengthening of a pre-existing collective dominant position. This may affect the question of how proof of collective dominance is established);[296]

(b) independent economic entities may hold a collective dominant position provided that they are united by economic links which enable them to present themselves as a collective entity and to adopt the same conduct on the market;

(c) the economic links may be contractual, structural (such as cross-shareholdings or common directorships), or provided by the structure of the market which ensures parallelism of behaviour between firms on an oligopolistic market.

(ii) Abuse of a Collective Dominant Position

The development of the concept of collective dominance in the context of the original EUMR ensured that the Commission had the power to prevent mergers which may later lead to tacit collusion on a market.[297] The issue that has to be dealt with under Article 102, however, is what, if anything, can be done about firms that *are* already collectively dominant. What conduct may amount to an abuse of a collective dominant position?[298] It will be seen in the discussion below that there are relatively few cases which address this matter and in what little jurisprudence there is the notion of abuse is rather narrowly defined. The section thus also explores how the concept of abuse may be developed or adapted to deal with specific problems which arise in the collective dominance context.

---

[293] Cases T-191 and 214–216/98, *Atlantic Container Line AB v Commission* [2003] ECR II-3275, paras. 595 and 631.

[294] Case T-193/02, *Laurent Piau v Commission* [2005] ECR II-209, para. 111.

[295] Case T-342/99, *Airtours plc v Commission* [2002] ECR II-2585.

[296] See Chap. 15.

[297] The fear that a merger might alternatively result in 'non-coordinated' effects but not dominance or collective dominance on the market led to the decision to alter the substantive test set out in the original Merger Reg., Reg. 4064/89 [1989] OJ L395/1, as amended by Reg. 1310/97 [1997] OJ L180/1, see Reg. 139/2004 [2004] OJ L24/1, Art. 2(2) and (3).

[298] See, e.g., P. Fernandez, 'Increasing Powers and Increasing Uncertainty: Collective Dominance and Pricing Abuses' (2000) 5 *ELRev* 645 and G. Monti, 'The Scope of Collective Dominance under Article 82' (2001) 38 *CMLRev* 131.

a. Overlap with Article 101?

In *Flat Glass*,[299] the Commission had concluded that the undertakings' communication of, for example, identical prices to customers and granting of identical discounts constituted abuses within the meaning of Article 102. However, the GC criticised the Commission for simply having recycled the facts of the Article 101 infringement to present an infringement of Article 102. Since then the Commission has sought to spell out the relevant market for the purposes of Article 102, the position of the undertakings on the market, and the abuses in the context of the express provisions of Article 102. The conduct alleged to be abusive in *French-West African Shipowners' Committee*, *CEWAL*, and *TACA* was nonetheless broadly the same as that which the Commission had already held to infringe Article 101 (the attempt by the members of the committee to eliminate effective competition from non-committee shipowners).[300]

b. Collective Abuses

In Chapter 7 it was seen that Article 102 has been used to condemn a range of conduct. It prohibits both exploitative practices (such as excessive pricing or inertia) and anti-competitive practices (such as predatory or discriminatory pricing, tying, refusals to supply, etc.). It is a crucial question whether or not these notions of abuse will be useful to control the behaviour of oligopolists that are not united by virtue of contractual or other formal links.

In this chapter we have seen that where there is no explicit collusion, a key competition concern in an oligopolistic market is that undertakings may engage in tacit collusion rather than price competition, setting their prices at a level which produces supra-competitive profits and restricts output (and that this conduct is not, in itself, caught by Article 101).[301] Could therefore this behaviour be caught by Article 102, which expressly provides that an abuse may consist of directly or indirectly imposing 'unfair selling prices'?

Exploitative Behaviour and Excessive Pricing

It is seen in Chapter 7 that Article 102 has, in fact, relatively rarely been used to condemn exploitative, unfair, or excessive prices. In practice it is very hard to establish that prices charged are excessive and the Commission has generally sought to avoid acting as price regulator.[302] Although therefore it might seem possible, in principle, for the Commission to condemn oligopolists that have engaged in parallel pricing at a level that the Commission considers to be 'excessive' it seems extremely unlikely that it would attempt to do so. In addition, it is arguably perverse to prohibit conduct which is 'natural' in some oligopolies as abusive and, consequently, to render the relevant undertakings open to large fines by way of penalties and/or to actions in national courts.[303] It seems more likely therefore that if Article 102 is to be useful, it should be applied to prevent conduct which excludes competitors and so facilitates or is liable to strengthen the potential for tacit collusion on a market.[304]

Other Collective Abuses

In the liner conference cases already discussed the Commission condemned behaviour that was targeted at eliminating competitors seeking to compete outside the liner conference. In *Compagnie*

---

[299] Cases T-68, 77, and 78/89, *Società Italiana Vetro SpA v Commission* ('Flat Glass') [1992] ECR II-1403.

[300] Although the Commission couched its analysis in terms of Art. 102 and was careful not to recycle the facts, the fact remains that much of the conduct was anyway condemned under Art. 101.

[301] M/524, *Airtours/First Choice* [2000] OJ L93/1, annulled on appeal Case T-342/99, *Airtours plc v Commission* [2002] ECR II-2585, discussed in Chap. 15.

[302] See Chap. 7.

[303] See R. Whish and B. Sufrin, 'Oligopolistic Markets and EC Competition Law' (1992) 12 *YEL* 59, 74–75. In condemning excessive prices of a monopolist, however, Art. 102 in the same sense also condemns natural or rational behaviour by a monopolist.

[304] See, e.g., R. Gjendemsjø, E. J. Helmeng, and L. Sørgard, 'Abuse of Collective Dominance: The Need for a New Approach' (2013) 36 *World Competition* 355.

Maritime Belge[305] the CJ upheld the Commission's finding of abuse in *CEWAL*, including the finding that the putting on of fighting ships by the undertakings was an abuse for the purposes of Article 102. In *TACA*[306] the Commission found that the members had abused their dominant position by (a) agreeing to place restrictions on the availability and content of service contracts[307] and (b) altering the competitive structure of the market so as to reinforce TACA's dominant position (in particular, by trying to ensure that any potential competitor wishing to enter the market would do so only after it had become a party to the TACA). Although the existence of the first abuse was upheld on the appeal, the GC found that on the facts the Commission had failed to demonstrate that the members had induced potential competitors to join the TACA by the measures referred to in the decision.[308] It is hard to envisage what other exclusionary abuses may be committed by undertakings indulging in parallel behaviour. It might be difficult to explain collective decisions refusing to supply an undertaking, or targeting a new entrant to the market, on the grounds of mutual interdependence.

It could be argued, however, that an abuse will have been committed by collectively dominant undertakings which are inefficient or which refuse to innovate.[309] Alternatively and additionally, it could arguably be abusive to engage in conduct which although not excluding new competitors, dampens competition and excludes rivalry between the collectively dominant firms perhaps by promoting the internal stability of the collusive arrangement, for example by collectively dominant firms incorporating certain vertical restraints into distribution arrangements (such as resale price maintenance, meeting competition, or most favoured nation clauses);[310] conduct which hinders the maintenance or growth of competition and so strengthens the collective dominant position. Indeed, it has been argued that:

> Article 102 represents a still underdeveloped tool with regard to collective dominance in oligopolistic markets. This is so because no consistent theory or abusive behaviour in such market has been developed.... In our view the legal standard formulated by the [CJ] provides a sufficient legal basis for intervention against any conduct with the object or effect of strengthening the collective dominant position.
>
> It should be noted that this reading of Article 102 does not imply that tacit collusion is to be regarded as an independent abuse. On the contrary, tacit collusion is an unavoidable consequence of the market structure and must be regarded as a consequent of the right of every undertaking to adapt intelligently to the strategy or perceived strategy of its competitors. However, the practices targeted under the approach advocated here amount to conduct strengthening the dominant position and thereby restricting competition by altering the competitive structure. This concept should be easily distinguishable from competition on the merits and from tacit collusion as such.[311]

c. Abuse by One of the Collectively Dominant Undertakings

In *Irish Sugar plc v Commission*[312] the GC held that an *individual* undertaking could engage in conduct which constitutes an abuse of its dominant position held collectively with one or more undertakings:

---

[305] Cases C-395 and 396/96 P, *Compagnie Maritime Belge Transports SA v Commission* [2000] ECR I-1365.

[306] COMP/35.134, [1999] OJ L95/1, on appeal, Case T-191/98, *Atlantic Container Line AB and Others v Commission* [2003] ECR II-3275.

[307] Contracts by which a shipper undertakes to provide a minimum quantity of cargo to be transported by the conference (conference service contracts) or by an individual carrier (individual service contracts) over a fixed period of time and the carrier or the conference commits to a certain rate or rate schedule as well as a defined service level.

[308] Cases T-191 and 212–214/98, *Atlantic Container Line v Commission* [2003] ECR II-3275.

[309] See Chap. 7.

[310] See Gjendemsjø, Helmeng, and Sørgard, n. 304. Such conduct may be likely to be caught by Art. 101(1) in any event, see Chaps. 4 and 11.

[311] Ibid., 371.

[312] Case T-228/97, [1999] ECR II-2969.

Whilst the existence of a joint dominant position may be deduced from the position which the economic entities concerned together hold on the market in question, the abuse does not necessarily have to be the action of all the undertakings in question. It only has to be capable of being identified as one of the manifestations of such a joint dominant position being held. Therefore, undertakings occupying a joint dominant position may engage in joint or individual abusive conduct.[313]

This finding was made in the context of a dominant position held jointly by a dominant undertaking and its distributor (on a vertical level). In this case Irish Sugar had such a close relationship with its distributor that it only narrowly failed to qualify as a single economic unit.[314] Had the Commission been able to make such a finding, it would of course have been unnecessary to invoke the concept of collective dominance. Further, the parties were clearly acting to safeguard their collective dominant position on the market.[315] The concept of an abuse has, however, been principally developed in a line of cases dealing with the conduct of a single dominant undertaking; in contrast, a different analysis may be required for identifying abusive conduct engaged in by one of a group of oligopolist. For example, it has been seen in Chapter 7 that the granting of loyalty rebates or discriminatory pricing by single dominant undertakings may unlawfully exclude competitors and be condemned under Article 102.[316] On an oligopolistic market, however, this type of conduct may indicate that price competition is in fact operating between the oligopolists.[317]

The concept of an individual abuse of a dominant position might nonetheless be useful in some situations, for example to preclude behaviour targeted by one of the members at a new entrant with the objective of protecting the oligopoly generally. In addition, it could be used to prevent price cuts targeted at a price-cutter that is destabilising tacit collusion on a tight oligopolistic market.[318] The implications of the *Irish Sugar* judgment are explored by G. Monti in an extract from his article.

G. Monti, 'The Scope of Collective Dominance under Article 82 EC' (2001) 38 *CMLRev* 131, 143

This is an important conclusion, which could apply to a variety of situations, horizontal and vertical. On a horizontal level, it may be deployed to catch a scenario like this: say there are three companies that enjoy collective dominance (e.g. because of membership in an export cartel). Let us now say that a fourth competitor attempts to penetrate the market and one of the three engages in predatory pricing or other exclusionary tactics not forbidden by Article [101]. In this scenario, the Commission is now empowered to find that undertaking liable under Article [102] for abusing the collective dominant position. It does not need to fine the other two undertakings. Moreover, and potentially more significantly, the *Irish Sugar* decision states that collective dominance can be held by undertakings in a vertical relationship, which entails that a non-dominant distributor who has sufficiently strong links with a dominant manufacturer has the same degree of responsibility not to hinder competition that the manufacturer has, thus any attempt to protect his market position (e.g. terminating a retailer who sells competing goods) may be found to be an abuse.

---

[313] Ibid., para. 66. In the case these included seven individual abuses on the market in granulated sugar intended for retail sale and for industry in Ireland and some abuses of a collective dominant position held with a distributor.

[314] Case T-228/97, *Irish Sugar plc v Commission* [1999] ECR II-2969, para. 28.

[315] Monti, n. 298.

[316] See, e.g., Case 85/76, *Hoffmann-La Roche v Commission* [1979] ECR 461, and Chap. 7. It should be noted that in the light of Case C-209/10, *Post Danmark A/S v Konkurrencerådet* EU:C:2012:172, selective price-cutting which is not predatory is more likely to be an abuse if the dominant position is a collective one, see Chap. 7, Section 8.I.

[317] See COMP/35.134, *TACA* [1999] OJ L95/6.

[318] In this case the predation may represent the 'punishment' mechanism which means that tacit collusion subsequently follows, see, e.g., the facts that arose in *Brooke Group Ltd v Brown & Williamson Tobacco Corp*, 509 US 209 (1993).

This vastly extends the jurisdiction of the Commission under Article [102]. While it is obviously a ruling which could be overturned by the CJ, it is submitted that the reasoning of the [GC] can be supported as consistent with well-established principles. Specifically, there is no need for a causal link between the dominant position and the abuse: the dominant position does not have to be used, so long as the conduct of a dominant firm has anti-competitive effects. This was established in *Continental Can* where the [CJ] said that 'the strengthening of the position of an undertaking may be an abuse and prohibited under Article [102], regardless of the means and procedure by which it is achieved' if it has anti-competitive effects. On this basis a contract clause that has an anti-competitive effects (e.g. SDL's product swap)[319] is a breach of Article [102] even if SDL is not individually dominant, because its effect was to consolidate the collective dominance by excluding potential competitors. This broad, effects-based application of Article [102] is in line with the 'special responsibility' imposed on dominant firms not to distort competition.

(iii) Conclusions

It appears that Article 102 applies to oligopolistic collective dominance. Even if Article 102 is applied to oligopolists linked only by their mutual interdependence, however, it has been seen that the concept of abuse, developed in relation to individually dominant firms, is not a mechanism ideally equipped to control the behaviour of oligopolists. It remains to be seen, however, whether the concept of individual or collective abuse might be further developed to prohibit practices which might facilitate collusion or contribute to the internal or external stability of a collusive strategy.

C. ALTERNATIVE METHODS FOR DEALING WITH OLIGOPOLISTIC MARKETS UNDER EU LAW

(i) Merger Regulation

Given that oligopolistic markets often do not function as effectively as ones in which free competition operates, and given the difficulties involved in applying either Article 101 or Article 102 to the conduct of undertakings operating on such markets, it may be that the Merger Regulation holds the key. Indeed, the EUMR prohibits mergers which are likely to significantly impede effective competition through either non-coordinated or coordinated effects on oligopolistic markets. If mergers are prohibited which cause market imperfections there will be less need for corrective measures under Article 101 or 102. It will be seen in Chapter 15, however, that it is difficult in practice for the Commission to demonstrate to the requisite standard that a merger is likely to lead to coordinated effects on a market.

(ii) Sector Inquiries

Article 12(1) of Regulation 17 gave the Commission a wide discretion to conduct sector inquiries and to decide whether or not to investigate markets that it considers to be malfunctioning. To conduct such an investigation the Commission did not have to have any evidence of, or even suspect, an infringement of either Article 101 or Article 102. Unfortunately the provision conferred no power on the Commission to take action to remedy any defects identified in an investigation and

---

[319] One of the abuses of a collective dominant position found by the Commission was that SDL, the distributor, had agreed with one retailer and one wholesaler to exchange its sugar for the sugar that the wholesaler and retailer had purchased from France.

was therefore, initially at least, rarely used. Whish and Sufrin argued that 'given the political will' the provision could form:[320]

[the] basis of a proper investigative system. Although there may be understandable concern about giving the Commission such large elements of discretion in respect of oligopolistic markets it is doubtful whether it is more worrying than the prospect of the Article [102] prohibition applied wholesale to the complex behaviour of oligopolies.

Article 17 of Regulation 1/2003 amended the Commission's powers but does not give it the broad basis called for by Whish and Sufrin.

Regulation 1/2003

Article 17

Investigations into sectors of the economy and into types of agreement

1. Where the trend of trade between Member States, the rigidity of prices or other circumstances suggest that competition may be restricted or distorted within the common market, the Commission may conduct its inquiry into a particular sector of the economy or into a particular type of [agreement] across various sectors. In the course of that inquiry, the Commission may request undertakings or associations of undertakings concerned to supply the information necessary for giving effect to Articles [101] and [102] of the Treaty.

The Commission may in particular request the undertakings or associations of undertakings concerned to communicate to it all agreements, decisions and concerted practices.

The Commission may publish a report on the results of its inquiry into particular sectors of the economy or of particular types of agreements across various sectors and invite comments from interested parties.

Article 17(1) thus provides the Commission with the powers to collect such information but does not confer power on the Commission to adopt remedies following such a report. Through such an inquiry, however, the Commission can obtain a broader view of the sector and examine more sector-wide practices than it would when concentrating on individual agreements concluded by firms operating on those markets. Having done this it could then take further action, perhaps under the competition, or other Treaty, rules. The powers may be particularly useful for investigating suspicious pricing or other practices in oligopolistic markets where the presence of a small number of players may incite concerted practices or for scrutinising agreements being used on the market that may shape the future competitive environment.

Since 2004 the Commission has used Article 12 of Regulation 17 on a number of occasions launching inquiries into, for example: the sale of sports rights to internet companies and to providers of the third generation (3G) of mobile phones services; roaming; leased lines; local loop; the energy, financial services and pharmaceutical sectors; and e-commerce.[321] The inquiries have been useful for identifying barriers to competition in the sectors generally.

---

[320] R. Whish and B. Sufrin, 'Oligopolistic Markets and EC Competition Law' (1992) 12 *YEL* 59, 83.

[321] See <http://ec.europa.eu/competition/antitrust/sector_inquiries.html>.

5. CONCLUSIONS

1. The Commission has wide investigative powers which it can use to unearth covertly operated cartels.

2. Where hardcore cartel activity is uncovered, heavy fines will be imposed by the Commission on the undertakings involved.

3. A number of Member States have criminalised cartel activity and/or set out criminal or civil sanctions for individuals involved in the conclusion of cartels.

4. The fight against cartels is now a core priority of the Commission. Whistle-blowers are encouraged and repeat offenders are punished particularly severely.

5. The Commission is trying to encourage consumers to seek compensation in the national courts from those engaged in hardcore cartel activity.

6. Article 101 prohibits joint conduct designed to supplement, or which facilitates, collusion between competitors (such as exchange of information, resale price maintenance, or meeting competition clauses).

7. Tacit collusion (or purely parallel behaviour) engaged in by firms operating on an oligopolistic market is not prohibited by Article 101(1). An agreement or some reciprocal direct or indirect contact between the undertakings operating on the market must be established (it also does not catch unreciprocated invitations to collude or public announcements which are not proved to form part of a concerted practice). The EUMR, however, prohibits mergers which may lead to an increase in price through coordinated effects on an oligopolistic market.

8. Article 102 may apply to oligopolists which collectively hold a dominant position on the market. Collective or individual actions designed to exclude new entrants into the market or to deter or to punish deviations from the cooperative structure might constitute abuses of a collective dominant position.

9. Article 17 of Regulation 1/2003 is an important mechanism for investigating concentrated markets or markets on which competition does not appear to be working well. The Commission uses it to identify problems on a market which can later be addressed through use of its powers under Articles 101, 102, 106, the EUMR, and/or the State aid rules.

10. Article 17 of Regulation 1/2003 does not provide such a broad basis for market investigation as does, for example, the UK's Enterprise Act, which provides for the investigation of markets where a feature or features of it appear to prevent, restrict, or distort competition. Where adverse effects on competition are identified in the UK following an investigation, remedies to deal with the problem may be imposed or recommended: for example, the total or partial termination of an agreement; that the prices to be charged for any specified goods or services on a market should be regulated; or that any business, or part of a business, be disposed of (by the sale of any part of an undertaking or assets or otherwise). In an investigation into aggregates, cement, and ready-mix concrete, for example, the UK competition authority required certain divestment remedies and said that it would implement remedy measures aimed at reducing transparency in the GB cement market, including a prohibition on generic cement price announcement letters to customers and restrictions on the disclosure and publication of GB cement market data.[322] It may also be suggested, or ordered, that measures should be taken by or against bodies other than the market players (for example, where it considers that the market rigidity has been caused, partly at least, by advertising restrictions or other legal or regulatory barriers).

11. Resort to such draconian remedies as price control and divestiture may not be a suitable means of dealing with the problems arising on oligopolistic markets. However, it can also be seen that a more flexible system may have advantages over one focusing exclusively on the abusive conduct, or

---

[322] Competition Commission Report of 14 January 2014.

the behaviour, of the undertakings on the market. Significant changes in the EU rules would need to be made before such a system could be operated by the Commission.

6. FURTHER READING

A. BOOKS

BISHOP, S., and WALKER, M., *The Economics of EC Competition Law: Concepts, Application and Measurement* (3rd edn, Sweet & Maxwell, 2009)

GERADIN, D., ZENGER, H., and STEPHAN, A., *EU Cartel Law and Economics* (Oxford University Press, 2016)

HARDING, C., and JOSHUA, J., *Regulating Cartels in Europe* (2nd edn, Oxford University Press, 2010)

B. ARTICLES

ALBORS-LLORENS, A., 'Horizontal Agreements and Concerted Practices in EC Competition Law: Unlawful and Legitimate Contacts between Competitors' [2006] 51 *Ant Bull* 837

CASTILLO DE LA TORRE, F., 'Evidence, Proof and Judicial Review in Cartel Cases' (2009) 32 *World Competition* 505

FRANZOSI, M., 'Oligopoly and the Prisoners' Dilemma: Concerted Practices and As If Behaviour' [1988] *ECLR* 385

GJENDEMSJØ, R., HELMENG. E. J., and SØRGARD, L., 'Abuse of Collective Dominance: The Need for a New Approach' (2013) 36 *World Competition* 355

JONES, A., '*Wood Pulp*: Concerted Practice and/or Conscious Parallelism' [1993] *ECLR* 273

KORAH, V., 'Concerted Practices' (1973) 36 *MLR* 260

MONTI, G., 'The Scope of Collective Dominance under Article 82' (2001) 38 *CMLRev* 131

VAN GERVEN, G., and VARONA, E. N., 'The *Wood Pulp* Case and the Future of Concerted Practices' (1994) 31 *CMLRev* 575

WERDEN, G. J., 'Sanctioning Cartel Activity: Let the Punishment Fit the Crime' (2009) 5 *European Competition Journal* 19

WHISH, R., AND SUFRIN, B., 'Oligopolistic Markets and EC Competition Law' (1992) 12 *YEL* 59

10

HORIZONTAL COOPERATION AGREEMENTS

1. CENTRAL ISSUES

1. Horizontal cooperation agreements may bring benefits to consumers, for example through enabling firms to share risk, pool know-how, resources, and skills, save cost, and/or achieve economies of scale. This may allow firms to bring new products or services to the market and/or to penetrate new markets.

2. Such arrangements may take a number of different forms ranging from loose cooperation arrangements to strategic alliances to the creation of a joint venture (JV) company. Although the form of cooperation does not generally affect the analysis of the conduct under Article 101, where the creation of a JV constitutes a 'concentration' with an EU dimension, the general rule is that the transaction is appraised under the EU Merger Regulation (EUMR), currently Regulation 139/2004, not Article 101. Over the years, the Commission has sought to ensure that the substantive assessment applicable to JVs under Article 101 and the EUMR respectively, is broadly consistent.

3. The Commission's policy towards horizontal cooperation agreements under Article 101 has evolved dramatically, from a time when a majority of such arrangements were found to infringe Article 101(1), but then more rigorously appraised, and frequently exempted, under Article 101(3),

to the present position where a more economic approach is adopted and a fuller assessment is made of whether the agreement infringes Article 101(1) at all.

4. Since the abolition of the notification and exemption system in 2004, undertakings have ordinarily had to 'self-assess' to determine whether their horizontal cooperation agreements infringe Article 101. As there is relatively little case law and decisional practice in this area, the Commission's 2010 Guidelines on horizontal cooperation agreements are of practical importance. They provide both general guidance and specific guidance in relation to six particular types of agreement: information exchanges (examined in Chapter 9), research and development (R&D), production (including specialisation), purchasing, commercialisation (including joint selling), and standardisation.

5. Two 'new generation' block exemptions cover R&D and specialisation agreements. They contain market share thresholds and lists of 'hardcore' restrictions. The current block exemption regulations were adopted in 2010 and expire at the end of December 2022. A third block exemption applies in relation to joint compilations, tables, and studies in the insurance industry.

2. INTRODUCTION

Horizontal cooperative arrangements (or arrangements between firms at the same level of the market) are extremely common. Such cooperation can take a variety of forms ranging from temporary arrangements at one level of activity, such as the research and development (R&D) stage, to 'strategic alliances',[1] to the creation of a separate joint venture (JV). Although the term JV could encompass a broad range of arrangements, it is normally used in the competition law context to describe an arrangement by which two or more undertakings (the 'parents'), in order to achieve a particular commercial goal, integrate part of their operations through the creation of an independent company or organisation, which they put under joint control. The parents also contribute resources into the enterprise, for example finance, intellectual property rights (IPRs), know-how, personnel, premises, or equipment. In the EU, the creation of certain JVs is subject to review under the EU merger rules rather than Article 101 (see Section 3 below).

Horizontal cooperation arrangements are not necessarily anti-competitive. On the contrary, in contrast to cartels discussed in Chapter 9, such cooperation may promote economic efficiency and integration by, for example: enabling firms to share risk, pool know-how, resources, and skills, save cost, and/or achieve economies of scale; facilitating the bringing of new products or services to the market; and/or enabling the penetration of new markets. Without cooperation firms may simply not have the resources to invest in, or capabilities to embark on, such a venture, in particular, in rapidly developing markets such as telecommunications, information technology, and the media. Although, therefore, a competition law system will wish to remain steadfast against cartels and other anti-competitive horizontal arrangements, it will not wish to deter the conclusion of beneficial cooperation arrangements. In determining whether horizontal agreements do adversely impact on competition, competition authorities will be concerned not only with reductions of competition between the parties themselves, but also with foreclosure effects on third parties and spill-over effects on to other markets (in particular, other markets in which the parents of a JV compete).

This chapter commences in Section 3 by considering some general issues in respect of horizontal cooperation, in particular jurisdiction and the evolution of competition policy in this area. It is seen in this section that, as in other areas examined in this book, EU competition policy towards horizontal cooperation has developed dramatically over the years. Consequently, older decisions and policy statements of the Commission must be approached with some caution. Indeed, following a review of its policy towards horizontal arrangements during the 1980s and 1990s,[2] the Commission adopted, in 2000, new-style block exemptions (Regulation 2658/2000 on specialisation agreements[3] and Regulation 2659/2000 on R&D agreements[4]) and published a set of Guidelines on the applicability of Article 101 to horizontal cooperation[5] which reflected its 'modernised' approach. These were replaced in 2010 with new block exemptions for R&D agreements and specialisation agreements, Regulations 1217/2010[6] and 1218/2010[7] respectively, and Guidelines on the applicability of Article 101 of the Treaty on the Functioning of the European Union to horizontal cooperation agreements (the Guidelines).[8] Sections 4–9 examine certain types of horizontal cooperation agreements, R&D, production (including specialisation), purchasing, commercialisation (including joint selling), and standardisation, and horizontal cooperation agreements in certain sectors.

---

[1] Commission, *XXIVth Report on Competition Policy* (1994), point 156 ('strategic alliances can be co-operative arrangements of varying scope involving the creation of several contractual and structural links, such as the creation of a joint venture, specialisation in certain markets, joint R&D, technology transfer, cross-supply agreements, commitments to co-operate in other fields in the future and the acquisition of cross-shareholdings'), see, e.g., COMP/34.607, *Banque Nationale de Paris/Dresdner Bank* [1996] OJ L188/37 and COMP/34.410, *Olivetti/Digital* [1994] OJ L309/24 and COMP/39.595, *Star Alliance: Continental/United/Lufthansa/Air Canada* 23 May 2013, nn. 10 and 62 and text.

[2] Commission, *XXVIIth Report on Competition Policy* (1997) paras. 46 and 47.

[3] [2000] OJ L304/3.

[4] [2000] OJ L304/7.

[5] [2001] OJ C3/2.

[6] [2010] OJ L335/36.

[7] [2010] OJ L335/43. See also, e.g., Reg. 267/2010 on the application of Article 101(3) to certain categories of agreements, decisions and concerted practices in the insurance sector [2010] OJ L83/1, nn. 158–160 and text.

[8] [2011] OJ C11/1.

It will be seen in this chapter that there are comparatively few judgments of the EU Courts in this area.[9] Pre-2004, undertakings rarely sought to challenge the Commission's actions before the EU Courts as beneficial cooperation was frequently permitted by the Commission through exemption or comfort letter (although sometimes only after requiring that the plans be amended). Similarly, post-2004, the Commission has principally dealt with concerns about horizontal cooperation, through commitments decisions.[10] Again, the result has been that relatively few cases find their way to the EU Courts giving the Commission a relatively free hand in the development of policy.[11]

3. APPRAISAL OF HORIZONTAL COOPERATION AND JOINT VENTURES: EVOLUTION OF POLICY

A. APPRAISAL UNDER THE EU MERGER REGULATION OR ARTICLE 101?

Horizontal cooperation agreements and joint ventures fall for substantive assessment either under Article 101 or, since a system of EU merger control came into force in 1990, under the EU Merger Regulation (EUMR).[12] This chapter deals with the substantive assessment of horizontal cooperation agreements conducted under Article 101. An important preliminary question, therefore, is which transactions, or JVs, fall for appraisal under Article 101 rather than the EUMR?

It will be seen in Chapter 15 that the general scheme of the EUMR is that concentrations with an EU dimension are appraised exclusively by the Commission under the provisions of the EUMR (they benefit from a one-stop shop appraisal under it). Such transactions have to be notified to the Commission and cannot be completed unless cleared, whether conditionally or unconditionally. The criteria for determining which JVs constitute a concentration has changed since 1990, and are described in Chapter 15. Broadly, however, the current position is that the EUMR applies to jointly-controlled 'full-function' JVs, that is JVs 'performing on a lasting basis all the functions of an autonomous economic entity'.[13]

A number of advantages have arguably followed for transactions constituting a concentration. For example, not only do concentrations with an EU dimension benefit from the one-stop EUMR appraisal by the Commission completed within tight statutory timetables,[14] but, in the early days of the EUMR at least, concentrations benefited from a more lenient substantive assessment. Carles Esteva Mosso,[15] Deputy Director-General Mergers at DG Comp, explains the problem that arose.

---

[9] Some of these have already been considered in Chap. 4, see, e.g., Case C-250/92, *Gøttrup-Klim Grovvareforening and Others v Dansk Landbrugs Grovvareselskab AmbA* [1994] ECR I-5641, Cases T-374, 375, 384, and 388/94, *European Night Services v Commission* [1998] ECR II-3141, Case T-112/99, *M6 v Commission* [2001] ECR II-2459, and Case T-328/03, *O2 (Germany) GmbH & Co OHG v Commission* [2006] ECR II-1231.

[10] Reg. 1/2003, Art. 9, see Chap. 13 and n. 21 and text.

[11] There have been more cases, however, in respect of purchasing and commercialisation.

[12] The original Merger Reg., Reg. 4064/89 [1989] OJ L395/1 was replaced in 2004 by the current EUMR, Reg. 1309/2004 [2004] OJ L24/1, see Chap. 15.

[13] EUMR, Art. 3(4).

[14] If such transactions meet the jurisdictional thresholds set out in the EUMR, they must ordinarily be notified to the Commission and cannot be completed until cleared by it.

[15] C. E. Mosso, 'The Contribution of Merger Control to the Definition of Harm to Competition', GCLC Conference, Brussels, February 2016.

Carles Esteva Mosso, 'The Contribution of Merger Control to the Definition of Harm to Competition', GCLC Conference, Brussels, February 2016

...[I]n the early years, the assessment of mergers was conceptually very different than the assessment under Article 101 of other types of agreements between undertakings, less structural in nature than mergers. Not only the substantive tests diverged: the 'creation or strengthening of a dominant position' was quite far apart from that of an agreement or practice 'having the object or effect of restricting competition'. Also the interpretation of both tests contributed further to the divergence of standards. In particular, under the previous, more form-based approach to the interpretation of 'restriction of competition', a large number of agreements were considered to be caught by the test of Article 101(1) and required exemption under Article 101(3), either by formal decision (rarely) or by comfort letter (more common). On the other hand, the dominance test in mergers was applied on the basis of the jurisprudence developed under Article 102 and found to be met in only a small proportion of the large number of mergers scrutinized by the Commission every year. Once dominance was found, no efficiency defence was considered to be available.

This divergence of standards, which in practice lead to a more lenient treatment of horizontal mergers than to collusive agreements between firms holding similar amounts of market power (also referred to as 'concentration privilege' 'Konzentrationsprivileg' in German), seems, with hindsight, difficult to explain. Why, let's say, a joint distribution agreement between companies holding a 30% market share could be caught by Article 101 while a merger between the same companies could be cleared unconditionally? This divergence of treatment could only be premised on an implicit presumption of efficiencies in mergers, which would justify the clearance of operations below the level of dominance. Such a general presumption, however, appears today as a very theoretical construct, difficult to support empirically.

It will be seen both in this chapter and Chapter 15 that the Commission has taken a series of steps to reform substantive assessment both under Article 101 and the EUMR, with the result that the assessment conducted under each has been brought more closely in line with the other. Indeed, the Commission states in the 2010 Horizontal Cooperation Guidelines:

21. The analysis of horizontal co-operation agreements has certain common elements with the analysis of horizontal mergers pertaining to the potential restrictive effects, in particular as regards joint ventures. There is often only a fine line between full-function joint ventures that fall under the Merger Regulation and non-full-function joint ventures that are assessed under Article 101. Hence, their effects can be quite similar.

Nonetheless, an acute problem which remains for parties whose transactions fall for assessment under Article 101, rather than the EUMR, is how they can deal with the loss of certainty that has resulted from the abolition of the notification and authorisation system set up by Regulation 17, and get comfort as to their transactions' compliance with Article 101. This may be particularly important in relation to transactions, such as partial-function production JVs, which 'require substantial investment and far reaching integration of operations, which makes it difficult to unravel them afterwards at the behest of a competition authority'.[16]

Although parties to agreements may, theoretically, seek an informal 'Guidance Letter' from the Commission,[17] or hope that the Commission will adopt a decision finding that Article 101 is

---

[16] White Paper on modernisation of the rules implementing Articles 85 and 86 [now 101 and 82] of the EC Treaty [1999] OJ C132/1 (White Paper), para. 79. Although the Commission proposed bringing a broader category of JVs within the EUMR (paras. 80 and 101), this proposal was eventually dropped, see Chap. 15.

[17] Commission Notice on informal guidance relating to novel questions concerning Articles 81 and 82 of the EC Treaty that arise in individual cases (guidance letters) [2004] OJ C101/78 (Informal Guidance Notice), see Chap. 13. One of the elements the Commission may take into account when deciding whether it is appropriate to issue a letter is 'the extent of the investments linked to the transaction in relation to the size of the companies concerned and

inapplicable to their agreement (see Regulation 1/2003, Article 10),[18] as at 1 July 2016, neither procedure had ever been used. The, reality, is therefore that in many cases parties will have to 'sell-assess' whether their agreement is compatible with Article 101. Given the relatively little jurisprudence in this sphere, the block exemption regulations, the Guidelines,[19] and the general Article 101(3) Guidelines[20] play a significant role. In some cases post-2004, however, the Commission has used the commitments decision process to close an investigation into a horizontal cooperation agreement, subject to commitments offered by the parties. Indeed, the use of this procedure in these circumstances seems to come close to replicating the functions previously performed under the old 'authorisation' system (and enabling the Commission to influence the content of cooperation arrangements (for example, in the financial services and airlines sector))[21] and has some parallels with conditional clearances under the EUMR.

B. THE DEVELOPMENT OF THE COMMISSION'S APPROACH TO THE ASSESSMENT OF HORIZONTAL COOPERATION UNDER ARTICLE 101

(i) General

Horizontal cooperation agreements[22] falling under Article 101 must be appraised to determine if they appreciably[23] restrict competition and, if so, whether they satisfy the conditions of Article 101(3).

Initially, the Commission took an interventionist approach to horizontal cooperation and JVs based on a fear of coordination between the parents and on the loss of potential competition. It took a broad view of what constituted a restriction of competition,[24] bringing many agreements within Article 101(1) and then assessing them under Article 101(3).[25] To deal with the practical difficulty

---

the extent to which the transaction relates to a structural operation such as the creation of a non-full function joint venture', ibid, para. 8(b).

[18] See Chap. 13.

[19] Guidelines, para. 6. The 2010 Guidelines apply irrespective of the level of integration involved and do not deal with JVs as a separate species of agreement, but consider them according to their provisions and effects in the light of the principles set out therein.

[20] Guidelines on the application of Article 81(3) [now Article 101(3)] of the Treaty (the Article 101(3) Guidelines) [2004] OJ C101/97, see Chap. 4.

[21] See n. 10, N. Dunne, 'Commitment Decisions in EU Competition Law' (2014) 10 J of Competition Law and Economics 399, 406–410 and, e.g., COMP 37.214, DFB 19 January 2005, n. 173 and text, COMP/38.173, Joint Selling of the Media Rights to the FA Premier League 22 March 2006, n. 173 and text, COMP 38.681, Cannes Agreement 4 October 2006, COMP/39.398, Visa MIF 26 February 2014, and COMP/39.595, Star Alliance 23 May 2013 (between Continental, United, Lufthansa, and Air Canada which was permitted subject to commitments), n. 62 and text.

[22] Once a JV has been formed the Commission in the past treated the parents and the JV as separate undertakings so arrangements between them would be caught by Art. 101. Although more recently the cases have suggested that the parents and the JV could be part of the same single economic entity for the purpose of imposing fines on entities within an infringing undertaking, it is questionable how this line of cases affects the question of whether an agreement between the entities falls within the scope of Art. 101 (see Chap. 3).

[23] See generally Chap. 4. The Notice on agreements of minor importance which do not appreciably restrict competition under Article 101(1) of the Treaty on the Functioning of the European Union (De Minimis Notice) [2014] OJ C291/01, provides that agreements between actual or potential competitors will not normally give rise to an appreciable restriction of competition where the parties' aggregate market share does not exceed 10%. Although the Notice does not normally apply to agreements incorporating hardcore restrictions, the Commission's guidance on by object sets out limited exceptions for certain joint purchasing, R&D, and specialisation agreements, see Staff Working Document on 'restrictions of competition "by object"', SWD(2014) 198 final, 2.1.2. See also Cases T-374–375, 384, and 388/94, European Night Services v Commission [1998] ECR II-3141, n. 35 and text.

[24] See especially Notice on cooperation agreements [1968] OJ C75/3 and Notice on the assessment of cooperative JVs pursuant to Article 101 [1993] OJ C43/2 (Notice on cooperative joint ventures).

[25] See further Chap. 4.

of exempting all such agreements, in 1985 it adopted two block exemption regulations, Regulation 417/85 on specialisation agreements[26] and Regulation 418/85 on R&D agreements,[27] which were rigid and consequently of limited utility.

The wide interpretation the Commission adopted to the concept of a restriction of competition, and its concern about the loss of potential competition, is vividly illustrated by its decision in *Vacuum Interrupters*.[28] In this case the Commission found that the formation of a JV for the development, production, and sale of a vacuum interrupter (to be incorporated into circuit-breakers) infringed Article 101(1) on the basis of the hypothetical possibility that, despite all the evidence to the contrary, the JV's parents (AEI and Reyrolle Parsons) *might each have proceeded* alone, and *might* each have ultimately produced a commercial product which they could have sold in other Member States in competition with each other if a market had developed for it there. In fact each had been individually researching the development of the product for ten years, but its construction and operation was complex and difficult and neither had been able to bring the product to the market. As the Commission noted:

Each of the companies found the cost of development was very substantial and each recognised that if vacuum interrupters were to be brought to commercial use at a price which would make them competitive with the conventional forms of switchgear, a collaboration and pooling of the resources available was essential in order that the heavy expenditure involved by the individual companies would be reduced.[29]

The Commission nonetheless concluded that the parties were potential competitors and that the object and effect of the agreement, which provided for the parents to cease independent work on the interrupter, was to restrict competition. As, however, it found that the joint venture scheme had obvious advantages and would not have been achieved by either party individually it went on to exempt it under Article 101(3).[30]

Decisions such as this were subject to significant criticism for finding restrictions of potential competition based on unrealistic assumptions. Further, the grant of an exemption seemed theoretically inconsistent with finding under Article 101(1). If the parents *were* able to enter the market independently, how could their coming together and the restrictions within the agreement be indispensable to the attainment of the agreement's (beneficial) objectives?

(ii) The Development of a More Economic Approach Towards the Application of Article 101 to Horizontal Cooperation

In 1983 the Commission started to re-evaluate its attitude towards the potential competition issue and in its *XIIIth Report on Competition Policy* signalled a new approach. It set out a checklist of questions it would ask in future in gauging whether there really was a restriction of potential competition.

The result of this change of heart was seen in a number of subsequent decisions starting with *Optical Fibres.*

COMP/30.320, *Optical Fibres* [1986] OJ L236/30

This concerned three joint ventures set up between a US company, Corning Glass Works, on the one hand and respectively BICC in the UK (a 50/50 unlimited partnership), Siemens in Germany (a joint venture company owned 50/50), and COFOCO in France (a joint venture company owned 40/60). The joint

---

[26] [1985] OJ L53/1.
[27] [1985] OJ L53/5.
[28] COMP/27.442, [1977] OJ L48/32.
[29] Ibid., para. 10.
[30] Ibid., para. 22.

ventures were set up to develop, produce, and sell optical fibres and optical cables for use in the European telecommunications market. Corning had experience in optical fibre manufacture but none in cables and the European partners had no experience in optical fibres. There were no clauses restricting competition between Corning and the other parties and they were all free to do independent R&D in optical fibres although in reality there was no prospect of the European companies doing this.

Commission

46. The individual joint venture agreements do not as such restrict competition between Corning and its partners. When the agreements were concluded, the parties were not actual or potential competitors in the market for optical fibres or optical cables. The production of optical fibres and optical cables are different activities. Corning had no experience in cable manufacture, while Corning's partners had no experience in glass manufacture which could have led to an invention competitive with Corning's. In spite of the parties' considerable financial resources, the entry by Corning into the optical cables market or by Corning's partners into the optical fibres market was not a natural and reasonably foreseeable extension of their respective business activities. The cooperation between Corning and its partners is rather of a complementary nature which does not give rise to restriction or distortion of competition at the level of the cooperating parties. Moreover, the agreements do not foreclose market access by third parties or have any other foreseeable anti-competitive impact on their activities. The various amendments made to the original agreements ensure that competition is maintained and that third parties do not suffer from discrimination or market partitioning. In addition, by virtue of the conditions and obligations attached to this Decision, competition is safe-guarded and the Commission is in a position to monitor future developments.

47. There is neither restriction nor distortion of competition between the parents and the joint venture. The agreements provide that the parents are free to engage in independent R&D of optical fibres. Furthermore, the individual joint venture agreements do not contain obligations which go beyond what would be admitted in simple licensing agreements between non-competitors. Thus the parties are free to engage in independent R&D of optical fibres, although in practice they depend on a continuous transfer of technology from Corning. In addition, there is no obligation on the joint ventures to grant exclusive licenses to Corning in respect of improvements or innovations.

48. The principal restrictions and distortions of competition in this case are to be found rather in the relationship between the joint ventures. The joint ventures have substantially the same business activity, namely the production and marketing of optical fibres. These joint ventures are therefore directly competing companies. The agreements taken together give rise to the creation of a network of inter-related joint ventures with a common technology provider in an oligopolistic market. Corning is one of the major producers and distributors of optical fibres in the world. Its partners are cable makers with large market shares in their respective home countries. The joint ventures therefore bring together companies with strong positions in the optical fibres and cables markets. Although the joint ventures are free to make active and passive sales into each other's territories, only passive sales are permitted in territories where Corning has an exclusive licensee. Corning has interests, whether through joint ventures, subsidiaries or licensees, in several Member States. Its financial stake and key technical and financial personnel representation in the joint ventures, the success of which depends on rapid access to Corning's technology, ensure that Corning is in a position to influence and coordinate the joint venture's conduct.

It can be seen from paragraphs 46 and 47 that the Commission did not find that there was a restriction of competition between Corning and its partners; neither partner was able to develop and put on to the market the JV product without the collaboration of the other, so the individual JV agreements fell outside Article 101(1). What concerned the Commission in this case was the setting up of the network of three JVs. This aspect of the operation *did* infringe Article 101(1) but was exempted (for 15 years), after modifications were made to the agreements to ensure competition between the JVs and to reduce Corning's control over them.[31]

Subsequently, in *ODIN*[32] the liberal policy led to a negative clearance (a finding that the agreement did not infringe Article 101(1) at all). Metal Box (UK) and Elopak (Norway) set up a 50/50 jointly owned company called ODIN. Metal Box manufactured a range of metal, plastic, and polythene containers, bottles, and other packaging, and various closures and seals. Elopak's expertise was in cartons for the dairy and food industries. The JV was to develop a new form of paperboard-based package with a separate laminated metal lid to be used for UHT-treated foods with a long shelf-life. The parties were not existing competitors and neither of them had all the technology required for the new product or the technical knowledge to develop it separately. The agreement did not contain ancillary restrictions beyond those necessary to make the JV work.

Similarly in *Konsortium ECR 900*[33] the Commission found that a JV between three undertakings for the development, manufacture, and distribution of a telecommunications system did not infringe Article 101(1). The undertakings could not have performed the tasks individually in the time demanded, the financial expenditure and staff resources required were too great for individual action, and as there were only 15 potential customers the parties could not have borne the financial risk individually.

The 1993 Notice on cooperative joint ventures[34] reflected this evolved approach, although the Commission was still criticised for sometimes continuing to conduct too formalistic analysis under Article 101(1) and reserving the more economic analysis for Article 101(3). In *European Night Services*,[35] the GC stressed that this approach was not acceptable; the Commission could not rely on granting exemption under Article 101(3) unless it had adequately established an infringement of Article 101(1).

In this case the Commission found that a JV between four railway companies to provide overnight passenger rail services between the UK and the Continent through the Channel Tunnel restricted competition between the parents, between the parents and the JV, and vis-à-vis third parties and that these effects were exacerbated by a network of JVs set up by the parents. Although the JV was exempted subject to conditions, the parties did not find these to be acceptable. The GC held that the Commission had not shown why Article 101(1) applied. It had not identified the relevant market properly, had not applied the appreciability criteria properly, and had demonstrated insufficient economic reasoning: for example, the holding that potential competition was restricted was based on 'a hypothesis unsupported by any evidence or any analysis of the structures of the relevant market from which it might be concluded that it represented a real, concrete possibility'.[36] The exemption conditions were flawed as well, as the Commission had applied the essential facilities concept inappropriately[37] and had given the exemption for too short a time in view of the long-term investment required.

The Commission subsequently defined, and further refined, its policy, first in the Guidelines on horizontal cooperation, published in 2001, and then in the current Guidelines.[38] It also reviewed

---

[31] See also COMP/31.340, *Mitchell Cotts/Solfitra* [1987] OJ L41/31 (parents neither actual nor potential competitors, but the distribution arrangements brought it within Art. 101(1) because they raised barriers to entry).

[32] COMP/32.009, *Metal Box/Elopak (ODIN)* [1990] OJ L209/15.

[33] COMP/32.668, [1990] OJ L228/31.

[34] [1993] OJ C43/2.

[35] Cases T-374–375, 384, and 388/94, *European Night Services v Commission* [1998] ECR II-3141; see further Chap. 4.

[36] Ibid., para. 142.

[37] See Chap. 7.

[38] In 2014, in COMP/39.822, 21 October 2014, the Commission issued a statement of objections to Honeywell and DuPont expressing concern that their cooperation in relation to the production of refrigerant for use in car air conditioning systems infringes Art. 101.

the block exemptions, in 2010, adopting Regulation 2658/2000 on specialisation agreements and Regulation 2659/2000 on R&D agreements. These were replaced in 2010 with Regulations 1218/2010 and 1217/2010 respectively.

(iii) The Horizontal Cooperation Guidelines

The current Guidelines clarify that they apply to cooperation of a 'horizontal' nature, that is, an agreement entered into between actual or potential competitors.[39] A company is treated as a potential competitor of another company if:[40]

> 10 . . . in the absence of the agreement, in case of a small but permanent increase in relative prices it is likely that the former, within a short period of time . . . would undertake the necessary additional investments or other necessary switching costs to enter the relevant market on which the latter is active. This assessment has to be based on realistic grounds, the mere theoretical possibility to enter a market is not sufficient (see Commission Notice on the definition of the relevant market for the purposes of Community competition law). . . .

In a footnote the Commission explains that 'short period of time' depends on the facts of the case in hand, its legal and economic context, and, in particular, whether the company in question is a party to the agreement or a third party. The question of whether the parties can be said to be potential competitors is crucial;[41] as if they are not the agreement is not a horizontal one and is unlikely to be problematic.[42]

The Commission explains its basic principles for Article 101 assessment in paragraphs 20–53, which are elaborated on in later sections dealing with six particular types of agreement: information exchanges (examined in Chapter 9), R&D, production (including specialisation), purchasing, commercialisation (including joint selling), and standardisation (unlike the 2000 Guidelines there is no separate section on environmental agreements).

The Guidelines start by providing general guidance on restrictions by object and effect in paragraphs 23–31 (but does not make specific reference to the doctrine of ancillary restraints referred to in the Article 101(3) Guidelines[43]). In this introductory section the Guidelines recite only that restrictions by object are those that by their very nature have the potential to restrict competition and that in assessing whether an agreement has an anti-competitive object regard must be had to the content, the objectives, and context of the agreement.[44] The later sections, however, make it clear that horizontal cooperation agreements, such as R&D, production, and joint purchasing agreements, which contain severe restraints (on price or output) will only restrict competition by object if they do not truly concern, for example, joint R&D, production, or joint purchasing, but serve as a tool to engage in a disguised cartel.[45] In other words such agreements are not ordinarily by their very nature (appreciably[46]) restrictive of competition, even if they provide for, for example, the joint

---

[39] Guidelines, para. 1.

[40] See also Case C-373/14 P, *Toshiba Corporation v Commission* EU:C:2016:26 (affirming the GC's upholding of the Commission's *Power Transformers* decision (COMP/39.129, 7 October 2009) and the finding that EEA and Japanese producers were actual or potential competitors in the market, see discussion of the case in Chap. 4).

[41] Ibid. See also, e.g., Case T-461/07, *Visa Europe Ltd v Commission* [2011] ECR II-1729 and COMP/39.226, *Lundbeck* 19 June 2013, IP/13/563 and IP/12/834, on appeal Case T-472/13, *Lundbeck v Commission* (judgment pending), discussed in Chap. 12.

[42] See n. 53 and text.

[43] See Chap. 4. The Guidelines do state, however, in the context of commercialisation and reciprocal distribution agreements, that such agreements are unlikely to give rise to competition concerns if objectively necessary to allow one party to enter a market (for example, consortia arrangements that allow companies to participate in projects that they would not be able to undertake individually), paras. 237–238, see Section 7.

[44] Guidelines, paras. 24–25 and Chap. 4.

[45] See, e.g., ibid., paras. 128, 160–161, and 205–206 (see Chap. 9) and discussion in Sections 4–6 below.

[46] See n. 23.

exploitation of possible future results, joint production, distribution, or selling. By way of example, paragraphs 160–161 of the Guidelines state in relation to production agreements:

160. Generally, agreements which involve price-fixing, limiting output or sharing markets or customers restrict competition by object. However, in the context of production agreements, this does not apply where:

- the parties agree on the output directly concerned by the production agreement (for example, the capacity and production volume of a joint venture or the agreed amount of outsourced products), provided that the other parameters of competition are not eliminated; or

- a production agreement that also provides for the joint distribution of the jointly manufactured products envisages the joint setting of the sales prices for those products, and only those products, provided that that restriction is necessary for producing jointly, meaning that the parties would not otherwise have an incentive to enter into the production agreement in the first place.

161. In these two cases an assessment is required as to whether the agreement gives rise to likely restrictive effects on competition within the meaning of Article 101(1). In both scenarios the agreement on output or prices will not be assessed separately, but in the light of the overall effects of the entire production agreement on the market.

This approach seems to accord with that required by the EU Courts and, in particular, with its requirement that object classification should be used sparingly and only for coordination that reveals in itself a sufficient degree of harm to competition;[47] consequently, it is inappropriate where (even severe) restraints are incorporated within what appears to be a beneficial horizontal cooperation agreement (rather, a closer examination of the effects of the agreement is required). Such an approach is also in line with that adopted in merger cases. No merger transactions are assumed to significantly impede effective competition (restrictions of competition by object have no equivalent in merger control). Rather, because it is assumed that mergers offer scope for efficiencies, a range of relevant factors, not just a contractual clause in isolation, are analysed to determine the likely impact of the merger on the main parameters of competition (price, output, quality, innovation, etc.).[48]

In paragraphs 28–29 the Commission explains when anti-competitive effects are likely to occur and how it will determine whether a particular agreement is likely to have those effects:

28. Restrictive effects on competition within the relevant market are likely to occur where it can be expected with a reasonable degree of probability that, due to the agreement, the parties would be able to profitably raise prices or reduce output, product quality, product variety or innovation. This will depend on several factors such as the nature and content of the agreement, the extent to which the parties individually or jointly have or obtain some degree of market power, and the extent to which the agreement contributes to the creation, maintenance or strengthening of that market power or allows the parties to exploit such market power.

29. The assessment of whether a horizontal co-operation agreement has restrictive effects on competition within the meaning of Article 101(1) must be made in comparison to the actual legal and economic context in which competition would occur in the absence of the agreement with all of its alleged restrictions (that is to say, in the absence of the agreement as it stands (if already implemented) or as envisaged (if not yet implemented) at the time of assessment). Hence, in order to prove actual or potential restrictive effects on competition, it is necessary to take into account competition between the parties and competition from third parties, in particular actual or potential competition that would have existed in the absence of the agreement. This comparison does not take into account any potential efficiency gains generated by the agreement as these will only be assessed under Article 101(3).

30. Consequently, horizontal co-operation agreements between competitors that, on the basis of objective factors, would not be able to independently carry out the project or activity covered by the co-operation,

---

[47] Case C-67/13 P, *Groupement des Cartes Bancaires v Commission* EU:C:2014:2204.

[48] Mosso, n. 15.

for instance, due to the limited technical capabilities of the parties, will normally not give rise to restrictive effects on competition within the meaning of Article 101(1) unless the parties could have carried out the project with less stringent restrictions . . .

A footnote to paragraph 30 refers to paragraph 18 of the general Article 101(3) Guidelines.

The Guidelines discuss how the 'nature and content of the agreement'[49] may limit competition. Three important potential competition concerns identified are: possible price increases (from a reduction in actual or potential competition between, or competition pressure on, the parties or the parties and the JV within the ambit of the JV);[50] the facilitation of coordination (within or outside the field of the cooperation);[51] and anti-competitive foreclosure.[52] These effects may result from, for example, terms which reduce competition between the parties or between the parties and third parties or which require the parties to share sensitive information. A restriction of competition is unlikely where the cooperation is between non-competitors (actual or potential) or could not be carried out by competitors independently.[53] In assessing effects it is necessary to consider the situation that would prevail in the absence of the agreement (i.e. the 'counter-factual').

As in other areas of competition law, the question of whether the undertakings concerned have market power plays a central role. The Guidelines thus include a section on 'market power and other market characteristics'.[54] They also provide that agreements in certain identified categories are unlikely to infringe Article 101 (because the parties are unlikely to be able to exercise and maintain market power) if the aggregate market shares of the parties do not exceed certain levels:

- 25 per cent, for R&D agreements;[55]
- 20 per cent, for production and specialisation;[56]
- 15 per cent, for purchasing,[57] commercialisation, and joint selling.[58]

This means that, in cases where agreements appear to span two or more of the categories, it may be important to identify the 'centre of gravity' of an agreement[59] so the applicable 'safe harbour' can be identified.

The Commission now seems to adopt a comparable methodology in its assessment of the anti-competitive effects of horizontal cooperation agreements as that adopted in relation to its appraisal of horizontal mergers. Indeed Mosso states that:

the concepts of 'restriction of competition' in Article 101 TFEU and of 'SIEC' in Article 2 of the Merger Regulation are today, arguably, substantially similar and should result in the same level of intervention. Furthermore ... both require a balancing of potential anti-competitive effects with likely efficiencies. While the fact that one of these tests is applied ex ante and the other normally ex post may undoubtedly be of practical relevance, it should have no bearing on the more conceptual question of whether or not both standards have actually converged.[60]

---

[49] Guidelines, paras. 32–38.

[50] Ibid., para. 34.

[51] Ibid., paras. 35–37.

[52] Ibid., para. 38. See also discussion of anti-competitive foreclosure in Chap. 7.

[53] See discussion of, e.g., *ODIN*, n. 32 and text.

[54] Guidelines, paras. 39–47 and see Chap. 1.

[55] Ibid., para. 134.

[56] Ibid., para. 169.

[57] Ibid., para. 208.

[58] Ibid., para. 240.

[59] Ibid., paras. 13–14.

[60] Mosso, n. 15, 7–8.

In the speech he identifies, as examples, three cases in which the effects of airline alliances were analysed by the Commission.

For instance, when assessing the Oneworld, Star Alliance and Skyteam airline alliances under Article 101 TFEU, the Commission looked at closeness of competition between the parties, their combined market shares and barriers to entry and carried out a price concentration analysis based on economic data. It also analysed foreclosure effects potentially resulting from the parties restricting access to connecting traffic. All these elements, in turn, formed a decisive part as well of the analysis conducted by the Commission in airline mergers cases such as Lufthansa/Austrian, Ryanair/Aer Lingus or British Airways/Iberia.[61]

In the airline alliance cases referred to, the Commission investigated revenue-sharing JVs between airlines for extensive cooperation on pricing, capacity, scheduling, and revenue-management coordination and designed to achieve efficiencies. The extract below from the *Star Alliance: Continental/United/Lufthansa/Air Canada*[62] decision illustrates the reasoning. Although the Commission's preliminary conclusion that the agreement restricted competition by object seems questionable,[63] the Commission did, as Mosso describes, go on to make a detailed analysis of the likely effects of the agreement, concluding that the agreement would appreciably restrict competition. The Commission also examined Article 101(3), accepting that the agreement would produce both in-market and out-of-market efficiencies, but concluding that the level was insufficient to outweigh the likely significant negative effects resulting from the elimination of competition. It thus accepted commitments (including, amongst other things, the release of landing and take-off slots) which the Commission concluded addressed the preliminary concerns set out in its preliminary assessment.

COMP/39.595, *Continental/United/Lufthansa/Air Canada* 23 May 2013

4.3.1. Application of Article 101(1) of the Treaty

4.3.1.1. Introduction

(34) While the A++ agreement creates a contractual joint venture, that joint venture does not conduct its business autonomously and at arm's length from its parents. On the contrary, it is directly managed by the parents and it uses the parents' assets as well as their marketing channels. Since the A++ joint venture does not qualify as 'full-function', the A++ agreement is subject to Article 101 of the Treaty rather than Council Regulation (EC) No 139/2004 of 20 January 2004 on the control of concentrations between undertakings ('the EU Merger Regulation').

(35) The A++ agreement is the latest element of the long-standing cooperation between AC, LH and UA on transatlantic routes. LH and UA and separately LH and AC had been operating joint ventures on transatlantic routes for more than a decade. The aim of the A++ agreement is full metal neutrality. The parties' definition of metal neutrality in the A++ agreement is 'a state of events in which each Party will be incentivised to treat all flying, regardless of airline, within the scope of the provisions of the A++ agreement as flying on its own network and in which customers will also become neutral to the choice among the parties as airlines and among itineraries on any given route'.

4.3.1.2. Restriction of competition by object

(36) The parties cooperate extensively in relation to key parameters of airline competition. In particular, they develop strategic network plans including capacity requirements, potential schedule patterns, new

---

[61] Ibid. He also states, 'This is even more evident in the assessment of joint ventures, an area where both merger control and antitrust play a significant role.'

[62] COMP/39.595, 23 May 2013.

[63] See nn. 44–48 and text.

projects and production shares; pursue joint revenue management activities; combine their pricing functions and align their pricing policy; coordinate on inventory management on transatlantic markets while
maintaining separate inventory management systems; coordinate their marketing activities; and align
their frequent flyer programmes ('FFP'). Moreover, the A++ agreement has provisions on the parties'
cooperation in relation to airport operations, quality management, IT and monitoring with the members
of the A++ joint venture and other non-member airlines.

(37) Based on the above, in its preliminary assessment, the Commission took the preliminary view that
the A++ agreement by its very nature aimed at, and had the potential of, restricting competition. This
is because the parties' cooperation in the joint venture completely eliminated competition between the
parties on key parameters of competition, such as price and capacity. Within the metal-neutral revenue-
sharing joint venture the parties undertook all possible means to eliminate their own incentives on the
market and focused on the common interest and benefit of the joint venture. The whole concept of
metal-neutrality conflicts patently with the concept inherent in the Treaty provisions relating to competition, since the parties substituted competition with full cooperation for the risk of competition that would
occur due to individual airlines' different incentives.

(38) Therefore, the Commission provisionally considered in the preliminary assessment that the A++
agreement that applies to a large number of transatlantic routes, was restrictive of competition by object
under Article 101(1) of the Treaty. Due to this qualification of the parties' cooperation in the A++ joint
venture, the restriction was also considered appreciable.

(39) Among the routes concerned by the A++ agreement, the Commission concentrated on those
routes where there was a high probability that the conditions of Article 101(3) of the Treaty would not be
met, and the preliminary assessment raised preliminary concerns on the Frankfurt–New York route for
premium passengers.

4.3.1.3. Restriction of competition by effect

(40) The Commission also examined whether the A++ agreement had the actual or potential effect of
appreciably restricting competition on the Frankfurt–New York route for premium passengers. As part of
this assessment, the Commission, first, examined whether the parties were actual or potential competitors in the relevant market. Secondly, the Commission identified the likely anti-competitive effects based
in particular on the key market characteristics, namely market shares, closeness of competition, demand
price elasticity, and buyer power. Finally, it considered whether competitors of the parties would be likely
to counter the likely anti-competitive effects of the parties' cooperation in the A++ joint venture by expanding their services.

Competitive conditions in the absence of the cooperation

(41) The Commission came to the preliminary conclusion that LH and CO would be actual competitors
in the absence of their cooperation in the A++ joint venture, operating independently their own non-stop
flights as they did before the implementation of the A++ agreement. Moreover, the parties have not made
the argument that in the absence of their cooperation in the A++ joint venture, LH or CO would exit the
market.

Loss of competition between the parties and market specific assessment

(42) In the preliminary assessment, the Commission's preliminary view was that prior to their cooperation
in the A++ joint venture, LH and CO had to consider each other's reaction to their own decisions on pricing, capacity or service levels. By joining forces, LH and CO no longer face competition from each other.
Due to that reduced degree of competition in the market and the stronger combined market position that
the parties gained as a result of their cooperation in the A++ joint venture, the Commission's preliminary
conclusion was that this cooperation is likely to be restrictive of competition by effect on the Frankfurt–
New York route for premium passengers.

(43) Prior to the parties' cooperation in the A++ joint venture, in 2009, LH held a market share of
64% and CO held a market share of 9% in the market for premium passengers on the Frankfurt–
New York route. That is a combined market share of 73%. In 2011, that combined market share was

slightly down at 71%. In 2011, Singapore Airlines had a 16% market share, Delta had 5%, and one-stop services accounted for 8%. The Commission has previously stated that high market shares are relevant to the competitive assessment. Specifically, when two parties eliminate competition on key parameters, such as price and capacity, between each other and hold a very large combined market share of 71%, it may at least be concluded that their cooperation is likely to produce 'appreciable' effects.

(44) The Commission also examined the closeness of competition between the various competitors' services and found evidence suggesting that CO is a closer competitor to LH on the Frankfurt-New York route for premium passengers than the rival airlines (namely, Delta and Singapore Airlines). Corporate customers most often named LH and CO as the two 'best choice' airlines on the route.

(45) The Commission also provisionally considered that premium passengers were relatively price inelastic. This circumstance was conducive to creating the likely anti- competitive effects, given the presence of other factors such as, for example, high market shares protected by high entry barriers. The vast majority of premium passengers were also found to lack sufficient buyer power in their dealings with CO and especially LH.

(46) By analysing key market characteristics, the Commission came to the provisional conclusion in its preliminary assessment that the situation in this case is leading to likely anti-competitive effects in the relevant market. The combined market share of the parties is very large, the parties' cooperation in the A++ joint venture eliminates competition on all key parameters, LH and CO are closer competitors with respect to each other than with respect to other competitors, and the customers are relatively price inelastic and largely deprived of significant buyer power.

Will competitors of the parties counter the likely anti-competitive effects?

(47) Finally, the Commission assessed whether competitors of the parties would be able to counter the likely anti-competitive effects on the Frankfurt–New York route for premium passengers. It considered barriers to entry and the parties' competitors' ability to replace the loss of competition between LH and CO through expanding their services.

(48) The preliminary assessment identified slot constraints on the Frankfurt–New York route, in particular at the two New York airports (namely, New York JFK and Newark Liberty). The Commission also provisionally established that while the fourth runway alleviated the slot constraints at Frankfurt at present, a new entrant might nevertheless encounter difficulties to obtain slots and infrastructure at peak times in the medium or long run. Moreover, the parties have much larger slot portfolios at Frankfurt and Newark Liberty airports than any other airline: in the summer 2012 season, the parties had approximately 67% of Frankfurt slots and 78% of Newark Liberty slots. Such a large portfolio gives them a unique ability to reshuffle their slots in a way that gives them optimal timings for their Frankfurt–New York flights. A new entrant and smaller competitor of the parties trying to expand would not have that flexibility.

(49) The Commission provisionally concluded that the parties' hub advantage acts as a substantial barrier for any new entrant or smaller competitor of the parties wishing to expand operations on the Frankfurt-New York route for premium passengers. Thanks to the hub advantage, a large operator at a given airport is able to reap benefits from (a) economies of scale, as it is able to spread its fixed costs at that airport over a large number of routes; (b) better brand name recognition; (c) attractiveness of its FFP among the local population; (d) feed traffic from its large network flowing through the airport in question; and (e) a better ability to attract corporate customers. The parties hold these advantages at both ends of the Frankfurt-New York route for premium passengers. At Frankfurt, LH operates its hub, while Newark Liberty airport is the hub for CO.

(50) As to the frequency gap between the parties' and their competitors' services post cooperation, the Commission provisionally considered it as a significant advantage that the parties' competitors are unable to bridge. Post-cooperation, the parties added a Frankfurt–New York frequency, for a total of five daily frequencies compared to a single daily frequency for each of Singapore Airlines and Delta. Therefore, the frequency advantage was provisionally considered as a significant barrier to entry and expansion for competitors of the parties. The relative number of frequencies of airlines on a route affects the attractiveness of each of these airlines in the eyes of customers, and especially premium passengers. Therefore,

adding frequencies results in a disproportionately larger amount of market share for the airline. This phenomenon is known as the 's-curve' effect.

(51) The ability of existing competitors of the parties to replace the loss of competition between LH and CO was provisionally considered as very limited, since neither Singapore Airlines nor Delta was considered as an airline able to significantly expand operations to counter the likely anti-competitive effects of the parties' cooperation in the A++ joint venture. Singapore Airlines is subject to regulatory constraints deriving from the Air Service Agreement concluded between Germany and Singapore. The Commission also provisionally considered that Delta does not appear to be willing and able to significantly expand operations.

(52) Given, among others, the short duration of the Frankfurt-New York flight, a high number of available non-stop flights, a low market share of one-stop flights (8%), one-stop services were provisionally not regarded as a competitive force that could counter the likely negative effects, just like the Commission did not identify any potential entrants that are planning likely, timely and sufficient entry on the Frankfurt–New York route for premium passengers.

4.3.1.4. Effect on trade between Member States

(53) In its preliminary assessment, the Commission provisionally concluded that the A++ agreement may appreciably affect trade between Member States within the meaning of Article 101(1) of the Treaty. The parties have significant operations and sales across the European Union. The A++ agreement covers all passenger services of the parties on transatlantic routes, namely those, among others, that link the European Union and North America and also services within the European Union connecting to or from transatlantic routes. The parties' cooperation in the A++ joint venture alters the manner in which their services on European Union-North American routes and intra-European Union routes that connect to these routes would be provided absent the A++ joint venture.

4.3.1.5. Conclusion on Article 101(1) of the Treaty

(54) The Commission took the preliminary view that the parties' cooperation in the A++ joint venture restricts competition in the premium market on the Frankfurt–New York route both by object and by effect. In particular, as regards the restriction of competition by effect, the Commission considered that the pre-cooperation competition that existed between LH and CO was eliminated and most likely could not be replaced by competition from the parties' competitors because they face substantial barriers to entry and expansion. This preliminary conclusion was not invalidated by evidence of some degree of residual competition from Singapore Airlines, Delta and one-stop competitors. The concern was that there was an appreciable reduction of competition and not that competition was being entirely eliminated.

Finally, the Guidelines clarify that even where there are restrictions by object or effect under Article 101(1), Article 101(3) may apply. Again, they refer to the general Article 101(3) Guidelines[64] and set out some guidance on the application of the block exemptions and the Article 101(3) criteria individually. A key point emphasised is that efficiencies which benefit consumers are most likely to be realised where the agreement allows the parties to combine complementary skills and assets[65] (and so to innovate or develop new goods or services[66] or to penetrate new markets[67] which they could have achieved independently).

50. In the area of horizontal co-operation agreements there are block exemption regulations based on Article 101(3) for research and development and specialisation (including joint production) agreements. Those Block Exemption Regulations are based on the premise that the combination of complementary

---

[64] Guidelines, para. 48.

[65] Ibid., paras. 48–52.

[66] Such as a new drug, COMP/28.796, *Beecham/Parke Davis* [1979] OJ L70/11.

[67] See, e.g., COMP/27.093, *De Laval-Stork* [1997] OJ L215/11.

skills or assets can be the source of substantial efficiencies in research and development and specialisation agreements. This may also be the case for other types of horizontal co-operation agreements. The analysis of the efficiencies of an individual agreement under Article 101(3) is therefore to a large extent a question of identifying the complementary skills and assets that each of the parties brings to the agreement and evaluating whether the resulting efficiencies are such that the conditions of Article 101(3) are fulfilled.

51. Complementarities may arise from horizontal co-operation agreements in various ways. A research and development agreement may bring together different research capabilities that allow the parties to produce better products more cheaply and shorten the time for those products to reach the market. A production agreement may allow the parties to achieve economies of scale or scope that they could not achieve individually.

52. Horizontal co-operation agreements that do not involve the combination of complementary skills or assets are less likely to lead to efficiency gains that benefit consumers. Such agreements may reduce duplication of certain costs, for instance because certain fixed costs can be eliminated. However, fixed cost savings are, in general, less likely to result in benefits to consumers than savings in, for instance, variable or marginal costs.

Assessment of the indispensability of any restrictions to achieve efficiencies is also a key part of any Article 101(3) assessment. In particular, the Commission will scrutinise non-competition clauses carefully where they prevent parents from competing with their JV after its termination.[68] In *Telefónica/Portugal Telecom*[69] the Commission imposed fines of €79 million on the parties for insertion of a non-compete clause in an agreement to dissolve a Brazilian JV, Vivo. The non-compete provision applied in Spain and Portugal (not Brazil) and the Commission considered that the agreement infringed Article 101(1) (the restraints were not ancillary to the JV) and did not satisfy the conditions of Article 101(3).

4. RESEARCH AND DEVELOPMENT AGREEMENTS

A. THE APPLICATION OF ARTICLE 101(1)

It has already been explained that the Guidelines set out guidance on six particular types of agreement, including R&D agreements and that there is a specific R&D block exemption, currently Regulation 1217/2010.

R&D is crucial to the competitiveness of the EU.[70] R&D agreements can take many forms, as the Guidelines recognise:

111. R&D agreements vary in form and scope. They range from outsourcing certain R&D activities to the joint improvement of existing technologies and co-operation concerning the research, development and marketing of completely new products. They may take the form of a co-operation agreement or of a jointly controlled company. This chapter applies to all forms of R&D agreements, including related agreements concerning the production or commercialisation of the R&D results.

As far as assessment under Article 101(1) is concerned, it has been seen that the Guidelines state that R&D agreements restrict competition by object only if they are really a tool for a disguised cartel. In true R&D cases therefore a detailed analysis of effects, and a consideration of the relevant market, will be required as a preliminary matter. The Guidelines state that the latter involves 'identifying 'those products, technologies or R&D efforts that will

---

[68] See, e.g., COMP/39.736, *Siemens/Areva* 18 June 2012.

[69] COMP/39.839, 23 January 2013, on appeal Cases T-208 and 216/13 (judgments pending) (amongst other things the appeals allege that the Commission wrongly applied Art. 101(1) as they had wrongly classed the parties as potential competitors and had failed to show that the agreement had as either its object or effect the restriction of competition).

[70] Recital 2 of the block exemption, Reg. 1217/2010, mentions Art. 179(2) TFEU which provides for the EU to encourage undertakings, including SMEs, in R&D and to support their cooperation efforts.

act as the main competitive constraints on the parties'.[71] An R&D agreement may be aimed at a change to existing products but may also be aimed at creating new products which may form an entirely new market; paragraphs 114–126 explain how relevant markets are defined in the latter circumstances. It may be necessary to define relevant upstream markets for technologies[72] or for innovation.[73] The calculation of market shares is particularly difficult where the agreement aims to develop a product which will create an entirely new demand, and this issue is dealt with in the block exemption.

Agreements which relate to cooperation in R&D at an early stage, far removed from exploitation of the results, will fall outside Article 101(1).[74] Further, agreements between non-competitors[75] and R&D cooperation which does not go as far as joint exploitation of possible results rarely infringes Article 101(1). The latter will do so only if the parties have market power on the existing markets and/or competition with respect to innovation is appreciably reduced.[76]

B. THE APPLICATION OF ARTICLE 101(3)

(i) The Block Exemption for R&D Agreements, Regulation 1217/2010

Where the agreement does fall within Article 101(1) the block exemption Regulation 1217/2010 may apply. The Regulation defines R&D agreements (Article 1), and provides an exemption for such agreements provided they meet certain conditions (Article 2). Article 3 sets out the conditions for exemption and Article 4 contains the market share threshold and the duration of the exemption, making a distinction between agreements between competitors and agreements between non-competitors. The exemption is more generous as regards the latter. Article 5 contains a list of 'hard-core' restrictions, the inclusion of which prevents the exemption applying, and Article 6 contains two 'excluded restrictions' which are not block exempted but do not take the rest of the agreement outside the protection of the Regulation.

Articles 1 and 2 clarify the scope of the exemption for R&D agreements. Note that paragraph 1(g) defines 'exploitation of the results' as 'the production or distribution of the contract products or the application of the contract technologies or the assignment or licensing of intellectual property rights or the communication of know-how required for such manufacture or application'. Article 2 clarifies that it also covers the assignment or licensing of intellectual property rights which is ancillary to the R&D agreement.

Article 1

Definitions

1. For the purposes of this Regulation, the following definitions shall apply:

   (a) 'research and development agreement' means an agreement entered into between two or more parties which relate to the conditions under which those parties pursue:

      (i) joint research and development of contract products or contract technologies and joint exploitation of the results of that research and development;

---

[71] Guidelines, para. 112.

[72] Ibid., paras. 116–118.

[73] Ibid., paras. 119–122.

[74] Ibid., para. 129 and, e.g., EUCAR, XXVIIIth Report on Competition Policy (1998), point 132.

[75] Guidelines, para. 130.

[76] Ibid, paras. 132–133.

(ii) joint exploitation of the results of research and development of contract products or contract technologies jointly carried out pursuant to a prior agreement between the same parties;

(iii) joint research and development of contract products or contract technologies excluding joint exploitation of the results;

(iv) paid-for research and development of contract products or contract technologies and joint exploitation of the results of that research and development;

(v) joint exploitation of the results of paid-for research and development of contract products or contract technologies pursuant to a prior agreement between the same parties; or

(vi) paid-for research and development of contract products or contract technologies excluding joint exploitation of the results . . .

Article 2

Exemption

1. Pursuant to Article 101(3) of the Treaty and subject to the provisions of this Regulation, it is hereby declared that Article 101(1) of the Treaty shall not apply to research and development agreements.

    This exemption shall apply to the extent that such agreements contain restrictions of competition falling within the scope of Article 101(1) of the Treaty.

2. The exemption provided for in paragraph 1 shall apply to research and development agreements containing provisions which relate to the assignment or licensing of intellectual property rights to one or more of the parties or to an entity the parties establish to carry out the joint research and development, paid-for research and development or joint exploitation, provided that those provisions do not constitute the primary object of such agreements, but are directly related to and necessary for their implementation.

In order to be covered by the block exemption an agreement within Article 1 must fulfil the conditions in Article 3. Broadly, this requires that all parties must have full access to the final results of the R&D, including any IPRs and know-how. There are two exceptions to this, one of which is to cover the position of universities, research bodies, and commercial research entities which are not in the business of exploitation. Further, joint exploitation can cover only results which are protected by IPRs or constitute know-how and are indispensable for the manufacture of the contract products or application of the contract technologies.

Article 4 sets out the applicable market share thresholds and duration of the exemption conferred. Article 4(1) applies to agreements between non-competitors, distinguishing between R&D agreements that extend into the exploitation stage and those which do not; the former are limited to seven years. Article 4(2) applies to agreements between competing undertakings. The effect of this latter provision is that where the parties' market shares exceed 25 per cent the exemption is not available. Further provisions about the calculation of market shares are set out in Article 7.

Article 4

Market share threshold and duration of exemption

1. Where the parties are not competing undertakings, the exemption provided for in Article 2 shall apply for the duration of the research and development. Where the results are jointly exploited, the exemption shall continue to apply for 7 years from the time the contract products or contract technologies are first put on the market within the internal market.

2. Where two or more of the parties are competing undertakings, the exemption provided for in Article 2 shall apply for the period referred to in paragraph 1 of this Article only if, at the time the research and development agreement is entered into:

    (a) in the case of research and development agreements referred to in point (a)(i), (ii) or (iii) of Article 1(1), the combined market share of the parties to a research and development agreement does not exceed 25 % on the relevant product and technology markets; or

    (b) in the case of research and agreements referred to in point (a)(iv), (v) or (vi) of Article 1(1), the combined market share of the financing party and all the parties with which the financing party has entered into research and development agreements with regard to the same contract products or contract technologies, does not exceed 25 % on the relevant product and technology markets.

3. After the end of the period referred to in paragraph 1, the exemption shall continue to apply as long as the combined market share of the parties does not exceed 25 % on the relevant product and technology markets.

Article 5 contains a list of hardcore restrictions: paragraph 5(a) deals with freedom to carry out independent R&D; paragraphs 5(b) and (c) target limitations on output or sales and fixing of prices, although important exceptions apply where joint exploitation is involved; paragraphs 5(d)–(g) deal with territorial restrictions.[77]

Article 5

Hardcore restrictions

The exemption provided for in Article 2 shall not apply to research and development agreements which, directly or indirectly, in isolation or in combination with other factors under the control of the parties, have as their object any of the following:

(a) the restriction of the freedom of the parties to carry out research and development independently or in cooperation with third parties in a field unconnected with that to which the research and development agreement relates or, after the completion of the joint research and development or the paid-for research and development, in the field to which it relates or in a connected field;

(b) the limitation of output or sales, with the exception of:

    (i) the setting of production targets where the joint exploitation of the results includes the joint production of the contract products;

    (ii) the setting of sales targets where the joint exploitation of the results includes the joint distribution of the contract products or the joint licensing of the contract technologies within the meaning of point (m)(i) or (ii) of Article 1(1);

    (iii) practices constituting specialisation in the context of exploitation; and

    (iv) the restriction of the freedom of the parties to manufacture, sell, assign or license products, technologies or processes which compete with the contract products or contract technologies during the period for which the parties have agreed to jointly exploit the results;

(c) the fixing of prices when selling the contract product or licensing the contract technologies to third parties, with the exception of the fixing of prices charged to immediate customers or the fixing of licence fees charged to immediate licensees where the joint exploitation of the results includes the joint distribution of the contract products or the joint licensing of the contract technologies within the meaning of point (m)(i) or (ii) of Article 1(1);

---

[77] See further discussion of territorial restraints in Chap. 11.

(d) the restriction of the territory in which, or of the customers to whom, the parties may passively sell the contract products or license the contract technologies, with the exception of the requirement to exclusively license the results to another party;

(e) the requirement not to make any, or to limit, active sales of the contract products or contract technologies in territories or to customers which have not been exclusively allocated to one of the parties by way of specialisation in the context of exploitation;

(f) the requirement to refuse to meet demand from customers in the parties' respective territories, or from customers otherwise allocated between the parties by way of specialisation in the context of exploitation, who would market the contract products in other territories within the internal market;

(g) the requirement to make it difficult for users or resellers to obtain the contract products from other resellers within the internal market.

Article 6 sets out 'Excluded restrictions'; restrictions which cannot be block exempted but which do not affect the exemption of the remaining provisions of the agreement. Article 6(a) deals with no-challenge clauses (although it is acceptable to provide for termination in the event of a challenge, see also Chapter 12), and Article 6(b) deals with the licensing of third parties.

Article 6

Excluded restrictions

The exemption provided for in Article 2 shall not apply to the following obligations contained in research and development agreements:

(a) the obligation not to challenge after completion of the research and development the validity of intellectual property rights which the parties hold in the internal market and which are relevant to the research and development or, after the expiry of the research and development agreement, the validity of intellectual property rights which the parties hold in the internal market and which protect the results of the research and development, without prejudice to the possibility to provide for termination of the research and development agreement in the event of one of the parties challenging the validity of such intellectual property rights;

(b) the obligation not to grant licences to third parties to manufacture the contract products or to apply the contract technologies unless the agreement provides for the exploitation of the results of the joint research and development or paid-for research and development by at least one of the parties and such exploitation takes place in the internal market vis-à-vis third parties.

(ii) The Individual Application of Article 101(3)

The Guidelines discuss the individual application of Article 101(3) in paragraphs 141–149 (giving worked examples in paragraphs 147–149). In theory Article 101(3) could be applied individually to agreements that do not satisfy the block exemption conditions. However, the Commission warns in paragraph 142 that it is unlikely that an agreement containing an Article 5 hardcore restriction would fulfil the 'indispensability' criterion in Article 101(3). Many R&D agreements will lead to efficiency gains by improvements to production or distribution or economic or technical progress, but the Commission will look closely at whether a fair share of the benefits is passed on to consumers.[78]

The Guidelines also consider the time element. Although Article 101(3) ceases to apply if the criteria were once fulfilled but no longer are, the Commission will take into account the need for the

---

[78] See, e.g., COMP/32.173, *Continental/Michelin* [1998] OJ L305/33, COMP/34.776, *Pasteur Mérieux-Merck* [1994] OJ L309/1 and COMP/33.863, *Asahi/Saint Gobain* [1994] OJ L354/87, Guidelines, para. 143.

parties to recoup sunk investments.[79] The Commission accepts that some R&D agreements are irreversible events in that once the agreement has been implemented the *ex ante* situation cannot be restored. In such a case the assessment is made on the basis of the facts at the time of implementation.[80]

5. PRODUCTION AGREEMENTS

A. GENERAL

Production agreements cover a number of scenarios: joint production of certain goods; subcontracting (where one party entrusts the other with production of certain goods); or specialisation, whereby the parties agree to specialise in manufacture by allocating the manufacture of certain products amongst themselves. In unilateral specialisation one party ceases production altogether, whereas in reciprocal specialisation each agrees to give up manufacturing certain products and leave it to the other.[81] If subcontracting is between parties at different stages of the market it is not covered by the Horizontal Guidelines but may be covered by the Verticals Guidelines[82] or by the Notice on subcontracting agreements.[83]

B. THE APPLICATION OF ARTICLE 101(1)

Production agreements, even those involving price-fixing, limiting production, or sharing markets or customers, will not be considered restrictive by object where (a) the parties agree on the output directly concerned by the production agreement and do not eliminate the other parameters of competition or (b) a production agreement providing for joint distribution of the jointly manufactured products envisages setting the sale price just for those products provided that the parties would not have had an incentive to enter the agreement otherwise.[84]

The Guidelines consider in paragraphs 162–182 when a production agreement is likely to have restrictive effects. Production agreements which also involve commercialisation functions, such as joint distribution or marketing, carry a higher risk of restrictive effects than pure production agreements, i.e. the closer to the consumer the agreement goes the more problematic it becomes.[85]

Restrictive effects are unlikely if the parties do not have market power,[86] but even where market power is present restrictive effects may still be low if the market is dynamic.[87] However, the Commission is concerned that there may be a collusive outcome if a production agreement between parties with market power increases their commonality of costs to a level which enables them to collude.[88]

---

[79] Guidelines, para. 145.

[80] Ibid., para. 146.

[81] See, e.g., COMP/26.437, *Jaz/Peter* [1969] OJ L195/5. Both parties manufactured clocks. Under the agreement Jaz in France was to continue making only electric clocks and domestic alarm clocks and Peter in Germany was to make large mechanical alarm clocks. They agreed that they would each supply the other with their products and spare parts, that they could both sell the whole range of the products in their respective territories, and that they would not buy the products covered by the agreement from third parties. See also COMP/30.863, *ICI/BP* [1984] OJ L212/1.

[82] [2010] OJ C130/1; and possibly by the Verticals Reg., see Chap. 11.

[83] [1979] OJ C1/2, see Chap. 11.

[84] See also n. 47, p. 723 and text.

[85] Guidelines, para. 167.

[86] Ibid., paras. 168–169.

[87] Ibid., para. 170.

[88] Ibid., paras. 175–176.

C. THE APPLICATION OF ARTICLE 101(3)

(i) The Block Exemption for Specialisation Agreements, Regulation 1218/2010

The block exemption, Regulation 1218/2010, applies to three types of specialisation agreement set out in Article 1. It is a less complex block exemption than Regulation 1217/2010 on R&D. It does not contain 'conditions' or 'excluded restrictions'. Article 2 states the exemption, Article 3 the market share threshold, Article 4 lists three hardcore provisions which prevent the exemption applying, and Article 5 explains the calculation of the market share threshold.

Articles 1 and 2 make it clear that the block exemption covers unilateral and reciprocal specialisation and joint production. The block exemption only applies to unilateral and reciprocal specialisation agreements which include obligations on the non-producing party to purchase the products from the other (unilateral) and on both parties to purchase from each other (reciprocal).

Article 2(2) makes it clear that IPR licensing and assignment provisions are covered by the exemption, but only to the extent that they are ancillary to a specialisation agreement. If they are the primary object then the regime governing technology transfer, not specialisation, applies.[89] Article 2(3)(a) allows the purchase or supply obligations mentioned in Article 1 to be exclusive and Article 2(3)(b) allows for joint distribution of the specialisation products.

Article 1

Definitions

1. For the purposes of this Regulation, the following definitions shall apply:

   (a) 'specialisation agreement' means a unilateral specialisation agreement, a reciprocal specialisation agreement or a joint production agreement;

   (b) 'unilateral specialisation agreement' means an agreement between two parties which are active on the same product market by virtue of which one party agrees to fully or partly cease production of certain products or to refrain from producing those products and to purchase them from the other party, who agrees to produce and supply those products;

   (c) 'reciprocal specialisation agreement' means an agreement between two or more parties which are active on the same product market, by virtue of which two or more parties on a reciprocal basis agree to fully or partly cease or refrain from producing certain but different products and to purchase these products from the other parties, who agree to produce and supply them;

   (d) 'joint production agreement' means an agreement by virtue of which two or more parties agree to produce certain products jointly. . . .

Article 2

Exemption

1. Pursuant to Article 101(3) of the Treaty and subject to the provisions of this Regulation, it is hereby declared that Article 101(1) of the Treaty shall not apply to specialisation agreements.

   This exemption shall apply to the extent that such agreements contain restrictions of competition falling within the scope of Article 101(1) of the Treaty.

2. The exemption provided for in paragraph 1 shall apply to specialisation agreements containing provisions which relate to the assignment or licensing of intellectual property rights to one or more of the

---

[89] See Chap. 12.

parties, provided that those provisions do not constitute the primary object of such agreements, but are directly related to and necessary for their implementation.

3. The exemption provided for in paragraph 1 shall apply to specialisation agreements whereby:

   (a) the parties accept an exclusive purchase or exclusive supply obligation; or

   (b) the parties do not independently sell the specialisation products but jointly distribute those products.

Article 3 sets the market share threshold at 20 per cent and Article 4 prohibits three basic hardcore provisions: price-fixing and limiting sales or output, but subject to exceptions, and market or customer allocation.

Article 3

Market share threshold

The exemption provided for in Article 2 shall apply on condition that the combined market share of the parties does not exceed 20 % on any relevant market.

Article 4

Hardcore restrictions

The exemption provided for in Article 2 shall not apply to specialisation agreements which, directly or indirectly, in isolation or in combination with other factors under the control of the parties, have as their object any of the following:

(a) the fixing of prices when selling the products to third parties with the exception of the fixing of prices charged to immediate customers in the context of joint distribution;

(b) the limitation of output or sales with the exception of:

   (i) provisions on the agreed amount of products in the context of unilateral or reciprocal specialisation agreements or the setting of the capacity and production volume in the context of a joint production agreement; and

   (ii) the setting of sales targets in the context of joint distribution;

(c) the allocation of markets or customers.

(ii) The Individual Application of Article 101(3)

Production agreements can provide efficiency gains in the form of costs savings or better production technologies.[90] The Commission considers parties to a production agreement are more likely to pass on variable costs savings to consumers than fixed costs savings.[91] Where the production agreement does not involve joint commercialisation, restrictions on the parties' competitive conduct outside the cooperation and joint setting of prices are not normally considered indispensable.[92]

The elimination of competition must be considered in relation to any possible spill-over markets and not just to the market on which the cooperation is occurring.[93] High market shares are

---

[90] Guidelines, para. 183.

[91] Ibid., para. 185.

[92] Ibid., para. 184.

[93] Ibid., para. 186.

not necessarily a bar to Article 101(3) exemption,[94] see, for example, *BPCL/ICI*,[95] *Philips/Osram*,[96] and *GEAE/P&W*.[97]

The Guidelines illustrate the possible application of Article 101(3) to production agreements in a series of examples.[98]

6. PURCHASING AGREEMENTS

A. THE NATURE OF JOINT PURCHASING AND ITS TREATMENT IN THE GUIDELINES

Joint purchasing agreements, carried out through a jointly controlled or owned company, contractual or other looser forms of cooperation,[99] or an 'alliance',[100] are generally aimed at creating buying power.[101] That can lead to lower prices or better quality products or services being passed on to consumers. Not only does the joint purchasing agreement itself have to be appraised for compatibility with Article 101, but vertical agreements concluded by the joint purchasers both with their suppliers and the individual members must also be scrutinised.[102]

Joint purchasing agreements may affect two markets, both the market(s) on which the joint purchasers buy (the purchasing, or procurement, market) and the downstream market(s) on which they sell. Markets must thus be defined for purchasing (defined from the supply side) and for downstream selling market (if the joint purchasers are competitors there).[103]

As a joint purchasing arrangement will not be found to restrict competition by object unless it is nothing but a disguised cartel, its actual or likely effects must ordinarily be assessed.[104] The arrangements are less likely to give rise to competition concerns when the parties do not have market power on the selling market(s):[105] indeed, the Guidelines state that a restriction on competition is unlikely where the parties do not exceed a combined 15 per cent market share on the purchasing market(s) *and* a combined market share of 15 per cent on the selling market(s). These are not absolute thresholds and market shares above these will not necessarily mean a restriction of competition will be found. In any event, where the combined market shares are below these figures it is likely that the Article 101(3) conditions are fulfilled.[106]

A core concern of the Commission is that buying power can have restrictive effects if it forecloses access to the market. Moreover, 'a high degree of buying power may indirectly affect the output, quality and variety of products on the selling market'.[107] However:

212. If . . . competing purchasers co-operate who are not active on the same relevant selling market (for example, retailers which are active in different geographic markets and cannot be regarded as potential

[94] See further Bellamy and Child (V. Rose and D. Bailey, eds.), *European Union Law of Competition* (7th edn, Oxford University Press, 2013), 6.060–6.061.

[95] COMP/30.863, [1984] OJ L212/1 (petroleum plastics).

[96] COMP/34.252, [1994] OJ L378/37 (lead glass).

[97] COMP/36.213, [2000] OJ L58/16 (aircraft engines).

[98] Guidelines, paras. 187–193.

[99] Ibid.

[100] Ibid., para. 196. See also COMP/38.064, *Covisint*, IP/01/1155 discussed in Chap. 9.

[101] Guidelines, para. 194, see further Chap. 9.

[102] See Chap. 11 and Guidelines, para. 196.

[103] Guidelines, paras. 197–199.

[104] Ibid., paras. 106–107. See also Case C-250/92, *Gøttrup-Klim* [1994] ECR I-5641, discussed n. 109 and text.

[105] Guidelines, para. 204.

[106] Ibid., paras. 208–209.

[107] Ibid., para. 210.

competitors), the joint purchasing arrangement is unlikely to have restrictive effects on competition unless the parties have a position in the purchasing markets that is likely to be used to harm the competitive position of other players in their respective selling markets.

Joint purchasing arrangements, involving exchange of commercially sensitive information, may also facilitate the coordination of the parties' behaviour on the selling market and lead to collusive outcomes.[108] However:

216 . . . If the information exchange does not exceed the sharing of data necessary for the joint purchasing of the products by the parties to the joint purchasing arrangement, then even if the information exchange has restrictive effects on competition within the meaning of Article 101(1), the agreement is more likely to meet the criteria of Article 101(3) than if the exchange goes beyond what was necessary for the joint purchasing.

There is no block exemption in respect of joint purchasing. Paragraphs 117–120 of the Guidelines provide general discussion as to how Article 101(3) may apply to joint purchasing arrangements before providing specific examples of how they may apply to certain agreements. They recognise that such agreements give rise to significant scope for efficiency gains, for example through cost saving, economies of scale, and facilitating qualitative efficiency gains, which may be passed on to consumers (perhaps through lower selling prices). The Guidelines recognise that in exceptional circumstances an obligation to purchase exclusively through cooperation may be indispensable to realise economies of scale.

B. CASES ON JOINT PURCHASING

Gøttrup-Klim,[109] discussed in Chapter 4, concerned joint purchasing of farming supplies such as fertilisers by a Danish cooperative association (DLG) on behalf of its members. The case arose following a challenge to DLG's rules, which precluded its members from belonging to any competing cooperative. The CJ held that the rules were not caught by Article 101(1) if they were necessary to ensure the proper functioning of the cooperative as a significant counterweight to the large multinational suppliers.

In *Métropole Télévision*[110] the Commission dealt with a joint purchasing agreement in respect of television rights to sporting events. It concerned the European Broadcasting Union (EBU), an association of radio and television organisations established in 1950, which exchanged programmes amongst members through Eurovision. To become an active member, a broadcasting organisation had to satisfy certain conditions, inter alia, as to its national coverage and the nature and financing of programmes. Métropole applied to become a member six times but its application was rejected each time. This battle between Métropole and the EBU surfaced several times before the EU Courts. In this case Métropole complained about EBU practices concerning the acquisition of TV rights to sporting events and challenged the Commission's exemption of its rules.[111] The GC annulled the decision on the ground that the Commission had not established that the final condition of Article 101(3) was satisfied.[112]

---

[108] Ibid., para. 213.

[109] Case C-250/92, [1994] ECR I-5641.

[110] COMP/32.150, [2000] OJ L151/18 and Cases T-185, 216, 299, and 300/00, *Métropole Télévision SA (M6) and others v Commission* [2002] ECR II-3805.

[111] COMP/32.150, [2000] OJ L151/18. It had successfully challenged exemption of the preceding EBU rules, COMP/32.150, [1993] OJ L179/23 and Cases T-528, 542, 543, and 546/93, *Métropole Télévision SA v Commission* [1996] ECR II-649.

[112] Other cases and decisions on joint purchasing include *National Sulphuric Acid Association* [1980] OJ L260/24 (Art. 101(3) applied after agreement amended) and COMP/297.958, *National Sulphuric Acid Association* [1989] OJ L190/22; Case 61/80, *Coöperatieve Stremsel- en Kleursfabriek v Commission* [1981] ECR 851 (the appeal from COMP/29.011, *Rennet* 5 December 1979) where the obligation of a group of over 90% of Dutch dairy producers to buy rennet exclusively from a cooperative was held to infringe Art. 101(1) and not satisfy Art. 101(3).

Cases T-185, 216, 299, and 300/00, *Métropole Télévision SA (M6) and others v Commission* [2002] ECR II-3805

The rules in question concerned granting access to Eurovision rights for pay-TV. The rules provided a 'sub-licensing scheme' which granted access to Eurovision rights to major sporting events to third parties who were competitors of EBU members. The Commission exempted EBU's rules for the sharing of jointly acquired sports TV rights on the grounds that the sub-licensing scheme guaranteed access to competitors and therefore avoided the elimination of competition in the market. The Commission did not settle on an exact definition of the market but contended that even on the basis of the narrowest possible definition (the acquisition of rights for a specific event such as the Football World Cup or the Summer Olympics) there was no elimination of competition. The GC accepted that the Commission's assertion that the market could consist entirely of major sporting events did not affect the analysis of whether Article 101(3) was satisfied. It then turned to consider whether in making that analysis the Commission had made a manifest error of assessment.

General Court

63. As regards the effects of the Eurovision system on competition, the contested decision shows (paragraphs 71 to 80) that there are two types of restrictions. First, the joint acquisition of television rights to sporting events, their sharing and the exchange of signal restricts or even eliminates competition among EBU members which are competitors on both the upstream market, for the acquisition of rights, and for the downstream market, for televised transmission of sporting events. In addition, that system gives rise to restrictions on competition as regards third parties since those rights, as set out in paragraph 75 of the contested decision, are generally sold on an exclusive basis, so that EBU non-members would not in principle have access to them.

64. While it is true that the purchase of televised transmission rights for an event is not in itself a restriction on competition likely to fall under Article [101(1)] and may be justified by particular characteristics of the product and the market in question, the exercise of those rights in a specific legal and economic context may none the less lead to such a restriction (see, by analogy, Case 262/101 *Coditel v Ciné-Vog Films* . . . paragraphs 15 to 17).

65. In that vein, the Commission states, in paragraph 45 of the contested decision, that 'the acquisition of exclusive TV rights to certain major sporting events has a strong impact on the downstream television markets in which the sporting events are broadcast'.

66. In addition, it appears from the analysis of the documents in the case and the arguments of the parties that the acquisition of transmission rights to a major international sporting event such as the Olympics or the football World Cup cannot fail to affect strongly the market in sponsorship and advertising, which is the main source of revenue for television channels which broadcast free-to-air, since those programmes attract a very wide audience.

67. Moreover, as pointed out by SIC, the effects which restrict competition for third parties as a result of the Eurovision system are accentuated, first, by the level of vertical integration of the EBU and its members, which are not merely purchasers of rights but also television operators which broadcast the rights purchased, and second, by the geographic extent of the EBU, whose members broadcast in all the countries of the European Union. As a result, when the EBU acquires transmission rights for an international sporting event, the access to that event is in principle automatically precluded for all non-member operators. By contrast, the situation appears to be different when the transmission rights for sporting events are acquired by an agency which buys those rights in order to resell them, or when they are bought by a media group which only has operators in certain Member States, since that group will tend to enter into negotiations with operators in other Member States in order to sell those rights. In that case, despite the exclusive purchase of the rights, other operators still have the opportunity to negotiate their acquisition for their respective markets.

68. In light of those facts—that is, the structure of the market, the position of the EBU in the market for certain international sporting events and the level of vertical integration of the EBU and its members— there is reason to determine whether the scheme for third-party access to the Eurovision system makes it possible to counterbalance the restrictions on competition affecting those third parties and thus to avoid their exclusion from competition.

. . .

73. However, even if it proves necessary, for reasons linked to exclusive transmission rights for sporting events and the guarantee of their economic value (see paragraph 60 above), for EBU members to reserve for themselves live transmission of the programmes acquired by the EBU, none of these reasons justifies their being able to extend that right to all the competitions which are part of the same event, even when they do not intend to broadcast all those competitions live.

. . .

83. All the information provided to the [General Court] thus goes to show that, contrary to what the Commission concludes in the contested decision, the sub-licensing scheme does not guarantee competitors of EBU members sufficient access to rights to transmit sporting events held by the latter on the basis of their participation in that purchasing association. Apart from a few exceptions, nothing in the rules or mode of implementation of the scheme enables competitors of EBU members to obtain sub-licences for the live broadcast of unused Eurovision rights. In reality, the scheme merely permits the acquisition of sub-licences to transmit roundups of competitions under extremely restrictive conditions.

7. COMMERCIALISATION AGREEMENTS

A. GENERAL

Commercialisation agreements involve cooperation between competitors in the selling, distribution, or promotion of their substitute products and cover a wide spectrum of agreements.

225. . . . At one end of the spectrum, joint selling agreements may lead to a joint determination of all commercial aspects related to the sale of the product, including price. At the other end, there are more limited agreements that only address one specific commercialisation function, such as distribution, after-sales service, or advertising.

Where the commercialisation forms part of another type of cooperation upstream, for example joint production or purchasing, the centre of gravity of the agreement must be determined and the analysis conducted accordingly.[113]

Like joint production, such agreements may have horizontal and vertical aspects, requiring an assessment of both the arrangements between the competitors and subsequent vertical agreements concluded for the sale and distribution of products.[114]

B. THE APPLICATION OF ARTICLE 101(1)

Commercialisation agreements between non-competitors do not infringe Article 101(1) in relation to their *horizontal* aspects, but may fall within Article 101(1) in respect of their *vertical* aspects. The Guidelines specifically say that there is no restriction of competition where undertakings submit a joint tender for projects for which they could not bid individually. The Commission states that in this situation the undertakings are not potential competitors for the tender.[115]

---

[113] Guidelines, para. 228. For 'centre of gravity' see n. 59 and text.
[114] Ibid., para. 227 and see Chap. 11.
[115] Ibid., para. 143.

The Commission is concerned that commercialisation agreements may result in price-fixing, output limitation, and/or market sharing. Further, that exchanges of strategic information, particularly in relation to marketing strategy and pricing and where there is joint advertising,[116] and increasing the parties' commonality of variable costs[117] may result in a collusive outcome on the market.[118]

Agreements limited purely to joint selling generally have the aim of coordinating the parties' pricing policies and so are likely to be restrictive by object even if the agreement is non-exclusive (so that the parties can sell outside the agreement).[119]

Where an analysis of effects is required, the Commission's view is that commercialisation agreements are normally unlikely to raise competition concerns if they are the only way that a party can enter the market.

6.3.3. Restrictive effects on competition

237. A commercialisation agreement is normally not likely to give rise to competition concerns if it is objectively necessary to allow one party to enter a market it could not have entered individually or with a more limited number of parties than are effectively taking part in the co-operation, for example, because of the costs involved. A specific application of this principle would be consortia arrangements that allow the companies involved to participate in projects that they would not be able to undertake individually. As the parties to the consortia arrangement are therefore not potential competitors for implementing the project, there is no restriction of competition within the meaning of Article 101(1).

238. Similarly, not all reciprocal distribution agreements have as their object a restriction of competition. Depending on the facts of the case at hand, some reciprocal distribution agreements may, nevertheless, have restrictive effects on competition. The key issue in assessing an agreement of this type is whether the agreement in question is objectively necessary for the parties to enter each other's markets. If it is, the agreement does not create competition problems of a horizontal nature. However, if the agreement reduces the decision-making independence of one of the parties with regard to entering the other parties' market or markets by limiting its incentives to do so, it is likely to give rise to restrictive effects on competition. The same reasoning applies to non-reciprocal agreements, where the risk of restrictive effects on competition is, however, less pronounced.

239. Moreover, a distribution agreement can have restrictive effects on competition if it contains vertical restraints, such as restrictions on passive sales, resale price maintenance, etc.

Again, a core issue in assessing restrictive effects is whether the parties have market power. It has been seen that a 'safe harbour' applies where the parties have a combined market share which does not exceed 15 per cent.[120]

C. THE APPLICATION OF ARTICLE 101(3)

As with joint purchasing, there is no block exemption on commercialisation. The Guidelines[121] recognise, however, that commercialisation may generate significant efficiency gains which may be passed on to consumers in the form of lower prices of better product quality or variety, for example

---

[116] Ibid., paras. 244–245.

[117] Ibid., paras. 242–243.

[118] Ibid., paras. 230–233.

[119] Ibid., paras. 234–235.

[120] Ibid., paras. 240–241. In para. 240 the Guidelines actually use the expression 'safe harbour' to describe this threshold.

[121] Ibid., paras. 246–251.

through cost savings resulting from integration of economic activities,[122] integration of marketing functions, or economies of scale or scope. 'However, if the joint commercialisation represents no more than a sales agency without any investment, it is likely to be a disguised cartel and as such unlikely to fulfil the conditions of Article 101(3).'[123] 'The question of indispensability is especially important for those agreements involving price fixing or market allocation, which can only under exceptional circumstances be considered indispensable.'[124]

Joint selling is frequently used in relation to media rights to sporting events[125] and in respect of rights to music and films.[126]

8. STANDARDISATION AGREEMENTS

A. STANDARDISATION AND STANDARD-SETTING

Standardisation agreements are those which 'have as their primary objective the definition of technical or quality requirements with which current or future products, production processes, services or methods may comply'.[127] The Guidelines do not apply to the provision of professional services[128] but do cover agreements on the environmental performance of products or production processes.[129]

Four relevant markets may be affected by a standardisation agreement: (a) that for the product(s) or service(s) to which the standard(s) relate; (b) the relevant technology market, if the standard-setting involves the selection of technology and IPRs are marketed separately from the products to which they relate; (c) the market for standard-setting (if a number of standard-setting bodies or agreements exist); and (d) a distinct market for testing and certification.[130]

Standardisation agreements usually have positive economic effects. However, they will be restrictive by object if used as part of a broader restrictive agreement aimed at excluding actual or potential competitors,[131] or if they influence prices charged to customers.[132] Further, the Commission is concerned that in specific circumstances there may be restrictive effects through a reduction in price competition, foreclosure of innovative technologies, and exclusion of, or discrimination against, certain companies by preventing effective access to the standard.[133]

In respect of standardisation agreements there is a particular concern over IPRs, in particular where a participant in the standard-setting which holds IPRs essential to the standard could obtain

---

[122] Ibid., para. 247 (the efficiency gains must not be savings which result only from the elimination of costs that are inherently part of competition, but must result from the integration of economic activities. A reduction of transport cost which is only a result of customer allocation without any integration of the logistical system can therefore not be regarded as an efficiency gain within the meaning of Art. 101(3)).

[123] Ibid., para. 248.

[124] Ibid., para. 249.

[125] See Section 9.

[126] See, e.g., COMP/30.566, UIP [1989] OJ L226/25 (discussed in Chap. 9) and COMP/38.698, CISAC 16 July 2008, largely annulled, Case T-442/08, International Confederation of Societies of Authors and Composers (CISAC) v Commission EU:T:2013:188, discussed in Chaps. 3 and 12.

[127] Guidelines, para. 257. Standardisation can range from the adoption of consensus standards by the recognised European or national standards bodies, through consortia or fora, to agreements between independent companies (Guidelines, para. 257, n. 1).

[128] Ibid., para. 258.

[129] Ibid., para. 257.

[130] Ibid., para. 261.

[131] As in COMP/35.691, Pre-Insulated Pipe Cartel [1999] OJ L24/1, para. 147. In Case 96/82 etc., IAZ v Commission [1983] 3369 it was held that the agreement between Belgian water companies and Belgian washing machine and dishwasher manufacturers in respect of conformity standards partitioned the market in excluding imports.

[132] Guidelines, paras. 273–276.

[133] Ibid., paras. 264–268.

control over the standard:[134] this could allow post-standardisation 'companies to behave in anti-competitive ways, for example by "holding-up" users after the adoption of the standard either by refusing to license the necessary IPR or by extracting excess rents by way of excessive . . . royalty fees thereby preventing effective access to the standard'.[135] The question of whether, and if so when, the holder of a standard-essential patent may abuse a dominant position through patent ambushes or other practices arising in the standard-setting context is discussed in Chapter 7.

In *EMC v Commission*[136] the GC affirmed the principle that a standard-setting agreement would not infringe Article 101(1) if the standard-setting was non-discriminatory, open, and transparent. The 2010 Guidelines provide detailed guidance on this issue.[137] They lay down four conditions to be fulfilled if a standard-setting agreement, which risks creating market power, is to fall outside Article 101(1). Agreements which do not comply with these principles are not presumed to fall within Article 101(1) but will necessitate a self-assessment to establish whether they do fall within Article 101(1) and, if so, whether Article 101(3) is satisfied.[138] The four conditions are unrestricted participation in the standard-setting; transparent procedure; no obligation to comply with the standard; and effective access to the standard on FRAND (fair, reasonable, and non-discriminatory) terms.

7.3.3. Restrictive effects on competition

Standardisation agreements

Agreements normally not restrictive of competition

280. Where participation in standard-setting is unrestricted and the procedure for adopting the standard in question is transparent, standardisation agreements which contain no obligation to comply . . . with the standard and provide access to the standard on fair, reasonable and non-discriminatory terms will normally not restrict competition within the meaning of Article 101(1).

281. In particular, to ensure unrestricted participation the rules of the standard-setting organisation would need to guarantee that all competitors in the market or markets affected by the standard can participate in the process leading to the selection of the standard. The standard-setting organisations would also need to have objective and non-discriminatory procedures for allocating voting rights as well as, if relevant, objective criteria for selecting the technology to be included in the standard.

282. With respect to transparency, the relevant standard-setting organisation would need to have procedures which allow stakeholders to effectively inform themselves of upcoming, on-going and finalised standardisation work in good time at each stage of the development of the standard.

283. Furthermore, the standard-setting organisation's rules would need to ensure effective access to the standard on fair, reasonable and non discriminatory terms . . .

284. In the case of a standard involving IPR, a clear and balanced IPR policy . . . adapted to the particular industry and the needs of the standard-setting organisation in question, increases the likelihood that the implementers of the standard will be granted effective access to the standards elaborated by that standard-setting organisation.

285. In order to ensure effective access to the standard, the IPR policy would need to require participants wishing to have their IPR included in the standard to provide an irrevocable commitment in writing to offer to license their essential IPR to all third parties on fair, reasonable and non-discriminatory terms ('FRAND commitment') . . . That commitment should be given prior to the adoption of the standard. At the same time, the IPR policy should allow IPR holders to exclude specified technology from the

---

[134] See Chap. 7.

[135] Guidelines, para. 269.

[136] Case T-432/05, [2010] ECR II-1629, appeal dismissed by Order, Case C-367/10, [2011] ECR I-46.

[137] Guidelines, paras. 280–291.

[138] Ibid., para. 279.

standard-setting process and thereby from the commitment to offer to license, providing that exclusion takes place at an early stage in the development of the standard. To ensure the effectiveness of the FRAND commitment, there would also need to be a requirement on all participating IPR holders who provide such a commitment to ensure that any company to which the IPR owner transfers its IPR (including the right to license that IPR) is bound by that commitment, for example through a contractual clause between buyer and seller.

286. Moreover, the IPR policy would need to require good faith disclosure, by participants, of their IPR that might be essential for the implementation of the standard under development. This would enable the industry to make an informed choice of technology and thereby assist in achieving the goal of effective access to the standard. Such a disclosure obligation could be based on ongoing disclosure as the standard develops and on reasonable endeavours to identify IPR reading on the potential standard . . . It is also sufficient if the participant declares that it is likely to have IPR claims over a particular technology (without identifying specific IPR claims or applications for IPR). Since the risks with regard to effective access are not the same in the case of a standard-setting organisation with a royalty-free standards policy, IPR disclosure would not be relevant in that context.

FRAND Commitments

287. FRAND commitments are designed to ensure that essential IPR protected technology incorporated in a standard is accessible to the users of that standard on fair, reasonable and non-discriminatory terms and conditions. In particular, FRAND commitments can prevent IPR holders from making the implementation of a standard difficult by refusing to license or by requesting unfair or unreasonable fees (in other words excessive fees) after the industry has been locked-in to the standard or by charging discriminatory royalty fees.

Where these principles are not fulfilled paragraphs 292–299 of the Guidelines set out the considerations which must be taken into account in assessing whether Article 101(1) applies. These are whether: (a) the members of the standard-setting organisation remain free to develop alternative standards or procedures; (b) the terms and conditions on which access to the standard is given; (c) whether participation in the standard-setting process is open; and (d) what are the market shares of the goods or services based on the standard ('although high market shares will not necessarily lead to the conclusion that the standard is likely to give rise to restrictive effects on competition').

If a standardisation agreement does fall within Article 101(1) there is no block exemption, but they may satisfy the Article 101(3) conditions.[139] Indeed the Guidelines recognise their considerable scope to achieve efficiencies to the benefit of consumers[140] through, for example: the creation of Union-wide standards which may facilitate market integration and allow companies to market their goods and services in all Member States; increasing consumer choice and decreasing prices; establishing technical interoperability and compatibility; reducing transaction costs for sellers and buyers; facilitating consumer choice and increasing product quality; reducing the time taken to bring a new technology to the market; and facilitating innovation by allowing companies to build on top of agreed solutions.[141] The Guidelines set out important information relating to the indispensability requirement:

316. Participation in standard-setting should normally be open to all competitors in the market or markets affected by the standard unless the parties demonstrate significant inefficiencies of such participation or recognised procedures are foreseen for the collective representation of interests . . .

---

[139] See, e.g., COMP/29.151, *Philips VCR*; COMP/31.458, *X/Open Group*; COMP/34.179 etc., *Dutch Cranes* [1995] OJ L312/79; COMP/39.416, *Ship Classification* Commitments Decision 14 October 2009.

[140] Guidelines, paras. 321–323 ('Where standards facilitate technical interoperability and compatibility or competition between new and already existing products, services and processes, it can be presumed that the standard will benefit consumers').

[141] Ibid., para. 308.

317. As a general rule standardisation agreements should cover no more than what is necessary to ensure their aims, whether this is technical interoperability and compatibility or a certain level of quality. In cases where having only one technological solution would benefit consumers or the economy at large that standard should be set on a non-discriminatory basis. Technology neutral standards can, in certain circumstances, lead to larger efficiency gains. Including substitute IPR . . . as essential parts of a standard while at the same time forcing the users of the standard to pay for IPR than technically necessary would go beyond what is necessary to achieve any identified efficiency gains. In the same vein, including substitute IPR as essential parts of a standard and limiting the use of that technology to that particular standard (that is to say, exclusive use) could limit inter-technology competition and would not be necessary to achieve the efficiencies identified.

318. Restrictions in a standardisation agreement making a standard binding and obligatory for the industry are in principle not indispensable.

319. In a similar vein, standardisation agreements that entrust certain bodies with the exclusive right to test compliance with the standard go beyond the primary objective of defining the standard and may also restrict competition. The exclusivity can, however, be justified for a certain period of time, for example by the need to recoup significant start-up costs . . . The standardisation agreement should in that case include adequate safeguards to mitigate possible risks to competition resulting from exclusivity. This concerns, inter alia, the certification fee which needs to be reasonable and proportionate to the cost of the compliance testing.

. . .

B. STANDARDISATION AGREEMENTS WITH ENVIRONMENTAL BENEFITS

Environmental agreements are no longer dealt with in a separate section in the Guidelines but there are cases in which the Commission has allowed standardisation agreements with environmental benefits, either because they fell outside Article 101(1) or because they satisfied Article 101(3). In *CECED*,[142] the Commission granted an exemption to an agreement between washing machine manufacturers to cease production and importation of less efficient machines despite such agreement being restrictive by object under Article 101(1). Its benefits were mainly collective environmental ones. The Commission also gave an individual exemption in *DSD*[143] in respect of exclusive service agreements which facilitated the collection and disposal of waste packaging. The *CECED* decision is not mentioned expressly in the Guidelines, but Example 5 in paragraph 329 appears to be based upon it.

C. STANDARD TERMS

The Guidelines also deal with standard terms. The standard terms may cover only a small part of the final contract or a very large part. When standard terms are used by most of the industry and/ or for most parts of the product or service it leads to a limitation or lack of consumer choice.[144] The effects of standard terms are felt on the downstream market where the companies using them compete for customers.[145] It is possible for standard terms to have restrictive effects on competition by limiting product choice and innovation and restricting price competition.[146] Standard terms which directly influence prices charged to customers are restrictive by object.[147] However, anti-competitive

---

[142] COMP/36.718, [2000] OJ L187/47 (discussed in Chap. 4). This decision was followed by approval of a similar agreement concerning dishwashers: see Commission Press Release IP/01/1659.

[143] COMP/34.493, [2001] OJ L319/1. An appeal by the undertaking against the obligations to which the exemption was subject was dismissed: Case T-289/01, *Der Grüne Punkt-Duales System Deutschland v Commission* [2007] ECR II-1691. Negative clearance was given to a waste disposal scheme in France in *Eco-Emballages* [2001] OJ L233/37.

[144] Guidelines, para. 259 and see Chap. 9. Standard terms play an important role in the banking and insurance sectors.

[145] Ibid., para. 262.

[146] Ibid., paras. 270–271.

[147] Ibid., para. 276.

foreclosure is unlikely if the standard terms are open for anyone to use.[148] When considering restrictive effects, therefore, the question is whether participation in the establishment of standard terms is unrestricted for competitors in the relevant market, and whether the established standard terms are non-binding and effectively accessible.[149]

As far as the application of Article 101(3) is concerned, the Commission view is that such agreements can entail economic benefits for consumers[150] through: making it easier for customers to compare the conditions offered and thus facilitating switching between companies; leading to savings in transaction costs; facilitating entry; and increasing legal certainty for the contract parties.[151] 'The higher the number of competitors on the market, the greater the efficiency gain of facilitating the comparison of conditions offered.'[152] Given that the risk of restrictive effects on competition and the likelihood of efficiency gains increase with the companies' market shares and the extent to which the standard terms are used, the Guidelines states that it is not possible to provide any general 'safe harbour' for standard agreements 'within which there is no risk of restrictive effects on competition or which would allow the presumption that efficiency gains will be passed on to consumers to an extent that outweighs the restrictive effects on competition'.[153]

9. AGREEMENTS IN PARTICULAR SECTORS

A. GENERAL

In this section we refer briefly to some cases arising in some particular sectors.[154]

B. INSURANCE

The Commission has in the past granted exemptions to horizontal cooperation agreements in the insurance sector; for example, in *Concordato Incendio* (fire insurance premiums)[155] and *Nuovo CEGAM* (basic premiums of engineering insurers).[156]

The Commission issued a block exemption, Regulation 358/2003, in the insurance sector to deal with, inter alia, common risk premium tariffs, non-binding standard policy conditions, and the common coverage of certain risks.[157] Although this Regulation was replaced in 2010 by Regulation 267/2010,[158] this Regulation expires at the end of March 2017 and the Commission is considering whether an industry-specific block exemption is still required or appropriate. The exemption covers the joint compilation and distribution of information necessary for calculating the average cost of covering a specified risk in the past, constructing tables on matters such as mortality

---

[148] Ibid., para. 272.

[149] Ibid., paras. 300–307.

[150] Ibid., para. 323 (certain efficiency gains, 'such as increased comparability of the offers on the market, facilitated switching between providers, and legal certainty of the clauses set out in the standard terms, are necessarily beneficial for the consumers').

[151] Ibid., para. 312.

[152] Ibid., para. 313.

[153] Ibid., para. 322.

[154] There have also been a number of cases involving airline alliances, see, e.g., nn. 21 and 64 and Bellamy and Child, n. 94, Chap. 6.

[155] COMP/32.265, [1990] OJ L15/25.

[156] COMP/30.084, [1984] OJ L99/29. But contrast COMP/30.307, *Fire Insurance* [1985] OJ L35/20 (exemption refused to recommendations by German property insurers about an increase in fire insurance rates), aff'd Case 45/85, *VdS v Commission* [1987] ECR 405.

[157] [2003] OJ L53/8, replacing Reg. 3932/92.

[158] [2010] OJ L83/1.

and illness, and the joint carrying out of studies on the probable impact of general circumstances external to the interested undertakings.[159] The exemption is subject to conditions (Article 3). The Regulation also exempts agreements for setting up and operating pools of insurance undertakings or reinsurance undertakings for the common coverage of a specific category of risks. The exemption is subject to market share thresholds (20 per cent combined market share for insurance pools and 25 per cent for reinsurance pools).[160]

C. PAYMENT SERVICES

In Chapter 9 it was seen that the Commission has been particularly concerned about anti-competitive agreements concluded in the financial sector. An important question has been how cooperation agreements should be analysed under Article 101. Chapter 9 examined the cases dealing with how payment systems incorporating multilateral interchanges fees (MIFs) have been assessed under Article 101. In Chapter 4 it was also seen that the CJ in *Groupement des Cartes Bancaires v Commission*,[161] found that the GC had erred in upholding a Commission decision finding that measures agreed by the French banks which increased the cost of issuing cards infringed Article 101(1) by object. The case has now been remitted to the GC to determine whether the Commission was correct to find that the effect of the agreement was to restrict competition (and did not satisfy the conditions of Article 101(3) as no efficiency gains or consumer benefits had been demonstrated).

D. SPORT

(i) General

Examples of cases involving sport have been examined throughout this book (in relation to Article 102 as well as Article 101) and it has been seen that the practice of sport (especially commercial exploitation of sport) falls within the scope of the competition law rules insofar as it constitutes an economic activity (only a very limited sporting exception applies).[162] An outline of some of the issues is also set out here as rules of sporting organisations often stem from horizontal agreements between their members or constituent bodies.[163]

Annex 1 to the Staff Working Document accompanying the Commission White Paper on Sport of July 2007[164] sets out examples of sporting rules which are likely and unlikely to comply with the competition rules. According to the Annex, rules that are more likely to comply include the selection criteria for competitions; 'home and away' rules;[165] transfer periods; nationality requirements in respect of national teams; prohibitions on multiple club or team ownership; anti-doping rules; and the basic rules of the game (such as duration, the off-side rule, the number of players, etc.). Rules less likely to comply include rules shielding sports associations from competition for commercial reasons; rules regarding professions ancillary to the sport itself (for example, football agents); and

---

[159] Ibid., Art. 2.

[160] Ibid., Art. 6.

[161] Case C-67/13 P, EU:C:2014:2204.

[162] See, e.g., Case C-519/04 P, *Meca-Medina and Majcen v Commission* [2006] ECR I-699; Case C-49/07, *Motosykletistiki Omospondia Ellados NPID (MOTOE) v Ellinkio Dimosi* [2008] ECR I-4863. For a summary of the application of the competition rules to sport, see Chap. 2. In 2014, the Commission rejected a complaint, on prioritisation grounds, in relation to UEFA's financial fair play rule, see COMP/40.105, 24 October 2014.

[163] But see, e.g., O. Budzinski and S. Szumanski, 'Are Restrictions of Competition by Sports Associations Horizontal or Vertical in Nature?' (2015) 11 *J of Competition Law and Economics* 409.

[164] The EU and Sport: Background and Context, SEC(2007) 935, accompanying the White Paper, COM(2007) 391 final. For a full discussion of Annex 1 see P. Kienapfel and A. Stein, 'The Application of Articles 81 and 82 EC in the Sports Sector' (2007) 3 *Competition Policy Newsletter* 6.

[165] See COMP/36.851, IP/99/365.

rules excluding legal challenges to sport associations' decisions before the ordinary courts. The Annex expressly does not take a view on the questions of UEFA's home-grown players rule, salary caps in professional football, and the release for national teams rule.[166]

(ii) Joint Buying

Joint buying of sports media rights is analysed in Annex 1 to the Staff Working Document. The Commission explained its concerns:

3.1.4 In the downstream markets joint buying arrangements may also be caught under Article [101(1)], in particular when the exclusive acquisition of sports media rights leads to foreclosure and output restrictions as a result of vertical restraints in agreements between seller and buyer or by horizontal agreements between different buyers. In cases where *ex ante* (single or collective) dominance exists at the acquisition market, under certain circumstances the acquisition and use of exclusive sports media rights could constitute an abuse of dominance by the buyer within the meaning of Article [102].

Foreclosure issues are especially relevant whenever exclusive rights constitute 'premium' content. In such situations (mostly concerning broadcasting rights for live football matches), competition may be adversely affected through the monopolisation of the acquisition of this premium content, if this content is an essential input for effective competition in the downstream market . . . In addition, because of insecurity about techno-logical developments, the existence of some substitution between different platforms and asymmetric value of rights, powerful operators on one retail market may seek to prevent players in neighbouring markets from acquiring meaningful rights. The acquisition of exclusive audiovisual rights for all platforms by a powerful retail operator in one downstream market (e.g., a pay-TV operator) may create additional anti-competitive *foreclosure effects in neighbouring markets* (e.g., 3G mobile telephony), thereby hampering the development of new services.

Output restrictions may occur when exclusive rights, which are either bought collectively by different op-erators or bought by a dominant firm for one or more downstream markets, are subsequently not exploited by the buyers.

The Commission may consider structural or behavioural remedies to address these concerns.[167]

(iii) The Joint Selling of Media Rights to Sporting Events

The Commission has been much concerned with the joint selling of commercial rights[168] to sport-ing events, particularly the collective selling of media rights by a football association or league on behalf of individual member football clubs. Broadly, it accepts that such joint selling[169] may be ben-eficial in principle. In the Helsinki Report on Sport in 1999 it stated:

Any exemptions granted in the case of the joint sale of broadcasting rights must take account of the ben-efits for consumers and of the proportional nature of the restriction on competition in relation to the legiti-mate objective pursued. In this context, there is also a need to examine the extent to which a link can be

---

[166] Annex 1, 2.3. The rule requiring football teams to release players required for national teams in interna-tional competition was before the CJ in a preliminary reference, Case C-243/06, *SA Sporting du Pays de Charleroi and Groupement des clubs de football européens v FIFA* but was removed from the register, [2009] OJ C69/30.

[167] Annex 1, 3.1.4.2.

[168] Media rights (radio, television, internet, and UMTS), sponsorship, suppliership, licensing, and IPRs, see, e.g., J. Faull and A. Nikpay (eds.), *The EU Law of Competition* (3rd edn, Oxford University Press, 2014), 14.63–14.69. It has also been concerned with the arrangements for selling tickets for sporting events, see, e.g., cases relating to, respec-tively, tickets sales for the 1990, 1998, and 2006 World Cups, e.g., COMP/33.384 and COMP/33.378, *The Distribution of Package Tours During the 1990 World Cup* [1992] OJ L326/31, COMP/36.888, *1998 World Cup Finals* [2000] OJ L5/55, and COMP/39.177, *Which?/DFB+Mastercard+FIFA*, IP/05/519.

[169] The consequences of football media rights being sold by individual clubs can be seen by looking at the posi-tion in Spain, where the rights are not sold collectively, and La Liga is dominated by two clubs. This is not to suggest that money is the only reason for Barcelona's success.

established between the joint sale of rights and financial solidarity between professional and amateur sport, the objectives of the training of young sportsmen and women and those of promoting sporting activities among the population. However, with regard to the sale of exclusive rights to broadcast sporting events, it is likely that any exclusivity which, by its duration and/or scope, resulted in the closing of the market, would be prohibited.[170]

An EU declaration on sport, based on the Helsinki Report, pronounced at the European Council in Nice in December 2000, recognised the social, educational, and cultural functions of sport and laid down principles with a view to preserving, inter alia, 'the cohesion and ties of solidarity that exist in sport at all levels' and fair competition. Of the sale of television rights it said:

As the sale of television broadcasting rights is one of the greatest sources of income for certain sports, the sharing of part of the corresponding revenue among the appropriate levels may be beneficial in order to preserve the principle of solidarity in sport.

The Commission generally accepts joint selling, however, only so long as certain conditions are satisfied (for example, that there is an open and transparent tender process, licences are granted for a limited duration, and the rights are broken into several packages to allow several competitors to acquire the rights, the so-called single buyer rule). The single buyer condition, however, has the result that viewers of sports channels often have to subscribe to more than one broadcaster in order to watch all the available matches in a particular league. For the ordinary sports fan the intervention of the Commission in the collective selling of football rights has created inconvenience and expense.

In particular, in its *UEFA* decision, the Commission stressed how valuable rights to screen football matches are.

In most countries football is not only the driving force for the development of pay-TV services but is also an essential programme item for free-TV broadcasters. Joint selling of free-TV and pay-TV rights combined with wide exclusive terms therefore has significant effects on the structure of the TV broadcasting markets as it can enhance media concentration and hamper competition between broadcasters. If one broadcaster holds all or most of the relevant football TV rights in a Member State, it is extremely difficult for competing broadcasters to establish themselves successfully in that market.[171]

This case concerned the arrangements for selling the media rights to the UEFA[172] Champions League. The Commission only exempted the arrangements following a lengthy negotiation and an agreement by UEFA to amend aspects of the arrangements.

The Commission adopted a commitments decision in respect of the German Bundesliga's joint selling of broadcasting rights,[173] which permitted joint selling on similar terms to those agreed in the *UEFA* case. The Bundesliga was to make several packages available to broadcasters and exclusivity was not to last longer than three years at a time. This was the first commitments decision taken under Article 9 of Regulation 1/2003.[174] The major leagues and international authorities consequently know that it is the norm for the Commission to be interested in their collective selling negotiations.

---

[170] Report from the Commission to the European Council with a view to safeguarding current sports structures and maintaining the social function of sport within the Community framework (The Helsinki Report on Sport), 10 December 1999, para. 4.2.1.3. See also Annex 1 to the Staff Working Document.

[171] *Joint selling of the commercial rights of the UEFA Champions League* [2003] OJ L291/25, para. 20.

[172] An association of national football associations and the regulatory authority of European football.

[173] COMP/ 37.214, *DFB* 19 January 2005. See also COMP/38.173, *Joint Selling of the Media Rights to the FA Premier League* 22 March 2006.

[174] See further Chap. 13.

10. CONCLUSIONS

1. The Commission's current policy towards horizontal cooperation agreements, as reflected in the Guidelines, is to take a realistic view, based on an economic analysis, of whether an agreement restricts competition. A consideration of market power is central to the inquiry.

2. The abolition of individual notification under Regulation 1/2003 poses considerable problems for parties entering into cooperation arrangements in that outside the scope of the R&D and production block exemptions they must 'self-assess' in respect of operations where the scale of the overall cooperation and the resources involved may be very large. The 2010 Guidelines are an attempt to give as much detailed guidance as possible, but all depends on the specific facts of the individual case.

3. There are increasing problems with standard-setting, particularly in the area of the digital economy, and the 2010 Guidelines constitute an important development in the Commission's policy towards them.

11. FURTHER READING

ARTICLES

BJÖRKROTH, T., 'Joint Purchasing Agreements in the Food Supply Chain: Who's in the Sheep's Clothing?' (2013) 9 *European Competition Journal* 175

BRODLEY, J., 'Joint Ventures and Antitrust Policy' (1982) 95 *Harvard LR* 1521

BROOKS, R., and GERADIN, D., 'Interpreting and Enforcing the Voluntary FRAND Commitment' (2011) 9 *International J of IT Standards and Standardization Research* 1

CAMESASCA, P., and SCHMIDT, A., 'New EC Horizontal Guidelines: Providing Helpful Guidance in the Highly Diverse and Complex Field of Competitor Cooperation and Information Exchange' (2011) 2 *JECLAP* 227

GERADIN, D., LAYNE-FARRAR, A., and PADILLA, A. J., 'Competing Away Market Power? An Economic Assessment of *Ex Ante* Auctions in Standard Setting' (2008) 4 *European Competition Journal* 443

KATTAN, J., 'Antitrust Analysis of Technology Joint Ventures: Allocative Efficiency and the Rewards of Innovation' (1993) 61 *Antitrust LJ* 937

KIENAPFEL, P., and STEIN, A., 'The Application of Articles 81 and 82 EC in the Sports Sector' (2007) 3 *Competition Policy Newsletter* 6

KITCH, E., 'The Antitrust Economics of Joint Ventures' (1987) 54 *Antitrust LJ* 957

MCAULEY, D., 'Exclusively for All and Collectively for None: Refereeing Broadcasting Rights Between the Premier League, the European Commission and BSkyB' [2004] *ECLR* 370

NITSCHE, I., 'Collective Marketing of Broadcasting by Sports Associations in Europe' [2000] *ECLR* 208

PIESIEWICZ, G., and SCHELLINGERHOUR, R., 'Intellectual Property Rights in Standard Setting from a Competition Law Perspective' (2007) 3 *Competition Policy Newsletter* 36

WILBERT, S., 'Joint Selling of Bundesliga Media Rights—First Commission Decision Pursuant to Article 9 of Regulation 1/2003' (2005) 2 *Competition Policy Newsletter* 44

11

VERTICAL AGREEMENTS

1. CENTRAL ISSUES

1. Vertical agreements provide the links in the distribution chain from raw material to the final consumer.

2. Vertical agreements are ordinarily concluded between firms which operate at different levels of the production and supply chain; the parties thus produce complementary products or services, not competing products or services. Vertical agreements are frequently pro-competitive.

3. In 1999, after consultation and debate, the Commission, accepting that vertical restraints are generally less harmful than horizontal ones and are unlikely to give rise to competition concerns unless there is insufficient competition at one or more levels of trade, overhauled and modernised the regime governing vertical agreements. It adopted a broad block exemption for vertical agreements and published accompanying Guidelines. The block exemption and Guidelines were reviewed and replaced in May 2010. The block exemption provides a safe harbour for many vertical agreements: in particular, where the parties' market shares do not exceed 30 per cent and where the agreement does not contain any 'hardcore' restraints.

4. Only if the block exemption does not apply is individual assessment of a vertical agreement required to determine whether or not it infringes Article 101(1) and, if it does, whether it satisfies the conditions of Article 101(3).

5. Agreements containing provisions which restrict competition by object (which the Commission equates with 'hardcore' restraints), are treated with suspicion and are unlikely to be found to be compatible with Article 101 in practice.

6. Neither the jurisprudence, nor the Guidelines, provide much guidance on how Article 101 analysis should be conducted in relation to newer forms of distribution practice, which have developed as online selling has continued to advance at breathtaking pace.

2. INTRODUCTION

A. GENERAL

A manufacturer of a product (or a supplier of a service) is not solely concerned with manufacturing. If it does not itself use that product as an input, it must also plan for its distribution. Generally, the manufacturer will wish to minimise the costs of distribution and to ensure that its products are distributed to customers in the most efficient manner. Broadly, this may be achieved either by distributing the product itself or by delegating the task to a third party (for example, an independent distributor or an agent). Similarly, a supplier of a service will need to decide how best to distribute its services.

This chapter starts by outlining the choices available to a supplier when deciding how best to market and sell its products or services to customers and the impact that the competition rules may have on a supplier's choice. The discussion focuses, however, on distribution agreements concluded between vertically related firms, for example a manufacturer and an independent wholesaler or retailer[1] (the terms supplier and distributor or dealer will generally be used to describe the up-stream and downstream parties respectively in this chapter), and the competition law problems that such agreements raise under Article 101.[2] These problems differ significantly from those raised in relation to horizontal agreements considered in prior chapters since the agreements are not usu-ally concluded by competitors (actual or potential), but by suppliers of complementary products or services; 'manufacturers and distributors are partners whose cooperation is essential to maxi-mizing both of their profits'. Consequently, 'normally (when neither have market power) their self-interested action leads to greater welfare to society. That is to say, when a manufacturer "restrains" its distributors, it normally does this because it expects that as a result sales will increase, and such an effect benefits manufacturer and distributor, and also consumers.'[3]

This first section outlines the main pro- and anti-competitive effects that may result from vertical restraints and the consequences that the debate about these competing effects has for an-titrust analysis. Section 3 charts the evolution in policy towards vertical restraints and, in particu-lar, the modernised approach heralded by the adoption in 1999 of a generic block exemption on vertical restraints,[4] together with accompanying Guidelines.[5] Following review and consultation,[6] these were replaced in 2010 by the current block exemption, Regulation 330/2010 (the Verticals Regulation)[7] and Guidelines on Vertical Restraints (the Guidelines).[8] In Sections 4 and 5 the applica-tion of Article 101(1) and Article 101(3) (including the Verticals Regulation) to vertical agreements is assessed. In Sections 6 and 7 subcontracting agreements and the possible application of Article 102 to distribution agreements are outlined. Section 8 concludes that some problems remain with the post-1999 regime. For example, not only does the existence of a broad block exemption regula-tion somewhat cloud the relationship between Article 101(1) and Article 101(3), but the rigid ap-proach to certain 'object' or 'hardcore' restraints may still be deterring the conclusion and operation of vertical agreements with efficiency-enhancing effects. Further, a clear picture is not yet emerg-ing as to how EU competition law governs new vertical models of distribution, including through online platforms, and how it should apply to a raft of newer contractual provisions impacting on online selling.

B. METHODS OF DISTRIBUTION

(i) Factors Affecting Choice

Essentially a supplier has the choice of distributing its product itself (through employees or a sub-sidiary), through the market using an independent distributor, or through a hybrid model using some other type of intermediary or an agent. The method of distribution selected by a supplier is likely to be determined after consideration of a wide range of factors. In particular, the relative costs of organising distribution internally compared with the costs of using the market or an agent, the nature of the product or service, the nature of the market, the size and resources of the supplier, and any tax or legal implications will be relevant to the assessment.

---

[1] An agreement between a manufacturer of a component and a producer of a product that uses that component is also a vertical agreement.

[2] Vertical restraints incorporated in contracts concluded by a dominant supplier are dealt with in Chap. 7.

[3] G. Monti, 'Restraints on Selective Distribution Agreements' (2013) 36 *World Competition* 489, 490.

[4] Reg. 2790/1999 [1999] OJ L336/21.

[5] [2000] OJ C291/1.

[6] A draft regulation and guidelines and the responses filed are available on DG Comp's website.

[7] [2010] OJ L102/1.

[8] [2010] OJ C130/10.

(ii) Vertical Integration

Whatever mode is selected, a supplier is likely to want to keep some control over how its products are distributed. It is likely to be able to retain maximum control by taking charge of distribution itself. This may be appealing to a supplier with considerable resources seeking to sell a highly complex product or to a supplier seeking to sell a high volume of low-margin product. The supplier may set up a distribution arm (internal growth) or may acquire an undertaking that is already in the distribution business (external growth).

A decision to move into distribution may, however, be impractical and/or an inefficient use of a firm's resources. There may not be a close fit between the supplier's product and the retailer's scope, the firm may become less efficient, and management may find it harder to keep track of what the firm's employees are doing as it grows, or the firm may simply not have the resources to move into retailing.

Retailers commonly secure economies of scope by offering the consumer under one roof dozens or even thousands of products, often gathered together from a diversity of manufacturers. It would be prohibitively costly for the manufacturer of paper towels, crescent wrenches, or antibiotics to establish its own retail distribution facilities in order to control the conditions under which its product is resold to consumers. And even when there is a reasonably close fit between manufacturer product line and retail outlets' scope, as in automobiles, major appliances, or photo supplies, the two stages require quite different skills, attitudes, and spans of managerial focus, and the advantages of specialization typically require that retailers be kept separate organizationally from their primary suppliers.[9]

In many cases a supplier may, therefore, consider it preferable to leave distribution to entities that are experienced in retailing and who know more about the markets and customers to be targeted. In particular, local distributors may be able to penetrate new markets more quickly and effectively.

(iii) Agency and Other Intermediaries

Whether or not a supplier decides to appoint a commercial agent or an independent distributor is likely to be dependent mainly on the independence it wishes the third party to be given, the risk it wishes to bear, and the responsibilities of the supplier on the termination of the relationship. Ordinarily, the functions of an agent are restricted and limited to negotiating sales or purchasing agreements on behalf of a principal. Indeed, the Commission defines agency agreements in the Guidelines as 'the situation in which a legal or physical person (the agent) is vested with the power to negotiate and/or conclude contracts on behalf of another person (the principal), either in the agent's own name or in the name of the principal, for the: purchase of goods or services by the principal, or sale of goods or services supplied by the principal'.[10] It thus typically operates as a marketing resource for the principal and bears little responsibility for the products it negotiates to sell. Agents usually receive either a commission based on the sales they make or a fixed salary.[11]

As the internet and online distribution has taken off, many suppliers now sell through intermediaries, such as online marketplaces or platforms which provide distribution (and other) services for a supplier in return for a fee or a sales commission. Indeed, the development of the internet generally

---

[9] F. M. Scherer and D. Ross, *Industrial Market Structure and Economic Performance* (3rd edn, Houghton Mifflin, 1990), 542.

[10] Guidelines, para. 12.

[11] If any agent appointed satisfies the definition of a 'commercial agent' set out in Council Dir. 86/653 on the coordination of the laws of the Member States relating to self-employed commercial agents [1986] OJ L382/17 (a self-employed intermediary who has continuing authority to negotiate the sale or purchase of goods on behalf of another person (his principal) or to negotiate and conclude such transactions on behalf of and in the name of the principal), that Directive contains provisions relating, for example, to the remuneration payable to it during the term of the agreement and as to indemnification or compensation on the termination or expiration of the agency contract, see Arts. 1(2) and 19, see, e.g., J. Goyder, *EU Distribution Law* (5th edn, Hart Publishing, 2011), 6.3.

has dramatically changed the way in which products and services are distributed to consumers. In the EU, a challenge is for competition agencies to consider how these new business practices should be analysed under Article 101.

(iv) Distribution through Independent Distributors

Alternatively, distribution may be left to an independent distributor that will itself sell, or use, the goods or supply the services. Where an independent undertaking is chosen, a distribution agreement will be necessary. A supplier may simply wish to ensure that its products or services are distributed through as many outlets as possible. Alternatively or additionally restrictions and obligations limiting the number or type of distributors or restricting the conduct of the distributors may be considered necessary to make the distribution agreement commercially viable and/or acceptable. Although restraints in vertical agreements were at one time treated with extreme suspicion in both the US and the EU, it is now recognised that they are frequently imposed for pro-competitive purposes and with the objective of minimising distribution costs, of ensuring efficient and effective distribution arrangements, and of enhancing sales of the supplier's product.[12] In short, they aim to bring a product or service to market in the most efficient manner. A supplier may, for example, wish to encourage consumers to purchase its product by requiring its distributors to provide specific services, to contribute to the creation of a brand image for the contract product or service, and/or to concentrate their selling efforts on the supplier's products. Additionally, the supplier may wish to conclude an agreement which allows it to exploit economies of scale in distribution.

A distributor may not be willing to incur the costs involved in providing specific services unless other distributors, who are not subject to similar promotional, servicing, and/or stocking obligation, are prevented from taking a free-ride on its promotional or other efforts (*free-riders*). The supplier may, therefore, only be able to influence the level of services furnished by its distributors by selecting or limiting the number of dealers it appoints and/or by limiting competition between them. The supplier may achieve this, for example, by:

- granting each dealer an exclusive sales territory (*exclusive distribution*) or allocating it an exclusive customer group (*exclusive customer allocation*). This may be reinforced by imposing restraints on the territories into which, or the customers to whom, the dealers, and the supplier itself, may sell the contract products or services (*territorial or customer restraints*). In the EU, it will be seen that a ban on internet selling is generally treated as a territorial restraint as it prevents a dealer from selling to a broader audience.

  Where the supplier is obliged or induced to sell the contract products only or mainly to one single buyer, there is an *exclusive supply agreement*. *Upfront access payments*, fixed fees that suppliers pay to distributors in order to get access to their distribution networks or to remunerate services provided to the suppliers by the retailers (such as slotting allowances and 'pay to stay' fees to ensure access to shelf-space), may induce a supplier to sell through only one distributor, or a limited number of distributors and so may operate like an exclusive supply agreement;

- specifying the price at which the products may be resold, for example a fixed or a minimum resale price (*resale price maintenance* (RPM)) or a maximum resale price (*maximum RPM*);

- selecting the type or number of outlets in which the supplier's products are sold and precluding dealers from selling to unauthorised distributors outside the network (*selective distribution*). 'Selective distribution is almost always used to distribute branded final products.'[13] An important issue which has arisen in the EU, is whether suppliers choosing a selective distribution system (SDS) can prevent online distribution of their products.

---

[12] See further n. 55 and text.
[13] Guidelines, para. 174.

In recent years, businesses have also started more frequently to incorporate most favoured nation clauses (MFNs) into their distribution agreements or concluded price relationship agreements or contracts that reference rivals' prices.[14] MFNs are a form of price relationship agreement under which a supplier constrains its ability to price discriminate amongst customers by promising to treat a customer no less favourably than other customers, for example that it will not provide its products to other customers at lower prices (and/or if it does it will also reduce the price to that customer) (wholesale MFNs) or that it will not sell its products on the agent's platform at a price higher than on which it sells on other platforms or which it sells itself (retail MFNs or Across Platform Parity Agreements (APPAs)).

MFNs, like exclusive distribution, territorial and customer restraints, RPM and SDSs, limit *intra-brand* competition (competition between distributors of the supplier's product or service) and may arguably be designed to encourage distributors to concentrate their selling efforts on the suppliers' products and so to increase *inter-brand* competition (competition between the supplier and producers of competing products).

In addition, and in order to ensure security of supply, purchase price and/or focused selling efforts, a vertical agreement may incorporate restraints which limit competition between the supplier and producers of competing goods and services and hence *inter-brand competition*. It may preclude or deter dealers from manufacturing, buying, marketing, or selling products which compete with the contract goods or services (through *non-competition provisions*, *quantity forcing*, or *requirements contracts*). For example:

- the distributor may be obliged, or have incentives, to purchase a specific brand of product exclusively from the supplier (in the Guidelines the Commission describes this kind of obligation as *exclusive sourcing*. Exclusive sourcing does not preclude the distributor from purchasing or selling competing goods or services from another supplier);[15]

- the distributor may be precluded from manufacturing, buying, marketing, and/or selling competing products or services (*non-compete* or *non-competition obligations*) or required to purchase a specific percentage or a specific amount of its requirements of a type of product from the supplier (*quantity forcing* or *requirements contracts*). The Commission describes agreements in which a buyer is induced to concentrate orders for a type of product with one supplier as *single branding* agreements.[16] Upfront access payments may operate like single branding provisions if widespread use of such payments creates barriers to entry for small entrants. Further *category management agreements*, by which the distributors entrust the supplier (the category captain) with the marketing of a category of products (including the suppliers' and its competitors' products), may foreclose other suppliers and operate like single branding agreements if the category captain is able to disadvantage the distribution of products of competing suppliers;[17]

- the distributor may be required to purchase a second distinct (tied) product as a condition of purchasing the first (tying) product (*tying*);

- distributors may be required not to open a competing business for a certain period after the distribution agreement has been terminated. Such an obligation may be of particular importance in, for example, a *franchising agreement* where a supplier, a franchisor, grants the right to a distributor, a franchisee, to exploit a franchise and to set up a business marketing specified

---

[14] In other price relationship agreements a supplier may require a reseller to set the resale price of its product at a price related to the price set for a competitor's product or offer a price match guarantee by which the price paid by the buyer is related to a price charged by a competitor for competing products.

[15] This eliminates arbitrage between distributors, Guidelines, para. 162. Exclusive sourcing is frequently backed by a non-compete obligation, a prohibition on selling competing products: see, e.g., Case C-234/89, *Delimitis v Henninger Bräu* [1991] ECR I-935, para. 10.

[16] Guidelines, para. 129.

[17] Ibid., paras. 129, 205, 209–210.

goods or services as part of a uniform business network established by the franchisor. The franchising agreement will ordinarily authorise the use of intellectual and industrial property rights, such as trade marks and know-how, to enable and to aid the franchisee to resell the goods and services. In addition, the franchisor usually provides the franchisee with commercial or technical assistance during the life of the agreement and requires a franchise fee for the use of the business method.

It is seen in Chapter 7 that single branding and tying provisions may create significant competition law problems where the firm imposing the provision is dominant.

C. COMPETITION RULES AND DISTRIBUTION

(i) The Impact of the Competition Rules on Methods of Distribution

The discussion below establishes that a decision to distribute products through an independent distributor raises most problems from an EU competition law perspective. This may therefore mean that competition law is a relevant factor when a business is deciding how to distribute its products or services. Arguably, this should not be the case. Rather, '[u]nless there is a good reason, businessmen should be left to select the most cost effective method with as little distortion as possible induced by the competition rules and other kinds of legal measure'.[18] In particular, if the competition rules on distribution are too severe when compared with the treatment of vertical integration there is a danger that this policy might sharply accelerate the trend towards vertical integration of the distribution process.[19]

(ii) Intra-undertaking Arrangements: Vertical Integration and Agency Agreements

a. Parent–Subsidiary Arrangements

In Chapter 3 it is seen that Article 101(1) does not apply to agreements concluded between entities forming part of the same economic unit (such as a parent supplier and its subsidiary distributor, where the conduct is considered to be the unilateral workings of an economic unit and not joint conduct). A supplier that sets up its own distribution arm is therefore unlikely to encounter difficulties with EU competition law unless (a) the integration is through external growth and the acquisition transaction is problematic under the EU merger rules (which is relatively rare);[20] and/or (b) Article 102 applies, because the undertaking is dominant on a relevant market.

b. Agency Agreements

The CJ has also held that the close economic links existing in an agency relationship mean that in some circumstances an agent is so closely interrelated with its principal that, as with the relationship between a parent and its subsidiary or employer and employee, the agent forms an integral part of the principal's business and the relationship is characterised by 'economic unity'. Thus under EU law:

- some agents operate as an 'auxiliary organ' 'forming an integral part of the principal's undertaking'[21] (an agent);

---

[18] V. Korah and D. O'Sullivan, *Distribution Agreements Under the EC Competition Rules* (Hart Publishing, 2002), 1.1. See also discussion of transaction cost economics and Coase theory in Chap. 1.

[19] In the US, the Supreme Court recognised that 'the *per se* illegality of vertical restraints would create a perverse incentive for manufacturers to integrate vertically into distribution', *Business Electronics Corp v Sharp Electronics Corp*, 485 US 717, 725, per Scalia J (1988).

[20] See Chap. 15.

[21] See Case 311/85, *ASBL Vereniging van Vlaamse Reisbureaus v ASBL Sociale Dienst van de Plaatselijke en Gewestelijke Overheidsdiensten* [1987] ECR 3801, paras. 19–20 and Case C-266/93, *Bundeskartellamt v Volkswagen AG and VAG Leasing GmbH* [1995] ECR I-3477, para. 19.

- whilst others operate as an independent economic operator so that the agency agreement is, like other vertical agreements, subject to Article 101(1).[22]

The jurisprudence makes it clear that it is not the parties' characterisation of the arrangement (the form) which is determinative to the question of whether the agent is to be treated as an independent undertaking or not but the 'economic reality'. Indeed, in a number of cases no 'genuine' agency agreement (as the Commission used to describe those falling outside Article 101(1)) has been found to exist, even though the parties had characterised it as one of agency.[23] It is for the Commission, or other person trying to prove a violation of Article 101(1), however, to establish whether an entity is in fact acting as an independent operator.[24]

In *Confederación Española de Empresarios de Estaciones de Servicio v Compañia Española de Petróleos (CEES)*[25] and *CEPSA Estaciones de Servicio SA v LV Tobar e Hojos SL (CEPSA)*,[26] the CJ provided guidance to national courts on the factors relevant to the assessment of whether 'agency' contracts fall within the ambit of Article 101(1). In both cases the compatibility with Article 101(1) of motor fuel agreements concluded with operators of Spanish service stations had arisen before the Spanish courts. The CJ held that:[27]

- vertical agreements are covered by Article 101 only where the operator is regarded as an independent economic operator and there is, consequently, an agreement between two undertakings;

- '[t]he decisive factor for the purposes of determining whether [an entity] is an independent economic operator is to be found in the agreement concluded with the principal and, in particular, in the clauses of that agreement, implied or express, relating to the assumption of the financial and commercial risks linked to sales of goods to third parties. The question of risk must be analysed on a case-by-case basis, taking account of the real economic situation rather than the legal categorisation of the contractual relationship in national law.'[28]

- Article 101 is not applicable where the operator bears only a negligible proportion of the risk.[29]

In determining whether an 'agent' accepts more than a 'negligible share' of the financial or commercial risks, the following 'risks' are relevant:

- risks which are directly related to the contracts concluded and/or negotiated by the agent on behalf of the principal. It may be important therefore whether, for example, the 'agent' takes possession of goods prior to selling them to a third party, assumes costs linked to distribution

---

[22] Guidelines, para. 21.

[23] See, e.g., COMP/26.876 and 26.894, *Pittsburgh Corning* [1972] OJ L272/35 (although an agency agreement had been selected for tax purposes the Commission decided that the parties were not in a relationship of economic dependency); Case 40/73, *Suiker Unie v Commission* [1975] ECR 1663, paras. 539–542 (parties, although technically commercial agents under German law, were found in fact to be powerful intermediaries which accepted the financial risks of the sales or of the performance of the contracts and operated at arm's length from their notional principals, and worked simultaneously as independent dealers for several undertakings); Case C-266/93, *Bundeskartellamt v Volkswagen AG and VAG Leasing GmbH* [1995] ECR I-3477, paras. 18–19 (the CJ rejected Volkswagen AG and VAG Leasing's argument that the German VAG dealers, as intermediaries of VAG Leasing, constituted exclusive agency agreements as the dealers bore some of the risks of leasing the contract vehicles. 'Representatives can lose their character as independent traders only if they do not bear any of the risks resulting from the contracts negotiated on behalf of the principal and they operate as auxiliary organs forming an integral part of the principal's undertaking').

[24] Case T-325/01, *DaimlerChrysler v Commission* [2005] ECR II-3319.

[25] Case C-217/05, [2006] ECR I-11987. See also Guidelines, paras. 12–21.

[26] Case C-279/06, [2008] ECR I-6681.

[27] Ibid., paras. 33–44, Case C-217/05, *Confederación Española de Empresarios de Estaciones de Servicio (CEES) v Compañia Española de Petróleos SA* [2006] ECR I-11987, paras. 38–63.

[28] Case C-279/06, *CEPSA* [2008] ECR I-6681, para. 36, relying on Case C-217/05, *CEES* [2006] ECR I-11987, para. 46.

[29] Case C-279/06, *CEPSA* [2008] ECR I-6681, para. 40, relying on Case C-217/05, *CEES* [2006] ECR I-11987, para. 61.

of goods, such as transport costs, maintains stocks at his own expense, assumes responsibility for any damage caused to the goods or by the goods to third parties, or bears the financial risk linked to the goods;[30]

- risks related to market-specific investments. These are investments specifically required for the type of activity for which the agent has been appointed by the principal and so to enable the agent to conclude and/or negotiate this type of contract. These include investments in premises, equipment, or advertising. Such investments are frequently sunk.[31]

The Commission states in its Guidelines that risks related to other activities required by the principal to be undertaken in the same product market are also relevant.[32]

In contrast, it seems that the following risks will not affect an entity's characterisation as a genuine agent: risks regarded as part and parcel of providing agency services (such as an agent's dependence on sales success for its income, an agent's investments in premises or personnel (which are not specific market investments),[33] and the ability of an agent to grant discounts from its commission); and risks accepted by the agent on another market (separate from the goods sold on behalf of the principal).[34] In *Mercedes Benz*,[35] for example, the Commission had rejected the argument that restrictions on the export of new Mercedes-Benz vehicles agreed between a supplier and German 'commercial agents' fell outside Article 101(1). It concluded that the Mercedes-Benz agents bore a number of risks, which went beyond the scope of a genuine commercial agent contract. On appeal, however, the GC annulled this aspect of the decision, holding that the German agents were agents so that an agreement between undertakings had not been substantiated.[36] On the facts, it found that Mercedes-Benz bore the risk associated with the contract and the purchase of new cars, not the commercial agents which operated, acting on the instructions of the principal, as an auxiliary organ integrated into the principal's business. Title in the cars passed direct from Mercedes-Benz to the customer and the agent had no authority to negotiate rebates except out of its own commission.[37] The fact that the agents bore responsibility for some activities and financial obligations on separate markets (such as transportation of the cars, purchase of demonstration cars, and provision of after-sales guarantee services) did not detract from this conclusion.

Although the Commission states in the Guidelines that the question of risk must be assessed on a case-by-case basis, it also states that Article 101(1) is unlikely to apply where the property in the contract goods bought or sold on behalf of the principal does not vest in the agent or the contract services are not supplied by the agent and where a number of other conditions are satisfied.

The focus on risk set out in recent cases appears to suggest that the appraisal is not affected by the question of whether the agent acts only for one, or for several, principals;[38] the same agent may form part of the same undertaking of one or more principals (and indeed it has been held that clauses preventing agents from acting for other principals may have to be assessed for their compatibility with Article 101(1)). Some older cases, however, indicate that agents can lose their character as independent traders only if they do not bear any of the risks and they operate as auxiliary organs forming an integral part of the principal's undertaking. For example, in *VZW Vereniging van Vlaamse Reisbureaus*

---

[30] Case 279/06, *CEPSA* [2008] ECR I-6681, para. 38, Case C-217/05, *CEES* [2006] ECR I-11987, paras. 50–61.

[31] Which means that upon leaving that particular field of activity the investment cannot be used for other activities or sold other than at a significant loss, Guidelines, para. 14.

[32] Ibid., para. 14.

[33] Ibid., para. 15.

[34] Case T-325/01, *DaimlerChrysler v Commission* [2005] ECR II-3319, paras. 99 and 113.

[35] COMP/36.264, [2002] OJ L257/1.

[36] Case T-325/01, *DaimlerChrysler v Commission* [2005] ECR II-3319.

[37] Ibid., paras. 93 and 94.

[38] Guidelines, para. 13.

v VZW Sociale Dienst van de Plaatselijke en Gewestelijke Overheidsdiensten[39] the CJ held that Flemish travel agents which observed travel prices set by tour operators and acted on behalf of a large number of tour operators, could not be regarded as an auxiliary part of the tour operators even though they contracted in the name of and on behalf of them. This issue and the question of how broadly the agency concept extends has become of increasing importance as more suppliers sell online, for example via platforms and following an agency model under which the platform is empowered to negotiate and/or conclude contracts on behalf of its principal, either in its own name or in the name of the principal, and is usually remunerated for the services by payment of a commission. In *e-books*,[40] for example, the Commission investigated a situation where five principal publishers agreed to sell their electronic books (e-books) directly to the consumer via an agent/platform using an agency, as opposed to a wholesale or reseller, model. In this case, however, the question of whether the vertical agency relationships were caught by Article 101(1) was not central to the case; rather, the Commission's concern was that the five publishers had engaged, with Apple, in a concerted practice to raise retail prices in breach of Article 101(1). In the end, the proceedings were concluded when the publishers agreed to terminate their agency agreements with Apple and offer other retailers the opportunity to end their agency agreements too.

Even if a relationship between a supplier and its distributor is characterised as one of agency, it will be remembered that a functional approach is taken to the concept of an undertaking. It is therefore only with regard to the market on which the agent offers its principal's goods or services to potential customers and obligations delineating the scope of that relationship that the principal and agent are considered to be acting unilaterally:[41] consequently, limitations of the territory into which, customers to whom, or prices and conditions at which the agent sells the goods or services and, possibly, exclusive agency provisions (provision preventing the principal from appointing other agents in respect of a given type of transaction, customer, or territory) may fall outside Article 101(1).

In contrast, the agent is normally regarded as an independent operator with regard to the market on which the agent offers its agency services to potential principals.[42] Thus even terms within a 'genuine' agency agreement may infringe Article 101(1) if they prevent the agent from acting as an agent or distributor of undertakings which compete with the principal (non-compete provisions) and so foreclose or lock up the relevant market,[43] or where they facilitate collusion.[44] In *Confederación Española de Empresarios de Estaciones de Servicio v Compañía Española de Petróleos* the CJ held that:[45]

> only the obligations imposed on the intermediary in the context of the sale of the goods to third parties on behalf of the principal fall outside the scope of that article. As the Commission submitted, an agency contract may contain clauses concerning the relationship between the agent and the principal to which that article applies, such as exclusivity and non-competition clauses. In that connection it must be considered that, in the context of such relationships, agents are, in principle, independent economic operators and such clauses are capable of infringing the competition rules in so far as they entail locking up the market concerned.

---

[39] Case 311/85, *VZW Vereniging van Vlaamse Reisbureaus v VZW Sociale Dienst van de Plaatselijke en Gewestelijke Overheidsdiensten* [1987] ECR 3801. See also n. 23.

[40] COMP/39.847, [2013] OJ C378/25. The Commission stated that its preliminary concerns did not relate to the legitimate use of the agency model and publishers were free to enter such agreements insofar as they do not infringe EU competition law.

[41] Guidelines, paras. 18–19.

[42] See Case C-279/06, *CEPSA* [2008] ECR I-6681, para. 41; Case C-217/05, *CEES* [2006] ECR I-11987, paras. 62–63; Guidelines, paras. 18–21.

[43] Such provisions may, however, meet the conditions of the Verticals Reg.

[44] E.g., when a number of principals use the same agents and collectively exclude others from using them, or when they use the agents to collude on marketing strategy or to exchange sensitive market information between the principals, Guidelines, para. 20.

[45] Case C-217/05, *CEES* [2006] ECR I-11987, para. 62.

The requirements set out in EU competition law are complex and stringent and are not easy to navigate in practice. This has led some to call for a more realistic approach to be taken which does not obscure the economic nature of agency relationships and is more in tune with it. If not, 'parties who wish to enter into benign agency agreements will likely renegotiate and choose alternative but less efficient contractual arrangements. Such contractual changes imposed solely on account of the law could lead to unintended consequences that could harm social welfare.'[46]

(iii) Distribution Agreements

a. Restraints on Conduct and Restrictions of Competition—The Problem

It has already been seen that vertical agreements concluded between suppliers and independent distributors operating at different levels of the supply chain generally contain restraints on the conduct or commercial freedom of one or more of the parties. A key question arising is whether or not these restraints restrict competition for the purposes of Article 101(1) and/or generate efficiencies cognisable under Article 101(3). Although economic theory supports a suspicion of horizontal agreements, '[e]conomists are much more equivocal about vertical agreements, between firms at different stages of the value-added chain'.[47]

b. The Positive Effects of Vertical Restraints

In the 1960s many commentators, especially members of the Chicago School, argued that competition law should rarely, if at all, be troubled by vertical restraints which lead to increased sales and to the minimisation of distribution costs. In particular, they propounded the view that a supplier will impose vertical restraints on intra-brand competition only where necessary to enhance sales of its product and to encourage inter-brand competition.

One of the main arguments is that vertical restraints on intra-brand competition are frequently necessary to enable a supplier to protect its distributors from free-riders. For example, vertical agreements imposing RPM, awarding a distributor an exclusive distribution territory, or restricting supplies to selected retailers may be essential to encourage distributors to provide additional services necessary to boost sales and to persuade consumers to purchase more of the supplier's product. In the absence of such restraints, distributors might be unwilling to incur the cost of providing additional services since other distributors would be able to take a 'free-ride' on their investment.[48]

Bork went further, arguing that not only was the rationale for the imposition of such vertical restraints[49] obvious, but their implications for economic efficiency were clear. A supplier would only ever impose vertical restraints in order to achieve distributive efficiency and to increase its output. If the supplier wrongly required distributors to provide services that customers did not want, or did not consider to be worth the increase in price, those consumers would purchase rival products instead. The market itself would provide retribution for a supplier's mistaken belief that a vertical restraint was desirable. Where it did not, the problem would be the monopoly power of the supplier, not the vertical restraint. This led to a greater focus on the positive effects that may result from vertical restraints on intra-brand competition, even price restraints imposing RPM, which might be necessary to encourage retailers to compete on non-price criteria, such as service and

---

[46] See A. H. Zhang, 'Toward an Economic Approach to Agency Agreements' (2013) 9 *J of Competition Law and Economics* 553.

[47] F. Fishwick, *Making Sense of Competition Policy* (Kogan Page, 1993), 56.

[48] See especially L. Telser, 'Why Should Manufacturers Want Fair Trade?' (1960) 3 *JL & Econ* 86; L. Telser, 'Why Should Manufacturers Want Fair Trade II?' (1990) 33 *J of Law and Economics* 409; R. A. Posner, 'The Next Step in the Antitrust Treatment of Restricted Distribution: Per Se Legality' (1981) 48 *Univ Chic LR* 1; F. H. Easterbrook, 'Vertical Arrangements and the Rule of Reason' (1984) 53 *Antitrust LJ* 135.

[49] See, e.g., R. H. Bork, 'The Rule of Reason and the Per Se Concept: Price Fixing and Market Division Part I' (1965) 74 *Yale LJ* 775; R. H. Bork, 'The Rule of Reason and the Per Se Concept: Price Fixing and Market Division Part II' (1966) 5 *Yale LJ* 373.

promotion, to protect a retailer's reputation for providing high-quality services and stocking high-quality products, to facilitate market entry by a new competitor or an undertaking producing a new product, and to protect the retailer from free-riding.

Comanor explains these free-rider and distributive efficiency arguments more fully.

W. S. Comanor, 'Vertical Price-fixing, Vertical Market Restrictions, and the New Antitrust Policy' (1985) 98 *Harvard LR* 983, 986–90

Building on earlier studies . . . Lester Telser offered a detailed explanation of why manufacturers benefit from resale price maintenance [L. Telser, 'Why Should Manufacturers Want Fair Trade? (1960) 3 *J.L. & E.* 86] As he observed, because the quantity sold of a manufacturer's product depends on the final price paid by consumers, the manufacturer normally stands to gain from competition among dealers that limits the distribution margin. Only if other factors intervene can the manufacturer benefit from restraints on competition among his dealers . . .

Telser's primary explanation centered on the distributor's role in furnishing 'services' along with the manufactured product. By 'services,' Telser referred not only to delivery, credit, and repair, but also to selling, advertising, and promotional activities . . . In short . . . all factors supplied by the distributor that may influence demand for the manufacturer's product. The provision of these services benefits the manufacturer as long as the positive effect on demand outweighs the depressing effect of the accompanying rise in price.

The manufacturer, however, can influence the level of services furnished only by limiting competition among his distributors. He cannot simply lower his price in the hope that distributors will use their increased revenues to finance the appropriate services. Even if some distributors will do so—recognizing that greater sales result from providing services jointly with the product—others will not, and might compete by setting a lower price. The result is the classic 'free rider' problem:

> Sales are diverted from the retailers who do provide the special services at the higher price to the retailers who do not provide the special services and offer to sell the product at the lower price. The mechanism is simple. A customer, because of the special services provided by one retailer, is persuaded to buy the product. But he purchases the product from another paying the latter a lower price. In this way the retailers who do not provide the special services get a free ride at the expense of those who have convinced consumers to buy the product . . .

In order to remain competitive with free riders, other distributors will cease to provide the requisite services . . . Thus, fewer services will be offered and total sales of the product will be lower than they would be otherwise . . . The solution, according to Telser, is for manufacturers to establish minimum retail prices, forcing retailers 'to compete by providing special services,' . . . and thereby eliminating the free-rider problem . . .

Telser's analysis explains why manufacturers would wish to impose vertical restraints. What it does not do, nor claim to do, is answer the question whether dealers' provision of additional services is efficient—that is, whether the additional services justify the higher price charged for the product . . .

Judge Bork wrote the first article directly addressing the implications of vertical restraints for economic efficiency [R. H. Bork, 'The Rule of Reason and the per se Concept: Price Fixing and Market Division (pt. 2)' (1966) 75 *Yale LJ* 373]. His test was simple: restrictions on output are anti-competitive, and increases in output are pro-competitive. Using this criterion, Bork concluded that all restraints imposed by manufacturers *must* be efficiency-enhancing and pro-competitive . . .

According to Bork, because a manufacturer will impose vertical restraints only if they lead to increased output and, in turn, to increased profits, such restraints must be pro-competitive . . . his position assumes that the interests of manufacturers and consumers fully coincide.

The reasoning behind Bork's theory, which appears to have gained acceptance among both lawyers and economists, is that manufacturers will not find it profitable to impose vertical restraints when customers do not find the value of the new services exceeds their incremental cost. Otherwise a rival manufacturer would surely offer the product without the additional services and lure customers away.

The government's . . . brief in *Spray-Rite* adopts precisely this position. Monsanto, the manufacturer whose products were distributed by Spray-Rite, believed that demand for its products was unnecessarily low because many potential customers understood neither which Monsanto herbicides were appropriate for particular farming needs, nor the proper method of applying the products. To spur the dissemination of information and avoid free-rider problems, the company initiated a policy of vertical restraints. The government argued that the restraints were pro-competitive:

> [A]lthough vertical restrictions increase both dealer costs and price, such restrictions will be unprofitable for the manufacturer unless they also increase the quantities of product that dealers sell. This is the critical, pro-competitive respect in which such vertical restrictions differ from a mere widening of dealer margins, which would increase price but *reduce* quantities of product sold. Indeed, the manufacturer usually will anticipate that its marketing program will enable its dealers to increase their prices, precisely so that they can recover their added costs. That is true whether the manufacturer uses restricted sales territories, location clauses, exclusive dealing arrangements, or some other vertical restriction. [Brief for the United States as Amicus Curiae in Support of Petitioner, *Spray-Rite* (No. 102-914)]

Inter-brand restraints limiting a purchaser's freedom to buy products from sources other than the seller or another specified supplier, such as exclusive dealing obligations, quantity-forcing provisions, requirements contracts, and tying arrangements, are also common practices, often with pro-competitive effect.[50] Single branding obligations, for example, may induce the dealer to concentrate its selling efforts on the promotion of the supplier's products, allow the seller to overcome free-rider issues (and give the seller an incentive to give dealers more support), reduce transaction costs, afford protection to the parties against price fluctuations, enable both parties to engage in long-term planning, and ensure a steady supply for the buyer and steady sales for the seller. Similarly, it has been argued that tying may achieve pro-competitive objectives through assurance of product quality,[51] achieving cost saving on the production or consumption side, the prevention of excessive charges for the tied product (avoiding the double marginalisation problem),[52] innovation, by incorporating new features into products, or enabling beneficial price discrimination between buyers by, for example, metering.

The Commission is fully aware of the benefits that vertical restraints may bring, recognising in its Guidelines that, '[f]or most vertical restraints, competition concerns can only arise if there is insufficient competition at one or more levels of trade, i.e. if there is some degree of market power at the level of the supplier or the buyer or at both levels. Vertical restraints are generally less harmful than horizontal restraints and may provide substantial scope for efficiencies.'[53] 'When a company has no market power, it can only try to increase its profits by optimising its manufacturing or distribution processes.'[54] Consequently, it accepts that vertical restraints may be essential to the realisation of efficiencies and the development of new markets and to ensure the optimal level of investment and sales. In paragraphs 106–109 it summarises the positive effects that vertical restraints on both intra- and inter-brand competition may bring, especially the promotion of non-price competition

---

[50] See further Chap. 7.

[51] Ensuring that its product is not used with another which will impair its performance and/or quality.

[52] See, e.g., B. Nalebuff, 'Bundling, Tying, and Portfolio Effects', DTI Economics Paper No. 1 (2003).

[53] Guidelines, para. 6.

[54] Ibid., para. 106.

and the improved quality of service. In particular, it lists the following justifications for the imposition of certain vertical restraints (a listing which does not purport to be complete or exhaustive):[55]

(a) to 'solve a "free-rider" problem', to prevent free-riding on pre-sales services, for example by the allocation of an exclusive territory to a distributor, or the imposition of a non-compete obligation;[56]

(b) to 'open up or enter new markets', to induce a distributor to engage in sufficient investment to enable a manufacturer to enter a new geographic market, for example by the allocation of an exclusive territory to a distributor;

(c) the 'certification free-rider issue', to introduce a new product on a market particularly by selling through retailers that have a reputation for selling only 'quality' products, for example by appointing an exclusive distributor or establishing a SDS;

(d) to deal with the 'hold-up problem' and encourage client-specific investment and innovation, for example a distributor may require exclusivity in distribution if it is to contribute to the cost of developing a manufacturer's new product;

(e) to deal with the 'specific hold-up problem that may arise in the case of transfer of substantial know-how', to protect know-how transferred under a distribution agreement, for example by the imposition of non-compete restrictions;

(f) the 'vertical externality' issue. The manufacturer may wish to ensure that retailers are not pricing too high or making too little sales efforts as increased sales also benefits manufacturers by bestowing a positive externality on it (if its wholesale price exceeds its marginal production costs). The negative externality of too high pricing by the retailer is sometimes called the 'double marginalisation problem' and it can be avoided by imposing a maximum resale price on the retailer. To increase retailer's sales efforts selective distribution, exclusive distribution, or similar restrictions may also be used;

(g) to enable a manufacturer to exploit 'economies of scale in distribution' and to realise lower prices, for example by using exclusive or selective distribution systems or quantity-forcing provisions;[57]

(h) to deal with 'capital imperfections', to provide security in respect of loans made in the terms of the agreement, for example through the use of exclusivity provisions; and/or

(i) to achieve 'uniformity and quality standardization', to increase sales by creating a brand image and increasing the attractiveness of a product to the final consumer, for example through the use of selective distribution or franchising agreements.

The Commission states in its Guidelines that these nine identified situations 'make clear that under certain conditions vertical agreement are likely to help realise efficiencies and the development of new markets and that these may offset possible negative effects'.[58]

c. The Negative Effects of Vertical Restraints

The fact that vertical restraints might provide positive effects does not, however, mean that the imposition of vertical restraints is always justified and that such restraints will inevitably result in distributive efficiency.[59] Rather, economists are generally 'cautious in their assessment of vertical

---

[55] Ibid., para.107.

[56] A supplier who funds a distributor's promotional expenses may also demand that the distributor purchase exclusively from it in order to prevent other suppliers free-riding or benefiting from its promotional effort.

[57] The limitation of the number of distributors within the system will reduce the costs of distribution and of monitoring any promotional efforts required of distributors.

[58] Guidelines, para. 104.

[59] Scherer and Ross, n. 9, 541.

restraints' and are unwilling 'to make sweeping generalisations' and to regard them 'as *per se* beneficial for competition'.[60]

Comanor, for example, criticised Bork's assumption that restraints would always lead to the most efficient result. The theory failed to attach sufficient importance to the different preferences of consumers for extra dealer-provided services and to distinguish between marginal and infra-marginal consumers.

The 'marginal consumer' is one whose valuation of the product approximates to its current price. This consumer is, therefore, sensitive to improvements leading to an increase in the market price of a product. He or she will purchase more of the product only if he considers that the improvement in service or quality of the product is worth the increase in its price. If he does not he will generally purchase less. In contrast 'infra-marginal consumers' are consumers that place a value on the product substantially higher than the original price. Such consumers are relatively insensitive to increases in price. They will, therefore, not refrain from purchasing the product on an increase in price even if, in their view, the improvement in the quality of the products did not merit that increase in price.[61]

In the view of Comanor 'societal gains or losses from changes in the product depend on the preferences of *all* consumers, not merely those at the margin. To the extent that such alterations fail to reflect the preferences of infra-marginal consumers, the interests of consumers in general may not be served.'[62] Vertical restraints which are profitable to a manufacturer may thus not always achieve economic efficiency but may lead to a reduction in consumer welfare as a whole. In particular, vertical restraints imposed to promote the sale of established products may induce distributors to supply an excessive level of information services. In contrast, where consumers must be persuaded to purchase new products vertical restraints are less likely to harm consumer welfare. Consumers will require more information to entice them to purchase the products.

W. S. Comanor, 'Vertical Price-fixing, Vertical Market Restrictions, and the New Antitrust Policy' (1984–1985) 98 *Harvard LR* 983, 992–9

Suppose, for example, that the service in question is the provision of information about how to use a product. Consumers who are 'ignorant' about the product value this information and are willing to pay more for it. For 'knowledgeable' consumers—those already familiar with the product—the opposite is true: this class of consumers is unwilling to pay the increased price for the product necessary to fund the information services.

Assume further that a large number of infra-marginal consumers are 'knowledgeable.' Many of the consumers in this class may be previous customers who originally learned about the product from outside sources or from advertising provided directly by the manufacturer. The 'ignorant' consumers, we may assume, are largely marginal. Perhaps they value the product less than 'knowledgeable' consumers do simply because they are uncertain of its merits.

Because marginal consumers desire the information services, the manufacturer will impose vertical restraints. But this action may not lead to an efficient result: the interests of 'knowledgeable' infra-marginal consumers must also be taken into account. If they are great in number, the harm caused by making them pay for unwanted services may exceed the benefit derived by marginal consumers. Thus, the mere fact that the services are profitable for the manufacturer is not sufficient evidence that all—or even

---

[60] European Commission, Green Paper on Vertical Restraints in EC Competition Policy, COM(96) 721, para. 54. See, e.g., W. S. Comanor, 'Vertical Price-fixing, Vertical Market Restrictions, and the New Antitrust Policy' (1984–1985) 98 *Harvard LR* 983 and J. J. Flynn, 'The "Is" and "Ought" of Vertical Restraints After *Monsanto Co v Spray-Rite Service Corp*' (1985–1986) 71 *Cornell LR* 1095.

[61] Comanor, ibid., 991.

[62] Ibid.

most—consumers benefit from their supply . . . In short, these services may be oversupplied in relation to the consumer optimum . . .

Economic theory alone cannot predict whether the imposition of vertical restraints—and dealers' provision of additional services—will benefit consumers and enhance efficiency. Whether consumers benefit depends on whether gains to marginal consumers outweigh losses to their infra-marginal counterparts. Because such losses may predominate—particularly when the restraints are used to support services for established products—consumer harm may result.

Several other concerns also cause scepticism about the necessity or legitimacy in all cases of vertical restraints, even those that limit only intra-brand competition. In the EU, there is a particular concern that agreements which impose territorial restrictions on dealers whilst restricting only intra-brand competition lead to the division of markets on national lines in contravention of the single market objective.[63] The extract from the Commission's Green Paper on Vertical Restraints[64] reinforces the importance of the 'wider objective of achieving an integrated internal market. Market integration enhances competition in the EU. Companies should not be allowed to recreate private barriers between Member States where State barriers have been successfully abolished.'[65]

Green Paper on Vertical Restraints in Competition Policy, COM(96) 721

70. The ongoing integration process of the Single Market adds an extra dimension to the analysis of vertical restraints. The 1992 programme was the result of a widely held conviction that the failure to achieve a single market has been costing European industry millions in unnecessary costs and lost opportunities. The exact title of the Cecchini Report, 'The cost of Non-Europe' . . . is a clear reflection of this. The efforts made since the entry into force of the EEC Treaty in 1958 had not exhausted by the mid-1980's all the potential gains to be expected from the full economic integration of the economies of the Member States. Now that more steps have been taken to eliminate the remaining obstacles to the free movement of goods, services and factors of production, it is still apparent that further efforts are necessary to achieve the maximum possible level of integration . . .

78. The EC experience shows that the removal of non-tariff barriers is not sufficient for the full development of parallel trade, arbitrage and changes in distribution across Europe. For the complete success of economic integration it is necessary that producers, distributors and consumers, find it profitable to move towards the new market situation and do not take actions to avoid or counteract the effects of the Single Market measures. The elimination of barriers to trade may not achieve its objectives if producers and/or distributors introduce practices contrary to integration. Unfortunately in many cases it is likely that they have strong incentives to do so.

The Commission's concerns about intra-brand restraints thus run more broadly. In particular, it places huge importance on the benefits of e-commerce for consumers and its development for achievement of the single market. The EU institutions have been hostile to restrictions on online sales incorporated within distribution agreements.[66] Indeed, in May 2015 the Commission

---

[63] See Chaps. 1, 4, and 7.

[64] Green Paper, n. 60, 721.

[65] Guidelines, para. 7. See also, e.g., L. Gyselen, 'Vertical Restraints in the Distribution Process: Strength and Weakness of the Free Rider Rationale under EEC Competition Law' (1984) 21 *CMLRev* 647.

[66] See e.g., G. Accardo, 'Vertical Antitrust Enforcement: Transatlantic Perspectives on Restrictions of Online Distribution under EU and US Competition Law' (2013) 9 *European Competition Journal* 225, especially 261–263.

launched, as a complement to actions launched within the framework of the Digital Single Market strategy,[67] an inquiry into the EU e-commerce sector[68] with the objective of identifying barriers erected by companies to cross-border online trade and what effects they have on competition and consumers. As the Commission's initial findings indicate that 'geo-blocking' is common for both consumer goods and digital content, it has stated that, where such geo-blocking results from agreements between suppliers and distributors, it will carefully consider whether such agreements restrict competition in the single market.[69] Further, it will be seen in the cases below that in addition to concerns that vertical restraints may foreclosure suppliers or dampen competition between them, there is an acute concern about restrictions on rivalry between, and foreclosure of, distributors, which has profoundly affected how vertical intra-brand restraints are assessed.

The Commission explains in the Guidelines that its anxieties about vertical intra- and inter-brand restraints are relatively broad.

Guidelines on Vertical Restraints

100. The negative effects on the market that may result from vertical restraints which EU competition law aims at preventing are the following:

(i)   anticompetitive foreclosure of other suppliers or other buyers by raising barriers to entry or expansion;

(ii) softening of competition between the supplier and its competitors and/or facilitation of collusion amongst these suppliers, often referred to as reduction of inter-brand competition;

(iii) softening of competition between the buyer and its competitors and/or facilitation of collusion amongst these competitors, often referred to as reduction of intra-brand competition if it concerns distributors' competition on the basis of the brand or product of the same supplier;

(iv) the creation of obstacles to market integration, including, above all, limitations on the possibilities for consumers to purchase goods or services in any Member State they may choose.

101. Foreclosure, softening of competition and collusion at the manufacturer's level may harm consumers in particular by increasing the wholesale prices of the products, limiting the choice of products, lowering their quality or reducing the level of product innovation. Foreclosure, softening of competition and collusion at the distributors' level may harm consumers in particular by increasing the retail prices of the products, limiting the choice of price-service combinations and distribution formats, lowering the availability and quality of retail services and reducing the level of innovation of distribution.

102. In a market where individual distributors distribute the brand(s) of only one supplier, a reduction of competition between the distributors of the same brand will lead to a reduction of intra-brand competition between these distributors, but may not have a negative effect on competition between distributors in general. In such a case, if inter-brand competition is fierce, it is unlikely that a reduction of intra-brand competition will have negative effects for consumers.

103. Exclusive arrangements are generally worse for competition than non-exclusive arrangements. Exclusive dealing makes, by the express language of the contract or its practical effects, one party fulfil all or practically all its requirements from another party. For instance, under a non-compete obligation the buyer purchases only one brand. Quantity forcing, on the other hand, leaves the buyer some scope to purchase competing goods. The degree of foreclosure may therefore be less with quantity forcing.

---

[67] One of the ten core priorities of the Commission, <http://ec.europa.eu/priorities/digital-single-market/index_en.htm>. The Commission wishes to ensure that there is better access to online goods and services in the EU and is examining a broad range of barriers to cross-border e-commerce.

[68] IP/15/4921.

[69] Initial findings were published on 18 March 2016, see <http://ec.europa.eu/competition/antitrust/sector_inquiries_e_commerce.html>, following the collection of information from a number of stakeholders. Geo-blocking which results from unilateral business decisions by a non-dominant undertaking falls outside the scope of EU competition law.

104. Vertical restraints agreed for non-branded goods and services are in general less harmful than restraints affecting the distribution of branded goods and services. Branding tends to increase product differentiation and reduce substitutability of the product, leading to a reduced elasticity of demand and an increased possibility to raise price. The distinction between branded and non-branded goods or services will often coincide with the distinction between intermediate goods and services and final goods and services.

105. In general, a combination of vertical restraints aggravates their negative effects. However, certain combinations of vertical restraints are better for competition than their use in isolation from each other. For instance, in an exclusive distribution system, the distributor may be tempted to increase the price of the products as intra-brand competition has been reduced. The use of quantity forcing or the setting of a maximum resale price may limit such price increases. Possible negative effects of vertical restraints are reinforced when several suppliers and their buyers organise their trade in a similar way, leading to so-called cumulative effects.[70]

3. THE EU APPROACH TO DISTRIBUTION AGREEMENTS—AN OVERVIEW

A. THE BACKGROUND: THE SINGLE MARKET PROJECT AND RESTRICTIONS ON ECONOMIC FREEDOM

The pro- and anti-competitive effects outlined above have caused many competition lawyers and economists to disagree vigorously about when and/or how often the different types of vertical restraint cause anti-competitive harm, how any such harm should be reconciled with the efficiencies that vertical restraints may generate, and how legal rules or standards should be constructed to identify and weigh the competing effects.

The Commission's historical approach to Article 101(1), and in particular to vertical distribution agreements, sparked huge controversy and intense debate. For many years it had broad concerns about vertical restraints and took the view, often without serious analysis of the effect of the agreement on the competitive process, that many restraints on parties' freedom of action, such as price or non-price restraints or non-compete clauses, amounted to restrictions of competition within the meaning of Article 101(1). Further, because it adopted a strict and formalistic approach when applying the Article 101(3) criteria and the block exemptions prior to 1999 were rigid and prescriptive, it intensely regulated the content of vertical agreements and imposed an enormous, and, arguably, unnecessary, burden on firms.[71]

The Commission received significant criticism for this approach, especially because it caused it to deal with agreements by category, applying certain rules to one type of agreement and different rules to others, and meant, with the host of accompanying drawbacks, that businesses felt the need to secure exemptions for their distribution agreements.[72] This may have deterred the conclusion and operation of many pro-competitive distribution arrangements.

In 1995, Hawk, in a seminal article,[73] fiercely criticised the Commission for its overbroad application of Article 101(1) (based on an incoherent rationale—notably the economic freedom

---

[70] In later sections, the Commission identifies more specific possible competition risks that arise from different types of restraints.

[71] It meant that in practice firms would often have to seek an individual exemption for their agreement, or, only a limited number of such decisions being rendered each year, more realistically, rely on a comfort letter: Green Paper, n. 60, 30.

[72] B. E. Hawk, 'System Failure: Vertical Restraints and EC Competition Law' (1995) 32 *CMLRev* 973, 985.

[73] Ibid., 973.

notion, the market integration objective, and the desire to protect small and medium-sized enterprises—and the consequent anaemic economic analysis which was inconsistent with Court judgments). He complained that the approach generated extraordinary legal uncertainty, led to a proliferation of block exemption and legal formalisms, analysis of agreements by categories, and a de-emphasis on or lack of substantive economic analysis. The approach, he contended, ultimately eliminated 'what should be the heart of the matter: and antitrust (i.e. economics/law) substantive analysis of a particular agreement or practice, i.e. its competitive harms and benefits'.[74] In short he claimed that the whole notification system had failed. This article is perceived to have been the straw (or at least one of them), which finally broke the camel's back and convinced the Commission that its approach to vertical restraints would have to change.

B. THE APPROACH SINCE 1999: THE BLOCK EXEMPTION AND REFORM

In 1996 the Commission issued a Green Paper on Vertical Restraints in which it discussed possible ways for developing and ameliorating its approach to vertical restraints. The Paper sought opinion upon possible options for reform. An additional option, to adopt a more realistic approach when assessing the agreement's compatibility with Article 101(1), was not discussed within the Paper but attracted much attention in the debate that followed.

Following the introduction of the Green Paper a follow-up document was published and several significant changes were introduced. On 22 December 1999, the Commission adopted a block exemption regulation for many vertical agreements that may fall within Article 101(1)[75] and published accompanying Guidelines on the appraisal of vertical agreements, setting out a more coherent approach to analysis under Article 101(1) and Article 101(3) based on the economic objective underpinning it. The block exemption (the Verticals Regulation) and Guidelines were revised and replaced following consultation in 2010. Although the scheme of the 1999 system was preserved, some modifications were introduced to deal, principally, with market changes, including increased retailer power and the growth of internet selling.

It has been seen that the Guidelines recognise that vertical restraints are generally less harmful than horizontal restraints as in vertical relationships the exercise of market power 'by either the upstream or downstream company would normally hurt the demand for the product of the other. The companies involved in the agreement therefore usually have an incentive to prevent the exercise of market power by the other.'[76] Indeed, under the scheme post-1999 many vertical agreements have been able to benefit from the safe harbour of the broader Verticals Regulation. The Guidelines clarify, however, that even agreements concluded between undertakings with more than 30 per cent of the relevant market (which cannot benefit from the block exemptions safe harbour) may not fall within Article 101(1).

C. METHODOLOGY

The Commission's modernised approach to vertical agreements signals, in line with the case law of the Court, that many such agreements will not infringe Article 101(1) at all. Further, that even if they do, or may, the Article 101(3) criteria are to be applied more flexibly.

---

[74] Ibid., 2.5.

[75] [1999] OJ L336/21.

[76] Guidelines, para. 98 and see n. 53 and text.

Logically, the first question that should be addressed in a verticals case is, does this agreement between undertakings infringe Article 101(1) at all? Many vertical agreements will fall outside Article 101(1) on account of their minor importance,[77] because they do not appreciably affect trade between Member States, and/or because they do have as their object or effect an appreciable restriction of competition. Practically, however, where an agreement appears to affect trade and competition appreciably, the parties may prefer to rely on the 'safe haven' of the block exemption rather than going through the full economic analysis required to determine whether or not the agreement has as its effect the restriction of competition. It is for this reason that the Commission states, in its Guidelines at paragraph 110, that the first question for undertakings to ask is whether the agreement falls within the block exemption, not whether the agreement actually falls within Article 101(1) and so requires scrutiny under Article 101(3).

(1) First, the undertakings involved need to establish the market shares of the supplier and the buyer on the markets where they [purchase] the contract products.

(2) If the relevant market share of the supplier and the buyer each do not exceed the 30 % threshold, the vertical agreement is covered by the Block Exemption Regulation, subject to the hardcore restrictions and conditions set out in that regulation.

(3) If the relevant market share is above the 30 % threshold for supplier and/or buyer, it is necessary to assess whether the vertical agreement falls within Article 101(1).

(4) If the vertical agreement falls within Article 101(1), it is necessary to examine whether it fulfils the conditions for exemption under Article 101(3).[78]

Although this approach clearly represents sensible, pragmatic advice, this methodology turns Article 101 on its head as undertakings should not need to comply with the block exemption or Article 101(3) criteria if the agreement does not infringe Article 101(1). In this chapter we thus start with the question of whether the agreement infringes Article 101(1) before going on to consider the terms of the block exemption and how Article 101(3) applies to vertical agreements which may violate Article 101(1) but do not benefit from the block exemption. It should be remembered, however, that, in practice, it may be preferable to sidestep the more complex Article 101(1) analysis and to start as the Commission suggests with the question: is this agreement covered by the block exemption and so exempted from Article 101(1) if within it?

It should also be remembered from Chapter 4 (see also Fig. 11.1) that a fundamentally different approach applies depending upon whether the agreement contains object restraints or restraints identified as hardcore restraints in the Verticals Regulation. Agreements which incorporate object restraints are presumed to be incompatible with Article 101, they are assumed to restrict competition appreciably, and the Commission's view is that they are presumed not to satisfy the conditions of Article 101(3) (for which reason the block exemption does not apply). The parties will have an uphill struggle to demonstrate that the conditions of Article 101(3) are met. In contrast, a large number of vertical agreements which do not incorporate such restraints are presumed to be compatible with Article 101, either because they fall outside Article 101(1) altogether on de minimis grounds or because they satisfy the conditions of the Verticals Regulation.

Because of these critical differences an important primary issue is whether an agreement incorporates a restraint which is likely to result in the agreement being characterised as restrictive of competition by object.

---

[77] Where the parties to the agreement do not have more than 15% of the relevant market, the agreement is likely to be de minimis so long as there are no network effects and it does not contain hardcore restraints, see Chap. 4.

[78] Guidelines, para. 110.

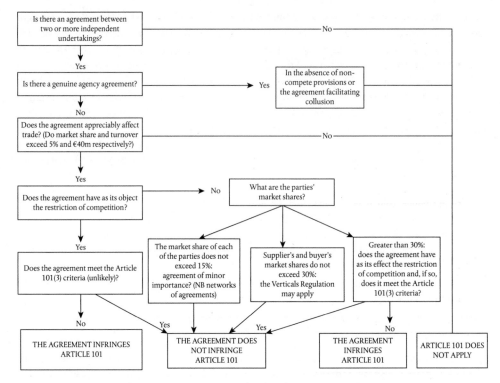

Figure 11.1 Analysis of vertical agreements under Article 101

4. DISTRIBUTION AGREEMENTS AND ARTICLE 101(1) OF THE TREATY

A. VERTICAL AGREEMENTS WHICH RESTRICT COMPETITION BY OBJECT

(i) Types of Restraints Which are Likely to be Characterised as Restrictive by Object

It was seen in Chapter 4 that in order to determine whether restraints are restrictive by object, 'regard must be had inter alia to the content of its provisions, the objectives it seeks to ascertain and the economic and legal context of which it forms part'.[79] Further, that the following 'vertical' restraints are highly likely to be found to be restrictive by object:

- RPM provisions (requiring buyers to observe fixed or minimum resale prices);
- restraints conferring absolute territorial protection (ATP) on a distributor or otherwise limiting parallel trade or partitioning national markets;
- selective distribution systems;

unless the context of the agreement suggests otherwise. It is seen in the discussion below that although the case law accepts that such vertical agreements may pursue a legitimate objective in exceptional contexts, this is extremely difficult to establish in practice.

---

[79] Case C-501/06 P, *GlaxoSmithKline Services Unlimited v Commission* [2009] ECR I-9291, para. 58.

(ii) Resale Price Maintenance

A number of cases establish that, where an agreement between the supplier and distributor can be established,[80] a provision fixing minimum resale prices to be charged by distributors (or indirectly operating as an RPM provision) will be found to be by its very nature injurious to competition. In *Pronuptia de Paris v Schillgallis* the CJ, in setting out guidelines on the compatibility of distribution franchises with Article 101(1), held that 'provisions which impair the franchisee's freedom to determine his own prices are restrictive of competition'.[81] In *Metro-SB-Grossmärkte GmbH v Commission (Metro I)*, the CJ stated that 'price competition is so important that it can never be eliminated',[82] and in *SA Binon & Cie v SA Agence et Messageries de la Presse* it held that 'provisions which fix the prices to be observed in contracts with third parties constitute, of themselves, a restriction on competition within the meaning of Article [101(1)]'.[83] The Commission's Guidelines indicate, however, that it is acceptable for a supplier to provide dealers 'with price-guidelines, so long as there is no concerted practice between the [parties] for the actual application of the prices'.[84] Further, a SDS in which 'price competition is not generally emphasized either as an exclusive or indeed as a principal factor' may not infringe Article 101(1). Indeed, the CJ has held that price competition 'does not constitute the only effective form of competition or that to which absolute priority must in all circumstances be afforded'[85] and maximum price setting may not infringe Article 101(1) so long as it does not operate as a 'focal point for the resellers' and which will be followed by them.[86] Recommended and maximum RPM and selective distribution may also be covered by the Verticals Regulation.[87]

(iii) ATP and Export Bans

Ever since *Société Technique Minière v Maschinenbau Ulm GmbH (STM)*[88] and *Établissements Consten SàRL & Grundig-Verkaufs-GmbH v Commission (Consten and Grundig)*[89] it has been clear that although appointing an exclusive distributor for a specific sales territory might not infringe Article 101(1), clauses in a distribution agreement which go beyond this and result in the isolation of a national market, and/or in maintaining separate national markets, are liable to be found to have as their object the

---

[80] Case T-208/01, *Volkswagen v Commission* [2003] ECR II-5141, *aff'd* Case C-74/04 P, [2006] ECR I-6585 (the GC quashed a Commission decision condemning RPM on the grounds that the Commission had failed to establish that the distributors had agreed to or acquiesced in the supplier's policy of RPM, see Chap. 4).

[81] Case 161/84, [1986] ECR 353, para. 25.

[82] Case 26/76, [1977] ECR 1875, para. 21.

[83] Case 243/83, [1985] ECR 2015, para. 44.

[84] Case 161/84, *Pronuptia de Paris GmbH v Pronuptia de Paris Irmgard Schillgallis* [1986] ECR 353, para. 25.

[85] Case 26/76, *Metro-SB-Grossmärkte GmbH v Commission (Metro I)* [1977] ECR 1875, para. 21, but see nn. 130 and 131 and text.

[86] Guidelines, para. 227.

[87] See Section 5.C.

[88] Case 56/65, [1966] ECR 235 (see extract set out in Chap. 4).

[89] Cases 56 and 58/64, [1966] ECR 299 (see extract set out in Chap. 4). See also, e.g., Case T-77/92, *Parker Pen v Commission* [1994] ECR II-549, Case C-501/06 P, *GlaxoSmithKline Services Unlimited v Commission* [2009] ECR I-9291, para. 61, Case T-360/09, *E.ON Ruhrgas AG v Commission* EU:C:2011:389, and see also Cases C-403 and 429/08, *Football Association Premier League Ltd and Others v QC Leisure and Others and Karen Murphy v Media Protection Services Ltd (Murphy)* EU:C:2011:631, paras. 137–139 (and Chap. 12) where the Grand Chamber of the CJ adopted a similar approach to that which it had adopted in *Consten and Grundig* 45 years earlier, when it distinguished between the situation where (a) a sole licensee was given an exclusive right to broadcast protected subject matter in a specified territory which was not anti-competitive by object and (b) agreements which went further, and partitioned national markets according to national borders (through clauses prohibiting broadcasters from effecting any cross-border provision of services) which tend to restore divisions between national markets and are liable to frustrate the Treaty's objective of achieving the integration of those markets through the establishment of a single market and must be regarded, in principle, as an agreement whose object is to restrict competition.

restriction of competition since they shelter the distributor from all intra-brand competition and lead to the division of national markets. In Chapter 4 it was seen that *Consten and Grundig* provides a clear example of the Court seeking to balance the EU policy of market integration against competition and efficiency.

G. Monti, 'Article 81 EC and Public Policy' (2002) *CMLRev* 1057–1099, 1065–1066

The more complex question is how to balance market integration with competition and efficiency, especially in the context of distribution agreement. The problem manifests itself because it has been argued (contrary to the Commission's position) that territorial protection is a means to increase competition in the market. This well-known argument can be summarized by reference to the decision in *Consten and Grundig*: Grundig's attempt to isolate the French market so as to give its exclusive distributor in France the opportunity to devote resources to market a new product was held unlawful, the CJ being deaf to the argument that without territorial protection, no reasonable distributor would have taken the risk of sinking costs into a new and uncertain market if he knew that a free rider would later enter and sell goods taking advantage of its marketing efforts.

Some economists would argue that in this situation, territorial protection is a necessary incentive to convince a distributor to market goods to remove the free-rider effect. Instead, under EC competition law, as Gyselen once memorably put it, the free rider is a 'hero' because he integrates markets by selling across borders. Paradoxically, this hard line may result in less competition and less integration: there would be less competition because firms might decide to integrate vertically, thus reducing the number of distributors in a Member State, to the possible disadvantage of new manufacturers who might find it harder to distribute their products; alternatively firms might decide not to export at all if they fear that commercial success will not materialize with an unprotected distributor, diminishing both competition and integration; or they might waste resources trying to find other means to prevent free riding without infringing competition provisions. These considerations suggest that territorial restrictions should be looked upon generously and that preference for market integration is counterproductive. However, economic learning and evidence from the United States suggests that absolute territorial protection does not *always* yield an efficient outcome. Comanor for example has argued that while with resale price maintenance agreements distributors are still able to compete against each other on things other than price, with territorial segregation all competition among rival distributors is lost, meaning that the increased prices set by distributors are not necessarily designed to recoup the costs of additional services provided to consumers, but are evidence of a welfare loss. Even in an integrated market like the United States, there is evidence that a lack of intra-brand competition can lead to anti-competitive results.

Therefore, economic evidence shows that it is impossible to state either that all territorial restraints by firms which lack market power are efficiency-enhancing (as some Chicago School lawyers would contend) nor that they are all inefficient (as *Consten and Grundig* suggests). This ambiguity poses a difficulty for competition authorities: the best approach would be to analyse territorial restrictions on a case-by-case basis to determine what the right amount of territorial protection is: however, this would lead to undesirable delay and uncertainty. The second-best solution is to devise some rule of thumb which draws a clear distinction between those territorial restrictions that are lawful and those that are unlawful which is a close as possible to the economic evidence but which allows parties to implement agreements speedily and with certainty. The rules of thumb deployed in the EC are stricter than those in the U.S. but,...the Commission has become increasingly willing to relax its tough stance against market partitioning agreement when this results in greater efficiencies.

As is the case for RPM, the Commission is concerned both about agreements which directly divide the EU market on territorial lines and those which do so indirectly through other measures or unilateral conduct by the supplier which is explicitly or tacitly accepted by the distributor,[90] for example:[91] where circulars are sent discouraging or prohibiting export;[92] where foreign customers are required to pay a deposit to the producer not required of national consumers;[93] where export is permitted but only if the consent of the producer is obtained;[94] where the producer must be contacted before exporting via the internet;[95] where goods are supplied to distributors but the invoice for supply bears the words 'export prohibited';[96] where insufficient quantities of goods are supplied with the objective of precluding export;[97] where performance bonuses are dependent upon dealers not exporting;[98] where exported products are bought back by the manufacturer;[99] where products supplied are marked so that parallel importers can be identified;[100] where guarantees are limited to the Member State in which the product was purchased;[101] where dual pricing is utilised to discourage export;[102] where an agreement requires a distributor to pass on any customer inquiries coming from outside the contract territory to the producer;[103] where a producer threatens to terminate or actually terminates contractual arrangements with distributors or dealers which sell outside their allotted territory;[104] or where financial support is contingent on products supplied to distributors being used only within a distributor's allotted territory.[105]

Further, in *Pierre Fabre v Président de l'Autorité de la concurrence*,[106] the CJ held that a requirement that a qualified pharmacist had to be present at a physical sales point operated as a *de facto* ban on internet selling which, in turn, considerably reduced the ability of a distributor to sell outside its territory and, so, was liable to restrict competition in that sector (see further the discussion of, and extract from, *Pierre Fabre* below). This approach accords with the view of the Commission that 'the promotion of online sales is extremely important for the internal market in Europe because it broadens

---

[90] See Chap. 3 and, in particular, Case T-41/96, *Bayer AG v Commission* [2000] ECR II-3383, *aff'd* Cases C-2 and 3/01 P, [2004] ECR I-23. In COMP/35.679, *Novalliance/Systemform* [1997] OJ L47/11 an export ban was prohibited even though stipulated to be applicable only 'unless prohibited by law'.

[91] See also the discussion of hardcore restraints prohibited by the Verticals Reg., n. 280 and text.

[92] See, e.g., COMP/31.503, *Konica* [1988] OJ L78/34.

[93] COMP/36.264, *Mercedes-Benz* [2002] OJ L257/1 (on appeal, Case T-325/01, *DaimlerChrysler v Commission* [2005] ECR II-3319, the GC found that the agreements were agency, see n. 36 and text).

[94] Case T-77/92, *Parker Pen v Commission* [1994] ECR II-549; Case 19/77, *Miller v Commission* [1978] ECR 131.

[95] COMP/37.975, *Yamaha* 16 July 2003.

[96] Case C-277/87, *Sandoz Prodotti Farmaceutici SpA v Commission* [1990] ECR I-45.

[97] See COMP/35.733, *Volkswagen* [1998] OJ L124/60, n. 116 and text.

[98] COMP/36.623, 36.820, and 37.725, *Peugeot* [2005] OJ L173/49, *aff'd* (but fine reduced) Case T-450/05, *Peugeot v Commission* [2009] ECR II-2533. In this case the discriminatory bonus system was backed up by a threat to reduce supplies to exporting dealers.

[99] Case T-38/92, *All Weather Sports Benelux v Commission* [1994] ECR II-211 and Case T-43/92, *Dunlop Slazenger v Commission* [1994] ECR II-441.

[100] COMP/32.948 and COMP/34.590, *Tretorn* [1994] OJ L378/45, COMP/25.757, *Hasselblad AG* [1982] OJ L161/18.

[101] COMP/1576, *Zanussi* 23 October 1978; Case 31/85, *ETA Fabriques d'Ébauches v DK Investments SA* [1985] ECR 3933. Guarantees can be limited to products sold by an authorised distributor within a selective distribution system, however, see Case C-376/92, *Metro v Cartier* [1994] ECR I-15, paras. 32–34.

[102] COMP/28.282, *The Distillers Co Ltd* [1978] OJ L50/16, on appeal Case 30/78, *Distillers Co v Commission* [1980] ECR 2229; and see COMP/30.228, *Distillers Co plc (Red Label)* [1983] OJ C245/3; COMP/32.390, *Newitt/Dunlop Slazenger International* [1992] OJ L131/32, on appeal Case T-38/92, *All Weather Sports Benelux v Commission* [1994] ECR II-211 and Case T-43/92, *Dunlop Slazenger v Commission* [1994] ECR II-441; and Case C-501/06 P, *GlaxoSmithKline Services Unlimited v Commission* [2009] ECR I-9291, see Chap. 4.

[103] Case T-175/95, *BASF Coating AG v Commission* [1999] ECR II-1581.

[104] COMP/35.733, *Volkswagen* [1998] OJ L124/60, n. 116 and text.

[105] COMP/35.918, *JCB* [2002] OJ L69/1, this aspect of the decision upheld, Case T-67/01, *JCB Service v Commission* [2004] ECR II-49, *aff'd* Case C-167/04 P, *JCB Service v Commission* [2006] ECR I-8935.

[106] Case C-439/09, EU:C:2011:277.

the market, improves the choices for customers, and generally speaking, enhances competition'.[107] Thus, generally, every distributor should be allowed to use the internet to sell its products; online selling constitutes a form of passive (not active) selling which can be restricted only in exceptional circumstances. A question which remains to be decided, however, is whether a prohibition of certain forms of internet selling (for example, via a platform or a price comparison site) constitutes a ban on passive selling—this issue has been raised in some cases arising before national competition authorities (NCAs).[108]

(iv) RPM and ATP Pursuing a Legitimate Objective?

In Chapter 4 it was seen that there is no such thing as a list of object restraints; both content and context must be considered before the precise purpose of the agreement can be said to restrict competition.[109] Indeed the CJ recognised in *Pierre Fabre*[110] that a SDS incorporating a ban, or *de facto* ban, on internet selling[111] would not constitute a restriction by object where it constituted a proportionate measure to achieve a legitimate aim.[112] Nonetheless, there is no EU Court judgment or Commission decision, involving an ordinary vertical agreement (rather than an intellectual property (IP) licensing agreement[113]) in which it has been accepted on the facts that either ATP or RPM is objectively necessary to achieve a legitimate aim. Rather the jurisprudence reflects an underlying presumption that RPM and parallel trade restrictions do have as their object the restriction of competition between dealers and are a disproportionate means to achieve any aims alleged to be sought by the parties to the agreement. Price competition is so important it should never be eliminated and restrictions on parallel trade frustrate the Treaty's objective of achieving the integration of national markets through the establishment of a single market.

In its Verticals Guidelines the Commission recognises that such an opportunity exists in the case of ATP, stating that such restraints will fall outside Article 101(1) for two years where a manufacturer needs to encourage substantial investments by a distributor in order to start developing a market.

61. A distributor which will be the first to sell a new brand or the first to sell an existing brand on a new market, thereby ensuring a genuine entry on the relevant market, may have to commit substantial investments where there was previously no demand for that type of product in general or for that type of product from that producer. Such expenses may often be sunk and in such circumstances the distributor may not enter into the distribution agreement without protection for a certain period of time against (active and) passive sales into its territory or to its customer group by other distributors. For example such a situation may occur where a manufacturer established in a particular national market enters another national market and introduces its products with the help of an exclusive distributor and where this distributor needs to invest in launching and establishing the brand on this new market. Where substantial investments by the distributor to start up and/or develop the new market are necessary, restrictions of passive sales by other distributors into such a territory or to such a customer group which are necessary for the distributor to recoup those investments generally fall outside the scope of Article 101(1) during the first two years that the distributor is

---

[107] 'Interview with Dr. Alexander Italianer, Director-General for Competition, European Commission', *theantitrustsource*, April 2011, 1, 6; Guidelines, paras. 52–54.

[108] See, e.g., the settlement reached by the Bundeskartellamt (the German NCA) following its investigation into *Adidas*, Case B3 137/12, 27 June 2014 (English summary available at <http://www.bundeskartellamt.de/SharedDocs/Entscheidung/EN/Fallberichte/Kartellverbot/2014/B3-137-12.pdf?__blob=publicationFile&v=2>).

[109] See Chap. 4.

[110] Case C-439/09, EU:C:2011:277.

[111] Ibid., para. 38.

[112] It was 'liable to restrict competition', ibid., para. 39.

[113] See Cases C-403 and 429/08, *Murphy* EU:C:2011:631 and discussion in Chap. 12.

selling the contract goods or services in that territory or to that customer group, even though such hardcore restrictions are in general presumed to fall within the scope of Article 101(1).

62. In the case of genuine testing of a new product in a limited territory or with a limited customer group and in the case of a staggered introduction of a new product, the distributors appointed to sell the new product on the test market or to participate in the first round(s) of the staggered introduction may be restricted in their active selling outside the test market or the market(s) where the product is first introduced without falling within the scope of Article 101(1) for the period necessary for the testing or introduction of the product.

These statements are not easy to reconcile with past case law (and in particular cases such as *Consten and Grundig* and *Distillers*[114]) where pleas that restrictions on parallel trade were required to enable the supplier to penetrate a new market fell on deaf ears. In addition, the Guidelines contain no similar statement in relation to RPM, suggesting (without explanation) that the Commission does not envisage circumstances in which it could be held that a pro-competitive objective pursued, might warrant a finding that RPM does not restrict competition by object. The Guidelines do accept, however, that in exceptional circumstances RPM might generate efficiencies cognisable under Article 101(3).[115] This approach is not easy to follow; in one situation the Commission suggests that efficiency justifications are cognisable and relevant characterisation under Article 101(1) and in another that (broadly the same) efficiency justifications are cognisable only under Article 101(3).

The uncertainty as to whether and if so when RPM or restrictions on parallel trade might be compatible with Article 101 means that it is risky to incorporate such restraints into an agreement. Indeed, in the past the Commission has been willing to impose significant fines on those engaged in such practices, for example: in *VW*[116] the Commission imposed fines of €102 million (reduced to €90 million on appeal)[117] in respect of a wide range of contractual practices designed to prevent distributors selling outside their contractual territory; in *Nintendo*[118] the Commission imposed a fine of €167.8 million on Nintendo and seven of its European distributors for colluding to prevent exports from low-priced to high-priced countries; and in *Yamaha*,[119] *JCB*,[120] and *Volkswagen*[121] it imposed fines in relation to RPM. In the latter two cases, however, the GC annulled the Commission's findings that an RPM policy had been implemented and agreed to, or acquiesced in, by the distributors.[122] In *Volkswagen*, the CJ[123] upheld the annulment ruling that a call by a manufacturer would only be prohibited by Article 101(1) if the Commission established concurrence of wills on the part of the parties to the dealership agreement.[124] Article 101 does not prevent a supplier from pursuing a policy of minimum resale prices if that policy is not accepted by its distributors.[125]

---

[114] See nn. 102 and 316 and text.

[115] See nn. 323–324 and text.

[116] COMP/35.733, *Volkswagen* [1998] OJ L124/60.

[117] Case T-62/98, *Volkswagen AG v Commission* [2000] ECR II-2707 (fine reduced), *aff'd* Case C-338/00 P, *Volkswagen AG v Commission* [2003] ECR I-9189.

[118] COMP/35.706 and 36.321, [2003] OJ L255/33, *aff'd* (but fines reduced), Case T-12/03, *Itochu v Commission* [2009] ECR II-909 and Case T-13/03, *Nintendo and Nintendo of Europe v Commission* [2009] ECR II-975, Case C-260/09 P, *Activision Blizzard Germany GmbH v Commission* EU:C:2011:62. See also COMP/39.154, *Apple/iTunes* 18 March 2008.

[119] COMP/37.975, *Yamaha* 16 July 2003.

[120] COMP/35.918, [2002] OJ L691.

[121] COMP/36.693, [2001] OJ L262/14 (imposing a fine of €30.96 million on Volkswagen).

[122] Case T-67/01, *JCB Service v Commission* [2004] ECR II-49, para. 130 (this finding was not challenged before the CJ, which broadly upheld the judgment of the GC, Case C-167/04 P, *JCB Service v Commission* [2006] ECR I-8935. Note that the agreement in *JCB* was originally notified to the Commission in June 1973!) and Case T-208/01, *Volkswagen v Commission* [2003] ECR II-5141, *aff'd* Case C-74/04 P, [2006] ECR I-6585, see Chap. 3.

[123] Case C-74/04 P, [2006] ECR I-6585.

[124] Ibid., paras. 39–56.

[125] For a discussion of unilateral conduct and agreements, see Chap. 3, Section 5.B.ii.

Although the Commission has not adopted an infringement decision involving a vertical agreement since 2005[126] (in June 2014, however, the EU commenced an investigation into territorial restrictions incorporated in broadcasting licensing agreements concluded between US film studios and EU broadcasters, see Chapter 12), a number of NCAs have been active in this area, in particular, fining undertakings found to have engaged in RPM or other practices designed to limit online sales.[127] Further, the Commission has made it clear that it is considering the extent to which barriers are being erected by companies to cross-border online trade in its e-commerce sector inquiry (focusing on sectors where e-commerce is most widespread such as electronics, clothing, shoes, and digital content) and what effects they are having on competition and consumers.[128] Enforcement action is likely to follow if unlawful restraints are uncovered during the course of this inquiry.

(v) Other Object Restraints, *Pierre Fabre* and *Allianz Hungária*

In Chapter 4 it is seen that there the category of object restraints includes all agreements whose content and context reveal in themselves a sufficient degree of harm to competition law. The Commission takes the view that all of the 'hardcore' restraints set out in Article 4 of the Verticals Regulation (which, in addition to RPM, includes, subject to limited exceptions, all restrictions on a buyer as to where (the territory) or to whom (the customers) the buyer can sell the contract products, actively and/or passively, restrictions on cross-selling by members of a SDS,[129] and certain restrictions on components suppliers)[130] are restrictive of competition by object, but the determination is of course for the EU Courts to make.

Further, two judgments of the CJ indicate that the category of vertical object restraints may be more expansive than had generally been thought. In particular, it will be seen in the discussion of SDSs below, that in *Pierre Fabre* the CJ held that such systems 'necessarily affect competition' and 'are to be considered, in the absence of objective justification, as restrictions by object'.[131] Thus SDSs which are not objectively justified—that is which 'aim at the attainment of a legitimate goal capable of improving competition in relation to factors other than price'[132]—automatically violate Article 101(1).

In *Allianz Hungária Biztosító Zrt, Generali-Providencia Biztosító Zrt v Gazdasági Versenyhivatal*,[133] the CJ also made it clear that as vertical restrictions could have particularly significant restrictive potential, the agreements, their objectives, and context had to be examined before the national court

---

[126] See COMP/36.623, 36.820, and 37.275, *Peugeot* [2006] OJ L173/20. But see COMP/39.771, 10 October 2012 (rejection of complaint brought against Oxford University Press, Burlington Books, and Pearson PLC alleging that restrictions had been imposed on their distributors' ability to sell English Language Teaching (ELT) books across borders and setting resale prices. Although the allegations related to 'hardcore' restrictions of competition, the Commission considered that an investigation would be disproportionate in the light of the limited impact that the conduct was likely to have on the functioning of the internal market, the complexity of the investigation required, the limited likelihood of establishing proof of a violation, and that the alleged infringement had ceased. This case could be taken as evidence of a more measured approach to hardcore restraints at EU level. On the other hand, the Commission's inactivity in this area could plausibly be attributed to a decision by it to focus resources elsewhere, combined with confidence that there is a healthy level of enforcement at the national level. Indeed, an important reason for rejecting the complaint relating to the distribution of ELT books was that the Greek competition authority had already dealt with the matter and would be well placed to deal with the alleged infringements).

[127] Especially the French and German NCAs.

[128] C(2015) 3026 final, see n. 69 and text.

[129] See Case 86/82, *Hasselblad v Commission* [1984] ECR 883, para. 46.

[130] See Staff Working Document, 'Guidance on restrictions of competition "by object" for the purposes of defining which agreements may benefit from the *De Minimis* Notice', SWD(2014) 198 final, s. 3.

[131] Case C-439/09, EU:C:2011:277, para. 39. For the view that the decision of the CJ to hold all SDSs to be restrictions by object is quite remarkable 'and probably a slip of the tongue. It is internally inconsistent because if one looks at the final holding of the Court, the restriction by object is only the ban on internet sales, not the use of selective distribution', see Monti, n. 3, 501.

[132] Case C-439/09, ibid., para. 40.

[133] Case C-32/11, EU:C:2013:160.

could determine whether a national court should classify a vertical agreement incorporating restraints as restrictive by object or not.[134] This case involved proceedings which had been brought by the Hungarian competition authority, GVH, in relation to a series of bilateral vertical agreements concluded annually between Hungarian insurance companies and car dealer/repairers. The GVH concluded that the arrangements had as their object the restriction of competition and imposed significant fines. Following judicial proceedings the Hungarian Supreme Court referred to the CJ the question of whether they were indeed restrictive of competition by object.

The CJ after repeating the general requirement that to determine if an agreement is restrictive of competition by object regard must be had to the content of its provisions, its objectives, and the economic and legal context of which it forms a part, held that account had to be taken of a number of facts, including that the agreements: linked the dealers' remuneration and the insurance broker function, were designed to increase the market shares of Generali and Allianz, and were concluded on the basis of 'recommended prices' established in decisions taken by GÉMOSZ. In particular, it held that the insurance companies by concluding agreements with GÉMOSZ could be treated as confirming the decision of GÉMOSZ to recommend prices, which had as its object the restriction of competition, and rendering those agreements as restrictive by object.

Case C-32/11, *Allianz Hungária Biztosító Zrt, Generali-Providencia Biztosító Zrt v Gazdasági Versenyhivatal* EU:C:2013:160

39. Concerning the agreements referred to in the question submitted, it should be noted that they relate to the hourly charge to be paid by the insurance company to car dealers, acting as repair shops, for the repair of cars in the event of accidents. They provide that that charge is increased in accordance with the number and percentage of insurance contracts that the dealer sells for that company.

40. Such agreements therefore link the remuneration for the car repair service to that for the car insurance brokerage. The linkage of those two different services is possible because of the fact that the dealers act in relation to the insurers in a dual capacity, namely as intermediaries or brokers, offering car insurance to their customers at the time of sale or repair of vehicles, and as repair shops, repairing vehicles after accidents on behalf of the insurers.

41. However, while the establishment of such a link between two activities which are in principle independent does not automatically mean that the agreement concerned has as its object the restriction of competition, it can nevertheless constitute an important factor in determining whether that agreement is by its nature injurious to the proper functioning of normal competition, which is the case, in particular, where the independence of those activities is necessary for that functioning.

42. Moreover, it is necessary to take account of the fact that such an agreement is likely to affect not only one, but two markets, in this case those of car insurance and car repair services, and that its object must be determined with respect to the two markets concerned.

43. In that regard, it must, first, be noted that, in contrast to the view apparently held by Allianz and Generali, the fact that both cases concern vertical relationships in no way excludes the possibility that the agreement at issue in the main proceedings constitutes a restriction of competition 'by object'. While vertical agreements are, by their nature, often less damaging to competition than horizontal agreements, they can, nevertheless, in some cases, also have a particularly significant restrictive potential. The Court has thus already held on several occasions that a vertical agreement had as its object the restriction of competition (see Joined Cases 56/64 and 58/64 *Consten and Grundig* v *Commission* [1966] ECR 429; Case 19/77 *Miller International Schallplatten* v *Commission* [1978] ECR 131; Case 243/83 *Binon* [1985] ECR 2015; and *Pierre Fabre Dermo-Cosmétique*).

---

[134] Ibid., para. 48.

44. Next, with regard to determining the object of the agreements at issue in the main proceedings with respect to the car insurance market, it should be noted that, by such agreements, insurance companies such as Allianz and Generali aim to maintain or increase their market shares.

45. It is not disputed that, if there was a horizontal agreement or a concerted practice between those two companies designed to partition the market, such an agreement or practice would have to be treated as a restriction by object and would also result in the unlawfulness of the vertical agreements concluded in order to implement that agreement or practice. Allianz and Generali dispute however that they acted in agreement or concert and claim that the contested decision found that there was no such agreement or practice. It is for the referring court to check the accuracy of those claims and, to the extent that it is enabled under domestic law, to determine whether there is enough evidence to establish the existence of an agreement or concerted practice between Allianz and Generali.

46. Nevertheless, even if there is no agreement or concerted practice between those insurance companies, it will still be necessary to determine whether, taking account of the economic and legal context of which they form a part, the vertical agreements at issue in the main proceedings are sufficiently injurious to competition on the car insurance market as to amount to a restriction of competition by object.

47. That could in particular be the case where, as is claimed by the Hungarian Government, domestic law requires that dealers acting as intermediaries or insurance brokers must be independent from the insurance companies. That government claims, in that regard, that those dealers do not act on behalf of an insurer, but on behalf of the policyholder and it is their job to offer the policyholder the insurance which is the most suitable for him amongst the offers of various insurance companies. It is for the referring court to determine whether, in those circumstances and in light of the expectations of those policyholders, the proper functioning of the car insurance market is likely to be significantly disrupted by the agreements at issue in the main proceedings.

48. Furthermore, those agreements would also amount to a restriction of competition by object in the event that the referring court found that it is likely that, having regard to the economic context, competition on that market would be eliminated or seriously weakened following the conclusion of those agreements. In order to determine the likelihood of such a result, that court should in particular take into consideration the structure of that market, the existence of alternative distribution channels and their respective importance and the market power of the companies concerned.

49. Finally, with regard to determining the object of the agreements at issue in the main proceedings with respect to the car repair service market, it is necessary to take account of the fact that those agreements appear to have been concluded on the basis of 'recommended prices' established in the three decisions taken by GÉMOSZ from 2003 to 2005. In that context, it is for the referring court to determine the exact nature and scope of those decisions (see, to that effect, Case C-260/07 *Pedro IV Servicios* [2009] ECR I-2437, paragraphs 78 and 79).

50. In the event that that court holds that the decisions taken by GÉMOSZ during that period in fact had as their object the restriction of competition by harmonising hourly charges for car repairs and that, by the agreements at issue, the insurance companies voluntarily confirmed those decisions, which can be assumed where the insurance company concluded an agreement directly with GÉMOSZ, the unlawfulness of those decisions would vitiate those agreements, which would then also be considered a restriction of competition by object.

51. In the light of all of the foregoing considerations, the answer to the question submitted is that Article 101(1) TFEU must be interpreted as meaning that agreements whereby car insurance companies come to bilateral arrangements, either with car dealers acting as car repair shops or with an association representing those dealers, concerning the hourly charge to be paid by the insurance company for repairs to vehicles insured by it, stipulating that that charge depends, inter alia, on the number and percentage of insurance contracts that the dealer has sold as intermediary for that company, can be considered a restriction of competition 'by object' within the meaning of that provision, where, following a concrete and individual examination of the wording and aim of those agreements and of the economic and legal context of which they form a part, it is apparent that they are, by their very nature, injurious to the proper functioning of normal competition on one of the two markets concerned.

In Chapter 4 it has been seen that there has been concern about the breadth of some of the statements and findings in this judgment (in particular those made in paragraph 48), but that the subsequent ruling of the CJ in *Groupement des Cartes Bancaires (CB) v Commission*[135] reiterates that (a) the category of object restrictions should be interpreted *restrictively* and reserved exclusively for agreements which inherently reveal a sufficient degree of harm to competition and (b) no detailed market analysis should be conducted in object cases; if such an assessment is required that suggests that a fuller effects analysis must be conducted.

An important question is how these judgments impact on a number of cases arising before the Commission and NCAs which raise the issue of how certain 'new' business practices which may resemble RPM, for example MFNs, price relationship agreements, or contracts that reference rivals, are to be characterised and analysed under Article 101 generally and, specifically, under Article 101(1).[136] Difficult issues to be decided include whether these (or any of these) types of clause should be analysed as a form of RPM (whether they are frequently incorporated either at the behest of a powerful buyer with the objective of raising rivals' costs of entry into the market or as a mechanism for facilitating collusion or dampening competition between sellers), whether wholesale and retail MFNs should be assessed differently and/or whether the analysis should be affected depending on whether the clauses relate to sales through physical stores or through a multi-sided platform. In particular, whether any such restraints are sufficiently deleterious to be treated as a restriction by object or whether, given the relative lack of experience with these provisions and their potential to give rise to significant efficiencies by, for example, facilitating customer investment or market entry and/or reducing transaction costs, effects analysis should be conducted to ensure a fuller understanding of the clauses is accumulated.[137]

A number of competition authorities have treated these types of provision with suspicion. For example, in *Tobacco*[138] the UK's NCA (then the Office of Fair Trading (OFT)) held that bilateral vertical agreements concluded between two tobacco manufacturers and their retailers, under which retailers agreed to set retail prices for cigarettes and other tobacco products in accordance with set 'parity and differential requirements' relating to competing linked brands, restricted competition by object (for the purposes of the Competition Act 1998, the UK equivalent of Article 101). It imposed significant fines, totalling £225 million, on the parties involved. On appeal, however, the Competition Appeal Tribunal annulled the decision because the OFT refined its case during the course of the appeal proceedings. It did not therefore have to rule on the important question of whether the OFT had been correct to categorise the restraints as restrictive by object.[139]

In *e-books*[140] it has been seen that the Commission was concerned about the distribution arrangements of five international publishers and Apple which had been switched from a wholesale to an agency model. The agency agreements incorporated MFNs, relating to the price at which the

---

[135] C-67/13 P, EU:C:2014:2204.

[136] See, e.g., a report published by the UK's Office of Fair Trading (OFT) and prepared by Laboratorio di Economia, Antitrust, Regolamentazione (LEAR), OFT 1438, 'Can "Fair" Prices be Unfair? A Review of Price Relationship Agreements', September 2012, <http://www.oft.gov.uk/shared_oft/research/OFT1438.pdf>.

[137] See, e.g., OFT 1438, ibid., J. P. van der Veer, 'Antitrust Scrutiny of Most-favoured-customer Clauses: An Economic Analysis' (2013) 6 *JECLAP* 501, 503–504, OECD, 'Vertical Restraints for On-line Sales', DAF/COMP(2013)13, 145–150, available at <http://www.oecd.org/competition/VerticalRestraintsForOnlineSales2013.pdf>, papers and reports at <http://www.oecd.org/daf/competition/competition-cross-platform-parity.htm>, A. Fletcher and M. Hviid, 'Retail Price MFNs: Are they RPM "At Its Worst"', CCP Working Paper 14-5, and 'The Digitisation of European Cinemas', IP/11/257. In the UK the OFT considered MFNs utilised in the online hotel sector operated like RPM provisions, see n. 141.

[138] Case CE/2596-03, *Tobacco* 15 April 2010.

[139] Cases 1160–1165/1/1/10 [2011] CAT 41. Given the complexity of the theory of harm involved, arguably this was conduct which should have been analysed more fully to assess its effects, see A. Jones and A. Turati, 'The UK Tobacco Case: Identifying Restrictions by Object in Vertical Agreements' (2012) 5 *JECLAP* 287.

[140] COMP/39.847, *e-books* [2012] OJ C73/17, see also Chap. 13 and the opinion of the Court of Appeals (2d Cir. 2015) in the US, *United States v Apple, Inc, and Others* 30 June 2015.

publishers would sell its products on competing platforms. The compatibility with Article 101 of the individual vertical agency agreements (and the MFNs within them) alone did not, however, directly arise in this case as the Commission focused on a suspected concerted practice between the publishers and Apple to raise retail prices. Although, therefore, the theory of harm did not relate specifically to the individual use of MFNs in the vertical contracts, but rather to the coordination between the publishers and Apple, the proceedings were brought to an end by commitments given by the parties both to terminate existing agency agreements and to refrain from adopting price MFNs.

Although the Commission is yet to adopt a decision involving MFNs in a purely vertical situation, a number of NCAs[141] have been scrutinising their use in contracts between hotels and online travel agents (OTAs, including Hotel Reservation Service (HRS), Booking.com and Expedia). Essentially, there has been concern about the use of broad MFNs in the hotel online booking sector, obliging hotels to commit not to offer lower rates or better conditions/availability either itself, or on other platforms, to those offered on the OTA's platform. In 2013, the German NCA (the Bundeskartellamt, or Federal Cartel Office (FCO)) adopted a decision finding that HRS's MFNs infringed competition law (both German and EU);[142] the FCO considered that the clauses restricted competition between the OTAs (preventing them from competing for the lowest commissions and best condition terms), made it more difficult for OTAs to enter the market and restricted competition between hotels, preventing them from competing for the best price of rooms. These anti-competitive effects were strengthened by the use of MFNs by the other major OTAs and the conditions of Article 101(3) were not met.[143] Although the FCO found at first glance that the free-riding argument raised to justify the clauses was persuasive, it did not find it to be supported by market data.

The FCO also continued to pursue proceedings against Booking.com, even after other NCAs, including the French, Italian, and Swedish authorities, accepted commitments from Booking.com, coordinated within the forum of the European Competition Network (ECN), to bring their proceedings against it to an end.[144] Essentially, these commitments allowed Booking.com to retain 'narrower' provisions, allowing the hotels to give OTAs parity in respect of rates and conditions published by the hotels online (but eliminating availability parity and price/condition parity against other OTAs or through offline channels of hotels and allowing hotels to offer lower rates to, for example, loyal customers).[145] These settlements are proving controversial however. Not only has the FCO not yet accepted that these narrow MFNs are compatible with Article 101, but in France the legislator has intervened to render unenforceable contractual provisions that prohibit hotels from displaying better deals for rooms on their own websites.[146]

There has been some concern expressed that the different approaches to MFNs create uncertainty for companies as to whether this type of conduct infringes Article 101. Although therefore the close level of cooperation between the authorities within the ECN in the hotel bookings case is unprecedented, and the variances in approach could be argued to be explicable by reason of the differing competitive dynamics of the national markets involved, it seems clear that greater coordination may be necessary in the future. Although the Commission did play a role in coordinating the national

---

[141] Including Austria, Belgium, Czech Republic, Denmark, France, Germany, Hungary, Ireland, Italy, Norway, Sweden, and the UK.

[142] 20 December 2013. This decision was upheld on appeal by the Higher Regional Court in Düsseldorf.

[143] It found that HRS's contractual terms could not be exempted under the Verticals Block Exemption Reg. (since the market share of the agent exceeded 30%) or individually under Art. 101(3). In particular, It was unclear how a fair share (of any established benefit) could be passed on to consumers since the hotels could not offer lower prices without offering them to all portals simultaneously.

[144] See N. Varona and A. Hernadez Canales, 'Online Hotel Booking', *CPI Antitrust Chronicle* May 2015.

[145] The NCAs hope that this will encourage competition between OTAs to compete for low commissions and encourage new entrants into the market.

[146] The Macron Law was passed in France in August 2015.

investigations, it has been questioned whether it should have intervened and taken the lead in cases involving a new kind of business practice.[147]

(vi) Object Restrictions—A Need for a Rethink?

Given a greater acceptance that vertical restraints on intra-brand competition (including ATP and RPM provisions) may be imposed for pro-competitive reasons, it may be questioned whether it is right to continue to treat these (or any) vertical restraints as object restraints, which are assumed to restrict competition. Rather, in the light of the potential of these restraints to enhance efficiency, can it really ever be said that they reveal in themselves a sufficient degree of harm to competition so that their precise purpose can be said to restrict competition?[148] Should it not be for the Commission, or other person trying to prove the same, to demonstrate the anti-competitive effects of the provisions before they are found to infringe Article 101(1)? Indeed, a leading economist has stated:

Theoretically, the only defensible position on vertical restraints seems to be the rule of reason. Most vertical restraints can increase or decrease welfare, depending on the environment. Legality or illegality per se thus seems unwarranted.[149]

In the US, challenges in the 1960s and the 1970s to the Supreme Court's rulings that many vertical intra-brand restraints, including minimum RPM,[150] maximum RPM,[151] and customer and territorial restraints,[152] were illegal per se under s. 1 of the Sherman Act led the Court to rethink and review the rules and, eventually, to disband each of the per se prohibitions. In 1977, in its landmark opinion in *Continental TV, Inc v GTE Sylvania*,[153] the Supreme Court overruled the per se rule against non-price intra-brand restraints and instated the rule of reason as the prevailing and presumptive standard of antitrust analysis. In so doing the Court accepted that the market impact of a vertical *non-price* intra-brand restriction (in that case, a location clause) was complex because of its ability simultaneously to reduce intra-brand competition and to stimulate inter-brand competition. The Court held that inter-brand competition was the primary concern of antitrust law,[154] emphasised the distribution efficiencies brought about by vertical restraints,[155] and concluded that any anti-competitive effects resulting from vertical non-price intra-brand restraints could adequately be identified and judged under the rule of reason.[156]

Subsequently, in *State Oil v Khan*,[157] the Court overruled the per se rule against maximum RPM and in *Leegin Creative Leather Products Inc v PSKS, Inc*[158] the Supreme Court held that fixed and

---

[147] The Commission declined to examine the case in June 2014. MLex later reported however that Commissioner Vestager had commented that this case illustrated that the EU should intervene earlier in new markets and that better coordination may be necessary in future cases, see further n. 345 and text.

[148] See Chap. 4.

[149] J. Tirole, *The Theory of Industrial Organization* (MIT Press, 1988), 186 (although the author accepts that this conclusion puts too heavy a burden on antitrust authorities and recognises the need for economic theorists to develop classifications and criteria to facilitate a determination of when such restraints are liable to harm social welfare).

[150] *Dr Miles Medical Co v John D Park & Sons Co*, 220 US 373 (1911).

[151] See *Keifer-Stewart Co v Joseph E. Seagram & Sons Inc*, 340 US 211 (1951) and *Albrecht v Herald Co*, 390 US 145 (1968).

[152] *United States v Arnold, Schwinn & Co*, 388 US 365, 376 (1967).

[153] 433 US 36 (1977).

[154] Ibid., n. 19.

[155] It thus indicated that non-competition factors, such as the protection of property rights and the autonomy of independent dealers, should not be relevant to the appraisal.

[156] On remand, the location clauses were found to be reasonable. The Ninth Circuit affirmed, stating that the plaintiff had to prove the unreasonableness of the restraint given its overall effect on intra- and inter-brand competition (simply proving a lessening of intra-brand competition does not shift the burden of justification to the defendant), *Continental TV Inc v GTE Sylvania Inc*, 694 F.2d 1132 (9th Cir. 1982).

[157] 522 US 3 (1997).

[158] 551 US 887 (2007). For a fuller analysis of the case, see, e.g., A. Jones, 'Resale Price Maintenance: A Debate About Competition Policy in Europe?' (2009) 5 *European Competition Journal* 479.

minimum RPM should also be analysed under the rule of reason. Very broadly, the majority[159] accepted that as the economics literature was 'replete' with pro-competitive justifications for a manufacturer's use of RPM (in particular, where necessary to stimulate inter-brand competition by, for example, preventing free-riding on a dealer's services or reputation, to allow suppliers to open up and enter new markets, to achieve a desired level of investment in retail services, to deal with demand uncertainty at the retail level, and/or to ensure high prices where such prices constitute part of a product's allure (to encourage higher prices for branded, luxury goods)),[160] the impact of RPM should be analysed under the rule of reason even though it might sometimes be anti-competitive.[161]

In stark contrast to the position that existed in 1976, therefore, minimum RPM, maximum RPM, and all non-price intra-brand restraints are illegal in the US only if proved to be in unreasonable restraint of trade under a rule of reason analysis. No violation of s. 1 will be established therefore if the plaintiff cannot establish that the agreement causes anti-competitive effects. Only then will the burden shift to the defendant(s) to establish a justification.

The dramatic evolution of US law in this area adds fuel to the debate about the strict approach against ATP, bans on online selling, and RPM in the EU. Indeed, the view could be taken that the economic arguments accepted by the majority in *Leegin* also suggest that these types of restraints are inappropriate for categorisation as restrictive by object. Rather, a fuller analysis should be required in each case to determine whether the effect of such conduct is in fact restrictive of competition (a theory of harm should be demonstrated). Even if normatively speaking this were considered to be correct, it seems most unlikely in reality that the CJ could be persuaded that such a change in approach would be desirable. It has been seen that, not only have vertical agreements containing ATP or RPM provisions been characterised time after time as restraints which have as their object the restriction of competition, but the CJ has consistently rejected arguments that the characterisation in a particular case should be contradicted by an argument that the parties pursued a legitimate object or did not in fact restrict competition.

Further, it seems most unlikely that the CJ would, more radically, be persuaded, as the US Supreme Court was in *Sylvania* and *Leegin*, that either restraint is no longer a suitable candidate for 'object' analysis. It only rarely reverses previous rulings and it seems doubtful that it would see fit to do so in relation to either of these situations. First, the EU cases express particular concern about protecting the process of rivalry between firms at the distributors', as well as the suppliers', level; restraints on intra-brand competition may therefore it seems be a concern even where inter-brand competition is intense.[162] Secondly, it has been seen that the internal market project gives the analysis in the EU a different dimension; agreements which erect private barriers to trade between Member States are problematic.

Further, in relation to RPM at least, it has been questioned whether or not the Supreme Court in *Leegin* was right to have dismantled the per se rule against it.[163] In particular, proponents of the per se rule (or at least a (rebuttable) presumption of illegality for RPM) have pointed to evidence that RPM may be used to facilitate, encourage, and/or allow collusion (explicit or tacit) between retailers or

---

[159] Roberts CJ and Scalia, Thomas, and Alito JJ joined in the Opinion.

[160] B. Orbach, 'Antitrust Vertical Myopia: The Allure of High Prices' (2008) 50 *Arizona LR* 261–287, Arizona Legal Studies, Discussion Paper No. 07-25.

[161] And not the per se rule which was confined to restraints that always or almost always tend to restrict competition, have manifestly anti-competitive effects, and lack any redeeming virtue.

[162] See Chap. 4.

[163] See, e.g., Comanor, n. 60; R. Pitofsky, 'In Defense of Discounters: The No-frills Case for a Per Se Rule Against Vertical Price Fixing' (1983) 71 *Geo LJ* 1487; M. L. Lao, 'Free Riding: An Overstated, and Unconvincing, Explanation for Resale Price Maintenance', Seton Hall Law School, Public Law and Legal Theory Research Paper Series, available at <http://ssrn.com/abstract=1024221>; and amici curiae brief filed by 37 states supporting the respondent before the Supreme Court in *Leegin*.

manufacturers,[164] leads to a rise in consumer prices,[165] eliminates innovative and dynamic competition from discounting retailers,[166] might be used to 'appease dealer interests in excess profits or the quiet life',[167] and/or may even produce anti-competitive effects in markets where there is competition upstream and downstream.[168] They have also raised concern that the free-rider argument, used to justify many vertical restraints on intra-brand competition, is frequently exaggerated and in fact applies only to relatively few products.[169] Indeed, concerns that RPM might cause anti-competitive effects with some regularity led four Justices in *Leegin* to dissent. Justice Breyer, writing for the minority, noted that US history provided empirical support for the view that RPM led to considerably higher retail prices[170] and that economists generally concurred on this point.[171] In contrast, he found no satisfactory answer to the question as to when and how often benefits, such as the prevention of free-riding, were likely to occur[172] and considered that courts would have extreme difficulty in identifying instances in which benefits were likely to outweigh harm. As antitrust law should be informed by economics but could not always replicate economists' (sometimes conflicting) views, he concluded that it would sometimes be acceptable to provide a rule of per se unlawfulness to a business practice which could at times produce benefits. The Commission, although recognising that RPM may sometimes lead to efficiencies which can be considered under Article 101(3), echoes these concerns about anti-competitive effects in its Guidelines and supports the view that RPM should be presumed to infringe Article 101(1). This view seems to be supported by many NCAs.[173] The Guidelines set out the Commission's core concerns about RPM.

224. RPM may restrict competition in a number of ways. Firstly, RPM may facilitate collusion between suppliers by enhancing price transparency in the market, thereby making it easier to detect whether a supplier deviates from the collusive equilibrium by cutting its price. RPM also undermines the incentive for the supplier to cut its price to its distributors, as the fixed resale price will prevent it from benefiting from expanded sales. This negative effect is in particular plausible if the market is prone to collusive outcomes, for instance

---

[164] See, e.g., D. O'Brien and G. Shaffer, 'Vertical Control with Bilateral Contracts' (1992) 23 *RAND J of Economics* 299; B. Jullien and P. Rey, 'Resale Price Maintenance and Collusion' (2007) 38 *RAND J of Economics* 983; P. Rey and T. Vergé, 'Resale Price Maintenance and Horizontal Cartel', CMPO Discussion Paper 02/047 (2004), and L. Peeperkorn, 'RPM and its Alleged Efficiencies' (2008) 4 *European Competition Journal* 1.

[165] M.-L. Allain and C. Chambolle, 'Anti-competitive Effects of Resale-below-cost Laws', Working Papers hal-00367492_vl (2007).

[166] If RPM is widespread, retailers engaging in significant price discounts will be eliminated from the market, consumers may be deprived of innovative retailing and price discounting so that prices may increase, price competition between suppliers may be softened, and tacit collusion between suppliers may result. See, e.g., T. R. Overstreet, *Resale Price Maintenance: Economic Theories and Empirical Evidence* (Federal Trade Commission Bureau of Economics staff report, November 1983) (indicating that the more widespread practice of RPM in Europe delayed the arrival of supermarkets).

[167] P. Areeda and H. Hovenkamp, *Antitrust Law: An Analysis of Antitrust Principles and Their Applications* (3rd edn, Aspen Publishers, 2004), 35. See also Scherer and Ross, n. 9, 550 and Guidelines, para. 224.

[168] See G. Shaffer, 'Anti-competitive Effects of RPM (Resale Price Maintenance) Agreements in Fragmented Markets', OFT report, February 2013.

[169] It applies only to pre-sales services (not post-sales services). Pre-sales services are unnecessary where consumers know what they want to buy (see the view of Comanor, n. 60 and text) and the free-rider argument is justified only in purchases of relatively high value, Scherer and Ross, n. 9, 552.

[170] Breyer J stated (551 US 877, 912 (2007)) that after the repeal of the Fair Trade Acts in the US (permitting RPM in many states), price surveys conducted by FTC staff indicated that RPM had in most cases increased the prices of products sold with RPM, Bureau of Economic Staff Report to the FTC, T. Overstreet, 'Resale Price Maintenance: Economic Theories and Empirical Evidence' (1983), 169.

[171] See, e.g., F. H. Easterbrook, 'Vertical Arrangements and the Rule of Reason' (1984) 53 *Antitrust LJ* 135 ('There is no such thing as a free lunch; the manufacturers can't get the dealer to do more without increasing the dealer's margin'); and amici curiae brief filed by 37 states supporting the respondent before the Supreme Court in *Leegin*.

[172] 'All this is to say that the ultimate question is not whether, but how much, "free riding" of this sort take place. And, after reading the briefs, I must answer that question with an uncertain "sometimes"', *Leegin*, 551 US 877, 916, Breyer J (2007).

[173] See n. 127 and text.

if the manufacturers form a tight oligopoly, and a significant part of the market is covered by RPM agreements. Secondly, by eliminating intra-brand price competition, RPM may also facilitate collusion between the buyers, i.e. at the distribution level. Strong or well organised distributors may be able to force/convince one or more suppliers to fix their resale price above the competitive level and thereby help them to reach or stabilize a collusive equilibrium. This loss of price competition seems especially problematic when the RPM is inspired by the buyers, whose collective horizontal interests can be expected to work out negatively for consumers. Thirdly, RPM may more in general soften competition between manufacturers and/or between retailers, in particular when manufacturers use the same distributors to distribute their products and RPM is applied by all or many of them. Fourthly, the immediate effect of RPM will be that all or certain distributors are prevented from lowering their sales price for that particular brand. In other words, the direct effect of RPM is a price increase. Fifthly, RPM may lower the pressure on the margin of the manufacturer, in particular where the manufacturer has a commitment problem, i.e. where he has an interest in lowering the price charged to subsequent distributors. In such a situation, the manufacturer may prefer to agree to RPM, so as to help it to commit not to lower the price for subsequent distributors and to reduce the pressure on its own margin. Sixthly, RPM may be implemented by a manufacturer with market power to foreclose smaller rivals. The increased margin that RPM may offer distributors, may entice the latter to favour the particular brand over rival brands when advising customers, even where such advice is not in the interest of these customers, or not to sell these rival brands at all. Lastly, RPM may reduce dynamism and innovation at the distribution level. By preventing price competition between different distributors, RPM may prevent more efficient retailers from entering the market and/or acquiring sufficient scale with low prices. It also may prevent or hinder the entry and expansion of distribution formats based on low prices, such as price discounters.

Finally, it is frequently argued there is not a need for such a dramatic change in EU approach, as unlike a finding of per se illegality (which does not allow any justifications for the conduct to be raised—there is a conclusive presumption of unreasonableness), a finding that an agreement is restrictive of competition by object does not prevent an argument that the agreement satisfies the conditions of Article 101(3). In Chapter 4 it was seen that there are problems with this argument. Not only does Article 101(3) not permit the parties to argue that the agreement does not restrict competition at all, but a perception has been built that object restrictions are most unlikely to satisfy the conditions of Article 101(3); the Commission has equated object restraints with a list of hardcore restraints which it considers are both presumed to violate Article 101(1) and presumed *not* to satisfy the conditions of Article 101(3).[174] Consequently, in the run-up to the adoption of the 2010 Verticals Regulation and Guidelines, one of the critical issues that arose was whether the Commission should relax its approach to hardcore restraints under Article 101(3) and, if so, how that change could be manifested.

In the light of these factor it seems unlikely that the Court will reconsider the existing case law on object restraints (it should, however, be more willing to consider context prior to object characterisation); more likely, the pressing issue will be whether the object category can be expanded to incorporate other practices (such as MFNs) which may operate like RPM and how efficiencies can be taken into account under Article 101(3).

B. ANALYSING THE RESTRICTIVE 'EFFECT' OF VERTICAL RESTRAINTS

(i) Introduction

Where an agreement does not have as its object the restriction of competition, it is necessary to look at the *effect* of the agreement. The sections below explore the cases that consider how this analysis is conducted in relation to specific types of vertical restraint. The Article 101(3) Guidelines interpret this case law as providing that it must be established that the agreement affects:

---

[174] See Chap. 4 and Section 5.E.ii.

- inter-brand, i.e. that it affects 'actual or potential competition to such an extent that on the relevant market negative effects on prices, output, innovation or the variety or quality of goods and services can be expected with a reasonable degree of probability';[175] or

- intra-brand competition—it restricts, without objective justification, distributors from competing with each other.[176]

Further that if, following these principles, the transaction is not restrictive of competition, restraints 'ancillary' to the main non-restrictive transaction also fall outside Article 101(1).[177]

Building on those principles, paragraphs 96–230 of the Vertical Guidelines, set out more specific guidance in relation to individual vertical agreements which will not benefit from the Verticals Regulation. The Commission states that it will adopt an economic approach in its application of Article 101. In paragraphs 111–121 the Commission sets out the factors it considers to be most important when assessing whether or not an agreement appreciably restricts competition under Article 101(1). The central inquiry focuses on the *market power* of the undertakings concerned:

111. . . . The following factors are in particular relevant to establish whether a vertical agreement brings about an appreciable restriction of competition under Article 101(1):

   a) nature of the agreement;

   b) market position of the parties;

   c) market position of competitors;

   d) market position of buyers of the contract products;

   e) entry barriers;

   f) maturity of the market;

   g) level of trade;

   h) nature of the product;

   i) other factors.

112. The importance of individual factors may vary from cases to case and depends on all other factors. For instance, a high market share of the parties is usually a good indicator of market power, but in the case of low entry barriers it may not be indicative of market power. It is therefore not possible to provide firm rules on the importance of the individual factors . . .

The importance of these factors on individual assessment is fleshed out in further detail in paragraphs 113–121.

Subsequent sections consider the case law, decisional practice, and guidance on the question of how Article 101(1) applies to specific types of vertical agreements and restraint. It is stressed again, however, that the complex analysis demanded in effect cases will ordinarily be circumvented where the parties' market shares do not exceed 30 per cent, since in most cases, absent hardcore restraints, the block exemption should apply.

---

[175] Article 101(3) Guidelines, para. 24. This could be because the agreement restricts actual or potential competition between the parties or between any one of the parties and third parties that could have existed absent the agreement, paras. 25–26.

[176] Thus according to the Commission two counterfactuals may need to be used—one to determine whether the agreement restricts inter-brand competition (whether the agreement restricts actual or potential competition that would have existed without the agreement) and one to determine whether it restricts intra-brand competition (whether the agreement restricts actual or potential competition that would have existed in the absence of the contractual restraints), see Chap. 4.

[177] Article 101(3) Guidelines, paras. 28–31 and see Chap. 4.

(ii) Single Branding Agreements and *Delimitis*

One of the most important of all of the Court's judgments in the context of distribution agreements is *Delimitis v Henninger Bräu*.[178] In this case the Court gave guidance to a national court asked to rule on the compatibility of a beer-supply agreement with Article 101(1). It will be remembered (from Chapter 4) that the contract obliged the café proprietor to obtain his beer requirements from the brewer, Henninger Bräu (although once a fixed quantity had been bought, Delimitis was free to purchase beer from other Member States). Agreements such as this which oblige a buyer to obtain all, most, or a certain percentage or amount of its requirements from a named supplier frequently lead to efficiencies in distribution. A supplier is enabled to plan the number of sales it will make with greater precision, and distributors are encouraged actively to promote the supplier's product. Further, suppliers often confer reciprocal benefits (such as loans at below market rates, training, business and financial advice) on distributors who agree not to purchase a competitor's products. Obviously the supplier will wish to ensure that these benefits are not used to assist sales of competitors' products.

Since, however, these non-compete or quantity-forcing agreements prohibit or deter distributors from handling competitors' products, there is a concern that these agreements, or networks of similar agreements, might tie up outlets and preclude competitors (actual and potential) from gaining access to distributors (they have a direct impact on inter-brand competition by foreclosing the market to competing and potential suppliers). This worry is particularly acute in markets where access to the market is not easy on account of the existence of barriers to entry, such as planning restrictions or licensing requirements. Further, there is a concern that such agreements may restrict inter-brand competition by softening competition and facilitating collusion between suppliers (especially in case of cumulative use) or through a loss of in-store inter-brand competition.[179]

In *Delimitis*[180] the CJ recognised that an obligation imposed on the café proprietor to purchase most of its beer requirements from the brewer entailed advantages for both the supplier and the reseller (the purpose/object of the agreement was not to restrict competition). It set out guidelines for the national court to determine whether or not the effect of such an agreement foreclosed access to the market and so restricted competition. This could be determined by, first, defining the relevant market and considering whether or not that market was foreclosed to other competitors or precluded expansion by existing competitors. If it was, secondly, it had to be determined whether or not the agreement in question restricted competition. It would only do so if the agreements concluded by that producer appreciably contributed to the foreclosure effect.

In this case the Court focused its inquiry on the important question whether or not the agreement, alone or in conjunction with a network of similar agreements, would lead to a restriction of inter-brand competition. It considered that only where the agreement contributed to the foreclosure of the market and to a restriction of inter-brand competition would it be found to restrict competition within the meaning of Article 101(1).

In a series of subsequent cases, the Commission dealt with single branding agreements notified to it for exemption; in some cases it found that such agreements did not infringe Article 101(1) at all,[181]

---

[178] Case C-234/89, *Delimitis v Henninger Bräu* [1991] ECR I-935 and see also discussion and extract set out in Chap. 4.

[179] See Guidelines, para. 130.

[180] See n. 178.

[181] See COMP/36.511, *Roberts/Greene King* 12 November 1998 (Greene King's network of agreements did not make a significant contribution to the foreclosure of the market of the distribution on beer in establishments selling alcoholic beverages for consumption on the premises in the UK, *aff'd* Case T-25/99, *Roberts v Commission* [2001] ECR II-1881) and, more remarkably, COMP/37.904, *Interbrew* 15 April 2003 (beer-supply agreements concluded by Interbrew, which had 56% of the Belgian Horeca market (Horeca (hotel/restaurant/catering) outlets are those that have concluded loan agreements or lease/sublease agreements with a brewer) did not, as amended, infringe Art. 101(1). Essentially the amended agreements gave Belgian Horeca outlets extended freedom to carry other beers not brewed by Interbrew as the non-compete obligations were limited to draught pils and, in the case of loan-tie agreements, could be terminated quite easily).

in some cases it found that the agreements infringed Article 101(1) but met the Article 101(3) criteria,[182] and in some it found that the agreements infringed Article 101(1) and did not meet the Article 101(3) criteria.[183] In *Van den Bergh Foods v Commission*,[184] for example, the GC upheld a finding that freezer exclusivity operated by HB in Ireland infringed Article 101(1) and did not meet the criteria of Article 101(3). In respect to the analysis required under Article 101(1), the GC reiterated the need for a *Delimitis*-type analysis.[185] It found that the freezer exclusivity had the same effect as outlet exclusivity (the freezer exclusivity had prevented retailers from stocking competing ice creams for which there was demand). The network of HB's agreements and their supply of exclusive freezer cabinets had 'a considerable dissuasive effect on retailers with regard to the installation of their own cabinet or that of another manufacturer and operate de facto as a tie on sales outlets that have only HB freezer cabinets'.[186] It thus concluded that it was 'clear from an examination of the entirety of the similar distribution agreements concluded on the relevant market, and other evidence of the economic and legal context of which those agreements form part, that the distribution agreements concluded by HB are liable to have an appreciable effect on competition for the purposes of Article [101(1)] of the Treaty and contribute significantly to a foreclosure of the market'.[187] The CJ also adopted a similar approach in *SIA 'Maxima Latvija' v Konkurences padome*.[188]

The Commission's approach in the Guidelines is consistent with the Court's case law.[189] In particular, the Commission stresses the central importance in the appraisal of single branding agreements of examining: the capacity of the obligation to result in anti-competitive foreclosure of competitors and the market position of the supplier (considering the market power of the supplier and the market position of its competitors and their ability to compete on equal terms for each individual customer's entire demand); and the extent to, and the duration for, which the supplier applies a non-compete obligation. The foreclosure will be more significant the greater the tied market share and the longer the duration of the non-compete obligation.[190] The Commission takes the view that non-compete obligations for under one year by non-dominant companies are in general not considered to give rise to appreciable anti-competitive effects, non-compete clauses in excess of five years are generally unnecessary and will outweigh claimed efficiencies, and clauses imposing non-compete obligations of between one and five years will require a proper balancing of the pro- and anti-competitive effects.[191]

The Commission states that it does not anticipate a single or cumulative anti-competitive effect where the market share of the largest supplier is below 30 per cent and the market share of the five largest suppliers is below 50 per cent.[192] The Commission states that it will also take into account entry barriers, countervailing buyer power, and the level of trade.[193]

---

[182] See, e.g., COMP/36.081, *Bass* [1999] OJ L186/1 and COMP/35.079, *Whitbread* [1999] OJ L88/26. But see the discussion of *Inntrepreneur Pub Co v Crehan* [2006] UKHL 38, in Chap. 14.

[183] See, e.g., COMP/34.072, *Langnese-Iglo GmbH* [1993] OJ L183/19, especially paras. 94–95 and 101, *aff'd* Case T-7/93, *Langnese-Iglo GmbH v Commission* [1995] ECR II-1533, and COMP/31.533 and 34.072, *Schöller Lebensmittel GmbH & Co KG* [1993] OJ L183/1, in which the Commission appeared to adopt an extremely narrow construction of the Court's judgment in Case C-234/89, *Delimitis v Henninger Bräu* [1991] ECR I-935,

[184] Case T-65/98, [2003] ECR II-4653, *aff'd* Case C-552/03 P, *Unilever Bestfoods v Commission* [2006] ECR I-9091.

[185] Case T-65/98, *Van den Bergh* [2003] ECR II-4653, para. 83, *aff'd* Case C-552/03 P, *Unilever Bestfoods* [2006] ECR I-9091, paras. 84–85.

[186] Case T-65/98, *Van den Bergh* [2003] ECR II-4653, para. 98.

[187] Ibid., para. 118.

[188] EU:C:2015:784 and see Chap. 4.

[189] See also Case C-214/99, *Neste Markkinointi Oy v Yötuuli* [2000] ECR I-11121.

[190] Guidelines, paras. 132–133.

[191] Ibid., para. 133 ('[s]ingle branding obligations are more likely to result in anti-competitive foreclosure when entered into by dominant companies').

[192] Ibid., para. 143.

[193] Ibid., para. 141.

(iii) Exclusive Distribution Agreements and *STM*

Exclusive distribution agreements, in which a manufacturer appoints a sole distributor for a particular area, have a number of positive effects and may consequently stimulate the competitive process. For example: efficiencies flow from the manufacturer's decision to deal only with one distributor in a particular territory; transaction costs are saved; customer feedback may be more easily obtained; and such an agreement may be essential to solve a free-rider problem. If the distributor is sheltered from intra-brand competition it will be encouraged to incur expenditure promoting and advertising the product, safe in the knowledge that other distributors will not be able to 'free-ride' on that expenditure.

The case law clearly recognises that benefits for the competitive process potentially flow from exclusive distribution agreements and that such agreements do not automatically infringe Article 101(1). In *STM*[194] the CJ held that exclusive distribution agreements will not restrict competition if the appointment of the exclusive distributor is necessary to enable the manufacturer to penetrate a new market. The Court also held that in assessing the impact of the agreement on competition it was necessary to take into account the products at issue, the market position and importance of the parties, the existence (or not) of parallel networks of similar agreements, and the severity of the clauses intended to protect the exclusive dealership. In its Vertical Guidelines the Commission reflects this ruling stating that when considering the effect of these agreements on competition, it looks at the market position of the supplier, the position of its competitors, barriers to trade, buying power, the maturity of the market, and the level of trade. It also recognises that 'the loss of intra-brand competition can only be problematic if inter-brand competition is limited. The stronger the "position of the supplier", the more serious is the loss of intra-brand competition.'[195] The Guidelines note, however, that such arrangements may also be problematic if they may soften competition and facilitate collusion, either at the suppliers' or distributors' level and/or foreclose or exclude distributors and reduce competition at the distribution level.[196]

It has already been seen that in drawing up an agreement varying degrees of immunity from intra-brand competition can be granted on top of the decision to appoint a sole distributor for the area. Further that if the agreement goes further and confers territorial or customer restraints to bolster it, the agreement is liable to be problematic under Article 101(1), whether or not the parties have market power and/or the ability to affect prices or output on the market. Although therefore *STM* accepts that a restraint necessary to persuade the distributor to take on the commercial risk inherent in the agreement does not constitute a restriction of competition within the meaning of Article 101(1), the EU Courts have not pushed this idea to its logical conclusion by accepting that even territorial restraints may be objectively necessary to the achievement of this objective. Rather, such restraints are liable in principle to be found to be restrictive of competition by object.

To encourage concentration of selling efforts exclusive distribution agreements are often combined with a single branding commitment. Single branding provisions can of course foreclose other suppliers. The Commission deals with the combination of exclusive distribution and single branding in its Guidelines.

161....[F]oreclosure of other suppliers does not arise as long as exclusive distribution is not combined with single branding. But even when exclusive distribution is combined with single branding anticompetitive foreclosure of other suppliers is unlikely, except possibly when the single branding is applied to a dense network of exclusive distributors with small territories or in case of a cumulative effect. In such a case it may be necessary to apply the principles on single branding set out in section 2.1. However, when the combination

---

[194] Case 56/65, [1966] ECR 235, see extract set out in Chap. 4.

[195] Guidelines, para. 153. The Commission notes, however, that if the number of competitors becomes small and their market position is rather similar, there is a risk of collusion, para. 154.

[196] Ibid., para. 151.

does not lead to significant foreclosure, the combination of exclusive distribution and single branding may be pro-competitive by increasing the incentive for the exclusive distributor to focus its efforts on the particular brand. Therefore, in the absence of such a foreclosure effect, the combination of exclusive distribution with non-compete may very well fulfil the conditions of Article 101(3) for the whole duration of the agreement, particularly at the wholesale level.

(iv) Selective Distribution Agreements and the *Metro* Criteria

A supplier wishing to project an image for its goods and/or to ensure that sales are accompanied by the provision of specific services may decide to establish a SDS. Under such a system the supplier will select its retailers, perhaps by number or by reference to quality or location of the distributor. Where the supplier wishes to portray and enhance a luxury image and to capitalise on consumers' desires to purchase a luxury product it may restrict supplies to retailers selling from a high-quality location. Alternatively, a supplier may agree only to supply retailers that will comply with certain obligations as to service, sales promotion, or regular ordering. It may wish to ensure that consumers purchasing its product receive a minimum level of pre-sales services and are fully informed about the product's qualities and capabilities. If such a system is to be effective both the supplier and the distributors will wish to ensure that non-authorised retailers, who will detract from the image they are attempting to create or which will free-ride on the pre-sales services provided, are not supplied.

A prohibition on the supply of retailers that have not been authorised to sell the products impacts on *intra-brand* competition and may be aimed at promoting inter-brand competition. In an ideal world a consumer who does not value the luxury image or the additional services imposed will purchase other competing products instead. Nonetheless, in some cases it may be arguable that the justifications for a SDS are not as strong as the supplier suggests and that, especially where a supplier has a degree of market power or networks of similar agreements are operated (in cases of cumulative effect), the practice may foreclose certain types of distributors, soften competition, and/or facilitate collusion between suppliers or buyers.[197]

Since *Metro I*[198] the CJ has recognised that certain simple, qualitative SDSs may escape the Article 101(1) prohibition.

Case 26/76, *Metro-SB-Grossmärkte GmbH v Commission (Metro I)* [1977] ECR 1875

SABA manufactured televisions, radios, and tape-recorders, which it distributed through a SDS, whereby only specialist dealers who met certain criteria sold the products. The Commission held that some aspects of the SDS were outside Article 101(1). Other provisions it held to be within Article 101(1) but it granted an exemption. Metro was a self-service dealer who SABA refused to admit to the network because it did not fulfil all the criteria. It appealed to the Court of Justice under Article 263 against the grant of the exemption to SABA.

Court of Justice

A Misuse of Powers

20. The requirement contained in . . . [Article 101] that competition shall not be distorted implies the existence on the market of workable competition, that is to say the degree of competition necessary to ensure the observance of the basic requirements and the attainment of the objectives of the Treaty, in particular

---

[197] Ibid., para. 175.

[198] Case 26/76, [1977] ECR 1875. The Court's judgment was given soon after the US Supreme Court's judgment in *Sylvania* which overruled *Schwinn*, see n. 153 and text.

the creation of a single market achieving conditions similar to those of a domestic market. In accordance with this requirement the nature and intensiveness of competition may vary to an extent dictated by the products or services in question and the economic structure of the relevant market sectors. In the sector covering the production of high quality and technically advanced consumer durables, where a relatively small number of large- and medium-scale producers offer a varied range of items which, or so consumers may consider, are readily interchangeable, the structure of the market does not preclude the existence of a variety of channels of distribution adapted to the peculiar characteristics of the various producers and to the requirements of the various categories of consumers. On this view the Commission was justified in recognising that selective distribution systems constituted, together with others, an aspect of competition which accords with Article [101(1)], provided that resellers are chosen on the basis of objective criteria of a qualitative nature relating to the technical qualifications of the reseller and his staff and the suitability of his trading premises and that such conditions are laid down uniformly for all potential resellers and are not applied in a discriminatory fashion.

21. It is true that in such systems of distribution price competition is not generally emphasised either as an exclusive or indeed as a principal factor. This is particularly so when, as in the present case, access to the distribution network is subject to conditions exceeding the requirements of an appropriate distribution of the products. However, although price competition is so important that it can never be eliminated, it does not constitute the only effective form of competition or that to which absolute priority must in all circumstances be accorded. The powers conferred upon the Commission under Article [101(3)] show that the requirements for the maintenance of workable competition may be reconciled with the safeguarding of objectives of a different nature and that to this end certain restrictions on competition are permissible, provided that they are essential to the attainment of those objectives and that they do not result in the elimination of competition for a substantial part of the Common Market. For specialist wholesalers and retailers the desire to maintain a certain price level, which corresponds to the desire to preserve, in the interests of consumers, the possibility of the continued existence of this channel of distribution in conjunction with new methods of distribution based on a different type of competition policy, forms one of the objectives which may be pursued without necessarily falling under the prohibition contained in Article [101(1)], and, if it does fall thereunder, either wholly or in part, coming within the framework of Article [101(3)]. This argument is strengthened if, in addition, such conditions promote improved competition inasmuch as it relates to factors other than prices.

The judgment throws interesting light on the Court's thinking. It indicates that certain restrictions in the SDS are not caught by Article 101(1) where necessary in pursuance of a desirable end. Further the CJ accepts that although selective distribution limits price competition, price competition does not necessarily constitute the only form of competition.[199] However, it is clear from this and subsequent judgments,[200] that such a reduction in price competition is only acceptable under Article 101(1) if certain conditions (explored further in the sections below) are satisfied:

(a) the characteristics or nature of the product in question necessitate a SDS;

(b) the distributors are chosen by reference to objective criteria of a qualitative nature which are set out uniformly and are not used arbitrarily to discriminate against certain retailers; and

(c) the criteria set out do not go beyond what is necessary for the product in question.[201]

---

[199] Case 26/76, *Metro I* [1977] ECR 1875, para. 21.

[200] See, e.g., Case T-19/92, *Leclerc v Commission* [1996] ECR II-1851, para. 112. See also Guidelines, para. 175.

[201] Case 31/80, *L'Oréal NV and L'Oréal SA v PVBA 'De Nieuwe AMCK'* [1980] ECR 3775 and Case T-19/91, *Société d'Hygiène Dermatologique de Vichy v Commission* [1992] ECR II-415. See, e.g., COMP/30.299, *Grohe* [1985] OJ L19/17 (restrictions must be objectively necessary to protect the quality of the products in question).

Further, even a simple SDS complying with these requirements may infringe Article 101(1) if the market is tied up with a network of similar agreements, leading to excessive rigidity and no room for other methods of distribution.[202]

Although this approach represents a welcome recognition that SDSs may enhance inter-brand competition,[203] the limitations set out by the Court are rather regulatory, limiting, and frustrating.[204] Indeed, the jurisprudence developed to this type of distribution is not easy to rationalise fully.[205] Although relatively clear, it has been criticised for ignoring the economic realities and effects of the arrangements and for engaging in 'unnecessary micro-management of the selective distribution relationship'.[206] For example, the requirement that the product should fall within one of two categories that the Court has ruled should be able to benefit from such a system may not always be appropriate or relevant. Even if true that the need for a SDS has sometimes been exaggerated, a producer operating on a competitive market will be punished by consumers if they do not believe that the product in question merits the system. Further, the requirement that retailers should be selected by reference only to *qualitative* criteria makes no economic sense. If a retailer has to comply with stringent qualitative criteria this may involve considerable expense which may demand that a quantitative limit on distributors is imposed. Apart from being economically indefensible, the requirement has also proved difficult to apply in practice and identical restrictions have sometimes been labelled as qualitative and in other cases as quantitative.

The net outcome has been that SDSs have arguably not, in the context of Article 101(1), adequately been assessed to determine whether or not they have led to an anti-competitive outcome on the market. This problem was rectified in the past by the Commission accepting that many quantitative restrictions, for example an obligation to engage in sales promotions, met the criteria of Article 101(3).[207] Now most SDSs, even quantitative systems where the criteria are not objectively justified by reference to the nature of product or service, may benefit from the more liberal regime set out in the Verticals Regulation.[208] Where the Verticals Regulation does not apply, however, guidance on the application of Articles 101(1) and 101(3) is still of importance.[209]

a. The Characteristics or the Nature of the Product

In *Metro I*[210] the Court stated that the operation of a SDS was justified in 'the sector covering the production of high quality and technically advanced consumer durables'. The case law accepts that two categories of products justify a SDS in order to protect the quality of the product and/or ensure its proper use: products which are sufficiently technically complex to justify a specialised distribution system[211] and luxury or branded products, where there is a need for the producer to preserve its brand image and to safeguard, in the mind of the consumer, the aura of exclusivity and prestige of the product has been assessed. In such cases appropriate marketing and a setting and presentation in line with the luxurious and exclusive nature and brand image of the product is essential.[212]

---

[202] See Case 75/84, *Metro-SB-Grossmärkte GmbH v Commission (Metro II)* [1986] ECR 3021.

[203] Especially prior to 1999 when no block exemption existed for SDSs.

[204] Hawk, n. 72, 985.

[205] See Case 75/84, *Metro II* [1986] ECR 3021; Case T-19/92, *Groupement d'Achat Édouard Leclerc (Leclerc) v Commission* [1996] ECR II-1851.

[206] Monti, n. 3, 492.

[207] See Case 26/76, *Metro I* [1977] ECR 1875; COMP/29.420, *Grundig* [1985] OJ L233/1, renewed [1994] OJ L20/15; COMP/33.542, *Parfums Givenchy* [1992] OJ L236/11.

[208] See Case C-158/11, *Auto24 SARL v Jaguar Land Rover France SAS* EU:C:2012:351.

[209] Guidelines, paras. 174–188.

[210] Case 26/76, [1977] ECR 1875.

[211] Case 75/84, *Metro II* [1986] ECR 3021.

[212] Case T-19/92, *Leclerc v Commission* [1996] ECR II-1851, para. 116.

Consequently, the following products have been found to justify such a system: televisions,[213] hi-fis,[214] cameras,[215] personal computers,[216] clocks and watches,[217] high-quality gold and silver products,[218] luxury cosmetics/perfumes,[219] dinner services,[220] and cars.[221]

It also seems that 'selective distribution systems which are justified by the specific nature of the products or the requirements for their distribution may be established in other economic sectors'.[222] In *SA Binon & Cie v SA Agence et Messageries de la Presse*,[223] for example, it was accepted that newspapers and periodicals would constitute a suitable product for selective distribution, partly because of the limited shelf-life which each had.

It may be hard to persuade the Commission or a court that a product merits a SDS if such a system is not operated in all jurisdictions in which the product is sold.

b. Qualitative Not Quantitative Criteria Applied Uniformly, and in a Non-discriminatory Manner

The Court in *Metro I* stated clearly that a SDS in which 'resellers are chosen on the basis of objective criteria of a qualitative nature relating to the technical qualifications of the reseller and his staff and the suitability of his trading premises and that such conditions are laid down uniformly for all potential resellers and are not applied in a discriminatory fashion'[224] would accord with Article 101. Any distributor satisfying the qualitative criteria should be supplied.

An immediate problem is to determine whether or not criteria are qualitative or quantitative in nature as qualitative restrictions inevitably lead to restrictions on the number of resellers selected. The purpose, however, appears to be to distinguish between criteria designed to select dealers on the basis of their objective suitability to distribute a particular kind of good (qualitative criteria) and criteria which 'more directly limit the potential number of dealers by, for instance, requiring minimum or maximum sales, by fixing the number of dealers, etc'[225] (quantitative criteria). The jurisprudence sheds some light on how this distinction applies.

It is clear from *Metro I* itself that criteria relating to the technical qualification of the reseller and its staff and the suitability of trading premises are of a qualitative nature. Further, so are obligations precluding the sale of goods that would detract from the product's brand image[226] and requiring dealers to provide after-sales services.[227] In some cases the Commission has found an obligation requiring a dealer to stock a wide or an entire range of products to be qualitative and in others it has

---

[213] Case 75/84, *Metro II* [1986] ECR 3021.

[214] COMP/29.420, *Grundig* [1985] OJ L233/1, renewed [1994] OJ L20/15.

[215] COMP/25.757, *Hasselblad* [1982] OJ L161/18, Case 86/82, *Hasselblad v Commission* [1984] ECR 883.

[216] COMP/30.849, *IBM* [1984] OJ L118/24.

[217] COMP/5715, *Junghans* [1977] OJ L30/10; cf. Case 31/85, *ETA Fabriques d'Ébauches v DK Investments SA* [1985] ECR 3933.

[218] COMP/30.668, *Murat* [1983] OJ L348/20.

[219] COMP/33.542, *Parfums Givenchy* [1992] OJ L236/11, partially annulled Case T-88/92, *Groupement d'Achat Édouard Leclerc v Commission* [1996] ECR II-1961; COMP/33.242, *Yves Saint Laurent* [1992] OJ L12/24, partially annulled Case T-19/92, *Leclerc v Commission* [1996] ECR II-1851. The *Yves Saint Laurent* selective distribution system now satisfies the terms of the Verticals Reg., see IP/01/713.

[220] COMP/30.665, *Villeroy & Bosch* [1985] OJ L376/15.

[221] COMP/14.650, *BMW* [1975] OJ L29/1, but see COMP/30.299, *Grohe* [1985] OJ L19/17 (unclear whether plumbing fittings are technically advanced products that necessitate a SDS).

[222] Case T-19/92, *Leclerc v Commission* [1996] ECR II-1851, para. 113.

[223] Case 243/83, [1985] ECR 2015, para. 32.

[224] Case 26/76, [1977] ECR 1875, para. 20.

[225] Guidelines, para. 175.

[226] COMP/33.542, *Parfums Givenchy* [1992] OJ L236/11, Case T-88/92, *Leclerc v Commission* [1996] ECR II-1961.

[227] COMP/29.420, *Grundig* [1985] OJ L233/1, renewed [1994] OJ L20/15; COMP/30.665, *Villeroy & Bosch* [1985] OJ L376/15.

found it to be quantitative; in such cases the classification appears to have turned upon the nature of the product involved.[228]

An obligation precluding members of the system from supplying unauthorised retailers does not infringe Article 101(1), since it is inherent in the SDS.[229] In contrast, provisions that protect approved network members from the competition of other retailers meeting the qualitative criteria will be quantitative, for example; a simple numerical limit placed on the number of distributors; clauses precluding cross-supplying between network members;[230] clauses restricting sales to specific types of stores;[231] or clauses requiring distributors to maintain specific amounts of stocks,[232] to promote the manufacturer's product, to stock an entire range of products,[233] or to have a minimum annual turnover.[234] Provisions setting out a difficult or lengthy procedure for retailers to join the network may also infringe Article 101(1).[235]

Article 101(1) will also apply if the supplier itself, acting in agreement with its distributors (and not unilaterally), refuses to supply those that meet these qualitative criteria. Thus suppliers (whether or not dominant) need to be careful which retailers they exclude from their SDS and refuse to deal with; the exclusion must be justified.[236]

c. The Criteria Must Not Go Beyond What is Necessary for the Product in Question

In *Metro I*[237] the CJ held that there must be a relationship between the goods protected by the SDS and the restrictions imposed on distributors: the restrictions are permissible provided that they are essential to protect the 'quality' of the relevant product. Restrictions that go beyond this will infringe Article 101(1). In *Vichy v Commission*,[238] for example, the GC held that 'the requirement of the status of dispensing chemist, which is a pre-condition for admission to the distribution network for Vichy products, is certainly not necessary for the proper distribution of those [cosmetic] products'. Rather such a requirement in relation to cosmetic products was 'entirely unnecessary' and 'disproportionate'.[239]

---

[228] Contrast *Grundig* ibid. (requirement that retailers had to carry and stock a whole range of products went beyond what was necessary for the distribution of products and was an impediment to competition (the agreement was, however, granted an exemption under Art. 101(3)) and *Villeroy & Bosch* ibid (the requirement that the retailer had to display and stock a sufficiently wide and varied range of products did not infringe Art. 101(1)—sales targets were not imposed, the requirement did not prevent retailers stocking competing products, and inter-brand competition was high). In the Guidelines, para. 187, the Commission states that an obligation requiring distributors to sell a certain range of the products is purely of a qualitative nature.

[229] Nor does a provision precluding wholesalers from supplying private customers, Case 26/76, *Metro I* [1977] ECR 1875, para. 27.

[230] In, e.g., COMP/25.757, *Hasselblad* [1982] OJ L161/18, Case 86/82, *Hasselblad v Commission* [1984] ECR 883, the supplier supplied only a few of those distributors which satisfied the criteria set out.

[231] Case T-19/92, *Leclerc v Commission* [1996] ECR II-1851 (it is not justifiable to have a provision precluding supermarkets or hypermarkets from becoming part of the network). See also Case T-19/91, *Société d'Hygiène Dermatologique de Vichy v Commission* [1992] ECR II-415.

[232] Case 26/76, *Metro I* [1977] ECR 1875.

[233] COMP/29.420, *Grundig* [1994] OJ L20/15.

[234] See, e.g., COMP/33.542, *Parfums Givenchy* [1992] OJ L236/11, partially annulled Case T-88/92, *Leclerc v Commission* [1996] ECR II-1961 and COMP/33.242, *Yves Saint Laurent* [1992] OJ L12/24, Case T-19/92, *Leclerc v Commission* [1996] ECR II-1851 (the GC annulled part of the decision which raised indirect obstacles to sale in supermarkets. The system was then modified to permit sales of perfume in multi-product sales points).

[235] Ibid.

[236] See Chap. 3. In Case T-24/90, *Automec v Commission (No. 2)* [1992] ECR II-2223, para. 51 the GC held that where a supplier is found to be operating a SDS in a discriminatory manner in breach of Art. 101(1), the Commission does not have power to order supply and to insist on contractual arrangements when other suitable means were available to ensure that the infringement was terminated. This aspect of *Automec (No. 2)* is discussed in Chap. 13. See also discussion of refusal to deal in Chap. 7.

[237] Case 26/76, [1977] ECR 1875.

[238] Case T-19/91, [1992] ECR II-415.

[239] Case T-19/91, *Vichy v Commission* [1992] ECR II-415, para. 69.

It has already been seen that although price competition is not emphasised in SDSs, it cannot be eliminated; provisions directly or indirectly aimed at RPM or preventing approved retailers from selling to each other (bans on cross-suppliers) or to consumers in other Member States (see also discussion of *Pierre Fabre* below) will be most unlikely to be considered necessary.[240]

d. Impact of the *Pierre Fabre* Judgment

The case law dealing with selective distribution has traditionally been interpreted as requiring its own rather specific analysis to determine whether restraints are necessary to achieve its objectives and so whether such a systems restricts competition within the meaning of Article 101(1). In *Pierre Fabre*,[241] however, the CJ interprets this line of cases as holding that if the *Metro I* criteria are not satisfied the agreement is restrictive by object.

Case C-439/09, *Pierre Fabre v Président de l'Autorité de la concurrence* EU:C:2011:277

Court of Justice

The classification of the restriction in the contested contractual clause as a restriction of competition by object

34. It must first of all be recalled that, to come within the prohibition laid down in Article 101(1) TFEU, an agreement must have 'as [its] object or effect the prevention, restriction or distortion of competition within the internal market'. It has, since the judgment in Case 56/65 LTM . . . been settled case-law that the alternative nature of that requirement, indicated by the conjunction 'or', leads, first, to the need to consider the precise purpose of the agreement, in the economic context in which it is to be applied. Where the anti-competitive object of the agreement is established it is not necessary to examine its effects on competition (see Joined Cases C-501/06 P, C-513/06 P, C-516/06 P and C-519/06 P *GlaxoSmithKline Services and Others v Commission and Others* . . . paragraph 55 and the case-law cited).

35. For the purposes of assessing whether the contractual clause at issue involves a restriction of competition 'by object', regard must be had to the content of the clause, the objectives it seeks to attain and the economic and legal context of which it forms a part (see *GlaxoSmithKline and Others v Commission and Others*, paragraph 58 and the case-law cited).

36. The selective distribution contracts at issue stipulate that sales of cosmetics and personal care products by the Avène, Klorane, Galénic and Ducray brands must be made in a physical space, the requirements for which are set out in detail, and that a qualified pharmacist must be present.

37. According to the referring court, the requirement that a qualified pharmacist must be present at a physical sales point de facto prohibits the authorised distributors from any form of internet selling.

38. As the Commission points out, by excluding de facto a method of marketing products that does not require the physical movement of the customer, the contractual clause considerably reduces the ability of an authorised distributor to sell the contractual products to customers outside its contractual territory or area of activity. It is therefore liable to restrict competition in that sector.

39. As regards agreements constituting a selective distribution system, the Court has already stated that such agreements necessarily affect competition in the common market (Case 107/82 *AEG-Telefunken v Commission* . . . paragraph 33). Such agreements are to be considered, in the absence of objective justification, as 'restrictions by object'.

---

[240] See Cases 228 and 229/82, *Ford-Werke AG and Ford of Europe Inc v Commission* [1984] ECR 1129; Case 32/78, *BMW v Commission* [1979] ECR 2435; COMP/24.055, *Kodak* [1970] OJ L142/24. Guarantees granted on sale in one Member State must be honoured by distributors in other Member States: Case 31/85, *ETA Fabriques d'Ebauches v DK Investments SA* [1985] ECR 3933.

[241] Case C-439/09, EU:C:2011:277.

40. However, it has always been recognised in the case-law of the Court that there are legitimate requirements, such as the maintenance of a specialist trade capable of providing specific services as regards high-quality and high-technology products, which may justify a reduction of price competition in favour of competition relating to factors other than price. Systems of selective distribution, in so far as they aim at the attainment of a legitimate goal capable of improving competition in relation to factors other than price, therefore constitute an element of competition which is in conformity with Article 101(1) TFEU (*AEG-Telefunken v Commission*, paragraph 33).

41. In that regard, the Court has already pointed out that the organisation of such a network is not prohibited by Article 101(1) TFEU, to the extent that resellers are chosen on the basis of objective criteria of a qualitative nature, laid down uniformly for all potential resellers and not applied in a discriminatory fashion, that the characteristics of the product in question necessitate such a network in order to preserve its quality and ensure its proper use and, finally, that the criteria laid down do not go beyond what is necessary (Case 26/76 *Metro* . . . paragraph 20, and Case 31/80 *L'Oréal* . . . paragraphs 15 and 16).

42. Although it is for the referring court to examine whether the contractual clause at issue prohibiting de facto all forms of internet selling can be justified by a legitimate aim, it is for the Court of Justice to provide it for this purpose with the points of interpretation of European Union law which enable it to reach a decision (see *L'Oréal*, paragraph 14).

43. It is undisputed that, under Pierre Fabre Dermo-Cosmétique's selective distribution system, resellers are chosen on the basis of objective criteria of a qualitative nature, which are laid down uniformly for all potential resellers. However, it must still be determined whether the restrictions of competition pursue legitimate aims in a proportionate manner in accordance with the considerations set out at paragraph 41 of the present judgment.

44. In that regard, it should be noted that the Court, in the light of the freedoms of movement, has not accepted arguments relating to the need to provide individual advice to the customer and to ensure his protection against the incorrect use of products, in the context of non-prescription medicines and contact lenses, to justify a ban on internet sales (see, to that effect, Deutscher Apothekerverband, paragraphs 106, 107 and 112, and Case C-108/09 *Ker-Optika* . . . paragraph 76).

45. Pierre Fabre Dermo-Cosmétique also refers to the need to maintain the prestigious image of the products at issue.

46. The aim of maintaining a prestigious image is not a legitimate aim for restricting competition and cannot therefore justify a finding that a contractual clause pursuing such an aim does not fall within Article 101(1) TFEU.

47. In the light of the foregoing considerations, the answer to the first part of the question referred for a preliminary ruling is that Article 101(1) TFEU must be interpreted as meaning that, in the context of a selective distribution system, a contractual clause requiring sales of cosmetics and personal care products to be made in a physical space where a qualified pharmacist must be present, resulting in a ban on the use of the internet for those sales, amounts to a restriction by object within the meaning of that provision where, following an individual and specific examination of the content and objective of that contractual clause and the legal and economic context of which it forms a part, it is apparent that, having regard to the properties of the products at issue, that clause is not objectively justified.

The CJ thus clearly states (a) that SDSs necessarily affect competition and 'are to be considered, in the absence of objective justification, as "restrictions by object"'; but (b) that they may be in conformity with Article 101 and justified insofar as they aim at the attainment of legitimate goals (such as the maintenance of a specialist trade capable of providing specific services as regards high-quality or high-technology products) where 'resellers are chosen on the basis of objective criteria of a qualitative nature, laid down uniformly for all potential resellers and not applied in a discriminatory fashion, that the characteristics of the product in question necessitate such a network in order to preserve its quality and ensure its proper use and, finally, that the criteria laid down do not go beyond what is necessary'.[242]

Although the narrow finding of the CJ—that the contractual clause at issue (prohibiting all forms of internet selling) was incompatible with Article 101(1)—is consistent with earlier precedent dealing with object restraints, the broader wording suggesting that *all* SDSs are restrictive by object unless 'objectively justified' is more surprising (and does not seem to have been strictly necessary for the ruling in question). Nonetheless, the CJ treats the *Metro I* criteria as a mechanism for distinguishing between SDSs which are restrictive by object and those which are objectively justified as they are necessary to achieve a legitimate aim and so not restrictive of competition in fact and outside Article 101 altogether. Not only is such an approach perhaps more reminiscent of that adopted in free movement[243] rather than Article 101 cases, but the CJ does not clearly link its approach with that adopted in other case law (and discussed in Chapter 4) which establishes that restrictions of competition essential to, or inherent in, the pursuit of a legitimate objective or objectively necessary for the existence of the agreement fall outside Article 101(1).[244] Further, although authority might support a statement that the aim of maintaining a prestigious brand is not a legitimate justification for an outright ban on passive sales, the broader suggestion of the Court that it is not a legitimate aim for restricting competition within SDSs is inconsistent with a consistent line of previous case law holding that such systems based on qualitative criteria in the luxury cosmetics sector may be compatible in principle with Article 101(1).[245] Georgio Monti comments on the judgment in the following extract.

G. Monti, 'Restraints on Selective Distribution Agreements' (2013) 36 *World Competition* 489

We can first comment on the specifics of the reasoning. First ... it puts a whole new gloss on *Metro 1*. The conventional reading of that judgment is that the CJ had realized that while selective distribution harms traders who are excluded, it is, overall, welfare enhancing because it serves to reduce transaction costs and addresses the free rider problem. The Court, paralyzed by the then absence of direct effect in Article 101(3) ruled that there had been no infringement. Now, the legal result after *Pierre Fabre* is the same: a restriction that is objectively justified by the defendant will be held to be one that does not infringe Article 101(1). However, the tone is more skeptical and the burden of justification seems stricter. Second, the Court appears to confuse the second and the third requirement of *Metro 1*. The second requirement is that the characteristics of the product make selective distribution necessary, and the third is that the criteria laid down do not go beyond what is necessary to achieve the second. However, when the Court holds that the maintenance of a prestigious image is not a legitimate aim, this jars with the previous case law where prestige had appeared to be a factor justifying restrictions. The Court should have rather directed the national court to consider whether the restriction on internet trade is proportionate in view of that objective. The Court also appears to misread the fundamental freedom case law in a similar way...

---

[242] Ibid., paras. 40 and 41 and see Monti, n. 3.

[243] The CJ relies on free movement cases (holding that the need to provide individual advice to a customer and to protect against incorrect use of products cannot justify a ban on internet sales of non-prescription medicines and contact lenses, in support of its conclusion that the aim of maintaining a prestigious brand is not a legitimate aim for restricting internet selling, Case C-108/09 *Ker-Optika* [2010] ECR I-12213, paras. 44–46).

[244] See the Opinion of Mazák AG who relies on Case C-309/99, *Wouters v Algemene Raad van de Nederlandse Order van Advocaten* [2002] ECR I-1577 for the view that the ban on internet selling would fall outside Art. 101(1) provided the limitations imposed were appropriate in the light of the legitimate objective (of a public law nature) sought and did not go beyond what was necessary, see para. 35.

[245] See, e.g., Case T-88/92, *Groupement d'Achat Édouard Leclerc v Commission* [1996] ECR II-1961, paras. 105–117.

More generally, by transposing reasoning from the internal market case law, the Court frustrates the more economics-based revolution in antitrust. In the *Ker-Optica* case, for example, there is no identification of how far the national measure impacts upon intra or inter-brand competition…

5. WHAT DRIVES THE CURRENT APPROACH?

In sum, what emerges from the analysis above is the following: first, there are some rules that protect retail outlets, but the anticompetitive effects of their exclusion are not always spelled out clearly. Second, and related, there remains a commitment to closely monitoring the way manufacturers manage internet distribution. Having provided a review of the present system, and indicating some of the mechanisms of regulatory intervention, we ask what might drive the present approach.

5.1 The Excessive Pursuit of Consumer Welfare

One possible explanation for the activism of competition authorities over selective distribution draws on this passage of the French NCA's commitment decisions for the selective distribution of cosmetics, where it explains the value of internet channels and the importance of the commitments offered.

As these are pro-competitive effects that may be expected from on line sale of products subject to selective distribution networks, the Council notes that the development of on line sales during the past ten years tends to show that high quality products can be sold through this channel without endangering neither their brand image, nor the advice offered to consumers. Furthermore, this kind of commercialization, allows to offer to consumers services that sales in shops does not allow, such as home delivery, or making available to the buyer, in real time, abundant information and thereby stimulating price competition, while incentivizing distributors to bring more services to attract clients or to render them loyal.

After this passage the decision moves on to consider how far the commitments offered by the parties remove the authority's competition concerns. The point to focus on here is that the authority points to procompetitive effects of the practice that the actors prevented. So the reason the agreement banning internet sales restricts competition is that there could be greater economic welfare absent that clause. In our view this approach goes beyond what antitrust law can do.

Antitrust law, generally, is not based upon proving that another way of acting would yield greater competition, or make markets work better for consumers. Rather, antitrust law is based on an act which reduces competition from what it was (or would be) before the act was carried out….

5.3 Industrial Policy

There is a related motivation for the approach taken here, which is based on industrial policy. If fostering the growth of the internet is in the public interest, this might explain why competition law is interpreted to facilitate that other EU objective. The Commission said as much in 2011 when commenting on Yves Saint Laurent's attempt to prevent its goods being distributed over the internet. Even if one agrees that competition law may be interpreted to sustain an industrial policy, it is not apparent how forcing all retailers to sell on the internet is somehow going to make a contribution to the EU's information technology agenda. It might be useful for the competition authorities to consider more closely how far promoting e-commerce by applying competition law makes this positive contribution.

It is worth noting that the US antitrust agencies and courts have hardly raised a finger against limitation on the use of the internet, and yet there seems to be more e-commerce in the US than in the EU. Of course such a blunt comparison is too simplistic but one has to wonder how significantly vertical restraints hamper e-commerce. One might also wonder whether simply pursuing e-commerce for all goods and services is desirable. E-commerce drives prices down, but this would also drive the image of certain products down. Many EU luxury brands are popular because of their brand image. Might stimulating e-commerce threaten the brand image and serve to reduce their popularity? And who would be making this trade-off? These complex policy questions require more analysis before one decides to claim that the approach in *Pierre Fabre* has a beneficial effect.

(v) Franchising Agreements and *Pronuptia de Paris*

The Commission describes franchise agreements in its Guidelines:

189. Franchise agreements contain licences of intellectual property rights relating in particular to trade marks or signs and know-how for the use and distribution of goods or services. In addition to the licence of IPRs, the franchisor usually provides the franchisee during the life of the agreement with commercial or technical assistance. The licence and the assistance are integral components of the business method being franchised. The franchisor is in general paid a franchise fee by the franchisee for the use of the particular business method. Franchising may enable the franchisor to establish, with limited investments a uniform network for the distribution of his products. In addition to the provision of the business method, franchise agreements usually contain a combination of different vertical restraints concerning the products being distributed, in particular selective distribution and/or non-compete and/or exclusive distribution or weaker forms thereof.

Franchising arrangements in which a franchisee, or franchisees, is appointed and established as part of a uniform business network, may have a positive impact on competition on a market. Franchise arrangements assist the entry of new competitors to a market and lead to an increase in inter-brand competition. They enable a franchisor to expand its reputation and network without engaging in substantial investment. A franchisee is also enabled to set up and to enter a market with the assistance of an entrepreneur whose business has already been tried and tested on the market.

In *Pronuptia de Paris GmbH v Pronuptia de Paris Irmgard Schillgallis*[246] the CJ recognised that franchise agreements do not in themselves interfere with competition and accepted that two categories of clauses, essential to their successful operation, did not constitute restrictions of competition for the purposes of Article 101(1).

Case 161/84, *Pronuptia de Paris GmbH v Pronuptia de Paris Irmgard Schillgallis* [1986] ECR 353

Court of Justice

14. The compatibility of franchise agreements for the distribution of goods with Article [101(1)[cannot be assessed in abstracto but depends on the provisions contained in such agreements …

15. In a system of distribution franchises of that kind an undertaking which has established itself as a distributor on a given market and thus developed certain business methods grants independent traders, for a fee, the right to establish themselves in other markets using its business name and the business methods which have made it successful. Rather than a method of distribution, it is a way for an undertaking to derive financial benefit from its expertise without investing its own capital. Moreover, the system gives traders who do not have the necessary experience access to methods which they could not have learned without considerable effort and allows them to benefit from the reputation of the franchisor's business name. Franchise agreements for the distribution of goods differ in that regard from dealerships or contracts which incorporate approved retailers into a selective distribution system, which do not involve the use of a single business name, the application of uniform business methods or the payment of royalties in return for the benefits granted. Such a system, which allows the franchisor to profit from his success, does not in itself interfere with competition. In order for the system to work two conditions must be met.

16. First, the franchisor must be able to communicate his know-how to the franchisees and provide them with the necessary assistance in order to enable them to apply his methods, without running the risk that that know-how and assistance might benefit competitors, even indirectly. It follows that provisions which are essential in order to avoid that risk do not constitute restrictions on competition for the

---

[246] Case 161/84, [1986] ECR 353.

> purposes of Article [101(1)]. That is also true of a clause prohibiting the franchisee, during the period of validity of the contract and for a reasonable period after its expiry, from opening a shop of the same or a similar nature in an area where he may compete with a member of the network. The same may be said of the franchisee's obligation not to transfer his shop to another party without the prior approval of the franchisor; that provision is intended to prevent competitors from indirectly benefiting from the know-how and assistance provided.
>
> 17. Secondly, the franchisor must be able to take the measures necessary for maintaining the identity and reputation of the network bearing his business name or symbol. It follows that provisions which establish the means of control necessary for that purpose do not constitute restrictions on competition for the purposes of Article [101(1)].

Because the franchisor had to be able (a) to communicate its know-how to franchisees and to protect it from use by competitors and (b) to maintain the identity and reputation of its network, the Court accepted that restraints on franchisees opening a shop of a similar nature during the period of the contract and for a reasonable period thereafter or selling the shop without the franchisor's consent might be essential to the contract and so fall outside Article 101(1). Further, clauses requiring the franchisee: to apply and to use the franchisor's business methods and know-how; to locate, lay out, and decorate the sales premises according to the franchisor's instructions; to gain the franchisor's approval prior to an assignment of the franchise; to sell only products supplied by the franchisor; and to gain the franchisor's approval for all advertising were unlikely to constitute restrictions.

The Court did not, however, totally embrace an economic approach to franchise agreements.[247] It would not accept that: (a) clauses effecting a division of territories between the franchisor and franchisees or between the franchisees *inter se*,[248] or that (b) clauses preventing price competition between them were essential to the operation of the franchise agreement. These are the types of clauses which in principle restrict competition by object and, it has been seen, are rarely considered to be objectively necessary to achieve a legitimate objective. Justifications for their imposition are generally considered only when determining their compatibility with Article 101(3).

Franchising agreements may therefore fall outside Article 101(1) altogether.[249] In many cases, however, they may incorporate clauses, in particular clauses involving market-sharing between the franchisor and franchisees or the franchisees *inter se*, which are liable to infringe Article 101(1). In such cases assessment of the agreement will need to be completed under Article 101(3).[250]

(vi) Tying

Although there have been relatively few cases which have dealt with tying under Article 101 (but see the discussion of the circumstances in which tying may constitute an abuse of a dominant position in Chapter 7), paragraphs 214–222 of the Guidelines deal with tying under Article 101. In particular, the Commission is concerned that tying may result in anti-competitive foreclosure on the tying and/or tied product markets. The Guidelines state that the main criteria for determining the effects of tying under Article 101 are: the market power of the supplier on the tying market; entry barriers; and the power of buyers on the market.

---

[247] See also Chap. 4.

[248] This has created difficulties since many franchisees are not willing to make the requisite investment without such protection.

[249] Guidelines, paras. 189–191.

[250] See, e.g., COMP/30.937, *Pronuptia* [1987] OJ L13/39, COMP/31.428–31.432, *Yves Rocher* [1987] OJ L8/49, COMP/32.358, *ServiceMaster* [1988] OJ L332/38 and COMP/31.697, *Charles Jourdan* [1989] OJ L35/31.

(vii) Other Restraints

The Commission's Guidelines also provide specific guidance on the compatibility of exclusive customer allocation (treated in a similar, but not identical, way to exclusive distribution), exclusive supply (i.e. where one distributor only is appointed within the EU and where the main competition risk of such agreement is foreclosure of other buyers), upfront access payments, and category management agreements with Article 101(1) and Article 101(3).[251]

5. ARTICLE 101(3)

A. GENERAL

The complex assessment required to determine whether or not an agreement infringes Article 101(1) or individually meets the Article 101(3) criteria, means that the Verticals Regulation is of enormous importance in practice.

B. THE OLD BLOCK EXEMPTIONS

Regulation 2790/1999, the first overarching block exemption for vertical agreements, replaced three 'old-style' block exemptions which applied to different categories of distribution agreement: Regulation 1983/83[252] (exclusive distribution agreements); Regulation 1984/83 (exclusive purchasing agreements (with special provisions for beer-supply and petrol agreements));[253] and Regulation 4087/88[254] (franchising agreements). These older block exemptions, which the Commission had used to mould and influence the content of distribution agreements and policy towards them, had a number of problems. Not only did agreements not always fit neatly within one of these identified categories so stultifying the variety of distribution arrangements that suppliers sought to use (for example, there was no block exemption for selective distribution), but they significantly curtailed the parties' freedom of contract. Each block exemption applied only if it related to goods for resale and set out categories of clauses that were permissible (a white list)[255] and categories of clauses that were not (a black list of hardcore restraints). Any restriction on conduct not specifically exempted by the Regulation would compromise and risk the validity of the agreement.[256] The 1999 block exemption sought to avoid these problems by operating on the basis that all vertical agreements concluded between parties meeting specified market share thresholds are exempted so long as specified conditions are met, including, in particular, that the agreements do not incorporate certain severe restraints. This basic format is also followed by the current 2010 Verticals Regulation.

---

[251] Guidelines, paras. 168–173, 192–202, 203–208, and 209–213 respectively.

[252] [1983] OJ L173/1.

[253] [1983] OJ L173/7. This and Reg. 1983/83 [1983] OJ L173/1 were the successors to Reg. 67/67 [1967] OJ Spec. Ed. 10.

[254] [1988] OJ L359/46.

[255] They did not therefore apply to agreements relating to services or to intermediate goods that the distributor had to finish or prepare for resale. The Verticals Reg. applies to goods (whether for resale or use by the distributor) and services.

[256] The impact of having a white list was that if the agreement contained any other clause there was a risk that the block exemption did not apply. In practice, therefore, parties would attempt to limit the restrictions on conduct and obligations imposed to the clauses explicitly permitted.

C. THE VERTICALS REGULATION—REGULATION 330/2010

(i) The Background

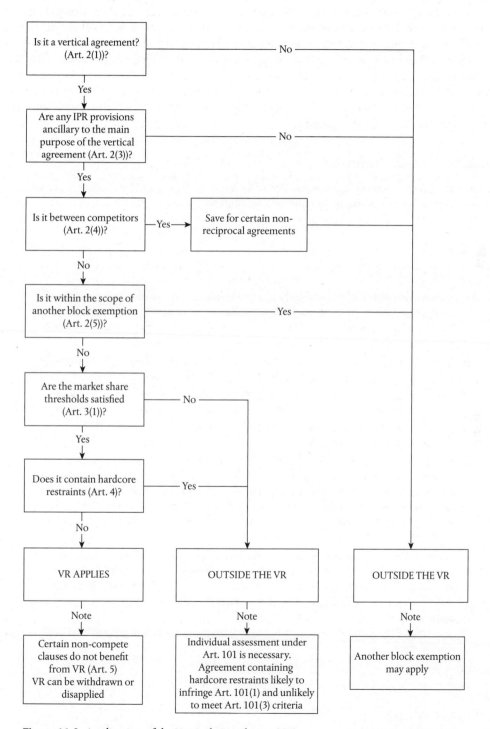

Figure 11.2 Application of the Verticals Regulation (VR)

The Verticals Regulation provides an umbrella block exemption which applies to vertical agreements generally (but see discussion of motor vehicle distribution agreements in Section 5.D). Regulation 330/2010 came into force on 1 June 2010, replacing Regulation 2790/1999. The recitals set out the background to the Regulation. In particular they explain that vertical agreements 'can improve economic efficiency within a chain of production or distribution' and that the 'likelihood that such efficiency-enhancing effects will outweigh any anti-competitive effects due to restrictions contained in vertical agreement depends on the degree of market power of the parties to the agreement'.[257] It thus operates as a safe harbour, setting out a presumption of legality for distribution agreements, whether for goods or services, which satisfy its market share thresholds and other provisions.[258]

The flowchart in Figure 11.2 outlines the working of the block exemption. The subsequent commentary sets out and explains the main provisions of the block exemption, drawing on the explanation set out in the Commission's Guidelines.

(ii) Article 1—Definitions

Article 1 defines core concepts to the application of the Verticals Regulation, for example what constitutes a vertical agreement or a non-competition obligation.

Article 1

1. For the purposes of this Regulation:

   (a) 'vertical agreement' means an agreement or concerted practice entered into between two or more undertakings each of which operates, for the purposes of the agreement or the concerted practice, at a different level of the production or distribution chain, and relating to the conditions under which the parties may purchase, sell or resell certain goods or services;

   (b) 'vertical restraint' means a restriction of competition in a vertical agreement falling within the scope of Article 101(1) of the Treaty;

   (c) 'competing undertakings' means actual or potential suppliers in the same product market; the product market includes goods or services which are regarded by the buyer as interchangeable with or substitutable for the contract goods or services, by reason of the products' characteristics, their prices and their intended use;

   (d) 'non-compete obligation' means any direct or indirect obligation causing the buyer not to manufacture, purchase, sell or resell goods or services which compete with the contract goods or services, or any direct or indirect obligation on the buyer to purchase from the supplier or from another undertaking designated by the supplier more than 80 % of the buyer's total purchases of the contract goods or services and their substitutes on the relevant market, calculated on the basis of the value of its purchases in the preceding calendar year;

   (e) 'selective distribution system' means a distribution system where the supplier undertakes to sell the contract goods or services, either directly or indirectly, only to distributors selected on the basis of specified criteria and where these distributors undertake not to sell such goods or services to unauthorised distributors within the territory reserved by the supplier to operate that system;

   (f) 'intellectual property rights' includes industrial property rights, know how, copyright and neighbouring rights;

---

[257] Verticals Reg., recitals 6 and 7.
[258] Case C-439/09, EU:C:2011:277.

(g) 'know-how' means a package of non-patented practical information, resulting from experience and testing by the supplier, which is secret, substantial and identified: in this context, 'secret' means that the know-how is not generally known or easily accessible; 'substantial' means that the know-how is significant and useful to the buyer for the use, sale or resale of the contract goods or services; 'identified' means that the know-how is described in a sufficiently comprehensive manner so as to make it possible to verify that it fulfils the criteria of secrecy and substantiality;

(h) 'buyer' includes an undertaking which, under an agreement falling within Article 101(1) of the Treaty, sells goods or services on behalf of another undertaking;

(i) 'customer of the buyer' is an undertaking not party to the agreement which purchases the contract goods or services from a buyer which is party to the agreement.

Article 1(2) makes clear that the terms undertakings, suppliers, and buyers in the Regulation also include their respective connected undertakings.

(iii) Article 2—The Main Exemption

a. An Umbrella Exemption Applying to all Vertical Agreements
Vertical Agreements

The Regulation exempts *all* vertical agreements (as defined in Article 1(1)(a), set out in Section 5.C.ii, p. 802) which meet its requirements, whether they relate to goods or services, and whatever their main objective (exclusive distribution, exclusive purchasing, franchising, selective distribution, or some other). The focus of the Regulation is thus more on the restrictive nature of the clause (substantive effect) than the type or form of the agreement involved.

Agreements Between Two or More Undertakings

The exemption applies to agreements and concerted practices concluded between two or more undertakings so long as each undertaking operates, for the purposes of the agreement, at different levels of the production or distribution chain (for example, supplier, wholesaler, and retailer or a supplier of a raw material which the other uses as an input).[259]

Agreements Relating to the Conditions Under Which the Parties may Purchase, Sell, or Resell Certain Goods or Services

The block exemption covers purchase and distribution agreements. These are agreements which:

[r]elate to the conditions under which the parties to the agreement, the supplier and the buyer, 'may purchase, sell or resell certain goods or services'. This reflects the purpose of the Block Exemption Regulation to cover purchase and distribution agreements. These are agreements which concern the conditions for the purchase, sale or resale of the goods or services supplied by the supplier and/or which concern the conditions for the sale by the buyer of the goods or services which incorporate these goods or services. For the application of the Block Exemption Regulation both the goods or services supplied by the supplier and the resulting goods or services are considered to be contract goods or services. Vertical agreements relating to all final and intermediate goods and services are covered. The only exception is the automobile sector, as long as this sector remains covered by a specific block exemption . . . The goods or services provided by the supplier may be resold by the buyer or may be used as an input by the buyer to produce his own goods or services.[260]

---

[259] It does not, therefore, apply to an agreement between a supplier and two wholesalers.
[260] Guidelines, para. 25.

The Regulation does not exempt agreements or restrictions or obligations that do not relate to the purchase, sale, or resale of goods or services, such as rent or leasing agreements or clauses preventing parties from carrying out independent research and development.[261]

b. Agreements between Competing Undertakings

Although the term vertical agreements encompasses agreements concluded between undertakings which for the purposes of the agreement operate at different levels of the production or distribution chain, Article 2(4) of the Verticals Regulation prevents the block exemption from applying to agreements concluded between competing undertakings[262] (even if operating for the purposes of the agreement at different levels of the production or distribution chain), except:

it shall apply where competing undertakings enter into a non-reciprocal vertical agreement and:

(a) the supplier is a manufacturer and a distributor of goods, while the buyer is a distributor and not a competing undertaking at the manufacturing level,[263] or

(b) the supplier is a provider of services at several levels of trade, while the buyer provides its goods or services at the retail level and is not a competing undertaking at the level of trade where it purchase the contract services.

A potential supplier is a supplier who could and would be likely to produce a competing product or service in response to a small and permanent increase in relative prices. A theoretical possibility of entering a market is not enough. The supplier should be able to make the necessary investments and enter the market within a period of one year.[264]

c. Association of Retailers of Goods

Article 2(2) provides that the block exemption applies to vertical agreements concluded between an association of retailers[265] (no member of which, together with its connected undertakings, has a total turnover of more than €50 million) and its members or its supplier—i.e. cooperation between retailers in the area of purchasing and selling. Any horizontal agreement concluded between the members (such as an obligation on members to purchase from the association) must however be assessed first and separately for its compatibility with Article 101.

d. Provisions Relating to the Assignment of Intellectual Property Rights

The assignment of intellectual property rights (IPRs), such as trademarks, copyright, or know-how, may be essential or extremely useful to the effective performance of a vertical agreement. Article 2(3) provides that the block exemption applies to vertical agreements containing provisions relating to the assignment to, or use by, the buyer of IPRs but only if they are ancillary (the provisions do not constitute the primary object of the agreement) and are directly related to the use, sale, or resale of goods or services by the buyer or its customers. The Verticals Regulation will not apply unless five conditions are fulfilled:[266]

(a) the agreement is a vertical one and not, for example, an assignment of IPRs for the manufacture of goods or licensing agreements;[267]

---

[261] Ibid., para. 26.

[262] See definition of competing undertaking in Art. 1 and set out in Section 5.C.ii, p. 802 (it includes actual or potential suppliers in the same product market, irrespective of whether or not they operate in the same geographic market).

[263] Dual distribution occurs where 'the manufacturer of particular goods also acts as a distributor of the goods in competition with independent distributors of his goods': Guidelines, para. 28.

[264] Ibid., para. 27.

[265] Retailers 'are distributors reselling goods to final consumers', ibid., para. 29.

[266] Ibid., para. 31.

[267] Reg. 772/2004 [2004] OJ L123/11, which applies to technology transfer agreements, may apply to such agreements; see Chap. 12. Para. 33 of the Guidelines sets out some examples of agreements which would not benefit from the Verticals Reg.

(b) the assignment or the licence of the IPRs must be made by the supplier to the buyer and not vice versa;

(c) the IPR provisions are ancillary to the implementation of the vertical agreement and not its primary object;

(d) the IPR provisions are directly related to the use, sale, or resale of goods or services by the buyer or its customers, for example where the licensing of a trade mark or know-how is necessary for the marketing of a good;

(e) the clauses relating to the IPRs must not have the same object or effect as restrictions that are not exempted under the Regulation. For example, territorial exclusivity, which is prohibited by Article 4, cannot be circumvented by arrangements involving licensing or assignment of IPRs.[268]

These conditions are of importance to all vertical agreements, but are particularly relevant to franchise agreements, which ordinarily involve the assignment or licensing of IPRs. Franchise agreements, dealt with in some detail in paragraphs 43–45 of the Guidelines, will ordinarily meet all five of the conditions set out in Article 2(3) as:

the franchisor provides goods and/or services, in particular commercial or technical assistance services, to the franchisee. The IPRs help the franchisee to resell the products supplied by the franchisor or by a supplier designated by the franchisor or to use these products and sell the resulting goods or services.[269]

Franchise agreements that do not fall within the block exemption on the ground that they principally concern the licensing of IPRs will be treated in a similar way to those dealt with under the block exemption. Paragraph 45 of the Guidelines sets out the types of obligations related to IPRs which are likely to benefit from the block exemption:

45. The following IPR-related obligations are generally considered to be necessary to protect the franchisor's intellectual property rights and are, if these obligations fall under Article 101(1), also covered by the Block Exemption Regulation:

(a) an obligation on the franchisee not to engage, directly or indirectly, in any similar business;

(b) an obligation on the franchisee not to acquire financial interests in the capital of a competing undertaking such as would give the franchisee the power to influence the economic conduct of such undertaking;

(c) an obligation on the franchisee not to disclose to third parties the know-how provided by the franchisor as long as this know-how is not in the public domain;

(d) an obligation on the franchisee to communicate to the franchisor any experience gained in exploiting the franchise and to grant it, and other franchisees, a nonexclusive licence for the know-how resulting from that experience;

(e) an obligation on the franchisee to inform the franchisor of infringements of licensed intellectual property rights, to take legal action against infringers or to assist the franchisor in any legal actions against infringers;

(f) an obligation on the franchisee not to use know-how licensed by the franchisor for purposes other than the exploitation of the franchise;

(g) an obligation on the franchisee not to assign the rights and obligations under the franchise agreement without the franchisor's consent.

e. Agreements Falling Within the Scope of Another Block Exemption

Article 2(5) states that the Verticals Regulation does not apply to vertical agreements the subject matter of which falls within the scope of another block exemption, unless otherwise provided for in such a regulation. For example, agreements potentially falling within the Technology Transfer

---

[268] See also Cases 56 and 58/64, *Consten and Grundig* [1966] ECR 299, para. 48.

[269] Guidelines, para. 44.

Regulation[270] or concluded in connection with horizontal agreements that may potentially benefit from a block exemption[271] are excluded. The exclusion applies to types of agreements so, for example, a technology transfer agreement which does not meet the criteria of the technology transfer block exemption cannot be exempted by virtue of the Verticals Regulation.[272] As it is of a different type it falls within the scope of the technology transfer regime, not the verticals regime.

(iv) Article 3—The Market Share Cap

a. The 30 Per Cent Threshold

A feature introduced by Regulation 2790/1999, which was not used in previous block exemptions (which applied, unless withdrawn, whatever the market shares of the parties), was the introduction of a market share cap of 30 per cent. Essentially, Regulation 2790/1999 applied where the supplier's market did not exceed 30 per cent. This reflected the Commission's view that vertical restraints were unlikely to pose competition problems, where inter-brand competition is strong and where imposed by a firm without significant market power.[273] The buyer's market share was relevant only where there was an exclusive supply obligation (where a supplier agrees to supply only one buyer inside the EU). When the block exemption was reviewed, however, the Commission decided to amend this provision to deal with potential competition problems arising from an increase in retailers' market power. Under Regulation 330/2010, therefore, the market share of both the supplier (on the market on which it sells the contract goods or services) and the buyer (on the market on which it purchases them) are now taken into account. In a multi-party situation (for example, an agreement between a supplier, wholesaler, and retailer), the market shares of the supplier and the wholesaler (on the markets on which they sell the contract goods or services) and the market shares of the wholesaler and the retailer (on the market on which they purchase the goods or services) are relevant. This additional requirement to take account of buyers' market shares adds an extra layer of uncertainty to the application of the Verticals Regulation. Article 3 provides:

1. The exemption provided for in Article 2 shall apply on condition that the market share held by the supplier does not exceed 30 % of the relevant market on which it sells the contract goods or services and the market share held by the buyer does not exceed 30 % of the relevant market on which it purchases the contract goods or services.

2. For the purposes of paragraph 1, where in a multi party agreement an undertaking buys the contract goods or services from one undertaking party to the agreement and sells the contract goods or services to another undertaking party to the agreement, the market share of the first undertaking must respect the market share threshold provided for in that paragraph both as a buyer and a supplier in order for the exemption provided for in Article 2 to apply.

b. Defining the Market

In addition to the Commission's general Notice on definition of the relevant market,[274] and the relevant jurisprudence, the Guidelines set out specific guidance on market definition and market share calculation issues, focused on distribution cases. Nonetheless, use of a market share test inevitably introduces an element of uncertainty into the block exemption which, arguably, is principally intended to provide legal certainty. Given the call for greater economic analysis in the approach to vertical restraints it is difficult, however, to be critical of the imposition of the market share cap.

---

[270] Reg. 772/2004 [2004] OJ L123/11, see Chap. 12.

[271] See Chap. 10.

[272] Broadly, patent, know-how, or software copyright licensing agreements or a mixed patent, know-how, or software copyright licensing agreement: Reg. 772/2004 [2004] OJ L128/11.

[273] But see n. 276 and text.

[274] See Chap. 1.

Arguably, however, a greater focus on the impact of potential market power to the Article 101(1) assessment might have been preferable.

c. Exceeding the Market Shares

Because of the inherent uncertainty which the market share test brings, it is important that the Guidelines recognise that even if the market share thresholds are (or may be) exceeded there is no presumption that the agreement either infringes Article 101(1) or does not satisfy the Article 101(3) criteria (unless the agreement contains object or hardcore restraints). The Regulation itself provides in Article 7 for the situation where the agreement satisfies the market share thresholds initially but subsequently exceeds them (see further below).

d. Portfolio of Products Distributed through the Same Distribution System

Where the supplier uses the same distribution system to distribute several goods or services some of which are, and some of which are not, in view of the market share thresholds, covered by the block exemption the block exemption exempts only the former.[275]

(v) Article 4—Hardcore Restrictions

a. The Block Exemption is Not Applicable to Vertical Agreements Containing Hardcore Restraints

Vertical agreements may, whatever restrictions or obligations they contain, benefit from the block exemption so long as they are not hardcore restraints prohibited by Article 4. The insertion of just one of these clauses precludes the entire vertical agreement from benefiting from the block exemption.[276] Article 4 focuses on clauses, such as those imposing price or territorial restraints, which restrict intra-brand competition. It will be remembered that there has been concern that EU competition law has treated these types of restraint too harshly (especially when compared to the position that exists in the US). Nonetheless, in the review of the Verticals Regulation and Guidelines the Commission never proposed removing these restraints from the list of hardcore restraints. Indeed, such a step would have resulted in a presumption of legality—which can only be withdrawn prospectively—for such restraints where incorporated in an agreement satisfying the market share thresholds. Arguably, this would be inappropriate, given their clear potential for serious anti-competitive effects.[277]

Article 4 prohibits all clauses which, directly or indirectly, have as their object certain restrictions specified in paragraphs (a)–(e) of the Article.

Article 4

Restrictions that remove the benefit of the block exemption— hardcore restrictions

The exemption provided for in Article 2 shall not apply to vertical agreements which, directly or indirectly, in isolation or in combination with other factors under the control of the parties, have as their object:

(a) the restriction of the buyer's ability to determine its sale price, without prejudice to the possibility of the supplier to impose a maximum sale price or recommend a sale price, provided that they do not amount to a fixed or minimum sale price as a result of pressure from, or incentives offered by, any of the parties;

---

[275] Guidelines, para. 72.

[276] Contrast the position for Art. 5 restraints, nn. 293–294 and text.

[277] They could, however, possibly have been classified as non-exempted rather than hardcore restraints.

(b) the restriction of the territory into which, or of the customers to whom, a buyer party to the agreement, without prejudice to a restriction on its place of establishment, may sell the contract goods or services, except:

   (i) the restriction of active sales into the exclusive territory or to an exclusive customer group reserved to the supplier or allocated by the supplier to another buyer, where such a restriction does not limit sales by the customers of the buyer,

   (ii) the restriction of sales to end users by a buyer operating at the wholesale level of trade,

   (iii) the restriction of sales by the members of a selective distribution system to unauthorised distributors within the territory reserved by the supplier to operate that system, and

   (iv) the restriction of the buyer's ability to sell components, supplied for the purposes of incorporation, to customers who would use them to manufacture the same type of goods as those produced by the supplier;

(c) the restriction of active or passive sales to end users by members of a selective distribution system operating at the retail level of trade, without prejudice to the possibility of prohibiting a member of the system from operating out of an unauthorised place of establishment;

(d) the restriction of cross-supplies between distributors within a selective distribution system, including between distributors operating at different level of trade;

(e) the restriction, agreed between a supplier of components and a buyer who incorporates those components, of the supplier's ability to sell the components as spare parts to end-users or to repairers or other service providers not entrusted by the buyer with the repair or servicing of its goods.

b. Article 4(a): Fixed or Minimum Sales Prices

Article 4(a) prohibits clauses resulting in the establishment of a fixed or minimum resale price or a fixed or minimum price level to be observed by the buyer. It is unclear whether this provision would prohibit MFN clauses but it seems unlikely that it would.[278] Recommended or maximum prices may be imposed so long as they do not amount to indirect means of achieving RPM.[279] Examples of price-fixing through indirect means and measures facilitating direct or indirect price-fixing are set out in paragraph 48 of the Guidelines:

an agreement fixing the distribution margin, fixing the maximum level of discount the distributor can grant from a prescribed price level, making the grant of rebates or reimbursement of promotional costs by the supplier subject to the observance of a given price level, linking the prescribed resale price to the resale prices of competitors, threats, intimidation, warnings, penalties, delay or suspension of deliveries or contract terminations in relation to observance of a given price level. Direct or indirect means of achieving price fixing can be made more effective when combined with measures to identify price-cutting distributors, such as the implementation of a price monitoring system, or the obligation on retailers to report other members of the distribution network that deviate from the standard price level. Similarly, direct or indirect price fixing can be made more effective when combined with measures which may reduce the buyer's incentive to lower the resale price, such as the supplier printing a recommended resale price on the product or the supplier obliging the buyer to apply a most-favoured-customer clause. The same indirect means and the same 'supportive' measures can be used to make maximum or recommended prices work as RPM. However, the use of a particular supportive measure or the provision of a list of recommended prices or maximum prices by the supplier to the buyer is not considered in itself as leading to RPM.

In paragraph 49 the Commission also objects, where agency agreements do fall within Article 101(1), to contractual provisions preventing or restricting the agent from sharing commission with the

---

[278] In the national cases dealing with MFNs, see nn. 142–146 and text, the parties' market share thresholds exceeded those permitted by the Verticals Reg. It did not have to be decided, therefore, whether or not the practices would have been block exempted or whether the MFNs could somehow be classified as prohibited hardcore price restraints.

[279] Guidelines, paras. 226–229.

customer. As the principal sets the price, the agent should be 'free to lower the effective price paid by the customer without reducing the income for the principal'.

c. Article 4(b): Restrictions of the Territory or the Customers to Whom the Buyer may Sell

Article 4(b) prohibits clauses that restrict the territory into which, or the customers to whom, the buyer party to the agreement or its customers may sell the contract goods or services. The provision prohibits both direct restrictions and indirect provisions that, in practice, prevent or deter a buyer or its customers from making sales outside specific territories or customer groups.

The hardcore restriction set out in Article 4(b) . . . concerns agreements or concerted practices that have as their direct or indirect object the restriction of sales by a buyer party to the agreement or its customers, in as far as those restrictions relate to the territory into which or the customers to whom the buyer or its customers may sell the contract goods or services. This hardcore restriction relates to market partitioning by territory or by customer group. That may be the result of direct obligations, such as the obligation not to sell to certain customers or to customers in certain territories or the obligation to refer orders from these customers to other distributors. It may also result from indirect measures aimed at inducing the distributor not to sell to such customers, such as refusal or reduction of bonuses or discounts, termination of supply, reduction of supplied volumes or limitation of supplied volumes to the demand within the allocated territory or customer group, threat of contract termination, requiring a higher price for products to be exported, limiting the proportion of sales that can be exported or profit pass-over obligations. It may further result from the supplier not providing a Union-wide guarantee service under which normally all distributors are obliged to provide the guarantee service and are reimbursed for this service by the supplier, even in relation to products sold by other distributors into their territory. Such practices are even more likely to be viewed as a restriction of the buyer's sales when used in conjunction with the implementation by the supplier of a monitoring system aimed at verifying the effective destination of the supplied goods, such as the use of differentiated labels or serial numbers. However, obligations on the reseller relating to the display of the supplier's brand name are not classified as hardcore. As Article 4(b) only concerns restrictions of sales by the buyer or its customers, this implies that restrictions of the supplier's sales are also not a hardcore restriction, subject to what is stated in paragraph (59) regarding sales of spare parts in the context of Article 4(e). . . . Article 4(b) applies without prejudice to a restriction on the buyer's place of establishment. Thus, the benefit of the Block Exemption Regulation is not lost if it is agreed that the buyer will restrict its distribution outlet(s) and warehouse(s) to a particular address, place or territory.[280]

Article 4 itself sets out four exceptions to the prohibition:

(1) Restrictions on Active Sales into Exclusive Territories or to an Exclusive Customer Group Reserved to Another

The first exception allows a supplier to restrict active sales by a buyer into an exclusive territory or to an exclusive consumer group reserved either to itself or to another buyer. It thus allows a supplier to reserve both exclusive territories and/or exclusive customer groups to a buyer and to preclude active selling by buyers into other territories or customer groups reserved to another.

The Regulation only permits the supplier to prohibit the buyer from making 'active' sales to another's customers or customers in another's territory. The Commission makes the corollary clear, a prohibition on the making of 'passive' sales into another's territory or to another's customer group is not permitted. The agreement must admit the possibility of some parallel trade in the goods or services. Given the importance of the distinction between active and passive sales, the issue is dealt with in some detail in the Guidelines. They explain that the prohibition on active sales is intended to prohibit a distributor from individually approaching customers, for example by mailing,

---

[280] Ibid., para. 50, but see Case T-67/01, *JCB Service v Commission* [2004] ECR II-49 (where distributors pay for the guarantee service it can be agreed that a distributor which sells outside its allotted territory must reimburse the distributor providing the service for the cost of the services plus a reasonable profit margin).

emailing, visiting, or targeting advertising on other customer groups or customers within another's territory.[281] No prohibition is permitted, however, on sales made in response to unsolicited requests from customers.

In the debate which led up to the adoption of the new Verticals Regulation in 2010 one of the core issues which arose for discussion, apart from the treatment of RPM, was the extent to which suppliers (especially those operating SDSs—see also discussion of Article 4(c) below) should be allowed to control or prevent sales by buyers over the internet (whether by 'click and brick'—brick and mortar stores which also sell over the internet—or 'pure players'—which sell only over the internet). Selling over the internet had grown exponentially between the two block exemption and Guidelines. Internet selling clearly offers enormous potential benefits for both sellers and consumers. It enables a distributor to target a broader range of customers than is possible through traditional sales methods as well as allowing it to provide 24-hour, and other, services not offered by traditional retailers. It may also intensify price competition,[282] allowing internet sellers to pass on their lower costs to customers, to overcome geographic barriers and provide customers with a broader range of outlets. A point which became of acute importance during the drafting of, and consultation on,[283] the 2010 Verticals Regulation and Guidelines was whether or not a requirement especially in the context of selective distribution, that dealers should have a brick and mortar shop, could be block exempted and/or whether exclusive dealers could be prohibited from selling or advertising on the internet—i.e. whether this amounts to active selling.

With regard to exclusive distribution, the Commission's starting point is that use of the internet constitutes passive selling so that a restriction on such sales and parallel trade is prohibited. The Guidelines provide some guidance on this issue but given how quickly methods of internet selling are evolving it seems likely that the guidance in this area at least will require updating in the near future. The Guidelines currently state:

The internet is a powerful tool to reach a greater number and variety of customers than by more traditional sales methods, which explains why certain restrictions on the use of the internet are dealt with as (re)sales restrictions. In principle, every distributor must be allowed to use the internet to sell products. In general, where a distributor uses a website to sell products that is considered a form of passive selling, since it is a reasonable way to allow customers to reach the distributor. The use of a website may have effects that extend beyond the distributor's own territory and customer group; however, such effects result from the technology allowing easy access from everywhere. If a customer visits the web site of a distributor and contacts the distributor and if such contact leads to a sale, including delivery, then that is considered passive selling. The same is true if a customer opts to be kept (automatically) informed by the distributor and it leads to a sale. Offering different language options on the website does not, of itself, change the passive character of such selling.[284]

Thus, agreeing that an exclusive distributor shall: prevent customers located in another exclusive territory from viewing its website; reroute customers to other distributors' websites; terminate consumers' transactions once their credit card data reveal an address that is not within the distributor's exclusive territory; limit the proportion of its overall internet sales; pay a higher price for products intended to be resold online are generally regarded by the Commission as hardcore restrictions on passive selling in view of their capability to limit the distributor's ability to reach

---

[281] Guidelines, para. 51.

[282] The French competition authority has brought a number of cases involving bans on internet selling within a selective distribution system (including *Pierre Fabre* itself) and in September 2012 published a report on an inquiry into online commerce which focused on the distribution of domestic appliances, luxury perfumes, and cosmetic and personal care products. The report concludes that as e-commerce often puts significant pressure on prices, offering consumers lower prices and more choice, vertical agreements should not generally curb the development of online sales. It has thus committed to keep a close eye on developments in this sector.

[283] See the Commission's initiatives in relation to online retailing, <http://ec.europa.eu/competition/sectors/media/online_commerce.html>.

[284] Guidelines, para. 52.

more and different customers.[285] The Commission does recognise, however, that some internet selling might constitute active selling which may be restricted, for example online advertising specifically addressed to certain customers, territory-based banners on third party websites, or paying a search engine to have its website found more easily in a particular territory or by a particular customer group.[286]

(2) Restrictions on Wholesalers

The second exception permits a prohibition on a buyer at the wholesale level of trade from making active or passive sales to end-users.

(3) The Restriction on Sales to Unauthorised Distributors by the Members of a Select Distribution System

This provision reiterates that where a SDS is operated it is possible to prohibit members of the system from selling (actively or passively) to unauthorised distributors. In the absence of such a provision the system would obviously break down. The way in which the Verticals Regulation applies to SDSs (especially Article 4(c) and (d)) is discussed below.

(4) Buyers of Components

A supplier may preclude a buyer of components for incorporation into another product from selling (actively or passively) to a customer who would use them to manufacture a product which competes with that produced by the supplier.

d. Articles 4(c) and 4(d): Restrictions in Selective Distribution Systems

The discussion of Article 4(b) establishes that as an exception to the rule that suppliers may not restrict the customers to whom, or the territories in which, the buyers sell the contract goods, members of a SDS can be precluded from making sales to unauthorised distributors outside the system and wholesaler members can be prohibited from making sales to end-users. Restraints can also be imposed on the location and nature of the distributors' premises.[287] Articles 4(c) and 4(d) also deal with the compatibility with Article 101 of sales restraints imposed on authorised members of the network. Article 4(c) prohibits restrictions on active or passive selling by retailers to end-users, but permits the prohibition of retailers operating out of an authorised place of establishment. In *Pierre Fabre*,[288] the CJ held that a requirement that cosmetic products could be sold only at a premises with a pharmacist present operated as a ban on passive selling for the purposes of Article 4(c): the contractual clauses prohibited *de facto* internet selling which had as its object the restriction of passive sales to end-users wishing to purchase online and located outside the physical trading area of the retailer. The Court rejected Pierre Fabre's argument that the ban on internet selling was simply equivalent to a prohibition on the retailer operating out of an authorised establishment. Article 4(d) provides that members of a system may not be precluded from making cross-supplies *inter se*.

It appears therefore that, insofar as a SDS is caught by Article 101(1) at all, the main constraints on the operation of a SDS under the block exemption are that:

- the supplier and buyer do not exceed the 30 per cent market share threshold set out;
- RPM is not directly or indirectly imposed;

---

[285] Ibid., subject to some exceptions (for example, a supplier may require, without limiting the online sales of the distributor, that the buyer sells at least a certain absolute amount of products offline to ensure an efficient operation of its brick and mortar shop).

[286] Guidelines, para. 53.

[287] Verticals Reg., Art. 4(c).

[288] Case C-439/09, EU:C:2011:277.

- retail members are not restrained from making sales to any end-user (active or passive and whether or not with the help of the internet). Suppliers may however require distributors to adhere to quality standards for the use of an internet site to resell goods and to have one or more brick and mortar shops or showrooms before engaging in online distribution. Obligations going beyond this, however, and designed to dissuade appointed dealers from using the internet to reach more and different customers will constitute hardcore restrictions;[289] and

- members are not restrained from making sales to another member of the network.[290] The members may not, therefore, be required to purchase products only from the supplier (exclusive sourcing).[291] Article 5 makes it clear, however, that non-compete obligations are permissible so long as they are not excessive in time and are not targeted at specific suppliers (see Section 5.C.vi, pp. 813–814).

The core difference to the assessment of SDS conducted under Article 101(1), therefore, is that it is not necessary to establish that the products concerned merit a SDS or that the members of the system are chosen only by reference to qualitative criteria—quantitative criteria may be used. The Guidelines provide that a SDS cannot be combined with exclusive distribution in the territory within which the supplier operates a SDS, as this would lead to a restriction of active or passive selling by dealers (although selected dealers can be prevented from running their business from different premises or from opening a new outlet in a different location).[292]

e. Article 4(e): Restrictions on Suppliers of Components

Where a supplier supplies a buyer with components which the latter incorporates into its goods, a restriction may not be imposed which prevents the supplier from selling the components to customers or repairers which have not been authorised by the buyer to repair or service its goods.

(vi) Article 5—Excluded Restraints: Severable, Non-exempted Obligations

a. Obligations which are Excluded (Not Exempted) But Which May Be Severable

Article 5, in comparison with Article 4, focuses on non-compete clauses[293] that are capable of foreclosing the market and directly restricting inter-brand competition. In contrast to the provision in Article 4, Article 5 provides only that where an agreement contains a non-compete obligation which goes beyond its provisions, that *clause* does not benefit from the block exemption—it does not, therefore, necessarily prevent the remaining provisions of the agreement benefiting from the Regulation. It will only do so where the offensive clauses violate Article 101 and are *not* severable from the remaining provisions of the agreement.[294]

---

[289] Guidelines, paras. 53–56 (they should be free to advertise and sell with the help of the internet).

[290] In COMP/37.709, *B&W Loudspeakers* 6 December 2000 (opening of proceedings) and IP/02/916, 24 June 2002 (comfort letter), the Commission objected to price restraints, restraints on cross-supplies between dealers, and restraints on distant selling via the internet in a selective distribution system notified to it under the old notification system. Eventually, however, it granted a comfort letter after the parties agreed to remove the hardcore restraints.

[291] Guidelines, para. 58.

[292] Ibid., para. 57.

[293] See the definition of non-compete obligations in the Verticals Reg., see Section 5.C.ii, p. 802.

[294] Whether or not the offending clauses can be severed is a question of national, not EU, law, see Chaps. 3 and 14.

Article 5

Excluded restrictions

1. The exemption provided for in Article 2 shall not apply to the following obligations contained in vertical agreements:

   (a) any direct or indirect non-compete obligation, the duration of which is indefinite or exceeds five years;

   (b) any direct or indirect obligation causing the buyer, after termination of the agreement, not to manufacture, purchase, sell or resell goods or services;

   (c) any direct or indirect obligation causing the members of a selective distribution system not to sell the brands of particular competing suppliers.

   For the purposes of point (a) of the first subparagraph, a non-compete obligation which is tacitly renewable beyond a period of five years shall be deemed to have been concluded for an indefinite duration.

2. By way of derogation from paragraph 1(a), the time limitation of five years shall not apply where the contract goods or services are sold by the buyer from premises and land owned by the supplier or leased by the supplier from third parties not connected with the buyer, provided that the duration of the non-compete obligation does not exceed the period of occupancy of the premises and land by the buyer.

3. By way of derogation from paragraph 1(b), the exemption provided for in Article 2 shall apply to any direct or indirect obligation causing the buyer, after termination of the agreement, not to manufacture, purchase, sell or resell goods or services where the following conditions are fulfilled:

   (a) the obligation relates to goods or services which compete with the contract goods or services;

   (b) the obligation is limited to the premises and land from which the buyer has operated during the contract period;

   (c) the obligation is indispensable to protect know-how transferred by the supplier to the buyer;

   (d) the duration of the obligation is limited to a period of one year after termination of the agreement.

   Paragraph 1(b) is without prejudice to the possibility of imposing a restriction which is unlimited in time on the use and disclosure of know-how which has not entered the public domain.

b. Article 5(1): Non-compete Obligations

Article 5(1) provides that the exemption does not apply to non-compete obligations imposed (or tacitly renewable) in excess of five years. An exception applies, however, where the buyer of the goods or services operates from premises owned by the supplier or leased by it from a third party not connected with the buyer. In this case the non-compete obligation can be imposed for the duration of the buyer's occupancy of the land. It thus seems, for example, that brewers leasing premises to a publican will be able to impose a non-compete obligation for the entire duration of the lease. The reason for this latter exception is that 'it is normally unreasonable to expect a supplier to allow competing products to be sold from premises and land owned by the supplier without its permission'. But '[a]rtificial ownership constructions . . . intended to avoid the five-year duration limit cannot benefit from this exception'.[295]

c. Article 5(3): Non-compete Obligations after the Termination of the Agreement

Article 5(3) states that the exemption does not apply to obligations imposed on the buyer which prevent it from manufacturing, purchasing, or selling or reselling goods or services after the termination of the agreement *unless* the prohibition: relates to competing goods or services; is limited to

---

[295] Guidelines, para. 67.

the premises and land from which the buyer has operated during the agreement; is indispensable to protect know-how[296] transferred by the supplier under the agreement; and is limited to a period of one year. A restriction which is unlimited in time may be possible, however, where essential to prevent the use or disclosure of know-how which has not entered the public domain.

d. Article 5(1)(c): Non-compete Obligations and Selective Distribution Systems

The block exemption covers 'the combination of selective distribution with a non-compete obligation, obliging the distributor not to resell competing brands in general'. Article 5(1)(c) provides, however, that the exemption will not apply where the supplier prevents distributors from buying products for resale from *specific* competing suppliers.

The objective of the exclusion of this obligation is to avoid a situation whereby a number of suppliers using the same selective distribution outlets prevent one specific competitor or certain specific competitors from using these outlets to distribute their products (foreclosure of a competing supplier which would be a form of collective boycott).[297]

(vii) Withdrawal of the Block Exemption by the Commission or the National Competition Authorities

The benefit of the block exemption can be withdrawn in relation to an agreement which, either in isolation or in conjunction with similar agreements, infringes Article 101(1) and does not in fact satisfy the conditions of Article 101(3).[298] The Commission has the exclusive power to withdraw the benefit of the block exemption in respect of vertical agreements restricting competition on a relevant geographic market which is wider than the territory of a single Member State, but concurrent jurisdiction with the NCAs where the relevant geographic market constitutes the territory of a single Member State, or a part thereof.[299] Where the Commission wishes to so withdraw the benefit of the Verticals Regulation it will have to prove that the agreement infringes Article 101(1) and does not fulfil one or several of the four conditions set out in Article 101(3). The Commission may, for example, wish to do so where foreclosure occurs as a result of parallel networks of vertical agreements. Responsibility for anti-competitive effects identified will be attributed to the undertakings which make an appreciable contribution to them.[300] A withdrawal does not apply retrospectively, however, it only has *ex nunc* effect, 'which means that the exempted status of the agreements concerned will not be affected until the date at which the withdrawal becomes effective'.[301]

(viii) Article 6—Non-application of the Regulation—Networks of Agreements

This provision allows the Commission to declare by regulation (applicable not to an individual undertaking but to all undertakings addressed) that the block exemption should not apply to agreements containing specified restraints in cases where more than 50 per cent of a relevant market is covered by networks of similar vertical restraints.[302] Any such regulation, fully restoring the

---

[296] Verticals Reg., Art. 1(1)(g).

[297] Guidelines, para. 69 providing the example of COMP/33.542, *Parfums Givenchy* [1992] OJ L236/11.

[298] See Reg. 1/2003, Art. 29(1)(2) and Verticals Reg., recital 15 (see Chap. 4).

[299] Guidelines, para. 78.

[300] Ibid., paras. 75–77.

[301] Ibid., para. 77.

[302] Ibid., para. 80, for example when parallel networks of selective distribution covering more than 50% of a market are liable to foreclose the market by using selection criteria which are not required by the nature of relevant goods or which discriminate against certain forms of distribution capable of selling such goods, para. 81.

application of Article 101 to the restraints and markets concerned,[303] could not take effect earlier than six months following its adoption[304] and does not affect the exempted status of the agreements concerned for the period preceding its coming into force.[305] When deciding whether to adopt a regulation the Commission will also consider whether withdrawal of the block exemption would be more appropriate. This will depend on the number of competing undertakings contributing to the cumulative effects and the number of affected geographic markets.[306]

Because the regulation must specify the scope of the regulation in relation both to the relevant product and geographic markets to which it applies and to the vertical restraints in respect of which the Verticals Regulation will not apply, the regulation may not apply to all agreements concluded on an affected market. Rather:

the Commission may modulate the scope of its regulation according to the competition concern which it intends to address. For instance, while all parallel networks of single-branding type arrangements shall be taken into account in view of establishing the 50 % market coverage ratio, the Commission may nevertheless restrict the scope of the disapplication regulation only to non-compete obligations exceeding a certain duration. Thus, agreements of a shorter duration or of a less restrictive nature might be left unaffected, in consideration of the lesser degree of foreclosure attributable to such restraints. Similarly, when on a particular market selective distribution is practised in combination with additional restraints such as non-compete or quantity-forcing on the buyer, the disapplication regulation may concern only such additional restraints. Where appropriate, the Commission may also provide guidance by specifying the market share level which, in the specific market context, may be regarded as insufficient to bring about a significant contribution by an individual undertaking to the cumulative effect.[307]

(ix) Articles 7, 8, and 9—Market Share, Turnover, and Transitional Provisions

Articles 7 and 8 contain provisions relating to the calculation of market share and turnover for the purposes of the Regulation. In particular, Article 7(d) makes provision to exempt agreements for a period of two consecutive calendar years which satisfy the 30 per cent threshold initially but subsequently rise above it (without exceeding 35 per cent). Article 9 provides that agreements already in force on 31 May 2010 and satisfying the provisions of Regulation 2790/1999, but not Regulation 330/2010, shall not be prohibited from 1 June 2010 to 31 May 2011.

(x) Article 10—Commencement and Expiry

Article 10 provides that the block exemption entered into force on 1 June 2010,[308] and expires on 31 May 2022. Whether the regime will need tweaking prior to this date to deal with e-commerce and new business practices (such as MFNs) remains to be seen.

D. THE MOTOR VEHICLE DISTRIBUTION BLOCK EXEMPTION

Until the end of May 2010, motor vehicle distribution agreements and agreements relating to repair, maintenance, and the supply of spare parts were not governed by the ordinary regime for vertical

---

[303] Ibid., para. 101.

[304] Art. 6(2).

[305] Guidelines, paras. 84–85.

[306] Ibid., para. 82.

[307] Ibid., para. 83.

[308] Except for the provision extending the application of the block exemption which has applied since 1 January 2000.

agreements but by Regulation 1400/02,[309] which recognised the special features of the motor vehicle sector. Before the block exemption was due to expire on 31 May 2010, the Commission, in 2008, evaluated its working. Following consultation on a future framework for motor vehicle agreements, the Commission concluded that motor vehicle manufacturers and dealers did not continue to require different treatment as compared to agreements in any other sector. In 2010, the Commission published a regulation, Regulation 461/2010, and Guidelines to replace Regulation 1400/2002.[310] This provided that from 31 May 2013, motor vehicle distribution agreements were brought within the ordinary regime for vertical agreements (subject to a three-year adaptation period). Repair and maintenance agreements, however, continue to be dealt with by a separate block exemption.

E. ARTICLE 101(3)—INDIVIDUAL ASSESSMENT

(i) Introduction

Where the parties cannot ensure that their agreement benefits from either the Verticals Regulation or the motor vehicle distribution block exemption, and the risk of infringing Article 101(1) is real, it may still be important to consider the application of Article 101(3) to an agreement. It will be remembered that any restrictive agreement is, in theory, capable of satisfying the criteria[311] but all four criteria must be satisfied.[312]

(ii) 'Hardcore' Restraints

A supplier or distributor may perceive territorial and/or price restraints to be essential to the operation of a distribution agreement. Prior to the 2010 Guidelines, the Commission appeared unwilling in both its decisional practice and the Guidelines to accept that agreements which confer RPM[313] or confer ATP on a distributor or which otherwise operate to prevent parallel imports meet the requirements of Article 101(3).[314] Rather, it generally took the view that such restraints are unlikely to benefit consumers or to be indispensable to achieve the efficiencies specific to the agreement (which are likely to be achievable by other practicable and less restrictive means).[315] In *Grundig*,[316] for example, it was the clauses resulting in Consten being granted the exclusive right to sell Grundig's products in France which caused the Commission to find that the agreement both infringed Article 101(1) and did not meet the Article 101(3) criteria (it refused an exemption). The result was that Grundig acquired Consten. Subsequently, the Commission has not proved receptive to any argument that these types of clauses may be essential to prevent free-riding on the distributors' services or to ensure that a product is successfully launched in a new market. Further, in 2003 in *Nintendo*,[317] the Commission relied on *Grundig* when it stated that agreements conferring ATP, would not meet the criteria of

---

[309] [2002] OJ L203/30. It entered into force in October 2002. In Case C-158/11, *Auto24 SARL v Jaguar Land Rover France SAS* EU:C:2012:351, the CJ gave a judgment which focused on the interpretation of specific provisions of Reg. 1400/2002 and the distinction set out therein between quantitative and qualitative selective distribution systems.

[310] See <http://ec.europa.eu/competition/sectors/motor_vehicles/legislation/legislation.html>.

[311] Case T-17/93, *Matra Hachette v Commission* [1994] ECR II-595, para. 85, see Chap. 4.

[312] The requirements are cumulative, Case T-528/93, *Métropole Télévision SA v Commission* [1996] ECR II-649, para. 86.

[313] See, e.g., COMP/37.709, *B&W Loudspeakers* 6 December 2000.

[314] See, e.g., COMP/35.733, *Volkswagen* [1998] OJ L124/60, on appeal Case T-62/98, *Volkswagen AG v Commission* [2000] ECR II-2707, the appeal to the CJ was dismissed, see Case C-338/00 P, *Volkswagen AG v Commission* [2003] ECR I-9189.

[315] See Chap. 4.

[316] COMP/3344, 23 September 1964. See also, e.g., COMP/28.282, *The Distillers Co Ltd* [1978] OJ L50/16, Case 30/78, *Distillers Co v Commission* [1980] ECR 2229, and COMP/223, *Transocean Marine Paint Associations* [1967] OJ L/10.

[317] COMP/35.706 and 36.321, [2003] OJ L255/33, *aff'd* Case T-12/03, *Itochu v Commission* [2009] ECR II-909, and Case T-13/03, *Nintendo and Nintendo of Europe v Commission* [2009] ECR II-975.

Article 101(3) (the provisions were not indispensable to realise the potential benefits of the exclusive distribution system).[318]

Nonetheless, the EU Courts have always made it clear that even object restraints are capable of meeting the Article 101(3) criteria. In Chapter 4 it was seen that in *GlaxoSmithKline Services Unlimited v Commission*,[319] the GC held that: the Commission's decision to refuse an exemption to a dual pricing system operated by Glaxo which prevented parallel trade was fundamentally flawed; and the Commission had not adequately discharged its duty under Article 101(3). Similarly, in *Binon*, the CJ indicated that the Commission might have to consider whether or not an agreement, where a publisher fixed the prices of its newspapers and periodicals, fulfilled the requirements of Article 101(3).[320]

Case 243/83, *SA Binon & Cie v SA Agence et Messageries de la Presse* [1985] ECR 2015

44. It should be observed in the first place that provisions which fix the prices to be observed in contracts with third parties constitute, of themselves, a restriction on competition within the meaning of Article [101(1)] . . .

45. In those circumstances, where an agreement which establishes a selective distribution system and which affects trade between Member States includes such a provision, an exemption from the prohibition contained in Article [101(1)] of the [EU] Treaty may only be granted by means of a decision adopted by the Commission in the conditions laid down by Article [101(3)].

46. If, in so far as the distribution of newspapers and periodicals is concerned, the fixing of the retail price by publishers constitutes the sole means of supporting the financial burden resulting from the taking back of unsold copies and if the latter practice constitutes the sole method by which a wide selection of newspapers and periodicals can be made available to readers, the Commission must take account of those factors when examining an agreement for the purposes of Article [101(3)].

In accordance with the case law and more modern economic thinking, the Commission was, therefore, when drafting the 2010 Guidelines, urged to ensure that the Guidelines reflected this position. The Commission has attempted to meet these calls, making it clear that even though the block exemption does not apply to hardcore restrictions and even if the agreement is assumed to restrict competition under Article 101(1), individual satisfaction of the Article 101(3) criteria is not excluded where there is convincing evidence of likely efficiencies:[321]

Including such a hardcore restriction in an agreement gives rise to the presumption that the agreement falls within Article 101(1). It also gives rise to the presumption that the agreement is unlikely to fulfil the conditions of Article 101(3), for which reason the block exemption does not apply. However, undertakings may demonstrate pro-competitive effects under Article 101(3) in an individual case. Where the undertakings substantiate that likely efficiencies result from including the hardcore restriction in the agreement and demonstrate that in general all the conditions of Article 101(3) are fulfilled, the Commission will be required to effectively assess the likely negative impact on competition before making an ultimate assessment of whether the conditions of Article 101(3) are fulfilled.

---

[318] 'Instead, in regard to the goods in question territories are hermetically sealed off, making interpenetrating of national markets impossible, thereby bringing to nought economic integration' COMP/35.706 and COMP/36.321, ibid., para. 338.

[319] Case T-168/01, [2006] ECR II-2969, *aff'd* Cases C-501, 513, 515, and 519/06, [2009] ECR I-9291, see further discussion of the case in Chap. 4.

[320] In neither case did the Court hold that the Art. 101(3) criteria were actually satisfied, however.

[321] Guideline, para. 47. See also para. 223.

The Guidelines except therefore that in exceptional circumstances parties may be able to plead 'an efficiency defence'[322] to justify territorial and price restraints. For example,[323] the Commission recognises that restraints on active sales by wholesalers in a selective distribution system may be necessary to protect promotional activities which must be conducted in wholesalers' own territories and that dual pricing arrangements (perhaps where the supplier charges higher prices for products to be sold online) may be justified where sales online lead to substantially higher costs for the manufacturer. In addition, the Commission states that efficiencies raised to justify RPM will be assessed under Article 101(3), for example:[324]

where a manufacturer introduces a new product, RPM may be helpful during the introductory period of expanding demand to induce distributors to better take into account the manufacturer's interest to promote the product. RPM may provide the distributors with the means to increase sales efforts and if the distributors on this market are under competitive pressure this may induce them to expand overall demand for the product and make the launch of the product a success, also for the benefit of consumers. Similarly, fixed resale prices, and not just maximum resale prices, may be necessary to organise in a franchise system or similar distribution system applying a uniform distribution format a coordinated short term low price campaign (2 to 6 weeks in most cases) which will also benefit the consumers. In some situations, the extra margin provided by RPM may allow retailers to provide (additional) pre-sales services, in particular in case of experience or complex products. If enough customers take advantage from such services to make their choice but then purchase at a lower price with retailers that do not provide such services (and hence do not incur these costs), high-service retailers may reduce or eliminate these services that enhance the demand for the supplier's product. RPM may help to prevent such free-riding at the distribution level. The parties will have to convincingly demonstrate that the RPM agreement can be expected to not only provide the means but also the incentive to overcome possible free riding between retailers on these services and that the pre-sales services overall benefit consumers as part of the demonstration that all the conditions of Article 101(3) are fulfilled.

Although the Commission does therefore now recognise that hardcore restraints may sometimes satisfy the conditions of Article 101(3), an extremely onerous burden rests on the parties who seek to demonstrate that efficiencies will result from including ATP or RPM in their agreement and to demonstrate also that the other conditions of Article 101(3) are fulfilled. Further the tendency of the Commission and NCAs to fine undertakings which incorporate these restraints in their contracts, combined with the limited and narrow examples provided in the Guidelines of the situations where the Article 101(3) conditions might be satisfied (and the lack of jurisprudence on this issue[325]), is, however, likely to make firms wary about incorporating these restraints into their agreements.[326] Indeed, it is not clear that the Commission has moved so far from the view expounded in the Article 101(3) Guidelines that hardcore restraints are unlikely to create objective economic benefits, to benefit consumers, or to be indispensable to the attainment of any efficiencies created by the agreement.[327] In particular, the 2010 Guidelines suggest that indispensability is likely to continue to present a problem to those seeking to rely on Article 101(3) to justify hardcore restraints as they will need to demonstrate that no other restraint would be sufficient to achieve the efficiencies alleged. Paragraph 109 makes this point clearly:

[a] large measure of substitutability exists between the different vertical restraints. As a result, the same inefficiency problem can be solved by different vertical restraints. For instance, economies of scale in distribution

---

[322] In addition, the Guidelines state at para. 60 that hardcore restrictions may be objectively necessary 'to align on a public ban on selling dangerous substances to certain customers for reasons of safety or health', see Chap. 4.

[323] Guidelines, paras. 61–64. See also discussion at n. 114 and text.

[324] Ibid., para. 225.

[325] But see the decision of the Australian Competition and Consumer Commission (ACCC) to grant authorisation to Tooltechnic to set minimum retail prices on Festool products until 31 December 2018, *Tooltechnic* 5 December 2014.

[326] It seems likely, however, that competition agencies do recognise that these provisions may sometimes be unproblematic and do not prioritise such cases for investigation.

[327] See Chap. 4.

may possibly be achieved by using exclusive distribution, selective distribution, quantity forcing or exclusive sourcing. However, the negative effects on competition may differ between the various vertical restraints, which play a role when indispensability is discussed under Article 101(3).

(iii) Other Restraints

In other cases, it is extremely important when drafting agreements to look at the jurisprudence and at both the Article 101(3) Guidelines[328] and at the Guidelines which set out how the Commission will enforce Article 101 in respect of individual agreements not covered by the block exemption (such as: single branding; exclusive distribution and customer allocation; selective distribution; franchising; exclusive supply; and/or recommended and maximum prices).[329] Article 5 of the Verticals Regulation also gives an indication of how Article 101(3) will apply to non-compete provisions. On occasion, however, it may be possible to argue that a non-compete provision for longer than that permitted in Article 5 is indispensable to the operation of the agreement.[330] When deciding whether or not an agreement meets the criteria of Article 101(3), in particular whether a restriction is indispensable to the operation of the agreement, the Guidelines make it clear that the determination must be made with regard to the *justification* for the vertical restraints (for example, whether or not it is necessary to help solve a free-rider problem, to create brand image, or to deal with a hold-up problem).

An example of a case in which a non-compete provision was found not to meet the criteria of Article 101(3) is *Van den Bergh Foods*.[331] In this case the GC rejected the applicants' assertion that the Commission had erred in law in applying Article 101(3), in particular by wrongly concluding that the restrictive effects of its freezer exclusivity agreements outweighed the advantages flowing from the distribution efficiency they produced. The GC held that as the agreement did not satisfy the first condition of Article 101(3), the Commission was entitled to refuse an exemption.[332] The advantages produced by the agreement were not objective ones but ensued to the parties to the agreement.[333]

Case T-65/98, *Van den Bergh Foods Ltd v Commission* [2003] ECR II-4653

General Court

138. The Court finds that, contrary to HB's submission in paragraph 123 above, it is clear from the contested decision that the Commission carried out a detailed analysis of the HB distribution agreement in

---

[328] [2004] OJ C101/97.

[329] See, especially, paras. 131–136 and 139–226.

[330] See, e.g., Guidelines, paras. 155 (longer periods may be possible where significant investment is required), and 158 and 171 (a non-compete provision may be permitted for the duration of an exclusive distribution agreement).

[331] Case T-65/98, *Van den Bergh Foods v Commission* [2003] ECR II-4653, aff'd Case C-552/03 P, *Unilever Bestfoods v Commission* [2006] ECR I-9091.

[332] The GC held that the review carried out in a case under the old notification and exemption system 'of the complex economic assessments undertaken by the Commission in the exercise of the discretion conferred on it by Article [101(3)] of the Treaty in relation to each of the four conditions laid down therein, must be limited to ascertaining whether the procedural rules have been complied with, whether proper reasons have been provided, whether the facts have been accurately stated and whether there has been any manifest error of appraisal or misuse of powers (see, to that effect, Joined Cases T-39/92 and T-40/92, *CB and Europay v Commission* [1994] ECR II-49, para. 109; Case T-17/93, *Matra Hachette v Commission* [1994] ECR II-595, para. 104; and Case T-29/92, *SPO and others v Commission* [1995] ECR II-289, para. 288). It is not for the [General Court] to substitute its own assessment for that of the Commission', Case T-65/98, *Van den Bergh Foods v Commission* [2003] ECR II-4653, para. 135. The judgment was aff'd Case C-552/03 P, *Unilever Bestfoods v Commission* [2006] ECR I-9091.

[333] Rather than improving distribution or promoting progress, the effect of the agreements was to strengthen the strong position of HB on the market.

the light of each of the four conditions laid down by Article [101(3)] of the Treaty (see recitals 221 to 254 of the contested decision).

139. As regards the first of those conditions, the agreements capable of being exempted are those which contribute to improving the production or distribution of goods or to promoting technical or economic progress. The Court would point out in that regard that it is settled law of the Court of Justice and of the [General Court] that the improvement cannot be identified with all the advantages which the parties obtain from the agreement in their production or distribution activities. The improvement must in particular display appreciable objective advantages of such a character as to compensate for the disadvantages which they cause in the field of competition (Joined Cases 56/64 and 58/64 *Consten and Grundig v Commission* . . . at 348, and *Langnese-Iglo*, paragraph 180).

140. The first condition is examined in recitals 222 to 238 of the contested decision. The Commission acknowledged in particular that the agreements whereby freezer cabinets are made available might secure some or all of the benefits described in the fifth recital to Regulation No. 1984/83 for HB itself and for the retailers who are the other parties to the agreements, and that the distribution method currently used by HB might offer it and its retailers certain advantages in terms of efficiency of planning, organisation and distribution. Therefore, the Commission held that those arrangements did not present appreciable objective advantages of such a character as to compensate for the disadvantages caused to competition. In support of that assertion, it pointed out that the freezer cabinet agreements in question considerably strengthened HB's position in the relevant market, especially vis-à-vis potential competitors. It rightly observed in that regard that the strengthening of an undertaking which is as important on the market as HB leads not to more but to less competition because the network of that undertaking's agreements constitutes a major barrier to the entry of others into the market, as well as to expansion within the market by its existing competitors (see in particular recitals 225 and 236 of the contested decision, and, by analogy, *Langnese-Iglo v Commission*, paragraph 182). It must also be pointed out that the level of foreclosure of the relevant market is in the order of 40 per cent (see paragraph 98 above) and not 6 per cent as HB submits . . .

141. Consequently, the Court finds that, contrary to HB's contention . . . the Commission rightly took into consideration the barriers to entry to the relevant market resulting from the exclusivity clause, and the consequent weakening of competition, when it assessed HB's distribution agreement in the light of the first condition laid down by Article [101(3)] of the Treaty (see, by analogy, *Consten and Grundig v Commission* at p. 348, and *Langnese-Iglo v Commission*, paragraph 180). It follows that the Court cannot accept HB's argument . . . to the effect that recitals 222 to 225 of the contested decision contain a fundamental logical flaw with regard to the relationship between Article [101(1)] and Article [101(3)] of the Treaty, as the Commission was obliged, pursuant to settled case-law on the subject, to ascertain whether there were objective advantages of such a character as to compensate for the disadvantages which an agreement creates for competition.

142. The Court also notes that HB's distribution agreements have two particular aspects, namely, first, they make freezer cabinets available without charge to retailers and, second, the retailers undertake to use those cabinets to stock HB ice creams only. The benefits ensured by the agreements in question are the result of the first aspect and can therefore be achieved even without the exclusivity clause.

143. The Court also accepts the Commission's argument in recital 227 of the contested decision that although the wide availability in outlets of freezer cabinets intended for the sale of impulse ice-creams, covering the entire geographic market and consisting mainly of HB's cabinets, could be considered an objective advantage in the distribution of those products in the public interest, it is nevertheless unlikely that HB would definitely cease to supply freezer cabinets to retailers, whatever the conditions, except in small number of cases, if its power to impose an obligation of exclusivity in respect of those freezers were to be restricted. HB has not shown that the Commission committed a manifest error in taking the view that business reality for a company such as HB, which wishes to maintain its position on the relevant market, is to be present in the maximum number of outlets possible (see recital 228 and paragraph 125 above). Contrary to HB's submission, the Commission did not merely assume continuity of provision by HB of freezer cabinets on the relevant market, but carried out a prospective analysis of the operation of

the market after the adoption of the contested decision. Furthermore, contrary to HB's argument (see paragraph 125 above), the Commission could validly rely on the argument that manufacturers competing with HB might adopt a policy of supplying freezer cabinets to sales outlets whose turnover in impulse ice-creams is too low to be of interest to HB, and do so upon more advantageous conditions than those which the retailers might expect to obtain themselves if HB ceased to supply freezer cabinets to certain sales outlets. Similarly, the Commission could validly point to the possibility that cabinets would be installed by independent resellers who would obtain supplies from various sources and satisfy demand from all the sales outlets from which HB had withdrawn its equipment or to which it decided not to supply equipment. HB cannot claim that the Commission's prospective analysis is vitiated by a manifest error of assessment unless it does so on the basis of concrete evidence, which HB has failed to adduce in the present case.

144. As HB's distribution agreements do not satisfy the first of the conditions laid down by Article [101(3)], the third plea must therefore be rejected and it is not necessary to consider whether the Commission committed a manifest error in regard to its assessment of the other conditions laid down by that provision. If any one of the four conditions is not satisfied, the exemption must be refused.

In *Telenor/Canal+/Canal Digital*,[334] the European Commission approved complex contractual arrangements providing for the exclusive distribution by Canal Digital of pay-TV premium content channels and pay-per-view and near-video-on demand (PPV/NVOD) channels in the Nordic region.[335] The agreements also imposed non-compete obligations which, broadly, prohibited Canal Digital from owning, operating, or retailing any other pay-TV premium content or PPV/NVOD channels.

In order to gain approval for the agreements the parties agreed to modify the agreements and: to mitigate foreclosure of potential entrants in the downstream DTH pay-TV market by reducing the duration and scope of Canal Digital's exclusivity; to alleviate foreclosure of potential entrants on the supply side in the upstream market for the wholesale supply of pay-TV by reducing the duration of the pay-TV non-compete obligations on Canal Digital; and to alleviate foreclosure of potential entrants on the supply side in the upstream market for the provision of transponder capacity for TV broadcasting by reducing non-compete obligations on Canal+.[336]

The Commission took the view that most of the clauses, even in their revised form, appreciably restricted competition within the meaning of Article 101(1).[337] Further, the Commission noted that the Verticals block exemption was not available to the parties, both because the primary purpose of the exclusivity and non-compete arrangement was the use by the buyer of IPRs and because of Canal+'s strong market position, which exceeded the 30 per cent threshold. The Commission stressed, however, that this did not mean that there was a presumption that the vertical agreement was illegal. 'Rather the agreements need individual examination by the Commission in the application of Article 101(3) of the Treaty.'[338]

[334] COMP/38.287, 29 December 2003.

[335] The notified agreements also related to the divestiture by Canal+ of its 50% shareholding in Canal Digital, previously jointly run with Telenor Broadband Services (TBS), and its acquisition by TBS. The distribution agreements related to the distribution by Canal Digital of Canal+ Nordic's pay-TV premium content channels and PPV/NVOD channels via direct-to-home (DTH) satellite platform, satellite master antenna television system networks (SMATV), and small cable networks in the Nordic region. Essentially, the agreements aimed to ensure continuity of the pay-TV content supply and distribution that had previously been secured within the vertically integrated company structure. Under the new arrangements there was a vertical relationship between the independent upstream supplier of pay-TV premium content, Canal+ Nordic, and an independent downstream DTH platform for the distribution of pay-TV to end consumers, Canal Digital.

[336] The parties also took steps to address horizontal cooperation concerns and to avoid foreclosure in related market segments.

[337] It granted negative clearance, however, to the clauses governing exclusive distribution by Canal Digital of Canal+ Nordic's PPV/NVOD channels, COMP/38.287, 29 December 2003, paras. 170–178.

[338] Ibid., para. 196.

The Commission found that the modified exclusivity and non-compete provisions generated efficiencies and contributed to the improvement in distribution and the promotion of economic progress within the meaning of Article 101(3) and that consumers received a fair share of the benefits. Although the Commission accepted that the provisions were indispensable to attain the efficiencies, this was only so subject to a strict limitation period, for example: of four years' duration for the pay-TV channel exclusivity provisions; and of three years in respect of the obligation on Telenor/Canal Digital not to own, operate, or distribute via DTH any other pay-TV premium content channels. The Commission concluded that the various contractual arrangements did not eliminate competition in the affected markets during the term of their validity. The cooperation for a limited period would maintain competition with the second satellite pay-TV distributor in the Nordic region, MTV/VIASAT and preserve the possibility of market entry in the Nordic pay-TV segments in the mid- to long-term. It thus granted an exemption to the provisions found to infringe Article 101(1) for a five-year period.[339]

6. SUBCONTRACTING AGREEMENTS

Subcontracting agreements, under which a contractor entrusts the manufacture of goods or the supply of services to a subcontractor, are vertical in nature.[340] Goods or services in subcontracting agreements are provided, on the instructions of the contractor, to that contractor or, on its behalf, to a third party. The arrangement may also involve a licence of IPRs from the contractor to the subcontractor.

A Commission Notice concerning the assessment of certain subcontracting agreements in relation to Article 101(1) of the Treaty (the 'Subcontracting Notice') recognises that these agreements are frequently pro-competitive. It thus indicates that certain clauses in subcontracting agreements are unlikely to restrict competition and infringe Article 101(1). For example, a requirement that: (a) technology or equipment provided by the contractor (i) may not be used except for the purposes of the subcontracting agreement and (ii) may not be made available to third parties; and (b) goods or services resulting from such technology or equipment may be supplied only to the contractor or performed on his behalf, will fall outside Article 101(1) on condition that the technology or equipment provided is necessary to enable the subcontractor to manufacture the goods or supply the services or to carry out the work in accordance with the contractor's instructions.[341] Further, paragraph 3 provides that the following provisions are unlikely to violate Article 101(1): (a) an obligation that a specified 'trade mark, trade name or get-up' provided under the contract be used by the subcontractor only as a means of identification in relation to the contract goods, services, or work; (b) an undertaking by either party not to reveal secret know-how (which has not become public knowledge) given by the other party during the negotiation and performance of the agreement; (c) an undertaking by the subcontractor not to make use, even after expiry of the agreement, of secret know-how (which has not become public knowledge) received during the currency of the agreement; and (d) an undertaking by the subcontractor to pass on to the contractor on a non-exclusive basis technical improvements or patentable inventions relating to improvements and/or new applications of the original invention, discovered during the currency of the agreement.

Where there is concern that the subcontracting agreements may violate Article 101(1), the agreement may be able to benefit from the Verticals Regulation.[342] It has been seen in the previous

---

[339] The Commission took due account of Telenor's/Canal Digital's and Canal+ Nordic's legitimate interest in achieving a reasonable return on their investment in their pay-TV business so far.

[340] See Notice of 18 December 1978 concerning its assessment of certain sub-contracting agreements in relation to Article [101(1)] (the Subcontracting Notice), [1979] OJ C1/2, para. 1.

[341] Subcontracting Notice, para. 2.

[342] Since the agreement is between undertakings which operate, for the purposes of the agreement, at different levels of the production or distribution chain, and the agreement relates to the conditions under which the parties may purchase, sell, or resell certain goods or services.

discussion, however, that this block exemption is not generally applicable if the agreement is between competitors or if the subject matter of the agreement falls within the scope of another block exemption. Further, it does not cover the licensing or assignment of IPRs unless they are assigned to the buyer, in this case, the *contractor*. In practice, therefore, although some subcontracting agreements may benefit from the Verticals Regulation, such as agreements between non-competitors whereby the contractor provides only specifications to the subcontractor describing the goods or services to be supplied, many will in fact fall outside its scope. Nonetheless, where the primary object of the agreement is to enable the subcontractor to use licensed technology exclusively for the production of products for the contractor, the technology transfer block exemption may apply (see Chapter 12). Alternatively, if the agreement is between competitors, and if any provisions concerning the assignment or use of IPRs do not constitute the primary object of the agreement, the subcontracting agreement might constitute a specialisation agreement (capable of benefiting from the specialisation block exemption) or a production agreement, dealt with in the Commission's Horizontal Cooperation Guidelines (see Chapter 10).

7. ARTICLE 102 AND DISTRIBUTION

Where the supplier has a market share approaching 40 per cent a finding of dominance within the meaning of Article 102 is possible. In such cases, it should be considered whether provisions within a vertical agreement, such as clauses imposing unfair or discriminatory selling prices, single branding provisions, or tying provisions, or granting discounts and rebates to purchasers, may infringe Article 102 as well as Article 101.[343] Conduct that amounts to an abuse of a dominant position is unlikely to meet the criteria of Article 101(3).

8. CONCLUSIONS

1. Figure 11.3 seeks to provide a broad summary of how vertical agreements are analysed under Article 101.

2. The Verticals Regulation and Guidelines indicate that the Commission adopts an economic approach to vertical agreements. An actual assessment of the effects of a vertical agreement occurs, however, only when a presumption of legality or a presumption of illegality does not apply.

3. The Verticals Regulation sets out a presumption that vertical agreements between undertakings whose market shares do not exceed the 30 per cent market share threshold and satisfy the other conditions of the Regulation are compatible with Article 101.

4. In contrast, agreements containing object or hardcore restraints are presumed to infringe Article 101. Experience indicates that that presumption is difficult to counter in practice. Indeed the lack of clarity on the question of exactly when Article 101 does not apply to such practices is likely to result in businesses continuing to be wary about incorporating such provisions in their agreements, even if they perceive them to be helpful, or even indispensable, to the efficient distribution of their products or services. This uncertainty is compounded by the fact that (a) some NCAs continue to fine firms that incorporate such restraints or other restraints on online selling within their distribution agreements; but, in contrast, (b) there is little concrete jurisprudence dealing with the application of Article 101(3) to these types of restraints.

5. The centrality of the Verticals Regulation and the Commission's recommended methodology of approach mean that the main focus of attention remains on a rather more mechanical application of clear presumptions of legality and illegality rather than a detailed assessment of whether

---

[343] See Chap. 7.

Restraints	Market shares			
	<=5%	5–15% (de minimis)	15–30% (within Verticals Regulation)	>30% (individual assessment necessary)
Agreements containing object restraints (for example RPM provisions, or conferring ATP on dealers or preventing cross-supplies between them)	Yes, if no appreciable effect on trade.	Assumed to restrict competition appreciably (Art. 101(1)). The Verticals Regulation generally does not apply and it will be difficult to establish that the criteria of Article 101(3) are met		
Agreement with non-compete provision	Yes, if no object restraints agreement unlikely to restrict competition or trade appreciably	Yes, if no object restraint unlikely to restrict competition appreciably so long as market not restricted by cumulative effect of agreements	Yes, except if certain non-compete provisions incorporated, only if compatible with Article 101 (Art. 5)	Individual application of Articles 101(1) and 101(3). If market shares over 40% may need to consider the application of Article 102—especially for single-branding, tying, and rebates
Exclusive distribution (including restrictions on passive selling to groups reserved to other)			Yes, but can only restrict *active* selling into territories/customer groups reserved to another (Art. 4(b), exception 1)	
Selective distribution			Yes, subject to a number of conditions set out in the block exemption (Arts. 4 and 5)	

Figure 11.3 Compatibility of vertical agreements with Article 101

the agreement in question restricts competition in the context in which it operates. NCAs have, however, been grappling with these issues when considering how Article 101 should be applied to MFNs and price parity clauses.

6. Although the Guidelines acknowledge that Article 101(1) may not apply even where the 30 per cent market share threshold set out in the Verticals Regulation is exceeded, no explanation is offered as to why such a broad overarching block exemption is necessary if a more economic approach is required at the Article 101(1) stage. Such an approach would suggest that most vertical agreements do not require block exemption at all. Even though therefore the Verticals Regulation is intended to operate as a safe harbour and provide legal certainty, its existence muddies the water when trying to rationalise and understand the analysis required under Article 101(1) and Article 101(3) respectively.

7. The Commission did not prioritise enforcement of Article 101 in relation to purely vertical agreements between 2005–2015. The last infringement decisions it adopted in this sphere were in 2005.[344] Although NCAs vary widely as to the level of their enforcement activity against vertical restraints, many of them (particularly the FCO) have regularly brought cases, in particular in relation to RPM and bans on internet selling and have been shaping EU policy in relation to newer forms of distribution practices and restraints (such as MFNs or restrictions on selling via certain online platforms) which they fear may be restricting competition to the detriment of consumers. Despite the obvious global character that these online practices have, the centre stage has been left by the Commission to the NCAs, which have then struggled to act consistently with one another and, so, adopt a uniform interpretation of EU competition law. The difficulties involved in such attempted coordination are illustrated by the events which unfolded in the online hotel booking cases. These events may have led the Commission to recognise the importance of it acting in this rapidly expanding area of e-commerce, where the same practice/business model is applied on a global basis. In particular, it is collecting data and other evidence in the context of its e-commerce sector inquiry,[345] launched within the framework of the Digital Single Market strategy. In the course of its

---

[344] See n. 126.

[345] C(2015) 3026 final and see nn. 67–69 and text.

inquiry, the Commission has identified that significant barriers have been erected by companies to cross-border online trade in a wide range of sectors. If the Commission finds that barriers to cross-border trade result from vertical agreements which restrict competition, enforcement action may follow. Consistently with this, in the *Hollywood Studios* case, the Commission is also investigating geo-blocking practices, that is whether restrictions preventing cross-border access to online pay-TV services, or satellite pay-TV services, incorporated in agreements concluded between US film studios and EU pay-TV broadcasters infringe Article 101 (see further Chapter 12).

8. Online selling, geo-blocking, and the role of platforms is also attracting the interest of a broader group of policy-makers and politicians. In particular, there is a growing view that competition law may not be able to deal with the multiplicity of issues arising and that, for example, regulation of online platforms or change of copyright and/or data protection rules may be required. Although Commissioner Vestager has urged caution in relation to *ex ante* regulation of online platforms, some of these issues are being considered by the Commission within the framework of the Digital Single Market strategy. Similarly, national legislators have indicated that, if they are unhappy with solutions reached by competition agencies, they may be prepared to intervene. In France, for example, the legislator acted to render unenforceable contractual provisions negotiated with the French NCA by investigated parties in a settlement in the online hotel bookings cases.

9. FURTHER READING

A. BOOKS

BORK, R. H., *The Antitrust Paradox: A Policy at War with Itself* (Basic Books, 1978, reprinted with a new Introduction and Epilogue, 1993), Chap. 14

GOYDER, J., *EU Distribution Law* (5th edn, Hart Publishing, 2011)

SCHERER, F. M., and ROSS, D., *Industrial Market Structure and Economic Performance* (3rd edn, Houghton Mifflin, 1990), Chap. 15

B. ARTICLES

ACCARDO, G., 'Vertical Antitrust Enforcement: Transatlantic Perspectives on Restrictions of Online Distribution under EU and US Competition Law' (2013) 9 *European Competition Journal* 225

COMANOR, W. S., 'Vertical Price-fixing, Vertical Market Restraints, and the New Antitrust Policy' (1984–1985) 98 *Harvard LR* 983

EASTERBROOK, F. H., 'Vertical Arrangements and the Rule of Reason' (1984) 53 *Antitrust LJ* 135

GYSELEN, L., 'Vertical Restraints in the Distribution Process: Strengths and Weaknesses of the Free Rider Rationale under EEC Competition Law' (1984) 21 *CMLRev* 647

HAWK, B. E., 'System Failure: "Vertical Restraints and EC Competition Law"' (1995) 32 *CMLRev* 973

JONES A., 'Resale Price Maintenance: A Debate About Competition Policy in Europe' (2009) 5 *European Competition Journal* 425

KORAH, V., 'Goodbye Red Label: Condemnation of Dual Pricing by Distillers' (1978) 3 *ELRev* 62

MONTI, G., 'Restraints on Selective Distribution Agreements' (2013) 36 *World Competition* 489

PITOFSKY, R., 'In Defense of Discounters: The No-frills Case for a Per Se Rule Against Vertical Price Fixing' (1983) 71 *Geo LJ* 1487

VENIT, J., '*Pronuptia*: Ancillary Restraints or Unholy Alliances?' (1986) 11 *ELRev* 213

ZHANG, A., 'Toward an Economic Approach to Agency Agreements' (2013) 9 *J of Competition Law and Economics* 553

12

LICENSING AGREEMENTS AND OTHER AGREEMENTS INVOLVING INTELLECTUAL PROPERTY RIGHTS

1. CENTRAL ISSUES

1. Intellectual property rights (IPRs), such as patents, trade marks, copyrights, and designs, grant the holder of the right an exclusionary, and sometimes exclusive, right to the exploitation of an emanation of the human intellect. They are designed to provide an incentive for innovation and invention.

2. IPRs are still generally granted at the national level (although there are some EU rights).

3. The existence and exercise of IPRs (especially national rights) has sometimes created tension with the EU rules both on free movement and competition.

4. This chapter considers agreements involving IPRs but focuses on the compatibility of intellectual property (IP) licensing agreements with Article 101.

5. As with vertical agreements, the Commission's policy towards IP licensing agreements has been a tumultuous one. The policy has evolved from a permissive approach, to a more interventionist one, to the current approach, reflected in the block exemption for technology transfer agreements and accompanying Guidelines, which the Commission states is based on a consumer welfare objective.

6. The 2014 technology transfer block exemption (the TTBER) provides a safe harbour for bilateral technology transfer agreements broadly where: the parties do not exceed specified market share thresholds; and the agreement does not contain specified hardcore restraints.

7. Given particular difficulties involved in assessing relevant markets (and market shares) in the context of transfer technology agreements, the framework for individual Article 101 analysis set out in the Technology Transfer Guidelines is also of utmost importance. These Guidelines set out general principles concerning Article 101 and IPRs, explain the provisions and application of the TTBER, and the application of Article 101(1) and Article 101(3) to technology transfer agreements outside of the scope of the TTBER.

8. Trade mark and copyright (except software copyright) licensing agreements are not technology transfer agreements and are not covered by the technology transfer block exemption or Guidelines.

2. INTRODUCTION

A. GENERAL

Intellectual property rights (IPRs) grant the holder of the right an exclusionary, and sometimes exclusive, right to the exploitation of the product of the human intellect. They are recognised and protected in some way in all developed countries and encompass a broad spectrum of different rights. For example, they safeguard the creators of aesthetic and artistic works from having their creations distorted and purloined by others, they provide an incentive for invention and innovation by enabling those who develop new products and processes to reap the financial rewards of their efforts, and they allow those who develop brand names to exploit the reputation attached to the brand. The importance of IPRs in the modern commercial world is incontrovertible, but their interaction with EU law is complex. They raise problems not only for competition law but also for the free movement of goods and services and the operation of the internal market. This is because of the following.

(a) Despite the introduction of some EU-wide rights[1] and growing international cooperation in relation to IP, IPRs are still typically granted by national laws and enforced on a national basis, conferring protection within national territories. This inevitably leads to a prima facie conflict with the EU provisions governing the free movement of goods and services since simple reliance on a national right could be used as a mechanism to prevent importation of a good or service from another Member State.

(b) IPRs may erect barriers to entry to a market and thus affect the determination of whether an undertaking is in a dominant position for the purposes of Article 102. In addition, the exercise by a dominant undertaking of its IPRs may constitute an abuse.[2]

(c) Transactions involving IPRs may be agreements falling within Article 101. Holders of IPRs often exploit their rights not by producing products or services exclusively themselves but, additionally or alternatively, by licensing others to use them (or assigning rights to them). The terms of such licences may involve restrictions of competition, including territorial restrictions which divide the internal market.

This chapter starts by looking at some of the different types of IPRs before outlining the relationship between IP and both EU competition law and the EU free movement rules. It focuses, however, on agreements involving IPRs, especially licensing agreements and their treatment under Article 101.

The application of Article 101 to IP licensing agreements has changed dramatically over the years and especially since modernisation in 2004. In particular, on 1 May 2004 a Technology Transfer Block Exemption, Regulation 772/2004 was adopted exempting certain 'technology transfer agreements' (patent, design, know-how, and/or software copyright licensing agreements) from Article 101(1).[3] It was accompanied by Technology Transfer Guidelines which explained in detail the Commission's approach to technology transfer agreements.[4] Following a review of the 2004 regime, a new Technology Transfer Block Exemption Regulation 316/2014[5] (TTBER) and accompanying Technology Transfer Guidelines[6] (the Guidelines) were adopted. The scheme of the 2004 regime was preserved although some significant changes were introduced. Section 3 of this chapter traces the development of EU competition policy to IP licensing agreements whilst Sections 4 and 5 examine the current TTBER and the Guidelines in close detail. Sections 6, 7, and 8 deal with trade mark licences, trade mark delimitation agreements, and copyright (other than software) licences

---

[1] See, e.g., the Trade Mark Dir., Dir. 2008/95/EC [2008] OJ L299/25, COM(2006)812; the Trade Mark Reg., Reg. 207/2009/EC [2009] OJ L78/1; the European Patent Convention of 1973 (the EPC, which allows companies to obtain multiple national (rather than EU) patents from the European Patent Office on a single application); Regulations establishing a Unitary Patent, Reg. 1257/2012/EU [2012] OJ L361/1 and Reg. 1260/2012/EU [2012] OJ L361/89; and Agreement on a Unified Patent Court which will provide the legal basis for the European Unitary Patent System, see EU Council Press Releases 17824/12 and 6590/13.

[2] See Chaps. 6 and 7.

[3] Regulation 772/2004 on technology transfer agreements [2004] OJ L123/11.

[4] Guidelines on the application of Article 81 of the EC Treaty to technology transfer agreements [2004] OJ C101/2.

[5] Regulation 316/2014 of 21 March 2014 on the application of Article 101(3) of the Treaty on the Functioning of the European Union to categories of technology transfer agreements (TTBER) [2014] OJ L93/17.

[6] Guidelines on the application of Article 101 of the Treaty on the Functioning of the European Union to technology transfer agreements (the Guidelines) [2014] OJ C89/3.

not covered by the TTBER and Guidelines. Section 9 outlines issues arising in cases involving IPRs under Article 102.

B. TYPES OF INTELLECTUAL PROPERTY RIGHTS

(i) The Nature of Intellectual Property Rights

IPRs give the holder an exclusionary, and sometimes exclusive, right to the exploitation of an emanation of the intellect. The nature of the right varies from one type of IP to another. IPRs vary in duration. Some arise only upon registration, while others arise from the act of creation itself. In the absence of harmonisation or harmonising measures, EU law does not regulate the conditions upon which national law grants IPRs,[7] although it may curtail the exercise of them.[8] This section very briefly outlines some of the main types of IPRs.[9]

(ii) Patents

Patents relate to inventions. The grant of a patent confers on the holder (the patentee), normally for a maximum period of 20 years,[10] a monopoly over a new and inventive product or process, and the right to prevent others from making, disposing of, using, or importing a product which is the subject of the patent or derived from it, or from using the patented process itself. Patents protect applied technology, not abstract ideas. Patents are granted in respect of the product or process disclosed in the specification when the patent is applied for, and on the expiry of the patent anyone else in the world may use the information contained in the specification.

(iii) Trade Marks

A trade mark is a mark or sign used to identify and differentiate a product or service. Registration of a trade mark gives the holder an exclusive right to use it as such, although if it is a non-invented word it does not take the word out of general use, but only prevents its use by others as a trade mark.[11] Other parties remain free to offer competing goods and services under other marks and brand names. If renewal procedures are complied with trade mark registration can continue indefinitely.

Marks and brand names which are not registered may also be protected by other means, for example through the law on passing-off (as in the UK) or laws on unfair competition (as in a number of Member States).

(iv) Copyright

Copyright protects 'works' such as literary, dramatic, musical, and artistic works, films, sound recordings, and broadcasts from unauthorised exploitation by third parties. Unlike a patent, copyright does not confer a monopoly because it prevents only *copying*: if a third party independently comes up with the same melody or words, he will not be liable for breach of copyright. Copyright does not

---

[7] See, e.g., Case 144/81, *Keurkoop v Nancy Kean Gifts* [1982] ECR 2853; Cases C-241–242/91 P, *RTE & ITP v Commission* [1995] ECR I-743, para. 49.

[8] Through, e.g., the application of the free movement and competition laws.

[9] There are also, e.g., plant breeders' rights, given in respect of the creation of new plant varieties, which are similar to patents in that they confer a monopoly (Council Regulation 2100/94 on plant variety rights created an EU plant variety right which coexists with national regimes [1994] OJ L227/1). See further, e.g., W. Cornish, D. Llewelyn, and T. Aplin, *Intellectual Property: Patents, Copyright, Trade Marks and Allied Rights* (8th edn, Sweet & Maxwell, 2013).

[10] The maximum 20-year term is common throughout the EU because of the European Patent Convention, n. 1.

[11] And the use of a similar mark or sign on identical or similar goods or services where there is a likelihood of confusion, Trade Mark Dir., n. 1, Art. 4(1)(b).

depend on registration or formal procedures but arises automatically when the work is set down or recorded in some form. Copyright in the EU lasts for the lifetime of the author plus 70 years.[12]

There are greater differences between the laws of EU Member States in respect of copyright than there are with other forms of IP. Common law notions of copyright emphasise the right of the author to prevent others exploiting their work for commercial gain whereas the civil law emphasises the right of the creator of a work to be recognised as such and to be morally entitled to protect its integrity. UK copyright law covers performers' rights and similar rights, but in most EU countries there is a distinction drawn between 'author's right' and 'neighbouring rights' (those accorded to sound recordings, broadcasts, and performers). Under UK law works created by the 'sweat of the brow', such as compilations of information, are accorded copyright protection, whereas civil law systems require a greater degree of creativity: this difference seemed to be a material issue in the Article 102 case on television listings, *Magill*.[13] The Information Society Directive has harmonised national laws on certain aspects of the protection of copyright owners' rights to control reproduction, distribution, and communication (primarily on the internet).[14]

(v) Databases

Although Member States' copyright laws differed according to the extent of the protection that was afforded to databases and software, the 1996 Database Directive[15] now creates a *sui generis* right for their protection and the Software Directive[16] requires Member States to protect software by way of copyright as a literary work within the meaning of the Berne Convention.[17]

(vi) Designs

Under the Berne Convention[18] countries are free to choose the way in which they protect industrial designs, for example whether through registered rights and/or through rules governing unregistered rights. The 1998 Directive on the legal protection of designs[19] dealt only with registered designs and is a partial harmonisation measure only. Under the Directive, protection is for 25 years and entitles the holder to prevent the making, offering, putting on the market, importing, exporting, and stocking of a product incorporating the design.

(vii) Know-how

Strictly speaking, know-how is not an IPR, but it often features in commercial transactions such as licensing arrangements to which Article 101 applies. Know-how is confidential, technical, commercially valuable information which is not patented or registered in any way.[20] Know-how is defined for the purposes of the TTBER[21] and is protected by contractual provisions and breach of confidence laws.

---

[12] Under Dir. 2006/116/EC [2006] OJ L372/12, on the term of protection of copyright and certain related rights (amended by Dir. 2011/77/EU [2011] OJ L265/1).

[13] Cases C-241–242/91 P, *RTE & ITP v Commission* [1995] ECR I-743; see Chap. 7. Specific protection is now accorded to databases under Dir. 96/9/EC [1996] OJ L77/20, see n. 15.

[14] Directive 2001/29/EC on Copyright and Related Rights in the Information Society [2001] OJ L167/10.

[15] Directive 96/9/EC on the legal protection of databases [1996] OJ L77/20.

[16] Council Directive 91/250/EEC on the legal protection of computer programs [1991] OJ L122/42, replaced by Dir. 2009/24/EC [2009] OJ L111/16.

[17] Software programs may also qualify for patent protection in all Member States.

[18] Berne Convention for the Protection of Literary and Artistic Works, 1886 (as subsequently revised).

[19] Dir. 98/71/EC [1998] OJ L289/28. See also Council Reg. 6/2002 on Community designs [2002] OJ L3/1.

[20] Usually because it does not fulfil the necessary criteria for patentability, but sometimes the creator chooses not to patent in order to keep the information out of the public domain.

[21] TTBER, Art. 1(1)(i), see n. 91 and text.

C. THE RELATIONSHIP BETWEEN INTELLECTUAL PROPERTY RIGHTS AND COMPETITION LAW

The relationship between IPRs and competition law has sometimes been an uneasy one. In the EU, this has particularly been the case in the (albeit rare) instances where competition law has interfered with the exercise of IPRs by dominant firms.[22] The underlying issue, however, is whether IPRs and competition law are fundamentally in conflict or whether they are different routes to the same goals. It appears to be generally accepted that IPRs and competition law do not have conflicting aims but, on the contrary, both pursue the promotion of consumer welfare. This view is set out in two extracts, one written by a Commission official, Luc Peeperkorn,[23] and the other by Anderman and Kallaugher in their book on technology transfer agreements.

L. Peeperkorn, 'IP Licences and Competition Rules: Striking the Right Balance' (2003) 26 *World Competition* 527, 527–528

II. Do IP and competition law have conflicting aims?

Recognising that early copying of an innovation and free riding on an innovator's efforts undermine the incentive to innovate, IP laws (intellectual property laws) grant the innovator a legal monopoly. They provide the innovator the right to exclusively exploit the innovation and exclude others from exploiting it. This legal monopoly may, depending on the availability of substitutes in the relevant market, in turn lead to market power and even monopoly as defined under competition law. This has given rise to the alleged source of conflict often mentioned: that competition law would take away what IP law is providing.

However, in principle this is only an apparent source of conflict. At the highest level of analysis IP and competition law are complementary because they both aim at promoting consumer welfare. The objective of IP laws is to promote technical progress to the ultimate benefit of consumers. This is done by striking a balance, hopefully the right one, between over- and under-protection of innovators' efforts. The aim is not to promote the individual innovator's welfare. The property right provided by IP laws is awarded to try to ensure a sufficient reward for the innovator to elicit its creative or inventive effort while not delaying follow-on innovation or leading to unnecessary long periods of high prices for consumers. A delay in follow-on innovation may result when the innovation consists of an improvement on earlier ideas that have been granted patent protection already. Unnecessary long periods of high prices will result when the innovation allows the IPR holder to obtain market power in the antitrust market(s) where the IPR is exploited and where the IPR protects this monopoly position longer than is required to elicit the innovative effort.

In order to correctly strike the balance between under- and over-protecting innovators' efforts, IPRs differ from and are usually less absolute than 'normal' property rights: they are often limited in duration (patents, copyright), not protected against parallel creation by others (copyright, know how) or lose their value once they become public (know how).

Competition policy aims at promoting consumer welfare by protecting competition as the driving force of efficient markets, providing the best quality products at the lowest prices. Companies under competitive pressure will be less complacent and will have more incentive to innovate and gain market share. Product market competition and a strict competition policy work as an effective stick to promote innovative effort. The relevant question is therefore not one of conflict but of complementarity and possibly adjustment in the individual case.

---

[22] See Chap. 7.

[23] Luc Peeperkorn was one of the officials responsible for conducting the review of the EU IP licensing regime which resulted in the adoption of a new block exemption on technology transfer agreements in April 2004, see nn. 3 and 4 and text.

S. D. Anderman and J. Kallaugher, *Technology Transfer and the New EU Competition Rules: IP Licensing after Modernisation* (Oxford University Press, 2006)

B. Background—the Relationship between Competition Law and IP

1.11 The introduction of the new [EU] paradigm comes at a time when advocates of competition policy and proponents of intellectual property have reached an accommodation that recognises that both competition law and IPRs legislation constitute complementary components of a modern industrial policy. Although both policies pursue the common aim of improving innovation and consumer welfare each does so using rather different means. Intellectual property rights legislation such as patent, copyright and design rights laws offer intellectual property right holders a period of exclusive rights to exploit their property right as both a reward to the individual and as an incentive to the wider process of innovation and R&D investment. Trademarks perform a different function. Their exclusivity is meant to protect the consumer as well as to reward the originator. Modern competition policy attempts to keep markets innovative and competitive by maintaining effective competition. The means it uses to pursue this aim include maintaining access to markets and preventing 'foreclosure' or monopolisation of markets.

1.12 At first sight there may seem to be a potential clash in the methods used by the two systems of legal regulation to achieve their common aim. The concern to maintain access to markets appears to be implacably opposed to the concept of exclusive rights to make, use and sell a product. And indeed, there was a period when the misunderstanding of the economic effects of IPRs led EC competition law and policy to attempt to place overly strict limits on the exercise of IPRs, particularly in the field of patent licensing. Today, however, the interrelationship between the two systems of law is characterised more by its accommodations than by its conflict. These accommodations tend to occur most often as an incidental result of the ordinary doctrines of each system. Thus, intellectual property laws make a contribution to effective competition and maintaining access to market by devices within their own internal doctrine that strive to maintain a balance between 'initial' inventors and creators and 'follow-on' invention and creation. Good examples are the 'fair use' doctrine in copyright laws, the doctrine of 'non-obviousness' and the provision of compulsory licensing in patent law and interoperability imperatives and decompilation rights in the computer program directive. On rare occasions, as in the [EU] database directive, the accommodation will be explicitly spelt out in the intellectual property law itself.

1.13 Within EC competition law the accommodation also tends to occur more owing to the incidental effect of the logic of the general doctrines of competition law rather that in the form of special treatment. When one looks at EC competition law the most obvious example of special treatment is the 'exceptional circumstances' test embedded within the abuse of refusal to supply under Article [102] . . .

1.14 This observation offers a good perspective for viewing the relationship between Article [101] and IP licensing under the new post-modernised legal framework. The accommodation with IPRs in the new Technology Transfer Block Exemption Regulation (TTBER) and Guidelines occurs almost entirely within the logic of the doctrines of competition law. Most of the accommodation takes place as an incidental benefit of the ordinary interpretation of Article [101] under the modernisation programme. In the Guidelines and Recitals there is evidence that the competition authorities have made a considerable effort to understand the nature of IPRs and their licensing. Thus, they acknowledge that the creation of IPRs often entails substantial investment and that it is often a risky endeavour. They state plainly that '[I]n order not to reduce dynamic competition and to maintain the incentive to innovate the innovator must not be unduly restricted in the exploitation of the IPR that turn out to be valuable'. In particular, they must be able to seek compensation for successful projects that takes failed projects into account. The Commission also acknowledges that technology licensing may require the licensee to make considerable sunk investment in the licensed technology and production assets necessary to exploit it. Moreover, the Guidelines have accepted that the great majority of licensing agreements are pro-competitive and compatible with Article [101].

1.15 This approach represents a conscious rejection of the argument that a special self-contained regime (like the old block exemptions) is necessary to satisfy the special requirements of IP licensing. As the Guidelines confidently proclaim '[in] assessing licensing agreements under Article [101], the existing analytical framework is sufficiently flexible to take due account of the dynamic aspects of technology licensing'. The new framework clearly harmonises the treatment of licensing agreements with that of other commercial agreements under Article [101] and, on the whole, this results in a reasonable treatment of IP licensing. However, as we shall see, the process of harmonisation has not been complete; the analytical framework has had to make certain adjustments to take due account of the special features of technology licensing.

D. THE RELATIONSHIP BETWEEN INTELLECTUAL PROPERTY RIGHTS AND THE FREE MOVEMENT RULES

Perhaps surprisingly for a document purporting to lay down the foundations for a single market, the TFEU itself contains very little about IP. Article 345 TFEU, however, contains a general rule about property rights:

The Treaties shall in no way prejudice the rules in Member States governing the system of property ownership.

EU law therefore recognises the existence and ownership of rights given by national law. Nevertheless, this recognition potentially creates conflict with the principle of the internal market. Article 34 TFEU, the basic provision on the free movement of goods, states:

Quantitative restrictions on imports and all measures having equivalent effect shall, without prejudice to the following provisions, be prohibited between Member States.

However, if widgets made in France by F cannot be imported into Germany because they would infringe G's German patent, the market is divided along national lines. Not only that, but G may wish to use its German patent to prevent its *own* widgets, which it has manufactured in the UK, from being imported into Germany by a parallel importer. In both these examples national IPRs can seriously impede the free circulation of goods.

IPRs are specifically dealt with in Article 36 TFEU, which provides a derogation from Article 34:

The provisions of Articles 34 and 35 shall not preclude prohibitions or restrictions on imports, exports or goods in transit justified on grounds of public morality, public policy or public security; the protection of health and life of humans, animals or plants; the protection of national treasures possessing artistic, historic or archaeological value; or the protection of industrial and commercial property.[24] Such prohibitions or restrictions shall not, however, constitute a means of arbitrary discrimination or a disguised restriction on trade between Member States.

EU law therefore accepts that restrictions on free movement may be justified to protect national IPRs so long as they do not to constitute 'a means of arbitrary discrimination or a disguised restriction' on inter-State trade. This proviso has been used to justify many of the limitations which the CJ has placed on the exercise of national IPRs.[25] Indeed, in a long line of cases, a series of rulings have

---

[24] Although at first sight the phrase 'industrial and commercial' property does not appear to cover copyright, the CJ has clarified that it does: see Case 78/70, *Deutsche Grammophon v Metro* [1971] ECR 487, and Cases 55 and 57/80, *Musik-Vertrieb Membran v GEMA* [1981] ECR 147. 'Intellectual property' is the generic phrase now used both at EU and international level.

[25] Art. 56 is the basic provision which governs free movement of services. The CJ has held that the principle in Art. 36 should be applied to it by analogy. Restrictions on the movement of services may therefore be justified by the need to protect IPRs in the same way as they are justified in respect of the movement of goods, see Case 62/79, *Coditel v Ciné Vog Films (Coditel I)* [1980] ECR 881; Case 262/81, *Coditel v Ciné Vog Films (Coditel II)* [1982] ECR 3381 and Cases C-403 and 429/08, *Premier League Ltd v QC Leisure* and *Murphy v Media Protection Services Ltd (Murphy)* EU:C:2011:631.

interpreted when a national measure can be so justified. That case law is not dealt with further in this book,[26] but very broadly, it has developed a number of interlinking concepts by which the Court has sought to reconcile the conflicting demands of the economic integration of the internal market and the protection of IPRs. In particular:

(a) it has drawn a dichotomy between the existence of IPRs and their exercise: the existence of rights is unaffected by the TFEU but their exercise may be;[27]

(b) it developed the idea that there is a 'specific subject matter' of each kind of IPR, the protection of which is justified even if it leads to restrictions on inter-Member State trade: the exercise of IPRs which partitions the market will be allowed insofar as it is necessary to protect the 'specific subject matter' of that right;

(c) it has built up a jurisprudence on the 'exhaustion of rights'. Broadly, once a rights holder has consented to the marketing of the protected product within the EU (and EEA),[28] the rights encompassed in the 'specific subject matter' are exhausted and the holder cannot rely on national rights to prevent the movement of the goods between Member States.

3. EXPLOITING INTELLECTUAL PROPERTY RIGHTS BY LICENSING

A. GENERAL

The owner of an IPR has a choice of ways in which to benefit from the right commercially. He may exploit it himself, assign it to a third party, or license it. The method chosen will depend on a number of factors. These include the resources available to the owner, the type of right concerned, the nature of the product and its life-cycle, manufacturing costs and complexity, the overall commercial strategy of the owner, local conditions in the territory in which the right is held, and taxation considerations. Some rights may be able to be carved up: for example, the owner of copyright in a book may deal separately with the rights to make a television programme of it, the rights to film it, the rights to serialise it in a newspaper, and the rights to make an audio tape or other recordings of it.

An *assignment* involves the outright transfer of the right to a third party. After transfer the original owner is excluded from using it without a licence from the new owner. An assignment may be gratuitous or by way of sale or swap. Rights are commonly sold on the transfer or take-over of a business, when they pass to the new owner along with the other assets. In contrast, a *licence* involves the owner of an IPR conferring permission upon another party to exploit the owner's legally protected exclusive right. The advantages of licensing include:

(a) the owner (the licensor) has continuing control of the use of the rights (insofar as this is not limited by competition law);

(b) the ability to carve up the rights is normally greater with licensing than assignment;

---

[26] But see, e.g., Bellamy and Child (V. Rose and D. Bailey, eds.), *European Union Law of Competition* (7th edn, Oxford University Press, 2013), Chap. 9.

[27] The distinction between the existence and exercise of rights (first introduced in Cases 56 and 58/64, *Consten and Grundig v Commission* [1966] ECR 299) is not convincing. A property right which cannot be exercised has no value, see the Opinion of Fennelly AG, para. 95 in Cases C-267 and 268/95, *Merck and Co Inc v Primecrown Ltd (Merck II)* [1996] ECR I-6285. IPRs are valuable because they enable the holder to exercise rights which prevent third parties from committing infringing acts. If EU law limits the holder's ability to control third parties then the value of the right is diminished, and the fact that the 'existence' of the right is untouched is of little comfort. Nonetheless the existence/exercise dichotomy has provided a flexible tool to enable the Court to develop policy in this area.

[28] The EEA (see Chap. 2) is the relevant area by virtue of Protocol 28 of the EEA Agreement, which provides for exhaustion throughout the EEA in accordance with the case law of the Court.

(c) the owner can obtain a continuing revenue stream from the exploitation and can benefit from the licensee's success;

(d) the owner can continue to exploit the right himself.

The TTBER treats certain assignments of patents, designs, know-how, and software copyright as licences where part of the risk associated with their exploitation remains with the assignor.

B. COMMERCIAL CONSIDERATIONS IN LICENCES

(i) General

A number of IPRs may be licensed together, for example patents, know-how, and trade marks. Whatever the licence consists of, the licensor will normally be concerned with maximising the financial return. The licensor may also wish to incorporate provisions in a licence agreement relating to, for example: safeguarding confidential information; ensuring quality control; supplying essential components or other goods to the licensee; ensuring (in the case of patents and know-how) that the licensor benefits from improvements made by the licensee; safeguarding the licensor from challenges by the licensee to the validity of the rights;[29] limiting what the licensee may do with the goods or services produced under the licence; ensuring that the licensee does not compete with the licensor; and providing for termination. Licensees will be concerned with the same issues but from the other side. How far such commercial requirements can be met will depend, in part, on competition law. In this section we look briefly at some of the terms commonly found in licensing agreements that may raise competition law concerns.

(ii) Royalties

Payment by the licensee for the licence will be by way of royalty obligations which may, for instance, take the form of lump sum payments, a percentage of the selling price, or a fixed amount for each product incorporating the licensed technology.[30] 'Running royalties' means royalties calculated on the basis of individual product sales. Where royalties are calculated on the basis of the licensee's products which incorporate the licensed technology the licensor may wish to stipulate that a minimum number are produced.

(iii) Territorial Restrictions on Production: Exclusive and Sole Licences

Licences can be exclusive, sole, or non-exclusive.

A licence is *exclusive* as regards a particular territory where it provides that the licensor will not grant further licences for that territory to other parties and will not itself exploit the licensed IPRs in the territory. It means that only the licensee can exercise the licensed rights in the territory covered by the licence.

A *sole* licence is where the licensor undertakes not to grant other licences for the territory but remains free to exploit the rights there itself. The rights can therefore be exploited in the territory by the licensor, the licensee, and no one else.

A *non-exclusive* licence is where the licensor remains free to grant other licences if it wishes and to exploit the licence in the territory itself.

Exclusive and sole licences are common phenomena. Licensees will often be interested in taking a licence only if they are assured of exclusivity. An undertaking may be interested in taking a licence

---

[29] With a patent, a licensee working it will be in the best position to identify the weaknesses in it.

[30] See Guidelines, 4.2.1.

of X's French patent, for example, only if it can be certain that having invested large resources in tooling up to exploit the patented process it will not face competition from other licensees in France or from the licensor itself operating in France. In the EU, however, clauses conferring such protection may raise serious concerns on account of the fact that they compartmentalise the single market. The concern will be particularly acute where they are coupled (as they frequently are) with territorial sales restrictions, whereby the licensor and/or the licensee are limited as to where they may *sell* the products produced with or incorporating the licensed technology.

(iv) Territorial Sales Restrictions and Customer Allocation

A licence may include restrictions as to where the licensor and/or licensee may sell (territorial restrictions) or to the customers or customer groups to whom they may sell (customer allocation). As with distribution agreements, sales restrictions can be active or passive (soliciting sales and responding to unsolicited sales respectively). Further restraints can be imposed directly or indirectly through, for example, quantity restrictions on output.

For instance, a licensee may be unwilling to take a licence unless she can be protected not only from the licensor and/or other licensees *producing* in the same territory as him, but also from them *selling* there. The rationale for a licensee being given territorial protection may be stronger than for giving territorial protection to a distributor (see Chapter 11), because the licensee may have to invest extremely heavily in order to tool up to exploit the licensed technology. Indeed in some cases a licensee may desire absolute protection from sales by the licensor and other licensees in its territory (absolute territorial protection, ATP). Similarly, the licensor may not be willing to disseminate its technology through licensing unless it can stop the licensees selling their production in territories where it sells itself.

(v) Field of Use Restrictions

Field of use restrictions confine the licensee to exploitation of the technology within certain technical fields of application. Technology may be exploited in different ways, for example a patented chemical may be used to produce both fertilisers and pesticides. A licensor may wish to grant a licence to exploit only one or some of the uses, or to grant licences for different uses to different licensees.

Field of use restrictions may be difficult to distinguish from, and have the same effect as, customer allocation as different customers may require the technology for different purposes. Thus in *French State/Suralmo*,[31] the Commission objected to provisions dividing the exploitation of engine technology for use in military equipment and use in civilian equipment respectively. The Commission explains the distinction in the Technology Transfer Guidelines.[32]

(vi) Tying and Bundling

Tying and bundling on the part of dominant undertakings was discussed in Chapter 7. In the context of the licensing of IPRs it is described in the Technology Transfer Guidelines as follows:

In the context of technology licensing tying occurs when the licensor makes the licensing of one technology (the tying product) conditional upon the licensee taking a licence for another technology or purchasing a product from the licensor or someone designated by it (the tied product). Bundling occurs where two technologies or a technology and a product are only sold together as a bundle. In both cases, however, it is a condition that the products and technologies involved are distinct in the sense that there is distinct demand

---

[31] Commission's *IXth Report on Competition Policy* (1979), part 114.
[32] Guidelines, 4.2.4.

for each of the products and technologies forming part of the tie or the bundle. This is normally not the case where the technologies or products are by necessity linked in such a way that the licensed technology cannot be exploited without the tied product or both parts of the bundle cannot be exploited without the other . . .[33]

The licensor may use tying and bundling in order to exercise quality control over the licensee's output and maintain standards by ensuring that the licensee uses only certain inputs in its production process. It may be necessary for the licensee to use these inputs to ensure the proper exploitation of the IPR. On the other hand it may also be a means of giving the licensor a guaranteed outlet for products not covered by IPRs and foreclosing competitors from the licensee's custom.

(vii) Non-compete Obligations

The licensor may wish to ensure that the licensee does not also use its own (or a third party's) technology to produce goods in competition with those produced under the licence. Limiting the licensee's ability to do this is one way of ensuring that the licensee produces a minimum amount under the licence and generates adequate royalties.

(viii) Non-challenge Clauses

The owner of a valid IPR is able to sue anyone who infringes its right. What amounts to an infringing act depends on the nature of the IPR. As already explained, a licence entitles another party to use the technology or other matter protected by the IPR without infringing. However, she can only use it in accordance with the terms of the licence and these will normally entail the payment of royalties. Were the IPR not valid she would be able to produce without payment and be free from the terms of the licence. A licensee exploiting licensed technology is in a good position to detect anything which might render the IPR invalid (for example, that the subject matter of a patent is obvious in the light of prior art and therefore not novel). Licensors, knowing this, often wish to insert 'non-challenge clauses' into licences which make it a breach of contract (and therefore actionable by damages) for the licensee to challenge the validity of the licensed IPR or even to challenge the validity of *any* of the licensor's IPRs. It should be noted, however, that it is not necessarily in the licensee's interest to establish the invalidity of the right because then anyone else may freely use the hitherto protected subject matter (although the licensee may have a great advantage on the market in being already tooled up and producing).

(ix) Improvements

While exploiting the licensed technology the licensee may well develop improvements or further know-how. These may be severable or non-severable. A severable improvement is one which can be exploited without infringing the licensed technology. Unless prevented by the terms of the licence therefore the licensee could continue using it after the licence has expired and/or could license or assign it to third parties. Licensors, however, frequently want exclusive access to the improvements and wish to incorporate terms in the licence which oblige the licensee to 'grant back' severable improvements. This enables them to improve their own technology, prevent third parties gaining access to the improvements, and, perhaps, prevent the licensee from becoming a stronger competitor. They may also want to 'feed-on' improvements made by one licensee to the others.[34]

---

[33] Ibid., para. 221.

[34] The dynamics of this are complex. Feed-on arrangements disseminate technology but licensees will only be happy with the arrangements if they are getting as much out of them as they put in. If one licensee does all the innovation and the others get the benefits while contributing little to the common knowledge the first licensee may lose the incentive to innovate and will certainly not be keen to reveal its improvements, see, e.g., Cornish, Llewelyn, and Aplin, n. 9.

Competition law may be concerned to limit the terms of severable improvements clauses. Non-severable improvements do not raise the same issues as they can be used only with the licensor's technology.

C. DEVELOPMENT OF COMPETITION POLICY TOWARDS LICENSING OF INTELLECTUAL PROPERTY RIGHTS

(i) Overview

The licensing of IPRs helps to disseminate new technology, brings new competitors on to the market, and increases the rewards for innovation. Its effects are generally pro-competitive and beneficial to consumer welfare. It can be argued that since a licence of IPRs allows a third party to exploit the rights, allowing it to do what would otherwise be unlawful, the grant of a licence opens up markets and does not restrict competition. It should not therefore infringe Article 101(1). However, it has been seen that licence agreements commonly contain provisions which go beyond a bare permission for the licensee to exploit the right. Competition law has to decide whether, and in what circumstances, these further obligations have the effect of restricting competition.

The Commission's policy on IP licensing agreements has developed and varied significantly over the years. Initially, a fairly permissive approach was adopted but, gradually, the Commission's attitude hardened and a more interventionist approach was taken. The 2004 TTBER and Technology Transfer Guidelines, however, heralded the start of a more economic approach to these types of agreements based on a consumer welfare objective.

The Commission has played an extremely influential role in the development of policy in this area, especially as there have been comparatively few Court decisions on licensing. This is due to a number of factors, in particular that: parties granted an Article 101(3) exemption had little incentive to challenge the decision (even if they had to change the agreement to obtain the exemption); and because from 1984 onwards block exemptions covered patent licences (and mixed patent/know-how licences and later pure know-how licences too). Therefore since 1984 parties have sought to enter into licensing arrangements which were covered by the block exemptions wherever possible. The importance of the block exemptions has meant that an enormous amount of lobbying and discussion has occurred whenever new block exemptions have been drawn up.

The few judgments of the Court which have been given, however, are of great importance and significance in the development not only of the law on licensing but also on the question of what amounts to a restriction of competition for the purposes of Article 101(1) generally.[35]

(ii) The Evolution of the Commission's Policy Towards Licensing Agreements

The Commission's early attitude, illustrated by its 1962 Notice on patent licensing agreements (the so-called Christmas Message)[36] was that even exclusive patent licensing agreements did not fall within Article 101(1) so long as the restrictions did not go beyond the 'scope of the patent'.[37]

Later, however, the Commission's attitude began to change and it moved towards the position that exclusive licences, unless de minimis, always fell within Article 101 and that many common

---

[35] See Chap. 4.

[36] 24 December 1962 [1962–1963] JO 2922/62, finally withdrawn in 1984 [1984] OJ C220/14. The same approach could be seen in Reg. 17, Art. 4(2)(b), [1959–1962] OJ Spec. Ed.87, as amended by Council Reg. 1216/1999 [1999] OJ L148/5, which classed a narrow category of licensing agreements as non-notifiable.

[37] See further S. Anderman, *EC Competition Law and Intellectual Property Rights* (Clarendon Press, 1998), 53–54.

non-territorial restraints also went beyond the scope of the patent and violated Article 101(1). This essentially led to the position that a patent (or other) licence which went beyond a simple right to exploit a patented invention against payment of royalties would violate Article 101(1) and require exemption.[38] The Commission's sharp change in attitude was triggered by the development of the exhaustion of rights doctrine and the elaboration of the existence/exercise dichotomy as more IPRs issues came before the Court and were notified to the Commission. Significant to this change was the CJ's judgment in *Consten and Grundig*[39] in which it dealt with a trade mark licence which had been used as a mechanism to create ATP for the distributor/licensee and to seal off the French market. The Commission became acutely conscious of the potential of exclusive licensing agreements for isolating markets. It was haunted by the idea that if the licensor had not given an *exclusive* licence it might have given a *non-exclusive* one, which would have led to competition between the different licensees in the same territory.

In the real world, however, licensees will frequently not entertain any licence but an exclusive (or at least a sole) one. The commercial risk is too great. The choice is often therefore between an exclusive licence and no licence, not between an exclusive and a non-exclusive one. The Commission was frequently criticised for considering matters with hindsight, *ex post*, rather than *ex ante*, as the parties would have done, when the transaction might well have looked risky. Nevertheless, throughout the 1970s the Commission held in a series of decisions that exclusive licences and many other restraints in licences restricted competition within the meaning of Article 101(1). Its approach to the latter restraints is exemplified, in particular, by *Windsurfing*.[40] In this case Windsurfing International (WI), an American company founded by Hoyle Schweitzer, granted a number of non-exclusive licences of its German patent for windsurfing equipment to firms within the EU. Litigation was current in Germany over whether or not the patent covered both the rig and the board, but the Commission proceeded on the basis that it covered only the rig. The Commission found that a number of provisions relating to quality control, tying, licensed-by notices, non-challenge clauses,[41] and royalty calculation infringed Article 101(1).

(iii) The Case Law of the Court

Although in *Windsurfing* the CJ took a formalistic approach, upholding the bulk of the Commission's findings in relation to Article 101(1)[42] and finding that the provisions went beyond the 'scope of the patent' and the 'specific subject matter of the patent',[43] the CJ never endorsed such a strict approach to exclusivity as that adopted by the Commission. This is illustrated by its important judgment in *Nungesser (Maize Seeds)*, the first judgment after *Consten and Grundig* in which it had to deal with an exclusive licence.

---

[38] See, e.g., the Commission's *IVth Report on Competition Policy* (1974), point 20.

[39] Cases 56 and 58/64, *Établissements Consten SA and Grundig-Verkaufs-GmbH v Commission* [1966] ECR 299. See discussion of case in Chap. 4.

[40] COMP/29.395, *Windsurfing International* [1982] OJ L229/1; Case 193/83, *Windsurfing International v Commission* [1986] ECR 611. Note that, despite a very different approach post-modernisation, the Commission cites *Windsurfing* in the Guidelines, para. 81, when explaining that price-fixing within the hardcore restriction list in Art. 4(1)(a) includes agreements whereby royalties are calculated on the basis of all product sales irrespective of whether the licensed technology is being used.

[41] The Commission took the view that non-challenge clauses restrict competition; it is in the public interest that invalid patents should be challenged.

[42] Except it held that the global calculation of royalties on the complete sailboard was not a restriction of competition on the sale of separate *rigs*, although it was on the sale of *boards*. As the agreements had not been notified to the Commission, the CJ did not have to rule on the compatibility of the agreement with Art. 101(3) and whether the Commission had been correct to hold that the agreement could not have been exempted.

[43] J. Venit, 'In the Wake of *Windsurfing*: Patent Licensing in the Common Market' [1986] *Fordham Corp L Inst* 517, 560–561 (the judgment as a whole is 'based on the assumptions that there is something inherently anti-competitive in the patent monopoly and that patent licenses [sic], even when arguably vertical in nature, differ fundamentally from distribution arrangements and warrant stricter treatment').

Case 258/78, *Nungesser v Commission* [1982] ECR 2015

INRA, a French State research institute, developed new strains of hybrid maize seed of great importance in European agriculture. Acting through FRASEMA, a French company set up to deal with INRA's seed varieties, it gave Kurt Eisele (later Nungesser KG) the exclusive right to produce and distribute INRA varieties in Germany. INRA agreed with Eisele not to import its seed into Germany itself and to prevent others from doing so. Eisele relied on the rights in Germany to prevent parallel importers from importing seed obtained from another source in France. One importer settled the action, but another complained to the Commission.

The Commission held that the exclusivity and territorial protection provisions were caught by Article 101(1) and could not be exempted. Eisele/Nungesser appealed.

Court of Justice

41. Th[e] synopsis of the German legislation shows that seeds certified and approved for marketing are subject to quality control on the part of the public authorities and that that control extends to the stability of the variety. However, breeders' rights are not intended to substitute for controls carried out by the competent authorities, controls carried out by the owner of those rights, but to confer on the owner a kind of protection, the nature and effects of which all derive from private law. From that point of view the legal position of a breeder of seeds is not different from that of the owner of patent or trade mark rights over a product subject to strict control by the public authorities, as is the case with pharmaceutical products.

. . .

43. It is therefore not correct to consider that breeder's rights are a species of commercial or industrial property right with characteristics of so special a nature as to require, in relation to the competition rules, a different treatment from other commercial or industrial property rights. That conclusion does not affect the need to take into consideration, for the purposes of the rules on competition, the specific nature of the products which form the subject-matter of breeders' rights.

. . .

48. The statement of reasons on which the decision is based refers to two sets of circumstances in order to justify the application of Article [101(1)] to the exclusive licence in question (II, No. 3). The accuracy of the facts thus stated has not been challenged.

49. The first set of circumstances is described as follows . . .

By licensing a single undertaking to exploit his breeders' rights in a given territory, the licensor deprives himself for the entire duration of the contract of the ability to issue licences to other undertakings in the same territory . . .

By undertaking not to produce or market the product himself in the territory covered by the contract the licensor likewise eliminates himself, as well as FRASEMA and its members, as suppliers in that territory.

50. Corresponding to that part of the statement of reasons is Article 1(b) of the decision, which in its first and second indents declares the exclusive nature of the licence granted by the 1965 contract to be contrary to Article [101(1) TFEU] in so far as it imposes: An obligation upon INRA or those deriving rights through INRA to refrain from having the relevant seeds produced or sold by other licensees in Germany, and an obligation upon INRA or those deriving rights through INRA to refrain from producing or selling the relevant seeds in Germany themselves.

51. The second set of circumstances referred to in the decision is described as follows:

The fact that third parties may not import the same seed [namely the seed under licence] from other [EU] countries into Germany, or export from Germany to other [EU] countries, leads to market sharing and deprives German farmers of any real room for negotiation since seed is supplied by one supplier and one supplier only.

52. That part of the statement of reasons is also reflected in Article 1 (b) of the decision, which in its third and fourth indents declares the exclusive nature of the licence granted by the 1965 contract to be contrary to Article [101(1) TFEU] in so far as it imposes:

An obligation upon INRA or those deriving rights through INRA to prevent third parties from exporting the relevant seeds to Germany without the licensee's authorization for use or sale there, and Mr Eisele's concurrent use of his exclusive contractual rights and his own breeder's rights to prevent all imports into Germany or exports to other Member States of the relevant seeds.

53. It should be observed that those two sets of considerations relate to two legal situations which are not necessarily identical. The first case concerns a so-called open exclusive licence or assignment and the exclusivity of the licence relates solely to the contractual relationship between the owner of the right and the licensee, whereby the owner merely undertakes not to grant other licences in respect of the same territory and not to compete himself with the licensee on that territory. On the other hand, the second case involves an exclusive licence or assignment with absolute territorial protection, under which the parties to the contact propose, as regards the products and the territory in question, to eliminate all competition from third parties, such as parallel importers or licensees for other territories.

54. That point having been clarified, it is necessary to examine whether, in the present case, the exclusive nature of the licence, in so far as it is an open licence, has the effect of preventing or distorting competition with the meaning of Article [101(1) TFEU].

55. In that respect the Government of the Federal Republic of Germany emphasized that the protection of agricultural innovations by means of breeders' rights constitutes a means of encouraging such innovations and the grant of exclusive rights for a limited period, is capable of providing a further incentive to innovative efforts.

From that it infers that a total prohibition of every exclusive licence, even an open one, would cause the interest of undertakings in licences to fall away, which would be prejudicial to the dissemination of knowledge and techniques in the Community.

56. The exclusive licence which forms the subject-matter of the contested decision concerns the cultivation and marketing of hybrid maize seeds which were developed by INRA after years of research and experimentation and were unknown to German farmers at the time when the co-operation between INRA and the applicants was taking shape. For that reason the concern shown by the interveners as regards the protection of new technology is justified.

57. In fact, in the case of a licence of breeders' rights over hybrid maize seeds newly developed in one Member State, an undertaking established in another Member State which was not certain that it would not encounter competition from other licensees for the territory granted to it, or from the owner of the right himself, might be deterred from accepting the risk of cultivating and marketing that product; such a result would be damaging to the dissemination of a new technology and would prejudice competition in the Community between the new product and similar existing products.

58. Having regard to the specific nature of the products in question, the Court concludes that in a case such as the present, the grant of an open exclusive licence, that is to say a licence which does not affect the position of third parties such as parallel importers and licensees for other territories, is not in itself incompatible with Article [101(1) TFEU].

59. Part B of the third submission is thus justified to the extent to which it concerns that aspect of the exclusive nature of the licence.

60. As regard to the position of third parties, the Commission in essence criticizes the parties to the contract for having extended the definition of exclusivity to importers who are not bound to the contract, in particular parallel importers....

61. The Court has consistently held (cf.... *Consten and Grundig* ...) that absolute territorial protection granted to a licensee in order to enable parallel imports to be controlled and prevented results in the artificial maintenance of separate national markets, contrary to the Treaty

...

76. It must be remembered that under the terms of Article [101(3) TFEU] an exemption from the prohibition contained in Article [101(1) TFEU] may be granted in the case of any agreement between undertakings which contributes to improving the production or distribution of goods or to promoting technical progress, and which does not impose on the undertakings concerned restrictions which are not indispensable to the attainment of those objectives.

77. As it is a question of seeds intended to be used by a large number of farmers for the production of maize, which is an important product for human and animal foodstuffs, absolute territorial protection manifestly goes beyond what is indispensable for the improvement of production or distribution or the promotion of technical progress, as is demonstrated in particular in the present case by the prohibition, agreed to by both parties to the agreement of any parallel imports of INRA maize seeds into Germany even if those seeds were bred by INRA itself and marketed in France.

78. It follows that the absolute territorial protection conferred on the licensee, as established to exist by the contested decision, constituted a sufficient reason for refusing to grant an exemption under Article [101(3) TFEU]. It is therefore no longer necessary to examine the other grounds set out in the decision for refusing to grant such an exemption.

In this judgment the CJ drew an important distinction between 'open' and 'closed' exclusive licences (paragraph 53); open licences pertain only to the position between licensor and licensee (the licensor agrees not to grant further licences in the same territory and not to operate there itself); whilst closed licences contain provisions which affect third parties and which create ATP. [44]

As far as open licences are concerned, the Court did not, as the Commission had done, conclude that the exclusivity provisions automatically infringed Article 101(1). Instead the Court looked at the licence in its economic context: if the exclusivity provisions were necessary to induce the licensee to enter the transaction then competition was not restricted. Its realistic approach was limited, however. Clauses leading to the imposition of ATP were held without consideration of their possible economic justifications,[45] to separate national markets artificially and to be automatically caught by Article 101(1), and not to qualify for exemption under Article 101(3).

The principles in *Nungesser* have been found to apply to other kinds of IPR licensing agreements, and not just to those involving the licensing of plant breeders' rights.[46] In particular, in *Premier League Ltd v QC Leisure* and *Murphy v Media Protection Services Ltd*[47] the Grand Chamber of the CJ distinguished, in the context of copyright licensing, between:

- a sole licence (granting the licensee an exclusive right to broadcast protected subject matter from a Member State)—which would not justify a finding that an agreement had an anti-competitive objective; and

- a licence aimed at partitioning national markets according to national borders—which was liable to frustrate the Treaty's objective of achieving the integration of those markets through the establishment of a single market and had to be regarded, in principle, as an agreement whose object is to restrict competition.

A licensing agreement conferring ATP will therefore be 'deemed to have as its object the restriction of competition, unless other circumstances falling within its economic and legal context justify the

---

[44] For further discussion of the distinction between open and closed licences, see M. Siragusa, 'EEC Technology Transfers—A Private View' [1982] *Fordham Corp L Inst* 95, 116–118 and, e.g., COMP/31.302, *Boussois/Interpane* [1987] OJ L50/30.

[45] See further Chap. 4.

[46] The general applicability of *Nungesser* to such transactions is manifest from the Court's rationale for holding the open exclusive licence outside Art. 101(1) (i.e. the need to provide incentives for investment by the licensee).

[47] Cases C-403 and 429/08, EU:C:2011:631, para. 139.

finding that such an agreement is not liable to impair competition'.[48] The EU Courts have only accepted such an argument in two cases, *Erauw-Jacquéry v La Hesbignonne*[49] and *Coditel v SA Ciné Vog Films (Coditel II)*.[50] In both cases the *nature* of the IPR appeared to be crucial to the Court's finding. *Erauw-Jacquéry* concerned basic seed, which can lawfully be used to propagate further seed, as distinct from the certified seed sold to produce crops. Plant breeders' rights in basic seeds are particularly vulnerable as they can easily be lost.[51]

Case 27/87, *Erauw-Jacquéry v La Hesbignonne* [1988] ECR 1919

The owner of plant breeders' rights licensed them to a cooperative on the terms that the cooperative could propagate basic seed and sell seed of the first or second generation but could not sell or export basic seed. The Court of Justice recognised the need for quality control and for assuring the proper handling of the basic seed by those allowed to propagate it. Advocate General Mischo likened the situation to one of a franchise, where the franchisor is justified in preventing its know-how benefiting competitors.

Court of Justice

8. In the first place the national court seeks to ascertain whether the provision prohibiting the holder of the licence for propagating basic seed from selling, assigning or exporting that seed falls within Article [101 1)].

9. The Commission and the breeder maintain that the provision prohibiting the sale and exportation of E2 basic seed, which is placed at the disposal of the growers only for the purposes of propagation, is not contrary to Article [101(1) TFEU]. Such a provision falls within the ambit of the plant breeder's rights.

10. In this respect, it must be pointed out that, as the Court acknowledged in its judgment of 8 June 1982 (in Case 258/78 *Nungesser v Commission* . . .), the development of the basic lines may involve considerable financial commitment. Consequently, a person who has made considerable efforts to develop varieties of basic seed which may be the subject-matter of plant breeders' rights must be allowed to protect himself against any improper handling of those varieties of seed. To that end, the breeder must be entitled to restrict propagation to the growers which he has selected as licensees. To that extent, the provision prohibiting the licensee from selling and exporting basic seed falls outside the prohibition contained in Article [101(1)].

11. Therefore, the answer to the first part of the question referred by the national court must be that a provision of an agreement concerning the propagation and sale of seed, in respect of which one of the parties is the holder or the agent of the holder of certain plant breeders' rights, which prohibits the licensee from selling and exporting the basic seed is compatible with Article [101(1) TFEU] in so far as it is necessary in order to enable the breeder to select the growers who are to be licensees.

The Court in this case stressed the need to protect the licensor's investment. The Court recognised the particularly fragile nature of basic seed (as compared with the certified seed at issue in *Nungesser*) and was prepared to hold that in these special circumstances ATP did not infringe Article 101(1).[52]

---

[48] Ibid.

[49] Case 27/87, [1988] ECR 1919.

[50] Case 262/81, [1982] ECR 3381.

[51] They were subject to cancellation if they ceased to be stable or uniform.

[52] The Commission emphasised the special nature of basic seeds in its comment on the case in its *XVIIIth Report on Competition Policy* (1989), part 103; in COMP/35.280, *Sicasov* [1999] OJ L4/27, the Commission applied *Erauw-Jacquéry* to another licence of basic seed.

In *Coditel II* the CJ had to consider whether an exclusive licence (amounting in effect to ATP) infringed Article 101(1). In *Coditel v Ciné Vog Films (Coditel I)*,[53] the CJ held, in relation to the same facts (a Belgian cable company relaying in Belgium the transmission of a film (Chabrol's *Le Boucher*) shown in Germany for which Ciné Vog had exclusive distribution rights in Belgium), that copyright in film was not exhausted by the first showing of the film because the specific subject matter of the right was the entitlement of the owner to charge each time the film was shown. In the subsequent Article 101 proceedings it also recognised the special nature of the rights concerned which were exploited through performance.

Case 262/81, *Coditel v SA Ciné Vog Films (Coditel II)* [1982] ECR 3381

Court of Justice

10. It should be noted, by way of a preliminary observation, that Article [36] permits prohibitions or restrictions on trade between Member States provided that they are justified on grounds, *inter alia*, of the protection of industrial and commercial property, a term which covers literary and artistic property, including copyright, whereas the main proceedings are concerned with the question of prohibitions or restrictions placed upon the free movement of services.

11. In this regard, as the Court held in its judgment of 18 March 1980 (*Coditel...*), the problems involved in the observance of a film producer's rights in relation to the requirements of the Treaty are not the same as those of which arise in connection with literary and artistic works the placing of which at the disposal of the public is inseparable from the circulation of the material form of the works, as in the case of books or records, whereas the film belongs to the category of literary and artistic works made available to the public by performances which may be infinitely repeated and the commercial exploitation of which comes under the movement of services, no matter whether the means whereby it is shown to the public be the cinema or television.

12. In the same judgment the Court further held that the right of the owner of the copyright in a film and his assigns to require fees for any showing of that film is part of the essential function of copyright.

13. The distinction, implicit in Article [36], between the existence of a right conferred by the legislation of a Member State in regard to the protection of artistic and intellectual property, which cannot be affected by the provisions of the Treaty, and the exercise of such right, which might constitute a disguised restriction on trade between Member States, also applies where that right is exercised in the context of the movement of services.

14. Just as it is conceivable that certain aspects of the manner in which the right is exercised may prove to be incompatible with Articles [56] and [57] it is equally conceivable that some aspects may prove to be incompatible with Article [101] where they serve to give effect to an agreement, decision or concerted practice which may have as its object or effect the prevention, restriction or distortion of competition within the common market.

15. However, the mere fact that the owner of the copyright in a film has granted to a sole licensee the exclusive right to exhibit that film in the territory of a Member State and, consequently, to prohibit, during a specified period, its showing by others, is not sufficient to justify the finding that such a contract must be regarded as the purpose, the means or the result of an agreement, decision or concerted practice prohibited by the Treaty.

16. The characteristics of the cinematographic industry and of its markets in the [EU], especially those relating to dubbing and subtitling for the benefit of different language groups, to the possibilities of television broadcasts, and to the system of financing cinematographic production in Europe serve to show that an exclusive exhibition licence is not, in itself, such as to prevent, restrict or distort competition.

[53] Case 62/79, [1980] ECR 881.

17. Although copyright in a film and the right deriving from it, namely that of exhibiting the film, are not, therefore, as such subject to the prohibitions contained in Article [101], the exercise of those rights may, none the less, come within the said prohibitions where there are economic or legal circumstances the effect of which is to restrict film distribution to an appreciable degree or to distort competition on the cinematographic market, regard being had to the specific characteristics of that market.

18. Since neither the question referred to the Court nor the file on the case provides any information in this respect, it is for the national court to make such inquiries as may be necessary.

19. It must therefore be stated that it is for national courts, where appropriate, to make such inquiries and in particular to establish whether or not the exercise of the exclusive right to exhibit a cinematographic film creates barriers which are artificial and unjustifiable in terms of the needs of the cinematographic industry, or the possibility of charging fees which exceed a fair return on investment, or an exclusivity the duration of which is disproportionate to those requirements, and whether or not, from a general point of view, such exercise within a given geographic area is such as to prevent, restrict or distort competition within the common market.

20. Accordingly, the answer to be given to the question referred to the Court must be that a contract whereby the owner of the copyright in a film grants an exclusive right to exhibit that film for a specific period in the territory of a Member State is not, as such, subject to the prohibitions contained in Article [101 TFEU]. It is, however, where appropriate, for the national court to ascertain whether, in a given case, the manner in which the exclusive right conferred by that contract is exercised is subject to a situation in the economic or legal sphere the object or effect of which is to prevent or restrict the distribution of films or to distort competition within the cinematographic market, regard being had to the specific characteristics of the market.

The Court therefore accepted that the exclusive right, which in this case precluded showing of the film by others during a specified period, was not *of itself* prohibited by Article 101(1), given the nature of the protected work and the characteristics of the film industry; in particular, the Court stressed that the essential function of the copyright in this case was to enable the owner of the copyright in a film and his assigns to require fees for any showing of that film. It did not, nevertheless, rule out the possibility that in certain circumstances the exercise of the exclusive right might have the effect of restricting competition. However, the criteria in the qualifications in paragraphs 17 and 19 of the judgment as to when exclusivity *will* infringe the prohibition (the exclusivity might create artificial and unjustifiable barriers to trade, lead to excessive prices, or be for an excessive duration) are imprecise and uncertain.[54]

Indeed, in *Premier League/Murphy*[55] the CJ, distinguishing *Coditel II*, declined to accept that prohibitions on parallel trade incorporated in licences to broadcast Premier League (PL) football matches fell outside Article 101(1). In this case, the Football Association Premier League Ltd (FAPL) licensed broadcasters the right to broadcast live PL football matches only in their licensed territory. Broadcasts are made by encrypted signals via satellite, and paying customers receive the broadcasts by use of a decoder card. Under the terms of the arrangements broadcasters outside the UK were prohibited from supplying their decoder cards for use in the UK. The proceedings in this case were brought by the FAPL against defendants alleged either to have supplied non-UK decoders in the UK or to have broadcast live PL football matches using a non-UK decoder.[56] One of the defences raised

---

[54] Para. 19 provides that a relevant factor is whether the rewards are excessive, although no indication is given of how the national court is to make such judgments in the context of the film industry.

[55] Cases C-403 and 429/08, *Murphy* EU:C:2011:631.

[56] See *The Football Association Premier League Ltd v QC Leisure* [2008] EWHC 44 (Ch), [2008] EWHC 1411 (Ch) and *Murphy v Media Protection Services Ltd* [2008] EWHC 1666 (Admin) (the latter case concerned criminal proceedings against the defendant for violation of the Copyright, Designs and Patents Act 1988, s. 297(1) (dishonestly receiving a programme included in a broadcasting service provided from a place in the UK with intent to avoid payment of any charge applicable to the reception of the programme)).

was that the territorial restraints preventing supply for use in the UK were in breach of Article 101. The claimants alleged, relying on *Coditel II*, that the restraints were compatible with EU law.

It has already been seen that following an Article 267 reference to it, the CJ drew an important distinction in its ruling between sole exclusive licences and licences which go further and restore divisions between national markets. Further, it went on to conclude that the FAPL licensing arrangements in this case did breach Article 101; they were restrictive of competition by object (the FAPL had not put forward any circumstances falling within the economic and legal context to justify a finding otherwise) and the clauses of the licence did not meet the Article 101(3) conditions. In so doing it entrenched the traditional stance to ATP adopted in the jurisprudence since *Consten and Grundig*, and, following the analysis it had conducted in relation to the EU free movement provisions, cursorily dismissed arguments relating to the cultural and economic aspects of the IPRs underlying the broadcast rights. In so doing, the CJ referred back to the paragraphs where, earlier in its judgment, it had dealt with the question of whether national legislation conferring legal protection on the contractual restrictions on cross-border broadcasting infringed free movement provisions (Article 56 TFEU). In that section the CJ held that as the legislation clearly constituted a restriction on the freedom to provide services, it was compatible with EU law only if it could be objectively justified by an overriding reason in the public interest; it had to be suitable for securing the attainment of that public interest objective and not go beyond what was necessary in order to attain it. It held, however, that the legislation in this case was not so justified, either by the need:

(a) to protect IPRs: the FAPL could not claim copyright in the PL matches themselves (sporting events were not 'works' within the meaning of the Copyright Directive); and the protection of sporting events guaranteed only appropriate remuneration (a premium to guarantee absolute territorial exclusivity—which would result in artificial price differences between the partitioned national markets—went beyond what is necessary to ensure appropriate remuneration for the rights holders). The Court distinguished *Coditel I* as in that case the cable television broadcasting companies communicated a work to the public without having, in the Member State of the place of origin of that communication, an authorisation from the rights holders concerned and without having paid remuneration to them. In the case before it the (non-UK) broadcasters carried out acts of communication to the public while having in the Member State of broadcast, which is the Member State of the place of origin of that communication, an authorisation from the rights holders concerned and by paying them remuneration—which, moreover, could take account of the actual and potential audience in the other Member States. In so ruling the Court referred to the developments of EU law that had resulted, in particular, from the adoption of the Television without Frontiers Directive and the Satellite Broadcasting Directive which are intended to ensure the transition from national markets to a single programme production and distribution market;[57] or

(b) to encourage the public to attend football stadiums by prohibiting broadcasting in the UK within closed periods (Saturday afternoons). The CJ considered that even if this was a legitimate objective, the contractual restrictions were not a proportionate means for achieving it. Rather it could be achieved by incorporating contractual limitations in the licence agreements under which the broadcasters would be required not to broadcast during these closed periods.[58]

---

[57] Cases C-403 and 429/08, *Murphy* EU:C:2011:631, paras. 85–121.
[58] Ibid., paras. 122–125.

Cases C-403 and 429/08, *Premier League Ltd v QC Leisure* and *Murphy v Media Protection Services Ltd* EU:C:2011:43

Court of Justice

134. By Question 10 in Case C-403/08 and Question 8 in Case C-429/08, the referring courts ask, in essence, whether the clauses of an exclusive licence agreement concluded between a holder of intellectual property rights and a broadcaster constitute a restriction on competition prohibited by Article 101 TFEU where they oblige the broadcaster not to supply decoding devices giving access to that right holder's protected subject-matter outside the territory covered by the licence agreement concerned.

135. First of all, it should be recalled that an agreement falls within the prohibition laid down in Article 101(1) TFEU when it has as its object or effect the prevention, restriction or distortion of competition. The fact that the two criteria are alternatives means that it is appropriate, first and foremost, to determine whether just one of them is satisfied, here the criterion concerning the object of the agreement. It is only secondarily, when the analysis of the content of the agreement does not reveal a sufficient degree of impairment of competition, that the consequences of the agreement should be considered, and for it to be open to prohibition it is necessary to find that those factors are present which show that competition has in fact been prevented, restricted or distorted to an appreciable extent (see, to this effect, Case C-8/08 *T-Mobile Netherlands and Others* . . . paragraph 28, and Joined Cases C-501/06 P, C-513/06 P, C-515/06 P and C-519/06 P *GlaxoSmithKline Services and Others v Commission and Others* . . . paragraph 55).

136. In order to assess whether the object of an agreement is anti-competitive, regard must be had inter alia to the content of its provisions, the objectives it seeks to attain and the economic and legal context of which it forms a part (see, to this effect, *GlaxoSmithKline Services and Others* v *Commission and Others*, paragraph 58 and the case-law cited).

137. As regards licence agreements in respect of intellectual property rights, it is apparent from the Court's case-law that the mere fact that the right holder has granted to a sole licensee the exclusive right to broadcast protected subject-matter from a Member State, and consequently to prohibit its transmission by others, during a specified period is not sufficient to justify the finding that such an agreement has an anti-competitive object (see, to this effect, ... *('Coditel II')* . . . paragraph 15).

138. That being so, and in accordance with Article 1(2)(b) of the Satellite Broadcasting Directive, a right holder may in principle grant to a sole licensee the exclusive right to broadcast protected subject-matter by satellite, during a specified period, from a single Member State of broadcast or from a number of Member States.

139. None the less, regarding the territorial limitations upon exercise of such a right, it is to be pointed out that, in accordance with the Court's case-law, an agreement which might tend to restore the divisions between national markets is liable to frustrate the Treaty's objective of achieving the integration of those markets through the establishment of a single market. Thus, agreements which are aimed at partitioning national markets according to national borders or make the interpenetration of national markets more difficult must be regarded, in principle, as agreements whose object is to restrict competition within the meaning of Article 101(1) TFEU (see, by analogy, in the field of medicinal products, Joined Cases C-468/06 to C-478/06 *Sot. Lélos kai Sia and Others* [2008] ECR I-7139, paragraph 65, and *GlaxoSmithKline Services and Others* v *Commission and Others*, paragraphs 59 and 61).

140. Since that case-law is fully applicable to the field of the cross-border provision of broadcasting services, as follows inter alia from paragraphs 118 to 121[59] of the present judgment, it must be held that, where a licence agreement is designed to prohibit or limit the cross-border provision of broadcasting services, it is deemed to have as its object the restriction of competition, unless other circumstances falling within its economic and legal context justify the finding that such an agreement is not liable to impair competition.

---

[59] See nn. 57 and 58 and text.

141. In the main proceedings, the actual grant of exclusive licences for the broadcasting of Premier League matches is not called into question. Those proceedings concern only the additional obligations designed to ensure compliance with the territorial limitations upon exploitation of those licences that are contained in the clauses of the contracts concluded between the right holders and the broadcasters concerned, namely the obligation on the broadcasters not to supply decoding devices enabling access to the protected subject-matter with a view to their use outside the territory covered by the licence agreement.

142. Such clauses prohibit the broadcasters from effecting any cross-border provision of services that relates to those matches, which enables each broadcaster to be granted absolute territorial exclusivity in the area covered by its licence and, thus, all competition between broadcasters in the field of those services to be eliminated.

143. Also, FAPL and others and MPS have not put forward any circumstance falling within the economic and legal context of such clauses that would justify the finding that, despite the considerations set out in the preceding paragraph, those clauses are not liable to impair competition and therefore do not have an anticompetitive object.

144. Accordingly, given that those clauses of exclusive licence agreements have an anticompetitive object, it is to be concluded that they constitute a prohibited restriction on competition for the purposes of Article 101(1) TFEU.

145. It should be added that while, in principle, Article 101(1) TFEU does not apply to agreements which fall within the categories specified in Article 101(3) TFEU, clauses of licence agreements such as the clauses at issue in the main proceedings do not meet the requirements laid down by the latter provision for reasons stated in paragraphs 105 to 124 of the present judgment and therefore the possibility of Article 101(1) TFEU being inapplicable does not arise.

146. In light of the foregoing, the answer to the questions referred is that the clauses of an exclusive licence agreement concluded between a holder of intellectual property rights and a broadcaster constitute a restriction on competition prohibited by Article 101 TFEU where they oblige the broadcaster not to supply decoding devices enabling access to that right holder's protected subject-matter with a view to their use outside the territory covered by that licence agreement.

(iv) Block Exemptions: 1996–2004

Although, prior to modernisation, the Commission was willing to exempt IP licensing agreements under Article 101(3)[60] so long as the parties were willing to modify the exclusivity clauses and other provisions held to be restrictions (such as tie-ins, non-challenge clauses, and grant backs of improvements), the broad, and rather uncertain, reach of Article 101(1) created a pressing need for some form of block exemption (given the inability of the Commission to grant many individual exemptions).[61] Despite the urgency, the path of the first block exemption was tortuous and contested and it was not adopted until 1984. Regulation 2349/84[62] applied to pure patent licensing agreements or to mixed patent and know-how licensing agreements where the patent was the predominant element. The second block exemption, Regulation 556/89,[63] applied to pure know-how licensing agreements and to mixed know-how and patent licensing agreements where know-how was the predominant element. The two Regulations were very similar: specifying the type of agreement covered and exempted and containing 'white lists' and 'black lists'.[64]

---

[60] See, e.g., COMP/17.545, 6.964, 26.858, 18.673, and 17.448, *Re the Agreements of Davidson Rubber Co* [1972] OJ L143/31; COMP/5.400, *Burroughs/Deplanque* [1972] OJ L13/50; COMP/26.813, *Raymond/Nagoya* [1972] OJ L143/39; COMP/28.967, *Bronbemaling v Heidemaatschappij* [1975] OJ L249/27; COMP/26.949, *AOIP v Beyrard* [1976] OJ L6/8.

[61] See Chaps. 2–4.

[62] [1984] OJ L219/15.

[63] [1989] OJ L61/1.

[64] See Chaps. 4 and 11.

Both Regulations were replaced in 1996 by a single block exemption, Regulation 240/96 on technology transfer agreements,[65] which encompassed any transaction in which the predominant element was the licensing of patents or know-how. Compared to the previous Regulations it had a shortened 'black list' of prohibited clauses and a longer 'white list'. On 1 May 2004, Regulation 772/2004 on technology transfer agreements[66] came into force which sought to avoid the formalistic, narrow, and 'straitjacketing' effect of the previous block exemptions in this sphere which were out of line with the approach of newer vertical, specialisation and research and development (R&D) block exemptions and the modernisation proposals more generally.[67] The path to the adoption of the 2004 technology transfer block exemption was also not a smooth one. Comments on an Evaluation Report[68] and a draft for a new block exemption[69] were critical of a number of features of the proposed reform, in particular: the proposal to introduce market share thresholds (market definition (and share) being notoriously difficult to assess in many IP licensing situations) which were argued to be an inappropriate and arbitrary indicator of the real competitive situation in technology markets;[70] the proposal for different thresholds to apply depending on whether the agreement was between 'competitors' or 'non-competitors';[71] the reduction in legal certainty, and concomitant greater risk of *ex post* challenges to agreements by the Commission, national competition authorities (NCAs) or (more likely) before national courts; the more severe list of hardcore restrictions; and the introduction of a list of 'excluded' restrictions.[72]

The Commission accepted some, but by no means all, of these criticisms when adopting the 2004 Regulation and Guidelines.[73] Above all, it adhered to its decision to impose market share thresholds:

The use of market share thresholds is mainly opposed because it is considered that market shares are of no relevance in high tech sectors, that the assessment of market shares throughout the life of the agreement decreases legal certainty and is costly and furthermore that relevant product and geographic markets are often difficult to define.

Let me first recall that the TTBER applies to all sectors not just high tech ones. It is fair to state that most sectors are mature and that even sectors that are in such a state of flux are so usually only for a limited period. Therefore in most sectors, and that also means in most sectors where licensing takes place, market shares do matter. In addition, usually licensing concerns products that either will continue to compete with existing products or that will replace existing products. There are not many products which cater to a human need for which nothing existed before. Therefore market definition in case of licensing will not be markedly more difficult than market definition for most other agreements.[74]

---

[65] [1996] OJ L31/2.

[66] [2004] OJ L123/11.

[67] Reg. 240/96 contained provisions (e.g., an opposition procedure) which would not have worked in a system without provision for the notification of agreements. The abolition of notification and exemption also meant that guidelines were desirable to assist undertakings make their own assessment of agreements outside the block exemption.

[68] Published on the Commission's website on 19 July 2002.

[69] Over 70 submissions were received see, e.g., speech of (then) Commissioner Mario Monti, 'The New EU Policy on Technology Transfer Agreements', Ecole des Mines, Paris, 16 January 2004.

[70] See, e.g., the submission of the International Chamber of Commerce to the Commission, available on the Commission's website, but cf. Monti, ibid.

[71] There was also concern that parties might start life as non-competitors but move into the competitor category during the lifetime of the agreement, with serious consequences for its validity.

[72] For example, the territorial and customer restrictions were stricter.

[73] Reg. 772/2004 [2004] OJ L123/11, Commission Guidelines on the application of Article 81 of the EC Treaty to technology transfer agreements [2004] OJ C101/2.

[74] See Monti, n. 69.

Although following the publication of a draft replacement TTBER and Guidelines for consultation[75] the 2004 block exemption and Guidelines were replaced in 2014, the general framework and scheme for analysing technology transfer agreements created in 2004 has, subject to some important refinements and changes to the detail, been preserved.[76]

D. THE 2014 TTBER AND THE TECHNOLOGY TRANSFER GUIDELINES

(i) Methodology

The 2014 TTBER was adopted, with accompanying Guidelines, in March 2014 and came into force on 1 May 2014. The TTBER and the Guidelines must be considered as a whole. Although the TTBER provides an important safe harbour for technology transfer agreements, the Guidelines go further, doing three things. First, they set out a framework of general principles concerning Article 101 and IPRs. Secondly, they explain the provisions and application of the TTBER. Thirdly, they explain the application of Article 101(1) and Article 101(3) to agreements outside the scope of the TTBER. This latter role is of utmost importance in the context of technology transfer agreements especially given the particular complexity involved in defining relevant markets in the context;[77] consequently, the Guidelines are the real centre piece. 'The central theme of the Guidelines is the need to identify competitive harm and to identify economic benefits that might outweigh those competitive harms in order to determine whether a licence agreement raised Article [101] issues…the…system demands a new type of legal and economic assessment of individual agreements.'[78]

As has been seen with the other block exemptions,[79] their existence turns the appraisal of the agreement under Article 101 on its head. It encourages undertakings to consider first whether their agreement falls (or can be made to fall) within their safe harbour even if they do not infringe Article 101(1). As the Guidelines explain:

many licence agreements fall outside Article 101(1) of the Treaty, either because they do not restrict competition at all or because the restriction of competition is not appreciable. To the extent that such agreements would anyhow fall within the scope of the TTBER, there is no need to determine whether they are caught by Article 101(1).[80]

Only if there is uncertainty as to whether the technology transfer agreement falls within the TTBER is it necessary to consider the application of Articles 101(1) and 101(3).

In the next sections the general principles applicable to IPRs and the framework for the assessment of technology transfer agreements set out in the Guidelines are considered. The provisions of the TTBER are then analysed prior to looking at how Article 101 applies to technology transfer agreements falling outside it.

---

[75] See IP/13/120; the documents are available at <http://ec.europa.eu/competition/consultations/2013_technology_transfer/index_en.html>.

[76] For a comprehensive discussion of the core changes between the two regimes see, e.g., S. Rab, 'New EU Technology Transfer Block Exemption: A Note of Caution' (2014) 5 *JECLAP* 136 (the TTBER includes, e.g., changes in relation to agreements incorporating non-challenge/termination clauses, passive sales restrictions (protecting exclusive licensees) and grant backs of improvements meaning that in some ways it is less permissive than the 2004 regime, and the Guidelines contain, e.g., greater analysis of settlement agreements and patent pools).

[77] S. D. Anderman and J. Kallaugher, *Technology Transfer and the New EU Competition Rules: IP Licensing after Modernisation* (Oxford University Press, 2006), 1.16.

[78] Ibid., 1.19–1.20.

[79] See Chaps. 10 and 11.

[80] Guidelines, para. 42.

(ii) General Principles: Application of Article 101 to Intellectual Property Rights

The Commission sets out the general principles by which it approaches the application of Article 101 to IPRs in part 2 of the Guidelines. This section of the Guidelines considers the value of IPRs and the relationship of IPRs and competition law. In particular, it notes that IP licensing is generally pro-competitive and compatible with Article 101.

Guidelines on the application of Article 101 of the Treaty on the Functioning of the European Union to technology transfer agreements

2. GENERAL PRINCIPLES

2.1. Article 101 of the Treaty and intellectual property rights

5. The aim of Article 101 of the Treaty as a whole is to protect competition on the market with a view to promoting consumer welfare and an efficient allocation of resources....

6. Intellectual property laws confer exclusive rights on holders of patents, copyright, design rights, trademarks and other legally protected rights. The owner of intellectual property is entitled under intellectual property laws to prevent unauthorised use of its intellectual property and to exploit it, for example, by licensing it to third parties. Once a product incorporating an intellectual property right, with the exception of performance rights, has been put on the market inside the European Economic Area (EEA) by the holder or with its consent, the intellectual property right is exhausted in the sense that the holder can no longer use it to control the sale of the product (principle of Union exhaustion). The right holder has no right under intellectual property laws to prevent sales by licensees or buyers of such products incorporating the licensed technology. The principle of Union exhaustion is in line with the essential function of intellectual property rights, which is to grant the holder the right to exclude others from exploiting its intellectual property without its consent.

7. The fact that intellectual property laws grant exclusive rights of exploitation does not imply that intellectual property rights are immune from competition law intervention. Article 101 of the Treaty is in particular applicable to agreements whereby the holder licenses another undertaking to exploit its intellectual property rights. Nor does it imply that there is an inherent conflict between intellectual property rights and the Union competition rules. Indeed, both bodies of law share the same basic objective of promoting consumer welfare and an efficient allocation of resources. Innovation constitutes an essential and dynamic component of an open and competitive market economy. Intellectual property rights promote dynamic competition by encouraging undertakings to invest in developing new or improved products and processes. So does competition by putting pressure on undertakings to innovate. Therefore, both intellectual property rights and competition are necessary to promote innovation and ensure a competitive exploitation thereof.

8. In the assessment of licence agreements under Article 101 of the Treaty it must be kept in mind that the creation of intellectual property rights often entails substantial investment and that this is often a risky endeavour. In order not to reduce dynamic competition and to maintain the incentive to innovate, the innovator must not be unduly restricted in the exploitation of intellectual property rights that turn out to be valuable. For these reasons the innovator should be free to seek appropriate remuneration for successful projects that is sufficient to maintain investment incentives, taking failed projects into account. Technology rights licensing may also require the licensee to make significant sunk investments (that is to say, that upon leaving that particular field of activity the investment cannot be used by the licensee for other activities or sold other than at a significant loss) in the licensed technology and production assets necessary to exploit it. Article 101 cannot be applied without considering such ex ante investments made by the parties and the risks relating thereto. The risk facing the parties and the sunk investment that must be committed may

thus lead to the agreement falling outside Article 101(1) or fulfilling the conditions of Article 101(3), as the case may be, for the period of time required to recoup the investment.

9. In assessing licensing agreements under Article 101 of the Treaty, the existing analytical framework is sufficiently flexible to take due account of the dynamic aspects of technology rights licensing. There is no presumption that intellectual property rights and licence agreements as such give rise to competition concerns. Most licence agreements do not restrict competition and create pro-competitive efficiencies. Indeed, licensing as such is pro-competitive as it leads to dissemination of technology and promotes innovation by the licensor and licensee(s). In addition, even licence agreements that do restrict competition may often give rise to pro-competitive efficiencies, which must be considered under Article 101(3) and balanced against the negative effects on competition. The great majority of licence agreements are therefore compatible with Article 101.

(iii) Points of General Importance in the Application of Article 101 to Technology Transfer Agreements

The appraisal of agreements falling outside the TTBER are discussed in Section 5. However, it is useful at the outset to note a few points of general importance. First, there is no presumption of illegality for a technology transfer agreement falling outside the TTBER so long as it does not contain hardcore restrictions on competition.[81]

Secondly, the Commission accepts that a technology transfer agreement, which does not contain hardcore restraints, is unlikely to infringe Article 101 where four or more independently controlled substitutable technologies exist in addition to those controlled by the parties.[82]

Thirdly, in paragraphs 10–18 of the Guidelines the Commission states, in line with its approach set out in the Article 101(3) Guidelines, that in applying Article 101(1) to technology transfer agreements it is concerned both with restrictions on inter-technology competition (competition between undertakings using different technologies) and restrictions on intra-technology competition (competition between undertakings using the same technology). This underpins the reliance upon *two* different 'counterfactuals', i.e. benchmarks against which the restriction of competition is measured.[83] The tests are set out paragraphs 12(a) and (b) of the Guidelines; restraints must be analysed in the light of both questions before it can be determined whether they restrict competition.

Paragraph 12(a) asks:

Does the licence agreement restrict actual or potential competition *that would have existed without the contemplated agreement?* If so, the agreement may be caught by Article 101(1). In making this assessment it is necessary to take into account competition between the parties and competition from third parties. For instance, where two undertakings established in different Member States cross licence competing technologies and undertake not to sell products in each other's home markets, (potential) competition that existed prior to the agreement is restricted. Similarly, where a licensor imposes obligations on its licensees not to use competing technologies and these obligations foreclose third party technologies, actual or potential competition that would have existed in the absence of the agreement is restricted. [emphasis added]

It can be seen that this paragraph deals with inter-technology competition, by asking whether the agreement restricts competition between existing technologies by, for example, sales bans in cross-licensing agreements between undertakings holding competing technologies or non-compete obligations.

---

[81] Ibid., paras. 9 and 156.

[82] Ibid., para. 157.

[83] See L. Peeperkorn, 'IP Licences and Competition Rules: Striking the Right Balance' (2003) 26 *World Competition* 527.

Paragraph 12(b) asks:

Does the licence agreement restrict actual or potential competition that *would have existed in the absence of the contractual restraint(s)*? If so, the agreement may be caught by Article 101(1). For instance, where a licensor restricts its licensees, who were not actual or potential competitors before the agreement, from competing with each other, (potential) competition that could have existed between the licensees in the absence of the restraints is restricted. Such restrictions include vertical price fixing and territorial or customer sales restrictions between licensees. However, certain restraints may in certain cases not be caught by Article 101(1) when the restraint is objectively necessary for the existence of an agreement of that type or that nature. Such exclusion of the application of Article 101(1) can only be made on the basis of objective factors external to the parties themselves and not the subjective views and characteristics of the parties. The question is not whether the parties in their particular situation would not have accepted to conclude a less restrictive agreement, but whether, given the nature of the agreement and the characteristics of the market, a less restrictive agreement would not have been concluded by undertakings in a similar setting. Claims that in the absence of a restraint the supplier would have resorted to vertical integration are not sufficient. Decisions on whether or not to vertically integrate depend on a broad range of complex economic factors, a number of which are internal to the undertaking concerned. [emphasis added]

Paragraph 12(b) focuses on restrictions on intra-technology competition. It looks at the competitive situation arising from the agreement and compares it with less restrictive alternatives. It is seen in Chapter 4 that the Article 101(3) Guidelines also state that Article 101(1) is applied to restraints on intra-brand competition unless 'objectively necessary' for the existence of an agreement of that type or nature (as in *Nungesser* itself). It does not ask, however, as paragraph 12(b) makes clear, whether these particular parties would have concluded a less restrictive agreement, but whether undertakings 'in a similar setting' would have done so. This is because the issue is what is *objectively* necessary.

This concern with intra-technology restrictions (and intra-brand competition more generally) distinguishes EU from US law.[84] This concern still supports a relatively interventionist approach to technology transfer agreements under Article 101 and influences the interpretation of both Article 101(1) and Article 101(3). The Commission appears unapologetic about this.[85]

L. Peeperkorn, 'IP Licences and Competition Rules: Striking the Right Balance' (2003) 26 *World Competition* 527, 538–539

The proposed new block exemption regulation and guidelines maintain a stricter EU approach, stricter than the United States, towards intra-technology restrictions contained in agreements between non-competitors. The reasons for this divergence with the United States are threefold:

First, territorial restrictions are paid more attention in particular because of the additional market integration objective which EC competition policy has. Secondly, it reflects the higher importance EC competition policy attaches to intra-brand and intra-technology competition in general. It is considered important to protect intra-brand and intra-technology competition as a useful and sometimes essential complement to inter-brand competition. For instance, production costs of licensees and distribution costs of distributors make up a good deal of the end price of most products and competition between licensees or distributors may help to reduce these costs. It is also recognition of the fact that restraints are

---

[84] See, e.g., M. Delrahim (US Deputy Assistant Attorney General), 'US and EU Approaches to the Antitrust Analysis of IP Licensing: Observations from the Enforcement Perspective', American Bar Association, Washington DC, 1 April 2004 and Department of Justice and Federal Trade Commission, 'Antitrust Guidelines for the Licensing of Intellectual Property' (1995).

[85] The extract above is from Peeperkorn's paper and contains the usual disclaimer that the views expressed are the author's and do not necessarily represent those of the Commission or DG Comp.

almost never only affecting intra-brand competition. There is no neat distinction between intra-brand and inter-brand restrictions. Reduced intra-brand competition may facilitate collusion and restrict inter-brand competition, especially in cases of cumulative use.

Thirdly, sales restrictions may be used to prevent arbitrage and support price discrimination between different markets, what economists call third degree price discrimination. This will in general lead to a loss of consumer welfare. While some consumers will pay a higher price and others will pay a lower price, collectively consumers will have to pay more to finance the extra profits obtained by the supplier (its motive to do price discrimination) and to cover the extra costs of supporting the price discrimination scheme and prevent arbitrage. Consumer welfare will also decline because of the loss of allocative efficiency because the marginal consumer in the high price market is willing to pay more than the marginal consumer in the low price market. Therefore consumer welfare will in general decline unless it can be clearly shown that otherwise the lower priced market would not be served at all and that therefore the price discrimination will lead to an undisputable increase of output. It is only in the latter case that consumer welfare may actually increase.

4. REGULATION 316/2014, THE TECHNOLOGY TRANSFER BLOCK EXEMPTION

A. GENERAL

The TTBER is both more flexible and stricter than the block exemptions that existed prior to 2004. In particular, it is more flexible as, like the other block exemptions adopted post-1999, it does not contain lists of 'white' or 'grey' clauses. All provisions which are not in the list of hardcore restrictions or the list of excluded restrictions are permitted. On the other hand, the incorporation of market share thresholds into the TTBER renders its application quite uncertain to many undertakings,[86] creating a risk that licensing agreements may be challenged for violation of Article 101.

B. THE SCHEME OF THE TTBER

The TTBER comprises 19 recitals and 11 Articles.

Article 1 contains definitions of the most important terms in the Regulation.

Article 2 contains the exemption for bilateral technology transfer agreements which fall within it.

Article 3 provides that technology transfer agreements can only benefit from the 'safe harbour' of the block exemption if specified market share thresholds are not exceeded.

Articles 4 and 5 contains lists of hardcore and excluded restrictions. The presence of a hardcore restriction removes the entire agreement from the protection of the block exemption.[87] In contrast, excluded restraints are not exempted by the TTBER but do not automatically remove the remainder of the agreement from the protection of the block exemption.

Articles 6 and 7 deal with withdrawal and disapplication of the TTBER.

Article 8 contains provisions about the calculation of the market share thresholds and provides for some marginal relief where market share increases during the lifetime of the agreement.

Article 9 provides that this Regulation shall not apply to licensing agreements which fall within the scope of other block exemption regulations relating to R&D or specialisation agreements.

---

[86] See Anderman and Kallaugher, nn. 77–78 and text.

[87] Pursuant to the judgment of the Court in Case C-234/89, *Delimitis* [1991] ECR I-935.

Article 10 contains the transitional provisions. Agreements in force on 30 April 2014 which satisfied the conditions for exemption in Regulation 772/2004 remained exempt from Article 101(1) until 30 April 2015. Otherwise agreements are not block exempted unless they comply with the 2014 TTBER. Undertakings were therefore given one year in which to examine existing licensing agreements.

Article 11 provides that the TTBER enters into force on 1 May 2014 and expires on 30 April 2026.

C. PRINCIPAL FEATURES OF THE TTBER

Certain features of the TTBER, elaborated on in greater detail in the sections below, should be noted at the outset:

- it covers patent and know-how licensing and licences of computer software and of designs so long as certain market share thresholds are not exceeded;
- throughout the TTBER a distinction is drawn between agreements between competitors and agreements between non-competitors. The market share thresholds, the hardcore restrictions, and the excluded restrictions differ depending on whether the agreement is between competitors or non-competitors;
- in respect of some types of provisions the TTBER draws a distinction between reciprocal and non-reciprocal obligations;
- in applying the TTBER two markets need to be taken into account: the *technology* market (consisting of the licensed technology and its substitutes) and the *product or service* market (consisting of the market for the product or service incorporating the licensed technology).

D. SCOPE OF THE TTBER

(i) Agreements to Which the TTBER May Apply

a. Article 2 TTBER

Article 2 of the TTBER exempts from Article 101(1) bilateral technology transfer agreements permitting the production of contract products. It states:

Article 2

Exemption

1. Pursuant to Article 101(3) of the Treaty and subject to the provisions of this Regulation, Article 101(1) of the Treaty shall not apply to technology transfer agreements.
2. The exemption provided for in paragraph 1 shall apply to the extent that technology transfer agreements contain restrictions of competition falling within the scope of Article 101(1) of the Treaty. The exemption shall apply for as long as the licensed technology rights have not expired, lapsed or been declared invalid or, in the case of know-how, for as long as the know-how remains secret. However, where know-how becomes publicly known as a result of action by the licensee, the exemption shall apply for the duration of the agreement.
3. The exemption provided for in paragraph 1 shall also apply to provisions, in technology transfer agreements, which relate to the purchase of products by the licensee or which relate to the licensing or assignment of other intellectual property rights or know-how to the licensee, if, and to the extent that, those provisions are directly related to the production or sale of the contract products.

---

b. Bilateral Technology Transfer Agreement

The definition of a technology transfer agreement is set out in Article 1(1)(c):

'technology transfer agreement' means:

(i) a technology rights licensing agreement entered into between two undertakings for the purpose of the production of contract products by the licensee and/or its sub-contractor(s),

(ii) an assignment of technology rights between two undertakings for the purpose of the production of contract products where part of the risk associated with the exploitation of the technology remains with the assignor;

The TTBER is thus limited to bilateral agreements (agreements between two undertakings).[88] When counting the parties to an agreement, however, each group of 'connected undertakings'[89] are counted as a single party. The two-party limitation does not prevent an agreement which affects third parties from falling within the TTBER however. For example, an agreement may require the licensee to impose obligations on resellers of the product produced under the licence.[90]

Article 1(1)(b) provides that 'technology rights' include know-how and/or patents, utility models, design rights, topographies of semiconductor products, supplementary protection certificates for medicinal products or other products for which such supplementary protection certificates may be obtained, plant breeders' certificates and software copyrights. Know-how is defined in Article 1(1)(i) as: a package of practical information, resulting from experience and testing, which is:

(i) secret, that is to say, not generally known or easily accessible,

(ii) substantial, that is to say, significant and useful for the production of the contract products, and

(iii) identified, that is to say, described in a sufficiently comprehensive manner so as to make it possible to verify that it fulfils the criteria of secrecy and substantiality;

The meanings of 'secret', 'substantial', and 'identified' are further elaborated upon in the Guidelines.[91] A technology transfer agreement can therefore comprise:

- a pure patent licensing agreement;
- a pure know-how licensing agreement;
- a pure software copyright licence (but not other forms of copyright licensing or trade mark licences);[92]
- a pure design licence;
- a 'mixed' agreement, by which two or more rights (patents, know-how, software copyright, designs) are licensed together (it is very common, for example, to license know-how together with a patent);
- provisions in technology transfer agreements relating to the licensing of other types of IP, such as trade marks and copyright, are covered only if, and to the extent that, they are directly related to the production or sale of the contract products (the rights serve to enable the licensee

---

[88] Council Reg. 19/65 [1965–1966] OJ Spec. Ed. Series I, 35, the relevant enabling regulation, only empowers the Commission to block exempt bilateral technology transfer agreements.

[89] TTBER, Art. 1(2). See also the discussion of the single economic entity doctrine in Chap. 3.

[90] Guidelines, para.55.

[91] Ibid., para. 45.

[92] Ibid., para. 48 ('The Commission will, however, as a general rule apply the principles set out in the TTBER and these guidelines when assessing licensing of copyright for the production of contract products under Article 101 of the Treaty') and see Section 8, p. 879.

to better exploit the licensed technology rights).[93] The TTBER also covers licences which contain provisions about the purchase of goods provided those provisions are directly related to the production or sale of the contract products.[94]

The TTBER only covers agreements whereby technology is *transferred*, where technology 'flows from one undertaking to another',[95] i.e. normally where the licensor grants a licensee the right to use its technology to produce contract goods against the payment of royalties. It also covers a sub-licence by the licensee for the exploitation of the technology.[96]

c. The Agreement Must Concern the Production of Contract Products

The licensing agreement or assignment must be 'for the purpose of the production of contract products', that is to use the licensed technology to produce goods or services (the word 'goods' is hereafter used in this chapter to denote both goods and services unless the context otherwise requires). The TTBER does not therefore cover:[97]

- 'technology pools' whereby two or more parties agree to pool their respective technologies and license them as a package;[98]
- master-licensing agreements, the primary object of which is sub-licensing;
- agreements whose object is to enable the licensee to carry out further R&D (rather than produce goods or services);
- agreements whose primary object is the sale and purchase of products (rather than their production).[99]

On the other hand the TTBER *does* cover, for example, agreements:

- which are entered into to settle disputes over IPRs within the scope of the TTBER ('settlement' agreements), including cross-licensing;[100]
- which are subcontracting agreements whereby the technology is licensed in order for the licensee to produce certain products exclusively for the licensor;[101]
- whereby the licensee has to carry out development work before obtaining a product or process that can be commercially exploited, provided that a contract product has been identified and the primary purpose of the agreement is not R&D.[102]

(ii) Relationship with Other Block Exemptions

Specialisation, R&D, and vertical agreements may involve the transfer of technology between the contracting parties. Paragraphs 70–78 of the Guidelines deal with the interface of the TTBER with the specialisation, R&D, and vertical block exemptions. Broadly:[103]

---

[93] Ibid., para. 47 and, e.g., COMP/32.736, *Moosehead/Whitbread* decision [1990] OJ L100/32, n. 211 and text.

[94] Guidelines, para. 46.

[95] Ibid., para. 51.

[96] Ibid., para. 60.

[97] Ibid., paras. 58–66.

[98] Ibid., para. 56. There is a lengthy section (4.4) in the Guidelines on technology pools: see Section 5, pp. 872–874. Such agreements are unlikely to be 'bilateral' and the parties are unlikely to meet the market share thresholds of the TTBER.

[99] Ibid., para. 61.

[100] Ibid., para. 53.

[101] Ibid., para. 64, see also Chap. 11.

[102] Ibid., para. 65.

[103] Ibid., paras. 70–79.

- Regulation 1218/2010,[104] the specialisation block exemption, not the TTBER, covers licensing in the context of a production joint venture (JV) (where the JV is licensed to exploit technology). It does not apply, however, to the situation where the JV engages in licensing technology to a third party. That amounts to a technology pool;

- Regulation 1217/2010, the R&D block exemption, and not the TTBER, covers licensing between parties and by parties to a joint entity in the context of an R&D agreement. Licensing of the fruits of the R&D to third parties might be covered by the TTBER, however; and

- the umbrella block exemption on vertical restraints, Regulation 330/2010, covers supply and distribution agreements. In Chapter 11 it was seen that it applies to vertical agreements involving licences of IP so long as the licence is ancillary to the vertical agreement and IPRs are assigned to the buyer for the purpose of using or selling the goods or services supplied under the agreement.[105] The Verticals Regulation may apply where a licensee sells products incorporating licensed technology to a buyer. Thus even though the TTBER will block exempt (within the safe harbour) a technology transfer agreement requiring a licensee to distribute the products in a particular way, for example through an exclusive or selective distribution system, such agreements will be vertical and subject to Regulation 330/2010 and the Verticals Guidelines.[106]

E. SAFE HARBOUR: THE MARKET SHARE THRESHOLDS

(i) The Market Share Thresholds

The block exemption applies on condition that specified market share thresholds are not exceeded on affected technology and/or product markets. Where the parties are competitors (actual competitors or potential competitors on the product market(s) and/or actual competitors on the technology market[107]) the relevant market share is 20 per cent (Article 3(1)). Where the parties are non-competitors the relevant market is 30 per cent (Article 3(2)). With regard to competitors it is the *combined* market share which is relevant, but in the case of non-competitors it is the market share of *each* of the parties on the affected relevant technology and product markets that is relevant.

If the parties' market shares are below the thresholds at the time the agreement is entered into, but subsequently increase so that they exceed it, the TTBER will continue to apply for two consecutive calendar years following the year in which the relevant threshold is first exceeded.[108]

In order to determine whether the TTBER applies it is therefore ordinarily necessary to identify the relevant markets, to calculate market shares, and to determine whether or not the parties are competitors.

(ii) Market Definition

The Guidelines provide guidance on specific issues which arise in the technology transfer context,[109] particularly as the relevant market means a combination of the relevant product or the technology market with the relevant geographic market.[110]

---

[104] [2000] OJ L304/3. See Chap. 10.

[105] See [1999] OJ L336/21, Art. 2(3) and (5).

[106] Guidelines, paras. 76–77.

[107] Ibid., para. 82.

[108] TTBER, Art. 8(e).

[109] Guidelines, para. 20.

[110] TTBER, Art. 1(1)(m).

a. The Technology Market

The technology market is the licensed technology and any other technology that the licensees consider to be interchangeable with, or substitutable for, the technology by reason of the technologies' characteristics, their royalties, and their intended use.[111] Paragraph 22 of the Guidelines states that the objective is therefore to identify competing technologies to which licensees could switch in response to a small but permanent increase in prices (which in this context means the royalties) (the SSNIP test).[112] It also provides 'an alternative approach' to defining the technology market, which looks to the market for products incorporating the licensed technology (see also paragraph 25 of the Guidelines).

b. The Product Market

The relevant product market comprises products regarded as interchangeable with or substitutable for the contract products incorporating the licensed technology (whether an interim or final product market) by reason of the products' characteristics, price, and intended use.[113] Occasionally, it may be necessary to define an innovation market, in particular where the agreement affects innovation aimed at creating new products and R&D poles can be identified.[114]

(iii) Market Shares

a. Means of Calculation

Where it is available, market share is to be calculated on the basis of market sales value data. Otherwise 'other reliable market information' including market sales volume data may be used.[115]

b. The Technology Market

The Guidelines suggest more than one method of calculating market shares on the technology market. One solution is to calculate the market shares by reference to the licensed technology and its substitutes. Market share can then be calculated on the basis of each technology's share of total licensing income from royalties. In practice, however, this test is hard to apply—especially as companies are unlikely to know the level of royalty income derived by their competitors. Article 8(d) thus provides that the market share can be defined with regard to the presence of the licensed technology on the relevant product market.

c. The Product Market

Market shares on the product market are assessed in the usual way, using sales data value if available.[116] The licensee's market share is the total sales of the licensee on the product market, i.e. products incorporating the licensor's technology and competing products. The licensor's sales (if any) on the product market must be included, but not those of other licensees.

(iv) The Distinction Between Competitors and Non-competitors

The provisions of the TTBER are based on the premise that agreements between competitors are likely to pose a greater risk to the competitive process than agreements between non-competitors.[117]

---

[111] Guidelines, para. 22.

[112] See Chap. 1.

[113] TTBER, Art. 1(1)(j) and Guidelines, para. 21.

[114] Guidelines, para. 26.

[115] TTBER, Art. 8(a). The calculation is on the basis of the preceding year, Art. 8(b).

[116] TTBER, Art. 8(a) and Guidelines, para. 92.

[117] Guidelines, para. 31.

Thus not only are the market share thresholds lower for agreements between competitors but a different, stricter set of hardcore restraints applies. Paragraph 28 of the Guidelines explains:

In order to determine the competitive relationship between the parties it is necessary to examine whether the parties would have been actual or potential competitors in the absence of the agreement. If without the agreement the parties would not have been actual or potential competitors in any relevant market affected by the agreement they are deemed to be non-competitors.

Article 1(1)(n) of the TTBER defines competing undertakings as undertakings that compete on the relevant technology market and/or the relevant product market.

'competing undertakings' means undertakings which compete on the relevant market, that is to say:

(i) competing undertakings on the relevant market where the technology rights are licensed, that is to say, undertakings which license out competing technology rights (actual competitors on the relevant market),

(ii) competing undertakings on the relevant market where the contract products are sold, that is to say, undertakings which, in the absence of the technology transfer agreement, would both be active on the relevant market(s) on which the contract products are sold (actual competitors on the relevant market) or which, in the absence of the technology transfer agreement, would, on realistic grounds and not just as a mere theoretical possibility, in response to a small and permanent increase in relative prices, be likely to undertake, within a short period of time, the necessary additional investments or other necessary switching costs to enter the relevant market(s) (potential competitors on the relevant market);

It can be seen from this definition that as far as product markets are concerned, both actual and potential competitors are treated as competitors. As far as technology markets are concerned, however, only actual competitors are relevant. If the licensor and licensee are both active on the same technology or product market, without infringing each other's IPRs, they are actual competitors on the market. On technology markets the parties will be considered actual competitors if they are both licensing substitutable technologies or the licensee is already licensing out its technology and the licensor enters the technology market by granting a licence for a competing technology to the licensee.[118] The parties are potential competitors on the product market if, in the absence of the agreement and without infringing IPRs, they would be likely to undertake the necessary investments required to enter the market within a short period (one to two years) in response to a small but permanent increase in price.[119] Outside the safe harbour of the TTBER potential competitors on the technology market are taken into account.[120]

The reference in Article 1(1)(n) to parties being competing undertakings only where they are both active on the technology market or product market 'without infringing each other's [IPRs]' means that if there is a one-way (one party cannot exploit its technology without infringing the other's IPRs) or two-way (neither party can exploit its technology without infringing the other's IPRs) blocking situation, the parties will *not* be characterised as competitors.[121] The Commission is, however, alive to the fact that the parties will usually prefer to be classified as non-competitors and blocking claims have to be examined carefully.[122]

The Guidelines state that in cases of 'drastic innovation' parties should be classed as non-competitors even though they produce competing products. This will be the case where the licensed technology represents such a technological breakthrough that the licensee's technology

---

[118] Ibid., paras. 30 and 35.

[119] Ibid., para. 27.

[120] See ibid., para. 81. This does not lead to the application of the hardcore list of restrictions relating to agreements between competitors.

[121] Ibid., para. 29.

[122] Ibid., para. 33.

becomes obsolete or uncompetitive (for example, the replacement of LP vinyl technology with CD technology).[123] Often, however, it will not be possible to draw this conclusion at the time the agreement is concluded. If it is *not* obvious at this time the parties will be classified as competitors initially but can be recognised as non-competitors later.[124]

It is extremely important when deciding whether the parties are competitors or non-competitors to remember that activities of their 'connected undertakings' must be taken into account.[125]

(v) Non-competitors Who Subsequently Become Competitors

What is the position if the parties are not competitors at the time the agreement is concluded but subsequently become competitors? Article 4(3) of the TTBER provides that the more liberal list of hardcore restrictions for agreements between non-competitors will apply during the full life of the agreement *unless* the agreement is subsequently amended 'in any material respect'. Where a material amendment occurs, including the conclusion of a new technology transfer agreement between the parties concerning competing technology rights, restraints previously block exempted may become hardcore restraints.[126] Paragraph 85 of the Guidelines explains, however, that the lower market share threshold will apply from the time that the parties become competitors:

Where the parties become competitors within the meaning of Article 3(1) TTBER at a later point in time, for instance where the licensee was already present, before the licensing, on the relevant market where the contract products are sold and the licensor subsequently becomes an actual or potential supplier on the same relevant market, the 20% market share threshold will apply from the point in time when they became competitors. However, in that case the hardcore list relevant for agreements between non-competitors will continue to apply to the agreement unless the agreement is subsequently amended in any material respect (see Article 4(3) of the TTBER and point (39) of these guidelines).

This suggests that the benefit of the TTBER will be lost where parties become competitors and their combined market shares exceed the 20 per cent threshold and that the two-year transitional relief provided by Article 8(e) does not apply in these circumstances.

F. HARDCORE RESTRICTIONS

(i) General

The scheme of the TTBER is that, subject to Article 5, if a contractual restraint is not prohibited, it is permitted. The presence of a 'hardcore' restraint, defined in Article 4, prevents the block exemption from applying. As is the case in the context of vertical agreements, a restraint will be hardcore whether achieved directly or *indirectly*. Indeed, the Commission's view is that hardcore restraints are restrictive of competition by object and are most unlikely even *individually* to satisfy the Article 101(3) conditions.[127]

As already noted, there are two separate lists of hardcore restrictions: those applying to agreements between competitors (Article 4(1)) and those applying to agreements between non-competitors (Article 4(2)). In addition, the list of hardcore restraints in agreements between competitors may differ depending upon whether the agreement is reciprocal or non-reciprocal. These terms are defined in Article 1(1)(d) and (e) of the TTBER. Essentially, an agreement is reciprocal where the parties cross-license competing technologies or technologies which can be used for the production of competing products.

---

[123] Ibid., para. 37.

[124] Ibid.

[125] See n. 89 and text.

[126] Guidelines, paras. 38–39.

[127] Ibid., paras. 94–96. See generally on this point Chap. 4.

(ii) Agreements Between Competing Undertakings

The list of hardcore restraints applicable to agreements between competitors is set out in Article 4(1). It focuses, subject to specified exceptions, on agreements which directly or indirectly have as their object: price-fixing; limitations of output; allocation of markets or customers; restrictions on the licensee's ability to exploit its own technology; and provisions restraining either party from carrying out R&D unless indispensable to prevent disclosure of the licensed technology.

a. Article 4(1)(a)—Price Restrictions

Article 4(1)(a) targets agreements incorporating a 'restriction of a party's ability to determine its prices when selling products to third parties'. An obligation on the licensee to pay a certain minimum royalty does not in itself amount to price-fixing.[128] However, indirect price restraints, for example through disincentives to deviate from an agreed price level or through provisions for the royalty rate to increase if prices are reduced below a certain level, are prohibited.[129]

b. Article 4(1)(b)—Output Limitations

Article 4(1)(b) applies to a 'limitation of output, except limitations on the output of contract products imposed on the licensee in a non-reciprocal agreement or imposed on only one of the licensees in a reciprocal agreement'. This means, in effect, that reciprocal output restrictions and output restrictions on the licensor in respect of its own technology constitute hardcore restrictions.[130] Provisions which have the effect of output restrictions, such as disincentives to produce more than a certain amount, are also caught.[131]

c. Article 4(1)(c)—Market or Customer Allocation

Article 4(1)(c) seeks to reconcile the need to ensure that competitors are not able to share markets between themselves with an acceptance that in certain circumstances a licensee will require an exclusive or sole licence and protection from sales into its territory.[132] It targets the allocation of markets or customers unless one of four exceptions[133] applies.

Article 4(1)(c)(i)

In a *non-reciprocal* licence both licensor and licensee can be restricted from producing within an exclusively territory reserved for the other, or selling *actively* and *passively* into an exclusive territory or to the exclusive customer groups, reserved for the other.

Article 4(1)(c)(ii)

In a *non-reciprocal* licence the licensee can be prohibited from making *active* (but *not* passive) sales into exclusive territories or to customer groups allocated to another licensee (so long as that other licensee was not a competitor of the licensor when it was given its licence). If the licensees agree among themselves not to sell actively or passively into each other's territories or to customers this clearly goes beyond what is permitted and indeed amounts to market-sharing, which is prohibited by Article 101.[134]

---

[128] A licensor is entitled to ensure that it obtains a certain minimum return for the licence.

[129] Guidelines, paras. 99–101.

[130] Ibid., para. 103.

[131] Ibid.

[132] It considers that agreements between competitors sharing markets or customers (such as reciprocal exclusive licensing between competitors) have as their object the restriction of competition, ibid., para. 105.

[133] The 2014 TTBER reduced the list of these exceptions by merging them and so simplifying the list. The Commission considers that this has not led to any change in substance.

[134] Guidelines, para. 110. 'Active' and 'passive' sales have the same meaning as in respect of vertical agreements (see Chap. 11).

Table 12.1 Table of permissible market or customer restraints in agreements between competitors under the TTBER

Restraint	Permitted in reciprocal agreement?	Permitted in non-reciprocal agreement?
Ban on production in territory, or active or passive selling into territory/customer group, reserved to other (licensor or licensee)	No	Yes
Ban on active selling into territory of, or to the exclusive customer group reserved to, another licensee	No	Yes, as long as other licensee was not a competitor of the licensor at time the agreement was concluded
Ban on passive selling into territory of, or to exclusive customer group reserved to, another licensee	No	No
Captive use restriction	Yes, so long as can sell as spare parts	Yes, so long as can sell as spare parts
Second source provision (obligation on licensee to produce for a single customer)	No	Yes, if the licence was granted specifically to create a source of supply for that customer

Article 4(1)(c)(iii)

This exception permits licensing where the licensee takes a licence in order to make products for its own use (known as captive use restrictions).[135] It enables the licensor to limit the licensee to making components to be incorporated into the licensee's own products and to prohibit it from selling them to others. The licensee must not, however, be restricted from selling the components as spare parts.

Article 4(1)(c)(iv)

A non-reciprocal licence granted specifically to create an alternative source of supply for a customer may restrict the licensee to producing the contract products only for that customer (a 'second source' provision); the whole point of the agreement is to provide a particular customer with an alternative source of the products. It is possible, however, for more than one licensee to be given a licence in respect of the same customer (so the latter gets a third or even fourth source of supply).[136]

The list of permissible market or customer restraints in agreements between competitors is summarised in Table 12.1.

d. Article 4(1)(d)—Limitations on Technology Exploitation or R&D

Whether the agreement is reciprocal or non-reciprocal, the licensee cannot be restricted from exploiting its own technology rights and neither party to the agreement can be restricted from carrying out independent R&D unless indispensable to prevent the licensed know-how from being disclosed to third parties (in which case the restriction must be necessary and proportionate).[137] In addition, the licensee must not be prevented from exploiting its own technology.

(iii) Agreements Between Non-competing Undertakings

Where the parties are non-competitors they are allowed more leeway. The list of hardcore restraints is briefer and less limiting. To some extent, it resembles the list contained in Article 4 of the Verticals

---

[135] Ibid., para. 111.

[136] Ibid., para. 112.

[137] Ibid., para. 115.

Regulation, focusing on restraints which directly or indirectly fix or impose minimum resale prices or which, subject to specified exceptions, restrict the territory into which, or the customers to whom, the licensee may sell the contract product.

a. Article 4(2)(a)—Price Restrictions

Article 4(2)(a) provides that 'the restriction of a party's ability to determine its prices when selling products to third parties' constitutes a hardcore restraint, but 'without prejudice to the possibility of imposing a maximum sale price or recommending a sale price'. The prohibition of resale price maintenance (RPM) does not, therefore, unlike the hardcore competitor list, cover maximum or recommended prices so long as they do not really amount to fixed or minimum prices. This clause is thus similar to that incorporated in the Verticals Regulation.

b. Article 4(2)(b)—Passive Sales Restrictions Imposed on the Licensee

This clause identifies, subject to five exceptions, the restriction of the territory into which, or of the customers to whom, the licensee may passively sell the contract products, as a hardcore restriction. This provision does not therefore blacklist any sales restrictions on the *licensor* or *active* sales restrictions on the *licensee* (but see discussion of Article 4(2)(c) below). The Commission explains:[138]

> The block exemption of restrictions on active selling is based on the assumption that such restrictions promote investments, non-price competition and improvements in the quality of services provided by the licensees by solving free rider problems and hold-up problems. In the case of restrictions of active sales between licensees' territories or customer groups, it is not necessary that the protected licensee has been granted an exclusive territory or an exclusive customer group. The block exemption also applies to active sales restrictions where more than one licensee has been appointed for a particular territory or customer group. Efficiency enhancing investment is likely to be promoted where a licensee can be sure that it will only face active sales competition from a limited number of licensees inside the territory and not also from licensees outside the territory.

Article 4(2)(b)(i)

The first exception allows a restriction on passive sales into an exclusive territory or to an exclusive customer group reserved for the licensor. If the licensor could not prevent this it might not disseminate the technology through licensing in the first place:

> It is presumed that up to the market share threshold such restraints, where restrictive of competition, promote pro-competitive dissemination of technology and integration of such technology into the production assets of the licensee.[139]

The 2004 block exemption also permitted a restriction on passive sales into an exclusive territory or to an exclusive customer group reserved to another licensee. Although this is no longer block exempted, the Commission does recognise that such restraints may fall outside Article 101(1) altogether for a certain duration where objectively necessary for the licensee to penetrate a new market (for example, where licensees have to commit substantial investments in order to start up and develop a new market).

> In such circumstances, it is often the case that licensees would not enter into the licence agreement without protection for a certain period of time against (active and) passive sales into their territory or to their customer groups by other licensees. Where substantial investments by the licensee are necessary to start up and develop a new market, restrictions of passive sales by other licensees into such a territory or to such a customer group fall outside Article 101(1) for the period necessary for the licensee to recoup those investments. In most cases a period of up to two years from the date on which the contract product was first put

---

138 Ibid., para. 120.
139 Ibid., para. 121.

on the market in the exclusive territory by the licensee in question or sold to its exclusive customer group would be considered sufficient for the licensee to recoup the investments made. However, in an individual case a longer period of protection for the licensee might be necessary in order for the licensee to recoup the costs incurred.[140]

Article 4(2)(b)(ii)

Article 4(2)(b)(ii) exempts captive use restrictions; 'an obligation to produce the contract products only for its own use provided that the licensee is not restricted in selling the contract products actively and passively as spare parts for its own products'.

Article 4(2)(b)(iii)

Article 4(2)(b)(iii) exempts second source provisions; 'the obligation to produce the contract products only for a particular customer, where the licence was granted in order to create an alternative source of supply for that customer'.

Article 4(2)(b)(iv)

This provision permits the maintenance of a distinction between wholesale and retail levels of trade, allowing 'the restriction of sales to end-users by a licensee operating at the wholesale level of trade'. The licensor can give the wholesale distribution function to a licensee and prohibit it from serving the end customers.

Article 4(2)(b)(v)

As under the Verticals Regulation,[141] this provision allows members of a selective distribution system to be restricted from selling to unauthorised distributors, thereby preserving the integrity of the system.

Table 12.2 below provides in tabular form the passive sales restraints that may be imposed on licensees in a licence agreement between non-competitors.

Table 12.2 Table of permissible restraints in the context of agreements between non-competitors on the territory into which or the customer to whom the licensee can passively sell the contract products

Restraint	Permissible?
Passive sales into an exclusive territory or to an exclusive customer group reserved to the licensor	Yes
Restriction on passive sales into an exclusive territory or to an exclusive customer group reserved to another licensee	No (although was permitted under the 2004 TTBER for 2 years after the licensee first starts selling the contract products)
Captive use restriction	Yes, the licensee can be required to produce the product only for its own use provided he can sell as spare parts to customers or third parties performing after-sales services
Second source provision	Yes, an obligation on the licensee to produce the products only for a specified customer is permissible where the licence was granted to create an alternative source of supply
Sales to end-users	Yes, where the licensee operates at the wholesale level
Sales to unauthorised distributors within a selective distribution system	Yes, but unless the licensee operates at the wholesale level, the licensee must be able to make sales (actively or passive) to end-users (see Article 4(2)(c))

---

[140] See ibid., para. 126.
[141] Reg. 330/2010, Art. 4(b).

c. Article 4(2)(c)—Active or Passive Sales Bans to End-users within Selective Distribution Systems

A licensee which operates at the retail level of a selective distribution system cannot be prevented from active or passive selling to any end-users without prejudice to the possibility of prohibiting a member of the system from operating out of an unauthorised place of establishment. Again, this is similar to the Verticals Regulation.[142]

G. EXCLUDED RESTRICTIONS

(i) Introduction

Article 5 sets out the 'excluded restrictions'. These are restrictions which are not exempted by the TTBER but the inclusion of which does not automatically remove the protection of the TTBER from the remainder of the agreement. Individual assessment is required to determine whether the excluded restraints infringe Article 101 and, if they do, whether they can be severed from the rest of the agreement.

(ii) Article 5(1)(a): Improvements; Exclusive Grant Backs

Article 5(1)(a) deals with improvements made by the licensee to the licensed technology, excluding from the benefit of the TTBER 'any direct or indirect obligation on the licensee to grant an exclusive licence or to assign rights, in whole or in part, to the licensor or to a third party designated by the licensor in respect of its own improvements to, or its own new applications of, the licensed technology'. It thus excludes exclusive grant backs (even if the grant or assignment is compensated). The Commission explains the reason for excluding such provisions from the TTBER:[143]

> An obligation to grant the licensor an exclusive licence to improvements of the licensed technology or to assign such improvements to the licensor is likely to reduce the licensee's incentive to innovate since it hinders the licensee in exploiting the improvements, including by way of licensing to third parties.

Article 5 does not cover (so the TTBER does cover) *non-exclusive* grant back provisions even if they are non-reciprocal (i.e. only imposed on the licensee) and where the licensor is entitled to feed-on improvements to other licensees.

> A non-reciprocal grant back obligation may promote the dissemination of new technology by permitting the licensor to freely determine whether and to what extent to pass on its own improvements to its licensees. A feed-on clause may also promote the dissemination of technology, in particular when each licensee knows at the time of contracting that it will be on an equal footing with other licensees in terms of the technology on the basis of which it is producing.[144]

(iii) Article 5(1)(b): Non-challenge and Termination Clauses

Article 5(1)(b) excludes certain non-challenge clauses, 'any direct or indirect obligation on a party not to challenge the validity of intellectual property rights which the other party holds in the Union,

---

[142] Ibid.

[143] Guidelines, para. 129. Under the 2004 regime licensors could require that non-severable improvements be licensed back. The change in 2014 is to encourage follow-on improvements by the licensee and so encourages disruptive innovation by it.

[144] Ibid., para. 131.

without prejudice to the possibility, in the case of an exclusive licence, of providing for termination of the technology transfer agreement in the event that the licensee challenges the validity of any of the licensed technology rights'.

The general rule is thus that non-challenge clauses are excluded from the scope of the block exemption. As licensees are normally in the best position to determine whether or not an IPR is invalid the Commission considers that it is in the interest of undistorted competition and in accordance with the principles underlying the protection of IP, that invalid IPRs (which stifle innovation) should be eliminated.[145] The Guidelines thus state that such clauses require careful individual assessment under Article 101 to balance the incentives of the licensor and licensee and the public interest in eliminating obstacles to competition.[146]

An exception exists, however (so the TTBER does not exclude), for termination clauses which apply to challenges made by an exclusive licensee to the licensed technology. The Commission, in seeking to balance incentives to innovate against the public interest in removing invalid IPR rights from the register, considers that such clauses are 'usually less likely on balance to have anticompetitive effects':[147]

Once the licence is granted, the licensor may find itself in a particular situation of dependency, as the licensee will be its only source of income as regards the licensed technology rights if royalties are dependent on production with the licensed technology rights, as may often be an efficient way to structure royalty payments. In this scenario, the incentives for innovation and for licensing out could be undermined if, for example, the licensor were to be locked into an agreement with an exclusive licensee which no longer makes significant efforts to develop, produce and market the product (to be) produced with the licensed technology rights ...

(iv) Limitations on Technology Exploitation or R&D

Although restrictions on the licensee's ability to exploit its own technology rights or on either party's ability to carry out R&D (unless such latter restriction is indispensable to prevent the disclosure of the licensed know-how to third parties) are not hardcore restraints in agreements between non-competitors, Article 5(2) provides that such restraints are excluded restraints and are not exempted by the TTBER.

H. WITHDRAWAL AND DISAPPLICATION OF THE BLOCK EXEMPTION

(i) Withdrawal

Article 29(1) of Regulation 1/2003 provides that the Commission has a general right to withdraw the benefit of a block exemption from any agreement which has effects which are incompatible with Article 101(3). Article 29(2) also confers power on the national authorities of the Member States to withdraw the benefit of the TTBER where the agreement has restrictive effects incompatible with

---

[145] Ibid., para. 134 (they also state that where the licensed technology is valuable such restraints are also likely to infringe Art. 101(1) and unlikely to fulfil the conditions of Art. 101(3). In contrast if the licensed technology is related to a technically outdated process which the licensee does not use, or if the licence is granted for free, no restriction of competition arises).

[146] Ibid., paras. 134–138.

[147] Ibid., para. 139. The 2004 TTBER permitted all terminate-on-challenge arrangements. Although the Commission proposed removing this exception entirely it accepted an intermediate position following consultation, see also discussion on *Windsurfing*, n. 40 and text.

Article 101(3) in the territory of their Member State. Article 6(1) of the TTBER states that withdrawal by the Commission may be appropriate in respect of technology transfer agreements where:

(a) access of third parties' technologies to the market is restricted, for instance by the cumulative effect of parallel networks of similar restrictive agreements prohibiting licensees from using third parties' technologies;

(b) access of potential licensees to the market is restricted, for instance by the cumulative effect of parallel networks of similar restrictive agreements prohibiting licensors from licensing to other licensees or because the only technology owner licensing out relevant technology rights concludes an exclusive license with a licensee who is already active on the product market on the basis of substitutable technology rights.

Withdrawal may only be made prospectively (it does not affect prior validity) and by way of an infringement decision (finding that the agreement infringes Article 101(1) *and* that it does not meet the conditions of Article 101(3)) or a decision making commitments binding on the undertakings concerned.[148]

(ii) Disapplication

As is the case for the Verticals Regulation, Article 7 of the TTBER provides that the Commission may, by regulation, exclude from the scope of the TTBER parallel networks of similar agreements containing specified restraints, which cover more than 50 per cent of a relevant market. The circumstances in which the Commission would consider exercising this power are discussed in paragraphs 149–155 of the Guidelines.

5. THE APPLICATION OF ARTICLE 101 TO LICENSING AGREEMENTS FALLING OUTSIDE THE TTBER

A. GENERAL PRINCIPLES

(i) Technology Transfer Agreements Outside the TTBER

Agreements may fall outside the TTBER because:

- they are not bilateral technology transfer agreements;
- they exceed the market share thresholds;
- they contain hardcore restrictions.

In addition, individual provisions may be outside the TTBER because they are excluded restrictions under Article 5.

The Guidelines provide guidance as to how Article 101 applies to agreements or provisions falling outside the TTBER. Although the principles applied in the TTBER and the Guidelines do not generally apply to agreements that do not constitute technology transfer agreements, the Guidelines indicate that these principles will apply by analogy to: technology transfer agreements to which more than two undertakings are party;[149] 'master licensing agreements';[150] and the licensing of copyright

---

[148] See Chap. 13.

[149] Guidelines, para. 57.

[150] Ibid., para. 60.

for the purposes of the production of contract products.[151] In the case of other licensing agreements, however, such as R&D subcontracting,[152] licensing of rental right and public performance rights protected by copyright,[153] and trade mark licences,[154] guidance must be sought from other sources: the case law of the Court, the Commission's decisional practice, and the Commission's Article 101(3) Guidelines.

(ii) No Presumption of Illegality

The general framework for analysis of technology transfer agreements falling outside the TTBER is set out in paragraphs 156–159 of the Guidelines. The basic principle is that there is no presumption of illegality for agreements that fall outside the TTBER provided they do not contain hardcore restrictions. In particular, there is no presumption that Article 101(1) applies just because the market share thresholds are exceeded.

(iii) The Second Safe Harbour

The Commission sets out in paragraph 157 of the Guidelines a 'second safe harbour':

In order to promote predictability beyond the application of the TTBER and to confine detailed analysis to cases that are likely to present real competition concerns, the Commission takes the view that outside the area of hardcore restrictions Article 101 of the Treaty is unlikely to be infringed where there are four or more independently controlled technologies in addition to the technologies controlled by the parties to the agreement that may be substitutable for the licensed technology at a comparable cost to the user …

The fact that the agreement falls outside the second safe harbour does not imply that the agreement is caught by Article 101(1) and, if so, that Article 101(3) is not satisfied. The safe harbour merely creates a presumption that, in the stipulated circumstances, the agreement is not prohibited.[155] The basis for determining whether the technologies are sufficiently substitutable is discussed in paragraph 157 of the Guidelines.

(iv) The Approach to the Analysis of Individual Agreements

The general approach to the application of Article 101 to technology transfer agreements is described in paragraphs 10–18 of the Guidelines.

The first question to be asked is, of course, whether or not an agreement falling within the scope of Article 101 has as its object or effect the restriction of competition. The Technology Transfer Guidelines seek to bring together the principles derived from the jurisprudence and to provide a coherent structure for the appraisal. It has already been seen that in determining what constitutes a restriction of competition for the purposes of Article 101(1), restraints on both inter-technology and intra-technology competition are relevant. The Commission is concerned that a licensing agreement will lead to negative effects from:

(a) reduction of inter-technology competition between the companies operating on a technology market or on a market for products incorporating the technologies in question, including facilitation of collusion, both explicit and tacit;

---

[151] Ibid., para. 48 (but not licensing of rental rights and public performance rights protected by copyright, in particular for films or music, which raise particular issues and may require assessment on the basis of other principles, para. 49 and see Section 8, p. 879).

[152] Ibid., para. 66.

[153] Ibid., para. 49.

[154] Ibid., para. 50.

[155] Ibid., para. 158.

(b) foreclosure of competitors by raising their costs, restricting their access to essential inputs or otherwise raising barriers to entry; and

(c) reduction of intra-technology competition between undertakings that produce products on the basis of the same technology.[156]

Agreements that restrict competition will be excepted from the Article 101(1) prohibition if they satisfy the Article 101(3) criteria. Although the Commission recognises in the Guidelines that even restrictive licence agreements will frequently produce pro-competitive effects in the form of efficiencies,[157] the Commission's general view is that hardcore restraints are most unlikely to satisfy the conditions of Article 101(3).[158]

The Guidelines also discuss factors which are particularly relevant to the application of Article 101 in individual cases, in particular:[159] the nature of the agreement; the market position of the parties, competitors, and buyers; entry barriers; and the maturity of the market. They also provide guidance on specific provisions.

B. SPECIFIC PROVISIONS

(i) Provisions Generally Not Restrictive of Article 101(1)

Paragraph 183 of the Guidelines sets out a list of obligations in licence agreements which are generally not restrictive of competition within the meaning of Article 101(1). These include:

(a) confidentiality obligations;

(b) obligations on licensees not to sub-license;

(c) obligations not to use the licensed technology rights after the expiry of the agreement, provided that the licensed technology rights remain valid and in force;

(d) obligations to assist the licensor in enforcing the licensed intellectual property rights;

(e) obligations to pay minimum royalties or to produce a minimum quantity of products incorporating the licensed technology; and

(f) obligations to use the licensor's trade mark or indicate the name of the licensor on the product.

(ii) Licensing Restrictions

The Guidelines provide guidance for assessment of restrictions in licensing agreements,[160] such as royalty provisions,[161] exclusive and sole licences, sales restrictions, output restrictions, field of use restrictions,[162] captive use restrictions, tying and bundling provisions, non-challenge clauses, and improvements. They thus consider not only when they might constitute hardcore or excluded

---

[156] Ibid., para. 169.

[157] Ibid., para. 174.

[158] See Chap. 4.

[159] Guidelines, para. 159.

[160] Ibid., 4.2.

[161] Royalty provisions, taking the form of a lump sum payment, a percentage of the selling price, or a fixed amount for each product incorporating licensed technology, are part and parcel of a licensing agreement and frequently fall outside Art. 101(1) and/or are block exempted where the TTBER market share thresholds are satisfied.

[162] Guidelines, 4.2.4 (field of use restrictions (in contrast to customer restrictions, restricting licensees from selling to specific identified customer groups which are hardcore restraints, Art. 4(1)(c) and. Art 4(2)(b)) are generally considered to be pro-competitive as they encourage the licensor to license its technology for applications that fall outside its main area of focus. Consequently, they are covered by the TTBER (they are not considered to be output restrictions). Outside the scope of the TTBER, field of use restrictions are most likely to be problematic where incorporated in agreements between competitors and where they result in the licensee ceasing to be a competitive force outside the licensed field of use).

restraints under the TTBER, but how they should be analysed under Article 101 more generally (what are the likely antitrust concerns raised by each restraint and how can they be weighed against likely pro-competitive justifications).

(iii) Settlement Agreements

The TTBER covers settlement agreements (involving a transfer of technology), designed to resolve disputes concerning the validity or scope of IP, insofar as they do not contain hardcore restrictions. Such agreements are common in patent-intensive industries, such as pharmaceuticals (where they are often concluded between the manufacturer of a patented (branded) drug and a generic provider of an equivalent drug). Such agreements may be beneficial, particularly where they put an end to infringements of valid patent rights without resorting to costly litigation. Outside the safe harbour, the general approach of the Commission is explained in the Guidelines:

234. Licensing of technology rights in settlement agreements may serve as a means of settling disputes or avoiding that one party exercises its intellectual property rights to prevent the other party from exploiting its own technology rights.

235. Settlement agreements in the context of technology disputes are, as in many other areas of commercial disputes, in principle a legitimate way to find a mutually acceptable compromise to a bona fide legal disagreement. The parties may prefer to discontinue the dispute or litigation because it proves to be too costly, time-consuming and/or uncertain as regards its outcome. Settlements can also save courts and/or competent administrative bodies effort in deciding on the matter and can therefore give rise to welfare enhancing benefits. On the other hand, it is in the general public interest to remove invalid intellectual property rights as an unmerited barrier to innovation and economic activity.

236. Licensing, including cross licensing, in the context of settlement agreements is generally not as such restrictive of competition since it allows the parties to exploit their technologies after the agreement is concluded. In cases where, in the absence of the licence, it is possible that the licensee could be excluded from the market, access to the technology at issue for the licensee by means of a settlement agreement is generally not caught by Article 101(1).

237. However, the individual terms and conditions of settlement agreements may be caught by Article 101(1). Licensing in the context of settlement agreements is treated in the same way as other licence agreements. In these cases, it is particularly necessary to assess whether the parties are potential or actual competitors.

Although the Commission recognises the importance and benefits of settlements, it has become concerned about pay-for restriction or pay-for-delay type settlement agreements (or 'reverse payments'),[163] which often do not involve the transfer of technology, but are based on a value transfer from one party in return for a limitation on the entry and/or expansion on the market of the other.[164]

In July 2009 the Commission concluded an inquiry into the pharmaceuticals sector.[165] In its report it found 'a number of structural shortcomings and problems in the companies' practices that potentially led to distortions of competition and delays to entry of new, innovative as well as cheaper generic medicines to the EU market'[166] and made a number of recommendations, including stronger enforcement of the competition rules, particularly in respect of patent settlements. In both its Preliminary and Final Reports,[167] the Commission indicated that patent settlement agreements

---

[163] Reverse payments because ordinarily when a patent infringement case is settled it is the alleged infringer that pays the patentee (not the other way round).

[164] Guidelines, para. 238. If they do involve a licensing of technology rights, then they would need to be assessed under the TTBER. Where the parties are actual or potential competitors the Commission will be particularly attentive to the risk of market sharing/allocation, para. 239.

[165] <http//:ec.europa.eu/competition/sectors/pharmaceuticals/inquiry/communication_en.pdf>.

[166] IP/09/1098; see also MEMO/09/321.

[167] Pharmaceutical Sector Inquiry, Preliminary Report, 28 November. 2008, Final Report, 8 July 2009. The Inquiry was launched under Reg. 1/2003, Art. 17, see <http://ec.europa.eu/comm/competition/sectors/pharmaceuticals/inquiry/index.html>.

concluded between originator and generic pharmaceutical companies might be restricting the ability of generic companies to market medicines or delaying entry into the markets.[168] The Report noted that just under half of the patent settlement agreements concluded in the EU, between January 2007 and July 2008, involved a limitation on generic entry (which it categorised as Type B settlements[169]) and that just under half of those agreements involved a value transfer from the originator to the generic company (Type B-II settlements) (in the form of a direct payment, a licence, a distribution agreement, or a side deal).[170] The Commission has since then been monitoring patent settlements,[171] so increasing awareness of antitrust issues and reducing the number of such settlement agreements being concluded.

Nonetheless, the Commission has remained concerned about settlements, particularly 'B-II' types. Like the Federal Trade Commission in the US, it is concerned that these agreements may eliminate potential competition and share the resulting profits between the parties, to the detriment of consumers.[172] It has conducted a number of investigations into such agreements[173] and has now adopted three infringement decisions in which it found that the agreements at issue infringed competition by object and imposed fines:

- in *Lundbeck*,[174] the Commission imposed fines on both an originator, Lundbeck (of €93.8 million), and producers of generic medicines (totalling €52.2 million), for delaying the market entry of cheaper generic products of Lundbeck's blockbuster antidepressant, citalopram. Under the agreements, the generic producers agreed not to enter the market in return for substantial payments and other inducements from Lundbeck (even though Lundbeck's patent over the active ingredient of the drug had expired);

- in *Johnson & Johnson/Novartis*,[175] the Commission fined Johnson & Johnson and Novartis for deterring the entry of a new generic drug by Novartis's subsidiary; and

- in *Servier/Périndopril*,[176] the Commission fined Servier[177] and five generic producers for restricting competition and excluding generic products from the market (in this case Servier's patent on perindropil had expired).

One controversial and contested issue is whether, and if so when, such agreements should be characterised as restrictive of competition by object; that is when they might be sufficiently deleterious that their precise purpose can be said to restrict competition.[178] Further, if they are not

---

[168] See Pharmaceutical Sector Inquiry, Preliminary Report, 28 November 2008, n. 167, 2.4.

[169] The Commission divided settlement agreements into three categories: Types A, B-I, and B-II. Type A settlements allow a generic to enter the market.

[170] Of 207 settlement agreements concluded in at least one Member State between January 2007 and June 2008, 99 contained limitation on generic entry and 45 of those involved a value transfer from the originator company (IP/12/210, the Commission closed the investigation into the question of whether AstraZeneca and Nycomed had engaged in individual or joint action to delay new market entry).

[171] See, e.g., 5th Monitoring Report, available at <http://ec.europa.eu/competition/sectors/pharmaceuticals/inquiry/patent_settlements_report5_en.pdf>.

[172] See, e.g., F. A. S. Bokhari, 'What is the Price of Pay-To-Delay Deals?' (2013) 9 *J of Competition Law and Economics* 739.

[173] See, e.g., IP/11/511, MEMO/08/734, IP/12/210, and N. Kroes, 'Five years of sector and antitrust inquiries', 3 December 2009.

[174] COMP/39.226, 9 June 2013, IP/13/563 and IP/12/834, on appeal Case T-472/13, *Lundbeck v Commission* (judgment pending).

[175] COMP/39.685, 10 December 2013.

[176] COMP/39.612, *Périndopril (Servier)* 9 July 2014, IP14/799, on appeal Case T-691/14, *Servier SAS v Commission* (judgment pending).

[177] It also fined Servier for abuse of a dominant position, in particular for inducing the conclusion of the settlement agreement and through acquiring competing technology to inhibit new entry, see Chap. 7.

[178] In the US the Supreme Court ruled in *Federal Trade Commission v Actavis, Inc,* 570 US 756 (2013) that, given their potential to lead to genuine adverse effects on competition, pay-for-delay settlements or reverse payment

restrictive of competition by object, what factors should be relevant to determine their effects on competition under Article 101(1) and Article 101(3) respectively.[179] In *Lundbeck*, for example, the Commission considered that the agreement was particularly problematic because the generics were (at least) potential competitors that were seeking to enter the market and that it was the reverse payment agreement (involving a significant transfer of value), rather than infringement of valid patents, that were precluding market entry. Given the complexity involved in even determining these issues in each case, however, it is arguable that object classification is inappropriate and that such classification has the potential to deter firms from concluding legitimate pro-competitive patent settlements (there being circumstances where pay-for-delay settlements may be either the only viable form of settlement or may lead to generics entering earlier into the market).[180] This issue will have to be decided by the GC, as Lundbeck has appealed on a number of grounds, including that the Commission wrongly concluded that Lundbeck and the generics were actual or potential competitors, wrongly assessed the relevance of the value transfers, and wrongly applied established principles on restrictions by object.

The Guidelines also contain guidance on settlement agreements whereby the parties cross-license each other and impose restrictions on the use of their technologies[181] and non-challenge clauses. Although cross-licensing provisions, which go beyond what is required to unblock blocking provisions may infringe Article 101(1), non-challenge clauses will frequently fall outside Article 101(1) since the whole point of the agreement is to settle disputes and avoid future ones.[182]

(iv) Technology Pools

The final part of the Guidelines deal at some length with agreements setting up technology pools,[183] 'arrangements whereby two or more parties assemble a package of technology which is licensed not only to contributors to the pool but also to third parties...the pool may allow licensees to operate on the market on the basis of a single licence'.[184] Technology pools are not covered by the TTBER (because the agreement establishing the pool does not allow the licensee to produce contract products) although the TTBER may cover a licence granted by a technology pool to a third party when not a multi-party agreement.[185]

Technology pools often, but do not necessarily, support a *de jure* or *de facto* industry standard and may be pro-competitive; facilitating dissemination of technology through one-stop licensing of pooled technologies and reducing transaction costs and limiting cumulative royalties.[186] They can create competition concerns, however, for example where they involve licensing of substitute technologies (creating a risk of price-fixing or market-sharing) or when they support or establish

---

settlement arrangements are subject to scrutiny under the antitrust laws. Such arrangements are not to be treated as per se illegal or even presumptively invalid, however. Rather, the complexity and variability of the practices required a rule of reason inquiry.

[179] See, e.g., S. de Margerie, '"Pay-for-Delay" Settlements: In Search of the Right Standard' (2013) 36 *World Competition* 85, F. Esposito and F. Montanaro, 'A Fistful of Euros: EU Competition Policy and Reverse Payments in the Pharmaceutical Industry' (2014) 10 *European Competition Journal* 499 and W. Choi, B. Den Uyl, and M. Hughes, 'Pay-For-Delay Practices in the Pharmaceutical Sector: *Lundbeck, Actavis,* and Others' (2014) 5 *JECLAP* 44.

[180] See Choi, Den Uyl, and Hughes, ibid and Chap. 4. But see Commission's *Lundbeck* decision, para. 639.

[181] Guidelines, paras. 240–241.

[182] Ibid., para. 242.

[183] Ibid., 4.4.

[184] Technology pools can be simple arrangements but may also be very elaborate, with the pooled technology entrusted to a separate entity, ibid., para. 244.

[185] Ibid., para. 247.

[186] Ibid., para. 245.

an industry standard and result in a reduction of innovation by foreclosing alternative, competing technologies.[187]

The competitive risks have to be balanced against their efficiency-enhancing potential taking account of: the nature of the pooled technologies, and whether they are (a) complementary[188] or substitutes[189] and (b) essential[190] or non-essential;[191] and the institutional framework of the pool.[192] The Commission states:

> The way in which a technology pool is formed, organised and operated can reduce the risk of it having the object or effect of restricting competition and provide assurances to the effect that the arrangement is pro-competitive. In assessing the possible competitive risks and efficiencies, the Commission will, inter alia, take account of the transparency of the pool creation process; the selection and nature of the pooled technologies, including the extent to which independent experts are involved in the creation and operation of the pool and whether safeguards against exchange of sensitive information and independent dispute resolution mechanisms have been put in place.[193]

Further detail of how this assessment is to be conducted is explained in paragraphs 249–265 of the Guidelines. The Commission's 2014 Guidelines provide more extensive discussion of this than their predecessors. In addition, with the objective of encouraging the conclusion of pro-competitive pools, they provide a safe harbour for the creation of certain technology pools and subsequent licensing out by them.[194]

> The creation and operation of the pool, including the licensing out, generally falls outside Article 101(1) of the Treaty, irrespective of the market position of the parties, if all the following conditions are fulfilled:
>
> (a) participation in the pool creation process is open to all interested technology rights owners;
>
> (b) sufficient safeguards are adopted to ensure that only essential technologies (which therefore necessarily are also complements) are pooled;
>
> (c) sufficient safeguards are adopted to ensure that exchange of sensitive information (such as pricing and output data) is restricted to what is necessary for the creation and operation of the pool;
>
> (d) the pooled technologies are licensed into the pool on a non-exclusive basis;
>
> (e) the pooled technologies are licensed out to all potential licensees on FRAND terms;
>
> (f) the parties contributing technology to the pool and the licensees are free to challenge the validity and the essentiality of the pooled technologies, and;

---

[187] Ibid., para. 246. See also, e.g., IP/06/139 (the Commission announced that it had closed an investigation into the practices of Philips Electronics which had offered European manufacturers of CD-recordable discs a joint portfolio licence which included both its own CD-recordable disc patents and those of Sony and Taiyo Yuden. The Commission closed the investigation once Philips undertook to discontinue the joint patent portfolio licence in Europe and to offer revised individual licences limited to its own patents).

[188] Both technologies are required to produce the product or carry out the process in question (see Guidelines, para. 250).

[189] Either technology allows the holder to produce the product or carry out the process.

[190] There are no substitutes for the technology inside or outside the pool and the technology in question constitutes a necessary part of the package of technologies for the purposes of producing the product(s) or carrying out the process(es) to which the pool relates. The draft Guidelines provided greater clarity on this issue.

[191] Guidelines, paras. 252. Broadly, the creation of a pool composed of only essential complementary technologies is likely to fall outside Art. 101(1). In contrast, a pool of substitute technologies will constitute a price-fixing arrangement which violates Art. 101(1) and is unlikely to satisfy the conditions of Art. 101(3). A pool comprising non-essential substitute technologies may foreclose third party competing technologies, Guidelines, para. 255.

[192] Factors such as whether participation in the pool is open, whether experts are involved, how information exchange is dealt with, and how disputes should be resolved are relevant, Guidelines, paras. 256–260.

[193] Ibid., para. 248.

[194] Ibid., para. 261.

(g) the parties contributing technology to the pool and the licensee remain free to develop competing products and technology.

Individual assessment will be required where the safe harbour does not apply. The Commission states that it applies four guiding principles when assessing individual restraints in licensing from the pool:[195]

In making its assessment of technology transfer agreements between the pool and its licensees the Commission will be guided by the following main principles:

(a) the stronger the market position of the pool the greater the risk of anti-competitive effects;

(b) the stronger the market position of the pool, the more likely that agreeing not to license to all potential licensees or to license on discriminatory terms will infringe Article 101;

(c) pools should not unduly foreclose third party technologies or limit the creation of alternative pools;

(d) the technology transfer agreements should not contain any of the hardcore restrictions listed in Article 4 of the TTBER (see section 3.4).

Where a technology pool compatible with Article 101 is created, provisions inherent in the establishment of the standard or pool, such as royalty provisions, also fall outside Article 101.[196] Where, however, the pool has a dominant position, closer scrutiny of the licensing provisions will be necessary and the Guidelines state, for example, that 'royalties and other licensing terms should be non-excessive and non-discriminatory and licences should be non-exclusive. These requirements are necessary to ensure that the pool is open and does not lead to foreclosure and other anti-competitive effects on down-stream markets.'[197] The Guidelines also seek to ensure that new technology is not foreclosed, for example by stating that restrictions on parties developing competing products or standards or on granting and obtaining licences outside the pool should not be incorporated.[198] They also provide that: grant back obligations should be non-exclusive and limited to essential or important developments; and pools should not be able to shield invalid patents through non-challenge and termination clauses between the pool and third parties.[199]

The Horizontal Cooperation Guidelines[200] contain separate guidance on the question of whether the agreement to establish an industry standard is compatible with Article 101—i.e. on standardisation agreements (agreements which 'have as their primary objective the definition of technical or quality requirements' for 'current or future products, production processes, services or methods'[201]) and on the licensing of IPRs essential for technology used to implement a standard on fair, reasonable, and non-discriminatory (FRAND) terms, see Chapter 10.

6. TRADE MARK LICENCES

A. GENERAL

There is no block exemption which specifically covers trade mark licences. In the discussion of the TTBER in Sections 4 and 5, however, it is seen that where the licence of a trade mark is ancillary to a licence of patents, know-how, designs, or software the TTBER may apply. Further, where a trade

---

[195] Ibid., para. 267.

[196] Ibid., para. 268.

[197] Ibid., para. 269.

[198] Ibid., para. 270.

[199] Ibid., paras. 271–272.

[200] Guidelines on the applicability of Article 101 of the Treaty on the Functioning of the European Union to horizontal co-operation agreements [2011] OJ C11/1 (Horizontal Cooperation Guidelines).

[201] Ibid., para. 257.

mark licence is directly related to the use, sale, or resale of goods or services (and does not constitute the primary object of the agreement) it may be ancillary to a vertical agreement, such as a franchising agreement and benefit from the Verticals Regulation.[202] In other situations, the principles developed in these Guidelines do *not* apply by analogy[203] and guidance will need to be sought from relevant jurisprudence. The paucity (and age) of the cases that exist, however, mean that it is not easy to determine the principles that apply.

In *Consten and Grundig*[204] it was held that an agreement seeking to confer ATP on the licensee of a trade mark would infringe Article 101(1). Further, in the Commission's two formal decisions relating to trade mark licences, *Campari*[205] and *Moosehead/Whitbread*,[206] it took a strict approach to exclusivity provisions[207] and applied broadly the same principles to trade mark licences as it did at the time in its decisions to patent and know-how licences. As the Commission's thinking has evolved considerably since this time, the reasoning in these cases, which support a formalistic approach to restraints on economic freedom, should be treated with some caution.

B. THE *CAMPARI* DECISION

The *Campari* transaction[208] is difficult to classify but the trade mark licence was a predominant element. The aperitifs Bitter Campari and Cordial Campari were made by mixing alcohol with a secret herbal concentrate. Campari-Milano set up a network of licensees to manufacture and sell its products in all EU countries except the UK and Ireland.[209] Under the agreements the licensees purchased the secret concentrate and colouring matter from the licensor and manufactured the drink in compliance with the licensor's instructions. The resulting bottles of aperitif were then sold under the licensor's Campari trade mark. The licences were exclusive, prevented the licensees from manufacturing or handling competing products or pursuing an active sales policy outside their territory, banned exports outside the common market, and provided that only the original Italian product could be supplied to certain customers/outlets. There were also provisions about manufacture only at approved sites, confidentiality, advertising, and non-assignment. The Commission held that the following provisions were outside Article 101(1): the ban on exports outside the common market, as in the circumstances there was little chance of this indirectly affecting inter-Member State trade; the restriction of the licence to those plants capable of guaranteeing the quality of the product; the obligation to follow the licensor's manufacturing instructions and to buy secret raw materials from the licensor, as this was central to the product being of proper 'Campari' quality;[210] the confidentiality of the know-how; the minimum advertising commitments; and the prohibition on assignment. Other clauses, including the exclusivity and the active sales ban, were held to infringe Article 101(1).

The Commission granted an exemption however. This part of the decision provides a good illustration of how the four criteria in Article 101(3) were applied. Note that in paragraph 71 the

---

[202] Guidelines, para. 50 and Chap. 11.

[203] Ibid., para. 50.

[204] Cases 56 and 58/64, [1966] ECR 299.

[205] COMP/171, 856, 172, 117, and 28.173, *Re the Agreement of Davide-Campari-Milano SpA* [1978] OJ L70/69.

[206] COMP/32.736, [1990] OJ L100/32.

[207] Even though this approach bore 'no relation to the reality that no lager brewer would contemplate developing and marketing a new brand in competition with one of its rivals', N. Green and A. Robertson, *Commercial Agreements and Competition Law* (2nd edn, Kluwer, 1997), 931.

[208] COMP/171, 856, 172, 117, and 28.173, *Re the Agreement of Davide-Campari-Milano SpA* [1978] OJ L70/69.

[209] The UK and Ireland were covered by a straightforward distribution agreement which fell within the block exemption then in force, Reg. 67/67 [1967] OJ Spec. Ed. 10.

[210] Certain other ingredients did not necessarily have to be bought from the licensor but had to be sourced on the basis of objective quality considerations.

Commission distinguishes between the effects of a non-competition clause in a trade mark licence and one in a patent licence.

COMP/171, 856, 172, 117, and 28.173, *Re the Agreement of Davide-Campari-Milano SpA* [1978] OJ L70/69

Commission

III APPLICABILITY OF ARTICLE [101(3)] . . .

. . .

A. The restrictions of competition mentioned at points 1 to 4 of item II A satisfy the tests of Article [101(3)].

1. The exclusivity granted by Campari-Milano contributes to improving the production and distribution of the products. By giving each licensee a guarantee that no other undertaking will obtain a licence within its allocated territory, and that in this territory neither Campari-Milano nor any other licensee may manufacture products bearing the licensor's trade mark this commitment confers upon each licensee an advantage in its allotted territory. This territorial advantage is such as to permit a sufficient return on the investment made by each licensee for the purpose of manufacturing the product bearing the trade mark under conditions acceptable to the licensor and holder of the trade mark, and it enables the licensee to increase its production capacity and constantly to improve the already long-established distribution network. In practice the exclusivity granted has allowed each licensee to improve its existing plant and to build new plant. It has also enabled each licensee to strengthen its efforts to promote the brand, doubling the total volume of sales in the Benelux countries and Germany over the last six years, and, by establishing a multistage distribution network, to secure a constantly increasing number of customers and thus to ensure supplies throughout the allotted territory.

2. The ban on dealing in competing products also contributes to improving distribution of the licensed products by concentrating sales efforts, encouraging the build-up of stocks and shortening delivery times.

The restriction on the licensees' freedom to deal in other products at the same time as the products here in question prevents the licensees from neglecting Campari in the event of conflict between the promotion of Campari sales and possible interest in another product. Although a non-competition clause in a licensing agreement concerning industrial property rights based on the result of a creative activity, such as a patent, would constitute a barrier to technical and economic progress by preventing the licensees from taking an interest in other techniques and products, this is not the case with the licensing agreements under consideration here. The aim pursued by the parties, as is clear from the agreements taken as a whole, is to decentralise manufacture within the EEC and to rationalise the distribution system linked to it, and thus to promote the sale of Campari-Milano's Bitter, manufactured from the same concentrates provided by Campari-Milano, according to the same mixing process and using the same ingredients, and bearing the same trade mark, as that of the licensor.

The prohibition on dealing in competing products, therefore, makes for improved distribution of the relevant product in the same way as do exclusive dealing agreements containing a similar clause, which are automatically exempted by Regulation 67/67/EEC; a declaration that the prohibition in Article [101(1)] is inapplicable to this clause is accordingly justified.

3. Distribution will also be improved by the prohibition against the parties engaging in an active sales policy outside their respective territories. This restriction on the licensees will help to concentrate their sales efforts, and provide a better supply to consumers in their territories for which they have particular responsibility, without preventing buyers elsewhere in the Community from securing supplies freely from any of the licensees. Application of the same restriction to Campari-Milano encourages the efforts made by . . . each territory allotted; the licensees thus have the benefit of a certain protection relative to Campari-Milano's strong market position.

4. The obligation on licensees to supply the original Italian product rather than that which they themselves manufacture, when selling to diplomatic corps, ships' victuallers, foreign armed forces and generally speaking all organisations with duty-free facilities, also helps to promote sales of Campari-Milano's Bitter. By restricting licensees' freedom to supply the products they manufacture themselves it makes sure that particular categories of consumers, who are deemed to be outside the licensee's territory and are usually required to move frequently from one territory to another, can always purchase the same original product with all its traditional features as regards both composition and outward appearance. Even though quality standards are observed, it is impossible in particular to avoid differences in taste between the products of the various manufacturers. This obligation is thus designed to prevent these consumers from turning to other competing products and to ensure that they continue to buy Bitter Campari, with the facility of being able to obtain stocks from their local dealer. Further, such consumers are not prevented from freely obtaining the licensees' own products even though any such purchase would be on the normal trading conditions applicable to non-duty free purchasers.

B. The licensing agreements have increased the quantities of Bitter Campari available to consumers and improved distribution, so that consumers benefit directly. There are other producers of bitter on the market, and effective competition will be strengthened by the growing quantities produced by Campari-Milano's licensees, so that it can be assumed that the improvements resulting from the agreements and the benefits which the licensees obtain from them are shared by consumers.

As buyers may secure supplies of Bitter from other territories through unsolicited orders, they are in a position to exert pressure on the prices charged by the exclusive licensee in their territory if these should be too high.

C. The restrictions of competition imposed on the parties must be considered indispensable to the attainment of the benefits set out above. None of the restrictions could be omitted without endangering the parties' object of promoting sales of Bitter Campari by concentrating the activities of the licensees on this product and offering the same original product to certain customers. In particular, none of the licensees and in all probability no other undertaking in the spirituous liquors industry would have been prepared to make the investment necessary for a significant increase in sales of Bitter if it were not sure of being protected from competition from other licensees or Campari-Milano itself.

D. The licensing agreements which are the subject of this Decision do not give Campari-Milano or its licensees the possibility of eliminating competition in respect of a substantial part of the Bitter products in question. In the EEC there exists a fairly large number of other well-known brands of bitter, which are all able to compete against Bitter Campari. Campari-Milano's licensees and Campari-Milano itself are also free to sell the Campari products in question within the Common Market but outside their territory for which they have particular responsibility.

C. THE *MOOSEHEAD/WHITBREAD* DECISION

This case concerned the manufacture in the UK of a lager produced by the Canadian brewer Moosehead.[211] According to the Commission, it had a taste typical of Canadian lagers.[212] Under the agreement Moosehead granted to the British brewer, Whitbread, the sole and exclusive right to produce and promote, market, and sell beer manufactured for sale under the name 'Moosehead' in the UK using Moosehead's secret know-how. Moosehead gave Whitbread an exclusive licence of its UK trade mark rights and agreed to provide it with all the relevant know-how (the know-how licence was non-exclusive) and to supply it with the necessary yeast. Whitbread agreed not to make active sales outside its territory, not to produce or promote any other beer identified as a Canadian beer, not to contest the ownership or validity of the trade mark, to comply with Moosehead's directions in relation to the know-how, and to buy the yeast only from Moosehead or a designated third party.

---

[211] COMP/32.736, *Moosehead/Whitbread* [1990] OJ L100/32.

[212] Ibid., para. 3.

The Commission held that the exclusivity provisions and the active sales ban in the trade mark licence were caught by Article 101(1). It did not consider the non-challenge clause to the *ownership* of the mark was caught because no matter whose name it was registered in, other parties would be prevented from using it. A non-challenge clause in respect of validity, however, was another matter. The Commission held that whether such clauses may infringe Article 101(1) would depend on the circumstances, but in this case it did not:

15.4. In relation to the trade mark non-challenge clause:

(a) in general terms, a trade mark non-challenge clause can refer to the ownership and/or the validity of the trade mark:

— The ownership of a trade mark may, in particular, be challenged on grounds of the prior use or prior registration of an identical trade mark.

— A clause in an exclusive trade mark licence agreement obliging the licensee not to challenge the ownership of a trade mark, as specified in the above paragraph, does not constitute a restriction of competition within the meaning of Article [101(1)]. Whether or not the licensor or licensee has the ownership of the trade mark, the use of it by any other party is prevented in any event, and competition would thus not be affected.

— The validity of a trade mark may be contested on any ground under national law, and in particular on the grounds that it is generic or descriptive in nature. In such an event, should the challenge be upheld, the trade mark may fall within the public domain and may thereafter be used without restriction by the licensee and any other party.

Such a clause may constitute a restriction of competition within the meaning of Article [101(1)], because it may contribute to the maintenance of a trade mark that would be an unjustified barrier to entry into a given market.

Moreover in order for any restriction of competition to fall under Article [101(1)], it must be appreciable. The ownership of a trade mark only gives the holder the exclusive right to sell products under that name. Other parties are free to sell the product in question under a different trade mark or trade name. Only where the use of a well-known trade mark would be an important advantage to any company entering or competing in any given market and the absence of which therefore constitutes a significant barrier to entry, would this clause which impedes the licensee to challenge the validity of the trade mark, constitute an appreciable restriction of competition within the meaning of Article [101(1)].

(b) In the present case Whitbread is unable to challenge both the ownership and the validity of the trade mark.

As far as the validity of the trade mark is concerned it must be noted that the trade mark is comparatively new to the lager market in the territory. The maintenance of the 'Moosehead' trade mark will thus not constitute an appreciable barrier to entry for any other company entering or competing in the beer market in the United Kingdom. Accordingly, the Commission considers that the trade mark non-challenge clause included in the agreement, in so far as it concerns its validity . . . does not constitute an appreciable restriction of competition and does not fall under Article [101(1)].

The Commission granted an exemption to the agreement, holding that the exclusivity provisions, active sales ban, and non-competition clauses met the Article 101(3) criteria, particularly in view of the amount of inter-brand competition on the UK beer market.

D. THE CURRENT POSITION

Although the Commission's decisions in *Campari* and *Moosehead* reflect the more formalistic approach to Article 101(1) it pursued prior to modernisation, they are useful in: (a) confirming that some types of clauses, such as non-challenge clauses, confidentiality provisions, and provisions dealing with quality control and manufacturing standards, may fall outside Article 101(1): and (b) setting out when provisions that may infringe Article 101(1) (such as exclusive licences, sales restraints, and non-compete provisions) are likely to satisfy the conditions of Article 101(3).

It must not be forgotten, however, that the Commission (or a national court or NCA) analysing a case today would now be likely to adopt a more economic approach, in particular when applying Article 101(1). Although case law could be interpreted to support the Commission's view that exclusive licences, especially if accompanied by sales restraints, violate Article 101(1), it is likely that fuller analysis would now be required before it could be determined whether other provisions restrict competition within the meaning of Article 101(1).

7. TRADE MARK DELIMITATION AGREEMENTS

Trade mark delimitation agreements are entered into in order to settle disputes.[213] They usually occur where one party opposes the other's application for, or use of, a mark on the ground that it is confusingly similar to one owned by the first party for similar products. The trade mark delimitation agreement may be adopted to settle protracted litigation. The CJ and Commission have made it clear that the provisions in such agreements may infringe Article 101(1)[214] in the same way as they might in any other agreement. The context in which the agreement is made does not therefore mean that it is immune from the application of Article 101(1). Delimitation agreements may restrict the class of products for which a party may use the mark, or the territories in which it may use the mark, or a party may accept a non-challenge obligation in relation to certain products or territories. In *BAT v Commission*[215] the Court took a more liberal attitude to delimitation agreements than the Commission had done previously. The position now appears to be that an agreement will be outside Article 101(1) if there is a genuine risk of confusion between the parties, and it is not just a ploy for market-sharing, and if the agreement does not divide markets within the EU (at least if there is no less restrictive means of dealing with the dispute).[216]

8. COPYRIGHT (OTHER THAN SOFTWARE) LICENCES

A. GENERAL

Software licences are 'technology transfer agreements' and are thus governed by the TTBER and the accompanying Guidelines. Licences of other types of copyright, however, do not benefit from the TTBER, or the Verticals Regulation, unless the licence is ancillary to a technology transfer or vertical agreement.[217] In discussing copyright licensing the Technology Transfer Guidelines distinguish between the licensing of copyright for the production of contract products and other rights related to copyright on the other. The principles set out in the TTBER and the Guidelines will, as a general rule, be applied to the former.[218]

---

[213] See n. 163 and text for non-assertion and settlement agreements in respect of IPRs potentially within the scope of the TTBER.

[214] See Case 65/86, *Bayer AG and Maschinenfabrik Hennecke v Heinz Süllhöfer* [1988] ECR 5249, concerning a non-challenge clause.

[215] Case 35/83, *BAT v Commission* [1985] ECR 363, the appeal from COMP/30.128, *Toltecs/Dorcet* [1982] OJ L379/19.

[216] See also COMP/27.879, *Sirdar/Phildar* [1975] OJ L125/27; *Hershey/Schiffers*, Commission Press Release IP/90/87; *Chiquita/Fyffes* IP(92)461.

[217] TTBER, Art. 1(1)(b).

[218] Guidelines, para. 49.

... On the other hand, the licensing of rental rights and public performance rights protected by copyright, in particular for films or music, is considered to raise particular issues and it may not be warranted to assess such licensing on the basis of the principles developed in these guidelines. In the application of Article 101 the specificities of the work and the way in which it is exploited must be taken into account. The Commission will therefore not apply the TTBER and the present guidelines by way of analogy to the licensing of these other rights.[219]

B. BROADCASTING LICENCES AND PERFORMANCE COPYRIGHT

Other than on the issue of exclusive licences there is almost no jurisprudence in this area. It has been seen that although the CJ held in *Coditel II*[220] that an exclusive licence (amounting in effect to ATP) did not in itself infringe Article 101(1), the scope of this exception is uncertain. Indeed, in the *Premier League/Murphy*[221] cases the CJ held that exclusive broadcast licences did violate Article 101. In *Film Purchases by German Television Stations*[222] the Commission also distinguished *Coditel II* but held that an exclusive broadcasting licence of MGM/UA films granted to a group of German TV stations for 15 years with a further 'selection period' which preceded this met the Article 101(3) criteria.[223] Although therefore the Commission held that the agreement was within Article 101(1) because of the number of films covered by the transaction[224] and the long duration of the arrangements which excluded third parties for a length of time which was described as 'disproportionate within the *Coditel II* judgment' and 'an artificial barrier to other undertakings',[225] it exempted the agreement after provision was made for third party broadcasters in Germany to apply for licences to show the films at times which did not clash with those of the licensees. The Commission considered that the arrangements as a whole allowed more films to be shown to German audiences and to be dubbed into German.

Broadcast licences and licensing of digital content is still an issue of acute interest to the Commission. It is currently investigating whether restrictions preventing cross-border access to online pay-TV services ('geo-blocking') or satellite pay-TV services incorporated in licensing agreements for audiovisual content, such as films, concluded between US film studios and EU pay-TV broadcasters infringe Article 101. Its current preliminary view is that such clauses prevent passive selling outside allocated territories and so grant absolute territorial exclusivity to the broadcasters

---

[219] Ibid., para. 50. This makes a change from the 2004 Guidelines which stated at para. 52: 'In the case of the various rights related to performances value is created not by the reproduction and sale of copies of a product but by each individual performance of the protected work. Such exploitation can take various forms including the performance, showing or the renting of protected material such as films, music or sporting events. In forms including the performance, showing or the renting of protected material such as films, music or sporting events. In the application of Article [101] the specificities of the work and the way in which it is exploited must be taken into account (see in this respect Case 262/81, *Coditel (II)* . . .). For instance, resale restrictions may give rise to less competition concerns whereas particular concerns may arise where licensors impose on their licensees to extend to each of the licensors more favourable conditions obtained by one of them. The Commission will therefore not apply the TTBER and the present guidelines by way of analogy to the licensing of these other rights.'

[220] Case 262/81, *Coditel II* [1982] ECR 3381.

[221] Cases C-403 and 429/08, EU:C:2011:631, n. 55 and text.

[222] COMP/31.734, [1989] OJ L284/36.

[223] In fact the Commission left open whether the transaction amounted to a licence 'in the legal and technical sense' or an assignment of rights for a limited period and to a limited extent. In either case the Commission considered that there was a restriction of competition: ibid., para. 41.

[224] And the fact that many of the films were important or noteworthy or had 'particular mass appeal such as the James Bond films': ibid., para. 43.

[225] Ibid., para. 44.

which, in the absence of an objective justification, infringes Article 101. [226] Indeed, Competition Commissioner Margrethe Vestager has stated:[227]

European consumers want to watch the pay-TV channels of their choice regardless of where they live or travel in the EU. Our investigation shows that they cannot do this today, also because licensing agreements between the major film studios and Sky UK do not allow consumers in other EU countries to access Sky's UK and Irish pay-TV services, via satellite or online. We believe that this may be in breach of EU competition rules. The studios and Sky UK now have the chance to respond to our concerns.

Further, the e-commerce sector inquiry[228] is designed to identify barriers erected by companies to cross-border online trade (including in digital content) and what effects they have on competition and consumers. In the context of the latter, the Commission's initial findings, from data gathered, indicate that such barriers do exist. It is now assessing the impact of such provisions on competition and consumers to determine the extent to which investments in the creation and distribution of content do depend upon any ATP or geo-blocking provisions.

There is almost no other precedent which indicates how *other* provisions in performance copyright licences will be appraised under Article 101. In 2004, the Commission indicated that it might be suspicious of favoured nation clauses incorporated in such contracts. In a press release, it reported that it had closed an investigation into contracts concluded by certain of the major Hollywood studios.[229] These contracts, providing for the sale of their entire film production to European pay-TV broadcasters, had originally included most favoured nation clauses, giving the studios the right to enjoy the most favourable terms agreed between a pay-TV company and any one of them. The Commission considered that the cumulative effect of these clauses was an alignment of prices paid to the studios for the broadcasting rights. It closed its investigation into the contracts of six of the studios after they withdrew the clauses.

C. COLLECTIVE LICENSING OF COPYRIGHT

As with technology pooling, the collective licensing of copyright may frequently be pro-competitive and necessary to the operation of an agreement.[230] Generally a benign approach has been taken (under Article 102 and Article 101) to the conduct of collecting societies which manage authors' rights in the musical works which they have created, in particular by licensing categories of rights to commercial users on behalf of the societies' members.[231] Collecting societies exist because of the impracticality of performers, musicians, etc. individually giving permission for their work to be performed or collecting royalties. Performers' rights societies are usually organised on a national basis and often have a *de facto* monopoly. Their activities have often given rise to competition law problems under Article 102. The Commission is concerned to address the issue of collecting societies as

---

[226] On 23 July 2015 the Commission sent a statement of objections to Sky UK and six major US film studios (Disney, NBC Universal, Paramount Pictures, Sony, Twentieth Century Fox, and Warner Bros) setting out the preliminary view that each of the six studios and Sky UK have agreed to prevent Sky UK from allowing EU consumers located elsewhere to access, via satellite or online, pay-TV services available in the UK and Ireland. On 22 April 2016 Paramount agreed to abandon its geo-blocking practices to end its part in the investigation.

[227] IP/15/4322.

[228] See <http://ec.europa.eu/competition/antitrust/sector_inquiries_e_commerce.html>, IP/15/4921 and IP/16/992.

[229] IP/04/1314.

[230] See discussion in Chaps. 4 and 9 and, e.g., COMP/37.398, *Joint selling of the commercial rights of the UEFA Champions League* [2003] OJ L291/25.

[231] See, e.g., Case T-224/95, *Tremblay v Commission* [1997] ECR II-2215, Case 395/87, *Ministère Public v Tournier* [1989] ECR 2521.

a whole and published a Communication on this in 2004.[232] In *Kanal 5 v STIM*[233] the CJ set out guidance on the question of when a copyright management organisation holding a dominant position might abuse that dominant position by engaging in excessive or discriminatory pricing practices.

Further, in *CISAC*,[234] the Commission became concerned about clauses in model contracts drawn up by the International Confederation of Societies of Authors and Composers (CISAC) and to be completed by contracting collecting societies. It declined, following market testing, to accept commitments offered by CISAC[235] and held that a number of clauses infringed Article 101(1) and that national territorial limitations (limiting the ability of each collecting society to offer services outside its domestic territory) resulted from a concerted practice which restricted competition between the collecting societies. On appeal, however, the GC[236] held that the Commission had not established, to the requisite legal standard, the existence of a concerted practice between the collecting societies to fix the national territorial limitations and had not put forward sufficient evidence to render implausible the collecting societies' explanation for their parallel conduct, based on the need to ensure the effectiveness of the fight against the unauthorised use of musical works. As no concerted practice was established the GC did not have to examine the argument put forward by CISAC that the national territorial limitations were not restrictive of competition but were necessary 'in order to avoid a race to the bottom with regard to royalties and to maintaining the existence of national one-stop-shops'.[237]

9. THE APPLICATION OF ARTICLE 102 TO INTELLECTUAL PROPERTY RIGHTS

There are two facets to the relationship between Article 102 and IPRs. First, there is the extent to which the ownership of IPRs puts the holder in a dominant position. Secondly, there is the question whether the holding, acquisition, or exploitation of IPRs can constitute an abuse of a dominant position and, if so, in what circumstances.

The application of Article 102 to IPRs is dealt with in Chapters 6 and 7 because it is impossible to divorce these questions about IPRs from the operation of Article 102 as a whole. Looking at them in isolation from other developments in Article 102 jurisprudence can lead to an incomplete and distorted picture. Reference should therefore be made to those chapters.

10. CONCLUSIONS

1. The TTBER and Guidelines seek to adopt an economic approach to IP licensing agreements. The TTBER sets out a presumption that technology transfer agreements which do not incorporate hardcore restraints and which are concluded between undertakings which do not exceed the market share thresholds are compatible with Article 101.

2. As with the approach to vertical agreements, the centrality of the TTBER means that the main focus of attention is still on whether or not a technology transfer agreement is compatible with

---

[232] Communication from the Commission to the Council, European Parliament and ESC on the Management of Copyright and Related Rights in the Internal Market, COM(2004) 261 final. See also, e.g., the commitments adopted in relation to the Cannes Agreement, see IP/06/1311.

[233] Case C-52/07, *Kanal 5 v STIM* [2008] ECR I-9275.

[234] COMP/38.698, *CISAC* 16 July 2008.

[235] Ibid.

[236] Case T-442/08, *International Confederation of Societies of Authors and Composers (CISAC) v Commission* EU:T:2013:188.

[237] Ibid., para. 183.

Article 101(3), not whether it is compatible with Article 101(1), i.e. whether it actually restricts competition.

3. In contrast with the position for vertical agreements, however, in practice it is likely to be much harder for firms to be sure about compliance with the provisions of the TTBER. Not only is it inherently more difficult to define technology markets but the hardcore and excluded restraints are more complex than those set out in the Verticals Regulation.

4. The practical reality is, therefore, that in many situations parties to IP licensing or IP agreements will have to rely on self-assessment to determine their agreement's compatibility with Article 101. As there is relatively little decisional practice and case law dealing with IP licensing agreements, reliance on the Technology Transfer Guidelines will be essential. These also provide important guidance on settlement agreements and technology pools. As trade mark and copyright licences are generally not covered by the TTBER and Guidelines, recourse to general Article 101 principles will be necessary in such cases.

11. FURTHER READING

A. BOOKS

ANDERMAN, S. D., *EC Competition Law and Intellectual Property Rights* (Clarendon Press, 1988)

ANDERMAN, S. D., and KALLAUGHER, J., *Technology Transfer and the New EU Competition Rules: IP Licensing after Modernisation* (Oxford University Press, 2006)

B. CHAPTERS IN BOOKS

IBÁÑEZ COLOMO, P., 'Copyright Licensing and the EU Digital Single Market Strategy' in R. D. Blair and D. D Sokol (eds.), *Handbook of Antitrust, Intellectual*

Property and High Technology (Cambridge University Press, 2016)

C. ARTICLES

AITMAN, D., and JONES A., 'Competition and Copyright: Has the Copyright Owner Lost Control?' [2003] *EIPR* 137

ANDERMAN, S. D., 'EC Competition Law and Intellectual Property Rights in the New Economy' (2002) 47 *Ant Bull* 285

BOKHARI, F. A. S., 'What is the Price of Pay-To-Delay Deals?' (2013) 9 *J of Competition Law and Economics* 739

CHOI, W., DEN UYL. B., and M. HUGHES, M., 'Pay-For-Delay Practices in the Pharmaceutical Sector: *Lundbeck, Actavis,* and Others' (2014) 5 *JECLAP* 44

DE MARGERIE, S., '"Pay-for-Delay" Settlements: In Search of the Right Standard' (2013) 36 *World Competition* 85

ESPOSITO, F., and MONTANARO, F., 'A *Fistful of Euros*: EU Competition Policy and Reverse Payments in the Pharmaceutical Industry' (2014) 10 *European Competition Journal* 499

IBÁÑEZ COLOMO, P., 'Article 101 TFEU and Market Integration' (2016) 12 *J of Competition Law and Economics* forthcoming

PEEPERKORN, L., 'IP Licences and Competition Rules: Striking the Right Balance' (2003) 26 *World Competition* 527

VENIT, J., 'In the Wake of *Windsurfing*: Patent Licensing in the Common Market' [1986] *Fordham Corp L Inst* 517

13

PUBLIC ENFORCEMENT BY THE COMMISSION AND THE NATIONAL COMPETITION AUTHORITIES OF THE ANTITRUST PROVISIONS

1. CENTRAL ISSUES

1. The EU's primary method for enforcing the competition rules is by a public enforcement system.

2. The system for enforcing Articles 101 and 102 was fundamentally changed on 1 May 2004 when Regulation 1/2003 replaced Regulation 17 of 1962. Regulation 1/2003 rendered Article 101(3) directly applicable and 'decentralised' the enforcement of the antitrust provisions so that the Commission and the national competition authorities (NCAs) have parallel competence to apply the rules. The European Competition Network (ECN) is the network of NCAs and the Commission working in close cooperation with one another.

3. The Commission's own powers of enforcement are set out in Regulation 1/2003. The Commission combines investigative, prosecutorial, and adjudicative functions in one body.

4. In investigating suspected breaches of the competition rules the Commission may require information and may carry out, inter alia, unannounced inspections at the premises of undertakings, and at private homes.

5. There are questions about the compatibility of some aspects of the Commission's procedures with fundamental rights as provided for in the European Convention on Human Rights (ECHR) and the EU Charter.

6. The Commission may take a number of decisions, including decisions ordering terminations of infringements, imposing fines, or accepting commitments. It can impose behavioural or structural remedies. Commitments decisions were introduced by Regulation 1/2003 and are an increasingly important instrument in the hands of the Commission.

7. The Commission pursues an aggressive policy towards the detection and punishment of cartels. It operates a 'leniency policy' whereby participants in cartels are given immunity or a reduced penalty in exchange for providing the Commission with information. The Commission imposes heavy fines on undertakings found to have committed serious breaches of the competition rules. It has a direct settlement procedure to enable it to dispose more quickly of cartel cases where the undertakings admit liability.

8. Commission decisions in competition cases are subject to judicial review by the EU Court. The extent of the compatibility of the judicial review with the ECHR and the EU Charter is a matter of controversy.

9. Decentralisation and the parallel enforcement competence of the NCAs mean that there are complex procedures and arrangements within the ECN for matters such as allocating cases and sharing information.

10. Complaints about breaches of the competition rules play an important role. The Commission has no duty to pursue complaints but is obliged to make a formal rejection of them—and this can be challenged before the EU Courts.

2. INTRODUCTION

The primary method of enforcement of the EU antitrust rules is public enforcement by the Commission and the competition authorities of the Member States (NCAs). A fundamental change in the enforcement system was made in 2004. The powers to enable the Commission to carry out its task of enforcing the competition rules are now contained in Council Regulation 1/2003,[1] which also confers enforcement powers on the NCAs.

In Section 3 of this chapter we explain the change in the enforcement regime which took place on 1 May 2004. In Section 4 we describe the system under Regulation 17 which applied before then and the reasons for, and salient features of, the 'modernisation' in Regulation 1/2003. In Sections 5, 6, and 7 the powers of the Commission are examined. In Section 8 we look at the role of the EU Courts. In Sections 9 and 10 we deal with enforcement by NCAs and the relationship between EU and national law. In Section 11 we consider the possibility of sanctions against individuals, and in Section 12 the position of those who make complaints about alleged infringements of the competition rules. Some conclusions are set out in Section 13.[2]

3. THE CHANGE TO THE ENFORCEMENT REGIME IN MAY 2004

Regulation 1/2003[3] is the linchpin of the 'modernised' enforcement regime. We have already seen that the modernisation of EU competition law has included a so-called 'more economic' approach to the substantive law[4] and a revised Merger Regulation (EUMR).[5] Regulation 1/2003 introduced fundamental changes to the way in which Articles 101 and 102 are enforced.

The previous implementing legislation, Regulation 17,[6] conferred the central role in the application and enforcement of EC competition law upon the Commission and the role of the NCAs and national courts was peripheral. Regulation 1/2003 'decentralised' application and enforcement and gave the NCAs a greater role. Furthermore, the reforms were designed to encourage more 'private' enforcement of competition law through litigation in the national courts of the Member States. 'Decentralisation' therefore means decentralisation to the national courts as well as to the NCAs. Private enforcement through civil litigation in the national courts is discussed in Chapter 14.

The post-modernisation enforcement of Articles 101 and 102 by the Commission has in practice become heavily reliant on negotiated procedures. This was not an (express) aim of the modernisation, but Regulation 1/2003 contains a procedure for 'commitments decisions'[7] of which the Commission makes great use in non-cartel cases. In respect of cartels the Commission introduced a

---

[1] [2003] OJ L1/1.

[2] For a detailed account of enforcement procedure, and practical considerations, reference should be had to practitioners' books. See, e.g., C. Kerse and N. Khan (Khan ed.), *EU Antitrust Procedure* (6th edn, Sweet & Maxwell, 2012); L. Ortiz Blanco, *EU Competition Procedure* (3rd edn, Oxford University Press, 2013); Bellamy and Child (V. Rose and D. Bailey, eds.), *European Union Law of Competition* (7th edn, Oxford University Press, 2013), Chaps. 13–16; J. Faull and A. Nikpay (eds.), *The EU Law of Competition* (3rd edn, Oxford University Press, 2014), Chap. 2 and Chap. 8, 8.95–8.444 (given that Faull and Nikpay is written by past and present Commission and NCA officials, its treatment of procedure is particularly valuable).

[3] [2003] OJ L1/1.

[4] See in particular Chaps. 4, 10, 11, and 12 in respect of Art. 101, and Chaps. 5–7 in respect of Art. 102.

[5] Reg. 139/2004 [2004] OJ L24/1, see Chap. 15.

[6] [1959–1962] OJ Spec. Ed. 87.

[7] Reg. 1/2003, Art. 9, see Section 7.E.iii, p. 945.

'settlement procedure' in 2008.[8] These developments changed Commission enforcement more radically than might have been anticipated in 2004.

Many Articles of Regulation 1/2003 are identical in effect (if not exact wording) to the Articles in Regulation 17. In respect of these the previous case law applies to the new provisions as to the old. In 40 years of pronouncing on the Commission's powers under Regulation 17 the EU Courts laid down and developed many important principles governing the exercise of the Commission's powers which also apply in the modernised system.

In extracts in this chapter containing references to Articles in Regulation 17 the original numbers have been left intact and the corresponding Articles in Regulation 1/2003 indicated where necessary.

4. MODERNISATION AND REGULATION 1/2003

A. THE OLD ENFORCEMENT REGIME SET UP BY REGULATION 17

Regulation 17[9] set up a system whereby an agreement falling within Article 101(1) could only escape via Article 101(3) if it was 'exempted'. The granting of an exemption was a 'constitutive act'. There were two ways of obtaining exemption. First, the parties could bring their agreement within a 'block exemption' regulation. It is still possible to do this.[10] Secondly, the parties could obtain an individual exemption from the Commission. Article 9(1) of Regulation 17 conferred 'sole power' on the Commission 'to declare Article [101(1)] inapplicable pursuant to Article [101(3)]'. From this simple monopoly enormous consequences flowed.[11] Parties to an agreement seeking an exemption had to notify it to the Commission and until they did so, no decision pursuant to Article 101(3) could be taken. Only notification gave the possibility of exemption.[12] Agreements could also be notified for 'negative clearance', i.e. a decision finding that an agreement did not infringe Article 101(1) at all.[13] Notification conferred immunity from fines.[14]

Notification required compliance with the requisite procedure.[15] Notification had to be made in the prescribed format.[16] Following notification there were no time limits within which the Commission had to give a decision.[17]

---

[8] Commission Notice on the conduct of settlement procedures [2008] OJ C167/1, see Section 7.F.

[9] [1959–1962] OJ Spec. Ed. 87.

[10] Block exemptions are an important part of the current system and are examined in various chapters of this book. For block exemptions generally, see Chap. 4.

[11] For an account of the workings of the Reg. 17 system, see J. Goyder and A. Albors-Llorens, *Goyder's EC Competition Law* (5th edn, Oxford University Press, 2009), Chaps. 4 and 5.

[12] Reg, 17, Art. 4(1). Certain 'non-notifiable' agreements, defined in Reg. 17, Art. 4(2), as amended could be exempted retrospectively to the date that the agreement was concluded irrespective of whether they had or had not been notified.

[13] Reg. 17, Art. 2. Negative clearance could also be sought in respect of Art. 102.

[14] Reg. 17, Art. 15(5). Immunity could be lifted under Reg. 17, Art. 15(6) following a preliminary examination.

[15] Antitrust Procedure (Applications and Notifications) Reg. 3385/94 [1994] OJ L377/28, replacing Reg. 27/62 [1959–1962] OJ Spec. Ed. 132 as amended; Reg. 2843/98 [1998] OJ L354/22 adopted a single form for notification of agreements within the transport sector.

[16] Form A/B, set out in Reg. 3385/94, which required extensive information. Some block exemptions contained an 'opposition procedure' whereby agreements not falling precisely within the terms of the block exemption could be notified to the Commission and allowed to benefit from the block exemption unless 'opposed' by the Commission within a specified time limit.

[17] Except that in 1993 a 'fast-track' was introduced for the treatment of structural joint ventures: Reg. 3385/94, Form A/B, Introduction, Section D.

Decisions granting individual exemption could be issued only for a specified period and could be made subject to conditions and obligations.[18] The decisions had to specify the date from which they ran and generally this could be no earlier than the date of notification.[19] A non-notified agreement which infringed Article 101(1) was therefore void pursuant to Article 101(2) even if, had it been notified, it would have merited exemption pursuant to Article 101(3).[20] Such an agreement was not, therefore, enforceable in a national court in respect of the period between the agreement coming into force and its notification. This was one reason for the large number of notifications the Commission received. In practice the Commission could not issue decisions granting exemption or negative clearance to all notified agreements. It granted a formal decision to a very small percentage of the notifications that it received.[21] The remainder were dealt with informally by administrative letter, a 'comfort letter'. This enabled the Commission to deal with notifications whilst giving priority to cases which raised greater concern from the Community perspective. The system was far from satisfactory however.[22]

The use of comfort letters rather than formal decisions meant that for many years prior to 1 May 2004 the notification-and-exemption procedure did not operate in practice as had been intended by Regulation 17.

B. THE MODERNISATION WHITE PAPER

In 1999 the Commission adopted a White Paper on modernisation of the rules implementing Articles 101 and 102.[23] The Commission wished to promote greater decentralisation of enforcement through the national courts and NCAs[24] but its exclusive right to grant individual exemptions under Article 101(3) made it difficult for national courts and NCAs to participate fully in the enforcement process.[25] Moreover, the widespread perception that the Commission alone enforced the competition rules meant that undertakings preferred to complain to the Commission rather than bring private proceedings before the national courts. The net result was that the Commission's limited resources were spent dealing with exemptions for essentially innocuous agreements leaving less available for the detection and prohibition of more serious violations of the rules. Moreover, the problem was about to worsen in view of the imminent further expansion of the EU.[26]

The Commission had consistently resisted the idea of reforming the system by conferring power on the NCAs to grant individual exemptions. The White Paper proposed a far more radical and fundamental change, namely complete abolition of the notification-and-exemption system. Article 101(3) should become a 'directly applicable exception'. The decision on whether or not an agreement fulfilled the criteria in Article 101(3) would no longer be taken by the Commission after notification. Rather, the decision would be made by a national court if the matter were relevant to litigation before it, or by an NCA or the Commission itself if the matter became of

---

[18] Reg. 17, Art. 8(1). Parties could apply for them to be renewed, and in certain circumstances they could be revoked or amended (Reg. 17, Art. 8(2), (3)).

[19] Reg. 17, Art. 6(1). There was an exception in respect of 'non-notifiable' agreements under Art. 4(2): see n. 12.

[20] Reg. 17, Art. 6(1), Art. 4(2).

[21] According to the White Paper on modernisation of the rules implementing Arts. 85 and 86 [1999] OJ C132/1 (the Modernisation White Paper), para. 34, 91% of cases (150–200 letters per year) were settled informally.

[22] For example, although assuring the parties that the Commission would not pursue the matter further, the letter was not a decision which could be applied by the national courts and consequently did not give the parties the same degree of legal certainty as a decision.

[23] Modernisation White Paper, n. 21.

[24] Private enforcement of EU competition law is discussed in Chap. 14.

[25] At the time of the Modernisation White Paper only half of the NCAs had power under their domestic law to enforce the EC competition rules.

[26] Ten new Member States acceded on 1 May 2004 and two more (Bulgaria and Romania) in January 2007.

concern. In other words, *ex ante* control would be replaced by *ex post* control.[27] Undertakings would, therefore, be deprived of the comfort of being able to notify and receive assurance of the compatibility of their agreement with Article 101. Instead they would be left to judge for themselves the legitimacy of their arrangements.[28] The White Paper called for 'intensified *ex post* control' in which the Commission's powers of inquiry would be strengthened and it would be easier to lodge complaints.[29]

The White Paper recognised the critical importance of ensuring that the consistent and uniform application of the competition rules was maintained and not jeopardised. The great advantage of the system set up by Regulation 17 was that it had left the application and enforcement of the competition rules in the hands of one body (subject only to review by the Court) which, by maintaining its iron grip, had directed the development of competition policy and ensured that the law was applied uniformly across the Community. The limited private litigation in national courts at least meant that this uniformity was not significantly compromised. The Commission was determined that its proposal for decentralisation should not be accompanied by divergent application among the various Member States. The White Paper thus proposed mechanisms and procedures to ensure continuing coherence and consistency.[30]

The Commission recognised that the abolition of the notification and authorisation system would entail greater responsibility on undertakings in ensuring that they complied with the competition rules. The Commission's official view was that 'undertakings are generally well placed to assess the legality of their actions in such a way as to enable them to take an informed decision on whether to go ahead with an agreement or practice and in what form'.[31]

The changes made in 2004 shifted the focus of the Commission's enforcement. The Commission now expends more of its resources on cartels and abuses of dominance rather than on vertical agreements (unless they involve price-fixing and market-sharing) and horizontal cooperation agreements.

C. REGULATION 1/2003 AND THE MODERNISATION 'PACKAGE'

(i) Regulation 1/2003, the Implementing Regulation, and the Modernisation Notices

After an extensive consultation exercise the Commission's proposal to abolish notification, render Article 101(3) a directly applicable exception, and decentralise the application and enforcement of the competition rules was accepted. The Council adopted Regulation 1/2003 on 16 December 2002[32] and it replaced Regulation 17 on 1 May 2004. Its adoption was accompanied by a number of Notices which flesh out the bare bones of the Regulation. A major concern was to establish mechanisms and procedures for the cooperation between the Commission and the

---

[27] In fact *ex post* control was already exercised in respect of cartel-type arrangements where the parties knew they were infringing the competition rules. They were most unlikely to notify and would be striving to keep their agreements secret.

[28] Unless the transaction was a partial-function production joint venture; see Modernisation White Paper, para. 79. This suggestion was ultimately abandoned.

[29] Ibid., para. 108.

[30] Coherence and consistency are not necessarily the same thing, see C. Townley 'Which Goals Count in Article 101 TFEU?: Public Policy and its Discontents' [2011] *ECLR* 441, 446.

[31] Commission Notice on informal guidance relating to novel questions concerning Articles 81 and 82 that arise in individual cases (Informal Guidance Notice) [2004] OJ C101/78, para. 3.

[32] [2003] OJ L1/1.

NCAs, without which the new decentralisation could not work. The creation of the European Competition Network (ECN) has been of great importance in this respect. The 'modernisation package' consisted of the following:

(a) Council Regulation 1/2003;

(b) Commission Regulation 773/2004 on the conduct of proceedings by the Commission pursuant to Articles 81 and 82 (the Implementing Regulation);[33]

(c) Commission Notice on cooperation within the network of competition authorities (the NCA Cooperation Notice);[34]

(d) Commission Notice on cooperation between the Commission and the courts of the EU Member States in the application of Articles 81 and 82 (the Cooperation Notice);[35]

(e) Commission Notice on the handling of complaints;[36]

(f) Commission Notice on informal guidance relating to novel questions concerning Articles 81 and 82 that arise in individual cases (Informational Guidance Notice);[37]

(g) Guidelines on the effect on trade concept contained in Articles 81 and 82;[38]

(h) Guidelines on the application of Article 81(3).[39]

(ii) Informal Guidance

Regulation 1/2003 abolished the notification and exemption procedure but recital 38 states:

Legal certainty for undertakings operating under the Community competition rules contributes to the promotion of innovation and investment. Where cases give rise to genuine uncertainty because they present novel or unresolved questions for the application of these rules, individual undertakings may wish to seek informal guidance from the Commission. This Regulation is without prejudice to the ability of the Commission to issue such informal guidance.

The Commission's Notice[40] sets out the circumstances in which it may be appropriate to issue informal guidance. It states that the new enforcement system 'is designed to restore the focus on the primary task of effective enforcement' by rendering Article 101(3) directly applicable and doing away with notification[41] and that undertakings are best placed to assess the legality of their actions, given the block exemptions, notices, case law, and case practice which are available to assist them.[42] Nevertheless, the Commission recognises that in some situations this may not be adequate. It will therefore provide informal guidance to individual undertakings 'in so far as this is compatible with its enforcement priorities'.[43]

---

[33] [2004] OJ L123/18, amended by Reg. 2015/1348 [2015] OJ L208/3.

[34] [2004] OJ C101/43.

[35] [2004] OJ C101/54, amended by [2015] OJ C256/4.

[36] [2004] OJ C101/65.

[37] [2004] OJ C101/78.

[38] [2004] OJ C101/101.

[39] [2004] OJ C101/96.

[40] Informal Guidance Notice.

[41] Ibid., para. 1.

[42] Ibid., paras. 3 and 4.

[43] Ibid., para. 7.

Commission Notice on Informal Guidance Relating to Novel Questions Concerning Articles 81 and 82 that Arise in Individual Cases (Informal Guidance Notice) [2004] OJ C101/78

5. Where cases, despite the above elements, give rise to genuine uncertainty because they present novel or unresolved questions for the application of Articles [101 and 102], individual undertakings may wish to seek informal guidance from the Commission . . . Where it considers it appropriate and subject to its enforcement priorities, the Commission may provide such guidance on novel questions concerning the interpretation of Articles [101 and/or 102] in a written statement (guidance letter). The present Notice sets out details of this instrument.

. . .

8. Subject to point 7, [the enforcement priorities of the Commission] the Commission, seized of a request for a guidance letter, will consider whether it is appropriate to process it. Issuing a guidance letter may only be considered if the following cumulative conditions are fulfilled:

(a) The substantive assessment of an agreement or practice with regard to Articles [101 and/or 102], poses a question of application of the law for which there is no clarification in the existing [EU] legal framework including the case law of the [Union judicature], nor publicly available general guidance or precedent in decision-making practice or previous guidance letters.

(b) A prima facie evaluation of the specificities and background of the case suggests that the clarification of the novel question through a guidance letter is useful, taking into account the following elements:

— the economic importance from the point of view of the consumer of the goods or services concerned by the agreement or practice, and/or

— the extent to which the agreement or practice corresponds or is liable to correspond to more widely spread economic usage in the marketplace and/or

— the extent of the investments linked to the transaction in relation to the size of the companies concerned and the extent to which the transaction relates to a structural operation such as the creation of a non-full function joint venture.

(c) It is possible to issue a guidance letter on the basis of the information provided, i.e., no further fact-finding is required.

The condition in paragraph 8(a) emphasises that guidance will be given only in respect of 'novel' questions. The Commission is the judge of the novelty, which must be in respect of hitherto unclarified law. In respect of the second condition, the 'usefulness' of the guidance, the first two indents in 8(b) show that an element of 'public interest' is relevant. The third indent specifically indicates that guidance letters may be forthcoming in certain cases involving non-full-function joint ventures.[44] The Commission will not issue a guidance letter if it would entail further fact-finding. It is entirely up to parties to provide the necessary information.[45]

Guidance letters will not be issued if the questions (identical or similar) are raised in a case pending before the EU Courts, or the agreement or practice in issue is subject to proceedings before the Commission, an NCA, or a national court in a Member State.[46] They will not be issued in respect of hypothetical questions or agreements or practices that are no longer being implemented. They will,

---

[44] In respect of which the abolition of notification was recognised in the White Paper as being particularly serious.

[45] Informal Guidance Notice, para. 8(c). There is no form or format on or in which the information must be provided, but para. 14 lists the matters which the memorandum accompanying a request for a guidance letter should contain.

[46] Ibid., para. 9.

however, be considered in respect of an agreement or practice which is envisaged but not yet imple-mented, so long as it has reached a sufficiently advanced stage.[47] Guidance letters do not prevent the Commission opening proceedings under Regulation 1/2003 with regard to the same facts (although it will take the letter into account),[48] do not prejudge any assessment by the EU Courts,[49] and do not bind the NCAs or national courts, although NCAs and national courts are entitled to take the Commission's views in the guidance letters into account 'in the context of a case'.[50] The letters are to be posted on the Commission's website.[51]

As at 5 February 2016 no guidance letters had been issued. The Staff Working Paper[52] in April 2009 said that the Commission had thitherto issued no letters because very few approaches had been made to it and, of those that had, none came near to fulfilling the conditions set out in the Notice.[53] Nevertheless the Commission 'remains firmly committed' to giving guidance on new or unresolved policy issues of general application which *do* fulfil the conditions.[54]

(iii) Regulation 1/2003

Broadly, Regulation 1/2003 deals with two matters. First, it renders Article 101(3) directly applicable and lays down the basic framework for the Commission, the NCAs, and the national courts to co-operate in the decentralised system. It effects the shift from *ex ante* to *ex post* control. Secondly, it pro-vides for the powers and procedures of the Commission in the investigation of competition matters.

Five years from the application of the Regulation the Commission had to report on its function-ing to the Council and the European Parliament and assess whether to propose any revisions.[55] The Commission's Report[56] concluded that overall Regulation 1/2003 was working well. There were a few matters which the Commission highlighted as meriting further evaluation but it left open the question as to whether any amendments were required.[57] The Commission adopted a further Communication in 2014, 'Ten Years of Antitrust Enforcement under Regulation 1/2003: Achievements and Future Perspectives'.[58] This concluded that the considerable achievements of the last ten years should be built on by strengthening the NCAs.[59]

(iv) Commission Regulation 773/2004

Regulation 773/2004[60] deals with the conduct of Commission proceedings in its application of the competition rules. It covers in more detail some of the matters provided for in Regulation 1/2003

---

[47] Ibid., para. 10.

[48] Ibid., paras. 11 and 24.

[49] Ibid., para. 23.

[50] Ibid., para. 24.

[51] Ibid., para. 21.

[52] Commission Staff Working Paper on the functioning of Regulation 1/2003, SEC (2009) 574 final.

[53] Informal Guidance Notice, para. 45.

[54] Commission Staff Working Paper, n. 52, para. 48.

[55] Reg. 1/2003, Art. 44.

[56] Communication from the Commission to the European Parliament and the Council, Report on the Functioning of Regulation 1/2003, COM(2009) 206 final; Press Release IP/09/683. It was accompanied by a Commission Staff Working Paper, SEC(2009) 574 final. They are available on the Commission website, <http://ec.europa.eu/competition/antitrust/legislation/regulations.html>.

[57] Report, para. 43. The views of the Commission on specific matters in Reg. 1/2003 are dealt with in this chapter in the appropriate sections.

[58] COM(2014) 453, accompanied by a Commission Staff Working Document, SWD (2014) 230 and SWD (2014) 231.

[59] See further Section 9.

[60] [2004] OJ L123/18, as amended by Commission Reg. 622/2008 [2008] OJ L171/3 on the conduct of settlement procedures in cartel cases, and by Reg. 2015/134 [2015] OJ L208/3.

(such as power to take statements, the handling of complaints, the exercise of the right to be heard,[61] and the right of 'access to the file').

(v) The Modernisation Notices

The Commission's Modernisation Notices are discussed and referred to throughout this book. The NCA Cooperation Notice,[62] the Notice on cooperation between the Commission and the courts of the EU Member States,[63] and the Commission Notice on the handling of complaints[64] are of particular relevance to this chapter and Chapter 14.

5. THE EUROPEAN COMPETITION NETWORK

The European Competition Network (ECN) is the network of NCAs and the Commission who under Regulation 1/2003 share competence to apply and enforce Articles 101 and 102. The close cooperation of the authorities is crucial to the effective operation of the decentralised system. This is dealt with further in Section 9.

6. THE BEST PRACTICES NOTICE AND THE MANUAL OF PROCEDURES

The Commission has published a Notice on 'Best Practices for the Conduct of Proceedings' (Best Practices) to give practical guidance on the Commission's procedure in respect of the enforcement of Articles 101 and 102.[65] The Notice seeks to 'increase understanding of the Commission's investigation process . . . and thereby enhance the efficiency of investigations and ensure a high degree of transparency and predictability in the process'.[66] The Commission has also issued a Staff Working Paper on 'Best Practices for the Submission of Economic Evidence'.[67]

In addition, the Commission has published its internal manual on procedures (the 'Antitrust ManProc').[68]

---

[61] Reg. 773/2004 replaced Reg. 2842/98 [1998] OJ L354/18.

[62] [2004] OJ C101/43.

[63] [2004] OJ C101/54.

[64] [2004] OJ C101/65.

[65] [2011] OJ C308/6.

[66] The Notice applies only to cases that were ongoing at the date of its publication, and to future ones: Best Practices, para. 6 and Case T-299/08, *Elf Aquitaine SA v Commission (Sodium chlorate)* [2011] ECR II-2149, para. 148.

[67] <http://ec.europa.eu/competition/antitrust/legislation/best_practices_submission_en.pdf>. It covers Arts. 101 and 102, and mergers.

[68] Available since 2012 on the DG Comp website, <http://ec.europa.eu/competition/antitrust/antitrust_manproc_3_2012_en.pdf>. Publication followed a complaint to the European Ombudsman about its previous non-disclosure, invoking the Transparency Regulation, Reg. 1049/2001 (see Section 7.D.v.d, p. 940): Complaint 297/2010/(ELB)GG, decision 26 September 2011. The Commission stresses that the ManProc only constitutes internal guidance to staff and does not in any way create or alter any rights or obligations under the competition rules. For a critique of the usefulness of publication of the ManProc, see J. Temple Lang, 'The Strengths and Weaknesses of the DG Competition Manual of Procedure' (2013) 1 *J of Antitrust Enforcement* 132.

7. ENFORCEMENT BY THE COMMISSION

A. GENERAL

(i) The Broad Powers of the Commission

In *Dansk Rørindustri* the CJ said:[69]

The supervisory task conferred on the Commission by Articles [101(1)] and [102] . . . not only includes the duty to investigate and punish individual infringements but also encompasses the duty to pursue a general policy designed to apply, in competition matters, the principles laid down by the Treaty and to guide the conduct of undertakings in the light of those principles.

The Commission may commence an investigation into alleged infringements of the competition rules on its own initiative or acting on a complaint.[70] In competition cases the Commission plays the parts of law-maker, policeman, investigator, prosecutor, judge, and jury, subject only to review by the EU Courts. This situation, which has been widely criticised but fiercely defended by the Commission,[71] was not changed by modernisation. The accumulation of functions in the Commission and the limited role of the EU Courts raise human rights issues but the EU Courts have approved the current situation.[72] The Commission has a margin of discretion to set priorities in enforcing the competition rules.[73] It has certain obligations when dealing with complaints[74] but otherwise can choose against whom, and when, to bring proceedings.[75]

Although Regulation 1/2003 abolished the notification procedure, it is recognised that in some novel cases guidance as to the compatibility of an agreement or practice with the rules may be necessary, perhaps to provide legal certainty to the parties[76] and/or to aid the consistent application of the competition rules in the decentralised system.[77] Regulation 1/2003 thus allows the Commission to adopt decisions of 'inapplicability'[78] and, as already mentioned, envisages that 'guidance letters' may be issued.[79] As at 5 February 2016 neither of these procedures had ever been used.

---

[69] Cases C-189, 202, 208, and 213/02 P, *Dansk Rørindustri A/S and others v Commission* [2005] ECR I-5425, para. 170, referring to Cases 100–103/80, *Musique Diffusion Française SA v Commission (Pioneer)* [1983] ECR 1825, para. 105; see also Case T-99/04, *AC-Treuhand AG v Commission* [2008] ECR II-1501, para. 163.

[70] This is clear from Reg. 1/2003, Art. 7 which gives the Commission power to take decisions when it has found an infringement; see also Best Practices, paras. 9–11. Many investigations in cartel cases are triggered by a leniency application. Complaints and the position of complainants are dealt with in Section 12 of this chapter.

[71] See A. Pera and M. Todino, 'Enforcement of EC Competition Rules: Need for a Reform?' [1996] *Fordham Corp Law Inst* 125, 144; F. Montag, 'The Case for Radical Reform of the Infringement Procedure under Regulation' [1998] *ECLR* 428; W. Wils, 'The Combination of the Investigative and Prosecutorial Function and the Adjudicative Function in EC Antitrust Enforcement: A Legal and Economic Analysis' (2004) 27 *World Competition* 201; I. Forrester, 'Due Process in EC Competition Case: A Distinguished Institution with Flawed Procedures' (2009) 34 *ELRev* 817; D. Slater, S. Thomas, and D. Waelbroeck, 'Competition Law Proceedings before the European Commission and the Right to a Fair Trial: No Need for Reform?' (2009) 5 *European Competition Journal* 97.

[72] In Cases T-548/08 etc., *Total SA v Commission* EU:T:2013:434 (on appeal Case C-597/13 P, EU:C:2015:613, judgment partially set aside on other grounds) the GC stated that the fact that the Commission is investigator, prosecutor, and decision-maker does not infringe the EU Charter.

[73] Case T-24/90, *Automec Srl v Commission (Automec II)* [1992] ECR II-2223.

[74] See Section 12.

[75] In Case T-219/99, *British Airways v Commission* [2003] ECR II-5917, for example, the GC dismissed the airline's plea that the Commission had infringed the principle of non-discrimination by bringing an Art. 102 action only against British Airways but not other airlines.

[76] See Reg. 1/2003, recital 38.

[77] See ibid., recital 14 and Informal Guidance Notice, para. 2.

[78] Reg. 1/2003, Art. 10, see Section 7.E.iv, p. 954.

[79] Reg. 1/2003, recital 38 and Informal Guidance Notice [2004] OJ C101/78, see Section 4.C.ii, p. 889.

(ii) The Two Stages of the Commission's Administrative Procedure and the Initiation of Proceedings

There are two distinct stages to the Commission's administrative procedure.[80] The first is the preliminary investigation stage, covering the period up until the notification of the statement of objections (SO), which is a period of fact-finding intended 'to enable the Commission to gather all the relevant information confirming or not the existence of an infringement of the competition rules and to adopt an initial position on the course of the procedure and how it is to proceed'.[81] The second, 'inter partes' or 'adversarial' stage, covers the period from the notification of the SO to the adoption of the final decision. The move from one stage to the other entails the 'initiation of proceedings'. The initiation of proceedings by the Commission is a formal act[82] by which the Commission indicates its intention to adopt a decision under Regulation 1/2003.[83] Under Article 11(6) of Regulation 1/2003 the initiation of proceedings by the Commission relieves the NCAs of their competence to apply Articles 101 and 102 in the case. National courts are not relieved of their competence, but they may not take a decision running counter to one adopted by the Commission.[84] Moreover, they must also avoid giving decisions which would conflict with a decision contemplated by the Commission.[85]

Article 2 of Regulation 773/2004 provides that the Commission may publicise the initiation of proceedings, in any appropriate way,[86] having previously informed the parties. Article 2(1) states:

The Commission may decide to initiate proceedings with a view to adopting a decision pursuant to Chapter III of Regulation (EC) No 1/2003 at any point in time, but no later than the date on which it issues a preliminary assessment as referred to in Article 9(1) of that Regulation, a statement of objections or a request for the parties to express their interest in engaging in settlement discussions, or the date on which a notice pursuant to Article 27(4) of that Regulation is published, whichever is the earlier.[87]

It is not necessary for the Commission to initiate proceedings before rejecting a complaint.[88]

---

[80] Case T-99/04, *AC-Treuhand* [2008] ECR II-1501.

[81] Ibid., para. 47; see also Cases C-238, 244–245, 247, 250, 251–252, and 254/99 P, *Limburgse Vinyl Maatschappij NV v Commission* [2002] ECR I-8375, paras. 181–183; Case C-105/04 P, *Nederlandse Federatieve Vereniging voor de Groothandel op Elektrotechnisch Gebied v Commission* [2006] ECR I-8725, paras. 37–38.

[82] See Case 48/72, *SA Brasserie de Haecht v Wilkin-Janssen* [1973] ECR 77, para. 16: 'the initiation of a procedure . . . obviously concerns an authoritative act of the Commission, evidencing its intention to take a decision'.

[83] NCA Cooperation Notice [2004] OJ C101/54, para. 52.

[84] Reg. 1/2003, Art. 16(1).

[85] See Chap. 14.

[86] See N. Petit and M. Rato, 'From Hard to Soft Enforcement of EC Competition Law—A Bestiary of "Sunshine" Enforcement Instruments', available at <http://ssrn.com/abstract=1270109>. Best Practices, para. 24, says that in cartel cases the opening of proceedings and the SO are normally simultaneous. It is customary for the Commission to issue a Press Release. The Commission must be careful what it says. The Ombudsman found that maladministration had occurred by the Commissioner making a number of public statements assuming the undertaking's guilt (e.g. 'The evidence we have collected is quite telling, so I'm pretty sure this investigation will not be closed without results') before the investigation was complete and nearly two years before the SO was sent: Decision of the European Ombudsman in an Inquiry into Complaint 1021/2014/PD, 11 November 2015. The case concerned the EIRD cartel.

[87] The preliminary assessment in Reg. 1/2003, Art. 9(1) is the initial view of the Commission that an infringement has occurred, although it may accept from the undertakings commitments which meet its concerns and therefore decide to take no further action (see Section 7.E.iii, p. 945). A statement of objections (SO) is the serving on the undertakings concerned of a notice setting out the Commission's case against them (see Section 7.D.iii, p. 931). An interest in engaging in settlement discussions is a reference to the settlement procedure in cartel cases (see Section 7.F, p. 956; Art. 2(1) was amended in 2008 to take account of the introduction of that procedure). An Art. 27(4) notice is the publication of a summary of the case and other details which must take place where the Commission intends to adopt a decision pursuant to Art. 9 (decisions making commitments binding) or Art. 10 (finding of applicability decision).

[88] Reg. 773/2004, Art. 2(4).

Article 2(3) of Regulation 773/2004 expressly states that the Commission may exercise its powers of investigation before initiating proceedings. This is vital as until the Commission has carried out an investigation it may not be in a position to issue an SO.

B. FUNDAMENTAL HUMAN RIGHTS

(i) General

The general position of fundamental human rights in EU law is described in Chapter 2.[89] The relevance and application of fundamental rights principles in respect of the enforcement of EU competition law is dealt with in context throughout this chapter. In this section, however, we make some general points.

Recital 37 to Regulation 1/2003 states:

This Regulation respects the fundamental rights and observes the principles recognised in particular by the Charter of Fundamental Rights of the European Union. Accordingly, this Regulation should be interpreted and applied with respect to those rights and principles.

As explained in Chapter 2, Article 52 of the Charter provides that where it contains rights corresponding to those in the European Convention on Human Rights (ECHR) their meaning and scope shall be the same as the latter (as a minimum).

The EU Courts have frequently emphasised the importance of ensuring that Commission enforcement proceedings respect what are known as 'the rights of the defence' as a fundamental principle. For example, in *Archer Daniels Midland*:[90]

It should be recalled that in all proceedings in which sanctions, especially fines or penalty payments, may be imposed, observance of the rights of the defence is a fundamental principle of Community law which must be complied with even if the proceedings in question are administrative proceedings (see, in particular, Case C-328/05 P *SGL Carbon v Commission*...paragraph 70).

As well as the rights of the defence (the right to a fair trial—effective judicial protection—and the consequent procedural rights) the EU Courts have recognised a number of rights relevant to the enforcement of the competition rules. These include the presumption of innocence, legitimate expectation, legal certainty, equal treatment, non-discrimination, privacy, non-retroactivity, proportionality, sound administration, and the protection of confidential information. Many of these rights are now enshrined in the Charter. The EU Courts are placing increasing emphasis on the compatibility of competition procedure with the Charter and the ECHR.

(ii) The Relevant Articles of the ECHR and the Charter

a. Article 6 ECHR and Article 47 of the Charter—Right to a Fair Trial

The principle of effective judicial protection is a fundamental right and a general principle of EU law to which expression is now given by Article 47 of the Charter, which corresponds to Article 6 ECHR.[91]

Article 6 ECHR, which applies to both natural and legal persons[92] provides the right to a fair trial and due process. It states:

1. In the determination of his civil rights and obligations or of any criminal charge against him, everyone is entitled to a fair and public hearing within a reasonable time by an independent and impartial

---

[89] Chap. 2, Section 6. For the ECHR, see Harris, O'Boyle, and Warbrick (D. Harris, M. O'Boyle, E. Bates, and C. Buckley, eds.), *Law of the European Convention on Human Rights* (3rd edn, Oxford University Press, 2014).

[90] Case C-511/06 P, *Archer Daniels Midland v Commission* [2009] ECR I-5843, para. 84.

[91] Case C-501/11 P, *Schindler v European Commission (The Elevators and Escalators Cartel)* EU:C:2013:522, para. 36; Case C-583/13 P, *Deutsche Bahn AG v Commission* EU:C:2015:404, para. 47.

[92] See, e.g., *Niemitz v Germany*, App. no. 1370/88 (1992) 16 EHRR 97. For the reasons why fundamental human rights are extended to corporate bodies see, e.g., A. Andreangeli, *EU Competition Enforcement and Human Rights* (Edward Elgar, 2008), 17–18.

tribunal established by law. Judgment shall be pronounced publicly but the press and public may be excluded from all or part of the trial in the interest of morals, public order or national security in a democratic society, where the interests of juveniles or the protection of the private life of the parties so require, or the extent strictly necessary in the opinion of the court in special circumstances where publicity would prejudice the interests of justice.

2. Everyone charged with a criminal offence shall be presumed innocent until proved guilty according to law.

3. Everyone charged with a criminal offence has the following minimum rights:

   (a) to be informed promptly, in a language which he understands and in detail, of the nature and cause of the accusation against him;

   (b) to have adequate time and the facilities for the preparation of his defence;

   (c) to defend himself in person or through legal assistance of his own choosing or, if he has not sufficient means to pay for legal assistance, to be given it free when the interests of justice so require;

   (d) to examine or have examined witnesses against him and to obtain the attendance and examination of witnesses on his behalf under the same conditions as witnesses against him.

Effective judicial protection—the right to a fair trial—includes the right to give evidence in one's own defence, to hear the evidence against oneself, to have the ability to examine and cross-examine witnesses,[93] and other matters of due process such as the privilege against self-incrimination.[94]

Article 47 of the Charter states:

Everyone whose rights and freedoms guaranteed by the law of the Union are violated has the right to an effective remedy before a tribunal in compliance with the conditions laid down in this Article.

Everyone is entitled to a fair and public hearing within a reasonable time by a fair and impartial tribunal previously established by law. Everyone shall have the possibility of being advised, defended and represented.

Legal aid shall be made available to those who lack sufficient resources in so far as such aid is necessary to ensure effective access to justice.

The CJ has stated that Article 47 secures in EU law the protection afforded by Article 6 ECHR, and that the principle of effective judicial protection laid down in Article 47 comprises various elements—in particular the rights of the defence, the principle of equality of arms, the right of access to a tribunal, and the right to be advised, defended, and represented.[95]

The first sentence of Article 6(1), providing for a hearing before an independent and impartial tribunal, applies to civil as well as criminal proceedings. Article 6(2) and (3) provides further rights in criminal proceedings. Article 47 contains no similar reference to civil and criminal matters.[96]

In respect of the civil/criminal distinction in Article 6 the case law of the European Court of Human Rights (ECtHR) establishes that the notion of a 'criminal charge' is an autonomous concept which is a matter of Convention law. The ECtHR has laid down principles for identifying a criminal charge, known as the 'Engel criteria'.[97] They are:

- the classification of the offence under national law;[98]

---

[93] *Jussila v Finland*, App. no. 73053/01 (2007) 45 EHRR 39. The right to examine witnesses laid down in Art. 6(1)(3)(b) does not require the Commission to give undertakings the opportunity, during the administrative process, to examine or cross-examine witnesses heard by the Commission: Cases C-239, 489, and 498/11 P, *Siemens AG, Mitsubishi Electric Corp and Toshiba Corp v Commission* EU:C:2013:866.

[94] *Saunders v UK*, App. no. 19187/91 (1997) 23 EHRR 313.

[95] Case C-199/11, *Europese Gemeenschap v Otis NV* EU:C:2012:684.

[96] See A.-L. Sibony, 'Casenote on *KME v Commission*' (2012) 49 *CMLRev* 1977.

[97] *Engel v Netherlands*, App. nos. 5101/71 etc. (1976) 1 EHRR 647.

[98] The classification of the offence as *not* criminal is not decisive, whereas the classification of it as being criminal is decisive, see *Özturk v Germany*, App. no. 8544/79 (1984) 6 EHRR 409.

- the nature of the offence;[99] and

- the nature and severity of the potential penalty.[100]

The second and third *Engel* criteria are alternatives but a cumulative approach is taken when a conclusion cannot be drawn on one of them alone.[101]

'Criminal' does not imply any particular degree of seriousness but the case law distinguishes between the 'hardcore' of criminal law and more minor offences not strictly belonging to the traditional categories of criminal law, such as traffic offences and tax surcharges.[102] The criminal-head guarantees do not necessarily apply with their full stringency to these 'minor offences'.[103]

In respect of civil proceedings ECtHR case law establishes that the right to a hearing before an impartial and independent tribunal does not preclude some matters of an administrative or professional disciplinary nature from being decided by administrative organs at the initial stage so long as they are subject ultimately to judicial control.[104] Similarly, 'later' judicial control is also possible in the case of minor 'non-core' criminal offences.[105] However, both civil and minor criminal offences must be able to come at some point to a public hearing before an independent and impartial judicial body with full jurisdiction.[106] In respect of 'core' criminal offences the right to the hearing in Article 6(1) applies to first instance proceedings. An initial decision by an administrative body is not sufficient.

The issues arising in respect of the enforcement of EU competition law by the Commission are therefore: (a) whether the proceedings are civil or criminal; (b) if they are criminal are they 'core' or 'minor' offences; and (c) do the procedures for making decisions in competition cases comply with the relevant requirements of the ECHR pertaining to the type of proceedings concerned. There has been a long-standing debate on these matters, in particular whether EU competition procedure satisfies Article 6 and, if it does not, how the system could be reformed.[107] The Commission cannot be classified as a 'tribunal' for the purposes of Article 6[108] and administrative proceedings before

---

[99] Matters taken into account in judging the 'nature of the offence' include whether the legal norm is generally applicable (*Bendenoun v France*, App. no. 12547/86 (1994) 18 EHRR 54); whether the sanctions have a deterrent and/ or punitive character (*Bendenoun*, para. 47, *Özturk*, App. no. 8544/79 (1984) 6 EHRR 409); whether the proceedings are instituted by a public body with statutory powers of enforcement (*Benham v UK*, App. no. 19380/92 (1996) 22 EHRR 293); whether the penalty is dependent on a finding of guilt (*Benham*, para. 56); and how other Council of Europe States classify comparable offences (*Özturk*, para. 53).

[100] This takes into account the maximum penalty for the offence and the stigma attaching to it, see *Özturk*, App. no. 8544/79 (1984) 6 EHRR 409, para. 54.

[101] *Bendenoun*, App. no. 12547/86 (1994) 18 EHRR 54, para. 47.

[102] *Jussila*, App. no. 73053/01 (2007) 45 EHRR 39, para. 43.

[103] Ibid., para. 43.

[104] *Le Compte, Van Leuven, and De Meyere v Belgium*, App. no. 6878/75 (1983) 5 EHRR 183.

[105] *Bendenoun* App. no. 12547/86 (1994) 18 EHRR 54; *Jussila*, App. no. 73053/01 (2007) 45 EHRR 39, para. 43.

[106] *Le Compte*, App. no. 6878/75 (1983) 5 EHRR 183, para. 29.

[107] See, e.g., A. Andreangeli, 'Towards an EU Competition Court: "Article-6-Proofing" Antitrust Proceedings before the Commission?' (2007) 4 *World Competition* 595; I. Forrester, 'Due Process in EC Competition Case: A Distinguished Institution with Flawed Procedures' (2009) 34 *ELRev* 817; D. Slater, S. Thomas, and D. Waelbroeck, 'Competition Law Proceedings before the European Commission and the Right to a Fair Trial: No Need for Reform?' (2009) *European Competition Journal* 97 and GCLC Working Paper 04/08; F. Castillo de la Torre, 'Evidence, Proof and Judicial Review in Cartel Cases' in C.-D. Ehlermann and M. Marquis (eds.), *European Competition Law Annual 2009: Evaluation of Evidence and its Judicial Review in Competition Cases* (Hart Publishing, 2011), 319; I. Forrester, 'A Bush in Need of Pruning: The Luxuriant Growth of "Light Judicial Review"' in C.-D. Ehlermann and M. Marquis (cited earlier in this note), 407; W. Wils, 'The Increased Level of Antitrust Fines, Judicial Review, and the European Convention on Human Rights' (2010) 33 *World Competition* 5; Editorial, 'Towards a More Judicial Approach? EU Antitrust Fines Under the Scrutiny of Fundamental Rights' (2011) 48 *CMLRev* 1405; W. Wils, 'EU Antitrust Enforcement Powers and Procedural Rights and Guarantees: The Interplay between EU Law, National Law, the Charter of Fundamental Rights of the EU and the European Convention of Human Rights' (2011) 2 *World Competition* 189; R. Nazzini, 'Administrative Enforcement, Judicial Review and Fundamental Rights in EU Competition Law: A Comparative Contextual-Functionalist Perspective' (2012) 49 *CMLRev* 971.

[108] The CJ has held that, see Cases 209–215 and 218/78, *Van Landewyck v Commission* [1980] ECR 3125, para. 81.

it cannot qualify as a public hearing before an 'independent and impartial tribunal'. The question, therefore, is whether the extent of the judicial review provided by the TFEU satisfies the requirements of Article 6(1) ECHR.[109]

Article 23(5)[110] of Regulation 1/2003 expressly states that decisions imposing fines (for either substantive or procedural offences) 'shall not be of a criminal law nature'. However, it is clear from the *Engel* criteria that such a statement cannot be conclusive of the matter for the purposes of the ECHR.[111] Moreover, even if the *fine* is not 'criminal' that does not mean that the *proceedings* concerned are not criminal.[112] In the EU it had already been generally accepted that the Commission's fining procedures were 'criminal' within Article 6 ECHR[113] and in *Menarini*[114] in 2011 the ECtHR held, in the context of a challenge to a sanction imposed by the Italian competition authority, that Italian competition law fines are of a criminal nature for the purposes of Article 6.[115] The ECtHR also held that decisions imposing fines could be taken by administrative, non-judicial competition authorities provided that the decisions were subject to full judicial review on matters of law and fact by independent courts with full jurisdiction. The Italian system at issue in the case was held to satisfy these criteria.[116] In *Schindler*[117] the CJ cited *Menarini* and, following the approach of the ECtHR as well as its own previous decision in *Chalkor*,[118] held that that the imposition of fines by the Commission rather than by a court was compatible with Article 6 ECHR and with Article 47 of the Charter as the power of review by the Court under Article 263 TFEU, and its unlimited jurisdiction to review fines under Article 261 TFEU and Article 31 of Regulation 1/2003 were sufficient to fulfil the requirements of the principle of effective judicial protection.[119]

The CJ has also held that it is not incompatible with Article 47 for the Commission to sue for damages in a national court in respect of an infringement of competition law which has been established

---

[109] See further Section 8.A.vii, p. 1000 and, e.g., Slater et al., n. 107; Wils, 'The Increased Level of Antitrust Fines, Judicial Review, and the European Convention on Human Rights', n. 107; Forrester, n. 107; Andreangeli, n. 107.

[110] Formerly Reg. 17, Art. 15(4).

[111] The fines imposed by the Commission for substantive offences can be up to 10% of the undertaking's turnover in the previous year (Reg. 1/2003, Art. 23(2)), can run into billions of euros, and serve as both sanction and deterrent. Fines for procedural offences (Reg. 1/2003, Art. 23(1)) and periodic penalty payments for non-compliance (Reg. 1/2003, Art. 24) can also be very heavy. Infringements of the competition rules, especially hardcore cartels, are excoriated in Commission press releases and speeches. All these factors are relevant to the second and third *Engel* criteria.

[112] Slater et al., n. 107.

[113] Either expressly or impliedly. See Judge Vesterdorf, acting as AG in Cases T-1–4 and 6–15/89, *Rhône-Poulenc and others v Commission* [1991] ECR II-867, 885; Léger AG in Case C-185/95 P, *Baustahlgewebe v Commission* [1998] ECR I-8417, para. 31 of the Opinion; Cases C-189/02 P etc., *Dansk Rørindustri* [2005] ECR I-5425, para. 202; Sharpston AG in Case C-272/09 P, *KME Germany AG v Commission* [2011] ECR I-12789, para. 64 of the Opinion. In Case C-199/92 P, *Hüls v Commission* [1999] ECR I-4287, para. 150 the CJ accepted that the presumption of innocence in Art. 6(2) applies to Commission proceedings that may result in fines.

[114] *Menarini Diagnostics SRL v Italy*, App No. 43509/08, judgment 27 September 2011, and see also *Société Bouygues Telecom v France*, App. no. 2324/08.

[115] In *Société Stenuit v France*, App. no. 11598/85 (1992) 14 EHRR 509 the European Commission on Human Rights had held in its Opinion that a fine imposed on undertakings by the French competition authorities was criminal in nature. *Stenuit* did not proceed to a judgment by the ECtHR as the applicant and the French authorities settled the matter, but the ECtHR referred approvingly to this finding in *Jussila v Finland*, App. no. 73053/01 (2007) 45 EHRR 39.

[116] Although there was a powerful dissenting opinion by Judge Pinto de Albuquerque. For comments on *Menarini*, see P. Oliver, 'Diagnostics—A Judgment Applying the European Convention of Human Rights to the Field of Competition' (2012) 3 *JECLAP* 163.

[117] Case C-501/11 P, *Schindler* EU:C:2013:522; repeated in Case C-295/12 P, *Telefónica SA v Commission* EU:C:2014:2062, paras. 51–57.

[118] Case C-386/10 P, *Chalkor AE Epexergasias Metallon v Commission* [2011] ECR I-13085; see also Case C-272/09 P, *KME* [2011] ECR I-12789.

[119] Case C-501/11 P, *Schindler* EU:C:2013:522, paras. 32–38. The nature and intensity of judicial review of Commission decisions and the application to it of Art. 6(1) ECHR and Art. 47 of the Charter are discussed further in Section 8.A.vii.

by its own infringement decision.[120] Again, the defendant's rights were held to be protected by the functions of the Court under Article 263 and Article 261, and also by it being the role of the national court in a damages action to assess causation and loss.[121] Consequently the Commission could not be regarded as judge and party in its own cause in breach of the *nemo iudex in sua causa* principle.[122]

The CJ has held that it is Article 41 of the Charter, rather than Article 47, which applies to the conduct of proceedings before the Commission.[123] Article 41 provides the right to good administration.

The issue of the compatibility with Article 6 of the EU position on self-incrimination is dealt with later in this chapter.[124]

b. Article 6 ECHR and Article 48 of the Charter—The Presumption of Innocence

The presumption of innocence in Article 6(2) ECHR appears in Article 48(1) of the Charter rather than in Article 47, and the rights of defence in Article 6(3) are guaranteed by Article 48(2). Article 48 states:

1. Everyone who has been charged shall be presumed innocent until proved guilty according to law.

2. Respect for the rights of the defence of anyone who has been charged shall be guaranteed.

c. Article 7 ECHR and Article 49 of the Charter—Non-retroactivity and Proportionality of Criminal Offences and Penalties

Article 7 ECHR provides for the non-retroactivity of criminal laws or penalties. Article 49 of the Charter replicates this almost exactly, but adds a provision (Article 49(3)) embodying one application of the EU principle of proportionality by stating that 'the severity of penalties must not be disproportionate to the criminal offence'.

d. Article 8 ECHR and Article 7 of the Charter—Privacy and the Inviolability of the Home

Article 8 ECHR states:

1. Everyone has the right to respect for his private and family life, his home and his correspondence.

2. There shall be no interference by a public authority with the exercise of this right except such as is in accordance with the law and is necessary in a democratic society in the interests of national security, public safety or the economic well-being of the country, for the prevention of disorder or crime, for the protection of health or morals, or for the protection of the rights and freedoms of others.

This guarantee is relevant to the Commission's powers to carry out inspections at premises (particularly unannounced 'dawn raids') under Articles 20 and 21 of Regulation 1/2003.[125]

The corresponding provision of the Charter is Article 7:

Everyone has the right to respect for his or her private and family life, home and communications.

Article 7 enshrines the general principle of EU law that there should be no arbitrary or disproportionate intervention by public authorities in the private sphere of any natural or legal person.[126]

---

[120] Case C-199/11, *Europese Gemeenschap v Otis NV* EU:C:2012:684 (concerning the Elevators and Escalators cartel, of which the Commission was a victim. Ultimately the Commission lost the case in the Brussels Commercial Court on the grounds that it had failed to prove the overcharging and the causality link).

[121] Ibid., paras. 62–65.

[122] Ibid., para. 67. The CJ reached a similar conclusion in respect of Art. 41 of the Charter in Case C-439/11 P, *Ziegler SA v Commission* EU:C:2013:513.

[123] Case C-439/11 P, *Ziegler* EU:C:2013:513, para. 154; Case C-109/10 P, *Solvay v Commission* [2011] ECR I-10329, para. 53.

[124] See Section 7.C.vi, p. 918 ff.

[125] See Section 7.C.iii and iv.

[126] Case T-135/09, *Nexans France SAS v Commission* EU:T:2012:596, para. 40.

e. Article 20 and Article 21 of the Charter—Equality Before the Law and Non-discrimination

Equal treatment is a general principle of EU law enshrined in Article 20:

Everyone is equal before the law

and in Article 21(1) on the prohibition of non-discrimination based on any ground such as sex, race, colour etc. (emphasis added). Discrimination on grounds of nationality is prohibited only within the scope of application of the Treaties (Article 21(2)).

Equal treatment means that comparable situations must not be treated differently and that different situations must not be treated in the same way unless such treatment is objectively justified.[127] The principle of equal treatment is particularly important in competition proceedings in respect of the calculation of the amount of the fine imposed upon different undertakings which have participated in the same infringement[128] and of the application of the leniency policy in cartel cases to different undertakings.[129]

f. Article 41 of the Charter—Right to Good Administration

Article 41 of the Charter provides:

1. Every person has the right to have his or her affairs handled impartially, fairly and within a reasonable time by the institutions, bodies, offices and agencies of the Union.

2. This right includes:

    –   the right of every person to be heard, before any individual measure which would affect him or her adversely is taken;

    –   the right of every person to have access to his or her file, while respecting the legitimate interests of confidentiality and of professional business secrecy;

    –   the obligation of the administration to give reasons for its decisions.

3. Every person has the right to have the Union make good any damage caused by its institutions or by its servants in the performance of their duties, in accordance with the general principles common to the laws of the Member States.

4. Every person may write to the institutions of the Union in one of the languages of the Treaties and must have an answer in the same language.

This Article covers a number of matters which are of crucial importance in the Commission's administrative procedure: impartiality, the right to be heard, access to the file, confidentiality and business secrecy, and the giving of reasons. The CJ considers that it is Article 41, rather than Article 47, which governs the administrative procedure before the Commission.[130] In *Ziegler* the CJ considered the requirement of impartiality in Article 41(1) in the context of a Commission infringement decision in respect of the *International Removals* cartel of which it was itself a victim (as it had reimbursed officials for removal expenses which were affected by the operation of the cartel).[131] The Court recognised the distinction between subjective and objective impartiality.[132] Subjective impartiality

---

[127] Case C-550/07 P, *Akzo Nobel Chemicals Ltd v Commission* [2010] ECR I-8301, paras. 54–55.

[128] In Case C-580/12 P, *Guardian Industries Corp v Commission* EU:C:2014: 2363, paras. 51–66, for example, Arts. 20 and 21 were applied to discrimination between vertically and non-vertically integrated undertakings.

[129] See Section 7.H.v.

[130] Case C-439/11 P, *Ziegler* EU:C:2013:513, para. 154; see also Case T-286/09, *Intel v Commission* EU:T:2014:547, para. 359.

[131] COMP/38543, *International Removal Services* 11 March 2008.

[132] The CJ upheld the GC (Case T-199/08, *Ziegler v European Commission* [2011] ECR II-3507) on the impartiality issue even though the GC (paras. 104–106 of the GC judgment) did not expressly make the distinction. The distinction is found in the jurisprudence of the ECtHR, see, e.g., *Micaleff v Malta*, App. no. 17056/06, judgment 15 October 2009 and Guide on Art. 6, <http://www.echr.coe.int/Documents/Guide_Art_6_ENG.pdf>.

requires that no member of the institution concerned who is responsible for the matter may show bias or personal prejudice, and objective impartiality requires that there are sufficient guarantees to exclude any legitimate doubt as to bias on the part of the institution concerned.[133] As far as the Commission's objective impartiality is concerned, that cannot be called into question merely because its departments (in *Ziegler* this was DG Comp on the one hand and those responsible for the administration of removals of officials and agents on the other) belong to the same organisational structure.[134] Moreover, since judicial review by the EU Courts satisfies Article 47 of the Charter the Commission is not to be regarded as the judge responsible for imposing the penalties.[135]

g. Article 50 of the Charter—*Ne Bis in Idem*

Article 50 enshrines the general principle of EU law against double jeopardy—*ne bis in idem*:

No one shall be liable to be tried or punished again in criminal proceedings for an offence of which he or she has already been finally acquitted or convicted within the Union in accordance with the law.

It is also contained in Article 4 of Protocol 7 ECHR.

C. THE INVESTIGATION STAGE OF THE ADMINISTRATIVE PROCEDURE: FACT-FINDING BY THE COMMISSION

(i) General

The Commission has extensive fact-finding powers under Articles 18–21 of Regulation 1/2003 (of which Articles 18 and 20 correspond respectively to Articles 11 and 14 of Regulation 17). The rights of the parties have been spelt out in the case law of the EU Courts when the Commission's actions have been challenged, often on the grounds that the Commission has acted in breach of the general principles of law or fundamental rights. The parties have no right to be heard before the investigatory stage, and the right to be heard does not apply fully until the statement of objections (SO). The principle of proportionality is of particular importance in respect of the Commission's fact-finding powers, as it requires that measures adopted by the EU institutions do not exceed what is appropriate and necessary to attain the legitimate objectives of the relevant legislation and, that where there is a choice between several appropriate measures, recourse must be had to the least onerous and the disadvantages must not be disproportionate to the aims pursued.[136]

Under Article 18 of Regulation 1/2003 the Commission may request undertakings (both those under investigation and others such as customers, competitors, or suppliers) to supply it with information. Where the Commission investigates suspected infringements of the competition rules it is often seeking information which the suspected parties are reluctant to disclose and may have taken active steps to conceal. The Commission may therefore also *demand* information by decision.

Article 20 enables the Commission to conduct inspections on the undertakings' premises. It can proceed directly to Article 20, and need not make a prior request for information under Article 18. Article 19 gives the Commission power to formally interview any natural or legal person who consents to be interviewed. Article 21 gives it power to carry out inspections at non-business premises.

---

[133] Case C-439/11 P, *Ziegler* EU:C:2013:513, para. 155.

[134] Ibid., para. 158,

[135] Ibid., para. 159.

[136] See, e.g., Case C-331/88, *Fedesa* [1990] ECR I-4023, paras. 8 and 14; Case C-189/01, *Jippes v Commission* [2001] ECR I-5689, para. 81.

(ii) Article 18 Requests for Information

Article 18(1) provides that the Commission 'may, by simple request or by decision, require under-takings and associations of undertakings to provide all necessary information'.[137] This includes requests for the disclosure of documents.[138] Under Article 18(3) the Commission can choose to re-quest information from undertakings by decision from the outset.[139] The Commission's choice of an Article 18(3) decision rather than an Article 18(2) simple request must be proportionate, in that the Commission must be in possession of sufficiently serious evidence to justify it. By Article 18(6) the governments of the Member States and the NCAs have to supply the Commission with all nec-essary information it requests. An Article 18 simple request or decision is not precluded by the Commission having already carried out an Article 20 inspection.[140] They are frequently used post-Article 20 inspections in cartel cases.

Article 18(2) provides that a simple request for information must:

state the legal basis and the purpose of the request, specify what information is required and fix the time-limit within which the information is to be provided, and the penalties provided for in Article 23 for supplying incorrect or misleading information.

There is no *duty* to comply with a simple request, although the intentional or negligent provision of *incorrect* or *misleading* information can be penalised with a fine under Article 23(1)(a) of Regulation 1/2003, and so the undertakings must be warned of this. A desire to cooperate with the Commission and not to make the situation worse also tends to be a spur to accuracy. The fact that ultimately the Commission can demand the information by adopting a decision under Article 18(3) is another reason for complying with an Article 18(2) request.[141]

A decision under Article 18(3) has to state, like a simple request, its legal basis and purpose, the information required, and the time limit. In addition to warning of Article 23 fines, it must also indicate or impose the periodic penalties under Article 24.[142] It must indicate that it can be reviewed by the Court. An Article 18(3) decision, like any other decision, must in accordance with Article 296 TFEU contain an adequate statement of reasons. The requirements of Article 18(3) in this regard were considered by the CJ in the *Cement and Related Products* cases, in which undertakings appealed against Article 18(3) decisions, inter alia on the ground that the Commission had not sufficiently set out the putative infringements it was investigating.[143] The GC upheld the decisions despite admit-ting that the statement of reasons was 'formulated in very general terms which would have ben-efited from greater detail and warrants criticism in that regard'.[144] However, the CJ set aside the GC

---

[137] See Kerse and Khan, n. 2, 3.013–3.030. The Commission now sends an email inviting the undertaking con-cerned to log on to the Commission's electronic investigative platform, eQuestionnaire, using a unique access code, and to answer the questions there electronically; see <http//:ec.europa.eu/competition/antitrust/information_en.html>.

[138] Case 374/87, *Orkem* [1989] ECR 3283, para. 14.

[139] Under Reg. 17, Art. 11 it had first to request it by a 'simple request' before moving on to a decision.

[140] Case 374/87, *Orkem* [1989] ECR 3283, para. 14. The Art. 18 powers can be used at any time throughout the Commission proceedings.

[141] See Case T-46/92, *The Scottish Football Association v Commission* [1994] ECR II-1039 for a case in which a reaction to a simple request for information which consisted of pained surprise, an explanation of the undertaking's policy, and a statement that the undertaking was 'happy' to meet the Commission at any time to explain its views was treated by the GC as a 'polite but explicit refusal to co-operate' (para. 33).

[142] See Section 7.H.iii, p. 959.

[143] Case T-292/11, *Cemex and Others* EU:T:2014:125; Case T-293/11, *Holcim (Deutschland) and Holcim* EU:T:2014:127; Case T-296/11, *Cementos Portland Valderrivas* EU:T:2014:121; Case T-297/11, *Buzzi Unicem* EU:T:2014:122; Case T-302/11, *HeidelbergCement* EU:T:2014:128; Case T-305/11, *Italmobiliare* EU:T:2014:126; Case T-306/11, *Schwenk Zement v Commission* EU:T:2014:123. The case concerned was COMP/39.520, *Cement and Related Products*.

[144] See, e.g., Case T-302/11, *HeidelbergCement* EU:T:2014:128, para. 42; Case T-306/11, *Schwenk Zement* EU:T:2014:123, para. 37.

judgments[145] and annulled the decisions. It held that the statement of reasons did not meet the requisite legal standard.[146]

Case C-247/14 P, *HeidelbergCement v Commission* EU:C:2016:149

Court of Justice

19. That obligation to state specific reasons is a fundamental requirement, designed not merely to show that the request for information is justified but also to enable the undertakings concerned to assess the scope of their duty to cooperate whilst at the same time safeguarding their rights of defence (see, by analogy, with respect to inspection decisions, judgments in *Dow Chemical Ibérica and Others* v *Commission*, 97/87 to 99/87,…, paragraph 26; *Roquette Frères*, C-94/00,…, paragraph 47; *Nexans and Nexans France* v *Commission*, C-37/13 P,…, paragraph 34; and *Deutsche Bahn and Others* v *Commission*, C-583/13 P,…, paragraph 56).

20. With respect to the obligation to state the 'purpose of the request', this relates to the Commission's obligation to indicate the subject of its investigation in its request, and therefore to identify the alleged infringement of competition rules (see, to that effect, judgment in *SEP* v *Commission*, C-36/92 P,…, paragraph 21).

21. In that regard, the Commission is not required to communicate to the addressee of a decision requesting information all the information at its disposal concerning the presumed infringements, or to make a precise legal analysis of those infringements, providing it clearly indicates the suspicions which it intends to investigate (see, by analogy, judgment in *Nexans and Nexans France* v *Commission*, C-37/13 P,…, paragraph 35 and the case-law cited).

22. That obligation may be explained, inter alia, by the fact that, as is apparent from Article 18(1) of Regulation No 1/2003 and recital 23 thereof, in order to carry out the duties assigned to it by that regulation, the Commission may, by simple request or by decision, require undertakings and associations of undertakings to provide 'all necessary information'.

23. As correctly noted by the General Court in paragraph 34 of the decision at issue, 'the Commission is entitled to require the disclosure only of information which may enable it to investigate presumed infringements which justify the conduct of the investigation and are set out in the request for information'.

24. Since the necessity of the information must be judged in relation to the purpose stated in the request for information, that purpose must be indicated with sufficient precision, otherwise it will be impossible to determine whether the information is necessary and the Court will be prevented from exercising judicial review (see, to that effect, judgment in *SEP* v *Commission*, C-36/92 P,…, paragraph 21).

25. The General Court also correctly held, in paragraph 39 of the judgment under appeal, that the adequacy of the statement of reasons of the decision at issue depends 'on whether or not the putative infringements that the Commission intends to investigate are defined in sufficiently clear terms'.

…

31. [The] statement of reasons does not make it possible to determine with sufficient precision either the products to which the investigation relates or the suspicions of infringement justifying the adoption of that decision. It follows that that statement of reasons does not enable the undertaking in question to check whether the requested information is necessary for the purposes of the investigation or the European Union judicature to exercise its power of review.

---

[145] In the cases which were further appealed. Some undertakings did not pursue the appeals as the Commission announced on 31 July 2015 that it had closed the investigation because the evidence was not sufficiently conclusive.

[146] Case C-247/14 P, *HeidelbergCement v Commission* EU:C:2016:149; Case C-248/14 P, *Schwenk Zement v Commission* EU:C:2016:150; Case C-267/14 P, *Buzzi Unicem v Commission* EU:C:2016:151; Case C-268/14 P, *Italmobiliare v Commission* EU:C:2016:152.

The CJ said that the question of whether a statement of reasons meets the requirements of Article 296 must be assessed with regard to its context as well as its wording and the relevant legal rules.[147] Here the context included the fact that the decision was adopted more than two years after the first Article 20 inspections, several months after the decision to initiate proceedings, and after the Commission had already sent a number of other requests for information. The Commission therefore had enough information to present a more precise account of the suspected infringements.[148] The CJ also noted the extensive amount of information the decision demanded.[149]

The question of what amounts to 'necessary information' was raised in the *Cement* cases. It is established that 'necessary information' must be interpreted by reference to the purposes for which the powers of investigation in question are conferred upon the Commission.[150] This is an application of the principles of proportionality and of protection against arbitrary and disproportionate intervention by public authorities in the sphere of any person's private activities.[151] The requirement for a correlation between the request for information and the presumed infringement is met if the request can be legitimately considered to be related to the presumed infringement in the sense that the Commission may reasonably suppose that the document will help to determine whether the alleged infringement has taken place.[152] Although it is not easy to show that the Commission has exceeded its leeway in the information it has requested, the Commission cannot go on a 'fishing expedition'.[153] One of the undertakings concerned in the *Cement* investigation[154] had, unlike the others, not been the subject of an Article 20 inspection before receiving the Article 18 decision, and claimed that the Commission was seeking to uncover information which might point to the existence of an infringement rather than checking on a situation about which it already had information. The GC reviewed the Commission decision by adopting measures of inquiry to examine exactly what information the Commission had in its possession at the time of the request. The GC concluded that the Commission was entitled to send the request in respect of all the putative infringements.[155]

Undertakings in the *Cement* cases also claimed that the requirement of 'necessity' was not met in respect of the excessive amount of information requested.[156] The GC said that the Commission need not have information *establishing* the existence of the infringement before sending the request; that it can request that the information be provided in a highly specific, detailed format;[157] and that it is not obliged at this stage to inform the undertakings what evidence is already in its possession. The Commission had demanded a high volume of information[158] which the GC admitted imposed a heavy workload to answer but held, nevertheless, that it was not disproportionate in

---

[147] Case T-302/11, *HeidelbergCement* EU:T:2014:128, para. 16.

[148] Ibid., para. 39.

[149] Ibid., para. 27.

[150] C-36/92 P, *SEP v Commission* [1994] ECR I-1911.

[151] Cases T-458/09 and T-171/10, *Slovak Telecom v Commission* EU:T:2012:145, para 81; Case T-296/11, *Cementos Portland Valderrivas v Commission* EU:T:2014:121, para. 39.

[152] Case C-36/92 P, *SEP* [1994] ECR I-1911, para. 21, approving Jacobs AG, para. 21; Cases T-458/09 and T-171/10, *Slovak Telecom* EU:T:2012:145, para. 40.

[153] See Case C-94/00, *Roquette Frères* [2002] ECR I-9011, paras. 54–55.

[154] COMP/39.520, *Cement and Related Products*.

[155] Case T-296/11, *Cementos Portland Valderrivas* EU:T:2014:121, paras. 40–60.

[156] Case T-292/11, *Cemex and Others* EU:T:2014:125; Case T-293/11, *Holcim (Deutschland) and Holcim* EU:T:2014:127; Case T-297/11, *Buzzi Unicem* EU:T:2014:122; Case T-302/11, *HeidelbergCement* EU:T:2014128; Case T-305/11, *Italmobiliare* EU:T:2014:126; Case T-306/11, *Schwenk Zement v Commission* EU:T:014:123.

[157] Such as being broken down on the basis of 37 parameters, see Case T-296/11, *Cementos Portland Valderrivas* EU:T:2014:121, para. 87.

[158] In *Cementos Portland Valderrivas*, one of the questions concerned all domestic purchases of five products over a ten-year period. There were 94 pages and 11 sets of detailed questions. In Case C-247/14 P, *HeidelbergCement* EU:T:2014128, para. 27 the CJ remarked that the Commission had demanded detailed information on domestic and international transactions in relation to 12 Member States over ten years.

the circumstances.[159] However, the time limit must be adequate for the undertaking to provide its reply and satisfy itself that it is supplying complete, correct, and not misleading information.[160] In the appeals Advocate General Wahl recommended the annulment of the decisions, inter alia on the grounds of lack of necessity and excessive burden[161] but as the CJ annulled the decisions and set aside the GC judgments because of the inadequacy of the statement of reasons, it did not directly address any other issues. The Commission may justifiably claim that the GC's confirmation of its powers remains, but the position is highly unsatisfactory.

Intel[162] raised the issue of an undertaking claiming that the Commission had failed to collect *sufficient* information, in that it had not obtained from the complainant certain documents Intel knew to be in the complainant's possession and which would have been exculpatory. The GC recognised that the principle of sound administration enshrined in Article 41 of the Charter required the Commission to examine all the relevant aspects of the individual case carefully and impartially. However, in principle it was for the Commission to decide how it wished to conduct the investigation and to decide what documents it needed to collect.[163] The Commission did not have an obligation to obtain as many documents as possible so as to ensure it had all potentially exculpatory evidence,[164] and had a margin of discretion in deciding whether to obtain documents requested by the undertaking under investigation.[165] Nevertheless, the GC held that in exceptional circumstances there may an obligation on the Commission to obtain documents at the request of the investigated undertaking. This would be where four cumulative conditions are fulfilled:[166]

- it is impossible for the undertaking to obtain the documents itself or disclose them to the Commission;

- the relevant documents are identified by the undertaking as precisely as possible;

- the documents are probably of considerable importance to the undertaking's defence; and

- the volume of documents at issue must not be disproportionate to their importance in the context of the investigation.

Article 18(4) of Regulation 1/2003 provides that lawyers may supply the information on behalf of their clients, although the client remains fully responsible if the information is incorrect, incomplete, or misleading. 'Best Practices for the Submission of Economic Evidence'[167] sets out the way in which the Commission prefers undertakings to present economic and econometric evidence in reply to requests for quantitative data.

The Commission has to send a copy of the request or decision to the NCA of the Member State in whose territory the seat of the undertaking concerned is situated and to the NCA of the Member State whose territory is affected.[168]

---

[159] Given the necessities of the inquiry and the extent of the putative infringements; see, e.g., Case T-296/11, *Cementos Portland Valderrivas* EU:T:2014:121, para. 89.

[160] Case T-306/11, *Schwenk* EU:T:014:123, para. 73. The GC held the two-week time limit to be 'disproportionate to say the least' (para. 92) and annulled the decision in respect of one set of questions. The Best Practices Notice, para. 38, says that the time limit is at least two weeks but will be set according to the length and complexity of the request. Schwenk had asked for an extension (as per para. 39 of Best Practices) but had been refused. The application of the amended *Heat Stabilisers* decision to Akzo Nobel was annulled because Akzo had insufficient time to reply, Case T-485/11, *Akzo Nobel v Commission* EU:T:2015:517.

[161] Opinion, EU:C:2015:694, 15 October 2015.

[162] Case T-286/09, *Intel v Commission* EU:T:2014:547, on appeal Case C-413/14 P, judgment pending.

[163] Ibid., para. 360.

[164] Ibid., para. 361.

[165] Ibid., para. 362.

[166] Ibid., paras. 375–382.

[167] See n. 65.

[168] Reg. 1/2003, Art. 18(5).

The questions of when undertakings may withhold documents from the Commission on the ground that they are legally privileged, and to what extent they can refuse to supply information on grounds of self-incrimination, are dealt with in Section 7.C.vii and Section 7.C.vi.

(iii) Article 20 Inspections of Undertakings

a. General

Article 20(1) gives the Commission powers to carry out 'all necessary inspections' of undertakings and associations of undertakings. This means investigations at the undertaking's premises. Inspections are carried out by officials and 'other accompanying persons authorised by the Commission'[169] such as IT experts.

Under Article 20(3) the Commission can carry out the inspection at the premises simply on production of a 'written authorisation'.[170] The officials may either give advance notice of their arrival or come without warning (although they have to give notice 'in good time before the inspection' to the NCA of the Member State in whose territory the inspection is conducted). So long as they carry only the Article 20(3) 'authorisation' an undertaking is under no legal obligation to submit to the inspection. Under Article 20(4), however, undertakings *must* submit to procedures ordered by a decision of the Commission.[171] The Commission cannot carry out inspections if the suspected agreement or concerted practice produces effects exclusively outside the internal market, as Articles 101 and 102 apply only to effects on inter-Member State trade. It can, however, examine documents relating to markets outside the EU in order to detect anti-competitive conduct which is liable to affect trade between Member States.[172]

In a 'dawn raid' the officials arrive without warning, armed with an Article 20(4) decision.[173] The CJ held in *National Panasonic*[174] that they are entitled to do this without going through the 'voluntary' (now Article 20(3)) procedure first. Despite the sobriquet 'dawn raids', unannounced inspections take place during normal business hours. There may be simultaneous surprise arrivals at undertakings across the EU where, for example, the Commission suspects the existence of a hardcore cartel.[175] The *Polypropylene* cartel investigation,[176] for example, involved ten simultaneous raids. Julian Joshua, at one time Deputy Head of the Cartel Unit in DG Comp, explained in 1983 why the apparently draconian powers of the Commission are necessary:[177]

More often, the most serious cartels are not modified at all. They are operated in conditions of strict secrecy. Communication between participants is kept to a minimum and knowledge of the arrangements confined to certain key employees. Meetings take place in safe countries or under the cover of a seemingly innocent trade association. There may even be emergency arrangements to shred documents and warn other participants by coded telex messages in the event of an investigation. Sometimes the cartel rules provide for

---

[169] Ibid., Art. 20(3), (5), and (6).

[170] This must contain the same or equivalent matters as required in respect of requests for information under Art. 18(2).

[171] Art. 20(4) decisions can be taken by the Commissioner responsible for competition as the delegation by the College of Commissioners is valid as it does not involve a matter of principle: Case 5/85, *AKZO v Commission* [1986] ECR 2585; Cases 46/87 and 227/88, *Hoechst AG v Commission* [1989] ECR 2859. The decision must contain the same or equivalent matters as required in respect of decisions under Art. 18(3). The form of authorisation carried by the inspectors executing a Decision is on DG Comp's website, see <http://ec.europa.eu/competition/antitrust/legislation/inspection_authorisation.pdf>. The Reg. 17 equivalents of Art. 20(3) and (4) were Art. 14(2) and (3) respectively.

[172] Case C-37/13 P, *Nexans France SA v Commission* EU:C:2014:2030, para. 40.

[173] The Commission may confirm by press release that dawn raids have taken place.

[174] Case 136/79, *National Panasonic v Commission* [1980] ECR 2033.

[175] The inspections may also be coordinated with similar inspections outside the EU by competition authorities in those countries.

[176] *Polypropylene Cartel* [1986] OJ L230/1.

[177] J. M. Joshua, 'The Element of Surprise' (1983) 8 *ELRev* 3, 5.

members to deny all knowledge of documents or their contents even when these are found in the safe. In such circumstances resort to surprise must be a legitimate and essential precaution.[178]

An Explanatory Note on the conduct of Article 20(4) inspections, setting out the Commission's view of its Article 20(4) powers, is published on DG Comp's website.[179]

In *National Panasonic* an undertaking subjected to the first unannounced dawn raid, under what was then Article 14(3) of Regulation 17, claimed that the procedure infringed its fundamental rights. It relied in particular on Article 8 ECHR on the inviolability of the home, and claimed that the principle of proportionality was infringed.

Case 136/79, *National Panasonic v Commission* [1980] ECR 2033

Commission officials arrived at Panasonic's offices in Slough at 10.00 a.m. The directors asked if the inspection could be delayed to await the arrival of their solicitor, who was in Norwich. The officials waited until 10.45 a.m. and then began. The solicitor did not arrive until 1.45 p.m. and the inspection finished at 5.30 p.m. Panasonic subsequently challenged the validity of the decision ordering the inspection in the CJ and asked that all the documents taken by the Commission should be returned or destroyed.

Court of Justice

17. The applicant then claims that by failing previously to communicate to it beforehand the decision ordering an investigation in question, the Commission has in this instance infringed fundamental rights of the applicant, in particular the right to receive advance notification of the intention to apply a decision regarding it, the right to be heard before a decision adversely affecting it is taken and the right to use the opportunity given to it under Article [278 TFEU] to request a stay of execution of such a decision. The applicant relies in particular on Article 8 of the European Convention for the Protection of Human Rights and Fundamental Freedoms of 4 November 1950 whereby 'everyone has the right to respect for his private and family life, his home and his correspondence'. It considers that those guarantees must be provided *mutatis mutandis* also to legal persons.

18. As the Court stated in its judgment of 14 May 1974 in Case 4/73, *J. Nold, Kohlen- und Baustoffgrosshandlung* v. *Commission of the European Communities* . . . at p. 507, fundamental rights form an integral part of the general principles of law, the observance of which the Court of Justice ensures, in accordance with constitutional traditions common to the Member States and with international treaties on which the Member States have collaborated or of which they are signatories.

19. In this respect it is necessary to point out that Article 8(2) of the European Convention, in so far as it applies to legal persons, whilst stating the principle that public authorities should not interfere with the exercise of the rights referred to in Article 8(1), acknowledges that such interference is permissible to the extent to which it 'is in accordance with the law and is necessary in a democratic society in the interests of national security, public safety or the economic well-being of the country, for the prevention of disorder or crime, for the protection of health or morals, or for the protection of the rights and freedom of others.'

20. In this instance, as follows from the seventh and eighth recitals of the preamble to Regulation No 17, the aim of the powers given to the Commission by Article 14 of that regulation is to enable it

---

[178] For a look at the inner workings of a cartel, see J. M. Griffin, 'An Inside Look at a Cartel at Work: Common Characteristics of International Cartels', Speech, 6 April 2000, available on the US DOJ website, <http://www.justice.gov/atr/speech/inside-look-cartel-work-common-characteristics-international-cartels>. The cartel concerned, the lysine (amino acids) cartel, also became the subject of an EC decision, [2001] OJ L152/24, on appeal to the GC, Case T-224/00, *Archer Daniels Midland v Commission* [2003] ECR II-2597, *aff'd* by the CJ, Case C-397/03 P, *Archer Daniels Midland v Commission* [2006] ECR I-4429 and was the subject of the 2009 Stephen Soderbergh film, *The Informant!* starring Matt Damon as the whistle-blower.

[179] <http://ec.europa.eu/competition/antitrust/legislation/explanatory_note.pdf>, last revised 11 September 2015.

to carry out its duty under the EEC Treaty of ensuring that the rules on competition are applied in the common market. The function of these rules is, as follows from the fourth recital of the preamble of the Treaty, Article 3[(1)(g) EC] and Articles [101 and 102 TFEU], to prevent competition from being distorted to the detriment of the public interest, individual undertakings and consumers. The exercise of the powers given to the Commission by Regulation No 17 contributes to the maintenance of the system of competition intended by the Treaty which undertakings are absolutely bound to comply with. In these circumstances, it does not therefore appear that Regulation No 17, by giving the Commission powers to carry out investigations without previous notification, infringes the right invoked by the applicant.

21. Moreover, as regard more particularly the argument that the application was in this instance denied the right to be heard before a decision was taken regarding it, it is necessary to state that the exercise of such a right of defence is chiefly incorporated in legal or administrative procedures for the termination of an infringement or for a declaration that an agreement, decision or concerted practice is incompatible with Article [101], such as the procedures referred to by Regulation No 99/63/EEC. On the other hand, the investigation procedure referred to in Article 14 of Regulation No 17 does not aim at terminating an infringement or declaring that an agreement, decision or concerted practice is incompatible with Article [101]; its sole objective is to enable the Commission to gather the necessary information to check…the actual existence and scope of a given factual and legal situation. Only if the Commission considers that the data for the appraisal thereof collected in this way justify the initiation of a procedure under Regulation No 99/63/EEC must the undertaking or association of undertakings concerned be heard before such a decision is taken pursuant to Article 19(1) of Regulation No 17 and to the provisions of Regulation No 99/63/EEC. Precisely this substantive difference between the decisions taken at the end of such a procedure and decisions ordering an investigation explains the wording of Article 19(1) which, in listing the decisions which the Commission cannot take before giving those concerned the opportunity of exercising their right of defence, does not mention that laid down in Article 14(3) of the same regulation.

22. Finally, the argument that the absence of previous information deprived the applicant of the opportunity of exercising its rights under Article [278 TFEU] to request the Court for a stay of execution of the decision in question is contradicted by the very provisions of Article [278]. That article presupposes in fact that a decision has been adopted and that it is effective whereas the previous notification, which the applicant complains that the Commission did not send it, should have preceded the adoption of the contested decision and could not have been binding.

23. In view of these considerations, the second submission is not well founded.

. . .

(D) The violation of the principle of proportionality

28. The applicant points out in addition that the principle of proportionality, as established by the case-law of the Court of Justice, implies that a decision ordering an investigation adopted without the preliminary procedure may only be justified if the situation is very grave and where there is the greatest urgency and the need for complete secrecy before the investigation is carried out. It points out, finally, that the contested decision violates such a principle by not indicating in the statement of the reasons upon which it is based that any of those facts exists.

29. The Commission's choice between an investigation by straightforward authorization and an investigation ordered by a decision does not depend on the facts relied upon by the applicant but on the need for an appropriate inquiry, having regard to the special features of the case.

30. Considering that the contested decision aimed solely at enabling the Commission to collect the necessary information to appraise whether there was any infringement of the Treaty, it does not therefore appear that the Commission's action in this instance was disproportionate to the objective pursued and therefore violated the principle of proportionality.

The CJ therefore rejected National Panasonic's claims and held that an unannounced inspection authorised by a decision is not a breach of the undertaking's fundamental rights.

Article 20 does not require the Commission to obtain any kind of judicial authorisation before adopting an inspection decision or carrying out the inspection unless the Commission has to call upon the assistance of national authorities under Article 20(6), in which case judicial authorisation may be necessary under national law. The lack of a need for judicial authorisation has been held by the CJ to be compatible with Article 8 ECHR because the lawfulness of the inspection decision is subject to review by the Court.[180]

Inspection decisions must be as precise as possible.[181] Inspections are intended to enable the Commission to gather documentary evidence to check the actual existence and scope of a given factual and legal situation about which *it already possesses certain information*. The Commission cannot use its Article 20(4) powers to go on 'fishing expeditions' and must have reasonable grounds for adopting an inspection decision. Decisions must indicate the subject and objective of the inspection, in order to show that the intervention is proportional and to enable the undertaking to understand the scope of its duty to cooperate with the Commission's inspectors, and preserve the rights of the defence.[182] However, the Commission is not required to communicate to the addressee all the information at its disposal concerning the presumed infringements, or make a precise legal analysis of those infringements, providing it clearly indicates the presumed facts which it intends to investigate.[183] It is not essential for the decision to define precisely the relevant market, set out the exact legal nature of the presumed infringements, or indicate the period over which those infringements were supposedly committed.[184] So in *Nexans*, where these principles were clarified and applied, the CJ upheld the GC's judgment[185] that an inspection decision covering suspected agreements and/or concerted practices which 'probably have a global reach' was sufficient delineation of its geographical scope.[186] However, the GC (partially) annulled the decision as the subject matter was described in a way that encompassed all electric cables, whereas it found that before the adoption of the decision the Commission had reasonable grounds for ordering an inspection only in respect of high-voltage underground and underwater cables.[187]

The prohibition on the Commission conducting fishing expeditions was further reinforced in *Deutsche Bahn*. In *Dow Benelux*[188] the CJ had held that if, in the course of an inspection, the Commission 'happened to obtain' evidence of an infringement which related to matters outside the subject matter of the investigation, it was not barred from initiating an inquiry into those matters in reliance on that evidence. In *Deutsche Bahn*[189] the CJ held that this applied only if the discovery of that evidence was purely fortuitous. It was otherwise where the Commission inspectors had been informed about a second complaint about the undertaking before an inspection relating to the first had been carried

---

[180] Case C-583/13 P, *Deutsche Bahn AG v Commission* EU:C:2015:404, paras. 18–36.

[181] Case C-94/00, *Roquette Frères* [2002] ECR I-9011, para. 83.

[182] Case C-37/13 P, *Nexans France* EU:C:2014:2030, para. 34; see also Cases 46/87 and 227/88, *Hoechst* [1989] ECR 2859, para. 29.

[183] Case C-37/13 P, *Nexans France* EU:C:2014:2030, para. 35; Case C-94/00, *Roquette Frères* [2002] ECR I-9011, para. 82; Case 97/87, *Dow Chemical Ibérica v Commission* [1989] ECR 3165, para. 46.

[184] Case C-37/13 P, *Nexans France* EU:C:2014:2030, para. 36.

[185] Ibid., *aff'g* Case T-135/09, *Nexans France SAS v Commission* EU:T:2012:596 (the *Electric Cables Cartel*). See A. Laghezza, 'From the *Nexans* Judgement to the "Next" Improvements of the EU Dawn Raid Rrocedure?' [2013] ECLR 214.

[186] Case C-37/13 P, *Nexans* EU:C:2014:2030, paras. 38–41.

[187] Case T-135/09, *Nexans* EU:T:2012:596, paras. 60–94. The evidence upon which the Commission took the decision to mount the dawn raid had mainly come from a leniency applicant. Nexans also challenged the inspection decision on the grounds that it had described the subject matter as 'the supply of electric cables…, including, amongst others, high voltage underwater electric cables, and, in certain cases, high voltage underground electric cables', whereas the Commission's real concern was high-voltage cables and it meant 'in particular' rather than 'including'. The GC accepted that the wording could have been 'less ambiguous' (para. 54) but nonetheless upheld the decision on this point.

[188] Case 85/87, *Dow Benelux NV v Commission* [1989] ECR 3137.

[189] Case C-583/13 P, *Deutsche Bahn AG v Commission* EU:C:2015:404.

out, and had based further inspection decisions on the material relating to that second complaint which was found during the first inspection. In annulling the further inspection decisions the CJ put aside the judgment of the GC finding that the Commission's actions were lawful.[190]

The stringency with which the EU Courts are prepared to review inspection decisions may reflect their current awareness of the need for proper judicial review of the Commission's decisions in order to satisfy the requirements of the Charter.[191]

b. The Powers of the Inspectors

The undertaking must actively and fully cooperate with the inspection.[192] However this duty exists only in connection with its activities in the sectors in respect of which the Commission has reasonable grounds for suspecting an infringement, as discussed earlier.[193]

Unlike challenges to the legality of the inspection decision, which can be challenged immediately in separate proceedings, the EU Courts may review disputes over procedural issues arising in the course of an inspection only as part of the review of the Commission's final decision in the case and not in a separate action, because they are only 'measures implementing the inspection decision'.[194] This can leave investigated undertakings in a difficult position. If they refuse to cooperate with the disputed measures during the inspection they are liable to be fined periodic penalty payments under Article 23(1) (at least they could challenge that decision immediately) although the Commission may instead wait and punish the obstruction by increasing any fine imposed in the final infringement decision.

It is standard procedure at the start of an inspection for the inspectors to request to block email accounts of key personnel, and set a new password known only to the inspectors. In *EPH* the Commission fined two Czech companies for modifying the password to one account during the inspection and for diverting all emails away from some blocked accounts.[195]

Under Article 20(2) inspections involve the following powers:[196]

The Power to Enter Any Premises, Land, and Means of Transport of Undertakings and Associations of Undertakings (Article 20(2)(a))

The extent of this power was set out by the CJ in *Hoechst*.[197] If the undertakings are willing to cooperate, the Commission officials have power to have shown to them the documents they request, and to enter such premises they choose and have shown to them the contents of particular furniture they indicate. They are *not* entitled forcibly to enter premises or furniture or carry out searches without the undertaking's consent. If the undertaking does not submit to the investigation Article 20(6) comes into play and the Commission has to rely on the assistance of the Member State.[198]

---

[190] This involved the CJ finding that the appeal against the GC's view that the Commission had valid reasons for telling the inspectors about the second complaint was an issue of law rather than of fact.

[191] See Section 7.B.ii.a, p. 895.

[192] Case 374/87, *Orkem SA v Commission* [1989] ECR 3283, paras. 22 and 27.

[193] Case C-37/13 P, *Nexans* EU:C:2014:2030, para. 34.

[194] Case T-135/09, *Nexans France SAS v Commission* EU:T:2012:596, para. 125. See also Case T-340/03, *France Télécom SA v Commission* [2007] ECR II-107. A complaint about the conduct of the inspection may be made only by the inspected party, unless the procedural regularity is likely to concern the other party directly: Case T-410/09, *Almanet v Commission* EU:T:2012:676.

[195] COMP/39.793, *EPH*, IP/12/319. The companies were fined €2.5 million under Reg. 1/2003, Art. 23(1)(c); upheld on appeal, Case T-272/12, *Energetický a průmyslový holding v Commission* EU:T:14 995; see MEMO/14/2181.

[196] For the detail and practicalities of inspections, see the Commission's Explanatory Note, n. 179; Kerse and Khan, n. 2, 3.072–3.138; Ortiz Blanco, n. 2, 8.28–8.95; Faull and Nikpay, n. 2, 8.343–8.387.

[197] Cases 46/87 and 227/88, *Hoechst v Commission* [1989] ECR 2859, paras. 31–32.

[198] See Section 7.B.iii.c, p. 912.

The Power to Examine Books and Other Records Related to the Business, Irrespective of the Medium on Which They Are Stored (Article 20(2)(b))

'Irrespective of the medium on which they are stored' encompasses all forms of information technology. The Explanatory Note elaborates on this and details what IT tools the inspectors can use. In *EPH* the Commission noted 'that over the last decade paper-based evidence has become less important and most of the documents collected nowadays during inspections are extracted from e-mail accounts and electronic files and that data stored in electronic format are much easier and quicker to destroy than paper files'.[199] The active duty to cooperate with the inspection means that the undertaking must do everything possible to assist the inspectors' access.

The Power to Take or Obtain in Any Form Copies of or Extracts from Such Books or Records (Article 20(2)(c))

The details of the Commission's practice in dealing with copies and extracts (which now will usually be mainly in electronic format) are provided in the Explanatory Note.[200] The Note was amended in 2013 after the GC *Nexans* judgment,[201] and again in September 2015. The 2015 amendments clarify and confirm the Commission's existing practices. The inspectors may search the 'IT-environment' (for example, servers, desktop computers, laptops, tablets, and other mobile devices) and all storage media, such as CD-ROMS, DVDs, USB-keys, external hard disks, backup tapes, and cloud services of the undertaking. It can also search private devices and media that are used for professional purposes when they are found on the premises.[202] At the end of the inspection collected data still to be searched is placed in a sealed envelope and taken back to Brussels or left with the undertaking for safe-keeping pending a further inspection visit.[203]

The Power to Seal Any Business Premises and Books or Records for the Period and to the Extent Necessary for the Inspection (Article 20(2)(d))

This power was expressly conferred on the Commission in Regulation 1/2003, although previously the Commission affixed seals when it thought it necessary. Seals should not normally be affixed for more than 72 hours.[204] Undertakings can be fined under Article 23(1)(e) for breaching seals. The Commission imposed a fine of €38 million on E.ON for breaching a seal during an inspection. The seal had been affixed overnight to the door of a room in which the inspectors had placed documents.[205]

The Power to Ask Any Representative or Member of Staff of the Undertaking or Association of Undertakings for Explanations on Facts or Documents Relating to the Subject Matter and Purpose of the Inspection and to Record the Answers

Under Article 20(2)(e) the inspectors may ask 'any representative or member of staff' for explanations on *facts and documents* relating to *the subject matter and purpose* of the inspection. This is wider

---

[199] *EPH*, Summary of decision [2012] OJ C316/8, para. 17.

[200] A demonstration of the way in which the Commission deals with electronic data during inspections is available on its website, <http://ec.europa.eu/competition/antitrust/information_en.html#inspections>.

[201] Case T-135/09, *Nexans France* EU:T:2012:596.

[202] Explanatory Note, para. 10.

[203] Ibid., paras. 14–18. The undertakings are invited to be present at the envelope opening.

[204] Reg. 1/2003, recital 25.

[205] Commission Decision 30.1.2008, COMP/39.326, Press Release IP/08/2008, Case T-141/08, *E.ON Energie AG v Commission* [2010] ECR II-5761, *aff'd* Case C-89/11 P, *E.ON Energie AG v Commission* EU:C:2012:738. Among E.ON's explanations for the damage to the seal was that it had been damaged by aggressive cleaning products and the cleaning lady wiping it with a damp cloth (see para. 84 of the decision). See also COMP/39.796, *Suez Environnement*, IP/11/632, where a fine of €8 million was imposed for breaching a seal, see C. Gauer, K. Bansard, and F. Christ, 'The *Suez Environnement* Case—Eur 8 Million Fine for Breaching a Commission Seal During an Inspection' (2011) 3 *Competition Policy Newsletter* 8.

than the previous power to ask for 'oral explanations on the spot' in Article 14(1) of Regulation 17. The answers can be recorded.[206] Article 23(1)(d) provides that the Commission may fine the undertaking up to 1 per cent of total turnover of the previous business year if in response to a question asked in accordance with Article 20(2)(e):

— they give an incorrect or misleading answer,

— they fail to rectify within a time-limit set by the Commission an incorrect, incomplete or misleading answer given by a member of staff, or

— they fail or refuse to provide a complete answer on facts relating to the subject-matter and purpose of an inspection ordered by a decision adopted pursuant to Article 20(4).

'They' in this paragraph refers to the undertaking, not to the individual member of staff. There are no powers under Regulation 1/2003 to impose fines on individuals.[207] The imposition of a fine for failure or refusal to rectify incomplete, incorrect, or misleading answers is elaborated upon in Article 4(3) of Regulation 773/2004 which provides:

In cases where a member of staff of an undertaking or of an association of undertakings who is not or was not authorised by the undertaking or by the association of undertakings to provide explanations on behalf of the undertaking or association of undertakings has been asked for explanations, the Commission shall set a time-limit within which the undertaking or the association of undertakings may communicate to the Commission any rectification, amendment or supplement to the explanations given by such member of staff. The rectification, amendment or supplement shall be added to the explanations as recorded pursuant to paragraph 1.[208]

It is clear from *Nexans*[209] that questioning employees is an 'implementing measure'. It is not a separately reviewable act that can be challenged earlier than any challenge to the final infringement decision.

c. The Role of the NCAs, the Member States, and the National Courts in Article 20 Inspections

Article 20(5) of Regulation 1/2003 provides that officials from the NCA on whose territory the inspection is conducted may actively assist the Commission officials (and have the Article 20(2) powers) if either the NCA or the Commission requests it. The role of the Member State becomes more important, however, if the undertaking does not submit to the investigation. The duty to submit to an Article 14(3) investigation was a continuing one, entailing both allowing the inspection to begin and cooperating thereafter, but the limited nature of the Commission officials' powers, and their reliance on national authorities and national procedures, was sharply demonstrated in the case of *Hoechst*.[210] Article 20(6)[211] provides:

Where the officials and other accompanying persons authorised by the Commission find that an undertaking opposes an inspection ordered pursuant to this Article, the Member State concerned shall afford them the necessary assistance, requesting where appropriate the assistance of the police or of an equivalent enforcement authority, so as to enable them to conduct their inspection.

---

[206] Under Reg. 773/2004, Art. 4(2) a copy of any recording made has to be made available to the undertaking after the inspection.

[207] The absence under EU law of liability on individuals is in contrast to the position in some Member States, including the UK.

[208] Under Reg. 773/2004, Art. 17(3) the time limit has to be at least two weeks.

[209] Case T-135/09, *Nexans France* EU:T:2012:596.

[210] Cases 46/87 and 227/88, *Hoechst AG v Commission* [1989] ECR 2859, in which Hoechst simply refused to admit the Commission inspectors when they arrived for a dawn raid in the course of the Commission's investigations into the PVC and polyethylene cartels, and the local district court initially refused to issue a search warrant.

[211] Replacing Reg. 17, Art. 14(6).

If the 'assistance' requires authorisation, under national law, from a judicial authority (for example, because national law requires a court to sanction coercive measures such as forcible entry) Article 20(7) provides that it must be applied for.[212]

Article 20(8) of Regulation 1/2003 sets out the role of the national court. The provision enacts, in effect, the judgment of the CJ in *Roquette Frères SA*.[213] It makes it clear that the lawfulness of the Commission decision may be reviewed only by the EU Courts.

Regulation 1/2003

Article 20

…

8. Where authorisation as referred to in paragraph 7 is applied for, the national judicial authority shall control that the Commission decision is authentic and that the coercive measures envisaged are neither arbitrary nor excessive having regard to the subject matter of the inspection. In its control of the proportionality of the coercive measures, the national judicial authority may ask the Commission, directly or through the Member State competition authority, for detailed explanations in particular on the grounds the Commission has for suspecting infringement of [Articles 101 and 102 TFEU], as well as on the seriousness of the suspected infringement and on the nature of the involvement of the undertaking concerned. However, the national judicial authority may not call into question the necessity for the inspection nor demand that it be provided with the information in the Commission's file. The lawfulness of the Commission decision shall be subject to review only by the Court of Justice.

Furthermore, the role of the national courts in the context of Commission inspections is spelt out again in the Notice on cooperation between the Commission and the courts of the EU Member States.[214]

d. The Application of Article 8 ECHR and Article 7 of the Charter

In *Hoechst*[215] the CJ stated that the principle of the inviolability of the home in Article 8 ECHR[216] (to which Article 7 of the Charter corresponds) did not apply to commercial premises. However, the ECtHR subsequently held in *Niemitz*[217] that 'private life' and 'home' in Article 8(1) included certain professional or business activities or premises, as otherwise unequal treatment could arise, in that self-employed persons may carry on professional activities at home and private activities at their place of work.[218] Nevertheless, the entitlement of public authorities contained in Article 8(2) to interfere 'in accordance with the law' on certain grounds, might be more far-reaching where professional or business activities were involved.[219] In *Roquette Frères*[220] the CJ finally recognised the outcome of *Niemitz* and was prepared to accept, in a departure from *Hoechst*, that the protection provided for in

---

[212] Reg. 1/2003, Art. 20(7). In the UK under the Competition Act 1998, the Competition and Markets Authority (CMA) has power to enter premises with a warrant from the High Court in England and Wales or the Court of Session in Scotland using reasonable force as necessary.

[213] Case C-94/00, *Roquette Frères* [2002] ECR I-9011. The powers and duties of the national court in this situation, which were not expressly mentioned under Reg. 17, were initially spelt out in *Hoechst*; and in *Roquette Frères* the CJ looked at the issue in the context of the general principles of Community law and the ECHR as developed since *Hoechst*.

[214] [2004] OJ C101/54, paras. 38–41.

[215] Cases 46/87 and 227/88, *Hoechst* [1989] ECR 2859, para. 18.

[216] See Section 7.B.ii.d, p. 899.

[217] *Niemitz v Germany*, App. no. 1370/88 (1993) 16 EHRR 97, para. 31. The case concerned a lawyer's office.

[218] For a discussion of the extension of fundamental human rights to corporate bodies see, e.g., Andreangeli, n. 92, 17–18.

[219] *Niemitz*, App. no. 1370/88 (1993) 16 EHRR 97, para. 31.

[220] Cited in n. 213, para. 29.

Article 8 ECHR may in certain circumstances be extended to cover business premises.[221] In recognising that extension, the CJ referred to the ECtHR case, *Colas Est*,[222] which concerned an inspection raid by the French competition authority. The ECtHR held that the rights guaranteed by Article 8 can apply to a company's head office, branch office, or place of business and that the inspections were disproportionate to the legitimate objectives being pursued. The French law at the time did not contain enough guarantees against abuse and Article 8 was therefore violated. One of the factors French law lacked was any provision for prior judicial authorisation or other judicial supervision. Although it was suggested at the time that in the light of this case Commission inspections do not comply with Article 8,[223] Commission officials strongly argued that they do, particularly in the light of the changes made by Article 20 of Regulation 1/2003.[224] In *Harju v Finland*[225] the ECtHR noted 'that the absence of a prior judicial warrant may be counterbalanced by the availability of an *ex post factum* judicial review'. In *Delta Pekárny*[226] the ECtHR ruled that a dawn raid by the Czech competition authority violated Article 8 because it was not subject to prior judicial authorisation and there was no effective *ex post* judicial review. In particular, the Czech court failed to review the actual process of the raid and the way in which the authority had exercised its powers. It is clear from the ECtHR cases, therefore, that where there is no prior judicial involvement (which appears to be the Court's preferred option), *ex post* judicial review must be stringent.

Article 20 does not require prior judicial authorisation unless the inspectors require the assistance of the Member State, in accordance with Article 20(6)–(8). It is therefore essential, if the inspection regime is to comply with Article 8 (and with Article 7 of the Charter), that there is effective and rigorous *ex post* review by the EU Courts. This was an issue in *Deutsche Bahn*,[227] in which the CJ upheld the GC's dismissal of the plea that the lack of prior judicial authorisation in EU law in respect of inspections was not remedied by effective *ex post* review. It approved the five categories of safeguards set out by the GC which must form the framework for the inspection decision and against which the legality of the decision must be measured: (a) the statement of reasons on which inspection decisions are based; (b) the limits imposed on the Commission during the conduct of inspections; (c) the impossibility for the Commission to carry out an inspection by force; (d) the intervention of national authorities; and (e) the existence of *ex post facto* remedies.[228] It held that the GC's detailed examination of the decision against that framework satisfied both the ECHR and EU law.

Case C-583/13 P, *Deutsche Bahn AG v Commission* EU:C:2015:404

Court of Justice

29. The detailed examination conducted by the General Court satisfies both the requirements of the ECtHR, as is apparent from the preceding paragraph herein, and the letter of Regulation No 1/2003 and the Court of Justice's case-law.

---

[221] In Cases T-305/94 etc., *Limburgse Vinyl Maatschappij* [1999] ECR II-931, the GC had considered that the evolution of the case law of the ECtHR since *Hoechst* had no direct impact on the latter and on appeal, Cases C-238, 244–245, 247, 250, 251–252, and 254/99 P, *Limburgse Vinyl Maatschappij NV v Commission* [2002] ECR I-8375, para. 251, the CJ did not find it necessary to rule on the matter.

[222] *Société Colas Est and others v France*, App. no. 37971/97, Judgment of 16 April 2002.

[223] J. Temple Lang and C. Rizza, 'The *Ste Colas Est and Others v France* Case: European Court of Human Rights Judgment of 16 April 2002' [2002] *ECLR* 417.

[224] K. Dekeyser and C. Gauer, 'The New Enforcement System for Articles 101 and 102 and the Rights of Defence' [2004] *Fordham Corp L Inst* 549, 556–557.

[225] App. no. 56716/09, Judgment of 15 February 2011, para. 44.

[226] *Delta Pekárny a.s. v The Czech Republic*, App. no. 97/11, Judgment of 2 October 2014.

[227] Case C-583/13 P, *Deutsche Bahn AG v Commission* EU:C:2015:404.

[228] Case T-289/11, *Deutsche Bahn AG v Commission* EU:T:2013:404, paras. 74–100.

30. On the one hand, it is apparent from Article 20(4) of Regulation No 1/2003 that the inspection decision must specify the subject-matter and purpose of the inspection, indicate the penalties incurred by the undertaking concerned and the undertaking's right to have the decision reviewed by the Court of Justice.

31. On the other hand, it is settled case-law that the Commission's powers of investigation are strictly defined, encompassing inter alia the exclusion of non-business documents from the scope of the investigation, the right to legal assistance, the preservation of the confidentiality of correspondence between legal counsel and clients, the obligation to state reasons for the inspection decision and the option of bringing proceedings before the EU courts (see, to that effect, judgment in *Roquette Frères,...*, paragraphs 44 to 50).

32. Moreover, as observed by the Advocate General in point 38 of his Opinion and as stated in paragraph 26 of this judgment, the presence of a post-inspection judicial review is considered by the ECtHR as capable of offsetting the lack of prior judicial authorisation and thus capable of constituting a fundamental guarantee in order to ensure the compatibility of the inspection measure in question with Article 8 of the ECHR (see inter alia ECtHR, judgment in *Delta Pekárny a.s. v. the Czech Republic*, no. 97/11, paragraphs 83, 87 and 92, 2 October 2014).

33. That is precisely the case under the system put in place in the European Union, as Article 20(8) of Regulation No 1/2003 states expressly that the lawfulness of the Commission decision is to be subject to review by the Court of Justice.

34. The review provided for by the Treaties means that the European Union courts carry out an in-depth review of the law and of the facts on the basis of the evidence adduced by the applicant in support of the pleas in law put forward (see, to that effect, judgments in *Chalkor* v *Commission*, C-386/10 P,..., paragraph 62, and *CB* v *Commission*, paragraph 44).

35. It follows that the General Court was correct in holding that the fundamental right to the inviolability of private premises, as protected by Article 8 of the ECHR, is not disregarded by there being no prior judicial authorisation.

36. Accordingly, it must also be concluded that no infringement of Article 7 of the Charter has been established.

In both *Deutsche Bahn* itself[229] and in *Nexans*,[230] the EU Courts have been at pains to demonstrate the comprehensiveness of their judicial review of inspections. It is clear that without prior authorisation of inspections the ECtHR demands much of *ex post factum* review and that the EU Courts appreciate this.

e. Legal Advice

Article 20, like Article 14 of Regulation 17, says nothing about an undertaking's right to have legal advisers present during the investigation. When conducting the unannounced investigation in *National Panasonic*[231] the Commission was prepared to wait for some time for the undertakings' legal advisers to arrive, but after a while proceeded in their absence. The CJ held that Panasonic's fundamental rights had not been infringed in the investigation, although it did not expressly avert to the legal adviser point. The Explanatory Note on inspections[232] says that the officials may enter the premises and occupy offices without waiting for the undertaking to consult its lawyer and will only accept a short delay before proceeding with the inspection. During any wait the undertaking's

---

[229] Where the CJ, on another point in the appeal, overruled the GC's finding that the second and third inspection decisions were valid, see Section 7.C.iii.a, p. 909.

[230] Cited in n. 185, see Section 7.C.iii.a, p. 909.

[231] Cited in n. 174.

[232] See n. 179, para. 6.

management has to ensure that business records remain as they were on the officials' arrival and the officials have to be allowed to enter and remain in the offices of their choice. In *Koninklijke Wegenbouw Stevin* an undertaking's refusal to allow the inspection to begin before the arrival of its external lawyer was held by the GC to constitute a refusal to submit to the inspection.[233]

(iv) Inspections on Private Premises Under Article 21

Regulation 1/2003 gives the Commission power to conduct inspections at private premises.[234] In other words, dawn raids may be conducted at the homes (and on the private vehicles) of directors and employees. Article 21(1) states:

If a reasonable suspicion exists that books or other records related to the business and to the subject-matter of the inspection, which may be relevant to prove a serious violation of Article [101] or Article [102]…are being kept in any other premises, land and means of transport, including the homes of directors, managers and other members of staff of the undertakings and associations of undertakings concerned, the Commission can by decision order an inspection to be conducted in such other premises, land and means of transport.

Recital 26 explains that the provision was introduced because '[e]xperience has shown that there are cases where business records are kept in the homes of directors or other people working for an undertaking'. In particular, the Commission is determined that its efforts to crack hardcore cartels are not frustrated by individuals keeping the incriminating evidence at home.[235] Unsurprisingly, the safeguards provided by Article 8 ECHR,[236] apply par excellence to Article 21. Moreover, the inspection may only take place with prior authorisation from the national judicial authority of the Member State concerned. The right of the national court to query the necessity for the inspection, however, is limited as in Article 20(8), so that the national judicial authority may not call into question the necessity for the inspection nor demand that it be provided with information in the Commission's file. In controlling that the Commission decision is authentic and that the coercive measures envisaged are neither arbitrary nor excessive, however, the national court should have regard to 'the importance of the evidence sought' and 'the reasonable likelihood that business books and records relating to the subject matter of the inspection are kept in the premises for which the authorisation is requested'.[237] In the light of the jurisprudence of the ECtHR there is doubt as to whether the limited functions of the national courts in respect of Article 21 inspections satisfy the ECHR requirements for prior judicial authorisation.[238] As in respect of Article 20, therefore, it will be the possibility of effective *ex post* judicial review by the EU Courts which needs to satisfy Article 8.

There is no provision in Article 21 for sealing private premises, or for questioning the person whose premises are being searched. Regulation 1/2003 does not impose penalties for opposing the inspection: there is no provision in Article 23 for the Commission to fine the undertaking concerned and nothing in Regulation 1/2003 puts any liability on individuals.[239] The position as regards

---

[233] Case T-357/06, *Koninklijke Wegenbouw Stevin BV v Commission* EU:T:2012:488 (the appeal, Case C-586/12 P, EU:C:2013:863, was on other grounds). When the lawyer arrived he refused to permit the inspectors to enter one particular office, which was also held to be a refusal to submit.

[234] This is an innovation in Reg. 1/2003. Reg. 17 did not contain such a power.

[235] See, e.g., *SAS/Maersk* [2001] OJ L265/15, in which documents relating to a market-sharing agreement were kept at home, although they were voluntarily surrendered a few days after the Reg. 17, Art. 14(3) inspection. A note of one meeting recorded a Maersk representative saying that 'all material on price agreements, market-sharing agreements and the like *had* to be destroyed before going home today. Anything that might be needed *had* to be taken home . . .' (*SAS/Maersk*, para. 89).

[236] See Section 7.B.ii.d, p. 899.

[237] Art. 21(3). See also Notice on cooperation between the Commission and the courts of the EU Member States [2004] OJ C101/54, para. 40.

[238] See Bellamy and Child, n. 2, 13.029; Kerse and Khan, n. 2, 3.142.

[239] It is possible, however, that penalties could be imposed under national law, see Faull and Nikpay, n. 2, 8.425.

forcible entry if provided for in national law is the same as in respect of Article 20.[240] The first dawn raid on a private home under Article 21 was carried out in 2007 in the UK in connection with the investigation of the *Marine Hoses cartel*.[241]

(v) The Power to Take Statements

Article 19 of Regulation 1/2003 gave the Commission a new power to 'take statements' by which it can conduct formal interviews with natural or legal persons. Such persons could include, for example, ex-employees, complainants, competitors, or employees of candidates for leniency.[242] It can be exercised only with the consent of the person concerned, and only to collect information in relation to the subject matter of an investigation. Article 19 states:

1. In order to carry out the duties assigned to it by this Regulation, the Commission may interview any natural or legal person who consents to be interviewed for the purpose of collecting information relating to the subject-matter of an investigation.

2. Where an interview pursuant to paragraph 1 is conducted in the premises of an undertaking, the Commission shall inform the competition authority of the Member State in whose territory the interview takes place. If so requested by the competition authority of that Member State, its officials may assist the officials and other accompanying persons authorised by the Commission to conduct the interview.

Article 3 of Regulation 773/2004 further provides:

1. Where the Commission interviews a person with his consent in accordance with Article 19 of Regulation (EC) No 1/2003, it shall, at the beginning of the interview, state the legal basis and the purpose of the interview, and recall its voluntary nature. It shall also inform the person interviewed of its intention to make a record of the interview.

2. The interview may be conducted by any means including by telephone or electronic means.

3. The Commission may record the statements made by the persons interviewed in any form. A copy of any recording shall be made available to the person interviewed for approval. Where necessary, the Commission shall set a time-limit within which the person interviewed may communicate to it any correction to be made to the statement.[243]

The interviewee is free not to accept the Commission's invitation to be interviewed, and there is no sanction for refusing. During the interview the person concerned can refuse to answer questions, refuse to give reasons for the refusal, and need not find documents, etc. There are no penalties for giving incorrect or misleading information under Article 19. This is in sharp contrast to Article 20(2)(e) (explanations on facts).

The GC considered the provisions of Article 21 and of Article 3 of Regulation 773/2004 in *Intel*.[244] It held that a distinction should be drawn between formal interviews conducted according to the requirements of Article 3, and informal interviews.[245] It is clear from recital 25 that the purpose of Article 19 is to supplement the Commission's other powers[246] and so the Commission retains its powers to conduct informal interviews and enjoys a discretion in deciding whether to make an interview subject to Article 3. Article 3 does not apply to all interviews relating to the subject matter

---

[240] See Section 7.B.iii.b, p. 913.

[241] COMP/39.406, 28 January 2009; IP/09/137 (decision partially annulled on appeal on the issue of economic continuity, Cases T-146/09 etc., *Parker ITR and Parker-Hannifin v Commission* EU:T:2013:258; judgment set aside by the CJ, Case C-434/13 P, *Commission v Parker Hannifin Manufacturing Srl* EU:C:2014:2456).

[242] See the discussion in Faull and Nikpay, n. 2, 8.320. For the leniency policy, see Section 7.G.v, pp. 983.

[243] The time limit is at least two weeks, Reg. 773/2004, Art. 17(3).

[244] Case T-286/09, *Intel* EU:T:2014:547, paras. 612–618.

[245] Ibid., para. 614.

[246] Ibid., para. 616.

of the investigation but only to the cases for which the Commission was pursuing the objective of obtaining both incriminating and exculpatory information on which it would be able to rely as evidence in its final decision.[247] However, although informal interviews are not covered by the recording requirements of Article 3, and there is no general duty on the Commission to establish a record of informal discussions, the principle of good administration (Article 41 of the Charter) may impose a duty in a particular case, depending on the circumstances and the content of the information. This is because addressees of SOs have a right to know the case against them, which includes a right of access to the Commission's file.[248] If the Commission does not make a record the addressee cannot access it. So in *Intel* the GC held that the Commission's failure to place on the file a succinct note of a five-hour interview with a senior executive of Intel's largest customer which contained the names of the participants and a brief summary of the subjects addressed breached the principle of good administration (which the GC was satisfied was later remedied).[249]

The Commission has used Article 19 regularly but 'experience has shown that the absence of penalties for misleading or false replies may be a disincentive to provide correct and complete statements'.[250] Interviewees are entitled to be accompanied by lawyers and interviews may take place on or away from business premises. The Antitrust ManProc says that nobody can be prevented by their current or former employer from giving an interview, unless he or she acts on behalf of the undertaking.[251]

(vi) The Privilege Against Self-incrimination

The Commission's wide powers to carry out inspections and ask for information under Articles 18, 20, and 21 of Regulation 1/2003 raises the issue of whether EU law recognises as part of the rights of the defence a privilege against self-incrimination.

The position in EU law is that the duty actively to cooperate with the Commission does not mean that the undertaking has to incriminate itself by admitting to infringements of the competition rules. However, the Commission may ask questions, or demand the production of documents, by means of which it can establish an infringement. This was first established in *Orkem*.

Case 374/87, *Orkem SA v Commission* [1989] ECR 3283

The Commission was investigating alleged cartels in the thermoplastics industry. The questions it required to be answered asked for: (a) factual information about a meeting, (b) clarification on 'every step or concerted measure which may have been envisaged or adopted to support such price initiatives', (c) the 'details of any system or method which made it possible to attribute sales or targets or quotas to the participants', and (d) 'details of any methods facilitating annual monitoring of compliance with any system of targets in terms of volumes or quotas'. The undertaking challenged the decision claiming that the Commission had infringed the general principle that no one may be compelled to give evidence against himself, a principle which was part of Community law as it was recognised by the Member States, by Article 6 ECHR, and by paragraph 3(g) of the International Covenant on Civil and Political Rights, 1966.

---

[247] Ibid., para. 615.

[248] Ibid., para. 620.

[249] Ibid., paras. 621–625. As it was remedied the *Intel* decision, COMP/37.990, was therefore not vitiated by procedural irregularity. The Ombudsman had earlier made a finding of maladministration (1935/2008/FOR) against the Commission for failing to take minutes of the meeting and therefore not to have placed a record on the file.

[250] Report on the Functioning of Reg. 1/2003, n. 56, para. 12; see also Faull and Nikpay, n. 2, 8.320.

[251] Antitrust ManProc (see n. 68), Module 8, para. 14.

Court of Justice

28. In the absence of any right to remain silent expressly embodied in Regulation 17, it is appropriate to consider whether and to what extent the general principles of Community law, of which fundamental rights form an integral part and in the light of which all Community legislation must be interpreted, require, as the applicant claims, recognition of the right not to supply information capable of being used in order to establish against the person supplying it, the existence of an infringement of the competition rules.

29. In general, the laws of the Member-States grant the right not to give evidence against oneself only to a natural person charged with an offence in criminal proceedings. A comparative analysis of national law does not therefore indicate the existence of such a principle, common to the laws of the Member-States, which may be relied upon by legal persons in relation to infringements in the economic sphere, in particular infringements of competition law.

30. As far as Article 6 of the European Convention is concerned, although it may be relied upon by an undertaking subject to an investigation relating to competition law, it must be observed that neither the wording of that Article nor the decisions of [the] European Court of Human Rights indicate that it upholds the right not to give evidence against oneself.

31. Article 14 of the International Covenant, which upholds, in addition to the presumption of innocence, the right (in paragraph 3(g)) not to give evidence against oneself or to confess guilt, relates only to persons accused of a criminal offence in court proceedings and thus has no bearing on investigations in the field of competition law.

32. It is necessary, however, to consider whether certain limitations on the Commission's powers of investigation are implied by the need to safeguard the rights of the defence which the Court has held to be [a] fundamental principle of the Community order (Case 322/102, *Michelin* v. *E.C. Commission* .

33. In that connection, the court observed recently in its judgment in Joined Cases 46/87 and 227/88 *Hoechst* v. *E.C. Commission*...that whilst it is true that the rights of the defence must be observed in administrative procedures which may lead to the imposition of penalties, it is necessary to prevent those rights from being irremediably impaired during preliminary inquiry procedures which may be decisive in providing evidence of the unlawful nature of conduct engaged in by undertakings and for which they may be liable. Consequently, although certain rights of the defence relate only to contentious proceedings which follow the delivery of the statement of objections, other rights must be respected even during the preliminary inquiry.

34. Accordingly, whilst the Commission is entitled, in order to preserve the useful effect of Article 11(2) and (5) of Regulation 17, to compel an undertaking to provide all necessary information concerning such facts as may be known to it and to disclose to it, if necessary, such documents relating thereto as are in its possession, even if the latter may be used to establish, against it or another undertaking, the existence of anti-competitive conduct, it may not, by means of a decision calling for information, undermine the rights of defence of the undertaking concerned.

35. Thus, the Commission may not compel an undertaking to provide it with answers which might involve an admission on its part of the existence of an infringement which it is incumbent upon the Commission to prove.

On this basis, the CJ annulled the decision in respect of all the questions listed except the first one. The Court drew a distinction (paragraphs 34 and 35) between a right to compel the undertaking to provide factual information which can be used to establish a breach of the rules, and a right to compel it to admit to the breach. The Commission has the former but not the latter right.[252]

---

[252] The privilege against self-incrimination is irrelevant to Art. 18(2) simple requests for information because there is no element of compulsion or sanction involved, see Case C-293/13 P, *Fresh del Monte Produce Inc v Commission* EU:C:2015:416, paras. 193–199.

The Court denied in *Orkem* (paragraph 30 of the extract) that Article 6 ECHR, guaranteeing the right to a fair trial,[253] included the right not to provide evidence against oneself. In *Funke* four years later, however, the ECtHR held that as a result of Article 6(1) a person charged with a criminal offence within the meaning of that Article had the right 'to remain silent and not . . . contribute to incriminating himself'.[254] In *Saunders v UK*,[255] however, the ECtHR said that the right not to incriminate oneself did not extend to 'material which may be obtained from the accused through the use of compulsory powers but which has an existence independent of the will of the suspect such as, inter alia, documents acquired pursuant to a warrant . . .'.[256] The concept of 'independent existence' is a difficult one and the jurisprudence of the ECtHR is still in a state of development.[257] However, it is clear that Article 6(1) does not require an absolute right to silence.[258]

The GC restated the *Orkem* position in *Mannesmannröhren-Werke AG*.[259] In that case the Commission was conducting an investigating into an alleged cartel.[260] The undertaking refused to reply to some requests for information under Article 11(4) of Regulation 17 relating to three sets of meetings. In respect of each of them the Commission asked for dates, places, names of participants, copies of all agendas, minutes, and records relating to them and (each time) 'in the case of meetings for which you are unable to find the relevant documents, please describe the purpose of the meeting, the decisions adopted and the type of documents received before and after the meeting'. Another set of questions related to four agreements. The undertaking was asked, inter alia, about the relationship of the agreements to another arrangement, and to what extent 'did the existence and implementation of these agreements influence the decisions adopted within the Europe-Japan Club and/or within the Special Circle?' On the undertaking's refusal to answer, claiming it was being asked to incriminate itself, the Commission adopted a decision under Article 11(5) of Regulation 17 demanding answers on pain of periodic penalty payments. The undertaking appealed against the decision. On appeal the GC held, on the basis of *Orkem*, that the last question in respect of each of the sets of meetings asked the undertaking about the 'purpose' of meetings, and the 'decisions' adopted. This went beyond mere factual information: 'it follows that requests of this kind are such that they may compel the applicant to admit its participation in an unlawful agreement . . .'.[261] The decision was therefore annulled in respect of the three last questions. The decision was also annulled in respect of the whole question about the agreements as '[a]nswering this question would require the applicant to give its assessment of the nature of those decisions'.[262] In *PVC Cartel II*[263] the CJ held that the developments in the ECtHR jurisprudence since *Orkem* did not alter the established position.

---

[253] See Section 7.B.ii.a, p. 895 and see, on the self-incrimination point, A. Riley, '*Saunders* and the Power to Obtain Information in Community and United Kingdom Competition Law' (2000) 25 *ELRev* 264.

[254] *Funke v France*, App. no. 10828/84 (1993) 16 EHRR 297, para. 44.

[255] *Saunders v UK*, App. no. 19187/91 (1997) 23 EHRR 313.

[256] Ibid., para. 69.

[257] See *JB v Switzerland*, App. no. 31827/96 [2001] Crim LR 748; *Heaney and McGuinness v Ireland*, App. no. 34720/97 (2001) 33 EHRR 12; *Jalloh v Germany*, App. no. 54810/00 (2007) 44 EHRR 32; *O'Halloran and Francis v UK*, App. no. 15809/02 (2008) 46 EHRR 21.

[258] See further Harris, O'Boyle, and Warbrick, n. 89, 259–264; M. Berger, 'Self-incrimination and the European Court of Human Rights: Procedural Issues in the Enforcement of the Right to Silence' (2007) 5 *EHRLR* 514; M. Redmayne, 'Rethinking the Privilege Against Self-incrimination' (2007) 27 *OJLS* 209; N. Andrews, 'Privilege Against Self-incrimination in the Human Rights Era' [2007] *CLJ* 47; A. Ashworth, 'Self-incrimination in European Human Rights Law—A Pregnant Pragmatism?' (2008–2009) 30 *Cardozo LR* 751; A.L.-T. Choo, *The Privilege Against Self-incrimination and Criminal Justice* (Hart Publishing, 2013).

[259] Case T-112/98, *Mannesmannröhren-Werke AG v Commission* [2001] ECR II-729. See P. R. Willis, '"You Have the Right to Remain Silent . . .", or Do You? The Privilege Against Self-incrimination Following *Mannesmannröhren-Werke* and Other Recent Decisions' [2001] *ECLR* 313.

[260] It culminated in the *Seamless Steel Tubes* decision in 1999, [2003] OJ L14/1.

[261] Case T-112/98, *Mannesmannröhren-Werke* [2001] ECR II-729, para. 71.

[262] Ibid., para. 74.

[263] Cases C-238/99 P etc., *Limburgse Vinyl Maatschappij* [2002] ECR I-8375.

In *Tokai Carbon* in 2004[264] the GC, although appearing to consider that it was following settled case law, nonetheless held that the Commission's request for documents in respect of meetings such as the protocols, working documents, preparatory documents, handwritten notes, planning and discussion documents, etc. was tantamount to requiring that the undertaking admit its participation. The GC reasoned that since, therefore, the undertaking concerned was not required to produce such documents on grounds of self-incrimination, if it *did* do so it must be regarded as doing so voluntarily and was thereby eligible for leniency under the Commission's leniency policy.[265] On appeal the Advocate General recommended that the GC's judgment be set aside. He considered that the law established by *Orkem* complied with the Article 6(1) as interpreted by the ECtHR and he stressed that there is a distinction between the protection conferred on natural persons and that conferred on legal persons.[266] The CJ said that the GC's judgment had weakened the principle that undertakings subject to an investigation have a duty to cooperate. The CJ re-established the position that undertakings cannot refuse to produce documents on grounds of self-incrimination.

Case C-301/04 P, *Commission v SGL Carbon* [2006] ECR I-5915

Court of Justice

39. It must be recalled first that, under Article 11(1) of Regulation No 17, in carrying out the duties assigned to it in the matter, the Commission may obtain all necessary information from the governments and competent authorities of the Member States and from undertakings and associations of undertakings. As set out in Article 11(4) thereof, the owners of the undertakings or their representatives and, in the case of legal persons, companies or firms, or of associations having no legal personality, the persons authorised to represent them by law or by their constitution are to supply the information requested.

40. As regards the Commission's powers to make such requests, it is important to note that, in paragraph 27 of the judgment in *Orkem* v *Commission*, the Court pointed out that Regulation No 17 does not give an undertaking which is being investigated under that regulation any right to evade the investigation and that, on the contrary, the undertaking in question is subject to an obligation to cooperate actively, which implies that it must make available to the Commission all information relating to the subject-matter of the investigation.

41. So far as concerns the question whether that obligation also applies to requests for information which could be used to establish, against the undertaking which provides the information, an infringement of the competition rules, the Court held, in paragraph 34 of that judgment that in order to ensure the effectiveness of Article 11(2) and (5) of Regulation No 17 the Commission is entitled to compel an undertaking, if necessary by adopting a decision, to provide all necessary information concerning such facts as may be known to it and to disclose to it, if necessary, such documents relating thereto as are in that undertaking's possession, even if the latter may be used to establish, against it or another undertaking, the existence of anti-competitive conduct.

42. By contrast, the situation is completely different where the Commission seeks to obtain answers from an undertaking which is being investigated by which that undertaking would be led to admit an infringement which it is incumbent upon the Commission to prove (see *Orkem* v *Commission*, paragraph 35).

43. It must be added that the Court of Justice, in paragraphs 274 to 276 of the judgment in *Limburgse Vinyl Maatschappij and Others* v *Commission*, observed that since the judgment in *Orkem* v *Commission* there have been further developments in the case-law of the European Court of Human Rights which

---

[264] Cases T-236, 239, 244–246, 251, and 252/01, *Tokai Carbon Co Ltd and others v Commission* [2004] ECR II-1181 (the appeal from the *Graphite Electrodes* cartel, [2002] OJ L100/1).

[265] Ibid., paras. 408–409. For the leniency policy, see Section 7.H.v, p. 983.

[266] Case C-301/04 P, *Commission v SGL Carbon* [2006] ECR I-5915, Geelhoed AG, paras. 56–69. He referred to *Niemitz v Germany*, App. no. 1370/88 (1992) 16 EHRR 97 which made this distinction in the context of Art. 8 ECHR.

the Community judicature must take into account when interpreting the fundamental rights. The Court of Justice stated however in that regard that those developments were not such as to put in question the statements of principle in *Orkem* v *Commission*.

44. It does not follow from that case-law that the Commission's powers of investigation have been limited as regards the production of documents in the possession of an undertaking which is subject to investigation. The undertaking concerned must therefore, if the Commission requests it, provide the Commission with documents which relate to the subject-matter of the investigation, even if those documents could be used by the Commission in order to establish the existence of an infringement.

45. It is important to point out also that the [General Court] itself, in paragraph 405 of the judgment under appeal, expressly referred to the principles stated in *Orkem* v *Commission* and to the fact that the Court of Justice has not reversed its previous case-law on the point.

46. The [General Court] found, however, in the course of its reasoning, that the Commission's request for information of 31 March 1999 was such as to require SGL Carbon to admit its participation in infringements of the Community competition rules.

47. That finding of the [General Court] misconstrues the scope of Article 11 of Regulation No 17, as interpreted by the Court of Justice, and therefore weakens the principle that undertakings subject to a Commission investigation must cooperate.

48. That obligation to cooperate means that the undertaking may not evade requests for production of documents on the ground that by complying with them it would be required to give evidence against itself.

49. In addition, as the Advocate General correctly observed in point 67 of his Opinion, while it is evident that the rights of the defence should be respected, the undertaking concerned is still able, either during the administrative procedure or in the proceedings before the Community Courts, to contend that the documents produced have a different meaning from that ascribed to them by the Commission.

50. Thus, the [General Court] made an error of law in holding that the conditions for a reduction in the fine by virtue of the Leniency Notice were fulfilled.

(vii) Legal Professional Privilege

a. The Extent of Legal Professional Privilege

Legal professional privilege (LPP) means the confidentiality attached to certain communications between a client and its lawyers. Regulation 1/2003, like Regulation 17, does not deal with the issue. In English law LPP means that confidential communications passing between lawyer and client with a view to giving or securing legal advice are privileged so far as the client is concerned, and protected from disclosure. In *AM&S* a UK undertaking argued that it was entitled to keep from the Commission correspondence with its legal advisers that would have been privileged under English law. There were two main issues: first, whether LPP applied in EC competition cases and, if so, whether it was a *Community* principle or a matter of recognising the rule in the Member State concerned; secondly, if legal privilege was recognised, how procedurally should it be dealt with? It is not attractive to the investigated undertakings for the Commission inspectors to look at documents and then decide they are to be disregarded, whatever 'Chinese walls' the Commission erects internally between the inspectors and those deciding on the existence or otherwise of an infringement.

Case 155/79, *AM&S Ltd v Commission* [1982] ECR 1575

On 20 February 1979 Commission officials arrived at the offices of AM&S in Bristol for an unannounced Article 14(2) inspection. At the end of two days the Commission inspectors left with copies of about 35 documents, leaving behind a written request for certain other documents to be supplied. The managing director sent a further seven files of documents on 26 March with a letter saying that certain of the requested documents were not being produced because the undertaking's lawyers considered they were covered by LPP. Without further communication the Commission adopted a decision on 6 July under Article 14(3) demanding that the undertaking submit to an inspection and in particular produce the excluded documents. In the preamble the Commission stated that although Community competition law did not provide for protection for legal papers nonetheless it was willing not to use certain communications between the undertaking and its lawyers as evidence and that '[w]hen the Commission comes across such papers it does not copy them'. It was for the Commission, subject to review by the Court, to decide whether a given document should be used or not. The Commission inspectors served the decision on 25 July and carried out a further inspection. The undertaking still refused to disclose all the disputed documents but finally, after a meeting with the Commission in Brussels, it disclosed all except one. On 4 October the undertaking commenced an action under Article 263 claiming that the decision of 6 July was void insofar as it required the disclosure of legally privileged documents.

Advocate General Warner presented in his Opinion a survey of the position on legal privilege in all Member States.

Court of Justice

15. The purpose of Regulation No 17 of the Council which was adopted pursuant to the first subparagraph of Article [103(1) TFEU] is, according to paragraph (2)(a) and (b) of that article, 'to ensure compliance with the prohibitions laid down in Article [101(1)] and in Article [102]' and 'to lay down detailed rules for the application of Article [101(3)]'. The regulation is thus intended to ensure that the aim stated in Article [3(1)(g) EC] is achieved. To that end it confers on the Commission wide powers of investigation and of obtaining information by providing in the eighth recital in its preamble that the Commission must be empowered, throughout the Common Market, to require such information to be supplied and to undertake such investigations 'as are necessary' to bring to light infringements of Articles [101] and [102].

16. In Articles 11 and 14 of the regulation, therefore, it is provided that the Commission may obtain 'information' and undertake the 'necessary' investigations, for the purpose of proceedings in respect of infringements of the rules governing competition. Article 14(1) in particular empowers the Commission to require production of business records, that is to say, documents concerning the market activities of the undertaking, in particular as regards compliance with those rules. Written communications between lawyer and client fall, in so far as they have a bearing on such activities, within the category of documents referred to in Articles 11 and 14.

17. Furthermore since the documents which the Commission may demand are, as Article 14(1) confirms, those whose disclosure it considers 'necessary' in order that it may bring to light an infringement of the Treaty rules on competition, it is in principle for the Commission itself, and not the undertaking concerned or a third party, whether an expert or an arbitrator, to decide whether or not a document must be produced to it.

(b) Applicability of the protection of confidentiality in Community law

18. However, the above rules do not exclude the possibility of recognizing, subject to certain conditions, that certain business records are of a confidential nature. Community law, which derives from not only the economic but also the legal interpenetration of the Member States, must take into account the principles and concepts common to the laws of those States concerning the observance of confidentiality, in particular, as regards certain communications between lawyer and client. That confidentiality serves the requirements, the importance of which is recognized in all of the Member States, that any person must be able, without constraint, to consult a lawyer whose profession entails the giving of independent legal advice to all those in need of it.

19. As far as the protection of written communications between lawyer and client is concerned, it is apparent from the legal systems of the Member States that, although the principle of such protection is generally recognized, its scope and the criteria for applying it vary, as has, indeed, been conceded both by the application and by the parties who have intervened in support of its conclusions.

20. Whilst in some of the Member States the protection against disclosure afforded to written communications between lawyer and client is based principally on a recognition of the very nature of the legal profession, inasmuch as it contributes towards the maintenance of the rule of law, in other Member States the same protection is justified by the more specific requirement (which, moreover, is also recognized in the first-mentioned States) that the rights of the defence must be respected.

21. Apart from these differences, however, there are to be found in the national laws of the Member States common criteria inasmuch as those law protect, in similar circumstances, the confidentiality of written communications between lawyer and client provided that, on the one hand, such communications are made for the purposes and in the interests of the client's rights of defence and, on the other hand, they emanate from independent lawyers, that is to say, lawyers who are not bound to the client by a relationship of employment.

22. Viewed in that context Regulation No 17 must be interpreted as protecting, in its turn, the confidentiality of written communications between lawyer and client subject to those two conditions, and thus incorporating such elements of that protection as are common to the laws of the Member States.

23. As far as the first of those two conditions is concerned, in Regulation No 17 itself, in particular in the eleventh recital in its preamble and in the provisions contained in Article 19, care is taken to ensure that the rights of the defence may be exercised to the full, and the protection of the confidentiality of written communications between lawyer and client is an essential corollary to those rights. In those circumstances, such protection must, if it is to be effective, be recognized as covering all written communications exchanged after the initiation of the administrative procedure under Regulation No 17 which may lead to a decision on the application of Articles [101] and [102] of the Treaty or to a decision imposing a pecuniary sanction on the undertaking. It must also be possible to extend it to earlier written communications which have a relationship to the subject-matter of that procedure.

24. As regards the second condition, it should be stated that the requirement as to the position and status as an independent lawyer, which must be fulfilled by the legal adviser from whom the written communications which may be protected emanate, is based on a conception of the lawyer's role as collaborating in the administration of justice by the courts and as being required to provide, in full independence, and in the overriding interests of that cause, such legal assistance as the client needs. The counterpart of that protection lies in the rules of professional ethics and discipline which are laid down and enforced in the general interest by institutions endowed with the requisite powers for that purpose. Such a conception reflects the legal traditions common to the Member States and is also to be found in [the] legal order of the Community, as is demonstrated by Article 17 of the Protocols on the Statutes of the Court of Justice of the EEC and the EAEC [European Atomic Energy Community], and also by Article 20 of the Protocol on the Statute of the Court of Justice of the ECSC [European Coal and Steel Community].

25. Having regard to the principles of the Treaty concerning freedom of establishment and the freedom to provide services the protection thus afforded by Community law, in particular in the context of Regulation No 17, to written communications between lawyer and client must apply without distinction to any lawyer entitled to practice his profession in one of the Member States, regardless of the Member State in which the client lives.

26. Such protection may be not be extended beyond those limits which are determined by the scope of the common rules on the exercise of the legal profession as laid down in Council Directive 77/249/EEC of 22 March 1977 (OJ L 78, p. 17), which is based in its turn on the mutual recognition by all the Member States of the national legal concepts of each of them on this subject.

27. In view of all these factors it must therefore be concluded that although Regulation No 17, and in particular Article 14 thereof, interpreted in the light of its wording, structure and aims, and having regard to the laws of the Member States, empowers the Commission to require, in the course of an investigation within the meaning of that article, production of the business documents the disclosure of which it considers necessary including written communications between lawyer and client, for proceedings in respect of any infringements of Articles [101] and [102], that power is, however, subject to a restriction imposed by the need to protect confidentiality, on the conditions defined above, and provided that the

communications in question are exchanged between an independent lawyer, that is to say one who is not bound to his client by a relationship of employment, and his client.

28. Finally, it should be remarked that the principle of confidentiality does not prevent a lawyer's client from disclosing the written communications between them if he considers that it is in his interests to do so.

(c) The procedures relating to the application of the principle of confidentiality

29. If an undertaking which is the subject of an investigation under Article 14 of Regulation No 17 refuses, on the ground that it is entitled to protection of the confidentiality of information, to produce, among the business records demanded by the Commission, written communications between itself and its lawyer, it must nevertheless provide the Commission's authorised agents with relevant material of such a nature as to demonstrate that the communications fulfil the conditions for being granted legal protection as defined above, although it is not bound to reveal the contents of the communications in question.

30. Where the Commission is not satisfied that such evidence has been supplied, the appraisal of those conditions is not a matter which may be left to an arbitrator or to a national authority. Since this is a matter involving an appraisal and a decision which affect the conditions under which the Commission may act in a field as vital to the functioning of the common market as that of compliance with the rules on competition, the solution of disputes as to the application of the protection of the confidentiality of written communications between lawyer and client may be sought only at Community level.

31. In that case it is for the Commission to order, pursuant to Article 14(3) of Regulation No 17, production of the communications in question and, if necessary, to impose on the undertaking fines or periodic penalty payments under that regulation as a penalty for the undertaking's refusal either to supply such additional evidence as the Commission considers necessary or to produce the communications in question whose confidentiality, in the Commission's view, is not protected in law.

32. The fact that by virtue of Article [278 TFEU] any action brought by the undertaking concerned against such decisions does not have suspensory effect provides an answer to the Commission's concern as to the effect of the time taken by the procedure before the Court on the efficacy of the supervision which the Commission is called upon to exercise in regard to compliance with the Treaty rules on competition, whilst on the other hand the interests of the undertaking concerned are safeguarded by the possibility which exists under Articles [278 and 279 TFEU], as well as under Article 83 of the Rules and Procedure of the Court, of obtaining an order suspending the application of the decision which has been taken, or any other interim measure.

The Court thus held that EU law does recognise LPP. This judgment, holding that the Community (now Union) legal order should recognise a principle contained in some form in nearly every Member State, is a famous example of the development of the jurisprudence on the general principles of law.[267] LPP in EU law is, however, a *Union* concept subject to two conditions. The first is that the protected communications must be made for the purposes and in the interests of the clients' rights of defence (paragraphs 21 and 23). The Court interpreted this broadly in *AM&S* itself, and in practice it has not caused difficulty, as the Commission accepts that communications, earlier than the initiation of proceedings but with a relationship to the subject matter of the proceedings, are covered. The second condition is that the communication must be with[268] an independent lawyer

---

[267] J. Temple Lang, 'The *AM & S* Judgment' in M. Hoskins and W. Robinson (eds.), *A True European—Essays for Judge David Edward* (Hart Publishing, 2004), Chap. 12. See generally, T. Tridimas, *The General Principles of EC Law* (2nd edn, Oxford University Press, 2006).

[268] The judgment is worded with reference to communications *from* the lawyer, but the privilege does encompass communications in both directions.

entitled to practise in one of the Member States, not an (in-house) lawyer bound to the undertaking by an employment relationship.

The limitation of privilege to 'independent' lawyers (paragraph 24) is based on the role of the lawyer as a collaborator in the administration of justice and the fact that in some Member States different rules of professional discipline apply once a lawyer is operating in an in-house employment relationship. Representations were made by in-house lawyers in submissions on the White Paper strongly arguing that privilege should be extended to them. In the system of non-notification brought in by Regulation 1/2003 undertakings are more heavily reliant on legal advice, and the lawyers said that such an extension would promote effective compliance with the competition rules. They argued that all lawyers must act ethically as defined in the rules of professional ethics and discipline.[269] Regulation 1/2003, however, contained no provision changing the position.

In *Akzo Nobel* in 2007 the issue was revisited. The undertaking concerned[270] argued, first, that the CJ in *AM&S* did not mean to attribute the notion of 'independent' only to external lawyers and that in-house lawyers could also be 'independent' and, secondly, in the alternative, that if it did mean to equate 'independent' with 'external' then both the evolution of EU competition law since 1982 (particularly the principle of equality and the reforms contained in Regulation 1/2003) and the evolution of the national legal systems required the solution in *AM&S* to be reconsidered. The GC[271] refused to depart from the law laid down in *AM&S* and continued to equate 'independent' with 'external'. It expressly rejected the argument that the abolition of the notification system was relevant to the question of LPP.[272] The undertaking appealed. The CJ upheld the GC.

Case C-550/07 P, *Akzo Nobel Chemicals Ltd v Commission* [2010] ECR I-8301

Court of Justice

45. As the Advocate General observed in points 60 and 61 of her Opinion, the concept of the independence of lawyers is determined not only positively, that is by reference to professional ethical obligations, but also negatively, by the absence of an employment relationship. An in-house lawyer, despite his enrolment with a Bar or Law Society and the professional ethical obligations to which he is, as a result, subject, does not enjoy the same degree of independence from his employer as a lawyer working in an external law firm does in relation to his client. Consequently, an in-house lawyer is less able to deal effectively with any conflicts between his professional obligations and the aims of his client.

46. As regards the professional ethical obligations relied on by the appellants in order to demonstrate Mr S.'s independence, it must be observed that, while the rules of professional organisation in Dutch law mentioned by Akzo and Akcros may strengthen the position of an in-house lawyer within the company, the fact remains that they are not able to ensure a degree of independence comparable to that of an external lawyer.

47. Notwithstanding the professional regime applicable in the present case in accordance with the specific provisions of Dutch law, an in-house lawyer cannot, whatever guarantees he has in the exercise of his profession, be treated in the same way as an external lawyer, because he occupies the position of an employee which, by its very nature, does not allow him to ignore the commercial strategies pursued by his employer, and thereby affects his ability to exercise professional independence.

---

[269] Summary of observations on the White Paper on reform of Reg. 17, published by the Commission, 29 February 2000, para. 7.7.

[270] Supported by various international and national Bar Associations including the Council of the Bars and Law Societies of the EU and the International Bar Association.

[271] Cases T-125 and 253/03, *Akzo Nobel Chemicals Ltd v Commission* [2007] ECR II-3523.

[272] Ibid., para. 172.

48. It must be added that, under the terms of his contract of employment, an in-house lawyer may be required to carry out other tasks, namely, as in the present case, the task of competition law coordinator, which may have an effect on the commercial policy of the undertaking. Such functions cannot but reinforce the close ties between the lawyer and his employer.

49. It follows, both from the in-house lawyer's economic dependence and the close ties with his employer, that he does not enjoy a level of professional independence comparable to that of an external lawyer.

50. Therefore, the General Court correctly applied the second condition for legal professional privilege laid down in the judgment in *AM & S Europe* v *Commission*.

...

54. It must be recalled that the principle of equal treatment is a general principle of European Union law, enshrined in Articles 20 and 21 of the Charter of Fundamental Rights of the European Union.

55. According to settled case-law, that principle requires that comparable situations must not be treated differently and that different situations must not be treated in the same way unless such treatment is objectively justified (see Case C-344/04 *IATA and ELFAA*. paragraph 95; Case C-303/05 *Advocaten voor de Wereld*. paragraph 56; and Case C-127/07 *Arcelor Atlantique et Lorraine and Others*, paragraph 23).

56. As to the essential characteristics of those two categories of lawyer, namely their respective professional status, it is clear from paragraphs 45 to 49 of this judgment that, despite the fact that he may be enrolled with a Bar or Law Society and that he is subject to a certain number of professional ethical obligations, an in-house lawyer does not enjoy a level of professional independence equal to that of external lawyers.

57. As the Advocate General stated, in point 83 of her Opinion, that difference in terms of independence is still significant, even though the national legislature, the Netherlands legislature in this case, seeks to treat in-house lawyers in the same way as external lawyers. After all, such equal treatment relates only to the formal act of admitting an in-house lawyer to a Bar or Law Society and the professional ethical obligations incumbent on him as a result of such admission. On the other hand, that legislative framework does not alter the economic dependence and personal identification of a lawyer in an employment relationship with his undertaking.

58. It follows from those considerations that in-house lawyers are in a fundamentally different position from external lawyers, so that their respective circumstances are not comparable for the purposes of the case-law set out in paragraph 55 of this judgment.

59. Therefore, the General Court rightly held that there was no breach of the principle of equal treatment.

...

71. As the General Court held, in paragraph 170 of the judgment under appeal, even though it is true that specific recognition of the role of in-house lawyers and the protection of communications with such lawyers under legal professional privilege was relatively more common in 2004 than when the judgment in *AM & S Europe* v *Commission* was handed down, it was nevertheless not possible to identify tendencies which were uniform or had clear majority support in the laws of the Member States.

72. Furthermore, it is clear from paragraph 171 of the judgment under appeal that a comparative examination conducted by the General Court shows that a large number of Member States still exclude correspondence with in-house lawyers from protection under legal professional privilege. Additionally, a considerable number of Member States do not allow in-house lawyers to be admitted to a Bar or Law Society and, accordingly, do not recognise them as having the same status as lawyers established in private practice.

73. In that connection, Akzo and Akcros themselves accept that no uniform tendency can be established in the legal systems of the Member States towards the assimilation of in-house lawyers and lawyers in private practice.

74. Therefore no predominant trend towards protection under legal professional privilege of communications within a company or group with in-house lawyers may be discerned in the legal systems of the 27 Member States of the European Union.

75. In those circumstances, and contrary to the appellants' assertions, the legal regime in the Netherlands cannot be regarded as signalling a developing trend in the Member States, or as a relevant factor for determining the scope of legal professional privilege.

76. The Court therefore considers that the legal situation in the Member States of the European Union has not evolved, since the judgment in *AM & S Europe* v *Commission* was delivered, to an extent which would justify a change in the case-law and recognition for in-house lawyers of the benefit of legal professional privilege.

...

83. Although it is true that Regulation 1/2003 has introduced a large number of amendments to the rules of procedure relating to European Union competition law, it is also the case that those rules do not suggest that they require lawyers in independent practice and in-house lawyers to be treated in the same way with respect to legal professional privilege, since that principle is not at all the subject-matter of the regulation.

84. It is clear from the provisions of Article 20 of Regulation No 1/2003 that the Commission may conduct all necessary inspections of undertakings and associations of undertakings, and in that context, examine the books and other records related to the business, irrespective of the medium on which they are stored, and also take or obtain in any form copies or extracts of such books or records.

85. That regulation, like Article 14(1)(a) and (b) of Regulation No 17, has therefore defined the powers of the Commission broadly. As it is clear from Recitals 25 and 26 in the preamble to Regulation No 1/2003, the detection of infringements of the competition rules is growing ever more difficult, and, in order to protect competition effectively and safeguard the effectiveness of inspections, the Commission should be empowered to enter any premises where business records may be kept, including private homes.

86. Thus, Regulation No 1/2003, contrary to the appellants' assertions, does not aim to require in-house and external lawyers to be treated in the same way as far as concerns legal professional privilege, but aims to reinforce the extent of the Commission's powers of inspection, in particular as regards documents which may be the subject of such measures.

87. Therefore, the amendment of the rules of procedure for competition law, resulting in particular from Regulation No 1/2003, is also unable to justify a change in the case-law established by the judgment in *AM & S Europe* v *Commission*.

...

92. It must be recalled that in all proceedings in which sanctions, especially fines or penalty payments, may be imposed observance of the rights of the defence is a fundamental principle of European Union law which has been emphasised on numerous occasions in the case-law of the Court (see Case C-194/99 P *Thyssen Stahl* v *Commission* . . . paragraph 30; Case C-289/04 P *Showa Denko* v *Commission* . . . paragraph 68; Case C-3/06 P *Groupe Danone* v *Commission* . . . paragraph 68), and which has been enshrined in Article 48(2) of the Charter of Fundamental Rights of the European Union.

93. By this ground of appeal, the appellants seek to establish that the rights of the defence must include the right of freedom of choice as to the lawyer who will provide legal advice and representation and that legal professional privilege forms part of those rights, regardless of the professional status of the lawyer concerned.

94. In that connection, it must be observed that, when an undertaking seeks advice from its in-house lawyer, it is not dealing with an independent third party, but with one of its employees, notwithstanding any professional obligations resulting from enrolment at a Bar or Law Society.

95. It should be added that, even assuming that the consultation of in-house lawyers employed by the undertaking or group were to be covered by the right to obtain legal advice and representation, that

would not exclude the application, where in-house lawyers are involved, of certain restrictions and rules relating to the exercise of the profession without that being regarded as adversely affecting the rights of the defence. Thus, in-house lawyers are not always able to represent their employer before all the national courts, although such rules restrict the possibilities open to potential clients in their choice of the most appropriate legal counsel.

96. It follows from those considerations that any individual who seeks advice from a lawyer must accept the restrictions and conditions applicable to the exercise of that profession. The rules on legal professional privilege form part of those restrictions and conditions.

97. Therefore, the argument alleging breach of the rights of the defence is unfounded.

The CJ also held that the GC's findings undermined neither the principle of legal certainty (paragraphs 100–108) nor the principle of national procedural autonomy (paragraphs 113–122).

The exclusion of in-house lawyers from LPP is a matter of great practical importance and remains a highly contentious issue.[273] Neither the GC nor the CJ in *Akzo Nobel* dealt with the further limitation of LPP to lawyers entitled to practise in one of the Member States.[274]

b. Procedure in Claims of LPP

The procedure for dealing with claims of LLP is derived from the judgments of the CJ in *AM&S* and the GC in *Akzo Nobel*,[275] and set out in Best Practices, paragraphs 51–58. Ultimately the determination as to whether any particular document is protected by LPP is a matter for the Court.

The undertaking claiming that documents are privileged should provide the inspectors with proof of that fact without revealing their contents. If the inspectors are not convinced the Commission may take a decision under Article 20(4) of Regulation 1/2003 requiring the production of the document or further evidence of its status. Such a decision may be challenged by the undertaking under Article 263 TFEU (with an application for interim measures under Articles 278 and 279 if appropriate). If the Commission officials cannot tell from a 'mere cursory look at the general layout, heading, title or other superficial features which would not reveal its content', whether a document is protected by LPP and there is a genuine doubt about its classification, they place the document in a sealed envelope and take it back to Brussels to await the outcome of any proceedings.[276] Disputes about whether documents are covered by LPP can be referred by the undertaking concerned to the Hearing Officer.[277] If the matter remains unresolved even after the Hearing Officer's recommendation the Commission can take a decision ordering the production of the document or the opening of the sealed envelope which the undertaking can then challenge before the GC.

The categorisation of particular documents into those protected by LPP and those not protected may be difficult. In *Hilti*[278] a report made and circulated within the undertaking of the legal advice received from an external legal adviser was held privileged. On the other hand, in *John Deere*[279] the Commission examined advice from in-house lawyers and concluded that the undertaking was aware that it was infringing Article 101. It took this into account when imposing the fine. A preparatory

---

[273] See M. Frese, 'The Development of General Principles for EU Competition Law Enforcement—The Protection of Legal Professional Privilege' [2011] *ECLR* 196; G. di Frederico, 'Casenote' (2011) 48 *CMLRev* 581.

[274] Although it was touched upon by Kokott AG, in para. 190 of her Opinion.

[275] Cases T-125 and 253/03, *Akzo Nobel* [2007] ECR II-3523, paras. 79–90. This issue was not appealed to the CJ.

[276] Ibid., paras. 81–83; Best Practices, para. 54.

[277] Decision on the function and terms of reference of the hearing officer [2011] OJ L275/29, Art. 4(2)(a); W. Wils, 'The Role of the Hearing Officer in Competition Proceedings before the European Commission' (2012) 35 *World Competition* 431, 448–450; for the functions of the Hearing Officer generally, see Section 7.D.iv, p. 933.

[278] Case T-30/89, *Hilti AG v Commission* [1990] ECR II-163.

[279] [1985] OJ L35/58.

document drawn up exclusively for the purpose of seeking advice from a lawyer in exercise of the rights of the defence may be covered by LPP.[280]

D. THE SECOND, 'INTER PARTES' OR 'ADVERSARIAL', STAGE OF THE PROCEDURE

(i) General: The Rights of the Defence and the Right to be Heard

At the end of the investigative phase the Commission may decide:

- to close the case;
- to proceed to a commitments decision if the parties are offering commitments at that stage;[281] or
- to open a formal procedure, if it finds evidence of an infringement and no commitments are being offered.

Before taking Regulation 1/2003 decisions finding an infringement, taking interim measures, or imposing fines or periodic payments the Commission must, by Article 27(1), grant the undertakings which are the subject of proceedings 'the opportunity of being heard on the matters to which the Commission has taken objection'.[282] Article 27(2) provides that 'the rights of defence of the parties concerned shall be fully respected in the proceedings' and they 'shall be entitled to have access to the Commission's file'.[283] The Commission may also hear other natural or legal persons. Article 27(4) provides for the hearing of interested third parties during the commitments decision procedure.[284]

The right to be heard in all proceedings initiated against a person which are liable to culminate in a measure adversely affecting that person is part of the rights of the defence and a fundamental principle of EU law which must be guaranteed even in the absence of any rules governing the proceedings in question.[285] The right to a hearing means in the first place that parties must be told the case against them.[286] This is now embedded in Article 27(1) which provides that '[t]he Commission shall base its decisions only on objections on which the parties concerned have been able to comment'. The Commission satisfies this requirement by sending the undertakings a document called the statement of objections (SO). The undertakings may then make submissions in reply and are offered the opportunity of an oral hearing.[287] The procedures are set out in Commission Regulation 773/2004.[288] If at the end of the proceedings the Commission finds that the competition rules have

---

[280] Cases T-125 and 253/03, *Akzo Nobel* [2007] ECR II-3523, para. 123. The GC refused to accept that the disputed document in issue met this description.

[281] For commitments decisions, see Section 7.E.iii, p. 945.

[282] Note that there is no duty to give parties a hearing where the Commission is simply replacing a decision ruled invalid for procedural defects at the final, authentication stage with another which relies on the same evidence as that which was annulled: see Cases C-238/99 P etc., *Limburgse Vinyl Maatschappij* [2002] ECR I-8375; Case C-109/10 P, *Solvay v Commission* [2011] ECR I-10329, para. 67. It is otherwise where the defects involved a failure to hear the parties in respect of the first decision, *Solvay*, paras. 68–71.

[283] For the application of this in an Art. 9 commitments decision, see Case C-441/07 P, *Commission v Alrosa* [2010] ECR I-5949, see Section 7.E.iii, p. 947.

[284] See Section 7.E.iii.

[285] Case C-32/95 P, *Commission v Lisrestal* [1996] ECR I-5373, para. 121 (a case on the European Social Fund).

[286] See Case 17/74, *Transocean Marine Paint Association v Commission (No. 2)* [1974] ECR 1063; Cases C-68/94 and 30/95, *France & SCPA v Commission* [1998] ECR I-1375, para. 174.

[287] The right to know the case against them does not entitle undertakings to examine for themselves the witnesses heard by the Commission: Cases C-239/11 P etc., *Siemens* EU:C:2013:866, para. 319.

[288] [2004] OJ L123/18, which replaced Reg. 2842/98 [1998] OJ L354/18, which in turn replaced Reg. 99/63 [1963–1964] OJ Spec. Ed. 47.

been infringed it may adopt a decision under Article 7 or 8 of Regulation 1/2003 and may impose a penalty under Article 23.

Considerable problems arise over the content of the rights of defence during these procedures, particularly where the rights of undertakings to know the case against them conflict with the Commission's duty to preserve the confidentiality of business secrets.

(ii) State of Play and Other Meetings

The Commission offers undertakings which are subject to proceedings the opportunity to attend 'State of Play' meetings with officials of DG Comp.[289] The meetings are not provided for in Regulation 1/2003 or in Regulation 773/2004 but have become an important part of Commission procedure. Best Practices says:[290]

Throughout the procedure the Directorate-General for Competition endeavours to give, on its own initiative or upon request, parties subject to the proceedings ample opportunity for open and frank discussions—taking into account the stage of the investigation—and to make their points of view known.

In this respect the Commission will offer State of Play meetings . . .

The meetings take place at the Commission's premises or, if appropriate, by telephone or videoconferencing and are normally chaired by senior DG Comp management.[291] Where several parties are being investigated the Commission offers a separate bilateral meeting to each one. The meetings are not offered to complainants except in certain circumstances[292] or to third parties. Normally, State of Play meetings are offered: (a) shortly after the opening of proceedings; (b) at 'a sufficiently advanced stage in the investigation' where the parties can be given the opportunity to understand the Commission's preliminary views; and (c) if an SO is issued, after the addressees have replied or after the oral hearing. The timing of State of Play meetings is different under the commitments decision procedure[293] and in cartel cases the undertakings are offered just one meeting, after the oral hearing.[294] The formalisation of State of Play meetings does not exclude the parties having discussions with the Commission on other occasions throughout the procedure.[295]

'Exceptionally' DG Comp may invite *all* the parties (and possibly the complainant and/or third parties too) to a 'triangular' meeting[296] before any SO is issued. Senior officers of parties subject to proceedings can ask for a discussion of the case with the Director-General or Deputy Director-General of DG Comp, or even the Commissioner.[297]

(iii) The Statement of Objections

By Article 10(1) of Regulation 773/2004[298] 'the Commission shall inform the parties in writing of the objections raised against them'. By Article 11(2), Commission decisions can deal only with objections in respect of which the parties have been able to comment. The SO sets out the facts as

---

[289] Best Practices, paras. 60–66; Antitrust ManProc, Module 10, paras. 21–27.

[290] Best Practices, paras. 60–61.

[291] Ibid., para. 61.

[292] Ibid., para. 65.

[293] Ibid., para. 65.

[294] Ibid., para. 65.

[295] Ibid., para. 66.

[296] Ibid., paras. 67–69; Antitrust ManProc, Module 10, paras. 28–30. Held if DG Comp believes it is desirable to hear the views of all of them in a single meeting (e.g. if two or more opposing views on key data or evidence have been advanced).

[297] Best Practices, para. 70.

[298] [2004] OJ L123/18. See Best Practices, paras. 81–91; Kerse and Khan, n. 2, 4.011–4.027.

understood by the Commission, a legal analysis explaining why it considers Article 101 or 102 to be infringed, and any proposed remedy the Commission is contemplating adopting.[299] The SO also indicates what remedies, if any, the Commission envisages imposing, in sufficient detail to allow the addressees to defend themselves on the necessity and proportionality of the remedies[300] and this detail includes the factors in the case which may affect the amount of the fine.[301] The SO must state the duration of the infringement.[302] The parties are invited to reply to the SO within a set time limit.[303] The Commission can send the parties fresh documents on which it intends to rely, after the initial SO[304] so long as it gives the necessary time for the parties to comment on them.[305] The Commission cannot fine parties in the ultimate decision unless it has expressed an intention to do so in the SO.[306] It cannot fine an undertaking for its direct and personal involvement in an infringement if the SO has referred only to its liability as a parent company for the conduct of its subsidiary as, if the undertaking does not know the capacity in which it is alleged to have committed an infringement, its ability to defend itself is compromised.[307] An undertaking which does not challenge a matter of law or fact in the SO during the administrative procedure is not barred from later challenging it before the GC.[308]

In order for the parties to make their views known, the Commission must reveal the documents on which it intends to rely. The SO therefore indicates the addressee's right of access to the file, so that the addressee can see the evidence on which the Commission has based its case.[309] However, it is not sufficient for the Commission to rely on items of evidence annexed to the SO which are not expressly referred to in the body of the SO as that infringes the rights of the defence.[310] The addressees may then exercise their rights to inspect the file, at least insofar as the documents are 'accessible'.[311] The current practical arrangements for this are contained in the Commission's 2005 Notice on access to the file.[312]

---

[299] See Antitrust ManProc, Module 11, 'Drafting of Statement of Objections'.

[300] Best Practices, para. 83.

[301] Ibid., para. 84.

[302] Cases 100–103/80, *Pioneer* [1983] ECR 1825.

[303] Reg. 773/2004, Art. 10(2). The minimum time set down in Reg. 773/2004 is four weeks, but the period is usually two months and may be longer, see Best Practices, para. 100, Antitrust ManProc, Module 11, paras. 48–56.

[304] A supplementary SO or 'letter of facts'. See Best Practices, paras. 109–111. A 'Letter of Facts' is sent where the new evidence merely corroborates previous evidence, rather than raising new objections.

[305] Case 107/82, *AEG-Telefunken v Commission* [1983] ECR 3151; Cases T-305/94 etc., *Re the PVC Cartel II: Limburgse Vinyl Maatschappij NV* [1999] ECR II-931, para. 497.

[306] In Cases T-25/95 etc., *Cimenteries CBR SA v Commission* [2000] ECR II-491 the GC annulled the fines on associations of undertakings where the Commission had not announced in the SO its intention to fine the associations as distinct from their individual members. On the other hand, the CJ annulled the fines on the individual members of a liner conference in Cases C-395 and 396/96 P, *Compagnie Maritime Belge and others v Commission* [2000] ECR I-1365, because the Commission had announced an intention to fine only the conference, not the individual shipping lines.

[307] Cases C-322, 327, and 338/07 P, *Papierfabrik August Koehler AG v Commission* [2009] ECR I-7191, paras. 34–48. The CJ annulled the fine. The GC had made the same finding about the SO but had not annulled the fine as it did not consider the error serious enough to vitiate the decision, Cases T-109/02 etc., *Bolloré and others v Commission* [2007] ECR II-947.

[308] Case C-407/08P, *Knauf Gips v Commission* [2010] ECR I-6375, paras. 88–92. The CJ overruled the GC on this point, citing the fundamental principles of the rule of law, the rights of the defence, and the right to an effective remedy and of access to an impartial tribunal guaranteed by Art. 47 of the Charter.

[309] If the addressee accompanies its reply to the SO with other documents the Commission can subsequently rely on them even though they were not referred to in the SO, Case T-11/89, *Shell v Commission* [1992] ECR II-757. See Case T-286/09, *Intel* EU:T:2014:547, discussed in Section 7.C.v, p. 918, for the duty of the Commission to place on the file an adequate record of informal interviews.

[310] Case C-511/06 P, *Archer Daniels Midland* [2009] ECR I-5843, paras. 74–96. The Commission relied on documents annexed to the SO but not referred to in it in order to establish that ADM was a leader of the cartel. This increased the fine (as an 'aggravating factor'). The CJ reduced the fine on this basis (from €39.6 million to €29.4 million).

[311] See Section 7.D.v, p. 933.

[312] [2005] OJ C325/7.

The SO is not a reviewable act against which an action for annulment can be brought, as it is only a preparatory act and can be challenged in an action brought against the act concluding the proceedings.[313] However, an *inadequate* SO amounts to a breach of an essential procedural requirement and so is a ground for annulment under Article 263.

The views set out by the Commission in the SO are not binding upon it and it is 'inherent in the nature of the statement of objections that it is provisional'.[314] The Commission is free to depart from the standpoint it has taken in the SO.[315] Findings of fact set out in the SO are not to be treated as established and so the Commission is free to depart from them in the final decision.[316]

(iv) The Hearing Officer

In 1982 the Commission decided to meet some of the criticisms of its position as investigator, prosecutor, and judge, and of the lack of objectivity in its decision-making process, by establishing the position of Hearing Officer.[317] Originally, his or her role was to preside over the oral hearing, but in 1994 it was extended to cover the whole of the Commission's administrative procedure. The role and functions are now governed by Commission Decision 2011/695[318] and are explained in this chapter at the relevant points. Since 1994 the Hearing Officer also has jurisdiction in relation to hearings provided for in the Merger Regulation.[319]

The rationale for creating the post in 1982 was to inject an element of disinterested objectivity into the Commission's decision-making process. He or she is attached, for administrative purposes, to the Competition Commissioner but the principle is that he or she is 'independent'.[320]

(v) Access to the File

a. General

Access to the Commission's file on which the SO is based is an important element of the parties' rights to know the case against them. The right of access to the file was developed in the case law[321]

---

[313] Case 60/81, *IBM v Commission* [1981] ECR 2639.

[314] Case C-328/05 P, *SGL Carbon AG v Commission* [2007] ECR I-3921, para. 62.

[315] Cases 142 and 156/84, *British American Tobacco Co Ltd and R. J. Reynolds Industries Inc v Commission* [1986] ECR 1899, para. 13.

[316] Case C-413/06 P, *Bertelsmann AG and Sony Corp of America v Commission (Impala)* [2008] ECR I-4951, paras. 63–67, holding that the GC had committed an error of law in finding otherwise, see Case T-464/04, *Independent Music Publishers and Labels Association (Impala) v Commission* [2006] ECR II-2289. See Chap. 15.

[317] See Commission's *XIth Report on Competition Policy* (1981), paras. 26 and 27 and the *XIIth Report* (1982), paras. 36 and 37. The original terms of reference of the Hearing Officer, [1982] OJ C215/2, were reformulated in 1990 because of the need to take on board hearings in transport cases: see EC Commission, *XXth Report on Competition Policy* (1990), 312–314, and revised in 1994: Commission Decision 94/810 on the terms of reference of hearing officers in competition procedures before the Commission [1994] OJ L330/67. See generally M. van der Woude, 'Hearing Officers and EC Antitrust Procedures; The Art of Making Subjective Procedures More Objective' (1996) 33 *CMLRev* 531; M. Albers and J. Jourdan, 'The Role of the Hearing Officers in EU Competition Proceedings: A Historical and Practical Perspective' (2011) 2 *JECLAP* 185; W. Wils, 'The Role of the Hearing Officer in Competition Proceedings before the European Commission' (2012) 35 *World Competition* 431.

[318] Decision of the President of the European Commission of 13 October 2011 on the function and terms of reference of the hearing officer in certain competition proceedings [2011] OJ L275/29 (the 'HO Terms of Reference'), replacing Commission Decision 2001/462/EC on the terms of reference of hearing officers in certain competition proceedings [2001] OJ L162/21.

[319] The EUMR, Reg. 139/2004 [2004] OJ L24/1. See the HO Terms of Reference, Art. 1(2).

[320] HO Terms of Reference, recitals 3–8 and Art. 2(2); 2001 Terms of Reference, recital 6 and Art. 2(2). It should be noted that the Hearing Officer does not appear on the chart of the organisation of DG Comp on its website. There are currently two Hearing Officers.

[321] See Cases 56 and 58/64, *Établissements Consten SA and Grundig-Verkaufs-GmbH v Commission* [1966] ECR 299; Cases 43 and 63/82, *VBVB and VBBB v Commission* [1984] ECR 19; Case C-51/92 P, *Hercules Chemicals NV v Commission (Polypropylene)* [1999] ECR I-4235, paras. 75–76; Case C-185/95 P, *Baustahlgewebe GmbH v Commission* [1998] ECR I-8471, para. 89; Cases T-10–12 and 14–15/92, *Cimenteries CBR SA v Commission* [1992] ECR II-2667, para. 38; Case T-30/91,

and Commission practice.[322] It is now provided for in Article 27(2) of Regulation 1/2003 which gives 'the parties concerned' a right of access. It is expanded upon in Regulation 773/2004 which also provides for access by complainants whose complaint is to be rejected (Article 8). The practical arrangements are contained in the Notice on access to the file.[323]

There are special provisions on access to leniency corporate statements. The Commission's leniency policy procedure involves the undertakings concerned making 'leniency corporate statements', i.e. presentations of their knowledge of the secret cartel and their role in it in return for immunity or leniency.[324] As we see in Chapter 14, the Damages Directive[325] was designed to facilitate damages actions but the Commission does not wish this to jeopardise the effectiveness of the leniency policy. Addressees of SOs have to be given access to the leniency corporate statement of other participants in the alleged cartel as part of their rights of defence[326] but they are strictly prohibited from using the information thereby gained for any purpose other than their defence in respect of Article 101 or Article 102 proceedings before the Commission, the EU Courts, or a national court in *directly* related proceedings. Regulation 773/2004 was amended in the wake of the Damages Directive to expressly provide this.

Regulation 773/2004 [2004] OJ L123/18, as amended by Regulation 2015/1348 [2015] OJ L208/3

LIMITATIONS TO THE USE OF INFORMATION OBTAINED IN THE COURSE OF COMMISSION PROCEEDINGS

Article 16a

1. Information obtained pursuant to this Regulation shall only be used for the purposes of judicial or administrative proceedings for the application of Articles 101 and 102 of the Treaty.

2. Access to leniency corporate statements within the meaning of Article 4a(2) or to settlement submissions within the meaning of Article 10a(2) shall be granted only for the purposes of exercising the rights of defence in proceedings before the Commission. Information taken from such statements and submissions may be used by the party having obtained access to the file only where necessary for the exercise of its rights of defence in proceedings:

   (a) before the European Union courts reviewing Commission decisions; or

   (b) before the courts of the Member States in cases that are directly related to the case in which access has been granted, and which concern:

      (i) the allocation between cartel participants of a fine imposed jointly and severally on them by the Commission; or

      (ii) the review of a decision by which a competition authority of a Member State has found an infringement of Article 101 TFEU.

Solvay SA v Commission [1995] ECR II-1775 and Case T-36/91, *ICI v Commission* [1995] ECR II-1847, aff'd Cases C-288 and 287/95 P, *Commission v Solvay* [2000] ECR I-2391; Cases T-305/94 etc., *Limburgse Vinyl Maatschappij* [1999] ECR II-931; Cases C-204, 205, 211, 213, 217, and 219/00 P, *Aalborg Portland A/S and Others v Commission* [2004] ECR I-123.

[322] Commission's *XXIInd Report on Competition Policy* (1982) parts 34 and 35.

[323] Commission Notice on the rules for access to the Commission file [2005] OJ C325/07 (replacing [1997] OJ C 23/3), as amended by [2015] OJ C256/7 to take account of the Damages Dir. (see n. 325); see also the Antitrust ManProc, Module 12. Access to the file can be granted in one or more of several ways: electronically, paper copies sent by mail, or examination of the accessible file at the Commission's premises: the choice is the Commission's, see Access Notice, para. 44. The whole accessible part of the file is often sent to the parties at the same time as the SO, by DVD or other electronic means.

[324] See Reg. 773/2004, Art. 4a(2). For the leniency policy, see Section 7.H.v and Chap. 9.

[325] Directive 2014/104/EU on certain rules governing actions for damages under national law for infringements of the competition law provisions of the Member States and of the European Union [2014] OJ L349/1.

[326] For the way in which this is done, see Section 7.H.v, p. 990.

Article 16(a) is reinforced by an amended paragraph 48 of the Access Notice[327] and an amended paragraph 34 of the Leniency Notice.[328]

Settlement submissions made in the course of the settlement procedure in cartel cases[329] are treated in respect of access to the file in the same way as leniency corporate statements.

The rules on allowing the parties access to the file reflect the principles originally enunciated in *Solvay*,[330] where the GC relied on the 'general principle of equality of arms' between the Commission and the undertakings being investigated. This means that the undertakings' knowledge of the file used in the proceedings should be the same as that of the Commission.[331] The principle is that undertakings must have disclosed to them documents which tend to exonerate them (exculpatory documents) as well as those which tend to incriminate them (inculpatory documents, failure to grant access to which will lead to the Commission being unable to rely on them as evidence of infringement[332]). It is not for the Commission alone to decide what documents are useful to the defence. The breach of the principle laid down in *Solvay* will not always lead to annulment of the decision. It will depend on whether, in the Court's view, the undertaking's ability to defend itself was prejudiced.[333] The undertaking does not have to show that if it had had access to the non-disclosed documents the Commission's decision would have been different in content, but only that those documents would have been useful in its defence.[334] The law was set out by the CJ in the final *Cement Cartel* appeals.

Cases C-204, 205, 211, 213, 217, and C-219/00 P, *Aalborg Portland A/S and Others v Commission* [2004] ECR I-123

Court of Justice

68. A corollary of the principle of respect for the rights of the defence, the right of access to the file means that the Commission must give the undertaking concerned the opportunity to examine all the documents in the investigation file which may be relevant for its defence (see, to that effect, Case T-30/91, *Solvay* v. *Commission* . . . paragraph 101, and Case C-199/99 P *Corus UK* v. *Commission* . . . paragraphs 125 to 128). Those documents include both incriminating evidence and exculpatory evidence, save where the business secrets of other undertakings, the internal documents of the Commission or other confidential information are involved (see Case 85/76, *Hoffmann-La Roche* v. *Commission* . . . paragraphs 9 and 11; Case C-51/92 P, *Hercules Chemicals* v. *Commission* . . . paragraph 75; and Joined Cases C-238/99 P, C-244/99 P,

---

[327] Access Notice, para. 48, as amended by OJ C256/3, says: 'Access to the file in accordance with this notice is granted on the condition that the information thereby obtained may only be used for the purposes of judicial or administrative proceedings for the application of the Union competition rules…The use of this information in breach of the limitations set out in Article 16a of Regulation (EC) No 773/2004 is in certain situations subject to penalties under national law…If the use for a different purpose or the breach of the said limitations occurred with the involvement of an outside counsel, the Commission may report the incident to the bar of that counsel, with a view to disciplinary action.'

[328] See Section 7.H.v, p. 990.

[329] See further Section 7.F, p. 956 and Chap. 9.

[330] Case T-30/91, *Solvay SA v Commission* [1995] ECR II-1775 and Case T-36/91, *ICI v Commission* [1995] ECR II-1847, applied in Cases T-305/94 etc., *Limburgse Vinyl Maatschappij* [1999] ECR II-931. For an interesting insight into the actual circumstances in *Solvay* see C.-D. Ehlermann and B. J. Drijber, 'Legal Protection of Enterprises: Administrative Procedure, in Particular Access to the File and Confidentiality' [1996] *ECLR* 375.

[331] For an interesting insight into the actual circumstances in *Solvay* see Ehlermann and Drijber, n. 330.

[332] See, e.g., Cases T-379 and 381/10, *Keramag Keramische Werke v Commission* EU:T:2013:457, paras. 115–116, and 264, on appeal Case C-613/13 P, judgment pending.

[333] See Cases C-238/99 P etc., *Limburgse Vinyl Maatschappij* [2002] ECR I-8375, paras. 315–328; Case C-51/92 P, *Hercules* [1999] ECR I-4235, paras. 75–101.

[334] Cases C-239/11 P etc., *Siemens* EU:C:2013:866, paras. 363–378.

C-245/99 P, C-247/99 P, C-250/99 P to C-252/99 P and C-254/99 P, *Limburgse Vinyl Maatschappij and Others* v. *Commission* . . . paragraph 315).

69. It may be that the undertaking draws the Commission's attention to documents capable of providing a different economic explanation for the overall economic assessment carried out by the Commission, in particular those describing the relevant market and the importance and the conduct of the undertakings acting on that market (see, to that effect, *Solvay* v. *Commission*, cited above, paragraphs 76 and 77).

70. The European Court of Human Rights has none the less held that, just like observance of the other procedural safeguards enshrined in Article 6(1) of the ECHR, compliance with the adversarial principle relates only to judicial proceedings before a tribunal and that there is no general, abstract principle that the parties must in all instances have the opportunity to attend the interviews carried out or to receive copies of all the documents taken into account in the case of other persons (see, to that effect, Euro. Court H.R., the *Kerojärvi* v. *Finland* judgment of 19 July 1995, Series A No 322, § 42, and the *Mantovanelli* v. *France* judgment of 18 March 1997, Reports of Judgments and Decisions 1997-II, § 33).

71. The failure to communicate a document constitutes a breach of the rights of the defence only if the undertaking concerned shows, first, that the Commission relied on that document to support its objection concerning the existence of an infringement (see, to that effect, Case 322/101, *Michelin* v. *Commission* . . . paragraphs 7 and 9) and, second, that the objection could be proved only by reference to that document (see Case 107/102 *AEG* v. *Commission* . . . paragraphs 24 to 30, and *Solvay* v. *Commission*, cited above, paragraph 58).

72. If there were other documentary evidence of which the parties were aware during the administrative procedure that specifically supported the Commission's findings, the fact that an incriminating document not communicated to the person concerned was inadmissible as evidence would not affect the validity of the objections upheld in the contested decision (see, to that effect, *Musique Diffusion française and Others* v. *Commission*, cited above, paragraph 30, and *Solvay* v. *Commission*, cited above, paragraph 58).

73. It is thus for the undertaking concerned to show that the result at which the Commission arrived in its decision would have been different if a document which was not communicated to that undertaking and on which the Commission relied to make a finding of infringement against it had to be disallowed as evidence.

74. On the other hand, where an exculpatory document has not been communicated, the undertaking concerned must only establish that its non-disclosure was able to influence, to its disadvantage, the course of the proceedings and the content of the decision of the Commission (see *Solvay* v. *Commission*, paragraph 68).

75. It is sufficient for the undertaking to show that it would have been able to use the exculpatory documents in its defence (see *Hercules Chemicals* v. *Commission*, paragraph 101, and *Limburgse Vinyl Maatschappij and Others* v. *Commission*, paragraph 318), in the sense that, had it been able to rely on them during the administrative procedure, it would have been able to put forward evidence which did not agree with the findings made by the Commission at that stage and would therefore have been able to have some influence on the Commission's assessment in any decision it adopted, at least as regards the gravity and duration of the conduct of which it was accused and, accordingly, the level of the fine (see, to that effect, *Solvay* v. *Commission*, paragraph 98).

76. The possibility that a document which was not disclosed might have influenced the course of the proceedings and the content of the Commission's decision can be established only if a provisional examination of certain evidence shows that the documents not disclosed might—in the light of that evidence—have had a significance which ought not to have been disregarded (see *Solvay* v. *Commission*, paragraph 68).

77. In the context of that provisional analysis, it is for the [General Court] alone to assess the value which should be attached to the evidence produced to it (see order of 17 September 1996 in Case C-19/95 P *San Marco* v *Commission* . . . paragraph 40). As stated at paragraph 49 of this judgment, its assessment of the facts does not, provided the evidence is not distorted, constitute a question of law which is subject, as such, to review by the Court of Justice.

The principles set out in *Aalborg* were followed and applied by the CJ in the appeal against the re-adopted *Solvay* soda-ash decisions.[335] In *Solvay* the GC upheld the decisions despite the Commission still not having given the undertaking access to all the documents, including those likely to be useful to its defence (five binders had gone missing).[336] The CJ set the judgment aside, saying that the rights of the defence, as explained in *Aalborg*, were now referred to in Article 41(2)(a) and (b) of the Charter.[337] The principles were also applied in *Intel* where the GC held that the undertaking had no right of access to documents which the Commission had no duty to procure.[338]

b. Confidentiality

There is a fundamental tension between the rights of the parties to know the case against them and the Commission's obligation to preserve confidentiality. A general duty of confidentiality is laid down in Article 339 TFEU:

> The members of the institutions of the Union, the members of committees, and the officials and other servants of the Union shall be required, even after their duties have ceased, not to disclose information of the kind covered by the obligation of professional secrecy, in particular information about undertakings, their business relations or their cost components.

Article 28 of Regulation 1/2003 on 'Professional Secrecy' provides that information collected pursuant to Articles 17–22 shall only be used for the purposes for which it is acquired. Article 28(2) addresses the matter of exchange of information within the network of competition authorities.[339] Article 30 provides that the publication of decisions shall 'have regard to the legitimate interest of undertakings in the protection of their business secrets'.[340]

Article 27(2) of Regulation 1/2003 states that the parties' right to have access to the Commission's file is 'subject to the legitimate interest of undertakings in the protection of their business secrets'. This is repeated in Article 15(2) of Regulation 773/2004 which provides that the right of access does not extend to 'business secrets or other confidential information'.[341] Further, Article 16(1) states:

> Information, including documents, shall not be communicated or made accessible by the Commission in so far as it contains business secrets or other confidential information of any person.

Confidentiality is a significant issue in competition proceedings as the Commission may obtain highly sensitive information during an investigation. 'Business secrets' comprise information about an undertaking's business activity disclosure of which could result in serious harm to the undertaking.[342] 'Other confidential information' is information other than business secrets

---

[335] Case C-109/10 P, *Solvay v Commission* [2011] ECR I-10329. See also Case T-161/05, *Hoechst GmbH v Commission* [2009] ECR II-3555, paras. 160–166; Case T-53/03, *BPB plc v Commission* [2008] ECR II-1333, paras. 43–45; Case T-240/07, *Heineken Nederland BV v Commission* [2011] ECR II-3355, para. 256; Cases C-239/11 P etc., *Siemens* EU:C:2013:866.

[336] Cases T-57/01 etc., *Solvay SA v Commission* [2009] ECR II-4621.

[337] Case C-109/10 P, *Solvay v Commission* [2011] ECR I-10329, para. 53. For Art. 41, the right to good administration, see Section 7.B.ii.f, p. 900.

[338] Case T-286/09, *Intel* EU:T:2014:547; see Section 7.C.ii, p. 905.

[339] See Notice on cooperation within the Network of Competition Authorities (the NCA Cooperation Notice) [2004] OJ C101/54. 'Professional secrecy' is a Community law concept (NCA Cooperation Notice, para. 28(a)).

[340] In Case T-474/04, *Pergan Hilfsstoffe für Industrielle Prozesse GmbH v Commission* [2007] ECR II-4225 the GC held that this should have prevented the Commission stating in a published decision (*Organic Peroxides* [2005] OJ L110/44) that an undertaking had been involved in the organic peroxides cartel but that it did not have sufficient evidence of its involvement (at a time that was not subject to the limitation period bar) to bring proceedings against it (the Hearing Officer had allowed it).

[341] Reg. 1/2003, Art. 27(2), and Reg. 773/2004, Art. 15(2) also exclude from the right of access certain Commission and NCA documents.

[342] Access Notice, para. 18; Case T-353/94, *Postbank NV v Commission* [1996] ECR II-921, para. 87. Examples given in the Notice are technical and/or financial information relating to an undertaking's know-how, methods

disclosure of which would significantly harm a person or undertaking.[343] This includes matters which would identify 'whistle-blowers',[344] complainants, or other third parties who have a justified wish to remain anonymous. The Notice recognises that the EU Courts have acknowledged that it is legitimate to refuse to reveal letters from an undertaking's customers which might expose the writers to retaliatory measures.[345]

The basic principle, laid down in *Hoffmann-La Roche*, is that the Commission cannot use to an undertaking's detriment facts or documents which it cannot disclose to it, where the absence of disclosure adversely affects the undertaking's opportunity to be heard.

Case 85/76, *Hoffmann-La Roche v Commission* [1979] ECR 461

Court of Justice

14. The said Article 20 [of Regulation 17] by providing undertakings from whom information has been obtained with a guarantee that their interests which are closely connected with observance of professional secrecy, are not jeopardized enables the Commission to collect on the widest possible scale the requisite data for the fulfilment of the task conferred upon it by Articles [101 and 102 TFEU] without the undertakings being able to prevent it from doing so, but it does not nevertheless allow it to use, to the detriment of the undertakings involved in a proceeding referred to in Regulation 17, facts, circumstances or documents which it cannot in its view disclose if such a refusal of disclosure adversely affects that undertaking's opportunity to make known effectively its views on the truth or implications of those circumstances on those documents or again on the conclusions drawn by the Commission from them.

Article 16 of Regulation 773/2004 puts the onus on addressees replying to an SO, complainants making their views known on an SO, persons with a sufficient interest making their views known, or complainants replying to a rejection letter, to identify confidential material which they do not want disclosed and provide a non-confidential version.[346] The Notice sets out the practical arrangements for giving access to the file while preserving confidentiality.[347] The Notice clarifies that access

---

of assessing costs, production secrets and processes, supply sources, quantities produced and sold, market shares, customer and distributor lists, marketing plans, cost and price structure, and sales strategy.

[343] Access Notice, para. 19.

[344] The Commission's notorious failure to conceal the identity of the whistle-blower Stanley Adams from Hoffmann-La Roche rendered the Commission liable to him in damages under Art. 340 (ex Art. 288(2), ex Art. 215(2)): Case 145/83, *Adams v Commission* [1985] ECR 3539.

[345] Access Notice, para. 19. In Case C-310/93 P, *BPB Industries and British Gypsum Ltd* [1995] ECR I-865 the CJ accepted that the Commission was entitled to keep such correspondence confidential because of the fear of retaliation from the dominant firm in an Art. 102 case. It has been argued (see M. Levitt, 'Commission Notice on Internal Rules of Procedure for Access to the File' [1997] *ECLR* 187) that whether the undertaking is in fact dominant may be one of the things which is in dispute and that the so-called 'economic or commercial pressure' may be no more than an unrealised fear of potential retaliation unrelated to the actual abuse allegation. In *Michelin II* (Case T-203/01, *Manufacture Française des Pneumatiques Michelin v Commission* [2003] ECR II-4071) the GC held that the Commission was justified, on account of the risk of retaliation, in withholding from Michelin the identity of the dealers who had answered its requests for information. Refusal by the Commission to reveal the identity of third parties has also been held justified in merger cases, see Case T-221/95, *Endemol v Commission* [1999] ECR II-1299; Case T-5/02, *Tetra Laval v Commission* [2002] ECR II-4381. In Case T-286/09, *Intel* EU:T:2014:547, paras. 683–684 the GC said that a customer of a dominant undertakings did not normally have an interest in wrongly accusing the undertaking of anti-competitive conduct and, if it did so, might suffer retaliation. Information given by a customer was therefore very unlikely to be incorrect.

[346] The non-confidential version and the description of the deleted information have to be such that any party with access to the file would be able to determine whether the deleted information is likely to be relevant for its defence and therefore to determine whether there are sufficient grounds for requesting access to the confidential information. DG Comp publishes informal guidance on making confidentiality claims on its website, <http://ec.europa.eu/competition/antitrust/information_en.html>.

[347] Access Notice, paras. 35–43.

to the file is granted only to addressees of SOs, and that other parties (complainants and other parties involved in merger cases) have a separate, more limited, right of access to specific documents.

The Notice distinguishes between 'accessible' and 'non-accessible' documents. Both business secrets and confidential information are 'non-accessible'. The Commission's internal documents are also 'non-accessible', as are those of the NCAs, correspondence between the Commission and the NCAs,[348] and correspondence between the NCAs *inter se* (insofar as this is in the Commission's file).[349] The Commission's rationale for the protection of internal documents is that they are not, by their nature, either incriminating or exculpatory and are not the sort of evidence on which the Commission can rely in its assessment of a case.[350] The CJ confirmed in *EnBW Energie Baden-Württemberg*[351] that the Commission may apply a general presumption that the disclosure of internal documents would undermine both the protection of the commercial interests of the undertakings involved and the protection of the purpose of the Commission's investigations.

The Notice sets out the procedure for resolving confidentiality and access to non-accessible information claims. In essence, if the Commission and the undertakings or other parties cannot agree, the matter is dealt with by the Hearing Officer.[352] In Best Practices the Commission sets out two practical possibilities for handling situations where otherwise undertakings would need to redact their submissions in relation to confidential information: a 'negotiated disclosure procedure'[353] and the 'data room' procedure.[354]

There are special provisions in respect of the protection of corporate statements made by applicants for leniency discussed in Section 7.H.v.

c. Confidentiality and Complainants

It was held in *AKZO*,[355] that business secrets are accorded 'very special protection' and cannot be disclosed to third parties who have lodged complaints, otherwise competitors could obtain access to other undertakings' secrets simply by lodging a complaint. In *AKZO* the Commission had sent a copy of the SO and a number of documents in the annexes to the complainant, and the CJ's order to the Commission to recover the documents meant that ECS was unable to rely on them in national proceedings.

---

[348] See Case T-623/13, *Unión de Almacenistas de Hierros de España v Commission* EU:T:2015:268.

[349] Reg. 1/2003, Art. 27(2), and Reg. 773/2004, Art. 15(2).

[350] Access Notice, para. 12. Examples of internal documents given in the Notice are drafts, opinions, memos, or notes from the Commission departments or other public authorities concerned. The Commission's correspondence with other public authorities (including, inter alia, with the NCAs and with competition authorities of non-Member States) are non-accessible (para. 15), although there are provisions for releasing non-confidential versions of some of these in exceptional circumstances (para. 16). For the production of the minutes of informal interviews, see Case T-286/09, *Intel* EU:T:2014:547, discussed in Section 7.C.v, p. 917 and Cases T-191 and 212–214/98, *Atlantic Container Line v Commission* [2003] ECR II-3275.

[351] Case C-365/12 P, *Commission v EnBW Energie Baden-Württemberg* EU:C:2014:112.

[352] Access Notice, paras. 42 and 47; HO Terms of Reference, Arts 7 and 8. In Case T-345/12 R, *Akzo Nobel v Commission* EU:T:2012:605, the President of the GC granted interim measures suspending a Commission decision which would have published a second, fuller version of the non-confidential version of the *Hydrogen and Perborate* cartel decision (2007). The Hearing Officer had rejected Akzo Nobel's claim for continued confidential treatment on the grounds, inter alia, that he could determine only whether the information might be disclosed because it contained business secrets or confidential information whereas the applicants were objecting to the second version solely because it contained information provided pursuant to the Leniency Notice.

[353] Whereby the party being granted access agrees bilaterally with interested parties to receive the entirety of the information they have provided to the Commission, including the confidential information rather than the redacted version. This involves the party granted access restricting its right to have access to the full file and the other party waiving confidentiality; Best Practices, para. 96.

[354] By which part of the file, including confidential information, is gathered in a room at the Commission's premises to which limited access is given under the Commission's supervision under strict conditions; see Best Practices on the disclosure of information in data rooms in proceedings under Articles 101 and 102 TFEU and under the EU Merger Regulation, 2 June 2015, <http://ec.europa.eu/competition/mergers/legislation/disclosure_information_data_rooms_en.pdf>.

[355] Case 53/85, *AKZO v Commission* [1986] ECR 1965.

Complainants, therefore, cannot have the same access to the file as alleged infringers. The rights of third parties[356] are limited to the right to participate in the administrative procedure.[357] This is embodied in paragraphs 30–31 of the Notice on access to the file. However, a complainant who has been told of the intention to reject his complaint may request access to the documents on which the Commission based the provisional assessment although he cannot have access to the confidential information or business secrets of the firm complained about, or those of any third parties, which the Commission has acquired in the course of its investigations.[358]

d. The Transparency Regulation

Article 2 of the Transparency Regulation, 1049/2001[359] provides that any citizen of the Union, and any natural or legal person residing or having its registered office in a Member State, has a right of access to documents of the institutions, subject to the principles, conditions, and limits defined in the Regulation.[360] This applies to all documents held by an institution, that is, documents drawn up or received by it and in its possession, in all areas of activity of the EU.[361] Exceptions to the right of access are set out in Article 4. Article 4(1) provides an absolute exception to disclosure and Article 4(2) and (3) provides for discretionary, or relative, exceptions where access to a document shall be refused unless there is an overriding public interest in disclosure.

The Article 4(1) exceptions cover the protection of: (a) the public interest as regards public security, defence and military matters, international relations, and the financial, monetary, or economic policy of the Community or a Member State; and (b) privacy and the integrity of the individual. Article 4(2) covers the protection of commercial interests of a natural or legal person including intellectual property, court proceedings and legal advice, and the purpose of inspections, investigations, and audits. Article 4(3) covers the undermining of the institution's decision-making process (even after the decision has been taken). The Article 4 derogations from the general principle are strictly construed.[362]

The question that arises is the relationship between these provisions of the Transparency Regulation on the one hand and the provisions of Regulation 1/2003 and Regulation 773/2004 on the other. If the Transparency Regulation trumps the specific competition provisions then not only can the carefully constructed provisions on confidentiality of the latter be subject to the more general regime of the former, but a wider category of persons than the undertakings concerned and complainants might be able to claim access. In particular the Transparency Regulation could be significant in respect of damages claims brought in national courts in the wake of infringement decisions, particularly Article 101 cartel decisions, where the undermining of an ongoing investigation is no longer an issue.[363]

In a number of cases the Commission's refusals to disclose have been overturned by the GC for lack of sufficient reasoning, a failure to demonstrate how exactly disclosure would undermine the interest protected by Article 4(2) or (3), and/or insufficient analysis of each document.[364] However,

---

[356] Laid down in Reg. 1/2003, Art. 27.

[357] Case T-17/93, *Matra Hachette SA v Commission* [1994] ECR II-595.

[358] Reg. 773/2004, Art. 8.

[359] Reg. 1049/2001 [2001] OJ L145/43, adopted pursuant to the principle in what is now Art. 15(1) TFEU that Union institutions and bodies, etc., shall conduct their work as openly as possible.

[360] Transparency Reg., Art. 2(1)

[361] Ibid., Art. 2(3).

[362] Case C-506/08 P, *Kingdom of Sweden v Commission* [2011] ECR I-75, para. 75.

[363] Chap. 14, Section 2.D, p. 1055 ff.

[364] See Case T-2/03, *Verein für Konsumenteninformation* [2005] ECR II-1121; Case T-437/08, *CDC Hydrogen Peroxide v Commission* [2011] ECR II-8251; Case T-181/10, *Reagens SpA v Commission* EU:T:2014:139 (in which one of the undertakings fined in the *Heat Stabilisers* cartel decision, COMP/38.589, 15 December 2011, wanted access to the non-confidential version of one of the other parties' application to have its fine reduced for inability to pay).

as we have seen, in *EnBW*[365] the CJ held that the Commission is entitled to apply a general presumption that access to documents in its file would harm the protection of the commercial interests of the undertakings involved in the proceedings and the protection of the purpose of the investigation.[366] The CJ considered that the Transparency Regulation and the access to the file provisions serve different purposes and that each had to be applied in a way which is compatible with the other. The general presumption may be rebutted by demonstrating that a specific document is not covered by the presumption, or that there is an overriding public interest in disclosure as provided in Article 4(2).[367] This is not satisfied by merely stating that disclosure was necessary for bringing a claim for damages in a national court.[368] The GC applied the *EnBW* judgment in *Schenker*,[369] where it held that the general rebuttable presumption against non-disclosure applied whether or not the case is closed, and in *AXA Versicherung* where the GC held that the Commission could not refuse to disclose the table of contents which included *references* to leniency statements.[370] The presumption also applies to proceedings of NCAs.[371]

The requested documents in *EnBW* included leniency statements. As we see in Chapter 14, the Damages Directive, designed to facilitate damages actions,[372] has special provisions about the disclosure of leniency corporate statements in national proceedings but Article 6(2) provides that nothing in the Directive affects access to documents under the Transparency Regulation.[373]

(vi) The Oral Hearing

The right to be heard is primarily exercised in writing, but Article 12 of Regulation 773/2004 gives the parties to whom an SO has been addressed the right to an oral hearing, if they request it in their written submissions.[374] The oral hearing is controlled and supervised by the Hearing Officer.[375] Third parties such as complainants may be heard in addition to the parties.[376] The oral hearing is not a formal 'trial'. It may last anything from a day to two or three weeks, depending on the complexity of the case. It is not heard in public and parties *may* be heard separately, having regard to their business secrets, etc.,[377] but there is no *right* to an *in camera* hearing, which is a matter for the discretion of

---

[365] Case C-365/12 P, *EnBW* EU:C:2014:112.

[366] The CJ had previously held this in respect to access to the file in merger cases (Case C-404/10 P, *Commission v Éditions Odile Jacob* EU:C:2013:808; Case C-477/10 P, *Commission v Agrofert Holding a.s.* EU:C:2012:394) and State aid cases (Case C-139/07 P, *Commission v Technische Glaswerke Ilmenau* [2010] ECR I-5885). In *EnBW* the CJ set aside the GC's judgment to the contrary, Case T-344/08, *EnBW Energie Baden-Württemberg v Commission* EU:T:2012:242.

[367] Case C-365/12 P, *EnBW* EU:C:2014:112, para. 117.

[368] Ibid., para. 132.

[369] Case T-534/11 P, *Schenker v Commission* EU:T:2014:854.

[370] Case T-677/13, *AXA Versicherung v Commission* EU:T:2015:473.

[371] Case T-623/13, *Unión de Almacenistas de Hierros de España v Commission* EU:T:2015:268.

[372] Dir. 2014/104/EU (see n. 325).

[373] See also recital 135 of the Directive, and Case T-677/13, *AXA* EU:T:2015:473, para. 135.

[374] See Best Practices, paras. 106–108; Antitrust ManProc, Module 3.3. The Commission does not breach the right to be heard if it refuses a hearing when it does not receive a request within the stipulated time limits, Case T-286/09, *Intel* EU:T:2014:547, paras. 325–326. There is no right to an oral hearing after the issue of a Letter of Facts (see n. 304), *Intel*, para. 327.

[375] HO Terms of Reference, Art. 10. See S. Durande and K. Williams, 'The Practical Impact of the Exercise of the Right to be Heard: A Special Focus on the Effect of Oral Hearings and the Role of the Hearing Officers' (2005) 2 *Competition Policy Newsletter* 22; W. Wils, 'The Oral Hearing in Competition Proceedings Before the European Commission' (2012) 35 *World Competition* 397.

[376] Reg. 773/2004, Art. 13.

[377] Ibid., Art. 14(6).

the Hearing Officer.[378] Article 14(5) of Regulation 773/2004 provides that the persons being heard may be 'assisted by' their lawyers.[379]

Article 14(8) of Regulation 773/2004 provides that the statements made at the hearing shall be recorded and the record made available to the persons who attended the hearing, regard being had to the protection of business secrets and confidential information. Business secrets and other confidential information are deleted.

The Hearing Officer is not a judge. It is not his or her function to come to a decision, but to make an interim report to the Competition Commissioner on the hearing and the conclusions to be drawn from it in respect of the right to be heard.[380] This report is not made available to the parties, who have no right to see it or comment on it. The Hearing Officer makes a final report which is attached to the draft decision submitted to the College of Commissioners[381] which is made known to the addressees of the decision and is published in the Official Journal together with the decision.[382] The limited nature of the Hearing Officer's role is relevant to the question of the compatibility of competition procedure with Article 6(1) ECHR.

E. COMMISSION DECISIONS

(i) General

The Commission may take a final decision ordering the termination of infringements of the competition rules and may take procedural decisions during the course of its investigation, as we have seen. It may also take interim measures in order to prevent irreparable damage occurring before it can come to a final decision. It was given two new powers under Regulation 1/2003: to take a decision making commitments binding but without making an infringement finding, and to take a 'positive' decision finding Article 101 or Article 102 inapplicable. It is usual to speak of 'the Commission' when discussing the conduct of EU competition policy, meaning the policy and actions of the Competition Directorate-General, DG Comp. However, it is important to remember that unless the taking of particular acts of management or administration has been delegated to a single Commissioner, decisions are collegiate acts of the whole Commission.[383] When the Commission adopts an infringement decision, therefore, the Commissioner responsible for competition lays the draft before the whole College and the measure is adopted by the College.[384]

This section deals with the content of decisions other than the imposition of fines: fines are dealt with in Section 7.H.

---

[378] Case T-384/09, *SKW Stahl-Metallurgie GmbH v Commission* EU:T:2014:27, on appeal Case C-154/14 P, *SKW Stahl-Metallurgie GmbH v Commission*, judgment pending.

[379] Not 'represented by' because it is necessary that someone from the undertaking itself (although that can be an in-house lawyer) is present to provide relevant information about the organisation, see Case 49/69, *BASF v Commission (Dyestuffs)* [1972] ECR 713. Persons 'invited to attend' may be represented by legal representatives, Reg. 773/2004, Art. 14(4).

[380] HO Terms of Reference, Art. 13(1).

[381] Ibid., Art. 14(1).

[382] Ibid., Art. 16.

[383] This aspect of decisions was stressed by the GC in the *Cement* appeal. Two of the applicants claimed a breach of the principle of impartiality, in that the same Commission official had carried out the investigation, acted as rapporteur, drawn up the SO, and prepared the draft decision. The GC held that the principle was not breached because the contested decision was actually taken by the College of Commissioners, not by the official: Cases T-25/95 etc., *Cimenteries* [2000] ECR II-491, para. 721.

[384] The failure of the College to adopt an authenticated version of the decision was one reason for the annulment of the *PVC* decision in Case C-137/92 P, *Commission v BASF and others* [1994] ECR I-2555: see Section 8.A.v, p. 997.

(ii) Final Decisions: Infringement Decisions under Regulation 1/2003, Article 7

a. Finding and Termination of Infringements

Article 7 of Regulation 1/2003[385] states:

> ### Finding and termination of infringement
>
> 1. Where the Commission, acting on a complaint or on its own initiative, finds that there is an infringement of Article [101] or of Article [102], it may by decision require the undertakings and associations of undertakings concerned to bring such infringement to an end. For this purpose, it may impose on them any behavioural or structural remedies which are proportionate to the infringement committed and necessary to bring the infringement effectively to an end. Structural remedies can only be imposed either where there is no equally effective behavioural remedy or where any equally effective behavioural remedy would be more burdensome for the undertaking concerned than the structural remedy. If the Commission has a legitimate interest in doing so, it may also find that an infringement has been committed in the past.
>
> 2. Those entitled to lodge a complaint for the purposes of paragraph 1 are natural or legal persons who can show a legitimate interest and Member States.

A decision finding an infringement may therefore order undertakings to bring the infringement to an end where it has not definitely been terminated already. These are called 'cease and desist orders'. The decision may also contain a 'like effects order' whereby the parties are prohibited from entering into similar arrangements.[386] The Court established in *Cementhandelaren* that the Commission is justified in taking a decision after an infringement has terminated so that the decision is in effect only a declaration that the past conduct did infringe.[387]

b. Behavioural and Structural Remedies

The corresponding provision to Article 7 in Regulation 17 was Article 3, which did not state whether the Commission could take decisions ordering the parties to take *positive* steps (i.e. adopt positive behavioural remedies) in order to bring the infringement to an end. The CJ, however, held in *Commercial Solvents* that it could:[388]

> [Article 3] must be applied in relation to the infringement which has been established and may include an order to do certain acts or provide certain advantages which have been wrongfully withheld as well as prohibiting the continuation of certain actions, practices or situations which are contrary to the Treaty.

In *Commercial Solvents* the dominant undertaking was ordered to supply a certain amount of raw material to the complainant, which involved the parties entering into contractual relations. Many

---

[385] Reg. 1/2003 [2003] OJ L1/1.

[386] See Case T-410/03, *Hoechst GmbH v Commission* [2008] ECR II-881, where the Commission decision prohibited future similar conduct although Hoechst had already left the market on which the infringement had been committed (sorbates). The GC upheld the decision, stating that the prohibition was preventive and did not depend on the undertaking's position at the time of the decision (the decision referred only to conduct on the sorbates market).

[387] Case 8/72, *Cementhandelaren v Commission* [1972] ECR 977; see also COMP/37.860, *Morgan Stanley/Visa International and Visa Europe*, upheld Case T-461/07, *Visa Europe and Visa International Service Association v Commission* [2011] ECR II-1729 where the infringement had ceased but the undertaking continued to deny it had done anything wrong.

[388] Cases 6 and 7/73, *Istituto Chemioterapico Italiano SpA and Commercial Solvents Corp v Commission* [1974] ECR 223, para. 45.

subsequent Article 102 cases on refusal to supply have involved ordering a dominant undertaking to supply or to share facilities.[389] The Commission may also order an undertaking to amend its contractual terms or its pricing policies. Article 7(1) of Regulation 1/2003 now expressly gives the Commission power to make positive orders by stating that it may impose 'any behavioural . . . remedies which are proportionate to the infringement committed and necessary to bring the infringement effectively to an end'. The overriding principle is proportionality. In *Automec*, an Article 101 case, the GC said that the Commission does not have the power to order a party to enter into a contractual relationship where there are other ways of making the party end the infringement.

In *Atlantic Container Line AB*[390] the Commission found that shipping companies had infringed Article 101(1) by an agreement which fixed prices and capacity. The decision, inter alia, required the parties to inform customers that they were entitled to renegotiate the terms of contracts concluded within the context of the agreement or to terminate them.[391] The GC annulled that part of the decision as it went beyond what was required to terminate the infringement:

> . . . [T]he Commission may specify the scope of the obligations imposed on the undertakings concerned in order to bring an end to the infringements identified. That power must however be implemented according to the nature of the infringement declared (see, by analogy, *Istituto Chemioterapico italiano and Commercial Solvents* v *Commission*, paragraph 45; *RTE and ITP* v *Commission*, paragraph 90; and Case C-279/95 P *Langnese-Iglo* v *Commission* . . . paragraph 74) and the obligations imposed must not exceed what is appropriate and necessary to attain the objective sought, namely re-establishment of compliance with the rules infringed (see *RTE and ITP* v *Commission*, paragraph 93).[392]

The problems of ensuring compliance with positive behavioural remedies are shown by *Microsoft*, in which the Commission ordered Microsoft to make available certain interoperability information (to remedy its refusal to supply) on fair and reasonable terms.[393] The decision provided for Microsoft to submit a proposal for the establishment of a mechanism, including the appointment of an independent monitoring trustee (IMT), to oversee Microsoft's compliance with the decision. The IMT was to be empowered to access Microsoft's information, documents, premises, and employees and also the source code of its relevant products. It provided for Microsoft to bear all the costs of the appointment of the IMT, including his remuneration. This part of the decision in respect of the remedy was annulled by the GC, which said that in effect the Commission was compelling Microsoft to grant to the IMT powers (without time limit) which the Commission was not itself authorised to confer on a third party. There was nothing in Regulation 17 to authorise such a remedy. The requirement for Microsoft to supply the interoperability information was left standing, however, and there was a dispute about whether Microsoft was providing access to the information in a satisfactory manner and about the rates of remuneration it was charging, culminating in a further decision in which the Commission imposed periodic penalty payments. In coming to the conclusion that the rates were unreasonable the Commission had to determine the 'economic value' of the information. It took into account the necessity of allowing competitors to compete viably with Microsoft while representing fair compensation for the value of the technology transferred. However, it excluded the value that derived from Microsoft's market power. The GC upheld the Commission.[394] In particular it said:

> . . . allowing Microsoft to charge remuneration rates reflecting the value resulting from the mere ability to interoperate with Microsoft's operating systems—in other words the strategic value stemming from Microsoft's

---

[389] See Chap. 7, Section 13.

[390] Case T-395/94, *Atlantic Container Line AB v Commission* [2002] ECR II-875.

[391] *Trans-Atlantic Agreement* [1994] OJ L376/1, Art. 5.

[392] Case T-395/94, *Atlantic Container Line* [2002] ECR II-875, para. 410.

[393] COMP/37.792, *Microsoft* 24 March 2004, upheld on the substantive issues Case T-201/04, *Microsoft v Commission* [2007] ECR II-3601.

[394] Case T-167/08, *Microsoft v Commission* EU:T:2012:323.

power in the client PC operating systems market or the work group server operating systems market—would in effect allow it to transform the benefits of the abuse into remuneration for the grant of licences.[395]

The power to order positive measures in appropriate cases in Article 3(1) of Regulation 17 did not appear to include a general power to order divestiture. Article 102 is infringed by an abuse, not by the dominant position per se and Article 3 of Regulation 17 provided only for the Commission to order the termination of the *infringement*. It did not give a power to restructure the market to prevent future abuses. However, in *Continental Can*[396] the Commission decision held that an undertaking had committed an abuse by acquiring another company and required the undertaking to dispose of it. The decision was annulled on substantive grounds, and so the order was never enforced. In this case, however, the order to divest related to the very subject matter of the abuse. Article 7(1) of Regulation 1/2003 now expressly provides for the Commission to take any structural remedies 'which are proportionate to the infringement committed and necessary to bring the infringement to an end'. The structural remedy can only be imposed where no behavioural remedy would be equally effective or where the behavioural remedy would be more burdensome for the undertaking concerned. Recital 12 of Regulation 1/2003 further states that changes to the structure of an undertaking as it existed prior to the infringement would only be proportionate 'where there is a substantial risk of a lasting or repeated infringement that derives from the very structure of the undertaking'.

The ability to impose a structural remedy, i.e. to order divestment or break up companies, is a powerful weapon in the hands of a competition authority and not one to be used lightly.[397] Since 2007 the Commission has turned to structural remedies with increasing frequency (because of its enforcement of the competition rules in the energy sector) but these have been obtained through commitments decisions rather than prohibition decisions.[398]

(iii) Final Decisions: Commitments Decisions under Regulation 1/2003, Article 9

a. General

Article 9 of Regulation 1/2003 enables the Commission to adopt decisions whereby, without a finding of infringement, commitments given by undertakings as to their future behaviour are made binding upon them.[399] This was a new provision in Regulation 1/2003. Previously the Commission could settle cases informally, but could not make any commitments binding.[400] Recital 13 of Regulation 1/2003 states that 'commitment decisions' are not suitable where the Commission intends to impose a fine and consequently the Commission does not apply the Article 9 procedure to secret cartels that fall under the Leniency Notice[401] or to other cases where the primary goal is

---

[395] Ibid., para. 142.

[396] Case 6/72, *Continental Can* [1973] ECR 215.

[397] The consequences of a competition authority deciding to restructure an industry can be seen in the saga of the UK beer sector following the Monopolies and Mergers Commission Report, *The Supply of Beer*, Cm. 651 (1989).

[398] The Competition Commissioner stressed the powers of the Commission to impose structural remedies for breaches of Arts. 101 and 102 when the Commission presented its report on its Reg. 1/2003, Art. 17 inquiry into the European gas and energy sectors, Communication from the Commission, COM(2006)851, 10 January 2007.

[399] See generally J. Temple Lang, 'Commitment Decisions and Settlements with Antitrust Authorities and Private Parties Under European Antitrust Law' [2005] *Fordham Corp L Inst* 265; C. Cook, 'Commitment Decisions: The Law and Practice under Article 9' (2006) 29 *World Competition* 209; W. Wils, 'Settlements of EU Antitrust Investigations; Commitment Decisions under Article 9 of Regulation 1/2003' (2006) 29 *World Competition* 345; W. Wils, 'The Use of Settlements in Public Antitrust Enforcement: Objectives and Principles' (2008) 31 *World Competition* 335; W. Wils, 'Discretion and Prioritisation in Public Antitrust Enforcement' (2011) 34 *World Competition* 353; N. Dunne, 'Commitment Decisions in EU Competition Law' (2014) 10 *J of Competition Law and Economics* 399; Commissioner Almunia SPEECH/13/210; A. Gautier and N. Petit, 'Optimal Enforcement of Competition Policy: The Commitments Procedure Under Uncertainty' (24 April 2015), <http://ssrn.com/abstract=2509729>; W. Wils, 'Ten Years of Commitment Decisions under Article 9 of Regulation 1/2003: Too Much of a Good Thing?' (15 June 2015) <http://ssrn.com/author=456087>.

[400] That power remains, see Section 7.G.

[401] Best Practices, para. 116. For the Leniency Notice see Section 7.H.v, p. 983.

to punish past behaviour.[402] However, Article 9 has been used in respect of what, if proved, would have been serious infringements of Article 102 where a heavy fine might have been expected to be imposed.[403] Commitments may involve behavioural or structural obligations and may go beyond what the Commission could impose in an Article 7 decision.[404] The Commission will not accept a mere commitment to comply with the competition rules in the future.[405] Behavioural commitments, such as those in *Microsoft* and those proposed in *Google*, may involve a monitoring trustee mechanism to ensure their implementation.[406]

Regulation 1/2003

Article 9

1. Where the Commission intends to adopt a decision requiring that an infringement be brought to an end and the undertakings concerned offer commitments to meet the concerns expressed to them by the Commission in its preliminary assessment, the Commission may by decision make those commitments binding on the undertakings. Such a decision may be adopted for a specified period and shall conclude that there are no longer grounds for action by the Commission.

2. The Commission may, upon request or on its own initiative, reopen the proceedings:

   (a) where there has been a material change in any of the facts on which the decision was based;

   (b) where the undertakings concerned act contrary to their commitments; or

   (c) where the decision was based on incomplete, incorrect or misleading information provided by the parties.

It will be noted that the power to take an Article 9 decision arises only where the Commission otherwise intends to adopt an Article 7 decision. However, it does not have to send an SO before taking an Article 9 decision. The Commission is only required to make a 'preliminary assessment'. The procedure is explained in Best Practices.[407] If the parties under investigation wish to avoid the issue of an SO they have to offer commitments early on, and the Commission may then issue a preliminary assessment rather than an SO.[408] If the Commission is minded to accept the commitments being offered, in that they meet its competition concerns, it puts them out for a 'market test' in accordance with Article 27(4) of Regulation 1/2003. It does this by publishing the proposed commitments in the Official Journal and inviting third party comments.[409] Following the responses the Commission may require amendments to the commitments or may drop the Article 9 procedure altogether and revert to the Article 7 procedure.[410] If the commitments finally offered are acceptable to the Commission it takes a decision under Article 9(1) and the undertaking is bound by them.

---

[402] 'To Commit or Not to Commit?' [2014] 3 *Competition Policy Brief* 1.

[403] For example, COMP/38.636, *Rambus*, IP/09/1897; COMP/39.530, *Microsoft* (tying), IP/13/2013; COM/39.692, *IBM Maintenance Services*, IP/11/1539; see Chap. 7. In Case 39.847, *e-books* [2013] OJ C73/17 and [2013] OJ C378/25, IP/12/1367 and IP/13/746, commitments were taken in a case which in effect involved price-fixing and resale maintenance.

[404] Case C-441/07 P, *Commission v Alrosa* [2010] ECR I-5949, para. 48.

[405] 'To Commit or Not to Commit?', n. 402.

[406] *Microsoft* (tying), IP/10/216, IP/13/2013; COMP/39.740, *Google*.

[407] Best Practices, paras. 115–133; Antitrust ManProc, Module 16.

[408] Although if an SO has already been sent the SO fulfils the requirements of the Preliminary Assessment.

[409] Best Practices, paras. 129–133. It may also actively contact third parties, see Faull and Nikpay, n. 2, 2.134.

[410] As happened in COMP/38.698, *CISAC*, on appeal Cases T-442/08 etc., *CISAC v Commission* EU:T:2013:188, and COMP/39.740, *Google*, IP/15/4780.

Article 9(2) gives the Commission power to reopen the proceedings in the circumstances listed therein[411] and a breach of an Article 9(1) decision may result in the Commission taking a decision imposing a fine under Article 23(2)(c) of Regulation 1/2003. A fine of €561 million was imposed on Microsoft for breaching its commitments in respect of the browser choice screen.[412] The Commission, however, is not *obliged* to act against a breach of commitments. It has the same discretion in deciding whether to take such action as it has in respect of any alleged anti-competitive conduct.[413]

The scope for the undertaking giving the commitments to appeal against an Article 9(1) decision is limited, and unlikely, although it could conceivably be done on procedural grounds.[414] Third parties may appeal, as happened in *Alrosa*,[415] and in particular complainants dissatisfied with the outcome of the case may challenge the decision[416] or complain that the commitments have been breached.[417] A commitments decision does not preclude an NCA from taking proceedings against the undertaking after the Article 9 procedure is over.[418]

b. The Nature of Commitments Decisions

The extent of the Commission's discretion and freedom of action under Article 9, and the nature of commitments decisions, was established in the *Alrosa* case in which the CJ overturned the GC's annulment of the Commission decision.

By an exclusive distribution agreement Alrosa undertook to sell a large proportion of its rough diamonds exclusively to De Beers. De Beers was the world's largest diamond producer and Alrosa the second. The agreement was notified to the Commission in 2001. The Commission considered Articles 101 and 102 might both apply to the agreement. In 2005 De Beers and Alrosa jointly offered commitments providing for a 'cap' on Alrosa's sales to De Beers. The Commission did not pursue the commitments after the market test produced negative responses.[419] De Beers (alone, as the dominant undertaking) then gave commitments to first phase out, and then cease completely, all direct and indirect purchases of rough diamonds from Alrosa. The Commission rendered these commitments binding by an Article 9(1) decision.[420]

Alrosa, considering itself seriously affected by the termination of its arrangements with De Beers, appealed. The GC annulled the decision on the grounds that it infringed the principle of proportionality and Article 9.[421] Moreover, Alrosa's right to be heard as a 'party concerned' under Article 27(2) had been infringed. The GC held that (a) although commitments arise from an offer made by the parties and accepted by the Commission that does not mean that the Commission is not the 'sole author' of the decision, which is binding *erga omnes*, and (b) the Commission cannot take a decision under Article 9(1) that it could not take as a final decision under Article 7(1). Only the most exceptional circumstances[422] could justify an Article 9(1) decision indefinitely prohibiting parties from entering into any contractual arrangements whatsoever. The principle of proportionality

---

[411] A material change in the facts; breach of the commitments; the decision was based on incomplete, incorrect, or misleading information supplied by the parties.

[412] COMP/39.530, *Microsoft*, IP/13/196.

[413] Case T-342/11, *Confederación Española de Empresarios de Estaciones de Servicio ('CEEES') v Commission* EU:T:2014:60.

[414] See Faull and Nikpay, n. 2, 2.143.

[415] Case C-441/07 P, *Commission v Alrosa* [2010] ECR I-5949.

[416] Case T-342/11, *CEEES* EU:T:2014:60; the appeal against the *Rambus* decision (COMP/38.636), Cases T-148 and 149/10, *SK Hynix v Commission* EU:T:2013:358, was withdrawn.

[417] Case T-76/14, *Morningstar Inc v Commission*, judgment pending.

[418] Case C-17/10, *Toshiba Corp* EU:C:2012:72, paras. 68–92; Case T-342/11, *CEEES* EU:T:2014:60, paras. 66–68.

[419] The third parties responding to the Art. 27(4) market test notice, [2005] OJ C136/32, thought the cap inadequate to meet the competition concerns.

[420] COMP/38.381, *DeBeers/Alrosa* [2006] OJ L205/24.

[421] Case T-170/06, *Alrosa v Commission* [2007] ECR II-2601.

[422] Such as possibly a collective dominance situation, which had not been established here.

would have been infringed if this had been an Article 7(1) decision, as there were less onerous options open to the Commission, so the principle of proportionality was equally infringed by the Article 9(1) decision.

The GC also held that Alrosa's right to be heard had been infringed as it had been unable to comment fully on De Beers' proposed commitments (its access to the file was insufficient). Although it was not 'an undertaking concerned' under Article 9(1) in respect of the Article 102 proceedings because it was not in a dominant position (paragraphs 89 and 90) it was more than a mere 'interested third party'. Until the Commission dropped the Article 101 proceedings and relied solely on Article 102 it *had* been 'an undertaking concerned' and these circumstances should have led to its being accorded the rights given to an undertaking concerned even though 'strictly speaking, it did not fall to be so classified' in the Article 102 proceedings. The right to be heard was a fundamental right, enshrined in Article 41(2) of the Charter.

On appeal the CJ set aside the GC judgment.[423] The CJ clarified that the principle of proportionality applies to Article 9(1) commitment decisions differently from Article 7 infringement decisions. It held that Article 9 was a new mechanism intended to provide a more rapid solution to competition problems identified by the Commission. Although the Commission is bound to respect the principle of proportionality in adopting commitment decisions, its task under Article 9 is confined to examining and possibly accepting commitments offered by the undertakings concerned in the light of problems identified by the Commission in its preliminary assessment. In contrast, Article 7 expressly provides that the Commission can only impose remedies on undertakings which are proportionate to the infringement committed and necessary to bring it effectively to an end. Undertakings offering commitments in Article 9 cases consciously accept that the concessions they make may go beyond what the Commission could impose on them in an Article 7 decision. In Article 9 cases the application of the principle of proportionality is therefore confined to verifying that the commitments offered addressed the concerns expressed, taking into consideration the interests of third parties.

The CJ also held that in holding that alternative solutions, which were less onerous than a complete ban on dealing, existed in this case, the GC had gone beyond considering whether the Commission had committed a manifest error of assessment and had wrongly substituted its own assessment for that of the Commission.

Case C-441/07 P, *Commission v Alrosa* [2010] ECR I-5949

Court of Justice

34. Under Article 9 of Regulation No 1/2003, where the Commission intends to adopt a decision requiring an infringement to be brought to an end, it may make the commitments offered by the undertakings concerned binding if they meet the competition concerns expressed in its preliminary assessment.

35. This is a new mechanism introduced by Regulation No 1/2003 which is intended to ensure that the competition rules laid down in the EC Treaty are applied effectively, by means of the adoption of decisions making commitments, proposed by the parties and considered appropriate by the Commission, binding in order to provide a more rapid solution to the competition problems identified by the Commission, instead of proceeding by making a formal finding of an infringement. More particularly, Article 9 of the regulation is based on considerations of procedural economy, and enables undertakings to participate fully in the procedure, by putting forward the solutions which appear to them to be the most appropriate and capable of addressing the Commission's concerns.

---

[423] See M. Kellerbauer, 'Playground Instead of Playpen: The Court of Justice of the European Union's *Alrosa* Judgment on Article 9 of Regulation 1/2003' [2011] *ECLR* 1.

36. As observed by the parties and by the Advocate General in point 42 of her Opinion, although Article 9, unlike Article 7 of Regulation No 1/2003, does not expressly refer to proportionality, the principle of proportionality, as a general principle of European Union law, is none the less a criterion for the lawfulness of any act of the institutions of the Union, including decisions taken by the Commission in its capacity of competition authority.

37. That being so, in the examination of acts of the Commission, whether in the context of Article 7 or of Article 9 of Regulation No 1/2003, the questions always arise, first, of the precise extent and limits of the obligations which flow from the observance of that principle and, second, of the limits of judicial review.

38. The specific characteristics of the mechanisms provided for in Articles 7 and 9 of Regulation No 1/2003 and the means of action available under each of those provisions are different, which means that the obligation on the Commission to ensure that the principle of proportionality is observed has a different extent and content, depending on whether it is considered in relation to the former or the latter article.

39. Article 7 of Regulation No 1/2003 expressly indicates the extent to which the principle of proportionality applies in situations covered by that article. In accordance with Article 7(1) of the regulation, the Commission may impose on the undertakings concerned any behavioural or structural remedies which are proportionate to the infringement committed and necessary to bring the infringement effectively to an end.

40. Article 9 of that regulation, by contrast, provides merely that in proceedings under that provision, as follows from recital 13 in the preamble to the regulation, the Commission is not required to make a finding of an infringement, its task being confined to examining, and possibly accepting, the commitments offered by the undertakings concerned in the light of the problems identified by it in its preliminary assessment and having regard to the aims pursued.

41. Application of the principle of proportionality by the Commission in the context of Article 9 of Regulation No 1/2003 is confined to verifying that the commitments in question address the concerns it expressed to the undertakings concerned and that they have not offered less onerous commitments that also address those concerns adequately. When carrying out that assessment, the Commission must, however, take into consideration the interests of third parties.

42. Judicial review for its part relates solely to whether the Commission's assessment is manifestly incorrect.

43. In the judgment under appeal, the General Court proceeded from the proposition that the application of the principle of proportionality has the same effect in relation to decisions taken under Article 7 of Regulation No 1/2003 as in relation to those taken under Article 9 of that regulation.

44. In paragraph 101 of the judgment under appeal, the General Court held that it would be contrary to the scheme of Regulation No 1/2003 for a decision which would, under Article 7(1) of the regulation, have to be regarded as disproportionate to the infringement that had been established to be taken by having recourse to the procedure laid down under Article 9(1) in the form of a commitment that is made binding.

45. That conclusion is not correct.

46. Those two provisions of Regulation No 1/2003, as noted in paragraph 38 above, pursue different objectives, one of them aiming to put an end to the infringement that has been found to exist and the other aiming to address the Commission's concerns following its preliminary assessment.

47. There is therefore no reason why the measure which could possibly be imposed in the context of Article 7 of Regulation No 1/2003 should have to serve as a reference for the purpose of assessing the extent of the commitments accepted under Article 9 of the regulation, or why anything going beyond that measure should automatically be regarded as disproportionate. Even though decisions adopted under each of those provisions are in either case subject to the principle of proportionality, the application of that principle none the less differs according to which of those provisions is concerned.

48. Undertakings which offer commitments on the basis of Article 9 of Regulation No 1/2003 consciously accept that the concessions they make may go beyond what the Commission could itself impose on them in a decision adopted under Article 7 of the regulation after a thorough examination. On the other hand, the closure of the infringement proceedings brought against those undertakings allows them to avoid a finding of an infringement of competition law and a possible fine.

49. Moreover, the fact that the individual commitments offered by an undertaking have been made binding by the Commission does not mean that other undertakings are deprived of the possibility of protecting the rights they may have in connection with their relations with that undertaking.

50. It must therefore be concluded that the Commission is right to submit that in the judgment under appeal the General Court wrongly considered that the application of the principle of proportionality must be assessed, in the case of decisions taken under Article 9 of Regulation No 1/2003, by reference to the way in which it is assessed in connection with decisions taken under Article 7 of that regulation despite the different concepts underlying those two provisions.

. . .

59. It should be recalled that the Commission examined the joint commitments after inviting third parties to submit observations and finding that the results of that public consultation were negative. From that it concluded that those commitments were not sufficient.

60. To answer the Commission's complaint and ascertain whether the General Court really did, as the Commission submits, infringe the discretion it has in connection with accepting commitments under Article 9 of Regulation No 1/2003, the extent of that discretion should first be defined.

61. Since the Commission is not required itself to seek out less onerous or more moderate solutions than the commitments offered to it, as was observed in paragraphs 40 and 41 above, its only obligation in the present case in relation to the proportionality of the commitments was to ascertain whether the joint commitments offered in the proceedings initiated under Article [101] were sufficient to address the concerns it had identified in the proceedings initiated under Article [102].

62. As the Advocate General observes in point 80 et seq. of her Opinion, the Commission concluded, after taking note of the results of the market test it had conducted, that the joint commitments were not appropriate for resolving the competition problems it had identified.

63. The General Court could have held that the Commission had committed a manifest error of assessment only if it had found that the Commission's conclusion was obviously unfounded, having regard to the facts established by it.

64. However, the General Court made no such finding.

65. Instead it examined other less onerous solutions for the purpose of applying the principle of proportionality, including possible adjustments of the joint commitments, in paragraphs 128, 129 and 137 to 153 of the judgment under appeal.

66. In paragraphs 129 to 136 of the judgment under appeal, the General Court expressed its own differing assessment of the capability of the joint commitments to eliminate the competition problems identified by the Commission, before concluding in paragraph 154 that alternative solutions that were less onerous for the undertakings than a complete ban on dealings existed in the present case.

67. By so doing, the General Court put forward its own assessment of complex economic circumstances and thus substituted its own assessment for that of the Commission, thereby encroaching on the discretion enjoyed by the Commission instead of reviewing the lawfulness of its assessment.

68. That error of the General Court in itself justifies setting aside the judgment under appeal.

Alrosa showed the GC and the CJ holding different conceptions of the nature of commitments decisions. The GC took what has been called a more 'public-law paradigm' view, whereby commitments decisions are part of an enforcement process 'epitomized by an authoritative, unilateral, top-down hierarchical command by the "State" '.[424] The CJ however, saw them as having more of a 'contract-law' character, where they are the outcome of a negotiation and agreement between parties of similar bargaining power able to safeguard their own interests.[425] The result of the CJ's conception of commitments decisions, it can be argued, is the marginalisation of judicial review and the sidelining of the principle of proportionality.[426] The CJ's judgment was an extreme example of the Court's willingness to defer to the Commission's discretion.

The CJ also held that the GC had misinterpreted the extent of Alrosa's 'right to be heard' in the Commission proceedings. As far as the Article 102 proceedings were concerned, Alrosa was not an 'undertaking concerned' for the purposes of Article 27(2) as it was not the dominant undertaking. Its rights were limited to those of an interested third party only.[427]

c. The Use of Article 9 Decisions

It quickly became apparent after Regulation 1/2003 came into force that commitments decisions would play a major role in the Commission's application of the competition rules and (outside hardcore cartels, where commitments decisions are not available) they have become the most common way the Commission deals with cases it wishes to pursue. In the ten years to 2014, the Commission took 34 commitments decisions but only 19 non-cartel Article 7 decisions.[428] At first the Commission used the procedure to dispose of a number of cases in which investigations had been opened before May 2004.[429] It has since been used to deal with a wide range of Article 101 non-cartel cases including, inter alia, airline alliances,[430] non-compete obligations in joint ventures,[431] multilateral exchange fees,[432] and limitations of price competition in *e-books*.[433]

The most striking use of Article 9, however, has been in respect of Article 102. Since 2007 a wide-ranging initiative against anti-competitive practices in the energy sector has seen a number of such decisions.[434] Structural remedies have been secured in some of these cases.[435] A particularly striking decision is *Bulgarian Energy Holding* in which the State-owned energy incumbent committed, inter alia, to set up a new power exchange with the assistance of an independent third party and transfer control of its ownership to the Bulgarian Finance Ministry.[436] Outside the energy sector a

---

[424] F. Wagner-Von Papp, 'Best and Even Better Practices in Commitment Procedures after *Alrosa*: The Dangers of Abandoning the "Struggle for Competition Law" ' (2012) 49 *CMLRev* 929, 933.

[425] Ibid., 933.

[426] See also F. Cengiz, 'Judicial Review and the Rule of Law in the EU Competition Law Regime after *Alrosa*' (2011) 7 *European Competition Journal* 127.

[427] Case C-441/07 P, *Commission v Alrosa* [2010] ECR I-5949, paras. 85–95.

[428] See [2015] 3 *Competition Policy Brief*, and the statistics presented in W. Wils, 'Ten Years of Commitment Decisions under Article 9', n. 399.

[429] COMP/37.214, *Deutsche Bundesliga* [2005] OJ L134/46 and COMP/38.173, *FA Premier League*, concerned the collective selling of media rights to football matches. COMP/38.681, *Cannes Extension Agreement*, IP/06/1311 concerned online music. COMP/38.348, *Repsol* [2006] OJ L176/104, was a move to open up the fuel distribution system in Spain, and involved a structural remedy.

[430] COMP/BA/AA/IB [2010] OJ C278/14; COMP/39.595, *Air Canada/Continental Airlines/Lufthansa/United* [2013] OJ C201/7; COMP/39.964, *AF-KL/DL/AZ* [2015] OJ C212/5.

[431] COMP/39.736, *Siemens/Areva* [2012] OJ C280/8.

[432] COMP/39.398, *Visa MIF* [2014] OJ C147/7.

[433] COMP/39.847, *e-books* [2013] OJ C73/17 and [2013] OJ C378/25.

[434] COMP/39.386, *EDF—Long Term Electricity Contracts in France*; COMP/37.966, *Distrigaz* [2008] OJ C9/8; COMP/39.316, *GDF, Gas market in France* [2010] OJ C57/13; COMP/39.388, *German Electricity Wholesale Markets* and COMP/39.389, *German Electricity Balancing Markets (E.ON)* [2009] OJ C36/8; COMP/39.402, *RWE—Gas Foreclosure* [2009] OJ C133/9; COMP/39.351, *Swedish Interconnectors* [2010] OJ C142/28; COMP/39.317, *E.ON (Gas)* [2010] OJ C278/9; COMP/39.315, *ENI* 29 September 2010; COMP/39.727, *CEZ* [2013] OJ C251/4; see further Chap. 7.

[435] See *Distrigaz, RWE, E.ON (Gas), ENI*, and *CEZ* cited in n. 434.

[436] COMP/39.767, 10 December 2015, IP/15/6289.

number of high-profile and sometimes controversial Article 102 cases have been settled by commitments, as discussed in Chapter 7.[437] In particular, the Commission developed the use of Article 102 in standard-essential patents (SEP) disputes by using Article 9[438] before finally making an Article 7 decision.[439]

The most notable attempt by the Commission to terminate a case with commitments was *Google*.[440] The Commission tried for over four years to obtain acceptable commitments from Google in respect of four particular search engine practices. Proceedings were opened in November 2010 after 17 undertakings had filed complaints,[441] and commitments offered by Google were finally put out to market test in April 2013.[442] The commitments were criticised by complainants and third parties and Google offered two sets of improvements, in October 2013 and in early 2014. The Commission announced in February 2014 that it intended to vote on adopting the third set,[443] but there was again much vociferous opposition, including from politicians[444] and the European Parliament.[445] The term of office of Commissioner Almunia, under whom the negotiations with Google had been conducted, finished at the end of October 2014, and under the new Commissioner, Margrethe Vestager, the Commission abandoned the Article 9 procedure and issued an SO to Google in April 2015 in respect of one of the practices ('comparison shopping') while continuing to 'actively investigate' the other three.[446]

d. The Advantages and Disadvantages of Commitments Decisions

Commitments decisions are an attractive procedure for the Commission. They enable it to terminate cases quickly while retaining control. The Commission has listed the advantages over Article 7 prohibition decisions as:[447]

- there is a quicker impact on the market and resolution of the competition concerns (the Commission considers this particularly important in markets in the process of liberalisation or in fast-moving markets);

- more effective remedies: commitments are forward-looking, more finely tuned, and can go beyond what could have been imposed under Article 7;[448]

- better and swifter implementation of structural and behavioural measures: the fact that the undertakings design the commitments themselves 'facilitates their implementation' and the threat of fines for their violation 'provides companies with an incentive to implement them properly'.

The advantages to the undertakings under investigation are that they avoid the more burdensome Article 7 procedure, with its lengthy oral and written adversarial proceedings, and that they have an

---

[437] Including *Rambus, Microsoft* (tying), and *IBM Maintenance Services*, cited in n. 403.

[438] COMP/38.636, *Rambus*, IP/09/1897; COMP/39.939, *Samsung* [2014] OJ C350/8; MEMO/14/322; IP/14/490.

[439] COMP/39.985 *Motorola* [2014] OJ C344/6; MEMO/14/322. The issue came before the CJ by way of an Art. 267 reference in Case C-170/13, *Huawei Technologies v ZTE* EU:C:2015:477, see Chap. 7, Section 14.C.ii, p. 549.

[440] COMP/39.740, IP/10/1624. For the substantive issues, see Chap. 7, Section 14.E, p. 553.

[441] IP/10/1624.

[442] IP/13/371, MEMO/13/383.

[443] IP/14/116, MEMO/14/87.

[444] See, e.g., *FT*, 21 May 2014, *New York Times*, 20 May 2014.

[445] See questions in the European Parliament, E-000261/2014, E-000261/2014, E-003673/2014, E-003691/2014, E-003673/2014, and E-004525/2014, and further R. Nazzini, '*Google* and the (Ever-stretching) Boundaries of Article 102 TFEU' (2015) 6 *JECLAP* 301, 304.

[446] IP/15/4780, MEMO/15/4780. Simultaneously the Commission opened proceedings in respect Google's Android mobile operating system, COMP/40.099, *Google Android*, IP/15/4780, MEMO/15/4782.

[447] [2015] 3 *Competition Policy Brief*.

[448] Because of Case T-170/06, *Alrosa v Commission* [2007] ECR II-2601, para. 48. The *Bulgarian Energy Holdings* remedy, for example, could not have been imposed under Art. 7.

input into the remedy. They avoid fines and may incur less bad publicity. An extremely attractive feature of commitments decisions is that they do not involve a finding of infringement, and therefore cannot be the basis of a follow-on action in a national court.[449] Undertakings in Article 9(1) proceedings do not have to admit guilt—in *Rambus* for example, the undertaking strongly disagreed with the Commission's assessment as regards both the factual and legal elements and denied the allegations against it.[450]

Third parties may be disadvantaged by Article 9 decisions, as shown in *Alrosa*. Although Alrosa was able to mount a challenge under Article 263 TFEU the wide discretion left to the Commission by the CJ's judgment ensured that Alrosa was unable to overturn the decision. The advantage for the investigated undertaking which is noted above—that there is no infringement decision on which to base a follow-on action—is a disadvantage for third parties. Moreover, although complainants have a right to a decision on their complaint[451] the wide discretion given to the Commission again makes this of doubtful use. However, third parties do have the benefit in the Article 9 procedure of being able to participate more fully than under Article 7 because of the 'market-testing' stage, and Google demonstrates how effective that participation may be.

It is also necessary to consider the effect of commitments decisions on the development of the law. The extensive use of Article 9 has shifted public enforcement from imposed infringement decisions to negotiated outcomes.[452] Although the Commission considers that it has to base a commitments decision on a coherent theory of harm[453] it can try out the application of Article 102 in novel situations without having to prove its case with extensive economic and legal analysis. Without an infringement decision there is no chance of review by the EU Courts, and the resultant diminution in jurisprudence may not be in the public interest.[454] For example, the Commission proclaimed the Microsoft internet browser commitments[455] as a great victory but its case was never put to the test, and had the Commission succeeded with its *Google* commitments, Article 102 would have been applied in a highly contentious way without the possibility of going to the GC.[456] The energy decisions, which have made extensive use of structural remedies, have been described as the Commission using Article 9 to pursue regulatory goals in furtherance of its liberalisation agenda,[457] again without going near the Courts. A member of the CJ has written, in a personal capacity, of a 'a growing and vocal disquiet within the EU competition law community concerning the European Commission's increasing recourse to commitment decisions':

Perhaps the strongest criticism levied against the Commission's practice of adopting commitment decisions is that they fail to sufficiently elucidate the law in novel and complex competition cases. This is due to the lack of a formal finding of infringement…in commitment decisions coupled with the fact that they provide limited opportunities for the solution adopted to be challenged before the General Court and the Court of Justice. While a commitment decision may offer 'legal comfort' to its addressee and rapidly restore competition in a given instance, it may provide less clarity and thus legal certainty for other actors than infringement decisions, which provide a more effective legal road map….

  [W]hile the paucity of precedent may be overstated [because of the incidence of preliminary references before the CJ], in my view, commitment decisions are a quick-fix solution the excessive recourse to which

---

[449] See Chap. 14.

[450] COMP/38.636, *Rambus*, IP/09/1897.

[451] See Section 12.F.iv, p. 1033.

[452] Although the Commission stresses that it does not enter a 'bargaining process' which allows undertakings to escape with insufficient commitments, see [2015] 3 *Competition Policy Brief*.

[453] Ibid.

[454] See Cengiz, n. 426; Wagner-Von Papp, n. 424.

[455] COMP/39.530, *Microsoft*, IP/10/216.

[456] See Nazzini, n. 445 and the discussion of *Google* in Chap. 7, Section 13.E, pp. 553.

[457] Cengiz, n. 426, 138.

may become undesirable over time, particularly if they are not interspersed with infringement decisions or if the Court of Justice has not had the opportunity to rule on related competition law questions.[458]

(iv) Final Decisions: Findings of Inapplicability

Under Article 10 of Regulation 1/2003 the Commission is able to take 'positive' decisions finding that Articles 101 and 102 are inapplicable to particular agreements or practices.

Regulation 1/2003

Article 10

Finding of inapplicability

Where the Community public interest relating to the application of Articles [101] and [102] so requires, the Commission, acting on its own initiative, may by decision find that Article [101] is not applicable to an agreement, a decision by an association of undertakings or a concerted practice, either because the conditions of Article [101(1)] are not fulfilled, or because the conditions of Article [101(3)] are satisfied.

The Commission may likewise make such a finding with reference to Article [102] of the Treaty.

In respect of Article 101, the finding may be that the conditions in Article 101(1) are not fulfilled or that the conditions in Article 101(3) are satisfied. The information required by the Commission could be acquired through the fact-finding procedures previously discussed or through the parties supplying it voluntarily. Article 10 refers to these decisions being made when the *[Union] public interest* so requires and says that the Commission will act *on its own initiative*, making it clear that the decisions are not intended (at least primarily) to be for the benefit of the parties. Recital 14 of Regulation 1/2003 says that Article 10 decisions will be adopted *in exceptional cases* 'with a view to clarifying the law and ensuring its consistent application throughout the [Union], in particular with regard to new types of agreements or practices that have not been settled in the existing case-law and administrative practice'. Nevertheless, Article 10 decisions are clearly advantageous to the parties as they are enforceable in national courts and give complete legal certainty. Further, Article 10 may be used by the Commission to pre-empt a decision by an NCA since Article 11(6) of Regulation 1/2003 provides that if the Commission initiates proceedings NCAs are relieved of their competence to act 'under the same legal basis against the same agreement(s) or practice(s) by the same undertaking(s) on the same relevant geographic and product market'.[459] As of 5 February 2016 no Article 10 decisions had been adopted. In the Working Paper[460] the Commission said of the (then) lack of such decisions that it was because Article 10 was designed to avoid being used as a replacement for the old exemption decisions and intended for truly exceptional cases only, and that the success of the ECN in promoting the coherent application of the competition rules had made its use to remove matters from the NCAs unnecessary to date.

(v) Procedural Decisions

As we have seen the Commission, in the course of its investigations, may take decisions about procedural matters. Thus, information may be demanded by decision under Article 18(3) of Regulation

---

[458] M. Wathelet, Editorial, 'Commitment Decisions and the Paucity of Precedent' (2015) 6 *JECLAP* 553, 554.

[459] Notice on cooperation within the Network of Competition Authorities [2004] OJ C101/43, para. 51. And see also para. 54(d).

[460] Working Paper, paras. 112–114.

1/2003 and an inspection may be ordered under Article 20(4). Failure to comply with such decisions may be penalised by fines.[461] The question of the confidentiality of documents is settled by a decision of the Hearing Officer.[462]

(vi) Interim Measures

Article 8 of Regulation 1/2003 gives the Commission power to take decisions ordering interim measures.

Regulation 1/2003

Article 8

1. In cases of urgency due to the risk of serious and irreparable damage to competition, the Commission, acting on its own initiative may by decision, on the basis of a prima facie finding of infringement, order interim measures.

2. A decision under paragraph 1 shall apply for a specified period of time and may be renewed in so far this is necessary and appropriate.

This was a new provision in Regulation 1/2003, given that Regulation 17 did not expressly provide powers for the Commission to take interim measures. However, case law established that the Commission *did* have such powers. The CJ recognised that otherwise there would be a serious lacuna, as Commission proceedings can be protracted and irreparable damage might occur before it could take a final decision under Article 3 of Regulation 17. The power to take interim measures was established in *Camera Care*,[463] in a striking example of the Court's teleological interpretative technique, and developed in subsequent cases, in particular *La Cinq*[464] and *IMS*.[465] The cases establish that certain conditions must be fulfilled before interim measures are taken:

- there must be a prima facie infringement of the competition rules;
- it must be a situation of proven urgency where there would otherwise be serious and irreparable damage to competition. Financial damage cannot, save in exceptional circumstances, be regarded as irreparable if it can ultimately be the subject of financial compensation unless the applicant can adduce evidence that would justify a prima facie finding that without the measures sought it would suffer losses that would threaten its survival.[466] Damage may also be

---

[461] See Section 7.H.ii, p. 960.

[462] The Hearing Officer terms of reference, Decision 2011/695, Art. 8 [2010] OJ L275/29. The jurisdiction of the Hearing Officer to take decisions in this respect means that the power to adopt a challengeable act has been delegated by the Commission to a single official. Such delegation is permitted where it does not involve a matter of principle: see Case T-450/93, *Lisrestal* [1994] ECR II-1177; M. van der Woude, 'Hearing Officers and EC Antitrust Procedures; The Art of Making Subjective Procedures More Objective' (1996) 33 *CMLRev* 531. Cf. the delegation of Reg. 1/2003, Art. 20(4) decisions to a single *Commissioner*: the validity of this in respect of Reg. 17, Art. 14(3) was confirmed in Case 53/85, *AKZO v Commission* [1986] ECR 1965.

[463] Case 792/79 R, *Camera Care v Commission* [1980] ECR 119.

[464] Case T-44/90, *La Cinq SA v Commission* [1992] ECR II-1; see also Cases 228–229/82 R, *Ford Werke AG v Commission* [1982] ECR 3091.

[465] Case T-184/01 R, *IMS Health v Commission* [2001] ECR II-3193, aff'd Case C-481/01 P (R), *NDC v IMS and Commission* [2002] ECR I-3401, the appeals against the interim decision, *NDC Health/IMS: Interim Measures* [2002] OJ L59/18, adopted by the Commission because it considered that the competitors refused permission to use the dominant undertaking's copyright might otherwise not survive on the market. For interim measures generally, see Antitrust ManProc, Module 17.

[466] Case T-184/01 R, *IMS Health v Commission* [2001] ECR II-3193, paras. 119–121.

irreparable if without the measures there are likely to be developments on the market which will be very difficult, or impossible, to reverse;[467]

- the measures must be of a temporary and conservatory nature only and restricted to what is required in the particular situation to preserve the status quo; the measures have to accord with the principle of proportionality;

- the legitimate rights of the party on which the measures are being imposed must be observed and the 'essential guarantees' provided for by Regulation 1/2003, especially Article 27 on the right to be heard, must be maintained;

- the measures must be in a form which is subject to review by the EU Courts, i.e. in the form of a reasoned decision.

A number of Commission decisions on refusal to supply as an abuse of a dominant position under Article 102 involved interim decisions. In *Boosey & Hawkes*[468] the interim measures ordered the dominant undertaking to maintain supplies to the complainant on the terms and conditions on which the parties had previously done business and in *Sealink/B&I*[469] the port authority was ordered to return to its previous published timetable. In *Sea Containers/Stena*[470] the Commission held that there was a prima facie case of abuse, but refused interim measures on the ground that there was not sufficient urgency as since the initial application the complainant had been offered and had accepted an offer of access so there was no danger of serious and irreparable harm occurring. The most notorious case of interim measures was the decision ordering an undertaking to license its copyright in *NDC Health/IMS: Interim Measures*.[471] The decision was suspended and ultimately withdrawn without a final decision being taken.[472] *NDC Health/IMS* was the last interim measures decision to be taken. As at 5 February 2016 none had been adopted under Article 8. Parties may prefer to seek interim relief in national courts or from NCAs.

F. THE SETTLEMENT PROCEDURE IN CARTEL CASES

Since 2008 the Commission has offered a 'direct settlement' procedure for cartel cases. It was established by an amendment to Regulation 773/2004[473] and is set out in the Notice on the conduct of settlement procedures (the Settlement Notice).[474] The aim of the settlement procedure is 'to simplify

---

[467] Ibid., paras. 128–129.

[468] BBI/*Boosey & Hawkes* [1987] OJ L286/36.

[469] IV/34.174, *Sealink/B&I Holyhead: Interim Measures* 11 June 1992; as in *Boosey & Hawkes* the case did not go to a final decision.

[470] [1994] OJ L15/8.

[471] [2002] OJ L59/18.

[472] Case T-184/01 R, *IMS Health v Commission* [2001] ECR II-3193, *aff'd* Case C-481/01 P (R), *NDC Health v Commission* [2002] ECR I-3401, see Section 8.A.x, p. 1012. For the substantive issues in this case see Chap. 7, Section 13.C.iv. The Presidents of the GC and CJ were concerned that, as IMS claimed, the decision went beyond the existing case law. The decision was therefore suspended on the ground that the status quo should be maintained pending the GC's judgment in the appeal. It was held that the balance of interests favoured preserving the copyright unimpaired during the appeal proceedings: there was potentially serious and irreparable harm to IMS in having to license its copyright and the copyright should not be devalued by reducing it to a purely economic right to receive financial compensation: the conditions for granting interim relief were therefore fulfilled.

[473] Reg. 773/2004 as amended by Reg. 622/2008 [2008] OJ L171/3, further amended by Reg. 2015/1348 [2015] OJ L208/3, Art. 10a.

[474] Commission Notice on the conduct of settlement procedures [2008] OJ C167/1, as amended by [2015] OJ C256/2. See M. L. Tierno Centella, 'The New Settlement Procedure in Selected Cartel Cases' [2008] 3 *Competition Policy Newsletter* 30; J. Tyler, 'Act of Settlement' (2008) 3 *CLI* 79; J. Joshua, K. Hugmark, and I. Daems, 'What's the Deal? Navigating the European Commission's 2008 Settlement Notice' [2009] *European Antitrust Rev* 2; R. Gamble, '"Speaking (Formally) with the Enemy"—Cartel Settlements Evolve' [2011] *ECLR* 449.

and speed up administrative procedures and to reduce the number of cases brought before the EU judicature, and thus to enable the Commission to handle more cases with the same resources'.[475] Leniency[476] and settlement can both be applied in the same case.

The procedure is for the Commission, on the conclusion of its investigation, to decide whether the case is suitable for settlement.[477] If it is, the Commission invites the parties concerned to reach an agreement with it. It informs them of the evidence and tells them its conclusions as to duration, seriousness, liability, and the likely fine. The parties have to make (orally or in writing[478]) a final settlement submission in which (Notice, paragraph 20) they acknowledge their liability 'in clear and unequivocal terms'; indicate the maximum fine they would accept in the framework of the settlement procedure; confirm that they have been informed of the case against them and that they have been given sufficient opportunity to make their views known; confirm that they do not envisage requesting access to the file or requesting to be heard orally again; and agree to accept an SO. The SO reflects the settlement submissions. The Commission then proceeds, without any further procedural steps, to adopt an Article 7 decision. Settlement submissions are protected from disclosure in the same way as are leniency corporate statements.[479]

According to paragraph 2 of the Settlement Notice the procedure is not a negotiation, in that the Commission 'does not negotiate the question of the existence of an infringement of Community law and the appropriate sanction...'. However, in *Timab* the GC said:

Admittedly, in point 2 of the settlements notice, it is stated that the Commission does not negotiate the question of the existence of an infringement of EU law or the appropriate penalty. However, that notice should not be an obstacle to discussions. The settlement procedure requires, by its very nature, an exchange of views between the parties. Accordingly, it is an inherent part of such a procedure that both the undertakings and the Commission should try to reach a common understanding of the situation (see, to that effect, point 17 of the settlements notice). If, taking account of the simplified nature of the settlement procedure, the undertaking at issue and the Commission cannot agree on a common assessment of the situation, only the standard procedure remains.[480]

The advantages to the Commission are obvious—a saving of time, resources, and appeals to the EU Courts. One advantage to the parties is that they receive a 10 per cent reduction (but only 10 per cent) on the fine that would otherwise have been imposed. They are saved the trouble of full-scale protracted cartel proceedings and may confine themselves to purely oral submissions. However, there are disadvantages for them. The procedure is totally in the control of the Commission, notwithstanding what the GC said in *Timab*. They lose some rights of defence (the oral hearing and access to the file) and have to assess what fine they think the Commission will accept (albeit in the light of the Commission's indication). The admission of liability may form the basis for future third party actions.[481] What is more, the Commission can decide right up to the end to revert to the normal procedure. Despite these drawbacks the procedure is popular among cartelists. The majority of cartel cases are now dealt with under the settlement procedure. *Car Parts* in January 2016 was the twentieth settlement decision.[482]

---

[475] Case T-456/10, *Timab Industries v Commission* EU:T:2015:296, para. 60, on appeal Case C-411/15 P, judgment pending.

[476] See Section 7.H.v, p. 983.

[477] The parties have no *right* to settlement, see Case T-270/12, *Panalpina World Transport (Holding) Ltd v Commission* EU:T:2016:109, paras. 209–210; Case T-267/10, *Deutsche Bahn AG v Commission* EU:T:2016:110, para. 418. For a discussion of the exercise of the Commission's discretion, see Case T-265/12, *Schenker v Commission* EU:T:2016:111, paras. 390–438.

[478] Reg. 773/2004, Art. 10a(2), third para., was amended by Reg. 2015/1348, to provide how oral statements can be made at the Commission's premises.

[479] See Section 7.D.v.a, p. 934.

[480] Case T-456/14/10, *Timab Industries* EU:T:2015:296, para. 117.

[481] See Chap. 14.

[482] COMP/40.028, IP/16/173.

The first settlement decision, in May 2010, was in respect of a cartel involving ten producers of DRAM memory chips.[483] The second was *Animal Feed Phosphates Producers*,[484] which was a 'hybrid' decision in which five undertakings followed the settlement route and one, Timab, withdrew from settlement after having been informed of the fine the Commission intended to impose.[485] However, the fine ultimately imposed after the case reverted to the standard procedure was higher than the maximum figure of the range envisaged during the settlement discussions.[486] On appeal[487] the GC ruled on the relationship between the settlement procedure and the standard procedure. It noted that the Commission had applied the same method (as laid down in the Fining Guidelines[488]) when calculating the range of fines in the settlement procedure and when it imposed the fine at the end of the standard procedure. It said that the calculation of a range of fines is an instrument solely and specifically related to the settlement procedure[489] and that once the case was proceeding under the standard procedure it would be illogical if the Commission was required to apply a range of fines falling within the scope of another procedure that had been abandoned.[490]

G. INFORMAL SETTLEMENTS

The Commission has sometimes not proceeded to a formal decision but terminated the matter informally. As we have seen, under the 'old' Regulation 17 regime notified agreements were often, and indeed usually, dealt with by way of comfort letter rather than by formal decision.[491] Cases have also been terminated informally because the Commission and the parties have come to a settlement, usually because the companies had made enough concessions to satisfy the Commission, and the latter considered that nothing would be gained by pursuing a formal proceeding any further. The settlements were reached both before and after the SO. Settlements often included the parties giving undertakings to the Commission. Several important cases were terminated in this way, such as *IBM*,[492] *Microsoft*,[493] *Digital*,[494] and *Deutsche Telekom Tariffs*.[495] Settlements were frequently publicised, in Commission press releases, in law reports, and in the Commission's annual reports, and inevitably they could attain the status of precedent. Clearly they were valuable guidance to other companies on what was acceptable to the Commission but by their nature they involved compromise and concession. Under Article 9 of Regulation 1/2003 the Commission acquired a new power to take decisions which make commitments offered by companies binding upon them and it has made extensive use

---

[483] COMP/38.511, *DRAMS*, IP/10/586. The investigation had commenced in 2002. The fines, totalling €331 million, included a reduction of 10% for the companies' acknowledgement of the facts.

[484] COMP/38.866, 20 July 2010, IP/10/985, OJ C111/19.

[485] COMP/39.792, *Steel Abrasives* [2014] OJ C362/8 and COMP/39.965, *Mushrooms* [2014] OJ C453/21 were also hybrid decisions.

[486] Because of the interaction between the reduction in the length of the cartel to which Timab admitted, the operation of the leniency programme, and the loss of the 10% settlement reduction. The leniency application was in respect of 1978–2004. During the resumed standard procedure Timab claimed that the evidence for 1978–1993 related to a separate cartel. The final decision was therefore in respect of 1993–2004 and not covered by leniency.

[487] Case T-456/10, *Timab Industries* EU:T:2015:296, on appeal Case C-411/15 P, judgment pending.

[488] See Section 7.H.g, p. 972.

[489] Case T-456/10, *Timab Industries* EU:T:2015:296, para. 100.

[490] Ibid., para. 105.

[491] See Section 4, p. 887.

[492] [1984] 3 CMLR 147.

[493] Commission Press Release IP/94/653.

[494] Commission Press Release IP/97/868.

[495] Commission's *XXVIIth Report on Competition Policy* (1997), part 77.

of this.[496] There is nothing in Regulation 1/2003 to prevent informal settlements but given the existence of Article 9 they are likely to be rare.[497]

H. FINES AND PERIODIC PENALTY PAYMENTS

(i) General

Regulation 1/2003 empowers the Commission to take decisions to impose fines on undertakings and associations of undertakings both for substantive infringements of the competition rules (Article 23(2)) and for procedural infringements (Article 23(1)). The Commission may also impose periodic penalty payments, in order to compel undertakings to do what the Commission requires by penalising defiance (Article 24). Regulation 1/2003 provides for fines and penalties to be levied only on *undertakings*: it does not impose liability on natural persons such as company directors and executives.

The Commission's multiplicity of roles in the enforcement regime means that the prosecutor determines guilt and fixes the fine. However, Article 261 TFEU[498] provides that regulations 'may give the Court of Justice of the European Union unlimited jurisdiction with regard to the penalties provided for in such regulations'. Pursuant to this Article 31 of Regulation 1/2003 states:

The Court of Justice shall have unlimited jurisdiction to review decisions whereby the Commission has fixed a fine or periodic penalty payment. It may cancel, reduce or increase the fine or periodic penalty payment imposed.

This jurisdiction is dealt with later in this chapter.[499]

The limitation periods for the imposition of penalties provided for in Article 25 of Regulation 1/2003 are three years in respect of procedural infringements (in connection with requests for information and inspections) and five years in respect of all other infringements. Time runs from the day the infringement was committed or on the day it ended in the case of a repeated or continuous infringement. Under Article 26 the time limit for the enforcement of penalties is five years from the date of the decision.[500]

Regulation 1/2003 uses turnover percentages rather than objective monetary amounts in setting maximum fines.[501]

---

[496] See Section 7.E.iii.

[497] J. Temple Lang, 'Commitment Decisions and Settlements with Antitrust Authorities and Private Parties under European Antitrust Law' [2005] *Fordham Corp L Inst* 265 (he suggests that informal settlements may still be used in 'small unimportant cases'); Kerse and Khan, n. 2, 6.091. There were informal settlements in *OMV/Gazprom*, IP/05/195 in 2005, *E.ON Ruhrgas/Gazprom*, IP/05/710 in 2005, and *Philips CD-Recordable Discrimination Patent Licensing*, IP/06/139 in 2006. The Commission reached an informal settlement with Apple over iTunes in 2008, IP/08/22.

[498] Ex Art. 229.

[499] See Section 8.A.vi, p. 998.

[500] In Case T-153/04, *Ferriere Nord SpA v Commission* [2006] ECR II-3889, the Commission had failed to pursue payment of the outstanding balance of one of the fines imposed in the *Welded Steel Mesh Cartel* [1989] OJ L260/1, after the decision was finally upheld by the CJ, Case C-219/95 P, *Ferriere Nord v Commission* [1997] ECR I-4411. Soon after the judgment the undertaking had twice asked the Commission to reconsider the amount of the fine because of, inter alia, the severe devaluation of the lira. The Commission did not reply until 2004. The GC held that the enforcement of the balance was time-barred since 2002, despite the existence of a bank guarantee which could have been called in at any time. The GC judgment was set aside, Case C-516/06 P, *Commission v Ferriere Nord SpA* [2007] ECR I-10685.

[501] Reg. 17 expressed the monetary amounts of fines and penalties in units of account but these were read as referring to euros after the introduction of the single currency (having previously become ECUs), pursuant to Council Reg. 1103/97 [1997] OJ L162/1, Art. 2(1).

(ii) Fines for Procedural Infringements

Article 23(1) of Regulation 1/2003 states:

The Commission may by decision impose on undertakings and associations of undertakings fines not exceeding 1 per cent of the total turnover in the preceding business year where, intentionally or negligently:

(a) they supply incorrect or misleading information in response to a request made pursuant to Article 17 or Article 18(2);

(b) in response to a request made by decision adopted pursuant to Article 17 or Article 18(3), they supply incorrect, incomplete or misleading information or do not supply information within the required time-limit;

(c) they produce the required books or other records related to the business in incomplete form during inspections under Article 20 or refuse to submit to inspections ordered by a decision adopted pursuant to Article 20(4);

(d) in response to a question asked in accordance with Article 20(2)(e),

— they give an incorrect or misleading answer,

— they fail to rectify within a time-limit set by the Commission an incorrect, incomplete or misleading answer given by a member of staff, or

— they fail or refuse to provide a complete answer on facts relating to the subject-matter and purpose of an inspection ordered by a decision adopted pursuant to Article 20(4);

(e) seals affixed in accordance with Article 20(2)(d) by officials or other accompanying persons authorised by the Commission have been broken.

Under this provision the Commission imposes fines of up to 1 per cent of turnover for failure to cooperate with, or obstructing, its investigations under Articles 17,[502] 18, and 20 of Regulation 1/2003 or for supplying incorrect, incomplete, or misleading information.[503]

(iii) Periodic Penalty Payments

Periodic penalty payments may be imposed at a daily rate for defiance of the Commission. The maximum is 5 per cent of average daily turnover. Article 24 of Regulation 1/2003 states:

1. The Commission may, by decision, impose on undertakings or associations of undertakings periodic penalty payments not exceeding 5 per cent of the average daily turnover in the preceding business year per day and calculated from the date appointed by the decision, in order to compel them:

(a) to put an end to an infringement of Article [101] or Article [102], in accordance with a decision taken pursuant to Article 7;

(b) to comply with a decision ordering interim measures taken pursuant to Article 8;

(c) to comply with a commitment made binding by a decision pursuant to Article 9;

(d) to supply complete and correct information which it has requested by decision taken pursuant to Article 17 or Article 18(3);

(e) to submit to an inspection which it has ordered by decision taken pursuant to Article 20(4).

2. Where the undertakings or associations of undertakings have satisfied the obligation which the periodic penalty payment was intended to enforce, the Commission may fix the definitive amount of the periodic penalty payment at a figure lower than that which would arise under the original decision. Article 23(4) shall apply correspondingly.

---

[502] The provision which provides for investigations into sectors of the economy and types of agreements: see Section 7.I.

[503] See Section 7.C.ii and Section 7.C.iii, pp. 902 ff.

Microsoft was the first undertaking to be fined for failing to comply with a decision. A long battle over its compliance with the 2004 decision requiring it to disclose interoperability information on 'fair and reasonable terms'[504] ended in two decisions imposing penalty payments. One was €280.5 million (€1.5 million per day from 16 December 2005 to 20 June 2006) for failing to disclose the required level of information.[505] The second was €899 million for failing to make the information available on 'fair and reasonable terms' but instead charging royalties until 22 October 2007 that were unreasonable.[506] The GC approved the imposition of a fine but reduced it to €860 million.[507] Microsoft then became the first undertaking to be fined (€561 million) under Article 24(1)(c) for failing to comply with a commitments decision under Article 9.[508]

(iv) Fines for Substantive Infringements

a. Regulation 1/2003, Article 23(2)

Article 23(2) of Regulation 1/2003, formerly Article 15(2) of Regulation 17, provides for the imposition of fines for substantive infringements:

2. The Commission may by decision impose fines on undertakings and associations of undertakings where, either intentionally or negligently:

   (a) they infringe Article [101] or Article [102]; or

   (b) they contravene a decision ordering interim measures under Article 8; or

   (c) they fail to comply with a commitment made binding by a decision pursuant to Article 9.

For each undertaking and association of undertakings participating in the infringement, the fine shall not exceed 10 per cent of its total turnover in the preceding business year.[509]

Where the infringement of an association relates to the activities of its members, the fine shall not exceed 10 per cent of the sum of the total turnover of each member active on the market affected by the infringement of the association.

3. In fixing the amount of the fine, regard shall be had both to the gravity and to the duration of the infringement.

4. When a fine is imposed on an association of undertakings taking account of the turnover of its members and the association is not solvent, the association is obliged to call for contributions from its members to cover the amount of the fine. Where such contributions have not been made to the association within a time-limit fixed by the Commission, the Commission may require payment of the fine directly by any of the undertakings whose representatives were members of the decision-making bodies concerned of the association.

After the Commission has required payment under the second subparagraph, where necessary to ensure full payment of the fine, the Commission may require payment of the balance by any of the members of the association which were active on the market on which the infringement occurred.

---

[504] COMP/37.792, *Microsoft*, upheld on appeal Case T-201/04, *Microsoft v Commission* [2007] ECR II-3601, see Chap. 7.

[505] Commission Decision of 12 July 2006, C(2006)4420, IP/06/076.

[506] C(2008) 764. The Competition Commissioner said (IP/08/318): 'Microsoft was the first company in fifty years of EU competition policy that the Commission has had to fine for failure to comply with an antitrust decision. I hope that today's Decision closes a dark chapter in Microsoft's record of non-compliance with the Commission's March 2004 Decision and that the principles confirmed by the General Court ruling of September 2007 will govern Microsoft's future conduct.'

[507] Case T-167/08, *Microsoft v Commission* EU:T:2012:323.

[508] COMP/39.530, *Microsoft*, IP/13/196.

[509] The 'preceding business year' to which the turnover relates means the last full business year of each of the undertakings concerned at the date of adoption of the decision. Cases T-25/95 etc., *Cimenteries* [2000] ECR II-491, para. 5009.

However, the Commission shall not require payment under the second or the third subparagraph from undertakings which show that they have not implemented the infringing decision of the association and either were not aware of its existence or have actively distanced themselves from it before the Commission started investigating the case.

The financial liability of each undertaking in respect of the payment of the fine shall not exceed 10 per cent of its total turnover in the preceding business year.

5. Decisions taken pursuant to paragraphs 1 and 2 shall not be of a criminal law nature.

This crucial provision, which confers upon the Commission its power to punish violations of the competition rules, says four things (apart from the trade association provisions in Article 23(4)):

- fines can only be imposed for intentional or negligent infringements;
- the maximum fine is 10 per cent of turnover in the preceding business year[510] (although it does not specify what turnover is to be taken into account);
- in fixing the fine regard is to be had both to the gravity of the infringement and to its duration;
- fines are not criminal penalties.

The concept of the 'single continuous infringement' is discussed in Chapter 3.[511] Whether cartel participants, for example, are charged with a single continuous infringement or a series of separate infringements can impact upon the amount of the fine (the maximum applies to each infringement and the duration will be affected).[512]

b. The Position of Trade Associations

Article 23 of Regulation 1/2003 provides for fines imposed on associations of undertakings. Article 15 of Regulation 17 did not provide that the members are jointly and severally liable, and this could prevent the collection of fines.[513] Article 23(4) provides that if the association is insolvent it must call upon its members for contributions to the fine. If that does not produce the fine within the time limit imposed the Commission may fine the members directly (up to 10 per cent of that undertaking's turnover) but only those which were implicated in the infringement.[514] The first fine on a professional body under this provision was imposed in ONP.[515]

c. Intentional or Negligent Infringement

Article 23(2) provides that the Commission may impose a fine only where the infringement was intentional or negligent. An undertaking, however, can act only through human agency and the intentions and negligence in issue are in effect those of its human directors and employees. EU competition law has not concerned itself with theories of vicarious liability or agonised over the imputation of the employees' conduct to the company. The position is that an undertaking is responsible for the conduct of its directors and employees and it should have in place, and enforce, a compliance programme to prevent infractions of the rules.[516]

---

[510] In Case T-33/02, *Britannia Alloys and Chemicals Ltd v Commission* [2005] ECR II-4973, para. 50, the GC confirmed that the Commission was correct to use the undertaking's last 'full' business year.

[511] Section 3.B.v.

[512] See, e.g., Case T-655/11, *FSL Holdings v Commission* EU:T:2015:383 where the GC reduced a fine because it held there was a single repeated infringement, not a single continuous infringement as the Commission had found in COMP/39.482, *Exotic Fruit (Bananas)* 12 October 2011.

[513] Commission's White Paper on Modernisation [1999] OJ C132/1, paras. 127–128, and see Cases T-213/95 and T-18/96, *SCK and FNK v Commission* [1997] ECR I-1739.

[514] See P. Callol, 'Mandatory Antitrust Liability under EU Competition Law of Trade Association Members in Case of Infringement by the Trade Association' [2015] *ECLR* 194.

[515] COMP/39.510, on appeal Case T-90/11, *Ordre National des Pharmaciens en France (ONP) v Commission* EU:T:2014:1049 the fine was reduced.

[516] See W. Wils, 'The Undertaking as Subject of EC Competition Law and the Imputation of Infringements to Natural or Legal Persons' (2000) 25 *ELRev* 99, 109–111. In Case C-338/00 P, *Volkswagen AG v Commission* [2004] ECR

'Intentional' means an intention to restrict competition, not an intention to infringe the rules. In *PVC Cartel II* the GC said:[517]

For an infringement of the competition rules of the Treaty to be regarded as having been committed intentionally, it is not necessary for an undertaking to have been aware that it was infringing those rules; it is sufficient that it could not have been unaware that its conduct was aimed at restricting competition.

Even if the infringement is not characterised as intentional it is likely to be held negligent. The EU Courts have never defined negligence for this purpose but the Commission and the Courts expect experienced commercial entities to understand what they are doing.[518]

Since both intention and negligence incur liability to fines it may be unnecessary to decide whether the infringement is intentional or negligent, except that intentional infringements tend to attract heavier fines and that committing an infringement negligently is an attenuating circumstance under the Fining Guidelines. It is rare for undertakings to enter into cartels 'negligently'.[519] It is no defence that the undertaking acted on legal advice or on a previous NCA decision that held its conduct did not infringe the competition provisions insofar as it could not be unaware of the anticompetitive nature of that conduct.[520]

There are rare instances where ignorance has led to non-imposition of a fine[521] and the Commission has sometimes considered that an undertaking has not been negligent where it condemned a practice as an infringement of the competition rules for the first time.[522] No fine was imposed in *Clearstream*[523] for abuse of a dominant position in the clearing and settlement markets, as the infringement had come to an end and there had been no previous case law or decisional practice dealing with the competition analysis of clearing and settlement, which was a novel economic activity. The Commission therefore adopted the decision in order to clarify the legal situation 'at a moment when cross-border trade in securities is becoming more important within the EU'.[524] It refused the same latitude in *Intel*, however, where it said that the economic activity concerned did not raise similar controversial issues or novel or specific circumstances.[525] No fine was imposed on Motorola in the first standard-essential patent decision.[526] No fine was imposed for an Article 102 infringement in *DSD*. No reason was given for this, but it is to be noted that the matter had originated

---

I-9189, paras. 94–98, the appellant argued that the Commission and GC should have identified the persons who acted improperly and were therefore to be treated as responsible for the infringement. The CJ held that this was unnecessary.

[517] Cases T-305/94 etc., *Re the PVC Cartel II* [1999] ECR II-931, para. 1111; see also Cases 100–103/80, *Pioneer* [1983] ECR 1825, para. 221; Case T-65/89, *BPB Industries and British Gypsum Ltd v Commission* [1993] ECR II-389, paras. 165–166; Case T-143/89, *Ferriere Nord v Commission* [1995] ECR II-917, para. 41.

[518] See Case 27/76, *United Brands v Commission* [1978] ECR 207, paras. 298–301 where the Court said the undertaking had been 'engaged for a very long time in international and national trade, has special knowledge of antitrust laws and has already experienced their severity', and Case C-277/87, *Sandoz Prodotti Farmaceutici SpA v Commission* [1990] ECR I-45 where the company had 'export prohibited' printed on its invoices.

[519] See H. de Broca, 'The Commission Revises its Guidelines for Setting Fines in Antitrust Cases' (2006) 3 *Competition Policy Newsletter* 1.

[520] Case C-681/11, *Bundeswettbewerbsbehörde and Bundeskartellanwalt v Schenker & Co AG* EU:C:2013:404, paras. 33–43.

[521] See *Bayer Dental* [1990] OJ L351/46; *Stainless Steel* [1990] OJ L220/28; and the other cases discussed by L. Gyselen in 'The Commission's Fining Policy in Competition Cases—"Questo è il catalogo"' in P. Slot and A. McDonnell (eds.), *Procedure and Enforcement in EC and US Competition Law* (Sweet & Maxwell, 1993), 63–75.

[522] See, e.g., *Vegetable Parchment* [1978] OJ L70/54. On the other hand, the arguable novelty of the developments in Art. 102 did not save United Brands (see n. 518), Hoffmann-La Roche in Case 85/76, *Hoffmann-La Roche v Commission* [1979] ECR 461, Tetra Pak in Case C-333/94 P, *Tetra Pak International SA v Commission (Tetra Pak II)* 1996 ECR I-5951, or AstraZeneca in Case C-457/10 P, *AstraZeneca AB and AstraZeneca plc v Commission* EU:C:2012:770, paras. 74–99. The Commission did not, however, impose a fine on Van den Bergh Foods when it held for the first time that freezer exclusivity was contrary to Art. 101 and an abuse under Art. 102: *Van den Bergh Foods Ltd* [1998] OJ L246/1, discussed in Chap. 7, and Chap. 11.

[523] COMP/38.096, *Clearstream* [2009] OJ C165/7, upheld Case T-301/04, *Clearstream Banking v Commission* [2009] ECR II-3155.

[524] Commission Press Release IP/04/705.

[525] COMP/37.990, *Intel* 13 May 2009, para. 1768, upheld Case T-286/09, *Intel* EU:T:2014:547, paras. 219–220 (first use of the concept of a 'naked restriction').

[526] COMP/39.986, *Motorola*, IP/12/345.

in a notification to the Commission.[527] In the *Organic Peroxide Cartel* decision the Commission imposed a fine of only €1,000 on a company which was the first it had ever fined for acting as a secretariat and facilitator while not being active itself on the market in question.[528]

d. Development of the Commission's Fining Policy

As can be seen from Article 23(2)[529] there is remarkably little guidance in the legislation about the level at which the Commission should set fines. There is just the ceiling and the references to gravity and duration. There is no indication in the Regulation whether the purpose of the fines is deterrence, punishment, ensuring that the offence does not pay,[530] or some combination of these and perhaps other factors. In 1983, however, the Commission said that the purpose was twofold: 'to impose a pecuniary sanction on the undertaking for the infringement and prevent a repetition of the offence, and to make the prohibition in the Treaty more effective'.[531] The Commission's fining policy has developed over the years in its decisional practice and in two sets of Guidelines, the first in 1998[532] and the second in 2006 (currently in force).[533]

The CJ has consistently held that the Commission is entitled to change its fining policy at any time.[534] Undertakings can have no legitimate expectation that infringing behaviour will attract only a certain level of fine.

The Commission first imposed a fine in 1969 in the *Quinine Cartel*.[535] The amount was 500,000 units of account. For the next ten years the level of fines was 'relatively light'.[536] Change came in 1979 when the Commission indicated in *Pioneer* that it intended to reinforce the deterrent effect of fines by raising their general level in cases of serious infringements. It fined one culprit over four million units of account.[537] The undertakings appealed and the CJ confirmed the legality of the Commission's policy and strategy.

Cases 100–103/80, *Musique Diffusion Française SA v Commission (Pioneer)* [1983] ECR 1825

Court of Justice

106. It follows that, in assessing the gravity of an infringement for the purpose of fixing the amount of the fine, the Commission must take into consideration not only the particular circumstances of the case but also the context in which the infringement occurs and must ensure that its action has the necessary

---

[527] [2001] OJ L166/1, upheld Case T-151/01, *Der Grüne Punkt—Duales System Deutschland GmbH v Commission* [2007] ECR II-1607, and Case C-385/07 P, [2009] ECR I-6155.

[528] COMP/37.857, on appeal Case T-99/04, *AC-Treuhand AG v Commission* [2008] ECR II-1501.

[529] Set out in Section 7.H.iv.a. It does not differ in any major respect from Reg. 17, Art. 15(2).

[530] Note that the former President of the GC considers that Reg. 1/2003 does not provide any basis for confiscating the possible illegal gains made by the infringement, and that for the Commission to use it as a means to confiscate would amount to an abuse of power, Bo Vesterdorf, 'The Court of Justice and Unlimited Jurisdiction: What Does It Mean in Practice?' <https://competitionpolicyinternational.com/assets/0d358061e11f2708ad9d62634c6c40ad/Vesterdorf-JUNE-09_2_.pdf>, n. 16. In *Devenish Nutrition Ltd v Sanofi-Aventis* [2008] EWCA Civ 1086, the UK Court of Appeal considered that the fines imposed by the Commission in the *Vitamins Cartel* [2003] OJ L6/1 decision might have included an account of the profits but, not having heard argument on this, left the point open, see para. 112 (Arden LJ).

[531] Commission, *XIIIth Report on Competition Policy* (1983), para. 62.

[532] Guidelines on the method of setting fines imposed pursuant to Reg. No. 17, Art. 15(2) and Art. 65(5) of the ECSC Treaty [1998] OJ C9/3.

[533] Guidelines on the method of setting fines imposed pursuant to Art. 23(2)(a) of Reg. No. 1/2003 [2006] OJ C210/2.

[534] See Cases 100–103/80, *Pioneer* [1983] ECR 1825; Cases C-189/02 P etc., *Dansk Rørindustri* [2005] ECR I-5425.

[535] [1969] OJ L192/5.

[536] Commission's *XIIIth Report on Competition Policy* (1983), para. 63.

[537] *Pioneer* [1980] OJ L60/21.

deterrent effect, especially as regards those types of infringement which are particularly harmful to the attainment of the objectives of the Community.

107. From that point of view, the Commission was right to classify as very serious infringements prohibitions on exports and imports seeking artificially to maintain price differences between the markets of the various member-States. Such prohibitions jeopardize the freedom of intra-Community trade, which is a fundamental principle of the Treaty, and they prevent the attainment of one of its objectives, namely the creation of a single market.

108. It was also open to the Commission to have regard to the fact that practices of this nature, although they were established as being unlawful at the outset of Community competition policy, are still relatively frequent on account of the profit that certain of the undertakings concerned are able to derive from them and, consequently, it was open to the Commission to consider that it was appropriate to raise the level of fines so as to reinforce their deterrent effect.

109. For the same reasons, the fact that the Commission, in the past, imposed fines of a certain level for certain types of infringement does not mean that it is estopped from raising that level within the limits indicated in Regulation 17 if that is necessary to ensure the implementation of Community competition policy. On the contrary, the proper application of the Community competition rules requires that the Commission may at any time adjust the level of fines to the needs of that policy.

. . .

119. Thus the only express reference to the turnover of the undertaking concerns the upper limit of a fine exceeding 1 000 000 units of account. In such a case the limit seeks to prevent fines from being disproportionate in relation to the size of the undertaking and, since only the total turnover can effectively give an approximate indication of that size, the aforementioned percentage must, as the Commission has argued, be understood as referring to the total turnover. It follows that the Commission did not exceed the limit laid down in Article 15 of the Regulation.

120. In assessing the gravity of an infringement regard must be had to a large number of factors, the nature and importance of which vary according to the type of infringement in question and the particular circumstances of the case. Those factors may, depending on the circumstances, include the volume and value of the goods in respect of which the infringement was committed and the size and economic power of the undertaking and, consequently, the influence which the undertaking was able to exert on the market.

121. It follows that, on the one hand, it is permissible, for the purpose of fixing the fine, to have regard both to the total turnover of the undertaking, which gives an indication, albeit approximate and imperfect, of the size of the undertaking and of its economic power, and to the proportion of that turnover accounted for by the goods in respect of which the infringement was committed, which gives an indication of the scale of the infringement. On the other hand, it follows that it is important not to confer on one or the other of those figures an importance disproportionate in relation to the other factors and, consequently, that the fixing of an appropriate fine cannot be the result of a simple calculation based on the total turnover. That is particularly the case where the goods concerned account for only a small part of the figure. It is appropriate for the Court to bear in mind those considerations in its assessment, by virtue of its powers of unlimited jurisdiction, of the gravity of the infringements in question.

This confirmed that the Commission was justified in suddenly raising the level of fines and in using fines to deter other undertakings from infringing.

It will be seen from paragraphs 120 and 121 of *Pioneer* that the Commission must take into account a number of factors, depending on the nature of the infringement and the circumstances of the case.[538] In paragraph 119 the Court said that 'turnover' in Article 15(2) (now Article 23(2))

---

[538] Para. 121 was repeated in Cases C-189/02 P etc., *Dansk Rørindustri* [2005] ECR I-5425, para. 243; Case C-397/03 P, *Archer Daniels Midland* [2006] ECR I-4429, para. 100; and described in Case C-580/12 P, *Guardian Industries Corp v Commission* EU:C:2014:2363, para. 54 as 'settled case law'.

meant the *total* turnover of the undertaking or group. Moreover, when the undertaking to which the infringement is attributed heads a group which constitutes an economic unit, the turnover of the group as a whole must be taken into account when calculating the 10 per cent upper limit.[539] The Commission does not have to prove that the undertakings form a single economic entity in the sense discussed in Chapter 3 as turnover for the purposes of Article 23(2) is a completely separate issue from whether each subsidiary determines its own conduct on the market for the purposes of attributing liability for infringements.[540] On the other hand, the Commission should have regard to the turnover in the products in respect of which the infringement was committed when fixing the fine, because that gives an indication of the scale of the infringement.[541] This remains the position after the adoption of the Fining Guidelines. The total turnover means total *worldwide* turnover.[542]

Pioneer gave the Commission a wide discretion, allowing it to 'individualise' the fine to each infringing undertaking.[543] The Commission increasingly took into account the Community turnover in the product concerned in the infringement and stated the importance of this factor in the *Cement Cartel* press release, where it said 'calculation is normally based on the Community turnover in the product concerned'.[544]

In 1992 the Commission announced that it would continue to move closer to the maximum fine laid down in Regulation 17[545] and that whenever it could ascertain the level of the ill-gotten gains from the infringement the calculation of the fine would take this as its starting point.[546] From the mid-1980s onwards the size of fines increased markedly.[547] In 1996 the Commission, in pursuance of its desire to obtain hard evidence of the existence of cartels, introduced a Notice offering leniency over fines to cartel participants which informed on the cartel to the Commission.[548]

The fining policy was criticised for its lack of transparency. It was said that the Commission appeared to pluck figures from the air in what could only be described as a lottery[549] and that the increasingly swingeing fines (particularly on cartelists) were based on no discernible methodology. The absence of a proper 'tariff', or to put it in the Commission's words, the rejection of 'a mathematical exercise based on an abstract formula' was contrasted unfavourably with the position in

---

[539] Case C-58/12 P, *Groupe Gascogne SA v Commission* EU:C:2013:770, para. 52.

[540] Ibid., para. 57.

[541] Cases 100–103, *Pioneer* [1983] ECR 1825, para. 121.

[542] The GC confirmed in Cases T-25/95 etc., *Cimenteries* [2000] ECR II-491, paras. 5022–5023, that only total turnover gives an approximate indication of the undertaking's size and influence on the market and that Reg. 17, Art. 15(2) (now Reg. 1/2003 Art. 23(2)) contained no territorial limit, so that the Commission could choose which turnover to take in terms of territory and products in order to determine the fine. See also Case C-289/04 P, *Showa Denko v Commission* [2006] ECR I-5859, paras. 16–18, and the 2006 Fining Guidelines, para. 18.

[543] The GC said in Case T-150/89, *Martinelli v Commission* [1995] ECR II-1165, para. 69, that the Commission could not be expected to apply a precise mathematical formula to fining calculations. And see also Case 322/81, *Nederlandsche Banden-Industrie Michelin v Commission* [1983] ECR 3461, paras. 17–21; Case T-53/03, *BPB plc v Commission* [2008] ECR II-1333.

[544] Press Release IP/1108 of 30 November 1994.

[545] Commission, *XXIst Competition Policy Report* (1992), para. 139.

[546] In Cases T-25/95 etc., *Cimenteries* [2000] ECR II-491, paras. 4884–4885 the GC explained that this did not mean that the Commission had taken it upon itself to establish in every case the financial advantage obtained, but merely that it would take it more into account where it could be assessed, albeit not precisely. But see the comments of Vesterdorf, cited in n. 530.

[547] In 1992 a fine of 75 million ECUs, approximately 2.5% of its overall turnover, was imposed on Tetra Pak for abuse of a dominant position, *Tetra Pak II* [1992] OJ L72/1, upheld on appeal Case T-83/91, *Tetra Pak International SA v Commission* [1994] ECR II-755 and Case C-333/94 P, *Tetra Pak* [1996] ECR I-5951: the fact that it was the first time that the Commission had held that an undertaking dominant on one market could abuse it by its conduct on the other did not reduce the size of the fine; in 1994 41 participants in the *Cement Cartel* were fined a total of 248 million ECUs, including one fine of over 32 million ECUs (some of these fines were reduced on appeal where the Commission had not proved the length of the infringement it alleged: Cases T-25/95 etc., *Cimenteries* [2000] ECR II-491).

[548] See Section 7.H.v, p. 983.

[549] See I. Van Bael, 'Fining à la Carte: The Lottery of EU Competition Law' [1995] *ECLR* 237.

other jurisdictions.[550] The debate about the desirability of more certainty in fining practice involves, inter alia, assessing which is the best deterrent, certainty or uncertainty. If undertakings know what infringements will cost them, will they engage in a cost–benefit analysis and, deciding that they will on balance gain or lose, then act accordingly? Will they be deterred only if they face unknown amounts? Such questions are not, of course, unique to competition law and there is a large literature on deterrence in criminal law and the economics of crime deterrence including work specifically on deterrence in competition law.[551]

Decisions levying fines can be challenged before the GC. As the Commission has to observe the normal general principles of EU law these decisions can be challenged on grounds, inter alia, of lack of adequate reasoning, lack of proportionality, and discrimination (the last is particularly relevant to the different treatment of cartel participants). A good example of the judicial attitude to fining policy was *Tréfilunion* in 1995[552] where one of the participants in the *Welded Steel Mesh Cartel*[553] claimed that the reasoning which led to the calculation of its fine was inadequate. The GC accepted that it should not be necessary for an undertaking to have to bring court proceedings in order to ascertain how the fine was calculated, but still upheld the decision. It also upheld the Commission's decision in *PVC Cartel II*, where some undertakings argued that the decision contained no specific information explaining the level of fines imposed on each of them and that the Commission had failed to specify the objective standards used to assess the liability of the undertakings and their respective importance. The GC held that in the light of the detailed account in the decision of the factual allegations made against the undertakings the decision did contain sufficient and relevant indications of the factors the Commission had taken into account.[554]

e. The Adoption of the Commission's 1998 Guidelines and 2006 Guidelines on the Method of Setting Fines

Conscious of the problems surrounding its fining policy the Commission published a Notice in January 1998, the Guidelines on the method of setting fines.[555] The Guidelines set out a methodology which still allowed the Commission a wide margin of discretion. The Notice did not mean that fines could henceforth be precisely calculated with mathematical accuracy and much of it, in particular as regards aggravating and attenuating (mitigating) circumstances, reflected the previous practice of the Commission and the rulings of the Court.

The Guidelines built on the two criteria stipulated in Regulation 17, gravity and duration, and based the calculation of fines on these. The Guidelines divided the gravity of infringements into 'minor',[556] 'serious',[557] and 'very serious'.[558] The fines for these were in the ranges €1,000 to €1 million,

---

[550] Ibid.

[551] See W. Wils, 'EC Competition Fines: To Deter or Not to Deter' (1995) 15 *YEL* 17 and the literature cited there; G. Becker, 'Crime and Punishment: An Economic Approach' (1968) 76 *J of Political Economy*; W. Landes, 'Optimal Sanctions for Antitrust Violations' (1983) 50 *Univ Chic LR* 652; R. Hardy, 'Casenote on Case C-510/06 P, *Archer Daniel Midlands*' (2009) 46 *CMLRev* 2095. The GC has said that too much predictability in the fine is undesirable, see Case T-53/03, *BPB plc v Commission* [2008] ECR II-1333, para. 336.

[552] Case T-148/89 etc., *Tréfilunion v Commission* [1995] ECR II-1063.

[553] [1989] OJ L260/1.

[554] Cases T-305/94 etc., *Re the PVC Cartel II* [1999] ECR II-931, para. 1179.

[555] Guidelines on the method of setting fines [1998] OJ C9/3.

[556] Trade restrictions, usually of a vertical nature, with a limited market impact and affecting only a substantial but relatively limited part of the Community market: 1998 Guidelines, para. 1.

[557] Horizontal or vertical restrictions of the same type as 'minor' infringements, but more rigorously applied, with a wider market impact, and with effects in extensive areas of the common market; and some abuses of a dominant position: 1998 Guidelines, para. 1.

[558] Horizontal restrictions such as price cartels and market-sharing quotas, or other practices jeopardising the proper functioning of the single market, such as the partitioning of national markets and clear-cut abuse of a dominant position by undertakings holding a virtual monopoly: 1998 Guidelines, para. 1. In Cases T-49 and 51/02, *Brasserie Nationale SA and others v Commission* [2005] ECR II-3033 (the *Luxembourg Brewers* cartel), para. 178, the GC appeared to consider that all horizontal cartels should be classified as 'very serious'.

€1 million to €20 million, and above €20 million respectively. It was provided that where it could be measured the actual impact on the market should be taken into account in the assessment of gravity. The starting figure was then increased according to the duration of the infringement: short (generally less than a year), no increase; medium (generally one to five years), up to 50 per cent increase; long (generally more than five years), up to 10 per cent per year increase. The gravity plus duration calculation gave the basic amount of the fine, which could then be increased where there were 'aggravating circumstances' or decreased where there were 'attenuating circumstances'. The Commission confirmed its freedom to apply different fines to undertakings involved in the same infringing conduct to take into account the 'real impact' of each undertaking's behaviour. This was particularly relevant to cartels. The Commission also stressed the necessity of producing a sufficient deterrent effect[559] and of taking account of an undertaking's capacity to cause damage to others.

Although the Guidelines brought a more systematic approach to the calculation of fines it was still impossible for undertakings to compute their liability exactly. The Notice contained many variables and many matters which were a matter of discretionary assessment by the Commission,[560] and the language of the Notice was imprecise—full of 'might be', 'generally speaking', 'in general', 'particularly'. Above all, the base figure from which the calculation flowed was in the discretion of the Commission. The result of this uncertainty was a flood of appeals to the Community Courts against the calculation of the fines imposed in infringement decisions, particularly in cartel cases.

The 1998 Guidelines were replaced by the 2006 Guidelines[561] in respect of cases where an SO was notified after 1 September 2006.[562]

f. The Legality and Legal Effect of the Fining Guidelines

In *Dansk Rørindustri*[563] the CJ confirmed that the Commission was legally empowered to adopt fining Guidelines and had not exceeded its discretion in so doing. The criteria of gravity and duration used in the Guidelines were those referred to in Article 15(2) of Regulation 17 (now Regulation 1/2003, Article 23(2)) and the Guidelines were therefore in conformity with the legal framework of penalties set out there. The Commission was not required by Article 15(2) to calculate the fines on the basis of the turnover of the undertakings concerned, although it was permissible to take turnover into account in order to assess the gravity of the infringement. However, disproportionate importance should not be attributed to turnover in comparison with other relevant factors.[564]

In a number of cases the Commission imposed fines calculated in accordance with the principles in the 1998 Guidelines in respect of conduct that took place before they were adopted. In *Dansk Rørindustri* the CJ held that the principles of legitimate expectation and non-retroactivity were not thereby infringed. Echoing the *Pioneer* (*Musique Diffusion*) judgment, it said that the Commission could at any time adjust fining levels in the light of the needs of competition policy.[565] The Commission had wide discretionary powers in the field of competition policy and the changes in fining policy

---

[559] The CJ recognises that the imposition of a 'deterrence multiplier' is justified, see, e.g., Case C-289/04 P, *Showa Denko v Commission* [2006] ECR I-5859 (one of the *Graphite Electrodes Cartel* appeals), paras. 28–39. The deterrent effect means that the fact that an undertaking did not benefit from an infringement cannot preclude the imposition of fines, so the Commission is not required to establish that the undertaking concerned profited from the infringement: Case T-143/89, *Ferriere Nord v Commission* [1995] ECR II-917; Cases T-25/95 etc., *Cimenteries* [2000] ECR II-491, para. 4881.

[560] See, e.g., the decision to add 20% for aggravating circumstances in *Volkswagen* [1998] OJ L124/60.

[561] Guidelines on the method of setting fines imposed pursuant to Article 23(2)(a) of Regulation No. 1/2003 [2006] OJ C210/5.

[562] 2006 Guidelines, para. 38. 'A' statement means that the Guidelines apply where a supplementary statement was notified after 1 September even if the first one was notified before, see H. de Broca, 'The Commission Revises its Guidelines for Setting Fines in Antitrust Cases' (2006) 3 *Competition Policy Newsletter* 1, 2.

[563] Cases C-189/02 P etc., *Dansk Rørindustri* [2005] ECR I-5425, the appeal from the judgments of the GC in the *Pre-Insulated Pipes Cartel* case.

[564] Cases C-189/02 P etc., *Dansk Rørindustri* [2005] ECR I-5425, paras. 250–258.

[565] See also Case C-3/06 P, *Group Danone v Commission* [2007] ECR I-1331, para. 90.

were reasonably foreseeable at the time of the infringements.[566] In considering the principle of non-retroactivity the CJ referred to the ECHR. It also made the point that although the legal basis of the fines was Article 15(2) rather than the Guidelines, the latter *were* relevant to the issue of retroactivity.

Cases C-189, 202, 208, and 213/02 P, *Dansk Rørindustri A/S and Others v Commission* [2005] ECR I-5425

Court of Justice

169. . . . [T]he [General Court] correctly observed that the fact that the Commission, in the past, imposed fines of a certain level for certain types of infringement does not mean that it is estopped from raising that level within the limits indicated in Regulation No 17 if that is necessary to ensure the implementation of Community competition policy. On the contrary, the proper application of the Community competition rules requires that the Commission may at any time adjust the level of fines to the needs of that policy (Joined Cases 100/80 to 103/80 *Musique Diffusion française and Others* v *Commission* . . . paragraph 109, and *Aristrain* v *Commission*, cited above, paragraph 101).

170. The supervisory task conferred on the Commission by Articles [101 and 102] not only includes the duty to investigate and punish individual infringements but also encompasses the duty to pursue a general policy designed to apply, in competition matters, the principles laid down by the Treaty and to guide the conduct of undertakings in the light of those principles (see *Musique Diffusion française and Others* v *Commission*, paragraph 105).

171. As the [General Court] appositely observed, traders cannot have a legitimate expectation that an existing situation which is capable of being altered by the Commission in the exercise of its discretionary power will be maintained (Case C-350/88 *Delacre and Others* v *Commission* . . . paragraph 33 and the case-law cited).

172. That principle clearly applies in the field of competition policy, which is characterised by a wide discretion on the part of the Commission, in particular as regards the determination of the amount of fines.

173. The [General Court] was also correct to infer that undertakings involved in an administrative procedure in which fines may be imposed cannot acquire a legitimate expectation in the fact that the Commission will not exceed the level of fines previously imposed, so that in the present case the applicants could not, in particular, found a legitimate expectation on the level of fines imposed in Commission Decision 94/601/EC of 13 July 1994 relating to a proceeding under Article [101] (IV/C/33.833—*Cartonboard*). As the Commission observes, it follows that a legitimate expectation cannot be based on a method of calculating fines either.

. . .

209 The Court has already held, in a judgment concerning internal measures adopted by the administration, that although those measures may not be regarded as rules of law which the administration is always bound to observe, they nevertheless form rules of practice from which the administration may not depart in an individual case without giving reasons that are compatible with the principle of equal treatment. Such measures therefore constitute a general act and the officials and other staff concerned may invoke their illegality in support of an action against the individual measures taken on the basis of the measures (see Case C-171/00 P *Libéros v Commission* . . . paragraph 35).

210 That case-law applies a fortiori to rules of conduct designed to produce external effects, as is the case of the Guidelines, which are aimed at traders.

211 In adopting such rules of conduct and announcing by publishing them that they will henceforth apply to the cases to which they relate, the institution in question imposes a limit on the exercise of its

---

[566] This point is also relevant to the application of the 2006 Guidelines.

discretion and cannot depart from those rules under pain of being found, where appropriate, to be in breach of the general principles of law, such as equal treatment or the protection of legitimate expectations. It cannot therefore be precluded that, on certain conditions and depending on their content, such rules of conduct, which are of general application, may produce legal effects.

. . .

213. The [General Court] was also correct to observe, at paragraph 418 of *HFB and Others* v *Commission* and paragraph 274 of *LR AF 1998* v *Commission*, that although the Guidelines do not constitute the legal basis of the contested decision, they determine, generally and abstractly, the method which the Commission has bound itself to use in assessing the fines imposed by the decision and, consequently, ensure legal certainty on the part of the undertakings.

214. Just as the admissibility of an objection of illegality raised against rules of conduct such as the Guidelines is not subject to the requirement that those rules constitute the legal basis of the act alleged to be illegal, the relevance of the Guidelines in the light of the principle of non-retroactivity does not presuppose that the Guidelines form the legal basis for the fines.

215. In that context, it is appropriate to refer to the case-law of the European Court of Human Rights on Article 7(1) of the ECHR, which, moreover, is cited by a number of the applicants (see, in particular, Eur. Court H.R., *S.W.* v *United Kingdom* and *C.R.* v *United Kingdom*, judgments of 22 November 1995, Series A Nos 335-B and 335-C, §§ 34 to 36 and §§ 32 to 34; *Cantoni* v *France*, judgment of 15 November 1996, *Reports of Judgments and Decisions*, 1996-V, §§ 29 to 32, and *Coëme and Others* v *Belgium*, judgment of 22 June 2000, *Reports*, 2000-VII, § 145).

216. It follows from that case-law that the concept of 'law' ('*droit*') for the purposes of Article 7(1) corresponds to 'law' ('*loi*') used in other provisions of the ECHR and encompasses both law of legislative origin and that deriving from case-law.

217. Although that provision, which enshrines in particular the principle that offences and punishments are to be strictly defined by law (*nullum crimen, nulla poena sine lege*), cannot be interpreted as prohibiting the gradual clarification of the rules of criminal liability, it may, according to that case-law, preclude the retroactive application of a new interpretation of a rule establishing an offence.

218. That is particularly true, according to that case-law, of a judicial interpretation which produces a result which was not reasonably foreseeable at the time when the offence was committed, especially in the light of the interpretation put on the provision in the case-law at the material time.

219. It follows from that case-law of the European Court of Human Rights that the scope of the notion of foreseeability depends to a considerable degree on the content of the text in issue, the field it is designed to cover and the number and status of those to whom it is addressed. A law may still satisfy the requirement of foreseeability even if the person concerned has to take appropriate legal advice to assess, to a degree that is reasonable in the circumstances, the consequences which a given action may entail. This is particularly true in relation to persons carrying on a professional activity, who are used to having to proceed with a high degree of caution when pursuing their occupation. They can on this account be expected to take special care in assessing the risks that such an activity entails (see *Cantoni* v *France*, cited above, § 35).

220. Those principles are also consistently reflected in the case-law of the Court to the effect that the obligation on the national court to refer to the content of the directive when interpreting the relevant rules of its national law is limited by the general principles of law which form part of Community law and in particular the principles of legal certainty and non-retroactivity (see Case 80/86 *Kolpinghuis Nijmegen* . . . paragraph 13).

221. According to that case-law, such an interpretation cannot lead to the imposition on an individual of an obligation laid down by a directive which has not been transposed or, a fortiori, have the effect of determining or aggravating, on the basis of the decision and in the absence of a law enacted for its implementation, the liability in criminal law of persons who act in contravention of that directive's provisions (see, in particular, *Kolpinghuis Nijmegen*, cited above, paragraph 14, and Case C-168/95 *Arcaro* . . . paragraph 42).

222. Like that case-law on new developments in case-law, a change in an enforcement policy, in this instance the Commission's general competition policy in the matter of fines, especially where it comes about as a result of the adoption of rules of conduct such as the Guidelines, may have an impact from the aspect of the principle of non-retroactivity.

223. Having particular regard to their legal effects and to their general application, as indicated at paragraph 211 of this judgment, such rules of conduct come, in principle, within the principle of 'law' for the purposes of Article 7(1) of the ECHR.

224. As stated at paragraph 219 of this judgment, in order to ensure that the principle of non-retroactivity was observed, it is necessary to ascertain whether the change in question was reasonably foreseeable at the time when the infringements concerned were committed.

225. In that regard, it should be noted that, as a number of the appellants have pointed out, the main innovation in the Guidelines consisted in taking as a starting point for the calculation a basic amount, determined on the basis of brackets laid down for that purpose by the Guidelines; those brackets reflect the various degrees of gravity of the infringements but, as such, bear no relation to the relevant turnover. The essential feature of that method is thus that fines are determined on a tariff basis, albeit one that is relative and flexible.

226. It is therefore necessary to consider whether that new method of calculating fines, on the assumption that it has the effect of increasing the level of fines imposed, was reasonably foreseeable at the time when the infringements concerned were committed.

227. As already stated at paragraph 169 of this judgment in connection with the pleas alleging breach of the principle of protection of legitimate expectations, it follows from the case-law of the Court that the fact that the Commission, in the past, imposed fines of a certain level for certain types of infringement does not mean that it is estopped from raising that level within the limits indicated in Regulation No 17 if that is necessary to ensure the implementation of Community competition policy. On the contrary, the proper application of the Community competition rules requires that the Commission may at any time adjust the level of fines to the needs of that policy.

228. It follows, as already held at paragraph 173 of this judgment, that undertakings involved in an administrative procedure in which fines may be imposed cannot acquire a legitimate expectation in the fact that the Commission will not exceed the level of fines previously imposed or in a method of calculating the fines.

229. Consequently, the undertakings in question must take account of the possibility that the Commission may decide at any time to raise the level of the fines by reference to that applied in the past.

230. That is true not only where the Commission raises the level of the amount of fines in imposing fines in individual decisions but also if that increase takes effect by the application, in particular cases, of rules of conduct of general application, such as the Guidelines.

231. It must be concluded that, particularly in the light of the case-law cited at paragraph 219 of this judgment, the Guidelines and, in particular, the new method of calculating fines contained therein, on the assumption that this new method had the effect of increasing the level of the fines imposed, were reasonably foreseeable for undertakings such as the appellants at the time when the infringements concerned were committed.

232. Accordingly, in applying the Guidelines in the contested decision to infringements committed before they were adopted, the Commission did not breach the principle of non-retroactivity.

The CJ confirmed the principles in the *Dansk Rørindustri* judgment in two *Archer Daniels Midland* judgments in 2006 and 2009.[567] These cases make it clear that the principle of equality is not infringed

---

[567] Case C-397/03 P, *Archer Daniels Midland Co v Commission* [2006] ECR I-4429 (lysine (amino acid) cartel) and Case C-510/06 P, *Archer Daniels Midland Co v Commission* [2009] ECR I-1843 (sodium gluconate cartel).

by the Commission changing its fining policy so that the same conduct is differently sanctioned depending on when it happens to take place.

The *Dansk Rørindustri* judgment is important in respect of the legal effect of the Fining Guidelines, and indeed of other Notices. Although they are not binding legislation,[568] it will be noted that in paragraphs 209–211 the CJ stated that by adopting Fining Guidelines the Commission imposes limits on its discretion, departure from which may involve a breach of the principles of equal treatment and legitimate expectation. Whilst not 'rules of law' which the administration is always bound to observe 'they nevertheless form rules of practice from which the administration may not depart in an individual case without giving reasons that are compatible with the principle of equal treatment'.[569] This principle is of great significance for all Commission Notices in respect of competition law.

In practice, appeals from Commission decisions imposing fines (on cartel participants in particular) now involve detailed arguments about whether the Commission correctly followed the Fining Guidelines (and the Leniency Notice)[570] more often than they involve arguments about whether or not there was an infringement in the first place.

g. The 2006 Fining Guidelines

The Commission adopted new Guidelines on the method of setting fines in June 2006 to remedy some perceived shortcomings in the 1998 methodology, to reflect the Commission's most recent practice, and to take on board recent case law.[571] The 2006 Guidelines follow a similar two-step methodology to the 1998 ones in providing first for a basic amount and secondly for an increase or decrease in the light of 'adjustment factors'—aggravating or attenuating circumstances.

Guidelines on the Method of Setting Fines Imposed Pursuant to Article 23(2)(A) of Regulation No. 1/2003 [2006] OJ C210/2

13. In determining the basic amount of the fine to be imposed, the Commission will take the value of the undertaking's sales of goods or services to which the infringement directly or indirectly . . . relates in the relevant geographic area within the EEA. It will normally take the sales made by the undertaking during the last full business year of its participation in the infringement (hereafter 'value of sales').

14. Where the infringement by an association of undertakings relates to the activities of its members, the value of sales will generally correspond to the sum of the value of sales by its members.

15. In determining the value of sales by an undertaking, the Commission will take that undertaking's best available figures.

---

[568] See Chap. 2.

[569] Case C-397/03 P, *Archer Daniels Midland Co v Commission* [2006] ECR I-4429, para. 91. In that case the CJ held that the GC had erred in law in allowing the Commission to breach the 1998 Guidelines in the way in which it had dealt with the undertaking's turnover, but nevertheless upheld the judgment as the GC, in an exercise of its unlimited jurisdiction (see Section 8.A.vi, p. 998), had ascertained that the fine would not have been different had the Commission taken account of the correct turnover, see Case T-224/00, *Archer Daniels Midland Co v Commission* [2003] ECR II-2597.

[570] See Section 7.H.v, p. 983.

[571] The Guidelines were amended because the Commission was dissatisfied in particular with the minor, serious, and very serious classification; accepted the criticisms of the lump sum base figures as vague and unsatisfactory; and wished to reinforce its policy with some more draconian elements. See Press Release, IP/06/857; de Broca, n. 562; Neelie Kroes, 'Delivering the crackdown: recent developments in the European Commission's campaign against cartels', SPEECH/06/595 (the Commissioner considered the effect of the 2006 Guidelines would be to increase the amount of fines by a factor of three); W. Wils, 'The European Commission's 2006 Guidelines on Antitrust Fines: A Legal and Economic Analysis' (2007) 30 *World Competition* 197. The Guidelines refer to the EEA rather than the EU because the competition rules apply to the whole EEA area, see Chap. 2.

16. Where the figures made available by an undertaking are incomplete or not reliable, the Commission may determine the value of its sales on the basis of the partial figures it has obtained and/or any other information which it regards as relevant and appropriate.

17. The value of sales will be determined before VAT and other taxes directly related to the sales.

18. Where the geographic scope of an infringement extends beyond the EEA (e.g. worldwide cartels), the relevant sales of the undertakings within the EEA may not properly reflect the weight of each undertaking in the infringement. This may be the case in particular with worldwide market-sharing arrangements.[572]

In such circumstances, in order to reflect both the aggregate size of the relevant sales within the EEA and the relative weight of each undertaking in the infringement, the Commission may assess the total value of the sales of goods or services to which the infringement relates in the relevant geographic area (wider than the EEA), may determine the share of the sales of each undertaking party to the infringement on that market and may apply this share to the aggregate sales within the EEA of the undertakings concerned. The result will be taken as the value of sales for the purpose of setting the basic amount of the fine.

B. Determination of the basic amount of the fine

19. The basic amount of the fine will be related to a proportion of the value of sales, depending on the degree of gravity of the infringement, multiplied by the number of years of infringement.

20. The assessment of gravity will be made on a case-by-case basis for all types of infringement, taking account of all the relevant circumstances of the case.

21. As a general rule, the proportion of the value of sales taken into account will be set at a level of up to 30 % of the value of sales.

22. In order to decide whether the proportion of the value of sales to be considered in a given case should be at the lower end or at the higher end of that scale, the Commission will have regard to a number of factors, such as the nature of the infringement, the combined market share of all the undertakings concerned, the geographic scope of the infringement and whether or not the infringement has been implemented.

23. Horizontal price-fixing, market-sharing and output-limitation agreements . . . which are usually secret, are, by their very nature, among the most harmful restrictions of competition. As a matter of policy, they will be heavily fined. Therefore, the proportion of the value of sales taken into account for such infringements will generally be set at the higher end of the scale.

24. In order to take fully into account the duration of the participation of each undertaking in the infringement, the amount determined on the basis of the value of sales (see points 20 to 23 above) will be multiplied by the number of years of participation in the infringement. Periods of less than six months will be counted as half a year; periods longer than six months but shorter than one year will be counted as a full year.

25. In addition, irrespective of the duration of the undertaking's participation in the infringement, the Commission will include in the basic amount a sum of between 15% and 25% of the value of sales as defined in Section A above in order to deter undertakings from even entering into horizontal price-fixing, market-sharing and output-limitation agreements. The Commission may also apply such an additional amount in the case of other infringements. For the purpose of deciding the proportion of the value of

---

572 The Commission applied para. 18 in COMP/39.406, *Marine Hoses Cartel*, where, 'given the global character of the cartel arrangements, the worldwide sales figures give the most appropriate picture of the participating undertakings' capacity to cause significant damage to other operators in the EEA' (para. 432), approved on appeal Cases T-146/09 etc., *Parker ITR and Parker-Hannifin v Commission* EU:T:2013:256, paras. 205–219, decision annulled on other grounds, Case C-434/13 P EU:C:2014:2456; see also COMP/39.180, *Aluminium Fluoride*, upheld Case T-406/08, *ICF v Commission* EU:T:2013:322, *aff'd* Case C-467/13, EU:C:2014:2274.

sales to be considered in a given case, the Commission will have regard to a number of factors, in particular those referred in point 22.

26. Where the value of sales by undertakings participating in the infringement is similar but not identical, the Commission may set for each of them an identical basic amount. Moreover, in determining the basic amount of the fine, the Commission will use rounded figures.

2. Adjustments to the basic amount

27. In setting the fine, the Commission may take into account circumstances that result in an increase or decrease in the basic amount as determined in Section 1 above. It will do so on the basis of an overall assessment which takes account of all the relevant circumstances.

A. Aggravating circumstances

28. The basic amount may be increased where the Commission finds that there are aggravating circumstances, such as:

— where an undertaking continues or repeats the same or a similar infringement after the Commission or a national competition authority has made a finding that the undertaking infringed [Article 101 or 102]: the basic amount will be increased by up to 100 % for each such infringement established;

— refusal to cooperate with or obstruction of the Commission in carrying out its investigations;

— role of leader in, or instigator of, the infringement; the Commission will also pay particular attention to any steps taken to coerce other undertakings to participate in the infringement and/or any retaliatory measures taken against other undertakings with a view to enforcing the practices constituting the infringement.

B. Mitigating circumstances

29. The basic amount may be reduced where the Commission finds that mitigating circumstances exist, such as:

— where the undertaking concerned provides evidence that it terminated the infringement as soon as the Commission intervened: this will not apply to secret agreements or practices (in particular, cartels);

— where the undertaking provides evidence that the infringement has been committed as a result of negligence;

— where the undertaking provides evidence that its involvement in the infringement is substantially limited and thus demonstrates that, during the period in which it was party to the offending agreement, it actually avoided applying it by adopting competitive conduct in the market: the mere fact that an undertaking participated in an infringement for a shorter duration than others will not be regarded as a mitigating circumstance since this will already be reflected in the basic amount;

— where the undertaking concerned has effectively cooperated with the Commission outside the scope of the Leniency Notice and beyond its legal obligation to do so;

— where the anti-competitive conduct of the undertaking has been authorized or encouraged by public authorities or by legislation.

C. Specific increase for deterrence

30. The Commission will pay particular attention to the need to ensure that fines have a sufficiently deterrent effect; to that end, it may increase the fine to be imposed on undertakings which have a particularly large turnover beyond the sales of goods or services to which the infringement relates.

31. The Commission will also take into account the need to increase the fine in order to exceed the amount of gains improperly made as a result of the infringement where it is possible to estimate that amount.

D. Legal maximum

32. The final amount of the fine shall not, in any event, exceed 10 % of the total turnover in the preceding business year of the undertaking or association of undertakings participating in the infringement, as laid down in Article 23(2) of Regulation No 1/2003.

33. Where an infringement by an association of undertakings relates to the activities of its members, the fine shall not exceed 10% of the sum of the total turnover of each member active on the market affected by that infringement.

E. Leniency Notice

34. The Commission will apply the leniency rules in line with the conditions set out in the applicable notice.

F. Ability to pay

35. In exceptional cases, the Commission may, upon request, take account of the undertaking's inability to pay in a specific social and economic context. It will not base any reduction granted for this reason in the fine on the mere finding of an adverse or loss-making financial situation. A reduction could be granted solely on the basis of objective evidence that imposition of the fine as provided for in these Guidelines would irretrievably jeopardise the economic viability of the undertaking concerned and cause its assets to lose all their value.

FINAL CONSIDERATIONS

36. The Commission may, in certain cases, impose a symbolic fine. The justification for imposing such a fine should be given in its decision.

37. Although these Guidelines present the general methodology for the setting of fines, the particularities of a given case or the need to achieve deterrence in a particular case may justify departing from such methodology or from the limits specified in point 21.

The main features of the 2006 Guidelines are therefore the following.

- Instead of categories of seriousness the basic amount is calculated on a proportion of the value of sales, depending on the degree of gravity of the infringement. Unlike the 1998 Guidelines the 2006 Guidelines do not provide for taking into account the actual impact on the market if it can be measured but that does not preclude the Commission from taking it into account if it can provide 'specific, credible and adequate evidence'.[573]

- The calculation uses the value of the undertaking's sales of goods or services to which the infringement directly or indirectly relates in the relevant geographic area within the EEA.[574] As a general rule the proportion of the value of the sales taken into account will be up to 30 per cent.[575] The value of the internal sales of vertically integrated undertakings should be

---

[573] Case T-286/09, *Intel* EU:T:2014:547, paras. 1624–1625.

[574] 2006 Guidelines, para. 13. 'Indirectly' encompasses situations such as horizontal price-fixing where the price of the product concerned then serves as a basis for the price of lower or higher quality products (para. 13 n. 1). In the case of worldwide cartels the Commission may take account of the value of sales in a relevant geographic area wider than the EEA (para. 18, relying on Cases T-236/01 etc., *Tokai Carbon* [2004] ECR II-1181, paras. 196–204 (aff'd Case C-289/04 P, *Showa Denko v Commission* [2006] ECR I-5859, paras. 16–18); Cases T-71, 74, 87, and 91/03, *Tokai Carbon Co Ltd and others v Commission* [2005] ECR II-10, para. 186).

[575] 2006 Guidelines, para. 21. In para. 37 the Commission reserves the right to depart from this limit in a particular case. This may be necessary, for instance, where no turnover figures are available at all, see *Competition Policy Newsletter*, n. 562.

taken into account as well as sales to independent third parties.[576] The Commission adopted the formula of value of sales multiplied by duration for the basic amount because it regards this as providing 'an appropriate proxy to reflect the economic importance of the infringement as well as the relative weight of each undertaking in the infringement'.[577] In *Intel* the Commission took 5 per cent of the value of the sales as the starting point.[578]

- The amount determined by the value of sales is multiplied by the number of years of participation in the infringement.[579]

- Duration therefore plays a greater role in the determination of the basic amount than it did under the 1998 Guidelines. This provision alone would result in heavier fines than previously. The duration of the infringement in *Intel* was held to be five years and three months so the basic amount was multiplied by 5.5 to give a total fine of €1.6 billion (there being no allowance for any mitigating circumstances).

- 'Entry fees'—in the case of horizontal price-fixing, market-sharing, and output-limitation agreements (i.e. cartels) the Commission will include as part of the basic amount of the fine a further sum of 15–25 per cent of the value of the sales simply as a punishment for having entered into the arrangement—an 'entry fee'.[580] The purpose is to deter cartelists at the outset by making participation expensive even for a short time. The Commission may impose the entry fee in respect of other infringements too.

- Recidivism is heavily penalised—it is expensive to be a repeat offender. One of the aggravating circumstances is for an undertaking to continue or repeat the same or similar infringements after having been found by the Commission or an NCA to have infringed previously.[581] Recidivism has long been considered an aggravating feature but in the 2006 Guidelines it is specifically provided that *each* subsequent infringement will increase ('uplift') the basic amount of the fine by up to 100 per cent. The 2006 Guidelines were applied in the *Calcium Carbide* cartel[582] where the fine on Akzo Nobel would have been increased by 100 per cent for having been fined four times previously had it not been granted immunity for whistle-blowing.[583]

---

[576] Case C-580/12 P, *Guardian Industries Corp v Commission* EU:C:2014:2363.

[577] 2006 Guidelines, para. 6.

[578] COMP/37.990, *Intel* 13 May 2009, upheld Case T-286/09, *Intel* EU:T:2014:547, paras. 1560–1638, on appeal Case C-413/14 P, judgment pending. The Commission explained: 'the Commission took into account the factors set out above, in particular the nature, the market share and the geographic scope of the infringement. In this specific case, the Commission also took into account additional factors, namely that while Intel's conducts vis-à-vis individual OEMs [original equipment manufacturers] constitute separate abuses, the Commission has also found Intel to have engaged in a single infringement. However, the intensity of that single infringement differs across the years. Most of the individual abuses concerned are concentrated in the period ranging from 2002 to 2005, whilst, after the end of 2005, at most two individual abuses occur simultaneously at any given point in time . . . The Commission also took into consideration that some of the individual abuses have a short duration. Further, the abuses differ in their respective likely anti-competitive impact. The Commission also took account of the fact that Intel took measures to conceal the conducts established in this Decision, which made it more difficult to detect and sanction them', *Intel*, para. 1785. For the facts of *Intel*, see Chap. 7.

[579] 2006 Guidelines, para. 24. Less than six months counts as half a year, and six to 12 months counts as a full year.

[580] 2006 Guidelines, para. 25.

[581] 'Similar' means the same kind of infringement, such as price collusion in cartel cases (see, e.g., COMP/38.638, *Butadiene Rubber and Emulsion Styrene Butadiene Rubber Cartel* [2008] OJ C7/11) or abusive loyalty-inducing discounts in the two *Michelin* cases, see Case T-203/01, *Manufacture Française des Pneumatiques Michelin v Commission (Michelin II)* [2003] ECR II-4071, paras. 283–288. The product or sector concerned is irrelevant. The infringements in *Michelin* were committed by two separate subsidiaries of the same parent. It does not matter that the previous infringement was under a different Treaty, see Case T-122/04, *Outokumpu Oyj v Commission* [2009] ECR II-1135, paras. 55–56 where the previous infringement was in respect of the prohibitions in the ECSC Treaty. For recidivism in the context of EU antitrust enforcement generally, see W. Wils, 'Recidivism in EU Antitrust Enforcement—A Legal and Economic Analysis' (2012) 35 *World Competition* 5. In practice recidivism causes difficult problems because of the attribution of liability to parent companies and to successor undertakings.

[582] COMP/39.396, [2009] OJ C301/18, IP/09/1169.

[583] Under the Leniency Notice, see Section 7.H.v, p. 983. The fine on Degussa was increased by 50% for recidivism.

It must always be remembered that the final amount of the fine cannot exceed the 10 per cent of turnover in the preceding business year laid down in Article 23(2) of Regulation 1/2003.[584] The 'entry fee' and the up to 100 per cent uplift for repeat offenders potentially make cartel participation much more expensive than previously. In paragraph 30 the Commission says that it may increase fines on undertakings which have a particularly large turnover beyond the value of sales to which the infringement relates in order to provide sufficient deterrence. This continues the 'deterrence multiplier' practice developed in the application of the 1998 Guidelines and approved by the CJ.[585] Paragraph 31 says that the Commission may increase the fine in order to exceed the benefits of the infringement where it is possible to estimate them.[586] That provision was also in the 1998 Guidelines but among the 'aggravating factors' rather than under a separate deterrence head.[587] Economists believe that, in general, financial penalties should be based on the harm caused rather than the gain obtained,[588] but it is not the purpose of paragraph 31 to force the Commission to make such an estimate of the gains or suggest that the Commission should systematically try to do so.[589]

Arguments that the discretion of the Commission over fines infringes Article 7(1) ECHR[590] continue to be dismissed:

... [T]he fact that a law confers a discretion is not in itself inconsistent with the requirement of foreseeability, provided that the scope of the discretion and the manner of its exercise are indicated with sufficient clarity, having regard to the legitimate aim in question, to give the individual adequate protection against arbitrary interference.[591]

In fact, although the thrust of the 2006 Guidelines is to increase the level of fines,[592] the application of the leniency policy in cartel cases means that many infringers end up paying nothing, and others have greatly decreased fines.[593]

---

[584] And previously in Reg. 17, Art. 15(2). In the course of the calculation the Commission may exceed the 10%, so long as the final sum imposed on the undertaking is below it. The 10% does not therefore apply to the intermediate calculations: Cases C-189/02 P etc., *Dansk Rørindustri* [2005] ECR I-5425, paras. 277–278. Where the undertaking has committed a number of infringements the ceiling applies to each one separately; in Case C-564/08 P, *SGL Carbon v Commission* [2009] ECR I-191 the undertaking claimed that the Commission had deliberately adopted four separate decisions for four separate infringements, thus evading the 10% cap. The CJ affirmed the GC's dismissal of this plea (Case T-68/04, *SGL Carbon v Commission* [2008] ECR II-2511).

[585] Case C-289/04 P, *Showa Denko v Commission* [2006] ECR I-5859, paras. 23–29. Note also the Commission's *Methylglucamine Cartel* decision [2004] OJ L38/18, para. 329 where the fine was increased as a deterrence measure, '[I]n order to ensure that the fine has a sufficient deterrent effect and takes account of the fact that large undertakings have legal and economic knowledge and infrastructures which enable them more easily to recognize that their conduct constitutes an infringement and be aware of the consequences stemming from it under competition law . . .'.

[586] 2006 Guidelines, para. 31.

[587] 1998 Guidelines, para. 2, fifth indent. The CJ approved of raising the fine to exceed the improper gains in Cases C-189/02 P etc., *Dansk Rørindustri* [2005] ECR I-5425, para. 294, and see the remarks of the CJ in *Pioneer* set out in Section 7.H.iv.d, p. 964.

[588] See W. Wils, 'The Commission's New Method for Calculating Fines in Antitrust Cases' (1998) 23 *ELRev* 252, 259; A. M. Polinsky and S. Shavell, 'Should Liability be Based on the Harm to the Victim or the Gain to the Injurer?' (1994) 10 *J of Law, Economics and Organization* 427. Victims of infringements seeking compensation need to bring private damages actions: see Chap. 14.

[589] According to de Broca, n. 562, 6. See C. Veljanovski, 'Penalties for Price Fixers: An Analysis of Fines Imposed on 39 Cartels by the EU Commission' [2006] *ECLR* 510 (analysing the 2008 Guidelines decisions).

[590] Which provides for non-retroactivity of criminal law and penalties, see Section 7.B.ii, p. 899. It follows from this that criminal offences and the relevant penalties must be clearly defined by law, so that the individual knows what acts and omissions make him criminally liable and what are the consequences.

[591] Case T-69/04, *Schunk GmbH v Commission* [2008] ECR II-2567, para. 33.

[592] 'These innovations are likely to increase average fines, particularly for long lasting infringements in large markets, where fines could well increase by a factor of three. I think all this will make potential cartelists think twice!', Neelie Kroes, 'Delivering on the crackdown: recent developments in the European Commission's campaign against cartels', SPEECH/06/595, 13 October 2006. For an analysis of the fines imposed on cartels from 2007 to 2011 see J. M. Connor, 'Cartel Fine Severity and the European Commission 2007–2011' [2011] *ECLR* 58.

[593] See Veljanovski, n. 589.

h. Particular Issues in the Application of the Fining Guidelines

A detailed examination of the application of the Commission's fining policy is outside the scope of this book and reference should be had to practitioner texts[594] but the following points should be noted.

Deterrence

The major theme of the Commission fining policy, in accordance with the duty identified back in 1983 in *Pioneer*, is deterrence. This encompasses not only specific deterrence (by sanctioning the undertaking concerned) but also general deterrence (deterring other undertakings).[595] Deterrence may involve imposing separate penalties for each of a number of multiple breaches.[596] The large fines imposed on cartels are part of a deliberate policy of the Commission to deter undertakings from entering into such arrangements, as explained in Chapter 9.[597]

Aggravating Circumstances

The list of aggravating circumstances in paragraph 28 of the Guidelines (recidivism, refusal to co-operate with the Commission's investigation and being the leader or instigator of the infringement, or having taken coercive or retaliatory measures) is not exhaustive. The issue of recidivism becomes a complex one where company restructuring and/or changes in ownership and control have taken place.[598] A fine may be increased for recidivism even if the previous infringement was in a different market so long as the type of infringement is similar. Aggravation in the form of non-cooperation during an inspection is illustrated by *Professional Videotape*[599] in which Sony's fine was increased by 30 per cent for failing to answer questions and shredding documents during the dawn raid. There are frequent arguments played out in appeals to the GC about whether or not an undertaking played a leadership or instigation role.[600] In *Nintendo*[601] the infringing agreement (to restrict parallel trade) was between a manufacturer and seven of its exclusive distributors. The manufacturer (Nintendo) was classified as the 'leader' and its fine increased accordingly. It argued that the leadership concept was relevant only in restrictive horizontal agreements because in vertical agreements the role of manufacturer and leader merge (in effect invariably rendering the manufacturer the 'leader' and so liable to the uplift in fine). The GC rejected this and refused to limit the leadership concept to horizontal cartels. The fact that leadership merged into the manufacturing role did not preclude it being an aggravating circumstance. It should be noted that although terminating an infringement when investigated is not a mitigating circumstance, continuing infringing conduct after the investigation has commenced is an *aggravating* circumstance.[602]

---

[594] See generally, Ortiz Blanco, n. 2, Chap. 11; Kerse and Khan, n. 2, Chap. 7; Bellamy and Child, n. 2, Chap. 14; see also D. Geradin and D. Henry, 'EC Fining for Competition Law Violations: An Empirical Study of the Commission's Decisional Practice and the Community Courts' Judgments' (2005) 1 *European Competition Journal* 401. For a detailed consideration of the application of the 2006 Guidelines see Case T-587/08, *Fresh Del Monte Produce Inc v Commission* EU:T:2013:129, *aff'd* on these points, Cases C-293/13 P, *Fresh Del Monte Produce Inc v Commission* EU:C:2015:416.

[595] 2006 Guidelines, para. 4; Case C-511/11, *Versalis SpA v Commission* EU:C:2013:386, para. 94.

[596] Case T-446/05 P, *Amann & Söhne GmbH & Co KG v Commission* [2010] ECR II-1255.

[597] See Chap. 9, Section 2.B, p. 656 ff.

[598] This is similar to the problem which arises over liability for the infringement and for the fine, see Chap. 3, Section 5.A.vi. p. 126; and see, e.g., Case C-511/11, *Versalis SpA v Commission* EU:C:2013:386.

[599] COMP/38.432. Sony's total fine was therefore over €47 million.

[600] See, e.g., Case T-15/02, *BASF AG v Commission* [2006] ECR II-497 (an appeal from the *Vitamins Cartel* decision, [2003] OJ L6/1) in which the GC cancelled the 35% increase in the basic amount imposed on BASF for being a leader or instigator or leader of the cartel in respect of two vitamins (C and D3) as the Commission had not sufficiently established this. The refusal of leniency under the 1996 Notice on the ground that it was not available to the leader or instigator therefore had to be re-examined too, but the GC held that BASF still did not qualify. ·

[601] COMP/35.387, *PO Video Games* [2003] OJ L255/33, on appeal Case T-13/03, *Nintendo v Commission*, [2009] ECR II-975 (the Commission had opened its investigation in 1995).

[602] See, e.g., *PO Video Games*, where Nintendo got a 25% increase for this, upheld by the GC, Case T-1/03, *Nintendo v Commission* [2009] ECR II-975.

Mitigating Circumstances

Undertakings commonly plead that they were merely 'passive' participants in cartels and therefore within the third indent of paragraph 29. It will be noted that paragraph 29 does not list as a mitigating factor the adoption of a compliance programme (that is, a set of measures put in place by an undertaking to ensure that none of its staff breach the competition rules thereby imposing liability on the undertaking). Before 1992 the Commission gave some fine reductions where the infringement was carried out in contravention of the undertaking's compliance programme but its current practice is not to do so.[603] In *PO Video Games*, where Nintendo had introduced a compliance programme after the infringement, the Commission said that, 'While the Commission does indeed welcome all steps taken by undertakings to raise awareness amongst their employees of existing competition rules, these initiatives cannot relieve the Commission of its duty to penalise their very serious infringement of competition rules.'[604] In *Professional Videotape* Sony claimed it was a junior employee who had shredded the documents during an inspection contrary to the company's compliance policy but the Commission still held this was an aggravating circumstance, 'it is the undertaking's responsibility to employ, instruct and control its employees, and to ensure that none of them obstructs or hampers the Commission's work during an inspection'.[605] It is not a mitigating circumstance to co-operate with the Commission by producing information in response to an Article 18(2) request.[606]

In the *Calcium Carbide* cartel one (Slovakian) company, NCZ, was fined an amount that nearly reached the maximum 10 per cent turnover ceiling despite pleading that its representatives at the meetings did not speak any foreign language fluently and so had on the whole to communicate through other cartel members, and that having emerged from a former Communist regime had no knowledge of competition law.[607]

Ability to Pay

Paragraph 35 of the 2006 Guidelines reflects the case law of the CJ that the Commission is not required to take into account the undertaking's ability to pay the fine, but may do so. The plea of inability to pay has become more frequent since the financial crisis. However, taking difficulty in paying into account may give 'unjustified competitive advantages to undertakings least well adapted to the market conditions'.[608] 'Specific social context' in paragraph 35 means the consequences which payment of a fine could have, in particular, by leading to an increase in unemployment or deterioration in the economic sectors upstream and downstream of the undertakings concerned.[609] Faull and Nikpay say that 'this exceptional treatment of companies in financial distress may even be a necessity for guaranteeing the social acceptance of EU competition policy'.[610] The last sentence of paragraph 35, 'irretrievably jeopardise the economic viability and cause its assets to lose all their

---

[603] See, e.g., Case T-53/06, *UPM-Kymmene v Commission* EU:T:2012:101, paras. 123–124. For the arguments around compliance programmes, see W. Wils, 'Antitrust Compliance Programmes and Optimal Antitrust Enforcement' (2013) 1 J of Antitrust Enforcement 52 and D. Geradin, 'Antitrust Compliance Programmes and Optimal Antitrust Enforcement: A Reply to Wouter Wils' (2013) 1 J of Antitrust Enforcement 1; A. Riley and D. Sokol, 'Rethinking Compliance' (2015) 3 J of Antitrust Enforcement 31. The Commission has published a guide, 'Compliance Matters: What companies can do better to respect EU competition rules', <http://ec.europa.eu/competition/antitrust/complianceen.html>.

[604] [2003] OJ L255/33, para. 451.

[605] COMP/38.432, para. 226.

[606] Case C-294/13 P, *Commission v Fresh Del Monte Produce Inc* EU:C:2015:416, paras. 167–188, where the CJ overturned the GC's reduction of a fine for cooperation.

[607] COMP/39.396, [2009] OJ C301/18, appeal dismissed, Case T-352/09, *Nováčke Chemické Závody v Commission* EU:T:2012: 673, para. 103.

[608] See Cases 96–102, 104, 105, 108, and 110/82, *IAZ International Belgium v Commission* [1983] ECR 3369, paras. 54–55; Cases C-189/02 P etc., *Dansk Rørindustri* [2005] ECR I-5425, para. 327; Case C-308/04 P, *SGL Carbon AG v Commission* [2006] ECR I-5977, paras. 105–106.

[609] Case C-308/04 P, *SGL Carbon AG* [2006] ECR I-5977, para. 106. The CJ was interpreting the 1998 Guidelines.

[610] Faull and Nikpay, n. 2, 8.696.

value...' was considered in *Novácke Chemické Závody*. The GC confirmed that the mere fact that the fine might cause the bankruptcy of the undertaking concerned was not alone enough to satisfy paragraph 35. Rather, it was a matter of looking at what would happen to the assets in such an event. If it was likely that the assets would not find a buyer, or be sold at a heavily reduced price, that could amount to losing all their value.[611] There is a concern to avoid an undertaking leaving the market because of an inability to pay, leaving another firm dominant (especially if the latter has received immunity under the Leniency Policy).[612]

The Commission gave a reduction for inability to pay in respect of one of the undertakings in the *International Removal Services Cartel*[613] but under paragraph 37 of the Guidelines rather than paragraph 35. On appeal the CJ held that an inability to pay under paragraph 35 cannot of itself give rise to a reduction under paragraph 37 but may be relevant to a reduction under paragraph 37.[614] It gave reductions in *Animal Feed Phosphates*,[615] *Prestressing Steel*,[616] *Bathroom Fixtures and Fittings*,[617] and *Retail Food Repackaging*.[618] The Commission has published an Information Note on Inability to Pay under paragraph 35, explaining its policy and methodology in dealing with such claims[619] and in Best Practices sets out the information an undertaking making the claim should provide.[620]

i. General Principles of Law

In imposing fines, as in all other aspects of competition procedure, the Commission must abide by the general principles of EU law. As well as non-retroactivity and legitimate expectation the Commission must, in setting fines, particularly heed the principles of proportionality, equal treatment, and sound administration.[621] As far as proportionality is concerned, the CJ stated in *Pioneer* that the upper limit on fines (10 per cent of turnover) was seeking to prevent fines from being disproportionate in relation to the size of the undertaking.[622] Equal treatment means that comparable situations must be treated in the same way and different situations treated differently, unless there is objective justification. Where a number of undertakings are involved in the same infringement—as in a cartel—the Commission applies weightings to reflect the differing impact of the undertakings' conduct. This may involve grouping the undertakings concerned.[623] The CJ confirmed in *Dansk Rørindustri* that the Commission does not have to ensure that the final amounts of the fines resulting from its calculations reflect any distinctions between them in terms of their turnover.[624]

---

[611] Case T-352/09, *Novácke Chemické Závody* EU:T:2012: 673, paras. 186–190.

[612] See Case T-392/09, *I.garantovaná v Commission* EU:T:2012:674.

[613] COMP/38.543, *International Removal Services* [2008] OJ C188/16 (70% reduction).

[614] Case C-439/11 P, *Ziegler v Commission* EU:C:2013:513, para. 171–174.

[615] COMP/38.866, 20 July 2010.

[616] COMP/38.344, 25 July 2012, on appeal Case T-438/12, *Global Steel Wire v Commission*, judgment pending (appeal on the ground of breach of the principle of non-discrimination by an undertaking which did *not* get a reduction).

[617] COMP/39.092, 23 June 2010, upheld on appeal by an undertaking which was not one of the five to be given a reduction, Case T-376/10, *Mamoli Robinetteria v Commission* EU:T:2013:442, on appeal Case C-619/13 P, judgment pending.

[618] COMP/39.563, 24 June 2015.

[619] SEC(2010)737/2.

[620] Best Practices, para. 88.

[621] For a case in which the principle of sound administration was breached, see Case T-410/03, *Hoechst GmbH v Commission* [2008] ECR II-881, where the Commission was embroiled in negotiations with two undertakings at the same time under the Leniency Notice.

[622] Cases 100–103/80, *Pioneer* [1983] ECR 1825, paras. 119–120; see Case T-33/02, *Britannia Alloys and Chemicals Ltd v Commission* [2005] ECR II-4973, para. 43.

[623] Case T-68/04, *SGL Carbon v Commission* [2008] ECR II-2511, aff'd Case C-564/08 P, *SGL Carbon AG v Commission* [2009] ECR I-191.

[624] Cases C-189/02 P etc., *Dansk Rørindustri* [2005] ECR I-5425, para. 312.

Appeals against fines on grounds of breach of the principles of proportionality and equal treatment are common. For example, in *Hoek Loos*[625] the fine imposed on one undertaking in the *Industrial Gases Cartel* decision[626] amounted to nearly 50 per cent of the total fines imposed in that case. The undertaking claimed that this was out of all proportion to its participation in the infringement or to its market share. The GC rejected this argument, saying that the final amount of a fine is not, in principle, an appropriate factor in assessing the possible lack of proportionality of the fine as regards the importance of the participants in the cartel. That final amount was set, inter alia, on the basis of various factors linked to the individual conduct of the undertaking in question, such as the duration of the infringement, the aggravating or attenuating circumstances, and the degree to which the undertaking cooperated.[627] On the other hand, in *Degussa*[628] the GC held that the Commission was wrong in applying the same deterrence multiplier to the applicant as to another of the cartelists despite the difference in the size of the two undertakings and reduced the fine from €118 million to €91.125 million. In *Guardian Industries*[629] the CJ held that the Commission breached the principle of non-discrimination by not taking internal sales into account when calculating the value of sales, because it resulted in an undertaking which made sales only to third parties receiving a disproportionately large fine relative to other cartel members who were vertically integrated.

j. Ne Bis in Idem

The principle of *ne bis in idem* (double jeopardy) means that a party cannot be prosecuted, tried, and convicted twice for the same (criminal) behaviour.[630] It is enshrined in Article 4 of Protocol 7 of the ECHR and in Article 50 of the EU Charter of Fundamental Rights and is a fundamental principle of Union law.[631] In respect of competition cases it precludes an undertaking from being found guilty or proceedings being brought against it a second time on the grounds of anti-competitive conduct in respect of which it has been penalised or declared not liable by a previous unappealable decision.[632] However, the principle did not prevent fines being imposed on four trade federations where three of them were members of the fourth.[633] Under the system for the allocation of cases within the ECN several NCAs may investigate in parallel the same matter in respect of the same undertakings.[634] However, no NCA could impose a fine on an undertaking in respect of the same matter in the same market.[635] The question has also arisen in relation to situations where fines have already been imposed outside the EU. The principle here is technically a corollary of *ne bis in idem*, as the undertakings are not pleading that the Commission had no right to take the proceedings, but only

---

[625] Case T-304/02, *Hoek Loos NV v Commission* [2006] ECR II-1887.

[626] [2003] OJ L84/1.

[627] Case T-304/02, *Hoek Loos* [2006] ECR II-1887, para. 85.

[628] Case T-279/02, [2006] ECR II-897. Degussa's further appeal against the fine was rejected, Case C-266/06 P, *Evonik Degussa GmbH v Commission* [2008] ECR I-81.

[629] Case C-580/12 P, *Guardian Industries Corp v Commission* EU:C:2014:2363.

[630] For the issue of whether competition proceedings are civil or criminal, see Section 7.B.ii, p. 895.

[631] Cases 18 and 35/65, *Gutmann v Commission of the EAEC* [1966] ECR 149; Commission Green Paper, 'On Conflicts of Jurisdiction and the Principle of *ne bis in idem* in Criminal Proceedings', COM(2005) 696 final; M. Wasmeier and N. Thwaites, 'The Development of *ne bis in idem* into a Transnational Fundamental Right in EU Law: Comments on Recent Developments' (2006) 31 *ELRev* 565; R. Nazzini, 'Fundamental Rights beyond Legal Positivism: Rethinking the *Ne Bis in Idem* Principle in EU Competition Law' (2014) 2 *J of Antitrust Enforcement* 225; A. Andreangeli, *EU Competition Enforcement and Human Rights* (Edward Elgar, 2008), 207–212.

[632] Cases C-238/99 P etc., *Limburgse Vinyl Maatschappij* [2002] ECR I-8375, para. 59. In that case the CJ confirmed that the Commission could readopt a decision annulled on procedural grounds without going through all the unimpeached parts of the procedure again.

[633] Cases C-101 and 110/07 P, *Cooperate de France Bétail et Viande and FNSEA v Commission* [2008] ECR I-10193.

[634] See Section 9.B.

[635] See W. Wils, 'The Principle of *Ne Bis in Idem* in EC Antitrust Enforcement: A Legal and Economic Analysis' (2003) 26 *World Competition* 131.

that it should have taken into account concurrent penalties concerning the same facts. The CJ held in *Archer Daniels Midland*[636] that the Commission was justified in refusing to take into account when fixing the fine that the undertaking had already been sanctioned in the US for the same cartel, at least where it had not been proved that the actions complained of were identical.[637] In *Showa Denko* the CJ explained that in applying competition law the Commission is protecting specific Community (Union) interests, that the objective of deterrence which the Commission is entitled to pursue when setting the fine is to ensure compliance with the competition rules, and that consequently 'when assessing the deterrent nature of a fine to be imposed for infringement of those rules, the Commission is not required to take into account any penalties imposed on an undertaking for infringement of the competition rules of non-member States'.[638] The CJ therefore holds that in competition cases *ne bis in idem* applies only when three conditions are fulfilled: identity of the facts, unity of the offender, and unity of the legal interest protected.[639]

k. Liability for Fines

The consequences of the single economic entity doctrine for the liability of parent companies for infringements by subsidiaries and the problems where an undertaking responsible for an infringement no longer exists (or no longer exists in an identical form) are discussed in Chapter 3.[640]

l. The Payment and Collection of Fines

The payment of fines is enforceable pursuant to Article 299 TFEU which provides that enforcement of decisions of the Council or Commission which impose a pecuniary obligation on persons other than States shall be governed by the rules of civil procedure in force in the State in the territory of which it is carried out. Member States must designate a relevant national authority for enforcement purposes.[641] Fines are normally expressed in euros. Decisions normally give the undertakings concerned three months in which to pay the fine and specify a bank account into which it is to be paid. They normally state that interest becomes payable after the specified time.[642] A challenge to the decision before the GC does not operate to suspend the payment of the fine but the Commission usually agrees to defer enforcing it pending the outcome of the appeal if the undertakings agree to pay interest on it and provide a bank guarantee. The question of whether fines are tax deductible arose in the Article 267 reference, *XBV*. While not expressly ruling on the tax deductibility of fines the CJ has clearly disapproved of it, saying that it might significantly reduce the effectiveness of the Commission decision.[643]

---

[636] Case C-397/03 P, *Archer Daniels Midland Co v Commission* [2006] ECR I-4429, paras. 46–53.

[637] Archer Daniels Midland had paid US$70 million for its involvement in the lysine cartel in the US and Canadian $16 million for its involvement in lysine (amino acid) and citric acid cartels in Canada. Moreover, its executives had been jailed in the US. See also Case T-410/03, *Hoechst GmbH v Commission* [2008] ECR II-881, paras. 597–606.

[638] Case C-289/04 P, *Showa Denko v Commission* [2006] ECR I-5859, para. 61.

[639] Cases C-204/00 P etc., *Aalborg Portland and others v Commission* [2004] ECR I-123, para. 338; Case C-17/10, *Toshiba v Úřad pro ochranu hospodářské soutěže* EU:C:2012:72, para. 97.

[640] Chapter 3.5.A.vi, p. 126.

[641] The UK has designated the High Court (the Court of Session in Scotland) pursuant to the European Communities (Enforcement of Community Judgments) Order 1972 (SI 1972/1590). Fines are enforced as if they were judgments of the UK courts.

[642] The payment of interest was approved by the CJ in Case 107/82, *AEG-Telefunken v Commission* [1983] ECR 3151; see also the GC in Case T-275/94, *Groupement des Cartes Bancaires 'CB' v Commission* [1995] ECR II-2169. In Case C-564/08 P, *SGL Carbon AG v Commission* [2009] ECR I-191, the CJ confirmed that the Commission could set a higher rate of interest than the market rate applicable to ordinary borrowers.

[643] Case C-429/07, *Inspecteur van de Belastingdienst v Commission* [2009] ECR I-4833, para. 39. The case was the first occasion on which the Commission intervened in national proceedings.

(v) The Leniency Policy in Cartel Cases

a. General

In Chapter 9 we discuss cartels and the problems in detecting them and in proving them to the standard required by the EU Courts, particularly where oligopolistic industries are concerned. The leniency policy (or 'programme') is the Commission's major weapon in the fight against cartels.[644]

Although it has the inspection powers described previously in this chapter, obtaining direct evidence of a cartel is much easier if participants can be induced to turn informer. This was demonstrated in *Cartonboard* in 1994 when one of the ringleaders 'spontaneously admitted' the infringement and provided detailed evidence to the Commission, receiving in return a greatly reduced fine.[645] In 1996 the Commission published a Notice (the Leniency Notice) putting the practice on a systematic footing.[646] It provided that in the event of participants in cartels giving information to the Commission and cooperating with it in the investigation they could expect a reduction in the fine which would otherwise be imposed, or even no fine at all.[647] It did not, however, *guarantee* full immunity to the first participant to come forward (as did the US and Canadian policies).[648]

The Commission therefore published an amended Notice in 2002[649] which, amongst other improvements, did guarantee immunity to the first undertaking to submit evidence which met certain criteria, if the undertaking fulfilled certain conditions. Some problems remained, but the increased certainty it offered, in particular the guaranteed 100 per cent immunity, made it an outstandingly successful tool in the fight against cartels.[650] Guaranteed immunity set the scene for the 'race to the Commission's door' as there can be only one grant of immunity per cartel.

The 2002 Notice was replaced by the current one in 2006.[651] The 2006 Notice (the Notice) is consistent with the ECN Model Leniency Programme (MLP) adopted to deal with the problems of divergences between national leniency policies.[652] Explicit legislative provision for the leniency policy was provided for the first time when Regulation 773/2004 was amended in 2015.[653] The details are still to be found in the Notice (as provided in Regulation 773/2004, Article 4a(1)).[654] The Commission

---

[644] See Chap. 9, Section 2.B, p. 656.

[645] [1994] OJ L243/1, para. 171. Its fine was reduced by two-thirds to ECU 11.25 million, representing 3% of its turnover in the Community cartonboard market for the relevant year, rather than the 9% suffered by the other ringleaders. See the discussion in the GC judgments in the appeals from the decision, e.g., Case T-319/94, *Fiskeby Board AB v Commission* [1998] ECR II-1331 paras. 86–104.

[646] Commission Notice on the non-imposition or reduction of fines in cartel cases [1996] OJ C204/14.

[647] The Leniency Notices only apply in cartel cases, Case T-13/03, *Nintendo v Commission* [2009] ECR II-975.

[648] The US policy only grants immunity. Reductions of fines are dealt with under a plea-bargaining process.

[649] Commission Notice on immunity from fines and reduction of fines in cartel cases [2002] OJ C45/3. For comments on the Notice, see, e.g., N. Levy and R. O'Donoghue, 'The EU Leniency Programme Comes of Age' (2004) 92 *World Competition* 75–99.

[650] See B. van Barlingen and M. Barennes, 'The European Commission's 2002 Leniency Notice in Practice' (2005) 3 *Competition Policy Newsletter* 6.

[651] Commission Notice on immunity from fines and reduction of fines in cartel cases [2006] OJ C298/11; Commission Press Release, IP/06/1705. See S. Suurnäkki and M. L. Tierno Centella, 'Commission Adopts Revised Leniency Notice to Reward Companies that Report Hardcore Cartels' (2007) 1 *Competition Policy Newsletter* 7. It applied from 8 December 2006 to all cases in which no undertaking had already contacted the Commission in order to claim leniency (except that the provisions on the protection of corporate statements (paras. 31–35) applied to all pending applications as well).

[652] <http://ec.europa.eu/comm/competition/ecn/model_leniency_en.pdf>; see Section 9.B.iii. There is no EU-wide system of leniency, and an application for leniency to the Commission does not count as an application to an NCA, see Case C-428/14, *DHL Express Italy srl and DHL Global Forwarding (Italy)* EU:C:2016:27, discussed in Section 9.B.iii, p. 1019.

[653] Reg. 2015/1348 [2015] OJ L208/3, Art. 1 inserted a new Art. 4a into Reg. 773/2004.

[654] The Notice was amended by [2015] OJ C256/1, in respect of the access to the file provision (para. 34); see Section 7.D.v, p. 933.

may not depart in an individual case from the rules of practice set out in the Notice without giving reasons compatible with the principle of equal treatment.[655] The leniency policy is not binding on the Member States.[656]

The EU leniency policy does not provide for what is known as 'Amnesty Plus' (or 'Leniency Plus')[657] whereby an applicant for leniency in respect of one cartel is further rewarded if it reveals another cartel in the course of the proceedings.[658]

Regulation 773/2004 [2004] OJ L123/18

Article 4a

The Commission's Leniency Programme

1. The Commission may set the requirements and cooperation conditions under which it may reward undertakings that are or have been party to secret cartels, for their cooperation in disclosing the cartel and facilitating the establishment of an infringement, with immunity from fines or a reduction in fines which would otherwise be imposed under Article 23(2) of Regulation (EC) No 1/2003 (the Commission leniency programme).

   Immunity from fines may be granted to the undertaking that is the first to submit evidence which in the Commission's view would enable it to carry out a targeted inspection or find an infringement of Article 101 of the Treaty in connection with the alleged cartel. A reduction in fines may be granted to undertakings which provide the Commission with evidence of the alleged infringement which represents significant added value with respect to the evidence already in the Commission's possession.

   The Commission will only grant immunity from or a reduction of the fine under its leniency programme if, at the end of the administrative proceedings, the undertaking has met the requirements and cooperation conditions set out in the leniency programme. Those may cover, among others, the type of information and evidence the undertakings are required to submit and the further cooperation expected from the undertakings during the administrative proceedings.

2. In order to qualify for immunity from or reduction of the fine which would otherwise be imposed, undertakings shall provide the Commission with voluntary presentations of their knowledge of a secret cartel and their role therein, which may be also in the form of voluntary presentations of the knowledge of former or current employees or representatives of the undertaking (leniency corporate statements). Such leniency corporate statements shall be drawn up specifically for submission to the Commission with a view to obtaining immunity from or reduction of fines under the Commission's leniency programme.

3. The Commission will offer parties appropriate methods of providing leniency corporate statements other than by written submission, including orally. Oral corporate statements may be recorded and transcribed at the Commission's premises. The undertaking shall be granted an opportunity to check the technical accuracy of the recording of its oral statement at the Commission's premises, and, where necessary, to correct the substance of the statement without delay. The rules in this Regulation on leniency corporate statements shall apply to such statements irrespective of the medium on which they are stored. Pre-existing information, i.e. evidence that exists irrespective of the Commission proceedings and that is submitted to the Commission by an undertaking in the context of its application for immunity from or reduction of the fine, is not part of a leniency corporate statement.

---

[655] Case C-510/11 P, *Kone Oyj v Commission* EU:C:2013:696, para. 29.

[656] Case C-557/12, *Kone AG v ÖBB-Infrastruktur AG* EU:C:2014:1317, para. 36.

[657] See D. McElwee, 'Should the European Commission adopt "Amnesty Plus" in its Fight Against Hardcore Cartels?' [2004] *ECLR* 558.

[658] The UK's NCA, the Competition and Markets Authority (CMA)) operates an amnesty plus system, set out in OFT 423, 'Guidance as to the appropriate amount of a penalty', paras. 3.21–3.22, as does the US. And see M. Martyniszyn, 'Leniency (Amnesty Plus): A Building Block or a Trojan Horse' (2015) 3 *J of Antitrust Enforcement* 391.

The Commission website has a section devoted to leniency which explains exactly how to apply for leniency and gives practical information.[659]

b. The Main Features of the Leniency Policy

- Immunity is guaranteed to the first undertaking to submit evidence sufficient for the Commission either to mount a targeted Article 20(4) inspection or to enable the Commission to find an infringement, if certain other conditions (i.e. full, continuous, and expeditious cooperation with the Commission, as set out in paragraph 12 of the Notice)[660] are fulfilled. The Notice sets out what type of information and evidence applicants need to submit to qualify for immunity: it links the threshold for immunity to what the Commission needs in order to carry out a 'targeted inspection'; it explains what applicants are and are not required to produce in their initial application; and it states explicitly that applicants need to disclose their participation in the cartel. In addition the undertaking has to end its involvement in the cartel. Immunity is not available to undertakings that have coerced others to participate in the infringement.

- Undertakings which approach the Commission later are eligible for a reduction in the fine that would otherwise have been imposed, subject to the same ongoing cooperation as for immunity applicants. However, nothing is guaranteed to them.

- A discretionary 'marker system' (first introduced in 2006) provides for an applicant for immunity to reserve its first place in the queue by initially providing only limited information.

- Corporate statements made by undertakings applying for leniency are protected from discovery procedures in civil actions for damages.

- The application of the Notice allows the Commission considerable discretion on crucial matters, such as what amounts to sufficient evidence and information to satisfy paragraphs 8(a) and 8(b) or qualifies as 'significant added value' under paragraph 26. However, this discretion is subject to an in-depth review of the law and the facts by the GC.[661]

c. Immunity

Commission Notice on Immunity from Fines and Reduction of Fines in Cartel Cases [2006] OJ C298/17

II. Immunity from Fines

A. Requirements to qualify for immunity from fines

(8) The Commission will grant immunity from any fine which would otherwise have been imposed to an undertaking disclosing its participation in an alleged cartel affecting the Community if that undertaking is the first to submit information and evidence which in the Commission's view will enable it to:

(a) carry out a targeted inspection in connection with the alleged cartel . . . or

(b) find an infringement of Article [101] EC in connection with the alleged cartel.

---

[659] <http://ec.europa.eu/competition/cartels/leniency/leniency.html>.

[660] In COMP/38.281, *Italian Raw Tobacco*, Deltafina applied for immunity under the 2002 Leniency Notice (the first undertaking to apply under that Notice). It was granted conditional immunity but later revealed at a meeting with the other cartelists, before the Commission had mounted investigations under Reg. 17, Art. 14(3) at the premises of the other undertakings, that it had confessed to the Commission and applied for immunity. The Commission withdrew the conditional immunity on the grounds that Deltafina had failed to cooperate continuously and expeditiously as such cooperation included refraining from taking any step which could undermine the Commission's ability to investigate and/or find the infringement (para. 432). The decision was upheld, Case C-578/11 P, *Deltafina SpA v Commission* EU:C:2014:1742.

[661] See eg Case C-510/11 P, *Kone* EU:C:2013:696; Case C-455/11 P, *Solvay SA v Commission* EU:C:2013:796.

(9) For the Commission to be able to carry out a targeted inspection within the meaning of point (8)(a), the undertaking must provide the Commission with the information and evidence listed below, to the extent that this, in the Commission's view, would not jeopardize the inspections:

(a) A corporate statement . . . which includes, in so far as it is known to the applicant at the time of submission:

— A detailed description of the alleged cartel arrangement, including for instance its aims, activities and functioning; the product or service concerned, the geographic scope, the duration of and the estimated market volumes affected by the alleged cartel; the specific dates, locations, content of and participants in alleged cartel contacts, and all relevant explanations in connection with the pieces of evidence provided in support of the application.

— The name and address of the legal entity submitting the immunity application as well as the names and addresses of all the other undertakings that participate(d) in the alleged cartel;

— The names, positions, office locations and, where necessary, home addresses of all individuals who, to the applicant's knowledge, are or have been involved in the alleged cartel, including those individuals which have been involved on the applicant's behalf;

— Information on which other competition authorities, inside or outside the EU, have been approached or are intended to be approached in relation to the alleged cartel; and

(b) Other evidence relating to the alleged cartel in possession of the applicant or available to it at the time of the submission, including in particular any evidence contemporaneous to the infringement.

(10) Immunity pursuant to point (8)(a) will not be granted if, at the time of the submission, the Commission had already sufficient evidence to adopt a decision to carry out an inspection in connection with the alleged cartel or had already carried out such an inspection.

(11) Immunity pursuant to point (8)(b) will only be granted on the cumulative conditions that the Commission did not have, at the time of the submission, sufficient evidence to find an infringement of Article [101] EC in connection with the alleged cartel and that no undertaking had been granted conditional immunity from fines under point (8)(a) in connection with the alleged cartel. In order to qualify, an undertaking must be the first to provide contemporaneous, incriminating evidence of the alleged cartel as well as a corporate statement containing the kind of information specified in point (9)(a), which would enable the Commission to find an infringement of Article [101] EC.

(12) In addition to the conditions set out in points (8)(a), (9) and (10) or in points (8)(b) and 11, all the following conditions must be met in any case to qualify for any immunity from a fine:

(a) The undertaking cooperates genuinely, fully, on a continuous basis and expeditiously from the time it submits its application throughout the Commission's administrative procedure. This includes:

— providing the Commission promptly with all relevant information and evidence relating to the alleged cartel that comes into its possession or is available to it;

— remaining at the Commission's disposal to answer promptly to any request that may contribute to the establishment of the facts;

— making current (and, if possible, former) employees and directors available for interviews with the Commission;

— not destroying, falsifying or concealing relevant information or evidence relating to the alleged cartel; and

— not disclosing the fact or any of the content of its application before the Commission has issued a statement of objections in the case, unless otherwise agreed;

(b) The undertaking ended its involvement in the alleged cartel immediately following its application, except for what would, in the Commission's view, be reasonably necessary to preserve the integrity of the inspections;

(c) When contemplating making its application to the Commission, the undertaking must not have destroyed, falsified or concealed evidence of the alleged cartel nor disclosed the fact or any of the content of its contemplated application, except to other competition authorities.

(13) An undertaking which took steps to coerce other undertakings to join the cartel or to remain in it is not eligible for immunity from fines. It may still qualify for a reduction of fines if it fulfils the relevant requirements and meets all the conditions therefor.

The applicant for immunity is required to make a leniency corporate statement containing the matters set out in paragraph 9. The threshold for immunity (paragraph 8 in the extract) is information and evidence which enables the Commission to carry out a targeted inspection or to find an Article 101 infringement. 'Targeted' inspection was a new concept in the 2006 Notice and means that the Commission is able to carry out a more focused Article 20 inspection with precise 'insider' information 'as to, for instance, what to look for and where in terms of evidence'.[662] The great problem for undertakings contemplating immunity applications is that at the time of the submission the Commission must not already have sufficient evidence to carry out the inspection or find an infringement, and the undertaking has to be the first participant to provide it. So there is no immunity if the Commission has already gathered the necessary evidence, or if the undertaking is not the first to approach the Commission. The threshold for evidence required under paragraph 8(a) is lower than that under paragraph 8(b) (contemporaneous and incriminating—a very high standard) in order to encourage undertakings to come forward early.[663]

Paragraph 12 sets out (in accordance with the case law on the earlier Notices) exactly what is involved in the required ongoing cooperation. The third indent (making employees and directors available for interview with the Commission) is a reference to Article 19 of Regulation 1/2003.[664] The Commission recognises that these individuals may not be keen on being interviewed, in the light of the criminal proceedings for cartel participation under the laws of some of the Member States,[665] but has said that the provisions in Article 12 on the exchange of information within the ECN[666] should be a sufficient safeguard for them.[667] The information the undertaking has to provide in its corporate statement—the confession which the leniency applicant has to make to the Commission—has to include, where necessary and as far as the applicant knows them, the home addresses of implicated individuals. This reflects the powers of the Commission under Article 21 of Regulation 1/2003 to carry out inspections at private premises.

The 2006 Notice introduced a 'marker' system by which an undertaking may reserve its place in the queue for immunity (but not for fine reduction) by making an application which gives limited information. It is then given a period of time (set at the Commission's discretion)[668] to 'perfect' the application by providing the additional evidence required to reach the immunity threshold.

Commission Notice on Immunity from Fines and Reduction of Fines in Cartel Cases [2006] OJ C298/17

II. Immunity from Fines

(15) The Commission services may grant a marker protecting an immunity applicant's place in the queue for a period to be specified on a case-by-case basis in order to allow for the gathering of the necessary information and evidence. To be eligible to secure a marker, the applicant must provide the Commission with information concerning its name and address, the parties to the alleged cartel, the

---

[662] MEMO/06/469, 7 December 2006. The quality of the applicant's submission is judged *ex ante*, and not in the light of what actually happens at the inspection.

[663] For a typical argument (under the 2002 Notice) of what constitutes sufficient evidence, see Case T-521/09, *Alstom Grid SAS v Commission* EU:T:2014:1000.

[664] See Section 7.C.v, p. 917.

[665] See Section 11, p. 1022.

[666] See the discussion of Art. 12, in Section 9.B.ii, p. 1016.

[667] MEMO/06/469. For the problems of the exchange of information within the ECN, see Section 9.B.ii and A. Andreangeli, 'The Impact of the Modernisation Regulation on the Guarantees of Due Process in Competition Proceedings' (2006) 31 *ELRev* 342.

[668] In MEMO/06/469 the Commission expressly refrained from giving any indication about the length of time; it 'will need to be decided based on the circumstances of each case'.

affected products(s) and territory(-ies), the estimated duration of the alleged cartel and the nature of the cartel conduct. The applicant should also inform the Commission on other past or possible future leniency applications to other authorities in relation to the alleged cartel and justify its request for a marker. Where a marker is granted, the Commission services determine the period within which the applicant has to perfect the marker by submitting the information and evidence required to meet the relevant threshold for immunity. Undertakings which have been granted a marker cannot perfect it by making a formal application in hypothetical terms. If the applicant perfects the marker within the period set by the Commission services, the information and evidence provided will be deemed to have been submitted on the date when the marker was granted.

(16) An undertaking making a formal immunity application to the Commission must:

(a) provide the Commission with all information and evidence relating to the alleged cartel available to it, as specified in points (8) and (9), including corporate statements; or

(b) initially present this information and evidence in hypothetical terms, in which case the undertaking must present a detailed descriptive list of the evidence it proposes to disclose at a later agreed date. This list should accurately reflect the nature and content of the evidence, whilst safeguarding the hypothetical nature of its disclosure. Copies of documents, from which sensitive parts have been removed, may be used to illustrate the nature and content of the evidence. The name of the applying undertaking and of other undertakings involved in the alleged cartel need not be disclosed until the evidence described in its application is submitted. However, the product or service concerned by the alleged cartel, the geographic scope of the alleged cartel and the estimated duration must be clearly identified.

It is still possible to make a formal application in 'hypothetical terms' but a marker cannot be perfected by a hypothetical application. The difference between a marker and a formal application in hypothetical terms has been explained by the Commission as follows:[669]

A marker and a hypothetical application cannot be combined due to their different purposes and features. The hypothetical application is available to allow companies to ascertain whether the evidence in their possession would meet the immunity threshold before disclosing their identity or the infringement. In a hypothetical application, the company is supposed to actually show the evidence liable to meet the relevant immunity threshold, although it can be done by means of edited copies with the data that could identify the company and the cartel at that stage deleted.

In contrast, a marker is granted to protect the place in the queue of an applicant which has not yet gathered the evidence necessary to formalise an immunity application. In order to protect the place in the queue without obtaining the relevant evidence in exchange, the Commission must be in a position to ascertain whether it already has a previous immunity application for the same cartel and ensure that the company is seriously engaged to provide the evidence. Therefore, in order to obtain a marker, a company is expected to provide certain data listed in the Notice, which include the identity of the applicant and some details on the cartel, but not the rest of the evidence required to meet the immunity threshold. This can be submitted later within a specified timeframe.

d. Reductions in the Fine

Undertakings which do not meet the criteria for immunity can get a reduction of the fine. How much reduction depends on their position in the queue: the first gets 30–50 per cent, the second

---

[669] MEMO/06/469. Hypothetical applications, which were introduced by the 2002 Notice, were often popularly referred to as 'markers', although this was misleading, see B. van Barlingen, 'The European Commission's 2002 Leniency Notice After One Year of Operation' (2003) 2 *Competition Policy Newsletter* 16, 18. The 2006 Notice makes it clear that putting down a marker and making a hypothetical application are different things.

20–30 per cent, and the subsequent ones up to 20 per cent. They are required to produce information of 'significant added value'[670] and comply with the same cooperation stipulations as are imposed on immunity applicants by paragraph 12. Obviously, the further down the queue an undertaking is, the more difficult it is to produce information of 'significant added value' to the Commission. There is no 'marker' system in respect of reductions.

Commission Notice on Immunity from Fines and Reduction of Fines in Cartel Cases [2006] OJ C298/17

III. Reduction of a Fine

A. Requirements to qualify for reduction of a fine

(23) Undertakings disclosing their participation in an alleged cartel affecting the Community that do not meet the conditions under section II above may be eligible to benefit from a reduction of any fine that would otherwise have been imposed.

(24) In order to qualify, an undertaking must provide the Commission with evidence of the alleged infringement which represents significant added value with respect to the evidence already in the Commission's possession and must meet the cumulative conditions set out in points 12(a) to 12(c) above.

(25) The concept of 'added value' refers to the extent to which the evidence provided strengthens, by its very nature and/or its level of detail, the Commission's ability to prove the alleged cartel. In this assessment, the Commission will generally consider written evidence originating from the period of time to which the facts pertain to have a greater value than evidence subsequently established. Incriminating evidence directly relevant to the facts in question will generally be considered to have a greater value than that with only indirect relevance. Similarly, the degree of corroboration from other sources required for the evidence submitted to be relied upon against undertakings involved in the case will have an impact on the value of that evidence, so that compelling evidence will be attributed a greater value than evidence such as statements which require corroboration if contested.

(26) The Commission will determine in any final decision adopted at the end of the administrative procedure the level of reduction an undertaking will benefit from, relative to the fine which would otherwise be imposed. For the:

— first undertaking to provide significant added value: a reduction of 30–50%,
— second undertaking to provide significant added value: a reduction of 20–30%,
— subsequent undertakings that provide significant added value: a reduction of up to 20%.

In order to determine the level of reduction within each of these bands, the Commission will take into account the time at which the evidence fulfilling the condition in point (24) was submitted and the extent to which it represents added value.

If the applicant for the reduction of a fine is the first to submit compelling evidence in the sense of point (25) which the Commission uses to establish additional facts increasing the gravity or the duration of the infringement, the Commission will not take such additional facts into account when setting any fine to be imposed on the undertaking which provided this evidence.

---

[670] For what amounts to 'significant added value' and the GC disagreeing with the Commission on this matter, see, e.g., Case T-186/06, *Solvay v Commission* [2011] ECR II- 2839, upheld Case C- 455/11 P, *Solvay SA v Commission* EU:C:2013:796; Case T-154/09, *Manuli Rubber Industries v Commission* EU:T:2013:260; Case T-406/09, *Donau Chemie v Commission* EU:T:2014:254.

e. Corporate Statements and Civil Litigation

As the Commission points out in the Notice[671] nothing in the leniency programme can protect an undertaking in a civil action brought by injured third parties.[672] This is an important consideration, as plaintiffs can rely on Commission decisions before national courts in the EU. It is possible that an increase in private damages actions in national courts may therefore serve as a disincentive to undertakings to take advantage of the leniency programme. Such damages actions have been facilitated by the Damages Directive[673] but, as explained in respect of access to the file,[674] the Commission does not want private litigation to discourage leniency applicants. Provisions in the Damages Directive,[675] and in the amended Regulation 773/2004, the amended Notice on access to the file, and the amended Leniency Notice itself, protect leniency corporate statements from being used in national proceedings. It is still possible, however, that an application to access to the statement under the Transparency Regulation could succeed.

In order to protect statements from possible discovery actions, the Commission has for some time allowed leniency applicants to make oral corporate statements[676] of which only the Commission retains a transcript. This procedure was formalised in the 2006 Notice. The Notice provides that a leniency applicant may make oral corporate statements at the Commission's premises which the Commission will record and transcribe, and which the applicant must then listen to and check.[677] The rationale is that if the transcript is part of the Commission's file, and access is limited only to addressees of an SO in the same case[678] under strict conditions,[679] and the applicant itself does not retain a copy of the statement, third parties will not be able to use discovery procedures to obtain it.

However, in *AKZO Nobel* the GC upheld the recent Commission policy of publishing less heavily redacted versions of its cartel decisions.[680] This increases the amount of useful information (much of it derived from leniency statements) that damages claimants can derive from the published decision and may decrease the attractiveness of leniency for undertakings.[681]

---

[671] 2006 Notice, para. 31.

[672] E.g., Aventis, given immunity in *Vitamins*, was subsequently sued for compensation along with its fellow conspirators. See Chap. 14 for actions in national courts.

[673] See n. 325.

[674] Section 7.D.v.

[675] Ibid.

[676] In the *Citric Acid Cartel* [2001] OJ L239/18 one undertaking for the first time obtained a 90% reduction on the basis of an oral statement. In Cases T-236/01 etc., *Tokai Carbon* [2004] ECR II-1181 and Case T-15/02, *BASF v Commission* [2006] ECR II-497, the GC held that (under the 1996 Notice) statements could be made to the Commission orally.

[677] 2006 Notice, para. 32. The Commission published new guidance 'Delivering Oral Statements at DG Competition' in October 2013, available on the Commission website, <http://ec/europa.eu/competition/cartels/leniency/oral_statements_procedure_en.pdf>. Only the description of the alleged cartel can be provided orally—other information such as product and market description, general market information, and publicly available information has to be submitted in writing (para. 2 of 'Delivering Oral Statements').

[678] Because of the rights of the defence: see Commission Notice on the rules for access to the Commission file [2005] OJ C325/7, see Section 7.D.v, p. 934.

[679] The other parties and their lawyers may not make any copy by any mechanical or electronic means and may use the information only 'for the purposes of judicial or administrative proceedings for the application of the Union competition rules' under pain of doing otherwise being counted as lack of cooperation under the Leniency Notice, and of having their fine increased (in the case of undertakings) and of being reported to their professional body (in the case of external lawyers), Leniency Notice, paras. 33 and 34 (as amended by [2015] OJ C256/1).

[680] Case T-345/12, *Akzo Nobel NV v Commission* EU:T:2015:50; see A. Kafetzopoulos, 'European Commission Policy on Publication of Cartel Decisions: The Latest Victory of Damage Claimants Against Leniency Applicants' [2015] *ECLR* 295.

[681] See C. Swaak and R. Wessling, 'Reconsidering the Leniency Option: If Not First In, Good Reasons to Stay Out' [2015] *ECLR* 346, who argue that the degree of exposure makes it particularly less attractive for undertakings who will merely qualify for a reduction, which may be quite small.

I. SECTOR INQUIRIES

As explained in Chapter 9,[682] Article 17 of Regulation 1/2003 provides for the Commission to conduct general inquiries into a sector of the economy. To this end the Commission has the powers to require information and carry out inspections contained in Articles 18, 19, and 20 (but not 21)[683] and to request the NCAs to carry out investigations under Article 22. It may impose fines and penalties under Articles 23 and 24 (for example, to sanction the provision of incorrect information).

J. THE POWERS OF THE COMMISSION AND DUE PROCESS

The preceding account of the enforcement system under Regulation 1/2003 shows the extent of the Commission's powers. We have already noted[684] the requirements of the relevant human rights instruments in respect of due process. The criticisms of the EU system of enforcement centres on the multiplicity of roles played by the Commission on the one hand and the limited role of the EU Courts in reviewing Commission decisions on the other. The main criticisms of the present position can be summed up as follows:

- there is no division between those who investigate, draft the decision, and propose the fine or other remedy;

- there is no hearing before an independent decision-maker on matters of substance, as the Hearing Officer's role is limited to overseeing the oral hearing (which is of a limited nature) and settling questions on procedural matters such as access to the file and confidentiality of documents;

- decisions imposing remedies and fines are ultimately taken by the entire College of Commissioners, which is political body of appointees. Severe sanctions are imposed on undertakings by people who have not heard or seen the parties or any of the evidence.

The increasing severity of the sanctions imposed with the blessing of the EU Courts has led to increased calls for reform.[685] Some proposals, such as strengthening the role of the Hearing Officer and separating the investigation, prosecution, and decision-making functions, could be achieved without any Treaty amendment. Others, such as having a separate 'competition court' as an independent first instance adjudicator, would be more radical.

---

[682] Chap. 9, Section 4.C.ii, p. 710.

[683] The power to carry out inspections on non-business premises. The first dawn raids under Art. 20 in a sector inquiry were conducted when the pharmaceutical sector inquiry was launched, IP/08/49, 16 January 2008.

[684] See Section 7.B, p. 895 ff.

[685] See, e.g., I. Forrester, 'Due Process in EC Competition Case: A Distinguished Institution with Flawed Procedures' (2009) 34 *ELRev* 817; B. Vesterdorf, 'Due Process Before the Commission of the European Union? Some Reflections Upon Reading the Commission Draft Paper on Best Practices in Antitrust Proceedings' (2010) 1 *CPI Antitrust Journal* April; D. Slater, S. Thomas, and D. Waelbroeck, 'Competition Law Proceedings before the European Commission and the Right to a Fair Trial: No Need for Reform?' (2009) *European Competition Journal* 97, 106; GCLC Working Paper 04/08; A. Andreangeli, 'Towards an EU Competition Court: "Article-6-Proofing" Antitrust Proceedings before the Commission?' (2007) 4 *World Competition* 595; R. Nazzini, 'Administrative Enforcement, Judicial Review and Fundamental Rights in EU Competition Law: A Comparative Contextual-Functionalist Perspective' (2012) 49 *CMLRev* 971. For a robust defence (mainly from those within the system), see F. Castillo de la Torre, 'Evidence, Proof and Judicial Review in Cartel Cases' (2009) 3 *World Competition* 505; P. Lowe, 'Cartels, Fines and Due Process' (2009) 2 *Global Competition Policy*; W. Wils, 'The Increased Level of Antitrust Fines, Judicial Review, and the European Convention on Human Rights' (2010) 33 *World Competition* 5; Sibony, see n. 96.

8. PROCEEDINGS BEFORE THE COURT OF JUSTICE OF THE EUROPEAN UNION

A. JUDICIAL REVIEW

(i) General

Commission competition decisions can be challenged in an action for annulment under Article 263 TFEU.[686] Since 1989 annulment actions have gone first to the GC with an appeal on a point of law to the CJ. Before the inception of the GC (originally the Court of First Instance) they went straight to the CJ. Although these actions are colloquially called 'appeals' they are in fact reviews of legality, i.e. judicial review proceedings. They do not entail a rehearing. The question of the intensity of the review in which the GC engages when reviewing Commission competition decisions is a burning issue. As the Commission is not a tribunal for the purposes of Article 6(1) ECHR or Article 47 of the Charter the supervision by the GC must satisfy the requirement for a fair and public hearing before an independent and impartial tribunal if the competition proceedings are to comply with the Convention and the Charter.[687]

Under Article 261 TFEU[688] the CJEU has 'unlimited jurisdiction' in respect of fines and penalties imposed by the Commission in competition cases.

The review process before the GC is often protracted.[689] In cartel cases, for example, there may be numerous parties who appeal to the GC, all claiming slightly different defects in the details of the Commission's procedure. There may then be an appeal to the CJ. By the end the argument may be about events which took place 20 years earlier.[690]

(ii) Article 263 TFEU

Article 263 states:

The Court of Justice of the European Union shall review the legality of legislative acts, of acts of the Council, of the Commission and of the European Central Bank, other than recommendations and opinions, and of acts of the European Parliament and of the European Council intended to produce legal effects vis-à-vis third parties. It shall also review the legality of acts of bodies, offices or agencies of the Union intended to produce legal effects vis-à-vis third parties.

It shall for this purpose have jurisdiction in actions brought by a Member State, the European Parliament, the Council or the Commission on grounds of lack of competence, infringement of an essential procedural requirement, infringement of the Treaties or of any rule of law relating to their application, or misuse of powers.

The Court shall have jurisdiction under the same conditions in actions brought by the Court of Auditors, by the European Central Bank and by the Committee of the Regions for the purpose of protecting their prerogatives.

---

[686] Ex Art. 230 EC.

[687] See Section 7.B.ii.a.

[688] Ex Art. 229 EC.

[689] The expedited procedure for cases of urgency (currently Rules of Procedure of the General Court [2015] OJ L105/45, Arts. 151–155) is not usually applicable to this kind of appeal.

[690] The limitation period laid down in Reg. 1/2003, Art. 25, runs only from the day the infringement ceases. In *Cement Cartel*, for example, the Commission commenced its investigations in 1989, and adopted the decision in 1994, [1994] OJ L343/1. It found infringements going back to January 1983. The GC judgment was delivered in 2000 (Cases T-25/95 etc., *Cimenteries* [2000] ECR II-491) and the CJ judgment in January 2004 (Cases C-204/00 P etc., *Aalborg Portland A/S and others v Commission* [2004] ECR I-12).

Any natural or legal person may, under the conditions laid down in the first and second paragraphs, institute proceedings against an act addressed to that person or which is of direct and individual concern to them, and against a regulatory act which is of direct concern to them and does not entail implementing measures.

Acts setting up bodies, offices and agencies of the Union may lay down specific conditions and arrangements concerning actions brought by natural or legal persons against acts of these bodies, offices or agencies intended to produce legal effects in relation to them.

The proceedings provided for in this Article shall be instituted within two months of the publication of the measure, or of its notification to the plaintiff, or, in the absence thereof, of the day on which it came to the knowledge of the latter, as the case may be.

The issues which arise from this provision in competition cases are:

- Is there a challengeable act?
- Does the natural or legal person wishing to make the challenge have standing to do so?
- Are there grounds for annulling the act?

There is a time limit (two months from publication or notification) for bringing an action. The limit is strictly applied.

(iii) *Locus Standi* —Who Can Bring an Action?

Under Article 263(4) a natural or legal person has limited standing, able only to challenge a decision actually addressed to them, an act which is of direct and individual concern to them, or a regulatory act of direct concern to them which does not entail implementing measures.[691]

The test formulated by the CJ for judging 'direct' and 'concern' is restrictive and generally makes it difficult for individuals to gain standing.[692] However, it has been more generously applied in competition cases. The CJ first allowed standing to a non-addressee of a decision in *Metro I*,[693] in respect of a party who had complained under Article 3(2)(b) of Regulation 17,[694] objecting to the granting of an exemption under Article 101(3). In *Metro II*[695] it widened the 'complainant' category to cover a party who had not *formally* complained but who had taken part in the Commission's proceedings and been recognised by the Commission as having a 'legitimate interest'. The applicant in both *Metro* cases was a retailer who was excluded by the provisions of an exempted selective distribution system from distributing the supplier's products. In *Métropole*[696] Antena 3 was refused admission to the European Broadcasting Union (EBU) as an active member before the Commission adopted a decision exempting the EBU's rules. Antena 3 brought an annulment action. It had not submitted observations.[697] The GC held that taking part in the administrative proceedings was not a prerequisite for being accorded standing, and that its application to join the EBU distinguished Antena 3 in the same way as if it were an addressee of the decision.

---

[691] Art. 263(4) appears not to have changed the situation under the corresponding provision in the EC Treaty, Art. 230(4) whereby a person could only challenge a decision which was of 'direct and individual concern' to it although in the form of a regulation or a decision addressed to *another* person. Legislation is not a 'regulatory act' within Art. 263(4): Case C-583/11 P, *Inuit Tapiiritt Kanatami v Parliament* EU:C:2013:625.

[692] It is whether the decision 'affects them by reason of certain attributes which are peculiar to them or by reason of circumstances in which they are differentiated from all other persons and by virtue of these factors distinguishes them individually just as in the case of the person addressed', Case 25/62, *Plaumann & Co v Commission* [1963] ECR 95.

[693] Case 26/76, *Metro SB-Grossmärkte GmbH v Commission (Metro I)* [1977] ECR 1875.

[694] Now Reg. 1/2003, Art. 7(2).

[695] Case 75/84, *Metro SB-Grossmärkte GmbH v Commission (Metro II)* [1986] ECR 3021.

[696] Cases T-528, 542, 543, and 546/93, *Métropole Télévision v Commission* [1996] ECR II-649.

[697] Following the publication of the Reg. 17, Art. 19(3) notice.

On the other hand, in *Kruidvat*[698] the Commission denied standing to a retailer who wished to challenge the Article 101(3) exemption of Givenchy's selective distribution network. It had taken no part in the Commission proceedings, had not complained to the Commission, had not applied to become a member of Givenchy's network, and did not wish to be one.[699] It was simply a competitor of Givenchy's authorised distributors. The GC agreed with the Commission's view that to grant Kruidvat standing would be to 'allow a practically limitless number of actions from unforeseeable sources to be brought' and said that individual concern could not be established on the basis that the legality of the decision might affect indirectly related national proceedings. Although there are no individual exemption decisions under Regulation 1/2003, it is possible that a third party might wish to challenge a 'finding of inapplicability' decision under Article 10.[700]

A non-addressee was allowed to challenge the Article 9 commitments decision in *Alrosa*.[701] Alrosa was directly and individually concerned by the decision: it was adopted at the conclusion of proceedings in which Alrosa had participated; it expressly referred to Alrosa; it was aimed at ending the long-standing trading relationship between Alrosa and the addressee; it was liable to have an appreciable effect on Alrosa's competitive position; and it produced direct and immediate effects on Alrosa's legal situation.

As far as representative bodies are concerned, the GC granted *locus standi* to the International Confederation of Societies of Authors and Composers in *CISAC*. The body was not an addressee of the decision but had been an addressee of the SO and the GC considered the decision was of direct and individual concern to it.[702]

(iv) Which Acts Can be Challenged?

It is not just formal decisions which can be challenged, but also other 'acts' taken by the Commission in the course of its procedures. The basic principle, laid down in *ERTA*,[703] is that Article 263 covers 'all measures adopted by the institutions which are intended to have legal force'. This was applied in *IBM*[704] where an undertaking wished to challenge the SO. The CJ said:

9. Any measure the legal effects of which are binding on, and capable of affecting the interests of, the applicant by bringing about a distinct change in his legal position is an act or decision which may be the object of an action under Article [263] for a declaration that it is void.

The test here is: does the act change the applicant's legal position? The SO does not do so; it is merely a preparatory act and any irregularity can be dealt with in a challenge to the act which concludes the proceedings. Although decisions authorising Article 20 inspections can be challenged, the *conduct* of an inspection may only be challenged in proceedings against any ensuing infringement decision, since the conduct amounts only to 'implementing measures'.[705]

---

[698] Case T-87/92, *BVBA Kruidvat v Commission* [1996] ECR II-1931.

[699] Its parent company was a member of a trade association which *had* participated, although the views of the association and of Kruidvat materially differed.

[700] See Section 7.E.iv, p. 954.

[701] Case T-170/06, *Alrosa v Commission* [2007] ECR II-2601, paras. 39–41; the judgment was set aside on appeal, Case C-441/07 P, *Alrosa* [2010] ECR I-5949, but the CJ did not deny Alrosa's right to standing (para. 90).

[702] Case T-442/08, *CISAC v Commission* EU:T:2013:188.

[703] Case 22/70, *Commission v Council, Re ERTA* [1971] ECR 263.

[704] Case 60/81, *IBM v Commission* [1981] ECR 2639.

[705] See Case T-135/09, *Nexans France* EU:T:2012:596, discussed in Section 7.C.iii. A challenge may be made to a fining decision under Art. 23(1) in respect of the undertaking's non-cooperation with the allegedly improper conduct of the inspection.

Interim decisions can be challenged.[706] Where complaints are concerned, 'Article 7' letters cannot be challenged but the final rejection of the complaint can be, even if it is only in the form of a letter.[707]

(v) The Grounds of Review

a. General

Article 263 provides four grounds of challenge, although they overlap and are in a sense all really encompassed in the third one, the infringement of the Treaties or of any rule of law relating to their application. Applicants often frame their cases in general terms. However, the infringement of an essential procedural requirement is a matter of public policy and must be raised by the Court of its own motion if it is not raised by the applicant[708] and so is lack of competence.[709] Otherwise the grounds can be considered only if they are raised by the applicant.[710] The fourth ground, misuse of powers (*détournement de pouvoir*) means that the Union institution has used its powers other than for the purpose for which they were conferred. A challenge on this ground very rarely succeeds as the burden on the applicant is a heavy one, and one has never succeeded in a competition case.[711]

b. Lack of Competence

Lack of competence covers: the lack of competence of the Union to act at all, because no Treaty provision has empowered it to do so; the lack of competence of the institutions to act under a particular empowering provision (incorrect legal basis); and the lack of competence of the particular institution or official to take the challenged act.

In the competition field the best example of the first situation is challenges made to the extraterritorial application of the competition rules. Undertakings outside the Union have argued that the EU rules could not be applied to them because they were outside the jurisdiction. These challenges have not hitherto succeeded.[712]

The second situation is exemplified in the challenges brought by Member States to directives adopted by the Commission on the basis of Article 106(3), discussed in Chapter 8.[713] In *British Airways*[714] the GC dismissed the undertaking's claim that the Commission had no competence to apply Regulation 17 to practices in the market for air travel agency services as it should have used Regulation 3975/87 on the air transport sector.[715] A number of cases arose from the expiry of the ECSC Treaty in 2002.[716] However, the GC upheld the readopted *Alloy Surcharge* decision of

---

[706] As in respect of the *IMS* decision, Case T-184/01 R, *IMS Health v Commission* [2001] ECR II-3193 (President of the GC), confirmed Case C-481/01 P (R), *NDC Health v Commission* [2002] ECR I-3401 (President of the CJ).

[707] See Section 12.F.

[708] Case C-272/09 P, *KME Germany AG v Commission* [2011] ECR I-12789, para. 101.

[709] Cases T-79/89 etc., *BASF and others v Commission* [1992] ECR II-315, para. 31.

[710] Case C-272/09 P, *KME* [2011] ECR I-12789.

[711] Although it has been pleaded: see, e.g., Case 5/85, *AKZO Chemie BV v Commission* [1986] ECR 2585; Case T-5/93, *Roger Tremblay v Commission* [1995] ECR II-185. In the merger case, Case T-145/06, *Omya AG v Commission* [2009] ECR II-145, the applicant claimed that the Commission had only requested extra information in order to suspend the time running. The GC stated that even if a decision had been taken for a purpose other than that for which the powers were conferred it would only invalidate the decision if no other proper ground for taking the decision was present.

[712] See Chap. 16.

[713] Chap. 8, Section 8.C, p. 645.

[714] Case T-219/99, *British Airways v Commission* [2003] ECR II-5917.

[715] [1987] OJ L374/1.

[716] The *Reinforcing Bars Cartel* decision, COMP/37.956, was annulled since the Commission had adopted it under Art. 65(1) ECSC post the expiry, Cases T-27/03 etc., *SP SpA v Commission* [2007] ECR II-4331. See Chap. 2. See also Case T-405/06, *Arcelor Mittal v Commission* [2009] ECR II-789, aff'd Case C-201/09 P, *Arcelor Mittal v Commission* [2011] ECR I-2239. The Commission readopted the *Concrete Reinforcing Bars* decision under Reg. 1/2003, 30 September 2009.

20 December 2006 in which the Commission used Regulation 1/2003 in respect of an infringement of Article 65(1).[717]

The third situation has arisen in competition cases where parties have alleged that the power to take decisions was unlawfully delegated. The delegation to the Commissioner responsible for competition of the power to take decisions ordering 'dawn raid' inspections under Article 14(3) of Regulation 17 was unsuccessfully challenged in AKZO,[718] and the delegation of the signing of documents such as SOs has been upheld.[719] However, a challenge to the adoption of a final decision finding an infringement by a single Commissioner succeeded in the first PVC Cartel case where a challenge to a decision on both competence and infringement of an essential procedural requirement grounds spectacularly succeeded.[720] The appointment of the monitoring trustee in the Microsoft decision was annulled because the Commission lacked authority to impose such measures.[721] British Airways claimed that the Commission had no competence to adopt the Virgin/BA decision of 14 July 1999[722] as, all the members of the Commission having resigned en bloc on 16 March 1999, they had authority only to deal with current business pending their replacement in September. The GC held that the Commissioners could exercise their normal powers until their resignations took effect on the date of their actual replacement.[723]

c. Infringement of an Essential Procedural Requirement

Infringement of an essential procedural requirement covers situations where a measure has been passed without complying with the legislative process laid down by the Treaties,[724] or with the rules of procedure of the relevant institution,[725] or with a general principle of law concerned with procedure,[726] or where the measure does not contain an adequate statement of reasons, contrary to Article 296 TFEU.

The GC annuls acts only for breach of an *essential* procedural requirement, and what amounts to such is a matter for the Court. A requirement is essential if the failure to observe it might have affected the final outcome of the act. On this basis the wrongful revelation of confidential material to the complainant in AKZO[727] was not a reason for annulling the Commission decision. An adequate statement of reasons is an essential procedural requirement. The CJ said in HeidelbergCement:

According to settled case-law, the statement of reasons required under Article 296 TFEU for measures adopted by EU institutions must be appropriate to the measure at issue and must disclose clearly and

---

[717] Case T-24/07, *ThyssenKrupp Stainless AG v Commission* [2009] ECR II-2309, aff'd Case C-352/09 P, *ThyssenKrupp Nirosta v Commission* [2011] ECR I-2359. For the reasons for the annulment of the original *Alloy Surcharge* decision, see n. 802.

[718] Case 5/85, *AKZO* [1986] ECR 2585.

[719] See Case 48/69, *ICI v Commission (Dyestuffs)* [1972] ECR 619.

[720] Cases T-79/89 etc., *BASF v Commission* [1992] ECR II-315, on appeal Case C-137/92 P, *Commission v BASF* [1994] ECR I-2555: see Section 8.A.v.c, p. 997.

[721] Case T-201/04, *Microsoft* [2007] ECR II-3601.

[722] [2000] OJ L30/1.

[723] Case T-219/99, *British Airways v Commission* [2003] ECR II-5917, paras. 55–57. The resignation of the entire Santer Commission in March 1999 to avoid a motion of censure of Parliament was a situation not foreseen by the EC Treaty. Art. 215 EC, which BA claimed prevented the resigned Commission transacting 'new' business, did not fit happily with what had happened in these rather extraordinary circumstances. Art. 215 was amended by the Treaty of Nice and is now Art. 246 TFEU.

[724] As where Parliament is not consulted: Case 138/79, *Roquette Frères v Council* [1980] ECR 3333.

[725] Case 68/86, *UK v Council* [1988] ECR 855; note the application of this in the *PVC Cartel* case: Case C-137/92 P, *Commission v BASF* [1994] ECR I-2555.

[726] Such as the *audi alteram partem* rule giving parties a right to a hearing: Case 17/74, *Transocean Marine Paint v Commission* [1974] ECR 1063.

[727] See Section 7.D.v.c, p. 939.

unequivocally the reasoning followed by the institution which adopted that measure in such a way as to enable the persons concerned to ascertain the reasons for it and to enable the competent court to review its legality. The requirements to be satisfied by the statement of reasons depend on all the circumstances of each case, in particular, the content of the measure in question, the nature of the reasons given and the interest which the addressees of the measure, or other parties to whom it is of direct and individual concern, may have in obtaining explanations. It is not necessary for the reasoning to go into all the relevant facts and points of law, since the question whether the statement of reasons meets the requirements of Article 296 TFEU must be assessed with regard not only to its wording but also to its context and to all the legal rules governing the matter in question (judgment in *Commission* v *Sytraval and Brink's France*, Case C-367/95 P,..., paragraph 63, and in *Nexans and Nexans France* v *Commission*, C-37/13 P,..., paragraphs 31 and 32 and the case-law cited).[728]

In competition cases, where the Commission has a wide margin of appreciation and power of appraisal, the reasoning is of fundamental importance because in reviewing the decision the Court must be able to establish whether the factual and legal matters upon which the exercise of the power of appraisal depended were present and whether the Commission has dealt properly with the parties' arguments.[729] The GC annulled the *Air Freight* cartel decision[730] because the decision was vitiated by contradictions between the statement of reasons (grounds) and the operative part and within the grounds themselves.[731]

Challenges to competition decisions frequently plead procedural defects as grounds for annulment, as seen earlier in this chapter. The GC annulled the *Soda-ash* decisions,[732] for example, on grounds that insufficient access to the Commission's file prejudiced the parties' right to be heard, and a significant part of the *TACA* decision[733] because the Commission had relied on an interpretation of a number of inculpatory documents upon which the undertakings had been given no opportunity to comment.[734] The most celebrated case of annulment on procedural grounds (and of lack of competence) is the *PVC I* case. There the GC found differences (going beyond corrections of grammar and syntax) in both the statement of reasons and the operative part of the decision, between the version adopted by the College of Commissioners at its relevant meeting and the version notified to the undertakings concerned. The Commission was unable to produce an authenticated version of the decision as adopted by the College. A draft in only three languages was available at the meeting, and the Competition Commissioner was authorised to adopt the measure in the other official Community languages, including those of undertakings to which the decision was addressed. Further, the Competition Commissioner whose signature appeared on the decision notified to all the addressees had left office some days before the notified version appeared to have been finalised. The GC considered these procedural defects, including the breach of the principle of collegiate responsibility, so serious that it did not merely annul the decision, it declared it *non-existent*.[735]

---

[728] Case C-247/14 P, EU:C:2016:149, para. 16, where the CJ annulled an Art. 18(3) decision because the vague statement of reasons did not allow the undertaking to check whether the requested information was necessary or the EU Courts to exercise their power of review, see Section 7.C.ii.

[729] In the *Net Book Agreement* case the CJ annulled a decision because the Commission had not adequately dealt with the evidence one party put forward about the benefits of RPM accepted by the UK courts, Case C-360/92 P, *Publishers' Association v Commission* [1995] ECR I-23 setting aside the GC judgment, Case T-66/89, *Publishers' Association v Commission* [1992] ECR II-1995.

[730] COMP/39.258, 9 November 2010.

[731] Cases T-9/11 etc., *Air Canada v Commission* EU:T:2015:994. The confusion concerned whether the Commission was finding a single continuous infringement or four separate single and continuous infringements.

[732] Cases T-30/91 etc., *Solvay SA v Commission (No. 2)* 1995] ECR II-1775; the readopted decisions were also annulled for lack of access to the file, Case C-109/10 P, *Solvay SA v Commission* [2011] ECR I-10329.

[733] [1999] OJ L95/1.

[734] Cases T-191 and 212–214/98, *Atlantic Container Line v Commission* [2003] ECR II-3275.

[735] Cases T-79/89 etc., *BASF* [1992] ECR II-315.

On appeal the CJ held that the flaws were not so fundamental as to render the act non-existent. It put aside the judgment of the GC, held that the decision existed, but annulled it.[736]

d. Infringement of the Treaties or Any Rule of Law Relating to Their Application

This ground is wide enough to cover the other three grounds as well. 'The Treaties' means the TEU and TFEU together with the Protocols, Acts of Accession, and the Charter of Fundamental Rights of the EU and any future amending Treaties. 'Any rule of law relating to their application' covers all the other binding provisions of the Union legal order, including the general principles of law and human rights developed in the Court's jurisprudence (many of which are now embedded in the Charter) and provisions of international law, particularly principles of customary international law and agreements the EU itself has concluded. It also covers ensuring that the Commission has followed any Notices or other measure to which it has committed itself, such as the Fining Guidelines and the Leniency Notice. Review under Article 263 entails ensuring that the Commission has properly interpreted the law.

The GC will therefore annul a decision where the Commission has committed an error of law or failed to abide by general principles of law such as proportionality, equality, non-discrimination, legitimate expectation, the presumption of innocence, or legal certainty.[737] This ground of annulment also covers the Court finding that the evidence relied on or the facts established by the Commission do not support its findings. This means that the GC does look at the facts,[738] not to rehear the case but to see whether the factual basis of the Commission decision was correct or sufficient and that the burden of proof was discharged. It annuls decisions where it finds that the Commission drew the wrong conclusions from the facts. The CJ said in *Kone* that the fact that the Court's analysis in an action for annulment had neither the object or effect of replacing a full investigation of the case in the context of an administrative procedure was inherent in the notion of a review of legality.[739]

(vi) Appeals Against Penalties: Article 261 TFEU

The Commission has a wide discretion in setting fines under Articles 23 and 24 of Regulation 1/2003.[740] It also has a discretion in respect of many matters in the Leniency Notice,[741] such as whether the conditions of paragraph 8 are met, whether information provided represents 'significant added value' under paragraph 24, or whether an undertaking coerced others under paragraph 13. Article 31 of Regulation 1/2003 gives the Court 'unlimited jurisdiction to review decisions whereby

---

[736] Case C-137/92 P, *Commission v BASF* [1994] ECR I-2555. The *LdPE cartel* [1989] OJ L74/21, was annulled on similar grounds in Cases T-80/89 etc., *BASF v Commission* [1995] ECR II-729. After the *PVC* judgment two of the undertakings concerned in the *Polypropylene Cartel*, who were challenging that decision in an action before the GC in which the oral proceedings had already been closed, asked the GC to reopen those proceedings so that they could enter pleas based on the *PVC* arguments. They claimed that the GC had wrongfully failed to raise those issues of its own motion. The GC refused and this was upheld by the CJ: see Case C-234/92 P, *Shell International Chemical Co Ltd v Commission* [1999] ECR I-4501, at paras. 66–68. The GC did, however, annul a Commission decision in Cases T-31–32/91, *Solvay v Commission* [1995] ECR II-1821 on non-authentication grounds. The applicants raised the plea after the close of the written procedure in the case, having read statements by Commission officials in the *Financial Times* and the *Wall Street Journal* that the Commission had been following the procedure condemned in the *PVC* case for the past 25 years. The annulment was upheld by the CJ, Cases C-286–288/95 P, *Commission v ICI* [2000] ECR I-2341. The Commission readopted the decisions eight months later, in December 2000, [2003] OJ L10/1.

[737] Legal certainty was cited in the *PVC I* judgments (see nn. 735 and 736) as being infringed when the Commission did not follow its own rules of procedure and could not produce the authenticated decision.

[738] It can play an active role by ordering measures of inquiry such as experts' reports. GC Rules of Procedure, 2015, Arts. 91–100.

[739] Case C-510/11 P, *Kone Oyj v Commission* EU:C:2013:696, para. 26.

[740] See Section 7.H, p. 959 ff.

[741] See Section 7.H.v, p. 983.

the Commission has fixed a fine or periodic penalty payment'. Article 31 is pursuant to Article 261 TFEU[742] which provides that regulations may give the Court unlimited jurisdiction with regard to penalties provided for in such regulations. The action under Article 261 cannot be used to circumvent the time limits laid down in Article 263 as it not an autonomous remedy but part of the Court's Article 263 jurisdiction.[743]

The distinction between the Court's powers under Article 261 and under Article 263 is that under the former the Court has *full jurisdiction*. It may actually change the Commission's decision. It may cancel, increase, or reduce the fine (but not impose one where the Commission has not). Although the EU Courts are not bound by the Fining Guidelines[744] they may derive guidance from them when exercising the unlimited jurisdiction.[745] This is particularly relevant when the Courts are dealing with the fine on one of several cartel participants as the exercise of the jurisdiction must not result in discrimination between the participants.[746] Under Article 263, however, the Court is limited to reviewing the legality of the decision and annulling all or part of it on the grounds laid down in the Article but cannot substitute its own judgment for that of the Commission. As with Article 263 itself, appeals against penalties go to the GC, with an appeal to the CJ. Where the CJ disagrees with the GC on a point of law the CJ can exercise the unlimited jurisdiction and adjust the fine confirmed, reduced, or increased by the GC, accordingly.[747]

The GC has been tolerant of the Commission's general approach to fining to a degree that has been criticised.[748] The CJ approved the change to higher fines for the sake of deterrence in *Pioneer*[749] and has not objected to the ever higher level of fines imposed since then. The GC will reduce or quash the fine, however, when it takes a different view to the Commission of such matters as the duration of an infringement[750] or of an undertaking's level of involvement in an infringement.[751] The Guidelines create legitimate expectations and the GC examines whether the Commission exercised its discretion in accordance with the methodology set out in the Guidelines and whether any departure from the Guidelines is supported by sufficient legal reasoning (which must be compatible with the principle of equal treatment).[752]

Many of the fiercest arguments about fines before the GC are now about the immunity or reductions which the Commission has accorded to cartel participants under the Leniency Notice. In the *Graphite Electrodes* appeal the GC *increased* the fine on an undertaking which, having been granted leniency for cooperation with the Commission, then argued about the facts before the GC.[753] In *BASF (Choline Chloride cartel)* the applicant's successful argument that the global and European cartel arrangements in which it was implicated could not be considered a 'single and continuous

---

[742] Ex Art. 229 EC.

[743] Case T-252/03, *Fédération nationale de l'industrie et des commerces en gros des viandes (FNICGV) v Commission* [2004] ECR II-3795.

[744] Case C-70/12 P, *Quin Barlo Ltd v Commission* EU:C:2013:351, para. 45.

[745] Case C-603/13 P, *Galp* EU:C:2016:38, para. 80.

[746] See C-441/11 P, *Verhuizingen Coppens* EU:C:2012:778, para. 80.

[747] See Case C-603/13 P, *Galp* EU:C:2016:38, where the fine was reduced by the GC and then again by the CJ.

[748] See, e.g., I. Forrester, 'A Bush in Need of Pruning: The Luxuriant Growth of "Light Judicial Review"' in C.-D. Ehlermann and M. Marquis (eds.), *European Competition Law Annual 2009: Evaluation of Evidence and its Judicial Review in Competition Cases* (Hart Publishing, 2011) (the author is now the UK judge at the GC). This is one aspect of the criticism of the intensity of the Court's judicial review of competition decisions generally.

[749] Cases 100–103/80, *Pioneer* [1983] ECR 1825.

[750] See, e.g., the GC judgment in the *Cement Cartel* cases, Cases T-25/95 etc., *Cimenteries* [2000] ECR II-491.

[751] Ibid., in respect of one undertaking's involvement in the white cement market cartel.

[752] See, e.g., Case C-70/12 P, *Quin Barlo* EU:C:2013:351, para. 53; Case T-116/04, *Wieland-Werke AG v Commission* [2009] ECR II-1087, paras. 29–33.

[753] Cases T-236/01 etc., *Tokai Carbon* [2004] ECR II-1181.

infringement' of Article 101(1) resulted in it losing the benefit of the leniency policy with the result that its fine was increased by its victory.[754]

In an Article 263 review the Commission cannot rely on evidence that was not in the decision.

(vii) Burden of Proof, Standard of Proof, and Standard of Review

The burden of proof is discussed in Chapter 3, Section 4.C (Article 101) and Section 5.C (Article 102). The EU Courts require that the Commission produces 'sufficiently precise and coherent proof' to support its case.[755] The meaning of that was explained by the GC in *Intel*.

Case T-286/09, *Intel v Commission* EU:T:2014:547

General Court

62. According to Article 2 of Regulation No 1/2003, in any proceedings for the application of Article [102], the burden of proving an infringement of that article rests on the party or the authority alleging the infringement, namely, in the present case, the Commission. Furthermore, according to well settled case-law, any doubt in the mind of the Court must operate to the advantage of the undertaking to which the decision finding an infringement was addressed. The Court cannot therefore conclude that the Commission has established the infringement at issue to the requisite legal standard if it still entertains any doubts on that point, in particular in proceedings for annulment of a decision imposing a fine (Joined Cases T-67/00, T-68/00, T-71/00 and T-78/00 *JFE Engineering and Others* v *Commission*..., paragraph 177, and Case T-112/07 *Hitachi and Others* v *Commission*..., paragraph 58).

63. In the latter situation, it is necessary to take account of the principle of the presumption of innocence resulting in particular from Article 6(2) of the European Convention for the Protection of Human Rights and Fundamental Freedoms (ECHR), signed in Rome on 4 November 1950, and from Article 47 of the Charter of Fundamental Rights of the European Union. Given the nature of the infringements in question and the nature and degree of severity of the ensuing penalties, the principle of the presumption of innocence applies in particular to the procedures relating to infringements of the competition rules applicable to undertakings that may result in the imposition of fines or periodic penalty payments (Case C-199/92 P *Hüls* v *Commission*..., paragraphs 149 and 150; and Case C-235/92 P *Montecatini* v *Commission*..., paragraphs 175 and 176; *JFE*, paragraph 62 above, paragraph 178).

64. Although the Commission must produce sufficiently precise and consistent evidence to support the firm conviction that the alleged infringement took place, it is important to emphasise that it is not necessary for every item of evidence produced by the Commission to satisfy those criteria in relation to every aspect of the infringement. It is sufficient if the body of evidence relied on by the institution, viewed as a whole, meets that requirement, as held by the case-law concerning the implementation of Article [101] (see, to that effect Joined Cases C-238/99 P, C-244/99 P, C-245/99 P, C-247/99 P, C-250/99 P to C-252/99 P and C-254/99 P *Limburgse Vinyl Maatschappij and Others* v *Commission*, paragraphs 513 to 523). That principle applies also in cases concerning the implementation of Article [102] (Case T-321/05 *AstraZeneca* v *Commission*]...('*AstraZeneca*'), paragraph 477).

---

[754] Cases T-101 and 111/05, *BASF v Commission* [2007] ECR II-4949, paras. 212–213. BASF had been granted leniency for its cooperation over the global cartel. As there was no single continuous infringement the proceedings in respect of the global, as distinct from the European, cartel were time-barred. It could not therefore be fined for the global cartel so leniency could not apply and the 10% reduction it had been given was removed.

[755] See, e.g., Cases 29 and 30/83, *CRAM and Rheinzink v Commission* [1984] ECR 1679, para. 20; Cases C-89/85 etc., A. Ahlström Oy v Commission (Wood Pulp II) [1993] ECR I-1307, para. 127; Case T-201/04, *Microsoft* [2004] ECR II-4463, para. 564.

In *Intel* the GC distinguished between two situations. The first is where the Commission finds an infringement on the basis that the established facts cannot be explained by anything other than anticompetitive behaviour, where the decision will be annulled if the undertakings can show another plausible explanation (the *Wood Pulp* cartel situation).[756] The second is where the Commission relies on evidence which in principle is sufficient to demonstrate existence of the infringement, when it is for the undertaking to call into question the probative values of that evidence.[757]

Continental Can was an early case where the decision was annulled because there the Commission had failed to establish why a particular type of container should be considered a relevant market. This meant there was no basis for its finding of dominance and the application of Article 102, even though the CJ confirmed the Commission's expansive interpretation of Article 102 to cover mergers.[758] In *Wood Pulp II*[759] the Court appointed experts to produce a report on parallelism of prices in the wood pulp industry, whether the documents relied on by the Commission justified their conclusions on the pricing, and whether there was a distinction between the documents gathered before and after the SO. A second experts' report into the structure and characteristics of the market was commissioned. These reports, particularly the finding that the market was oligopolistic, were crucial to the Court's judgment and it (largely) annulled the decision.

The GC was established largely to relieve the CJ of having to deal with complex issues of fact. An early example of an assiduous examination of the factual basis of a competition decision was the *Wood Pulp* cartel case already noted, and another was its treatment of the *Italian Flat Glass* decision in *Società Italiana Vetro*[760] where the GC submitted the documentary evidence to careful scrutiny and in the main found it seriously wanting. Two other examples of annulment are *Métropole*[761] and *European Night Services*.[762] However, it became established that the GC undertook only a limited review of what are termed matters of 'complex economic assessment' in which the Commission has a 'margin of appreciation'. The CJ stated in *Aalborg* that '[E]xamination by the Community judicature of the complex economic assessments made by the Commission must necessarily be confined to verifying whether the rules on procedure and on the statement of reasons have been complied with, whether the facts have been accurately stated and whether there has been any manifest error of appraisal or misuse of powers'.[763] *Microsoft*, discussed in Chapter 7, is a prime example of the GC wrestling with the inherent problems of engaging in only a limited review in an Article 102 case. The GC explained that its role where 'complex' economic *and technical* appraisals were concerned was 'necessarily limited to checking whether the relevant rules on procedure and on stating reasons have been complied with, whether the facts have been accurately stated and whether there has been any manifest error

---

[756] Cases C-89/85 etc., *Wood Pulp II* [1993] ECR I-1307.

[757] Case T-286/09, *Intel* EU:T:2014:547, paras. 65–67.

[758] Case 6/72, *Continental Can* [1973] ECR 215.

[759] Cases C-89/85 etc., *Wood Pulp II* [1993] ECR I-1307; see Chap. 9.

[760] Cases T-68/89 etc., *Società Italiana Vetro SpA v EC Commission* [1992] ECR II-1403.

[761] Cases T-528/93 etc., *Métropole Télévision* [1996] ECR II-649, where the Commission had not properly examined whether the fourth criterion for Art. 101(3) exemption relating to the indispensability of restrictions was satisfied, and had taken into account the criteria in Art. 106(2) TFEU (see Chap. 8) despite having decided that Art. 106(2) did not apply.

[762] Cases T-374–375, 384, and 388/94, *European Night Services v Commission* [1998] ECR II-3141, where, inter alia, the Commission had not analysed whether there was a restriction of competition, had applied the de minimis test in too mechanistic a manner, and had applied the essential facilities doctrine without explaining why the resources at issue could be considered essential facilities; see Chap. 4.

[763] Cases C-204/00 P etc., *Aalborg Portland* [2004] ECR I-123, echoing Case 42/84, *Remia v Commission* [1985] ECR 2545. Reference is often made to the Commission's 'discretion' or 'margin of discretion' in this respect but it has been cogently argued that it is a 'margin of appreciation' rather than discretion (in that discretion involves choosing the standards according to which power is exercised or a decision made, while a margin of appreciation involves weighing up the evidence and assessing whether a given standard is reached, see O. Odudu, 'Article 101(3), Discretion and Direct Effect' [2002] *ECLR* 17; D. Bailey, 'Scope of Judicial Review Under Article 101 EC' (2004) 41 *CMLRev* 1327). Nevertheless the EU Courts seem to use the terms interchangeably (although 'appreciation' certainly sounds more suitable when applied to technical assessments).

of assessment or a misuse of powers' and that the Commission's appraisals were 'in principle sub-ject to only limited review by the Court'.[764] It then, nevertheless, proceeded to examine the facts in considerable detail:

However, while the Community Courts recognise that the Commission has a margin of appreciation in eco-nomic or technical matters, that does not mean that they must decline to review the Commission's interpreta-tion of economic or technical data. The Community Courts must not only establish whether the evidence put forward is factually accurate, reliable and consistent but must also determine whether that evidence contains all the relevant data that must be taken into consideration in appraising a complex situation and whether it is capable of substantiating the conclusions drawn from it (see, to that effect, concerning merger control, Case C-12/03 P *Commission v Tetra Laval* . . . paragraph 39).[765]

The reference to *Tetra Laval* is to the merger case in which the CJ first set out the rigour with which the EU Courts should deal with complex economic assessments.[766]

There are also matters which do not necessarily involve complex economic assessments but where the Commission has a margin of discretion. These include applying the Fining Guidelines, applying the Leniency Notice, deciding to accept commitments,[767] and rejecting complaints.

Limiting the role of judicial review to 'manifest errors of appraisal' in situations of complex eco-nomic (and technical) assessments and in other situations where the Commission has a 'margin of discretion' raises difficulties.[768] The pervasive problem is the Commission's multifaceted role and how far EU competition procedures are compliant with Article 6(1) ECHR and Article 47 of the Charter.[769] The Commission is not a tribunal within Article 6, as its decisions are those of an admin-istrative authority[770] but the GC has held itself to be an independent and impartial court, established in order particularly to improve the judicial protection of individuals by making a close inspection of complex facts[771] and so it has been held that the requirements of Article 6(1) are satisfied by the right of the parties to challenge Commission decisions in that Court. However, the leeway given to the Commission by 'light touch judicial review' in limiting the review to 'manifest errors of ap-praisal' where some of the most contentious findings of the Commission are concerned raises seri-ous doubts as to the adequacy of the EU's procedures. Decisions emerging from a process whereby investigation, prosecution, and decision-making are rolled into one body are subjected to limited scrutiny in a system which many argue is deeply flawed.[772] In 2011 the EU system was challenged directly in appeals from the GC in respect of the fines in the *Copper Plumbing Tubes* cartel.[773] The un-dertakings argued, inter alia, that their right to effective judicial protection had been compromised

---

[764] Case T-201/04, *Microsoft* [2007] ECR II-3601, paras. 87 and 88.

[765] Ibid., para. 89.

[766] Case C-12/03 P, *Commission v Tetra Laval* [2005] ECR I-987, para. 39, discussed in Chap. 15. Bellamy and Child, n. 2, 13.147 set out a (non-exhaustive) list of matters which can be discerned from the case law as involving 'com-plex economic assessments': the application of Art. 101(3); certain aspects of merger control; the definition of the relevant market; the extent of market foreclosure; the legitimate duration of a non-compete clause on the sale of a business; the choice of relevant cost standards; and the choice of econometric instruments to use in non-horizontal merger assessments.

[767] See Case C-441/07 P, *Alrosa* [2010] ECR I-5949 (nn. 283 and 701), discussed in Section 7.E.iii, where the CJ overturned the GC for interfering too much with the Commission's discretion in respect of a commitments decision.

[768] Moreover, it has been pointed out that the extension of this in *Microsoft* to 'technical matters' exacerbates the matter: Forrester, n. 748.

[769] See Section 7.B.

[770] Cases 209–215 and 218/78, *Van Landewyck v Commission* [1980] ECR 3125, para. 81; Cases 100–103/80, *Pioneer* [1983] ECR 1825, para. 7; Case T-11/89, *Shell v Commission* [1992] ECR II-757, para. 39.

[771] Case T-348/94, *Española v Commission* [1998] ECR II-1875, paras. 57–63; Cases T-25/95 etc., *Cimenteries* [2000] ECR II-491, paras. 718–719.

[772] For a critical analysis of the present situation, see Forrester, n. 748 and the literature cited in n. 685.

[773] COMP/38.069, 3 September 2004.

by the GC's review of the decisions[774] in that the GC had violated their fundamental right to full and effective judicial review by failing to examine the arguments thoroughly, i.e. that the GC had deferred too much to the Commission's discretion and fallen short of the standard demanded by Article 6(1) ECHR and Article 47 of the Charter. The CJ judgments *KME*[775] and *Chalkor*[776] were given less than three months after the ECtHR judgment in *Menarini* had held that the Italian competition system did comply with the ECHR.[777]

In the judgments the CJ said that the EU system of review by the GC under Article 263 and Article 261 did provide effective judicial protection which satisfied Article 47. However, the CJ did not refer to a 'manifest error of appraisal'. Instead it talked of the 'in-depth' review which the GC conducts. The *Copper Tubes* judgments were followed by similar ones in the appeals from the *Elevators and Escalators* decision,[778] *Schindler*,[779] *Otis*,[780] and *Kone*.[781] In *Kone* the GC had said that it had to determine whether the Commission had manifestly gone beyond its margin of assessment (in respect of the undertaking's cooperation under the Leniency Notice).[782] The CJ accepted that this was not enough to meet the standard required by Article 47 of the Charter, which needed an in-depth review.[783] However, the CJ upheld the judgment on the basis that whatever the GC *said* it was doing, it had in fact examined the decision in sufficient depth.[784]

The following extract is from the appeal in the Article 102 margin squeeze case, *Telefónica*, in which the Court set out the position reached in the judgments mentioned above and proclaimed again the compliance of EU law with the ECHR and the Charter. The review standard is now described as 'in-depth'.

Case C-295/12 P, *Telefónica SA v Commission* EU:C:2014:2062

Court of Justice

40. The principle of effective judicial protection is a general principle of EU law to which expression is now given by Article 47 of the Charter of Fundamental Rights of the European Union ('the Charter') and which corresponds, in EU law, to Article 6(1) of the ECHR (see Case C-386/10 P *Chalkor* v *Commission*…, paragraph 51; Case C-199/11 *Otis and Others*…, paragraph 47; and Case C-501/11 P *Schindler Holding and Others* v *Commission*…, paragraph 36).

41. Whilst, as Article 6(3) TEU confirms, fundamental rights recognised by the ECHR constitute general principles of EU law and whilst Article 52(3) of the Charter requires rights contained in the Charter which correspond to rights guaranteed by the ECHR to be given the same meaning and scope as those laid down by the ECHR, the latter does not constitute, as long as the European Union has not acceded to

---

[774] Case T-127/04, *KME Germany v Commission* [2009] ECR II-1167; Case T-25/05, *KME Germany AG v Commission* [2010] ECR II-91; Case T-21/05, *Chalkor v Commission* [2010] ECR II-1895.

[775] Case C-272/09 P, *KME Germany AG v Commission* [2011] ECR I-2789 and Case C-389/10 P, *KME Germany v Commission* [2011] I-13125.

[776] Case C-386/10 P, *Chalkor AE Epexergasias Metallon v Commission* [2011] ECR I-13085.

[777] A. *Menarini Diagnostics SRL v Italy*, App No. 43509/08, judgment 27 September 2011; see Section 7.B.ii.a, p. 898.

[778] COMP/38.823, 2 February 2007.

[779] Case C-501/11 P, *Schindler Holdings v Commission* EU:C:2013:522.

[780] Case C-199/11 P, *Otis and Others v Commission* EU:C:2012:684.

[781] Case C-510/11 P, *Kone Oyj v Commission* EU:C:2013:696. See also the EFTA Court judgment, Case E-15/10, *Posten Norge v EFTA Surveillance Authority*, 18 April 2012. J. Temple Lang, 'Judicial Review of Competition Decisions under the European Convention on Human Rights and the Importance of the EFTA Court: The *Norway Post* Judgment' (2012) 37 ELRev 464, considered the Court's statements in that case to be clearer than the judgments of the CJ in the *Copper Plumbing Tubes* cases, and broader in their implications.

[782] Case T-151/07, *Kone v Commission* [2011] ECR II-5313, paras. 85 and 95.

[783] Case C-510/11 P, *Kone* EU:C:2013:696, paras. 23–24.

[784] Ibid., para. 43.

it, a legal instrument which has been formally incorporated into EU law (see *Schindler Holding and Others* v *Commission*..., paragraph 32).

42. According to established case-law, EU law provides for a system of judicial review of Commission decisions relating to proceedings under Article 102 TFEU which affords all the safeguards required by Article 47 of the Charter (see, to that effect, *Chalkor* v *Commission*..., paragraph 67, and *Otis and Others*..., paragraphs 56 and 63). That system of judicial review consists in a review of the legality of the acts of the institutions for which provision is made in Article 263 TFEU, which may be supplemented, pursuant to Article 261 TFEU, by the Court's unlimited jurisdiction with regard to the penalties provided for in regulations.

43. As regards review of the legality of Commission decisions in competition matters, the first and second paragraphs of Article 263 TFEU provide that the Court of Justice is to review the legality of acts of the Commission intended to produce legal effects vis-à-vis third parties and, to that end, it has jurisdiction in actions brought on grounds of lack of competence, infringement of an essential procedural requirement, infringement of the Treaties or of any rule of law relating to their application, or misuse of power. Under Article 256 TFEU, the General Court has jurisdiction to review at first instance the legality of Commission decisions in competition matters, as provided for in Article 263 TFEU.

44. That review of legality is supplemented, in accordance with Article 261 TFEU, by the Court of Justice's unlimited jurisdiction with regard to the fines and periodic penalty payments imposed by the Commission for infringement of the competition rules. Article 17 of Regulation No 17, replaced by Article 31 of Regulation No 1/2003, provides that the Court of Justice is to have unlimited jurisdiction to review decisions whereby the Commission has fixed a fine or periodic penalty payment, which means that it may cancel, reduce or increase the fine or periodic penalty payment imposed.

45. It follows from the foregoing that the scope of judicial review extends to all Commission decisions relating to a proceeding under Article 102 TFEU, whereas the scope of the unlimited jurisdiction conferred by Article 31 of Regulation No 1/2003 is confined to the parts of such decisions imposing a fine or a periodic penalty payment.

46. Since the fifth part of the fifth ground of appeal concerns parts of the contested decision relating to the establishment of the infringement, the appellants' argument alleging that the General Court failed to have regard to the obligation to carry out a review exercising its powers of unlimited jurisdiction for the purpose of Article 47 of the Charter must be understood as referring to the review of legality carried out by the General Court in the present case, as provided for in Article 263 TFEU.

47. In essence, the appellants contend that the General Court failed to have regard to its obligation to carry out a review exercising its powers of unlimited jurisdiction for the purpose of Article 47 of the Charter in its assessment of the abuse and its effects on competition. In particular, the appellants take issue with the General Court for rejecting their arguments after concluding that there was no manifest error on the part of the Commission, at paragraphs 211, 220, 223, 244, 251 and 263 of the judgment under appeal. The appellants make three complaints in that regard.

48. By their first complaint, the appellants maintain that the General Court's review was limited to a manifest error of assessment of factors which did not give rise to complex economic assessments.

49. By their second complaint, the appellants contend that the General Court was incorrect to confine itself to reviewing the manifest error of assessment, thus avoiding examining whether the evidence adduced by the Commission substantiated the conclusions it drew from its assessment of the complex economic situation, in accordance with the judgment in Case C-12/03 P *Tetra Laval*..., paragraph 39.

50. By their third complaint, the appellants claim that the General Court is required, even when dealing with complex economic questions, to exercise its powers of unlimited jurisdiction for the purpose of Article 6 of the ECHR, as interpreted by the European Court of Human Rights in. *A. Menarini Diagnostics S.rl v. Italy*, no 43509/08 of 27 September 2011, in which the manifest error of assessment test has no place.

51. According to the case-law of the European Court of Human Rights, the obligation to comply with Article 6 of the ECHR does not preclude, in an administrative procedure, a 'penalty' being imposed in the first instance by an administrative authority. For this to be possible, however, decisions taken by administrative authorities which do not themselves satisfy the requirements laid down in Article 6(1) of the ECHR must be subject to subsequent review by a judicial body endowed with unlimited jurisdiction (judgments of the European Court of Human Rights, *Segame SA v. France*, no 4837/06, § 55, ECHR 2012, and *A. Menarini Diagnostics v. Italy*, § 59).

52. It is also apparent from the case-law of the European Court of Human Rights that the characteristics of a judicial body endowed with unlimited jurisdiction include the power to quash in all respects, on questions of fact and law, the decision at issue. Such a body must in particular have jurisdiction to examine all questions of fact and law relevant to the dispute before it (see, inter alia, the judgment of the European Court of Human Rights, *A. Menarinin Diagnostics v. Italy*, § 59; and *Schindler Holding and Others v Commission*…, paragraph 35).

53. It is established case-law that the review of legality provided for in Article 263 TFEU involves review by the European Union judicature, in respect of both the law and the facts, of the arguments relied on by applicants against the contested decision, which means that it has the power to assess the evidence, annul the decision and to alter the amount of the fine (see, to that effect, *Schindler Holding and Others v Commission*…, paragraph 38 and the case-law cited).

54. Accordingly, the Court of Justice has already stated that, whilst, in areas giving rise to complex economic assessments, the Commission has a margin of discretion with regard to economic matters, that does not mean that the EU judicature must refrain from reviewing the Commission's interpretation of information of an economic nature. The EU judicature must, among other things, not only establish whether the evidence put forward is factually accurate, reliable and consistent, but must also determine whether that evidence contains all the relevant data that must be taken into consideration in appraising a complex situation and whether it is capable of substantiating the conclusions drawn from it (*Commission v Tetra Laval*…, paragraph 39; *Chalkor v Commission*…, paragraph 54; and *Otis and Others*…, paragraph 59).

55. Moreover, failure to review the whole of the contested decision of the court's own motion does not contravene the principle of effective judicial protection. Compliance with that principle does not require that the General Court—which is indeed obliged to respond to the pleas in law raised and to carry out a review of both the law and the facts—should be obliged to undertake of its own motion a new and comprehensive investigation of the file (*Chalkor v Commission*…, paragraph 66, and *Kone and Others v Commission* …, paragraph 32).

56. Accordingly, the EU judicature must carry out its review of legality on the basis of the evidence adduced by the applicant in support of the pleas in law put forward and it cannot use the Commission's margin of discretion as regards the assessment of that evidence as a basis for dispensing with the conduct of an in-depth review of the law and of the facts (see, to that effect, *Chalkor v Commission*…, paragraph 62, and *Schindler Holding and Others v Commission*…, paragraph 37).

57. Given those characteristics, the review of legality provided for by Article 263 TFEU satisfies the requirements of the principle of effective judicial protection enshrined in Article 6(1) of the ECHR, which corresponds in EU law to Article 47 of the Charter (see, to that effect, *Chalkor v Commission*…, paragraph 67; *Otis and Others* EU:C:2012:684, paragraph 56; and *Schindler and Others v Commission*…, paragraph 38).

58. In the present case, the appellants simply claim, by means of general assertions alleging that the General Court erred in law in its examination of the evidence adduced by the Commission, and do not specifically identify the nature of any such error, inter alia by reference to the requirements set out at paragraph 54 above. Accordingly, they do not maintain that the General Court failed to establish whether the evidence put forward is factually accurate, reliable and consistent or that the evidence reviewed by that court does not contain all the relevant data that must be taken into consideration in appraising a complex situation. Moreover, they fail to explain how the General Court erred in law in the conclusions set out at paragraphs 211, 220, 223, 244, 251 and 263 of the judgment under appeal and in the reasons given for those conclusions.

> 59. In any event, it should be noted that, in carrying out the review of legality provided for in Article 263 TFEU, the General Court did not merely ascertain whether there were any manifest errors of assessment but carried out an in-depth review, as regards questions of both fact and law, of the contested decision in the light of the pleas in law put forward by the appellants, thus satisfying the requirements of an unrestricted review for the purpose of Article 47 of the Charter (see, to that effect, *Chalkor* v *Commission*..., paragraph 82, and Case C-272/09 P *KME and Others* v *Commission*..., paragraph 109).

It is notable that the CJ lays great store on the 'unlimited jurisdiction' in Article 261. That relates only to penalties, as the CJ in a subsequent case has been at pains to stress:

By contrast, the scope of that unlimited jurisdiction is strictly limited, unlike the review of legality provided for in Article 263 TFEU, to determining the amount of the fine ...

It follows from this that the unlimited jurisdiction enjoyed by the General Court on the basis of Article 31 of Regulation No 1/2003 concerns solely the assessment by that Court of the fine imposed by the Commission, to the exclusion of any alteration of the constituent elements of the infringement lawfully determined by the Commission in the decision under examination by the General Court.[785]

Furthermore, some of the most contentious decisions of the Commission in respect of Article 102 have imposed remedies that have had far greater consequences for the undertakings concerned than the payment of even the largest fine.

The view of the CJ, however, is that EU competition law is fully compliant with the Charter and the ECHR. This depends, however, on the GC not using the Commission's margin of discretion (either in respect of complex economic matters or other matters) as a basis for dispensing with the conduct of an in-depth review of the law and of the facts.[786] In all these recent cases the CJ was satisfied that the GC did carry out a sufficiently in-depth review. It was not satisfied, however, in *Groupement des Cartes Bancaires*[787] where it set aside the judgment of the GC in a case concerning the pricing measures of a payment card system.[788] The CJ criticised the GC, inter alia, for failing to adequately examine the Commission's conclusion that the measures should be categorised as restrictive by object.

(viii) Annulment

Article 264 TFEU states that if the action is well founded 'the Court of Justice of the European Union shall declare the act concerned to be void'. The finding of defects in a decision does not necessarily lead to annulment of the whole if the defects relate only to ancillary components which do not alter the substance of the decision: if the defective parts can be severed the rest of the decision will stand.[789] The parts that are not annulled definitively form part of the Union legal structure and produce all their legal effects and therefore, for example, in *Compagnie Maritime Belge* annulling the fine for procedural reasons did not affect the legality of the rest of the decision finding the infringement.[790]

---

[785] Case C-603/13 P, *Galp* EU:C:2016:38, paras. 76–77.

[786] Case C-386/10 P, *Chalkor* [2011] ECR I-13085, para. 56; Case C-501/11 P, *Schindler* EU:C:2013:522, para. 37; Case C-295/12 P, *Telefónica* EU:C:2014:2062, para. 56. Case T-151/07, *Kone* [2011] ECR II-5313 shows that it is what the GC does, rather than what it says it is doing, that matters.

[787] Case C-67/13 P, *Groupement des Cartes Bancaires v Commission* EU:C:2014:2204, see Chap. 4.

[788] See Chap. 4, Section 3.B.iv, p. 202 ff.

[789] Case C-441/11 P, *Commission v Verhuizingen Coppens* EU:C:2012:778, paras. 36–38; Case C-603/13 P, *Galp Energía España SA v Commission* EU:C:2016:38, para. 86.

[790] Case T-276/04, *Compagnie Maritime Belge v Commission* [2008] ECR II-1277. The original fines on the shipping lines were annulled because the Commission had announced an intention to fine only the conference, not the individual shipping lines, Cases C-395 and 396/96 P, *Compagnie Maritime Belge* [2000] ECR I-1365.

In *Verhuizingen Coppens* the CJ overruled the GC for wrongly annulling the *International Removal Service* decision in respect of Coppens entirely instead of partially.[791]

A decision finding an infringement of the competition rules addressed to a number of undertakings (as is common in cartel cases) is in effect a bundle of individual decisions. The decision can therefore be annulled only as regards the addressees who have successfully challenged it. Twenty-eight of the 36 addressees of the *Wood Pulp* decision[792] brought an action for annulment. The CJ annulled or reduced the fines imposed on the appellants.[793] The CJ upheld the Commission's refusal to refund the other addressees: they had not challenged the decision within the two-month time limit and it continued to be valid and binding on them.[794] In *CISAC*[795] 21 of the addresses brought a successful action for annulment on the grounds of insufficient evidence of a concerted practice. One undertaking brought an appeal on different grounds, which failed, and the GC did not allow it to adopt at the hearing stage the other appellants' submissions.[796]

The EU Courts cannot substitute their own decision for that of the Commission. So, in *European Night Services*[797] the GC refused to annul the conditions which the Commission had attached to the Article 101(3) exemption and leave the applicants with an unconditional decision. It annulled the decision completely.[798]

Article 266 TFEU says:

The institution or institutions whose act has been declared void or whose failure to act has been declared contrary to the Treaties shall be required to take the necessary measures to comply with the judgment of the Court of Justice of the European Union.

This includes repaying any fine that has been paid, including default interest. Where the fine is partially reduced the relevant proportion and interest must likewise be repaid.[799] Where decisions are annulled for procedural defects the Commission often readopts them. The Commission responded to the final annulment of the *PVC I* decision[800] by adopting a new one six weeks later. The undertakings again appealed, inter alia on the grounds that this breached the principle of double jeopardy, *ne bis in idem*, and that the Commission had denied them the right to be heard by not sending a new SO and holding new hearings. The CJ held that *ne bis in idem* did not apply when the annulment was only on procedural grounds, and that given that the Court had not found any defects in the preparatory stages of the Commission's procedure, there was no need to repeat those stages. A right to be heard was necessary only in respect of matters which were not in the original decision.[801] The Commission's practice is, consequently, to readopt decisions annulled for procedural reasons, and the triumph of those who win on procedural grounds can be short-lived.[802]

---

[791] Case C-441/11 P, *Verhuizingen Coppens* EU:C:2012:778. The decision, COMP/38.543, 11 March 2008 should have been upheld in respect of the infringement which the GC still found.

[792] [1985] OJ L85/1.

[793] Cases C-89/85 etc., *A. Ahlström Oy v Commission (Wood Pulp II)* [1993] ECR I-1307.

[794] Case C-310/97 P, *Commission v AssiDomän* [1999] ECR I-5363.

[795] Case T-442/08, *CISAC v Commission* EU:T:2013:188.

[796] Case T-451/08, *Föreningen Svenska Tonsättares Internationella Musikbyrå u.p.a. (Stim) v Commission* EU:T:2013:189.

[797] Cases T-374–375, 384, and 388/94, *European Night Services v Commission* [1998] ECR II-3141.

[798] In Case T-168/01, *GlaxoSmithKline Services Unlimited* [2006] ECR II-2696, para. 320, the GC annulled the part of the decision refusing GlaxoSmithKline's request for an individual exemption under Art. 101(3) after that procedure had been abolished by Reg. 1/2003. The GC told the Commission to rule on the request for exemption insofar as GSK was still requesting it, as the annulment had retrospective effect. The Commission has now quietly dropped the matter.

[799] Case T-53/03, *BPB v Commission* [2008] ECR II-1333.

[800] Case C-137/92 P, *Commission v BASF* [1994] ECR I-2555.

[801] Cases C-238/99 P etc., *Limburgse Vinyl Maatschappij (PVC II)* [2002] ECR I-8375, paras. 59–76.

[802] For two further examples of decisions readopted after annulments for procedural reasons, see COMP/38.907, *Steel Beams* [2008] OJ C235/4, undertaking fined €10 million (original decision (adopted under the

(ix) Appeals from the General Court to the Court of Justice

An appeal lies from the GC to the CJ on a point of law.[803] This means that the appeal is limited to the grounds of lack of competence of the GC, a breach of procedure before it adversely affecting the interests of the applicant, or the infringement of EU law by the GC.[804] An error of law includes the legal characterisation of facts by the GC and the legal conclusions it draws from them.[805] The appellant has to state the errors of law alleged to have been made by the GC.[806] It is not sufficient for it simply to repeat the arguments it raised before the GC[807] and it may not adduce new arguments. The CJ will not entertain arguments whereby the appellant is really trying to argue about the facts found in the original decision rather than identify errors committed by the GC. In a number of cases the CJ has been highly critical of appeals where it has struggled to identify the grounds. This was so in *Telefónica*,[808] for example, where the CJ said:

30. Accordingly, a ground of appeal supported by an argument that is not sufficiently clear and precise to enable the Court to exercise its powers of judicial review, in particular because essential elements on which the ground of appeal is based are not indicated sufficiently coherently and intelligibly in the text of the appeal, which is worded in a vague and ambiguous manner in that regard, does not satisfy those requirements and must be dismissed as inadmissible (see, to that effect, Case C-194/99 P *Thyssen Stahl* v *Commission* ..., paragraphs 105 and 106, and Case C-520/09 P *Arkema* v *Commission* ..., paragraph 61 and the case-law cited). The Court has also held that an appeal lacking any coherent structure which simply makes general statements and contains no specific indications as to the points of the order under appeal which may be vitiated by an error of law must be dismissed as clearly inadmissible (see the order in Case C-107/07 P *Weber* v *Commission* ..., paragraphs 26 to 28).

31. As regards the appeal brought in the present case, it should be noted, as observed by the Commission, that it contains a great many grounds and arguments that must be regarded as inadmissible. However, the present appeal cannot be regarded as inadmissible in its entirety. Some of the grounds of appeal identify with the requisite degree of precision the contested elements of the judgment under appeal and set out with sufficient clarity the legal arguments relied on. As a consequence, notwithstanding the shortcomings identified below, the plea of inadmissibility raised by the Commission in respect of the appeal in its entirety must be rejected.

The CJ has explained the respective roles of the CJ and the GC on many occasions. The following is an extract from *Siemens*.[809]

ECSC Treaty) annulled in Case C-176/99 P, *Arbed SA v Commission* [2003] ECR I-10687 as the decision had not been addressed to the same addressee as the SO) and COMP/39.234, *Alloy Surcharge* 20 December 2006, undertaking fined €3,168,000 (original decision annulled in Cases C-65 and 73/02 P, *ThyssenKrupp Stainless AG v Commission* [2005] ECR I-6773 as ThyssenKrupp was fined without being explicitly invited to give its views of the cartel behaviour of Thyssen Stahl, who had merged with another company after the infringement to form ThyssenKrupp).

[803] Art. 256 TFEU.

[804] Art. 58 of the Statute of the Court of Justice.

[805] Case C-67/13 P, *Groupement des Cartes Bancaires* EU:C:2014:2204, para. 41. The CJ set aside the GC's judgment because it had, inter alia, failed to carry out a sufficiently in-depth review, showed defective reasoning, and misinterpreted and misapplied Art. 101(1)

[806] See Case C-295/12 P, *Telefónica SA v Commission* EU:C:2014:2062.

[807] Case C-19/95 P, *San Marco v Commission* [1996] ECR I-4435.

[808] Case C-295/12 P, *Telefónica* EU:C:2014:2062; see also Case C-603/13 P, *Galp* EU:C:2016:38, 'The arguments ... do not identify, with the required precision, any error of law on the part of the General Court, but consist of general and unsubstantiated statements, with the result that they must be rejected as inadmissible' (para. 45).

[809] The appeals in the *Gas Insulated Switchgear* cartel, COMP/38.899, 24 January 2007, upheld on appeal.

Cases C-239, 489, and 498/11 P, *Siemens AG and others v Commission* EU:C:2013:866

Court of Justice

38. First of all, it must be borne in mind that, in an appeal, the Court of Justice has no jurisdiction to establish the facts or, in principle, to examine the evidence which the General Court accepted in support of those facts. Provided that the evidence has been properly obtained and the general principles of law and the rules of procedure in relation to the burden of proof and the taking of evidence have been observed, it is for the General Court alone to assess the value which should be attached to the evidence produced to it. Save where the evidence adduced before the General Court has been distorted, the appraisal therefore does not constitute a point of law which is subject to review by the Court of Justice (Joined Cases C-403/04 P and C-405/04 P *Sumitomo Metal Industries and Nippon Steel* v *Commission*..., paragraph 38 and the case-law cited).

39. The jurisdiction of the Court of Justice to review the findings of fact by the General Court therefore extends, inter alia, to the substantive inaccuracy of those findings as apparent from the documents in the file, the distortion of the evidence, the legal characterisation of that evidence and the question whether the rules relating to the burden of proof and the taking of evidence have been observed (*Sumitomo Metal Industries and Nippon Steel* v *Commission*, paragraph 39 and the case-law cited).

40. By contrast, contrary to what Siemens maintains, the Court's power of review in the context of an appeal cannot extend to the alleged infringement of purported principles derived from experience, such as those claimed by Siemens, concerning, inter alia, established knowledge relating to the functioning of the memory and the psychology of witnesses, or the fact that individuals from an undertaking involved in the cartel may themselves have an interest in maximising the unlawful conduct of competitors and minimising their own liability.

41. Review of an infringement of that nature requires a factual assessment which is fundamentally different from the marginal review which the Court carries out when an appellant complains, in a sufficiently detailed manner, that the General Court distorted the evidence.

42. It should be pointed out that, according to settled case-law, the distortion must be obvious from the documents in the Court's file, without there being any need to carry out a new assessment of the facts and the evidence (see, inter alia, Case C-260/09 P *Activision Blizzard Germany* v *Commission*..., paragraph 53 and the case-law cited).

...

44. Next, it should be borne in mind that the review carried out by the Court in order to assess a ground of appeal alleging the distortion of evidence is restricted to ascertaining that, in relying on that evidence to make a finding that an undertaking participated in a cartel, the General Court did not manifestly exceed the limits of a reasonable assessment of that evidence. The task of the Court of Justice is not, therefore, to assess independently whether the Commission has established such participation to the requisite legal standard and thus discharged the burden of proof necessary to show that the rules of competition law were infringed, but to determine whether, in finding that that was actually so, the General Court misconstrued the evidence in a manner manifestly at odds with its wording (see, to that effect, *Activision Blizzard Germany* v *Commission*, paragraph 57).

The correction of a manifest error by the GC was made in *Aalborg*.[810] The GC had included within the calculation of the fine to be imposed on one of the participants in the cement cartel the turnover of its Belgian subsidiary. However, at the time of the infringement the undertaking concerned

---

[810] Cases C-204/00 P etc., *Aalborg Portland* [2004] ECR I-123.

had not yet assumed control of the Belgian company. This was apparent from the *Cement Cartel* decision itself.[811] The CJ reduced the fine by nearly €3 million as it considered it had the necessary evidence to give judgment itself. It was entitled to do this because Article 61 of the Statute of the Court of Justice provides that if an appeal is well founded the CJ must quash the GC's decision and may either refer the matter back to the GC or, 'where the state of proceedings so permits', itself give final judgment in the matter. The effect of this was nicely illustrated by CJ's judgment in *PVC Cartel II*. It held that the GC had wrongly refused to consider, on procedural grounds, Montedison's plea that its right of access to the file had been infringed, and its plea about the Commission's power to fine in the circumstances of the case.[812] The CJ therefore partially annulled the GC's decision. However, it decided that this was a case in which it could give final judgment itself. It therefore considered Montedison's pleas and rejected them, leaving Montedison in the same position as it was after the GC judgment.[813]

Errors of law do not lead to the setting aside of a judgment where it is upheld on other grounds.[814]

In a number of cases applicants have claimed that proceedings before the GC were of such an excessive length that their right to a fair trial within a reasonable period under Article 6(1) ECHR and (now) Article 47 of the Charter was infringed. The CJ considers the length of the proceedings in the light of the complexity of the case.[815] If the CJ concludes that the delay was unreasonable but did not prejudice the outcome of the case the judgment is not set aside. Rather, the remedy is for the appellant to bring an action for damages before the GC (differently constituted if the GC itself was responsible for the delay).[816] In this matter the CJ has changed its previous approach, which was to reduce the fine in such cases.[817] The new Rules of Procedure of the GC which entered into force on 1 July 2015[818] are intended to strengthen the Court's capacity to deal with cases in a reasonable time in accordance with Article 47.

Where appeals against judgments of the GC on fines are concerned the CJ has held that it is for the GC to examine how the Commission assessed the gravity of the infringement and to decide whether the fine should be changed. The CJ will not substitute its own assessment for that of the GC. It stated in *Ferriere Nord*:[819]

---

[811] [1994] OJ L343/1.

[812] The peculiarities of the proceedings against the PVC cartel, which resulted in a first annulled decision being replaced by a second one, are described in Section 8.A.v.c, p. 997.

[813] Cases C-238/99 P etc., *Limburgse Vinyl Maatschappij* [2002] ECR I-8375, paras. 355–379, 416–428, and 647–698.

[814] As in, e.g., Case C-501/06 P, *GlaxoSmithKline Services Unlimited v Commission* [2009] ECR I-9291; Case C-113/07 P, *SELEX Systemi Integrati SpA v Commission* [2009] ECR I-2207. For instances where the GC judgment was set aside completely see, e.g., the GC upholding the Commission decision in the *Net Book Agreement* case, Case C-360/92 P, *Publishers' Association v Commission* [1995] ECR I-23; replacing the GC's finding of a non-existent act in *PVC I* with a finding of an act which should be annulled: Case C-137/92 P, *Commission v BASF* [1994] ECR I-2555; setting aside the GC judgment against the Commission in Case C-310/97 P, *AssiDomän Kraft Products AB and others* [1999] ECR I-5363; and the overturning of the GC in Case C-441/07 P, *Alrosa* [2010] ECR I-5949.

[815] E.g., Case C-185/95 P, *Baustahlgewebe GmbH v Commission* [1998] ECR I-8417; Case C-194/99 P, *Thyssen Stahl AG v Commission* [2003] ECR I-10821; Cases C-403 and 405/04 P, *Sumitomo Metal Industries Ltd v Commission* [2007] ECR I-729.

[816] Case C-40/12 P, *Gascogne Sack Deutschland v Commission* EU:C:2013:768, paras. 86–90; Case C-50/12 P, *Kendrion v Commission* EU:C:2013:771, paras. 91–95; Case C-58/12 P, *Groupe Gascogne* EU:C:2013:770, paras. 80–84; Case C-295/12 P, *Telefónica* EU:C:2014:2062, paras. 66–67; Case C-603/13 P, *Galp* EU:C:2016:38, paras. 55–58. The length of the proceedings in *Galp* was almost five years nine months, including a period of over four years, without any procedural acts, between the end of the written procedure and the hearing.

[817] In Case C-185/95 P, *Baustahlgewebe GmbH v Commission* [1998] ECR I-8417 the CJ reduced the fine of three million ECUs by 50,000 ECUs.

[818] [2015] OJ L105/1.

[819] Case C-219/95, *Ferriere Nord v Commission* [1997] ECR I-4411; see also Case C-310/93 P, *BPB Industries and British Gypsum Ltd v Commission* [1995] ECR I-865, para. 34; Case C-185/95 P, *Baustahlgewebe* [1998] ECR I-8417, paras. 128–129; Case C-359/01 P, *British Sugar v Commission* [2004] ECR I-4933, paras. 47–48; Cases C-189/02 P etc., *Dansk Rørindustri* [2005] ECR I-5425, paras. 244–246 and 302.

31. As regards the allegedly unjust nature of the fine, it is important to point out that it is not for this Court, when ruling on questions of law in the context of an appeal, to substitute, on grounds of fairness, its own assessment for that of the [General Court] exercising its unlimited jurisdiction to rule on the amount of fines imposed on undertakings for infringements of Community law (Case C-310/93 P, *BPB Industries and British Gypsum v E.C. Commission* . . .). In contrast, the Court of Justice does have jurisdiction to consider whether the [General Court] has responded to a sufficient legal standard to all the arguments raised by the appellant with a view to having the fine abolished or reduced.

(x) Interim Measures by the Court under Article 278 TFEU

Bringing an Article 263 action for annulment does not automatically suspend the contested act. However, Article 278 TFEU states:

Actions brought before the Court of Justice of the European Union shall not have suspensory effect. The Court may, however, if it considers that circumstances so require, order that application of the contested act be suspended.

Also, Article 279 TFEU provides that in any cases before it, the Court may prescribe any necessary measures. The President of the GC normally hears applications for suspension.[820] His or her decision may be appealed to the CJ.

In order for a decision to be suspended the applicants must show that the main action is admissible and that suspension is urgently needed to prevent them suffering irreparable damage which could not be remedied in the event of their winning the main action. On this basis suspension was ordered, inter alia, in *United Brands*,[821] *Magill*,[822] *Net Book Agreement*,[823] *Adalat*,[824] *Atlantic Container Line*,[825] *Van den Bergh*,[826] and *IMS*.[827] Suspension was refused in *Microsoft* on the grounds that the undertaking had failed to show the likelihood of serious and irreparable damage.[828] The Commission's intention to publish a revised 'non-confidential version' of a final decision was suspended in *Akzo Nobel*.[829]

The President has to balance the harm to the applicant from non-suspension (foreseeable with a sufficient degree of probability)[830] with any harm which will be suffered by other parties if the suspension is granted. In *Adalat*, for example, the President considered that as a result of the order the applicant, Bayer, might be obliged to lower the prices of the drug in issue, risking major and irrecoverable losses of profit, and that there was a risk that the pharmaceutical base of one subsidiary 'might be deprived of its economic basis, resulting in the dismissal of many employees'. He considered this would be disproportionate in relation to the interests of wholesalers in Spain and France in increasing their exports.[831] Moreover, he was concerned that the Commission's interpretation of the

---

[820] For the procedure before the GC, see GC Rules of Procedure (2015), Arts. 156–161.

[821] Case 27/76 R, *United Brands v Commission* [1976] ECR 425.

[822] Cases 76–77 and 91/89 R, *RTE and others v Commission* [1989] ECR 1141.

[823] Case 56/89 R, *Publishers' Association v Commission* [1989] ECR 1693.

[824] Case T-41/96 R, *Bayer v Commission* [1996] ECR II-381.

[825] Case C-149/95 P (R), *Commission v Atlantic Container Line and others* [1995] ECR I-2165.

[826] Case T-65/98 R, *Van den Bergh Foods Ltd v Commission* [1998] ECR II-2641.

[827] Case T-184/01 R, *NDC Health v Commission* [2001] ECR II-3193 (President of the GC), Case C-481/01 P (R), *IMS Health v Commission* [2002] ECR I-3401 (President of the CJ).

[828] Case T-201/04 R, *Microsoft v Commission* [2004] ECR II-4463.

[829] Case T-345/12 R, *Akzo Nobel NV v Commission* EU:T:2012:605; the publication was finally allowed by the GC in Case T-345/12, *Akzo Nobel NV v Commission* EU:T:2015:50.

[830] Case C-280/93 R, *Commission v Germany* [1993] ECR I-3667.

[831] [1996] ECR II-407 at paras. 59–60.

law (i.e. its view of what constitutes an 'agreement' for the purposes of Article 101) was questionable (as, indeed it proved to be).[832]

The suspension in *IMS* was of an interim decision. Again, as with *Adalat*, the President of the GC was concerned about the legal basis of the Commission's decision (the compulsory licensing of a copyright).[833] The GC may suspend the obligation to give a bank guarantee ensuring payment of the fine but this is done only in very exceptional circumstances.[834] The GC (and on appeal, the CJ) refused to do it in respect of one of the shipping lines fined in *TACA*.[835]

B. ACTIONS FOR DAMAGES UNDER ARTICLE 340 TFEU

Article 340 TFEU provides for damages for non-contractual liability:

In the case of non-contractual liability, the Union shall, in accordance with the general principles common to the laws of the Member States, make good any damage caused by its institutions or by its servants in the performance of their duties.

This raises the possibility that where a decision of the Commission is overturned by the EU Courts the undertakings concerned may be able to sue the Commission for any damage caused to it by the defective decision.

Actions under Article 340 are notoriously difficult for plaintiffs to win.[836] The Union institution must have committed a sufficiently serious breach of a superior rule of law intended to confer rights on individuals, and the test for 'sufficiently serious' is whether the institution manifestly and gravely disregarded the limits on its discretion.[837] These conditions were held not to be fulfilled in *Holcim* where the GC excused the Commission on the grounds, inter alia, of the difficulties it had faced in the case, which was one of the *Cement Cartel* appeals.[838]

Stanley Adams, however, did succeed in a damages claim under Article 340 when the Commission's negligent breach of confidentiality in revealing his identity to Hoffmann-La Roche led to his imprisonment in a Swiss jail.[839] Airtours (now MyTravel) commenced proceedings against the Commission in respect of the prohibition decision of its merger with First Choice which was annulled by the GC,[840] as did Schneider Electric in respect of the *Schneider/Legrand* annulled merger decision.[841]

As explained in Section 8.A.ix, the CJ considers that an action for damages is the proper remedy for unreasonable delays in proceedings before the GC.

---

[832] The Commission's decision was annulled in Case T-41/96, *Bayer v Commission* [2000] ECR II-3383, confirmed by the CJ, Cases C-2 and 3/01 P, *Bundesverband der Arzneimittel-Importeure EV and the Commission v Bayer AG* [2004] ECR I-23, see Chap. 3.

[833] The suspension was confirmed by the President of the CJ. Case C-481/01 P (R), *NDC Health v Commission* [2002] ECR I-3401. The decision was ultimately withdrawn and a final decision not adopted, see Section 7.E.vi, p. 956 and Chap. 7.

[834] See Case T-295/94 R, *Buchmann v Commission* [1994] ECR II-1265.

[835] Case C-364/99 P (R), *DSR-Senator Lines v Commission* [1999] ECR I-8733.

[836] See P. Craig and G. de Búrca, *EU Law: Text, Cases, and Materials* (6th edn, Oxford University Press, 2015), Chap. 16.

[837] Case C-352/98 P, *Bergaderm and Goupil v Commission* [2000] ECR I-5291.

[838] Case T-28/03, *Holcim v Commission* [2005] ECR II-1357, aff'd by the CJ, Case C-282/05 P, *Holcim (Deutschland) AG v Commission* [2007] ECR I-2941. The undertaking was claiming damages in respect of the charges it had incurred in providing for the bank guarantee for the fine pending the appeal. The GC held that the claim was, in any case, barred on limitation grounds, as it had not been brought within five years of the guarantee being provided. The five years did not run from the date that the GC had annulled the decision.

[839] Case 53/84, *Stanley Adams v Commission* [1985] ECR 3595.

[840] Case T-212/03, [2008] ECR II-1967.

[841] Case C-440/07 P, *Commission v Schneider Electric* [2009] ECR I-6413, largely setting aside Case T-351/03, [2007] ECR II-2237, see Chap. 15.

9. ENFORCEMENT BY THE NATIONAL COMPETITION AUTHORITIES WITHIN THE EUROPEAN COMPETITION NETWORK

A. GENERAL

As discussed previously[842] the NCAs have, since 1 May 2004, played a much more significant role in the enforcement of the EU competition rules. Regulation 1/2003 creates a system of parallel competences in which the competition rules are enforced by a network of competition authorities (through the ECN), as well as by the national courts. Article 5 of Regulation 1/2003 provides that the 'competition authorities of the Member States shall have power to apply Articles 101 and 102' in individual cases.[843]

Regulation 1/2003

Article 5

Powers of the competition authorities of the Member States

The competition authorities for the Member States shall have the power to apply Articles [101 and 102 TFEU] in individual cases. For the purpose, acting on their own initiative or on a complaint, they may take the following decisions:

— requiring that an infringement be brought to an end,
— ordering interim measures,
— accepting commitments,
— imposing fines, periodic penalty payments or any other penalty provided for in their national law.

Where on the basis of the information in their possession the conditions for prohibition are not met they may likewise decide that there are no grounds for action on their part.

Article 5 was interpreted by the CJ in *Tele2 Polska*[844] in a way which seriously limits the powers of the NCAs.[845] The CJ held that Article 5 does not permit NCAs to adopt decisions finding that Article 102 has not been infringed. An NCA may decide that Article 102 *has* been infringed and may decide that there are no grounds for action. It cannot, however, actually take a non-infringement decision. The CJ further held in *Bundeswettbewerbsbehörde v Schenker*[846] that the NCAs do not have power to adopt a decision concluding that there is no infringement of Article 101 either. On the other hand, NCAs should only exceptionally refrain from imposing a fine where an undertaking has intentionally or negligently infringed Article 101(1) (such as where a national leniency programme is applied).

---

[842] See Sections 3 and 5, and Chap. 2.

[843] The designation of the bodies responsible for the application of the rules is left to the Member States, Reg. 1/2003, Art. 35. The individual websites of each NCA are accessible through a link from the Commission's website, <http://ec.europa.eu/competition/ecn/competition_authorities.html>, some of them in more than one language. Many of them are available there in English.

[844] Case C-375/09, *Prezes Urzędu Ochrony Konkurencji i Konsumentów v Tele2 Polska sp. z o.o., now Netia SA* [2011] ECR I-3055.

[845] See S. Brammer, 'Casenote on *Prezes Urzędu Ochrony Konkurencji i Konsumentów v Tele2 Polska sp. z o.o., now Netia SA*' (2012) 49 *CMLRev* 1163.

[846] Case C-681/11, *Bundeswettbewerbsbehörde and Bundeskartellanwalt v Schenker & Co AG* EU:C:2013:404, para. 42.

Regulation 1/2003 leaves the Member State to determine which body will enforce the rules and what mechanisms for investigating infringements and enforcing decisions will apply. It does not demand any particular arrangement, so long as an NCA is designated[847] and the provisions of the Regulation can be complied with. There is no further attempt at harmonisation. Article 35 of Regulation 1/2003 provides that the designated authorities may include courts. The Commission's current moves to consider more harmonisation in the operation and procedures of NCAs are discussed in Section D.[848]

The creation of a network of authorities responsible for enforcing the same rules obviously creates a number of potential difficulties, in particular, how work is to be allocated between the respective authorities,[849] whether information collected by one authority can be passed on to another, where an application for leniency should be made, whether one authority can conduct inspections on behalf of another, and how a uniform and consistent approach in the interpretation and application of the provisions can be maintained. These, and other matters, are dealt with in Regulation 1/2003 itself (especially Articles 11–16) and more fully in the Commission's Notice on cooperation within the Network of Competition Authorities (the NCA Cooperation Notice). Each NCA has signed a statement acknowledging the principles set out in the Notice and agreeing to abide by the principles.

In January 2010 the Commission inaugurated the publication five times a year of the 'ECN Brief', designed to keep the reader informed of the activities of the ECN and disseminate news of enforcement and other activities of the NCAs.[850]

B. DIVISION OF WORK

(i) Case Allocation—Which Authority is Well Placed to Deal with a Case?

Chapter IV of Regulation 1/2003 deals with cooperation, including cooperation between the Commission and the competition authorities of the Member States. Further, a Joint Statement of the Council and the European Commission on the Functioning of the Network of Competition Authorities (the Joint Statement)[851] sets out the main principles governing the ECN, whilst the Commission's NCA Cooperation Notice provides fuller and more specific detail of cooperation and division of work. Article 101 and 102 cases can be dealt with by:

- a single NCA (possibly with the assistance of others);
- several NCAs acting in parallel;[852] or
- the Commission.[853]

The basic principles are that a case should be dealt with by the authority best placed to deal with it and able to restore or maintain competition in the market, and that cases should be allocated according to a predictable process and as soon as possible in the procedure.[854]

---

[847] Reg. 1/2003, Art. 35.

[848] Section 9.D, p. 1020.

[849] The principles on work allocation set out in this Notice are of critical importance to a complainant seeking to lodge its complaint with the authority best placed to deal with the case.

[850] Available on the Commission's ECN page at <http://ec.europa.eu/competition/ecn/index_en.html>.

[851] Joint Statement of the European Council and the European Commission on the functioning of the network of competition authorities, 10 December 2002, available at <http://ec.europa.eu/competition/ecn/joint_statement_en.pdf>.

[852] Cases should be dealt with by a single authority where possible.

[853] NCA Cooperation Notice [2004] OJ C101/43, para. 5.

[854] Joint Statement, paras. 11–14.

In order for an authority to be well placed, there must be a material link between the infringement and the territory of the authority (the conduct has substantial direct actual or foreseeable effects in the territory), the authority must be able to bring the entire infringement effectively to an end (either on its own or in parallel with another authority), and the authority must be able to gather the evidence required (whether or not with the assistance of another authority). Where two or more NCAs are well placed to act, then one NCA only should act where the action of one would be sufficient to bring the entire infringement to an end. If it would not, then two or more NCAs should act. The authorities should coordinate their action and where possible designate a lead authority for the case.[855] The guidance in the NCA Cooperation Notice in this respect is relatively limited and does not deal with the question of what is to happen in the event of a dispute as to which NCA should act and/or which NCA should take the lead in an investigation.

The Commission is likely to be best placed to deal with an agreement or practice where: it has effects on competition in three or more Member States; the conduct is linked with other Union provisions which may be exclusively or more effectively applied by the Commission; or the Union interest requires it (to develop competition policy or to ensure effective enforcement).[856]

The determination as to which authority deals with the case may be of critical importance to the undertakings investigated, the complainant (if any), and the authorities themselves as modernisation did not entail harmonisation of procedure, sanctions, or judicial review between the Member States or between the Member States and the Commission. Even where Regulation 1/2003 did make provision for the handling of certain matters within the ECN, problems remain.[857] The allocation principles are set out with examples in the NCA Cooperation Notice.[858]

In order to ensure that allocation takes place as quickly as possible, and normally within a period of two months,[859] Article 11(3) of Regulation 1/2003 imposes an obligation on the NCAs to inform the Commission and other NCAs 'before or without delay after commencing the first formal investigative measure'. Further, the Commission is obliged to transmit copies of documents to the NCAs that it has collected pursuant to its powers of investigation under Articles 18–21 of Regulation 1/2003. Once a case has been initially allocated the case should not ordinarily be reallocated unless the facts known about the case change materially during the course of the proceedings.[860] Article 13 of Regulation 1/2003 specifically provides that an authority (the Commission or an NCA) may suspend proceedings or reject a case that is being, or has been, dealt with by another competition authority.[861] This provision was applied in *easyJet* where the Commission rejected a complaint on the grounds that an NCA had already dealt the matter.[862]

Decisions of NCAs to terminate or open proceedings are challengeable only under their national laws.[863]

---

[855] Ibid., para. 18.

[856] Ibid., para. 19.

[857] See, e.g., R. Nazzini, *Concurrent Proceedings in Competition Law* (Oxford University Press, 2004); S. Brammer, 'Concurrent Jurisdiction under Regulation 1/2003 and the Issue of Case Allocation' (2005) 42 *CMLRev* 1383; A. Andreangeli, 'The Impact of the Modernisation Regulation on the Guarantees of Due Process in Competition Proceedings' (2006) 31 *ELRev* 342.

[858] Paras. 8–15.

[859] Cooperation Notice [2004] OJ C101/43, para. 18.

[860] Ibid., para. 19.

[861] The Commission can also reject a complaint which lacks Union interest or which fails to substantiate an allegation, see Section 12.F, p. 1029. National provisions may also provide an alternative basis for suspending a complaint.

[862] Case T-355/13, *easyJet v Commission* EU:T:2015:36.

[863] But see Reg. 1/2003, Art. 11(6) discussed in Section 9.C, p. 1019.

(ii) Transfer of Information

Where an authority does suspend national proceedings or reject a complaint on the grounds that it is being dealt with by another authority, that authority is permitted to transfer information, including confidential information, to the authority which is dealing with the case. Article 12(1) of Regulation 1/2003 provides generally for the Commission and the NCAs to provide one another with and use in evidence 'any matter of fact or of law, including confidential information'.[864] In order to protect the interests of individuals and undertakings, safeguards exist against the use and exchange of this information in certain circumstances. In particular, the competition authorities are bound by an obligation of professional secrecy, the information transferred can be used only for the purposes of applying Article 101 or 102 (and in certain circumstances national competition law) and in respect of the subject matter for which it was collected,[865] and the information can only be used to impose sanctions on *natural* persons where the law of the transmitting authority foresees sanctions of a similar kind in relation to the infringement, or the information has been collected in a way that affords the person the same level of protection of rights provided for under the rules of the receiving authorities. Thus, by Article 12(3), an NCA which may not impose sanctions on individuals, may not transfer information to an NCA which may, unless: (a) the information was collected in a way which respects the rights of defence afforded to the individuals by the rules of the receiving authority (but custodial sanctions can be imposed only where both the transmitting and the receiving authority can impose such a sanction); or (b) the receiving authority does not use the information in proceedings against an individual but only in proceedings against an undertaking. The safeguards are explained more fully in paragraph 28 of the NCA Cooperation Notice.

It has been argued that, despite these provisions, serious doubts remain as to how well the rights of the defence are safeguarded by the exchange of information provided for by Article 12(1).[866] There is a particular problem, for instance, in the divergence between the Member States' legal systems in the protection given to certain classes of information, such as what is covered by legal professional privilege.[867] This could result in an NCA using information it would have been unable to collect under the rules of its own jurisdiction.[868] There are particular problems in respect of the exchange of information connected with leniency applications, as discussed in Section 9.B.iii. The Commission's 2009 Report on the Functioning of Regulation 1/2003[869] suggested that the provisions in Article 12(3) about information and criminal sanctions are 'too far-reaching and an obstacle to efficient enforcement' and might appropriately be re-examined.[870]

(iii) Leniency Applications

Both in Chapter 9 and in Section 7.H.v. of this chapter, the importance of leniency regimes in the fight against cartels has been stressed, and the Commission's leniency regime discussed. As at 5 February 2016 all the Member States except Malta operated leniency programmes. However,

---

[864] The information must of course have been collected in a legal manner by the transmitting authority.

[865] Reg. 1/2003, Art. 12(2).

[866] A. Andreangeli, 'The Impact of the Modernisation Regulation on the Guarantees of Due Process in Competition Proceedings' (2006) 31 *ELRev* 342.

[867] For the position on legal professional privilege in EU law, see Section 7.C.vii, p. 922 ff.

[868] Andreangeli, n. 866, 354–356; B. Vesterdorf, 'Legal Professional Privilege and the Privilege Against Self-incrimination in EC Law: Recent Developments and Current Issues' [2004] *Fordham Corp L Inst* 19; see, e.g., the UK, where legal professional privilege extends to communications with in-house lawyers as compared to the position in EU law, discussed in Section 7.C.vii.

[869] COM(2009) 206 final.

[870] Ibid., para. 27, see also the Staff Working Paper on the functioning of Regulation 1/2003, SEC (2009) 574 final, paras. 244–245.

because there is no EU-wide system 'an application for leniency to a given authority is not to be considered as an application for leniency to any other authority'.[871] An undertaking contemplating a leniency application therefore has to consider making an application to *all* authorities which have competence to apply Article 101 in the territory affected by the infringement (which have leniency policies) and which are likely to be considered to be well placed to deal with the infringement (even if the infringement takes place in three or more Member States the applicants may not be sure that the Commission will take jurisdiction). In view of the importance of timing in leniency applications (total immunity is usually available only to the first to come forward) it will usually be advisable to make simultaneous applications. An authority considering opening an investigation as a result of a leniency application has a duty to inform other members of the ECN.[872] Information submitted to the network in this way may not, however, be used by the receiving authorities as a basis for starting an investigation on their own behalf. Further, information will, generally,[873] only be transmitted pursuant to Article 12 with the consent of the leniency applicant that has submitted the information voluntarily.[874]

Given the Commission's belief that leniency plays an important part in the fight against cartels, the inability for firms to file a single 'EU' leniency application was a notable omission from the NCA Cooperation Notice. Even though fewer Member States operated leniency programmes in 2004 it would have been possible, for example, to have established the Commission as the central recipient and coordinator of NCAs which did have such programmes or to have provided that NCAs may receive leniency applications on behalf of another NCA. The modernisation programme did not make such provision, however. The Commission was anxious that the efficacy of leniency should not be undermined by decentralisation[875] but the post-May 2004 position had clear deficiencies from the view of both the competition authorities and the (potential) applicant.[876]

In the light of these problems the Competition Commissioner announced in April 2005 that she was consulting on the idea of a 'one-stop shop' for leniency applications.[877] In the event, the ECN considered various ways of dealing with the difficulties.[878] First, a system of mutual recognition could have been established, by which immunity or a reduction of fines granted by one authority would be recognised by all other members of the ECN. Secondly, a fully centralised 'one-stop shop' could have been established, by which all leniency applications would be made to the Commission: if the case was later allocated to an NCA (or NCAs) the leniency application would go with the allocation. Thirdly, the ECN considered a system analogous to the regime established by the Merger Regulation,[879] whereby jurisdictional criteria would be developed for allocating cases between authorities and the applicants would approach those which would be dealing with their case. All these ideas presented serious difficulties and were rejected.

Instead the ECN turned to harmonisation. In September 2006 it adopted the ECN Model Leniency Programme (MLP). The aim was to produce a model setting out the minimum standards with which

---

[871] NCA Cooperation Notice, para. 37.

[872] Reg. 1/2003, Art. 11.

[873] But see NCA Cooperation Notice, para. 41 for exceptions to this.

[874] Ibid., paras. 39–42.

[875] S. Blake and D. Schnichels, 'Leniency Following Modernisation: Safeguarding Europe's Leniency Programmes' [2004] *ECLR* 765.

[876] See C. Gauer and M. Jaspers, 'Designing a European Solution for a "One Stop Leniency Shop"' [2006] *ECLR* 685.

[877] Neelie Kroes, 'The First Hundred Days', Speech, Brussels, 7 April 2005, available on DG Comp's website.

[878] Gauer and Jaspers, n. 876.

[879] Reg. 139/2004 [2004] OJ L24/1, see Chap. 15.

all ECN policies should be aligned.[880] It is without prejudice to an NCA adopting a more favourable stance towards applicants. The explanatory notes to the programme stated:

8. While it is highly desirable to ensure that all CAs [competition authorities] operate a leniency programme, the variety of legislative frameworks, procedures and sanctions across the EU makes it difficult to adopt one uniform system. The ECN Model Programme therefore sets out the principal elements which, after the soft harmonisation process has occurred, should be common to all leniency programmes across the ECN. This would be without prejudice to the possibility for a CA to add further detailed provisions which suit its own enforcement system or to provide for a more favourable treatment of its applicants if it considers it to be necessary in order to ensure effective enforcement.

The MLP (revised in November 2012) provides for immunity (Type 1 applications: Type 1A is immunity before inspections, Type 1B is immunity after inspections, corresponding to paragraphs 8(a) and 8(b) of the Commission's 2006 Notice),[881] subject to conditions; and for a reduction in fines (Type 2 applications),[882] subject to conditions. It also contains procedural requirements, including a 'marker' system (as under the Commission's 2006 Notice)[883] and the acceptability of oral applications.[884] It provides for NCAs to accept 'summary applications' for immunity or leniency containing more limited information than normally required, where the applicant has filed, or is in the process of filing, an immunity application with the Commission.[885] The explanatory notes exhort those Member States which can impose sanctions on individuals to ensure that employees and directors of applicants for leniency are protected, in order to ensure the efficient working of corporate leniency programmes.[886]

In 2009 the Commission published a report, ECN Model Leniency Programme: Report on Assessment of the State of Convergence.[887] This reported that the adoption of the MLP had encouraged Member States to introduce and/or develop their own leniency policies. It also reported on the divergences which remained and concluded that it should form the 'basis for reflections whether any further convergence is needed'.[888]

Problems arose over the operation of leniency programmes from the judgments of the CJ in Pfleiderer[889] and Donau Chemie[890] which are discussed in Chapter 14. In both cases litigants before national courts sought to obtain from the NCAs in the Member States copies of leniency statements made by the defendants.[891] This issue has now been dealt with by the provisions of the Damages Directive.[892] However, in the course of the Pfleiderer judgment the CJ held that neither the NCA

---

[880] Or, in the case of Member States without a leniency programme, adopted and aligned. In some Member States the adoption of, or alterations to, a leniency programme required legislation or some other form of lawmaking not under the control of the NCA, which meant that the wish of the NCA to have such a programme was not definitive of the matter.

[881] (MLP), <http://ec.europa.en/competition/ecn/mlp_revised_2012_en.pdf, paras. 5–8>.

[882] Ibid., paras. 9–12.

[883] Ibid., paras. 16–18.

[884] Ibid., paras. 28–30.

[885] Ibid., paras. 22–25 (November 2012 amendment). Previously only the applicant for Type 1 immunity could submit a summary application to NCAs. See 'European Competition Network refines its Model Leniency Programme', MEMO/12/887. The ECN page on the DG Comp website contains a list of NCAs which accept summary applications, see <http://ec.europa.eu/comm/competition/ecn/accepting_nca.pdf>. As at 22 November 2012 all 26 Member States with a leniency policy accepted summary applications.

[886] Explanatory Notes to the MLP, para. 15.

[887] Available at <http://ec.europa.eu/competition/ecn/model_leniency_programme.pdf>, and see MEMO/09/456.

[888] Leniency Report, para. 66.

[889] Case C-360/09, Pfleiderer AG v Bundeskartellamt [2011] ECR I-5161.

[890] Case C-536/11, Bundeswettbewerbsbehörde v Donau Chemie AG EU:C:2013:366.

[891] See S. Völcker, 'Casenote on Pfleiderer AG v Bundeskartellamt AG v Bundeskartellamt' (2012) 49 CMLRev 695.

[892] Dir. 2014/104/EU, see n. 325, and Chap. 14.

Cooperation Notice, the Leniency Notice, nor the MLP are binding on the courts and tribunals of the Member States.[893]

The CJ dealt a further blow to the MLP in *DHL*.[894] We have already seen that the MLP contains provision for 'summary applications' for immunity or leniency to an NCA where the applicant has filed, or is in the process of filing, an immunity application with the Commission.[895] In *DHL* the Italian court asked the CJ whether an NCA could deviate from the MLP and about what legal links exist between the main application for immunity to the Commission and the summary application to an NCA.[896] The CJ ruled that the MLP is not binding on NCAs and that there is no legal link between an application submitted to the Commission and the summary application to an NCA. The NCA is not required to assess the summary application in the light of the application to the Commission and is not required to contact the Commission in order to obtain information on the purpose and results of the Commission procedure in the case. This is because the Commission's leniency programme and those of the Member States coexist and each of the programmes is autonomous.

C. CONSISTENT APPLICATION OF ARTICLES 101 AND 102

(i) General

It has been explained that, despite the creation of a network of authorities, the Commission has sought to retain its central role 'as the guardian of the Treaty' having 'the ultimate but not the sole responsibility for developing policy and safeguarding consistency when it comes to the application of EC competition law'.[897]

(ii) Mechanism of Cooperation

Article 11 of Regulation 1/2003 deals with cooperation between the Commission and the competition authorities of the Member States, providing that the NCAs and Commission should apply the EU competition rules in 'close cooperation'.[898] It has already been seen that it provides for the Commission and NCAs respectively to inform each other when acting under Article 101 or 102,[899] and for the early allocation of cases. Article 11(4) also provides for the NCAs to inform the Commission[900] 30 days prior to the adoption of a decision applying Article 101 or 102 and requiring that the infringement be brought to an end.[901] The Commission may then make written observations on the case before the adoption of the decision by the NCA, or may decide itself to initiate proceedings. Article 11(6) of Regulation 1/2003 provides that the initiation of proceedings by the Commission relieves the NCAs of their competence to apply Articles 101 and 102. 'This means that once the Commission has opened proceedings, NCAs cannot act under the same legal basis against

---

[893] Case C-360/09, *Pfleiderer* [2011] ECR I-5161, paras. 21–22.

[894] Case C-428/14, *DHL Express (Italy) Srl and others v Autorità Garante della Concorrenza e del Mercato* EU:C:2016:27.

[895] MLP, paras. 22–25.

[896] The undertaking claimed that its summary application to the NCA and its application to the Commission should have given it precedence over another undertaking's application to the NCA. The case arose from much confusion about what sectors subject to the cartel the various applications covered.

[897] NCA Cooperation Notice, para. 43.

[898] Reg. 1/2003, Art. 11(1).

[899] NCAs informed the Commission of 180 new case investigations in 2005 (Commission's *XXXVth Report on Competition Policy* (2006), para. 210).

[900] The information may also be shared with the NCAs, Reg. 1/2003, Art. 11(4).

[901] Art. 11(5) states that the NCAs may consult the Commission on any case involving the application of Community (now Union) law. This may be useful, e.g., where the NCA wishes to adopt a decision rejecting a complaint or closing a procedure, etc.

the same agreement(s) or practice(s) by the same undertaking(s) on the same relevant geographic and product market.'[902] The existence of Article 11(6) is thus a powerful weapon in the hands of the Commission and gives it considerable leverage over an NCA when it disapproves of the decision it is about to adopt. The Commission deals with the full consequence of its Article 11(6) power in its Cooperation Notice. The Notice indicates that it will only rarely initiate proceedings where a case has initially been allocated to another NCA.

D. FURTHER STRENGTHENING OF THE NCAS AND THE ECN

In its Report on the Functioning of Regulation 1/2003 in 2009[903] the Commission said that Member States' enforcement systems still diverge on matters such as fines, criminal sanctions, liability of groups of undertakings, succession of undertakings, prescription periods, the standard of proof, structural remedies, and priority setting, and that 'this aspect may merit further examination and reflection'.[904] In its 2014 Communication 'Ten Years of Antitrust Enforcement under Regulation 1/2003'[905] the Commission returned to this theme and focused on the NCAs and the workings of the ECN. In particular it was concerned with the large degree of flexibility EU law leaves to the Member States in the design of their competition regimes. It noted that the 'achievements made to date remain fragile and can be rolled back at any time'.[906] It contrasted this unfavourably with related policy areas such as telecoms and energy where EU law provides for a number of requirements regarding the independence and financial and human resources of the national supervisory authorities. The Commission wants in particular to: further guarantee the independence of NCAs and ensure they are adequately resourced; ensure they have a complete set of effective investigative and decision-making powers; and ensure that they have powers to impose effective and proportionate fines, have well-designed leniency programmes, and have measures to avoid disincentives for corporate leniency applicants.[907] Further to these conclusions the Commission launched a public consultation exercise in November 2015, *ECN Plus, Empowering the national competition authorities to be more effective enforcers*, to get feedback on these issues.[908]

10. THE RELATIONSHIP BETWEEN EU AND NATIONAL COMPETITION LAW

Articles 101 and 102 and the domestic competition rules of the Member States can be applied concurrently. The applicability of Articles 101 and 102 has not precluded the application of the national competition provisions.[909] The fact that the rules may apply concurrently obviously leads to the possibility that their joint application may not always achieve the same outcome. Important questions which have arisen therefore are whether an NCA or national court could, for example: (a) authorise an agreement or practice prohibited by Article 101 or 102; or (b) condemn conduct which is not

---

[902] NCA Cooperation Notice, para. 51.

[903] See n. 869.

[904] Report on the Functioning of Regulation 1/2003, n. 869, para. 33; see also the accompanying Staff Working Paper, n. 870, paras. 200–207.

[905] COM(2014) 453, http://ec.europa.eu/competition/antitrust/legislation/antitrust_enforcement_10_years_en.pdf.

[906] Ibid., para. 28.

[907] Ibid., para. 46.

[908] IP/15/5998. The consultation closed on 12 February 2016.

[909] Case 14/68, *Walt Wilhelm v Bundeskartellamt* [1969] ECR 1.

prohibited by EU law (for example, because an agreement does not infringe Article 101(1) or meets the criteria of Article 101(3)).

In the context of the EUMR, the allocation of jurisdiction over mergers between the EU and national authorities is defined by the Regulation itself.[910] In contrast, Regulation 17 did not deal with this situation. Rather, case law developed which provided, in accordance with the principle of supremacy[911] and Article 10 EC (now Article 4 TEU),[912] that national law could be applied so long as its application did not 'prejudice the full and uniform application of Community law or the effects of measures taken or to be taken to implement it'.[913] The case law made it clear that a national authority could not authorise an agreement or conduct prohibited by Community law,[914] but was less clear on the question of whether, and if so when, national rules could be used to prohibit an agreement authorised at the Community level. The position is now more clearly dealt with in Article 3 of Regulation 1/2003.

Regulation 1/2003

Article 3

Relationship between Articles [101] and [102] of the Treaty and national competition laws

1. Where the competition authorities of the Member States or national courts apply national competition law to agreements, decisions by associations of undertakings or concerted practices within the meaning of Article [101(1) TFEU] which may affect trade between Member States within the meaning of that provision, they shall also apply Article [101 TFEU] to such agreements, decisions or concerted practices. Where the competition authorities of the Member States or national courts apply national competition law to any abuse prohibited by Article [102 TFEU], they shall also apply [Article 102 TFEU].

2. The application of national competition law may not lead to the prohibition of agreements, decisions by associations of undertakings or concerted practices which may affect trade between Member States but which do not restrict competition within the meaning of Article [101(1) TFEU], or which fulfil the conditions of Article [101(3) TFEU] or which are covered by a Regulation for the application of Article [101(3) TFEU]. Member States shall not under this Regulation be precluded from adopting and applying on their territory stricter national laws which prohibit or sanction unilateral conduct engaged in by undertakings.

3. Without prejudice to general principles and other provisions of Community law, paragraphs 1 and 2 do not apply when the competition authorities and the courts of the Member States apply national merger control laws nor do they preclude the application of provisions of national law that predominantly pursue an objective different from that pursued by Articles [101 and 102 TFEU].

It can be seen from this that Article 3(1) provides that where an NCA or national court applies national competition law to conduct which constitutes an agreement, decision, or concerted practice within the meaning of Article 101 or an abuse prohibited by Article 102, which affects trade

---

[910] See Chap. 15.

[911] Case 6/64, *Costa v ENEL* [1964] ECR 585.

[912] See Chap. 8, Section 3.

[913] Case 14/68, *Walt Wilhelm v Bundeskartellamt* [1969] ECR 1, para. 9.

[914] Ibid., para. 9. The fact that an agreement had been authorised at the national level did not preclude the Commission from subsequently finding that the agreement in fact infringes Art. 101: see Case C-360/92 P, *Publishers' Association v Commission* [1995] ECR I-23.

between Member States,[915] it *shall* also apply Article 101 or Article 102.[916] National authorities are thus obliged when applying national law to agreements and abusive conduct that affect trade between Member States to also apply EU law. We mentioned Article 11(6) of Regulation 1/2003 in Section 9.C.ii. In *Toshiba v Úřad pro ochranu hospodářské soutěže*[917] the CJ held that the combined effect of that provision with Article 3(1) is that the Commission's initiation of proceedings deprives NCAs of their competence to apply Articles 101 and 102 and national competition laws until the Commission proceedings are concluded.

In order to provide a level playing field,[918] Article 3(2) deals with the relationship between EU and national law and, specifically, with when national authorities may apply stricter national laws to agreements or conduct. The position differs depending upon whether Article 101 or Article 102 applies. If an agreement is authorised by Article 101, either because it does not restrict competition within the meaning of Article 101(1), it fulfils the criteria of Article 101(3), or satisfies the conditions of a block exemption, it cannot be prohibited by national law. The national authorities are, however, free to apply national competition laws which are stricter than Article 102 to unilateral conduct. They may therefore prohibit or impose sanctions on unilateral conduct engaged in by undertakings which does not constitute an abuse of a dominant position.[919] The Commission has intimated that it would like to revisit Article 3(2) as it is swayed by complaints that 'diverging standards fragment business strategies that are typically formulated on a pan-European or global basis'.[920]

Article 3(2) does not deal with the position where conduct is prohibited by Article 101 or Article 102. However, the principle of supremacy of Community law means that such an agreement or conduct cannot be permitted under national law.

Article 3(3) makes it clear that neither Article 3(1) nor Article 3(2) applies where the authority wishes to apply national merger control rules or national provisions that predominantly pursue a different objective to agreements or conduct. An NCA applying national merger rules to an acquisition or joint venture which is not a concentration with a Community dimension (or which has a Community dimension but has been referred back to the NCA) does not have to apply Article 101 or Article 102. Further, the Regulation does not preclude the implementation of more onerous 'national legislation, which protects other legitimate interests provided that such legislation is compatible with general principles and other provisions of Community law'.[921] This means that regulators applying sectoral powers which pursue a predominantly different objective to Articles 101 and 102, are not obliged to apply Article 101 or Article 102. To the extent that they are applying national competition rules or sectoral powers pursuing the same objective, however, they are obliged to apply Articles 101 and 102 and to comply with Article 3(2).

11. CRIMINALISATION AND SANCTIONS AGAINST INDIVIDUALS

EU competition law does not impose criminal liability or any type of sanction on natural persons, i.e. it does not punish individuals. The conduct of employees, directors, and officers by which an

---

[915] For the meaning of an effect on trade between Member States, see Chap. 3 Section 5.E and Chap. 5, Section 5.E.

[916] Reg. 1/2003, Art. 3(1).

[917] In Case C-17/10, *Toshiba v Úřad pro ochranu hospodářské soutěže* EU:C:2012:72.

[918] Reg. 1/2003, recital 8.

[919] In the UK, the competition authorities may investigate a market and impose remedies under the Enterprise Act 2002.

[920] Report, n. 869, para. 22, Staff Working Paper, n. 870, para. 181.

[921] Reg. 1/2003, recital 9.

undertaking infringes the competition rules results in fines for the undertaking and not in penalties for those individuals.[922]

As we saw in Chapter 9 there is, however, a global trend for criminalising some forms of 'hardcore' cartel conduct. An increasing number of jurisdictions do impose criminal liability on individuals for cartel behaviour.[923] The most notorious of these is the US, where the Sherman Act may be enforced by the DOJ through both civil and criminal processes.[924] In practice only clear, intentional violations, mostly cases of explicit price-fixing or bid-rigging, are the subject of criminal proceedings,[925] but prosecutions in this type of case are pursued as a matter of determined and aggressive policy.[926] Individual directors and executives are imprisoned[927] and extradition sought of those who have moved out of the jurisdiction.[928] The argument in favour of criminalising competition law infringements is that it has a deterrent effect way beyond that produced by sanctions against undertakings.[929] There is evidence that the possibility of prison in the US leads some international cartels to 'carve out' the US, i.e. to collude in respect of the rest of the world but not the US.[930] However, there is also a great deal of debate about how real the deterrence actually is. In order to deter there has to be knowledge of the sanction and a likelihood of detection and punishment. These factors are not always present in the cartel context. Furthermore, in democratic societies there needs to be acceptance of cartel conduct as criminal behaviour and there are considerable practical difficulties in many jurisdictions in formulating an offence in terms which fit into the criminal law system. All these matters, and others, have produced a large body of literature on the subject of criminalisation.[931]

---

[922] See the discussion of fines, in Section 7.H, p. 959 ff. Where individuals give misleading or incorrect information in the course of an inspection under Art. 20, for instance, the fine for the procedural offence is levied on the undertaking. Although the Commission now has power to conduct an inspection on the homes of individuals under Art. 21, it is still only the undertaking that is responsible for what is found there. Of course, indulging in anti-competitive practices may amount to a breach of contract meriting dismissal, particularly if the undertaking has a proper compliance programme in place. There are now instances where undertakings have commenced proceedings against employees whose unauthorised conduct has resulted in fines being imposed on the undertaking.

[923] In C. Beaton-Wells and C. Parker, 'Justifying Criminal Sanctions for Cartel Conduct: A Hard Case' (2013) 1 *J of Antitrust Enforcement* 198, 199 the figure is given as more than 30. See the list in Chap. 9, Section 2.B.i.d, p. 569. In December 2015, however, the New Zealand Government announced it was dropping plans to criminalise cartel conduct, saying that it would have had a chilling effect on pro-competitive behaviour.

[924] The Federal Trade Commission, in contrast, has no criminal jurisdiction.

[925] H. Hovenkamp, *Federal Antitrust Policy: The Law of Competition and its Practice* (4th edn, West, 2011), 643.

[926] Including pursuing individuals overseas by way of extradition proceedings, see n. 928, and Chap. 16.

[927] For example, Alfred Taubman, the billionaire who invented the shopping mall concept, spent nearly a year in prison as a result of the price-fixing agreement between Sotheby's and Christie's, and in 1999 executives from Archer Daniels Midland were convicted in connection with the lysine cartel and sentenced to prison terms of 24–30 months.

[928] As in the case of Ian Norris, *Norris v Government of the US* [2008] UKHL 16, [2008] 1 AC 920.

[929] See G. Werden, S. Hammond, and B. Barnett, 'Deterrence and Detection of Cartels: Using all the Tools and Sanctions', DOJ Speech, 1 March 2012, available at <http://www.justice.gov/atr/public/speeches/283738.pdf>.

[930] M. Bloom, 'Immunity/Leniency/Financial Incentives/Plea Bargaining', 11th EUI Competition Law and Policy Workshop, 2006; S. Hammond, 'Charting New Waters in International Cartel Prosecutions', 2 March 2006, available at <http://www.justice.gov/atr/public/speeches/214861.htm>. Applications for immunity under the DOJ leniency programme are usually accompanied by leniency applications from the individuals implicated.

[931] See, e.g., K. Cseres, M. Schinkel, and F. Vogelaar (eds.), *Criminalization of Competition Law Enforcement: Economic and Legal Implications for the EU Member States* (Edward Elgar, 2006); Beaton-Wells and Parker, n. 923 (which includes the results of an empirical Australian project); C. Beaton-Wells and A. Ezrachi (eds.), *Criminalising Cartels: Critical Studies of an International Regulatory Movement* (Hart Publishing, 2011); C. Harding, 'A Pathology of Business Cartels: Original Sin or the Child of Regulation?' (2010) 1 *NJECL* 44; A. Stephan, 'Survey of Public Attitudes to Price-fixing and Cartel Enforcement in Britain' (2008) 5 *Competition Law Review* 123; P. Whelan, 'A Principled Argument for Personal Criminal Sanctions as Punishment under EC Cartel Law' (2007) 30 *World Competition* 197; I. Lianos and I. Kokorris (eds.), *The Reform of Competition Law: Towards an Optimal Enforcement System* (Kluwer International, 2010); P. Grodecki and S. Maxwell, 'Alternative Approaches to Sentencing in Cartel Cases: The European Union, Ireland and the United States' (2013) 9 *European Law Journal* 341; P. Whelan, *The Criminalization of European Antitrust*

The problems of criminalisation in practice have been demonstrated in the UK where the Enterprise Act 2002 originally set out a statutory criminal offence for an individual who 'dishonestly' engages in price-fixing, market-sharing, and bid-rigging arrangements.[932] Individuals are liable to a sentence of up to five years' imprisonment and/or a substantial fine. The standard for 'dishonesty' was the standard laid down in the normal criminal law[933] but the House of Lords held in *Norris* (in the context of rejecting the possibility of considering price-fixing as a conspiracy to defraud at common law) that a mere charge of price-fixing, without aggravating circumstances, does not show dishonesty.[934] Prosecutions under s. 188 of the Enterprise Act 2002 proved very hard to bring and the UK Government removed the dishonesty requirement from 1 April 2014 and replaced it with statutory exclusions and defences.[935]

In the UK the CMA and sectoral regulators have power to seek a disqualification order against a director of a company that has committed a breach of the competition rules (which includes both Article 101 and Article 102 TFEU and their domestic equivalents)[936] and whose conduct makes him unfit to be concerned in the management of a company.[937] It has been cogently argued that disqualification orders may be a more effective route to securing compliance with competition rules than criminal sanctions.[938]

Liability on individuals for breach of the EU competition rules could only be imposed across the EU by a harmonisation measure which would entail each Member State making it an offence within its jurisdiction. Such a measure would need to go through the Council and EU-wide individual liability is therefore not an imminent prospect. In the meantime, the disparity between members of the ECN in matters of individual liability can lead to difficulties.[939]

12. COMPLAINTS

A. GENERAL

An entity which believes that an undertaking has committed, or is committing, a breach of EU competition law may wish to take action against that undertaking. It may wish to stop the infringement but may also hope to recover in respect of any loss suffered in consequence of the breach of the rules.

Enforcement: Theoretical, Legal, and Practical Challenges (Oxford University Press, 2014); A. Jones and R. Williams, 'The UK Response to the Global Effort Against Cartels: Is Criminalization Really the Solution' (2014) 2 *J of Antitrust Enforcement* 100; A. Stephan, 'Four Key Challenges to the Successful Criminalization of Cartel Law' (2014) 2 *J of Antitrust Enforcement* 333;. There is also a massive US literature, see, e.g., the references in the Werden, Hammond, and Barnett speech, n. 929.

[932] Penalties may also be imposed on individuals for certain procedural offences under the Competition Act 1998, ss. 42–44. The CMA has power to issue 'no-action' letters to 'whistle-blowers' confirming that an individual who meets certain stipulated conditions will not be prosecuted, Enterprise Act 2002, s. 190(4).

[933] *R v Ghosh* [1982] 2 All ER 689.

[934] *Norris v Government of the US* [2008] UKHL 16, [2008] 1 AC 920.

[935] See Enterprise Act 2002, ss. 188A–188B, as amended by the Enterprise and Regulatory Reform Act 2014. The first (and up to 5 February 2016 the only) person convicted (Nigel Snee) pleaded guilty to the dishonesty offence in respect of a cartel in the supply of galvanised steel water storage tanks. He was sentenced on 14 September 2015 to six months' imprisonment, suspended, and 120 hours of community service. Two others, who pleaded not guilty, were cleared after the jury were not convinced that they had acted 'dishonestly'. Their defence was that they had acted to maintain a sensible, sustainable profit and avoid redundancies and insolvency.

[936] Competition Act 1998, Chap. I and Chap. II prohibitions.

[937] Enterprise Act 2002, s. 204. The provisions amend the Company Directors Disqualification Act 1986.

[938] See A. Khan, 'Rethinking Sanctions for Breaching Competition Law: Is Director Disqualification the Answer?' (2012) 35 *World Competition* 77.

[939] See B. Perrin, 'Challenges Facing the EU Network of Competition Authorities: Insights from a Comparative Criminal Law Perspective' (2006) 31 *ELRev* 540.

Such an entity essentially has two possibilities. It may complain to a public enforcer, the Commission, or one of the NCAs, and hope that the authority acts on the complaint, or it may commence proceedings before a national court seeking a declaration that an agreement infringes the competition rules and is unenforceable, an injunction to prevent future breaches, and/or other remedies in respect of a breach. It may both complain *and* bring an action. Both Articles 101 and 102 are directly applicable and confer rights on individuals that can be relied on before a national court. Complainants thus play an important part in the enforcement process. Not only may they draw breaches of the competition rules to the attention of the competition authorities, but they may privately enforce the rules through civil litigation.

In many cases an aggrieved person may prefer to complain to the Commission or an NCA than to commence private proceedings. It is cheaper and more convenient. The Commission and many of the NCAs are encouraging greater private enforcement of the competition rules at the national level[940] but that may encourage rather than deter complaints from potential litigants who want an infringement decision from which to launch a 'follow-on' action. It is more difficult to bring an action in a national court in the absence of a prior finding of infringement by a competition author-ity (a 'stand-alone' action). However, the Commission wishes, in particular, to preserve its resources for cases in which a point of particular EU interest is raised. It may, therefore, decline to act on the complaint.

Regulation 1/2003 envisages that complaints may be made both to the Commission and to NCAs.[941] Article 7 provides that the Commission may, acting on a complaint or on its own initiative, find an infringement of Article 101 or Article 102 and that complaints may be lodged by 'natural or legal persons that can show a legitimate interest' and Member States. Further, Article 33 pro-vides that the Commission shall be authorised to take measures as to the form, content, and other details of complaints lodged and of the procedure for rejecting complaints. In pursuit of this objec-tive Chapter IV of the Implementing Regulation, Regulation 773/2004,[942] deals with the handling of complaints and the Commission has issued a Notice on the handling of complaints that is intended to provide guidance to those seeking relief from infringements of the competition rules. Article 5 of Regulation 1/2003 provides that an NCA, acting on a complaint or its own initiative, may take deci-sions ordering an undertaking to bring an infringement of Article 101 or Article 102 to an end and Article 13 provides that the Commission and NCAs may reject a claim which is being, or has been, dealt with by another competition authority.

One of the difficulties of encouraging complaints is that, in many cases, they may be lodged by disgruntled entities losing out in the competitive process rather than by those suffering as a result of anti-competitive conduct infringing the competition rules.

B. WHERE TO COMPLAIN

In Section 12.A it was seen that complaints can be made both to the Commission and to NCAs. An initial difficulty for a potential complainant is to decide to whom they should complain, the Commission, one or more NCAs, or to all of these authorities.

---

[940] See Chap. 14.

[941] Although Reg. 17 recognised that a complaint could be lodged with the Commission, the procedures gov-erning complaints developed informally under this system. The Commission understood the importance of com-plaints which became an established part of the enforcement procedure. In its White Paper on Modernisation, the Commission considered that complaints should play a fuller part in a directly applicable system. One of the objec-tives of the new rules was to encourage and facilitate the lodging of complaints and to draw the competition au-thorities' attention to serious infringements of the rules. In the White Paper the Commission estimated that almost 30% of new cases it dealt with resulted from complaints and that many of its own-initiative investigations began with information sent to the Commission informally, White Paper on Modernisation [1999] OJ C132/1, para. 117.

[942] [2004] OJ 123/18.

The Commission's Notice on the handling of complaints indicates that the complaint should be made to the 'authority most likely to be well placed to deal with their case'.[943] In determining who is best placed, guidance can be obtained from the Commission's NCA Cooperation Notice,[944] which deals with work-sharing between the Commission and NCAs inside the ECN.[945] The authorities inform each other of investigations being made following a complaint, and members of the network seek to ensure that the correct authority is put in charge of the case.

Commission Notice on the Handling of Complaints by the Commission under Articles 81 and 82 of the EC Treaty [2004] OJ C101/65

23. Within the European Competition Network, information on cases that are being investigated following a complaint will be made available to the other members of the network before or without delay after commencing the first formal investigative measure. Where the same complaint has been lodged with several authorities or where a case has not been lodged with an authority that is well placed, the members of the network will endeavour to determine within an indicative time-limit of two months which authority or authorities should be in charge of the case.

24. Complainants themselves have an important role to play in further reducing the potential need for reallocation of a case originating from their complaint by referring to the orientations on worksharing in the network set out in the present chapter when deciding on where to lodge their complaint. If nonetheless a case if reallocated within the network, the undertakings concerned and the complainant(s) are informed as soon as possible by the competition authorities involved.

25. The Commission may reject a complaint in accordance with Article 13 of Regulation 1/2003, on the grounds that a Member State is dealing or has dealt with the case. When doing so the Commission must, in accordance with Article 9 of Regulation 773/2004 inform the complaint without delay of the national competition authority which is dealing or has already dealt with the case.

C. STANDING

Regulation 1/2003 provides that 'natural or legal persons who can show a legitimate interest' and Member States (which are deemed to have a legitimate interest for all complaints they lodge) have standing to complain about a breach of the competition rules.[946]

Any applicant who is directly and adversely affected, or will be so affected, as a result of the infringement will have standing. It has been held, for example, that an entity which has been excluded, or threatened with exclusion, from a distribution network;[947] which believes that it was negotiating with members of a cartel;[948] or which believes itself to be a victim of abusive behaviour by a dominant undertaking,[949] has a legitimate interest within the meaning of Article 3(2). Further, in *BEMIM*

---

[943] Commission Notice on the Handling of Complaints by the Commission under Articles 81 and 82 of the EC Treaty [2004] OJ C101/65, para. 21 (the Complaints Notice).

[944] [2004] OJ C101/54, especially points 8–15.

[945] Complaints Notice, paras. 19–25.

[946] Art. 7(2). This is similar to the language previously used in Reg. 17, Art. 3.

[947] Case 210/81, *Demo-Studio Schmidt v Commission* [1983] ECR 3045.

[948] See, e.g., *Building and Construction Industry in the Netherlands* [1992] OJ L92/1 (a complaint about collusive tendering lodged by a local authority).

[949] See, e.g., Cases 6 and 7/73, *Istituto Chemioterapico Italiano SpA and Commercial Solvents Corp v Commission* [1974] ECR 223, complaint by Zoja, *Zoja-CSC/ICI* [1972] OJ L299/51; Case C-62/86, *AKZO Chemie BV v Commission* [1991] ECR I-3359, complaint lodged by ECS; see Chaps. 6 and 7).

v Commission[950] the GC held that a trade association had a legitimate interest where the conduct complained of was liable to affect adversely the interests of the members that it was entitled to represent. The Complaints Notice provides further guidance on this matter, providing examples of entities which would have a legitimate interest such as consumer associations. Paragraph 38 says that those acting purely *pro bono publico* do not have a legitimate interest.

Commission Notice on the Handling of Complaints by the Commission under Article 101 and 102 of the EC Treaty [2004] OJ C101/65

35. The [General Court] had held that an association of undertakings may claim a legitimate interest in lodging a complaint regarding conduct concerning its members even if it not directly concerned, as an undertaking operating in the relevant market, by the conduct complained of, provided that, first, it is entitled to represent the interests of its members[951] and secondly, the conduct complained of is liable to adversely affect the interests of its members. Conversely, the Commission has been found to be entitled not to pursue the complaint of an association of undertakings whose members were not involved in the type of business transactions complained of.[952]

36. From this case law, it can be inferred that undertakings (themselves or through associations that are entitled to represent their interests) can claim a legitimate interest where they are operating in the relevant market or where the conduct complained of is liable to directly and adversely affect their interests. This confirms the established practice of the Commission which has accepted that a legitimate interest can, for instance, be claimed by the parties to the agreement or practice which is the subject of the complaint, by competitors whose interests have allegedly been damaged by the behaviour complained of or by undertakings excluded from a distribution system.

37. Consumer associations can equally lodge complaints with the Commission.[953] The Commission moreover holds the view that individual consumers whose economic interests are directly and adversely affected insofar as they are the buyers of goods or services that are the object of an infringement can be in a position to show a legitimate interest.[954]

38. However, the Commission does not consider as a legitimate interest within the meaning of Article 7(2) the interest of persons or organizations that wish to come forward on general interest considerations without showing that they or their members are liable to be directly and adversely affected by the infringement (*pro bono publico*).

39. Local or public authorities may be able to show a legitimate interest in their capacity as buyers or users of goods or services affected by the conduct complained of. Conversely, they cannot be considered as showing a legitimate interest within the meaning of Article 7(2) of Regulation 1/2002 to the extent that they bring to the attention of the Commission alleged infringements *pro bono publico*.

40. Complainants have to demonstrate their legitimate interest. Where a natural or legal person lodging a complaint is unable to demonstrate a legitimate interest, the Commission is entitled, without prejudice to its right to initiate proceedings of its own initiative, not to pursue the complaint. The Commission may ascertain whether this condition is met at any stage of the investigation.

---

[950] Case T-114/92, [1995] ECR II-147; see in particular para. 28.

[951] See, e.g., Case T-114/92, *BEMIM v Commission* [1995] ECR II-147, para. 28.

[952] See, e.g., Cases T-133 and 204/95, *IECC v Commission* [1998] ECR II-3645, paras. 79–83.

[953] See, e.g., Case T-37/92, *BEUC v Commission* [1994] ECR II-285, para. 36.

[954] This point was raised in Cases T-213 and 214/01 as seen in the next extract.

In *Österreichische Postsparkasse* the GC took a broad view of those having a 'legitimate interest' under Article 3(2) of Regulation 17, the antecedent of Article 7(2) of Regulation 1/2003. It extended this to any final consumer who can show that his economic interests have been harmed.

Cases T-213 and 214/01, *Österreichische Postsparkasse v Commission* [2006] ECR II-1601

The case was an appeal against two decisions of the Hearing Officer to send to an Austrian political party (FPÖ) the non-confidential version of the SO in the investigation which culminated in the *Lombard Club* decision.[955] The FPÖ complained to the Commission in June 1997 about certain practices of a group of Austrian banks. In February 1998 the Commission informed the FPÖ that it intended to reject its complaint, stating that it did not have a legitimate interest within Article 3(2) of Regulation 17. In fact, the Commission had already started an investigation on its own initiative in May 1997, before it had received the complaint. In due course the Commission sent the banks an SO and informed them that it intended to send a non-confidential version to the FPÖ. The banks protested but the Hearing Officer overruled their objections.[956] The banks claimed that the FPÖ did not have sufficient 'legitimate interest' under Article 3(2) to merit receiving the SO. The copy of the SO was duly sent, and its contents were disclosed to the press. The banks carried on with an appeal to the General Court, claiming, *inter alia*, that the FPÖ's status as a customer of banking services did not constitute a 'legitimate interest' under Article 3(2).

General Court

114. The [General Court] considers that there is nothing to prevent a final customer who purchases goods or services from being able to satisfy the notion of legitimate interest within the meaning of Article 3 of Regulation No 17. The Court considers that a final customer who shows that his economic interests have been harmed or are likely to be harmed as a result of the restriction of competition in question has a legitimate interest within the meaning of Article 3 of Regulation No 17 in making an application or a complaint in order to seek a declaration from the Commission that Articles [101 and 102] have been infringed.

115. It should be pointed out in this respect that the ultimate purpose of the rules that seek to ensure that competition is not distorted in the internal market is to increase the well-being of consumers. That purpose can be seen in particular from the wording of Article [101]. Whilst the prohibition laid down in Article [101(1)] may be declared inapplicable in the case of cartels which contribute to improving the production or distribution of the goods in question or to promoting technical or economic progress, that possibility, for which provision is made in Article [101(3)], is inter alia subject to the condition that a fair share of the resulting benefit is allowed for users of those products. Competition law and competition policy therefore have an undeniable impact on the specific economic interests of final customers who purchase goods or services. Recognition that such customers—who show that they have suffered economic damage as a result of an agreement or conduct liable to restrict or distort competition—have a legitimate interest in seeking from the Commission a declaration that Articles [101 EC and 102] have been infringed contributes to the attainment of the objectives of competition law.

116. Contrary to the claims made by the applicants, this finding does not effectively render the notion of legitimate interest meaningless by making it excessively broad or pave the way for an alleged '*actio popularis*'. Acknowledging that a consumer who can show that his economic interests have been harmed as a result of a cartel complained of by him may have a legitimate interest in this regard within the meaning of Article 3(2) of Regulation No 17 is not the same as considering that any natural or legal person has such an interest.

---

[955] [2004] OJ L56/1, substantially upheld by the GC in Cases T-259, 264, and 271/02, *Raiffeisen Zentralbank Österreich AG v Commission* [2006] ECR II-5169, *aff'd* Case C-125/07, *Erste Bank AG (formerly Erste Bank der österreichischen Sparkassen) v Commission* [2009] ECR I-8681.

[956] In Case T-213/01 R, *Österreichische Postsparkasse v Commission* [2001] ECR II-3963, the President of the GC rejected a request to suspend the Hearing Officer's decision.

An individual who does not have a legitimate interest within the meaning of Article 7(2) of Regulation 1/2003 even after *Österreichische Postsparkasse*, or for some reason does not want to make an official complaint, may still draw the Commission's attention informally to market information which indicates that conduct may be in breach of the competition rules. Once the conduct has been drawn to its intention the Commission is, of course, free to commence proceedings on its own initiative if it considers it appropriate to do so.

D. THE PROCEDURE

A formal complaint must be submitted in compliance with Form C,[957] available on DG Comp's website.[958] Form C requires the complainant to provide information regarding itself, details of the alleged infringement and evidence, an explanation of the findings sought from the Commission, the grounds on which a legitimate interest is claimed, and details of any approach made to another competition authority or lawsuits brought before a national court. In certain circumstances, the Commission may waive the need for submission of some of the comprehensive information and supporting documentation required.[959]

E. THE THREE-STAGE PROCEDURE

On receipt of a complaint the Commission is bound to collect information which enables it to determine whether it should reject the complaint or conduct an investigation.[960]

During the first stage of the procedure it collects information from the complainant, gives an initial reaction to the case, and allows the complainant an opportunity to expand on its allegations.[961]

During the second stage it investigates further to determine whether to initiate proceedings or to reject the complaint.[962] Before the Commission rejects a complaint, it must give the complainant an opportunity to make its views known on the Commission's provisional intention to reject, within a specified time limit.[963] This is known as sending the complainant an 'Article 7(1) letter'.[964] The complainant may also be provided with access to non-confidential documents on which the Commission has based its provisional assessment. The Article 7(1) letter is not in itself capable of being challenged before the GC.

Taking cognisance of the views of the complainant the Commission, in the third stage, either initiates proceedings or rejects the complaint.[965]

F. REJECTION OF THE COMPLAINT

(i) Introduction

The Commission may on investigation consider that no breach of the EU competition rules has occurred. Alternatively, it may consider that a breach might have occurred but that the case is of insufficient Union interest to warrant the time and resources that would be involved in investigation.

---

[957] Reg. 773/2004 [2004] OJ L123/18, Art. 5, and Annex.

[958] The Commission encourages electronic submission.

[959] Reg. 773/2004 [2004] OJ L123/18, Art. 5(1).

[960] See Section 12.F and the Complaints Notice, para. 54.

[961] Complaints Notice, para. 55.

[962] Ibid., para. 56. The procedure prior to rejecting a complaint is set out in Best Practices, paras. 139–141.

[963] Reg. 773/2004 [2004] OJ L123/18, Art. 7(1).

[964] I.e., ibid., Art. 7(1).

[965] Complaints Notice, para. 57.

It may also consider that another NCA within the ECN would be better placed to deal with the case. Although the Commission has a duty 'to examine carefully the facts and points of law brought to its notice by the complainant in order to decide whether they disclose conduct liable to distort competition in the [internal] market and affect trade between Member States'[966] it does not have a duty to proceed to a final decision on the alleged breach of the rules. The Commission must, however, examine the case carefully in order to assess the Union interest in further investigation of the case.[967]

(ii) The Union Interest and the Right to Prioritise

In *Automec Srl v Commission (Automec II)*[968] the GC held that the Commission is entitled to prioritise cases before it. As a public enforcer it has a margin of discretion to set priorities in its enforcement activity. It may reject a complaint on the ground that it does not raise a sufficient Union interest. Save where the subject matter of the complaint falls within the exclusive purview of the Commission,[969] the rights conferred upon complainants do not, therefore, include a right to obtain a decision as regards the existence or otherwise of the alleged infringement. Rather, the Commission, in fulfilling its functions, is bound to apply different degrees of priority to the cases arising before it. The Commission is therefore entitled to assess whether the complaint raises sufficient Union interest to warrant an investigation.

Case T-24/90, *Automec Srl v Commission (Automec II)* [1992] ECR II-2223

A complaint was lodged by Automec Srl, in respect of the refusal by BMW to renew Automec's distributorship of BMW cars in Treviso, Italy. Automec brought proceedings before the national courts to compel BMW to continue the contractual relationship and subsequently, in 1988, lodged a complaint with the Commission. In particular, it contended that BMW was obliged to supply it with vehicles and spare parts on the terms applicable to other dealers. The Commission sent Automec a letter stating that it had no power to grant its application. Automec commenced judicial review proceedings before the GC seeking annulment of the letter and damages from the Commission in respect of loss suffered in consequence of the Commission's failure to commence proceedings against BMW (*Automec I*). Subsequently, further letters were exchanged between the Commission and Automec. In February 1990 the Commission sent Automec a letter rejecting the complaint, stating that there was not a sufficient Community interest to justify examining the facts raised by the complaint. Automec brought further proceedings before the GC seeking annulment of the February 1990 decision.

General Court

71. The Court considers that the question raised by this plea asks in substance what the Commission's obligations are when it receives an application under Article 3 of Regulation No 17 from a natural or legal person.

72. It is appropriate to point out that Regulations Nos 17 and 99/63 confer procedural rights on persons who have lodged a complaint with the Commission, such as the right to be informed of the reasons for which the Commission intends to reject their complaint and the right to submit observations in this connection. Thus the Community legislature has imposed certain specified obligations upon the Commission. However, neither Regulation No 17 nor Regulation No 99/63 contain[s] express provisions

---

[966] Case T-575/93, *Koelman v Commission* [1996] ECR II-1, para. 39.

[967] Complaints Notice, para. 42.

[968] Case T-24/90, [1992] ECR II-2223.

[969] E.g., the withdrawal of a block exemption in an individual case, see Reg. 1/2003, Art. 29.

relating to the action to be taken concerning the substance of a complaint and any obligations on the part of the Commission to carry out investigations.

73. In determining the Commission's obligations in this context, the first point to note is that the Commission is responsible for the implementation and orientation of Community competition policy (see the judgment of the Court of Justice in Case C-234/89 *Delimitis* v. *Henninger Bräu AG* . . .at 991). For that reason, Article [101(1)] gave the Commission the task of ensuring that the principles laid down by Articles [101] and [102] were applied, and the provisions adopted pursuant to Article [103] have conferred wide powers upon it.

74. The scope of the Commission's obligations in the field of competition law must be examined in the light of Article [101(1)], which, in this area, constitutes the specific expression of the general supervisory task entrusted to the Commission by Article [17(1) TEU]. However, as the Court of Justice has held with regard to Article [258 TFEU] in Case 247/87 *Star Fruit* v. *Commission* . . . at 301, that task does not mean that the Commission is bound to commence proceedings seeking to establish the existence of any infringement of Community law.

75. In that regard, the Court observes that it appears from the case-law of the Court of Justice (judgment in *GEMA* . . . at 3189) that the rights conferred upon complainants by Regulations Nos 17 and 99/63 do not include a right to obtain a decision, within the meaning of Article [288 TFEU], as regards the existence or otherwise of the alleged infringement. It follows that the Commission cannot be required to give a decision in that connection unless the subject-matter of the complaint falls within its exclusive purview, as in the case of the withdrawal of an exemption granted under Article [101(3)].

76. As the Commission is under no obligation to rule on the existence or otherwise of an infringement it cannot be compelled to carry out an investigation, because such investigation could have no purpose other than to seek evidence of the existence or otherwise of an infringement, which it is not required to establish. In that regard, it should be noted that, unlike the provision contained in the second sentence of Article [105(1)] in relation to applications by Member States, Regulations Nos 17 and 99/63 do not expressly oblige the Commission to investigate complaints submitted to it.

77. In that connection, it should be observed that, in the case of an authority entrusted with a public service task, the power to take all the organizational measures necessary for the performance of that task, including setting priorities within the limits prescribed by the law—where those priorities have not been determined by the legislature—is an inherent feature of administrative activity. This must be the case in particular where an authority has been entrusted with a supervisory and regulatory task as extensive and general as that which has been assigned to the Commission in the field of competition. Consequently, the fact that the Commission applies different degrees of priority to the cases submitted to it in the field of competition is compatible with the obligations imposed on it by Community law.

78. That assessment does not conflict with the judgments of the Court of Justice in *Demo-Studio Schmidt* . . . in Case 298/83 *CICCE* v. *Commission* . . . and in Joined Cases 142 and 156/84 *BAT and Reynolds* v. *Commission* . . . In the judgment in *Demo-Studio Schmidt*, the Court of Justice held that the Commission 'was under a duty to examine the facts put forward' by the complainant, without prejudging the question whether the Commission could refrain from investigating the complaint because, in that case, the Commission had examined the facts set out in the complaint and had rejected it on the ground that there was nothing to suggest the existence of an infringement. Likewise this question did not arise in the later cases of *CICCE* (cited above) and *BAT and Reynolds* (cited above).

79. However, although the Commission cannot be compelled to conduct an investigation, the procedural safeguards provided for by Article 3 of Regulation No 17 and Article 6 of Regulation No 99/63 oblige it nevertheless to examine carefully the factual and legal particulars brought to its notice by the complainant in order to decide whether they disclose conduct of such a kind as to distort competition in the common market and affect trade between Member States (see the judgments in *Demo-Studio Schmidt*, *CICCE* and *BAT and Reynolds*, cited above).

. . .

84. The next point to consider is whether it is legitimate, as the Commission has argued, to refer to the Community interest in a case as a priority criterion.

85. In this connection, it should be borne in mind that, unlike the civil courts, whose task is to safeguard the individual rights of private persons in their relations *inter se*, an administrative authority must act in the public interest. Consequently, the Commission is entitled to refer to the Community interest in order to determine the degree of priority to be applied to the various cases brought to its notice. This does not amount to removing action by the Commission from the scope of judicial review, since, in view of the requirement to provide a statement of reasons laid down by Article [296 TFEU], the Commission cannot merely refer to the Community interest in the abstract. It must set out the legal and factual considerations which led it to conclude that there was insufficient Community interest to justify investigation of the case. It is therefore by reviewing the legality of those reasons that the Court can review the Commission's action.

86. In order to assess the Community interest in further investigation of a case, the Commission must take account of the circumstances of the case, and in particular of the legal and factual particulars set out in the complaint referred to it. The Commission should in particular balance the significance of the alleged infringement as regards the functioning of the common market, the probability of establishing the existence of the infringement and the scope of the investigation required in order to fulfil, under the best possible conditions, its task of ensuring that Articles [101] and [102] are complied with.

At paragraph 44 of the Complaints Notice,[970] the Commission sets out some of the criteria, taken from the case law, which it uses to assess whether or not a particular case now has a Union interest:[971]

— The Commission can reject a complaint on the ground that the complainant can bring an action to assert its rights before national courts.

— The Commission may not regard certain situations as excluded in principle from its purview under the task entrusted to it by the Treaty but is required to assess in each case how serious the alleged infringements are and how persistent their consequences are. This means in particular that it must take into account the duration and the extent of the infringements complained of and their effect on the competition situation in the Community.

— The Commission may have to balance the significance of the alleged infringement as regards the functioning of the common market, the probability of establishing the existence of the infringement and the scope of the investigation required in order to fulfil its task of ensuring that Articles [101 and 102 TFEU] are complied with.

— While the Commission's discretion does not depend on how advanced the investigation of a case is, the stage of the investigation forms part of the circumstances of the case which the Commission may have to take into consideration.

— The Commission may decide that it is not appropriate to investigate a complaint where the practices in question have ceased. However, for this purpose, the Commission will have to ascertain whether anti-competitive effects persist and if the seriousness of the infringements or the persistence of their effects does not give the complaint a Community interest . . .

— The Commission may also decide that it is not appropriate to investigate a complaint where the undertakings concerned agree to change their conduct in such a way that it can consider that there is no longer a sufficient Community interest to intervene . . .

The Commission applied these principles when rejecting a complaint about Athens airport, particularly the first and third indent, and was upheld on appeal.[972] The rejection of a complaint about the

---

[970] [2004] OJ C101/65.

[971] After *Automec* the Commission dealt with the question of whether a particular case had a Community interest in its old Notice on cooperation between national courts and the Commission in applying Articles 85 and 86 [81 and 82] of the EEC [EC] Treaty [1993] OJ C39/6, see especially paras. 13–15. The Notice has now been replaced by the 2004 Notice on the cooperation between the Commission and the courts of the EU Member States.

[972] Case T-306/05, *Scippacercola and Terezakis v Commission* [2008] ECR II-4 (COMP/38.469, *Athens International Airport*) upheld by order, Case C-159/08 P, [2009] ECR I-46. See also Case T-60/05, *Union Française de l'Express v Commission (UFEX)* [2007] ECR II-3397 (Commission should consider seriousness of infringement even when

prices increases of a German electricity supplier (E.ON) resulted in a complaint to the Ombudsman about the Commission's refusal to open proceedings. The Ombudsman held that the Commission had acted within the limits of its discretion in declining to open proceedings.[973]

It is clear, however, from paragraphs 79–86 of *Automec II*, that before rejecting a complaint the Commission must carefully examine the factual and legal particulars brought to its notice; set out the legal and factual considerations which led it to the conclusion of insufficient Union interest; and take account of the circumstances of the case.[974] It must examine the complaint diligently and impartially in accordance with the principle of sound administration as confirmed in the Charter of Fundamental Rights.[975] In *CEAHR*[976] the GC held that the Commission had committed manifest errors of assessment in dealing with a complaint from luxury watch repairers about the practices of luxury watch manufacturers in that it had wrongly defined the market[977] and had given inadequate reasons for limiting the size of the relevant market and the territories it covered before concluding that there was insufficient Union interest.

The Commission said in the Report on Regulation 1/2003 that it wanted to examine further how it can streamline the handling of complaints that are not a priority case.[978] The obligations imposed by the case law (see the next extract, from *Guérin*) mean that non-priority cases nevertheless create an administrative burden.[979]

(iii) Investigation by Another Competition Authority

As already indicated, the Commission is entitled to reject a complaint under Article 13(2) of Regulation 1/2003 on the grounds that an NCA is dealing, or has dealt, with the case.[980] The meaning of this was explored in *easyJet*.[981] The airline lodged a number of complaints about charges at Schiphol airport with the Netherlands competition authority, NMa. The NMa rejected all of them, having examined the charges in the light of Article 102. The airline then lodged a complaint with the Commission, again alleging that the charges were excessive and discriminatory and contrary to Article 102. The Commission rejected the complaint on the basis, inter alia, that an NCA had already dealt with it. easyJet appealed, claiming that having been rejected, its complaints had not been 'dealt with'. The GC held that a complaint has been dealt with in the meaning of Article 13(2) if an NCA has rejected it on the basis of a review carried out in the light of the EU competition rules.

(iv) The Commission is Obliged to Make a Formal Rejection of the Complaint

Where the Commission decides not to act on a complaint, has communicated this to the complainant, and given it an opportunity to make its views known by the sending of an Article 7(1) letter,

---

terminated and without continuing anti-competitive effects); Case T-74/11, *Omnis v Commission* EU:T:2013:283 (there is no obligatory or limited list of criteria the Commission has to apply, it depends on the circumstances of the individual case).

[973] Complaint 1142/2008/(BEH)KM.

[974] Case T-432/05, *EMC Development AB v Commission* [2010] ECR II-1629, paras. 59–60, appeal dismissed Case C-367/10 P, [2011] ECR I-46.

[975] Case T-54/99, *max.mobil v Commission* [2002] ECR II-313, paras. 56–57.

[976] Case T-427/08, *Confédération européenne des associations d'horlogers-réparateurs (CEAHR) v Commission* [2010] ECR II-5865.

[977] See Chap. 1, Section 15.B.vii.e, p. 72.

[978] Report on Regulation 1/2003, para. 16.

[979] See Staff Working Paper, n. 870, para. 117.

[980] Reg. 1/2003, Art. 13.

[981] Case T-355/13, *easyJet v Commission* EU:T:2015:36.

the Commission is bound either to initiate a procedure or to reject the complaint by decision under Article 7(2) of Regulation 773/2004.[982]

> ### Case T-186/94, *Guérin Automobiles v Commission* [1995] ECR II-1753
>
> **General Court**
>
> 34.... [I]t should be emphasized that, having submitted within the time stipulated in the letter of 13 June 1994 comments in response to the Article [7] notification, the applicant is henceforth entitled to obtain a definitive decision from the Commission on its complaint; and that decision may, if the applicant sees fit, be challenged in an action for annulment before this court ...

Although, therefore, the Commission cannot be required in every case to proceed to a final decision on the compatibility of the conduct complained of with the competition rules it must, if it is not going to investigate, formally reject the complaint by decision, stating reasons, before closing its file. This decision is subject to appeal before the GC.

G. ACTING ON A COMPLAINT

If the Commission considers it to be worthwhile to initiate proceedings, it may do so by issuing an SO. It can take an infringement decision even if the complaint has been withdrawn in the meantime.[983] The Commission's fact-finding powers and the opening of a formal procedure are discussed in Sections 7.C and 7.D. A few points of importance to a complainant are, however, highlighted here. First, since the Commission is bound by a general duty of confidentiality the complainant should be sure to mark any business secrets or other confidential information which it does not wish the Commission to disclose. Secondly, if the Commission initiates proceedings and issues an SO relating to a matter in respect of which it has received a complaint, it must provide a non-confidential version of the SO to the complainant and give it an opportunity to make its views known in writing. This does not apply in respect of the SO in the cartel settlement procedure.[984] Where appropriate, non-confidential versions of the replies to the SO can be given to the complainant, provided that business secrets are not disclosed and the suppliers of the information have been consulted[985] and, where appropriate, non-confidential versions of the complainants' comments may be sent to the undertakings complained of.[986] Thirdly, the complainant may also be given the opportunity to make submissions at the oral hearing if it so requests.[987] Fourthly, the complainant cannot specifically request that the Commission adopt interim measures. According to Article 8 of Regulation 1/2003 the Commission may order interim measures *on its own initiative* where there is the risk of serious and irreparable damage to *competition*. The Commission takes the view that requests for interim measures should be brought before the national courts—which are better placed to decide on such measures.[988] Fifthly, if the Commission does find that an undertaking has

---

[982] Reg. 773/2004 [2004] OJ L123/18, Art. 7(2). Case T-64/89, *Automec Srl v Commission (Automec I)* [1990] ECR II-367.

[983] COMP/37.860, *Morgan Stanley/Visa International and Visa Europe*, on appeal Case T-461/07 [2011] ECR II-1729.

[984] Introduced by Reg. 622/2008. Nor is the complainant entitled to see the settlement submissions.

[985] Antitrust ManProc, Module 21, para. 17.

[986] Ibid., Module 21, para. 18.

[987] Reg. 773/2004 [2004] OJ L123/18, Art. 6. Complaints Notice, paras. 64–67.

[988] Complaints Notice, para. 80.

infringed Article 101 or Article 102 it cannot compensate an entity which has suffered loss in consequence of a breach.[989] Compensation must be pursued through private action in a national court, as discussed in Chapter 14.

H. JUDICIAL REVIEW PROCEEDINGS

(i) An Omission to Act

Where the Commission is in breach of an obligation to act it is possible, under Article 265, to bring proceedings in respect of its failure to act.[990] Before such proceedings can be brought it is essential that the Commission should have been called upon to act and have failed to adopt a measure in relation to the complainant which that complainant was legally entitled to claim by virtue of the rules of EU law. Since a complainant cannot insist that the Commission should commence an investigation it cannot bring proceedings under Article 265 in respect of its failure to launch such an investigation. However, the complainant can challenge the failure to issue an Article 7(1) letter within a reasonable time.[991] Because the Commission is obliged to issue a formal rejection of a complaint, a complainant can bring Article 265 proceedings where such a final decision has not been taken. Once the Commission informs a complainant that it has decided to close its file and has formally rejected a complaint that complainant may, if it so wishes, bring judicial review proceedings under Article 263 TFEU challenging the validity of that decision.

(ii) Review of Acts

A complainant may wish to bring proceedings to annul a Commission decision rejecting its complaint or any decision made subsequent to an investigation. If an individual has standing to complain to the Commission, it is considered that it will also have standing to institute proceedings where its complaint is rejected. In *Metro v Commission* the CJ held that it was essential that a person with a legitimate interest 'should be able, if their request is not complied with either wholly or in part, to institute proceedings in order to protect their legitimate interests. In those circumstances, the applicant must be considered to be directly and individually concerned within the meaning of the second paragraph of Article [263], by the contested decision.'[992]

The formal rejection of a complaint is a reviewable act within the meaning of Article 263.[993] However, the Commission's initial letters (such as the Article 7(1) letter) and preliminary investigations are not reviewable, and may not be challenged. In some cases it may be difficult to determine whether or not the Commission has actually given a final decision which is susceptible to challenge under Article 263.[994]

I. COMPLAINTS AND THE MERGER REGULATION

The rights of third parties under the EU Merger Regulation are dealt with in Chapter 15.

---

[989] The fine goes into the EU coffers.

[990] See Craig and de Búrca, n. 836, p. 537 ff.

[991] See Cases T-190/95 and T-45/96, *Sodima v Commission* [1999] ECR II-3617.

[992] Case 26/76, *Metro SB-Grossmärtke GmbH & Co KG v Commission* [1977] ECR 1875, para. 13.

[993] See Section 8.A.iv, p. 994.

[994] See, e.g., Case T-37/92, *BEUC* [1994] ECR II-285 and Case C-39/93 P, *SFEI v Commission* [1994] ECR I-2681.

13. CONCLUSIONS

1. Regulation 1/2003 made fundamental changes to the way that Articles 101 and 102 are enforced, with the principal objective of strengthening enforcement of those rules. The changes have had significant effects on the Commission, NCAs, and undertakings. The operation of the ECN has so far been highly successful, but the judgment in *Tele2 Polska* underlined the fact that NCAs are junior partners to the Commission.

2. The Commission gained new powers under Regulation 1/2003 to facilitate its task of detecting and punishing breaches of Articles 101 and 102. It pursues an increasingly aggressive policy, particularly towards cartels, with draconian fines. Its actions against cartels are heavily dependent on the leniency policy and the settlement procedure allows the Commission to save time and resources.

3. The Commission's extensive use of the commitments decision procedure in Article 9, and the use of the settlement procedure in cartel cases, have to a large extent changed the nature of the Commission's enforcement strategy. Top-down enforcement has been replaced by negotiated outcomes. This is advantageous to the Commission and may be convenient for the parties, but commitments decisions in particular are prejudicial to the development of the law as what may be novel and controversial points of law, and remedies which would not be possible under Article 7, are taken away from the possibility of review by the EU Courts. The development of the law on Article 102 in particular, therefore, may come to depend more on preliminary references from the national courts.

4. The extensive powers of the Commission in competition cases and the (limited) role of the EU Courts are questionable in the light of the human rights guarantees provided in the EU's own legal order, and in the ECHR which it reflects and to which the EU is, under the Treaty of Lisbon, committed to acceding. The CJ has approved the enforcement system as compliant with the Charter, and changed the terms in which the intensity of the GC's review is described, but it has not put an end to criticisms of the system. The question remains as to whether the investigation and prosecutorial functions of the Commission should be separated from adjudication.

14. FURTHER READING

A. BOOKS

AMATO, G., *Antitrust and the Bounds of Power* (Hart Publishing, 1997), Chap. 8

ANDREANGELI, A., *EU Competition Enforcement and Human Rights* (Edward Elgar, 2008)

BEATON-WELLS, C., and EZRACHI, A. (eds.), *Criminalising Cartels: Critical Studies of an International Regulatory Movement* (Hart Publishing, 2011)

BEATON-WELLS, C., and TRAN, C., *Anti-cartel Enforcement in a Contemporary Age: Leniency Religion* (Hart Publishing, 2015)

BELLAMY and CHILD (V. Rose and D. Bailey, eds.), *European Union Law of Competition* (7th edn, Oxford University Press, 2013 and Supplement by L. John and J. Turner, 2015), Chaps. 13–15

BUHART, J., and HENRY, D., *Leniency Regimes* (5th edn, Sweet & Maxwell, 2015)

EHLERMANN, C.-D., and ATANASIU, I. (eds.), *European Competition Law Annual 2000: The Modernisation of EC Antitrust Policy* (Hart Publishing, 2001)

EHLERMANN, C.-D., and ATANASIU, M. (eds.), *European Competition Law Annual 2001: Effective Enforcement of EC Antitrust Law* (Hart Publishing, 2003)

EHLERMANN, C.-D., and MARQUIS, M. (eds.), *European Competition Law Annual 2008: Antitrust Settlements Under EC Competition Law* (Hart Publishing, 2010)

EHLERMANN, C.-D., and MARQUIS, M. (eds.), *European Competition Law Annual 2009: The Evaluation of Evidence and its Judicial Review in Competition Cases* (Hart Publishing, 2011)

EHLERMANN, C.-D., and MARQUIS, M. (eds.), *European Competition Law Annual 2010: Merger Control in European and Global Perspective* (Hart Publishing, 2013)

FAULL, J., and NIKPAY, A., *The EU Law of Competition* (3rd edn, Oxford University Press, 2014), Chap. 2 and Chap. 8, 8.95–8.725

KERSE, C., and KHAN, N. (Khan ed.), *EU Antitrust Procedure* (6th edn, Sweet & Maxwell, 2012)

Lianos, I., and Geradin, D. (eds.), *Handbook on European Competition Law (Enforcement and Procedure)* (Edward Elgar, 2013)

Lianos, I., and Kokorris, I. (eds.), *The Reform of Competition Law: Towards an Optimal Enforcement System* (Kluwer, 2010)

Merola, M., and Derenne, J., *The Role of the Court of Justice of the European Union in Competition Law Cases* (Bruylant, 2012)

Nazzini, R., *Concurrent Proceedings in Competition Law* (Oxford University Press, 2004)

Nazzini, R., *Competition Enforcement and Procedure* (Oxford University Press, 2016)

Nihoul, P., and Skoczy, T. (eds.), *Procedural Fairness in Competition Proceedings* (Edward Elgar, 2015)

Ortiz Blanco, L., *EU Competition Procedure* (3rd edn, Oxford University Press, 2013)

Simonsson, I., *Legitimacy in EU Cartel Control* (Hart Publishing, 2010)

Tridimas, T., *The General Principles of EC Law* (2nd edn, Oxford University Press, 2006)

Van Bael, I., *Due Process in EU Competition Proceedings* (Kluwer, 2011)

Wardhaugh, B., *Cartels, Markets and Crime: A Normative Justification for Criminalization of Economic Collusion* (Cambridge University Press, 2014)

Wesseling, R., *The Modernisation of EC Antitrust Law* (Hart Publishing, 2000)

Whelan, P., The Criminalization of European Antitrust Enforcement: Theoretical, Legal, and Practical Challenges (Oxford University Press, 2014)

Wils, W., *The Optimal Enforcement of EC Antitrust Law: Essays in Law and Economics* (Kluwer Law International, 2002)

B. CHAPTERS IN BOOKS

Forrester, I., 'A Bush in Need of Pruning: The Luxuriant Growth of "Light Judicial Review"' in C.-D. Ehlermann and M. Marquis (eds.), *European Competition Law Annual 2009: The Evaluation of Evidence and its Judicial Review in Competition Cases* (Hart Publishing, 2010), 407

Lianos, I., 'Is the Availability of "Appropriate" Remedies a Limit to Competition Law Liability under Article 102 TFEU? The Mischiefs of "Discretionary Remedialism" in Competition Law' in F. Etro and I. Kokkoris (eds.), *Competition Law and* the Enforcement of Article 102 (Oxford University Press, 2010), Chap. 10

Pace, L. F., and Seidel, K., 'The Drafting and Role of Regulation 17: A Hard-Fought Compromise' in K. K. Patel and H. Schweitzer (eds.), *The Historical Foundations of EU Competition Law* (Oxford University Press, 2013), 54

Temple Lang, J., 'The AM&S Judgment' in M. Hoskins and W. Robinson (eds.), *A True European—Essays for Judge David Edward* (Hart Publishing, 2004), Chap. 12

C. ARTICLES

Albers, M., and Jourdan, J., 'The Role of Hearing Officers in EU Competition Proceedings: A Historical and Practical Perspective' (2011) 2 *JECLAP* 185

Amory, B. E., and Desmedt, Y. N., 'The European Ombudsman's First Scrutiny of the EC Commission in Antitrust Matters' [2009] *ECLR* 205

Andreangeli, A., 'The Impact of the Modernisation Regulation on the Guarantees of Due Process in Competition Proceedings' (2006) 31 *ELRev* 342

Andreangeli, A., 'Towards an EU Competition Court: "Article-6-Proofing" Antitrust Proceedings before the Commission?' (2007) 4 *World Competition* 595

Bailey, D., 'Scope of Judicial Review Under Article 101 EC' (2004) 41 *CMLRev* 1327

Beaton-Wells, C., and Parker, C., 'Justifying Criminal Sanctions for Cartel Conduct: A Hard Case' (2013) 1 *J of Antitrust Enforcement* 198

Berghe, P., and Dawes, A., '"Little Pig, Little Pig, Let me Come In": An Evaluation of the European Commission's Powers of Inspection in Competition Cases' [2009] *ECLR* 407

Billiet, P., 'How Lenient is the EC Leniency Policy? A Matter of Certainty and Predictability' [2009] *ECLR* 14

Blake, S., and Schnichels, D., 'Leniency Following Modernisation: Safeguarding Europe's Leniency Programmes' [2004] *ECLR* 765

Brammer, S., 'Concurrent Jurisdiction under Regulation 1/2003 and the Issue of Case Allocation' (2005) 42 *CMLRev* 1383

Bronkers. M., and Vallery, A., 'No Longer Presumed Guilty: The Impact of Fundamental Rights on Certain Dogmas of EU Competition Law' (2011) 43 *World Competition* 535

Callol, P., 'Mandatory Antitrust Liability under EU Competition Law of Trade Association Members in Case of Infringement by the Trade Association' [2015] *ECLR* 194

Castillo de la Torre, F., 'Evidence, Proof and Judicial Review in Cartel Cases' (2009) 32 *World Competition* 505

CENGIZ, F., 'Multi-level Governance in Competition Policy: The European Competition Network' (2010) 35 *ELRev* 660

CENGIZ, F., 'Judicial Review and the Rule of Law in the EU Competition Law Regime after *Alrosa*' (2011) 7 *European Competition Journal* 127

CONNOR, J. M., 'Cartel Fine Severity and the European Commission 2007–2011' [2011] *ECLR* 58

DEKEYSER, K., and GAUER, C., 'The New Enforcement System for Articles 101 and 102 and the Rights of Defence' [2004] *Fordham Corp L Inst* 549

DUNNE, N. 'Commitment Decisions in EU Competition Law' (2014) 10 *J of Competition Law and Economics* 399

EHLERMANN, C.-D., 'Reflections on a European Cartel Office' (1995) 32 *CMLRev* 471

FORRESTER, I., 'Due Process in EC Competition Case: A Distinguished Institution with Flawed Procedures' (2009) 34 *ELRev* 817

FORRESTER, I., 'A Challenge for Europe's Judges: The Review of Fines in Competition Cases' (2011) 36 *ELRev* 185

GAUER, C., and JASPERS, M., 'Designing a European Solution for a "One Stop Leniency Shop"' [2006] *ECLR* 685

GAUTIER, A., and PETIT, N., 'Optimal Enforcement of Competition Policy: The Commitments Procedure Under Uncertainty', 24 April 2015, <http://ssrn.com/abstract=2509729>

GERADIN, D., 'Breaking the EU Antitrust Enforcement Deadlock: Re-empowering the Courts?' (2011) 36 *ELRev* 457

GERADIN, D., 'Antitrust Compliance Programmes and Optimal Antitrust Enforcement: A Reply to Wouter Wils' (2013) 1 *J of Antitrust Enforcement* 1

GERADIN, D., and HENRY, D., 'EC Fining for Competition Law Violations: An Empirical Study of the Commission's Decisional Practice and the Community Courts' Judgments' (2005) 1 *European Competition Journal* 401

GERADIN, D., and PETIT, N., 'Judicial Remedies under EC Competition Law: Complex Issues Arising from the "Modernisation" Process' [2005] *Fordham Corp L Inst* 393

GERBER, D., 'Modernising European Competition Law: A Developmental Perspective' [2001] *ECLR* 122

GRODECKI, P., and MAXWELL, S., 'Alternative Approaches to Sentencing in Cartel Cases: The European Union, Ireland and the United States' (2013) 9 *European Law Journal* 341

TER HAAR, M., 'Obstruction of Investigation in EU Competition Law: Issues and Developments in the European Commission's Approach' (2013) 2 *World Competition* 247

HARDING, C., 'A Pathology of Business Cartels: Original Sin or the Child of Regulation?' (2010) 1 *NJECL* 44

HEIMLER, A., and MEHTA, K., 'Violations of Antitrust Provisions: The Optimal Level of Fines for Achieving Deterrence' (2012) 35 *World Competition* 103

HEMPEL, R., 'Access to DG Competition's Files: An Analysis of Recent EU Court Case Law' [2012] *ECLR* 195

HOLLES, B., 'The Hearing Officer: Thirty Years Protecting the Right to Be Heard' (2013) 36 *World Competition* 5

JONES, A., and WILLIAMS, R., 'The UK Response to the Global Effort Against Cartels: Is Criminalization Really the Solution' (2014) 2 *J of Antitrust Enforcement* 100

JOSHUA, J., 'The Element of Surprise' (1983) 8 *ELRev* 3

KAFETZOPOULOS, A., 'European Commission Policy on Publication of Cartel Decisions: The Latest Victory of Damage Claimants Against Leniency Applicants' [2015] *ECLR* 295

KATSOULACOS, Y., and ULPH, D., 'Optimal Enforcement Structures for Competition Policy: Implications of Judicial Reviews and of Internal Error Correction Mechanisms' (2011) 7 *European Competition Journal* 71

KELLERBAUER, M., 'Playground Instead of Playpen: The Court of Justice of the European Union's *Alrosa* Judgment on Article 9 of Regulation 1/2003' [2011] *ECLR* 1

KHAN, A., 'Rethinking Sanctions for Breaching Competition Law: Is Director Disqualification the Answer?' (2012) 35 *World Competition* 77

LEVY, N., and O'DONOGHUE, R., 'The EU Leniency Programme Comes of Age' (2004) 27 *World Competition* 75

MELÍCIAS, M. J., '*Did They Do It?* The Interplay Between the Standard of Proof and the Presumption of Innocence in EU Cartel Investigations' (2012) 35 *World Competition* 471

MONTAG, F., 'The Case for Radical Reform of the Infringement Procedure under Regulation 17' [1996] *ECLR* 428

MURPHY, G., 'Is It Time to Rebrand Legal Professional Privilege in Article 82 EC Law?' [2009] *ECLR* 125

NAZZINI, R., 'Administrative Enforcement, Judicial Review and Fundamental Rights in EU Competition Law: A Comparative Contextual-Functionalist Perspective' (2012) 49 *CMLRev* 971

NAZZINI, R., 'Fundamental Rights Beyond Legal Positivism: Rethinking the *Ne Bis In Idem* Principle in EU Competition Law' (2014) 2 *J of Antitrust Enforcement* 225

OLIVER, P., 'Diagnostics—A Judgment Applying the European Convention of Human Rights to the Field of Competition' (2012) 3 *JECLAP* 163

PEREK, M., and LEFÈVRE, S., 'Competition Litigation Before the General Court: Quality if not Quantity' (2016) 53 *CMLRev* 65

PETIT, N., and RATO, M., 'From Hard to Soft Enforcement of EC Competition Law—A Bestiary of

"Sunshine" Enforcement Instruments', 2008 <http://ssrn.com/abstract=1270109>

RILEY, A., '*Saunders* and the Power to Obtain Information in Community and United Kingdom Competition Law' (2000) 25 *ELRev* 264

RILEY, A., 'EC Antitrust Modernisation: The Commission Does Very Nicely—Thank You! Part One: Regulation 1 and the Notification Burden' [2003] *ECLR* 604

RILEY, A., 'EC Antitrust Modernisation: The Commission Does Very Nicely—Thank You! Part Two: Between the Idea and the Reality: Decentralisation under Regulation 1' [2003] *ECLR* 657

RILEY, A., 'The Modernisation of EU Anti-cartel Enforcement—Will the Commission Grasp the Opportunity?', CEPS Special Report, January 2010

RILEY, A., and SOKOL, D., 'Rethinking Compliance' (2015) 3 *J of Antitrust Enforcement* 31

RIZZA, C., 'The Duty of National Competition Authorities to Disapply Anti-competitive Domestic Legislation and the Resulting Limitations on the Availability of the State Action Defence (Case C-198/01 *CIF*)' [2004] *ECLR* 126

RODGER, B., 'The Commission White Paper on Modernisation of the Rules Implementing Articles 101 and 102 of the EC Treaty' (1999) 24 *ELRev* 653

SIBONY, A.-L., 'Casenote on *KME v. Commission*' (2012) 49 *CMLRev* 1977

SLATER, D., THOMAS, S., and WAELBROECK, D., 'Competition Law Proceedings Before the European Commission and the Right to a Fair Trial: No Need for Reform?' (2009) 5 *European Competition Journal* 97

SLOT, P. J., 'Does the *Pfleiderer* Judgment Make the Fight Against International Cartels More Difficult?' [2013] *ECLR* 197

STEPHAN, A., 'An Empirical Assessment of the European Leniency Notice' (2009) 5 *J of Competition Law and Economics* 537

STEPHAN, A., 'Four Key Challenges to the Successful Criminalization of Cartel Law' (2014) 2 *J of Antitrust Enforcement* 333

SWAAK, C., and WESSLING, R., 'Reconsidering the Leniency Option: If Not First In, Good Reasons to Stay Out' [2015] *ECLR* 346

TEMPLE LANG, J., 'Commitment Decisions and Settlements with Antitrust Authorities and Private Parties Under European Antitrust Law' [2005] *Fordham Corp L Inst* 265

TEMPLE LANG, J., 'Judicial Review of Competition Decisions under the European Convention on Human Rights and the Importance of the EFTA Court: The *Norway Post* Judgment' (2012) 37 *ELRev* 464

TEMPLE LANG, J., 'The Strengths and Weaknesses of the DG Competition Manual of Procedure' (2013) 1 *J of Antitrust Enforcement* 132

TEMPLE LANG, J., and RIZZA, C., 'The *Ste Colas Est and Others v. France* Case: European Court of Human Rights Judgment of 16 April 2002' [2002] *ECLR* 417

TIERNO CENTELLA, M. L., 'The New Settlement Procedure in Selected Cartel Cases' (2008) 3 *European Policy Newsletter* 30

VARONA, E. N., 'The Undertaking as Subject of EC Competition Law and the Imputation of Infringements to Natural or Legal Persons' (2000) 25 *ELRev* 99

VARONA, E. N., 'The Combination of the Investigative and Prosecutorial Function and the Adjudicative Function in EC Antitrust Enforcement: A Legal and Economic Analysis' (2004) 27 *World Competition* 201

VARONA, E. N., and DURÁTEZ, H. G., 'Interim Measures in Competition Cases Before the European Commission and the Courts' [2002] *ECLR* 512

VESTERDORF, B., 'Legal Professional Privilege and the Privilege Against Self-incrimination in EC Law: Recent Developments and Current Issues' [2004] *Fordham Corp L Inst* 107

VESTERDORF, B., 'The Court of Justice and Unlimited Jurisdiction: What Does It Mean in Practice?' (2009) 2 *Global Competition Policy* (June)

VÖLCKER, S., 'Casenote on *Pfleiderer AG v Bundeskartellamt*' (2012) 49 *CMLRev* 695

WAGNER-VON PAPP, F., 'Best and Even Better Practices in Commitment Procedures After *Alrosa*: The Dangers of Abandoning the "Struggle for Competition Law"' (2012) 49 *CMLRev* 929

WALSH, D. J., 'Carrots and Sticks—Leniency and Fines in EC Cartel Cases' [2009] *ECLR* 30

WASMEIER, M., and THWAITES, N., 'The Development of *Ne Bis in Idem* into a Transnational Fundamental Right in EU Law: Comments on Recent Developments' (2006) 31 *ELRev* 565

WATHELET, M., Editorial, 'Commitment Decisions and the Paucity of Precedent' (2015) 6 *JECLAP* 553

WESSELING, R., 'A Principled Argument for Personal Criminal Sanctions as Punishment under EC Cartel Law' (2007) 30 *World Competition* 197

WESSELING, R., 'Legal Certainty and Cartel Criminalisation within the EU Member States' [2012] *CLJ* 677

WESSELING, R., and VAN DER WOUDE, M., 'The Lawfulness and Acceptability of Enforcement of European Cartel Law' (2012) 35 *World Competition* 569

WHELAN, P., 'Cartel Criminalization and the Challenge of "Moral Wrongfulness"' (2013) 33 *OJLS* 535

WHELAN, P., 'Cartel Criminalisation and Due Process: The Challenge Imposing Criminal Sanctions Alongside Administrative Sanctions within the EU' (2013) 64 *Northern Ireland Legal Quarterly* 143

WILS, W., 'Self-incrimination in EC Antitrust Enforcement: A Legal and Economic Analysis' (2003) 26 *World Competition* 567

WILS, W., 'The Principle of *Ne Bis in Idem* in EC Antitrust Enforcement: A Legal and Economic Analysis' (2003) 26 *World Competition* 131

WILS, W., 'The European Commission's 2006 Guidelines on Antitrust Fines: A Legal and Economic Analysis' (2007) 30 *World Competition* 197

WILS, W., 'The Use of Settlements in Public Antitrust Enforcement: Objectives and Principles' (2008) 31 *World Competition* 335

WILS, W., 'The Increased Level of Antitrust Fines, Judicial Review, and the European Convention on Human Rights' (2010) 33 *World Competition* 5

WILS, W., 'Discretion and Prioritisation in Public Antitrust Enforcement' (2011) 34 *World Competition* 353

WILS, W., 'Recidivism in EU Antitrust Enforcement: A Legal and Economic Analysis' (2012) 35 *World Competition* 5

WILS, W., 'The Oral Hearing in Competition Proceedings Before the European Commission' (2012) 35 *World Competition* 397

WILS, W., 'The Role of the Hearing Officer in Competition Proceedings Before the European Commission' (2012) 35 *World Competition* 431

WILS, W., 'Antitrust Compliance Programmes and Optimal Antitrust Enforcement' (2013) 1 *J of Antitrust Enforcement* 52

WILS, W., 'Ten Years of Commitment Decisions under Article 9 of Regulation 1/2003: Too Much of a Good Thing?', 2015 <http://ssrn.com/author=456087>

WOUDE, M., VAN DER, 'Hearing Officers and EC Antitrust Procedures: The Art of Making Subjective Procedures More Objective' (1996) 33 *CMLRev* 531

14

PRIVATE ENFORCEMENT

1. CENTRAL ISSUES

1. In Chapter 13 it is seen that the Commission and the national competition authorities play a crucial role in detecting, halting, deterring, and punishing violations of EU competition law.

2. This chapter focuses on private civil actions which may achieve corrective justice by allowing victims to obtain compensation. Private enforcement also relieves enforcement pressure on public agencies by helping to ensure infringements of the rules are brought to an end, violations are deterred, and that the law is developed and clarified. Private litigants may therefore supplement public enforcement by allowing Article 101 or 102 to be used either as a shield, or as a sword, in civil proceedings before a national court.

3. For a number of years the EU Courts have made it clear that EU law requires national courts to:

   (a) apply directly effective provisions of EU law, including Articles 101 and 102;

   (b) ensure that their decisions do not run counter to those adopted by the Commission;

   (c) render provisions in an agreement that contravene Article 101 (and it seems Article 102) void and unenforceable; and

   (d) ensure effective judicial protection of rights conferred by Articles 101 and 102 and that effective remedies are available to protect them. In particular, damages, entailing full compensation, must, in principle, be available to those that have suffered loss in consequence of a breach of Article 101 or 102. Further, in certain circumstances injunctions must be available to protect putative EU rights.

4. In the absence of EU harmonising measures, national rules of procedure, evidence, and substance govern any such proceedings to protect EU rights before the national courts. Such rules are, however, subject to the overriding requirement that they must not be less favourable than those relating to similar claims of a domestic nature and must not make it virtually impossible or excessively difficult to exercise the right that the national courts are obliged to protect (the principles of equivalence and effectiveness).

5. Despite the imposition of these clear obligations on national courts, the Commission has been concerned about the relatively low amounts of antitrust litigation which have been brought by private individuals before national courts in the EU, especially actions for damages. Even though the amount of private litigation has begun to grow in some Member States, the Commission has taken a series of steps to encourage such litigation further, particularly damages actions, in a way that will complement, but not jeopardise, public enforcement.

6. Following extensive consultation and debate, the Commission, in June 2013, published a range of measures designed to facilitate damages claims by victims of antitrust violations and to optimise the interaction between public and private enforcement, including: a proposal for a directive designed to remove a number of practical difficulties confronted by victims of infringements of the EU antitrust rules when instigating damages claims; a Recommendation of non-binding principles for collective redress mechanisms for Member States; and a practical guide on the quantification of harm for damages to assist national courts. A Damages Directive was finally adopted in November 2014 and has to be transposed by the Member States into their national laws by 27 December 2016.

2. INTRODUCTION

In order for the objectives of a competition law system to be achieved, effective enforcement of the rules must take place. Without it, the meaning of the law will not be developed and elucidated, breaches of the rules will not be halted, punished, or deterred, and victims of violations will not be compensated;[1] 'deterrence, compensation, and remediation'[2] will not be ensured. A critical issue to be determined when designing or developing a competition law system is therefore how effective enforcement mechanisms can be established.

Chapter 13 examines public enforcement through the European competition network (the Commission and the national competition authorities (NCAs)). Public enforcers, however, have limited resources, which they may concentrate predominantly on ensuring that serious violations which cause widespread harm to consumer welfare (such as cartels) are brought to an end and deterred. Accordingly they are not able to root out and prevent all violations of the rules or to ensure compensation for victims. Indeed, in the EU the Commission does not have power to award damages to those that have suffered loss in consequence of an antitrust infringement,[3] although it has been active in trying to facilitate private actions by victims for compensation. Civil enforcement of the rules, through claims made by private litigants in the national courts and tribunals of the individual Member States (the national courts), may consequently also play a fundamental part in ensuring effective enforcement of the competition law rules. This chapter concentrates on private enforcement of the rules by those specifically affected by a competition law violation in the EU and considers what its principal function is, or should be, whether, and if so how, it should be encouraged and facilitated, and how it may be balanced with public enforcement.

The chapter commences in Section 3 by examining the way in which private antitrust litigation may contribute to effective enforcement of competition law and the core function, or functions, it may fulfil. In particular, it scrutinises the private enforcement system in the US where the legislature seems to have made a conscious policy choice, at the time of adopting the antitrust laws there, to encourage private litigants to participate in their enforcement.[4] It is seen that over time, and combined with other elements of, and developments in, the US system, the net result of this choice has been that, uniquely in the world, a vast majority of antitrust enforcement in the US (approximately 90 per cent of cases[5]) emanates from private litigation rather than public enforcement. Such actions

---

[1] W. Wils, 'The Relationship Between Public Antitrust Enforcement and Private Actions for Damages' (2009) 32 *World Competition* 3. See also N. Dunne, 'The Role of Private Enforcement within EU Competition Law' (2013–2014) 16 *Cambridge Yearbook of European Legal Studies* 143 (conceptualising competition law as rules to correct public wrongs, private wrongs, or market failures).

[2] See A. I. Gavil, 'Designing Private Rights of Action for Competition Policy Systems: The Role of Interdependence and the Advantages of a Sequential Approach' in P. Lowe and M. Marquis (eds.), *European Competition Law Annual 2011: Integrating Public and Private Enforcement Competition Law—Implications for Courts and Agencies* (Oxford: Hart Publishing, 2014) (remediation provides means for halting offensive conduct and perhaps correcting for its adverse competitive effects, as with equitable and injunctive relief) and A. Komninos, 'Private Enforcement in the EU with Emphasis on Damages Actions' in I. Lianos and D. Geradin (eds.), *Handbook on European Competition Law: Enforcement and Procedure* (Edward Elgar, 2013).

[3] But see, e.g., OFT Press Release 88/06, 'Independent Schools agree settlement', 19 May 2006 (where the UK competition authority accepted a settlement whereby the schools which had engaged in price-fixing agreed to make an ex gratia payment into a fund for the benefit of the victims of the infringement) and the provisions on voluntary redress in the UK's Consumer Rights Act 2015, Sch. 8. See further Wils, n. 1, 12; Gavil, n. 2, 6 and n. 204.

[4] See now especially Clayton Act 1914, s. 4 (superseding and expanding provisions set out in the Sherman Act 1890) and s. 16 and Section 3 below.

[5] See, e.g., H. J. Hovenkamp, 'Quantification of Harm in Private Antitrust Actions in the United States', University of Iowa Legal Studies Research Paper, <http://ssrn.com/abstract=1758751>. or <http://dx.doi.org/10.2139/ssrn.1758751>, Report for the European Commission, 'Making antitrust damages actions more effective in the EU: welfare impact and potential scenarios', DG COMP/2006/A3/012D, 28 and D. Crane, *The Institutional Structure of Antitrust Enforcement* (Oxford University Press, 2011), 163. It is difficult to get completely precise statistics relating to the ratio of private to public enforcement however (e.g., because many separate private action cases may be filed in relation to the same case before consolidation there may be over-counting of private actions. In contrast, as many public cases may be resolved before a case is filed, there may be under-counting of government actions).

have been argued by some to play a crucial function, decentralising decision-taking, democratising antitrust policy, affirming the rule of law, deterring violations, and ensuring that victims obtain compensation. The system has encouraged such high volumes of litigation, however, that it has been felt necessary, through a series of steps, to adjust the system to limit and curtail litigation and ensure that some of its perceived excesses are moderated;[6] in particular, to ensure that unmeritorious litigation is not encouraged which may have the potential to chill pro-competitive behaviour and so undermine the objectives of the antitrust laws.[7]

Section 4 then examines the EU system, the obligations that EU law imposes on national courts, the different factors that have operated over time as barriers to private litigation in the EU Member States, and the package of measures that has been adopted to overcome these obstacles. In this section it is seen that the EU position contrasts starkly with that which exists in the US. The Treaty contains no specific provision governing private rights of action for damages or injunctions following a violation of the EU competition law rules. Further, although private proceedings in the national courts have been possible by virtue of the fact that Articles 101 and 102 have direct effect and a key objective of Regulation 1/2003[8] was to allow a more decentralised enforcement system to emerge with the national courts (and NCAs) participating more actively within it, a number of factors have combined to preclude private actions from developing evenly across the EU. Even though, therefore, litigation has grown rapidly in some Member States, particularly the UK, the Netherlands, and Germany,[9] significant barriers to private antitrust actions continue to exist in others.

For many years the Commission has taken the view that the EU situation is unsatisfactory and more needs to be done, whilst avoiding the problems that have confronted the US system, to stimulate and harmonise national rules governing private enforcement which could then contribute to promoting a culture of competition: 'The overall enforcement of the EU competition rules is best guaranteed through complementary public and private enforcement.'[10] In 2013, after extensive debate and discussion as to whether, and if so how, to develop a European approach to private enforcement,[11] the Commission proposed a package of measures on private antitrust actions including:

- a Recommendation of non-binding principles for collective redress mechanisms for Member States;[12]

---

[6] '[T]he conventional wisdom in the international competition community [is] that U.S.-style private enforcement has been a disaster', R. H. Lande, 'The Proposed Damages Directive: The Real Lessons from the United States' (2014) 2 *CPI Antitrust Chronicle* 1, 1.

[7] But see, e.g., Lande, ibid. and Section 3 below.

[8] See n. 60 and text.

[9] See, e.g., M. Kuijpers, S. Tuinenga, S. Wisking, K. Dietzel, S. Campbell, and A. Fritzsche, 'Actions for Damages in the Netherlands, the United Kingdom, and Germany' (2015) 6 *JECLAP* 129.

[10] Commission, 'Proposal for a Directive of the European Parliament and the Council on certain rules governing actions for damages under national law for infringements of the Competition law provisions of the Member States and the European Union', COM(2013) 404 final, Explanatory Memorandum 1.2.

[11] They focus on damages actions (but see n. 12), see especially: a study prepared for DG Comp by Ashurst on damages actions before national courts of the then 25 Member States, D. Waelbroeck, D. Slater, and G. Even-Shoshan, 'Ashurst Study on the conditions of claims for damages in case of infringement of EC competition rules: Comparative Report' (2004) (The Ashurst Report); Commission, 'Green Paper on Damages Actions for Breach of the EC Antitrust Rules', COM(2005) 672 final, Commission, 'Staff Working Paper, Annex to the Green Paper on Damages Actions for Breach of the EC Antitrust Rules', SEC(2005) 1732; and Commission, 'White Paper on Damages Actions for Breach of the EC Antitrust Rules', COM(2008) 165 final.

[12] Commission Recommendation 2013/396/EU of 11 June 2013 on common principles for injunctive and compensatory collective redress mechanisms in the Member States concerning violations of rights granted under Union Law [2013] OJ L201/60 (enabling consumers, by joining claims with others, to get access to justice and pursue infringements of competition law, where the cost of individual action may otherwise have acted as a deterrent, see recital 9). (Although the Commission originally intended to incorporate provisions on collective redress within the Damages Dir. this proposal caused controversy, especially in the European Parliament.) The Recommendation applies not only in the field of competition law but also horizontally to consumer protection, environmental protection, data protection, financial services, and other areas where claims for injunctions or damages in respect of breaches of EU law are relevant, recital 7.

- a practical guide on the quantification of harm for damages to assist national courts;[13] and
- a draft directive[14] designed to facilitate damage claims by removing the main obstacles to full compensation for victims of antitrust violations and ensuring that private and public enforcement operate harmoniously together.

The final directive on certain rules governing actions for damages under national law for infringements of the competition law provisions of the Member States and of the EU (the Damages Directive) was signed into law on 26 November 2014 and must be transposed into national law by 27 December 2016.[15]

The analysis set out in Sections 3 and 4 provides the critical backdrop to an examination of the provisions contained in the EU reform package, in particular in the Damages Directive. The chapter considers what has been done to overcome the obstacles to private litigation that exist in the EU, whether the package is likely to achieve its objectives, what pitfalls might be anticipated, and/or what further developments and clarifications are likely to be required in the future. Section 5 concludes that although the package of reforms constitutes a courageous and innovate step to draw private litigants throughout the EU into the enforcement process without encouraging unmeritorious actions and over-enforcement of the rules, a question which remains is whether sufficient has been done to boost and facilitate private damages actions and to create the level playing field across the EU sought by the Commission. Not only does the Directive not institute a completely harmonised framework, leaving a number of potential obstacles to national actions and areas of legal ambiguity outstanding, but some of the Directive's provisions are liable to introduce considerable complexities into national proceedings. Further, scope for some significant divergences between national rules remains; such differences are likely to continue to affect where litigants choose to commence their actions and to result in forum-shopping.

3. THE ROLE OF PRIVATE ANTITRUST LITIGATION AND ITS RELATIONSHIP WITH PUBLIC ENFORCEMENT: THE EXPERIENCE IN THE US

Private civil actions provide a mechanism for achieving corrective justice by allowing compensation of victims. They thus have an important 'compensation function'—to compensate those harmed by the competition law infringement. Further, private enforcement (for example, in the form of actions for damages, restitution, and/or an injunction) may provide the springboard for the law to be developed, relieve enforcement pressure on public enforcement agencies, fill public enforcement gaps,[16] and result in violations of the rules being brought to an end and/or deterred (through exposing those in violation to liability for damages). Indeed, if violations are sufficiently deterred, the need for actions for compensation will be reduced. Private litigation may, like public enforcement, thus serve a variety of important functions, including remediation and 'deterrent' functions—to deter the violation of the competition rules and to punish the perpetrators;[17] it is interdependent with and

---

[13] Commission, 'Staff Working Document—Practical Guide on Quantifying Harm in Actions for Damages Based on Breaches of Article 101 or 102 of the Treaty on the Functioning of the European Union', SWD(2013) 205.

[14] Commission Proposal, n. 10.

[15] Directive 2014/104/EU on certain rules governing actions for damages under national law for infringements of the competition law provisions of the Member States and of the European Union [2014] OJ L349/1.

[16] S. Weber Waller, 'Towards a Constructive Public–Private Partnership to Enforce Competition Law' (2006) 29 *World Competition* 367.

[17] See A. P. Komninos, 'Public and Private Antitrust Enforcement in Europe: Complement? Overlap?' (2006) 3 *Competition Law Review* 1, 9; R. Nazzini, and A. Nikpay, 'Private Actions in EC Competition Law' (2008) 4 *Competition Policy International* 107, 109.

complementary to public enforcement requiring public and private enforcement to be combined harmoniously.[18]

If private enforcement is to play a meaningful part in the enforcement process, however, important issues to be resolved are what the primary function of private enforcement should be—for example, should it be deterrence[19] of public wrongs that distort competition and harm society as a whole or compensation of specific victims harmed by an antitrust infringement and whose private rights have been infringed—and how can the optimal balance between private and public enforcement be achieved?

In the US, private enforcement seems to have been designed to compensate victims but also, specifically, to act as a deterrent. Indeed, the Clayton Act[20] itself encourages private enforcement of the antitrust laws by providing, for: treble damages for those injured by reason of anything forbidden in the antitrust laws;[21] injunctive relief against threatened loss or damage by a violation;[22] the use of judgments entered against the defendant as prima facie evidence against that defendant;[23] clear limitation periods;[24] and successful plaintiffs (claimants) to recover costs, including reasonable attorney's fees, contrary to the ordinary rule in the US that each party bears its own attorney fees and costs.[25]

Although these provisions did not trigger significant volumes of private antitrust litigation on their own, different individual features of the US system have combined and developed sequentially[26] to allow such actions to play a significant role in the enforcement process. In the 1960s and 1970s private litigation began to burgeon. Partly, this growth reflected the development of a more interventionist antitrust policy between the 1940s and 1960s, underpinned by a scepticism about the ability of firms and the markets to provide a successful economic outcome and a mistrust of big business and concentrated markets.[27] Especially during the Warren Court era, the Supreme Court[28] adopted broad interpretations of the antitrust statutes (for example, making wide use of per se rules and applying lenient procedural, substantive, and evidential burdens of proof[29]), which made it relatively easy for plaintiffs to win cases.[30] Combined with the facts that:[31]

- wide-ranging pre-trial discovery powers exist in the US which assist the collection of relevant and essential evidence;

---

[18] OECD (2011), 12; A. Komninos, *EC Private Antitrust Enforcement: Decentralised Application of the EC Competition Law by National Courts* (Hart Publishing, 2008), 9; R. Van den Bergh, 'Private Enforcement of European Competition Law and the Persisting Collective Action Problem' (2013) 20 *Maastricht J of European and Comparative Law* 12, 15; S. Campbell and T. Feunteun, 'Designing a Balanced System: Damages, Deterrence, Leniency and Litigants' Rights—A Claimant's Perspective' in Lowe and Marquis, n. 2, 27, 28–29; W. Kovacic, 'Private Rights of Action and the Enforcement of Public Competition Laws' in C. Baudenbacher (ed.), *Current Developments in European and International Competition Law: 17th St Gallen International Competition Law Forum ICF 2010* (Helbing & Lichtenhahn, 2011), 421.

[19] G. Becker and G. Stigler, 'Law Enforcement, Malfeasance and Compensation of Enforcers' (1974) 3 *J of Legal Studies* 1, 14. See also G. Becker, 'Crime and Punishment: An Economic Approach' (1968) 76 *J of Political Economy* 169.

[20] See n. 4.

[21] Clayton Act 1914, s. 4.

[22] Ibid., s. 16.

[23] Ibid., s. 5(a).

[24] The ordinary limitation period of four years also gets suspended during government enforcement proceedings, ibid., ss. 4B and 5(i).

[25] Ibid., s. 5(a).

[26] See, e.g., Gavil, n. 2.

[27] See, e.g., E. Levi, 'The Antitrust Laws and Monopoly' (1974) 14 *Univ Chic LR* 153, C. Kaysen and D. Turner, *Antitrust Policy* (Harvard University Press, 1959).

[28] At this time the Chief Justice was Earl Warren (1953–1969).

[29] For example, courts have applied lesser burdens of proof as to the amount of damages in antitrust cases, e.g. *Zenith Radio Corp v Hazeltine Research*, 395 US 100 (1969).

[30] H. Hovenkamp, *The Antitrust Enterprise: Principle and Execution* (Harvard University Press, 2005), 1.

[31] See Gavil, n. 2 (explaining that 'the field of *complex litigation*' did not develop until mid-century).

- federal rules allow for consolidation of antitrust claims and for the bringing of opt-out class actions;[32]
- lawyers regularly accept antitrust cases on a contingency fee (no win, no fee) basis;
- most antitrust cases are tried by jury[33] (so conferring an element of 'unpredictability' to antitrust trials); and
- defendants, as joint tortfeasors, are jointly and severally liable for any damage caused with no right to contribution from co-defendants;[34]

private litigation was able to flourish. Further, as US public enforcement agencies have never adopted such a central role in antitrust enforcement as has their European counterpart, the Commission, those injured by an antitrust violation have frequently had little choice but to litigate if they wish the infringement to be brought to an end.

In 1968 and 1977 the Supreme Court also handed down two important judgments, *Hanover Shoe Inc v United Shoe Machine Corp*[35] and *Illinois Brick Co v Illinois*,[36] which facilitated private litigation and clearly seemed to elevate the remediation and deterrent functions served by private enforcement higher than its 'compensation function'. These cases hold that: the possibility that a claimant might have recouped some of an anti-competitive overcharge by passing it on to its customers is *not* relevant in the assessment of antitrust damages cases;[37] and claims brought by *indirect* purchasers (who may have been harmed by an overcharge being passed on to them) should generally be refused[38] (indirect purchaser actions are however possible in a number of states under state law[39]). Although these principles might be criticised on the grounds that they may deny compensation to the real victims of the anti-competitive activity and allow direct purchasers to collect a windfall, they do concentrate antitrust claims in the hands of those most likely to sue, simplify damages litigation by allowing difficult issues of remoteness and tracing of injury to be sidestepped, and reduce the process costs of litigation.[40] In contrast, provision for apportionment of recovery through the distribution chain would increase the overall costs of recovery through injecting extremely complex issues into the case; at the same time such an apportionment would reduce the benefits to each plaintiff by dividing the potential recovery among a much larger group and reduce the incentive to sue.[41]

By enlisting in these ways the help of those most directly affected by anti-competitive conduct in the enforcement of the law, numerous antitrust cases have been privately litigated, providing the platform for some of the most significant principles of antitrust law to be developed, the rapid evolution of the law, the plugging of enforcement gaps, and offsetting of periods of lax government

---

[32] So permitting small claimants to spread costs and aggregate similar claims, making them easier and more economical to bring, see Federal Rules of Civil Procedure (FRCP), Rule 23 (defining the standards for bringing class actions).

[33] Criminal antitrust proceedings always involve trial by jury (US Const., Fifth Amendment) and both the plaintiff and the defendant can demand a jury trial in civil cases (US Const., Seventh Amendment).

[34] *Texas Industries v Radcliff Materials, Inc*, 451 US 630 (1981).

[35] *Hanover Shoe Inc v United Shoe Machine Corp*, 392 US 481 (1968).

[36] *Illinois Brick Co v Illinois*, 431 US 720 (1977).

[37] Otherwise such claims would become excessively complicated, private actions would be deterred, and a wrongdoer in breach would be able to retain his unlawful profits and the fruits of his own illegality. See also extract from A. Jones and D. Beard, 'Co-contractors, Damages and Article 81: The ECJ Finally Speaks' [2002] ECLR 246, n. 152 and text.

[38] If the fact that loss has been passed on by the purchaser may not be taken into account *defensively* in a claim between the seller and the purchaser, it should not be open to an indirect purchaser to use the passing on principle *offensively* in damages proceedings. The court set out three exceptions to this position.

[39] Such rules are not pre-empted by federal law, *California v ARC Corp*, 490 US 93 (1989).

[40] In addition, from the defendant's perspective, they preclude a multiplicity of claims and the risks of duplicate recovery from arising, but see n. 39 and text.

[41] But see the position now adopted in the Damages Dir., nn. 193 and 194 and text.

enforcement and disputes between private parties to be resolved privately (without drawing public agencies within them).[42]

It is well known, nonetheless, that the virtues of the US private enforcement system are not universally extolled and that its benefits have been hotly debated. Widespread concern has been articulated that features of the system have encouraged overinvestment in private litigation (motivated by private profit rather than public-interest considerations), over-enforcement, and over-deterrence[43] and that, especially in the 1960s to 1970s and in relation to class actions, damages actions got 'out of control'[44]—the system became prone to error and encouraged 'anaemic' claims to be brought and settled by defendants eager to avoid protracted and expensive litigation. In addition, there has been concern that private actions might actually undermine public enforcement and deterrence, by discouraging leniency applications.

Although not all might agree with these, or all of these, criticisms, these types of anxiety have led to a dramatic recalibration of the US system. Not only has the legislator stepped in in order to diminish the disincentive of submitting amnesty applications, by de-trebling antitrust damages for corporations that participate in the amnesty programme and cooperate with claimants,[45] but the Supreme Court has expressed concerns about the 'coercive'[46] elements of the antitrust system, the risk of false positives they create, and has handed down a series of opinions which, collectively, limit the types of antitrust claim that can successfully be brought and appreciably raise the bar for antitrust claimants.[47] The courts have thus been supportive of efforts to safeguard against antitrust claims having a chilling effect on competition through the use of evidential, procedural, and substantive rules.[48] The developments relating to procedure have, in particular, made it easier for antitrust defendants to escape a full antitrust trial either on the basis that the complaint fails to state a claim upon which relief can be granted[49] or following discovery on the basis that 'there is no genuine issue as to any material fact' so that 'the moving party is entitled to judgment as a matter of law'.[50] Further, and crucially, there seems little doubt that the perceived 'excesses' of the treble damages system have been an important factor influencing the Supreme Court in its decision over the last 35 years to rein in the substantive reach of the antitrust laws, making it now extremely difficult for

---

[42] An important issue which has arisen is whether claimants that have suffered loss in consequence of a cartel operated worldwide or internationally can pursue a US class action in respect of cartelised products purchased from the companies but delivered outside the US, that is encompassing claimants whose case does *not* arise from the *US effect* of the anti-competitive conduct. In *F. Hoffmann-La Roche Ltd v Empagran SA*, 542 US 155 (2004) the Supreme Court held they may *not* do so in respect of injuries flowing exclusively from foreign effects of allegedly anti-competitive global conduct, where the foreign effects are independent of, and not intertwined with, the US effects, see further Chap. 16.

[43] W. Landes and R. Posner, 'The Private Enforcement of Law' (1975) 4 *J of Legal Studies* 1.

[44] Especially, for example, the right to treble damages, the fact that the defendant never gets its costs, even if it wins, the fact that liability is joint and several with no right to contribution from co-defendants, and the expansive use by the Supreme Court of per se rules in the 1960s and 1970s. These difficulties were exacerbated by the fact that the costs of discovery may be astronomical (and are likely to be mainly borne by the defendant) and the opt-out class action system encourages huge volumes of litigation and multiple procedures being launched against alleged antitrust infringers.

[45] The Antitrust Criminal Penalty Enhancement and Reform Act 2004.

[46] See, e.g., *Bell Atlantic Corp v Twombly*, 550 US 554, 557 (2007) and F. H. Easterbrook, 'Discovery as Abuse' (1989) 69 *Boston Univ LR* 635.

[47] Gavil, n. 2.

[48] See, e.g., ibid.; *Brunswick Corp v Pueblo Bowl-O-Mat, Inc*, 429 US 477 (1977); *Monstanto Co v Spray-Rite Service Corp*, 465 US 752 (1984); *Matsushita Electric Industrial Co v Zenith Radio Corp*, 475 US 574 (1986); *Daubert v Merrell Dow Pharmaceuticals, Inc*, 509 US 579 (1993); *Verizon Communications Inc v Law Offices of Curtis V. Trinko LLP*, 540 US 398 (2004); *Bell Atlantic Corp v Twombly* 550 US 554, 557 (2007); *Leegin Creative Leather Products Inc v PSKS, Inc*, 551 US 877 (2007).

[49] A FRCP 12(b)(6) motion results in the dismissal of claims that do not allege the facts necessary to sustain a cause of action. It requires 'a short and plain statement of the claim showing that the pleader is entitled to relief', FRCP 8(a)(2).

[50] FRCP 56(c).

private plaintiffs not only to bring antitrust actions but to 'win' them.[51] The Supreme Court has repeatedly expressed fear that enforcement should not be permitted to 'chill the very conduct the antitrust laws are designed to protect'[52] and this concern has influenced its efforts to

scale back the application of the U.S. antitrust laws. The consequence of getting it wrong—or false positives—is much greater when a firm is exposed to treble, rather than single, damages for its alleged wrongdoing...These combination of factors has led our Supreme Court to craft increasingly tough liability rules for antitrust offences and increasingly high hurdles for plaintiffs to move beyond the pleadings stage or to survive summary judgment or a directed verdict to get to a jury. The concern is not just that juries will get it wrong, but that the fear of false positives will chill business behaviour that may benefit consumers.[53]

There is now some concern however that the pendulum has swung too far in the opposite direction in the US; rules are so rigorous and provide so little certainty that meritorious litigation may be being discouraged. As antitrust law has shifted away from clear rules the costs of deciding antitrust cases have been increased without concern

for the loss of certainty that had been associated with now abandoned per se rules and lenient burdens of proof and the increased party and institutional costs associated with reliance on more demanding standards of proof. Neither has it been concerned with the possibility that the incidence of false negatives could increase due to cost and lack of access to the necessary proof.[54]

Indeed, following an important study of 60 private US antitrust cases,[55] Professors Davis and Lande[56] published a paper 'defying conventional wisdom', rejecting some or the more anecdotal and unsubstantiated concerns about private enforcement, and concluding that the private actions studied demonstrated that they had played an important role both in compensating victims and deterring violations. They found not only that the cases analysed (47 of which were opt-out class actions brought through lawyers working for a contingency fee) demonstrated that significant amounts of cash (in excess of $33.8 billion) was returned to victims of anti-competitive behaviour,[57] but it was clear that they had uncovered violations which might otherwise have been undiscovered; a third of the cases examined were stand-alone actions, actions which did not follow-on from public enforcement, and a number of the follow-on cases extended significantly beyond the parameters of the original government case. This complemented and bolstered their views, articulated in a separate paper, that private antitrust actions deter anti-competitive conduct more effectively even than criminal cartel proceedings pursued by the Department of Justice.[58]

The long experience of the US provides some important lessons for other jurisdictions. Not only does it illustrate how private actions can play an important role in the enforcement process and in ensuring that its compensatory, remediation, and/or deterrence functions are achieved, but it

---

[51] W. Kolasky, 'Different Roads' (2008) 11 *Global Competition Review* 17, 17.

[52] *Matsushita Electric v Zenith Radio Corp*, 475 US 574, 594 (1986); *Monsanto Co v Spray-Rite Service Corp*, 465 US 752, 762–764 (1984).

[53] Kolasky, n. 51, 19.

[54] Gavil, n. 2, 7–8.

[55] See R. H. Lande and J. P. Davis, 'Benefits from Private Antitrust Enforcement: An Analysis of Forty Cases' (2008) 42 *Univ San Francisco LR* 879, and J. P. Davis and R. H. Lande, 'Toward an Empirical and Theoretical Assessment of Private Antitrust Enforcement (2013) 36 *Seattle Univ LR* 1269.

[56] J. P. Davis and R. H. Lande, 'Defying Conventional Wisdom: The Case For Private Enforcement' (2013) 48 *Georgia LR* 1.

[57] They found that recovery levels were much higher in cases involving direct purchasers and that only 11 of the cases involved indirect purchasers.

[58] R. H. Lande and J. P. Davis, 'Comparative Deterrence from Private Enforcement and Criminal Enforcements of the US Antitrust Laws' (2011) *Brigham Young Univ LR* 315, but see G. J. Werden, S.D. Hammond, and B. A. Bartlett, 'Deterrence and Detection of Cartels: Using All The Tools and Sanctions' (2011) 56 *Ant Bull* 207 and R. H. Lande and J. P. Davis, 'The Extraordinary Deterrence of Private Antitrust Enforcement: A Reply to Werden, Hammond and Barnett' (2013) 58 *Ant Bull* 173.

illustrates that a number of pitfalls exist. Further, that in developing a system of private enforcement a number of issues should be addressed, including how to: (a) craft rules in a way that will achieve, and balance, the competing objectives pursued and which will minimise error costs; and (b) ensure that it does not undermine public enforcement.

Because of the close connection between private and public enforcement, many public enforcement agencies take a keen interest in the development of private enforcement. Indeed, it has already been seen that, in the EU, it has been the Commission which has spearheaded the campaign to encourage greater private enforcement of the EU antitrust laws, whilst at the same time stressing that it should not adversely impact on public enforcement. The Commission has been facilitated in this task by its unique and unusual position of having separate and central roles within the EU legal order both as a competition enforcement agency and as the EU institution which ordinarily formulates legislative proposals (including those to promote the effective application of competition law).

4. PRIVATE ENFORCEMENT IN THE EU

A. OVERVIEW: EFFECTIVE JUDICIAL PROTECTION AND THE PRINCIPLE OF NATIONAL PROCEDURAL AUTONOMY

In contrast to the position in the US, the EEC Treaty, the EC Treaty, and the TFEU have all been silent on the question of whether private rights of action for damages or injunctions must follow from a violation of the EU competition law rules; until the Damages Directive was adopted in 2014, no EU legislation specifically addressed private rights of action. Rather, such rights derive from the jurisprudence of the CJ[59] which has developed only in a gradual and piecemeal fashion. The slow evolution of this strand of cases has been partly due to the fact that, until Regulation 1/2003 came into force in 2004, national courts could not apply Article 101(3). Until then, the Commission's exclusive right to grant exemptions under Article 101(3), coupled with its wide interpretation of Article 101(1), meant that the Commission exercised tight control over enforcement[60] and national courts were excluded from playing a full role in antitrust cases.

Since 1974 it has been clear that private actions are possible by virtue of the fact that Articles 101 and 102 have direct effect (see *Belgische Radio en Televisie v SV SABAM*[61]). Further, in a series of subsequent cases the CJ has established that national courts[62] must provide effective judicial protection of the rights which individuals derive from directly effective provisions of EU law, and give them precedence over conflicting principles of national law.[63] These principles, combined with Article 3 of Regulation 1/2003,[64] mean that national courts, like NCAs: have an obligation to apply EU law in combination with national law to conduct which affects trade between Member States; cannot

---

[59] Which are now affirmed in Reg. 1/2003 on the implementation of the rules on competition laid down in [Arts. 101 and 102 TFEU] (Reg. 1/2003) [2003] OJ L1/1 (providing that national courts must have the power to apply Arts. 101 and 102 and for cooperation between the national courts and the Commission and consistency in interpretation of the provisions by all decision-takers).

[60] The conferral by Reg. 17 of 1962 [1959–1962] OJ Sp. Ed. 87, of the exclusive right on the Commission to rule on the compatibility of an individual agreement with Art. 101(3) made it difficult for the national courts to take part in the enforcement process; consequently, the central role in enforcing Arts. 101 and 102 was played by the Commission.

[61] Case 127/73, [1974] ECR 51, para. 16 ('As the prohibitions of Articles [101(1) and 102] tend by their very nature to produce direct effects in relations between individuals, these articles create direct rights in respect of the individuals concerned with the national courts must safeguard').

[62] See also now Reg. 1/2003, Art. 3(1).

[63] See Case 14/68, *Walt Wilhelm v Bundeskartellamt* [1969] ECR 1, para. 9.

[64] [2003] OJ L1/1.

apply national law to authorise conduct prohibited by EU law; can only apply national competition law more strictly in the circumstances specified by Regulation 1/2003; and must ensure effective remedies are available to protect EU rights.

Where an individual seeks to vindicate or protect his EU rights before a national court, the general principle is that of 'national procedural autonomy':

in the absence of Community rules on this subject, it is for the domestic legal system of each Member State to designate the courts having jurisdiction and to determine the procedural conditions governing actions at law intended to ensure the protection of rights which citizens have from the direct effect of [EU] law.[65]

Although the protection given to EU rights is thus dependent on the procedural, evidential, and substantive rules applicable in each particular Member State, the national courts have a duty of sincere cooperation to ensure the availability of adequate remedies sufficient to guarantee real and *effective* judicial protection for EU rights and to comply with the principles of equivalence and effectiveness—national rules (a) must not be less favourable than those relating to similar claims of a domestic nature (the principle of equivalence); and (b) must not make it virtually impossible or excessively difficult to exercise the rights that the national courts are obliged to protect (the principle of effectiveness).[66] Although these obligations may leave a national court freedom to determine how best to protect those rights,[67] in some cases it may require it to grant one of two or more possible remedies[68] or even a specific remedy to rectify a specific wrong.[69] For example, the CJ has held that a Member State is obliged, in defined circumstances, to compensate individuals who have been injured by its breach of EU law (*Francovich v Italy*)[70] and to repay charges it has levied in breach of EU law.[71] National courts are not required to grant *new* remedies,[72] but this obligation means that national rules may have to be adapted or extended to ensure that a remedy is available where required by EU law. National defences and procedural limitations to such a claim apply insofar as they comply with the principles of equivalence and effectiveness (the *acquis communautaire*).

In the context of Articles 101 and 102, these principles have combined to require national courts to ensure that:

(a) they do not take decisions that run counter to those adopted by the Commission (see Section B);

(b) individual *clauses* in an agreement affected by the Article 101(1)—and Article 102—prohibition are held to be void (see Section C);

(c) interim relief is available where necessary to protect putative EU rights (see Section D);

(d) full compensation is, in principle, available to those that have suffered loss in consequence of a breach of Article 101 or 102 (see Section D);

(e) defences and limitations to such rights/actions are only applied insofar as the principles of equivalence and effectiveness are respected (see Section D).

---

[65] Case 33/76, *Rewe-Zentralfinanz eG and Rewe-Zentral AG v Landwirtschaftskammer für das Saarland* [1976] ECR 1989.

[66] See Case 14/83, *Von Colson and Kamann v Land Nordrhein-Westfalen* [1984] ECR 1891, especially para. 23 and Case 33/76, *Rewe-Zentralfinanz*, ibid., para. 5.

[67] Case 34/67, *Lück v Hauptzollamt Köln* [1968] ECR 245.

[68] See Case C-271/91, *Marshall v Southampton and South-West Hampshire Area Health Authority (Teaching) (No. 2)* [1993] ECR I-4367.

[69] See, e.g., Case 199/82, *Ammistrazione delle Finanze dello Stato v San Giorgio SpA* [1983] ECR 3595 (the applicant's right to restitution is a 'consequence of and an adjunct to' the rights conferred on that individual by EU law).

[70] See Cases C-6 and 9/90, [1991] ECR I-5357.

[71] See, e.g., Case C-242/95, *GT-Link A/S v De Danske Statsbaner (DSB)* [1997] ECR I-4449.

[72] Case 158/80, *Rewe-Handelsgesellschaft Nord mbH v Hauptzollamt Kiel* [1981] ECR 1805.

Further constraints on the autonomy of national systems will come into place when the harmonising measures of the Damages Directive come into effect (see Section D). As the Directive does not harmonise all aspects of national law governing such claims the principle of national procedural autonomy will continue to have importance in relation to the issues following outside the scope of the Directive.

B. UNIFORM AND CONCURRENT APPLICATION OF ARTICLES 101 AND 102

(i) Cooperation Between the Commission and National Courts

A key concern which may follow from decentralising enforcement of Articles 101 and 102 is that the Commission, the individual NCAs, and national courts respectively may adopt inconsistent interpretations and applications of the rules. When applying Articles 101 and 102, the national courts are obviously bound to interpret those provisions in accordance with that adopted by the CJ and to respect the principle of primacy of EU law. Article 267 provides an important mechanism for national courts struggling with the interpretation of EU law. Further, the CJ has held that the duty of cooperation requires the Commission to assist national courts in their application of EU law and vice versa.[73]

Both Regulation 1/2003 itself and the Commission's Notice on cooperation with courts of the EU Member States in the application of [Articles 101 and 102 TFEU] (the Cooperation Notice)[74] explain how that cooperation may manifest itself. For example, Article 15 of Regulation 1/2003 envisages that the Commission should act as amicus curiae to the national courts. Not only does it provide that the national courts might request the Commission to provide information or an opinion on the application of the EU competition rules but it provides that the Commission may, where 'the coherent application of Article [101] or Article [102] so requires', submit written observations to the national courts and also, with their permission, make oral observations.[75] Any opinion so provided is published but does not have binding effect on the courts (although it may have persuasive impact).[76] The procedural framework, dealing with how the submissions should be provided, is governed by national law. Regulation 1/2003 also provides how the national courts must assist the Commission in the fulfilment of its tasks. In addition to providing the Commission and NCAs with the documents necessary for preparing written or oral observations to the courts, Member States must forward to the Commission 'a copy of any written judgment of national courts deciding on the application of Articles [101] or Article [102]' without delay.[77] The Commission publishes these judgments on its website according to the Member State of origin.[78]

(ii) Judgments Contrary to Decisions of the Commission

Article 11(6), which relieves NCAs of their competence to apply Articles 101 and 102 following initiation of proceedings by the Commission, does not apply to national courts. Nonetheless, the CJ has held that the duty of cooperation set out in EU law requires a national court to follow a Commission

---

[73] See, e.g., Case 234/89, *Delimitis v Henninger Bräu* [1991] ECR I-935, para. 53.

[74] [2004] OJ C101.

[75] Reg. 1/2003, Art. 15(3) (NCAs are also entitled to submit written observations to the national courts of their Member State and oral observations with permission).

[76] These observations are available at <http://ec.europa.eu/competition/court/antitrust_amicus_curiae.html>. See, e.g., Case C-429/07, *Inspecteur van de Belastingdienst v X BV* [2009] ECR I-4833 (the CJ upheld the Commission's ability to intercede under Art. 15(3) in national proceedings where the outcome of the dispute was capable of impairing the effectiveness of the penalty it had imposed).

[77] Art. 15(2).

[78] See the National Court Cases Database, <http://ec.europa.eu/competition/elojade/antitrust/nationalcourts/>.

decision dealing with the same parties and the same agreement in the same Member State.[79] Further, in order to ensure a uniform application of Articles 101 and 102, Article 16 of Regulation 1/2003 provides that the national courts must not adopt decisions contrary to a previous Commission decision and must avoid giving decisions that would conflict with a decision contemplated by the Commission.[80] Regulation 1/2003 does not deal with the impact of decisions of NCAs within the European Competition Network on national courts. Although the Commission proposed that NCAs' decisions should be given similar effect, the final Damages Directive provides only that NCA decisions should be binding in their home jurisdiction.[81]

Where the Commission has initiated proceedings but not determined a case, a national court must not, therefore, adopt a decision which will conflict with that which will be adopted by the Commission. The Commission will provide the national court with information as to whether it has initiated proceedings, the progress of proceedings, and the likelihood of a decision. Unless the national court cannot doubt the Commission's contemplated decision or the Commission has already decided on a similar case, it should ordinarily stay the proceedings before it.[82] Where this occurs the Commission will endeavour to give the case priority. Where the Commission has already decided on the case, however, the Commission's decision is binding on the national court, without prejudice to the interpretation of EU law by the CJ.[83] If the national court does not agree with the decision of the Commission it must either await the outcome of an appeal, if any, from its decision, or refer the question to the CJ for a preliminary ruling.[84] Where the national court does stay proceedings in the context of parallel or consecutive proceedings, it should consider whether it should impose interim measures in order to safeguard the interests of the parties involved.[85]

In *Inntrepreneur Pub Co v Crehan*[86] the UK's House of Lords (now the Supreme Court) adopted a narrow interpretation of the national court's duty of sincere cooperation and its obligation not to adopt decisions contrary to those in a previous Commission decision. This ruling was the last in a saga which commenced in 1993 and saw the parties endure 13 years of litigation before the High Court, the Court of Appeal, the CJ, back to the High Court, the Court of Appeal, and, finally, before the (then) House of Lords. Although the case led, before the CJ, to clarification of an EU right to damages in competition cases,[87] the final outcome of the case eventually turned upon the question of whether an English court was bound to adopt the same approach to the question of how Article 101(1) applied to a beer tie agreement concluded by a UK brewer and a publican as that which had been adopted by the Commission in similar cases, but involving different parties. In a number of decisions, such as *Whitbread*, *Bass*, and *Scottish & Newcastle*,[88] the Commission had held that extremely similar agreements concluded by other UK brewers foreclosed the UK market for the distribution of beer in on-licensed premises and violated Article 101(1). Further, although it did not actually adopt a decision, the Commission had indicated that the Inntrepreneur leases (the leases at issue) were also in breach of Article 101. Nonetheless, when the *Crehan* case reverted to the

---

[79] See, e.g., Case C-344/98, *Masterfoods v HB Ice Cream Ltd* [2000] ECR I-11369 and Case 234/89, *Delimitis v Henninger Bräu* [1991] ECR I-935.

[80] See also Cooperation Notice, n. 74, paras. 11–13.

[81] Commission Proposal, n. 10, Art. 9 and see n. 201 and text.

[82] See, e.g., Case 234/89, *Delimitis v Henninger Bräu* [1991] ECR I-935, paras. 43–55. See *AAH Pharmaceuticals Ltd and Others v Pfizer Ltd and UniChem Ltd* [2007] EWHC 565 (Ch).

[83] Case 314/85, *Foto-Frost v Hauptzollamt Lübeck-Ost* [1987] ECR 4199, paras. 12–20.

[84] Ibid., para. 12.

[85] Case C-344/98, *Masterfoods v HB Ice Cream Ltd* [2000] ECR I-11369, para. 58.

[86] [2006] UKHL 38. See, e.g., J. Temple Lang, '*Inntrepreneur* and the Duties of National Courts under Article 10 EC' [2006] *Comp Law* 231.

[87] See n. 115 and text.

[88] COMP/35.079, *Whitbread* [1999] OJ L88/26, aff'd Case T-13/99, *Shaw v Commission* [2002] ECR II-2023, COMP/36.081, *Bass* [1999] OJ L186/1, and COMP/35.992, *Scottish and Newcastle* [1999] OJ L186/28.

High Court following the CJ's ruling, Park J held that the beer tie agreements did not infringe Article 101(1).[89] Although accepting that he should give the Commission decisions weight, he did not consider himself to be bound by them. In so ruling, the judge departed from the approach taken not only by the Commission,[90] but also by the UK authorities,[91] and other English courts in their analysis of beer tie agreements in the UK market. Although on appeal the Court of Appeal held, noting that the judge should have given greater deference to previous Commission decisional practice,[92] that the lease incorporating the beer tie did infringe Article 101(1),[93] the House of Lords held that the judge was not bound by the Commission's assessment. The duty of sincere cooperation did not require the English court to accept the factual basis of a decision reached by an EU institution when considering an issue arising between different parties in respect of a different subject matter. The judge was thus bound to consider the factual evidence presented to him and to analyse it giving particular attention to those points on which he differed from the Commission. To have done otherwise would have been an abdication of the judicial function.

Had the Court of Appeal's opinion prevailed in this case, companies might have felt compelled to intervene in and challenge decisions addressed to other parties which might have affected their interests in the future. The House of Lords opinion, however, undoubtedly leaves the slightly uncomfortable and unsatisfactory position that 'because the English courts did not ask the Commission for submissions, breweries to which Commission decisions were addressed were put in a different position from Inntrepreneur, and there is no obvious way of resolving this inconsistency'.[94]

C. THE ENFORCEABILITY OF AGREEMENTS INFRINGING ARTICLE 101 OR 102

(i) Article 101

In Chapter 3 it was seen that Article 101 itself provides that agreements or decisions prohibited by Article 101(1) are void if the agreement does not satisfy the conditions of Article 101(3) (Article 101(2)).[95] Further, that despite the wording of Article 101, the CJ has held that the nullity provided for in Article 101(2) in fact applies only to individual clauses in the agreement affected by the Article 101(1) prohibition.[96] The agreement as a whole is thus void only where those clauses are not severable from the remaining terms of the agreement.[97] In *Manfredi v Lloyd Adriatico Assicurazioni SpA* the CJ clarified that the invalidity of the agreement (or affected clauses) is absolute—the agreement has no effect as between the contracting parties and cannot be invoked against third parties.[98]

---

[89] *Crehan v Inntrepreneur Pub Co* [2003] EWHC 1510 (Ch). Applying the test set out by the CJ in Case C-234/89, *Delimitis* [1991] ECR I-935 (discussed in Chap. 4) he considered that the UK market for the distribution of beer in on-licensed premises was not foreclosed.

[90] See the discussion in Chaps. 4 and 11.

[91] See, e.g., *The Supply of Beer: a report on the supply of beer for retail sale in the United Kingdom* (Cm. 651, 1989).

[92] *Crehan v Inntrepreneur Pub Co CPC* [2004] EWCA Civ 637, para. 97.

[93] Ibid., para. 78 ('[i]t is a striking feature of this case that, as Inntrepreneur very properly accepts, if the judge were right, the Commission has been consistently wrong for many years in its view of the foreclosure of the United Kingdom market ...').

[94] Temple Lang, n. 86, 234.

[95] A plea that an agreement infringed Art. 101 and was void caused acute difficulties in the cases that arose prior to 2004 under the old Reg. 17 system on account of the national courts' inability to apply Art. 101(3) to individual cases, see Case 234/89, *Delimitis v Henninger Bräu* [1991] ECR I-935.

[96] Case 56/65, *Société La Technique Minière v Maschinenbau Ulm GmbH* [1966] ECR 234, 250.

[97] Ibid. and Case 319/82, *Société de Vente de Ciments et Bétons de l'Est SA v Kerpen & Kerpen GmbH & Co KG* [1983] ECR 4173, see Chap. 3.

[98] See Cases C-295–298/04, [2006] ECR I-6619, para. 57.

Although the effect of Article 101(2) has been spelt out by the CJ, the question of whether the prohibited clauses can actually be severed from the remaining provisions in the contract is a matter for national law.[99] Under English law, for example, the position is, broadly, that the courts will sever parts of a contract only where sufficient consideration remains to support the agreement and it is possible to sever by running a blue pencil through that offending part.[100] The courts will not make a new contract or rewrite the contract for the parties, for example by adding or rearranging words. Nor will a court strike out words of a contract if, in so doing, a contract of an entirely different scope or intention would be left.[101]

The English courts have also found[102] that not only are contractual provisions offending Article 101(1) void, but they are *illegal* for the purposes of the (English) *in pari delicto* rule (a principle of public policy which prevents a court from lending 'its aid to a man who founds his cause of action upon an immoral or illegal act').[103] The compatibility of the plea of illegality with EU law is discussed in greater detail in Section 4.D below.

An agreement infringes Article 101 only if all of the elements of Article 101(1) are satisfied and the four conditions of Article 101(3) are not met. It is possible, therefore, that, as events change over a period of time, an agreement which does not infringe Article 101(1) will subsequently be found to do so or vice versa. Suppose, for example, a small, local undertaking concludes an agreement which does not infringe Article 101(1) on account of its minor importance (the undertaking has an extremely small share of the market). Suppose further, that that undertaking is subsequently taken over by a larger undertaking so that the agreement now does have an appreciable effect on competition and trade, does not meet the conditions of a block exemption, and does not fulfil the conditions of Article 101(3). The agreement which previously fell outside Article 101(1) (and was valid) now becomes subject to its prohibition (and void). In *Passmore v Morland plc*[104] the reverse scenario occurred and the English Court of Appeal held that the reverse can occur: an agreement which was initially void can become valid (and possibly void again) as the agreement falls within and without the Article 101(1) prohibition.

A further crucial question which arises is whether contracts concluded in implementation, or in consequence, of an illegal agreement might be vitiated, for example a contract for sale at prices inflated in consequence of a cartel agreement entered into by the seller or sales contracts made in consequence of an invalid beer tie. In certain circumstances EU law makes it clear that a contract confirming an illegal contract is also in violation of Article 101.[105] Otherwise, it seems it is for national law,[106] subject to the principles of equivalence and effectiveness, to determine whether or not a contract concluded with a third party on the basis of a void agreement should also be tainted by the illegality and 'regarded as springing from or founded on the agreement rendered illegal'.[107]

---

[99] This means that the enforceability of a contract will vary depending on which Member State's rules are applicable and will not necessarily be uniform throughout the EU, see, e.g., R. Whish, 'The Enforceability of Agreements under EC and UK Competition Law' in F. Rose (ed.), *International Commercial Law* (LLP, 2000).

[100] See, e.g., *Chemidus Wavin Ltd v TERI* [1978] 3 CMLR 514, 520.

[101] See, e.g., *Goldsoll v Goldman* [1914] 2 Ch 603.

[102] *Gibbs Mew plc v Gemmell* [1999] 1 EGLR 43.

[103] *Holman v Johnson* (1775) 1 Cowp 341, 343, per Lord Mansfield.

[104] [1999] 3 All ER 1005.

[105] See, e.g., discussion of Case C-32/11, *Allianz Hungária Biztosító Zrt, Generali-Providencia Biztosító Zrt v Gazdasági Versenyhivatal* EU:C:2013:160 in Chap. 11.

[106] Case 319/82, *Société de Vente de Ciments et Bétons de l'Est SA v Kerpen & Kerpen GmbH & Co KG* [1983] ECR 4173.

[107] *Courage v Crehan* [2004] EWCA Civ 637. See also, e.g., the view of the Swedish Supreme Court in *Boliden Mineral AB v Birka*, OCL 057 (SE 2004) and C. Cauffman, 'The Impact of Voidness from Infringement of Article 101 TFEU on Related Contracts' (2012) 8 *European Competition Journal* 95.

(ii) Article 102

Article 102 contains no declaration of nullity equivalent to that set out in Article 101. This omission is not surprising since Article 102 does not explicitly prohibit agreements but focuses on a wider range of conduct.[108] Nevertheless, the Article implicitly prohibits many contracts and contractual terms and the effect in relation to sanctioned agreements is, despite being couched in different terms, similar to that of Article 101. It is to be expected, therefore, that Article 102 should render a contract, or severable terms of a contract, affected by its prohibition void[109] or, at the very least, unenforceable.[110] The former view was taken by the High Court of England and Wales in *English Welsh & Scottish Railway Ltd v E.ON UK plc*[111] where it held that the effect of finding by a UK regulator (the Office of Rail Regulation, the ORR) that a contractual provision violated Article 102,[112] is that the offending contractual provision is illegal and void and the agreement as a whole is void if the prohibited clauses cannot be severed from the remaining terms of the agreement. On the facts, Field J held that the exclusionary aspects of the contract, being in breach of Article 102, had been illegal and void since execution. Further that, as severance of the exclusionary terms would leave a contract of a fundamentally different nature, the effect of the ORR's decision was that the entire Coal Carriage Agreement was void and unenforceable.

D. REMEDIES: INJUNCTIONS AND DAMAGES

(i) EU Remedies

a. An EU Right to an Injunction

For many years a lack of clarity surrounded the question of what *exact* rights Articles 101 and 102 conferred upon individuals and what remedies had to be available to protect them. In *R v Secretary of State for Transport, ex parte Factortame Ltd*,[113] however, the CJ made it clear that a national court must ensure that interim measures are available where necessary to protect putative EU rights:[114]

19. In accordance with the case-law of the Court, it is for the national courts, in application of the principle of cooperation laid down in Article [10] of the [EC] Treaty, to ensure the legal protection which persons derive from the direct effect of provisions of Community law . . .

20. The Court has also held that any provision of a national legal system and any legislative, administrative or judicial practice which might impair the effectiveness of Community law by withholding from the national court having jurisdiction to apply such law the power to do everything necessary at the moment of its application to set aside national legislative provisions which might prevent, even temporarily, Community rules from having full force and effect are incompatible with those requirements, which are the very essence of Community law. . . .

---

[108] See Chaps. 5 and 7.

[109] See, e.g., the view of the Swedish Court of Appeal, *Scandinavian Airlines System (SAS) v Swedish Board of Aviation* (unreported), T. Pettersson and J. Aswall, 'Discriminatory Pricing: Comments on a Swedish Case' [2003] *ECLR* 295, U. Bernitz, 'The Arlanda Terminal 2 Case: Substantial Damages Awarded on the Basis of Article 82 TEC' [2004] 1 *Comp Law* 195, and R. Whish, 'The Enforcement of EC Competition Law in the Domestic Courts of the Member States' in J. Lonbay (ed.), *Frontiers of Competition Law* (Wiley, 1994), Chap. 5. In many cases an agreement concluded by a dominant undertaking which incorporates a contractual clause infringing Art. 102 is likely also to infringe Art. 101(1).

[110] See, e.g., *Gibbs Mew plc v Gemmell* [1999] 1 EGLR 43.

[111] [2007] EWHC 599 (Comm).

[112] And the UK equivalent, Chap. II of the Competition Act 1998.

[113] Case 213/89, [1990] ECR I-2433.

[114] An individual suffering in consequence of a breach of the competition rules might request an injunction, final or interim (pending resolution of the final dispute), to prevent the undertaking or undertakings committing a breach of the rules in future. The availability of an interim injunction will be of particular importance to an undertaking which believes that it is being driven out of the market by, e.g., exclusionary conduct infringing Art. 102.

21. . . . [T]he full effectiveness of Community law would be just as much impaired if a rule of national law could prevent a court seized of a dispute governed by Community law from granting interim relief in order to ensure the full effectiveness of the judgment to be given on the existence of the rights claimed under Community law. It follows that a court which in those circumstances would grant interim relief, if it were not for a rule of national law, is obliged to set aside that rule.

It was not until 2001, in *Courage Ltd v Crehan*, however, that the question of whether damages were required to protect rights derived under Articles 101 and 102 was finally resolved.

b. Development of an EU Right to Damages

The question of whether there is any EU right to damages was decided by the CJ following a reference to it of questions by the English Court of Appeal using the Article 267 procedure. The reference was made in the course of hearing conjoined appeals in the case of *Courage Ltd v Crehan*.[115] The case concerned two leases of public houses that had been concluded between Inntrepreneur Estates (CPC) Ltd (owned equally by Grand Metropolitan plc and Courage Ltd) and Mr Crehan and which required Mr Crehan to purchase minimum quantities of various beers for resale at the leased premises from Courage, and no other person. The proceedings involved an action brought by the brewers for the recovery of £15,266, alleged to be the price of beers sold and delivered to Mr Crehan. By way of defence Crehan alleged, amongst other things, that the beer tie in the lease was in breach of Article 101. He counterclaimed for damages and/or restitution. The case thus raised the compatibility of the beer ties and the leases with Article 101 and the impact of any such incompatibility on the claims and counterclaims made by the parties.

Courage Ltd v Crehan was one of a series of cases that had arisen before the English courts, raising the compatibility of leases containing beer ties with Article 101 and the ability of tenants to recover in respect of their loss suffered in consequence of the void beer tie (the actions were based on the brewer's breach of statutory duty)[116] or to recover the payments made pursuant to the void contract (the restitutionary claim).[117]

By the time the *Crehan* case reached the Court of Appeal, authority established that the case must fail. The English courts had given short shrift to the claims which had been rejected as 'hopeless'. Although a whole host of different reasons had been given for the rejection of the claims,[118] the most significant obstacle to the actions had been that the claims were based on an illegal act. The English courts have generally refused to assist a claimant whose action is founded on an illegal act: *ex turpi causa non oritur actio*[119] and to allow a party to a prohibited contract either to enforce that contract or to bring any other action based upon it: *in pari delicto potior est conditio defendentis*.[120] Although the Court of Appeal in *Courage Ltd v Crehan* agreed with the first instance judge that English law would not afford a remedy of damages to a party to an agreement prohibited by Article 101,[121] it recognised

---

[115] [1999] EuLR 834.

[116] They therefore claimed the difference between the contract price of the beer and its market value and other consequential loss, see, e.g., *Gibbs Mew plc v Gemmell* [1998] EuLR 588 and *Trent Taverns v Sykes* [1999] EuLR 492.

[117] In many cases the restitutionary claims were eventually abandoned, see, e.g., A. Jones, *Restitution and EC Law* (LLP, 2000), Chap. 6 and A. Jones and B. Sufrin, *EC Competition Law: Text, Cases, and Materials* (Oxford University Press, 2001), Chap. 15, 991–1002.

[118] The courts questioned whether, in the context of a breach of Art. 101, any tortious action for damages for breach of statutory duty lies at all (see *Inntrepreneur Estates (CPC) plc v Milne*, unreported, 30 July 1993, *Matthew Brown plc v Campbell* [1998] EuLR 530).

[119] 'No court will lend its aid to a man who founds his action upon an immoral or illegal act.'

[120] 'Where both parties are equally wrongful the position of the defendant is stronger', *Holman v Johnson* (1775) 1 Cowp 341, 343. The rule is a principle not of justice but of policy which discourages all contracts that are contrary to public policy. 'For an agreement to be illegal it need not be in breach of the criminal law', *Gibbs Mew plc v Gemmell* [1999] 1 EGLR 43, 49, [1998] EuLR 588.

[121] *Courage Ltd v Crehan* [1999] EuLR 834.

that there might be sound policy arguments in favour of accepting that a party to a prohibited agreement has a right to sue for damages.[122] Further, that a party to a prohibited agreement such as that before it, might have rights by virtue of Article 101 that were protected by EU law which might supersede any principle of English law denying the right. The Court of Appeal thus made a reference to the CJ essentially asking whether EU law required a national court to provide a remedy of damages to claimants injured by a breach of Article 101, even if it was a party to the prohibited contract.

Case C-453/99, *Courage Ltd v Crehan* [2001] ECR I-6297

Court of Justice

19. It should be borne in mind, first of all, that the Treaty has created its own legal order, which is integrated into the legal systems of the Member States and which their courts are bound to apply. The subjects of that legal order are not only the Member States but also their nationals. Just as it imposes burdens on individuals, Community law is also intended to give rise to rights which become part of their legal assets. Those rights arise not only where they are expressly granted by the Treaty but also by virtue of obligations which the Treaty imposes in a clearly defined manner both on individuals and on the Member States and the Community institutions (see the judgments in Case 26/62, *Van Gend en Loos* [1963] ECR 1, Case 6/64, *Costa* [1964] ECR 585 and Joined Cases C-6/90 and C-9/90, *Francovich and Others* [1991] ECR I-5357, para. 31).

20. Secondly, according to Article 3(g) of the EC Treaty (now, after amendment, Art. 3(1)(g) EC), Article [101 TFEU] constitutes a fundamental provision which is essential for the accomplishment of the tasks entrusted to the Community and, in particular, for the functioning of the internal market (judgment in Case C-126/97, *Eco Swiss* [1999] ECR I-3055, para. 36).

21. Indeed, the importance of such a provision led the framers of the Treaty to provide expressly, in Article [101(2) TFEU], that any agreements or decisions prohibited pursuant to that article are to be automatically void (judgment in *Eco Swiss*, cited para. 36).

22. That principle of automatic nullity can be relied on by anyone, and the courts are bound by it once the conditions for the application of Article [101(1)] are met and so long as the agreement concerned does not justify the grant of an exemption under Article [101(3) TFEU] (on the latter point, see, *inter alia*, Case 10/69, *Portelange* [1969] ECR 309, para. 10). Since the nullity referred to in Article [101(2)] is absolute, an agreement which is null and void by virtue of this provision has no effect as between the contracting parties and cannot be set up against third parties (see the judgment in Case 22/71, *Béguelin* [1971] ECR 949, para. 29). Moreover, it is capable of having a bearing on all the effects, either past or future, of the agreement or decision concerned (see the judgment in Case 48/72, *Brasserie de Haecht II* [1973] ECR 77, para. 26).

23. Thirdly, it should be borne in mind that the Court has held that Article [101(1) TFEU] and Article [102] produce direct effects in relations between individuals and create rights for the individuals concerned which the national courts must safeguard (judgments in Case, 127/73 *BRT and SABAM* [1974] ECR 51, para. 16, (*BRT I*) and Case C-282/95 P, *Guérin Automobiles v Commission* [1997] ECR I-1503, para. 39).

24. It follows from the foregoing considerations that any individual can rely on a breach of Article [101(1) TFEU] before a national court even where he is a party to a contract that is liable to restrict or distort competition within the meaning of that provision.

25. As regards the possibility of seeking compensation for loss caused by a contract or by conduct liable to restrict or distort competition, it should be remembered from the outset that, in accordance with

---

[122] Referring to the US Supreme Court's opinion in *Perma Life Mufflers Inc v International Parts Corp*, 392 US 134 (1968) (the illegality defence did not bar an action brought by a party to an anti-competitive agreement that was in an economically weaker position and not equally at fault (*in pari delicto*)—private suits important to antitrust enforcement and furthering the public policy in favour of competition).

settled case-law, the national courts whose task it is to apply the provisions of Community law in areas within their jurisdiction must ensure that those rules take full effect and must protect the rights which they confer on individuals (see, *inter alia*, the judgments in Case 106/77, *Simmenthal* [1978] ECR 629, para. 16, and in Case C-213/89, *Factortame* [1990] ECR I-2433, para. 19).

26. The full effectiveness of Article [101 TFEU] and, in particular, the practical effect of the prohibition laid down in Article [101(1)] would be put at risk if it were not open to any individual to claim damages for loss caused to him by a contract or by conduct liable to restrict or distort competition.

27. Indeed, the existence of such a right strengthens the working of the Community competition rules and discourages agreements or practices, which are frequently covert, which are liable to restrict or distort competition. From that point of view, actions for damages before the national courts can make a significant contribution to the maintenance of effective competition in the Community.

28. There should not therefore be any absolute bar to such an action being brought by a party to a contract which would be held to violate the competition rules.

29. However, in the absence of Community rules governing the matter, it is for the domestic legal system of each Member State to designate the courts and tribunals having jurisdiction and to lay down the detailed procedural rules governing actions for safeguarding rights which individuals derive directly from Community law, provided that such rules are not less favourable than those governing similar domestic actions (principle of equivalence) and that they do not render practically impossible or excessively difficult the exercise of rights conferred by Community law (principle of effectiveness) (see Case C-261/95 *Palmisani* [1997] ECR I-4025, para. 27).

30. In that regard, the Court has held that Community law does not prevent national courts from taking steps to ensure that the protection of the rights guaranteed by Community law does not entail the unjust enrichment of those who enjoy them (see, in particular, Case 238/78, *Ireks-Arkady v Council and Commission* [1979] ECR 2955, para. 14, Case 68/79, *Just* [1980] ECR 501, para. 26, and Joined Cases C-441/98 and C-442/98, *Michailidis* [2000] ECR I-7145, para. 31).

31. Similarly, provided that the principles of equivalence and effectiveness are respected (see *Palmisani*, cited above, para. 27), Community law does not preclude national law from denying a party who is found to bear significant responsibility for the distortion of competition the right to obtain damages from the other contracting party. Under a principle which is recognised in most of the legal systems of the Member States and which the Court has applied in the past (see Case 39/72, *Commission v Italy* [1973] ECR 101, para. 10), a litigant should not profit from his own unlawful conduct, where this is proven.

. . .

36. Having regard to all the foregoing considerations, the questions referred are to be answered as follows:

— a party to a contract liable to restrict or distort competition within the meaning of Article [101 TFEU] can rely on the breach of that article to obtain relief from the other contracting party;

— Article [101 TFEU] precludes a rule of national law under which a party to a contract liable to restrict or distort competition within the meaning of that provision is barred from claiming damages for loss caused by performance of that contract on the sole ground that the claimant is a party to that contract;

— Community law does not preclude a rule of national law barring a party to a contract liable to restrict or distort competition from relying on his own unlawful actions to obtain damages where it is established that that party bears significant responsibility for the distortion of competition.

It can be seen from this extract that the Court stresses the new legal order created by the EU, the rights the Treaty provisions confer on individuals, the centrality of the competition rules to the EU project, and the direct effect of Article 101(1). The Court did not hesitate to conclude that *any* individual is entitled to rely on a breach of Article 101(1) and the nullity set out in Article 101(2) before a national court, even a party to a prohibited contract.

The Court then goes on to underline the obligation of national courts to ensure that EU rules take full effect and to protect the EU rights those provisions conferred on individuals[123] and highlights the importance of private actions to the enforcement of EU law.[124] The Court thus concluded that there should be no absolute bar to a damages claim, even to one brought by a party to a contract violating the competition rules. Insofar as the English principle of illegality provides an absolute bar to a claim for damages commenced under Article 101 it is therefore undoubtedly incompatible with EU law. Application of the English illegality rule might be compatible with EU law, however, where it respects the EU principles of equivalence and effectiveness; for example, where a right to obtain damages is denied to a contracting party found to bear *significant responsibility* for the distortion of competition.[125] The CJ deals with the meaning of significant responsibility in paragraphs 32–35 of its judgment.[126]

Case C-453/99, *Courage Ltd v Crehan* [2001] ECR I-6297

Court of Justice

32. In that regard, the matters to be taken into account by the competent national court include the economic and legal context in which the parties find themselves and, as the United Kingdom Government rightly points out, the respective bargaining power and conduct of the two parties to the contract.

33. In particular, it is for the national court to ascertain whether the party who claims to have suffered loss through concluding a contract that is liable to restrict or distort competition found himself in a markedly weaker position than the other party, such as seriously to compromise or even eliminate his freedom to negotiate the terms of the contract and his capacity to avoid the loss or reduce its extent, in particular by availing himself in good time of all the legal remedies available to him.

34. Referring to the judgments in Case 23/67, *Brasserie de Haecht* [1967] ECR 127 and Case C-234/89, *Delimitis* [1991] ECR I-935, paras. 14–26, the Commission and the United Kingdom Government also rightly point out that a contract might prove to be contrary to Article [101(1) TFEU] for the sole reason that it is part of a network of similar contracts which have a cumulative effect on competition. In such a case, the party contracting with the person controlling the network cannot bear significant responsibility for the breach of Article [101], particularly where in practice the terms of the contract were imposed on him by the party controlling the network.

35. Contrary to the submission of Courage, making a distinction as to the extent of the parties' liability does not conflict with the case-law of the Court to the effect that it does not matter, for the purposes of the application of Article [101 TFEU], whether the parties to an agreement are on an equal footing as regards their economic position and function (see, *inter alia*, Joined Cases 56/64 and 58/64, *Consten and Grundig v Commission* [1966] ECR 382). That case-law concerns the conditions for application of Article [101 TFEU] while the questions put before the Court in the present case concern certain consequences in civil law of a breach of that provision.

The judgment thus clearly establishes that: (a) Article 101 confers rights on individuals, even parties to a contract in breach (illegality cannot constitute an absolute bar to a claim); and (b) any breach of Article 101 is sufficiently serious to trigger an EU right to damages. The ruling thus creates

---

[123] Case C-453/99, [2001] ECR I-6297, para. 26.

[124] Ibid., para. 27.

[125] Ibid., para. 31. In these circumstances the principle of EU law that a litigant should not profit from his own unlawful conduct would be respected, Case 39/72, *Commission v Italy* [1973] ECR 101, para. 10.

[126] On remission of the case to the English court, this factor led Park J and the Court of Appeal to hold that the tenant's claim could not be barred by the principle of illegality or significant responsibility, but see discussion of the case in n. 89 and text.

a new 'Euro-tort'[127] along the lines of *Francovich*;[128] individuals must, in principle, be entitled to claim damages for loss caused by an agreement or conduct that restricts competition; whatever the position in national law, a right to claim damages to compensate breaches of both Article 101 and Article 102 must be available under national law.[129] Until the harmonising measures incorporated within the Damages Directive are implemented, national rules exclusively[130] govern the recovery claim, subject to the principles of equivalence and effectiveness.

The ruling in *Crehan* is of significance to all damages claims, not just those involving co-contractors. The CJ reiterated this view in *Manfredi v Lloyd Adriatico Assicurazioni SpA*[131] where it stated that the practical effect of the Article 101(1) prohibition would be put at risk if it were not open to any individual to claim damages for loss caused to him by a contract or by conduct liable to restrict or distort competition. 'It follows that any individual can claim compensation for the harm suffered where there is a causal relationship between that harm and an agreement or practice prohibited under Article [101].'[132] In this case, the Court was also asked whether Article 101 had to be interpreted as requiring national courts to award 'punitive' damages, greater than the advantage obtained by the offending operator, thereby deterring the adoption of prohibited agreements.[133] The CJ stressed that the right to claim damages was designed to strengthen the working of the EU competition rules and to discourage prohibited agreements but that the question of whether to award punitive damages was, in the absence of EU rules governing the matter, for the domestic legal system of each Member State to determine, provided that the principles of equivalence and effectiveness are observed. It thus stated that:

(a) it must be possible to award punitive damages if such damages may be awarded pursuant to similar actions founded on domestic law. However, EU law did not prevent national courts from taking steps to ensure that protection of EU rights does not entail unjust enrichment of those who enjoy them; and

(b) the right to seek compensation must include compensation not only for actual loss but also for loss of profit plus interest.[134]

Damages claims in the EU are not necessarily restricted to claimants in a vertical chain with the defendant (for example, a direct or indirect purchaser from the defendant), so long as it can be established that the loss caused to the claimant resulted in consequence of the infringing conduct. This point was confirmed by the CJ in *Kone AG v ÖBB-Infrastruktur AG*.[135] In this case the claimant alleged

---

[127] N. Dunne, 'Antitrust and the Making of European Tort Law' (2015) 36 *OJLS* 1, 3.

[128] See Cases C-6 and 9/90, [1991] ECR I-5357 and n. 70 and text.

[129] Although the Court did not specifically deal with Art. 102 it referred to the need to compensate those who have suffered loss caused to them by a contract *or* by conduct liable to restrict or distort competition.

[130] The principle of national procedural autonomy will remain important even afterwards as the Directive only seeks to harmonise selected aspects of national law governing competition law damages claims (minimum harmonisation). The Commission recognises in its Notice on cooperation with the national courts the particular difficulties that may arise in consequence of the fact that there is no harmonisation of procedures in the Member States, see the Cooperation Notice, n. 74, paras. 9–10.

[131] Case C-295–298/04, [2006] ECR I-6619, para. 60.

[132] Ibid., para. 61. In English law a claimant has to establish that the breach caused the loss complained of, i.e. that the damage would not have occurred but for the breach.

[133] Ibid., paras. 83–100. In the UK, contrast *Devenish Nutrition Ltd v Sanofi Aventis SA* [2007] EWHC 2394 (Ch) (exemplary damages not available where the Commission has imposed a fine in relation to the same offence), aff'd [2008] EWCA Civ 10 with Case 1178/5/7/11, *2 Travel Group plc (in liquidation) v Cardiff City Transport Services Ltd* [2012] CAT 19 (exemplary damages awarded). See also Case 1166/5/10, *Albion Water Ltd v Dwr Cymru Cyfyngedig* [2013] CAT 6.

[134] The Commission recognises in its Notice on cooperation with the national courts the particular difficulties that may arise in consequence of the fact that there is no harmonisation of procedures in the Member States, see the Cooperation Notice, n. 74, paras. 9–10.

[135] Case C-557/12, EU:C:2014:1317. See also, e.g., F. Maier-Rigaud, 'Umbrella Effects and the Ubiquity of Damage Resulting from Competition Law Violations' (2014) 5 *JECLAP* 247.

before an Austrian court that it had been harmed by the market-sharing cartel at issue in the elevators and escalators market which had enabled suppliers (which were not themselves in the cartel) to raise their prices. Austrian law did not, however, permit such a claim, because the alleged loss resulted from an independent business decision of the non-cartelist.

The CJ concluded that the full effectiveness of Article 101 would be put at risk if it were not open to any individual to claim damages for loss caused to him by infringing conduct. A person was thus entitled to claim compensation for the harm suffered where a causal link with an agreement or practice prohibited under Article 101 could be established. Because market price was one of the main factors taken into consideration by an undertaking when determining the price at which it will offer its goods or services, it could not be ruled out that a competing undertaking, outside the cartel in question, might choose to set the price of its offer at an amount higher than it would have chosen in the absence of that cartel where the cartel resulted in artificially high prices for particular goods. The victim of such 'umbrella pricing' should consequently be able to obtain compensation for such loss from the members of a cartel, 'where it is established that the cartel at issue was, in the circumstances of the case and, in particular, the specific aspects of the relevant market, liable to have the effect of umbrella pricing being applied by third parties acting independently, and that those circumstances and specific aspects could not be ignored by the members of that cartel'.[136]

c. The Principle Underpinning the EU Right to Damages

The question of how national rules must be applied and developed to comply with the requirements of EU law has been a matter of some debate. In particular, the answer is dependent partly on how the principle of effectiveness stressed in the CJ's judgments is to be interpreted and especially whether it suggests that the principal purpose of private enforcement is the attainment of corrective justice[137]—with deterrence operating merely as a socially beneficial by-product of such actions[138]—or whether private enforcement is simply a tool to increase enforcement and deter violations[139] (that is, whether the primary function of the private action is seen to be one of compensation or deterrence). Nebbia, for example, considers that uncertainty on this issue stems from an ambiguous understanding of the notion of 'effectiveness' relied on by the CJ in *Courage*.[140] He analyses the notion of 'effectiveness' by reference to the EU's *acquis communautaire* before concluding that private enforcement should ultimately be about effective judicial protection of individual rights and compensation.

P. Nebbia, 'Damages Actions for the Infringement of EC Competition Law: Compensation or Deterrence?' (2008) 33 ELRev, 23, 35–36

Which principle of 'effectiveness' for Courage?

It is here submitted that the notion of 'effectiveness' on which the *Crehan* decision relies is that of 'effective judicial protection', rather than 'effective enforcement' First and foremost, *Crehan* is commonly considered as the logical extension of the same principle that generated *Francovich* and *Brasserie du Pêcheur.* As noted at the outset, the Commission acknowledges that: [T]he existence of a Community law remedy of damages against individuals for breach of Articles 81 and 82 EC follows from the same principles [as those

---

[136] Case C-557/12, EU:C:2014:1317, para. 34.

[137] P. Nebbia, 'Damages Actions for the Infringement of EC Competition Law: Compensation or Deterrence?' (2008) 33 *ELRev* 23, 28.

[138] K. Roach and M. J. Trebilcock, 'Private Enforcement of Competition Laws' (1996) 34 *Osgoode Hall LJ* 461, 496.

[139] F. Hoseinian, 'Passing-on Damages and Community Antitrust Policy—An Economic Background' (2005) 28 *World Competition* 3, 7.

[140] Nebbia, n. 137, 23, 28.

that give rise] to such a remedy against Member States for breaches of other provisions of Community law. This principle is, as discussed above, predominantly based on 'effective judicial protection'.

Secondly, the wording of the *Crehan* decision is very similar to that of *Brasserie du Pêcheur*. After highlighting that 'Community law is intended to give rise to rights which become part of [individual] legal assets', the [CJ] reaffirms the principle that: [T]he full effectiveness of Article 85 [now 101] of the Treaty would be put at risk if it were not open to any individual to claim damages for loss caused to him by a contract or conduct liable to restrict or distort competition.

The subsequent paragraph is then devoted to the 'enforcement' argument, and acknowledges the contribution that such a right would give 'to the maintenance of effective competition in the Community'. This argument, however, seems to be used to reinforce, rather than to establish, the basis of liability.

This emerges more clearly in the *Manfredi* decision. In that case, the [CJ] affirmed more explicitly than in *Crehan* the existence of a Community-based right to compensation for the infringement of antitrust law but, in so doing, only echoed the part of the *Crehan* judgment that dealt with judicial protection . . .:

[I]t should be recalled that the full effectiveness of Article [101] and, in particular, the practical effect of the prohibition laid down in Article [101(1)] would be put at risk if it were not open to any individual to claim damages for loss caused to him by a contract or by conduct liable to restrict or distort competition (*Courage and Crehan*. . . para. 26).

The 'enforcement' argument can only be found much later, where the CJ deals with the question of whether punitive damages should be awarded.

If the reasoning here developed is correct, it is clear that the [EU] context is remarkably different from that of the United States: the primary aim of private enforcement should be compensation, and any measure proposed to enhance its operation should take this priority into account. In this respect, the conclusions drawn here have significant practical implications as different views on which objective should be prioritised may imply quite different (but not necessarily conflicting) policy agendas.

Wils also supports what he describes as a 'separate-tasks approach'.[141] Nazzini, in contrast, concludes that the principle of effectiveness means effectiveness of EU law—which supports the deterrence approach.

R. Nazzini, 'The Objective of Private Remedies in EU Competition Law' (2011) 4 *Global Competition Litigation Review* 131, 139–140

(iii) The case law on the right to damages for breach of art. 101 or 102 TFEU

When the court was required to address the core question of whether those who have been harmed by a breach of art.101(1) TFEU have a right to damages, the enforcement rationale becomes more evident.

In *Crehan*, the Court of Justice was called upon to decide whether the English law rule *ex turpi causa non oritur actio* was incompatible with EU law in so far as it prevented a party to an agreement prohibited by art.101(1) TFEU from recovering damages from the other party. The court said that the full effectiveness of art.101 of the Treaty and, in particular, the practical effect of the prohibition laid down in art.101(1) would be put at risk if it were not open to any individual to claim damages for loss caused to him by a contract or by conduct liable to restrict or distort competition. The court added that the existence of such a right strengthens the working of the EU competition rules and discourages anti-competitive

---

[141] Wils, n. 1, 12–13, relying on the 2008 White Paper on Damages, n. 10. In its 2005 Green Paper, n. 11, 2.7, however, the Commission stated that damages actions and public enforcement serve the same deterrence objective.

agreements or practices. Finally, the court said that actions for damages before the national courts can make a significant contribution to the maintenance of effective competition in the European Union. The enforcement rationale could not be more clearly articulated.

In the subsequent case of *Manfredi*, the court repeated almost verbatim paras. 26 and 27 of the *Crehan* case. The court was ruling on whether art.101 TFEU must be interpreted as requiring national courts to award punitive damages, greater than the advantage obtained by the defendant, thereby deterring agreements or concerted practices prohibited under that article. The question explicitly linked the award of punitive damages to deterrence. It was, therefore, important for the court to make it clear that the fact that EU law does not require the award of punitive damages does not mean that the right to damages for loss caused by a breach of art.101 or 102 TFEU is any less important in ensuring the effectiveness of EU competition law.

Although strictly not required to do so, the court went on to determine the content of the right in light of its function of ensuring the full effectiveness of EU competition law. The court considered that the effectiveness of EU competition law and the right to seek compensation required that the claimant be entitled to 'full compensation', including actual loss, loss of profit and interest, but leaving the award of punitive damages to national law subject to the principle of equivalence. In determining the damages recoverable, the court relied both on the principle of effectiveness and on the right to seek compensation. In doing so, the court applied a test similar to that set out in *Brasserie du Pêcheur SA and Factortame*, whereby the remedies available for the protection of the right are determined according to both the requirement of full effectiveness of EU law and the requirement of effective judicial protection.

Applying the three-stage framework proposed in this chapter, it would appear that, in the first stage, the EU right to damages for breach of art.101 or 102 TFEU is recognised based entirely upon the enforcement rationale. In the second stage, the principle of full effectiveness of EU law applies, in conjunction with the principle of effective judicial protection, to determine the content of the right. Finally, in the third stage, under the doctrine of procedural autonomy, the principles of full effectiveness of EU law and effective judicial protection apply to assess whether national rules on remedies and procedure are compatible with EU law. . . .

Some appear to argue that the objective of the EU law right to damages for breach of the competition provisions is compensation and not the effectiveness of the regime. However, it is necessary to distinguish between the content of the right, on the one hand, and its legal basis and function, on the other. The discussion so far has demonstrated that full compensation as the content of the right is consistent with the objective of ensuring the effective enforcement of EU competition law. Furthermore, the competition law cases of *Crehan* and *Manfredi* clearly articulate in unambiguous language an enforcement rationale for the conferral of the right to damages.

The enforcement rationale which underpins the right to damages for breach of art.101 or 102 TFEU is further demonstrated by the absence of the 'protective purpose' doctrine under EU law. The protective purpose doctrine is well established under German tort law, where the claimant is only entitled to compensation if he suffers harm as a consequence of the violation of a norm the purpose of which was to protect a person in the position of the claimant from the harm in question. The concept is not alien to English tort law where the claimant, to recover damages for breach of statutory duty, must establish that he is within the category of person the statute intended to protect from the harm in question. The Court of Justice in *Manfredi* appears to have rejected, albeit implicitly, the protective purpose doctrine. The court said that art.101 TFEU must be interpreted as meaning that any individual can rely on the invalidity of an agreement or practice prohibited under that article and, where there is a causal relationship between the latter and the harm suffered, claim compensation for that harm.

The absence of the protective purpose doctrine in EU competition law is consistent with an enforcement rationale. If the legal basis of the right to damages for breach of art.101 or 102 TFEU were to protect individual interests, it would follow that the claimant would have to prove that he belongs to the category of person that art.101 or 102 TFEU intends to protect and that the harm suffered is of the type that those provisions intend to prevent. . . .

Although most might agree that private actions can fulfil a dual-objective which may be inextricably linked, the question of which objective predominates becomes crucial, as seen below, where they pull in different directions.[142]

d. The Principle of National Procedural Autonomy; Bringing an EU Damages Claim Before the National Courts

The question of which national court, or courts, has jurisdiction to hear an antitrust claim is governed by the (now recast) Brussels Regulation, Regulation 1215/2012 on jurisdiction and the recognition and enforcement of judgment in civil and commercial matters. Very broadly, it allows tortious proceedings to be brought in the courts of the Member State where the defendant is domiciled or the harm occurred.[143]

Prior to the Damages Directive taking effect, the principle of national procedural autonomy has conferred considerable latitude on the national systems and the national courts in dealing with an antitrust damages claim. The protection given to EU rights has, consequently, been heavily dependent on the procedural, evidential, and substantive rules governing civil litigation applicable in each individual Member State and how EU law—in particular the principles of equivalence and effectiveness—is considered to constrain their operation.[144] Considerable opacity has surrounded a multiplicity of questions arising at the national level, including how national claims should be framed (and whether fault should or can be a constituent element of the cause of action), how causation can be established and damages calculated, whether national courts are required to award 'punitive' damages and whether other national rules governing the claim comply with EU law, and, especially, the principle of effectiveness; for example, rules relating to standing, remoteness, illegality, a passing on defence, or setting out limitation periods.

It has been seen that the CJ has been requested to give rulings on some of these issues, including on the availability of punitive damages and the compatibility of the English principle of illegality with the EU principle of effectiveness.[145] In *Manfredi v Lloyd Adriatico Assicurazioni SpA*[146] the CJ was also asked for guidance on the question of whether a national limitation period was compatible with EU law. The relevant limitation period in that case began to run from the day on which that prohibited agreement or practice was adopted. The CJ held that such a national rule could make it practically impossible to exercise the right to seek compensation for the harm caused by that prohibited agreement or practice, particularly if that national rule also imposed a short limitation period which is not capable of being suspended. It noted that in the case of continuous or repeated infringement, it was possible in these circumstances that the limitation period would expire even before the infringement was brought to an end. The principles of equivalence and effectiveness

---

[142] R. Nazzini and A. Nikpay, 'Private Actions in EC Competition Law' (2008) 4 *Competition Policy International* 107, 110.

[143] [2012] OJ L351/1 (its predecessor, Reg. 44/2001, [2001] OJ L12/1 applies only to proceedings instituted prior to 10 January 2015). A number of EU and national judgments deal with the question of its interpretation, see, e.g., Case C-352/13, *Cartel Damage Claims v Akzo Nobel NV* EU:C:2015:335, *Provimi v Aventis* [2003] EWHC 961 (Comm), and *Cooper Tire & Rubber v Shell Chemicals* [2009] EWHC 2609 (Comm), [2010] EWCA Civ 864. The Lugano Convention (signed by the EU, Iceland, Norway, Denmark, and Switzerland) contains rules based on the Brussels Reg.

[144] See obstacles identified by the Commission in its Green Paper, n. 11 and n. 176 and text As many national cases settle it is not easy to draw a picture of how national courts are resolving these issues, K Coates, 'Cartels and Follow On Damages Actions', Competition Law Lecture Series, Lincoln's Inn, 24 November 2014 ('That highlights one of the problems we have to deal with: although there are a number of points of law that will inevitably require clarification, there are a lot of judgment calls being made in the shadows').

[145] For example, in Case C-453/99, *Courage Ltd v Crehan* [2001] ECR I-6297, para. 31, the CJ held that although the illegality of the agreement cannot operate as a general bar to claims brought between parties to a contract concluded in breach of Art. 101(1), it can do so where the claimant co-contractor can be said to bear 'significant responsibility' for the breach, see n. 125 and text. See also Case C-295-298/04, *Manfredi* [2006] ECR I-6619.

[146] Case C-295–298/04, [2006] ECR I-6619.

thus require national rules which render nugatory the right to compensation, to be struck down, or disapplied.[147]

Where no specific judgment exists, however, the position remains subject to differing interpretations and, accordingly, uncertainty. For instance, the question of whether EU law demands that indirect purchasers should have standing to bring antitrust proceedings and/or whether defendants should be able to raise a passing on defence, would appear to depend on how the principle of effectiveness stressed in the CJ's *Crehan* and *Manfredi* judgments is to be construed: specifically, whether it suggests that the principal purpose of private enforcement is the attainment of corrective justice (this is the view adopted in the Damages Directive[148]) or whether it is simply a tool to increase enforcement and to bring to an end and deter violations.[149] Although the Court has stressed the importance of private actions to the strengthening of the working of the competition rules and to the maintenance of effective competition,[150] in *Manfredi* the CJ also clarified 'that any individual can claim compensation for the harm suffered where there is a causal relationship between that harm and an agreement or practice prohibited under Article [101]'.[151] In the extract below, Jones and Beard[152] explore when national rules on standing and on the acceptance of a passing on defence are likely to be compatible with EU law.

A. Jones and D. Beard, 'Co-contractors, Damages and Article 81: The ECJ Finally Speaks' [2002] *ECLR* 246, 253–255

Quantification of loss and other issues

The judgment in *Crehan* recognises that a Community right to damages should in principle be available to compensate breaches of Article [101] or Article [102] for two main reasons. First, to ensure that individuals are compensated in respect of loss caused by anti-competitive conduct ('the compensatory principle'). Secondly, to strengthen the working of the Community competition rules and to discourage anti-competitive practices—private actions contribute to the maintenance of effective competition in the Community ('the deterrence principle'). Both principles are closely linked to the need to ensure the effectiveness of the competition rules within the Community.

The recognition of a Community right to damages will mean that many national rules of procedure and substance may have to be tested for their compatibility with Community law. Two specific problems that are liable to arise in many damages actions are: who is entitled to claim? and how will loss be quantified? For example, take a cartel or monopolist that sells its goods at supra-competitive prices. A direct purchaser from the cartel or monopolist (say a wholesaler) will clearly suffer in consequence of paying a price that is in excess of the competitive price. However, the direct purchaser may be able to pass on some of the loss to the next purchaser in the chain, a retailer or a consumer. Ultimately, at least part of the inflated price may be passed on to the consumer. This leads to two related questions. First, if the direct purchaser brings a damages claim, should the national court take account . . . [of] the fact that some of that loss has been passed on to other purchasers along the line? Second, should indirect purchasers, further down the chain, also be entitled to bring damages actions to compensate them in respect of their loss?

In the US the courts have already had to grapple with these, and other, difficult questions....[153]

---

[147] Case C-536/11, *Bundeswettbewerbsbehörde v Donau Chemie* EU:C:2013:366, para. 32.

[148] See nn. 193 and 194 and text.

[149] See, e.g., Hoseinian, n. 139, 7, Nebbia, n. 137, 28, R. Nazzini, 'The Objective of Private Remedies in EU Competition Law' (2011) 4 *Global Competition Litigation Rev* 131, 139–140.

[150] Case C-295-298/04, *Manfredi* [2006] ECR I-6619, para. 91.

[151] Ibid., para. 61.

[152] Jones and Beard, n. 37.

[153] See discussion nn. 35 and 36 and text.

A national court will not of course be bound by US case law. Rather it will instead have to reach its own conclusions, ensuring that the rules it applies are compatible with the Community principles of equivalence and effectiveness.

Passing on

At first sight, it would appear that the Community rules should not prevent a national court from taking into account the fact that loss has been passed on to another purchaser further down the line. The compensatory principle would, on its face, appear to suggest that a claimant should recover only that which he has lost in consequence of an infringement. Further, the Court of Justice has consistently held that Community law does not prevent national courts from ensuring that the protection of rights guaranteed by Community law does not entail the *unjust enrichment* of those who enjoyed them and the Court specifically stated this in *Crehan*. Arguably, a claimant would be unjustly enriched if he could recover damages even though he had been able to pass some of the loss on to others.

However, the position is not quite so simple. First, even if it were accepted that theoretically the fact that losses have been passed on to customers should be taken into account, the quantification of loss then becomes fraught with difficulty. In many cases it will be difficult to determine whether or not the loss has actually been passed on. Even if this can be established, the cost of the increased price of the product can only be passed on through a price rise to customers. In most cases, this will mean a decline in sales. These types of difficulties have caused the English Court of Appeal to hold, in the context of a private claim for restitution (based on the principle of unjust enrichment), that a defence of passing on is not available.

Secondly, the possibility that such arguments might be raised by a defendant and the complications involved in the assessment might deter private actions by direct purchasers. It may, therefore, interfere with the important . . . Community objective of encouraging private proceedings to strengthen the working of the competition rules. In other words, if the operation of compensatory principle enunciated by the Court in *Crehan* were invoked to justify the recognition of a passing on defence in national law, it may be argued that the rule would undermine the operation of the deterrence principle and the principle of effectiveness upon which the Court also relied.

Thirdly, the acceptance of a passing on argument would frequently allow the *wrongdoer* to benefit and to retain some of the fruits of its wrong since in a great majority of cases indirect purchasers, to whom some of the higher prices have been passed on, will not sue. In a case like *Crehan*, for example, the publican-tenants may have passed some of their loss down the chain to their customers. It seems unlikely, however, that even the most hardened drinkers would contemplate their losses being sufficient to make proceedings against the brewers worthwhile. In the UK the Government's proposals to facilitate damages actions on behalf of consumers might encourage claims by indirect purchasers. Nonetheless, the Government accepts that it will be an uphill struggle to encourage actions to be brought in intractable cases such as these.

Indirect purchasers

It has already been mentioned that the rule in *Illinois Brick*, precluding claims by indirect purchasers, has been subjected to considerable criticism in the US. In some states the rule has even been reversed through legislation. The most obvious argument in support of the rule is that it precludes duplicate recovery from a defendant (full recovery from the direct purchaser and recovery in respect of the part passed on by the indirect purchaser). Coupled with the *Hanover Shoe* rule, the *Illinois Brick* rule means that wrongdoers will face damages actions from those most directly affected by their conduct and will ensure that wrongdoers are stripped of the fruits of their wrongdoing (thus deterring anti-competitive behaviour). However, it is clearly arguable that the application of such a rule by a national court would be inconsistent with [the] direct effect of Articles [101] and [102] and would undermine the operation of the principle that an individual who has suffered loss in consequence of a breach of the competition rules is entitled to compensation. In some cases, the application of the rule may allow the direct purchaser to retain at least part of the fruits of the seller's wrongdoing whilst those further down the chain, who have also suffered loss, are not compensated.

Such potential outcomes might militate against the application in national, and EC, law of the *Illinois Brick* rule. Indeed, the UK's government's proposal to foster representative claims on behalf of consumers seems to indicate that it would not be in favour of the adoption of such a rule. Arguably, the risk of double recovery is outweighed by the public interest in ensuring that anti-competitive behaviour is deterred and that those who suffer loss as a result are properly compensated. In the following extract, Clifford Jones recognises that the Court of Justice will have some difficult policy decisions to make in the future.

The theoretical possibility of double recovery is inherent if defensive passing-on is not allowed but offensive passing-on is allowed. However, if defensive passing on is allowed and fewer than all indirect purchasers sue, then the wrongdoer retains at least some of the fruits of his violation. Both major alternatives have aspects which are unsatisfactory. At bottom, the [CJ] will have to choose the approach which it considers best serves fair and effective Community law.

A further matter which has arisen, and which is even less clear-cut and more controversial, is the extent to which EU law can require Member States more positively or proactively to facilitate damages claims and to put in place measures, or reform institutions in a way, which would ensure an effective enforcement framework.[154] In particular, the existence, or not, of specialist competition law tribunals or courts, the speed of litigation and individual national rules governing access to information and evidence, litigation costs, funding and cost rules, follow-on actions, mechanisms for collective redress, and remedies for final consumers are all factors which may dramatically affect the culture of competition in each Member State and the feasibility of successfully launching private litigation there. Thus, even if, for example, it were clear that EU law demands that indirect purchasers should be able to seek compensation before a national court, such a right might be worthless in a State where the national tools are inadequate to allow that right to be effectively exercised—perhaps because procedural mechanisms do not allow for actions to be grouped together collectively or for relevant evidence to be uncovered, collected, or appropriately processed and assessed. In some jurisdictions individuals may simply be less litigious than in others.[155]

It seems clear that a combination of these types of features of the national litigation systems in the individual Member States have been deterring or constraining EU claimants. In particular:

- the cost and risk of litigation frequently operates as a deterrent, especially where claimants have not suffered much loss individually and where class or other consolidated actions and contingency fees are not available[156] or where national cost rules provide disincentives to litigation (for example, where claimants are obliged to pay the defendant's legal costs if unsuccessful);[157]

- it is extremely difficult for claimants to gather the requisite evidence under many national systems. The question of when national courts can order disclosure vary considerably between Member States;[158]

---

[154] See Dunne, n. 1.

[155] For a discussion of the position in the Member States on many of these issues see B. Rodgers (ed.), *Competition Law: Comparative Private Enforcement and Collective Redress Across the EU* (Wolters Kluwer, 2014), especially Chap. 2. For the view that individuals in Lithuania are less litigious because, historically, the clutches of the Soviet Union precluded the Lithuanian legal system from development, see J. Malinauskaite, 'Private Enforcement of Competition Law in Lithuania: A Story of Underdevelopment' (2013) 3 *Global Competition LR* 123, 133.

[156] Only 0.4% of the 1,268 antitrust judgments decided between 1999–2012 identified in Rodgers, n. 155, 162 were aggregated/class consumer cases. Class actions may not only facilitate relief for certain victims but may produce external benefits for society as a whole, W. B. Rubenstein, 'Why Enable Litigation? A Positive Externalities Theory of the Small Claims Class Action', Public Law and Legal Theory Research Paper Series, UCLA School of Law, No. 06-10, <http://www.ssrn.com/abstract=890303>.

[157] See, e.g., J. Peysner, 'Costs and Financing in Private Third Party Competition Damages Actions' (2006) 3 *Competition Law Review* 97.

[158] Disclosure is recognised in the UK but does not exist in many civil law systems. National courts may ask the Commission to transmit to them information in its possession or its opinion on questions concerning the application of the EU competition law rules, see Reg. 1/2003, Art. 15(1).

- proceedings may be being deterred in some States by uncertainty over the weight to be given to decisions of NCAs;

- many national courts have limited experience dealing with antitrust arguments and may not, consequently, be the most appropriate or understanding forum for the hearing.[159]

Finally, a matter of specific contention in the EU has been the relationship between public and private enforcement which has become strained. In particular, tensions have arisen between the need to ensure, on the one hand, the effectiveness of the right to compensation available to victims of anti-competitive practices and, on the other, the effectiveness of the leniency programme, which constitutes a key tool for the Commission in its fight against cartels and, consequently, to public enforcement.

Litigants in the EU have frequently sought access to leniency evidence in national proceedings under disclosure rules (as well as separately through seeking access to a competition agency's file or by filing a claim under EU transparency rules, see Chapter 13[160]). Although the Commission, supported by some NCAs and Advocate General Mazák, has taken the view that access should *not* be granted to self-incriminating statements voluntarily provided by leniency applicants as this could substantially reduce the attractiveness of the leniency programme and, in turn, the effective enforcement of Article 101,[161] in *Pfleiderer* the CJ favoured a more balanced approach to be taken by national courts to the question of when access to leniency documents should be granted under national disclosure rules.

Case C-360/09 *Pfleiderer AG v Bundeskartellamt* [2011] ECR I-5161

Court of Justice

19. It must be recalled at the outset that the competition authorities of the Member States and their courts and tribunals are required to apply Articles 101 TFEU and 102 TFEU, where the facts come within the scope of European Union law, and to ensure that those articles are applied effectively in the general interest (see, to that effect, Case C-439/08, *VEBIC* . . . para. 56).

20. Neither the provisions of the EC Treaty on competition nor Regulation No 1/2003 lay down common rules on leniency or common rules on the right of access to documents relating to a leniency procedure which have been voluntarily submitted to a national competition authority pursuant to a national leniency programme.

. . .

23. . . . [E]ven if the guidelines set out by the Commission may have some effect on the practice of the national competition authorities, it is, in the absence of binding regulation under European Union law on the subject, for Member States to establish and apply national rules on the right of access, by persons adversely affected by a cartel, to documents relating to leniency procedures.

24. However, while the establishment and application of those rules falls within the competence of the Member States, the latter must none the less exercise that competence in accordance with European

---

[159] See, e.g., Gavil. n. 2 and Malinauskaite, n. 155, 133.

[160] See Regulation 1049/2001 regarding public access to European Parliament, Council and Commission documents (Transparency Reg.) [2001] OJ L145/43, Case T-2/03, *Verein für Konsumenteninformation* [2005] ECR II-1121, Case T-437/08, *CDC Hydrogen Peroxide v Commission* [2011] ECR II-8251, and Ombudsman Decision 3699/2006/ELB, 2010.

[161] Case C-360/09, *Pfleiderer AG v Bundeskartellamt* [2011] ECR I-5161, Mazák AG, paras. 38-42. In his view an interference with the injured parties' right to an effective remedy and a fair trial was justified by the legitimate aim of ensuring the effective enforcement of Art. 101 by NCAs and ultimately private litigants' possibility of obtaining an effective remedy.

Union law (see, to that effect, the judgment of 12 November 2009 in Case C-154/08, *Commission v Spain*, para. 121 and the case-law cited). In particular, they may not render the implementation of European Union law impossible or excessively difficult (see, to that effect, Case C-298/96, *Oelmühle and Schmidt Söhne . . .*, paras. 23 and 24 and the case-law cited) and, specifically, in the area of competition law, they must ensure that the rules which they establish or apply do not jeopardise the effective application of Articles 101 TFEU and 102 TFEU (see, to that effect, *VEBIC*, para. 57).

25. However, as maintained by the Commission and the Member States which have submitted observations, leniency programmes are useful tools if efforts to uncover and bring to an end infringements of competition rules are to be effective and serve, therefore, the objective of effective application of Articles 101 TFEU and 102 TFEU.

26. The effectiveness of those programmes could, however, be compromised if documents relating to a leniency procedure were disclosed to persons wishing to bring an action for damages, even if the national competition authorities were to grant to the applicant for leniency exemption, in whole or in part, from the fine which they could have imposed.

27. The view can reasonably be taken that a person involved in an infringement of competition law, faced with the possibility of such disclosure, would be deterred from taking the opportunity offered by such leniency programmes, particularly when, pursuant to Articles 11 and 12 of Regulation No 1/2003, the Commission and the national competition authorities might exchange information which that person has voluntarily provided.

28. Nevertheless, it is settled case-law that any individual has the right to claim damages for loss caused to him by conduct which is liable to restrict or distort competition (see Case C-453/99, *Courage and Crehan* [2001] ECR I-6297, paras. 24 and 26, and Joined Cases C-295/04 to C-298/04, *Manfredi and Others* [2006] ECR I-6619, paras. 59 and 61).

29. The existence of such a right strengthens the working of the Community competition rules and discourages agreements or practices, frequently covert, which are liable to restrict or distort competition. From that point of view, actions for damages before national courts can make a significant contribution to the maintenance of effective competition in the European Union (*Courage and Crehan*, para. 27).

30. Accordingly, in the consideration of an application for access to documents relating to a leniency programme submitted by a person who is seeking to obtain damages from another person who has taken advantage of such a leniency programme, it is necessary to ensure that the applicable national rules are not less favourable than those governing similar domestic claims and that they do not operate in such a way as to make it practically impossible or excessively difficult to obtain such compensation (see, to that effect, *Courage and Crehan*, para. 29) and to weigh the respective interests in favour of disclosure of the information and in favour of the protection of that information provided voluntarily by the applicant for leniency.

31. That weighing exercise can be conducted by the national courts and tribunals only on a case-by-case basis, according to national law, and taking into account all the relevant factors in the case.

32. In the light of the foregoing, the answer to the question referred is that the provisions of European Union law on cartels, and in particular Regulation No 1/2003, must be interpreted as not precluding a person who has been adversely affected by an infringement of European Union competition law and is seeking to obtain damages from being granted access to documents relating to a leniency procedure involving the perpetrator of that infringement. It is, however, for the courts and tribunals of the Member States, on the basis of their national law, to determine the conditions under which such access must be permitted or refused by weighing the interests protected by European Union law.

The CJ thus held that a national court had, in deciding whether to grant access to leniency documents, to weigh, according to national law and taking into account all the relevant factors in the case,[162] the respective interests of the leniency applicant (to have voluntarily submitted corporate

---

[162] Case C–360/09, *Pfleiderer* [2011] ECR I–5161, para. 31.

statements protected) and the claimant (to have access to documents which would facilitate the claim).[163] Further, in *Bundeswettbewerbsbehörde v Donau Chemie*,[164] the CJ held that an Austrian law which prohibited disclosure to third parties of court files on public law competition proceedings, unless all parties to the proceedings agreed, was not compatible with the principle of effectiveness and so conflicted with EU law. '[I]n competition law . . . any rule that is rigid, either by providing for absolute refusal to grant access . . . or for granting access as a matter of course . . . is liable to undermine the effective application of . . . Article 101'.[165] The CJ thus reiterated that the national court should have the opportunity to consider the issues on a case-by-case basis weighing the competing interests. Although both of these cases stressed that the national court should have the opportunity to consider the issues on a case-by-case basis weighing the competing interests, in *EnBW*[166] the Court did, in the context of proceedings relating to the Transparency Regulation, recognise that access should be required only in cases of absolutely necessity where relevant evidence was not available from alternative mechanisms. In addition, from the end of 2017 the Damages Directive makes it clear that national courts will not be able to give access to leniency statements (or settlement submissions) under national disclosure rules.[167]

e. A Need for Clarification and Harmonization: The EU Package and Damages Directive

The previous discussion establishes that damages must in principle be available to compensate breaches of Articles 101 and 102 but that the principle of national procedural autonomy means that relevant national rules retain significant impact on the likelihood of a claim's success or failure. In 2005 the Commission expressed its view that as a result of this the system of damages for infringements of competition law of the Member States presented 'a picture of "total underdevelopment"'.[168] Further, even though private enforcement has steadily been increasing, from approximately 54 decided judgments within the EU in 1999 to 146 in 2011,[169] the Commission still concluded in 2013 that '[d]espite some recent signs of improvement in a few Member States, to date most victims of infringements of the EU competition rules in practice do not obtain compensation for the harm suffered';[170] victims only commenced private actions in 25 per cent of cases where antitrust infringement decisions had been adopted by the Commission.

Although not all might agree that this picture indicates that steps should be taken to stimulate private enforcement,[171] or that EU measures are required, desirable, and/or practicable,[172] it has been seen that the Commission has been considering for some time whether measures can, and should, be adopted to amend and/or harmonise national procedural and substantive rules governing damages claims, for example on costs, access to evidence, limitation periods, standing, class or representative actions, fault, and/or defences, such as the passing on defence.

In its 2005 Green Paper on Damages actions for breach of the EC antitrust rules[173] the Commission stated its view that '[s]ignificant obstacles exist in the different Member States to the effective

---

[163] Ibid., para. 30.

[164] Case C-536/11, EU:C:2013:366.

[165] Case C-536/11, *Bundeswettbewerbsbehörde v Donau Chemie* EU:C:2013:366, para. 31.

[166] Case C-365/12 P, *Commission v EnBW Energie Baden-Württemberg AG* EU:C:2014:112.

[167] See n. 199.

[168] Green Paper, n. 11, 1.2. This view was based on the Ashurst Report, n. 11.

[169] See Rodgers, n. 155, 87. Only 31% of all the cases analysed were damages claims.

[170] Commission Proposal, n. 10, Explanatory Memorandum, 1.2 and ibid.

[171] See, e.g., W. Wils, 'Should Private Antitrust Enforcement be Encouraged?' (2003) 26 *World Competition* 473 (but see now Wils, n. 1, 3), F. Jacobs, 'Civil Enforcement of EEC Antitrust Law' (1984) 82 *Mich LR* 1364 and Dunne, n. 127.

[172] Although final judgments are relatively low, these do not take account of the numerous cases that are settled, see, e.g., speech by Coates, n. 144 ('Many of these cases settle. I was talking to an economist a few months ago who had advised on—he thought approximately—50 damages calculations. Not one of the cases went to final judgment').

[173] COM/2005/0672/final.

operation of damages actions for infringement of Community antitrust law'.[174] The Green Paper, and an accompanying Commission Staff Working Paper,[175] thus sought: (a) 'to identify the main obstacles to a more efficient system of damages claims and to set out different options for further reflection and possible action to improve both follow-on actions (for example, cases in which the civil action is brought after a competition authority has found an infringement) and stand-alone actions (that is to say, actions which do not follow on from a prior finding by a competition authority of an infringement of competition law);'[176] and (b) to invite a discussion on obstacles identified and options formulated for overcoming them and allowing a competition culture to develop. Following the receipt of comments on its Green Paper, the Commission published further proposals in its White Paper on Damages actions (which has to be read together with a Commission Staff Working Document and an Impact Assessment Report)[177] which recommended a broad range of measures aimed to ensure that all victims of anti-competitive behaviour are able to obtain full compensation (but not punitive or multiple damages) for harm suffered but that unmeritorious claims are not encouraged.[178] It recognised, however, that '[i]mproving compensatory justice would . . . inherently also produce beneficial effects in terms of deterrence of future infringements and greater compliance with [EU] antitrust rules. Safeguarding undistorted competition is an integral part of the internal market and important for implementing the Lisbon strategy. A competition culture contributes to better allocation of resources, greater economic efficiency, increased innovation and lower prices.'[179] It thus concluded that EU instruments *were* requisite to overcome barriers to litigation and to stimulate and harmonise damages actions,[180] and to balance it with public enforcement. In its view the new measures adopted 'will democratise enforcement and empower the victims of antitrust infringements to receive effective compensation . . .'.[181]

In considering what EU measures should be enacted the Commission had a tortuous path to navigate, both politically and legally.[182] Not only did it have to convince the Parliament[183] and the Council that EU legislation was required which encroaches on national litigation systems and entrenched principles developed within them,[184] but it had to reflect on an array of factors when considering what those measure should look like and what they should cover. In addition to considering how to overcome national obstacles to litigation, it has thus had to consider: what legislative proposals would realistically be accepted, how it should balance the potential deterrent, compensatory, and other functions of private actions; how it should balance private and public enforcement; whether it should adopt a more holistic, all-encompassing, or a more gradual, sequential approach; and how to encompass lessons emerging from the US experience and to safeguard against an unleashing

---

[174] Ibid., 1.2.

[175] Commission Staff Working Paper, Annex to the Green Paper, n. 11.

[176] Green Paper, n. 11, 1.3.

[177] COM(2008) 165 final, SEC(2008)404, and SEC(2008)405, available at <http://ec.europa.eu/comm/competition/antitrust/actionsdamages/documents.html>.

[178] SEC(2008)404, paras. 2, 12, and 16.

[179] COM(2008) 165 final.

[180] See section 1. The Commission has not proposed specific measures to stimulate other sorts of private enforcement actions.

[181] Speech J. Almunia, 'Looking back at five years of competition enforcement in the EU', Global Antitrust Enforcement Symposium, Washington DC, 10 September 2014.

[182] See, e.g., Dunne, n. 127.

[183] A first Directive proposed by the Commission in 2009 was based on Art. 103 TFEU and would have excluded the Parliament from the legislative procedure. In the end the Directive was adopted under Arts. 103 and 114, so requiring use of the co-decision procedure.

[184] In some Member States, e.g. Germany, there has been resistance to the introduction of disclosure rules on the basis that litigation proceeds on the basis that it is for the claimant to prove its case, see A. Howard, 'Too Little, Too Late? The European Commission's Legislative Proposals on Anti-trust Damages Actions' (2013) 4 *JECLAP* 455, 460. The author is suspicious that the extent of compromises in the Directive and the rather timid selection of the procedural issues is linked to political concerns regarding the sanctity of national procedural autonomy, ibid. 464.

of some of the excesses connected with the litigation culture developed there.[185] It has therefore had to exercise caution to ensure that, in seeking to bolster and encourage private enforcement in the EU, rules are not made so claimant friendly that antitrust litigation gets out of control and encourages undeserving claims to be commenced (creating the risk of false positives).[186] Were that to occur, courts might become inclined to adopt narrow constructions of substantive and procedural rules making it harder for public enforcement agencies,[187] as well as private litigants, to establish violations.

An examination of the package of EU measures illustrates how the Commission and the legislature have sought to resolve the issues and how it will alter private enforcement in the Member States (see also Table 14.1 below). A first (obvious) point is that the Commission has taken the view that legislation governing damages action was required to clarify and harmonise certain issues (only, minimum harmonization). Although, therefore, some matters have been dealt with primarily through soft recommendations and guidance, others (many relating to procedural change) have been dealt with through harmonising legislation, the Damages Directive. Article 1 explains that the Directive 'sets out certain rules necessary to ensure that anyone who has suffered harm caused by an infringement of Article 101 or 102 of the Treaty or of national competition law, can effectively exercise the right to full compensation for that harm' and designed to foster undistorted competition, to ensure equivalent protection for those who have suffered antitrust harm throughout the EU, and to coordinate public and private enforcement. Some important definitions are set out in Article 4.

Secondly, in line with the approach set out in its White Paper, the Directive has generally embraced the compensatory approach,[188] reflecting the Commission's articulated view that public and private enforcement should pursue different, albeit complementary, objectives and that *all* victims of antitrust violations, including small and medium-sized enterprises (SMEs) and consumers, should be able to obtain damages. Consequently, Article 3 mandates national courts to ensure that *any* natural or legal person who has suffered harm caused by a competition law infringement is able to claim and to obtain full compensation—for actual loss and for loss of profit, plus the payment of interest.[189] The Directive establishes a rebuttable evidential presumption of harm (but no specific amount of harm) in cartel (but not other) cases[190] and empowers national courts to estimate the amount of harm in cases where precise quantification is impossible or excessively difficult.[191] The Commission's practical guide on the quantification of harm for damages is designed to assist national courts in this sphere.[192] It also specifies that such actions shall *not* lead to overcompensation, for example by means of punitive or multiple damages.

---

[185] See, e.g., the responses to the Commission's Green Paper, n. 11.

[186] A choice may have to be made as to whether false positives or negatives are worse.

[187] See, e.g., W. E. Kovacic, *Private Participation in the Enforcement of Public Competition Laws* (15 May 2003), available at <http://www.ftc.gov/speeches/other/030514biicl.shtm>.

[188] But see also nn. 198 and 199 and text.

[189] Dir. 2014/104/EU, Art. 3(2). The basis is tortious—to ensure that the compensation puts the person who suffered harm in the position that it would have been had the infringement of competition law not been committed, ibid.

[190] Ibid., Art. 17(2), pushing the burden onto the defendant to rebut the presumption by providing evidence to establish there was in fact no overcharge. See also Art. 17(3) (NCAs shall on request assist national court with respect to the determination of quantum of damages). Some NCAs are now going out of their way to provide evidence of effects and quantum of harm in their cartel decisions and, consequently, to facilitate private enforcement, see B. Veronese, 'European Public and Private Antitrust Enforcement: It Takes Two to Tango' (2014) 5 *JECLAP* 563.

[191] Ibid., Art. 17(1). The Directive also incorporates provisions on consensual dispute resolution. Economics is consequently bound to play an ever increasing role in private enforcement cases, Veronese, n. 190, and E. Clark and R. Sanders, 'Navigating the Quantum Minefield in Cartel Damages Cases' (2015) 6 *JECLAP* 153.

[192] SWD(2013) 205, n. 12. See also, e.g., an external study prepared for the Commission, Oxera, 'Quantifying antitrust damages. Towards non-binding guidance for courts. Study prepared for the European Commission' (Publications Office of the European Union, 2010); and Commission, 'Draft Guidance Paper—Quantifying Harm in Actions for Damages based on Breaches of Article 101 or 102 of the Treaty on the Functioning of the European Union (June 2011), available at <http://ec.europa.eu/competition/consultations/2011_actions_damages/draft_guidance_paper_en.pdf>.

Article 3

Right to full compensation

1. Member States shall ensure that any natural or legal person who has suffered harm caused by an infringement of competition law is able to claim and to obtain full compensation for that harm.

2. Full compensation shall place a person who has suffered harm in the position in which that person would have been had the infringement of competition law not been committed. It shall therefore cover the right to compensation for actual loss and for loss of profit, plus the payment of interest.

3. Full compensation under this Directive shall not lead to overcompensation, whether by means of punitive, multiple or other types of damages.

Articles 12 and 14 clarify that indirect, as well as direct, purchasers can sue (and indeed in some cases overcharges are presumed to be passed on to them by direct purchasers)[193] and Article 13 states, in line with the principle that overcompensation must not ensue, national courts must ensure the passing on defence is available to defendants.[194] These provisions, which will demand rigorous economic analysis to determine the appropriate level of damages, widen the pool of claimants beyond those permitted under federal antitrust rules in the US.

CHAPTER IV THE PASSING-ON OF OVERCHARGES

Article 12

Passing-on of overcharges and the right to full compensation

1. To ensure the full effectiveness of the right to full compensation as laid down in Article 3, Member States shall ensure that, in accordance with the rules laid down in this Chapter, compensation of harm can be claimed by anyone who suffered it, irrespective of whether they are direct or indirect purchasers from an infringer, and that compensation of harm exceeding that caused by the infringement of competition law to the claimant, as well as the absence of liability of the infringer, are avoided.

2. In order to avoid overcompensation, Member States shall lay down procedural rules appropriate to ensure that compensation for actual loss at any level of the supply chain does not exceed the overcharge harm suffered at that level.

3. This Chapter shall be without prejudice to the right of an injured party to claim and obtain compensation for loss of profits due to a full or partial passing-on of the overcharge.

4. Member States shall ensure that the rules laid down in this Chapter apply accordingly where the infringement of competition law relates to a supply to the infringer.

5. Member States shall ensure that the national courts have the power to estimate, in accordance with national procedures, the share of any overcharge that was passed on.

Article 13

Passing-on defence

Member States shall ensure that the defendant in an action for damages can invoke as a defence against a claim for damages the fact that the claimant passed on the whole or part of the overcharge resulting from the infringement of competition law. The burden of proving that the overcharge was passed on shall be on the defendant, who may reasonably require disclosure from the claimant or from third parties.

---

[193] Dir. 2014/104/EU., Arts. 12 and 14.
[194] Ibid., Art. 13.

Article 14

Indirect purchasers

1. Member States shall ensure that, where in an action for damages the existence of a claim for damages or the amount of compensation to be awarded depends on whether, or to what degree, an overcharge was passed on to the claimant, taking into account the commercial practice that price increases are passed on down the supply chain, the burden of proving the existence and scope of such a passing-on shall rest with the claimant, who may reasonably require disclosure from the defendant or from third parties.

2. In the situation referred to in paragraph 1, the indirect purchaser shall be deemed to have proven that a passing-on to that indirect purchaser occurred where that indirect purchaser has shown that:

   (a) the defendant has committed an infringement of competition law;

   (b) the infringement of competition law has resulted in an overcharge for the direct purchaser of the defendant; and

   (c) the indirect purchaser has purchased the goods or services that were the object of the infringement of competition law, or has purchased goods or services derived from or containing them.

This paragraph shall not apply where the defendant can demonstrate credibly to the satisfaction of the court that the overcharge was not, or was not entirely, passed on to the indirect purchaser.

Recognising the complexity that is likely to follow for national courts in applying a passing on defence, the Directive provides that '[t]he Commission shall issue guidelines for national courts on how to estimate the share of the overcharge which was passed on to the indirect purchaser'.[195]

Thirdly, the Directive has sought to tackle some (but not all) of the practical difficulties which have been confronting victims of EU antitrust infringements, to encourage damages actions and to establish certain minimum standards for litigation throughout the EU. In Article 5 it addresses the problem of information asymmetry and that disclosure is not widely available in some Member States by providing that, subject to certain conditions, national courts must be able to order a defendant (or claimant) to disclose relevant evidence under its control where a request is accompanied by a reasoned justification sufficient to support its plausibility.[196] National courts must however limit disclosure of evidence to that which is proportionate[197] and must protect confidential information and give full effect to legal professional privilege.

Article 5

Disclosure of evidence

1. Member States shall ensure that in proceedings relating to an action for damages in the Union upon request of a claimant who has presented a reasoned justification containing reasonably available facts and evidence sufficient to support the plausibility of its claim for damages, national courts are able to order the defendant or a third party to disclose relevant evidence which lies in their control, subject to the conditions set out in this Chapter. Member States shall ensure that national courts are able, upon request of the defendant, to order the claimant or a third party to disclose relevant evidence. This paragraph is without prejudice to the rights and obligations of national courts under Regulation (EC) No 1206/2001.

---

[195] Ibid., Art. 16.

[196] It also provides for disclosure from third parties and competition agencies.

[197] See, e.g., the approach of Roth J in the English High Court in *National Grid Electricity Transmission Plc v ABB Ltd* [2012] EWHC 869 (Ch).

2. Member States shall ensure that national courts are able to order the disclosure of specified items of evidence or relevant categories of evidence circumscribed as precisely and as narrowly as possible on the basis of reasonably available facts in the reasoned justification.

3. Member States shall ensure that national courts limit the disclosure of evidence to that which is proportionate. In determining whether any disclosure requested by a party is proportionate, national courts shall consider the legitimate interests of all parties and third parties concerned. They shall, in particular, consider:

   (a) the extent to which the claim or defence is supported by available facts and evidence justifying the request to disclose evidence;

   (b) the scope and cost of disclosure, especially for any third parties concerned, including preventing non-specific searches for information which is unlikely to be of relevance for the parties in the procedure;

   (c) whether the evidence the disclosure of which is sought contains confidential information, especially concerning any third parties, and what arrangements are in place for protecting such confidential information.

4. Member States shall ensure that national courts have the power to order the disclosure of evidence containing confidential information where they consider it relevant to the action for damages. Member States shall ensure that, when ordering the disclosure of such information, national courts have at their disposal effective measures to protect such information.

5. The interest of undertakings to avoid actions for damages following an infringement of competition law shall not constitute an interest that warrants protection.

6. Member States shall ensure that national courts give full effect to applicable legal professional privilege under Union or national law when ordering the disclosure of evidence.

7. Member States shall ensure that those from whom disclosure is sought are provided with an opportunity to be heard before a national court orders disclosure under this Article.

8. Without prejudice to paragraphs 4 and 7 and to Article 6, this Article shall not prevent Member States from maintaining or introducing rules which would lead to wider disclosure of evidence.

In order to ensure that such actions do not disrupt public enforcement, however, the Directive overrides the case law of the CJ[198] and limits national rules governing disclosure by providing an absolute bar on the disclosure of leniency statements and settlement submissions.[199]

Article 6

Disclosure of evidence included in the file of a competition authority

1. Member States shall ensure that, for the purpose of actions for damages, where national courts order the disclosure of evidence included in the file of a competition authority, this Article applies in addition to Article 5.

2. This Article is without prejudice to the rules and practices on public access to documents under Regulation (EC) No 1049/2001.

3. This Article is without prejudice to the rules and practices under Union or national law on the protection of internal documents of competition authorities and of correspondence between competition authorities.

---

[198] In both Case C–360/09, *Pfleiderer* [2011] ECR I–5161, paras. 23–24 and Case C-536/11, *Donau Chemie* EU:C:2013:366, paras. 25–27 the CJ recognised that national courts could only apply, subject to EU law and particularly the principle of effectiveness, their national rules on the right of access to documents, if no binding regulation under EU law on the subject applied. For the position under the Transparency Reg. see Chap. 13.

[199] Dir. 2014/104/EU, Art. 6(6).

4. When assessing, in accordance with Article 5(3), the proportionality of an order to disclose information, national courts shall, in addition, consider the following:

(a) whether the request has been formulated specifically with regard to the nature, subject-matter or contents of documents submitted to a competition authority or held in the file thereof, rather than by a non-specific application concerning documents submitted to a competition authority;

(b) whether the party requesting disclosure is doing so in relation to an action for damages before a national court; and

(c) in relation to paragraphs 5 and 10, or upon request of a competition authority pursuant to paragraph 11, the need to safeguard the effectiveness of the public enforcement of competition law.

5. National courts may order the disclosure of the following categories of evidence only after a competition authority, by adopting a decision or otherwise, has closed its proceedings:

(a) information that was prepared by a natural or legal person specifically for the proceedings of a competition authority;

(b) information that the competition authority has drawn up and sent to the parties in the course of its proceedings; and

(c) settlement submissions that have been withdrawn.

6. Member States shall ensure that, for the purpose of actions for damages, national courts cannot at any time order a party or a third party to disclose any of the following categories of evidence:

(a) leniency statements; and

(b) settlement submissions.

7. A claimant may present a reasoned request that a national court access the evidence referred to in points (a) or (b) of paragraph 6 for the sole purpose of ensuring that their contents correspond to the definitions in points (16) and (18) of Article 2. In that assessment, national courts may request assistance only from the competent competition authority. The authors of the evidence in question may also have the possibility to be heard. In no case shall the national court permit other parties or third parties access to that evidence.

8. If only parts of the evidence requested are covered by paragraph 6, the remaining parts thereof shall, depending on the category under which they fall, be released in accordance with the relevant paragraphs of this Article.

9. The disclosure of evidence in the file of a competition authority that does not fall into any of the categories listed in this Article may be ordered in actions for damages at any time, without prejudice to this Article.

10. Member States shall ensure that national courts request the disclosure from a competition authority of evidence included in its file only where no party or third party is reasonably able to provide that evidence.

11. To the extent that a competition authority is willing to state its views on the proportionality of disclosure requests, it may, acting on its own initiative, submit observations to the national court before which a disclosure order is sought.

Article 7

Limits on the use of evidence obtained solely through access to the file of a competition authority

1. Member States shall ensure that evidence in the categories listed in Article 6(6) which is obtained by a natural or legal person solely through access to the file of a competition authority is either deemed to be inadmissible in actions for damages or is otherwise protected under the applicable national rules to ensure the full effect of the limits on the disclosure of evidence set out in Article 6.

2. Member States shall ensure that, until a competition authority has closed its proceedings by adopting a decision or otherwise, evidence in the categories listed in Article 6(5) which is obtained by a natural

or legal person solely through access to the file of that competition authority is either deemed to be inadmissible in actions for damages or is otherwise protected under the applicable national rules to ensure the full effect of the limits on the disclosure of evidence set out in Article 6.

3. Member States shall ensure that evidence which is obtained by a natural or legal person solely through access to the file of a competition authority and which does not fall under paragraph 1 or 2, can be used in an action for damages only by that person or by a natural or legal person that succeeded to that person's rights, including a person that acquired that person's claim.

The Directive also clarifies that:

- a finding of an infringement by an NCA or a review court should be irrefutably established for the purposes of damages claims based on it before a national court in that State (so in these follow-on actions a claimant will have to establish only causation, loss, and the quantum of damages,[200] not the existence of the breach);[201]

- national limitation periods must not be less than five years and cannot commence to run before the infringement has ceased and the claimant knows, or can reasonably be expected to know, of it (it must also be suspended or interrupted until public enforcement proceedings are terminated);[202] and

- undertakings responsible for an infringement through joint behaviour should (except for certain SMEs and immunity recipients) be jointly and severally liable for the infringement.[203]

CHAPTER III EFFECT OF NATIONAL DECISIONS, LIMITATION PERIODS, JOINT AND SEVERAL LIABILITY

Article 9

Effect of national decisions

1. Member States shall ensure that an infringement of competition law found by a final decision of a national competition authority or by a review court is deemed to be irrefutably established for the purposes of an action for damages brought before their national courts under Article 101 or 102 TFEU or under national competition law.

2. Member States shall ensure that where a final decision referred to in paragraph 1 is taken in another Member State, that final decision may, in accordance with national law, be presented before their national courts as at least prima facie evidence that an infringement of competition law has occurred and, as appropriate, may be assessed along with any other evidence adduced by the parties.

3. This Article is without prejudice to the rights and obligations of national courts under Article 267 TFEU.

---

[200] Although, of course, these may be formidable obstacles to overcome.

[201] Dir. 2014/104/EU, Art. 9 (although currently in some Member States decisions of their NCAs bind their national courts, in a majority of States NCA decisions do not have any binding effect). The Commission's original proposal that decisions of NCAs were to constitute full proof before civil courts that an infringement occurred provoked considerable debate and was not adopted in the final Directive, see n. 81 (although such decisions may be presented before the national courts of another Member State as at least prima facie evidence of a competition law infringement).

[202] Ibid., Art. 10 (this means in practice that proceedings may commence many years after an infringement has ended).

[203] Ibid., Art. 11.

Article 10

Limitation periods

1. Member States shall, in accordance with this Article, lay down rules applicable to limitation periods for bringing actions for damages. Those rules shall determine when the limitation period begins to run, the duration thereof and the circumstances under which it is interrupted or suspended.

2. Limitation periods shall not begin to run before the infringement of competition law has ceased and the claimant knows, or can reasonably be expected to know: (a) of the behaviour and the fact that it constitutes an infringement of competition law; (b) of the fact that the infringement of competition law caused harm to him; and (c) the identity of the infringer.

3. Member States shall ensure that the limitation periods for bringing actions for damages are at least five years. 4. Member States shall ensure that a limitation period is suspended or, depending on national law, interrupted, if a competition authority takes action for the purpose of the investigation or its proceedings in respect of an infringement of competition law to which the action for damages relates. The suspension shall end at the earliest one year after the infringement decision has become final or after the proceedings are otherwise terminated.

Article 11

Joint and several liability

1. Member States shall ensure that undertakings which have infringed competition law through joint behaviour are jointly and severally liable for the harm caused by the infringement of competition law; with the effect that each of those undertakings is bound to compensate for the harm in full, and the injured party has the right to require full compensation from any of them until he has been fully compensated.

2. By way of derogation from paragraph 1, Member States shall ensure that, without prejudice to the right of full compensation as laid down in Article 3, where the infringer is a small or medium-sized enterprise (SME) as defined in Commission Recommendation 2003/361/EC, the infringer is liable only to its own direct and indirect purchasers where: (a) its market share in the relevant market was below 5 % at any time during the infringement of competition law; and (b) the application of the normal rules of joint and several liability would irretrievably jeopardise its economic viability and cause its assets to lose all their value.

3. The derogation laid down in paragraph 2 shall not apply where: (a) the SME has led the infringement of competition law or has coerced other undertakings to participate therein; or (b) the SME has previously been found to have infringed competition law.

4. By way of derogation from paragraph 1, Member States shall ensure that an immunity recipient is jointly and severally liable as follows: (a) to its direct or indirect purchasers or providers; and (b) to other injured parties only where full compensation cannot be obtained from the other undertakings that were involved in the same infringement of competition law. Member States shall ensure that any limitation period applicable to cases under this paragraph is reasonable and sufficient to allow injured parties to bring such actions.

5. Member States shall ensure that an infringer may recover a contribution from any other infringer, the amount of which shall be determined in the light of their relative responsibility for the harm caused by the infringement of competition law. The amount of contribution of an infringer which has been granted immunity from fines under a leniency programme shall not exceed the amount of the harm it caused to its own direct or indirect purchasers or providers.

6. Member States shall ensure that, to the extent the infringement of competition law caused harm to injured parties other than the direct or indirect purchasers or providers of the infringers, the amount of any contribution from an immunity recipient to other infringers shall be determined in the light of its relative responsibility for that harm.

Finally, the Directive incorporates provisions relating to, and designed to incentivise, consensual dispute resolution.[204] The Directive does not, however, deal with a number of factors which might impact on the success of a national claim, for example causation, remoteness, the availability of class actions (this issue is dealt with only by a Recommendation), cost rules or rules governing admissibility of expert evidence, motions to dismiss, or summary judgment.

Table 14.1 The impact of the Damages Directive on private antitrust actions in the EU Member States

	The position prior to the implementation of the Damages Directive	The position once the Damages Directive is implemented
Statutory provision governing private rights of action?	No statutory provision but principles developed by the CJ. Essentially EU right to compensation/injunction governed by national law *subject to it being compatible with EU principles of equivalence and effectiveness (in particular rules must not render exercise of rights practically impossible or excessively difficult)*	Directive: requires Member States to set out rules necessary to ensure that anyone who has suffered harm caused by a competition law infringement can obtain full compensation (Art. 1) Directive does not deal with right to an injunction
Compensatory principle? Punitive or multiple damages?	Governed by national law *subject to EU principles of equivalence and effectiveness* (punitive damages must be available if available in equivalent situations under national law, *Manfredi*)	Compensation for action loss and loss of profit, plus interest. Full compensation shall not lead to over compensation whether by means of, e.g., punitive or multiple damages (Art. 3)
Standing and remoteness	Governed by national law *subject to EU principles of equivalence and effectiveness*	Compensation for any person that has suffered harm but no provision as to how rules of remoteness to be applied
Passing on and indirect purchasers	Governed by national law *subject to EU principles of equivalence and effectiveness*	Indirect purchaser actions expressly permitted and passing on defence mandated (Arts. 12 and 14)
Application of illegality defence, *in pari delicto* doctrine	Governed by national law but principle of effectiveness requires damages unless claimant bears significant responsibility for the breach (*Crehan*)	
Follow-on cases: weight of public law finding	Commission decisions binding but impact of NCA decisions governed by national law (Reg. 1/2003, Art. 16)	Commission decisions binding and decisions of NCA or review court binding on national courts in that Member State (Art. 9)
Causation, harm, and quantification	Governed by national law *subject to EU principles of equivalence and effectiveness*	Evidential presumption of harm in cartel cases—national courts to estimate harm (Art. 17)
Limitation periods	Governed by national law *subject to EU principles of equivalence and effectiveness*—litigation in some Member States (see, e.g., *Manfredi* and UK), especially as to when limitation periods start to run	Limitation periods must not be less than 5 years—stipulation of when periods can start to run (Art. 10)
Availability of class actions	Governed by national law *subject to EU principles of equivalence and effectiveness*—but Recommendation for Member States to adopt opt-in class actions	
Legal costs	Governed by national law—some Member States apply loser pays principle	

(Continued)

---

[204] Ibid., Arts. 18 and 19. Art. 18(3) provides that a competition authority may consider compensation paid as a consensual settlement prior to its decision imposing a fine to be a mitigating factor.

Table 14.1 Continued

	The position prior to the implementation of the Damages Directive	The position once the Damages Directive is implemented
Disclosure of evidence	Governed by national law—disclosure not widely available in civil systems although recognised by common law systems (e.g. UK/Ireland)	Subject to some exceptions, provision for disclosure of evidence supported by plausible claim (Art. 5)
Impact on leniency	National court must balance competing interests of claimant and defendant when deciding when to order disclosure of leniency documents—no absolute rule against or in favour of disclosure permitted	Absolute bar on disclosure of leniency documents and settlement decisions (Art. 6) Modification of rules governing joint and several liability for leniency applicants
Joint and several liability	Governed by national law *subject to EU principles of equivalence and effectiveness*	Joint and several liability for co-infringers with exceptions for certain SMEs and leniency applicants
Admissibility of expert evidence	Governed by national law *subject to EU principles of equivalence and effectiveness*	
Motions to dismiss and summary judgment	Governed by national law *subject to EU principles of equivalence and effectiveness*	

5. CONCLUSIONS

1. The Commission's modernisation programme was designed to allow the Commission to refocus its scarce resources and to encourage greater enforcement of the rules at the national level. The Commission has not only sought to enlist the aid of NCAs in the enforcement of the rules, but also is eager that private actions should be used more frequently to bolster public enforcement. Both the Commission and a number of Member States are now actively taking steps to encourage private enforcement, particularly damages actions.

2. The abolition of the Commission's exclusive right to rule individually on the compatibility of an agreement with Article 101(3) removed a fundamental barrier to the courts' participation in the enforcement process. Further, the CJ's ruling in *Courage Ltd v Crehan* has given national courts clearer guidance on their obligations when hearing damages claims. Nonetheless, litigants in competition cases have continued to face a number of major hurdles to their claims. The new Damages Directive and package is designed to overcome those impediments and to stimulate private litigation, which is beginning to emerge in some Member States, across the EU.

3. An examination of the Damages Directive indicates that over-enforcement cannot be anticipated as a consequence of the current reforms. Although in some respects EU law goes further than US federal antitrust law (expanding to umbrella and indirect purchaser claims), the US 'toxic cocktail', consisting of, in particular, class actions, contingency fee arrangements, favourable attorneys' fees rules, treble damages, broad discovery, jury trials, and the rule of joint and several liability, with no right of contribution, are not provided for in the Directive.[205] Rather, the Directive provides for full—but not over—compensation, seeks to avoid fishing exercises by restricting disclosure to scenarios where a request for evidence is plausible, provides for joint and several liability (but with some limits and no bar on a right to contribution), and does not deal with attorney fees, jury trials, or class actions (the latter being dealt with only by a Recommendation). Although one

---

[205] See, e.g., Gavil, n. 2.

concern could be that as substantive EU antitrust laws are interpreted more broadly than their US counterparts in some areas, such as vertical restraints and unilateral conduct, there is a danger that greater volumes of private action will create a risk of false positives, the EU package does not provide huge additional incentives to the launch of these types of claim. Rather, many of its more detailed provisions focus on measures designed to stimulate actions in cartel damages cases; indeed, its provisions seem likely to have greatest impact in follow-on cases. Further, it could be argued that these are areas where litigation *should* be encouraged, as few competition agencies have sufficient resources to dedicate towards enforcement in these spheres.

4. Greater concern may thus centre on the issue of whether the reforms have done enough to overcome the impediments to litigation and to achieve the Commission's objectives of increasing, and harmonising, private damages actions across the EU. Three core problems seem potentially to exist. First, because the Commission has not adopted a holistic approach, attempting to introduce a completely harmonised framework,[206] a number of significant obstacles to national actions and areas of legal ambiguity appear to remain. For example, the Directive does not contain provisions dealing with the admissibility of economic evidence, causation, remoteness, and quantification of damages (dealt with only in the form of a non-binding practical guide). These rules will consequently continue to be governed by national law, subject to their compliance with the principles of effectiveness and equivalence. Further, although the Commission hopes that the introduction of a set of common principles in the field of collective redress will help to ensure that effective compensation is obtained by final consumers and SMEs in mass-harm situations, its ability to bolster the position of such consumers is uncertain. Not only does the Recommendation on collective redress take the form of 'soft law', but the Recommendation is simply that collective redress systems should, as a general rule, be based on the 'opt-in' principle (under which claimant parties are formed through directly expressed consent of their members).[207] A valid concern may therefore be that such classes will encompass only a small percentage of antitrust victims.[208]

Secondly, even where harmonising rules have been adopted, there still seems to be significant scope for divergence in national rules in some areas.[209] For example, given different national approaches to disclosure it seems possible that different interpretations will be adopted to the Directive's requirements relating to the plausibility and proportionality of a request for disclosure. Further, the Directive leaves Member States the opportunity to introduce more favourable national rules in some situations. It seems likely that a number of Member States will take opportunities to facilitate private actions, for example by adopting more generous rules relating to disclosure, limitation periods, and class actions. The question of how private actions should be encouraged has also been discussed by some of the Member States. Indeed the UK Government, for example, introduced

---

[206] Howard, n. 184, 456 ('At first glance, the proposed Directive appears to be a random selection of minimum procedural requirements that lack coherence or structure. This is not a blueprint set of procedural rules that govern damages actions from start to finish'). Although the Directive is based on both Arts. 103 and 114 TFEU, n. 183 (to ensure that the differences in the liability regimes applicable in the Member States do not negatively affect both competition and the proper functioning of the internal market), arguably it simply provides a guarantee that a minimum set of rules will govern actions across the EU rather than providing a set of harmonised rules.

[207] The Commission had considered including an opt-out class procedure in the Damages Dir. but it became apparent that this proposal would be unlikely to be accepted by the Parliament, see, e.g., Dunne, n. 127, G. Barling, 'Collective Redress for Breach of Competition Law—A Case for Reform?' [2011] *Comp Law* 5, A. Andreangeli, *Private Enforcement of Antitrust: Regulating Corporate Behaviour through Collective Claims in the EU and the US* (Edward Elgar, 2014), and M. Ioannidou, *Consumer Involvement in Private EU Competition Law Enforcement* (Oxford University Press, 2016).

[208] See Lande, n. 6, 6 (recovery in the EU will also be severely limited if lawyers are not allowed to receive contingency fees; 'the vast majority of consumer-victims and small business-victims' may therefore 'continue to be uncompensated').

[209] E.g., although Directive 2004/48/EC of the European Parliament and of the Council of 29 April 2004 on the enforcement of intellectual property rights [2004] OJ L157/70 provides effective means of enforcement of intellectual property rights, principally through private litigation and requires Member States to ensure minimum procedural standards, evidence indicates that the concepts within the Directive have been subject to different interpretation at the national level, see Dunne, n. 127, 11.

changes to competition legislation in 2015 designed to facilitate private litigation.[210] The existence of national differences is therefore likely to continue to affect where litigants choose to commence their actions and to result in forum-shopping.

Thirdly, a legitimate anxiety may be that the working of a number of the Directive's provisions will introduce considerable complexities into national proceedings (for example, as the courts grapple with the intricate rules applicable to limitation, joint and several liability, and passing on) so detracting from its goal of facilitating them.

5. Despite some concerns, it is clear that the Commission and the EU legislature have taken a bold first step in the journey towards encouraging damages claims throughout the EU and the development of a coherent EU system governing them. Indeed, it arguably constitutes the 'most complete vertical example of European tort law to date'.[211] The Commission has worked hard to avoid the pitfalls experienced in the US and the new framework lays the foundations for the law in this area to develop sequentially as the EU and national courts interpret and assess the full implications of the provisions in cases arising before them. It is to be expected, therefore, that private actions in Europe will gradually become more commonplace. Whether the package of reforms will be a significant success, however, and/or whether further measures will be required, remains to be seen.

6. FURTHER READING

A. BOOKS

ANDREANGELI, A., *Private Enforcement of Antitrust: Regulating Corporate Behaviour through Collective Claims in the EU and the US* (Edward Elgar, 2014)

BERGSTRÖM, M., IACOVIDES, M., and STRAND, M. (eds.), *Harmonising EU Competition Litigation: The New Directive and Beyond* (Hart Publishing, 2016)

IOANNIDOU, M., *Consumer Involvement in Private EU Competition Law Enforcement* (Oxford University Press, 2016)

JONES, A., *Restitution and European Community Law* (LLP, 2000), Chap. 6

KOMNINOS, A. P., *EC Private Antitrust Enforcement: Decentralised Application of EC Competition Law by National Courts* (Hart Publishing, 2008)

LOWE, P., AND MARQUIS, M. (eds.), *European Competition Law Annual 2011: Integrating Public and Private Enforcement of Competition Law—Implications for Courts and Agencies* (Hart Publishing, 2014)

RODGERS. B. (ed.), *Competition Law: Comparative Private Enforcement and Collective Redress Across the EU* (Wolters Kluwer, 2014)

WILS, W., *Principles of European Antitrust Enforcement* (Hart Publishing, 2005), Chap. 4

B. ARTICLES

BREALEY, M., 'Adopt *Perma Life* but follow *Hanover Shoe* to Illinois? Who Can Sue for Damages for Breach of EC Competition Law' [2002] 1 *Comp Law* 127

DRAKE, S., 'Scope of *Courage* and the Principle of "Individual Liability" for Damages: Further Development of the Principle of Effective Judicial Protection by the Court of Justice' (2006) 30 *ELRev* 841

DUNNE, N., 'The Role of Private Enforcement within EU Competition Law' (2013–2014) 16 *Cambridge Yearbook of European Legal Studies* 143

DUNNE, N., 'Antitrust and the Making of European Tort Law' (2015) 36 *OJLS* 1

HODGES, C., 'Competition Enforcement, Regulation and Civil Justice: What is the Case?' (2006) 43 *CMLRev* 1381

---

[210] See the Consumer Rights Act 2015 and the OFT's Discussion Paper, OFT 916, 'Private Actions in competition law: effective redress for consumers and business' (April 2007) and subsequent recommendations to the Government (OFT916resp), BIS, 'A Competition Regime for Growth: A Consultation on Options for Reform' (March 2011), and BIS, 'Private Actions in Competition Law: A consultation on options for reform—government response' (January 2013).

[211] Dunne, n. 127, 19 (although the author notes that completeness is not exactly a characteristic of European tort law as such).

HODGES, C., 'European Competition Enforcement Policy: Integrating Restitution and Behaviour Control. An Integrated Enforcement Policy, Involving Public and Private Enforcement with ADR' (2011) 34 *World Competition* 383

JACOBS, F. G., 'Civil Enforcement of EEC Antitrust Law' (1984) 82 *Mich LR* 1364

JONES, A., and BEARD, D., 'Co-contractors, Damages and Article 81: The ECJ Finally Speaks' [2002] *ECLR* 246

ODUDU, O., 'Developing Private Enforcement in the EU: Lessons from the Roberts Court' (2008) 53 *Ant Bull* 873

ODUDU, O., and EDELMAN, J., 'Compensatory Damages for Breach of Article 81' (2002) 27 *ELRev* 327

RODGER, B., 'Competition Law Litigation in the UK Courts: A Study of All Cases to 2004', Parts I, II, and III [2006] *ECLR* 241–248, 279–292, and 341–350

RODGER, B., 'Why Not Court? A Study of Follow-on Actions in the UK' (2013) 1 *J of Antitrust Enforcement* 104

TEMPLE LANG, J., '*Inntrepreneur* and the Duties of National Courts under Article 10 EC' [2006] *Comp Law* 231

VAN GERVEN, W., 'Of Rights, Remedies and Procedures' (2000) 37 *CMLRev* 501

WILS, W., 'Should Private Antitrust Enforcement be Encouraged?' (2003) 26 *World Competition* 473

WILS, W., 'The Relationship Between Public Antitrust Enforcement and Private Actions for Damages' (2009) 32 *World Competition* 3

15

MERGERS

1. CENTRAL ISSUES

1. Prior to 1990, the Commission had to rely on its power to apply Articles 102 and 101 to prevent one firm from taking over or acquiring shares in another.

2. In 1989 the Council adopted a European Merger Control Regulation (EUMR) to regulate changes in market structure in the EU. The Regulation came into force in 1990. This Regulation was amended in 1997 before being amended again and consolidated into a new regulation in 2004, Regulation 139/2004.

3. The 2004 EUMR declares incompatible with the internal market 'concentrations' with a 'Community dimension' (or an 'EU' dimension) which would significantly impede effective competition in the internal market or a substantial part of it, in particular as a result of the creation or strengthening of a dominant position.

4. A 'concentration' occurs where two or more undertakings on a market 'merge', where one or more undertakings acquire 'control' over another, or where a full-function joint venture is created.

5. The concept of an EU dimension aims to ensure that mergers creating structural changes which impact beyond the national borders of a Member State are appraised by the Commission under the EUMR. It is a quantitative test based on the turnover of the undertakings concerned.

6. The general scheme of the EUMR is that, subject to certain important exceptions:

   (a) concentrations with an EU dimension are appraised exclusively by the Commission under the provisions of the EUMR (they benefit from a 'one-stop shop');

   (b) concentrations without an EU dimension are appraised exclusively at the national level.

A case referral system applies, however, allowing for the transfer of cases (or aspects of cases) between the Commission and national authorities in exceptional defined circumstances.

7. Concentrations with an EU dimension must generally be notified to the Commission for appraisal prior to completion and are suspended pending investigation under the tight statutory timetable set out in the EUMR.

8. Mergers are frequently motivated by the desire of the merging parties to increase efficiency. Nonetheless, horizontal mergers (between competitors) reduce the number of players on the market, increase the market share of the post-merger firm, and may significantly impede effective competition on a market by enabling the post-merger firm to exercise market power either individually, or collectively, through collusion or coordination with other firms operating on the market (unilateral or coordinated effects may occur).

9. Non-horizontal mergers are less likely to cause competition concerns and provide significant scope for efficiencies. There is concern, however, that where one of the parties to such a merger has market power in at least one market, vertical and conglomerate mergers may harm competition through:

   (a) foreclosure of a distinct upstream, downstream, or related market; or

   (b) changing the structure of competition on a market in such a way that the firms operating on it are likely to coordinate their behaviour.

10. Merger analysis also requires assessment of factors which are likely to counteract the merged firm's ability to exercise market power, such as countervailing buyer power or new entry.

11. Efficiencies achieved by the merger may also offset any anti-competitive consequences. Where one of the merging parties is failing, the merger may not be the cause of any anti-competitive harm arising on the market.

12. A controversial issue is whether, and if so when, public interest (or non-competition) factors may be taken into account when deciding whether to prohibit or authorise a merger and how such interests should be balanced against competition considerations.

2. INTRODUCTION

A. WHAT IS A MERGER?

A merger is generally defined as occurring where two or more formerly independent entities unite. A number of different transactions and agreements concluded by undertakings could result in a unification of independent undertakings' decision-making process. Every jurisdiction needs, therefore, to adopt a definition of what constitutes a merger for the purposes of their merger control legislation. The European Union Merger Regulation (the EUMR)[1] applies to 'concentrations'. Broadly, there is a concentration where two or more previously independent undertakings merge their businesses, where there is a change in control of an undertaking (sole or joint control of an undertaking being *acquired* by another undertaking or undertakings), or where a full-function joint venture (JV) is created.[2]

B. THE PURPOSES OF MERGER CONTROL

The purpose of merger control is to enable competition authorities to regulate changes in market structure by deciding whether two or more commercial companies may merge, combine, or consolidate their businesses into one. It has been seen that the EU competition authorities are hostile to anti-competitive agreements concluded between independent undertakings.[3] Mergers naturally create a more permanent and lasting change on the market than agreements.[4] It might be expected, therefore, that many mergers, especially horizontal mergers, would be forbidden. However, mergers also give the owner of a business the opportunity to sell it. Without this possibility, entrepreneurs might be reluctant to start a business. Further, mergers provide significant efficiency opportunities.

The reasons for not making mergers unlawful per se or for not even coming anywhere near such a rule are plain. Widespread prohibition of mergers would impose serious, if not intolerable, burdens upon owners of businesses who wished to liquidate their holdings for irreproachable personal reasons. Moreover, economic welfare is significantly served by maintaining a good market for capital assets . . . Most importantly, a policy of free transferability of capital assets tends to put them in the hands of those who will use them to their utmost economic advantage, thus tending to maximize society's total output of goods and services.

Growth by merger . . . will often yield substantial economies of scale—in production, research, distribution, cost of capital and management. Entry by merger . . . may stimulate improved economic performance in an industry characterized by oligopolistic lethargy and inefficiency. Finally, acquisition of diversified lines of business, by stabilizing profits, may minimize the risk of business failure and bankruptcy.[5]

The task of the competition authorities is consequently to identify and to prohibit those mergers which have such an adverse impact on competition that any benefits resulting from them are outweighed. A further issue is whether, and if so when, public interest (or non-competition) factors should be relevant to the assessment of a merger and permitted to override the competition law assessment.

---

[1] Reg. 139/2004 [2004] OJ L24/1 (the EUMR).

[2] EUMR, Art. 3, discussed in Section 3.A.

[3] See especially Chap. 9.

[4] See, e.g., K. Hüschelrath and F. Smuda, 'Do Cartel Breakdowns Induce Mergers? Evidence From EC Cartel Cases' [2013] *European Competition Journal* 407.

[5] D. Turner, 'Conglomerate Mergers and Section 7 of the Clayton Act' (1965) 78 *Harvard LR* 1313, 1317.

(i) The Motives for, and Advantages of, a Merger

a. Efficiency

In many cases the parties may state that the main motivation for their merger is to realise efficiencies. Indeed, the market for corporate control plays an important role in disciplining the management of companies and driving economic efficiency.[6] Not only do mergers provide the opportunity for management innovation,[7] the purchase of weak firms, and the movement of capacity from declining to growth sectors, but they may allow the merging firms to engage in consolidation, to increase productivity, and to deliver technological innovation and efficiencies, for example through achieving marketing efficiencies,[8] pooling research and development (R&D) skills, complementarities, economies of scale, and scope.

Mergers may, therefore, promote economic growth by raising the efficiency of resources, total factor productivity, and by enabling undertakings to increase efficient levels of manufacture, R&D, and distribution more rapidly and more cheaply than they could by internal growth.

b. Barriers to Exit

It has already been noted that few people would go to the trouble to set up a business if they could not sell it when they had had enough or when they wished to realise capital profits from it.

c. Failing Undertakings, Unemployment, and/or Industry Stability

A merger may also provide an escape route for a company facing an otherwise inevitable liquidation. In these circumstances, the possibility of selling the business to another may mean that assets are kept in production, that creditors, owners, and employees are protected from the adverse consequences of the undertaking's failure, and/or that stability is preserved in a critical industry sector (for example, the financial sector).

d. Cross-border Mergers

In recent years, cross-border mergers, through foreign direct investment (FDI),[9] have increased dramatically in response to technological change, global competition, and the liberalisation of markets.[10] FDI has played a key role in the process of global economic integration and has been 'positively correlated with growth';[11] for developed countries 'the limited evidence available indicates fairly consistently that the productivity of domestically owned firms is positively related to the presence of foreign firms'[12] and 'that FDI triggers technology spillovers, assists human capital

---

[6] See, e.g., R. S. Ruback and M. C. Jensen, 'The Market for Corporate Control: The Scientific Evidence' (1983) 11 J of Financial Economics 5.

[7] By ensuring that the most productive assets are managed by the most efficient managers (the merger may bring new and superior management to the business). The simple threat of a take-over may encourage the incumbent management of a company to strive for efficiency (rigid control of mergers will remove or greatly reduce this perceived threat).

[8] E.g., from broader product lines, streamlining of the sales force, the use of common advertising, etc.

[9] A company may invest in another country either by merging, setting up a joint venture (JV) with, or acquiring control over or a shareholding in, a business already registered in that country, or by setting up its own business or subsidiary there (greenfield investment).

[10] See Almunia, SPEECH/13/360, 'The evolutionary pressure of globalisation on competition control', ICN 12th annual conference, Warsaw, 24 April 2013 (FDI 'passed from 6.5% of world GDP in 1980 to over 30% before the onset of this long [financial and economic] crisis').

[11] IMF Working Paper, Middle Eastern Department, WP/Ol/175, 'Determinants of, and the Relation between, Foreign Direct Investment and Growth: A Summary of the Recent Literature', Prepared by Ewe-Ghee Lim, November 2001; OECD, *Economic and Other Impacts of Foreign Corporate Takeovers in OECD Countries* (2007), 68–70 (cross-border openness may also contribute to national security and regional or international stabilisation). See also, e.g., A. Nourry and N. Jung, 'Protectionism in the Age of Austerity—A Further Unlevelling of the Playing Field' (2012) 8 *Competition Policy International* 1.

[12] Ibid. For a discussion of some of the benefits which have resulted in the UK from high amounts of inward and outward FDI, see speech of A. Chisholm, 'Public interest and competition-based merger control: An agency

formation, contributes to international trade integration, helps create a more competitive business environment and enhances enterprise development'.[13]

Cross-border mergers may also facilitate EU market integration. '[E]xternal growth by means of mergers and acquisitions can be a means of quickly realizing potential cost savings and integration gains offered by the internal market.'[14]

e. National or European Champions

Mergers affect the structure of a market and questions of industrial policy inevitably arise. The desire to increase the scale of national and European companies may be a goal of national, or European, industrial policy. The ability to restructure or to create national or European champions may, for example, mean that the parties can, in combination, survive and compete more effectively on international markets, contribute to technical and economic progress, and/or facilitate cross-border trade.

(ii) The Adverse Consequence of Mergers and the Need for Merger Control

Despite the potential for mergers to produce benefits, there is concern that many mergers in fact fail to realise the efficiencies and innovation predicted and, consequently, the increase in value for shareholders.[15] Indeed, one report commissioned by the Commission concluded that even if mergers do sometimes create efficiencies there seemed to be 'no empirical support for a general presumption' that they do so.[16] Although most competition systems do not seek to second-guess and to identify in advance those mergers that will, or will not, work out for the company, the economy, and shareholders,[17] they do generally encompass rules which allow competition agencies to assess whether an adverse impact on efficiency, resulting from a lessening of competition, can be anticipated to result from it. In addition, many jurisdictions are sensitive about capital flows in and out of their States and the costs and benefits of inward FDI. Accordingly, some States have rules which allow competition agencies or politicians to assess the impact of takeovers (especially foreign ones)[18] on national security, businesses perceived to be of national strategic importance, technological capabilities, jobs, and exports.

a. A Damaging Effect on Competition

There is a danger that undertakings may wish to merge in order to achieve or to strengthen their market power.

In horizontal mergers, and especially in the massive consolidations that took place [in the US] around the turn of the [20th] century, the desire to achieve or strengthen monopoly power played a prominent role. Some 1887–1904 consolidations gained monopoly power by creating firms that dominated their industries. Others fell short of dominance, but transformed market structures sufficiently to curb the tendencies toward

---

perspective on the lessons from evolution of the current regime', Fordham Competition Law Institute Annual Conference, 12 September 2014, 8–9.

[13] Given the appropriate host-country policies and a basic level of development, OECD, *Foreign Direct Investment for Development: Maximising Benefits and Minimising Costs* (2002) (concluding that the macroeconomic benefits of inward FDI in most cases outweigh the costs. See also OECD, n. 11.

[14] European Commission, 'Competition and Integration: Community Merger Policy' (1994) 57 *European Economy* vii.

[15] See, e.g., M. Monti, SPEECH/02/252, 'Review of the EC Merger Regulation—Roadmap for the Reform Project', Speech to British Chamber of Commerce, Brussels, 4 June 2002 and Chisholm, n. 12.

[16] See L.-H. Röller, J. Stennek, and F. Verboven, 'Efficiency Gains From Mergers', European Economy, no. 5/2001, Brussels and speech by Monti, ibid.

[17] See, e.g., Chisholm, n. 12.

[18] Although economic theory is neutral as to the form FDI takes, governments tend to be more welcoming of FDI through greenfield investment (see n. 9) and more suspicious of FDI through foreign mergers, OECD, n. 11, 70–71.

price competition toward which sellers gravitated in the rapidly changing market conditions of the time. As Thomas Edison remarked to a reporter concerning reasons for the formation of the General Electric Company in 1892:

Recently there has been sharp rivalry between [Thomson-Houston and Edison General Electric], and prices have been cut so that there has been little profit in the manufacture of electrical machinery for anybody. The consolidation of the companies . . . will do away with competition which has become so sharp that the product of the factories has been worth little more than ordinary hardware.

Those were days when businesspeople were not yet intimidated by the wrath of trustbusters or public opinion. Now they are more circumspect, and evidence of monopoly-creating intent is harder to find. Also, vigorous antitrust enforcement in the United States and, more recently, abroad has done much to curb competition-inhibiting mergers.[19]

Even if dominance or the acquisition of market power is not the motive for a merger, it may be its effect.

Horizontal Mergers

A horizontal merger is one which occurs between undertakings operating at the same level of the economy. As Hovenkamp points out, such mergers have two important implications for the market on which the merging firms operate:

Because the horizontal merger involves two firms in the same market, it produces two consequences that do not flow from vertical or conglomerate mergers: 1) after the merger the relevant market has one firm less than before; 2) the post-merger firm ordinarily has a larger market share than either of the partners had before the merger.[20]

The reduction in the number of firms active on the market and the increase in concentration may raise competition concerns where it allows the merging parties to acquire individual market power which might be exploited at the expense of customers and protected by anti-competitive behaviour (unilateral or non-coordinated effects). Alternatively, it may lead to a substantial increase in the concentration of a particular industry and enable the merging parties to raise prices and restrict output, through explicit or tacit coordination of their behaviour with other firms operating on the market (coordinated effects).

Vertical Mergers

A vertical merger is one concluded between firms at different levels of production in the economy. The motive for vertical mergers is frequently to achieve efficiencies and/or to obtain a secure supply of a raw material or to secure an outlet for the sale of products. They may, however, raise competition concerns. The predominant fear is that where the merging firms have market power at one or more vertical level, vertical mergers may 'foreclose' the market or a source of supply to competitors. For example, a merger between a manufacturer of a product and a supplier of an essential component for that product (backward integration) may have severe implications for competing manufacturers. The foreclosure effect will be acute where there are few or no other suppliers of the essential components. Similarly, the acquisition by a manufacturer of a distributor (forward integration) could make it more difficult for competitors to gain access to distributors. A vertical merger may also increase price transparency or facilitate collusion between firms operating on the market.

---

[19] F. M. Scherer and D. Ross, *Industrial Market Structure and Economic Performance* (3rd edn, Houghton Mifflin, 1990), 160.

[20] 'Merger policy is the most powerful weapon available in the American antitrust arsenal for combating tacit collusion or Cournot style oligopoly. Since we cannot go after oligopoly directly under [section 1 Sherman Act], we do the next best thing. We try to prevent (taking efficiencies and other factors into account) the creation of market structures that tend to facilitate Cournot or collusion-like outcomes', H. Hovenkamp, *Federal Antitrust Policy: The Law of Competition and its Practice* (5th edn, West, 2016), 12.1b, 668.

Conglomerate Mergers

Conglomerate mergers are concentrations which have no horizontal or vertical effect. As such mergers do not result in horizontal overlaps or vertical effects, they do not obviously raise competition problems. Rather they may frequently be motivated by innocuous objectives from a competition perspective, such as the need for risk reduction. An undertaking may, for example, wish to expand into another market where it is operating in a declining or cyclical industry or where it simply wishes to spread risk. However, where post-merger a firm will have market power in one market there could be concern that it will use its power in that market to foreclose competition in a neighbouring or related market, for example by engaging in tying or by cross-subsidising or predating in that market.[21] This may be more likely where the relevant markets are closely related and the merged undertakings will be able to offer a portfolio of products.

Alternatively there may be a fear that conglomeracy will lead to a loss of potential competition. A merger of firms operating in different product or geographic markets may cause a loss of potential competition. Any threat that they may enter each other's markets is eliminated. This may be of particular importance where the undertakings operate in the same product but a different geographic market or where they operate in neighbouring product markets. In the EU, the elimination of a potential competitor is identified as a horizontal issue,[22] but it will be seen in the discussion below that the Commission has also displayed concerns about purely conglomerate mergers.

b. Other public policy concerns

Mergers may cause other concerns, apart from purely competition ones. For example:

Fear of Big Business

Some commentators believe that conglomeracy, or mergers that would create large businesses, have implications for the freedom of society more generally. It is feared that too great an economic concentration is anti-democratic and restricts individual freedom and enterprise or that it has an adverse effect on the distribution of wealth.[23]

In Chapter 1 it was seen that it has been argued that one of the goals of competition laws should be the diffusion of economic power and the protection of individual freedom.

Private power can cross economic boundaries and poses the threat of an 'extra market' power which can change the rules of the game in favour of the dominant corporations. In such a situation, where relationships between firms and their socio-economic environment constitute a mixture of market and non-market bonds, the authorities aim at the dispersion of private power. Even if this entails some loss of economic efficiency, such a choice would not necessarily be irrational, because such costs may be outweighed by social or political advantages.[24]

Further, and in particular following the 2008 financial and economic crisis, one question which arose was whether care should be taken to ensure that no firm is allowed to become so large that it is 'too big to fail' and, if so, whether merger rules should play any role in enforcing such a policy.[25]

---

[21] See Chap. 7.

[22] Guidelines on the assessment of horizontal mergers under the Council Regulation on the control of concentrations between undertakings (the Horizontal Merger Guidelines) [2004] OJ C31/5, para. 5. ('A merger with a potential competitor can generate horizontal anti-competitive effects . . . if the potential competitor significantly constrains the behaviour of the firms active in the market').

[23] A. Cairncross et al., *Economic Policy for the European Community* (Macmillan, 1974).

[24] A. P. Jacquemin and H. W. de Jong, *European Industrial Organisation* (Macmillan, 1997), 198–199.

[25] See, e.g., J. T. Rosch, 'Implications of the Financial Meltdown for the FTC', Speech at the New York Bar Association Annual Dinner, New York, 29 January 2009 ('if a merger creates a firm whose failure is likely to have a catastrophic effect on the market as a whole, because it is so integral to the market, the end result may be a substantial lessening of competition. It would arguably be better to avoid the creation of such firms in the first place through merger instead of having the Treasury Department bail them out').

Special Sectors and Fear of Overseas Control

It may be believed that tighter control should be exercised over, and a broader range of factors taken into account in relation to, mergers which occur in particularly sensitive sectors. For example, interests of democracy may require the preservation of the 'plurality of the press' or national security may require that the ownership of certain industries, such as oil and defence equipment, does not pass overseas. Indeed, in recent years, there have been numerous instances, both within and outside the EU, in which the impact of a proposed merger on the national interest has provoked debate. In particular, popular backlash against foreign control of key national businesses has sometimes led to calls for national governments to protect industry and have raised the potential for differences in opinion as to how the benefits and costs of the respective transactions should be assessed and weighed and a clash between proponents of the principle of an open market economy and proponents of greater protectionism.[26]

Unemployment

Mergers may mean asset-stripping, profits to shareholders, rationalisation, and loss of jobs. Mergers which occur in depressed regions or in areas in which unemployment is already high may, therefore, cause concern and lead to pressure on politicians to intervene.

Personal Data

An increasing concern in the information economy is the impact of transactions on personal data and the extent to which the use, or protection, of such data should be a relevant factor impacting on, or subsumed within, substantive merger assessment.[27] Indeed, the acquisition of a data-advantage may be a motivation for mergers in businesses where firms rely on personal data as a key input, in particular 'two-sided markets; companies offer consumers free services with the aim of acquiring valuable personal data to assist advertisers to better target them with behavioral ads'.[28]

C. THE HISTORY OF THE EUROPEAN MERGER CONTROL REGULATION

(i) The Initial Lacuna and the Drive for Merger Control at the EU Level

The original EEC Treaty, unlike the ECSC Treaty, did not contain any specific provision for controlling mergers.[29] The Commission recognised the crucial need for rules specifically focused on mergers which effect a lasting change to the structure of the market (rather than the behaviour of firms)

---

[26] See, e.g., Pfizer's proposed acquisition of AstraZeneca discussed in A. Jones and J. Davies, 'Merger Control and the Public Interest: Balancing EU and National Law in the Protectionist Debate' (2014) 10 *European Competition Journal* 453.

[27] See Chap. 1 and, e.g., F. Costa-Cabral and O. Lynskey, 'The Internal and External Constraints of Data Protection on Competition Law in the EU', LSE Law, Society and Economy Working Papers 25/2015 and D. Sokol and R. E. Comerford, 'Does Antitrust Have a Role to Play in Regulating Big Data?' in R. D. Blair and D. Sokol (eds.), *Cambridge Handbook of Antitrust, Intellectual Property and High Tech* (Cambridge University Press, 2016).

[28] M. Stucke and A. Grunes, 'Debunking the Myths Over Big Data and Antitrust' (2015) 5 *CPI Antitrust Chronicle* 1.

[29] Explanations for the different approach may be that: the ECSC was a *traité-loi* whilst the EEC was a *traité-cadre* (a framework document, to be fleshed out by implementing legislation) and, most likely, that it was easier to agree on a rule which would affect only the specific industries perceived to be of vital importance given their political and military significance, see Art. 66(7) of the ECSC Treaty and S. Bulmer, 'Institutions and Policy Change: The Case of Merger Control' (1994) 72 *Public Administration* 423, 427–428. Conversely it may have been considered that the objectives set out in EEC Treaty, Art. 2 (of economic expansion) might be achieved by concentrating economic power rather than prohibiting mergers.

from early on[30] and adopted its first legislative proposal for a merger control regulation in 1973.[31] Any regulation on merger control had, however, to be passed unanimously by the Council[32] and, for a long time, there was no consensus amongst the Member States as to: whether EU merger control was necessary at all; whether power to control changes in industrial structure in their territories should be ceded to the Commission; and/or what substantive criteria should be used to appraise mergers and, in particular, whether only the effects on competition should be relevant, or whether social and industrial policy considerations should also be taken into account. There were, therefore, two major sticking points:

(a) jurisdiction—whether, and if so at what point, control should be relinquished by the Member States to the Commission and what the relationship between EU and national law should be; and

(b) appraisal criteria—should factors other than competition be taken into account in assessing whether a particular merger was compatible or incompatible with the common market?

(ii) The Catalysts for the EUMR

Frustrated by the lack of a specific provision enabling it to control mergers the Commission sought not only to persuade the Council to enact a specific merger control provision but applied its existing tools to prevent them: it utilised Articles 102 and, subsequently, 101 TFEU to prevent take-overs and acquisitions of shareholdings in other undertakings.

It has been seen in Chapter 7 that in *Europemballage Corp and Continental Can Co Inc v Commission*[33] the CJ upheld the Commission's view that Article 102 could be used to prevent a dominant undertaking from abusing its dominant position by acquiring a competitor and thereby strengthening its dominant position. Article 102 proved to be a reasonably effective weapon against mergers, but its use is, of course, limited by the fact that the acquiring company must have a dominant position before Article 102 can apply; it may not therefore apply where two or more undertakings merge to create a dominant position[34] or where a dominant undertaking is acquired by a non-dominant undertaking.

Although Article 101, in contrast, does not appear to be particularly suitable for controlling mergers[35] (it strikes principally at *agreements* between independent undertakings so it might be artificial to try and deal with many types of mergers under its provisions, for example hostile take-overs which are opposed by the target undertaking), the Commission did seek to apply it to merger situations. In *BAT and Reynolds v Commission*[36] the CJ confirmed that Article 101 might apply to the acquisition by an undertaking of a minority shareholding in another. The difficulties raised, and the ambiguities left unresolved, by the judgment led to widespread concern in industry which 'were fully exploited by the Commission and the resulting uncertainty was used skillfully...to persuade Member States to return to the negotiating table on a new draft of a merger control regulation...'.[37]

---

[30] See *Memorandum on the Concentration of Enterprises in the Common Market*, EEC Competition Series Study No. 3 and, e.g., C. Overbury, 'Politics or Policy? The Demystification of EC Merger Control' [1992] *Fordham Corp L Inst* 561.

[31] In the period between 1973 and 1989 a series of draft regulations was proposed and rejected by the Council: see [1973] OJ C92/1, [1982] OJ C36/3, [1984] OJ C51/8, [1988] OJ C130/4, [1989] OJ C22/141.

[32] The legal basis for the EUMR is Arts. 103 and 352 TFEU.

[33] Case 6/72, *Europemballage Corp and Continental Can Co Inc v Commission* [1973] ECR 215, see Chap. 5.

[34] '[O]nly the strengthening of dominant positions and not their creation can be controlled under Art. [102]': Case T-102/96, *Gencor Ltd v Commission* [1999] ECR II-753, para. 155; and see Case 6/72, ibid, para. 26.

[35] See Commission's *Memorandum on the Concentration of Enterprises in the Common Market*, EEC Competition Series Study No. 3 (published in 1966), para. 58.

[36] Cases 142 and 156/84, [1987] ECR 4487, paras. 36–39.

[37] C. J. Cook and C. S. Kerse, *EC Merger Control* (5th edn, Sweet & Maxwell, 2009), 1-003. Soon after this judgment the green light was given to the Commission to put forward another proposal for a merger regulation, see also Section 3.E, p. 1122.

The internal market programme also led to industry calls for EU merger control. Business re-structuring was a natural result of the programme and an increasing number of EU-wide mergers were completed in the lead-up to 1992,[38] and firms called for a level playing field and to have to comply with only *one* set of merger rules.

A combination of Commission support, pressure from industry, the internal market programme, and increasing numbers of mergers led to the eventual realisation that a system of European merger control was inevitable.

(iii) The Original Merger Control Regulation—Council Regulation (EEC) 4064/89

The original Merger Control Regulation was adopted by the Council of Ministers on 21 December 1989[39] and came into force on 21 September 1990. It set out jurisdictional, procedural, and substantive rules. The procedural requirements were fleshed out by Regulation 447/98[40] and numerous Commission Notices set out guidance on how the Commission interpreted various aspects of the regulations.

Although the Regulation was reviewed[41] and then amended by Council Regulation 1310/97,[42] the Commission has constantly kept the working and operation of the Regulation, especially its juris-dictional thresholds,[43] under review. A persistent concern of the Commission has been whether the jurisdictional thresholds are drawn correctly and, in particular, whether an important number of transactions with significant cross-border effects remain outside the scope of the EUMR.[44] In 2001, however, the Commission embarked on a more comprehensive review of the Regulation, publish-ing a Green Paper[45] mooting wide-ranging changes to its substantive and procedural provisions as well as jurisdictional ones. This led, following consultation, to a proposal for a package of meas-ures to reform the provisions and working of the EUMR and an entire new consolidated merger regulation.[46]

(iv) The Current Merger Control Regulation, Council Regulation (EC) 139/2004

After fairly intensive negotiation and discussion, political agreement for a new text of the EUMR was agreed leading to the adoption of the current, recast, EUMR,[47] Regulation 139/2004. Essentially, it incorporates elements of the original 1989 Regulation and amendments

---

[38] L. Tsoukalis, *The New European Economy Revisited* (2nd edn, Oxford University Press, 1993), 103 (115 mergers in 1982–1983, 492 by 1988–1989, and 622 in 1989–1990).

[39] Council Reg. (EEC) 4064/89 of 21 December 1989 on the control of concentrations between undertakings [1989] OJ L395/1.

[40] Commission Reg. 447/98 [1998] OJ L61/1 (replacing Reg. 2367/90).

[41] Community Merger Control, COM(96) 19 final.

[42] Council Reg. 1310/97 of 30 June 1997 [1997] OJ L180/1 (it, e.g., introduced an additional (lower) jurisdictional threshold, and changed the rules dealing with JVs).

[43] It had an obligation to report to the Council on the jurisdictional thresholds, the old EUMR, Art. 1(4).

[44] See the Report to the Council on the application of the Merger Regulation Thresholds, COM(2000) 399 final.

[45] 2001 Green Paper on the Review of Council Regulation (EEC) No. 4064/89, COM(2001) 745/6 final.

[46] COM(2002) 711 final, OJ [2003] C20/4.

[47] In the interest of legal certainty, the Commission recast the Regulation, adopting a single legislative text to make the desired amendments, see the Inter-institutional agreement of 28 November 2001 on a more structured use of recasting technique for legal acts [2002] OJ C77/1.

introduced in both 1997 and 2004. The 2004 Regulation is, like its predecessor, supplemented by an implementing regulation[48] and a number of Commission Notices which provide guidance as to the interpretation of various of its provisions. In particular, the following Notices are of importance:[49]

(a) Commission Consolidated Jurisdictional Notice[50] (the 'Jurisdictional Notice', replacing and consolidating into a single Notice previous Notices on the concept of a concentration, undertakings concerned, the calculation of turnover, and on the concept of full function joint ventures);

(b) Notice on simplified procedure for the treatment of certain concentrations;[51]

(c) Notice on remedies;[52]

(d) Notice on restrictions directly related and necessary to concentrations;[53]

(e) Notices on the appraisal of both horizontal and non-horizontal mergers;[54]

(f) Commission Notice on Case Referral in respect of concentrations;[55]

(g) Notice on access to the file.[56]

The Commission has also published Best Practice Guidelines on the conduct of EUMR proceedings and Economic Evidence (how best to present economic and empirical evidence)[57] and model texts for divestiture commitments and trustee mandates.[58]

(v) Subsequent Review

The EUMR provided for mandatory review of the jurisdictional thresholds and provisions dealing with pre-notification reasoned submissions,[59] and the Commission continues to monitor the working of the rules more generally.

One concern of the Commission has been to ensure that the regulatory burden imposed by the Regulation is not excessive or disproportionate. In 2013, it thus launched a review[60] which led to changes to the simplified procedure[61] (for non-problematic mergers) and the publication of a 2014

---

[48] Reg. 802/2004.

[49] The Commission's Notice on market definition is also crucial, see Chap. 1 and n. 338 and text.

[50] [2008] OJ C95/1, replacing Notices on: the concept of concentration [1998] OJ C66/5; on the concept of undertakings concerned [1998] OJ C66/14; on calculation of turnover [1998] OJ C66/25; and on the concept of full-function joint ventures [1998] OJ C66/1.

[51] See Commission Notice of 5 December 2013 on a simplified procedure for treatment of certain concentrations under Council Regulation (EC) No. 139/2004 (Notice on Simplified Procedure) [2013] OJ C366/5.

[52] [2008] OJ C267/1.

[53] [2005] OJ C56/24.

[54] [2004] OJ C31/5 and [2008] OJ C265/6.

[55] [2005] OJ C56/2.

[56] [2005] OJ C325/7. See also decision on the terms of reference of Hearing Officers [2001] L162/21, Chap. 13.

[57] 17 October 2011. See also OECD Best Practice Roundtable, *Economic Evidence in Merger Ananlysis*, DAF/COMP(2011) 23.

[58] Available with the other legislation on DG Comp's website at: <http://ec.europa.eu/competition/mergers/legislation/legislation.html>.

[59] EUMR, Art. 1(4).

[60] See IP/13/584, Commission Staff Working Document, Towards more effective EU merger control.

[61] See nn. 51 and 119–120 and text.

White Paper,[62] consulting on ideas for, for example: improving the jurisdictional provisions; ensuring the effectiveness and smoothness of the case referral system;[63] simplifying procedures; and fostering coherence of, and convergence between, merger rules in the EU. Although the White Paper makes it clear that the Commission considers there is an enforcement gap in relation to acquisitions of non-controlling minority interests not covered by the EUMR, it also recognises the need to strike a balance between meeting competition concerns and the procedural burden that plugging the gap would impose on business.[64]

D. SCHEME OF THE EUROPEAN UNION MERGER REGULATION

The EUMR applies to concentrations with a 'Community'—an EU—dimension. The concept of an EU dimension allocates responsibility over concentrations between the Commission and the Member States and imposes an external limit on merger transactions caught within its jurisdiction. Broadly, with certain limited (but important) exceptions, concentrations that do not have an EU dimension are assessed under any applicable national competition legislation (no EU competition law applies), whilst concentrations with an EU dimension are assessed under the provisions of the EUMR. In the latter case, the Commission's decision under the terms of the EUMR is decisive and, as a general rule, no other national or EU competition law applies to the transaction; such concentrations benefit from a 'one-stop shop'. A case referral system applies, however, to ensure that, in defined circumstances, cases can be transferred between the EU and national authorities as appropriate.

Concentrations with an EU dimension must be notified to the Commission and must, in general, be suspended until the Commission's final decision either clearing (conditionally or unconditionally) or prohibiting the merger. The Commission's decision must be taken within tight timetables.[65] There is a right of appeal from Commission decisions[66] to the GC and a further appeal, on a point of law, to the CJ. Despite the recognition of a particular need for speed in merger cases, the expedited appeals procedure applies only in exceptional cases.[67]

The basic scheme of the EUMR is illustrated in Fig. 15.1 below. Section 3 deals more fully with the EUMR's jurisdictional provisions. Section 4 considers procedure whilst Section 5 examines substantive appraisal of EU mergers. Sections 6, 7, and 8 deal respectively with merger statistics, judicial review, and international issues, whilst Section 9 sets out some conclusions.

---

[62] White Paper, Towards more effective EU merger control, COM/2014/0449 final (see also accompanying Staff Working Document and Impact Assessment, available at <http://ec.europa.eu/competition/mergers/publications_en.html>).

[63] Although the Commission considers that further improvements could be made to the jurisdictional thresholds it believes that they do largely provide an appropriate legal framework for allocating cases between the EU level and the Member States, see Commission Report to Council on the functioning of Regulation 139/2004, 18 June 2009, COM(2009) 281 final.

[64] See further, nn. 87–89 and text.

[65] Delays in review should not hamper the flexibility of undertakings seeking to engage in industrial restructuring.

[66] But not a decision by the Commission to open Phase II proceedings, see n. 273.

[67] See Section 7 and Chap. 13.

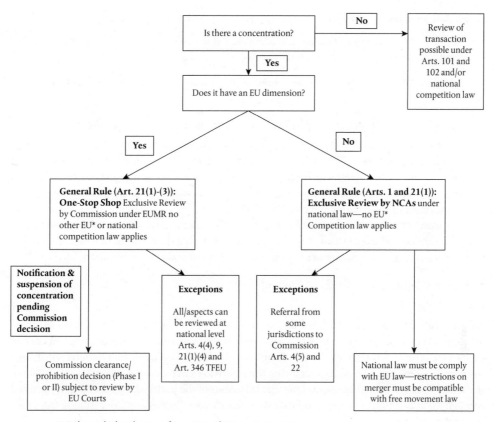

Figure 15.1 Scheme of the EUMR

3. JURISDICTION

A. CONCENTRATIONS

(i) Definition

Subject to specified exceptions, the EUMR applies to concentrations with an EU dimension. The concept targets operations resulting in 'a lasting change in the control of the undertakings concerned and therefore in the structure of the market'.[68] Article 3 of the EUMR defines concentration. Article 3(1) provides:

A concentration shall be deemed to arise where a change of control on a lasting basis results from:

   (a) the merger of two or more previously independent undertakings or parts of undertakings, or

   (b) the acquisition, by one or more persons already controlling at least one undertaking, or by one or more undertakings whether by purchase of securities or assets, by contract or by any other means, of direct or indirect control of the whole or parts of one or more other undertakings.

---

[68] EUMR, recital 20.

Article 3(4) provides:

The creation of a joint venture performing on a lasting basis all the functions of an autonomous economic entity shall constitute a concentration within the meaning of paragraph 3(1)(b).

The Commission's Jurisdictional Notice provides guidance on how the Commission interprets Article 3.[69]

a. Article 3(1)(a)—Mergers between Previously Independent Undertakings

The Regulation does not define the term 'merge'. A broad economically oriented interpretation of the term would render Article 3(1)(b) otiose. The purpose appears, therefore, to be that merger is defined narrowly to catch undertakings which have fused their businesses ('legal' mergers), that is where two or more undertakings amalgamate into one business and cease to exist as separate legal entities or where one undertaking acquires and completely absorbs another undertaking (which subsequently ceases to exist), for example the merger between SmithKline Beecham and Glaxo Wellcome to create GlaxoSmithKline.[70] The distinction is relevant, to the extent that the question of whether there has been a merger, or merely a change in control, affects who must make the notification.[71]

b. Article 3(1)(b)—Acquisition of Control

Decisive Influence

Article 3(1)(b) applies where there is a change in control of an undertaking,[72] for example: where an undertaking acquires sole control of another or two or more undertakings acquire *joint* control of another. Article 3(2) clarifies that the Regulation is intended to catch transactions which lead to an undertaking or undertakings acquiring the ability to exercise *decisive influence* over another— the ability to control the strategic commercial behaviour of the undertakings concerned (acquired through the acquisition of property rights, assets, shareholders' agreements, or resulting from economic dependence):[73]

Control shall be constituted by rights, contracts or any other means which, either separately or in combination and having regard to the considerations of fact or law involved, confer the possibility of exercising decisive influence on an undertaking, in particular by:

(a) ownership or the right to use all or part of the assets of an undertaking;

(b) rights or contracts which confer decisive influence on the composition, voting or decisions of the organs of an undertaking.

Sole Control

Sole control is acquired if one undertaking alone can exercise decisive influence on an undertaking. It can be acquired both where the one undertaking enjoys the power to determine strategic commercial decisions of the other or where a shareholder is able to veto strategic decisions in an undertaking but does not have the power to impose such decisions (negative sole control). It can be acquired on a *de jure* or *de facto* basis.

---

[69] The Commission Consolidated Jurisdictional Notice [2008] OJ C95/1 (the Jurisdictional Notice).

[70] See Jurisdictional Notice, para. 9. Para. 10 of the Notice states that a merger may also occur where, in the absence of a legal merger, the combining of the activities of previously independent undertakings results in the creation of a single economic unit.

[71] See Section 4.

[72] It does not matter whether control is acquired in one, two, or more stages or by means of one or more transactions, provided the end result constitutes a single concentration. Thus a concentration may be deemed to arise where a number of formally distinct legal transactions are interdependent so that none of them would be carried out without the others and the result consists in conferring on one or more undertakings direct or indirect economic control over the activities of another, see Case T-282/02, *Cementbouw Handel & Industrie BV v Commission* [2006] ECR II-319, paras. 104–109.

[73] Jurisdictional Notice, para. 16.

Sole control, or decisive influence, is ordinarily acquired on a legal basis through an acquisition of more than 50 per cent of the share capital and with it, more than 50 per cent of the voting rights of another undertaking.[74] However, it will always be necessary to look at other factors. Even an undertaking with more than 50 per cent of the share capital will not acquire sole control if, for example, it does not have control of a majority of the voting rights or where a supermajority of voting rights is required for strategic decisions. In such circumstances the acquisition of a simple majority may lead to a scenario of negative or joint control.[75]

Sole control may also be gained where a share of considerably less than 50 per cent is acquired (a minority shareholding),[76] for example it may be acquired on: a legal basis where special rights are attached to the preferential shareholding (a majority of the voting rights are nonetheless conferred on the shareholder or the shareholder has power to appoint more than half of the management team); a *de facto* basis where the remainder of the shares are widely dispersed,[77] the shareholder is likely to get a majority of votes at a shareholders meeting,[78] or an agreement confers an option to purchase shares in the near future.[79] The analysis in each case is fact-specific and it is important to consider a number of factors, including all shareholdings, special rights, and veto rights attached to the shareholding or set out in a management or shareholding agreement. In *Yara/Kemira GrowHow*,[80] for example, the Commission considered that the acquisition of 30.05 per cent of the shares in GrowHow constituted an acquisition of control. In practice, based on attendance at the last three AGMs, Yara would be able to control a majority of votes at a shareholders meeting.

Negative sole control exists where a sole shareholder has enough voting rights to veto all strategic decisions.[81] Such a shareholder does not have joint control as although it can block strategic decisions, no other shareholder enjoys the same level of influence and the shareholder exercising negative control does not necessarily have to cooperate with other shareholders in determining the strategic behaviour of the controlled undertaking.[82] Decisive influence and hence control is acquired because of the ability of the shareholder to produce a deadlock situation.

In *Ryanair/Aer Lingus*,[83] the Commission concluded that Ryanair's acquisition of a 25 per cent stake in Aer Lingus did *not* constitute acquisition of control. Although it prohibited the proposed merger (a hostile public bid by Ryanair for the remaining *entire* share capital of Aer Lingus), the Commission concluded it could not require Ryanair to divest this non-controlling stake it had already acquired. The GC upheld the Commission's decision that Ryanair's shareholding did not confer control or amount to partial implementation of a concentration.[84]

Although in the end the UK competition authority required Ryanair in this case to sell most of its stake using powers conferred by UK law,[85] the Commission has been reflecting on the questions of whether: (a) its inability to review acquisitions of non-controlling minority shareholdings constitutes a serious lacuna or gap in its powers to regulate transactions which have potential to cause significant

---

[74] Ibid, paras. 18–34 (it can also be acquired on a contractual basis or through the acquisition of assets).

[75] Ibid, para. 56. See M.17, *MBB/Aerospatiale* 25 February 1991 (Aerospatiale and MBB had joint control of a joint venture formed to carry out their helicopter businesses. Although Aerospatiale received 60% of equity (and MBB only 40%), all strategic decisions for the joint venture required unanimous consent of both partners).

[76] Ibid, para. 57, M.258, *CCIE/GTE* 25 September 1992 and M.4994, *Electrabel/CNR* 29 April 2008, *aff'd* Case T-332/09, *Electrabel v Commission* EU:T:2012:672 (Electrabel's holding of 49.94% of CNR's capital and 47.92% of its voting right amounts to sole control), Case C-84/13P, EU:C:2014:2040.

[77] See, e.g., M.25, *Arjomari/Wiggins Teape* 10 December 1990 (39% shareholding conferred sole control since no other entity had more than a 4% shareholding).

[78] See, e.g., M.343, *Société Générale de Belgique/Générale de Banque* 3 August 1993 and Case T-332/09, *Electrabel v Commission* EU:T:2012:672, *aff'd* Case C-84/13P, EU:C:2014:2040.

[79] Case T-2/93, *Air France v Commission* [1994] ECR II-323 and Jurisdictional Notice, paras. 59–60.

[80] M.4730, 21 September 2007.

[81] Jurisdictional Notice, paras. 54 and 57.

[82] Ibid, para. 54.

[83] M.4439, 27 June 2007.

[84] Case T-411/07, *Aer Lingus Group v Commission* [2010] ECR II-3691.

[85] See Case No. 1219/4/8/13, *Rynair Holdings v CMA* [2014] CAT 3, *aff'd* [2015] EWCA Civ 83.

harm to competition (through unilateral or coordinated effects);[86] and (b) Article 8(4) should be amended to allow it to 'require the dissolution of partially implemented transactions declared incompatible with the internal market in line with the scope of the suspension obligation . . .'.[87] The Commission has concluded that it would like to have jurisdiction over such transactions (believing that Articles 101 and 102 do not provide suitable alternatives), and has proposed a targeted transparency system in its White Paper.[88] Nonetheless, it recognises that it will be a challenge to design a system of control without imposing an unnecessary and disproportionate regulatory burden and cost on companies and competition agencies. Indeed, Commissioner Vestager made it clear that such a system would require time to design correctly and that '[t]here is no need to rush. What counts is that the new rules—when they are introduced—work well and are proportionate to the problem'.[89]

Joint Control

The Commission explains joint control, where two or more undertakings have the possibility of exercising decisive influence over another, in its Jurisdictional Notice.[90]

Jurisdictional Notice [2008] OJ C95/1

62. Joint control exists where two or more undertakings or persons have the possibility of exercising decisive influence over another undertaking. Decisive influence in this sense normally means the power to block actions which determine the strategic commercial behaviour of an undertaking. Unlike sole control, which confers upon a specific shareholder the power to determine the strategic decisions in an undertaking, joint control is characterized by the possibility of a deadlock situation resulting from the power of two or more parent companies to reject proposed strategic decisions. It follows, therefore, that these shareholders must reach a common understanding in determining the commercial policy of the joint venture and that they are required to cooperate.

63. As in the case of sole control, the acquisition of joint control can also be established on a *de jure* or *de facto* basis. There is joint control if the shareholders (the parent companies) must reach agreement on major decisions concerning the controlled undertaking (the joint venture).

Joint control may thus be acquired where two parents hold the voting rights equally and also in the absence of equality (for example, where minority shareholders have additional rights which allow them to veto decisions which are essential for the strategic commercial behaviour of the joint venture). It is necessary to consider not only the size of the undertakings' shareholdings but also factors such as the voting rights attached to the shareholdings and shareholder and management agreements, veto rights, and the ability of two or more undertakings to jointly exercise the majority of voting rights.[91]

Changes in the Quality of Control

The EUMR applies to operations leading to change in the quality of control[92] catching transactions leading to: a change from sole control to joint control; a change in joint control (by the entrance

---

[86] See Commission's White Paper, n. 62, and, e.g., OFT 1218, *Minority Interests in Competitors: A Research Report prepared by DotEcon Ltd*, March 2010 and A. Ezrachi and D. Gilo, 'EC Competition Law and the Regulation of Passive Investments Among Competitors' (2006) 26 *OJLS* 327.

[87] Commission Staff Working Document, Towards more effective EU merger control, 20 June 2013, 21–22.

[88] See nn. 62 and 89 text and, e.g., G. Motta, 'White Paper for a More Effective EU Merger Control: How to Review the Acquisition of Non-controlling Minority Shareholdings' (2015) 6 *JECLAP* 253 and N. Levy, 'EU Merger Control and Non-controlling Minority Shareholdings: The Case Against Change' [2013] *European Competition Journal* 721.

[89] See speech by Commissioner Vestager, 'Thoughts on merger reform and market definition', 12 March 2015.

[90] See also, in particular, the GC's judgment in Case T-282/02, *Cementbouw Handel & Industrie BV v Commission* [2006] ECR II-319.

[91] Jurisdictional Notice, paras. 64–82.

[92] Ibid, paras. 83–90 and, e.g., M.23, *ICI/Tioxide* 28 November 1990.

of a new shareholder, by replacement of an existing shareholder, or possibly by a reduction in the number of jointly controlling shareholders); or a change from joint control to sole control. It thus covers: (a) an entrance of one or more new controlling shareholders irrespective of whether or not they replace existing controlling shareholders; and (b) a reduction of the number of controlling shareholders (although the simplified procedure is likely to apply where a party is to acquire sole control of an undertaking over which it already has joint control).[93]

(ii) Joint Ventures

a. Introduction

The creation of a separate JV is dealt with under the EUMR only where it amounts to a 'concentration'. Where it does constitute a concentration with an EU dimension it will, like other concentrations, generally benefit from a '*one-stop shop*' appraisal by the Commission under the EUMR (national competition rules do not apply).[94] In contrast, if the JV falls to be assessed under Article 101, the application of national law (subject to Article 3 of Regulation 1/2003) is not precluded and an authorisation decision is most unlikely (self-assessment is generally required). Further, the JV agreement is valid only insofar as the agreement satisfies the conditions of Article 101 both at the time the agreement is concluded and in the future.[95]

The differences in treatment of JVs under the EUMR and Article 101 respectively, have led the Commission to make a number of changes to its approach over the years. Not only has it sought to ameliorate the way in which it deals with JVs under Article 101,[96] but in 1998 the definition of JV set out in the EUMR was expanded to bring more JVs within its scope.

b. 'Full-function' Joint Ventures

Article 3(4)[97] provides that the creation of a JV constitutes a concentration only if the JV is jointly controlled by two or more undertakings and it is 'full-function'. The full-functionality criterion, which does *not* apply where joint control of an undertaking with market presence is *acquired* from a third party or parties,[98] requires that the JV is formed on a lasting basis to carry out the functions of an autonomous economic entity. It must therefore be autonomous from an operational point of view, have sufficient resources to operate independently on a market, and be intended to operate on a lasting basis.[99] It must have 'a management dedicated to its day-to day operations and access to sufficient resources including finance, staff, and assets (tangible and intangible) in order to conduct on a lasting basis its business activities within the area provided for in the joint-venture agreement'.[100] It will not be full-function if it simply takes over one specific function for its parents.

Jurisdictional Notice [2008] OJ C95/1

95. A joint venture is not full-function if it only takes over one specific function within the parent companies' business activities without its own access to or presence on the market. This is the case, for example, for joint ventures limited to R&D or production. Such joint ventures are auxiliary to their parent companies' business activities. This is also the case where a joint venture is essentially limited to the distribution or sale of its parent

---

[93] Notice on Simplified Procedure, para. 5(d), see Jurisdictional Notice, para. 84.

[94] See Section 3.C, p. 1109.

[95] See Chap. 10.

[96] Ibid.

[97] Old EUMR, Art. 3(2).

[98] Jurisdictional Notice, para. 91. But see, e.g., L. Rudolf and B. Leupold, 'Joint Ventures—The Relevance of the Full Functionality Criterion under the EU Merger Regulation' (2012) 3 *JECLAP* 439.

[99] Jurisdictional Notice, paras. 91–109.

[100] Ibid, para. 94.

companies' products and, therefore, acts principally as a sales agency. However, the fact that a joint venture makes use of the distribution network or outlet of one or more of its parent companies normally will not disqualify it as 'full-function' as long as the parent companies are acting only as agents of the joint venture.

96. A frequent example where this question arises are joint ventures involved in the holding of real estate property, which are typically set up for tax and other financial reasons. As long as the purpose of the joint venture is limited to the acquisition and/or holding of certain real estate for the parents and based on financial resources provided by the parents, it will not usually be considered to be full-function as it lacks an autonomous, long term business activity on the market and will typically also lack the necessary resources to operate independently. This has to be distinguished from joint ventures that are actively managing a real estate portfolio and who act on their own behalf on the market, which typically indicates full-functionality.

Another relevant factor in the determination of full-functionality may be whether the parent companies make sales or purchases to or from the JV. Where sales are made to the parent companies, the main issue to be determined is whether, regardless of these sales, the JV can play an active role on the market and be considered economically autonomous from an operational viewpoint.[101] Further, a JV is unlikely to be full-function where it operates like a joint sales agency purchasing from its parents and adding little value to the products or services concerned.[102]

The Jurisdictional Notice also states that the fact that the agreement contains a clause providing for the dissolution of the JV, for example on its failure or on disagreement between the parents, does not necessarily mean that the JV has not been established on a lasting basis. In addition, a JV created for a finite period but long enough to affect the structure of the market will also be established on a lasting basis, but one established for a short finite period will not.

Jurisdictional Notice [2008] OJ C95/1

103. Furthermore, the joint venture must be intended to operate on a lasting basis. The fact that the parent companies commit to the joint venture the resources described above normally demonstrates that this is the case. In addition, agreements setting up a joint venture often provide for certain contingencies, for example, the failure of the joint venture or fundamental disagreement as between the parent companies. This may be achieved by the incorporation of provisions for the eventual dissolution of the joint venture itself or the possibility for one or more parent companies to withdraw from the joint venture. This kind of provision does not prevent the joint venture from being considered as operating on a lasting basis. The same is normally true where the agreement specifies a period for the duration of the joint venture where this period is sufficiently long in order to bring about a lasting change in the structure of the undertakings concerned, or where the agreement provides for the possible continuation of the joint venture beyond this period.

104. By contrast, the joint venture will not be considered to operate on a lasting basis where it is established for a short finite duration. This would be the case, for example, where a joint venture is established in order to construct a specific project such as a power plant, but it will not be involved in the operation of the plant once its construction has been completed.

105. A joint venture also lacks the sufficient operations on a lasting basis at a stage where there are decisions of third parties outstanding that are of an essential core importance for starting the joint venture's business activity. Only decisions that go beyond mere formalities and the award of which is typically uncertain qualify for these scenarios. Examples are the award of a contract (e.g., in public tenders), licences (e.g., in the telecoms sector) or access rights to property (e.g., exploration rights for oil and gas). Pending the decision on such factors, it is unclear whether the joint venture will become operational at all. Thus, at that stage the joint venture cannot be considered to perform economic functions on a lasting basis and consequently does not qualify as full function. However, once a decision has been taken in favour of the joint venture in question, this criterion is fulfilled and a concentration arises.

---

[101] Ibid, paras. 98–100.
[102] Ibid, para. 97.

The Notice deals at paragraphs 106–109 with the position if the parents enlarge the scope of the JV's activities in the course of its lifetime. Such enlargement may constitute a concentration requiring notification, in particular where it entails the acquisition of the whole or part of another undertaking from the parents that would, considered in isolation, qualify as a concentration.

The Relevance of Coordination of Competitive Behaviour

The original EUMR provided that a JV which has as its object or effect the coordination of the competitive behaviour of undertakings which remain independent could not constitute a concentration. This *negative* condition was removed in 1997 so that the complex determination required by it no longer has to be made at the jurisdictional stage. It is still of importance, however, as a different *substantive* appraisal applies. Although the basic appraisal made in the case of each JV will be the same as in respect of all other concentrations, the coordinative aspects of JVs are assessed additionally for their compatibility with the internal market in accordance with the criteria set out in Article 101 TFEU.[103]

(iii) Article 3(5) and Warehousing Arrangements

Article 3(5) of the EUMR sets out several circumstances in which a concentration shall be deemed not to arise. These deal with shares held by financial institutions on a temporary basis, the acquisition of control by liquidators or other administrators, and operations carried out by financial holding companies.[104] It is unclear whether, and if so when, the exception for shares held by financial interests can apply to temporary shareholdings acquired in warehousing structures (where an ultimate purchaser seeking to acquire another does so through a third party, interim purchaser, which holds the shares on a temporary basis). The Commission's view, set out in the Jurisdictional Notice, is that such structures do not benefit from the exemption if the interim transaction forms part of a broader, single concentration,[105] that is where:

an undertaking is 'parked' with an interim buyer, often a bank, on the basis of an agreement on the future onward sale of the business to an ultimate acquirer. The interim buyer generally acquires shares 'on behalf' of the ultimate acquirer, which often bears the major part of the economic risks and may also be granted specific rights. In such circumstances, the first transaction is only undertaken to facilitate the second transaction and the first buyer is directly linked to the ultimate acquirer . . . no other ultimate acquirer is involved, the target business remains unchanged, and the sequence of transactions is initiated alone by the sole ultimate acquirer. . . . [T]he Commission will examine the acquisition of control by the ultimate acquirer, as provided for in the agreements entered into by the parties. The Commission will consider the transaction by which the interim buyer acquires control in such circumstances as the first step of a single concentration comprising the lasting acquisition of control by the ultimate buyer.[106]

Where the interim buyer's purchase forms part of the concentration with the ultimate acquirer, the EUMR's notification and suspensory provisions are therefore triggered.

Prior to the publication of the Jurisdictional Notice, however, in *Lagardère/Natexis/VUP*,[107] the Commission applied Article 3(5)(a) to a scenario in which Lagardère, the ultimate buyer, agreed to take the assets out of the hands of VUP and parked the shares with a bank prior to obtaining clearance for the transaction. Had the bank's acquisition formed part of the concentration between Lagardère and VUP there would have been a breach of the stand-still obligation. Éditions Odile, one of the competing bidders for VUP, brought an appeal before the GC and CJ. Neither the

---

[103] EUMR, Art. 2(4)(5), discussed in Section 5.E, pp. 1191–1194.
[104] Jurisdictional Notice, paras. 110–118.
[105] Ibid., para. 114.
[106] Ibid., para. 35.
[107] M.2978, 7 January 2004.

GC nor the CJ had to decide the warehousing point directly as it did not affect the legality of the Commission's clearance decision (this issue affected only the question of whether the suspensory obligation had been breached and whether the parties could have been fined).[108] Although the GC[109] indicated that Lagardère had not acquired control at the time of the bank's interim acquisition, as it could not exercise control over the target at this time, the CJ made it clear that these statements had not been necessary to the ruling but had merely 'been made for the sake of completeness'.[110] If the temporary and ultimate acquisitions of the shares do not form part of the same concentration, then, unless Article 3(5) applies, the interim transaction will constitute a separate concentration.

(iv) Abandonment of a Concentration

If the Commission initiates Phase II proceedings following notification of a concentration to it, it must close the proceeding by means of a decision adopted under Article 8 of the EUMR 'unless the undertakings concerned have demonstrated to the satisfaction of the Commission that they have abandoned the concentration'.[111] In *MCI WorldCom/Sprint*,[112] for example, the Commission issued a decision prohibiting a concentration even though the parties stated that they had abandoned the merger. On appeal, however, the GC annulled the Commission's decision, holding that the Commission had exceeded its powers by adopting a prohibition decision when the notifying parties had formally withdrawn their notification and informed it of the abandonment of the concentration in the form envisaged in the notification.

Where the Commission indicates that it is likely to prohibit a merger the reality is that the parties may prefer to abandon it rather than to receive a prohibition decision.[113] The Commission's Jurisdictional Notice now sets out guidance as to how the parties may demonstrate that the transaction has been abandoned. General guidance, set out in paragraphs 119–120, is followed by specific guidance of the type of proof that is required depending upon whether the original concentration takes the form of a binding agreement, a good faith intention to conclude an agreement, a public announcement of a public bid or of the intention to make a public bid, or an implemented concentration.

B. EU DIMENSION

(i) A Bright-Line Jurisdictional Test and Simplified Procedure

The concept of an EU dimension is designed to catch concentrations which create significant structural changes the impact of which extends beyond the national borders of any one Member State.[114] Broadly, whether or not a merger has an EU dimension is assessed by reference to the *turnover* of the parties involved.[115] Since the notification to the Commission of such concentrations is compulsory,

---

[108] Cases C-551, 553, and 554/10, *Éditions Odile Jacob v Commission* EU:C:2013:809, paras. 34–38.

[109] See Case T-279/04, *Éditions Odile Jacob v Commission* [2010] ECR II-185 on appeal, Cases C-551/10 etc., ibid., paras. 34–38.

[110] Cases C-551/10 etc., ibid., para. 40.

[111] EUMR, Art. 6(1)(c).

[112] M.1741, 28 June 2000, on appeal Case T-310/00, *MCI v Commission* [2004] ECR II-3253.

[113] See, e.g., M.7419, *TeliaSonera/Telenor/JV* (withdrawn) and speech of Commissioner Vestager, 'Competition in Telecoms Markets', 42nd Conference on International Antitrust Law and Policy, Fordham University, 2 October 2015.

[114] EUMR, recital 8.

[115] 'Turnover is used as a proxy for the economic resources being combined in a concentration, and is allocated geographically in order to reflect the geographic distribution of those resources', Jurisdictional Notice, para. 124.

the jurisdictional test incorporated within the EUMR is intended to be a bright-line test which can be applied relatively simply, objectively, and easily.[116]

The corollary of having a simple quantitative jurisdictional test is that:[117] jurisdiction over EU mergers is not always allocated appropriately as between the Commission and the Member States; and concentrations between undertakings which obviously will not raise competition problems may be brought within the regulation and subject to mandatory notification (the impact of the transaction on competition is relevant only to the substantive assessment).[118] In order to deal with these limitations the Commission has sought:

- to ensure that flexible mechanisms exist for referral of cases as between the Commission and national competition authorities (NCAs) where appropriate; and

- to reduce inconvenience and cost by introducing a simplified procedure for the treatment of concentrations that do not raise competition concerns.[119] In such cases it is possible to submit a short-form notification.[120] Where the Commission is satisfied that the concentration qualifies for the simplified procedure it normally adopts a short-form decision. In 2013 this procedure was extended to a greater category of 'non-problematic' mergers and the information requirements were reduced/streamlined. Commissioner Vestager stated that:

Around 10% of cases have moved from the normal procedure to the simplified procedure. Also, the pre-notification stage has become shorter for both normal and simplified cases. These are steps in the right direction.[121]

Nonetheless, the Commission is still considering how notification requirements can be further reduced, cutting costs and administrative burden for business.[122]

(ii) Article 1(2)

The primary test is that set out in Article 1(2). Only if this test is *not* satisfied is it necessary for an undertaking to consider whether or not the thresholds set out in Article 1(3) are satisfied.

Article 1

1. Without prejudice to Article 4(5) and Article 22, this Regulation shall apply to all concentrations with a Community dimension as defined in this Article.

2. A concentration has a Community dimension where:

    (a) the combined aggregate worldwide turnover of all the undertakings concerned is more than EUR 5,000 million; and

    (b) the aggregate Community-wide turnover of each of at least two of the undertakings concerned is more than EUR 250 million

    unless each of the undertakings concerned achieves more than two-thirds of its aggregate Community-wide turnover within one and the same Member State.

---

[116] In some States, jurisdiction may be determined by reference to the market shares of parties, see, e.g., Spain, and Portugal. In these States even the question of whether the merger should be notified may be a complex one to determine.

[117] It also catches some mergers between non-EU undertakings whose business is principally carried on outside the EU, see Section 8, p. 1203.

[118] For the view that because more than half of the mergers notified do not give rise to competition concerns at the EU level alternative jurisdictional delimitations should be considered, see M. Broberg, 'Improving the EU Merger Regulation's Delimitation of Jurisdiction: Re-defining the Notion of Union Dimension' (2014) 5 *JECLAP* 261.

[119] See n. 51.

[120] See Short Form for the notification of a concentration pursuant to Reg. 139/2004, attached to Reg. 802/2004.

[121] See speech by Commissioner Vestager, n. 89.

[122] See White Paper, n. 62.

This test looks to the combined worldwide turnover of the undertakings concerned and the EU-wide turnover of at least two of the undertakings involved in the concentration. Even where the thresholds are met, jurisdiction is denied if the *proviso* applies—if each of the undertakings concerned achieves more than two-thirds of its EU turnover within one and the same Member State. The purpose of the proviso is to exclude concentrations the effects of which are felt primarily in one Member State. The Commission has, however, had some concerns about the operation of the two-thirds rule, as it can mean that consolidations between large national players escape scrutiny under EU rules even though they produce effects on competition across the EU.[123] No change to this rule is currently envisaged however.

(iii) Article 1(3) of the EUMR

Although the Commission would have preferred (and has proposed) lower thresholds than those set out in Article 1(2),[124] the compromise eventually reached was to add Article 1(3).[125] This provides that a concentration which satisfies lower worldwide and EU-wide turnovers than those set out in Article 1(2) may be caught if two additional criteria are satisfied. Broadly, these aim to catch concentrations where the undertakings concerned, jointly and individually, have a minimum level of activities in three or more Member States and which are therefore likely to be subject to the merger rules of those three or more Member States.[126] Like Article 1(2), paragraph 3 contains a proviso excluding concentrations where two-thirds of the EU-wide turnover of all of the undertakings involved is achieved in one and the same Member State.[127]

Article 1(3)

A concentration that does not meet the thresholds laid down in paragraph 2 has a Community dimension where:

(a) the combined aggregate worldwide turnover of all the undertakings concerned is more than EUR 2 500 million;

(b) in each of at least three Member States, the combined aggregate turnover of all the undertakings concerned is more than EUR 100 million;

(c) in each of at least three Member States included for the purpose of point (b), the aggregate turnover of each of at least two of the undertakings concerned is more than EUR 25 million; and

(d) the aggregate Community-wide turnover of each of at least two of the undertakings concerned is more than EUR 100 million

unless each of the undertakings concerned achieves more than two-thirds of its aggregate Community-wide turnover within one and the same Member State.

---

[123] See Commission Report to Council on the functioning of Regulation 139/2004, COM(2009) 281 final, para. 16, Green Paper on Community Merger Control, COM(96) 19 final, para. 48, N. Kroes, SPEECH/06/60, Speech before the EP Economic and Monetary Affairs Committee, 31 January 2006. The Commission had been particularly concerned about the application of the two-thirds rule in cases arising in the energy sector, and as to whether some Member States have been willing to authorise mergers which may reduce competition within the EU on public policy grounds, see e.g., nn. 209–210 and text. The two-thirds rule can also mean that competing bids for a company are assessed under different regimes, see e.g.: Lloyds' bid for the take-over of Midland Bank (UK jurisdiction), HSBC's bid assessed under the EUMR, M.213, 21 May 1992; Gas Natural's (Spain's largest gas operator) bid for Spanish electricity operator, Endesa did not have an EU dimension because of the two-thirds rule (Endesa's appeal against the Commission's refusal to take jurisdiction was rejected, Case T-417/05, *Endesa v Commission* [2006] ECR II-2533) whilst E.ON's and ENEL/Acciona's bids did, see Cases M.4110 and M.4685 and discussion of cases at n. 201 and text.

[124] The original EUMR anticipated a review, and a lowering, of the thresholds by the end of 1993 but this was not done at this stage for fear of severe opposition from a number of Member States, including Germany, the UK, and France.

[125] Introduced by Council Reg. 1310/97.

[126] Reg. 1310/97 [1997] OJ L180/1, Art. 1(1)(a) and (b).

[127] See n. 129 and accompanying text.

(iv) Rethinking the Thresholds

Periodically the Commission has to report to the Council on the operation of the jurisdictional thresholds.[128] The Commission recognises that they are not perfect and, in particular, that a number of transactions with significant cross-border effects are not caught by them.[129] Although it has mooted change,[130] ultimately it has opted instead to focus on ensuring that simple and streamlined 'corrective' mechanisms operate to reallocate cases effectively where necessary.[131]

A further issue that has arisen is whether the Commission should be able to review deals where the target does not have a large turnover but the transaction value is high (see, for example, the merger between *Facebook/Whatsapp*).[132]

(v) Concentrations, Undertakings Concerned, and Calculation of Turnover

In order to apply the Article 1(2) and (3) tests, it is first necessary to identify the number of concentrations involved. In simple cases, such as the acquisition of B by A, there will usually be only one. In more complex cases, such as the division of an existing JV company between its parents, there may however be more than one concentration.[133] Once the appropriate concentration(s) is identified it is necessary to determine (a) the undertakings concerned and (b) their turnover. In spite of the aim of the Regulation to provide a clear, simple jurisdictional test these steps are not always straightforward. The meaning of 'undertakings concerned' and 'turnover' is consequently clarified in the Jurisdictional Notice.

The Notice seeks, guided by prior cases, to identify undertakings concerned in most typical situations. Paragraphs 134–153 provide detailed analysis of who the undertakings concerned are in acquisition of control cases (for example, acquisition of sole control, part or joint control change from joint to sole control or of controlling shareholders, etc.).

Jurisdictional Notice [2008] OJ C95/1

2. MERGERS

132. In the case of a merger, the undertakings concerned are the merging undertakings.

3. ACQUISITION OF CONTROL

133. In the remaining cases, it is the concept of 'acquiring control' that will determine which are the undertakings concerned. On the acquiring side, there can be one or more undertakings acquiring sole or joint control. On the acquired side, there can be one or more undertakings as a whole or parts thereof. As a general rule, each of these undertakings will be an undertaking concerned within the meaning of the Merger Regulation.

---

[128] The old EUMR, Art. 1(4).

[129] See, e.g., the Report to the Council on the application of the Merger Regulation Thresholds, COM(2000) 399 final.

[130] Green Paper on the Review of Council Regulation (EEC) No. 4064/89, COM(2001) 745/6 final, paras. 24–28.

[131] See, e.g., Commission Report to Council on the Functioning of Regulation 139/2004, COM(2009) 281 final.

[132] M.7217, 3 October 2014 (the transaction did not have an EU dimension because Whatsapp's turnover was too low but was referred to the Commission under EUMR, Art. 4(5) because the concentration was capable of notification in three or more Member States). See speech of Commissioner Vestager, n. 89. For the view that the notification thresholds should be reviewed more fundamentally, see e.g., Broberg, n. 118.

[133] See, e.g., M.197, *Solvay/LaPorte* [1992] OJ C165/26 (notification of the division of a JV, between the parties. The Commission concluded that this was two separate concentrations. The Solvay concentration had an EU dimension but the Laporte concentration did not).

Once the undertakings concerned have been identified their turnover must be calculated. Article 5(1) defines turnover as 'the amount derived by the undertakings concerned in the previous financial year from the sale of products and provision of services falling within the undertaking's ordinary activities' (i.e. net sales—ordinarily assessed from audited accounts from the last financial year).[134] Article 5(2) provides that where the concentration consists of an acquisition of part or parts, of one or more undertakings (such as a subsidiary or a division), only the turnover of the relevant parts which are the subject of the concentration shall be taken into account with regard to the seller or sellers.[135] Article 5(3) sets out special turnover rules which apply, for example, to credit and financial institutions and insurance undertakings. Article 5(4) provides (subject to Article 5(2)) that turnover is calculated by reference not only to those undertakings concerned but also to the turnover of all those entities which they control or by which they are controlled, and to other connected undertakings. The operation of Article 5(4) is explained in the Jurisdictional Notice.

Jurisdictional Notice [2008] OJ C95/1

175. Where an undertaking concerned by a concentration belongs to a group, not only the turnover of the undertaking concerned is considered, but the Merger Regulation requires to also take into account the turnover of those undertakings with which the undertaking concerned has links consisting in the rights or powers listed in Article 5(4) in order to determine whether the thresholds contained in Article 1 of the Merger Regulation are met. The aim is again to capture the total volume of the economic resources that are being combined through the operation irrespective of whether the economic activities are carried out directly by the undertaking concerned or whether they are undertaken indirectly via companies and undertakings with which the undertaking concerned possessed the links described in Article 5(4).

176. The Merger Regulation does not delineate the concept of a group in a single abstract definition, but sets out in Article 5(4)(b) certain rights or powers. If an undertaking concerned directly or indirectly has such links with other companies, those are to be regarded as part of its group for purposes of turnover calculation under the Merger Regulation.

177. Article 5(4) of the Merger Regulation provides the following:

Without prejudice to paragraph 2 [acquisition of parts], the aggregate turnover of an undertaking concerned within the meaning of Article 1(2) and (3) shall be calculated by adding together the respective turnovers of the following:

(a) the undertakings concerned;

(b) those undertakings in which the undertaking concerned directly or indirectly;

    (i) owns more than half the capital of business assets, or

    (ii) has the power to exercise more than half the voting rights, or

    (iii) has the power to appoint more than half the members of the supervisory board, the administrative board or bodies legally representing the undertakings, or

    (iv) has the right to manage the undertaking's affairs;

(c) those undertaking which have in an undertaking concerned the rights or powers listed in (b);

(d) those undertakings in which an undertaking as referred to in (c) has the rights or powers listed in (b);

(e) those undertakings in which two or more undertakings as referred to in (a) to (d) jointly have the rights or powers listed in (b).

An undertaking which has in another undertaking the rights and powers mentioned in Article 5(4) (b) will be referred to as the 'parent' of the latter in the present section of the Notice dealing with the calculation of turnover, whereas the latter is referred to as 'subsidiary' of the former. In short, Article 5(4)

---

[134] Jurisdictional Notice, paras. 157–174.

[135] Acquisitions of parts between the same persons or undertakings in a series of transactions within a two-year period are treated as one and the same concentration, EUMR, Art. 5(2).

therefore provides that the turnover of the undertaking concerned by the concentration (point (a)) should include its subsidiaries (point (b)), its parent companies (point (c)), the other subsidiaries of its parent undertakings (point (d)) and any other subsidiary jointly held by two or more of the undertakings identified under (a)–(d) (point (e)).

Note that with the aim of providing greater legal certainty, the definition of control in Article 5(4) is different from, and more tightly defined than, the definition of control set out in Article 3(2).[136] In general, the whole turnover of undertakings identified in Article 5 is taken into account. However, for JVs between two or more undertakings concerned, turnover of the JVs is apportioned equally amongst the undertakings concerned.[137] Further, in practice, the Commission allocates turnover for JVs between undertakings concerned and third parties on a per capita basis according to the number of undertakings exercising joint control.[138]

Examples

The following examples seek to clarify, through an examination of transactions carried out by entities within a larger group of companies, how Article 5 applies to identify the undertakings whose turnover is taken into account for the purposes of calculating EU dimension.

Group A

A is a wholly owned subsidiary of W. A has two wholly owned subsidiaries, X and Y. Y and a third party, TP, jointly control Z.

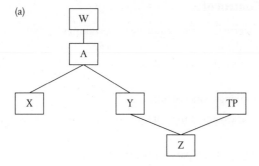

(a)

Group B

B is company jointly owned by J and K. K has a wholly owned subsidiary L. B has a wholly owned subsidiary, M.

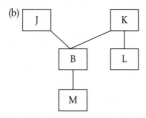

(b)

---

[136] Although the Commission invited comments as to whether the differences between the two meanings of control was problematic, no harmonisation of the rules was made, see 2001 Green Paper on the Review of Council Regulation (EEC) No. 4064/89, COM(2001) 745/6 final.

[137] EUMR, Art. 5(5)(b).

[138] Jurisdictional Notice, para. 187.

Group C

C is a company jointly controlled by D and E. E is a wholly owned subsidiary of F.

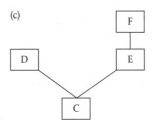

(c)

1. A Acquires B

The undertakings concerned are A and B.

The aggregate turnover for the purposes of Article 1(2) and (3) is calculated by adding together the respective turnovers of A, X, Y, Z (50 per cent), and W in Group A and B and M (in Group B) That is:

a. A and B (the undertakings concerned);

b. X, Y, and M (subsidiaries) and Z (half of the turnover, since it is a company jointly controlled with a third party);

c. W (A's parent) but not J and K (B's parents, because only an acquisition of part of seller (Article 5(2)).

2. C Acquires Sole Control of A

The undertakings concerned are the acquiring undertakings, C, and the target company, A. The aggregate turnover for the purposes of Article 1(2) and (3) is calculated by adding together the respective turnovers of C, D, E, and F in Group C and A, X, Y, and Z (50 per cent) in Group A. That is:

a. C and A (the undertakings concerned);

b. X and Y (the subsidiaries) and Z (half of the turnover, since it is a company jointly controlled with a third party);

c. D and E (C's parents) and F (C's parent's parent) but not W (A's parent because only an acquisition of part of seller (Article 5(2)).

3. J Acquires Sole Control of B (a Change from Joint Control with K to Sole Control by J)

The undertakings concerned are J and B. K, the existing shareholder (as seller) is not an undertaking concerned.

The aggregate turnover for the purposes of Article 1(2) and (3) is calculated by adding together the respective turnovers of J, B, and M. That is:

a. J and B (the undertakings concerned);

b. M (B's subsidiary). To avoid double counting the turnover of J has to be calculated without the turnover of the JV, B.[139]

---

[139] The turnover of B's parents are not included. K's turnover is excluded because it is an acquisition of part and to avoid double counting the turnover of the joint venture has to be taken without the turnover of the acquiring shareholder, J.

4. A and B Acquire joint Control of C

The undertakings concerned are A and B (the undertakings acquiring joint control) and C (the pre-existing acquired undertaking).

The aggregate turnover for the purposes of Article 1(2) and (3) is calculated by adding together the respective turnovers of A, X, Y, Z (50 per cent), and W in Group A; B, J, K, and L in Group B; and C in Group C. That is:

a. A, B, and C (the undertakings concerned);

b. X, Y, and M (the subsidiaries) and Z (half of the turnover, since it is a company jointly controlled with a third party);

c. W, J, and K (A and B's parents), but not D, E, or F (because only acquisition of part (Article 5(2));

d. L (a subsidiary of B's parent K).

C. CONCENTRATIONS WITH AN EU DIMENSION: A ONE-STOP SHOP?

(i) Exclusive Competence of the Commission under the EUMR

Article 21(1)–(3) provides:

1. This Regulation alone shall apply to concentrations as defined in Article 3, and Council Regulations (EC) No 1/2003, (EEC) No 1017/68, (EEC) No 4056/86 and (EEC) No 3597/87[140] shall not apply, except in relation to joint ventures that do not have a Community dimension and which have as their object or effect the coordination of competitive behaviour of undertakings that remain independent.

2. Subject to review by the Court of Justice, the Commission shall have sole jurisdiction to take the decisions provided for in this Regulation.

3. No Member State shall apply its national legislation on competition to any concentration that has a Community dimension . . .

Article 21 encompasses the 'one-stop shop' principle; the general rule is that the EUMR, and no other EU or national competition law, applies to concentrations with an EU dimension and the Commission has sole jurisdiction over such transactions. Further it sets out the general rule (combined with Article 1) that no EU competition law applies to concentrations that do not have an EU dimension.

(ii) Case Referrals

The financial criteria relevant to the assessment of an EU dimension generally serve as effective proxies for identifying transactions with an EU dimension. The EUMR jurisdictional mechanism is, however, flexible allowing cases to be referred to or from the Member States,[141] consistently with the principles of subsidiarity and one-stop shop appraisal for EU mergers.[142] The EUMR[143] thus provides

---

[140] Reg. 3597/87 has essentially been repealed by Reg. 411/2004 [2004] OJ L68/1.

[141] Commission Notice on Case Referral in respect of concentrations (Notice on case referral) [2005] OJ C56/2, para. 3.

[142] Ibid., para. 5.

[143] See also, e.g., Art. 346 TFEU, n. 187 and text.

for circumstances in which, at the initiative, or invitation, of the Commission, the Member State, or the parties:

- a concentration with an EU dimension, or aspects of it, may be referred to a national authority for assessment under its domestic law;
- a concentration without an EU dimension may be referred to the Commission.[144]

The Commission's Notice on Case Referral in respect of concentrations (the 'Notice on case referral')[145] describes the rationale underlying the system, provides practical guidance on its mechanics (including guiding principles and specific guidance on each provision) and best practices on cooperation and dialogue between the Commission and NCAs. In its 2014 White Paper[146] the Commission has proposed further modifications to the referral provisions to ensure its operates optimally.

Commission Notice on Case Referral in respect of concentrations [2005] OJ C56/2

Guiding principles

8. The system of merger control established by the Merger Regulation, including the mechanism for re-attributing cases between the Commission and Member States contained therein, is consistent with the principle of subsidiarity enshrined in the EC Treaty. Decisions taken with regard to the referral of cases should accordingly take due account of all aspects of the application of the principle of subsidiarity in this context, in particular the suitability of a concentration being examined by the authority more appropriate for carrying out the investigation, the benefits inherent in a 'one-stop shop' system, and the importance of legal certainty with regard to jurisdiction. These factors are inter-linked and the respective weight placed upon each of them will depend upon the specificities of a particular case. Above all, in considering whether or not to exercise their discretion to make or accede to a referral, the Commission and Member States should bear in mind the need to ensure effective protection of competition in all markets affected by the transaction.

More appropriate authority

9. In principle, jurisdiction should only be re-attributed to another competition agency in circumstances where the latter is the more appropriate for dealing with a merger, having regard to the specific characteristics of the case as well as the tools and expertise available to the agency. Particular regard should be had to the likely locus of any impact on competition resulting from the merger. Regard may also be had to the implications, in terms of administrative effort, of any contemplated referral.
10. The case for re-attributing jurisdiction is likely to be more compelling where it appears that a particular transaction may have a significant impact on competition and thus may deserve careful scrutiny.

One-stop shop

11. Decisions on the referral of cases should also have regard to the benefits inherent in a 'one-stop shop' system, which is at the core of the Merger Regulation. The provision of a one-stop shop is beneficial to competition authorities and businesses alike. The handling of a merger by a single competition agency normally increases administrative efficiency, avoiding duplication and fragmentation of enforcement

---

[144] And/or in which Arts. 101 and 102 can be applied to a concentration by the Commission itself or by a national court or NCA.

[145] [2005] OJ C56/2. See also 'Best Practices on Cooperation between the EU National Competition Authorities', available at <http://ec.europa.eu/competition/ecn/nca_best_practices_merger_review_en.pdf>.

[146] See n. 62.

effort as well as potentially incoherent treatment (regarding investigation, assessment and possible remedies) by multiple authorities. It normally also brings advantages to businesses, in particular to merging firms, by reducing the costs and burdens arising from multiple filing obligations and by eliminating the risk of conflicting decisions resulting from the concurrent assessment of the same transaction by a number of competition authorities under diverse legal regimes.

12. Fragmentation of cases through referral should therefore be avoided where possible, unless it appears that multiple authorities would be in a better position to ensure that competition in all markets affected by the transaction is effectively protected. Accordingly, while postal referrals are possible under Articles 4(4) and 9, it would normally be appropriate for the whole of a case (or at least all connected parts thereof) to be dealt with by a single authority.[147]

Legal certainty

13. Due account should also be taken of the importance of legal certainty regarding jurisdiction over a particular concentration, from the perspective of all concerned. Accordingly, referral should normally only be made when there is a compelling reason for departing from 'original jurisdiction' over the case in question, particularly at the post-notification stage. Similarly, if a referral has been made prior to notification, a post-notification referral in the same case should be avoided to the greatest extent possible.

14. The importance of legal certainty should also be borne in mind with regard to the legal criteria for referral, and particularly—given the tight deadlines—at the pre-notification stage. Accordingly, pre-filing referrals should in principle be confined to those cases where it is relatively straightforward to establish, from the outset, the scope of the geographic market and/or the existence of a possible competitive impact, so as to be able to promptly decide upon such requests.

Concentrations with an EU dimension, or aspects of such a concentration, may be dealt with by an NCA pursuant to Article 9 or Article 21(4) of the EUMR, Article 346 TFEU, or following a reasoned submission by a party to a concentration (Article 4(4)).

(iii) Article 9—Distinct Markets

a. Objective of Article 9

Article 21(3), paragraph 2 states that the prohibition on a Member State applying its national competition legislation to a concentration with an EU dimension is 'without prejudice to any Member State's power to carry out any enquiries necessary for the application of Articles 4(4), 9(2) or after referral, pursuant to Article 9(3) first subparagraph, indent (b), or Article 9(5), to take the measures strictly necessary for the application of Article 9(8)'.

Article 9 of the EUMR was included at the particular insistence of Germany (hence it is often known as the 'German clause'). Germany was initially opposed to the introduction of EU merger control and, in particular, it feared that the Commission's action might be less rigorous than national merger control and that local or regional issues might not be sufficiently addressed.[148] Article 9 was added at a late stage in the negotiations to meet the Germans' objections over loss of control. It provides for the referral, at the request of a national authority, of a merger, or aspects of it (i.e. total or partial referrals), to that authority where the concentration threatens competition in a 'distinct' market in that authority's State.

---

[147] See, e.g., M.2389, *Shell/DEA* 20 December 2001 and M.2533, *BP/E.ON* 20 December 2001 (referral to Germany of all of the markets for downstream oil products, 6 December 2001, but retention by the Commission of the parts of the cases involving upstream markets) and M.2706, *P&O Princess/Carnival* 24 July 2002 (Commission did not refer part of the case to the UK, because it wished to avoid a fragmentation of the case, see IP/02/552).

[148] EUMR, Art. 2 only permits the Commission to take action against concentrations which would impede competition in 'the common market or in a substantial part of it'.

The Notice on case referral recognises that the objective of Article 9 is to ensure, subject to the principle of the one-stop shop and legal certainty, that an NCA should deal with a case when it is in the best position to do so.[149]

b. The Article 9 Procedure

Council Regulation (EC) No. 139/2004 of 20 January 2004 on the Control of Concentrations between Undertakings [2004] OJ L24/1

Article 9

1. The Commission may, by means of a decision notified without delay to the undertakings concerned and the competent authorities of the other Member States, refer a notified concentration to the competent authorities of the Member State concerned in the following circumstances.

2. Within 15 working days of the date of receipt of the copy of the notification, a Member State, on its own initiative or upon the invitation of the Commission, may inform the Commission, which shall inform the undertakings concerned, that:

   (a) a concentration threatens to affect significantly competition in a market within that Member State, which presents all the characteristics of a distinct market, or

   (b) a concentration affects competition in a market within that Member State, which presents all the characteristics of a distinct market and which does not constitute a substantial part of the common market.

3. If the Commission considers that, having regard to the market for the products or services in question and the geographical reference market within the meaning of paragraph 7, there is such a distinct market and that such a threat exists, either:

   (a) it shall itself deal with the case in accordance with this Regulation, or

   (b) it shall refer the whole or part of the case to the competent authorities of the Member State concerned with a view to the application of that State's national competition law.

   If, however, the Commission considers that such a distinct market or threat does not exist, it shall adopt a decision to that effect which it shall address to the Member State concerned, and shall itself deal with the case in accordance with the Regulation.

   In cases where a Member State informs the Commission pursuant to paragraph 2(b) that a concentration affects competition in a distinct market within its territory that does not form a substantial part of the common market, the Commission shall refer the whole or part of the case relating to the distinct market concerned, if it considers that such a distinct market is affected.

Article 9 is not triggered unless a Member State makes a request, either on its own initiative or on the invitation of the Commission, for a reference back within 15 working days (WDs) of receipt of the copy of the notification from the Commission.

Where the Commission receives a request from a Member State in accordance with Article 9(2)(a), the Commission must determine whether the requesting State has prima facie demonstrated that (a) a distinct market exists[150] and (b) the concentration threatens to affect significantly competition

---

[149] Notice on case referral, paras. 9–13 and 37 and EUMR, recital 11.

[150] Whether a distinct market exists is determined with regard to the market for the products or services in question and, in particular, the geographical reference market; an area 'in which the undertakings concerned are involved in the supply and demand of products or services, in which the conditions of competition are sufficiently homogeneous and which can be distinguished from neighbouring areas because, in particular, conditions of competition are appreciably different in those areas', Art. 9(7).

within that Member State. Even where these conditions are satisfied, the Commission has a discretion to deal with the case itself rather than making a (total or partial[151]) referral.[152] It is only in
Article 9(2)(b)[153] cases where the Member State has provided preliminary evidence establishing that
the concentration affects competition in a distinct market which does not constitute a substantial
part of the internal market (markets with a narrow geographic scope)[154] that the Commission *must*
refer the whole or part of the case relating to the distinct market.

Article 9 thus concedes little authority to the Member States; except in Article 9(2)(b) cases, the
Commission is the arbiter of whether or not the matter should be referred to the Member State.
Nonetheless, the Commission and NCAs work together to ensure that their respective competences
are applied in close cooperation, 'using efficient arrangements for information-sharing and consultation, with a view to ensuring that a case is dealt with by the most appropriate authority, in the
light of the principle of subsidiarity and with a view to ensuring that multiple notifications of a given
concentration are avoided to the greatest extent possible'.[155] This means that in a majority of cases
a partial or full referral back is made after an Article 9 request (only around 10 per cent of requests
have been refused by the Commission).[156]

c. A Reference Back

The Commission's decision to refer, or not, must generally be taken within 35 WDs of notification,
or 65 WDs where Phase II proceedings have been initiated.[157] If the Commission does make a reference to the national authority that authority must decide the case 'without undue delay' and, in any
event, must inform the undertakings concerned of the result of the preliminary competition assessment and what further action it proposes to take within 45 WDs of the Commission's referral (or
national notification if requested).[158]

Insofar as a reference is made, the Commission delegates power to investigate the aspects of
the merger that affect competition in that distinct market. However, the Member State may only
take 'measures strictly necessary to safeguard or restore effective competition on the market
concerned'.[159]

d. Examples of Article 9 Decisions

Although a reference back under Article 9 is not guaranteed,[160] it may be likely to result in a case
(or aspects of it) being referred to a NCA where, for example, it raises specific issues in a Member
State[161] or regional[162] or local[163] markets. In *ProSiebenSat.1/RTL/JV*[164] the Commission even made a

---

[151] See M.180, *Steetley plc/Tarmac* discussed in n. 166 and accompanying text.

[152] EUMR, Art. 9(3). Notice on case referral [2005] OJ C56/2, para. 37.

[153] Notice on case referral, ibid., paras. 38–41.

[154] It is thus a relatively narrow provision. The first Art. 9(2)(b) reference made was M.2446, *Govia/Connex South Central* 20 July 2001. See also M.2730, *Connex/DNVBVG* 24 April 2001 and M.3130, *Arla Foods/Express Dairies* 10 June 2003.

[155] EUMR, recital 14.

[156] See <http://ec.europa.eu/competition/mergers/statistics.pdf>. Although, e.g., in 2013–2015, most Art. 9 requests were refused.

[157] EUMR, Arts. 9(4) and 10(1). See M.330, *McCormick/CPC/Ostmann* 29 October 1993.

[158] Ibid., Art. 9(6).

[159] Ibid., Art. 9(8).

[160] See, e.g., M.165, *Alcatel/AEG Kabel* 18 December 1991; M.238, *Siemens/Philips* (subsequently abandoned), M.7000, *Liberty Global/Ziggo* 25 June 2014, and M.7018 *Telefónica Deutschland/E-Plus* 30 January 2014.

[161] See, e.g., M.5996, *Thomas Cook/CGL and Midland* 6 January 2011.

[162] See, e.g., M.3373, *Accor/Barrière/Colony* 4 June 2004 and M.3905, *Tesco/Carrefour* 22 December 2005.

[163] See, e.g., M.2533, *BP/E.ON* 6 September 2001, and M.2730, *Connex/DNVBVG* 24 April 2001.

[164] M.5881, 24 September 2010.

partial reference back of aspects of the concentration to *two* authorities—the German and Austrian agencies—who it considered were well placed to investigate the impact of the transaction in their respective national markets.

In many cases a decision to make a reference to a national authority may cause concern to the notifying parties as the reference is unlikely to be requested unless the concentration is considered to pose particular risks for the distinct national market affected.[165]

The first case in which the Commission agreed to make a reference back was *Steetley plc/Tarmac*.[166] In this case competing bids had been made for Steetley plc by Tarmac and Redland. Only the Tarmac bid had an EU dimension (the Redland bid fell to be assessed in the UK).[167] This concentration would have pooled the building materials activities of the undertakings and conferred very high market shares on the merged entity for bricks and clay tiles in some regions of England. The Commission accepted that the concentration would lead to particular local problems in the market for the manufacture and sale of bricks in the north-east and south-west of England and in relation to the manufacture of clay tiles throughout Great Britain.[168] As the brick markets were regional and trade flows in clay tiles between Great Britain and the rest of the EU were low, the economic implications were substantially limited to the UK. The Commission issued a decision referring these aspects of the merger back to the UK and a decision finding that the remaining aspects of the concentration were compatible with the internal market.[169]

An Article 9 case which provides an illustration of the difficulties that can result from dual scrutiny in derogation of the one-stop shop principle is *SEB/Moulinex*.[170] This case concerned a proposal by SEB to purchase Moulinex, which was in the midst of bankruptcy proceedings. Both companies were French and operated in the small household electrical appliances business. The Commission appraised the concentration insofar as it affected 14 countries,[171] but made a partial reference to the French authorities (under Article 9(2)(a)) as the primary effects of the merger were to be felt in France. Although the Commission cleared the merger subject to commitments (rejecting the failing firm defence[172]), the French authorities went on to unconditionally clear the merger, applying its 'failing firm' defence, even though the combined entity would achieve an average of 60–70 per cent market share on segments of the French small electrical household appliances market.

Two competitors of the parties, BaByliss and Royal Philips, challenged the decisions. The challenge to the Commission's appraisal of the aspects of the transaction it considered was successful, but the appeal against its decision to refer the concentration to the national authority was not.[173]

---

[165] See M.2044, *Interbrew/Bass* [2000] OJ C293/11, in the UK, Interbrew SA and Bass plc: *A report on the acquisition by Interbrew SA of the brewing interests of Bass plc* (Cm. 5014, 2001). But see M.460, *Holdercim/Cedest* [1994] OJ C211/5, (the French authorities cleared aspects of a concentration which had been referred to it under Art. 9), M.3130, *Express Dairies/Arla Foods* 10 June 2003 (cleared by the UK authorities: DTI Press Release, 15 October 2003), M.4298, *Aggregate Industries/Foster Yeoman* (the OFT accepted undertakings from the parties in lieu of a reference to the Competition Commission), and discussion of *SEB/Moulinex* in n. 180 and accompanying text.

[166] M.180, 12 February 1992. A number of Art. 9 referrals have involved the building or construction industries, see also, e.g., M.4298, *Aggregate Industries/Foster Yeoman* 6 September 2006.

[167] Then the UK's Fair Trading Act 1973 (FTA) (the provisions have, however, now been repealed and replaced by the Enterprise Act 2002, Part 3).

[168] The Commission also considered the fact that a competing bid was being assessed at the domestic level.

[169] M.180, 12 February 1992, [1992] OJ C50/25.

[170] M.2621, IP/02/22.

[171] Ibid., annulled on appeal Case T-119/02, *Royal Philips Electronics v Commission* [2003] ECR II-1433 (insofar as it had cleared the concentration without commitments in five Member States). The Commission subsequently reopened the case and again cleared it unconditionally.

[172] Ibid. For a discussion of the failing firm defence, see Section 5.D.vii, pp. 1168–1172. The next application for an Art. 9 reference by the French authorities was rejected, see M.2978, *Lagardère/Natexis/VUP*, IP/03/808.

[173] Case T-119/02, *Royal Philips Electronics v Commission* [2003] ECR II-1433.

The GC was not at liberty to rule on the compatibility of the French authority's decision with the Commission's approval decision (or with EU law), *only* on whether the Commission was entitled to refer the concentration to the French authorities, i.e. whether the conditions of Article 9(2)(a) were satisfied and, if so, whether the Commission had properly exercised its discretion. The Court held that the Commission was not entitled to make such a reference where the authority was not capable of acting so as to maintain or restore effective competition or if the reference would undermine the Commission's decision, including commitments, in respect of the parts not referred back. However, this determination had to be made at the time the reference back decision was made and not with the benefit of hindsight and the result of national proceedings. The fact that the referral fragmented the examination of the concentration and interfered with the one-stop shop principle did not affect the conclusion since 'a fragmented assessment undermining the "one-stop shop" principle is inherent in the referral procedure'.[174]

The surprising outcome in this case was, therefore, that—despite the objectives of Article 9 (to allow Member States to look at mergers where the effects are likely to be particularly acute in the national market)—'in contrast to the Commission, which approved the concentration in question only after the commitments relating to the Moulinex trade market had been offered, the French competition authorities . . . approved the concentration with respect to its effects on the relevant markets in France without imposing commitments relying on the "failing firm" doctrine'.[175] Eventually, however, the French administrative court (Conseil d'Etat)[176] annulled the French authorities' authorisation of the merger, holding that the failing firm conditions had not in fact been fulfilled.

The Commission has to exercise its discretion carefully, if it is not to rob the one-stop shop principle of its substance and add to the length and cost of the review unnecessarily;[177] and the GC has made it clear that such references should only be made in exceptional circumstances.[178] In a series of cases the Commission has made it clear that it will be reluctant to make references back in the telecommunications sector, given the importance of that sector and movements in it to development of competition in the EU.[179] In particular, it considers it is better placed to deal with cases in the mobile sector because of its experience in assessing such mergers and the need for a consistent application of merger control rules.[180]

(iv) Article 4(4) Request for Referral to a National Competition Authority

Article 4(4) (discussed in Section 4) allows notifying parties, instead of notifying a concentration with an EU dimension to the Commission, to make a reasoned submission that a concentration may significantly affect competition in a distinct market in a Member State and should be examined in whole or in part by that Member State. In contrast with an Article 9 request it is thus lodged *by* the parties themselves and *prior* to notification.

---

[174] Ibid., para. 355. See also Cases T-346 and 347/02, *Cableuropa v Commission* [2005] ECR II-4251.

[175] Case T-119/02, *Royal Philips Electronics v Commission* [2003] ECR II-1433, para. 345.

[176] No. 249627, 6 February 2004.

[177] [2005] OJ C56/2.

[178] Case T-119/02, *Royal Philips Electronics v Commission* [2003] ECR II-1433.

[179] See, e.g., M.7000, *Liberty Global/Ziggo* 25 June 2014.

[180] The Commission rejected Germany's request to review the merger between Telefónica and E-Plus, see M.7018, *Telefónica Deutschland/E-Plus* 30 January 2014.

(v) Article 21(4)—Legitimate Interests

Article 21(4) recognises that there are some matters which are so sensitive to the national interest that the Member States should be entitled to retain control over them. Under Article 21(4), a Member State may take steps to protect 'legitimate interests' not protected under the EUMR itself:

Notwithstanding paragraphs 2 and 3, Member States may take appropriate measures to protect legitimate interests other than those taken into consideration by this Regulation and compatible with the general principles and other provisions of EU law.

Public security, plurality of the media and prudential rules shall be regarded as legitimate interests within the meaning of the first subparagraph.

Any other public interest must be communicated to the Commission by the Member State concerned and shall be recognised by the Commission after an assessment of its compatibility with the general principles and other provisions of EU law before the measures referred to above may be taken. The Commission shall inform the Member State concerned of its decision within 25 working days of that communication.

A few important points about Article 21(4) should be noted.

First, to date, it has only been used defensively—to enable a Member State to protect its legitimate interests by scrutinising, and, if necessary, *prohibiting* mergers which raise concerns other than pure competition ones (even were the Commission to consider that the merger was compatible with the internal market). It does not seem to allow a Member State to act, as it can where the EUMR does not apply,[181] to authorise a merger on public interest grounds (even if it is problematic from a competition perspective).[182]

Secondly, in cases of uncertainty as to whether one of the recognised legitimate interests set out in Article 21(4) applies, whether such measures conform with EU law,[183] or where a Member State wishes to act to protect '[a]ny other public interest', the Member State must notify it to the Commission.[184] The Commission may thus consider whether the narrow criteria of Article 21(4) are satisfied. Not only does it require that, if the interest to be protected is not one of the recognised interests, it must be a 'public' interest which is not protected by the EUMR itself (it is not a 'competition' interest), but, crucially, that measures taken are compatible with EU law, particularly the rules on freedom of establishment and free movement of capital, Articles 49 and 63 TFEU. These provisions impose substantial constraints on the ability of a Member State to impose 'restrictions' on free movement, for example through prohibiting, submitting to conditions, or prejudicing, investments through shareholding, mergers, and acquisitions. Such measures are incompatible with EU law unless the Member State can show that the measure is both: (a) justifiable, either on the basis of one of the specific Treaty-based exceptions or the Court-recognised justifications—the overriding requirements of public interest; and (b) proportionate.[185]

An inextricable and important link thus exists between 'legitimate interests', within the meaning of Article 21(4), and the exceptions and justifications that apply to the free movement of capital and freedom of establishment rules. If the national rules 'restrict' free movement of capital and/or freedom of establishment and do not fall within one of the exceptions or justifications to those rules, it will not be permitted under Article 21(4); the legitimate interest pursued must therefore constitute a valid public interest justification within the meaning of those free movement rules. The close link between the concept of legitimate interest under Article 21(4) and the free movement provisions is reinforced by the fact that the recognised interests (public security,

---

[181] See nn. 208–209 and text.

[182] This is the Commission's view and is consistent with case law holding that the principle of supremacy of EU law precludes a Member State from authorising a transaction which has been prohibited under the EU Treaty competition provisions, see Jones and Davies, n. 26.

[183] See, e.g., M.1616, *BSCH/A.Champaliaud* [1999] OJ C306/37, para. 66.

[184] EUMR, Art. 21(4) and M.1616, ibid., para. 27.

[185] See Jones and Davies, n. 26.

plurality of the media, and prudential rules) are concepts whose specific meaning have been developed under that law.

In a number of cases the Commission has accepted that Member States may take action to: protect defence policy or military security[186] (the Member States also have a general right, set out in Article 346 TFEU, to act to protect national security[187]); maintain diversified sources of information, plurality of opinion, and a multiplicity of views in media markets;[188] or safeguard 'prudential rules' (aiming to ensure, for example, capital adequacy requirements (solvency) and the good repute and honesty of those running the company concerned).[189] In *Newspaper Publishing*,[190] for example, although the proposed acquisition of Newspaper Publishing plc (publisher of the *Independent*) by Promotora de Informaciones SA, Editoriale l'Espresson SpA, and Mirror Group Newspapers plc fell within the scope of the EUMR, the UK was able to take steps to protect its legitimate interests, in this case the plurality of the media.[191] Any measures adopted by the UK authorities had, however, to be objectively the least restrictive to achieve the end pursued (to comply with the EU principle of proportionality). In *Thomson CSF/Racal (II)*[192] the UK authorities also stated an intention to consider the public security aspects of a concentration impacting on 'defence electronics' markets under Article 21(4) and in *Sun Alliance/Royal Insurance*[193] the Commission accepted that the UK authorities could apply UK insurance legislation to the transaction.

By analogy with the free movement rules, it also seems that public security would encompass proportionate measures to counter a genuine and sufficiently serious threat to the security of supplies of a product or service which is of fundamental importance for the existence of, or survival of those in, that Member State (such as oil, gas, water, electricity, telecommunications)[194] or of vital or

---

[186] See, e.g., M.1858, *Thomson CSF/Racal (II)* 15 June 2000 (impacting on defence electronics markets), M.336, *IBM France/CGI* 19 May 1993 (involving IT businesses, including hardware, software, and services), M.3418, *General Dynamics/Alvis* 26 May 2004 (involving British armoured combat vehicles), M.3720, *BAE Systems/AMS* 14 March 2005 (involving defence and commercial aerospace systems and BAE's communications and avionics business), and M.4561, *GE/Smiths Aerospace* 23 April 2007 (involving Smiths Groups' aerospace division).

[187] EUMR, recital 19 makes it clear that the Regulation (and in particular Art. 21(4)) does not affect a Member State's ability to act under Art. 346 TFEU. A list of arms referred to by Art. 346 TFEU was adopted by the Council (Decision 255/58), see Bellamy and Child (V. Rose and D. Bailey, eds.), *European Union Law of Competition* (7th edn, Oxford University Press, 2013), Vol. II, A7. When acting under Art. 346 TFEU, Member States, instead of acting in addition to the Commission under the EUMR (as is the case under EUMR, Art. 21(4)), have generally instructed firms not to notify the exclusively military aspects of the deal to the Commission at all, see e.g., M.528, *British Aerospace/VSEL* 24 November 1994 and M.529, *GEC/VSEL* 7 December 1994. If the Commission considers that a Member State is making improper use of these powers it may take the matter directly before the Court under Art. 348 TFEU.

[188] See, e.g., M.423, *Newspaper Publishing* 14 March 1984 and M.5932, *NewsCorp/BSkyB* 21 December 2010, paras. 304–309.

[189] See the Commission's Notes on Council Regulation (EEC) 4064/89, available at <http://ec.europa.eu/competition/mergers/legislation/notes_reg4064_89_en.pdf> (prudential interests should be understood to cover, e.g., measures to ensure the good repute of individuals managing such undertakings, the honesty of transactions, and the rules of solvency) and M.1724, *BSCH/A.Champalimaud* 20 July 1999, para. 36 (EU harmonising provisions should also be taken into account to determine the EU notion of prudential interest which should include interests protected by harmonising directives).

[190] M.423, 14 March 1984.

[191] A number of States consider that media ownership may require a different approach from that ordinarily applicable in domestic competition law.

[192] M.1858, 15 June 2000. See also, e.g., M.4561, *GE/Smiths Group* 23 April 2007 where the Commission approved GE's proposed acquisition of Smiths Group's aerospace division. The UK Secretary of State intervened under EUMR, Art. 21(4), IP/2007/60 but eventually accepted undertakings from the parties relating to the protection of sensitive information rather than referring it to the UK's Competition Commission.

[193] M.759, [1996] OJ C225/12.

[194] See Case 72/83, *Campus Oil* [1984] ECR 2727. In M.567, *Lyonnaise des Eaux SA/Northumbrian Water Group* [1996] OJ C11/3, for example, the Commission accepted, following a notification from the UK, the right for the UK authorities to apply the provisions of the Water Industry Act to the concentration to protect public security. Contrast M.1346, *Edf/London Electricity* 27 January 1999 (no need for a derogation under Art. 21(4), IP/99/49).

essential interest for the population's health.[195] In *Lyonnaise des Eaux SA/Northumbrian Water Group*,[196] for example, the Commission accepted that the regulation of the UK water industry constituted a legitimate interest. In accepting the legitimate interests of the UK, however, the Commission stressed that the UK authorities should not, in their scrutiny of the concentration, take account of factors properly falling for assessment by the Commission.[197]

Thirdly, although, to ensure the *effet utile* of the EUMR, non-recognised interests must be notified to the Commission, in some cases Members States have not complied with the notification and stand-still obligation in circumstances where the Commission believes that the conditions of Article 21(4) are not satisfied. An important ruling therefore is *Portuguese Republic v Commission*,[198] where the Court confirmed that, even if no communication is made by the Member State to the Commission, the Commission is still entitled to adopt a decision under Article 21 assessing whether measures taken by a Member State are compatible with Article 21(4) and requiring a Member State to withdraw measures which it finds are not. Otherwise, Member States could easily avoid the scrutiny of the Commission and national measures could irretrievably prejudice a merger with an EU dimension.[199]

In practice, therefore, where the Commission believes that a Member State has violated the exclusivity provisions of the EUMR, it communicates this preliminary view to the Member State and gives it a chance to respond, before issuing an Article 21 decision.[200] For example, it went into battle with the Spanish authorities over their actions in relation to competing bids for Spanish electricity operator, Endesa. The background to the case was that the Commission had cleared E.ON's and ENEL/Acciona's respective bids under the EUMR[201] (a third bid (which was supported by the Spanish Government) by Spanish Gas Natural, did not have an EU dimension and was appraised by the Spanish competition authorities). Nonetheless, the Spanish authorities imposed conditions on the potential investors under regulatory powers. In its Article 21 EUMR decisions,[202] the Commission found that the actions were not justified by a need to protect the security of supply risks alleged and were contrary to the capital and establishment provisions and required Spain to withdraw them without delay.[203] Public security could be relied on only if there were a genuine and sufficiently serious threat to a fundamental interest of society, for example if measures were necessary to ensure a minimum level of energy supplies in the event of a crisis. As the measures were not withdrawn, the Commission eventually brought enforcement proceedings against Spain under Article 258 TFEU; the Court confirmed that, by not withdrawing conditions to the E.ON merger, Spain had failed to fulfil its Treaty obligations.[204]

---

[195] See the Commission's Notes on Council Regulation (EEC) 4064/89, n. 189.

[196] M.567, [1996] OJ C11/3. Following the privatisation of the UK water industry, the water authority in the UK seeks to maintain competitive pressures on water suppliers (which enjoy a monopoly in the provision of local or regional services) by making comparisons of, for example, the relative operating and capital costs of the different water enterprises. In order to achieve this task a sufficient number of independent providers must be maintained. Contrast M.1346, *EDF/London Electricity* 27 January 1999.

[197] M.567, [1996] OJ C11/3.

[198] Case C-42/01, *Portuguese Republic v Commission* [2004] ECR I-6079.

[199] Ibid., para. 55.

[200] 'Our line is clear: if interference by any Member State—is not justified by a legitimate public interest, the Commission will continue to condemn such national measures': SPEECH/07/301, N. Kroes, 'European competition policy facing a renaissance of protectionism—which strategy for the future?', Speech to the St Gallen International Competition Law Forum, 11 May 2007. Where a Member State fails to comply with this decision, the Commission may bring proceedings under Art. 258 for failure to fulfil their Treaty obligations, see e.g. n. 204 and text.

[201] Cases M.4110 and M.4197, *E.ON/Endesa* 25 April 2006, 26 September, and 20 December 2006, Case T-200/06, *Iberdrola v Commission* (appeal withdrawn) and M.4685, *ENEL/Acciona/Endesa* 5 July 2007.

[202] See *E.ON/Endesa* ibid. (decisions in September and December 2006) and *ENEL/Acciona/Endesa* ibid. (decision in December 2007, IP/07/1858, Case T-65/08, *Spain v Commission* [2008] ECR II-69 (application withdrawn)).

[203] 26 September 2006.

[204] Case C-196/07, *Commission v Spain* [2008] ECR I-41 and see n. 200. Eventually the ENEL/Acciona bid did prevail.

In *BSCH/A.Champalimaud*,[205] the Commission also found that Portugal had improperly applied Article 21(4) of the EUMR to a transaction, this time in the insurance sector. In this case the Portuguese Minister of Finance relied on measures restricting a foreign firm from acquiring in excess of 20 per cent of domestic insurance firms to prohibit a proposed concentration with an EU dimension between Banco Santander Central Hispano (BSCH), a Spanish banking group, and Champalimaud (which was ultimately cleared by the Commission). The Portuguese authorities had not communicated any public interest to the Commission but in press statements had stated that they had acted to protect national interests and strategic sectors for the national economy. The Commission considered that the Government should have notified its actions to it and that the protection of national interests and strategic sectors for the national economy could not constitute a legitimate interest within the meaning of Article 21(4). Further, it entertained considerable doubt as to whether the actions were really based on prudential rules rather than constituting a discriminatory measure designed to prevent the opening of the financial services sector to non-nationals. The Commission thus ordered the Republic of Portugal to suspend the measures adopted and to notify them to it as required. In the end, the Portuguese authorities agreed to modified arrangements which were also cleared by the Commission under the EUMR.

Following the *Champalimaud* case, then Competition Commissioner Mario Monti stressed the importance of the Commission's intervention in this case to the safeguarding of the internal market and that it should serve as a reminder that Member States should not try and prevent the opening of their markets to non-nationals and that operations which did not raise competition concerns should in principle be able to proceed.[206]

The discussion above indicates that although there have been a number of cases in which Member State have successfully relied on recognised interests to scrutinise a merger for its impact on non-competition factors, recognition of other legitimate interests have been rare.

D. CONCENTRATIONS WITHOUT AN EU DIMENSION

(i) National Law Applies

Article 21(1) provides that the EUMR alone applies to 'concentrations' and disapplies Regulation 1/2003 and the other implementing regulations that confer power on the Commission and NCAs to implement Articles 101 and 102. The general principle is thus that national competition law *only* applies to concentrations which do not have an EU dimension.[207]

The application of national merger rules must, however, be compatible with EU law more generally, and must not impose restrictions on freedom of establishment and free movement of capital unless justifiable and proportionate (see the discussion in the section on Article 21(4) above).[208] The free movement rules are, however, triggered only by restrictions and do not, therefore, appear to preclude a Member State from, for example, exercising regulatory *approval* of mergers between domestic companies on public interest grounds (as is permitted in a number of Member States), even

---

[205] See Cases M.1616, M.1680, and M.1724, *BSCH/A.Champaliaud* (1999), IP/99/669, IP/99/772, IP/99/774 and IP/99/818, IP/00/296 (withdrawing the EUMR, Art. 21 proceedings).

[206] See also, e.g., *Cimpor*, C(2000)3543 Final (challenge to the actions of Portugal, in relation to a proposed acquisition of Portuguese cement business, Cimpor, a former State-owned entity) and M.3894, *Unicredito/HVB*, IP/05/1299 (infringement of Art. 21 by Poland in relation to a merger which had been cleared by the Commission but in which the Polish Treasury Minister intervened in order to protect the 'privatisation' process of Polish banks and to ensure the de-monopolisation of, and the protection of competition in, the financial and banking services, M.4125, IP/06/277).

[207] The prohibition, in Art. 21(3), on a Member State applying its national legislation on competition applies only where the concentration has an EU dimension. But see discussion in Section 3.E, p. 1122 on the residual role of Arts. 101 and 102 TFEU.

[208] See Jones and Davies, n. 26.

if the application of such rules might result in the creation of a national champion at the expense of competition and the interest of consumer welfare within the EU. Indeed, there has been concern in some cases that Member States may have applied national law to permit mergers without an EU dimension (most likely because of the two-thirds rules) which are nonetheless liable to harm competition throughout the EU.

For example, the German Government's decision to overrule the decision of the German NCA and authorise a merger between energy companies E.ON/Ruhrgas[209] and the creation of a national champion, caused considerable consternation and anxiety. Further, during the 2008 financial crisis, the UK Government stepped in to support and permit a merger which did not have an EU dimension (and so fell to be assessed under UK merger rules) between Lloyds TSB and HBOS.[210] Controversially, the Government considered that the public interest in the stability of the UK financial system outweighed the concerns of the competition agency that the merger might substantially lessen competition in relation to banking services and the provision of mortgages in the UK.

(ii) Joint Ventures

Article 21(1) itself makes it clear that there is an exception, for full-function JVs with coordinative aspects, to the general position that no EU competition law applies to concentrations which do not have an EU dimension.[211]

(iii) Article 22, Referrals to the Commission

a. Background

Article 22, known as the 'Dutch clause',[212] also derogates from the general rule that concentrations without an EU dimension are appraised only at the national level:

1. One or more Member States may request the Commission to examine any concentration as defined in Article 3 that does not have an EU dimension within the meaning of Article 1 but affects trade between Member States and threatens to significantly affect competition within the territory of the Member State or States making the request.

Such a request shall be made at most within 15 working days of the date on which the concentration was notified, or if no notification is required, otherwise made known to the Member State concerned.

The Article provides a mechanism by which a Member State can ask the Commission to apply the provisions of the EUMR to a concentration which does not have an EU dimension but which, nonetheless, affects trade between Member States and where it has been prima facie established that the concentration significantly affects competition within the territory of the requesting State.[213] Although the original provision was included to enable Member States without merger control rules to refer particularly troublesome concentrations, from a competition perspective, to the Commission,[214] 27 of the 28 Member States now have merger

---

[209] See, e.g., NERA Energy Regulation Brief, <http://www.nera.com/extImage/5483.pdf>.

[210] 31 October 2008, see OFT, *Anticipated acquisition by Lloyds TSB plc of HBOS plc Report to the Secretary of State for Business Enterprise and Regulatory Reform* (2008).

[211] See Chap. 10.

[212] The clause having been inserted at the request of the Dutch.

[213] Notice on case referral, paras. 42–45.

[214] Indeed three of the first four Art. 22 references were made by Member States which did not have merger control rules and all three of these concentrations were prohibited by the Commission, see M.553, *RTL/Veronica/Endemol* [1996] OJ L294/14 (*aff'd* Case T-221/95, *Endemol Entertainment Holding BV v Commission* [1999] ECR II-1299), M.784, *Kesko/Tuko* [1997] OJ L174/47 (request by the Finnish NCA. The Commission prohibited the concentration and, as the acquisition had already taken place, ordered Kesko to divest itself of the Tuko business, *aff'd* Case T-22/99, *Kesko Oy v Commission* [1999] ECR II-3775), and M.890, *Blokker/Toys'R'Us* [1998] OJ L316/1. The fourth was made

control rules.[215] Consequently the provision is most likely to be used for cases which are primarily of EU interest which cannot adequately be dealt with under national law; particularly where the Commission is better placed to review its cross-border effects. *Promatech SpA/Sulzer AG*[216] was the first case of a joint referral to the Commission made by the authorities of Spain, Italy, the UK, Germany, France, Portugal, and Austria and a number of joint referrals have been made subsequently, see for example, *GEES/Unison*,[217] *GE/AGFA NDT*,[218] *Omya/Huber*,[219] *Caterpillar/MWM*,[220] and *Sara Lee (Insecticides and Airfresheners)*.[221] The Commission states that referrals should only be made where specific criteria are met:

45. As post-notification referrals to the Commission may entail additional cost and time delay for the merging parties, they should normally be limited to those cases which appear to present a real risk of negative effects on competition and trade between Member States, and where it appears that these would be best addressed at the EU level. The categories of cases normally most appropriate for referral to the Commission pursuant to Article 22 are accordingly the following:

— Cases which give rise to serious competition concerns in a market/s which is/are wider that national in geographic scope, or where some of the potentially affected markets are wider than national, and where the main economic impact of the concentration is connected to such markets.

— Cases which give rise to serious competition concerns in a series of national or narrower than national markets located in a number of countries of the EU, in circumstances where coherent treatment (regarding possible remedies but also, in appropriate cases, the investigative efforts as such) is considered desirable, and where the main economic impact of the concentration is connected to such markets.

b. The Article 22 Procedure

A Member State making an Article 22 request, on its own initiative or at the invitation of the Commission, must do so within 15 WDs of the date on which the concentration was notified, or otherwise made known, to it. The procedure does not, therefore, prevent the parties from having to make national notifications (and perhaps multiple ones) prior to the request or requests being made.[222]

Where a request is made by a Member State under Article 22, the Commission must inform the competent authorities of all the Member States and the undertakings concerned of the request without delay. At this time all applicable national time limits are suspended and, to the extent that the concentration has not been implemented, the suspensory provisions in Article 7 apply.[223] Once such a notice is received the other Member States have 15 WDs to decide if they would like to join the initial request. If a Member State decides not to join the request and informs the Commission the suspension of its national time limit ends.

by Belgium which wished the Commission to intervene in the *British Airways/Dan Air* merger (M.278, 17 February 1993, cleared unconditionally). The Belgian authorities did not have jurisdiction to preclude a merger between two UK companies.

[215] Only Luxembourg does not have merger control rules.

[216] M.2698, IP/02/1140.

[217] M.2738, *GEES/Unison*, IP/02/578 (referral requests from the authorities of Germany, France, Spain, Italy, the UK, and Greece—the merger was cleared by the Commission on 14 April 2002).

[218] M.3136, *GE/AGFA NDT*, IP/03/1666 (Art. 6 clearance subject to conditions and obligations).

[219] M.3796, IP/06/1017.

[220] M.6106, 26 January 2011 (full referral), 19 October 2011.

[221] Cases M.5969, 9 May 2011 and M.5828, 31 March and 17 June 2010. As the Commission has cleared a number of these unconditionally it has been speculated that the Commission may be accepting these requests too readily and where the exceptional circumstances envisaged by Art. 22 do not exist, see, e.g., G. Drauz, S. Mavroghenis, and S. Ashall, 'Recent Developments in EU Merger Control' (2012) 3 *JECLAP* 52, 65.

[222] But see Art. 4(5) (enabling parties to make a reasoned submission to the Commission *prior* to notification at the national level), discussed in Section 4.B, p. 1125.

[223] See Section 4.C, p. 1126.

Within 25 WDs of informing the Member States and undertakings of the initial request, the Commission may decide to examine the concentration (if it does not adopt a decision within this time period it is deemed to accept the request). If it does accept the request the referring Member States retain no control over the Commission's investigation[224] and they may no longer apply their national competition rules (jurisdiction ceases). The Commission may require notification from the parties. If so, the time periods set out in Article 10[225] run as usual from notification. Where notification is not required the time periods run from the WD after the Commission informs the undertakings that it has decided to examine the concentration. Although the Commission is empowered to proceed as if the merger itself had an EU dimension, it is also possible that the transaction may be scrutinised at the national level by Member States that did not join in the referral. With the aim of better implementing the one-stop shop principle, the 2004 EUMR sought to simplify and clarify the Article 22 procedure (and to deal with its procedural and operational weaknesses).[226] The Commission has, however, made further proposals aimed at streamlining Article 22 and to give the Commission EEA-wide jurisdiction over cases referred under it.[227]

(iv) Article 4(5), Request for a Referral to the Commission

Article 4(5) (discussed in Section 4) provides a mechanism for parties to a concentration which does not have an EU dimension and which is capable of being reviewed under the national competition laws of at least three Member States, to request that the Commission should examine the concentration *prior* to national notification.

E. A RESIDUAL ROLE FOR ARTICLES 101 AND 102 OF THE TREATY

(i) The Relevance of Articles 101 and 102 TFEU

It has been seen that prior to the enactment of the EUMR the Commission made use of both Articles 102 and 101 to prohibit transactions which would now amount to a 'concentration'. Further, that subject to certain provisos and exceptions, the general rule is that the EUMR alone should apply to concentrations which have an EU dimension and that national law alone should apply to concentrations which do not. The purpose is to exclude the possible application of Article 101 or Article 102 to concentrations altogether.

The difficulty is that the Regulation cannot disapply Articles 101 and 102, Treaty provisions; it disapplies only the implementing legislation, which delegates responsibility for the enforcement of the rules to the Commission.

(ii) Application in the National Courts

As both Articles 101 and 102 are directly effective in their entirety, it is possible (unless the CJ were to find that the provisions of the EUMR somehow deprived Articles 101 and 102 of their direct effect) that a private individual might be able to challenge the compatibility of a concentration with Article 101 or Article 102 TFEU before a national court. In practice such a challenge would be most likely to occur where the concentration has an EU dimension (as an interested third party is able to challenge any Commission decision to clear the merger).

---

[224] Case T-221/95, *Endemol Entertainment Holding BV v Commission* [1999] ECR II-1299, para. 42.

[225] See Section 4.D, p. 1127.

[226] See 2001 Green Paper on the Review of Council Regulation (EEC) No. 4064/89, COM(2001) 745/6 final, 25–26 and EUMR, recital 12.

[227] White Paper, n. 62, para. 63.

(iii) The Commission and National Competition Authorities

A question which also arises is whether either the Commission or a NCA could apply Articles 101 and 102, using residual powers set out in Article 105 and Article 104 TFEU respectively.[228] Article 105 authorises the Commission to investigate a breach of Article 101 or Article 102 on its own initiative or at the request of a Member State. Thus it could, in theory, investigate a breach of these provisions in respect of a concentration which does not have an EU dimension.[229] Because, however, the implementing regulations are suspended the Commission would have to operate without the powers set out therein, for example the power to request information and the power to impose fines on those found to be in breach. The Commission has never made use of Article 105 in this way and it seems unlikely that it would do so.

Article 104 also authorises the competition authorities of the Member States to act when no implementing legislation applies.[230] Where a concentration does not have an EU dimension then generally neither the provisions of the EUMR nor those of Regulation 1/2003 apply.[231] Where, however, a concentration has an EU dimension it seems that, since the parties are obliged to notify such concentrations to the Commission, the jurisdiction of the Member States is denied.[232]

4. PROCEDURE

A. NOTIFICATION

The EUMR requires, to ensure effective control,[233] the notification of concentrations with an EU dimension[234] within the time period set out in Article 4.

Article 4

1. Concentrations with a Community dimension . . . shall be notified to the Commission prior to their implementation and following the conclusion of the agreement, the announcement of the public bid, or the acquisition of a controlling interest.

    Notification may also be made where the undertakings concerned demonstrate to the Commission a good faith intention to conclude an agreement or, in the case of a public bid, where they have publicly announced an intention to make such a bid, provided that the intended agreement or bid would result in a concentration with a Community dimension.

Parties may therefore notify any time prior to the implementation of an agreement, public bid, or acquisition of a controlling interest even where an agreement or public bid has not actually been made—provided that it can be demonstrated 'that their plan for that proposed concentration is sufficiently concrete, for example on the basis of an agreement in principle, a memorandum of understanding, or a letter of intent signed by all undertakings concerned, or, in the case of a public bid, where they have publicly announced an intention to make such a bid'.[235]

---

[228] These provisions are discussed in Chap. 2.

[229] If the concentration does have an EU dimension it will in any event be examining the transaction under the provisions of the EUMR.

[230] The competent national authorities' power to apply Arts. 101 and 102 TFEU by Reg. 1/2003, Art. 5 is disapplied.

[231] Consequently it seems that both Arts. 101 and 102 could be applied.

[232] See Chap. 2.

[233] EUMR, recital 17.

[234] Although the Commission is obliged to publish the fact of notification, the Commission must take account of the legitimate interest of the undertakings in the protection of their business secrets and is bound by a general duty of confidentiality, see EUMR, Arts. 4(2) and 17(2) and Chap. 13.

[235] EUMR, recital 34. The relevant date for establishing jurisdiction (the date of the conclusion of a binding legal agreement, the announcement of the public bid, the acquisition of a controlling interest, or the date of filing, whichever date is earlier) is crucial to the calculation of turnover, Jurisdictional Notice, paras. 154–156.

Which parties to the concentration are obliged to notify is dependent on the type of transaction that occurs. Broadly, joint notification must be made by the merging parties in true merger cases or by those acquiring control in other cases.[236] The implementing regulation, Regulation 802/2004[237] and Form CO set out how notification should be made and the information and documents which must be furnished to the Commission (unless the simplified procedure for certain concentrations that do not raise competition concerns applies, in which case a Short Form, also attached to the implementing regulation, is used[238]).

Form CO is not a form but a pattern, divided into sections, which prescribes how the information requested must be presented. A large amount of information is required (to enable the Commission to comply with the tight deadlines imposed on it). Thus the form requires a description of the concentration, information about the parties, details of the concentration, information about ownership and control, supporting documentation (which includes information bringing about the concentration and also copies of all analyses, reports, studies, surveys, and any comparable documents submitted to, or prepared by or for, any member(s) of the board of directors for the purposes of assessing or analysing the concentration with respect to market shares, competition condition, competitors, the rationale of the concentration, potential for sales growth),[239] information on market definitions and affected markets, overall market context and efficiencies, and cooperative effects of a JV. The notification must be accompanied with a declaration signed by representatives of the undertakings.

It can be seen from this description that notification is costly and time-consuming to complete. Failure to recognise the time and effort involved in the notification could disrupt the completion of the deal. Further, if all the requisite information is not supplied the notification will be 'incomplete' and a decision from the Commission will be delayed.[240] Pre-notification discussions with the Commission are always possible and in practice are ordinarily essential and extensive and play 'an important part of the whole review process'.[241] Pre-notification discussions may minimise the possibility of an incomplete notification and may lead to a reduction in the amount of information that the parties are required to provide in a notification. The Commission's Best Practices Guidelines provide guidance on pre-notification contacts and the preparation of a draft and final Form CO.

In *Gencor/Lonrho*[242] the Commission took the view that the parties' notification of the concentration to it meant that they had submitted to the EU jurisdiction.[243]

B. REASONED SUBMISSIONS

(i) Background

It has been explained that there has been a consistent concern that the simple turnover thresholds set out in Article 1(2) and (3) do not correctly divide jurisdiction between the Commission and NCAs in all cases. The EUMR thus provides flexible mechanisms for the transfer of such cases between the Commission and the national authorities and, since 2004, has enabled the parties to provide input into the determination of jurisdiction through the submission of reasoned submissions to the Commission *prior* to notification at the EU or national level (as relevant). Such submissions

---

[236] EUMR, Art. 4(2).

[237] [2004] OJ L133/1, especially Art. 3(2).

[238] See also nn. 119–120 and text.

[239] Form CO, s. 5(4). This information can sometimes be damaging.

[240] The tight time limits do not start to run until notification is complete.

[241] DG Comp, Best Practices on the conduct of EC merger control proceedings, para. 5. Section 3 of the form deals with pre-notification.

[242] M.619, [1997] OJ L11/42.

[243] See discussion in Section 8, pp. 1203–1205 and Chap. 16.

are made on Form RS, attached to the implementing regulation. The Commission's Notice on case referral[244] provides guidance on the system and practical guidance relating to its working.

The procedure may also enable the parties to speed up the reference procedure and may preclude the need for a notification to an authority which is simply going to refer the case to another.

(ii) Article 4(4), Request for Referral to a National Competition Authority

Article 4(4) provides that where a concentration has an EU dimension the notifying parties may, prior to notification to the Commission, make a reasoned submission that a concentration may significantly affect competition in a distinct market in a Member State and should be examined in whole or in part by that Member State. Where such a submission is made the Commission must inform the relevant Member State without delay and that State has a period of 15 WDs to express agreement or disagreement with the request to refer the case.

Unless the Member State disagrees the Commission has a period of 25 WDs from receiving the reasoned submission to determine whether or not to refer the case.[245] In deciding whether or not to make a reference the Commission, consider guiding principles[246] and in particular whether the national authority (or authorities), taking account of the likely locus of the competitive effects, is the most appropriate authority for dealing with the case.[247]

Where the Commission decides to refer the whole of the case *no* notification to the Commission is required and national competition law applies, subject to the conditions set out in Article 9.[248] Although Article 4(4) requests may occur where the parties anticipate that an Article 9 request will be made by a Member State, the Commission recognises that it is a problem that the parties essentially have to 'self-incriminate' themselves by claiming that the transaction may significantly affect competition in a market. It has thus proposed that this should no longer be a requirement, and the parties should simply have to show that the transaction is likely to have its main impact in a distinct market in the Member State.[249]

(iii) Article 4(5), Request for a Referral to the Commission

Article 4(5) provides that parties to a concentration which does not have an EU dimension, and which is capable of being reviewed under the national competition laws of at least three Member States, may, prior to national notification, make a reasoned submission that the concentration should be examined by the Commission. The parties may not implement the concentration while the Commission is considering it under Article 4(5). The Commission must transmit such submissions to the Member States without delay. The Member States then have a period of 15 WDs within which to express their disagreement with the procedure. The procedure is terminated if one Member State disagrees. Where, however, no Member State disagrees the concentration is deemed to have an EU dimension. It becomes notifiable to the Commission and *no* Member State is permitted to apply its national competition law to the concentration.

The advantage of the Article 4(5) procedure is apparent: if no Member State objects the parties may be saved multiple notifications and the transaction may be deemed to have an EU dimension. The risks are also obvious: if just one Member State objects the procedure is terminated.

---

[244] [2005] OJ C56/2.

[245] A decision to refer is deemed if it fails to adopt a decision within this time period.

[246] [2005] OJ C56/2, paras. 8–14.

[247] Ibid., paras. 19–23.

[248] See EUMR, Art. 9(6)–(9).

[249] White Paper, n. 62, para. 75.

This would mean that the parties may, having already made a reasoned submission, then have to make multiple notifications to the national authorities (and still risk the possibility that some of the Member States may then make an Article 22 reference to the Commission, making a notification necessary).[250] In order to minimise this risk and to encourage the use of Article 4(5) the Commission's Notice on case referral[251] provides guidance on the question of when a referral of the case to the Commission is likely to be considered the most appropriate authority for dealing with the case.[252]

Given that vetoes by the Member States have been rare in practice, the Commission has proposed modification of Article 4(5) to facilitate its use. In particular, it has suggested allowing the parties to notify immediately to the Commission (so abolishing the need to make a reasoned submission) and for the Commission to have jurisdiction unless a Member State (which is prima facie competent to review it) opposes it.[253]

C. SUSPENSION

Article 7(1) provides that a concentration with an EU dimension, or to be examined by the Commission pursuant to Article 4(5), is not to be implemented 'either before its notification or until it has been declared compatible with the internal market pursuant to a decision under Articles 6(1)(b), 8(1) or 8(2), or on the basis of a presumption according to Article 10(6)'. The suspensory obligation prohibits 'gun jumping', closing a transaction prior to notification or implementing a transaction which has been notified prior to obtaining clearance from the Commission. As a general rule therefore parties must take care not to take steps towards implementation of the merger *and* not to engage in information-sharing or other conduct which might infringe the competition law rules before clearance has been obtained, for example, through: coordinating their commercial activities; integrating business expertise; coordinating price, production, or research strategies; and/or engaging in joint marketing or advertising.[254]

The Commission may permit derogations from this suspensory effect following a request (and has occasionally used this power to allow rescue operations requiring quick closure during a financial or economic crisis)[255] and Article 7(2) provides an automatic derogation for public bids[256] 'or a series of transactions in securities including those convertible into other securities admitted to trading on a market such as a stock exchange, by which control is acquired from various sellers, provided that'[257] (a) the concentration is notified to the Commission without delay and (b) the acquirer does not exercise its voting rights or does so only to maintain the full value of its investments (based on an express derogation by the Commission).

---

[250] See, e.g., M.6502, *London Stock Exchange/LCH Clearnet Group* 14 July 2012.

[251] [2005] OJ C56/2.

[252] Ibid., paras. 25–32.

[253] White Paper, n. 62, 4.2.1.

[254] Such actions may not only breach the EUMR but also constitute a violation of Art. 101 TFEU, see e.g., M.4734, *Ineos/Kerling* 30 January 2008 (suspected infringement of the stand-still obligation investigated through unannounced inspections), see, e.g., F. Depoortere and S. Lelart, 'The Standstill Obligation in the ECMR' [2010] *World Competition* 103.

[255] EUMR, Art. 7(3). See, e.g., M.4956, *STX/Aker Yards* 5 May 2008, M.5363, *Santander/Bradford & Bingley* 17 December 2008, and M.7184, *Marine Harvest* 23 July 2014.

[256] See, e.g., M.2283, *Schneider/Legrand* 10 October 2001 (Schneider make a public exchange offer in respect of the shares held in Legrand and acquired 98.7% of the shares in Legrand prior to the Commission's final decision prohibiting the merger (and ordering the separation of Schneider and Legrand (see EUMR, Art. 8(4), (5) in Section 4.E, p. 1129)). The Commission's decision was annulled on appeal, Case T-310/01, *Schneider Electric SA v Commission* [2002] ECR II-4071 and Schneider subsequently brought proceedings against the Commission in respect of its loss, see Section 7.

[257] See, e.g., M.4730, *Yara/Kemira GrowHow* 21 September 2007.

The Commission has power under Article 14(2)(a) of the EUMR to impose fines, not exceeding 10 per cent of the aggregate turnover of the undertakings concerned, on a party that, intentionally or negligently, fails to notify a concentration in accordance with Articles 4 and 22(3) prior to its implementation and, under Article 14(2)(b), to impose penalties not exceeding 10 per cent of the aggregate turnover on those, intentionally or negligently, breaching the suspensory provisions. The validity of any such transaction closed in breach of the notification and/or suspensory provisions is dependent upon a clearance decision of the Commission.[258]

The Commission first imposed a fine of ECU 33,000 (at this time the amount of the fine could not exceed ECU 50,000)[259] on an undertaking, Samsung, which had failed to notify a concentration, its acquisition of control over an American firm, AST Research Inc, in due time.[260] In subsequent cases, however, and since the fining thresholds have increased, fines have been larger.[261] Indeed, in both *Electrabel*[262] and *Marine Harvest*,[263] the Commission imposed fines of €20 million for gun-jumping. In the latter case the Commission found that Marine Harvest, a salmon farmer and processor, had acquired, through the purchase of a 48.5 per cent stake, *de facto* sole control over its rival Morpol without prior EUMR authorisation and that the exception to notification provided for by Article 7(2) of the EUMR did not apply. The Commission concluded that the €20 million fine reflected (a) the serious nature of the breach both generally (given the importance of the stand-still obligation to ensuring permanent and irreparable damage is not done to effective competition) and specifically in this case (given the serious competition problems raised by the case which combined two of the largest farmers and primary processors of Scottish salmon);[264] and (b) mitigating factors, including that Marine Harvest had not exercised its voting rights in Morpol and had informed the Commission through pre-notification contacts shortly after closing the transaction.

D. PHASE I INVESTIGATION

The Commission must examine notifications as soon as they are received.[265] The time limits for initiating proceedings and decisions are set out in Article 10. The implementing regulation provides further information on the operation of the EUMR time limits and compliance with them.[266]

Phase I decisions must generally be taken within 25 WDs following receipt of complete notification. The period is extended to 35 WDs in Article 9 cases or cases where commitments designed to render the concentration compatible with the internal market are offered[267] (so long as the commitments are offered within 20 WDs of notification).[268] Details of notification must be published in the Official Journal in order to give third parties the opportunity to react.[269]

At the end of the 25- or 35-WD period the Commission must adopt a decision under Article 6. This may take one of several forms.

---

[258] EUMR, Art. 7(4).

[259] The fines that can be imposed were significantly increased by Reg. 139/2004.

[260] M.920, [1999] OJ L225/12.

[261] See, e.g., M.969, *AP Moller* [1999] OJ L183/29.

[262] Electrabel acquired control over Compagnie Nationale du Rhône (France's second largest electricity producer) in 2003 without notification, MEMO/09/267, Case T-332/09, *Electrabel v Commission* EU:T:2012:672 (dismissing Electrabel's appeal), *aff'd* Case C-84/13P, EU:C:2014:2040.

[263] M.7184, IP/14/862.

[264] The Commission only authorised the transaction subject to conditions, M.6850, IP/13/896.

[265] EUMR, Art. 6(1).

[266] Reg. 802/2004, Arts. 7–10.

[267] EUMR, Art. 10(1).

[268] Reg. 802/2004, Art. 19(1).

[269] EUMR, Art. 4(3).

(i) Article 6(1)(a)

Where the notified transaction does not in fact fall within the EUMR at all, it does not amount to a concentration with an EU dimension, the Commission may issue a decision to that effect. Such decisions are understandably rare in practice (less than 1 per cent of all notifications).[270]

(ii) Article 6(1)(b)

The Commission may declare the notified concentration to be compatible with the internal market either unconditionally or conditionally (subject to the acceptance of commitments by the parties[271]). Clearance decisions are deemed to cover restrictions directly related and necessary to the implementation of the concentration.[272]

(iii) Article 6(1)(c)

Where the Commission has serious doubts about the concentration's compatibility with the internal market it must issue a decision to that effect and initiate proceedings launching a second-phase investigation. In-depth reviews occur in less than 5 per cent of all notified cases.

Where such proceedings are launched then, without prejudice to Article 9, unless the undertakings can demonstrate to the satisfaction of the Commission that they have abandoned their concentration, the proceedings must be closed by virtue of a final decision under Article 8 decision. An Article 6(1)(c) decision initiating proceedings is not an appealable decision.[273]

(iv) Article 10(6)

Where the Commission fails to adopt a decision within the prescribed periods the concentration 'shall be deemed to have been declared to be compatible with the common market'.

E. PHASE II

The Commission has a period of 90 WDs from the day following the initiation of proceedings in which to make its assessment in Phase II proceedings.[274] This time period can be extended by 15 WDs where commitments are offered by the parties *after* the 54th WD (commitments must generally be offered within 65 WDs).[275] Further, it is possible that the period can be extended up to a total of 20 WDs either by the parties or at the request of the Commission with the consent of the parties.[276] This means that in complex cases the time period may be extended to a maximum of 125 WDs. Occasionally, however, the time periods may be expanded even beyond this statutory timetable if the Commission 'stops the clock' on account of the parties' failure to respond to requests for information by a stipulated time period.[277]

---

[270] See <http://ec.europa.eu/competition/mergers/statistics.pdf>.

[271] EUMR, Art. 6(2), see discussion of commitments in Section 5.G, p. 1195.

[272] See Section 5.F, p. 1194.

[273] See Case C-188/06 P, *Schneider Electric SA v Commission* [2007] ECR I-35. The CJ upheld the GC's view that a challenge to a decision opening a Phase II merger investigation was inadmissible since the decision was not a challengeable act but an intermediary act, to assist the Commission in reaching a final decision. The parties had therefore to wait to contest the final decision of the Commission determining the outcome of the case (in fact the parties abandoned the merger).

[274] EUMR, Art. 10(3).

[275] Reg. 802/2004, Art. 19(2).

[276] EUMR, Art. 10(3), second paragraph.

[277] See, e.g., M.2282, *Schneider/Legrand*, IP/01/408 (the Commission stopped the clock on account of the failure of the parties to respond to 322 questions within 12 calendar days (5 WD), *aff'd* Case T-310/01, *Schneider Electric SA*

Again, if no decision is taken within the prescribed period the concentration is deemed to be compatible with the internal market.[278]

At the end of the proceedings the Commission may under Article 8 of the EUMR either:

(a) declare the concentration to be compatible with the common market;

(b) declare that the concentration, following modification and/or subject to commitments, is compatible with the common market;[279]

(c) declare the concentration to be *incompatible* with the common market.[280]

In Article 8(1) and (2) cases the clearance decision is deemed to cover restrictions related and necessary to the concentration.[281] Where the concentration is prohibited but the parties have already completed the transaction the Commission has comprehensive powers, including the power to take interim measures or to take restorative measures.[282] These powers can also be exercised where a concentration is implemented in breach of a condition or obligation.

F. CONDUCT OF MERGER INVESTIGATIONS

When making its assessment, within the short periods stipulated, the Commission has power under Articles 11 and 13 of the EUMR to obtain information from the parties, or third parties (such as customers, suppliers, or competitors), by means of a request, either by a simple request or decision,[283] or by an inspection (including unannounced on-the-spot investigations).[284] Third parties play an important role in the merger proceedings. The investigation is ordinarily conducted in the form of requests for information to customers, suppliers, or competitors but may also be addressed to the notifying parties. It may also seek the views of these parties orally. The Commission's powers of investigation were extended by the current Regulation to bring them more closely into line with the Commission's corresponding powers under Regulation 1/2003.

The Commission has power under Articles 14 and 15 to impose both fines, not exceeding 1 per cent of the aggregate turnover of the undertakings concerned, and periodic penalty payments for a number of offences, such as intentionally or negligently failing to respond to an Article 11 letter or supplying incorrect or misleading information in a notification or following a request for information.[285] In *BP/Erdölchemie*,[286] for example, the Commission imposed a fine of €35,000 on Deutsche BP for having omitted to identify important information in its Form CO (the maximum fine was then €50,000 but is now 1 per cent of the turnover of the undertaking concerned). A decision adopted on the basis of incorrect information for which one of the undertakings is responsible may be revoked.[287]

State of play meetings are generally held during the process with the objective of contributing to the quality and efficiency of the decision-making process and of ensuring transparency and

---

v Commission [2002] ECR II-4071, para. 100; the GC held that a request for information was reasonable given the circumstances of the case and the requirement for speed which characterises the overall scheme of the EUMR). See also, e.g., Case T-145/06, *Omya v Commission* [2009] ECR II-145 and, e.g., M.7095, *SOCAR/DESFA*.

[278] EUMR, Art. 10(6).

[279] EUMR, Art. 8(6). It may also revoke decisions which are based on incorrect information.

[280] EUMR, Art. 8(2). Commitments are discussed in Section 5.G, p. 1195.

[281] See Section 5.F, p. 1194.

[282] EUMR, Art. 8(4) and (5), see e.g. M.2416, *Tetra Laval/Sidel* 30 October 2001, M.2283, *Schneider/Legrand* 10 October 2001 and 30 January 2002, M.890, *Blokker/Toys'R'Us* 26 June 1997 and M.784, *Kesko/Tuko* 19 February 1997.

[283] EUMR, Art. 11.

[284] EUMR, Arts. 12 and 13, see M.4734, *Ineos/Kerling* 30 January 2008. The power to carry out dawn raids is equivalent to those set out in Reg. 1/2003 [2003] OJ L1/1, discussed in Chap. 13.

[285] EUMR, Art. 14(1), COMP/29.895, *Telos* [1982] OJ L58/19.

[286] M.2624, [2004] OJ L91/40.

[287] EUMR, Arts. 6(3) and 8(6).

communication between DG Comp and the parties. If Phase II proceedings are initiated there are usually state of play meetings at five different points in the procedure. Occasionally, voluntary 'triangular' meetings involving the parties and third parties are held.

In the course of Phase II investigations a statement of objections (SO) may be served on the notifying parties. This lets the parties know the Commission's objections to the concentration.[288] Parties then have an opportunity to respond to the statement in writing by a specified date (the Commission is not obliged to take account of comments received after the expiry of the specified time limit);[289] they have a right of access to the file[290] and to attend and speak at the oral hearing, which is conducted by the Hearing Officer in full independence.[291] Further, other involved parties[292] and third parties, including customers, suppliers, competitors, members of the administrative or management bodies of the undertakings concerned or the recognised representative of their employees, and consumer associations where the proposed concentration concerns products or services used by end consumers,[293] may have a right to receive the SO, to respond to it, to have access to the file,[294] to attend the oral hearing, and to speak at it. If disputes arise in the course of this procedure, the issue can be raised with the Hearing Officer.

The Court takes the procedural obligations of the Commission very seriously. In *Schneider Electric SA v Commission*[295] the GC was critical of the Commission's substantive analysis of the case but annulled the decision on account of procedural irregularities committed by the Commission, in particular denial of the rights of defence. The GC found that the SO had not adequately stated the Commission's case against the parties. In its final decision, the Commission took account of the conglomerate effects of the merger whilst the SO had identified only horizontal effects. The GC held that although the Commission was able to add to or revise its arguments identified in the SO, the SO had to state objections in a sufficiently precise way to enable the parties to rebut the case against them and/or to devise or present remedies capable of saving the merger.[296]

Concentrations are initially investigated and appraised by merger units within DG Comp. In Phase II investigations an independent 'panel' is appointed with the task of scrutinising the case team's conclusions with a fresh pair of eyes at key points of the inquiry (devil's advocate process).[297] This step was added to deal with the criticism that the case team was often convinced of its own arguments at the end of Phase I, and that this affected the outcome of the second-phase investigations. The Advisory Committee on Concentrations must be consulted before a final decision is taken.[298] The final decision is made by the College of Commissioners[299] save, where delegated,[300] where it is adopted by a single Commissioner (usually the Competition Commissioner).

---

[288] Ibid., Art. 18(1) and (2).

[289] Ibid., Art. 18(3), Reg. 802/2004, Art. 13(2)(3).

[290] Ibid., Art. 18(3), Reg. 802/2004, Art. 17(1).

[291] Reg. 802/2004, Arts. 14 and 15.

[292] Parties to the transaction other than the notifying parties.

[293] See, e.g., Reg. 802/2004, Art. 11(1)(b)(c). See also on the rights of third parties, Cases C-68/94 and 30/95, *France v Commission, Société Commerciale des Potasses et de l'Azote (SCPA) v Commission* [1998] ECR I-1375.

[294] Third parties may also seek access to Commission documents using the Transparency Reg., see Cases C-404/10 P, *Commission v Éditions Odile Jacob*, and C-477/10 P, *Commission v Agrofert Holding* EU:C:2012:393 and Chap. 13.

[295] Case T-310/01, [2002] ECR II-4071.

[296] In Case T-5/02, *Tetra Laval v Commission* [2002] ECR II-4381 (GC rejected Tetra Laval's arguments that the Commission had failed to respect Tetra's rights to access to the file).

[297] See M. Monti, SPEECH/02/545, 'Merger Control in the European Union: a radical reform', European Commission/International Bar Association, Brussels, 7 November 2002. Representatives from the staff of the Chief Competition Economist participate in this panel.

[298] It must also be consulted, for example, before a decision imposing a fine or penalty or ordering divestment is taken.

[299] See n. 610 and text.

[300] Phase I decisions are usually delegated.

G. SUMMARY

Figure 15.2 sets out an outline summary of the EUMR's merger procedure provisions.

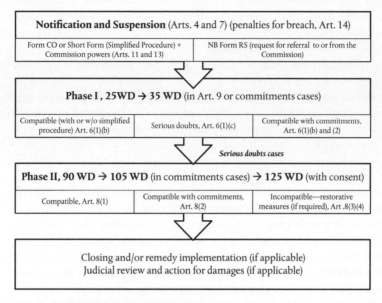

Figure 15.2 EUMR's merger procedure provisions

5. SUBSTANTIVE APPRAISAL OF CONCENTRATIONS UNDER THE EU MERGER REGULATION

A. BACKGROUND

The *original* EUMR[301] adopted a 'dominance' test for substantive appraisal, providing in Article 2(3) that:

A concentration which creates or strengthens a dominant position as a result of which effective competition would be significantly impeded in the common market or in a substantial part of it shall be declared incompatible with the common market.

In its 2001 Green Paper,[302] however, the Commission launched a debate as to whether there should be a move from this standard to the 'substantial lessening of competition' (SLC) test. Procedural and substantive arguments both arguably favoured such reform. The gist of the procedural argument was that alignment of the test with the SLC test used in a number of jurisdictions, including the US,[303] would lead to greater international convergence in the application of merger rules. The Commission was not entirely convinced, however, partly because of the uncertainty that switching to a new substantive test for appraisal would create, and partly because of the inconsistency it would cause in the EU where many Member and acceding States had modelled their merger rules on the dominance test.

---

[301] The substantive test was not amended by Reg. 1310/97 [1997] OJ L180/1.

[302] 2001 Green Paper on the Review of Council Regulation (EEC) No. 4064/89, COM(2001) 745/6 final, especially paras. 160–167.

[303] The test is also used, e.g., in Canada, Australia, the UK, and Ireland.

The substantive reasons advanced hinged on the relative flexibility of the SLC test, in particular when dealing with mergers in concentrated markets. It will be seen in the discussion below that, despite initial doubt, it was gradually established that the old EUMR applied, not only to mergers leading to the creation or strengthening of a dominant position held by a single undertaking, but to mergers leading to the creation or strengthening of a collective dominant position (that is, a dominant position held by the merging parties and another or other undertakings operating on the market, mergers resulting in *coordinated effects*).[304]

Advocates of the adoption of the SLC test[305] took the view that in spite of this development, the dominance test was not broad enough to capture and prevent all problematic mergers occurring on a concentrated market. For example, a merger between the second and third largest competitors on a market with only three players might not lead to the creation of a single dominant position, it might not lead to the coordination of the competitive behaviour of the firms remaining on the market, but it might substantially lessen competition and lead to higher prices on the market (through *unilateral effects*) by eliminating the rivalry between the merging firms and the competitive constraint that they had exercised both on each other and on the market leader. The EUMR was thus argued to include a 'blind spot' or gap. Indeed, this gap appeared to have contributed to the Commission's problems in the *Airtours* case discussed below.[306]

A classic example given of this gap situation was the US 'baby food' case.[307] In this case Heinz, the third largest producer of baby food in the US, wished to acquire Milnot Holding Corp, whose subsidiary, Beech-Nut, was the second largest producer of baby food in the US. Following the merger the parties would have acquired around 33 per cent of the relevant market, whilst Gerber would have retained 65 per cent of the prepared baby food market. The merger clearly would not have given the merging parties a 'dominant' position. Nonetheless the Federal Trade Commission (FTC) was concerned not only that the merger would lead to coordinated effects on the market (e.g., tacit coordination of prices by the merged entity and Gerber) but also that the merger would lead to a substantial lessening of competition on the market since the merging parties competed vigorously to be chosen as the number two supplier in supermarkets and in innovation in product development and differentiation. The merger would thus eliminate substantial competition between Heinz and Beech-Nut and eliminate Beech-Nut as a substantial, independent, and competitive force in the market. This competition also placed competitive pressure on Gerber with respect to both prices and innovation. Although the challenge to this merger led to its eventual abandonment, it was argued that, had the same facts arisen in the EU, the EU authorities would have been powerless to prevent the merger unless collective dominance (or coordinated effects) could be established.

Although the Commission indicated in its Green Paper that it thought this so-called 'gap' was more hypothetical than real, it launched a debate which raged until the last moments before the text for the new EUMR was finally agreed.[308]

---

[304] See also the discussion of collective dominance in Chap. 9.

[305] See, e.g. J. Vickers, 'Competition Economics and Policy' [2003] *ECLR* 95, R. Whish, 'Substantive Analysis under the EC Merger Regulation: Should the Dominance Test be Replaced by "Substantial Lessening of Competition"' in *EU Competition Law & Policy: Developments & Priorities* (Hellenic Competition Commission, 2002), 45 and Z. Biro and M. Parker, 'A New EC Merger Test? Dominance v Substantial Lessening of Competition' [2002] 1 *Comp Law* 157.

[306] M.1524, *Airtours/First Choice* [2000] OJ L93/1, annulled on appeal, Case T-342/99, *Airtours v Commission* [2002] ECR II-2585, see discussion especially n. 463 and text. See also J. Vickers, 'How to reform the EC merger test', Speech at the EC/IBA merger control conference, Brussels, 9 November 2004.

[307] *FTC v HJ Heinz Co*, 246 F.3d 708 (DC Cir. 2001), 116 F. Supp.2d 190 (2000).

[308] E.g., the UK, Irish, and Swedish delegations were in favour of the SLC test (see submissions to the Commission's 2001 Green Paper, available on DG Comp's website) whilst the German delegation favoured retention of the dominance test (see also, e.g., submissions of Italy, the Netherlands, and the European Parliament). Some Member States (e.g., Portugal and Denmark) favoured a retention of the dominance test, but with a clarification of how the test applied on oligopolistic markets whilst France and Spain supported a dual test combining features of the SLC and dominance tests.

B. REFORM AND THE NEW SUBSTANTIVE TEST

Given the need for unanimous agreement in the Council the end result of the reform process was a classic, yet ingenious, European 'compromise' designed to meet the arguments of those in both the SLC and dominance camps. The substantive test *was* altered but the SLC test was *not* adopted. The decision was made to utilise, but reorganise, the wording of the original EUMR. Article 2(3) of the current Regulation states:

A concentration which would significantly impede effective competition in the common market or in a substantial part of it, in particular as a result of the creation or strengthening of a dominant position, shall be declared incompatible with the common market.

The new 'SIEC' test is thus broader than the old test; a merger may be prohibited even if it does not create or strengthen a dominant position if it would lead to a significant impediment to effective competition (SIEC). By referring to the creation or strengthening of a dominant position, however, the EUMR preserves the previous decisional practice and case law of the CJ. Horizontal Merger Guidelines[309] were also adopted with the objective of clearly and comprehensively articulating the analytical approach under the new test.

The twin objectives, of broadening the test whilst at the same time preserving the case law on the meaning of dominance, are explained in recitals 25 and 26 of the EUMR. In particular, recital 25 makes it crystal clear that the new substantive test is designed to catch mergers that will result in non-coordinated effects on an oligopolistic market even though a position of single or collective dominance may not be established.

(25) In view of the consequences that concentrations in oligopolistic market structures may have, it is all the more necessary to maintain effective competition in such markets. Many oligopolistic markets exhibit a healthy degree of competition. However, under certain circumstances, concentrations involving the elimination of important competitive constraints that the merging parties had exerted upon each other, as well as a reduction of competitive pressure on the remaining competitors, may, even in the absence of a likelihood of coordination between the members of the oligopoly, result in a significant impediment to effective competition. The Community courts have, however, not to date expressly interpreted Regulation (EEC) No 4064/89 as requiring concentrations giving rise to such non-coordinated effects to be declared incompatible with the common market. Therefore, in the interests of legal certainty, it should be made clear that this Regulation permits effective control of all such concentrations by providing that any concentration which would significantly impede effective competition, in the common market, or in a substantial part of it, should be declared incompatible with the common market. The notion of 'significant impediment to effective competition' in Article 2(2) and (3) should be interpreted as extending, beyond the concept of dominance, only to the anti-competitive effects of a concentration resulting from the non-coordinated behaviour of undertakings which would not have a dominant position on the market concerned.

Arguably, the adoption of this new substantive test has, over the years, enabled the Commission both 'to move away from an excessively structuralist analysis in merger control towards a more effects based one and to close a gap with respect to cases leading to unilateral effects in a non-collusive oligopoly'[310] and to bring the standard for substantive assessment more closely into line with that adopted under Article 101. 'The SIEC test does not require the finding of dominance but a lower level of market power and focuses on the likely impact of the merger in the main market competition parameters (price, output, innovation,...)'.[311]

---

[309] [2004] OJ C31/5, para. 5. The Non-Horizontal Merger Guidelines were adopted subsequently.

[310] Speech of Deputy Director-General (Mergers) at DG Comp, Carles Esteva Mosso, 'The Contribution of Merger Control to the Definition of Harm to Competition', GCLC Conference, Brussels, February 2016.

[311] Ibid.

Article 2(1) sets out the criteria to be used in appraising concentrations.

Concentrations within the scope of this Regulation shall be appraised in accordance with the objectives of this Regulation and the following provisions with a view to establishing whether or not they are compatible with the common market.

In making this appraisal, the Commission shall take into account:

(a) the need to maintain and develop effective competition within the common market in view of, among other things, the structure of all the markets concerned and the actual or potential competition from undertakings located either within or outwith the Community;

(b) the market position of the undertakings concerned and their economic and financial power, the alternatives available to suppliers and users, their access to supplies or markets, any legal or other barriers to entry, supply and demand trends for the relevant goods and services, the interests of the intermediate and ultimate consumers, and the development of technical and economic progress provided that it is to consumers' advantage and does not form an obstacle to competition.

Article 2(4) and (5) set out an additional test applying the criteria of Article 101 to the aspects of a full-function JV that may appreciably restrict competition between undertakings that remain independent. Section 5.D examines how the Commission applies the substantive test for assessment.

C. BURDEN AND STANDARD OF PROOF AND COUNTERFACTUAL

The burden is on the Commission to establish that the merger is either compatible or incompatible with the internal market. In making the determination, the merger must be assessed in the context of the position that would exist were the merger not to be completed (the counterfactual). Thus to establish a SIEC, it is necessary to demonstrate a causal link between completion of the merger and the competitive harm.

9. In assessing the competitive effects of a merger, the Commission compares the competitive conditions that would result from the notified merger with the conditions that would have prevailed without the merger. In most cases, the competitive conditions existing at the time of the merger constitute the relevant comparison for evaluating the effects of a merger. However, in some circumstances, the Commission may take into account future changes to the market that can reasonably be predicted. It may, in particular, take account of the likely entry or exit of firms if the merger did not take place when considering what constitutes the relevant comparison.[312]

Although mergers are normally assessed against the competitive conditions existing at the time of the merger, assessing the counterfactual may be more complex in some scenarios, for example where two mergers take place close together in time in the same industry or relevant market. In this situation the Commission now seems to favour assessing the first merger without regard to the second but the second taking account of the first (giving priority to the transaction notified first).[313] In *Western Digital/Viviti*,[314] the Commission thus applied the first come, first served rule assessing that transaction taking into account the *Seagate/Samsung*[315] merger (also affecting the market for hard disk drives) which had been notified one day earlier.[316] It has, however, sometimes assessed both, taking into account the impact of the other on the market.[317]

---

[312] Horizontal Merger Guidelines, para. 9. See also discussion of the failing firm defence in Section 5.D.vii.

[313] See J. Almunia, SPEECH 11/561, 'Policy Objectives in Merger Control', 8 September 2011.

[314] M.6203, *Western Digital Ireland/Viviti Technologies* 23 November 2011.

[315] M.6214, 19 October 2011.

[316] The proposed transaction would, after the Seagate/Samsung merger, reduce the number of suppliers in the market to three, and in some markets to two.

[317] Compare, e.g., Cases M.2533, *BP/E.ON* 20 December 2011 and M.2389, *Shell/DEA* 20 December 2011 with Cases M.4601, *KarstadtQuelle/MyTravel* 4 May 2007 and M.4600, *TUI/First Choice* 4 June 2007 (transactions assessed in the light of the competitive situation that prevailed at the time of the respective filings. The first filing was thus assessed

It seems clear that, whether or not the Commission clears or prohibits a merger, the standard of proof is the balance of probabilities[318] (there is no general presumption that the merger is either compatible or incompatible with the internal market).[319] In a series of cases it has been made clear that the GC will rigorously review the Commission's decisions and, although it recognises that the Commission has a margin of discretion with regard to economic matters, it will consider whether the evidence relied upon by the Commission is correct, reliable, and consistent, and is capable of substantiating the conclusions it has drawn—i.e. whether the reasoning and evidence relied upon provides a proper factual basis for the conclusions and all the information which must be taken into account in order to assess a complex situation.[320]

This burden imposes an acute burden on the Commission which must examine how a concentration might, in the future, alter the factors determining the state of competition on a market in order to establish whether it would lead to a SIEC and envisage 'various chains of cause and effect with a view to ascertaining which of them is the most likely'.[321] If the Commission does not meet the appropriate standard the GC will annul its decision. Indeed, in 2002 the GC annulled three Commission decisions in a series of judgments given in close succession.[322] Since then, as Anne Witt notes in the following extract, the Commission has worked hard to strengthen its decision-making processes, to improve the quality and quantity of evidence and economic analysis set out in its merger decisions.[323]

5.3.3. *Burden and standards of proof*

Another central point of criticism in all three annulment judgements from 2002 was that the Commission's assessments did not meet the required stand of proof because they failed to provide convincing factual evidence in support of key assumptions. A comparison of these decisions with the Commission's decisional practice post-reform shows a dramatic improvement in the quality and quantity of evidence used by the Commission. In *Ryanair/Aer Lingus*, the Commission collated evidence to an unprecedented degree, carried out an in-depth market investigation (comprising the views of scheduled airlines, charter airlines, airports, customer, slot coordination authorities, civil aviation authorities and transport authorities) and produced several econometric studies. It used this wealth of evidence painstakingly to support its factual assumption, and published in its entirety in several annexes to the final decision.

This trend is not specific to merger review . . . One side effect of this commitment is that it has considerably increased the length of the Commission's prohibition decisions . . .

---

independently from the second) and see generally G. Drauz, S. Mavroghenis, and S. Ashall, 'Recent Developments in EU Merger Control' (2012) 3 *JECLAP* 52, 72–75 (the Commission initially favoured the combined approach—especially in coordinated effects analysis—but is now more inclined to adopt the priority rule approach).

[318] Thus if there is appreciable uncertainty about the merger's incompatibility on the part of the Commission, it appears that the merger should be approved, Case C-12/03 P, *Commission v Tetra Laval BV* [2005] ECR I-987, Tizzano AG, paras. 76–77. See further, e.g., Cook and Kerse, n. 37, 7-008 and Lindsay and Berridge, *The EU Merger Regulation: Substantive Issues* (4th edn, Sweet & Maxwell, 2012), 2.5(b).

[319] See Case C-413/06 P, *Bertelsmann and Sony Corp v Commission* [2008] ECR I-4951, paras. 46–48, Case T-87/05, *EDP v Commission* [2005] ECR II-3745, para. 61, and Case C-12/03 P, *Commission v Tetra Laval BV* [2005] ECR I-987. The parties, however, may need to provide evidence which may be material to the decision and, for example, to support a view that there are few barriers to entry to the market, that one of the firms is failing, or that the merger will achieve significant efficiencies, see e.g., discussion in A. Lindsay and A. Berridge, n. 318, 2.5(a) and (b).

[320] But see further Chap. 13. The tight time constraints that the Commission is operating under is, however, relevant to the assessment of the appraisal conducted, see, e.g., Case T-151/05, *Nederlandse Vakbond Varkenshouders v Commission* [2009] ECR II-1219 (the Commission cannot be expected to verify the accuracy to the last detail of all the information it receives in the course of Phase I proceedings).

[321] Case C-12/03 P, *Commission v Tetra Laval* [2005] ECR I-987, para. 43 and Case C-413/06 P, *Bertelsmann and Sony Corp v Commission* [2008] ECR I-4951, para. 47.

[322] See Case T-342/99, *Airtours v Commission* [2002] ECR II-2585; Case T-310/01, *Schneider Electric SA v Commission* [2002] ECR II-4071; and Case T-5/02, *Tetra Laval v Commission* [2002] ECR II-4381.

[323] A. C. Witt, 'From *Airtours* to *Ryanair*: Is the More Economic Approach to EU Merger Law Really About More Economics?' (2012) 49 *CMLRev* 217. See also Speech by M. Monti, 'Merger Control in the European Union: A Radical Reform', 7 November 2002.

Although the complexity of the theory of competitive harm put forward does not appear to affect the standard of proof, it is an important factor which is taken into account when assessing the plausibility of the various consequences that the merger might have.[324] In *Tetra Laval BV v Commission* the CJ stated:[325]

Case C-12/03 P, *Tetra Laval BV v Commission* [2005] ECR I-98739

39. Whilst the Court recognises that the Commission has a margin of discretion with regard to economic matters that does not mean that the Community Courts must refrain from reviewing the Commission's interpretation of the information of an economic nature. Not only must the Community Courts, *inter alia*, establish whether the evidence relied on is factually accurate, reliable and consistent but also whether that evidence contains all the information which must be taken into account in order to assess a complex situation and whether it is capable of substantiating the conclusions drawn from it. Such a review is all the more necessary in the case of a prospective analysis required when examining a planned merger with conglomerate effect.

40. Thus, the [GC] was right to find . . ., that the Commission's analysis of a merger producing a conglomerate effect is subject to requirements similar to those defined by the Court with regard to the creation of a situation of collective dominance and that it calls for a close examination of the circumstances which are relevant for an assessment of that effect on the conditions of competition on the reference market.

41. Although the [GC] stated, in paragraph 155, that proof of anti-competitive conglomerate effects of a merger of the kind notified calls for a precise examination, supported by convincing evidence, of the circumstances which allegedly produce those effects, it by no means added a condition relating to the requisite standard of proof but merely drew attention to the essential function of evidence, which is to establish convincingly the merits of an argument or, as in the present case, of a decision on a merger.

42. A prospective analysis of the kind necessary in merger control must be carried out with great care since it does not entail the examination of past events—for which often many items of evidence are available which make it possible to understand the causes—or of current events, but rather a prediction of events which are more or less likely to occur in future if a decision prohibiting the planned concentration or laying down the conditions for it is not adopted.

43. Thus, the prospective analysis consists of an examination of how a concentration might alter the factors determining the state of competition on a given market in order to establish whether it would give rise to a serious impediment to effective competition. Such an analysis makes it necessary to envisage various chains of cause and effect with a view to ascertaining which of them are the most likely.

44. The analysis of a 'conglomerate-type' concentration is a prospective analysis in which, first, the consideration of a lengthy period of time in the future and, secondly, the leveraging necessary to give rise to a significant impediment to effective competition mean that the chains of cause and effect are dimly discernible, uncertain and difficult to establish. That being so, the quality of the evidence produced by the Commission in order to establish that it is necessary to adopt a decision declaring the concentration incompatible with the common market is particularly important, since that evidence must support the Commission's conclusion that, if such a decision were not adopted, the economic development envisaged by it would be plausible.

45. It follows from those various factors that the [GC] did not err in law when it set out the tests to be applied in the exercise of its power of judicial review or when it specified the quality of the evidence which the Commission is required to produce in order to demonstrate that the requirements of Article 2(3) of the Regulation are satisfied.

46. With respect to the particular case of judicial review exercised by the [GC] in the judgment under appeal, it is not apparent from the example given by the Commission, which relates to the growth in the

---

[324] Case C-413/06 P, *Bertelsmann and Sony Corp v Commission* [2008] ECR I-4951, para. 51.
[325] Case C-12/03 P, [2005] ECR I-987.

use of PET packaging for sensitive products, that the [GC] exceeded the limits applicable to the review of an administrative decision by the Community Courts. Contrary to what the Commission claims, paragraph 211 of the judgment under appeal merely restates more concisely, in the form of a finding by the [GC], the admission made by the Commission at the hearing, which is summarised in paragraph 210 of the judgment, that its forecast in the contested decision with regard to the increase in the use of PET for packaging UHT milk was exaggerated. In paragraph 212 of the judgment under appeal, the [GC] gave the reasons for its finding that the evidence produced by the Commission was unfounded by stating that, of the three independent reports cited by the Commission, only the PCI report contained information on the use of PET for milk packaging. It went on, in that paragraph, to show that the evidence produced by the Commission was unconvincing by pointing out that the increase forecast in the PCI report was of little significance and that the Commission's forecast was inconsistent with the undisputed figures on the use of HDPE contained in the other reports. In paragraph 213 of the judgment under appeal, the [GC] merely stated that the Commission's analysis was incomplete, which made it impossible to confirm its forecasts, given the differences between those forecasts and the forecasts made in the other reports.

47. Amongst the other examples given by it, the Commission challenges the [GC]'s finding, in paragraph 289 of the judgment under appeal, that 'fresh milk is not a product for which the marketing advantages offered by PET have any particular importance' and its conclusions as to the cost of PET in comparison to that of carton, which are set out in paragraphs 288 and 328 of the judgment under appeal. It should be noted that these are findings of fact, which are not subject to review by the Court in appeal proceedings. It is therefore unnecessary to give a ruling on the merits of those findings by the [GC] and it need be stated only that the [GC] was able to base those findings on various items in the contested decision.

48. It follows from these examples that the [GC] carried out its review in the manner required of it, as set out in paragraph 39 of this judgment. It explained and set out the reasons why the Commission's conclusions seemed to it to be inaccurate in that they were based on insufficient, incomplete, insignificant and inconsistent evidence.

49. In doing so, the [GC] observed the criteria to be applied in exercising the Community Courts' power of judicial review and, accordingly, complied with Article [263 TFEU].

50. Consequently, the above analyses do not show that the [GC] infringed Article 2(2) or (3) of the Regulation.

51. It follows from all of the above considerations that the first ground of appeal is unfounded.

D. A SIGNIFICANT IMPEDIMENT TO EFFECTIVE COMPETITION

(i) General

The EUMR aims to preserve effective competition on a market, and to deliver benefits to consumers in the form of low prices, high-quality products, a wide selection of goods and services, and innovation. By prohibiting mergers that would lead to a SIEC, the EUMR seeks to prevent mergers that would deprive customers of these benefits by significantly increasing the market power of firms.[326] 'By "increased market power" is meant the ability of one or more firms to profitably increase prices, reduce output, choice or quality of goods and services, diminish innovation, or otherwise influence the parameters of competition.'[327] This could result from unilateral or coordinated effects which result from the merger and which are not offset by countervailing factors or efficiencies.

---

[326] This inevitably involves a comparison of the existing competitive conditions with the conditions that will exist post-merger.

[327] Horizontal Merger Guidelines [2004] OJ C31/5, para. 8. See also paras. 1 and 4 ('The creation or the strengthening of a dominant position is a primary form of such competitive harm' and provides 'an important indication as to the standard of competitive harm that is applicable when determining whether a concentration is likely to impede effective competition to a significant degree').

Decisional practice, EU case law, and the Commission's Horizontal and Non-Horizontal Merger Guidelines[328] clarify and explain the appraisal process.[329] Although the Commission is bound by its guidelines (insofar as they do not depart from the TFEU or the EUMR), they describe an analytical approach to be followed and do not provide a mechanical checklist requiring application of all the mentioned factors in each and every case.[330] Rather, the Commission enjoys a degree of discretion in determining whether or not to take account of certain factors in a given case.[331]

(ii) Market Power and Market Definition

a. The Role of Market Definition

Because merger assessment focuses on the question of whether the merger will increase the market power of firms, market definition frequently plays an important role; in particular, it enables meaningful information regarding market power and how competition operates on the market to be acquired. 'The main purpose of market definition is to identify in a systematic way the immediate competitive constraints facing the merged entity.'[332]

Although market definition is not 'an end in itself but a tool to identify situations where there might be competition concerns',[333] and it will be seen that some have questioned whether it is required at all in certain merger cases (see discussion of pricing pressure indices below[334]), the CJ has held that:

a proper definition of the relevant market is a necessary precondition for any assessment of the effect of a concentration on competition.[335]

In some Phase I clearance decisions, however, the Commission does not need to make a final determination of the relevant market because it will not affect the outcome of the case,[336] whichever way the market is defined.[337]

b. The Commission's Notice on Market Definition and Previous Decisional Practice

In Chapter 1 it was seen that the Commission's Notice on the definition of the relevant market[338] sets out how the Commission goes about determining the relevant market for the purposes of its merger decisions. Further, that the Notice explains that it uses the SSNIP test where possible, 'postulating a hypothetical small, non-transitory change in relative prices and evaluating the likely reaction of customers to that increase'.[339] Indeed, the test is frequently helpful in the application of the merger rules since the practical problem presented by the *cellophane fallacy* (especially relevant in Article 102 cases) does not ordinarily apply.[340]

---

[328] Available on DG Comp's website. The Commission commissioned and published on its website an *ex post* review of Merger Control Decisions, prepared by LEAR.

[329] EUMR, recital 28.

[330] Case T-282/06, *Sun Chemical Group v Commission* [2007] ECR II-2149, para. 55.

[331] Ibid., para. 57.

[332] Horizontal Merger Guidelines, para. 10.

[333] M. Monti, 'Market Definition as a Cornerstone of EU Competition Policy', Speech at Workshop on Market Definition, Helsinki Fair Centre, 5 October 2001.

[334] See nn. 380–381 and text.

[335] Cases C-68/94 and 30/95, *France v Commission, Société Commerciale des Potasses et de l'Azote (SCPA) v Commission* [1998] ECR I-1375, para. 143. See also Mosso, n. 310, 4 ('To assess market power, you need a relevant market').

[336] See M.232, *PepsiCo/General Mills* [1992] OJ C228/6.

[337] See M.833, *The Coca-Cola Co/Carlsberg A/S* [1998] OJ L145/41.

[338] [1997] OJ C372/5, discussed in Chap. 1. For a comprehensive discussion of market definition in merger cases, see, e.g., Lindsay and Berridge, n. 318, Chap. 3.

[339] See Chap. 1.

[340] The Commission's practice in defining markets for the purposes of the EUMR is the inspiration behind the SSNIP test set out in the Notice.

There are also now a significant number of merger (and Article 102[341]) decisions which may provide useful indications of how market definition might be approached in particular spheres (merger cases are grouped on DG Comp's website by reference to NACE code (i.e. industry sector)[342]). Nonetheless, some caution needs to be exercised with old cases, particularly where developments and technological change have led to market changes. Indeed, case law makes it clear that market definition must be freshly addressed in every case.[343] Some important points about the limited 'precedent' value of market definition in merger cases are made by Mosso, Deputy Director-General (Mergers) in DG Comp:[344]

However, I should also add that market definitions in merger decisions should be taken 'with a grain of salt' before they are imported into an antitrust case. First, the 'cellophane fallacy' (according to which the hypothetical monopolist test cannot be applied to a market where prices are already above competitive level) is more likely to occur in antitrust cases than in merger cases. The Market Definition Notice recognises this point. Second, since antitrust is often about the past, we can often directly observe the parties' behaviour and deduce the relevant market from that, if needed. For example, a market-sharing agreement defines its own relevant market. In such cases, trying to further analyse the relevant market runs the risk of putting theory ahead of practical experience.

In fact, market definitions in merger decisions should be also taken 'with a grain of salt' before they are 'imported' into subsequent merger cases: our exercise of market definition is very much facts-driven and we stand ready to adapt our previous conclusions to the new prevailing circumstances, where markets have evolved, for instance by widening in scope.

In many cases the parties to a merger may prefer a broad product market in which their market shares are lower. It will be harder for the parties to persuade the Commission to clear a merger affecting a narrowly defined market in which they have, say, a 70 per cent market share than in a wider one in which they have, for example, a 30 per cent market share. On some occasions, however, a narrower product market definition may work to the parties' advantage, since this could result in a finding that there is no, or less, significant horizontal overlap in the products they produce.[345]

It will also frequently be the case that the parties will wish to argue for as broad a geographic market as possible in order to diminish their market shares.[346] It may therefore be argued that the geographic market is a wide, or even global, one so the creation of a national or EU champion to compete on that market should be allowed. The Commission will scrutinise such arguments carefully and will not allow a merger which would significantly impede effective competition in the EU and damage consumers within it.

A drawing of a 'worldwide' market may be possible in the case of highly technical products involving significant R&D and large capital and manufacturing costs[347] or where a product is very valuable, internationally traded, and relatively cheap to transport. In *Gencor/Lonrho*,[348] for example, the Commission identified worldwide markets for various metal products, including platinum, which

---

[341] In M.2416, *Tetra Laval/Sidel* 30 October 2001, e.g., the market definition adopted in Case C-333/94 P, *Tetra Pak II* [1996] ECR I-5951, was followed.

[342] Nomenclature générale des Activités économiques dans les Communautés Européennes.

[343] Cases T-125 and 127/97, *Coca-Cola v Commission* [2000] ECR II-1733 (as market definitions change with market circumstances a previous market definition finding is not binding upon the Commission). See P. McGeown and A. Barthélemy, 'Recent Developments in EU Merger Control' (2015) 6 *JECLAP* 440, 440.

[344] Mosso, n. 310, 4–5.

[345] See, e.g., M.1578, *Sanitec/Sphinx* [2000] OJ L294/1, M.7284 *Siemens/John Wood/Rolls-Royce Combined ADGT Business/RWG* 4 August 2014 and M.7259, *Carphone Warehouse/Dixons* 25 June 2014.

[346] Even if a more narrowly drawn geographic market will not result in horizontal overlaps the Commission may be prepared to characterise a merger between parties present on the same product market but in neighbouring geographic product markets, as having horizontal effects in consequence of their being 'potential' competitors.

[347] See, e.g., M.269, *Shell/Montecatani* [1994] OJ L332/48.

[348] M.619, [1997] OJ L11/30.

were traded on a global basis at publicly quoted prices. Further, in *Aérospatiale/Alenia/de Havilland*[349] the Commission concluded that the geographic market for the commuter aircraft[350] was worldwide, excluding China and Eastern Europe. There were no tangible barriers to the importation of these aircraft into the EU and negligible costs of transportation.[351]

(iii) Competitive Assessment of Horizontal Mergers

a. Introduction and Overview

Mergers between undertakings that are competitors, or potential competitors, on the same market may, by eliminating a competitive restraint on the market, lead to the firms' gaining or enhancing their market power. Form CO thus requires the parties to provide data in relation to affected markets where 'two or more of the parties to the concentration are engaged in business activities in the same relevant market and where the concentration will lead to a combined market share of 20 % or more'.[352]

The Horizontal Merger Guidelines[353] clarify that market share and concentration thresholds are used as a preliminary 'rule of thumb' to identify potentially problematic mergers.[354] The Commission examines, however, the likelihood that the merger will result in anti-competitive effects on the market, through either non-coordinated or coordinated effects.[355] It then considers whether or not countervailing factors, such as buyer power, new entry, or efficiencies would counteract the potentially harmful effects identified.[356] It also considers that a concentration may be permitted where the anti-competitive effects result from the failure of a firm rather than the merger.[357]

b. Market Shares, Concentration Levels, and GUPPI

In 1982 the US competition agencies advocated use of a concentration index to make preliminary assessments of the legitimacy of a horizontal merger and the reduction in competition it will cause on a particular market. The Herfindahl–Hirschman index (the HHI) seeks to identify the concentration of a particular market by using numerical distinctions[358] which reflect both concentration levels on the market generally and the degree to which larger firms are dominant in the market. It operates by adding together the squares of the market shares of each of the undertakings operating in the market.[359] The degree of concentration on the market is assessed by reference to the sum of those market shares (it thus gives greater weight proportionately to the market shares of the larger firms).

The Commission's Horizontal Merger Guidelines explain that it relies on concentration ratios as well as market shares to aid its *preliminary* assessment of a horizontal merger case. 'Market shares and concentration levels provide useful first indications of the market structure and of the

---

[349] M.53, [1991] OJ L334/42. See also M.877, *Boeing/McDonnell Douglas* [1997] OJ L336/16.

[350] The Commission relied on the evidence of customers and competitors to conclude that there was not just one market for all aircraft of between 20 and 70 seats but three separate turbo-prop commuter aircraft markets for: commuters with 20–39 seats; 40–59 seats; and 60+ seats, each of which attracted different categories of buyers.

[351] M.53, *Aérospatiale/Alenia/de Havilland* [1991] OJ L334/42, para. 20.

[352] Form CO, s. 6.3.

[353] [2004] OJ C31/5, para. 5.

[354] Horizontal Merger Guidelines [2004] OJ C31/5, part III.

[355] Ibid., part IV.

[356] Ibid., parts V–VII.

[357] Ibid., part VIII.

[358] The HHI has some serious limitations, see S. Bishop and M. Walker, *The Economics of EC Competition Law: Concepts, Application and Measurement* (3rd edn, Sweet & Maxwell, 2010), 3-016–3-019.

[359] 'Although it is best to include all firms in the calculation, lack of information about very small firms may not be important because such firms do not affect the HHI significantly.' Horizontal Merger Guidelines, para. 16.

competitive importance of both the merging parties and their competitors.'[360] The Commission states that where the market share of the undertakings concerned does not exceed 25 per cent the merger is not liable to impede effective competition and is presumed to be compatible with the internal market. Further the Notice on simplified procedure applies if the parties' combined market share is less than 20 per cent or if the merger leads only to a small incremental increase in market share.[361] Conversely, a market share of over 50 per cent may in itself be evidence of the existence of a dominant market position.[362] The Commission accepts, however, that high market shares cannot necessarily be equated with market power. An adverse finding may not result, for example, where they are met by rigorous competition from an active competitor on the market,[363] where the increase in market share is insignificant or market shares are declining,[364] where they will be counteracted by buyer power[365] or new entry,[366] or market shares are volatile.[367]

The Commission also looks to the overall concentration level in a market, for useful information about the competitive situation, an indication of the market structure, and of the competitive importance of the merging parties and their competitors.[368] Like market shares, the HHI is used as an initial indicator of the absence of competition concerns, but 'do not give rise to a presumption of either the existence or the absence of such concerns'.[369] The Guidelines state that the Commission is *unlikely* to identify competition concerns in a market:[370]

- with a post-merger HHI below 1,000;

- with a post-merger HHI between 1,000 and 2,000, where the change in the HHI (the delta) is below 250;

- with a post-merger HHI above 2,000, where the delta is below 150;

except where special circumstances exist, for example: one of the firms is a potential entrant or an important innovator; one of the firms is a maverick likely to disrupt coordinated conduct; one of the firms has a pre-merger market share of 50 per cent or more; cross-shareholdings exist between the market participants; or there is evidence of past coordination of facilitating practices on the market.

---

[360] Ibid., para. 14.

[361] [2013] OJ C366/4, II.

[362] Horizontal Merger Guidelines, paras. 17–18 and see, e.g., M.6166, *Deutsche Börse/NYSE Euronext* 1 February 2012, *aff'd* Case T-175/12, *Deutsche Börse v Commission* EU:T:2015:148. See also later discussion of market shares and entry analysis and Case C-62/86, *AKZO Chemie BV v Commission* [1991] ECR I-3359, para. 60 (in the context of an Art. 102 case, the CJ reiterated that: 'very large shares are in themselves, and save in exceptional circumstances, evidence of the existence of a dominant position . . . That is the situation where there is a market share of 50%', see Chap. 6.

[363] See, e.g., M.68, *Tetra Pak/Alfa Laval* [1991] OJ L290/35, 38–39; M.12, *Varta/Bosch* [1991] OJ L320/26 (the merged entity held 44% of the German battery market but a competitor, with only 5–10% of the market would provide strong competition on account of its reputation and resources); M.4, *Renault/Volvo* [1990] OJ C281/2 (Renault would acquire 54% of the French market but Mercedes, which had only 18%, had the reputation and resources to be able to exercise sufficient competitive restraint on Renault); and M.4533, *SCA/P&G* 5 September 2007 (European facial tissue business) (market shares of 80–90% would not enable the merged entity to exercise market power because of vigorous competition from private labels). However, some competitors may not provide effective competition and may be unlikely to do so in the future: M.190, *Nestlé/Perrier* [1992] OJ L356/1.

[364] See, e.g., McGeown and Barthélemy, n. 343, 444.

[365] See, e.g., M.1225, *Enso/Stora* [1999] OJ L254/9 and M.4617, *Nutreco/BASF* 25 September 2007.

[366] M.42, *Alcatel/Telettra* [1991] OJ L122/48 and see Section 5.D.v.

[367] See, e.g., Case T-79/12, *Cisco Systems Inc v Commission* EU:T:2013:635, n. 373 and text, M.354, *American Cyanamid/Shell* [1993] OJ C273/6 ('an analysis focusing on market shares alone is not particularly probative in a dynamic and R&D-intensive industry') and M.7217, *Facebook/WhatsApp* 3 October 2014.

[368] Horizontal Merger Guidelines, paras. 14–21.

[369] Ibid., para. 21.

[370] Ibid., paras. 19–21.

In *Sun Chemical Group v Commission*[371] the GC had to consider the importance of these preliminary tools to the robustness of a Commission decision authorising a merger between Apollo and Akzo Nobel (the first and second players in the market). The appellants argued that the Commission had failed (a) to draw the right conclusions from the fact that the merger between Apollo and Akzo Nobel would result in a combined market share of 40–50 per cent (indicative of dominance) and (b) to consider concentration levels which would have indicated real concern. The GC held that the analysis of market shares did not in itself show the existence of dominance.[372] Further, that the Commission's failure to make an HHI calculation did not affect the finding on dominance (even if, as the applicants alleged, the calculation indicated that the effects of the merger exceeded the Commission's stipulated thresholds). Exceeding the HHI thresholds did not give rise to a presumption of the existence of competition concerns. On the contrary, market shares and concentration levels, whilst providing useful first indications, did not have to be assessed in every decision.

In *Cisco Systems Inc v Commission*,[373] the GC similarly rejected the claimant's action seeking an annulment of the Commission's decision clearing the *Microsoft/Skype* merger on the grounds that the combination of a very high market share and HHI concentration degree (of 7,340) provided, at the very least, a 'strong indicia of the existence of competition concerns warranting additional scrutiny'.[374] Again the Court stressed that these factors provided only a starting point in the assessment; 'market shares may only be used as indicia of competition concerns …'.[375] The Court noted that in this case the markets shares were very unstable, particularly as the sector (consumer communications) was a recent and fast-growing one characterised by short innovation cycles in which 'large market shares may turn out to be ephemeral. In such a dynamic context, high market shares are not necessarily indicative of market power and, therefore, of lasting damage to competition which Regulation No 139/2004 seeks to prevent.'[376] The GC also referred to a number of features of the market which meant that the market shares and concentration ratio could not be said to be 'indicative of a degree of market power which would enable the new entity to significantly impede effective competition in the internal market'.[377]

Some competition agencies now supplement or substitute traditional analysis based on market definition, market shares, and concentration measures with other tools, such as pricing pressure indices (PPIs)—especially for mergers in differentiated product markets where the competitive effect depends more upon the closeness of competition between the merging parties than on market shares—and merger simulation,[378] based on oligopoly models.[379] 'Upward pricing pressure' (UPP) seeks to measure the incentives of the merged firm to increase the price of its products post-merger and is calculated on the basis of diversion ratios and price/cost margins.[380] For example, the US Horizontal Merger Guidelines state:[381]

In some cases, where sufficient information is available, the Agencies assess the value of diverted sales, which can serve as an indicator of upward pricing pressure [UPP] on the first product resulting from the merger. Diagnosing unilateral price effects based on the value of diverted sales need not rely on market

---

[371] Case T-282/06, [2007] ECR II-2149.

[372] Ibid., paras. 133–142.

[373] Case T-79/12, EU:T:2013:635.

[374] Ibid., para. 56.

[375] Ibid., para. 65. It held that the same is true for concentration ratios.

[376] Ibid., para. 69.

[377] Ibid., para. 74.

[378] See, e.g., n. 399 and text.

[379] See, e.g., OECD Roundtable on Market Definition, Discussion paper, DAF/COMP(2012) 13, and Chap. 1.

[380] See, e.g., J. Farrell and C. Shapiro, 'Antitrust Evaluation of Horizontal Mergers: An Economic Alternative to Market Definition' (2010) 10 *B.E. J of Theoretical Economics* (Policies perspectives) and A. Oldale and J. Padilla, 'EU Merger Assessment of Upward Pricing Pressure: Making Sense of UPP, GUPPI and the Like' (2013) 4 *JECLAP* 375.

[381] US DOJ and FTC, Horizontal Merger Guidelines, 19 August 2010 (2010 Guidelines), 6.1.

definition or the calculation of market shares and concentration. The Agencies rely much more on the value of diverted sales than on the level of the HHI for diagnosing unilateral price effects in markets with differentiated products. If the value of diverted sales is proportionately small, significant unilateral price effects are unlikely.

As, unlike UPP, this approach does not take account of efficiencies or other factors that would create downward pricing pressure,[382] it is generally described as the 'gross upward pricing pressure index', or GUPPI.

Although the Commission still considers traditional assessment based on market shares, etc. to provide an 'important and strong' first indication of market power in many markets (such as mature, basic industries in which firms produce relatively homogenous products)[383] and does not refer to UPP or GUPPI in its guidelines, analysis of UPP is starting to form an integral part of its 'quantitative merger assessment' (see, for example, *Hutchinson 3G Austria/Orange Austria*,[384] *Telefónica Deutschland/E-Plus*,[385] and *Hutchison 3G UK/Telefónica Ireland*[386]).[387] Indeed, in unilateral effects cases it takes account of UPP through assessing diversion ratios and the profit margins of firms when determining the closeness of competition between the merging firms.[388]

c. Possible Non-coordinated Anti-competitive Effects

Where a merger removes important competitive constraints on the merging firms those firms may acquire greater market power. The merged entity may then be able to increase price or reduce quality, choice, or innovation irrespective of the response of its competitors.[389] Generally, such market power will be acquired, and the merger will give rise to non-coordinated effects, where the merger creates or strengthens the dominant position of a single firm which, typically, acquires a larger market share than the next competitor post-merger. The Horizontal Merger Guidelines also make it clear, however, that non-coordinated effects may arise outside this classic scenario where the merger occurs on an oligopolistic market.[390]

25. Generally, a merger giving rise to such non-coordinated effects would significantly impede effective competition by creating or strengthening the dominant position of a single firm, one which, typically, would have an appreciably larger market share than the next competitor post-merger. Furthermore, mergers in oligopolistic markets involving the elimination of important competitive constraints that the merging parties previously exerted on each other together with a reduction of competitive pressure on the remaining competitors may, even where there is little likelihood of coordination between the members of the oligopoly, also result in a significant impediment to competition. The Merger Regulation clarifies that all mergers giving rise to such non-coordinated effects shall also be declared incompatible with the common market.

---

[382] It is not a means for assessing entry, buyer power, or efficiencies etc.

[383] M.6471, *Outokumpu/Inoxum* 7 November 2012, paras. 315 and 360.

[384] M.6497, 12 December 2012, see n. 425 and text.

[385] M.7018, 2 July 2014, see n. 426 and text.

[386] M.6992, see n. 427 and text.

[387] See L. Wiethaus and R. Nitsche, 'Upward Pricing Pressure Analysis: Critical Issues in Recent Applications' (2015) 6 *JECLAP* 48 and G. Drauz, P. McGeown, and B. Record, 'Recent Developments in EU Merger Control' (2013) 4 *JECLAP* 146, 153.

[388] See ibid., n. 394 and text, and e.g., S. Thomas, 'Close Competitors in Merger Review' (2013) 4 *JECLAP* 391 ('[a]lthough the analysis of closeness of competition is an important enhancement of substantive merger appraisal, it is not appropriate to waive market definition as such').

[389] If other firms on the market follow, then the anti-competitive effects will be felt throughout the market. In contrast with coordinated effects cases, however, the ability of the merged entity to increase price is not dependent upon the reaction of other undertakings in the market.

[390] Horizontal Merger Guidelines, para. 25. See also the discussion of *T-Mobile/tele.ring*, nn. 420–424 and accompanying text.

The Guidelines set out a non-exhaustive list of factors that the Commission considers may influence its decision as to whether significant non-coordinated anti-competitive effects are likely to result from the merger:

The Market Shares Held by the Merging Firms and the Closeness of Competition Between Them

It has been seen[391] that the larger the combined market shares and the increase in market share the more likely it is that the merger will lead to a significant increase in market power.[392] The discussion above, however, provides an important reminder that market shares are just one factor in a dominance or unilateral effects assessment. Whilst being an important factor, a high market share will not constitute 'decisive proof that the merged group will hold market power';[393] assessment of other factors, including the nature of the product and industry, is also vital. Another critical factor in non-coordinated effects cases is the closeness of competition between the merging parties, often tested by the Commission through the use of questionnaires sent to customers and competitors of the merging parties and/or through quantitative analysis and the measurement of diversion ratios.

Where products are differentiated on a market, some will be closer substitutes for each other than others:[394]

28. Products may be differentiated within a relevant market such that some products are closer substitutes than others. The higher the degree of substitutability between the merging firms' products, the more likely it is that the merging firms will raise prices significantly. For example, a merger between two producers offering products which a substantial number of customers regard as their first and second choices could generate a significant price increase. Thus, the fact that rivalry between the parties has been an important source of competition on the market may be a central factor in the analysis. High pre-merger margins may also make significant price increases more likely. The merging firms' incentive to raise prices is more likely to be constrained when rival firms produce close substitutes to the products of the merging firms than when they offer less close substitutes. It is therefore less likely that a merger will significantly impede effective competition, in particular through the creation or strengthening of a dominant position, when there is a high degree of substitutability between the products of the merging firms and those supplied by rival producers.

The competition between firms may also be more intense the more proximately located the competitor.

S. Bishop and M. Walker, *The Economics of EC Competition Law: Concepts, Application and Measurement* (3rd edn, Sweet & Maxwell, 2010)

Mergers involving differentiated products

7.026 Potential variations in the 'closeness' of competition between competing firms that arises from product or geographical differentiation raises a number of additional complications in applying the traditional approach to assessing whether a merger gives rise to unilateral effects . . . [I]t is often argued that defining the relevant market is much more problematic in industries characterized by a high degree of differentiation, But . . . the Hypothetical Monopolist Test is well-suited to addressing such issues. This implies that any additional complications that arise in industries with highly differentiated goods and services relate to the interpretation that can be drawn from market shares rather than the definition of the

---

[391] Ibid., paras. 27–30.

[392] See, e.g., M.6663, *Ryanair/Aer Lingus* 27 February 2013 (discussed from n. 401 and text), M.4404, *Universal/BMG* 22 May 2007; M.4523, *Travelport/Worldspan* 21 August 2007; M.4381, *JCI/FIAMM* 10 May 2007; and M.4734, *INEOS/Kerling* 30 January 2008.

[393] Horizontal Merger Guidelines, para. 27.

[394] Ibid., para. 28.

relevant market. Interpreting market shares in highly differentiated industries is rendered more difficult since the very essence of competition between differentiated products implies that consumers do not consider all products to be equally substitutable. In consequence, products do not all impose the same strength of competitive constraint on each other. Where this is the case, market shares provide a poor proxy for discriminating 'close' competitors and 'not so close' competitors.

A competitor will be said to be, loosely speaking, 'close' if following a relative price increase a significant proportion of the resulting lost sales would be gained by that competitor. The concept of 'closeness of competition' when a merger concerns highly differentiated products can be thought of in terms of product characteristics and geographical location. For example, a premium ice cream, say, is likely to face 'closer' competition from another supplier of a premium ice cream brand than from a supplier of an own-label product. Similarly, when transportation costs are important, a supplier is likely to face 'closer' competition from suppliers located nearby than from those located far away.

The concept of 'closeness' of competition is illustrated in the following example. Suppose there are four firms, A, B, C, and D, each with sales of 100. Suppose that if A raises its price by 5 per cent, it will lose 20 per cent of its sales, which makes the price rise unprofitable. These sales would be diverted to the other three firms as shown in Table 7.2. This table shows that 15 consumers divert from A to B, three divert to C and two divert to D. In this sense, B is a closer competitor to A than either C or D; the extent to which consumers would divert from A to B is understated by B's market share. If A and B were to merge, then an increase in the post-merger price of products supplied by A would lead to the combined firm, AB, losing only five units of sales. In consequence, increasing the price of A by 5 per cent is more likely to be profitable than a merger between A and D, where the same increase in the price of products supplied by A would lead to the loss of 18 units of sale.

Table 7.2 An illustration of Unilateral Effects

Firm	Sales at current prices	Sales if A raises price 5 per cent
A	100	80
B	100	115
C	100	103
D	100	102
AB	**200**	**195**

This example illustrates that the degree to which a merger in a differentiated product market might result in a unilateral price increase depends on the relative 'closeness' of the merging firms to one another. Based on market shares alone, B, C and D all appear to be providing an equally strong competitive constraint on A. However, examination of the diversion of sales from A to these firms shows that in this hypothetical example, B provides a much stronger pre-merger competitive constraint on A than either C or D since most of A's lost sales went to B, indicating that A and B are in some sense particularly 'close' competitors.

However, it is important to understand that the concept of closeness of competition cannot be divorced entirely from an assessment of market shares. In the above example, B is said to represent a particularly close competitor because the proportion of sales lost to B exceeds that predicted by market share alone; on the basis of market shares, we would predict that six to seven units would be diverted to B whereas in reality the number of units diverted (in the hypothetical example) would be 15. Assessing whether a merger will result in a reduction in the effectiveness of competition therefore requires an assessment of whether market shares provide a good proxy for the degree of pre-merger competitive constraint or whether they understate or overstate the importance of that competitive constraint. In the case where market shares understate the competitive constraint, we can properly consider two firms to be 'close' competitors.

When assessing closeness of competition, it is important that the source of that closeness is clearly articulated and closely examined. All too often, it is asserted that two firms are particularly close competitors without reference being made to the alleged source of that closeness. Assessing whether two firms represent particularly close competitors is an empirical question and cannot (or should not) be determined solely with reference to physical or geographical attributes of the firms concerned. For example, consider a straight road on which four petrol stations are located. On one level, it might appear intuitive that the petrol stations adjacent to one another provide 'closer' competitive constraints than no-adjacent petrol stations. But that is not necessarily the case. If all potential consumers drive past all of these four petrol stations on their way to work from home then all the petrol stations could be equally close. Similarly, the fact that two firms have more similar offerings than some other competitors cannot by itself be determinative that they represent particularly close competitors.

In cases where the parties are found not to be close competitors, such as *Facebook/WhatsApp*,[395] an unconditional clearance decision is likely. In contrast a merger between firms which produce products with a high degree of substitutability is more likely to produce anti-competitive consequences and either be prohibited or cleared only subject to commitments. In *Volvo/Scania*[396] the Commission, in assessing the effect of Volvo's acquisition of a controlling stake in Scania, was influenced by the fact that in various markets Volvo and Scania (active on the heavy trucks markets) had similar market positions and that their products were each other's closest substitutes. The loss of competition between them would significantly increase the merged entity's advantage over its competitors.[397]

In *GE/Instrumentarium*[398] the Commission was concerned about the proposed acquisition by GE Medical Equipment of a Finnish-based company, Instrumentarium, which was a leading manufacturer of hospital equipment. The merger would bring together two of the four leading players in Europe in patient monitors, markets characterised by differentiated products with competition taking place through tenders. In particular, the Commission considered that the merger would lead to the merged entity acquiring high market shares in a number of national EU markets for perioperative monitors, used by anaesthesiologists to monitor patients during operations. The Commission conducted a series of statistical analyses and relied on bidding data and win-loss analysis[399] to establish that the parties were particularly close competitors, at least on some markets, so that the merger would significantly increase their market power.[400] Analysis showed that each of the parties was likely to charge a lower price where the other took part in the bidding contest. In the end the concentration was cleared subject to a package of remedies designed to remove the horizontal overlaps in the perioperative monitoring market.

---

[395] M.7217, 3 October 2014. In M.7259, *Carphone Warehouse/Dixons* 25 June 2014 the Commission accepted that the businesses were not close competitors, partly because they operated very different business models.

[396] M.1672, [2001] OJ L143/74.

[397] Ibid., paras. 31–70 and 107 (the geographical scope of the market was crucial in this case. If, as the parties alleged, the market was an EU or EEA market the parties' market shares would have been diluted since they did not have such a significant presence on markets outside four Nordic countries and Ireland. The Commission concluded that for these five countries the relevant geographic markets were still national in scope).

[398] M.3083, [2004] OJ L109/1.

[399] The analysis considered the closeness of competition between the merging parties by analysing the ranking of the other party in contracts won by one of them. Other mechanisms such as diversion rations, survey evidence, merger simulation, econometric techniques, shock analysis, and internal documents may also be used to measure closeness of competition between the merging parties, see, e.g., Lindsay and Berridge, n. 318, 7.3 and, e.g., M.3765, *Amer/Salomon* 12 October 2005.

[400] M.3083, IP/03/1193, paras. 131 ff. But contrast, e.g., M.3765, ibid.

The closeness of competition between the merging parties was a critical factor in the Commission's first decision[401] prohibiting Ryanair's hostile take-over bid for Aer Lingus.[402] This was a controversial case, not only as it was the first merger prohibition since 2004 but also because it was the first time that the Commission has prohibited a merger between airlines.[403] The Commission defined the relevant market as point-to-point scheduled air transport services between cities (each route having its own point of origin and own point of destination). On this basis, the Commission found that the proposed transaction would lead to actual overlaps between the merging parties on 35 routes. The Commission also prohibited a subsequent attempt by Ryanair to take over Aer Lingus in 2013.[404]

In assessing the competitive effects of the first Ryanair/Aer Lingus merger attempt, the Commission found not only that the parties would have very high combined market shares on a large number of routes as they would acquire a monopoly position on 22 of the routes and more than 60 per cent market share on 13 more routes[405] (when reviewing the merger in 2012 the Commission found these figures to have increased to 28 and 18 respectively (i.e. a total of 46 routes with very high market shares)) but that the merger would eliminate competition between the two closest competitors on the routes and that barriers to entry into the markets were high. Ryanair argued that it and Aer Lingus were not close competitors. On the contrary, they were very different and occupied distinctive spaces in the markets in which they operated. In particular, Ryanair argued that it targeted customers whose alternative was not to fly with another airline but rather not to fly at all. It claimed that its low cost base was such that no other airline was capable of targeting these passengers. Accordingly, Ryanair was not constrained in its pricing by other airlines but rather by the price sensitivity of its passengers.[406] Ryanair also sought to distinguish its service from that offered by Aer Lingus, arguing that Aer Lingus was a 'mid-frills' operator offering seat allocation and flying to more centrally located airports,[407] whilst Ryanair was a 'no-frills' operator.

The Commission did not find Ryanair's arguments supported by its in-depth analysis and its decision was upheld by the GC. Rather, it found evidence to establish that Aer Lingus, although a former national flag carrier, had adjusted its business model to become increasingly similar to Ryanair[408] and that Aer Lingus sought to compete with the no-frills airlines rather than to differentiate itself in terms of quality.[409] In addition, both airlines flew point-to-point,[410] i.e. directly between individual

---

[401] The transaction was notified three times, see M.4439, 27 June 2007 (prohibited), M.5434 (withdrawn in January 2009), and M.6663, 27 February 2013 (prohibited).

[402] M.4439, 27 June 2007; Case T-342/07, *Ryanair v Commission* [2010] ECR II-3457; Case T-411/07, *Aer Lingus v Commission* [2010] ECR II-3457 (both appeals were dismissed); M.6663, *Ryanair/Aer Lingus* 27 February 2013; and see A. Witt, 'From *Airtours* to *Ryanair*: Is the More Economic Approach to EU Merger Law Really About More Economics?' (2012) 49 *CMLRev* 217.

[403] See IP/07/893, see also M.5830, *Olympic Air/Aegean Airlines I* 26 January 2011, n. 509 and text. Contrast, e.g., M.5335, *Lufthansa/SN Airholding (Brussels Airline)* 14 April 2010, M.5747, *Iberia/British Airways* 14 July 2010, and M.6447, *IAG/bmi* 30 March 2012 (cleared subject to commitments to give up airport slots) and for a review of a number of airline mergers, see, e.g., G. Drauz, T. Chellingsworth, and H. Hyrkas, 'Recent Developments in EC Merger Control' (2010) 1 *JECLAP* 12, 14–17

[404] See n. 401.

[405] M.4439, 27 June 2007, para. 342.

[406] Ibid., paras. 52, 53, 432, and 433.

[407] Ibid., para. 353.

[408] The Commission noted that there was a range of airlines offering different levels of service so that, at one end of the spectrum, would be 'full-service' airlines offering, e.g., seat reservation, online check-in, last-minute bookings, customer loyalty schemes, free baggage handling, business lounges, free drinks and food on board, etc. and, at the other end of the spectrum, would be the 'no-frills' airlines offering a rudimentary level of service encompassing few, if any, of the above, ibid., para. 49.

[409] E.g., Aer Lingus had adopted its marketing slogan ('Low Fares—Way Better'). This slogan appeared to constitute a direct response to Ryanair's slogan: 'The Low Fares Airline', ibid., para. 367, Case T-342/07, [2010] ECR II-3457, paras. 92–93.

[410] M.4439, ibid., paras. 47–48.

airports, rather than on a hub-and-spoke model where traffic flows through a central hub.[411] Both operated out of, and were based at, Dublin airport[412] and had a combined share of about 80 per cent of all scheduled European traffic to and from Dublin.

The Commission also found evidence establishing that each party closely monitored the other's marketing campaigns and price changes and constrained each other's behaviour in relation to both price and other parameters of competition (e.g. frequencies, capacity load factors, expansion of networks, advertising, and pricing of ancillary services).[413] These findings were corroborated by a price regression analysis, together and a specifically designed passenger survey.[414] The analyses established that Ryanair did constrain Aer Lingus's prices generally in a way that other carriers did not, and that customers did consider Aer Lingus or Ryanair to be closer substitutes for one another than from other carriers.[415] The Commission thus found the parties to be each other's closest actual competitor[416] and that the merger would eliminate competition on these routes and give the merged entity significantly increased market power. Consequently it could be predicated that, post-merger, both carriers would have an incentive to set higher fares (or reduce the number of flights) for Aer Lingus since most customers lost as a result would be captured by Ryanair. Further, the merger would take away incentives for the airlines to increase quality and to innovate.[417]

In 2012 and 2013 the Commission also blocked mergers between: *Deutsche Börse/NYSE Euronext*[418] which would have led to parties acquiring extremely high market shares in a number of exchange-traded financial derivatives markets; and *UPS/TNT Express*,[419] a so-called gap case. In *UPS/TNT* the Commission concluded that the parties were close competitors and that the merger, which would have created a stronger number 2 player in the express delivery services market (behind DHL), would result in UPP which was not offset by efficiency benefits.

In addition, the Commission has been concerned about mergers in mobile telecoms markets, especially where they may eliminate a new or maverick player from the market. In *T-Mobile/tele.ring*,[420] the Commission assessed a merger between the second (T-Mobile Austria) and fourth (tele.ring) players in the Austrian mobile telephony services market. Post-merger, Mobilkom would remain the market leader so that, despite an increase in market shares, the merged entity would remain the number two player on the market. The Commission was nonetheless concerned about the removal of tele.ring from the already concentrated market. Although it did not explicitly rely on the particular closeness of competition between the merging parties, it did consider that tele.ring had exerted significant competitive pressure on both Mobilkom and T-Mobile and that its removal from

---

[411] In contrast to previous airline cases decided by the Commission which involved network carriers operating at different airports in different countries, see, e.g., M.3940, *Lufthansa/Eurowings* 22 December 2005, M.3280, *Air France/KLM* 11 February 2002, *aff'd* Case T-177/04, *easyJet v Commission* [2006] ECR II-1913.

[412] Where they concentrate their operations and the point from where a majority of their flights begin and end. It is also the place of: overnighting aircraft; maintenance, customer care, and ground-handling services; stand-by planes; and where staff are based, M.4439, 27 June 2007, paras. 404–407.

[413] Ibid., para. 434 ff.

[414] A price regression analysis is a specific tool for understanding the relationship between two or more variables, see e.g., M. de la Mano, E. Pesaresi, and O. Stehman, 'Econometric and survey evidence in the competitive assessment of the Ryanair-Aer Lingus merger' (2007) 3 *Competition Policy Newsletter* 73.

[415] M.4439, 27 June 2007, paras. 79–80.

[416] Ibid., para. 431.

[417] Ibid., para. 491. The Commission was also concerned about the impact the merger would have on potential competition. As the airlines were the main carriers operating on routes to/from Dublin, the merger would eliminate the most likely entrant on routes out of that airport currently served by only one of them.

[418] M.6166, 1 February 2012, *aff'd* Case T-175/12, *Deutsche Börse v Commission* EU:T:2015:148. The Commission rejected the parties' claim that extensive efficiencies would outweigh the negative effects of the merger, see especially n. 533 and text.

[419] M.6570, 30 January 2013.

[420] M.3916, 26 April 2006.

the market would result in non-coordinated effects.[421] In particular, tele.ring was a relatively new entrant to the market which had quickly gained market share through vibrant competitive practices and the offering of low prices;[422] it was an aggressive and innovative competitor.[423] The Commission thus approved the merger only after specific remedies designed to strengthen the position of smaller players on the market were agreed.[424]

Subsequently, the Commission has investigated other mergers in, for example, the Austrian,[425] German,[426] Irish,[427] and Danish[428] mobile-telecoms markets (considering in each case that the geographical markets are national). In *Hutchison 3G UK/Telefónica Ireland*, the Commission was also worried that the merger, which would reduce the number of mobile network operators in Ireland from four to three, would eliminate the newest and an aggressive or innovative competitor from the market. In the end the merger was cleared subject to commitments.

The Commission has reviewed each of these telecom mergers on a case-by-case basis assessing each in the context of the national market in which it operates and stressing that there is no magic 'acceptable' number of mobile network operators in a given country. Commissioner Vestager has also made it clear that although such mergers may be argued to stimulate investment, the Commission takes the view that companies usually have strongest incentives to invest and innovate in competitive markets. In general therefore it seeks to ensure that mergers do not weaken competition. In the context of telecoms:

So far, I have not seen compelling evidence that would support the existence of a trade-off between competition and investment.

Research seems to suggest that a reduction of the number of players from four-to-three in a national mobile market in the EU can lead to higher prices for consumers. But not that it leads to more investment per subscriber. In other words, it does not seem to lead to significantly higher overall investment by carriers.

And we should not forget that consumers ultimately do not benefit from investment as such. It is the impact of investment on parameters of competition such as quality and price that leads to consumer benefit.[429]

In many of the cases discussed in the section above, the emphasis has been on the impact of the reduction of competition on price. In some markets, however, it may be necessary to consider

---

[421] The s. 6(1)(c) document raised concerns about both coordinated and non-coordinated effects but the former were not pursued in the final decision.

[422] The Commission described tele.ring as a 'maverick', normally a more important issue in coordinated effects cases, see Section 5.D.iii.d pp. 1152-1161 and Horizontal Merger Guidelines, para. 42.

[423] For the view that 'the Commission appears to be exploring alternative ways of describing and assessing closeness of competition', including by describing 'one or more of the merging parties as "particularly aggressive or innovative"', see McGeown and Barthélemy, n. 343, 448.

[424] The merging parties agreed to divest UMTS frequencies and mobile telephony sites off to smaller players, such as Hutchison 3G. These commitments were designed to enable Hutchison 3G to expand its Austrian network without being dependent on its current national roaming agreement with Mobilkom.

[425] M.6497, *Hutchison 3G Austria/Orange Austria* 12 December 2012 (merger that would reduce the number of players on the Austrian market from four to three was cleared subject to commitments. The Commission declined to make a reference back to the Austrian authorities under Art. 9). See also subsequent *ex post* evaluations of the impact of the merger, <http://www.bwb.gv.at/Documents/BWB2016-re-Ex-post%20evaluation%20of%20the%20mobile%20telecommunications%20market.pdf> and <https://www.rtr.at/de/inf/Analysis_merger_H3G_Orange/Ex_post_analysis_merger_H3G_Orange_RTR.pdf> and M.7612, *Hutchison 3G UK/ Telefónica UK*, 11 May 2016 (prohibited).

[426] M.7018, *Telefónica Deutschland/E-Plus* 2 July 2014.

[427] M.6992, *Hutchison 3G UK/Telefónica Ireland* 28 May 2014.

[428] M.7419, *TeliaSonera/Telenor/JV* (withdrawn). The parties abandoned this merger, which would have created the largest mobile network operator in Denmark and a highly concentrated market structure (the merged entity and TDC would have had around 80% of the market), when it became clear that the Commission was likely to reject the remedies offered by the parties and prohibit it. The Commission was concerned that the merger would have both anti-competitive unilateral effects and coordinated effects and negatively affect the favourable conditions for competition that existed in Denmark. It was not clear how these would be offset by greater investment, see speech of Vestager, n. 113.

[429] See Vestager, n. 113, and discussion of efficiencies below.

the impact of the transaction on the quality of the products/services offered or consumer choice post-merger, for example, in markets where consumers particularly value the quality of the product or service provided (over price) or, in the information economy, where consumers may especially value privacy and security issues (as a form of non-price competition[430]), for example the quality of data protection offered to them. These non-price or quality effects are much more difficult to assess and many competition agencies may not possess the analytical economic tools to do so in all cases.[431]

The Ability of Customers to Switch

Customers unable to switch, for example because of the limited availability of alternative suppliers or because of significant switching costs, are particularly vulnerable to price rises.[432] In contrast, where customers are able to switch, any attempt by the merging parties to raise price would be likely to be counteracted. In *Votorantim/Fischer*,[433] for example, the Commission cleared a concentration between two global orange juice producers. A number of other suppliers existed and customers could easily switch between them.

The Likelihood That Competitors Will Increase Supply

If competitors cannot increase output (or to not have the incentive to do so), it may be easier for the merging firms to restrict output themselves and to benefit from price rises:[434]

When market conditions are such that the competitors of the merging parties are unlikely to increase their supply substantially if prices increase, the merging firms may have an incentive to reduce output below the combined premerger levels, thereby raising market prices. The merger increases the incentive to reduce output by giving the merged firm a larger base of sales on which to enjoy the higher margins resulting from an increase in prices induced by the output reduction.[435]

Conversely, where rival firms have significant spare capacity and are likely to find it profitable to expand output sufficiently, the Commission is unlikely to find that the merger will create or strengthen a dominant position or otherwise significantly impede effective competition.[436]

In merger cases it is therefore important to assess competitors' ability to increase output in response to a price rise, and their incentives to do so. The former might be limited by capacity constraints, the cost of increasing capacity, or 'barriers to expansion'.[437] Such barriers may originate from the merging firms themselves,[438] for example as a result of their controlling or influencing the supply of essential inputs, access to distribution channels, and access to intellectual property rights (IPRs), or where the merged entity would have the ability and incentive to raise costs or decrease the quality of service to rivals in markets where interoperability between different infrastructures or platforms is important (e.g., in energy, telecommunications, and communications industries).[439]

---

[430] See Stucke and Grunes, n. 28 and, e.g., M.7217, *Facebook/WhatsApp* 3 October 2014.

[431] Stucke and Grunes, n. 28, 5. See also, e.g., Costa-Cabral and Lynskey, n. 27.

[432] Horizontal Merger Guidelines, para. 31 and see, e.g., M.4381, *JCI/FIAMM* 10 May 2007.

[433] M.5907, 4 May 2011.

[434] See, e.g., M.4525, *Kronospan/Constantia* 19 July 2007.

[435] Horizontal Merger Guidelines, para. 32.

[436] Ibid., para. 33. See, e.g., M.7230, *Bakaert/Pirelli Steel Tyre Cord Business* 30 July 2014.

[437] The inability of competitors to expand capacity is most likely to be problematic where products are homogenous, but it may also be important when suppliers produce differentiated products, Horizontal Merger Guidelines, para. 35.

[438] Ibid., para. 36.

[439] The fact that such behaviour might constitute an abuse of a dominant position is one factor that must be taken into account, see nn. 563–568 and following text.

In *MCI Worldcom/Sprint*,[440] the Commission prohibited a proposed merger of two global communications companies, MCI Worldcom Inc and Sprint Corp. It considered that the combination of the merged firms' extensive networks and customer base would lead to such a powerful force that both competitors and customers would have been dependent upon them to obtain universal internet connectivity. In particular, it would create a

super-tier provider of global internet connectivity. strong position due to its absolute and relative size compared to its competitors. Given the size of the merged entity, it will be able to control the prices of its competitors and customers. It will also be in a position to control technical developments. The combined entity will be able to sustain such behaviour due to its capacity to discipline the market notably through the threat of selective degradation of its competitors internet connectivity offering . . . and also through its essential ability to determine and agree any new technical development to enable advance internet services . . .[441]

In *GE/Instrumentarium*[442] the Commission also feared that the parties would be able to foreclose other perioperative monitor suppliers from the market by making its anaesthesia machines incompatible with rival monitors. This would, of course, have made it difficult for the competitors to respond to an increase in price by increasing capacity.

In addition to considering evidence of competitors' ability to expand output, the Commission may also assess whether competitors would have the incentive to expand output sufficiently, that is to say whether they would find it profitable to expand output so as to offset a likely price increase by the merged entity. In *INEOS/Solvay JV*,[443] for example, the Commission considered that as, post-merger, three firms by sales would hold more than 80–90% of sales, the market would be highly concentrated so that a price increase from the newly created JV would shift some demand to competitors and reduce the competitive pressure on those competitors.

(1024) When faced with an increase in demand following a price increase by the JV, therefore, the Notifying Parties' competitors would generally respond by increasing their price and expanding production or redirecting their output into [North Western Europe], or possibly both. Reactions by rivals of the merging parties in a concentrated market can therefore generally be expected not to be sufficiently strong to make a price increase unprofitable for the JV.

(1025) This prediction remains applicable also in the presence of spare capacity pre-Transaction. In particular, in an oligopolistic market, competitors do not necessarily have an incentive to expand output up to the full capacity utilization, as it can often happen that the profit maximizing level of output is below maximum capacity. Even in markets which are characterised by levels of spare capacity at the industry level such as in this case, therefore, a merger which leads to a substantial consolidation of production capacities can be expected to lead to significant non-coordinated effects, as described at Paragraph 24 of the Horizontal Merger Guidelines.

(1026) Thus, in a mature, concentrated market where the degree of product homogeneity is very high…reactions by rivals of the merging parties even in the presence of spare capacity can generally be expected not to be sufficiently strong to make a price increase unprofitable for the JV.

(1027) In this case, therefore, non-merging parties…can most likely be expected to benefit from the reduction of competitive pressure between INEOS and Solvay, which will result from the Transaction. Those rivals are therefore expected to refrain from making full use of their spare capacity, when available, to expand output so as to offset a price increase by the JV post-Transaction. Conversely, they would likely expand output to some extent and increase their prices

(1028)…[T]he Notifying Parties' competitors will have no incentive, as well as no ability, to expand output sufficiently so as to offset a likely price increase by the JV post-Transaction…[444]

---

[440] M.1741, 28 June 2000, annulled, Case T-310/00, *MCI v Commission* [2004] ECR II-3253.

[441] M.1741, *MCI Worldcom/Sprint* 28 June 2000, para. 146.

[442] M.3083, IP/03/1193.

[443] M.6905, 8 May 2014.

[444] Ibid.

The Competitive Force Eliminated by the Merger

The merger is more likely to cause concern where the merger is with a firm that is likely to change the competitive dynamics of a market more than its market share suggests, e.g. if the merger involves a new entrant or an important innovator in the market (for example, where two companies have new competing products in the pipeline).[445]

In *Boeing/McDonnell Douglas*[446] the Commission was concerned that the merger would strengthen Boeing's already dominant position in the markets for large commercial aircraft and for narrow-body and wide-body aircraft. Although McDonnell Douglas's market share had been declining, responses from airlines indicated that its competitive influence had been greater than that reflected in its market share. Its participation in the competitive process and influence on competition was of significant importance leading, it appeared, to a reduction of over 7 per cent in the realised price. In the end the Commission cleared the merger subject to the parties complying with specified commitments.

In *Danone/Numico*[447] the Commission examine a merger between two major players on the French, Belgian, and Dutch markets for baby milk, meals, snacks, cereals, and drinks. In the French infant milk market, for example, the parties were close competitors and owned a high number of must-have brands. Numico had played an important role in making the market competitive, keeping prices down, and introducing innovative products. The Commission considered that the merger would lead to the removal of a strong competitive constraint on prices. In the end, the merger was cleared at the end of Phase I, subject to a commitment to divest the Numico baby milk business in France and a package of other remedies.

d. Possible Coordinated Anti-competitive Effects—Collective or Joint Dominance

The Horizontal Merger Guidelines deal separately with the question of how mergers leading to 'coordinated effects' or the creation of strengthening of a 'collective dominant position' can be identified.

Horizontal Merger Guidelines

39. In some markets the structure may be such that firms would consider it possible, economically rational, and hence preferable, to adopt on a sustainable basis a course of action on the market aimed at selling at increased prices. A merger in a concentrated market may significantly impede effective competition, through the creation or the strengthening of a collective dominant position, because it increases the likelihood that firms are able to coordinate their behaviour in this way and raise prices, even without entering into an agreement or resorting to a concerted practice within the meaning of Article [101] TFEU. A merger may also make coordination easier, more stable or more effective for firms, that were already coordinating before the merger, either by making the coordination more robust or by permitting firms to coordinate on even higher prices.

40. Coordination may take various forms. In some markets, the most likely coordination may involve keeping prices above the competitive level. In other markets, coordination may aim at limiting production or the amount of new capacity brought to the market. Firms may also coordinate by dividing the market, for instance by geographic area or other customer characteristics, or by allocating contracts in bidding markets.

---

[445] Horizontal Merger Guidelines, paras. 37–38 and see discussion of the mobile mergers, nn. 420-429 and text.

[446] M.877, [1997] OJ L336/16.

[447] M.4842, 31 October 2007.

In concentrated markets the Commission thus examines mergers to determine whether or not they will make coordination more likely to emerge in markets through the creation or strengthening of a collectively held dominant position. The Guidelines state that coordination is more likely to emerge in markets where it is relatively simple for the firms to reach a common understanding on terms of coordination and:

- the coordinating firms are able to monitor whether the terms of coordination are being adhered to;
- there is some form of credible deterrent mechanism to ensure discipline; and
- the reaction of outsiders, customers, or competitors will not jeopardise the results expected from the coordination.[448]

These conditions derive from case law developed under the old EUMR on the meaning of a collective dominant position, and in particular the GC's judgment in *Airtours*.

Background

It was seen in Chapter 9 that Article 101 prohibits explicit, but not tacit, collusion, but that explicit collusion is hard to detect. Further, that Article 102 provides less than an ideal tool for controlling tacit collusion. Given these difficulties, it is critical that the EUMR should be applicable to *prevent* mergers that might lead to collusion (whether explicit or tacit) on a market; otherwise the system would be seriously flawed.[449]

The old EUMR only allowed the Commission to prohibit mergers leading to the creation or strengthening of a dominant position. An important question was thus whether its scope was broad enough to prevent mergers which would lead to the creation or strengthening of a dominant position held collectively[450] by two or more independent entities united together by 'economic links'. Even though the old EUMR provided *no* textual support for such an approach,[451] the Commission took the view that it did,[452] a view which was affirmed in a series of judgments of the EU Courts.

The CJ first clarified, interpreting the original EUMR in accordance with 'its purpose and general structure',[453] that 'collective dominant positions do not fall outside the scope of the Regulation'[454] in *France v Commission*.[455] In this case the Commission had concluded that the merger led to the creation of a market-leading duopoly in the EU (except Germany) market for potash enjoyed by: Kali und Salz (K+S)/MdK (the merging parties) and Société Commerciale des Potasses et de l'Azote (SCPA) but cleared it, subject to commitments which affected not only the merging parties, but also SCPA. On the facts, the CJ annulled the Commission's decision, finding that it had not established

---

[448] Horizontal Merger Guidelines, para. 41. See also discussion of explicit and tacit collusion in Chap. 9.

[449] See Commission's *XVIth Report on Competition Policy* (1986), 285.

[450] Cases T-68 and 77–78/89, *Società Italiana Vetro (SIV) v Commission* [1992] ECR II-1403, see Chap. 9.

[451] Although Art. 102 refers to a dominant position held by 'one or more' undertakings, the old EUMR simply referred to concentrations which lead to the creation or strengthening of *a* dominant position, see the arguments raised in Case T-102/96, *Gencor Ltd v Commission* [1999] ECR II-753, report for the hearing, paras. 110–127 and D. Ridyard, 'Economic Analysis of Single Firm and Oligopolistic Dominance' [1994] *ECLR* 255, 258.

[452] It introduced the concept in M.165, *Alcatel/AEG Kabel* [1992] OJ C6/23 but nonetheless cleared the merger. In M.190, *Nestlé/Perrier* [1992] OJ L356/1 the Commission first took commitments as a condition for clearing a concentration (between Nestlé and Perrier) which it considered would 'create a duopolistic dominant position which would significantly impede [the] effective competition position on the French bottled water market'.

[453] In so doing, the CJ stressed that a textual and historical examination of the Regulation was not conclusive. Rather, an interpretation in accordance with its underlying objective (to prevent mergers which would prove incompatible with the system of undistorted competition envisaged by the Treaty) precluded a narrow interpretation which would deprive the Regulation of its intended effect, Cases C-68/94 and 30/95, *France v Commission, Société Commerciale des Potasses et de l'Azote (SCPA) v Commission* [1998] ECR I-1375, paras. 165–177.

[454] Ibid., para. 178.

[455] Ibid.

that the concentration would in fact give rise to a collective dominant position on the market.[456] Nonetheless, it confirmed the important point that the EUMR precluded mergers leading to the creation or strengthening of a dominant position and that the key to collective dominance was the parties' ability to adopt a common policy on the market and to act independently of their competitors, customers, and consumers.

In *France v Commission* the CJ did not (as in *Flat Glass*[457]) expressly state whether a collective dominant position could be held by parties which had no contractual or other links between them. However, the judgments of *Gencor Ltd v Commission*,[458] *Airtours plc v Commission*,[459] and *Impala*,[460] spelled out that a collective dominant position could be held by members of a 'tight oligopoly'.

Gencor[461] concerned a decision by two companies, Gencor Ltd (a South African company) and Lonrho Plc (a UK company), to merge their business activities in the platinum group metal (PGM) sector. Although the platinum businesses were both based in South Africa (and the South African Competition Board did not consider that the operation gave rise to competition policy concerns under South African law), the Commission nevertheless issued a decision prohibiting it. It considered that the merger would create a duopoly between the merged entity and Anglo American Corporation of South Africa Ltd (AAC), which, through its associated company, Amplats, was the remaining competitor on the market. Further, the anti-competitive effects of that duopoly would be felt on the relevant markets within the EU and EEA.[462] No contractual or other structural links existed between the parties.

The applicant sought annulment of the Commission's decision. After reiterating that 'collective dominant positions do not fall outside the scope of the Regulation' the Court rejected the applicant's claim that, in order that a finding of collective dominance be made, formal 'structural' links had to exist between the undertakings involved.

Case T-102/96, *Gencor Ltd v Commission* [1999] ECR II-753

General Court

273. In its judgment in the *Flat Glass* case, the Court referred to links of a structural nature only by way of example and did not lay down that such links must exist in order for a finding of collective dominance to be made.

274. It merely stated . . . that there is nothing, in principle to prevent two or more independent economic entities from being united by economic links in a specific market and, by virtue of that fact, from together holding a dominant position *vis-à-vis* the other operators on the same market.

. . .

276. Furthermore, there is no reason whatsoever in legal or economic terms to exclude from the notion of economic links the relationship of interdependence existing between the parties to a tight oligopoly within which, in a market with the appropriate characteristics, in particular in terms of market concentration, transparency and product homogeneity, those parties are in a position to anticipate one another's behaviour and are therefore strongly encouraged to align their conduct in the market, in particular in such

---

[456] This was the first case in which the CJ annulled a Commission decision under the EUMR. Following the annulment, the Commission re-examined the concentration and cleared it in Phase I proceedings.

[457] Cases T-68 and 77–78/89, *Società Italiana Vetro (SIV) v Commission* [1992] ECR II-1403.

[458] Case T-102/96, *Gencor Ltd v Commission* [1999] ECR II-753.

[459] Case T-342/99 [2002] ECR II-2585.

[460] Case T-464/04 [2006] ECR II-2289, Case C-413/06 P, *Bertelsmann and Sony Corp v Commission* [2008] ECR I-4951.

[461] Case T-102/96, *Gencor Ltd v Commission* [1999] ECR II-753.

[462] See also Section 8 and Chap. 16.

a way as to maximise their joint profits by restricting production with a view to increasing prices. In such a context, each trader is aware that highly competitive action on its part designed to increase its market share (for example a price cut) would provoke identical action by the others, so that it would derive no benefit from its initiative. All the traders would thus be affected by the reduction in price levels.

277. That conclusion is all the more pertinent with regard to the control of concentrations, whose objective is to prevent anti-competitive market structures from arising or being strengthened. Those structures may result from the existence of economic links in the strict sense argued by the applicant or from market structures of an oligopolistic kind where each undertaking may become aware of common interests and, in particular, cause prices to increase without having to enter into an agreement or resort to a concerted practice.

278. In the [present] case, therefore, the applicant's ground of challenge alleging that the Commission failed to establish the existence of structural links is misplaced.

279. The Commission was entitled to conclude, relying on the envisaged alteration in the structure of the market and on the similarity of the costs of Amplats and [Implats/LPD], that the proposed transaction would create a collective dominant position and lead in actual fact to a duopoly constituted by those two undertakings.

The case is illuminating. By referring to *Flat Glass* when considering the links required between undertakings before a finding of collective dominance can be made, the Court clearly envisages that collective dominance has the same meaning for the purposes of both Article 102 and the EUMR.[463]

In addition, the Court establishes that the contractual links given as examples of economic links in *Flat Glass* are not necessary to support a finding of collective dominance. Although the Court does not fully explain the difference between the 'structural' and 'economic links' it refers to in its judgment, it is clear that the market structure itself (the relationship of interdependence existing between parties to a tight oligopoly) suffices to establish the links required.

The next opportunity for the GC to rule on collective dominance followed the Commission's decision in *Airtours/First Choice*.[464] Here the Commission adopted a controversial decision prohibiting the acquisition by Airtours of First Choice. It held that the concentration would lead to the creation or strengthening of a collective dominant position on the UK short-haul foreign package holiday (FPH) market. The dominant position would be held by Airtours/First Choice (32 per cent), Thomson (27 per cent), and Thomas Cook (20 per cent). The remainder of the market was highly fragmented, and this meant that no effective restraint on the competitive conduct of the larger players would be exercised.

In reaching its decision the Commission appeared to expand the concept of collective dominance. The Commission held at paragraph 54 of its decision that it was not necessarily essential to show that the parties would adopt a common policy on the market. Rather, it appeared to take the view that the ability to engage in explicit or tacit coordination is not essential. It was sufficient that each individual undertaking operating on the oligopolistic market had sufficient market power to enable it to act independently (arguably therefore this was a 'gap' case). Nonetheless the Commission did consider that tacit coordination between the parties would occur. That tacit coordination would, however, not occur in relation to price but in relation to output or capacity on the market.

On appeal the GC annulled the Commission's decision in a judgment that was highly critical of the Commission's economic reasoning. It held that the Commission's analysis had not been based

---

[463] See Chaps. 6 and 9.

[464] M.1524, *Airtours/First Choice* [2000] OJ L93/1, annulled, Case T-342/99, *Airtours v Commission* [2002] ECR II-2585.

on cogent evidence and that the decision was vitiated by a series of errors of assessment as to factors fundamental to any assessment of whether a collective dominant position might be created. Building upon the judgments in *France v Commission* and *Gencor v Commission*, however, it set out the conditions necessary for a finding of a collective dominant position.

Case T-342/99, *Airtours plc v Commission* [2002] ECR II-2585

62. As the applicant has argued and as the Commission has accepted in its pleadings, three conditions are necessary for a finding of collective dominance as defined:

— first, each member of the dominant oligopoly must have the ability to know how the other members are behaving in order to monitor whether or not they are adopting the common policy. As the Commission specifically acknowledges, it is not enough for each member of the dominant oligopoly to be aware that interdependent market conduct is profitable for all of them but each member must also have a means of knowing whether the other operators are adopting the same strategy and whether they are maintaining it. There must, therefore, be sufficient market transparency for all members of the dominant oligopoly to be aware, sufficiently precisely and quickly, of the way in which the other members' market conduct is evolving;

— second, the situation of tacit coordination must be sustainable over time, that is to say, there must be an incentive not to depart from the common policy on the market. As the Commission observes, it is only if all the members of the dominant oligopoly maintain the parallel conduct that all can benefit. The notion of retaliation in respect of conduct deviating from the common policy is thus inherent in this condition. In this instance, the parties concur that, for a situation of collective dominance to be viable, there must be adequate deterrents to ensure that there is a long-term incentive in not departing from the common policy, which means that each member of the dominant oligopoly must be aware that highly competitive action on its part designed to increase its market share would provoke identical action by the others, so that it would derive no benefit from its initiative (see, to that effect, *Gencor v Commission*, paragraph 276);

— third, to prove the existence of a collective dominant position to the requisite legal standard, the Commission must also establish that the foreseeable reaction of current and future competitors, as well as of consumers, would not jeopardise the results expected from the common policy.

The GC thus requires proof of three criteria in collective dominance cases which are echoed by the Commission in paragraph 41 of its Guidelines:[465]

- sufficient market transparency to enable each member of the dominant oligopoly to know how the other members are behaving and to monitor whether or not they are adopting a common policy;

- the ability to sustain the situation of tacit coordination over time, i.e. the existence of deterrents to ensure that there is a long-term incentive not to depart from the common policy; and

- the common policies must not be at risk from the foreseeable reaction of competitors or consumers.

These three requirements were reiterated by the GC in *Independent Music Publishers and Labels Association (Impala) v Commission*.[466] Although on appeal the CJ expressed the collective dominance test in slightly different terms, the wording is similar and not inconsistent with the test adopted by the GC. Both formulations accord with the economists' views of the conditions required for

---

[465] See n. 447 and text.

[466] Case T-464/04, [2006] ECR II-2289, para. 254.

coordinated effects (i.e. the ability of firms to reach a tacit understanding as to which parameters of competition they will moderate, the ability of firms to sustain any tacit understanding (monitoring adherence to and deviations from the tacit understanding and punishing deviations), and immunity from destabilising reactions from firms outside the coordinating group).[467] The CJ stresses however that a too mechanical approach should not be adopted; rather a more rounded approach to the theory of harm is required.

Case C-413/06 *P Bertelsmann and Sony Corp v Commission* [2008] ECR I-4951

120. In the case of an alleged creation or strengthening of a collective dominant position, the Commission is obliged to assess, using a prospective analysis of the reference market, whether the concentration which has been referred to it will lead to a situation in which effective competition in the relevant market is significantly impeded by the undertakings which are parties to the concentration and one or more other undertakings which together, in particular because of correlative factors which exist between them, are able to adopt a common policy on the market (see *Kali & Salz*, paragraph 221) in order to profit from a situation of collective economic strength, without actual or potential competitors, let alone customers or consumers, being able to react effectively.

121. Such correlative factors include, in particular, the relationship of interdependence existing between the parties to a tight oligopoly within which, on a market with the appropriate characteristics, in particular in terms of market concentration, transparency and product homogeneity, those parties are in a position to anticipate one another's behaviour and are therefore strongly encouraged to align their conduct on the market in such a way as to maximise their joint profits by increasing prices, reducing output, the choice or quality of goods and services, diminishing innovation or otherwise influencing parameters of competition. In such a context, each operator is aware that highly competitive action on its part would provoke a reaction on the part of the others, so that it would derive no benefit from its initiative.

122. A collective dominant position significantly impeding effective competition in the common market or a substantial part of it may thus arise as the result of a concentration where, in view of the actual characteristics of the relevant market and of the alteration to those characteristics that the concentration would entail, the latter would make each member of the oligopoly in question, as it becomes aware of common interests, consider it possible, economically rational, and hence preferable, to adopt on a lasting basis a common policy on the market with the aim of selling at above competitive prices, without having to enter into an agreement or resort to a concerted practice within the meaning of Article [101] and without any actual or potential competitors, let alone customers or consumers, being able to react effectively.

123. Such tacit coordination is more likely to emerge if competitors can easily arrive at a common perception as to how the coordination should work, and, in particular, of the parameters that lend themselves to being a focal point of the proposed coordination. Unless they can form a shared tacit understanding of the terms of the coordination, competitors might resort to practices that are prohibited by Article [101] in order to be able to adopt a common policy on the market. Moreover, having regard to the temptation which may exist for each participant in a tacit coordination to depart from it in order to increase its short-term profit, it is necessary to determine whether such coordination is sustainable. In that regard, the coordinating undertakings must be able to monitor to a sufficient degree whether the terms of the coordination are being adhered to. There must therefore be sufficient market transparency for each undertaking concerned to be aware, sufficiently precisely and quickly, of the way in which the market conduct of each of the other participants in the coordination is evolving. Furthermore, discipline requires that there be some form of credible deterrent mechanism that can come into play if deviation is detected. In addition, the reactions of outsiders, such as current or future competitors, and also the reactions of customers, should not be such as to jeopardise the results expected from the coordination.

---

[467] Bishop and Walker, n. 358, 7.049–7.053.

124. The conditions laid down by the [GC] in paragraph 62 of its judgment in *Airtours v Commission*, which that court concluded, in paragraph 254 of the judgment under appeal, should be applied in the dispute before it, are not incompatible with the criteria set out in the preceding paragraph of this judgment.

125. In applying those criteria, it is necessary to avoid a mechanical approach involving the separate verification of each of those criteria taken in isolation, while taking no account of the overall economic mechanism of a hypothetical tacit coordination.

126. In that regard, the assessment of, for example, the transparency of a particular market should not be undertaken in an isolated and abstract manner, but should be carried out using the mechanism of a hypothetical tacit coordination as a basis. It is only if such a hypothesis is taken into account that it is possible to ascertain whether any elements of transparency that may exist on a market are, in fact, capable of facilitating the reaching of a common understanding on the terms of coordination and/or of allowing the competitors concerned to monitor sufficiently whether the terms of such a common policy are being adhered to. In that last respect, it is necessary, in order to analyse the sustainability of a purported tacit coordination, to take into account the monitoring mechanisms that may be available to the participants in the alleged tacit coordination in order to ascertain whether, as a result of those mechanisms, they are in a position to be aware, sufficiently precisely and quickly, of the way in which the market conduct of each of the other participants in that coordination is evolving.

Establishing Coordinated Effects or the Existence of a Collective Dominant Position

The Commission has an onerous burden to discharge to establish that a collective dominant position has been created or strengthened and that coordinated effects on a market would result. In both *France v Commission*[468] and *Airtours plc v Commission*[469] the CJ and GC respectively annulled the Commission's decision on the ground that this burden had not been discharged. In *France v Commission* the CJ found that the Commission had not shown to the necessary legal standard that the concentration would give rise to a collective dominant position. In particular, a market share of 60 per cent (which would be held by K+S/MdK and SCPA after the concentration, they had 23 per cent and 37 per cent shares respectively) did not of itself point conclusively to the existence of a collective dominant position on the part of the undertakings. Further, the structural links between K+S and SCPA were not as tight or as binding as the Commission had sought to make out, and the Commission had not succeeded in showing that there was no effective competitive counterweight to the grouping allegedly formed by K+S/MdK and SCPA. Similarly, it has been seen that the GC in *Airtours* held that the Commission had not presented cogent evidence in support of its analysis and conclusion.

These cases make it clear that a finding by the Commission of collective dominance, or coordinated effects, will have to be rigorously supported by evidence other than that relating to market shares. Since then the Commission has cleared mergers, even where the number of players on the market will reduce from four to three[470] or from three to two,[471] where no coordinated (or unilateral) effects seem likely. Indeed, in 2014, the Commission concluded in *Holcim/Cemex West*[472] and *Cemex/*

---

[468] Cases C-68/94 and 30/95, *France v Commission, Société Commerciale des Potasses et de l'Azote (SCPA) v Commission* [1998] ECR I-1375. The French Government and SCPA submitted that, if the Regulation did apply to collective dominant positions, the Commission's reasoning concerning the alleged creation of a dominant duopoly had been based on an assessment which was wrong in fact or law and which was inadequate. The CJ upheld this limb of the appeal, see in particular, paras. 179–250.

[469] Case T-342/99, [2002] ECR II-2585.

[470] See, e.g., M.4523, *Worldspan/Travelport* 21 August 2007, M.4601, *KarstadtQuelle/MyTravel* 4 May 2007.

[471] See, e.g., M.4662, *BSG/Universe* 4 December 2007 and M.4600, *TUI/First Choice* 4 June 2007. See also nn. 420–428 and text.

[472] M.7009, 5 June 2014.

Holcim Assets[473] that, despite preliminary concerns about coordination in cement markets in parts of Germany, Spain, and Belgium, the mergers were unlikely to make potential coordination easier, more stable, or more effective.

In *Gencor/Lonrho* the Commission carefully set out the factors supporting its finding that a collective dominant position would be created on the platinum market. For example, it stated at paragraph 141 of its decision:

141. (a) on the demand side, there is moderate growth, inelastic demand and insignificant countervailing buyer power. Buyers are therefore highly vulnerable to a potential abuse;

(b) the supply side is highly concentrated with high market transparency for a homogenous product, mature production technology, high entry barriers (including high sunk costs) and suppliers with financial links and multi-market contacts. These supply side characteristics make it easy for suppliers to engage in parallel behaviour and provide them with incentives to do so, without any countervailing checks from the demand side.

On appeal[474] the GC affirmed that these factors had been correctly relied upon and upheld the finding of collective dominance. Obviously the relevant factors may vary from market to market. This checklist, however, seems to 'be based upon the standard "textbook" characteristics which are thought to facilitate tacit collusion in a market'.[475]

In its Horizontal Merger Guidelines, the Commission devotes 13 paragraphs[476] to the market features that are likely: (a) to enable the firms to reach terms of coordination; (b) to monitor deviation; (c) to provide a deterrent mechanism; and (d) to prevent outsiders jeopardising the outcome of the expected coordination.

Given the difficulties involved in proving collective dominance or the likelihood of coordinated effects, an interesting twist in events was the GC's judgment in *Independent Music Publishers and Labels Association (Impala) v Commission*[477] in which it annulled a Commission decision unconditionally *clearing* a merger between two of the five music majors, Sony and BMG.[478] In its decision, the Commission, despite indicating otherwise in its SO, made a dramatic U-turn, concluding that the merger would not lead either to the strengthening or the creation of a collective dominant position in the physical or digital recorded music markets.[479] With regard to the physical recorded music market, for example, the Commission found that there was no strengthening of a dominant position as the market was not characterised by features facilitating coordinated behaviour. Not only was there no evidence of parallel pricing, but the Commission considered that the market was not transparent, the heterogeneity of the products made coordination unlikely, and there was no evidence of past cheating or retaliation against deviations from a collusive strategy. Further, there was nothing to suggest that a reduction in the number of players, from five to four, would change the position such that a collective dominant position would be created.

The GC annulled the Commission's decision on the grounds that the Commission's reasoning was inadequate and contained manifest errors of assessment. It concluded that the Commission had failed to contain a sufficient statement of reasons for its finding that the market was not conducive to collective dominance. The Commission's finding that the market was not transparent was not

---

[473] M.7054, 9 September 2014.

[474] Case T-102/96, *Gencor Ltd v Commission* [1999] ECR II-753.

[475] The Lexecon *Competition Memo* of November 1999. See Chap. 9.

[476] Horizontal Merger Guidelines, paras. 45–57.

[477] Case T-464/04, [2006] ECR II-2289 and Case C-413/06 P, *Bertelsmann and Sony Corp v Commission* [2008] ECR I-4951.

[478] M.3333, 3 October 2007. The Commission therefore had to reconsider the merger and, after a very thorough investigation, again cleared the transaction in 2007. Although Impala recommended proceedings before the GC (Case T-229/08) these proceedings were abandoned when Sony purchased Bertelsmann's share of the joint venture, M.5272, *Sony/SonyBMG* 15 September 2008.

[479] M.3333, 3 October 2007.

supported and was vitiated by a failure to rely on data supporting the conclusion. Further, the reliance on the absence of previous instances of retaliation was vitiated by an error of law, or at the very least by manifest errors in the assessment.

In its assessment of whether a position of collective dominance existed, the Commission had focused on the question of whether the *Airtours* conditions existed. The GC indicated that in the case of a strengthening of an *existing* dominant position, the Commission, instead of proving the *Airtours* criteria in the traditional way through recourse to theoretical analysis, could have established satisfaction of the *Airtours* criteria by reference to 'indicia and items of evidence relating to the signs, manifestations and phenomena inherent in the presence of a collective dominant position'.[480]

Case T-464/04, *Independent Music Publishers and Labels Association (Impala) v Commission* [2006] ECR II-2289

General Court

250. The determination of the existence of a collective dominant position must be supported by a series of elements of established facts, past or present, which show that there is a significant impediment of competition on the market owing to the power acquired by certain undertakings to adopt together the same course of conduct on that market, to a significant extent, independently of their competitors, their customers and consumers.

251. It follows that, in the context of the assessment of the existence of a collective dominant position, although the three conditions defined by the [GC] in [Case T-342/99] *Airtours v Commission* [[2002] ECR II-2585], which were inferred from a theoretical analysis of the concept of a collective dominant position, are indeed also necessary, they may, however, in the appropriate circumstances, be established indirectly on the basis of what may be a very mixed series of indicia and items of evidence relating to the signs, manifestations and phenomena inherent in the presence of a collective dominant position.

252. Thus, in particular, close alignment of prices over a long period, especially if they are above a competitive level, together with other factors typical of a collective dominant position, might, in the absence of an alternative reasonable explanation, suffice to demonstrate the existence of a collective dominant position, even where there is no firm direct evidence of strong market transparency, as such transparency may be presumed in such circumstances.

253. It follows that, in the present case, the alignment of prices, both gross and net, over the last six years, even though the products are not the same (each disc having a different content), and also the fact that they were maintained at such a stable level, and at a level seen as high in spite of a significant fall in demand, together with other factors (power of the undertakings in an oligopoly situation, stability of market shares, etc.), as established by the Commission in the [contested decision], might, in the absence of an alternative explanation, suggest, or constitute an indication, that the alignment of prices is not the result of the normal play of effective competition and that the market is sufficiently transparent in that it allowed tacit price coordination.

The GC thus suggested that when assessing whether a collective dominant position already exists, it may be possible, or necessary, for the Commission, instead of relying on prospective analysis of the probable development of the market or theoretical analysis, to determine, using past or present facts, that a number of undertakings have power to adopt the same course of conduct.

---

[480] Case T-464/04, [2006] ECR II-2289, para. 251. The GC also quashed the Commission's finding that the merger would not lead to the *creation* of a collective dominant position on the basis that the examinations carried out by the Commission were too 'succinct' and 'superficial' to satisfy its obligation to carry out a prospective analysis, see paras. 525–528.

On appeal, the CJ reversed the judgment of the GC (and remitted the case back to it)[481] but did not overrule this statement. Rather, it stated that 'the investigation of a pre-existing collective dominant position based on a series of elements normally considered to be indicative of the presence of the likelihood of tacit coordination between competitors cannot therefore be considered to be objectionable of itself. However . . . it is essential that such an investigation be carried out with care and, above all, that it should adopt an approach based on the analysis of such plausible coordination strategies as may exist in the circumstances.'[482]

(iv) Countervailing Buyer Power

The Horizontal Merger Guidelines stress that a competitive constraint can be exercised over possible non-coordinated or coordinated anti-competitive effects identified not only by competitors (actual and potential) but by customers with countervailing buyer power.[483] Such a buyer may have the incentive[484] to credibly threaten to find an alternative source of supplier, perhaps by changing supplier, vertically integrating, or persuading/sponsoring new entry, were the supplier to increase price.[485] In such cases, the countervailing buyer power may neutralise the market power of the parties.[486] It is only in a relatively few cases that the defence has been decisive. Rather, fairly exceptional market conditions have to be satisfied for the countervailing buyer power to tilt the balance.[487]

In *Enso/Stora*[488] the Commission considered that even though the merging parties would acquire a market share of 60 per cent in the market for liquid packaging board the merger would not be problematic since they would face a very concentrated buying situation. In particular, Tetra Pak purchased 60 per cent of the packaging board and would be likely to set up an alternative source of supply if the new entity sought to exploit its position of market power.

Countervailing purchaser power was also relevant in *Alcatel/Telettra*.[489] In this case the Commission cleared a merger which gave the parties market shares of 83 per cent. The Commission considered that Telefónica, the only purchaser, would be able to exert a downward pressure on prices.[490] Further, the Commission's initiative to erode barriers to cross-border trade in this sphere meant that Telefónica would seek products elsewhere if the concentration sought to charge excessive prices (high market shares in a market are unlikely to be significant in an opening market).

(v) Entry Analysis and Barriers to Entry

The Commission will not be concerned with a horizontal merger if the parties' decision to raise prices or reduce quality, variety, or innovation will be frustrated by new entry into the market.

---

[481] Broadly on the grounds that the Commission's reasoning was, on the facts of the case and in the light of tight time constraints under which the Commission had to act, adequate.

[482] Case C-413/06 P, *Bertelsmann and Sony Corp v Commission* [2008] ECR I-4951, para. 129. See also M.6458, *Universal/EMI Music* 21 September 2102 (clearance, subject to commitments of a merger which would reduce the number of major players on the wholesale market for digital music by record companies from four to three).

[483] Although buyer power may be relevant where the merger will create or strengthen buyer power in a way which will lead to a SIEC, its consideration as 'countervailing' buyer power is more common, see e.g., A. Ezrachi and M. Ioannidou, 'Buyer Power in European Union Merger Control' [2014] *European Competition Journal* 69.

[484] It may not if, for example, it can pass on the price increases to its customers, see, e.g., M.1225, *Enso/Stora* [1999] OJ L254/9, para. 91.

[485] *Enso/Stora* [1999] OJ L254/9, para. 65.

[486] M.833, *The Coca-Cola Co/Carlsberg A/S* [1998] OJ L145/41.

[487] See Ezrachi and Ioannidou, n. 483.

[488] M.1225, [1999] OJ L254/9. See also, e.g., M.4057, *Körsnäs/AssiDomän Cartonboard* 12 May 2006, especially paras. 57–64 and M.1630, *Air Liquide/BOC* [2004] OJ L92/1.

[489] M.42, [1991] OJ L122/48. See also, e.g., M.3732, *Procter & Gamble/Gillette* 15 July 2005.

[490] See also M.4, *Renault/Volvo* [1990] OJ C281/2 where the Commission found that large fleet buyers would exercise downward pressure on truck and bus prices.

For entry to be considered a sufficient competitive constraint on the merging parties, it must be shown to be likely, timely and sufficient to deter or defeat any potential anti-competitive effects of the merger.[491]

Clear evidence that a position of market strength will only be temporary and will be quickly eroded because of a high probability of strong and timely market entry will thus lead to a finding that the concentration is compatible with the internal market.[492] In *HP/Compaq*,[493] for example, the Commission cleared a merger in which the parties would gain market shares of between 85 and 95 per cent on the basis that timely and sufficient new entry was likely.

The Commission may also take account of constraining competition from manufacturers operating outside the geographic market.[494] The Commission will therefore consider a great variety of factors in its assessment of barriers to entry such as whether: legal or regulatory barriers to entry exist;[495] the ownership of patents, other IPRs, or data[496] operate as a barrier to entry into a market, particularly in technology markets[497] (in *Tetra Pak/Alfa Laval*[498] the Commission relied on a number of factors, including Tetra Pak's ownership of patents, to conclude that new entry was not likely in the market for aseptic carton packaging machines[499]); and/or other technical factors will inhibit entry. In *The Coca-Cola Co/Carlsberg*,[500] for example, the Commission considered that new entry into the carbonated soft drinks markets (CSDs)[501] in Denmark and Sweden was not likely on account of severe barriers to entry which included access to brands, access to a distribution network, access to shelf space, the need for a sales and service network, brand image, customer loyalty, and (sunk) advertising costs.[502]

Factors such as the evolution of the market (entry is less likely to be profitable in a mature market than a dynamic one), scale economies, and network effects are also relevant.[503] In making the assessment, the Commission considers only potential competitors which are likely to enter the market within a relatively short time frame (although 'timeliness' is dependent upon the characteristics or dynamics of the market, entry must generally occur within two years)[504] and whether market entry will be on a sufficient scale to deter or defeat the anti-competitive effects of the merger.[505]

In *Aérospatiale/Alenia/de Havilland*[506] the Commission held that countervailing factors would not prevent the anti-competitive effects that would result from the parties acquiring very

[491] Horizontal Merger Guidelines, para. 68 and Chap. 1.

[492] See, e.g., M.477, *Mercedes-Benz/Kässbohrer* [1995] OJ L211/1; cf. M.774, *Saint Gobain/Wacker-Chemie/NOM* [1997] OJ L247/1.

[493] M.2609, 31 January 2002.

[494] M.315, *Mannesmann/Vallourec/Ilva* [1994] OJ L102/15.

[495] See, e.g., M.1430, *Vodafone/Airtouch*, 21 May 1999 (the need for a licence to provide mobile telephony communications services).

[496] See, e.g., M.4854, *TomTom/Tele Atlas* 14 May 2008.

[497] See, e.g., M.269, *Shell/Montecatani* [1994] OJ L332/48, para. 32.

[498] M.68, [1991] OJ L290/35, point 3.4.

[499] See also Chap. 6.

[500] M.833, [1998] OJ L145/41.

[501] Although the Commission considered that the market could be defined more narrowly, to include different flavours of CSDs, the exact definition did not affect the outcome of this case, ibid., para. 43.

[502] M.833, *The Coca-Cola Co/Carlsberg* [1998] OJ L145/41, paras. 72–75 (it was very unlikely that anyone other than the existing international brand owners would be able to launch a new international CSD).

[503] Horizontal Merger Guidelines, para. 73.

[504] Ibid., para. 74.

[505] Ibid., para. 75 and, e.g., M.1157, *Skanska/Scancem* [1999] OJ L183/1, para. 184.

[506] M.53, [1991] OJ L334/42, para. 53.

large shares on the commuter aircraft market generally. The high risks involved in entering the market on account of the high sunk costs that would be required and the maturity of the market reduced the likelihood of new entry.[507] Further any new entry into the commuter aircraft market was likely to occur only after a period of time and too late to catch an expected period of high demand.

In *Ryanair/Aer Lingus*, the Commission also concluded that significant barriers to entry meant that new entry was most unlikely. In particular, other airlines did not have a large base in Dublin, and they faced significant entry costs and capacity constraints in terms of obtaining slots at Dublin and destination airports. Further, Ryanair had a reputation of reacting aggressively against new entrants.[508] This view was reinforced by the fact that easyJet, another major low-cost carrier present in Europe, had tried and failed to enter routes in competition with Ryanair.[509] In *Olympic Air/Aegean Airlines I*[510] the Commission also considered that new entry was not likely, even if slots were available at Athens airport.

(vi) Efficiencies

a. An Efficiency Defence?

A merger may lead to efficiencies which increase competition between the merging parties and the other undertakings on the market. A further important question, however, is whether merger analysis admits, or should admit, an 'efficiency defence'. Such a defence would redeem a concentration which increases concentration and market power, but which results in significant cost savings and economies of scale (which favour restructuring).

Horizontal mergers can create substantial efficiencies even as they facilitate collusion or enlarge market power. Courts and other policy makers have entertained three different positions concerning efficiency and the legality of mergers:

(1) mergers should be evaluated for their effect on market power or likelihood of collusion, and efficiency considerations should be largely irrelevant;

(2) mergers that create substantial efficiencies should be legal, or there should be at least a limited 'efficiency defence' in certain merger cases;

(3) mergers should be condemned because they create efficiencies, in order to protect competitors of the post-merger firm.[511]

b. An Increase in Consumer Welfare

In the US the authorities are receptive to arguments based on the efficiencies and cost savings of a merger.[512] Such a defence is justifiable on grounds of strict economic theory, since the costs savings give rise to an increase in consumer welfare as a whole. The argument raised in support of such a defence is outlined by Hovenkamp.

---

[507] Ridyard, n. 450, 256.

[508] Ryanair had a history of responding to third parties attempting to run services in competition with them by starting aggressive fare wars until the third party withdrew from the route, M.4439, *Ryanair/Aer Lingus* 27 June 2007, para. 515, *aff'd* Case T-342/07, [2010] ECR II-3457, para. 286.

[509] M.4439, ibid., para. 514.

[510] M.5830, 26 January 2011, the merger was eventually cleared, however, see n. 541 and text.

[511] Hovenkamp, n. 20, 12.2, 674–675.

[512] Department of Justice and Federal Trade Commission, Horizontal Merger Guidelines (2010), §10 (the onus of proving qualifying efficiencies rests on the parties).

H. Hovenkamp, *Federal Antitrust Policy: The Law of Competition and its Practice* (5th edn, West, 2016), 12.2b1

12.2b1. The Welfare 'Tradeoff' Model

Today the idea that mergers should be condemned because they create efficiency has been abandoned. While the Supreme Court itself has never recognized an 'efficiencies defense' to a prima facie unlawful merger, both the Merger Guidelines and several of the Circuits have done so. Importantly, the query into efficiencies comes into play *only* after the merger has been found presumptively anticompetitive by structural and behavioral analysis. If a merger poses no competitive threat to begin with, then analysis of possible efficiencies is unnecessary.

The argument for an 'efficiency defense' in merger cases is suggested by Figure 1 which illustrates a merger which gives the post-merger firm measurably more market power than it had before the merger. As a result, the firm reduces output from Q1 to Q2 on the graph, and increases price from P1 to P2. Triangle A1 represents the monopoly 'deadweight loss' that results from reduced output.

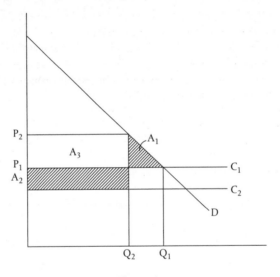

Figure 1

At the same time, the merger produces measurable economies, which show up as a reduction in the firm's costs from C1 to C2. Rectangle A2 represents efficiency gains that will result from these economies. If A2 is larger than A1 the merger produces a *net* efficiency gain, even though it permits the firm to raise its price from the pre-merger level. Further, Figure 1 suggests that A2 can be larger than A1. The efficiency gains illustrated by A2 are spread over the entire output of the post-merger firm. The deadweight losses in A1 is spread over only the reduction in output. If the post-merger firm reduced its output by 10%, each of the 90% of units still being produced would contribute to the efficiency gains; the deadweight loss, however, would accrue over only the 10% reduction.

By his own admission, Williamson's analysis was highly simplified and it is vulnerable to some criticism...

Broadly, Williamson establishes that in some cases mergers which enable the parties to acquire market power and, consequently, to restrict output and raise prices may nonetheless lead to an increase in consumer welfare. Although consumers lose output (and deadweight loss occurs) in some cases, where efficiency gains are large, that loss is offset by a greater gain in cost or resource savings. To determine whether or not this is the case a comparison must be made in each case of deadweight loss relative to cost savings.

Although the importance of Williamson's conclusions remains, Hovenkamp identifies a number of significant limitations of the welfare trade-off model.[513] For example, that the theory may underestimate the social costs of the merger and does not work effectively when applied to mergers occurring on oligopolistic markets (in oligopolistic markets, the achievement of efficiencies may provoke more aggressive competition between the players on the market by destabilising the tacit coordination). Further, the theory treats all efficiency gains in the same way no matter who gets the benefit; a merger which has an overall efficient effect (increasing total welfare) may nonetheless result in an actual output reduction and still lead to an increase in price for consumers (in such case the benefits accrue to the merging parties).[514] Another acute difficulty lies in the practical application of the defence. Not only can it be difficult to determine whether or not the efficiencies pleaded could be obtained by means other than merger, but courts (and competition agencies) may not be able to make the measurements that its analysis would require. 'Our knowledge that mergers can produce both economies and monopoly pricing is fairly secure. However, quantifying either of these in a particular merger case is impossible. Most mergers found illegal under current law probably create efficiencies. They are condemned, however, because no court is capable of balancing the increase in market power of the potential for collusion against the economies achieved.'[515]

Others have suggested that even if the comparison *could* be made, it *should* not. Huge cost savings would be necessary to offset any associated price increases[516] and, in contrast, a rigorous merger policy would be more likely to bring about an increase in economic welfare. Public policy should thus concentrate on preserving and fostering competition for the ultimate benefit of consumers.

c. Background—Efficiencies and the EUMR

Initially doubt was expressed as to whether the wording of the EUMR left scope for the trade-off of efficiencies where a concentration significantly impedes effective competition. Although Article 2(1)(b) allows for 'technical and economic progress' to be taken into account as part of the appraisal, it is only 'provided it is to consumers' advantage and does not form an obstacle to competition'; this might be difficult to establish if the consumer would have to pay supra-competitive prices post-merger.[517]

Indeed, some commentators alleged that (in the past at least) the Commission's decisions were actually more reflective of an 'efficiency attack' or 'offence', a fear that mergers which would enable the parties to achieve significant economies of scale or scope may be more likely to result in a finding that the merger is incompatible with the internal market as the parties will have even greater advantages over their nearest competitors.[518] For example, in some cases involving conglomerate mergers, the Commission does seem to have accepted that efficiencies resulting from a merger would

---

[513] Hovenkamp, n. 20, 12.2b1, 678.

[514] See the discussion of total welfare and consumer welfare in Chap. 1. The US Merger Guidelines require that efficiencies are sufficient to reverse the harm to consumers, by preventing price increases in the market, 2010 Guidelines, §10.

[515] Hovenkamp, n. 20, 12.2b4, 683.

[516] Scherer and Ross, n. 19, 174: statistical evidence supporting the hypotheses that profitability and efficiency increase following mergers is at best weak.

[517] See, e.g., A. Jacquemin, 'Mergers and European Policy' in P. H. Admiral (ed.), *Merger and Competition Policy in the European Community* (Blackwell, 1990), 36.

[518] In M.53, *Aérospatiale-Alenia/de Havilland* [1991] OJ L334/42, e.g., the parties claimed that efficiency gains that arose from the merger appeared to have 'merely strengthened the Commission's view that the merged group would enjoy benefits that would be out of the reach of its competitors. If anything, the "efficiency defence" seems in this case to have reduced the chances of clearance for the deal', Ridyard, n. 451, 256–257.

enable the merging parties to lower their prices and so damage competitors. In *GE/Honeywell*[519] the Commission was particularly concerned that the merged entity would be able to offer low bundled prices for those that purchased both its aircraft engines and its avionics and non-avionics systems. The focus that the Commission placed on the harm that would result to the new entity's competitors led some commentators to take the view that the decision was indicative of a hostile approach to mergers that create efficiencies and as protective of competitors rather than competition.

d. The Horizontal Merger Guidelines

In view of the confusion over the part played by efficiency considerations in EU merger cases, the Commission invited discussion in its 2001 Green Paper of the proper role and scope that such considerations should play.[520] Most respondents considered that, as part of a sound economics-based merger control policy, the Commission should take account of efficiencies in its analysis of the overall effects likely to be produced by a proposed merger. Further, that guidance should be produced on the proper scope of the defence. Recital 29 of the EUMR now provides that it 'is possible that the efficiencies brought forward by the concentration counteract the effects on competition, and in particular the potential harm to consumers, that it might otherwise have and that, as a consequence, the concentration would not significantly impede effective competition, in particular as a result of the creation or strengthening of a dominant position' and the Commission deals with efficiencies in its Horizontal Merger Guidelines.[521]

In the Guidelines it is recognised that, in making its substantive appraisal, it takes account of the development of technical and economic progress,[522] and that 'efficiencies generated by the merger are likely to enhance the ability and incentive of the merged entity to act pro-competitively for the benefit of consumers, thereby counteracting the adverse effects on competition which the merger might otherwise have'.[523] The burden is on the parties to establish the efficiency defence.[524] The Commission will thus only take account of substantiated efficiencies which: (a) benefit consumers; (b) are merger specific;[525] and (c) are verifiable.[526] Thus

efficiencies brought about by a merger may counteract its possible anti-competitive effects and thus not lead to a SIEC—in a very similar way to an agreement or practice meeting the test of Article 101(3) TFEU … In both instances,

- the restriction of competition according to Article 101(1) must be necessary to obtain them, or respectively, the efficiencies must be 'merger-specific';

- the restriction of competition must allow 'consumers a fair share of the resulting benefit', or respectively, the efficiencies resulting from the merger must be 'passed on to consumers';

- finally, while under Article 101(3) a restriction of competition may not afford the parties 'the possibility of eliminating competition in respect of a substantial part of the products in question', the Horizontal Merger Guidelines state that a merger resulting in a near-monopoly is unlikely to product efficiencies large enough to exclude a SIEC.[527]

---

[519] M.2220, 3 July 2001, *aff'd* Cases T-209 and 210/01, *Honeywell v Commission* and *General Electric Co v Commission* [2005] ECR II-5527 and 5575. See the discussion of this case in Section 5.D.ix, pp. 1181–1184. But see refutation of Mario Monti, then Commissioner for Competition, 'Antitrust in the US and Europe: A History of Convergence', General Counsel Roundtable American Bar Association, Washington DC, 14 November 2001.

[520] 2001 Green Paper on the Review of Council Regulation (EEC) No. 4064/89, COM(2001) 745/6 final. See also, e.g., L. Roller, J. Stennek, and F. Verboven, 'Efficiency Gains from Mergers', The Research Institute of Industrial Economics, Working Paper No. 543, 2000.

[521] [2004] OJ C31/5, para. 5. Form CO also has a section on efficiency gains.

[522] Horizontal Merger Guidelines, para. 76.

[523] Ibid., para. 77.

[524] Case T-175/12, *Deutsche Börse v Commission* EU:T:2015:148.

[525] Ibid., para. 85.

[526] Horizontal Merger Guidelines, paras. 77–88.

[527] Mosso, n. 310 (in each the burden of proof is on the parties—the same is true for the objective justification of otherwise abusive conduct).

Benefit to Consumers

Consumers should not be worse off as a result of the merger. The merger must thus bring timely efficiencies that will result, for example, in lower prices (perhaps through reduction in variable or marginal costs) or in new or improved products or services (for example, from efficiency gains in the sphere of R&D). In the context of coordinated effects, efficiencies may lead to incentives to increase production and reduce output and disincentives to coordinate behaviour.

The greater the market power acquired by the undertakings the more difficult it will be to show that benefits will result which will be passed on to consumers. Further, the Commission states that the efficiencies should in principle benefit consumers in the market where the competition problems arise.

Merger Specificity

Paragraph 85 of the Horizontal Merger Guidelines explains the requirement of merger specificity.

Efficiencies are relevant to the competitive assessment when they are a direct consequence of the notified merger and cannot be achieved to a similar extent by less anti-competitive alternatives. In these circumstances, the efficiencies are deemed to be caused by the merger and thus, merger specific. It is for the parties to provide in due time all the relevant information necessary to demonstrate that there are no less anti-competitive, realistic and attainable alternatives of a non-concentrative nature (e.g., a licensing agreement, or a cooperative joint venture) or of a concentrative nature (e.g., a concentrative joint venture, or a differently structured merger) than the notified merger which preserve the claimed efficiencies. The Commission only considers alternatives that are reasonably practical in the business situation faced by the merging parties having regard to established business practices in the industry concerned.

Verifiability

A difficult task for the parties will be to verify the efficiencies 'such that the Commission can be reasonably certain that the efficiencies are likely to materialize, and be substantial enough to counteract a merger's potential harm to consumers'.[528] The Commission states that the parties should quantify the efficiencies where possible or otherwise identify the positive impact on consumers.

Cases

Although efficiencies have not yet been given as a decisive factor for a merger clearance it was given as one of them in *Körsnäs/AssiDomän Cartonboard*.[529] In this case the Commission accepted that synergies resulting from the merger between two of the three main players active in the worldwide market for the production of liquid carton packaging board were likely to be passed on to consumers. The Commission also considered, however, that countervailing buyer power as well as competition from EnsoStora,[530] suppliers outside the EU, and suppliers of other board materials, were likely to constrain the behaviour of the merged parties.

In both *UPS/TNT Express*[531] and *Ryanair/Aer Lingus*[532] the Commission also carefully scrutinised efficiencies submitted by the parties. In *UPS/TNT*, the Commission recognised a number of them but prohibited the merger because it considered that they would not outweigh the price increases likely

---

[528] Horizontal Merger Guidelines, para. 85. See, e.g., D. Gerard, 'Merger Control Policy: How to Give Meaningful Consideration to Efficiency Claims?' (2003) 40 *CMLRev* 1367.

[529] M.4057, 12 May 2006, especially paras. 57–64. See also, e.g., M.3732, *Procter & Gamble/Gillette* 15 July 2005; M.3664, *Repsol Butano/Shell Gas* 2 March 2005; and M.4000, *Inco/Falconbridge* 4 July 2006 (the parties' efficiencies claims were rejected) and, e.g., P. Lowe, 'A more economic approach to competition law enforcement—making it operational', CRA International Annual Conference, Brussels, 15 December 2005.

[530] See n. 479 and accompanying text.

[531] M.6570, 30 January 2013. See also, e.g., M.6360, *Nynas/Shell/Habrug Refinery Assets* 2 September 2013 and M.6166, *Deutsche Börse/NYSE Euronext* 1 February 2012, *aff'd* Case T-175/12, *Deutsche Börse v Commission* EU:T:2015:148.

[532] M.4439, *Ryanair/Aer Lingus* 27 June 2007, *aff'd* Case T-342/07, *Ryanair v Commission* [2010] ECR II-3457, para. 443.

to result from it. In *Ryanair/Aer Lingus* the Commission rejected the argument that offsetting efficiencies would be brought about by the merger. Rather, it found that the efficiencies that would result from a reduction of Aer Lingus's operating costs constituted more of a general assertion than a verifiable claim and were not merger-specific (since it appeared that they could be generated by Aer Lingus simply applying Ryanair's business plan). Further, given that the Commission had established that the merged entity would face little, if any, competition on a number of routes and that many of the claimed efficiencies related to fixed costs, the Commission considered there to be little incentive for any cost savings made to be passed on to consumers—the efficiencies were of insufficient benefit to consumers to outweigh a merger to monopoly on some routes.[533] The GC upheld the Commission's decision and rejected Ryanair's allegation that the Commission had set the bar to establish efficiencies too high. The conclusion reached in this case lends support to the view set out in paragraph 84 of the Horizontal Merger Guidelines that it is highly unlikely that a merger leading to a market position approaching monopoly can be declared compatible with the internal market on the ground that the efficiency gains would be sufficient to counteract its potential anti-competitive effects.[534]

(vii) The Failing Firm Defence or Rescue Mergers

The failing firm defence, well established in US antitrust practice,[535] provides an escape route for a merger involving a firm facing an otherwise inevitable liquidation. Historically, it appears to have been adopted in the US to ensure the protection of the creditors, owners, and/or employees of small businesses; it was therefore concerned not with efficiency but with distributive justice. Nonetheless, a narrowly applied failing company 'could be efficient when it (1) enables a failing firm and its creditors to avoid the high administrative costs of bankruptcy; and (2) it keeps on the market productive assets that are worth keeping in production and would likely to be taken out of production were it not for the merger.'[536]

In the EU, a failing firm defence was first recognised in *Kali und Salz/MdK/Treuhand*[537] which raised the question whether or not an undertaking with large market shares could combine activities with its only, or main, failing competitor. It has been seen that the case concerned the combination of the potash and rock-salt activities of K+S and MdK. Although the Commission found that the concentration would acquire enormous shares on the potash market in Germany and the magnesium products market of 98 per cent and 100 per cent respectively, it concluded that it was not the merger that could be said to be the cause of the deterioration in the competitive structure. Even if the merger was prohibited, the acquiring undertaking would inevitably achieve or reinforce its dominant position to the same extent. The parties established (the onus being on them to do so) that:

- the acquired undertaking would in the near future be forced out of the market if not taken over by another undertaking (MdK would inevitably have been forced out of the market as it was in a critical economic position following the collapse of the relevant markets);

- the acquiring undertaking, K+S, would inevitably acquire the market share since it was the only other relevant participator on the respective markets; and

- no less anti-competitive purchase was possible (although tenders had been invited, all other alternatives had practically been ruled out).

---

[533] Ibid., para. 1151, *aff'd* Case T-342/07, ibid., para. 443.

[534] See also M.6166, *Deutsche Börse/NYSE Euronext* 1 February 2012 and Mosso, n. 310.

[535] 2010 Guidelines, §11. See also OECD, 'Failing Firm Defence' (2009), available at <http://www.oecd.org/daf/competition/mergers/45810821.pdf>.

[536] 2010 Guidelines, para. 12.9, 545.

[537] M.308, [1994] OJ L186/30; on appeal Cases C-68/94 and C-30/95, *France v Commission, Société Commerciale des Potasses et de l'Azote (SCPA) v Commission* [1998] ECR I-1375. The Commission had rejected the defence in M.53, *Aérospatiale/Alenia/de Havilland* [1991] OJ L334/42. See G. Monti and E. Rousseva, 'Failing Firms in the Framework of the EC Merger Regulation' (1999) 24 *ELRev* 38.

The French Government challenged the decision to authorise a concentration leading to the creation of a monopoly without imposing conditions but the CJ upheld the Commission's decision, confirming that if a concentration is not the cause of the significant impediment to competition it must be declared compatible with the internal market.[538]

Cases C-68/94 and C-30/95, *France v Commission, Société Commerciale des Potasses et de l'Azote (SCPA) v Commission* [1998] ECR I-1375

Court of Justice

111. It appears from point 71 of the contested decision that, in the Commission's opinion, a concentration which would normally be considered as leading to the creation or reinforcement of a dominant position on the part of the acquiring undertaking may be regarded as not being the cause of it if, even in the event of the concentration being prohibited, that undertaking would inevitably achieve or reinforce a dominant position. Point 71 goes on to state that, as a general matter, a concentration is not the cause of the deterioration of the competitive structure if it is clear that:

— the acquired undertaking would in the near future be forced out of the market if not taken over by another undertaking,

— the acquiring undertaking would gain the market share of the acquired undertaking if it were forced out of the market,

— there is no less anti-competitive alternative purchase.

112. It must be observed, first of all, that the fact that the conditions set by the Commission for concluding that there was no causal link between the concentration and the deterioration of the competitive structure do not entirely coincide with the conditions applied in connection with the United States 'failing company defence' is not in itself a ground of invalidity of the contested decision. Solely the fact that the conditions set by the Commission were not capable of excluding the possibility that a concentration might be the cause of the deterioration in the competitive structure of the market could constitute a ground of invalidity of the decision.

113. In the present case, the French Government disputes the relevance of the criterion that it must be verified that the acquiring undertaking would in any event obtain the acquired undertaking's share of the market if the latter were to be forced out of the market.

114. However, in the absence of that criterion, a concentration could, provided the other criteria were satisfied, be considered as not being the cause of the deterioration of the competitive structure of the market even though it appeared that, in the event of the concentration not proceeding, the acquiring undertaking would not gain the entire market share of the acquired undertaking. Thus, it would be possible to deny the existence of a causal link between the concentration and the deterioration of the competitive structure of the market even though the competitive structure of the market would deteriorate to a lesser extent if the concentration did not proceed.

115. The introduction of that criterion is intended to ensure that the existence of a causal link between the concentration and the deterioration of the competitive structure of the market can be excluded only if the competitive structure resulting from the concentration would deteriorate in similar fashion even if the concentration did not proceed.

116. The criterion of absorption of market shares, although not considered by the Commission as sufficient in itself to preclude any adverse effect of the concentration on competition, therefore helps to ensure the neutral effects of the concentration as regards the deterioration of the competitive structure of the market. This is consistent with the concept of causal connection set out in Article 2(2) of the Regulation.

---

[538] Cases C-68/94 and C-30/95, *France v Commission, Société Commerciale des Potasses et de l'Azote (SCPA) v Commission* [1998] ECR I-1375, para. 110.

117. As to the criticism of the Commission that it failed to show that if the concentration did not proceed MdK would inevitably have been forced out of the market, it should be observed that the Commission stated in point 73 of the contested decision that, even though MdK had been restructured by 1 January 1993, that undertaking continued to make considerable losses in the first six months of the year. According to the Commission, MdK's serious economic situation was essentially a result of its obsolete operating structure and the crisis in sales attributable primarily to the collapse of markets in eastern Europe. MdK also lacked an efficient distribution system (see points 74 and 75 of the contested decision).

118. In point 76 of the contested decision, the Commission observed that MdK had been able to continue operating until now only because Treuhand had consistently covered its losses. The Commission added, however, that Treuhand could not cover MdK's losses in the long term from public aid, since that was in any case incompatible with the Treaty provisions on State aid.

119. In the light of the foregoing, the Commission cannot be criticised for finding that MdK was no longer economically viable and for considering that it was probable that, on its own, MdK would continue to accumulate losses even if Treuhand provided the funds envisaged for restructuring purposes in the proposed concentration.

120. In those circumstances, the Commission's forecast that MdK was highly likely to close down in the near future if it were not taken over by a private undertaking cannot be regarded as unsupported by a consistent body of evidence.

121. Finally, with respect to the condition concerning the absence of an alternative, less anti-competitive method of acquiring MdK, it should be noted that the French Government's complaint is that the Commission, because of the lack of transparency in the tendering procedure, failed to show that that condition was in fact satisfied.

122. Suffice it to note that the French Government has merely observed that the MdK trade unions pointed to a lack of transparency in the tendering procedure, without providing any details as to what constituted the alleged lack of transparency.

123. In the absence of any details of that complaint, it cannot be upheld.

124. It follows from the foregoing that the absence of a causal link between the concentration and the deterioration of the competitive structure of the German market has not been effectively called into question. Accordingly, it must be held that, so far as that market is concerned, the concentration appears to satisfy the criterion referred to in Article 2(2) of the Regulation, and could thus be declared compatible with the common market without being amended. Consequently, contrary to the French Government's assertion, it is not possible without contradicting that premise to require the Commission, with respect to the German market, to attach any condition whatever to its declaration of the concentration's compatibility.

Since *Kali and Salz* the Commission has been prepared to apply the failing firm defence or the concept of the 'rescue merger' more broadly. The defence has been pleaded in a number of cases[539] and was developed in *BASF/Pantochim/Eurodiol*.[540] This concentration was likely to lead to the acquisition of high market shares on certain base chemical markets. In applying the failing firm defence the Commission stressed that the approach taken by the CJ in its *Kali and Salz* judgment was wider than the criteria set out in the Commission's own decision in that case. The key requirement for a merger to be regarded as a rescue merger was that the competitive structure resulting from the concentration would deteriorate in a similar fashion even if the concentration did not proceed, i.e. even if the concentration was prohibited. Thus the essential conditions are that the undertaking to be acquired can be regarded as a 'failing firm' and that the merger will not be the *cause* of the deterioration of

---

[539] It has been rejected in a number of cases, see, e.g., M.774, *Saint-Gobain/Wacker-Chemie-NOM* [1997] OJ L247/1.

[540] COMP/M.2314, IP/01/984. See also M.2876, *Newscorp/Telepiù*, IP/03/478, K. Joergens, 'Anderson and the "Failing Firm"' (2003) 26 *World Competition* 363 and I. Kokkoris, 'Failing Firm Defence in the European Union: A Panacea for Mergers?' [2006] *ECLR* 494.

the competitive structure. The Commission does not therefore require that the acquiring company would inevitably acquire the entire market share of the acquired undertaking if it were forced out of the market, but only that the acquired company's assets would inevitably exit the market were the firm not taken over.

M.2314, *BASF/Pantochim/Eurodiol*

Commission

(140) In general terms, the concept of the 'rescue merger' requires that the undertakings to be acquired can be regarded as 'failing firms' and that the merger is not the cause of the deterioration of the competitive structure. Thus, for the application of the rescue merger, two conditions must be satisfied:

    (a) the acquired undertaking would in the near future be forced out of the market if not taken over by another undertaking; and

    (b) there is no less anti-competitive alternative purchase.

(141) However, the application of these two criteria does not completely rule out the possibility of a takeover by third parties of the assets of the undertakings concerned in the event of their bankruptcy. If such assets were taken over by competitors in the course of bankruptcy proceedings, the economic effects would be similar to a takeover of the failing firms themselves by an alternative purchaser.

Thus it needs to be established in addition to the first two criteria, that the assets to be purchased would inevitably disappear from the market in the absence of the merger.

(142) Given this general framework, the Commission regards the following criteria as relevant for the application of the concept of the 'rescue merger':

    (a) the acquired undertaking would in the near future be forced out of the market if not taken over by another undertaking;

    (b) there is no less anti-competitive alternative purchase; and

    (c) the assets to be acquired would inevitably exit the market if not taken over by another undertaking.

(143) In any event, the application of the concept of the 'rescue merger' requires that the deterioration of the competitive structure through the merger is at least no worse than in the absence of the merger.

The approach is followed in the Horizontal Merger Guidelines.

Guidelines on the Assessment of Horizontal Mergers under the Council Regulation on the Control of Concentrations between Undertakings [2004] OJ C31/5

VIII. Failing firm

89. The Commission may decide that an otherwise problematic merger is nevertheless compatible with the common market if one of the merging parties is a failing firm. The basic requirement is that the deterioration of the competitive structure that follows the merger cannot be said to be caused by the merger. This will arise where the competitive structure of the market would deteriorate to at least the same extent in the absence of the merger.

90. The Commission considers the following three criteria to be especially relevant for the application of a 'failing firm defence'. First, the allegedly failing firm would in the near future be forced out of the market because of financial difficulties if not taken over by another undertaking. Second, there is no

less anti-competitive alternative purchase than the notified merger. Third, in the absence of a merger, the assets of the failing firm would inevitably exit the market.

91. It is for the notifying parties to provide in due time all the relevant information necessary to demonstrate that the deterioration of the competitive structure that follows the merger is not caused by the merger.

The criteria set by the Commission in the cases and guidelines are high and have, in spite of the financial and economic crisis, only been met in relatively few cases, for example *Aegean/Olympic II*[541] and *Nynas/Shell Harburg Refinery Assets*.[542] In *Aegean/Olympic II*, the Commission, despite having prohibited the merger a couple of years before (because it would lead to a merger with Aegean's closest competitor and a monopoly on several domestic routes),[543] approved the merger unconditionally, accepting that Olympic was failing and would be forced to leave the market. The ongoing Greek crisis meant that demand for domestic air travel was continuing to drop significantly. Further, no less anti-competitive purchase was credible. As, absent the merger, Olympic's assets were likely to leave the market completely, the merger would have no additional adverse effect on competition.

In *Nynas/Shell*, the Commission approved Nynas's acquisition of Shell's Harburg refinery assets finding that, absent the merger, the refinery (producing naphthenic base and process and transformer oils) was likely to be closed. Such a closure would reduce production capacity and increase prices in the EEA.

The Commission has not ruled out the possibility of the defence applying where only part of the firm is failing. It appears, however, that the defence, and lack of causality between the merger and the adverse effect on competition, will be much harder to establish in such cases.[544]

(viii) Assessing Mergers in Network Industries and in Two-sided Markets

Appraisal of mergers in network markets, prone to 'tipping', or in 'two-sided' markets, may in certain circumstances require some different substantive merger assessment. The extract from Bishop and Walker explains some of the difficulties involved in appraising such mergers.

S. Bishop and M. Walker, *The Economics of EC Competition Law: Concepts, Application and Measurement* (3rd edn, Sweet & Maxwell, 2010)

Assessing Mergers in Network Industries

7.082 In some industries, the value that consumers place on a firm's product offering depends on the number of other consumers that are using that firm's product. Where this is the case, in general, an increase in the number of consumers using the firm's product increases the value consumers place on that product and hence the more attractive the product becomes, at given prices. Such industries are termed 'network industries'.

---

[541] M.6796, 9 October 2013, see e.g., A Komninos and J. Jeram, 'Changing Mind in Changed Circumstances: Aegean/Olympic II and the Failing Firm Defence' (2014) 5 *JECLAP* 605.

[542] M.6360, 2 September 2013.

[543] M.5830, 26 January 2011, Case T-202/11 *Aeroporia Aigaiou Aeroporiki v Commission* (proceedings discontinued), see n. 510.

[544] See M.1221, *Rewe/Meinl* [1999] OJ L274/1 and M.2876, *Newscorp/Telepiù*, IP/03/478, I. Kokkoris and R. Olivares-Caminal, *Antitrust Law Amidst Financial Crises* (Cambridge University Press, 2010), 109, and E. F. Clark and C. E. Foss, 'When the Failing Firm Defence Fails' (2012) 3 *JECLAP* 317.

The existence of network effects raises the possibility that a merger will give rise to *tipping* or *snowball effects*. *Tipping* refers to the phenomenon whereby network effects can sometimes lead to the market being dominated by just one product (e.g., Microsoft Windows). The basic argument of such theories is as follows. Due to the existence of network effects, if two networks were to merge, this will make that network more attractive to consumers and as a result more consumers would be attracted to the network, thereby further enhancing its competitive position. Such a virtuous circle, it is then alleged, can lead to the market tipping as all consumers drift towards the largest network operator, ultimately resulting in total monopoly.

This line of argument has been applied by the Commission in a number of cases, including *MCI/Worldcom, Vodafone/Mannesman* and *Microsoft Liberty Media/Telewest* . . .

The Commission's analysis in each of these cases can be heavily criticized for a reliance on speculative market analysis that placed too much weight on the theoretical possibility of tipping effects without subjecting those theories to empirical reality . . .

Finally, it is important to distinguish between the possibility that network effects are strong enough to lead to tipping and the apparent assumption that network effects inevitably lead to monopoly. To see that monopoly is not the inevitable outcome of network effects, consider the video games market. Although this market is arguably characterised by network effects it has not tipped to monopoly. There are currently three main players: Sony, Microsoft and Nintendo.

. . .

Assessing Mergers in Two-Sided Markets

7.084 A number of industries can be considered to be 'two-sided'. For a market to be described in economic terms as 'two-sided' two conditions must hold. First, the product at the centre of the analysis is a 'platform' that allows or facilitates the interaction of two distinct groups of customers. Secondly, the benefit that customers in one group derive from the interaction is larger the greater the number of customers on the other side of the platform (the platform creates indirect network externalities). Examples of markets with two-sided features include the media (where advertisers and audience/readership 'interact' through newspapers or television channels) and credit cards (interaction between merchants and customers).

In two-sided markets, a firm's bargaining strength with one group of customers can affect its bargaining strength with the group of consumers on the other side of the market. This raises the possibility that a change in market structure brought about by a merger could lead to adverse outcomes for one or both groups of customer. By strengthening the merged entity's position on one side of the market, it may be able to raise prices to consumers on the other side of the market.

In a traditional one-sided market, economic theory predicts that when a firm raises price this has two conflicting effects on the profits of the firm. On one side, it increases the firm's revenues on each unit sold. On the other side, higher prices induce some customers to switch to competing products, thereby reducing the firm's volume of sales. A horizontal merger may give rise to unilateral effects because, post-merger, some of the sales lost as a result of a price increase are captured by the other merging party, mitigating the loss of sales compared to the pre-merger situation and therefore creating an incentive to raise prices. In a two-sided market these conflicting incentives also exist, but the mechanism is more complicated due to the interaction between the two sides of the market. If a supplier raises its price to customers on one side of the market (call them 'downstream'), it may induce some of those customers to switch to its competitors. This would lead to a reduction in the volume of sales made through that firm and therefore reduces revenues. Moreover, the reduction in the number of downstream customers means that the firm would become less attractive to customers on the other side of the market (call them 'upstream') and this may weaken the firm's bargaining position vis-à-vis these customers. This additional feedback 'interaction' between the downstream and the upstream side of the market, which is a specific characteristic of two-sided markets, reinforces the competitive constraints existing on suppliers but may also create opportunities for suppliers to 'leverage' market power from one side of the market to the other side.

(ix) Competitive Assessment of Non-Horizontal Mergers

a. The Non-Horizontal Merger Guidelines

The Commission's merger decisions have over the years reflected concerns with significant impediments to effective competition resulting from vertical, and/or conglomerate, mergers. Some of these decisions, in particular those adopted in *GE/Honeywell*[545] and *Tetra Laval/Sidel*,[546] have been extremely controversial. In 2007, however, the Commission adopted, following consultation on an earlier draft,[547] Non-Horizontal Merger Guidelines designed to provide clear and predictable guidance to companies as to how the Commission will analyse the impact of non-horizontal mergers on competition. These Guidelines aim to complement the Commission's guidance on horizontal mergers and, no doubt, to meet the challenges, standards, and demands required of it by EU Courts in non-horizontal merger cases.

The Non-Horizontal Merger Guidelines accept that non-horizontal mergers are generally less likely to lead to a SIEC than horizontal mergers. Not only do vertical and conglomerate mergers not entail the loss of direct competition between the merging parties in the same relevant market but it is recognised that they provide substantial scope for efficiencies, particularly through the integration of complementary activities and the reduction of transaction costs.[548]

Non-Horizontal Merger Guidelines

12. First, unlike horizontal mergers, vertical or conglomerate mergers do not entail the loss of direct competition between the merging firms in the same relevant market. As a result, the main source of anti-competitive effect in horizontal mergers is absent from vertical and conglomerate mergers.

13. Second, vertical and conglomerate mergers provide substantial scope for efficiencies. A characteristic of vertical mergers and certain conglomerate mergers is that the activities and/or the products of the companies involved are complementary to each other. The integration of complementary activities or products within a single firm may produce significant efficiencies and be pro-competitive. In vertical relationships for instance, as a result of the complementarity, a decrease in mark-ups downstream will lead to higher demand also upstream. A part of the benefit of this increase in demand will accrue to the upstream suppliers. An integrated firm will take this benefit into account. Vertical integration may thus provide an increased incentive to seek to decrease prices and increase output because the integrated firm can capture a larger fraction of the benefits. This is often referred to as the 'internalisation of double mark-ups'. Similarly, other efforts to increase sales at one level (e.g. improve service or stepping up innovation) may provide a greater reward for an integrated firm that will take into account the benefits accruing at other levels.

14. Integration may also decrease transaction costs and allow for a better co-ordination in terms of product design, the organisation of the production process, and the way in which the products are sold. Similarly, mergers which involve products belonging to a range or portfolio of products that are generally sold to the same set of customers (be they complementary products or not) may give rise to customer benefits such as one-stop shopping.

---

[545] M.2220, *General Electric/Honeywell* 3 July 2001, *aff'd* Cases T-209 and 210/01, *Honeywell Intl v Commission* [2005] ECR II-5527 and 5575.

[546] M.2416, 30 October 2001, annulled on appeal Case T–5/02, [2002] ECR II–4381, *aff'd* Case C-12/03 P, [2005] ECR I-987.

[547] On 13 February 2007, the Commission launched a public consultation on the draft guidelines (see IP/07/178). Feedback on the consultation is available on DG Comp's website, <http://ec.europa.eu/comm/competition/mergers/legislation/non_horizontal_consultation.html>. See also Report for DG Competition, European Commission prepared by Jeffrey Church (University of Calgary, Canada), September 2004, *The Impact of Vertical and Conglomerate Mergers on Competition* (available at <http://bookshop.europa.eu/is-bin/INTERSHOP.enfinity/WFS/EU-Bookshop-Site/en_GB/-/EUR/ViewPublication-Start?PublicationKey=KD7105158>).

[548] Non-Horizontal Merger Guidelines, paras. 11–13.

The Commission is nonetheless still concerned that both types of mergers may lead to a SIEC on a market by giving rise to non-coordinated effects (principally through foreclosure) and/or coordinated effects (through changing the nature of competition so the firms are significantly more likely to coordinate and raise prices). The Commission makes it clear in its Guidelines, however, heeding perhaps the criticism it faced following its decision in *GE/Honeywell*, that it focuses on the effects of the merger on the customers to which the merged entity and its competitors are selling. 'Consequently, the fact that a merger affects competitors is not in itself a problem. It is the impact on effective competition that matters, not the mere impact on competitors at some level of the supply chain. In particular, the fact that a rival may be harmed because a merger creates efficiencies cannot in itself give rise to competition concerns.'[549]

b. Market Shares and Concentration Levels

The Commission considers that non-horizontal mergers pose no threat to effective competition unless the merged entity has a significant degree of market power in at least one of the markets affected by the merger. Market shares and concentration levels provide useful *first indications* of market power (a significant degree of market power is a necessary, but not sufficient, condition for competitive harm). The Non-Horizontal Merger Guidelines state that the Commission is unlikely to have concerns with non-horizontal mergers where the market share post-merger of the new entity in each of the markets concerned is below 30 per cent[550] and the post-merger HHI is below 2,000.[551] Indeed, the simplified procedure applies where the market share of the new entity in each of the markets concerned is less than 30 per cent.[552]

c. Assessment of Vertical Mergers

A number of cases examined carefully by the Commission have raised vertical foreclosure concerns, including a number in the energy[553] and media sectors. *AOL/Time Warner*,[554] for example, concerned a merger between Time Warner, a media and entertainment company, and AOL, the leading internet access provider in the US. The merger would create the first internet vertically integrated content provider and would be able to distribute Time Warner content (music, news, and films) through AOL's internet distribution network. AOL would also have access to Bertelsmann content in consequence of a JV it had with the latter in Europe. The Commission was concerned that AOL would be able to dominate the emerging market for internet music delivery online through its becoming the gatekeeper to the nascent market. In the end the Commission cleared the merger subject to a 'remedy package' which essentially required AOL to sever its links with Bertelsmann. This would leave Europe's largest media company free to compete and prevent the merged entity from dominating the market. In the Non-Horizontal Merger Guidelines the Commission states that it appraises both the possible anti-competitive effects of vertical mergers and pro-competitive effects stemming from substantiated efficiencies.

---

[549] Ibid., paras. 16 and 27.

[550] This percentage accords with the market share threshold included in the Verticals Block Exemption, see Chap. 11.

[551] The Commission will extensively investigate such cases only where 'special circumstances' exist: (a) the merger involves a company that is likely to expand in the near future; (b) there are significant cross-shareholdings or cross-directorships among market participants; (c) one of the merging parties is a firm which is likely to disrupt coordinated conduct; or (d) where indications of prior or ongoing facilitating practices are present, Non-Horizontal Merger Guidelines, paras. 25–26.

[552] Notice on Simplified Procedure, 5(c)(ii). See also Form CO, 6.3 and 6.4.

[553] See, e.g., M.3440, *EDP/ENI/GDP* (*aff'd* Case T-87/05, *EDP v Commission* [2005] ECR II-3745) and M.3696, *E.ON/MOL*. See also Chap. 11.

[554] M.1845, *Time Warner/AOL*, IP/00/1145. See also, e.g., M.4504, *SFR/Télé 2 France*.

Non-coordinated Effects: Foreclosure

With regard to the danger of non-coordinated effects, the focus is on foreclosure:[555] whether actual or potential rivals' access to supplies or markets is materially hampered or eliminated as a result of the merger, thereby reducing those companies' ability to compete and so allowing the merging parties—and possibly some of its competitors as well—profitably to increase the price charged to consumers. This may result from:

(a) input foreclosure—where the merger will restrict access to an important input raising down-stream rivals' costs; and/or

(b) customer foreclosure—where vertical integration forecloses upstream rivals by foreclosing their access to a sufficient customer base.

In each case, the Commission assesses: the *ability* of the merging parties to foreclose access to inputs or customers;[556] the *incentive* to do so; and the overall *likely effect* on competition (taking into account efficiencies that benefit consumers are merger-specific and verifiable where they 'are likely to enhance the ability and incentive of the merged entity to act pro-competitively for the benefit of consumers, thereby counteracting the adverse effects on competition which the merger might otherwise have').[557] These three factors are closely intertwined and are generally considered together.

In the context of input foreclosure, it seems unlikely that these conditions will be satisfied unless the input is sufficiently important, the firm has market power in the upstream market, the foreclosure will be profitable to the merged entity, and foreclosure will result in a SIEC in the downstream market (through, for example, increasing costs of downstream rivals and raising barriers to entry to potential competitors). In *TomTom/Tele Atlas*,[558] for example, the Commission cleared an acquisition by TomTom, a Personal Navigation Device (PND) manufacturer with a leading position, of Tele Atlas (one of two producers of navigable digital maps, an essential input for PND manufacturers). Although the Commission had been concerned that the duopoly in the upstream market for navigable digital maps, combined with TomTom's strong position on the market for PNDs, would lead to a SIEC, following an in-depth examination it concluded that the merged entity would not have the ability to increase the costs of other PND manufacturers for navigable digital maps or to limit their access to these maps. Its ability to restrict access to digital maps for others would be limited by the presence of an upstream competitor, Navteq. Further, it found that the merged company would have no incentive to restrict access to digital maps because the sales of digital maps lost by Tele Atlas would not be compensated by additional sales of PNDs.[559]

The ability or incentive to foreclose may also be affected by legislation or regulation.[560] These were discussed in both *Google/Motorola*[561] and *Lenovo/Motorola Mobility*.[562] In the former the Commission considered that Google's open-source Android OS, one of the most popular mobile operating

---

[555] The Commission is also concerned that non-coordinated effects may occur where the merged entity may, by vertically integrating, gain access to commercially sensitive information regarding the upstream or downstream activities of rivals and that the merger may also put competitors at a competitive disadvantage, thereby dissuading them from entering or expanding in the market, Non-Horizontal Merger Guidelines, para. 78.

[556] In particular, where the merger involves an important input for the downstream product and the merged firm has market power in the upstream market or where the downstream merging party is an important customer in the downstream market and there are significant economies of scale or scope in the input market.

[557] E.g., internalisation of double mark-ups; improved coordination of the production and distribution process; and alignment of incentives for investments in new products, new production processes, and marketing, Non-Horizontal Merger Guidelines, paras. 55–57.

[558] M.4854, 14 May 2008.

[559] The Commission also investigated the proposed acquisition of Tele Atlas's main competitor, Navteq, by Nokia, M.4942, 2 July 2008 (notified shortly after TomTom/Tele Atlas.

[560] See, e.g., M.7268, *CSAV/HGV/Kühne Maritime/Hapag-Lloyd AG* 11 September 2014.

[561] M.6381, 13 February 2012.

[562] M.7202, 26 June 2014.

systems (OS), and a number of Motorola's 'standard essential' patents (SEPs)[563] were key inputs in smart mobile devices (Motorola, being a leading player in the development of smart phones and tablets). In the end, however, the merger was cleared unconditionally in Phase I proceedings. With regard to the SEPs, the Commission did not consider that the merger would significantly change the current position and was also influenced by Google's 'legally binding' and 'irrevocable' letter to standard-setting organisations to honour Motorola's pre-existing commitment to license them on fair, reasonable, and non-discriminatory (FRAND) terms. Further, it did not consider that Google would have the incentive to prevent Motorola's competitors from using its OS as that would stifle the spread of its other services. In the latter, it considered the Lenovo's ability to foreclose access to SEPs would be constrained by FRAND commitments which bound it, its inability to enforce an injunction against a willing licensee, and the fact that it had widely licensed SEPs in the past.

The Commission will also consider countervailing factors (such as buyer power and potential competition) and assess efficiencies resulting from the merger (such as the internalisation of double mark-ups, better coordination of the production and distribution process, and alignment of parties' incentives).

Incentives to Foreclose and Article 102 TFEU

In considering incentives to foreclose, the Commission is required, in both vertical and conglomerate effects cases, to take into account the possibility that the foreclosing conduct might be illegal (under Article 102 TFEU). The question of the extent to which the existence of Article 102 can be expected to affect the incentive of the merged entity to engage in a course of conduct in breach of it (i.e. is the merger appraisal affected by the fact that foreclosure of the downstream, upstream, or related market would, or might, constitute an abuse of a dominant position?) arose in *GE/Honeywell*[564] and *Tetra Laval/Sidel*[565] (both of which involved potential vertical *and* conglomerate effects).

In *Tetra Laval* the GC[566] stressed the importance of the Commission basing its analysis of the likelihood of engaging in anti-competitive behaviour in the future on sufficiently convincing, plausible, and cogent evidence. It held that it could not be assumed that a dominant firm would automatically commit abuses of a dominant position and that its conduct would not be constrained by the existence of the competition rules. Rather, when the Commission sought, in assessing the likely effects of the merger, to rely on foreseeable conduct which was likely to constitute such an abuse, it was also required to assess whether, despite the prohibition, it was nonetheless likely that the entity would act in such a way or whether the illegal nature of the conduct and/or the risk of detection would make such a strategy unlikely. Although it was right to take into account the incentives to act illegally, therefore, the Commission should also have taken into account the extent to which the incentives would be eliminated, as a result of the illegality of the conduct, the likelihood of its detection, action taken by competent authorities, and the financial penalties which could ensue.

On appeal, the Commission alleged that such a burden would be impossible to comply with in practice. The CJ[567] appeared to agree, finding that although the Commission must make some assessment of the Article 102 position, the extent of the obligation imposed by the GC was excessive. It held that although the likelihood of the merged entity engaging in a specific course had to be

---

[563] For a discussion of anti-competitive conduct in the context of standard-setting organisations, see also Chaps. 7 and 12.

[564] M.2220, 3 July 2001, *aff'd* Cases T-209 and 210/01, *Honeywell v Commission* [2005] ECR II-5527 and 5575. With regard to the vertical effects, however, the GC considered that the Commission had committed a manifest error of assessment and had failed to prove that the practices would in fact create or strengthen a dominant position. In particular, the Commission had been concerned that the merged entity would have an incentive not to supply engine starters to rival manufacturers of jet engines.

[565] M.2416, 30 October 2001, annulled on appeal Case T-5/02, [2002] ECR II-4381, *aff'd* Case C-12/03 P, [2005] ECR I-987.

[566] Case T-5/02, ibid., especially para. 159.

[567] Case C-12/03 P, [2005] ECR I-987.

examined comprehensively, taking account of both the incentives to adopt such conduct and the factors liable to reduce or even eliminate those incentives, it would run counter to the purpose of the merger rules to require the Commission to examine in every merger case the extent to which the incentives to adopt anti-competitive conduct would be reduced or eliminated as a result of the unlawfulness of the conduct in question, the likelihood of its detection, the action taken by the competent authorities, both at EU and national level, and the financial penalties which could ensue. Such an investigation would require too speculative an assessment about how Article 102 would apply to hypothetical future events.[568]

Case C-12/03 P, *Commission v Tetra Laval BV* [2005] ECR I-987

Court of Justice

74. Since the view is taken in the contested decision that adoption of the conduct referred to recital 364 in that decision is an essential step in leveraging, the [GC] was right to hold that the likelihood of its adoption must be examined comprehensively, that is to say, taking account, as stated in paragraph 159 of the judgment under appeal, both of the incentives to adopt such conduct and the factors liable to reduce, or even eliminate, those incentives, including the possibility that the conduct is unlawful.

75. However, it would run counter to the Regulation's purpose of prevention to require the Commission, as was held in the last sentence in paragraph 159 of the judgment under appeal, to examine, for each proposed merger, the extent to which the incentives to adopt anti-competitive conduct would be reduced, or even eliminated, as a result of the unlawfulness of the conduct in question, the likelihood of its detection, the action taken by the competent authorities, both at Community and national level, and the financial penalties which could ensue.

76. An assessment such as that required by the [GC] would make it necessary to carry out an exhaustive and detailed examination of the rules of the various legal orders which might be applicable and of the enforcement policy practised in them. Moreover, if it is to be relevant, such an assessment calls for a high probability of the occurrence of the acts envisaged as capable of giving rise to objections on the ground that they are part of anti-competitive conduct.

77. It follows that, at the stage of assessing a proposed merger, an assessment intended to establish whether an infringement of Article [102 TFEU] is likely and to ascertain that it will be penalised in several legal orders would be too speculative and would not allow the Commission to base its assessment on all of the relevant facts with a view to establishing whether they support an economic scenario in which a development such as leveraging will occur.

78. Consequently, the [GC] erred in law in rejecting the Commission's conclusions as to the adoption by the merged entity of anti-competitive conduct capable of resulting in leveraging on the sole ground that the Commission had, when assessing the likelihood that such conduct might be adopted, failed to take account of the unlawfulness of that conduct and, consequently, of the likelihood of its detection, of action by the competent authorities, both at Community and national level, and of the financial penalties which might ensue. Nevertheless, since the judgment under appeal is also based on the failure to take account of the commitments offered by Tetra, it is necessary to continue the examination of the second ground of appeal.

79. With respect to the argument that the [GC] departed from the approach taken by it in the Gencor judgment, it must be held that, contrary to what the Commission claims, the [GC] did not depart from the position taken by it in paragraph 94 of that judgment, namely that there will be a significant impediment to effective competition if there is a lasting alteration of the structure of the relevant markets as a result

---

[568] It also held that the Commission was required to take account of behavioural undertakings that would prevent that conduct, see discussion of remedies in Section 5.G, p. 1195.

of a concentration having the direct and immediate effect of creating conditions in which abusive conduct is possible and economically rational.

80. The situation in the Gencor case was entirely different from that addressed in the contested decision. As is clear from paragraph 91 of the judgment in that case, the concentration would have led to the creation of a dominant duopoly in the platinum and rhodium markets, as a result of which effective competition would have been significantly impeded in the common market.

81. It was therefore the concentration which would have given rise to a lasting alteration of the structure of the relevant markets in that case and thus would have made abuses possible and economically rational.

82. In the present case, it is true that the notified merger was capable of slightly altering the structure of the market for carton inasmuch as the merged entity could strengthen the dominant position which Tetra had held for some time on that market and which, moreover, had been the subject of a Commission decision pursuant to Article [102 TFEU]. However, it was not effective competition on the carton market which the Commission intended to protect by prohibiting the merger but competition on the market for PET equipment, in particular that for low and high capacity SBM machines used for sensitive products.

83. The structure of that market would not have been immediately and directly affected by the notified merger but it could have been so affected only as a result of leveraging and, in particular, abusive conduct by the merged entity on the carton market.

84. It follows from the above considerations that the situation examined in the Gencor case is not sufficiently comparable to that on which the [GC] ruled by the judgment under appeal for that court to have been able to draw any useful inferences from it. The structure of the market on which the Commission intended, by the contested decision, to preserve effective competition was, in the Gencor case, directly altered by the merger whereas, in the present case, it could be altered only by leveraging.

85. With respect to consideration of the behavioural commitments offered by Tetra, the [GC] was right to hold, in paragraph 161 of the judgment under appeal, that the fact that Tetra had, in the present case, offered commitments relating to its future conduct was a factor which the Commission had to take into account when assessing the likelihood that the merged entity would act in such a way as to make it possible to create a dominant position on one or more of the relevant markets for PET equipment.

The inquiry demanded by the CJ thus appears to be a pragmatic one, proportionate to the fact that the Commission is investigating a merger under constrained time limits. Indeed, in *General Electric v Commission* the GC suggests that a summary, not detailed, analysis of this issue is required.[569] The GC does not, however, address the concern raised by the CJ in *Tetra Laval* that this issue should not have an adverse impact on the EUMR's preventative function.

Case T-210/01, *General Electric Co v Commission* [2005] ECR II-5575

General Court

73. It follows from the foregoing that the Commission must, in principle, take into account the potentially unlawful, and thus sanctionable, nature of certain conduct as a factor which might diminish, or even eliminate, incentives for an undertaking to engage in particular conduct. That appraisal does not, however, require an exhaustive and detailed examination of the rules of the various legal orders which might be applicable and of the enforcement policy practised within them, given that an assessment intended to

---

[569] See also Case T-209/01, *Honeywell v Commission* [2005] ECR II-5527.

establish whether an infringement is likely and to ascertain that it will be penalised in several legal orders would be too speculative.

74. Thus, where the Commission, without undertaking a specific and detailed investigation into the matter, can identify the unlawful nature of the conduct in question, in the light of Article [102] or of other provisions of Community law which it is competent to enforce, it is its responsibility to make a finding to that effect and take account of it in its assessment of the likelihood that the merged entity will engage in such conduct (see, to that effect, *Commission* v *Tetra Laval*, paragraph 60 above, paragraph 74).

75. It follows that, although the Commission is entitled to take as its basis a summary analysis, based on the evidence available to it at the time when it adopts its merger-control decision, of the lawfulness of the conduct in question and of the likelihood that it will be punished, it must none the less, in the course of its appraisal, identify the conduct foreseen and, where appropriate, evaluate and take into account the possible deterrent effect represented by the fact that the conduct would be clearly, or highly probably, unlawful under Community law.

The Commission seeks to synthesise the obligations imposed on it in these cases in its Non-Horizontal Merger Guidelines when it states:

46. In addition, when the adoption of a specific course of conduct by the merged entity is an essential step in foreclosure, the Commission examines both the incentives to adopt such conduct and the factors liable to reduce, or even eliminate, those incentives, including the possibility that the conduct is unlawful. Conduct may be unlawful inter alia because of competition rules or sector-specific rules at the EU or national levels. This appraisal, however, does not require an exhaustive and detailed examination of the rules of the various legal orders which might be applicable and of the enforcement policy practised within them. Moreover, the illegality of a conduct may be likely to provide significant disincentives for the merged entity to engage in such conduct only in certain circumstances. In particular, the Commission will consider, on the basis of a summary analysis: (i) the likelihood that this conduct would be clearly, or highly probably, unlawful under EU law, (ii) the likelihood that this illegal conduct could be detected, and (iii) the penalties which could be imposed.

Other Non-coordinated Effects and Coordinated Effects in Vertical Mergers

The Commission has not ordinarily been concerned with vertical mergers which have no foreclosure effects. However the Non-Horizontal Merger Guidelines state that vertical mergers may also cause concern where the merged entity gains access to commercially sensitive information regarding the upstream or downstream activities of rivals through vertical integration, or where vertical integration changes the nature of competition in such a way that firms that previously were not coordinating their behaviour are significantly more likely to coordinate and raise price or otherwise harm competition. A vertical merger may also make coordination easier, more stable, or more effective for firms which were coordinating prior to a merger. For example, the Non-Horizontal Merger Guidelines state that a vertical merger, by reducing the number of effective competitors in a market, may make it easier for the firms concerned to reach a common understanding on the terms of coordination. Such a merger may also increase the level of market transparency between firms (for example, through access to sensitive information on rivals or by making it easier to monitor pricing) and reduce the scope for outsiders to destabilise the coordination by increasing barriers to enter the market.

In *J&J/Pfizer*[570] the Commission had concerns about non-coordinated effects that would result from the acquisition of Pfizer's Consumer Healthcare (PCH) division by Johnson & Johnson (J&J). Through the proposed transaction, J&J would acquire PCH's Nicorette business. As a result, J&J would own a leading Nicotine Replacement Therapy (NRT) patch brand (PCH's Nicorette) and

---

[570] M.4314, 11 December 2006.

would be the sole supplier of nicotine patches to its principal downstream competitor, GSK. The Commission considered that there was a risk that this vertical relationship would give the merged entity the ability and incentive to foreclose GSK from the market for nicotine patches/NRT products by making it harder for it to obtain supplies under similar prices and conditions as would be available absent the merger. This would advantage the merged entity's Nicorette business and lead to harm to consumers (a risk of input foreclosure). Further, there was a risk that the merged entity would gain access to confidential information about GSK which it could use post-merger to the benefit of the acquired Nicorette business. In order to resolve the vertical concerns, J&J offered to divest part of its international nicotine patch manufacturing business. It also agreed to transfer relevant supply agreements, trade marks, and technology and to provide manufacturing capacities and technical assistance to the purchaser until the latter became fully operational. The proposed remedies would therefore structurally eliminate the vertical relationship.

d. Assessment of Conglomerate Mergers

Despite the adoption of some controversial decisions on conglomerate effects, the Commission confirms in its Non-Horizontal Merger Guidelines that the majority of conglomerate mergers will not lead to any competition problems. In certain cases, however, where the companies are active in closely related markets (for example, complementary products or products belonging to a range of products purchased by the same set of customers for the same use)[571] harm may arise. As in its assessment of vertical effects, the Commission considers both the possible anti-competitive effects arising from conglomerate mergers and the possible pro-competitive effects stemming from substantiated efficiencies.

GE/Honeywell *and* Tetra Laval/Sidel

The approach taken in the Guidelines is, no doubt, an attempt to meet the challenges set by the EU Courts in appeals from the Commission's decisions in *GE/Honeywell*[572] and *Tetra Laval/Sidel*[573] respectively. In both cases the Commission prohibited mergers, principally on account of their conglomerate effects, and on the basis that the mergers would create incentives for the merged firms to leverage market power between related markets. In both cases the Courts were extremely critical of the Commission's analysis. The Commission's right to intervene in mergers resulting in conglomerate effects was, however, upheld.

In *GE/Honeywell*[574] the Commission prohibited the proposed acquisition of Honeywell Inc by General Electric Co even though it had been cleared by the US antitrust authorities.[575] Essentially, the Commission was concerned that the $42 billion merger would strengthen GE's already dominant position in the markets for jet engines for large commercial aircraft and regional aircraft and create a dominant position in avionics, non-avionics, and corporate jet engines (Honeywell was the leading supplier of these products). In particular, the Commission considered that it would allow the merged entity to leverage its market power by engaging in bundling or strategic price cuts, thereby strengthening the dominant position in the large commercial jet engine market and creating dominant positions in the corporate jet engine market and avionics/non-avionics market.[576]

---

[571] Non-Horizontal Merger Guidelines, paras. 90–91.

[572] M.2220, 3 July 2001, *aff'd* Cases T-209 and 210/01, [2005] ECR II-5527 and 5575.

[573] M.2416, 30 October 2001, annulled on appeal Case T-5/02, [2002] ECR II-4381, *aff'd* Case C-12/03 P, [2005] ECR I-987. See also M.794, *Coca-Cola Enterprises/Amalgamated Beverages* [1997] OJ L218/15; M.833, *The Coca-Cola Co/Carlsberg A/S* [1998] OJ L145/41; M.938, *Guinness/Grand Metropolitan* [1998] OJ L288/24.

[574] M.2220, 3 July 2001, *aff'd* Cases T-209 and 210/01, [2005] ECR II-5527 and 5575. See, e.g., G. Drauz, 'Unbundling GE/Honeywell' [2003] *ECLR* 115.

[575] See, e.g., F. D. Platt Majoras, 'GE-Honeywell: The US Decision', Remarks before the Antitrust Law Section, State Bar of Georgia, 29 November 2001. For the extraterritorial aspects of this decision see Chap. 16.

[576] It was also concerned that the aircraft financing arm of GE, GECAS, would specify Honeywell equipment in its aircraft purchases.

The anticipated outcome of the bundling or strategic price costs was that, although prices would reduce in the short term, the pricing policy would drive competitors from the market so that, eventually, prices could be expected to rise and product quality and service would reduce.[577] The speculative nature of this prediction triggered a 'firestorm of criticism', particularly in the US, 'not just from the US antitrust authorities, senior [US] administration officials, but also from the business community generally and from leading economists, antitrust legal scholars, and editorial writers'.[578]

The criticism centred on the notion that the EU authorities had prohibited a merger which was to lead to a reduction in prices and increase in output. The anti-competitive effect would only result if the other competitors could not match the merged firm's offerings. In the US, the authorities went out of their way to stress that they would not prohibit a merger which would make a firm more efficient, because of fears that it might force competitors from a market: antitrust laws 'protect competition, not competitors'. In their view a competition authority should be very cautious about adopting a merger policy that sacrificed short-term efficiencies in the name of maintaining competition.[579]

W. J. Kolasky, 'Conglomerate Mergers and Range Effects: It's a Long Way from Chicago to Brussels', Address before George Mason University Symposium Washington, DC, 9 November 2001

At a minimum, before applying such a policy, we should make certain we have a high degree of confidence that the trade-off we are making will ultimately benefit consumers. This would require quantifying the efficiencies and determining the likely duration of the competitive round that will occur before less efficient rivals are forced from the market. It would also require a high degree of confidence that the rivals will in fact be forced from the market—that they will not be able to develop counter-strategies that will enable them to become more efficient themselves in order to survive. Indeed, any business strategy that did not take into account competitive counter-strategies would fail the test for the Nash equilibrium . . . It would also require us to estimate the size of the price increases likely to occur once the merged firm gains market power to determine whether, taking into account the efficiencies, future prices to consumers are likely to be higher or lower than they would be in a market populated by several less efficient firms. Finally we would have to determine the likely duration for the monopoly period—which would be dependent on entry conditions at the time the monopoly is finally achieved.

In the United States, we have very little confidence in our ability to make these judgments which would necessarily involve predictions far out into the future. We believe . . . that we need to 'be humble.' We have more confidence in the self-correcting nature of the markets. This confidence is especially strong when the markets are populated by strong rivals and strong buyers, who will usually find ways to protect themselves from an aspiring monopolist. Our strong belief in markets and our humility in our predictive abilities lead us to be skeptical of claims by rivals that a merger will lead to their ultimate demise and to demand strong empirical proof before we will accept such claims.

---

[577] See D. Giotakos, L. Petit, G. Garnier, and P. De Luyck, 'General Electric/Honeywell—An Insight into the Commission's Investigation and Decision' (2001) 3 *Competition Policy Newsletter* 5.

[578] See W. J. Kolasky, 'Conglomerate Mergers and Range Effects: It's a Long Way from Chicago to Brussels', Address before George Mason University Symposium Washington DC, 9 November 2001. See also M. Pflanz and C. Caffarra, 'The Economics of GE/Honeywell' [2003] *ECLR* 115.

[579] See Kolasky, n. 578. See also the disagreement over the *Oracle/Sun Microsystems* case in which the DOJ published a press release backing the merger on the same date that the Commission launched Phase II proceedings.

In the appeal from the Commission's decision the GC[580] upheld the Commission's decision but *only* on the basis that its analysis of horizontal effects (the creation of a monopoly in the market for engines for large regional jets) provided a sufficient basis to prohibit the merger. With regard to the leveraging theory, the Court considered that the Commission had made a manifest error of assessment and had failed to provide evidence to substantiate its claim that bundling between engines and avionics/non-avionics was possible or feasible. The Commission had not established that the merged entity had an economic incentive to bundle and consequently it had the burden of putting forward other evidence to suggest that the merged entity would make the strategic decision to sacrifice profits in the short term with a view to reaping larger profits in the future. This could be done, for example, through economic studies or the production of internal documents showing that GE's directors had that objective on the launch of their bid for Honeywell.[581]

The GC thus carefully scrutinised the Commission's decision to determine whether it had been established that the merged entity would have the capability of engaging in the alleged bundling practices, whether it was likely to do so, and if, in consequence, anti-competitive harm would occur (a dominant position would have been created or strengthened on one or more of the relevant markets in the relatively near future).[582]

Case T-210/01, *General Electric Co v Commission* [2005] ECR II-5575

General Court

399. The Commission stated in essence in the contested decision that, following the merger, the merged entity would have the ability, unlike its competitors, to offer its customers packages for large commercial aircraft, large regional aircraft and corporate aircraft, encompassing both engines and avionics and non-avionics products. It also held that such behaviour would clearly be in the commercial interests of the merged entity and would thus probably be engaged in after the merger had taken place (recitals 350 to 404, 412 to 416, 432 to 434, 443 and 444 and 445 to 458). As a consequence, a dominant position would have been created for Honeywell on the markets for avionics and non-avionics products and GE's dominant positions would have been strengthened, particularly on the market for large commercial jet aircraft engines (recital 458 of the contested decision).

400. The Commission's case is based on the fact that jet engines, on the one hand, and avionics and non-avionics products, on the other, are complementary, since all these products are indispensable in the construction of an aircraft. The final customer, the operator of the aircraft, must therefore purchase all of them, directly or indirectly, from their manufacturer. The Commission held in the contested decision that on the whole the customers are essentially the same for all those products and that the latter could therefore be bundled. The Commission also observes that the applicant's group is financially very strong, both compared with its main competitors on the engines markets and with its competitors on the markets for avionics and non-avionics products (see, as regards the latter, recitals 302 to 304, 323 and 324 of the contested decision; see also recital 398 et seq.). The merged entity would thus be in a position to reduce its profit margins on avionics and non-avionics products with a view to increasing its market share and making larger profits in the future.

401. It should be noted, as a preliminary point, that the way it is predicted that the merged entity will behave in the future is a vital aspect of the Commission's analysis of bundling in the present case. It

---

[580] Cases T-209 and 210/01, *Honeywell v Commission* and *General Electric Co v Commission* [2005] ECR II-5527 and 5575, see D. Howarth, 'The Court of First Instance in *GE/Honeywell*' [2006] *ECLR* 485.

[581] Case T-210/01, [2005] ECR II-5575, para. 466.

[582] The case was decided under the old EUMR (the dominance not the SIEC test). See also Case T-209/01, *Honeywell v Commission* [2005] ECR II-5527.

follows from the fact that the applicant had no presence on the markets for avionics and non-avionics products prior to the merger, together with the fact that Honeywell had no presence on the market for large commercial jet aircraft engines before the merger, that the merger would have had no horizontal anti-competitive effect on those markets. Thus, the merger would, prima facie, have had no effect whatsoever on those markets.

402. Moreover, in so far as the Commission predicts, at recitals 443 and 444 of the contested decision, that bundling will have an impact on the market for engines for corporate jet aircraft, it should be noted that the applicant's pre-merger share of that market was only [10–20]%, in terms of the installed base, whilst Honeywell's was [40–50]%, and only [0–10]%, in terms of the installed base on those aircraft still in production, as compared with Honeywell's [40–50]% share (recital 88 of the contested decision). In those circumstances, even if it were shown that the merged entity would bundle those engines with avionics and non-avionics products after the merger, there would be no causal link between the merger and the bundled offers, except in the small minority of cases in which the engine was a product of the former GE. Moreover, it is not suggested in the contested decision that either of the parties to the merger manu-factures engines for small regional aircraft. It follows that any bundling which might be engaged in by the merged entity on the market for regional aircraft would in any event concern only large regional aircraft.

403. The Commission held in the contested decision that each avionics product for regional and cor-porate aircraft constitutes a market in itself and that there is a market for each non-avionics product for all types of aircraft, including large commercial aircraft. Accordingly, its reasoning with regard to the creation, by means of bundling, of dominant positions on the markets for the different avionics products cannot be accepted in relation to the markets for each of the various avionics products for corporate and regional aircraft. Indeed, on the assumption that it actually becomes a reality after the transaction, any bundling attributable to the merger will affect only one segment of those markets, the large regional aircraft segment. In the same way, the Commission's reasoning is undermined (albeit to a lesser degree) in relation to non-avionics products, for which the Commission defined an individual market for each specific product, irrespective of the size and other features of the aircraft equipped.

404. It is therefore, in principle, in the sector for large commercial aircraft, for which the Commission has defined distinct markets both for jet engines and for each avionics product, that the Commission's case on bundling could conceivably be sustained.

405. In relation to the possible impact of the merger on (i) the markets for jet engines for large com-mercial aircraft and large regional aircraft, (ii) those for avionics products for large commercial aircraft and (iii) those for non-avionics products, the Court must determine whether the Commission has established that the merged entity would not only have the capability to engage in the bundling practices described in the contested decision but also, on the basis of convincing evidence, that it would have been likely to engage in those practices after the merger and that, in consequence, a dominant position would have been created or strengthened on one or more of the relevant markets in the relatively near future (*Tetra Laval* v *Commission*, paragraph 58 above, paragraphs 146 to 162).

Notwithstanding the general controversy the Commission's decision in *GE/Honeywell* provoked, in *Tetra Laval/Sidel*[583] the Commission prohibited another merger which it considered would enable the merged entity to leverage its market power in one market into another. This case concerned a public bid by Tetra Laval SA for shares in Sidel SA. Tetra, part of the Tetra Pak company, is the world market leader in the area of liquid food carton packaging. In contrast, Sidel is involved in the production of packaging equipment and systems and is a worldwide leader for the production and supply of stretch blow moulding (SBM) machines, used in the production of polyethlylene terephthalate (PET) plastic bottles. The Commission considered that the merger would strengthen Tetra's dominant

---

[583] M.2416, 30 October 2001. See also M.2283, *Schneider/Legrand* 10 October 2001, annulled as the Commission had not identified its conglomeracy concerns in the SO, see n. 667, Case T-310/01, *Schneider Electric SA v Commission* [2002] ECR II-4071.

position in the market for aseptic carton packaging machines and cartons and create a dominant position in the market for PET packaging equipment. The Commission made findings of horizontal and vertical effects and held that the merger would enable the merged entity to exploit its dominant position on the carton markets by leveraging into the market for PET packaging equipment in order to dominate it. The Commission set out its reasons for concluding that the market structure was particularly conducive to leverage effects at paragraph 359 of its decision.

- There would be a common pool of customers requiring both carton and PET packaging systems to package sensitive liquids.

- Tetra has a particularly strong dominant position in aseptic carton packaging with more than 80–90 per cent of the market and a dependent customer base.

- Tetra/Sidel would start from a strong, leading, position in PET packaging systems and in particular SBM machines with a market share in the region of 60–70 per cent.

- Tetra/Sidel would have the ability to target selectively specific customers or specific customer groups as the structure of the market enables price discrimination.

- Tetra/Sidel would have a strong economic incentive to engage in leveraging practices. As carton and PET are technical substitutes, when a customer switches to PET he/she is a lost customer on the carton side of the business either because he/she partially switched *from* carton or because he/she did not switch some of the production *to* carton from other packaging materials. This creates an added incentive to capture the customer on the PET side of the business to recover the loss. Therefore, by leveraging its current market position in carton, Tetra/Sidel would not only enhance its market share on the PET side but defend or compensate its possible loss on the carton side.

- Competitors of Tetra/Sidel in both the carton and the PET equipment markets would be much smaller, with the largest competitor having no more than 10–20 per cent share in the market for carton packaging machines or SBM machines.

The Commission considered that the leveraging would foreclose competitors from the rest of the SBM machine market and turn Sidel's leading position on the market into a dominant one. On appeal, the GC annulled the Commission's decision, finding the pleas alleging lack of horizontal, vertical, and conglomerate anti-competitive effects were well founded.[584] The GC's judgment was upheld by the CJ on appeal.[585] The GC devoted more than half of its judgment to the plea that the Commission had failed to establish foreseeable conglomerate effects,[586] concluding that the decision did not establish that the merger would give rise to significant anti-competitive conglomerate effects to the requisite legal standard.[587]

The GC accepted that the EUMR can apply to merger transactions having horizontal, vertical, or conglomerate effects so long as the conditions set out in Article 2(3) are met[588] and drew a distinction between mergers where the conglomerate effects would be structural (arising directly from the economic structure created)[589] and those where they might be behavioural, in the sense that they arise only if the new entity created engages in certain commercial practices.[590] *Tetra Laval* was of the

---

[584] Case T-5/02, [2002] ECR II-4381, *aff'd* Case C-12/03 P, [2005] ECR I-987. When the Commission re-examined the merger, it cleared it subject to a commitment that Tetra Laval license the new technology for making PET bottles to third parties.

[585] Case C-12/03 P, [2005] ECR I-987.

[586] Case T-5/02, [2002] ECR II-4381, paras. 142–336.

[587] Ibid., para. 226. In the end the Commission cleared the merger, M.2416, 13 January 2003.

[588] Ibid., paras. 146–152.

[589] I.e. where the new entity would immediately and automatically create a second dominant position which the new entity could abuse.

[590] Case T-5/02, [2002] ECR II-4381, para. 147.

latter type. It was therefore necessary to determine whether the merger would have anti-competitive effects by, in all likelihood, allowing the new entity to obtain, in the relatively near future, a dominant position on a market in which one of the parties held a leading position, as a result of leveraging from a market in which the other party was already dominant.[591] In a case involving prospective analysis of conglomerate effects, the GC stated that the Commission must establish that competition will be significantly impeded in the near future:[592] the parties must have both the ability and incentive to leverage and the consequences of leveraging must be particularly plausible and must in all likelihood occur in the very near future.

The judgment stressed the importance of the Commission basing its analysis of the likelihood of leveraging, and of the consequences of such leveraging, on sufficiently convincing, plausible, and cogent evidence.

Case T-5/02, *Tetra Laval BV v Commission* [2002] ECR II-4381

General Court

146. It should be observed, first, that the Regulation, particularly at Article 2(2) and (3), does not draw any distinction between, on the one hand, merger transactions having horizontal and vertical effects and, on the other hand, those having a conglomerate effect. It follows that, without distinction between those types of transactions, a merger can be prohibited only if the two conditions laid down in Article 2(3) are met (see paragraph 120 above). Consequently, a merger having a conglomerate effect must, like any other merger (see paragraph 120 above), be authorised by the Commission if it is not established that it creates or strengthens a dominant position in the common market or in a substantial part of it and that, as a result, effective competition will be significantly impeded.

. . .

155. The Commission's analysis of a merger producing a conglomerate effect is conditioned by requirements similar to those defined by the Court with regard to the creation of a situation of collective dominance (*Kali & Salz*, paragraph 222; and *Airtours v Commission*, paragraph 63). Thus the Commission's analysis of a merger transaction which is expected to have an anti-competitive conglomerate effect calls for a particularly close examination of the circumstances which are relevant for an assessment of that effect on the conditions of competition in the reference market. As the Court has already held, where the Commission takes the view that a merger should be prohibited because it will create or strengthen a dominant position within a foreseeable period, it is incumbent upon it to produce convincing evidence thereof (*Airtours v Commission*, paragraph 63). Since the effects of a conglomerate-type merger are generally considered to be neutral, or even beneficial, for competition on the markets concerned, as is recognised in the present case by the economic writings cited in the analyses annexed to the parties' written pleadings, the proof of anti-competitive conglomerate effects of such a merger calls for a precise examination, supported by convincing evidence, of the circumstances which allegedly produce those effects (see, by analogy, *Airtours v Commission*, paragraph 63).

The CJ rejected the Commission's appeal from this judgment in its entirety. Although it did find that the GC had in some respects erred in the law, it held that these errors did not call into question the judgment insofar as it annulled the Commission's decision.[593] The judgment sheds light on a

---

[591] Ibid., para. 148.

[592] Ibid., para. 153.

[593] Case C-12/03 P, [2005] ECR I-987. See Tizzano AG, para. 123 ('the [GC] correctly found that, just as the Commission had assessed the economic incentives for engaging in such conduct, so it ought to have taken into consideration the possible disincentives in that respect of the unlawful nature of the conduct in question . . . or of the commitments into which that company had offered to enter').

number of important issues, including the standard of proof in merger cases and the impact that the illegality of the conduct has on the incentives of the merged entity to adopt any abusive conduct. In particular, the CJ stressed that the prospective analysis required in merger control had to be carried out with great care: it required an analysis not of past events but of a prediction of the future, making it necessary to envisage various chains of cause and effect with a view to ascertaining which of them was most likely. The quality of evidence relied upon by the Commission in such circumstances is particularly important.[594]

Non-coordinated Effects—Foreclosure

In its Guidelines the Commission states that its analysis of non-coordinated effects focuses on the possibility of foreclosure:[595] the possibility that the merger will confer on the merged entity the ability and incentive to leverage a strong market position from one market to another by means of tying or bundling or other exclusionary practices.[596] The Commission will examine intertwined factors to determine whether the merged firm would have the ability to foreclose its rivals (which is unlikely unless, for example, one of the products is viewed by many customers as particularly important and there is a common pool of customers for the individual products concerned), whether it would have the economic incentive to do so (which is dependent on the profitability of the strategy and the extent to which the incentive to adopt such conduct is reduced or eliminated by, for example, the possibility that the conduct is unlawful), and whether a foreclosure strategy would have a significant detrimental effect on competition causing harm to consumers.

The Non-Horizontal Merger Guidelines indicate concern that bundling or tying may reduce sales by single-component rivals by affecting their ability or incentive to compete and allowing the merged entity subsequently to acquire market power (in the market for the tied or bundled good) and/or maintain market power (in the market for the tying or leveraging good). The effect on competition is assessed in the light of substantiated efficiencies, for example lowering margins on the sale of complementary goods[597] and costs savings in the form of economies of scope.[598] In *Google/DoubleClick*[599] the Commission investigated but ruled out various foreclosure scenarios that might result from the acquisition by Google (a leading player in search advertising and a major provider of online advertising space and intermediation services for online advertisements) of DoubleClick, the leading supplier of ad serving technology.

Portfolio Power and Foreclosure

Prior to the adoption of the Non-Horizontal Merger Guidelines, in *Guinness/Grand Metropolitan*[600] the Commission had to examine a concentration which had an impact on certain separate spirits markets. Although there was some horizontal overlap in the relevant markets in which the parties operated, the merger also led to an extension of the complementary products and range of spirits offered. The Commission displayed concern about 'portfolio power'.

---

[594] See Section 7.

[595] Non-Horizontal Merger Guidelines, paras. 93–118.

[596] The Commission accepts that tying and bundling as such are common practices that often have no anti-competitive consequences, Non-Horizontal Merger Guidelines, para. 92.

[597] The Cournot effect, i.e. the merged firm has an incentive to lower margin on one product to boost sales of a complementary product.

[598] The Guidelines state, however, that '[s]uch economies of scope . . . are necessary but not sufficient to provide an efficiency justification for bundling or tying. Indeed, benefits from economies of scope frequently can be realized without any need for technical or contractual bundling', Non-Horizontal Merger Guidelines, para. 118.

[599] M.4371. See, e.g., J. Brockhoff, B. Jehanno, V. Pozzato, C. Buhr, P. Eberl, and P. Papandropoulos, 'Google/DoubleClick: The First Test for the Commission's Non-Horizontal Merger Guidelines' (2008) 2 *Competition Policy Newsletter* 53.

[600] M.938, [1998] OJ L288/24.

M.938, *Guinness/Grand Metropolitan* [1998] OJ L228/24

Commission

40. The holder of a portfolio of leading spirit brands may enjoy a number of advantages. In particular, his position in relation to his customers is stronger since he is able to provide a range of products and will account for a greater proportion of their business, he will have greater flexibility to structure his prices, promotions and discounts, he will have greater potential for tying, and he will be able to realize economies of scale and scope in his sales and marketing activities, Finally, the implicit (or explicit) threat of a refusal to supply is more potent.

41. The strength of these advantages, and their potential effect on the competitive structure of the market, depends on a number of factors, including whether the holder of the portfolio has the brand leader or one or more leading brands in a particular market; the market shares of the various brands, particularly in relation to the shares of competitors; the relative importance of the individual markets in which the parties have significant shares and brands across the range of product markets in which the portfolio is held; and/or the number of markets in which the portfolio holder has a brand leader or leading brand.

The Commission concluded that the merger in that case would have portfolio effects. The effect was particularly acute on the Greek market where the merged entity would have a dominant position in the gin, brandy, and rum markets and where it would be able to supply the leading brands, with the exception of vodka. Through portfolio effects the dominant position in these markets would be reinforced.[601] This decision received criticism not for its adoption of the concept of portfolio power but for failing to identify with sufficient clarity what is wrong with an undertaking's acquisition of a wider portfolio of products. For example, some paragraphs, including paragraph 40, of the Commission's decision indicate that the Commission objected to the economies of scale and scope offered to the parties from the increased range of products that the merger allowed.[602] Such benefits would, however, not harm but benefit consumers and intervention on these grounds would give the Commission a broad discretion. An objection to portfolio power on the ground that it would give the merged entity greater power to tie products is less controversial.[603]

The Guidelines clarify that the fact that the merged entity will have a broad range or portfolio of products does not, as such, raise competition concerns but that this factor may be relevant when determining whether the merged entity will have the ability to foreclose the market. In such circumstances, customers may have a strong incentive to save transaction costs by buying the range of products from a single source rather than from many.

In *Nestlé/Gerber*[604] the Commission unconditionally cleared Nestlé's acquisition of Novartis's Gerber baby food business. Although the activities of the parties overlapped in several segments of manufactured baby food (baby meals, drinks, and cereals) in certain Member States, the Commission found these did not give rise to competitive concerns. In the course of its investigation, the Commission considered possible portfolio effects in the context of the relative strength of competitors' brands and their portfolios. In some markets, Nestlé would become, post-merger, a full-range supplier of baby foods with strong brands in other food markets. Some respondents to the Commission's market test considered that Nestlé would be able to use its portfolio power to prevent

---

[601] M.938, ibid., paras. 90–118. The Commission permitted the merger only once the parties agreed to end the distribution arrangements for Bacardi rum in Greece even though the merger did not increase the parties' market shares on this market.

[602] Ibid., para. 40.

[603] See, e.g., Bishop and Walker, n. 358, 8.030–8.032.

[604] M.4688, 27 July 2007.

new entry or to impede the expansion of existing 'single-brand' competitors (by, for example, limiting the access of competitors to distribution channels and reducing their shelf space).

In assessing conglomerate effects, however, the Commission drew a distinction between a 'pure portfolio effect' (an incentive on customers to buy the range of products from a single source rather than from many suppliers because it entails efficiencies) and a strategic use of portfolio and financial leverage, such as product bundling, targeted discounts, and discriminatory across-the-board promotions.[605] The Commission considered that the former, although conferring a competitive advantage on suppliers, is not necessarily regarded as anti-competitive. It clarified that conglomerate effects result in a significant impediment to effective competition when the merged entity decides to condition its sales in a particular and strategic way in order to disadvantage its competitors or potential entrants. On the facts, the Commission found no evidence that Nestlé would have opportunity or incentive, post-merger, to adopt an anti-competitive bundling strategy. The Commission was also concerned about possible bundling and technical tying of security products and services (made by McAfee) with Intel's central processing units and chipsets in *Intel/McAfee*.[606] In the end, however, the merger was cleared in Phase I proceedings after commitments were offered to allay the Commission's concerns. The Commission also rejected concerns about tying in *Microsoft/Skype*.[607]

Coordinated Effects

The Non-Horizontal Merger Guidelines state that conglomerate mergers may, in certain circumstances, facilitate anti-competitive coordination in markets, for example by reducing the number of effective competitors, where foreclosed rivals choose not to contest the situation of coordination and/or by increasing the scope and effectiveness of a disciplining mechanism by increasing the extent and importance of multi-market competition.

119. Conglomerate mergers may in certain circumstances facilitate anticompetitive co-ordination in markets, even in the absence of an agreement or a concerted practice within the meaning of Article [101 TFEU]. The framework set out in Section IV of the Notice on Horizontal Mergers also applies in this context. In particular, co-ordination is more likely to emerge in markets where it is fairly easy to identify the terms of co-ordination and where such co-ordination is sustainable.

120. One way in which a conglomerate merger may influence the likelihood of a coordinated outcome in a given market is by reducing the number of effective competitors to such an extent that tacit coordination becomes a real possibility. Also when rivals are not excluded from the market, they may find themselves in a more vulnerable situation. As a result, foreclosed rivals may choose not to contest the situation of co-ordination, but may prefer instead to live under the shelter of the increased price level.

121. Further, a conglomerate merger may increase the extent and importance of multi-market competition. Competitive interaction on several markets may increase the scope and effectiveness of disciplining mechanisms in ensuring that the terms of co-ordination are being adhered to.

(x) Industrial, Social, and Other Policy

a. General

An important question is whether non-competition factors can, should be, or are/have been taken into account when appraising mergers under Article 2. Could, for example, the fact that a merger is advantageous from an industrial or social policy perspective be relied on as a basis for finding that an otherwise problematic merger is nonetheless compatible with the internal market? Alternatively, could non-competition factors be relied upon to prohibit a merger which is otherwise unproblematic from a competition perspective?

---

[605] Ibid., para. 35.

[606] M.5984, 26 January 2011.

[607] M.6281, 7 October 2001, Case T-79/12, *Cisco Systems Inc v Commission* EU:T:2013:635.

b. Other Policies as a Countervailing Factor

Industrial policy, for example, could support industrial restructuring where it is necessary for the undertakings to compete in a global market, to encourage cross-border concentration, to encourage technical progress, to protect certain industries, or to protect employment, even where a concentration might lead to a SIEC. In the run-up to the adoption of the original EUMR some Member States feared that EU industrial policy, aimed at safeguarding and ensuring 'the competitiveness of European industry', might be permitted to support the creation of a Euro champion in circumstances where that Euro champion would be dominant.

Article 2 of the EUMR does not at first sight appear to permit non-competition factors to be taken into account as part of the appraisal process;[608] it permits technical and economic progress to be taken into account but only 'provided that it is to the consumers' advantage and does not form an obstacle to competition'. Recital 23 of the EUMR does, however, state that the Commission must place its appraisal within the general framework of the fundamental objectives of the Treaties.[609] Further, the final decision to clear or prohibit a concentration following a Phase II merger investigation is made by the College of Commissioners[610] and not simply by the Commissioner responsible for competition.[611] This means that in controversial or politically charged cases lobbying of the Commissioners takes place.[612]

Nonetheless, it does not appear that industrial or other EU policies, or lobbying, has, in recent years at least,[613] affected the final outcome of merger decisions. Thus, although some high-profile merger cases, such as the merger between NYSE Euronext and Deutsche Börse or other proposed concentrations which might have created a European or national[614] champion, may have caused public clashes between advocates of industrial policy and supporters of a competition policy based strictly on competition factors alone, in most cases the Commission has resolutely opposed mergers which are not to the consumers' advantage or which form an obstacle to competition. It adheres to the view that EU rules allow firms to search for the best scale and size to compete globally, but ensures that they face sufficient competition to secure performance in international markets. Indeed,

---

[608] Subject to a teleological interpretation being given to the provision, see Chaps. 2 and 4.

[609] See Chap. 2. Recital 13 to the original EUMR also stated that the appraisal should be made within the general framework of the fundamental objectives referred to in Art. 2 of the EC Treaty, including the strengthening of the EU's economic and social cohesion, see also Case T-12/93, *Comité Central d'Enterprise de la Société Anonyme Vittel v Commission* [1995] ECR II-1247, paras. 38–40.

[610] See, e.g., W. Sauter, *Competition Law and Industrial Policy in the EU* (Clarendon Press, 1997), 140.

[611] See Chap. 2.

[612] For example, prior to the Commission's decision in M.7018, *Telefonica Deutschland/E-Plus* 2 July 2014, Angela Merkel and Jean-Claude Juncker (now President of the Commission) expressed their view that the Commission should make it easier for telecom operators to merge so that they can compete more effectively in international markets. Decisions of the Commission must, of course, be taken on legitimate grounds and be adequately justified and reasoned. A decision which is not so taken may be subject to annulment in judicial review proceedings before the Court, see Section 7, p. 1201 and Chap. 13.

[613] In M.315, *Mannesmann/Vallourec/Ilva* [1994] OJ L102/1, e.g., it appears that the College of Commissioners authorised a merger which DG Comp wished to prohibit on the ground that it would lead to the creation of a collective dominant position on the Western European market for seamless steel tubes. The case was strongly supported by the Commissioner responsible for industry. It is believed that the College of Commissioners was deadlocked so that, since the Commission had not voted to prohibit the merger, the decision was rewritten to avoid clearance by default (which would have occurred had the Commissioners failed to deliver a formal decision in time). The fear that this type of thing could happen has led in the past to a call for an independent European Cartel Office to be created, which would be seen to operate independently and free from political constraints, see also Chap. 13.

[614] See, e.g., IP/04/501, 'The Commission puts industry centre stage and reinforces competitiveness in an enlarged European Union', M.469, *MSG Media Service GmbH* 9 November 1994, M.1672, *Volvo/Scania* [2001] OJ L143/74, M.53, *Aérospatiale-Alenia/de Havilland* [1991] OJ L334/42 (it seems that although the French and Italian Governments, the (then) Commissioner for Industry, Martin Bangemann, and the then President of the Commission, Jacques Delors, supported the concentration, others, including the then Competition Commissioner, Sir Leon Brittan, opposed it, believing that it would lead to the creation of a dominant position. The Commission's decision to prohibit the merger was controversial).

the decisions to block the mergers in *MSG/Media Services GmbH*[615] and *Volvo/Scania*[616] were controversial. In practice, therefore, the College of Commissioners ordinarily accept the decisions prepared by DG Comp overseen by the Commissioner for Competition.[617]

During the 2009 financial and economic crisis, the Commission also came under some pressure both from businesses and politicians to relax the application of the competition rules and to subordinate pro-market policies to industrial and other policies supportive of struggling businesses. The Commission took the view, however, that the recession was 'no time to relax the rules'; it was 'business as usual in cartels, mergers and antitrust'.[618]

c. Other Policy Where the Concentration Does Not Significantly Impede Effective Competition

A concentration which does not significantly impede effective competition must be declared to be compatible with the internal market.[619] Further, it has been seen that although steps may be taken by the Member States to preclude an EU concentration where necessary to protect their 'legitimate interests' or 'essential interests of security', the Commission polices the exercise of such powers carefully and tackles 'nationalistic' or 'protectionist' measures by Member States by bringing proceedings against them where national rules, or actions based upon them, breach EU law.[620]

Even though it is possible that things might change in the future, Competition Commissioners have, to date, worked hard to send the message that industrial and other 'non-competition' criteria do not prevail in EU merger policy.

E. ARTICLE 2(4), (5), JOINT VENTURES

The review of JVs[621] under the EUMR[622] is potentially bipartite. It is first necessary to determine whether the creation of the JV itself leads to a SIEC.[623] Secondly, it is necessary to determine whether the JV will lead to the coordination of the competitive behaviour of undertakings which remain

---

[615] M.469, 9 November 1994.

[616] M.1672, [2001] OJ L143/74.

[617] It is noteworthy, however, that in 2012 then Commission President Barroso asked Commissioner Almunia to give early advance notice of cases with a dimension going beyond the scope of competition policy which might impact on other EU policies, see minutes of the 2022nd meeting of the Commission, PV(2012)2022 final. Further the Commission structure under Commission President Juncker, emphasises cooperation and coordination between the Commissioners, see Chaps. 1 and 2.

[618] N. Kroes, 'Competition, the crisis and the road to recovery', 30 March 2009, available at <http://ec.europa.eu/competition/speeches/index_2009.html>.

[619] EUMR, Art. 2(2). Some concern has been expressed that the Commission's willingness to adopt an expansive approach to the concept of an undertaking and single economic unit in the context of State-owned enterprises heightens the risk of EU merger review and distorts merger assessment involving, for example, Chinese companies, see e.g., A. Zhang, 'The Single Entity Theory: An Antitrust Time-bomb for Chinese State-owned Enterprises' (2012) 8 J of Competition Law and Economics 805. The Commission has stressed however that it applies the same criteria to all transactions, wherever the inward investment originates from, see speech by then Commissioner Almunia, SPEECH/11/561, 'Policy Objectives in Merger Control', Fordham Competition Conference, New York, 8 September 2011. The EUMR also affords no grounds for applying less favourable rules, and for retaliating against, companies of third countries that discriminate against EU companies in their own merger control or foreign investment legislation (see, EUMR, Art. 24, n. 724 and text).

[620] See discussion of EUMR, Art. 21(4) and especially e.g., n. 200 and text.

[621] From 1998 to April 2002, Art. 2(4) cases were designated as 'JV' cases and were often handled outside the then Merger Task Force. Since April 2002 they have been designated and have been handled like other merger cases within the merger network.

[622] All jointly controlled full-function joint ventures established on a lasting basis which have an EU dimension fall for assessment under the EUMR.

[623] EUMR, Art. 2(2) and (3). See G. A. Zonnekeyn, 'The Treatment of Joint Ventures Under the Amended EC Merger Regulation' [1998] *ECLR* 414 and J. Temple Lang, 'International Joint Ventures under Community Law' [1999] *Fordham Corporate L Inst* 465.

independent on any market, in particular, an upstream or downstream market or in the market of the JV itself. If it may lead to the coordination of the independent undertakings' behaviour Article 2(4) and (5) of the EUMR provides that these coordinative aspects of the JV will be appraised in accordance with criteria set out in Article 101:

4. To the extent that the creation of a joint venture constituting a concentration pursuant to Article 3 has as its object or effect the co-ordination of the competitive behaviour of undertakings that remain independent, such co-ordination shall be appraised in accordance with the criteria of Article [101(1)] and (3) [TFEU], with a view to establishing whether or not the operation is compatible with the common market.

5. In making this appraisal, the Commission shall take into account in particular:

— whether two or more parent companies retain, to a significant extent, activities in the same market as the joint venture or in a market which is downstream or upstream from that of the joint venture or in a neighbouring market closely related to this market,

— whether the co-ordination which is the direct consequence of the creation of the joint venture affords the undertakings concerned the possibility of eliminating competition in respect of a substantial part of the products or services in question.

These provisions thus require the Commission to consider whether two or more parent companies retain significant activities in the same market as the JV or in downstream, upstream, or neighbouring markets (the identification of candidate markets), and whether any coordination which is the direct consequence of the creation of the JV affords the undertakings concerned the possibility of eliminating competition in respect of a substantial part of the products or services in question. There must therefore be a causal link between the setting up of the JV and the appreciable restriction of competition on the market.[624]

There is no specific Commission guidance on the application of Article 2(4) and (5) to JV cases although decisional practice and the guidance on the application of Article 101 to horizontal co-operation agreements[625] are helpful. The Commission's decisions under the EUMR have been welcomed for displaying an economically realistic approach to the Article 101 assessment required.[626] In *Telia/Telenor/Schibsted*,[627] for example, the parties notified a JV for the provision of various internet services. The Commission considered that the parents remained active on two markets in which coordinated behaviour might be possible. In particular both Telia and Telor remained present on the market to provide 'dial-up' internet access. Although the parents already had joint market shares of between 35 per cent and 65 per cent of the market it was concluded that coordinated behaviour between the parents was not likely. These market shares were not significant on the growing market for dial-up internet access in Sweden. The market was characterised by high growth, low barriers to entry, and low switching costs. On the other market, the website production market, the parent companies and the JV had less than 10 per cent of the market. Any coordination on such a market would not amount to appreciable restriction of competition.[628]

Nonetheless the Commission has, in some cases, dealt with coordination concerns. In *Fujitsu/Siemens*,[629] for example, the parties' agreement to create a JV to develop, manufacture, distribute, market, and sell desktop computers did not have a significant impact on competition. The Commission was worried, however, about the effect that the merger would have on the parents' activities in a number of upstream and downstream markets. In particular, the structure of the 'financial workstation'[630] market made coordination between the parents in financial workstations likely.

---

[624] See, e.g., JV.2, *ENEL/DT/FT* [1999] OJ C178/15.

[625] See Chap. 10.

[626] See Chaps. 4 and 10.

[627] JV.2, [1999] OJ C178/15.

[628] See Chaps. 4 and 13.

[629] Case IV/JV.22, [1999] OJ C318/15.

[630] ATMs and cash dispensers.

The parties, however, proposed a remedy to resolve the problem identified and the Commission cleared the concentration subject to conditions and obligations.

Case IV/JV.22, *Fujitsu/Siemens*

Commission

63. For the reasons set forth below, the financial workstations market displays several structural characteristics, which make co-ordination between the parents in financial workstations likely. First, the market is highly concentrated with NCR, Siemens and Fujitsu accounting for a share of sales of approximately 70 per cent. Second, NCR and Siemens together with Fujitsu have roughly symmetrical market shares. Third, the remaining competitors all have market shares, which do not exceed 10 per cent. Fourth, the technology for financial workstations is relatively mature, as the technology needed to operate financial workstations tends to be standard personal computer-based technology.

64. Any co-ordination between the parent companies would furthermore be appreciable. Both parties will jointly hold a share of sales of [20–40] per cent and will be the second biggest competitor next to NCR, which accounts for [30–40] per cent of the financial workstations market. In light of the almost symmetrical market shares of the two major groups in the financial workstations market and the resulting relationship of interdependence existing between NCR and Siemens/Fujitsu, taken as a group, any co-ordination between the parties appears likely to cause the elimination of competition in respect of a substantial part of the financial workstations market.

65. Co-ordination between the parent companies will also have an effect on trade between Member States. Both Siemens and Fujitsu are EEA-wide operators in financial workstations with activities covering all the major Member States of the EEA. Any alteration of their competitive behaviour would have an effect on intra-Community trade in financial workstations.

66. When these concerns were communicated to the parties, Siemens offered a remedy in order to remove the competitive concerns raised by the operation with regard to the EEA-wide financial workstations market.

67. In two letters dated 15 and 23 September 1999, respectively, Siemens undertakes the following:

(i) Siemens announced, in November 1998 its intention to sell off its retail and banking systems business. This will be done through the sale of all its shares in Siemens Nixdorf Retail and Banking Systems GmbH (based in Paderborn) and the sales of all respective business activities abroad to be carved out of regional legal entities (the 'Retail and Banking System Business') . . .

Siemens commits itself to selling the Retail and Banking Systems Business . . .

. . .

69. The undertaking given by Siemens removes the Commission's concern that the creation of the JVC has as its effect the co-ordination of the competitive behaviour of Siemens and Fujitsu in the financial workstations market. The undertaking to divest Siemens' Retail and Banking Systems Business within . . . removes the incentive to co-ordinate its behaviour with that of Fujitsu . . . . After divestment . . . the financial workstation market will no longer be a candidate market for co-ordination within the meaning of Article 2(4) of the Merger Regulation.

The methodology adopted by the Commission seems thus to be to consider (a) whether or not the creation of the JV has the object of coordinating the behaviour of the parents; and (b) if it does not, whether or not this is its effect. In making this latter determination the Commission identifies candidate markets, considers whether coordination is likely on those markets, and whether the coordination would appreciably restrict competition. The Commission did not consider Article 101(3) elements in *Fujitsu/Siemens* as the parties put forward remedies to deal with the Article 101(1) problems identified.

F. RESTRICTIONS DIRECTLY RELATED AND NECESSARY TO THE CONCENTRATION

Ancillary restraints are clauses the presence of which are vital to the particular concentration since the transaction, in its absence, would not take place. For example, it is usually a condition of a sale of a business that the vendor covenants not to compete with the business for a period of time. Otherwise the goodwill of the business may be rendered valueless.[631] Similarly, in JVs the parents may agree to license IPRs to the JV and perhaps not to compete with the JV. Both the old and current EUMR have made it clear that restrictions directly related and necessary to the implementation of the concentration ('ancillary restraints') may be cleared along with the concentration.[632] To the extent that the restrictions are ancillary, the EUMR alone thus applies to them.[633] By contrast, Articles 101 and 102 remain applicable to restrictions that cannot be considered to be ancillary.

Prior to 2001 the Commission used to clear ancillary restraints in its decision to clear the concentration as a whole. In 2001, however, the Commission issued a Notice regarding restrictions directly related and necessary to concentrations[634] making it clear that the Commission did not intend to make an assessment of restrictions directly related and necessary to the concentration in its merger decisions any longer, and tightening its interpretation of ancillary restraints. Although the GC held in *Lagardère SCA* and *Canal+SA v Commission*[635] that the practice of not assessing the restraints in individual cases was not consistent with the Commission's obligations under the original EUMR, the wording of the new EUMR has been altered to legitimise this practice. It now provides that the Commission's clearance decisions (under both Phase I and Phase II) 'shall be deemed to cover' ancillary restraint.[636]

The Commission's Notice[637] is consequently of critical importance since it provides guidance as to when ancillary restraints are automatically covered by the Commission's clearance decisions.[638] It sets out both general principles[639] and principles applicable to commonly encountered restrictions in cases of acquisition of an undertaking,[640] and JV cases.[641]

With regard to restrictions agreed in relation to the transfer of an undertaking the Commission states, for example, that non-competition obligations on the vendor are generally justified for periods of up to two or three years (three, where both goodwill and know-how are included in the transfer).[642] Non-competition clauses are not considered necessary when the transfer is limited to physical assets or to exclusive industrial and commercial property rights.[643] Any non-competition clause should ordinarily be limited to the products and services forming the economic activity of the undertaking transferred and the geographical area in which the vendor offered them.[644] Licences

---

[631] See also, e.g., the discussion of ancillary restraints in Chap. 4.

[632] EUMR, Art. 8(2). See also Art. 6(1).

[633] EUMR, Art. 21(1).

[634] [2001] OJ C188/5.

[635] Case T-251/00, [2002] ECR II-4825.

[636] EUMR, Arts. 6(1)(b) and 8(1) and (2) and recital 21. The Commission states that '[t]his reflects the intention of the legislator not to oblige the Commission to assess and individually address ancillary restraints', July 2004, para. 2.

[637] Notice of Ancillary Restraints [2005] OJ C56/24.

[638] If the Notice does not provide guidance on a particular restraint and there is no other guidance to be found, the parties may apply to the Commission for individual assessment of a case which presents 'novel and unresolved questions giving rise to genuine uncertainty', ibid., paras. 3–6 (and EUMR, recital 21).

[639] Notice of Ancillary Restraints, part II.

[640] Ibid., part III.

[641] Ibid., part IV.

[642] Ibid., para. 20. The Commission evaluates non-solicitation and confidentiality clauses in the same way as non-competition clauses, para. 26.

[643] Ibid., para. 21.

[644] Ibid., paras. 22–23.

of patents, similar rights, or know-how, and purchase and supply obligations, may also be considered necessary to the implementation of the concentration.[645]

In the context of JV agreements, the Commission considers that non-competition obligations between the parent undertakings and a JV may be ancillary to the concentration for the lifetime of the JV where the obligations correspond to the products, services, and territories covered by the JV agreement or its by-laws.[646] Further, it may be legitimate for the parents to grant IP licences to the JV (whether granted exclusively, for a period of time, or whether a field of use restriction is incorporated), for licences to be granted by the JV to one of the parents, for cross-licences to be granted, or for purchase and supply agreements to be concluded by the parent undertakings and the JV. Licence agreements between the parents are not ancillary to the implementation of the JV.[647]

G. COMMITMENTS OR REMEDIES

(i) Legal Basis and Time Periods

In some cases the parties may propose modifications to the original concentration plan and offer commitments to the Commission in order to allow it to clear the transaction. It is crucial, however, that the commitments offered are full and effective and satisfy the Commission that the remedies are sufficient to restore the conditions of effective competition on a permanent basis.[648]

The EUMR makes it clear that the Commission 'may attach to its decision . . . conditions and obligations intended to ensure that the undertakings concerned comply with the commitments they have entered into vis-à-vis the Commission with a view to rendering the concentration compatible with the common market'[649] in both Phase I, prior to initiation of proceedings, and in Phase II proceedings. Commitments must be offered (on Form RM) within specified timetables; 20 WDs of notification in Phase I proceedings and within 65 WDs of the initiation of proceedings in Phase II proceedings.[650] Any such offer extends the time period for examining the concentration by 10 WD (in Phase I) and 15 WD (in Phase II).[651] In very complex cases, a further extension of up to 20 WDs may be agreed in Phase II.[652] As the time periods are extremely tight, the possibility of offering commitments should be considered very early on in the procedure and, generally, prior to notification.

If offered in Phase I, the commitments will have to be sufficient to rule out clearly any of the Commission's 'serious doubts' within the meaning of Article 6(1)(c). Clearly, the Commission has significant bargaining power at this first stage of the proceedings, and the parties may have to be prepared to give up more at this juncture if they wish to prevent the transaction being taken through to second-phase proceedings. Nonetheless a significant number of cases are resolved through Phase I commitments each year.[653] In Phase II cases, it is for the Commission to communicate its competition concerns, for the parties to formulate appropriate remedies proposals (the Commission cannot impose them), and for the Commission, if it wants to reject the commitments, to demonstrate that the remedies offered do not resolve the competition concerns identified. It is not, therefore, for the parties to prove that their commitments eliminate the competition concerns identified (although

---

[645] Ibid., paras. 27–35.

[646] Ibid., para. 36.

[647] Ibid., paras. 42–43.

[648] The Commission does not, otherwise, have power to authorise a concentration which has been found to be incompatible with the internal market.

[649] EUMR, Arts. 6(2) and 8(2).

[650] Reg. 802/2004, Art. 19(1) and (2).

[651] Only if offered after the 54th WD.

[652] See n. 276.

[653] Since 2001 more Phase I commitments decisions have been taken than the number of Phase II proceedings launched, see <http://ec.europa.eu/competition/mergers/statistics.pdf>.

they must provide the relevant information necessary for the assessment).[654] The parties' ability to influence the outcome of the decision is, therefore, significant. In cases raising serious competition problems, however, the commitments may have to substantially modify the terms and conditions of the transaction.

The Commission tests the commitments submitted by taking them to the market. Indeed, the Regulation specifically provides that transparency must be maintained and Member States and interested third parties should be consulted.[655] Third parties, competitors, suppliers, and customers are, therefore, heavily involved in the process.

In *Oracle/SunMicrosystems*[656] the Commission cleared a transaction subject, not to formal commitments, but taking account of public announcements of a series of pledges made by Oracle to customers, users, and developers.

(ii) The Commission's Notice on Remedies Acceptable under the EUMR

In 2008, the Commission issued a revised Notice on remedies[657] acceptable, which following consultation in the light of a study it published in 2005 on the implementation and effectiveness of remedies[658] and other developments, replaced a 2001 notice.[659] 'The notice sets out the general principles applicable to remedies acceptable to the Commission, the main types of commitments that may be accepted . . . the specific requirements which proposals of commitments need to fulfil in both phases of the procedure, and the main requirements for the implementation of commitments.'[660]

(iii) Types of Commitments

Commitments concluded may relate to the *structure* of the concentration or to the *behaviour* of the parties. A structural remedy ordinarily requires divestiture of the activities of an existing viable business that can operate on a stand-alone basis. Alternatively, a behavioural commitment might have a sufficient effect on the market to restore effective competition, for example to terminate exclusive agreements or to grant competitors access to infrastructure, platforms, key technology, production, or R&D facilities, or to license IPRs.

In practice a structural solution, such as a commitment to sell a subsidiary, may be preferable, since the commitment may prevent (and could be the only solution to prevent[661]) the SIEC arising and it does not require medium- or long-term monitoring measures.[662] Further, behavioural remedies may be difficult to control and enforce.[663] Nonetheless, either are acceptable so long as they

---

[654] See, e.g., Case T-87/05, *EDP v Commission* [2005] ECR II-3745, paras. 65–69.

[655] EUMR, recital 30. See also Cases C-68/94 and C-30/95, *France v Commission, Société Commerciale des Potasses et de l'Azote (SCPA) v Commission* [1998] ECR I-1375.

[656] M.5529. 21 January 2010, Case T-292/10, *Monty Program AB* (appeal withdrawn). See D. Zimmer, 'The Merger Between Oracle and Sun' (2010) 1 *JECLAP* 315 and the discussion of *Google/Motorola*, n. 561 and text.

[657] Remedies Notice [2008] OJ C267/1.

[658] IP/05/1327.

[659] [2001] OJ C6/3. See also the Commission's Merger Remedies Study, IP/05/327, available at <http://ec.europa.eu/competition/mergers/legislation/remedies_study.pdf>.

[660] Remedies Notice, para. 3.

[661] See M.469, *MSG Media Service GmbH* [1994] OJ L364/1, para. 99.

[662] Case T-102/96, *Gencor Ltd v Commission* [1999] ECR II-753, para. 319.

[663] See M.490, *Nordic Satellite Distribution* [1990] OJ L53/21 where the Commission rejected the undertakings offered by the parties on these grounds.

ensure the effective competitive structure of the market and 'are capable of rendering the notified transaction compatible with the common market'.[664]

In some situations, no remedy may be adequate to deal with the adverse effects identified or may be so complex that the Commission cannot determine with the required degree of certainty that effective competition will be restored.[665] In *Deutsche Börse/NYSE Euronext*,[666] for example, not only was the Commission concerned about the sufficiency of the remedies proposed, but it was concerned about their workability and effectiveness. Although in *Schneider/Legrand*,[667] the Commission twice rejected remedies submitted by the parties, the second time on the ground that they were too complex and did not address the Commission's concerns, on appeal, the GC considered that the Commission had not clearly identified its concerns with the transaction in its SO. Consequently, the parties had been unable to put forward proposals for divestiture capable of rendering the concentration compatible with the internal market. The effect of the Commission's irregularities was particularly serious as the Commission had made it clear that remedies were the only means of preventing the concentration falling under Article 2(3) of the Regulation and being declared incompatible. The decision was thus vitiated by the infringement of the rights of defence and annulled.[668]

(iv) Divestiture

The most effective means of restoring effective competition is through divestiture of a subsidiary or production facilities and the creation of a new competitive entity or the strengthening of existing competitors.[669] The divestiture gives a new or existing competitor the possibility of gaining access to the market. In such cases the Commission will wish to ensure that the activities, consisting of a viable business which can operate on a stand-alone basis and compete effectively with the merged entity on a lasting basis, are divested to a suitable purchaser within a specified time period. Sometimes the Commission may require the parties to find a buyer prior to completion of the notified operation (an upfront buyer or fix-it-first (where a buyer is identified and a binding agreement is concluded prior to the Commission's clearance decision)).[670] The sale of the entity may itself amount to a notifiable concentration.

Usually tight deadlines are set within which the divestiture must occur and the commitments will set out specific details and procedures relating to the Commission's oversight of the divestiture, in particular, approval of the trustee and approval of the purchaser and purchase agreement.[671]

The Commission sometimes accepts alternative remedies packages, recognising that the parties' preferred divestiture option may be uncertain or difficult to complete. It may therefore accept a preferred divestiture package on condition that an alternative is available which is equally effective. The Commission explains alternative divestiture commitments and 'crown jewels' in its Remedies Notice:

1.4 Alternative Divestiture commitments: Crown Jewels

In certain cases, the implementation of the parties' preferred divestiture option (of a viable business solving the competition concerns) might be uncertain in view, for example, of third parties' pre-emption rights

[664] Case T-102/96, *Gencor Ltd v Commission* [1999] ECR II-753, para. 318. See also Case C-12/03 P, *Tetra Laval BV v Commission* [2005] ECR I-987, paras. 85–89.

[665] Remedies Notice, paras. 31–32.

[666] M.6166, 1 February 2012, *aff'd* Case T-175/12, *Deutsche Börse v Commission* EU:T:2015:148.

[667] M.2283, 10 October 2001.

[668] Case T-310/01, *Schneider Electric SA v Commission* [2002] ECR II-4071, paras. 421–463.

[669] Remedies Notice, para. 22, see, e.g., M.6471, *Outokumpu/Inoxum* 7 November 2012, M.6503, *La Poste/Swiss Post/JV* 4 July 2012,

[670] See Remedies Notice, paras. 53–57 and, e.g., M.6570, *UPS/TNT Express* 30 January 2013.

[671] Ibid., part IV deals with requirements for the implementation of commitments. See also the Best Practice Guidelines which provide standard model texts for divestiture commitments and for trustee mandates.

or uncertainty as to the transferability of key contracts, intellectual property rights, or the uncertainty of finding a suitable purchaser. Nevertheless, the parties may consider that they would be able to divest this business to a suitable purchaser within a very short time period. In such circumstances, the Commission cannot take the risk that, in the end, effective competition will not be maintained. Accordingly, the Commission will only accept such divestiture commitments under the following conditions: (a) absent the uncertainty, the first divestiture proposed in the commitments would consist of a viable business, and (b) the parties will have to propose a second alternative divestiture which the parties will be obliged to implement if they are not able to implement the first commitment within the given time frame for the first divestiture. Such an alternative commitment normally has to be a 'crown jewel', i.e. it should be as least as good as the first proposed divestiture in terms of creating a viable competitor once implemented, it should not involve any uncertainties as to its implementation and it should be capable of being implemented quickly in order to avoid that the overall implementation period exceeds what would normally be regarded as acceptable in the conditions of the market in question. In order to limit the risks in the interim period, it is indispensable that interim preservation and holding separate measures apply to all assets included in both divestiture alternatives. Furthermore, the commitment has to establish clear criteria and a strict time-table as to how and when the alternative divestiture obligation will become effective and the Commission will require shorter periods for its implementation.

If there is uncertainty as to the implementation of the divestiture due to third party rights or as to finding a suitable purchaser crown jewel commitments and up-front buyers as discussed below in paragraphs 54 address the same concerns, and the parties may therefore choose between both structures.

Divestiture commitments may also be used for removing links between the parties and competitors where these links contribute to competitive concerns raised by the merger.[672]

(v) Other Remedies: Access Remedies, Behavioural Commitments, and 'Remedy Packages'

Divestiture is not the only acceptable remedy.

Nevertheless, a general distinction can be made between divestitures, other structural remedies, such as granting access to key infrastructure or inputs on non-discriminatory terms, and commitments relating to the future behaviour of the merged entity. Divestiture commitments are the best way to eliminate competition concerns resulting from horizontal overlaps, and may also be the best means of resolving problems resulting from vertical or conglomerate concerns. Other structural commitments may be suitable to resolve all types of concerns if those remedies are equivalent to divestitures in their effects, as explained in more detail below. Commitments relating to the future behaviour of the merged entity may be acceptable only exceptionally in very specific circumstances. In particular, commitments in the form of undertakings not to raise prices, to reduce product ranges, or to remove brands, etc., will generally not eliminate competition concerns resulting from horizontal overlaps. In any case, those types of remedies can only exceptionally be accepted if their workability is fully ensured by effective implementation and monitoring in line with the considerations set out in paragraphs 13–14, 66, and 69 of the Remedies Notice, and if they do not risk leading to distorting effects on competition.

Other commitments, such as access remedies and change of long-term exclusive contracts, may also be offered and accepted.[673] The thrust of such commitments is often aimed at opening the market for competitors, through giving access to infrastructure[674] or key technology. The parties

---

[672] See, e.g., M.492, *VEBA/Degusa* [1994] OJ C303/5; M.3653 and M.1845, *Time Warner/AOL* 11 October 2000.

[673] M.877, *Boeing/McDonnell Douglas* [1997] OJ L336/16. Further, the Commission also required Boeing to make some of its IPRs available, through licences, to competitors. These types of remedies may be particularly relevant in telecommunications and media cases.

[674] See, e.g., JV.37, *BSkyB/Kirsch* 21 March 2000.

may also have to make commitments as to 'interoperability'. In *GE/Instrumentarium*,[675] for example, the Commission was concerned about the effect of the merger in the perioperative monitors market and also that the parties could take steps to ensure that competitors' critical care and patient monitors could not interoperate with its anaesthesia equipment. GE adopted a package of measures, the divestiture of a company, and a series of supply agreements with its acquirer, to deal with the horizontal overlaps and to ensure the emergence of an effective competitor to the merged entity on the perioperative monitors market. It also undertook to provide the electrical and mechanical interface for third parties' patient monitors to be able to interconnect with its own anaesthesia equipment.

In the Remedies Notice the Commission states, 'non-structural types of remedies, such as promises by the parties to abstain from certain commercial behaviour (e.g. bundling products), will generally not eliminate the competition concerns resulting from horizontal overlaps. In any case, it may be difficult to achieve the required degree of effectiveness of such a remedy due to the absence of effective monitoring of its implementation . . . Therefore, the Commission may examine other types of non-divesture remedies, such as behavioural promises, only exceptionally in specific circumstances, such as in respect of competition concerns arising in conglomerate structures.'[676]

Behavioural commitments have in some cases been offered to deal with problems arising in coordinated effects or conglomerate cases. In *Kali und Salz/MdK/Treuhand*,[677] for example, the parties to the concentration offered to sever links with its main competitor, SCPA (which were considered to facilitate anti-competitive behaviour on the oligopolistic market).[678] Further, in both *GE/Honeywell*[679] and *Tetra Laval/Sidel*[680] the parties offered commitments to abstain from certain commercial behaviour (for example, bundling products) to deal with the Commission's concerns. In the latter cases the Commission rejected the commitments on the grounds that they were pure promise and would involve excessive monitoring. In the *GE/Honeywell* appeals,[681] the GC did not need to rule on the correctness of the Commission's actions in this regard as it considered that its competition assessment of the conglomerate effects contained manifest errors of assessments. In *Commission v Tetra Laval BV*,[682] however, the CJ held that as the Commission had rejected the commitments as a matter of principle the GC had been correct to find that this was a factor that the Commission should have taken into account when assessing the likelihood that the merged entity would act in such a way as to make it possible to create a dominant position on one or more of the relevant markets for PET equipment. In *Intel/McAfee*,[683] in contrast, the Commission accepted a range of behavioural remedies to deal with its concerns both about bundling and technical tying in a conglomerate merger case and foreclosure of competing security solution providers.

(vi) Other Cases

The broad range of packages accepted often requires the parties to be 'inventive' and to propose remedy packages which will resolve the competition problems identified by the Commission. In

---

[675] M.3083, IP/03/1193.

[676] Remedies Notice, para. 69.

[677] M.308, [1994] OJ L186/30; on appeal Cases C-68/94 and C-30/95, *France v Commission, Société Commerciale des Potasses et de l'Azote (SCPA) v Commission* [1998] ECR I-1375.

[678] Their imposition was one of the factors which caused SCPA and France to challenge, successfully, the legitimacy of the Commission's decision.

[679] M.2220, 3 July 2001.

[680] M.2416, 30 October 2001, annulled on appeal Case T-5/02, [2002] ECR II-4381, *aff'd* Case C-12/03 P, [2005] ECR I-987.

[681] Cases T-209 and 210/01, *Honeywell v Commission* and *General Electric Co v Commission* [2005] ECR II-5527 and 5575.

[682] Case C-12/03 P, [2005] ECR I-987, paras. 85–89.

[683] M.5984, 26 January 2011.

some cases the Commission has accepted alternative remedies packages. For example, in *Nestlé/ Ralston Purina*[684] the Commission was concerned about the impact of the concentration in the Spanish markets for dry dog food, dry cat food, and snacks and treats for cats and in the Italian and Greek markets for dry cat food. With regard to Spain, the party undertook to divest itself of its 'Friskies' brand, through the grant of exclusive licences for a substantial period and to divest itself of a Spanish production plant or, if not implemented within a specified time period, alternatively, to remove the overlap in Spain by divesting itself of Ralston Purina's 50 per cent shareholding in the JV, Gallina Blanca Purina.

In some cases a concentration has been saved by a third party to the transaction. In *Alcatel/ Telettra*,[685] for example, the Spanish telecommunications company, Telefónica, agreed to sell its interests in the parties to the concentration in order to persuade the Commission that the undertakings' potential market power would be counteracted by the countervailing exercise of monopolistic demand.

(vii) Breach of a Condition or Obligations

Commitments consist of both 'conditions' and 'obligations'. The Commission may take a decision prohibiting the concentration where it finds that it has been implemented in contravention of a condition attached to a decision.[686] Further, it may revoke a decision where the undertakings concerned commit a breach of an obligation, relating to the steps necessary to implement the commitment, attached to the decision.[687] In addition, the Commission may impose fines of up to 10 per cent of the aggregate turnover of the undertakings concerned that have failed to comply with conditions or obligations imposed,[688] and periodic penalty payments on undertakings for delay caused by failure to comply with an obligation.[689]

(viii) Modification and Waiver of Commitments

In some exceptional cases the Commission has been prepared to modify or waive certain commitments which had been attached to a clearance decision.[690]

6. EUMR STATISTICS

DG Comp publishes statistics, which it updates monthly, setting out what happens to merger notifications.[691] These are revealing and provide important information on, for example, the number of notifications (including notifications under the simplified procedure) (see Fig. 15.3), the number of referrals, Phase II proceedings, Phase I and II clearances (conditional or unconditional), and prohibitions (see Fig. 15.4).

---

[684] M.2337, IP/01/1136.

[685] M.42, *Alcatel/Telettra* [1991] OJ L122/48.

[686] EUMR, Art. 8(7).

[687] EUMR, Arts. 6(3) and 8(6).

[688] EUMR, Art. 14(2)(d).

[689] EUMR, Art. 15(1)(c).

[690] See M.950, *Hoffmann-La Roche/Boehringer Mannheim* 3 May 2011.

[691] <http://ec.europa.eu/competition/mergers/statistics.pdf>.

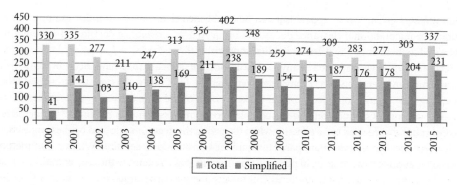

Figure 15.3 Number of notifications 2000–2015

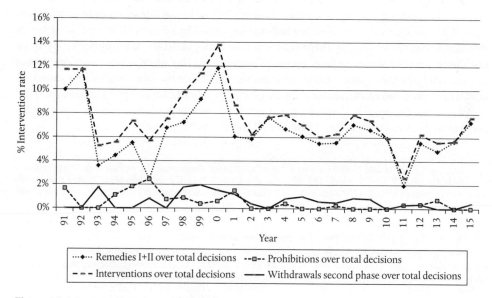

Figure 15.4 Interventions in notified concentrations

7. JUDICIAL REVIEW AND OTHER PROCEEDINGS BEFORE THE EU COURTS

The EUMR itself provides the CJ with unlimited jurisdiction to review penalties imposed by the Commission and to cancel, reduce, or increase any such fine imposed.[692] The ordinary provisions in the TFEU also authorise the review of institutions' acts and failure to act. A party to a concentration may, therefore, institute proceedings against a final merger decision under Article 263 TFEU.[693] Further, third parties (such as a competitor of the merging parties[694] or a third party affected by

---

[692] EUMR, Art. 16.

[693] Most likely a prohibition decision, see e.g., Case C-188/06 P, *Schneider Electric SA v Commission* [2007] ECR I-35, para. 67 and n. 273.

[694] See e.g., Case T-2/93, *Air France v Commission* [1994] ECR II-323; Case T-119/02, *Royal Philips Electronics v Commission* [2003] ECR II-1433; and Case T-177/04, *easyJet Airline Co Ltd v Commission* [2006] ECR II-1931.

commitments given)[695] may appeal if it can be established that the decision (for example, a conditional or unconditional clearance decision[696] or an Article 9 reference decision[697]) although not addressed to them 'is of direct and individual concern' to them.[698]

Sections 1–5 have discussed many of the important appeals that have been brought from Commission merger decisions. It has been seen that the EU Courts consistently stress that when reviewing the Commission's decisions they take account of the wide discretion that the Regulation imposes upon the Commission and the complex economic assessments required.[699] Nonetheless, the Court has shown itself to be effective when reviewing the decisions adopted by the Commission and, where necessary, has been prepared to annul the Commission's decision. Where a Commission decision is annulled, in whole or in part, the Commission has to examine the concentration 'afresh' in the light of current market conditions. This means that the parties must put in a new notification or a supplement to the original notification, or, where the notification has not become incomplete, a certification stating that there are no changes. The ordinary Phase I time procedure runs from the WD following the receipt of the new notification, supplementary notification, or certification.[700]

The appeals procedure is discussed more fully in Chapter 13. An important issue which arises, especially in merger cases, however, is whether there should be a fast-track procedure. Although the Commission has to proceed within very tight time limits, under the Regulation itself it may be years before a review of its decision is conducted by the Court. This, of course, puts the Commission in a powerful position.[701] Since 2001[702] an expedited procedure has been available for cases (not limited to competition cases) capable of being resolved by abbreviated written procedures and a full oral procedure. The procedure, which ordinarily takes between nine and 12 months, was used, for example, in the *Philips*,[703] *Schneider*,[704] *Tetra Laval*,[705] and *Impala*[706] appeals.[707]

---

[695] See Cases C-68/94 and C-30/95, *France v Commission, Société Commerciale des Potasses et de l'Azote (SCPA) v Commission* [1998] ECR I-1375, paras. 173–175. See also Case T-464/04, *Independent Music Publishers and Labels Association (Impala) v Commission* [2006] ECR II-2289; Case C-413/06 P, *Bertelsmann and Sony Corp v Commission* [2008] ECR I-4951; Case T-79/12, *Cisco Systems Inc v Commission* EU:T:2013:635.

[696] Ibid.

[697] See, e.g., Case T-119/02, *Royal Philips Electronics v Commission* [2003] ECR II-1433.

[698] No direct and individual concern was established in, e.g., Case T-350/03, *Wirtschaftskammer Kärnten and best connect Ampere Strompool v Commission* [2006] ECR II-68; Case T-96/92 R, *CCE de la Société générale des grandes sources and others v Commission* [1995] ECR II-1213. Proceedings have also been brought by employees and shareholders of one of the undertakings concerned, see e.g. Case T-83/92, *Zunis Holding v Commission* [1993] ECR II-1169.

[699] See, e.g., Cases C-68/94 and C-30/95, *France v Commission, Société Commerciale des Potasses et de l'Azote (SCPA) v Commission* [1998] ECR I-1375, paras. 223–224; and Case T-221/95, *Endemol Entertainment Holding BV v Commission* [1999] ECR II-1299.

[700] EUMR, Art. 10(5). In the second investigation into the *Tetra Laval/Sidel* merger, M.2416, 13 January 2003, the merger was eventually cleared subject to commitments. Following a launch of a further Phase II investigation in the *Schneider* case, however, the merger was eventually abandoned.

[701] This fact may encourage the undertakings involved to give commitments to persuade the Commission to authorise the merger. Further, the parties will have to observe a prohibition or commitments imposed until the Commission's decision is suspended or annulled.

[702] [2000] OJ L322.

[703] Case T-119/02, *Royal Philips Electronics v Commission* [2003] ECR II-1433. See also, e.g., Case T-87/05, *EDP v Commission* [2005] ECR II-3745.

[704] Case T-310/01, [2002] ECR II-4071.

[705] Case T-5/02, [2002] ECR II-4381.

[706] Case T-464/04, *Independent Music Publishers and Labels Association (Impala) v Commission* [2006] ECR II-2289, Case C-413/06 P, *Bertelsmann and Sony Corp v Commission* [2008] ECR I-4951. Although this case was run under the expedited procedure, judgment was not handed down until 19 months after the Commission's decision had passed. The GC was critical of the way that Impala had handled the case, having requested the expedited procedure, and this fact was reflected in the costs order it made, see paras. 544–554.

[707] Schneider agreed to cut back its case so that the expedited procedure could be used. In both *Schneider* and *Tetra Laval* the GC gave judgment within a period of about a year from the Commission's decision. See C. Chibnall, 'Expedited Treatment of Appeals against EC Competition Decisions under the EC Merger Control Regulation' [2002] *Comp Law* 327.

In both *My Travel* (previously *Airtours*) and *Schneider*, claimants launched damages proceedings against the Commission in respect of the loss suffered in consequence of the wrongful prohibition of their proposed acquisitions (under Article 340(2) TFEU, dealing with the non-contractual liability of the EU).[708] My Travel's claim was dismissed and although the GC in *Schneider v Commission* awarded Schneider damages in respect of two of the categories of loss claimed (having found that some of the Commission's failures had manifestly and gravely disregarded the limit on its discretion), the CJ set aside the judgment insofar as it ordered the Commission to make good the loss claimed as a result of the reduction in the sale price of Legrand. It thus significantly reduced the sum awarded, holding that the Commission was only liable to pay compensation to Schneider to cover costs incurred in respect of the resumed merger control procedure. The sum of €50,000 eventually awarded was significantly less than the €1.6 billion originally claimed.

8. INTERNATIONAL ISSUES

A. THE LONG ARM OF THE EUMR

The quantitative jurisdictional tests incorporated within the EUMR look not to the effect of the concentration on inter-State trade or on competition but to the size of the undertakings involved. This means that they may encompass: mergers between non-EU undertakings even though the undertakings' business is principally carried on outside the EU and/or the merger is completed outside the EU; a JV set up by non-EU parents even though it has no activities in the EU;[709] a transaction which has no or little impact on competition within the EU; and even if the transaction has been cleared in another jurisdiction. As there is no exemption for mergers occurring outside the EU or any requirement that any of the undertakings involved is established or has substantial operations in any part of the EU,[710] the Commission's scrutiny of some mergers has been extremely politically sensitive in nature.

In 1997, for example, the Commission considered a merger announced in December 1996 between Boeing and McDonnell Douglas, neither of which had facilities or assets in the EU.[711] The merger was instigated with the encouragement of the US authorities (the Clinton administration) and was not challenged by the US FTC in July 1997.[712] Although the Commission had concerns about the merger, in the end a political storm was saved by Boeing's offer of acceptable commitments to the Commission. In *Gencor/Lonrho*,[713] however, the Commission prohibited a concentration concluded between a South African (Gencor) and UK (Lonrho) company merging business activities based in South Africa even though the South African Competition Board did not consider that the operation gave rise to competition concerns under South African law. Similarly, in *GE/Honeywell*,[714] the Commission prohibited a merger which had been permitted by the US authorities.

---

[708] Case T-212/03, *MyTravel v Commission* [2008] ECR II-1967 and Case T-351/03, *Schneider v Commission* [2007] ECR II-2237; Case C-440/07 P, [2009] ECR I-6413, see D. Arts, '"Schneider" and the Non-contractual Liability of the European Community in the Field of Merger Control' (2010) 1 *JECLAP* 27. For a discussion of Art. 340 (ex Art. 288 EC) see, e.g., T. Hartley, *The Foundations of European Union Law* (7th edn, Oxford University Press, 2010), Chap. 16.

[709] If the parent companies, or other connected undertakings within the group, satisfy the worldwide and EU-wide turnover thresholds, the JV transaction will have an EU dimension even if the JV created is not established in the EU, does not have activities in or make sales into the EU, and it is not foreseeable that the JV will produce any direct and substantial effects in the EU.

[710] In earlier EUMR drafts it was a requirement that at least one of the undertakings was established in the EU and had substantial operations in one of the Member States: see [1973] OJ C92/1, Art. 1(1), [1982] OJ C36/3, [1988] OJ C130/4.

[711] M.877, [1997] OJ L336/16. The extraterritorial aspects of this case are discussed in greater detail in Chap. 16.

[712] See US FTC Press Releases of 1 July 1997: 'FTC Allows Merger of the Boeing Company and McDonnell Douglas Corporation', 23 September 1997.

[713] M.619, [1997] OJ L11/30.

[714] M.2220, 3 July 2001, *aff'd* Cases T-209 and 210/01, ECR II-5527 and 5575.

It can be seen from these examples that a number of important issues arise in the application of the EUMR. The first is to what extent the Commission has *jurisdiction* to apply the EUMR extraterritorially to concentrations between foreign entities. The second relates to whether the provisions of the EUMR can be enforced against merging parties and third parties located outside the EU.[715] The third relates to comity and what steps have been taken to cooperate with the competition authorities of other States involved in the investigation of the same case, to exchange information where possible, and to avoid conflicting decisions being taken. This has become an increasingly important issue as the number of jurisdictions around the world with merger control regimes has grown and as parties to international merger transactions more frequently have to make multi-jurisdictional filings. The Commission now often cooperates, through formal and more informal arrangements, successfully with other agencies, particularly the US ones, to coordinate their merger reviews, insofar as is possible, to ensure consistency in remedies where required. In *Deutsche Börse/NYSE Euronext* and *Intel/McAfee*[716] for example, the Commission cooperated closely with the US DOJ and FTC respectively, in *UPS/TNT Express*[717] it cooperated closely with both the US and Canadian authorities and in *Thermo-Fisher/Life Technologies*[718] and *GE/Alstom*[719] it cooperated with a large number of agencies across the globe.

In *Gencor Ltd v Commission*[720] the GC had to deal with an argument which raised the right of the Commission to assert jurisdiction over the JV which Gencor alleged had no activities within the EU, was not implemented within the EU,[721] and did not have an immediate, direct, and substantial effect within the EU. The GC upheld the legality of the Commission's prohibition decision, ruling that the Commission's assertion of jurisdiction was not inconsistent with the EUMR, other EU case law, or the rules of public international law.[722] Indeed, the GC made it clear that even where there is doubt about the legality of the assertion of jurisdiction under the EUMR, compulsory notification of such transactions is justifiable, as the Commission must be in a position to assess whether or not a transaction falls within its purview.[723] These issues, and this aspect of the GC's judgment in *Gencor*, are discussed in Chapter 16.

B. RECIPROCITY

Article 24 of the EUMR makes provision for the Member States to inform the Commission 'of any general difficulties encountered by their undertakings with concentrations . . . in a non-member country'. Further it provides for the Commission to draw up reports on this issue.

---

[715] Neither the EUMR itself nor the implementing regulation explicitly deals with the limits of enforcement jurisdiction. Rather, the provisions apply broadly. Further, the Commission has in practice used the powers to request information from parties and even third parties located outside the EU and to prohibit, or to clear subject to compliance with conditions or obligations, transactions between non-EU firms. See Chap. 16.

[716] Cases M.6166, 1 February 2012 and M. 5984, 26 January 2011 and see revised best practices for US–EU cooperation in merger investigations (14 October 2011). See also, ICN Practical Guide to International Enforcement Cooperation in Mergers available at <www.internationalcompetitionnetwork.org/working-groups/current/merger.aspx>.

[717] M.6570, 30 January 2013.

[718] M.6944, 26 November 2013.

[719] M.7278, 8 September 2015.

[720] Case T-102/96, *Gencor Ltd v Commission* [1999] ECR II-753.

[721] Arguably, as the structural changes in *Gencor* were not implemented within the EU, the implementation test expounded in *Wood Pulp* had not been satisfied. For the view that both cases endorse the effects doctrine, see Mosso, n. 310, 7 (see Chap. 16).

[722] Further, that the principles of non-interference or proportionality did not require the Commission to refrain from exercising jurisdiction where another authority had authorised but not required the transaction.

[723] The parties may be spared the inconvenience of a full notification in this situation as the short-form notification and simplified procedure is likely to apply, see nn. 119–120 and text.

Where it appears that certain non-Member States do not permit or otherwise make it difficult for EU undertakings to carry out mergers in circumstances in which undertakings in that State would be permitted to carry out a merger in the EU, 'the Commission may submit proposals to the Council for an appropriate mandate for negotiation with a view to obtaining comparable treatment for EU undertakings'.[724]

9. CONCLUSIONS

1. In the relatively short period since the EUMR first came into force, the Commission has developed an effective and well-respected system of merger control.

2. The Commission has not shied away from adopting decisions involving complex and difficult analysis within the stringent time periods prescribed by the EUMR. It seems clear that the rigorous economic approach adopted routinely in merger cases, has impacted on and encouraged the development and modernisation of the Commission's analysis under Articles 101 and 102.

3. The Commission regularly reviews the operation and working of the EUMR, considering how to improve procedures and substantive analysis as well as tackling the complex jurisdictional problems that the EUMR provokes.

4. The challenge for the Commission remains to conduct the rigorous analysis demanded of it by the GC, within the tight time periods set out in the EUMR.

10. FURTHER READING

A. BOOKS

COOK, C. J., and KERSE, C. S., *EC Merger Control* (5th edn, Sweet & Maxwell, 2009)

HOVENKAMP, H., *Federal Antitrust Policy: The Law of Competition and its Practice* (5th edn, West, 2016)

LINDSAY, A., and BERRIDGE, A., *The EU Merger Regulation: Substantive Issues* (4th edn, Sweet & Maxwell, 2012)

LOWE, P., and MARQUIS, M. (eds.), *European Competition Law Annual 2010: Merger Control in European and Global Perspective* (Hart Publishing, 2013)

B. ARTICLES

BAILEY, D., 'Standard of Proof in EC Merger Proceedings: A Common Law Perspective' (2003) 40 *CMLRev* 845

BRITTAN, L., 'The Law and Policy of Merger Control in the EEC' (1990) 15 *ELRev* 351

COATE, M. B., 'Did the European Union's Market Dominance Policy Have a Gap? Evidence from Enforcement in the United States' (2009) *European Competition Journal* 655

HACKER, N., 'The *Kali+Salz* Case—the Re-examination of a Merger After an Argument by the Court' (1998) 3 *Competition Policy Newsletter* 40

HOWARTH, D., 'The Court of First Instance in *GE/Honeywell*' [2006] *ECLR* 485

LEVY, N., 'The EU's SIEC Test Five Years On: Has It Made a Difference?' [2010] *European Competition Journal* 211

MEZZANOTTE, F. E., 'Direct versus Indirect Proof of the *Airtours* Criterion in *Impala*' (2009) 31 *World Competition* 253

MONTI, G., and ROUSSEVA, E., 'Failing Firms in the Framework of the EC Merger Regulation' (1999) 24 *ELRev* 38

MOTTA, M., 'EC Merger Policy and the *Airtours Case*' [2000] *ECLR* 199

RÖLLER, L. H., and DE LA MANO, M., 'The Impact of the New Substantive Test in European Merger Control' [2006] *European Competition Journal* 9

---

[724] EUMR, Art. 24(3).

SIMONS, S., and COATE, M. B., 'Upward Pressure on Price Analysis: Issues and Implications for Merger Policy' [2010] *European Competition Journal* 377

TURNER, D., 'Conglomerate Mergers and Section 7 of the Clayton Act' (1965) 78 *Harvard LR* 1313

WERDEN, G. J., 'Economic Reasoning in Merger Cases and How Courts Should Evaluate It' [2009] *European Competition Journal* 701

WHISH, R., 'Substantive Analysis Under the EC Merger Regulation: Should the Dominance Test be Replaced by "Substantial Lessening of Competition"?' *EU Competition Law & Policy: Developments & Priorities* (Hellenic Competition Commission, 2002)

WITT, A., 'From *Airtours* to *Ryanair*: Is the More Economic Approach to EU Merger Law Really About More Economics?' [2012] *CMLRev* 217

16

INTERNATIONAL ASPECTS

1. CENTRAL ISSUES

1. In a globalised marketplace the effects of anti-competitive conduct can be felt far from where they originate and mergers frequently involve undertakings from different jurisdictions or multinational companies that operate worldwide. Very many States now have competition law regimes but although trade and competition are global, competition laws remain national (or supranational in the case of the EU).

2. It was the US which first developed concepts to deal with jurisdictional problems in competition law. The US formulated the 'effects doctrine' whereby US antitrust laws apply to conduct which has a direct, substantial, and reasonably foreseeable effect in the US.

3. The US can be an attractive jurisdiction to foreign plaintiffs. Damages actions for competition injury are more common in the US than in Europe and many aspects of US litigation are plaintiff friendly. Recent US cases, however, have limited the use of the US courts by foreign plaintiffs.

4. The EU's single economic entity doctrine has brought many foreign companies within its jurisdiction. The EU has also formulated an 'implementation' doctrine and a 'qualified effects' doctrine. The Merger Regulation takes jurisdiction over undertakings anywhere in the world on the basis of the amount of their turnover in the EU.

5. The EU has entered into a number of agreements, including dedicated bilateral cooperation agreements on competition, with other States.

6. Plans for international competition regimes or rules, for instance within the WTO, have not progressed. However, there is a great deal of international cooperation in competition law matters and very successful 'soft law' developments going on stemming from cooperation between competition agencies from around the world, in particular the International Competition Network (ICN).

2. INTRODUCTION

Trade and competition are increasingly global. Restrictions on competition and anti-competitive conduct which affect trade between Member States may originate outside the EU. Firms established outside the EU may, for example, fix prices in the EU or divide the single market between them. A firm established outside the EU may hold a dominant position in the single market and may engage in behaviour which is an abuse under Article 102. Further, concentrations involving non-EU undertakings may have consequences for competition inside the EU. But how far does the jurisdiction of the EU competition authorities reach?

As the globalisation of the world economy advances it becomes increasingly difficult to isolate the effects of transactions which take place on that global market. A company like Microsoft or Google has a dominant position throughout the world. Consumers anywhere can be injured by global conspiracies and one issue of current concern is in which jurisdiction(s) the victims can sue for compensation. The two most pressing matters are dealing with multinational mergers and international cartels, neither of which are confined within one jurisdiction. A number of remedies have been proposed or put in place, including the conclusion of bilateral and multilateral international arrangements and dealing with competition policy within the framework of existing international organisations (such as the World Trade Organization (WTO)). The EU has been an enthusiastic proponent of international cooperation in competition law matters.

In this chapter we look first at the question of extraterritoriality in international law; secondly, at competition law and extraterritoriality in respect of the EU and the US; and, thirdly, at the 'internationalisation' of competition law and the moves which have been made towards dealing with competition issues on a global footing to match the global operations of undertakings on world markets.

3. INTERNATIONAL LAW

The matter of the rights of States to take jurisdiction outside their territory is known as *extraterritoriality*. Extraterritoriality is a complex topic in international law.[1] International law traditionally distinguishes between two types of jurisdiction. On the one hand there is what is called *prescriptive* (or *subject-matter* or *legislative*) jurisdiction, which is the right of States to make their laws applicable to persons, territory, or situations. On the other hand there is *enforcement* jurisdiction, which is the capacity to take executive action to enforce compliance with those laws.[2]

The two undoubted bases for jurisdiction in international law are nationality and territory.[3] There are two aspects to territorial jurisdiction: subjective and objective. *Subjective territoriality* gives a State jurisdiction over acts which originated within its territory but were completed abroad. *Objective territoriality* gives a State jurisdiction over acts which originated abroad but were completed, at least partially, within its own territory. Objective territoriality was recognised by the Permanent Court of International Justice (PCIJ) in the *Lotus* case.[4] Further possible principles of jurisdiction are the passive personality principle, by which States claim jurisdiction over aliens who have committed acts abroad harmful to their nationals, and the protective or security principle[5] by which they claim jurisdiction over aliens for acts committed abroad which harm the security of the State. The latter principle is capable of indefinite expansion and could potentially be used to justify jurisdiction over economic acts.

It is the application of the objective territoriality principle which gives rise to the greatest controversy in competition law. Objective territoriality was developed in respect of physical actions

---

[1] There is an enormous literature on jurisdiction in international law, a complex issue of which the question of jurisdiction in competition law is but a small part. See, e.g., M. Akehurst, 'Jurisdiction in International Law' (1972–1973) 46 *BYIL* 145; F. A. Mann, 'The Doctrine of International Jurisdiction Revisited After Twenty Years' (1984) 156 *RdC* 9; F. A. Mann, 'The Doctrine of Jurisdiction in International Law' (1964) 111 *RdC* 3; D. W. Bowett, 'Jurisdiction: Changing Problems of Authority over Activities and Resources' (1982) 53 *BYIL* 1; J. Crawford, *Brownlie's Principles of Public International Law* (8th edn, Oxford University Press, 2012), Chap. 21; R. Jennings and A. Watts (eds.), *Oppenheim's International Law* (9th edn, Oxford University Press, 2008), Vol. 1, 472–478; O. Schachter, *International Law in Theory and Practice* (Nijhoff, 1991), Chap. XII; R. Higgins, *Problems and Process* (Oxford University Press, 1994), Chap. 4. With particular reference to antitrust law, see K. M. Meessen, 'Antitrust Jurisdiction under Customary International Law' (1984) 78 *AJIL* 783; P. J. Slot and E. Grabandt, 'Extraterritoriality and Jurisdiction' (1986) 23 *CMLRev* 545; P. M. Roth, 'Reasonable Extraterritoriality: Correcting the "Balance of Interests"' (1992) 41 *ICLQ* 245.

[2] See the Opinion of Darmon AG in Cases 89, 104, 114, 116, 117, and 125–9/85, A. *Ahlström Oy v Commission* [1988] ECR 5193 (*Wood Pulp I*), paras. 19–32 and 47–58 of the Opinion.

[3] See, e.g., *Brownlie's Principles of Public International Law*, n. 1; *Oppenheim's International Law*, n. 1; Akehurst, n. 1, 177.

[4] (1927) PCIJ Ser. A, No. 10, 23. However, there is continuing uncertainty about what *Lotus* actually decided. The case arose from a collision on the high seas between a French ship and a Turkish ship which led to Turkey instituting criminal proceedings against the officers of the watch on the French ship when it put into a Turkish port. The PCIJ held that international law did not *prevent* Turkey instituting proceedings: it was not asked whether international law *authorised* it to do so. See J. Griffin, 'Reactions to US Assertions of Extraterritorial Jurisdiction' [1998] *ECLR* 64, 68.

[5] See the *Cutting* case (1886), in J. B. Moore, *Digest of International Law*, Vol. II (US Government Printing Office, 1906). A further principle, not relevant here, is the universality principle, where jurisdiction is taken over aliens as a matter of international public policy for crimes such as piracy or aircraft hijacking.

(the weapon fired across the frontier scenario), not economic activities. While most States agree (officially at least) that actions such as murder are criminal behaviour deserving of punishment, the belief that anti-competitive behaviour is also contrary to the public good depends on the acceptance of a certain set of economic and political beliefs.[6] Moreover, even in States with competition law regimes, the objectives of the laws may vary, or the authorities' application of them in a specific situation may differ. For example, the EU and US authorities have had different views on some transactions despite the close cooperation between the two jurisdictions in competition matters and the existence of similar laws. Moreover, if States apply their competition laws extraterritorially undertakings may find themselves subject to a number of competing and irreconcilable actions, there may be conflict between national authorities, and other States may feel that their sovereignty is infringed.

For a State applying its competition law extraterritorially merely taking prescriptive jurisdiction may not be enough. Often it also needs enforcement jurisdiction whereby its authorities can conduct investigations, collect evidence, serve proceedings, and recover penalties abroad. The distinction between prescriptive and enforcement jurisdiction was explored by the Advocates General in the EU cases, *Dyestuffs*[7] and *Wood Pulp I*.[8] They considered that the mere imposition of a pecuniary sanction is a matter of prescriptive jurisdiction, enforcement jurisdiction being involved only when steps are taken for its recovery, because only then is the State taking coercive measures in the territory of a foreign sovereign. A number of international instruments provide for cooperation between jurisdictions, in particular with regard to the recognition and enforcement of judgments, and the taking of evidence abroad,[9] but the extraterritorial enforcement of a State's competition law is another matter, and one which is highly contentious as we see, for example, in the UK's Protection of Trading Interests Act 1980.[10]

A major question in this area is whether the US 'effects doctrine', discussed in Section 4, whereby the US asserts jurisdiction based on 'direct, substantial and reasonably foreseeable' effects within the United States is in conformity with the principle of objective territoriality in international law or is an illegitimate extension of it which is inconsistent with the principle of the sovereignty of nations. The US Government considers that it does comply with international law. Some other States disagree.[11] We see in discussing the position of extraterritorially in EU law in Section 5 that the EU Courts have been careful to state that the principles they have crafted are in accordance with international law.

4. US LAW

A. GENERAL

It is necessary to look at extraterritoriality in US law before considering EU competition law because as the Sherman Act dates from 1890 its extraterritorial reach became an issue before the EEC even existed.[12] The 'effects doctrine' propounded in the US courts has provided the central concept

---

[6] See Chap. 1.

[7] Opinion of Mayras AG in Case 48/69, *ICI v Commission (Dyestuffs)* [1972] ECR 619, 695.

[8] Opinion of Darmon AG in Cases 89/85 etc., *Wood Pulp I* [1988] ECR 5193, paras. 28–30.

[9] See the Hague Convention on the Recognition and Enforcement of Judgments on Civil and Commercial Matters, 1971, and the Hague Convention on the Taking of Evidence Abroad in Civil or Commercial Matters, 1970. It should be noted that private international law (conflict of laws), as well as public international law, is relevant to jurisdiction questions in competition cases. Private international law attempts to regulate whether a particular State has jurisdiction to try an issue and which law will be applied in determining it, see e.g. Dicey, Morris, and Collins, *The Conflict of Laws* (15th edn, Sweet & Maxwell, 2014).

[10] Discussed in Section 4.C.

[11] See Griffin, n. 4, 68.

[12] See R. Y. Jennings, 'Extraterritorial Jurisdiction and the United States Antitrust Laws' (1957) 33 *BYIL* 146.

around which the discussion of extraterritoriality in competition law is conducted. The extraterritorial application of US antitrust law has long been controversial, not just as a matter of principle but because of the features of US antitrust litigation. US law provides, for example, for the recovery of 'treble damages' for breaches of the antitrust laws,[13] for far-ranging pre-trial discovery, and for 'opt-out' class actions. In recent years the attractions to litigants of pursuing in US courts competition law claims with only an indirect connection to the US have led to a lively debate about the jurisdiction of US courts in antitrust cases.[14]

Two points about US law should be noted at the outset. First, there is a multiplicity of actors in antitrust law. The two federal agencies, the Department of Justice (DOJ) and the Federal Trade Commission (FTC) are not primarily decision-makers as is the European Commission, as antitrust law is enforced in the ordinary courts. Different courts of equal authority can (and do) come to different conclusions on the same issues which can sometimes render it difficult to make general statements about US law.[15] Secondly, extraterritoriality in antitrust law is but one aspect of the long arm of US law.[16]

B. THE EFFECTS DOCTRINE

At first the US courts were diffident about applying the Sherman Act[17] extraterritorially. In the *American Banana* case[18] Justice Oliver Wendell Holmes said in the Supreme Court that 'the general and almost universal rule is that the character of an act as lawful or unlawful must be determined wholly by the law of the country where the act is done'. Later cases retreated from this self-denying ordinance,[19] and in the *Alcoa* case[20] in 1945, which concerned a cartel of aluminium producers based in Switzerland which fixed production quotas to boost prices, Judge Learned Hand laid down what is known as the 'effects doctrine'. He said that the Sherman Act *did* apply to agreements concluded outside the US which were intended to affect US imports and did actually affect them:

… it is settled law that any State may impose liabilities, even upon persons not within its allegiance, for conduct outside its borders which has consequences within its borders which the State reprehends; and these liabilities other States will ordinarily recognise.[21]

In 1982 the Foreign Trade Antitrust Improvements Act (FTAIA) amended the Sherman Act. The FTAIA stipulates that as regards foreign commerce other than import commerce the antitrust laws will not apply unless the conduct has a *direct*,[22] *substantial, and reasonably foreseeable* effect on US

---

[13] Clayton Act, 15 USC s. 15. However, see the Antitrust Criminal Penalty Enhancement and Reform Act 2004 (see n. 55).

[14] See *F. Hoffmann-La Roche Ltd v Empagran*, see Section 4.D, p. 1216.

[15] See the varying views of the different Circuits which culminated in the *Empagran* case, see Section 4.D, p. 1215.

[16] See, e.g., legislation such as the Iran–Libya Sanctions Act 1996, later the Iran Sanctions Act 2006, and the Iran Freedom and Counter-Proliferation Act 2012, and the Alien Tort Statute 1789. The Alien Tort Act was considered by the Supreme Court in *Sosa v Alvarez-Machain*, 542 US 2004, a case in which an arrest was effected in Mexico by US federal agents. However, the Supreme Court has reaffirmed the principle that there is a presumption against extraterritoriality in that '[w]hen a statute gives no indication of an extraterritorial application, it has none', *Morrison v National Australia Bank Ltd*, 130 S.Ct 2869 (2010) (concerning the Securities and Exchange Act 1934), *EEOC v Arabian American Oil Co*, 499 US 244 (1991).

[17] 15 USC, 2 July 1890.

[18] *American Banana Co v United Fruit Co*, 213 US 347, 356, 29 S.Ct 511, 512 (1909).

[19] See *United States v Sisal Sales Corp*, 274 US 268, 47 S.Ct 592 (1927). The *American Banana* case has been limited to its facts and read in a limited way.

[20] *United States v Aluminum Co of America*, 148 F.2d 416 (2d Cir. 1945).

[21] Ibid., 444. See further M. Winerman and W. Kovacic, 'Learned Hand, *Alcoa* and the Reluctant Application of the Sherman Act' (2013) 79 *Antitrust LJ* 295, <http://ssrn.com/abstract=2417338>.

[22] The 'direct' condition was interpreted very narrowly by the 7th Circuit Court of Appeals (Judge Richard Posner) in *Motorola Mobility v AU Optronics*, 7th Circuit, 28 March 2014.

commerce or on US exports and such effect gives rise to a claim under the Sherman Act or FTC Acts. In other words, the FTAIA exempts export transactions from the Sherman Act unless they injure the US economy. This provision has inevitably come to be seen as a statutory formulation of the effects doctrine. In *Hartford Fire Insurance* Justice Souter, delivering the majority opinion of the Supreme Court, held that 'it is well established by now that the Sherman Act applies to foreign conduct that was meant to produce and did in fact produce some substantial effect in the United States'.[23] He looked to the FTAIA formulation as expressing the effects doctrine.

Not surprisingly, the extraterritorial application of US antitrust laws has met with hostility from other States. The US courts are sensitive to this. In *Timberlane*[24] the Ninth Circuit Court of Appeals considered the notion of 'international comity'. 'Comity' means living peacefully with other nations in mutual respect and accommodating their interests or, as one authority puts it, the 'rules of politeness, convenience and goodwill observed by States in their mutual intercourse without being legally bound by them'.[25] In *Timberlane* the court recognised the effects doctrine as laid down in *Alcoa*, but considered that its application had to be balanced against the interests of international comity. Judge Choy said that three questions had to asked.

Timberlane Lumber Co v Bank of America, 549 F.2d 597 at 613 (9th Cir. 1976), Judge Choy

Despite its description as 'settled law', ALCOA's assertion has been roundly disputed by many foreign commentators as being in conflict with international law, comity and good judgment. Nevertheless American courts have firmly concluded that there is some extra-territorial jurisdiction under the Sherman Act. Even among American courts and commentators, however, there is no consensus on how far the jurisdiction should extend . . .

There is no agreed black-letter rule articulating the Sherman Act's commerce coverage in the international context . . . The effects test by itself is incomplete because it fails to consider the other nation's interests; nor does it expressly take into account the full nature of the relationships between the actors and this country . . .

A tripartite analysis seems to be indicated. As acknowledged above, the antitrust laws require in the first instance that there be *some* effect—actual or intended—on American foreign commerce before the federal courts may legitimately exercise subject-matter jurisdiction under those statutes. Second, a greater showing of burden or restraint may be necessary to demonstrate that the effect is sufficiently large to present cognizable injury to the plaintiffs and therefore a civil violation of the antitrust laws . . . Third, there is the additional question, which is unique to the international setting, of whether the interests of and links to the United States, including the magnitude of the effect on American commerce, are sufficiently strong, *vis-à-vis* those of other nations, to justify an assertion of extra-territorial authority . . .

In answering this third question, which was necessary because 'at some point the interests of the United States are too weak and the foreign harmony incentive for restraint too strong to justify an extraterritorial assertion of jurisdiction', he said that the following factors should be taken into account: the degree of conflict with foreign law or policy, the nationality or allegiance of the parties and the locations or principal places of business of corporations, the extent to which enforcement by either State can be expected to achieve compliance, the relative significance of effects on the United States as compared with those elsewhere, the extent to which there is explicit purpose to

---

[23] *Hartford Fire Insurance Co v California*, 509 US 764, 796, 113 S.Ct 2891 (1993).

[24] *Timberlane Lumber Co v Bank of America*, 549 F.2d 597 (9th Cir. 1976).

[25] *Oppenheim's International Law*, n. 1, Vol. 1, 34; see J. R. Paul, 'Comity in International Law' (1991) 32 *Harvard Int'l LJ* 1.

harm or affect American commerce, the foreseeability of such effect, and the relative importance to the violations charged of conduct within the United States as compared with conduct abroad. The criteria were expanded in *Mannington Mills*.[26]

Timberlane and *Mannington Mills* do not deny jurisdiction to the US courts in the interests of comity, but merely hold that it should not be exercised where the interests of the US in asserting jurisdiction are outweighed by the interests of comity.[27]

In *Hartford Fire Insurance*[28] the Supreme Court recognised the claims of comity, but took a robust approach to applying the effects doctrine. Justice Souter held that the court should first decide whether it had jurisdiction. Then it could be determined whether jurisdiction should be declined on comity grounds. In this case there was no reason to decline it. He took the view that although the UK *allowed* the conduct in issue, it did not *compel* it.[29] There was therefore no conflict between British and American policy, and no reason for comity concerns to override the effects doctrine. The problem is, however, that if international comity is only to prevent the US taking jurisdiction in such narrowly drawn conflict situations it will rarely prevail.[30]

Justice Scalia dissented in *Hartford Fire Insurance*. He considered that comity is an integral part of determining whether the court has jurisdiction in the first place, rather than something to be taken into account when deciding whether to *exercise* jurisdiction.[31] Hovenkamp comments that antitrust law expresses the substantive economic policy of the United States and 'American "public" policy is entitled to be given as much weight by an American court as is the policy of a foreign sovereign, at least where American interests covered by the policy are substantially affected'.[32]

In 1995 the DOJ and the FTC issued a revised set of Antitrust Enforcement Guidelines for International Operations.[33] These explain, inter alia, that the agencies will take comity into account when deciding to bring an action or seek particular remedies. The Guidelines list a number of factors[34] that will be considered when making the decision. Once the decision is made, however, this represents 'a determination by the Executive Branch that the importance of antitrust

---

[26] *Accord Mannington Mills Inc v Congoleum Corp*, 595 F.2d 1287 (3rd Cir. 1979). The additional criteria were: the possible effect on foreign relations if the court exercises jurisdiction; if the relief is granted, whether a party will be put in the position of being forced to perform an act illegal in either country or be under conflicting requirements by both countries; whether an order for relief would be acceptable in the US if made by a foreign nation under similar circumstances; whether a treaty with the affected nations has addressed the issue.

[27] Such a balancing act had earlier been advocated by Kingman Brewster, who called it a 'jurisdictional rule of reason' in *Antitrust and American Business Abroad* (McGraw-Hill, 1958). And see the argument in H. Hovenkamp, *Federal Antitrust Policy* (4th edn, West, 2011), 833, that comity should be decisive only when the conflict with the foreign government is strong (without amounting to an Act of State or foreign sovereign compulsion defence).

[28] *Hartford Fire Insurance Co v California*, 509 US 764, 113 S.Ct 2891 (1993).

[29] The 'foreign sovereign compulsion defence' (i.e. the US courts do not hold private individuals liable for acts they were compelled to perform by a foreign sovereign on that sovereign's territory) therefore did not apply. The US also recognises 'foreign sovereign immunity' (the Act of State defence) whereby foreign governments have immunity in the courts, although usually only for commercial activities (see the Foreign Sovereign Immunities Act 1976).

[30] When dealing with internal inconsistencies between federal antitrust law and the laws of US states, it is accepted that immunity from the former may sometimes arise as a consequence of the latter, even where the individual or undertaking concerned could comply with both, see A. Robertson and M. Demetriou, '"But That Was in Another Country . . .": The Extraterritorial Application of US Antitrust Laws in the US Supreme Court' (1994) 43 ICLQ 417, 421–422. The issue of another jurisdiction which merely permits rather than compels is demonstrated by the EU merger case, Case T-102/96, *Gencor Ltd v Commission* [1999] ECR II-753, discussed at Section 5.D, p. 1224.

[31] See also the minority opinion by Judge Adams in *Mannington Mills*, 595 F.2d 1287 (3d Cir. 1979).

[32] Hovenkamp, n. 27, 827. And see F. A. Mann, 'The Doctrine of International Jurisdiction Revisited After Twenty Years' (1984) 186 RdC 9, who considers that if a court has jurisdiction it must exercise it. If, on the other hand, international law says it has no jurisdiction that is the end of the matter. One cannot, however, have a court which has a discretion whether or not to exercise its own jurisdiction.

[33] Available at <www.justice.gov/atr/public/international/index.html>.

[34] Similar to those in *Timberlane*, 549 F.2d 597 (9th Cir. 1976).

enforcement outweighs any relevant foreign policy concerns'. The Guidelines warn that the courts should not 'second-guess' its judgment 'as to the proper role of comity concerns under these circumstances'.[35]

The effects doctrine was applied in *Nippon Paper*,[36] where the DOJ commenced criminal proceedings under the Sherman Act against a Japanese company for a cartel fixing the price at which fax paper should be sold in the US.[37] The conspirators were all Japanese and all the activities of the cartel—the meetings, monitoring, and the sales to distributors with instructions about the resale price in the US—took place in Japan. In contrast to the position in *Hartford Fire Insurance* the conduct was illegal under Japanese law. The First Circuit Court of Appeals held that the US courts did have jurisdiction. It said that *Hartford Fire* had 'stunted' the concept of comity in antitrust cases and considered that the Japanese undertakings should not, in these circumstances, be sheltered from prosecution by principles of comity:

We see no tenable reason why principles of comity should shield [the Japanese undertakings] from prosecution. We live in an age of international commerce, where decisions reached in one corner of the world can reverberate around the globe in less time than it takes to tell the tale. Thus, a ruling in [the Japanese undertakings'] favor would create perverse incentives for those who would use nefarious means to influence markets in the United States, rewarding them for enacting as many territorial firewalls as possible between cause and effect.[38]

This was the first case in which extraterritorial criminal jurisdiction had been taken under the Sherman Act. In *Motorola Mobility v AU Optronics*[39] the Seventh Circuit Court of Appeals considered the doctrine of comity at length and referred to the resentment of foreign countries at the US trying to act as the world's policeman and to the Supreme Court's warning against 'rampant extraterritorial application' of US laws in *Empagran* (where comity played a large role)[40] before dismissing the plaintiff's appeal against the dismissal of its claims.

C. ENFORCEMENT AND THE REACTIONS OF OTHER STATES

Particular problems arise where the US wishes to take enforcement action extraterritorially. A stark example of the conflicts that can arise is *United States v ICI Ltd*.[41] A US court ordered, on the grounds of infringement of the Sherman Act, the cancellation of agreements between ICI and Du Pont by which Du Pont assigned to ICI certain patents which were to be registered in the UK. ICI was ordered to reassign the patents to Du Pont. ICI, however, had already contracted to license the patents to a UK company which sued in the English courts to enforce its contractual rights. Danckwerts J granted a decree of specific performance, saying that the US judge 'was applying an enactment of Congress, which has no application to the United Kingdom'.[42]

---

[35] For the application of comity in a discovery request see *Société Nationale Industrielle Aérospatiale v United States District Court for the Southern District of Iowa*, 482 US 522.

[36] *United States v Nippon Paper Industries Co*, 109 F.3d 1 (1st Cir. 1997).

[37] See R. M. Reynolds, J. Sicilian, and P. S. Weliman, 'The Extraterritorial Application of the US Antitrust Laws to Criminal Conspiracies' [1998] ECLR 151; Griffin, n. 4, 68.

[38] *Nippon Paper*, 109 F.3d 1, 9 (1st Cir. 1997).

[39] See n. 22. The case was an action in respect of mobile phones sold in the US into which had been incorporated components sold outside the US which had been the subject of a price-fixing cartel. The same scenario gave rise to the *InnoLux* case (see n. 117) in the EU, discussed in Section 5.F, p. 1233. See further *The Antitrust Counselor*, Vol. 84, 2014 (published by the ABA). The Supreme Court refused to hear the appeal, 15 June 2015.

[40] *F. Hoffmann-La Roche Ltd v Empagran*, 542 US 155 (2004), see Section 4.D, p. 1215.

[41] 105 F. Supp. 215 (1952).

[42] *British Nylon Spinners Ltd v ICI Ltd* [1955] Ch 37.

US pre-trial discovery confers wide-ranging powers on US plaintiffs wishing to search abroad for evidence of antitrust violations. In *Rio Tinto Zinc*[43] letters rogatory requested the High Court to require directors and employees of a British company to give oral evidence before an examiner in London and to require the company to produce the documents contained in a lengthy schedule. The request was in connection with a private antitrust suit in Virginia. The House of Lords decided that the US Court's request for assistance fell within the exceptions to the obligation to assist in requests for discovery by foreign courts contained in the Evidence (Proceedings in Other Jurisdictions) Act 1975, and consequently refused discovery.

The UK subsequently passed the Protection of Trading Interest Act 1980 to 'block' the enforcement of any foreign international trade laws, but in reality largely directed at US antitrust laws. First, the Act enables the Secretary of State to direct a person carrying on business in the UK not to comply with the orders of a foreign court or authority affecting international trade which threaten to damage the trading interests of the UK.[44] Secondly, the Secretary of State is empowered to prohibit persons within the UK from complying with demands by foreign tribunals and authorities for commercial documents or information not located within the jurisdiction of the State concerned.[45] Thirdly, defendants in UK courts are protected from the enforcement of punitive treble damages claims. Section 5 describes such awards as 'penal' and forbids their enforcement in UK courts under the usual reciprocal enforcement procedures.[46] Section 6 provides a 'clawback' provision enabling British citizens or companies or persons carrying on business in the UK to bring an action in the UK courts to recover the non-compensatory part of any such damages they have paid. Other States have also passed such 'blocking' statutes.[47]

Violation of s. 1 of the Sherman Act is a criminal offence, and individuals who participate in cartel arrangements are liable to criminal prosecution, fines, and imprisonment.[48] However, executives can escape US jails by lurking in countries which will not extradite to the US for antitrust offences. That was true of the UK until s. 191 of the Enterprise Act 2002 introduced the 'cartel offence' into UK law.[49] The offence is extraditable[50] which means a person may be extradited to another country for an equivalent offence. Section 191 is not retrospective and so does not apply to conduct prior to June 2003. An attempt by the US Government to extradite Ian Norris, the ex-Chief Executive of Morgan Crucible, to face trial in the US for violation of the Sherman Act prior to 2003 by arguing that price-fixing was an offence of conspiracy to defraud at common law, failed in the House of Lords.[51] However, the Supreme Court (as the House of Lords had become in the meantime) later held that he could be extradited on charges of obstructing justice (as that would have been an offence in the UK at the time of the alleged conduct in the US).[52]

---

[43] *Rio Tinto Zinc Corp v Westinghouse Electric Corp* [1978] AC 547.

[44] Protection of Trading Interest Act 1980, s. 1.

[45] Section 2. Note that in the current spirit of international cooperation the UK favours the ability to exchange information in order to further the enforcement of competition laws. The Enterprise Act 2002, s. 243 sets out the circumstances in which a UK public authority could disclose information to an overseas public authority, including a competition authority. The UK/US Mutual Assistance Treaty now covers criminal infringements of competition law (UK/US Mutual Legal Assistance Treaty, 2001 (Cm. 5375)).

[46] See Chap. 14. Section 5 was applied by the Scottish Court of Session in *Service Temps Inc v MacLeod* [2013] CSOH 162.

[47] See generally A. V. Lowe, *Extraterritorial Jurisdiction* (Grotius Publications, 1983).

[48] For the criminalisation of cartel arrangements generally, see Chap. 13, Section 11, p. 1022.

[49] Enterprise Act 2002, s. 188.

[50] Enterprise Act 2002, s. 191.

[51] *Norris v Government of the United States of America* [2008] UKHL 16, see Chap. 13, Section 11, p. 1024.

[52] *Norris v Government of the United States of America* [2010] UKSC 9.

D. FOREIGN PLAINTIFFS IN US COURTS

In Chapter 14 we saw that private litigation of antitrust cases is far more common in US courts than it is in the EU. As well as the differences in the systems of enforcement there are various features of the US legal system which make it easier or more attractive for plaintiffs in the US to bring actions.[53] In brief, these are:

- very broad discovery rules;[54]

- class actions (in which, moreover, injured parties need not join in at the start of the case, i.e. they are 'opt-out' actions);

- contingent attorneys' fees;

- treble damages;[55]

- unsuccessful plaintiffs do not pay the defendant's costs.

Furthermore, in the US actions are heard before juries, which can be very generous in awarding damages to those they see as wronged by big corporations.

Overseas litigants often look with envy at the sight of US plaintiffs winning large damages awards in US courts. Some of these have been in respect of major international cartels which had effects in numerous countries. Overseas victims of international cartels therefore started litigating in US courts in respect of harm suffered outside the US. At first sight these actions seemed unlikely to succeed because of the FTAIA's stipulation that as regards foreign commerce the antitrust laws will not apply unless the conduct has a direct, substantial, and reasonably foreseeable effect on US commerce. However, various US Courts of Appeals differed in their reactions to claims over harm overseas. The matter went to the Supreme Court in *F. Hoffmann-La Roche Ltd v Empagran*.[56]

There were two strands of argument in *Empagran*. The first was a matter of statutory construction of the FTAIA in the light of international comity. The second was a matter of statutory construction in the light of its legislative history. The issue was whether the US could or should act as a kind of world policeman, welcoming litigants from all over the world who have been injured abroad by cartels which have also caused injury inside the US. In *Empagran* itself the plaintiffs were, inter alia, Ukrainian, Ecuadorean, and Panamanian buyers, while the defendant sellers were German and Swiss. One argument for the US courts taking jurisdiction was that global cartels do not really 'take place' in any particular territory. When foreign purchasers contract with a multinational corporation the contract could be sourced anywhere, and there is no reason why a party's ability to recover should depend on how the multinational structures its transactions. Further it is argued that global cartels do harm US consumers, because in a globalised world there is no such thing as domestic price-fixing: the important thing to do is to deter cartel behaviour by making it too expensive (e.g. by allowing the victims to sue in US courts). The DOJ argued in its amicus curiae brief to the Supreme Court in *Empagran* that, in particular, the taking of jurisdiction by US courts would undermine the DOJ's leniency programme by expanding the scope of the cartellists' potential civil liability, and would undermine cooperation with other competition authorities.

The Supreme Court held that the FTAIA excluded foreign plaintiffs from seeking damages in the US where the harm flowed exclusively from the foreign effects of the conduct which infringed the

---

[53] But note the Commission Recommendation on collective redress mechanisms of 11 June 2013 and the Damages Dir., discussed in Chap. 14.

[54] Although, as noted in Chap. 14, the narrower discovery rules in European jurisdictions (very much narrower in some Member States) may be bypassed where the litigant is able to rely on the information laid out in a Commission decision (which may well have been uncovered by a Commission inspection under Reg. 1/2003, Art. 20).

[55] The Antitrust Criminal Penalty Enhancement and Reform Act 2004 limits the damages recoverable from a corporate amnesty applicant which also cooperates with private plaintiffs in their damages actions against remaining cartel members to the damage actually inflicted by the amnesty applicant's conduct.

[56] 542 US 155 (2004).

Sherman Act. It considered the question of comity. Several foreign governments (including the UK) submitted briefs to the Supreme Court arguing against the US courts taking jurisdiction, and the Supreme Court gave these considerable weight.

F. Hoffmann-La Roche Ltd v Empagran SA, 542 US 155 (2004), 14 June 2004

Opinion of the Supreme Court

Justice Breyer

IV

We turn now to the basic question presented, that of the exception's application. Because the underlying antitrust action is complex, potentially raising questions not directly at issue here, we reemphasize that we base our decision upon the following: The price-fixing conduct significantly and adversely affects both customers outside the United States and customers within the United States, but the adverse foreign effect is independent of any adverse domestic effect. In these circumstances, we find that the FTAIA exception does not apply (and thus the Sherman Act does not apply) for two main reasons. *First*, this Court ordinarily construes ambiguous statutes to avoid unreasonable interference with the sovereign authority of other nations. See, *e.g., McCulloch* v. *Sociedad Nacional de Marineros de Honduras*, 372 U.S. 10, 20–22 (1963) (application of National Labor Relations Act to foreign-flag vessels); *Romero* v. *International Terminal Operating Co.*, 358 U.S. 354, 382–383 (1959) (application of Jones Act in maritime case); *Lauritzen* v. *Larsen*, 345 U.S. 571, 578 (1953) (same). This rule of construction reflects principles of customary international law—law that (we must assume) Congress ordinarily seeks to follow. See Restatement (Third) of Foreign Relations Law of the United States §§403(1), 403(2) (1986) (hereinafter Restatement) (limiting the unreasonable exercise of prescriptive jurisdiction with respect to a person or activity having connections with another State); *Murray* v. *Schooner Charming Betsy*, 2 Cranch 64, 118 (1804) ('[A]n act of Congress ought never to be construed to violate the law of nations if any other possible construction remains'); *Hartford Fire Insurance Co.* v. *California*, 509 U.S. 764, 817 (1993) (SCALIA, J., dissenting) (identifying rule of construction as derived from the principle of 'prescriptive comity').

This rule of statutory construction cautions courts to assume that legislators take account of the legitimate sovereign interests of other nations when they write American laws. It thereby helps the potentially conflicting laws of different nations work together in harmony—a harmony particularly needed in today's highly interdependent commercial world.

No one denies that America's antitrust laws, when applied to foreign conduct, can interfere with a foreign nation's ability independently to regulate its own commercial affairs. But our courts have long held that application of our antitrust laws to foreign anti-competitive conduct is nonetheless reasonable, and hence consistent with principles of prescriptive comity, insofar as they reflect a legislative effort to redress domestic antitrust injury that foreign anti-competitive conduct has caused. See *United States* v. *Aluminum Co of America*, 148 F. 2d 416, 443–444 (CA2 1945) (L. Hand, J.); 1 P. Areeda & D. Turner, *Antitrust Law* ¶236 (1978).

But why is it reasonable to apply those laws to foreign conduct insofar as that conduct causes independent foreign harm and that foreign harm alone gives rise to the plaintiff's claim? Like the former case, application of those laws creates a serious risk of interference with a foreign nation's ability independently to regulate its own commercial affairs. But, unlike the former case, the justification for that interference seems insubstantial. See Restatement §403(2) (determining reasonableness on basis of such factors as connections with regulating nation, harm to that nation's interests, extent to which other nations regulate, and the potential for conflict). Why should American law supplant, for example, Canada's or Great Britain's or Japan's own determination about how best to protect Canadian or British or Japanese customers from anti-competitive conduct engaged in significant part by Canadian or British or Japanese or other foreign companies?

We recognize that principles of comity provide Congress greater leeway when it seeks to control through legislation the actions of American companies, see Restatement §402; and some of the anti-competitive price-fixing conduct alleged here took place in America. But the higher foreign prices of which the foreign plaintiffs here complain are not the consequence of any domestic anti-competitive conduct that Congress sought to forbid, for Congress did not seek to forbid any such conduct insofar as it is here relevant, i.e., insofar as it is intertwined with foreign conduct that causes independent foreign harm. Rather Congress sought to release domestic (and foreign) anti-competitive conduct from Sherman Act constraints when that conduct causes foreign harm. Congress, of course, did make an exception where that conduct also causes domestic harm. See House Report 13 (concerns about American firms' participation in international cartels addressed through 'domestic injury' exception). But any independent domestic harm the foreign conduct causes here has, by definition, little or nothing to do with the matter.

We thus repeat the basic question: Why is it reasonable to apply this law to conduct that is significantly foreign insofar as that conduct causes independent foreign harm and that foreign harm alone gives rise to the plaintiff's claim? We can find no good answer to the question . . .

. . .

Respondents reply that many nations have adopted antitrust laws similar to our own, to the point where the practical likelihood of interference with the relevant interests of other nations is minimal. Leaving price fixing to the side, however, this Court has found to the contrary. See, e.g., *Hartford Fire*, 509 U.S. at 797–799 (noting that the alleged conduct in the London reinsurance market, while illegal under United States antitrust laws, was assumed to be perfectly consistent with British law and policy); see also, e.g., 2 W. Fugate, Foreign Commerce and the Antitrust Laws §16.6 (5th ed. 1996) (noting differences between European Union and United States law on vertical restraints).

Regardless, even where nations agree about primary conduct, say price fixing, they disagree dramatically about appropriate remedies. The application, for example, of American private treble-damages remedies to anti-competitive conduct taking place abroad has generated considerable controversy. See, e.g., 2 ABA Section of Antitrust Law, Antitrust Law Developments 1208–1209 (5th ed. 2002). And several foreign nations have filed briefs here arguing that to apply our remedies would unjustifiably permit their citizens to bypass their own less generous remedial schemes, thereby upsetting a balance of competing considerations that their own domestic antitrust laws embody . . .

These briefs add that a decision permitting independently injured foreign plaintiffs to pursue private treble-damages remedies would undermine foreign nations' own antitrust enforcement policies by diminishing foreign firms' incentive to cooperate with antitrust authorities in return for prosecutorial amnesty . . . Respondents alternatively argue that comity does not demand an interpretation of the FTAIA that would exclude independent foreign injury cases across the board. Rather, courts can take (and sometimes have taken) account of comity considerations case by case, abstaining where comity considerations so dictate. Cf., e.g., *Hartford Fire*, supra, at 797, n. 24; *United States* v. *Nippon Paper Industries Co.*, 109 F. 3d 1, 8 (CA1 1997); *Mannington Mills, Inc* v. *Congoleum Corp*, 595 F. 2d 1287, 1294–1295 (CA3 1979).

In our view, however, this approach is too complex to prove workable. The Sherman Act covers many different kinds of anti-competitive agreements. Courts would have to examine how foreign law, compared with American law, treats not only price fixing but also, say, information-sharing agreements, patent-licensing price conditions, territorial product resale limitations, and various forms of joint venture, in respect to both primary conduct and remedy. The legally and economically technical nature of that enterprise means lengthier proceedings, appeals, and more proceedings—to the point where procedural costs and delays could themselves threaten interference with a foreign nation's ability to maintain the integrity of its own antitrust enforcement system. Even in this relatively simple price-fixing case, for example, competing briefs tell us (1) that potential treble-damage liability would help enforce widespread anti-price-fixing norms (through added deterrence) and (2) the opposite, namely that such liability would hinder antitrust enforcement (by reducing incentives to enter amnesty programs). Compare, e.g., Brief for Certain Professors of Economics as Amici Curiae 2–4 with Brief for United States as Amicus Curiae 19–21. How could a court seriously interested in resolving so empirical a matter—a matter potentially related to impact on foreign interests—do so simply and expeditiously?

> We conclude that principles of prescriptive comity counsel against the Court of Appeals' interpretation of the FTAIA. Where foreign anti-competitive conduct plays a significant role and where foreign injury is independent of domestic effects, Congress might have hoped that America's antitrust laws, so fundamental a component of our own economic system, would commend themselves to other nations as well. But, if America's antitrust policies could not win their own way in the international marketplace for such ideas, Congress, we must assume, would not have tried to impose them, in an act of legal imperialism, through legislative fiat.

The Supreme Court then considered the legislative history of the FTAIA and concluded that its 'language and history suggest that Congress designed the FTAIA to clarify, perhaps to limit, but not to expand in any significant way, the Sherman Act's scope as applied to foreign commerce'.[57]

The Supreme Court based its judgment on the assumption that the foreign effects of the cartel were quite independent of its effects in the US. It left open the question of what would be the position if the foreign and domestic effects could be shown to be intertwined, for example if the prices abroad would have been lower had it not been for the effects in the US. However, in *Re Monosodium Glutamate Antitrust Litigation* the US Court of Appeals for the 8th Circuit upheld a ruling excluding foreign plaintiffs from bringing a class action against manufacturers involved in a cartel. The court said that 'the domestic effects of the price fixing scheme—increased US prices—were not the direct cause of the appellants' injuries. Rather it was the foreign effects of the price fixing scheme—increased prices abroad'.[58] The court set a high standard of proof for any effect on US commerce and rejected claims that a worldwide conspiracy in which prices must be inflated in every market (to avoid arbitrage) could satisfy the standard.

E. THE EFFECTS DOCTRINE AND FOREIGN CONDUCT AFFECTING EXPORTS

The FTAIA provides that the Sherman Act only applies to export commerce where the conduct has a direct, substantial, and reasonably foreseeable effect on US commerce. It can be argued, however, that if US exports are injured by being denied access to foreign markets there may be a disadvantageous effect on commerce inside the US. Taking jurisdiction where conduct of foreign actors abroad affects the US *export* trade is true extraterritoriality. Although the US agencies consider that they do in theory have jurisdiction over conduct abroad which affects exports,[59] they do not usually take action against it.[60] Indeed, the practical enforcement problems are very great. In the *Fuji* case the US tried to use trade rather than competition law to advance the interests of its exporters. Kodak alleged that it was unable to penetrate the Japanese market because of anti-competitive activities there, in particular on the part of Fuji's distributors, despite the existence of Japanese anti-monopoly laws. Kodak brought a section 301 Trade Act 1974 petition in the US and the US Trade Representative referred the Japanese Government's conduct in tolerating the anti-competitive behaviour to the WTO. Access to the WTO dispute resolution process is limited to governments. The WTO panel held that the WTO rules apply only to governments and that it is not open to governments to attack private measures in this way.[61] This showed that the WTO rules cannot be used to force open foreign markets which are obstructed by private conduct.

---

[57] On remand, the DC Circuit ruled for the defendants, 417 F.3d 1267 (DC Cir. 2005).

[58] 477 F.3d 535 (8th Cir. 2007).

[59] Antitrust Enforcement Guidelines for International Operations, para. 3.1222.

[60] But see *United States v Pilkington* (1994–1992) Trade Cases 70, 482.

[61] *Japan—Measures Affecting Consumer Photographic Film and Paper*, WT/DS44/R, 31 March 1998.

5. EU LAW

A. GENERAL

Articles 101 and 102 are silent on the question whether or not they apply extraterritorially. At first the development of the single economic entity doctrine[62] precluded the need for resolving the issue. However, the point finally had to be dealt with in *Wood Pulp I*[63] and is an important aspect of *Intel*.[64] The Merger Regulation, the EUMR,[65] while not expressly addressing the extraterritoriality question, contains a jurisdiction threshold which may catch concentrations between undertakings based outside the EU.[66] Because the Articles 101 and 102 cases and the EUMR case, *Gencor*, reference each other we discuss the cases in chronological order in this section. The jurisdiction point in *Intel* is on appeal and the CJ's judgment should be of the utmost importance on this issue.

B. THE *DYESTUFFS* CASE AND THE SINGLE ECONOMIC ENTITY DOCTRINE

In the *Dyestuffs* case[67] the question whether there is an effects doctrine in EEC law was raised for the first time.[68] The Commission found a cartel among aniline dyes producers. The participants included ICI, a company incorporated and having its headquarters in the UK which was not at the time a member of the EEC. It was found to have engaged in concerted practices contrary to Article 101(1) by virtue of the instructions it had given to its Belgian subsidiary. The Commission imposed a fine of 50,000 units of account on ICI.[69] In the Decision the Commission asserted jurisdiction over ICI on the basis of 'effects':

Under Article [101(1)] . . . all agreements between undertakings, all decisions by associations of undertakings and all concerted practices which may affect trade between Member States and the object or effect of which is to prevent, restrict or distort competition within the Common Market shall be prohibited as incompatible with the Common Market. The competition rules of the Treaty are, consequently, applicable to all restrictions of competition which produce within the Common Market effects set out in Article [101(1)]. There is therefore no need to examine whether the undertakings which are the cause of these restrictions of competition have their seat within or outside the Community.[70]

The ICI appealed, inter alia on the jurisdiction point. It claimed that the Commission had no power to apply the competition rules to an undertaking established outside the EEC. In reply the Commission relied both on an elaboration of the effects point and on the claim that, although the subsidiaries within the Community had separate legal personality in law, the reality was that they were merely carrying out the parent's orders, so that the subsidiaries appeared 'as mere extensions of ICI in the Common Market'.[71]

---

[62] See Chap. 3, A.vi, p. 125 ff.

[63] Cases 89, 104, 114, 116, 117, and 125–129/85, *A. Ahlström Oy v Commission* [1988] ECR 5193.

[64] Case T-286/09, *Intel v Commission* EU:T:2014:547, on appeal Case C-413/14 P, judgment pending.

[65] Council Reg. 139/2004 [2004] L24/1.

[66] See Chap. 15.

[67] Case 48/69, *ICI v Commission (Dyestuffs)* [1972] ECR 619.

[68] Earlier, Case 22/71, *Béguelin Import Co v GL Import Export* [1971] ECR 949 concerned the distribution arrangements of a Japanese manufacturer with its French distributor which compartmentalised the common market on national lines. As one of the parties to the agreement was clearly within the Community, and in the context of the case the imposition of a penalty on the Japanese undertaking did not arise, jurisdiction could be asserted without the question of extraterritorially having to be addressed.

[69] *Re the Cartel in Aniline Dyes* [1969] OJ L195/11.

[70] Ibid., para. 28.

[71] Case 48/69, *ICI v Commission (Dyestuffs)* [1972] ECR 619, 627.

Advocate General Mayras recommended upholding the Decision on the basis of the 'effects doctrine'. He reviewed the national laws of the Member States on this issue, the international law arguments, and US law. He said that the conditions necessary for taking extraterritorial jurisdiction were that the agreement or concerted practice must create a *direct and immediate* restriction of competition, that the effect of the conduct must be *reasonably foreseeable*, and that the effect produced on the territory must be *substantial*. The Advocate General justified this adoption of what amounted to an effects doctrine not just by reference to principle, but also on grounds of pragmatism.[72]

However, as already mentioned, he drew a distinction between prescriptive and enforcement jurisdiction.[73] He was prepared to accept that the decision taken by the Commission might not be capable of enforcement:

the courts or administrative authorities of a State—and, *mutatis mutandis*, of the Community—are certainly not justified under international law in taking coercive measures or indeed any measure of inquiry, investigation or supervision outside their territorial jurisdiction where execution would inevitably infringe the internal sovereignty of the State on the territory of which they claimed to act.[74]

In its judgment the CJ did not take up its Advocate General's espousal of an effects doctrine. Instead it upheld the Commission's decision on the basis of nationality by applying what has become known as the single economic entity doctrine. It is explained in Chapter 3 that EU law developed this doctrine by which parents and subsidiaries are considered to be one undertaking for the purposes of the application of the competition rules. In *Dyestuffs* the Court relied on this concept to impute the conduct of the subsidiary to the parent and to hold that the Commission did have jurisdiction over the UK company.

Case 48/69, *ICI v Commission (Dyestuffs)* [1972] ECR 619

Court of Justice

130. By making use of its power to control its subsidiaries established in the Community, the applicant was able to ensure that its decision was implemented on that market.

131. The applicant objects that this conduct is to be imputed to its subsidiaries and not to itself.

132. The fact that a subsidiary has separate legal personality is not sufficient to exclude the possibility of imputing its conduct to the parent company.

133. Such may be the case in particular where the subsidiary, although having separate legal personality, does not decide independently upon its own conduct on the market, but carries out, in all material respects, the instructions given to it by the parent company.

134. Where a subsidiary does not enjoy real autonomy in determining its course of action in the market, the prohibitions set out in Article [101(1)] may be considered inapplicable in the relationship between it and the parent company with which it forms one economic unit.

135. In view of the unity of the group thus formed, the actions of the subsidiaries may in certain circumstances be attributed to the parent company.

136. It is well-known that at the time the applicant held all or at any rate the majority of the shares in those subsidiaries.

---

[72] See in particular, ibid. at 696.

[73] See Section 3, p. 1208.

[74] Case 48/69, *Dyestuffs* [1972] ECR 619, 695.

137. The applicant was able to exercise decisive influence over the policy of the subsidiaries as regards selling prices in the Common Market and in fact used this power upon the occasion of the three price increases in question.

138. In effect the Telex messages relating to the 1964 increase, which the applicant sent to its subsidiaries in the Common Market, gave the addressees orders as to the prices which they were to charge and the other conditions of sale which they were to apply in dealing with their customers.

139. In the absence of evidence to the contrary, it must be assumed that on the occasion of the increases of 1965 and 1967 the applicant acted in a similar fashion in its relation with its subsidiaries established in the Common Market.

140. In the circumstances the formal separation between these companies, resulting from their separate legal personality, cannot outweigh the unity of their conduct on the market for the purposes of applying the rules on competition.

141. It was in fact the applicant undertaking which brought the concerted practice into being within the Common Market.

142. The submission as to lack of jurisdiction raised by the applicant must therefore be declared to be unfounded.

The CJ therefore held here that the subsidiary did not have 'real autonomy' but acted on its parent's instructions, so that the infringing conduct in the EEC could be treated as having been committed by the subsidiary as an agent of the parent.[75]

At the time of *Dyestuffs* the UK Government disputed the disregarding of the legal separation between parent and subsidiary, but has since dropped its hostility to this concept and the Competition Act 1998 received it fully into UK law, along with the other jurisprudence on the competition rules.[76] However, it is worth noting that many countries continue to have particular concerns about the application of a similar concept in US law. As Griffin explains:[77]

Nearly all nations agree that nationality can be a valid basis for asserting extraterritorial jurisdiction. However, U.S. assertions of jurisdiction based upon the control exercised by an American parent over a subsidiary incorporated and operating abroad are not accepted as valid under international law by a number of nations. These nations contend that despite the American parent's majority ownership or its possession of effective working control, under international law nationality is properly determined by the place of incorporation . . . Moreover, according to one knowledgeable British official,[78] 'even where nationality is a legitimate basis for extraterritorial jurisdiction it must remain subject to the primacy of the laws and policies of the territorial state.' . . . U.S. officials typically respond to these contentions with the assertion that they cannot permit 'technicalities' such as the place of incorporation and inconsistent policies of host states to be used by American companies to evade their obligations under U.S. law . . .

In *Dyestuffs* the CJ neither approved nor disapproved the Advocate General's views on the effects doctrine. It preferred to proceed on the other, less controversial, ground. Its silence on the point, however, encouraged the Commission's belief that Community law did recognise the effects doctrine.

---

[75] F. A. Mann argued that the facts of the case did not support this conclusion: 'Dyestuffs Case in the Court of Justice of the European Communities' (1973) 22 *ICLQ* 35 and 'Responsibility of Parent Companies for Foreign Subsidiaries' in C. Olmstead (ed.), *Extra-territorial Application of Laws and Responses Thereto* (ESC Publishing, 1984), 156.

[76] Competition Act 1998, s. 60.

[77] Griffin, n. 4, 69.

[78] The reference is to William M. Knighton, 'Nationality and Extraterritorial Jurisdiction: US Law Abroad', Remarks before the International Law Institute of the Georgetown University Law Center, 13 August 1981.

C. THE *WOOD PULP* CASE AND THE IMPLEMENTATION DOCTRINE

In *Wood Pulp I*[79] the jurisdiction issue had to be faced in a situation where the single economic entity doctrine could not be applied. The Commission found a price-fixing cartel in the wood pulp industry.[80] All 43 producers and trade associations concerned had their registered offices outside the EEC although most, if not all, of the producers had 'branches, subsidiaries, agencies or other establishments within the Community'.[81] Many of the addressees appealed, inter alia on the ground that the Commission had no jurisdiction to apply its competition law to them. The CJ heard the jurisdiction plea first.[82]

Advocate General Darmon engaged in a lengthy survey of the relevant international and US law and the scholarly literature and concluded that the Community was entitled to take, and should take, jurisdiction in this case on the basis of the effects doctrine, which was not contrary to international law:

57. . . . [T]here is no rule of international law which is capable of being relied upon against the criterion of the direct, substantial and foreseeable effect. Nor does the concept of international comity, in view of its uncertain scope, militate against the criterion either.

58. In the absence of any such prohibitive rule and in the light of widespread State practice, I would therefore propose that in view of its appropriateness to the field of competition, it be adopted as a criterion for the jurisdiction of the Community.

The CJ, however, couched its judgment in different terms.

Cases 89, 104, 114, 116, 117, and 125–129/85, *A. Ahlström Oy v Commission* [1988] ECR 5193

Court of Justice

11. In so far as the submission concerning the infringement of Article [101] itself is concerned, it should be recalled that that provision prohibits all agreements between undertakings and concerted practices which may affect trade between Member States and which have as their object or effect the restriction of competition within the Common Market.

12. It should be noted that the main sources of supply of wood pulp are outside the Community, in Canada, the United States, Sweden and Finland and that the market therefore has global dimensions. Where wood pulp producers established in those countries sell directly to purchasers established in the Community and engage in price competition in order to win orders from those customers, that constitutes competition within the Common Market.

13. It follows that where those producers concert on the prices to be charged to their customers in the Community and put that concertation into effect by selling at prices which are actually coordinated, they are taking part in concertation which has the object and effect of restricting competition within the Common Market within the meaning of Article [101].

---

[79] Cases 89, 104, 114, 116, 117, and 125–9/85, *A. Ahlström Oy v Commission* [1988] ECR 5193 (*Wood Pulp I*).

[80] *Woodpulp* [1985] OJ L85/1, see Chap. 9.

[81] Only some of them did according to para. 79 of the Decision, [1988] OJ L85/1, but later, in its rejoinder before the Court, the Commission stated that all of them did: see W. van Gerven, 'EC Jurisdiction in Antitrust Matters: The *Wood Pulp* Judgment' [1989] *Fordham Corp L Inst* 451, 464.

[82] For the appeal on the concerted practices issue, see Cases C-89, 104, 114, 116, 117, and 125–129/85, *A. Ahlström Osakeyhtiö v Commission (Wood Pulp II)* [1993] ECR I-1307, and Chaps. 3 and 9.

14. Accordingly, it must be concluded that by applying the competition rules in the Treaty in the circumstances of this case to undertakings whose registered offices are situated outside the Community, the Commission has not made an incorrect assessment of the territorial scope of Article [101].

15. The applicants have submitted that the decision is incompatible with public international law on the grounds that the application of the competition rules in this case was founded exclusively on the economic repercussions within the Common Market of conduct restricting competition which [was] adopted outside the Community.

16. It should be observed that an infringement of Article [101], such as the conclusion of an agreement which has had the effect of restricting competition within the Common Market, consists of conduct made up of two elements, the formation of the agreement, decision or concerted practice and the implementation thereof. If the applicability of prohibitions laid down under competition law were made to depend on the place where the agreement, decision or concerted practice was formed, the result would obviously be to give undertakings an easy means of evading those prohibitions. The decisive factor is therefore the place where it is implemented.

17. The producers in this case implemented their pricing agreement within the Common Market. It is immaterial in that respect whether or not they had recourse to subsidiaries, agents, sub-agents, or branches within the Community in order to make their contacts with purchasers within the Community.

18. Accordingly the Community's jurisdiction to apply its competition rules to such conduct is covered by the territoriality principle as universally recognized in public international law.

19. As regards the argument based on the infringement of the principle of non-interference, it should be pointed out that the applicants who are members of KEA have referred to a rule according to which where two States have jurisdiction to lay down and enforce rules and the effect of those rules is that a person finds himself subject to contradictory orders as to the conduct he must adopt, each State is obliged to exercise its jurisdiction with moderation. The applicants have concluded that by disregarding that rule in applying its competition rules the Community has infringed the principle of non-interference.

20. There is no need to enquire into the existence in international law of such a rule since it suffices to observe that the conditions for its application are in any event not satisfied. There is not, in this case, any contradiction between the conduct required by the United States and that required by the Community since the Webb–Pomerene Act[83] merely exempts the conclusion of export cartels from the application of United States antitrust laws but does not require such cartels to be concluded.

21. It should further be pointed out that the United States authorities raised no objections regarding any conflict of jurisdiction when consulted by the Commission pursuant to the OECD Council Recommendation of 25 October 1979 concerning co-operation between Member Countries on Restrictive Business Practices affecting International Trade . . .

22. As regards the argument relating to disregard of international comity, it suffices to observe that it amounts to calling in question the Community's jurisdiction to apply its competition rules to conduct such as that found to exist in this case and that, as such, that argument has already been rejected.

23. Accordingly it must be concluded that the Commission's decision is not contrary to Article [101] or to the rules of public international law relied on by the applicants.

The judgment avoided talking about 'effects' and instead talked about 'implementation' (paragraphs 16 and 17). Given the terms in which the Commission decision, the arguments before the Court, and the Advocate General's Opinion had been couched, the avoidance of specific reference to the effects doctrine must have been deliberate. Indeed, in *Intel* the GC said that it meant that where jurisdiction can be established on the basis of implementation it is unnecessary to examine if there were any effects.[84]

---

[83] The Webb–Pomerene Act 1918 is a US statute which allows American exporters to act together in export markets in ways which would otherwise violate the Sherman Act.

[84] Case T-286/09, *Intel v Commission* EU:T:2014:547, para. 238.

It will be noted that the judgment (the extract comprises the entirety of the section on jurisdiction) falls into distinct parts. First, paragraphs 11–14 deal with whether or not the Commission infringed *the Treaty* by applying the competition rules to the individual undertakings.[85] The CJ held that it had not, as it had correctly assessed the territorial scope of Article 101. Secondly, paragraphs 15–18 consider whether the Commission had infringed *international* law. The CJ held that it had not done this either, as the taking of jurisdiction was covered by the 'universally recognized' territoriality principle (paragraph 18). Thirdly, paragraphs 19–22 reject the argument based on a possible 'non-interference' principle by saying that the US legislation did not *require* export cartels to be entered into, but merely tolerated them. This is the same position as that reached by the Supreme Court in *Hartford Fire* in respect of the UK legislation.[86]

In paragraph 16 the Court divided the infringing conduct into two elements, the formation of the agreement and its implementation. It did not matter where the formation of the agreement took place: the decisive factor was the place where it was 'implemented'. The crucial question is what is meant by 'implementation'. The first thing to note is that the CJ said in paragraph 17 that it was immaterial whether or not the producers used subsidiaries, agents, sub-agents, or branches inside the Community. This means that 'implementation' covers direct sales to EU purchasers and does not depend on the sellers establishing some form of marketing organisation within the EU. Jurisdiction is taken simply because of sale into the EU. Some commentators believe that this is not justified in international law.[87] However, the satisfaction of the criterion as to implementation by mere sale was confirmed in both *Gencor* and *Intel*.[88] A second point to note is that the preponderant view is that 'implementation' would not cover negative behaviour such as agreements concluded outside the EU by which undertakings agree not to sell within the EU, or agree not to purchase from EU producers.[89] Such conduct could, it is argued, fall within the effects doctrine.[90]

In *Wood Pulp*, therefore, the Court confirmed that Article 101[91] could be applied extraterritorially, but did so by enunciating a Community (now EU) concept of extraterritorial jurisdiction based on implementation rather than by adopting the effects doctrine as developed in US law.

D. THE *GENCOR* CASE

(i) The Terms of the Merger Regulation

As explained in Chapter 15, the EU Merger Regulation (EUMR)[92] provides that the Commission has sole jurisdiction[93] over concentrations with an 'EU dimension'.[94] The meaning of this is set out in Article 1.

---

[85] As far as the applicant trade association, KEA, was concerned, the CJ annulled the decision because it held that KEA had not played a separate role in the implementation of the price-fixing agreements: [1988] ECR 5193, paras. 24–28.

[86] See Section 4B., p. 1212.

[87] See Van Gerven, n. 81, 470.

[88] Case T-102/96, *Gencor* [1999] ECR II-753, para. 87; Case T-286/09, *Intel* EU:T:2014:547, para. 241.

[89] See, e.g., Griffin, n. 4; Van Gerven, n. 81. Van Gerven's view is also that any attempt to encompass such conduct within 'implementation' would be contrary to international law as there would not be a sufficiently close link to support jurisdiction.

[90] Griffin, n. 4.

[91] And presumably also Art. 102.

[92] Reg. 139/2004 [2004] L24/1 (replacing Reg. 4064/89 [1989] OJ L395/1). For the EUMR generally, see Chap. 15.

[93] Subject to certain exceptions, discussed in Chap. 15, such as Art. 9, which allows for concentrations to be referred back to national authorities.

[94] For a full analysis of the 'Union dimension' see M. Broberg, *The European Commission's Jurisdiction to Scrutinise Mergers* (4th edn, Wolters Kluwer, 2013).

Article 1 does not, however, expressly say anything about where the undertakings concerned are incorporated, or carry on business, or whether the undertakings must have assets in the EU. Its criteria relate only to a worldwide turnover figure and a much smaller EU-wide turnover figure. Article 5, which deals with the calculation of turnover, says that '[t]urnover in the [Union] or in a Member State, shall comprise products sold and services provided to undertakings or consumers, in the [Union] or in that Member State as the case may be'.[95] The main reason for the original Merger Regulation not directly addressing the jurisdiction issue seems to be that the Council Working Group was dealing with the details of the regulation at the time *Wood Pulp I* was before the CJ. In the light of the problems raised in that case express references to jurisdiction were deleted from the final version.[96]

As a result of the EU dimension test it was inevitable that undertakings established abroad would be drawn into the net of EU merger control by involvement in transactions with EU undertakings. The formulation of the Union dimension threshold, however, can also catch transactions which involve *only* undertakings located outside the EU with few assets inside it, and transactions which have minimal impact inside the EU. The broad jurisdiction is unlikely to cause great problems in most cases, in that the concentration concerned will clearly not be incompatible with the internal market under the test in Article 2 of the EUMR.[97] Even so, non-EU undertakings may object to the Commission's jurisdiction, particularly where the Commission is unhappy about a concentration.

(ii) The *Gencor* Judgment

In *Gencor/Lonrho* the Commission prohibited a merger in the South African platinum and rhodium industry,[98] on the ground that it would create a position of oligopolistic dominance. One of the parties appealed, inter alia on the ground that the Commission had no jurisdiction over the transaction.[99]

The case concerned a proposed merger between the platinum and rhodium mining interests in South Africa of Gencor and LPD. Both were companies incorporated in South Africa, although LPD was a subsidiary of Lonrho, which was incorporated in London. LPD's sales worldwide were made through Lonrho's Belgian subsidiary. Platinum group metal (PGM) was sold throughout the world, mainly in Japan (approximately 50 per cent of world demand), and North America and Western Europe (approximately 20 per cent each).[100] Approximately 70–75 per cent of the world supply of PGM came from South Africa and 22–25 per cent from Russia[101] (although South Africa has 90 per cent of the world reserves). In South Africa the largest producer was Anglo-American, which was also incorporated there. It appears that Anglo-American probably had 35–50 per cent of world sales and LPD and Gencor 15–17 per cent each.[102]

---

[95] Merger Reg., Art. 5(1), second para.

[96] C. J. Cook and C. S. Kerse, *EC Merger Control* (3rd edn, Sweet & Maxwell, 2000), 11–12.

[97] And will receive their Art. 6(1) clearance within a month, see Chap. 15, Section 4.

[98] M.619, [1997] OJ L11/30.

[99] Once the Commission had blocked the merger there was no possibility of the transaction going ahead, since under the agreement between the parties it was a condition precedent that clearance from the Commission should be obtained by a certain date. The entire purchase agreement had therefore lapsed. Nevertheless, the GC held that the action for annulment was still admissible since the applicant had an interest in having the legality of the decision addressed to it examined by the Community judicature: Case T-102/96, *Gencor* [1999] ECR II-753, paras. 40–46.

[100] For the exact figures from 1991 to 1995 see Table 5 in M.619, *Gencor/Lonrho* [1997] OJ L11/30.

[101] *Gencor/Lonrho* [1997] OJ L11/30, Table 2.

[102] The companies' sales figures were redacted from the published decision as business secrets, but see the figures extrapolated from the information in the decision in E. Fox, 'The Merger Regulation and its Territorial Reach' [1999] *ECLR* 334, 334.

All of Gencor's and LPD's production was in South Africa. The proposed merger was notified to the South African authorities, which found that there were no competition problems.[103] The merger had a Community dimension because of the worldwide and Community-wide turnover of Gencor and Lonrho. The Commission found the merger to be incompatible with the common market on account of the effect which the creation of the dominant duopoly position would have on *sales* of PGM in the Community.

Gencor contested the assumption of jurisdiction before the GC. It argued[104] that the EUMR is applicable only if the activities forming the subject matter of the concentration are located within the Community. The location of the concentration was South Africa, and if the *Wood Pulp* test was applied the concentration was implemented in South Africa, not the EEC. South Africa had approved the merger. Moreover, even if the test for jurisdiction *was* whether the merger had an immediate and substantial effect on competition within the EEC, that test was not satisfied either: 'the Commission cannot claim jurisdiction in respect of a concentration on the basis of future and hypothetical behaviour in which undertakings in the relevant market might engage and which might or might not fall within its purview under the Treaty'.[105] The GC, however, upheld the Commission's decision.

Case T-102/96, *Gencor Ltd v Commission* [1999] ECR II-753

General Court

78. The Regulation, in accordance with Article 1 thereof, applies to all concentrations with a Community dimension, that is to say to all concentrations between undertakings which do not each achieve more than two-thirds of their aggregate Community-wide turnover within one and the same Member State, where the combined aggregate worldwide turnover of those undertakings is more than ECU 5000 million and the aggregate Community-wide turnover of at least two of them is more than ECU 250 million.

79. Article 1 does not require that, in order for a concentration to be regarded as having a Community dimension, the undertakings in question must be established in the Community or that the production activities covered by the concentration must be carried out within Community territory.

80. With regard to the criterion of turnover, it must be stated that, as set out in paragraph 13 of the contested decision, the concentration at issue has a Community dimension within the meaning of Article 1(2) of the Regulation. The undertakings concerned have an aggregate worldwide turnover of more than ECU 10 000 million, above the ECU 5000 million threshold laid down by the Regulation. Gencor and Lonrho each had a Community-wide turnover of more than ECU 250 million in the latest financial year. Finally, they do not each achieve more than two-thirds of their aggregate Community-wide turnover within one and the same Member State.

81. The applicant's arguments to the effect that the legal bases for the Regulation and the wording of its preamble and substantive provisions preclude its application to the concentration at issue cannot be accepted.

82. The legal bases for the Regulation, namely Articles [103 and 352 TFEU], and more particularly the provisions to which they are intended to give effect, that is to say Articles 3(g) [EC] and [101 and 102 TFEU], as well as the first to fifth, ninth and eleventh recitals in the preamble to the Regulation, merely point to the need to ensure that competition is not distorted in the common market, in particular by concentrations which result in the creation or strengthening of a dominant position. They in no way exclude

---

[103] The Deputy Foreign Minister told the Commission that he would not contest the Commission's policy, but that the South African Government considered that two equally matched competitors (as Anglo-American and Gencor/Lonrho would be) were preferable to the prevailing situation of one dominant firm (Anglo-American), *Gencor/Lonrho* [1997] OJ L11/30, para. 19.

[104] Case T-102/96, *Gencor Ltd v Commission* [1999] ECR II-753, paras. 48–63.

[105] Ibid., para. 61.

from the Regulation's field of application concentrations which, while relating to mining and/or production activities outside the Community, have the effect of creating or strengthening a dominant position as a result of which effective competition in the common market is significantly impeded.

83. In particular, the applicant's view cannot be founded on the closing words of the 11th recital in the preamble to the Regulation.

84. That recital states that 'a concentration with a Community dimension exists . . . where the concentrations are effected by undertakings which do not have their principal fields of activities in the Community but which have substantial operations there'.

85. By that reference, in general terms, to the concept of substantial operations, the Regulation does not, for the purpose of defining its territorial scope, ascribe greater importance to production operations than to sales operations. On the contrary, by setting quantitative thresholds in Article 1 which are based on the worldwide and Community turnover of the undertakings concerned, it rather ascribes greater importance to sales operations within the common market as a factor linking the concentration to the Community. It is common ground that Gencor and Lonrho each carry out significant sales in the Community (valued in excess of ECU 250 million).

86. Nor is it borne out by either the 30th recital in the preamble to the Regulation or Article 24 thereof that the criterion based on the location of production activities is well founded. Far from laying down a criterion for defining the territorial scope of the Regulation, Article 24 merely regulates the procedures to be followed in order to deal with situations in which non-member countries do not grant Community undertakings treatment comparable to that accorded by the Community to undertakings from those non-member countries in relation to the control of concentrations.

87. The applicant cannot, by reference to the judgment in *Wood Pulp*, rely on the criterion as to the implementation of an agreement to support its interpretation of the territorial scope of the Regulation. Far from supporting the applicant's view, that criterion for assessing the link between an agreement and Community territory in fact precludes it. According to *Wood Pulp*, the criterion as to the implementation of an agreement is satisfied by mere sale within the Community, irrespective of the location of the sources of supply and the production plant. It is not disputed that Gencor and Lonrho carried out sales in the Community before the concentration and would have continued to do so thereafter.

88. Accordingly, the Commission did not err in its assessment of the territorial scope of the Regulation by applying it in this case to a proposed concentration notified by undertakings whose registered offices and mining and production operations are outside the Community.

2. Compatibility of the contested decision with public international law

89. Following the concentration agreement, the previously existing competitive relationship between Implats and LPD, in particular so far as concerns their sales in the Community, would have come to an end. That would have altered the competitive structure within the common market since, instead of three South African PGM suppliers, there would have remained only two. The implementation of the proposed concentration would have led to the merger not only of the parties' PGM mining and production operations in South Africa but also of their marketing operations throughout the world, particularly in the Community where Implats and LPD achieved significant sales.

90. Application of the Regulation is justified under public international law when it is foreseeable that a proposed concentration will have an immediate and substantial effect in the Community.

91. In that regard, the concentration would, according to the contested decision, have led to the creation of a dominant duopoly on the part of Amplats and Implats/LPD in the platinum and rhodium markets, as a result of which effective competition would have been significantly impeded in the common market within the meaning of Article 2(3) of the Regulation.

92. It is therefore necessary to verify whether the three criteria of immediate, substantial and foreseeable effect are satisfied in this case.

93. With regard, specifically, to the criterion of immediate effect, the words 'medium term' used in paragraphs 206 and 210 of the contested decision in relation to the creation of a dominant duopoly position are, contrary to the applicant's assertion, entirely unambiguous. They clearly refer to the time when it is envisaged that Russian stocks will be exhausted, enabling a dominant duopoly on the part of Amplats and Implats/LPD to be created on the world platinum and rhodium markets and, by the same token, in the Community as a substantial part of those world markets.

94. That dominant position would not be dependent, as the applicant asserts, on the future conduct of the undertaking arising from the concentration and of Amplats but would result, in particular, from the very characteristics of the market and the alteration of its structure. In referring to the future conduct of the parties to the duopoly, the applicant fails to distinguish between abuses of dominant position which those parties might commit in the near or more distant future, which might or might not be controlled by means of Articles [81] and/or [82] of the Treaty, and the alteration to the structure of the undertakings and of the market to which the concentration would give rise. It is true that the concentration would not necessarily lead to abuses immediately, since that depends on decisions which the parties to the duopoly may or may not take in the future. However, the concentration would have had the direct and immediate effect of creating the conditions in which abuses were not only possible but economically rational, given that the concentration would have significantly impeded effective competition in the market by giving rise to a lasting alteration to the structure of the markets concerned.

95. Accordingly, the concentration would have had an immediate effect in the Community.

96. So far as concerns the criterion of substantial effect, it should be noted that, as held in paragraph 297 below, the Commission established to the requisite legal standard that the concentration would have created a lasting dominant duopoly position in the world platinum and rhodium markets.

97. The applicant cannot maintain that the concentration would not have a substantial effect in the Community in view of the low sales and small market share of the parties to the concentration in the EEA. While the level of sales in western Europe (20 per cent of world demand) and the Community market share of the entity arising from the concentration (. . .) per cent in respect of platinum) were already sufficient grounds for the Community to have jurisdiction in respect of the concentration, the potential impact of the concentration proved even higher than those figures suggested. Given that the concentration would have had the effect of creating a dominant duopoly position in the world platinum and rhodium markets, it is clear that the sales in the Community potentially affected by the concentration would have included not only those of the Implats/LPD undertaking but also those of Amplats (approximately 35 per cent to 50 per cent), which would have represented a more than substantial proportion of platinum and rhodium sales in western Europe and a much higher combined market share held by Implats/LPD and Amplats approximately (. . .) per cent to 65 per cent).

98. Finally, it is not possible to accept the applicant's argument that the creation of the dominant position referred to by the Commission in the contested decision is not of greater concern to the Community than to any other competent body and is even of less concern to it than to others. The fact that, in a world market, other parts of the world are affected by the concentration cannot prevent the Community from exercising its control over a concentration which substantially affects competition within the common market by creating a dominant position.

99. The arguments by which the applicant denies that the concentration would have a substantial effect in the Community must therefore be rejected.

100. As for the criterion of foreseeable effect, it follows from all of the foregoing that it was in fact foreseeable that the effect of creating a dominant duopoly position in a world market would also be to impede competition significantly in the Community, an integral part of that market.

101. It follows that the application of the Regulation to the proposed concentration was consistent with public international law.

102. It is necessary to examine next whether the Community violated a principle of non-interference or the principle of proportionality in exercising that jurisdiction.

103. The applicant's argument that, by virtue of a principle of non-interference, the Commission should have refrained from prohibiting the concentration in order to avoid a conflict of jurisdiction with the South African authorities must be rejected, without it being necessary to consider whether such a rule exists in international law. Suffice it to note that there was no conflict between the course of action required by the South African Government and that required by the Community given that, in their letter of 22 August 1995, the South African competition authorities simply concluded that the concentration agreement did not give rise to any competition policy concerns, without requiring that such an agreement be entered into (see, to that effect, *Wood Pulp*, paragraph 20).

104. In its letter of 19 April 1996 the South African Government, far from calling into question the Community's jurisdiction to rule on the concentration at issue, first simply expressed a general preference, having regard to the strategic importance of mineral exploitation in South Africa, for intervention in specific cases of collusion when they arose and did not specifically comment on the industrial or other merits of the concentration proposed by Gencor and Lonrho. It then merely expressed the view that the proposed concentration might not impede competition, having regard to the economic power of Amplats, the existence of other sources of supply of PGMs and the opportunities for other producers to enter the South African market through the grant of new mining concessions.

105. Finally, neither the applicant nor, indeed, the South African Government in its letter of 19 April 1996 have shown, beyond making mere statements of principle, in what way the proposed concentration would affect the vital economic and/or commercial interests of the Republic of South Africa.

106. As regards the argument that the Community cannot claim to have jurisdiction in respect of a concentration on the basis of future and hypothetical behaviour, namely parallel conduct on the part of the undertakings operating in the relevant market where that conduct might or might not fall within the competence of the Community under the Treaty, it must be stated, as pointed out above in connection with the question whether the concentration has an immediate effect, that, while the elimination of the risk of future abuses may be a legitimate concern of any competent competition authority, the main objective in exercising control over concentrations at Community level is to ensure that the restructuring of undertakings does not result in the creation of positions of economic power which may significantly impede effective competition in the common market. Community jurisdiction is therefore founded, first and foremost, on the need to avoid the establishment of market structures which may create or strengthen a dominant position, and not on the need to control directly possible abuses of a dominant position.

107. Consequently, it is unnecessary to rule on the question whether the letter of 22 August 1995 from the South African Competition Board constituted a definitive position on the concentration, on whether or not the South African Government was an authority responsible for competition matters and, finally, on the scope of South African competition law. There is accordingly no need to grant the application for measures of organisation of procedure or of inquiry made by the applicant in its letter of 3 December 1996.

108. In those circumstances, the contested decision is not inconsistent with either the Regulation or the rules of public international law relied on by the applicant.

109. For the same reasons, the objection, based on Article [241] of the Treaty, that the Regulation is unlawful because it confers upon the Commission competence in respect of the concentration between Gencor and Lonrho must be rejected.

It can be seen from this extract that in paragraphs 78–88 the GC looked first at the EUMR itself. It concluded that it does not matter where the PGM production took place, because not only does Article 1 not require that the production should take place in the Community (now Union) (paragraph 79), it actually accords greater importance to sales. In the second half of paragraph 87 it returned to the *Wood Pulp* judgment and said that the criterion of the implementation of an agreement is satisfied by mere sale in the Community. Therefore the Commission had jurisdiction under the EUMR on the basis that the concentration would be implemented in the Community.

In paragraphs 89–111, the GC considered whether the decision was in accordance with public international law. It concluded that it was. In paragraph 90, the GC says, in words redolent of the effects doctrine, that the application of the EUMR is justified in international law 'when it is foreseeable that a proposed concentration will have an immediate and substantial effect in the Community'. The GC did not appear to expressly adopt the effects doctrine, but rather examined whether taking jurisdiction on grounds of implementation in this case conformed with the criteria which it identified as required by international law. However, as we see in the next extract, in *Intel* the GC said that in *Gencor* relied solely on 'qualified effects'.[106]

Gencor is a striking demonstration of the implications of extraterritoriality. The EC forbade a merger involving producer undertakings in a non-Member State because of the sales of the product (less than a quarter of the worldwide total) in the Community. The GC examined the matter in light of the principles of non-interference and proportionality (paragraphs 102–108) but concluded that there was no conflict with the interests of South Africa because South Africa did not require the transaction to take place. There is no conflict of jurisdiction between a State which prohibits something and a State which allows it (rather than requires it). The difficulty with this is that merger control invariably operates only to forbid certain concentrations, not to require them, and the prohibiting jurisdiction will always trump the other. However, in *Gencor* the transaction was likely to have a more serious impact on the economy of South Africa than on consumers in the EC.[107]

E. INTEL AND THE QUALIFIED EFFECTS DOCTRINE

The substance of *Intel* is discussed in Chapter 7. It is seen there that the abuses found by the Commission were exclusivity rebates and so-called 'naked restrictions' whereby Intel paid computer manufacturers to delay or cancel the marketing of products containing their competitor's (AMD) x86CPUs. On appeal Intel, inter alia, challenged the jurisdiction over the transactions with two manufacturers, Acer and Lenovo, on the grounds that their manufacturing facilities were in China and Taiwan and that few of the affected computers would have been sold in the EEA. The GC confirmed that there is a 'qualified effects' doctrine in EU law.

Case T-286/09, *Intel v Commission* EU:T:2014:547

General Court

231. First of all, it should be noted that, in the case-law of the Court of Justice and the General Court, two approaches have been followed in order to establish that the Commission's jurisdiction is justified under the rules of public international law.

232. The first approach is based on the principle of territoriality. That approach was followed in Joined Cases 89/85, 104/85, 114/85, 116/85, 117/85 and 125/85 to 129/85 *Ahlström Osakeyhtiö and Others* v *Commission*, 'Woodpulp'). In paragraph 16 of that judgment, the Court held that it was necessary to distinguish two elements of conduct, namely the formation of the agreement, decision or concerted practice and the implementation thereof. If the applicability of prohibitions laid down under competition law were made to depend on the place where the agreement, decision or concerted practice was formed, the result would obviously be to give undertakings an easy means of evading those prohibitions. The Court therefore held that the decisive factor is the place where it is implemented.

233. The second approach is based on the qualified effects of the practices in the European Union. That approach was followed in Case T-102/96 *Gencor* v *Commission* 'Gencor'. In paragraph 90 of that

---

[106] Case 286/09, *Intel* EU:T:2014:547, para. 240.

[107] See E. Fox, 'The Merger Regulation and its Territorial Reach' [1999] *ECLR* 334, for a critique of *Gencor* on these grounds.

judgment, the Court held that application of Council Regulation (EEC) No 4064/89 ... on the control of concentrations between undertakings ..., is justified under public international law when it is foreseeable that a proposed concentration will have an immediate and substantial effect in the European Union.

234. By submitting that where trade with third countries is involved, even where implementation of the practices at issue takes place within the European Union, the Commission must also prove the existence of immediate, substantial, direct and foreseeable effects within the European Union, the applicant's reasoning amounts to an assertion that implementation and qualified effects in the European Union are cumulative conditions.

235. The Commission stated, at the hearing, that, in the present case, its jurisdiction was justified, first, under the doctrine of implementation of the practices at issue in the EEA, which was followed in *Woodpulp*, paragraph 232 above, and, second, under the effects doctrine, which was followed in *Gencor*, paragraph 233 above.

236. In that regard, the Court would point out that demonstrating the implementation of the practices at issue in the EEA or demonstrating qualified effects are alternative and not cumulative approaches for the purposes of establishing that the Commission's jurisdiction is justified under the rules of public international law.

237. In *Woodpulp*, paragraph 232 above, the Court of Justice relied solely on the implementation of the conduct at issue in the territory of the European Union.

238. The applicant may not rely on the fact that Advocate General Darmon stated, in point 82 of his Opinion in *Woodpulp*, paragraph 232 above, that it would be for the Court 'to ascertain whether the effects of the conduct alleged by the Commission were substantial, direct and foreseeable in order to determine whether the Commission was right in exercising jurisdiction over the applicants'. The Advocate General proposed that the Court should rely on the effects of the conduct at issue in the territory of the European Union in order to establish the Commission's jurisdiction. The Court did not follow the Advocate General's proposal and relied on the implementation of the agreement in the European Union. It therefore follows from the judgment of the Court in that case that, where the Commission's jurisdiction can be established on the basis of the implementation of the conduct at issue in the European Union, it is not necessary to examine whether there were any effects in order to establish the Commission's jurisdiction.

239. The applicant relies in that context also on *Gencor*, paragraph 233 above.

240. However, in *Gencor*, paragraph 233 above (paragraphs 89 to 101), the General Court relied solely on the qualified effects in order to establish that the Commission's jurisdiction was justified under the rules of public international law.

241. It is indeed true that, in paragraph 87 of that judgment, the Court observed that, according to *Woodpulp*, paragraph 232 above, the criterion as to the implementation of an agreement is satisfied by mere sale within the European Union. However, paragraph 87 forms part of the reasoning of the Court by which the latter held that Regulation No 4064/89 did not, for the purpose of defining its territorial scope, ascribe greater importance to production operations than to sales operations (*Gencor*, paragraph 233 above, paragraphs 85 to 88). In that context, the Court rejected an argument of the applicant based on *Woodpulp*, paragraph 232 above, by holding that, according to that judgment, the criterion as to the implementation of an agreement is satisfied by mere sales. The Court therefore rejected the applicant's argument that it follows from *Woodpulp*, paragraph 232 above, that greater importance is ascribed to production activities than to sales activities.

242. Next, the Court examined, in paragraphs 89 to 101 of *Gencor*, paragraph 233 above, whether the application of Regulation No 4064/89 in that case was consistent with public international law. In that context, the Court confined itself to examining whether the criteria of immediate, substantial and foreseeable effect were satisfied.

243. It therefore follows from *Gencor*, paragraph 233 above, that, in order to justify the Commission's jurisdiction according to the rules of public international law, it is sufficient that the criteria of immediate, substantial and foreseeable effect in the European Union be satisfied.

244. It follows from the foregoing that, in order to justify the Commission's jurisdiction under public international law, it is sufficient to establish either the qualified effects of the practice in the European Union or that it was implemented in the European Union.

245. In another connection, it should be noted that, in the contested decision, the Commission does not deal expressly with the question whether the Commission's jurisdiction is justified under the rules of public international law. In that regard, the Commission states that it dealt, at recitals 1749 to 1753 of the contested decision, with the question whether trade was affected between Member States.

246. Furthermore, the Commission states, without being contradicted on that point by the applicant, that, during the administrative procedure, the applicant never questioned the Commission's international jurisdiction.

247. In that context, the Court notes that the wording of Article [102] contains two elements which relate to a link with the territory of the European Union. First, Article [102] requires the existence of a dominant position 'within the common market or in a substantial part of it'. Second, it requires that trade between Member States be capable of being affected by the conduct in question. In the contested decision, the Commission established the existence of a dominant position by the applicant at a worldwide level, which includes the common market. Moreover, at recitals 1749 to 1753 of that decision, it expressly examined the effect on trade between Member States.

248. It is true that the question whether the Commission's jurisdiction is justified under public international law is a question separate from that of the criteria laid down by Article [102]. In that regard, it should be observed that the criterion of the effect on trade between Member States is intended to define the sphere of application of Community rules in relation to national laws (see, to that effect, Joined Cases 6/73 and 7/73 *Istituto Chemioterapico Italiano and Commercial Solvents* v *Commission* ..., paragraph 31).

...

251. ...[T]he Court would point out that the Commission is not obliged to establish the existence of actual effects in order to justify its jurisdiction under public international law. The criteria of immediate, substantial and foreseeable effects do not mean that the effect must also be actual. It is for the Commission to ensure that competition within the common market is protected against threats to the effective functioning thereof.

252. Accordingly, the view cannot be taken that the Commission is required to confine itself to pursuing and punishing abuse which achieved the intended result and in respect of which the threat to the functioning of competition materialised. The Commission cannot be expected to adopt a passive position where there is a threat to the effective competition structure in the common market and may therefore intervene also in cases in which the threat did not materialise or has not yet materialised.

The GC then proceeded to examine whether on the facts the effects were indeed substantial, immediate,[108] and foreseeable.[109] The main issue was substantiality, as the effects were not just foreseeable but intended, and the fact that Intel itself did not sell into the EEA did not make the effects of Intel's conduct indirect because it did directly concern its customers' sales.[110] On substantiality the GC said that it is not necessary for the EEA to be more affected than other regions in the world, and that the EEA constitutes a significant part of the world market.[111] The effects do not have to be actual, so that the Commission can act to prevent a threat to the effective competition structure.[112] Moreover, weakening Intel's sole significant competitor at the worldwide level was

[108] The GC seems to use 'immediate' and 'direct' synonymously, although in para. 234 it mentions both together.
[109] Case 286/09, *Intel* EU:T:2014:547, paras 259–296.
[110] Ibid., para. 279.
[111] Ibid., paras. 261–262.
[112] Ibid., para. 251.

capable of having repercussions on the competitive structure of the common market.[113] Another element in proving substantiality was the treatment of Intel's various abuses as 'a single continuous infringement' rather than as a number of separate abuses.[114]

In this judgment the GC identified two bases on which the Commission can take jurisdiction: implementation and qualified effects ('qualified' meaning the immediate, substantial, and foreseeable criteria). These are alternative, not cumulative, approaches which are both justified under international law (paragraph 236) so that is sufficient to establish either the qualified effects of the practice in the EU or that it was implemented in the EU (paragraph 244). If qualified effects are established it is not necessary to also establish that the conduct was implemented in the EU although 'for the sake of completeness' the GC did proceed to do that.[115])

The case is on appeal to the CJ.[116]

F. THE *INNOLUX* CASE AND THE CALCULATION OF FINES

The appeal to the CJ in *InnoLux*[117] concerned the calculation of the fine imposed on the appellant undertaking for its participation in the worldwide *LCD Panels* cartel.[118] For the purpose of calculating the value of sales under paragraph 13 of the Fining Guidelines[119] the Commission took into account the value of sales in the EEA of 'transformed products', i.e. products into which the vertically integrated cartelist had incorporated the cartelised product in China and Taiwan. The GC upheld this,[120] but Advocate General Wathelet,[121] having surveyed the EU case law on extraterritoriality, considered that:

44....unless further evidence can be furnished that the cartel creates qualified effects in the EEA, the Commission goes too far if it fines cartels relating to products manufactured and sold outside the EEA for the sole reason that those products are subsequently 'transformed' or incorporated into other products which (either wholly or in part) arrive in the EEA.

...

48....[T]he only justification for the Commission's having jurisdiction with regard to the sales at issue must arise in this case from application of the 'qualified effects' test.

He did not consider that the Commission had produced sufficient evidence of such effects.

The CJ, however, did not concern itself with the extraterritorial issue. It did not mention qualified effects or the arguments of the Advocate General. It noted that according to *Wood Pulp I* there was no question about its jurisdiction over the LCD cartel itself. It saw this as being simply about the amount of the fine:

...It would, however, be contrary to the goal pursued by Article 23(2) of Regulation No 1/2003 if the vertically-integrated participants in a cartel could, solely because they incorporated the goods the subject of the infringement into the finished products outside the EEA, expect to have excluded from the calculation of the fine the proportion of the value of their sales of those finished products in the EEA that are capable of being regarded as corresponding to the value of the goods the subject of the infringement.[122]

---

[113] Ibid., para. 275.

[114] Ibid., paras. 267–272.

[115] Ibid., paras. 297–314.

[116] Case C-413/14 P, judgment pending.

[117] Case C-231/14 P, *InnoLux Corp v Commission* EU:C:2015:451.

[118] COMP/39.309, 8 December 2010. The US case *Motorola Mobility* (n. 22) arose from the same cartel.

[119] See Chap. 13, Section 7.H.iv.g, p. 972 ff.

[120] Case T-91/11, *InnoLux v Commission* EU:T:2014:92.

[121] Case C-231/14 P, EU:C:2015:292, para. 44.

[122] Case T-91/11, *InnoLux v Commission*, para. 55. For a comment on the extraterritorial implications of this case, see S. S. H. Chan, '*InnoLux Corp v Commission*: Establishment of the Effects Doctrine in Extraterritoriality of EU Competition Law?' [2015] *ECLR* 463.

G. ENFORCEMENT JURISDICTION

In many cases problems of enforcement jurisdiction against non-EU undertakings may be avoided by the single economic entity doctrine. Requests and demands for information under Regulation 1/2003, Article 18 may be addressed to the branch or subsidiary of a non-EU undertaking which is situated within the EU and final decisions may be served on and enforced against EU subsidiaries, as was done in *Dyestuffs*.[123]

It appears that a statement of objections (SO) may be served on a branch or subsidiary within the EU.[124] However, it is sufficient for the purposes of EU law for the Commission to send the SO in a registered letter by post direct to the non-EU undertaking's address outside the EU. The CJ merely requires that the undertaking receives the SO in circumstances which enable it to take cognisance of the case against it.[125]

Matters are more difficult where the Commission cannot rely on the single economic entity doctrine. There appears to be no objection to sending an Article 18(2) request for information to an undertaking outside the EU as it does not entail any element of compulsion but it is otherwise with an Article 18(3) demand by decision and the better view is that the Commission cannot do this,[126] although it is permissible for the Commission to require information from an undertaking in a Member State pertaining to a period before that Member State acceded to the EU.[127] It is generally thought inconceivable that the Commission could mount an Article 20 or 21 inspection outside the EU although it might ask the competition authorities in a non-Member State for help in its investigation. If a trade association has a presence in the EU it cannot resist an Article 20 inspection on the grounds that some of its members are outside the EU.[128] As with an SO, a final decision may be served directly on a non-EU undertaking and it is sufficient that the undertaking receives it and can take cognisance of it, even if it returns it without reading it.[129] Whilst decisions imposing fines can be sent to undertakings outside the EU[130] they cannot be enforced unless the undertaking has assets inside the EU which can be seized.

6. INTERNATIONAL COOPERATION

A. GENERAL

Faced with the globalisation of the economy and with the problems of the application and enforcement of competition laws already discussed, attention is currently focused on the desirability of international agreements as at least a partial solution. Agreements in place at the moment are mainly bilateral ones between major trading partners, but there are also some multilateral regional trading arrangements which contain competition provisions.[131] The EU commonly insists on the

---

[123] Case 48/69, *Dyestuffs* [1972] ECR 619.

[124] C. Kerse and N. Khan (Khan ed.), *EU Antitrust Procedure* (6th edn, Sweet & Maxwell, 2012), 4-023.

[125] Case 52/69, *Geigy v Commission* [1972] ECR 787 (one of the *Dyestuffs* cases). The SO was sent to Geigy's address in Switzerland. Geigy returned it arguing that this infringed both Swiss and public international law and thus vitiated the proceedings. The CJ rejected this.

[126] Art. 18(5) provides for a copy of both an Art. 18(2) request and an Art.18(3) decision to be forwarded to the NCA of the Member State in which the undertaking's seat is situated, which would be impossible in the case of a non-EU undertaking, but this would not necessarily affect the possibility of using Art. 18(2) given the lack of coercion.

[127] Cases T-458/09 and T-171/10, *Slovak Telecom v Commission* EU:T:2012:145, para. 134.

[128] *Ukwal* [1992] OJ L121/45.

[129] Case 6/72, *Europemballage Corp and Continental Can Co Inc v Commission* [1973] ECR 215.

[130] As happened in, e.g., *Wood Pulp* [1985] OJ L85/1.

[131] See C. Noonan, *The Emerging Principles of International Competition Law* (Oxford University Press, 2008), 13.2.3.

insertion of competition law provisions in trade agreements and has particular arrangements with countries which are candidates for possible Accession. There is also significant activity at the level of international organisations and increasingly important international cooperation. In particular, national competition agencies cooperate with each other closely. In its 2014 Competition Report the Commission stated that it currently works with agencies outside the EU in 64 per cent of its abuse of dominance cases, 58 per cent of its complex merger investigations, and 78 per cent of cartel decisions. In merger cases, where the Commission normally tries to establish contact with the relevant other authorities as soon as it becomes aware that approval will also be required in other jurisdictions, it is standard practice for the Commission to ask the parties for a confidentiality waiver, to allow the agencies to exchange information. The parties are normally happy to agree in order to smooth the path of the transaction.[132]

B. EU BILATERAL AGREEMENTS

(i) The EU–US Cooperation Agreements

a. The Content of the 1991 and 1998 Agreements

In 1991 the Commission concluded an agreement with the US authorities on cooperation over the enforcement of their competition laws.[133] The authority of the Commission to enter into the agreement was subsequently challenged by France, supported by Spain and the Netherlands, and the CJ found that the Commission did not have the power to conclude (as distinct from negotiate) agreements with foreign countries.[134] The agreement was finally approved by means of a joint decision of the Council and Commission in 1995.[135]

The Agreement provides for: the reciprocal notification of cases under investigation by either authority, where they may affect the important interests of the other party (Article II); exchanges of information and periodic meetings between competition officials from each country (Article III); and rendering each other assistance and coordinating their enforcement activities (Article IV). The most significant provisions, however, are Articles V and VI. Article V is the 'positive comity' Article, providing the possibility for one authority to request the other to take enforcement action, and Article VI provides for 'traditional' or 'negative' comity, i.e. for each authority to take into account the important interests of the other in the course of its enforcement activities.

The Competition Commissioner, writing in the *XXVIIIth Report on Competition Policy* said that this amounted to 'a commitment by the EU and the USA to cooperate with respect to antitrust enforcement, and not to act unilaterally and extraterritorially unless the avenues provided by comity have been exhausted'.[136]

The successful operation of the Agreement persuaded the parties to strengthen the positive comity provisions and in 1998 they signed the EU–US Positive Comity Agreement[137] which entered into force on 4 June 1998. This spells out more clearly the circumstances in which a request for positive comity will be made and the manner in which such requests should be treated (Article III). Article IV provides for investigations by the requesting party to be deferred or suspended in reliance on the requested party's enforcement. The effect of the 1998 Agreement is to create a presumption,

---

[132] See J. Faull and A. Nikpay (eds.), *The EU Law of Competition* (3rd edn, Oxford University Press, 2014), 5.318–5.330. See in particular the relationship with the US agencies, Section B.i.b.

[133] Agreement between the Government of the US and the Commission of the European Communities regarding the application of their Competition Laws, 23 September 1991.

[134] Case C-327/91, *France v Commission* [1994] ECR I-3641.

[135] [1995] OJ L95/47.

[136] Commission's *XXVIIth Report on Competition Policy* (1998), foreword, 5.

[137] [1998] OJ L173/28.

as described by the Commission in its report on the application of the cooperation agreement for 1998.[138]

The 1998 EC/US Positive Comity Agreement, like the 1991 Agreement, does not alter existing law, nor does it require any change in existing law. However, it does create a presumption that when anti-competitive activities occur in the whole or in a substantial part of the territory of one of the parties and affect the interests of the other party, the latter 'will normally defer or suspend its enforcement activities in favour of' the former. This is expected to happen particularly when these anti-competitive activities do not have a direct, substantial and reasonably foreseeable impact on consumers in the territory of the party deferring or suspending its activities.

The presumption of deferral will only occur if the party in the territory of which the restrictive activities are occurring has jurisdiction over these activities and is prepared to deal actively and expeditiously with the matter. When dealing with the case that party will keep its counterpart closely informed of any developments in the procedure, within the limits of its internal rules protecting confidentiality.

The 1998 Agreement constituted an important development, since it represents a commitment on the part of the EU and the US to cooperate with respect to antitrust enforcement in certain situations, rather than to seek to apply their antitrust laws extraterritorially.

It is important to note that because the EU merger rules do not allow for the deferral or suspension of action which the Agreement envisages the EU merger rules are not within the 1998 Agreement.[139] However, the EU and US have established a merger working group which in 2002 adopted a set of 'Best Practices' on cooperation in merger investigations where the same transaction is being investigated in both jurisdictions. This was revised in 2011.[140]

b. The Application of the Agreements

The EU and US authorities consider that their cooperation works well and has made a positive contribution to competition law enforcement. The authorities have a very close relationship. The 1991 procedures worked particularly successfully, for example, in respect of the investigation into Microsoft in 1994.[141] One drawback in the operation of the agreement is that Articles VII of the 1991 Agreement and V of the 1998 Agreement provide for the maintenance of the confidentiality of information acquired by the authorities in the course of their investigations. Further, Articles IX and VII respectively provide that nothing in the Agreements is to be interpreted in a manner which is inconsistent with the parties' existing laws. This limits the information which the authorities may exchange although, as already mentioned, in merger cases particularly the parties normally agree to confidentiality waivers. Notably, in the 1994 Microsoft investigation, the undertaking was happy to have the US and EU investigations combined as it was easier for the company to deal with the two authorities together, so it agreed to waive its rights to confidentiality and to allow information exchanges between the Commission and the DOJ. The EU's 2013 cooperation agreement with Switzerland is innovative in enabling the competition authorities to exchange information.

The existence of the EU–US cooperation agreement did not prevent the 1997 dispute over the *Boeing/McDonnell Douglas* merger[142] or the *GE/Honeywell* row,[143] In *Boeing/McDonnell Douglas*, for

---

[138] At para. 3. See the Commission's *XXVIIIth Report on Competition Policy* (1998), 315.

[139] Art. II(4)(a).

[140] Available at <http://ec.europa.eu/competition/mergers/legislation/international_cooperation.html>.

[141] Although because of the case brought by France (see Section 6.B.i.a) the agreement was not officially in force.

[142] M.877, [1997] OJ L336/16, see Chap. 15, Section 8.A. See further A. Bavasso, 'Boeing/McDonnell Douglas: Did the Commission Fly Too High?' [1998] *ECLR* 243; A. Schaub, 'International Co-operation in Antitrust Matters: Making the Point in the Wake of the Boeing/MDD Proceedings' (1998) 1 *Competition Policy Newsletter* 2, 3–4; B. Bishop, 'Editorial, The Boeing/McDonnell Douglas Merger' [1997] *ECLR* 417; A. Kaczorowska, 'International Competition Law in the Context of Global Capitalism' [2000] *ECLR* 117, 118. A. Burnside, 'GE, Honey I Sank the Merger' [2002] *ECLR* 107; D. Giotakos, L. Petit, G. Garnier, and P. De Luyck, 'GE/Honeywell—An Insight into the Commission's Investigation and Decision' (2001) 3 *Competition Policy Newsletter* 5.

[143] M.2220 upheld by the GC, Case T-210/01, *General Electric v Commission* [2005] ECR II-5575; see Chap. 15 see A. Burnside, 'GE, Honey I Sank the Merger' [2002] *ECLR* 107; D. Giotakos, L. Petit, G. Garnier, and P. De Luyck, 'GE/Honeywell—An Insight into the Commission's Investigation and Decision' (2001) 3 *Competition Policy Newsletter* 5.

instance, the authorities did consult each other. In accordance with the provisions of the Agreement the Commission and the FTC carried out the necessary notifications and consultations, and the Commission took into account the US concerns over its defence interests. In the end, however, as the Director General recognised, '[p]rocedures of notification and consultation and the principles of traditional and positive comity allow us to bring our respective approaches closer in cases of common interest but there exist[s] no mechanism for resolving conflicts in cases of substantial divergence of analysis'.[144] Nevertheless, these cases of conflict between the EU and US are rare. When adopting the 2002 Merger Best Practices the authorities recognised that 'cooperation is most effective when the investigation timetables of the reviewing agencies run more or less in parallel'. The 2011 Best Practices[145] state that 'cooperation between DG Competition and the US agencies is beneficial not only for the agencies, but also for merging parties and third parties, as it increases the efficiency of the respective investigations, reduces the burden on merging parties and third parties, and increases the overall transparency of the merger review process'.[146] Best Practices encourages undertakings to allow the EU and US agencies to exchange information which they have submitted during the course of an investigation and to allow joint EU/US interviews. The document identifies key points at which consultations between the agencies are likely to be particularly useful and says that consultations between senior officials in the respective agencies may be appropriate at any time.

(ii) Other Dedicated Bilateral Competition Cooperation Agreements

Encouraged by the success of its agreement with the US, the EU entered into a similar agreement with Canada which came into force on 29 April 1999. In particular, the Agreement contains (Articles V and VI), provisions similar to Articles V and VI of the 1991 Agreement including the principle of positive comity.[147] In June 2003 it entered into an agreement with Japan. Again, the principal elements are mutual information, coordination of enforcement activities, and exchange of non-confidential information. In March 2016 the Commission reached agreement with the Japanese Fair Trade Commission to start negotiating an update of this agreement. The EU signed a cooperation agreement with South Korea in May 2009 which came into force on 1 July 2009. It provides for the reciprocal notification of cases, the possibility of coordination by the two authorities of their enforcement activities, taking enforcement action at the request of the other and taking into account the interests of the other party during enforcement activity, the exchange of non-confidential information, and regular bilateral meetings.

The cooperation agreement signed with Switzerland in May 2013[148] was hailed by Commissioner Almunia as 'unprecedented' and described as going beyond the EU's existing agreements with other third countries. In particular it contains innovative provisions on the exchange of information. It is planned that the updated agreement with Japan will include similar provisions on sharing information, which would be in line with an OECD recommendation of September 2014 encouraging legal measures to permit such sharing.

DG Comp signed a Memorandum of Understanding on Cooperation with the competition authorities in Brazil (2009), Russia (2011), and India (2013). The EU agreed to establish the EU–China competition policy dialogue in 2003 whereby the Commission and the Chinese authorities shared experience and views on competition matters and the EU provided technical and capacity-building. This culminated in a Memorandum of Understanding on Cooperation in September 2012 between

---

[144] Schaub, n. 142.

[145] Available at <http://ec.europa.eu/competition/mergers/legislation/eu_us.pdf>.

[146] Best Practices, para. 2.

[147] [1999] OJ L175.

[148] IP/13/44.

DG Comp and the Chinese competition authorities and Practical Guidance for Merger Cooperation in October 2015.

The texts of all these dedicated agreements are available on the Commission website.[149]

(iii) Other Bilateral Cooperation Arrangements

The EU enters into bilateral trade and development agreements with many other countries, including developing countries and/or those with economies in transition. It is usual for these to contain competition provisions and/or (where relevant) to provide for the adoption by the other party of competition rules. There are certain groups of agreements containing similar provisions: agreements with candidate countries or countries of the Western Balkans (Stabilization and Association Agreements); those with other countries formerly part of the USSR (Partnership and Cooperation Agreements); and Euro-Mediterranean Agreements establishing an association with countries of the southern Mediterranean.

Although not strictly bilateral, the African Caribbean and Pacific (ACP) agreement, the Cotonou Agreement, should be noted. The agreement, between the EU and a number of developing countries, replaced the Lomé Agreement. It came into force in 2003 and will last for 20 years. It contains provisions on political cooperation, trade links, and development assistance and also a provision on competition, Article 45.

The deeply controversial Transatlantic Trade and Investment Partnership Agreement (TTIP) between the EU and the US, which has been in the course of negotiation since 2013, includes a chapter on competition.

C. MULTILATERAL COOPERATION

(i) General

There are now well over a hundred countries in the world with some form of competition laws, many of which were adopted under pressure from, or under the influence of, the EU, often as a result of the bilateral trade agreements already mentioned.[150] US law has been extremely influential but it is the EU 'model' which is the one most commonly adopted. This is not only because of pressure from the EU but because other countries prefer to copy the public enforcement system rather than the litigation model which is the product of a particular and singular legal system. One distinguished American commentator considers that the EU model has 'trumped' the US as the model for the world because it resonates with developing and transitional countries as it deals with the emergence from statism and the development of a single market while displaying qualities such as openness, transparency, and non-discrimination. Moreover, the ECN provides a model of how regional cooperation in competition policy can work.[151]

There is a continuing discourse about the suitable form and content of competition laws for developing and transitional economies and the way in which both the substantive and procedural rules need to take account of local political and cultural conditions.[152] A discussion on this is outside the scope of this book, but reference should be made to the further reading at the end of the chapter. There have been initiatives within various international fora aimed at formulating mechanisms for increasing cooperation over competition laws and avoiding conflicts. These are briefly described

---

[149] <http://ec.europa.eu/competition/international/bilateral/>.

[150] International bodies such as the IMF have also played a role, on occasion making loans conditional on the adoption of competition rules (e.g., Indonesia).

[151] Professor Eleanor Fox speaking at the EU Competition Forum, 2 February 2012.

[152] For an interesting discussion of the relationship between Islam and competition law and policy, for example, see M. Dabbah, *Competition Law and Policy in the Middle East* (Cambridge University Press, 2007), Chap. 2.

here. We consider the problems inherent in such multilateral international arrangements and ask whether it is possible to envisage the creation of a multilateral international competition law mechanism at present.

(ii) UNCTAD and the OECD

The United Nations' Set of Multilaterally Agreed Equitable Principles and Rules for the Control of Restrictive Business Practices were adopted in 1980 under the auspices of UNCTAD[153] but provide only a voluntary, non-binding Code. In 1967 the OECD (Organisation for Economic Co-operation and Development) adopted a Recommendation that its member countries should cooperate with each other in the enforcement of their national competition laws.[154] This provides: for one country to notify another when the latter's important interests are affected by the former's investigation or enforcement; for countries to share information and to consult; for them to coordinate parallel investigations; for countries to assist one another in obtaining information inside each other's territory; and for countries to consider dealing with anti-competitive behaviour affecting their interests but occurring in another country's territory by requesting the latter's authorities to take action (positive comity). The bilateral agreements described in Section 6.B reflect these provisions but the 1991 EC–US Agreement was the first to include the 'positive comity' principle. In May 1998 the OECD Committee of Competition Law and Policy adopted a recommendation on hardcore cartels, aimed at strengthening the effectiveness and efficiency of the member countries' enforcement of their competition laws against such cartels. In 2006 the OECD issued a report, 'Competition Law and Policy in the EU'.[155] The Commission cooperates closely with the competition authorities of other OECD member countries based on the 1995 OECD recommendation. There is a direct link from the Commission website to the OECD Competition Committee. The Competition Committee holds regular roundtable meetings to which the Commission contributes and its submissions to the Working Parties are available on the website.[156] Those in 2015 included oligopoly markets, liner shipping, and public and private antitrust enforcement.

(iii) The WTO

When the WTO was being negotiated in 1993 a Draft International Antitrust Code was drawn up by a group of experts at the Max Planck Institute. This would have established an international antitrust regime.[157] The parties to the WTO did not agree to its adoption, however, and no agreement on international competition law was annexed to the WTO Charter. Promoted by the EU, the matter was later taken up at the First Ministerial Conference of the parties to the WTO in Singapore in 1996 and a Working Group on Trade and Competition Policy was set up in 1997. The first Chair of this Group was Professor Jenny of the French competition authority, who was Chair of the OECD Competition Law and Policy Committee.

In 1997 and 1998 the Working Group worked on a checklist of issues, of which the main elements were: the relationship between the objectives, principles, concepts, scope, and instruments of trade and competition policy and their relationship with development and economic growth; stocktaking and analysis of existing instruments, standards, and activities regarding trade and

---

[153] The United Nations Conference on Trade and Development.

[154] Amended, inter alia, in 1995: OECD Doc. C(95)130/FINAL.

[155] Available on the Commission's website, <http://ec.europa.eu/comm/competition/international/multilateral/oecd.html>, and on the OECD website, <http://www.oecd.org/dataoecd/7/41/35908641.pdf>.

[156] <http://ec.europa.eu/competition/international/multilateral/oecd_submissions.html>.

[157] For the details, see C. Cocuzza and M. Montini, 'International Antitrust Co-operation in a Global Economy' [1998] *ECLR* 156, 160–161; E. U. Petersmann, 'International Competition Rules for Governments and for Private Business' (1996) 30 *J of World Trade* 5.

competition policy, including experience with their application; and the interaction between trade and competition policy. In 1999 the Group examined three further topics: the relevance of the fundamental WTO principles of national treatment, transparency, and most favoured nation treatment to competition policy and vice versa; approaches to promoting cooperation and communication among members, including in the field of technical cooperation; and the contribution of competition policy to achieving the objectives of the WTO, including the promotion of international trade.

Ultimately, the question which has to be addressed is whether a multilateral framework on competition policy should be set up under the auspices of the WTO. The US has been reluctant to go down that path whereas the EU advocated working through the WTO to achieve this. The EU's views were set out in a Discussion Document in March 1999, in preparation for the 1999 WTO Ministerial Conference in Seattle. In the event, the WTO meeting at Seattle collapsed. However, the US agreed to explore the idea of a multilateral framework within the WTO. The Fourth WTO Ministerial Conference at Doha in November 2001 adopted a Declaration which contained three paragraphs on competition policy. The Declaration recognised the case for a multilateral framework to enhance the contribution of competition policy to international trade and development and said that negotiations on trade and competition should take place after the Fifth Ministerial Conference at Cancun in 2003. Competition was one of the so-called 'Singapore Issues' (the others were trade facilitation, transparency in government procurement, and the relationship between trade and investment).

The meeting at Cancun was abruptly terminated amid much disagreement. Although there was certainly dispute over the 'Singapore Issues', including competition, many members of the WTO had grievances over a range of issues and there were complex reasons for the collapse of the meeting.[158] The agricultural subsidies offered by the EU and the US Government to their home producers were a cause of dissension and many developing countries had become unhappy with the concept of 'free trade' which seemed previously to have become universally accepted as the remedy for the world's ills. The WTO, like the World Bank, is seen in many quarters as part of the problem, not the remedy. The idea of a multilateral competition framework was a victim of the spirit of the times.[159] In 2004 the General Council of the WTO abandoned any attempt to work on a set of antitrust rules.[160] It appears that this was partly due to the fears of the small or developing nations but the marked reluctance of the US was also a factor.[161]

(iv) The International Competition Network

While attempts to put competition on the map at the WTO ran into difficulties, competition authorities from around the world have quietly been getting on with setting up procedures and mechanisms through which they can cooperate. In October 2001 the International Competition Network was established. The EU is a member. The impetus for this came from the US IPAC report (International Competition Policy Advisory Committee) in February 2000.[162] According to its website[163] the ICN 'provides antitrust agencies from developed and developing countries with a focused network for addressing practical antitrust enforcement and policy issues of common concern.

---

[158] See F. Jenny, 'Competition Trade and Development Before and After Cancun' [2003] *Fordham Corp L Inst* 631.

[159] For an entertaining account (with a serious message) of Cancun, see F. Jenny, 'WTO Core Principles and Trade/Competition, Policies' [2003] *Fordham Corp L. Inst* 703, in which he tells the tale in the guise of the plot of the film *The Third Man* (with the EU Trade Commissioner as Holly Marten and 'Trade Consensus' as Harry Lime).

[160] Doha Work Programme Decision, 1 August 2004.

[161] See E. Elhauge and D. Geradin, *Global Competition Law and Economics* (2nd edn, Hart Publishing, 2011) 1242–1247, for a discussion of this.

[162] US DOJ: available at <http://www.usdoj.gov/atr/icpac/finalreport.htm>.

[163] <http://www.internationalcompetitionnetwork.org>.

It facilitates procedural and substantive convergence in antitrust enforcement and merger control through a results-oriented agenda and informal, project-driven organization'. The ICN has proved an extremely useful and productive organisation. It has five active working groups including the Merger Working Group, which has adopted 'guiding principles and recommended practices' which competition authorities should abide by when analysing mergers across several jurisdictions; and the Cartels Working Group, which organises annual cartel workshops and has produced a number of reports on anti-cartel policy and a cartel enforcement manual, including a template for ICN member agencies to set out their rules governing cartel enforcement.

This 'soft law' harmonisation is highly effective and the ICN is a particularly valuable resource for competition agencies from developing countries and those which have only recently adopted competition laws.

(v) A Global Competition Law Regime?

The WTO remains the most obvious framework for the establishment of some type of international competition regime and its existing dispute settlement mechanism provides a possible model. However, the problems facing the WTO vividly demonstrate how difficult it is to reach international consensus in the economic field when States are in such different stages of development and have such different interests. The requirement of the WTO is that all Member States, except the very poorest, subscribe to its rights and obligations in exchange for trade liberalisation. Prominent among the organisation's shortcomings, however, is that its rules do not sufficiently allow for socio-cultural and environmental criteria to be considered and it is argued that it is essential to take account of socio-cultural divergences in any set of competition rules which are adopted at an international level.[164] Some developing countries have come to view the WTO as a 'rich man's club', run for the benefit of the world's most powerful trading blocs. Both caution and pragmatism would suggest that the present problems in the WTO need to be dealt with before a competition law element is added. However, as more and more countries adopt competition law regimes the capacity for conflict between them, should they all take extraterritorial jurisdiction, increases exponentially, at least in theory.

In the meantime competition authorities across the world have learned to cooperate to their mutual advantage. At present it appears that soft law instruments, particularly within the ICN, are producing successful convergence and cooperation and spreading best practice between competition authorities. The EU is committed to these processes, which seem to hold out more promise for the globalised economy than attempts to produce international regulatory structures.

7. CONCLUSIONS

1. Traditional concepts of extraterritorial jurisdiction are not well suited for use in competition law situations. However, like some other jurisdictions, the EU has developed rules for taking extraterritorial jurisdiction which it considers are in conformity with international law. These include the 'implementation doctrine' and the 'qualified effects' doctrine.

2. Plaintiffs are understandably keen to sue in US courts when they have been victims of international cartels but the US courts are not welcoming at present and this coincides with the attempts in the EU described in Chapter 14 to develop better ways of facilitating damages actions in Europe.

3. Ideas for international competition regimes are unrealistic and overambitious. Bilateral agreements and friendly and cooperative relations between enforcers seem a better way ahead. While

---

[164] W. Pape, 'Socio-cultural Differences and International Competition Law' (1999) 5 *European Law Journal* 438.

there are occasional high-profile differences, much work has been done in building up an international consensus. The best way forward at present is through soft law instruments.

4. Competition laws are now a global phenomenon. It is crucial to recognise the international dimensions of competition law and to see the EU system in a global perspective.

8. FURTHER READING

A. BOOKS

Cook, P., Fabella, R. V., and Lee, C. (eds.), *Competitive Advantage and Competition Policy in Developing Countries* (Edward Elgar, 2007)

Crawford, J., *Brownlie's Principles of Public International Law* (8th edn, Oxford University Press, 2012), Chap. 21

Dabbah, M., *The Internationalisation of Antitrust Policy* (Cambridge University Press, 2003)

Dabbah, M., *Competition Law and Policy in the Middle East* (Cambridge University Press, 2007)

Dabbah, M., *International and Comparative Competition Law* (Cambridge University Press, 2010)

Elhauge, E., and Geradin, D., *Global Competition Law and Economics* (2nd edn, Hart Publishing, 2011)

Epstein, R., and Greve, M. (eds.), *Competition Laws in Conflict: Antitrust Jurisdiction in a Global Economy* (AEI Press, 2004)

Furse, M., *Antitrust Law in China, Korea and Vietnam* (Oxford University Press, 2009)

Gerber, D., *Global Competition: Law, Markets, and Globalization* (Oxford University Press, 2010)

Higgins, R., *Problems and Process: International Law and How We Use It* (Clarendon Press, 1994)

Jennings, R. Y., and Watts, A. (eds.), *Oppenheim's International Law* (9th edn, Longman, 1992)

Jones, C. A., and Matsushita, M., (eds.), *Competition Policy in the Global Trading System* (Kluwer, 2002)

Kennedy, K., *Competition Law and the World Trade Organization: The Limits of Multilateralism* (Sweet & Maxwell, 2001)

Noonan, C., *The Emerging Principles of International Competition Law* (Oxford University Press, 2008)

Olmstead C. (ed.), *Extra-territorial Application of Laws and Responses Thereto* (ESC Publishing, 1984), 156

Papadopoulos, A., *The International Dimension of EU Competition Law and Policy* (Cambridge University Press, 2010)

Ryngaert, C., *Jurisdiction in International Law* (Oxford University Press, 2008)

Schachter, O., *International Law in Theory and Practice* (Nijhoff, 1991), Chap. XII

Stiglitz, J., *Globalization and its Discontents* (Penguin, 2002)

Zäch, R., and Heinemann, A. (eds.), *The Development of Competition Law Global Perspectives* (Edward Elgar, 2010)

Zanettin, B., *Cooperation Between Antitrust Agencies at the International Level* (Hart Publishing, 2002)

B. CHAPTERS IN BOOKS

Swan, A. C., 'The Hartford Insurance Company Case; Antitrust in the Global Economy' in J. Bhandari and A. Sykes (eds.), *Economic Dimensions in International Law* (Cambridge University Press, 1997)

Wood, D. P., 'The Trade Effects of Domestic Antitrust Enforcement' in J. Bhandari and A. Sykes (eds.), *Economic Dimensions in International Law* (Cambridge University Press, 1997)

C. ARTICLES

Akehurst, M., 'Jurisdiction in International Law' (1972–1973) 46 *BYIL* 145

Bavasso, A., 'Boeing/McDonnell Douglas: Did the Commission Fly Too High?' [1998] *ECLR* 243

Bishop, B., 'Editorial, The Boeing/McDonnell Douglas Merger' [1997] *ECLR* 417

Botteman, Y., and Patsa, A., 'The Jurisdictional Reach of EU Anti-cartel Rules: Unmuddling the Limits' (2012) 8 *European Competition Journal* 365

Bowett, D. W., 'Jurisdiction: Changing Problems of Authority over Activities and Resources' (1982) 53 *BYIL* 1

Burnside, A., 'GE, Honey I Sank the Merger' [2002] *ECLR* 107

Cocuzza, C., and Montini, M., 'International Antitrust Co-operation in a Global Economy' [1998] *ECLR* 156

Collins, L., 'Blocking and Clawback Statutes' [1986] *JBL* 372

DAVIDOW, J., and SHAPIRO, C., 'The Feasibility and Worth of a WTO Competition Agreement' (2003) 37 J of World Trade 49

DI FREDERICO, G., 'The New Anti-monopoly Law in China from a European Perspective' (2009) 32 World Competition 249

DURAND, B., FONT GALARZA, A., and MEHTA, K., 'The Interface Between Competition Policy and International Trade Liberalisation. Looking into the Future: Applying a New Virtual Anti-trust Standard' (2004) 27 World Competition 3

FOX, E., 'Towards World Antitrust and Market Access' (1997) 91 AJIL 1

FOX, E., 'The Merger Regulation and its Territorial Reach' [1999] ECLR 334

GERVEN, W. Van, 'EC Jurisdiction in Antitrust Matters: The Wood Pulp Judgment' [1989] Fordham Corp L Inst 451

GERVEN, Y. Van, and HOET, L., 'Gencor: Some Notes on Transnational Competition Law Issues' (2001) 28 LIEI 195

GREWLICH, A. S., 'Globalisation and Conflict in Competition Law' (2001) 24 World Competition 367

GRIFFIN, J., 'Reactions to U.S. Assertions of Extraterritorial Jurisdiction' [1998] ECLR 64

GUZMAN, A., 'The Case for International Antitrust' (2004) 22 Berkeley J of Int'l Law 355

HOFFET, F., and BREI, G., 'The First and Second Generation Competition Enforcement Co-operation Treaty: Free Flow of Information Between Switzerland and the EU?' [2014] ECLR 157

JENNINGS, R. Y., 'Extraterritorial Jurisdiction and the United States Antitrust Laws' (1957) 33 BYIL 146

JENNY, F., 'Competition, Trade and Development Before and After Cancun' [2003] Fordham Corp L Inst 631

JENNY, F., 'Competition Law and Policy: Global Governance Issues' (2003) 26 World Competition 609

KACZOROWSKA, A., 'International Competition Law in the Context of Global Capitalism' [2000] ECLR 117

LANGE, D. F. G., and SANDAGE, J. B., 'The Wood Pulp Decision' (1989) 26 CMLRev 137

LIANOS, I., 'The Contribution of the United Nations to the Emergence of Global Antitrust Law' (2007) 15 Tulane J of International and Comparative Law 145

LIPSKY, JR., A. B., 'Competition and the WTO: Beyond Cancun' [2003] Fordham Corp L Inst 657

MANN, F. A., 'The Doctrine of Jurisdiction in International Law' (1964) 111 RdC 1

MANN, F. A., 'Casenote' (1973) 22 ICLQ 35

MANN, F. A., 'The Doctrine of International Jurisdiction Revisited After Twenty Years' (1984) 186 RdC 9

MEESSEN, K. M., 'Antitrust Jurisdiction under Customary International Law' (1984) 78 AJIL 783

MITCHELL, A. D., 'Broadening the Vision of Trade Liberalisation' (2001) 24 World Competition 367

PAPE, W., 'Socio-cultural Differences and International Competition Law' (1999) 5 European Law Journal 438

PARISI, J., 'Enforcement Co-operation Among Antitrust Authorities' [1999] ECLR 133

PETERSMANN, E. U., 'International Competition Rules for Governments and for Private Business' (1996) 30 J of World Trade Law 5

PETERSMANN, E. U., 'WTO Core Principles and Trade/Competition' [2003] Fordham Corp L Inst 669

PITOFSKY, R., 'Competition Policy in a Global Economy' (1999) 3 JIEL 403

REYNOLDS, R. M., SICILIAN, J., and WELLMAN, P. S., 'The Extraterritorial Application of the US Antitrust Laws to Criminal Conspiracies' [1998] ECLR 151

ROBERTSON, A., and DEMETRIOU, M., '"But That Was in Another Country": The Extraterritorial Application of US Antitrust Laws in the US Supreme Court' (1994) 43 ICLQ 417

ROTH, P. M., 'Reasonable Extraterritoriality: Correcting the "Balance of Interests"' (1992) 41 ICLQ 245

SLOT P. J., and GRABANDI, E., 'Extraterritoriality and Jurisdiction' (1986) 23 CMLRev 545

TAY, A., and WILLMAN, G., 'Why (no) Global Competition Policy is a Tough Choice' (2005) Quarterly Rev of Economics and Finance 312

TORREMANS, P., 'Extraterritorial Application of EC and US Competition Law' (1996) 21 ELRev 280

VANDERGRIFT, S., and LUCAS, J., 'The GE/Honeywell Saga? Ehh, What's Up Doc? A Comparative Approach Between US and EU Merger Control Proceedings Almost 15 Years Later' [2014] ECLR 172

WHELAN, P., 'Resisting the Long Arm of Criminal Antitrust Laws: Norris v. US' (2009) 72 MLR 272

WOOD, D. P., 'Soft Harmonization Among Competition Laws: Track Record and Prospects' (2003) 48 Ant Bull 305

INDEX